WILLIAM F. MAAG LIBRARY
YOUNGSTOWN STATE UNIVERSITY

COMMUNICATION SERIALS

*"An international guide to periodicals
in communication, popular culture,
and the performing arts"*

1992 / 1993 Edition

Published by SovaComm, Inc.
SAN 250-9180

Copyright © 1992, SovaComm, Incorporated

All rights reserved. Reproduction of this reference work, in whole or in part, without permission of the publisher is strictly prohibited.

International Standard Book Number 0-929976-00-2

International Standard Serial Number 1041-7893

Printed and bound in the United States of America

No payment is either solicited or accepted for the inclusion of periodical entries in this publication. Every possible precaution has been taken to ensure that the information it contains is accurate, and the publishers cannot accept any liability for errors or omissions however caused.

Trade marked names are editorially used throughout this publication. Rather than place a trademark symbol next to each occurrence, we state that these names are used only in an editorial fashion and to the benefit of the trademark owner, and that there is no intention of trademark infringement.

COMMUNICATION SERIALS

"An international guide to periodicals in communication, popular culture, and the performing arts"

1992 / 1993 Edition

Harry W. Sova, Ph.D.
Patricia L. Sova, M.A.

This page intentionally blank

Table of Contents

Acknowledgements vii
Introduction ix
Guidelines for Filing xi
User Guidelines xiii
Communication Serials 1

INDICES

    Abstracts 699
    Associations 717
    Columnists 743
    Departments 775
    International 875
    ISSN 883
    Publishers 897
    Subject Headings
        Guide to Definitions 923
        Medium by Subject 929
    Subtitle 985
    Varies 1,011
    VFOT (Varying Form of Title) 1,029

Note: to provide a more logical search procedure, some indices are integrated into the main annotated section of this publication.

This page intentionally blank

Acknowledgements

This reference book is the result of over twenty years research and compilation. Along the way, the authors have been blessed with the generous giving of time, suggestions, and advice of numerous professionals in the information science and communication fields.

The initial impetus for this work came from discussions with graduate students, Christopher Sterling and David McFarland in Madison, Wisconsin during Winter 1968/1969. It was in these entrepreneurial idea sessions that the concept for this volume was first discussed and in the ensuing months took root. Those evenings of creative discussion remain vibrant memories for the author.

At Indiana University, friends Lisa and John Hanrahan, and Dr. Keith Mielke, Chairman of the Department of Radio-Television-film, encouraged continuation of research. Friend and doctoral advisor, Dr. Joseph Berman at Ohio University, shared the author's interests in history, technology, and serials, and gave encouragement both in exploring historical research and completion of dissertation. His zest for learning, teaching, and living remains influential.

Dr. George Mastroianni, Chairman of the Radio-Television-Film program at California State University at Fullerton, provided the author his first teaching position. Both he and his wife, Nancy, furnished many evenings of spirited conversation. Colleagues Dr. Larry Ward, Dr. Ron Dyas and Dr. Edward Trotter, provided constructive feedback and were always willing to help the author maintain sanity by removing him from the library stacks to the sand and surf of Southern California. A special note of thanks to Dr. Ted Smythe, the "professors' professor," for his dedication and love of communication historiography, and guidance in these initial stages.

Three years of advertising agency ownership preceeded the next teaching position at Southern California College. At SCC, the project continued with the support and encouragement of President Wayne Kraiss, Academic Dean Dr. Lewis Wilson, and Librarian Dean Tracy. It was here that the co-authors met, married, and initiated working together on this volume in 1979. Patricia, after a suitable honeymoon period, began the rigorous task of editing the developing manuscript, while maintaining her faculty position at Cerritos College in Norwalk, California.

Numerous Southern California librarians (notably at the libraries of the University of Southern California, the University of California at Los Angeles, California State University at Fullerton, Orange Coast College, the University of San Diego, the University of California at Berkeley, and Southern California College) provided valued guidance, and essential research facilities.

After Southern California College, the author joined the College of Communication at Regent University, where colleagues gave of their time and talents to review, critique, and refine the final version for publication. Our appreciation is extended to colleagues Dean Dr. David Clark, and Associate Dean Dr. Eugene Elser of the College of Communication; Chair of the Institute of Performing Arts Dr. Gillette Elvgren; Dr. Benson Fraser, Dr. Darlene Graves, Chair of the School of Communication Studies Dr. Michael Graves; Dr. John Keeler, Dr. Clifford Kelly, Professor John Lawing, Dr. Terry Lindvall, Professor Donald Piper, Professor Charles Pollak, Professor Andrew Quicke, Chairman of the School of Radio-TV-Film, Dr. Robert Schihl; Chair of the School of Journalism Dr. Douglas Tarpley; Dr. Elaine Waller, and Dr. Glanel Webb.

Deserving of special recognition at Regent University are Dean of Libraries, Lois Lehman, and Associate Dean Dr. Eva Kiewitt, along with Associate Librarians S. Leanne Gardner, Patricia Luman, and Bob Sivigny. Over the past six years these professionals have provided critiques, suggestions, and contacts necessary for the completion of this book. Their help, friendship, and encouragement has been greatly appreciated.

When the project seemed quagmired, it was the encouragement of these Regent University colleagues who gave strength and vision to "stay the course." A special note of thanks is extended to Regent University Provost W. George Selig for his support in the granting of a sabbatical, and bringing new meaning to the phrase "carrot and the stick."

Numerous research trips have been made to local, regional, public, private, academic and national libraries. These reference librarians have been helpful in their willingness to share their frustrations, quests and desires for a serials reference work, and thus shaped the nature of this book. For these professionals who so willingly gave of their time and knowledge, we offer our grateful appreciation. The content, structure, indices, and features of this work is a direct response to these informative sessions. It is our sincere desire that this volume will make their formidable daily tasks a bit easier.

In particular, we wish to thank the library staffs at the University of Oregon, the University of Virginia, the New York Public Library, the British National Musuem, the British Film Institute, American Film Institute, Indiana University, Ohio University and the University of Wisconsin for their help in accessing their serial collections, and making arrangements for a quiet work room. We wish also to acknowledge Librarian Francis Wilhoit at Indiana University for her comments and critique of the work in progress and Dolores Jenkins, librarian at the University of Florida, Gainesville, and chair of the Mass Communication Bibliographers Division of the Association for Education in Journalism and Mass Communication, for her encouragement to complete the project.

A special thank you is extended to the dedicated staff of the Library of Congress, whose devotion oftentimes went beyond the expected. The authors are indebted to Lawrence Boyer, and James Stewart, Head Librarian, Social Science Reading Room for their help in finding a room, table, nook or cranny to operate a laptop computer in the midst of organized chaos as the Jefferson building was undergoing rennovation and the Adams building Social Science Reading Room was continuously squeezed for space and facilities.

We wish to also recognize the talented professional staff of the National Serials Data Program at the Library of Congress. Julia C. Blixrud, Section Head, and Regina R. Reynolds, Assistant Head have been most helpful in their incredibly difficult task of education, monitoring, and recording the very important ISSN records associated with various American serials. On numerous occasions their staff has aided the authors' quest to resolve conflicting, or misprinted ISSN numbers. Their help has been most appreciated.

For Jonathan Lewis Sova and Courtney Michelle Sova, who have come to believe that their father was born with a computer permanently fixed to his lap, and their mother an editing pencil in hand, we offer our love and the promise of that special trip.

Finally, we thank you for the purchase of this work, and encourage your correspondence with suggestions and comments concerning improvement. We look forward to many productive years ahead with you.

Patricia Sova
Harry Sova

January, 1992
Virginia Beach, VA

Introduction

Communication Serials is a unique reference work encompassing over 2,700 annotated communication-related periodical titles from the early 1800s to the present. It has been specifically designed to facilitate research of serials from a variety of approaches.

Scope

To be considered for inclusion, a serial must:

- Be published in the English language (English summary page minimum).

- Possess an unique title.

- Have a semiyearly or more frequent publication schedule.

- Be published on a regular interval basis.

- Minimally contain two articles or sections.

- Fall within one or more of the following topic areas of communication:

Advertising
Animation
Audio
Audio-Visual
Cable Television
Comics and Cartoons
Communication Law
Communication Research
DBS
Direct Mail
Drama
Electronics
Film
Forensics & Debate
Graphic Arts
Instructional Communication
Interactive Media
International Short-Wave
Interpersonal Communication
Journalism
Labor Unions and Guilds
Magazines
Marketing
Motion Pictures
Newspapers
Photography
Printing
Promotion
Public Relations
Publishing
Radio
Satellite Communication
Sound Recording
Speech
Telecommunication
Telephone
Telegraphy
Television
Theatre
Vaudeville

Excluded from this reference work are monographs, catalogs, directories, bibliographies, and other non-"magazine" publications. Also excluded are mass media program guides of a local community nature, and program guides which are event-oriented. In addition, foreign language publications consisting only of an English-language contents page were not included.

Some serials have been incorporated into this volume whose editorial content is not of a communication nature at present, but which in its day had provided critical information and/or forums for discussion of issues leading to development of latter-day forms of communication. Similarly, some present day serials have been excluded as their content, form, and function have removed them from the general communication arena. When reference is made to such serials, one of the following codes will explain its exclusion from the work:

- [NF] This publication has a published frequency of less than twice per year (semiyearly).

- [NC] This periodical does not have a communication orientation.

- [NE] This publication is not printed in English.

Considerations in Data Entry

Several challenges were met in the assembly of this work, and are noteworthy for their impact upon the entry process. Chief among these was the challenge of clarifying serial lineage, as serials often changed titles, publishing schedules and content over time.

For a variety of reasons, it has become evident that at times publishers did not fully appreciate the neccessity for specific information about historical lineage, with some earlier publishers claiming one lineage change, and latter publishers claiming a different path to current form. Also, library staff may have been called upon to catalog a given serial with only minimal information available. For any given serial with multiple title, editorial or publisher changes, small misperceptions could and have easily resulted in multiple catalogue records for one publication.

To the best of our ability we have attempted to clarify this problem of lineage by several different methods:

- The consolidation of continuing serials into their respective publication groups.

- The identification of specific serial titles by unique ISSN numbers.

- The examination of sample periodical issues at time of change in title, content, or publisher.

The process of tracing serial lineage has been facilitated by the OCLC on-line cataloging system for North American member libraries, which holds individual records for each serial title held in member library collections. Prior to January 1, 1981 cataloguers had the option of entering serials either under ALA (American Library Association) Cataloging Rules, that of Latest Entry Cataloging, or by AACR (Anglo-American Cataloging Rules) of Successive Entry Cataloging. Only the latter system (Successive Entry Cataloging) has been allowed since January 1, 1981.

Guidelines for Filing

- **Titles** are entered in all CAPS. Serials with a unique set of upper and lower case letters (e.g. AmeriCanadian TeleViews) will be readily apparent within the serial description.

- **Titles** are filed alphabetically from A - Z.

- **Titles** that are proceded by special characters (such as #, %, or *) are filed before the letter A.
    - #1 Video Dealer
    - *Wars Association Monthly
    - ABC Bulletin of Photography

- **Numbers** (with the exception of indices), are filed as spelled out. Thus *8 MM Magazine* would be filed as *Eight Millimeter Magazine*.
    - Eigamen's Typographical Courier
    - Eight Millimter Magazine
    - Every Man's Theatrical Fare

- **Hyphens** (-) and **diagonal slashes** (/) are filed as spaces.
    - Film-Store Quarterly
    - Film Storywriter
    - Film/Style Videography

- **Apostrophes** ('), **colons** (:), **semicolons** (;) and markings other than hyphen and slash are ignored in filing.
    - Printer's Exchange
    - Printers; Publishers; Advertising
    - Printers Publish: Quarterly Report

- **Initials** and **abbreviations** within main titles are treated as a single whole word. Periods, spaces, and other markings are removed and filed alphabetically. Thus, *A. D. F. Association Journal* is filed as *ADF Association Journal*. Note: both the acronym and title would be fully spelled out within the VFOT (Varying Form of Title) Index, such as: *American Designer Foundation Association Journal*.
    - Adapting New Technology
    - ADF Association Journal
    - Alabama Journalist

- **Foreign language serial titles** are normally entered under their foreign language title, letters and diacritics shown and filed according to their plain language English equivalents. Rules for hyphen, diagonal slashes, apostrophes, colons, semicolons, and other markings apply here as well. The English title equivalent (when available), is entered within VFOT (Varying Form of Title) under SPAN. For example, a German language publication *Rundfunk Woche* with English summaries would be entered under the title *RUNDFUNK WOCHE*, with the English translation *Broadcasting Weekly* entered within VFOT under SPAN.

    The exception to this rule is when a foreign language title or edition is also published. Under this circumstance, the English-language title is the main-entry title of the serial; the foreign language title is entered within FOREIGN TITLE, and a foreign edition title within FOREIGN EDITION, both items under SPAN. The relationship between these serials is explained within the description section.

    For example, let us say that *Rundfunk Woche* is a German-language only serial with NO English summaries, but that this publisher also issues an equivalent English edition titled *Broadcasting Weekly*. The main-entry title would read *BROADCASTING WEEKLY*. Under FOREIGN EDITIONof SPAN would be entered: *Rundfunk Woche*. This FOREIGN EDITION line may also include ISSN record numbers as described elsewhere.

- **Initial articles** (A, An, The), and foreign equivalents are placed at the end of their respective titles. Thus, *The Public and an Author* would be entered and filed as: *Public and an Author, The*.
    - Portland Vaudevillian
    - Public and an Author, The
    - Public Author, A

- **Variations in English spelling** have been maintained from the original serial. Thus, the following are valid both in title and text applications:
    - Color
    - Colour
    - Theater
    - Theatre

- In those instances where organizations and government agencies act as publishers, some cataloguers will provide the complete agency name and serial title (separated by periods) as serial title. For example:

    UNITED STATES GOVERNMENT. DEPARTMENT OF TRANSPORTATION. USING MEDIA WISELY.

    Since most readers will search for a key title rather than full organization name, this publication has filed the Main-Entry Title to read:

    USING MEDIA WISELY

    Under SPAN/VFOT would be entered: --*United States Government. Department of Transportation. Using Media Wisely.* This full organizational title will also be found within the Varying Form of Title Index.

- Variances exist in placement of apostrophe (') as possessive or non-possessive (e.g. *Printers Ink, Printer's Ink,* or *Printers' Ink*). In those instances where apostrophe usage cannot be clearly defined, NO apostrophe is used in the main title entry, with varying apostrophe usage shown in the VFOT (Varying Form of Title) Index.

- A more difficult situation resides in determining whether a publisher established a leading article at the beginning of a serial title, (e.g. *Printers Monthly* versus *The Printers Monthly*). Numerous instances existed where publishers utilized leading articles during a given time span, dropped them, and once again utilized these articles as part of the main-entry title. In these instances where such variation in usage exists, NO leading article is used in the Main Entry Title, but is referenced within the VFOT.

User Guidelines

[Main Entry Title - Page xiv] →

[Subtitle - Page xiv] →

[Publisher - Page xiv] →

[Description - Page xiv] →

[Department - Page xiv] →

[Typical - Page xv] →

[Schedule - Page xv] →

[Span - Page xv] →

[Library/Cong - Page xvi] →

[Dewey # - Page xvii] →

[ISSN # - Page xvii] →

[Abstracts - Page xvii] →

ADVERTISING TRENDS AND COMMUNICATION

SUB: "The journal of newspaper publishing and advertising."

SUB: "A national magazine of sales and business-building ideas." (Apr 9,1925 - Jul 9, 1925).

PUBL: American Advertiser Publishing Co., 1455 Fifth Ave., New York, NY 10012-3456.

DESC: Although most sources show *American Adverpaper* to be a varying title of *Advertising Trends and Communication*," there appears to have been a major difference in the content and purpose of the two serials. *American Adverpaper* was aimed at the editor and publisher of the weekly or daily newspaper. Articles described successful tactics of circulation, union negotiations, qualities sought in an editor, and other topics of importance to newspaper advertising management. A distinct change took place with the serial by the early 1900's, with a more news-style format of late-breaking stories, and a growing emphasis on the advertising side of print. By 1945, the transformation was complete, and *Advertising Trends and Communication* became an authoritative business weekly for the advertising community. Some graphics; magazine format.

DEPT: "Mechanical Department," 'A learning session'; "Editorial," "Class and Trade Journalism," "Letter-Writers' Symposium." (8-1893). "Some Successful Advertising Men," profiles; "Mechanical Department," "Some Personal Notes," by John Smith. (8/9-04). "Editorial." (1-22-25). "Adver-Letters," letters; "Corporate," profile; "Buying Media," column by Robert Jackson; "Taking a Stand," editorial; "The Time is Ripe," commentary. (1-89).

TYPL: "Essential Departments of the Trade Journal," "The Story of a New Jersey County Weekly." (8-1893). "Editor Gets Farming Land," "Wild Publisher's Wildest Dream." (8/9-04). "Vital Problems at Detroit," "Agency Conspiracy Suit False," "Cross Word Puzzle Lotteries." (1-22-25). "Targeting the Upscale Reader," "Whatever Happened to Cold Calls?," "Computerized Data Bases Mean Profit." (1-89).

SCHL: Monthly [irregular at times] (1892 - Jun, 1895); Bimonthly (Aug, 1895 -Oct 11, 1906); Biweekly (Oct 25, 1906 - Jun 3, 1945); Monthly (Jul, 1945+), 85 pp.

SPAN: Mar, 1892 - Jul, 1989//
FOREIGN TITLE
--Advertize Stille (ISSN: 1236-9803).
VARIES
--Vol 1 - 40, No. 5 as American Adverpaper (ISSN: 0202-2367)
--Jan 15, 1906 - Sep 28, 1907 as AA News.
--? - ? as News-Paper.
WITH SUPPLEMENT???
--Market, The (ISSN: 2220-3949), Jun 3, 1955 - Mar 1,1971.
ABSORBED
--Caxton Caveat, Jan 9, 1902.
MERGED WITH
--Today's Advertiser and Publisher (ISSN: 4443-4959) (to form) Advertising Publisher (ISSN: 3939-0333), Sep, 1989.

LC: PN 4700.A25

DD: 621.3/5/3327

ISSN: 7415-2940

ABST: World Guide to Media Serials
Magazine Reader Index.

NOTE: Data contained in this example is ficticious, and was designed to demonstrate various possible entries for a given serial.

[Main Entry Title]

This is the "name" of the publication, and is entered as shown by the publisher, within the publisher's statement of editorial office, publication schedule, ISSN number, etc. It is significant that at times the cover title is not the same as the official publication title of a serial.

All currently published titles are preceded by the symbol ✤. This allows the user to quickly locate those serials with a current publishing status. A complete listing of current serial titles, and current serial titles listed by subject area are available in the indices. A typical entry for a current serial might appear as:

✤ NEWS OF THEATRE, FILM AND TELEVISION

SUB:

The subtitle is almost exclusively found on the front cover, under the masthead, or on the title page of the serial, and provides additional information, sometimes in slogan form, to the Main Entry Title. A start, stop, or inclusive dates for subtitle usage is provided within parentheses. All subtitles are sorted and indexed in the Subtitle Index provided at the end of this work.

PUBL:

The publisher line reflects the current publisher and address (sometimes subscription address), or in the case of ceased serials, the last known publisher and address at time of cessation. Certain address abbreviations may be used as shown below:

Aly.	Alley	Gdns.	Gardens
Arc.	Arcade	Grv.	Grove
Ave.	Avenue	Hts.	Heights
Bldg.	Building	Hwy.	Highway
Blvd.	Boulevard	Inc.	Incorporated
Br.	Branch	Ln.	Lane
Byp.	Bypass	Ltd.	Limited
Co.	Company	Mnr.	Manor
Cswy.	Causeway	Pl.	Place
Cir.	Circle	Plz.	Plaza
Cres.	Crescent	Pt.	Point
Ct.	Court	PO Box	Post Office
Ctr.	Center	Rd.	Road
Dr.	Drive	Sq.	Square
Expy.	Expressway	St.	Street
Fwy.	Freeway	Ter.	Terrace

DESC:

The description segment is designed to provide a succinct descriptive evaluation of the serial including items of historical lineage, layout design, editorial content, and unique aspects of the publication. Many annotations also indicate the shape, size, paper quality, presence of graphics, or other unique features of the publication which would be noteworthy.

Recognizing that a serial may change editorial purpose, layout design, and function a number of times during its publication span, the authors have attempted whenever possible to preserve individual DESCriptions as characterizes the publication at those unique stages. Through these multiple descriptions, the reader will more clearly understand the evolution, purpose, and style of the serial as it progressed through time. Each multiple description segment bears the VARIES title in bracketed italics.

The size of a sampled serial is presented as (Width x Height inches / Width x Height mm) in both Imperial and Metric units. The first measurement in inches, is rounded off to the nearest ⅛ inch mark. The second measurement in millimeters, again is rounded off to the nearest 5 mm interval. When the publication span covers a significant segment of time, more than one measurement may be provided, with the year of publication preceding the Imperial and Metric figures. It is important to note that these are approximate measurements, owing to the fact that paper and trimming procedures may provide a slight variance in serial size from one issue to another.

DEPT:

This section lists regular departmental features from sample issues. The authors have endeavored to list ALL regular departmental features with the exception of classified advertisements. Departmental titles which are self-explanatory (such as "Letters to the Editor"), are entered as is. Those departmental features which are not self-explanatory may contain a several word explanation, the most often used phrase being "newsbriefs." Some departmental features possess their own subtitle, which is included in single quote marks.

Dates of sample issues examined are shown as single digit numbers. January, 1985 would be listed as (1-85). Year dates before 1901 are listed in full, such as Jun, 1892 which would be entered as (6-1892). The designators "u" or "?" used within or in place of dates indicates an unknown value. All departmental titles are sorted and indexed under the Departments Index. Additionally, the Columnist Index provides an alphabetical list of columnists' names as they appeared in the DEPT section.

While the authors have undertaken to separate out Departmental titles from Typical article titles, instances exist where only a single issue of the serial was available for examination. In these situations, a "best guess" was made between what was a regular departmental feature, and a typical article. A Departmental listing being extracted from a single issue may not always accurately reflect the flavor or content of the publication.

TYPL:

Oftentimes a serial title, and even a detailed description is insufficient in describing the complexity or content of articles to the reader. To further the reader's evaluation three to five typical article titles are listed from sample issues. At times special punctuation and other typographical symbols or elements used within article titles have been removed for reasons of clarity, and printing restrictions. Also, some publishers follow the convention of shortening, , or rewriting article titles for placement on the title page. Thus, while the majority of article titles presented in this work have come from the title page, there are occasions when that information was taken from the editorial pages itself. Dates are inscribed in the same format as for departmental titles.

SCHL:

The Schedule section details the frequency of publication, changes in frequency, and any exceptions to the publishing schedule. Exception data is placed within brackets. Inclusive dates for specific frequencies (when known), are placed within parentheses. The approximate number of pages in the sampled issue follows the frequency of publication. Page number counts above 25 are rounded up to the next five-page count. Months are abbreviated to a three-letter format.

Considerable confusion exists concerning the application of "semi-" and "bi-" to publication frequency. In this work the traditional dictionary definitions are utilized, that the word "Semi" means "half of something," and thus a serial with a semimonthly schedule would be published every half-month, or two issues per calendar month. In a similar fashion, the word "Bi" indicates "two of something," and therefore a serial published bimonthly, would be created once in every two month calendar period, or every two months. Publication frequencies and their definitions are as follows:

Daily	One issue per day
Semiweekly	Two issues per week
Weekly	One issue per week
Biweekly	One issue every two weeks
Semimonthly	Two issues every month
Monthly	One issue per month
Bimonthly	One issue every two months
Quarterly	One issue every three months
Semiyearly	Two issues per year
Yearly	One issue per month
Biyearly	One issue every two years

SPAN:

The publication span section details the lineage of the periodical. Publication span dates can take several forms. The starting date always reflects the earliest lineage, the first VARIES title under SPAN. A serial currently published is noted with a plus (+) sign. A serial which has ceased publication will be noted by a set of double slashes (//) following the cessation date. Single digits which remain unknown will be shown by a lower-case letter "u," while full dates which are in doubt will be noted by the use of a question mark (?) following the unverified date.

Other elements of the span section are:

EDITION

This is most often utilized to list various regional editions of the serial appearing under the same Main Title. Examples of this form include:

--North American.
--Ontario.
--Western States.

FOREIGN EDITION

This section is present when a foreign language serial has a counterpart English language edition, the latter being entered as the Main Entry Title, and the foreign language edition title(s) appearing here. Note that the English-language edition may not contain all editorial content found in the original language serial.

FOREIGN TITLE

This span section appears when a serial shares the same title in different languages. The most common occurrence of this situation is in multiple-language serials, whereby the editorial content remains the same for all countries, the only difference being the serial title, presented in the native language of the country of distribution. In this instance, the English title is the Main Title entry and any foreign language titles, along with their associated ISSN designations, are listed here.

VARIES

This lists prior lineage of the current serial by inclusive dates, title, ISSN number, and any OCLC record numbers associated with that key title. This section only lists serials shown to be CONTINUED BY a later serial which is shown to have continued volume numbering or the cessation date of the prior publication.

WITH SUPPLEMENT, SUPPLEMENT TO

WITH SUPPLEMENT lists all supplements to this parent publication, associated ISSN and OCLC record numbers, and inclusive dates. SUPPLEMENT TO also lists ISSN, OCLC and inclusive date information and the parent publication for which this annotated serial was a supplement.

Publication titles which are not applicable to the communication field, and therefore were not annotated are signified by the notation [NA]. Publication titles which were not located by press time are indicated as "Not Found," using the symbol [NF]. Either symbol will be located at the very end of the title line. These notations will also be found under ABSORBED, ABSORBED BY, SPLIT OFF WITH, SPLIT INTO, MERGED WITH, and FROM MERGER OF span segments.

ABSORBED, ABSORBED BY

Absorption pertains to a serial ceasing publication and being absorbed into an existing periodical. ISSN numbers, if available, are listed, along with the date of absorption, if it differs from the date of cessation.

SPLIT OFF WITH, SPLIT INTO

This section details publications which have split into two or more separate periodicals, with corresponding ISSN numbers, and the date of the split, if available.

MERGED WITH, FROM MERGER OF

Two or more periodicals which have merged together to form a new parent publication are listed here, again along with corresponding ISSN numbers, and the date of the merger, if available.

SUSPENDED

Periodicals which have suspended publication show inclusive suspension dates here.

CONTINUED, CONTINUED BY

This indicator is present ONLY when the succeeding serial title is [NA] (published less than semi-yearly), [NC] (not communication-oriented), or [NE] (not published in English language).

LC:

This Library of Congress number is present ONLY when the serial in question is at that facility, and an LC number has been assigned. Local library LC numbers are not utilized.

DD:

The Dewey Decimal Classification Number is shown ONLY when the serial in question is at the National Library of Canada, or has been verified from other sources.

ISSN:

The ISSN (International Standard Serial Number) is a unique eight-digit code (including a check digit) assigned to a SPECIFIC key serial title by a network of ISDS (International Serials Data System) centers throughout the world. A change in title requires assignment of a new ISSN number. Additionally, a different ISSN is assigned to each language edition of a separately published serial, both the parent serial title and its supplement title, and a main title series and each of its subseries. In the United States, assignment of ISSN numbers for American published serials is made within the National Serials Data Program at the Library of Congress in Washington, DC.

The program began in 1971, and all current periodicals since that date have been assigned ISSN numbers by the Washington, DC center. In addition, publishers who can demonstrate clear lineage through previous titles, can, at their request, also have individual ISSN numbers assigned to those previous titles.

All serial publishers are urged to participate in this important program to assign unique ISSN numbers to each published serial. Publishers who desire ISSN assignments to their serial publications may easily do so by contacting the Library of Congress, National Serials Data Program, Washington, DC 20540. The telephone number is (202) 707-6452. There is no charge for this valuable service which benefits publisher, library, and the public.

ABST:

This is a non-inclusive listing of known abstracting and indexing services connected with a given serial. ISSN numbers associated with the publication are provided when known. The reader is directed to individual abstract and indexing resources to determine inclusive dates for a given serial.

This page intentionally blank

Annotated Serial Listings

This page intentionally blank

✣ A & E PROGRAM GUIDE

PUBL: Arts & Entertainment Network, Hearst/ABC/NBC, 555 Fifth Ave., New York, NY 10017.
DESC: "Arts and Entertainment" is not merely an avocation of the Arts & Entertainment [cable television] network; it is a passion. This monthly program guide celebrates the diversity, quality, and the fullness of life contained in each of us, wherever we happen to live, in whatever culture we might be. One sampled issue for December, 1990 explored "Diana: The Making of a Princess," "Sacrifice at Pearl Harbor," "The Legend of Valentino," and a wonderful profile of "Unlikely Legends," the Gables, Monroes, Hepburns, Fields, and Mae Wests of Hollywood fame. Classic motion pictures, a cornucopia of musical treats, hilarious comedy and a few farces for good measure all add up to pleasureable, informative, and stimulating viewing for American cable television subscribers. Other general program guides simply cannot match the quality of the *A&E Program Guide*, sufficient reason to be on any impassioned television viewer's reading list. Some advertising, lavish full-color pages in a stapled magazine format on coated paper stock (8 1/8 x 10 7/8 inches / 205 x 275 mm).
DEPT: "[Month] Highlights," "Close-Up," "[Month] Booklist," review; "[Month] Primetime Grid," "[Month] Listings." (12-90).
TYPL: "Hansel and Gretel," "The Vienna Boys' Choir," "Unlikely Legends: An Appreciation," "The Avengers," "Bells, Bells, Bells." (12-90).
SCHL: Monthly, 45 pp.
SPAN: Jan?, 1986+

A-D

SUB: "An intimate journal for art directors, production managers and their associates."
PUBL: A-D Publishing Co., 130 W 46th St., New York, NY.
DESC: A small format serial designed to demonstrate printing techniques and creative graphics design in the print media, most pages display variances in typefaces or printing paper samples as they apply to specific advertising campaigns. The small format placed some restrictions on creative design. Numerous graphics, paper and color content to fit serial's purpose. An announcement in the April/May, 1942 issue that publication would suspend for the "duration" [world war II], apparently became cessation.
DEPT: "Books & Pictures," reviews; "A-D Shorts," newsbriefs.
TYPL: "The Ethics and Aesthetics of Type and Typography." (4/5-42).
SCHL: Monthly (Sep, 1934 - Nov, 1937); Bimonthly (Dec, 1937+), 50 pp.
SPAN: Sep, 1934 - Apr/May, 1942//
VARIES
--Sep, 1934 - May, 1940 as PM.
WITH SUPPLEMENT
--Design and Paper, ? - ?
LC: Z119.A15

✣ AAP MONTHLY REPORT

SUB: "A newsbulletin for members of the Association of American Publishers."
PUBL: Association of American Publishers, 1718 Connecticut Avenue, N.W., Washington, DC 20009.
DESC: This organizational newsletter of the Association of American Publishers, is designed to inform members of trends, news, and emerging issues in the field of publishing. Articles run the gamut of Washington, D.C. political issues, to the academic community selling complimentary copies, to marketing research on the issues of retail sales and consumer demand. The Association of American Publishers requires a minimum of five titles published per year to qualify for membership. For the sampled issue of 1990: black ink editorial content with blue spot ink on uncoated paper stock in folded newsletter format no graphics or advertising (8 1/2 x 11 inches / 215 x 280 mm).
DEPT: "News From Washington," "News From the Paperback Publishing Division," "News From the Higher Education Division," "News from the School Division," "News from the General Publishing Division." (4-90).
TYPL: "High Praise for Washington Meeting; Board Votes to Return in '92," "Copyright Office Looking at Automatic Renewal," "AAP Supports Bill to End 'Propaganda' Labeling on Imported Books and Films," "Critical Issues Committee to Sponsor 'Teleseminar'," "AAP/PEN Program Looks at Acquisitions in a Changing World of Publishing." (4-90).
SCHL: Monthly, 4 pp.
SPAN: Sep, 1984+
FROM MERGER OF
--AAP Capital Letter (ISSN: 0162-3303) (and) Trade Voices (and) AAP International News and Notes (and) Paperback Publishing Division Information Bulletin (and) AAP School Division Newsletter (and) Higher Education Division Information Bulletin (and) AAP Professional and Scholarly Division Newsletter (and) School Higher Education Trade Voices Paperback Publishing News and Notes, Sep, 1984.
DD: 070 11
ISSN: 0748-8173

✤ AB BOOKMAN'S WEEKLY

SUB: "For the specialist book world."
SUB: "The only weekly journal of bookselling."
SUB: "The specialist book trade weekly."
PUBL: AB Bookman Publications, Inc., PO Box AB, Clifton, NJ 07015.
DESC: "Each weekly issue contains articles, news notes, book fair calendar, trade reviews, display ads, and a classified books wanted and books for sale section, as well as other departments of importance and interest to all antiquarian and specialist booksellers. Nearly half of *AB*'s weekly issues are devoted to subjects that pertain to the specialist dealer. *AB*'s Special Subject Issues are unique. They are practical resource tools as well as invaluable annual references for the book trade. Each one focuses on a specialty and contains informative articles on past and present publishing and bookselling within that field. Articles may range from nuts-and-bolts bookselling articles, definitive bibliographies or historical surveys by leading specialists or scholars in the field to interviews with booksellers or publishers, or histories of centuries-old publishing houses. Roundups of the current publishing in the specialty are also an important feature of our special issues." Special topical issues for 1990 included such diverse areas as Cartography, Western Americana, Photographica, Fine Arts, Music & Performing Arts, Auction, Crime, Law & Mystery, Medical, and Military History. A fascinating weekly publication in which extensive advertising matter holds equal interest. Must reading for librarians, collectors, and historians in all fields. For the sampled 1990 issue: Stapled magazine format, numerous black/white graphics and editorial content on uncoated paper stock, with two-color cover on coated paper stock (8 1/8 x 10 3/4 inches / 205 x 275 mm).
DEPT: "Editor's Corner," column by Jacob L. Chernofsky; "New Catalogues," of antiquarian and specialist booksellers; "Exhibition Notes," current displays related to antiquarian/specialist books; "Book Fair Calendar," upcoming events. (6-18-90).
TYPL: "The Next Decade: Issues, Strategies and Opportunities for Special Collections in the 1990s," "Librarians and Booksellers: Forming a Durable Bond," "Buying O.P. Books: A Guide for Librarians." (6-18-90).
SCHL: Weekly, 100 pp.
SPAN: Jan 3, 1948+
VARIES
--Jan 3, 1948 - May 29, 1967 as Antiquarian Bookman.
ISSN: 0001-0340
ABST: --Book Review Index (ISSN: 0524-0581)
--Library Literature (ISSN: 0024-2373)
--Reference Sources (ISSN: 0163-3546)

✤ ABC NEWS BULLETIN

PUBL: Audit Bureau of Circulation, 900 North Meacham Rd., Schaumburg, IL 60195.
DESC: Function of this four to six page newsletter is to keep Audit Bureau of Circulation subscribers apprised of recent changes in ABC monitoring program. News items tend to be brief, with special showcases for new Audit Bureau of Circulation publications.
DEPT: None. (7-78). None. (10-81).
TYPL: "'How to Read' ABC Reports to Be Featured in Series on New Cassettes, Booklets," "Schedule Test Audits Unslective Coverage of Free Publications," "Planned Study of Coupon Rule as Applied to Magazines." (7-78). "Business Eligibility Change Approved," "Circulation Seminars Scheduled for Chicago," "Approved ZIP Code Proposal." (10-81).
SCHL: Monthly (? - ?); Quarterly (?+), 6 pp.
SPAN: 1914+
LC: HF 5801.A
ISSN: 0001-0448

✤ ABC WEEKLY

PUBL: Australian Broadcasting Commission, Box 3906, G.P.O, Sydney, Australia.
DESC: The *ABC Weekly* began publication in 1939 amidst a storm of protest by commercial station owners over what they viewed as competition to their own listener publications. In its first editorial, the serial took great pains to champion its own independence not only from these station-publications, but also to state its freedom from government propaganda and other issues of a political or nationalistic flavor. The focus was and still is on providing a schedule of broadcasts for Australian license holders, and some accompanying articles detailing programs, artists, and other items of interest. Early issues favored reprinting highlights from many Australian Broadcasting Commission broadcasts, giving way to a more newsworthy design by the late 1940s. As of the last issue examined in December, 1950, all coverage concerned radio. Numerous photographs; newsprint small magazine format.
DEPT: "Editorial Introductions," "Curent Opinion," newsbriefs; "Picked Up on the Air," anecdotes; "Pinpoints from the ABC Talks," "World Wags," newsbriefs; "Selected Books," "Odds and Ends," anecdotes; "Mainly About Women," "The Music Page," "Science and Medicine," "Page of Sport," "What's On the Air," (12-16-39). "Letters to the Editor," "Radio Newsreel," pictures; "Interval," column by Lindley Evans; "Book Review," "Radio Plays for Next Week," "Films," reviews; "Show Business," column by Peter Woodruff; "Victorian A.B.C. Highlights," "Radio Round & About," "The Little Theatre in Australia," "Sport," (12-23-50).
TYPL: "Trotsky in Exile," "B.B.C. Barnstorming," "Sound Detectors in War," "Duke of Kent's Children," (12-16-39). "Great Grandson to Witness Re-Enactment of Sturt's 1830 Expedition," "Sydney Symph. Orchestra Makes Its First Commercial Recording," "Theatre Television Started Twenty Years Ago," (12-23-50).
SCHL: Weekly, 50 pp.
SPAN: Dec 2, 1939+?

LC: TK 6540 .A13

ABCA Bulletin, The
1969 - Dec, 1984//
(ISSN: 0001-0383)
SEE: BULLETIN OF THE ASSOCIATION FOR BUSINESS COMMUNICATION, THE

Abels Photographic Weekly
Dec 7, 1907 - Jan, 1934//
SEE: PROFESSIONAL PHOTOGRAPHER, THE

About Music & Writers
? - ?//
SEE: BMI: MUSICWORLD

About Music and Writers
Oct, 1964//
(ISSN: 0740-8382)
SEE: BMI: MUSICWORLD

✣ ABSOLUTE SOUND, THE
PUBL: Absolute Sound, Box 115, Sea Cliff, NY 11579.
DESC: In the premiere issue, the editors described *Absolute Sound* as a serial designed not for audio aficionados, but for those who wished to hear fine music played through a home audio system. As such, the emphasis was to be on music; with some articles detailing technological developments for the home. By the second issue, however, the editorial content of *Absolute Sound* (as it continues to present), concerned an advanced audiophile discussion of new technology. Articles are always well informed, and well written for a sophisticated audio audience. Of special note are detailed discussions concerning new models of audio equipment released for the consumer market. Numerous graphics; small format.
DEPT: "Viewpoints," editorial; "The Sound," equipment review; "Second Thoughts," concerning past equipment reviews; "The Passing Parade," comment; "Records and Tapes," reviews; "The Market Place," reader equipment responses. (fall-73). "Viewpoints," editorial; "Controversies and Letters," "Press Commentary," "Controversies," "Think Pieces," "The Sound," reviews; "Full Reviews," "Considerations," equipment reviews; "Editor's Choice," special equipment review; "Manufacturer's Corner," response; "The Music," "Marks Barks," record reviews; "Audiophile Recordings," reissues; "Classical Music," "The Parting Shot," comment. (summer-85).
TYPL: "The High End at CES: Almost Like a Family Reunion," "The Politics of Record Players," "The Dilemma of Digital: Questions and Paradoxes." (summer-85).

SCHL: Quarterly, 170 pp..
SPAN: Feb, 1973+
LC: TK 7881.4
DD: 621.389/3/05
ISSN: 0097-1138

✣ ABU NEWSLETTER
PUBL: Asia-Pacific Broadcasting Union, Sydney, Australia.
DESC: One year after its 1964 founding, the Asian Broadcasting Union began this monthly newsletter for its broadcast membership. The newsletter was designed to be a forum for news and discussion of issues of common importance. Early issues were typewritten (often on different typewriters), leading in later years to a standardized typewritten format with graphics. Latter issues also began to feature articles concerning broadcasters and broadcast organizations outside of the A.B.U. sphere. Magazine format.
DEPT: "Changes in Personnel," "Topics of Technical Interest," "News from Secretariat," (10-65). "Just a Few Lines," newsbriefs; "Sport Scene," "People," (10-72).
TYPL: Newsbriefs, (10-65). "NHK's New Complex Operative in July," "BBC Celebrates its 50th Anniversary," "Broadcast Fredom: 'This Monument to Our Liberties,'" "Extensive Training for Asian Broadcasting," (10-72).
SCHL: Monthly, 50 pp.
SPAN: Apr, 1965+?
LC: HE 8689.9 .A7

✣ ABU TECHNICAL REVIEW
SUB: "Published bimonthly by the Asian Broadcasting Union."
PUBL: Asia-Pacific Broadcasting Union, NHK Broadcasting Centre, 2-2-1 Jinnan, Shibuya-ku, Tokyo 150 Japan.
DESC: Similar in nature to its European Broadcasting Union cousin, the *ABU Technical Review* is designed to be a forum for news and discussion concerning technological developments in broadcast technology for its membership. Early issues necessarily had to serve as introductory text material to television developments. Latter issues concerned more technologically oriented discussions of equipment, with the inclusion of schematics and formulas, and assumed a more knowledgeable readership. Numerous graphics, charts, schematics, and other materials pertinent to discussion of technological issues.
DEPT: "Development News," newsbriefs; "Review of Technical Publications," "Question Box," (9-69). "Editorial," "Development News," "Broadcast Equipment Design," "CCIR Papers Reviewed," "Review of Technical Publications," "Personalities and Posts." (11-78).
TYPL: "Unattended Operation of MF Transmitting Stations," "Shading Correction Generator," "Broadcasting Developments in the ABU Region," (9-69). "Signal

Assignment System for TV Studios," "Low-Cost Satellite Receiving Techniques," "International Broadcasting Convention," (11- 78).
SCHL: Bimonthly, 60 pp.
SPAN: Mar, 1969+
LC: TK 6630 .A1A84
DD: 621.38/05
ISSN: 0126-6209
ABST: --Computer & Control Abstracts (ISSN: 0036-8113)
--Electrical & Electronics Abstracts (ISSN: 0036-8105)
--Physics Abstracts. Science Abstracts. Series A. (ISSN: 0036-8091)

ABWA Bulletin

May, 1937 - May, 1967//
SEE: BULLETIN OF THE ASSOCIATION FOR BUSINESS COMMUNICATION, THE

✢ ACA BULLETIN

PUBL: Association for Communication Administration, 5105 Backlick Rd., #E, Annendale, VA 22003.
DESC: Serving as a valuable resource for college and university communication administration, the *ACA Bulletin* provides a wide variety of stimulating articles on the administration of communication departments, schools, and colleges. Articles run the gamut from faculty salaries to course loads to linking the divergent fields of communication together into one academic discipline. Considering the breadth of the communication field, and the myriad ways in which such programs have historically developed, the *ACA Bulletin* is an excellent resource for both academic management and pedagogical applications. For the sampled 1991 issue: black ink on beige uncoated paper stock in perfect-bound magazine format (8 ½ x 11 inches / 215 x 280 mm).
DEPT: "Notes from the President." (8-84). None. (4-91).
TYPL: "Top Third/Bottom Third: A Humane Approach to Merit Pay for Academic Departments," "Theatre Faculty in the United States: Background and Past Analysis," "Administrative Burnout: A Women's Perspective," "Chairman Burnout and Productivity: An Inverse Relationship," "Communication, Climate, and Administrative Burnout: A Technique for Relieving Some of the Pressure," "Close-Outs in Communication Courses: the Student's Perspective." (8-84). "Speaking Across the Curriculum: Threat, Opportunity or Both?," "Preparing for the Future: Faculty Development Issues in the Year 2000," "An Intradisciplinary Perspective, Multiple Methods of Inquiry and Faculty Development - Point of View," "Planning for the Year 2000: Women in Academe," "Report on the Perceptions of Communication and Relationship During the Dissertation Process by Speech Communication Doctoral Advisors and Advisees." (4-91).
SCHL: Quarterly, 100 pp.
SPAN: Oct, 1972+

VARIES
--Oct, 1972 - Apr, 1975 as Bulletin of the Association of Departments & Administrators in Speech Communication.
LC: PN 4073.A8512
DD: 808.5/07/1173
ISSN: 0360-0939
ABST: --Current Index to Journals in Education (ISSN: 0011-3565)

Academy of Motion Picture Arts and Sciences. Bulletin

1928 - 1946//
SEE: BULLETIN

ACCESS

SUB: "Concerning media reform and citizen access to telecommunications."
SUB: "The journal of telecommunications reform."
PUBL: Telecommunications Research and Action Center, PO Box 12038, Washington, DC 20005.
DESC: Perhaps the best description of *Access* was contained in its subscription application: "I want to stay fully informed about the issues, the agencies, and the people affecting media reform and citizen access to telecommunications." This was a gutsy, challenging publication dealing with what the editors felt was the monolithic nature of media and government in the United States, and the need for citizen vigilence in gaining or maintaining access to those media, hence the name of the publication. This periodical covered issues of gender, sex, violence, children, minorities and government regulation of broadcast media. Of interest, the sampled 1981 issue indicated that Ralph Nader and Nicholas Johnson served on the board of directors. Note: the Telecommunications Research and Action Center was formerly known as the National Citizens Committee for Broadcasting. For the sampled issue of 1981: folded tabloid newspaper format, black ink with spot color on newsprint, some advertising (11 x 14 ½ inches / 280 x 365 mm).
DEPT: "FCC Docket," "Hardcopy," book reviews; "Feedback," letters; "Viewpoint," "Networking," similar public service minded organizations. (5-84).
TYPL: "Changing Telephone Numbers," "Prime Time Fantasies," "Cable Compromise Reached," "Communications Future: Democratic, Small 'd'." (5-84).
SCHL: Biweekly [except last two weeks of Aug and Dec] (1975 - 1976); Monthly (1977+), 8 pp.
SPAN: Jan 13, 1975 - 1985//
ISSN: 0149-9262

Access Reports

Jun 16, 1975 - 1981//
SEE: ACCESS REPORTS/FREEDOM OF INFORMATION

✣ ACCESS REPORTS/FREEDOM OF INFORMATION

SUB: "A biweekly newsletter on freedom of information and privacy."
PUBL: Access Reports, Inc., 417 Elmwood Ave., Lynchburg, VA 24503.
DESC: "*Access Reports-FOI* is a bi-weekly newsletter that reports on the latest developments in the freedom of information field." This unique 16-page newsletter ably produced by Editor/Publisher, Harry A. Hammitt, provides information important to the working journalist concerning the relative freedom of obtaining access to government materials and information. The newsletter provides a strong emphasis on legal aspects of the Freedom of Information Act, and the flow of information from these governmental agencies. Typical of the articles in 1991 were "Leahy Introduces FOIA Legislation," "CISPES Informant Denied Records," "GAO Faults FDA FOIA Operations," "Bill Would Subject Congress, President to FOIA," and "Buckley Amendment Violates First Amendment." For the sampled 1991 issue: single sheet, stapled, newsletter format, black ink with spot-color cover on uncoated paper stock, no advertising (8 ½ x 11 inches / 215 x 280 mm).
DEPT: "In Brief." (12-9-81). "News From Canada," freedom of information column by Tom Riley; "Views From the States," state roundup of news concerning freedom of information; "In Brief." (12-11-91).
TYPL: "Senator Hatch Reverses Position on FOI Ammendments," "Environmental Impact of Nuclear Plant is Classified, High Court Rules," "Chrysler Guarantee Loan Board Not an Agency Under Sunshine Act," "Political Action Committee makes Plea for Guaranteed Air Time," "Historian Loses Bid for JFK Assassination Papers." (12-9-81). "Court Orders Vaughn in Exemption 7(A) Case," "'Agency Records': Brevity Over Clarity," "Discovery Allowed in PROFS Case." (12-11-91).
SCHL: Biweekly, 16 pp.
SPAN: Jun 16, 1975+
VARIES
--Jun 16, 1975 - 1981 as Access Reports.
LC: JK 468.S4A64
DD: 323.44/5/0973
ISSN: 0364-7625

✣ ACES

PUBL: Acme Press, Ltd., 391 Coldharbour Lane, London, SW9 8LQ, England.
DESC: *Aces* provides a wonderful English-translation window to the comic strip world of various European creative talents. Consisting primarily of their ongoing comic strip series, Editor/Designer Cefin Ridout creates a quality showcase for their works, as well as interesting profiles of the artists, their backgrounds, breaks, and the hard work necessary for these professionals to have "arrived" in their careers. Editor/Designer Ridout has provided a dynamic layout format that makes for a pleasurable reading experience. All in all, *Aces* contributes to a wider deserved recognition to comic strip artists on the European continent. Stapled magazine format, black/white editorial content on uncoated paper stock, cover is full-color on coated paper stock, no advertising (8 ⅜ x 11 inches / 210 x 275 mm).
DEPT: None. (10-88).
TYPL: "Hollywood Eye," "Hardboiled Hollywood," "Foreign Interest," "Air Mail," "Continental Update," "Morgan." (10-88).
SCHL: Bimonthly, 35 pp.
SPAN: Apr/May, 1988+

✣ ACTF / PAC NEWS

PUBL: American College Theater Festival, University of California, Department of Theater, Film and Television, 405 Hilgard Ave., Los Angeles, CA 90024-1622.
DESC: "The ACTF/PAC NEWS is published quarterly by the Playwriting Awards Committee and the Playwriting Awards Development Committeee to further the purpose of the American College Theatre Festival and the Playwriting Awards Program." This 12-page newsletter functions to encourage, provide news of, and information on competitions for collegiate playwrights. Of special import is the large section, "Reports from the Regions," which provides highly detailed information on individuals, activities, productions, and other events of note which contribute to the healthy status of theatre on college campuses. Newsletter format; black/white graphics.
DEPT: "Reports from the Regions." (spring-88).
TYPL: "Two Original One Acts Chosen," "Some Bad News...Some Good News...," "Selection Team Report," "Theatre Bonding." (spring-88).
SCHL: Quarterly, 12 pp.
SPAN: ?+

✣ ACTION

SUB: "World Association for Christian Communication Newsletter."
PUBL: World Association for Christian Communication, 122 Kings Rd., London SW3 4TR, England.
DESC: *Action* is an eight-page newsletter designed to highlight news developments and provide a forum for ideas within the world Christian community which is involved in or planning to use different forms of mass communication. Each issue contains international news on the use of a variety of media, problems encountered in implementing or gaining access to media, and success stories of individual groups. Note: publication shows ISSN: 0413-3253, although other sources indicate this may be in error. For sampled issue of 1991: folded loose-leaf-style newsletter for-

mat, black ink with blue spot color on uncoated paper stock, three-hole-punched (8 ¼ x 11 ¾ inches / 210 x 295 mm).
DEPT: "Courses-Conferences," international schedule; "Books-Monographs," review; "People," newsbriefs. (7-84).
TYPL: "UK Churches Take Lead in Local Television," "Indian Exhibit Draws 30,000," "Latin Americans Urged to Write," "Lutherans Boost Young Writers," "AV Student Plans Community Training," "Cartoons Communicate." (7-84).
SCHL: Ten issues per year, 8 pp.
SPAN: Jul, 1975+

ACTION!
SUB: "The magazine of the Directors Guild of America."
PUBL: Directors Guild of America, Inc., 7950 Sunset Blvd., Hollywood, CA 90046.
DESC: Beginning with the first issue, *Action!* was a rather brash periodical exploring areas and issues that were not being spoken of in the trade press concerning the role, and function of the director concerning motion picture and television product. *Action!* was especially important for providing insight into the realities of directing. One sample issue provided articles on how a cinematographer views directors, a profile of a director of B horror films, an interview with Norman Lear concerning the "Family Hour," and the process of directing "Murder by Death," by situation comedy director Robert Moore. Camera technique, film economics, and general function of the director were subjects that found emphasis in early issues before suspending publication for a period of 18 months. A redesigned *Action!* appeared in January, 1978 but lacked the bite and zest of earlier editorship. The serial ceased publication one year later. For the sampled issue of 1976: stapled magazine format with editorial content mixture of black/white spot- and full-color pages with full-color cover on coated paper stock (8 ½ x 11 inches / 215 x 280 mm).
DEPT: "The Action Forum," letters; "News of the Guild," newsbriefs. (1/2-67). "Callboard," items of interest to DGA members; "New Products and Processes," "Outtakes," described as 'heavy and light industry gossip unavailable elsewhere'. (1-78).
TYPL: "Destination Vietnam," "Make Way for the Kids," "It's Time We Junked the Model-T Techniques," "A Star Discusses Directors in General and Wyler in Particular," (1/2-67); "Gross Behavior: How to Get Your Percentage Back," "The Cutting Edge of Verna Fields," "TV West-Don't Sensationalize the Dead Gopher," "Through a Shot Glass Darkly: How Raymond Chandler Screwed Hollywood." (1-78).
SCHL: Bimonthly, 60 pp.
SPAN: Sep/Oct, 1966 - Nov/Dec, 1978//
SUSPENDED
--Jul/Aug, 1976 - Nov/Dec, 1977.
LC: PN 1995.9 .P7A25
ISSN: 0567-8390

✤ ACTION FILMS
SUB: "Check it out, dude!"
PUBL: CFW Enterprises, Inc., 4201 Vanowen Place, Burbank, CA 91505.
DESC: *Action Films*, a quarterly consumer serial, showcases the action motion pictures for fans of this film genre. Numerous full-page action scenes from these films grace the pages, some in black/white. One sample issue for Summer, 1990 provided articles on Jamie Lee Curtis, Lou Diamond Phillips, Steven Seagal, Rutger Hauer and Jean Claude Van Damme. For the sampled issue of 1990: stapled magazine format with black/white and full color graphics and cover on coated paper stock, limited advertising (8 x 10 ¾ inches / 200 x 275 mm).
DEPT: None. (summer-90).
TYPL: "The Ten Best Action Films in Home Video," "Teenage Mutant Ninja Turtles," "Jean Claude Van Damme -- First Action Star of the 90's." (summer-90).
SCHL: Monthly (Jan, 1981 - ?); Quarterly (?+), 65 pp.
SPAN: Jan, 1981+
VARIES
--Jan, 1981 - Oct, 1982 as Martial Arts Movies (ISSN: 0744-8430).

ACTOR ILLUSTRATED, THE
SUB: "A monthly review of the stage."
SUB: "The magazine for professional and amateur."
PUBL: Actor Illustrated, 9, Arundel St., Strand, London WC, England.
DESC: *The Actor Illustrated* was a curious monthly serial for the "professional and amateur," which contained its own monthly supplement, *The Amateur Actor Illustrated*. Despite a supplement devoted to amateurs, many of the articles in the primary serial were also dedicated to amateur actors, stage reviews, and plays. Throughout these articles was an interesting thread of how stage professionals had affected stage amateurs, and an examination of the rise of the amateur actor to professional status. If there was a watchword for this serial, it would be "encouragement," for *The Actor Illustrated* believed that the professional actor of the London stage had his/her roots in the humble beginnings of Britain's amateur country theatres. Of special note was the monthly inclusion of a full duotone centerfold featuring a major actor or actress. Magazine format; numerous graphics.
DEPT: "A Review of the Month." (3-05).
TYPL: "Clever Village Actors," "Mr. Tree's Dramatic School," "Can Actresses Afford to be Athletes?," "Mr. Bart Kennedy's Life as a Property Man," "Famous Actors Who were Amateurs." (3-05).
SCHL: Monthly, 25 pp.
SPAN: Jan, 1905 - Jan, 1906//
WITH SUPPLEMENT
--Amateur Actor Illustrated, The,, Jan, 1905 - ?

ACTORS BY DAYLIGHT

SUB: "And pencilings in the pit" (Mar 3, 1838 - Nov 17, 1838).
SUB: "And miscellany of the drama, music and literature. Containing correct memoirs of the most celebrated London performers; original tales, poetry, and criticisms" (Nov 24, 1838 - Mar 16, 1839).
PUBL: J. Patie, 4 Brydges St., Catherine St., London, England.
DESC: "As dramatic criticism is the main object of our publication, we trust a word or two upon the subject, by way of preface, will not be deemed irrelevent in our first number. Error, mis- statement, and often palpable falsehood, stain our daily press, and are fast rendering criticism a nonentity, and the name of a critic an object of ridicule, derision, and contempt." Little appears to have changed since that first editorial appeared in *Actors by Daylight* on March 3, 1838. This weekly, small-format serial took theatrical criticism seriously, providing encouragement and compliments to those deemed worthy, and barbed poems (among other items) for those the editor (and it was hoped the reader) felt needed to be chided. As example, a poem in the June 16, 1838 issue took actor Charles Kean to task, calling him a "vain boy." Each issue carried a series of small articles detailing recent banquets, new theatrical fare, anecdotes of the famous and infamous. Of special note were detailed biographies of actors, producers and other theatrical individuals. Publication ceased after the editor took ill and could no longer maintain any regular publishing schedule. One full page woodcut graced the cover of each weekly issue of four pages, moving to a 16-page edition by 1839. A marvelous resource for the study of British theatre.
DEPT: "Notes of a Reader," "Works in the Press," "Notices to Correspondents," "Paris Theatricals," Theatrical activities; "Dramatic Incidents and Notes Theatrical and Miscellaneous." (1-12-1839).
TYPL: "Mr. Charles Mathews," "The 'National' Theatre," "Our Miscellany," (4-21-1838); "Memoir of M. Bihin," "The Crimes of Richard Hawkins," "Illustration of a Passage in 'King John," "Shakesperian Characters and Their Representatives." (1-12-1839).
SCHL: Weekly, 16 pp.
SPAN: Mar 3, 1838 - Mar 16, 1839//
LC: PN 2001.A4

Actors by Gaslight

Apr 21, 1838 - Dec 29, 1838//
SEE: ODDFELLOW, THE

Actor's Cues

Sep 30, 1941 - 1948//
(ISSN: 7800-0081)
SEE: SHOW BUSINESS

ACTORS FORUM

PUBL: Emmett Groseclose, Box 164, New York, NY.
DESC: "*Actors Forum* is the result of protracted and often intense discussion among a small group of young actors and actresses who have for many years felt the need for a medium through which actors could express their views on the many problems which face them in a chaotic industry. We have seen from our own experiences and those of numerous others that an incalculable amount of waste motion takes place in New York, Hollywood, and elsewhere that goes by the name 'persuing an acting career.' Naturally, whatever we say in this regard about actors is equally true of singers, dancers, writers, musicians, directors, and other artists of the entertainment industry." *Actors Forum* was designed to be an independent voice, fully separate from other actor publications which were "official voices" of their respective guilds and unions. This was a serial of the legitimate stage which basically ignored other media, using the argument that actors do form stage companies, but rarely buy a film or television stage complex. Editor Groseclose firmly believed that theatre via government funding was absolutely critical to the prosperity of live theatre, and such views are found within the serial's pages. Sample copies viewed (Nov, 1956 - Feb, 1957), were mimeographed typewritten publications without graphics. Commencing with the second issue (Dec, 1956), *Actors Forum* contained the statement "Published by the Actors Forum Group."
DEPT: "The Readers Write." (1-57).
TYPL: "Acting (The Semi-Career)," "Let's Organize--What For?," "Off-Broadway, the Junior Broadway." (1-57).
SCHL: Monthly, 7 pp.
SPAN: Nov, 1956 - Feb, 1957?//?

✧ ACUSTICA

SUB: "International journal on acoustics."
PUBL: S. Hirzel Verlag GmbH & Co., Birkenwaldstraße 44, Postfach 10 22 37, D-7000 Stuttgart 10, Federal Republic of Germany.
DESC: An excellent theoretical journal devoted to scientific developments in the international field of acoustics. Articles are submitted and printed in one of three host languages: English, French, or German, with accompanying article summaries in all three languages. Book reviews, letters, and miscellaneous sections printed in the submitted language have no translations. Numerous technical schematics, graphs and charts accompany each article. An excellent journal for acoustics research. For the sampled issue of 1990: Stapled magazine format, black ink editorial content on coated paper stock, with black ink cover on coated blue paper stock, with limited advertising (8 ¼ x 11 ⅝ inches / 210 x 295 mm). Assumes advanced technical knowledge of acoustics.
DEPT: "Letter," "Book Reviews," "Miscellaneous," newsbriefs and errata. (1-90).

TYPL: "New Three-Dimensional Models for the Piezoceramic Characterization," "A Detailed Investigation of Effective Geometrical Parameters for Weakly Focussed Ultrasonic Transducers. Part I: Optimisation of Experimental Procedures," "On the Concentration of Aerosol Particles by Means of Drift Forces in a Standing Wave Field," "The Influence of the Spectral Content and the Decay Time of Impulse Noise on Asymptotic Threshold Shift." (1-90).
SCHL: Monthly, 95 pp.
SPAN: Jan, 1951+
WITH SUPPLEMENT
--Akustische Beihefte (ISSN: 0516-3668), 1951 - 1963.
LC: QC221 .A5
ISSN: 0001-7884
ABST: --Biological Abstracts (ISSN: 0006-3169)
--CIS Abstracts (ISSN: 0302-7651)
--Communication Abstracts
--Computer & Control Abstracts (ISSN: 0036-8113)
--Electrical & Electronics Abstracts (ISSN: 0036-8105)
--Energy Information Abstracts (ISSN: 0147-6521)
--Energy Research Abstracts (ISSN: 0160-3604)
--Engineering Index Annual (ISSN: 0360-8557)
--Engineering Index Bioengineering Abstracts (ISSN: 0736-6213)
--Engineering Index Energy Abstracts (ISSN: 0093-8408)
--Engineering Index Monthly (1984) (ISSN: 0742-1974)
--Engineering Index Monthly (ISSN: 0013-7960)
--Excerpta Medica
--International Aerospace Abstracts (ISSN: 0020-5842)
--Life Sciences Collection
--Mathematical Reviews (ISSN: 0025-5629)
--Nuclear Science Abstracts (ISSN: 0029-5612)
--Physics Abstracts. Science Abstracts. Series A. (ISSN: 0036-8091)
--RILM Abstracts (ISSN: 0033-6955)

Ad Art Techniques
Nov, 1968 - Aug, 1970//
SEE: ADVERTISING AND GRAPHIC ARTS TECHNIQUES

AD Assistant
Sep, 1965 - Oct, 1968//
(ISSN: 0567-3607)
SEE: ADVERTISING AND GRAPHIC ARTS TECHNIQUES

Ad Forum
Jun, 1980 - May?, 1985//
(ISSN: 0274-6328)
SEE: ADWEEK'S MARKETING WEEK

✣ AD • MENTOR, THE
SUB: "An unabashed attempt to inspire advertising agency account executives."
PUBL: DCK & Associates, 3289 Winterberry Circle, Marietta, GA 30062.
DESC: There are magazines for advertising executives, production managers, media buyers, creative teams, technologists, office staff and even the mailroom. But until *The Ad • Mentor* came on the scene, there really was no publication for the advertising agency account executive where "the rubber truly meets the road." That's the beauty and value of this wonderful newsletter. Information and sales strategies are explained in clear, concise language for the newly-arrived or "stuck in neutral" sales team at any agency. Articles in the sampled issue explained how account executives will prosper as the agency prospers, a refreshing perspective which allows that agency principals are also of the human race, an excellent chart of the television spot commercial process, and equally informative articles concerning media planners subtitled "Planners are passionate people;" and the process of planning in order to succeed each and every day. In the decade of the 90s, in the mad rush to accomplish tasks, there seems to be less time than ever before to explain, instruct, and motivate the agency sales team to go out there and accomplish one more for the "gipper." *The Ad • Mentor* is not just nice to have around the agency, it is truly REQUIRED reading for any member of the agency sales team, and for any agency who wishes to profitably succeed in the coming years. To any and all involved in advertising agency sales: get this one and fast! For sampled issue of 1991: three-hole punched newsletter format, printed on recycled paper (8 ½ x 11 inches / 215 x 280 mm).
DEPT: None. (6-91).
TYPL: "Profiting from Agency Profitability," "Interview with Steve Kopcha," "Television Commercial Production," "Media...More Than Just By the Numbers," "Adapting to Evolving Client Needs." (6-91).
SCHL: Monthly, 6 pp.
SPAN: ?+

Ad-School, The
Jan, 1901 - Mar, 1902//
SEE: COMMON SENSE

AD SENSE
SUB: "A journal of advertising and business methods."
SUB: "A magazine for business builders."
PUBL: Ad Sense Co., 92-98 State St., Chicago, IL.
DESC: The format of this serial changed dramatically over its publication span, but not so its focus; that of providing anecdotes useful for advertising copywriters, halftones of noteworthy graphics, and short editorial-cum-anecdotes about the state of current advertising in America. Beginning with the January, 1906 issue

(first issue to include the recently merged/absorbed *Ad Writer* of St. Louis), *Ad Sense* provided lengthy, if not in-depth articles of interest to a wider audience in the advertising and manufacturing fields. Few trade ads appeared in early issues, giving way to numerous advertisements and graphics in later numbers.
DEPT: "As They Appear to Me," editorial; "By the Ad Sense Man," advertising trends; (2-1901); "As Viewed by the Managing Editor," "The Man in the Cage," comment; "Headlines and Phrases," 'from the pens of those who know how to pull business'; "The Advertisers' Round Table," 'Current retail advertising criticised'; "Rate Department," detailed rate cards for various publications. (3-06).
TYPL: "Piccolo Letter to Salesmen," "How to Get Results from Business Shows," "Hints on the Effectiveness of Window Displays, for the Manufacturer," "The Decentralization of the Weekly." (3-06).
SCHL: Monthly, 120 pp.
SPAN: 1896 - Aug, 1906//
ABSORBED
--Mail Order Bulletin, Jan, 1901.
--Ad Writer (St. Louis), Jan, 1906.
LC: HF 5801 .A2

AD WEEKLY

PUBL: Mercury House Publications, 110 Fleet St., E.C. 4, London, England.
DESC: This 50-page weekly periodical covers advertising agency trade news in England and selected world centers. Although some critical articles can be found, this periodical is primarily newsbriefs about agencies winning and losing accounts, new campaigns proposed, and the general state of international advertising. As is typical with advertising reviews, a great number of photographs are included.
DEPT: "Comment," editorial; "The Weeks Campaigns at A-Glance," excellent but brief overview of current advertising campaigns in Great Britain; "Accounts," briefs of ads and public relations; "News About People," lengthy personnel segments; "Media News Digest," media campaigns; "Off the Cuff," latest confidential news and gossip; "Letters," large section; "Perspective," comment; "Ad Weekly International," ad news. (6-5-70).
TYPL: "'Top Job or I Form My Own Agency'--Gearon," "Print Man Follows Bishop at BBBPC," "TV and Cinema for Hairspray," "Producers and Clients Clash Over Future of Sponsored Films," "New Subsidiary for IPC Business Press." (6-5-70).
SCHL: Weekly, 60 pp.
SPAN: ? - ?//
LC: HF 5801.A

Ad Weekly

Jun 6, 1969 - Oct 6, 1972//
SEE: ADWEEK

✤ ADVANCED IMAGING

SUB: "The voice of the imaging industry."
PUBL: PTN Publishing Co., 445 Broad Hollow Rd., Melville, NY 11747.
DESC: PTN Publishing and its editorial staff have always believed in the importance of the imaging science role in research, problem solving, new product development, and the corporate manufacturing production line. In December, 1968 when the first issue of *Technical Photography* was unveiled, imaging science meant only still photography. Then came the role of video in the early 1980s, and a whole host of new scientific and computer media which brought a merger between *Technical Photography* and *Functional Photography* into *Tech Photo Pro Imaging Systems*. Even this new publication title fell short of the explosive growth experienced in the late 1980s, and hence the move to the current *Advanced Imaging* title. Individuals who have not seen this publication for a while are in for something of a shock, for the field of imaging science now includes designs, equipment, and techniques (many of which are communication elements) that are on the cutting edge of technology. This publication is especially important for corporate media departments, whose task it may be not just to videotape a manufacturing process, but by means of graphic database, high-speed video shutter cameras, optical storage, and media presentation; explain what actually happens in the manufacturing process. An excellent publication for the scientific study of materials and processes via communication media, and for the quickly changing field of information science for corporate communication, sending, receiving, and storage. Magazine format, full color graphics throughout (7 7/8 x 10 3/4 inches / 200 x 275 mm).
DEPT: "From the Editor," "Events," calendar; "People," personnel newsbriefs; "Update," newsbriefs; "Comment," "Products," review; "Letters to the Editor." (9-89). "People," 'News of people who make the imaging industry'; "Updates," 'The latest imaging news in brief'; "Comment," "Products," 'What's new in imaging-related products'; "Events," 'Upcoming conferences, shows, seminars'; "Off the Shelf," column by Lee J. Nelson; "ROI," column by Leonard R. Yencharis; "What's in Store," column by Hugh Green; "Getting the Picture," column by Don Lake. (2-91).
TYPL: "DEC and Imaging," "The 1989 Imaging Chip Survey," "Automated License Plate Reading," "Satellite SAR Imaging on the Way," "'Erasable' Disks at Work in Remote Sensing." (9-89). "Audio Buttresses Medical Imaging," "Postal Inspection with Multiple Cameras," "Standard Platform Image Analysis Software," "Color Imaging Based on Just Two Colors," "Multimedia's Encounter with Image Processing." (2-91).
SCHL: Monthly, 75 pp.
SPAN: Jun, 1988+
FROM MERGER OF
--Functional Photography (ISSN: 0360-7216) (and) Technical Photography (ISSN: 0040-0971).

VARIES
--Jun, 1988 - Sep?, 1988 as Tech Photo Pro Imaging Systems (ISSN: 1040-0141).
DD: 770
ISSN: 1042-0711

Advertiser, The

Jul, 1933//
SEE: ADVERTISER MAGAZINE, THE

ADVERTISER MAGAZINE, THE

SUB: "Monthly for those who use and create art in advertising."
SUB: "Monthly in the interest of good advertising."
SUB: "The nation's advertisers--they ALL read The Advertiser."
PUBL: Advertiser Publishing Co., 11 West 42nd St., New York, NY.
DESC: The publishers, citing a "crying need for a Common Ground on which the Advertiser and the Advertising Artist may meet," developed this glossy meeting ground for artistic discussion on the technique and profitability of advertising art. Launched in the midst of the Great American Depression, general reader support showed gratitude for the serial's varied articles on visual graphics. Pages are in black and white with irregular use of color covers in the early years of publication. Latter issues moved into broader issues and media (most notably television).
DEPT: "Editorial Page," "Publisher's Page," opinion; "Advertising Art News," newsbriefs. (2-31). "Publisher's Report," "Reporter's Notebook," column by Charles Sievert; "Ad Agency Activities," "London Report," "Lithography, Printing & Production," column by Milton Rich; "Editorial Page," "AD-Lib," column by Ben Duffy; "Guest Editor," "TV Advertisers," "With the Broadcasters," "Publishers & Publications," "Newspaper Ad Activities," "Letters to the Editor," "With the Reps." (8-53).
TYPL: "Billing the 'Greatest Show on Earth,'" "Coordination of Art with Copy makes Fisher Body Corporation Advertisements an Outstanding Success," "Every Advertiser's 'FRONT PAGE' and How to Illustrate It." (2-31). "National Ad Consistency Builds Greater Institutional Value," "Brand Identification is NOT Brand Accepance," "Capable Management Assures UHF-TV Profits," "NBC: Maintaining Leadership is the Sarnoff Tradition." (8-53).
SCHL: Monthly, 50 pp.
SPAN: Oct, 1930 - 195u//
VARIES
--Oct, 1930 - Jun, 1933 as Artist & Advertiser, The.
--Jul, 1933 as Advertiser, The.
LC: HF 5801.A

ADVERTISER'S DIGEST

SUB: "Presenting a condensed summary of the best material--written and spoken--on advertising and sales merchandising."
SUB: "Presenting a condensed summary of the best material written and spoken, about the modern business scene."
PUBL: Executive Review Publishers, 224 S. Michigan Ave., Chicago, IL 60604.
DESC: A condensation-type serial which reprints, in the opinion of its editor, the very best articles on "advertising and sales merchandising." Sample issues from 1940 show about a dozen such articles per issue. No graphics.
DEPT: None. (10-40).
TYPL: "Low Pressure Selling," "Publishing a House Organ for Distributors' Salesmen," "Let's Keep Our Heads," "Paperwork in Sales Control." (10- 40).
SCHL: Monthly, 35 pp.
SPAN: Dec, 1935 - ?//?
LC: HF 5801.A24

ADVERTISERS GAZETTE

SUB: "A journal devoted to the interests of advertisers."
PUBL: George P. Rowell, No. 41 Park Row, New York, NY.
DESC: The *Advertiser's Gazette* defined its purpose in the first issue: "We shall in our next number commence the publication of a complete list of all the newspapers published in the United States, the value of such a list being long felt, and difficult to supply." This was a serial directed to the potential or active newspaper advertiser, providing information on technical, graphic, press, telegraph, and other elements designed to improve newspaper advertising in the United States. Unlike other serials of this time and ilk, the *Advertiser's Gazette* had fewer pages, but definitely more graphics devoted to advertising practices. Of special note were occasional listings of publication opportunities for advertisers. One such example was a March 23, 1876 listing of "Religious and Agricultural Weeklies." Small format.
DEPT: "Newspaper Intelligence," data on new, suspended, and ceased publications; "General Newspaper Items," newsbriefs; "Advertisers Interviewed," profile; "Editorial," "Advertisements," small display rate cards. (10-14-1875). "Newspaper Intelligence," "General News Items," "Centennial Exhibition--What Folks Say," "Editorial," "Advertisements." (3-23-1876).
TYPL: "Fallacious and True Reasoning," "Medical Advertising," "A Muzzled Press," "Pertinacity," "And Yet Another," "Badly Bitten--and Rightly So," "Bismarck and the Press," "How Large to Make an Advertisement." (10-14-1875). "Difference Between Men and Money," "The Woes of the Editors," "A Parting Word," "The Law of Libel," "Ingenious Advertisements." (3-23-1876).
SCHL: Monthly (Nov, 1866 - Jan, 1871); Weekly (Feb, 1871 - ?); Quarterly (? - Dec, 1873); Monthly (Jan, 1874 - Mar, 1875); Weekly (Apr 1, 1875 - ?), 16 pp.

SPAN: Nov, 1866 - 1888//
VARIES
--Nov, 1866, as Geo. P. Rowell & Co's Advertising Agency Circular.
--Dec, 1866 - Dec, 1870 as Advertiser's Gazette.
--Jan, 1871 - ? as American Newspaper Reporter and Advertiser's Gazette.
--? - ? as American Newspaper Reporter.
MERGED WITH
--Newspaper Reporter (to form) Printers Ink, 1888.

Advertiser's Gazette

Dec, 1866 - Dec, 1870//
SEE: ADVERTISERS GAZETTE

✤ ADVERTISERS GUIDE

SUB: "A magazine devoted to the interests of advertisers and newspaper publishers."
PUBL: A. W. Ayer and Son, 733 Sansom St., Philadelphia, PA.
DESC: The *Advertiser's Guide* began at an auspicious time, coinciding with the Philadelphia Centennial Exhibition, and the rise of newspaper advertising. N.W. Ayer and Sons' purpose in publishing this small format serial was noted in the first issue: "We shall aim to disseminate a more general knowledge of newspaper advertising and the advantages to be gained by it..." In effect, this promotional serial's purpose was to enlighten and cajole readers to utilize N.W. Ayer's service to place such advertisements, they being (according to their own articles), the best possible agency to utilize. During 1876, the *Advertiser's Guide* richly borrowed articles from the 1876 Centennial Exhibition, always proposing a means of advertising the merchandise described. It is also valuable for its criticisms of newspaper operation during this time, bringing to the reader's attention the "good, bad, and the ugly" of journalism practice. Of special note is the "Advertisements" section which comprises over half of each issue and is composed of self-serving hype, display and rate card information by a variety of American newspapers. No graphics except for newspaper mastheads within Advertisement section. Also of interest were lists of specialty newspapers such as the March, 1877 issue which carried "N.W. Ayer & Son's Select List of One Hundred and Thirty Religious Papers."
DEPT: "Journalistic Incidents," very brief news items; "Educational Intelligence," educational newsbriefs; "Fractional Currency," homespun sayings; "What Folks Say," Positive comments concerning the N.W. Ayer & Sons Company; "Advertisements," large 30-plus page of individual newspaper rate cards. (3-1877).
TYPL: "The Business Outlook," "Curious Facts About Insurance," "Turn on the Heat," "Concerning Titles," "Bambooing Corrupt Officials." (3-1877).
SCHL: Quarterly, 50 pp.
SPAN: Jun, 1876+?

Advertisers Magazine

Oct, 1907 - Sep, 1910//
SEE: ADVERTISING ADVOCATE

ADVERTISERS' WEEKLY

SUB: "A journal dedicated to service for the advertiser and space buyer regarding newspapers and markets."
PUBL: Advertisers' Weekly, 420 Lexington Ave., New York, NY.
DESC: *The Advertisers' Weekly* brought hard newspaper market data to the buyer of print space. Articles were filled with tables of information detailing circulation, lineage rates, consumer buying habits, paper supplies, and a number of retail dealers (from art goods to upholsterers) in any given newspaper market in the United States. The serial believed in strongly-worded factual articles with an absolute minimum of illustrations.
DEPT: "Editorials," "Basic Facts," tables of facts. (2-23-24). "Account Changes," "The Advertising Gallery," sample ads; "Recommended Newspaper List," "Creative Analysis," unique content analysis of a newspaper; "Review of Business Facts and Trends," "Talk of the Week," newsbriefs. (4-28-24).
TYPL: "Daily Newspapers of Over 100,000 Circulation," "Public Service Advertising," "Side Lights on Merchandising," "Are Rates Too High?" (2- 23-24). "Parke, Davis & Co. Enters the Ranks of National Advertisers," "Advertised Toilet Articles Show Large Ratio of Fast Sellers," "Denney Offers a New Idea in Measuring Advertising Expenditures," "How the Talking Machine Industry was Brought Back to Popularity," (4-28-28).
SCHL: Weekly, 30 pp.
SPAN: Jan 5, 1924 - May 19, 1928//
VARIES
--Jan 3, 1925 - Sep 26, 1925 as Jason Rogers' Advertisers' Weekly.
MERGED WITH
--Sales Management (to form) Sales management and Advertisers Weekly.
LC: HF 5801.A

Advertisers Weekly

1913 - May 30, 1969//
SEE: ADWEEK

ADVERTISING

SUB: "The journal of newspaper publishing."
SUB: "The journal of newspaper publishing and advertising."
SUB: "A national magazine of sales and business-building ideas." (Apr 9, 1925 - Jul 9, 1925).
PUBL: Newspaper Advertiser Publishing Co., New York, NY.

DESC: Although most sources show *Newspaperdom* to be a varying title of *Advertising*, there appears to be a substantial difference in content and purpose in the two serials. *Newspaperdom* was aimed at the editor and publisher of the weekly or daily newspaper. Articles described successful tactics of circulation, union negotiations, sought-out qualities of an editor, and other topics of importance to administrators. A distinct change took place with the serial by the early 1900s, with a more news-style format of late-breaking stories, and a growing emphasis on the advertising side of print. By the 1920s, this transformation to advertising was complete, and a name change to *Advertising* confirmed the change in focus. The emphasis now was on advertising across all media. Some graphics; magazine format.
DEPT: "Advertising Department," "Mechanical Department," "Editorial," "Class and Trade Journalism," "Letter-Writers' Symposium." (8-1893). "Some Successful Advertising Men," "Some Personal Notes." (8-1-04). "Editorial." (1-22-25).
TYPL: "How a Binghamton Newspaper Succeeded," "Essential Departments of the Trade Journal," "The Story of a New Jersey County Weekly." (8-1893). "Disturb Neighbors," "Editor Gets Farming Land," "Wild Publisher's Wildest Dream." (8-11-04). "Vital Problems at Detroit," "Agency Conspiracy Suit False," "Cross Word Puzzle Lotteries." (1-22-25).
SCHL: Monthly [irregular at times] (1892 - Jun, 1895); Weekly (Aug, 1895 - Oct 11, 1906); Biweekly (Oct 25, 1906 - Jul 9, 1925); 25 pp.
SPAN: Mar, 1892 - Jul 9, 1925//
VARIES
--Vol 1-40, No. 5 as Newspaperdom.
ABSORBED
--Caxton Caveat, Jan 9, 1902.
ABSORBED BY
--Editor & Publisher.
LC: PN 4700.A25
ABST: --Public Affairs Information Service Bulletin (ISSN: 0033-3409)

Advertising

Summer, 1978 - Winter, 1979/1980//
(ISSN: 0141-8920)
SEE: ADVERTISING MAGAZINE

Advertising Abroad

Dec, 1928 - Dec, 1929//
SEE: EXPORT ADVERTISER

ADVERTISING ADVOCATE

SUB: "An advertiser's magazine."
SUB: "A journal of information for advertisers and mail order dealers."
SUB: "A magazine for business men who advertise."
SUB: "A journal for the business man who advertises."
PUBL: ?, New York, NY.
DESC: "Chalk off your route ahead and then REACH THE GOAL! Let not obstacles, real or imaginary, turn you from your way. Persist! --and the end of the journey is soon in sight! ... Start the task right--THEN PERSIST! You'll finish with the winners!" These words from the first issue's editorial told the reader in no uncertain terms that *Advertisers' Magazine* would be persistently upbeat in its approach to finding ever-better advertising premiums and techniques for its readers' consideration. The serial was closely allied with the Associated Advertising Clubs of America, and strongly suported its purposes as the "keynote of success" in any business. *Advertisers' Gazette* dealt with all print media, providing thoughtful ideas on new advertising strategies; critiquing recent advertisements; and prodding its readers on to new heights of quality and subsequent profits. Some latter issues featured a particular segment of advertising such as May, 1910: "New England States and Publicity," or the September, 1910 issue: "Railroad and Municipal Advertising." Small format with numerous illustrations.
DEPT: "Editorial," short positive encouragements; "Daily Newspaper Notes," newsbriefs; "Magazine Notes," newsbriefs. (4-08). "Editorial," "Literature of Business," new books and magazines concerning advertising; "Magazine Notes," "Newspaper Notes," "Personals." (9-10).
TYPL: "A Striking Success in Selling Women's Apparel by Mail," "The Future's Correspondence Schools," "Direct or Through an Agent," "The Power of Suggestion," "Some Good Dairy Advertising." (4-08). "Out for Tourist Traffic," "The Cities that We Hear About," "What Makes an Advertisement Pull," "The Science of Mail-Order Merchandising," "Easy to See Why Some Men Succeed." (9-10).
SCHL: Monthly, 80 pp.
SPAN: 1902 - 1911?//?
VARIES
--1902 - Sep, 1907 as Western Monthly [Kansas City].
--Oct, 1907 - Sep, 1910 as Advertisers Magazine.
LC: HF 5801.A

✢ ADVERTISING AGE

SUB: "Where the world gets the word on marketing."
SUB: "The international newspaper of marketing."
SUB: "Crain's international newspaper of marketing."
PUBL: Crain Communications, Inc., 220 East 42nd St., New York, NY 10017.
DESC: Publisher Joe Cappo in describing the merits of *Advertising Age* called it a "...primary source of news for the marketing and advertising businesses, not only in the country but internationally. Our idea...is to reaffirm to everybody that *Ad Age* is by far the largest and most influential marketing publication in the world. We are telling our readers, who are mostly on the client side of the business, that there is still nobody who is close to us in terms of the kind of worldwide

influence that we [exert] in the industry." One of a group of "must read" serials, *Advertising Age* has dispensed timely marketing and advertising news to agencies, marketing managers, and their clients since 1930. Well-known in the trade for concise, detailed, and graphic coverage, this tradenews weekly provides news of advertising strategies, campaigns, production houses, personnel changes, international developments, regulatory items and industry news. Special note is made of the wide use of print layouts and film stills of new commercial campaigns, especially the use of four-color printing. An excellent source of new advertising developments for any creative budget or department. *Advertising Age* is published in two disinct sections on a weekly basis, with special issues the fourth week of January, and the fourth week of September. For sampled issue of 1991: stapled tabloid format with dynamic layout design, full color pages throughout on coated paper stock (11 x 14 ½ inches / 280 x 370 mm).

DEPT: "AdBeat," advertising news shorts; "Photo Revue," highlights of current advertising. (?-76). "Brady," column by James Brady; "Brady's Bunch," personnel observations; "Calendar," "Direct Marketing," "Editorials," "For the Record," account and trade newsbriefs; "Forum," guest commentary; "Garfield," comment column by Bob Garfield; "Global Gallery," 'Creative advertising from around the world'; "Letters," "MediaWorks," ratecard and editorial changes; "New Products Roundup," "People," newsbriefs; "PeopleWorks," profiles; "Photo Review," "Public Relations Beat," "Slices," column by Joe Winski; "The Next Trend," column by Lenore Skenazy; "Words," column by Michael Gartner; "Con-Sid-erations," column by Sid Bernstein. (12-5-88).

TYPL: "McMahan Selects the '100 Best' Television Commercials of 1976," "Cross-Ruff Promos Gaining Popularity as Marketing Tool," "Focus Selling Efforts on Life Styles, Retailers Told." (?-76) "How Burnett Built Billings to $3 Billion," "RJR's Brands: Bidding Begins," "NBC to Cut Olympic Clutter," "Software Publisher Tries Brand Strategy." (12-5-88).

SCHL: Weekly (? - ?); Semiweekly (? - ?); Weekly (?+), 90 pp.

SPAN: 1930+
VARIES
--Jan 3, 1958 - Aug 29, 1958 as Advertising Agency [Bristol, CT], Sep, 1958.
ABSORBED
--Promotion, May 13, 1974.

LC: HF 5801.A276
DD: 659.105
ISSN: 0001-8899
ABST: --ABI/Informer
--Business Periodical Index (ISSN: 0007-6961)
--InfoBank
--Predicasts
--Trade and Industry Index

Advertising Age [Electronic Media Edition]

May 3, 1982 - Jul ?, 1982//
(ISSN: 0744-6675)
SEE: ELECTRONIC MEDIA

Advertising Age and Mail Order Journal, The

Apr, 1916 - Aug, 1921//
SEE: NATIONAL ADVERTISING

Advertising Age/Europe

Jan, 1979 - Dec, 1981//
(ISSN: 0197-2359)
SEE: FOCUS

ADVERTISING AGENCY

SUB: "The publication."
PUBL: Agency Publishing Co., 400 Madison Ave, New York, NY.
DESC: *Advertising Agency* burst upon the advertising community as a fresh approach to promotion and sale of ideas and merchandise. This serial was almost as much a celebration of the artistic side of the medium as it was an exploration of new concepts. Covers, layout design, and even advertisements used color and typography in ever-changing formulas to find a new approach to the age-old quest for consumers. This was not a serial for the latest news in the field of advertising, but rather one of thoughtful consideration for new campaigns.
DEPT: "From the Publisher," "Crumbs from Other Tables," gleaned news items; "A Word to the Wise," "Federal Trade Commission Says." (12-37).
TYPL: "Radio Goes to College," "I Married into Advertising," "The Better to See You." (12-37).
SCHL: Monthly (at times Bimonthly), 150 pp.
SPAN: Sep/Oct, 1936 - Mar/Apr, 1938?//?
LC: HF 5801.A2765

ADVERTISING AGENCY

SUB: "Markets, merchandising, and media."
SUB: "Devoted to the professional practice of advertising." (Oct 4, 1954 - Apr 4, 1955).
SUB: "The magazine of agency operations and management." (Apr 29, 1955 - Dec 20, 1957).
PUBL: Moore Publishing Co., 48 West 38th St., New York, NY.
DESC: *Advertising Agency* provided a forum of thoughtful articles concerning advertising technique. This was not a serial concerned with burning issues of the day, although articles of that type were included within its pages, especially at the start of publication when the

serial was known as *Advertising Fortnightly*. It was obvious that by spring, 1958, (several months before its demise) that this publication was in trouble. Articles were short, when compared to other publications of this ilk, and problems of double-printed pages (May 9, 1958 sample issue) did not help matters. Numerous illustrations, especially in the area of newsbriefs, concerning advertising agency changes.

DEPT: "Page Five--The Late News," newsbriefs; "The Editorial Page," "The 8-pt Page," column by Odds Bodkins; "Written by Our Readers," readers comment; "EOW," observations. (6-6-23). "Letters from Readers," "The Peeled Eye," column by Dick Neff; "TV & Radio," "Barometer," "Copy Clinic," "For Creative Men," "Agencies Ask Us," Q&A; "Current Campaigns," "Industrial Advertising," "Inside the Agencies," newsbriefs; "Account Changes," "Media Report," "Starch Newspaper Scores," "Market Studies," "Agency Bookshelf," "Newspaper Ad Trends," "Calendar," "In Our Opinion." (5-9-58).

TYPL: "Making a Merchandising Policy 100 Per Cent Efficient," "What the Agricultural Market Buys," "The Measurements of Advertising," "Try This Plan if Your Sales Force Doesn't Follow Inquiries." (6-6-23). "Media Research," "Industrial Ads Fail to Sell Engineers," "To Land New Accounts," "Wyatt Earp Rides High," "10 Time-Buying Yardsticks." (5-9-58).

SCHL: Monthly (Apr, 1923 - Apr, 1924); Weekly (May 7, 1924 - Apr 21, 1926); Monthly (May, 1926 - Jan, 1953); Weekly (Feb, 1953 - Apr 4, 1955); Biweekly (1955+); 50 pp.

SPAN: Apr, 1923 - Aug 29, 1958//
FROM MERGER OF
--Advertising Fortnightly (and) Advertising & Selling.
VARIES
--May 7, 1924 - Apr 21, 1926 as Advertising and Selling Fortnightly.
--May, 1926 - Aug, 1948 as Advertising & Selling.
--Sep, 1948 - Apr, 1949 as Advertising and Selling and the Advertising Agency.
--May, 1949 - Sep, 1954 as Advertising Agency and Advertising & Selling.
--Oct 4, 1954 - Apr 4, 1955 as Advertising Agency.
--Apr 29, 1955 - Dec 20, 1957 as Advertising Agency Magazine.
WITH SUPPLEMENT
--Advertising Arts, Nov, 1923 - Sep, 1933.
--Advertising Agency, The, Jul, 1948 - ?
ABSORBED BY
--Advertising Age (ISSN: 0001-8899), 1958.

LC: HF 5801.A29
DD: 659.1/05
ABST: --Industrial Arts Index

Advertising Agency

Oct 4, 1954 - Apr 4, 1955//
SEE: ADVERTISING AGENCY

Advertising Agency [Bristol, CT]

Jan 3, 1958 - Aug 29, 1958//
SEE: ADVERTISING AGE

Advertising Agency and Advertising & Selling

May, 1949 - Sep, 1954//
SEE: ADVERTISING AGENCY

Advertising Agency Magazine

Apr 29, 1955 - Dec 20, 1957//
SEE: ADVERTISING AGENCY

Advertising Age's Focus

Jan, 1982 - Jan, 1985//
(ISSN: 0264-1755)
SEE: FOCUS

ADVERTISING ALERT

PUBL: United States Federal Trade Commission, Washington, DC.
DESC: A short four to six-page typewritten serial designed to alert readers to actions proposed, and actions taken by the United States Federal Trade Commission. Primary function of the monthly publication was to list advertising offenders prohibited from future commercial work in a specific area, such as aluminum siding installation, catalog merchandising, sewing machine sales, beauty products, food, carpeting, etc. No graphics; small format, moving to magazine-size format (April 7, 1967), and again (?) back to small format size.
DEPT: None.
TYPL: "FTC Issues Public Statement on Possible Shrinkage of Preshrunk Fabrics When Dried in Automatic-Dryer; Invites Written Views on Subject," "FTC Calls for Fair Packaging in the Toy Industry," "Orders Issued by FTC in Litigated Cases." (7-31-67).
SCHL: Monthly, 4 pp.
SPAN: Nov 6, 1961 - Nov 10, 1965?//?
LC: HF 5813.U6 A615

✤ ADVERTISING AND GRAPHIC ARTS TECHNIQUES

SUB: "A quarterly review of the communications business."
PUBL: ADA Publishing Co., 10 East 39th St., New York, NY 10016.
DESC: This publication concentrates on the creative art director. Several individuals from print and television areas are interviewed about their particular styles. Pictures and/or storyboards of their work are dis-

played within each profile. Although an interesting publication, none of the graphics in this 35-page periodical are in color. No advertising.
DEPT: "Literature and Supplies," new products; "Book Reviews," new art techniques books; "Easy Way," pasteup design shortcuts. (10-77).
TYPL: "Cover Profile: Mark Kozlowski," "Glowering Success," "Macy's Revivified." (10-77).
SCHL: Monthly, except July and August, 35 pp.
SPAN: Sep, 1965+
VARIES
--Sep, 1965 - Oct, 1968 as AD Assistant (ISSN: 0567-3607).
--Nov, 1968 - Aug, 1970 as Ad Art Techniques.
--Sep, 1970 - Mar, 1983 as Advertising Techniques (ISSN: 0001-0235).
SUSPENDED
--1977 - Spring, 1978.
ISSN: 0747-3168
ABST: --InfoBank

✤ ADVERTISING AND MARKETING

PUBL: Advertising and Marketing, Mercury House, Waterloo Rd., London, SE1, England.
DESC: This small-format magazine covers British advertising and marketing, and does it well. There are no color pages, but advertising stills from print and TV spots are used extensively. Some research, but little in the area of statistical research. A nice overview of current British advertising trends.
DEPT: "Book Reviews," rather extensive critiques of internationally published books on advertising and marketing. (Autumn-77).
TYPL: "Who Really Owns the Copyright in Advertisements," "Teenagers: Startling Facts About the New Affluent Market," "Selling Swimwear Became a Revelation of the Naked Truth," "Advertisers Who Do Not Match Their Beliefs with Their Money." (Autumn-77).
SCHL: Quarterly, 60 pp.
SPAN: 1964+
LC: HF 5801.A
ISSN: 0001-8902

ADVERTISING AND MARKETING MANAGEMENT

SUB: "Official journal of the incorporated Advertising Managers Association."
SUB: "A magazine of marketing communications."
PUBL: Advertising Management, Ltd., Pergamon Press, 61-67 North St., Portslade, Sussex, England.
DESC: A modest publication covering advertising strategy, campaigns, and philosophy in the British Isles. Emphasis is on advertising campaigns using interviews and numerous graphics.

DEPT: "Ad-Man's Diary," newsbriefs; "In Code," essay; "What's New," newsbriefs; "Review," "Letters to the Editor," "IAMA," presidents column; "People on the Move," newsbriefs; "Aspects of Advertising," editorial; (1-68). "Ad-Man's Diary," newsbriefs; "Review," "Bunbury," column; "What's New," newsbriefs; "News About Jobs," "Book Reviews," "President's Column," "IAMA News," (5-70).
TYPL: "How This Bore Got on Television," "When St. Michael Came to Belfast," "Changing the Pin-Stripe Image," (1-68). "Management Science and Marketing-Not All Models are Mathematical," "The Proof of the Pudding," (5-70).
SCHL: Monthly, 34 pp.
SPAN: 1964 - Jul, 1970//
VARIES
--1964 - Dec?, 1969 as Advertising Management.

Advertising and Newspaper News

? - ?//
(ISSN: 0001-8929)
SEE: ADVERTISING NEWS

Advertising & Sales Promotion

May, 1961 - Dec, 24, 1973//
(ISSN: 0001-8937)
SEE: PROMOTION

ADVERTISING & SELLING

SUB: "The national journal of modern merchandising." (? - Feb, 1922).
SUB: "The national journal of the advertising industry." (Mar, 1922 - ?).
SUB: "For the business of advertising."
PUBL: Advertising & Selling Co., 253 Broadway, New York, NY.
DESC: In an initial editorial the publisher observed: "*Advertising & Selling* is the consolidation of *Profitable Advertising* and the *Selling Magazine*. It will cover the fields of both, broadened to include all phases and developments of the processes of marketing." While *Advertising & Selling* lost the sense of humour previously displayed by *Profitable Advertising*, it gained a new vitality in its examination of the techniques, legalities, opportunities, and expense/profit side of the field. Articles demonstrated an honest attempt at quality research, with some tables of figures, and numerous graphics pertaining to articles. At times, special issues, (such as September 1909 on New England) appeared within the serial. Of special note in early issues was a directory of advertisers. An increased emphasis on radio advertising by the 1940s. Two-color covers with remainder black/white; small format at the start of publication, moving into a large magazine format by 1920s, and some color pages by 1940s.

DEPT: "The Editorial Point of View." (10-09). "Advertising, [year]--and After," column by Alan Reilly; "Clay Feet," current ad critiques column by Leroy Fairman; "Men Who Make Advertising," profile; "Editorial Comment," "Trade Editors Analyze Business Conditions," "Agencies," "Business Papers," "Magazines," "Advertisers," "Newspapers," "Convention Dates." (6-22). "Advertising's Month," media comparison; "To the Editor," "Editorial," "Peeled Eye," newsbriefs column by James Tyler; "Copy Clinic," column by E.B. Smith; "The News Digest of Accounts and Personnel," "Faces and Footnotes," personnel newsbriefs; "The Last Word," newsbriefs. (11-40).
TYPL: "A 'Horrible Example' Title Page Reformed and Reset," "Advertising and Copyright," "Booklets for Railroads and Hotels," (10-09). "How Big Can Your Business Grow," "Selling the Surface by Making the Surface Sell," "Big Doings at Milwaukee." (6-22). "And Now, Let's Look at Contests," "But How Does Mrs. O'Grady Like Premiums," "The 10 Commandments of Copy Writing." (11-40).
SCHL: Monthly (1909 - Dec, 1920); Weekly (Jan 15, 1921 - Aug 6, 1921), 50 pp.
SPAN: Jun, 1909 - Apr, 1924//
FROM MERGER OF
--Profitable Advertising (and) Selling Magazine, May, 1909.
VARIES
--Jan 15, 1921 - Aug 6, 1921 as Advertising & Selling Magazine.
WITH SUPPLEMENT
--Advertising Arts (ISSN: 0737-4232), 1930? - Mar, 1931?
ABSORBED
--Business World, The, Dec, 1910.
--Advertising News, Sep, 1918.
--Advertising Arts (ISSN: 0737-4232), May, 1935.
MERGED WITH
--Advertising Fortnightly (to form) Advertising & Selling Fortnightly}.
LC: HF 5801.A28

Advertising & Selling
May, 1926 - Aug, 1948//
SEE: ADVERTISING AGENCY

Advertising and Selling and the Advertising Agency
Sep, 1948 - Apr, 1949//
SEE: ADVERTISING AGENCY

Advertising and Selling Fortnightly
May 7, 1924 - Apr 21, 1926//
SEE: ADVERTISING AGENCY

Advertising & Selling Magazine
Jan 15, 1921 - Aug 6, 1921//
SEE: ADVERTISING & SELLING

ADVERTISING DISPLAYS
SUB: "A monthly magazine for national advertisers."
PUBL: Advertising Displays Publishing Co., 299 Madison Ave., New York, NY.
DESC: This is a most unusual serial in the advertising field, being exclusively devoted to window display. *Advertising Displays* attempted to look as good as the displays it critiqued, by use of art deco lettering and layout style. The value of this publication lay in the technique and style of compelling the street shopper to stop and consider the merits of products within the storefront window. Numerous graphics.
DEPT: "Editorial," "Gallery of Advertising Displays," "Installation Directory," pertaining to companies which installed window displays. (10-30).
TYPL: "How to Make Window Displays Produce Orders," "Science Does New Tricks for Advertisers," "What do Buyers and Sellers of Displays Think About Speculation," "How Miller Rubber Solved a Display Problem." (10-30).
SCHL: Monthly, 35 pp.
SPAN: May, 1930 - 1932//
LC: HF 5801.A295

ADVERTISING EXPERIENCE
SUB: "An illustrated monthly magazine for advertisers."
SUB: "A magazine devoted to the exposition of advertising." (Sep, 1902 - Dec, 1902).
PUBL: W.G. Souther, 1526 Marquette Bldg., Chicago, IL.
DESC: New editor and publisher Irving McColl took over *Advertising Experience* in May, 1897 (labeled Vol. V, No. 1), and described a host of new features soon to be found in this advertising publication. Among the new elements would be quality articles concerning the advertising industry accomplished through the expansion of special departments, guest writers, and new explorations in the area of graphics and graphic design. This was not a news and issues serial as much as a publication that provided encouragement, comment, and samples of advertising technique to its readers. A ten to 20-page section completed each serial containing advertisements for various print publications. Just prior to its demise, the serial consisted almost entirely of special departments with very few feature articles in the editorial section.
DEPT: "Editorial," "What We Hear About Advertisers," newsbriefs; "Of a Personal Nature," personnel newsbriefs. (2-1898). "Matters of Current Comment," "About the Magazines," "Outdoor Publicity, Etc.," "Doings of Those Concerned," "Publishers Who Will Substantiate Their Circulation Claims." (10-02).

TYPL: "Advertisement Illustrations," "Things Talked About," "Photography in Advertising," "How Publishers Advertise," "Advertisements, Booklets and Catalogues." (2-1898). "'Collier's Weekly' Excursion," "Helps for the Catalogue Maker." (10-02).
SCHL: Monthly, 50 pp.
SPAN: 1894 - Dec, 1902//
ABSORBED BY
--Judicious Advertising and Advertising Experience.
LC: HF 5801.A

ADVERTISING IDEAS

SUB: "A practical manual for the busy advertising man in dry goods stores and newspaper offices."
PUBL: Advertising Ideas, 239 West 39th St., New York, NY.
DESC: This was a very unique serial for a very narrow target audience, the dry goods store advertising manager. While it provided some techniques and "tricks of the trade," primary function was to present so-called "thumb-nail" sketches of full page newspaper ads, and their accompanying sample layout for fictitious and real department stores. In that manner, *Advertising Ideas* acted more as an ongoing instructional manual than a vehicle of news developments in the field. An important serial for the many pages devoted to sample advertisements, their makeup and psychology. Numerous graphics; very clean layout style.
DEPT: "Copy Clipped from Here and There," sample copy items. (9-21).
TYPL: "September--The Bigger Business Month," "Practice Pages for Beginners in Copy Writing," "Six Original Layouts a Month in Advance," "Making a Campaign Out of a Business Birthday," "Examples of Brief and Direct Appeals," "Now for a Little Baby Talk." (9-21).
SCHL: Monthly, 50 pp.
SPAN: ? - ?//
LC: HF 5801.A335

✢ ADVERTISING MAGAZINE

SUB: "A quarterly review of the communications business."
SUB: "A critical and professional review."
PUBL: Advertising Association, Abford House, 15 Witton Rd., London SW1V 1NJ, England.
DESC: A scholarly review of advertising in Great Britain, which publishes current research, criticism, and news of the advertising industry. This quarterly provides a considered exploration of the field of advertising, at times via quantitative measurement, and at times by means of descriptive and historical treatment. All forms of media are examined, historical and contemporary, as they relate to the general advertising field. A worthy publication for the scholarly arena.
DEPT: "In the Margin," commentary; "New Books," reviews. (winter 70/71). "In the Margin," "Bookshelf," (summer-81).
TYPL: "What is the Future for ITV?," "Commercial Radio and the Advertiser," "Monopoly and Advertising: A Case Study," "Advertising and Market Power." (winter-70/71). "We Must Reverse the Gentrification of Britain," "Profitability and Intangible Assets," "How the Standard was Raised in Scotland," "Direct Mail: At Last We Can Have Accurate Statistics." (summer-81).
SCHL: Quarterly, 45 pp.
SPAN: Autumn, 1964+
VARIES
--Autumn, 1964 - 1977 as Advertising Quarterly.
--Summer, 1978 - Winter, 1979/1980 as Advertising (ISSN: 0141-8920).
LC: HF 5801.A
ISSN: 0001-8961
ABST: --Public Affairs Information Service Bulletin (ISSN: 0033-3409)

Advertising Management

1964 - Dec?, 1969//
SEE: ADVERTISING AND MARKETING MANAGEMENT

ADVERTISING NEWS

SUB: "As the name indicates, is a guide to all publishers--and the newspaper fraternity in general."
PUBL: Advertising News Company, 117 East 24th St., New York, NY.
DESC: Early issues of this serial (under the title of *The Publishers' Guide*), had targeted the commercial publisher who desired information which would help him to substantially increase his advertising lineage each year. Each issue began with a profile of a major newspaper publisher. Additional articles, many of them newsbriefs with a terse one to three word headline, provided news of importance to publishers, with an emphasis on advertising. Of special note is that the majority of these newsbriefs were listings of "deadbeat" advertisers, bad experiences with advertising agencies, and advertisers judged to be of no repute at all. In 1916, a change of editor and title moved editorial content to a more clearly defined objective, newspaper advertising. Articles during this two-year time span discussed issues of newspaper/agency/advertiser relationships, and the growing emphasis on advertising campaigns. Indeed, a number of issues were devoted to campaign case studies printing complete portfolio examples for its readers, and details on the campaigns. Magazine format.
DEPT: "Among the Agencies," accounts; "New Advertisers," to newspapers; "Newspaper Gossip," "Shy People," 'Firms no longer advertising, and deadbeat advertisers'. (9-1898). "Editorial," "Observations as We Pass Along," "Mainly About People in the Advertising Business," "Retail Advertising and Advertising Men." (6-15-18).
TYPL: "Harrison Gray Otis," "Bargain Counter Plates," "The Roberts Agency." (9-1898). "An American Trademark for Our Goods," "The Advertisement as an

Artistic Design," "Graphic Methods for Presenting Facts," "The Ludicrous in Technical Advertising." (6-15-18).
SCHL: Monthly (? - ?); Weekly (? - ?); Monthly (?+), 35 pp.
SPAN: 1893 - Sep 21, 1918//
VARIES
--1893 - Jul 28, 1916 as Publishers' Guide, The.
--Aug 4, 1916 - Aug 11, 1916 as Publishers' Guide and the Advertising News.
--Aug 18, 1916 - Aug 25, 1916 as Advertising News and the Publishers' Guide, The.
ABSORBED BY
--Advertising & Selling Sep, 1918.
LC: HF 5801.A34

✢ ADVERTISING NEWS

SUB: "The big magazine for agencies and advertisers."
PUBL: Yaffa Publishing Group, GPO Box 606, Sydney, N.S.W. 2001, Australia.
DESC: *Advertising News* is a trade news publication for agencies, advertisers and general media organizations of Australia. A bright, lively format provides many newsbriefs and some feature articles concerning current business activities, trend analysis, and societal/regulatory developments which might impact the Australian advertising community. Liberal use of ad reprints and promotional activities enhance the content of the publication. A good resource for the status of advertising in Australia and the Asian-Pacific region.
DEPT: "Opinion," editorial; "News," briefs; "Marketing Trends," "Campaigns," varied group of ad reprints; "Media Buyers Bulletin," briefs of media buyers. (8-78).
TYPL: "Housewife Superstar Adds Sparkle to $1.5 Malleys Campaign," "The Upward Trend in Sales Tracking," "Budget: Ups and Downs in Federal Ad Spending." (8-78).
SCHL: Biweekly, 20 pp.
SPAN: 1928+
VARIES
--? - ? as Newspaper News and Advertising News?.
--? - ? as Advertising and Newspaper News (ISSN: 0001-8929).
ABSORBED
--Newspaper News, ?
--Advertising in Australia, ?
--Advertisers Monthly, The, ?
--Radio and Television News, ?
LC: PN 4700.N

Advertising News and the Publishers' Guide, The

Aug 18, 1916 - Aug 25, 1916//
SEE: ADVERTISING NEWS

ADVERTISING OUTDOORS

SUB: "A monthly journal devoted to outdoor advertising."
SUB: "You stick to me, and I'll stick to you."
SUB: "An illustrated monthly magazine devoted to poster advertising and poster art."
SUB: "The national journal of outdoor advertising and poster art." (1910? - Jan, 1930).
SUB: "A magazine devoted to the interests of the outdoor advertiser." (Sep, 1930 - Dec, 1931).
PUBL: Outdoor Advertising Association of America, 165 West Wacker Drive, Chicago, IL.
DESC: In the first issue of *The Bill Poster* on February 22, 1896, the editors defined that serial as "a trade journal, devoted to the interests of the Associated Bill Posters' Association and the Outdoor Advertisers of this country," with "a stock in trade of sound, practical sense, plain words, persuasive pictures and their judicious application to Outdoor Advertising. *The Bill Poster* will spare no endeavor to obtain and provide news interesting to business men throughout the United States in all that appertains to outdoor advertising." This was at a time when bill posters were mainly concerned with circuses and other traveling shows. As bill posters began to include display advertising, the name of the serial also changed; to *The Bill Poster and Display Advertising*, and in 1910 to *The Poster*. *Advertising Outdoors*, which succeeded *The Poster*, providing numerous examples of the potential of the new outdoor advertising industry. New techniques of color application, sheet size, mechanical and electrical displays all received their due. Numerous graphics of both ad concepts and actual billboards were featured. Stating that, "For the present at least, *Advertising Outdoors* has reached the end of its effectiveness," the serial ceased publication with the December, 1931 issue.
DEPT: "Editorial," "The Outdoor Industry Abroad." (8-30).
TYPL: "Outdoor Advertising Sells Checker Cab Service," "An American Art Director Looks at Europe's Outdoor Advertising," "Old West Lives Again on Rio Grande Posters," "New Radio Programs Introduced by Outdoor Advertising." (8-30).
SCHL: Monthly, 35 pp.
SPAN: Feb 22, 1896 - Dec, 1931//
VARIES
--Feb 22, 1896 - ? as Bill Poster, The.
--? - 1910 as Bill Poster and Display Advertising, The.
--1910 - Jan, 1930 as Poster, The.
LC: HF 5843.A15

Advertising Quarterly

Autumn, 1964 - 1977//
SEE: ADVERTISING MAGAZINE

Advertising Requirements

Feb, 1953 - Apr, 1961//
SEE: PROMOTION

ADVERTISING RESULTS MAGAZINE

SUB: "The magazine on the science of advertising" (Aug, 1909).
SUB: "The clearing house of advertising facts and figures." (Sep/Oct, 1909).
PUBL: R. R. Lawson Co., 70 Fifth Ave., New York, NY.
DESC: Editor Robert Kennedy noted in the first issue: "The purpose of this magazine is to reduce advertising to a science--to eliminate all guess work and to get one hundred cents worth of value out of every dollar spent." Readers certainly got their money's worth from this small format serial that stressed technique of, and case-studies of advertising. This was, indeed, a common-sense approach, with a 30-page initial issue greatly enlarged in the second (and unfortunately last) issue of Sep/Oct, 1909 to 50 pages. Numerous graphics, especially magazine covers of note.
DEPT: "Who's Who in Advertising," profiles. (9/10-09).
TYPL: "A Mortality Table on Advertising," "Advertising Results of Food and Food Products," "From Little Acorns Great Oaks Grow," "The Horsepower of Advertising." (9/10-09).
SCHL: Monthly (Aug, 1909); Bimonthly (Sep/Oct, 1909), 50 pp.
SPAN: Aug, 1909 - Sep/Oct, 1909//
LC: HF 5801.A35

ADVERTISING REVIEW

PUBL: St. Bride's Press, Carlisle House, 8 Southampton Row, London WC1, England.
DESC: In its first issue, the editors noted that the British had admired other nations' advertising long enough; that England had much to teach the world, and would explore advertising issues and techniques through the pages of this new journal. Advertising campaigns, rather than late-breaking news was the focus, with numerous sample advertisements featured, some of which were in color. Of special note is the irregular use of two different paper stocks to emphasize different sections of each issue, and in-depth profiles of British advertising executives. Twenty-five-plus articles per issue.
DEPT: "Editorial," "Australian Newsletter." (spring-55). "Editorial," "Marketing Today." (9/10-58).
TYPL: "Public Relations for Advertising," "Moving Pictures--The Advertising Film," "Sales Management Personalities and Practice," "The Schweppesman Conquers America." (spring-55). "First Aid for Art Directors," "Trade Marks and Their Infringement," "The Printer Speaks." (9/10-58).
SCHL: Quarterly [Irregular at times], (1954 - 1957); Bimonthly, (1958); 50 pp.
SPAN: Summer, 1954 - Nov/Dec, 1958//
LC: HF 5801.A36
DD: 659.105
ISSN: 0515-491X

Advertising Statistical Review

1972 - 1975//
(ISSN: 0065-3640)
SEE: PRESS STATISTICAL REVIEW

Advertising Statistical Review of Press and Television Expenditures

? - 1972//
SEE: PRESS STATISTICAL REVIEW

Advertising Techniques

Sep, 1970 - Mar, 1983//
(ISSN: 0001-0235)
SEE: ADVERTISING AND GRAPHIC ARTS TECHNIQUES

Advertising World

1974? - Jun, 1985//
(ISSN: 0163-9412)
SEE: INTERNATIONAL ADVERTISER

✦ ADVISER UPDATE

PUBL: Dow Jones Newspaper Fund, PO Box 300, Princeton, NJ 08543-0300.
DESC: The *Adviser Update* lacks a subtitle, but if one were to submit one for this quarterly publication, it could be "Absolutely indespensible for today's scholastic publications adviser." The Dow Jones Newspaper Fund continues to generously contribute to the print field with this outstanding publication detailing the state of press freedom, layout design trends, and employment opportunities for journalism students in high schools in the United States. Pedagogical advisers are seen as critical to the process of journalistic quality and furtherance of the craft. Articles are a wonderful blend of both encouragement (in the form of teaching and publication awards), as well as the political/economic reality of producing an independent publication at any academic level. Certainly one favorite section of each issue is "These Struck Our Fancy," in which articles and photographs from high school publications are reprinted for the enjoyment and instruction of other journalism advisers. Those that believe "high school" publications are synonymous with ditto machines and mimeo masters are in for a surprise with the dynamic journalistic examples reprinted in the *Adviser Update*. This is truly "MUST" reading for today's high school journalism adviser. Sampled issue for 1991: stapled magazine format with different spot color utilized each issue, excellent graphics and examples of newspaper layout on coated paper stock (8 ½ x 11 inches / 215 x 280 mm).
DEPT: "Newsmakers," people, projects in the news; "These Struck Our Fancy," outstanding showcase for the best in scholastic newspaper journalism. (summer-91).

TYPL: "Student Press Freedom Bill Would Protect Advisers Who Encourage Free Expression," "N.J. Judge Rules Student Press Rights Protected," "Poynter Study Challenges Opinion of What Attracts Reader to the News Page," "Looking to the Future in High School Publications," "Self-Censorship: Red Light? Green Light?" (summer-91).
SCHL: Quarterly, 12 pp.
SPAN: ?+

ADVISOR

SUB: "A journal specially devoted to the interests of advertisers." (Feb, 1899 - Aug, 1899).
SUB: "A magazine devoted to the interests of advertisers." (Sep, 1899 - Dec, 1902).
PUBL: Phillips and Co., 1133 Broadway, New York, NY.
DESC: In its initial issue of February, 1899, the editors set the tone for future issues: "There is no journal published in the United States at the present time devoted exclusively to the interests of the advertisers of America-- hence the birth of *The Advisor*." The editors took great pains to point out that other such advertising serials were partial to, or exclusively under the control of newspapers, but not *The Advisor*, which would represent the interests of the advertiser. *The Advisor* enjoyed strong support from magazine and newspaper publishers, and sometimes the advertising section outweighed the serial's editorial area. Articles were very short, oftentimes only one-third column long. The majority of some issues were single sentence observations about some aspect of advertising, such as what approach a particular advertiser was using this month. Few graphics; small format.
DEPT: None. (8-02).
TYPL: "Outdoor Advertising Posterizing in Particular," "The Attractiveness of Color," "Trade Paper Advertising," "Mail Order Monthlies as Advertising Mediums." (8-02).
SCHL: Monthly, 114 pp.
SPAN: Feb, 1899 - Dec, 1902//
LC: HF 5801.A4

✦ ADWEEK

SUB: "A journal for all who advertise and all who ought to advertise at home and overseas." (? - Apr 4, 1919).
SUB: "The journal of advertising and marketing."
SUB: "Organ of British Advertising."
PUBL: Mercury House Publications, Mercury House, Waterloo Rd., London SE1, England.
DESC: In the 1950s, *Advertisers Weekly* was a news magazine-style serial devoted to late-breaking news of the advertising field. Short articles and numerous graphics made up the bulk of reading material. Advertisements were primarily by print media extolling the virtues of their respective vehicles to reach British consumers. Pages in the late 1950s were still on newsprint due to post-war shortages. By the mid-1970s the title changed to *Adweek*, the format to a tabloid newsprint-style publication. The function remained that of reaching the British advertising community, delivering to them a significant amount of late-breaking news in 50-some pages each week. A primary emphasis continued to be industry news with succinct articles in a six-column format. Numerous graphics, especially those featuring people and advertising campaigns. Quality reporting and editing are an obvious hallmark in this trade paper.
DEPT: "This Week in Advertising," "Good Ideas for Advertisers," "Men of Mark in Advertising," profiles; "Letters from Our Readers," "Law Reports," "We Hear." (9-26-19). "Letters to the Editor," "Club News," ad association newsbriefs; "News About People," "Editorial," "Display & Commercial Art," "Mainly Personal," "New Books Reviewed," "Current Advertising," "Media Space Record," "We Hear," newsbriefs. (2-23-50). "Diary," comment; "Letters," "Television," column by Alice McKay; "Press," column by Doug Vickers; "Adweek Digest Top 50," agency facts and figures; "Adweek Digest," activity by agency; "People," "In Brief," "Adweek Piggyback Register," proposed marketing surveys; "Appointments," "The Admen's Guide to Advertising Services," "Rumour." (1-10-75)
TYPL: "What do Advertisers Pay For?," "Advertisers--Follow Up Where Our Soldiers Went," "Putting the 'Clincher' into the Copy." (9-26-19). "How Newspapers will Tell the General Election Story," "Compliance with Code Made New Condition of Agency Recognition," "Newspaper society and I.I.P.A. Reach Agreement on Cancellations." (2-23-50). "Marsteller Beats 3 to Mercedes," "Agencies Lose Charity Slices," "DPBS Gives Up Austin Reed Account," "Media Man Quits for New Shop," "IPA Scraps Radio Deal with Equity." (1-10-75).
SCHL: Weekly, 40 pp.
SPAN: 1913+
VARIES
--1913 - May 30, 1969 as Advertisers Weekly.
--Jun 6, 1969 - Oct 6, 1972 as Ad Weekly.
LC: HF 5801.A273
DD: 659.1/05
ISSN: 0001-8880

✦ ADWEEK

SUB: "Media, Agencies, Clients." (Feb 2, 1959 - ?).
SUB: "National monthly issue."
SUB: "The chronicle of advertising in the west."
SUB: "Media, Agencies, Clients." (Jan 7, 1965 - ?).
SUB: "Advertising's first and only semi-weekly." (Jan 7, 1965 - ?).
SUB: "Marketing / Advertising / Communication."
PUBL: A/S/M Communications, 5757 Wilshire Blvd., Suite M110, Los Angeles, CA 90036
DESC: This remains required reading material for all advertising agencies and many West Coast corporate advertising directors. News items, while brief, comprehensively address the changing state of accounts, agencies, media buys, and those accounts

which were up for review. *MAC*, (and all of its other various titles) remains a major news source for the advertising community. The new format under the *Adweek* banner provides longer articles and features on the advertising market, especially details concerning unique campaigns, agency ownership, and other news affecting the west coast.

DEPT: "MiniMACs," newsbriefs. (7-6-67). "On the Move," agency change of address; "MiniMACs," personnel promotions and changes. (2-76).

TYPL: "Samsonite Backs Record Push with $1 Million+ Allocation," "News is Most Important Commodity--Should be Effective Sales Tool: Motley." (7-6-67). "Broadcast Effort Supports Pentel Pens," "Great Western Corp Reviews Agencies for $2 Million Billing," "PICAM Products Int'l to Bow Multimedia Effort." (2-76).

SCHL: Weekly [except first and last weeks of the year], 30 pp.

SPAN: Dec, 1951+
VARIES
--Dec 19, 1951 - Jul 10, 1967 as Media, Agencies, Clients.
--Jul 13, 1967 as MAC/WA.
--Jul 17, 1967 - Dec 21, 1967 as MAC.
--Dec 28, 1967? - Jan 4, 1970? as MAC/WA.
--Jan 12, 1970 - Mar 2, 1970 as MAC/Western Advertising.
--Mar 9, 1970 - Nov 17, 1980 as MAC/Western Advertising News (ISSN: 0194-4789).
--Apr 12, 1982 as Adweek/West.
ABSORBED
--Western Advertising, Jul 6, 1967.

LC: HF 5801.M
ISSN: 0199-4743
ABST: --InfoBank

Adweek [National Marketing Edition]

Jul 1, 1985 - Sep 1, 1986//
(ISSN: 0888-3718)
SEE: ADWEEK'S MARKETING WEEK

Adweek/West

Apr 12, 1982//
SEE: ADWEEK

✤ ADWEEK'S MARKETING WEEK

SUB: "For consumer marketing management."
PUBL: A/S/M Communications, 49 East 21st St., New York, NY 10010.
DESC: [*Adweek's Marketing Week*]: A subscription postcard bound into a July, 1991 issue exclaimed to readers: "Big Brands. Big Ideas. Yes! Start my subscription to *Adweek's Marketing Week* and keep me informed about America's biggest brands and biggest marketing ideas." Without a doubt, that is the form, function, and value of this well-executed weekly publication of marketing for North American advertising agencies. Bold colors combine with succinct articles throughout this weekly concerning the latest news of brand-name product promotion for the world consumer community. One sampled issue provided articles on medical endorsements, the New York City Consumer Affairs Commissioner's attempts to bring minorities into advertisements, a retrospective review of advertising's classic commercials, and a series of excellent articles on corporations who have revived their market shares through innovative marketing measures. Most articles have subheads, such as "Cover Story," "American Pulse," "Retailing," "Corporate Profile," "Comebacks," or "Critique," that aid in fast recall of pertinent facts. Of special note is an excellent (and separately numbered) classified advertising section designed for unique North American editions with the following subsections: "Advertising Services," "Media Contacts," "Business Opportunities," and "Employment Opportunities." This is "MUST" reading for anyone immersed in the fast-changing arena of product marketing and promotion. Indeed, *Adweek's Marketing Week* provides an unusual guarantee to potential subscribers: "If you're employed by an agency or client company and are disappointed by *Adweek's Marketing Week* at any time, we'll refund the entire subscription price, no questions asked." Sampled issue for 1991 consisted of stapled magazine format, full-color pages throughout on coated paper stock (8 3/8 x 10 7/8 inches / 210 x 275 mm).

DESC: [*Ad Forum*]: This was a magazine for the corporate marketing executive, detailing successful and not so successful campaigns in bringing new products to the consumer market. Special emphasis was placed upon the use of advertising within these new marketing campaigns. Typical topics included marketing the cruise line industry, new opportunities for magazines and cable; the marketing value of daytime television; use of personal computers in marketing services; pitching of new services by hotels; and the return of one-sponsor television specials. For the sampled issue of 1983: perfect-bound magazine format, mixture of black ink, spot- and full-color pages all on coated paper stock (8 x 10 3/4 inches / 205 x 275 mm).

DEPT: "From the Editors," "Outlook," "Your Marketing Instincts," "Legal Watch," "Marketing Update," "Ed Forum," "Worldwatch," "Roper's America," "Product Alert," "Ad Impact," "Video Update," "Campaign," "The Marketer's Economist," "Management Moves," "Bibliofiles." (9-84). "News Briefs," "Signing On," new product marketing review; "Consumer Data," American consumer demographics; "Account Activity," news of winning and losing agencies; "Editor's Note," editorial column by Rinker Buck; "Letters," "Tie-In Network," companies seeking or offering promotional opportunities; "New Product Watch," "Calendar," extensive listing of upcoming events, workshops, and seminars for advertising, marketing, and media professionals; "People," newsbriefs; "Re-

sources," helpful listing of potential materials and people; "Corridor Talk," marketing, media and advertising tidbits column by Kevin Kerr. (7-29- 91).
TYPL: "The Trouble with Sports Advertising," "Timex and VALS Engineer a Psychographic Product Launch," "Cigarette Makers Turn to Packaging in Fight for Share," "Business Joins Government to Sell America Abroad." (9-84). "Marcus Welby, Brand Manager," "Drink Boxes Hit TV... the New 'Cracker-Chips'," "Bully Tactics for Political Gain," "Fashion Comes to Scuba," "Mervyn's Wows Miami." (7-29-91).
SCHL: Monthly (Jun, 1980 - May?, 1985); Weekly [except semiweekly last week of Mar, Jun, Sep, and Dec; no issue in last week of Dec] (Jul 1, 1985 - Sep 1, 1986), 30 pp.
SPAN: Jun, 1980+
EDITION
--National Marketing Edition.
VARIES
--Jun, 1980 - May?, 1985 as Ad Forum (ISSN: 0274-6328).
--Jul 1, 1985 - Sep 1, 1986 as Adweek [National Marketing Edition] (ISSN: 0888-3718).
SUSPENDED
--Jul, 1981.
LC: HF 5801.A43
DD: 659.1/0973
ISSN: 0892-8274
ABST: --ABI/Informer
--Business Periodical Index (ISSN: 0007-6961)
--Management Contents

AEG Progress

? - 1967//
SEE: AEG-TELEFUNKEN PROGRESS

AEG-TELEFUNKEN PROGRESS

PUBL: AEG Telefunken Zentralabteilung Firmenverlag, Hohenzollerndamm 150, 1000 Berlin 33, Federal Republic of Germany.
DESC: This English language edition encompassed a highly technical review of electronics developments by the AEG-Telefunken organization headquartered in Berlin, West Germany. Articles covered a multitude of industries, among which were the diverse fields of mass communication technologies. Engineering knowledge was assumed; numerous graphics and schematics. Note: an all-German language edition was also published under the ISSN: 0040-1447.
DEPT: None. (#4-75).
TYPL: "TV Translators with Common Vision and Sound Signal Transmission," "A New Series of Parabolic 3-m-Antennas," "Tomorrow's Television Picture Reproducing Systems." (#4-75).
SCHL: Quarterly, 40 pp.
SPAN: ? - #2, 1982//
VARIES
--? - 1967 as AEG Progress.

LC: TK 3.A22
ISSN: 0001-107x
ABST: --Communication Abstracts
--Coal Abstracts (ISSN: 0309-4979)
--Energy Research Abstracts (ISSN: 0160-3604)
--Engineering Index Annual (ISSN: 0360-8557)
--Engineering Index Energy Abstracts (ISSN: 0093-8408)
--Engineering Index Monthly (ISSN: 0013-7960)

AEJ Newsletter, The

1968? - ?//
(ISSN: 0278-8179)
SEE: AEJMC NEWS

✣ AEJMC NEWS

SUB: "The newsletter of the Association for Education in Journalism and Mass Communication."
PUBL: Association for Education in Journalism and Mass Communication, 1621 College St., USC, Columbia, SC 29208-0251.
DESC: Supplementing AEJMC's scholarly works (*Journalism Quarterly* and *Journalism Monographs*), is *AEJMC News*, providing news of association schools, individuals, and association activities throughout the school year. News items include grant opportunities, news of upcoming workshops or conventions, publication activities, journalism program development and other items of interest to college-level faculty and staff. Of special note is the ongoing departmental feature "Placement Service," listing pedagogical opportunities at colleges and universities. For the sampled issue of 1988: magazine format (8 ½ x 11 inches / 215 x 280 mm); some graphics.
DEPT: "From the President," "Association Briefs," newsbriefs; "News Notes," extensive section detailing AEJMC member individual and school activities; "Placement Service," news of academic employment opportunities. (summer-88).
TYPL: "Members Enjoy Portland Convention's Diversity," "Program Offers Grants to Journalism Faculty," "PF&R Evaluates 1986-87 Divisions," "Convention Papers Can Be Ordered." (summer-88).
SCHL: Quarterly (? - ?); Ten issues per year (? - ?); Six issues per year [Sep - Jun] (?+), 20 pp.
SPAN: 1968?+
VARIES
--1968? - ? as AEJ Newsletter, The (ISSN: 0278-8179).
--198u - Jul, 1983 as AEJMC Newsletter, The.
DD: 070
ISSN: 0747-8909

AEJMC Newsletter, The

198u - Jul, 1983//
SEE: AEJMC NEWS

AERT Journal
Oct, 1956 - May, 1957//
SEE: PUBLIC TELECOMMUNICATIONS REVIEW

✣ AES
SUB: "Journal of the Audio Engineering Society."
SUB: "Audio/Acoustics/Applications."
SUB: "Audio, acoustics, applications."
PUBL: Audio Engineering Society, 60 East 42nd St., New York, NY 10017.
DESC: "The Audio Engineering Society is organized for the purpose of: uniting persons performing professional services in the audio engineering field and its allied arts; collecting, collating, and disseminating scientific knowledge in the field of audio engineering and its allied arts; advancing such science in both theoretical and practical applications; and preparing, publishing, and distributing literature and periodicals relative to the foregoing purposes and policies." Designed for the audio engineer with a focus on new technological developments in audio for all media applications. Well-illustrated with maps, graphics, and photos. Most authors are working professionals preeminent in their individual fields. Assumes some professional background, and knowledge of the technology of audio. For the sampled issue of 1991: black ink with full-color advertisements on coated paper stock, cover consisting of black/blue inks on coated paper stock, advertising, in stapled magazine format (8 1/4 x 11 inches / 210 x 280 mm).
DEPT: "Standards," new proposed and accepted standards by the Acoustical Society of America; "Review of Acoustical Patents," "News of the Sections," chapter briefs; "Sound Track," news briefs; "Shopping the Audio Market," product news. (11-78). "Engineering Reports," "Standards and Information Documents," "Review of Acoustical Patents," "News of the Sections," "Upcoming Meetings," "Sound Track," personnel changes and news; "New Products and Developments." (11-91).
TYPL: "Computer-Aided Loudspeaker Design: Synthesis Using Optimumization Techniques," "Audio Recording Tapes Based on Iron Particles," "A Study of Theater Loudspeakers and the Resultant Development of the Shearer Two-Way Horn System," "Considerations on Providing Audio Coverage in Television Production Studios." (11-78). "Minimally Audible Noise Shaping," "Low-Frequency Performance of Listening Rooms for Steady-State and Transient Signals," "Challenges to the Successful Implementation of 3-D Sound," "A Monolithic Dual Switch for Professional Audio Applications." (11-91).
SCHL: Quarterly (Jan, 1953 - 1968); Bimonthly (1969 - 1970); Monthly [except Jan/Feb and Jul/Aug when issued bimonthly] (1970+), 85 pp.
SPAN: Jan, 1953+
VARIES
--Jan, 1953 - Dec, 1985 as Journal of the Audio Engineering Society.
ABST: --Applied Science and Technology Index (ISSN: 0003-6986)
--Computer & Control Abstracts (ISSN: 0036-8113)
--Electrical & Electronics Abstracts (ISSN: 0036-8105)
--Engineering Index Annual (ISSN: 0360-8557)
--Engineering Index Bioengineering Abstracts (ISSN: 0736-6213)
--Engineering Index Energy Abstracts (ISSN: 0093-8408)
--Engineering Index Monthly (1984) (ISSN: 0742-1974)
--Engineering Index Monthly (ISSN: 0013-7960)
--Nuclear Science Abstracts (ISSN: 0029-5612)

✣ AEU
SUB: "Electronics and Communication."
PUBL: S. Hirzel Verlag GmbH & Co., Postfach 347, 7000 Stuttgart 1, Federal Republic of Germany.
DESC: Highly technical in its approach, this publication stands as an important journal in the field of electronics research and theory. German articles have English abstracts: English articles likewise print German abstracts at the end of each article. Numerous scientific graphs and notations. Assumes advanced knowledge of electronics and German language. Text in English and German. For the sampled issue of 1990: Stapled magazine format, minimal advertising, editorial content consisting of black ink on coated paper stock, cover is black/yellow inks on coated paper stock (8 1/4 x 11 3/4 inches / 210 x 295 mm).
DEPT: "Letters," "Conferences," "Miscellaneous," "Bookreviews." (1-71). "Book Reviews," "Conferences." (1/2-90).
TYPL: "Investigations on GaAs:GaAlAs Single-Heterostructure Light Emitting Diodes for Optical Communication Systems," "Error Rates for Fading PSK Signals Subject to Generalized Noise," "A Contribution to the Optimization of Roundoff-Noise in Recursive Digital Filters." (12-75). "Analysis of Different Antenna Feed Models for the Calculation of the Input Impedance of a Waveguide-to-Microstrip Transition," "Reliability Estimation for Symbols Detected by Trellis-Decoders," "Fast Block Implementation of Two-Dimensional Recursive Digital Filters via VLSI Array Processors." (1/2-90).
SCHL: Monthly (? - ?); Bimonthly (?+), 65 pp.
SPAN: Jul/Aug, 1947+
VARIES
--Jul/Aug, 1947 - Dec, 1970 as Archiv der Elektrischen Ubertragung (ISSN: 0374-2393).
LC: TK 7800.A22
ISSN: 0001-1096
ABST: --Energy Research Abstracts (ISSN: 0160-3604)
--Engineering Index Annual (ISSN: 0360-8557)
--Engineering Index Bioengineering Abstracts (ISSN: 0736-6213)

--Engineering Index Energy Abstracts (ISSN: 0093-8408)
--Engineering Index Monthly (1984) (ISSN: 0742-1974)
--Engineering Index Monthly (ISSN: 0013-7960)
--Excerpta Medica
--International Aerospace Abstracts (ISSN: 0020-5842)
--ISMEC Bulletin (ISSN: 0306-0039)
--Pollution Abstracts with Indexes (ISSN: 0032-3624)
--Safety Science Abstracts Journal (ISSN: 0160-1342)

✤ AFA JOURNAL

SUB: "Promoting the Judeo-Christian ethic of decency in the American society with primary emphasis on television."
PUBL: American Family Association, PO Box 2440, Tupelo, MS 38803.
DESC: The values, concepts, and purpose of the National Federation for Decency are maintained through the new organizational name of the American Family Association, and the *AFA Journal*, respectively. Articles concentrate on perceived "wrongs" and problems with current or upcoming programming on national American television networks. Most articles include a plan of action for readers in order to respond to the objectionable program elements, usually through the sponsorship of such programs. Of note is a bound section "Christians & Society Today," which is "A supplement for local bulletins and newsletters." For the sampled 1991 issue: black ink with spot color on coated paper stock, advertising (8 ¼ x 10 ⅞ inches / 210 x 275 mm).
DESC: [*NFD Journal*]: "The NFD is a citizens organization promoting the Judeao-Christian ethic of decency in the American Society, with primary emphasis on television. The NFD seeks constructive television programming. By constructive television programming, we mean television which adds to man's cultural, social, mental, emotional and spiritual heritage in an informative and entertaining manner, and which does not appeal to, nor exploit man's prurient nature." As stated, primary emphasis is on cleaning up television programming with national advertisers targeted in write-in campaigns by NFD members. Copies of letters sent to national advertisers are often reprinted. Replies of major television advertisers are also published.
DEPT: None. (1-79). "Television Reviews," "News of Interest," newsbriefs; "Media," "Family." (11/12-91).
TYPL: "Miles Reply Called Deceptive; Sponsorship Continues," "Readers urged to Write Noxema," "NFD Efforts named 1978 Number One Religious News Story in Mississippi," "Incest to be Subject of CBS Program." (1-79). "NBC Says It Will Hold Universal Studios Reponsible for Advertising Losses on Program," "Congress Closer to Stopping NEA Funding of Filth," "AFA Asks One Million Christian Households to Join Kmart Boycott," "Hollywood Abandons Religion, Censors Religious Characters From TV, Movies," "When No News is Biased News." (11/12-91).
SCHL: Monthly (May?, 1979 - ?); Bimonthly (? - ?); Monthly [except bimonthly Jul/Aug and Nov/Dec] (Oct, 1984 - ?); Monthly [except bimonthly Nov/Dec] (?+), 24 pp.
SPAN: May?, 1979+
VARIES
--May?, 1979 as Newsletter of the National Federation for Decency
--Jun, 1979 - Jul, 1979 as NFD Newsletter.
--Aug, 1979 as National Federation for Decency Newsletter.
--Sep, 1979 - ? as NFD Newsletter.
--? - Sep, 1983 as NFD Informer.
--? - ? as NFD Journal.

AFFS Newsletter
? - ?//
SEE: CRITIC

AFI EDUCATION NEWSLETTER

PUBL: American Film Institute, Education Services, 2021 North Western Ave., PO Box 27999, Los Angeles, CA 90027.
DESC: This was a newsletter for the radio-television-film academic community designed to update instructors on developments in legal areas, new publications, resources, academic jobs, and new archive acquisitions, especially that of film and video product saved through AFI and other organizational efforts. An excellent resource for both teaching and research, *AFI Education Newsletter* challenged the academic community to develop excellence in teaching, and to nurture a realistic appreciation of the film/television industry as well. Of special note was the "Course File," a series of "model syllabi" for instructors within the film and television field. Early sample issues were printed brown ink on yellow paperstock. Some sample issues from 1983 were photocopied.
DEPT: "Announcements," news of grants, seminars and archive acquisitions; "In print," new film-video publications; "Resources," available materials; "Calendar," upcoming film and media festivals, seminars, and conventions; "Jobs," academic marketplace; "Course File," detailed model syllabi. (5/6-82).
TYPL: "Charleton Heston on Acting," "Television in School," "The Philadelphia Film Study Seminars: A Model." (10/11-68). "Rockefeller Funds Summer Institute for Humanists," "AFI Feldman Library Acquisitions," "Janus Copyright Decision," "LOC Television Archives Conference." (6-78)
SCHL: Bimonthly, 14 pp.
SPAN: Mar/Apr, 1978 - Sep/Oct, 1982//
DD: 791 11
ISSN: 0883-6213
ABST: --Film Literature Index (ISSN: 0093-6758)

AFI Report
Winter, 1973? - Summer, 1974//
SEE: AMERICAN FILM INSTITUTE. QUARTERLY.

AFRO-ASIAN JOURNALIST
PUBL: Afro-Asian Journalists Association, Djakarta, Indonesia.
DESC: "Anti-Imperialism," "Anti-Colonialism," "Revolutionary Journalism," and "Yankee Dogs" are oft used phrases within this serial of African/Asian revolutionary journalism. The editors viewed these journalistic efforts as one means of throwing off the yokes of oppressed peoples throughout the world. A significant amount of editorial content was anti-American, anti-British, and anti-NATO. Later issues showed a distinct move away from the serial's original journalism focus to that of general political activity. Magazine format; early issues on newsprint; some graphics.
DEPT: "Editorial," "What Our Papers Say," "News and Views," newsbriefs. (4-64). "Editorial," "AAJA Activities," "News in Brief," "From Our Colleagues," letters. (12-71).
TYPL: "Japanese Journalists Struggle for Freedom," "Pakistani Journalists Oppose Gun Boat Diplomacy," "South Africa: Land of Censorship, Death and Struggle," "One People, One Struggle, One Enemy: Imperialism." (4- 64). "World People's Victory, U.S. Political Bankruptcy," "Revolutionary Storm Gathering in India," "Social-Imperialism's Ignominious Failure Inevitable." (12-71).
SCHL: Monthly (Mar, 1964 - Apr, 1964); Bimonthly (May/Jun, 1964); Monthly (Jul, 1964); Bimonthly (Aug/Sep, 1964 - ?), 25 pp.
SPAN: Mar, 1964 - 1974//?
LC: PN 5450.A38

AFTER DARK
SUB: "The national magazine of entertainment."
SUB: "Movies, theatre, music, art, fashions, travel and dining out."
PUBL: Dandad Publishing Co., Inc., 10 Columbus Circle, Suite 1455, New York, NY 10019.
DESC: Describing their readers in a 1977 issue, Dandad Publishing stated they were "...affluent, successful and single. With no strings to tie them down. And the time and money to live it up, any chance they get. Every month 360,000 *After Dark* readers turn to their favorite magazine. Because it covers their scene--the entertainment scene--like nobody else. Shares their enthusiasm for the latest talents and newest trends. Percolates with ideas for adding more fun and enjoyment to their leisure hours." *After Dark* covered the arts worldwide, but focused on the New York City area, and specifically the media of dance, theatre, and music in that city. *After Dark* had a wonderful vitality that mirrored the performing arts pulse of New York, bringing the excitement that was Broadway, Off-Broadway, and other special events to the reader through creative writing, and dynamic pictures of stage productions. Stapled magazine format, black/white and color editorial content throughout on coated paper stock (8 ½ x 10 ¾ inches / 220 x 275 cm).
DEPT: "Editorial," "Broadway Buzz," column by Brant Mewborn; "Art Scene," column by James Alan Nash; "Classical Scene," column by John David Richardson; "On the Town," column by Mark Zweigler; "Behind Both Screens," column by Norma McLain Stoop; "London," city review column by Michael Leech; "Germany West," city review column by Horst Koegler; "Vienna," city review column by Ron Dobrin; "Los Angeles," city review column by Viola Hegyi Swisher; "Las Vegas," city review column by Morag Veljkovic; "San Francisco," city review column by James Armstrong; "Dallas-Ft. Worth," city review column by Larry Holden; "D.C.," city review column by Noel Gillespie; "Montreal," city review; "Boston," city review column by Michael McDowell; "Reviews: Theater On Broadway and Off," column by Patrick Pacheco; "Off Off and Away," theatre review column by Rob Baker; "Other Stages," theatre review column by Glenn Loney; "Films," review column by Norma McLain Stoop; "More Films," review column by Martin Mitchell; "TV Spotlight," review column by Norma McLain Stoop; "Recordings: Classical," review column by John David Richardson; "Rock," review column by Ron Baron; "Pop," music review column by Chris Huizenga; "Book Bits," review column by Chris Huizenga; "Dining Out," column by Louis Miele; "Letters," "Highlights," picture and news page. (7-77).
TYPL: "The Entrances and Exits of Hector Mercado," "New York's Wild, Wild West Side," "Oregon Shakespearean Festival: Rousing Repertory in the Middle of Nowhere," "Singing the Dance Electric," "Peter Lobdell: The Marriage of Myth and Mime." (7-77).
SCHL: Monthly, 110 pp.
SPAN: May, 1968 - Jan, 1983//
VARIES
--Feb, 1960 - Mar, 1968 as Ballroom Dance Magazine.
--Apr, 1968 as Ballroom After Dark.
LC: PN 1560.A42
ISSN: 0002-0702
ABST: --Media Review Digest (ISSN: 0363-7778)

✤ AFTERIMAGE
SUB: "Photography / Independent Film / Video / Visual Books."
PUBL: Visual Studies Workshop, 31 Prince St., Rochester, NY 14607.
DESC: "The '80s was a period of tremendous growth and expansion in the media arts. *Afterimage* was at the center of this creative explosion in film, video, photography, and alternative publishing, bringing our readers interviews with leading artistic and critical figures, features on the work of emerging artists and the latest developments in cultural theory, and

groundbreaking scholarly essays. We closely followed changes in the field, providing reviews of exhibitions, films, tapes books, and conferences and insightful news coverage. Articles published in *Afterimage* helped to define the decade in media arts and have become standard critical references, widely anthologized and cited. As we move into the '90s the world of media arts is raising ever more complex aesthetic, social, and ethical issues. You can count on *Afterimage* to continue to provide independent critical commentary on education, arts funding policy, and censorship. At the same time we will explore the boundaries of the media arts, with challenging and provocative discussions of the computer imaging technologies that will shape the visual culture of the twenty-first century." The focus in this tabloid-size publication is visual anthropology. The media of still photography, motion picture film and video are explored primarily from a creative viewpoint, without technical descriptions. A large portion of the publication, therefore, reviews visual artists' works, with many illustrations from their portfolios. Notes co-editors Grant Kester and Nadine L. McGann: "*Afterimage* is a nonprofit publication that covers photography, independent film and video, and alternative publishing. In addition to the topics explored in 'Youth, Representation, Power,' we consistently investigate underrecognized or controversial artists, the politics of race, gender, and sexuality, issues of censorship and arts funding, emerging media technologies, and other concerns. *Afterimage* reaches across disciplinary boundaries, making connections not just within the visual arts but between the visual arts and other fields. We periodically publish special issues that exclusively emphasize particular themes. In the recent past we have focused on 'youth', 'labor', and 'technology'; ... *Afterimage* also has the most comprehensive free notices section in the country, including job listings, funding and exhibition opportunities, and other services." Printed on high-quality newsprint, the visual imagery in this publication is indeed seen as art-form (11 ½ x 17 ⅜ inches / 290 x 440 mm).

DEPT: "Correspondence," city news; "Reviews," in-depth, illustrated reviews of new books and films; "Products and Processes," the one segment given to technical aspects of visual imagry; "News Notes," briefs; "Sources," literature and software; "Notices," an unusually long and detailed section listing upcoming workshops and seminars. (4-78). "Reviews," "Notices." (1-90).
TYPL: "In Visual Anthropology, Objectivity is Still the Question," "Video Reviews: Tapes by CAPS Recipients," "Repairing a Half-Tone Positive for Photo-Etching," "The Films of Taka Iimura." (4-78). "Public Agendas, Private Lives," "Burning With Desire: The Birth and Death of Photography," "Guilty Objects, Unattainable Desires." (1-90).
SCHL: Monthly [Except Jun, Jul, Aug, and Sep], 24 pp.
SPAN: 1972+
LC: TR 640.A2
DD: 770/.5
ISSN: 0300-7472
ABST: --Art Index (ISSN: 0004-3222)
--Book Review Index (ISSN: 0524-0581)
--Film Literature Index (ISSN: 0093-6758)
--Repetoire International de la Litterature de l'Art (ISSN: 0145-5982)

AFTERIMAGE

PUBL: Afterimage Publishing, Ltd., 1 Birnam Rd., London N4 3LJ England.
DESC: Small-format periodical with an emphasis on film criticism, especially in the area of underground and third-world works. Utilizes numerous production stills to enhance text. Focus of publication is confusing at times, with some whole issues devoted to particular themes such as film and politics, avant-garde film, third-world approaches to cinema, etc. Publication schedule varied greatly during the nine-issue publication span.
DEPT: None. (4-70). None. (winter-82/83).
TYPL: "The Aesthetics of Violence," "British Sounds, Pravda," "The Inner Space Project." (4-70). "Michael Snow: a Filmography," "Seeing is Believing: Wavelength Recondsidered," "Snowbound: A Dialogue With a Dialogue." (winter-82/83).
SCHL: Quarterly [Irregular at times], 80 pp.
SPAN: Apr, 1970 - Spring, 1981//
LC: PN 1993.A52
DD: 791.43/05
ISSN: 0261-4472

✤ AFTERNOON TV

PUBL: Laurant Publishing, Inc., 300 West 43rd St., New York, NY 10036.
DESC: *Afternoon TV* is a video star magazine which concentrates on afternoon soap operas, an area of television programming long overlooked by other publications devoted to television viewing. Like its counterparts, *Afternoon TV* is printed with a number of photos, and newly discovered "secrets" of the stars, and shows both backstage and "at-home" lives of these daytime artists. A significant number of current motion picture and primetime television artists got their start in daytime soap opera programming, a fact well known by those devoted to this television genre.
DEPT: "Soap Bubbles," five pages of the hottest info on television's afternoon stars; "From the Editor's Desk," a reader interest column by Harry Shorten. (3-79).
TYPL: "Happiness isn't a Worthwhile Goal," "Rosehill Residents Show Their Love of Party-Life," "Joe Gallison-Sexiest Rogue in Town," "Guiding Light on Location: Two Roads Diverge," "Six Stars Share Their Secrets for Staying Slim." (3-79).
SCHL: Eight times per year, 70 pp.
SPAN: 1969+
ISSN: 0164-6508

✣ AFVA BULLETIN

SUB: "Official periodical of the Educational Film Library Association, Inc."
PUBL: American Film and Video Association, 920 Barnsdale Rd., Suite 152, La Grange Park, IL 60525.
DESC: [*EFLA Bulletin*]: Typewritten newsletter for the Educational Film Library Association, detailing developments in the broad audio-visual field, especially software and equipment as it affects libraries. Articles tended to be brief with no graphics. This was a new series for the *EFLA Bulletin* and was "...issued inbetween issues of its sister publication, *Sightlines*."
DESC: [*Sightlines*]: *Sightlines* was published quarterly by the Educational Film Library Association, "...a non-profit educational corporation, serving libraries, universities, schools, museums, and other community agencies that utilize film." It unquestionably promoted the use of film for instructional and educational functions, and to both instruct and entertain. Articles on current films and filmmaking dominated, with few historical or nostalgic overviews. Emphasis was on the educational and instructional motion picture.
DEPT: "Voice Over," commentary; "Video Playback," developments in video; "Book Reviews," "Recent Film/Video Releases," software reviews; "New Publications," directories, books and periodicals; "News Notes," newsbriefs; "Calendar," "Traveling Shots," newsbriefs on film and filmmakers. (fall/winter, 80). "Notes on People," personnel briefs; "TV/Video Corner," newsbriefs; "Calendar." (3-81).
TYPL: "Islam on Film," "Hollywood and the Third World--Some Positive Images," "Hispanic Films from the Chicano Film Festival," "Germany Awake: Propaganda in Nazi Cinema," "The Great Film Bazzar: Best-Selling Educational Films of the '70s." (fall/winter-80). "Twenty-Third American Film Festival Update," "Kodak Raises Its Prices," "Archives and Preservation; the American Archives of the Factual Film," "French Law Requires Film Deposits," "Social Science Film Laboratory." (3-81).
SCHL: Bimonthly (1967 - 1969); Five issues per year (1970 - 1974); Quarterly (1975 - Summer, 1977); Monthly (? - ?); Quarterly (?+), 45 pps.
SPAN: Sep/Oct, 1967+
FROM MERGER OF
--EFLA Bulletin (and) Filmlist (ISSN: 0015-1602) (and) Film Review Digest (ISSN: 0428-3708).
VARIES
--Sep/Oct, 1967 - Summer?, 1987? as Sightlines (ISSN: 0037-4830).
WITH SUPPLEMENT
--EFLA Bulletin, Summer, 1977 - #3/4, 1987//
ABSORBED
--Film Library Quarterly (ISSN: 0015-1327), 1985.
ABST: --Film Literature Index (ISSN: 0093-6758)
--Library Literature (ISSN: 0024-2373)
--Media Review Digest (ISSN: 0363-7778)

✣ AGAINST THE GRAIN

PUBL: Against the Grain, Citadel Station, Charleston, SC 29409.
DESC: *Against the Grain* is a wonderful title for this publication that explores the symbiotic relationship of library, vendor, and publisher in the United States. These three areas depend on each other in order to function and thrive. Since publisher, librarian, and vendor must often set their proprietary interests aside for the common good, this may, and often does "go against the grain" of competitive business practices and trends in library management, vendor distribution, and book/magazine publishing. *Against the Grain* provides a marvelous forum for the discussion of the thorny issues in these three areas. At times such forthright comment is cloaked under the nom de plume of "anonymous." Issues are presented in a frank, sometimes cutting, sometimes witty approach that makes one eager for each new issue. This serial is MUST reading for any acquisitions librarian, bookseller/distributor/vendor, or publisher. *Against the Grain* supports the work of the Publisher/Vendor/Library Relations Committee (PVLR) of the American Library Association. For the sampled issues of 1990: magazine format, three-hole punched, black ink on cream-color uncoated paper stock; some graphics with advertising (8 ½ x 11 inches / 215 x 280 mm).
DEPT: "If Rumors Were Horses," newsbriefs; "The Pilgrim's Scrip," commentary; "Publisher's Profile," "Issues in Library-Vendor Relations," "The Meyers Connection," column by Barbara Meyers; "Bet You Missed It!," summary of recent articles of interest. (6-90).
TYPL: "And They Were There," "There's No Biz Like Acq Biz," "The Quotable Nemesis," "If You're Hot You're Hot." (6-90).
SCHL: Five issues per year, 40 pp.
SPAN: Mar, 1989+
ISSN: 1043-2094

✣ AGENCY

SUB: "A publication of the American Association of Advertising Agencies."
PUBL: Act III Publishing, 401 Park Avenue South, New York, NY 10016, on behalf of the American Association of Advertising Agencies, 666 Third Ave., New York, NY 10017.
DESC: American Association of Advertising Agencies' President, John E. O'Toole, set the tone for this new, dynamic publication: "We intend *Agency* to be a magazine that interests the people who work in advertising agencies, keeps them informed about what's really going on in their industry, and helps them excel at their jobs. That's Objective Number One. The extent to which we accomplish it will determine whether or not we attain Objective Number Two: Getting across to our members, particularly those below the CEO level, the rich and unparalleled resources available to them at the AAAA. We want the younger people in our member agencies to know how

we can help them become more productive and more professional. ...*Agency* will be the only medium delivering advertising-agency professionals exclusively--38,000 intelligent, educated trendsetters who plan, create, place--and believe in--American advertising" (premiere issue for Spring, 1990). A quality, issues-oriented serial for the American advertising agency community, complete with numerous full color graphics and media advertisements targeted at agency print buyers. Magazine format; an excellent resource for advertising.
DEPT: "Presidential Address," AAAA Presidents' column; "Editor's Note," "Top of Mind," noteworthy advertising newsbriefs; "Pressue Points," 'Readers find answers to some sensitive questions about the agency business'; "Law Review," column by Sandra Salmans; "The Right Thing," "The Question Is," "Figures," "Calendar," "The AAAA Recommends," 'Our best bets for some new products and services'. (spring-90).
TYPL: "Pitch Time: One Client's View," "Pitch Time: Three Agencies' View," "Stunts." (spring-90).
SCHL: Quarterly, 90 pp.
SPAN: Spring, 1990+

AGRICULTURAL ADVERTISING
SUB: "Pertaining to agricultural newspaper advertising."
SUB: "Newspaper, magazine, mail order, street car, and outdoor advertising."
SUB: "A journal of publicity and merchandising plans."
PUBL: Long-Critchfield Publishing House, Brooks Building, Chicago, IL.
DESC: *Agricultural Advertising* began as a trade journal for advertisers desiring to reach the American farmer. By 1918, however, the title of the serial was a misnomer, as the content was more concerned with broad aspects of the advertising industry, the least attention being provided that area known as "agriculture." As the subtitle implies, this was a serial of technique, a how-to manual for advertising campaigns of all sorts, and a compendium of short articles reporting such activities throughout the industry. Noteworthy for its attack on poor quality advertising, the advertisements which are themselves reproduced for the reader's consideration. Small format.
DEPT: "Railroad Advertising," "A Solicitors Tale," by Carew. (2-00). "Editorial," "Through the Enlarging Glass," 'The further adventures of Alice in Advertising-Land'; "The Harpoonist," ad critique; "In the Advertising Workshop," ad critique by Adcraft; "The New York Listening Post," column by Father Knickerbocker; "The Net o' Things," newsbriefs. (6-18).
TYPL: "Agricultural Prosperity," "Selling Fertilizer," "Chicago Poultry Show," "The Sensible Farmer." (2-00). "New Support for the Cause of Trademark Righteousness," "Along the Eastern Trail," "War Work Done by Advertising Men," "German Propaganda in Anti-Advertising Talk?" (6-18).
SCHL: Monthly, 60 pp.
SPAN: 1893 - Dec, 1918//

LC: HF 6161.A3A2

AID
SUB: "For Education and Training."
PUBL: Institute of International Research and Development, Inc., P.O. Box 4456, Lubbock, TX.
DESC: The focus of this small publication is use of mass media in education and training. Few pages, but some relatively good articles concerning use of such media in the instructional arena.
DEPT: "Research Report," newsbriefs of recently published research into instructional media; "Newsbriefs," "Opinion and Fact," a forum for opinions concerning use of instructional media; "Workshops," upcoming. (3-63).
TYPL: "Programmed Courses Lead Curriculum as Delta Presents Enrichment Classes," "New Media Involves Multiple Elements," "The Integration of Programmed Media into a Total Training Package." (3-63).
SCHL: Monthly, 10 pp.
SPAN: 1961 - 1963//

AIGA Journal
1947 - 1953//
(ISSN: 0197-6907)
SEE: AIGA JOURNAL OF GRAPHIC DESIGN

✤ AIGA JOURNAL OF GRAPHIC DESIGN
PUBL: American Institute of Graphic Arts, 1059 Third Ave., New York, NY 10021.
DESC: The American Institute of Graphic Arts was founded in 1914 for graphic arts professionals. The *Journal* began in November, 1965 and the early issues provided a mixture of articles and graphic arts examples, usually via competition, exhibition, or theme. Latter issues (early 1970s) had basically dropped the articles, and now consisted primarily of examples of creative graphics, with an unusual degree of care taken in the printing process. The journal in its latter stages functions as a fine resource for graphic artists. Journal format; numerous graphics.
DEPT: "News Notes," "AIGA Calendar of Events." (#3-66). "Book Reviews," "News Notes." (#27-75).
TYPL: "Doomsday in Dogpatch: The McLuhan Thesis Examined," "New Definitions and New Ways in Print Making," "New Research in Legibility." (#3-66). "Comics." (#27-75).
SCHL: Five issues per year (1947 - 1953); Three issues per year (? - ?); Quarterly (Jun, 1982+), 50 pp.
SPAN: 1947+
VARIES
--1947 - 1953 as AIGA Journal (ISSN: 0197-6907).
--1965 - ? as Journal of the American Institute of Graphic Arts (ISSN: 0065-8820).

SUSPENDED
--May, 1949 - Oct, 1950.
ISSN: 0736-5322

✣ AIM REPORT

SUB: "Your watchdog of the news media."
SUB: "For fairness, balance and accuracy in news reporting."
PUBL: Accuracy in Media, 1275 K St., NW, Suite 1150, Washington, DC 20005.
DESC: "AIM (Accuracy in Media) is America's media watchdog. It works for you. Your job, business, reputation, peace of mind, and even your freedom can be endangered by irresponsible media actions. Do our media sometimes distort and twist the facts? Do they sometimes suppress important news or tell only half the story? You know it! Suing for libel is almost the only legal protection Americans have against media abuse. It is an expensive, slow and uncertain remedy. Moreover, it offers no protection whatever against misinformation that misleads the public but does not defame an individual or institution. There is another way to combat media distortion and abuse -- the AIM way." This statement of purpose from a promotional pamphlet defines the form and function of the twice-monthly newsletter from Accuracy in Media. Editor Reed Irvine has earned numerous kudos for his work, including comments from Victor Lasky who stated, "Reed Irvine is a modern-day David fighting Goliath--the most powerful institution in America today--the media." Charles Seib, former ombudsman at the *Washington Post*, said, "It sticks in my craw, but I'll say it, Irvine and his AIM are good for the press." Detractors might claim a rather conservative, "Republican- style" of investigative journalism is present within the pages of the *AIM Report*, but no matter on which side of the political media fence one sits, there is more than sufficient material in each semimonthly issue for impassioned discussion. The value of the publication is the bringing to light of journalistic issues deserving of reasoned discussion and thought. Newsletter format, limited graphics with spot color (8 ½ x 11 inches / 215 x 280 mm).
DEPT: "Notes From the Editor's Cuff," editorial column by Reed Irvine. (12-B- 90).
TYPL: "PBS Perverts Korean War Story," "Who Started the War?," "Germ Warfare Disinformation," "A War Without Winners." (12-B-90).
SCHL: Monthly (1972 - May, 1983); Semimonthly (Jun, 1983+), 8 pp.
SPAN: Aug, 1972+
DD: 070
ISSN: 0738-7792

AIR LAW REVIEW

SUB: "Official journal of the American section of the International Committee on Wireless Telegraphy." (Jan, 1930 - Apr, 1930).
SUB: "Official journal of the American section of the International Committee on radio of the American Academy of Air Law." (Apr, 1931 - 1941).
SUB: "International in scope and interest."
PUBL: School of Law, New York University, New York, NY.
DESC: "It is the purpose of the *AIR LAW REVIEW* (including aeronautical and radio law) to publish matter presenting a view of merit on subjects of interest to the legal profession, to the industries concerned and to the public at large." The *AIR LAW REVIEW* is, at first glance, a curious mixture of aeronautical and radio law which came out of the 1929 American Bar Association convention, specifically the Committee on Aeronautical Law, and the Committee on Radio Law, the latter renamed as the Committee on Communications. The journal, therefore, shared dual interests during its 11-year publication span. Early issues mixed both aeronautical and radio fields, but as radio broadcasting grew in size and stature, articles of radio and television interest were placed apart from issues of aeronautical concern. In the final issue of October, 1941, Editor-in-Chief, Alison Reppy told readers: "When the *AIR LAW REVIEW* was organized it was contemplated that the time might come when the decisions and legislation affecting aeronautics and radio might become stabilized and, therefore, the continuation of the publication beyond that point would be without useful purpose. While many important problems remain for solution in both fields, it is thought that the law with regard to each is approaching the period of stability, after which the changes therein will not be rapid." A secondary cessation factor was the entrance of the United States into the world war, the "current emergency" as the publication put it. An outstanding resource for the legal development of American electronic communications. For the sampled issues of 1930 and 1941: journal format, black ink on uncoated paper stock, some illustrations, no advertising (6 x 9 inches / 155 x 230 mm).
DEPT: "Book Reviews." (1-30). "Legislative and Administrative Activities," comments on radio law and legislation; "Notes: Radio," case notes from recent legal proceedings; "Quarterly Review of Decisions," "Check List of Current Books and Monographs," radio issues review; "Table of Cases," brief listing of legal cases 'reported, noted, commented upon or digested'. (10-41).
TYPL: "International Rights of a Radio Station," "Legal Aspects of Radio Broadcasting," "Radio Legislation Pending Before Congress," "Standard of Public Interest, Convenience or Necessity as Used in the Radio Act of 1927," "Unification of Communications Service." (1-30). "Civil Liability of Aircraft Carriers Under the Canadian Law," "Exclusion Clauses in Insurance Policies Relative to Aeronautics." (10-41).
SCHL: Quarterly, 100 pp.
SPAN: Jan, 1930 - Oct, 1941//

✤ AIR TIME

PUBL: National Association of Broadcasters, Office of Community Affairs, 1771 N Street, No. 708, Washington, DC.
DESC: Highlighting minority broadcast developments in the United States, this bimonthly newsletter emphasizes black employment opportunities in the industry. Articles brought to the forefront the issues of minority opportunities, and development of broadcast media and black access to those media.
DEPT: "Dates and Deadlines," conference and convention information of interest to black broadcasters and journalists. (2-77).
TYPL: "In Actuality: A Talk with Four Black Owners," "FCC and EEO," "Washington Association of Black Journalists," "Satellite technology and the Continent of Africa: An Argument for Increased Participation in the Development of Policies." (2-77).
SCHL: Bimonthly, 10 pp.
SPAN: ?+

✤ AIRBRUSH ACTION

PUBL: Airbrush Action, 400 Madison Ave., Lakewood, NJ 08701.
DESC: "If it's happening in art, you'll read about it in *Airbrush Action*. From highbrow to high-tech, we cover it all. From innovative features on commercial illustration, graphic design, and fine art, to exclusive interviews with artists like Robert Risko, Michael Cacy, Olivia, Mark Fredrickson, Tom Nikosey, and David Kimble. *Airbrush Action* keeps you on the cutting edge of the art world--offering comprehensive coverage of airbrush art through T-shirts, sign painting, modern ceramics, and hobby applications. And we're not just full of hot air--we provide the most practical, up-to-date information and reviews on studio equipment, new products, and the business of art in general." *Airbrush Action* provides a first-rate showcase for professional artistic product, the technique of same, and new technologies to hone the artisan's craft. For the 1990 sampled issue: Stapled magazine format, full-color and black ink editorial content with full-color cover all on coated paper stock (8 ⅛ x 10 ⅞ inches / 210 x 275 mm).
DEPT: "New Products," review; "Tech Corner," "Air Report." (5/6-90).
TYPL: "Five and Counting," "T-Shirt Pricing Guidelines," "Showing 'Em in the 'Show Me' State." (5/6-90).
SCHL: Quarterly (1985 - summer, 1986); Six issues per year (Sep/Oct, 1986 - Jan/Feb, 1988); Five issues per year (Mar/Apr, 1988+), 80 pp.
SPAN: May/Jun, 1985+
LC: NC 915.A35 A38
DD: 751.4/94/05
ISSN: 1040-8509

✤ AIRWAVES

SUB: "The quarterly journal of the IBA."
PUBL: Independent Broadcasting Authority, 70 Brompton Rd., London SW3 1EY, England.
DESC: "This journal of opinion discusses broadcasting policy, the IBA's process of decision-making, and other significant radio and television topics." Published quarterly, *Independent Broadcasting*, provided a lively forum for the activities of Britain's Independent Broadcasting Authority with a strong emphasis on program fare and the relationship between IBA and the viewing public. Under the banner of *Airwaves*, it emerged into a well-designed full-color magazine layout, with informative articles about programs, their producers, and the workings of the Independent Broadcasting Authority itself. Typical topics in 1986 included women in broadcasting; researching the medium of direct broadcast satellite services; and the ever-present issues of taste and decency. For the sampled issues of 1986: stapled magazine format, black ink and full-color graphics on coated paper stock (8 x 11 ½ inches / 205 x 295 mm).
DEPT: None. (6-84).
TYPL: "Advertising Standards and the IBA," "Sounds Educational," "How Broadcasters Serve the Consumer," "Math on Television: Doing or Viewing?," "Bringing You the New Programmes," "Dallas in Dorking." (6-84).
SCHL: Quarterly, 24 pp.
SPAN: Aug, 1974+
VARIES
--Aug, 1974 - Nov, 1984 as Independent Broadcasting (ISSN: 0305-6104).
LC: HE 8689.9.G7 I528
DD: 384.55/4/0941 19
ISSN: 0267-3789

AISLE VIEW

SUB: "The newsletter of tips, tactics and how-tos for small exhibitors."
PUBL: Exhibitor Publications, Inc., 745 Marquette Bank Bldg., Rochester, MN 55904.
DESC: In the highly competitive arena of sales, marketing, and advertising, small vendors were often overshadowed by large-budget competitors. This was especially true in the area of convention/exposition exhibiting, where exhibit booths could cost $15 per square foot and up. The small exhibitor fortunately had a street-wise ally in *Aisle View*, a monthly newsletter published by *Exhibitor*; "the magazine of trade show marketing." Within its pages were a host of informative articles for the smaller vendor, all designed to elicit excitement, strategies, and sales objectives for a given exhibition. Of note was a two-page section, "Show Calendar," which listed upcoming exhibitions, number of estimated attendees, number of booths, and cost per square foot. Pictures provided examples of successful booth designs, displays and operations. The emphasis was on projecting a "class

act" image. This newsletter was required reading for any vendor wishing to communicate a marketing / advertising / sales message to potential buyers of their services. Unfortunately it ceased publication as of July 15, 1991. In the words of Lee Knight, Publisher and Editor of parent *Exhibitor Magazine*, "Even good ideas are often ahead of their time." Stapled newsletter format on coated paper stock, three hole punched (8 ⅜ x 11 inches / 210 x 275 mm).
DEPT: "Tip of the Month," "Promotion," "On the Scene," "Exhibit Planning," "Exhibit Selling," "Show Calendar," "The Resource Guide," new products and services. (4-91).
TYPL: "Setting Objectives: Your First Step to a Successful Show," "Self-Promotion Pays Off," "Making the Most of Consumer Shows," "Give Your Staffers Some Selling Space!," "Learning the Ropes: Mistakes and Lessons." (4-91).
SCHL: Monthly, 8 pp.
SPAN: ? - Jul 15, 1991//

✣ AKASHVANI

SUB: "Incorporating the Indian Radio Times."
SUB: "English program journal of all India."
SUB: "Features of lasting value."
PUBL: All India Radio, Akashvani Group of Journals, PTI Bldg., Parliament St., New Delhi 110001, India.
DESC: Patterned after the BBC's *Radio Times*, this publication also provides radio schedules, and a variety of articles associated with topics from those programs. Some graphics; Newsprint; Text in English.
DEPT: "Pick of the Week," "Selected Air Programmes," "Selected Doordarshan Programmes." (11-25-79).
TYPL: "New Agricultural Technology," "Indian Monsoons and Cyclones," "It is an Art to Say 'No,'" "Public Sector Management." (11-25-79).
SCHL: Semimonthly (? - ?); Weekly (?+), 50 pp.
SPAN: 1936+
VARIES
--? - ? as Indian Listener.
LC: PN 1991.A42

✣ ALABAMA JOURNALIST

PUBL: University of Alabama, Department of Journalism, Box 1482, University, AL 35486.
DESC: This tabloid newspaper produced by University of Alabama journalism students, is designed to detail activities within U of A's journalism department. It provides a noteworthy link between the academic and professional communities.
DEPT: None. (1-76).
TYPL: "Communication Students, Faculty Retreat to Cheaha," "NBC's Brokaw Says Access to White House Still Limited," "APA Meets Thursday in Mobile." (1-76).
SCHL: One issue per semester?, 8 pp.
SPAN: ?+

✣ ALBUM

PUBL: 70 Princedale Rd., London W11, England.
DESC: "A gallery of photographic works" might aptly convey the contents of this serial dedicated to showcasing the talents of several photographers each issue. Printed on quality paper stock, *Album* usually highlights the work of both early and contempory photographers, displaying some 5-20 prints per artist. Of special note are quality historical articles about lifestyles, society, and profiles of showcased photographers. Also, accompanying text is noteworthy for critical, condensed commentary concerning each artist. No advertising; well recommended.
DEPT: None.
TYPL: "Note on Photographic non- representation," "Daguerreotypes by Louis Daguerre," "Lewis W. Hine, a Camera and a Social Conscience." (5-70).
SCHL: Monthly, 50 pp.
SPAN: Feb, 1970+
LC: TR 640.A3
DD: 770/.5
ISSN: 0002-4937

ALBUM, THE

SUB: "A journal of photographs of men, women, and events of the day."
PUBL: Ingram Brothers, London, England.
DESC: This, in many ways, was an early British version of pictorial *Life* magazine of the 1930s and 40s. *The Album* was primarily interested in presenting quality photographs of British royalty, governmental figures, blue collar workers, and general society. For today's scholar, this serial provides an unequaled photographic gallery of major political, entertainment, and societal figures of the late 19th and early 20th centuries. Feature articles oftentimes accompanied photographs, at times for biographical information; more often, one senses, to provide some reading material within the issue. Quality printing; large magazine format.
DEPT: "Mere Gossip," "The Artistic Home," "The Inevitable Interviewer," "A Letter from Abroad," "The Life of Childhood," "Our Art Supplement." (11-4-1895).
TYPL: None.
SCHL: Weekly (Feb 4, 1895 - Dec 9, 1895); Monthly (Jan, 1896+).
SPAN: February 4, 1895 - Mar, 1896//
LC: AP 4.A352

All About Television

Summer, 1927//
SEE: TELEVISION

✣ ALL-STAR ACTION HEROES

PUBL: Jacobs Publications, 475 Park Avenue South, New York, NY 10016.

DESC: This full-color serial pays tribute to the action-adventure hero (and heroine) of the American silver screen. Although *All-Star Action Heroes* sounds similar to a host of Hollywood pulp and hype publications, this one stands out for its literate writing and attention to layout design and color printing. Articles are keyed to current motion picture releases and their star properties; but *All-Star Action Heroes* moves on to provide a retrospective (including color shots of past performances) of each star covered. The second issue of this semiyearly serial featured a dozen films, including stars Jack Nicholson, Don Johnson, Kevin Costner, Patrick Swayze, Rutger Hauer, Sean Connery, Mel Gibson, and Goldie Hawn. The sample issue viewed also contained two double-sided posters (15.5" x 21" / 39.37 x 53.34 mm). This is a very satisfying consumer publication for action stories on the motion picture screen. No advertising except by Starlog Communications International, of which Jacobs Publications is a group member. Magazine format with full-color graphics throughout.
DEPT: None. (#2-90).
TYPL: "Arnold Schwarzenegger," "RoboCop," "Dick Tracy," "War is Easy." (#2-90).
SCHL: Semiyearly, 70 pp.
SPAN: ?, 1989?+

ALL-WAVE RADIO
SUB: "The journal of world radio." (Apr, 1936 - Jun, 1938).
SUB: "Official organ of the Radio Signal Survey League." (Feb, 1937 - Jun, 1938).
PUBL: Manson Publications Corporation, 200 Fifth Ave., New York, NY.
DESC: "This is a magazine for the radio listener and experimenter and no one else." So began *All-Wave Radio* in its initial issue for September, 1935. Interest in amateur and experimental radio was strong in America, with thousands of young men wanting to "tinker" with the electronic medium. It was for this audience that *All-Wave Radio* was designed, providing articles on new equipment, new "home-brew" apparatus by readers, news of short-wave development in other nations, and always a number of technical schematics for its readers. Numerous illustrations and graphics.
DEPT: "Dial Light," publisher comment; "Globe Girdling," "Roses and Razzberries," critical commentary; "Channel Echoes," British news; "The Footloose Reporter," "Radio Proving Post," new equipment; "Backwash," 'Readers Forum'; "In Writing for Veries," 'Addresses of principal short-wave stations by country'; "Short-Wave Station List." (11-35).
TYPL: "Review of 1936 All-Wave Receivers," "Reinartz S.W. Rotary Beam Aerial," "Design of Transformers for Amateurs." (11- 35). "Now It's Recording," "Building the 'Streamliner,'" "Modern Rack and Panel C.W. & Fone Transmitter." (6-38).
SCHL: Monthly, 50 pp.
SPAN: Sep, 1935 - Jun, 1938//
SUSPENDED
--Oct, 1935.
--Jun, 1936.
ABSORBED BY
--Radio News.
LC: TK 6540.A45
DD: 621.38405

✢ ALPHA AND OMEGA FILM REPORT
SUB: "Film & video reviews--from a Christian perspective."
PUBL: Alpha-Omega Productions, PO Box 58843, Renton, WA 98058.
DESC: This monthly newsletter concentrates (as the subtitle indicates) on film and video product, industry trends, and consumer approaches to these media from a Christian perspective. In the sample issue reviewed (Oct, 1989), the majority of the issue was devoted to film and video reviews, with one major article providing general criticism and critique. An interesting publication, and one of a growing number of Christian newsletters devoted to criticism and review of American mass media. Dot-matrix printed with line graphics; newsletter format.
DEPT: "At the Theater," large section of film and video reviews from a Christian perspective; "On Video," new videocassette releases; "Last Page," film and video newsbriefs. (10-89).
TYPL: "A Christian Perspective on Film: Part II." (10-89).
SCHL: Monthly, 8 pp.
SPAN: Jan, 1985?+

ALPHABET AND IMAGE
SUB: "A quarterly of typography and graphic arts."
PUBL: Art and Technics, 58 Frith St., Soho, London W1, England.
DESC: A fascinating, short-lived serial that explored the function and beauty of typefaces and graphic illustration. Scholarly articles concerning typefaces provided many reprints of mastheads, posters, book passages, and other historical works to provide an always fascinating account of British publication history. Equally pleasing to the senses were full-color, illustrated stories (oftentimes with color page foldout sections), which provided scholarly historical accounts of the development of British graphic arts. A special "Stop Press" supplement to issue #8 (Dec, 1948), announced that the serial henceforth would be split into two publications: *Alphabet* to be issued annually, the serial to concentrate on typographical matters; and *Image I*, a quarterly publication dealing with graphic arts. A quality resource journal for print and illustration research.
DEPT: None.
TYPL: "Times Roman: a Revaluation," "News Bills: a Retrospectus," "Draughtsmen of the Early 'Daily Graphic.'" (9-46). "The River Books of Robert Gibbings," "17th Century Trade-Cards," "Charles Keene: The Last Phase." (12-48).

SCHL: Quarterly.
SPAN: 1946 - Dec, 1948//
SPLIT INTO
--Alphabet [NA] (and) Image (ISSN: 0046-8649).
LC: Z 119.A1 A4
DD: 655.05
ISSN: 0361-8366

✧ ALTERNATIVE THEATRE

PUBL: Alternative Theatre, the Theatre Project, 45 West Preston St., Baltimore, MD 21201.
DESC: "The reason we call our paper *Alternative Theatre* is that the theatre we are most interested in is called that. The term is in the air or will probably last until whatever theatre it means to be alternative to calls itself alternative theatre. Useful language gets used up quickly. After all, everything in the arts that sucks calls itself 'experimental' or 'innovative' or such. 'Happenings' lasted until every chi-chi event became one. Broadway has already absorbed 'environmental theatre.' The 'new' is now old before it is fully publicized. So we don't mean to define alternative theatre, or prescribe eligibility for admission to the club. We prefer to describe, inform and comment on 'alternative theatre' while it is still alive and forming, before it becomes a convenient label for instant-self identification." This fascinating newsprint tabloid was anti-anything that smacked of established theatre structure, be it acting, unions, staging, or sources of financial support. The focus was on developing theatre, of unconventional approaches to the art and craft of theatre.
DEPT: "Comment," "Alternative Theatre Directory," extensive national workshop listing by state. (1/2-76).
TYPL: "Native American Theatre: The Play Chelsea Didn't Produce," "Spider Woman Theatre Workshop," "Power and Lunch with Andre Gregory," "Theatre Repression in Brazil," "Mabou Mimes: From Beckett to Breuer." (1/2-76).
SCHL: Bimonthly, 16 pp.
SPAN: Sep/Oct, 1975+

✧ ALUMNI NEWSLINE

PUBL: Dow Jones Newspaper Fund, Inc., PO Box 300, Princeton, NJ 08543-0300.
DESC: This four-page quarterly newsletter "...is provided free to Alumni, directors and supporters of Newspaper Fund programs" connected with the Dow Jones Newspaper Fund. The publication, which began as a two-page issue in Fall, 1988 and is now four pages in length, details activities of those journalistic alumni, and provides a valuable job information feature in a variety of geographically diverse newspapers, and college teaching positions. Sampled issue for 1991: four-page folded newsletter format on light-beige uncoated paper stock, no advertising (8 ½ x 11 inches / 215 x 280 mm).

DEPT: "Peopleline," Newspaper Fund alumni newsbriefs; "Jobsline," employment opportunities. (winter-91).
TYPL: "Editing Interns Receive Summer Assignments," "LA Times' Shaw, Sharpe of GNS Win Pulitzers," "Internships Can Lead to Editing Jobs." (winter-91).
SCHL: Quarterly, 4 pp.
SPAN: Fall, 1988+

✧ AM

PUBL: Mercury House Publications, London, England.
DESC: Primary function of this British publication is to promote the use of advertising and marketing by industrial concerns. The fact that this periodical did not attract sufficient revenue or article submissions led to a format change in March, 1971 to a smaller format and increased editorial content. Few graphics.
DEPT: "Editorial," "Marketing Pointers," newsbriefs; "Around the Agencies," newsbriefs; "Industrial Marketing News," newsbriefs; "Eye on the Press," newsbriefs; "Exhibition Diary." (11/12-70).
TYPL: "A Small Company Fights the Take-Over Bid," "Britain's Low Budget Films Can Boost Sales," "Tomorrows Technology, the Key to the Aviation Industry," "It's the Clients Turn to Decide," "Sometimes the Big Boys Make Big Mistakes." (11/12-70).
SCHL: Monthly (May, 1964 - Fall, 1975); Quarterly (?+), 40 pp.
SPAN: May, 1964+
VARIES
--May, 1964 - Fall, 1975 as IAM.

AM-FM Television

Mar, 1954 - Apr, 1954//
SEE: RCA BROADCAST NEWS

✧ AMATEUR ACTOR ILLUSTRATED, THE

PUBL: ?, England.
DESC: With an eye to amateur acting, primarily in the English provinces, *The Amateur Actor Illustrated* provided a most interesting monthly supplement to the parent publication, *The Actor Illustrated*, the latter of which was dedicated to both the professional and amateur actor. While the parent serial contained an interesting mixture of both amateur and professional articles, this supplement was exclusively amateur, with an emphasis on acting societies, and cast names. Each issue contained a number of photographs of current productions, and some reproductions of advertising posters for these productions.
DEPT: "What the Societies are Doing," 'News of the amateur companies in and about London'; "In the Provinces," newsbriefs. (3-05).
TYPL: "Amateur at Cambridge," "The Triumph of a Rejected Play." (3-05).
SCHL: Monthly, 10 pp.

SPAN: Jan, 1905+
SUPPLEMENT TO
--Actor Illustrated, The, Jan, 1905 - ?

Amateur Movie Maker
? - ?//
SEE: EIGHT MM MOVIE MAKER AND CINE CAMERA

Amateur Movie Makers
Dec, 1926 - May, 1928//
SEE: MOVIE MAKERS

✧ AMATEUR PHOTOGRAPHER
SUB: "Published every Wednesday."
PUBL: IPC business Press, Ltd., Surrey House, 1 Throwley Way, Sutton, Surrey SM1 4QQ England.
DESC: "As the name of the journal implies we cater mainly for amateurs although we are well aware that most dealers and manufacturers as well as many professionals are regular readers. Our aim is simple -- to inform, to instruct and to entertain. We inform by bringing you full details of new apparatus, new materials and new techniques, and our test reports are eagerly studied by trade and consumer alike. We instruct with many practical articles written by staff or by leading photographers, while beginners as well as advanced workers are catered for. We entertain, we hope, with features of general interest and countless reproductions of photographs in black and white or colour as well as interviews with the famous. Above all we try to make you feel that this is your magazine so you have the opportunity to use it as a forum through our correspondence columns and to use it as a yardstick for measuring your progress by entering our monthly competitions, which we particularly commend to beginners." Sampled issue for 1975 was a mixture of coated and uncoated paper stock, primarily black/white editorial content with several full-color pages. The sampled issue also reflected an editorial philosophy which placed some 50 pages of advertising at the front of the issue with another 50 pages of advertising at the back of the magazine, and most editorial content in the middle. Magazine format, stapled (8 ½ x 11 ⅝ inches / 215 x 295 mm).
DEPT: "Next Week," upcoming editorial content; "Readers Write," letters to the editor; "Test Report," equipment review; "Practically Speaking," column by Ronald Spillman; "Notes for Novices," column by R. H. Mason; "Make Mine Movies," 'A series of help and advice for the non-expert film-maker' column by Peter Dean; ."Cameravaria," photographic potpourri column by Victor Blackman; "Sound and Picture," column by Ray Beaumont-Craggs; "AP Tested," test bench review column by Allan Shriver; "What's New." (12-24-75).
TYPL: "Salon in the City of Light," "Picturing the Curious Onges," "The Spirit of Christmas," "With Shaker Simplicity," "Keeping Static at Bay." (12-24-75).
SCHL: Weekly, 165 pp.
SPAN: Jun 19, 1918+
FROM MERGER OF
--Photography and Focus (and) Amateur Photographer and Photographic News, The.
VARIES
--Jun 19, 1918 - Jul 27, 1927 as Amateur Photographer and Photography, The.
--Aug 3, 1927 - Jun 13, 1945 as Amateur Photographer & Cinematographer, The.
ABSORBED
--New Photographer, Aug 1, 1928.

Amateur Photographer & Cinematographer, The
Aug 3, 1927 - Jun 13, 1945//
SEE: AMATEUR PHOTOGRAPHER

Amateur Photographer and Photography, The
Jun 19, 1918 - Jul 27, 1927//
SEE: AMATEUR PHOTOGRAPHER

AMATEUR PHOTOGRAPHER'S WEEKLY, THE
SUB: "A journal designed to create and foster a desire for picture making with the camera." (Jul 26, 1912 - ?).
SUB: "The journal that teaches Photography." (? - Oct 17, 1919).
SUB: "Official organ of the Camera Club of New York."
SUB: "Official organ of the Photo Pictorialists of Buffalo."
SUB: "Official organ of the Boston Photo Clan."
PUBL: J. C. Abel, 401 Caxton Bldg., Cleveland, OH.
DESC: This weekly serial provided clear instructions for amateur photographers, from lens selection to film printing. Articles were written in a basic "how-to" style, and included numerous examples of technique, and readers' mastery of the subjects. In consideration of the restricted nature of photographic supplies available to the membership, many articles gave specific instructions on mixing chemicals from readily available drugstore materials in the community. Also construction of darkrooms, photographic platforms, and other items necessary to full photographic application were combined with schematics and instructions for their assembly. An interesting serial for the basics of amateur photography.
DEPT: "Perplexities," Q&A column. (9-6-12). "Reader's Criticism," "Local Manipulation," comment. (10-10-19).

TYPL: "Small Negatives for Enlarging," "Avoiding Shadows When Photographing Small Objects." (9-6-12). "Houses as a Specialty," "Photography in the Mountains," "A One-Solution Metol-Hydro Developer." (10-10-19).
SCHL: Weekly, 24 pp.
SPAN: Jul 12, 1912 - Oct 17, 1919//
ABSORBED
--Photoisms, Aug, 1912.
ABSORBED BY
--American Photography.
LC: TR1.A43
ISSN: 0097-577x

AMATEUR POINTER FOR AMATEUR PHOTOGRAPHERS, THE

PUBL: Anthony & Scovill Co., 122-124 Fifth Ave., New York, NY.
DESC: The three-year span of this 16-page monthly serial provided articles pertaining to the art and technique of photography, and was split into two sections, one for amateurs and one for advanced photographers. Its small size and life span provide mute testimony to the highly competitive market for amateur photographic serials at this time, and *The Amateur Pointer for Amateur Photographers* simply could not compete with other, more successful works. The February, 1902 issue announced that it was to be "incorporated into the *Photographic Times* under the name of *The Photographic Times and Amateur Pointer*.
DEPT: "Answers to Correspondents." (8-01).
TYPL: "Composing the Picture--Notes for the Beginner," "Seashore Photography," "Care and Storage of Negatives." (8-01).
SCHL: Monthly, 14 pp.
SPAN: Jan, 1899 - Feb, 1902//
ABSORBED BY
--Photographic Times, The.
LC: TR 1.A45

Amateur Radio

Jan, 1977 - ?//
SEE: CQ

AMATEUR RADIO DEFENSE

SUB: "In the interests of Amateur Radio Defense Association."
PUBL: Pacific Radio Publishing Co., San Francisco, CA
DESC: "*Amateur Radio Defense* is being published to foster a greater use of amateur radio operators and equipment in the defense of our nation. Its primary purpose is to create a better understanding and encouragement of the amateur's ability to meet emergencies arising from disruption of normal communication facilities by acts of war. This purpose, incidentally, is not being effectively accomplished by any other agency." The United States government, not being at war in November, 1940, could not, of course, address the proposed problem, even though it was a matter of daily conversation among the general public. The editors, like the American public, foresaw war to be a natural development of the time, and prepared their readers for what they felt was a prime opportunity for amateur radio operators to participate in the defnese of the United States. Articles provided latest news and gossip about the possibilities of war, and technical articles on boosting power, range, and quality of transmissions. Numerous schematics and illustrations.
DEPT: "Chats With the Editors," letters; "The Editor's CQ," comment; "News from Washington," "Engineering Applications." (3-41).
TYPL: "A.R.D.A. and the Seattle Black-Out Test," "High-Power Screen-Grid Transmitter," "The War and the Radio Amateur." (3-41).
SCHL: Monthly (Nov, 1940 - Mar, 1941); Bimonthly (Apr/May, 1941 - Jun/Jul, 1941); 55 pp.
SPAN: Nov, 1940 - Jun/Jul, 1941//
LC: TK 6540.A56

Amateur Tape Recording

1959 - ?//
SEE: HI-FI SOUND

Amateur Tape Recording & Hi-Fi

Feb, 1961 - 1963//
SEE: HI-FI SOUND

Amateur Tape Recording, Video & Hi-Fi

1963? - Nov, 1967//
SEE: HI-FI SOUND

Amateur Wireless and Electrics

No. 1 - 331//
SEE: AMATEUR WIRELESS AND RADIOVISION

AMATEUR WIRELESS AND RADIOVISION

PUBL: Bernard Jones Publications, Ltd., London, England.
DESC: Guglielmo Marconi, from his yacht Elletra cabled "Good Wishes" to the staff of *Amateur Wireless and Electrics*, providing an auspicious start to this publication. Amateur radio and broadcasting were still relatively new media in 1922, and articles attest to that in providing both basic and more advanced technical information. This was a serial for the experimenter, the basement "tinkerer" ready and willing to put to-

gether his own radio set and listen to the world. The title *Radiovision*, which replaced *Electrics*, was an early term for television. Numerous graphics and schematics for this exciting era of radio. Unfortunately, printed on newsprint.
DEPT: "Broadcasting and the Public," news. (7-22-22). "News and Gossip of the Week," "Listeners' Letters," "Full Size Blueprints," "My Broadcasting Diary," "Postcard Radio Literature." (12-29-34).
TYPL: "Marconi Patents and the Amateur," "The Nature of the Ether," "Protecting the Aerial from Lightning." (7-22-22). "Microphone Manipulation," "Coil Making Made Easy," "Listen to India on Short Waves." (12-29-34).
SCHL: Weekly, 50 pp.
SPAN: Jun 10, 1922 - Jan 19, 1935//
VARIES
--No. 1 - 331 as Amateur Wireless and Electrics.
MERGED WITH
--Practical Wireless (to form) Practical and Amateur Wireless.
LC: TK 6540.A6

✤ AMAZING CINEMA

PUBL: Cinema Enterprises, 12 Moray Court, Baltimore, MD 21236.
DESC: *Amazing Cinema* is a horror "fanzine" with a unique approach to this film genre; not only does the publication showcase current film product (both silver screen and video releases), but also provides readers with interesting articles on "home" productions, and insights as to how the Hollywood professionals accomplish a certain effect. A sampled issue for 1981 had a color cover and black/white editorial content with an editorial promise by Editor and Publisher Don Dohler to build a dramatic increase in pages, a letters column (to be called "Reader Viewpoint"), and expanded coverage of the "amazing" side of cinematic entertainment in the months to come. Articles concerning effects were quite informative, oftentimes illustrating how readers might attempt to duplicate Hollywood effects on a small budget. For example, one feature on animating physical objects such as a cereal box or bottle, provided very explicit information on lenses, lighting, film speed, zooms, and other technical details necessary for the home producer to arrive at a satisfactory effect. Editorial layout was well executed with spot color on some pages. Magazine format on coated paper stock (8 ½ x 11 inches / 215 x 280 mm).
DEPT: "Production Slate," 'New Films Coming Your Way'; "Pittaro's Clinic," 'Questions & Answers on Film & Effects' column by Ernie Pittaro; "Product Guide," 'New Items to Aid or Entertain' books and other reviews; "Classic Film Salute," column by Don Leifert; "Amazing Video," 'Capsule Reviews of Current Video Fare'. (6-81).
TYPL: "The Triceratops Vs. Aunt Gertie," "Tabletop Scenery: You Don't Have to be an Artist to Get Realistic, Believable Results," "Animating Physical Objects," "Fiend: A New Low-budget Thriller that Strives for Story & Acting, Rather than Blood & Guts." (6-81).
SCHL: Ten issues per year, 35 pp.
SPAN: May, 1981+

✤ AMAZING HEROES

PUBL: Fantagraphics Books, Inc., 7563 Lake City Way, Seattle, WA 98115.
DESC: "Some magazines offer news... Some magazines offer interviews... some magazines offer previews...but only one magazine offers you all of the above, plus an exciting variety of columns, essays, and special features--all published every other week and wrapped up with covers by your favorite pros! ...So if you love comic books, you'll certainly want to subscribe to fandom's only bi-weekly magazine about comics! And for extra thrills, check out those back issues for special features on comics you read and creators whose work you collect!". This semimonthly is an interesting mixture of comic industry news, trends, lawsuits, and a comic fandom's paradise of new and fascinating comic art product, all served up with a liberal selection of comic art from past, current, and to-be-released product. In the first issue of June, 1981, J. Michael Catron noted; "And so, *Amazing Heroes*. A magazine that likes to play hooky from daily reality. Here in our pages, you'll be treated to the delights of that playground." Ten years later in a June, 1991 10th anniversary issue, contributor Kevin Dooley stated, "...Alfred North Whitehead put it best with 'Art flourishes where there is a sense of adventure, a sense of nothing having been done before, of complete freedom to experiment; but when caution comes in, you get repetition, and repetition is the death of art'. I feel this is one of the few ways we're going to prevent comics from becoming mere landfill. Naysayers aver comics won't be around in 10 years. We'll be here. We may be a completely different animal, but that depends on what we do today. It's time for heroes to grow in a different direction. Not toward a sanitized, goody two-shoes wimpo, but not any further toward the sadistic, fists-first, hate 'em and kill 'em all machismo. Yes, a little pacifism, yes, a little more understanding, yes, a lot more optimism." Well said, and typical of the quality essays, news reporting, and commentary found within this long-running publication. Magazine stapled format; black/white editorial content on newsprint with full-color cover on coated paper stock, limited advertising (6 ⅝ x 10 ¼ inches / 170 x 260 mm).
DEPT: "Editorial," "Perspective," "Newsline," "Coming Distractions," upcoming releases; "Backstage," column by Andy Mangels; "Video Views," column by Nancy Collins; "Doc's Bookshelf," column by Dwight R. Decker; "Small Talk," column by Edd Vick; "Comics

in Review," "Amazing Readers," letters; "The Cartoonist," column by Teri S. Wood; "Strom's Index," column by David Strom. (7-15-89).
TYPL: "Welcome to the Xenozoic Age," "King of the Seven Seas," "10 Best Super-Team Team-Ups." (7-15-89).
SCHL: Monthly (Jun, 1981 - Mar, 1983); Semimonthly (Apr, 1983+), 140 pp.
SPAN: Jun, 1981+
ISSN: 0745-6506

AMERICAN ADVERTISER
SUB: "The advertiser's problem is the problem."
SUB: "Devoted to the problems of the advertiser in the belief that anything helpful to him is helpful to all whose line of work relates to advertising."
SUB: "Oldest advertising journal in the world."
PUBL: M. L. Starke, Tribune Bldg., New York, NY.
DESC: "As the *American Advertiser* is published solely in the interests of advertisers, it is our duty to show up any evils which militate against the advertisers' interests. The greatest of these is that the advertiser receives only sixty cents' worth of advertising for each dollar spent in newspapers." This statement from the January, 1905 issue set the tone for this important trade journal for advertisers. The editors of *American Advertiser* were crusaders against advertising agencies, newspaper and magazine publishers, when it was discovered that the advertiser was receiving something less than full value for his advertising dollars. The serial explored new publications, advertising techniques (one issue discussed advertising to dentists), and had an ongoing series of articles which served to introduce publishers, sales agents, and advertising agency owners to readers via line drawing caricature or steel-engraved photograph. That the editors succeeded with all parties is witnessed to by a 290-page issue for January, 1906 with numerous advertisements by media seeking clients. One will find little humor within these pages, but a bounty of serious approaches to the science and art of advertising. In the February, 1906 issue, editor and publisher M. Lee Starke noted he was retiring as of this issue. He purchased the serial in September, 1904, but stated that he would rather let it cease publication than to change editorial content under the same title, and thus no more issues were published following his retirement. Small magazine format.
DEPT: "Our Department of Criticism," commentary; "Concerning Foreign Markets," "Department for Retailers," "Type-ology," 'For the advancement of technical printing knowledge among non-printer advertisers'; "Making Retail Advertisements." (4-05).
TYPL: "Machine Made Advertising," "Why Good Advertising Does Not Always Pay," "Curtains as an Advertising Medium," "Rate Raising Without Reason." (4-05).
SCHL: Monthly, 200 pp.
SPAN: Jan, 1905 - Feb, 1906//
LC: HF 5801.A6

✤ AMERICAN ADVERTISER
SUB: "How to advertise a retail stock."
PUBL: Merchants Publishing Co., Clark and Lake Sts., Chicago, IL.
DESC: This serial had an interesting approach, as stated on its editorial page: "This paper tells how to advertise with success, and furnishes the advertisements ready written." The *American Advertiser* was 16 pages of ready-to-use engravings, copywriting ideas, and even complete ads, where all one needed to do was add the company name to the bottom of the column. A fascinating historical record of graphic cuts and advertising approaches.
DEPT: "The Window Dresser," techniques; "Locals," 'original and catchy write ups'; "General Advertisements," "Editorial Siftings," (8-1890).
TYPL: None.
SCHL: Monthly, 16 pp.
SPAN: Feb, 1887+?
LC: HF 5801.A62

AMERICAN ADVERTISER REPORTER
SUB: "A journal in the interest of newspaper publishers and advertising managers."
SUB: "A publication for publishers and advertising managers."
SUB: "A bi-weekly journal devoted to the interest of publishers and advertising managers, containing certain information respecting advertisers in the United States and Canadian Provinces."
PUBL: New York Reporter Printing Co., 234 - 235 Broadway, New York, NY.
DESC: Newspaper publishers and their respective sales managers received their bi-weekly trade news through the *American Advertiser Reporter*, a small format serial with brief newsworthy articles. There were few articles in each 12-page issue; no illustrations; some advertisements for publishing supplies. By 1893, each issue was eight pages in length with virtually no advertisements remaining.
DEPT: "Relating to Advertisers," newsbriefs; "Things at Hand," comment; "The Country Over," individual press news; "Personal," "Legal," "New Ratings." (2-1-1888).
TYPL: "The Royal Baking Powder Company," "Mississippi Valley Farmer," "An Agents' Association," "Discontented Watch Buyers." (2-1-1888).
SCHL: Biweekly (1886 - 1889); Weekly (1890 - 1893), 12 pp.
SPAN: 1886 - Sep 13, 1893?//
LC: HF 5801.A65

AMERICAN AMATEUR PHOTOGRAPHER AND CAMERA & DARKROOM

SUB: "An illustrated monthly magazine devoted to amateur photography in all its phases and developments." (Jul, 1889 - ?).
SUB: "A monthly review of amateur photography." (Jul, 1889 - ?).
PUBL: American Photographic Publishing Co., New York, NY.
DESC: Publisher W. H. Burbank set out to produce a serious magazine for the amateur photographer, remarking that he would leave the humor to publications like *Judge* that had already shown the amateur photographer to be just that, an amateur in approach and demeanor. This small-format serial provided news on new technical developments, building home darkrooms, experimental chemicals, lenses, and the printing of what the editors felt were outstanding examples of serious amateur photography. Numerous line drawings and reproduced photographs. In the June, 1907 issue, the publishers announced that they had acquired the *Photo-Beacon*, which would be merged with the *American Amateur Photographer and Camera & Darkroom* to form a new serial to be known as *American Photography* commencing with the July, 1907 issue. Small format.
DEPT: "Editorial Notes," "Our Portfolio," "Society News," concerning camera clubs; "Our Table," book reviews; "Letters to the Editors," "Answers to Correspondents." (6-07).
TYPL: "The Portland Camera Club," "Preserving Glass Negatives," "Ordinary Room Portraiture," "The Working of Gaslight Papers," "How to Make a Single Transfer Carbon Print." (6-07).
SCHL: Monthly, 40 pp.
SPAN: Jan, 1907 - Jun, 1907//
FROM MERGER OF
--American Amateur Photographer (and) Camera and Dark Room.
MERGED WITH
--Photo Beacon (to form) American Photography, Jul, 1907.
LC: TR 1.A5

✤ AMERICAN CINEMATOGRAPHER

SUB: "The international journal of motion picture production techniques."
SUB: "The magazine of motion picutre photography."
SUB: "International journal of motion picture photography and production techniques."
PUBL: ASC Holding Corporation, 1782 North Orange Drive, Los Angeles, CA 90028.
DESC: It is all that the subtitle indicates, and more. Published since 1920 by the American Society of Cinematographers this remains "the" publication for the behind-the-scene's "how-to" of film production. The serial is famed for quality authoritative articles on the technique and technology of movie-making. Here the reader will learn of production problems and solutions as they occurred on-location or soundstage. The accomplishment of special effects, lighting, sound, and cinemagraphic approaches to the art and industry of film are often shown only in this publication. Long a reading staple of the industry professional, *American Cinematographer* remains unique in its field. Highly recommended. Magazine format, perfect bound on coated paper stock, color pages throughout (8 3/8 x 10 7/8 inches / 215 x 275 mm).
DEPT: "Cinema Workshop," interesting production concepts; "Questions & Answers," provides advice on professional film questions; "Profile: ASC," profiles one outstanding ASC member; "Bookshelf," reviews of better film and television publications. (11-77). "Electronic Imagery," separate videography section; "Letters," "What's New," products; "The Bookshelf," reviews; "From the Clubhouse," newsbriefs; "The Last Page," commentary. (11-86). "Letters," "Ask ASC," questions and comments column by David Heuring; "What's New," production techniques, products, and trends; "The Bookshelf," book review column by George L. George; "The Last Page," ASC picture page. (4-91).
TYPL: "Behind the Camera on 'Valentino,'" "Metal Halide Lighting Parameters Reassessed," "Spectacular Visual Effects for 'Damnation Alley." (11-77). "American Cinematographers in Britain," "Du Art Labs: Important Part of Indy Survival," "Lighting for Drama: The Color of Money." (11-86). "Alibi: Gangsters Take on Talkies," "The Josephine Baker Story: From Squalor to Glory," "High Tech Noir Look for Writer's Block," "Miller Beer Commercials--Bigger Than Life." (4-91).
SCHL: Semimonthly (Nov 1, 1920 - Mar 1, 1922); Monthly (Apr 1, 1922+), 105 pp.
SPAN: Nov 1, 1920+
SUSPENDED
--Nov, 1958.
LC: TR 845.A55
ISSN: 0002-7928
ABST: --Art Index (ISSN: 0004-3222)
--Film Literature Index (ISSN: 0093-6758)

✤ AMERICAN CINEMEDITOR

SUB: "Official publication of American Cinema Editors, Inc."
SUB: "A publication of the honorary professional society--American Cinema Editors, Inc."
PUBL: American Cinema Editors, Inc., PO Box 26082, Encino, CA 91426-2082.
DESC: As *Cinemeditor*, this brief newsletter served to provide timely information on ACE (American Cinema Editors) activities, festivals, and current projects of ACE membership. Under the later title of *American Cinemeditor*, the subtitled indicated that "The Cinemaeditor is sponsored and published quarterly by American Cinemaeditors, Inc., the honorary profes-

sional society of film editors, and is devoted to film editing and allied television and motion picture news." This previous 20- and now 50-page publication continues to provide fascinating insight into the often misunderstood art, technique and technology of entertainment product editing. What began as an exclusively motion picture film stock medium, has now dynamically evolved into an organization and publication which views motion picture entertainment as the medium, and with film, videotape, optical disk, and other recording vehicles as the technological means to an artistically successful end. Several motion picture projects are featured in each issue, along with considered discussions of visual philosophies, member profiles, and the potential application of new technologies to this traditional film field. An excellent resource. For sampled issue of 1991: stapled magazine format, black ink and full color mixed pages throughout on coated paper stock (8 1/8 x 10 7/8 inches / 210 x 280 mm).
- DEPT: "American Cinema Editors Current Assignments." (10-61). "The Answer Print," Q&A format on editing items. (winter-73/74). "From the Editor," editorial column by Howard Kunin; "Trim Bin," who is editing what listing, column by Bob Bring; "Scene and Heard," editors in the news, column by Denise Abbott; "In Memoriam," obituaries. (spring-91).
- TYPL: "New ACE Awards Plan Adopted," "A.C.E. Represented at UFPA Berkeley Conclave," "The TVola for Videotape." (10-61). "A Bit of London in Los Angeles," "Sea Gulls on the Cutting-Room Floor," "The Creative Experience of Editing Jonathan Livingston Seagull," "An Evening with a Cine Society." (winter-73/74). "George Lucas: His First Love is Editing," "Sound: Digital Vs. Analog," "Special Report: Electronic Editing," "There's a Bottom Line Below the Line: Hollywood's Post-Production Entrepreneurs," "E-Trax Brings Multi-Channel Audio Editing to Nonlinear Post-Production." (spring-91).
- SCHL: Quarterly (? - ?); Monthly (? - Summer, 1971); Quarterly (Fall, 1971+), 50 pp.
- SPAN: Winter, 1950+
  VARIES
  --Winter, 1950 - Summer, 1971 as Cinemeditor (ISSN: 0069-4169).
- LC: TR 899.A54
- DD: 778.5/35/05 19
- ISSN: 0044-7625

AMERICAN CLASSIC SCREEN
- PUBL: American Classic Screen, PO Box 7150, Overland Park, KS 66207.
- DESC: Originally the official publication of the Bijou Society which later became the National Film Society, *American Classic Screen* mirrors the intent of its organization, that of dedication to the great and near-great of early Hollywood film. The broad appeal of this serial is oftentimes most noticeable in articles that range from fan magazine level, to a serious study of film star lives and historical product. Some issues feature rare publicity and production stills. Primary target audience is the movie fan, and film historians.
- SCHL: Bimonthly (Sep/Oct, 1976 - Jul/Aug, 1979); Quarterly (Fall, 1979 - Spring, 1980); Bimonthly (Summer, 1980+).
- SPAN: Sep/Oct, 1976 - Nov/Dec, 1984//
- LC: PN 1993.A615
- DD: 791.43/05
- ISSN: 0195-8267
- ABST: --Film Literature Index (ISSN: 0093-6758)

✦ AMERICAN DEMOGRAPHICS
- SUB: "Consumer trends for business leaders."
- SUB: "The magazine of consumer trends and lifestyles."
- SUB: "The magazine of consumer markets."
- PUBL: American Demographics, Inc., 127 West State St., Ithaca, NY 14850.
- DESC: "If you've been looking for a magazine that can breathe life, substance and meaning into statistics, a magazine that can keep you posted on the latest demographic research, analyze and interpret the findings for you, relate them to your areas of concern and report them to you without the usual sociological jargon, you should get to know *AMERICAN DEMOGRAPHICS*, The Magazine of Consumer Trends and Lifestyles." Every once in a while there comes a periodical so valuable, so applicable, so in touch with the times that not to subscribe is like turning out the lights in the board room and hoping to succeed in the dark. *AMERICAN DEMOGRAPHICS* is an absolute must for any American business, and perhaps even more valuable to the international business community in explaining and exploring the fickle tastes and trends of the American consumer public. Subscribers treasure their subscriptions with statements such as "I have three people on my research staff--and *AMERICAN DEMOGRAPHICS* is the fourth," or "*AMERICAN DEMOGRAPHICS* adds 'flesh' to the bare framework of census data. It is clear, concise, and a pleasure to read. You make numbers come to life for marketing application." It is difficult to conceive of the advertising agency, marketing department or corporation that relies on consumer purchasing which would not be a loyal subscriber and user of the authoritative data found in this monthly publication. Magazine format (8 3/8 x 11 inches / 215 x 280 mm), stapled, full color throughout on coated paper stock.
- DEPT: "Editor's Note," column by Brad Edmondson; "Seasons," column by Judith Waldrop; "Spending Money," column by Thomas Exter; "Letters," "Demographic Forecasts," column by Thomas Exter; "The Lincoln Sample," a cross-country odyssey column by Tom Parker. (3-91).
- TYPL: "A Place in the Country," "The Legacy of the 1980s," "The Information Empire," "The Future of the Family," "How to Avoid Big Mistakes." (3-91).
- SCHL: Monthly [with combined Jul/Aug and Nov/Dec issues] (Jan, 1979 - Sep, 1981); Monthly [with combined Jul/Aug issue] (Oct, 1981+), 60 pp.

SPAN: Jan, 1979+
WITH SUPPLEMENT
--Numbers News (ISSN: 0732-1597), ?+
ISSN: 0163-4089
ABST: --ABI/Informer
--Business Periodical Index (ISSN: 0007-6961)
--Energy Information Abstracts (ISSN: 0147-6521)
--Environment Abstracts (ISSN: 0093-3287)
--InfoBank
--Management Contents
--Population Index (ISSN: 0032-4701)
--Predicasts
--Public Affairs Information Service Bulletin (ISSN: 0033-3409)

American Federation of Film Societies. Newsletter
Oct, 1956 - Jun, 1957//
SEE: CRITIC

✤ AMERICAN FILM
SUB: "Journal of the film and television arts." (Oct, 1975 - Dec/Jan, 1979).
SUB: "Magazine of the film and television arts." (Feb, 1979+).
SUB: "Film, video and television arts."
PUBL: Billboard Publications, 3 East 54th St., New York, NY 10022.
DESC: *American Film* is concerned with a broad range of motion picture topics, including the production, direction, acting, promotion, and preservation side of film product in the United States and Europe. If a philosophical approach is present, it is to promote motion picture film, by examining past classics of the silver screen, current trends, the role of director, international production companies, and the relationship of film to society in general. The American Film Institute has been a major partner in the long-overdue effort to save early nitrate film prints for future generations, an effort aided by ongoing articles concerning preservation and reviews of past product. Readers will not find deep theoretical/philosophical approaches here; rather, this is a serial which celebrates film as social comment, business enterprise, and entertainment medium. Written for a lay audience with knowledge or love of the visual arts. Of special note are articles by name industry professionals. Also the sampled issue for 1979 contained the special section, "Dialogue on Film," an interview with noted film producer Joeseph E. Levine. For sampled issue of 1979: stapled magazine format, mixture of black ink and full-color pages on coated paper stock (8 ⅛ x 11 inches / 210 x 280 mm). Sampled issue for 1987: stapled magazine format, full color throughout on coated paper stock (8 ⅛ x 10 ¾ inches / 205 x 270 mm).
DEPT: "Comment," 'A forum for diverse views on the media'; "Letters," "Lehman at Large," commentary column by Ernest Lehman; "Festival Report," "Focus on Education," column by Jonathan Rosenbaum; "About Television," column by Martin Mayer; "Books," reviews; "AFI News," 'A newsletter about film and television activities of special interest to the American Film Institute members', edited column by Brynda Pappas; "Periodicals," resourceful listing of current comments in various publications. (9-79). "Newsreel," newsbriefs; "Dialogue on Film," unique interviews; "Preservation," of historic films; "Independents," "Books," "Trailers," films in progress; "From the Director," editorial. (10-84). "Editing Room," editorial; "Letters," "Illuminations," 'notes and essays from around the world'; "Television," "Dialogue on Film," "Screenings," review of new film product; "Video Classics," review; "New Video Releases," review; "AFI Calendar," American Film Institute events; "Bravo Program Guide," cable television programming guide; "Epilogue." (7/8-89).
TYPL: "The Remarkable Visions of Peter Ellenshaw," "TV's Fall Offensive: The Tent-Pole Strategy," "The Greatest Movies Never Made," "Recycling Jerry Lewis." (9-79). "The Natural," "Sunday in the Country With Bertrand," "Big Heads," "Gunga Duke," "On the Edge," "Collector's Choice: Gremlins to Go." (10-84). "Knocking on Hollywood's Door," "Pals," "Film School Confidential," "The Hottest Dead Man in Hollywood." (7/8-89).
SCHL: Monthly (Oct, 1975 - Sep, 1979 with combined Dec/Jan and Jul/Aug issues); Monthly [with combined Jan/Feb, Jul/Aug issues] (Oct, 1979+), 75 pp.
SPAN: Oct, 1975+
ABSORBED
--Dialogue on Film, May/Jun, 1975.
LC: PN 1993.A617
DD: 791.43/05
ISSN: 0361-4751
ABST: --Art Index (ISSN: 0004-3222)
--Book Review Index (ISSN: 0524-0581)
--Film Literature Index (ISSN: 0093-6758)
--Humanities Index (ISSN: 0095-5981)
--Index to Book Reviews in the Humanities (ISSN: 0073-5892)
--Magazine Index
--Media Review Digest (ISSN: 0363-7778)
--Popular Magazine Review (ISSN: 0740-3763)
--Reference Sources (ISSN: 0163-3546)

✤ AMERICAN FILM INSTITUTE. QUARTERLY.
PUBL: American Film Institute, the John F. Kennedy Center for the Performing Arts, Washington, DC 20566.
DESC: "The American Film Institute is an independent, non-profit organization. . .to advance the art of film and television in America." As such, the *AFI Report*, later renamed *American Film Institute Quarterly* (winter-73), is primarily concerned with past motion pictures and television programming, discussion of same, and means of preserving historical records dealing with

those productions. Many historical stills are included in each issue with significant academic community contributions.
DEPT: "Books on View," reviews. (winter-73).
TYPL: "The Rise and Fall of Women in the Movies," "New American Cinema, the First Thirty Years," "The War We Watched on Television," "D. W. Griffith and the Moral Landscape." (winter-73).
SCHL: Bimonthly (Jun, 1970 - Aug, 1970); Monthly (Feb, 1971 - ?); Quarterly (?+), 50 pp.
SPAN: 1967?+?
VARIES
--Jun, 1970? - Fall, 1973 as American Film Institute Report (ISSN: 0044-7684).
--Winter, 1973? - Summer, 1974 as AFI Report.
WITH SUPPLEMENT
--American Film Institute. Education Newsletter, ? - ?
LC: PN 1993.A512

American Film Institute Report
Jun, 1970? - Fall, 1973//
(ISSN: 0044-7684)
SEE: AMERICAN FILM INSTITUTE. QUARTERLY.

✢ AMERICAN JOURNALISM
SUB: "The publication of the American Journalism Historians Association."
PUBL: American Journalism, Department of Journalism, School of Communication, University of Alabama, PO Box 1482, University, AL 35486.
DESC: Providing an historical forum for the discovery, critique, and review of American journalism, the American Journalism Historians Association provides scholars with a unique publication for considered thought. Articles are of a scholarly nature, fully footnoted, and chosen in a refereed manner. This is an important work in the ever-widening search for the historical roots of journalism, and a better understanding of how the American system of journalism developed. Articles provide a fascinating insight to development of American journalism. At times special issues are published, such as the second issue of 1989 which contained "...the historical works deemed the three best submitted to the 1988 paper competition of the American Journalism Historians Association." Of special note is an excellent section devoted to book reviews of new publications in journalism history. For the sampled issue of 1989: Perfect bound journal format, no graphics, editorial content being black ink on uncoated paper stock with black ink on heavy gray uncoated paper stock cover (6 x 9 ⅛ inches / 150 x 230 mm).
DEPT: "Book Reviews." (Vol 6, #2-89).
TYPL: "A Last Hurrah for the Frontier Press," "George Seldes and the Winter Soldier Brigade: The Press Criticism of 'In Fact', 1940 - 1950," "'Purse and Pen': Party-Press Relationships, 1789 - 1816." (Vol 6, #2-89).
SCHL: Semiyearly (? - ?); Quarterly (?+), 75 pp.
SPAN: Summer, 1983+
LC: PN 4700.A39
DD: 071/.3/09
ISSN: 0882-1127

AMERICAN JOURNALIST, THE
SUB: "A magazine for professional writers."
PUBL: American Journalist Printing and Publishing Co., St. Louis, MO.
DESC: In launching this periodical on September 15, 1883, the editors noted that, "The journalistic profession is the only one existing at the present time that is without a medium of intercourse between its respective members...*The Journalist* is therefore sent out to represent the interests of the working writers of the press throughout the land; to bring into communion him who does his work on the Atlantic coast with his contemporary laborer on the shores of the Pacific, and to constitute such a medium as will give to the toilers with the pen just recognition for the services they are devoting to mankind." This publication very quickly served its stated function by providing news of new technology for the sending of news stories, the status of the average newspaper reporter/writer, and it served as a clearing house and forum for news from individual press clubs throughout the country. No illustrations, except advertising cuts.
DEPT: "Legal Decisions," "Press Clubs," "Gossip of Itinerants," 'told by the nomads of journalism'; "Newspaper Notes," "National Editorial Directory," complete list of newspaper managers and primary staff members. (7-1884).
TYPL: "Pioneer and Recent Journalism in Houston, Texas," "A Woman Journalist," "An Hour in Silence." (7-1884).
SCHL: Monthly, 30 pp.
SPAN: Sep 15, 1883 - Jun, 1885//
LC: PN 4700.A4

AMERICAN LITERARY GAZETTE AND PUBLISHERS' CIRCULAR
SUB: "A monthly record of works published in America, England, Germany and France; with a review of the current literature of the day; contents of leading American and English periodicals; advertisements of the trade, etc., etc." (Jan, 1852? - Sep 1, 1855).
PUBL: George W. Childs, 600 Chestnut St., Philadelphia, PA.
DESC: The "Book Trade" was the primary audience for this publication, first published in September, 1855. Its function was to provide a listing of recent books published, newsnotes of publishers, and developments within the industry. First issues for 1855 were magazine-size serials, moving to a small format by 1871 with numerous line drawings and advertisements at the back of each issue. Sample issues for 1872 show paucity of articles, with listing of new

books being primary. There was an interesting lineage (although not clearly defined), connected with this and prior publications. Some sources indicate that a George W. Childs of Philadelphia bought in 1855 what had previously been *Norton's Literary Gazette and Publishers' Circular* and changed that publication to the *American Publishers' Circular and Literary Gazette*, which had been a publishers advertising forum for the purpose of promoting and selling books. This *Gazette* absorbed *The Criterion* in 1856 and Charles R. Rode, editor of that publication, became editor of the *Circular*. The *Circular*, in turn, changed its title (in 1863), to *American Literary Gazette and Publishers' Circular*. A fascinating publication for early book publishing and distribution.
DEPT: "Literary Intelligence," newsbriefs; "Books Received," "List of Announcements," publishers booklists. (9-15-1855).
TYPL: "Trade Sales," "Publisher's Association." (9-15-1855).
SCHL: Weekly (Sep, 1855 - Jun, 1861); Monthly (Jul, 1861 - Dec, 1862); Semimonthly (1863 - Jan 15, 1872); 12 pp.
SPAN: Nov 2, 1863 - Jan 15, 1872//
VARIES
--May, 1851 - Jan, 1852 as Norton's Literary Advertiser.
--Jan, 1852 - Sep 1, 1855 as Norton's Literary Gazette and Publishers' Circular
--Sep 1, 1855 - Oct 15, 1863 as American Publishers' Circular and Literary Gazette.
ABSORBED
--Criterion, The, Jul 12, 1856.
ABSORBED BY
--Publishers' and Stationers' Weekly Trade Circular.
LC: Z 1219.P978

✦ AMERICAN MOVIE CLASSICS MAGAZINE

PUBL: Crosby Vandenburgh Group, 150 Crossways Park West, Woodbury, NY 11797.
DESC: With dynamic layout design, full color graphics, and spritely writing, this program guide for the American Movie Classics cable television network is a winner. The cable network features Hollywood motion pictures of the past, and this programming guide is designed not only to whet one's appetite through interesting articles, but also to inform about films being shown, and date/time of broadcast. Approximately six to eight films are exhibited each day. Magazine format (8 x 10 ¾ inches / 205 x 275 mm); full color graphics.
DEPT: "Great American Cinemas," wonderful section concerning restored cinema theatres; "Festival Highlights," special film showings for the upcoming month; "This Month on AMC," 'Easy-to-read calendar and alphabetical descriptions for this month's AMC programming'; "It Was Rumored," film stars of yesteryear; "Letters," 'With Bob Dorian'. (2-90).

TYPL: "Gene Tierney: Behind the Glamorous Mask," "A Princess's Progress-- Grace Kelly's Screen Debut." (2-90).
SCHL: Monthly, 16 pp.
SPAN: Jan, 1988+

✦ AMERICAN NEWSPAPER BOY, THE

SUB: "Rain and shine and sleet and snow; it's all the same to us, you know." (Nov, 1936 - ?).
SUB: "Published monthly for all newspaper boys." (Nov, 1936 - ?).
PUBL: American Newspaper Boy Press, 416-20 North Marshall St., Winston-Salem, NC.
DESC: "Sold in bulk to newspapers for free distribution to their carrier and salesboy organizations," *The American Newspaper Boy* was a newsprint tabloid filled with positive sales techniques, woodpulp "dime-novel" adventure stories, and just plain Horatio Algier stories of newsboys who made good during Depression-era America. Throughout this monthly tabloid, newsboys were encouraged to increase subscriptions by industry, honesty, and dedication to task. Sayings, such as "Don't tease children. Remember, their mothers and fathers are your customers," or "A carrier should read HIS paper--after he has delivered his route," were peppered between columns of jokes, cartoons, and articles on stamp collecting, adventure, baseball and other articles of interests to this group. A fascinating promotional serial issued by American newspaper publishers.
DEPT: "Sparks," short positive advice on building subscribers column by J. W. Triplett; "Sales," positive advice column by Charles Rohleder; "World of Science in Pictures," "Pluggy's Letter," column; "Laugh Lighters," jokes. (5-37).
TYPL: "The Captain's Folly," "The Winged Alarm," "May Days--Profit Days," "Newspaper Reading Habits Change Often," "Rules Successful Salesmen Follow." (5-37).
SCHL: Monthly, 8 pp.
LC: AP 201.A57

American Newspaper Reporter

? - ?//
SEE: ADVERTISERS GAZETTE

American Newspaper Reporter and Advertiser's Gazette

Jan, 1871 - ?//
SEE: ADVERTISERS GAZETTE

American Newspapers and Printers Gazette

? - ?//
SEE: WOODCOCK'S PRINTERS' AND LITHOGRAPHERS' WEEKLY GAZETTE AND NEWSPAPER REPORTER

✢ AMERICAN PHOTO

PUBL: Diamandis Communications, Inc. 1633 Broadway, New York, NY 10019.
DESC: The word for this magazine is "class." It is a highly professional serial concerned with unusual concepts in photography. The art and technique of imagry is explored via individual artists, reviews of famous portfolios, unusual photo essays, strong historical features on the development of the medium, and truly fascinating features concerning photography in cities and countries throughout the world. Of special note are challenges to readers to submit photographs reflecting a particular theme, such as "Hearts and Flowers," or "Mirrors and Windows." After 11 years of publication, publisher Diamandis Communications shortened the serial's title, and moved it to a bimonthly publishing schedule. The layout design had a more "European look," with the new design debut in Jan/Feb, 1990. In short, a very classy magazine of photography, where even the book review covers are printed in full color. Printed on heavy quality paper stock, without the usual plethora of camera store ads. Sampled issue for 1990: (8 ⅞ x 10 ¾ inches / 225 x 275 mm).
DEPT: "In Camera," newsbriefs together with photographs of interesting items; "Exhibitions," detailed synopses; "Books," lengthy reviews; "Latent Images," fascinating feature printing some bygone photos; "Contact," stories and contact prints; "Assignment," readers are challenged to send in photos embodying a challenge theme; "Flash," unusual...; "Gallery," photo essay; "Letter," excellent letters detailing the status of photography in a world city; "Monitor," story behind a photojournalism project; "By Request," printing of 'to be seen again' photos; "Listings," Gallerys and current exhibitions; "Tech Notes," "Inside Advertising," Ad projects; "Parting Shots," readers letters. (3-79). "Editor's Note," column by David Schonauer; "In Camera," news of note; "Monitor," contributed pictures; "I, Witness," fascinating first-person photographers report; "State of the Art," "Photofile," 'A roundup of new and noteworthy products' column by Ruyssell Hart; "Field Test," "Books," review; "Tech Tips," 'A user's guide to know-how'; "On Location," back-page photo. (7/8-90).
TYPL: "Portfolio: Richard Kalbar," "Photo Essay: Genesis of an Island," "Abe Witkin Sampler," "History: Face of Our Fathers." (3-79). "The Advertising Game," "Everyone Agrees on Six Factors that are Shaping Advertising Photography," "The Image Index," "When Bad Ideas Happen to Good Photography." (7/8-90).
SCHL: Monthly (Jun, 1978 - Dec, 1989); Bimonthly (Jan/Feb, 1990+), 115 pp.
SPAN: June, 1978+
 VARIES
 --Jun, 1978 - Dec, 1989 as American Photographer (ISSN: 0161-6854).
LC: TR1 .A568
DD: 770/.5 20
ISSN: 1046-8986

American Photographer

Jun, 1978 - Dec, 1989//
(ISSN: 0161-6854)
SEE: AMERICAN PHOTO

AMERICAN PHOTOGRAPHY

PUBL: American Photographic Publishing Co., New York, NY.
DESC: *American Photography*, formed from the merger of three individual serials, produced in latter years a photography magazine of some repute. The long list of absorbed periodicals attests to the strength of this serial amongst serious photographers, both amateur and professional. Issues for 1907 varied little from its predecessors both in scope and interest. Issues for 1917 demonstrated a much larger editorial content, and improved quality printing of pictures; while 1942 issues brought the serial to its zenith with well-presented full-page pictures and technical articles concerning photographic equipment and process. This was and remains a quality publication for the art and science of photography. Note: lineage on this publication is in dispute.
DEPT: "Hints to Beginners," "Editorial Note and Comment," "Correspondence," "Our Portfolio," "Society News," "Our Table," "Recent Photographic Patents." (9-07). "Practical Hints," "The Editor's Point of View," "For the Beginner," "Notes and News." (12-42).
TYPL: "The Photo-Pictorialists of Buffalo," "A Method of Measuring Shutter Speeds," "Photographing for Profit." (9-07). "High Resolution Emulsions," "On the Question of Print Size," "Three Dimensional Photography." (12-42).
SCHL: Monthly, 35 pp.
SPAN: Jul, 1907 - Jul, 1953//
 FROM MERGER OF
 --American Amateur Photographer and Camera & Darkroom (and) Photo-Beacon, Jul, 1907.
 ABSORBED
 --Camera Notes, Jan, 1909.
 --Popular Photography [Boston], Jan, 1917.
 --Amateur Photographers Weekly, Nov, 1919.
 --Photo-Craft, Feb, 1920.
 --Photo-Era Magazine (ISSN: 0097-5885), Apr, 1932.
 --Photo Miniature, Oct, 1939.
 --Photo Technique (ISSN: 0097-5893), Jan, 1942.
 --Camera Craft (ISSN: 0527-3919), Apr, 1942.
 ABSORBED BY
 --Photography, Jul, 1953.
LC: TR 1.A58
DD: 770.5

ISSN: 0097-577x

✤ AMERICAN PREMIERE

SUB: "The magazine of the film industry."
PUBL: American Premiere Ltd., 8421 Wilshire Blvd., Suite 205, Beverly Hills, CA 90211.
DESC: A very nicely produced serial that discusses Hollywood product as business, one which cuts through cultural nostalgia to present film and television as a major industry worthy of serious business discussion. Publisher Susan Royal and editor Michael Firmature combine hard information with feature style writing. Special issues are featured from time to time, such as the May/June, 1991 "Cannes Film Festival Issue," which included an excellent resource section entitled "Annual Directory of Film Festivals & Markets." For sampled issue of 1991: stapled magazine format, full-color pages throughout on heavy coated paper stock, advertising primarily targeted to film and video producers (8 ½ x 11 inches / 215 x 280 mm). Note: this publication is made available on a gratis basis to all members of the Academy of Motion Picture Arts and Sciences.
DEPT: "Quoteables," "Reader's Comments," "Premiere Salutes," "TV Film," "Hollywood Remembered," "The Bookshelf," "CloseUps," profiles; "The Screening Room." (5-81). "Resources," "Location Shooting: Who's Shooting Where," column by Casey Barnett; "Film Expositions & Conventions," listing. (5/6-91).
TYPL: "Independent Producers," "The Landaus: Trailblazers and Innovators," "Straight Talk: Two Television Independents Speak Out," "Premiere's Guide to Film Financing." (5-81). "Irwin Winkler Takes on Blacklisting in His Directorial Debut: Guilty by Suspicion," "The Hollywood Who Done It," "An Interview with Geena Davis Starring in Thelma & Louise." (5/6-91).
SCHL: Monthly [except Feb and Aug] (Sep, 1980 - ?, 1984); Quarterly (Winter, 1984 - ?); Bimonthly (?+), 35 pp.
SPAN: Sep, 1980+
VARIES
--Sep, 1980 - Mar, 1981 as Premi'ere (ISSN: 0274-7766).
SUSPENDED
--Apr, 1981.
LC: PN 1993.5 .U6 A877
DD: 384/.8/0973
ISSN: 0279-0041

AMERICAN PRESS

SUB: "A monthly journal devoted to the interests of printers, publishers, lithographers, paper dealers, bookbinders, electrotypers, engravers & kindred trades." (Apr, 1889 - ?).
SUB: "The magazine for newspaper production."
SUB: "The monthly feature magazine for newspaper management."
PUBL: American Press Magazine, 651 Council Hill Rd., Dundee, IL 60118.
DESC: Since its first issue, this was a serial for newspaper management, providing information on new technologies, paper supplies, printing presses, and personnel news of interest to subscribers. With extensive advertising throughout attesting to the industry readership of this publication, *American Press* explored current operations management, examined new trends, and analyzed the changing nature of daily newspapers in American society and consumer demand for same. In the October, 1972 issue, publisher Walter Strong announced that beginning with the first issue of volume 91, *The American Press* would be combined with the *Newspaper Edition* of *Printing Management* magazine and would appear under the new title of *Newspaper Production*.
DEPT: "Editorial Notes," "Things Worth Knowing," "Among the Fraternity," "Items of Interest." (5-25-1889). "So It Seems," comment; "Offset," news concerning; "People," "Briefs," "Product Report," "Worth Reading," "Newsmonth," newsbriefs. (5-72).
TYPL: "Now for Cheap Type," "Public Printer Palmer," "Ethics of Journalism." (5-25-1889). "'Word Processing': Next Step in Newspaper Composing," "Advertising Color: a New Approach for Weeklies," "Preprints: Problems and Opportunities." (5-72).
SCHL: Monthly, 35 pp.
SPAN: 1882 - Oct, 1972//
MERGED WITH
--Printing Management [Newspaper Industry Edition] (to form) Newspaper Production (ISSN: 0148-9631).
LC: PN 4700.A55
ISSN: 0003-0600

✤ AMERICAN PRINTER

SUB: "The graphic arts managers magazine."
PUBL: Maclean Hunter, 29 North Wacker Dr., Chicago, IL 60606-3298.
DESC: One of the "granddaddies" of periodicals pertaining to the production side of American printing, for almost 100 years, *American Printer* and its predecessors have been providing new information on production techniques, shortcuts, equipment developments and printing standards. This is a publication whose purpose is to instruct, encourage, and extoll those elements of printing management which lead to a successful profitable operation. Numerous advertisements.
DEPT: "Newspaper Operations," a special section; "In-Plant Operations," a special section; "Pointers for Printers," "Photomechanical," "Quick Printing," "New Equipment," "New Literature." (9-81). "Letters to the Editor," "Editor's Desk," column by Jill Roth; "Business/Management Newsletter," excellent late breaking news column; "Let's Get the Facts," unique reader questionaire feature; "Industry News Roundup," newsbriefs; "Perspective," commentary; "Direct Mail/Sales Promotion," from a printer's point-of-view; "Sales & Marketing," printing promotion; "Pointers for Printers," techtips; "Prepress Connec-

tions," "Quality Control," "Product Profile," application/review of new products; "New Equipment," review; "Large Plant Management," 'special section for plants with 10 or more employees'. (6-89).
TYPL: "Typesetting's Swift Evolution Accelerates," "Focus on the Non- Heatset Web Market," "Discipline Spells Large Scale Profits," "One Man's Dreams are Milestones in Printing," "Moving Paper Up to the Press is Now a Breeze." (9-81). "Solving Production Puzzles," "Making Color Worth-While," "Data Entry with the Wave of a Wand," "Management with Flair," "This 'Evergreen' Grows Sales Leads." (6-89).
SCHL: Monthly, 145 pp.
SPAN: Nov, 1958+
FROM MERGER OF
--Inland Printer, The (and) American Printer & Lithographer.
VARIES
--Nov, 1958 - Jul, 1961 as Inland and American Printer and Lithographer, The (ISSN: 0096-2562).
--Aug, 1961 - Dec, 1978 as Inland Printer, American Lithographer (ISSN: 0020-1502).
--Jan, 1979 - Dec, 1981 as American Printer and Lithographer (ISSN: 0192-9933).
WITH SUPPLEMENT
--Prepress Links, ?+
LC: Z 119.I56
DD: 686.2/05
ISSN: 0744-6616
ABST: --Abstract Bulletin of the Institute of Paper Chemistry (ISSN: 0020-3033)
--Business Periodical Index (ISSN: 0007-6961)
--Communication Abstracts
--Predicasts
--Printing Abstracts (ISSN: 0031-109x)
--Trade and Industry Index

American Printer and Lithographer

Jan, 1979 - Dec, 1981//
(ISSN: 0192-9933)
SEE: AMERICAN PRINTER

American Publishers' Circular and Literary Gazette

Sep 1, 1855 - Oct 15, 1863//
SEE: AMERICAN LITERARY GAZETTE AND PUBLISHERS' CIRCULAR

American Society of Magazine Photographers Newsletter

? - ?//
SEE: ASMP BULLETIN

American Society of Magazine Photographers. News

Aug, 1950 - Jan, 1952//
(ISSN: 0361-9168)
SEE: ASMP BULLETIN

AMERICAN TELEGRAPH MAGAZINE

SUB: "Canst thou send lightnings, that they may go and say unto thee, here we are?--Job." (Oct, 1852 - Jul 15, 1853).
SUB: "I'll put a girdle 'round the earth in forty minutes.--Shakespeare." (Oct, 1852 - Jul 15, 1853).
PUBL: Donald Mann, New York, NY.
DESC: A short-lived, but important serial in the development of the American telegraph system. Printed in small magazine format with 6 - 8 point type, publisher Donald Mann produced an incredible number of articles in a small volume. One issue for July 15, 1853 contained over 100 brief articles for readers covering topics from "Notes on History and Principles of Telegraphing," to "Compact of 1847, between Morse Patentees, for Settling Difficulties with O'Rielly," to "Number and Course of the Journals whose Agents Demand Equal Rights in Telegraphing." A fascinating, and valuable resource. Editor Mann in the July 15, 1853 issue announced that *Shaffner's Telegraph Companion* (of which two issues had been published in Louisville) was to be absorbed (some sources say "merged") into the *American Telegraph Magazine* starting with the next issue.
DEPT: None.
TYPL: "American Patent System and Abuses Thereof," "Municipal Telegraph for Police and Fire Alarms," "Claims and Disclaimers of Professor Morse," "Experimental Line Between Washington and Baltimore," "Hints to Telegraphers--Need for Increased Care." (12-15-1852).
SCHL: Monthly (Oct, 1852 - Jan, 1853); Bimonthly (Feb/Mar, 1853); Monthly (Jul 15, 1853); 70 pp.
SPAN: Oct, 1852 - Jul, 1853//
SUSPENDED
--Apr, 1853 - Jun, 1853.
LC: TK 1.A66

AMERICAN TELEPHONE JOURNAL, THE

PUBL: American Telephone Journal Co., New York, NY.
DESC: Function of this biweekly publication was to provide late-breaking news of technical development within the telephone industry in America, and the general status of telephone business. This was primarily a serial for management, although an occasional issue provided technical schematics that required some previous electronics knowledge. In this pre-amplification (Triode) era, the bulk of articles concerned business

expansion, aesthetics of telephone booths and switchboards, and communication lines. Graphics; magazine format.
DEPT: "Opinion and Comment," "The Week's Messages," newsbriefs; "Problems--Queries," "Patents," "The Law." (1-11-02).
TYPL: "Something About Repeating Coils," "The Telephone Situation in Maine," "The Passing of Telephone Poles," "Telephone Finance." (1-11-02).
SCHL: Weekly, 16 pp.
SPAN: 1900 - Aug 29, 1908//
ABSORBED
--Sound Waves, Feb, 1908.
ABSORBED BY
--Telephony (ISSN: 0040-2656), Sep, 1908.
LC: TK 1.A67

✤ AMERICAN THEATRE
PUBL: Theatre Communications Group, American Theatre, 355 Lexington Ave., New York, NY 10017.
DESC: The status of American live stage performance is not only "alive and well," but vibrant, dynamic, and challenging. One only needs to read through several issues of *American Theatre* to experience the geographic, philosophical, and ethnic diversity that is live stage performance. The editorial stance is to meet current issues in bold and considered fashion, e.g., "A New Generation of Black Theatres," "A Gay Life in the Theatre," and a very extensive departmental section entitled "Government," with eight to ten pages devoted to the love/hate relationship between regulatory/funding bodies and the stage artist's desire for freedom of expression. This feature often provides stimulating discussion on elements of censorship, legal developments, funding trends, and regulatory reform. Of special note is the inclusion of the complete texts of plays, along with the playwright's profile and other information concerning production of same. Numerous newsbriefs, articles, and photographs announce theatrical events across the United States. An excellent resource in magazine format (8 ½ x 11 inches / 215 x 280 cm), spot color employed on covers, editorial content black/white on coated paper stock.
DEPT: "Letters to the Editor," "Editorial," "Frontlines," guest commentary; "Stages," "Government," excellent feature on government and theatre; "In Print," book reviews; "Notes From Abroad," international and world theatre news; "Trends," "Awards," "People," profile and newsbriefs; "Entrances & Exits," personnel newsbriefs; "In Memoriam," "Plays & Playwrights," "On Stage," state-by-state listing of current theatrical fare. (11-90).
TYPL: "An Eye on Tomorrow," "A Gay Life in the Theatre," "Scenes From a Censored Life," "A 'No' to Restrictions, a 'Yes' to NEA Reform," "Out of the Shadows and into the Swan." (11-90).
SCHL: Monthly [combined Jul/Aug issue], 80 pp.
SPAN: Jan, 1973+
VARIES
--Jan, 1973 - Mar, 1979 as Theatre Communications Group Newsletter (ISSN: 0163-9137).
--Apr, 1979 - Mar, 1984 as Theatre Communications (ISSN: 0275-5971).
LC: PN 2000.A52
DD: 792/.0973
ISSN: 8750-3255

✤ AMPERSAND'S COLLEGE ENTERTAINMENT GUIDE
PUBL: Alan Weston Communications, Inc., 303 North Glenoaks Blvd., #600, Burbank, CA 91502.
DESC: Encompassing motion pictures, television, and music entertainment, this quarterly full-color guide to today's hottest media product provides a viable means of hunting the elusive advertising quarry: the affluent college student. With a decided emphasis on motion pictures, this magazine provides interviews with current stars, capsule summaries of new film product, and a general overview of what is "hot" on today's American college campus. For the 1986 sampled issue: Stapled magazine format, full color graphics and cover on coated paper stock, distributed free of charge on selected college campuses (8 ⅛ x 10 ¾ inches / 205 x 275 mm).
DEPT: "Quick Takes," 'Previews of major upcoming films, groups on tour and television events, plus some inside scoop on personalities you like to watch', column by Jimmy Summers (with Greg Ptacek, Victor Davis and Sharon J. Pang); "Movie Roundup," new film releases column by Bart Mills. (fall-86).
TYPL: "David Lynch: Wizard of Odd," "Max Attack!," "Cruisin'." (fall-86).
SCHL: Quarterly, 24 pp.
SPAN: Fall, 1977+

✤ AMUSEMENT BUSINESS
SUB: "The international newsweekly for sports & mass entertainment."
PUBL: BPI Communications, Inc., 49 Music Square West, Nashville, TN 37203.
DESC: For those whose livlihood is derived from an appreciative public, whether the setting be sports stadium, arena, theme park, auditorium, stage show, carnival or circus, *Amusement Business* covers the news that management needs to effectively compete in todays entertainment field. The trade newspaper, issued on a weekly basis, is filled with news items concerning the economic health, development, and public response to specific entertainment media in geographic North American locations. The contents of each issue are divided into eight distinct entertainment-specific subject segments: "Promotions," "Talent," "Auds & Arenas," "Pro-Am Athletics," "Food & Drink," "Parks & Attractions," "Fairs & Expos," and "Shows." One wonderful trademark of *Amusement Business* is the large number of photographs found in any given issue,

providing a means in bringing together the people and personalities of this geographically diverse, and often transient entertainment field. Of special note are several unique departmental features. The first of these is "Boxscore," subtitled "Top concert grosses reported through [selected week]," providing a detailed listing under the headings of "Gross Ticket Sales," "Headliner, Support Act(s)," "Total Attendance," "Total Capacity & Number of Show(s)," "Ticket Scale," "Promoter," "Venue, City, Date(s)." The "Calendar" of upcoming events provides an informative listing of meetings, conventions and other events. The sampled issue for June, 1991 listed almost 60 such upcoming events, trade shows, association gatherings, and conventions for groups as diverse as the International Country Music Buyers Association, The League of Historic American Theatres, the International Association of Auditorium Managers, and the British Association of Leisure Parks, Piers & Attractions. Finally, a special department titled "Routes," lists the upcoming tours and show cities for North American carnivals and circuses. Show dates listed are for approximately one month in advance. In short, *Amusement Business* covers the business and people news of a host of diverse entertainment media, and does so in its own entertaining, informative, and newsworthy style. This is a magazine not to be missed for entertainment management. Large format, stapled magazine/newspaper style, black/white editorial content with some full-color advertisements, cover uses two-color ink, numerous pictures and other graphics (11 x 14 inches / 280 x 355 cm).

DEPT: "Up Front," brief review of current issue; "T. P. on Amusement Business," column by Tom Powell; "Retrospect," from the pages of Amusement business ten and twenty years ago; "Up Close & Personal," artist or business profile column by Ray Waddell; "Letters," "Management," newsbriefs concerning changes or promotions; "Lifelines," marriage announcements and 'Final curtains' obituaries; "Calendar," upcoming events; "Nashville Notes," column by Lisa Zhito; "AB Stock Index," selected stock activities; "Commentary," "Promotions," "Talent & Celebrities," news and publicity; "On Record," interview; "Boxscore," 'Top concert grosses reported' and detailed information column by Marie Ratliff; "Billboard Top 25 Singles," "Auds & Arenas," auditorium and arena news; "Pro/Am Athletics," news; "Food & Drink," merchandise and food preparation news; "Parks & Attractions," news and information; "Fairs & Expos," news and information; "Routes," unique roadshow itinerary for carnivals and circuses; "Jackpots," picture page. (6-10-91).

TYPL: "24,000 Country Fans Flock to Music City," "Brown M&Ms? No Problem for Most Acts Today; Contract Riders Becoming Simpler," "Indonesia's Dreamland a Study in Contrasts," "LPs, Concerts, Radio, TV Projects: What Next for Riders in the Sky?," "Madison Square Garden to Take Food & Merch Operation In-House." (6-10-91).

SCHL: Weekly [except first week in Jan], 40 pp.

SPAN: Jan 9, 1961+
FROM MERGER OF
--Show News and Funspot, Dec 31, 1960.
LC: GV 1851.A3 A55
DD: 338.7/61/79006805
ISSN: 0003-2344

Andy Warhol's Interview

1972 - Feb, 1977//
(ISSN: 0020-5109)
SEE: INTERVIEW

✧ ANIMAFILM

SUB: "The journal of animated film."
SUB: "Official organ of the ASIFA."
SUB: "Le journal du cinema d'animation, organe officiel de l'ASIFA."
SUB: "The international quarterly of animated film."
PUBL: Centro Internazionale per il Cinema di Animazione, corso Cairoli 6, 10123 Turin Italy.
DESC: Published originally in Poland by the Polish Film Makers' Association, events in that country brought this serial in January, 1984 under the editorial leadership of the Centro Internazionale per il Cinema di Animazione, in Turnin, Italy. In its initial editorial for 1984, the editors stated: "During theoretical, critical and historiographic debate, animation suffers from an incomprehensible isolation. One of the principal aims of this publication shall be to oppose that very tendency, almost inborn, which reveals itself in studies and research dealing with 'frame by frame'. *Animafilm* thus will act as a hyphen between animation and the other aspects of the film world and of the figurative art." The serial is clearly divided into two sections: 1) aesthetic and historical essays, documents, technical approaches and interviews; and 2) a timely news section (entitled *AnimaNews*), detailing festivals, grants, workshops, new animation product, etc. *Animafilm* articles are in English or French, with summaries in the alternating language.
DEPT: "Editorial," "Calendar of Events," "Festival Report," "Education and Workshop," "Books and Reviews," "ASIFA News," newsbriefs of the International Animated Film Association; "Telex," newsbriefs. (1-84).
TYPL: "The Films of Zbigniew Rybczynski, or the Calculated Vision," "An Interview with Kihashiro Kavamoto," "Felix the Cat, Betty Boop, Casper the Friendly Ghost and Their Creators." (1-84).
SCHL: Quarterly, 35 pp.
SPAN: 1979+

✧ ANIMATION MAGAZINE

SUB: "All the news that's fit to animate."
PUBL: Animation Magazine, PO Box 25547, Los Angeles, CA 90025.

DESC: Publisher/Editor Terry Thoren in the premiere issue for Fall, 1986 stated: "During the past year, We have received more than 20,000 requests from people who have seen the 19th Tournee asking for more information on the world of animation. The *Animation News* was created to provide a consistent source of news about the world of animation in all its varied forms." The first preview issue consisted primarily of news regarding the Los Angeles International Animation Celebration and related events. Future issues promised to "...include book reviews, film reviews, film festival dates and deadlines, interviews, industry news and information on the latest home video releases." For six months under the title of *Animation News* (as a newsprint tabloid), and then as *Animation Magazine*, this serial had been designed "...to celebrate achievers and achievements, remember past accomplishments, commemorate today's top talents and watch for tomorrow's innovators." The move to magazine status was a welcome one, allowing quality reproduction of animation cells, and providing the durability that newsprint cannot. Format of *Animation News* was small tabloid with black/white graphics. Under banner of *Animation Magazine*, magazine format, black/white graphics on quality newsprint, moving by Fall, 1989 to clay-coated paper stock, black/white graphics.

DEPT: None. (fall-86). "Home Video Directory," a large section detailing releases; "Student Animation Workshops," "Book Reviews." (1/2-87). "News," "Festivals/Calendar," "Jim Korkis' Animation Anecdotes," "Film Review," "Book Review," "Profile." (fall-89).

TYPL: "Science Fiction Author Ray Bradbury Hosts Animation Celebration Salute to World Famous Cartoonist Chuck Jones," "Festival of Claymation to Premiere During Holiday Season," "Bob Clampett Cels Help to Raise Funds for Student Scholarship." (fall-86). "Steven Spielberg: Producing Animation for a New Audience," "'Get a Job,' Full Time Work for Caslor," "No Downtime for Today's Computer Wizards." (1/2-87). "'The Simpsons' Marks the Return of Prime Time Adult Animation," "John Canemaker: Animation's Renaissance Man," "Disney Swims Into Underwater Animation." (fall-89).

SCHL: Bimonthly (Jan, 1987 - Jul, 1987); Quarterly (Aug, 1987+), 60 pp.
SPAN: Jan, 1987+
VARIES
--Jan, 1987 - Jul, 1987 as Animation News.
LC: NC 1766.U5A48
DD: 741.5805
ISSN: 1041-617x

Animation News
Jan, 1987 - Jul, 1987//
SEE: ANIMATION MAGAZINE

Animation Newsletter
Jan, 1978? - ?, 1983?//
SEE: ANIMATOR

✦ ANIMATIONS
SUB: "A review of puppets and related theatre."
SUB: "A review of the arts of animation in theatre, film and television."
PUBL: Puppet Centre Trust, 156 Lavender Hill, London SW11 5RA, England.
DESC: "The Puppet Centre is a registered charity formed in 1974 to promote and further the arts of puppetry and animation in all their forms and to serve the needs of anyone involved or interested in professional, amateur, educational and therapeutic puppetry." As animated and innovative as the stories it covers, *Animations* is a delight to read, and encouraging in the support brought to this long-established theatrical form. The emphasis is on the art and technique of puppetry, through extensive showcasing of current projects in review, ongoing work to broaden public support, and always interesting profiles of amateur and professional puppeteers. Crisp black/white graphics printed on quality paper enhance an alreadyvaluable publication. For the 1989 sampled issue: Stapled magazine format, black ink on coated paper stock, limited advertising (8 ¼ x 11 ¾ inches / 210 x 300 mm).
DEPT: "Centrenews," of the Puppet Centre Trust; "Home News," British puppet-related news; "International News," of puppetry; "What's On," extensive international event calendar of puppet theatre programs; "Spotlight," on innovation; "Letters," "OnScreen," puppetry on television or film; "Critical Reviews," "Reviews," "Bookworm," book reviews; "The Right of Reply," 'Readers' answers to last issue's review'; "Extra... Extra...," "Punchlines," column by John Styles. (10/11-89).
TYPL: "A Puppetmaster Remembered," "A Puppet and Mask Centre for Scotland," "Brazil and the Mamulengo Tradition," "Disney Buys Henson Associates." (10/11-89).
SCHL: Bimonthly, 20 pp.
SPAN: Oct/Nov, 1977+
ISSN: 0140-7740

✦ ANIMATO!
SUB: "The animation fan's magazine."
PUBL: Animato, PO Box 1240, Cambridge, MA 02238.
DESC: *Animato* is an interesting collage of articles, newsbriefs, essays, and historical profiles of animators and their film product. With a decidedly American focus, the Massachusetts-based periodical appears to favor profiles of animators and the historical development of their craft. Articles are intelligently written, and are targeted at more than the casual Saturday morning cartoon aficionado, often providing insight into an industry that has been long ignored by the entertain-

ment industry. Early issues were photocopied; later issues printed; small stapled journal format. Reproduction of animation cels varies greatly. For sampled issue #18 for spring, 1989: stapled magazine format, editorial content consists of black ink on newsprint, with two-color blue and black ink cover on coated paper stock (8 ⅛ x 10 ¾ inches / 205 x 270 mm).
DEPT: "Editorial," "Fanmail From Some Flounder," letters; "Koko Komments," column by G. Michael Dobbs; "Harlequin," trivia column by Jim Korkis; "Flipbooks," "Toons on Tape," videocassette releases; "Short Subjects," "The Fox Report," 'Animation news from John Cawley'. (winter-87/88). "Praxinoscope," 'Animato's melange of news, commentary, and more'; "Short Subjects," 'reviews of recent films, books, and television programs, including a look at the current Saturday-morning season'; "Toons on Tape," "Animatorial/Fan Mail," "Koko Komments," "Jim Korkis's Animation Anecdotes," 'Jim Korkis's roundup of tidbits and trivia about animation past and present'; "A Little Birdie Told Me," 'Thelma Scumm, animation's most prominent society reporter, tells all about everybody who's anybody'. (spring-89).
TYPL: "In the Temple of the Muses," "My Youth in Cartoonia," "Uncle Scrooge vs. He-Man." (winter-87/88). "An Interview with Friz Freleng," "The Triumph of Termite Terrace." (spring-89).
SCHL: Quarterly (1983 - Fall, 1987); Three issues per year (Winter, 1987/1988+), 40 pp.
SPAN: 1983+
DD: 741 11
ISSN: 1042-539x

✥ ANIMATOR

SUB: "Your guide to the world of animation."
PUBL: Filmcraft Publications, 13 Ringway Rd., Park St., St. Albans, Herts AL2 2RE England.
DESC: Designed for the British animation industry, this publication is part trade-news, and part promotional for the spectrum of creative animation work. Historical animator profiles and studio histories, while not foreign to this serial, are not the primary focus; rather, this publication concentrates on today's animation industry, with animator profiles, technical developments, and excellent pieces concerning current projects in production. Significant care is taken for quality reproduction of animation cells, including color when required. Of special note are excellent articles on the technique of drawing animated characters. This publication appears to be connected with the British section of ASIFA (International Animated Film Association), and should be an important publication for every student of the art and technique of animation.
DEPT: "News Round-Up," newsbriefs; "Editorial," "The USA Scene," animation news from the States column by John Crawley. (1-88). "News Round-Up," "The USA Scene," "Book Reviews." (7-89).
TYPL: "Postscript to Snow White," "The Great Animation Debate," "Owning Part of Your Dream," "The Best of British Animation," "Animating in Turkey." (1-88). "Over My Shoulder," "Paul Driessen Workshop," "Animation and Art," "Ray Fields Workshop." (7-89).
SCHL: Semiyearly, 35 pp.
SPAN: Jan, 1978?+
VARIES
--Jan, 1978? - ?, 1983? as Animation Newsletter.

ANPA NEWS RESEARCH REPORT

SUB: "An ANPA News Research Center study."
SUB: "A report for editors provided in coordination with the newspaper readership council."
PUBL: ANPA News Research Center, P.O. Box 17407, Dulles International Airport, Washington, DC 20041.
DESC: This monograph-type serial provides summarized findings of newspaper research funded by the American Newspaper Publishers Association. One study is published per issue; three-hole punched; no graphics.
DEPT: None. (4-12-77).
TYPL: "Content, Appearance and Circulation." (4-12-77).
SCHL: Irregular, 4 pp.
SPAN: Apr 8, 1977 - Dec, 1983//
VARIES
--? - 1976 as News Research Bulletin (ISSN: 0734-9238).
LC: PN 4700.A14a
DD: 071/.305
ISSN: 0195-8585

ANPA Newspaper Information Service Newsletter

? - ?//
(ISSN: 0569-6712)
SEE: ANPA PUBLIC AFFAIRS NEWSLETTER

✥ ANPA PUBLIC AFFAIRS NEWSLETTER

PUBL: American Newspaper Publishers Association, Dulles International Airport, P.O. Box 17407, Washington, DC 20041.
DESC: Short newsletter designed to keep ANPA members apprised of association-related events and news.
DEPT: None. (6-76).
TYPL: "ANPA has Initiated Two New Technical Research Projects," "Speeches Available," "ANPA Convention Readership Panel Cites Methods for Building Circulation." (6-76)
SCHL: Monthly, 8 pp.
SPAN: ?+
VARIES
--? - ? as ANPA Newspaper Information Service Newsletter (ISSN: 0569-6712).

Anti-Nazi News
1936 - Mar, 1937//
SEE: HOLLYWOOD NOW

Antiquarian Bookman
Jan 3, 1948 - May 29, 1967//
SEE: AB BOOKMAN'S WEEKLY

✢ ANTIQUE RADIO CLASSIFIED
SUB: "The national publication for buyers and sellers of old radios and related items."
PUBL: John V. Terrey, 498 Cross St., PO Box 2, Carlisle, MA 01741.
DESC: "*Antique Radio Classified* is published for people involved in the radio collecting hobby. Its purpose is to stimulate growth of the hobby through the buying, selling and trading of radios and related items, and to provide a monthly forum for the interchange of ideas and information. This may include articles, book reviews, photos, information on upcoming radio events, meetings, antique radio organizations, radio auctions and price reports, sources of old radio and restoration supplies, and other related and interesting material." This small booklet-styled publication is an excellent resource for the area of antique radio collection. Majority of each issue is devoted to an extensive "Classified Advertisements" section with wants/needs of collectors throughout the United States. Other articles showcase individual collectors, exhibitions, the care and cleaning of antique radios, and any and all resources in support of one's superheterodyne receiver. As entertaining for the articles and classified advertisements as it is for the numerous pictures of early wireless equipment. A wonderful resource for the antique radio enthusiast and collector.
DEPT: "Editor's Comments," "With the Collectors," antique radios held by collectors; "Restoration Topics," care and cleaning of antique radios; "Photo Review." (1-90).
TYPL: "The Earthquake: October 17, 1989; Can Your Collection Survive the Big One?," "The 'Pudding Quake' of '89," "The Earthquake and Our Vulnerable Collections." (1-90).
SCHL: Monthly, 75 pp.
SPAN: Jan, 1984+
ISSN: 8750-7471

✢ ANYMATOR
SUB: "The ASIFA-East newsletter."
PUBL: The International Animated Film Society-East, c/o The Optical House, 25 West 45th St., New York, NY 10036.
DESC: The "NY" in ANY*mator* stands for the East chapter of the International Animated Film Society, for whose members this newsletter is published. Function is primarily to alert readers to upcoming festivals, exhibitions, screenings, and other animation events in the region. Other regional ASIFA chapters exist in the United States, some of which also have their own local newsletter. Typewritten; loose pages.
DEPT: "International News," extensive section of animation newsbriefs; "Screenings," upcoming animation. (10-89).
TYPL: "Animation Archive Opens at New York University." (10-89).
SCHL: Monthly, 8 pp.
SPAN: ?+

✢ AP BROADCASTER
SUB: "News for broadcast members of the Associated Press."
PUBL: AP Broadcast News Center, 1825 K St., N.W., Washington, DC 20006-1253.
DESC: Begun under the banner of *Network News*, the function of this bimonthly newsletter is to provide association news and developments for AP Broadcast Service affiliates. Issues are comprised of personnel changes, association news items, operation of individual AP Broadcast News centers, and development of news items sent to these affiliated members. Magazine format; graphics.
DEPT: "Broadcast Life," "The News Doctor," journalistic advice column by Chuck Wolf; "Letters." (5/6-86). "AP People," personnel briefs; "TV Direct" television news; "AP Network News," "AP Sports," "Newsworthy," commentary; "Letters." (3/4-88).
TYPL: "AP Network News to Feature President Reagan in Liberty Minutes," "APTV Enhancement Debuts at NAB," "Never Ending Phone Call Makes AP's Libya Coverage Matchless," "Electronic Carbons Aid San Francisco Bureau." (5/6-86). "Covering Calgary," "Health & Medicine Hits Home With Listeners," "The Russians are Listening," "Animated Election Graphics Available." (3/4-88).
SCHL: Bimonthly, 16 pp.
SPAN: 1982+
VARIES
--1982 - ? as Network News.

✢ APERTURE
PUBL: Aperture Foundation, Inc., 20 East 23rd St., New York, NY 10010.
DESC: "Aperture, Inc. is a non-profit, educational organization publishing a quarterly of photography, portfolios, and books to communicate with serious photographers and creative people everywhere." This quality forum for the serious art/culture-related photographer was founded by Ansel Adams, Dorothea Lange, Beaumont and Nancy Newhall, Barbara Morscap and Minor White. Often one issue is dedicated to a particular photographer, or portfolio in monograph form. Other issues are themed, such as the May, 1990 issue on "Cultures in Transition," which grew out of a 1988 symposium on "The World's Reality," sponsored in

part by the Aperture Foundation: "During the course of this four-day gathering, photographers, anthropologists, filmmakers, and others discussed issues involved in depicting cultures in a changing world. Several essays in this issue highlight topics that were central to the symposium's debates: In any photographic exchange, who decides what will be depicted, and how it will be shown? Who are the pictures being made for? In studying another culture, does the observer--whether photographer or anthropologist--have a responsibility beyond simply making a record, to attempt to influence or arrest the change?" This statement is typical of the care, concern, and charge of *Aperture*: to explore the nature of visual imagry, and its relationship both to the reality of the world, and to the inquisitive nature of the reader. Pictures are often placed one to a page, the entire contents printed on heavy coated paper stock, with advertising relegated to the back section of the quarterly. For anyone who has pondered the role of visual media in this world, *Aperture* provides stimulating thought, and a delightful photographic adventure. For the sampled issue of 1990: Square magazine format (9 5/8 x 11 3/8 inches / 240 x 290 cm).
DEPT: "People & Ideas." (5-90).
TYPL: "The Unveiled: Algerian Women," "A House Divided: South Africa's Hostels," "Sobriety and Variation: Notes on Brazilian/Yoruba Sacred Altars," "The Past Becoming Future: Who Lives an Image, For Whom an Image Lives," "Native Visions: The Growth of Indigenous Media." (5-90).
SCHL: Quarterly (Apr, 1952 - 1975); Irregular (1976 - ?); Quarterly (1983+), 85 pp.
SPAN: Apr, 1952+
LC: TR 1.A62
DD: 770/.5
ISSN: 0003-6420
ABST: --Art Index (ISSN: 0004-3222)

✧ APERTURE, THE

SUB: "Workshop publication for 16 mm film producers."
PUBL: Calvin Co., 1105 Truman Rd., Kansas City, MO.
DESC: This eight-page publication is a promotional release of Calvin Communications, Inc., a producer, laboratory and sales group for 16mm film equipment.
DEPT: "CCI Newsletter." (12-75).
TYPL: "Multiple Choice: A Test About Survival," "Ektachrome Reversal Prints Now Available," "7240 Video News Film, a Status Report." (12-75).
SCHL: Irregular, 8 pp.
SPAN: May, 1959+?
LC: PN 1995.9 .P7A55

✧ APPLIED ARTS QUARTERLY

PUBL: Applied Arts, Inc., 885 Don Mills Rd, suite 324, Don Mills, Ontario Canada M3C 1V9.
DESC: With a $12.50 (spring, 91) cover price, this is not a magazine for the casual reader. But for the practicing design professional, this is a "Class Act" of fascinating reading, new insights, stunning photography, and the art and craft of printing which pushes the outer envelope of what is technologically feasible in the "ink on paper" field. *Applied Arts* brings together a creative blend of what is both new and of quality in the field of typography, layout design, visual graphics, and paper stocks. Articles are written by professionals for professionals, and critically examine current advertising fare, as well as provide some instructional pages on current trends and developments. The quarterly showcases outstanding applied arts, most often advertising vehicles in the form of print, billboard, and television advertisements. A sampling of typical articles for mid-1991 included creative annual reports, the handlettering professional in the computer age of typography, the means by which one artist designs type on a desktop computer, a look at what is new in the field of stock photography, an analysis of Canadian advertising regulations, and numerous profiles pertaining to artists of note. Printed products including creative photography are reproduced with great care. This is an excellent publication for working professionals; for ideas, concepts, trends and technologies which continue to change and shape our perceptions of what constitutes "quality" imagry. Large perfect-bound magazine format, full-color pages throughout on heavy coated paper stock, and specialty printing stock furnished by various paper manufacturers (9 5/8 x 12 3/4 inches / 245 x 325 mm).
DEPT: "Noteworthy," 'Briefs from the applied arts'; "Letters," "Hot & Cold" critical look at contemporary advertising; "Reel Talk," profile; "Opinion," "Fresh Faces," new artists on the applied arts scene. (spring-91).
TYPL: "You Can Go Home Again," "Designs for a Richly Imagined Future," "An End to Extravagance," "The Finishing Touch," "Start From Scratch and Win." (spring-91).
SCHL: Quarterly, 70 pp.
SPAN: Spring, 1986+
DD: 741.6/0971
ISSN: 0829-9242
ABST: --Canadian Periodical Index (ISSN: 0008-4719)

APPLIED PHOTOGRAPHY

SUB: "A magazine of noteworthy examples of photography as applied to the major problems of industrial management and market development."
PUBL: Eastman Kodak Co., 343 State St., Rochester, NY 14650.
DESC: It would be difficult for anybody to look at this superior publication, and not become excited about its content and form. It is a full color treatment of advertising agencies' and professional photographers' works in preparation for advertisements, corporate reports, and other applied techniques. Of special note is a brief description explaining each printed photo, a

problem, and how the problem was resolved; along with photo credits of the client, advertising agency, photographer, and account executive or art director. It is highly recommended.
DEPT: None.
TYPL: "The Industrial Photographer's Assignment: Mission Impossible," "Fresh Looks at Familiar Subjects," "Interpreting the Usual," "Beating Dead Horses. . .Successfully," "The Corporate Image." (No. 61).
SCHL: Two issues per year [Irregular at times], 40 pp.
SPAN: May, 1931 - 1975//
SUSPENDED
--Apr, 1936 - 1954.
SUPPLEMENT TO
--Commercial Camera Magazine, The, May, 1931 - Mar, 1936.
WITH SUPPLEMENT
--Commercial Camera (ISSN: 0414-0303), 1954 - 1969.
LC: TR 690.A1A6
ISSN: 0003-6943

APR
SUB: "The Australasian Photo-Review."
PUBL: Kodak (Australasia) Pty., Ltd., Sydney, Australia.
DESC: A relatively short, small-format, monthly serial to provide photographic news to professionals in Southeast Asia. Articles detailed problems of working under adverse conditions, new laboratory techniques, new product releases, and other similar topics. Issues in the 1950s contained duotone covers and some duotone pictures with articles. *APR* came close to being an ideal promotional serial for a company such as Kodak, but by 1956 that company felt that there was no longer a need for a general publication of photography, and *APR* ceased as of the December, 1956 issue.
DEPT: "Notes from Magazines," photographic news culled from other publications; "Editorial Notes," "The Photographic Societies," newsbriefs. (1-47). "The Photographic Societies," "Notes from the Magazines." (11-56).
TYPL: "Processing in the Tropics," "Colour Filters in Photomicrography," "Underwater Photography with Kodachrome." (1-47). "Enlarging--An Inexpensive Method," "Factors Affecting Print Quality," "Springtime and the Camera." (8-56).
SCHL: Monthly, 70 pp.
SPAN: 1894 - Dec, 1956//
LC: TR 1.A14

Archiv der Elektrischen Ubertragung
Jul/Aug, 1947 - Dec, 1970//
(ISSN: 0374-2393)
SEE: AEU

✤ ARK
SUB: "Comic news, interviews, reviews, strips."
SUB: "The comics magazine."
PUBL: Titan Books, Paul Duncan, 15 Tregullan Rd., Exhall, Coventry, CV7 9NG England.
DESC: Editor Paul Duncan stated there were several reasons why he wanted "...to put comics out on the stands. The first reason is that I see a lot of talent about that doesn't have the proper outlet to show the world what they can do. They don't fit into somebody else's ideas about comics. Secondly, I am in contact with a lot of creators who have not quite developed to their full potential and they need guidance and support. Getting them into print will help. Thirdly, each comic or magazine will contain a complete story so that you will get the satisfaction of reading the whole thing." Showcasing new and promising talent, *Ark* fulfills the promise of Editor Duncan with ample cartoon work, and interesting profiles of the artists themselves. The artwork is at times lavish, at times harsh, but always compelling. The philosophical, technical, and storytelling approaches to the cartoon work of these artists is fascinating. These artisans oftentimes provide the reasoned thought behind their printed works, enticing the reader to study the cartoon artwork, read the artist's intention, and again return to the cartoon panels. Editorial care is evident in the reproduction of artwork within the pages of *Ark*, and the use of a "bright-white" uncoated paper stock for printing. Full color covers with black/white editorial content (8 ¼ x 10 ¾ inches / 210 x 270 cm).
DEPT: "News and Reviews," 'From Around the World'; "Reviews," of current comic, strips, and graphic work; "UK News," current work by artist and corporate group; "USA News," current work by artist and corporate group; "New Zealand News," current products and artist news; "Germany / France," comic and artist news; "Torture Garden," enlightened comment on good and not so good comic releases, column by Mark D. Sard. (#26- 88).
TYPL: "A Midsummer Day's Conversation with Charles Vess," "Terry Austin & Mark Farmer," "Peter Kuper," "Chris Reynolds." (#25-88).
SCHL: Bimonthly, 65 pp.
SPAN: Sep/Oct?, 1984?+

ARS TYPOGRAPHICA
SUB: "A quarterly miscellany of the printing art."
PUBL: Marchbanks Press, 114 E. 13th St., New York, NY.
DESC: A lavish but briefly published periodical devoted to the art of typography. Beautifully illustrated with woodcuts, half-tones and line art. The 15-year publication tended to explore historical developments from the middle-ages to the twentieth century. Printed one column in 14 point type. An excellent historical resource.
DEPT: "The Editors Workshop," commentary; "Publishers Page," editorial combined with letters. (spring-20).

TYPL: "Old and New Fashions in Typography," "Initial 'G' from Plantim's Printing Office," "Le Bonheur de ce Monde," "Hand-Press Printing," "The Happiness of this World," "Printing as an Art." (spring-20).
SCHL: Quarterly, 50 pp.
SPAN: Spring, 1918 - Autumn, 1934//
SUSPENDED
--Summer, 1920 - Spring, 1925.
--Fall, 1926 - Summer, 1934.
LC: Z 119.A78
DD: 655.05

✣ ARSC JOURNAL

PUBL: Association for Recorded Sound Collections, c/o Les Waffen, Exec. Sec., Box 1643, Manassas, VA 22110.
DESC: "Because the field of sound recordings covers so very many facets of human experience, represented by such disciplines as anthropology, orinthology, history, theatre, music--each in turn supporting a multitude of specialized associations, the Association for Recorded Sound Collections has its own particular role to play, which is that of helping make the sound recordings medium work more effectively in both its informational and experiential functions." Emphasis is on past recordings via the medium of the phonograph cylinder and record, with some articles detailing archive efforts via magnetic audio tape. Note: officially published three times per year, although certain issues were combined during 1987 - 1989 period. Small format; limited graphics.
DEPT: "Discographies," "Bibliography," "Reviews of Records." (#3-81).
TYPL: "The Mapleson Cylinder Project," "A Provisional Mapleson Cylinder Chronology," "The Times as Reflected in the Victor Black Label Military Band Recordings from 1900 to 1930." (#3-81).
SCHL: Three issues per year, 130 pp.
SPAN: Winter, 1967/1968+
VARIES
--Winter, 1967/1968 - 1985? as Journal (ISSN: 0004-5438).
LC: ML 1.A84
ISSN: 0004-5438
ABST: --MLA International Bibliography of Books & Articles on the Modern Languages and Literatures (ISSN: 0024-8215)
--Music Index (ISSN: 0027-4348)
--RILM Abstracts (ISSN: 0033-6955)

✣ ART & CINEMA

SUB: "A periodical review of films and videotapes made by artists and about the arts."
PUBL: VRI Arts Publishing, PO Box 1208, Imperial Beach, CA 92032.
DESC: "Art + Cinema,...is the only magazine which devotes itself exclusively to information on and critical review of art-related films and videotapes. It fills a major bibliographical void, reporting on available works selected in consultation with artists, critics and art educators and historians for their aesthetic importance or their educational value in the classroom, museum, or wherever a better understanding is sought of the creative arts of our time." Issues vary greatly in content (indeed, some ignore film altogether for discussion of theatre, musicals, and dance), but primary focus is on providing an informational forum for new ideas of merging art and cinematic film/videotape. Some articles provide schematics to indicate camera/talent positions.
DEPT: "Editor's Page," "Review." (12-78).
TYPL: "Hollywood and the Hollywood Group," "Thirty Years of Film Poetry," "Art and the Technological Imperative," "Holography: Revolution in Space." (12-78).
SCHL: Three issues per year, 50 pp.
SPAN: Jan, 1973+
LC: N 72.M6 A77
DD: 700
ISSN: 0363-2911

✣ ART & DESIGN NEWS

SUB: "The authority on new products and services for commercial artists and graphic designers.
PUBL: Grady Publishing Company, PO Box 871, Saint Petersburg, FL 33731.
DESC: As the title suggests, this large-tabloid serial showcases new products for the graphic arts industry, having a majority of editorial content reviewing those new items for the graphic designer. Each issue contains several articles profiling the work of leading graphic designers for product design, and application of graphic products within the workplace. Tabloid format enhanced by full color graphics.
DEPT: "From the Publisher," "Books," "Videotapes," "Brochures," "Catalogs," "Calendar." (9/10-88).
TYPL: "Taking the Plunge into Computer Graphics," "Burnout," "Tips on Toting." (9/10-88).
SCHL: Bimonthly, 55 pp.
SPAN: Jan/Feb, 1979+
VARIES
--Jan/Feb, 1979 - Nov/Dec, 1990 as Art Product News (ISSN: 0163-7460).
DD: 760
ISSN: 1055-2286

✣ ART DIRECTION

SUB: "The magazine of visual communication."
SUB: "The magazine of visual communication, serves the field of advertising art, photography, typography and related graphic arts field."
PUBL: Advertising Trade Publications, Inc., 10 E. 39th St., New York, NY 10016.
DESC: Primarily print oriented, Art Direction sets out to cover what is new and interesting in all visual media. Reproductions of current ad campaigns (full size in many cases), and interviews with interesting new

illustrators, photographers and other visual artists are of special interest to the reader. For the graphic designer, this is an excellent resource to explore ideas, concepts, and finished work of a variety of fellow colleagues work across America. The advertisements included in each issue are those that display an unusual spark of creativity in photography, illustration, concept or layout design. Also a prime outlet for paper manufacturers' new ideas on visual design. Magazine format; numerous black/white and color graphics; various paper stocks in each issue according to advertiser campaigns. Sampled issue for 1988: (8 3/8 x 11 inches / 215 x 280 cm).

DEPT: "Trade Talk," one-line report of personnel changes; "Business News," briefs; "Literature and Supplies," new products; "TV Cuts," "Spot Agency News," "Seen and Noted," currently running ads of note; "Best," current ads of outstanding quality; "Upcoming Illustrator," profile; "Upcoming Photographer," profile. (11-74). "Letters," "Joint Ethics," news of the Joint Ethics Committee; "Trade Talk," personnel newsbriefs; "News," recent ad campaigns; "Late News," recent ad campaigns; "TV Cuts," shotboards of recent video advertising campaigns; "Design," graphics projects; "Just Breaking," new advertising campaigns; "Best," outstanding advertising campaigns; "Seen and Noted," ad campaigns; "Swipefile," great graphic design ideas; "Portfolio," artist showcase; "Upcoming Photographer," profile; "Regional News," ad campaigns from various American cities; "Book Reviews," "Upcoming Illustrator," profile; "Calendar," "Literature & Supplies," "Looking Back," Art Direction graphics of yesteryear; "In Brief." (6-88).

TYPL: "Warner Brothers Ads," "New DirecReport," "The New York Blitz." (11-74). "Marathoners," "Some Room to Spread Out." (6-88).

SCHL: Monthly, 70 pp.

SPAN: Winter, 1942+
VARIES
--Winter, 1942 - Jun, 1950 as Studio News.
--Jul, 1950 - Dec, 1955 as Art Director & Studio News.

LC: NC 997.A1A684

DD: 741.6/05

ISSN: 0004-3109

ABST: --Art Index (ISSN: 0004-3222)
--Book Review Index (ISSN: 0524-0581)
--InfoBank

Art Director & Studio News
Jul, 1950 - Dec, 1955//
SEE: ART DIRECTION

✧ ART DYNAMO
SUB: "Boston / New England area arts."
SUB: "Alternative Spaces."
PUBL: Art Dynamo, 24 Benedict St., Somerville, MA 02145.

DESC: In a 1991 editorial Publishers/Editors Gary Rattigan and Sandy Rattigan asked "Where are the independent arts and artists of Boston? ... This is what we will try to be about -- bringing together a forum of the arts from the Boston and New England region so there might be another place for people to see the enormous amount of activity that is going on. Most of this work remains out of sight not by choice, but because most people either don't know what these people are doing (and this is largely the case) or they feel that what these people are doing is irrelevant to their lives. But it isn't. ... Art Dynamo was started in response to this non-responsiveness to the artists of this region. It is not only an attempt to give another voice to the 'arts community' but also to try and expose some of the lesser known elements like the experimental music/sound underground who often refer to themselves as 'home tapers'. But all disciplines are welcome; painters, sculptors, actors, directors, producers, writers, musicians, filmmakers, performance artists, dancers and any others you can name." This is a showcase for new creative talent in the Boston/New England region. True to its word, the Summer issue for 1991 contained news and articles on each of the artistic areas described in the lead editorial, from an opera "...that is rooted more in the 'flux' of performance art rather than theater's 'definitive production'"; to a profile of two ensemble theater groups built on a heritage of black theater companies in Boston since the 1700s. An article on a collaborative team of 8/16 mm filmmakers and their current projects; and one on the Chop Shop on sculptural experimental "Sound materials fed through reactive speaker constructions" also provided informative reading concerning the state of the arts in the Northeastern quadrant of the United States. For sample issue of 1991: stapled magazine format, black/white editorial content on uncoated paper stock, cover consists of two-color red/black ink on coated paper stock, limited advertising (8 5/8 x 11 inches / 220 x 280 mm).

DEPT: None. (summer-91).

TYPL: "Mobius," "'Dance of the Spiders': An 'Opera' by Actor/Director Rusty Smart," "Black Folks Theater and E&J Productions," "Filmakers," "'Experimental Sound' at the Chop Shop." (summer-91).

SCHL: Quarterly?, 65 pp.

SPAN: Summer, 1991?+

ART IN ADVERTISING
SUB: "An illustrated monthly for business men."
PUBL: Art in Advertising Co., 50 - 56 East 19th St., New York, NY.
DESC: Always sporting an embossed gold foil front and back cover, this serial "practiced what it preached;" that quality artwork in a publication pays dividends in reader interest and commerce. One of the more interesting aspects of this monthly was the editor's regular critique of publications crossing his desk. The better of the lot were displayed in *Art in Advertising*. The lesser examples were lambasted by name and listing

of problems perceived. The nature of the periodical provided what its readers desired, a critical eye on contemporary art and layout design. Numerous graphics; small format.

DEPT: "A Review of Recent Advertising," "Things Well Done," "Random Notes." (3-1898).
TYPL: "Circulation--Tribulation--Consolation," "In the Cars," "Flotsam and Jetsam of Advertising," "Seedsmen's Advertising." (3-1898).
SCHL: Monthly, 70 pp.
SPAN: Mar, 1890 - Feb, 1899?//
LC: HF 5801.A8

✤ ART PAPERS

PUBL: Atlanta Art Papers, Inc., PO Box 77348, Atlanta, GA 30357.
DESC: In the July/August, 1991 issue was a reprinted article by previous *Art Papers* editor Laura Lieberman, who described the publications' development: "*Art Papers* was formed and fostered by an active artists' space, the Atlanta Art Workers Coalition, an artists' union which began in 1975... The artists responsible saw the publication as an extension of that alternative space. We were missionaries; we believed in the importance of a shared network of information, factual information--where to show, who was showing, what studio spaces, jobs, services, etc. were available. We also believed in the absolute necessity of serious informed critical attention for the development of a strong professional arts community. ... A great deal has changed in the southeastern arts community since we began our missionary work. Governmental support on all levels has become increasingly conservative. Despite what appears to be a future as problematic as the past, I firmly believe that *Art Papers* will continue to serve the art and artists of the Southeast." Past editor Lieberman's comments still ring true in the form, function, and élan of this bimonthly large-format magazine of Southeastern United States arts. In one sampled issue, 45 of the 56 articles were reviews of current media, events, festivals, and assorted media works in a variety of artistic fields, providing a dynamic forum, a network for information concerning new artists, new works, and the relationship of these to government/societal regulation, judgement, and perhaps most important, the issue of funding. Indeed, the best description of *Art Papers* was provided by current editor Glenn Harper, who in introducing the Lieberman farewell editorial, noted that "...little has changed, seemingly, in the struggle to provide the services to artists and the public that only the alternative arts press can provide." Editor Harper continued with this Walter Benjamin quote: "...that writers 'must nurture the inconspicuous forms that better fit influence in active communities than does the pretentious, universal gesture of the book.' The alternative arts press is just such a form: its importance is its engagement in active communities that may be geographic or may be based on a shared medium (like performance art, video, or photography) or shared interests and goals. The immediacy of the alternative magazines makes them able to respond quickly and directly to the artists and audiences that are our communities and the reason for our existence." Large stapled magazine format, black/white editorial content on uncoated paper stock, cover is one-color ink on textured uncoated paper stock. Excellent layout design that contributes to the format of the publication (10 x 13 ½ inches / 255 x 345 mm).

DEPT: "Reviews," extensive section; "Book Review," "Newsbriefs," "Letters," "Information," 'Services for artists'. (7/8-91).
TYPL: "Some Notes on Alternative Arts Publications," "On the Limitations of the Missionary Position," "Paranoia, Politics, & Provincialism at the Arts Journal: Ex-Editor of Troubled Regional Arts Rag Tells All," "Points of Departure: Origins in Video," "Places with a Past: Spoleto Festival." (7/8-91).
SCHL: Bimonthly, 85 pp.
SPAN: 1976+
  VARIES
  --1976? - Nov/Dec, 1980? as Atlanta Art Workers Coalition Newspaper.
  FROM MERGER OF
  --Contemporary Art/Southeast (ISSN: 0147-6297) (and) Atlanta Art Papers (ISSN: 0271-2083).
LC: NX 506 .A77
ISSN: 0278-1441
ABST: --Abstrax
  --Art Bibliographies Modern (ISSN: 0300-466x)

Art Product News

Jan/Feb, 1979 - Nov/Dec, 1990//
(ISSN: 0163-7460)
SEE: ART & DESIGN NEWS

✤ ARTHURIAN THEATRE MAGAZINE, THE

PUBL: Arthurian Theatre Magazine, 52 Belham Park Rd., London, S.W., England.
DESC: One of the better promotional pieces for the legitimate stage, *The Arthurian Theatre Magazine* promoted, covered, and extolled the British public to attend the plays featured by the ten theatre chain owned by Robert Arthur. Theatre sites included London, Liverpool, Newcastle, Nottingham, Aberdeen, and Dundee. Some individual issues were on specific themes, such as issue #3 on Shakespeare, but more typically, issues featured several Arthurian playbills for the public's consideration. Interestingly, nestled within these promotional pieces were also articles on photography, humour, and other non-theatrical fare. Numerous graphics; magazine format with duotone covers.
DEPT: "Celebrities of the Stage," actor profiles; "London Theatres at a Glance," playbill. (5-05).

TYPL: "A Stage Record--David Garrick," "Should the Theatre Amuse?," "The Art of Photography," "Phases of Theatre Management," "An Up-to-Date London Theatre," "A Novelty in Picture Post-Cards." (5-05).
SCHL: Monthly, 25 pp.
SPAN: Feb, 1905+

Artist & Advertiser, The

Oct, 1930 - Jun, 1933//
SEE: ADVERTISER MAGAZINE, THE

✤ ASCAP IN ACTION

SUB: "A publication of the American Society of Composers, Authors and Publishers."
PUBL: American Society of Composers, Authors and Publishers, ASCAP Bldg., One Lincoln Plaza, New York, NY 10023.
DESC: Printed in full-color with a dynamic layout design, *ASCAP In Action* showcases all the right reasons why an artist would desire to license their music through the American Society of Composers, Authors and Publishers. Focus of the quarterly publication is to profile, promote, and inform about the membership and the function of the Society. An excellent promotional piece by a renowned licensing organization. For the sampled issue of 1988: perfect-bound magazine format, full-color graphics/pages throughout on coated paper stock, no advertising (8 x 10 ¾ inches / 205 x 275 mm).
DEPT: "President's Page," editorial column by Morton Gould; "Legal Wrap-Up," newsbriefs; "Inside ASCAP," staff profiles; "New Members," "ASCAP Foundation," news items; "Meet and Greet," pictures; "Steppin' Out," ASCAP events. (fall-88).
TYPL: "The Spectre of Source Licensing," "The Cry of the Ancient Pentameter," "The Joy of Bernstein," "The Changing Face of Country, 65 Years of Being 'In', 'Out', and In-Between," "What Members Want to Know." (fall-88).
SCHL: Quarterly, 75 pp.
SPAN: Fall, 1979+
VARIES
--? - 1967 as ASCAP News (ISSN: 1043-3791).
--1967 - Summer, 1979? as ASCAP Today (ISSN: 0001-2424).
LC: ML 27.U5 A83445
DD: 338.4/778/0973
ISSN: 0197-7849

ASCAP News

? - 1967//
(ISSN: 1043-3791)
SEE: ASCAP IN ACTION

ASCAP Today

1967 - Summer, 1979?//
(ISSN: 0001-2424)
SEE: ASCAP IN ACTION

✤ ASIAN ADVERTISING & MARKETING

SUB: "The magazine for communication executives."
PUBL: Travel & Trade Publishing Asia, Ltd., 16th Floor, Capitol Centre, 5-19 Jardine's Bazaar, Causeway Bay, Hong Kong.
DESC: Decidedly upbeat in its narrative, informative in its approach, and accompanied by a dynamic layout design; these elements of a quality publication all come together in this Hong Kong monthly designed to report on advertising and marketing news in the greater Asian sphere. Articles discuss governmental regulation, cultural and geographic diversities, the role/effect of Asian advertising and marketing on a global scale, and the impact of international marketing and advertising efforts within these Asian consumer markets. Editor-in-Chief Susan P. Girdwood serves up a very nice balance of various media, their products, and their successes. One sampled issue discussed an international air carrier's marketing efforts to Asian business and consumer travelers, the potential for a Malaysian music star's own brand of soda products, how Asian-Americans are challenging American marketers, and a special feature on "Europe in Asia," about the European Community of 1992. Full-color graphics are excellent, often accompanied by graphs, charts, and other visual elements. Articles are very informative, giving specific details (both successes and failures) of campaigns, publications, and marketing efforts, often quoting currency both in national and United States dollar figures. This authoritative publication should be required reading for all who competitively strive to bring product to/from the Asian marketplace. Stapled magazine format, full-color throughout on coated paper stock, with a wide variety of international advertisers (8 ¼ x 11 ¼ inches / 210 x 285 cm).
DEPT: "Letters," "Dateline," advertising and marketing newsbriefs; "Stop Press," late-breaking news of special importance; "Media Mix," news and comment; "Sales Promotion," "Direct Talk," comment and analysis; "Opinion," "Campaigns," profile; "People," newsbriefs concerning changes and promotions; "Parting Shot," inside back cover comment. (5- 91).
TYPL: "Dramatic Event Aims to Life Airline Blues," "Multi-Cultural Agencies Avoid Ethnic Marketing's Pitfalls," "The European Publishing Affair," "Singapore Gets Its First Taste of Satellite TV," "Is Sudi the Real Thing?" (5-91).
SCHL: Monthly, 65 pp.
SPAN: Jan, 1986+
ISSN: 0257-893x

✧ ASIAN JOURNAL OF COMMUNICATION

PUBL: Asian Mass Communication Research and Information Centre (AMIC), 39 Newton Rd., Singapore 1130, Republic of Singapore.

DESC: From the foreward to the premiere issue of September, 1990: "Among a community of scientists and scholars, journals are one of the main channels of reporting advances in their fields of knowledge. It not only provides a forum for publication of research work but also helps to forge links among scholars for the fruitful exchange of views and findings that cumulatively build the body of knowledge of their discipline. There are very few journals in Asia that provides such an opportunity for communication scholars to report their research findings and forge links with the rest of the scholarly community in Asia. We do hope that the *Asian Journal of Communication* would provide this opportunity. The *Journal* represents a joint effort of the Asian Mass Communication Research and Information Centre and the Department of Mass Communication, National University of Singapore." An accompanying flyer continues the description: "The *Asian Journal of Communication* is a research publication with the objective of advancing the understanding of the process of communication in the Asia-Pacific region. The AJC Editorial Board comprising eminent academics and communication researchers oversees the publication. The *Journal* aims to advance understanding of the process of communication in the Asia-Pacific region by publishing articles that develop communication theory, report empirical research and describe advances in research methodology." This is an excellent journal of serious research focusing on a long overlooked segment of world communication. The excellent editorial advisory team is drawn from a variety of Asian-Pacific universities, plus representation from the United States, and the Netherlands. The premiere issue for September, 1990 contained a number of charts and graphs depicting statistical information. Perfect-bound journal format, no advertising, editorial content is black ink on uncoated paper stock, cover consists of blue and red ink on uncoated paper stock (5 ¾ x 8 ¾ inches / 150 x 220 mm).

DEPT: "Research Notes," "Book Review." (9-90).

TYPL: "Communication and Revolution in the Islamic World: An Essay in Interpretation," "Communication, Culture and the Growth of the Individual Self in Third World Societies," "The Political Economy of International News Coverage: A Study of Dependant Communication Development," "Implication of Technological Change for Scientific Communication in the Third World," "Prosocial Effects of Entertainment Television in India." (9-90).

SCHL: Semiannually, 150 pp.
SPAN: Sep, 1990+
ISSN: 0129-2986

✧ ASIFA NOUVELLES

PUBL: International Animated Film Association, Folioscope a.s.b.l., Rue Americaine 78, 1050 Bruxelles, Belgium.

DESC: Recognizing the explosive growth of animation worldwide, the International Animated Film Association decided in May, 1988 to create this news magazine, and to place sister serial *Animafilm* on an annual publication status to showcase animated works "...less directly related to current events." Printed in three languages (English, French, and Russian), each *ASIFA News* article takes up three times as much space as normal, and thus the number of articles to appear in any one given issue is quite limited. On the other hand, there is a certain excitement attached to a publication in which the majority of the world's population is reading the same trade-news articles at the same time, a global animated news stand of sorts.

DEPT: "Editorial," "Festivals," news of upcoming events; "ASIFA International," newsbriefs; "Calendar," upcoming events; "News," world newsbriefs. (5-88).

TYPL: "Zagreb's 8th Festival of Animated Films," "[Interview with] Keith Griffiths," "A European Office of Film Distribution," "Graphic Memory of Animation Cinema in Lausanne Sponsored by ASIFA." (5-88).

SCHL: Quarterly, 16 pp.
SPAN: May, 1988+

✧ ASMP BULLETIN

SUB: "ASMP journal of photography in communications."
PUBL: American Society of Magazine Photographers--The Society of Photographers in Communications, 60 East 42nd St., New York, NY 10017.

DESC: [Infinity]: Browsing through this high-quality magazine, you wish it would go on much longer than its 25 pages. It is a meeting point for outstanding magazine photography, providing excellent reviews of classic photographers and their subjects, and new data on upcoming photographers as well. The focus is on the art and technique of photography; not technology. Sampled issue for 1990: magazine format (8 ½ x 10 ⅞ inches / 215 x 275 cm).

DESC: "ASMP was established in 1944 to promote high professional and artistic standards in photography and to further the professional interests of its membership by disseminating information on a range of subjects and concerns." Articles within this professional trade publication concentrate on the role, problems and opportunities of the professional magazine photographer. "...membership in ASMP is much more than a *Bulletin* or Handbooks. It is ASMP that makes it possible for all of us to keep track of the industry, that tempers the desires of the buying public, and that educates members. Without ASMP there would be little or no equilibrium and buyers would control the business; it wouldn't matter where you lived." Every professional photographer who sells photographs to serial publications can benefit by this excellent trade organization. Magazine format; color covers with black/white editorial content.

DEPT: "On the Beat with the Editors," newsbriefs; "Those Young Pros," a continuing feature profiling one new photographer; "Business," issues and problems. (8-71). "President's Report," "Executive Director's Desk," "Aerial Safety," "Legal," "Cross Country." (6-90).
TYPL: "Victor Keppler: Photography as I See It," "The Video Cassette Dream," "One Day in the Life of Ivan Denosovitch," (8-71). "Parade, Parks and Unpaid Photographers," "Tracking Stock Sales," "Image Appropriation-- and Misappropriation," "Distinguished Panel of Editors Sought for Ten Thousand Eyes," "Aerial Photography." (6-90).
SCHL: Monthly [Irregular at times] (? - ?); Ten issues per year (? - ?); Monthly (?+), 16 pp.
SPAN: ?+
VARIES
--? - ? as American Society of Magazine Photographers Newsletter.
--? - Jul, 1950 as ASMP News.
--Aug, 1950 - Jan, 1952 as American Society of Magazine Photographers. News (ISSN: 0361-9168).
--Feb, 1952 - Mar, 1973 as Infinity (ISSN: 0019-9583).
--? - ? as Bulletin. ASMP (ISSN: 0361-9168).
ISSN: 0744-5784

ASMP News

? - Jul, 1950//
SEE: ASMP BULLETIN

AT&T Bell Laboratories Technical Journal

Jan, 1984 - Dec, 1984//
(ISSN: 0748-612x)
SEE: AT&T TECHNICAL JOURNAL

AT&T MAGAZINE

SUB: "A medium of suggestion and a record of progress."
PUBL: American Telephone and Telegraph Co., 195 Broadway, New York, NY 10017.
DESC: [Bell Telephone Magazine]: Beginning with its publication in 1922 (and a former title of *Bell Telephone Quarterly*), this periodical has been subtitled "A medium of suggestion and a record of progress." The subtitle was dropped in later issues, but the spirit of that earlier quest remains in the new format. This is still a periodical that charts where Bell Telephone and societal progress are at the present. A large number of factual articles including maps and diagrams will be found in the *Quarterly* format. Later issues under the *Magazine* masthead are more essay oriented.
DEPT: None. (1-30). "Commentary," "Reviews," books; "Vox Populi," letters. (winter-78).
TYPL: "Communication Facilities in the Making," "Operating Features of the Straight-Forward Trunking Method," "Communications for Aviation," "International Radio Technical Conference at the Hague." (1-30). "Reorganization by Product: A Question of Who is Really in Charge, and Whether or Not the Answer Really Matters," "Should the Regulatory Dragon Be Pulled Out of Broadcasting?," "Minority Business Enterprise: a Handup, Not a Handout." (winter-78).
SCHL: Quarterly (Feb, 1941 - Dec?, 1966); Bimonthly (1967 - 1983); Three issues per year (1984); Four issues per year (1985), 50 pp.
SPAN: Apr, 1922 - 1985//
VARIES
--Apr, 1922 - Oct, 1940 as Bell Telephone Quarterly (ISSN: 0270-5869).
--Feb, 1941 - 1983? as Bell Telephone Magazine (ISSN: 0096-8692).

✛ AT&T TECHNICAL JOURNAL

SUB: "Devoted to the scientific and engineering aspects of electrical communication."
SUB: "A journal of the AT&T companies."
PUBL: American Telephone and Telegraph Co., 195 Broadway, New York, NY 10017.
DESC: [Bell System Technical Journal]: Since 1922, the *Bell System Technical Journal* has been in the forefront of communications research technology. Many early concepts for radio, television, film, signal transmission, and home communications systems, were first explored in detail in this journal. Technical in nature, primary audiences are those interested in technological developments and who possess technical background to understand these rather scientific articles. Many scientific notations, graphs and charts are used.
DEPT: None. (10-77).
TYPL: "A Quasioptical Feed System for Radio Astronomical Observations at Milimeter Wavelengths," "Analysis of Longintudinal Stress Imparted to Fiber in Twisting an Optical Communication Cable United," "An Evaluation of Two Simple Methods for Detecting Tones over Telephone Lines," "Some Experiments in Adaptive and Predictive Hadamard Transform Coding of Pictures." (10-77).
SCHL: Quarterly, (1922 - 1941); Irregular, (1942 - ?); Monthly, [except for May/Jun and Jul/Aug combined issues] (1985); Bimonthly (1986+), 200 pp.
SPAN: Jul, 1922+
VARIES
--Jul, 1922 - Dec, 1983 as Bell System Technical Journal (ISSN: 0005-8580).
--Jan, 1984 - Dec, 1984 as AT&T Bell Laboratories Technical Journal (ISSN: 0748-612x).
LC: TK 1.B425
DD: 621.38/05
ISSN: 8756-2324
ABST: --Applied Science and Technology Index (ISSN: 0003-6986)
--Mathematical Reviews (ISSN: 0025-5629)

✧ AT&T TECHNOLOGY

SUB: "Devoted to research development in the field of communications."
SUB: "A monthly magazine of information for members of Bell Telephone Laboratories, Incorporated."
DESC: [Bell Laboratories Record]: As the subtitle suggests, this is a publication dealing in research developments for mass communications and for point-to-point communications. Since a great deal of communications technology comes from Bell Laboratories, this remains an important periodical for all areas of media development. It is very well illustrated, with extraordinary graphics.
DEPT: "50 and 25 Years Ago in the Record," paragraph-long reprinted stories from 25 and 50 years ago.
TYPL: "Lightwave Communications Passes Its First Test," "New Dimensions in Color Picture Coding," "What's New at the End of Data Channels." (12- 76).
SCHL: Monthly (Sep, 1925 - ?, 1961); Eleven issues per year (?, 1962 - ?, 1980); Monthly [except May/Jun, and Jul/Aug combined issues] (1981 - 1986); Bimonthly (1986+), 30 pp.
SPAN: Sep, 1925+
VARIES
--Sep, 1925 - May/Jun, 1983 as Bell Laboratories Record (ISSN: 0005- 8564).
--Jul/Aug, 1983 as Record [Bell Laboratories] (ISSN: 0743-0205).
--Sep, 1983 - Mar, 1986 as Record [AT&T Bell Laboratories] (ISSN: 0749- 8152).
LC: TK 1.B4
DD: 621.385
ISSN: 0889-8979
ABST: --ABI/Informer
--Applied Science and Technology Index (ISSN: 0003-6986)
--Computer & Control Abstracts (ISSN: 0036-8113)
--Electrical & Electronics Abstracts (ISSN: 0036-8105)
--Engineering Index Annual (ISSN: 0360-8557)
--Engineering Index Bioengineering Abstracts (ISSN: 0736-6213)
--Engineering Index Energy Abstracts (ISSN: 0093-8408)
--Engineering Index Monthly (1984) (ISSN: 0742-1974)
--Engineering Index Monthly (ISSN: 0013-7960)
--International Aerospace Abstracts (ISSN: 0020-5842)
--Physics Abstracts. Science Abstracts. Series A. (ISSN: 0036-8091)

Atlanta Art Workers Coalition Newspaper

1976? - Nov/Dec, 1980?//
SEE: ART PAPERS

Atlas

Mar, 1961 - Apr, 1972//
(ISSN: 0004-6930)
SEE: WORLD PRESS REVIEW

Atlas World Press Review

May, 1974 - Feb, 1980//
(ISSN: 0161-6528)
SEE: WORLD PRESS REVIEW

✧ ATR

SUB: "Australian Telecommunication Research."
PUBL: Telecommunication Society of Australia, Box 1802Q, Melbourne 3001, Victoria, Australia.
DESC: A highly technical journal of electronic telecommunication research, with a strong emphasis on electronics development. Numerous graphics and schematics; assumes considerable electronic engineering knowledge.
DEPT: None. (Vol 18, #1-84).
TYPL: "An Overview of the MELBA Automatic Code Generation Project," "Propagation at 500 MHz for Mobile Radio," "Comments on a Property of the Equivalent Random Method." (vol 18, #1-84).
SCHL: Semiannual, 68 pp.
SPAN: Nov, 1967+
LC: TK 5101 .A1 A17
ISSN: 0001-2777
ABST: --Computer & Control Abstracts (ISSN: 0036-8113)
--Electrical & Electronics Abstracts (ISSN: 0036-8105)
--Engineering Index Bioengineering Abstracts (ISSN: 0736-6213)
--Engineering Index Energy Abstracts (ISSN: 0093-8408)
--Engineering Index Monthly (1984) (ISSN: 0742-1974)
--Engineering Index Monthly (ISSN: 0013-7960)
--International Aerospace Abstracts (ISSN: 0020-5842)
--Physics Abstracts. Science Abstracts. Series A. (ISSN: 0036-8091)

✧ AUDIO

SUB: "The world of sound."
SUB: "The authoritative magazine about high fidelity."
PUBL: CBS Magazines, 1515 Broadway, New York, NY 10036.
DESC: "Audio" and its predecessors are designed for the audio professional or the lay consumer with sufficient technical knowledge. Accordingly, articles are more concerned with the technical nature of the medium rather than the creative-aesthetic side. Always well-written and illustrated, there is decided emphasis on new technical developments and product comparisons such as tape recorders, quadraphonic disc systems, amplifiers, and turntables. The advanced amateur, or individual with some electronics background would

find this a most valuable publication both for new technical developments, as well as for engineering clinics. Sampled issue for 1982: magazine format (8 x 10 ⅝ inches / 205 x 270 cm). For sampled issue of 1990: stapled magazine format with full-color pages throughout on coated paper stock (8 x 10 ½ inches / 205 x 265 mm).

DEPT: "Equipment Profiles," unusually long section providing full technical performance data; "Classical Record Reviews," "Canbys Capsules," "Weingarten Looks at. . .," jazz and blues reviews; "Whats New in Audio," product reviews; "Audio Clinic," technical Q&A column by Joseph Giovanelli; "Tape Guide," specific tape Q&A column by Herman Berstein; "Dear Editor," letters; "Behind the Scenes," production column by Bert Whyte; "Editors Review," news items. (7-72). "Classical Reviews," "The Column," music; "Folkbag," reviews; "Top of the Pile," record releases; "Audio, Etc.," column by Edward Tatnall Canby; "What's New in Video," "What's New in Audio," "Audioclinic," Q&A column by Joseph Giovanelli; "Tape Guide," Q&A column by Herman Burstein; "Behind the Scenes," comment column by Bert Whyte; "Video Scenes," comment column by Bert Whyte; "That's the Way It Was," historical ph`os. (2-82). "Signals & Noise," letters; "What's New," new products; "Audioclinic," column by Joseph Giovanelli; "Tape Guide," column by Herman Burstein; "Behind the Scenes," column by Bert Whyte; "Spectrum," column by Ivan Berger; "Audio Etc," column by Edward Tatnall Canby. (2-90).

TYPL: "Horn Enclosure for Custom Installations," "Flexible Tone Control Circuit," "Twin-Triple Resistance Decader and Bridge." (9-53); "Discrete Vs. SQ Matrix Quadraphonic Discs," "Test Reports: Two Decoder Amplifiers," "Dollars for Tape Contest." (7-72). "Understanding Equalization and Time Constants," "The CX Noise-Reduction System for Records." (2-82). "The Audio Interview: Doc Pomus," "Statistics in A/B Testing: By the Numbers," "Sound From Space: Digital Broadcasts, Digital Components." (2-90).

SCHL: Monthly, 130 pp.
SPAN: Jan, 1917+
SUSPENDED
--Jun, 1917 - Dec, 1919.
--Apr, 1947.
VARIES
--Jan, 1917 - Oct, 1921 as Pacific Radio News.
--Nov, 1921 - Feb/Mar, 1947 as Radio.
--May, 1947 - Feb, 1954 as Audio Engineering (ISSN: 0275-3804).
ABSORBED
--Radio Journal, Jan, 1926.
--Modern Radio, Jul, 1933.
--R-9, Jan, 1936.
LC: TK 6540.R17
DD: 621
ISSN: 0004-752x
ABST: --Applied Science and Technology Index (ISSN: 0003-6986)
--Consumers Index to Product Evaluations and Information Sources (ISSN: 0094-0534)
--Magazine Index
--Popular Magazine Review (ISSN: 0740-3763)

✤ AUDIO AMATEUR, THE

SUB: "The journal for audiophile crafts."
PUBL: Audio Amateur, PO Box 576, Peterborough, NH 03458-0576.
DESC: A truly unique publication for the experimenting electronics engineer, *The Audio Amateur* "...is published five times per year in the interests of high quality audio reproduction." The emphasis, thus, is on current and future audio technologies for the home audiophile. Sufficient audio engineering background is required to fully utilize the technical schematics and understand some articles. This is a indeed a serial for the technical audiophile who wishes to improve current equipment, and be informed on new product developments. Quality graphics, schematics, and step-by-step instructions.
TYPL: "The Super Buff: Mating Hostile Impedances," "Modifying the Audio Research SP6 Series," "Revising Preamp Power Regulators," "Home Built Heatsinks," "Adding a tower for FM." (1981).
SCHL: Quarterly (Winter, 1970 - Summer, 1982); Five issues per year (Oct, 1982 - ?); Quarterly (Jan, 1985+), 80 pp.
SPAN: Winter, 1970+
LC: TK 7881.7 A9
DD: 621.389/3/05
ISSN: 0004-7546

Audio & Video News

Jan, 1973 - Dec, 1973//
(ISSN: 0362-1162)
SEE: AUDIOVIDEO INTERNATIONAL

✤ AUDIO CRITIC, THE

PUBL: Audio Critic, Inc., Bronxville, NY.
DESC: An unusual publisher's statement began this serial: "Before you get involved in our equipment reviews or anything else in our first issue, read this introduction to our philosophy. And keep it in mind as the plot thickens in future issues." This introduction to the premiere issue, which required three full pages, described a serial that "...is an advisory service and technical review for consumers of high-priced audio equipment." It carried no advertising and therefore was beholding to no one. Articles were technically specific and succinct without requiring a significant background in electrical engineering. Of note was the two-column, 10-12 point type body text style employed throughout the publication; no illustrations. Also of note was the departmental feature, "The Admonitor," which took audio newspaper and magazine

advertisements to task. The publication succumbed to a very irregular schedule with the last issue labeled "Spring through Fall, 1980." In that last sampled issue the publisher promised readers that commencing in January, 1981, a new *Audio Critic*, in newsletter format would be published biweekly. No information is available as to that new venture.
DEPT: "Records & Recording," "The Admonitor," "Box 392: Letters to the Editor." (7/8/9-77).
TYPL: "Sophisticated Speaker Systems, Large and Small: a Comparative Survey," "Cartridge, Arm and Turntable vs. the Groove: Who's Winning?" "The Realities of Noncommercial Audio Journalism." (7/8/9-77).
SCHL: Bimonthly (Jan/Feb, 1977 - May/Jun, 1977); Quarterly (Jul/Aug/Sep, 1977 - Winter, 1977/78); Irregular ("spring through fall, 1978"+?), 70 pp.
SPAN: Jan/Feb, 1977+?
LC: TK 7881.4 .A9
ISSN: 0146-4701

Audio Engineering
May, 1947 - Feb, 1954//
(ISSN: 0275-3804)
SEE: AUDIO

AUDIO LEAGUE. REPORT.
PUBL: Audio League, PO Box 55, Pleasantville, NY.
DESC: A typewritten serial whose function it was to provide critical evaluation of new audio equipment. It was evident that the editors had a problem with then existing audio serials: "The popular magazines are designed to satisfy the interests of a diversified readership, and are frequently filled with human interest articles, information on home construction of mediocre equipment designed by hack writers, and boring repetitions of the most obvious elementary facts and platitudes." Readers of *The Audio League Report* would not find a single platitude within its covers, but would discover a host of critical evaluations (with performance graphs and curves) to back up the evaluative process.
DEPT: None.
TYPL: None. All articles composed of equipment evaluations.
SCHL: Monthly; Irregular at times, 10 pp.
SPAN: Oct, 1954 - Jun, 1957.
ABSORBED BY
--High Fidelity, Jun, 1957.
LC: TK 7882.H5 A8

✛ AUDIO PRODUCTION FOR BROADCAST
SUB: "Applications of today's state-of-the-audio-art in broadcasting."
PUBL: Recording-Engineer/Producer, P.O. Box 2449, Hollywood, CA 90028.
DESC: Published by the same staff as the quality periodical, *Recording Engineer/Producer*, *Audio Production for Broadcast*, concerns state-of-the-art equipment as applied to broadcasting. The editors are careful to note that this does NOT inlcude audio equipment built for broadcast applications. Publication includes articles on production techniques, new equipment, and production facilities.
DEPT: None.
TYPL: "A Comparision of Operational and Broadcast Production Philosophies," "Recording and Post-Production of a Commercial Music and Effects Library," "The Grand Ole Opry Broadcast Production Complex," "Recording and Production Techniques for Networked Live Music Broadcasts." (Fall-82).
SCHL: Semiyearly, 50 pp.
SPAN: Spring, 1982+

✛ AUDIO/VIDEO INTERIORS
SUB: "Style and technology in harmony."
PUBL: CurtCo Publishing, Warner Plaza VI, 21700 Oxnard St., Suite 1600, Woodland Hills, CA 91367.
DESC: "When was the last time an electronics magazine made it to your coffee table? Every two months, *Audio/Video Interiors* brings you a new perspective on home-entertainment electronics: a perspective that shows the true potential of audio and video technology in the home; a perspective that culminates in the modern media system, a successful blending of interior design and electronic craftsmanship." This coffee / drafting table serial showcases the very best in audio/video technology, and the means by which that technology is incorporated into the home. Price is no object in the wonderful feature articles demonstrating the classy blending of technology and form. For those able to afford such surroundings this becomes a wonderful resource for planning and execution: for others it is a wonderful adventure into the realm of the possible for today's home consumer. Outstanding color graphics of homes architectually designed for state-of-the-art entertainment. For the sampled issue of 1990: Perfect-bound magazine format on heavy clay-coated paper, full-color printing throughout (8 ¼ x 10 ⅞ inches / 210 x 275 mm).
DEPT: "Editorial Perspective," column by Christopher J. Esse; "Designers," audio/video designer profile column by Sam Burchell; "Home Theater," column by Mark Fleischmann; "Digital By Design," column by Peter Mitchell; "Form & Function," column by Doug Patton; "Components," new product review. (7/8-90).
TYPL: "New York Party Penthouse," "Puttin' On the Ritz," "Technology's Artisans," "Unsung Heroes." (7/8-90).
SCHL: Bimonthly, 150 pp.
SPAN: Feb/Mar, 1989+
ISSN: 1041-5378

✧ AUDIO VISUAL

SUB: "Incorporating The Industrial Screen and BIFA Bulletin."
SUB: "For all engaged in the screening of information, education, and entertainment."
SUB: "Incorporating Film User (established 1946) and Industrial Screen."
PUBL: Maclarens, PO Box 109, Davis House, 69-77 High St., Croydon, Surrey CRZ 1QH England.
DESC: Under the original banner of *Film User*, this British publication was devoted to individuals in the industrial, educational, and instructional fields whose primary medium was film. It claimed to be the first British journal to give full recognition to the media of film strips and sponsored films. Twenty-two years later (in January, 1972), the periodical incorporated *Industrial Screen* magazine, and continued to promote industrial-educational use of film, with increasing recognition of video. Some feature articles appeared in latter stages of the *Film User*, with initial content of *Audio Visual* magazine concerning the basics of AV media: overhead projectors, slide systems and film projectors. Later issues in the 1970s delved into new fields: multi-image slide projection and videotape equipment. Articles are informative and pertain specifically to issues of interest to AV management. Some articles discuss international conventions and trends.
DEPT: "Register of Releases," 16 MM documentary, educational, factual and industrial films, 8 mm cassettes and filmstrips and entertainment guide; "Audio-Visual News," briefs; "Shorts," new product news. (12-71). "Commentary," "AV News," "Media," "Filter," "Literature." (6-78).
TYPL: "When Your Face is a Visual Aid," "On the Screen in Ninety Seconds," "Sponsored Spools," (1-50); "Kenneth Myer Discusses Films and Newspapers," "Twenty-Nineth Salon International Photo-Cinema Optique." (12-71). "Winter's Tale: Progress of the ITVA," "A-V at the Science Museum," "Video Within BOC," "OHP-Making Charts." (6-78).
SCHL: Monthly, 40 pp.
SPAN: Nov, 1946+
VARIES
--Nov, 1946 - Oct, 1947 as 16 MM Film User.
--Nov, 1947 - Nov, 1971 as Film User (ISSN: 0015-1459).
ABSORBED
--Industrial Screen (ISSN: 0446-0855), Jan, 1964.
LC: TS 2301.A7 A78
DD: 384
ISSN: 0305-2249

✧ AUDIO-VISUAL BULLETIN

PUBL: Audio-Visual Bureau, Brooklyn College, Brooklyn, NY.
DESC: An early post-war approach to new developments in audio-visual instruction and equipment. Produced by the Audio-Visual Bureau of Brooklyn College, this 20-page mimeographed publication provided discussion of new ideas, and listings of new product at Brooklyn College.
DEPT: None.
TYPL: "Foreign Films, a Challenge for Language Teaching," "Short Films in the Classroom." (vol 3, # 1).
SCHL: Monthly (except Jul - Aug), 20 pp.
SPAN: Mar, 1948+?
LC: LB 1043.A79

Audio-Visual Communication Review
Winter, 1953 - Nov/Dec, 1963//
(ISSN: 0885-727x)
SEE: EDUCATIONAL COMMUNICATION AND TECHNOLOGY

Audio Visual Communications
May, 1967 - Jun, 1989//
(ISSN: 0004-7562)
SEE: AVC

Audio Visual Directions
Nov/Dec, 1980 - Jan, 1984//
(ISSN: 0746-8989)
SEE: AV VIDEO

Audio-Visual Education
Apr, 1957 - Jan/Mar, 1966//
SEE: NIE JOURNAL

AUDIO-VISUAL GUIDE

SUB: "Including photoplay and radio studies." (1936 - 1942).
SUB: "Radio and newspapers, film and theater." (1942).
PUBL: Educational & Recreational Guides, Inc., 1630 Springfield Ave., Newark, NJ.
DESC: *Audio-Visual Guide* had humble beginnings in monthly (sometimes irregular) discussion guides concerning one current motion picture release. The concept was a simple one; group viewing and intellectual discussion of a major motion picture. These small format booklets ranged in size from 12 pages for Fred Astaire's "Damsel in Distress," to a 30-page booklet for the film epic, "The Good Earth." By 1942 that format included radio programs, as well as newspapers and theatre. In 1947 *Audio-Visual Guide* changed to magazine size format, and developed a new editorial policy of excluding all media except that for the educational classroom. A motion picture guide (similar to earlier issues) was issued as a supplement to some issues. Numerous graphics in all formats.
DEPT: "News of Latest A-V Materials and Equipment," "Recommended New Books," "A-V Industry News." (3-53).

TYPL: "Seeing the World by Filmstrips, Films, and Picture Sets," "Kindergarten Education with Sound Slides," "Phonograph Records and the Librarian." (3-53).
SCHL: Monthly [except Jul - Aug] (Feb, 1936 - Sep, 1942); Monthly [except Jun - Sep] (Oct, 1942+), 40 pp.
SPAN: Feb, 1936 - Jun, 1956//
VARIES
--Feb, 1936 - Jun, 1942 as Group Discussion Guide.
--Oct, 1942 - Jun, 1945 as Film and Radio Discussion Guide.
--Oct, 1945 - Jun, 1947 as Film & Radio Guide.
ABSORBED
--Photoplay Studies, 1940.
MERGED WITH
--Educational Screen (to form) Educational Screen & Audio-Visual Guide
LC: PN 1993.A8
DD: 791.405
ISSN: 0091-360x

AUDIO VISUAL JOURNAL

PUBL: University of Minnesota, Audio Visual Library, 2037 University Ave., S.E., Minneapolis, MN 55455.
DESC: Designed for Minnesota public schools and patrons of the Audio Visual Library Service at the University of Minnesota, this serial provides news of new films, filmstrips, videotapes, and other instructional media which had arrived at the library, and which the staff wished its readers to understand better.
DEPT: "Editorial," "Judy's Column," news items; "What's New on Videotape," "Jan's Potpourri," newsbriefs; "Pearson's Corner," essay. (winter-76).
TYPL: "American Poets--Audio Tape Programs," "The Behavior in Business Film Series." (winter-76).
SCHL: Five issues per year (Sep, 1966 - May, 1971); Three issues per year (Sep, 1971 - May, 1971), 70 pp.
SPAN: ? - Spring, 1978//
VARIES
--? - 1966 as Look, Listen, Learn.
LC: LB 1043.A816
ISSN: 0004-7570

Audio-Visual Media

Spring, 1967 - Mar, 1971//
(ISSN: 0571-8716)
SEE: EDUCATIONAL MEDIA INTERNATIONAL

Audio Visual Product News

Fall, 1978 - Sep/Oct, 1980//
(ISSN: 0164-6834)
SEE: AV VIDEO

Audiocraft

Nov, 1955 - May, 1957//
SEE: AUDIOCRAFT FOR THE HI-FI HOBBYIST

AUDIOCRAFT FOR THE HI-FI HOBBYIST

SUB: "The how-to-do-it magazine of home sound reproduction." (Nov, 1955 - ?).
SUB: "For the Hi-Fi hobbyist." (Jun, 1957 - Nov, 1958).
SUB: "The magazine for the Hi-Fi hobbyist." (Jun, 1957 - Nov, 1958).
PUBL: Audiocom, Great Barrington, MA.
DESC: Here was a audio magazine for the true "do-it-yourselfer," with pages of building ideas for constructing speaker systems, house installation, and equipment cabinets. *Audiocraft* assumed that one was not satisfied with buying off-the-shelf components, and that the reader had carpentry skills sufficient to see any project through to fulfillment. Numerous graphics, schematics, and "blueprints" for construction.
DEPT: "The Grounded Ear," 'what's new in sound reproduction;' "Book Reviews," "Audionews," "Electronic Firsts," basic electronics; "Editorial," "Readers' Forum," "Tape News and Views," "Sound-Fancier's Guide," "Audio Aids." (7-58).
TYPL: "Stereo System Techniques," "Using Test Instruments," "Puzzlements." (7-58).
SCHL: Monthly, 50 pp.
SPAN: Jun, 1957 - Nov, 1958//
VARIES
--Nov, 1955 - May, 1957 as Audiocraft.
MERGED WITH
--High Fidelity (ISSN: 0735-925x) (to form) High Fidelity & Audiocraft.
LC: TK 9956.A76
DD: 621.389/332/05
ISSN: 0519-4229

✧ AUDIOPHILE WITH HI-FI ANSWERS

PUBL: Haymarket Magazines, Ltd., 38-42 Hampton Road, Teddington, Middlesex TW11 0JE England.
DESC: *Audiophile with Hi-Fi Answers* is a common meeting-ground for those serious about performance, quality, and purity in their audio equipment, recordings, and listening sessions. Articles cover mid to high-range quality and cost factors in the audio field. Reviews are thorough, with an opportunity for vendor disagreement in the departmental feature, "Right of Reply;" aptly subtitled "We relax and let the manufacturers hold forth." Authors and reviewers are knowledgeable, and sufficiently opinionated to provide a stimulating discussion forum, whether the product is a new CD release, technological breakthrough, or re-examination of audiophile norms. Of special note is the supplement, *Hi-Fi Answers*, published in a separate yellow-page section (15 pages in the sampled copy). It emphasizes audio equipment of British and European origin. Full color throughout enhances an excellent editorial content for today's advanced audiophile. Magazine format (8 1/4 x 11 3/4 inches / 210 x 300 mm).

DEPT: "Head to Head," competitive review; "News," audio newsbriefs; "Auditorium," letters; "Questions & Answers," audio-related problems from readers; "Dealer Visit," unique vendor interaction with reader problems and inquiries; "Audiophile Selection," equipment guide; "Right of Reply," unique vendor replies to previous reviews; "Audiogenic," guest commentary. (12-90).
TYPL: "The State of the Art," "Flouting the Rules," "Cables and Tables," "Preamp Cabling," "Audio Research LS1 and Classic 60." (12-90).
SCHL: Monthly, 125 pp.
SPAN: May, 1990?+
WITH SUPPLEMENT
--Hi-Fi Answers, ?+
ISSN: 0959-7697

AudioVideo
Jan, 1974 - Nov, 1974//
(ISSN: 0093-6499)
SEE: AUDIOVIDEO INTERNATIONAL

✤ AUDIOVIDEO INTERNATIONAL
SUB: "An international review of the electronics world." (Jan, 1973 - Oct, 1973).
SUB: "The international electronics review." (Jan, 1974+).
PUBL: Dempa Publications, 400 Madison Ave., New York, NY 10017.
DESC: New electronics for the consumer market is the focus of this retail- based publication. It is a showcase for new products, and the new technologies, distribution systems, and sales strategies connected with those new consumer products. The magazine educates the retailer, and hopefully floor sales personnel about new technological developments, while providing electronics manufacturers a positive promotional forum by which electronic trends and issues can be discussed in a business setting. Articles are authoritative, often written by industry manufacturing staff members, and provide significant technical detail to compare merits of similar marketplace items. Other articles look at retail sales strategies, covering issues from special sales events, to floor displays, to "fast-track" training of new sales staff at the retail level. This is an excellent resource for any retail electronics store. Sampled issue for 1991: stapled magazine format, full-color pages throughout on coated paper stock (8 ¼ x 10 ⅞ inches / 205 x 275 mm).
DEPT: "International News," "Marketing Trends," "Product Review and Preview." (10-73). "International News," "Washington Focus," "Marketing Trends," "Around the Nation," "Product Roundup," "People Chatter." (7-76). "The AudioVideo View," editorial comment; "World News," "Sales Leaders Retail Survey," "Washington Focus," "Marketwatch," new technology; "Point of Sale," retail strategies and commentary column by Marc Horowitz; "People," personnel newsbriefs. (1-91).
TYPL: "How to Become a Better Retail Salesman," "Videodiscs spinning Ahead in Europe," "Audio Blooms in Arizona Department Stores," "Sanyo Grows Via Worldwide Production and Sales Bases." (10-73). "A Look at the TV Picture," "Selling with a Classical Touch," "What the Vertical FET is All About," "A Dynamic Department Store." (7-76). "Television: The Progress of HDTV," "Home Audio: 'Deck-nologies' View for Dealer Notice," "Blank Tape: The High-Grade Push is On," "How to Use DAT Technology to Sell DAT Recorders," "Retail Management Primer." (1-91).
SCHL: Quarterly (Jan, 1973 - Oct, 1973); Monthly (Jan, 1974+); 115 pp.
SPAN: Jan, 1973+
VARIES
--Jan, 1973 - Dec, 1973 as Audio & Video News (ISSN: 0362-1162).
--Jan, 1974 - Nov, 1974 as AudioVideo (ISSN: 0093-6499).
LC: TK 7800.A83
DD: 621.38/05
ISSN: 0362-1162

Audiovisual Instruction
Oct, 1956 - May, 1978//
(ISSN: 0004-7635)
SEE: TECHTRENDS

Audiovisual Instruction with/Instructional Resources
Sep, 1978 - Dec, 1979//
(ISSN: 0191-3417)
SEE: TECHTRENDS

✤ AUSTRALASIAN PRINTER
SUB: "Journal of the graphic arts."
PUBL: Calmor & Associates, 26 Arthur St., North Sydney, NSW 2060, Australia.
DESC: Generalized trade periodical concerning print management operations in Australia. Articles are decidedly broader than just management, however, with special features on technology, production room, sales, and quality controls. Emphasis is on the elements and technique of printing which generate profits. Printed in black/white with some duotone advertisements.
DEPT: "Magazine Print Focus," "Magazine Print Scope," pre-press developments; "Magazine Spotlight," "Print Happenings," newsbriefs; "News and Views," "Print Talk," "Print Scene," "Shop Talk," "People," "Print Out," new product review; "Around the World Print News," industry newsbriefs; "News from Suppliers."

TYPL: "The Importance of Plate Bending in Web Offset," "Automating Post-press Work," "The Future of Newspapers-Free or Paid?," "Computers and the Printing Industry." (6-81).
SCHL: Monthly, 80 pp.
SPAN: 1950+
LC: Z119 .A89
ISSN: 0004-8453
ABST: --CIS Abstracts (ISSN: 0302-7651)
--Printing Abstracts (ISSN: 0031-109x)

Australian Film Guide
Jun, 1966 - 1967//
SEE: FILM INDEX

AUSTRALIAN JOURNAL OF SCREEN THEORY
PUBL: University of New South Wales, School of Drama, PO Box 1, Kennsington, NSW 2033, Australia.
DESC: "The *Australian Journal of Screen Theory* is an interdisciplinary film journal, which, while an Australian publication, is oriented towards an international English-speaking market. The *Journal* has the principle objective of providing regular interdisciplinary reflection on the increasingly complex body of film theory at a level suited to the many film courses springing up at the tertiary and senior secondary level. As the *Journal* is a response to the complaint of Australian tertiary and secondary teachers that there is a gap between the needs of their students and the hermeticism of existing journals of film theory, we want, in *Screen Theory*, to challenge that polarisation by explicating theories of film via detailed film analysis, thereby, we hope, avoiding an undue emphasis on meta-theory in the abstract. Above all, we want our articles to be readible by people who are not necessarily specialists in the specific theory under consideration." Primary emphasis was on film, with some issues or articles dedicated to television. It is an important serial of film criticism. Film publication schedule, and city of publication varied greatly due to financial reasons, although serial claimed semiannual schedule.
DEPT: None. (#3-77).
TYPL: "In St. Louis: Smith or the Ambiguities," "Douglas Sirk and Melodrama," "Minelli and Melodrama," "Twenty Thousand Years in Sing-Sing," "Structural Ambiguity in 'Ode to Billie Joe.'" (#3-77).
SCHL: Semiannual [Irregular at times], 90 pp.
SPAN: 1976 - 1984//
LC: PN 1993.A
ISSN: 0313-4059
ABST: --Australian Public Affairs Information Service (ISSN: 0005-0075)
--Film Literature Index (ISSN: 0093-6758)

Australian Media Notes
Dec, 1975//
SEE: MEDIA INFORMATION AUSTRALIA

✤ AUSTRALIAN PHOTOGRAPHY
SUB: "A contemporary view."
PUBL: Globe Publishing, 381 Pitt St., Sydney, Australia.
DESC: This popular photography magazine of amateur photographers in Australia contains typical articles of new equipment, techniques in photography, contests, and a wide selection of reader submissions in black/white and color. Sampled issues in late 1960s were still printed all black/white, moving to color pages in 1970s. Primary emphasis is on photo technique for the amateur.
DEPT: "Colour Clinic," technical advice; "Talkabout," column by John Carnemolla; "What's News?," new products; "Any Questions?," Q&A; "Letters," "Candid Shots from the Editor," editorial; "Scoreboard," magazine contest winners; "Scoreboard Competition," details on monthly winners; "New Products," "Australia Photography Test Report," "Movies," (2-75).
TYPL: "No Road," "Facsimilie Colour," "Magic of Dusk," "Factors in Depth of Field," "Grainless Super Blow-Ups," (2-75).
SCHL: Monthly, 75 pp.
SPAN: 1950+
LC: TR1.A
ISSN: 0004-9964

✤ AUTHOR, THE
PUBL: The Society of Authors, 84 Drayton Gardens, London, SW109SD, England.
DESC: This is a small but spirited publication for British authors. The format averages 40 pages per quarter, but articles tend to be on point, and are useful to both beginning and professional writers. Issues explored are the same for all writers; publications, copyright problems, working with publishers, how to break into media, average charges for work performed and how to improve one's skills. There are no illustrations.
DEPT: "Bookshelf," reviews; "On the Side," quarterly scrapbook of newsbriefs; "To the Editor," unusually long letters dealing with writers complaints; "Diary," brief summaries of major writing group meetings.
TYPL: "Economic Alarms," "Collective Copyright Licensing-Surrender or Safeguard?" "The Cassette Revolution," "Playwright Prospects." (winter- 74).
SCHL: Monthly (May, 1890 - 1900); Monthly [except Aug - Sep] (1901 - Jul, 1917); Irregular (Oct, 1917 - Apr, 1919); Monthly (May, 1919 - ?); Quarterly (?+), 40 pp.
SPAN: 1948+?
VARIES
--May 15, 1890 - Sep, 1926 as Author, The.

--Oct, 1926 - Winter, 1948 as Author, Playwright and Composer.
LC: PN 101.A8
DD: 808/.025/05
ISSN: 0005-0628
ABST: --Library Information Science Abstracts (ISSN: 0024-2179)

AUTHOR, THE
SUB: "A monthly magazine to interest and help all literary workers."
SUB: "A monthly magazine for literary workers."
PUBL: William H. Hills, P.O. Box 1905, Boston, MA.
DESC: This rather early literary magazine was designed to help writers enter and compete in contemporary media. Like most publications of this (pre-1900) era, there were few, if any, illustrations. Typical issues however, are identical to contemporary writing magazines. The focus is on how successful authors achieved success, perfecting one's writing skills, the future of certain media, and news of what people were selling, and for what amount of money. Of special note observed in one particular issue (1889), was a unique feature, "Personal Gossip About Writers," which was not only avant-garde for its time period, but also significantly predated the Hollywood "fanzines" of the 1930s through today.
DEPT: "Queries," Q&A format for the neophyte writer; "Personal Gossip About Writers," human-interest insight into famous authors; "Literary News and Notes," information concerning upcoming publications.
TYPL: "Peculiarities of Genius," "The Future of Diction," "Why that Manuscript Came Back." (10-1889).
SCHL: Monthly, 15 pp.
SPAN: Jan 15, 1889 - Jan 15, 1892//
LC: PN 101.A

Author, The
May 15, 1890 - Sep, 1926//
SEE: AUTHOR, THE

Author, Playwright and Composer
Oct, 1926 - Winter, 1948//
SEE: AUTHOR, THE

✦ AUTO SOUND & SECURITY
PUBL: McMullen Publishing, Inc., 2145 West La Palma Ave., Anaheim, CA 92801-1785.
DESC: Dazzling color highlights most pages in this bimonthly publication dedicated to both the best in sound and auto security systems for American automobile owners. It showcases sophisticated system installations and their operation in contemporary and classic automobiles. Articles have a wonderful stylistic approach that speaks to both those new to the field, and to those who have worked with automobile sound and security systems for years. One article "Ohm, Ohm on the Range," subtitled "Clearing the Air on the Mysteries of Electrical Impedance," explores the basics with the caveat, "Basic stuff here--propeller heads needn't waste their time reading this section." Pictures of products and automobile installations are of excellent quality, and certainly contribute to the classy character of this bimonthly under the direction of editorial director Bob Clark. For those individuals who believe their automobile sound and security systems are as important as the vehicles they drive, this is a great resource. For the 1991 sampled issue: full-color pages on coated paper stock in stapled magazine format (8 x 10 ⅞ inches / 205 x 275 mm).
DEPT: "Sound Off," column by DG Leadbetter; "Feedback," letters; "Watts New," new product section; "Audio Glossary," "Music Review." (8-91).
TYPL: "All in One Accord," "Doctor, We Have a Pulse!," "Behold, the Equalizer!," "Ohm, Ohm on the Range," "Cellular Basics." (8-91).
SCHL: Bimonthly, 105 pp.
SPAN: Jan/Feb, 1990+

AV Communication Review
Spring, 1964 - Winter, 1977//
(ISSN: 0001-2890)
SEE: EDUCATIONAL COMMUNICATION AND TECHNOLOGY

✦ AV GUIDE
SUB: "The learning media magazine."
SUB: "The learning media newsletter."
PUBL: Educational Screen, Inc., 380 East Northwest Hwy, Des Plaines, IL 60016-2282.
DESC: This four-page newsletter describes new trends, equipment, and software in the AV field. In earlier issues, page one was dedicated to news; page two to film and filmstrip releases; page three to new equipment; and page four to recent books. Current issues present news in varied position within the publication. For the sampled issues of 1978 and 1991: black ink with spot-color cover on uncoated paper stock in newsletter format (8 ½ x 11 inches / 215 x 280 mm).
DEPT: "Films and Filmstrips," new releases; "New Equipment," reviews; "Books," reviews. (9-81). None. (12-91).
TYPL: "Circulation System Designed for Libraries Serving Handicapped," "Mr. Rogers Series Chosen for 'International Year of Disabled Persons.'" (9-81). "State Court System Videotape Series Wins Silver Screen Award," "World of Science Brought to the Classroom," "Laser Multi-Disc Player Offers Improved Audio and Video Performance," "Entertaining Series Looks at Space Exploration," "New Videos for Home EC Fields." (12-91).
SCHL: Monthly [except Jul and Aug] (Sep, 1956 - Nov, 1971); Monthly, 4 pp.
SPAN: Sep, 1956+

	FROM MERGER OF
	--Educational Screen (and) Audio-Visual Guide
	VARIES
	--Sep, 1956 - Nov, 1971 as Educational Screen and Audio-Visual Guide.
	SUSPENDED
	--Mar, 1973 - Dec, 1973.
LC:	LB 1044.A2E4
DD:	371.33/05
ISSN:	0091-360x.
ABST:	--Education Index (ISSN: 0013-1385)

✣ AV VIDEO

SUB:	"The what's new and how to magazine for the AV communicator." (Fall, 1978 - Sep/Oct, 1980).
SUB:	"New directions in production and presentation technology."
SUB:	"Production and presentation technology."
PUBL:	Montage Publishing, Inc., 25550 Hawthorne Blvd., Suite 314, Torrance, CA 90505.
DESC:	It would be difficult to find a better magazine of production technology or technique for the so-called corporate and/or professional audio-video field. Editor Sam Stalos has acquired a well-deserved reputation for "telling it like it is," no matter whose toes, including that of current advertisers, get stepped on. This editorial stance, in conjunction with superb explanatory articles on the technical side of production by well-known author Peter Utz, provides one of the more valuable trade periodicals of its kind. "Tips to Clip," a special departmental feature by Dick Reizner of *AV Video*, addresses issues on the care and wear of equipment. Cecil Smith, in "The Technical Smithy," provides excellent explanations of everyday problems plaguing the production professional. Technical articles are enhanced by full color graphics and schematics. In all, this is an outstanding publication for the small production house owner, corporate video chief, technician, or layman trying to understand the technician. Magazine format on coated paper stock, color graphics throughout (8 1/8 x 10 3/4 inches / 205 x 275 mm).
DEPT:	"Up Front," commentary; "News Briefs," "Tips to Clip," "Technical Smithy," "TARGA SIG," special interest group column; "Under the Covers," interview; "Product Focus," "Showbill," upcoming events; "Art Gallery," graphic art portfolios. (1-89). "Tips to Clip," column by Dick Reizner; "Technical Smithy," column by Cecil Smith; "Media Management," excellent section concerning the business of video; "Under the Covers," computer graphics column by Howard Goldstein; "Amiga Niches," column by Matt Drabick; "TGA SIG," computer column by Bob Gillman; "PC Plus," column by F. D. Miller; "Product Close-Ups," "Up Front," editorial columnb by Phil Kurz; "Letters," "Product Focus," "Art Gallery." (2-91).
TYPL:	"Bah Humbug," "Videotaping with Scan Converters: As Easy as One-Two-Three," "Repairing VTRs," "Waveform Monitors," "The 2-Inch Still-Video Format--A Failure to Communicate." (1-89). "Military's Commitment to Interactive Video Spells Potential Boon," "24-Bit Amiga Technology," "Dupe Prices Tumble," "A New Family of Control," "PC Titling Comes of Age." (2-91).
SCHL:	Quarterly (fall, 1978 - ?, 1980); Five issues per year (?, 1980 - ?); Seven issues per year (1980 - 1981); Nine issues per year (1982 - ?); Monthly (Feb, 1984+), 115 pp.
SPAN:	Fall, 1978+
	VARIES
	--Fall, 1978 - Sep/Oct, 1980 as Audio Visual Product News (ISSN: 0164-6834).
	--Nov/Dec, 1980 - Jan, 1984 as Audio Visual Directions (ISSN: 0746-8989).
	ABSORBED
	--Video Management, Dec, 1989.
ISSN:	0747-1335
ABST:	--Electronics and Communications Abstracts Journal (ISSN: 0361-3313)
	--Exceptional Child Abstracts
	--ISMEC Bulletin (ISSN: 0306-0039)
	--Pollution Abstracts with Indexes (ISSN: 0032-3624)
	--Safety Science Abstracts Journal (ISSN: 0160-1342)

✣ AVC

SUB:	"Presentation technology & applications."
PUBL:	PTN Publishing Co., 445 Broad Hollow Rd., Melville, NY 11747.
DESC:	[*Audio-Visual Communications*]: *Audio-Visual Communications* is concerned primarily with the broad AV field including multi-media shows, instructional television and film, corporate AV, and training devices. Its strength lies in concentrating on applications of these media to the audio-visual forum, be it corporate boardroom, classroom, interactive instruction, conferencing, or the annual stockholders' meeting. Articles profile successful configurations of various multi-media equipment, problems, and success stories of same. Many articles do not assume prior production experience, and thus *Audio-Visual Communications* remains an especially good publication for those who are new to the AV field. For the sampled issue of 1977: stapled magazine format with full-color pages and cover on coated paper stock (7 7/8 x 10 5/8 inches / 200 x 270 mm).
DESC:	[*AVC*]: The audio-visual field, which just a few short years ago consisted primarily of multi-projector slide shows has now been transformed into a "high-tech, high-touch (interactive)" medium that utilizes laser discs, computers, high-definition video, and computer-generated slides with vibrant colors, dazzling displays, and computer-generated artwork. Articles within *AVC* describe major corporate sales demonstrations, training, and large-hall presentations via these media. Every issue includes a "Slide Showcase," where graphic artists' best work is displayed in full color. Two new departments began in January, 1991. The first is "Presenting Management," described as a "...series to help you new and would be supervisors feel more comfortable, confident and competent with your new role, as well as strengthen the skills of

veterans." The second department, "Forum," "...is a soapbox for industry and related speakers to challenge thought and spirit with new ideas or twists on old ones." *AVC*, after 30 years of publication, remains an excellent resource for the technology of audio-visual presentations. As publisher PTN put it, "As technology improves, leading us into fresh new ways of creating exciting presentations, *AVC* will, as always, be there to keep you informed about the latest trends, and about the communicators using them." Magazine format, full color throughout (7 ⅞ x 10 ¾ inches / 200 x 275 mm).
DEPT: "Communications Digest," newsbriefs; "Calendar," "Business Briefs," "Reference File," available publishers materials; "People," "Equipment and Materials." (4-82). "Letters," "Business Briefs," "Slide Showcase," sample portfolios; "Commentary," "Association Update," news of various media trade groups; "Software," product reviews; "Equipment & Materials," product reviews; "Calendar." (5-89). "Business Briefs," "Production Spotlight," "New Products," "Video," column by Ken Jurek; "Analog Presentations," column by Dona Meilach; "Computer Graphics," column by Helena Powell; "Forum," "Audio," column by Ken French; "Presenting Management," "Slide Showcase." (2-91).
TYPL: "Video: Notes from Underground," "Mobile AV: A Video Van Plan," "Training: Audio-Visuals Aloft." (11-77); "Slides: Special Effects Showcase," "Videotape Production Facilities and Services," "Audio: Making Do with Two Tracks," "What Every AV Client Should Know." (4-82). "Double Technowhammy," "Putting It to Work," "Spreading the Word," "Media Primer Part Two," "Anatomy of a Show." (5-89). "Don't Diss the Discs; Real World Adventures with Optical Media," "Hi8 Hits the Acquisition Trail," "Interactive Disks Deliver Sales," "Corporate TV on a PC," "Leading Edge Sound Tools." (2-91).
SCHL: Annual (1961 - 1967); Quarterly, (Feb, 1967); Bi-monthly, (1968 - ?); Monthly (?+); 50 pp.
SPAN: May, 1961+
SUSPENDED
--Mar, 1967 - Apr, 1967.
VARIES
--May, 1961 as Industrial Film and Audio-Visual Annual [NF].
--May, 1962 - ? as Film and Audio-Visual Annual [NF].
--Feb, 1967 as Film and Audio-Visual Communications.
--May, 1967 - Jun, 1989 as Audio Visual Communications (ISSN: 0004-7562).
LC: TS 2301.A7 F472
DD: 621.389/7/05 20
ISSN: 1045-6910
ABST: --Business Periodical Index (ISSN: 0007-6961)
--Reference Sources (ISSN: 0163-3546)
--Trade and Industry Index

✢ AWA TECHNICAL REVIEW

PUBL: Amalgamated Wireless (A/SIA) Ltd., Sydney, Australia.
DESC: This journal, which averaged three articles per issue, provided a highly technical review of current research in wireless telecommunications. Many schematics; assumed advanced electronics knowledge.
DEPT: None. (4-38). None. (6-75).
TYPL: "Equipment for the Measurement of Loudspeaker Response," "Precision Frequency-Control Equipment Using Quartz Crystals," "The Effect of a Thunderstorm on the Upper Atmosphere." (4-38). "Coherent Multi- Regenerated Communication," "Silicon p-i-n Photodectectors," "A Simple Optical-Fibre Digital Coupler." (6-75).
SCHL: Quarterly, 40 pp.
SPAN: Mar, 1935+?
SUSPENDED
--Jan, 1937
--Apr, 1937
LC: TK 6540.A15
ISSN: 0001-2920
ABST: --Engineering Index Annual (ISSN: 0360-8557)
--Engineering Index Monthly (ISSN: 0013-7960)

✢ AWRT NEWS AND VIEWS

SUB: "The newsletter of American Women in Radio and Television, Inc."
PUBL: American Women in Radio and Television, 1101 Connecticut Ave., N.W., Suite 700, Washington, DC 20036.
DESC: *News & Views* inform American Women in Radio and Television members about developments of their organization. Speaking to the company executive on why it makes good business sense to support AWRT: "The communictions environment continues to change rapidly, but some things do not change: the need to have well-connected employees who are confident and well trained; the need to make your company's views known; and most importantly, coming on the heels of recent surveys about the glass ceiling for women in the broadcast industry, the need to show your company's support for EEO and the continued advancement of women. We are part of a dynamic organization that provides vital training and development that makes women more promotable--a real benefit to employers. We also provide great marketing opportunities for companies who want access to women opinion leaders." It includes news about people at local, regional, and national levels; and educational and career opportunities provided through speakers' bureaus, scholarships, and conventions. Newsletter format in early issues moving to large tabloid news format in late 1980s; graphics.
DEPT: None. (4-80). "President's Message," "Careerline," employment opportunities. (9/10-89).
TYPL: "Meet Anne Pomex-Addison," "AWRT Supports Dereg--with Reservations," "To Help You Up the Career Ladder," "So You Want to Own Your Own Station."

(4-80). "Women's Issues Report," "AWRT Advocates Women's Preferences; Opposes Lottery," "San Diego Chapter Finds Programming, Personal Contact Essential for Success." (9/10-89).
SCHL: Bimonthly, 4 pp.

SPAN: 1982?+
VARIES
--? - ? as News & Views.
DD: 384
ISSN: 1040-497x

✤ BACK STAGE

SUB: "The complete service weekly for the communications and entertainment industry."
SUB: "The performing arts weekly."
PUBL: Back Stage Publications, Inc., 330 W. 42nd St., New York, NY 10036.
DESC: *Backstage* is a fast-breaking news tabloid for both those who work "on" and "back stage" in the production of motion pictures, television, audio and legitimate stage product. *Back Stage* accomplishes much in its coverage of business, new equipment, productions in progress, regulatory actions, and union and guild activities. Primary emphasis is on New York area media involved with the production of advertisements, but readers will also find significant national coverage, especially of production center activity in special features; "West," "Texas," "Midwest," "England," and "Florida." Of special interest is ongoing advertisement promotions for independent producers and directors, and a large and varied classified advertising section detailing opportunities, positions desired, and upcoming casting calls. Numerous production stills contribute to a breezy format. *Back Stage* comes close to being a national newspaper of the overall entertainment industry. In July, 1990 an editorial change took place, moving the focus of the magazine to actors and artistic expression of the theatre, television and motion picture fields. At the same time, a new publication, *Back Stage/SHOOT* began to provide news of the commercial film and video field.
DEPT: "Publishers Place," newsbriefs; "TV Commercial Production," briefs; "Sponsored Field," spot news; "Tape Topics," "Stop Action," "Syndicators Directory," a continuing update on TV syndicators and their properties; "Main Street," personality column by Ted Green; "Radio Dial," radio briefs; "Syndication Story," briefs about syndicated materials; "Backstage--Chicago and Midwest," Windy City news; "Business and Home TV Screen," updated information to supplement Business Screen Magazine; "Allen on the Avenue," personality column by Ben Allen; "Sound Waves," audio briefs; "Backstage--West," production briefs of the west coast; "The Reel West," column by Bob Harris; "On the Un-Coast," column by Ted Compton; "Chicago Report," column by Mel Miles; "Film Casting," opportunity briefs. (12-77). "TV Commercial Production," "Ad Agency News & Views," "Book News," column by George L. George; "AICP/SF Report," column by Marianne Lucchesi; "AICP/Atlanta Report," column by Lynn Hoffman-Keating; "Animation Spot," column by Howard Beckerman; "Main Street," column by Ted Green; "Music Notes," "West," "Texas," "Midwest," "New England," "Florida," "Computer Visuals," "Facilities," "Equipment News." (3-27-87).
TYPL: "Tape Tops in Spots," "Greenhouse Repeats as AFTRA Prexy," "Snows: A California Bonus." (12-77). "How to Choose a Scout," "Sony Unveils New Product Line-Up," "The Advantages to Shooting in Australia," "HDTV Shoots for Palisadium, SIE & Brokers." (3-27-87).
SCHL: Weekly, 45 pp.
SPAN: Dec 2, 1960+
WITH SUPPLEMENT
--Business Screen, Jan 14, 1977 - Nov, 1977.
--Business and Home TV Screen, Jan, 1978 - Feb, 1979.
--Back Stage Magazine Supplement/Business Screen, Mar, 1979? - ?
--Business Screen, ?+.
ABSORBED
--Business Screen, Jan 14, 1977.
LC: PN 2000.B128
DD: 792
ISSN: 0005-3635

Back Stage Magazine Supplement/Business Screen

Apr, 1979 - Jun, 1980//
SEE: COMPUTER PICTURES

✤ BACK STAGE/SHOOT

SUB: "The world's leading newsweekly for commercial production."
PUBL: Back Stage Publications, Inc., 330 West 42nd St., New York, NY 10036.
DESC: The news in *Back Stage/Shoot* is fresh and dynamic, a mirror reflection of the volatile commercial film and video production industry in America today. The weekly, 100-page stapled tabloid contains an even mix of news, opinion, and advertisements by producers, studios, and other support establishments, all keyed to the production of commercials within film and video media. Beyond the general news section, articles are placed into three additional categories: "State of the Art," concerning equipment; "Business Shoot," commercial production news within the corporate world; and "Tracks," post audio houses and other production facilities. *Back Stage/SHOOT* was born as a result of an editorial shift in focus of parent publication *Back Stage* in July, 1990. At that point *Back Stage* reverted to its original editorial stance of covering news of actors in the theatre, television and film industries; while new publication *Back Stage/SHOOT* covered news stories in the spot com-

mercial production field. Both are excellent serials, with a decided emphasis on the New York City area. Large magazine format, stapled tabloid, with spot color and full color on uncoated paper stock (11 x 14 ½ inches / 275 x 370 mm).
DEPT: "Ad Nauseam," editorial column by Mary Knox; "Action," 'Late-Breaking News'; "Street Talk," "Letters to the Editor," "News," 'Creative, Production, Post Production'; "Agency People on the Move," "Spotlight," "State of the Art," "On the Market," column by Tom Soter; "Business Shoot," "Some of Your Business," "Tracks," "House Beat," "Allen Asks," column by Ben Allen. (4-12-91).
TYPL: "Opinions on the AICP: Why Some Production Companies Stay on the Outside Looking In," "Manufacturers at NAB: Analyzing the Trends," "HBO Studio Uses D1 for USA Network," "Digipix Offlines Corporate Show in PAL on Avid Nonlinear System," "Public Rhythm Off to Good Start in Boston." (4-12-91).
SCHL: Weekly [except for last week in Dec], 100 pp.
SPAN: Jul 6, 1990+
DD: 792
ISSN: 1055-9825

✤ BAKER'S NEWS

SUB: "Latest releases from Broadway, Off Broadway, the West End, and the regionals."
SUB: "New texts on theatre performance, design, and production."
PUBL: Baker's Plays, 100 Chauncy St., Boston, MA 02111.
DESC: The Baker's Plays firm is synonymous with literary resources for the American stage. Housed on the third floor of a Boston business building, any given day will find dozens of individuals going through the "Baker Stacks" looking for published plays, and other books concerning stagecraft and acting. This promotional tabloid newspaper serves to announce new works of merit carried by Baker which are available for sale to the general public. Each issue carries an article concerning the theatre, and innovative play material. For one sampled issue, reviews included new award-winning plays, theatre resource and reference books, a wide variety of audition material, and "Plays For and About Women." For sampled issue of 1991: tabloid newspaper, black ink on newsprint (11 ½ x 14 ½ inches / 290 x 365 mm).
DEPT: "Award-Winning Plays & Playwrights," "New Theatre Books," "New Audition Material." (winter-91).
TYPL: "Where are New Plays Coming From and Does Anyone Want to See Them?: An Interview with Living Playwright Werner Trieschmann," "Plays For and About Women." (winter-91).
SCHL: Quarterly, 4 pp.
SPAN: Winter, 1989+

✤ BALLETT INTERNATIONAL

SUB: "Europe's bilingual cultural magazine."
PUBL: Ballett International, Verlags-GmbH, Richard-Wagner-Str. 33, PO Box 270443, D-5000 Cologne 1 Germany.
DESC: The additonal letter, "T," on "Ballett" is a key to the German origin of this internationally acclaimed journal of ballet and modern dance. Tri-lingual in nature, the publication focuses on Germany, France, and the United States. Two distinct supplements are present. The first is an all-German supplement *Ballett Info*, also referred to as the "German section." A second quarterly supplement, *Journal Français*, appeared for the first time in the February, 1986 issue, and provided four articles in French. Working often in the midst of controversy, Editor in Chief Rolf Garske had this to say about an ongoing series concerning the merits and evaluation of different styles and modes of dance in the three nations: "Our editorial interest lies, as always, in reliable information, informed reportage, constructive engagement for innovation and unusual questions and solutions. The bilingual nature of *Ballett International* has allowed for a direct dialogue unhampered by political and aesthetic boundaries since 1982, and has shed a decisive light on dance-related institutions, theatre managers, critics, dancers and choreographers, above all in the USA and in many socialist countries." Articles vary in the number of the three language translations provided. Graphics of productions and dancers are very well executed, and care is taken to ensure their proper placement and format. For the sampled issue of 1986: magazine format, full color cover with black/white editorial content on coated paper stock (8 ¼ x 11 ¾ inches / 210 x 295 mm), center stapled.
DEPT: "Editorial," "Press Review," "Report," "News," "Media: Books," "Calendar," "Schools." (2-86).
TYPL: "The Art of Being Properly Understood," "French Dance Theatre in the Federal Republic," "The BAM Symposium on Dance Theatre in the FRG and Postmodern Dance in the USA," "Lin Hwai-min's Taipei Contemporary Dance Theatre," "Working with a Gong in Therapy." (2-86).
SCHL: Monthly, 85 pp.
SPAN: Jan, 1978+
WITH SUPPLEMENT
--Ballett Info (ISSN: 0171-7995) [NE], Jan, 1988+.
--Journal Français [NE], Feb, 1986+.
LC: GV 1787 .B2743
DD: 792.8/05
ISSN: 0722-6268

Ballroom After Dark
Apr, 1968//
SEE: AFTER DARK

Ballroom Dance Magazine
Feb, 1960 - Mar, 1968//
SEE: AFTER DARK

BAND LEADERS

SUB: "Pictures and stories of the top-flight band leaders."
PUBL: Comic Corporation of America, 215 Fourth Ave., New York, NY.
DESC: Frank Sinatra, Mary Small, Helen Forrest, Paul Warner, Bonnie Baker, Freddy Martin, Jerry Wald, Paul Whiteman, Tommy Dorsey, Stan Kenton, and dozens of other big band leaders and featured singers had their tours, lives, and fortunes made available to readers of this promotional magazine of the 1940s. For the sampled issue of 1943, wartime conditions had a major impact on layout design and availability of newsprint, but publisher Comic Corporation of America produced a magazine of vitality and substantial size in *Band Leaders*. Front and back covers, both inside and outside, featured full page photos of major band personalities. The 1943 issue included cover girl Dinah Shore, Kay Kyser, Louis Armstrong, and Benny Goodman. Most articles were rather brief, but very big on printed photographs with a mixture of candid photography, and pictures, some of which appeared to have been touched up a bit too much in the darkroom process. Articles spanned the realm of music entertainment, from one article concerning the Ringling Brothers-Barnum and Bailey's band, to the wartime activities of radio and singing star, Dinah Shore. Ms. Shore was described as the "...Blues-Singing Idol of the A.E.F.'s, and America's One-Woman Entertainment Industry." Other articles included an interview with Jimmy Dorsey, and a description of singing sensation Frank Sinatra's early years. Of special note was the departmental feature, "Hollywood Bandstand," which provided pictures and information on the latest motion picture releases which included big band elements. Columnist Paul Vandervoort had a wonderful writing style, as demonstrated by these opening words: "Greetings Customers--gather 'round the bandstand and dig the dope from Hollywood. The glamour burg is really jumping, what with bands buzzing on and off the movie lots. Hollywood is hep--and from what I hear around the studios--it's only the beginning kids." Perfect-bound magazine format; black/white editorial content on uncoated paper stock; cover consisted of two-color ink on coated paper stock, limited advertising (8 ½ x 11 ¼ inches / 215 x 285 mm).
DEPT: "Did You Know That," personality chit-chat; "Hollywood Bandstand," big bands and personalities in Hollywood motion pictures, column by Paul Vandervoort; "Behind the Midwest Baton," 'News of the band world out Chicago way', column by Dixon Gayer; "Waxing Wise," musical commentary column by Dave Fayre. (11-43).
TYPL: "Nice to Come Home to," "All This and Betty, Too," "Conversation with Jimmy," "Rhythm in a Top-Hat," "Idol of the A.E.F." (11-43).
SCHL: Bimonthly, 50 pp.
SPAN: Nov, 1942 - ?//

✤ BASELINE

SUB: "International Typographics magazine."
PUBL: TSI Ltd., St. George's House, 195-203 Waterloo Rd., London, SE1, England.
DESC: *Baseline* is a publication concerning typeface design, typography and typographic news, with an emphasis on TSI's own Letraset products. Printed in separate English, French and German editions, *Baseline* features the introduction of new type fonts, the process of developing those fonts, and the application of same in advertisements and other art production. These are issues to be saved on the reference shelf, partly for the detailed historical descriptions of individual design fonts which provide interesting insights into development of the typographical set; and also for the sample applications of those typographical designs. This great company publication for current typefont usage contains numerous graphics. For the 1981 sampled issue: stapled magazine format, black with spot color ink on coated paper stock (8 ¼ x 11 ¾ inches / 210 x 300 mm).
DEPT: "Letters to the Editor," "Newsline," TSI newsbriefs; "Further Information," where to write. (#3-81). "Newsline." (#4-81).
TYPL: "Brighton," "Bramley," "The Wizardry of Oz," "Typography in Japan." (#3-81). "Adrian Frutiger," "Caxton," "Baskerville--Then and Now," "Corporate Typefaces." (#4-81).
SPAN: 1981?+?

BBC Empire Broadcasting

? - Sep 17, 1939//
SEE: BBC WORLD SERVICE LONDON CALLING

BBC ENGINEERING

SUB: "Including Engineering Division monographs."
SUB: "A record of BBC technical experience and developments in radio and television broadcasting."
PUBL: BBC Publications, 34 Marylebone High Street, London W1M 4AA, England.
DESC: This was a highly technical journal, designed to publicize advancements in radio/television engineering at the British Broadcasting Corporation. Most articles had schematics, and assumed advanced electronics knowledge. However, some articles were written at the layman's level and provided an historical chronology of various broadcast developments. Printed on heavy high-gloss stock.
DEPT: None.
TYPL: "Experience in the Operation of Colour Studios," "BBC Television News--Alexandra Palace and the Television Centre Spur," "Twelve Years of Videotape." (1-70). "Direct Broadcasting by Satellite for the United Kingdom," "Digital Coding of the Composite PAL Colour Television Signal for Transmission at 34 Mbit/s." (9-80).
SCHL: Quarterly, 50 pp.

SPAN: 1955? - Jul, 1980//
VARIES
--1955? - 1969 as BBC Engineering Monographs (ISSN: 0005-2817).
LC: TK 6630.A1 B16
DD: 621.388/05
ISSN: 0308-2369

BBC Engineering Monographs

1955? - 1969//
(ISSN: 0005-2817)
SEE: BBC ENGINEERING

BBC London Calling

Apr, 1963 - Jun, 1981//
SEE: BBC WORLD SERVICE LONDON CALLING

BBC QUARTERLY, THE

SUB: "A journal for those interested in the art and science of broadcasting."
PUBL: British Broadcasting Corporation, London, England.
DESC: This is a quality journal about radio and television programming, criticism, and developments. A number of articles have pictorial and graphics support. Quarterly issues oftentimes present an historical review of broadcast development, making this an important periodical for early broadcast research.
DEPT: None.
TYPL: "Reflections on Television," "The Survival of Sound Broadcasting in the United States," "Incidental Music on the Wireless," "Radio and James Joyce," "The Acoustical Design of a New Sound Broadcasting Studio for General Purposes," "The Impedance Specification of a Television Transmitting Aerial." (Summer-54).
SCHL: Quarterly, 70 pp.
SPAN: Apr, 1946 - Autumn, 1954//
LC: HE 8690.B72

✤ BBC WORLD SERVICE LONDON CALLING

PUBL: BBC World Service, PO Box 76, Bush House, London WC2B 4PH London, England.
DESC: Beginning under the banner of *BBC Empire Broadcasting*, the purpose of this newsprint tabloid weekly was to provide radio program listings on short-wave broadcasts to British empire service listeners. The majority of each was a listing of program times and descriptions, but accompanying those schedules were several pages of feature articles oftentimes highlighting a series of upcoming programs, or providing a behind-the-scenes look at BBC studios. Under the title of *London Calling* was a listener tabloid newspaper for BBC international short-wave service, providing a mixture of program listings, and articles concerning those upcoming broadcasts. During the war years, issues ran to 20+ pages of pictures, articles and program listings. By 1962, issues dwindled to eight pages, of which two were dedicated to program notes. *London Calling* was designed as a tabloid format on light-weight newsprint for the purpose of international postal requirements. By 1981, both title (*BBC London Calling*), and format changed to 16-page magazine format, with the first six pages devoted to program descriptions, and the remainder of the serial to program guides, world service frequencies, and language broadcasts. Numerous black/white graphics in all of these series.
DEPT: "What Other Listener's Think," letters; "Around the Studios," program newsbriefs. (8-8-37). "London Letter," column by Douglas Macdonald Hastings; "Programmes for the BBC's North American Transmission," "Programmes for the BBC's Pacific and Central Transmissions," "Schedule of the BBC's Foreign Language Services." (1-19-41). "Personalities of the Week." (12-13-62). "Features," program descriptions; "Music," "Drama," "Day to Day," program schedule; "Sport," sports schedule; "Learn," 'English by radio'; "At a Glance," regular program schedule; "World Service Frequencies," "Language Broadcasts." (3-81).
TYPL: "The Proms--from Music-Hall to Music," "Musicians-Magicians- Microphones." (8-8-37). "German Art Under Hitler," "The National Anthems of the Allies," "Denmark Under Nazi Rule--a Dane Speaks Out." (1-19-41). "A Language in Common," "Impressions of Malaya," "Dame Edith at Home," "Jack Hobbs, Octogenarian." (12-13-62). "Fear, Horror and Aversion--The Story of Phobias," "The Study of Man," "Moments of Being." (3-81).
SCHL: Weekly (? - Mar 23, 1963); Monthly (Apr, 1963+).
SPAN: ?+
VARIES
--? - Sep 17, 1939 as BBC Empire Broadcasting.
--Sep 24, 1939 - Mar 23, 1963 as London Calling (ISSN: 0024-600x).
--Apr, 1963 - Jun, 1981 as BBC London Calling.

✤ BEA NEWSLETTER

PUBL: Broadcast Education Association, Department of Communication at the University of Dayton, 300 College Park, Dayton, OH 45469.
DESC: Produced by the Courses & Curricula Committee (now a division) of the Broadcast Education Association, this four-page newsletter is designed to update members on news, trends, ideas, software, and other resources for the development and refinement of college curricula for broadcast education. This is a dynamic group desirous of tackling the always difficult, but important task of adapting pedagogical ideas and structure to a localized situation, all to properly prepare students for the broadcast industry. Newsletter format (8 ⅜ x 11 inches / 215 x 280 mm), printed black ink on color paper, no advertising.

DEPT: "Personals." (12-90).
TYPL: "Notes from Chairman Bob," "Town Meeting Report," "PC Notes," "Report From Task Force #3." (12-90).
SCHL: Quarterly?, 4 pp.
SPAN: Dec, 1987+

Beacon
1889? - 1892?//
SEE: PHOTO-BEACON, THE

BEHIND THE SCENE
SUB: "The magazine you can believe in."
PUBL: JB Publishing Corporation, 157 West 57th St., New York, NY.
DESC: Among the Hollywood "fanzines" of the 1950s, *Behind the Scene* was one of the more sexually-oriented, star expose-style publications available on the newstand. With titles such as, "What Makes Hollywood Think xxxxxxx is Queer?;" and "I was a Calendar Girl!," the latter subtitled, "My fee is higher when I pose with clothes on..." *Behind the Scene* prided itself on publishing articles, cartoons, jokes and pictures that other similar serials felt were "too hot" for publication. *Behind the Scene* also published informative articles about the entertainment industry, such as "Tricks of a Hollywood Make-Up Man." Articles such as "What They Don't Dare Tell You About X- Rays;" or "America's Secret Terror Weapon," about development of germ warfare; were often ahead of their times. Articles were interesting, and oftentimes carried shock value as well. For the sampled issue of 1957: editorial content was black ink on newsprint, with two-color red/black ink cover on coated paper stock (8 ⅜ x 10 ½ inches / 215 x 265 mm), stapled magazine format
DEPT: "The Readers Scene," letters; "Too Hot to Print," adult cartoons not accepted by other publications; "Jokes the TV Censors Killed." (11-57).
TYPL: "Why Marilyn Monroe is Afraid to Have a Baby!," "When Van Heflin Tried to Make an 'Honest Woman' of Diana Barrymore," "How to Put a Babe on Your Expense Account," "Why Barbara Hutton's Boy is Bashful in the Boudoir!" (11-57).
SCHL: Bimonthly, 70 pp.
SPAN: Aug, 1954 - ?//

Bell Laboratories Record
Sep, 1925 - May/Jun, 1983//
(ISSN: 0005-8564)
SEE: AT&T TECHNOLOGY

Bell System Technical Journal
Jul, 1922 - Dec, 1983//
(ISSN: 0005-8580)
SEE: AT&T TECHNICAL JOURNAL

Bell Telephone Company of Pennsylvania News, The
//
SEE: TELEPHONE NEWS, THE

Bell Telephone Magazine
Feb, 1941 - 1983?//
(ISSN: 0096-8692)
SEE: AT&T MAGAZINE

Bell Telephone Quarterly
Apr, 1922 - Oct, 1940//
(ISSN: 0270-5869)
SEE: AT&T MAGAZINE

Bertha Landers Film Reviews
Jun 1, 1956 - 1959//
SEE: LANDERS FILM REVIEWS

✤ BEST OF FILM & VIDEO
PUBL: Selwood Press, Ltd., Suite C, Elsinore House, 43 Buckingham St., Aylesbury, Bucks HP20 2NQ, England.
DESC: In the premeiere issue for Mar/Apr, 1990, editor Richard Mansfield told new readers that the *Best of Film & Video* was "...the new magazine all about film entertainment--on the big screen and on video. And we mean entertainment. This magazine is all about the movies that the majority like. It's not an art film magazine, or a highbrow intellectual look at the deep inner meanings of the latest film from the Balkan States. It's about the new films that set out to entertain. And the stars who appear in them. It's for everyone who enjoys going to the pictures and seeing a good film." This new serial is a public relations/marketing dream: it is an exciting, upbeat vehicle for motion picture enthusiasts showcasing new product for the large screen, and the home video front. Each review and artist interview (with over 50 such articles in the premiere issue), is flanked by numerous pictures, both production stills and informal shots. Editorial content is informative, and thoroughly enjoyable. This is one serial bound to deliver the all important target audience, the motion picture enthusiast, into the laps of film marketers worldwide. Well-recommended for broad coverage of current popular film fare on both sides of the Atlantic. For the sampled issue of 1990:

stapled magazine format, black ink, spot and full color graphics and full-color cover on coated paper stock (8 ⅜ x 11 ¾ inches / 210 x 300 mm).
DEPT: "In & Out," extensive section detailing perceived stars rise and fall with their publics; "Hot From Hollywood," gossip column by Al Jackson; "On Video," new releases; "Music on Video," new releases; "Coming Attractions," forthcoming videocassette releases. (3/4-90).
TYPL: "Live Duo in Cartoon Cop Action," "Fat Man, Little Boy," "Pooch in Paradise," "A Bad Year for the Roses." (3/4-90).
SCHL: Bimonthly, 65 pp.
SPAN: Mar/Apr, 1990+
ISSN: 0958-9147

Bestseller Business
Mar, 1972 - ?//
SEE: MAGAZINE & BOOKSELLER

Bestsellers
Oct, 1960 - ?//
(ISSN: 0005-9730)
SEE: MAGAZINE & BOOKSELLER

✢ BETTER BROADCASTS NEWS
PUBL: American Council for Better Broadcasts, 120 E. Wilson St., Madison, WI 53703.
DESC: "The American Council for Better Broadcasts is a national, non-profit organization coordinating the efforts of concerned individuals and local, state and national groups to improve by educational means the quality of radio and television." This newsletter is a means of informing its members of activities, upcoming programming events, and efforts to persuade the radio and television industry to adapt their programming more to the ACBB viewpoint.
DEPT: "Promising Programs," upcoming; "Thoughts For the Critical Viewer," 'A collection of notes and quotes;' "Suggested Reading." (10/11-79).
TYPL: "Ferret Out Implications in News Reports," "Hints to Teachers of English," "Art on Television," "Television Programming for Children." (10/11-79).
SCHL: Six issues per year, 8 pp.
SPAN: Oct, 1955+
VARIES
--Oct, 1955 - ? as Better Broadcasts Newsletter (ISSN: 0409-283x).
ISSN: 0006-0054

Better Broadcasts Newsletter
Oct, 1955 - ?//
(ISSN: 0409-283x)
SEE: BETTER BROADCASTS NEWS

BETTER EDITING
PUBL: American Business Press, 205 E. 42nd St., New York, NY 10017.
DESC: A spritely publication designed for the Association of Specialized Business Publications, its target readership was editors and publishers of business publications. Articles provided toolskills on such topics as increasing readership, layout design, and an especially large section detailing success stories of other member publications. Several full color pages per issue.
DEPT: "What Goes On," newsbriefs; "Books," reviews. (fall-71).
TYPL: "How'd You Like to Raise Your Readership 85%?," "Before You Begin a Readership Study," "How We Create Our Covers," "Putting out Bell Magazine," "Editing an Ethnic Business Magazine." (fall-71).
SCHL: Quarterly, 23 pp.
SPAN: Fall, 1965 - Mar/Apr, 1974//
ABSORBED BY
--Folio (ISSN: 0046-4333).
LC: PN 4700.B
ISSN: 0006-0119

✢ BETTER LISTENING
SUB: "Through high fidelity."
PUBL: St. Regis Publications, 7 West 44th St., New York, NY.
DESC: This promotional serial, emblazoned with the local audio dealer's name on the front cover, was sent to customers to inform about, and hopefully stimulate future sales of audio high-fidelity equipment. *Better Listening* covered most of the brand-name items that an average audio retailer might stock; stereo components, records, tapes, and even kits for the home enthusiast. Square magazine format; numerous graphics.
DEPT: "Music for Your Pleasure," review; (fall-61).
TYPL: "Life-saving for Your Records," "Better Stereo by Air," "The Technique of Multiplex," "A Personal Note on Music History." (fall-61).
SCHL: Monthly, (Jul, 1955 - May, 1959); Quarterly, (Summer, 1959 to date); 20 pp.
SPAN: Jul, 1955+?
VARIES
--? - ? as Better Listening Through High Fidelity.
LC: TK 7881.7 .B49
DD: 621.389/332/05
ISSN: 0198-7240

Better Listening Through High Fidelity
? - ?//
SEE: BETTER LISTENING

✥ BETTER RADIO AND TELEVISION

PUBL: National Association for Better Broadcasting, 7918 Naylor Ave., Los Angeles, CA 90045.
DESC: Published by the National Association for Better Radio and Television, this eight-page newsletter provides quarterly updates on NAFBRAT members' advancements in the area of improving American radio and television programming. Much of the editorial content consists of recent Federal Communications Commission (FCC), and Congressional actions affecting broadcasting; and critical analysis of specific television programs, especially as they relate to what the publisher believes is the promotion of sex and violence within network programming.
DEPT: "Editorial," "Letters," "Recommended Radio and Television Programs." (winter-63/64). "Book Review." (summer-83).
TYPL: "NAFBRAT Testimony Supports FCC Action," "Dangers of Courtroom TV Cited in Association Policy Statement," "What the Broadcasters Say," "Too Many Spots?" (winter- 63/64). "Leading Schools Using Book on Broadcast Rights for Consumers," "Is the He-Man Children's Show a Half-Hour Commercial?," "Congress Leaders are 'Deeply Troubled' by Fowler's Excesses." (summer-83).
SCHL: Quarterly, 8 pp.
SPAN: Winter, 1960+
   VARIES
   --? - ? as Newsletter.
   --Summer, 1960 - Summer, 1963 as NAFBRAT Quarterly.
   ABSORBED
   --Television For the Family.
ISSN: 0006-0194

✥ BEYOND THE RATINGS

PUBL: Arbitron Ratings Company, 4320 Ammendale Rd., Beltsville, MD 20705.
DESC: This corporate promotional newsletter provides a wealth of information concerning Arbitron radio and television ratings systems, as well as broad information on ratings operations in general. Articles explain current operations, new concepts, and reports on latest research on the elusive quest for radio and television household listening and viewing patterns. For the sampled issue of 1985: folded loose-leaf newsletter format, black and blue ink on coated paper stock, no advertising (8 ½ x 11 inches / 215 x 280 mm).
DEPT: None. (6-82). "Commentary from the Council," ongoing dialogue between Arbitron and the Arbitron Radio Advisory Council; "Calendar," "Arbitron People," personnel briefs. (5-85).
TYPL: "CBS FM Program Directors Confer at rbitron," "Fall Television: New Procedures for High Density Black Areas," "Getting Public Response to Surveys," "Religious Format Radio Audience Younger Than Expected." (6-82). "Arbitron Offers Free Computer-Assisted Training Program," "Product Target AID a Success in Omaha," "Television Advisory Council Meets." (5-85).
SCHL: Monthly, 8 pp.
SPAN: Mar, 1978?+?
DD: 384
ISSN: 0749-7466

✥ BEYOND THE RATINGS/RADIO

SUB: "A magazine for the radio industry."
PUBL: Arbitron Ratings Company, 142 West 57th St., New York, NY 10019.
DESC: Providing information for its radio subscribers, *BTR/Radio* provides a quarterly roundup of what's new in Arbitron research, trends in audience analysis, and problems peculiar to broadcast radio. It is similar in nature to sister publication, *Beyond the Ratings/Television*.
DEPT: "Buying & Selling Strategies," "Inside the Ratings," newsbriefs about Arbitron subscribers; "Arbitron People," personnel briefs; "TV Picture," news items concerning Arbitron and its rating service. (2-89).
TYPL: "Viva Arbitron!," "Samples in Focus," "Radio Market Fingerprint." (2- 89).
SCHL: Quarterly.
SPAN: ?+

✥ BEYOND THE RATINGS/TELEVISION

SUB: "A magazine for the television industry."
PUBL: Arbitron Ratings Company, 142 West 57th St., New York, NY 10019.
DESC: This is a promotional publication, providing a quarterly report on Arbitron, its television ratings services, and the clients served by that corporation. Articles emphasize new services offered by Arbitron, and their potential application by broadcast member stations. This is similar in nature to sister publication, *Beyond the Ratings/Radio*.
DEPT: "Inside the Ratings," news of clients and the Arbitron company; "Arbitron People," personnel newsbriefs; "Radio Update," information from the radio side of ratings systems. (4-88). "Inside the Ratings," "Arbitron People," "Radio Talk." (10-89).
TYPL: "Dick and Jane See Spot Run, But Could They Classify It?," "How Your Station Can Get Lucky with the Lottery," "Why AID is the 'Primary' Way to Target the Voter," "Managing Spot Activity Now Made Easy with Market Manager." (4-88). "Electronic Commercial Tracking," "Success in a Bottle with CTA," "What's in a Zip Code?" (10-89).
SCHL: Monthly, 16 pp.
SPAN: ?+

✧ BIG REEL, THE

SUB: "The exciting world of film collecting."
PUBL: Empire Publishing, Drawer B, Summerfield, NC 27358.
DESC: This is a true subscription bargain for those interested in the sale, rental or trade of old films, or videocassettes. The 100+ page tabloid newspaper carries over one hundred advertisements from individual collectors desiring a rare print, or offering a unique series to individuals. Nestled within the ads are a series of nostalgic articles about motion pictures and television. Some articles are reprinted from other publications. *The Big Reel* is a collector's dream for video, 8 MM films, 16 mm films, records, movie stills, pressbooks, publications, collectable cards, posters, comics, slides, and photos.
DEPT: "The Bookshelf," "Breezing Along With the B's," B movie nostalgia column; "In The Nick of Time," 'The Movie Serial in the Sound Era;' "Obituaries," "Video Parade," Films available on video cassette; "The Mail Box," letters; "Meet the Collectors," "Previews of Coming Atractions," upcoming events; "Lines and Splices," editorial. (3- 80).
TYPL: "Up to Date With Ava Gardner," "An Interview with Lois January," "Collecting Nostalgia Records." (3-80).
SCHL: Monthly, 105 pp.
SPAN: Jun, 1974?+
ISSN: 0744-723x

BIJOU

SUB: "The magazine of the movies."
PUBL: Baronet Publishing, 509 Madison Ave., New York, NY 10022.
DESC: Publisher Norman Goldfind, in an editorial column for 1977, expressed his feeling as a jogger watching the motion picture "Rocky": "My body tingled, and my head soared to unimaginable heights. A remembered scene from a movie had brought me to this extraordinary state, this incomparable feeling. Maybe that's what movies are really all about. When those flickering images on a screen lift your soul, or bring tears to your eyes, or make you roar with laughter, or cause your heart to pound, or make you feel differently about things, then they have achieved their goal. In the final analysis, it may be that a film is worth the $4.00 now charged by first-run movie houses when its story, its performances, and its production converge magically to create that elusive thing we call 'entertainment'. Directorial nuances, camera angles, symbolic gestures--these are rightfully the province of the film scholar. But the sheer entertainment of the movies belongs to every moviegoer." This is the key to understanding *Bijou*, a wonderful motion pictures publication, which, unfortunately lasted but for a very short time. Typical articles celebrated the joy of motion pictures, both current releases for fan attendance, and past "orchid and onion" productions for rememberence. Editorial content was an interesting mixture of both newsprint and coated paper stock, with both front/back inside covers devoted to promotional graphics. One very nice feature of each issue was a centerfold pull-out, full-color reproduction of a motion picture lobby poster ready for framing. This was a spritely publication which deserved a longer publishing run than just two years. For the sampled issue from 1977: stapled magazine format, editorial content consisting of a mixture of black ink on newsprint paper stock and coated paper stock, plus full-color pages on coated paper stock, cover was of full-color on coated paper stock (8 ¼ x 10 ⅞ inches / 210 x 275 mm).
DEPT: "The Editor's Page," editorial column by Ted Sennett; "Sparklers and Fizzlers," orchids and onions survey column by Curtis F. Brown; "Publisher's Page," editorial column by Norman Goldfind; "Looking Ahead with Bijou," commentary column by Bill O'Connell; "Bijou Books," review column by Foster Hirsch; "Talk About Movies," discussion and commentary column by Ted Sennett; "Bijou Quiz Corner," 'The movie scene: from mirth to mayhem'; "Movies Then/Movies Now," fascinating dual look at movies past and present, column by Curtis F. Brown and Will Holtzman. (8-77).
TYPL: "Filming the Deep," "A Conversation with Ellen Burstyn," "How to Win an Academy Award for the Wrong Reasons," "Elliott Gould on Barbra, Booklyn, Ingmar Bergman, Bert Lahr, M*A*S*H and...," "The Big Apple on film." (8-77).
SCHL: Bimonthly, 75 pp.
SPAN: Apr/May, 1977 - 1978//

Bill Poster, The

Feb 22, 1896 - ?//
SEE: ADVERTISING OUTDOORS

Bill Poster and Display Advertising, The

? - 1910//
SEE: ADVERTISING OUTDOORS

✧ BILLBOARD

SUB: "The international music-record-tape newsweekly."
SUB: "The world's foremost amusement weekly."
SUB: "Music-phonograph merchandising, radio-TV programming, coin machine operating."
SUB: "The international newsweekly of music and home entertainment."
SUB: "If it's here, it plays."
PUBL: BPI Communications, Inc., 1515 Broadway, New York, NY 10036.
DESC: Authoritative, thorough, and current are descriptors easily applied to this outstanding business weekly for the music and home entertainment industry. The large magazine format is filled with news, personality profiles, playlists, and business indicators critical to the

entertainment field. Departmental columns have become staple reading for music/entertainment executives, and production personnel as well. This publication lives up to all of its subtitles, containing general news trends, business developments, and new recording stars. Above all, *Billboard* is known for its valuable weekly top-music and video playlists. Printed in large magazine format, early issues were on newsprint, while current issues are printed on coated paper stock. This trade weekly is "must" reading for anyone in the music and home entertainment industry. For the sampled issue of 1987: stapled magazine format, black ink, spot- and full-color pages on coated paper stock (10 ¾ x 13 ¼ inches / 275 x 335 mm).

DEPT: "Executive Turntable," executive moves; "Market Quotations," major music organizations; "Billboard Singles Radio Action," top moving records on regional and national basis; "Billboard Album Radio Action," "Rack Singles Best Sellers," playlist; "Rack LP Best Sellers," playlist; "Easy Listening," top-50 playlist; "Signings," new contracts; "Talent in Action," talent reviews; "Sound Waves," audio column by John Woram; "Studio Track," studio column by Bob Kirsch; "Discos," "Disco Action," playlist; "Disco Mix," column by Tom Moulton; "Jazz," "Jazz LP," playlist; "Tape-Audio-Video," hardware news; "Record Rack," briefs; "Tape Duplicator," convention briefs; "Hot Soul Singles," playlist; "Soul LPs," playlist; "Hot Country LPs," playlist; "Nashville Scene," news column by Coleene Clarke; "Hot Country Singles," playlist; "International," world news; "Hot Latin LPs," playlist; "Latin Scene," briefs; "Canada," Canadian recording news; "From the Music Capitols of the World," briefs; "Hits of the World," international playlist; "Top Album Picks," annotated review of 50 major albums; "Top Single Picks," similar annotation; "Top LPs and Tape," playlist; "Inside Track," industry gossip. (2-76). "No. 1 in Billboard," front cover chart; "Executive Turntable," executive moves; "Chart Beat," column by Paul Grein; "Letters to the Editor," "Commentary," "Radio," "Washington Roundup," radio news column by Bill Holland; "Vox Jox," column by Sean Ross; "Newsline...," newsbriefs; "Networks and Syndication," column by Craig Rosen; "Billboard's PD of the Week," radio program director profile; "Promotions & Marketing," column by Phyllis Stark; "YesterHits," 'Hits from Billboard 10 and 20 Years Ago This Week'; "Album Rock Tracks," "Modern Rock Tracks," "Power Playlists," 'Current playlists of the nation's largest and most influential top 40 radio stations'; "Hot R&B Playlists," 'Sample playlists of the nation's largest urban radio stations'; "Top R&B Albums," "The Rhythm and the Blues," column by Janine McAdams; "Hot R&B Singles," "Hot Rap Singles," "Hot R&B Singles Sales & Airplay," "Terri Rossi's Rhythm Section," column by Terri Rossi; "Hot R&B Singles Action," "Hot Dance Music," club play and 12-inch singles sales; "Dance Trax," column by Larry Flick; "Artist Developments," dance music newsbriefs; "Hot Dance Breakouts," chart; "Talent," "The Beat," column by Thom Duffy; "Words & Music," talent column by Irv Lichtman; "Boxscore," 'Top concert grosses' compiled by Amusement Business; "Nashville Scene," country music news; "Hot Country & Single Tracks," 'Compiled from a national sample of monitored country radio by Broadcast Data Systems'; "Top Country Albums," "Country Corner," column by Marie Ratliff; "Retail," marketing, promotion, and sales; "Retail Track," column by Geoff Mayfield; "Grass Route," retail news; "Album Releases," "Home Video," "Top Video Rentals," "The Hollywood Reporter Box Office," "Store Monitor," home video column by Earl Paige; "Top Music Videos," "2nd Features," 'This weekly column is provided as a guide through the wilderness of unfamiliar feature video titles' column by Michael Dare; "Top Video Sales," "Laser Scans," home video column by Chris McGowan; "Top Videodisc Sales," "Audio Track," pro audio production news by city; "Studio Action," production credits; "The Eye," music video column by Melinda Newman; "The Clip List," "Video Track," music video production news by city; "New Videoclips," "New Products & Services," "Top Jazz Albums," "Top Contemporary Jazz Albums," "Hot Latin Tracks," "Latin Notas," column by Carlos Agudelo; "Jazz Blue Notes," column by Jeff Levenson; "Classical Keeping Score," column by Is Horowitz; "Top Classical Albums," "Top Crossover Albums," "International," "Hits of the World," international playlist; "Maple Briefs," Canadian newsbriefs; "Album Reviews," "Single Reviews," "Hot 100 Singles," famed Billboard playlist compiled from retail stores, one-stop sales reports and radio playlists; "Lifelines," births, marriages and deaths; "For the Record," ommissions and corrections; "Calendar," "Hot 100 Singles Spotlight," column by Michael Ellis; "Hot 100 Singles Action," "Hot 100 Sales & Airplay," "Hot Adult Contemporary," "Crossover Radio Airplay," "Top Pop Albums," "Inside Track," news and trends column by Irv Lichtman; "Newsmakers," picture page. (11-10-90).

TYPL: "Copyright Revision Bill Passed by Senate; Mechanical Royalty 2.5 cents," "More Small Top 40s Adopt Tighter Playlist," "Single Sales a Headache for Top U.S. Superstars." (2-76). "Rock Losing Grip as Other Genres Gain," "Labels Weighing Video Cost Vs. Gains," "Oldies Get a New Twist Via Compact Disc," "Senate Says OK to Vid Game Rental," "Software Groups Want DAT Royalty." (11-10-90).

SCHL: Monthly (Nov, 1894 - May, 1900); Weekly [except for last week of December] (Jun, 1900+), 110 pp.

SPAN: Nov, 1894+
VARIES
--Nov, 1894 - Mar, 1897 as Billboard Advertising.
--Apr, 1897 - Dec 26, 1960 as Billboard, The.
--Jan 9, 1961 - Dec 22, 1962 as Billboard Music Week.
WITH SUPPLEMENT
--Show News, ? - Dec 31, 1960.

LC: PN 2000.B5
ISSN: 0006-2510
ABST: --InfoBank
--Music Index (ISSN: 0027-4348)

--Trade and Industry Index

Billboard, The
Apr, 1897 - Dec 26, 1960//
SEE: BILLBOARD

Billboard Advertising
Nov, 1894 - Mar, 1897//
SEE: BILLBOARD

Billboard Music Week
Jan 9, 1961 - Dec 22, 1962//
SEE: BILLBOARD

BILLBOARD TV PROGRAM AND TIME AVAILABILITIES, THE
PUBL: Billboard Publishing Co., 1564 Broadway, New York, NY.
DESC: A fascinating resource for advertising agencies and their clients, providing a monthly compendium of data on network television and spot TV sales and of great value to the media buyer; this serial provided CPMs on "best buys", national spot campaigns, syndicated films, television sales representatives (TV reps), and participating programs. The last issue was February, 1958 when the television section of this serial was sold to *Television Age*, the latter publisher which agreed only to continue the features and editorial content of the serial rather than its massive directory of spot TV data.
DEPT: "Best Buys in Network Television," "New TV Spot Campaigns," "Pulse Syndicated Film Ratings," "ARB's Top 10 Films in 15 Key Markets," "Pulse Local Ratings," "TV Station Representatives," "Monthly Guide to Local Participating Program Availabilities." (1-58).
TYPL: "Local Live Shows Use 10% of Station Time," "Highlights of Survey on Local Live Shows," "What Advertisers Should Know About Local Shows," "Over 200 Clients Now Use Local Live Shows." (1-58).
SCHL: Monthly, 60 pp.
SPAN: ? - Feb, 1958//
VARIES
--? - ? as TV Availabilities.
LC: HE 8690.B5

BIOMEDICAL COMMUNICATIONS
PUBL: United Business Publications, 750 Third Ave., New York, NY 10017.
DESC: If "Immune Complex Complement Mediated Pathogenesis" sounds like the name of a new foreign film, then this may not be the publication you are seeking. Indeed, *Biomedical Communications* is designed for the communications staff at hospitals and clinics; for nurses, doctors and dentists. Some medical expertise is expected for readers of this publication. Focus of these instructionally-oriented articles primarily concern the media of still photography and video and their relationship to the medical field for information, instruction, and business operation.
DEPT: "Communications Review," upcoming events; "AV Clinic," specific problem solving; "Book Reviews," "Bed and Bored," patient education.
TYPL: "Total Recall: Using the IPR Method and Video to Teach Dental Students." (11-77).
SCHL: Bimonthly, 60 pp.
SPAN: Jan, 1973 to date.
LC: W 1.BI838W.
ISSN: 0092-8607
ABST: --Hospital Literature Index (ISSN: 0018-5736)
--ISMEC Bulletin (ISSN: 0306-0039)
--Pollution Abstracts with Indexes (ISSN: 0032-3624)
--Safety Science Abstracts Journal (ISSN: 0160-1342)

BIOSCOPE, THE
SUB: "The independent film trade paper."
PUBL: Bioscope Publishing Company, Ltd., Faraday House 8-10 Charing Cross Rd., London W.C.2, England.
DESC: *Bioscope* was one of three very early motion picture trade journals published in England. Among its publishing "firsts" were the first film reviews to be published in a British trade paper, and whose reference is to be found in the British Film Institute Film Title Index. Articles emphasized exhibition, technical advances, and film reviews. Among its exhortations to *Bioscope* readers was to prepare for the coming of sound to the silent motion picture.
SCHL: Weekly.
SPAN: Sep 18, 1908 - May 4, 1932//
ABSORBED
--Amusement World, The, ?
--Novelty News, The, ?
WITH SUPPLEMENT
--Films Week By Week, ? - ?

BKSTS Journal, The
Jan, 1974 - Jun, 1986//
(ISSN: 0305-6996)
SEE: IMAGE TECHNOLOGY

✤ BLACK JOURNALISM REVIEW
SUB: "There is already enough ignorance."
PUBL: BJR Publishing Co., 664 North Michigan Ave., Chicago, IL 60611.

DESC: *Black Journalism Review* provides a status report of how blacks, especially those prominent in executive media positions, are reported, described, and discussed. An early issue noted that "The absence of significant black input in either mass-communications, or even the agencies which monitor the media is part of what spawned the birth of *BJR*." This tabloid publication is printed on quality newsprint.
DEPT: "Media News," newsbriefs concerning blacks in media positions; "Ad Lines," similar briefs concerning advertising; "Last Pages," BRJ comments on other media.
TYPL: "Should the Word 'Nigger' be Used in the Media?" "Newsroom Ethics Code for Blacks," "Did Angola Get a Fair Trial?" (Fall-76).
SCHL: Quarterly, 25 pp.
SPAN: Summer, 1976+?

Black oracle

Mar, 1969 - Summer/Fall?, 1978//
(ISSN: 0045-2246)
SEE: CINEMACABRE

✤ BLACK RADIO EXCLUSIVE

PUBL: Black Radio Exclusive, 6353 Hollywood Blvd., Hollywood, CA 90028-6363.
DESC: For over fifteen years, *Black Radio Exclusive* has provided a central forum for the showcasing and promotion of black radio station formats and artists in the United States. Utilizing a dynamic, upbeat layout design, this weekly serial covers the black radio field in a thorough, authoritative manner. The majority of each issue contains playlists, and indicators of individual artist's strengths for a given time period. For the sampled 1990 issue: stapled magazine format with black ink and full color graphics on coated paper stock (8 ¾ x 11 ¾ inches / 220 x 300 mm).
DEPT: "Singles Chart," weekly listing; "Front Page," news concerning black format radio; "In Brief," "Exec Stats," black radio personnel changes; "Quote of the Week," "Short Takes," newsbriefs; "BRE Music Report," top of the weekly chart singles and albums; "BRE-Flicks," black radio personality pictures; "In Other Media," black news item column by Alan Leigh; "The British Invasion," newsbriefs about British black artists column by Dotun Adebayo; "The Carolinas Report," black radio playlist; "The Ohio Valley Report," black radio playlist; "The Mid-Atlantic Report," black radio playlist; "The Mid-South Report," black radio playlist; "The Midwest Report," black radio playlist; "The Southeast Report," black radio playlist; "The Northeast Report," black radio playlist; "The West Report," black radio playlist; "On Stage," black artists in live performance column by LarriAnn Flores; "Canadian Report," newsbrief column on Canadian black artists column by Norman Richmond; "Tech Notes," technical radio column by Billy Paul; "Albums Chart," weekly black radio format listing; "Jazz Profile," "Jazz Chart," weekly radio playlist; "In the Mix," studio news of black artists column by Elaine Stepter; "Rappin' It Up," rap records column by LarriAnn Flores; "Music Reviews," "New Record Releases," "Grapevine," "The Prophet," horoscope. (1-12-90).
TYPL: "Nominees Named For 2nd Annual Dance Music Awards," "NAB Urges FCC to Make Changes for Better AM Radio," "Paula Abdul, Totally Opposite Attraction." (1-12-90).
SCHL: Weekly [except one week in Jun, Thanksgiving, Christmas and two weeks at New Years], 55 pp.
SPAN: Jan 1, 1976?+
 VARIES
 --Jan 1, 1976? - ? as Sidney Miller's Black Radio Exclusive (ISSN: 0161-1526).
LC: ML 3478 .B5
DD: 780/.8996073 19
ISSN: 0745-5992

BLACK STARS

PUBL: Johnson Publishing Co., 820 S. Michigan Ave., Chicago, IL 60605.
DESC: This glossy periodical is designed for the black community interested in black recording, legitimate stage, radio, television, and film stars. Articles profile these artists/personalities, including details of their rise to stardom, current activities, and plans for the future. Consumer oriented, with numerous publicity photos.
DEPT: "Black Stars Letters," letters; "Starscope," horoscope; "Movie Review," "Let's Talk--Music," column by Julie Ellis; "Following the Stars," column by Charles Hobson.
TYPL: "The Inspiration Behind the Hit Making Pen of Nickolas Ashford," "LaWanda Page: a Cinderella Story," "Scat Man Crothers: a Star at Last!," "Who the Stars View as Being Heroes and Heroines." (12-77).
SCHL: Monthly, 74 pp.
SPAN: Nov, 1950 - Jul, 1981//
 VARIES
 --Nov, 1950 - Sep, 1952 as Tan Confessions.
 --Nov, 1952 - Oct, 1971 as Tan (ISSN: 0039-9345).
LC: PN 1560.B5
DD: 791./092/2
ISSN: 0163-3007

BLACK THEATRE

SUB: "A periodical of the black theatre movement."
PUBL: New Lafayette Publications, Rm 103, 200 West 135th St., New York, NY 10030.
DESC: Conceived during a period of national conscienceness-raising, *Black Theatre* provided a clear commentary on the state of Black thought and society expressed through the medium of on-stage performance. Printing and graphics were stark black/white imagry to correspond to the "revolutionary" tone of this serial. Unfortunately published on newsprint.
DEPT: "News," "Black Theatre Notes," "Reviews." (#1-68).

TYPL: "Cultural Nationalism and Black Theatre," "An Interview with Leroi Jones," "The Electronic Nigger Meets the Gold Dust Twins." (#1- 68).
SCHL: Three issues per year, 35 pp.
SPAN: 1968 - 1972//
LC: PN 2270 .A35 B58
ISSN: 0006-4270

✤ BLOCKBUSTER VIDEO MAGAZINE

PUBL: BLOCKBUSTER Entertainment Corporation, 901 East Las Olas Blvd., Ft. Lauderdale, FL 33301.
DESC: A promotional publication for BLOCKBUSTER video locations in the United States, this full-color magazine highlights rental videocassettes of feature motion pictures, documentaries, and off-television projects available to the consumer. The "Holiday Issue" provided a gift catalog of hot videotapes for the holiday season as well. With a phenomenal growth record (6.5 million members in December, 1989), and an eye to innovative marketing techniques, this well-done complimentary publication should continue to grow in stature through the coming years. Full color magazine format (8 ⅜ x 10 ⅞ inches / 210 x 275 cm); numerous film graphic stills.
DEPT: "Spotlight Special," special priced rentals; "New Releases," "Cinema Scope," highlights past production credits associated with current hit films; "Readers' Choice," reader poll; "Blockbuster Picks," film rental suggestions; "Blockbuster Crossword," "Kids' Clubhouse," children's fare. (12-89).
TYPL: "Red Hot," "Dealing With the Joker," "Murray Mania." (12-89).
SCHL: Monthly, 40 pp.
SPAN: 1989+

BLUE PENCIL MAGAZINE

PUBL: Blue Pencil Club, 9 Spruce St., New York, NY.
DESC: The Blue Pencil Club "...is home of the best known newspaper men and artists, whose work is known all over these United States, and who are all possessed of the true Bohemian instincts that are only to be found on the island of Manhattan." In other words, this serial contained the copy, cartoons, and biting satire that newspaper editors refused to print. This was a caustic journal of societal comment, oftentimes aiming barbs at a favorite target, the newspaper editor. Indeed, an entire series of satirical cartoons appearing in this magazine was about editors at local New York City newspapers. Typical of this wonderful serial was one small article entitled "Answers to Correspondents," in which an author wrote: "No, sir; your reckoning is entirely wrong. With one fare on the cable car you may carry your one child of six years of age, or your six children of one year of age (if you happen to be built that way); but for a child of one year of age to carry six fathers has never been done successfully outside of Paris." An always fascinating, oftentimes hilarious presentation of the underground side of journalism. Long, narrow format; numerous ink drawings and caricatures.
DEPT: None. (9-1900).
TYPL: "How the 'Scooper' was Scooped," "A Barnyard Interlude," "Mr. Nimble Abandons Newspaper Writing," "Mickey Finn Sketches." (9-1900).
SCHL: Monthly, 30 pp.
SPAN: Feb, 1900 - Nov, 1901//
LC: AP 2.B632

BM/E

Jan, 1965 - May, 1988//
(ISSN: 0005-3201)
SEE: BME'S TELEVISION ENGINEERING

BM/E's World Broadcast News

Jan, 1978 - Jan, 1990//
SEE: WORLD BROADCAST NEWS

BME For Technical and Engineering Management

Jun, 1988 - Jan, 1990//
(ISSN: 1043-7487)
SEE: BME'S TELEVISION ENGINEERING

BME'S TELEVISION ENGINEERING

SUB: "The technical magazine for the nineties." (Feb, 1990).
SUB: "For technical and engineering management."
SUB: "The magazine of broadcast management/engineering."
PUBL: Act III Publishing, 401 Park Avenue South, New York, NY 10016.
DESC: An outstanding publication for those interested in broadcast technology, *BM/E* was created to bridge the gap between engineering and management personnel at broadcast stations, no small task in an age of tightening budgets, and advancing technology. A redesigned format in June, 1988 added four new special departmental features: "Crosstalk--an ongoing journal for engineering management," "Tech Watch--which explores the future of technology," "Compute--discussions relative to PC's and peripherals," and "Spectrum--which explores and analyzes the regulatory environment." In February, 1990, Act III Chairman and CEO Norman Lear (publisher of the serial) noted that, "As we approach a new century, TV and radio have become separate markets. What's more, TV technology is about to enter the era of advanced and high-definition television, which promises more change and innovation than anything since the invention of the medium itself." With that in mind,

a title and editorial content change commenced with the February, 1990 issue placing *BME's Television Engineering* squarely into television. In Fall, 1990 Act III Publishing placed the publication on the sales block, and it was absorbed by rival serial, *Television Broadcast*, effective with the October, 1990 issue. This was a magazine of new and applied technology, written to inform a technically-minded engineering staff, while giving lay readers the basics of engineering and technology. During its publication span this publication was "must" reading in television engineering and management. Magazine format (8 x 10 ⅞ inches / 205 x 275 cm), full color graphics.

DEPT: "Broadcast Industry News," large number of industry newsbriefs; "Radio Programming and Production for Profit," a valuable feature sharing successful programming items; "BM/E's Program marketplace," lengthy profile of program suppliers; "TV Programming and Production for Profit," successful video productions; "Great Idea Contest," the technical minded vie for prizes with new engineering concepts; "FCC Rules and Regulations," superb interpretations of current rules and regulations by leading broadcast legal authorities. (2-78). "Radio News," "Viewpoint," editorial; "Feedback," letters; "Update," "Crosstalk: an Engineering Management Journal," "Tech Watch," "Compute," "Spectrum: the Regulatory Environment," "New Equipment," "Business Briefs," "Currents: A Guest Editorial." (4-89). "Viewpoint," editorial; "Update," industry newsbriefs; "Business Briefs," "ATV Watch," advanced television developments; "Audio for Video," "New Products," review; "Currents: A Guest Editorial." (3-90).

TYPL: "Digital Audio: This Year an Industry Begins to Form," "Fresh Though Pays on Radio Air," "Digital Technology's Impact on Television Post-Production," "KSTP-TV's 'Country Day:' A New Approach to an Old Idea." (2-78). "ATV: High Stakes, Tough Choices," "The Digital Audio Workstation Dilemma," "What's New in Radio Transmitters?" (4-89). "Switching to Digital," "Camera Angles," "Decisions: To Buy or Not to Buy." (3-90).

SCHL: Monthly, 115 pp.
SPAN: Jan, 1965 - Sep, 1990//
VARIES
--Jan, 1965 - May, 1988 as BM/E (ISSN: 0005-3201).
--Jun, 1988 - Jan, 1990 as BME For Technical and Engineering Management (ISSN: 1043-7487).
ABSORBED BY
--Television Broadcast (ISSN: 0898-767x), Oct, 1990.
DD: 384 11
ISSN: 1049-4588

✤ BMI: MUSICWORLD

PUBL: BMI Corporate Relations Dept., 320 West 57th St., New York, NY 10019.
DESC: *BMI: MusicWorld* is a promotional piece by the BMI Corporate Relations Department, and quite naturally pertains to the artists whose work is licensed through the Broadcast Music Incorporated organization. The magazine is filled with numerous pictures of these artists, brief descriptions of their backgrounds, and lists their current projects. Some pictures in color.

DEPT: "Hither and Yon," BMI newsbriefs; "On the Scene," artist profiles; "In Concert," newsbriefs; "Update," artist projects; "Kudos," awards; "Music People," artist pictures and newsbriefs; "On Copyright," column. (summer-89).

TYPL: "Street Music: The Sounds of a New Generation," "BMI Pop Awards Light Up the Night," "Grusin Takes Top Honor at BMI Film/TV Awards," "Scandinavian Scene Heats Up," "You Can Always Go 'Downtown'." (summer-89).

SCHL: Monthly (1964 - 1972); Quarterly (1973+), 65 pp.
SPAN: 1962+
VARIES
--? - ? as About Music & Writers.
--Oct, 1964 as About Music and Writers (ISSN: 0740-8382).
--Nov, 1964 - Fall, 1987 as Many Worlds of Music, The (ISSN: 0045-317x).
LC: ML 3469 .M9
DD: 781.64/05
ISSN: 1042-6736

✤ BOARD REPORT FOR GRAPHIC ARTISTS

SUB: "Continuing publications for American professional graphic artists."
PUBL: Board Report, PO Box 1561, HBG, PA 17105.
DESC: What graphic artist, advertising or marketing executive has not "run out of creative ideas" at some point? *Board Report for Graphic Artists* is a cornucopia of creative ideas, graphics, trends, and concepts to fire the imagination (and profitability) of individuals on the creative side of media. Each monthly issue consists of several unique sections. First is the four-page typewritten newsletter, a collection of creative ideas, trends, and promotions ripe for immediate application. Ideas here cover the broad range of advertising and marketing. One article provided historical insight as to how a few simple typos changed the course of history. Another covered how designers could reduce their production costs. Still another provided a fascinating look into a left-brain approach for creating successful brochures. Also included is a group of supplemental materials, "Designer's Compendium," which is four or five graphics idea sheets on a mixture of coated and uncoated paper stock. Ideas range from annual reports to unusual folds. Indeed, the alphabetical index consisted of some 75+ topics including matchbooks, film and TV art, foil stamping, record jackets, calendars, package designs, billboards, greeting cards, themography, silk-screening, line conversions, logos, coupons, direct mail, and posterizations. Each of the segments includes full pictorial instruction on the process and technique of design, with sample materials, construction schematics, and other pertinent information. This is an excellent resource for

design, advertising or marketing individuals interested in staying creative, competitive, and profitable in today's advertising/promotion field. All materials printed on coated and uncoated paper stock, three-hole punched with instructions for placement in a binder (8 ½ x 11 inches / 215 x 280 cm). Highly recommended.
DEPT: "Call for Entries," "Upcoming Seminars & Workshops." (9-90).
TYPL: "Original Party Animal Loses Trademark to a Cracker," "63% Direct Mail Response Falls Short of Goal," "Mature Market Relies More on Newspaper Print Advertising," "Use This Color When You Don't Want to Get Noticed," "Bored Drivers Become Moving Market." (9-90).
SCHL: Monthly, 4 pp.
SPAN: ?+

BOLEX REPORTER, THE
SUB: "For all movie makers."
PUBL: Paillard Products, Inc., 100 6th Ave, New York, NY.
DESC: A very well organized public relations piece, *Bolex Reporter* is printed two-color on glossy stock. A great deal of amateur and professional news is packed into its 25-page quarterly format. A large number of illustrations show use of Bolex equipment. It is written for lay and professional audience.
DEPT: "Bolex Showcase," product reviews; "Bolex-pressions," letters.
TYPL: "Bolex Eclipses the Sun," "Bolex Used by Western Union D&R for First Color Motion Picture," "Operative 3-D in Proctology," "Twenty-One Days Behind the Iron Curtain," "TV News Filming," "You Too can Film a Dramatic TV Show." (Fall-54).
SCHL: Quarterly (1950-1960); Semiannual (1961+), 25 pp.
SPAN: Dec, 1950 - 1974//
LC: TR 845.B6
DD: 778.5/05
ISSN: 0006-6516

✤ BOMB MAGAZINE
SUB: "Artists, writers, actors, directors."
PUBL: New Art Publications, 177 Franklin St., New York 10013.
DESC: "*BOMB* is dedicated to presenting the work in its own light. Our purpose is to develop and expand the parameters of original work. The magazine's contents are predicated upon the discourse between artists. This discourse dictates its form--original art, fiction and extensive interviews between professionals in art, literature, poetry, theater and film. There is no other magazine which serves as a forum for artists and writers to speak for themselves." This large format (270 x 370 cm) publication provides a very unique opportunity for personal expression; printed black/white on quality paper, with large amounts of white-space contributing to an uncluttered layout design. The emphasis is on the artistic side of media, with the individual artist (unencumbered by the medium of the critic) providing full discourse on the emotional, economic, political and creative processes leading to completion of individual projects. Great care is taken in reproduction and placement of graphics. Most articles are structured in interview- style. An excellent publication for expression by artists, writers, actors and directors. Large format magazine format.
SCHL: Three issues per year, 95 pp.
SPAN: Spring, 1981+
LC: NX 458 .B65
DD: 700/.9/04 19
ISSN: 0743-3204

✤ BONDAGE
SUB: "The James Bond 007 Fan Club is dedicated to the memory of Ian Fleming and his work."
PUBL: James Bond 007 Fan Club, PO Box 414, Bronxville, NY 10708.
DESC: On the masthead page of this semiannual publication is stated, "The James Bond 007 Fan Club is dedicated to the memory of Ian Fleming and his work." *Bondage* is a fanzine of quality printed on heavy coated paper stock, with very little advertising, and with front and back covers of full-color pictures of James Bond actors and actresses. Articles provide a fascinating look into the life of Ian Fleming and his famous James Bond creations. Two sampled issues covered a three-part series on an Ian Fleming gold hunt in the Indian ocean, Fleming's early involvement in development of the television series, "The Man From U.N.C.L.E.;" location settings for Bond motion pictures, and a wonderful segment on musicians' contributions to the history of James Bond productions. *Bondage*, along with newsletter, *Bondage Quarterly*, is part and parcel of membership in the James Bond 007 Fan Club. Stapled magazine format, black/white editorial content with full-color cover on coated paper stock, limited advertising pertaining to James Bond collectibles (8 ½ x 11 inches / 215 x 280 mm).
DEPT: "Pen Pals," listing. (winter-89).
TYPL: "Treasure Hunt in Eden," "The Soundtracks to the Novels," "Report from the Set of License to Kill," "Timothy Dalton Revisited." (winter-89).
SCHL: Semiannual, 30 pp.
SPAN: 1973+

Book and Magazine Production
Nov/Dec, 1980 - May, 1982//
(ISSN: 0273-8724)
SEE: HIGH VOLUME PRINTING

✤ BOOK MARKETING UPDATE
PUBL: Ad-Lib Publications, 51 North Fifth St., PO Box 1102, Fairfield, IA 52556-1102.

DESC: Readers like what they see in *Book Marketing Update*: "Your newsletter proved quite rewarding to this small publisher who is head to head with the giants. We have been holding our own for 38 years, and I hope your good words, ideas and observations will keep us in business for many years to come. Your newsletter seems more useful than the other one in the field, as it deals with more practical subjects that can be applied immediately." Kudos have also been expressed by other publishers: "As each issue comes, I think 'There's no way you can top this' --and your next one does;" and "I have joined the legions that stand in awe of your vacuum-cleaner ability to glean the stuff of publishing." This three-hole punched newsletter of 30-plus pages is sent first class in order that readers may implement ideas and resources in a timely manner. It is a resource listing opportunities for the marketing of books, be that through distribution, marketing, or promotion. Numerous outlets are provided, along with the important consideration of the names, titles, telephone numbers, and business addresses of key promotion individuals in radio, television, and print media. At $48 per year (for 1990), this is an excellent, highly usable resource for any independent book publisher desirous of improving the marketing side of book publishing. Three-hole-punched stapled newsletter format (8 ½ x 11 inches / 215 x 280 cm), some pages two-color, no illustrations.
DEPT: "Media Notes: Magazines," "Media Notes: Radio Talk Shows," "Media Notes: National Television Shows," "Our Readers Write," letters. (1/2-90).
TYPL: "The Environment--The Hot Topic for the 1990's," "Software and Other Reviews," "The 30 Timeless Direct Marketing Principles," "Top Independent Booksellers," "New Books to Help You Do Your Job Better." (1/2-90).
SCHL: Bimonthly, 35 pp.
SPAN: Dec, 1986+
ISSN: 0891-8813

Book Production Industry & Magazine Production
? - Sep/Oct?, 1980//
(ISSN: 0192-2874)
SEE: HIGH VOLUME PRINTING

✤ BOOK PROMOTION HOTLINE
PUBL: Ad-Lib Publications, 51 North Fifth St., PO Box 1102, Fairfield, IA 52556-1102.
DESC: "Each issue of the newsletter features from 75 to 100 key media and book marketing contacts. All information contained in each issue is verified the same week the newsletter is published, so you are guaranteed that the names and addresses are not only accurate but also actively seeking information about new books and authors. But *Book Promotion Hotline* is more than just a listing of contacts. As a subscriber, you should consider us your own personal research assistant. Just tell us what you want to know, and we'll do the research -- whether you want to know about a new television show, track down the address of a syndicated columnist, get a list of wholesalers who sell garden books, or update magazines which cover a special topic of interest to you. Whatever you want to know, we'll do the footwork and print the results of our investigations in the next available issue of the newsletter." This weekly newsletter removes much of the hard work of book promotion; the eternal search for current names, addresses, telephone numbers, and other data associated with promotional opportunities in American print and electronic media. Listings provide concise information. For print media, listings include names of editors, columnists and their departmental column names. For electronic media, listings include the type, length, nature, and broadcast time of radio-television programming conducive to promotional activities. The annual subscription cost of $150 (for 1990), provides a unique, cost-effective service for book publishers. For the sampled issue of 1990: four-page black/white newsletter format, no illustrations or advertising.
DEPT: "Syndicated Columns." (1-5-90). "Cancelled Magazines," "Deleted Wholesalers," "Wholesalers." (5-11-90).
TYPL: "Magazines -- The Seven Sisters Plus One," "Houston Newspapers," "Creative Mind," "New Children's Bookstores." (1-5-90). "New Age Magazines," "Twin Cities Radio," "Tribune Media Service." (5-11-90).
SCHL: Weekly, 4 pp.
SPAN: Jan 5, 1990+
DD: 010
ISSN: 1049-4456

Book Research Quarterly
Spring, 1985 - Winter, 1990/1991//
(ISSN: 0741-6148)
SEE: PUBLISHING RESEARCH QUARTERLY

BOOKS AND FILMS
SUB: "A monthly publication devoted to library film cooperation."
PUBL: Ina Roberts and Anthony Belle, Cleveland Public Library, Cleveland, OH.
DESC: An interesting mimeographed publication whose purpose was to "...increase book and information service to its public through featuring the worthwhile books connecting with worthwhile films." Editors Roberts and Belle provided critical commentary for the Hollywood product based upon library holdings, in essence evaluating the success with which the Hollywood Producers faithfully reproduced the book history, novel, or biography. An interesting serial that promoted library use through association with major motion picture releases.
DEPT: "Current," film releases; "Coming Releases," "In Production," "Future Films." (4-36).

TYPL:	"Stills for Shorts," "Film Courses in Adult Education," "Cooperation with Lighter Films." (4-36).
SCHL:	Monthly, [except Jul - Aug], 6 pp.
SPAN:	Oct, 1935 - Oct, 1938//
	ABSORBED BY
	--Hollywood Spectator, Oct, 1938.
LC:	PN 1993.B55

✣ BOOKS & RELIGION

SUB:	"A monthly review."
PUBL:	Duke University, Divinity School, P.O. Box 3000, Dept. LL, Denville, NJ 07834.
DESC:	"For more than a decade, *Books & Religion* has been the only publication offering timely and dependable coverage of the broad range of American religious thought and scholarship--Protestant, Catholic and Jewish, conservative and liberal, popular and scholarly." While the primary emphasis is on the more than 2,000 religious-oriented books published each year, this tabloid-size newspaper also provides some articles on other mass communication fields as well. An excellent resource for books and publishing activities of America's religious community. Numerous graphics; printed on quality newsprint.
DEPT:	"B&R Reviews," book reviews; "First Impression," new books; "Hot Type," guest commentary; "Foolscap," cartoon comment. (5/6-86).
TYPL:	"God's Choice: The Total World of a Fundamentalist Christian School," "Scholars Off on a New Quest for the Historical Jesus," "Only the News that's Fit to Print: When Christ Ran the Newsroom." (5/6-86).
SCHL:	Monthly (except Aug and Dec); 20 pp.
SPAN:	Jan/Feb, 1985+
	FROM MERGER OF
	--New Book Review (ISSN: 0028-4297) (and) Review of Books and Religion, The, 1976.
	VARIES
	--Sep, 1976 - Jun, 1980 as New Review of Books and Religion, The (ISSN: 0146-0609).
	--Sep, 1981 - Sep/Oct, 1984 as Review of Books and Religion, The (ISSN: 0732-5800).
LC:	BL 1.N48
DD:	200
ISSN:	0890-0841
ABST:	--Index to Religious Periodical Literature (ISSN: 0019-4107)
	--Religion Index One (ISSN: 0149-8428)

✣ BOOKSTORE JOURNAL

SUB:	"Official publication of Christian Booksellers Association."
PUBL:	Christian Booksellers Association, 2620 Venetucci Blvd., Colorado Springs, CO 80906-4000.
DESC:	"The purpose of *Bookstore Journal* is to help Christian retailers and suppliers raise their standard of excellence and develop more effective ministries by providing them business solutions to business problems. We accomplish this goal by encouraging communication and cooperation among all industry entities and by providing management, marketing, and merchandising information as well as relevant industry and product news." *Bookstore Journal* provides an excellent resource for this niche in publishing and retailing. Articles cover retail operations, new trends in advertising/marketing, store operations, purchasing, trends in publishing of books, music recordings, and other materials. Of special merit is the value of the extensive music, book, and material reviews designed to help the store manager decide what to stock in the store at any given time. For the sampled issue of 1989: magazine format (8 ¼ x 10 ⅞ inches / 210 x 280 cm); numerous graphics.
DEPT:	"Best-Seller Lists," "Between the Lines:," profiles; "Book Notes," "Book Reviews," "Books to Come," "CBA News," news of the Christian Booksellers Association; "Center Stage:," music and video profile; "Music News," "Music Reviews," "Open Forum," letters; "Reference Shelf," "Store News," "Supplier News," "Video Reviews," "What's New," new product information. (10-89).
TYPL:	"Kid Conscious: Making Young Customers Feel Welcome," "CD's--A Sound Investment," "Print Music--How to Nurture an Endangered Species," "Creating Hearty Displays for Valentine's Day." (10-89).
SCHL:	Monthly, 140 pp.
SPAN:	Jun, 1968+
LC:	Z 479 .B65
DD:	381/.45/070573
ISSN:	0006-7563

✣ BOOKTALKER, THE

SUB:	"A newsletter containing booktalks, news, and other information of interest to booktalkers."
PUBL:	HW Wilson Co., 950 University Ave., Bronx, NY 10452.
DESC:	This five-issue-per-year supplement to the *Wilson Library Bulletin* is an informative description of recent works designed for the American library market. *The Booktalker* fills in often-missing information from standard critiques by providing a capsule summary of the plot action to be found primarily within works of a fictionalized nature. The summaries are written with a nice touch of wit and enthusiasm, and are a joy to read. There are no graphics, but the book descriptions more than adequately fire the visual imaginations of those individuals who receive this wonderful publication. Stapled newsletter format, black and spot-color ink on tinted uncoated paper stock, no advertising (8 x 11 inches / 205 x 280 mm).
DEPT:	"From the Editor," editorial column by Joni Bodart. (5-91).
TYPL:	"Booktalking the Bluebonnets." (5-91).
SCHL:	Five issues per year, 20 pp.
SPAN:	Sep, 1989+
	SUPPLEMENT TO
	--Wilson Library Bulletin (ISSN: 0043-5651), Sep?, 1988+.

Boston Dramatic Review

? - Nov 25, 1899//
SEE: DRAMATIC REVIEW, THE

✤ BOX OFFICE

SUB: "The pulse of the motion picture industry."
SUB: "The national film weekly."
PUBL: RLD Communications, Inc., Boxoffice Data Center, PO Box 25485, Chicago, IL 60625.
DESC: *Boxoffice* is published in a national executive edition, as well as in nine regional editions. It is a trade periodical for the motion picture exhibitor, emphasizing new product releases and promotion. *Boxoffice* provides an excellent news vehicle in which to share ideas and issues of film exhibition. Large studio advertisements highlight each issue. In addition, monthly *Boxoffice* features "The Modern Theater," a supplement concerning motion picture house construction, equipment, concessions and maintenance.
DEPT: "Motion Pictures Rated by the Code and Rating Administration," assigned rating codes; "Hollywood Report," news of upcoming films; "Boxoffice Barometer," economic ratings of major motion pictures in 20 cities; "Broadway," "Washington," "Buffalo," "Philadelphia," "Pittsburgh," "Baltimore," "Denver," "Tuscon," "Manilla," "Salt Lake City," "Kansas City," "Chicago," "St. Louis," "Atlanta," "Jacksonville," "Miami," "New Orleans," "Dallas," "Houston," "San Antonio," "Oklahoma City," "Minneapolis," "Des Moines," "Detroit," "Louisville," "Boston," "Hartford," "Rhode Island," "Vermont," "Maine," "New Haven," "Calgari," "Vancouver," "Ottawa," "St. John," and "Toronto," "Hollywood Happenings," newsbriefs; "Review Digest and Alphabetical Index," superb section of all currently-released motion pictures with information and titles, types, distributors, issue reviews, and rating via the Hollywood Reporter, Box Office, Variety, Parents Magazine, and the New York Daily News; "Feature Chart," release data by studios; "Feature Reviews," excellent lengthy reviews of current productions, with two unique subsections: 'Exploitips,' promotion information, and 'Catchlines,' slogans usable for promotion. (The following special articles are featured in the Modern Theater section of Boxoffice:) "Projection and Sound," "Refreshment Service," subtitled as 'added income opportunities for progressive exhibitors;' "New Equipment and Developments," new product briefs; "About People and Product."
TYPL: "American Multi-Cinema Announces 24 New Screens for Spring, 1978," "Gala Boston Premiere for 'Bridge Too Far,'" "Press Luncheon Gives Opportunity to See Realism of 'Choir Boys' Set." (from Modern Theater section:) "Creative Showmanship, Hard Work Boost Off-Season Ozoner Business," "Manager Must Take Burglary Precautions," "Cinema Radio's Innovative Sound System like Small Radio Stations." (6-77).
SCHL: Weekly (? - ?); Monthly (Jul, 1984+), 70 pp.
SPAN: 1920+
ABSORBED
--Boxoffice [Eastern Edition], 1977.
--Boxoffice [Southeast Edition], 1977.
--Boxoffice [Southwest Edition], 1977.
--Boxoffice [National Executive Edition], 1977.
WITH SUPPLEMENT
--Modern Theater, The, ? - ?
LC: PN 1993.B6
DD: 791 11
ISSN: 0006-8527
ABST: --Film Literature Index (ISSN: 0093-6758)
--InfoBank

BOXOFFICE

SUB: "The pulse of the motion picture industry."
SUB: "The national film weekly."
PUBL: Associated Publications, Inc., 4704 East 9th St., Kansas City, MO.
DESC: This "Southeastern" edition served the states of Texas, Oklahoma, Arkansas, Tennessee, Louisiana, Alabama, Mississippi, Georgia, Florida, North and South Carolina. One of seven separate regional editions, it provided a mixture of local exhibitor news, and national information as it applied to local operations. It also reported on how national events affected local operation in this eleven-state area. A number of weekly departments merited the attention of the local showman. "Local Releases" listed films that completed three successive days of first-run engagements at regular admission prices. "Reviews" provided clear story synopses, cast listings, and film ratings in adult, family, or juvenile audience categories. "Exploitips" provided "Selling Angles," and advertising "Catchlines" keyed to current film releases. Of special aid to the local showman was the section, "Selling Seats." This two-page section with graphics had ideas for promotion and tie-ins for use on a local level, these included a six a.m. "Milkman's Matinee" in Washington, DC; a Burlington Railroad 150 mile excursion fare into Denver to see a motion picture; and a Houston, Texas appeal to parents that a two-hour film was an effective ten cent babysitter were among the suggestions proposed to the local motion picture exhibitor. For the sampled issue of 1935: magazine format (9 ¼ x 12 ⅜ inches / 235 x 315 mm) on coated paper stock. Two-color covers with several ads in two-color printing as well.
DEPT: "Photo Summary of Week's News for Southern Showmen," "Local Releases," "First Runs," week's gross; "Outstanding in the Week's News," newsbriefs; "Reviews," 'Opinions on current feature productions'; "Exploitips," 'Suggestions for selling the picture - ad aids'; "Short Subject Reviews," "Feature Index," 'A check-up on current product'; "Selling Seats," 'Practical ideas by practical showmen'; "Nuggets," publicity ideas for exhibitors; "Hollywood," 'News and views of the productiooon center'; "Clearing House," 'Sells and buys equipment, theatres, services'. (3-23-35).

TYPL: "Availability Decision is Upheld," "Children Honor 'Dad' Shaw," "From Celler to Culkin and to Pettengill Goes Allied's Hand," "Cite Minimum Wage Clause," "Text of Pettengill Bill." (3-23-35).
SCHL: Weekly, 30 pp.
SPAN: Dec 1, 1920? - 1977//
EDITION
--Southeast.
ABSORBED BY
--Box Office (ISSN: 0006-8527), 1977.

✤ BPME IMAGE MAGAZINE

SUB: "The magazine of the Broadcast Promotion & Marketing Executives."
PUBL: Broadcast Promotion & Marketing Executives, Inc., 402 East Orange St., Lancaster, PA 17602.
DESC: "Broadcast Promotion and Marketing Executives is the international professional association for those people who care about and are involved in all aspects of the advertising, promotion, marketing and publicizing of television, radio and cable." Provided free to BPME members, *Image* provides monthly case studies of promotions that worked; detailing problem solving, comparison of media, campaign strategies, and how to successfully reach the target audience. Sample print campaigns are included, and BPME members have access to the BPME Resource Center in Los Angeles with more than 20,000 print advertisements, video promotionals and audio commercial spots within the collection. For the 1987 sampled issue: stapled magazine format, black/white editorial content with full-color advertising pages and full-color cover on coated paper stock (8 x 11 inches / 205 x 280 mm).
DEPT: "Letters to the Editor," "Profile," "My Turn," guest editorial; "Management Tips," "Interchange," BPME membership news; "Roster Changes," personnel briefs; "Afterthoughts," commentary. (3-87).
TYPL: "Finding and Using Outside Resources," "Dealing with the Music Makers," "If It Sells It's Good--If Not It's Art," "Working with a Consultant," "BPME Drug Ads." (3-87).
SCHL: Monthly [except Nov], 60 pp.
SPAN: ?+
VARIES
--? - ? as Newsletter / Broadcasters Promotion Association.

Brains

Jan, 1905 - Aug 28, 1912//
SEE: RETAIL EQUIPMENT AND MERCHANDISE

BRIGHT LIGHTS

SUB: "The magazine of American film."
SUB: "For the film director."
PUBL: Gary Morris, Box 26081, Los Angeles, CA 90026.

DESC: *Bright Lights* is a motion picture review magazine; a commentary on historical Hollywood product concentrating on talent, the role of director and the visual style within motion pictures. It is printed on high-gloss paper with lavish use of production stills. The serial followed a very irregular publication schedule: a total of nine issues were published during its four year span.
DEPT: "Book Review." (#1-80).
TYPL: "Bette Davis: a Talent for Hysteria," "'Love is the Exception to Every Rule, is it Not?,' The Films of Vincente Minnelli & Allen Jay Lerner," "Tex Avery: Archradicalizer of the Hollywood Cartoon," "Woody Allen's Love Letter to Diane Keeton." (#1-80).
SCHL: Irregular (Quarterly), 34 pp.
SPAN: Fall, 1974 - #1, 1980//
ISSN: 0147-4049
ABST: --Film Literature Index (ISSN: 0093-6758)

✤ BRITISH BOOK NEWS

SUB: "The British Council's monthly survey for bookbuyers throughout the world."
SUB: "A monthly selection of recent books."
SUB: "A monthly review of new books."
PUBL: British Council, 65 Davies St., London W1Y 2AA England.
DESC: Targeted to librarians, this monthly magazine is produced by the Booksellers Association of Great Britain and Ireland, and is designed to review current trends and developments in the book publishing field, as well as showcase new British and Irish publications. Each issue carries approximately five articles, with the focus being concise reviews of new works in the "Forthcoming Books" section, under subtitles such as "Engineering and Technology," "Medicine," "Pure Sciences," "Social Sciences," "History, Biography and Travel," "Language and Literature," "Arts," "General Reference and Information Science," and "Secondary School Textbooks." An excellent column, "Notes and News from the Book Trade in Britain," provides interesting details on late-breaking developments and people in the news. In the sampled issue for April, 1991 articles in this departmental feature concerned the Bookseller's Association annual conference, new publishing imprints, a newly formed UK book trade standards group, literary awards, and the rapidly developing issue of data protection. An excellent resource for publisher, bookseller, and library information professional alike. Note: some issues were accompanied by supplements, plus special issues such as number 53a "British Wartime Books for Young People." For sampled issue for 1991: stapled magazine format, black/white editorial content on uncoated paper stock, with full-color cover on coated paper stock (8 ¼ x 11 ¾ inches / 210 x 295 mm).
DEPT: "Notes and News from the Book Trade in Britain," current events column by Nicholas Clee and Jane Murray; "Around Books," "Book Survey," "Periodicals and Serials," 'Reviews of new titles'; "Com-

pany Profile," "Publishing," "British Books Abroad," 'The British Council Overseas'; "Forthcoming Books," brief descriptions and information. (4-91).
TYPL: "BA Conference: Leaner and Fitter," "Data Protection: UK Urges Rethink," "The Play's the Thing: Spotlight on Theatre Studies," "IOP Publishing," "Distance Education: A Survey of the Current Literature." (4-91).
SCHL: Monthly, 85 pp.
SPAN: Mar, 1940+
VARIES
--Mar, 1940 - Apr, 1941 as Selection of Recent Books Published in Great Britain.
WITH SUPPLEMENT
--Children's Books (ISSN: 0264-5637), 1983 - 1988.
LC: Z 1035 .B838
DD: 016
ISSN: 0007-0343
ABST: --Book Review Index (ISSN: 0524-0581)
--Library Information Science Abstracts (ISSN: 0024-2179)
--Reference Sources (ISSN: 0163-3546)

BRITISH COMMUNICATIONS AND ELECTRONICS

SUB: "The journal of the electronics industry."
PUBL: Heywood, 161/166 Fleet St., London E.C.4, England.
DESC: A technical journal of new developments in electronics, articles cover a broad definition of communication and electronics; and oftentimes concern basic research. Some news is featured about research careers, salaries, and profiles of British research facilities. Provides state- of- industry news as well.
DEPT: "Highlights," newsbriefs; "Comments of the Month," "News from SIMA," "Patents in Prospect." (1-65).
TYPL: "The Design of Thin Film Microcircuits," "A Thin Film I.F. Amplifier," "Measuring Intense R.F. Radiation." (1-65).
SCHL: Monthly, 80 pp.
SPAN: May, 1955 - Aug, 1965//
VARIES
--Oct, 1954 - Apr, 1955 as Communications and Electronics.
ABSORBED BY
--Industrial Electronics (ISSN: 0537-5185).
LC: TK 7800.B7
DD: 621.3805
ISSN: 0524-5753

✤ BRITISH INSTITUTE OF RECORDED SOUND. BULLETIN.

PUBL: British Institute of Recorded Sound, 38 Russell Square, London WCI, England.
DESC: "The *Bulletin*, which will be circulated to Friends of the Institute from time to time, will include information about acquisitions of special interest and will give particulars of functions arranged by the Institute. It will also contain 'discographies' -- bibliographies of records -- and articles on subjects related to the objects of the Institute including: record archives; the care of records and technical matters; and on valuable sounds of all kinds worthy of preservation in recorded form." This mimeographed publication focuses on describing the 25,000 (1956 holdings) records of the Institute.
DEPT: "Book Review." (autumn-58).
TYPL: "Ignace Jan Paderewski--Discography," "Language Learning and Audio-Visual Aids." (autumn-58).
SCHL: Quarterly, 25 pp.
SPAN: Summer, 1956+?

British Institution of Radio Engineers. Journal

1939 - Dec, 1962//
SEE: ELECTRONICS & COMMUNICATIONS ENGINEERING JOURNAL

✤ BRITISH JOURNAL OF PHOTOGRAPHY

SUB: "Technical, professional, scientific."
PUBL: Henry Greenwood & Co., 24 Wellington St., London WC2E 7DH, England.
DESC: The *British Journal of Photography* began in 1854 as *The Liverpool Photographic Journal*, at a time when photographers of serious intent had to mix their own chemicals and oversee the entire photographic process from start to finish. Those first issues (small magazine format) dealt with photographic exhibitions, new chemical compounds, and societies who existed to give recognition to members, and further the craft. Current issues of *BJP* still serve the "photographer of serious intent," but in a current format and layout style on heavy clay-coated paper stock. The photographic print is treated with loving care, with elements of layout design, font, and editorial content designed to support the visual process. Typical articles from sample issue of February, 1990 included such topics as professional photographer profiles, use of computer-driven imagery/processing, the manufacture of holograms, issues of privacy, and a survey of professional enlargers. For 130+ years, this serial has provided quality news and promotion to the craft and art of photography; and what is especially amazing is that *British Journal of Photography* has been published WEEKLY for some 125 years! Of special historical note are the interesting letters to the editor submitted in 1854, presenting issues that were a forum for new ideas in photography. Some engravings in 1854 issues; well recommended for the serious photographer. For the sampled issue of 1990: stapled magazine format with black/white and color pages and full-color cover on coated paper stock (9 x 11 ¾ inches / 230 x 300 mm).

DEPT: "Correspondence." (2-11-1854). "Comment," "Letters," "News," "Pinboard," newsbriefs. (6-26-87). "Comment," "News," extensive section of photographic newsbriefs; "Products," newsbriefs; "Pinboard," news capsules of photographic interest; "Letters," "Diary," event calendar; "Imaging Technology," excellent technical feature; "Books," review; "Collectables," historical cameras; "Review," new exhibitions; "Buyers Guide," equipment listing. (2-22-90).
TYPL: "[Minutes from] Liverpool Photographic Society," "The Exhibition of Photographs and Daguerreotypes, by the London Photographic Society." (2-11-1854). "'True Stories and Photofictions' at Fotogallery, Cardiff." (6-26-87). "About Face for Skrebneski," "Photograph and Computer," "The Business of Embossing," "The Invasion of Privacy." (2-22-90).
SCHL: Monthly (Jan, 1854 - 1856); Semimonthly (Jan, 1857 - Jun, 1864); Weekly (Jul, 1864+); 40 pp.
SPAN: Jan, 1854+
VARIES
--Jan, 1854 - Dec?, 1856 as Liverpool Photographic Journal.
--Jan, 1857 - Dec?, 1858 as Liverpool and Manchester Photographic Journal.
--Jan, 1859 - Dec, 1859 as Photographic Journal.
WITH SUPPLEMENT
--British Journal of Photography Annual, The [NA] Dec 15, 1859+.
--Lantern Record, The, Oct, 1892 - Dec, 1901.
--Colour Photography, Jan, 1907 - 1934.
LC: TR1.B8
ISSN: 0007-1196
ABST: --Art Index (ISSN: 0004-3222)
--Computer & Control Abstracts (ISSN: 0036-8113)
--Electrical & Electronics Abstracts (ISSN: 0036-8105)
--Physics Abstracts. Science Abstracts. Series A. (ISSN: 0036-8091)
--Printing Abstracts (ISSN: 0031-109x)
--World Surface Coating Abstracts (ISSN: 0043-9088)

British Kinematography

194u - Dec, 1965//
(ISSN: 0007-1358)
SEE: IMAGE TECHNOLOGY

British Kinematography, Sound and Television

Jan, 1966 - Dec, 1973//
(ISSN: 0373-109x)
SEE: IMAGE TECHNOLOGY

BRITISH LITHOGRAPHER

SUB: "A journal for lithographers, artists, draughtsmen, phototypers, steel & copper-plate engravers, etc." (Oct/Nov, 1891 - ?).
PUBL: Raithby, Lawrence & Co., Ltd., De Montfort Press, Queen St., Leicester, England.
DESC: What better way to start publication of a serial on lithography than to provide a frontispiece engraving of Senefelder (the father of lithography), and a full-color lithographic cover, as *British Lithographer* did for its first issue of Oct/Nov, 1891! The publisher provided typical news of new technology and technique. Of special note were bound lithographic prints of color checks, calendars, vegetable labels, and other ordinary uses for lithography. These made this serial such an important historical resource. Numerous illustrations, many in color.
DEPT: "Book Notes," "Trade Reports." (2/3-1895).
TYPL: "The Three-Colour Printing Process," "The Revival of Lithography as an Artistic Process," "Made in England or Abroad?," "German Collotype Printers." (2/3-1895).
SCHL: Bimonthly, 35 pp.
SPAN: Oct/Nov, 1891 - Aug/Sep, 1895//
ABSORBED BY
--British Printer, Sep, 1895.
LC: NE 2250.B7

✤ BRITISH PRINTER

SUB: "Official journal of the British Typographia." (Vol 1 - 4).
SUB: "Leading technical journal of the printing industry."
SUB: "A journal for the printing trades."
PUBL: Maclean-Hunter, 30 Old burlington St., London W1X 2AE, England.
DESC: Glossy news monthly for the production rooms of the British printing industry. A focus on new equipment, current technology and technique is evident in this lively periodical. A significant number of articles highlight economics, sales, and other management fuctions.
DEPT: "Leader," editorial; "Commentary," "Printers Bookshelf," "Research Notes," newsbriefs on new equipment; "New Machinery, Equipment and Materials," "Memories of a Journeyman," "Printing Industry News," newsbriefs. (3-71).
TYPL: "BSI Metric Type Measurement Standard," "When All Else Fails, Try Selling!," "Improved Machine Control and Faster Etching Times Metal and Chemicals," "The Cost of Plant Leasing," "Letter Spacing and Legibility." (3-71).
SCHL: Monthly, 130 pp.
SPAN: 1888+
ABSORBED
--British Bookmaker, Apr, 1894.
--British Lithographer, Oct, 1895.
--Printers' International Specimen Exchange, 1895.
LC: Z 119.B86
ISSN: 0007-1684
ABST: --Abstract Bulletin of the Institute of Paper Chemistry (ISSN: 0020-3033)
--Printing Abstracts (ISSN: 0031-109x)

✣ BROADCAST

SUB: "The industry's news magazine."
SUB: "For the new age of broadcasting."
SUB: "Incorporating Television Weekly."
PUBL: International Thomson Business Publishing, Central House, 27 Park St., Croydon CR0 1YD England.
DESC: *Broadcast* is a superb business tabloid providing thorough coverage of British broadcast and cable television activities in the fields of programming, regulation, technology, and economics. Each weekly issue thoroughly reports on the state of British communication while providing a rather unique international viewpoint to future trends in technology, programming, and distribution. While the majority of news concerns British communication, a more than fair look is afforded international broadcasting as well. One sampled issue included articles on the United States, Sweden, France, Germany, Australia, Canada, Netherlands, and Japan. Of special consideration are two departmental features. The first, "British Top 100," provides ranked program episode ratings for the preceeding week, including the previous week's rank, channel, day of air, audience (in millions) and the TVR. The second feature, "Ratings," expands the analysis into 11 categories (for a sampled March, 1991 issue), including "Hours of Viewing," "Audience Reach," "ITV Day/Night," "BBC 1," "BBC 2," "ITV," "Channel 4," "S4C All Viewers," S4C Welsh Speaking," "Breakfast Television," and "BBC Day/Night." An excellent resource for the state of the British broadcast arts. For the sampled issue of 1991: tabloid format (10 ¾ x 15 ¾ inches / 275 x 400 cm), numerous graphics, published on coated paper stock.
DEPT: "Comment," editorial; "News Focus," commentary; "Headliners," profile; "Letters," "Talkback," "In Production," "Technology," "Radio," "Creatives," "Broadcast Analysis," "Notebook," column by Sean Day-Lewis; "Monthly Ratings," "Events," calendar; "British Top 100," record chart; "Viewing Summary," ratings data. (9-9-88). "Newslines," newsbriefs; "Headliners," profile; "Franchise File," fascinating programming profile; "News Focus," "Letters," "Radio," "Technology," "Facilities," "Off Air," commentary; "Programming," "British Top 100," top 100 television programs for the week; "Ratings," detailed accounting for the preceeding week. (3-8-91).
TYPL: "United Cable Leads Super Channel Bid," "ACTT Rebels Talk to EETPU," "ITV and BBC Told Price is Not Right," "Radio Row in Jersey," "Yorkshire Snaps Up TWI Sports Show," "World Service Job Cuts to Continue, Says BBC," "Drama Out of a Crisis." (9-9-88). "Granada Joins Forces with Border for Tyne Tees Bid," "Independent Chases Big Five Licence," "Ealing Comedies for Sale," "Dromgoole to Quite Position in HTV Rejig," "Religious Code Reversed." (3-8-91).
SCHL: Weekly, 30 pp.
SPAN: 1973+
VARIES
--? - ? as Television Mail.
ABSORBED
--Television Weekly (ISSN: 0264-2905), ?
WITH SUPPLEMENT
--Invision (ISSN: 0951-5968), ?+.
ISSN: 0040-2788

✣ BROADCAST ACCOUNTING ALERT

PUBL: Miller, Kaplan, Arase & Co., Certified Public Accountants, 10911 Riverside Dr., North Hollywood, CA 91602.
DESC: Most media activities involve issues of selling and buying, profit and loss, but these are issues often missing in the trade press. Fortunately there is *Broadcast Accounting Alert*, a promotional newsletter by the firm of Miller, Kaplan, Arase & Company, Certified Public Accountants in North Hollywood, California. In one single four-page issue were discussions on overcoming price resistance, reduction of royalty fees for "Talk & Music" stations, radio formats which have shown dynamic upward profit trends, media loans, health group insurance, and the ever important topic of receivables. The broadcast clients of Miller, Kaplan, Arase & Company are well served by this most informative publication for broadcast management. Newsletter format; no graphics.
DEPT: None. (4-90).
TYPL: "Market Aging Recipients Experience 40% Decline in 90 Day and Over Receivables," "Oldies and Soft-Lite AC Formats Post Power Ratio Gains," "Television Programming--A Strategic Approach," "Full Service AM Stations Taking Steps to Cut Royalty Fees." (4-90).
SCHL: Monthly, 4 pp.
SPAN: ?+

✣ BROADCAST + TECHNOLOGY

SUB: "Keeping the broadcast professional informed."
PUBL: Diversified Publications, 6 Farmers Lane, Box 420, Bolton, Ontario L0P 1A0, Canada.
DESC: The primary focus of early issues under the title of *Broadcast Technology* was the Canadian broadcast technician. Articles covered a wide field of technical issues, problems and news in Canada. Of special note was the departmental feature, "Associations," providing brief activity summaries of members within Canadian engineering associations. The current *Broadcast + Technology* functions as an excellent business magazine of contemporary Canadian broadcasting; providing detailed news articles concerning topics from marketing to broadcast tower maintenance; radio programming to sales campaigns; Canadian legislative information to changing societal entertainment values. Of special note within *Broadcast + Technology* are a number of special departmental reports for Canadian trade associations, including the Central Canada Association of Broadcast Engineers, and the Canadian Institute for Theatre Technology. An excellent business publication for those interested in Canadian broadcasting and related enter-

tainment fields. For the sampled issue of 1991: stapled magazine format, full-color pages throughout on coated paper stock (8 ⅛ x 10 ⅞ inches / 205 x 275 mm).
DEPT: "Technitopics," column; "The Phil Stone Report," "Associations," "Stations in the News," "Ad-Lib!," newsbriefs; "Broadcast Beat," column; "Appointments," "New Products," "Business Report," "CRTC," legal decisions from Canadian Radio and Television Commission. (5/6- 83). "Calendar," "Industry News," newsbriefs; "Stations in the News," "CCBE Newsletter," news of the Central Canada Association of Broadcast Engineers, column by Bob Findlay; "Jerry Fairbridge," column by Jerry Fairbridge; "Howard Christensen," column by Howard Christensen; "Atlantic Airwaves," column by Sandra Porteous; "Broadcast Beat," column by Phil Stone; "Programming," column by Howard English; "SMPTE," report; "Discover," column by Howard English; "Theatre Technology," CITT news of the Canadian Institute for Theatre Technology, column by Paul Court; "The Phil Stone Report," column by Phil Stone; "Lighting Technology," STLD information column by Alf Hunter; "Associations," "Ad Lib!," column by Jacquie Loney; "Cable + Satellite News," "Broadcast Business," "People." (11/12-91).
TYPL: "Broadcast Teletext Signal Processing," "AM Stereo with Directional Arrays," "CCBE Engineering Newsletter," "Light Source," "First Use of Fibre Optics by CBC Television," "Can AM and FM Find Common Ground?" (5/6-83). "Montreal Graphic Designers Congress," "Promotion Overcomes Downtown Apathy--This Time," "Cinar Expands Montreal Facilities," "Understanding Your Research: What NOT to do," "Networking Rejuvenates Tired Marketing Practices." (11/12-91).
SCHL: Bimonthly, 70 pp.
SPAN: Sep/Oct, 1975+
VARIES
--Sep/Oct, 1975 - Dec, 1979 as Broadcast Equipment Today (ISSN: 0383-9338).
--Sep/Oct, 1979 - Sep, 1986 as Broadcast Technology (ISSN: 0709-9797).
DD: 384.54/0971
ISSN: 0709-9797

Broadcast Bibliophile Booknotes
Nov, 1969 - Aug, 1973//
(ISSN: 0045-3188)
SEE: COMMUNICATION BOOKNOTES

✢ BROADCAST CABLE FINANCIAL JOURNAL
SUB: "The official publication of the Institute of Broadcasting Financial management."
SUB: "The official publication of the Broadcast Financial Management Association."
PUBL: Broadcast Cable Financial Management Association, Suite 1010, 701 Lee St., Des Plaines, IL 60016.

DESC: "The Broadcast Cable Financial Management Association is a not-for-profit corporation organized in 1961 which is comprised of over 1,200 of broadcasting's and cable's top financial, MIS and personnel people, station general managers and other broadcasting and cable management people as well as associate members in the allied fields of auditing, data processing, sales and the law." In the commercial broadcast and cable industries where the bottom line means success or failure, the Broadcast Cable Financial Management Association and its publication, *Broadcast Cable Financial Journal*, are strong allies in the daily struggle not just to "make it," but to thrive amongst competitors. This is "the" publication for anyone working on the financial side of broadcast and cable operations. Expect well-written, well-illustrated reading on broadcast/cable economics, financing and accounting procedures. For the 1981 sampled issue: black ink on uncoated paper stock with three-color ink cover also on uncoated paper stock. For the 1988 sampled issue: black ink on uncoated paper stock with three-color ink cover on coated paper stock with some color advertising. Size for both issues: (8 ½ x 11 inches / 215 x 280 mm).
DEPT: None. (3-80). "BCA Update," news of Broadcast Credit Association; "BFM Member News," news of Broadcast Financial Management Association members. (1/2-88).
TYPL: "Survey of TV Station Business Automation Shows 85 Per Cent Rate it 'Good' or 'Excellent,'" "Business Automation Systems: They all do it Differently and They're All Busy Enhancing," "Ratings: an Aid to Programming and Purchase of TV Properties." (3-76). "Internship: Find Future Station Employees," "The Measure of Regulation: It's Expensive," "Debt: Get It Off the Balance Sheet." (3-80). "Trade and Barter, a Discussion of Internal Controls," "PC--Plenty Chaos," "Legal Preventive Maintenance," "Human Resources Management in Broadcasting." (1/2-88).
SCHL: Ten issues per year, 50 pp.
SPAN: Mar, 1972+
VARIES
--Mar, 1972 - ? as Broadcast Financial Journal (ISSN: 0161-9063).
LC: HE 8689.B74
DD: 384.54/3/0973

Broadcast Communications
? - Sep, 1983//
(ISSN: 0164-999x)
SEE: TELEVISION BROADCAST

✢ BROADCAST EDUCATOR NEWS NOTES
SUB: "BEA's individual membership newsletter published in September, December and March."
PUBL: Broadcast Education Association, 1771 N St., NW, Washington, DC 20036-2891.

DESC: This informal newsletter is for college/university faculty teaching in the area of radio and television. These readers also belong to and participate in the primary pedagogical association, the Broadcast Education Association. Majority of sample issue contained announcements of positions available at colleges and universities for the forthcoming academic year. Typewritten, photocopied newsletter format (8 ½ x 11 inches / 215 x 280 cm), stapled in corner; no graphics.
DEPT: None (4-90).
TYPL: "BEA Elections for Board of Directors Results," "Faculty Summer Internship Offered By Legend Communications' Larry Patrick," "BEA Committees Changes to Divisions." (4-90).
SCHL: Three issues per year [Sep, Dec, Mar], 15 pp.
SPAN: Sep, 1987?+

✣ BROADCAST ENGINEERING

SUB: "The journal of the broadcast communications industry."
PUBL: Intertec Publishing Co., PO Box 12901, Overland park, KS 66212.
DESC: Reflecting upon its thirtieth anniversary of publication, *Broadcast Engineering* noted its original May, 1959 editorial: "In this day of rapid technical developments, it is difficult to keep informed of the many technical phases of the industry. The goal of *Broadcast Engineering* is to bring to its readers as much technical information on current developments as possible so that all may benefit from these ideas, and to make that information available to everyone who desires it." Providing faithful service to the broadcast engineering community, *Broadcast Engineering* has provided a professional forum for the discussion of new technology, problem solving concerning current technology, and the development of a professional engineering staff. Of special note is the professional caliber of departmental features "FCC Update," "Strictly TV," "Re: Radio," "Satellite Technology," "Circuits," "Troubleshooting," and "Management for Engineers." Some articles assume considerable technical knowledge. For the sampled issue of 1989: well-illustrated with schematics, magazine format (8 x 10 ⅞ inches / 205 x 275 cm).
DEPT: "Direct Current," Washington, DC newsbriefs; "Industry News," briefs; "SBE News," communications column for members of the Society of Broadcast Engineers; "Globecasting," news of world-international broadcast developments; "People in the News," briefs; "Radio Workshop," unique articles concerning radio engineering. (4-78). "News," briefs; "Editorial," "FCC Update," "Strictly TV," "Re: Radio," "Satellite Technology," "Circuits," "Troubleshooting," "Management for Engineers," "Field Report," "SBE Update," "People," personnel briefs; "Business." (5-89).
TYPL: "Lighting is Your Best Shot at Better Production," "Digital VTRs: They Could Come as Early as 1980," "How to Make Automation a 'Genie,' Instead of a 'Ogre,'" "RENG: Creating Visual Images With Sound." (4-78). "Milestones in the Evolution of Technology," "Five Decades of Magnetic Tape," "The Future for Fiber," "AM Radio: Regrouping for the 21st Century," "UHF-TV: Breaking New Efficiency Records." (5-89).
SCHL: Monthly, 170 pp.
SPAN: May, 1959+
LC: TK 6540.B8433
ISSN: 0007-1994

BROADCAST ENGINEERS' JOURNAL, THE

SUB: "Official publication of the National Association of Broadcast Employees and Technicians."
PUBL: National Association of Broadcast Engineers and Technicians, Suite 1009, Investment Bldg., Washington, DC.
DESC: This serial provided a news, research, and issue forum for NABET members concerning broadcast engineering and union topics. Each issue supplied several articles pertaining to engineering or broadcast developments, but the majority of each 40 page monthly was devoted to membership news. Numerous graphics; some schematics.
DEPT: "Chapter Chatter," individual 'letters' detailing chapter events and news. (11-44).
TYPL: "DuMont Demonstrates Confidence in Television," "The Magnetically Focussed Radial Beam Vacuum Tube," "Summary of NABET-Petrillo Dispute," "Cleveland Chapter Shoots the Works." (11-44).
SCHL: Monthly, 40 pp.
SPAN: 1934 - Oct, 1952//
LC: TK 6540.B8435

Broadcast Equipment Exchange

Jul, 1977 - Jun, 1980//
(ISSN: 0194-2190)
SEE: RADIO WORLD

Broadcast Equipment Today

Sep/Oct, 1975 - Dec, 1979//
(ISSN: 0383-9338)
SEE: BROADCAST + TECHNOLOGY

Broadcast Financial Journal

Mar, 1972 - ?//
(ISSN: 0161-9063)
SEE: BROADCAST CABLE FINANCIAL JOURNAL

Broadcast News

Oct, 1931 - Feb, 1954//
SEE: RCA BROADCAST NEWS

Broadcast News

May, 1954 - Feb, 1968//
SEE: RCA BROADCAST NEWS

✤ BROADCAST PIONEERS LIBRARY REPORTS

SUB: "An occasional newsletter."
SUB: "A quarterly newsletter."
PUBL: Broadcast Pioneers Library, 1771 N St., N.W., Washington, DC 20036.
DESC: The newsletter of the Broadcast Pioneers Library may be published "quarterly, more or less," but its arrival is of great importance to broadcast historians as a means of showcasing new acquisitions at the BPL facility, discussing projects in progress, and the state of the library itself. A very unusual feature of the publication provides paragraph-long discussions of why individuals used the library facilities in the past quarter, thereby demonstrating the breadth of the holdings, while also reporting on projects of library patrons. Of special note are biographies of broadcast pioneers who have recently donated materials to the library. Some graphics of acquisitions. An important publication for broadcast historiography.
DEPT: "Editor's Essay," "Readers Tell Us," "Errata," "BPL Helped," Broadcast Pioneers Library users; "Gifts," "Other Friends," "Donors," "Volunteers," "Preservation," "Circulation," "Membership." (fall-89).
TYPL: "BPL's Oral Historian at Large," "BPL's Special Correspondent John Hickman Reports," "When ABC was Blue." (fall-89).
SCHL: Quarterly, 60 pp.
SPAN: Spring, 1975+
VARIES
--Spring, 1975 - ?, 1987? as Reports.

BROADCAST PROGRAMMING AND PRODUCTION

SUB: "The magazine of competitive radio-television broadcasting."
PUBL: Recording and Broadcast Publications, 1850 N. Whitley Ave., Suite 220, Box 2449, Hollywood, CA 90028.
DESC: This bimonthly is devoted to radio-TV production, covering areas of creativity, resources, marketing, and general "how-to" approaches. Typical issues include articles on producing radio-TV programs, or specific craft areas such as audio engineering for the Johnny Carson Tonight Show. Of special note is a continuing series, "More Basics of Competitive Production," providing "technical tricks of the trade." A most valuable publication for broadcast programmers and production staff.
DEPT: "Market Memoranda," individual market surveys concerning a particular programming format; "New Products and Services," news briefs; "Broadcast Buffoonery," broadcast cartoon series noteworthy as it is created column by Robert W. Morgen.
TYPL: "Dave Hull and Danny Dark on Commercial Voice-Overs," "Creative Programming with Automation," "Producing the Bob Newhart Show." (9-77).
SCHL: Bimonthly, 85 pp.
SPAN: Apr, 1975 - ?//
LC: PN 1992.75 .B75
DD: 384.54/05
ISSN: 0191-4898

BROADCAST REPORTER

PUBL: Broadcast Reporter, Inc., Barr Bldg., Washington, DC.
DESC: *Broadcast Reporter* supplied an interesting mixture of weekly news, programming developments, and personality columns covering the growth industry of radio and television during the American Depression. The tone of this serial was always upbeat, but also took errant broadcasters to task for illegal or immoral operations. This was a serial for the radio management team, and served its readers well.
DEPT: "Commission Docket for forthcoming Month," "Hearings During Past Week." (12-5-31). "Highlights of the News," "Trend of Radio Broadcasting," "Along Studio Street," 'program ideas for stations and advertisers'; "News of Radio Broadcasting," "Letters." (5-15-33).
TYPL: "Hoover, Charter Member of Radio Family, Retains Interest in Broadcasting," "Grounds Cited for Denying Columbia Booster Station," "30,000 Domestic Problems Submitted to Sisters of Skillet." (12-5-31). "Loud as Life and Twice as Natural," "Supreme Court Defines Authority of Federal Radio Commission," "There's an Audience Awaiting Novel Radioizations." (5-15-33).
SCHL: Weekly, (Nov 7, 1931 - Jan 2, 1933); Semimonthly, (Jan 15, 1933 - Jun 15, 1933), 40 pp.
SPAN: Nov 7, 1931 - Jun 15, 1933//
VARIES
--Nov, 1931 - Oct 8, 1932 as National Broadcast Reporter.
--Oct 17, 1932 - Jun, 1933 as Broadcast Reporter.
ABSORBED BY
--Broadcasting, Jul 1, 1933.
LC: TK 6540.B 845

Broadcast Reporter

Oct 17, 1932 - Jun, 1933//
SEE: BROADCAST REPORTER

Broadcast Sound

198u - Feb, 1985//
(ISSN: 0263-5682)
SEE: BROADCAST SYSTEMS ENGINEERING

✤ BROADCAST SYSTEMS ENGINEERING

PUBL: Link House, Dingwall Ave., Croydon CR9 2TA, England.
DESC: With a focus on technology and communication engineering, this international publication provides a good world view of new developments in equipment, problem solving, and production area design, form and function. Many articles profile actual facilities, providing detailed technical information of immediate use to readers. It maintains a continuing overview of new equipment developments at trade fairs and conventions world-wide, but its emphasis is on Great Britain. Articles assume technical knowledge.
DEPT: "Diary," 'Dates, locations and addresses of the important events this year'; "Spectrum," radio and audio newsbriefs; "Audio Equipment," new developments; "Scan," 'News, contracts and people from the TV and video industries'; "Video Equipment," reviews; "Test Report," test bench report. (3-87).
TYPL: "Signal Routing in a Digital Audio Studio," "Digital Video Effects," "Signal Processing," "The Digital Video Recorder." (3-87).
SCHL: Monthly.
SPAN: Oct, 1974?+
VARIES
--1982? - 198u as Professional Video (ISSN: 0264-1321).
--198u - Feb, 1985 as Broadcast Sound (ISSN: 0263-5682).
ISSN: 0267-565x

✤ BROADCAST SYSTEMS INTERNATIONAL

PUBL: Link House, Dingwall Ave., Croydon CR9 2TA England.
DESC: "*Broadcast Systems International* is published monthly and is available internationally to ...those being management and technical personnel professionally engaged in broadcasting, telecommunications and film or video post-production in any part of the world." Another in the quality lineup of Link House publications, "*Broadcast Systems International* provides in-depth coverage of current news, trends and developments within the professional television and sound broadcasting industries and allied fields." Like a number of other "international communication" publications, news coverage is international in scope, but with a decided domestic philosophical stance, which looks at international news developments from "domestic-colored glasses." This is an excellent publication for any broadcast professional, and indeed required reading in this day and age of international communication media. Glued-spine magazine format (8 ¼ x 11 ⅝ inches / 210 x 295 mm), full color throughout on coated paper stock.
DEPT: "Editorial," "Industry News," "Company News," "User Profile," "Focus," "The Barry Fox Column," column by Barry Fox; "Company Profile," "Product Update," "Comment." (3-91).
TYPL: "Astra 1B Launch Success Further Threatens D-MAC," "HDTV: Uncoding the World's Standards," "War News by Satellite," "Matsushita--The Sleepy Giant Wakes," "European HDTV." (3-91).
SCHL: Monthly, 60 pp
SPAN: ?+
ISSN: 0959-5813

Broadcast Technology

Sep/Oct, 1979 - Sep, 1986//
(ISSN: 0709-9797)
SEE: BROADCAST + TECHNOLOGY

✤ BROADCASTER

SUB: "The magazine for communicators."
SUB: "Canada's communications magazine."
SUB: "Serving Canada's Communications Industry."
PUBL: Southam Business Communications, Inc., 1450 Don Mills Rd., Don Mills, ON M3B 2X7 Canada.
DESC: Founded by Richard G. Lewis in 1942, *Broadcaster*, the Canadian news monthly, covers the business side of broadcasting. Corporate changes, networks, sales, programming, and other elements that contribute to the profit margin are covered here, as well as news of state-run communication systems. This is a publication for management, providing thorough coverage on the events of the present, and the possibilities for the future of Canadian broadcasting and cable television. Commencing with the March, 1991 issue, *Broadcaster* is under a new publisher with a new layout design and a significant number of spot color and full-color pages. Articles often appear under a variety of subtitled topics including, "Facilities," "Markets," "Analysis," and "Technology." Editorially speaking, the issue of American/Canadian competition is never far from the surface of many articles. Editor Ted Davis, in the newly redesigned March, 1991 issue, spoke of "culture taxes" being levied in the fight to retain Canadian identity against the onslaught of American media. This is one issue certain to stir passions on both sides of the border, and *Broadcaster* serves an important function in airing the elements of that continuing struggle to raise American consciousness, retain cultural purity, and enlarge opportunities for Canadian nationals in the finite broadcast programming schedule. For this and other reasons *Broadcaster* is an important publication to today's North American broadcaster. For sampled issue of 1991: stapled magazine format, spot and full-color pages on coated paper stock (8 ⅛ x 10 ⅞ inches / 205 x 275 mm).

DEPT: "News," briefs; "Roundup," station news; "Engineering and Equipment," "On the Move," personnel briefs; "Sales Report," equipment sales; "CRTC Decisions," briefs of Canadian Radio-TV Commission; "Cable," newsbriefs; "People-Promo," briefs. (6-77). "Editorial," "Your Turn," guest editorial; "Special Events," calendar; "Short-Takes," newsbriefs; "Update," newsbriefs; "Programming," newsbriefs; "New Products," "People," personnel briefs; "Industry Clips," news items; "See, Hear," commentary column by John Porteous. (3-87). "Special Events Calendar," "Editorial," column by Ted Davis; "Tech Talk," newsbriefs; "New Products," reviews; "Broadcast News," newsbriefs. (3-91).

TYPL: "His English Friends are cautious. . .His French Friends Don't Have the Money," "Video Cassettes Show Greatest Market Potential," "West Germany Debates Electronic Newspapers," "Advocacy Advertising. . . the Hot Issue." (6-77). "Trends and Tastes," "Brave New Airwaves," "Research--the C-Fax Edge," "Westwood One Canada," "Troiano on Television." (3-87). "Radio Repatriation: Canadian Border Stations Try to Woo Listeners and Advertisers Away From U.S. Broadcasters," "Maritime Make-Over: California Architecture Characterizes the New Home of Two East Coast Radio Stations," "Welcome to Hog High: Toronto's CHOG Radio Lures a Youthful Audience with 'Maximum Grunt' Programming," "Syndication Sentence: A Recent Survey Points to the Probable Future of Syndicated Radio Programs Under the New FM Regulations." (3-91).

SCHL: Monthly, 35 pp.
SPAN: Jan, 1942+
VARIES
--Jan, 1942 - Sep, 1969 as Canadian Broadcaster, The (ISSN: 0319-1389).
WITH SUPPLEMENT
--Playlist, The, ? - ?
LC: HE 8699.C
ISSN: 0008-3038
ABST: --Canadian Business Index (ISSN: 0227-8669)

Broadcasters News Bulletin
? - Mar 4, 1933//
SEE: NARTB MEMBER SERVICE

✢ BROADCASTING
SUB: "The weekly newsmagazine of radio."
SUB: "The newsweekly of broadcasting and allied arts."
SUB: "The news magazine of the fifth estate."
SUB: "The businessweekly of radio and television."
PUBL: Broadcasting Publications, Inc., 1705 DeSales Street NW, Washington, DC 20036.
DESC: "*Broadcasting* subscribers already know that each issue opens the door to a world of news, interviews, commentary and more. You get the unmatched experience and perspective of *Broadcasting*, with its almost 60 years of experience covering the hard news of the industry, combined with an award-winning design that's easy on the eye." *Broadcasting* long ago emerged as "The" authoritative voice of newsworthy developments in the broadcast and allied arts field. Begun as a semimonthly radio trade paper in 1931, publisher Sol Taishoff soon promoted it as the news magazine of the fifth estate. *Broadcasting* became a weekly publication in 1941, and expanded into the new media of television, and cable. This remains an authoritative business weekly publication which reports communication news and important issues of the day in a clear, concise manner, a journalistic tradition which has earned it the title of "the" business news magazine of the broadcast industry. Of special note among a myriad of industry "must-reads" are "Closed Circuit," a wonderful resource for what is being said around town; "Datebook," one of the most extensive events calendars in the electronic media field; "Changing Hands," a very informative record of purchase/sales information concerning broadcast outlets; and "For the Record," subtitled "filings, authorizations and other FCC actions." Very highly recommended. For sampled issue of 1991: stapled magazine format, full- color pages throughout on coated paper stock (8 ⅛ x 10 ⅞ inches / 205 x 275 mm).

DEPT: "The Week in Brief," news outline for the reader short on time; "Closed Circuit," billed as 'insider report, behind the scene, before the fact;' "Business Briefly," "Monday Memo," guest column on advertising; "Where Things Stand," an excellent feature billed as a 'status report on major issues in electronic communications;' "Open Mike," letters column important for responses; "Changing Hands," radio-TV stations sold; "Playlist," popular song playlist; "Fates and Fortunes," personnel briefs; "For the Record," detailed FCC actions for the week; "Stock Index," over 100 publicly-held companies listed; "Profiles," of a major broadcast executive. (1/89).

TYPL: "Radio and TV Moving Toward Home-Grown Ratings Service," "Black Eyes for ABC, CBS at Sports Hearings," "Money's the Real Problem say Comments on FCC 45-Day Proposal," "Cable to Put It's Best Foot Forward in San Diego." (11-77). "ESPN Gets to 'Play Ball' for $400 Million," "Dingell Reintroduces Fairness Doctrine Bill," "Independents: Upbeat and Giving No Ground," "Harnessing Radio's Strengths for Television." (1-89).

SCHL: Semimonthly (Oct 15, 1931 - Jan, 1941); Weekly (Jan 13, 1941 to date, with a combined issue at year's end), 70 pp.
SPAN: Oct 15, 1931+
VARIES
--Oct 15, 1931 - Feb 1, 1933 as Broadcasting.
--Feb 15, 1933 - Jun 15, 1936 as Broadcasting, Combined With Broadcast Advertising.
--Jul 1, 1936 - Nov 19, 1945 as Broadcasting, Broadcast Advertising.
--Nov 26, 1945 - Oct 7, 1957 as Broadcasting, Telecasting.
ABSORBED
--Broadcast Advertising, Feb 15, 1933.

--Broadcast Reporter, Jul 1, 1933.
--Television, Oct, 1968.
LC: TK 6540.B85
DD: 621 11
ISSN: 0007-2028
ABST: --ABI/Informer
--Biography Index (ISSN: 0006-3053)
--Business Periodical Index (ISSN: 0007-6961)
--InfoBank
--Predicasts
--Public Affairs Information Service Bulletin (ISSN: 0033-3409)
--Trade and Industry Index

Broadcasting
Oct 15, 1931 - Feb 1, 1933//
SEE: BROADCASTING

✤ BROADCASTING ABROAD
SUB: "Covering the international media world: TV, radio cable and satellites."
PUBL: Broadcasting Publications, Inc., 1705 DeSales St., NW, Washington, DC 20036.
DESC: What *Broadcasting* does for the American broadcast community, *Broadcasting Abroad* very capably accomplishes for the international field; thorough, reliable coverage of international electronic media. The emphasis here is on people, the "movers and shakers" of the corporate electronic world; what they and their corporate staffs are accomplishing in the ever-competitive bid to be first and best. Interviews are interspersed with news of business deals and dealings, both successful and not. Also prominent are news items concerning regulation, advertising, programming, and technology. This is crisp, authoritative journalism. *Broadcasting Abroad* utilizes the same format style as sister publication, *Broadcasting*. For the sampled issue of 1991: stapled magazine format (8 ⅛ x 11 inches / 205 x 275 mm) on coated paper stock with numerous color pages throughout.
DEPT: "Fates & Fortunes," personnel newsbriefs; "Distant Signals," newsbriefs. (5-91).
TYPL: "What Cable Could Be in 2000: 500 Channels," "Market is Key in UK Telco-Cable Debate," "International Program Market Shows Industry's Underlying Strengths," "Prime Time Network Schedulers," "Canadian Broadcasting Corporation's Gerard Veilleux: Setting the Course." (5- 91).
SCHL: Monthly, 65 pp.
SPAN: Jan, 1989+

✤ BROADCASTING AND THE LAW
SUB: "Reports and interprets current court and FCC rulings affecting broadcasting practice and operations."
SUB: "A report on broadcast rules and regulations presented by Broadcasting and the Law, Inc., a wholly owned company of the partners of Leibowitz & Spencer, a law firm practicing in the area of communications law."
PUBL: Broadcasting and the Law, 3050 Biscayne Blvd., Suite 501, Miami, FL 33137.
DESC: "A twice-a-month newsletter that reports and interprets current court and FCC rulings affecting broadcasting practice and operations." This is an excellent legal newsletter for the communications industry, reporting on new developments affecting radio, television and cable operations. A unique question-and-answer (Q&A) format makes for a very readable publication, and at times almost seems like the reader is having a private conversation with his legal representative. For the sampled issue of 1988: three-hole punched newsletter format, black ink on color uncoated paper stock, no advertising (8 ½ x 11 inches / 215 x 280 mm). A valuable asset for communications management.
DEPT: None. (12-15-88).
TYPL: "Contests: Has the FCC Adopted a New Rule Governing Contests Conducted by Broadcasters?," "Posting Operating Instructions: Where Must Instructions to 'Lesser Grade Operators' as to Proper Transmitter Operation be Posted?," "Announcements of Effective Radiated Power: Are FM Stations Allowed to Add the Powers of Vertical and Horizontal Polarization and Announce the Sum as the Station's Operating Power?" (10-76). "AM Overhaul," "Foreign Lanaguage Programs," "Low Power Television," "Ownership Rules." (12-15-88).
SCHL: Semimonthly, 4 pp.
SPAN: 1971+
VARIES
--1971 - Dec 1, 1984 as Perry's Broadcasting and the Law (ISSN: 0161-5823).
LC: KF 2801.A3 P47
DD: 343.73/09945
ISSN: 0161-5823

Broadcasting, Broadcast Advertising
Jul 1, 1936 - Nov 19, 1945//
SEE: BROADCASTING

Broadcasting, Combined With Broadcast Advertising
Feb 15, 1933 - Jun 15, 1936//
SEE: BROADCASTING

Broadcasting Systems & Operations
1978 - Mar, 1980//
SEE: INTERNATIONAL BROADCASTING

Broadcasting, Telecasting
Nov 26, 1945 - Oct 7, 1957//
SEE: BROADCASTING

✣ BROADSIDE
SUB: "Newsletter of the Theatre Library Association."
PUBL: Theatre Library Association, 111 Amsterdam Ave., New York, NY 10023.
DESC: "Broadside" serves as a newsworthy resource for librarians specializing in the field of legitimate theatre. The four-page quarterly provides details on collectables, seminars and changes in personnel within the organization. This is a reliable resource for historians and contemporary researchers alike. Focus of the publication is on member news, activities, and especially management of collections. Typical articles drawn from the 1984 - 1986 time period included an off-off Broadway exhibition; a report on Shakespeare's lost years; a new home for London's Raymond Mander and Joe Mitchenson Theatre Collection; and the process of managing theatre collections. Issue emphasis is on book reviews for adoption consideration. An excellent resource and association for those concerned with managing information materials of current and historical theatre. For the sampled issues of 1981: black ink on color uncoated paper stock. The sampled issue of 1987: black ink on coated paper stock with numerous pictures of collections and association activities. Both sampled issues were (8 ½ x 11 inches / 215 x 280 mm).
DEPT: "Books Received," "People," "Book Reviews," "Exhibitions." (spring-84).
TYPL: "TLA Presents Book Awards at Gala Celebration," "1984 American Film Festival." (spring-84).
SCHL: Quarterly, 4 pp.
SPAN: May, 1940+
DD: 026.792
ISSN: 0068-2748

Broadway Magazine
Apr, 1898 - Nov, 1907//
SEE: HAMPTON MAGAZINE

BROADWAY SIGN POST
SUB: "The sign post shows all the roads--the choice lies with the traveler." (Feb 5, 1949 - ?).
SUB: "A monthly review of current plays and motion pictures." (Feb 5, 1949 - ?).
PUBL: D.F. Mendola, 236 West 55th St., New York, NY.
DESC: As befits its subtitle, the purpose of this small format, mimeographed serial was to provide short reviews of current theatrical plays and motion pictures. The focus was on theatre, always with a special section listing current offerings by theatre, telephone number, curtain time, etc. No graphics, except front cover.
DEPT: "Broadway at a Glance," theatre listings. (3-49).

TYPL: None.
SCHL: Weekly [Oct - May] (Oct 30, 1930 - May, 1948); Monthly, 16 pp.
SPAN: Oct 30, 1930 - ?//?
VARIES
--Oct 30, 1930 - May, 1948 as Margaret Wentworth's Sign Post.
SUSPENDED
--Jun, 1948 - Jan, 1949.
--Jun, 1950 - Oct, 1951.
LC: PN 2000.B7

✣ BROADWAY WEEKLY
SUB: "The most beautiful weekly paper in the world." (Feb 18, 1903 - ?).
PUBL: Broadway Magazine Co., 121 West 42nd St., New York, NY.
DESC: This is another example of the "Broadway" magazines that addressed a mixture of Broadway theatrical performers and plays, as well as scenes of New York City societal life. As the editors stated in their initial offering: "*Broadway Weekly* has but one definite object in view--to fitly represent the busy, pulsating life of the metropolis...It will mirror New York life--but only its interesting, beautiful and amazing sides." That segment devoted to the Broadway stage served up quality treatment in full-size photos and flattering reviews of performers and performances. At the least, this was an interesting serial of the co- status of New York society and the legitimate stage. Numerous graphics; large magazine format.
DEPT: "Heard Along Broadway," gossip; "Plays and Players of the Week," "At the Theatres," listing. (4-16-03).
TYPL: "An Intimate Interview with Marie Cahill," "The Truth About Klaw & Erlanger and Martin Harvey." (4-16-03).
SCHL: Weekly, 20 pp.
SPAN: Feb 18, 1903+?
LC: AP 2.B843

✣ BULGARIAN FILMS
SUB: "Organ of the Bulgarian Cinematography State Corporation." (1983+).
PUBL: Bulgarian Cinematography State Corporation, 135-A Rakovski St., Sofia, Bulgaria.
DESC: *Bulgarian Films* emphasizes the Bulgarian film industry, with film reviews, talent/director profiles, interviews and information on new product releases. Initial issues were consumer oriented, with latter issues being letter-press printed, some color photographs, and a move from consumer-orientation to film criticism and comment. Quality of printed pictures leaves much to be desired. Editions in English, French, Russian and Spanish.
DEPT: "Comments from Abroad," lengthy letters; "Interview," "New Releases."

TYPL: "How We Made Films," "First Lesson," "Cartoon Films," "Foreign Comments on Bulgarian Films." (#1-60). "1983 Problems and Prospective Results," "A Surge of Tenderness," "Destiny," "Last Wishes." (#1-83).
SCHL: Eight issues per year, 20 pp.
SPAN: 1960+
DD: 791
ISSN: 0204-8884

✤ BULGARSKO FOTO
SUB: "A journal of photographic art, technique, and photo-journalism."
PUBL: Komitet za Izkustvo i Kultura, 39, Dondukov Blvd., Sofia, Bulgaria.
DESC: Most sources indicate that this publication provides "Summaries in English, French, German, and Russian." In the sampled issues, these summaries were very brief: one page contained all four language summaries for all the articles. Summaries oftentimes were no more than two sentences in length. A wide array of photographs beautifully printed on high-gloss paper that needs no language accompaniment is part of the serial.
SCHL: Ten issues per year.
SPAN: 1966+
LC: TR 1.B835
ISSN: 0007-4012

✤ BULLETIN
PUBL: Academy of Motion Picture Arts and Sciences, 8949 Wilshire Blvd., Beverly Hills, CA 90211.
DESC: "The Bulletin of the Academy of Motion Picture Arts and Sciences is designed to provide information about the full range of Academy activities and other newsworthy developments in the film world." The four-page newsletter is liberally enhanced with photos.
DEPT: None.
TYPL: "Friedkin to Produce 49th Awards Show," "Academy's Film Collection Store in Hollywood Hills," "Four Student film Awards Set for May 15." (Winter-77).
SCHL: Irregular, 4 pp.
SPAN: 1928+
VARIES
--1928 - 1946 as Academy of Motion Picture Arts and Sciences. Bulletin.
SUSPENDED
--Apr, 1981+

Bulletin
? - Spring, 1979//
SEE: CSPAA BULLETIN

Bulletin
1945? - Dec?, 1957?//
SEE: JOURNALISM EDUCATOR, THE

Bulletin. ASMP
? - ?//
(ISSN: 0361-9168)
SEE: ASMP BULLETIN

Bulletin d'Informations
May, 1949 - Oct, 1965//
SEE: FIEJ-BULLETIN

Bulletin of ALPSP
1977 - ?//
(ISSN: 0260-9428)
SEE: LEARNED PUBLISHING

BULLETIN OF PHOTOGRAPHY
SUB: "A weekly magazine for the professional photographer." (Aug 14, 1907 - ?).
SUB: "The portrait and commercial weekly." (? - Jun 24, 1931).
SUB: "Oldest photographic weekly in America." (? - Jun 24, 1931).
SUB: "The business magazine for portrait, commercial and industrial photographers." (? - Jun 24, 1931).
PUBL: 636 Franklin Square, Philadelphia, PA.
DESC: The *Bulletin of Photography* was published for the professional photographer, and furnished commentary and essays on sales, place of business, office configuration, retail sales, etc. The usual technical talks about chemicals, papers, lenses, and other apparatus is not in this serial. If there was an emphasis, it was on the portrait photographer, and professional photographer of industrial, and societal scenes. The publisher took care not to print on opposite pages of the serial when a photograph or other important item was printed. Numerous graphics.
DEPT: "News and Notes." (10-16-07). "The Chief's Column," "The Conventions to Come," "Print Analysis Department," critique; "Items of Interest," 'by an old timer;' "Necrology." (5-6-31).
TYPL: "Some Remarks on Pictures by Garo," "It is So Safe to Condemn a Photograph," "Broad Lighting-Perfection Lamp-Luxo Powder." (10-16-07). "The Woman Photographer's Point of View," "Another Automatic Studio is Invented," "In Which Somebody--Not You--Gets a Scolding." (5-6-31).
SCHL: Weekly, 25 pp.
SPAN: Aug 14, 1907 - Jun 24, 1931//
ABSORBED
--Photographer, The, Nov, 1907.
--St. Louis & Canadian Photographer, Jan, 1910.

ABSORBED BY
--Camera, The, Jul, 1931.
LC: TR 1.B85

✤ BULLETIN OF THE AMERICAN SOCIETY OF NEWSPAPER EDITORS, THE

PUBL: American Society of Newspaper Editors, 11600 Sunrise Valley Drive, Reston, VA 22091.
DESC: The *Bulletin* provides a forum through which society members learn of news developments, personnel changes, and the art/technique of newspaper editing. Articles never lack for critical bite in approaching such diverse topics as hiring minorities, press freedom, and other issues of interest to ASNE (American Society of Newspaper Editors) membership. Typical articles during 1991 included the impact of 900 telephone numbers on newsrooms and reporting; how newspaper organizations are coping with "Repetitive Stress Injuries"; the nurturing of minority students within graphics departments; first amendment freedoms; and the ways in which personal computers may aid reporting skills. For the sampled issue of 1991: stapled, square-magazine format, black ink on coated paper stock, cover consisting of black ink with spot color (8 x 9 ⅞ inches / 205 x 250 mm).
DEPT: "Books and Speeches," reviews; "The Bulletin Board," letters and newsbriefs; "A Shot Across the Masthead," opinion; "The Back Page," guest column. (12-87).
TYPL: "Newspaper Reporter Added to Press Pool--but Problems Persist," "Journalist Groups Arguing Over Need for Strong Ethics Codes," "Keep Your Eyes Open; You'll Know Unethical Behavior When You See It." (12- 87).
SCHL: Monthly [except May/Jun, Jul/Aug, and Sep/Oct] (? - ?); Nine issues per year (?+), 30 pp.
SPAN: 1923+
LC: PN 4700 .A58
ISSN: 0003-1178

✤ BULLETIN OF THE ASSOCIATION FOR BUSINESS COMMUNICATION, THE

SUB: "A publication of the American Business Communication Association."
PUBL: American Business Communication Association, University of Illinois, English Building, 608 S. Wright St., Urbana, IL 61801.
DESC: The *ABCA Bulletin* and its successor, *Bulletin of the Association for Business Communication*, hold interest for working professionals desirous of developing their writing, teaching and speaking skills. The focus is on the process of communication within the corporate arena, the means and style by which individuals create written materials for circulation or public offering. Topics include personalized business letters, corporate annual reports, committee papers, writing memorandums and other research functions important to a successful organization. Some articles are aimed at those involved in the educational process. For the sampled 1978 issue: perfect-bound magazine format, black ink on uncoated paper stock with black ink on various color uncoated paper stock for cover, no advertising (8 ¼ x 10 ¾ inches / 205 x 275 mm).
DEPT: "Purrs and Growls," comment; "News and Notes," "Bulletin Board." (3- 83).
TYPL: "Managing the Large Business Communication Class," "Use Numbers to Demonstrate the Control of Emphasis in Written Messages," "Coping with Communication Anxiety: Strategies to Reduce Writing Apprehension," "A Collobrative Learning Model: The Rhetorical Situation as a Basis for Teaching Business Communication." (3-83).
SCHL: Eight issues per year (May, 1937 - May, 1959); Six issues per year (Oct, 1959 - May, 1967); Quarterly (1969+), 60 pp.
SPAN: May, 1937+
SUSPENDED
--Jun, 1967 - 1968?
VARIES
--May, 1937 - May, 1967 as ABWA Bulletin.
--1969 - Dec, 1984 as ABCA Bulletin, The (ISSN: 0001-0383).
DD: 658
ISSN: 8756-1972

Bulletin of the Association of Departments & Administrators in Speech Communication

Oct, 1972 - Apr, 1975//
SEE: ACA BULLETIN

Bulletin of the Columbia Scholastic Press Advisors Association

Summer, 1979 - ?//
SEE: CSPAA BULLETIN

BURR MCINTOSH MONTHLY, THE

PUBL: Burr McIntosh Co., 20 W. 33rd St., Manhattan, NY.
DESC: This is, quite simply, a long- format magazine of McIntosh photos. It is meant to be a photographic feast of society portraits, landscapes, and other items of interest. In its only editorial copy, the editors note that "some of our readers, or maybe they are just 'lookers,' have criticized our lack of reading matter. Personally, I think it is a waste of good material to print reading matter on this costly paper, when it is possible to receive our beautiful reproductions."
DEPT: None.

TYPL: None.
SCHL: Monthly, 25 pp.
SPAN: Apr, 1903 - May, 1910//
LC: TR 1.B9

BUSINESS ADVERTISING

SUB: "Published by the Printers' Ink Network of magazines."
PUBL: Decker Communications, 501 Madison Ave., New York, NY 10022.
DESC: This serial contributed answers to an area long neglected by the advertising community; how to effectively market and advertise industrial products to the industry one serves. Readers will find no consumer preference surveys, or societal trend essays in these pages. *Business Advertising* was dedicated to the premise of explaining, supporting, and stimulating industrial advertising; that a transistor can look just as appealing as a can of baked beans. An excellent resource for the industrial marketing manager. graphics; magazine format.
DEPT: "Trendletter," "Media News and Views," "Publisher's View," "Messner on Business Ads," critique column by Fred Messner; "Editorials," "After Hours," guest column. (4-67).
TYPL: "Dilemma of Business Papers: Too Good for Their Own Good?," "New Research Method Measures Effect of Business-Paper Ads," "Sporty Cars Spark Spritely Ads." (4-67).
SCHL: Monthly, 50 pp.
SPAN: Mar, 1964 - Aug, 1967//
LC: HF 5801.B8

Business and Home TV Screen

Jan, 1978 - Feb, 1979//
SEE: COMPUTER PICTURES

✤ BUSINESS AND THE MEDIA

PUBL: The Media Institute, 3017 M St., N.W., Washington, DC 20007.
DESC: This thrice-yearly newsletter provides updates on news of the Media Institute, which is "...an independent, nonprofit research foundation based in Washington, D.C., working for more comprehensive, analytical and balanced media coverage of business and economic affairs. The Media Institute publishes studies analyzing media coverage of major issues. The Institute also sponsors and participates in numerous other programs encouraging open discussion of media-related issues, both domestic and international."
DEPT: "Making News," newsbriefs; "Staff Changes," "Upcoming Projects." (winter-85/86).

TYPL: "Time to Abolish Cable Franchise Process, New Issue Paper Argues," "TV Coverage of Budget Debate Lacked Comprehensiveness, Balance, Study Finds," "Monograph Explores New Communications Technologies." (winter-85/86).
SCHL: Three issues per year, 4 pp.
SPAN: Fall, 1979+
VARIES
--Fall, 1979 as Newsletter - Media Institute (ISSN: 0270-3564).
LC: HD 59 .B869
DD: 302.2/34
ISSN: 0270-3572

✤ BUSINESS COMMUNICATIONS REVIEW

PUBL: BCR Enterprises, Inc., 950 York Rd., Hinsdale, IL 60521.
DESC: To paraphrase a well-known saying, the business of *Business Communications Review* IS business communications; from pbx systems to voice messaging, Local Area Networks (LANs), ISDN, pricing structures, international developments, consultants, tests and trends. The focus of this telecommunication publication is on the process and application of corporate business communication via electronic means. An excellent review of the current status of business communications both on a domestic and international basis.
DEPT: "Doing Business Electronically," column by John McQuillan; "Washington Perspective," column by Victor J. Toth; "Net Management Directions," column by James Herman; "Consultant's Corner," column by richard A. Kuehn; "Memo From the Publisher," "Editorial," "Briefing," excellent compilation of late-breaking news in business communication; "Buyer's Blueprint," "Technology Trends," "New Products," "Messaging," voice message applications and commentary; "BCR Seminars," upcoming. (10-89).
TYPL: "Centrex--Caterpillar or Butterfly?," "Is ISDN Too Little, Too Late?," "Planning for Battle: Network Services Agreements," "The EIA's New Cabling and Building Architectural Standards." (10-89).
SCHL: Monthly, 105 pp.
SPAN: Jan?, 1971+
LC: HF 5717.B87
DD: 658.4/5/05
ISSN: 0162-3885
ABST: --ABI/Informer

✤ BUSINESS INFORMATION ALERT

SUB: "What's new in business publications, databases and research techniques."
PUBL: Alert Publications, Inc., 399 West Fullerton Parkway, Chicago, IL 60614.

DESC: For the specialized field of business library and information management, *Business Information Alert* comes highly recommended for describing monthly "what's new in business publications, databases and research techniques." This area of information management has developed into an almost obligatory "data-on-demand" setting for most American- based corporations. Information is valuable, and perhaps even critical to the corporate bottom line, as long as the location of that data and method of accessibility is known to the special business librarian. The value of *Business Information Alert* is its concise, informative, and readily applicable information about resources for any corporate environment. New publication or service reviews, which are the heart of this monthly newsletter, consist of thoughtful, considered critiques accompanied by the contributor's evaluation of the publication to the business workplace. The back page lists names, addresses and telephone numbers for publishers of reviewed items in each issue. A most helpful resource in the race to maintain the "corporate edge." Subscription price for 1991: $135 per year. Three- hole punched and stapled magazine format, two-color blue and black inks on uncoated paper stock, no advertising (8 ½ x 11 inches / 215 x 280 mm).
DEPT: "From the Editor," "For Your Information," "Database Report," "New Publications," extensive and helpful review section; "Calendar," upcoming events of interest to special librarians. (5-91).
TYPL: "Information Sources for the Green Market," "Legal Advice for Managers," "Traveler's Rights Video," "Chicago Tribune on CD-ROM," "New Political Libraries Inaugurate Campaign Season on NEXIS." (5-91).
SCHL: Ten issues per year, 12 pp.
SPAN: Jan, 1989+
DD: 025
ISSN: 1042-0746

✦ BUSINESS MARKETING

SUB: "The newsmonthly of advertising and selling to business, industry and the professions."
PUBL: Crain Communications, Inc., 740 Rush St., Chicago, IL 60611.
DESC: Heralding the name change from *Industrial Marketing* to that of *Business Marketing*, Editor Bob Donath told readers in the April, 1983 issue, "We changed our name because of you readers. You are selling new ideas and new technologies, and using more sophisticated tools to do it." This updated title continued the same fine tradition of "business-to-business" marketing begun by G. D. Crain Jr., as founder of Crain Communication and *Industrial Marketing* magazine. For corporations whose livlihoods depends upon the marketing of their products and services to other businesses, this periodical remains a prime resource in the promotion, marketing, and sale of business products. For the sampled issue of 1991: full-color pages and cover on coated paper stock, advertising (8 ⅛ x 10 ⅞ inches / 205 x 275 mm).

DESC: [Industrial Marketing]: As the title implied, this periodical detailed how American industries promoted themselves through various print and electronic media. Emphasis was on the advertising of industrial products and image, with other articles covering in-house and non-advertising media.
DEPT: "Newsbriefs," "Meetings," "Market Info," briefs; "Marketing Mix," media briefs; "Copy Chasers," features concerning unique copy approaches; "Perspectives," column; "International Newsletter," news review; "Books," review. (2-83). "FrontTALK," managing editor column by Steve Yahn; "Marketing Monitor," newsbriefs; "Business Media Update," new publications; "Forum," guest commentary. (12-91).
TYPL: "European Ads have Improved IM's Young Tells EurAm Meeting," "Nippon Electric Hits Jackpot with Color Ads," "Communicating with Business Markets in Latin America," "IPC Uses a Craftsmanship Theme to Sell Custom Capabilities." (2-83). "Conner Cracks a Tough Nut," "A Really Big Show," "The New European Order," "Copy Chasers," "Key Players." (12-91).
SCHL: Monthly, 70 pp.
SPAN: Jan, 1915+
VARIES
--Jan, 1915 - Feb, 1927 as Class.
--Mar, 1927 - Jun, 1933 as Class & Industrial Marketing.
--Jun, 1935 - Mar, 1983 as Industrial Marketing (ISSN: 0019-8498).
SUSPENDED
--Jul, 1933 - May, 1934.
SUPPLEMENT TO
--Advertising, Jul, 1933 - May, 1935.
LC: HF 5801.I45
DD: 658.8/005
ISSN: 0745-5933
ABST: --ABI/Informer
--Accountants' Index. Supplement. (ISSN: 0748-7975)
--Business Periodical Index (ISSN: 0007-6961)
--Industrial Arts Index
--InfoBank
--Management and Marketing Abstracts (ISSN: 0308-2172)
--Predicasts

✦ BUSINESS OF FILM, THE

SUB: "Finance, distribution, marketing."
PUBL: Brook Press Ltd., 56 Grosvenor St., London W.1, England.
DESC: An excellent British serial designed with the premise that the business of motion pictures and television production is profit, this monthly London-based magazine stands as an informative news medium of developments, trends, and personnel changes in a volatile industry. This is a publication which tackles contemporary business issues and trends. Subjects have included "Violence and the Media -- In-depth study of the effects of violence in the movies. Should we have a responsibility?;" "I.S.A.'s -- International

Sales Agents. Who are they? How do they operate? How are they financed?;" and "Tax Incentives World-Wide -- Tax incentives available to filmmakers around the world." The sampled issue for June/July, 1991 was a special tribute to black filmmakers worldwide. *The Business of Film* provided excellent profiles of blacks working at all levels of the industry under articles such as "Reversing Stereotypes," Innovators," "Behind Cameras," "Legal Framework," and "Product Profile." This special issue of consciousness- raising clearly points to the important positions held by blacks throughout the motion picture world. Available by subscription only, a one year (for 1991) order costs £90 sterling for the UK and Europe, £130 sterling for Australia, Middle and Far East, and $175 for American and Canadian subscribers. While this may appear to be a steep price for four issues, the timely, insightful information found here will more than pay for itself in today's very competitive world entertainment market. In short, for any production firm or producer, *The Business of Film* is not an option. For sampled issue of 1991: stapled magazine format, editorial content is black ink on uncoated paper stock, black ink cover on coated paper stock (8 ⅜ x 11 ¾ inches / 210 x 300 mm).
- DEPT: "Comment," editorial commentary by Elspeth Tavares and Lloyd Shepherd; "Business Diary," newsbriefs of film events, personnel, and developments; "Business Briefs," news items; "International Briefs," news items; "TV Briefs," news items; "On Release," analysis of current box office receipts in various international cities; "People in the News," personnel newsbriefs; "Finance Briefs," financial news concerning motion picture production and distribution; "Contact Numbers for Your Diary," excellent resource listing for industry professionals. (6/7-91).
- TYPL: "The Art of the Deal: Simon Olswang and David St. John White Discuss the Rudiments of a successful partnership Between East and West Producers," "The New Genre: Black Filmmakers in the 90's," "European TV: Towards a Homogeneous Market," "Sunny Side of the Doc," "Cultural Impact: Through the Medium of Cinema, Directors are Confronting the Black Experience Head On." (6/7-91).
- SCHL: Monthly, 80 pp.
- SPAN: Nov, 1982+

Business Screen
1938 - Mar 1, 1946//
SEE: COMPUTER PICTURES

Business Screen
October 1, 1968 - Nov, 1977//
SEE: COMPUTER PICTURES

Business Screen
Aug, 1980? - Dec?, 1982?//
(ISSN: 0160-7294)
SEE: COMPUTER PICTURES

Business Screen Magazine
Apr 23, 1946 - Aug 15, 1968//
SEE: COMPUTER PICTURES

BUSINESSTV VIDEO 8 GUIDE
- PUBL: BusinessTV, Inc., PO Box 6250, Altadena, CA 91001-9958.
- DESC: "Like the lightweight and easy-to-use Video Walkman of the 1990's, the magazine is designed for busy business people who never know where and when they will view their business videos. Video 8 tapes, playback equipment, and the *Guide* are designed to be carried in your pocket or briefcase, while you travel. They can be used on one's lap, on airplane or train tray tables, in the hotel room, or in the home. Each issue, *BusinessTV Video 8 Guide* will begin with a feature story on how business is using 8mm videos. The main section of the *Guide* contains listing of programs available on 8mm videotape with an index to suppliers at the end of the magazine" (from premiere issue of Mar/Apr, 1990). Each 8mm video listing within the guide includes running time, preview, rental and purchase/license fee for end users. The first three issues of this small format serial were a special supplement to *Telespan's BusinessTV* publication. Small format size; some graphics.
- DEPT: "Video 8 Programming," large section guide to business applications video. (3/4-90).
- TYPL: "Not All 8mm Video Equipment at JC Penny Is 'For Sale'." (3/4-90).
- SCHL: Bimonthly, 14 pp.
- SPAN: Mar/Apr, 1990 - Aug, 1990//?
  SUPPLEMENT TO
  --Telespan's BusinessTV (ISSN: 0896-3142), Mar/Apr, 1990 - Aug, 1990//.

✦ BUYERS GUIDE
- PUBL: Industrial Marketing Advisory Services, Inc., 5827 Columbia Pike, Suite 310, Falls Church, VA 22041.
- DESC: Earlier issues of this supplement to *Radio World* existed as a separate newspaper tabloid section. The current supplement appears at end of *Radio World*, which is published as a stapled tabloid. *Buyers Guide* is pure engineering/technical information for the radio station engineering management team, detailing new equipment on the market, engineering trends, and advances in radio technology. Assumes reader has significant technical knowledge in radio broadcast field. Stapled tabloid newspaper format with graphics and schematics.

DEPT: "User Report," "Buyers Brief," short product review; "Industry Roundup," "Tuned In," corporate changes newsbriefs; "Technology Update," "Consultants," professional cards. (11-22-89).
TYPL: "Continental Debuts at WJVS," "FM Solid State Still on Horizon," "Target Tuning Hits the Mark With SCAs," "Increasing to 6kW: What Will It Cost?" (11-22-89).
SCHL: Quarterly?, 15 pp.
SPAN: ?+

SUPPLEMENT TO
--Radioworld (ISSN: 0274-8541), ?+.

Buyer's Guide for Comic Fandom, The
1971 - Feb 4, 1983//
SEE: COMICS BUYER'S GUIDE

✤ C: JET

SUB: "Leading the way in secondary school journalism."
SUB: "Journalism education today."
SUB: "Leading the way in secondary school journalism and media education."
PUBL: Journalism Education Association of the United States, 4933 17th Pl., Lubbock, TX 79416.
DESC: "*Communication: Journalism Education Today* is primarily established to meet the challenge of an evolving highschool curriculum, a constantly changing world, and a gradual alteration in the pattern of highschool publications. The magazine is written particularly for journalism, English, speech, social science, art, publications, and audio-visual teachers." Careful writing is a hallmark of this quarterly. Information can be readily applied to a classroom situation. Good graphics and layout.
DEPT: "Forum," letters.
TYPL: "Try a Retreat," "Not Enough is Known About the Press," "Teaching License for Journalism," "Materials for Quality Journalism," "Books for Mass Media." (spring-76).
SCHL: Quarterly, 25 pp.
SPAN: 1967+
VARIES
--1967 - Summer?, 1977 as Communication: Journalism Education Today (ISSN: 0010-3535).
ABSORBED
--JEA Digest, ?
LC: PN 4788.C65
DD: 373.18/97
ISSN: 0198-6554

✤ C-O-N-N-E-C-T-I-O-N-S

SUB: "The Southern States Communication Association Newsletter."
PUBL: Southern States Communication Association, Speech Communication, The University of Southern Mississippi, Southern Station, PO Box 5131, Hattiesburg, MS 39406-5131.
DESC: In the Fall, 1991 newsletter, SSCA President Howard Dorgan noted; "In the last twenty years SSCA has experienced considerable growth through an openness to change: it is no longer the Southern 'Speech' Communication Association; it has dropped one division (Theatre), added four (Applied Communication, Freedom and Responsibilities of Speech, Gender Studies, and Intercultural Communication), and changed the names of four (Speech Pathology and Audiology to Language Behavior, Forensics to the Southern Forensic Association, Oral Interpretation simply to Interpretation, and Radio-TV-Film to Mass Communication)." These changes plus a reformatted journal and a move "...from a fairly tight focus upon speech function studies, performance studies, and historical/rhetorical studies to an exceptionally broad examination of all communication media, problems, and issues," makes for a dynamic organization and sufficient cause for publication of this information-filled newsletter concerning member activities within the Southern States Communication Association. For sampled copy of 1991: stapled newsletter format, black ink with spot color on cover, all on uncoated paper stock (8 ½ x 11 inches / 215 x 280 mm).
DEPT: "Academic Openings," employment opportunities; "News & Notes: SSCA Members on the Move!," newsbriefs; "Calendar," upcoming events; "Executive Secretary's Corner." (fall-91).
TYPL: "During Periods of Change, Honor Your Past," "San Antonio: The Best Time, Every Time," "Celebrating Sixty-One Years," "A Tribute to Sara Lowrey: A Pioneer," "Editor Nominations Sought." (fall-91).
SCHL: Three issues per year, 12 pp.
SPAN: ?+

✤ C-SPAN IN THE CLASSROOM

SUB: "A newsletter for professors."
PUBL: C-SPAN Department of Educational Services, 400 North Capitol St., NW, Suite 650, Washington, DC 20001.
DESC: This informative newsletter "...is a bimonthly publication of the C-SPAN Department of Educational Services. It has been created as a forum for program members to exchange ideas about C-SPAN's teaching applications, to seek input from other members, and to share professional experiences and accomplishments." Focus of the newsletter is application of C-SPAN satellite cable television programming within the educational process, from elementary to postgraduate levels of education. Articles detail both program information and classroom application. For sampled issue of 1991: loose-leaf newsletter style, black ink with spot color, limited advertising (8 ½ x 11 inches / 215 x 280 mm).
DEPT: None. (10/11-91).
TYPL: "Seminar Application Deadline: October 30," "Internships Available for College Students," "New Compilation Tapes Available From Purdue," "C-SPAN Helps Create Communication Futures Courses," "Incorporating C-SPAN Into Education Courses." (10/11-91).
SCHL: Bimonthly, 6 pp.
SPAN: Aug/Sep, 1989+

✤ C-SPAN UPDATE

SUB: "The newspaper of America's network."
PUBL: C-Span Update, PO Box 75298, Washington, DC 20013.
DESC: "C-SPAN, the Cable Satellite Public Affairs Network, is a non-profit cooperative of the cable television industry. The network's on-air debut in 1979 coincided with the inauguration of live telecasts from the floor of the House of Representatives. At that time, C-SPAN's programming consisted solely of live, gavel-to-gavel telecasts of House proceedings, and its potential audience comprised 3.5 million households. Today, C-SPAN's programming is available in more than 54 million households via 4,038 affiliated cable systems. The core of C-SPAN's programming continues to be live, unedited telecasts of the House. These proceedings, however, account for only 15 percent of the network's schedule." *C-SPAN Update* is an informative newspaper filled with listings for current and future program dates, as well as news items and events connected with C-SPAN programming. For the sampled issue of 1991: tabloid newspaper format, printed black ink, with additional spot color employed throughout the publication on uncoated quality paper stock, numerous graphs, charts, and pictures, no advertising (11 3/8 x 16 inches / 290 x 410 mm).
DEPT: "Viewer Mail," letters; "International Programming," "Inside C-SPAN," "Programming," listing; "Program Highlights," "Booknotes," review. (10-27-91).
TYPL: "Viewer Calls in '91 Already Surpass '90 Total," "Queen Opens New Session of Parliament," "Connecticut Representative Hopes to Bring 'Question Time' to America," "Pomp and Circumstance Precede Queen Elizabeth II's Speech," "Art Case Pits First Amendment Against Copyright Law." (10-27-91).
SCHL: Weekly [except first week of January and June], 8 pp.
SPAN: ?+
ISSN: 0746-3812

CA

1959 - 1966//
SEE: COMMUNICATION ARTS

CA Magazine

1967 - 1969//
(ISSN: 0884-0008)
SEE: COMMUNICATION ARTS

Cable Communications

Jun/Jul, 1973 - Apr, 1979//
(ISSN: 0824-8435)
SEE: CABLE COMMUNICATIONS MAGAZINE

Cable Communications

? - ?//
SEE: COMMUNICATIONS

✤ CABLE COMMUNICATIONS MAGAZINE

SUB: "Serving Canadian telephone and cable television systems."
SUB: "The authoritative international cable television publication."
SUB: "The authoritative cable television publication covering news, views, issues & developments in North America and around the world."
PUBL: Ter-Sat Media Publications, 4 Smetana Drive, Kitchener, Ontario N2B 3B8, Canada.
DESC: *Cable Communications* maintains an international scope while most articles are written by Canadians and address primarily Canadian issues. This serial does well in rendering (in the early 1970s) a dual emphasis on Canadian telephone and cable television topics, although (even then), cable television received the bulk of editorial attention and advertisements. The current serial is a good overview of cable television's status, with topics of primary interest to cable managers and vendors.
DEPT: "Review and Forecast," guest commentary; "Tele-Views," newsbriefs. (12-71/1/72). "Cable Comments," "Calendar of Events," "Tele-News," "Cable Programming," "Industry Notes," "Marketing," of cable services; "Dateline USA," "Dateline Europe," "Dateline U.K.," "Tele-Views." (9-86).
TYPL: "The Mini-Network Cablecasting," "Canadian Independent Telephone Association--Convention Report." (12-71/1-72). "Report of the Task Force on Broadcasting Policy: A passive role for Cable," "Cherry Picking for Profits--or How to Customize Service to Beat SMATV Competition and Increase Subscriber Penetration." "Cable Penetration Gains Rekindle Investor Interest." (9-86).
SCHL: Quarterly (May, 1934 - 1968); Five issues per year (1969+); 40 pp.
SPAN: May, 1934?+
VARIES
--May, 1934? - Dec, 1965 as Canadian Telephone Journal, The (ISSN: 0318-0050).
--Spring, 1966 - Apr/May, 1973 as Canadian Telephone and Cable Television Journal (ISSN: 0008-5162).
--Jun/Jul, 1973 - Apr, 1979 as Cable Communications (ISSN: 0824-8435).
LC: HE 8700.7 .C6C36
DD: 384.55/56/0971
ISSN: 0318-0069

✤ CABLE GUIDE, THE

SUB: "America's cable magazine."
PUBL: TVSM, Inc., 309 Lakeside Dr., Horsham, PA 19044.

DESC: Mixing national cable television schedules with regional cable system channel assignments has made *The Cable Guide* an indispensable guide to cable programming for American consumers. Feature stories, which are not time-critical, are printed in full color. Actual programming schedules which are both time-critical, and system-sensitive, are printed within the large newsprint section in the middle of this periodical. Commencing with the October, 1990 issue, the publication moved from digest size to standard magazine size (7 ⅝ x 10 ⅝ inches) with expanded features. "In announcing the changed format, Editor Jay Gissen noted, "Television is big, bright and colorful, and we think a magazine that covers television should be the same. That's why we're expanding *The Cable Guide* from digest size to a large magazine format." As part of the format change, *The Cable Guide* also added a new, 12-page monthly feature, "Teaching with Television." Editor Gissen noted that the publication is "committed to helping parents use TV as a positive force in children's lives."
DEPT: "Guest Star," column; "Highlights," for the upcoming month; "Channel Directory," for this region; "Cablevision Information," for this region; "Pay-Per-View Calendar," upcoming broadcasts; "Programming Index," "Title Index," of television shows. (1-89).
TYPL: "Cable Plays Its ACE," "Taking Stock of Michael Douglas," "Third Annual Readers Poll." (1-89).
SCHL: Monthly, 200 pp.
SPAN: 1980?+
VARIES
--1980 - 1982 as Great TV Entertainment.
ABSORBED
--Cable Today, 1983?

✥ CABLE LIBRARIES

PUBL: C. S. Tepfer Publishing Co., Inc., PO Box 565, Ridgefield, CT 06877.
DESC: This is an eight-page typewritten serial (issued by the American Society for Information Service, Washington, DC), that informs libraries about utilizing cable television and videotape. The editors normally report on cable-access opportunities, regulatory developments, library usage, and public response to program offerings. This unique newsletter is for public librarians who see video and cable as important developments in serving patrons. It provides interesting news stories of video programs and services offered by libraries, oftentimes through their local CATV outlet. Also noteworthy are news items concerning copyrights, new technology, and tape exchanges. No graphics.
DEPT: None. (10-76). "Regulatory Roundup," "Mediagraphy," reviews; "Meetings," upcoming events. (2-81).
TYPL: "Ocean County Library uses Public Relations as Port of Entry to Cable," "National Survey of Libraries Offering Video Services," "Two-Way Cable TV Study in Pennsylvania Expanded." (10-76). "Videotape Cassette Project at the Ferguson Library Stamford, Connecticut." (2-81).
SCHL: Monthly, 8 pp.
SPAN: May, 1973+
LC: Z 716.8 .C32
DD: 021/.28
ISSN: 0161-7605

✥ CABLE LINES

PUBL: CBN Cable Network, Virginia Beach, VA 23463.
DESC: A promotional newspaper for the 6,000-plus cable systems who regularly carry CBN Family Channel cable television programming, this tabloid newsprint format carries articles on new programs, schedule changes, promotional campaigns, and other developmental news concerning the cable network.
DEPT: None. (12-4-85).
TYPL: "CBN Cable Tops 30 Million Mark," "Fresh Look at News, Finances Slated," "Regular Programming in Spirit of the Season," "Impact is Aim of New Unit of CBN Sales." (12-4-85).
SCHL: Quarterly, 8 pp.
SPAN: Jan, 1985+

CABLE MARKETING

SUB: "The marketing/management magazine for cable television executives."
PUBL: Associated Cable Enterprises, 352 Park Avenue South, New York, NY 10010.
DESC: After a successful nine-year publication span, this magazine ceased publication in summer, 1990. Preeminent within this quality publication was the emphasis on the marketing of cable services to individual systems. A large-format, full-color style contributed to the authoritative articles concerning the important business of gaining/retaining subscribers, and the usage of cable programming product in developing a successful marketing strategy. The serial took stock of emerging technology, new equipment, and some aspects of programming, but the emphasis remained on marketing. In essence, this was a serial comprised of professional writing and considerate thought to the profit-side of economics. Reflecting the development of local and national marketing efforts by local cable systems, the magazine was redesigned and "relaunched" in May, 1990 with greater emphasis on marketing and advertising sales. In August, 1990, Jobson Publishing Company announced that it was ending the newly revamped serial, citing difficulties in publishing a "stand alone title." For the sampled issue of 1989: large-format, stapled magazine design, mixture of black ink and full-color graphics with full-color cover on coated paper stock (10 ¾ x 13 ⅞ inches / 275 x 355 mm).
DEPT: "Cable Scan," newsbriefs; "Cable Tech," newsbriefs; "Opinion & Comment," "Ad Strategy," critique; "Studio Strategies," production; "Marketing Services,"

newsbriefs; "Cable Ticker," cable management; "Employee Dyamics," advice; "Cable People." (3-86). "Cable Scan," newsbriefs; "Cable Tech," new technology; "Sales Management," column by Kevin Dorr; "Employee Dynamics," column by Gayla Kalp; "Programming Clips," newsbriefs; "Product Marketplace." (10-88).
TYPL: "Pricing: Will Cable Operators Kill the Golden Goose?," "The Changing Economics of Addressability," "Making the Most of Telemarketing," "Improving Cable Marketing Effectiveness Through Segmentation." (3-86). "A New Role for Regionals," "The Home Satellite Enigma," "Growing Basic Penetration by 20% in Less Than a Year (in a Desert)," "High Subscriber Values Boost Headend Sales," "Pushing Cable Publicity into its Prime." (10-88).
SCHL: Monthly, 80 pp.
SPAN: Feb, 1981 - Aug?, 1990//
MERGED WITH
--MSO (to form) MSO's Cable Marketing, Sep/Oct, 1990.
LC: HE 8700.7 .C6C333
DD: 384.55/563/0973
ISSN: 0279-8891

Cable Strategies

Oct, 1987 - Aug?, 1989//
(ISSN: 1044-2820)
SEE: MSO'S CABLE MARKETING

Cable Television Business Magazine

Oct?, 1982 - Sep 15, 1989//
(ISSN: 0745-2808)
SEE: CABLE TV BUSINESS MAGAZINE

✧ CABLE TELEVISION ENGINEERING

SUB: "Journal of the Society of Cable Television Engineers."
PUBL: Society of Cable Television Engineers, 10 Avenue Rd., Dorridge, Solihull, West Midlands B93 8LD, England.
DESC: Appearing in the United States as a supplement ("magazine-within-a-magazine") to *International Cable*, this journal of the Society of Cable Television Engineers in the UK provides four to five primarily technical articles on installation, maintenance, and new technologies as they relate to the cable television field. The 16-page, separately numbered section has no advertising. Articles range from news and information concerning British and European cable to highly technical articles on signal transmission and routing. For the sampled issue of 1991: black ink editorial copy, full-color cover all on coated paper stock (8 ½ x 10 ⅞ inches / 215 x 275 mm).
DEPT: "Random Reflections," news item column by Tom Hall. (6/7-91).
TYPL: "Future Standards," "The local(est) Loop," "Radio Frequency Transmission Lines," "American Products Successfully Marketed in Europe." (6/7-91).
SCHL: Three issues per year, 16 pp.
SPAN: 1971+
VARIES
--? - ? as Relay Engineer.
SUPPLEMENT TO
--International Cable, ?+
LC: TK 6675.C
ISSN: 0048-718x

Cable Television Review

Mar, 1965 - Aug, 1967//
SEE: VUE

✧ CABLE TV ADVERTISING

PUBL: Paul Kagan Associates, Inc., 126 Clock Tower Place, Carmel, CA 93923-8734.
DESC: One of a series of outstanding Paul Kagan Associates trade newsletters, *Cable TV Advertising* covers the emerging field of spot advertising through cable television systems. The serial covers spot advertising sales at the local cable level, national cable systems sales, ad inventories, availabilities, and news of cable television advertising in the United States. Well recommended for any sales or corporate office connected with the burgeoning field of cable television spot sales. Typewritten with some graphics.
DEPT: "Cable Ad-Dendums." (6-30-89).
TYPL: "Cable Network Billings: The Good Times Roll On," "Local Ad Inventory Expands," "Examining Local Break Times," "Interconnect Activity in High Gear," "Starting Local Ad Sales: Better Late Than Never." (6-30-89).
SCHL: Monthly, 10 pp.
SPAN: Jun, 1975?+
ISSN: 0270-885x
ABST: --Predicasts

✧ CABLE TV AND NEW MEDIA LAW & FINANCE

PUBL: Leader Publications, 111 Eight Ave., New York, NY 10011.
DESC: With an editorial group and Board of Contributors that reads like a "who's who" of the electronic media legal profession, *Cable TV and New Media Law & Finance* is an excellent publication for the ever-changing, ever-challenged standards of electronic regulation. Articles are both timely and highly informative, containing reasoned opinion concerning contemporary events and future trends within this volatile field. Typical topics during 1991 included the growth of European cellular radio; the results of cable operator

overbuilding; applying state sales tax to cable television service; the cost and impact of fiber optic information networks to management and consumer; pay-per-view programming; and asset sale contracts in cable television. The 1991 yearly subscription price of $195 is a bargain in the electronics media field. It is difficult to imagine any cable or new media management team that wouldn't significantly benefit from a subscription to this informative newsletter. For the sampled issue of 1991: stapled newsletter format, black ink with spot-color on uncoated paper stock, no advertising (8 ½ x 11 inches / 215 x 280 mm).
DEPT: "F.C.C. Watch," commission developments column by Robert R. Bruce; "Video People: Recent Deals," news column by John Sarna. (11-91).
TYPL: "Right to Operate Upheld Despite Renewal Denial," "Broadband Fiber to the Home: Strategies for Cable & Telcos," "FCC Proposes a Video Dialtone Policy," "AT&T Could Become 'the Phone Company' Again," "No Surprises in Time Warner Deal." (11-91).
SCHL: Monthly, 8 pp.
SPAN: ?+
ISSN: 0736-489x

CABLE TV BUSINESS MAGAZINE

SUB: "The professional journal of cable system operations."
SUB: "Professional journal of the cable television industry."
PUBL: Cardiff Publishing, 6300 South Syracuse Way, Suite 650, Englewood, CO 80111.
DESC: *Cable Television Business*, and later, *Cable tv Business Magazine* (note use of small *tv* in latter title), was a publication whose name had mirrored the ever-changing cable television industry, continuing to revise its masthead to match the current status of the medium. This serial brought its focus to bear on the business aspects of cable television, reporting with a professional journalistic style the important issues facing this newly deregulated industry. This was a quality resource for the business-side of American cable television. Note: Although publication changed title from *Cable Television Business Magazine* to *Cable tv Business Magazine*, the same ISSN (0745-2808) was maintained over full publication span of both titles. For the sampled issue of 1990: mixture of black ink and full-color pages and cover on coated paper stock (8 x 10 ¾ inches / 200 x 275 mm).
DEPT: "Commentary," "Editorial Comment," "Letters," "In the News," "Business Notes," "Correspondent's Column," "People," "Financial Notes." (04-15- 84) "Commentary," "Denver Journal," "Calendar," "Executive Digest," "Association Update," cable association news; "In the News," "People," profiles; "Financial Notes." (12-15-88).
TYPL: "Cable's Role in DBS," "Mass Marketing Security," "Banking on Business," "Who's Minding the Store?" (04-15-84). "Cable at the Turning Point," "Networks Grow in '88," "The March Toward Oligopoly," "Fiber, HDTV Pace 1988." (12-15-88).

SCHL: Monthly (Jul, 1976 - Sep, 1978); Semimonthly (Oct 1, 1978 - Nov 15, 1978); Semimonthly [plus additional May issue] (Dec?, 1978+), 95 pp.
SPAN: Jan, 1964 - Jan 4, 1991//
VARIES
--Jan, 1964 - Dec, 1966 as TV & Communications.
--Jan, 1967 - Jun, 1976 as TV Communications (ISSN: 0039-8519).
--Jul, 1976 - Oct?, 1982 as TVC (ISSN: 0164-8489).
--Oct?, 1982 - Sep 15, 1989 as Cable Television Business Magazine (ISSN: 0745-2808).
ABSORBED
--Cable Tech (ISSN: 0090-4376), Jul, 1976.
--Vue, Oct 1, 1978.
LC: TK 6675.T2
DD: 384.55/56/05

✧ CABLE TV PROGRAMMING

PUBL: Paul Kagan Associates, Inc., 126 Clock Tower Place, Carmel, CA 93923-8734.
DESC: This Paul Kagan Associates newsletter covers programming in the cable television industry, and provides the same thorough, reliable coverage found in other Kagan publications. Topics cover programming budgets, audience growth (especially vis a vis established broadcast television networks), innovative programming concepts, new offerings, and programming trends among the numerous cable networks. Quality publication; typewritten newsletter format with graphics.
DEPT: "Network Notes," (7-31-89).
TYPL: "Cable Program Budgets: Bucks Buy Clout," "All Eyes are on Movietime," "Off-Network Hours Still Landing on Cable," "Nostalgia Network Receives Bid," "Peeking at Cable Network Cumes." (7-31-89).
SCHL: Biweekly, 12 pp.
SPAN: Sep 25, 1981+
DD: 384 11
ISSN: 0278-503x
ABST: --Predicasts

✧ CABLE WORLD

PUBL: Cable World Associates, 1905 Sherman St., Suite #1000, Denver, CO 80203.
DESC: "Cable television is an international business. A Belgian firm is helping finance construction of the cable system in Hong Kong. Managers from Philadelphia are running cable systems in the United Kingdom. Financiers from Connecticut are backing cable construction in Poland. Canadian banks are lending to American system operators. CNN is carried in Moscow and the House of Commons is seen in Chicago. No trade publication in the world covers cable around the world better than *Cable World*. So, wherever in the world you live, if you are in cable you need *Cable World*." *Cable World* "...is organized the way a modern cable system works, with sections on operations, technology, finance, advertising, marketing and pro-

gramming." This excellent newsweekly provides late breaking information in each of these primary areas in a concise, quick-read format. It serves the busy cable executive who needs to know what is happening THIS week in cable television. Of special note is the supplement, *Marketing New Media*, the outstanding Paul Kagan Associates newsletter on the marketing side of emerging communication media. The eight-page newsletter is published on salmon-colored, uncoated paper stock, and is included in *Cable World* issues the third week of each month. Magazine format (8 ¼ x 10 ¾ inches / 210 x 270 mm), with numerous color graphics.

DEPT: "Newswire," late breaking news items; "Operations News," "Programming News," "Advertising News," "Marketing News," "Technology News," "People," "A Look Ahead," calendar; "Financial News," "Marketplace," cable and the stock market. (4-10-89). "Newswire," "And Another Thing," column by Thomas P. Southwick; "Operations," "Technology," "Marketing," "Programming," "Advertising," "People," personnel newsbriefs; "A Look Ahead," calendar; "Hot Dates," 'Editor's pick of top upcoming events'; "Cable World Business Extra," excellent 2nd section on the business of cable television operation; "Market Diary," stock performance of selected cable television companies. (9-17-90).

TYPL: "TCI's On-Home Box May Stir a Revolution," "Wider Metered Ratings Data Arms Cable with New Sales Muscle," "NCTA Won't Challenge Syndex Rule in Court." (4-10-89). "With Cable Industry Divided, Cable Legislation Moves Ahead," "Drive Consumer Demand at Your Own Risk, Operators Tell Networks," "Faroudja Goes Commercial," "Second Sets: No Free Lunch," "N.C. Operator Relies on Fiber to Reduce Long Amplifier Runs." (9-17-90).

SCHL: Weekly, 80 pp.
SPAN: Jan 9, 1989+
WITH SUPPLEMENT
--Marketing New Media (ISSN: 0743-2178), ?+
DD: 384 11
ISSN: 1042-7228

✢ CABLEAGE

PUBL: Television Editorial Co., 1270 Avenue of the Americas, New York, NY 10020.
DESC: "*CableAge* is the only cable industry publication with an in-depth overview, in every issue, of cable's six vital information fronts: Programming, Equipment, Marketing, Advertising, Finance, Regulation." While *CableAge* certainly is a valuable resource in each of the above named areas, it may of particular value in its coverage of cable television programming. In the December 10, 1984 issue, Publisher S. J. Paul told readers: "We are announcing an expansion of our service to both readers and advertisers starting with the January 7 [1985] issue of the publication. *CableAge* will be published as a separate entity within the covers of one issue which will contain *Television/Radio Age* and *CableAge*. Those readers who wish to continue to receive *CableAge* on an individual basis can continue to do so. With the combination of the two publications in each issue, *CableAge* will adapt a lively new format. It will initiate a new section, titled 'Newsfront'. It will continue with the concise informative coverage that it has been known for--informative, interpretative trend stores, regular financial departments and features, advance listings of motion pictures on pay services and 'Appointments' section designed to keep readers updated on personnel changes." *CableAge* ran as a second section of *Television/Radio Age* from January 7, 1985 until May 27, 1985. Publisher Paul noted: "In view of recent developments in cable, we are restructuring *CableAge* to keep pace with the growth of that industry. ...The new *CableAge* will concentrate on important pillars of the cable industry--programming, the raw material out of which business is fashioned; financial, the monetary aspects of an expanding industry; and advertising, the fastest segment of growth potential." *CableAge* took a one issue (June 10, 1985) hiatus and returned in the July 8, 1985 issue in a redesigned second section format. The December 23, 1985 issue appears to be the last to include *CableAge*, although no publisher's announcement to that end was viewed in succeeding issues of *Television/Radio Age*. For the sampled issues of 1984: magazine format, black ink with black ink, blue spot-color cover and full-color advertisement pages on coated paper stock (8 x 10 ¾ inches / 200 x 275 mm).

DEPT: "Wall Street Analysis," "Corporate Profile," "London Letter," "Programming," "Advertising," "Production," "Marketing," "Operations," "Networks," "Technology," "A Closer Look," "Appointments." (9-3-84).
TYPL: "Southeast Cable Operators Turn to State Legislatures," "Cable Contracters Regroup for Declining Workload," "FCC Ruling Won't Bring Dramatic Basic Rate Hikes," "On-the-Job Safety Gets Enhanced MSO Attention," "RF Converter Security Versus Digital TV Mulled." (9-3-84).
SCHL: Biweekly, 60 pp.
SPAN: May 18, 1981+
SUPPLEMENT TO
--Television/Radio Age (ISSN: 0040-277x), Nov 21, 1983+.
LC: HE 8700.72.U6 C36
DD: 384.55/47/0973 19
ISSN: 0279-4004

Cablecasting and Educational Television

Sep, 1967 - Oct, 1968//
(ISSN: 0574-9905)
SEE: E-ITV

✣ CABLEVISION

SUB: "The news and features weekly of the cable television industry."
SUB: "The premium entertainment magazine."
SUB: "Information and analysis for cable television management."
PUBL: Capital Cities Media, Inc., 825 7th Ave., New York, NY 10019.
DESC: This business weekly serves the needs and interests of the American cable television management community very well. It is a gutsy, no-nonsense business periodical covering the areas of regulation, technology, city-cable relationships, and general audience trends. Articles appear under one of two headings; information or analysis, providing considerate thought to the problems of the present, and the potential of the future for profitable cable television operation. Information is authoritative, and very applicable to whatever size of cable system being managed. In one sampled issue articles addressed original cable programming, trends and issues in direct broadcast satellite, billing software, the theory and reality of tiering, and helpful tips for the cable sales team, subtitled "How to attract new advertisers and sell up existing ones, tap into co-op dollars, tie network promotions in a neat little bow and...sell pizza too." Numerous graphics, charts. Sampled issue for 1990: (8 ⅜ x 10 ⅞ inches / 210 x 275 mm).
DEPT: "Between the Lines," editorial; "CableScope," newsbriefs; "News Wire," newsbriefs; "Update," "Leading the Week," "Programming," "Advertising," "Government & Law," "CableVision Plus," "Financial Services Chart," "Business," "Technology," "Events," "People," "From Washington," "Cable Stats," "Parting Words." (8-1-83). "Information," news column; "Programming," "Management," "Operations," "Advertising," "Money," "People," "Calendar," "Catalogue," new product review; "From Washington," column by Lisa Stein. (3-27-89).
TYPL: "CAB Sets Sights on Capturing Madison Avenue," "Cities Stand by Compromise," "Beermaker Gets Stake in Pay-TV," "New York Signs On," "Showtime Jangles Wichita Lines," "Pace Quickens in U.K.," "HBO's Situation Comedy." (8-1-83). "MultiPort Gains Support," "Penney's Plans for Shop TV," "Anixter Adjusts Fiver Strategy," "Construction Surge Continuing," "In Search of the Right Avails." (3-27-89).
SCHL: Biweekly (? - ?); Weekly [except last week of December] (Jul 14, 1980 - Mar 29, 1982); Fifty-one issues per year (Apr 5, 1982 - Mar 18, 1985); Weekly (Mar 25, 1985 - Apr 29, 1986); Biweekly (May 5, 1986+), 90 pp.
SPAN: 1975+
LC: HE 8700.7.C6 C334
DD: 384.55/47
ISSN: 0361-8374

CAHIERS DU CINEMA IN ENGLISH

PUBL: Cahiers Publishing Co. Inc., 635 Madison Ave., New York, NY 10022.
DESC: "What was it about *Cahiers du Cinema* that excited some of us so much? Partly, I suppose, it was a case of *Cahiers* releasing our cultural inhibitions the way Paris traditionally has released the sexual inhibitions of backward Anglo-Saxons. Not that there is more sin and sex in Paris than anywhere else, simply more *savoir-faire*, more *elan vital*, more *joie de vivre*, and, what is more important, more sensual complicity in the language itself." Thus, editor Andrew Sarris set forth the intentions of this English language translation of the international film favorite, *Cahiers du Cinema*. In its relatively brief two-year publication span, *Cahiers du Cinema in English* provided a real service for non-French speaking film enthusiasts, with accurate translations of film articles of major import.
DEPT: "Small Talk," current Hollywood news column by Axel Madsen; "New York Openings," theatre listing; "Editor's Eyrie," column by editor Andrew Sarris. (#4-66).
TYPL: "Jerry Lewis," "New Canadian Cinema," "Carl Dreyer." (#4-66).
SCHL: Bimonthly, 70 pp.
SPAN: Jan, 1966 - Dec, 1967//
LC: PN 1993.C
ISSN: 0575-0954

✣ CALIFORNIA PUBLISHER

PUBL: California Newspaper Publishers Association, 1127 11th St., Suite 1040, Sacramento, CA 95814.
DESC: The official publication of the California Newspaper Publisher's Association, this monthly tabloid's function is to keep its membership advised on organizational activities, media growth, and association developments in general. Most issues contain thought pieces and issue-oriented discussions.
DEPT: "Looking Back," twenty-five years ago in California newspapers; "-- 30--," obit column; "People," newsbriefs; "Newspapers," newsbriefs concerning changes in member publications. (11-77).
TYPL: "CNPA Captures 28 NNA Awards," "Tips on Selling Advertising," "Newspapers Must be Fit to Survive." (11-77).
SCHL: Monthly, 8 pp.
SPAN: 1918+
LC: PN 4700.C34
DD: 071.94
ISSN: 0008-1434
ABST: --ABI/Informer

✣ CAMCORDER

SUB: "The complete magazine of video photography."
PUBL: Miller Magazines, Inc., 2660 East Main St., Ventura, CA 93003.

DESC: Designed for the lay and "semi-professional" consumer, *Camcorder* provides information on trends in video camera-recorder units (camcorders), instruction on the technique of production, and applications for same. One sample issue provided the latest news in camcorders from the Consumer Electronics Show (CES), a new home party game utilizing a video camera and recorder, economic opportunities in legal videography, the workings of time base correctors (TBCs), and the emerging realm of desktop video. The emphasis remains on the camcorders themselves, with readers receiving full value for their newstand purchases. For the samled issue of 1990: stapled magazine format, full, and spot color graphics throughout on coated paper stock including cover (8 x 10 ¾ inches / 205 x 275 mm).
DEPT: "Video Trends," column by Rod Woodcock; "Camcorder Tests," test bench reviews column by Rod Woodcock. (8-90).
TYPL: "NEW Concepts in Video," "Hollywood Playback," "Amiga Power," "Laying Down a Soundtrack," "TBC." (8-90).
SCHL: Bimonthly, 85 pp.
SPAN: Jan, 1985+
VARIES
--Jan, 1985? - Mar, 1989? as Super Television.
--Apr, 1989 - Nov, 1989 as Camcorder Report (ISSN: 1047-8787).
LC: TR 882 .C36
DD: 778.59/9 20
ISSN: 1048-8804

Camcorder Report
Apr, 1989 - Nov, 1989//
(ISSN: 1047-8787)
SEE: CAMCORDER

✣ CAMCORDER USER
SUB: "The video-making magazine."
PUBL: WV Publications, Ltd., 57/59 Rochester Place, London NW1 9JU, England.
DESC: "*Camcorder User* is the UK's leading creative magazine for the camcorder enthusiast. Colourful and informative, *Camcorder User* gives readers the latest equipment news and hints on what goes into making the best movies." Designed for the camcorder user/owner, this serial concentrates on the elements of production; highlighting technology, shooting scripts, casting sessions, filters, special effects; and shooting outdoors, i.e., everything from birds in the wild to whales under the sea. Some articles pertain to the post-production process of editing, but most focus on the art and technique of videography for the British home enthusiast. For the sampled issue of 1990: perfect-bound magazine format, numerous graphics and advertisements in spot- and full-color all on coated paper stock (8 ¼ x 11 ⅝ inches / 210 x 295 mm).
DEPT: "Your Letters," "Eyeview," column by Ian MacQuillin; "Ray Smith," column by Ray Smith; "Club Contact," 'John Wright on what's happening around the country's video clubs'; "Still Video," 'Steve Parker investigates the latest developments'; "Movie Master Class," "Helpline," Q&A column by Terry James; "Best Buy Guide," "Closing Shots." (3-90).
TYPL: "Preparing for a Video Birdwatch," "Making the Most of the Video Craft," "Video Record of a Revolution," "The Art of Crashing." (3-90).
SCHL: Monthly, 150 pp.
SPAN: ?+

CAMERA
SUB: "Official organ of FIAP (International Federation of Photographic Art)."
SUB: "International magazine for photography."
SUB: "International magazine for photography and cinematography."
PUBL: C. J. Bucher Ltd., CH-60002 Lucerne, Switzerland.
DESC: "...*Camera* is a unique publication read by both professionals and advanced amateurs. Its quality reproduction and format is directed to the reader's aesthetic enjoyment, visually as well as factually and it provides the reader with a source of ideas on new photo techniques, new equipment and the total excitement of what's happening in the international world of photography." This publication in English, French, and German concerned the fine-arts aspect of still camera photography, and did so with élan, and verve in a very classic layout/publication style. It is difficult to overstate the quality inherent in this magazine, with heavy coated paper stock covers to single pictures filling an entire page, themed articles on different paper stock and tinted paper dividers within single issues. Photographers throughout the world were represented in the publication, both established and promising new talent alike. Of special note in an already unique publication was the special department, "Technical Round-Up," which provided a succinct description of new technology applied to this field. For over 50 years *Camera* had delighted audiences, showcased photographer's work, and bridged the international cultural gap. It was indeed a sad day when this publication folded in December, 1981. For the sampled issue of 1970: perfect-bound magazine format, mixture of black/white and full-color printing throughout on a variety of media, in a very dynamic layout design (8 ¾ x 11 ⅜ inches / 225 x 290 mm). Commencing with the March, 1957 issue, *Camera* was published in an English edition replacing the trilingual (French, German, English) editions published before this date.
DEPT: "Technical Round-Up," new photographic developments column by L. A. Mannheim; "Books," review; "Photo News in Brief," new product review; "Exhibitions and Announcements." (1-70). "Camera: Then," historical briefs from early Camera issues; "Photo: Now," international newsbriefs of new products; "Agenda," upcoming international photography seminars and workshops.

TYPL:	"Violence," "Water," "Marché aux Puces," "People," "The Civil War." (1-70). "Portals, Passages, and Portraits," "Eugene Atget," "Who was Eugene Atget, a Biography." (3-78).
SCHL:	Monthly, 50 pp.
SPAN:	Jan, 1922 - Dec, 1981// ABSORBED BY --Fotomagazin.
LC:	TR 1.C115
DD:	770/.5
ISSN:	0366-7073

✢ CAMERA, THE

SUB:	"The photographic journal of America."
PUBL:	Camera, 636 Franklin Square, Philadelphia, PA.
DESC:	Editor Frank V. Chambers in a 1938 issue said this about his publication: "*THE CAMERA* is not a photographic text book, nor is photography, as practised by a large majority, an exact science. As we conceive it, it is an art-science. Certainly, photography, more than any other art, depends for its effects on the studious application of certain scientific principles, and hence, its appellation. While such principles are immutable--as are all principles--it is evident that when all photographers are inevitably committed to a single method of their application, photography will necessarily cease to be an art, and will enter the roll of the sciences. Which of the two, we wonder, would our readers prefer? ... *THE CAMERA* is an unbiased photographic magazine and, as such, will always offer its pages as an open forum for the expression of various opinions, whether some of these be contradictory, or not. All that we require of our contributions is that they reveal some evidence of their author's possession of a modicum of plain horse sense." Caustic and supportive, technical and artistic, these seemingly contradictory approaches to the field of photography are evident in this excellent publication for the professional and advanced-technique photographer. Within the cream-colored pages of *THE CAMERA* is provided a stimulating round-table discussion of whatever is pertinent to the field of photographic art, technique and science. One of the many fascinating aspects of the monthly magazine is the often-caustic critiques of reader-submitted pictures, many of which were submitted by novices. The publication offered an interesting subscription "two-fer" to readers, providing a second photographic subscription in addition to *THE CAMERA* for one low combined price. Similar in nature to many other magazines of the era, advertising is confined to the front and back sections, with editorial content in the middle. All photographs are printed with some amount of white space, and set off from text on the page. Perfect-bound magazine format, black/white editorial and cover on coated paper stock. Separate 20 page section of advertising matter (7 ¾ x 10 ¾ inches / 200 x 275 mm).
DEPT:	"Print Analysis Department," column by David B. Edmonston; "Pictorial Print Analysis," column by Konrad Cramer; "Just Between You and Me," editorial column by Frank V. Chambers; "News and Notes," photographic newsbriefs; "U.S. Patents Relating to Photography," excellent resource section 'Compiled from Patent Office Gazette'; "Clubs, Contests, and Exhibitions," 'Clubs, societies and associations of photographers like to know how other clubs are doing'; "Diminutive Camera Technique and Practice," commentary and technique column by Norris W. Harkness; "Along the Main Stem," commentary column by Paul David Steele; "Modern Color Photography," technique and technology column by Herbert C. McKay; "Print Criticism Department," highly critical and insightful column concerning reader submitted pictures; "Newest Additions to the Bookshelves," "Questions and Answers," extensive technical Q&A section; "Pictorial Salon Calendar," upcoming exhibitions calendar. (2-38).
TYPL:	"Publicity for Camera Clubs," "Photography as a Means of Self Expression," "Stalking Salon Prints in Europe," "A Novel 'Dodging' Device," "Tricks of the Press Photographer." (2-38).
SCHL:	Monthly, 150 pp.
SPAN:	?+?

Camera
Jul, 1897 - Feb, 1949//
SEE: CAMERA MAGAZINE

Camera Owner
1963? - Jul, 1967//
SEE: CREATIVE CAMERA

CAMERA & CAMCORDER MONTHLY

PUBL:	Aceville Publications, Ltd., Castle House, 97 High St., Colchester, Essex CO1 1TH, England.
DESC:	In the world of current photographic periodicals, the quality of printing, paper and layout design is as important as the editorial content itself. *Camera & Camcorder Monthly* was, in some ways, a victim of consumer expectations. The articles themselves were well-written, and format design was in the process of improving, but contemporary subscribers oftentimes expect more articles, and full utilization of heavy clay-coated stock in printing. Here was a publication which focused primarily on the still film camera, with some forays into darkroom procedures, and video. Articles ranged from cave photography to film stock, color processing, to photographing wildlife. The emphasis was on the technical side of photography, providing consumers with clear facts on improving technique, or suggestions for new adventures. Editor Steve Wright, in the last issue for March, 1990 stated that the publication would be suspended for "...the foreseeable future," and it can only be hoped that

"suspension" does not become "cessation." For the 1990 sampled issue: Stapled magazine format, numerous black/white and color graphics, including full-color cover on coated paper stock (8 ¼ x 11 ¾ inches / 210 x 300 mm).
DEPT: "On Test," equipment review; "Secondhand Scene," classic film cameras reviewed; "Portfolio," photographer showcase; "Hot Shots," outstanding photo submissions; "Focal Point," photo submissions; "Photo Clinic," Q&A column by Rod Ashford; "Books," review. (3-90).
TYPL: "Chris the Cave-Dweller," "Konica Print Films," "Soft Focus: The Hard Facts," "Fixed Lens or Zoom?" (3-90).
SCHL: Monthly, 65 pp.
SPAN: ? - Mar, 1990//

CAMERA AND DARK ROOM

SUB: "Official organ of the New York Society of Amateur Photographers." (Feb, 1899 - ?).
PUBL: American Photographic Publishing Co., 361 Broadway, New York, NY.
DESC: More than a membership serial, *Camera and Dark Room* informed about camera technique, and dark room science and artistry for amateur photographers. The badge of "amateur" was worn with pride, as articles extolled the virtues of experimentation with lighting, lenses, and darkroom facilities. The focus changed in latter years to a mixture of amateur and professional work with an emphasis on the technique of accomplishing professional results. Indeed, an ongoing special department (until its December, 1906 demise) was labeled: "Photography for Amateurs, by a Professional." Small format; numerous photographs.
DEPT: "On Developing," "Light Topics," "Editorials," "Query Department." (4-1899). "Photographic Items of Interest," "Picture Criticism," "Query Department." (11-06).
TYPL: "Slow Plates and Large Stops," "How I Tried to be a Professional," "Photographing Infants." (4-1899). "Backgrounds and Their Influence on the Portrait," "Portrait Lighting in the Studio," "Gelatino-Chloride Emulson for Making a Slow Gaslight Paper." (11-06).
SCHL: Monthly, 25 pp.
SPAN: Feb, 1899 - Dec, 1906//
ABSORBED
--Pictorial Photographer and Developer, Sep, 1899.
MERGED WITH
--American Amateur Photographer, The (to form) American Amateur Photographer and Camera & Darkroom.
LC: TR 1.C23

✤ CAMERA & DARKROOM PHOTOGRAPHY

SUB: "The magazine for creative photographers."
SUB: "Officially endorsed by the Photography Instructors Association."
PUBL: LFP, Inc., 9171 Wilshire Blvd., Suite 300, Beverly Hills, CA 90210.
DESC: [*Darkroom Photography*]: "The need (for this periodical) stems from the basic fact that in photography, 'taking the picture' is only the beginning. It is a most critical beginning, but still it is only the first step in the chain of events leading to an enjoyable photograph. The steps after 'taking the picture' are 'developing' and 'printing'...two significant areas most often neglected by current photographic publications. It is this void that *Darkroom Photography* will fill. *Darkroom Photography* will concentrate on well-written and well-researched articles, but our most important credo is: 'Photography is Fun!'" This excellent publication (officially endorsed by the Photography Instructors Association), instructs about technique of the darkroom, and provides a forum for discussion on the artistic approach to completed products. As an in-magazine advertisement stated: "*Darkroom Photography* guides you through the fascinating but complex world of photography. Whether you approach the medium from a technical or visual end, we cover it all!" Numerous black/white and color graphics.
DESC: [*Camera & Darkroom*]: In a promotional advertisement for early 1991, publisher LFP said of the new title: "We've changed our name. But our great coverage stays the same!" Indeed, to their credit, the coverage expanded while maintaining the authoritative stance always associated with the serial. The artistic side of photography gets significant attention, but the focus is on technique. As the advertisement told potential subscribers; "Get the most from the latest techniques, equipment and supplies. There's a world of photographic information waiting for you each month in *Camera & Darkroom Photography* magazine!" Of special note is the usage of *Photography* in advertisements and the front cover of the magazine, although the word is dropped in the official masthead and contents page. Magazine format (8 x 10 ⅞ inches / 205 x 275 mm), numerous graphics in black/white and full color throughout on coated paper stock.
DEPT: "Bender on Black-and-White," "Larger Formats," "Special Effects," "Product Probe," "Color Corner," "Making Money," "Mailbox," "Grabshots," "Readers Tips," "Hot Shots," "Q&A," "Product Review," "Photographers Marketplace," "Calendar," "Final Frame." (12-83). "Editors Page," "Mailbox," "Q&A," "Grab Shots," column by Norma Edwards; "Product Update," "Readers Tips," "Final Frame," last editorial page picture. (8-90).
TYPL: "Suburban Windows," "Re-Imagined Images," "Tanks for the Memories," "Printing Big," "Darkroom Discoveries." (12-83). "The Perfect Moment: Viewing the Robert Mapplethorpe Exhibit," "Paper Fingers From an Unmarked Grave," "David Fahleson: F/8 Creates a Photojournalist," "W. Eugene Smith," "The Magic of Flash." (8-90).
SCHL: Eight issues per year (? - ?); Monthly (?+), 75 pp.

SPAN: Mar/Apr, 1979+
VARIES
--? - Nov, 1990 as Darkroom Photography (ISSN: 0163-9250).
LC: TR 287.D37
DD: 770/.28/305
ISSN: 1056-8484

CAMERA ARTS

PUBL: Ziff-Davis Publishing Co., 1 Park Ave., New York, NY 10016.
DESC: A number of elements combined in the late 1970s to bring forth a host of fine photography magazines. *Camera Arts* is one of these. The Ziff-Davis publication showcases professional work, in a variety of applications. One sample issue addressed photographing in the heat and humidity of the tropics, and photographing church interiors through the technique of "painting with light," along with articles on the life and work of a documentarian, British scenes of everyday life, and one photographer's collage of junkyard castoffs. *Camera Arts* has a fine editorial eye for both present and historical photography, and presents in a format worthy of the images, oftentimes one photograph to a page. Note: some sources indicate that the issue for November/December, 1980 was labeled "Premiere Issue," with actual publication schedule beginning in November/December, 1982. For the sampled 1983 issue: stapled magazine format, with numerous black/white and color graphics and cover all on coated paper stock (8 x 10 ¾ inches / 205 x 275 mm).
DEPT: "Editor's Journal," "Correspondence," "Books," "Perspective," "End Paper," back-page commentary; "New & Noteworthy," "Photographic Exhibitions." (2-83).
TYPL: "In the Heat of the Night," "The Human Factor," "The Body English," "Alter Pieces," "Time Frames." (2-83).
SCHL: Bimonthly (Nov/Dec, 1980 - Jul/Aug, 1982); Monthly (Sep, 1982+), 95 pp.
SPAN: Nov/Dec, 1980 - Jul, 1983//
LC: TR 640 .C35
DD: 770/.5 19
ISSN: 0271-1583

CAMERA CRAFT

SUB: "Official organ of the Photographers' Association of California." (Nov, 1922 - Jan, 1925).
SUB: "A photographic monthly."
PUBL: Camera Craft Publishing Co., Claus Spreckles Bldg., San Francisco, CA.
DESC: This was an excellent publication for its time (for publishing span of 1900 through 1942). Early issues were rather short, but displayed a remarkably creative layout design unique to this magazine. Later issues detailed work in commercial and professional photography of both portrait and product sessions. Articles were well-illustrated with interesting information on how certain photographic essays were shot, and technical features on home projects and new equipment. A group of artistic photos were mixed with human-interest pictures, ranging from flowers to nudes, from dogs to landscapes. It was printed on good quality paper. Periodical was official organ of Photographers' Association of California from November, 1922 to January, 1925.
DEPT: "Questions and Answers," "Monthly Competition," "Club Notes," extensive section discussion photo club activities in the United States; "Notes and Comments," newsbriefs; "Or Bookshelves," paragraph-length reviews. (5-37).
TYPL: "Photographing under Difficulties," "Searching for Unknown Indians," "Photometery in Medical Science," "Photography and the Sequoias," (5- 1900); "The Perfect Negative," "Modern Photography," "Photography and the Eye," "Night Movies Without Electricity." (5-37).
SCHL: Monthly, 60 pp.
SPAN: May, 1900 - Mar, 1942//
ABSORBED
--Western Camera Notes, Jan, 1908.
ABSORBED BY
--American Photography (ISSN: 0097-577x), Apr, 1942.
LC: TR 1.C3
ISSN: 0527-3919

CAMERA MAGAZINE

SUB: "A practicle magazine for photographers."
SUB: "Photography's how-to-do-it magazine."
SUB: "Official organ of Columbia Photographic Society." (Jul, 1897 - Feb, 1900).
PUBL: Camera Magazine, Baltimore, MD.
DESC: [Camera]: *Camera* began as a humble eight-page serial for the members of the Columbia Photographic Society, headquartered in Philadelphia. It was purely a membership publication. By February, 1898, the editors began printing one duotone photograph on each month's cover, but retained the same editorial content. The *Camera Magazine* of the 1950s was a far different serial, providing 100-plus pages of articles, and several color pages per issue. Articles still focused on the consumer side of photography concerning equipment, technique, and new technology. Interestingly, *Camera Magazine* also had some articles about home filmmakers, and Hollywood motion picture equipment.
DEPT: "For the Beginner," "Pinholes," one sentence comments. (12-1897). "Editorial Comment," "Was My Face Red," reader submitted mistakes; "The Camera Forum," Q&A; "Modern Color Methods," "Lighting Angles," "Legal Problems in Photography," "What's New," "The Camera Club News," various club news-briefs; "Modern Movie Methods," "Here's How," "Fotofile," "Inside the Camera." (6-53).
TYPL: "The Landscape Exhibit," "C.P.S. Excursion Through Western Maryland." (12-1897). "Mighty Miniature," "Portraits in the Park," "How to Make Picture Stories." (6-53).

SCHL: Monthly, 110 pp.
SPAN: Mar, 1949 - Jul, 1953//
VARIES
--Jul, 1897 - Feb, 1949 as Camera.
ABSORBED
--Photographic Journal of America, The, Jul, 1923.
--Bulletin of Photography, Jul, 1931.
ABSORBED BY
--Photography, Aug, 1953.
ISSN: 0097-5818

✤ CAMERA OBSCURA

SUB: "A journal of feminism and film theory."
PUBL: Camera Obscura, Rush Rhees Library, University of Rochester, Rochester, NY 14627.
DESC: From a distinctly feminist's point-of-view, the motion picture is examined, dissected, evaluated and critiqued. Discussions are theoretical and philosophical, exploring the issues which constitute the "ideas" inherent in motion picture product, ideas which often move into the political realm. This thrice-yearly serial brings together an unique combination of evaluative elements which makes for interesting reading, and thoughtful consideration of film format and intent on the parts of the cinematographer, director, and producer. Some previous issues are theme-oriented, such as "Feminism, Fiction & Avant-Garde," "Jean-Luc Godard," "Television & The Female Consumer," "Male Trouble," and "The Spectatrix." An excellent journal for exploration of feminist issues within the broad spectrum of the moving visual image. For sampled issue of 1990: perfect-bound journal format, black ink and graphics on uncoated paper stock, cover consisting of black ink on coated paper stock (5 ½ X 8 ½ inches / 140 x 215 mm).
DEPT: "Women Working," current status of various projects. (fall-77). "Editorial," "Reviews." (1-90).
TYPL: "The Avant-Garde and Its Imaginary," "Hitchcock, The Enunciator," "Introduction to Arnold Schoenberg's 'Accompaniment for a Cinematographic Scene': Straub/Huillett: Brecht: Schoenberg," "Jeanne Dielman, 23 Quai du Commerce, 1080 Bruxelles," "La Femme du Gange." (fall-77). "Feminism and Film History," "Reformers and Spectators: The Film Education Movement in the Thirties," "Adventures of Goldilocks: Spectatorship, Consumerism and Public Life," "Melodrama and Social Drama in the Early German Cinema," "Female Power in the Serial-Queen Melodrama: The Etiology of an Anomaly." (1-90).
SCHL: Three issues per year [irregular at times], 175 pp.
SPAN: Fall, 1976+
LC: PN 1995.9.W6 C28
DD: 791.43/088042 19
ISSN: 0270-5346
ABST: --Alternative Press Index (ISSN: 0002-662x)
--Arts and Humanities Citation Index (ISSN: 0162-8445)
--Film Literature Index (ISSN: 0093-6758)
--International Index to Film Periodicals (ISSN: 0000-0038)

CAMERA 35

SUB: "Magazine of miniature photography." (spring, 1957 - ?).
SUB: "The number one authority on photography."
PUBL: Popular Publications, 150 East 58th St., New York, NY 10022.
DESC: At first published by U.S. Camera Publishing Corporation, and later by Popular Publications, *Camera 35* provided up-to-date information on emerging product in the 35mm field, and was a showcase for the talents of its readers and professional photographers. The very first issue of Spring, 1957 was devoted to convincing a rather skeptical audience that 35 mm photography had arrived for professional and amateur alike. Columnist Will Connell in that issue extolled the virtues of the new format, while photographer Fritz Henle disparaged the new upstart photographic medium. Early issues were primarily instructive, moving some 20 years later to an appreciation of its readers' relative sophistication in the 35mm camera field. The 1970s held a fascination for the female form, as various features showcased photographers' talents. Latter issues were an even mixture of features and technical topics, with significant color pages. For the sampled issue of 1957: stapled magazine format, primarily black/white editorial content with some color pages and full-color cover on coated paper stock (9 x 12 inches / 230 x 305 mm). Commencing with the Spring, 1958 issue a different format size was implemented: (8 ¼ x 11 ⅛ inches / 215 x 285 mm). For the sampled issue of 1977: stapled magazine format, mixture of black/white and full-color pages and cover on coated paper stock (8 x 10 ¾ inches / 205 x 275 mm).
DEPT: "Lens Lines," 'Commentary by the editors on things seen and heard'; "Technical Topics," column by Arthur Kramer; "Comments on Color," column by Phillip Leonian. (fall-57). "Editor's Notebook," "Letters," "Critic's Corner," column by Michael Edelson; "The Third Eye," column by Lief Ericksenn; "Photpourri," "Tips from a Pro," column by Jim Elder; "On Color," column by Ed Scully; "A Humanist View," column by Lou Stettner; "Books in Review," "Ad Lib." (5-78).
TYPL: "Faces in Sports," "Lightning in the Lab," "Fiesta in Cuba," "My First Roll of Film," Filing Negatives." (#2-57). "Reincarnations," "The Face of Courage," "The Lower East Side," "Reproducing Pictures." (5-78).
SCHL: Monthly, 60 pp.
SPAN: Spring, 1957 - May?, 1978//
MERGED WITH
--Photo World (ISSN: 0091-2778) (to form) Camera 35 With Photo World, Jun?, 1978.
LC: TR 1.C46
ISSN: 0008-2171

CAMERA 35 INCORPORATING PHOTO WORLD

PUBL: Sahadi Publications, Inc., PO Box 239, Palisades, NY 10964.
DESC: This monthly publication (title on front cover reads *Camera 35*, but *Camera 35 Incorporating Photo World* on the masthead/publication page), was designed for the 35 mm professional serious about his/her craft. While feature articles covered a wide range of topics, the focus of this monthly was on a wonderful assemblage of departmental columnists, photographic professionals in their own right, who wrote authoritative columns on a wide variety of subjects. These columns provided information, commentary, opinion and facts, often with witty, urbane prose. In one sampled issue, columnists explored a myriad of new photographic books on the Christmas gift-giving market; another looked back on the year in review and wondered what the marketing geniuses would convince the consumer to buy next; another article showcased a man who rented exotic automobiles for professional shoots; and a fascinating article concerning idea thievery for photographic subjects. For the sampled issue of 1981: mixture of black/white and full-color pages and cover on coated paper stock (8 x 10 ¾ inches / 200 x 270 mm).
DEPT: "Editor's Notebook," editorial column by Lief Ericksenn; "Letters to the Editor," 'Kudos, challenges, criticisms and ideas from our readers'; "Light Readings," column by A. D. Coleman; "The 40th Frame," column by Jim Elder; "Behind the Scenes," column by Casey Allen; "Safelight," column by Bob Nadler; "Books in Review," column by Joe Novak; "Positives & Negatives," column by Hugh Birnbaum; "The Third Eye," column by Lief Ericksenn. (12-81).
TYPL: "Radiant Light Forms," "Two For the Road," "Messing Up the Signals," "A Short Look at a Long Lens," "A Song and a Dance." (12-81).
SCHL: Monthly, 85 pp.
SPAN: Jun, 1978 - Apr, 1982//
FROM MERGER OF
--Camera 35 (and) Photo World (ISSN: 0091-2778).
VARIES
--Jun, 1978 - Jul, 1978 as Camera 35 With Photo World.
--Aug, 1978 - Feb, 1979 as Camera 35 Photo World.
--Mar, 1979 - Jun, 1979 as Camera 35 With Photo World.
LC: TR 1.C46
DD: 770/.5
ABST: --Consumers Index to Product Evaluations and Information Sources (ISSN: 0094-0534)

Camera 35 Photo World

Aug, 1978 - Feb, 1979//
SEE: CAMERA 35 INCORPORATING PHOTO WORLD

Camera 35 With Photo World

Jun, 1978 - Jul, 1978//
SEE: CAMERA 35 INCORPORATING PHOTO WORLD

Camera 35 With Photo World

Mar, 1979 - Jun, 1979//
SEE: CAMERA 35 INCORPORATING PHOTO WORLD

Camera World

Jun, 1955 - Apr, 1958//
SEE: 35MM PHOTOGRAPHY

✧ CAMERART

SUB: "The international magazine of Japanese photography."
SUB: "All the news about cameras and photography."
PUBL: CamerArt, C.P.O. Box 20, Tokyo, Japan.
DESC: Still, motion picture, and video media all receive their due review in this Japanese publication. Although written in English, the focus is Japanese, with many pictures of Japan, and promotional discussion of Japanese products. Of special note are in-depth articles pertaining to emerging Japanese products.
DEPT: "Editor's Album," "What's New in Photo Products," "Snapshots: Photo News in Brief," "Aids to Help You in Photo and Video," "Video News." (11-85).
TYPL: "Eye-Catching Cameras Today," "Tokyo Map," "Still Camera Report," "Japanese Video Industry Slowed by 8mm Video." (11-85).
SCHL: Monthly, 60 pp.
SPAN: Spring, 1958+
LC: TR 1.C55
DD: 770
ISSN: 0008-2082

✧ CAMPAIGN

SUB: "The specialist weekly for the communicators."
SUB: "The only national weekly serving the advertising, journalistic, printing and allied fields, including newspapers, magazines, trade press, outdoor publicity, commercial films, TV and radio, direct mail, advertising production and press and public relations."
SUB: "The Communications Newspaper."
SUB: "The national weekly of the communications business embracing advertising, marketing, newspapers and magazines, film and television."
PUBL: Haymarket Publishing, Regent House, 54-62 Regent St., London W1A 4YJ, England.
DESC: For over fifty years, *Campaign* and its various titles has been "the" resource for news of advertising placement, strategies, campaigns, techniques, and politics within the British advertising community. Similar in nature to the American *Adweek* series, it informed

well about ad campaigns, the status of agencies, and their corporate clients. Of ongoing interest in earlier years was the relative health of British media, especially as advertising vehicles. Early issues were mostly print-oriented, with somewhat short articles (moving to longer features concerning all media in latter issues), with an emphasis upon personel changes, securing of new accounts, and media campaign purchases. The current serial, *Campaign*, is a large-format, glossy publication which has greatly expanded the scope of its predecessor, "Worlds Press News and Advertisers Review." *Campaign* covers British advertising and publication news primarily, but also includes international advertising coverage, especially campaigns in and from America. As befits a publication of its nature, a great number of photos and ad reprints are featured in a breezy format. Large magazine format in early issues, moving September 8, 1961 to a slightly smaller format, and now back to a large tabloid format; numerous graphics, especially of print advertisements.

DEPT: "News Extra," late-breaking newsbriefs; "Christiansen's Column," "News from Manchester," "Don Iddon from New York," comment; "Lancashire-West," "Nine to Five-Thirty," advertising comment; "Dr. Syntax Presents Good Writing Points," "Conference Planning," "International News," "Commonwealth Press," status; "Ad Eye by Hermes," personnel changes; "Campaign Briefs," "Focus on Fleet Street," "Captain Video's," TV column. (7-1-60). "Marketing," comment column by John Winkler; "PR Affairs," column by Robert Gavin; "Adlib," advertising commentary; "Commonwealth Press," status; "Press," column by Sir Linton Andrews; "Cover 2," personnel newsbriefs. (7-26-68). "International News," briefs; "Outline," gossip briefs; "Account Changes," "Leader," editorial; "The Grapevine," gossip; "Phil Klineman," commentary on agencys; "TV Ratings," of prior weeks broadcasts; "Monday's Newcomers," 'A review of the weeks commercials;' "Michael Jackson," newspaper comment; "Sellers on Style," format comment; "Campaign Medals," onions and roses for recent campaigns; "The Printer's Devil," 'Giving printers a hot time each week. . .printbuyer Terry Snow of Hobson, Bates;' "Mediagraph," publications data in chart form. (6-24-77).

TYPL: "Westminster Press to Pay 15% Agency Commission," "David Ogilvy Wins 16 Million $ Shell Oil Account from J.W.T.," "Ad Clutter Code May be Extended to Scotland," "Outdoor Ad Contractors' Petition to House of Lords Succeeds." (7-1-60). "Way Open for Other PR Groups," "'E Mail' Gives Ad Rates," "Festival Controversey Rages: Pearl Replies," "Television Ad Society: Working Party Set Up." (7-26-68). "Mail Revives Color Supplement Idea," "More Trouble for GBO Agency," "Admen Blaze a Trail Beyond the Iron Curtain," "Its Your Baby, Say Agencies," "One Revolution the Press Should Join," (10-4-68); "Unions Fair List: Agencies Unscathed," "Charity Slams Ban on Radio Commercial," "Colgate Splashes Out on Liquid Detergent," "Major City Agencies Set New Buying Trend," (6-24-77).

SCHL: Weekly, 75 pp.
SPAN: 1929+
VARIES
--1929 - Oct, 1935 as World's Press News.
--Nov, 1935 - Aug, 19, 1937 as World's Press News and Advertising.
--1944 - Nov 13, 1964 as World's Press News and Advertiser's Review,
--Nov 20, 1964 - Sep 4, 1968? as WPN and Advertisers' Review.
ABSORBED
--Advertising World, Nov, 1935?
WITH SUPPLEMENT
--Printing (ISSN: 0032-8618), 1932 - May, 1934.
--Sign and Display Advertising, 1933 - 1936.
--Design & Art Direction, ? - Jan 17, 1986.
--Direction, Feb 14, 1986+.
LC: PN 4701.W62
DD: 659
ISSN: 0008-2309
ABST: --Management and Marketing Abstracts (ISSN: 0308-2172)
--Management Contents
--Predicasts
--Printing Abstracts (ISSN: 0031-109x)

CAMPUS BROADCASTERS

SUB: "The campus membership of National Religious Broadcasters."
PUBL: Intercollegiate Religious Broadcasters, CN 1926, Morristown, NJ 07960.
DESC: This short newsletter is for Christian colleges with communications departments and membership in the Intercollegiate Religious Broadcasters, the academic arm of National Religious Broadcasters.
DEPT: None.
TYPL: "LBC Kicks Off New Year," "Northwestern Starts New Station," "Evangelizing Through Drama," "NRB Offers Personnel Service." (11-83).
SCHL: Irregular, 8 pp.
SPAN: ? - ?//

Canadian Broadcaster, The

Jan, 1942 - Sep, 1969//
(ISSN: 0319-1389)
SEE: BROADCASTER

Canadian Cinematography

1961 - May/Jun, 1967//
(ISSN: 0576-4823)
SEE: CINEMA/CANADA

Canadian Film and TV Bi-Weekly

May 26, 1965 - Dec 24, 1969//
(ISSN: 0383-0233)
SEE: CANADIAN FILM DIGEST

CANADIAN FILM DIGEST

SUB: "Voice of the Canadian motion picture industry."
SUB: "Voice of the entertainment industry."
PUBL: Canadian Film-TV Bi-Weekly, 175 Bloor St., East, Toronto 5, Ontario Canada.
DESC: This ten-page biweekly provides exhibitor and studio information on the Canadian film industry. Topics of interest include new products, exhibitor growth, and new promotion and technological developments. As with other film industry counterparts, a large number of promotional/publicity photos are used.
DEPT: "Our Business," industry comment column by N.A. Taylor; "News Notes," briefs; "On the Square," comment column by Hye Bossin; "Short Throws," briefs; "Films in Production," data on Canadian product. (7-15-53). "Looking Ahead," new upcoming product; "Its My Bag," personality column by Ed Hocura; "News Clips," briefs. (11-26-59).
TYPL: "Screen Ads Stronger in Country," "Drive-In Total Now 130 as Five More Open," "Hypo Promotion for MGM Films," (7-15-53). "Twentieth-Century Fox Report Has Sad Sound of Music," "No Cause for Gloom at Walt Disney Studio," "Explosion to Premiere in B.C. at Thirteen Theaters." (11-26-69).
SCHL: Weekly (1936 - May 12, 1965); Biweekly (May 26, 1965+), 10 pp.
SPAN: 1936 - Dec, 1976//
VARIES
--1936 - May 12, 1965 as Canadian Film Weekly (ISSN: 0383-0225).
--May 26, 1965 - Dec 24, 1969 as Canadian Film and TV Bi-Weekly (ISSN: 0383-0233).
--Jan 14, 1970 - May 29, 1970 as Canadian Film Weekly (ISSN: 0590-7918).
SUSPENDED
--May, 1974 - Nov, 1976.
ABSORBED
--Canadian Moving Picture Digest, ?
LC: PN 1993.C33
DD: 338.4/7/791430971
ISSN: 0008-3569

Canadian Film Weekly

1936 - May 12, 1965//
(ISSN: 0383-0225)
SEE: CANADIAN FILM DIGEST

Canadian Film Weekly

Jan 14, 1970 - May 29, 1970//
(ISSN: 0590-7918)
SEE: CANADIAN FILM DIGEST

✤ CANADIAN JOURNAL OF COMMUNICATION

SUB: "Research, analysis and comment on communication and mass media."
PUBL: Canadian Journal of Communication, PO Box 272, Station R, Toronto, Ontario M4G 3T0 Canada.
DESC: "Research, analysis and comment on communication and mass media. Published quarterly for media practitioners, academics, students and the general public." A typewritten magazine format periodical that covers academic research, criticism, and activities of Canadian media. Few graphics; some article reprints.
DEPT: None. (spring-78).
TYPL: "Interactive Cable Communication Services," "Themes of Innis and Marx Compared," "Community Groups and Media," "TV Ontario Founded for Learning," "Proxemics and Television--the Politician's Dilemma." (spring-78).
SCHL: Quarterly, 45 pp.
SPAN: Mar, 1974+
VARIES
--Mar, 1974 - Summer, 1977 as Media Probe (ISSN: 0384-1618).
LC: P 87
DD: 301.16/1/0971
ISSN: 0705-3657
ABST: --Canadian Business Index (ISSN: 0227-8669)

✤ CANADIAN PHOTOGRAPHIC JOURNAL, THE

SUB: "Devoted to the interests of the professional and amateur photographer." (Feb, 1892 - ?).
PUBL: G. Gilson, Toronto, Canada.
DESC: This serial resembles a host of other amateur/professional photography publications of the era, except that it is targeted to the Canadian reader with topics of national interest. Each issue contained assorted articles pertaining to equipment, darkroom technique, composition, exhibitions, and other items of interest to readers. Of special note was the inclusion (at least in early issues) of a mounted photograph on thick cardboard that prefaced each issue. Editor and publisher George Gilson hand autographed his own picture, mounted in the end-of-the-year issue for January, 1893. Small format.
DEPT: "Books Received," "Trade Catalogues Received." (1-1893).
TYPL: "Lantern Slides of Life and Character," "Kodaks at the World's Fair," "The Amateur Question," "Good Work for Women." (1-1893).
SCHL: Monthly, 40 pp.
SPAN: Feb, 1892+?
LC: TR 1.C6

✤ CANADIAN PRINTER

SUB: "Devoted to the interests of the printers and publishers of Canada."

SUB: "Maclean-Hunter national monthly of the Canadian graphic arts industries."
SUB: "The monthly magazine read by everyone in the Canadian printing industry."
PUBL: Maclean-Hunter, Ltd., 777 Bay St., Toronto, Ontario M5W 1A7, Canada.
DESC: [*Canadian Printer & Publisher*]: Designed for the pressman and manager, *Canadian Printer and Publisher* has had a fine record of bringing new developments in technology and technique to its subscribers' attention. This serial speaks both to the everyday problems in producing quality product, as well as managerial problems of marketing, sales, and office management. Of special note were inclusions of sample printing on unique papers or using advanced techniques. One prime example of this was the inclusion of a 3-dimensional printed card of the Last Supper in the June, 1968 edition.
DEPT: "Typothetae Activities," "Cross-Canada News," "Trade News." (7-22). "Things I Hear," newsbriefs; "Direction," comment; "News Scene," "Materials Handling," "New Patents," "Manufacturing & Supply," "Graphic Arts Financial," newsbriefs; "Appointments," "Dates for Your Diary," "Printing File," newsbriefs; "People in Publishing." (6-68).
TYPL: "Paper Box Manufacturing," "Radio Epidemic in Alberta," "Offset Printing Explained," "Building a Weekly Newspaper." (7-22). "Instant Estimating gives Costs by Adding Two Figures," "Production Control System Cuts Out Dependence on Memory," "3-D Printing is Making its Move to Capture New Markets," "Copyright Laws Don't Protect the Author and Publisher." (6-68).
SCHL: Monthly, 70 pp.
SPAN: 1891+
  VARIES
  --? - ? as Printer & Publisher (ISSN: 0317-1213).
  --? - Aug, 1989 as Canadian Printer & Publisher (ISSN: 0008-4816).
LC: Z 119.C3
DD: 338.4/76862/0971 20
ISSN: 0849-0767
ABST: --Abstract Bulletin of the Institute of Paper Chemistry (ISSN: 0020-3033)
  --Canadian Business Index (ISSN: 0227-8669)
  --Printing Abstracts (ISSN: 0031-109x)

Canadian Printer & Publisher

? - Aug, 1989//
(ISSN: 0008-4816)
SEE: CANADIAN PRINTER

Canadian Telephone and Cable Television Journal

Spring, 1966 - Apr/May, 1973//
(ISSN: 0008-5162)
SEE: CABLE COMMUNICATIONS MAGAZINE

Canadian Telephone Journal, The

May, 1934? - Dec, 1965//
(ISSN: 0318-0050)
SEE: CABLE COMMUNICATIONS MAGAZINE

✤ CANEWS

SUB: "Publication of Christians in the Arts Networking."
PUBL: Christians in the Arts Networking, Inc., PO Box 1941, Cambridge, MA 02238-1941.
DESC: A typewritten, legal-sized page newsletter designed to provide a quarterly report on the activities of Christians and Christian groups in the performing arts. "CAN exists to strengthen Christ-centered art and its makers by encouraging communication and fellowship, and by gathering and spreading information." Sampled issue for 1991: two legal-size sheets of paper, typewritten black ink on light-yellow uncoated paper stock, no advertising (8 ½ x 14 inches / 215 x 355 mm).
DEPT: "CAN Opening," performing arts opportunities; "Networking," news of productions and personnel; "The CANdid Report: A Living Stone Collection," news column by Karen Mulder. (winter-89).
TYPL: "Network with Asian Christian Artists and Image Magazine," "Playwright/Actor Tom Key to Perform in Off-Broadway Theater," "Behind the Bamboo Curtain," "Biennial Visual Arts Conference." (winter-89).
SCHL: Quarterly, 2 pp.
SPAN: ?+

✤ CANTRILLS FILMNOTES

SUB: "An irregular publication in which Arthur and Corinne Cantrill print anything in cinema which interests them."
SUB: "A review of independent cinema and video."
PUBL: Arthur and Corinne Cantrill, Box 1295 L, G.P.O. Melbourne, Victoria 3001, Australia.
DESC: The two sub-titles above describe quite well the variations in format and philosophy that *Cantrill's Filmnotes* went through from the first mimeograph issue to later, glossy issues in the 1970s. This is a periodical of alternative cinema and video, with emphasis on developments in Australian and New Zealand media. Poetry, film and video criticism, introduction of new directors, and recent productions in the alternative media field are featured. A striking number of graphic illustrations are in each issue.
DEPT: "Editor's Notes," "Letters," "New Books," reviews. (7-76).
TYPL: "Propositions and Thoughts in Pictures," "Jeff Keen and the Theatre of Doctor Goz," "Energy Field Films," "Ant Farm in Australia." (7-76).
SCHL: Bimonthly (1971 - 1972); Quarterly (1973 - 1974); Semiyearly (1975 - 1980); Fortnightly, 70 pp.
SPAN: Mar, 1971+
LC: PN 1993.C333
DD: 791.43/05
ISSN: 0158-4154

ABST: --Film Literature Index (ISSN: 0093-6758)

Canyon Cinemanews
Jan, 1963 - Sep/Oct, 1976//
(ISSN: 0008-5758)
SEE: CINEMANEWS, THE

Captain George's Whizzbang
Nov/Dec, 1968? - Vol 1, #6?//
SEE: NEW CAPTAIN GEORGE'S WHIZZBANG, THE

✤ CAR AUDIO AND ELECTRONICS
PUBL: CurtCo Publishing, Warner Plaza VI, 21700 Oxnard St., Suite 1600, Woodland Hills, CA 91367.
DESC: "...*Car Audio and Electronics* is the automotive accessory that combines the pleasure of music, a sense of security, and the power of communication. ...Each issue includes: simple articles explaining the latest technologies; overviews covering the equipment on the market; a new product section bringing machines to life; comparison test reports that really help people buy; columns by experts to help readers get the most out of their electronics when they're in their cars." An imaginative layout design enhances understanding of equipment, and installation of same within individual automobiles. For the 1990 sampled issue: full color graphics throughout, including cover on coated paper stock in perfect-bound magazine format (8 x 10 ⅞ inches / 205 x 275 mm).
DEPT: "Hot News," 'on car audio, security, cellular phones, or other auto electronics'; "Letters," "New Machines," product review; "Installations," showcase; "Choices," unique applications; "Down the Road," column by Bill Neill; "Troubleshooting," column by David Navone; "Street Security," column by Barnet C. Fagel; "Tunes to Go," column by Doug Newcomb; "Test Report." (7-90).
TYPL: "The Best of the Year," "Thank You, Mr. Ohm," "Six Cassette Radios Under $350." (7-90).
SCHL: Monthly, 135 pp.
SPAN: Jul, 1988+
DD: 621 11
ISSN: 0898-3720

✤ CAR STEREO REVIEW
SUB: "From the editors of Stereo Review."
PUBL: Diamandis Communications, Inc., 1633 Broadway, New York, NY 10019.
DESC: Upscale automobile owners will be informed about upscale audio and electronics products in this bimonthly publication by the editors of *Stereo Review*. Although topics are diverse (such as extensive buying guides on cellular telephones, radar devices, CBs, and other electronics), the primary emphasis remains on high-quality, high-tech audio equipment and related products. Publication assumes understanding of audio system basics. Indicative of the type of reader drawn to this bimonthly are the specific automobiles utilized for representative systems such as the Porsche Carrera 4, Nissan 240SX Coupe, and the Mustang GT. Graphics are first-rate, and the articles are authoritative and informative, contributing to the publishing success of this serial. Magazine format (7 ⅞ x 10 ½ inches / 200 x 265 mm); numerous full color graphics; extensive advertising.
DEPT: "The Front End," editorial; "Sound Off," letters; "New For the Road," new product review; "Close-Up," comment and observations; "Tool Aid," 'Tools and accessories for professional installers and the do-it-yourselfer' column by Pat Turnmire; "Security & Communications," column by Joseph Palenchar; "Car Tunes," Music review column by Chris Giancola and Mike Mettler; "The Fast Lane," column by Ralph Hodges; "Wire Service," electronic wiring column by Wayne Harris; "Back Seat," observations; "Test Reports," extensive test bench reports; "User's Evaluations," unique equipment review. (7/8-90).
TYPL: "Systems: The Mustang that took IASCA," "Systems: New Problems and Solutions in the 1990 Porsche Carrera 4," "Design and Conquer: Subwoofer Boxes and the Pursuit of Amazing Bass," "Scales of Justice: Weighing the Options in High-End Security," "Insider Report: System Building: Four Systems for the 1990 Nissan 240SX Coupe." (7/8-90).
SCHL: Quarterly (? - spring, 1988); Bimonthly (Jul/Aug, 1988+), 150 pp.
SPAN: Fall, 1987+
DD: 621 11
ISSN: 0894-3443

✤ CARDOZO ARTS & ENTERTAINMENT LAW JOURNAL
PUBL: Benjamin N. Cardozo School of Law, Yeshiva University, New York, NY 10003.
DESC: This is one of a growing group of quality law journals of recent publication vintage which examines the relatively new field of communication law and regulation. Journal articles reflect decisions handed down in major court tests, and provide an historical or sociological review of a particular communications issue. Well recommended for exploration of contemporary issues of communication ethics, regulation, economics, and freedom-of-information. A publication of the Benjamin N. Cardozo School of Law at Yeshiva University. For the sampled issue of 1990: black ink on uncoated paper stock in perfect-bound journal format, with cover consisting of dark blue ink on uncoated paper stock (6 ¾ x 10 inches / 170 x 255 mm).
DEPT: "Book Review." (#1-84). "Notes." (#1-90).

TYPL: "The Widening Gyre: Are Derivative Works Getting Out of Hand?," "Antitrust Issues in the New Video Media," "Summary Judgement in Copyright: From Cole Porter to Superman," "New York Artists' Authorship Rights Act of 1983: Waiver and Fair Use," "Old Wine in New Bottles: Replacing the Fairness Doctrine with an Enforcable Diversity in the Media," "Coming to a Theatre Near You: Movie Distributors Challenge Exhibitor Instigated Anti-Blind Bidding Statutes." (#1-84). "An Antitrust Paradox for the 1990s: Revisiting the Role of the First Amendment in Cable Television," "Author, User, Scholar, Thief: Fair Use and Unpublished Works," "University of New York v. Fox--The Dawn of a New Age of Commercial Speech Regulation of Tobacco and Alcohol," "Painting a Dark Picture: The Need for Reform of IRS Practices and Procedures Relating to Fine Art Appraisals," "Trial by Docudrama: Fact or Fiction?" (#1-90).
SCHL: Semiannual, 270 pp.
SPAN: Spring, 1982+
LC: K 3.A687
DD: 344.73/097/05
ISSN: 0736-7694
ABST: --Legal Resource Index

Carleton Drama Review

1955? - May?, 1957//
(ISSN: 0161-3936)
SEE: TDR

✤ CARTOONIST PROFILES

PUBL: Cartoonist Profiles, PO Box 325, Fairfield, CT 06430.
DESC: A truly fascinating, quarterly journal of cartoon art and profiles of their creative professionals. Although there are numerous examples of popular culture and fanzine elements within any given issue, it is a publication for the working professional. Even the advertisements (which are predominently that of syndicated services) are trade-oriented. Editor Jud Hurd has created a wonderful meeting place where working cartoonists can come together for a discussion of cartoonist backgrounds, strip histories, legal developments, economic considerations, and virtually any other element which is important to the field. In one sampled issue for 1990, cartoonist Jerry Scott described how a character balloon company transferred his "Nancy" character from the printed page to that of parade character balloon. Another article provided an interview with a comics syndicate editor that discussed the process of selecting new strips for syndication. Other articles detailed how to develop a running gag, techniques of cel animation, and an excellent information section on "Important Children's Book Information for Cartoonists." Also of importance was a cartoon and caricature collector who provided a fascinating insight into the means by which unscrupulous collectors or sales agents manage to obtain original cartoon work. Of note is a special section at the end of the issue devoted to news from the Museum of Cartoon Art in Rye Brook, New York, a institution with over 60,000 individual pieces of artwork. For the working professional, *Cartoonist Profiles* is an outstanding reference source. For the sampled issue of 1990: stapled magazine format, editorial and advertising content is black ink on quality uncoated paper stock, cover consists of two-color ink on uncoated paper stock, advertising is targeted to the working professional cartoonist (8 ½ x 11 inches / 215 x 280 mm).
DEPT: None. (9-81). "Ask Leo," Q&A column by Leo Stoutsenberger; "News and Events," from the Museum of Cartoon Art. (3-90).
TYPL: "Jim Henson's Muppets by Guy and Brad Gilchrist," "Jack Markow," "War Correspondent, Syndicate President, Oil Painter, Cartoonist!," "Animation for a Broadway Musical," "The Yellow Kid," "A Limited Edition Comic Art from Famous Fine Art Publisher, " "Denis Gifford's British TV Game Show." (9-81). "A 55-Foot 'Nancy'," "Syndicate Comics Editor," "Glenn Bernhardt--Magazine Cartoonist," "Development of a Gag," "Could You Send an Original?" (3-90).
SCHL: Quarterly, 85 pp.
SPAN: Winter, 1969+
LC: NC 1300.C35
DD: 741.5/0973
ISSN: 0008-7068

✤ CASTING CALL

SUB: "Where show business begins."
PUBL: Mel Pogue Enterprises, 3365 Cahuenga, Hollywood, CA 90068.
DESC: For over 15 years *Casting Call* has been a Hollywood resource for motion pictures, television, print, theatre, and other projects requiring actors and actresses. Editorial content is typed and layout is pasted in traditional fashion. Personality columns are wonderful sources of news in a variety of production markets, but it is probably the "Auditions" items which command the greatest attention from subscribers. Stapled magazine format. Editorial content black/white on uncoated paper stock, with coated paperstock cover (8 ½ x 11 inches / 215 x 280 mm).
DEPT: "Auditions," "Wardrobe," column by Hy Fashion; "Las Vegas Casting," column by Polly Peluso; "Stargazing," "Palm Springs," 'Show Biz' column by Breena Alane; "Hollywood Reporting," column by Jean Doran; "Lee Hartgrave's Show Buzz," column by Lee Hartgrave. (5-16-91).
TYPL: None. (5-16-91).
SCHL: Biweekly, 12 pp.
SPAN: Jan 17, 1976+

✤ CASTING NEWS

SUB: "New England's most complete guide to opportunities in the performing arts."
PUBL: Casting News Publications, PO Box 201, Boston, MA 02134.
DESC: A one year subscription (for 1991) to *Casting News* is $45, a wise investment for anyone interested in professional performing arts employment in the greater Boston/New England region. This monthly magazine covers it all, from an outstanding article on how to assemble the proper headshots and resumes to a poignant rememberence of New England actress Lee Remick. A column entitled "The Voice Doctor" provides practical advice on approaching the recording session, with informative counsel on insuring the successful recording session. The "Curtain Calls" review section serves up wonderful details on current productions from the performing artist and craftsperson point-of-view, a refreshing approach! Despite these wonderful editorial content items, the raison d'être remains the extensive listing section which may occupy half of any given issue. Listed here is a solid core of audition and contact information for a variety of performing arts positions, including sections for "Actors," "Musicians," "Dancers," "Variety Artists," and a rarely seen section for "Staff" positions. Three additional sections, "Films & Video Tapes," "Funding," and "Scripts" provide current information on festivals, competitions, and opportunities for performing arts producers. For the sampled issue of 1991: stapled magazine format, black ink typewritten editorial content with various pictures on uncoated paper stock, cover consisting of two-color red and black ink on coated paper stock (8 3/8 x 11 inches / 215 x 280 mm).
DEPT: "The Voice Doctor," column by Jeannie Deva; "Curtain Calls," column by John Chatterton and D. M. Colucci; "Crossword," puzzle; "Broadway Box Office," current show statistics; "Local Pop Music," review column by Michael Cohen and Debbie Catalano; "Actors," extensive upcoming auditions listing; "Musicians," needed for upcoming productions; "Top 20 Albums," record statistics; "Films & Video Tapes," distribution and festival listing; "Top 20 Films," current statistics; "Top 20 Video Rentals," current statistics; "Word Puzzle," "Funding," grants, awards, and fund information; "Scripts," wanted, and production company contacts; "Dancers," auditions listing; "Variety Artists," auditions and needed; "Staff," performing arts staff positions available. (8-91).
TYPL: "Headshots & Resumes," "New England Stars: Lee Remick," "Promising New Act: The Industrial Gypsies." (8-91).
SCHL: Biweekly, 35 pp.
SPAN: Aug 1, 1988?+

CASTLE OF FRANKENSTEIN

PUBL: Gothic Castle Publishing, 509 Fifth Ave., New York, NY 10017.
DESC: At first "trance," the reader might assume that *Castle of Frankenstein* would appeal only to devotees of ghouls, ghosts and goblins. However, it is a nostalgic and current lay pictorial covering everything from Japanese science fiction films to current television programs (circa early 1960s), such as "Twilight Zone," and "Men in Space." Like most fan magazines, it has numerous photos and large type format. Newsprint.
DEPT: "Ghostal Mail," v-e-r-y unusual letters to the editor; "The Melting Pot," reviews of amateur fantasy and monster press.
TYPL: "'The Mummy' Through the Ages," "George Pal's 'The Time Machine,'" "Have Rocket--Will Travel," "Jack the Ripper," "Greetings Honorable Monster--Take Me to Your Emperor." (2-61).
SCHL: Quarterly (? - ?); Bimonthly (?+); Irregular at times, 70 pp.
SPAN: ?, 1959 - ?, 1974//
VARIES
--?, 1959 - Dec?, 1961 as Journal of Frankenstein, The.
LC: None.

✤ CAT NEWS

PUBL: International Communication Association, Communication and Technology Division, PO Box 9589, Austin, TX 78766.
DESC: This brief newsletter details current news and developments of the Communication and Technology Division of the International Communication Association. The Spring, 1991 issue consisted exclusively of news pertaining to an upcoming ICA convention; papers to be presented, a list of reviewers and information on bylaws. For the sampled issue of 1991: typeset black ink on uncoated paper stock, stapled single sheets, no advertising (8 1/2 x 11 inches / 215 x 280 mm).
DEPT: None. (spring-91).
TYPL: "1991 Chicago ICA Convention," "Communication and Technology Sessions." (spring-91).
SCHL: Semiyearly?, 6 pp.
SPAN: ?+

Catholic Film Newsletter

1964 - Dec 30, 1975//
(ISSN: 0008-8021)
SEE: FILM & BROADCASTING REVIEW

✤ CATHOLIC JOURNALIST

SUB: "The official organ of the Catholic Press Association of the United States."
PUBL: Catholic Press Association, 119 N. Park Ave., Rockville Centre, NY 11570.

DESC: The American Catholic church has always had strong roots in print media. Therefore, it was only natural that the *Catholic Journalist Newsletter* was begun to serve a community of diocesan newspapers and independent publishers affiliated with the Catholic community. Early newsletters were typewritten with some photographs in an eight-page format. Later issues, dropping the word *newsletter*, went to typeset newsprint tabloid format. Primary audience remains the 500- plus publishers of diocesan materials, with some articles exploring radio, television, and satellite distribution.
DEPT: "In the Spotlight," personnel newsbriefs; "Publishers Newsbriefs," "Books for Journalists," reviews. (8-68).
TYPL: "1968 Catholic Press Directory is Published; Shows Circulation Jump for Catholic Papers," "Conference Exploring Religious Journalism to be Held Next Month at Northwestern University." (8-68). "CPA Tells Archbishop Laghi Catholic Journalists are Loyal, Faithful," "Catholic New York to Publish First Issue September 17," "Father McBrien Urges Church to Change with Modern World." (6-81).
SCHL: Monthly, 8 pp.
SPAN: 1945+
VARIES
--? - ? as Catholic Journalist Newsletter.
LC: PN 4700
ISSN: 0008-8129

Catholic Journalist Newsletter
? - ?//
SEE: CATHOLIC JOURNALIST

CATHOLIC SCHOOL EDITOR
SUB: "Official publication of the Catholic School Press Association."
PUBL: Catholic School Press Association, Marquette College of Journalism, 1135 W. Kilbourn Ave., Milwaukee, WI 53233.
DESC: A rather small constituency was served by this publication; Catholic gradeschools, highschools, and colleges with publications programs. Although it had a long publishing span (beginning in 1922), the magazine did not remain current with its audience, and ceased publication in June, 1975. The black/white glossy format provided interesting articles, but one which typically could have also been in other secular magazines.
DEPT: None.
TYPL: "Step Up Advocacy, Song-Peddle Authority," "Let Your Students Carry the Ball," "Our Quicksilver Words: Use Them With Care and With Love," "How and Why to Make Readers Care About Reviews." (3-74).
SCHL: Quarterly, 15 pp.
SPAN: 1922 - Jun, 1975//
LC: PN 4700.C

ISSN: 0008-834x

CATV
Aug 14, 1967 - Oct 18, 1976//
(ISSN: 0574-9204)
SEE: VUE

✤ CAUCUS QUARTERLY, THE
SUB: "The caucus for producers, writers, & directors."
PUBL: The Caucus for Producers, Writers & Directors, 760 N. La Cinega Blvd., Los Angeles, CA 90069.
DESC: "Welcome to *The Caucus Quarterly*, the newest voice of the people who create, write, produce and direct what you see on television. It is a voice that needs to be raised...and that needs to be heard, in studio boardrooms, in network brainstorming sessions, in Congressional regulatory hearings." This statement from the premiere issue describes the *Caucus Quarterly*, the vocal conscience of the television industry, from the point of view of those who work within the television field. It is a hard-working forum for discussion of tough issues facing television programming and related fields. The back of each issue has the stated "Aims and Objectives" of the Caucus, the preamble of which reads: "We, a concerned group of producers, writers and directors--representing a broad spectrum of the creative community--have organized THE CAUCUS FOR PRODUCERS, WRITERS & DIRECTORS for the purpose of assuming a more direct reponsibility to the American viewing public in television programming and related fields, and to protect our integrity as creative artists. THE CAUCUS is concerned with fundamental issues that transcend the specific interests and functions of industry guilds and unions." Following is a list of 22 specific aims and objectives of this dynamic organization. This is "must" reading for television producers, writers and directors in America. Highly recommended; booklet size format with no graphics, black ink on uncoated paper stock, cover is two-color red and black ink on uncoated paper stock (5 7/8 x 9 inches / 150 x 230 mm).
DEPT: None. (4-83). None. (2-89).
TYPL: "Invisible America," "Network Power ande the Deregulation Scam," "Murder by Alcohol." (4-83). "Let's Start Over, This isn't Working," "A Profusion of Pundits," "Television that Solves Problems," "Two Views on Language." (2-89).
SCHL: Quarterly, 12 pp.
SPAN: April, 1983+

✤ CAVERNE COMMUNICATION, THE
SUB: "Cinema and video environmental review news exchange."
SUB: "Cinema and video environmental reference network exchange."

PUBL: Caverne Publishing, 1429 East Fourth St., Long Beach, CA 90802.
DESC: The purpose of *The Caverne Communication* "...is to address two aspects of cinema and video others have ignored: 1) translating in-depth technical information into simple understandable language and, 2) the art of human survival in adverse environments (natural and/or man- made). *The Caverne Communication* will speak of things technical in words understandable to non-technicians and will share knowledge based on hard-earned experience culled from years of trial and error in the field. All of which enable a reader to use equipment to greater advantage and cope with various location situations that may be encountered. As a result a person will work smarter and with more confidence in his or her own abilities." This is a unique publication with an advisory board drawn from the areas of art, emulsion, law, lighting design, math and physics, medical and television engineering. It is recommended for the practicing professional using the technology of mass media. Magazine format; numerous graphics and schematics.
DEPT: "Editorial." (6-87).
TYPL: "The Lighmaker Ballast," "Art Galleries," "Up in the Clouds," "What is an Independent Contractor?," "Going Abroad." (6-87).
SCHL: Monthly [except Jan and Jul], 16 pp.
SPAN: Jun, 1987+

✤ CB LIFE

SUB: "The magazine of personal communications."
PUBL: Twentieth Century Publications, Inc., PO Box 547, Chatsworth, CA 91311.
DESC: The emphasis in this consumer-read publication is on the technology of Citizens' Band Radio and the people who use it. Articles detail late-breaking technology, new trends in equipment, and the workbench means of adapting CB equipment for personal application. Numerous product reviews are included with full information on installation and operation. Other articles look at the people-side of CB, profiling CB users, their equipment, and application of same, oftentimes for the benefit of the local community. Of special note are the "do-it-yourself" feature articles, many of which include step-by-step photographs and instructions on installation, modification, or operation of CB equipment. For sampled 1977 issue: stapled magazine format with black/white editorial content and some spot color advertising, and full-color cover, all on coated paper stock (8 ⅛ x 10 ⅞ inches / 205 x 275 mm).
DEPT: "From My 10-20," column by Byron G. Wels; "Seatcovers," column by Ladybug; "Tappan on Sideband," column by Mel Tappan; "CB Afield," column by V. Lee Oertle; "CB Life Afloat," column by Jim Martenhoff; "Ch. Two-Four," column by Ormel duke; "Buyer's 10-14," 'Regarding what's new in CB'. (1-77).
TYPL: "The Bob Conrad Story...Star of 'Baa Baa Blacksheep' is Active CBer on SSB," "VHF/UHF Scanning Monitor Receivers: When the Channels are Dead, Try a Scanner," "Burglar-Proofing Your Mobile--If You Can't Prevent It, Do Make It Harder," "Rockhounding and CB...How to Use Your CB Rig Effectively When Prowling Wild Country," "Those Dual Antenna Systems: Do They Really Work on Small Vehicles?" (1-77).
SCHL: Monthly, 70 pp.
SPAN: ?+?

CBC TIMES

PUBL: Canadian Broadcasting Corporation, 354 Jarvis St., Toronto, Canada.
DESC: This is a radio and TV counterpart to America's TV Guide for Canadian viewers and listeners. A selection guide to radio-TV programs is provided on a yellow paper middle section, surrounded by in-depth reviews of upcoming programs to arouse viewer interest. Utilizes small format with no advertising.
DEPT: None. (1-70).
TYPL: "Shoe Full of Stones," "Looking Back," "Growing Up Male." (1-70).
SCHL: Weekly, 20 pp.
SPAN: 1948 - Jan, 1970//
LC: TK 6548.C

CCJA Journalist

Summer, 1983//
SEE: COMMUNITY COLLEGE JOURNALIST

✤ CD REVIEW

PUBL: WGE Publishing, Inc., Forest Rd., Hancock, NH 03449.
DESC: The masthead section of any magazine (the six-point type font area which lists publisher, ISSN number, staff members names, subscription address, etc.) is not usually fascinating reading; except for, of course, the publisher, the librarian, and postal authorities. But at the bottom of the masthead in *CD Review* was this gem: "Legal Contract: Merely reading this constitutes a legal, binding contract with publisher Wayne Green to help in the fight against Satan. It is obviously Satan, and the major label propaganda machine, which has prevented you from buying Greener Pastures Records GPR-001, the incredible Joplin CD played by Scott Kirby. Fight Satan, call 800-CD-GUILT and order it." That is no ordinary masthead, and *CD Review* is no ordinary review of compact discs. Coverage of recent CD releases is thorough, and thought-provoking. Lucid commentary is sparked with just a tinge of irreverence for the concept that every CD release is a milestone in musical history. The letters departmental feature ("Readers' Forum") indicates broad subscriber support for this editorial philosophy, and is fascinating reading itself. A marketing plea to potential advertisers in one sampled issue cites a recent reader survey that subscribers spend $30 million a

month on CDs, and $23 million each month on audio equipment. As the advertisement went on to state: "Find out what an incredible bunch of buying fanatics we've managed to put together for you. If you can't make big money with this bunch, you'd better look for a teaching or government job. You're just not cut out for marketing." A wonderful publication for today's upscale audio home consumer, it puts fun back into the compact disc field.
DEPT: "The First Word," editorial column by David Vernier; "Current Samples," "Worth a Look," column by Daniel Kumin and Edward Murray; "New Release Spotlight," column by David Vernier; "The 17th Bit," column by Daniel Kumin; "CD & Beyond," column by Bryan Brewer; "CD Business," column by Elliot Blair Smith; "What's New on CD," new releases column by Lou Waryncia; "Readers' Forum," letters; "The Last Word," editorial column by Wayne Green. (3-88). "The First Word," editorial column by Larry Canale; "Current Samples," news items column by Robin Chalmers; "Top Ten," current hits in pop/rock, jazz, and classical categories; "Worth a Look," new equipment column by Mary Kate Bourn; "Pop/Rock Reviews," "Disc of the Month," "Capsule Critiques," music review column by Larry Canale; "Jazz Reviews," "Blues Reviews," "New Age Reviews," "Classical Reviews," "FYI," artist profiles; "Country Reviews," "World Reviews," "Stage & Screen Reviews," "What's New on CD?," "Readers' Forum," letters; "Vox Pop," 'A collection of comments compiled from our reader CD rating cards'; "The Last Word," editorial column by Wayne Green. (1-91).
TYPL: "Cream of the Crop II," "1988 Winter Consumer Electronics Show," "Magnificent Modern Maestro," "Digital Audio 101," "Mitsubishi DP-311R: Keeping a Low Profile." (3-88). "Music's Obvious Child," "CD Review Hall of Fame," "Basic 50 Blues CD Library," "It Takes Two." (1-91).
SCHL: Monthly, 110 pp.
SPAN: Sep, 1984+
VARIES
--Sep, 1984 - ? as Digital Audio & Compact Disc Review (ISSN: 0743-619x).
--? - ? as Digital Audio's CD Review (ISSN: 1041-8342).
LC: ML 156.9 .D525
DD: 780.26/6/05
ISSN: 1044-1700

✤ CD-ROM
SUB: "The magazine of compact-disc data storage."
PUBL: CW Communications, Peterborough, Inc., Elm St., Peterborough, NH.
DESC: The age of CD-ROM (compact disc-read only memory), and CD/I (compact disc/interactive) is indeed upon us. Some view the CD-ROM as a major breakthrough in data storage and retrieval, providing pictures, clip-art, article indices, and encyclopedic segments all designed to benefit the publishing industry. Others have mixed reactions to CD/I technology, designed to be stand-alone information/entertainment-on-demand fixtures next to (and understandably competing with) stereo, radio programming, or cable, broadcast, and videotape television systems. CD-ROM is designed to explain the technology, the potentials and hazards associated with this rapidly developing field. Magazine format.
DEPT: "Editorial," "CD-ROM Report: News," "Glossary," 'CD-ROM buzzwords you should know'; "CD-ROM Report: Products," "Q&A." (9-86).
TYPL: "Making Miracles," "Getting It All on Disc," "CD-ROM Goes to Work," "How High is Up?," "The Impact of CD-ROM on On-Line Data Bases." (9-86).
SCHL: Monthly?, 90 pp.
SPAN: Sep?, 1986+

✤ CD-ROM LIBRARIAN
SUB: "The largest circulation optical media review for information professionals."
SUB: "The optical media review for information professionals."
PUBL: Meckler Corporation, 11 Ferry Lane West, Westport, CT 06880.
DESC: Another in the excellent series of Meckler publications for information professionals, CD-ROM Librarian provides late-breaking news and thoughtful critiques concerning both on-line database information services and new CD-ROM (Compact Disc-Read Only Memory) products of value to today's "CD-ROM Librarian." That librarian, more often than not, is a member of the Special Libraries Association, a dynamic organization of information professionals who manage corporate, or large organizational library operations where the watchword phrase is "I need all the information that can be found, and fast!" Fast and thorough information searches are synonymous with on-line services and CD-ROM server systems, and this excellent publication provides the latest information on what is available, what systems the search engine software is compatible with, costs, release dates, etc. It is an informative resource for this burgeoning field of information-on-demand. Sampled issue for 1991: stapled magazine format, black/white editorial content with full-color cover on coated paper stock (8 ½ x 11 inches / 215 x 280 mm).
DEPT: "Editorial," column by Norman Desmarais; "Optical News," extensive news column by Carol Kelley; "Optical Product Review," column by Peter Brueggeman and Carol Reed; "Supplement to CD-ROMS in Print," update compiled column by Norman Desmarais. (5-91).
TYPL: "CD-ROM 1990: The Year in Review," "Attica Exhibits New CD-ROM Products at Computers in Libraries International," "Optical Product Review: Hydrodata: Water Resources Information for the United States and Canada," "Optical Product Review: Climatedata Summary of the Day and Climatedata Hourly Precipitation." (5-91).
SCHL: Bimonthly (Jan/Feb, 1987 - Nov/Dec, 1987); Monthly [with combined Jul/Aug and Nov/Dec issue] (Jan, 1988+), 45 pp.

SPAN: Jan, 1987+
VARIES
--? - Dec, 1986 as Optical Information Systems Update / Library & Information Center Applications (ISSN: 0886-019x).
LC: Z 681.3.067 C3
DD: 025
ISSN: 0893-9934
ABST: --Computer & Control Abstracts (ISSN: 0036-8113)
--Electrical & Electronics Abstracts (ISSN: 0036-8105)
--Physics Abstracts. Science Abstracts. Series A. (ISSN: 0036-8091)

CELEBRITY

PUBL: Magazine Management Co., 575 Madison Ave., New York, NY 10022.
DESC: *Celebrity* is a popular consumer serial concerned with celebrities in the arts, in government, in society, or in the news. Most often, the focus is on people within media, as the magazine attempts to provide the "backstage" view of what "personality X" is really like. Many photos; early issues mixed newsprint with high gloss pages.
DEPT: "Cindy Says," newsbriefs column by Cindy Adams; "Letters to the Editor," "Who's News," "Clebrity Exclusive," interview; "Offguard," pictures the celebrities wish not had been taken; "Celebrity Horoscope," "Then and Now," nostalgia; "Celebrity Profiles," "Special Feature," "Celebrity Salutes," tribute essay; "We Name for Fame," prediction; "Fun and Games." (10-77).
TYPL: "Steve Lawrence & Eydie Gorme--Still in Tune," "George Masters--Sharing His Beauty Secrets," "Twelve Celebrities Tell How They Gained Self-Confidence," "Star Wars' Stars--They're Really Spaced Out." (10-77).
SCHL: Monthly, 70 pp.
SPAN: Jun, 1975 - ?//.
LC: AP 2 .C3565
DD: 051 19
ISSN: 0163-8378

Celebrity Focus

Jan, 1987 - Feb, 1988//
(ISSN: 0896-8225)
SEE: CELEBRITY PLUS

✢ CELEBRITY PLUS

PUBL: Globe Communications, 441 Lexington Ave., New York, NY 10017-3910.
DESC: Here the focus is on the media celebrity, and every issue is packed with news stories, interviews, profiles, and exposes of the suddenly and longterm-famous. The sampled issue for 1989 included such well-knowns as Oprah Winfrey, Monty Python, Cybill Shepherd, Jane Wyman, Sophia (no last name necessary), John Candy, Rodney Dangerfield, and a host of others, along with a "whatever happened to" the various Woodstock Music Festival performers. An article, "Growing Up in Hollywood," explored the lives of Hollywood families, while a Monty Python 20th anniversary celebration provided current news of the Python gang of film and video fame. The "Plus" in the publication's title refers to some non-media articles, such as (in the sampled issue) a reader's poll on current issues, "New Hope for Headache Sufferers," and "Vitamin Guide for the Whole Family." For sampled issue of 1989: stapled magazine format, black/white and color pages on coated paper stock (8 x 10 ⅞ inches / 205 x 275 mm).
DEPT: "Letters," "Spice," celebrity column by Malcolm Boyes; "Reader's Poll Results," on current issues; "Star Treks," celebrity news by Jae-Ha-Kim; "Celebrities I've Met," fan close-encounters; "Rave and Grave Reviews," concerning books, records and videos, column by Anne M. Raso and Jae-Ha-Kim. (6-89).
TYPL: "Woodstock Music Festival Revisited," "Oprah Winfrey's Secrets," "Growing Up in Hollywood," "Looking Back on Zany Monty Python's 20th Anniversary," "Hollywood Mystery Death: The Curse of the Barrymores." (6-89).
SCHL: Monthly, 60 pp.
SPAN: Jan, 1987+
VARIES
--Jan, 1987 - Feb, 1988 as Celebrity Focus (ISSN: 0896-8225).
LC: PN 1993.C36
DD: 791.43/028/05
ISSN: 0897-4381

✢ CELLULOID NIGHTMARE

SUB: "A magazine of sleaze film culture!"
PUBL: Celluloid Nightmare Production, 7605 Santa Monica Blvd., Suite 641, West Hollywood, CA 90046.
DESC: There are magazine promotional advertisements, and there are MAGAZINE PROMOTIONAL ADVERTISEMENTS such as this one from the Fall, 1990 issue of *Celluloid Nightmare*: "...I want to have film festivals and bring to the public what I didn't have. I want to put on shows and entertain people with the lowest form of cinematic magic that ever was. And I think that L.A. needs it. I think that L.A. wants it. ...I have faith in the L.A. public and want to give this town the face lift that it so desperately needs, that it so desperately crys out for in the endless void of big budget filth not worth of the title pond scum. Join me in the fight to save L.A. from being over run by big movie corporations. Help me bring the Sleaze back into the sleaziest city alive. It's all here, help me to uncover it. Write in and voice your opinion and pledge your support to a dying breed. This is a publication which champions the "Sleazy B-Movies" of America, specifically those of Hollywood. There are no "main stream" big box-office stars, motion pictures, or officially licensed wind-up dolls in full-color glossy

pages in this fanzine. Instead, readers and authors discuss the merits of "Curse of the Queerwolf," "Revenge of the Scream Queen," "Nightmare Sisters," "Slave Girls From Beyond Infinity," "Transylvania Twist," "Vampire Cop," "Invisible Maniac," "Poor White Trash II," and "Sorority Babes in the Slimeball." Each issue has several pages of interesting letters to the editor, informative interviews with stars, producers, and others working in this film genre, and news of new releases (often videocassettes) both in the United States and on the international market. This is NOT a journal of academic study on the aesthetics and theory of filmmaking. Some pictures of a sexual nature and text may offend some readers. For sampled issue of 1990: stapled magazine format, cover and editorial content consists of black ink on uncoated paper stock, limited advertising, no pagination (8 ½ x 11 inches / 215 x 280 mm).
DEPT: "Editorial," 'Editor/Publisher Dude' column by Tony Biner; "Letters From the Fringe Few!," extensive pasionate letter section; "Book Reviews." (fall-90).
TYPL: "Bustin' It Up With: Brinke Stevens," "Other Mags to Pass the Time," "In London with Bal Crotchi Checking Out: Psychotronic Video Shop," "The Legend Continues," "Melissa Talks Some Moore." (fall-90).
SCHL: Irregular, 55 pp.
SPAN: ?, 1990+?

✤ CENSORSHIP NEWS
SUB: "A newsletter of the National Coalition Against Censorship."
PUBL: National Coalition Against Censorship, 2 West 64th St., New York, NY 10023.
DESC: Censorship in media is the theme of this membership newsletter of the National Coalition Against Censorship. In a typical issue, topics ranged from motion pictures to grade school text books, the FBI library program, and student journalism. This is, in a very pure sense, a NEWSletter, providing late-breaking news items, and updates on continuing censorship of ideas and media. Amongst the distinguished Council of Advisors are Shana Alexander, Isaac Asimov, and Robert Wise. Typewritten newsletter format; no graphics.
DEPT: None. (fall-88).
TYPL: "Milpitas and the California State Education Department," "Students Press for Free Press," "Student Appeals Press Censorship," "Congress Considers Federal Obscenity Legislation." (fall-88).
SCHL: Quarterly, 8 pp.
SPAN: Spring, 1980+
DD: 363 11
ISSN: 0749-6001

Central States Speech Journal
Nov, 1949 - 198u//
(ISSN: 0008-9575)
SEE: COMMUNICATION STUDIES

CEPN
Jan, 1975 - ?//
SEE: CONSUMER ELECTRONICS PRODUCT NEWS

CETO News
Oct?, 1963? - Jan, 1967?//
SEE: MEDIA IN EDUCATION AND DEVELOPMENT

✤ CHANNEL ONE
PUBL: ATV Corporation, 1229 N. Highland Ave., Hollywood, CA 90038.
DESC: This unique full-color magazine is sent free to Zenith television service contract members. Excluding the non-media articles on Baja road adventures and consumer advice, the reader may be pleasantly surprised by the TV-Guide-type articles on broadcast history, engineering and programming; all written for the lay audience.
DEPT: None.
TYPL: "Requiem for Wrestlers and Fender Benders," "Spencer's Pilots Rev Up for TV," "Island in the Sky."
SCHL: Quarterly, 32 pp.
SPAN: ?+?

CHANNELS
SUB: "The business of communications."
PUBL: Act III Publishing, 401 Park Avenue South, New York, NY 10016.
DESC: "[This] magazine sprang from an awareness that television is too important a social, political, and cultural force in America to be covered by a press that has historically viewed the medium as a competitor, or as a wellspring of celebrity features and gossip." On its fifth anniversary, *Channels* was purchased by Norman Lear's Act III Publishing, and rededicated itself to continuing its distinguished record for evaluating the role of video in world society. This publication of considered thought generated new insights into this 65-year old medium, but failed in generating sufficient revenue to escape the ravages of the magazine industry during 1990, and by fall, 1990 was shut down. As editor Les Brown noted, "Where previously (television) was driven by technology, today it is powered by business and finance." *Channels* was an important publication for the expanding role of television in society. For the sampled issues of 1981 and 1988: perfect-bound magazine format, mixture of black/white and full-color pages with full-color cover on coated paper stock, advertising (8 x 10 ⅝ inches / 200 x 270 mm).
DEPT: "The Business Side," "The Public Eye," "Private Eye," "Hollywood, Inc.," "On Air," "Program Note," "Sound Bites," "Running the Numbers." (03-86). "Reports," newsbriefs; "Editor's Note," "Letters," "What's On," 'a monthly calendar'; "Advertising," "The Public Eye," "The Business Side," "Market

Eye," "Media Deals," "Sound Bites," "Running the Numbers," "Database," communication industry facts and figures column by Michael Burgi. (9-88).
TYPL: "Talk Show," "Reports," "Going Fourth," "The Stuart Karl Workout," "In Focus: Cable." (03- 86). "Now Cosby's Campaign," "Here Come the News Punks," "Who is Christopher Skase?," "Muddling Through the Must-Carry Mess," "The New TV Viewer." (9-88).
SCHL: Bimonthly (? - Jan/Feb, 1986); Ten issues per year (Mar, 1986 - ?); Monthly (? - Mar, 1990); Biweekly (Apr, 1990+), 70 pp.
SPAN: Apr/May, 1981 - Dec 17?, 1990//
VARIES
--Apr/May, 1981 - Jul/Aug, 1986 as Channels of Communications (ISSN: 0276-1572).
LC: PN 1992.6 .C514
DD: 384.55/4/05 19
ISSN: 0895-643x
ABST: --Readers Guide Abstracts (ISSN: 0886-0092)
--Readers Guide to Periodical Literature (ISSN: 0034-0464)

Channels of Communications

Apr/May, 1981 - Jul/Aug, 1986//
(ISSN: 0276-1572)
SEE: CHANNELS

Charles Austin Bates Criticisms

Jan, 1897 - Mar, 1900//
SEE: CURRENT ADVERTISING

CHICAGO JOURNALISM REVIEW

PUBL: Association of Working Press, 6037 N. Monticello, Chicago, IL 60659.
DESC: A very irreverent, certainly critical viewpoint of mass communications journalism in the greater Chicago area, its black/white format lends a stark reality to its contents. *Chicago Journalism Review* is a product of many journalists, some of whom prefer anonymity. It is a very unique outlet for commentary, rumor, and critical evaluation of Chicago media, and never fails to inform, enlighten, and entertain.
DEPT: "Letters," caustic, humorous and important reader viewpoints; "News on the March," newsbriefs on Chicago journalism scenes.
TYPL: "That Singer Crowd...Simply Not Chicago Style," "Redlining: Bleed Thy Neighbor." (3/4-75).
SCHL: Monthly, 16 pp.
SPAN: Oct, 1968 - Sep, 1975//
LC: PN 4700.C5
DD: 070/.05
ISSN: 0009-3580
ABST: --ABI/Informer

✤ CHRISTIAN ADVERTISING FORUM

SUB: "An exchange of ideas and opinions."
PUBL: Wike Associates, 5007 Carriage Dr., 2nd Floor, Roanoke, VA 24018.
DESC: In the premiere issue of Spring, 1981, Publisher Stephen Wike told readers: "Before I decided to publish *Christian Advertising Forum*, I talked with some of the experts in the field. ...Everyone agreed that the need existed for a publication aimed specifically at people in the Christian advertising profession." This periodical is one of several new publications devoted to the expanded role of the Christian marketplace. *Christian Advertising Forum* has two main functions: 1) a tutorial on advertising; 2) a forum of news and views within the unique Christian advertising and marketing field. Both goals are well acomplished within the bimonthly periodical. For the sampled issues of 1985: mixture of black ink, spot- and full-color pages and cover on coated paper stock, in stapled magazine format (8 ¼ x 10 ¾ inches / 210 x 275 mm).
DEPT: "Industry News," newsbriefs; "Magazine Comparison," ad pages, circulation and CPM figures on 40+ Christian periodicals.
TYPL: "Copy & Design: Breaking the Rules," "Attacking the Networks Via Madison Avenue," "Sam Moore, Thomas Nelson Publishers." (12/1-82).
SCHL: Bimonthly, 30 pp.
SPAN: Apr/May, 1981+
ISSN: 0744-4370

Christian Broadcaster

Oct, 1953 - Apr, 1968?//
(ISSN: 0577-9960)
SEE: MEDIA DEVELOPMENT

CHRISTIAN DRAMA

PUBL: Malone College, 515 25th St., NW, Canton, OH 44709.
DESC: In the first issue of October, 1977, Editor Nonna Childress Dalan of Evangel College told readers that the purpose of *Christian Drama* was: "To serve as a clearing house for sources of dramatic material that directors have found effective in particular situations for the church and the Christian college, [and] to serve as an announcement sheet for workshops, special performing groups, activities, and happenings in Christian drama." Majority of each issue was devoted to the printing of a short dramatic work suitable for performance within a college or church setting. Cessation apparently occurred with the January, 1986 issue following the death of founding Editor Dalan in late 1985. For the sampled issues of 1985: photocopied on single, stapled sheets, some graphics (8 ½ x 11 inches / 215 x 280 mm).
DEPT: "Pot Pour Ri," newsbriefs; "College," "Missions." (1-84).

TYPL: None. (1-84).
SCHL: Quarterly [Oct, Jan, Apr, Jul], 4 pp.
SPAN: October, 1977 - January, 1986//?

✣ CHRISTIAN FILM & VIDEO

SUB: "A bimonthly review & resource guide."
PUBL: Curtis Mark Communications and the Wheaton College Graduate School of Communications, Box 3000, Dept. Y, Denville, NJ 07834.
DESC: This bimonthly newsletter was designed to review films/videotapes, and explored issues of importance to the church community, such as the effect of electronic media on the church, Christian film/video producers, buying and using media equipment, and the use of video for community outreach. It has two sections: "Clips," news and articles; and "Reviews," in-depth reviews of new film/videotape releases. For the sampled issues of 1989: loose-leaf newsletter format, three-hole punched, black ink with spot-color on uncoated paper stock with graphics, limited advertising (8 ½ x 11 inches / 215 x 280 mm).
DEPT: "News and New Releases," "Clips," "Reviews." (3/4-87).
TYPL: "Video Libraries in the Church? It's Coming, Coming, Came," "Bringing a Redemptive Message to Theater Screens." (3/4-87).
SCHL: Bimonthly, 8 pp.
SPAN: Jan/Feb?, 1984+
DD: 200 11
ISSN: 0890-3387

✣ CHRISTIAN REVIEW

SUB: "An evangelical magazine reviewing the best in Christian books and recordings."
PUBL: 6080 New Peachtree Rd., P.O. Box 47058, Atlanta, GA 30340.
DESC: *Christian Review* provides a much broader range of media products (those which are sold through religious bookstores nationwide) than the subtitle would suggest, although the primary emphasis is books and audio recordings. Not all items may be reviewed, as noted in the publisher's statement: "Our policy is never to criticize questionable works but simply not to represent them in this magazine." A large amount of advertising by media producers is present, along with numerous promotional graphics.
DEPT: "News," newsbriefs; "Special Features," book reviews; "Pick of Books," "Recordings," review. (11-82).
TYPL: "Interview with John Sherrill," "Mother's Song," "The Sacred Journey," "Christmas Joys," "Classic Feature." (11-82).
SCHL: Monthly, 36 pp.
SPAN: Jan, 1973+

CHRONICLE OF INTERNATIONAL COMMUNICATION

PUBL: International Communication Projects, Inc., PO Box 2596, Washington, DC.
DESC: "The Chronicle of International Communication is produced by International Communication Projects, Inc., (ICPI), an independent non-profit corporation--501(c)(3) IRS Code--concerned with the public policy aspects of international communication, education, news and data flow, media trends, broadcasting, information and cultural exchange. The Chronicle monitors current American plans and policy on relevant issues and foreign relationships." Articles for the final year of publication covered a wide variety of topics including: "Measuring Telecommunications Trade Trends," "INTELSAT in Transition," "Pride, Protocol and Press Ploys," "Communications Development Issues Occupy Ad Hoc Policy Group," and "Blocking Scientific-Technical Data Exports." For the sampled issues of 1985: black ink on uncoated paper stock in newsletter format, no advertising (8 ½ x 11 inches / 215 x 280 mm).
DEPT: "Books & Documents," review. (7/8-84).
TYPL: "Tune Up for Term Two," "Turn Down for Worldtel," "The Coordinator at Work," "Democracy & Associates, Inc.," "A Touch of Trauma," "Tale of Two Cities." (7/8-84).
SCHL: Semiyearly (1980); Ten issues per year [combined issues Jan/Feb, Jul/Aug] (1982+), 10 pp.
SPAN: Jan, 1980 - Sep/Oct, 1985//
    MERGED WITH
    --Transnational Data Report (ISSN: 0167-6962) (to form) Transnational Data and Communications Report (ISSN: 0892-399x), Oct, 1985.
LC: P 96.I52 U63
DD: 384
ISSN: 0278-0011

✣ CINE-KODAK NEWS, THE

SUB: "Published monthly in the interests of amateur motion pictures by the Eastman Kodak Company, Rochester, NY."
SUB: "For both 8mm and 16mm movie makers." (Mar/Apr, 1941 - ?).
PUBL: Eastman Kodak Co., Rochester, NY.
DESC: In keeping with the fine publication history of this company, the *Cine-Kodak News* is a classy publication, a first-rate promotional serial designed to showcase Kodak products at the same time that it promotes home movie making. As expected, the photography is superb, and the advice is both detailed and succinct. Of special note were the reproductions and resolutions of typical problems.
DEPT: None. (8-24). "Cine-Chat," letters. (6-40).
TYPL: "How to Make Your Own Titles," "Back Lighting Effects with Your Cine-Kodak," "Let the Plot Thicken." (8-24). "Of All Wedding Gifts--the Finest,"

"Cinematography's Seven League Boots," "Cavalcade of Color," "Each Blossom--Many Times Larger than Life." (6-40).
SCHL: Monthly, 12 pp.
SPAN: Jun, 1924+?
LC: TR 845.C5

✤ CINE NEWS

SUB: "A publication of the Council on International Nontheatrical Events."
PUBL: Council on International Nontheatrical Events, 1001 Connecticut Ave., NW, Washington, DC 20036.
DESC: Founded in 1957, the Council on International Nontheatrical Events publishes the *CINE NEWS*, a newsletter designed to report on news events, trends, and to generally aid in stimulating production of "non-theatrical" film and video productions in the United States. As of early 1991 the *CINE NEWS*, "...has a circulation of 11,000 which includes industry professionals, independent and student filmmakers, production companies, distributors, and film schools." For the sampled premiere issue of 1991: folded loose-leaf newsletter format, black ink on uncoated paper stock, advertising (8 ½ x 11 inches / 215 x 280 mm).
DEPT: "Cine Calendar," upcoming festivals and competitions for nontheatrical product. (#1-91).
TYPL: "Ken Burns Guest of CINE at the National Archives," "1991 Showcase Moves to Willard Intercontinental," "CINE Films Nominated for Academy Awards," "CINE Welcomes New President," "CINE Films Win in Foreign Festivals." (#1-91).
SCHL: Three issues per year [May, Sep, and Nov], 8 pp.
SPAN: May?, 1991+

✤ CINEASTE

SUB: "America's leading magazine of the arts and politics of the cinema."
SUB: "America's leading magazine on the art and politics of the cinema."
PUBL: Cineaste Publishers, Inc., 200 Park Avenue South, New York, NY 10003.
DESC: Critics often remark that the way to tell the difference between film and broadcast journals is to compare their respective sizes: film people love to talk at greater length about film. This is certainly evident in this well-edited, quarterly journal of motion pictures. *Cineaste* is not concerned with major American studio releases, but with international film, underground film, and the independent filmmaker. Extensive critical comment is provided on a wide variety of film topics. Articles are well thought out and organized. Highly recommended for American and international film. For the sampled issue of 1990: stapled magazine format, numerous black/white production stills, and black ink editorial content on heavy coated paper stock with two-color blue/black cover on coated paper stock as well (8 ¼ x 11 inches / 210 x 280 mm).
DEPT: "Film Reviews," covering both domestic and international releases; "Film Guide," capsule descriptions of current film fare. (fall-76). "Editorial," "Letters," "Independents," filmmaker profiles; "Books," reviews; "Festivals," "Lost and Found," review of overlooked films; "A Second Look," reviews with the aid of the passage of time; "Home Video," new product releases; "Interview," insightful information; "Film Reviews," extensive, detailed reviews of current film product. (#4-90).
TYPL: "The Oberhausen Film Festival--Whither the Short Film?" "Cinema in Revolutionary Portugal--An Interview with Fernando Lopes," "What does a Film Archivist do, anyway?" (fall-76). "Renewing the African-American Cinema: The Films of Spike Lee," "What Might Have Been: DEFA Films of the Past and the Future of German Cinema," "Great Belles of Fire: Southern Women on the Screen," "Isabelle Adjani: The Actress as Political Activist," "Reflections on 'Roger & Me', Michael Moore and His Critics." (#4-90).
SCHL: Quarterly, 70 pp.
SPAN: Summer, 1967+
LC: PN 1993.C5177
DD: 791
ISSN: 0009-7004
ABST: --Alternative Press Index (ISSN: 0002-662x)
--Film Literature Index (ISSN: 0093-6758)
--Media Review Digest (ISSN: 0363-7778)

✤ CINEFAN

SUB: "Science fiction, fantasy & horror in films."
SUB: "The review journal of obscure, popular, independent, and foreign horror and fantasy cinema."
PUBL: Fandom Unlimited Enterprises, PO Box 70868, Sunnyvale, CA 94086.
DESC: "*Cinefan* is devoted to the serious study of the motion picture, with particular emphasis on the fantastic cinema." Indeed, this serial was almost exclusively devoted to the area of "science fiction, fantasy & horror in films," as a later subitle attested. Editor and publisher Randall Iarson provides a quality typewritten publication with a large number of film graphics, most of which are publicity stills. Some profiles of actors/actresses; complete credits of profiled films.
DEPT: "The Editor's Page," "Classified Ads," "Recent Films in Review," lengthy reviews. (#2-1980).
TYPL: "Vampire Circus; a Critical Analysis," "Don Dohler and the Alien Factor," "The Fantasy Film Music of Bernard Herrmann." (#2-1980).
SCHL: Irregular, 65 pp.
SPAN: Jul, 1974+
LC: PN 1995.9 .F36C55
DD: 1796246
ISSN: 0095-1447

✤ CINEFANTASTIQUE

SUB: "The magazine with a 'sense of wonder.'"

SUB: "The review of horror, fantasy, and science fiction films."
PUBL: Cinefantastique, PO Box 270, Oak Park, IL 60303.
DESC: Here is an excellent publication which is "...devoted to the serious study of horror, fantasy and science fiction films." From its very first issue in fall, 1970 to the present, *Cinfeantastique* has kept its promise by exploring special effects, the weird, strange, and just plain mystifying aspects of motion picture product. Great emphasis is placed on behind-the-scenes work by special effects personnel and their work. Spritely layout with numerous graphics, many in color.
DEPT: "Letters," "The Score," music for motion pictures; "News and Notes," newsbriefs; "Short Notices," upcoming films. (summer-71). "Coming," new film product; "A Few Minutes With," interview; "Reviews," "Film Ratings," "Letters." (12/1-83/84).
TYPL: "Oriental Fantasy from Daiei," "Portrait of Jennie: A Retrospect." (summer-71). "The Films of David Cronenberg," "Stephen King," "The Right Stuff," "Brainstorm," "Space Ace." (12/1-83/84).
SCHL: Quarterly (1970? - ?); Five issues per year (Sep, 1981 - ?, 1982); Bimonthly (May/Jun, 1982 - ?); Five issues per year (Dec/Jan, 1983/1984+), 64 pp.
SPAN: Fall, 1970+
LC: PN 1995.9 .H6C48
ISSN: 0145-6032
ABST: --Film Literature Index (ISSN: 0093-6758)
--Media Review Digest (ISSN: 0363-7778)

✤ CINEFEX

SUB: "The journal of cinematic illusions." (Mar, 1980+).
PUBL: Cinefex, PO Box 20027, Riverside, CA 92516.
DESC: *Cinefex* is one of those truly outstanding serials that one enjoys for the great color pictures of special effects, and the detailed articles on techniques of creating the effects. Articles are amazingly detailed down to the last resolved item of putting together the crew, the concept, the mechanical "what-ever," film, lighting, movement, lens, computer-control system, and a host of other items that all contribute to the final look of the film. Editor and publisher Don Shay obviously enjoys what he does, and his work under the title of *Cinefex* can be highly recommended to anyone interested in special effects for motion pictures. For the sampled issue of 1990: stapled magazine format with black/white and stunning color pages throughout on coated paper stock, limited advertising (9 x 8 inches / 230 x 205 mm).
DEPT: None.
TYPL: "Tauntauns, Walkers, and Probots," "Walter Murch--Making Beaches Out of Grains of Sand," "The Microcosmic World of Ken Middleham." (12-80). "Behind the Lines of 'Enemy Mine,'" "Der Trickfilm--a Survey of German Special Effects," "Fright Night." (2-86). "The Thrill of the Hunt," "Beneath Perfection," "Star Trek V -- Sharing the Pain." (5-90).
SCHL: Quarterly, 70 pp.
SPAN: Mar, 1980+
LC: TR 858.C45

DD: 778.5/345/05
ISSN: 0198-1056
ABST: --Film Literature Index (ISSN: 0093-6758)

✤ CINEGRAM

SUB: "The magazine of film and video."
PUBL: Cinegram Inc., and the Ann Arbor Film Cooperative, 512 S. Main, Ann Arbor, MI 48114.
DESC: Volume 3, Number 1 (Summer, 1978), reestablished the publication schedule of this magazine which bills itself as "The only publication geared to popular non-technical know-how and news of film and video." True to its word, articles are non-technical and entertaining. Video articles tend to concentrate on non-network software and hardware for the home and independent producer, including such topics as script submissions, trends in independent distribution and exhibition, and helpful information on how to "break into the industry." Published in large format with numerous illustrations; editorial pages on newsprint.
DEPT: "Whats Hot," upcoming projects and people; "Tech," technical newsbriefs; "Homescreen," information concerning home software- hardware; "Film Music," "Festivals," upcoming events and reviews of recent screenings. (summer-78).
TYPL: "Eyes Director Irvin Kershner," "Women In Love With Film," "The Show Stealers," "Columbus Arrives," "Animation Gold," "Herzog and Wenders." (summer-78).
SCHL: Bimonthly, 38 pp.
SPAN: Mar/Apr, 1976+
LC: PN 1993.C5178
DD: 791.43/05
ISSN: 0145-3483

CINEMA

SUB: "The magazine for discriminating movie-goers."
PUBL: Avant Film Publications, 8066 Beverly Blvd., Hollywood, CA.
DESC: The short three-issue span of this periodical concentrated on major motion pictures as a cultural medium. Topics included articles on film music, directing, and issues current to the year 1947, such as juvenile delinquency and post-war development. By its third issue, a format change was taking place in which the special department, "Little Cinema," was becoming a significant section of the publication.
DEPT: "Film Scene," paragraph-length news on the industry; "File Scene International," letters from London; "Little Cinema," news on art, documentary, religious and educational releases.
TYPL: "The World of the Actor," "Hollywood Music," "Movies and Society." (8-47).
SCHL: Monthly, 20 pp.
SPAN: Jun, 1947 - Aug, 1947//
LC: PN 1993.C

CINEMA

PUBL: Spectator International, 307 N. Rodeo Drive, Beverly Hills, CA 90210.
DESC: *Cinema* was a quality, large-size, glossy format magazine with numerous pictures and excellent graphics to complement well-written articles on film. Articles covered a broad range of topics from interviews with directors and film criticism to a refreshing look at how new technology might affect future filmmaking. Of note were special supplements, such as one noted in a sample issue: "The New Ballgame: The Cartridge Revolution," written by a major studio executive.
DEPT: "Review," critical reviews of current films.
TYPL: "Ozu Spectrum," "Renoir, a Progress Report," "The New Documentaries of Frederick Weisman." (No. 1-70).
SCHL: Three times per year; at times irregular.
SPAN: 1962 - 1976//
SUSPENDED
--1975.
LC: PN 1993.C518
DD: 791.43/05
ISSN: 0009-7047

CINEMA

SUB: "A quarterly magazine published from 12-13 Little Newport St., London, WC2H 7JJ."
PUBL: Cinema Rising, Ltd., 12-13 Little Newport St., London, WC2H 7JJ, England.
DESC: A relatively brief, but scholarly look at cinema as art and societal reflector. Some ten articles each issue emphasize major and experimental filmmakers and their product. Numerous black/white graphics.
DEPT: None.
TYPL: "A George Melies Scrapbook," "Death Plays & Wax Works," "Celluloid Apocalypse," "Film Directors; a Revolution." (#9-71).
SCHL: Quarterly, 45 pp.
SPAN: Dec, 1968 to date.
LC: PN 1993.C519

Cinema

Jul, 1921 - Nov, 1922//
SEE: SCREEN INTERNATIONAL

✤ CINEMA AND THEATRE

SUB: "The journal for the film industry and the cinema trade."
PUBL: Hutchinson Co., 10 Grade Queens St., London WC2, England.
DESC: This paperback-sized periodical is filled with information concerning studio and exhibition news within England. Focus is on studio utilization, technical equipment, exhibition news, and the general status of the British film product. A large number of illustrations are used, considering its size and 50-page length. A good source of British cinema production news.
DEPT: "Production Scene," briefs of films and shooting schedules; "The Films We See," 'reviews of recent reviews;' "From a Managers Notebook," exhibitor commentary; "People," newsbriefs. (3-48).
TYPL: "British Pictures and Foreign Competition," "The New Warner Studios at Teddington," "Unusual Features of Carpenter Projector," "Will There be Censorship for 16 MM Screenings?" (3-48).
SPAN: 1932+?
LC: PN 1993.C

✤ CINEMA/CANADA

SUB: "The magazine of the Canadian Society of Cinematographers."
SUB: "Canada's first magazine of motion picture cinematography."
PUBL: Canadian Society of Cinematographers, PO Box 398, Station Outremont, Montreal, PQ H2V 4N3 Canada.
DESC: Originally founded by the Canadian Society of Cinematographers, *Cinema Canada* is now published by an independent foundation covering news of interest to individuals working within the Canadian film industry. Articles survey the fields of film and film in television, various trade organizations, general commentary on the relationship between filmmakers and the Canadian government, and the status of Canadian film in general. Many news articles and graphics. This periodical began publication in 1961 with a rather low-key format, changing to a more modern style and expanded editorial content in Jul/Aug 1972. A large format newsprint format change occurred in Mar, 1981, transforming *Cinema Canada* into a modern business news serial for Canadian cinema. For the sampled issue of 1989: stapled large magazine format, editorial content consisting of black ink on uncoated paper stock with full-color cover on coated paper stock (10 ⅝ x 14 ⅛ inches / 270 x 360 mm).
DEPT: "Short Ends," newsbriefs; "Cinematography Assignments," listing; "Questions and Answers," concerning film technique. (11/12-63). "Editorial," "Canadian Film News," "Technical News," "Film Reviews," "NABET-AMC Local-700," newsbriefs; "CSC Assignments," "CFE News," "Directors Guild of Canada," newsbriefs; "Opinion," "Book Review," "Reverb," letters. (12/1-72/73). "News," "Editorial/Letters," "People," "Production Guide," "Reviews." (10-83). "Letter," "People," "Appointments," personnel briefs; "On Location," films in progress; "Events," upcoming items; "Festivals," "On (Experimental) Film," column by Mike Hoolboom; "Film Reviews," large detailed section; "Mini- Reviews," column by Pat Thompson; "Trade News," "Prairie Pulse," commentary column by Greg Klymkiw; "Shoot Alberta," column by Linda Earl and Charles Mandel; "Eastern Wave," column by Chris Majka; "Fronts West," column by Mark O'Neill; "Distribu-

tion Notes," newsbriefs; "Bookshelf," review column by George L. George; "Production Guide," column by Jim Levesque. (9-89).
TYPL: "Championship Golf Shooting Keeps Cameramen Alert," "The World of Process Projection Photography," "A Film Editor Comments on Film Making." (11/12-63). "Student Film Festival," "British Independent Cinema," "Women in Canadian Film," "Nothing Changes Much." (12/1-72/73). "Canada and Coproductions, 1963 - 1983: a Retrospective," "Jayne Eastwood: Actress at the Crossroads," "Introducing the Godmother of Canadiana Independence," "Electronic Flyspecks." (10-83). "Donald Brittain Remembered," "The Bethune Myth: Man and Movie," "Montreal Doing the Cannes Thing." (9-89).
SCHL: Bimonthly (1961 - Jan/Feb, 1981); Monthly (Mar, 1981+), 60 pp.
SPAN: 1961+
VARIES
--1961 - May/Jun, 1967 as Canadian Cinematography (ISSN: 0576-4823).
ABSORBED
--Cinemag (ISSN: 0709-5635) Mar, 1981.
LC: PN 1993.5 .C2 C5
DD: 791.43/05
ISSN: 0009-7071
ABST: --Canadian Periodical Index (ISSN: 0008-4719)
--Film Literature Index (ISSN: 0093-6758)
--Magazine Index
--Media Review Digest (ISSN: 0363-7778)

✦ CINEMA FRANCAIS

PUBL: Unifrance Film, 77 Champs-Elysees, 75008 Paris, France.
DESC: "This monthly magazine will be published in several languages with the purpose of: providing a complete guide on French productions so that they may be brought to the attention of foreign countries, informing them of those responsible of creating, planning, producing, and exporting them...This magazine will proudly and fervently attempt to place the French cinema on an universal standing." As other periodicals of this promotional genre, *Cinema Francais* offers interviews with talent, directors, and producers of French film product. Printed on high-gloss stock with numerous production stills. Text in English and French.
DEPT: "In Production," newsbriefs. (#8-77).
TYPL: "Joseph Losui," "Isabelle Adjani." (5-76). "An Actor-Producer Who Loves Challenge," "Rene Gilson Films the Events of 1936," "Inspecteur la Pavure: A Detective Comedy." (10-80).
SCHL: Eleven issues per year, 44 pp.
SPAN: May, 1976+
ISSN: 0041-6746

CINEMA HALL-MARKS
SUB: "Honest, justice and an interest in the other fellow."
PUBL: ?, Hollywood, CA.
DESC: "Hall-Marks accepts no advertising. There are no holdup numbers, no special editions, no paid publicity!! All it costs to read Hall-Marks every week (including the pertinent, timely and exclusive commentary of John C. Moffitt, Esq) is five bucks, the gold standard notwithstanding." That statement set the tone for the breezy manner of this four-page weekly newsletter on Hollywood cinema. Editor Howard Hall noted that his policy was: "...to encourage creative ability and ambitions, to enlighten those too busy to notice, and to entertain those engaged in the cinema." To that extent, it was a combination of gossip news, and interesting commentary on the status of Hollywood motion pictures. A most interesting newsletter on Hollywood doings.
DEPT: "Critic on the Hearth," column by John Moffitt.
TYPL: "From Frying Pan (Apparently Berman) into Fire!," "The Lady is Willing, but Harry Cohen is Not!," "Twentieth Century Deceives Exhibitors." (3-5-34).
SCHL: Weekly, 4 pp.
SPAN: Jul, 1933 - ?//
LC: PN 1993.C

✦ CINEMA JOURNAL
PUBL: Society for Cinema Studies, University of Illinois Press, 54 East Gregory, Champaign, IL 61820.
DESC: "A learned society founded in the spring of 1959, the Society for Cinema Studies is composed of college and university educators, film makers, historians, critics, scholars, and others concerned with the study of the moving image." In *Cinema Journal*, "...America's leading film scholars approach such diverse film and television topics as criticism, aesthetics, history, theory, directing, acting, writing, production, economics, and teaching." The society seeks to encourage the publishing of articles on the form and function of motion picture film, some three to eight features appearing in any given issue. In one sampled issue, articles ranged from an essay on the motion picture "Fort Apache," to the study of pornography vs. the practice of film theory, and finally, visual aesthetics and verbal expression in "23rd Psalm Branch." Of special note is the very valuable practice of providing contents page article synopses for each issue; a practice that many readers wish their scholarly journals utilized. A most thoughtful and considered scholarly publication in journal format. For the sampled issue of 1988: black/white graphics on glossy cover and back-of-issue advertising section, no graphics viewed in editorial section (5 ⅞ x 8 ⅞ inches / 150 x 225 mm).
DEPT: "Cinema Journal Book Reviews," unusually long reviews. (spring-77). "President's Report," "Dialogue," considered replies to past articles; "Professional Notes." (winter-88).
TYPL: "Toward a Historiography of American Film," "Alexander Black's Picture Plays: 1893 - 1894," "Rene Clair, Le Million, and the Coming of Sound." (Spring-77). "'All I Can See is the Flags': Fort Apache and the

Visibility of History," "The Pornographic Image and the Practice of Film Theory," "Words and Images in Stan Brakhage's 23rd Psalm Branch." (winter-88).
SCHL: Annual (1966/1967 - 1967/1968); Semiannual [Nov and Apr], (Fall, 1968 - Fall, 1984); Quarterly (Spring, 1985+), 90 pp.
SPAN: Fall?, 1961+
VARIES
--? - ? as Society of Cinematologists. Journal..
LC: PN 1993.S62
DD: 791.43/05
ISSN: 0009-7101
ABST: --Art Index (ISSN: 0004-3222)
--Arts and Humanities Citation Index (ISSN: 0162-8445)
--Film Literature Index (ISSN: 0093-6758)
--International Index to Film Periodicals (ISSN: 0000-0038)
--MLA International Bibliography of Books & Articles on the Modern Languages and Literatures (ISSN: 0024-8215)
--Writings on American History (ISSN: 0364-2887)

Cinema News and Property Gazette

1911 - Jul, 1921//
SEE: SCREEN INTERNATIONAL

Cinema News and Property Gazette, The

May, 1923 - Feb, 1928//
SEE: SCREEN INTERNATIONAL

✤ CINEMA NOW

SUB: "Perspectives on American underground film." (#1-1968 - ?).
PUBL: University of Cincinnati, Cincinnati, OH.
DESC: The editor's "Purpose is to provide for the future a documented understanding of developments in the art form that communicates what is happening now," the point of view in this case being that the underground film best provides that communication. The majority of the sample issue viewed (#1, 1968) consisted of transcripts and interviews of underground filmmakers at the University of Cincinatti at an April, 1967 conference. Virtually the entire serial consists of filmmakers' introspectives on the art of the personal film (as transcribed from the seminar). Wide format; graphics.
DEPT: None.
TYPL: No titles listed.
SCHL: ?
SPAN: 1968+?
LC: PN 1995.9 .E96C54
DD: 791.43/05

✤ CINEMA PAPERS

PUBL: Cinema Papers Pty, Ltd., 644 Victoria St., North Melbourne, Australia 3051.
DESC: With an emphasis on the Australian film community, *Cinema Papers* covers news of international film directors, talent, and new products. Most articles have an international flavor, while departments within the magazine concentrate on the Australian film industry. A large-format publication; unfortunately printed on newsprint. Of special note are articles on historical development of Australian cinema.
DEPT: "In Production," "Letters." (4-74). "The Quarter," news of film regulation; "Letters," "Picture Preview," "Film Censorship Listings," status; "Box-Office Grosses," "Production Survey," "Film Reviews," lengthy. (5/6-83).
TYPL: "The Censor Speaks," "Dirty Pix," "Not Suitable for Children," "A State of False Conscienceness," "National Film Theatre of Australia," "Between the Wars: Production Report." (4-74). "Sydney Pollack," "The Dismissal," "Denny Lawrence," "Stereoscopic Film," "Alex Stitt." (5/6-83).
SCHL: Quarterly (Jan, 74 - ?); Bimonthly (?+), 68 pp.
SPAN: Jan, 1974+
ABSORBED
--Filmviews (ISSN: 0158-3778), 1989.
LC: PN 1993.5.A8 C56
DD: 791.43/05
ISSN: 0311-3639
ABST: --Australian Public Affairs Information Service (ISSN: 0005-0075)
--Film Literature Index (ISSN: 0093-6758)
--Media Review Digest (ISSN: 0363-7778)

✤ CINEMA PERSPECTIVES

PUBL: Cinema Products Corporation, 2037 Granville Ave., Los Angeles, CA 90025.
DESC: The primary intention of this extraordinary public relations publication is to showcase the use of Cinema Products' 16 and 35 mm motion picture cameras used by professionals. Every page of this classy publication is printed in full color with lively interviews and applications of Cinema Products equipment. Useful information and the professional activities of news and feature cinematographers is found in this little magazine.
DEPT: None. (winter-75).
TYPL: "How We Boosted the Efficiency of Our TV-News-Film Operation," "The Filming of 'Hey Good Looking'," "A Return to Creative News-Documentary Filming," "A Conversation with Harry W. Wolfe, A.S.C." (winter-75).
SCHL: Quarterly, 24 pp.
SPAN: ?+?

CINEMA PROGRESS

SUB: "The film and life."

SUB: "Publication of the Cinema Appreciation League."
PUBL: American Institute of Cinematography, 3551 University Ave., Los Angeles, CA.
DESC: "During this past summer (1935), some thirty persons interested in the teaching of motion picture appreciation and experimentation with motion picture technics felt the need for an organization through which they might share and exchange their experiences and problems, and derive source materials for the appreciation of motion pictures." As a result of that meeting, the National Cinema Workshop and Cinema League, later called the Cinema Appreciation League, developed a periodical designed to explore the appreciation of film in society, education, and entertainment. This well-edited publication went through several format changes beginning in 1935 as a small format with no illustrations, to tabloid style in 1938, filled with a great number of illustrations and copy. The magazine explored primarily the Hollywood motion picture, behind-the-scenes production stories, and use of film in the classroom. Other articles dealing with non-theatrical use in everyday matters were also included, such as dentists using motion picture film for study. Written for a lay audience.
DEPT: "Picture Parade," lengthy reviews.
TYPL: "Wanted: A Story Specialist," "Censorship and the Story," "Crime by formula," "Will Television Affect our Movies?" "Television Eyes for the Radio Drama." (1-39).
SCHL: Irregular, 35 pp.
SPAN: Dec, 1935 - Jun/Jul, 1939//
VARIES
--Dec, 1935 - Jul, 1936 as National Cinema Workshop and Appreciation League Bulletin.
LC: PN 1993.C53

Cinema Quarterly

Autumn, 1932 - Summer, 1935//
SEE: DOCUMENTARY FILM NEWS

CINEMA STUDIES

SUB: "Journal of the Society for Film History Research."
PUBL: Society for Film History Research, 1 Dane St., High Holborn, London WC1, England.
DESC: This unique journal worked within a narrow definition of film history, publishing articles of limited reader appeal. Editor Neville March Hunnings wrote in the first issue: "It is the purpose of this journal, and of this Society, to encourage the basic research necessary to enable the history of the cinema, especially in Britain, to be adequately written." Inadequate financial resources brought the society and the journal to a close in 1968.
SCHL: Semiannual (1960-1964); Irregular (1965-1967).
SPAN: Mar, 1960 - Sep, 1967//
LC: PN 1993 .56133

✤ CINEMA THE WORLD OVER

PUBL: National Cinema Development Corporation, c/o K. S. Hosain, 204-205 Hotel Metropole, Karachi, Pakistan.
DESC: In its initial issue the publisher proclaimed no particular manifestoes of intent or purpose. "We do, however, hold fast to certain truths concerning the central importance of cinema as an art form, and as an instrument of social and cultural change. We shall not hesitate to discern these truths, to proclaim them by indirection or example." *Cinema the World Over* had two very strong intentions: 1) to bring news of world cinema to its national readers; and 2) to stimulate the Pakistani film industry to new freedoms and expression in filmmaking. It succeeds by use of numerous still pictures from world releases, and interviews with renowned filmmakers of international and Pakastani scope. An unfortunate aspect of the serial was its policy to mix newsprint pages with high-gloss paper.
DEPT: "From the Publisher," "Editorial," (2/3-76).
TYPL: "A Note on French Cinema," "Antonioni Talks," "The New Canadian Cinema," "History of Pakistan Cinema: 1949-1953, the Years of Groping," "Entertainment in the United Arab Emirates." (2/3-76).
DESC: Text is in English.
SCHL: Bimonthly, 60 pp.
SPAN: Jul, 1975+
LC: PN 1993 .C535
DD: 791.43/05

Cinema TV Today

Nov 13, 1971 - Aug, 1975//
SEE: SCREEN INTERNATIONAL

✤ CINEMA, VIDEO & CABLE MOVIE DIGEST

SUB: "An easy-to-read guide to movie enjoyment."
PUBL: Movie Digest, Inc., 7002 West Butler Pike, #100, Ambler, PA 19002.
DESC: "*CINEMA, VIDEO & CABLE MOVIE DIGEST* serves as your handy source to current releases on the big and little screens. For the busy person it provides a simple monthly guide to the world of movies available at theaters and on video or TV in easy to follow format. For quick reference the magazine is divided into three sections and an index." Section 1 is labeled "CINEMA," and lists full-page descriptions of current and about-to-be released motion picture product. The second section, "VIDEO RENTALS," notes what's new at local video rental stores, along with charts and graphs indicating popularity of current fare. "CABLE MOVIES," the third section of the magazine, provides an alphabetical listing of cable television motion pictures in the upcoming month on ten specific cable television channels. Finally, a detailed index provides an "A to Z" listing of all motion picture product by category (drama, comedy, fantasy, adventure, mystery, or thriller). An excellent guide to available mo-

tion picture product whether on the silver screen, cable television channel, or video cassette rental. For the sampled issue of 1991: black ink on newsprint with full-color cover on coated paper stock, limited advertising, in perfect-bound magazine format (8 x 10 ½ inches / 205 x 265 mm).
DEPT: "On Location," 'Short previews of feature films in progress'; "Celebrity Corner," 'New and familiar faces on the big screen'; "New Cinema," 'A round-up of the new cinema releases'; "Showcase," 'Stars of the month' profile; "New Videos," 'A review of the new video releases'; "Top 10 Videos," 'Rental and sales charts'; "Kiddie Cassettes," 'Cheaper than a babysitter and twice as reliable. What's available for the under-12 set'; "Vintage Video," "Ask the Expert," video Q&A column by Myron Berger; "Celebrity Crossword," 'Pencil games for the movie enthusiast'; "Cable Movie Calendar," 'What's playing on the movie channels for each day in [month]'; "Cable Movie Highlights," 'An A to Z listing with a story line for each cable movie'; "Horoscope Highlights." (6-91).
TYPL: "Kevin Costner, a Movie Hero for the '90s," "John Candy," "Top 50 Video Rentals of 1990," "Ginger Rogers: a Toast," "Literary Lives." (6-91).
SCHL: Monthly, 110 pp.
SPAN: May, 1991+

CINEMA VISION INDIA
SUB: "India's first professional cinema quarterly."
PUBL: Cinema Vision India, 1 Geetika, Swami Vivekenanda Rd., Santacruz (West), Bombay 400 054, India.
DESC: This small-format serial (printed on a light-lavendar color paper), provides fascinating insight into the history and industry of film in India. Each issue centers on a single topic such as: "Is There a New Cinema Movement," "The Rise of the Indian Film Song," "View from the Other Side," and "The Golden Age of Hindi Film Music." Articles serve to educate world readers about India's film industry.
DEPT: None. (1-82).
TYPL: "Indian Film: At the Crossroads?," "Underestimated Cinema," "The Easiest Place in the World to Make Films?," "Unfamiliarity Breeds Contempt," "World Cinema Scene: Survival of the Fattest." (1-82).
SCHL: Quarterly (1980); Annual (?); 85 pp.
SPAN: Jan, 1980 - Jan, 1983//
LC: PN 1993.5 .I8C54
DD: 384/.8/0954
ISSN: 0250-6998

✢ CINEMACABRE
SUB: "An appreciation of the fantastic."
SUB: "An appreciation of fantastic films."
PUBL: George Stover, PO Box 10005, Baltimore, MD 21285.
DESC: *Cinemacabre* is truly a first-class publication, beautifully layed out on coated paper stock, with gorgeous full-color and black/white pictures throughout. It fosters "An appreciation of the fantastic" as publisher George Stover put it, and makes one want to save and savor the contents of each issue over and over again. Interviews and filmographies are superb, but it is the reprinting of movie posters and lobby cards (many of which are in full color) which really sets this publication apart. It is obvious that Editor/Publisher Stover takes great care in securring the best possible copies of these items, AND in reprinting them. Articles are intelligently written and very informative. The sampled issue for 1988 consisted of a Leslie Nielsen interview, a profile/interview with director Reginald LeBorg, and an equally fascinating "Bridging the Bride of Frankenstein," subtitled "An examination of the cut scenes from 'The Bride of Frankenstein' in an effort to close the gaps in one of the finest horror films ever produced." Bravo to the editorial team for an excellent publication of the cinema macabre. For the sampled issue of 1988: stapled small journal format, an exquisitely printed magazine, full color throughout on coated paper stock, with outstanding black/white and color picture reproduction, no advertising (5 ½ x 8 ⅜ inches / 140 x 210 mm).
DEPT: "Editorial," "Letters to the Editor," "Bookrack," reviews; "Soundtrack," column by Steve Vertlieb; "Film Reviews," "Cinemacabre Video," reviews. (fall-88).
TYPL: "Minimacabre," "Cinemacabre Interview: Leslie Nielsen," "Bridging the Bride of Frankenstein," "Cinemacabre Interview: Reginald LeBorg," "Reflections." (fall-88).
SCHL: Semiyearly (? - ?); Three issues per year (?+), 65 pp.
SPAN: Mar, 1969+
VARIES
--Mar, 1969 - Summer/Fall?, 1978 as Black oracle (ISSN: 0045-2246).
ISSN: 0198-1064

CINEMAGES
PUBL: Group for Film Study, 3951 Gouverneur Ave., New York, NY.
DESC: "*Cinemages*'s main purpose is to impart to the viewer of the films shown some sense of their significance; to provide a background of historical and critical facts; to assist the film student in establishing his own criteria for judging a motion picture by giving the reasons for its production and the theories involved; to create, eventually, a discriminating audience for a better screen product." Each mimeographed issue coincided with Group for Film Study screenings in New York City. What this publication lacks in visuals, it makes up for in thoughtful analysis and historical background for the surveyed films.
DEPT: None.
TYPL: No titles listed.
SCHL: Irregular, 40 pp.
SPAN: Mar, 1955 - 1958//

```
             VARIES
             --? - Feb, 1955? as Film Study.
LC:          PN 1994.C53
ISSN:        0412-5479
```

✦ CINEMAGIC

SUB: "The guide to fantastic filmmaking."
PUBL: O'Quinn Studios, 475 Park Ave., South, New York, NY 10016.
DESC: From a 1981 subscription promotion: "If you are a young filmmaker with a special interest in science fiction, special effects and the limitless magic of the cinema... This is your magazine. *Cinemagic* will feature: How to produce professional titles that move, change color, melt, sparkle, burst into flames, zoom into space...all for a few bucks! Tired of square screens? Learn about inexpensive lenses and devices to make your picture W-I-D-E-S-C-R-E-E-N. Breakaway props for realistic fight scenes. ...Reviews of new equipment, lenses and optical gadgets for creating special effects! Readers' forum--letters and questions exchanging techniques and production secrets! Step-by-step illustrated articles detailing methods you can use to create visual effects, makeup and sound FX." *Cinemagic* is a techniques magazine aimed at the science fiction-filmmaker enthusiast. Articles provide basic "how to" instructions on special effects, such as how to create cobwebs, makeup or unusual lighting. Some electronic schematics for special projects. Many graphics. For the sampled issue of 1981: stapled magazine format with full-color inside/outside covers on coated paper stock (8 1/8 x 11 inches / 205 x 275 mm).
DEPT: "Editors Bench," "Producers Bulletin Board," "Electronic Special Effects," "Filmmakers Forum." (#1-83).
TYPL: "Spin Your Own Spiderwebs," "I was a High School Werewolf," "Melies Tribute Seen on Cable TV," "Three Simple Lighting Devices." (#1-83).
SCHL: Quarterly (#1 - #7); Bimonthly (#8); Monthly (#9 - #11); Bimonthly (#12 - ?); Quarterly (? - ?); 36 pp.
SPAN: Winter, 1972+
       SUSPENDED
       --1975 - 1979.
LC: TR 858.C462
DD: 778.5/345
ISSN: 0090-3000
ABST: --Film Literature Index (ISSN: 0093-6758)

CINEMANEWS, THE

PUBL: Foundation for Art in Cinema, Box 1112, Larkspur, CA 94939.
DESC: Weird, strange, underground, poetic, and independent are some ways to describe this serial of the Independent California Canyon Cinema News Co-op. Beginning publication in the early 1960s, *Canyon Cinemanews* (later entitled *The Cinemanews*), provided an atypical forum for discussion ("rapping"), concerning independent (underground) filmmakers, their film product, and noteworthy worldwide festivals to showcase their projects. The publication format itself is nothing short of remarkable, oftentimes changing size, paper, ink color, and content every issue. Contributing to the confusion over format and publication schedule was the latter practice of publishing six issues a year, with up to five of those issues being a combined "super" issue. Finally, by 1977, *The Cinemanews* settled into a standardized magazine format, while retaining its original spunky editorial stance toward established films and their audiences. Within the typical issue, the reader will find everything the underground or independent filmmaker would need or desire to read: used buses for sale, poetry, comment on the Vietnamese (or any other) war, lively reviews (sometimes spiked with four-letter words), articles by the editor as to where to find the cheapest wines in the San Francisco Bay area, news of filmmakers, children's essays, government oppression, readers' doodles, and always the rallying cry to overthrow the established cinema. The mixture may seem strange, but the purpose remained true: to advance the state of independent filmmaking, and to maintain contact between geographically diverse individuals and their co-ops. Many of the early issues were mimeographed or typewritten/offset, and lack any feature or article titles, the news items simply appearing one after another.
DEPT: "Letters," "New Films," "Independent Film Review." (# 6-78).
TYPL: "Harry Smith," "Unlimited Filmic Opportunities," "Signifying Blues," "Brakhage Uncensored," "Wind, Decay, Rewind." (#6-78).
SCHL: Bimonthly, 30 pp.
SPAN: Jan, 1963 - 1980?//?
       VARIES
       --Jan, 1963 - Sep/Oct, 1976 as Canyon Cinemanews (ISSN: 0008-5758).
ISSN: 0198-7305

CINEMATOGRAPHY AND BIOSCOPE MAGAZINE

SUB: "The world's headquarters for animated photography."
PUBL: The Warwick Trading Company, 4 & 5, Warwick Ct., Holborn, London WC, England.
DESC: In the premiere issue of this free promotional "serial" for the trade, the editor noted that "The genesis of the trade circular is more or less wrapped in mystery. In common with all good things, some authorities affirm that the idea is of American origin, whilst others hold that it is a gradual and necessary outcome of the monthly price list. Which ever suggestion is correct, is to us little consequence; what does interest us more is the conclusion we have come to, namely, that it affords an excellent means of intercommunication between buyer and seller, and keeps the one in closer touch with the other." This small trade circular pro-

vided in-depth reviews of latest films distributed by the Warwick Trading Company, including complete descriptions and numbering of scenes, incidents within each scene, footage, and price information. Still pictures from recent releases commenced in the second issue. Of special interest in the May, 1906 issue was the first offering of San Francisco Earthquake pictures, and the Warwick Trading Company where great pains were taken to convince the reader that their footage was real, not the fake material conjured up by other less-reputable companies.

DEPT: "News in brief," "Latest Films," extensive reviews; (4-06).
TYPL: "The Educational Value of the Cinematograph," (4-06).
SCHL: Monthly (Apr, 1906 - Jun, 1906); Quarterly (Jul/Sep, 1906 - Jan/Mar, 1907); 16 pp.
SPAN: Apr, 1906 - Jan/Mar, 1907//

Cinemeditor

Winter, 1950 - Summer, 1971//
(ISSN: 0069-4169)
SEE: AMERICAN CINEMEDITOR

✣ CINEMONKEY

SUB: "A serious film journal."
SUB: "The magazine of science fiction people."
PUBL: Cinemonkey, PO Box 8502, Portland, OR 97207.
DESC: *Cinemonkey* takes the art of filmmaking seriously, providing thoughtful essays on the meaning of film as an art forum and showing the techniques and intentions of filmmakers. Intermingled are considered discussions of the impact of current film exhibition on society. Each issue covers international filmmakers, with a considerable number of still pictures.
DEPT: "Reviews," "Books," "Music." (fall-78).
TYPL: "Rules of the Game: Martin Scorsese's *Mean Streets*," "Jean- Luc Godard & Jean-Paul Gorin's *Letter to Jane*," "Contemporary Film Noir: Questing in *Chinatown's* Maze." (fall-78).
SCHL: Quarterly, 60 pp.
SPAN: Winter, 1975+
VARIES
--Winter, 1975? - 1978? as Scintillation (ISSN: 0147-5789).
LC: PN 1993.C546
DD: 791.43/05
ISSN: 0162-0126
ABST: --Film Literature Index (ISSN: 0093-6758)

✣ CIPA NEWS

PUBL: California Intercollegiate Press Association, Peperdine University, Malibu, CA.
DESC: A short newsletter of the California Intercollegiate Press Association which is mostly newsbriefs of local CIPA chapters and upcoming activities. No graphics.

DEPT: None.
TYPL: "A Slight Plan Change," "CIPA? What's That?" "Mustang Daily Suspended," (11-77). "Journalists to Converge on Goleta," "CIPA Calls for Print Mail-In Entries," (1-82).
SCHL: Monthly, 4 pp.
SPAN: ?+?

Class

Jan, 1915 - Feb, 1927//
SEE: BUSINESS MARKETING

Class & Industrial Marketing

Mar, 1927 - Jun, 1933//
SEE: BUSINESS MARKETING

Classic

Sep, 1922 - Jan, 1924//
SEE: MOVIE CLASSIC

CLASSIC IMAGES REVIEW

PUBL: Muscatine Journal, 301 E. 3rd St., Muscatine, Iowa 52761.
DESC: In one advertisement, the publisher calls *Classic Images Review* the "Junior Version" or "Appetizer" to the senior publication, *Classic Images*. Indeed, this spritely tabloid newsprint quarterly is a reprint of selected articles from the senior publication, along with numerous advertisements of vendors selling old motion pictures, TV shows, documentaries, and other programming fare on either 16 mm film or videotape stock. Don't look for any logic in the kind of articles selected; remember that this publication is only intended to "whet your appetite" for *Classic Images*.
DEPT: None.
TYPL: "Marx Bros. 'Forgotten' TV Pilot Discovered by Gaines '16' Films," "Dialogue With Pat O'Brien," "The Lucky Man: Hoot Gibson," "The Full-Length Animated Film is Alive and Well." (8-81).
SCHL: Quarterly, 64 pp.
SPAN: Nov, 1979 - ?, 1981//
ISSN: 0199-9486

Classic Pictorial of Screen and Stage

Feb, 1924 - Aug, 1924//
SEE: MOVIE CLASSIC

✣ CLIO AMONG THE MEDIA

SUB: "Newsletter of the AEJMC history division."

PUBL: Association for Education in Journalism and Mass Communication, History Division, Department of Communication, University of Utah, Salt Lake City, UT 84112.
DESC: Scholarly historical work in the print media is very much alive and well thanks to the efforts of the History Division of the Association for Education in Journalism and Mass Communications. It is this group of individuals who publish *Clio Among the Media*, a wonderful serial that makes history both enlightening and entertaining. What makes this periodical so valuable is that not only does each issue contain a considerable number of articles on print history, but also a fair number of articles concerning news about current research projects, available fellowships and grants, and news on the general state of historical scholarship in America. It makes media history relevant to today's industry and society. Black/white magazine style, with numerous historical line-drawings (8 3/8 x 11 inches / 213 x 280 mm).
DEPT: "Editor's Notes," "Letter to the Editor," "Upcoming Meetings," "Other Meetings of Interest," "Fellowships and Grants," "People & Projects." (1/88). "Division Head Speaks," "Awards," "Papers & Conferences," upcoming; "Announcements From Around the World," journalism history newsbriefs. (10-89). "Editorial Notes," "Inside the Division," "Coming Events, Manuscript Calls, Deadlines." (winter-90).
TYPL: "The Secondary Literature Problem in Journalism History," "On Using a Diagnostic Test Before Teaching Journalism History," "Some Thoughts about Press Freedom and Our Research," "Printing and Proselytizing." (1/88). "Matching Birthdays Provides Personal Stake in History," "Minutes of History Division Business Meeting," "Exploring Intellectual and Cultural Approaches to History." (10-89). "History as Adventure," "Call for Bicentennial Ideas," "Honors Course Uses More than Standard Tools," "Will Geraldo Rivera Get His Wings?" (winter-90).
SCHL: Quarterly, 12 pp.
SPAN: Fall, 1969?+

Clio Devoted to Commercials
Oct, 1968 - ?//
SEE: CLIO MAGAZINE

CLIO MAGAZINE
SUB: "Devoted to commercials." (Oct, 1968 - ?).
SUB: "Quarterly for mass communications."
PUBL: CLIO Awards Enerprises, 30 E. 60th St., New York, NY 10022.
DESC: *Clio* was devoted to commercial production primarily in New York City (according to the sample issues reviewed). It centered on the process of producing national television spots, with input from copywriters, directors, agency managers, and clients. *Clio* provided the forum for professionals to discuss and explore their craft. Numerous graphics, especially spot stills.
DEPT: "Letters," "Product Analysis," "Scene/Agencies," "Scene/Production," "Scene/Festivals," "TvB Report," "Scene/and Heard," "RAB Report," "Scene/Technical," "Scene/World," "People Mix," "If You Ask Me," "Copy Points," "Rod Allen's Own Thing," column. (3-69).
TYPL: "Openers--New Commercials," "The New Visuals," "One-Stop Shopping," "See How They Ran." (3-69).
SCHL: Monthly (? - ?); Quarterly (? - ?, 1976//?); 80 pp.
SPAN: Oct, 1968 - ?, 1976//?
VARIES
--Oct, 1968 - ? as Clio Devoted to Commercials.

CLOSE-UP
SUB: "A newsletter for members and friends of AFI."
PUBL: American Film Institute, John F. Kennedy Center for the Performing Arts, Washington, DC 20566.
DESC: In its premiere issue, *Close-Up* was said to "...be designed to acquaint you with the breadth of the institute's activity and to advise members about new benefits." *Close-Up* described on-going archival, media, and institutional activities within the American Film Institute. Articles ranged from an East German film tour; a rediscovered Lon Chaney film previously thought to have been lost; AFI public service programs; an AFI/USIA Chinese exchange program; and update information about the National Center for Film and Video Preservation. For the sampled issues of 1983: two-color ink on uncoated paper stock in folded newsletter format (8 ½ x 11 inches / 215 x 280 mm). For the sampled issues of 1984 and 1987: tabloid newspaper format, black ink with spot-color on newsprint (11 x 14 ¾ inches / 280 x 365 mm).
DEPT: None. (fall-82). None. (fall-85).
TYPL: "'The Rogue Song' Sings Again," "Contempory Films of China," "New Learning Opportunities About Film and Television," "American Viewers Meet Hungarian Films," "Snapshots of Fonda." (fall-82). "AFI Selected for California State Bond Program," "New Television Workshop Announced at Institute," "National Board Meets to Establish Preservation Priorities." (fall- 85).
SCHL: Quarterly [Irregular at times], 6 pp.
SPAN: Fall, 1982 - Spring, 1987//
SUSPENDED
--1986.
ISSN: 0742-2105

CLOSE-UP
SUB: "Devoted to the art of films."
PUBL: POOL, London, England.
DESC: "Fifty odd years hasn't done so badly in getting an art into the world that fifty more will turn into THE art, but now, after somewhat magnificent growth, one feels here is its critical age." So began this celebrated

film periodical in July, 1927. Continuing its short run till its demise in 1933, *Close-Up* provided an international viewpoint for the development of film as an art. It began as a monthly, moving later into a quarterly and larger format. Articles were always fascinating if not lengthy on subjects ranging from silent films to talkies, from domestic to international awareness of film as an entertainment, art and political medium. Like many small magazines of this era the world depression called a halt to its publishing schedule.
DEPT: "Comment and Review," (#2-27). "Criticism and Achievement," variety of viewpoints; "Book Reviews."
TYPL: "Mrs. Emerson," (by Gertrude Stein); "The Real Danger of the Cinema," "Portrait Photography," "British Solecisms," (#2-27). "A Mining Film," "Facts for Finance," "At the Boundary of Film and Theatre," "Four Films from Germany," "Notes from America," "Young Workers Film Their Own Life." (3-32).
SCHL: Monthly (Jul, 1927 - 1930); Quarterly (1931 - Dec, 1933); 75 pp.
SPAN: Jul, 1927 - Dec, 1933//
LC: PN 1993.C62
DD: 791.43/05

✦ CLOSE-UP

PUBL: Corporate Communications Group, Polaroid Corporation, 549 Technology Square, Cambridge, MA 02139.
DESC: A quality corporate promotional magazine detailing uses and users of Polaroid photo equipment. Issues are always well balanced between technical use by the scientific community, profiles of professional photographers, and the introduction or discussion of Poloroid techniques. Beautiful layout; printed on high quality paper.
DEPT: "Poloroid Technology," "Techphoto Applications," "Recent Publications and Exhibitions," "New Products," "Hot Line," Q&A column.
TYPL: "Preparing for the Next Big One," "Lucien Aigner, Master of Photography," "Light Dialogues," "Cows, Hills, Barns, and People of Point Reyes, California." (#1-81).
SCHL: Quarterly, 35 pp.
SPAN: Sep, 1970+
LC: TR 1.C
ISSN: 0740-5545

✦ CLOSE-UP

SUB: "The magazine of the film forum."
PUBL: Film Forum, 421, Hind Rajasthan Centre, Bombay-14 DD, India.
DESC: This film discussion review encompasses both Indian and world film product. International articles sometimes consist of reprints from other international film serials. Film product is the focus of all articles. The psychology of filmmaking is more important than the technology or technique of motion picture production. Emphasis is on the international director with remainder of publication devoted to issues of the Indian film industry, such as distribution, exhibition, regional cinema, and the ever-present issue of censorship in all cultures. Square magazine format; oftentimes printed on various papers and various colors. Some graphics.
DEPT: "Editorial," "Reviews." (#7/8-71).
TYPL: "The Art and Films of Satyajit Ray," "Fonda on Easy Rider," "Antonioni on Antonioni." (#7/8-71).
SCHL: Quarterly, 70 pp.
SPAN: Jul, 1968+
LC: PN 1993.C598
DD: 791.43/0954

✦ CLOSEUP

SUB: "Network services and equipment."
PUBL: CMP Publications, Inc., 600 community Dr., Manhasset, NY 11030.
DESC: *Closeup* is a supplement to *CommunicationsWeek*, and provides service and technological information about point-to-point communication operation. Each issue reviews one topic in depth. Like its parent publication, *Closeup* is tabloid size on glossy paper; numerous color graphics.
DEPT: None. (5-2-88).
TYPL: "Will the Nations Become United?," "National Profiles," "Gloomy View." (5-2-88).
SCHL: ?, 12 pp.
SPAN: ?+
SUPPLEMENT TO
--CommunicationsWeek (ISSN: 0746-8121), ?+

✦ CMA NEWSLETTER

PUBL: College Media Advisers, Memphis State Univesity, MJ-300, Memphis, TN 38152.
DESC: This newsletter matches the vibrancy of the organization it serves; college faculty who are advisers to campus media and students. Editor Richard Lytle and Associate Editor Jean Pietrobono, together with their College Media Adviser colleagues, have wisely chosen to publish a newsletter whose editorial content is primarly special departmental articles submitted by some one-dozen CMA members. This variety of authors inform, excite, and are truly representative of the thoughts and trends of the organization at large. This is must reading for pedagogues whose daily duties bring them into the role of adviser to students and campus media activities. Of special note is the pleasant practice of printing the authors' pictures alongside articles. For the 1990 sampled issue: stapled single-sheet newsletter format, black ink editorial content with graphics on uncoated paper stock (8 ½ x 11 inches / 215 x 280 mm).
DEPT: "From the Editor," column by Richard Lytle; "CMA Calendar," of upcoming events; "CMA Shorts," newsbriefs; "From the President," column by Lesley Marcello; "From the Vice President," column by Laura Widmer; "From the Vice President for Member Serv-

ices," column by Terry Vander Heyden; "Yearbook," column by Linda Puntney; "Newspaper," column by Bob Adams; "Electronic Media," column by Adele Lanan; "Press Law," column by Louis Ingelhart; "Black and White and Red All Over," column by Martin L. 'Red' Gibson; "Magazine," column by Janet Terry; "Technology," column by John Slothower; "Newspaper," column by Brent Bates; "Advertising/Business," column by Kevin Schwartz; "Jobs," "CMA People," personnel newsbriefs. (2-90).
TYPL: "Pros Highlight Spring Convention," "Committee Co-Sponsors Survey of Minority Faculty, Advisers," "Total Alertness Helps Prevent Ridiculous Homophone Errors," "Magazine Committee is Developing New National Media Buying Guide." (2-90).
SCHL: Quarterly (? - ?); Ten issues per year (?+), 18 pp.
SPAN: ?+
VARIES
--? - ? as Newsletter.

CODE NEWS

PUBL: Code Authority, National Association of Broadcasters, 1771 N Street N.W., Washington, DC 20036.
DESC: A four to eight-page newsletter of monthly developments in the National Association of Broadcasters (NAB), Code of Good Programming Practices. To a great extent the publication serves to clarify current standards in broadcast programming.
DEPT: "Subscriber Status," radio-TV code station additions and deletions.
TYPL: "Commercials for Securities Need Careful Reviews, Legal Counsel to Assure Compliance with Existing Laws," "Motion Picture Ads Reviewed by Code," "Emergency-Type Procedures When Used in Advertising are Questionable Under Penumbra of code and Legal Issues."
SCHL: Monthly, 4 pp.
SPAN: Mar, 1968 - ?//
FROM MERGER OF
--TV Code News (ISSN: 0494-4267) (and) Radio Code News, Mar, 1968.
LC: HE 8690.N32
DD: 384.5
ISSN: 0547-3861

COLLEGE & UNIVERSITY JOURNAL

SUB: "Official monthly publication of the American College Publicity Association."
PUBL: American College Public Relations Association, Washington, DC.
DESC: *College Public Relations Quarterly* provided encouragement, education, critique, and counsel for the higher education public relations director. Published by the American College Public Relations Association, it was a forum for discussion of college issues, and provided examples of public relations applications which could aid in resolving those issues. Topics covered the gamut of academic activities, from sports to admissions, from publicity to fund raising, and were presented in a lucid, scholarly manner. It was in journal format with no illustrations. In its final issue for May, 1974, the editor reflected that "The chief purpose of the *Journal* was to explore the concerns that would be affecting higher education and, more importantly, that would have considerable impact upon the institutional advancement program." To that end, *College and University Journal* provided thoughtful essays on public relations philosophy, and case studies in successfully relating to a sometimes sceptical public. Other articles were administration-oriented, pertaining to important issues facing every college president. In Spring, 1974, the American College Public Relations Association merged with the American Alumni Council and a new serial emerged to serve both. Some graphs and charts; magazine format.
DEPT: "Editorials," "Professional Book Shelf, The." (1-50). "Professional Book Shelf, The." (4-56). "Book Reviews," "Research Report." (fall-62). "Comments & Trends." (5-74).
TYPL: "A Study of P.R. in Catholic Colleges," "The Sixteen Millimeter Screen--Manysided Medium," "Athletics, Key Public Relations Tool." (1-50). "Some Fundamentals of University Development," "Scripts is Where You Find 'Em," "Have You Dedicated a College Recently?" (4-56). "What is a University," "Issues in College Admissions," "The Christian Liberal Arts College," "The Free Spirit in the Free University." (fall-62). "Knowledge Renewal with Innovation," "Gone are the Whitewashers," "Getting to Know the Corporation.")(5-74).
SCHL: Monthly [Sep - Jun] (1917 - May/Jun, 1946); Monthly [Oct - Jun] (Oct, 1947 - May/Jun, 1949); Five issues per year (?+), 45 pp.
SPAN: 1917 - May, 1974//
VARIES
--1917 - Jul, 1942 as College Publicity Digest, The.
--Sep, 1942 - May/Jun, 1946 as Publicity Problems.
--Oct, 1947 - May/Jun, 1949 as College Public Relations.
--Oct, 1949 - Jul, 1956 as College Public Relations Quarterly.
--Jan, 1957 - Jun, 1961 as Pride (ISSN: 0032-8197).
LC: LB 2300.C53
DD: 378
ISSN: 0010-0927

✤ COLLEGE BROADCASTER

SUB: "A publication of the National Association of College Broadcasters."
PUBL: National Association of College Broadcasters, PO Box 1955, Brown University, Providence, RI 02912.
DESC: "Respected by students and professionals alike, *College Broadcaster* is read at nearly every college radio and television station and communications department in the country. The magazine provides a comprehensive mix of articles, department features and

special listings covering the needs of college radio and TV managers and staff in every department at the station. The magazine makes readers aware of changes occurring in both the professional and college media world and how these developments interact. The magazine is NACB's primary means of communication with the college electronic media community." This membership publication of the National Association of College Broadcasters covers activities of college/university radio and television stations. Some twenty-plus years ago, that meant carrier- current radio stations faced with the difficult task of sending their radio program signals through 60 Hz electrical current wires into dormitory basements, and seemingly spending most hours attempting to route signals around fluorescent light fixtures, large electrical motors, and other obstacles. Today, college radio and television operations use fiber optic cable, automated operations, and even U-Net, the "first university-programmed, national satellite network." An interesting, nicely designed publication for student-operated college radio and television services. Magazine format (8 3/8 x 11 inches / 215 x 280 mm), numerous graphics.

DEPT: "Book Reviews," "Editorial," "Engineering," "Equipment Reviews," "Faculty Advisor," written by faculty advisors to college campus radio and television operations; "Government & Industry News," "Letters to the Editor & to NACB," "Music Charts & Reviews," "NACB News," news of National Association of College Broadcasters; "Station Profiles." (9-89). "Editorial," "User Review," "Letters," "Record Label Servicing," "Radio Ratings," college stations compared to other radio media in market; "U-Net Program Profile," "NACB News," news of the National Association of College Broadcasters; "Government & Industry News," "Conferences & Events," calendar of upcoming events; "Legal," "Product Releases," "Book Review," "Music Charts and Playlists," "Music Reviews," "Station Profiles." (2-91).

TYPL: "Get the 'WORD' Out," "NACB's 1st Annual Station T-Shirt Contest," "New Music Seminar 10," "Radio: More Than Coursework," "College Media's Christian Alternative: IRB." (9-89). "Live Assistant at KCCU," "KUHF Edits Audio Digitally with Studer-Dyaxis," "Free Music and Videos Are a Call Away," "Pirate Radio Stations: Tuning in to Underground Broadcasts," "Formats and Conformity." (2-91).

SCHL: Eight issues per year, 35 pp.
SPAN: Sep, 1988+

✣ COLLEGE MEDIA REVIEW

SUB: "Devoted to opinion and research on the student communications media and related areas."
PUBL: College Media Advisers, Inc., Journalism Department, Memphis State University, Memphis, TN 38152.
DESC: Continuing the tradition of *College Press Review*, this serial provides news, advice, and case studies in faculty management of college media: campus newspapers, radio, television, and public relations activities. Information is practical, useful, and very applicable to the ever-present academic struggle of budget vs. student media activities vs. academic freedom and policy. This is a forum where management ideas and concepts take root in the dual function of offering media outlet opportunities for communication students, while recognizing the unique nature of operating such activities under academic sponsorship, censorship and encouragement. Primary focus of the quarterly publication is on campus journalism, and more specifically the student college newspaper. Magazine format (8.5 x 11 inches / 215 x 280 mm), printed black/white on coated paper stock, graphics, with minimal advertising.

DESC: [College Press Review]: This compact journal is designed for college- level journalism, graphics and advertising instructors; in short, it is a medium of opinion and information for college personnel who oversee or publish a campus newspaper. Typical articles cover the economics of publishing/advertising, the training of professional journalists, rights of campus newspapers, and success campaigns of individual programs. Several format changes were evident during publication span of this title. For the sampled issues of 1978 through 1980: black ink on uncoated paper stock, cover consisting of black ink on coated paper stock with occasional spot-color on cover (8 1/4 x 10 3/4 inches / 210 x 275 mm). Issues for Fall, 1980 through Spring, 1981 were black ink on uncoated paper stock with covers being black ink on coated paper stock, one with additional spot-color silver ink (5 1/8 x 8 3/8 inches / 130 x 215 mm). And for the sampled issue of late 1981 (undated, but numbered as volume 20, #5): black ink on uncoated paper stock with green-color ink cover in bound journal format (5 1/8 x 8 3/4 inches / 130 x 225 mm). Sampled issues for January, 1982 through Spring, 1983 were in a stapled, square-magazine format, black ink on uncoated paper stock, with black ink cover on coated paper (8 1/4 x 10 7/8 inches / 210 x 280 mm).

DEPT: "Articles Pertinent to the Campus Press," bibliography of current articles. (spring-75). "Book Reviews." (winter-86). "Editor's Note." (spring-90).

TYPL: "The Indiana Collegiate Press Association: Service and Cooperation," "Future Careers in Environmental Journalism," "Covering the State Legislature," "Teaching Ad Copy and Layout." (spring-75). "Revival in Decatur," "Bringing Radio News Home," "The Trouble with Fools," "The Ideal Internship." (winter-86). "From Sources to Resources: Managing to Survive," "How are We Doing? Evaluating Staff & Product," "What's Out There? Ask the Right Stuff," "A Public Affairs Reporting Class & the Newsroom," "Getting Campus Journalism Back to its Roots." (spring-90).

SCHL: Quarterly, 24 pp.
SPAN: Summer, 1983+
VARIES
--1956 - Spring, 1983? as College Press Review (ISSN: 0010-1117).

ISSN: 0739-1056
ABST: --Reference Sources (ISSN: 0163-3546)

College Press Review
1956 - Spring, 1983?//
(ISSN: 0010-1117)
SEE: COLLEGE MEDIA REVIEW

College Public Relations
Oct, 1947 - May/Jun, 1949//
SEE: COLLEGE & UNIVERSITY JOURNAL

College Public Relations Quarterly
Oct, 1949 - Jul, 1956//
SEE: COLLEGE & UNIVERSITY JOURNAL

College Publicity Digest, The
1917 - Jul, 1942//
SEE: COLLEGE & UNIVERSITY JOURNAL

College Radio
1964 - 1969//
SEE: JOURNAL OF COLLEGE RADIO

✤ COLLEGIATE JOURNALIST
PUBL: Society for Collegiate Journalists, c/o Douglas Tarpley, National Executive Director, Regent University, Virginia Beach, VA 23463.
DESC: This is the official publication of the Society for Collegiate Journalists, originally founded in 1909 as Pi Delta Epsilon, and later called Alpha Phi Gamma (1919). It is a news and general information vehicle for individual campus chapters throughout the United States. Articles concern press freedom issues, subscriptions, photography, journalistic career and technology trends, and the state of collegiate journalism at small and large institutions. Editor Richard Gotshall in his first issue (fall-87) called for a "...blend of both broad and specific articles that chapters and their publications can use, and also to make the magazine fun to read so students will read it." It appears that *The Collegiate Journalist* has accomplished both in fine style. Numerous black/white graphics; magazine format.
DEPT: None.
TYPL: "Showbiz Journalism: Whose Fault?," "What's Happening in Your Chapter," "Three Days in Charleston," "Change: the Constant of Education." (fall-87).
SCHL: Semiannual, 20 pp.
SPAN: Fall, 1963+
ISSN: 0010-1214

✤ COLOPHON
PUBL: Adobe Systems Inc., 1585 Charleston Rd., PO Box 7900, Mountain View, CA 94039-7900.
DESC: "*Colophon* is the news publication of Adobe systems Incorporated. It features news about Adobe's products, the PostScript page-description language, PostScript language software applications, and PostScript printers." Produced as a large format magazine, this self-promotional for Adobe type provides interesting "how-to" articles on type usage, layout and design ideas, and showcases Adobe type for desktop publishing at the same time. For the 1988 sampled issue: large magazine stapled format, red spot color used throughout with black ink on coated paper stock (11 x 15 inches / 280 x 380 mm).
DEPT: None. (3-88).
TYPL: "New Gray-Scale Scanners, Better Halftones, and the EPSF Advantage," "Get Control From any Perspective," "A Timely Solution to a Technical Problem," "The Stone Family of Typefaces." (3-88).
SCHL: Quarterly?, 25 pp.
SPAN: ?+?

✤ COLORADO EDITOR
SUB: "Official publication of the Colorado Editorial Association, issued for, and devoted to the best interests of Colorado editors and the dissemination of news of interest to the publishers of the Centennial State."
PUBL: Colorado Press Association, 1336 Glenarm Pl., Denver, CO 80204.
DESC: For over a hundred years, the *Colorado Editor* has provided its readers news and views on the state of the Colorado Press Association. It is interesting to note that many of the topics found in the issues from the early 1920s are many of the same topics to grace the trade publications of current-day newspaper management; issues of personnel, subscriptions, technical problems, and topics related to the local community. Graphics.
DEPT: "Just Among Ourselves," newsbriefs; "From Our Letter Box," "From the Field Manager's Office," (10-1-27). "Blood in the Ink," editorial; "We Get Letters," "FYI," newsbriefs; "FOI Boxscore," newsbriefs. (6-79).
TYPL: "Music News Bureau Admits Space Grafting," "Care and Treatment of Type Casting Metals," "What the National Advertiser Wants to Know about Your Paper." (10-1-27). "Colorado Editors Asked to Aid 1st Amendment Fight," "Newswomen Find Promotion Rough," "Paper Execs Help Circulation Improve." (6-79).
SCHL: Monthly, 12 pp.
SPAN: 1926+
VARIES
--?, 1926 - Mar, 1942 as Colorado Editor and the Intermountain Press.
LC: PN 4700.C6
DD: 070.5
ISSN: 0162-0010

Colorado Editor and the Intermountain Press

?, 1926 - Mar, 1942//
SEE: COLORADO EDITOR

✣ COLOUR

SUB: "An international broadcast engineer's publication."
PUBL: ?, London, England.
DESC: It is believed that *Colour* is a supplement to *International Broadcast Engineer*, although the sampled issue (1971) did not provide any such lineage information. Articles cconcentrated on elements of color television technology, including camera automation, portable cameras, on-location videotrucks, and video tape recorders (VTRs), which comprise the bulk of editorial content.
DEPT: None. (?-71).
TYPL: "A Choice of Continental-European Colour Cameas," "Mobile Colour," "Helical Scan," "Developments in Decca Colour." (?-71).
SCHL: Semiyearly?, 30 pp.
SPAN: ?+
LC: TK 6670.C585

✣ COLUMBIA JOURNALISM REVIEW

SUB: "National media monitor: press, radio, TV."
SUB: "To assess the performance of journalism, to help stimulate continuing improvement in the profession, and to speak out for what is right, fair, and decent."
PUBL: Columbia University Press, Graduate School of Journalism, 700 Journalism Bldg., New York, NY 10027.
DESC: *"Columbia Journalism Review* is published bimonthly under the auspices of the faculty, alumni and friends of the School of Journalism, Columbia University. The *Review* is published for two considerations: First, to meet the need to assess the performance of journalism in all its forms, to call attention to its shortcomings and its strengths and to help define or redefine standards of honest, responsible service. Second, the obligation that falls on a serious professional school--a graduate institution, national in character--to help stimulate continuing improvement in its profession and to speak out for what it considers right and fair and decent." Recognized as an authoritative periodical for the field of journalism ethics, *CJR* provides fascinating insight into the field of broadcast and print journalism in the United States. Articles plunge into controversies surrounding "checkbook journalism," the elements of newsgathering and ethics of same, and the ongoing struggle between government, the public, and the news media. This is a trade journal of great repute, both for the public, and the reporters working in the trenches; and is well recommended. Magazine format (8 ⅛ x 10 ⅞ inches / 205 x 275 mm). Note: Volume 1, Number 1 issue for spring, 1962 was preceded in fall, 1961 by a "pilot issue."
DEPT: "Chronicle," newsbriefs; "At Issue," editorial; "Books," review; "Briefing," review; "Unfinished Business," letters; "The Lower Case," comic comment. (7/8-84). "Chronicle," "Darts and Laurels," onions and orchids handed out to news media; "Capital Letter," "Opinion," "Judgment Call," "Books," "Letters," "The Lower Case," print faux pas. (9/10-90).
TYPL: "George McGovern: The Target Talks Back" "Black Reporters, White Press--and the Jackson Campaign," "Readers Digest: Who's in Charge?," "Warning: CIA Censors at Work," "Is CBS Going Gee-Whiz?" (7/8-84). "Investigative Reporting: CNN Goes for the Gold," "Has Success Spoiled NPR?," "Retail Stores and Big-City Newspapers," "Pack Journalism, Japanese Style," "Steven Brill Builds an Empire." (9/10-90).
SCHL: Quarterly (Spring, 1962 - Winter, 1966); Bimonthly (Jul/Aug, 1978+), 65 pp.
SPAN: Fall, 1961+
ABSORBED
--*More* (ISSN: 0047-8091), Jun, 1978.
LC: PN 4700.C64
DD: 070/.05
ISSN: 0010-194x
ABST: --ABI/Informer
--Book Review Digest (ISSN: 0006-7326)
--Book Review Index (ISSN: 0524-0581)
--Energy Information Abstracts (ISSN: 0147-6521)
--Environment Abstracts (ISSN: 0093-3287)
--Film Literature Index (ISSN: 0093-6758)

✣ COMBROAD

SUB: "The bulletin of the Commonwealth Broadcasting Conference." (Dec, 1966 - ?).
SUB: "A quarterly journal."
PUBL: Commonwealth Broadcasting Association, Broadcasting House, London W1A 1AA, England.
DESC: The Commonwealth Broadcasting Association consists of some 50-plus member nations stretching across the alphabet (in the sampled issues), from Antigua & Barbuda to Zimbabwe. The emphasis is on the broadcasting activities of member nations, and the primary host, Great Britain. Initial issues were typewritten, long format, without graphics. Current issues are magazine format with numerous graphics of member activities. An interesting forum for developments in international broadcasting.
DEPT: "Members Report." (6-69). "Notebook," comment by the Secretary-General; "About Our Members," profiles; "Books," "Equipment Review." (10-86).
TYPL: None. (6-69). "Television: The First Fifty Years," "Regional Broadcasting and Community Radio in Sri Lanka," "Pioneering with B-MAC in Australia," "Violence on Television in Britain." (10-86).
SCHL: Semiannual (Jan, 1967 - Jan, 1970); Quarterly (Apr/Jun, 1971+), 50 pp.
SPAN: Jan, 1967+

VARIES
--Jan, 1967 - Apr/Jun, 1974 as Commonwealth Broadcasting Conference.
LC: HE 8689 .C6613
DD: 384.55/4/09171241
ISSN: 0951-0826
ABST: --Recently Published Articles (ISSN: 0145-5311)

COMIC CELLAR, THE

SUB: "Exclusive interviews, short stories, photos, strips, art, and so much more."
PUBL: Fifer International, 50 Hanover Rd SW, Calgary, Alberta T2V 3J4 Canada.
DESC: This was a serial of the Canadian comic industry, but one which may have only had a two-issue publication span, beginning with the first issue sometime during 1980, and the announced "final issue" for summer, 1982. There was a sense throughout the summer, 1982 issue that here for the first time was a magazine of the Canadian comic industry, and one designed for and targeted to the Canadian reader; a "fanzine" which was not to be determined by American comic publications. Letters to the editor strongly supported this view. Unfortunately, for reasons of time (Publisher Fifer was about to enter Southern Alberta Institute of Technology), or subscriber support, there appears to have been no issues past that of summer, 1982. Articles showcased Canadian talent and news, with the majority of the sample issue devoted to the demise of Canada's own "Captain Canuck" comic series developed in Calgary. Interviews with artists, publishers, and fans, plus numerous panels of black/white graphic comic art adorned the periodical. For the 1982 sampled issue: stapled magazine format, editorial content consisting of black ink on newsprint, with full-color cover on coated paper stock (7 5/8 x 10 3/4 inches / 195 x 275 mm).
DEPT: "Editorial," "Art Gallery," 'Contributions from our talented readers'; "Letter Page," 'The pros speak'. (summer-82).
TYPL: "Callista, Queen of the World," "Ken Ryan Interview," "Captain Canuck," "Strip Collecting." (summer-82).
SCHL: Quarterly?, 90 pp.
SPAN: 1980 - Summer, 1982//?
SUSPENDED
--?, 1980 - Spring, 1982?

✣ COMIC FANDOM'S FORUM

SUB: "The comics opinion and comics review."
SUB: "The voice of the direct market."
PUBL: New Media Publishing, Inc., 1518 East Fowler Ave., Tampa, FL 33612.
DESC: The September, 1982 issue concerned a new name change effective with that issue in which the editor noted, "This magazine is your platform, a platform from which you can express and share your thoughts with other readers. It is also a showcase for your talents--both in writing and in art. Plus we will continue to offer in-depth interviews with the people who have made the Alternative Market/Direct Market a strong and quickly growing segment of the graphic story industry." Thus, *Comic Fandom's Forum* concerns graphics and graphic artists not associated with mainstream comic products (e.g., newspaper, comic books, etc). It has numerous graphics, and extensive writing pertaining to the analysis and appreciation of comic art and artists. For the 1982 sampled issue: black ink on newsprint with full-color cover on coated paper stock (8 1/2 x 10 3/4 inches / 215 x 275 mm).
DEPT: "Editorial," "Fandom's Forum," extensive discourse on comics; "Signed... Sealed... Delivered!," letters. (9-82).
TYPL: "Sex and/or the Batman," "Unfamiliarity Breeds Stupidity," "I am the Law," "Fandom Spotlight on First Comics, Inc.," "Cinderella was an Englishwoman." (9-82).
SCHL: Monthly, 80 pp.
SPAN: ?+
VARIES
--? - ? as LOC.

✣ COMIC INFORMER

SUB: "News! Reviews! All new fan strips."
PUBL: Comic Informer Enterprises, Inc., 7152 Kernal, Houston, TX 77087.
DESC: "People are finding out that comics mean more than talk. They're finding out that comics still mean entertainment, as well as a source of quick and insightful commentary. They're finding out that the *Comic Informer* is bringing them the best in new strips, as well as articles and reviews which make the world of comics a safer place to visit..." Editor-in-Chief Michael Wolff presented his seven-point editorial policy/philosophy in the Jan/Feb, 1983 issue including such points as, "The comic book reader is usually more intelligent than some people think," and "Moosehead is the official beer of this magazine," at least according to self-proclaimed teetotaler Wolff. But it is the first editorial policy item which sets the tone for this serial: "Above all, comics are a medium of entertainment. There are a handful of people out in the world who aren't happy unless they're constantly elevating comics to the intellectual equivalent of Plato's Retreat." *Comic Informer*, provided news and comment on the comic industry, but with special emphasis on fan-submitted comic artwork in the unique backsection called "Informal Comics," which began with the Jan/Feb, 1983 issue. For the 1983 sampled issue: stapled magazine format, editorial content consisting of black ink on newsprint with full-color cover (8 3/8 x 11 inches / 215 x 280 mm).
DEPT: "Tales of the Flying Desk," editorial column by Michael Wolff; "Infograms," 'Late breaking news from the comics industry and related media'; "The Lion's Den," column by Gene Phillips; "The Voided Snoid," 'Video column by Mike Betker'; "Guest Editorial," "Fanzine Update," fanzine reviews column by Dave

Patterson; "Informer Reviews," 'Critiques on all media'; "Informal Comics," 'Showcase for the best in fan strips'. (1/2-83).
TYPL: "Kerry Gammill," "Double Visions," "Marvel and the Batman," "Watched Any Good Comics Lately?" (1/2-83).
SCHL: Bimonthly, 65 pp.
SPAN: Oct/Nov, 1981+

✦ COMIC READER, THE

PUBL: Street Enterprises, PO Box 255, Menomonee Falls, WI 53051.
DESC: This small journal-format magazine is designed to provide information of new comic book products, changes in same, and other data of interest to collectors and readers. Although there was nary an article in the the sampled issue for 1976, it was packed with typewritten information within numerous departmental columns, each one quickly identifiable by the production company and its brand-name comic book product. The typewritten text for that sampled issue was photocopy-reduced to pack a great deal of editorial content concerning the comic book industry into some 30 pages. Commencing with the December, 1976 issue *The Comic Reader* sported a two-color ink (red and black) cover, and center advertising section. Each page contains at least two examples of comic book covers or artwork, which adds greatly to the reading pleasure and value of the publication. Small journal format, stapled with photocopy-reduced typewritten copy on mixture of newsprint and uncoated paper stock, cover and middle advertising section comprised of two color ink on uncoated paper stock, some advertising (5 ½ x 8 inches / 140 x 205 mm).
DEPT: "DC News," newsbriefs concerning DC Comic products; "Warren Coming Comics," product newsbriefs; "Marvel News," product newsbriefs; "TCR Message," editorial; "Media News," newsbriefs; "TCR Mailboat," letters; "Comment," "Western News," newsbriefs; "Et Al," miscellaneous news items; "Gold Key News," product newsbriefs; "Coming Comics," release data; "Visual Publications," product newsbriefs; "Continuity Associates," product newsbriefs; "Harvey Coming Comics," "Marvel Coming Comics," "DC Coming Comics." (12-76).
TYPL: None. (12-76).
SCHL: Monthly (Jul, 1978 - Mar?, 1984); Every Six Weeks (Apr, 1984+), 30 pp.
SPAN: Jul, 1978?+?
ISSN: 0747-3575

✦ COMIC RELIEF

SUB: "Proudly published monthly in Humbold County, California.
SUB: "The cutting edge of what's funny."
SUB: "The monthly topical humor review."
SUB: "The lighter side of life. Fewer calories than a newspaper. More laughs per pound."
PUBL: Page One Publishers & Bookworks, Inc., PO Box 6606, Eureka, CA 95502.
DESC: "The *Comic Relief* Pledge: *Comic Relief* is an equal-opportunity offender, and promises to make fun of all social, political & religious orientations equally, as long as it's funny! Any seeming liberal bias is due to the presence of a conservative administration. If the liberals were in power, you can bet we'd be making fun of them too. OK?" From outward appearances, this successful magazine is more than OK with the American public, dishing out a venerable feast of caustic comic comment on the "good, bad, and the ugly" of American government and society. In the sampled issue for September, 1991 over 150 wonderful editorial cartoons were reprinted covering everything from war to the Supreme Court, from the economy to religion, world politics to landfills, health care, presidential campaigns, race, religion, and unemployment. Some 53 pages of editorial cartoons, strips, panels, and humorous columns were followed by samplings of "Maxine," "President Bill," "Sylvia," "Washingtoon," "Off the Mark," "Life in Hell," "Angriest Dog in The World," "Twisted Image," "Doonesbury," "Outland," and "Calvin & Hobbes." Who could ask for more? For the sampled issue of 1991: stapled magazine format, editorial content is black/white on newsprint, with full-color cover on coated paper stock, fascinating advertisements tied to the comics field (7 ¾ x 10 ¾ inches / 195 x 270 mm).
DEPT: "Funny Stuff," editorial column by Perry Bradford-Wilson and Michael Kunz; "The Scorecard," 'In stereo where available' and 'Subtitled in Esperanto' humor newsbriefs; "Letters," extensive commentary by readers; "This Month in Cartoons," outstanding section showcasing best editorial cartoons; "Weird News," 'Real news items from the mainstream press'; "Ask Dr. Science," wonderful Duck's Breath Mystery Theatre column concerning the mysteries of life; "Drawing Board," 'a forum for new and aspiring humorists'; "Dave Barry," humor column by Dave Barry; "Ian Shoales," humor column by Ian Shoales; "Joe Bob Briggs," humor column by Joe Bob Briggs; "Stephanie Brush," humor column by Stephanie Brush. (9-91).
TYPL: "Garbage In, Genius Out," "Presential Candidate Barry Gets His Priorities Straight," "Small Talk in a Big Country," "Save America's Dives--Its Vanishing Heritage," "Wanted for Illegal Possession Of, Uh, ... Testosterone???" (9-91).
SCHL: Monthly, 75 pp.
SPAN: May, 1989+
 VARIES
 --Jun, 1989 - ? as Comic Relief Magazine (ISSN: 1042-1556).
DD: 741
ISSN: 1055-9639

Comic Relief Magazine

Jun, 1989 - ?//
(ISSN: 1042-1556)
SEE: COMIC RELIEF

✧ COMIC SHOP NEWS

PUBL: ParaGraphics, 1353 Gray Rock Drive, Marietta, GA 30066.
DESC: This newsprint weekly tabloid is a wonderful promotional vehicle for upcoming comic book releases, and educates the comic aficionado about the lesser known artists and their products. Four of the eight pages are in full color, and as an added bonus, each issue contains two ongoing Batman stories, one strip printed in black/white, the other in color. It mainly showcases upcoming comic book talent and product before it hits the newsstands. Articles discuss the creators of selected comic product, the characters they created, and additional information concerning the about-to-be released comic books. This gratis publication fulfills a real need for promotion by the local retail comics dealer. Newsprint tabloid format, display size folded: (7 ½ x 11 ⅜ inches / 190 x 290 mm); reading size folded: (11 ⅜ x 15 inches / 290 x 380 mm); numerous black/white and color graphics of comic book releases, and comic strips. Note: first issue preceded by special dated April 10, 1987, and numbered as Volume 1, Number 0.
DEPT: "CSN Checklist," checklist of upcoming comic book releases. (8-15-90).
TYPL: "Wolverine Gets a Hot-Headed Partner," "Eclipse Finds Avengers Very Ap-Peel-ing," "Rovers Ramble On to Mindgame Gallery," "Enemy Ace Has Trouble Taking Off," "New Writers for New Mutants." (8-15-90).
SCHL: Weekly, 8 pp.
SPAN: Jul 1, 1987+

✧ COMICS BUYER'S GUIDE

SUB: "Serving the world of comics every week."
SUB: "Reaching all serious comic art fans and collectors."
PUBL: Krause Publications, Inc., 700 East State St., Iola, WI 54990.
DESC: "New Collectibles, Comic Books - Comics Memorabilia, find them every week in *Comics Buyer's Guide.* Your love of comics and your knowledge of collecting will make you a natural in your hot new hobby! And you'll find all the comics information you need in *Comics Buyer's Guide.* Especially for the beginning comics collector, *Comics Buyer's Guide* means: You find comics collectibles in the hobby's largest, wildest marketplace!; You get inside comics news from editors who live the hobby they write about!" For one who believes that comic books and associated memorabilia are just for kids, a single reading of *Comic Buyer's Guide* will quickly change one's mind. Each issue is 80 full tabloid newsprint pages comprised of publishers' announcements of new comic book series, articles on the ways and means of collecting same, and numerous advertisements by dealers willing to sell the mundane for 50 cents, to the rarefied, where classic issues command from 50 to 100 dollars, or more! In between articles are a generous serving of comic strips, comic book cover art, and sample panels from forthcoming releases. A fascinating weekly publication, and must reading for any serious collector, dealer, or publisher of comic books. Tabloid newspaper format published on newsprint; numerous black/white graphics. Display stand fold: (8 ½ x 11 ⅜ inches / 215 x 290 mm). Readers fold: (11 ¼ x 17 inches / 285 x 430 mm).
DEPT: "Editorial," "Oh, So?," letters; "Information Please," requests by comic book collectors; "Obituaries," "But I Digress," commentary column by Peter David; "Animation News," column by Darrell McNeil; "Fanzine Guide," column by Timothy R. Corrigan; "Comics Guide," column by Don Thompson; "Dan T's Inferno," column by Dan Tyree; "Publisher Marketshares," comics ordered for month. (8-24-90).
TYPL: "'Batman 3-D' has New Byrne Story," "'Aliens Vs. Predator' Sells 400,000 Copies," "Captain America Joins War on Drugs," "'Metal Bikini' Mini-series is 'Good-Girl Manga'." (8-24-90).
SCHL: Semimonthly (? - ?); Monthly (? - ?); Weekly (?+), 80 pp.
SPAN: 1971+
VARIES
--1971 - Feb 4, 1983 as Buyer's Guide for Comic Fandom, The.
ISSN: 0745-4570

✧ COMICS CAREER NEWSLETTER

SUB: "The monthly magazine for aspiring comics professionals."
PUBL: OffBeat Productions, 2012 West Ash, M-10, , Columbia, MO 65203.
DESC: It is realitivly rare to find a publication like *Comics Career Newsletter*, a newsprint tabloid dedicated to instruction, critique, and encouragement for "aspiring comics professionals." With dynamic layout, authoritative articles, and of course, generous amounts of cartoon/comic art, Editor/Publisher Kirk Chritton creates a work of love each month. It's all here: articles on what to charge; addresses and contacts of major comic publishers; profiles of those publishers and their submission guidelines; interviews with successful artists; news of industry issues and trends, stories of specific cartoon development, and professional critiques of reader submitted material. No "aspiring" comic artist should be without this tabloid! Small tabloid format, display fold: (7 ⅝ x 11 ½ inches / 195 x 290 mm); opened for reading: (11 ¼ x 15 ¼ inches / 290 x 385 mm); printed two color covers and black/white editorial content on newsprint paper stock; many examples of cartoon and comic art throughout each issue.

DEPT: "News Briefs...," "Graphic Guides," how-to via cartoons by DCR; "Editorial," "Hot Topics," "Comics Career Portfolio," "Back Talk," reader response. (7-90).
TYPL: "Hot Summer 1990: Comics Sales Skyrocket," "Judge Says Revolutionary Can Print New Kids Bio," "Fantagraphics Comes Out of the Closet," "Pitting Art Against Entertainment Creates a Dangerous Dichotomy," "Panel by Panel, Comic Strips are a Different Animal." (7-90).
SCHL: Monthly, 24 pp.
SPAN: Apr, 1988+

✤ COMICS FANDOM EXAMINER

SUB: "Your guide to creator-owned small press and independent comics."
SUB: "The comics fandom examiner."
PUBL: MU Press, 5014-D Roosevelt Way NE, Seattle, WA 98105.
DESC: "...Your publication opened a whole new subculture of comics for me. Small press and self-publishing seems to be a way to get material that might not be considered 'commercial' to an audience who might be more receptive and interested in it. ... The point of these small press publications seems not to be necessarily to make money (although I'm sure that would be nice), but rather to have the satisfaction of getting it seen and read by other people. (letter to editor)." This is a marvelous resource for, by, and about small press publishers of comic product, those artists who seek to have their comic art seen and appreciated, but who have not been successful in securing normal commercial channels of publishing, marketing, and distribution. Another way to define "Small Press" is that it encompasses those publishers of small press runs who oftentimes photocopy their work in black/white and self-distribute/sell their artistic product to the public. Articles and artwork are dynamic, oftentimes fascinating, and always informative, especially about how the "alternative network" of small press publishers functions. If there is new talent to be discovered, encouraged, and launched into the comic-book field, it will probably have its origins herein. An excellent resource for news, industry trends, and the status of the small press industry. Serial librarians should be aware that the running title of this serial is *Comics F/X*, while the official published title is *Comics Fandom Examiner*. For the 1990 sampled issue: small tabloid newspaper format (11 ½ x 17 ½ inches / 290 x 445 mm), published on newsprint; black/white graphics and editorial copy throughout.
DEPT: "Tel's From the Crypt," column by Terry Hooper; "Comix Wavola," column by Clay Geerdes; "Kyle," column by Andrew J. Kyle; "The Alternative Forum," column by Chris Lightfoot and Edd Vick; "F/X Comics," a page of comics; "Critiques F/X," 'Reviews'; "Op-Edd Page," 'Opinions, editorials, and your letters'. (4/5-90).
TYPL: "Phoebe Lives! Siergey is New Artist," "Comics Not 'Art' Claims German Zine Editor," "Small Press Distribution Network Planned," "A Conversation with Larry Blake," "Cartoonist Squad on the Loose." (4/5-90).
SCHL: Bimonthly, 32 pp.
SPAN: Apr, 1988+
DD: 741 11
ISSN: 0898-3119

✤ COMICS FEATURE

PUBL: New Media Publishing, Movie Publishers Services, Inc., Suite 208, 8399 Topanga Canyond Blvd., Canoga Park, CA 91304.
DESC: "*Comics Feature* is the fastest growing magazine about comic books. If you're interested in following the adventures of comics characters, read what the leading professionals have to say about their work and the industry, and keep up with the news, then *Comics Feature* is just the magazine for you." This is the sister publication to *Comic Fandom's Forum*, which concentrates on alternative media; while *Comics Feature* is more likely to concentrate on the more mainstream comics available to the American public. As another advertisement states, "Comic books, animation, newspaper strips, superhero role-playing games-- Like no other magazine, *Comics Feature* covers it all. Written exclusively by professionals, printed on the best paper and loaded with full, vibrant color, *Comics Feature* is truly unique. *Comics Feature* is the only magazine that's universally trusted by the creators, publishers and producers of comic and animation art to accurately and fairly report on their activities." The sampled issue for 1985 consisted of magazine format (8 ⅛ x 10 ¾ inches / 205 x 270 mm); black/white graphics on newsprint; later issues had full-color center section for selected comic reproductions.
DEPT: "Opening Notes," "Headlines," "End Notes." (6-81). "Editorial," "News," "Letters," "Listings," 'Comic consumer guide'; "Publisher's Picks," of new releases. (11-85).
TYPL: "An Interview with Bill Mantlo," "World's Finest Mediocrity," "Dark Phoenix and the Prime-Time Vixens." (6-81). "Walt & Louise Simonson," "Stan Lee Speaks!," "The X-Factor," "Animated Antics." (11-85).
SCHL: Monthly, 60 pp.
SPAN: Mar, 1980+
ISSN: 0199-7459

✤ COMICS INTERVIEW

SUB: "We let the industry speak for itself."
PUBL: Fictioneer Books, Ltd., Suite 301, 234 Fifth Ave., New York, NY 10001.
DESC: "*Interview* is unique among comics magazines. Our slogan says it all: 'We let the industry speak for itself'. We print interviews, all interviews, and only interviews. Indeed, as I said in my editorial for the very

first issue of *COMICS INTERVIEW*: 'The idea is to provide a place where comics fans and professionals can get to know one another as people. Some of the other fanzines do a very good critical job ... but in this case people will speak for themselves'. You can learn a lot by reading *INTERVIEW* -- it's like taking a course in every aspect of the comics industry. Each issue is a cornucopia of information from a surprisingly diverse array of sources, among them publishers, production artists, colorists, letterers, retailers and others. Professionals. Talking about what they know best: comics." Small magazine format; newsprint with numerous black/white graphic art from the comic industry. Fascinating resource for the workings of this entertainment medium. For the 1989 sampled issue: stapled magazine format with black ink on newsprint editorial content with full-color cover on coated paper stock (6 7/8 x 10 1/8 inches / 175 x 255 mm).

DEPT: "Up Front," editorial column by David Anthony Kraft; "The Last Word," letters. (#70-89).
TYPL: "Sam Hamm," "Steve Englehart," "Batman the Movie," "Bob Kane." (#70-89).
SCHL: Monthly, 100 pp.
SPAN: ?, 1983+

✤ COMICS JOURNAL, THE

SUB: "The collector's guide to comics, science fiction, fantasy, and art."
SUB: "The magazine of news & criticism."
PUBL: Fantagraphics Books, Inc., 1800 Bridgegate St., #101, Westlake Village, CA 91361.
DESC: "Once every four weeks, thousands of readers around the world turn to *The Comics Journal* to keep up with the world of comics. They realize that only in the *Journal* can they find the stimulating mixture of fact and opinion, news and reviews, articles and columns, interviews and editorials, that have kept the *Journal* on the cutting edge of comics for the better part of a decade. Every issue, the *Journal*'s battery of critics, columnists, and journalists take you on a round-the-world trip of the exciting comics medium--through no-holds-barred critiques, informative historical pieces, in-depth news reporting, idiosyncratic columns, and, of course, the *Journal*'s legendary interviews--exhaustive raps with the men who make the comics." A fascinating 100+ page monthly newsprint magazine that covers the comics in-depth, with an interesting mixture of serious scholarly work and irreverent humor; filled, of course, with numerous examples of the cartoonist's pen. *The Comics Journal* must possess one of the most interesting copyright notices ever placed in a publication: "Be nice and don't illegally reprint any of the neat stuff in this issue, okay? Please. Pleeeeez...Or we'll knock your [deleted] teeth down your throat and sue you 'till you're dead and buried. Thank you much." Anyone with an interest in the poetic, the personalities of, or the profit side of comics should have this publication (both back issues and current). Stapled magazine format, editorial content is black ink on newsprint, with full-color cover on coated paper stock (8 3/8 x 10 7/8 inches / 215 x 275 mm).

DEPT: "Newswatch," very large section of latebreaking news concerning comics industry; "Blood and Thunder," letters to editor. (4-85). "Opening Shots," comment; "Editorial," "Newswatch," "International Newswatch," "Miscellania," newsbriefs; "New Comics News," new releases; "Blood & Thunder," letters; "Funny Book Roulette," detailed critiques of current releases; "Comics Library," review; "Dramas of the Mind," column by Kenneth Smith. (9-90).
TYPL: "Newave Comics Survey," "Word and Image," "From Off the Streets of Cleveland," "Leering or Laughing?" (4-85). "Textbooks From Cartoon U," "The Cheapening of the Comics," "Cartooning is Alive and Well," "Creator Vs. Corporate Ownership," "A Bill of Rights for Comics Creators." (9-90).
SCHL: Every six weeks (? - ?); Monthly (Mar, 1979 - ?); Ten issues per year (Mar, 1981 - Oct, 1983); Monthly [except Feb, Apr, and Jun] (Nov, 1983 - ?); Bimonthly (? - ?); Monthly (?+), 125 pp.
SPAN: Jun?, 1974+
VARIES
--Jun?, 1974 - Dec, 1976 as Nostalgia Journal.
DD: 741
ISSN: 0194-7869

Comics Review
1983 - 1985//
SEE: COMICS REVUE

✤ COMICS REVUE

PUBL: Fictioneer Books, Ltd., Suite 301, 234 Fifth Ave., New York, NY 10001.
DESC: For those too busy to read their daily newspaper comic strips, or for those individuals who like to read the entire story plot in a single sitting, *Comics Revue* is wonderful. Although some issues feature interviews with the creators of these comic heroes, the majority of each magazine is devoted to the strips. One sampled issue for 1989 included "Bloom County," "The Phantom," "Popeye," "Latigo," "Flash Gordon," "Hagar the Horrible," "Modesty Blaise," "Steve Canyon," and "Gasoline Alley." Most reprinted strips are within ten years of original publication. For the sampled issue of 1989: stapled magazine format (8 1/2 x 11 inches / 215 x 275 mm), full color covers, editorial content published on newsprint.
DEPT: "A Letter from Rick," editorial column by Rick Norwood. (vol 2, #2-89).
TYPL: None. (Vol 2, #2-89).
SCHL: Monthly, 65 pp.
SPAN: 1983+
VARIES
--1983 - 1985 as Comics Review.

✣ COMICS SCENE

PUBL: Starlog Communications International, Inc., 475 Park Avenue South, New York, NY 10016.
DESC: Publisher Starlog Communications International (which also publishes *Gorezone, Toxic Horror, Fangoria,* and *Starlog*) calls *Comics Scene* "The magazine that explores the four color world with exciting previews of new comics and fascinating interviews with comics creators, plus exclusive news of the latest comic book movies & TV shows!" It is certainly all that and more, with selected comics rendered in full four-color splendor. Articles and interviews are handled in a literate, articulate manner, and provide significant insight into the development of comic characterization, plot, and profit of comic characters in a variety of unique media. It has a quality layout design in a magazine format with numerous graphics. Note that subscriptions to *Comics Scene* are for six bimonthly issues; the two "Special Spectacular" issues for July and September being outside the normal subscription. For sampled issue of 1982: stapled magazine format with mixture of black ink and full-color pages on uncoated paper stock, cover consisting of full-color on coated paper stock (8 x 10 7/8 inches / 205 x 275 mm).
DEPT: "Word Balloons," editorial column by Robert Greenberger; "Lettering," letters; "Comics Reporter," news; "Loose Cruse," column by Howard Cruse; "Guest Spot," guest commentary; "Ed. Notes," editorial column by Howard Zimmerman. (1-82). "Word Balloons," editorial; "Lettering," letters; "Comics Reporter," news; "Comics Screen," comic characters in development for other media. (8-90).
TYPL: "2 1/2 Carrots Tall, TV's First Animated Cartoon Star: The Stories of Crusader Rabbit," "Elfquest Book 2: A Special Look at the New Collection of Stories," "The Ultimate Team Player: A Look at the Career and Art of George Perez," "The Short Life of Sally Cruikshank," "What Are Direct Sales?" (1-82). "Return to the Mutant Planet," "The Scribe Strikes!," "The Wild Wild West," "Gray Morrow," "Crimestopper's Heritage." (8-90).
SCHL: Eight issues per year [including two special issues in Jul & Sep], 75 pp.
SPAN: Jan/Feb, 1981+
VARIES
--Jan/Feb, 1981 - ?, 1982 as Starlog Presents Comics Scene (ISSN: 0732-5622).

✣ COMICS WEEK

PUBL: Paragon Q Publishing, PO Box 1146, Maplewood, NJ 07040.
DESC: Editor Mark Waid, in the premiere issue, set forth the reason for *Comics Week*'s publication: "...Because the field has grown to accommodate over 100 comics publishers, it's more important than ever to have a magazine that gives complete, thorough, and unbiased coverage of all types of comics news, from who's pencilling 'Captain America' to how the various companies are dealing with issues such as censorship, creator's rights, penetration into the non-comics market, and so forth. There has to be a new, contemporary way to cover news in the field. *Comics Week* has locked on to that new approach." This news weekly of the comic book publishing industry; provides information, shipping schedules, critiques, and trends in the field and is both entertaining and informative. For the 1987 sampled issue: large, square, stapled magazine format, numerous graphic drawings in black ink with some full-color pages, including full-color cover on coated paper stock (9 7/8 x 12 inches / 255 x 305 mm).
DEPT: "Editorial," "What's New," comic books recently shipped to retailers; "News," "Random Samplings," column by R. A. Jones; "Reviews," critique of new releases column by Jeff Kapalka. (8-17-87).
TYPL: "Blue and White and Red All Over," "Vic and Blood: The Chronicles of a Boy and His Dog," "The Chicago Tea Party." (8-17-87).
SCHL: Weekly, 35 pp.
SPAN: Jul 13, 1987+?

Comixscene
Nov/Dec, 1972 - Sep/Oct, 1973//
SEE: PREVUE

Comm/Ent, A Journal of Communications and Entertainment Law
Fall, 1977 - Summer, 1983//
SEE: HASTINGS COMMUNICATIONS AND ENTERTAINMENT LAW JOURNAL

Comm/Ent, Hastings Journal of Communications and Entertainment Law
Fall, 1983 - Summer, 1988//
SEE: HASTINGS COMMUNICATIONS AND ENTERTAINMENT LAW JOURNAL

✣ COMMENT ON THE MEDIA

PUBL: Seton Hall University, Department of Communications, South Orange, NJ.
DESC: This well-designed workshop publication of the Department of Communications at Seton Hall University in New Jersey is similar to publications at other colleges. *Comment on the Media* publishes articles of news, whimsy, thought, and opinion, with a sprinkling of graphics throughout.
DEPT: "Briefs," "Music," reviews; "Books," reviews. (spring-79).

TYPL: "Self-Help Magazines: New Subscription Drugs," "ASCAP: Pennies From Heaven," "Sex and the Game Shows: When TV Becomes a Four-Letter," "Back Page Blues." (spring-79).
SCHL: Quarterly?, 38 pp.

COMMERCIAL CAMERA

SUB: "For the commercial photographer." (Oct/Nov, 1947 - Aug, 1953?).
PUBL: Eastman Kodak Company, Rochester, NY.
DESC: [Commercial Camera Magazine]: Kodak published this classy "how-to" serial for the professional photographer, showing clearly how the professional could expand knowledge, business, and profits through product shoots, studio applications, and other advertising/marketing concepts. Much of this serial featured full-color pictures, and provided a showcase for Kodak materials not found elsewhere. Printed on heavy stock; numerous full color graphics.
DEPT: "Comments." (12-50).
TYPL: "Wrap Her in Moonlight," "The Six Ways to Color," "They Float through the Air," "Photographic Packaging." (12-50).
SCHL: Monthly, 30 pp.
SPAN: May, 1931 - 1969//
SUSPENDED
--Apr, 1936 - 1954.
WITH SUPPLEMENT
--Applied Photography (ISSN: 0003-6943), May, 1931 - Mar, 1936.
SUPPLEMENT TO
--Applied Photography (ISSN: 0003-6943), 1954 - 1969.
VARIES
--Oct/Nov, 1947 - Aug, 1953? as Commercial Camera Magazine.
MERGED WITH
--Studio Light (to form) Studio Light/Commercial Camera, 1969.
ISSN: 0414-0303

Commercial Camera Magazine

Oct/Nov, 1947 - Aug, 1953?//
SEE: COMMERCIAL CAMERA

COMMERCIAL PHOTOGRAPHER, THE

SUB: "A journal for commercial industrial, press and microphotographers and all connected with the profession." (Oct, 1925 - ?).
SUB: "Official journal the Photographers' Association of America."
PUBL: C. Abel, Loraine, OH.
DESC: Devoted to the craft of commercial photography, this small format serial published articles of interest to the trade (the commercial division of the Photographers' Association of America), for almost 25 years. Craft concerns over service advertising, use of flash, negative handling, darkroom techniques, and the care and handling of client were addressed. Conservative in layout design and advertising, *The Commercial Photographer* succumbed with the last issue of March, 1950; and was combined with its sister publication, *The Professional Photographer*. Of special note in early issues was the inclusion of "The Bulletin of the Commercial Section," for the Photographers' Association of America.
DEPT: "Just at Random," newsbriefs; "Aerial Photography," "The Microscopic Eye," for photo-micrographers; "Editorials." (9-26). "What's Wrong with this Photograph?," analysis; "How to Light Commercial Photographs," "New Books," reviews; "Just at Random," newsbriefs. (1-50).
TYPL: "Photographing Snowflakes," "Orthochromatic Photography," "Photographing Church Interiors." (9-26). "Three Men on a Camera," "Shooting for a 'Jackpot,'" "Press Photographer on Wheels." (1-50).
SCHL: Monthly, 35 pp.
SPAN: Oct, 1925 - Mar, 1950//
ABSORBED BY
--Professional Photographer, The (ISSN: 0749-0119).
LC: TR 690.A1C6

COMMERCIAL PHOTOGRAPHIC NEWS, THE

PUBL: R. Walzl, Baltimore, MD.
DESC: "While it shall be the principle aim of *The Photographer's Friend* to set its readers photographically right, *The Commercial Photographic News* will endeavor to attend to that part pertaining to the financial success of our fraternity." Publisher Richard Walzl produced this supplement to *The Photographer's Friend* for ten months, during which time it primarily discussed chemical formulas and news of international photographic associations. By October, 1872, Walzl decided to greatly enlarge *The Photographer's Friend*, move its publication schedule from quarterly to bimonthly; and terminated *The Commercial Photographic News*. Small format; no graphics.
DEPT: "Price Bulletin," listing of photographic chemicals sold by R. Walzl. (7-1872).
TYPL: "The Standard Formulas," "Financial and Commercial," "Photographing Colors." (7-1872).
SCHL: Quarterly, 16 pp.
SPAN: Jan, 1872 - Oct, 1872//
SUPPLEMENT TO
--Photographer's Friend, The, Jan, 1872 - Oct, 1872.
LC: TR 1.P72

Commercials Monthly

1977 - 1982//
(ISSN: 0194-5114)
SEE: ENTERTAINMENT MONTHLY

COMMON SENSE
SUB: "A practical advertiser." (Jan, 1901 - Mar, 1902).
SUB: "A monthly journal devoted to an era of better publicity."
PUBL: Common-Sense Publishing Co., Page Bldg., Michigan Avenue and 40th St., Chicago, IL.
DESC: *Common Sense* was conceived to provide basic information on the art and technique of print advertising. The editors advised their readers that they would find only the most practical of information on advertising: "For sentiment or theories, puffs or grievances, we have no room." An interesting aspect of this publication was that it took its own advice to heart in selling subscriptions, for spaced throughout each issue were premium incentives (cuckoo clocks, Morris chairs, crystal glassware, etc.) designed to entice the reader to extend subscriptions. The serial met its demise in 1910 among a final-issue flurry of subscription incentives which almost outmatched editorial content. An interesting serial for the psychology of print advertising at the turn of the century.
DEPT: "What Our Philosopher Has to Say," comment; "Timothy Seed's Letters to His Son Who Writes Advertisements," home-spun advice; "Answers to Correspondence," "How to Write Advertisements," 'A department devoted to practical suggestions.' (5-01). "Editorials," "Advertising Talk," "Book Reviews." (12-10).
TYPL: "Theater Program Advertising," "Advertisement Writing as an Educator," "To the Man Who Says He is Too Poor." (5-01). "Stories Told by Stage People," "Bonds, but Not Gowns," "The Problem of Keeping Love Alive." (12-10).
SCHL: Monthly, 30 pp.
SPAN: Jan, 1901 - Dec, 1910//
VARIES
--Jan, 1901 - Mar, 1902 as Ad-School, The.
LC: HF 5801.C6

Commonwealth Broadcasting Conference
Jan, 1967 - Apr/Jun, 1974//
SEE: COMBROAD

✢ COMMUNICATE
SUB: "The magazine of RCA."
PUBL: Radio Corporation of America, 30 Rockefeller Plaza, New York, NY 10020.
DESC: This is a slick house magazine designed as a showcase public relations piece for RCA and its varied subsidiaries. Articles in *Communicate* tend to focus on individuals within the many companies which make up the RCA family. Numerous illustrations.
DEPT: "Communiquotes," quotes from RCA personnel appearing before public groups.
TYPL: "How Customers Use RCA," "The Joys of Engineering," "Globcom's Globe trotter." (4/5-77).
SCHL: Bimonthly, 26 pp.
SPAN: ?+

✢ COMMUNICATION
PUBL: Gordon and Breach Science Publishers, 41-42 William IV St., London WC2, England.
DESC: "*Communication* is devoted to fresh conceptual-theoretical-philosophical approaches to the role of communication in human affairs, or to fresh reasessments of approaches little known or long forgotten." Each issue is devoted to a specific theme, such as: "Communication and Community," "Philosophies of Communication," "Ethics in Communication," "International Communication: Bias and Balance," and "Communication and Politics." No graphics.
DEPT: None. (5-82).
TYPL: "Communication and Community," "Community Television: A Tool for Community Action?," "Communication and Political Agendas," "Too Clever By Far: Communications and Community Development." (5-82).
SCHL: Semiyearly (Jun, 1974? - 1983); Quarterly (1985+), 100 pp.
SPAN: Jun, 1974+
LC: P 87.C5973
DD: 001.5/05
ISSN: 0305-4233
ABST: --Language and Language Behavior Abstracts (ISSN: 0023-8295)
--Psychological Abstracts (ISSN: 0033-0202)
--Social Welfare, Social Planning / Policy and Social Development (ISSN: 0195-7988)

Communication
Jul, 1972 - Sep, 1984//
(ISSN: 0882-4088)
SEE: WORLD COMMUNICATION

COMMUNICATION AND BROADCAST ENGINEERING
SUB: "The journal of world communication." (Oct, 1934 - Mar, 1937).
PUBL: Bryan Davis Publishing Co., 19 East 47th St., New York, NY.
DESC: The popularity and excitement of broadcast and international short-wave communication were evident in this serial during the height of the American Depression. This was a periodical for the practicing engineer, consisting of technical developments, schematics, and advice on equipment repair and maintenance. Publisher Bryan Davis included topics of radio telegraphy and telephony, wired cable telegraphy and telephony, broadcast transmission, carrier and beam transmission; marine, police and aeronautical radio; television, and facsimile. Numerous graphics and schematics; assumed engineering knowledge.

DEPT: "Telecommunication," 'panorama of progress in the fields of communication and broadcasting;' "Federal Communication Commission Reports," "Veteran Wireless Operators Association News," "Over the Tape," 'News of the radio, telegraph and telephone industries;' "Editorial," "Commercial Radio Trends." (1-35).
TYPL: "A Method of Continuous Aural Frequency Monitoring," "Temporary Vertical Radiator," "Low-Power Broadcast Stations," "Pre-Amplifier Design." (1-35).
SCHL: Monthly, 35 pp.
SPAN: Oct, 1934 - Aug, 1937//
MERGED WITH
--Broadcast Engineer (and) Radio Engineering (to form) Communications (ISSN: 0161-374x), Sep, 1937.
LC: TK 6540.C6

✦ COMMUNICATION ARTS

SUB: "The journal of commercial art and design."
SUB: "The journal of the communication arts."
PUBL: Communication Arts, PO Box 10300, 410 Sherman Ave., Palo Alto, CA 94303.
DESC: Leafing through *Communication Arts*, it is easy to believe that you have come across the guidebook to a major art museum. Large, full-color reproductions of television spots, billboards, company reports, magazines, and special print projects are featured, as well as excellent interviews with leading designers. In the sampled issue for 1990, a promotional subscription page talks about *CA*'s eight issues per year: "They carry about 60% more editorial pages than the next largest design magazine. There are other reasons why we have been the circulation leader for over twenty years, but we suppose there isn't much we could tell you about *CA* that you don't already know. ... The care and extra preparation we utilize assures superior reproduction quality as well as the fidelity to the original piece. We follow that up with 175-line screen printing by one of the finest printers in the United States. Doing it better is expensive, but we believe the results are worth it." *Communication Arts* is a feast of innovative, dynamic ideas showcasing the very best in the art, and process of communication. At times, it focuses on advertising, at times promotion, and other times on avenues of communicating ideas; all through the visual media of television, outdoor advertising, and print. A high quality publication. Some issues also serve as annuals, including for calendar year 1990: July Illustration Annual, August Photography Annual, November Design Annual, and the December Advertising Annual. Each of these special issues average 250 pages. Perfect-bound magazine format on quality paper stock, full-color throughout with numerous paper manufacturer sample inserts (8 ⅝ x 10 ⅞ inches / 220 x 275 mm).
DEPT: "Books," new releases; "Club News," graphic arts organizations. (1-77). "Editor's Column," editorial comment column by Patrick Coyne; "Design Technology," column by Wendy Richmond; "Opinion / Commentary," column by Philip B. Meggs; "Free- Lance," column by Barbara Gordon; "Exhibit," communication showcase; "Book Reviews," "Materials," product review; "Clubs, Conferences, Seminars," calendar. (3/4-90).
TYPL: "Geoffrey Moss," "Lock-Pattersen," "Bruce Wolfe," "David Lance Goines." (1-77). "Michael Brock," "Great Moments in Design Tools," "The Ball WCRS Partnership," "Madsen and Kuester," "Chiat/Day: The Book." (3/4- 90).
SCHL: Monthly (Aug, 1959 - Aug, 1962); Bimonthly (Sep/Oct, 1962 - ?); Eight issues per year (? - ?); Seven issues per year (Mar/Apr, 1984 - ?); Eight issues per year (?+), 150 pp.
SPAN: Aug, 1959+
VARIES
--1959 - 1966 as CA.
--1967 - 1969 as CA Magazine (ISSN: 0884-0008).
ABSORBED
--Annual Exhibition of Communication Art [NA].
LC: NC 997.A1 C2
DD: 741.6/05 19
ISSN: 0010-3519
ABST: --Art Index (ISSN: 0004-3222)

✦ COMMUNICATION BOOKNOTES

SUB: "Recent titles in telecommunications, information and media."
PUBL: Center for Advanced Study in Telecommunications (CAST), The Ohio State University, 210E Baker Systems, 1971 Neil Ave., Columbus, OH 43210.
DESC: "*Communication Booknotes* provides early information about new publications (chiefly books, monographs, reports and documents) on telecommunications, mass communication and information. Comments are mainly descriptive to allow users to make order decisions. Where possible, comparative and evaluative comments are included as well. It is designed chiefly for an academic, research, and library readership." This is one "must" publication for anyone wishing to keep up with the voluminous number of books, periodicals and special publications in the mass media field. Founding editor Chris Sterling and a quality group of contributors provide excellent critical commentary on publications in broadcasting, foreign media, print, photography, music and other fields. Regional contributors provide information on new publications from Australia, Britain, Canada, France, Germany, Italy, and Spain. In addition, topical contributors provide editorial material in the areas of film, popular culture, and telecommunication technology. Each monthly issue highlights 30-plus new books and publications. For the sampled issue of 1990: square magazine format (8 ½ x 8 ½ inches / 215 x 215 mm), printed two-color on uncoated paper stock.
DEPT: "Book of the Month," best of the review group. (7/8-90).
TYPL: No Article Titles.

SCHL: Monthly (1969 - 1986); Bimonthly (1986+), 30 pp.
SPAN: Nov, 1969+
VARIES
--Nov, 1969 - Aug, 1973 as Broadcast Bibliophile Booknotes (ISSN: 0045-3188).
--Sep, 1973 - Jan, 1982 as Mass Media Booknotes (ISSN: 0740-6479).
ISSN: 0748-657x
ABST: --Media Review Digest (ISSN: 0363-7778)

✤ COMMUNICATION BRIEFINGS

SUB: "A monthly idea source for decision makers."
SUB: "Ideas that work."
PUBL: Encoders, Inc., 140 South Broadway, Pitman, NJ 08071.
DESC: The purpose of *Communication Briefings* is "...to provide subscribers with down-to-earth communication ideas and techniques they can put into action to persuade clients, influence peers and motivate employees; to help them earn approval, command respect, spur productivity, gain recognition and win public support." Publisher Don Bagin, in a recent promotional stated: "Don't confuse *Communication Briefings* with the average newsletter. It's more like an ongoing education on every phase of communicating." This upbeat monthly does both educate readers about the essence of written and oral communication, as well as provide ideas, news tips, success stories and anecdotal items which can be applied in various fields. In the process, readers become better communicators, a most coveted skill in today's competitive marketplace. Well recommended. Two-color typeset newsletter format (8 ½ x 11 inches / 215 x 280 mm); no graphics viewed in sample issues.
DEPT: "Tips of the Month," short communicator suggestions. (Vol 8, #2). "Tips of the Month," short communicator suggestions; "Read 'Em and Reap," resources; "Blooper Brigade," "Quote of the Month." (Vol 8, #9).
TYPL: "What Managers Don't Know," "Creating a Credible Report," "Why You Should be a Risk Taker," "How to Get and Keep Quality," "A Guide to Customer Service." (Vol 8, #2). "Those Gold-Collar Workers," "Coping with Someone's Anger," "Getting Your Views Accepted," "Selecting the Right Committee," "How Younger Managers Work," "When Delegating, Don't Dump." (Vol 8, #9).
SCHL: Monthly, 8 pp.
SPAN: Dec, 1981+
DD: 658
ISSN: 0730-7799

✤ COMMUNICATION EDUCATION

SUB: "A publication of the Speech Communication Association."
PUBL: The Speech Communication Association, 5105 Backlick Rd., Annandale, VA 22003.

DESC: From the Guidelines for Submissions: "*Communication Education* publishes the best scholarship available on topics related to communication in instructional settings. Materials published in the journal are not restricted to any particular methodology, approach, or setting. Articles in *CE* focus primarily on the role of communication in the instructional process and teaching communication in traditional academic environments. However, manuscripts related to teaching communication or the role of communication in the instructional process in non-traditional settings (e.g., training in business, health, and legal settings) are strongly encouraged." It continues by noting that manuscripts "...providing practical suggestions for classroom teachers of communication, previously published in the *Instructional Practices* section of *CE*, should be submitted to our sister publication, *Speech Communication Teacher*. However, manuscripts reporting formal tests of such methods should be submitted to *CE*." Target audience is faculty for speech and related communication classes, with a primary emphasis on improved teaching methods through articles of pedagogical research. It is a well-edited publication; no graphics. Some issues revolve around special topics, such as the July, 1991 issue entitled, "Managing Multicultural Communication Education." For sampled issue of July, 1991: perfect-bound journal format, black ink on uncoated paper, cover is two-color black/blue ink on coated paper stock (6 ⅜ x 10 inches / 170 x 255 mm).
DEPT: "Forum," letters; "ERIC Report," "Reviews of Teaching/Learning Resources." (7-84). "Master Syllabi," classroom application; "Teaching Aid Reviews," "Book Reviews," major review section. (7-91).
TYPL: "The Role of Inner Speech in Human Communication," "The Concept of Inner Speech and Its Implications for Integrated Language Arts Curriculum," "The Role of Speech in Self Development, Self-Concept, and Decentration," "Memoirs and Journals as Maps of Intrapersonnel Communication," "The Case for a Developmental Pragmatics Approach to Assessing Language Proficiency." (7-84). "Building Shared Meaning: Implications of a Relational Approach to Empathy for Teaching Intercultural Communication," "Communication Curricula in the Multicultural University," "Managing Multiracial Institutions: Goals and Approaches for Race-Relations Training," "Minorities and Mentoring: Managing the Multicultural Institution," "Taming the Beast: Designing a Course in Intercultural Communication." (7-91).
SCHL: Quarterly, 90 pp.
SPAN: Jan, 1952+
VARIES
--Jan, 1952 - Nov, 1975 as Speech Teacher, The (ISSN: 0038-7177).
LC: PN 4071 .S74
DD: 808.5/05
ISSN: 0363-4523
ABST: --Current Index to Journals in Education (ISSN: 0011-3565)
--Engineering Index

--Language and Language Behavior Abstracts (ISSN: 0023-8295)
--Media Review Digest (ISSN: 0363-7778)
--MLA International Bibliography of Books & Articles on the Modern Languages and Literatures (ISSN: 0024-8215)
--Reference Sources (ISSN: 0163-3546)

COMMUNICATION ENGINEERING

SUB: "Devoted to frequency modulation." (Nov, 1940).
SUB: "The complete and authoritative source of information on frequency modulation." (Dec, 1940 - Oct, 1941).
SUB: "Radio broadcast, communications & Television Engineering and design practice." (Nov, 1941 - Mar, 1942).
SUB: "The journal of wartime radio-electronic development, engineering & manufacturing." (Apr, 1942).
SUB: "The journal of radio communication."
PUBL: Great Barrington, MA.
DESC: [*FM*]: Initial issues dealt almost exclusively with FM broadcasting. Within a year, however, an editorial move was under way towards the mobile radio field, and last issues of this serial (under a variety of names, formats, and probably readership), moved exclusively into the mobile radio area. Of special note were articles by pioneering inventors, most notably FM "father" Edwin Armstrong; and television development achieved by Klaus Landsberg. A marvelous reference for development of FM for broadcast and two-way communication. Numerous graphics; schematics.
DEPT: "Spot News," "Radio Design Practice," new design newsbriefs; "Comments," from readers. (11-41).
TYPL: "Television Camera Equipment," "What the FM Broadcasters Have to Say," "Zenith Engineers Built Station W51C." (11-41).
SCHL: Monthly, 50 pp.
SPAN: Nov, 1940 - Mar, 1954//
 VARIES
 --Nov, 1940 - Feb, 1942 as FM.
 --Mar, 1942 - Apr, 1942 as FM Electronic Equipment Engineering & Design Practise.
 --May, 1942 - Feb, 1943 as FM Radio-Electronic Engineering and Design.
 --Mar, 1943 - Mar, 1944 as FM Radio Electronics.
 --Apr, 1944 - Oct, 1948 as FM and Television.
 --Nov, 1948 - Jan, 1950 as FM-TV.
 --1950 - 1951 as FM-TV Radio Communication.
 --1952 as FM-TV.
 ABSORBED
 --Applied Electronic Engineering, Mar, 1942.
 --Television Engineering (ISSN: 0495-0372), May, 1952.
 ABSORBED BY
 --Radio-Electronic Engineering (1643890), Apr, 1954.
LC: TK 6540.C63
ISSN: 0414-1121

Communication: Journalism Education Today

1967 - Summer?, 1977//
(ISSN: 0010-3535)
SEE: C: JET

✤ COMMUNICATION LAW & POLICY NEWSLETTER

SUB: "Special interest group of the International Communication Association (ICA)."
PUBL: International Communication Association, Communication Law and Policy Interest Group, PO Box 9589, Austin, TX 78766.
DESC: The *Communication Law & Policy Newsletter* represents the interests, and presents news of events concerning members of the Communication Law and Policy Interest Group of the International Communication Association. In the group's second newsletter, Professor Sandra Braman sought to define the scope of this new assemblage: "The inception of a new interest group in the International Communication Association carries with it the burden of what we know about relationships between institutional form, intellectual currents, and the state. From the perspective of the sociology of knowledge, it denotes a new grouping of sufficient import that disciplinary boundaries shift. In the birth of the Communication Law and Policy (CLAP) interest group, we certainly see demonstration of this, for policy issues have now become so central to any analysis of the information environment--and sufficiently distinct from law--that they need to be separately identified, explored, and the relationships between law and policy analyzed." For the sampled issue of 1991: black ink on uncoated paper stock, stapled single sheet format, no advertising (8 ½ x 11 inches / 215 x 280 mm).
DEPT: "From the Chair," chair's column by John L. Huffman; "From the Editor," editorial column by Paul E. Kostyu. (9-91).
TYPL: "New Interest Group Carries Burden," "How Do We Reach a Definition?," "Reinterpretation of First Amendment Underway," "Charter Provides Start for CLAP," "Communication Law and Policy Bylaws." (9-91).
SCHL: Annual (1990); Quarterly (Sep, 1991+), 6 pp.
SPAN: Nov, 1990+

✤ COMMUNICATION MONOGRAPHS

PUBL: Speech Communication Association, 5105 Backlick Rd., Annandale, VA 22003.
DESC: Editor Judee K. Burgoon, in her inaugural issue of March, 1990, described the form and function of this long revered journal: "Traditionally, *Communication Monographs* has been devoted to 'publishing the best original scholarship that advances theory and research on human communication processes'. As the name

also implies, monographs are typically articles of greater length, and presumably, in justification of that greater length, ones of substantial significance. ...Communication Monographs is, first, devoted to publishing only those works that propose, test, modify, or amplify human communication theories, models, and constructs. This means that the central aim of a manuscript must be explication of communication phenomena. Moreover, the manuscript must make some original and noteworthy contribution to theory development or to methods which will enable theory development. *Communication Monographs* is, second, a social science journal. This means that the work being submitted must be open to scientific scrutiny and test. It does not mean that only empirical or quantitative work is acceptable. ...*Communication Monographs* is, third, a journal intended to represent a broad cross-section of the scholarly interests of the Speech Communication Association membership." *Communication Monographs* is a scholarly journal long recognized for its authoritative approach to communication theory and application. For the sampled issues of 1974, 1984 and 1990: journal format (6 ¾ x 10 inches / 170 x 255 mm), black ink on uncoated paper stock, some graphics.

DEPT: None. (6-84). "Editor's Remarks." (3-90).
TYPL: "The Affinity-Seeking Function of Communication," "Effects of Experience on Radio Language Performance," "Age, Social- Cognitive Development, and the Use of Comforting Strategies," "Style, Meaning and Message Effects," "A Model of Social Interaction: Phase III: Tests in Varying Media Situations." (6-84). "Reconstructing <Equality>: Culturetypal and Counter-Cultural Rhetorics in the Martyred Black Vision," "Efficacy of Inoculation Strategies in Promoting Resistance to Political Attack Messages: Application to Direct Mail," "The Dialectic of Marital and Parental Relationships within the Stepfamily," "The Cunning Rhetor, the Complicitous Audience, the Conned Censor, and the Critic." (3-90).
SCHL: Quarterly, 80 pp.
SPAN: 1934+
VARIES
--1934 - Winter?, 1975 as Speech Monographs (ISSN: 0038-7169).
LC: PN 4077.S6
ISSN: 0363-7751

✤ COMMUNICATION QUARTERLY

SUB: "A publication of the Eastern Communication Association."
SUB: "Journal of the Eastern Communication Association."
PUBL: Eastern Communication Association, Department of Communication, SUNY-Geneseo, Geneseo, NY 14454.
DESC: "*COMMUNICATION QUARTERLY* is a scholarly, academic journal sponsored by the Eastern Communication Association that is committed to publishing referred manuscripts relating directly to the understanding of human communication. The journal is philosophically committed to an eclectic approach to scholarship and the publication of articles of the highest quality regardless of their type, orientation, or origin. ...Manuscripts may be philosophical, theoretical, methodological, critical, applied, pedagogical, or empirical in nature." The focus of this communication serial is within the areas of academic theory and research. The whole area of communication studies is well represented. For the sampled issues of 1991: perfect-bound journal format, black ink on uncoated paper stock, cover consisting of red/brown ink on coated paper stock, limited advertising (7 x 10 inches / 180 x 255 mm).

DEPT: "Reviews," very lengthy book reviews. (fall-77). "Book Reviews," "Editor's Page." (fall-91).
TYPL: "South of the Border: the NBC and CBS Radio Networks and the Latin American Venture, 1930 - 1942," "Commercial vs. Public Television Audiences: Public Activities and the Watergate Activities," "Freedom of Expression and the Law Enforcement Officer." (fall-77). "The Relationship of Interprersonal Communication Variables to Academic Success and Persistence in College," "College Teacher Misbehaviors: What Students Don't Like About What Teachers Say and Do," "The Dark Side of Trust: Conceptualizing and Measuring Types of Communicative Suspicion," "Expectancy Violation and Student Rating of Instruction," "The Communication Investigator: Teaching Research Methods to Undergraduates." (fall-91).
SCHL: Semiyearly (1953); Quarterly (1954+), 85 pp.
SPAN: Apr, 1953+
VARIES
--Apr, 1953 - Fall, 1975 as Today's Speech (ISSN: 0040-8573).
LC: PN 4071.T6
DD: 001.5/05
ISSN: 0146-3373
ABST: --Current Index to Journals in Education (ISSN: 0011-3565)
--Education Index (ISSN: 0013-1385)
--Humanities Index (ISSN: 0095-5981)
--Language and Language Behavior Abstracts (ISSN: 0023-8295)

✤ COMMUNICATION REPORTS

PUBL: Western Speech Communication Association, Department of Communication Studies, California State University, Los Angeles, CA 90032.
DESC: "*Communication Reports* publishes short, data-based articles relating to the field of communication as defined broadly. These reports of research may address theoretical, methodological, or applied issues, and the scope of these articles should be limited. Submissions must devote a substantial amount of space to the reporting and analysis of the data on which the research was based. *Communication Reports* is open to all scholarly research methodologies, whether social, scientific, or humanistic. When appro-

priate to the methodology, the data may be illustrative, rather than systematically collected. Articles which are purely speculative or theoretical as opposed to data analytic are not acceptable." For the sampled issues of 1991: editorial content and cover consisting of black ink on coated paper stock, limited advertising, in stapled journal format (6 x 9 inches / 150 x 230 mm).
DEPT: "Issues of Concern." (winter-90).
TYPL: "Imagined Interaction and Interpersonal Communication," "The Ideal Communicator as the Basis for Competence Judgments of Self and Friend," "Iran/Contra and the Defeat of Accountability," "'No Japs Allowed': Negation and Naming as Subject-Constituting Strategies Reflected in Contemporary Stories of Japanese American Internment," "Academic Achievement: a Study of Relationships of IQ, Communication Apprehension, and Teacher Perception." (winter-90).
SCHL: Semiannually, 55 pp.
SPAN: Winter, 1988+
DD: 001
ISSN: 0893-4215

Communication Reports
Dec, 1984//
SEE: WORLD COMMUNICATION

❖ COMMUNICATION RESEARCH
PUBL: Sage Publications, 275 S. Beverly Drive, Beverly Hills, CA 90212.
DESC: From Information for Authors section: "Communication processes are a fundamental part of virtually every aspect of human social life. *Communication Research* publishes articles that explore the processes, antecedents, and consequents of communication in a broad range of societal systems. These include, but are not limited to, international, organizational, political, legal, family, and health systems. Of equal interest is the role of both traditional mass media and the new information technologies in these and other communication systems. The editorial goal of *Communication Research* is to publish articles that significantly advance our theoretical understanding of human communication processes. Within this general framework, the editors invite manuscript submissions that develop theory, report research, and describe new developments in methodology. The field of communication utilizes several alternative methods to generate understanding, insight, and knowledge. Each submitted manuscript is evaluated in terms of how well it meets the canons of excellence for the genre of inquiry that it utilizes. Emphasis is placed on quality, not orthodoxy." A strong focus on research across common communication topics makes this international refereed journal a favorite among academic researchers. Of special note is the use of slightly larger type, and other layout techniques which provide an unusually clean style for an academic journal of this nature. Perfect-bound journal format, black ink on uncoated paper stock. Cover for sampled issue of August, 1991 was two-color black and pink ink on coated paper stock, limited advertising (6 x 9 inches / 150 x 230 mm).
DEPT: "Review Essay," extended communications reviews. (10-77). "Review Essays." (8-91).
TYPL: "The Analysis and Significance of Communication Effect Gaps," "Mass Media Use and the 'Revolution of Rising Frustrations,'" "Television Market Shares, Station Characteristics, and Viewer Choice." (10-77). "Psychological Predictors of Television Viewing Motivation," "Modeling Dynamic Communication Processes with Event History Analysis," "Organizational Colleagues, Media Richness, and Electronic Mail: A Test of the Social Influence Model of Technology Use," "An Information-Processing Model of Jury Decision Making," "Family Communication Patterns: An Epistemic Analysis and Conceptual Reinterpretation." (8-91).
SCHL: Bimonthly (? - ?); Quarterly (?+), 145 pp.
SPAN: Jan, 1974+
LC: P 91 .C56
DD: 001.5
ISSN: 0093-6502
ABST: --Current Index to Journals in Education (ISSN: 0011-3565)
--Humanities Index (ISSN: 0095-5981)
--Psychological Abstracts (ISSN: 0033-0202)
--Social Sciences Index (ISSN: 0094-4920)

❖ COMMUNICATION RESEARCH REPORTS
PUBL: World Communication Association, Pan American University, Edinburg, TX 78359.
DESC: From the Guidelines for Submission: "*Communication Research Reports* is committed to publishing brief articles that either (1) report research findings directly related to human communication or (2) discuss a particular methodological issue (e.g., experimenter-wise error). Theoretical rationale should receive only modest coverage in research reports." Typical articles from 1990 covered a wide area of human communication processes including, "David Letterman, His Audience, His Jokes and Their Relationship," "The Effects of Gender-Role Expectations Upon Perceptions of Communicative Competence," "Regional Speech Rates in the United States: A Preliminary Analysis," and "Recall of Corporate Advertising Slogans in Nigeria." The majority of articles in the sampled issues were authored by American academics. For the sampled issues of 1990: black ink on uncoated paper stock with one-color ink cover on coated paper stock, no advertising (7 x 10 inches / 175 x 255 mm).
DEPT: None. (12-90).
TYPL: "Development and Construct Validation of the Sensitivity to Feedback Scale," "Ritual Versus Logic in Significance Testing in Communication Research," "Assessing Two Domains for Communicating Romance: Behavioral Context and Mode of Interaction," "Media Technology Hardware and Human Sensory

Channels: Cognitive Structures in Multidimensional Space," "The Construct Validity of Trait-Based Measures of Interpersonal Competence." (12-90).
SCHL: Semiyearly [Jun and Dec], 65 pp.
SPAN: Dec, 1984+
ISSN: 0882-4096

✦ COMMUNICATION RESEARCH TRENDS

SUB: "A quarterly information service from the Centre for the Study of Communication and Culture."
PUBL: Communication Research Trends, 221 Goldhurst Terrace, London NW6 3EP, England.
DESC: The Centre for the Study of Communication and Culture in London provides this quarterly newsletter as "...an international service for communication research." *Communication Research Trends* serves as a clearinghouse publication for currently published research from the international scholarship field, focusing on one research theme per issue. Of special note are the departments, "Current Research on...," and "Additional Bibliography on...;" providing additional topical information. The Centre for the Study of Communication and Culture was established by the Jesuits in 1977. Notable to researchers is the practice of *Communication Research Trends* to provide, in accompaniment to themed issues, a detailed bibliography of references utilized within the issue; a bibliography of resources not used for the issue, but of scholarly importance; and a valuable listing of named researchers and their current research projects related to the themed issue (also libraries and archives of note are included). For the sampled issues of 1991: black ink on cream-colored uncoated stock in stapled magazine format (8 ¼ x 11 ¾ inches / 210 x 300 mm).
DEPT: "Current Research on," review; "Additional Bibliography on," review. (#2-84). "Book Reviews." (#1-91).
TYPL: "Communication Technology and the Transformation of Culture," "Communication Media in Perspective: the History of Technology," "Assessing the Present and Forecasting the Future," "Critical Research and Social Transformation," "Technology and Freedom." (#2-84). "Televangelism and the Religious Uses of Television," "Religion in the History of Broadcasting," "The Sawdust Trail: Revivalism in America," "The Character of Televangelism," "Televangelism in Context: Religion and Broadcasting in General." (#1-91).
SCHL: Quarterly, 35 pp.
SPAN: Spring, 1980+
VARIES
--? - ? as CSCC Newsletter.
ISSN: 0144-4646
ABST: --Film Literature Index (ISSN: 0093-6758)

✦ COMMUNICATION STUDIES

PUBL: Central States Communication Association, Department of Communication, Purdue University, West Lafayette, IN 47907.
DESC: "The *Central States Speech Journal* is the official publication of the Central States Speech Association. *Central States Speech Journal* publishes articles representative of the several areas comprising the field of communications studies. These generally are identified as Rhetorical Studies (history, theory, criticism); Communications Studies (theory and research); Applied and Educational Communications Studies (theory, research and pedagogy); Media Studies (mass communication theory and research, radio-TV-film history, criticism, regulation and pedagogy); Aesthetic Communications Studies (oral interpretation, theatre, and other artistic theory and research); and Forensic Studies (descriptive, historical, critical, advisory and pedagogical works)." Although the publication changed title to *Communication Studies*, the focus of this scholarly journal remains the same: articles of research comprising the broad field of communication studies. For the sampled issues of 1968: perfect-bound journal format, black ink on coated paper stock, cover consisting of black ink on uncoated paper stock (5 ⅞ x 9 inches / 150 x 230 mm). For the sampled issues of 1987: perfect-bound journal format, black ink on uncoated paper stock, cover consisting of one-color on coated paper stock, advertising (6 ½ x 9 ⅞ inches / 165 x 250 mm).
DEPT: "Research Reports," "News and Notes." (spring-68). None. (fall-83). None. (winter-89).
TYPL: "Stokely Carmichael: Two Speeches on Black Power," "The Effects of Intensional and Extensional Audiences on Communicator Anxiety," "Forensic Activities at Trinity College, Dublin, In the Eighteenth Century," "Specialization and the Speech Associations," "Interviewing in Speech Pathology and Audiology." (spring-68). "The Discourses of TV Quiz Shows or, School + Luck = Success + Sex," "Dynasty: the Dialectic of Feminine Power," "Ideology and Television News: a Metaphoric Analysis of Political Stories," "Robert Schuller: the American Dream in a Crystal Cathederal." (fall-83). "Organizing and the Social Psychology of Organizing," "Organized Improvisation: 20 Years of Organizing," "Negotiation and Organizing: Two Levels within the Weickian Model," "Organizational Rhetoric and the Public Sphere," "Comic Strategies and the Amcrican Covenant." (winter-89).
SCHL: Quarterly, 80 pp.
SPAN: Nov, 1949+
VARIES
--Nov, 1949 - 198u as Central States Speech Journal (ISSN: 0008-9575).
LC: PN 4001.C45
DD: 302.2/05
ISSN: 1051-0974
ABST: --Current Index to Journals in Education (ISSN: 0011-3565)

--Language and Language Behavior Abstracts (ISSN: 0023-8295)
--Psychological Abstracts (ISSN: 0033-0202)
--Social Science Citation Index (ISSN: 0091-2887)

✤ COMMUNICATION THEORY

PUBL: International Communication Association, PO Box 9589, Austin, TX 78766-9589.
DESC: "*Communication Theory* is an international, interdisciplinary forum for theory and theoretically oriented research on all aspects of communication. Open to all views, *Communication Theory* is designed to sustain a scholarly dialogue across disciplinary, methodological, and geographical boundaries. Original theoretical work on human communication has rapidly grown in quantity, distinction, and international prominence in recent years. *Communication Theory* will be a showcase for the best of this work from the broad spectrum of communication studies. Whatever the topic or methodological approach, articles in this important new journal will make a significant contribution to communication theory. But, communication theory is not yet an established, well defined field of scholarship. Paradoxically, even as theoretical work on communication has grown and matured, the scope of communication theory as well as its proper forms and functions have become increasingly uncertain and controversial. The fragmentation of communication theory across disciplines and subdisciplines challenges those who would proclaim communication an emerging discipline. Tangled and often rancorous debates over the methodological and political premises of communication inquiry challenge those who would proclaim this field a science. ...Holding up a mirror to the field of communication in all its diversity, stimulating reflection and dialogue on issues of interdisciplinary significance, encouraging innovation and experimentation, at times provoking controversy, *Communication Theory* will engage its readers in the reconstruction of an academic discipline at a crucial juncture in its history." An important new journal from the International Communication Association.
DEPT: "Editorial," column by Robert T. Craig; "Forum," "Book Reviews." (2-91).
TYPL: "The Biological Origins of Automated Patterns of Human Interaction," "Is Comparative Communication Theory Possible/Desirable?," "Comparative Theory Reconceptualized: From Entities and States to Processes and Dynamics," "Contingency, Irony and Solidarity," "Communication and Power in Organizations: Discourse, Ideology and Domination." (2-91).
SCHL: Quarterly.
SPAN: Feb, 1991+
ISSN: 1050-3293

✤ COMMUNICATION WORLD

PUBL: International Association of Business Communicators, 870 Market St., Suite 940, San Francisco, CA 94102.
DESC: [*IABC News*]: The goal of the eight-page monthly is to "provide information about the profession of organizational communication and news of IABC." Emphasis is on news affecting business communicators, with liberal examples of recent publications.
DEPT: "Photo Technique," an analysis of current photo communications; "The Look of the Book," critique and suggestions on publication design.
TYPL: "Photojournalism is Alive and Well--In a Brochure!!," "Legal Restrictions on Horizon?," "Economic Gloom Lifts for Communicators."
SCHL: Monthly (Winter?, 1971/1972? - Dec, 1985); Eleven issues per year (Jan, 1986+), 8 pp.
SPAN: Winter?, 1971/1972?+
SPLIT OFF WITH
--Journal of Organizational Communication (from parent) IABC Notebook.
VARIES
--Winter?, 1971/1972 - May?, 1982 as IABC News (ISSN: 0744-7612).
DD: 659
ISSN: 0744-7612
ABST: --ABI/Informer
--Management Contents

✤ COMMUNICATIONS

PUBL: Bohlau Verlag, Koln, Federal Republic of Germany.
DESC: [*International Journal of Communication Research*]: This international journal of mass communication research prints articles in the original language of German (host language), French, or English; with summaries in the other two languages. In an early issue the publisher noted that "Research appears in connexion [sic] with communications media in diverse situations with different functions at any given time. The satellite-like accompaniment of all communications phenomena by various research activities is characteristic. In this relation, the association with science is not so unequivocal as in other fields such as modern technology, which in its main designs is always dependent upon previous ongoing basic research." Scholarly, thoughtful articles within an international forum. Journal format; no graphics.
DEPT: None. (1. Jahrgang, Heft 2, 1974).
TYPL: "Die Regenbogenpresse, Inhalt - Leserschaft - Wirkung," "Models for a Sociology of Language," "The Mass Media and Nation-Building: Testing a Hypothesis in Multi-National Yugoslavia," "Etude diachronique des posters publicitaires de la Firme Levi's en Europe." (1. Jahrgang, Heft 2, 1974).
SCHL: Three issues per year.
SPAN: 1974+
VARIES
--1974 - ? as International Journal of Communication Research (ISSN: 0340-0158).

LC: P 87 .I56
DD: 001.51/05
ISSN: 0341-2059
ABST: --ABI/Informer
--Computer & Control Abstracts (ISSN: 0036-8113)
--Electrical & Electronics Abstracts (ISSN: 0036-8105)
--Language and Language Behavior Abstracts (ISSN: 0023-8295)
--Physics Abstracts. Science Abstracts. Series A. (ISSN: 0036-8091)
--Psychological Abstracts (ISSN: 0033-0202)
--Social Welfare, Social Planning / Policy and Social Development (ISSN: 0195-7988)

✤ COMMUNICATIONS

SUB: "The professional journal of business communications."
SUB: "For the professional in land mobile radio."
PUBL: Cardiff Publishing, 6430 South Yosemite, Englewood, CO 80111.
DESC: The boom in land mobile communications led to the popularity of this magazine, which covers everything from automobile telephones to walkie-talkies, from medical communications to management of point-to-point systems. Interviews and features concerning users and applications for land-mobile dominate. Numerous advertisements.
DEPT: "Comment," editorial; "Washington News," "Association Events," "NMRA News," "Business News," "Over the Counter," sales tips; "Product News," "From the Bench," readers technical suggestions.
TYPL: "The Megawatt Syndrom: Warfare with a Broadcaster," "Business Radio Needs Its Fair Share," "How to Make Advertising Work for You," "Emergency Medical Communications in the Grand Canyon," "Peak Deviation and Density: Keys to Proper Modulation." (11/81).
SCHL: Monthly, 125 pp.
SPAN: 1964+
VARIES
--? - ? as Cable Communications.
LC: TK 5101.A1C629
DD: 384/.05
ISSN: 0010-356x

Communications

Sep, 1937 - Dec, 1949//
(ISSN: 0161-374x)
SEE: TELEVISION ENGINEERING

Communications and Electronics

Oct, 1954 - Apr, 1955//
SEE: BRITISH COMMUNICATIONS AND ELECTRONICS

✤ COMMUNICATIONS AND THE LAW

PUBL: Meckler Publishing, 520 Riverside Ave., Westport, CT 06880.
DESC: "Expanding technologies, aggressive use of the media by business, censorship, public opinion formation by government: these and scores of communication issues have daily impact on legislative, legal, and judicial affairs. *Communications and the Law* is devoted to the study and discussion of such issues." Editor-in-Chief, Theodore R. Kupferman, added, "It would be difficult to find any area of human activity in our normal relationships which is not in some way affected by law and legislation. We will endeavor through articles, guest editorials, symposia, reviews and commentaries, to analyze those aspects which affect the law in the area of communications. This will involve a broad range of issues from censorship to new technological uses. Every phase of the law involving communications, from a picket's shout to a publicist's release, in business or entertainment or government, will be grist for our literary mill. We will not only cover communications law, we will consider the means by which the law is communicated." A valuable bimonthly journal for the study of legal issues in the ever-expanding field of mass communications. For the sampled issues of 1979 and 1986: perfect-bound journal format, black ink on uncoated paper stock (5 ½ x 8 ¾ inches / 140 x 225 mm).
DEPT: "Book Review." (8-84).
TYPL: "Obtaining the Photojournalist's Work Product Via Warranted Searches and Subpoenas," "Copyright and the Federal Government: Ghosts of Protection for Authors," "Retraction's Role Under the Actual Malice Rule," "Don't Give the First Amendment a Bad Name." (8-84).
SCHL: Quarterly (Winter, 1979 - 1987?); Bimonthly (1987?+), 70 pp.
SPAN: Winter, 1979+
LC: K3 .O39
DD: 343/.73/09905
ISSN: 0162-9093
ABST: --ABI/Informer
--Computer & Control Abstracts (ISSN: 0036-8113)
--Electrical & Electronics Abstracts (ISSN: 0036-8105)
--Index to Legal Periodicals (ISSN: 0019-4077)
--Legal Resource Index
--Physics Abstracts. Science Abstracts. Series A. (ISSN: 0036-8091)

✤ COMMUNICATIONS CONCEPTS

SUB: "The best ideas in print for professional communicators."
PUBL: Communications Concepts, Inc., 2100 National Press Building, Suite 202, Washington, DC 20045.
DESC: "*Communications Concepts* is an 8-page monthly newsletter--a 'mini-seminar' that helps you sort through the flood of information to quickly find the

'gems'--the methods that work, the best ideas. *Communications Concepts* will show you how to use professional communications methods to do your job better, and get the recognition you deserve. ... *Concepts* is an original newsletter, packed with valuable, in-depth information. All our editorial material is written by professional writers, communicators and successful practitioners. The *Concepts* editors interview numerous top communicators--the results of those exclusive interviews appear only in *Concepts*." The accolades are numerous and well-deserved for this wonderful resource: "Of all the newsletters that cross my desk, *Communication Concepts* is the only one I read word for word," "Great balance/blend of useful information...you publish the best, most useful newsletter in the business," and "An outstanding job of spotting the essentials others miss. Concise, focused style." Each monthly issue contains a feature story followed by a series of articles within the following categories: "Communications Management," "Writing & Editing," "Ideas That Work," "Time $avers & Money Makers," "Publication Design & Production," "Desktop Concepts," and "Letters & Notes." This is a treasure trove of workable, creative ideas for the workplace and marketplace. Well worth the 1990 subscription price of $99 per year. For anyone in the business of communicating through the medium of print, *Communications Concepts* is a "must" subscription. Loose-leaf newsletter format (8 ½ x 11 inches / 215 x 280 mm), printed two color on uncoated paper stock.

DEPT: "Communications Management," "Writing & Editing," "Ideas That Work," "Time $avers & Money Makers," "Publication Design & Production," "Desktop Concepts," "Letters & Notes," letters to the editor plus newsbriefs. (12-90).
TYPL: "Successful Newsletters Carry News to Use," "Executive Branch P.R. Requires Special Planning," "Sight and Sound Often Outweigh Words in Video Scripts," "Take Time Out to Study Time Management Techniques," "Computers Can Help Publication Programs Many Ways." (12-90).
SCHL: Monthly, 8 pp.
SPAN: May, 1984+
ISSN: 0741-0069

✤ COMMUNICATIONS ENGINEERING & DESIGN

SUB: "Reporting the technologies of broadband communications."
SUB: "Published for the Society of Cable Television Engineers."
PUBL: Capital Cities/ABC, New York, NY.
DESC: [*Communications/Engineering Digest*]: An excellent publication covering cable television communications hardware and other broadband technology. Articles are aimed at the magazine's primary audience--cable television engineers--and mainly concentrate on problems, techniques, and innovations of getting a signal from the head end to the home. Articles are enhanced by excellent documentation and explanatory graphics.
DEPT: "Bulletin Board," current broadband news; "Proof of Performance," a how-to, when-to technical construction series. (12-75).
TYPL: "Satellite Communications, Cable Television, and the Advent of the International Communications Grid," "Proposed National Standard for CATV Graphic Symbols," "CATV Earth Stations: an Amplifier Update." (12-75).
SCHL: Monthly, 60 pp.
SPAN: Oct, 1975+
VARIES
--Oct, 1975 - ? as Communications/Engineering Digest (ISSN: 1046-574x).
ISSN: 0191-5428

Communications/Engineering Digest

Oct, 1975 - ?//
(ISSN: 1046-574x)
SEE: COMMUNICATIONS ENGINEERING & DESIGN

✤ COMMUNICATIONS INDUSTRIES REPORT, THE

SUB: "The newsletter of NAVA, the International Communications Industries Association."
SUB: "The newspaper of the International Communications Industries Association."
SUB: "Video, multimedia, audio-visual, interactive systems, industry, government."
PUBL: The International Communications Industries Association (ICIA), 3150 Spring St., Fairfax, VA 22031.
DESC: "For over half a century, the International Communications Industries Association (ICIA) has served the communications industry as the trade association for professionals involved in the sales and use of communications products, equipment and services. An alliance of over 1,400 leading audio-visual, video and computer companies, ICIA is an organization that has proven its ability to keep up with the fast-paced, ever-changing industry it represents." *Communications Industries Report* is a wonderfully dynamic publication, mirroring the vitality of the organization. Articles cover a number of areas of communication including, video, multimedia, audio-visual, interactive systems, industry, and government. A major premise of this membership publication is to keep subscribers apprised of new technologies, their impact on current media, and government regulatory trends and developments concerning those technologies. *Communications Industries Report*, along with membership in the International Communications Industries Association, is a "must" for any vendor or primary user of video, multimedia and audio-visual equipment. Large magazine (loose-leaf) format (10 x 14 inches / 255 x 350 mm), two color throughout, advertising.

DEPT: "Calendar," "Books / Publications / Videos," reviews; "Selected Shorts," 'The following from news services, press releases, and newspapers reflect recent items of interest'; "New Products," review; "Products Plus," detailed production introductions; "Industry News," personnel and corporate newsbriefs; "Government News," excellent regulatory review. (4-91).
TYPL: "Four of Six FCC-Tested Systems Will be Digital," "HD Video Debuts in Renovated Ed Sullivan Theater," "Perot Needles Bureaucrats, Berates Politicians and Praises Troops at FOSE Show," "Amiga Uses for Video Businesses," "ICIA Legislative Committee Meets with Senate Small Business Committee Rep." (4-91).
SCHL: Monthly, 25 pp.
SPAN: 1946+
VARIES
--1946 - Aug, 1983 as NAVA News.
WITH SUPPLEMENT
--Market Monitor (1983+).

✧ COMMUNICATIONS LAWYER

SUB: "The journal of media, information and communications law."
SUB: "Publication of the Forum on Communications Law."
PUBL: American Bar Association, Forum on Communications Law, 750 North Lake Shore Drive, Chicago, IL 60611.
DESC: *Communications Lawyer* is aimed at attorneys and other communications specialists who devote a major portion of their practice to broadcasting, cable television, satellites, newspapers, magazine and book publishing, telecommunications, common carrier, entertainment, intellectual property law, and related areas. It endeavors to provide current practical information, as well as public policy and scholarly viewpoints that it believes to be of professional and academic interest to its members and other readers." This is an excellent resource and membership benefit for members of the Forum on Communications Law of the American Bar Association. Articles are timely in reflecting societal and legislative changes in communication, and informative in their coverage of late-breaking events and analysis. Of special consideration is the "Current Bibliography" section which provides articles and book titles of note under the subtitles of "Mass Media," "Television & Radio," "Telecommunications," "Newspapers," "Libel," and "Freedom of Press." This section alone would justify cost of division membership for ABA members. For sampled issue of 1991: black ink with spot color on uncoated paper stock in stapled magazine format, no advertising (8 ½ x 11 inches / 215 x 280 mm).
DEPT: "From the Chair," chair commentary column by Patricia M. Reilly; "Books," review; "Courtside," recent communication legal decisions, column by Timothy Dyk and Barbara McDowell; "Current Bibliography," articles and books of interest. (spring-91).

TYPL: "The First Amendment: A Rock on Which to Stand," "The First Amendment: A Global Perspective," "Balancing Legitimate Rights: Freedom of the Press and Other Rights in French Law," "Press Freedom vs. National Security in South Korea," "Prior Restraint of the Press in New Zealand." (spring-91).
SCHL: Quarterly, 40 pp.
SPAN: Winter, 1983+
ISSN: 0737--7622

✧ COMMUNICATIONS NEWS

SUB: "Combined with Wire & Radio Communications."
PUBL: Edgell Communications, Inc., Cleveland, OH.
DESC: "It is edited for those in all business and industry responsible for the design, engineering, construction, operation and maintenance of communications systems." This large format magazine highlights new voice, signal and data communications equipment, and news covering all aspects of communications hardware industry.
DEPT: "Hot Line," Washington, D.C. news; "Lab Report," new developments in communications technology.
TYPL: "ITT Proposes Domestic Digital Data Network," "Bell Labs Sees Two Important Trends," "Intercity Relay System Supports Extensive Broadcast-Translator Complex."
SCHL: Monthly, 75 pp.
SPAN: Oct, 1964+
ABSORBED
--Wire & Radio Communications, Mar, 1965.
LC: TK 5101.A1 C64
DD: 621 11
ISSN: 0010-3632
ABST: --Business Periodical Index (ISSN: 0007-6961)
--Electronic Publishing Abstracts (ISSN: 0739-2907)
--Management and Marketing Abstracts (ISSN: 0308-2172)
--Predicasts
--Trade and Industry Index

✧ COMMUNICATIONS TECHNOLOGY & POLICY NEWS

PUBL: Association for Education in Journalism and Mass Communication, Communications Technology and Policy Interest Group, University of South Carolina, Columbia, SC 29208.
DESC: In a quest for division status within the Association for Education in Journalism and Mass Communication, the August, 1991 newsletter put forth these objectives for the Communications Technology and Policy Interest Group: "The mission of the Communications Technology and Policy Division will be three-fold: to foster research in communications technology and policy, to both broaden and strengthen the teaching of communications technology and policy in journalism schools, and to strengthen linkages between journalism and mass communication educators

and professionals in media industries." The newsletter reflects this mission, reporting on membership activities within the communications technology and policy field. For the sampled 1991 issue: photocopied black ink on beige-colored uncoated paper stock (8 ½ x 11 inches / 215 x 280 mm).
DEPT: None. (8-91).
TYPL: "ComTech Events Continue at Boston AEJMC," "Petition to Establish the Communications Technology and Policy Division," "Proposed Bylaws." (8-91).
SCHL: ?, 2 pp.
SPAN: ?, 1988+

✤ COMMUNICATIONS WORLD

SUB: "Official guide to AM, FM, TV and worldwide SW."
PUBL: Davis Publications, Inc., 380 Lexington Ave., New York, NY 10017.
DESC: The amateur radio operator is in a unique class, often working in the same electronics industry that one practiced as a hobby; shortwave radio. Since the beginning of American radio broadcasting, there has always been a number of serials devoted to this area, and *Communications World* is among the best. Articles provide three services to readers: up-to-date listings of operating stations world-wide; a showcase for reader's equipment; and information on new radio advancements. There is a much stronger connection to broadcast activities within the pages of this serial than may first be assumed. Editorial content changed when the serial went to an annual publication schedule, providing more basic articles on radio. Of special note is the inclusion of *White's Radio Log*, a large compendium of AM, FM, TV, and shortwave stations by call letters, frequency, and location. It had a small size format for the first two years of publication, moving to standard magazine format in Fall/Winter, 1975. For the sampled issue of Mar/Apr, 1975, under the *Elementary Electronics* title: perfect-bound magazine format with black ink editorial content on newsprint with some spot-color employed, cover consisting of full-color on coated paper stock (8 ¼ x 10 ⅞ inches / 210 x 275 mm). For the sampled issue of Fall/Winter, 1975 under the title of *Communications World*: stapled magazine format, editorial content being black ink on newsprint with full-color cover on coated paper stock (8 ⅛ x 10 ⅞ inches / 205 x 280 mm).
DEPT: "White's Radio Log," "New Products," "Literature Library," "Ask Hank, He Knows!," Q&A; "Action Band Receivers," equipment review. (fall/winter, 75). "White's Radio Log," "New Products," "Ask Hank," "Literature Library." (81).
TYPL: "The World Above 30 Megs," "A Closer Look at the Bands," "Spanish ABCs," "Bird's-Eye View of the Higher Hertz." (fall/winter, 75). "Location of the SWBC Bands," "What to Look for in a SW Receiver," "How to Get QSL's," "Radio Clubs You Can Join plus Foreign DX Club Listing." (81).
SCHL: Bimonthly (196u - May/Jun, 1981); Semiannual (spring/summer, 1973 - ?); Annual (?+); 125 pp.
SPAN: 196u+?
VARIES
--196u - Jan/Feb, 1981 as Elementary Electronics (ISSN: 0013-595x).
--Mar/Apr, 1981 - May/Jun, 1981 as Science & Electronics (ISSN: 0279-585x).
--Jul/Aug, 1981 - ? as Computers and Programming (ISSN: 0279-070x) [NC].
LC: TK 6540.C663
DD: 621.3841/05
ISSN: 0095-4063

✤ COMMUNICATIONSWEEK

SUB: "The newspaper for the communications industry"
PUBL: CMP Publications, Inc., 111 East Shore Rd., Manhasset, NY 11030.
DESC: One of the fastest growing areas of technology worldwide is the field of telephony for voice and digital communication, and *CommunicationsWeek*, a newsprint tabloid, provides late-breaking news in this area, especially as it relates to competitive events, governmental actions, and the ever-fluid actions of the communications marketplace. Early issue emphasis appeared to be on digital switching equipment, and "telephone" handsets, but contemporary issues have broadened coverage to include computer transmission (Local Area Networks included), fiber optics, and other forms of point-to-point communication media.
DEPT: "AT&T Monitor," "BOC Monitor," "Business File," "Business & Finance," "Career Opportunities," "CloseUp," "Data Communication & Networks," "Data Network," "Equipment," "Equipment: Central Office," "Equipment: CPE," "Equipment: Transmission," "Marketing & Distribution," "People & Careers," "Personnel File," "Pipeline," "Services: Enhanced," "Services: Local," "Services: Long Distance," "Usage & Applications," "Washington Watch." (7-30-84). "Analyst's Portfolio," "BOC Monitor," newsbriefs; "Convergence," newsbriefs; "Forum," 'Editorial, perspective, comment, letters'; "ISDN Monitor," newsbriefs concerning integrated services digital networks; "PC Connections," "Pipeline," comment; "Public Policy," newsbriefs. (5-2-88).
TYPL: "Decline Reported in Rate Increases Granted to Telcos," "AT&T Pulling Out All Stops to Land Key Equipment Pacts," "Zilog & Excelan Sign Licensing Deal for Ethernet Processor." (7-30-84). "New Data Czar at AT&T," "DEC & Siemens Seek LAN Links," "Health-Care Industry Lags in Technology," "FCC Rules Get Mixed Reviews." (5-2-88).
SCHL: Biweekly [except combined issue in Jan/Feb] (Feb 1, 1984 - Aug 5, 1985); Weekly (Aug 19, 1985+), 60 pp.
SPAN: Feb 1, 1984+
WITH SUPPLEMENT
--Closeup, ?+
DD: 384 11
ISSN: 0746-8121

✤ COMMUNICATOR

SUB: "Bulletin of the Radio Television News Directors Association."
SUB: "The magazine of the Radio-Television News Directors Association."
PUBL: Radio Television News Directors Association, Suite 615, 1717 K St., NW, Washington, DC 20006.
DESC: This official publication of the Radio-Television News Directors Association, details current broadcast news issues and items concerning the operation of a radio-television newsroom in the United States. Major issues in earlier issues included freedom of the press, right to privacy, fairness, and professional news standards. Later issues (under current title) include these topics, plus case stories of news gathering, the competitive nature of today's professional news operation, and the explosive impact of new technology on broadcast journalism. Also featured are newsbriefs on Radio Television News Directors Association (RTNDA) members and organizational activities. Excellent resource on the state of broadcast journalism today. Magazine format.
DEPT: "Communique," reprint of recent topical news speeches; "Clear Channels," newsbriefs of personnel changes; "Jobs," unusual section listing job openings and RTNDA members seeking job changes. (2-77). "Book Beat," "From the Chairman," "News Directions," personnel changes; "News Practices," column by Emerson Stone; "Reporting for Radio," "Straight from the Shoulder," guest commentary; "Word-Watching," writing style how-to; "You're On!," guest commentary. (10-89).
TYPL: "Don't Ban Execution Coverage, But Use Good Taste, Schultz Says," "More Women Reporting News on the Air," "RTNDA Helps Devise New Plan for Release of Nixon Tapes." (2-77). "Government, Not Media, Lost Vietnam, Army Study Says," "Electronic Paint Systems Tell the Story Pictorially," "Computer-Generated News Opens Catch Viewers' Attention," "Interviewing: How to Do It and Get the Information You Need." (10-89).
SCHL: Monthly, 40 pp.
SPAN: Jan, 1947?+
VARIES
--Jan, 1947? - Nov, 1952 as NARND Bulletin.
--Dec, 1952? - Dec, 1970 as RTNDA Bulletin.
--1971 - Jul, 1988 as RTNDA Communicator (ISSN: 0033-7153).
DD: 384
ISSN: 1041-7117

✤ COMMUNICATOR, THE

PUBL: Association of Visual Communicators (AVC), 900 Palm Ave., Suite B, South Pasadena, CA 91130.
DESC: Published as a supplement/insert to *Video Manager*, *The Communicator* is designed to report on member activities of the Association of Visual Communicators (formerly called the IFPA). Articles in this lively publication provide member profiles, new technologies, and the news behind winning entries in AVC competitions. For the 1988 sampled issue: black/white editorial content with numerous graphics on uncoated paper stock in stapled magazine format (8 x 11 inches / 205 x 280 mm).
DEPT: "From the President," "Executive Director's Report," "News from National," "Calendar." (4-88).
TYPL: "Douglas Mesney: Keeping the Future in Motion," "'Interact' System Makes Training Worth Investigating," "'The 928S4 Experience--What it Means to Video Producers Today." (4-88).
SCHL: Bimonthly (? - ?); Quarterly (?+), 20 pp.
SPAN: 1973+
SUPPLEMENT TO
--Video Manager (ISSN: 0149-6832), ?+?
ISSN: 0099-1090

COMMUNIQUE

SUB: "Serving the sun belt's advertising-marketing industry."
SUB: "Journal of Florida publications, broadcasting, advertising, public relations."
PUBL: Worth International Communications, Box 2226, Hollywood, FL 33022.
DESC: This advertising and marketing periodical features the latest news and developments in the southern states. It is similar to other such regional publications on the West Coast, Chicago, or New York.
DEPT: "Worth Quoting," newsbriefs of special interest to those in advertising and marketing; "At Deadline," newsbriefs; "Sunbelt Rap," briefs on the following areas: account action, client news, ad agencies, newspapers, magazines, kudos, television, radio, promotion, associations, film/tape, and classified. (6-78).
TYPL: "How Have Record Sales Affected Bacardi's Target Marketing Goals?," "The Survival of Frogs, Freedom, and Small Furniture Manufacturers," "Who Says Auto Dealership Spots Have to be Bad to be Good?" (6-78).
SCHL: Monthly, 35 pp.
SPAN: 1919 - ?//
VARIES
--192u - Oct, 1947 as Florida Newspaper News.
--Nov, 1947 - Dec, 1969 as Florida Newspaper News and Radio Digest.
LC: P 87.F56
DD: 001.5/05
ISSN: 0015-4180

✤ COMMUNIQUÉ

PUBL: University of Wyoming, Department of Communication and Mass Media, PO Box 3904, Laramie, WY 82701-3904.
DESC: *COMMuniqué* is a promotional newsletter for the students, faculty, alumni, and friends of the Department of Communication and Mass Media at the University of Wyoming. Articles cover current activities of the department, profile faculty members, and pro-

vide news of departmental alumni. Four-page newsletter, black ink on light-grey uncoated paper stock (8 ½ x 11 inches / 215 x 280 mm).
DEPT: "Alumni News." (fall-90).
TYPL: "Millar Takes Charge," "1990-91 Co/MM Faculty Members," "Budget Cutters Spare Department So Far," "Scholarship fund Set Up in Photojournalism," "Journalism Scholarship Winners Named." (fall-90).
SCHL: Semiyearly, 4 pp.
SPAN: ?+

✥ COMMUNIQUÉ

SUB: "Philosophy of Communication Division Newsletter."
PUBL: International Communication Association, Philosophy of Communication Division, PO Box 9589, Austin, TX 78766.
DESC: In this newsletter of the Philosophy of Communication (Philcom) Division of the International Communication Association, editor Lisa Henderson in a 1991 issue provided a partial description of its function: "We typically include conference programs, calls for papers, announcements of members' current research, the syllabus exchange, information about upcoming ICA elections, etc." Of special interest to academics is the departmental feature, "Syllabus Exchange," providing samples for adoption consideration. For the sampled issue of 1991: typewritten single sheet format, no advertising (8 ½ x 11 inches / 215 x 280 mm).
DEPT: "Syllabus Exchange." (fall-91).
TYPL: "Call for Papers," "The Future of Communiqué," "Canadian Mail Strike," "New Journals." (fall-91).
SCHL: Semiyearly, 6 pp.
SPAN: ?+?

✥ COMMUNITY COLLEGE JOURNALIST

SUB: "The official publication of the Community College Journalism Association."
PUBL: Community College Journalism Association, Southwestern College, 900 Otay Lakes Rd., Chula Vista, CA 92010.
DESC: [Community College Journalist]: This serial serves as a communication forum for journalism instructors at the community college level, and deals with issues affecting those campus publications. It is also a serial in search of a stable publication schedule. From inception, *Community College Journalist* has struggled to find a sufficient number of articles, and a publishing schedule that is right for its membership (the Community College Journalism Association), moving from quarterly, to semiannual, to a three-times-per-year publication schedule. Magazine format.
DEPT: None. (winter-76). "Editor's Note," "Book Review." (spring-86).
TYPL: "Read Ad Contracts in Detail or You May Not Get Paid!," "Grad Programs Lack Creative Initiative," "Is Your Campus Ready for a Magazine?," "Wanted: Broadcasters with Degree and Writing Skills for Texas Stations." (winter-76). "Attitudes of Two-Year vs. Four-Year College Advisers," "Taking the Fear Out of Calculating Percentages," "In Arizona: Educators, Professionals Join to Seek Journalism Education Improvements." (spring-86).
SCHL: Three issues per year (1974 - ?); Quarterly (1977+), 14 pp.
SPAN: Summer, 1972+
VARIES
--Summer, 1972 - Spring/Summer, 1974 as Junior College Journalist.
--Fall, 1974 - Summer, 1981 as Community College Journalist.
--Fall, 1981 - Spring, 1983 as Journalist.
--Summer, 1983 as CCJA Journalist.

Community College Journalist

Fall, 1974 - Summer, 1981//
SEE: COMMUNITY COLLEGE JOURNALIST

Community Theatre Bulletin

Mar, 1955? - Sep, 1960//
(ISSN: 0414-1520)
SEE: THEATRE JOURNAL

Community Video Report

Summer, 1973 - Autumn, 1974//
SEE: TELEVISIONS

✥ COMPUTER PICTURES

SUB: "The visual communications magazine."
SUB: "Back Stage Supplement."
SUB: "For creators and producers of graphic presentations."
SUB: "A-V communications linking the whole community."
PUBL: Knowledge Industry Publications, Inc., 701 Westchester Ave., White Plains, NY 10604.
DESC: The evolution of *Business Screen* into *Business Screen Magazine*, *Business Screen*, and finally *Computer Pictures*, has been a fascinating one. Whereas the lineage of most publications concentrates in one area of communication, these publications have covered a variety of disciplines. In the beginning was *Business Screen*, an ongoing supplement to *Back Stage*, which furnished news of interest to three specific groups: audio-visual buyers and users, media producers, and distributors. As a supplement, it was designed for a "quick read" to provide late breaking news, and to showcase activities of A/V, industrial, or corporate media organizations. Next in line was *"Business and Home TV Screen"* devoted to providing facts, ideas and analysis helpful to executives engaged in the business of using and sponsoring, producing and distributing films, video tapes and other A-V

media for industry, government, and other organizations, as well as for the newest A-V medium: home video." The emphasis in this serial was on the creation, packaging, distribution and reception of the message of the medium. Numerous stories and production sources were provided, and were uniquely segmented into three cross-referenced areas: 1) AV use; 2) production; and 3) distribution. Finally, the emphasis in the current *Computer Pictures* concerns computerized creation, enhancement, and transmission of graphics for mass media application. The breadth of this medium is apparant from the variety of articles covering topics ranging from FBI criminal investigations of missing children, to desktop publishing, broadcast electronic effects, and full color print advertising. Many of the advertisements are as valuable for their display of new technology as are the articles, which provide in-depth reviews of same. Whether the reader is concerned with photography, advertising, public relations, television, film animation, or print, *Computer Pictures* is "the" serial for high tech computer generated graphics. Well recommended with numerous full-color graphics (8 ¼ x 10 ¾ inches / 205 x 275 mm).

DEPT: "Camera Eye," comment column by Ott Coelln; "Off-screen," production profile column by Bob Harris; "Paradox," production comment column by Stanford Sobel. (11-77). "Conventions," "Events," "Changes," "Money," "Promotion," "Software," "Hardware," "How To," "Services." (3-78). "Editorial," "Graphics Update," newsbriefs; "Making of the Covers," how front cover was created. (11/12-87). "Editor's View," "News Briefs," "Graphics Update," "Shopping Digest," "Graphics Creations," "Products Showcase," "Graphics Calendar." (2/3-90).

TYPL: "Cutting Location Red Tape," "Stock Film Library," "The Independent Filmmaker," "Corporate Videotape," "Slides are Flexible, Effective and Affordable." (11- 77). "Getting the Citibank Family Together," "Super Eight on the Run," "Psychodrama Sells," "Creating Multi-Media," "Mono-Key Multi-Images." (3-78). "How the Fortune 1000 Use Computer Graphics," "The FBI Gets a Face Lift," "Electronic Studio: Post Perfect," "New Desktop Publishing Series," "The Broadcast Designers." (11/12-87). "Video Establishment Sees Multimedia as Way to Grow," "Leaders 'Crystal Ball' Computer Graphics in the 1990s," "Truevision Art Winners Tell All." (2/3-90).

SCHL: Ten issues per year (1938 - ?); Eight issues per year (? - Aug 15, 1968); Bimonthly (1972? - 1976); Monthly (Jan, 1977 - Mar, 1977); Bimonthly (May, 1977+), 90 pp.

SPAN: Jan/Feb, 1983+
VARIES
--1938 - Mar 1, 1946 as Business Screen.
--Apr 23, 1946 - Aug 15, 1968 as Business Screen Magazine.
--October 1, 1968 - Nov, 1977 as Business Screen.
--Jan, 1978 - Feb, 1979 as Business and Home TV Screen.
--Apr, 1979 - Jun, 1980 as Back Stage Magazine Supplement/Business Screen.
--Aug, 1980? - Dec?, 1982? as Business Screen (ISSN: 0160-7294).
SUPPLEMENT TO
--Back Stage, Jan 14, 1977 - Jun, 1980?
ABSORBED
--See and Hear, Jan, 1954.

ISSN: 0883-5683
ABST: --Media Review Digest (ISSN: 0363-7778)
--Trade and Industry Index

✤ COMPUTER PUBLISHING

PUBL: Pacific Magazine Group, 513 Wilshire Blvd., Suite 344, Santa Monica, CA 90401.

DESC: Designed for the desktop publishing professional, *Electronic Publishing and Printing* (new fall, 1990 title of *Computer Publishing*), provides fresh, practical information for this burgeoning new field of publishing and printing. Equipment for this rapidly changing technology is reviewed, along with new promising software, and advice for surviving and thriving in the competitive field of publishing. In one sample issue reviewed were articles that spanned subjects such as type design and leading principles, new technologies in the color scanner field, and a wide variety of software utilities designed to enhance current desktop publishing opperations. Each issue holds instruction for the novice, and pragmatic information for the largest corporate information manager. Full color throughout with numerous graphics; an excellent resource in magazine format.

DEPT: "Behind the Desk," editorial column by Kurt Luchs; "Letters," "News & Notes," newsbriefs; "Type Style," typography column by Edward F. Henninger; "Software Corner," column by Dave Brambert; "Washington Update," column by Wilson Dizard; "Peoplescape," personnel changes; "Installations," equipment recently installed; "Electronic Art World," 'For the art & design professional' column by Jan V. White; "Product Update," "Literature Exchange," "The Last Desktop," back cover commentary column by James Cavuoto. (4-90).

TYPL: "Scanning the Horizon: A Look at Desktop Color Scanners," "Low-Rent Utilities: Affordable Software That Adds EP&P Value," "Color Panel Do's and Don'ts for EP&P Designers," "E = EP&P: Einstein Meets Electronic Publishing." (4-90).

SCHL: Nine issues per year, 70 pp.
SPAN: Jan/Feb, 1986+
VARIES
--Jan/Feb, 1986 - Aug/Sep, 1990 as Electronic Publishing & Printing (ISSN: 1044-0852).
DD: 686
ISSN: 1054-0415

COMPUTERS & ELECTRONICS
SUB: "World's largest-selling electronics magazine." (Jan, 1974 - Oct, 1982).
PUBL: Ziff-Davis Publishing Co., PO Box 2774, Boulder, CO 80302.
DESC: This was a publication of news concerning electronics (and later computer applications of same), as well as resources for electronics projects (complete with schematics, parts lists, and instructions). In addition, equipment tests of home electronics items (everything from stereos to test bench equipment, to intruder/fire alarms) were featured. To round out each issue was news of trends in electronics, and commercial applications of such equipment. For sampled issue of 1971: perfect-bound small magazine format (6 ½ x 9 inches / 165 x 230 mm) on coated paper stock. For the sampled issue of 1980: perfect- bound magazine format, mixture of black and spot-color inks with full- color pages and cover on coated paper stock (8 x 10 ¾ inches / 205 x 275 mm).
DEPT: "Direct & Current," editorial column by Milton S. Snitzer; "Interface," letters; "New Literature," "Electronics Library," book review; "New Products," review; "Stereo Scene," column by J. Gordon Holt; "Opportunity Awareness," 'Thoughtful reflections on your future' column by David L. Heiserman; "Communications," technical column by Leslie Solomon; "The Product Gallery," technical review; "Solid State," technical column by Lou Garner. (12-71). "Solid State Developments," column by Forrest M. Mims; "Experimenter's Corner," column by Forrest M. Mims; "Project of the Month," column by Forrest M. Mims; "Entertainment Electronics," column by Harold A. Rodgers; "Computer Bits," column by Carl Warren; "Computer Sources," column by Leslie Solomon; "Editorial," "Audiophile Recordings," review column by Harold A. Rodgers. (12-80).
TYPL: "Distortionless Audio Compressor," "What's Happened to Educational TV?," "Build a Mini-Pyramidal UHF TV Antenna," "Giant Billboard Antennas for Space-Age Radars," "Hi-Fi Amplifier Module." (12-71). "PE Examines Cordless Telephones," "An Inexpensive Expansion to TRS-80 Memory," "Electronic Games: Space-Age Leisure Activity," "English Broadcasts Audible in North America," "A Low-Cost Emergency Broadcast System Monitor." (12-80).
SCHL: Monthly, 110 pp.
SPAN: Oct, 1954 - Apr, 1985//
VARIES
--Oct, 1954 - Dec, 1971 as Popular Electronics (ISSN: 0032-4485).
--Jan, 1972 - Dec, 1973 as Popular Electronics, Including Electronics World.
--Jan, 1972 - Oct, 1982 as Popular Electronics (ISSN: 0032-4485).
ABSORBED
--Electronics World (ISSN: 0013-5232), Jan, 1972.
LC: TK 9900.P6
DD: 621.381/05
ISSN: 0745-1458
ABST: --Abridged Readers' Guide to Periodical Literature (ISSN: 0001-334x)
--Computer & Control Abstracts (ISSN: 0036-8113)
--Consumers Index to Product Evaluations and Information Sources (ISSN: 0094-0534)
--Electrical & Electronics Abstracts (ISSN: 0036-8105)
--Magazine Index
--Micro Computer Index (ISSN: 8756-7040)
--Physics Abstracts. Science Abstracts. Series A. (ISSN: 0036-8091)
--Popular Magazine Review (ISSN: 0740-3763)
--Readers Guide to Periodical Literature (ISSN: 0034-0464)

Computers and Programming
Jul/Aug, 1981 - ?//
(ISSN: 0279-070x)
SEE: COMMUNICATIONS WORLD

✦ COMSAT TECHNICAL REVIEW
PUBL: Communications Satellite Corporation, 22300 Comsat Drive, Clarksburg MD 20871.
DESC: This serial features a host of highly-technical articles dealing with satellite communications. In particular, technical protocols in using Comsat Satellites provide the bulk of information. Most issues include French and Spanish language abstracts. Technical knowledge is assumed; small journal format.
DEPT: None.
TYPL: "New Types of Waveguide Bandpass Filters for Satellite Transponders," "A Model for Nonpenetrating Proton Damage to Silicon Solar Cells." (fall-71). "Multipath Fading Characterization of L-Band Maritime Mobile Satellite Links," "A Bound on Diurnal Error in Predicted Ranges of Nearly Geostationary Satellites." (fall-86).
SCHL: Semiannual, 150 pp.
SPAN: Fall, 1971+
LC: TK 5104 .C64
DD: 621.38/0422
ISSN: 0095-9669
ABST: --Communication Abstracts
--Computer & Control Abstracts (ISSN: 0036-8113)
--Electrical & Electronics Abstracts (ISSN: 0036-8105)
--Engineering Index Annual (ISSN: 0360-8557)
--Engineering Index Bioengineering Abstracts (ISSN: 0736-6213)
--Engineering Index Energy Abstracts (ISSN: 0093-8408)
--Engineering Index Monthly (1984) (ISSN: 0742-1974)
--Engineering Index Monthly (ISSN: 0013-7960)
--International Aerospace Abstracts (ISSN: 0020-5842)
--Physics Abstracts. Science Abstracts. Series A. (ISSN: 0036-8091)

✦ CONGRESSIONAL QUARTERLY'S EDITORIAL RESEARCH REPORTS

PUBL: Congressional Quarterly, Inc., 1414 22nd St., N.W., Washington, DC 20037.
DESC: Since 1923, *Editorial Research Reports* has provided an outstanding weekly resource for members of the radio, television, newspaper and magazine editorial community by publishing timley interpretations of world and domestic political/sociological events. Each small format issue includes charts, graphs, and maps to accompany main interpretive articles.
DEPT: None.
TYPL: "Presidential Race Ideology, Demographics," "Voter Targeting an American Tradition," "Religious Ingredients in This Campaign," "Assessing the Gender Gap and Yuppies," "Regional Profile of Nation's Voting Traits." (9-14-84).
SCHL: Weekly, 15 pp.
SPAN: ?+
VARIES
--Jan, 1924 - Dec 26, 1986 as Editorial Research Reports (ISSN: 0013-0958).
LC: H 35.E35
DD: 300/.973
ISSN: 0013-0958
ABST: --Coal Abstracts (ISSN: 0309-4979)
--Energy Research Abstracts (ISSN: 0160-3604)
--Nexis
--Public Affairs Information Service Bulletin (ISSN: 0033-3409)

✦ CONNECT

SUB: "Teaching with television."
PUBL: The Crosby Vandenburgh Group, 420 Boylston St., Boston, MA 02116-4000.
DESC: This is a publication for teachers wishing to integrate educational cable television programming into their classroom curricula. *Connect* facilitates the joinder between these two entities by showcasing upcoming cable television product. Program listings are arranged by subject matter (and time zones), making *Connect* an invaluable resource. Magazine format; numerous graphics.
DEPT: "The Connect Survey," comprehensive survey of upcoming cable television educational programs; "The Connect Study Guide," "The Connect Report," 'programming of note'; "The Connect Locater," 'teaching materials and where to find them'. (10-89).
TYPL: "Watching China," "Fulfilling the Promise," "Get the Picture," "Real Pictures, Real Learning." (10-89).
SCHL: Monthly [with combined Jul/Aug issue], 50 pp.
SPAN: Oct, 1989+
DD: 371 11
ISSN: 1047-7268

✦ CONSUMER ELECTRONICS

SUB: "Featuring office at home: the electronic workplace."
PUBL: CES Publishing Corp., 345 East 75th St., New York, NY 10021.
DESC: Virtually any new electronic product for the home market can be found in this serial. Designed for the trade, this periodical profiles and promotes what local dealers should be carrying in their consumer stores, and the product line includes almost everything from bathroom telephones to the customary electronic "kitchen sink." This is the ideal publication for communication futurists, where next year's "hot" product is displayed. Of special note is the ongoing series entitled *Mystery Shopper*, in which a team explores electronic retail shops in a different city each issue, and then writes up often hilarious/depressing (depending upon whether one is the owner/vendor/distributor) stories of how sales people handled the sales session. This departmental feature alone is worth the price of subscription to see how the best marketing plans at headquarters often go awry on the retail battle front. For the sampled issue of 1987: perfect-bound magazine format with editorial content mixture of black/white, spot- and full-color graphics on coated paper stock (8 ⅛ x 10 ⅞ inches / 205 x 275 mm).
DEPT: "Probe," editorial; "Input," comment; "People," "Bits and Pieces," newsbriefs; "General News," "Ten Years Ago," "Man in Japan," business newsbriefs; "Ad Watch," critique; "Fast Forward," comment column by Bob Gerson; "Outtakes," comment column by Seth Goldstein; "Mystery Shopper," "The Last Word," comment column by Mel Buchwald. (5-86).
TYPL: "Summer Stock: Price and Availability Head CES Concerns," "Lazer Sound Writing Retailing Hit with CD Software Specialization," "Furniture at CES: Aiming at New Upscale Market," "Suppliers Play Out Yen/Dollar Hand with Price Hikes, CES No-Shows." (5-86).
SCHL: Monthly, 180 pp.
SPAN: 1972+
VARIES
--? - ? as Consumer Electronics Monthly.
LC: HD 9696.A3 U532
DD: 338.4/7/62130973
ISSN: 0362-4722

Consumer Electronics Monthly
? - ?//
SEE: CONSUMER ELECTRONICS

✦ CONSUMER ELECTRONICS PRODUCT NEWS

SUB: "The product magazine for the consumer electronics market." (Jan, 1975 - ?).
PUBL: St. Regis Publications, 25 W. 45th St., New York, NY 10036.

DESC: This is another in a series of trade publications for the consumer electronics retailer. Smaller in scope and editorial content than *Consumer Electronics*, this serial nonetheless provides a wealth of material on new products. Of special interest is a new series of articles commencing with the March, 1977 edition entitled *Retail Manager's Sales Training Guide*, which provided specific instructions on how to sell a particular brand of product. This is an important feature for the novice salesperson about to meet his/her first customer. Numerous graphics.
DEPT: "Components," "Television," "Personal Communications," cb equipment; "Tape Recorders & Tape," "Autosound." (3-77).
TYPL: "Learn How Young Speaker Lines Get the Market to Listen," "Sales Handouts Provide Free Lunch," "Merchandise VTR and Expand Your TV Marketing." (3-77).
SCHL: Monthly, 56 pp.
SPAN: Jan, 1975+
VARIES
--Jan, 1975 - ? as CEPN.
LC: HD 9696.A3 U533
DD: 338.4/7/62130973
ISSN: 0097-8329

CONTEMPORARY PHOTOGRAPHER

PUBL: Contemporary Photographer, 132 Amory St., Brookline, MA 02416.
DESC: As befits its title, this publication focuses on avant-garde photography, contemporary photo-journalism, and photo-essays. Several articles preface each issue, with photos reflecting the new-found photo freedoms of the 1960s taking up the remainder of the publication. Printed on high-quality coated paper stock with few captions. In the sampled issue, only black/white photos were used.
DEPT: "Editorial," "Letters From," news of contemporary photography from Boston, New York, Japan, Minneapolis and other centers; "New Contributors."
TYPL: "An Idealistic Picture of the Photojournalist," "Charles Harbutt: the Multi-Level Picture Story," "Two Recent Exhibits at the Smithsonion Institution," "Profile of Poverty, Another View." (1-68).
SCHL: Bimonthly (May/Jun, 1960 - ?); Quarterly (?+), 85 pp.
SPAN: May/Jun, 1960 - Fall, 1971//
LC: TR 1.C76
DD: 770
ISSN: 0010-7506

CONTRAST

SUB: "The television quarterly."
PUBL: British Film Institute, 81 Dean St., London W1, England.
DESC: Editor Peter Black, writing the foreword in the premiere issue for Autumn, 1961 said in part, "...television seems so exciting that it becomes a marvel how dull most of it is in fact. This is a useful attitude to television, this constant pull of wonder and impatience against the inertia and complacency, inside and outside television, that seem very serious threats to television's development. Both sides, commercial and BBC, have in a sense had things too easy--a factor that they should remember when counting the heads of the audience for a particular show. *CONTRAST* will try to reflect this sense of wonder, impatience, critical concern, as it is among the 30 million who look at television and the few hunmred thousand who put it on for them to look at. Specifically the object is to provide comment on television programmes and on trends and developments in television. It will naturally concentrate on British Television but will be international in outlook and will acquire its own overseas correspondents." *CONTRAST* lived up to its promise of exploring the issues of the medium and its relationship to society at large. Articles not only spoke of current programming fare, but also took viewers "back stage" to see the process of production, and showcased the individuals who were part of the British television industry. For the sampled issue of 1961: editorial content consisted of black ink on coated paper stock with two-color ink cover on coated paper stock, limited advertising (6 7/8 x 9 1/2 inches / 175 x 245 mm).
DEPT: "Editorial," column by Peter Black. (summer-62).
TYPL: "Year of the New Brooms," "Donnybrook Fare," "Is TV Unfair Enough?," "Granada's Camino Real," "How to Make a Bonanza." (summer-62).
SCHL: Quarterly, 80 pp.
SPAN: Autumn, 1961 - 1966//
LC: PN 1992.C768
ISSN: 0589-5758

✤ CORPORATE TELEVISION

SUB: "The journal of the International Television Association."
SUB: "The official magazine of the International Television Association."
PUBL: Media Horizons, Inc., 50 West 23rd St., New York, NY 10010.
DESC: [*International Television*]: "*International Television* is not about video, it's about you and your professional use of this exciting and challenging medium. Depending on your current position-entrepreneur, corporate executive, government employee or academician-how you profit from television and the commercial and communication opportunities it can provide will be determined by how well you have mastered the technology." So began the letter from the publisher in the first issue of *International Television* in June, 1983. This Ziff-Davis publication was produced with editorial advisement by the International Television Association, a trade organization of non-broadcast television executives, producers and directors. While *International Television* did provide some news of the ITVA, primary emphasis was on the

technique and corporate management of current television operation. This was a very welcome addition to the non-broadcast video field.
DESC: [*Corporate Television*]: In its initial issue, editor Carl Levine noted: "Each issue of *Corporate Television* will focus on a specific topic of critical importance. This theme will be thoroughly covered in Continuing Reports, which appear regularly, and in the Special Reports for each issue. Our goal is to provide essential management and leading-edge technology information necessary for the successful operation of private television operations as well as the utilization of outside services." Tossing aside the yoke of stereotyped "industrial television," this serial reflects the new and powerful emergence of "corporate television," with facilities and operating budgets eclipsing that of traditional production houses and program suppliers. Corporate television is a business associate of the corporate community; with a function to support internal/external activities of its workforce, and the marketing of that company's product through a variety of media. To that end *Corporate Television* serves its readers well. Magazine format.
DEPT: "Guest Editorial," "Story-Board," unique production profile; "Creatively Thinking," ideas; "What's the Problem," "Your Business," "ITVA Today," "FYI," upcoming events; "In the News," newsbriefs; "Internationally Speaking," ITVA world news; "New Products," review. (11-83). "Guest Editorial," "Creative Techniques," "Story-Board," "What's the Problem?," "Your Business," "ITVA Today," "In the News," "FYI," column by David Hosansky. (7-85). "Editor's Note," "Corporate Imagery," animation and graphics; "Letters," "In-House Production," "Teleconference Update," "Research Report," "ITVA Report," news concerning International Television Association; "Facility Forum," "Regional Report," ITVA chapter news; "In Print," review; "Perspective," commentary. (3-87).
TYPL: "Video Networks: Sending Video Overseas," "Network Day-to-Day Management," "A Guide to Time Base Correction," "Effective Marketing Via Video," "Controlling Audio Levels Automatically." (11-83). "Planning an Interactive Program," "Long-Range Planning," "Signal Quality of VCRs." (7-85). "Designing an Editing Suite," "Buyers Speak Out," "The New Technical Choices," "NAB Corporate Directory," "Broadcast news: a Corporate Media Frontier." (3-87).
SCHL: Bimonthly (Jun, 1983 - ?); Monthly (Mar, 1985 - ?); Bimonthly (?+), 90 pp.
SPAN: Jun, 1983+
VARIES
--Jun, 1983 - Jul, 1986 as International Television (ISSN: 0737-3929).
LC: TK 6630.A1 C67
DD: 384.55/05 19
ISSN: 0889-4523

CORPORATE VIDEO DECISIONS

PUBL: Act III Publishing, Technical Group, 401 Park Avenue South, New York, NY 10016.
DESC: *Corporate Video Decisions* mirrored the explosive growth in the field of corporate video that had developed in the latter part of the 1980s. With facilities and budgets often outstripping their commercial kin, corporate video departments had become a medium unto its own. This publication, with a lively journalistic flair, explored the management, technology, production, and distribution of product for the corporate video community. It was considered especially valuable for its articles on successful management techniques applied to the corporate video field. Articles described corporate studios, operations, maintenance, and application of video to corporate needs and perceptions. In September, 1990 Act III Publishing sold the publication to PSN which absorbed it into its trade magazine, *Videography*. Magazine format (8 x 10 ⅞ inches / 205 x 275 mm), numerous color graphics.
DEPT: "Editor's Notes," "News," newsbriefs; "Outside Services," outside support suppliers; "Management Strategies," "Video Conferencing," "Presentation Graphics," "New Products," "Executive Outlook," application. (5-89). "Editor's Notes," editorial column by James Kaminsky; "News," "Outside Services," available production resources, news and trends; "Management Strategies," "Screening Room," 'A critical look at the latest business videos'; "New Products," "Executive Outlook," interview. (8-90).
TYPL: "Chargeback: Who Foots the Bill?," "Playback Decks Move to Center Stage," "Fast-Food Order: Video, Well-Done," "Detroit: Motown Production Isn't Just Motors Anymore." (5-89). "Where Does Video Fit in the Communications Mix?," "The Communications Blitz: Preparing for a High-Tech Revolution," "Corporations Stay Out of the Digital Domain," "Publishing: The Printed Word Meets the Moving Image," "Dallas: Survival in the Lone Star State." (8-90).
SCHL: Monthly, 65 pp.
SPAN: Sep, 1988 - Aug, 1990//
ABSORBED BY
--Videography (ISSN: 0363-1001), Sep, 1990.
DD: 384 11
ISSN: 1050-8287

✛ COSMEP NEWSLETTER

SUB: "Committee of Small Magazine Editors and Publishers."
SUB: "The international association of independent publishers."
PUBL: COSMEP, Inc., PO Box 703, San Francisco, CA 94101.
DESC: "With more than 1,300 current members, COSMEP is the largest organization of publishers in the United States. Established in Berkeley, California in 1968, by the editors of forty presses and literary magazines, the organization has grown to its current size and international membership... COSMEP services include net-

working the large and diverse membership through publication of a monthly newsletter. The newsletter includes extensive coverage of publishing and marketing opportunities both in this country and abroad, as well as providing a forum for the exchange of problems and solutions among the members of COSMEP, many of whom are recognized authorities in their own fields of publishing." Membership in COSMEP is open "...to any publisher who is not a member of a publishing conglomerate." A fascinating newsletter for the small, independent publisher, providing a forum for discussion, news of the industry, and potential trends for publishing in the future, it is well worth the $50 membership fee. For the sampled 1991 issues: black ink on beige uncoated paper stock in stapled newsletter format; no graphics or advertising (8 ½ x 11 inches / 215 x 280 mm).

DEPT: "News Notes," newsbriefs from members concerning publishing; "Dear Deborah," legal Q&A on publishing column by Deborah Michelle Sanders; "Letters," "News of Members," from this international association of independent publishers. (6-90).

TYPL: "COSMEP 23rd Annual Publishers' Conference," "Literary Market Place 'Small Presses' Listings," "Joys of Book Publishing," "Book Marketing: Gaining an Edge." (6-90).

SCHL: Monthly, 8 pp.

SPAN: Mar, 1981+
VARIES
--Aug, 1969 - May, 1980 as COSMEP Newsletter (ISSN: 0007-8832).
--Jun, 1980 - Feb, 1981 as Independent Publisher, The.

ISSN: 0007-8832

COSMEP Newsletter

Aug, 1969 - May, 1980//
(ISSN: 0007-8832)
SEE: COSMEP NEWSLETTER

CPB Memo

1970? - Aug 23, 1974//
SEE: REPORT

CPB Report

? - May 10, 1982//
SEE: REPORT

✣ CQ

SUB: "The radio amateur's journal."
SUB: "A magazine of, by and for commercial radio operators and technicians."
SUB: "Serving amateur radio since 1945."
SUB: "Amateur Radio."

DESC: A subscription promotion says it all: "Tune in with *CQ*, The Ham's Magazine. All year long *CQ* brings you the best writers. . .the best reading in Amateur Radio. Written and edited to be enjoyed as much as you enjoy Ham Radio itself. Not just good. It's the best!" A photo-filled monthly designed for the American radio amateur, there are articles on new equipment, new techniques for improving signals and news of basic electronics. The focus concerns pictures and news items of radio amateurs and their equipment. All articles are written by current operating radio amateurs. Articles provide practical information on purchasing, setting up, and operating amateur radio equipment, and serve to tie geographically diverse ham operators through reports on regional club activities and individual installations. The friendliness and helpful attitude connected with ham radio operators is evident. For anyone interested in this fascinating field of amateur radio, *CQ* is indeed "the best!" Issues for Jul/Aug, 1970 were combined. For sampled issue of 1972: stapled journal format, primarily black ink with spot and full-color pages and full-color cover on coated paper stock (5 ⅞ x 9 inches / 150 x 230 mm). For sampled issue of 1991: Stapled magazine format with mixture of black ink, spot and full-color pages and full-color cover on coated paper stock (8 ⅛ x 10 ⅞ inches / 205 x 275 mm).

DEPT: "Announcements," club notes; "Contest Calendar," "DX," news of international radio amateurs; "Ham Clinic," Q&A on equipment; "Ham Shop," classifieds; "Letters," "Novice," news of the novice group; "Propagation," atmospheric conditions; "QSL Contest," "RTTY," "Side Band," "Space Communications," "USA-CA," "VHF," "YL," "Zero Bias," editorial. (2-63). "Announcements," club notes; "Contest Calendar," column by Frank Anzalone; "DX," news of international radio amateurs, column by Jerry Hagen; "Our Readers Say," letters; "Propagation," column by George Jacobs; "Q&A," technical reader-submitted questions, column by Wilfred M. Scherer; "The Awards Program," column by Ed Hopper; "F.M.," column by Glen E. Zook; "Math's Notes," column by Irwin Math; "Surplus Sidelights," unusual military surplus equipment column by Gordon Eliot White. (9-72). "Awards," 'News of certificate and award collecting' column by Hugh S. Unger; "Propagation," 'The science of predicting radio conditions' column by George Jacobs; "Contest Calendar," 'News/views of on-the-air competition' column by John Dorr; "DX," 'News of communication around the world' column by Chod Harris; "Bill's Basics," 'How-to for the newcomer to amateur radio', column by Bill Welsh; "Washington Readout," 'Regulatory happenings from the world of amateur radio', column by Frederick O. Maia; "CQ Showcase," new products; "VHF Plus," 'All about the world above HF', column by Joe Lynch; "Radio FUNdamentals," 'Things to learn, projects to build, and gear to use', column by Bill Orr; "Zero Bias," editorial; "Announcements." (8-91).

TYPL: "The Overtone-Harmonic Crystal Oscillator," "Automatic RTTY and C.W. With Multi-Gates," "A 'G-Line' For UHF," "Taming the Diode Field Strength Meter," "The Care and Feeding of TV Rotators." (2-63). "Slow-Scanning Color," "SSTV: Electrostatic Deflection CR Tubes," "FM: ARRL 220 and 420 MHZ Band Plans Criticized," "Identifying Unmarked Surplus Digital IC's." (9-72). "Building the Ultimate Rotating Tower," "How to Build a Remotely Controlled Bridge for Impedance Matching," "Build a Mini HF KW Dummy Load," "Tuning Antennas Without a Transceiver," "Packet User's Notebook: The Future of Digital Communications." (8-91).
SCHL: Monthly, 130 pp.
SPAN: Jan, 1945+
VARIES
--Jan, 1977 - ? as Amateur Radio.
ABSORBED
--Ham Radio, Jun, 1990.
LC: TK 6540.C18
DD: 621.38405
ISSN: 0007-893x
ABST: --Computer & Control Abstracts (ISSN: 0036-8113)
--Electrical & Electronics Abstracts (ISSN: 0036-8105)
--Physics Abstracts. Science Abstracts. Series A. (ISSN: 0036-8091)

✣ CRC NEWSLETTER

PUBL: Communications Research Center, College of Communications, University of Tennessee, Knoxville, TN 37916.
DESC: This four-page newsletter by the College of Communications, University of Tennessee, provides briefs of current communications research. The briefs are drawn from current trade and academic journals with sources cited.
DEPT: "Broadcasting Research," "Journalism Research," "Advertising Research," "Current Research in the College of Communications."
TYPL: "The Fate of PR Releases to Radio," "Consumers are Skeptical About Discount Ads," "Wire Editors Know Their Readers."
SCHL: Irregular, 4 pp.
SPAN: Jan, 1975+

✣ CREATIVE CAMERA

SUB: "Art, images, ideas."
PUBL: Creative Camera, Battersea Arts Centre, Old Town Hall, Lavender Hill, London SW11 5TF, England.
DESC: *Creative Camera* appears to have existed in two very distinct, unique, and commendable formats, each one providing a serious showcase for different needs and issues in photography. Early pre-1980 issues were exclusively black/white graphics on coated paper stock. This photographic serial demonstrated exquisite care in editing and publishing that manifested itself in picture reproduction, typography, and layout design. Sections showcased the works of historical and current professionals, and provided commentary on the general state of professional photography. Publisher Colin Osman even informed the reader when picture negatives were both shot and printed by the named photographer, a commendable effort to maintain purity within the total creative process. The sampled issues for 1991 indicate a slight change in format design and the inclusion of color, both in the presented photographs, and in the cover. Editor David Brittain has maintained the integrity of early classic issues, but has expanded international contributions and interviews with those artists. No matter whether early or contemporary issues are at hand, *Creative Camera* remains a celebration of the beauty and vitality of life as seen through the photographic lens. An excellent publication for those serious about photography as art and as medium of expression. For the sampled issues of 1991: black/white and full-color pages and cover on coated paper stock in stapled magazine format (8 ¼ x 11 inches / 210 x 280 mm).
DEPT: "Views," comment; "Gallery," 'guide, products, news'. (9-71). "News/Listings," "Talkback," editorial column by David Brittain; "Letters," "Books in Brief," "Reviews." (8/9-91).
TYPL: "Bill Brandt Photograph," "John Benton-Harris Boot Camp," "Howard Selina Pieces of America." (9-71). "Film as Crime," "The Garden," "CC Profile," "Of Nature," "Inscribed Sights." (8/9-91).
SCHL: Monthly, 50 pp.
SPAN: 1963+?
VARIES
--1963? - Jul, 1967 as Camera Owner.
--Aug, 1967 - Jan, 1968 as Creative Camera Owner.
LC: TR 640.C74
DD: 770/.5
ISSN: 0011-0876
ABST: --Art Index (ISSN: 0004-3222)

Creative Camera Owner
Aug, 1967 - Jan, 1968//
SEE: CREATIVE CAMERA

✣ CRITIC

PUBL: American Federation of Film Societies, 144 Bleecker St., New York, NY 10012.
DESC: "*Film Critic* is intended to be a critical film magazine. Hopefully, a good critical film magazine. In any event, a highly un'conventional' critical film magazine. 'Conventional' criticism still suffers heavily from the fact that its practitioners are heirs to the failings of the Two-Cultures Syndrome: they 'still,' as C.P. Snow points out, 'like to pretend that the traditional culture is the whole of culture.'" With that introductory editorial, *Critic* went on to showcase critical film journalism, especially from "young campus critics." Departmental features from *Critic*'s predecessor, *Film Society Review*, were continued in the new publication. Some graphics; small format.

DEPT: "News," "Television," "Press," "International," "Commentary," "Books," "Letters." (11/12-72).
TYPL: "Karlovy Vary--the Persistence of (re)Vision," "Vichy Cinema: the 'Official Myths' of the Nazi Occupation Years." (11/12-72).
SCHL: Nine issues per year (1963 - Mar/May, 1972); Bimonthly (?+), 85 pp.
SPAN: Oct, 1956?+
VARIES
--Oct, 1956 - Jun, 1957 as American Federation of Film Societies. Newsletter.
--? - ? as AFFS Newsletter.
--? - Winter, 1962? as For Film.
--1963 - Apr, 1965 as Film Society Newsletter.
--Sep, 1965 - Mar/May, 1972 as Film Society Review (ISSN: 0015-1408).
LC: PN 1993.C78
DD: 791.43/05
ISSN: 0090-9831

✦ CRITICAL STUDIES IN MASS COMMUNICATION

SUB: "A publication of the Speech Communication Association."
PUBL: Speech Communication Association, 5105 Backlick Rd., #E, Annandale, VA 22003.
DESC: "*Critical Studies in Mass Communication* provides a forum for cross-disciplinary research and welcomes a wide range of theoretical orientations and methodological approaches. Our focus is broad and includes the evolution, organization, control, economics, administration, and technological innovations of mass communication systems; the form and structure of mass media content; the relationship between culture and mass commuication; and the analysis or illustration of mass media criticism." A later issue noted that "*Critical Studies in Mass Communication* is a cross-disciplinary forum for the study of mass communication. While the Journal encourages diverse theoretical and methodological orientations, material submitted should be critically framed by addressing (1) the significance to mass communication scholarship of the phenomenon studied, and (2) the relevant epistemological and ideological questions raised in studying that phenomenon. The subject matter studied, whether represented by original research and/or theory and/or literature analysis, should be revealed as an illustration of a larger critical problem." This journal has become a standard in the academic communication community for considered analysis, commentary, and research, and is highly recommended for those interested in this dynamic field. For sampled issue of 1991: journal format, editorial content consisting of black ink on uncoated paper stock with graphs, charts, and schematics in support of articles, cover is two-color blue and black ink on coated paper stock (6 3/8 x 10 inches / 170 x 255 mm).
DEPT: "CSMC Booknotes," (12-86). "CSMC Booknotes," reviews. (9-88).
TYPL: "Television: Polysemy and Popularity," "A Window on the World?: Foreign Coverage by a British Radio Current Affairs Program," "Demythologizing Media: Recent Writings in Critical and Institutional Theory," "Conceptualizing Culture as Commodity: The Problem of Television." (12- 86). "Work Songs, Hegemony, and Illusions of Self," "The Homology Hypothesis: Pornography on the VCR," "The Audience as Nuisance," "The Real World of Audiences," "Researching Televangelism." (9-88).
SCHL: Quarterly, 95pp.
SPAN: Mar, 1984+
LC: P 87 .C73
DD: 302.23/05 20
ISSN: 0739-3180

CSCC Newsletter

? - ?//
SEE: COMMUNICATION RESEARCH TRENDS

CSPAA BULLETIN

PUBL: Columbia Scholastic Press Advisers Association, Box 11, Central Mail Room, Columbia University, New York, NY 10027.
DESC: For over 55 years, the *CSPAA Bulletin*, with its various titles, provided succinct news for those individuals supervising journalism programs at schools and colleges. It was for this common goal that the Columbia Scholastic Press Association was formed. The first *Bulletin* was mimeographed from 1930 to October, 1942 when it was suspended "for the duration," like many other printed publications throughout the world. The *Bulletin* resumed publication with the December, 1946 issue with the premise: "Through its pages advisers should be kept informed of changing trends and current problems. It should perform a two-fold function of presenting the viewpoint of the Association and of serving as a medium of expression for our problems and our ideas." With the October, 1950 issue the format moved from mimeographed newsletter to "cold type" small journal format, and finally to lithographic process in the early 1970s. In March, 1986 the Association determined to once again contain the editorial content of the *CSPAA Bulletin* within the pages of the Association magazine, *The School Press Review*, which previously had been the case during the late 1930s. For the 1986 sampled issue: black ink on uncoated paper stock in stapled magazine format with purple ink on uncoated paper stock cover (5 1/2 x 8 3/8 inches / 140 x 215 mm).
DEPT: "Current Literature Reviews." (summer-86).
TYPL: "A Judge Gives Today's Newspapers a Critique," "As a Teacher, I Find Myself Serving as That Editing Partner with My Students," "Former Yearbook Editor Suggests How to Avoid Those Terrible Photographs." (summer-86).
SCHL: Quarterly, 20 pp.
SPAN: Summer?, 1930 - Summer, 1986//

VARIES
--? - ? as The Advisers Bulletin.
--? - Spring, 1979 as Bulletin.
--Summer, 1979 - ? as Bulletin of the Columbia Scholastic Press Advisors Association.
ISSN: 0010-1990
ABST: --Current Index to Journals in Education (ISSN: 0011-3565)

✥ CTVD

SUB: "A quarterly review of the serious, foreign-language cinema-TV-press." (winter, 1961/62 - ?).
SUB: "Cinema, TV digest."
PUBL: Hampton Books, Route 1, Box 202, Newberry, SC 29108.
DESC: "*CTVD* is to fill a need that has long existed...to bring together into one place the current thought of the best film critics and film students, whose work is for most of us locked up in the cells of languages other than English. It is our task to break open those cells and let out the treasure. Let us make clear one point right now and forever--*CTVD* reports what the film critics say--*CTVD* does not criticize. We are, on what we hope is a high plane, a 'news magazine.' We give the news of what is going on in the highest intellectual reaches of cinema: we do not make that news." This is an outstanding resource for any film researcher, distributor, or producer on the state of international film product production and consumption. Primarily intended for an academic audience. Small journal format.
DEPT: "The Hot & Cold Eye," film reviews; "Books." (fall-63). "News," 'What's happening or shouldn't have;' "Television," "Hot & Cold Eye." (winter-1972/73).
SCHL: Quarterly (irregular at times), 30 pp.
SPAN: Winter, 1961/1962+
LC: P 87 .C25
DD: 791.43/7
ISSN: 0007-9219

✥ CURRENT

SUB: "For people in public telecommunications."
PUBL: Current Publishing Committee, 2311 18th St., NW, Washington, DC 20009.
DESC: *Current* is a spritely tabloid newspaper designed to keep public radio and television station staff members abreast of the latest news in public telecommunications. Replacing the early educational viewpoint days are articles that deal with ratings, money, programming, audiences, and again (inevitably) money, without which public programming cannot survive. This is a lively newspaper reflecting the exciting changes in public programming. Graphics; published on newsprint.
DEPT: "Current Commentary," "Calendar," "Current People," newsbriefs; "Awards and Grants," "M Street Law," 'The law in public broadcasting'; "Program Pipeline," "Radio Intelligence," 'Research news and knowledge you can use;' "Current Monitor." (12-22-87).
TYPL: "Public Broadcasting Trust Fund Killed," "NPR Board Endorses Unbundling Plan," "Congress Agrees on 1990 Money," "'Kids America' Goes Off the Air." (12-22-87).
SCHL: Monthly (? - Mar, 1979); Semimonthly (Mar 15, 1980+), 24 pp.
SPAN: 19uu+
VARIES
--19uu - 1964 as National Association of Educational Broadcasters Newsletter (ISSN: 0027-8610).
--1964 - Mar, 1979 as NAEB Letter.
--Apr/May, 1979 - Jan/Feb, 1980 as Public Telecommunications Letter.
ISSN: 0739-991x

CURRENT ADVERTISING

PUBL: Charles Austin Bates, 132 Nassau St., New York, NY.
DESC: In January, 1903, upon the sale of *Current Advertising*, advertising statesman Charles Austin Bates told his readers: "When I started *Charles Austin Bates Criticisms* in 1897, it was chiefly with the idea of having fun with it. I wanted a place in which I could say whatever I pleased about anything and anybody." Bates oftentimes took friend and foe alike to task for advertising layout, design, or editorial philosophy. Latter issues traded advertising space for Bate's spicy commentary, and the reader was wiser for it. Numerous graphics.
DEPT: "Printed Things," "Magazine Publicity," "Trade Papers." (12-02).
TYPL: "Epistles from St. Paul," "A Striking Circular," "A Good Example of a Bad Card." (2-1898). "Mail Order Possibilities," "Advertising in New Zealand." (12-02).
SCHL: Monthly, 70 pp.
SPAN: Jan, 1897 - Jan, 1903//
VARIES
--Jan, 1897 - Mar, 1900 as Charles Austin Bates Criticisms.
ABSORBED BY
--Profitable Advertising.
LC: HF 5801.C8

Curtain

Oct, 1969 - ?//
SEE: DRAMATICS

✥ CWA NEWS

PUBL: Communications Workers of America, 1925 K ST., N.W., Washington, DC 20006.
DESC: As the official publication of the Communications Workers of America, this 12-page, small-format newspaper's primary function is to disseminate infor-

mation among union members. News concerns the current state of the union, strikes, talks, issues, conferences and conventions.
DEPT: "Communique," CWA president's column; "Opinion," editorial; "Consumers Corner."
TYPL: "Drive Launched for Texas State Workers," "CWA Opens Talks with the Bell System," "CWA's Denver Meeting an Historic Event," "First Public Employee Conference Held." (6-80).

SCHL: Monthly, 12 pp.
SPAN: May, 1941+
VARIES
--May, 1941 - Jun, 1947 as Telephone Worker.
SUSPENDED
--Apr, 1947 - May, 1947.
LC: HD 6350.T23C2
ISSN: 0007-9227

D

DA

Jan, 1943? - #3, 1977//
(ISSN: 0011-4693)
SEE: PRINTING PAPER

✧ DAILY VARIETY

SUB: "News of the show world."
PUBL: Daily Variety, Ltd., 5700 Wilshire Blvd., Los Angeles, CA 90036.
DESC: *Daily Variety* a well-renowned publication, is one of "The" sources for information on the very competitive media of film and television. And it emanates from Hollwood, California, where the "deal" is still made and the product produced that will grace silver and black-matrixed screens world-wide. Like its weekly counterpart, *Daily Variety*, which is published daily, covers both the hard news and the "talk-around-town" concerning motion pictures, radio-TV, records, and legitimate stage. Unlike its weekly counterpart, however, *Daily Variety* is more likely to use standard journalistic English. It is a superb source for both reliable and "hearsay" information of the mass communications industry. Highly recommended for all those on the "for-profit" side of the industry.
DEPT: "Pix, People, Pickups," news of new productions just signed; "Just for Variety," news bits about personalities; "Showbiz Stock Transactions," yesterday's stock quotations; "Film Review," Variety's famed critical review of new releases; "Obituaries," also well-known section for its in-depth information usually not found elsewhere.
TYPL: "Wiley Doubts Public Would Benefit from Reducing TV Reruns to Boost H'Wood Jobs," "Eleven AFTRA Locals Agree to New Commercials Pact," "Film Biz Figures are Expected to be Called in Tax Investigation." (2-76).
SCHL: Daily except Saturday, Sunday, and holidays, with a special edition the last week in October, 12 pp.
SPAN: 1933+
LC: PN 1993.D3
ISSN: 0011-5509

✧ DAREDEVILS

SUB: "Adventure films and television."
SUB: "Presenting the most important interviews, guides and reviews of daredevils in movies on television and print."
SUB: "The magazine of adventure."
PUBL: New Media Publishing, Inc., 1518 East Fowler Ave., Tampa, FL 33612.
DESC: In an inner-cover promotion for the magazine, Publisher/Editor Hal Schuster noted the editorial philosophy of *Daredevils*: "Regularly featuring Star Trek Guide featuring the original TV series that started it all in the most complete guide ever printed. (Prepared by *Enterprise Incidents* Editor James Van Hise). James Bond Movies, presenting the complete information on everyone's favorite spy. (Prepared by America's expert on British features, John Peel, Editor of *Fantasy Empire*). The Stars, gives complete filmographies and intimate looks at your favorite actors and actresses... those people who bring adventure to life. Plus looks at the latest in the media, reviews of important television shows and much more." Letters from readers are enthusiastic about the form and content of this monthly publication devoted to adventure in film and television. Coming in for special recognition is the continuing practice of printing several program episode profiles per issue, listing program title, writers' credits, television network air date, primary crew and cast members, plot synopses, and a very helpful episode analysis that provides insight into the episode vis a vis the entire series. At least one black/white episode picture accompanies each description. Articles are unusually detailed and not only cover specific series, but Editor Schuster graciously promotes other publications and/or membership organizations relevant to the motion picture or television series under discussion. Layout design is professional and printed black/white on quality uncoated paperstock, with full-color cover on coated paperstock. Stapled magazine format (8 ⅜ x 10 ⅞ inches / 215 x 275 mm).
DEPT: "Editorial," "Daredevil Newsbits," "Daring Comments," letters. (8-84).
TYPL: "The Neverending Story," "Will the Real James Bond Please Stand Up," "Riptide," "Star Trek Season Guide," "The Fan From Uncle." (8-84).
SCHL: Monthly, 55 pp.
SPAN: Nov, 1983+?

✧ DARKROOM AND CREATIVE CAMERA TECHNIQUES

PUBL: Preston Publications, 7800 North Merrimac Ave., Niles, IL 60648.
DESC: For the photographer serious about his/her craft from picture-taking, through darkroom processing, to final mounting and exhibition; *Darkroom and Creative Camera Techniques* provides a wealth of information, with creative examples of the art and craft of photography. It is a treasure-chest of authoritative information on the technique and technical side of the

photographic field. Typical articles from the 1980s included special-effect filters, color bleaches, prints from slides and infrared photography, the future of densitometry, a photographer's guide to film and paper, curing agitation woes, black and white exhibition papers, and copying old photographs. One of the wonderful aspects of this periodical is the side-by-side comparisons of variations in technique, allowing the reader to decide which process to follow. All photographs provide full details on camera, film, processing, and other techniques utilized. As the publisher stated, "Each bimonthly issue brings you in-depth practical information and innovative ideas to help you develop a higher level of competence in picture-taking and picture-making." We couldn't agree more. Magazine format (8 1/8 x 10 7/8 inches / 205 x 275 mm), full color throughout on coated paper stock.

DEPT: "Photograms," letters; "Photo Flashes," newsbriefs; "Photochemistry Question and Answer," technical column by Robert Chapman; "Questions on Photography," column by Ron Jegerings; "Product Proofs," very detailed new product reviews. (9/10-90).
TYPL: "Zone System Contraction," "C-Print Contrast Reduction," "Divided Developer for Cibachrome," "Professional Portfolio: Coloring Every Moment," "VC Paper and Exhibition-Quality Prints." (9/10-90).
SCHL: Quarterly (Fall, 1979 - 1982); Bimonthly (1983+), 80 pp.
SPAN: Jan, 1979+
VARIES
--Fall, 1979 - Nov/Dec, 1983 as Darkroom Techniques (ISSN: 0195-3850).
ISSN: 0195-3850

✣ DARKROOM PHOTOGRAPHY

SUB: "The magazine for creative photographers." (? - Oct, 1984).
PUBL: Sheptow Publishing, One Hallidie Plaza, San Francisco, CA 94102.
DESC: In the premiere issue of March/April, 1979, Publisher Paul M. Sheptow told new readers of the desire for a magazine concerning darkroom photography: "The need stems from the basic fact that in photography, 'taking the picture' is only the beginning. It is a most critical beginning, but still it is only the first step in the chain of events leading to an enjoyable photograph. The steps after 'taking the picture' are 'developing' and 'printing' ...two significant areas most often neglected by current photographic publications. It is this void that *DARKROOM PHOTOGRAPHY* will fill. *DARKROOM PHOTOGRAPHY* will concentrate on well-written and well-researched articles, but our most important credo is: 'photography is fun!'." Articles for the first year of publication included, "A 6-Step Recipe for Posterization," "Diary of a Darkroom Improvisor," "Table Salt Printing on Fabric," "The Pleasures of Platinum," and "A Candid Guide to Print Washers." Early issues often contained a full-color centerfold poster. For the sampled issues of 1979 and 1984: mixture of black/white and full-color pages and cover on coated paper stock, advertising (7 3/4 x 10 3/4 inches / 195 x 275 mm).

DEPT: "Editor's Page," editorial column by Kimberly Torgerson; "Product Probe," "Larger Formats," column by Bobby Adams; "Color Corner," column by George Post; "Basics," of photography column by George Schaub; "Making Money," in photography, column by Maria Piscopo; "Special Effects," column by Nick Steadman; "Q&A," reader-submitted questions; "Grab Shots," newsbriefs; "Mailbox," letters; "Readers Tips," photographic shortcuts; "Final Frame," 'reserved for images that have been altered in some way'. (12-84).
TYPL: "Photogifts," "Artful Ties," "Ticket to Danger," "Color Printing Handbook," "Darkroom Discoveries." (12-84).
SCHL: Eight issues per year [Bimonthly Jan - Aug, and monthly Sep - Dec], 85 pp.
SPAN: Mar/Apr, 1979+?
ISSN: 0163-9250

Darkroom Photography

? - Nov, 1990//
(ISSN: 0163-9250)
SEE: CAMERA & DARKROOM PHOTOGRAPHY

Darkroom Techniques

Fall, 1979 - Nov/Dec, 1983//
(ISSN: 0195-3850)
SEE: DARKROOM AND CREATIVE CAMERA TECHNIQUES

✣ DARKSLIDE

PUBL: National Press Photographers Association, Region 7, The Wichita Eagle, DayBreak Section, 820 East Douglas, Wichita, KS 67201.
DESC: An outstanding quarterly membership publication of Region 7 National Press Photographers Association members, this is primarily a showcase for member photographs. These are news photographs, at times poignant, at times startling, but each one providing a clear, strong message. Some articles describe on-going issues of importance to press photographers, while other sections detail chapter news. By far the largest segment of the serial is listed under "Clips," a showcase for member photographs. Note: no publication date, volume or issue number information was present in sample issue. Magazine format; black/white graphics.
DEPT: "Opinions," "Clip Standings," "Chapter News," "Clips." (4-90).
TYPL: "Death as a Fact of Life in the Community," "Activists Expect the World to be Watching," "The Class of 2000." (4-90).
SCHL: Quarterly, 24 pp.
SPAN: ?+

✣ DASH WORLD

SUB: "A publication for the international recording community."
PUBL: Sony Broadcast & Communications, Jays Close, Viables, Basingstoke, Hampshire RG22 4SB, England.
DESC: This is a well-produced, self-promotional "newsletter" by Sony Broadcast & Communications for their proprietary audio recording DASH format. Employing vivid color and imaginative layout design, this semiyearly tabloid proclaims the Sony audio format through interviews with studio owners, artists, engineers, and recording studio owners worldwide. Indeed, in the Spring, 1990 issue *Dash World* even provided a chart of "Worldwide DASH Multi-Track Sales at the Time of Going to Press." For the 1990 sampled issue: small tabloid stapled format, full color graphics and editorial content throughout on coated paper stock, sample issues distributed as an insert to *Studio Sound* magazine (9 ½ x 13 inches / 240 x 330 mm).
DEPT: None. (spring-90).
TYPL: "Changing the Nashville Skyline," "Germany Unified Behind DASH," "Bob Clearmountain--Editing Digitally with DASH." (spring-90).
SCHL: Semiyearly, 8 pp.
SPAN: Winter, 1990+

✣ DAYTIME TV

SUB: "Twenty years the authority."
PUBL: Sterling's Magazines, 355 Lexington Ave, New York, NY 10017.
DESC: For the daytime television fan, life begins after morning news, and ends with local station programming during late afternoon drive time. In between, there is a myriad of quiz shows, network reruns, and soap operas to please the audience of *Daytime TV*. It is the "soaps" that attracts these readers, with behind-the-scenes and on-camera stories that at times suggest that lives on and off- screen are pretty much the same. For over 15 years, *Daytime TV* has provided thorough coverage of daytime television programming, and has won the support of the American consumer public. Numerous graphics; printed on quality newsprint (8 x 10 ⅞ inches / 205 x 275 mm).
DEPT: "Latest News," "Soap Opera Festival," meeting stars in person; "Nighttime Soap News," "Plotline Hotline," plot developments; "Inside Hollywood," newsbriefs; "Letters to Editor," "Latest Cast Lists," of soap operas; "Readers Poll." (6-86). "Latest News," column by Anne Marie Allocca; "Soap Opera Festival," column by Joyce Becker; "Inside Hollywood," 'Daytime TV's West coast woman in the know!' column by Janet DiLauro; "You the Viewer," letters; "Fan Club Listings," "Role Call," 'Complete cast lists of all the shows'; "Readers' Poll," "Nielsen Ratings," "Soap Doctor," 'We answer your questions'; "Birthdays of the Stars!" (3-90).
TYPL: "Will Frisco Fade-Out Forever?," "John Travolta Will Dance at Our Wedding," "I'll Help You Remember the Love We Shared," "A Little Hot Hate Brought Us Together." (6-86). "True to Life," "They Worked Hard for the Money," "America the Beautiful," "The Frisco Kid Returns," "Courting Success." (3-90).
SCHL: Bimonthly, 90 pp.
SPAN: Winter, 1970+
LC: PN 1992.8 .S4D39
DD: 051
ISSN: 0011-7129

Daytimers

198u - 198u//
(ISSN: 0744-3935)
SEE: REAL LIFE/DAYTIMERS

✣ DB

SUB: "The sound engineering magazine."
SUB: "Serving: recording, broadcast and sound contracting fields."
PUBL: Sagamore Publishing Co., 1120 Old Country Rd., Plainview, NY 11803.
DESC: *db* magazine serves the technical side of audio recording, and is written for the professional audio-engineer. Articles emphasize the behind-the-scenes aspects of professional audio recording today, dealing with new technology, applications of same, case studies, road reports, and studio operation. For over 20 years *db* has served the recording engineer community with practical advice, new applications, and discussions on the state of the recording industry. Later issues are split into two sections, The Recording Engineer (and) The Broadcast Engineer. With well-illustrated schematics, knowledge of electronics assumed. For the sampled issues of 1991: black ink, with spot-color pages, advertising and cover in full-color on coated paper stock in perfect-bound magazine format (8 ¼ x 10 ⅞ inches / 210 x 280 mm).
DEPT: "Theory and Practice," "Computer Audio," "Digital Audio," "Sound Reinforcement," "Letters," "Editorial," "New Products and Services," "People, Places, Happenings." (6-84). "Letters," "Editorial," "New Products," "People, Places, Happenings." (11/12-86).
TYPL: "Problems with CDs--Real or Imagined," "A Soundmixer's Guide to Videodisc," "Development of a New Studio Artificial Head," "The Golden Age of Radio Returns." (6-84). "Looking into the Future to Improve the Past," "Mastering Digital Broadway," "Recording Techniques: Sampling, Sequencing, and MIDI," "Asset Disposition." (11/12-86).
SCHL: Monthly (? - ?); Bimonthly (?+), 60 pp.
SPAN: 1967+
DD: 621
ISSN: 0011-7145
ABST: --Applied Science and Technology Index (ISSN: 0003-6986)
--Computer & Control Abstracts (ISSN: 0036-8113)
--Electrical & Electronics Abstracts (ISSN: 0036-8105)
--Physics Abstracts. Science Abstracts. Series A. (ISSN: 0036-8091)

✧ DBS NEWS

SUB: "Including DBS radio, HDTV, SMATV, and TVRO."
PUBL: Phillips Publishing, Inc., 7811 Montrose Rd., Potomac, MD 20854.
DESC: In a back-page panel of this monthly publication, the editors told prospective subscribers, "In today's numerous and diverse video markets you need in-depth and reliable information. Phillips Publishing's Video Group publications will give you dependable and original news, reporting, research, analysis and forecasts you will use to gain a competitive advantage." Even at a 1991 subscription price of $347 per year, *DBS News* is a "must-read" publication for those in the electronic communication field whose livlihoods demand they stay up to date on regulatory, economic, and technological developments in the direct broadcast satellite industry. Senior Managing Editor Susan J. Aluise, Senior Editor David Bross, and Editor Britton Manasco compile a very compact, succinct summary of news events. The use of several news pictures each issue (rare in newsletter publications), serves to enhance an already valuable news medium. It is excellent for those who need to know what is happening in the satellite television field; representative of the quality approach to communication news found in all Phillips publications. Printed black ink on gold uncoated paper stock with graphics (8 ½ x 11 inches / 215 x 280 mm).
DEPT: "Regulation," "DBS Radio," "International," "DBS in Brief," "Legal." (4-91).
TYPL: "Skypix Corporation Receives $30 Million Investment from HSN," "Cable Unveils Fall HDTV Plans; First Medium to Offer Technology," "Cable Rereg Back on Capitol Hill; Program Access in the Crossfire," "DAB TAsk Force Cheers Eureka; Dissenters Say Test Unimportant," "Eutelsat's Pre-Europesat Satellite: Signatories Endorse the Project." (4-91).
SCHL: Monthly, 10 pp.
SPAN: Sep, 1982+
SUSPENDED
--Jul, 1988 - Jul, 1990.
DD: 384
ISSN: 0733-9739
ABST: --Predicasts

DEALERSCOPE

SUB: "The people magazine of the home electronics, appliance and personal electronics industry."
SUB: "The industry magazine for appliances, consumer electronics, and home entertainment."
PUBL: Bartex Publishing Group, Inc., 115 2nd Ave., Waltham, MA 02154.
DESC: Providing trade news for the electronics retailer is the primary function of this 60-page publication. New product introductions are showcased, along with marketing advice on current staples. One important element of this trade serial is to analyze future directions of trade, manufacturing, and the fickle nature of the American buying public. Numerous graphics.
DEPT: "Viewpoint," "LIFO," new product newsbriefs; "Far Forward," product promotion; "20 Years Ago," "People," "On the Floor," sales floor tactics; "Cellular Parade," "Software Sampler," "New Products," "News," "Portfolio," electronic industry stocks; "StatWatch," statistics. (10- 84).
TYPL: "Superstore Retailers," "Tis the Season for Computers," "Mass Merchandising Video Software." (10-84).
SCHL: Monthly, 56 pp.
SPAN: ? - Feb, 1986//
MERGED WITH
--Merchandising (ISSN: 0362-3920) (to form) Dealerscope Merchandising (ISSN: 0888-4501).
LC: HD 9971.U6D4
DD: 338.4/768383/0973
ISSN: 0011-7218

✧ DEBUT

SUB: "The educational programs and services newsletter."
PUBL: Academy of Television Arts & Sciences, Educational Programs and Services Committee, 3500 West Olive Ave., Suite 700, Burbank, CA 91505.
DESC: Published by the Educational Programs and Services Committee of the Academy of Television Arts & Sciences, *Debut* profiles the educational activities and opportunities available to those interested in a career in television. One sampled issue described summer Hollywood internships, international interns, news of successful prior Academy interns, production awards, and intern "Alumni News." This is a welcome publication for the television professional, academic, and potential Academy intern. Two color, loose-leaf newsletter format on coated paper stock (8 ½ x 11 inches / 215 x 280 mm), no advertising.
DEPT: "From the President," "From the Editors," "Academy Calendar," upcoming events; "Damon Romine Goes Behind the Scenes," column by Damon Romine; "Alumni News," status of previous Academy interns. (spring-91).
TYPL: "Academy Honors Student Winners in 12th Annual College TV Awards," "Summer Internships Opening Doors in Hollywood," "Student Interns Mingle with Pat Mitchell," "TV Academy Hosts Interns From Abroad," "Student-Produced Anti-Drug Messages to Air Nationwide." (spring-91).
SCHL: Semiannual, 8 pp.
SPAN: Spring, 1988+

✧ DEEP RED

SUB: "Horror from Hollywood."
SUB: "The movies your mother wouldn't take you to see."
PUBL: FantaCo Enterprises, Inc., 21 Central Ave., Albany, NY 12210-1391.
DESC: *Deep Red* Editor Charles Balun described the nature of this jugular- grabbing publication by reminding readers that the big studio era was over; that the era of successful independent producing had arrived. "So, even if your little backyard Godzilla pic never ever

plays in even one theatre, you'll still have an opportunity for your film to be seen by thousands of horror fans the world over. You won't get rich, but maybe your work will be appreciated and celebrated and you might even make enough money to get to do it again and again. *Deep Red* is committed to encouraging and promoting the NEW BLOOD on the block. We know you don't have a $250,000 advertising budget; so, send us the info or clips about your production and we'll do our best to get the word out." Of special note are featured departments, "News Slashes," providing the latest details on upcoming features and their creators; and the "Gore Scoreboard," a splendid review section of the best and worst of horror film genre productions. Among the films reviewed or advertised in one sample issue were "I Dismember Mama," "Chainsaw Honeymoon," "Hollywood Chainsaw Hookers," subtitled "They charge an arm and a leg!;" "I Was a Zombie for the FBI," "Psychos in Love," and the four-skull rated "Hammer: The Studio that Dripped Blood." Numerous graphics, editorial content in the sampled issue printed on uncoated paperstock in black/white (a real break for the faint-of-heart), with a blood-red black/white cover on coated paperstock. It is a well-produced publication for this genre of motion picture films and videocassettes. In the words of competitor publication *Fangoria Magazine*, "This little masterpiece...is hilarious. The man is a genius...every review is witty and some are downright hysterical. Balun tells it like it is. You gotta like this guy." Note: the December, 1987 premiere issue was preceded by a 20-page "promotional issue" in 1986. Stapled magazine format (8 ½ x 11 inches / 215 x 280 mm).
DEPT: "Editorial," "Fan Zone," 'Letters to the Editor'; "News Slashes," horror film newsbriefs column by Charles Balun; "Gore Scoreboard," unique four-skull horror film rating system; "Video Dog House," horror films in videocassette release. (3-88).
TYPL: "Redneck Zombies," "Mark Shostrom: Nightmare Maker," "Leatherface in Love: 'Post-Chainsaw Dating Etiquette'," "Here's Blood In Your Eye: 'I, Zombie'." (3-88).
SCHL: Quarterly, 65 pp.
SPAN: Dec, 1987+
DD: 791 11
ISSN: 0896-4513

✥ DEMOCRATIC JOURNALIST

SUB: "The journal of the International Organization of Journalists."
PUBL: International Organization of Journalists, Parizka 9, 110 01 Prague 1, Czechoslovakia.
DESC: This Czechoslovakian publication, printed with English, French, Russian and Spanish editions, concerns itself with media topics primarily within what was previously called the Soviet bloc, or allied nations, and is written with that viewpoint in mind. Prior to the thawing of the "cold war" era, the *Democratic Journalist* was unique in providing the reader with a rare view into the workings and philosophy of such media. Of special interest is a long, annotated list of newly published Soviet books on the function and operation of mass media.
DEPT: "New Books," most of which are Moscow published.
TYPL: "The Thoughts of a Journalist on the Development of Mass Communication Media," "What is the Austrian Radio Coming To?," "Romanian Revolutionary Journalist--a Participant in the October Revolution," "The Ideas of October and the Czechoslovak Press." (11-77)
SCHL: Monthly [irregular at times], 25 pp.
SPAN: Nov, 1953+
LC: PN 4701.D4
DD: 070
ISSN: 0011-8214

✥ DESIGN

SUB: "The journal of the society of newspaper design."
PUBL: Society of Newspaper Design, The Newspaper Center, PO Box 17290, Dulles International Airport, Washington, DC 20041.
DESC: *Design* is published by "The Society of Newspaper Design [which] was formed in January, 1979 to contribute through design to the improvement of newspapers." The need for such a publication was evident after the premiere issue of March, 1980 went to the membership. Letters arrived back shortly thereafter, and Editor Richard Curtis in the second issue noted that much had already been learned: "That there is a tremendous need out there among newspaper people for more information on how they can do their jobs as communicators more effectively; That progress in making newspapers better is being made, though sometimes painfully slowly, on all fronts, and in all sizes of newspapers. That there appears to be a consensus of opinion that 'newspaper design'--and that term is defined in any number of ways--has suddenly become important, for whatever reasons; and that there is no end to the willingness of dedicated professionals to nurture better newspapers by communicating their ideas through journals such as this." This is a quality resource, not only for art and design directors, but also for publishers, editors; managing and city editors as well. Issues contain numerous illustrations of newspaper format "make-overs" with accompanying information concerning the "make-over" process, the effect of readability, circulation changes, advertising increases, etc. Some issues contain special sections, such as the April, 1991 issue, "Graphics Go to War," a 24-page special report on graphic design concerning the Persian Gulf War. For the sampled issues of 1980: black ink on coated paper stock, no advertising, in stapled magazine format (8 ½ x 11 inches / 215 x 280 mm). For the sampled issues of 1991: editorial content consists of black ink with spot- and full-color pages, and full-color cover on coated paper stock, limited advertising, in stapled magazine format (8 ½ x 11 inches / 215 x 280 mm).

DEPT: None. (3-81). "Editor's Note," editorial column by Ed Kohorst; "Directly Speaking," commentary. (1-91).
TYPL: "Other Voices: Unconventional Solutions to Conventional Problems," "Reading Between the Lines: Visual Contracts," "Good Illustrations in Forty Inches of Rain: A Report From the Soggy Northwest," "One Artist, One Newspaper," "Sunday Comics: Fitting More Into the Same." (3-81). "The Los Angeles Times: The Surf and the Competition are Up in Hot Orange County," "What Other Publications Say About Newspaper Design," "Get Ready to Break Traditions in Newspaper Workshops," "How Do Americans Read Newspapers? What Do They Read?," "Color Study: The Pallette Thickens." (1-91).
SCHL: Quarterly, 25 pp.
SPAN: Mar, 1980+

Design & Art Direction
? - Jan 17, 1986//
SEE: DIRECTION

✦ DESKTOP COMMUNICATIONS
PUBL: International Desktop Communications, Ltd., 48 East 43rd St., New York, NY 10017.
DESC: "*DESKTOP COMMUNICATIONS* is the one-stop publishing guide to improving business communications. It will help you organize effective presentations, standardize your design formats to speed the creation of reports and proposals, and select the best software for your business needs. Reap the rewards of the 'next step' in computer technology that is revolutionizing business communications. Learn how to create more powerful, more persuasive presentations, proposals and reports--before your competition does. All with a little help from *DESKTOP COMMUNICATIONS*, your indispensable 'how-to' guide to the power of well-designed business communications." This dynamic serial stands out from a group of similar publications by its focus on desktop applications to the "real world" of business. Articles offer solutions to typical business problems. For example, one sampled issue contained a number of articles for immediate application; how to use caption dingbats, developing a network for desktop stations, how a major communication publisher keeps track of materials for weekly magazines, how to judge a typeface, the new generations of page description languages, and desirable features in new software releases. Also of special note, and of significant benefit is the ongoing department, "Vertical Markets," which explores successful desktop operations in unique business operations, real estate or sales/marketing. Best of all, the publication "practices what it preaches," having full layout and design created through desktop publishing technology. That alone speaks well for the state of the art in contemporary desktop publishing. This is a marvelous resource for those whose livelihoods depend upon this new means of communication. For sampled issue of 1991: stapled magazine format with full-color pages throughout on heavy coated paper stock (8 ⅛ x 11 inches / 205 x 280 mm).
DEPT: "Editorial," "Letters to the Editor," "From the Font," column by Keith Baumann; "Trade Secrets," column by Daniel Will-Harris; "Corporate View," column by Pauline Ores; "Vertical Markets," column by Mayrose Wood; "Network Publishing," column by Theo Anderson; "Bookshelf," reviews column by Katherine Shelly Pfeiffer; "Desktop Paper," column by Warren Struhl; "Gallery," reader submissions. (9/10-90).
TYPL: "Color Printers: What Will Work for You?," "Font Freedom: Have It Your Way," "The Need for Speed," "Send In the Clones," "Putting on Weight." (9/10-90).
SCHL: Bimonthly, 80 pp.
SPAN: Mar/Apr, 1989+
VARIES
--Mar/Apr, 1989 - Mar/Apr, 1990? as ITC Desktop (ISSN: 1042-3923).
DD: 070
ISSN: 1050-1800

DEVELOPER, THE
PUBL: American League of Amateur Photographers, 56 Vesey St., New York, NY.
DESC: "It should be understood by this time that *The Developer* aims to be more of a news medium than a technical journal; and while it proposes to lay before its readers the latest results in the various fields of photographic inquiry and research, it is anxious to become the means of communications and the vehicle for news among amateurs." True to its word, articles explain the intricacies of photography, how to build basic darkrooms, and give techniques for the photographic amateur. A fair number of photos are printed on fine-quality paper (commencing with volume II); and, a number of illustrations for blueprints for building projects and chemical compositions so necessary to this era of early photography are included as well.
DEPT: None.
TYPL: "In the Camera Man's Interest," "The Combined Toning and Fixing Bath," "Fine Work from New Orleans," "Some Samples of Mats," "Lantern Slides at Night by Reduction," "Pyrogallic Acid." (7-1893).
SCHL: Monthly, 30 pp.
SPAN: 1893 - Jan, 1896//
LC: TR 1.D

DIALOGUE ON FILM
PUBL: American Film Institute, J. F. Kennedy Center for the Performing Arts, Washington, DC.
DESC: "An inquiry into the arts and crafts of filmmaking through interview seminars between Fellows and prominent filmmakers held at Greystone, under the auspices of the American Film Institute's Center for Advanced Film Studies." An in-depth interview publication with numerous graphics concerning one or several filmmakers per issue. A list of typical persons

interviewed included Richard Zanuck, David Brown, Robert Wise, Robert Towne, Ingmar Bergman, and William Wyler.
DEPT: None.
TYPL: None.
SCHL: Ten issues per year, 15 pp.
SPAN: 1972 - May/Jun, 1975//
CONTINUED BY
--Discussion (ISSN: 0046-0346).
ABSORBED BY
--American Film (ISSN: 0361-4751), Oct, 1975.
LC: PN 1993.D

✤ DIGEST

PUBL: University Film Association, Department of Drama and Communications, University of New Orleans, Lakefront, New Orleans, LA 70122.
DESC: *Digest* is a typewritten newsletter with brief news items for members of the University Film Association. Typical areas of interest are current film research, academic film positions available, research papers, and film archives.
DEPT: "Research in Progress," brief listings of known academic and commercial research projects. (3-77)
TYPL: NA (too brief in nature).
SCHL: ?, 10 pp.
SPAN: ?+?

✤ DIGEST OF THE UNIVERSITY FILM AND VIDEO ASSOCIATION

PUBL: University Film and Video Association, University of North Texas, Division of Radio, Television and Film, Denton, TX 76203.
DESC: This community-style newsletter provides news of association activities, along with occasional articles concerning equipment usage and application; but is best known among film and video faculty for its large section of teaching positions available at colleges and universities. Articles are reprinted as received by contributors, resulting in a variety of type styles and formats. Some graphics; newsletter format (8 ½ x 11 inches / 215 x 280 mm).
DEPT: "Jobs," "News From Members," "Sustainer News," "Summer Seminars," "Competitions," "Conferences," "MOMA News," newsbriefs from Museum of Modern Art. (3-89).
TYPL: "UFVA Conference," "Notes From Your President," "About Lavalier Microphones." (3-89).
SCHL: Bimonthly [irregular at times] (? - ?); Monthly (?+), 8 pp.
SPAN: ?+
VARIES
--? - Sep, 1981 as Digest of the University Film Association.

Digest of the University Film Association
? - Sep, 1981//
SEE: DIGEST OF THE UNIVERSITY FILM AND VIDEO ASSOCIATION

Digital Audio & Compact Disc Review
Sep, 1984 - ?//
(ISSN: 0743-619x)
SEE: CD REVIEW

Digital Audio's CD Review
? - ?//
(ISSN: 1041-8342)
SEE: CD REVIEW

✤ DIGITAL DOMAIN DIGEST

SUB: "A digital audio newsletter from Lexicon Inc."
PUBL: Lexicon, Inc., 100 Beaver St., Waltham, MA 02154.
DESC: This four-page, black/white promotional newsletter is a supplement to the major trade journal, *Pro Sound News*. Lexicon uses this quarterly supplement to update users and potential buyers about new products, and industry applications of current products. Graphics of products and their applications accompany most articles. Newsletter format (8 ½ x 11 inches / 215 x 280 mm), black/white on coated paper stock, bound with rubber cement into issues of *Pro Sound News* for easy removal.
DEPT: "What's New at Lexicon." (winter-91).
TYPL: "Two Decades of Digital Audio," "Looking Back Proudly," "Commercial Recording Goes Digital with OPUS," "Audio Groups Make Exception for THX." (winter-91).
SCHL: Quarterly, 4 pp.
SPAN: Fall, 1990+
SUPPLEMENT TO
--Pro Sound News (ISSN: 0164-6338), Fall, 1990+

✤ DIGITAL EVOLUTION MAGAZINE

SUB: "North America's most informative professional video equipment magazine."
PUBL: Castlestone Publishing, Ltd., 3214 Wharton Way, Mississauga, Ontario Canada L4X 2C1.
DESC: Publisher Ray Lockhart makes this statement of objective in the masthead of his magazine: "To share knowledge with professional video equipment users. To provide a targeted medium for instructing, advising, announcing and advertising. To generally provide a communication tool at the 'grass roots' level of the professional video equipment industry. To maintain an easy to read format, filled with quality and useful information. To always place the readers' needs first by listening to their requests for knowledge and en-

deavoring to fulfill them accordingly." In the rapidly developing field of digital video, one is confronted with a myriad of products applicable to various visual applications. *Digital Evolution Magazine* helps to cut through the product maze by profiling and showcasing new products for the field. One innovative approach provided product listings by "inexpensive," "mid range," "upper mid range," and "high end" categories. Printed primarily black ink on coated paper stock, certain advertisements and editorial content in full color (8 ⅛ x 11 inches / 205 x 275 mm).
DEPT: "Product Feature FYI," equipment profile; "Inexpensive," chart and products; "Mid Range," chart and products; "Upper Mid Range," chart and products; "The High End," chart and products; "Industry News," 'New products, services, business closures, etc.'. (3-91).
TYPL: "Digital Video Effects," "Not Strictly DVE's," "The Video Toaster and Its Friends," "Glossary of DVE Terminology." (3-91).
SCHL: Monthly, 40 pp.
SPAN: Jul, 1989+
ISSN: 1181-7917

✤ DIGITAL MEDIA

PUBL: Seybold Publications, Inc., PO Box 644, Media, PA 19063.
DESC: A subscription promotion entitled, "The word from A to D," explains both form and function of this outstanding Seybold Publications periodical: "No, we haven't forgotten the rest of the alphabet. *Digital Media: A Seybold Report* chronicles the transition of print, graphic arts, sound, music, photography, video and film from A to D (analog to digital) technology. It also examines how people use digital and transitional technology--the advantages, the shortcomings and the ethical implications." Publisher Jonathan Seybold and Editor Denise Caruso have created an informative, newsworthy, easy-to-understand publication which delivers fully on the subscription promise noted above. This Seybold report is noteworthy for the succinct manner in which difficult technologies are explained, new concepts (both software and hardware issues) are explored; and the manner in which the reader is updated about emerging trends in the digital field. An outstanding publication worthy of its 1991 subscription fee of $395; one which is "must" reading for those involved with information and instructional technologies in the digital communication arena. For the sampled issue of 1991: black ink on uncoated paper stock with cover consisting of black ink with purple and yellow spot inks also on uncoated paper stock, limited advertising (8 ⅝ x 11 inches / 220 x 280 mm).
DEPT: "I/O," 'Readers respond' with letters; "Events," calendar of upcoming conferences, workshops, and other related gatherings. (9-16-91).

TYPL: "Content: The Promise of New Media," "Interactive Markets: There is No There, There (Yet)," "Publishing Today: The Electronic Piñata," "Expansive HDTV," "If It Worked for Print Publishing," "Adobe Buys Super-Mac's ReelTime." (9-16-91).
SCHL: Monthly, 25 pp.
SPAN: Jun, 1991+
ISSN: 1056-7038

✤ DIGITAL RADIO NEWS

SUB: "Surviving in the digital age."
PUBL: DRN, Inc., PO Box 18373, Washington, DC 20036-8373.
DESC: "Surviving in the digital age" describes the present situation in digital radio, and "thriving and profiting in the digital age" is an apt description for *Digital Radio News*, a semimonthly newsletter for North American radio broadcasters. With a focus on the digital audio realm, the newsletter covers satellite, mobile audio services, innovative spectrum utilization, CD channels, and other technological, regulatory, and business elements connected with the developing field of digital radio. A one year subscription (1991) is $250, and is also available more quickly via fax for $350 per year (1991). International fax subscriptions are also available. Printed black ink (with spot color on cover) on yellow uncoated paper stock (8 ½ x 11 inches / 215 x 280 mm).
DEPT: "Product Watch," digital radio newsbriefs. (4-14-91).
TYPL: "Satellite CD Radio Changes DAB Plan," "DAB Task Force Targets L-Band," "Strother Joins Satellite Arena; Plans to Propose DAB by Sat," "DAB Scorecard: Status Report on Players," "Digital Storage is the Surprise of NAB Show." (4-14-91).
SCHL: Semimonthly, 4 pp.
SPAN: Nov 3, 1990+

Direct Advertising

Spring, 1935 - Jan, 1943//
(ISSN: 0740-9265)
SEE: PRINTING PAPER

Direct Advertising and Sample Book of Mill Brand Papers

1911 - Winter, 1934//
(ISSN: 0740-9249)
SEE: PRINTING PAPER

✤ DIRECT MARKETING

SUB: "The magazine of direct mail."
SUB: "Advertising and selling by letters, folders, booklets, blotters, house magazines, catalogs, etc."
SUB: "A monthly forum devoted to business communications in selected markets."

SUB:	"The Reporter of Direct Mail Advertising."
SUB:	"The art/science of selling to consumer and business markets." (? - Dec, 1989).
SUB:	"Using direct response advertising to enhance marketing database." (? - Dec, 1989).
SUB:	"The monthly magazine for direct marketing professionals." (Jan, 1990+).
PUBL:	Hoke Communications, 224 Seventh St., Garden City, Long Island, NY 11530-5726.
DESC:	*Direct Marketing* recognizes "...the total activity of direct mail users in employing all media to acquire and identify customers and prospects; then to communicate directly with them regardless of medium." A variety of marketing problems and success stories concerning direct mail campaigns grace this monthly format. Emphasis is on new technology and new techniques to reach the mass consumer with advertising messages, and proven strategies for sales. Since 1927, *Direct Marketing* has been at the forefront of this unique advertising medium, and it has kept current. The latest update occurred with the January, 1990 issue with a format redesign, and new categorization of editorial content into six distinct departments: "--three devoted to case histories and three devoted to how-to type articles. Mail Order, Retail and Lead Generation constitute the case history section and the how-to's focus on the subjects of Creative Strategies, Lists & Databases and Media Management." It is always a delight. Sampled issue for 1978: perfect-bound magazine format, with mixture of black ink, spot color and full color pages on coated paper stock, with some advertising pages on special paper (8 ¼ x 11 ⅛ inches / 210 x 285 mm).
DEPT:	"Short Notes," direct mail ideas and news items; "Whats New," pictorial display of recent direct mail items; "Newsmakers," "Upgrading Letter Copy," advice column by Paul Bringe; "Ideas for Retailers," advice column by Murray Raphel; "Direct Response," advice column by John Caples; "Canadian Memo," newsbriefs column by Vic Baker; "Cassette Reports," an interesting section detailing new audio cassettes of speakers and workshops in direct mail; "Marketing Viewpoints," advice column by Luther Brock. (11-76). "Direct Marketing News," "What's New," "Newsmakers," "Letter to Editor," "Club News," of regional marketing clubs; "Calendar," "Editorial," "Canadian Memo," column by Vic Baker; "Marketing Viewpoint International," column by Luther Brock; "Telemarketing," column by Peg Kuman; "Legal Outlook," column by Robert Posch; "Foundations for the Future," column by Laurie Spar. (1-86). "Editor's Notebook," "Direct Intelligence," newsbriefs; "DM Data," 'Pieces of mail by class'; "Agency Action," personnel newsbriefs; "Canadian Memo," column by Robert T. Stacey; "List News," direct mail list news; "DM People," 'Promotions & Newcomers'; "Calendar/Associations," "Noted & Quoted," '...a slightly irreverent look at some of the stories that beg for a less than serious tack'; "Career Directions," column by Karen Gillick; "Legal Outlook," column by Robert Posch; "Rapp Around the World," column by Stan Rapp. (1-90).
TYPL:	"Direct Marketing Relates to the Consumer Market," "Seafood Processor Plunges into Direct Mail Waters," "There's a Friend at Chase Using Direct Mail Methods." (11-76). "Direct Mail Applications of Small Area Demographics," "Writing Copy for Loose Deck Cards," "IIA Addressing Rapid changes in Electronic Realm," "Twenty-Two Rules for Successful Self-Promotion." (1-86). "Food By Mail: Beyond the Fruitcake," "How to Get A-Head in Direct Mail," "The New Age of Radio," "What's New in Letter-Writing Techniques." (1-90).
SCHL:	Monthly, 100 pp.
SPAN:	Sep, 1927+ FROM MERGER OF --Mailbag, The (and) Postage. VARIES --Sep, 1927 - Nov, 1937 as Postage and the Mailbag. --May, 1938 - Apr, 1968 as Reporter of Direct Mail Advertising, The. SUSPENDED --Dec, 1937 - Apr, 1938.
LC:	HF 5861.R4
DD:	659.13/3/05
ISSN:	0012-3188
ABST:	--ABI/Informer --Business Periodical Index (ISSN: 0007-6961) --InfoBank --Management Contents --Predicasts

✦ DIRECT RESPONSE SPECIALIST, THE

SUB:	"The dollars & sense of direct marketing."
SUB:	"The mail marketer's newsletter of effective response/profit techniques."
PUBL:	Stilson & Stilson, PO Box 1075, Tarpon Springs, FL 34688.
DESC:	"Every issue of *TDRS* brings you understandable, applicable response/profit tips, tricks, and techniques that will help you achieve your response/profit goals. YOU GET the how-to's, when-to's, why-to's, and what-if's of mail marketing." This typewritten newsletter is designed to dramatically improve direct-mail marketing efforts through dynamic copy, premiums, and other aspects of this advertising medium. Sentences are short and to the point, packing a considerable amount of information into the eight-page newsletter format. Stilson & Stilson also publishes guidebooks to better direct-mail pieces and consultation services. Subscription rate in December, 1988 was $77 for 12 monthly issues. Typewritten, three-hole punched newsletter format (8 ½ x 11 inches / 215 x 280 mm), no graphics.
DEPT:	None. (12-88).

TYPL: "Get to Know ... Secretaries," "Make Self-Mailers Personal," "How to Sell to Middle Management (and Below)," "Helpful Copyfitting Charts," "How to Make Your Publication Ads More Effective." (12-88).
SCHL: Monthly, 8 pp.
SPAN: Feb, 1987?+
　　　VARIES
　　　--? - ? as Mail Order Connection.

✤ DIRECTION

PUBL: Navy Internal Relations Activity, Office of the Chief of Information, Department of the Navy, Crystal Plaza Six, Room 1044, Washington, DC 20360.
DESC: *Direction* is targeted to public relations offices, officers, and others in leadership positions within the United States Navy. Individuals outside of the armed forces will also find it valuable for its well-presented guidelines on news releases, interviews, contacts, and other ways in which there is regular contact with the mass media. Of special interest are profiles of successful Navy PR campaigns.
DEPT: None.
TYPL: "Successful News Conference: Journey into Time and Space," "Interviews: Results Through Personal Contact," "The Don'ts of Photo Releases." (1/2-79).
SCHL: ?, 55 pp.
SPAN: 1965+

✤ DIRECTION

SUB: "Where art meets the real world."
SUB: "Circulated with Campaign only in the U.K."
PUBL: Direction, 22 Lancaster Gate, London W2 3LY, England.
DESC: "Where art meets the real world" defines this quality trade serial for the British advertising/marketing designer, providing outstanding color renditions and text on quality paper stock. Within the pages of this monthly are a wide variety of advertising examples, from the packaging of lemons to audio album covers; from a discussion of forthcoming British satellite television to the application of computer graphics to the design process. Television titles, cereal boxes, collage photography, print ads, showcards, menues, bottle labels, video spots and bookcovers; and a fair number of designer profile interviews are included as well. Quality layout design (as would be expected), graphics and editorial content make this required reading for today's professional designer. For the sampled 1990 issue: perfect-bound magazine format, with black/white and full-color graphics and full-color cover on coated paper stock (9 ⅛ x 12 inches / 235 x 305 mm).
DEPT: "Briefing," outstanding full-color section of recent ads; "Showcase," designer profile; "Choice," favorite ad designs; "Computer Graphics," technology column by Barry Smith; "Preview," upcoming events in graphic design; "Adwatch," column by Jim Davies; "Vidbeat," column by Chrissy Iley; "Viewpoint," letters; "Day by Day," unique 'captains log' tracks designer day activities. (3-90).
TYPL: "On the Spot," "Work Hard, Play Hard," "TV Talents," "Titles Fight." (3-90).
SCHL: Monthly, 70 pp.
SPAN: ?+
　　　VARIES
　　　--? - Jan 17, 1986 as Design & Art Direction.
　　　SUPPLEMENT TO
　　　--Campaign (ISSN: 0008-2309), ?+
LC: NC 998.6.G7 D48
DD: 741.6/0941 19

✤ DISCOURSE & SOCIETY

SUB: "An international journal for the study of discourse and communication in their social, political and cultural contexts."
PUBL: Sage Publications, Ltd., 28 Banner St., London EC1Y 8QE, England.
DESC: Editor Teun A. Van Dijk, in the premiere issue for July, 1990, provides a succinct discourse as to the reasons and challenges which brought about publication of this journal. After describing several decades of expanded discourse studies in the humanities and social sciences, he stated, "The time has come for a change. *Discourse & Society* (D&S) has been founded to stimulate this change, and to publish the increasing number of studies that focus on the social, political and cultural dimensions of discourse. Since not only forms of text and talk but full communication processes are involved in these dimensions, the journal also pays attention to similar developments in various subdisciplines of communication studies, which are slowly merging with discourse analysis. The same is true for the social and cultural study of language use, both in sociolinguistics and in the ethnography of speaking. Whereas much of the earlier work on language use and discourse has a linguistic bias, *Discourse & Society* provides a more socio-political emphasis. This does not mean that the theoretical and methodological sophistication that resulted from two decades of linguistic grammars and systematic discourse analysis will be ignored. On the contrary, it needs to be shown that these advances are also relevant for the analysis of social, political and cultural problem areas. Conversely, the new journal must also show that serious discourse and communication analysis is at best fragmentary without the integration of, and contribution to, thorough theory formation in the social and political sciences." With an emphasis on theoretical, empirical, and methodological research, *Discourse & Society* steps out boldly into this new and burgeoning field of discourse and communication in "...their social, political and cultural contexts." It is an outstanding publication for this field, and another in the expanding field of quality journals by Sage. For the sampled issue of 1990: perfect-bound

journal format, black ink on uncoated paper stock, cover is in green ink on coated paper stock, limited advertising (6 x 9 ¼ inches / 150 x 235 mm).
DEPT: None. (7-90).
TYPL: "Stacking the Cards of Ideology: the History of the *Sun Souvenir Royal Album*," "US Media Discourse on South Africa: the Development of a Situation Model," "'Thank God I Said No to Aids': On the Changing Discourse of AIDS in Uganda," "Not Just 'Doctors Orders': Directive-Response Sequences in Patients' Visits to Women and Men Physicians." (7-90).
SCHL: Quarterly, 115 pp.
SPAN: Jul, 1990+
LC: P 302 .D5476
DD: 401/.41/05
ISSN: 0957-9265

✤ DISNEY ADVENTURES

SUB: "The magazine for kids."
SUB: "Official Publication: The Disney Afternoon."
PUBL: W.D. Publications, Inc., 500 South Buena Vista St., Tower Building, 29th Fl., Burbank, CA 91521.
DESC: Targeted to children ages seven to 14, *Disney Adventures* is designed for tie-in with the "Disney Afternoon" show that premiered in fall, 1990. That cartoon-filled program slot consists of "Chip 'n' Dale Rescue Rangers," "Tale Spin," and "Ducktales," all three of which have comic sections within this monthly digest. One additional show in the afternoon lineup (without comic section in the premiere issue) is the "Gummi Bears." Other departments and articles provide showcases for a variety of Disney product, including Roger Rabbit, Walt Disney theme parks, family-oriented motion picture products, and news/adventure/science items of interest to this age group. Most articles average one-page in length. Digest-sized magazine (5 ¼ x 7 ⅜ inches / 130 x 190 mm) in full color.
DEPT: "Zip Code," letters; "Disney Beat," Disney production-related items; "Street," 'What's happening'; "Chip 'n Dale Rescue Rangers," comic section; "Tale Spin," comic section; "Cyber," 'Kidtech and science'; "Ducktales," comic section; "Impulse," 'Action guide'; "Roger Rabbit," comic section; "Xoxxox," 'Puzzles, games and activities'. (11-12-90).
TYPL: "Backpack: A Guide to the World," "The Wild West," "Ranch Life: 2000," "Blazing Buffalo Bill," "Western Gear and More." (11-12-90).
SCHL: Biweekly, 130 pp.
SPAN: Nov 12, 1990+
DD: 051
ISSN: 1050-2491

✤ DISNEY CHANNEL MAGAZINE, THE

PUBL: The Disney Channel, 3800 West Alameda Ave., Burbank, CA 91505.
DESC: This program guide for the Disney Channel provides articles of upcoming programming, a special kids' section with games and puzzles, and, of course complete listings of Disney programming for the month ahead. It is unique in the liberal use of Disney characters throughout each monthly guide. Magazine format; color graphics throughout.
DEPT: "Behind the Scenes," "Mickey's Just for Kids Section," "Get Involved," letters. (12-83). "Disney Beat," "Archives," 'Disney facts, films and trivia'; "Families," "Disney Night Time," highlights; "Program Highlights," "What's Next," following month highlights; "What's On," schedule. (11/12-89).
TYPL: "Home for the Holidays," "Mom, the Mousketeer," "A Disney Channel Christmas," "Happy Holidays from Walt Disney World." (12-83). "The Making of The Little Mermaid," "That Tireless, Traveling Man, Mr. Hope," "Ready Steady Go! The '60s Musical Celebration," "Seoul '88: 16 Days of Glory." (11/12-89).
SCHL: Monthly, 65 pp.
SPAN: Jan, 1983+
ISSN: 0747-4644

✤ DM NEWS

SUB: "The newspaper of direct marketing."
PUBL: Mill Hollow Corporation, 19 West 21st St., New York, NY 10010.
DESC: Whether the medium is the telephone, mail, or a variety of other media, direct marketing has become a major player in advertising strategies to reach consumers. *DM News* reports on developments in the direct mail field, its semimonthly publication schedule and newspaper tabloid format allowing for a number of late-breaking stories to be timely upon delivery. Issues of database management, telephone solicitation, new concepts in postal pieces, and direct mail success stories abound in this publication. Tabloid size on newsprint.
SCHL: "Late News," "Agency Leaders Survey," column by C. James Schaefer; "Hardware and Software," column by Gary Beck and Gill Winograd; "Martin Gross on Creative," "Fenvessy on Fulfillment," column by Stanley Fenvessy; "DM Views," letters; "Agency Beat," "Careers," "Package Inserts," "Space Beat," Direct mail and print media; "Calendar." (12-1-88).
TYPL: "Laws Barring DR Fax Advertising Could be Enacted by Two States," "Marriott, Amtech Joint Venture to Put Video Kiosks in Airports," "Deliverability Study Due to USPS; Auditor Already Asking Questions," "Newspaper Agency Mail Effort Captures 11 Percent Response." (12-1-88).
SCHL: Monthly (Sep, 1979 - May, 1987); Semimonthly (Jun 1, 1987+), 70 pp.
SPAN: Sep, 1979+
LC: HF 5415.126 .D6
DD: 658.8/4 19
ISSN: 0194-3588

✣ DOCTOR WHO MAGAZINE

PUBL: Marvel Comics, Ltd., 23 Redan Place, Queensway, London W2 4SA, England.

DESC: There is only a handful of science fiction television programs that can boast of their own dedicated fan organizations and magazines. Doctor Who fans can claim their own magazine (courtesy of Marvel Comics, Ltd.), one with a passionate world-wide following interested in the stories and characters of this television series. The strength of fan support for the Doctor Who program was seen in mid-1985, when the British Broadcasting Corporation announced they were mandating an 18-month rest for the program. Fans were outraged at the thought. Much of the editorial content of this monthly is centered on series episodes, especially new story twists, and the creative talent that produces the series. For the 1991 sampled issue there were several noteworthy items: "Doctor Who?," "The Dominators," and "Party Animals," well-executed cartoon features; "Pick of the Penguin," a fascinating letter section; and "Continuity Queries," plot faux pas. Mention also needs to be made of the numerous full-color pictures found throughout the serial. Stapled magazine format, full color and black/white graphics on coated paper stock, limited advertising (8 3/8 x 11 inches / 210 x 280 mm).

DEPT: "Doctor Who Letters," "Gallifrey Guardian," "Matrix Data Bank," series newsbriefs; "On Target," product review; "Comic Strip," unique comic strip rendition of a Dr. Who story. (8-85). "Controversy Corner," column by Richard Landen; "Into the Vortex," "Gallifrey Guardian," 'All ashore that's going ashore in the Who world'; "Clubs," news; "Off the Shelf," video and fanzine review column by Gary Russell; "Pick of the Penguin," letters; "Continuity Queries," reader Q&A. 5-91).

TYPL: "Interview: Paul Trerise, Catherine Davies, Dinah Collin," "Interview: Pip and Jane Baker," "Interview: Sarah Hellings." (8-85). "Lies, Lies, Lies," "Pathfinders," "Writing Doctor Who," "The Years Tapes," "Enlightening." (5-91).

SCHL: Monthly, 45 pp.

SPAN: 1985?+?
VARIES
--1985? - ? as Official Doctor Who Magazine, The.

DOCUMENTARY FILM NEWS

SUB: "Incorporating Cinema Quarterly." (Apr, 1936 - ?).

PUBL: Film Centre, London, England.

DESC: The serial began as *Cinema Quarterly* in Autumn, 1932, as a Scottish film aesthetics publication, and included among its writers such notables as Paul Rotha, Rudolph Arnheim, and Herman Weinberg. Editor Norman Wilson noted in the first issue: "Whatever else Cinema Quarterly stands for, it stands for sincerity. With all the vigor it can muster, it will attack the empty masquerade of sham sentiments and false emotions that is the stock-in-trade of most commercial movies." By the end of its four-year publication span, the serial could boast of contributing authors in the United States, France, Sweden, Netherlands, Italy, Belgium, Hungary, India, South Africa, Australia, Ireland, and Japan. The Summer, 1935 issue indicated that the serial would appear in a new form for Autumn, 1935 under the title, *World Film News and Cinema Quarterly*, a monthly magazine. The first new issue, however, did not appear until April, 1936, under the title of *World Film News and Television Progress*, with a subtitle of "Incorporating *Cinema Quarterly*." In that first issue of the new series, the editors stated: "*World Film News* is the *Cinema Quarterly* in new dress...*Cinema Quarterly* was successful. It circulated widely through the film societies...*Cinema Quarterly*, had, by necessity, to rely on theory. *WFN* has more information, and less theory. In the film world there is an excellent service of commercial and trade news, and an excellent service for fans. There is no service which reports on creative people and creative efforts in the many branches of cinema. *WFN*, is, in this sense, a necessary paper." This two-year publication had its center in London, with most of its content focusing on that metropolis. It was an interesting publication due to the variety of articles, and if there existed a foreign emphasis, it was the American motion picture. Some articles concentrated on long film reviews of new releases: others concerned themselves with the life story of current film stars; and still others provided interesting production stories. It is definitely a lay publication. Recognition of the new medium of television in 1938 brought about three new title changes before arriving in its final form, *Documentary News Letter* (in January, 1940). This initially typewritten serial "...continues the policy and purpose of *World Film News* by expressing the documentary idea." Remainder of issues were printed news-tabloid style. Articles championed the documentary film form, and its myriad applications including education, instruction, propaganda, promotion, etc. An excellent resource for propaganda documentaries produced during the war years. Few graphics.

DEPT: "Nederlandesche Filmiga Bulletin," "The Miscellany," letters to the editor; "The Cinema Library," book reviews; "Films of the Quarter," reviews; "The Film Society of Glasgow," "Wanted: Scenerios," (winter- 32). "Miscellany," "Films of the Quarter," "Film Societies," "The Independent Film-Maker." (spring-34). "Films Reviewed," reprint of newspaper critics reviews; "Movie Theater Management," problems and opportunities of the exhibitor, a column by Basil Clavering; "This Months Releases," one-line look at British and American releases; "Cockalorum," pertaining to industry newsbriefs; "Film Guide," listing of British film theaters and current programs; "Television," new feature beginning in Aug, 1938 column by Thomas Baird. (8-38). "Notes of the Month," "Story Film of the Month," "Children's Film of the Month," "British Documentary Activity," "Documentary in the United States," "Non-Theatrical Distribution in Great Britain," "Film Catalogue of the Month," "New Documentary Films," "Film Society

News," "Book Review," (2- 40). "Notes of the Month," "Depropaganda Fide," "New Documentary Films," "Film of the Month," "Film Society News," "News from USA," "MOI Five Minute Films," "Short Film Bookings for," "Film Libraries." (9-41).
TYPL: "Documentary," "The Misconception of 'Montage,'" "Significant Speech," "The Film in Czechoslovakia," (winter-32). "The Spectator," "Poetry and Film," "The Art of Disney," "The Symphonic Film," "Whither Colour?," "Ethics or Movie?," "Germany on the Screen," (spring-34). "The Public My Partner, Says Laughton," "Time Marches On," "At a Chaplain Film with Chaplain," (4-36). "Grandma's Boy: The Comedies of Harold Lloyd," "The Sheik Rides Again; The Return of Rudolph Valentino," "European Storm Center: 'The March of Time' on Czechoslovakia," "Time and the Cowboys." (8-38). "Films at the New York Worlds Fair," "Public Reaction: The Lion has Wings," "Non-Theatrical Distribution in Great Britain," "Non- Theatrical Film Libraries," "Dutch Documentary," (2-40). "First Principles," "Whither Film Societies?," "Celuloid Circus," "Behind the Box-Office," "Films for Primitive Peoples," "Commercial Television in U.S.A.," (9-41).
SCHL: Quarterly (Autumn, 1932 - Spring, 1935); Monthly (? - ?); Monthly (Jan, 1940 - Dec, 1945); Bimonthly (Jan/Feb, 1946 - Aug/Sep, 1947); Monthly (Oct, 1947); Bimonthly (Nov/Dec, 1947), 15 pp.
SPAN: Autumn, 1932 - Jan, 1949//
VARIES
--Autumn, 1932 - Summer, 1935 as Cinema Quarterly.
--Apr, 1936 - ? as World Film News.
--?, 1936 - Jan, 1937 as World Film News and Television Progress.
--Feb, 1937 - Aug, 1938 as World Film News.
--Sep, 1938 - Nov, 1938 as SEE; World Film News.
--Jan, 1940 - Nov/Dec, 1947 as Documentary News Letter.

Documentary News Letter
Jan, 1940 - Nov/Dec, 1947//
SEE: DOCUMENTARY FILM NEWS

Documentation and Information Bulletin of the International Broadcasting Organization
Feb, 1960? - ?//
SEE: RADIO AND TELEVISION

Documentation List
Jan, 1972 - Jul/Oct, 1973//
SEE: MEDIA ASIA

✜ DOW JONES NEWSPAPER FUND NEWSLETTER
PUBL: Dow Jones Newspaper Fund, PO Box 300, Princeton, NJ 08543-0300.
DESC: This eight-page, two-color newsletter reports on trends, status of, and promising reporters in the high-school and college journalism fields. Articles cite outstanding faculty and their involvement in academic journalism, along with announcements of competition winners in unique categories such as the "National Urban Writing Competition" sponsored by the Dow Jones Newspaper Fund. The Fund seeks the encouragement, strengthening, and preparation of students into the journalistic field, a necessary endeavor for the development of a democratic society. Two-color newsletter in a stapled magazine format (8 ½ x 11 inches / 215 x 275 mm). Graphics, but no advertising.
DEPT: None. (winter-87).
TYPL: "Cutsinger and Harkrider Chosen Fund's 1987 Teachers of the Year," "Supreme Court Hears Arguments in Hazelwood Case," "Student Law Center Offers Services for Scholastic Press," "These Struck Our Fancy." (winter-87).
SCHL: Quarterly, 8 pp.
SPAN: Spring, 1960?+
VARIES
--Spring, 1960? - Nov, 1982 as Newspaper Fund Newsletter.

✜ DOWN BEAT
SUB: "The contemporary music magazine."
SUB: "Every other Thursday since 1934."
SUB: "On newsstands throughout the world."
SUB: "Readers in 142 countries."
SUB: "Jazz, blues & beyond."
PUBL: Maher Publishing, 180 West Park Ave., Elmhurst, IL 60126.
DESC: For almost 50 years, *Down Beat* magazine has dispensed news, comment, instruction, and general information on the music field to a subscriber base throughout the world. The biweekly publication (issued Thursdays) covers music recording, live stage, (and the art and technique of this form); and a myriad of applications, with everything from hard rock to Mancini, from street musicans to night club jazz, from film/television post recording to industry issues on the changing nature of the industry. Each issue features several interviews with major music artists, and is definitely one of the major trade publications for the music field. The 1970 issue employed some spot color, but primarily black/white editorial content. Issue for 1990: stapled magazine format with mixture of black/white and full-color pages all on coated paper stock (8 ¼ x 10 $E7/8 inches / 205 x 275 mm).
DEPT: "The First Chorus," column by Charles Suber; "Chords & Discords," 'A forum for readers'; "Record Reviews," "Blindfold Test," "Caught in the Act," live show showcase; "Music Workshop," "Strictly Ad Lib," music notes from international cities. (3-5-70).

"On the Beat," column by John Ephland; "Chords & Discords," letters; "News," "Riffs," "Record & CD Reviews," extensive listing; "Blindfold Test," "Caught," review; "Ad Lib," "Pro Shop," product showcase; "Pro Session," "Auditions," 'Young musicians deserving recognition'. (12-90).
TYPL: "Della Reese: 'Why Not Now'," "Mancini's Movie Music Manifesto," "'Monterey Pop' Revisited." (3-5-70). "Charlie Parker: Golden Bird," "55th Annual DB Readers Poll," "Los Lobos: The Wolf Prospers," "Don Grolnick: Dreamweaver." (12-90).
SCHL: Biweekly [except monthly Jul - Sep], 45 pp.
SPAN: Jul, 1934+
LC: ML 1 .D72
DD: 780/.5
ISSN: 0012-5768
ABST: --Book Review Index (ISSN: 0524-0581)
--Jazz Index (ISSN: 0344-5399)
--Magazine Index
--Music Index (ISSN: 0027-4348)
--Popular Magazine Review (ISSN: 0740-3763)
--Readers Guide Abstracts (ISSN: 0886-0092)
--Readers Guide to Periodical Literature (ISSN: 0034-0464)
--RILM Abstracts (ISSN: 0033-6955)

✤ DRAMA
SUB: "A monthly record of the theatre in town and country at home & abroad."
SUB: "The quarterly theatre review."
PUBL: British Theatre Association, 9 Fitzroy Square, London W1P 6AE, England.
DESC: The purpose of *Drama* has been to cover British dramatic arts, a task well accomplished since the appearance of the first issue in 1919. Sample issues from 1937 show a small, square format serial, letter-press printed; and thus few graphics were included. The current *Drama* is a totally different experience: it is magazine-size format with extensive editorial content, and numerous graphics; all set in an exciting layout design. Today's *Drama* goes outside the boundaries of the British Isles to cover international news, interviews, and fascinating reviews of world drama; whether on stage, radio, television, or film. But the emphasis is on the theatre, and readers will find this to be a marvelous resource for its study.
DEPT: "Recent Books," "News from North and South." (4-37). "Plays in Performance," world-wide reviews; "An Actor's Diary," "Plays in Print," "Books." (#3-85).
TYPL: "Plays of the Month," "Does the Screen Need Acting?," "The Proscenium on the Amateur Dramatic Stage," "The English School Theatre." (4-37). "Michael Redgrave Remembered," "Writing Pravda," "The Real Lindsay Kemp," "The Arts Funding Debate." (#3-85).
SCHL: Monthly (? - ?); Quarterly (?+); 60 pp.
SPAN: Jul, 1919+
VARIES
--Jul, 1919 - Jul/Sep, 1939 as Drama.
--Winter?, 1939/1940? - Apr?, 1945 as War-Time Drama.
--May, 1945 - Jul, 1945 as VE-Time Drama.
--Oct, 1945 as VJ-Time Drama.
--Nov, 1945 - Spring?, 1946 as Interim Drama.
LC: PN 2001.D64
DD: 792.0941
ISSN: 0012-5946
ABST: --Abstract of English Studies (ISSN: 0001-3560)
--Book Review Index (ISSN: 0524-0581)
--Index to Book Reviews in the Humanities (ISSN: 0073-5892)
--International Index to Periodicals
--Subject Index to Periodicals

DRAMA, THE
SUB: "A daily register of histrionic performances on the Dublin stage; and critical review of general dramatic literature. By two gentlemen of the Dublin University."
PUBL: W. Underwood, 19 St. Andrew St., Dublin, Ireland.
DESC: "Two gentlemen of the Dublin University" is the only information provided as to the identification of the editors of this *daily* four- page, pocket-sized critique of Dublin theatre in 1821. And a lively daily critique it was, as each evening's theatrical fare was analyzed, promoted, and chastized; sometimes with a reprinting of the musical lyrics; and at times with thoughtful essays on the relationship of theatre to Irish society and culture. Primarily, however, this serial's raison d'etre resided in reviewing the play itself, taking actor and audience to task for performances on both sides of the curtain. In the Friday, November 16, 1821 issue commenting on the performance by a veteran actress, the editors noted: "From this Lady's high name we expected a good piece of acting last night, but we are sorry to confess ourselves much disappointed. Her voice is strong and coarse, without melody or variation--there are not three tones in it. Her declamation is swelled and lengthened into an unnatural cant, falling periodically on the ear with a most disagreeable effect." An excellent resource for early Irish theatre. Small format; no graphics.
DEPT: None. (10/30-1821).
TYPL: "The Belle's Stratagem, and Harlequin and Friar Bacon." (10/30-1821).
SCHL: Daily (Monday through Friday), 4 pp.
SPAN: Oct 23, 1821 - Dec 10, 1821//
LC: PN 2001.D65

Drama
Jul, 1919 - Jul/Sep, 1939//
SEE: DRAMA

DRAMA & THEATRE
SUB: "A quarterly of new drama." (winter-61/62 - ?)

PUBL: State University College, Department of English, Fredonia, NY 24063.
DESC: Within its front cover, the purposes of *Drama & Theatre* are clearly stated: "to offer new plays of outstanding quality; to bring new playwrights to the attention of theatrical producers throughout the world; to offer and encourage a free exchange of ideas and criticism on the techniques, practices and problems of the contemporary theatre." Its major contribution is the printing of new dramatic plays in their entirety. Here for the theatrical producer/director is an opportunity to see a work before committing to the playwright's agent for performance rights. Presentation of the four to six plays each issue also provides an interesting barometer as to the content and style of contemporary aspiring and professional playwrights. Some plays typewritten; no graphics.
DEPT: "Drama Forum." (spring-62). "Book Reviews." (spring-75).
TYPL: "Theory and Practice for the Playwright." (spring-62). "The Off-Off Broadway Theatre," "An Interview with Richard Foreman," "The Paris Theatrical Season." (spring-75).
SCHL: Quarterly (winter-61/62 - ?); Semiannual (? - ?); 90 pp.
SPAN: Winter, 1961/1962 - Spring, 1975//
VARIES
--Winter, 1961/1962 - Winter, 1967/1968 as First Stage (ISSN: 0885-047x).
LC: PN 6111.D7
DD: 808.82/04
ISSN: 0012-5954
ABST: --Annual Bibliography of English Language and Literature (ISSN: 0066-3786)

DRAMA LEAGUE MONTHLY

PUBL: The Drama League of America, Mount Morris, IL.
DESC: Buoyed by the success of sponsoring a nation-wide celebration of the Shakespeare Tercentenary, the Drama League of America launched this serial in April, 1916 to continue what the editors called "...a fermentation of interest in drama which promises a great dramatic revival on American soil." The Drama League used its monthly publication to promote new American plays, provide a forum for discussion of the American dramatic art form, and reported on dramatic activities of Drama League members throughout the country. Small format; no graphics.
DEPT: "Bulletined Plays," listings by city; "News from Centres," "Educational Department." (10-17).
TYPL: "Drama League War Work," "Organizing the Social and Recreational Life of Communities Near Camps," "5,000 Sailors See The Wanderer." (10-17).
SCHL: Monthly [except Jun - Aug]; 25 pp.
SPAN: Apr, 1916 - May, 1919//
VARIES
--Apr, 1916 as Monthly Bulletin.
ABSORBED BY
--Drama, The [Chicago].
LC: PN 2016.D64

✦ DRAMA-LOGUE

SUB: "America's foremost casting newspaper."
PUBL: Drama-Logue, Inc., 1456 North Gordon St., Los Angeles, CA 90028.
DESC: A long-time favorite of aspiring and working actors/actresses, *Drama-Logue* continues to showcase opportunities in the live stage, motion picture, audio and television fields. Primary emphasis is on Southern California, with justifiably famous reviews of productions in those media, and an extensive "now-casting" section segmented into numerous categories. "Union Film & TV," for example, has listings in the media of "Feature Films," "Film," "Television," and "Commercials," under segment titles "Now Casting," "What's Happening," "In Development," and "Talent Agencies." The "Casting Notices," section has sub-segments of "Stage- Equity," "AEA 99-Seat Plan," "Non-Union Theatres," "Films-Non-Union," "Student," "Commercials," "Music Video," "Grad Student," "TV/Video," "Music," "Singers," "Dance," "Writers," "Tech" for stage, film and video, "Teachers," "Variety," and "Game Shows." Columnists provide current information about these media in a variety of cities and settings. For the working professional, *Drama Logue* is a necessary, informative and entertaining publication, and well worth the $50 yearly subscription price (May, 91). Stapled large magazine format (11 ⅞ x 15 inches / 295 x 380 mm), black/white editorial content with two- color cover, all published on coated paperstock. Numerous pictures and advertisements by vendors catering to the acting community.
DEPT: "Theatre Beat," column by Bruce Feld; "Screen Scene," column by Tom Provenzano; "Theatre Reviews," extensive West Coast stage productions; "Critics' Choices," top-rated productions; "So. Calif. Opening Nights," theatre listing; "Union Film & TV," now casting; "Casting Notices," extensive listing; "Film Reviews," "New York, New York," column by Michael Sander; "Cabaret Corner," column by Jason McCloskey; "Las Vegas Desert Spiel," column by Neil Hoffman; "Performance Art," column by Lucia Dewey; "Community Theatre," column by Gene Warech and Lynn Warech; "Dance Spectrum," column by Lucia Dewey; "The Underground Astrologer," column by Barry Brownlee; "San Francisco Scene," column by Dean Goodman. (5-16-91).
TYPL: "Long Beach CLO Says Hello to 'Bye Bye Birdie'," "Down-to-Earth Casting Director James F. Tarzia Offers Skies-the-Limit Advice to Ambitious Actors," "Celebrity Acution for Outreach," "Falk Roasted for LIFE," "Plotting to Be a Scriptwriter." (5-16-91).
SCHL: Weekly [except last week in Dec], 35 pp.
SPAN: Jan, 1970?+
ISSN: 0272-2720

DRAMA MAGAZINE, THE

SUB: "A quarterly review." (Feb, 1911 - ?).

SUB: "A quarterly review of dramatic literature." (Feb, 1911 - May, 1919).
SUB: "A monthly review of dramatic literature." (Oct, 1919 - May, 1925).
SUB: "A review of the allied arts of the theatre." (Oct, 1925 - May, 1930).
SUB: "In combination with the Little Theatre Monthly." (Oct, 1930 - Jun, 1931).
PUBL: The Drama Corporation, 15 West 44th St., New York, NY.
DESC: *The Drama Magazine* began as a quarterly review of theatre. During its first season of publication, a complete play was offered each issue, oftentimes consuming over one-half of the contents of the 220 pages offered. In addition, articles provided a state-of-drama report in major world cities, and a forum of discussion for readers. The serial made major changes in October, 1930, moving to a magazine-size format of 30 pages per monthly issue. The editors excised the printing of full-length plays, and substituted two-page, one-act plays instead. This editorial change brought a new vitality to the serial, providing expanded topical areas; especially in the areas of radio broadcasts and puppet shows. Also beginning with the October, 1930 issue was a new supplement, *Little Theatre Monthly*, covering "Little theatres and community theatres, university, college, school and high school dramatics, religious drama, and settlement drama."
DEPT: "Editorial." (5-11). "Moments with the New Books," "Popular Study Course," "In the Realm of the Dance," "The Travel Department," "College Drama News," "The Drama League of America," newsbriefs; "The Puppet Department." (2-31).
TYPL: "The Dramatic Season and the Spirit of the Time," "The Drama in London," "The Formula of the American Drama." (5-11). "Towards an Adult Theatre," "Censorship in the United States," "Broadway Plays Pass in Review," "Chamber Theatre in South America." (2-31).
SCHL: Quarterly (Feb, 1911 - May, 1919); Monthly (Oct, 1919 - Jun, 1924); Eight issues per year (Oct, 1924+), 40 pp.
SPAN: Feb, 1911 - Jun, 1931//
VARIES
--Feb, 1911 - May, 1930 as Drama, The [Chicago].
ABSORBED
--Drama League Monthly, Jun, 1919.
--Little Theatre Monthly, May, 1925.
LC: PN 1601.D6

Drama Review, The
Spring, 1968 - Winter, 1987//
(ISSN: 0012-5962)
SEE: TDR

DRAMA SURVEY
SUB: "A review of dramatic literature & the theatrical arts." (May, 1961 to date?).
PUBL: Bolingbroke Society, Inc., 800 Washington Avenue S.E., Minneapolis, MN 55414.
DESC: "A flourishing theatre has always been one of the principal attributes of a flourishing culture, and like the other arts, the theatre can flourish only when it is subjected to constant critical scrutiny." This, plus the construction of the new Tyrone Guthrie Repertory Theatre, and the belief "...that the foundation of this new theatre in the center of the continent rather than in New York is an event of major significance," provided the stimulus for the publication of this serial. Typically, each issue had three segments; articles, theatre surveys, and book reviews. International in scope, it is published in journal format; no graphics.
DEPT: "Theatre Survey," "Book Reviews." (10-61).
TYPL: "Magnanimous Despair," "A Half Century of Scandinavian Drama," "New Dimensions in German Comedy." (10-61).
SCHL: Three issues per year, 125 pp.
SPAN: May, 1961 - Winter, 1968/1969//
LC: PN 1601.D65
DD: 792
ISSN: 0419-7127
ABST: --Annual Bibliography of English Language and Literature (ISSN: 0066-3786)
--Social Science and Humanities Index (ISSN: 0037-7899)

Drama, The [Chicago]
Feb, 1911 - May, 1930//
SEE: DRAMA MAGAZINE, THE

DRAMATIC CENSOR, THE
SUB: "Or weekly theatrical report." (Jan, 1800 - Jun 28, 1800).
SUB: "Or critical and biographical illustration of the British stage for the year 1811, involving a correct register of every night's performances at our metropolitan theatres, and published with a view to sustaining the morality and dignity of the drama." (Jul, 1800 - Jun, 1801).
SUB: "Or monthly epitome of taste, fashion, and manners." (Jul, 1800 - Jun, 1801).
PUBL: J. Roach and C. Chapple, London, England.
DESC: Editor J. M. Williams served up an interesting periodical of the British stage in *The Dramatic Censor*. Conforming to the publishing style of the 18th century, there are no article titles, nor departmental items to be found within a given issue. Instead, each issue is comprised of stage production reviews, noting the date of performance, the theatre, playwright and production title. The function of this publication was criticism, which was ably accomplished. About "The Honest Welchman," at the Covent-Garden on Saturday, March 29, 1800: "It is, in every sense of the word, so contemptible a performance, that criticism will scarcely deign to honour it even with reprehension, but spurns it, as unworthy of her serious notice." On

the positive side, the "Egyptian Festival" at the Drury-Lane theatre on Monday, March 31, 1800 drew this response: "Mr. Hoare is above the common level of modern stage writers. His productions are distinguished by neat humour and elegant diction. He possesses, likewise, the faculty, which few authors of musical pieces can boast, of incorporating his songs with the plot, and rendering the verse and the diologue mutually subservient to each other." Of note in the sampled issue of 1800 was an "Historical Retrospect of the Public Controversy, and Collateral Proceedings Relative to, and Connected with, the Theatrical Insurrection of the 'Glorious Eight'," a play which had its debut in January, 1800 at Covent-Garden. The article provided a very detailed record of events, statements, and segments of the play which were found to be objectionable by the public and the authorities. By the end of 1800, pagination had increased some 14 pages to a total of 40. Other changes noted were general inclusion of cast and character lists connected with each theatrical critique, general commentary concerning theatrical issues (such as "General Retrospect of the Performances of Mr. Cooke"), and a fascinating series of open letters written to raise the standards of theatrical production and management. In the December, 1800 issue there was a "Letter to Richard Brinsley Sheridan, Esq., on the Conduct and Proceedings of the New Manager of Drury-Lane Theatre." This is an excellent resource of early London theatre.

DEPT: None. (4-5-1800).
TYPL: None. (4-5-1800).
SCHL: Weekly (Jan, 1800 - Jun 28, 1800); Monthly (Jul, 1800+), 26 pp.
SPAN: Jan 4, 1800 - Jul, 1801//

DRAMATIC MAGAZINE, THE

PUBL: Dramatic Magazine Press, Chicago, IL.
DESC: In its last issue for August, 1900, the publisher ironically extolled the virtues of his serial, telling readers: *"The Dramatic Magazine* is the only publication of the kind in the United States. It is exclusively devoted to Theatrical, Operatic and Musical matters. Its illustrations are, without exception, superior to those of any monthly on the newsstands." Despite these statements, it is probable that subscribers held a differing view, and *The Dramatic Magazine* ceased publication in August, 1900 after three brief years of publication. In the years between the first issue (Aug, 1897) and the last, it promoted the virtues of midwestern (and especially Chicago-style) theatre. Articles covered orchestra, plays, stage equipment, costumes, and even "powder rooms." But this serial focused on the actor, providing profiles (but never criticism) of new and established members of the stage. Numerous graphics printed on quality paper.
DEPT: "Chicago Summer Attractions," "Dramatic Chat," "From the July Magazines," "New Books," "New Music." (8-1897). "Stage Chat," "Musical Chat." (2-1900).
TYPL: "Dramatic Artists in Vaudeville," "Stock Companies of Today," "An American Baritone in Grand Opera," "A Group of Stage Celebrities." (8- 1897). "Sailors of the Stage," "The Decline of the Drama," "The Pan-American Exposition," "The Terre Haute Play House." (2-1900).
SCHL: Monthly, 150 pp.
SPAN: Aug, 1897 - Aug, 1900//
LC: PN 2000.D7.

DRAMATIC MAGAZINE, THE

SUB: "Embellished with numerous engravings of the principal performers."
PUBL: Whittaker, Treacher and Co., Ave Maria Lane, London, England.
DESC: In their first issue of March 2, 1829, the editors rued the fact that the likes of Churchill, Lloyd and others did not have the advantage of possessing copies of *The Dramatic Magazine* for their enlightenment and enjoyment of the theatre: "Now had a Theatrical Review been established, giving an exact report of all theatrical proceedings, it would not only have been a great source of amusement to the public, but have proved of most essential service to the actor; for there are many minute circumstances in the exhibition of a character upon the stage, which do not appear from reading the poet, but must be supplied by the player from his own observation of human life. These minute circumstances may be preserved in a Theatrical Review, as a gallery of pictures, in the dresses of the times, gives us a lively idea of the appearance of our ancestors." This serial is a venerable treasure-trove of British theatre from March 2, 1829 to its (assumed) demise with the January 1, 1831 issue. Theatrical scholars will especially appreciate the ongoing series of articles detailing current and historical reviews of British playwrights, criticism, costume, and general dramatic development. American scholars should note an interesting letter to the editor (dated November 1, 1830), in which a gentleman purports to give the history of British dramatic emigration to the American colonies. *The Dramatic Magazine* is filled with saucy wit, criticism, history, and the joy of the London and provincial theatres of the early 1800s. Small journal format; one or two metal engravings per issue of current actors and actresses in costume.
DEPT: "Miscellanies," "Provincial Intelligence," "Poetry and Songs." (5-1-1829). "Theatrical Journal," detailed happenings in Drury Lane, Covent Garden, Haymarket, and minor theatres; "Provincial Intelligence." (11-1-1830).
TYPL: "Covent Garden Theatrical Fund Dinner," "Coincidences and Imitations Among Dramatic Writers," "The English Drama, Ancient and Modern," "Memoir of the Late Mr. Macready." (5-1-1829). "Illustrated Memoirs of Our Early Actors and Actresses," "Notices of the Lives and Writings of Our Early Dramatists." (11-1-1830).
SCHL: Monthly, 30 pp.
SPAN: Mar 2, 1829 - Apr, 1831//

LC: PN 2001.D7

DRAMATIC MIRROR, THE

SUB: "Gazing at the Stars."
SUB: "The show news weekly."
SUB: "All the news."
SUB: "Music, pictures, drama, vaudeville, stock."
SUB: "Cartoon reviews of bills, picture programs."
PUBL: Dramatic Mirror Co., 1639 Broadway, New York, NY.
DESC: This dynamic weekly publication under Managing Editor Louis R. Reid provided a detailed review of what was important and upcoming in drama, vaudeville, and motion pictures. With an emphasis on the greater New York City area, the publication was evenly divided among the three entertainment areas, with a wealth of information contained in each. For example, in the sampled issue for 1919, the "Dramatic" section provided status news of a number of Broadway stars, including Eddie Cantor, DeWolf Hopper, Ed Wynn, Marie Dressler, and Helen Ferguson. The "Vaudeville" section reviewed numerous current variety acts, including Thurston the Magician, Al Jolson, Mae West, Joe Laurie, Frank Crumit and the Vatican Singers. The "Pictures" section provided a full picture page covering "Who's Wife," a new film release, along with other current fare, "His Majesty--the American," "The Right to Happiness," "Broken Commandments," and "The Market of Souls." Full-page advertisements by music concerns, motion picture producers, vaudevillians and Broadway theatrical entrepreneurs added to each issue's content. One slogan seen throughout the publication was "Gazing at the Stars," a phrase which neatly sums up the delightful approach to entertainment which the staff of *The Dramatic Mirror* maintained for over 40 years. This remains a wonderful resource for historical research in the Broadway, vaudeville, and motion picture fields. Stapled large magazine format, black ink on uncoated paper stock, cover for sampled issue of September 25, 1919 was two-color dark blue and orange ink on coated paper stock, extensive advertising for the trade (10 ⅛ x 13 ¼ inches / 255 x 335 mm).
DEPT: "The Broadway Time Table," current theatrical fare in New York City; "No Man's Land," news items concerning Broadway celebrities, column by Mlle Rialto; "About Stock Plays and Players in Many Cities," selected theatre review; "How the Shows are Doing on the Road," road report; "Where Shows Are," short location information; "Where'll We Go?," New York City restaurant guide; "Deaths," "Vaudeville Volleys," review of current vaudeville fare; "In the Song Shop," music on Broadway and in Vaudeville, column by E. M. Wickes; "Where the Acts are Next Week and How They Did This Week," American vaudeville fare; "Without Fear or Favor," 'By an old exhibitor', entertainment commentary; "Is That So!," film personnel newsbriefs; "Broadway Picture Programs and Music," very unique and extensive information on music and programs accompanying motion pictures, column by M. M. Hansford; "Picture First Showings Reported by Wire," telegraph box office reports; "Songs that Scored in Vaudeville This Week," brief listing; "First Showings by Wire Summary of Last Two Weeks." (9-25-19).
TYPL: "Members of the Lambs to Have Club in Adirondacks Next Year," "Theater Tickets Raised to $2.50," "Jazz Dominates Palace Program," "Mae West, Joe Laurie and the Nagyfys in New Acts," "Strike in California Studios." (9-25-19).
SCHL: Weekly (Jan 26, 1889 - Jan 7, 1922); Monthly (Mar, 1922+), 35 pp.
SPAN: 1879 - Apr, 1922//
VARIES
--1879? - ? as New York Mirror.
--Jan 26, 1889 - Feb 10, 1917 as New York Dramatic Mirror, The.
--Feb 17, 1917 - Feb 1, 1919 as Dramatic Mirror of the Stage and Motion Pictures.
--Feb 8, 1919 - Oct 9, 1920 as Dramatic Mirror.
--Oct 16, 1920 - Dec 24, 1921 as Dramatic Mirror and Theatre World.

Dramatic Mirror

Feb 8, 1919 - Oct 9, 1920//
SEE: DRAMATIC MIRROR, THE

DRAMATIC MIRROR AND LITERARY COMPANION, THE

SUB: "Devoted to the stage and the fine arts."
PUBL: Turner & Fisher, 52 Chatham St., New York, NY.
DESC: Editor James Rees in the first issue for August 14, 1841, speaks of a beleagured theatre, one that has become the target of crusades originating from city church pulpits, and weakened from within by "starring systems." The purpose of this serial was to battle these demoralizing forces and encourage the New York City theatre industry via critique and box office support. Intermingled with dramatic critiques were literary works of serialized fiction, poetry, and essays. Of special note was the inclusion of theatrical reports from several cities each issue, such as Cincinnati, Boston, Philadelphia, Baltimore, New Orleans; and, of course, New York City. Dramatic scholars will find much rich and varied material within these pages. No graphics, save masthead woodcut; 3-column, 7 point type in magazine format.
DEPT: "Items," newsbriefs; "Popular Songs," lyrics. (1-1-1842).
TYPL: "The Southern Stage, Actors and Authors," "My First and Last Appearance on Any Stage," "The Stage and Peerage." (1-1-1842).
SCHL: Weekly, 8 pp.
SPAN: Aug 14, 1841 - May 7, 1842//
LC: PN 2000.D75

Dramatic Mirror and Theatre World
Oct 16, 1920 - Dec 24, 1921//
SEE: DRAMATIC MIRROR, THE

Dramatic Mirror of the Stage and Motion Pictures
Feb 17, 1917 - Feb 1, 1919//
SEE: DRAMATIC MIRROR, THE

DRAMATIC REVIEW, THE
PUBL: Review Company, 45 Winter St., , Boston, MA.
DESC: Vaudeville and legitimate stage activity in greater Boston was the scope of this weekly dramatic events diversion. Each 16-page issue was aimed at the actors as much as at the audience at large. Duotone covers (beginning with Dec 9, 1899 issue), and numerous photographs of performers.
DEPT: "About Current Plays," "Gossip," "The Grumbler," commentary; "Heard on the New York Rialto," from the New York office. (3-31-1900).
TYPL: None.
SCHL: Weekly, 16 pp.
SPAN: Dec 2, 1899 - Aug 4, 1900?//
VARIES
--? - Nov 25, 1899 as Boston Dramatic Review.
LC: PN 2000.D8

✤ DRAMATICS
SUB: "Published by the International Thespian Society."
PUBL: The International Thespian Society, 3368 Central Park Way, Cincinnati, OH 45225.
DESC: "We think *Dramatics* serves an important function in theatre. For many people--probably for most of our readers--*Dramatics* is a first introduction to what theatre is all about: what functions it serves; what kind of people do it, and why; why it should be taken seriously. Recognizing that most of our readers won't go on to careers in theatre, our goal has been to instill in them a lifelong love of theatre. And we have included liberal doses of career counseling--something no other theatre magazine in this country does--for those of our readers determined to try their hand at one of the riskiest of all professions." *Dramatics* for six years also included an internal organization publication, *Dramatics Curtain Edition*, which ceased publication in September, 1984. The *Curtain Edition* was merged into the general readership *Dramatics* magazine. For the sampled issue of 1992: stapled magazine format, black ink editorial content with full-color cover on coated paper stock, advertising (8 ¼ x 10 ⅞ inches / 210 x 275 mm).
DEPT: None. (9-84). "Journal," news items; "Theatre Talk," column by Paul Steiner; "Books," lengthy reviews; "Video," new product review; "Festivals and Conferences," 'A schedule of theatre festivals and conferences sanctioned by the Educational Theatre Association'. (1-92).
TYPL: "Scott Glenn, Food for the Soul, and More," "If You Become a Critic," "Advice to Hamlet's (Student Players)," "Play Publishers/Leasing Agents and You," "Embossed Leather Masks." (9-84). "German Theatre, Then and Now," "Full House: California Cottage Theatre Makes Plays at Home," "The Press Rep: Filling the Seats," "Love, Death and the Prom: Six Short Plays by Jon Jory." (1-92).
SCHL: Monthly (Oct, 1948 - ?); Bimonthly (? - May, 1981); Monthly [except Jun - Aug] (Apr, 1986+), 50 pp.
SPAN: Jan, 1929+
EDITION
--Curtain Edition.
VARIES
--Oct, 1929 - May, 1944 as High School Thespian.
--Oct, 1944 - May, 1948 as Dramatics.
--Oct, 1969 - ? as Curtain.
--Feb, 1981 - Sep?, 1981 as Dramatics' Curtain.
ISSN: 0012-5989

Dramatics
Oct, 1944 - May, 1948//
SEE: DRAMATICS

Dramatics' Curtain
Feb, 1981 - Sep?, 1981//
SEE: DRAMATICS

✤ DRIVING AMBITION
SUB: "The hi-fi choice guide to in-car entertainment."
PUBL: Dennis Publishing, Ltd., 14 Rathbone Place, London W1P 1DE England.
DESC: Based on a highly successful layout and content design of parent publication, *Hi-Fi Choice*, this supplement to the home audiophile, monthly covers audio components, installation, and operation of quality audio components in automobiles. In the sampled 1991 supplement, articles detailed a luxury sound system installed in the S-Class Mercedes; four automobile radio/CD player units (two of which were "Recommended"); how the British RDS (Radio Data System) was quickly becoming the world standard for car radio transmission/reception; and a thoughtful commentary on whether the term "in-car hi-fi" is a "...valid concept, or merely an awkward contradiction in terms." Like its parent publication, *Driving Ambition* displays a crisp, dynamic layout design which makes it a pleasure to read. Supplement for 1991 is stapled magazine format, black/white and color editorial content on coated paper stock (8 ¼ x 11 ¾ inches / 210 x 295 mm).
DEPT: "The Reviews," extensive audio reviews for the car. (7-91).

TYPL: "Surround Sound," "Taming the Airwaves," "In at the Deep End." (7-91).
SCHL: ?, 16 pp.
SPAN: ?+
SUPPLEMENT TO
--Hi-Fi Choice (ISSN: 0955-1115), ?+

✥ DWB

SUB: "Doctor Who Bulletin."
SUB: "The British journal of telefantasy."
PUBL: Gary Leigh, PO Box 1015, Brighton BN2 2YU, England.
DESC: For the numerous fans of the "Doctor Who" television series, *DWB* provides complete details on the series, including the actors; and stories on producers, directors, and other behind-the-camera staff. Advertisements offer merchandise, and black/white production stills from the series, as well as promotion of other publications in a like vein. While the emphasis is on "Doctor Who," there is a fair amount of review material concerning other science fiction themes, including "Star Trek" on British satellite, and a host of printed works of a reference and serial nature. This is a publication that science fiction fans can appreciate for the wealth of detail, interesting interviews, and program series provided in every issue. For the sampled issue of 1988: the publication was typewritten, primarily black/white editorial content with some spot color. Two short years later, for the sampled issue of 1990: stapled magazine format, typeset editorial content, with mixture of black/white and full-color pages on coated paper stock (8 ¼ x 11 ¾ inches / 210 x 295 mm).
DEPT: "Editorial," "WHO News," news of Doctor Who television series; "Briefly," newsbriefs; "Video Review," "Letters," "News," "Preview," "In * Print," review; "Interview," "Retrospective." (7-90).
TYPL: "Cinema Verity Hot Favourites for Independent 'WHO' Production," "Memory Cheats 'The Brain of Morbius'," "Power Photos Proof of Troughton's Versatility," "Star Trek Takes Off on Sky," "Peter Grimwade: The Final Interview." (7-90).
SCHL: Monthly, 20 pp.
SPAN: ?+

E

E-ITV

SUB: "The magazine of closed-circuit and community antenna TV."
SUB: "The techniques magazine for professional video."
PUBL: Broadband Publications, 295 Madison Ave., New York, NY 10017.
DESC: With basic treatment of new equipment and techniques in educational and industrial (corporate) television, this publication was especially helpful to individuals new to the corporate video field, a field which had witnessed phenomenal growth in previous decades. Publication defined the role of corporate video, and championed its existence as a separate medium apart from broadcast, cable and other video media. Of special note were in-depth facility profiles. For the sampled issues of 1988: mixture of black/white, spot- and full-color pages and cover on coated paper stock with advertising in perfect-bound magazine format (7 7/8 x 10 3/4 inches / 200 x 270 mm).
DEPT: "Newsbeat," "Production House News," "The Screening Room," reviews; "Teleconferencing Report." (9-86). "Dateline," "Newsbeat," "Teleproduction Journal," "Screening Room," "Points of View," letters. (12-87).
TYPL: "Eliminating Interactive Barriers," "Case Studies Prove Cost-Effective Benefits of Interactivity," "A Dollars and Sense Approach to the Interactive Videodisc." (9-86). "Rapid Response: Video Meets the Retail and Fashion Challenge," "In Pursuit of Excellence in Corporate Video." (12-87).
SCHL: Bimonthly (Aug, 1965 - Jun/Jul, 1967); Monthly (?+), 55 pp.
SPAN: Aug, 1965 - Feb/Mar, 1988//
VARIES
--Aug, 1965 - Jun/Jul, 1967 as View.
--Sep, 1967 - Oct, 1968 as Cablecasting and Educational Television (ISSN: 0574-9905).
--Nov, 1968 - 1971 as Educational Television (ISSN: 0424-6101).
--1972 - May, 1983 as Educational & Industrial Television (ISSN: 0046-1466).
LC: LB 1044.7 .E364
DD: 371.3/358/05
ISSN: 0743-7773
ABST: --Education Index (ISSN: 0013-1385)
--Hospital Literature Index (ISSN: 0018-5736)
--Media Review Digest (ISSN: 0363-7778)
--Predicasts

EBU Bulletin
1954 - 1957//
SEE: EBU REVIEW. TECHNICAL.

EBU Documentation and Information Bulletin
1950 - 1953//
SEE: EBU REVIEW. TECHNICAL.

EBU Review. Part A: Technical
Jan, 1958 - Dec, 1971//
(ISSN: 0423-9865)
SEE: EBU REVIEW. TECHNICAL.

EBU Review. Part B: General and Legal
Feb, 1958 - Nov, 1971//
(ISSN: 0012-7493)
SEE: EBU REVIEW. PROGRAMMES, ADMINISTRATION, LAW.

✣ EBU REVIEW. PROGRAMMES, ADMINISTRATION, LAW.

PUBL: European Broadcasting Union, Geneva, Switzerland.
DESC: *EBU Review. Part B: General and Legal* began publication in February, 1958. This superb publication covered virtually every aspect of broadcast production in member nations of the European Broadcasting Union, and has been recognized for its thoroughness, and bringing together news items, new programming concepts, production facilities, legal reports, and articles concerning audience acceptance of international programs. January, 1972 saw the serial change names to *EBU Review. Radio and Television Programmes, Administration, Law*, continuing the same fine tradition as its predecessors (Parts A and B) of covering indepth new program concepts, production facilities, legal issues and administrative-management problems in the European Broadcasting Union. It is well-written and illustrated. A sampling of articles from 1990 included, "The Broadcasting of a Colourized Version of a Film," "Metered Television Audience Measurement in Finland," "What Kind of Future for Radio Drama," "HDTV Changes Production Ground-Rules," and "The Demand for Television Programmes--Europeanization or Americanization." Well recommended to anyone interested in world (national), or international broadcasting. For the sampled issues of 1978: black ink with some spot-color pages and two-color cover on coated paper stock, no advertising (8 x 10 7/8 inches / 200 x 275 mm). A format

change took place effective with the January, 1983 issue: editorial content consisted of black ink with spot-color and two-color cover on coated paper stock, some pages consisting of black ink on color uncoated paper stock with no advertising. Issues for late 1990 included a significant number of full- and spot-color pages and limited advertising. Issues for 1983 and 1990: (8 x 11 ½ inches / 200 x 290 mm).
DEPT: "Legal Notebook," in-depth articles on current broadcast issues. (11-71). "EBU Newsreel," upcoming events; "Personalia," personnel briefs; "Legal Notebook," in-depth legal discussions. (1-77). "Book Reviews." (11-90).
TYPL: "Cooperation in Program Planning and Presentation: a New Trend in the ARD's Radio Programs for Children and Young People," "Young Japanese in Today's Society 'With Teenagers,'" "Italian Broadcasting and its Young Audiences--New Approaches in Children's Television," "Matching the Programs to Modern Youth: New Trends in Finland," "Serving Youth: CBS Spotlight in Youth Problems and Aspirations." (11-71). "Direct Broadcasting to the Home Via Satellite; Possible Applications in the United Kingdom," "A Footnote to the General Assembly of the International Radio-Television University (URTI), Two Testimonies," "Twenty Years of Television in Span: Organization and Structure of the Service," "Why Four Weeks Without Television?" (1-77). "Flashback on the 1990 World Football Cup: The Television Production Model for the World Cup," "The Europe Coproduction Association is Five Years Old. Towards a European TV Drama Industry?," "Broadcasting Re-Regulation in Europe--Citizenship and Consumerism," "Problems and Outlook for a Broadcasting Service's Music Library," "Welte-Mignon--A Cofinanced Project for Radio." (11-90).
SCHL: Bimonthly, [alternating with Part A] (Feb, 1958 - Nov, 1971); Bimonthly (Dec, 1971+), 45 pp.
SPAN: Feb, 1958+
SPLIT OFF WITH
--EBU Review. Part A: Technical (ISSN: 0423-9865) (from parent) EBU Bulletin.
VARIES
--Feb, 1958 - Nov, 1971 as EBU Review. Part B: General and Legal (ISSN: 0012-7493).
--Jan, 1972 - 1982 as EBU Review. Radio and Television Programmes, Administration, Law.
LC: PN 1991.3 .E8E2
DD: 384.54/094
ISSN: 0012-7493

EBU Review. Radio and Television Programmes, Administration, Law

Jan, 1972 - 1982//
SEE: EBU REVIEW. PROGRAMMES, ADMINISTRATION, LAW.

✤ EBU REVIEW. TECHNICAL.

PUBL: EBU Technical Center, European Broadcasting Union, Geneva, Switzerland.
DESC: For almost 40 years, *EBU Review - Technical* has provided a quality engineering forum for the discussion of electronic developments and their application to European broadcasting. Lay readers will be able to understand and comprehend most technical articles, although some segments require technical knowledge. A clean layout style enhances readability; graphics.
DEPT: "Editorial," "Calendar of International Technical Meetings," "Abstracts and Reviews," "EBU Technical Meetings." (10-84).
TYPL: "Planning Considerations for the Second Session of the VHF/FM Planning Conference: the Method of Foremost Priority," "A Computerized Frequency Assignment Method Based on the Theory of Graphs," "European Sound and Television Broadcasting Stations." (10-84).
SCHL: Bimonthly, 50 pp.
SPAN: 1950+
SPLIT OFF WITH
--EBU Review. Part B: General and Legal (from parent) EBU Bulletin.
VARIES
--1950 - 1953 as EBU Documentation and Information Bulletin.
--1954 - 1957 as EBU Bulletin.
--Jan, 1958 - Dec, 1971 as EBU Review. Part A: Technical (ISSN: 0423-9865).
LC: TK 6540.E22
DD: 621.3841/05
ABST: --Computer & Control Abstracts (ISSN: 0036-8113)
--Electrical & Electronics Abstracts (ISSN: 0036-8105)
--Engineering Index Annual (ISSN: 0360-8557)
--Engineering Index Bioengineering Abstracts (ISSN: 0736-6213)
--Engineering Index Energy Abstracts (ISSN: 0093-8408)
--Engineering Index Monthly (1984) (ISSN: 0742-1974)
--Engineering Index Monthly (ISSN: 0013-7960)
--Physics Abstracts. Science Abstracts. Series A. (ISSN: 0036-8091)

✤ ECHO BUSS

SUB: "Users group newsletter."
PUBL: Fostex Corporation of America, 15431 Blackburn Ave., Norwalk, CA 90650.
DESC: A corporate promotional publication aimed at current and prospective owners of Fostex audio equipment, this eight-page quarterly provides case stories, applications, and updates on new equipment and software releases by Foxtex. Graphics.
DEPT: "Thru the Grapevine," recent projects using Fostex equipment. (summer-88).
TYPL: "You Don't Have to be a Rock Star to Make Money with Your Music," "RM Monitors." (summer-88).

SCHL: Quarterly, 8 pp.
SPAN: Winter, 1986?+?

EDISON KINETROGRAM
PUBL: Edison Manufacturing Co., Ltd., Edison Works, Willesden Junction, London NW, England.
DESC: This large-format serial was a trade promotional for recently released Edison films in Great Britain. The editorial content of each issue was devoted to lengthy descriptions and promotional features of each film, the film number, telegraph cable code, copyright date, release date, and length of film (expressed in feet). Each review included a description of the film type; industrial, comedy, or dramatic. Many of the reviews contained several still pictures from the releases. Some reviews included production details. Of special note in the March 1, 1911 issue was an article by Thomas Edison in which he stated, "When I invented the modern moving picture, in the summer of 1899, I sought to do for the eye what the phonograph had done for the ear." Also beginning in that issue was a special feature called the "Critics' Page," with the subtitle, "On which is shown, in the order of its release, a criticism on each Edison film by some one of the several reviewers for the film and dramatic press." Beginning with the May 15, 1911 issue, individual film casts were listed along with reviews. And beginning with the March 1, 1913 issue, all films included the statement "This film has been passed by the British Board of Film Censors."
DEPT: "Critics' Page," "Press Comments on Edison Films," "Questions and Answers," letters to editor; (3-1-11).
TYPL: individual film reviews.
SCHL: Semimonthly (Apr 15, 1910 - Mar 1, 1911); Biweekly (Mar 1, 1911 - Apr 1, 1913), 16 pp.
SPAN: Apr 15, 1910 - Apr 1, 1913//

✢ EDITOR AND PUBLISHER
SUB: "The fourth estate."
SUB: "Spot news and features about newspapers, advertisers and agencies."
SUB: "The only independent weekly journal of newspapering."
PUBL: Editor and Publisher, 11 West 19th St., New York, NY 10011.
DESC: *Editor and Publisher*, The Fourth Estate, bills itself as "The oldest publishers and advertisers newspaper in America," superseding five previous publications back to *The Journalist*, established in 1884. Whether or not it is the oldest continuously published journal is a matter for editorial debate: the fact is that *Editor and Publisher*, known for in-depth coverage and trusted reporting, easily claims the title of dominant business news publication for the American newspaper industry. This is a news magazine which is concerned with the financial and regulatory health of its member publishers. Sampled issue for August 3, 1991 was stapled magazine format, black/white editorial content with mixture of black/white and color page advertising, all on coated paper stock, advertising (8 x 10 ⅞ inches / 205 x 275 mm).
DEPT: "Catch-Lines," interesting news briefs concerning reporters, pressroom workers, etc.; "Circulation," "Plant and Equipment," "Advertising." (10-77). "The 4th Estate," comment; "Editorial Workshop," "Letters to the Editor," "Newspeople in the News," "Obituaries," "Technical Briefs," "Syndicates," "Shop Talk at Thirty," commentary. (3-7-87).
TYPL: "Reporters Group Declines Payment for Pike Report," "District Sales Managers Sell Non-Subscribers," "Chicago Newspaper Ad Sales Survey Probed." (10-77). "Think Tank Under Fire," "Battling Against JOAs," "Labor Lawyer Warns Newspapers," "Special Kids Publish Special Newspapers." (3-7-87).
SCHL: Weekly, (Jun 29, 1901 - 1944); Weekly [with an additional issue in Jan, later Feb] (Jan 6, 1945 - Apr 19, 1958); Weekly (Apr 26, 1958+), 50 pp.
SPAN: Jun 29, 1901+
 VARIES
 --Jun 29, 1901 - Jun 3, 1911 as Editor and Publisher.
 --Jun 10, 1911 - Apr 15, 1916 as Editor and Publisher and Journalist.
 ABSORBED
 --Journalist, Jan 26, 1907.
 --Advertising, Jul, 1925.
 --Fourth Estate, Dec, 1927.
LC: PN 4700.E4
DD: 070.4
ISSN: 0013-094x
ABST: --ABI/Informer
 --Business Periodical Index (ISSN: 0007-6961)
 --InfoBank
 --Printing Abstracts (ISSN: 0031-109x)
 --Trade and Industry Index

Editor and Publisher
Jun 29, 1901 - Jun 3, 1911//
SEE: EDITOR AND PUBLISHER

Editor and Publisher and Journalist
Jun 10, 1911 - Apr 15, 1916//
SEE: EDITOR AND PUBLISHER

EDITORIAL
SUB: "Published for the dissemination of the best editorial thought of the day."
SUB: "For people who think."
PUBL: Editorial Publishing Co., South Whitley, IN.
DESC: Here was a review used by both the literate public and the newspaper editor. "Papers from every part of the Union are carefully perused for editorial utterances on vital and interesting topics. The best are selected and so arranged and classified that the reader may readily find just the subject that appeals to him. The complete

editorial is reproduced, so that the full connection is displayed, while it is left to the reader's intelligence to make his own deductions." This was quite an amazing effort, considering that some 50 pages of small-type was produced each week. A good resource for historians as well as current-day editors.
DEPT: "Calendar of the News," newsbriefs; "Condensed Thoughts," humorous comment. (8-19-16).
TYPL: "Scense in the Wake of Palaver," "When Past Sixty or Seventy," "Honest, Courageous, True!" (8-19-16).
SCHL: Weekly, 50 pp.
SPAN: May 6, 1915 - Apr 14, 1917//
LC: AP 2.E255

✤ EDITORIAL EYE, THE
SUB: "Focusing on publications standards and practices."
PUBL: Editorial Experts, Inc., 5905 Pratt St., Alexandria, VA 22310.
DESC: A spritely eight-page typewritten newsletter that serves to inform, test, and prick the conscience of journalism editors throughout the nation, this is not a newsletter with weighty matters of opinion: rather its short articles and news briefs point out typical grammatical errors, standards of publication and editorial judgement.
DEPT: "Test Yourself," unique self-exam on editing judgement; "Black Eyes," Bad examples; "Calendar," "Usage Forum." (5-14-79).
TYPL: "Computer Takes on Editors' Tasks," "Proverbs for Proofreading," "What's Happening to American English?" (5-14-79).
SCHL: Twenty issues per year, 8 pp.
SPAN: 1978+
ABSORBED
--Freelancer's Newsletter (ISSN: 0016-0636), Feb, 1979.
ISSN: 0193-7383

✤ EDITORIAL NEWSLETTER
PUBL: Standard Gravure Co., Louisville, KY.
DESC: If one were a newspaper editor, then *Editorial Newsletter* would be like a kindly, knowledgable uncle dispensing friendly, professional advice on improving your work. Editor Angus Perkerson provides practical instruction and encouragement on editorial style and content. This is indeed a "newsman's newsletter." This is appeal to the intellect, without typeset copy, color pictures, screaming advertisements, or loose "blow-in" cards. *Editorial Newsletter* is as informative as it is enjoyable to read.
DEPT: "A Quick Look at the Locally Edited Magazines." (11-66).
TYPL: "Color Shot a Year in Advance," "Why Can't there be More Simultaneous Publication?," "Idea Came from Weekly Story Conference," "Elephant Hunting in Indiana." (11-66).
SCHL: Monthly, 25 pp.
SPAN: ?+?
LC: PN 4784.L6L6

Editorial Research Reports
Jan, 1924 - Dec 26, 1986//
(ISSN: 0013-0958)
SEE: CONGRESSIONAL QUARTERLY'S EDITORIAL RESEARCH REPORTS

EDITORIAL REVIEW
PUBL: The Editorial Review Co., New York, NY.
DESC: This was a review (by reprint) of major newspaper editorials of the day. Of special note was the section, *Contemporary Journalism*, within which one major newspaper would be historically profiled each issue. This remains an interesting look at the quality, stature, and content of newspaper editorials in pre-World War I America.
DEPT: "Contemporary Journalism," "Literary Notes." (2-10).
TYPL: "Our Seagoing Marine," "'Conservation' the Fad of the Year 1909," "Equal Pay for Equal Work," "Taxation, Conservation, and the Cost of Living," "Rapid Transit Problems in New York City." (2-10).
SCHL: Monthly, 100 pp.
SPAN: Aug, 1909 - Aug, 1912//
ABSORBED BY
--Current Literature, Aug, 1912.
LC: AP 2.E26

✤ EDITORIALIST, THE
SUB: "Professional journal of the National Broadcast Editorial Association."
SUB: "Journal of the National Broadcast Editorial Association."
PUBL: National Broadcast Editorial Association, 6223 Executive Blvd., Rockville, MD 20852.
DESC: Issued bimonthly, this serial provides news of activities and the members of the National Broadcast Editorial Association, "...the only organization devoted to heightening the impact of broadcast editorials in both the general community and the field of journalism." The amount of editorial content varies widely from issue to issue, with the largest number of editorial pages appearing in post-convention publications. Articles cover the process of broadcast editorials, from fact gathering to presentation, and the difficulty of the editorialist in structuring the broadcast editorial in a meaningful, fair and accurate manner. Magazine format (8 ½ x 11 inches / 215 x 280 mm), with graphics.
DEPT: "From the President." (1/2-86). "From the President." (9/10-88).
TYPL: "You'll Know Madison Winner by His Work," "Writer Still Yearns for Adventure on the Shuttle," "The Gospel...According to Managers." (1/2-86). "A Propitious Time to Take the Helm," "Convention Gets Political Kickoff," "Ralph Renick Receives James Madison Award," "Journalists, Politicians Debate Character Issue," "Final Panel Explores Progress of Civil Rights." (9/10-88).

SCHL: Bimonthly, 12 pp.
SPAN: Sep/Oct, 1974+

✧ EDITOR'S WORKSHOP

SUB: "The newsletter to help you improve your publication."
SUB: "The newsletter that's guaranteed to improve your publication."
PUBL: Lawrence Ragan Communications, Inc., 407 south Dearborn St., Chicago, IL 60605.
DESC: Deserving of being on every newsletter publisher/editor's desk is this fine publication from Lawrence Ragan Communications, a guide to improvement and a treasure chest of ideas for corporate and organizational publications. A sampling of submitted newsletters are reproduced, evaluated, and complimented (when appropriate) on design, format, writing style, and content. For individuals who publish the company/organization newsletter, *Editor's Workshop* will revitalize and stimulate them to take their newsletter to new heights of quality, interest, and respectability. Some article titles planned for future issues include: "Sell Copy Using Headlines, Leads, Blurbs, and Breakout Quotes," "Avoid the Ten Mortal Sins of the Organizational Press," "How to Turn Your Mugshots into Powerful Photographs," "Why You Must Know Your Audience--and How to Analyze an Audience You've Never Met," and "Humor--It Can be the Only Way to Win Over a Hostile Reader." The ideas contained in a single issue are alone well worth the 1991 yearly subscription cost of $119. Highly recommended. For the sampled issue of 1991: primary publication consisting of black ink on uncoated paper stock in stapled magazine format, with center section "The Editor's Desk," printed two-color ink on uncoated paper, no advertising (8 ½ x 11 inches / 215 x 280 mm).
DEPT: "Short Spots," design column by Ed Arnold; "Shoptalk," "Profile," "Letters," "The Editor's Desk," "Trends," "EW Report Card," "Working Words." (12-91).
TYPL: "Use a Calendar to Get More Names and Pictures in Print," "A Good Story Idea: Show the Evolution of Your Company's Logo," "Sometimes Photographs Show Too Much," "A Dollar Bill is a Useful Gauge for Spacing Elements," "Best Idea of the Month and VPs on Forklifts." (12-91).
SCHL: Monthly, 20 pp.
SPAN: ?+

Educational & Industrial Television
1972 - May, 1983//
(ISSN: 0046-1466)
SEE: E-ITV

EDUCATIONAL BROADCASTING

SUB: "The international journal of audio and visual learning."
PUBL: Barrington Publications, 825 S. Barrington Ave., Los Angeles, CA 90049.
DESC: The field of educational and instructional media is finally seeing the type of public recognition that has been long overdue. Unfortunately, it has arrived too late for *Educational Broadcasting*. This serial took a broad look at the entire educational/instructional field, including production, management, and instructional radio-television for school and industry; with a decided emphasis on production for broadcast. Articles were enhanced by graphics, and assumed some knowledge of video production.
DEPT: "Press Conference," news briefs; "On the Move," appointments and promotions in the ITV world; "Equipment Spectrum," new technology; "New Literature," sales and other print materials.
TYPL: "Instructional Television Rationale," "Designing Sets for Television," "Audio Technology: Audio Recording," "ENG: Not for News Gathering Only." (11/12-76).
SCHL: Monthly (1971 - ?); Bimonthly (?+), 45 pp.
SPAN: Jun, 1971 - Mar/Apr, 1977//
VARIES
--1968 - May, 1971 as Educational-Instructional Broadcasting (ISSN: 0013-1776).
LC: LB 1044.E36
DD: 371.33
ISSN: 0046-1474
ABST: --Education Index (ISSN: 0013-1385)

Educational Broadcasting International
Mar, 1971 - Sep, 1981//
(ISSN: 0013-1970)
SEE: MEDIA IN EDUCATION AND DEVELOPMENT

Educational Broadcasting Review
Oct, 1967 - Jun, 1973//
(ISSN: 0013-1660)
SEE: PUBLIC TELECOMMUNICATIONS REVIEW

EDUCATIONAL COMMUNICATION AND TECHNOLOGY

SUB: "A journal of theory, research and development."
PUBL: Association for Educational Communications and Technology, 1126 16th St., N.W., Washington, DC 20036.
DESC: In Winter, 1953, a new serial entitled *Audio-Visual Communication Review* was inaugurated, and included a forthright editorial: "The launching of this *Audio-Visual Communication Review* is a sign that we are seriously interested in audio-visual research

and communication. We are concerned with communication; we are interested in the answer to the question, 'What does it mean to communicate?'" For 35 years, scholars debated that editorial question posed in that initial edition. Research published within *AV Communication Review* reflected the growth and maturity of communication research during this time period, moving from a somewhat simplistic descriptive research of audio-visual classroom presentations to complex quantitative studies on a variety of media. Final form of this important educational serial came in 1978: "*ECTJ* welcomes papers on theory, development and research related to technological processes in education." The emphasis was on applied technology to the education field, which oftentimes meant instructional communication media. The periodical averaged two articles per issue, before its demise in 1988. No graphics.
DEPT: "World Communication," "Book Reviews," "Film Reviews," "Research Abstracts." (spring-53). "Comment," "Letters," "Book Reviews," "Research Abstracts." (winter-77). "International Review," "Book Review," "Research Abstracts." (summer-84).
TYPL: "Audio-Visual Research in the U.S. Air Force," "Teacher Competence in the Use of Audio-Visual Materials," "Needed Research in Audio-Visual Methods." (spring-53). "Educational Technology and Human Values," "Pictorial Organization Versus Verbal Repetition of Children's Prose: Evidence for Processing Differences," "Television Programs as Socializing Agents for Mentally Retarded Children." (fall-77). "The Proper Study of Instructional Technology," "Two Experiments on the Effects of Mnemonic Strategies: Is it Mode or Cognitive Function that Influences Learning?" (summer-84).
SCHL: Quarterly (Winter, 1953 - Summer, 1962?); Bi-monthly (Nov/Dec, 1962+), 60 pp.
SPAN: Winter, 1953 - ?, 1988//
VARIES
--Winter, 1953 - Nov/Dec, 1963 as Audio-Visual Communication Review (ISSN: 0885-727x).
--Spring, 1964 - Winter, 1977 as AV Communication Review (ISSN: 0001-2890).
MERGED WITH
--Journal of Instructional Development (ISSN: 0162-2641) (to form) Educational Technology, Research and Development (ISSN: 1042-1629), 1989.
LC: LB 1028.3 .E2
DD: 378/.17/078
ISSN: 0148-5806
ABST: --Current Index to Journals in Education (ISSN: 0011-3565)
--Education Index (ISSN: 0013-1385)
--Predicasts
--Psychological Abstracts (ISSN: 0033-0202)
--Reference Sources (ISSN: 0163-3546)

Educational-Instructional Broadcasting
1968 - May, 1971//
(ISSN: 0013-1776)
SEE: EDUCATIONAL BROADCASTING

✤ EDUCATIONAL MEDIA INTERNATIONAL
SUB: "Official journal of the International Council for Educational Media."
SUB: "The official quarterly journal of the International Council for Educational Media."
PUBL: International Council for Educational Media, 29 Rue D'Ulm, 75230 Paris, France.
DESC: "This Council was founded in 1950 under the name of the International Council for Educational Films, to encourage cooperation in the field of educational media. The name was changed in 1966 to International Council for the Advancement of Audio-Visual Media, and in 1970 to the International Council for Educational Media (ICEM), also named Conseil International des Moyens D'Enseignement (CIME)." This journal highlights educational media by member nations, with a focus on primary and secondary school systems in those member nations, and is primarily a publication for use by educators and education managers. Each quarterly issue is themed, such as these 1991 topics, "The Challenge of Information Technology and Mass Media for Small Linguistic Societies," "Media in Elementary Schools," and "Media Efficiency--the Vienna Conference." Note: some issues of *Audio-Visual Media* were produced in English and French language text. For the sampled issues of 1991: black ink editorial content with two-color cover on coated paper stock, no advertising, in stapled magazine format (7 ⅜ x 9 ⅝ inches / 185 x 245 mm).
DEPT: "Obituary," "News and Views," 'Publications on audio-visual aids and educational technology published in member countries, other activities, exhibitions, conferences, equipment testing;' "General News," newsbriefs. (10-78). "Editorial," column by Tom Fox; "ICEM News," information concerning the International Council for Educational Media; (9-91).
TYPL: "ICEM and the Economics of New Educational Media," "Economic Analysis of Educational Media," "Lessons of Experience in the Use of Media," "Success or Failure of Communication Technology in the Third World." (10-78). "State Broadcasting and Minority Languages: the Case of Irish in Ireland," "Developing School Media Libraries for the Autonomy of Linguistic Minorities," "Television--Challenge or Threat to Social Identity in Small Language Communities?," "The Icelandic Language, Modern Technology and Satellite Television," "Types of Small Linguistic Communities and the Challenges They Face in the Field of Educational Media." (9-91).
SCHL: Quarterly, 60 pp.
SPAN: Mar, 1971+

VARIES
--Spring, 1967 - Mar, 1971 as Audio-Visual Media (ISSN: 0571-8716).
LC: LB 1043.E325
ISSN: 0004-7597
ABST: --Education Index (ISSN: 0013-1385)
--Excerpta Medica

EDUCATIONAL SCREEN
SUB: "The independent magazine devoted to the new influence in national education." (Feb, 1922 - ?).
SUB: "The audio-visual magazine."
PUBL: The Educational Screen, 5200 Harper Ave., Chicago, IL.
DESC: "The purpose of *The Educational Screen* is single and emphatic. This magazine intends to get at the truth about visual education--in all its phases and in its broadest aspects--and serve it up in a form palatable to thinking Americans. *The Educational Screen* is not the official organ of anything or anybody. It is published to give American educators, and every American who believes education important, the thing they have needed ever since the so-called 'visual movement' started--namely a magazine devoted to the educational cause and to no other; a magazine distinctly intellectual and critical, rather than commercial and propagandist; a magazine written and produced exclusively by those whose scholarly training, experience and reputation qualify them to discuss educational matters." This was a journal designed to explore the new visual media, and consider how these media could be harnessed for the purposes of American education. Early sample issues from 1922 indicate small journal size; no graphics.
DEPT: "Editorials," "From Hollywood," developments; "School Department," use of AV in the classroom; "Theatrical Film Critique," reviews; "Announcements." (2-22).
TYPL: "Musings on the Movies," "Teaching by the Cinema in France," "Among the Magazines." (2-22).
SCHL: Monthly [except Jul and Aug], 20 pp.
SPAN: Jan, 1922 - Sum, 1956//
ABSORBED
--Moving Picture Age, Jan, 1923.
--Visual Education, Jan, 1925.
--Visual Instruction News, Apr, 1932.
MERGED WITH
--Audio-Visual Guide, (to form) Educational Screen & Audio-Visual Guide, Summer, 1956.
LC: LB 1044.A2E4
ISSN: 0013-1946
ABST: --Education Index (ISSN: 0013-1385)

Educational Screen and Audio-Visual Guide
Sep, 1956 - Nov, 1971//
SEE: AV GUIDE

Educational Television
Nov, 1968 - 1971//
(ISSN: 0424-6101)
SEE: E-ITV

Educational Television International
Mar, 1967 - Dec, 1970//
SEE: MEDIA IN EDUCATION AND DEVELOPMENT

Educational Theatre Journal
Oct, 1949 - Dec, 1978//
(ISSN: 0013-1989)
SEE: THEATRE JOURNAL

Educators Guide to Media & Methods
Nov, 1967 - May, 1969//
(ISSN: 0013-2063)
SEE: MEDIA & METHODS

EFLA BULLETIN
PUBL: Educational Film Library Association, 43 West 61st St., New York, NY 10023.
DESC: After *EFLA Bulletin* merged with *Film Review Digest* and *Filmlist* to form *Sightlines*, the *EFLA Bulletin* was published once again, from 1977 to 1987, as a supplement to, and between issues of *Sightlines*. In this supplemental format it was a typewritten newsletter for the Educational Film Library Association, detailing developments in the broad audio-visual field, especially software and equipment as it affects libraries. Articles tended to be brief with no graphics.
SPAN: Summer, 1977 - #3/4, 1987//
SUPPLEMENT TO
--Sightlines (ISSN: 0037-4830), Summer, 1977 - # 3/4, 1987.
LC: LB 1044.A2E44

EIGHT MM MOVIE MAKER AND CINE CAMERA
PUBL: Fountain Press, 46-47 Chancery Lane, London WC2, England.
DESC: Amateur movies were reaching their zenith in the late 1950s to 1960s, when Fountain Press launched this publication. Admitting that this serial was similar in nature to its sister publication, *Amateur Cine World*, the publishers promised many easy "how-to" articles for a hobby that was presented as being fun for the entire family. Through its publication span, *Amateur Movie-Maker* remained true to its promise of providing the best "how-to" articles possible for the world of 8mm film. Numerous graphics; latter issue covers in color.

DEPT: "Pick of the Post," letters; "Test Department," "Enquiry Desk." (2-58). "News of the Month," "Reader's Letters," "Test Department," "Commentary," "Camera Clinic," "Other People's Pictures." (1-67).
TYPL: "Filming Winter Sports," "My First Movie," "Cartooning in Clay." (2-58). "How to Film a Party," "Special Effects with Commentary," "Beginners' Guide to Animation." (1-67).
SCHL: Monthly, 75 pp.
SPAN: ? - Feb, 1967//
VARIES
--? - ? as Amateur Movie Maker.
--Oct, 1957 - 1964? as 8 MM Movie-Maker.
ABSORBED
--Cine Camera.
MERGED WITH
--Amateur Cine World (ISSN: 0365-1282) (to form) Movie Maker (ISSN: 0027-2701), Mar, 1967.
ISSN: 0422-7840

✤ ELECTRICAL COMMUNICATION

SUB: "Official technical journal of ITT."
PUBL: International Telephone and Telegraph Co., 190 Strand, London WC2R 1DU, England.
DESC: "*Electrical Communication* is the technical journal of the ITT System reporting the research, development, and production achievements of its affiliates worldwide." A quality technical publication restricted to ITT employee contributions, it assumes significant electronic engineering experience. Of special note are full color graphs and charts for unique clarity.
DEPT: None. (#3-85).
TYPL: "Adaptive Echo Canceling for Baseband Data Transmission," "Trends in Single-Chip Programmable Digital Signal Processors," "Coding of Video Signals." (#3-85).
SCHL: Quarterly, 100 pp.
SPAN: Aug, 1922+
SUSPENDED
--Sep, 1922 - Dec, 1922.
LC: TK 1.E26
DD: 621.38/05
ISSN: 0013-4252
ABST: --Computer & Control Abstracts (ISSN: 0036-8113)
--Electrical & Electronics Abstracts (ISSN: 0036-8105)
--Energy Research Abstracts (ISSN: 0160-3604)
--Engineering Index Annual (ISSN: 0360-8557)
--Engineering Index Bioengineering Abstracts (ISSN: 0736-6213)
--Engineering Index Energy Abstracts (ISSN: 0093-8408)
--Engineering Index Monthly (1984) (ISSN: 0742-1974)
--Engineering Index Monthly (ISSN: 0013-7960)
--International Aerospace Abstracts (ISSN: 0020-5842)
--ISMEC Bulletin (ISSN: 0306-0039)
--Physics Abstracts. Science Abstracts. Series A. (ISSN: 0036-8091)
--Pollution Abstracts with Indexes (ISSN: 0032-3624)
--Safety Science Abstracts Journal (ISSN: 0160-1342)

Electrical Engineering

Jan, 1931 - Dec, 1963//
(ISSN: 0095-9197)
SEE: IEEE SPECTRUM

Electrical Engineering and Telephone Magazine

Aug, 1898 - Dec, 1899//
SEE: TELEPHONE MAGAZINE

Electrical Engingeering

Jun, 1893 - Jul, 1898//
SEE: TELEPHONE MAGAZINE

✤ ELECTRICAL REVIEW

PUBL: Business Press International, Ltd., 35 Perrymount Rd., Haywards Heath, Sussex RH16 3BR, England.
DESC: "We need not dwell upon the importance of the applications of Electricity. It would be better to review the position that the chief branch -- Telegraphy, a science itself -- occupies in relation to the Public. The arrangement of the affairs of commerce is so intimately concerned with the progress of Telegraphy, that it is remarkable there exists no Journal considering both the scientific and the commercial aspects of the science." *The Telegraphic Journal*, started on November 15, 1872, emphasized the most practical electrical application of that era; telegraphy. This was a scientific journal devoted to the topic of electricity and magnetism. It reported on experiments and new developments in electrical apparatus. It was remarkable for its day in the considerable use of mathematical equations, electrical design schematics, and graphic line-cuts of various equipment. One hundred years later, the approach to electrical devices as communication medium is gone and today's *Electrical Review* is exclusively a serial of electrical power; its design, generation, transmission, and control. Early issues were journal format; latter issues were magazine format.
DEPT: "Students' Column," "Papers for Junior Students," "Proceedings of Societies," "Electrical Science in Foreign Journals," "Notices of Books," "Correspondence," "City Notes," (5-15-1873).
TYPL: "Employment for Women," "Multiple Transmission by the Same Wire," "Duration and Multiple Character of Flashes of Lightning," "On the Intensity of an Induced Galvanic Current." (5-15-1873).
SCHL: Semi-Monthly (Nov 15, 1872 - Dec, 1881); Monthly (Nov, 1872 - May, 1873); Weekly (1882+); 50 pp.
SPAN: Nov 15, 1872+?

VARIES
--Nov 15, 1872 - Dec, 1872 as Telegraphic Journal and Monthly Illustrated Review of Electrical Science.
--Jan, 1873 - Dec, 1891 as Telegraphic Journal and Electrical Review.
--? - ? as Electrical Review International.
ABSORBED
--Electrical Journal, The, Mar 2, 1962.
LC: TK 1.E44
ISSN: 0013-4384
ABST: --CIS Abstracts (ISSN: 0302-7651)
        --Coal Abstracts (ISSN: 0309-4979)
        --Computer & Control Abstracts (ISSN: 0036-8113)
        --Electrical & Electronics Abstracts (ISSN: 0036-8105)
        --Energy Research Abstracts (ISSN: 0160-3604)
        --Metals Abstracts (ISSN: 0026-0924)
        --Physics Abstracts. Science Abstracts. Series A. (ISSN: 0036-8091)
        --Predicasts
        --Ship Abstracts (ISSN: 0346-1025)
        --World Aluminum Abstracts (ISSN: 0002-6697)

Electrical Review International

? - ?//
SEE: ELECTRICAL REVIEW

Electrical Worker, The

1902? - Jul, 1914//
SEE: IBEW JOURNAL

Electrical Worker, The

May, 1901? - Jul, 1914//
SEE: JOURNAL

Electrical Workers' Journal, The

Jan?, 1948 - Dec, 1971//
SEE: IBEW JOURNAL

Electrical Workers' Journal, The

?, 1893 - Apr, 1901//
SEE: JOURNAL

Electrical Workers' Journal, The

1948 - Dec, 1971//
SEE: JOURNAL

ELECTRONIC AGE

SUB: "Research, manufacturing, communications, broadcasting."
SUB: "Research, manufacturing, communications, broadcasting, television."
PUBL: Radio Corporation of America, New York, NY.
DESC: *Radio Age* began publication at about the same time America entered WW II. Wartime issues emphasized RCA's contribution to the war effort through innovations in manufacturing and electronics. Curiously, several articles about programming on the NBC Radio Blue Network were always included, but articles concerning the Red Network were not found (in sample issues for 1942-43). *Electronic Age* was a large-format sized serial with an energized layout style of splashy graphics and full page pictures. This serial, which unfortunately ended in 1971, was a very dynamic promotional vehicle for RCA, providing many thoughtful articles with the David Sarnoff "what if" approach to the future of electronics.
DEPT: None. (4-43). "For the Records," new RCA releases; "Books at Random," reviews; "This Electronic Age," cartoon comment; "Electronically Speaking," RCA newsbriefs. (summer-70).
TYPL: "Women in War Jobs," "Old Tubes Made New," "Radio Adds to the Story of Religion," "Paul Whiteman Joins Blue," "Sarnoff Urges Charter for Business." (4-43). "Technology: Challenge and Promise," "Pop Music--Hit Sound of the Recording Industry," "The Huntley-Brinkley Bandwagon," "Crime and Computers." (summer-70).
SCHL: Monthly (? - ?); Quarterly (? - Fall, 1971); 40 pp.
SPAN: Oct, 1941 - Fall, 1971//
        VARIES
        --Oct, 1941 - ?, 1957 as Radio Age.
LC: TK 6540.R22
ISSN: 0013-4783
ABST: --International Aerospace Abstracts (ISSN: 0020-5842)

Electronic & Radio Engineer

Jan, 1957 - Dec, 1959//
SEE: INDUSTRIAL ELECTRONICS

✤ ELECTRONIC DESIGN

SUB: "For engineers and engineering managers -- worldwide."
PUBL: Hayden Publishing co., Rochelle Park, NJ.
DESC: "*Electronic Design's* function is: To aid progress in the electronics manufacturing industry by promoting good design; To give the electronic design engineer concepts and ideas that make his job easier and more productive; To provide a central source of timely electronics information; To promote communication among members of the electronics engineering community." Target audience for this publication is "...those individuals in the United States and Western Europe who function in design and development engineering in companies that incorporate electronics in their end product and government or military agencies involved in electronics activities." *Electronic Design* showcases new electronic components to the engi-

neering designer for consideration of inclusion into assembled electronic devices for government, industry and consumer application. Technical expertise in electronic components and their application is assumed. For sampled issue of 1979: perfect-bound magazine format, typeset editorial content with mixture of black/white, spot and full-color pages throughout on coated paper stock (8 x 10 ⅞ inches / 205 x 275 mm). Note: while a full publication schedule did not commence until December, 1953, an "introductory number" issue was published in December, 1952 and numbered as volume A, #1.
DEPT: "Reader Feedback," "Previews," "News & Technology," "Briefs," technological items; "From Washington," regulatory news; "Editorial," column by Larry Altman; "Engineering," "Design Engineering," "Ideas for Design," "New Products," review; "Evaluation Samples," "New Literature," "Technical Management," "Vantage Point." (8-16-79).
TYPL: "Measuring Optical-Fiber Attenuation," "PROM-Pinout Schemes," "Math Transform Bridges," "In-Circuit Emulators," "Vantage Point: European Instruments Invade the U.S." (8-16-79).
SCHL: Biweekly [three issues in Jul], 165 pp.
SPAN: Dec, 1952+
ISSN: 0013-4872

Electronic, Electro-Optic and Infrared Countermeasures

? - Apr?, 1977//
(ISSN: 0148-6373)
SEE: MILITARY ELECTRONICS / COUNTERMEASURES

✤ ELECTRONIC ENGINEERING

SUB: "The world's first television journal." (Mar, 1928 - Jan, 1935).
SUB: "Official organ of the Television Society." (1928 - May, 1932).
SUB: "The first television journal in the world."
PUBL: Hulton Press, Ltd., 43-44 Shoe Lane, London, England.
DESC: This publication began on March, 1928 as the official organ of the Television Society in London, within two years of the formal debut of television by John Logie Baird. Articles feature "how-to" advice on building a television receiver, and watching irregularly scheduled London telecasts. Current issues are closely tied to contemporary applications of video, audio and other communications media to world problems.
DEPT: "Recent Developments," "News Brevities," (12-40).
TYPL: "Optical Projection," "The Birth of the Television Society," "Television in Warfare," "Commercial Television: When May We Expect It?," "How to Make a Simple Televiser." (3-28). "Aeroplane 'Spotting' by Electro- Acoustical Methods," "Design for Audio-frequency Generator," "Prevention of 'Dark' Current in Electron Multipliers," (12-40).
SCHL: Monthly, 40 pp.
SPAN: Mar, 1928+?
VARIES
--Mar, 1928 - Jan, 1935 as Television.
--Feb, 1935 - Sep, 1939 as Television and Short-Wave World.
--Oct, 1939 - May, 1941 as Electronics and Television & Short-Wave World.
LC: TK 6630.A1T45
ISSN: 0013-4902
ABST: --Applied Science and Technology Index (ISSN: 0003-6986)
--British Technology Index (ISSN: 0007-1889)
--CIS Abstracts (ISSN: 0302-7651)
--Communication Abstracts
--Computer & Control Abstracts (ISSN: 0036-8113)
--Electrical & Electronics Abstracts (ISSN: 0036-8105)
--Electronic Publishing Abstracts (ISSN: 0739-2907)
--Energy Information Abstracts (ISSN: 0147-6521)
--Engineering Index
--Engineering Index Bioengineering Abstracts (ISSN: 0736-6213)
--Engineering Index Energy Abstracts (ISSN: 0093-8408)
--Engineering Index Monthly (ISSN: 0013-7960)
--International Aerospace Abstracts (ISSN: 0020-5842)
--Metals Abstracts (ISSN: 0026-0924)
--Physics Abstracts. Science Abstracts. Series A. (ISSN: 0036-8091)
--Predicasts
--Ship Abstracts (ISSN: 0346-1025)

✤ ELECTRONIC MEDIA

PUBL: Crain Communications, 740 North Rush St., Chicago, IL 60611.
DESC: "Authoritative, thorough, and professional" mark Crain publications, and *Electronic Media* continues that tradition in reporting on the visual electronic media (television, video, cable) in America. The large, tabloid-size publication is a concise means of understanding the problems, status, and potential of electronic media. Technical innovations, advertising concepts, methods of management, program development, legal actions, and the constant competitive desire to be "number one" are all part of this quality publication. Well recommended reading for managers of all media. Sampled issue for 1991: large stapled magazine format, full color throughout on coated paper stock (11 x 14 ½ inches / 280 x 370 mm).
DEPT: "News Summary," "Briefly Noted," "Calendar," "Industry Beat: Cable," "Industry Beat: Syndication," "Letters to the Editor," "Season-to-Date TV Ratings," "Technology/Equipment," "Videotech Update," "Viewpoint," "Who's News." (10-27-83). "News Summary," "Briefly Noted," "Calendar," "Finance," "The Insider," industry topics under discussion; "Letters to the Editor," "News of Record," FCC actions; "Quick Takes," short opinions; "Season-to-Date Ratings," "Syndication Standings," "Technology," "Viewpoint," "Who's News." (1-30-89).

TYPL: "Realism Sobers Up Videotex Industry," "Nielsen vs. Arbitron," "ABC Football Helps CBS Gain in Ratings," "Phone Company Seeks Cable Franchise," "Slow Marketing of Players Hurts Sales for Compact Discs." (10-27-83). "Q&A: Cable's Top News Boss," "Fox Stations Call for New Kids' Block," "Court Blocks 24-Hour 'Indecency' Law," "NBC Gambles Big on New Businesses," "TV Quality in Spotlight at SMPTE." (1-30-89).
SCHL: Weekly, 50 pp.
SPAN: Aug 5, 1982+
VARIES
--May 3, 1982 - Jul ?, 1982 as Advertising Age [Electronic Media Edition] (ISSN: 0744-6675).
ISSN: 0745-0311

✢ ELECTRONIC PRODUCTS

PUBL: Hearst Business Communications, UTP Division, 645 Steward Ave., Garden City, NY 11530.
DESC: For the busy electronics design engineer, a periodical resource for what is new in the electronics field, and potential application of same would prove to be a valuable ally indeed: *Electronic Products* is such an ally. This is a publication concerning electrical components, newly emerging technologies, testbench approaches to quality control, and creative applications of these components for new electronic products. For the sampled issue of 1974, four major articles were included, with the vast majority of the issue devoted to subject areas such as "Test Measuring," "Displays Subassemblies," "Circuit Components," and "Controls, Switches, Drives." For that sampled issue: perfect-bound magazine format, mixture of black/white, spot and full-color pages, along with full-color cover all on coated paper stock, extensive advertising of new products and technologies (8 ¼ x 11 inches / 210 x 280 mm).
DEPT: "IC Update," "Test Measurement," "Inter-Connection Packaging," "Computer Systems," "Controls, Switches, Drives," "Power Sources," "Displays Subassemblies," "Circuit Components." (12-16-74).
TYPL: "Product Perspective: Capacitors," "Ribbon Cable Wraps Up Interconnection Problems," "Digital IC Tester--Engineering Tool or Production Necessity?," "Choosing IC's for Serial Data Communication." (12-16-74).
SCHL: Monthly (1958? - Jan, 1969); Fourteen issues per year (Feb, 1969 - May, 1970); Nineteen issues per year (Feb 7, 1984 - Jan 1, 1985); Fifteen issues per year (Jan 11, 1982 - Jan 11, 1984); Fourteen issues per year (Mar, 1981 - Dec, 1981); Semimonthly (Jan 15, 1985+), 140 pp.
SPAN: 1958+
VARIES
--1958? - ?, 1962 as Electronic Products Magazine & Clip File.
--Sep, 1962 - May, 1970 as Electronic Products (ISSN: 0738-2553).
--Jun, 1970? - Feb?, 1981 as Electronic Products Magazine.
LC: TK 7870 .E543

DD: 621
ISSN: 0013-4953
ABST: --Predicasts

Electronic Products

Sep, 1962 - May, 1970//
(ISSN: 0738-2553)
SEE: ELECTRONIC PRODUCTS

Electronic Products Magazine

Jun, 1970? - Feb?, 1981//
SEE: ELECTRONIC PRODUCTS

Electronic Products Magazine & Clip File

1958? - ?, 1962//
SEE: ELECTRONIC PRODUCTS

✢ ELECTRONIC PUBLISHER

PUBL: Innes Publishing Co., P.O. Box 368, Northbrook, IL 60065.
DESC: A monthly supplement to *In-Plant Printer & Electronic Publisher*, this 20-page segment showcases the new "desk-top publishing" process and its application to the traditional print plant operation. "*Electronic Publisher* covers typesetting, text and graphic processing, electronic printing and paste-up." This supplement adds vitality to a traditionally conservative industry, and in the process not only promotes a new kind of publishing, but encourages those who fear new technological inroads to traditional means of printing. See: *In-Plant Printing & Electronic Publisher* for further information. Numerous graphics.
DEPT: "Developments," news; "Case Study," "Electronics Forum," commentary; "Products," "Literature." (6-87).
TYPL: "Desk-Top Publishing in the In-Plant." (6-87).
SCHL: Monthly, 20 pp.
SPAN: ?+
SUPPLEMENT TO
--In-Plant Printer & Electronic Publisher (ISSN: 0019-3232), ? to date.

Electronic Publishing & Printing

Jan/Feb, 1986 - Aug/Sep, 1990//
(ISSN: 1044-0852)
SEE: COMPUTER PUBLISHING

Electronic Servicing

? - ?//
(ISSN: 0013-497x)
SEE: ELECTRONIC SERVICING & TECHNOLOGY

✤ ELECTRONIC SERVICING & TECHNOLOGY

SUB: "TV - AM - FM - sound."
SUB: "The professional radio-TVman's magazine."
SUB: "Reaching every radio TV service firm owner in the USA."
PUBL: Intertec Publishing Corp., PO Box 12901, Overland Park, KS 66215-9981.
DESC: [*Radio-Television Service Dealer*]: This publication was designed for those whose livlihoods depended upon concise information regarding installation, maintenance, and repair of a myriad of home consumer electronic entertainment and leisure devices. As one promotional page put it, "A typical issue covers Video Speed Servicing Systems, Rider's 'TV Field Service Manual' data sheets, latest TV installation and maintenance techniques for VHF and UHF, auto radio installation and service, advanced data on new circuitry, production changes and field service data on receivers, new tubes, new test equipment operation and application, hi-fi installation and service, new developments, such as transistors, color, UHF, etc., news of the trade, service short cuts & shop notes, explanation of difficult circuits, and many more exclusive, original, authoritative, timely, fully illustrated subjects that can only be read in *Service Dealer*." One significant feature of this publication has to be the extensive array of equipment schematics for the working serviceman, providing possible answers (with technical graphics) to a number of workbench problems. Most articles, and of course the schematics, assumed a working knowledge of consumer electronics for that era. For the sampled issue of 1954: stapled magazine format, editorial content consisting of black ink (some red spot-color on various pages) on coated paper stock with red/black ink cover (8 ¼ x 11 ¼ inches / 210 x 285 mm).
DEPT: "Circuit and Service Forum," "Answer Man," technical fixit column by Bob Dargan; "The Work Bench," column by Paul Goldberg; "Rider TV Field Manual Service Data Sheets," removable schematics; "Video Speed Servicing Systems," "Editorial," column by S. R. Cowan; "New Products," "Trade Flashes," new technologies newsbriefs; "Association News." (7-54).
TYPL: "Horizontal and High Voltage Color Circuitry," "Tape Recorder Servicing Series, Part 1," "True and False Color Concepts," "A Special Purpose Tube Tester," "Sell and Service Radio-Controlled Garage Door Operators." (7-54).
SCHL: Monthly, 50 pp.
SPAN: Apr, 1940+
VARIES
--Apr, 1940 - Jan, 1944 as Radio Service Dealer.
--Feb, 1944 - Apr, 1944 as Radio & Electrical Appliance Dealer.
--May, 1944 - Jul, 1950 as Radio Service Dealer.
--195u - 195u as Radio-Television Service Dealer.
--? - ? as Electronic Servicing (ISSN: 0013-497x).
ABSORBED
--Electrical Appliance Retailing, ?
--Electronic Technician/Dealer (ISSN: 0192-7175), Apr, 1982.
LC: TK 7870.E547
DD: 621.381/028/8
ISSN: 0278-9922

Electronic Technican

Nov, 1956 - Dec, 1967//
(ISSN: 0013-4988)
SEE: ELECTRONIC TECHNICAN/DEALER

ELECTRONIC TECHNICAN/DEALER

SUB: "World's largest electronic trade circulation."
PUBL: Harcourt Brace Jovanovich Publications, New York, NY.
DESC: [*Electronic Technician*]: The letters to the editor column was filled with accolades for this technical publication. From the Philippines: "We wish to congratulate your wonderful electronic trade magazine for its rare, direct and non-biased articles." From San Jose, California: "...your Circuit Digest is of outstanding value; [it] means money in my pocket," and from Rockville, Indiana: "I certainly do enjoy your magazine. ...One thing I have observed and appreciate: the articles are written in the language of the average technician. I can understand it. This is something many present-day magazines cannot boast of." *Electronic Technican* was an excellent resource for the local radio-television-electronics servicing center, providing very practical advice to solve electronic circuitry problems in specific equipment models. Of special note was the "Circuit Digests" section, a series of foldout blueprint schematics detailing three to five models of television receivers, radio sets, and high-fidelity stereo components. This was an excellent publication for its time, and should remain a wonderful resource for collectors of earlier electronics equipment. For sampled issue of 1963: perfect-bound magazine format, spot-color and black/white editorial content on coated paper stock, ciruit schematics were blue ink on uncoated paper stock, folded once, schematic size unfolded: (13 ½ x 10 ¾ inches / 345 x 275 mm), cover consisted of spot color on coated paper stock (8 x 11 inches / 205 x 280 mm).
DEPT: "Letters to the Editor," "Manufacturers Technical Digest," technical information for servicing; "ET Viewpoint," editorial; "News of the Industry," newsbriefs; "New Products," showcase; "Calendar of Events," "Circuit Digests," full technical schematics of home

electronic equipment; "'Tough Dog' Corner," 'Difficult service jobs described by readers'; "Shop Hints," 'Tips for home and bench service'. (2-63).
TYPL: "Test Instruments for Bench and Caddy," "Selecting Sound System Components," "Take a Closer Look at the Control Grid," "Solving TV Sound and Alignment Problems," "Soldering Irons for Transistor Circuitry." (2-63).
SCHL: Monthly, 70 pp.
SPAN: Sep, 1953 - Mar, 1982//
SPLIT OFF WITH
--Mart (ISSN: 0025-4061) (from parent) Television Retailing, Aug, 1953.
VARIES
--Sep, 1953 - Dec, 1953 as Technician.
--Jan, 1954 - Jul, 1956 as Technician & Circuit Digests.
--Aug, 1956 - Oct, 1956 as Technician.
--Nov, 1956 - Dec, 1967 as Electronic Technican (ISSN: 0013-4988).
ABSORBED
--Service, Nov, 1958.
ABSORBED BY
--Electronic Servicing & Technology.
DD: 621.3888/7/05
ISSN: 0192-7175

Electronic Technology

Jan, 1960 - Sep, 1962//
SEE: INDUSTRIAL ELECTRONICS

✤ ELECTRONICS

SUB: "The worldwide technology weekly."
PUBL: Penton Publishing, Inc., 611 Route #46 West, Hasbrouck Heights, NJ 07604.
DESC: For 54 years, under a variety of banners, *Electronics* has been "the" publication of the electronics industry; providing the latest news on emerging technologies for design engineers and executives. *ElectronicsWeek* continued the 54 year tradition of *Electronics*, providing a weekly news report of emerging technology for the electronics design engineer and executive. And in spring of 1984, the serial returned once again to its original title of *Electronics*. All issues contained numerous news stories of new components for use in new communications products, and graphics along with technical schematics. Certain technical knowledge is assumed. Of note concerning the sampled issue for 1966: departmental sections, "Electronics Newsletter" and "Washington Newsletter," were on newsprint for emphasis; other editorial material was mixture of black/white, spot and full-color ink on coated paper stock (8 ⅛ x 11 ⅛ inches / 205 x 280 mm). A full layout design makeover was evident in the sampled issue for 1990, as well as a broader editorial outlook; including electronics elements such as computer-based applications, automation, computer design, multimedia, and other practical uses. The use of full-color pages, and an exciting layout design make for a dynamite publication for the electronics design engineer. As a promotional page put it, "*Electronics*, the magazine that gives its readers the best perspective on vital issues and trends is also the place to communicate every month with engineers who manage their companies. And the right place to reach those successful engineers who are overseeing their company's technology-related functions." Of special note in the 1990 sampled issue was the supplement, "Executives on the Go," subtitled, "A lifestyle supplement to Penton publications: travel, lodging, resorts, recreation, leisure." Perfect-bound magazine format, full-color pages on coated paper stock (8 x 10 ¾ inches / 200 x 275 mm).
DEPT: "Readers Comment," letters; "People," personnel newsbriefs; "Meetings," calendar of upcoming events; "Meeting Preview," scheduled events and speakers at forthcoming events; "Editorial," "Electronics Newsletter," latebreaking news items; "Washington Newsletter," latebreaking regulatory news items; "New Products," "New Books," "Technical Abstracts," from recent presentations; "Electronics Review," newsbriefs; "Probing the News," newsbriefs; "Electronics Abroad," newsbriefs. (5-16-66). "Electronics," "Washington," "International," "Engineers," "Products," "Highlights," "Editor's Letter," "Readers Comments," "People," "Editorial," "Meetings," "News Updates," "Business Activities." (7-12-84). "Up Front," editorial column by Jonah McLeod; "Letter From London," column by Peter Fletcher; "Management Edge," column by David Sylvester; "Electronics Index," outstanding full-color status check of the electronics industry; "News Roundup," "Products to Watch," "European Observer," "News Front," "Worldwide News," "Buses," "Factory Automation," "Solid State," "Systems," "Newsmakers." (2-90).
TYPL: "Multipurpose Chips Cut Costs of F-M Receiver," "Lenses Guide Optical Frequencies to Low-Loss Transmission," "The War that Needs Electronics," "For Want of a Beacon, a Brigade Moved Out," "War Brings On-the-Spot Research." (5-16-66). "IBM Eyes Niche in Burgeoning Supercomputer Market," "Motorola Takes High-Speed, Low-Power Road to 32-Bit Microprocessor Market with 68020," "IR Sensors Shrunk for Target System," "Bipolar Transistors Pick Up Speed," "Kiosk Data Service Expands Nationwide." (7-12-84). "Special Multimedia Report: Who Will Dominate the Desktop in the '90s?," "Hypertext Tackles the Information Glut," "Risky Business: Where RISC Meets CISC," "Say Hello to VFEQ, Potentially the Single Open-Bus Standard of the Future: After VMEBUS, What?," "Riding the Next Consumer Wave." (2-90).
SCHL: Monthly (1930 - ?); Biweekly (May 26, 1977 - ?); Biweekly [except last week of Dec] (1983 - ?); Weekly (Sep 10, 1984 - ?); Biweekly (Jul 10, 1986+), 105 pp.
SPAN: Apr, 1930+

VARIES
--Apr, 1930 - Jul 12, 1984 as Electronics (ISSN: 0013-5070).
--Jul 23, 1984 - Jun 10, 1985 as ElectronicsWeek (ISSN: 0748-3252).
WITH SUPPLEMENT
--Executives on the Go, ?+
LC: TK 7800 .E4384
DD: 621.381
ISSN: 0883-4989
ABST: --Abstract Bulletin of the Institute of Paper Chemistry (ISSN: 0020-3033)
--Applied Science and Technology Index (ISSN: 0003-6986)
--Computer & Control Abstracts (ISSN: 0036-8113)
--Electrical & Electronics Abstracts (ISSN: 0036-8105)
--Engineering Index Annual (ISSN: 0360-8557)
--Engineering Index Bioengineering Abstracts (ISSN: 0736-6213)
--Engineering Index Energy Abstracts (ISSN: 0093-8408)
--Engineering Index Monthly (ISSN: 0013-7960)
--Excerpta Medica
--Fluidex
--Industrial Arts Index
--International Aerospace Abstracts (ISSN: 0020-5842)
--Magazine Index
--Nexis
--Physics Abstracts. Science Abstracts. Series A. (ISSN: 0036-8091)
--Predicasts
--Trade and Industry Index

Electronics

Apr, 1930 - Jul 12, 1984//
(ISSN: 0013-5070)
SEE: ELECTRONICS

ELECTRONICS AND COMMUNICATIONS

SUB: "Official journal of the New Zealand Electronics Institute."
SUB: "Television, communications, service, sound,"
SUB: "Electricity, communications, service, sound."
PUBL: Magazine Press, Auckland, New Zealand.
DESC: This serial was something of a national forum, being the official journal of The New Zealand Electronics Institute, the New Zealand Radio and Television Manufacturers' Federation, the New Zealand Radio and Electrical Traders' Federation, and the New Zealand Radio, TV and Electrical Association (as of Mar, 1954 issue). The magazine had wide-ranging content and readership, with articles encompassing topics from how to fix a home steam iron to the latest phase inverters for broadcast use. Later 1960s issues narrowed the focus to more of an applied electronics nature. Numerous drawings, pictures and schematics. Small magazine format.
DEPT: "Editorial," "For the Serviceman," "Publications Received," "Trade Winds," "New Products," "Letters to the Editor," (3-54). "Letters," "Listening Post," shortwave; "Book Reviews," "New Products," (3-67).
TYPL: "An Easily Constructed Multi-meter," "Using the Harmonic Signal Generator for Receiver Alignment," "A Short History of Television," (3-54). "The Operation of VHF and UHF Transistors," "Field Effect Transistors in Audio Amplifiers," "High Frequency Crystal Filters," (3-67).
SCHL: Monthly, 35 - 50 pp.
SPAN: Apr, 1946 - Oct/Nov, 1974//
VARIES
--Apr, 1946 - Apr, 1954 as Radio and Electronics.
--May 1, 1954 - Apr 1, 1964 as Radio and Electrical Review.
--May 1, 1964 - Dec 1, 1971 as Radio, Electronics and Communications.
ABSORBED BY
--Automation and Control (ISSN: 0110-6295) [NC].
ISSN: 0112-9775

ELECTRONICS & COMMUNICATIONS

SUB: "The engineering journal of the Canadian electronics industry."
PUBL: Southam Communications Ltd., 1450 Don Mills Rd., Ontario M3B 2X7, Canada.
DESC: "Editorial purpose: to bring new product information to the electronics design engineer and other potential users of electronic equipment in industry, government, science, medicine, education, the professions, and research and development. To report through regular departments: national and international news; state-of-the-art; product applications; and other matters of interest to the Canadian electronics community." Numerous graphics.
DEPT: "Business Briefs & Trends," "The Editor's Space," "Editorial," "New Products," "Book Reviews," "Letters to the Editor." (1/2-55). "Distributor News," "New Products," "Profile," "Dates," "Industry News." (10-81).
TYPL: "Electronics for Defense," "F.M. Radio Network," "High Speed Electronic Teleprinting System." (1/2-55). "The Electronic Cottage," "Microelectronics & Telecommunications," "DTMF Communications." (10- 81).
SCHL: Seven issues per year, 50 pp.
SPAN: Mar/Apr 1953 - Feb, 1984//
LC: TK 7800.E43857
ISSN: 0013-5100
ABST: --Canadian Business Index (ISSN: 0227-8669)
--Computer & Control Abstracts (ISSN: 0036-8113)
--Electrical & Electronics Abstracts (ISSN: 0036-8105)
--Physics Abstracts. Science Abstracts. Series A. (ISSN: 0036-8091)
--Predicasts

✤ ELECTRONICS & COMMUNICATIONS ENGINEERING JOURNAL

SUB: "Official organ of the British Institution of Radio Engineers."
SUB: "The journal of the Institution of Electronic and Radio Engineers."
PUBL: Institution of Electrical Engineers, Savoy Place, London WC2R OBL England.
DESC: From the Guide to Authors: "*Electronics & Communication Engineering Journal* is pitched in the middle tier of the IEE's three-tier publishing structure and is aimed at the graduate-level practising professional engineer involved in electronics and communications. It seeks to keep its readers up-to-date by providing coverage of new developments in a serious technical, but not overformal or academic, manner at a level which will be informative to other workers in the area and also accessible to engineers active in other fields of electronics and communications. ...Detailed mathematical analysis is not encouraged but it is quite appropriate to include basic formulas which will help the reader to make a quantitative assessment of the subject and summarise basic principles." The scope of this excellent publication includes the following areas of electronics and communication engineering: "Components and devices; Circuit design, simulation and CAD; Measurement and instrumentation; Signal and image processing, coding; Microwaves, antennas and radio propagation; Optoelectronics; TV and sound broadcasting; Medical and biological electronics; Telecommunication networks; Radio and satellite communications; Radar, sonar and navigation systems; Avionics; [and] Electromagnetic compatibility." There is a very practical application of spot color in graphs, charts, and schematics within this journal, which aids immeasurably to clarity. This remains an outstanding journal for the field of electronics and communication engineering, and one which would benefit any working professional who requires current research data and knowledge of important trends in the field. While a working knowledge of electronics is assumed, articles are editorially engineered to be readable by non-engineering communication professionals. Highly recommended. For sampled issue of 1991: stapled magazine format, spot and full-color employed throughout publication on coated paper stock, numerous graphs, charts and schematics in a well-designed format (8 3/8 x 11 3/4 inches / 210 x 300 mm).
DEPT: "Book Review," "Calendar," of upcoming international events and conventions. (2-91).
TYPL: "Experiences with the University of London Interactive Video Education Network," "Passive Millimetre Wave Imaging," "Networks and Their Architectures," "Model-Based Coding of Videophone Images," "Speech Recognition Techniques." (2-91).
SCHL: Irregular (1934 - 1948); Monthly (1949 - ?); Bimonthly (Jan/Feb, 1989+), 50 pp.
SPAN: Oct, 1926+
VARIES
--Oct, 1926 - 1939 as Proceedings, The.
--1939 - Dec, 1962 as British Institution of Radio Engineers. Journal.
--1963 - Nov/Dec, 1984 as Radio and Electronic Engineer, The (ISSN: 0033-7722).
--Jan, 1985 - Dec?, 1988 as Journal of the Institution of Electronic and Radio Engineers, The (ISSN: 0267-1689).
ISSN: 0954-0695

Electronics and Television & Short-Wave World

Oct, 1939 - May, 1941//
SEE: ELECTRONIC ENGINEERING

Electronics & Wireless World

Oct, 1983 - Sep, 1989//
(ISSN: 0266-3244)
SEE: ELECTRONICS WORLD + WIRELESS WORLD

ELECTRONICS ILLUSTRATED

SUB: "Consistently the best in hobby electronics."
PUBL: Fawcett Publications, Inc., Fawcett Bldg., Greenwich, CT 06830.
DESC: "Where the action is! In electronics...that's where it's happening! And *Electronics Illustrated* puts you right in the middle with the fundamentals of the hobby along with the latest in news and construction projects in stereo, amateur and Citizens Band radio, servicing, shortwave listening and home projects." Individual issues placed articles under a number of subheadings: "Special Audio Section," "Amateur Radio," "Citizens Band," "Shortwave Listening," "Service," "Theory & Practice," "Electronics in Wartime," "Your Library," "Kit Report," "New Products," and "Hobby & Business Opportunities." While aimed at the electronics hobbiest, a certain technical knowledge level was expected. It provided detailed schematics and electronics formulas for a variety of electronics applications. Editorial content for the 1971 sampled issue was spot-color on coated paper stock, stapled journal format, full-color cover on heavy paper stock (6 5/8 x 9 1/4 inches / 170 x 235 mm).
DEPT: "Feedback From Our Readers," letters; "Uncle Tom's Corner," technical Q&A column by Tom Kneitel; "Tips," "Electronic Marketplace," new products; "Service Tips," column by Art Margolis; "CB Corner," column by Len Buckwalter; "The EI Ticker," latebreaking newsbriefs; "Good Reading," 'Books, pamphlets, booklets, flyers, bulletins and application notes' column by Tim Cartwright; "EI Kit Report," review; "Electronics in the News," product applications; "The Listener," column by C.M. Stanbury; "The Ham Shack," column by Wayne Green. (11-71).

TYPL: "The Strange Saga of Ivan the Terrible," "Super-Mod Speakers for All Budgets," "Big Noise in Four Channel," "2-Meter Beam for 2 Bucks," "Update on Semiconductors." (11-71).
SCHL: Bimonthly (May, 1958 - Sep, 1958); Monthly (Oct, 1958 - Dec, 1959); Bimonthly (Jan, 1960+), 110 pp.
SPAN: May, 1958 - 1972//
ABSORBED BY
--Mechanix Illustrated (ISSN: 0025-6587) [NC].
LC: TK 7800 .E439
DD: 621.381
ISSN: 0013-5178

✣ ELECTRONICS LETTERS

SUB: "An international publication."
PUBL: Institution of Electrical Engineers, Michael Faraday House, Six Hills Way, Stevenage, Herts SG1 2AY, England.
DESC: From the Guide to Authors: "*Electronics Letters* is intended to provide a rapid means of communicating new information and results on important topics of current interest. ...The subject field of *Electronics Letters* embraces science and engineering, telecommunications and optoelectronics. Contributions of a theoretical nature should show a specific application in one of these fields; generalizations are not acceptable. Where such contributions are mathematical, the author is expected to explain in English and in detail the application of the mathematics." *Electronics Letters* packs a tremendous amount of engineering research data into each biweekly issue. For the sampled issue of March 28, 1991 some 40 articles or "letters" were published under specific subheadings of: "Communications & Signal Processing, Electromagnetic Waves, Filters, Image Processing, Information Theory, Memories, Microwave Devices, Neural Networks, Optical Communications, Optical Fibres, Optics, Optoelectronics, Semiconductor Devices & Materials, Semiconductor Lasers, [and] Telecommunications." While remarkably succinct, a significant number of graphs, charts, schematics and pictures (all in black/white) accompany most articles. This is an excellent resource for the communication engineering field, one which is truly international in scope and importance. For sampled issue of 1991: stapled magazine format, editorial content is black/white with numerous graphs, charts and schematics on uncoated paper stock, cover is spot-color on coated paper stock (8 ³⁄₈ x 11 ¾ inches / 210 x 300 mm).
DEPT: None. (3-28-91).
TYPL: "Design of a Discrete Cosine Transform Based Speech Scrambler," "Doppler Optimised Mismatched Filters," "Calculating Nonlinear Microwave Circuits with Undersampled Time Signals," "Simple Method to Improve Dynamic Range of Optical Amplifiers in Coherent Optical Communication Systems with Heterodyne Receivers," "New Construction for Classes of Majority Logic Decodable Codes with Even Minimum Distances." (3-28-91).
SCHL: Monthly (Mar, 1965 - Apr, 1976); Biweekly (May, 1976 - Mar, 1982); Biweekly [except for one issue in Dec] (Apr, 1982+), 70 pp.
SPAN: Mar, 1965+
LC: TK 7800 .E4395
DD: 621.381/05
ISSN: 0013-5194
ABST: --Computer & Control Abstracts (ISSN: 0036-8113)
--Electrical & Electronics Abstracts (ISSN: 0036-8105)
--Engineering Index Bioengineering Abstracts (ISSN: 0736-6213)
--Engineering Index Energy Abstracts (ISSN: 0093-8408)
--Engineering Index Monthly (1984) (ISSN: 0742-1974)
--Engineering Index Monthly (ISSN: 0013-7960)
--Engineering Index Annual (ISSN: 0360-8557)
--International Aerospace Abstracts (ISSN: 0020-5842)
--Mathematical Reviews (ISSN: 0025-5629)
--Metals Abstracts (ISSN: 0026-0924)
--Nuclear Science Abstracts (ISSN: 0029-5612)
--Physics Abstracts. Science Abstracts. Series A. (ISSN: 0036-8091)
--World Aluminum Abstracts (ISSN: 0002-6697)

ELECTRONICS WORLD

SUB: "Circulation larger than that of any other radio publication."
SUB: "Radio's greatest magazine."
SUB: "First in radio."
SUB: "First in radio electronics."
SUB: "World's leading electronics magazine." (Aug, 1948 - Mar, 1957).
SUB: "Leading technical magazine in the electronics world."
SUB: "First in radio-television-audio-electronics."
PUBL: Ziff-Davis Publishing Co., One Park Ave., New York, NY 10016.
DESC: For over 50 years *Electronics World* had covered developing electrical communication technologies; first under famed Hugo Gernsback's editorship with the Experimenter Publishing Company banner; and then as an equally famous Ziff-Davis publication, *Electronics World* (including previous title variations), well-known for its clear explanations of what was new in communications. Articles covered everything from tubes to transistors, transformers, photocells, switching, meters, and a whole host of other electronic developments. In 1926, typical articles consisted of new developments in vacuum tubes, how world weather conditions changed reception, and novel applications for radio apparatus. In 1958, articles were on transistors, how videotape recorders worked, citizen radio, and "Hi-Fi" product news. Each issue contained numerous schematic circuits (parts lists and instructions) for current and proposed electronics projects. Knowledge of electronics was assumed. The popularity of its sister publication, *Popular Electronics*, forced a merger in December, 1971. Note: some issues during the period 1943 - May,

1955 included a separately paged and numbered section, entitled *Radionics*, during 1943; and *Radio-Electronic Engineering* thereafter. This supplement was availabe to any subscriber in 1948 for $6 per year, or $4 for *Radio News* without supplement. The *Radio-Electronic Engineering* section was also separately issued during the period of Aug, 1954 - May, 1955. Contents of the sampled 1926 issue were: stapled magazine format, black ink on coated paper stock, full-color cover, significant advertising (8 ¾ x 11 ⅝ inches / 220 x 295 mm). For the 1948 sampled issue: stapled magazine format, black and spot-color ink on newsprint and coated paper stock, significant amount of advertising material, and full-color cover on coated paper stock (8 ½ x 11 ⅛ inches / 215 x 285 mm). For the sampled 1958 issue: magazine format; spot color throughout; many graphics, and advertisements (8 ½ x 11 inches / 215 x 280 mm).
- DEPT: "The DX Listener," editorial column by Hugo Gernsback; "Radio Happenings of the Month Illustrated," column by George Wall; "Radio Developments Shown in Pictures," "International Radio," radio news by nation; "Radio Set Owner's Information," reader Q&A by specific model; "New Developments in Radio Apparatus," column by William J. Griffin; "List of Broadcast Stations in the United States," "Radio Wrinkles," newsbriefs; "Radiotics," humorous misprints concerning radio; "Correspondence From Readers," letters; "Standard Hook-Ups," how-to; "Radio Set Directory," "Radio News Laboratories," new products; "I Want to Know," technical Q&A column by Joseph Bernsley; "Book Reviews." (4-26). "For the Record," editorial column by Oliver Read; "Spot Radio News," 'Presenting latest information on the radio industry' column by Fred Hamlin; "Within the Industry," personnel newsbriefs; "Short-Wave," column by Kenneth R. Boord; "RN Circuit Page," 'circuit diagrams and parts lists'; "What's New in Radio," product review; "New Receivers," product review; "Technical Books," review; "Letters From Our Readers." (2-48). "Behind the Scenes in Publishing," editorial; "Spot News," 'Latest information on the electronic industry'; "Calendar of Events," "Sound on Tape," review column by Bert Whyte; "Certified Record Revue," column by Bert Whyte; "Mac's Service Shop," technical column by John T. Frye; "Test Bench Puzzler," column by Art Margolis; "Service Association of the Month," "Antenna News," "Service Industry News," "Service Notes," "Letters From Our Readers," "Within the Industry," newsbriefs; "Technical Books," review; "What's New in Radio." (11-58). "For the Record," editorial; "EW Lab Tested," "Antennas and Grounds," column by John Frye; "Test Equipment Product Report," "Coming Next Month," "Letters From Our Readers," "Radio & TV News," "Book Reviews," "New Products," "Manufacturers' Literature." (3-64). "For the Record," "Letters." (12-71).
- TYPL: "A New and Convenient Method of Assembling Radio Sets," "More About Vacuum Tubes," "Static Forecasts Forest Fires," "Changes in the Polarization of Radio Waves," "Round the World in a Radio-Equipped Lifeboat." (4-26). "Build Your Own Magnetic Tape Recorder," "Understanding the Wire Recorder," "The FreModyne FM Detector," "Television Installation," "Converting a Brush Tape Recorder for Broadcast Use." (2-48). "Basics of Preset Counters," "Loading the Phono Cartridge," "Transistor Superregen FM Tuner," "X-Rays From TV Sets: Are They Harmful?," "Scope Calibrator and Pulse Generator." (11-58). "Traveling-Wave Tubes," "Voltage-Divider Nomogram," "The Integrated Amplifier-Speaker," "New Look in Transformers," "Transistors for Music." (3-64). "Optical Communications with Semiconductor Light Sources," "Channel Electron Multipliers," "Facsimile via Telephone." (12-71).
- SCHL: Monthly, 70 pp.
- SPAN: Jul, 1919 - Dec, 1971//
  VARIES
  --Jul, 1919 - Jun, 1920 as Radio Amateur News.
  --Jul, 1920 - Jul, 1948 as Radio News.
  --Aug, 1948 - Mar, 1957 as Radio & Television News.
  --Apr, 1957 - Apr, 1959 as Radio and TV News (ISSN: 0097-6660).
  WITH SUPPLEMENT
  --Radio-Electronic Engineering, 1943 - Jul, 1948 [irregular schedule].
  --Radionics, 1943 [irregular schedule].
  ABSORBED
  --Radio Call Book Magazine and Technical Review, Dec, 1932.
  --All-Wave Radio, Aug, 1938.
  --TV and Radio Engineering, Dec, 1953.
  --Communication Engineering, Apr, 1954.
  --Radio-Electronic Engineering, Jun, 1955.
  ABSORBED BY
  --Popular Electronics, Including Electronics World, Jan, 1972.
- LC: TK 6540.R668
- DD: 621.381/05
- ISSN: 0013-5232
- ABST: --Readers Guide to Periodical Literature (ISSN: 0034-0464)

✦ ELECTRONICS WORLD + WIRELESS WORLD

- SUB: "Covering every wireless interest."
- SUB: "Radio, Television, and Electronics."
- PUBL: Reed Business Publishing, Ltd., Quadrant House, The Quadrant, Sutton, Surrey SM2 5AS England.
- DESC: [*Wireless World*]: From its debut in 1913, this serial has been a standard for individuals working at the electronics level of wireless radio, television, facsimile and other non-wired communications. It is known for its in-depth discussions of electronic theories and apparatus. Excellent graphics, diagrams, tables and schematics allow even the inexperienced to grasp new developments in media. It covers a wide range of

topics, from radar to navigation systems, from radio to facsimile, from television to long play records. Tremendous number of advertising pages.
DESC: [*Electronics World + Wireless World*]: The above description of this excellent electronics design publication still holds true, with new topics exploring computers and electronics, sophisticated analyses of circuits, new ideas in technology, and worldwide competition in the electronic design and technology field. Serial contains numerous graphs, schematics, charts, and graphics, many of which are in color. Assumes well-founded knowledge of electronics and design applications (8 1/4 x 11 5/8 inches / 210 x 295 mm).
DEPT: "Editorial Comment," "World of Wireless," newsbriefs on international technical developments; "Societies and Clubs," 'List of Radio Groups in the British Isles;' "Manufacturers Products," "Unbiased," personality column by Free Grid; "Letters to the Editor," "Random Radiations," column by Diallist. (1-51). "Comment," "Research Notes," "Update," "Circuit Ideas," "Pioneers," excellent historical profiles; "Letters," "Applications," "RF Connections." (8-90).
TYPL: "Ribbon Loudspeaker," "Temporary Vision Aerial," "Vector Diagrams," "Radio-Controlled Launch," "British Long-Playing Records," "Double Super Heterodyne Communications Receiver," "Navagitional Track Guide," "Flyback E.H.T. Booster." (1-51). "Single Chip Micros--An Overview," "Going to the Proms," "Audio Preamplifier Design," "Interfacing With C," "Designing Fractals to Order." (8-90).
SCHL: Weekly (Apr, 1922 - Sep, 1939); Monthly (Nov, 1939+), 95 pp.
SPAN: Apr, 1922+
FROM MERGER OF
--Radio Review, The (and) Wireless World, The, Mar, 1922.
VARIES
--Apr, 1922 - Jun, 1932 as Wireless World and Radio Review, The.
--Jul, 1932 - Sep, 1983 as Wireless World, The (ISSN: 0043-6062).
--Oct, 1983 - Sep, 1989 as Electronics & Wireless World (ISSN: 0266-3244).
LC: TK 5700 .W55
DD: 621.38/05 20
ISSN: 0959-8332
ABST: --Applied Science and Technology Index (ISSN: 0003-6986)

ElectronicsWeek

Jul 23, 1984 - Jun 10, 1985//
(ISSN: 0748-3252)
SEE: ELECTRONICS

Elementary Electronics

196u - Jan/Feb, 1981//
(ISSN: 0013-595x)
SEE: COMMUNICATIONS WORLD

✤ EMMY

SUB: "The magazine of the Academy of Television Arts and Sciences."
PUBL: Academy of Television Arts and Sciences, 3500 West Olive Blvd., Suite 700, Burbank, CA 91505.
DESC: Upon the completion of its first year of publication, *Emmy* observed that "...we envisioned *EMMY* as a general-interest magazine designed to serve both the television industry and the intelligent television viewer. At the time we felt there was a real need for such a magazine. We still do." Holding fast to that premise, *Emmy* turns a quality, thought-provoking, critical eye on the American television industry. Articles cover programming, directors, production trends, biographies of media pioneers, and the American television viewer. This remains an excellent, thought-provoking publication in a very dynamic layout design, and is highly recommended. Typical articles during 1991 included a post production house profile; the programming philosophy of the Family Channel; day in the life of a program publicist; and the debate concerning rerun revenues. For the sampled issues of 1991: editorial content consisting of black ink, with full-color advertisement and cover pages on coated paper stock in stapled magazine format (8 1/2 x 11 inches / 215 x 280 mm).
DEPT: "Editorial," "Off the Record," "Viewpoint." (fall-79). "President's Message," "Update," "Letters," "Viewpoint," "Innerviews," "Below the Line," "Focus," "Books," "New Tech," "Ways and Means," "Finnigan's File," column by Joseph Finnigan; "Academy News," "Outtakes." (3/4-87). "President's Message," "Letters," "Viewpoint," "Innerviews," "Below the Line," "Books," "Academy News," "Finnigan's File," column by Joseph Finnigan; "Ways and Means," "Outtakes." (5/6-89).
TYPL: "Roundtable: On Programming for Children," "Profile: Goodson-Todman," "Pat Weaver: Visonary or Dilettante?," "Rating the TV Critics." (fall-79). "Hollywood in Hindsight," "Backstage at Wolf Trap," "The Flops That Shouldn't Have," "Suffering with Success," "The Ultimate Viewer." (3/4-87). "Blair Brown's Molly Dodd: A New Lease on Lifetime," "Cable Plays for Keeps," "True-Life TV: Cable's Discovery Channel," "Head of the Class-nost." (5/6-89).
SCHL: Quarterly (Winter, 1979 - ?); Bimonthly (Mar/Apr, 1983+), 80 pp.
SPAN: Winter, 1979+
LC: PN 1992.3 .U5E45
DD: 791.45/05
ISSN: 0164-3495

✤ EMPIRE

SUB: "The modern guide to screen entertainment."
PUBL: EMAP Metro, 42 Great Portland St., London W1N 5AH, England.

DESC: *Empire* has a copyright statement that warns of dire consequences should the reader have conniving thoughts about putting the serial to "other uses." It continues with "Liposuction, eh? Why don't they just eat less?" *Empire* is an irreverent "...modern guide to screen entertainment" for British moviefans. With an odd mixture of the serious and the hilarious, *Empire* matches the mood, the product, and the denizens of Hollywood in their quests for fame, fortune, funding, and a good script. One sampled issue provided articles on film star salaries, interviews with Tom Cruise and Oliver Stone, the success story of Disney studios, Hollywood stalkers after stars, and how a film preview for "Steel Magnolias" was conducted. The large square magazine format lends itself well to quality color/black- white production stills that are combined in a breezy design. Some 30-plus pages of each issue is contained within the section labeled "Empire Directory," where regular departments of video, book reviews, letters to the editor, and new films can be found. Some British film product is discussed, but primary focus is on American film. Well recommended as an excellent guide to the artists, the process and the product of Hollywood. For the 1990 sampled issue: black/white and full-color graphics with cover on coated paper stock in perfect-bound magazine format (9 x 11 ¾ inches / 230 x 300 mm).
DEPT: "The Front Desk," 'A monthly digest of news, information, stories, production details and the occasional slice of madness.'; "In Production," film project details; "The Hollywood Kids," hot gossip, Hollywood-style; "Obituaries," quality tributes of Hollywood artists; "Charts," Box-office rankings in Los Angeles, London, Australia; "New Films," "Videos to Rent," "Videos to Buy," "Books," review; "Letters," "Classic," one-page lookback at classic films. (3-90).
TYPL: "You Too Can Have a Body Like This," "This Charming Man," "What Would Happen to Tom Cruise If...," "Hi-Ho, Hi-Ho, It's Off to Work He Goes..." (3-90).
SCHL: Monthly, 100 pp.
SPAN: Jul, 1989+

✦ ENTERTAINER, THE
SUB: "Your monthly cable magazine."
PUBL: TV Host, Inc., 3201 Northeast Loop, 820, Suite 150, Fort Worth, TX 76137.
DESC: This monthly program guide is provided to Warner cable subscribers, providing several pages of national articles and essays on television programming. The bulk of the magazine consists of program listings for each Warner cable system printed on newsprint. Magazine format.
DEPT: "Alphabetical Movie Listings," "Cable News Network," "Channel Directory," "C-SPAN," "MTV," "Program Listings," "Subscribers Corner." (4-89).
TYPL: "This Month, Look for the Best that Cable Has to Offer," "Something Funny's Going On Around Here," "Matthew Broderick Doesn't Suffer from Biloxi Blues," "Roy Firestone: ESPN's Ace in the Hole." (4-89).

SCHL: Monthly, 100 pp.
SPAN: Sep, 1982+
ISSN: 8750-0280

✦ ENTERTAINMENT AND SPORTS LAWYER, THE
PUBL: American Bar Association, Forum Committee on the Entertainment and Sports Industries, 750 North Lake Shore Drive, Chicago, IL 60611.
DESC: "*The Entertainment and Sports Lawyer* is directed at lawyers who devote a major portion of their practice to entertainment, sports, intellectual property law, and other related areas. It endeavors to provide current, practical information as well as public policy and scholarly viewpoints that it believes to be of professional and academic interest to Forum members and other readers." This outstanding publication covers important issues of litigation in the volatile arena of entertainment media and sports. A sampling of typical articles include: "A Basic Approach to Securing Event Sponsorship Rights," "Key Entertainment and Sports Law Provisions in the New Immigration Law," "Financing Motion Pictures Under Nonpublic and Limited Offering Exemptions from Federal Securities Laws," "New Developments in Recording Contract Negotiations: Reflections of a Changing Economic Profile," and "Redefining the Rights and Obligations of Publishers and Authors." Highly recommended. The premiere issue of spring, 1982 was followed by issue #2 for fall, 1982. For the sampled issues of 1982 and 1991: black ink with spot-color on uncoated paper stock, no advertising, in stapled magazine format (8 ½ x 11 inches / 215 x 280 mm).
DEPT: "Chairman's Column," column by Robert G. Woolf; "Editor's Column," column by David Nochimson; "Division News." (fall-82). "Editor's Column," column by David M. Given. (summer-91).
TYPL: "The Ownership and Protection of Performers' Names," "New Tax Law Offers Several Options for Obtaining the Tax Benefits of Motion Picture Films." (fall-82). "Miramax Films Corp. v. Motion Picture Ass'n of Amer., Inc: The Ratings System Survives, For Now," "Record Lyrics and Labelling," "Interview with Frank Zappa," "'Son of Sam' Terrorizes Publishing Industry," "Un-Ban the Banned Band: A First Amendment Perspective on Banning Concerts." (summer-91).
SCHL: Quarterly, 35 pp.
SPAN: Spring, 1982+
LC: KF 4290.A15E57
DD: 344.73/099
ISSN: 0732-1880

✦ ENTERTAINMENT CONNECTION MAGAZINE
SUB: "It's the difference that makes us different."
PUBL: Entertainment Connection Magazine, 6430 Sunset Blvd., Suite 522, Los Angeles, CA 90028.

DESC: This is primarily a black talent-oriented publication that showcases new, promising, and established stars in a variety of entertainment fields; including motion pictures, television, on-stage performance, sports and music. The focus of *Entertainment Connection Magazine* is music, providing detailed coverage of recording sessions, new production companys, stage reviews, and numerous artist profiles. This is also a magazine of encouragement. As Editor-in-Chief and Publisher Janie Bradford noted in the sampled issue, "Oftentimes, the bridge that we build to lead us to our dream, may get washed away by some unexpected tide of events. But there is always an alternate route to arrive at any destination we may design. The alternate choice may take us longer, but it will still take us there. As you see, you are in an endurance race, the trophy is not given to the swiftest, but to whomever holds out to the end. Keep thinking success and you will succeed. If the elevator stops--take the stairs." For the sampled issue of 1991: stapled magazine format, black/white editorial content and full-color cover on coated paper stock (8 ½ x 11 inches / 215 x 280 mm).

DEPT: "Portraits," profile; "Shining Star," "Night Prowl," "For the Record," column by Marilyn McLeod; "On the Scene," column by Nicole Hobbs; "On Stage," "Gospel Truth," "Living Legend," "Movie Notes," column by Ernestine Mancha; "Astrology & Poetry," "Nikki's Poetry Corner," column by Nikki; "Short Takes," newsbriefs; "Inside Moves," "Salute to Blues & Jazz," "Theatre Ticket," "Locker Room," "Country Cooking." (8-91).

TYPL: "Fantasy Records Salutes Blues and Jazz," "Alice Coltrane, Keeper of the Vision," "A New Music Phenomenom With a Golden Touch," "Newly Formed International Marketplace Studios and Mint Records Announces Inaugural Slate of Motion Picture and Television Projects," "World's Most Popular Children's Book, 'Charlotte's Web', Brought to Life by Serendipity Theatre Co." (8-91).

SCHL: Monthly, 35 pp.
SPAN: ?+

✤ ENTERTAINMENT MONTHLY

SUB: "The magazine serving the commercial broadcast production industry."
PUBL: Entertainment Monthly, 8721 Sunset Blvd., Suite 305, Los Angeles, CA 90069.
DESC: This is a periodical aimed at a most unique segment of the production industry, those who produce and participate in the making of television commercials. As such, advertisements tend to be display boards for talent agencies, with selected rosters of talent. Articles focus on current productions, status of commercial spot production studios and sharing of successful campaigns.
DEPT: "Editorial," "BAPSA: (Broadcast Advertising Producers Society of America), a Forum for Creative Exchange," news; "VO News," briefs on voice-over work; "Production News," lengthy segment on East/West Coast activities; "Commercial Talent Directory," listing of New York, Chicago, Los Angeles agencies.
TYPL: "Recipe for the Successful Commercial Production Company," "The AICP (Association of Independent Commercial Producers), an Idea Whose Time Has Come," "The War on Clutter--Making Your Spot Stand Out." (3/4-79).
SCHL: Monthly, 60 pp.
SPAN: 1977+
VARIES
--1977 - 1982 as Commercials Monthly (ISSN: 0194-5114).
ISSN: 0744-8775

✤ ENTERTAINMENT REVUE

SUB: "Florida film and television."
SUB: "Hooray for HollyWorld™."
PUBL: World Perspective Communications, Inc., 3443 Parkway Center Court, Orlando, FL 32808.
DESC: "Every month *Entertainment Revue* will be your inside guide to the dynamic film and TV industries in Central Florida and the Southeast. Designed for industry professionals, as well as cheering audiences, *Entertainment Revue* covers it all: Movies, TV Shows, Stage Productions, Concerts and Clubs and a lot more! We'll take you behind the scenes and show you the real, working world of Florida entertainment as you've never seen it before. There's no business like show business." This is a dynamic trade publication for the ever-growing Florida film and television production community, indicating projects-in- progress, new resources, and observations on the status of Florida media production. It also provides pragmatic industry advice on the mechanics and techniques of executing productions. The square format magazine (300 cm high x 250 cm wide) contains the monthly supplement, *Inside Entertainment*, designed to provide late-breaking news on Florida production. Square magazine format (9 ⅞ x 11 ⅞ inches / 250 x 300 mm).
DEPT: "Publisher's Note," "Wide Angles," Florida production news; "Around Florida," locations of note; "Auditions," "Above the Line," "Below the Line," "Outside Looking In," out-of-staters survey the Florida production scene; "Inside Looking Out," Florida production observations; "Career Profile," "In Brief," legal insight to film and video production; "Brass Tacks," production observation and instruction; "Financing Films," excellent monetary status of project financing; "Book Reviews," "The Last Word," editorial comment; "Eye on Television," column by David B. Horowitz; "Eye on Film," column by Donald E. Barnhorst. (10-89).
TYPL: "Master Class: Gregory Peck, a Giant Among the Corn," "Quick! I Need a Star," "Baby Wranglers," "Commercial Producers: a Baker's Dozen of the Best," "Fool-Proof Corporate Video." (10-89).
SCHL: Monthly, 55 pp.
SPAN: Apr, 1988+

WITH SUPPLEMENT
--Inside Entertainment, ?+

✦ ENTERTAINMENT WEEKLY

PUBL: Entertainment Weekly, Inc., 1675 Broadway, New York, NY 10019.

DESC: "America's hot new magazine with your very best bets in... Movies, Music, Books, TV, Videos, Home Electronics & More. With so many entertainment options and so little free time, you need help making the best choices. That's why we created *Entertainment Weekly*. Brash, browsable, opinionated, fun--*Entertainment Weekly* is your best all-in- one source for Entertainment News, Reviews, Previews, Behind-the-Scenes Reports, The Truth and Nothing But The Truth about what's worth your time and money--and what's not." The American media consumer has waited a long time for a magazine which covers the major entertainment media, and Time, Incorporated has produced it in award-winning layout design, form and function. The publishers of *Entertainment Weekly* have recognized that people seem to have less leisure time than ever before. Therefore, a magazine of this caliber needs to guide the consumer around the shoals of "flash and trash," to the better media products. Of special note is the wonderful tear-out card-page, appropriately called the "Cue Card;" which provides a neat capsule listing of what is notable to watch, read and listen to in the upcoming week. Above all, *Entertainment Weekly* is informative in a creative, entertaining way, or as parent publisher Time stated: "It's the hot new magazine that's fast, feisty and fun. It's your best single source for the very best bets in movies, TV, books, music, videos, home electronics and more." Amen! An excellent resource for current American media. For the 1990 sampled issue: stapled magazine format with numerous color graphics and full-color cover on coated paper stock, and special weekly media guide printed in full-color on uncoated card stock (8 x 10 ¾ inches / 205 x 275 mm).

DEPT: "Television Reviews," column by Ken Tucker; "News & Notes," television newsbriefs; "Capsules," 'Other notable programming'; "Sports," "The Ratings," televisions' top and bottom five; "Movie Reviews," column by Owen Gleiberman; "News & Notes," film newsbriefs; "Box Office," economically speaking; "Critical Mass," 'Current releases rated by reviewers across the country'; "Capsules," 'Short takes on pictures still playing'; "Print Reviews," critique; "News & Notes," print newsbriefs; "Specialty:," reviewing one aspect of the print medium; "Best-Sellers," list of fiction & non-fiction; "Capsules," 'Other new and notable titles in hardcover and paperback'; "The Book Browser," 'Opening lines from five new books'; "Music Reviews," column by Greg Sandow; "News & Notes," music newsbriefs; "The Music Charts," Top selling albums; "Capsules," 'Other new recordings'; "Specialty:," reviewing a unique music form; "Video Reviews," critique; "News & Notes," video newsbriefs; "Critical Mass," 'How movie critics across the country rated some of this week's new video releases and top rentals during their theatrical runs'; "Top Tapes," "Capsules," 'Other new releases and reissues'; "Specialty:," unique video formats; "Kids Reviews," various media; "Critic on the Loose," comment column by Jeff Jarvis; "Cue Card," 'Our carry-along, week-at- a-glance list of what's new and avilable in film, TV, video, music, books, and for kids--plus a postcard'; "Everybody's a Critic," letters. (4-27-90).

TYPL: "Holy Roles," "Last But Not Least," "The Fright Stuff," "Beta's Last Stand." (4-27-90).

SCHL: Weekly [except two combined year-end issues], 85 pp.

SPAN: Feb 16, 1990+

DD: 790 11

ISSN: 1049-0434

ENTERTAINMENT WORLD

SUB: "The trade weekly for all the entertainment industry." (Oct, 1969 - May 29, 1970).

PUBL: Entertainment World, 6548 Sunset Blvd., Hollywood, CA 90028.

DESC: Here was a short-lived serial that deserved better treatment from its subscribers. In its initial issue, the editors promised "...to present a weekly magazine whose content is significant, meaningful, and helpful to every executive, every personality, every participant in the entertainment industry." To that end, *Entertainment World*, succeeded admirably in its "industry-to-make-a-profit" approach. Where it failed was the idea that a weekly serial of this scope could compete against stiff competition emanating from serials such as *Hollywood Reporter* and *Variety*. Despite the fact that articles fairly sparkled with insight and media witicisms, it could not succeed at the newstand, and in May, 1970 merged with sister publication, *Show*, "Magazine of Films and the Arts," and moved from monthly to biweekly publishing status. Large format; numerous graphics.

DEPT: "Letters to the Editor," "News in Brief," "EW Reports," newsbriefs; "Motion Pictures," reviews; "Television & Radio," reviews; "Music & Recording," reviews; "Night Life," reviews; "Theatre," reviews; "Production and Casting Logs," listing; "EW List of Entertainment Stocks." (3-70).

TYPL: "Gene Kelly: Is There a Future for the Hollywood Musical?," "Rx Rewrite: Script Doctor John T. Kelley Talks About His Profession," "Bookmakers: From Soft Cover to Hard Cash with Harold Robbins and Irving Wallace." (3-70).

SCHL: Weekly, 40 pp.

SPAN: Oct 3, 1969 - May 29, 1970//
ABSORBED BY
--Show (ISSN: 0037-4296), Jun, 1970.

LC: PN 1560.E5

ISSN: 0531-7991

✧ EPI-LOG

- SUB: "The television magazine of science fiction, fantasy, and adventure."
- SUB: "The television fanzine of science fiction, fantasy, and adventure."
- PUBL: Epi-Log, PO Box 1322, Dunlap, TN 37327.
- DESC: "Each issue of our fan-produced magazine features 76 to 100 pages packed full of photos (some in full color) and episode guide reviews of sci-fi, fantasy, horror, suspense, and adventure TV series!" This fanzine provides very detailed episode information (episode number, initial airdate, plot description, guest cast, writer and director) for each television series featured in the issue. This is an important resource for media historians exploring the episodic nature of television programs in the "science fiction, fantasy, and adventure" field. Some issues (such as the November, 1991 "Special All-British Issue!"), are themed. For sampled issue of 1991: stapled magazine format, editorial content consisting of black ink on uncoated paper stock, full-color cover on coated paper stock (8 1/4 x 10 7/8 inches / 210 x 275 mm).
- DEPT: "Editorial," column by Bill Anchors. (11-91).
- TYPL: "Dr. Who (seasons 14 - 26)," "H. G. Well's Invisible Man," "Captain Scarlet," "The Secret Service," "Hitchhiker's Guide to the Galaxy." (11-91).
- SCHL: Monthly (Oct, 1990 - Feb?, 1992); Bimonthly (Mar/Apr?, 1992+), 80 pp.
- SPAN: Dec, 1990+

EPIEGRAM

- SUB: "The educational consumer's newsletter."
- PUBL: EPIE Institute, Box 620, Stoney Brook, NY 11790.
- DESC: This short, concise critical newsletter evaluates educational products for American school systems. Evaluations range from textbooks to training services, microcomputers to audio- visual software and hardware. Sister publications include *EPIE gram Materials*, dedicated to software evaluations, and *EPIE gram Equipment*.
- DEPT: None.
- TYPL: "Administrators Fail Materials Test," "Teachers Report on Materials Use," "Learning to Read in Schools--Part II." (11-81).
- SCHL: Monthly (Oct - Jun), 8 pp.
- SPAN: Oct, 1972 - Jun, 1977//
  SPLIT INTO
  --EPIEgram. Equipment (ISSN: 0884-5239) (and) EPIEgram. Materials (ISSN: 0884-5247).
- LC: LB 1043.E
- ABST: --Consumers Index to Product Evaluations and Information Sources (ISSN: 0094-0534)
  --Education Index (ISSN: 0013-1385)

✧ EPIEGRAM

- SUB: "The newsletter about educational materials and technology."
- PUBL: Sterling Harbor Press, PO Box 28, 146 Sterling Ave., Greenport, NY 11944.
- DESC: Continuing the course set by the original *EPIEgram*, this new version also reports, evaluates, and describes new technologies, software and programming products designed for, or applicable to the education process. Includes both "hardware" and "software" items recently coming to market. Most issues contain an "EPIEgram Feedback Form," allowing subscribers an opportunity "...to respond to any article in *EPIEgram* or to tell us of a materials- or equipment-related problem or satisfaction." For the sampled issues of 1988: color ink on uncoated paper stock, no advertising, loose-leaf style newsletter. For the 1991 sampled issues: black ink with spot-color on beige uncoated paper stock, loose-leaf newsletter style. Both samples: (8 1/2 x 11 inches / 215 x 280 mm).
- DEPT: "Research & Reports," news items. (#2-91).
- TYPL: "For Teachers, a High-Tech Center," "Schools Need Copyright Policy," "Publishers Consider Electronic Book," "TV Program to Teach Viewing Skills," "Kids Network Expands Programs." (#2-91).
- SCHL: Nine issues per year, 12 pp.
- SPAN: 1987+
  FROM MERGER OF
  --EPIEgram. Equipment (ISSN: 0884-5239) (and) EPIEgram. Materials (ISSN: 0884-5247), ?, 1987.

✧ EPISODES

- SUB: "Exclusive from the studios of ABC."
- PUBL: ABC Daytime Circle, Inc., 77 West 66th St., New York, NY 10023.
- DESC: After the Mar/Apr, 1990 premiere issue, readers wrote: "Bravo!!! I have just finished my first issue of *Episodes* and am absolutely thrilled with this magazine!," and: "...I love it. Because I only watch the soaps on ABC, this magazine is perfect for me. I read my copy from cover to cover;" and finally, "The articles were well written, and the photography was among the finest I've seen in any magazine." This is a sample of the high praise lavished on the ABC television magazine targeted at ABC daytime soap opera fans, and if these letters are any indication of fan loyalty, then ABC television and their advertisers are doing well indeed. This is a quality publication from its full color photography to well-executed layout design with articles providing a nice mixture between character/show stories, and the artistic talent off-stage at play. Publisher, ABC Daytime Circle, utilizes an interesting approach to subscriptions: $3.00 per year, either by check/money order or simply by calling a 900 number, and charging the subscription fee to one's telephone bill. This is one magazine where all benefit: ABC television, advertisers, and especially ABC daytime television soap opera fans. Magazine format (8 1/8 x 10 3/4 inches / 210 x 275 mm), full color graphics throughout on coated paper stock.
- DEPT: "Soap Dish," 'Wit and whimsy from your favorite stars'; "Soap Snaps," picture section; "In the Kitchen," "Fan Tales," "You Tell Us," reader input; "Around the

Dial," at ABC daytime television; "Are You Watching," 'Test your soap smarts'; "Director's Notes," editorial; "Soap Box," letters; "Sweepstakes," reader contest. (5/6-90).
TYPL: "Off the Set: The Passion of AMC's Ruth Warrick Bridges Two Worlds," "Family Album: OLTL's Erika Slezak Carries on the Slezak Dynasty," "Peek Behind-the-Scenes: What Really Happens When a Soap Goes on the Road," "Beauty Notebook: Dressing the tresses of LOV's Linda Cook," "Scene on Day TV: Quick Takes From Some Recent Soap Stories." (5/6-90).
SCHL: Bimonthly, 85 pp.
SPAN: Mar/Apr, 1990+

✤ EQ

SUB: "The creative recording magazine."
PUBL: Miller Freeman Publications, 500 Howard St., San Francisco, CA 94105.
DESC: "*EQ* is the ... magazine that covers the real-life world of today's recording studio. From recording techniques to studio and career management, from programming and performing to hands-on and how-to, *EQ* is for engineers, producers, and musicians who are serious about recording. Each and every bi-monthly issue is packed with pages and pages of: Hard-hitting reviews of today's hottest new recording gear, MIDI equipment, software, and more; Fascinating visits to artists' and producers' studios, as well as commercial and home facilities all over the US and the world; Audio-For-Video - you'll learn the inside workings of music video, film and television sound production; Workshops and clinics, on everything from Arranging in The Studio to Digital Recording, will give you the competitive edge." An upbeat, colorful publication dedicated to production sound and the technology and technique for same. Informative, professional, technological and entertaining, *EQ* should become a favorite of recording engineers everywhere. Magazine format (8 ¼ x 10 ⅞ inches / 210 x 275 mm); dynamic layout design and color graphics.
DEPT: "Editor's Notes," column by Brent Hurtig; "Reflections," letters; "Line In/Line Out," information for corresponding; "Guest Editorial," "Update," 'News & notes from the world of modern recording and knob twisting'; "How It Works," detailed lay explanation; "Studio Reference Series," excellent technical series; "Future Watch," column by Linda Jacobson; "The Sharp Angle," column by J.D. Sharp; "Across the Board," column by Roger Nichols; "It's About Time," Creative Workshop column by Norman Weinberg; "Hands-On Production," Creative Workshop column by Michael Marans; "In the Pocket," Down to Business column by Steve Harlan; "Studio Clinic," Tech Support column by Richie Moore; "Film & Video Sound," Visual Media column by Larry Blake; "The Big Picture," Visual Media column by Rolbert Wait. (9/10-90).

TYPL: "In Profile: Craig Dory, Record Producer Banks on Custom Cable, Purist Miking, & Digital Technology," "Crank It Down: You Have a Mild High- Frequency," "In Profile: Roma Baran, Renaissance Woman in an Avant- Garde World," "Life at the Edge of the Boom: Microphone Techniques." (9/10-90).
SCHL: Bimonthly, 85 pp.
SPAN: Mar/Apr, 1990+
DD: 789 11
ISSN: 1050-7868

✤ ERNST & YOUNG ENTERTAINMENT BUSINESS JOURNAL

PUBL: Ernst & Young Entertainment Industry Group, 787 Seventh Ave., New York, NY 10019.
DESC: This journal of the executive side of "show business" is published by the distinguished firm of Ernst & Young, a well-known professional services organization in the entertainment industry. The journal reflects the issues discussed by communication executives, who oftentimes are, in turn, the clients of Ernst & Young through their principle offices in New York, Los Angeles, Toronto and London. Articles are devoid of flashy layout design and graphics, but provide thorough quality discussions of the entertainment issues at hand; the kind of information today's media executive requires to remain efficient and effective. For the 1989 sampled issue: black ink with spot-blue ink color on coated paper stock (8 ½ x 11 inches / 215 x 280 mm).
DEPT: None. (summer-89).
TYPL: "For the Entertainment Industry 1992 is Already Here," "It's a Glamor Profession: Executives vs. Stars," "Grant Tinker: An Interview With the Entertainment Journal," "Computers: The Quiet Revolution in the Entertainment Business," "Q and A: Entertainment Tax Highlights." (summer-89).
SCHL: Quarterly, 20 pp.
SPAN: Spring, 1989?+

✤ ETI

SUB: "The electronics, science & technology monthly."
SUB: "Electronics today international."
PUBL: Argus Specialist Publications, Argus House, Boundary Way, Hemel Hempstead HP2 7ST, England.
DESC: *ETI* is for the electronics experimenter, with a host of electronics ideas, discussions, and schematics for the creation of various electronic projects. In the sample issue for March, 1990, the issue contained projects as diverse as a bass guitarist's amplifier, an automatic plant waterer, a super siren, a Valentine's heart-buzzer, and an electronic oscilloscope. Articles in that sample issue discussed ground communication, the basic elements of radio communication, and usage of frequency meters and power supplies. The only drawback to this two-color serial is that it is published on newsprint, although an announcement was made to

look for full color center pages in the near future. Numerous schematics, diagrams, and graphics. For the 1990 sampled issue: stapled magazine format, black ink with green spot-color ink on uncoated paper stock with full-color cover on coated paper stock (8 ¼ x 11 ¾ inches / 210 x 295 mm).
DEPT: "News," new electronic products; "Open Channel," commentary; "Blueprint," 'Blueprint is a column intended to provide suggested answers to readers electronics design problems'; "Review," "Insight," "Tech Tips," reader ideas; "Oooooops!," schematic corrections; "PCB Foil Patterns." (3-90).
TYPL: "The Business Amp," "Earth Current Signalling," "Elements of Radio," "Fluorescents." (3-90).
SCHL: Monthly, 70 pp.
SPAN: Jan, 1972?+
ISSN: 0142-7229

✦ ETV NEWSLETTER

SUB: "The biweekly news report of educational and instructional television."
PUBL: C.S. Tepfer Publishing Co., 51 Sugar Hollow Rd., Danburry, CT 06810.
DESC: This is an eight-page typewritten newsletter designed for quick-breaking news on educational and instructional television. Newsbriefs cover corporations, new products, software, and personnel changes.
DEPT: "Software News," reviews; "Positions Open," employment opportunities; "People in the News," personnel briefs; "Recommended Reading," new materials; "Calendar of Upcoming Events." (12-28-81).
TYPL: "The Reagon Administration Has, for All Intents and Purposes, Washed Its Hands...," "Learning Tech Fair in NYS," "New Videotape Company," "The Videodisc as a Filing System," "Student Video Competition." (12-28-81).
SCHL: Biweekly, 8 pp.
SPAN: Dec, 1966+
LC: LB 1044.7 A
ISSN: 0012-8023

✦ ETV REPORTER

SUB: "The complete news service for the educational TV and related industries."
PUBL: Industry Reports, 514 10th St., N.W., Washington, DC 20004.
DESC: In this 12-page, typewritten newsletter whose primary function is to report fast-breaking news in educational television; emphasis is on equipment and funding for ETV projects, as well as reporting news of a variety of United States governmental agencies which deal with ETV or ITV areas. No graphics.
DEPT: "Recent FCC Actions," newsbriefs on FCC rulings concerning ETV. (2-6-70).
TYPL: "PTV Managers Approve Environmental Programming Reponsibility," "Macy Urges Prompt Return of ETV Coverage-Expense Forms," "UHF tuning Mechanisms Must Match VHF Tuning Capability," "Broadcast Engineers to Study Transmitter Icing Problems." (2-6-70).
SCHL: Biweekly, 12 pp.
SPAN: 1967+
LC: LB 1044.7 E115
ISSN: 0424-0197

✦ EUROPEAN JOURNAL OF COMMUNICATION

PUBL: Sage Publications, London, England.
DESC: "The *European Journal of Communication* will be a non-sectarian publication, representing the best of communication theory and research in Europe in all its diversity. Articles will be chosen for excellence and significance and will primarily be by European authors on European topics. The journal will thus be genuinely international, promoting interchange among European scholars of different intellectual traditions and national backgrounds. The *European Journal of Communication* will be open to the ideas of young scholars (as well as already established Europeans in the field) and to thoughtful contributions from media professionals. In keeping with its cross-national character, the journal is particularly interested in comparative communication analysis and research and in comparisons between Europe and other parts of the world. The policy dilemmas resulting from the introduction of new technologies into the fast-changing European media scene is another likely focus. The journal will regularly provide useful information features, such as periodic reviews, country-by-country, of recent national communication literatures; communication policy developments; and trends in media organization and audience behaviour." This is another excellent Sage publication, which describes, informs, and illuminates changes, structure, and trends in European media. Articles consist of a pleasing mixture of historical and current topics, including in recent issues, "History as a Comnnunication Event: the Example of the French Revolution," "The Media-Sport Production Complex: American Football in European Societies," "Bloodhounds or Missionaries: Role Definitions of German and British Journalists," and "Media Logic and Party Logic: The Italian General Election of 1983." Both the editorial board and corresponding editors' list consists of individuals from diverse academic institutions and professional media organizations throughout Europe. A wonderful resource for individuals interested in the changing role of media and society throughout the continent. Its issues are periodically theme-oriented. For the sampled issue of 1991: perfect-bound journal format, editorial content printed black ink on uncoated paper stock, cover consists of maroon ink on coated paper stock, limited advertising, graphs and charts used to support issue articles (5 ¼ x 8 ½ inches / 135 x 215 mm).

DEPT: "Editorial," "Reviews," of current books and publications; "Abstracts, Resumes, Zusammenfassungen," Article abstracts in author's original language. (3-91).
TYPL: "The Internationalization of Television," "The Role of the Alternative Press in the Agenda-building Process: Spill-over Effects and Media Opinion Leadership," "The Contagiousness of Mass-mediated Terrorism," "Knowledge Gaps Revisited: Secondary Analyses," "Public Television in Crisis: Critiques Compared in Norway and Britain." (3-91).
SCHL: Quarterly, 130 pp.
SPAN: Mar, 1986+
ISSN: 0267-3231

✦ EUROPEAN TRANSACTIONS ON TELECOMMUNICATIONS AND RELATED TECHNOLOGIES

PUBL: Associazione Elettrotecnica ed Elettronica Italiana, Viale Monza, 259 - 20126 Milano, Italy.
DESC: *European Transactions on Telecommunications and Related Technologies* provides a highly technical discussion of electronics theory and application from a European perspective. Published with the support of the Commissioin of the European Communities, the quarterly publication replaces *Alta Frequenza* and *ntzArchiv* as of the beginning of 1990. The magazine is published by the Associazione Elettrotecnica ed Elettronica Italiana, in cooperation with Asociación Electrotécnica y Electrónica Española, Association des Ingénieurs Electriciens sortis de l'Institut Montefiore, Consulting Committee of the Professional Electroengineers' Organizations in Finland, Koninklijk Instituut van Ingenieurs Afd elektrotechniek, Schweizerischer Elektrotechnischer Verein, Societé Royale Belge des Electriciens, Koninklijke Belgische Vereniging der Elektrotechnici, and the Verband Deutscher Elektrotechniker. Articles for the sampled issue of November/December, 1990 issue ranged from discussion of mathematical/theoretical approaches to electronic design, to the application of new technologies. Each article includes an article abstract and information/picture of the contributor(s). Articles contain a large number of charts, graphs, schematics and scientific notations, and readers are assumed to have knowledge of electronic theory, design and application. It also provides interesting insight into the developing sense of family within the European Community, and the changes which may occur within the electronics industry in the next few years. Perfect-bound tall magazine format, black/white editorial content on uncoated paper stock, two-color cover on coated paper stock, no advertising (8 1/4 x 11 3/4 inches / 210 x 295 mm).
DEPT: "Contributors," author pictures and biographies; "News from CEC Information Technology and Telecommunications." (#6-90).
TYPL: "Custom Integrated Circuits for Audio Processing and Signaling in Vehicular Units," "An Example of a New VLSI Design Style Based on Systolic Macrocells: a High-Speed Single-Chip Transversal Filter for Signal Processing Applications," "A New ARQ Scheme Using a Go-Back-N Protocol," "A Unified Analysis for the Multiple-Site Diversity Outage Performance of Single / Dual - Polarized Communication System," "Mathematical Approaches to Electron Device Modelling for Non-Linear Microwave Circuit Design: State of the Art and Present Trends." (#6- 90).
SCHL: Bimonthly, 70 pp.
SPAN: Jan/Feb, 1990+
FROM MERGER OF
--Alta Frequenza (ISSN: 0002-6557) (and) NTZ Archiv (ISSN: 0170-172x), Jan, 1990.
LC: TK 5101.A1 E975
DD: 621.382/05
ISSN: 1120-3862

✦ EUROPEAN TRASH CINEMA

PUBL: European Trash Cinema, PO Box 5367, Kingwood, TX 77325.
DESC: In a 1990 editorial, founding editor Craig Ledbetter tells subscribers: "If you've noticed lately, Euro-genre films and filmmakers are getting a lot more coverage, both in the fan and glossy publications. Part of this is due to the fact that a lot of fans are getting real bored with the U.S. film scene. After you have seen all the sequels, the shot-on-video atrocities, the big budget sleaze you realize everyone is stuck in neutral. So you start looking elsewhere, overseas for instance, for something different." *European Trash Cinema* is that "something different" for fans of the underground film distribution circuit. Written with wit and verve, *ETC* provides coverage of motion picture/video product not commonly covered in the popular national press. Publisher Tom Weisser has assembled a quality staff and contributing writers to cover such overlooked European film subjects as erotica, westerns, Mondo "flicks" and other low-budget films with a European origin. Filmographies are well-documented, and often include invitations to readers to submit additions and corrections. Numerous black/white graphics are included of production stills, lobby posters, advertising layouts, and publicity pictures of production talent. Black/white cover on coated paper stock, with black/white editorial content on uncoated paper stock, minimal advertising, small journal format (5 1/2 x 8 1/2 inches / 140 x 215 mm).
DEPT: "Editorial," "European Trash Comments," letters; "The View From Twin Shore," 'A biased look at European Trash Cinema', column by Pompano Joe Torrez; "News From Spain," column by Dale Pierce. (vol 2, #2).
TYPL: "Periodicals," "Antonio Margheriti, a Complete Filmography," "The Immoral Tales of Walerian Borowczyk," "Beyond Good and Evil; an Interview with Riccardo Freda," "Sergio Corbucci and the Italian Western." (Vol 2, #2).

SCHL: Quarterly, 50 pp.
SPAN: ?, 1990?+

✤ EXECUTIVES ON THE GO

SUB: "A lifestyle supplement to Penton Publications: travel, lodging, resorts, recreation, leisure."
PUBL: Penton Publishing, 611 Route #46 West, Hasbrouck Heights, NJ 07604.
DESC: This full-color supplement to *Electronics* magazine which provides information on "travel, lodging, resorts, recreation, [and] leisure" for busy electronics executives. In the sampled issue for February, 1990, the single article was titled "Super Spa," aptly subtitled "Fitness resorts recharge executives and shape lifestyle changes." The full-color pages indicate that life exists apart from the test benches and competitive pressure-cooker of corporate life, emphasising the advantages of weekend jaunts to places of a recreational and leisurely nature. Similar to parent publication, *Electronics*, this supplement consists of full-color pages on coated paper stock (8 x 10 ¾ inches / 200 x 275 mm).
DEPT: "What's Happening," calendar of upcoming non-electronics related events. (2-90).
TYPL: "Super Spa." (2-90).
SCHL: ?, 8 pp.
SPAN: ?+?
SUPPLEMENT TO
--Electronics (ISSN: 0883-4989), ?+

Exhibitor's Herald and Moving Picture World

Jan 7, 1928 - Dec 29, 1928//
SEE: EXHIBITORS HERALD WORLD

EXHIBITORS HERALD WORLD

SUB: "The independent film trade journal."
PUBL: Quigley Publishing Co., 407 South Dearborn St., Chicago, IL.
DESC: Always at the forefront of motion picture business, the *Exhibitors Herald World* championed the entire industry, from production studio through distribution, promotion, and exhibition. During the publication span of 1928 to 1930, the focus was on sound: how to install, finance, and operate a quality sound system, one which would promote the theatre and sound film product alike. Beginning in December, 1929, Martin J. Quigley, Publisher and Editor of the *Exhibitors Herald World*, awarded plaques for "Better Film Reproduction" to "...exhibitors in cities and towns of all sizes." Many letters from industry officials heartily approved of the award and Quigley's efforts to boost the installation of quality sound systems in American film theatres. Many departments merited attention. "What's in a Name," a column by Douglas Fox, provided wry comment on film people in the news. "Sound Pictures" offered detailed descriptions of sound system technology, installation and operation. Based on a Q&A format, the question for December 7, 1929 was: "Explain just what anology [sic] there is as between a spring in mechanics and a condenser in electrics. Name some of the mechanical things which are very similar to a condenser in their action." In conjunction with this extensive section was a weekly listing of Western Electric sound installations, listed by city with house capacity. The departmental feature, "Music and Talent," detailed the many theatrical houses that still produced live stage shows and musical reviews. The inroads made by sound pictures could be seen in the leading article, "Public Still Wants Its Stage Acts." "What the Picture Did For Me," a longtime Quigley staple, provided firsthand exhibitor feedback on current films in release. "J.C. Jenkins--His Colyum," chronicled the cross-country travels of the *Exhibitors Herald-World* columnist. His commentary on motion picture exhibition in a "city of the week" format, descriptively indicated the health of the film business on a local level. Finally, there was the "Quick Reference Picture Chart," tabulated by each studio's current film releases; with a key to plot category, sound (all talking, musical score, talking sequences, sound effects, or singing), show length, and release date. Serial contained supplement, *Better Theatres*, "devoted to construction, equipment and operation of theatres," which was published every fourth week. Beginning at some point in 1930, certain elements of film product were placed into a supplment entitled *Film Buyer*, issued with separate supplement, *Better Theatres*. Both supplements were called "Section Two" of *Exhibitors Herald World*. *Film Buyer* would later be bound as supplement to *Product Digest*, but with separate pagination. Magazine format (235 cm wide x 310 cm high). Published on coated paper stock with many studio film advertisements in spot and full-color.
DEPT: "Broadway," New York City exhibition news column by Peter Vischer; "Motion Picture Finance," column by Laurence Stern; "Securities Price Range," for film organizations on Chicago and New York Stock Markets; "Pictorial Section," 'Film news in pictures; stories told by the camera'; "What's in a Name," marvelous personal column by Douglas Fox; "Sound Pictures," new technology column by F. H. Richardson; "The Studio," production and business news; "News Notes," production newsbriefs; "New York Showings," review and comment; "The Short Feature," production news of film shorts; "Newspictures," title and content listing; "Short Features With Sound," title, plot, release date; "The Theatre," new technologies and management technique; "Service Talks," 'Incorporated in this department of the Herald-World, which is a department containing news, information and gossip on current productions, is the Moving Picture World department: Through the Box Office Window' by T.O. Service; "Music and Talent," live stage elements; "Russell Says," live stage news column by W.S. Russell; "Hollywood Tunes," music

news column by Madame Octave; "Stage Shows," extensive reviews; "Sid Says About Songs," best selling sheet music and comment column by Sid Bermann; "Organ Solos," live stage/theatre programs; "Up and Down the Alley," music news and personalities column by E.T. Dawson; "Quick Reference Picture Chart," very extensive listing of current film releases; "The Voice of the Industry," 'Letters from readers'; "What the Picture Did For Me," 'Verdicts on films in language of exhibitor'; "J.C. Jenkins--His Colyum," traveling film commentary column by J. C. Jenkins; "New Pictures," 'The Exhibitors Herald-World presents in concise form information on current and forthcoming attractions'; "Chicago Personalities," Chicago exhibition column by Joe Fisher. (12-7-29).
- TYPL: "Industry Watches U.S. Suits Against Fox and the Warners," "Pathe Tests Sound Censorship by Starting Suit in U.S. Court," "New Arbitration Plan Centers on Rental Information Bureau," "Murray Roth Film Started on New $300,000 Vitaphone Stage," "Star Singing Three Languages is a Solution of Sound Shorts." (12-7-29).
- SCHL: Weekly, 75 pp.
- SPAN: Jan 7, 1928 - Dec 27, 1930//
  FROM MERGER OF
  --Exhibitors Herald (and) Moving Picture World.
  VARIES
  --Jan 7, 1928 - Dec 29, 1928 as Exhibitor's Herald and Moving Picture World.
  WITH SUPPLEMENT
  --Better Theatres, Jul 7, 1928 - Sep 29, 1928.
  --Film Buyer, ? - ?
  MERGED WITH
  --Motion Picture News (ISSN: 0748-5921) (to form) Motion Picture Herald (ISSN: 0027-1616).
- LC: PN 1993.E78

EXHIBITORS' TIMES

- SUB: "The motion picture newspaper." (May 17, 1913 - Aug 30, 1913).
- SUB: "The motion picture weekly." (Sep 13, 1913 - Sep 27, 1913).
- PUBL: W. A. Johnston, New York, NY.
- DESC: "As its name implies, this paper addresses the Exhibitor. The success of the Exhibitor rests upon the picture. By 'the picture' we mean pictures which *are* pictures. Every film made and released is not necessarily a picture. That is the trouble of the pictures of the United States, if not the world, to-day. A great many of them should have never been made, or, if made, never released; or if released, never shown. The harm done to the public by the exhibition of unsuitable pictures is incalculable." *Exhibitors' Times* crusaded for quality in film projection, management, production, and marketing; and took those to task who did not meet minimimum criteria for the professional exhibitor. This serial remains a real treasure of articles concerning motion picture theatre management, the marketing of said product, and the handling of the viewing public. Many special departments bear noting: "Right Off the Reel," providing strong industry criticism; "Motion Picture Theatre Construction Department," detailed schematics and drawings of the mechanical side of exhibition; "Music and the Picture," use of music within the theatre; "Advertising the Picture," marketing ideas for local promotion; "Appearance and Manners," discussion of interior design and function; and "Licensed Release Dates," picture titles, release date, and production company. Published weekly. A great resource for early film exhibition. Magazine format; numerous graphics on quality paper.
- DEPT: "Right Off the Reel," "Chicago Notes," "On the Road," "The Operators Forum and Question Box," Q&A; "Appearance and Manners," "Philadelphia Notes," "Answers to Correspondents," "Licensed Release Dates," "Exclusive Supply Release Dates," "Universal Release Dates," "Mutual Releases." (8-16-13).
- TYPL: "How Motion Pictures are Made," "Thirteen Thousand Motion Picture Cameras in Constant Use," "Film War Scene on Lubin Estate Attracts Thousands," "Seven and a Half Cents a Foot: Regrettable Price Cutting Amongst the Independent Factions." (8-16-13).
- SCHL: Weekly, 34 pp.
- SPAN: May 17, 1913 - Sep 27, 1913//
  ABSORBED BY
  --Moving Picture News.
- LC: PN 1993.E8

EXHIBITORS TRADE REVIEW

- SUB: "Of, for, and by the motion picture exhibitor."
- PUBL: Exhibitor's Trade Review, Inc., Knickerbocker Bldg., Forty-Second St., and Broadway, New York, NY.
- DESC: Perfectly fitting its title, this weekly serial reviewed the exhibition news, promotion news, and product of the American motion picture industry. The exhibition industry was justifiably proud of the quality and variety of theatrical houses for the public. Exhibitors were "showmen," and *Exhibitors Trade Review* reported on numerous conventions, publicity "stunts," and distributor/studio news as it pertained to the local business side of film. Successful exhibitors were profiled, often within the context of reporting on regional or state conventions. Those that criticized the industry, especially "movie fan magazines" that told lurid tales, were singled out for their negative impact on what exhibitors viewed as a family entertainment medium. Several features were noteworthy. The "Reviews of Independent Production" furnished extensive story summaries, and other information on cast and crew members. "Live News of the West Coast" provided studio and independent production news. "The Campaign Formula" presented pictures of example promotional efforts by local exhibitors, along with their merchant "tie-ins," ideas transferable to other cities. Pictures of storefront windows, flyers, newspaper advertisements, billboards, posters, mechanical dis-

plays, puzzles, and other implements were showcased for others to utilize. "The Voice of the Box Office" provided information from exhibitors on the "Exploitation" value of the film, the "Short Subjects" shown in conjunction with same, and "Press Comment" from various newspaper and magazine publications. Finally, "Illustrated Screen Reports" presented a unique full one-column review of current film fare. Each review contained four production stills, and the following labeled paragraphs: "Cast and Synopsis," "Points of Appeal," "Cast," and "Photography, Lighting, Direction." A valued serial for the American motion picture exhibitor. Large magazine format (235 cm wide x 310 cm high), with two- color covers.

- DEPT: "The News of the Week," motion picture developments; "State Rights," 'All the news of activities in the territories'; "Reviews of Independent Productions," lengthy reports; "Short Subjects and Serials," reviews; "Reviews of Current Short Subjects," "Live News of the West Coast," Hollywood trade news column by Renee Beeman; "Exploitorials," newsbriefs regarding exhibitor promotion column by Tom Kennedy; "Making the Theatre Pay," "Exploiting the Picture," "Equipping the Theatre," "The Campaign Formula," picture story of successful promotions; "The Voice of the Box Office," 'How the latest releases are being received throughout the country'; "What They Give the Public," exhibition program at various theatres; "First Runs on Broadway," 'Their presentation and press comments by various New York dailies'; "Illustrated Screen Reports," edited column by George T. Pardy and James M. Davis; "Better Screen Results," 'A department devoted to projection' column by T. O'Conor Sloane; "Theatre Construction News," 'This department is devoted to theatre building news and publishes the earliest news obtainable concerning projected theatres, schools, etc., where motion picture equipment will be used'; "Schedule of Exhibitor Conventions." (4-21-23).
- TYPL: "Steffes Boom is Launched," "Indiana Endorsers Hold Convention," "Public Relations Committee Officially Thanks Hays Organization for Co-operation," "Newspapers Hail Picture Progress," "Flaherty Guest at Notable Dinner." (4-21-23).
- SCHL: Weekly, 65 pp.
- SPAN: Dec 9, 1916 - Apr 17, 1926//
- LC: PN 1993.E85

EXPERIMENTAL CINEMA

- SUB: "A monthly projecting important international film manifistations."
- PUBL: Experimental Cinema, 919 Locust St., Philadelphia, PA.
- DESC: "*Experimental Cinema*, published by the Cinema Crafters of America, is the only magazine in the United States devoted to the principles of the art of the motion picture. It believes there is profound need at this time for a central organ to consolidate and orient those individuals and groups scattered throughout America, Europe and U.S.S.R. that are working to liberate the cinema from its stereotyped symbolism. It believes the time has come for wide critical and creative support of these isolated movements not only from the point of view of the spectator but also from the point of view of the creator, and it is the intention to experiment with new forms and to introduce to the spectator and creator the leading ideas and principles of the new film world." There was a revolutionary fervor espoused by the editors of this publication, to whom cinema was a "means to an end," a tool for the revolutionary forces of the world, a catalyst for discussion of new ideas. Cinema, in their opinion, was not mere entertainment. A short-lived, but important forum for film analysis and discussion. Some graphics.
- DEPT: "Hollywood Bulletin," newsbriefs. (#3-31).
- TYPL: "The Problem of the New Film Language," "One Hour with G. Seldes," "Turksib and the Soviet Fact," "Position of the Soviet Cinema," "On a Theory of 'Sources.'" (#3-31).
- SCHL: Irregular, 40 pp.
- SPAN: Feb, 1930 - Jun, 1934//
- LC: PN 1993.E87
- DD: 791.43/05

Experimental Wireless

Oct, 1923 - Aug, 1924//
SEE: INDUSTRIAL ELECTRONICS

Experimental Wireless & the Wireless Engineer

Sep, 1924 - Aug, 1931//
SEE: INDUSTRIAL ELECTRONICS

EXPORT ADVERTISER

- SUB: "A journal devoted to the interests of American companies advertising in foreign countries." (Dec, 1928 - ?).
- PUBL: Advertising Abroad Publishing Co., 67 West 44th St., New York, NY.
- DESC: This serial came into existence because "Those who are in any way connected with the marketing of American products abroad find themselves greatly handicapped by the lack of definite information on a host of questions. *Advertising Abroad* will endeavor to supply this need...by publishing news of the foreign media situation, rates, circulation figures, class and appeal; articles by recognized authorities on correct advertising and merchandising procedure; information on how best to translate, print and distribute booklets, folders, catalogues and display material; and by answering questions submitted to us on any subject related to foreign business." These goals aside, it was the beginning of the Great Depression in the United States, and the editorial content mirrored the uncertainty of manufacturing and advertising of that time.

There no longer was a need for a serial with this emphasis by mid-1932. Small format; numerous graphics.
DEPT: "Editorials." (7-31).
TYPL: "Tapping South American Markets by Radio Broadcast Advertising," "Trade Rivalry Keen in Argentina Competitive Trade Survey Shows," "Hurdling the Customs Barriers with Your Foreign Samples." (7-31).
SCHL: Monthly, 50 pp.
SPAN: Dec, 1928 - Jun, 1932//
VARIES
--Dec, 1928 - Dec, 1929 as Advertising Abroad.
ABSORBED BY
--Business Abroad and Export Trade.
LC: HF 5801.E8

✣ EXPOSURE

SUB: "Journal of the Society for Photographic Education."
PUBL: Society for Photographic Education, PO Box BBB, Albuquerque, NM 87196.
DESC: "*Exposure* is the quarterly journal published by and for the members of the Society for Photographic Education (SPE). The Society is a non-profit educational corporation which exists to promote high standards of photographic education. SPE attempts to increase the public's awareness of photography and will cooperate with all other organizations having similar aims." Sample issues for 1975 were published in a wide magazine format with most editorial content dedicated to news and activities of the Society. Latter issues (samples from 1982) show a small, square magazine format in which lengthy articles feature the works and philosophies of various photographic professionals. This current approach showcased numerous photographs of Society members. A thought-provoking and fascinating serial.
DEPT: "From the Editor," "Reviews," "Letters." (#4-81).
TYPL: "Images," "Imo's Photographers," "Stieglitz and Autochrome: Beginnins of a Color Aesthetic," "Teaching: A Bibliography on Photography for the Undergraduate Library." (#4-81).
SCHL: Quarterly, 60 pp.
SPAN: 1963+
LC: TR 1.E93
DD: 770/.5
ISSN: 0098-8863

✣ EXTRA!

SUB: "A publication of FAIR (Fairness & Accuracy in Reporting)."
SUB: "The newsletter of FAIR (Fairness & Accuracy in Reporting)."
PUBL: FAIR, Fairness & Accuracy in Reporting, 175 Fifth Ave., Suite 2245, New York, NY 10010.
DESC: "*FAIR* is the national media watch group offering well-documented criticism in an effort to correct bias and imbalance. *FAIR* focuses public awareness on the narrow corporate ownership of the press, the media's persistent Cold War assumptions and their insensitivity to women, labor, minorities and other public interest constituencies. *FAIR* seeks to invigorate the First Amendment by advocating for greater media pluralism and the inclusion of public interest voices in national debates. While FAIR does not pull punches when it comes to criticizing the mainstream press, our intention is not to vilify or harangue specific journalists. The main problem, as we see it, has less to do with individual reportorial bias than a far more ominous development: the increasing concentration of the US media in fewer and fewer corporate hands. Our sympathies lie with the working press; in this spirit we distribute *Extra!* to thousands of media professionals in an effort to encourage hard-hitting, aggressive journalism, which may at times conflict with the priorities of corporate media owners." This is a lively, informative critique by professional journalists concerning professional journalists. Two-color newsletter format (8 ½ x 11 inches / 215 x 280 mm); graphics.
DEPT: None. (5/6-88). None. (3/4-90).
TYPL: "The Media and the Environment: Redefining National Security," "Moscow Summit Media-Go-Round: US Press Could Use Some Glasnost of Its Own," "The Greening of Ted Turner--An Interview with the Chief of CNN," "SOS From Independent Public Broadcasting Producers," "Jesse Jackson as Media Critic." (5/6-88). "The Press Slices Up the Peace Dividend," "CIA Chief Bush Suppresses the News," "Mandela's Walk to Freedom," "Acquaintance Rape and the Media." (3/4-90).
SCHL: Monthly (Jul, 1987 - Aug, 1988); Eight issues per year (Sep/Oct, 1988+), 16 pp.
SPAN: Jul, 1987+
DD: 070 11
ISSN: 0895-2310

F

✧ FA

SUB: "Britain's premier comics fanzine."
PUBL: Trident Comics, Unit 3, 28 Canal St., South Wigston, Leicester, LE8 2PL, England.
DESC: This monthly publication consists of a two and three-column typewritten (flush left-ragged right) format in black ink on uncoated paper stock, and contains a generous amount of news, information, interviews, and profiles concerning the British, and some American comic book industry. Editor Martin Skidmore has successfully overcome the potential problems of typewritten material through the use of comic panel reproductions and crisp reproductions of same on a brilliant white paper stock. Of special note is the "Letters" section, which allow extensive discourse by readers on a variety of topics from new comic debuts to changes in favorite comic characters. This publication is interesting reading as well as an excellent resource concerning news, developments, and trends in the British comic book industry. Cover consists of full-color on heavy coated paper stock, limited advertising by comic book publishers and retail stores (8 ⅛ x 11 ¾ inches / 210 x 295 mm).
DEPT: "Report: Comics," extensive news section concerning British/American comic publications; "Reviews: Comics," "Creator Overview," profile; "Reviews: Books," "Interview," "Viewpoint," commentary; "Letters," very extensive section. (3-89).
TYPL: "Trident Comics: The Hype Article," "Osamu Tezuka Obituary," "Peter Bagge Interview," "Bill of Rights," "No Man's Land." (3-89).
SCHL: Monthly, 50 pp.
SPAN: ?+

✧ FACETS FEATURES

PUBL: Facets Multimedia, 1517 W. Fullerton Ave., Chicago, IL 60614.
DESC: "*Focus:Chicago* [was] published six times a year by FACETS MULTIMEDIA,...a non-profit, tax-exempt cultural organization dedicated to the propogation of cinematic, plastic, performing, graphic and literary arts." The emphasis was on Chicago film, or Chicago-style commentary concerning external (read non-Hollywood) activities. This free publication (to FACETS members) provided an interesting look at avant-garde and experimental films of both independent and foreign producers. Issues beginning with May/Jun, 1976 moved from typewritten to typeset copy.
DEPT: "Editor's Desk," "Letters," "Forum Schedule," "Books," "Coming Events." (6/7-76).
TYPL: "Focus on World Film Events," "Walt Disney Presents...(or is it Roy?)," "High School Filmmakers." (6/7-76).
SCHL: Bimonthly (? - ?), Monthly (?+), 30 pp.
SPAN: 1967+
VARIES
--Feb, 1967 - Spring/Summer, 1973 as Focus: Chicago (ISSN: 0362-0905).
ISSN: 0736-3745

FACTS ABOUT FILM FINLAND

SUB: "Bulletin of the Finnish Film Foundation."
PUBL: The Finnish Film Foundation, Kaisaniemenkatu 3 B 25, Sf-00100 Helsinki, Finland.
DESC: This quarterly statistical report of the Finnish film industry was concerned with production lists, attendance figures, and other statistics pertinent to motion picture production and exhibition. Later issues, notably 1976-77, included occasional articles concerning the Finnish film industry. Some production stills are included.
DEPT: "News Briefs," "Letters to the Editor." (#3-77).
TYPL: "Report of the Film Archives or Group," "Towards the History of Finnish Film Research," "The Pioneers of Finnish Film," "Early Stages of Finnish Puppet Films." (#3-77).
SCHL: Quarterly, 56 pp.
SPAN: 1972? - 1978//
ABSORBED BY
--Finland Filmland (ISSN: 0355-1539), 1978.
ISSN: 0355-1520

✧ FACTSHEET FIVE

PUBL: Hudson H. Luce, 244 West McMicken St., #1, Cincinnati, OH 45214.
DESC: This is "absolutely the world's greatest" resource for magazines (Zine's), newsletters, audio/video tapes, T-shirts, posters, buttons, armbands, and Moebius strips that range from what former Editor/Publisher Mike Gunderloy called "young, to the left, and environmentally and/or musically oriented;" to another "substantial portion [which] is on the right," a group he called "Goldwater libertarians." Over 700 such non-mainstream "publications" are abstracted in each bimonthly issue, including from one sampled issue: *Achoo! Service*, designed for a pilot hospital "...where hope and humor help in healing," and published by the Gesundheit Institute; *Ecco*, a magazine on Mondo films, with portrayal of cannibalism and torture; *Decalcomania*, a club newsletter for collectors of radio station posters, stickers and airchecks; *Trash 'O' Rama*, a review of trashy films; *Tencton Times*, for fans of the Fox TV series Alien Nation; *The Shake-*

speare Oxford Society Newsletter, whose readers postulate that Edward deVere, rather than the Bard was responsible; *New Plays & Playwrights*, for Midwest theatre professionals; *NAAPM Newsletter*, from the National Association for the Advancement of Perry Mason; *Lies of Our Times*, for segments of society who have a very difficult time believing what they read in the New York Times; *Skinned Alive*, for horror film fans; *Shots*, a magazine devoted to improving photographic talents; and (in random order), *Small Press Review, Sticky Carpet Digest, Psychotronic Video, No More Censorship Fact Sheet, Mentertainment, Housewife-Writer's Forum,* and *The Off Hollywood Report*. Publications, audio/video tapes, poetry, cartoons, comics, and "you name it" all appear in the 135-plus newsprint pages of this marvelous resource. Of special note are ongoing articles instructing readers on the joys and problems of self-publishing newsletters and magazines. Most reviews are written by multi-talented Editor and Publisher Michael A. Gunderloy, and are fascinating entertainment. From *The Optimistic Pezzimist*, for collectors of Pez candy dispensers; to the *Eraser Carvers Quarterly*; to *The Fillmore Bungle*, a serial of the "Society for the Preservation and Enhancement of the Recognition of Millard Fillmore, Last of the Whigs," (a group, which is "dedicated to mediocrity"); readers will be constantly surprised by the breadth of serials for anyone's political, sexual, educational, cultural, or psychological leanings. It is outstanding for the study of contemporary society, culture, and communication. In magazine format, it is published on newsprint. "Zines" are primarily American, with representative items from Britain, Canada, Australia, and European nations. NOTE: a change of publishers took place in mid-August, 1991, with final issue edited by founding publisher Mike Gunderloy, numbered 44, and shipped in early August, 1991. Issue #45, under new publisher Hudson H. Luce, was to be shipped in November, 1991 with a Jan/Feb, 1992 cover date. Various black/white graphics (cartoons, drawings, etc.) are printed. Some listed items, advertisements and/or graphics contain sexually explicit material. Sampled issue for mid-1991: cover consisted of three-color inks on uncoated paper stock, editorial content black ink on newsprint (8 ¼ x 10 ¾ inches / 210 x 275 mm).

DEPT: "Columnist and Artist Addresses," "Factsheet Five Projects," 'News of books you can buy from us, sales of our mailing list (and how to avoid getting your name sold), the FF index and t-shirts, and ways you can get pounds of zines for only the cost of postage'; "Dead Zines," 'Alas, another list of people who have recently ceased publishing'; "Hall of Shame," "Calendar Reviews," "T-Shirt Reviews," "Game Reviews," "Artifact Reviews," 'Artifacts are things that have a presence beyond being carriers of print--buttons, stickers, armbands, Moebius strips and other goodies'; "Noted But Not Seen," 'Zines which sent us advertising instead of copies'; "Editorial," "Publishers' Choice," "Zine Reviews," "Music Zine Reviews," "Comics Reviews," "Poetry Reviews," "One-Shot Reviews," "Software Reviews," "Important Events," "Mail Art Contacts," "Miscellaneous News," "Stars on One," media commentary column by Anni Ackner; "Experioddica," column by Bob Grumman; "Video Reviews," "NTSC Cyberbeat," media column by Belka Stamas; "The Fishing Hole," publishing column by Joe Lane; "Conspiracy Corner," column by Kerry Thornley; "Curmudgeon Corner," column by Garry De Young; "Why Publish," 'In which several publishers answer this curious question'; "The Abandoned Stone Quarry," "Audio Reviews," "Book Reviews," "Letters," 'The readers talk back, with a few pot shots from the editor'. (#38, 9-90).
TYPL: "The Warm Fuzzy of Utopian Possibility Vs. the Cold Prickly of Militarized Industrialism." (#38, 9-90).
SCHL: Bimonthly, 135 pp.
SPAN: Jul, 1982+
DD: 028
ISSN: 0890-6823

✤ FALLING FOR STARS

PUBL: El' Jon Publications, 410 Broadway, Santa Monica, CA 90401.
DESC: "The Stuntmen of America are those professional men and women who add the action to the shows and films of the Television and Movie Industry. The story may be make-believe -- but the stunts are real! In virtually every movie ever filmed there is that one moment of extraordinary action which is the focal point of the entire movie, a moment seldom forgotten by the public. That special feat of daring which mystifies and thrills the audience is generally done by a stuntman. We shall be writing and reporting on all the action shows, with stories and pictures of how it was done way back when -- the Silents; the early talkies; the serials of Republic, Columbia and Universal -- plus present-day filmmaking and current Television shows. We'll have them all in *Falling for Stars Magazine*." Beginning as a newsletter in 1965, and moving to magazine status with the premiere issue for July/August, 1974, *Falling for Stars* is a labor of love, a tribute to those who "gave their all" (sometimes their lives) to the entertainment industry. *Falling for Stars* dispels all myths about stuntmen of brawn rather than brains: this was and is a business for the intelligent strategist, the quick-witted, and quick-acting man or woman who doubles for the stars and starlets of Hollywood, and in so performing as professionals, makes the dangerous and difficult seem easy. What the premiere issue lacked in layout design and finesse, it made up for in fascinating stories and pictures of this vital aspect of the entertainment field. For the 1974 sampled issue: stapled magazine format, black ink editorial content with numerous black/white graphics, and three-color yellow/red/black ink cover all on coated paper stock, limited advertising (8 ½ x 11 inches / 215 x 280 mm).
DEPT: "Letters." (7/8-74).

TYPL: "Harvey Parry Strikes Back," "Saga of Jock Mahoney," "Spy Smasher--a Republic Serial," "Cauliflower Alley's Awards Banquet," "Project Concept: Hollywood Stuntmen's Hall of Fame, Inc." (7/8-74).
SCHL: Ten issues per year, 35 pp.
SPAN: 1965+
VARIES
--1965 - May/Jun, 1974 as Falling for Stars News.

Falling for Stars News

1965 - May/Jun, 1974//
SEE: FALLING FOR STARS

FAME

PUBL: Fame Magazine Group, Inc., 140 West 22nd St., New York, NY 10011.
DESC: This was one of the best publications ever to grace the American newstands for profiling and extolling fame. With an unusual, square magazine format, *FAME* went beyond what many other similar publications covered; recognizing other arenas where personalities excelled, played and reflected: it featured individuals from live theatre, radio and television, politics, society, music, and business. Articles were informative and entertaining, with photography and layout design that was trend-setting in the 1990s. In one sampled issue, articles ranged from a loving tribute to Rose Kennedy on her one hundredth birthday to the show business acumen of Bill Cosby. Also included were a profile of Brigitte Bardot, a discussion on the mixing of drugs and sex, observations on foreign divorce, remembering literary giant Walker Percy, New York fashions for fall, and a comprehensive rememberence (numerous pictures) of famous Studio 54. This is a wonderful publication for its "breadth and depth" in covering todays' personalities. Note: regular publication commenced with the November, 1988 issue, although a pilot issue was published in June, 1988 and was labeled as volume 1, Number 0. Magazine format (9 x 10 ⅞ inches / 230 x 275 mm); numerous high quality color graphics on coated paper stock.
DEPT: "Editor's Letter," column by Gael Love; "Contributors," unique pictorial attribution; "Past Perfect," enduring personality profile; "The New ... and the Observed," 'Hot flashes, fresh faces, and things you never knew you couldn't live without'; "Exposures," full color pix and personality profile; "Health," "Surviving Success," column by Herbert J. Freudenberger; "Love and the Law," column by Raoul Lionel Felder; "Voyeur," 'We like to watch' a column of pictures and observations; "FAME Says It All About Hollywood," column by Dana Kennedy; "FAME Says It All About Film," column by Carrie Rickey; "FAME Says It All About Books," column by Phil McCombs; "FAME Says It All About Society," column by Diane Goldner. (8-90).
TYPL: "Cybill Disobedience," "Partying Glances," "And God Created Bardot," "Don't Mess With Bill." (8-90).

SCHL: Monthly [except Jan and Jul], 130 pp.
SPAN: Jun, 1988 - Dec, 1990//
DD: 051
ISSN: 0898-6940

✤ FAMOUS MONSTERS OF FILMLAND

SUB: "Incorporating Monster World."
SUB: "The world's first monster fan magazine."
PUBL: Warren Publishing Co., 145 E. 32nd St., New York, NY 10016.
DESC: A layman's pictorial guide to every ghoul and goblin to grace the Hollywood screen, and written rather tongue-in-cheek; *Famous Monsters* is filled with a large number of publicity stills from current and old releases. The full-color covers are outstanding, and entice the reader to a generous selection of movie monster-themed articles, a sampling of which included (from past issues): "When Dracula Invaded England," "Boris Karloff in the Magic Castle," "Phantom of the Opera," "How They Made Godzilla," and "The World Explodes When Frankenstein Meets the Wolfman." Most issues have a central theme, often indicated by cover picture, and some issues have a horror-themed comic section as well. The letters column, appropriately called "Fang Mail," has the unusual policy of printing reader-submitted pictures of themselves. "You Axed For It" pertains to reader-requested pictures of their favorite horror movie scenes. Finally, special note must be made of news reports concerning current monster club activities in the United States, or as the publisher puts it: "the neck's bite is mine!." This wonderful magazine for the horror-movie fan presents the broad array of horror films produced since the turn of the century, but stops short of academic examination of the aesthetic, philosophical, and societal elements of the motion picture. For the sampled issue of 1969: editorial content was black ink on newsprint, cover was full-color on coated paper stock, limited advertising (8 ⅛ x 10 ⅞ inches / 205 x 275 mm).
DEPT: "Monster Club Section," monster youth club news; "Monster Club Members," listing of names and hometowns of new members; "Monstorama Quiz." (4-59). "The Shape of Things to Come," 'As seen thru the terror tell-us-scope'; "You Axed For It," 'An extra generous helping of extra special reader-requested fotos'; "Fang Mail," 'Growls from the monster mail bag'. (1-69).
TYPL: "Frankenstein from Space," "Just Ghost to Show You," "No Ghoul Like an Old Ghoul," "You Axed for It." (4-59). "The Horror in the Lighthouse," "Mystery Photo," "Castle of Terror," "Face #1001," "Hammer of Horror." (1-69).
SCHL: Nine per year, 70 pp.
SPAN: 1958+?
ABSORBED
--Monster World, ?
LC: PN 1995.9 .H6F3
ISSN: 0014-7443

FANFARE

SUB: "The magazine of popular culture and the arts."
PUBL: Fanfare, 329 North Avenue 66, Los Angeles, CA 90042.
DESC: "*Fanfare* is a successor-in-interest to a limited circulation effort called *Graphic Story Magazine* and, before that, *Fantasy Illustrated*. It dealt with experimental comics and interviews with comic creators, and in that aim it was considered by quite a few people to be the best of its kind. *GSM* only went so far, however, and after 16 issues the format was wearing thin. Comic books are nifty ...but there are other things in life. We think *GSM* has undergone the same change that many comic book fans experience. After immersing themselves in funnybook fandom, many fans grow bored, possibly because of the lack of diversification that comic books have to offer. Specialization is not always an asset, especially in an art form that has so many crannies left undelved. So those fans often move on to other things, as has *GSM*, encompassing common interests like movies, television, comedy records, animation and so on. Scratch a hardcore comics fan and the chances are you'll find a media freak underneath." This statement by publishers/editors Bill Spicer and Mark Evanier describes the background, and events leading up to *Fanfare*, a magazine broadly based in popular culture and performing arts. There appears to have been a two to three year suspension between the last issue of *Graphic Story Magazine* in 1974, and the first issue of *Fanfare*, possibly in early 1978; and a second suspension of approximately one year between the first and second issue of 1978. Terminating in 1983, it is a real loss of a fine serial of popular culture. Articles had "something for everyone." One issue contained anecdotes about Harry Cohn, and Orson Welles, a wonderful article entitled "Why Magazine Writers Get Migraines," detailing the problems of securing enough information to publish an article on the "Golddiggers;" a reprinted article from the Washington Post on videotaping the Tonight Show, and commentary on the comeback of the Popeye cartoon series. Paper stock was good quality, uncoated material, and was used for extensive reprinting of black/white graphics, as well as color graphics of motion picture art and television production stills in the sampled issue. Some magazines maintain their editorial distance from their readers, but not *Fanfare*. Letters to the editor and their VERY extensive replies required seven full pages (four columns) in the sampled issue, and were as entertaining, informative, and thought provoking as the primary features themselves. Magazine format (8 ⅜ x 10 ⅞ inches / 215 x 275 mm), black/white and color graphics.
DEPT: "Short Subjects," 'From here, there and everywhere'; "Fanfare Forum," editorial and letters. (winter-78).
TYPL: "Film Noir and Comic Books," "Whatever Happened to the Golddiggers?," "The Magic of Middle-Earth," "The Movie Poster Art of Frank Frazetta," "Groucho and Us." (winter-78).
SCHL: Three-Four issues per year [irregular at times], 65 pp.
SPAN: 1964 - 1983//
VARIES
--? - ? as Fantasy Illustrated.
--1964? - 1974 as Graphic Story Magazine.

✤ FANGORIA

SUB: "Horror in entertainment."
PUBL: Starlog Communications International, Inc., 475 Park Avenue South, New York, NY 10016.
DESC: "The magazine of movie chills and terror, featuring page after page of bloody good color photos, scenes from new splatter films, interviews with stars, special effects make-up artists, directors, writers, actors--all the news of horror!" While *Fangoria* will not become a coffee table staple, it certainly has a niche in the full-color realm of the bizarre, berserk, and bananas in motion picture entertainment. Each issue is a demented Transylvanian laboratory scientist's dream come true, as mutant transformations of human and alien forms appear in all their glory, oftentimes up close and perhaps a bit too personal. This quality publication of the horror genre motion picture has fascinating interviews with the special effects/modeling experts, directors, actors, and producers whose diligent efforts bring our worst fears to fruition. Readers will be pleasantly surprised by the industry articles, including a very informative article about MPAA ratings in the sample issue reviewed. As *Fangoria* succinctly put it: "So beat the heat--we've got the meat!" For the 1990 sampled issue: stapled magazine format, with full-color graphics and cover on coated paper stock, some black ink editorial content, advertising (8 x 10 ⅞ inches / 205 x 275 mm).
DEPT: "Elegy," 'Assault of the killer editorial'; "Postal Zone," letters; "Monster Invasion," 'The Fangoria fright file of up-to-the-minute newsbreaks and other horrible happenings!'; "Dr. Cyclops," videocassette reviews; "Nightmare Library," book reviews; "The Wasteland." (8-90).
TYPL: "Brad to the Bone," "Arachnophobia Spins Its Web," "Pittsburgh and the Pendulum," "Masters of Metal," "It's Not Over Till the Fat Lady Splits." (8-90).
SCHL: Bimonthly (?, 1979 - Jan?, 1982); Eight issues per year (Feb, 1982 - Jul?, 1985); Nine issues per year (Aug, 1985 - ?); Ten issues per year [not published in Jan and Mar] (?+), 70 pp.
SPAN: 1979+
ISSN: 0164-2111

✤ FANTASTIC FILMS

SUB: "The magazine of visual fantasy and science fiction."
SUB: "The magazine of fantasy & science fiction in the cinema."
SUB: "The magazine of imaginative media."
PUBL: Fantastic Films, Inc., 2020 Lincoln Park West, Chicago, IL 60614.

DESC: "Each issue is loaded with dozens of full color photos, lively interviews, controversial articles, fascinating and unusual special effects features, with easy-to-understand explanations, plus letters, movie news, book reviews and behind-the-scenes information. *Fantastic Films* is your complete guide to imaginative media." For the motion picture fan fascinated with the science fiction/adventure genre, *Fantastic Films* provides detailed coverage of current film fare in the areas of star profiles, production, director/producer interviews, special effects, and story development; among other items. Utilizing Helvetica type in a four-column format, a large amount of editorial material accompanies the numerous black/white and color production stills seen throughout this serial. This entertaining publication stimulates the reader to view the film on the large screen. Of special note are literate interviews with production personnel. In the sampled issue, interviews included Director George Miller of "Mad Max Beyond Thunderdome," Director Tobe Hooper of "Lifeforce," Director Richard Donner of "The Goonies," Director Richard Fleischer of "Red Sonja," and Director Ron Howard of "Cocoon." Magazine format (8 1/8 x 10 7/8 inches / 210 x 275 mm), numerous black/white and color graphics on coated paper stock.
DEPT: "Databank," 'A look at what's happening in the world of films, theater, literature, conventions and fandom' column by Sharon Williams; "Readout," 'Reviews of some of the newer SF literary releases'; "Cinemasneak," 'Advance production information and first photos from forthcoming attractions' column by Priscilla Kitt; "Starscan," 'A closer look at some of your favorite film personalities'; "Filmfax," 'Interviews and information focusing on the latest developments in state-of-the-art cinema'. (8-85).
TYPL: "Tina Turner Becomes Auntie Entity in 'Mad Max Beyond Thunderdome'," "'Robotech:' Robots, Romance and Real Good animated Adventure," "On Location with Director Ron Howard During the Filming of His New SF Fantasy 'Cocoon'," "Action, Adventure and Just Plain Fun were the Secret Passwords for Director Richard Donner & Co. During the Filming of Steven Spielberg's Newest: 'The Goonies'," "'Red Sonja': Newcomer Brigitte Nielsen Stands Strong and Tall in Her Role as the Fiery Blade-Wielding Beauty on a Quest for Revenge." (8-85).
SCHL: Bimonthly (Jan, 1982 - ?); Nine issues per year (?+), 60 pp.
SPAN: Jan, 1982+
ISSN: 0273-7043

✣ FANTASTIC TELEVISION!

PUBL: Videosonic Arts, 11225 Magnolia Blvd., Suite 200, North Hollywood, CA 91601.
DESC: American video stars of yesteryear are given royal treatment in *Fantastic Television!* Television has rarely received this kind of authoritative, in-depth treatment in periodical form, which makes it a particular delight. Each article includes full production bibliography (no matter what medium), with numerous black/white production and publicity pictures. Some articles concerning television series provide a complete cast/title episode listing, including directorial and writing credit. Finally, these retrospective articles detail current projects or status of the featured individual. A wonderful publication, but unfortunately contains no publishing schedule or lineage information other than issue number. Stapled black/white magazine format on unocated paper stock with two-color cover (8 1/2 x 11 inches / 215 x 280 mm).
DEPT: None. (#2-?).
TYPL: "Dick Tracy on TV," "The Mysterious Korla Pandit," "TV of the Future," "A Few Words on a Tucker They'll Never Make a Movie About," "Bela Lugosi on TV," "Interview: Dave deCocteau." (#2-?).
SCHL: ?, 55 pp.
SPAN: ?+?

Fantasy Illustrated

? - ?//
SEE: FANFARE

✣ FANTASY ZONE

SUB: "The media guide to fantasy and science fiction!"
PUBL: Marvel Comics, Ltd., Arundel House, 13/15 Arundel St., London WC2R 3DX, England.
DESC: Marvel Comics of Great Britain provides an excellent vehicle for the fantasy/science fiction fan in the form of *Fantasy Zone*, a serial of "other worlds" populated by heroes and anti-heroes. It looks at the grotesque and beguiling nature of the human form, of society gone wrong, and the triumph of good over evil on earth or in a galaxy long ago and far away. It is for the aficionado of this particular art form, and serves as a forum to discuss genres, trends, artists, directors, and other aspects of this unique entertainment medium. It is not a magazine that revels in detailed explanations of special effects (which are considerable in film products of this kind). While articles explaining special effects do appear from time to time, the publisher has wisely understood his audience: it is sufficient on occasion to have a quick peak at the wizard behind "the green curtain," without explaining how the curtain was made, hung and operated. Distinctive on many different levels, including minimal advertising. For 1990 sampled issue: black/white and full-color pages (including cover) all on coated paper stock in stapled magazine format, with numerous graphics, primarily production stills (8 1/4 x 11 inches / 210 x 280 mm).
DEPT: "News," news items concerning fantasy and science fiction film/video product; "Newsreel," newsbriefs; "Previews," new film/video reviews; "Reviews," current fantasy product; "Books," reviews; "Videos," previews, new releases and best buys. (2-90).
TYPL: "Back With a Vengeance," "Man Friday," "Super Heroes For Reel," "Man of a Thousand Faces." (2-90).
SCHL: Monthly?, 40 pp.
SPAN: ?+

ISSN: 0957-5340

Far East Film News
Jun, 1953 - May, 1959//
SEE: MOVIE/TV MARKETING

Far East Film News
Jul, 1959 - Dec, 1961//
SEE: MOVIE/TV MARKETING

Far East Film News and TViews
May, 1953//
SEE: MOVIE/TV MARKETING

✤ FAST FORWARD
SUB: "The truth comes out."
PUBL: Home Entertainment Products Department, 3M Center, St. Paul, MN 55144.
DESC: This promotional newsletter is for the home videophile, with information tidbits on enjoying home videocassette machines. Articles cover most facets of home video camera/VCR combinations.
DEPT: "Product Close-Up," brief comparison of new video products; "Ask Video Phil," Q&A by readers; "Why Didn't I Think of That," techniques and other suggestions sent in by readers.
TYPL: "Video Clubs: Strength in Numbers." (#2-81).
SCHL: Quarterly, 6 pp.
SPAN: 1980+

✤ FCC WEEK
SUB: "An exclusive weekly report on the FCC, the Executive Branch, and Congress."
PUBL: Dawson-Butwick Publishers, 1001 Connecticut Ave., N.W., Suite 301, Washington, DC 20036.
DESC: This eight-page typewritten newsletter covers news of communication rules and regulations in Washington, DC from the prior week. News is divided into convenient subcategories of "Broadcast," "Cable TV," "International," "Common Carrier," and "General." The no-nonsense approach, with the timeliness of a newsletter format makes this a most important resource for studying the federal communications regulation process. For the sampled issues of 1983: loose-leaf, three-hole-punched newsletter format, black ink with spot-color on uncoated paper stock, typewritten, no advertising (8 ½ x 11 inches / 215 x 280 mm).
DEPT: "In Brief." (10-4-82).
TYPL: "Commission Hikes ENFIA by $5 and Sets Rules for Counting Minutes Next Time," "Dispute Between OGC and Broadcast Bureau Delays Attribution and 7-7-7 NPRMs," "AT&T Formally Rejects Notion of Bidding for New International Telecommunications Services." (10-4-82).
SCHL: Weekly [48 issues per year], 8 pp.
SPAN: 198u+
ISSN: 0738-5714

Federal Communications Bar Journal
Mar, 1937 - 1976//
(ISSN: 0014-9055)
SEE: FEDERAL COMMUNICATIONS LAW JOURNAL

✤ FEDERAL COMMUNICATIONS LAW JOURNAL
PUBL: UCLA School of Law, 405 Hilgard Ave., Los Angeles, CA 90024-3712.
DESC: The premiere issue of the publication for March, 1937, under the former title of *Federal Communications Bar Journal*, informed readers that the publication's purpose was "...to serve as a medium primarily for the dissemination of information relating to the activities of the Association, and secondarily, and to the extent permitted by the resources of the Association, information of value to lawyers practicing before the Federal Communications Commission." Early issues of the *Journal* contained news of the association as well as articles on regulation, comment and litigation. Several format changes were executed. The size of the sampled issues for 1937 were: (6 ⅛ x 9 ⅛ inches / 155 x 230 mm). A format design change occurred with the first issue of 1976 to (5 ¾ x 8 ¾ inches / 145 x 200 mm). Commencing with the winter, 1977 issues: (6 x 9 inches / 150 x 230 mm). A final design change was implemented with the winter, 1978 issues to: (6 ½ x 10 inches / 165 x 255 mm). All issues from 1937 to date consist of black ink on uncoated paper stock, perfect-bound journal format, limited advertising in latter issues. The *Federal Communications Law Journal* is split into two distinct sections, articles concerning FCC issues and commentary on FCC actions. Each issue is edited by the UCLA School of Law and follows normal scholarly legal format. Typically one to three articles and commentary are published per issue. An excellent resource for the communications regulatory area.
DEPT: "Book Reviews," "Articles Digest." (winter-81). "Book Review," "Articles Digest." (7-91).
TYPL: "Alien Ownership and the Communications Act," "Judge David Bazelon: Making the First Amendment Work," "The Computer Inquiries: Mapping the Communications/Data Processing Terrain," "In the Wake of Chandler vs. Florida: a Comprehensive Approach to the Implementation of Cameras in the Courtroom." (winter-81). "Assignments and Transfers of Control of FCC Authorizations Under Section 310(d) of the Communications Act of 1934," "Defending the 'Time Culture': The Public and Private Interests of Media Corporations," "Austin v. Michigan Chamber of

Commerce: The Supreme Court Takes a 'Less Speech, Sounds Great' Approach to Corporate Political Expression." (7-91).
SCHL: Three issues per year, 180 pp.
SPAN: Mar, 1937+
VARIES
--Mar, 1937 - 1976 as Federal Communications Bar Journal (ISSN: 0014-9055).
SUSPENDED
--Dec, 1945 - Feb, 1948.
LC: K6.E29
DD: 343/.73/099405
ISSN: 0163-7606
ABST: --Index to Legal Periodicals (ISSN: 0019-4077)
--Legal Resource Index
--Management Contents

✤ FEED-BACK

SUB: "The California journalism review."
SUB: "The journalism report and review for northern California."
PUBL: San Francisco State University, Journalism Department, 1600 Holloway, San Francisco, CA 94132.
DESC: This is a journalism review which concentrates on northern California print media, with a small section on radio-TV journalism. Articles appear to be written by San Francisco State journalism students, members of Sigma Delta Chi. A well-produced publication.
DEPT: "Precede," late breaking media news; "Post," most interesting letters; "Type-Lice," typos and fluffs in area media; "Courts," California legislation affecting journalism; "Broadcast," broadcast journalism review; "Kick Back," an interesting section of the magazine devoted to the magazine ombudsman. (winter-77).
TYPL: "The King of Trash," "The Fight to Sell the Oakland Tribune," "The San Francisco Progress: Every Throwaway has its Price." (winter-77).
SCHL: Quarterly, 60 pp.
SPAN: Oct, 1974+
LC: PN 4700.F42
DD: 071/.94
ISSN: 0145-6261

✤ FEEDBACK

PUBL: Broadcast Education Association, 1771 N. St., N.W., Washington, DC 20036.
DESC: "Published quarterly for members of the Broadcast Education Association and others with professional interest in broadcast education," Feedback "...serves to facilitate communication among educators and broadcast professionals, enhancing mutual appreciation of goals and demands associated with the education and employment of students in telecommunications fields." Feedback provides a valuable forum both for the discussion of pedagogical issues, and is a means by which readers are informed about Broadcast Education Association (BEA) membership activities. Beginning with the winter, 1989/1990 issue, Feedback moved from small journal to standard magazine-sized format "...to make the publication more readable and visually appealing." Editor Philip Kipper used that opportunity to tell readers: "My goal for Feedback is to make it a lively and vital publication that investigates the key issues facing broadcasting and other forms of electronic communication." Describing the ideal article, Kipper went on to say, "I invite contributors to take risks with respect to the ideas and subjects they bring up. Feedback should be a forum where broadcast educators, as well as professionals, propose and investigate new concepts. What better way for Feedback to fulfill its purpose, which is to serve as an intellectual liaison between the educational and professional worlds." An excellent resource and idea forum for educator and professional alike. Sampled issue for 1990: magazine format (8½ x 11 inches / 215 x 280 mm); black/white graphics on heavy clay-coated paper.
DEPT: "Personal Notes," academic changes, awards, grants. (11-76). "Book Review," "Membership Report." (summer-88). "Book Reviews," "Membership Reports." (winter-89).
TYPL: "Broadcasting and the FCC--a Candid Talk with Mr. Wiley," "Dual-Track Video Tape Recorder used to Teach Television News Directing," "Broadcast Education Needs Re-Emphasis on Liberal Arts." (11-76). "Put the Roper Survey on the Shelf--We Have Our Own Agenda," "The 'Electronic Media Career Preparation Study' as Research," "Bashing Academia Again: The Roper Study." (summer-88). "Corporate Television Industry Open to Working with Colleges," "A Survey of Broadcast Job Placement," "Personality Type Indicators as a Tool in Teaching Television Production." (winter-89).
SCHL: Quarterly, 25 pp.
SPAN: Fall, 1960?+
LC: PN 1990.83 .F38
DD: 384.54/05
ISSN: 0147-4871

✤ FEMINIST SCHOLARSHIP INTEREST GROUP NEWSLETTER OF THE INTERNATIONAL COMMUNICATION ASSOCIATION

PUBL: International Communication Association, Feminist Scholarship Interest Group, PO Box 9589, Austin, TX 78766.
DESC: For an upcoming themed conference of "Communication and New Worlds," the newsletter stated in part: "FSIG encourages creative and challenging explorations of the conference theme, including (but not limited to) submissions on what constitutes a new world within feminist theory: workplace, families, technologies, local and international networking, global activism, cross-cultural exchange; and the in-

ter-relatedness of gender, class, race, sexuality, age, region, ability, and ethnicity in informing our understanding of possible ideal and actual new worlds. FSIG also welcomes entries that develop feminist theory, criticism, and methodology in all areas of communication scholarship." The newsletter in many ways mirrors these same concerns, and encourages participation of members in exploring and defining the scope, form and function of same. For the sampled issue of 1991: (5 ½ x 8 ½ inches / 140 x 215 mm).
DEPT: None. (fall-91).
TYPL: "Call For Papers," "Paper Reviewers Sought for FSIG," "Television, Video and Feminist Studies," "AEJMC Call For Papers," "FSIG News Flash." (fall-91).
SCHL: Semiyearly?, 10 pp.
SPAN: ?+

FIEJ-BULLETIN

PUBL: Federation Internationale des Editeurs de Journaux et Publications, (International Federation of Newspaper Publishers), 6, rue du Faubourg Poissonniere, 75010 Paris, France.
DESC: Since its first issue in 1949, FIEJ has published a dual language (French/English) serial to inform, stimulate, and provide a forum for discussion of issues affecting newspaper publication throughout the world. A typical issue may discuss new technology (and its probable impact), press freedom, labor unions, marketing, advertising and reporters; in short, all of the elements that make up the newspaper industry, which in this case is seen from a world viewpoint. Printed on quality paper; but printed pictures are at times of minimal standards. This remains an important serial for an understanding of the state of world newspaper publishing today.
DEPT: "In a Few Lines," newsbriefs; "Latest Books," "FIEJ Throughout the World," newsbriefs. (10-52). "In a Few Lines." (1-79).
TYPL: "Are We Reading Fewer Newspapers?," "Press and the Fiscal Policies," "Collective Agreements and Arbitration." (10- 52). "Times Newspapers Halted," "The Electronic Editing Systems," "A Look at a Chinese Da ly," "Bring the Written Press Out of the Dark." (1-79).
SCHL: Three issues per year (1949 - 1950); Quarterly (1951 to date); 40 pp.
SPAN: Mar, 1949 - Jun, 1986//
VARIES
--May, 1949 - Oct, 1965 as Bulletin d'Informations.
LC: Z284.I4
ISSN: 0046-3531
ABST: --Printing Abstracts (ISSN: 0031-109x)

Fifth Mode, The
198u - 1988?//
SEE: SCSC XEROX PIPELINE

✤ FILM
SUB: "Monthly journal of the BFFS."
SUB: "The film society magazine."
SUB: "The magazine of The Federation of Film Societies."
PUBL: British Federation of Film Societies, 81 Dean St., London W1, England.
DESC: Dedicated to the premise that a well-structured and energetic film society can bring new dynamics to the film viewing experience, *Film* provides news, encouragement, and instruction for same on behalf of the British Federation of Film Societies. Each 12-page issue is a venerable celebration of the motion picture, with articles detailing new film releases for society showings, programming ideas, suggestions for themed film festivals, books, festival events, and excellent instruction for what makes for an outstanding film society in Great Britain. Financially assisted by the British Film Institute, the British Federation of Film Societies through their publication, *Film*, accomplishes much to enhance the marriage of consumer to the medium of motion picture film. For the 1990 sampled issue: black/white editorial content with two-color cover on coated paper stock in stapled magazine format (8 ¼ x 11 ¾ inches / 210 x 295 mm).
DEPT: "Film Society News," "Awards," "Film News," feature film newsbriefs; "Book Reviews," "Coming Up," British film society events. (2-90).
TYPL: "Hollywood Goes to College," "An Exploration of Russian Films," "Colouring the Picture," "Let's Put on a Good Show." (2-90).
SCHL: Quarterly (1954 - 1963); Three issues per year (1964 - 1972); Monthly (1972+); 12 pp.
SPAN: Oct, 1954+
SUSPENDED
--Fall, 1972 - Mar, 1973.
LC: PN 1993.F
ISSN: 0015-1025
ABST: --Film Literature Index (ISSN: 0093-6758)
--Media Review Digest (ISSN: 0363-7778)

Film
Spring, 1933//
SEE: FILM ART

Film
Nov, 1961 - Feb, 1962//
SEE: FILM BULLETIN

✤ FILM ALBUM MAGAZINE
SUB: "A quarterly presentation of your film favorites old and new, featuring exciting portraits and personal biographies." (Summer, 1948 - ?).
PUBL: Select Publications, Inc., 350 Fifth Ave, New York, NY.

DESC: Despite the fact that a newsprint shortage was very real in 1948, the editors saw fit to launch this "moviefan" quarterly designed to show the lives of the famous and infamous of Hollywood. There was no place for production stories, or Hollywood parties in this serial. Every page (and no advertising!) was filled with pictures and brief prose of some 30 Hollywood thespians.
DEPT: "Glamour Gallery," "Slated for Success," "We Present," "Album Specials." (fall-48).
TYPL: "Tough 'n Terrific," "The Girl's Got Sparkle!," "Crosby is Never Anybody Else," "Sultry Sirens," "Charming Menace," "Sitting Pretty." (fall-48).
SCHL: Quarterly, 50 pp.
SPAN: Summer, 1948+?
LC: PN 1993.F415

Film and Audio-Visual Annual [NF]

May, 1962 - ?//
SEE: AVC

Film and Audio-Visual Communications

Feb, 1967//
SEE: AVC

FILM & BROADCASTING REVIEW

SUB: "A biweekly publication of the U.S. Catholic Conference."
PUBL: United States Catholic Conference, 1011 First Ave., Suite 1300, New York, NY 10022.
DESC: Ranging in size from four to eight pages per issue, *Film & Broadcasting Review* provided capsule commentary on current American film and video offerings. Primarily, this serial sought to provide analysis of programming content vis a vis widely held Christian values of morality, decency, etc. In alternating issues the editors provided a complete listing of current films with moral suitability ratings. Analysis was always thoughtful, and oftentimes provided interesting commentary on societal norms. A lack of subscribers forced cessation on September 1, 1980. Two-color newsletter style; some graphics.
DEPT: "Cinecapsules," film reviews; "Television," reviews; "In Focus," film newsbriefs. (3-15-76).
TYPL: "James Whitmore's Rousing One-Man Show." (3-15-76).
SCHL: Biweekly, 8 pp.
SPAN: 1964 - Sep 1, 1980//
VARIES
--1964 - Dec 30, 1975 as Catholic Film Newsletter (ISSN: 0008-8021).
LC: PN 1995.F457
DD: 791.43/7
ISSN: 0362-0875

✤ FILM & HISTORY

PUBL: Historians Film Committee, New Jersey Institute of Technology, Newark, NJ 07102.
DESC: "The Historian's Film Committee exists to further the use of film sources in teaching and research, to disseminate information among film and film use to historians and other social scientists, to work for an effective system of film preservation so that scholars may have ready access to film archives, and to organize periodic conferences and seminars dealing with film." This is an excellent resource that brings together two often overlooked areas (film and history), of scholarly research and study. Some issues contain similarly themed articles such as the September, 1990 issue: "Three Periods of French Resistance Films: The Case of 'The Red Poster'," and "Born to Kill: S. Kubrick's 'Full Metal Jacket' as Historical Representation of America's Experience in Vietnam." Typewritten, small-format publication dedicated to exploring the role of film in history, and the portrayal of history through the film medium. Sampled issues for 1979 and 1982: (7 x 8 ½ inches / 180 x 215 mm).
DEPT: "Film and History News," "Film Reviews," "Source Notes," "Letters." (Vol 2-# 1). "Film Review." (12-90).
TYPL: "Motion Pictures and the Study of Attitudes: Some Problems for Historians," "Documentary Film for Historians: An Appreciation of Public Television." (Vol 2-# 1). "The Santa Fe Trail, John Brown, and the Coming of the Civil War," "Crisis on the Eastern Front, 1941 - 42: A Comparative Analysis of German and American Newsreel Coverage," "Bearing Witness: Michael Lesy and Photography as Historical Resource." (5-83). "Boundaries of Participation: The Problem of Spectatorship and American Film Audiences, 1905 - 1930," "'The Captain of Kopenick: A Faitfhul Adaptation?." (12-90).
SCHL: Quarterly, 30 pp.
SPAN: Mar, 1971+
VARIES
--Mar, 1971 - Dec, 1971 as Newsletter - Historians Film Committee.
LC: PN 1995.2 .F54
DD: 791.43/09/09358
ISSN: 0360-3695
ABST: --America, History and Life (ISSN: 0002-7065)
--Historical Abstracts. Part A. Modern History Abstracts. (ISSN: 0363-2712)
--Historical Abstracts. Part B. Twentieth Century Abstracts. (ISSN: 0363-2725)
--Recently Published Articles (ISSN: 0145-5311)
--Writings on American History (ISSN: 0364-2887)

Film and Radio Discussion Guide

Oct, 1942 - Jun, 1945//
SEE: AUDIO-VISUAL GUIDE

Film & Radio Guide
Oct, 1945 - Jun, 1947//
SEE: AUDIO-VISUAL GUIDE

Film and Television Daily
Mar 18, 1968 - Nov 14, 1969//
SEE: FILM TV DAILY

FILM AND THEATRE TODAY
PUBL: Saturn Press, London, England.
DESC: Recognizing a new post-war resurgence in British theatre, editors Montagu Slater and Christopher Lee set out in 1946 to produce a serial to meet the renewal of public interest in live theatre performance. This was not to be a serial of current dramatic offerings (although there are such features within some issues), but rather a publication with two distinct purposes: one, to tackle major issues affecting British drama; and two, to provide a forum (called the "Green Room") for philosophical discussion concerning the contemporary state of the theatre. Often *Film and Theatre Today*, and its predecessor, *Theatre Today*, attained those goals. Pages were a mixture of newsprint (editorial content), and coated paper stock (pictures and editorial pages).
DEPT: "Editorial," "Books on the Theatre." (#7-49).
TYPL: "Money, Money, Money," "This Opera Business," "Blast Actor Managers," "The Bristol Experiment," "The Abominable Foote," "Theatre Project," "As Actor to Actor." (#7-49).
SCHL: Irregular, 70 pp.
SPAN: Mar, 1946 - 1949//
VARIES
--#1 - 7 as Theatre Today.
ABSORBED
--Film Today, 1948.
LC: PN 2001.F5
DD: 792.05

✧ FILM & VIDEO
SUB: "The production magazine."
PUBL: Optic Music, Inc., 8455 Beverly Blvd., Suite 508, Los Angeles, CA 90048.
DESC: The excitement of on-location or studio film/video productions is evident in *Film & Video*, a serial with separate monthly sections for teleproductions, motion pictures, music videos, commercials, special effects, facilities, and audio. It holds special interest for the industry professional, whether he/she is a "below the line" crew member, with articles detailing production case histories, new technical advancements, and production logistics; or a producer/director with articles concerning budgets, industry trends, and news of state-of-the-art post facilities. There is strong emphasis on the individual production company (and its respective associates)--who they are, where they're located, and what facilities are available. Of special note are extensive advertisements by equipment rental/sales vendors, and film commissions, attesting to the strong industry readership of this publication. Well recommended for both below/above-the-line readers. Full color throughout on heavy-coated paper stock (8 ½ x 11 inches / 215 x 280 mm).
DEPT: "Equipment News," "Music Video Production Listings," "Music Video Production Listings Breakdown," "Production Companies." (12-87). "Production News," "News," "New Equipment," "Music Video Production Listings," "Production Companies," "Film Commission News," news of state film commission activities. (3-89). "Production News," column by Katharine Stalter; "Post Production News," column by Katharine Stalter; "Motion Pictures," "Commercials," "Teleproductions," "Music Videos," "Facilities," "New Equipment," "Music Video Production Listings," projects in progress; "Production Companies," "Film Commission News," "Calendar." (1-91).
TYPL: "Graphic Facilities Within Post Production Companies--A Growing Trend Across the Country," "Dominic Sena--Directing Liza Minnelli for Estee Lauder and AC&R Advertising," "The Cinematographer Reveals His Craft," "The XVth Winter Olympics--ABC Reveals the Task of Broadcasting the Games." (12-87). "Executive Producers David Chase, Diane English, Peter Jones, David Paulsen and Marty Ryan Reveal the Secrets Behind Their Successful Television Series," "FYI--Producer Paul Flattery and Director Jim Yukich Find Success with Their Own Music Video House," "The Gemini Process--A New System for Transferring D-1 Video to 35 mm Film is Developed by The Post Group and Pacific Title," "Anderson Video--The New Electronic Post House Prepares for a Move onto the Universal City Studios Lot." (3-89). "Prime-Time Production and Post Breakdown--A Show by Show Directory of the 1990-91 Television Season," "Trends in Prime-Time Production--Television's Movers and Shakers Downplay the Importance of Trends as They Seek to Create Unique Programming," "Animation in Commercials--Computer Graphics and Cel Animation Develop into Sophisticated Solutions for Agency Producers," "What's It Really Like to Shoot a Music Video? Red Car Director D.J. Webster's Day-by-Day Account of the Making of Jeffrey Osborne's 'I'm Only Human' Provides the Answer." (1-91).
SCHL: Monthly, 75 pp.
SPAN: Feb, 1984+
VARIES
--Feb, 1984 - May, 1987 as Optic Music (ISSN: 0889-5651).
--Jun, 1987 - Oct, 1988 as Opticmusic's Film & Video Production (ISSN: 0894-4423).
DD: 791 11
ISSN: 1041-1933

FILM & VIDEO NEWS

SUB: "World wide news of documentary and educational motion pictures." (Dec, 1940 - ?).
SUB: "The international review of AV materials and equipment."
SUB: "Official organ of the Educational Film Library Association."
SUB: "The newsmagazine of films, filmstrips, television, recordings."
PUBL: Gorez Goz Publishing Company, 1058 Eighth St., La Salle, IL 61301.
DESC: Since 1939, *Film News* has been "for users of films, filmstrips, ETV and equipment." As such, *Film News* was a vehicle for news of new educational media releases, and trade news concerning the Association for Educational Communication and Technology. During WW II, the emphasis was on world-wide documentary production and the use of film for propaganda purposes. In the 1980s the emphasis remained on world-wide film, (with specific focus on educating children, and the world community). The periodical ceased publication in 1981, and resumed with an April, 1984 issue and the new name of *Film & Video News*, to reflect the growing number of titles in the videotape area. In the 1980s, with the noticeable move to videocassettes, *Film News* made note of the availability of such product in that format. This remains a marvelous resource for individuals interested in documentary and educational films. For the sampled issues of 1981 and 1984: black ink on coated paper stock with various covers from black ink with spot-color to full-color on coated paper stock (8 1/8 x 11 1/4 inches / 205 x 285 mm).
DEPT: "Sponsored Films." (4-42). "Previews and Reviews," assorted in-depth reviews of new releases; "Film and TV Press," reviews of publications concerning media; "Magazine Rack, The," news of new periodicals; "What They are Showing," film festival calendar. (02-71). "Editorially Speaking," "Book Reviews," "Film/Video Reviews." (fall-81). "Comment," "Profiles," "Language Arts," "Classroom & Community," "Nutrition," "History & Current Events," "Art." (04-84).
TYPL: "Washington Awaits New Film Plans," "Schools Produce Films," "Films for War Workers," "Films from Down Under." (4-42). "AECT One in Philadelphia," "Critical Moments in teaching," "Films from Poland." (2- 71). "Frederick Wiseman: From Titicut Follies to Model," "The Year the Films Came Off the Shelves," "An Interview with Sally Heckel," "Our Uncongenial Environment as Film Teachers." (fall-81). "Movies: Classroom Discussion in Italian, Japanese, Spanish, French, German, Etc." (04-84).
SCHL: Bimonthly (Dec, 1939 - Apr, 1940); Ten issues per year (May, 1940 - Winter, 1957/1958); Weekly (Apr, 1958 - Sep 1, 1958); Quarterly (1960 - 1963); Six issues per year (1964 - 1973); Five issues per year (1974 - 1979); Quarterly (1980+), 50 pp.
SPAN: Dec, 1939 - Apr, 1984//
VARIES
--Dec, 1939 - Apr, 1940 as News From the American Film Center, Inc..
--May, 1940 - Winter, 1957/1958 as Film News (ISSN: 0015-1343).
--Apr, 1958 - Sep 1, 1958 as Film/AV News (ISSN: 0737-2582).
--Oct, 1960 - Fall, 1981 as Film News (ISSN: 0195-1017).
ABSORBED
--Learning Resources (ISSN: 0318-0077), Jan, 1978.
SUSPENDED
--Dec, 1942 - May, 1943.
--Jul, 1958 - Sep, 1960.
WITH SUPPLEMENT
--Sponsored Films, Jan, 1942 - ?
LC: PN 1993 .F62
DD: 791.43/53/05
ISSN: 8750-068x
ABST: --Film Literature Index (ISSN: 0093-6758)
--Media Review Digest (ISSN: 0363-7778)

FILM ART

SUB: "Review of the advance-guard cinema." (Summer, 1933 - Winter, 1934).
SUB: "An independent quarterly devoted to the serious film." (Autumn, 1935 - Spring, 1937).
PUBL: The Studios, 5 Steynings Way, London N12, England.
DESC: "The commercialization of any art is its downfall, for commercialism disregards any aesthetic significance, and judges a product by its popularity in the field it caters for. The present day universally shown film is a totally unimaginative performance. A film is not to be despised because it makes money. The film to despise (and it forms the bulk of present day cinema) is that in which characters and incidents are given a vulgar glamour which is unlike life, and which is an insult to any standard of intelligence. The public which is potentially interested in good films and which, furthermore, does not want to see inferior films at all, requires a certain amount of organization and and a guide. This, we feel, is part of our job. *Film* is not going to devote a certain amount of incidental space to good cinema, but is going to be entirely devoted to the film as an art. We shall seek a film-forum, and attempt to solve problems which prevent a realization of that film-forum." The editors made it clear they would attempt to provide an unbiased forum for film discussion, and that only those motion pictures which fit the description of "art" would be included. Articles were long-essay form in this intellectual guide. Some graphics; small format, single-column layout. NOTE: the February, 1935 issue of *Film* informed its readers that "Publication will be roughly quarterly--at certain intervals, even more frequently." Soon thereafter, the serial was published by number, rather than calendar notation. Also note that issue #1, a preview issue for spring, 1933 is entitled *Film*. Beginning with regular issue #1 for summer, 1933, the title of the serial was *Film Art*.

DEPT: "Film Review," "Comment," newsbriefs; (spring-33). "Films of the Quarter," "Books of the Quarter," "Correspondence," (autumn-36).
TYPL: "The Principles of the Film," "Montage," "Film Societies, a Suggestion," "Individualism and the Documentary Film," (spring-33). "On Film Criticism," "Psychopathia Cinema Sexualis," "Printed Scenarios," "Some Film Elements and Their Synthesis," "Cinema Art," "America's Golden Days," (autumn-36).
SCHL: Quarterly (Spring, 1933 - Winter, 1934); irregular (Winter, 1934 - Spring, 1937); 35 pp.
SPAN: Spring, 1933 - Spring, 1937//
VARIES
--Spring, 1933 as Film.
SUSPENDED
--Winter, 1934 - Autumn, 1935.
LC: PN 1993.F

FILM ARTISTE
SUB: "Stills and stories of the films."
PUBL: Film Artistes' Association, 61 Marloes Rd., Kensington, London W8, England.
DESC: Here is an unusual serial; one which is published by a trade union (the Film Artistes' Association), but written and designed for the British general public. The primary purpose is to showcase new films through limited discussion and publicity stills of the motion picture cast members. This serial maintains its focus on the Film Artistes' Association cast members within their film roles. Numerous production stills grace this very readable publication.
DEPT: "Film Artistes Newsreel & Production Guide," member newsbriefs; "Mailbag." (#2-68).
TYPL: "Battle of the Battle of Britain Film," "You Only Live Twice," "Man for All Seasons," "Night of the Generals." (#2-68).
SCHL: Quarterly, 40 pp.
SPAN: 1964 - 1974//
LC: PN 1993.F418
ISSN: 0015-1122

Film/AV News
Apr, 1958 - Sep 1, 1958//
(ISSN: 0737-2582)
SEE: FILM & VIDEO NEWS

✢ FILM BULLETIN
PUBL: Film Polski, 6/8 Mazowiecka, Warszawa, Poland.
DESC: These 60-odd pages of double-spaced mimeographed material serve primarily to describe and review recent Polish film releases intended for world-wide distribution. Most issues contain one or two interviews with filmmakers or actors; some contain world press clippings on Polish film product. In addition, each issue publishes one or two pages of glossy photo sheets containing publicity stills from recent releases. Mimeographed.
DEPT: "An Interview With...," "Features," reviews; "New Shorts." (2-62).
TYPL: None. (2-62).
SCHL: Monthly, 60 pp.
SPAN: May, 1961+
VARIES
--Nov, 1961 - Feb, 1962 as Film.
FOREIGN TITLE
--Film Polski.
ABST: --Film Literature Index (ISSN: 0093-6758)
--Media Review Digest (ISSN: 0363-7778)

FILM BUYER
SUB: "A quick reference picture chart."
PUBL: Quigley Publishing Co., 407 South Dearborn St., Chicago, IL.
DESC: This separately bound serial was issued with another supplement, *Better Theatres*, together as "Section Two," and issued every four weeks to parent publication, *Exhibitors Herald World*, the parent magazine being called "Section One." *Film Buyer* contained most information required by independent exhibitors to make reasoned decisions about renting films. The "Quick Reference Chart for Buyers and Bookers" listed titles by studio; providing information on film category (comedy, drama, western, operetta, etc.), time length, release date, and (important to this time period), whether the title was released in silent, sound or both versions. Some titles also offered a choice between sound-on-disc or sound-on-film. Of special note was the department, "Song Hits in Current Films," which listed music publishers' properties and the films in which they appeared. That list of several hundred musical properties spanned everything from "If I Had a Talking Picture of You" (from a Fox film, "Sunnyside Up"), to the "Boop Boop A Doopa Doo Trot," also from a Fox project entitled "Let's Go Places." *Film Buyer* continued in later years as an in-magazine supplement (with separate pagination and editorial control) to *Motion Picture Herald*. Magazine format (235 cm wide x 310 cm high), published on coated paper stock. Black/white editorial content, no graphics. Advertising appeared only on the cover in two-color form.
DEPT: "Alphabetical Listing of Pictures," new releases; "Quick Reference Chart for Buyers and Bookers," extensive listing of new feature films; "The Short Feature," extensive section listed by producer; "Song Hits in Current Films," very unique index by film title, and producer. (6-28-30).
TYPL: No Article Titles. (6-28-30).
SCHL: Every four weeks, 25 pp.
SPAN: ? - Dec 27, 1930?//
SUPPLEMENT TO
--Exhibitors Herald-World, Jan 6, 1928 - Dec 27, 1930?

✤ FILM COMMENT

SUB: "A journal of film comment." (Spring, 1962 - Summer, 1962).
PUBL: Film Society of Lincoln Center, 140 W. 65th St., New York, NY 10023.
DESC: This bimonthly publication of the Film Society of Lincoln Center serves several functions: to educate the public about motion picture industry norms, to explore new concepts in film product, to provide commentary on current offerings, and to showcase numerous interviews and reviews of past films and stars. Each issue provides an unique "Midsection," which consists of an in-depth treatment of a specific issue. Typical "Midsection" themes are: "The Video Revolution," "The Producers," "Celebrities," "Novels & Film," "Dueling Genres." Well-written with a multi-faceted target audience. Magazine format (8 ⅜ x 10 ⅞ inches / 210 x 275 mm), numerous graphics.
DEPT: "Journals--London & New York," column by Jonathan Rosenbaum; "Journals--Australia," column by Jan Dawson; "Guest Column," "Midsection," "Book Marks," comment column by Richard T. Jameson; "Books," reviews; "Back Page," film newsbriefs. (7/8-76). "Books," "Bulletin Board." (5/6-82). "Letters." (7/8-90).
TYPL: "Billy Wilder, Closet Romanticist," "Stokeo," "Three Blue Birds," "In All Directions," "Britannia Waves the Rules." (7/8-76). "John Milius & Guilty Pleasures," "Gay Films, Straight Movies," "The Names Behind the Titles," "Acting English," "Assignment: Berlin," "Bracketting Wilder," "Hollywood Lays an Egg," "Steven Spielberg Interview." (5/6-82). "Smart Women, Foolish Choices," "Angst for the Memories," "Auteurism is Alive and Well," "Preminger's Brass." (7/8-90).
SCHL: Quarterly (Spring, 1962 - Summer, 1972); Bimonthly (Sep/Oct, 1972+), 85 pp.
SPAN: Spring, 1962+
VARIES
--Spring, 1962 - Summer, 1962 as Vision.
LC: PN 1993.F438
ISSN: 0015-119x
ABST: --Art Index (ISSN: 0004-3222)
--Book Review Index (ISSN: 0524-0581)
--Film Literature Index (ISSN: 0093-6758)
--Humanities Index (ISSN: 0095-5981)
--Magazine Index
--Media Review Digest (ISSN: 0363-7778)
--Popular Magazine Review (ISSN: 0740-3763)
--Readers Guide to Periodical Literature (ISSN: 0034-0464)

✤ FILM CRITICISM

PUBL: Film Criticism, Box 825, Edinboro, PA 16412.
DESC: The function of *Film Criticism* is to provide serious examination and commentary on the film arts. Scholary articles (usually by academic authors), cover both popular and other more artistic film product in both American and world markets. The publisher has stated that "*Film Criticism* ...resolve(s) to publish the best writing on film we can find, regardless of critical approach." Published three times per year, most issues are themed such as the fall, 1990 "Modern British Cinema," and the spring, 1991 "Book Review Issue." For the sampled issues of 1991: black ink on uncoated paper stock, two-color cover on coated paper, no advertising (5 ½ x 8 ½ inches / 140 x 215 mm).
DEPT: "Editor's Notes," "Books." (winter-84).
TYPL: "Breaker Morant and the Melodramatic Treatment of History," "Politics and Ethnography: Ramparts of Clay," "Music and Emotion in the Classic Hollywood Film: The Case of the Best Years of Our Lives," "The Symbolism of Hiroshima Mon Amour," "Return of the Jedi: the End of the Myth." (winter-84).
SCHL: Three issues per year, 80 pp.
SPAN: Spring, 1976+
LC: PN 1993.F4183
DD: 791.43/75/05
ISSN: 0163-5069
ABST: --Book Review Index (ISSN: 0524-0581)
--Film Literature Index (ISSN: 0093-6758)
--MLA International Bibliography of Books & Articles on the Modern Languages and Literatures (ISSN: 0024-8215)

✤ FILM CULTURE

PUBL: Film Culture Non-Profit, Box 1499, G.P.O. New York, NY 10001.
DESC: *Film Culture* is a small format periodical devoted to the serious task of film criticism and culture, especially from an historical viewpoint. Articles emphasize the "artistic film" field (experimental and avant-garde), and the producers / directors herein. This is "must" reading for cinematographers and patrons of the avant-garde film product. For the sampled issue of 1983: perfect-bound journal format, black ink on uncoated paper stock, numerous graphics pertaining to motion pictures and cultural elements, no advertising (5 ¼ x 7 ⅞ inches / 130 x 200 mm), rather erratic publication schedule.
DEPT: "Received and Noted," reviews. (#70/71-83).
TYPL: "A Movie House is an Enlarged Camera Obscura for the Sale of Popcorn," "Christopher Maclaine--Approaching 'The End,'" "Excerpts from Discussions with Ernie Gehr," "James Herbert Filmography," "Program Notes for a Walter Gutman Retrospective in 1981." (#70/71-83).
SCHL: Erratic [bimonthly at times] (? - ?); Quarterly (?+), 250 pp.
SPAN: Jan, 1955+
LC: PN 1993.F44
DD: 791.4305
ISSN: 0015-1211
ABST: --Art Index (ISSN: 0004-3222)
--Film Literature Index (ISSN: 0093-6758)
--Media Review Digest (ISSN: 0363-7778)

Film Daily, The
Jan 1, 1922 - Mar 17, 1968//
SEE: FILM TV DAILY

✤ FILM DIRECTIONS
SUB: "A film magazine for Ireland." (Dec?, 1977 - ?).
PUBL: Arts Council of Northern Ireland, 181a Stranmillis Rd., Belfast 9, Northern Ireland.
DESC: "*Film Directions* is a cultural magazine, for which we make no apology at all. Film and television/video...have arguably had the greatest influence on 20th century culture, and the most fundamental attitude that *Film Directions* will hold is that going to the cinema (or watching television) is not just a pleasant way of spending one's time." This is a thoughtfully written and composed serial, with one foot firmly planted in philosophical thought, and the other in the realities of popular culture. Magazine format; graphics.
DEPT: "Book Reviews." (5-80).
TYPL: "An Active Film Culture," "When I See an Elephant Fly," "Hitchcock, a Tribute," "Berlin Festival Report," "Science Fiction--in Search of meaning." (5-80).
SCHL: Quarterly, 25 pp.
SPAN: 1977+
LC: PN 1993.5 .I85F54
DD: 791.43/05

✤ FILM FAMILIES
PUBL: Ideal Publishing Co., 2 Park Ave., New York, NY 10016.
DESC: This is a Hollywood star magazine concentrating on families of the celebrities, and features the hot news, gossip and photos which the American consumer has come to love. The added twist of family ties provides a unique approach. A large number of nostalgic family stills are featured.
DEPT: None. (3-79).
TYPL: "Super Mix and Match Puzzle: Reunite Parent and Child," "Children of the Stars: Do They Really Have it Made?," "The Hollywood Epidemic which Tears its Children Apart," "When Acting Becomes a Family Tradition." (3-79).
SCHL: Quarterly, 75 pp.
SPAN: 1978+

FILM FAN MONTHLY
SUB: "Including Profile."
PUBL: Film Fan Monthly, 77 Grayson Place, Teaneck, NJ 07666.
DESC: *Film Fan Monthly* was designed for the collector of 8mm and 16mm releases of major American sound and silent motion pictures. Each 30-page issue (small serial format) provided data on filmographies of past actors/actresses, directors, producers, and other pertinent information. Among the many supporting actors profiled were: Bennie Barnes, Ellen Corby, Dorothy Morris, Dan Dailey, Helene Thimig, Dwight Frye, Jayne Meadows, and Roddy McDowall. Each issue was filled with advertisements offering new product releases by numerous companies. Early issues were printed from typewritten copy on newsprint, with latter issues typeset and coated paperstock, which greatly enhanced the reproduction quality of the numerous production stills. By June, 1975 publisher Leonard Maltin could no longer continue issuing the serial and it ceased publication. This remains a rich historical source of film releases to private collectors, especially of the "B" movies of the 1930s and 1940s. Sampled issue for 1968: stapled small-journal format, black ink-typewritten editorial content on coated paper stock with limited advertising (5 ⅜ x 8 ½ inches / 135 x 215 mm).
DEPT: "Book Reviews," "Davy on 16 MM," column by Daryl Davy; "The Collecting Scene," extensive section on available motion picture product for collectors. (11-68). "Book Reviews," "Classified," film offerings; "Odds and Ends," column by Tony Clifford. (9-74).
TYPL: "Rex Ingram," "Franchot Tone," "Ida Lupino: Director," "Tom & Jerry: The Aesthetics of Violence." (11-68). "Madeleine Carroll," "Ruth Etting Today." (9-74).
SCHL: Monthly (Jul/Aug issues combined); 30 pp.
SPAN: 1961 - Jun, 1975//
ISSN: 0015-1238

FILM FORUM REVIEW
SUB: "Devoted to the use of motion pictures in adult education."
PUBL: Institute of Adult Education, Columbia University Teachers College, New York, NY.
DESC: In its initial offering, the publishers noted that this serial "...represents an attempt to describe and analyze films and film forum programs from the point of view of their fitness both to increase the store of general knowledge available to the public and to sharpen and define issues of current interest, national and international. The *Review* will encourage the development of high standards in the utilization of a new and fascinating medium of education. Although recognizing the fact that motion pictures comprise an important medium for the education of children, the *Review* will be concerned primarily with the exploration and development of motion pictures devised for mature minds." Journal format; no graphics.
DEPT: "Editorial," "Index of Films." (fall-47).
TYPL: "Street Films for Unity," "Training Leaders for Film Forums," "The Motion Picture in Adult Education," "Films for Forums on Intergroup Relations, Housing, Health and Community Organization." (fall-47).
SCHL: Quarterly, 70 pp.
SPAN: Spring, 1946 - Winter, 1948/49//
LC: LB 1044.A2F5
DD: 371.3352305

✧ FILM FUN

PUBL: Film Fun Publishing Co., 28-30 East 32nd St., New York, NY.
DESC: Most of the starlets featured in the picture pages of this monthly magazine appear to be dressed in bathing, bedroom, or various degrees of undergarment attire. At times it featured true stars of the Hollywood film community, and at times beautiful women who had a more distant connection with Hollywood or the motion picture industry. If nothing else, *Film Fun* was certainly creative in matching a bevy of beautiful women with a series of motion picture themes, even if some of those themes may have been a bit far fetched. In the August, 1940 issue, for example, the "Girls From the Film Fun Band" featured six New York models attired in lingerie, playing various instruments with photo cutlines such as "Honest, fellows, she has more musicians than she can shake a stick at. And they all have heard that the hardest part of a gold-digger's job is making a big gun shell out." Each month's issue featured a center-foldout of a Hollywood star or starlet, an ongoing movie fact quiz, and an innovative film rating system ranging from one ("feeble") to four ("tops") "cigars" per current release. This magazine contained little reading material, but that's not what the predominantly male audience bought it for. As one article title put it, "Corset's Nice!," which left little doubt as to the form, the function, and the popularity of this tinseltown picture publication. It provides a fascinating look back at the beautiful women of Hollwood and the saucy liberties taken with social norms of the period. For sampled issue of 1940: stapled magazine format, black/brown ink duotone printing on uncoated paper stock, with full-color cover on coated paper stock (8 ½ x 11 ⅜ inches / 215 x 290 mm).
DEPT: "Talkie Tips," rated reviews of current film fare; "Talkie Tidbits," picture page; "The Girl on the Cover," picture profile; "Prettiest Extra Girl of the Month," "Cartoon Comics," "Clips From the Cutting Room," news of Hollywood stars and starlets; "Girls Make News," Hollywood stars and starlets in the news; "Quizzical Culture," 'Film Fun's quiz of movie hits and misses'; "Favorite Film Fun Models." (8-40).
TYPL: "Legs of Nations," "Girls From the Film Fun Band," "Make Mine Villainy," "Movie Memories...in the Star Spangled Manner," "Showgirl Revue." (8-40).
SCHL: Monthly, 55 pp.
SPAN: ?+?

✧ FILM GUIDE

SUB: "Devoted to the cause of good cinema."
SUB: "Reviews, comment, criticism."
PUBL: Rising Sun Press, 192 Canterbury Rd., Canterbury, Victoria, Australia.
DESC: Broadcast television made its appearance in Canterbury in 1956, the same year an editorial in *Film Guide* commented on the new medium: "...our main reaction to date is an apprehensive shake of the head." This serial was designed for and devoted to the cause of *good cinema*, those elements of the theatre and moving film experience which television (at least at this point in time) could only hope to achieve some day. Articles in this small journal format publication interspersed international authors with film news and issues of a uniquely Australian flavor. Numerous graphics; printing quality was, at times, less than satisfactory.
DEPT: "Editorials," "Correspondence," "Review of New Films," "Books on the Film," "Spotlight on Documentary," "News and Views," "Sydney Notes," newsbriefs. (summer-56).
TYPL: "The Cult of Bigness," "Gina Lollobrigida--Beauty of Cinema," "Outlook in Europe," "Remakes in Reich Studios," "Heresies and Evangelical Inspirations," "If I Were Zanuck," "New Australian Film a Competent Job," "Need for Film Archives in Australia." (summer-56).
SCHL: Quarterly, 38 pp.
SPAN: ?+?
SUSPENDED
--Oct, 1958 - Mar, 1962.
LC: PN 1993.F53

FILM HERITAGE

PUBL: University of Dayton, College of Liberal Arts, Dayton, OH 45469.
DESC: This critical review of cinema in America, with strong contributions from the academic community, had two to five articles per issue; with graphics; and interviews with cinematographers, directors, and historical reviews of past creative filmmakers.
DEPT: "Film Reviews." (spring-77).
TYPL: "There is No Set Pattern," "You Learn from Old Masters." (spring-77).
SCHL: Quarterly, 50 pp.
SPAN: Fall, 1965 - Spring, 1977//
LC: PN 1993.F55
DD: 791.43/05
ISSN: 0015-1270
ABST: --Historical Abstracts. Part B. Twentieth Century Abstracts. (ISSN: 0363-2725)

✧ FILM INDEX

PUBL: John H. Reid, 47 Osborne Rd., Manly, N.S.W. 2095, Australia.
DESC: "*Film Index* is limited to United States sound cinema. Nothing Else. Since some 70 percent of films seen on Sydney television were of American sound product," making this primarily a compilation of motion picture reviews concerning product shown on Australian television. Published 12 times per year, the small format magazine was printed at first on coated paper stock and provided numerous production stills. At times, special features were included, such as interviews with Hollywood directors, producers, and American actor biographies. Beginning with issue #35 (circa

1977?), *Film Index* evolved into a small, square format on newsprint, providing photo reproductions of less than quality nature, and moved from typeset to typewritten editorial content. The last sample issue reviewed (#53, circa April, 1979), provided some dozen reviews in ten pages with several production stills. Cast credits, running time, and other pertinent information was always included with each review.
DEPT: None.
TYPL: No Article Titles.
SCHL: Monthly, 10 pp.
SPAN: Jun, 1966+?
VARIES
--Jun, 1966 - 1967 as Australian Film Guide.
LC: PN 1993.F59
DD: 791.43/05
ISSN: 0015-1289

FILM JOURNAL

PUBL: New Melbourne Film Group, Mount Albert, Australia.
DESC: *Film Journal* began as many other contemporary periodicals of film criticism/review, first as a mimeographed small-format magazine, gradually moving into a printed format with graphics. Unfortunately, *Film Journal* never succeeded in circulation or support to move beyond an initial 30 pages per issue, and ceased publication in 1965. A publication of the Melbourne Film Society, *Film Journal*'s emphasis was on foreign motion pictures, specifically French, German, and American.
DEPT: None. (12-65).
TYPL: "Joseph Von Sternberg: A Study," "Berlin, 1965," "The Evolution of the Western," "The Western Mythology." (12-65).
SCHL: Quarterly, 30 pp.
SPAN: 1958 - 1964//
LC: PN 1993.F

FILM JOURNAL, THE

PUBL: Thomas Atkins, Box 9602, Hollins College, VA 24020.
DESC: "The *Film Journal* will contain new source material about film--not the kind of topical essays or current movie reviews that are available in abundance today, but original documents and critical evaluations that will be useful to scholars, teachers, students, or anyone seriously interested in film. With the help of a consulting board of editors and many other writers and film professionals, the *Film Journal* will print documentation about significant films of all types, contemporary and historical, American and foreign; scholarly appraisals from a wide variety of disciplines and viewpoints; filmographies, biographies, bibliographies and other pertinent information about film sources and publications. Films are documents born in a certain time and place, and we hope to provide some of the basic data and primary material for understanding this history." Printed on quality paper with numerous graphics.
DEPT: "Books." (spring-71).
TYPL: "The Making of 'The Revenge'-Teenagers Western Style," "A Sampling of Films from the Youth Film Distribution Center," "Politics by Magic: Glauber Rocha's Antonio Das Mortes," "Cinematographer Karl Freund: A Profile." (spring-71).
SCHL: Quarterly (Spring, 1971 - 1975); Two-three issues per year (1975 to date), 88 pp.
SPAN: Spring, 1971 - 1975?//
SUSPENDED
--1975 - ?
LC: PN 1993.F613
DD: 791.43/05
ISSN: 0046-3787
ABST: --Film Literature Index (ISSN: 0093-6758)
--International Index to Film Periodicals (ISSN: 0000-0038)

✦ FILM JOURNAL, THE

SUB: "Trade paper for exhibitors of motion pictures."
SUB: "Devoted to the best interests of the motion picture industry."
PUBL: Pubsun Corp., 244 West 49th St., New York, NY 10019.
DESC: From 1937 to the present, whether under the current banner, *The Film Journal*, or the earlier *Independent Film Journal*, this trade publication successfully champions the commercial interests of the independent motion picture exhibitor. Emphasis is on current and future releases and elements of theatre operation and management. Articles provide helpful analyses of marketing factors, box office appeal, theatrical plant and other considerations which comprise the managerial realm of the local exhibitor. Each issue of *The Film Journal* is divided into two major sections, "Features" and "Theatres & Equipment." The former covers five to ten current feature releases and provides thoughtful commentary on the box office value and appeal of this new film product targeted to the American movie-going public. The "Theatres & Equipment" section is devoted to technology, plant operation, projection, concession, ticketing, and other managerial functions critical to the "bottom line" segment of exhibition. Numerous advertisements for projection equipment, concession food and drink items, sound systems, and management-oriented computer systems attest to the success in reaching this targeted audience. Convention issues, such as that for February, 1991 greatly expand the size and scope of this valuable trade journal. For sampled issue of 1991: editorial content was black/white, with numerous advertisements and cover in full color, all on coated paper stock, stapled magazine format (8 ½ x 11 inches / 220 x 280 mm).
DEPT: "Financial Notes," economic news of the industry; future films; "Buying and Booking Guide," unusually detailed descriptions of current or soon to be released

motion pictures; "Calendar of Feature Releases," distributors and dates of their release; "Newsgram," late breaking news briefs. (11-78). "In Focus," editorial column by Robert Sunshine; "Reel News in Review," newsbriefs; "New Posts," personnel newsbriefs; "Tips From TEA," exhibition advice from TEA members; "Film Company News," extensive news section divided by major studio. (2-91).
TYPL: "Twentieth Fox Halts Open Bidding; Myers Cites Exhibitor Apathy," "See's Music Hall Claim Upheld; Sergeant Battle Ready for Court," "Editors Mailbag: In Defense of Small Town Theaters." (11-78). "Vincent & Theo, Agenda Put Hemdale on a Roll," "Movie Audiences Made the Hits in 1990," "Fox and Friends Ad Company Thrives on Theatrical Campaigns," "Targeting an Upscale Movie Audience," "Advertising Current Attractions Crucial for Box Office Success." (2-91).
SCHL: Biweekly (1937 - 1979); Monthly (? - ?); Bimonthly (? - ?); Monthly [with combined Apr/May and Nov/Dec issues] (?+), 125 pp.
SPAN: 1937+
VARIES
--1937 - Nov, 1979 as Independent Film Journal (ISSN: 0019-3712).
ISSN: 0199-7300

FILM LIBRARY QUARTERLY
PUBL: Film Library Information Council, 139 Amity St., Brooklyn, NY 11201.
DESC: *Film Library Quarterly* was a well-written, small-format, publication for members of the Film Library Information Council, a non-profit organization of film librarians. Several film reviews and interviews with film-makers are featured in each quarterly issue. Some discussion of video is also provided, especially as video applies to art.
DEPT: "Projections," upcoming events; "Book Reviews," "Film Reviews," "Video Reviews."
TYPL: "How the Myth was Made; New Film on Robert Flaherty," "Frederick Wisemans Cinema of Alienation," "Video in Public Library Service: a FLIC Workshop Report." (fall- 78).
SCHL: Quarterly, 60 pp.
SPAN: Winter, 1967/68 - 1985//
VARIES
--Winter, 1967/1968 - Fall, 1971 as Film Library Quarterly (ISSN: 0015-1327).
--Winter, 1971/1972 - ? as FLQ (ISSN: 0160-7316).
ABSORBED BY
--EFLA Bulletin, 1985.
LC: Z 692.M9F5
DD: 791.43/05
ISSN: 0015-1327
ABST: --Film Literature Index (ISSN: 0093-6758)
--International Index to Film Periodicals (ISSN: 0000-0038)
--Library Literature (ISSN: 0024-2373)
--Media Review Digest (ISSN: 0363-7778)

Film Library Quarterly
Winter, 1967/1968 - Fall, 1971//
(ISSN: 0015-1327)
SEE: FILM LIBRARY QUARTERLY

FILM MAKING
SUB: "The magazine for movie makers, film & Video Collectors."
PUBL: Penblade Publishers, Ltd., 15-23 Porteus Rd., London W2 1UT, England.
DESC: This was an interesting home-consumer magazine which provided "how-to" information concerning amateur filmmaking, plus general reviews of recent film and video releases. The emphasis was on film, primarily 8mm product; with many articles on producing one's own film epic, especially the techniques of shooting and post-production elements. Numerous graphics.
DEPT: "Editorial," "Editor's Post Box," "Starting from Scratch," "Coming Cine Events," "The Smaller Screen," dealing with television; "The Club Scene," "Technical Course," "Guide to...," "Sound Matters." (8-62). "Newsreel," newsbriefs; "Letters," "Answers," Q&A; "In Camera," commentary. (8-80).
TYPL: "Town and Country Filming," "Film Classics: Programme Notes on Three of Charlie Chaplin's Best." (8-62). "A to Zk of Cine," "How to Get Into the Movies," "Make Your Own Sci-Fi Fantasy," "Big Budget Locations on a Sheet of Glass." (8-80).
SCHL: Monthly 70 pp.
SPAN: 1962? - Oct, 1980//
VARIES
--1962? - Apr?, 1969? as 8mm Magazine.
--May, 1969 - Aug, 1970 as 8 MM.
ABSORBED BY
--Movie Maker (ISSN: 0027-2701), Oct, 1980.
LC: TR 845.E5
ISSN: 0013-2543
ABST: --Film Literature Index (ISSN: 0093-6758)

FILM MEDIA
SUB: "The magazine for sponsors of industrial, business, television films." (Jun, 1957 - ?).
SUB: "The magazine for sponsors of business, educational, television films." (? - ?).
PUBL: Photography in Business, 10 East 40th St., New York, NY.
DESC: "It is *Film Media*'s stated objective to publicize successful case history experiences of leading company executives...who have solved varied and complex business problems with the specific help of film media. More than that, we will try to measure film critically in hard, business-like, comparative terms. For if a film program accomplishes its specified tasks well, we have a strong case for film versus competitive

media." This serial was interested in promoting film, whether industrial film production, industry trade shows, advertising, or in-house training.
DEPT: "News Notes," 'doings and data on the film scene'; "Letters to the Editor," "Sponsors Want to Know," "New Equipment," "Editorial," "Opinion." (10-59).
TYPL: "Film Teaches New Life-Saving Technique," "Centennial Film Touts State's Economic Growth," "Magazine Ad Brought to Life," "Film Spurs Support for Social Work." (10-59).
SCHL: Monthly (? - ?); Quarterly (? - ?); 35 pp.
SPAN: Jun, 1957 - Jan/Mar, 1960//
LC: HF 5844.F49

✦ FILM MONTHLY

SUB: "The magazine that loves movies."
PUBL: Argus Specialist Publications, Argus House, Boundary Way, Hemel Hempstead HP2 7ST, England.
DESC: *Film Monthly* is a wonderful guide to motion picture product (both silver screen and videocassette), currently available to the British home consumer. This full-color monthly has numerous reviews of actors, their motion picture product, and auxilliary items such as music videos, and motion picture releases on home video cassette. Sample issue for March, 1990 provided artist interviews and profiles with Kathleen Turner, Paul Newman, Tom Cruise, Andy Garcia, Kelly Lynch, Al Pacino, and Ellen Barkin; all accompanied by an excellent "Review Section" detailing current releases, new videos, and other films of note. Film reviews consist of descriptions, a reasonable "verdict," cast credits, and critics' ratings for these new motion picture releases. A good resource for film fans. For the 1990 sampled issue: stapled magazine format with screen tint and full-color pages on coated paper stock with full-color cover (8 ¼ x 11 ¾ inches / 210 x 300 mm).
DEPT: "From the Editor to You," "Your Points of View," letters; "Scene & Heard," film news column by Ken Ferguson; "Insider," 'Tony Crawley reports the latest screen chat'; "Review Section," extensive segment of current film fare; "Video View," '*Film Monthly*'s guide to the latest video releases'; "Movie Trax," 'Paul Cliff reports on the new soundtrack releases'; "Nostalgia," '*Film Monthly* looks back'; "Hollywood Hotline," 'Boze Hadleigh reports from Beverly Hills'. (3-90).
TYPL: "What Movie Sex Appeal Means to Kathleen Turner," "Newman at 65," "The Transformation of Tom Cruise," "The Big Switch: a Turn Off or a Turn On?" (3-90).
SCHL: Monthly, 50 pp.
SPAN: Jan, 1950?+
VARIES
--Jan, 1950? - Dec, 1985? as Photoplay Movies & Video.
--Jan, 1986 - Mar, 1989 as Photoplay.
ISSN: 0956-0890

Film News
May, 1940 - Winter, 1957/1958//
(ISSN: 0015-1343)
SEE: FILM & VIDEO NEWS

Film News
Oct, 1960 - Fall, 1981//
(ISSN: 0195-1017)
SEE: FILM & VIDEO NEWS

Film News
? - ?//
SEE: NATIONAL EXHIBITOR, THE

✦ FILM QUARTERLY

PUBL: University of California Press, 2120 Berkeley Way, Berkeley, CA 94720.
DESC: [*Hollywood Quarterly*]: The role of motion pictures in the post-war world of 1945 was not far from the minds of the editors of this new publication in October, 1945. In an editorial statement they asked, "What part will the motion picture and the radio play in the consolidation of the victory, in the creation of new patterns of world culture and understanding? The editors of the *Hollywood Quarterly* are not so incautious as to attempt an answer to this question. Rather, the purpose of the magazine will be to seek an answer by presenting the record of research and exploration in motion pictures and radio in order to provide a basis for evaluation of economic, social, aesthetic, educational, and technological trends." That first year of publication produced such article titles as, "The Hollywood War Film: 1942 - 1944," "Eisenstein and the Historical Film," "Radio Plays as Literature," "Television and Motion-Picture Sound Processes," "A Novelist Looks at Hollywood," "Educational Broadcasting: The Cleveland Plan," "The Copyright Dilemma of the Screen Composer," and "The Interpretive Camera in Documentary Films." Articles under the publication banner of *Hollywood Quarterly* included a significant number concerning radio and television programming. For the sampled issues of 1945: stapled journal format, black ink on uncoated paper stock (6 x 9 inches / 150 x 230 mm).
DESC: *Film Quarterly*, published by the University of California Press, is a scholary criticism-commentary on international film product. Emphasis is on sociological examination of motion pictures, especially major or classic films and filmmakers. Articles are written primarily by academics, and importantly reflect a somewhat detached viewpoint from that of the commercial production industry product. This remains an excellent resource, a critical consideration of the aesthetic, the commercial, and the mundane concerning the film and television industry. *Film Quarterly* has

changed format several times, the most recent being a large format and full-graphic cover in fall, 1981; black-white graphics throughout.
DEPT: "Notes and Communications," "Book Reviews." (#1-46). "Reviews," films; "Controversy and Correspondence," "Books." (fall-81). "Reviews," detailed descriptions; "Book Reviews," "Controversy & Correspondence," opinion and letters. (spring-91).
TYPL: "Television and the Motion Picture Industry," "Character, Personality, and Image: A Note on Screen Acting," "A Costume Problem: From Shop to Stage to Screen," "The Improbability of Radio Criticism," "Psychiatry and the Films." (#1-46). "Narrative Pleasure: Two Films of Jacques Rivette," "Lost Harmony: Tarkovsky's 'The Mirror' and 'The Stalker,'" "The Right of Re-Vision: Michelle Citron's Daughter Rite," "Chaplin: The Antagonism of the Comic Hero." (fall-81). "The Civil War: 'Did It Not Seem Real?'," "Moods Indigo," "Illuminations: An Interview with Andrew Noren," "GoodFellas," "Taxi Blues." (spring-91).
SCHL: Quarterly, 70 pp.
SPAN: Oct, 1945+
SUSPENDED
--Fall, 1948 - Summer, 1949
--Fall, 1957 - Summer, 1958.
VARIES
--Oct, 1945 - Summer, 1951 as Hollywood Quarterly.
--Fall, 1951 - Summer, 1957 as Quarterly of Film, Radio, and Television, The.
LC: PN 1993.H457
ISSN: 0015-1386
ABST: --Art Index (ISSN: 0004-3222)
--Biography Index (ISSN: 0006-3053)
--Book Review Index (ISSN: 0524-0581)
--Film Literature Index (ISSN: 0093-6758)
--Humanities Index (ISSN: 0095-5981)
--Magazine Index
--Media Review Digest (ISSN: 0363-7778)
--Readers Guide to Periodical Literature (ISSN: 0034-0464)

✤ FILM REVIEW

SUB: "Britain's best selling movie monthly."
SUB: "The mag the megastars talk to."
SUB: "The movie mag that's for reel."
PUBL: Orpheus Publications, 4th Floor, Centro House, Mandela St., London NW1 0DU, England.
DESC: The motion picture is focal in this 50+ page monthly designed to review the latest releases, and the motion picture stars that are featured in those films. Approximately one-half of the sample issue viewed (March, 1990) consisted of interviews/profiles with such stars as Paul Newman, Joe Dante, Sarah Douglas, Tom Conti, Theresa Russell, Timothy Hutton and James Wilby. The other half of *Film Reviews*' editorial content reviewed motion pictures, including "War of the Roses," "Harlem Nights," "Renegades," "The Fabulous Baker Boys," "Sea of Love," and "Born on the Fourth of July." *Film Review* sported a new layout design beginning with the June, 1991 issue which really propelled this publication into the "must read" category for anyone interested in the motion picture entertainment medium. This "new look" includes extensive graphics, especially of production stills and publicity pictures; enhanced use of color; and editorial content in a clean 4-5 column layout. It's a winning combination for "Britain's best monthly movie magazine." For sampled issue of 1991: stapled magazine format, mixture of black/white and color editorial content with full-color cover on coated paper stock, numerous black/white and color pictures (9 ⅛ x 11 ¾ inches / 235 x 300 mm).
DEPT: "Film Reviews," "Circuit Breakers," 'The movies doing this months rounds'; "Gossip," 'Hot reviews, hot gossip from the movie scene'; "Video Guide," 'The critical guide to this months major rental releases'; "Your Questions Answered," column by David McGillivray; "Film Reviews Extra," "Films to Come," 'A sneak photo-preview of pix in the pipeline'; "Book Reviews," 'The latest film-flavoured hard- and paper-backs'; "Film Crossword," "Starcast," 'What the stars hold in store this month'. (3-90). "Worldwide Movie Making," 'Who's making what, with who and where', excellent production status column by Kathryn Kirby; "Set Pieces," 'Star news from film and video'; "Film Reviews," extensive section; "Film Crossword," "Who's Dating Who," 'All this month's celebrity clinching, partner pinching and relationship lynching' column by Fiona Cullinan; "Video Reviews," "Stop Press," late-breaking video releases; "Retro," retrospective profile; "Star Struck," star birthdays and astrological signs; "Film Fax," 'Your questions answered by David McGillivray, our man with all the answers' column by David McGillivray; "Tales From the Script," 'This month's movie books reviewed', column by Howard Maxford. (6-91).
TYPL: "Gone to Blaze's: Paul Newman--the New York Interview," "Douglas, Vile of Man," "Conti-nental Drift," "Murphy's Pryor Engagement." (3-90). "Oscars Wild!," "Up Over From Down Under," "Like Lambs to the Slaughter," "Meet Hannibal the Cannibal," "Muddy Realism--And No Green Tights!" (6-91).
SCHL: Monthly, 55 pp.
SPAN: 1951+
VARIES
--Jun, 1990 - Jul, 1990 as Film Review Now.
ABSORBED
--Films and Filming (ISSN: 0015-167x), Apr, 1990.
LC: PN 1993 .F6243
DD: 791.43/05

Film Review Now

Jun, 1990 - Jul, 1990//
SEE: FILM REVIEW

Film Society Newsletter
1963 - Apr, 1965//
SEE: CRITIC

Film Society Review
Sep, 1965 - Mar/May, 1972//
(ISSN: 0015-1408)
SEE: CRITIC

Film Spectator, The
Mar, 1926 - Jun 13, 1931//
SEE: HOLLYWOOD SPECTATOR

Film Study
? - Feb, 1955?//
SEE: CINEMAGES

Film Teacher
Summer, 1952 - ?//
SEE: SCREEN

✤ FILM THREAT
SUB: "The other movie magazine."
PUBL: LFP, Inc., 9171 Wilshire Blvd., Suite 300, Beverly Hills, CA 90210.
DESC: Editor-in-Chief Chris Gore, in a November, 1991 editorial noted, "*Film Threat* originally began as a student newsletter at Wayne State University in Detroit. The first issue, published in February, 1985, was six pages of xeroxed punk rantings about how bad contemporary Hollywood films were. I started *Film Threat* because I wanted to write about the movies I liked that never seemed to get any press ...And I'm tired of hearing about the same filmmakers: Scorsese, Coppola and Spielberg are not the only people making movies. The real story of how the film industry works is not a pretty one. But rest assured that *Film Threat* is here to document it in all its ugliness." This unique magazine takes an irreverent look at the "movies," probing the strange, the independent, the wacky and wonderful side of motion picture product and production. Lead-off departmental feature is "Hate Mail," subtitled, "Pranksters please note: Letter bombs will be returned undetonated." Letters, including signatures, are reproduced as sent. Various sections of the magazine feature interesting film review synopses with rankings of "Politics" (anarchist, liberal, moderate, republican, fascist), "Reality Check" (fantasy, surreal, fiction, drama, documentary), and "Demographics" (geriatric, baby boomer, baby buster, teenage, adolescent). Each review also contains a number-ranked emotion chart (laught, scream, cry, orgasim, think) on each reviewed picture. The sampled issue contained both an excellent feature article concerning child stars, as well as a full-color mockup advertisement for Blump's Farm Fresh Pork Juice with Pulp. While this magazine may at times defy categorization, it certainly has attracted a loyal audience, and continues to explore the film medium as few other publications have. For sampled issue of 1989 published in Royal Oak, Michigan: stapled magazine format, editorial content of black/white pages on uncoated paper stock with full-color cover on coated paper stock (8 ⅜ x 10 ¾ inches / 210 x 275 mm). For the sampled issue of 1991: full-color content and cover on coated paper stock in stapled magazine format (8 x 10 ⅞ inches / 205 x 275 mm).
DEPT: "Editorial," column by Christian Gore; "Hate Mail," letters; "Popcorn," movie-connected news items; "Review," films; "Coming Attractions," upcoming film product; "Underground," independent cinema review column by David E. Williams; "Comics." (11-91).
TYPL: "The Fashions of Hollywood Boulevard," "Child Stars: Temptations, Tragedies and Triumphs," "The Dark Backward," "Director's Diary," "The Frigid 50: The Coldest People in Hollywood." (11-91).
SCHL: Bimonthly, 65 pp.
SPAN: Feb, 1985+
DD: 791
ISSN: 0896-6389

✤ FILM TV DAILY
SUB: "The international newspaper of motion pictures & broadcasting."
SUB: "Intimate in Character; international in scope; independent in thought."
SUB: "The Bradstreet of filmdom."
SUB: "The daily newspaper of motion pictures."
SUB: "Independent reviews of feature films." (Jun 1, 1916 - May 2, 1918).
PUBL: 1501 Broadway, New York, NY.
DESC: Under the banner of *Film and Television Daily*, this New York based publication covered the business side of American show business, and especially film and television corporations based in New York City. The magazine-format "newspaper" published articles of legal, corporate, and especially economic matters of film and television media. Articles tended to be concise, designed to fit within the daily four-page publication schedule. Of special import was the featured segment, "Reviews of New Films," providing production details and story synopses on current releases. Published daily in New York, the four to eight-page serial provided timely information on legal, financial, regulatory and boxoffice issues that are the lifeblood of the industry. An excellent historical resource for the American motion picture industry, and an important business resource in today's highly competitive entertainment market. Large magazine format with graphics.

DEPT: "The Mirror," 'a column of comment'; "Financial," data; "The Industry Date Book," calendar of events; "Explitettes," 'a clearing house for tabloid exploitation ideas'; "Along the Rialto," column by Phil M. Daly; "Timely Topics," 'A digest of current opinion'; "Hollywood Flashes," newsbriefs; "MPTOA Sidelights." (3-11-31). "Coming and Going," personnel briefs; "Winners' Corner," Boxoffice champs; "Population Explosion," "Wedding Bells," "Reviews of New Films." (12-23-68). "Wall St. Report," "Winners' Corner," boxoffice receipts; "Film Reviews," "Music & Recordings," newsbriefs; "Obituaries." (2-10-70).

TYPL: "Score Charges Again to be Slashed," "Exhibs Seek Hays Office Aid in Combatting Non-Theatricals," "Consol. Film Assets Up, Common Dividend Passed," "Popularity of Travel films Threatened, Says E. M. Newman." (3-11-31). "TV Rebs at Government Quiz," "Mo. Station Rebuts 'Opry' Suit Claims," "UA Pix in 272 N.Y. Theatres for Holidays," "20th-Fox Sets Redemption of its 5 3/4% Debentures." (12-23-68). "Nixon Moves into B'Casting," "Low-Cost H'wood Pix to Get IATSE Break," "Putting TV Pic into Theatres Means More Money for Members of Guilds," "Pessimism Not Valid in Pix Biz: Schenck." (2-10-70).

SCHL: Daily (Except Sat and Holidays) (Jan 1, 1922 - Mar 17, 1968), 8 pp.
SPAN: Oct 14, 1915+
VARIES
--Oct 14, 1915 - May 25, 1916 as Wid's Films and Film Folk.
--Apr 27, 1916 as Films by Wid.
--Jun 1, 1916 - May 2, 1918 as Wid's.
--May 8, 1918 - Dec, 31, 1921 as Wid's Daily.
--Jan 1, 1922 - Mar 17, 1968 as Film Daily, The.
--Mar 18, 1968 - Nov 14, 1969 as Film and Television Daily.
LC: PN 1993.F45

Film User

Nov, 1947 - Nov, 1971//
(ISSN: 0015-1459)
SEE: AUDIO VISUAL

✤ FILM WITNESS

PUBL: Regent University, College of Communication, Virginia Beach, VA 23464.
DESC: This informative newsletter is produced by film students in the School of Radio-TV-Film, College of Communication at Regent University, a graduate-level institution. Articles describe current projects, commentary on the role of film and Christianity, and the status of film graduates. Film activities reported give strong testimony to the varied oportunities afforded film majors at the university. Produced via desktop publishing (DTP), photocopied in small square magazine format.

DEPT: "Terry Lindvall's Sprocket Holes," film commentary column by Terry Lindvall; "From the Editor," editorial; "Letters." (12-89).
TYPL: "The Canon of Imagination: William Blake's Legacy for Fantasy Filmmakers," "The Bible in Horror Films," "Memoirs of a Space Cadet." (12-89).
SCHL: Four issues per year, 8 pp.
SPAN: 1984?+

Film World

Feb, 1945 - Sep, 1951//
SEE: FILM WORLD AND A-V NEWS MAGAZINE

Film World

1964 - Jul, 1975?//
(ISSN: 0015-1475)
SEE: FILMWORLD

FILM WORLD AND A-V NEWS MAGAZINE

SUB: "The basic magazine of the 16 mm. industry."
SUB: "Non theatrical 16mm film magazine." (Feb, 1945 - ?).
PUBL: 6060 Sunset Blvd., Hollywood, CA.
DESC: "*Film World* is a monthly trade magazine devoted to the interests of the 16mm movie industry. Especially emphasized is news of interest to producers, distributors, exhibitors, film libraries, visual education departments in schools, churches, clubs, and all other fields in which 16mm films are used." In many ways *Film World* was the *Motion Picture Herald* of the 16mm film industry, providing trade news, production techniques, distribution plans, and lengthy release reviews. Graphics.
DEPT: "Editorial," "Reviews of New Releases," "Association News," "16mm Film Booking Chart," "Late Films." (6-45).
TYPL: "Companies Announce Production of 16mm Features," "Differences in Distribution Methods--An Analysis," "Churches Reveal Increased Use of Films," "Television Studios Will Have a 16 mm Camera Department." (6- 45).
SCHL: Monthly, 25 pp.
SPAN: Feb, 1945 - Jun, 1966//
VARIES
--Feb, 1945 - Sep, 1951 as Film World.
--Oct, 1951 - May, 1960 as Film World and A-V World News Magazine.
ABSORBED
--Business Films, 1948
--School Films, 1948.
--16 MM Reporter, 1949
--Church Films, 1952
LC: PN 1993.F64

Film World and A-V World News Magazine

Oct, 1951 - May, 1960//
SEE: FILM WORLD AND A-V NEWS MAGAZINE

✣ FILMFARE

PUBL:	Bennett Coleman & Co., Times of India, 7 Bahadur Shah Zaffar Marg, New Delhi 110002, India.
DESC:	The love of Indian people for motion pictures is manifested in *Filmfare*, a newsprint (Sunday magazine-style) periodical that promotes Indian actors, actresses, and films. International film product is mentioned, but is not dominant. There are numerous color and black/white pictures of Indian film stars, both on and off-screen, and full discussion of the large number of motion pictures produced each month by the Indian film industry.
DEPT:	"Movie Montage," newsbriefs; "News in Pix," "Reviews," "JS Johar's Question Box," Q&A; "Behind the Screen," profiles; "Film Letter from Hollywood," "From the Film Centres," "Post Box." (2-22-63).
TYPL:	"My Memorable Roles," "Johnny Walker: Has Cycle, Will Travel." (2-22-63).
SCHL:	Biweekly, 70 pp.
SPAN:	1952+
LC:	PN 1993.F642
ISSN:	0015-1548

✣ FILMFAX

SUB:	"The magazine of unusual film & television."
PUBL:	Filmfax, PO Box 1900, Evanston, IL 60201.
DESC:	*Filmfax* is described in its own subscription advertisement as "...the modern magazine that helps you keep pace with the past! [containing articles on] Horror, Science Fiction, B-Movies, Animation, Film Noir, Biker/J.D./Exploitation, Exclusive Interviews, Comedy Classics, 1950s TV, Mystery and Monster Movies, Reviews of the latest video and filmbook releases," and more. Monsters, ghouls, and general silver screen mayhem are featured in each bimonthly issue, with articles written in an informative and articulate nature. Numerous black/white photographs provide a pictorial foray into the world of the unique and unusual. A wonderful resource for this film/video genre; color cover on coated paper, remainder on newsprint paper stock. Sampled issue for 1990: (8 ½ x 11 inches / 215 x 280 mm).
DEPT:	"Re:Edits," 'Opinions, ideas and announcements'; "Cinema Sourcebook," 'The newest in filmbook literature'; "Videoscan," 'Rare and unusual video releases'; "Wax Museum," 'The latest news on record collectibles'. (1-90).
TYPL:	"The Phantom Ghoul (a.k.a. The Ghoul Goes West)," "Bring Me the Brain of the Head of the Thing That Wouldn't Die," "Roland Winters: The Last Charlie Chan," "An Interview With Keye Luke." (1-90).
SCHL:	Bimonthly, 100 pp.
SPAN:	Jan/Feb, 1986+
ISSN:	0895-0393

FILMING

SUB:	"A quarterly journal of filmic art."
PUBL:	Dipok Dey, 107/2 Amherst St., Calcutta 9, India.
DESC:	*Filming* began as a wonderful effort to preview, analyze, and comment on world and Indian film product. It held great promise as an international film review, but unfortunately only the premiere issue was ever published. The quarterly provided over 70 pages of current motion picture synopsis, a variety of production stories, and news of the Indian film industry as well. The second issue was to have been exclusively devoted to censorship. Graphics; square magazine format.
DEPT:	"Editorial." (1-69).
TYPL:	"Czechoslovak Film To-Day," "Behind the Screen," "The Fourth Chicago International Film Festival," "The Development and Progress of Sound Recording in Indian Motion Picture." (1-69).
SCHL:	Quarterly, 70 pp.
SPAN:	Jan, 1969//
LC:	PN 1993.F645
ISSN:	0533-1056

FILMIS

SUB:	"Missionary bulletin of the International Catholic Film Office."
PUBL:	Missionary Secretariat, 117, Quattro Fontane, Rome, Italy.
DESC:	This was both a serial and, at times, a catalog of missionary films, described by the International Catholic Film Office as "films produced in general by religious congregations to publicize their achievements in the mission countries and thus to awaken the interest of various groups, in the different problems encountered in countries where these congregations have carried out their work of evangelization." The editorial content was primarily film reviews, with several articles per issue pertaining to the "missionary film." Mimeographed; no graphics.
DEPT:	None. (7-62).
TYPL:	"The True Light," "The Cinema--Instrument of the Apostolate," "Cinema and TV--Reflection of Man," "Christianity and Creativity in Films and TV." (7-62).
SCHL:	Irregular, 40 pp.
SPAN:	?, 1969? - ?, 1979?// CONTINUED BY --Filmis Index Cards [NA].
LC:	BV 1535.4 .F54

✣ FILMLAND

SUB:	"Hundreds of new and intimate pictures!"
PUBL:	Red Circle Magazines, Inc., 655 Madison Ave., New York, NY.

DESC: With feature articles divided by subject headings ("Personal to You," "Star Life," "Seeing Stars"), *Filmland* successfully utilized a formula which promoted the better side of Hollywood stars, their careers, and abundant pictures of same at home and play. Even in the television boom times of the early 1950s, *Filmland* stayed the course of covering primarily new motion picture releases and their stars. Of special note was a series of articles written by Hollywood celebrities in the "Personal to You" subheading. The sampled issue of 1953 included "I Like Sexy Girls" by Tab Hunter; "What My Wife Knows" by John Derek; "Should a Man Be the Boss?" by Virginia Mayo;" and "My Marriage," by John Barrymore, Jr. The section, "Star Life," portrayed the semi-private lives of the rich and famous, while "Seeing Stars" provided a showcase of stars on-camera, and off-stage,often connected with a recent motion picture release. Each issue contained a generous number of Hollywood-themed pictures, related film advertising, and star information. For sampled issue of 1953: perfect-bound magazine format, editorial content is black/white on newsprint, with full-color cover on coated paper stock (8 ½ x 10 ⅞ inches / 215 x 275 mm).
DEPT: "Hello, Friends," editorial column by Bessie Little; "Hollywood Secrets," 'Here's the inside on all the gossip' column by Edith Gwynn; "Hollywood Tattletale," personality column by The Insider; "For the Love of Mike," personality column by Denny Shane; "Filmland Reviews," motion picture review column by Lillian Smith; "Filmland Forum," letters column. (6-53).
TYPL: "June Haver Says Goodbye," "Who's Kissing Whom in Hollywood?," "Calamity Jane Rides Again," "Gentleman Beachcomber," "Liz isn't Lonely Any More." (6-53).
SCHL: Bimonthly, 80 pp.
SPAN: 1951+?

Filmmakers

Oct, 1978//
(ISSN: 0194-4339)
SEE: FILMMAKERS FILM & VIDEO MONTHLY

Filmmakers

Feb, 1980 - ?, 1982//
(ISSN: 0194-4339)
SEE: FILMMAKERS FILM & VIDEO MONTHLY

FILMMAKERS FILM & VIDEO MONTHLY

SUB: "Film and video monthly."
SUB: "The magazine for habitual filmmakers."
PUBL: Suncraft International, Inc., P.O. Box 607, Andover, MA 01810.

DESC: "The *Filmmakers Newsletter* is the only national publication devoted exclusively to supplying hard-core information for the independent-student, avantguarde, experimental, and teaching-filmmaker. We run articles on, by, and about filmmakers; comments on everything from films and film books to distributors and festivals." In September, 1978 the serial became *Filmmakers Monthly*, and with the new masthead came a new purpose: "*Filmmakers Monthly* is a magazine for professionals and semi-professionals working in film and videotape in studios, independent production houses, university film departments, TV stations and corporations." Final form of this publication was as *Filmmakers Film & Video Monthly*, which lasted until early 1982. In all formats, the emphasis was on equipment and production technique, with one major filmmaker profiled each issue. Information on new techniques and equipment, festivals, seminars and sources for financing of independent film projects were also featured. Magazine format; black/white editorial content with two-color covers. Sampled issue for 1976 (8 ½ x 11 inches / 220 x 280 mm), on coated paper stock.
DEPT: "Equipment News," "Film Feedback," a Q&A column on technique; "Building Cine Stuff," constructing your own; "Filmmaker's Notebook," technique instruction; "Festivals," calendar. (2-70). "What's Happening," "Cinescenes," newsbriefs; "Film Nut News," column by Alan Oddie; "Equipment News," "Building Cine Stuff," column by L. Bruce Holman; "Videotape," "Superserious-8," column by Raul da Silva; "Making $$$ in Filmmaking," "Filmmakers Notebook," column by Elinor Stecker; "Animation Kit," column by Howard Beckerman; "New Books," review column by John Belton; "Product Report," review column by Steven T. Smith; "Festivals," "Letters," "Lens Caps," comment and observations. (9-76). "What's Happening," calendar; "Future Festivals," "Used Equipment," "Bulletin Board," wantads. (7/8-81).
TYPL: "Notes on a Mixed Media Environment," "Millennium," "East Goes West." (2-70). "Jack Ofield and 'Don't Tread On Me'," "Filming the Great Plains Buffalo," "Observations on the Making of 'The Last Hard Men'," "Making and Selling 'The Omen'." (9-76). "Animation Special," "Raiders of the Lost Ark," "Oil and Gas Industry," "Superserious 8: Myths That Do Us No Good," "Animation on Broadway." (7/8-81).
SCHL: Monthly, 80 pp.
SPAN: Nov, 1967 - Jan/Feb, 1982//
VARIES
--Nov, 1967 - Mar, 1968 as NY Filmmakers Newsletter.
--Apr, 1968 - Sep, 1978 as Filmmakers Newsletter (ISSN: 0015-1610).
--Oct, 1978 as Filmmakers (ISSN: 0194-4339).
--Nov, 1978 - Jan, 1980 as Filmmakers Monthly.
--Feb, 1980 - ?, 1982 as Filmmakers (ISSN: 0194-4339).
LC: PN 1993.F64715

Filmmakers Monthly

Nov, 1978 - Jan, 1980//
SEE: FILMMAKERS FILM & VIDEO MONTHLY

Filmmakers Newsletter

Apr, 1968 - Sep, 1978//
(ISSN: 0015-1610)
SEE: FILMMAKERS FILM & VIDEO MONTHLY

FILMO TOPICS

PUBL: Bell and Howell, 1842 Larchmont Ave., Chicago, IL.
DESC: This 15-page quarterly was an interesting promotional publication produced by the Bell and Howell Company and mailed to purchasers and users of Filmo brand motion picture cameras. Its editorial content, therefore, informed the reader about the many ways of using their Filmo motion picture camera through special techniques, new ideas, and newly developed attachments. A well-accomplished promotional piece.
DEPT: "Motion Pictures in Industry," newsbriefs of the use of film equipment; "Motion Pictures in Education," same; "Questions and Answers," basic Q&A cinema technique format; "Missing Equipment," unique feature detailing serial numbers of reported missing film equipment.
TYPL: "Rodeo," "Hunting with a Movie Camera," "Summer Title Making," "Tricks to Dress Up Your Summer Movies." (summer-39).
SCHL: Quarterly, 15 pp.
SPAN: 1925 - ?//?
LC: TR 845.F5
DD: 778.5/3/05

FILMOGRAPH

SUB: "For people who like movies."
PUBL: Murray Summers, Orlean, VA 22128.
DESC: "This periodical is devoted to the history of the film..." began *Filmograph*. This serial was created and maintained with loving care, and produced a considered examination of the Hollywood of a bygone era, when silent stars were indeed stars (no income taxes at this time), and the Saturday morning serials kept throngs of young children happy through boxes of popcorn, candy and soda. *Filmograph* demonstrated to the reader time and time again the essence of what was termed the "Golden Age" of Hollywood, an almost magical era in which the motion picture and the star reigned supreme on silver screens throughout America, no matter the economic climate or state of war/peace existing at the time. This most enjoyable serial both informed and entertained. Journal style on yellow-color paper; with publicity stills.
DEPT: "Books & Periodicals," reviews; "And Selected Short Subjects," newsbriefs. (1-71).
TYPL: "The Film Career of Patsy Ruth Miller," "The Falcon Film Series," "Kermit Maynard as Western Star and Stunt Man," "Roots of Film Realism in a Griffith One-Reeler," "A Filmography of Phyllis Diller." (1-71).
SCHL: Quarterly, 50 pp.
SPAN: Spring, 1970 - Summer, 1976//
LC: PN 1993.F64716
ISSN: 0015-1629

Filmograph

May?, 1923 - 1929//
SEE: HOLLYWOOD FILMOGRAPH

FILMS

SUB: "A quarterly of discussion and analysis."
PUBL: Kamin Publishers, 15 West 56th St., New York, NY.
DESC: This short-lived quarterly of the international film industry and its product was a forum for the intellectual and pragmatic discussion of film. Noted contributers included Harry Potamkin, James Agee, Paul Strand, Paul Rotha, Budd Schulberg, Kurt London, and Kenneth Arnold. It was a journal of intellect encompassing film aesthetics, theory, and genres; but interestingly, also a journal of reality, providing a pragmatic look at Hollywood studio unions, film distribution, and the fickle tastes of the "movie-going" audience. It deserved a better fate than its four-issue publication span. The first issue, cover dated as November, 1939 was later considered to be the Winter, 1939 number. No graphics.
DEPT: None. (spring-40).
TYPL: "A Channel for Democratic Thought," "History in American Films," "Life Goes to the Pictures," "A Year of the Motion Picture Herald," "America at the Movies." (spring-40).
SCHL: Quarterly, 95 pp.
SPAN: Nov, 1939 - Winter, 1940//
LC: PN 1993.F64724
DD: 791.43/05

FILMS AND FILMING

SUB: "Britain's most established screen monthly."
SUB: "Incorporating Focus on Film."
PUBL: Orpheus Publications, Fourth Floor, Centro House, Mandela St., London NW1 0DU, England.
DESC: This was a wonderful British consumer guide to current American and British film releases, and the talent that lay within. It had well-written, intelligent film reviews and profiles of box-office personalities. Some segments presented information concerning film festivals, collectors, music, and video. One sampled issue for 1962 included an interview with Jose Ferrer, a George Raft profile, an interview with Bessie Love, an extensive series on the films of Howard Hawks; and as always, in-depth reviews of current film re-

leases. Commencing with the August, 1962 issue a new "Film Guide" section was included as a "pull-out" feature, printed on tinted uncoated paper stock. In that debut, editor Peter G. Baker noted: "We believe that our critics are constantly aware of what film-makers are trying to do because they are closely in touch with the creative and technical problems of filming. We believe that they are also closely in touch with that informed public opinion that rejects the insincere but responds, on a variety of levels, to all kinds of films, big and small, irrespective from where they come, providing they are good of their kind. ...Good criticism stimulates ideas; it does not attempt to tell other people how and what to think." It produced distinctive, informed and enjoyable reading, but perhaps, fell short of commercial success, resulting in a March, 1990 cessation by Orpheus Publications. Subsequently, *Films and Filming* was absorbed by *Film Review*, an outstanding publication in its own right. Signed reviews; numerous black/white and color graphics; magazine format. Sampled issue for 1962: stapled magazine format, black ink editorial copy, two-color cover, all on coated paper stock (8 ⅜ x 10 ⅞ inches / 210 x 275 mm).

DEPT: "Film of the Month," "Revival," "In Production," "In Camera," newsbriefs; "Films and Filming in Hollywood," "Films and Filming Abroad." (10-54). "Editorial," "Newsreel," newsbriefs; "Denis Gifford's Flavour of the Month," TV releases; "F & F Interview," "Reviews," "Pin Up of the Past." (10-83). "Short Takes," newsbriefs; "World Wide Movie Making," excellent current projects and prospects column by Kathryn Kirby; "Now You Know," reader Q&A; "Review," large segment detailing film releases, video view, books, and film music; "Retro," comment. (2-90).
TYPL: "Italy and London," "The Battle of the Systems," "The Brooder," "Designer of Dreams," "Song and Dance." (10-54). "Luis Bunuel," "Carole Lombard," "Joseph Lewis," "Don't Look Now, It's Not There Anymore." (10-83). "Single Frame Trickery," "A Capital Festival," "Ardent Ardant," "The Return of Al Pacino." (2-90).
SCHL: Monthly, 70 pp.
SPAN: Oct, 1954 - Mar, 1990//
VARIES
--? - ? as Films & Filming Incorporating Focus on Film.
ABSORBED
--Focus on Film (ISSN: 0015-5128), 1981.
ABSORBED BY
--Film Review, Apr, 1990.
LC: PN 1993.F64725
DD: 791.43/05
ISSN: 0015-167x

Films & Filming Incorporating Focus on Film
? - ?//
SEE: FILMS AND FILMING

Films by Wid
Apr 27, 1916//
SEE: FILM TV DAILY

FILMS ILLUSTRATED
SUB: "The magazine that loves movies."
PUBL: Independent Magazines, 181 Queen Victoria St., London EC4V 4DD, England.
DESC: This indeed was a serial that "loves movies," evident in its thoughtful analyses of film product for general public entertainment. The accent here was on current films, with numerous publicity stills, filmographies, and profiles of actors and actresses. Enjoyable reading.
DEPT: "Letters," "Background," 'news and views on the best of the months films'; "Film Guide." (9-71). "Up Front," reviews; "Books." (9-81).
TYPL: "Haven't We Met Somewhere Before?," "Retrospective: The Gingerbread Man," "Technical Hitch." (9-71). "Mapping Out the Road to Camelot," "Escape to Victory," "Words as Good as His Bond." (9-81).
SCHL: Monthly, 35 pp.
SPAN: Jul, 1971 - ?//
ABSORBED BY
--Photoplay Movies & Video Monthly, ?
LC: PN 1993.F64727
DD: 791.43/05
ABST: --Film Literature Index (ISSN: 0093-6758)

✤ FILMS IN REVIEW
SUB: "The National Board of Review Magazine."
PUBL: National Board of Review of Motion Pictures, PO Box 589, New York, NY 10021.
DESC: "*Films in Review* is a publication of the National Board of Review of Motion Pictures, Inc., a non-profit, independent organization of public-spirited citizens founded in 1909 to represent the interests of the motion picture public. Since the National Board maintains the responsibility for good motion pictures is not the industry's alone, but also the public's, it reviews, classifies and disseminates information about films and organizes audience support for them. The National Board further assists the development of the motion picture as entertainment, and as art, by providing media for the expression of the public's opinions about films and their cultural and social affects." *Films in Review* is the means by which the National Board of Review of Motion Pictures disseminates information about motion picture product in the international marketplace. The small-format,

black-white publication (5 ½ x 7 ½ inches / 140 x 190 mm), has an emphasis on motion picture stars, directors and producers, and interviews of same.

DEPT: "Ad Glib," comment; "The Sound Track," "The Television Scene," "The Collecting Scene," "Book Reviews," "Films in Release," with an entertainment value system; "Letters," "Letter From the Editor." (1-82). "The Television Scene," column by Alvin H. Marill; "Book Reviews," column by John Nangle; "The Sound Track," column by Page Cook; "Letters." (10-84). "Video-Syncrasy," column by Alan G. Barbour; "The Television Scene," column by Chris Buchman; "Book Reviews," column by William K. Everson; "The Sound Track," column by Page Cook; "Obituaries," column by Billy H. Doyle; "Letters." (10-90).

TYPL: "1981 David Wark Griffith Awards," "Bob Balaban," "Charles Durning," "The Australian Cinema," "Henry Fonda," "Marcos Imhoof." (1-82). "Renaissance on 53rd St. The Museum of Modern Art Reopens," "Fritz Lang: The Maker of Metropolis," "The New Sound of Music," "Lubitsch Returns to Berlin," "James Ivory: An Interview." (10-84). "Clarence Brown," "Margaret Rutherford," "Who's in Town," "Document of the Dead." (10-90).

SCHL: Monthly (Feb, 1926 - Dec, 1928); Monthly [except no issues Jun - Aug] (Jan, 1929 - Jan, 1942); Monthly [except bimonthly Jun/Jul and Aug/Sep] (Feb, 1942+), 65 pp.

SPAN: Feb, 1926+
FROM MERGER OF
--Exceptional Photoplays (and) Film Progress (and) Photoplay Guide to the Better Pictures, Feb, 1926.
VARIES
--Feb, 1926 - Jan, 1942 as National Board of Review Magazine.
--Feb, 1942 - Jan/Feb, 1949 as New Movies, The.

LC: PN 1993.F6473
DD: 791.43/7
ISSN: 0015-1688
ABST: --Art Index (ISSN: 0004-3222)
--Book Review Index (ISSN: 0524-0581)
--Film Literature Index (ISSN: 0093-6758)
--Index to Book Reviews in the Humanities (ISSN: 0073-5892)
--Media Review Digest (ISSN: 0363-7778)
--Reference Sources (ISSN: 0163-3546)

FILMWORLD

SUB: "A current study of international films and filmfolk." (Oct, 1964 - ?).
SUB: "The complete movie monthly."
PUBL: Film World International Publications, A-15 Anand Nager, Juhu Tara Rd., Bombay 400054, India.
DESC: "The object of this publication is to promote understanding, friendship and collaboration among filmfolk and movie fans living in all parts of the world." International in scope, *Film World* (later *Filmworld*) began to showcase, profile, and critique international film product from a cultural, intercultural and aesthetic point of view. Indeed, the first issue was comprised of articles submitted by various authors from 26 nations. By the 1980s, however, the editorial stance had moved from international, to an all-Indian, all movie-fan oriented magazine. This placed *Filmworld* more akin to the American Hollywood fan magazines than to a serious journal of film thought and analysis. Numerous color graphics.

DEPT: None. (10-64). "Your Point of View," letters; "Teasers n Trailers," comic comment; "Blow Hot, Blow Cold," gossip; "Sugar n Spice," readers comments; "Cultural Scene," newsbriefs; "Around Filmdom," pictures; "Goings On," gossip. (2-83).

TYPL: "Bright Prospects Along the Nile," "India Beckons Hollywood Moghuls," "Entertainment Tax Removal Helps Industry," "Bergman's New Film Creates Stir." (10-64). "Revealed: Raakhee's Secret Complaint Against Indian Men," "Smita Reveals All About Loneliness Love & Raj Babbar," "Amjad Blasts the Censors." (2-83).

SCHL: Monthly, 75 pp.
SPAN: Oct, 1964 - 1983?//
VARIES
--1964 - Jul, 1975? as Film World (ISSN: 0015-1475).

✣ FINELINE

SUB: "The newsletter on journalism ethics."
PUBL: Billy Goat Strut Publishing, Inc., 600 East Main St., Louisville, KY 40202.
DESC: "*FineLine*, the monthly Newsletter on Journalism Ethics, brings you practical solutions to ethical problems...real answers from real people. It's the only publication dedicated to helping the journalism professional caught between a tough call and a tight deadline. So, the next time you're torn between maintaining a public trust and revealing a private tragedy...when naming names could mean ruining lives -- only *FineLine* tells you how your colleagues have dealt with similar problems." The professional journalistic community has waited a long time for a publication of this caliber, a monthly forum for the discussion of journalism ethics. This is not theoretical journalism. The articles discussed are real events and were oftentimes written by the journalists involved in the story. It makes for sobering (but enlightened) consideration of managing today's newsroom organization. With a 1991 subscription fee of $49 for ten issues, it is difficult to imagine any news operation that would not benefit from the information contained within a single issue of this newsletter; especially in this age of public suspicion and litigation. Very highly recommended for all professional journalists. Newsletter format, three-hole punched; some supporting graphics, black ink with spot color on coated paper stock (8 ½ x 11 inches / 215 x 280 mm).

DEPT: None. (10-89).
TYPL: "How to Handle Suicide Threats," "Red Flag for Badgering," "Have I Got a Deal for You!, the Line Between Cooperation and Collusion." (10-89).

SCHL: Monthly (Apr, 1989 - ?); Ten issues per year (?+), 8 pp.
SPAN: Apr, 1989+
DD: 174 11
ISSN: 1044-7407

Finland Filmland

1978 - ?//
(ISSN: 0355-1539)
SEE: FINNISH FILMS

✤ FINNISH FILMS

SUB: "Facts about film in Finland."
PUBL: ?, Kaisaniemenkatu 3 B 25, SF-00100 Helsinki 10, Finland.
DESC: This is a public relations periodical by the Finnish Film Foundation, whose primary purpose is to promote and inform world readers of the status of motion picture production in Finland. Numerous graphics accompany the typewritten format which introduces new Finnish filmmakers, films in production, and general Finnish film news of interest to international readers. Certainly one of the better publications in this field.
DEPT: None.
TYPL: "Finnish Amateur Film Makers," "An Addressography of Finnish Film Photographers," "Armas Vallasvuo--Veteran," "Film Prizes in Finland," "New Films." (#2-79).
SCHL: Quarterly (? - ?); Annual (?+), 60 pp.
SPAN: 1970?+
VARIES
--1978 - ? as Finland Filmland (ISSN: 0355-1539).
ABSORBED
--Facts About Film Finland (ISSN: 0355-1520), 1978.

First Stage

Winter, 1961/1962 - Winter, 1967/1968//
(ISSN: 0885-047x)
SEE: DRAMA & THEATRE

✤ FLAKE

SUB: "Scott Bruce's cereal box collecting magazine."
PUBL: Mr. Cereal Box, PO Box 481, Cambridge, MA 02140.
DESC: This is no academic journal of marketing, but a publication that returns us to our past, to that golden age of growing up amidst a mountain of grocery store cereal boxes, and the never-ending quest to find that free something that the manufacturer always managed to place at the very bottom of the box. *Flake* is about cereal boxes, their contents, and the advertising/marketing effort that was invested in them. In the premiere issue, Publisher Scott Bruce stated, "Personally, I think the selling of kids' cereal was, and still is, one of the greatest stick-ups in business. *FLAKE*'s job is to return to the scene of this crime!" Publisher Bruce has fun as he details decades of manufacturers and their advertising agencies pushing whole-grain, sugar-coated-grain, and mystery-grain cereals at the American public with every sort of free premium imaginable. Lest one thinks that Mr. Bruce is a lone voice crying in the wilderness, be aware that the first two issues have generated some very passionate responses of individuals who also collect cereal boxes, or are very interested in the historical media connection between cartoon/radio/television stars and this food product. Stapled magazine format, black/white editorial content on uncoated paper stock, cover on coated paper stock (8 ½ x 10 ¾ inches / 215 x 275 mm).
DEPT: "Editorial," "Letters," "Discoveries," new cereal boxes and giveaways recently found; "Boxography," historical cereal box lineage; "Review." (#2-90).
TYPL: "Jay Ward: The Emperor of the Grain Ghetto," "More Than a Snack," "Big D Round Up." (#2-90).
SCHL: ?, 25 pp.
SPAN: ?, 1990+

✤ FLASH

SUB: "The magazine for creative information."
PUBL: Macmillan Creative Services Group, 212 West Superior St., Suite 203, Chicago, IL 60610.
DESC: "*Flash* magazine is unique in its ability to provide national coverage of the advertising and graphic design industries as well as news and information about the forces affecting the reader's own market." It's easy to see why art directors, advertising executives, and production managers would be drawn to this exceptional publication of creative communication. Here is a showcase of advertising genius, a gallery of outstanding advertising campaigns, printed with loving care on thick clay-coated paper. Innovative ideas are applicable to other media. Profiles are thorough and informative. Columns and departmental features cover the gamut of street news of agency accounts, to prepress/postpress forums, product showcases, trends in technology, and the symbiotic relationship between film and video in today's commercial field. *Flash* is published in three separate editions: New York/East, Chicago/Midwest, and Los Angeles/West; each concentrating on local and regional agency news, with a majority of articles appearing nationally in all three editions. Subscription price (for 1990) is $36 per year for seven issues, or $8.00 per copy at the newstand. An excellent resource for today's advertising team. Magazine format (8 ½ x 11 inches / 215 x 280 mm), full color graphics throughout, printed on heavy clay-coated paper stock.
DEPT: "First Draft," editorial column by R. Patricia Herron; "Street Talk," advertising agency and business news by selected cities; "Graphics People," profiles; "Creative Pulse," "Creative Spotlight," "Tear Sheets," samples; "One on One," profile; "Design Project," case study; "Film Campaign," "Tangents," column by Vince Kamin; "Technology Update," "Product Showcase," "Calendar of Events," "Film and Video Views,"

column by Mark Androw; "Printing Forum," column by Dennis J. Castiglione; "Final Copy," column by Jack Reznicki. (9/10-90).
TYPL: "Creative Spotlight: Booting Up Competition in Home PCs," "Design Project: Synthesis Concepts Promotes Itself with a Game," "One on One: Mike Moser," "Film Campaign: Ogilvy & Mather/New York Sends Eastern's Image Flying," "Prepress in the Creative Continuum." (9/10-90).
SCHL: Bimonthly, 110 pp.
SPAN: Jul/Aug, 1990+
FROM SPLIT OF
--Chicago/Midwest Flash (ISSN: 0882-1925) (into) Flash [Los Angeles/West Edition] (ISSN: 1055-3142, (and) Flash [Chicago/Midwest Edition], (and) Flash (New York/East Edition], Jun, 1990.
EDITION
--New York/East.
--Chicago/Midwest.
--Los Angeles/West.
ISSN: 0882-1925

✤ FLASHBACK

SUB: "The all-talking, all-singing, all-dancing magazine."
PUBL: Pentragram Publications, P.O. Box 567, Bookline Village, MA 02147.
DESC: This lay-audience publication began during the American nostalgia craze, and as the title implies, *Flashback* takes the reader back in time. Like many lay periodicals, this one has a large number of motion picture stills and movie posters. Articles are well-written, and aimed at those who have an interest in Hollywood's past.
DEPT: "Nostalgia Newsfront," sort of a 'whatever happened to' news feature; "The Soundtrack," record albums with nostalgic themes; "Vintage Catalog," other mailorder items of a similar nature.
TYPL: "1941: It was a Very Good Year," "The Movie Cowboy," "Lon Chaney: How I Broke into the Movies." (9-72).
SCHL: Bimonthly, 70 pp.
SPAN: 1972+?

Florida Newspaper News

192u - Oct, 1947//
SEE: COMMUNIQUE

Florida Newspaper News and Radio Digest

Nov, 1947 - Dec, 1969//
SEE: COMMUNIQUE

✤ FLORIDA REEL

SUB: "Film, television, video."
PUBL: Take 5 Publishing, Inc., 800 North Magnolia Ave., Suite 1200, Orlando, FL 32803.
DESC: In a December, 1989 open letter, publisher Dennis Zink commented: "Florida, you have a lot to offer, but you're a well kept secret. You're more than just a location, you're fast becoming a production destination. You're still young and building for the future. To compete worldwide, you will need to have the best resources -- the best facilities, and the best people in the film industry. You will prove yourself with hard work and dedication. Other states will look to you as an example of excellence. You will be known across the country as the production center of choice." With reference to the motion picture, "Field of Dreams," publisher Zink noted, "If we build it ... they will come." The Florida production boom is on, and *Florida Reel* functions to extoll, report, and comment on film, television, and video developments in the state. It is a producer's resource, indicating in both editorial content and advertising by professional services that Florida has "arrived" as a production center. The magazine is upbeat, with a sense of breaking new ground each issue, much in the same way that Hollywood was during the dawning of its golden age. Never far from the surface of most articles is the reality that Florida is a "right to work" state, and the impact this represents in state services and operations. For the 1989 sampled issue: full-color and spot-color graphics on heavy coated paper stock in a stapled magazine format, advertising (8 $\frac{1}{8}$ x 10 $\frac{7}{8}$ inches / 205 x 275 mm).
DEPT: "Publisher's Letter," "Editor's Letter," "In Print," review; "Reel News," 'Industry news'; "Focus," 'A close-up of a company'; "In the Spotlight," profile; "Spots," 'Statewide commercial production'; "On Location." (12-89).
TYPL: "Pennies to Pesos," "Colleges Tackle Filmmaking," "Southbound: Who's Moving to Florida?," "Selling Your Script," "A Conversation on Right to Work," "HDTV: To Be or Not to Be." (12-89).
SCHL: Bimonthly, 60 pp.
SPAN: Oct/Nov, 1989+
DD: 338 11
ISSN: 1046-0489

FLQ

Winter, 1971/1972 - ?//
(ISSN: 0160-7316)
SEE: FILM LIBRARY QUARTERLY

FM

Nov, 1940 - Feb, 1942//
SEE: COMMUNICATION ENGINEERING

FM and Television

Apr, 1944 - Oct, 1948//
SEE: COMMUNICATION ENGINEERING

FM Electronic Equipment Engineering & Design Practise

Mar, 1942 - Apr, 1942//
SEE: COMMUNICATION ENGINEERING

FM Radio-Electronic Engineering and Design

May, 1942 - Feb, 1943//
SEE: COMMUNICATION ENGINEERING

FM Radio Electronics

Mar, 1943 - Mar, 1944//
SEE: COMMUNICATION ENGINEERING

FM-TV

Nov, 1948 - Jan, 1950//
SEE: COMMUNICATION ENGINEERING

FM-TV

1952//
SEE: COMMUNICATION ENGINEERING

FM-TV Radio Communication

1950 - 1951//
SEE: COMMUNICATION ENGINEERING

FOCUS

SUB: "The international newspaper of marketing."
SUB: "The European journal of advertising and marketing."
SUB: "Advertising Age's spotlight on pan-European marketing."
PUBL: Crain Communications, 740 Rush St., Chicago, IL 60611.
DESC: *Advertising Age/Europe* (later *Focus*), is identical in layout style to its sister Chicago publication with one major difference: the typical international issue usually contains less editorial content. Here is a publication that provides fascinating professional insights into the European advertising process. Ad concepts, techniques, and industry norms taken for granted in one nation may not be acceptable to another. It is large format with numerous graphics. A magazine "prototype issue" was published in Summer, 1981, with full publication schedule taking effect with the January, 1982 issue. An excellent resource for the study of international advertising and marketing.
DEPT: "Agency Account Changes," "European News Roundup." (10-81).
TYPL: "Taxes, Ad Bans Slow Cigarettes," "Eurobrand: a New Approach to Marketing," "French Radio Wrangle: Ad Freedom vs. Control," "Sweden: KF Struggles to Push No-Name Products." (10-81).
SCHL: Ten issues per year (? - ?); Eleven issues per year (? - ?); Monthly (?+), 16 pp.
SPAN: Jan, 1979 - Jul, 1987//
VARIES
--Jan, 1979 - Dec, 1981 as Advertising Age/Europe (ISSN: 0197-2359).
--Jan, 1982 - Jan, 1985 as Advertising Age's Focus (ISSN: 0264-1755).
LC: HF 5801.A293
DD: 659.1/094
ABST: --Predicasts

Focus: Chicago

Feb, 1967 - Spring/Summer, 1973//
(ISSN: 0362-0905)
SEE: FACETS FEATURES

✢ FOCUS!

SUB: "Chicago's movie journal."
PUBL: Documentary Film Group, University of Chicago, Chicago, IL.
DESC: *Focus!* was a forum for thoughtful criticism of international film product, with broad issue coverage of historical motion pictures, current product, and film reviews. *Focus!* seemed to delight in profiles of film cinematographers, producers, directors, and editors; the above- the-line personnel whose personal philosophical stamp is so evident in film product. Articles were typewritten with numerous graphics.
DEPT: None.
TYPL: "Probing the Limits of a new Art," "The Westerns of Richard Brooks," "Documentaries of the 30s," "Emulsion Compulsion: Jerry Lewis' The Nutty Professor.'" (autumn-72).
SCHL: Quarterly, 65 pp.
SPAN: Oct, 1969?+?
LC: PN 1993.F7

FOCUS ON FILM

PUBL: Tantivy Press, 136-148 Tooley St., London SE1 2TT, England.
DESC: An unusual serial in an unique short/wide format, *Focus on Film* provided a refreshing approach to film research, analysis and comment. Editor Allen Eyles, in the first issue, noted his intentions were to provide a scholarly, but not-too-serious look at international film, and he quite successfully did so. This British publication made for both enjoyable and enlightening reading, as the motion picture was probed and analyzed by some of the best minds in film criticism. Some issues were devoted to single subject areas; numerous graphics.

DEPT: "Focus on the New Films," large film review section; "Book Spread," "Best Cartoons on 16mm," reviews; "Focus on Sponsored Cinema," reviews. (autumn-72). "In Print," book reviews; "Video," "16mm News," "Sponsored Scene." (12-79).
TYPL: "Sir Alec Guinness," "Old Westerns," "Walter Newman." (autumn-72). "The Art of Art Direction," "Gracie Fields," "Chaplin's A Woman of Paris," "Will Hay & Co." (12-79).
SCHL: Quarterly (Jan/Feb, 1970 - 1973); Three times per year (1974 - Jan/Feb, 1979); Irregular (1980 - 1981).
SPAN: Jan/Feb, 1970 - 1981//
ABSORBED BY
--Films and Filming (ISSN: 0015-167x), 1981.
LC: PN 1993.F72
DD: 791.43/05
ISSN: 0015-5128
ABST: --Film Literature Index (ISSN: 0093-6758)

✤ FOCUS ON FOX

PUBL: Twentieth Century-Fox Film Corporation, 10201 West Pico Blvd., Los Angeles, CA 90035.
DESC: This slick monthly serves as a communications vehicle for the employees of Twentieth Century Fox. Spot colors are utilized to enhance articles on Fox film activities, information concerning Fox subsidiaries, employee advancements, retirements, and other related events. Tabloid format; large number of photos.
DEPT: "People," newsbriefs concerning additions, retirements and other personnel notes; "Spotlight," Fox briefs; "Anniversary Dates," detailing years of services of Fox employees.
TYPL: "Company Achieves Record Earnings in 1978," "Fox's New Comedy Series 'Billy' Airs Sundays on CBS," "Second International Marketing Meeting Stresses Team Spirit," "Fox Television Reports New Production Activities," "Prop Foreman Wermich Reminisces About Studio Career." (2- 79).
SCHL: Monthly, 8 pp.
SPAN: Feb, 1976+

FOI DIGEST

SUB: "Published by the Freedom of Information Center, School of Journalism, University of Missouri."
PUBL: University of Missouri School of Journalism, Freedom of Information Center, PO Box 858, Columbia, MO 65201.
DESC: An eight-page, bimonthly news digest of activities concerning freedom of information in the United States, especially in the journalism field; *FOI Digest* editors report on state news, legal opinions, and requests by journalists for "freedom of information" in government agencies. Of special note are the departments, "Periodical Articles," "Law Review Articles," and "Books," which cover newly published material in the freedom of information field. Note: although the "premiere" issue labeled volume one, number one was published in May/June, 1959, the editors pointed out that the premiere issue was actually "...a continuation of unnumbered mimeographed sheets bearing that title issued by The National Editorial Association since 1955." In the November/December, 1985 issue Editor Sue Corbett informed readers that "After 27 years, the FoI Center folds its publications arm effective with this issue of the *Digest*. Center reports of note will have an avenue for publication through another University effort entitled *Ideas*. The *Digest* will appear, in abbreviated form, as part of the quarterly *IRE Journal*." For the sampled issues of 1959 and 1984: black ink on uncoated paper with red ink spot-color masthead, in loose-leaf newsletter format, no advertising (8 ½ x 11 inches / 215 x 280 mm).
DEPT: "FOI In the States," state news roundup; "Events Abroad," newsbriefs; "Articles and Books," reviews. (9/10-60). "Periodical Articles," review; "Law Review Articles," review; "Books," review. (5/6-84).
TYPL: "Court Strikes Down Movie Censorship Statute," "FCC Policy Statement Calls It Program Evaluation, Not Control," "Law Renders Payola Not Proper," "Moss Counsel Submits New FOI Proposal," "Newsman Unions Form Inter-American Group." (9/10-60). "All Out Censorship Plan in Effect Despite Legislation to Prevent It," "Supreme Court Bars Media from Court Files," "Upholding Cuba Visa-Denial Law Prompts Court Action by ACLU," "Child Pornographers Face Bigger Penalties," "Efforts Designed to Exempt Security Files from FOIA." (5/6-84).
SCHL: Bimonthly, 8 pp.
SPAN: May/June, 1959 - Nov/Dec, 1985//
VARIES
--May 25, 1954 - Apr, 1959 as Freedom of Information News Digest.
DD: 323.4405
ISSN: 0015-5349

✤ FOLIO:

SUB: "The magazine for magazine management."
PUBL: Hanson Publishing Group, Inc., Six River Bend Center, 911 Hope St., PO Box 4949, Stamford, CT 06907-0949.
DESC: This monthly publication for professional magazine management covers numerous topics of interest, such as cost, modernization, diversification, circulation analysis and development. It's hard to consider any topic left untouched by these editors, including such items as salary schedules, postage regulations, promotional campaigns, fullfillment issues, and paper supply or cost. These articles provide thorough news on current developments, and the application columns provide pragmatic advice. These outstanding columns authored by magazine professionals offer practical information on the everyday management of magazine publication: they are efficacious, entertaining, and to the point, and are much of what sets *Folio:* apart from other trade publications. Magazine publishers need *Folio:* for issues, trends, and other data that will

ensure a healthy bottom line profit for their operation. Magazine format (8 x 11 inches / 205 x 275 mm), full color throughout with numerous graphics.
DEPT: "Publisher's Notes" personal observations; "Update," news briefs; "Publisher's Marketplace," a white-pages listing of services useful to magazine management. (11-77). "Briefings," latebreaking news; "Hanson on Magazines," column by J. J. Hanson; "Letters," "Update," news briefs; "Magazine People," personality profile; "Management," personnel briefs; "Ad Marketing," personnel briefs; "Editorial," personnel briefs; "Circulation," personnel briefs; "Production," personnel briefs; "Awards," "Magazine Watch," "Mergers/Acquisitions," "Miscellany," "Milestones," "List Watch," "Conferences," "John Peter on Design," column by John Peter; "Jeff Parnau on Production," column by Jeff Parnau; "Eliot Schein on Circulation Direct Marketing," column by Eliot Schein; "Ron Scott on Single-Copy Sales," column by Ron Scott; "William Abbott on Ad Marketing," column by William Abbott; "Point of View," commentary. (4-86).
TYPL: "Success is coming to Success Unlimited," "Getting into the Book Business: A Compatible Operation for the Magazine Publisher," "The Magazine-Mail order Marriage." (11-77). "Promotion Design that Works," "There's a New Newsweekly Style," "Planning for In-House Fulfillment," "Promotion Budgets: Tightening the Belt," "Publishers Eye Ad Potential in Loose Enclosures." (4-86).
SCHL: Monthly, 155 pp.
SPAN: Jun, 1972+
ABSORBED
--Better Editing (ISSN: 0006-0119), Mar/Apr, 1974.
LC: PN 4734.F65
DD: 658/.91/070572
ISSN: 0046-4333
ABST: --Public Affairs Information Service Bulletin (ISSN: 0033-3409)

✤ FOLLOW FOCUS

PUBL: Professional Film and Video Equipment Association, PO Box 9436, Silver Spring, MD 20906-0436.
DESC: *Follow Focus* was begun in 1973 by manufactures, dealers and distributors of professional film equipment. The Professional Film and Video Equipment Association (PFVEA) works together to: 1) print the "Equipment of Questionable Origin," a list of allegedly stolen equipment; 2) work with the SMPTE (Society of Motion Picture and Television Engineers) organization on equipment standardization; 3) set standards for booth exhibition at major trade shows; 4) provide equipment workshops and seminars; and 5) operate a "security committee" for SMPTE conventions. *Follow Focus*, as the official publication of PFVEA, explores these concerns by providing a news and discussion forum for film/video equipment manufacturers. Of special import is the "Equipment of Questionable Origin," a listing of allegedly purloined production equipment listed with serial number and description. This feature should be required reading for all production managers. This interesting serial has no equal in the film and video production community. Sampled issue for 1989: (8 ½ x 11 inches / 215 x 280 mm).
DEPT: "Member Update," newsbriefs; "Equipment of Questionable Origin," important section listing possible stolen items; "Technical Corner." (spring-89).
TYPL: "Putting Insurance Into Focus," "Who Needs the Assistant Cameraman Anyway?," "Rechargeable Power Supplies," "The 65mm Question," "HDTV-To Be Or Not To Be," "Selection and Use of Lavaliers." (spring-89).
SCHL: Semiannual, 35 pp.
SPAN: 198u+
VARIES
--? - ? as Newsletter.

✤ FOR ADVERTISERS

PUBL: South Wind Publishing Co., 4551 W. 107th St., Suite 343, Overland Park, KS 66207.
DESC: This one-page insert is a supplement to *Magazine Design & Production*, and is "...directed to advertisers, ad agencies, and ad prospects." Articles promote the medium of magazines to ad agency media planners and buyers, and highlight articles within the parent serial which would be of special interest to the advertising agencies.
DEPT: None.
TYPL: "Magazines Getting Fatter," "The Evidence is Right Before You," "Circulation Expands Reach," "June Issue to be Colorful." (3-88).
SCHL: Monthly, 1 p.
SPAN: ?+
SUPPLEMENT TO
--Magazine Design & Production (ISSN: 0882-049X).

For Film
? - Winter, 1962?//
SEE: CRITIC

✤ FORDHAM ENTERTAINMENT, MEDIA & INTELLECTUAL PROPERTY LAW FORUM

PUBL: Fordham School of Law, New York City, NY.
DESC: Publication of this new law journal for entertainment media and sports litigation came at the time of the sesquicentennial celebration of the Fordham University Law School. The first issue covered such interesting topics as freedom of speech for trial lawyers, a detailed history of musical and entertainment satire, an examination of legal rights in "sing-alike, look-alike" celebrity advertisements, and the ongoing debate over the guidelines established by sports leagues and associations to retain control over an athlete's eligibility to compete on the sports field. For the premiere issue of Autumn, 1990: perfect-bound jour-

nal format, black ink on uncoated paper stock, cover consisting of blue ink on textured uncoated paper, limited advertising (6 ¾ x 10 inches / 170 x 255 mm).
DEPT: "Notes." (Autumn-90).
TYPL: "The Free Press-Fair Trial Conflict--What's a Lawyer to Say?," "Stranger in Parodies--Weird Al and the Law of Musical Satire," "Federal Preemption of the Right of Publicity," "Anti-Trust & Professional Sports Eligibility Rules: The Past, the Present, and the Future." (autumn-90).
SCHL: Semiyearly, 90 pp.
SPAN: Autumn, 1990+

✣ FORECAST
PUBL: Baker & Taylor Books, a GRACE Distribution Company, 652 East Main St., PO Box 6920, Bridgewater, NJ 08807-0920.
DESC: "*Forecast* keeps you ahead of patron demand by providing prepublication information on titles we've purchased for inventory. Our buyers have recognized the potential appeal that each of the titles included here will have to your library. By including a title in *Forecast*, we're giving you information your patrons will be asking about in the months to come. Titles from more than 14,000 publishers are available from Baker & Taylor Books. We stay in close contact with all the major publishing houses in an effort to secure the most complete information available to pass on to you in *Forecast*." A wonderful resource for acquisitions librarians. Magazine format; numerous promotional advertisements by publishers; black/white graphics.
DEPT: "What's New," commentary column by Hal Hager; "Focus On," "Soon to be Bestsellers," "Publisher's Place," guest editorial; "Publicity News," upcoming titles, author tours, book club sales, and media tie-ins; "Friends Forum," news and information by Friends of Libraries, USA; "Focus," on recently published and forthcoming titles by topic; "Adult Books," listing; "Children's Books," listing; "Author Index," "In Demand," 'This list represents titles most in demand by librarians'; "Conference Calendar." (7-90).
TYPL: None. (7-90).
SCHL: Monthly, 105 pp.
SPAN: Apr, 1975+
ISSN: 0098-213x

✣ FORUM
PUBL: Public Relations Student Society of America, Department of Journalism, Western Kentucky University, Bowling Green, KY 42101.
DESC: This national newsletter of the Public Relations Student Society of America, covers current PRSSA news and upcoming events. News items include opportunities for public relations majors, ongoing programs at participating colleges and universities, and analysis of trends in the field of public relations.
DEPT: "From the Chair," PRSSA Chairman's column; "PR Briefs," news notes.
TYPL: "Focus 77, Theme of National Conference," "A Well-Rounded Education a Plus, Says PRSA Northeast District Chairman," "A Tribute to the Immediate Past Chairperson." (summer-77).
SCHL: Quarterly, 10 pp.
SPAN: 1969+

✣ FORUM
SUB: "Council on church and media."
PUBL: Council on Church and Media, a forum of Brethren in Christ, Church of the Brethren, and Mennonite churches, PO Box 483, Goshen, IN 46526-0483.
DESC: "CCM is organized to facilitate and enhance communication, professional enrichment, fellowship, and development among its members. Membership is open to professional communicators and those interested in communication issues who are related to one of the sponsoring denominations." This is a thrice-yearly newsletter devoted to communication issues within the Bretheren in Christ, Church of the Brethren and Mennonite church community. For the sampled issues of 1991: black in on uncoated paper stock in newsletter format with graphics (8 ½ x 11 inches / 215 x 280 mm).
DEPT: "News Briefs," information concerning Mennonite Brethren communication developments; "Editorial." (11-89).
TYPL: "Into the Mind of the Member," "The Meaning of 'Mennonite'," "Shunning the Telephone," "Television: the Unpopular View." (11-89).
SCHL: Three issues per year, 8 pp.
SPAN: Spring, 1988?+

✣ FORUM
SUB: "An occasional publication promoting information exchange."
PUBL: International Communication Association, Council of Communication Libraries, PO Box 9589, Austin, TX 78766.
DESC: The Council of Communication Libraries and its associated newsletter, *Forum*, have been long-awaited events for those interested in the research, preservation, cataloging, and locating of pertinent materials to the communication field. Since 1984, (and prior to bestowing of council status in 1990 by the ICA), the forum has "...dealt with issues and strategies involved in database searching, uses made of the electronic media trade press by communication scholars, the future directions of communication publishing, European communication journals and their editorial policies, and ...the relationship between broadcast archives and communication scholarship. The Council forums have featured expert participants and have addressed issues relevant to both information professionals and communication scholars." Continuing on, newsletter Editor Carolyn Martin Spicer noted; "What struck us all at these meetings is how rich, but rela-

tively unexplored, the issues and pressures are that converge at the points of access to the materials that form the substance of much communications scholarship. Although the organization and services of communication libraries, resource centers, and other information providers vary according to institutional affiliation, user orientation, budgetary support, and format of material provided, it is clear that shared interests and problems revolve around a common purpose: to facilitate communications study and research. It is to this end that the Council is committed." This is an excellent organization whose time has come, and one certain to gain in importance as international scholars vie for a bewildering array of information resources in the quest for new fields of research, commentary and historiography as befits international media development. Membership in the Council (through the auspices of the International Communication Association) is certainly a "must" proposition for all agencies engaged in the preservation, cataloging, and accessability of such material to the public. For the sampled issue of 1991: typeset black ink on uncoated paper stock, no advertising, single sheet stapled (8 ½ x 11 inches / 215 x 280 mm).

DEPT: None. (fall-91).
TYPL: "Council of Communication Libraries Comes On-line," "Broadcast Archives and Communication Scholarship," "European Communication Journals-- Meet the Editors," "Editorial Statements from Ten European Scholarly Communication Journals." (fall-91).
SCHL: Two to Three Issues Per Year, 14 pp.
SPAN: Fall, 1991+

✢ FOUR A NEWSLETTER

PUBL: American Association of Advertising Agencies, Inc. 666 Third Ave., New York, NY 10017.
DESC: In this American Association of Advertising Agencies newsletter detailing organization activities, personalities, events, and other items affecting the general advertising industry, the emphasis is on the service side of AAAA to its constituency. Typical articles include changes and trends in societal buying habits, the role and function of advertising agencies within the corporate scheme, and guest commentary on current and future advertising trends in America. For the 1989 sample issue: stapled newsletter format with numerous graphics utilizing spot-color and black ink editorial content, no advertising, on coated paper stock (8 ½ x 11 inches / 215 x 280 mm).
DEPT: "President's Message," "Letters," "Guest Editorial," "Clip File," "Calendar of Events." (3-89).
TYPL: "A is for Apple; G is for Greenbrier," "Hal Shoup to Head Washington Office," "Eleven Chairmen Honor One President." (3-89).
SCHL: Monthly, 12 pp.
SPAN: ?+

✢ 4A'S WASHINGTON NEWSLETTER, THE

PUBL: American Association of Advertising Agencies, Inc. 1899 L St., NW, Washington, DC 20036.
DESC: The American Association of Advertising Agencies (AAAA) publishes this monthly compendium of regulatory news concerning advertising practices. There is no wasted space, advertising, or self-promotion of any kind in this serial, whose purpose is simply to report late breaking Washington, DC events which affect the advertising industry. Small magazine format (5 ½ x 8 ½ inches / 140 x 215 mm); no graphics or advertising.
DEPT: "Editorial," "Washingtonia," newsbriefs; "Quoted as Saying," mid-speech quotes. (4-87).
TYPL: "Congress Pushes for 'Fairness' Law," "Florida Commission Recommends Taxing Network Advertising," "Advertising Tax Deductibility," "Ad Ban Update," "FTC Reauthorization." (4-87).
SCHL: Monthly?, 8 pp.
SPAN: ?+?

✢ FOUR COLOR

SUB: "For comic book connoisseurs." (Nov/Dec, 1986+).
PUBL: Paragon Q Publishing, PO Box 1146, Maplewood, NJ 07040.
DESC: "*Four Color* is aimed at a collector with a knowledge of the direct sales market. The magazine covers the major comic book companies, the independents and, as much as possible, the growing black and white market. ... Each month we will bring you the latest news, reviews and the finest articles written on the field. We chose our name to set us apart from other publications that service the market. *Four Color* is the name of the comic book medium and it also emphasizes our pro-hobby position and our belief that comics are a legitimate art form" (Nov/Dec, 1986 premiere issue). The comic medium has treated its fans somewhat poorly, oftentimes printing fanzines on the same deteriorating newspulp as the originals were published. Not so in *Four Color*, a classy serial on heavy clay-coated stock, where the talented artwork of numerous graphic artists can be showcased, and, since it is NOT newsprint, will endure. This is truly a collector's piece for the comic book connoisseur, offering an intelligent, thoughtful approach to the serious and not-so-serious side of the comic industry. Graphics are a delight, often in full color, and full page size. Articles range from a discussion of the spirit of Christmas, in an imaginative layout style; to a discussion of new marketing techniques of aiming super heroes to an older, more demanding reader. Among all the industry reviews on this unqiue medium, *Four Color* stands out from the competition for its quality; distinctive, thought-provoking articles and superior four-color reproduction. For the premiere 1986 issue: stapled magazine format, black/white and color graphics throughout on heavy coated paper stock (8 ½ x 10 ¾ inches / 215 x 275 mm).

DEPT: "Point Blank," 'The responsibility of publishing is discussed'; "Letters," "News," "Reviews," "On the Racks," new comic product reviewes column by Barry Dutter; "Forthcoming," 'A look at *Four Color* to come'. (1-87).
TYPL: "Catch the Spirit," "The Short, Happy Life of the Black-and-Whites," "Forum: The Never-Ending Super Hero Cycle." (1-87).
SCHL: Monthly, 70 pp.
SPAN: Nov/Dec, 1986+

✦ 4SIGHT MAGAZINE

PUBL: National Press Photographers Association, Region 4, PO Box 1146, Durham, NC 27702.
DESC: This bimonthly publication by Region 4 of the National Press Photographers Association is filled with member photographs of newsworthy/public interest events in the states that make up the fourth region. Here, the professional photojournalists' work is seen and described as it happened in the field. While the publication (for very practical reasons) does not showcase television station news videographers' work, there are articles by working television journalists on problems and issues they encounter. Of special note is the reprinting of full page photographic essays from regional newspapers, allowing the reader to savor both the photography and layout design that combine for unforgettable journalism. Magazine format (8 ½ x 11 inches / 215 x 280 mm), black/white graphics throughout; minimal advertising.
DEPT: "Director's Column," "Associate Director's Column," "Regional News," "A Point of View," "Regional Clips." (9/10-89).
TYPL: "A Family of Photographers," "Is it Tougher for a Woman to be a Photo Manager?," "Quayle Hunt: When Indiana's 'Favorite Son' Becomes US Vice-President, Accessibility isn't Quite as Easy as it Once Was," "Covering Vice-President Bush Wasn't Any Easier...Especially for Dayton, Ohio's WKEF News Photographer Ali Ghanbari, Who Was Born in Iran." (9/10-89).
SCHL: Bimonthly, 35 pp.
SPAN: Mar/Apr, 1983+
ISSN: 0746-9837

FOURTH ESTATE

SUB: "A weekly newspaper for advertisers and newspaper makers." (? - Nov 26, 1927).
SUB: "A weekly newspaper for the makers of newspapers." (Mar 1, 1894 - ?).
SUB: "A weekly newspaper for publishers, advertisers, advertising agents and allied interests."
PUBL: The Fourth Estate, 25 West 43rd St., New York, NY.
DESC: For some 30 years, *The Fourth Estate* provided definitive late-breaking news of advertising and newspaper publishing activities throughout the United States. Billing itself as a "newspaper," *The Fourth Estate* dispensed the facts of business, and let other publications deal in promotion, layout design, and other vagaries of the "downstairs shop." This serial was for the publisher, and championed the process of publishing a newspaper for profit. It was only right, therefore, that at the time of its demise, *The Fourth Estate* was absorbed by another business publication, *Editor and Publisher*. Magazine format; narrow four-column layout style with small graphics
DEPT: "Newspaper News," newsbriefs; "Note and Comment," newsbriefs; "Purely Personal," personal briefs; "Obituary Notes." (4-5-1894). "Up Through A Century," newspaper history profiles; "Romance in American Journalism," publisher profile; "About the Ad Women," newsbriefs; "News from Here and There--and Short News Flashes," "Live News and Notes of the International Advertising Association." (11-12-27).
TYPL: "One of the Oldest," "Brooklyn's Strike," "An Important Case," "The Newspaper and the Magazine." (4-5-1894). "Newspaper Advertising Brings Prompt Sales Response," "Country Newspaper Fills the Gap in National Advertising," "Advertising in French Canada," "Advertising and Trade Marks." (11-12-27).
SCHL: Weekly, 30 pp.
SPAN: Mar 1, 1894 - Nov 26, 1927//
ABSORBED BY
--Editor and Publisher (ISSN: 0013-094x).
LC: PN 4700.F6

✦ 4TH MEDIA JOURNAL, THE

SUB: "The monthly journal for interactive communications."
PUBL: Virgo Publishing, Inc., PO Box 5400, Scottsdale, AZ 85261.
DESC: With an April, 1990 debut, publisher Robert Titsch began this serial of the 900 telephone service industry, or is termed "the fourth medium," with a question: What is this new medium of applied telephony? Publisher Titsch: "..we think it is what you create when you marry the audiotex industry to the voice response industry and take that creation and marry it to the media industry. You now have a new industry--the 4th media." Whatever the applied description, there is little doubt that this is an exciting new medium of advertising and marketing opportunities for a very wide spectrum of American industries. The 900 telephone service is a cooperative, innovative effort between common-carrier telephone companies and marketing/promotion/sales firms. The individual caller is billed (via monthly home telephone bills) for each telephone call, usually a basic rate for the first minute, plus a reduced rate for each minute of interaction beyond the first minute. The resulting monies are then divided between the cooperating telephone company and its partner. In the relatively short period of time such services have been offered, they have proven to be a successful and, at times, lucrative enterprise for the cooperative partners. Services and costs-per-minute are as diverse as the individuals participating at any given moment in time. A public

broadcast station uses 900 services to generate new members. A newspaper syndicator uses 900 services to distribute "hot" news of new television programs. A rental agent uses the service to list owners of vacation rental properties. An entertainment employment service lists new openings. One issue for January, 1991 listed over 150 service bureau companies that were capable of offering 900 services to the American consumer. This medium has quickly attained wide favor among the various publics. Magazine format, full color throughout on coated paper stock (8 1/8 x 10 7/8 inches / 205 x 275 mm).
DEPT: "Editor's Letter," editorial column by Joyce Hemmen; "Washington Line," regulatory news and information column by Danny E. Adams; "Profile," of a successful 900 telephone service company; "Bulletin Board," extensive newsbriefs on 900 telephone service trends and developments; "Application," of 900 telephone service; "Resource Guide," product guide. (1-91).
TYPL: "Service Bureaus: Different Visions of a Dynamic Industry," "State Attorneys General Continue Examination of 900 Services," "Advertising--Don't Start Your Line Without It," "Walk 'n' Roll, Shoe Maker Puts Sole Into Concert Line." (1-91).
SCHL: Monthly, 95 pp.
SPAN: Apr, 1990+
DD: 384
ISSN: 1053-6213

Frame By Frame
Dec, 1982 - ?//
SEE: PENCIL TEST

✤ FREE SPEECH
PUBL: Commission on Freedom of Speech, Speech Communication Association, 5101 Backlick Rd., #E, Annandale, VA 22003.
DESC: This thrice-yearly newsletter is published by a subdivision of the Speech Communication Association dealing with the issue of freedom of speech in the United States. One or two articles per issue are featured, along with news notes concerning the Commission on Freedom of Speech of the SCA. A caveat is noted on each of the sampled issues from Fall, 1987 to Spring, 1990 that "*FREE SPEECH* is published as frequently as submitted and solicited material allows." Some issues represented special editions, such as the spring, 1990 publication, which Editor John Llewellyn described as "...a preponderance of scholarly opinion and commentary with less emphasis on current events of note." The sampled issue for 1987 was typewritten, photocopied on uncoated paper stock in stapled single-sheet format. The sampled issue for 1990 was typeset, black ink on single-sheet beige-color, uncoated paper stock. Both issues were: (8 1/2 x 11 inches / 215 x 280 mm).
DEPT: "Editor's Notes." (10-83). None. (Fall-89).

TYPL: "Emma Goldman, Ardent Anarchist," "Current Social and Political Trends and Their Implications for Future Litigation." (10-83). "Seen and Noted," "Court Actions," "Flag Matters," "Art For Art's Sake?" (fall-89).
SCHL: Three issues per year, 14 pp.
SPAN: 1970?+?

Freedom of Information News Digest
May 25, 1954 - Apr, 1959//
SEE: FOI DIGEST

✤ FRENDX
PUBL: North American Short Wave Association, 45 Wildflower Rd., Levittown, PA 19057.
DESC: This small-format periodical provides detailed information on the world of shortwave broadcasting, primarily for listeners of international radio broadcasts. Articles are reprinted from a variety of sources and include a section on the status (as reported by readers), of international shortwave stations. Some typewritten segments have photocopied graphics of varying quality. For the sampled issues of 1981 and 1986: various mixtures of typewritten and typeset copy on uncoated paper stock (some issue pages in color ink, and spot color on colored paper stock) in stapled journal format (5 1/4 x 8 1/2 inches / 135 x 215 mm).
DEPT: "Shortwave Center," newsbriefs; "SWC Computer Corner," "Contact," "Technical Topics," "Pappas on Programming," "Listeners Notebook," "QSL Reports," "Scoreboard," "Update," "Log Report." (9-84).
TYPL: "NIVI-NIVI: Hoax or Satire," "The Home Computer as an Aid to the Visually Impaired DXer," "DXing in Europe." (9-84).
SCHL: Monthly, 50 pp.
SPAN: ?+
ISSN: 0160-1989

✤ FRESH!
SUB: "The main motion in rock & video."
PUBL: Ashley Communications, Inc., PO Box 91878, Los Angeles, CA 90009.
DESC: *Fresh!* is a fanzine with a primary focus on today's black entertainer and celebrity. It is promotional, with an upbeat, positive coverage of top black entertainment talent; as well as an important means for new talent to become recognized in the radio, television, motion picture, and recording fields. Coverage on today's hottest performers is very thorough, with a large number of full-color pages on coated paper stock. Minimal advertising, which is very surprising for the quality and breadth of coverage within this serial published on a every-three-weeks schedule. Magazine format (8 x 10 7/8 inches / 205 x 275 mm), full color covers and star photo inserts, editorial content printed black/white on uncoated paper stock.

DEPT: "Spotlight," star newsbriefs; "Letters," "Profile," star biography; "Pen Pals," 'Find the friend you've been wanting'; "Fresh Facts," 'Here's your chance to find out everything you need to know about how to succeed in show business'; "Person to Person," advice column; "Photo of the Month," "Just Asking," questions posed to celebrities; "Hollywood Now," news and information column by Debi Fee; "Hot Off the Press!," unusual back-cover information page on black celebrities. (3- 17-90).
TYPL: "What Makes Hammer Happy?," "Janet & Bobby: What Makes Them so Special?," "Eric Gable Does Soul Train! You are There!," "Just Chillin' with Slick Rick," "The Wit and Widom of Watley--Jody, That is!" (3-17-90).
SCHL: Every three weeks, 65 pp.
SPAN: Jan 1, 1985+
VARIES
--? - ? as Record Review (ISSN: 0198-8573).
DD: 789
ISSN: 0886-9596
ABST: --Music Index (ISSN: 0027-4348)

FUNCTIONAL PHOTOGRAPHY

PUBL: The Press Centre Limited, 9-10 Old Bailey, London EC4, England.
DESC: *Functional Photography* featured the unique application of photography to industry. Articles were quite often of a technical nature, providing detailed (sometimes at the microscopic level), pictures concerning discussed issues. Subscriptions over the five-plus years of publication continued to build, but advertising revenues dropped to an unacceptable level by March, 1955 and *Functional Photography* came to an end. Editor Norman Hall informed readers that The Press Centre's more popular serial, *Photography*, would attempt to devote several pages each issue to "...subjects specially covered by this journal." Small magazine format.
DEPT: "Progress," "One Man's Work," profile; "New Products," "News Page," newsbriefs. (10-50).
TYPL: "Advances in Film Studio Lighting," "Developing the Latent Image," "Hospital Photography," "Photography at Dunlop's Research Centre." (10- 50).
SCHL: Bimonthly (? - Oct, 1950); Monthly (Dec, 1950 - Mar, 1955); 35 pp.
SPAN: 1949 - Mar, 1955//
LC: TR 1.F76

FUNCTIONAL PHOTOGRAPHY

SUB: "The magazine of photographic applications in science, technology & medicine."
SUB: "Visual documentation & communication in science, technology & medicine."
PUBL: PTN Publishing Co., 210 Crossways Park Drive, Woodbury, NY 11797.
DESC: This was a trade serial for photographers working in the professional application fields of science, technology, and medicine. Articles showcased unique photography equipment and applications. Typical features from one sampled issue included the means by which Skylab monitored climate change through aerial photography, or how NASA (National Aeronautics & Space Administration) utilized aerial photography of Nicaragua to "...evaluate its use for disaster assessment, support of relief efforts, reconstruction planning and geological analysis" connected with the early 1970s earthquake in that nation. Articles could also be highly technical in nature, as "A Color Schlieren System," editorially described as "Development of the system for use in conjunction with studies of separated compressible fluid flows; it is felt that the use of a color Schlieren will aid interpretation of the observed phenomena." It is an interesting "how-to" publication for the professional in this specialized photographic field. For sampled issue of 1974: stapled magazine format, black/white, spot and full-color pages (including cover), all on coated paper stock, advertising (8 ¼ x 11 ¼ inches / 210 x 285 mm).
DEPT: "New Products." (1-74). "Newsbeat," "New Products," "Book Reviews," "Micro/Macro Focus," unique photographic equipment; "Audio-Visual On-Line," production tips and comment. (1/2-88).
TYPL: "Skylab Monitors Climate Change," "Aerial Photography for Disaster Assessment and Damage," "A Color Schlieren System," "Telecentric Camera," "Ten Years of NASA Aerial Photography." (1-74). "Science Museum Features Unique Cell Wall," "The Reverse Projection Technique in Forensic Photogrammetry," "Zero Hazardous Photo Waste is Company Goal." (1/2-88).
SCHL: Quarterly? (Winter, 1966/1967 - Spring, 1968); Bimonthly (?+), 46 pp.
SPAN: Winter, 1966/1967 - May?, 1988//
VARIES
--Winter, 1966/1967 - Spring, 1968 as Photographic Applications in Science and Technology (ISSN: 0031-871x).
--Summer, 1968 - Jul, 1975 as Photographic Applications in Science, Technology and Medicine (ISSN: 0098-8227).
MERGED WITH
--Technical Photography (ISSN: 0040-0971) (to form) Tech Photo Pro Imaging Systems (ISSN: 1040-0141), Jun, 1988.
LC: TR 692.P5
DD: 778.3/05
ISSN: 0360-7216
ABST: --Computer & Control Abstracts (ISSN: 0036-8113)
--Electrical & Electronics Abstracts (ISSN: 0036-8105)
--GeoRef
--International Aerospace Abstracts (ISSN: 0020-5842)
--Physics Abstracts. Science Abstracts. Series A. (ISSN: 0036-8091)

FUNNYWORLD

SUB: "The world of animated films and comic art."
PUBL: ?, PO Box 1633, New York, NY 10001.
DESC: "*Funnyworld* is an amateur, non-profit magazine devoted to comic books, comic strips and animated cartoons, and is pubished at irregular intervals by Mike Barrier..." The relaxed editorial stance of the publication was evident from the masthead which invited readers to call the publisher anytime during the day where he was employed at the Arkansas Gazette. For the reader, *Funnyworld* was "the" authority for the latest news and always fascinating profiles of current and promising cartoonists and illustrators. For historians of this medium, this remains a venerable treasure chest of fascinating interviews, pictures, and sample strips of cartoonists and their works up through 1981. Issues up through May, 1969 were typewritten, and mimeographed with special inserts in stapled newsletter format on uncoated mimeograph paper stock. Beginning with the summer, 1970 issue: typeset black ink on uncoated paper stock in stapled newsletter format. Latter issues were black ink on uncoated paper stock, advertising, with full-color covers on heavy coated paper stock in stapled (some issues perfect-bound) magazine format. All issues shared same format size of (8 ½ x 11 inches / 215 x 280 mm).
DEPT: "The Funniest Animal: or, What Passes for *Funnyworld*'s Editorial Page," "Reviews," "Letters." (summer-70). "Letters." (spring-72). "Editorial and Letters," "Reviews." (fall-79).
TYPL: "Notes on the Underground," "Bob Clampett: an Interview," "Carl Barks Bibliography." (summer-70). "All in Color for Seventy-Five Cents," "A Vision of Katzenjammers," "Ub Iwerks, 1901 - 1971." (spring-72). "Screenwriter for a Duck," "Bambi and the Goof," "Destination: Animation." (fall-79).
SCHL: Quarterly 50 pp.
SPAN: Oct, 1966 - Apr, 1981//
LC: PN 6725.F86
DD: 741.5/973
ISSN: 0071-9943

ABST: --Film Literature Index (ISSN: 0093-6758)

✧ FUTUREHOME TECHNOLOGY NEWS

SUB: "The executive report on information and entertainment media."
PUBL: Phillips Publishing, Inc., 7811 Montrose Rd., Potomac, MD 20854.
DESC: "Are you missing out on profit-making opportunities in the marketplace for new residential products and services? Will the impending conference of audio, data and video leave you behind? Not if you subscribe to Phillips Publishing's *FUTUREHOME TECHNOLOGY NEWS*." This advertisement succinctly describes the biweekly newsletter; one that reports on the status and trends of home entertainment and information systems. The typewritten articles detail late-breaking developments under the departmental titles of: "Futurehome," general news; "Mergers & Acquisitions," corporate actions; "Washington," regulatory news; "Technology," "Legal," "Consumer Electronics," "On-Line Services," detailing on-line (via modem) computerized information services; and other news items in "News in Brief." The $395 yearly subscription rate (1990) is justified in today's highly competitive electronics industry. Typewritten, some graphics in a newsletter format.
DEPT: "Futurehome," "Mergers & Acquisitions," "Washington," "Technology," "Legal," "Consumer Electronics," "News in Brief," "On-Line Services." (10-8-90).
TYPL: "GTE Tests Fiber Optic-Based Prototype Video-On-Demand System," "Matsushita Joins Sony in Hollywood Gold Rush," "Is Cable Reregulation Dead? Not So Fast," "Digital Radio Laboratories Inks Tuner Pact With Hitachi," "DAT Legal Battles Threaten Tandy Recordable CD." (10-8-90).
SCHL: Biweekly, 8 pp.
SPAN: Sep 10, 1990+
ISSN: 1051-9971

G

✤ GAMBIT

SUB: "International Theatre Review."
PUBL: John Calder, Ltd., 18 Brewer St., London W1R 4AS, England.
DESC: *Gambit* is a fascinating publication for the theatrical field, structured by unique themed issues, and deriving much of its dynamic energy from contemporary playwrights, critics, producers, directors, and production companies. A sampling of previous themes included "Sartre on Theatre," "Theatre Censorship," "Children's Theatre," "German Theatre," "Theatre Subsidy Issue," "Television," and a "Young British Dramatists Issue." For the sampled issue of 1977, a back-cover synopsis provided a succinct overview of that issue's contents: "*Gambit* 31 is devoted to a consideration of Political Theatre in Britain, currently seeing a remarkable resurgence of plays that examine the political problems of Britain and of the world. A discussion between a group of directors and writers brings out many of the present preoccupations and problems. This issue also contains the full text of an important play by Howard Barker, 'That Good Between Us', set in a future Britain where a Labour government finds itself obliged to behave in a frighteningly authoritarian way. There are also articles and reviews of recent productions." A wonderful resource and thinking-person's guide to contemporary theatre. For the sampled issue of 1977: perfect-bound journal format, black ink on uncoated paper, with reddish-brown ink on coated paper stock for the cover, some advertising (5 ½ x 8 ½ inches / 140 x 215 mm).
DEPT: "Editorial," "Reviews of Plays," "Reviews of Opera," "Reviews of Books," "Theatre Diary," news and happenings column by Burbage. (#31-77).
TYPL: "Political Theatre in Britain Today," "That Good Between Us." (#31-77).
SCHL: Quarterly, 150 pp.
SPAN: ?+
ISSN: 0016-4283

✤ GANNETT CENTER JOURNAL

PUBL: Gannett Foundatioon Media Center and the Gannett Foundation, Columbia University, 2950 Broadway, New York, NY 10027.
DESC: "The *Gannett Center Journal* is a quarterly forum for scholars, practitioners and informed commentators to discuss topical themes of enduring importance to the mass media and the public." This journal of international repute is published by "The Gannett Foundation Media Center, an operating program of the Gannett Foundation, [which] is an institute for the advanced study of mass communication and technological change. Through a variety of programs, it seeks to enhance media professionalism, foster greater public understanding of how the media work, strengthen journalism education and examine the effects on society of mass communication and communications technology." An outstanding forum for serious discussion of numerous issues, *Gannett Center Journal* focuses on the continuing evolution of global media, and their varied impacts upon international cultures, nations, societies, and individuals. One sampled issue explored the world's 20 most important newspapers, the development of global television service, third world press, and the "art of international advertising." Graphics are included when appropriate; journal format on uncoated paper stock (6 x 9 inches / 150 x 225 mm). Well recommended.
DEPT: "Book Review." (fall-90).
TYPL: "Media Globalism in the Age of Consumer Sovereignty," "The Business of a Free Press," "Singlethink: Thoughts on the Havel Episode," "They Don't Teach Survival Skills: Journalism Education in Africa," "Decline of a Polemical Press: The Case of France." (fall-90).
SCHL: Quarterly, 150 pp.
SPAN: Spring, 1987+
LC: P 87 .G36
DD: 001.51/05
ISSN: 0893-8342
ABST: --Public Affairs Information Service Bulletin (ISSN: 0033-3409)

✤ GANNETTEER

SUB: "A magazine for Ganett Group people."
PUBL: Gannett Company, 55 Exchange St., Rochester, NY 14614.
DESC: In this in-house publication for the workers of the large-based Gannett communications chain, articles profile employees' work, and participation in community activities. A dynamic layout design enhances the articles about the Gannett Company and its employees.
DEPT: "Short Takes," briefs of individual Gannett newspapers; "Changing Roles for Gannetteers," job promotions and changes; "Gannett News Highlights," corporate news briefs.
TYPL: "How 'First Place' Spot was Captured," "Drama Looms in Falls Rescue," "A Political Drama Stuns the Country." (11-73).
SCHL: Monthly, 40 pp.
SPAN: Jan, 1955+
DD: 070
ISSN: 0437-163x

✤ GAZETTE

SUB: "The international journal for mass communication studies."
PUBL: Institute of the Science of the Press, Box 269, The Hague, Netherlands.
DESC: A 1984 publication noted, "The *Gazette* is now entering its 30th year of publication, and is known as one of the best international periodicals in the field of mass communication. It provides a forum for scientific discussion that includes the international exchange and comparison of ideas for editors and journalists as well as for all those who are interested in public relations, politics, government information services, economics, and advertising." A sampled issue for 1991 stated the editorial philosophy in more formal terms: "The Editorial Board of *GAZETTE* has chosen to develop the editorial policy with respect to the following central fields: --the role of communication in international relations and in international understanding; --communication and development; --legal and socio-cultural aspects of new information technologies with special attention to 'integration'; [and] --communication policy and communication planning." The text of earlier issues was in English, French, and German; latter issues in English only. For sampled issues of 1991: black ink editorial content and cover on uncoated paper stock (cover on coated paper), limited advertising in perfect-bound journal format (6 ¼ x 9 ½ inches / 160 x 240 mm).
DEPT: "Book Review." (#3-84). None. (5-91).
TYPL: "Modernization and the Media in China," "The Nicaraguan Press: Revolutionary, Developmental or Socially Responsible?," "'A Little Good News:' The Treatment of Developmental News in Selected Third World Newspapers," "Ownership Patterns of Nigerian Newspapers," "Foreign Correspondents and the New World Information Order." (#3-84). "Media Reform in China Since 1978: Background Factors, Problems and Future Trends," "Contraceptive Social Marketing in the Third World: A Case of Multiple Transfer," "Contradictions in Brilliant Eyes," "Space WARC: A New Regulatory Environment for Communication Satellites?" (5-91).
SCHL: Quarterly (? - #2-84); Bimonthly (#3-84+), 90 pp.
SPAN: Jan, 1955+
LC: PN 4699.G3
ISSN: 0016-5492

General Electric Company Review

Mar 2, 1903 - Apr, 1907//
SEE: GENERAL ELECTRIC REVIEW

GENERAL ELECTRIC REVIEW

PUBL: General Electric Company, Schenectady, NY.
DESC: The *General Electric Review* "...is distributed to scientists and engineers throughout industrial, consulting, educational, professional society, and government groups, both domestic and foreign." The *Review* began as a technical manual in the early 1900s, becoming in later years a more general guide to technological developments in General Electric. Early issues remain an excellent resource for historical studies. From May 1907 - Nov, 1923 this periodical was published by the General Electric Publications Department: from Dec, 1923 - Nov, 1925 it was published by the General Electric Publicity Department.
DEPT: "Book Review," (1912). "Editorial," (9-58).
TYPL: "The Nature of Transients in Electrical Engineering," "Some Special Applications of Gasoline-Electric and Storage Battery Automobile Equipment," "Alternating Current Apparatus Troubles," "Synchronous Motors in Preference to Induction Motors for Low Speed Work." (3-12). "Space Technology Spurs New Development Philosophies," "Engineering Headlights for Safer Driving," "How Television is Helping to Improve Education," "What is the Future of Radiation Chemistry in Industrial Processing." (9-58).
SCHL: Monthly (1903-1951); Bimonthly (1952+), 50 pp.
SPAN: Mar 2, 1903 - Nov, 1958//
VARIES
--Mar 2, 1903 - Apr, 1907 as General Electric Company Review.
LC: TK 1.G5
ISSN: 0095-9480
ABST: --Engineering Index
--Industrial Arts Index

General Radio Experimenter, The

Jun, 1926 - Oct/Dec, 1970//
(ISSN: 0095-9499)
SEE: GR TODAY

Geo. P. Rowell & Co's Advertising Agency Circular

Nov, 1866,//
SEE: ADVERTISERS GAZETTE

Get Animated

Feb, 1985 - ?, 1986//
SEE: GET ANIMATED! UPDATE.

✤ GET ANIMATED! UPDATE.

PUBL: John Cawley, PO Box 1582, Burbank, CA 91507.
DESC: Editor/Publisher John Cawley has created a work of love in *Get Animated!*, a newsletter about the business and creative sides of animation, with a specific emphasis on the artists, the motivations, and developing trends in commercial animation. Editorial staff credentials were briefly mentioned in the February, 1985 premiere issue, detailing their extensive commercial experience. Editorial staff members have worked

commercially for almost every animation center in Southern California, and this expertise is apparent in the quality of the publication. Articles in sample issues ranged from proper seating arrangements to avoid backaches, to philosophical approaches to "He-Man & the Masters of the Universe;" from commercial international news of England, Australia, and Spain, to a profile of Australian animation studios; and the ongoing issue of "Offshore Animation." After a nine month period of suspension, the publication emerged once again in Nov, 1986 as a monthly newsletter, minus the reviews, articles and artwork of earlier issues, and featuring "The World of Animation from cartoons to television, to computers, to puppets, to video." This is a publication for those who want to know what is occurring in the commercial animation industry, a goal accomplished with enthusiasm, an eye to detail, and a search for accuracy in editorial content. "Must" reading for today's commercial animator. Magazine format; black/white graphics.

DEPT: "Checking," commentary column by John Cawley; "GA! Newsreel," animation newsbriefs; "The Foreign Desk," world animation news; "Notes From New York," animation news column by Jerry Beck; "The Wayback Machine," historical newsnotes column by Jim Korkis; "Reviews," "Recent Home Video Titles," "GA! Feature Guide," feature animated films in progress. (11-85).
TYPL: "Animation: An Evolution for the Eighties," "A Modest Look at Cosgrove-Hall," "Offshore Animation." (11-85).
SCHL: Bimonthly (Feb, 1985 - ?); Monthly (Nov, 1986 - ?); Every six weeks (?+), 16 pp.
SPAN: Feb, 1985+
VARIES
--Feb, 1985 - ?, 1986 as Get Animated!
SUSPENDED
--Jan, 1986 - Oct, 1986.
DD: 791 11
ISSN: 0892-5968

✤ GF MAGAZINE

PUBL: Gannett Foundation, 1101 Wilson Blvd., Arlington, VA 22209.
DESC: The Gannett Foundation, founded by the Rochester-based Gannett Company, a major media conglomerate, is dedicated to the premise of a better society for all American citizens. A segment of that premise is based upon the professionalism and responsibility of the mass media. Hence, the reason for this quarterly publication, a showcase of social community programs that work, and an exploration of the quest by news media to create a better society. The "Letters to the Editor" column provides strong testimony to the value and impact of this publication. For the sampled issue of 1989: stapled magazine format with full-color spot and black-ink editorial content in a very effective layout design on coated paper stock (9 x 11 inches / 230 x 280 mm).

DEPT: "Giving," "Communities," "Literacy," "Media," "Profile." (winter-89).
TYPL: "Cheat Charity," "A Voice They Can Trust," "The Invisible Minority." (winter-89).
SCHL: Quarterly, 25 pp.
SPAN: Spring?, 1989+

Glenn Hauser's Independent Publication

? - ?//
SEE: REVIEW OF INTERNATIONAL BROADCASTING

Global Movie Marketing

Jan, 1962//
SEE: MOVIE/TV MARKETING

✤ GOLDEN AGE OF COMICS

PUBL: New Media Publishing, Inc., 1518 East Fowler Ave., Tampa, FL 33612.
DESC: "*The Golden Age of Comics* is the only magazine which regularly presents uncut reprints of the stories from the best years of comics, when they were fresher and less restrained...when they were learning just what comics were really about and didn't have the time to present stale old cliches...every story in every book was fresh and exciting and many of them were better than anything we have ever seen since. *The Golden Age of Comics* gathers the best selection of stories from these spectacular years and presents them on white paper with careful reproduction. And *The Golden Age of Comics* fleshes out the subject with carefully researched and well written articles and interviews which help to illuminate the stories in their proper perspective. The true comic book fan will not want to miss these gems; the comic book reader will never be able to afford the fine collection here offered for less than a dollar per story; and the comic book historian will find the material invaluable reference." Publisher Hal Schuster has performed a true public service in reproducing these wonderful cartoons from the 1940s era for a whole new generation to read and appreciate. The sampled issue contained three articles, the majority of the publication given over to reproducing the comic pages themselves. Articles are well-written, articulate and informative. A three-part series on Walt Kelly and the Pogo comic strip was one of a number of articles that was very well done. Great care has been taken to reproduce comics from "best available" copies, but at times one must recognize the technical problem of transferring color comic pages with little original contrast to a black/white print medium that demands greater contrast range. The authenticity is maintained, but at a price. Despite this problem, *Golden Age of Comics* is an excellent resource for "stripographies," comic character development, and the philosophy behind the artwork. Stapled

magazine format, black/white editorial content on uncoated paper stock with full-color cover on coated paper stock (8 ½ x 11 inches / 215 x 280 mm).
DEPT: None. (1-84).
TYPL: "Unreality, Fancy An' Fantasy," "Doc Savage," "MLJ Comics," "Mankillers," "Commando in Mufti." (1-84).
SCHL: Monthly, 55 pp.
SPAN: Jun?, 1982+

✤ GOOD NEWS: CHRISTIANS IN JOURNALISM

PUBL: Crown Communications, PO Box 11626, Saint Paul, MN 55111-0626.
DESC: In the premiere issue of January, 1987, Editor Steven M. Deyo told readers that this publication was "...for Christians who are journalists, for journalists interested in the issues of media ethics, for students considering a career in journalism, and all who seek excellence in mass communications." The January, 1988 issue went on to report that "its purpose is to encourage and inform Christian professionals and students in the field of journalism, especially those working in the secular mass media." Two or three articles per issue on a wide variety of topics linking Christianity together with media are featured. For the sampled issues of 1987 and 1988: single-sheet stapled, photocopied pages, black ink on uncoated paper stock (8 ½ x 11 inches / 215 x 280 mm).
DEPT: "News File," "Clipping Comment," "Correspondence." (4-87).
TYPL: "James Whalen: Teaching the Write Stuff," "Dangerous Denny." (4-87).
SCHL: Quarterly?, 8 pp.
SPAN: Jan, 1987+?

✤ GOOD OLD DAYS

SUB: "The magazine that remembers the best."
SUB: "Featuring stories, photos, illustrations of the happy days gone by."
PUBL: House of White Birches, 306 East Parr Rd., Berne, IN 46711.
DESC: "Relive the days when you could kick up your heels and live life to its fullest! Remember wonderful times and places. Take a nostalgic glance at the way things were in America from 1900 to 1949 with *Good Old Days* magazine. The essence of yesteryear is captured in the stories, photos, comics and features in every issue of *Good Old Days*! Read about the early days of radio and television. Look back to the marvelous time-honored days that your grandparents loved and lived in." This is a wonderful piece of historic and nostalgic work concerning everyday life for the first 50 years of the twentieth century. One sampled issue covered such media items as the Marx Brothers, carnivals, pulp novels, western film serials featuring a Roy Rogers interview, comic strips, "hootchy-kootchy" shows, sheet music, and a day (all-day for the younger set) at the movies, circa 1930s. For the 1990 sampled issue: stapled magazine format, full color cover; editorial content black ink on newsprint (8 x 10 ¾ inches / 205 x 275 mm). Despite the problem of newsprint, this is a magazine that is enjoyable to read, and a multifaceted resource on the public's use of media and the performing arts from 1900 through 1949.
DEPT: "Letters to the Editor," "Country Store," "The Passing Scene," celebrities remembered; "Good Old Days in the Kitchen," recipes and rememberences; "Walkin' in the Past," "Old Time Music," reprinted sheet music; "Nostalgia Quiz," "Looking Hollywood Way," film entertainment of yesteryear; "Nostalgic News," 'Excerpts from--old time newspapers across the nation-- early 1900s'; "Old Time Comic," reprinted comic strip; "Country Things," explained and remembered. (8-90).
TYPL: "The Skinny-Dip My Brother Never Forgot," "King of the Cowboys," "Dead as a Doornail?," "Catching Up with Jesse Owens," "General Pershing and the New Shoes." (8-90).
SCHL: Monthly, 65 pp.
SPAN: 1964+
ISSN: 0046-6158

✤ GOREZONE

SUB: "America's #1 horror magazine."
SUB: "All the splatter that matters!"
SUB: "Can you take it?"
PUBL: Starlog Communications International, Inc., 475 Park Avenue South, New York, NY 10016.
DESC: "Devoted to horror films and TV. Interviews and articles on Freddy, Jason, Leatherface and all your favorites! Dozens of yummy (and yucky!) photos! Plus horror fiction! Each issue also contains four, giant, fold-out posters, measuring a horrifying 16 x 22 inches! Guaranteed to make your teeth chatter and your flesh crawl! *Gorezone* is the mag that weeds out the wimps from the horror readership. Each issue is packed with the profiles, reviews, previews, giant posters, makeup FX how-to, fiction and assorted goodies every splatter fiend demands!" With almost every page running red with simulated blood and gore, it would be difficult to argue with this premise. *Gorezone* is indeed NOT for the faint of heart, with graphics that display the fascinating (time consuming and artistic) craft of makeup, creature development, and cinematography that makes the "steak tartre" in all of us reach for the ceiling. For fans of this entertainment genre, *Gorezone*, is a wonderful adventure, showcasing the work of talented artists; and informing readers of new horror product about to appear on their neighborhood silver screens. Magazine format (8 x 10 ⅞ inches / 205 x 275 mm), with more-than-full color graphics throughout.

DEPT: "Gut Reactions," letters; "Makeup FX Lab," fascinating how-to makeup series; "HorrorScope," what's new in horror films; "Video Watchdog®" video releases column by Tim Lucas; "Future Shock," upcoming articles. (7/8-90).
TYPL: "Profile: Joe Dante," "Piece O' Mind," "Profile: Steve Johnson," "Review: 'Dr. Caligari'," "Blood Fest." (7/8-90).
SCHL: Bimonthly, 70 pp.
SPAN: May, 1988+
DD: 791 11
ISSN: 0896-8802

✧ GOSSIP

SUB: "Movies, parties, television."
PUBL: Laufer Publishing Co., 7060 Hollywood Blvd., Hollywood, CA 90028.
DESC: "Most people only dream about meeting their favorite celebrities. Now, thanks to Our Ms. Rona you can see and even go steady with the stars once a month by subscribing to *Rona Barrett's GOSSIP* magazine! You'll get a parade of Superstars. Exclusive Scoops, Full Color Photos and even more Colorful quotes;" and "Treat yourself to an 'addiction' that isn't fattening, expensive, or in any other way dangerous to your health. Thousands of readers constantly write us to tell Rona that her magazine is so juicy and so entertaining that they're 'positively addicted'! But--unlike cigarette smoking and other nasty addictions-- the Surgeon General hasn't declared RBG 'hazardous to your health'." The playful spirit of this serial of the stars reflects the "don't take it too seriously" philosophies of Executive Editor Rona Barrett and Publisher Charles Laufer. Cutlines, pictures, and articles celebrate the crazy, wacky world of the Hollywood and media celebrities; including Burt Reynolds, Dinah Shore, Glenda Jackson, Patricia Neal, Robert Shaw, Ryan O'Neal, Lee Majors, Sean Connery and a host of others. While the majority of the sampled issues were published on newsprint (some two-color), other editorial pages were in full-color on coated paper stock. Minimal advertising. Sampled issue for May, 1976: (8 1/8 x 10 7/8 inches / 205 x 275 mm).
DEPT: "Inside Gossip," inside front cover page; "Rona Barrett's Gossip," 'Our Ms. Rona with the latest--and the best!' column by Rona Barrett; "One Minute Interview," "Global Gossip," 'Whether it's happening in Paris, London, or even Timbuktu, Our Man is on the scene to give you the lowdown on the swinging jet-setters!'; "Rona's Would You Believe?," 'Unbelieveable tidbits from Rona!' column by Rona Barrett; "Bulletin Board," 'Swap star stuff with other readers!'; "For the Record," "Lowdown on the music scene' column by Dianne Bennett; "Dear Rona," 'What you have to say to our Ms. Rona!' column by Rona Barrett; "Couplings," 'Hollywood's newest twosomes--and a few untwosomes'; "Channel to Channel," 'What's happening behind the TV scene'; "Nothing But the Truth," 'You ask it--we'll tell you the truth'; "Rona's Bonus Scrapbook," 'Nostalgic photos from Rona's own album' column by Rona Barrett; "Close Up," star profile; "Up the Mailbox," 'What you have to say about the stars!'; "Rona's Odds & Ends," 'So odd--it'll be the end of you!'. (5-76).
TYPL: "Tatum O'Neal Says She's NOT 'Growing Up Too Fast'!," "Alfred Hitchcock's 'The Family Plot'," "John Wayne Digs Garbage!?," "Robert Conrad: Shake Hands and Come Out Fighting," "Kate Hepburn Flashes at Fan with Flashbulbs!" (5-76).
SCHL: Monthly, 85 pp.
SPAN: May, 1972?+
VARIES
--May, 1972? - Dec, 1980 as Rona Barrett's Gossip (ISSN: 0199-1590).
ISSN: 0273-7493

✧ GR TODAY

PUBL: General Radio Co., Concord, MA.
DESC: "To supplement the technical information already contained in the leading radio magazines, the *General Radio Experimenter* will be issued every month to provide the experimenter with reliable data and helpful suggestions which may be put to good use in the home laboratory." (Jun, 1926). This was a promotional publication for General Radio Company products, providing explanations of components, applications, and suggestions for future developments. Issues of the 1970s moved from home experimentation to business and educational applications.
DEPT: None.
TYPL: "A Discussion of Condenser Plate Shapes." (3-27). "A Big Little-Brother Preamplifier," "Expansion in the Resistor Family," "Solid-State, Programmable Attenuators." (10/12-70).
SCHL: Monthly (? - ?); Quarterly (? - ?); 4 pp.
SPAN: Jun, 1926+?
VARIES
--Jun, 1926 - Oct/Dec, 1970 as General Radio Experimenter, The (ISSN: 0095-9499).
SUSPENDED
--Sep, 1926 - Apr, 1928.
LC: TK 6540.G4

✧ GRAFFITI

SUB: "A bimonthly review of film and video animation."
SUB: "The newsletter of ASIFA - Hollywood."
PUBL: International Animated Film Society/ASIFA-Hollywood, 11442 Marquette Lane, Pomona, CA 91766.
DESC: This bimonthly newsletter by the ASIFA-Hollywood chapter of the International Animated Film Society provides news and information on ASIFA members through profiles and interviews, newsbriefs concerning projects in production and related events, plus general news of the animation community in Hollywood and other ASIFA chapters world wide. This is a publication for the working professional, detailing issues such as client relationships, contracts, guild/union activities, new technology, and trends in anima-

tion. Numerous black/white graphics provide both reference to animated product and creator alike. An interesting and informative serial. Magazine format.
DEPT: "The Wisdom of Solomon," column by Charles Solomon; "Animation Profiles," column by Harry Love; "Newsreel," animation newsbriefs. (vol 8, #2).
TYPL: "Raisin Eyebrows in Advertising," "Follow Your Nose," "Engineering Entertainment." (vol 8, #2).
SCHL: Monthly (Oct, 1979 - Nov, 1981); Bimonthly (Dec, 1981+), 15 pp.
SPAN: ?+
DD: 791 11
ISSN: 0748-6324

✤ GRAMOPHONE
SUB: "News and reviews."
PUBL: General Gramophone Publications, 177-179 Kenton Rd., Harrow, Middlesex HA3 0HA, England.
DESC: This is a publication of reviews; reviews of new music, spoken word, and special collections; reviews of new audio equipment; and reviews of talented rising stars in the non-pop music world. While all three areas are covered very nicely, the emphasis is placed squarely on music reviews. Page after page of 3-column compact type critique each new recording. Historical antecedent, philosophical musings, aesthetics of tonal and spatial qualities all receive their due from a faculty of informed, erudite reviewers. Reading a single issue is an education in itself, and makes for a more informed listener, more appreciative of the care and toil which is invested in recordings. Bravo to both publisher, Anthony Pollard, and to a most delightful, informed editorial staff dedicated to bringing all the news and views associated with non-popular music recordings and audio equipment for the contemporary consumer. For sampled issue of 1989: perfect-bound magazine format, full-color throughout on coated paper stock (8 ½ x 11 inches / 215 x 280 mm).
DEPT: "Editorial Notes," "Correspondence," "Commentary," "Equipment Reviews," "New Products." (5-80). "Correspondence," letters; "Editorial," "News & Views," "A Quarterly Retrospect," 'The gramophone and the voice' column by John Steane; "Record Reviews," "Audio," product review; "New Releases," 'A listing of new compact disc, cassette and LP releases scheduled to appear this month'. (4-89).
TYPL: "New Record and Cassette Releases," "A quarterly Retrospect," "Here and There...". (5-80). "Andrew Litton," "Hi-Fi 89: Ivor Humphreys Reports From the Bristol Show," "DAT From Nakamichi," "Music We Thought We Knew," "Recording a Career." (4-89).
SCHL: Monthly, 100 pp.
SPAN: Apr, 1923+
VARIES
--Apr, 1923 - ? as Gramophone (ISSN: 0017-310x).
--? - ? as Gramophone Including Compact Disc News and Reviews.
ABSORBED
--Vox, Dec, 1930.
--Radio Critic, Dec, 1930.
--Broadcast Review, Dec, 1930.
LC: ML 5.G65
DD: 789.9/13/05
ISSN: 0017-310x
ABST: --Music Index (ISSN: 0027-4348)

Gramophone
Apr, 1923 - ?//
(ISSN: 0017-310x)
SEE: GRAMOPHONE

Gramophone Including Compact Disc News and Reviews
? - ?//
SEE: GRAMOPHONE

GRAND ILLUSIONS
SUB: "The journal of the Emerson College Film Society."
PUBL: Emerson Film Society, 148 Beacon St., Boston, MA 02116.
DESC: This Boston-based publication, a project of Emerson College students, is an excellent review of motion pictures past and present. Patterned after Renoir's La Grande Illusion, the magazine notes that it is "devoted to cinema, our most intimate medium, with a universality that is the beauty of the art." Of special note are exclusive interviews with noted filmmakers. Many varied production stills.
DEPT: "Works in Progress," an unusual section detailing major film studio activity as 'shooting,' 'post-production,' and 'future projects;' "Independent Cinema," news on independent filmmakers.
TYPL: "Michael Ritchie's America," "Robert Wise: Part One; The RKO Years," "Tay Garnett: An American Classic." (winter-77).
SCHL: Quarterly, 50 pp.
SPAN: Feb, 1977 - Summer, 1980//

✤ GRAPHIC
SUB: "An industry promotion quarterly."
PUBL: Graphic Arts Association of Michigan, 320 Lafayette Blvd., Detroit, MI.
DESC: This trade periodical provided interesting profiles of publishers, and general commentary on the graphics trade in the state of Michigan. This was a serial of encouragement and a showcase for sample products, not a vehicle for late-breaking industry news and opinion. Valued for its approaches to innovative printing techniques.
DEPT: "Editorial." (summer-55).
TYPL: "Four Sides of Customer Satisfaction," "Giant Among the Mailers," "Printing Services for the Suburbs," "The True Larceny Artists." (summer-55).
SCHL: Quarterly, 35 pp.

SPAN: Summer, 1955+?
LC: NC 1.G73

✢ GRAPHIC ANTIQUARIAN

SUB: "The magazine for collectors of photographica."
SUB: "For historians and collectors of photographic paraphernalia and images."
PUBL: Blake Enterprises, 4213 Princess Place Drive, Wilmington, NC 28401.
DESC: For the photographic historian and collector of same, *Graphic Antiquarian* provides a marvelous forum for historical review, and current-day collectors and equipment. Mass communication scholars will discover a valuable resource in the detailed articles and reproductions of very early photographs and accompanying equipment. Stereoscopes, magic lanterns, glass plates, collectors, inventors, and manufacturers all receive their due.
DEPT: "Antiquarian Activities and Letters," "Information Please," 'about collector's items that aren't completely identifiable;' "Meet the Collectors," "Equipment Showcase," "Editor's Desk." (10-70).
TYPL: "Photographed by Brady," "Where Camera Buffs Compete," "Nadar--Darling of the Boulevards," "Gas Lights, Bicycles and Cameras," "Processing for Permanence." (10-70).
SCHL: Quarterly 30 pp.
SPAN: Jul, 1970+
LC: TR 250.G73
ISSN: 0017-3274

✢ GRAPHIC ARTS

SUB: "Supplement to Industrial and Commercial Photographer."
PUBL: Distinctive Publications, Ltd., Croydon, England.
DESC: "Covering the uses of equipment and materials in small offset printing, plan copying, photocopying, microfilming, photo-composition, print circuit manufacture, etc." This 25-page supplement published six times yearly, provided a special section for the trade aspects noted above. This was a specialized supplement for the shop manager and technicians providing news of techniques and new equipment.
DEPT: "What's New in Graphic Arts." (2-71).
TYPL: "Recent Advances in Direct Screen Separation Techniques," "How to Obtain Well-Shaped Dots from Grainy Films on Enlargers." (2-71).
SCHL: Bimonthly 25 pp.
SPAN: ?+?
LC: TR 925.G77

GRAPHIC ARTS, THE

SUB: "For printers and users of printing." (Vol 1 - 3).
SUB: "A magazine for printers and users of printing."
SUB: "The monthly magazine of the craftsmanship of advertising."
PUBL: The Graphic Arts Company, 516 Atlantic Ave., Boston, MA.
DESC: "*The Graphic Arts* is to deal with the business of printing. Example is always so much more convincing than text, that new printing establishments and other equipment will be fully illustrated, with critical comment upon the important features. ...By the same treatment of printing press products--instead of reviews, the latest developments in all the reproductive arts, in typography and design will be demonstrated by actual exhibits. This will constitute reference material upon which new work can be based." True to its word, each issue of *The Graphic Arts* was a lavish showcase of the printing art, providing not only details on printed samples, but also the weight, name and other characteristics of the serial's paper stock as well. All of the better printed samples have tissue overlays; overall, a quality serial for the printing and publishing trade.
DEPT: "Business Notes," "Editorial." (3-11). "Editorial," "Pamphlet Cover," samples. (5-15).
TYPL: "An Achievement in Two-Color Printing," "Efficient Catalogue Illustration," "Concrete Buildings for the Printing and Publishing Business," "Getting Out of the Cow Paths." (3-11). "An Innovation in Catalogue Making," "Combination Reductions in All-Over Half-Tone Screen," "The Remarkable Amount of Overland Automobile Advertising." (5-15).
SCHL: Monthly (Irregular Jul/Aug, 1912 - May/Jun, 1913); 40 pp.
SPAN: Jan, 1911 - Jun, 1915//
VARIES
--Jan, 1911 - Apr, 1911 as Graphic Arts for Printers and Users of Printing.
LC: Z 110.G86

Graphic Arts for Printers and Users of Printing

Jan, 1911 - Apr, 1911//
SEE: GRAPHIC ARTS, THE

✢ GRAPHIC ARTS MONTHLY

SUB: "The magazine of the printing industry."
PUBL: Cahners Publishing Co., 249 West 17th St., New York, NY 10011.
DESC: This business monthly has a primary focus at the production level of a printing plant. Articles and advertisements speak to technical problems, new developments in equipment, quality standards, and the general state of production room operation. Articles are aimed at production, management and sales in commercial printing operations involving such media as newspapers, books, screen and package printing, and other forms of lithography. Editorially, the purpose of *Graphic Arts Monthly* is "...to provide readers with technological advances and provide information to help them lower costs, increase productivity, en-

hance quality and maximize safety." Numerous advertisements and articles profiling equipment and printing plants are included.
DEPT: "Mailbox," letters; "Calendar," "News Notes," "Editors Notebook," editorial; "Publishers Perspective," editorial; "Equipment/Supplies," "Literature/Samples," "Meetings/Conventions," "People," "Companies," "Washington Newsletter," column by Bob Kling; "Hows Your Advertising?," column by George Griffin; "Selling," column by Kenneth Garner; "Estimating," column by Gerald Silver; "Paper," column by William Bureau; "Composing Room," column by Frank Higgason; "Phototopography," column by Carl Palmer.
TYPL: "Surge of Product Introductions Greets New Year," "Printing Industry Rates High in Agency Competition," "International Printing Shows Impress Visitor," "Standards in Graphic Arts: Early Plate Specs." (1-81).
SCHL: Monthly (except June), 140 pp.
SPAN: Jan, 1938+
FROM MERGER OF
--Graphic Arts Monthly, The (and) Printing Industry.
VARIES
--Jan, 1938 - Oct, 1987 as Graphic Arts Monthly and the Printing Industry (ISSN: 0017-3312).
ABST: --ABI/Informer
--Abstract Bulletin of the Institute of Paper Chemistry (ISSN: 0020-3033)
--Art and Archaeology Technical Abstracts (ISSN: 0004-2994)
--Business Periodical Index (ISSN: 0007-6961)
--Communication Abstracts
--Printing Abstracts (ISSN: 0031-109x)
--Trade and Industry Index

Graphic Arts Monthly and the Printing Industry

Jan, 1938 - Oct, 1987//
(ISSN: 0017-3312)
SEE: GRAPHIC ARTS MONTHLY

Graphic Arts Review

Jan, 1938 - ?//
SEE: MID-ATLANTIC GRAPHIC ARTS REVIEW

Graphic Arts Unionist

Nov, 1964 - Nov/Dec, 1977//
(ISSN: 0017-3363)
SEE: GRAPHIC COMMUNICATOR

✣ GRAPHIC COMMUNICATOR

SUB: "The newspaper of the Graphic Communications Union."
SUB: "Official organ of Lithographers and Photoengravers International Union."
PUBL: Graphic Arts International Union, 1900 L St., N.W., Washington, DC 20036.
DESC: This serial served as official news organ for members of the Lithographers and Photoengravers International Union. Unlike other similar union publications, *Graphic Arts Unionist* also provided instruction on craft techniques to the readership through an informative series of articles. Magazine format.
DEPT: "The Craft at Work," unique section of craft techniques; "News of General Interest." (11-64).
TYPL: "Newspaper Publishers and Unions Launch Joint Technological Study," "The Impact on Lithography of Web Offset," "Running Lightweight Paper," "The Use of the New Lateral Reverse Film." (1-65).
SCHL: Eleven times per year [except August], (? - ?); Bi-monthly (? - Nov/Dec, 1977); Monthly [except Jan and Sep] (Feb, 1978 - Jun 30, 1983); Nine issues per year (Jan, 1987+), 50 pp.
SPAN: Nov, 1964+
FROM MERGER OF
--American Photo Engraver, The (ISSN: 0097-3297), (and) Lithographers Journal, Nov, 1964.
VARIES
--Nov, 1964 - Nov/Dec, 1977 as Graphic Arts Unionist (ISSN: 0017-3363).
--Feb, 1978 - Jun 30, 1983 as Union Tabloid (ISSN: 0275-8342).
DD: 331
ISSN: 0746-3626

✣ GRAPHIC DESIGN: USA

SUB: "News, ideas & trends for America's largest audited circulation of graphic designers and art directors."
PUBL: Kaye Publishing Corp., 120 East 56th St., New York, NY 10022.
DESC: *Graphic Design: USA* is, in many ways, more of a "happening" than a news-filled publication of graphic design. It functions to show what is new, fresh, and innovative in graphic design support resources, which includes paper stock, markers, type, stat cameras, inks, and other items relevant to the design process. *Graphic Design: USA* stimulates the senses with a broad representation of sample product, from logo design, to advertisement concepts, packaging, letterhead, and corporate identification. Advertiser support is very evident in numerous inserts of special paper stock, and other sample products. An excellent publication for the graphic design professional (8¼ x 11 inches / 210 x 280 mm).
DEPT: "Graphics Update," newsbriefs column by Gordon D. Kaye; "Graphics Action," agency account activity; "Graphic Design People," personnel newsbriefs. (10-89).
TYPL: "Landor Associates Docks at Young & Rubicam; Price Could Reach $50 Million," "Newest in Creative Production Ideas," "GAA, GASF Instruct Printing Buyers." (10-89).
SCHL: Monthly, 115 pp.

SPAN: May, 1980+
FROM MERGER OF
--Graphics: New York (ISSN: 0436-3264) (and) Graphics: USA (ISSN: 0017-3428).
VARIES
--May, 1980 - Jun, 1983 as Graphics Design, USA (ISSN: 0274-7499).
LC: NC 998.5 .A1 G67
DD: 741/6/0973

Graphic Story Magazine

1964? - 1974//
SEE: FANFARE

Graphics Design, USA

May, 1980 - Jun, 1983//
(ISSN: 0274-7499)
SEE: GRAPHIC DESIGN: USA

GRAPHICS: U.S.A.

PUBL: Graphics: USA, 211 E. 43rd St., New York, NY 10017.
DESC: *Graphics: U.S.A.* is primarily an advertising vehicle for manufacturers of graphic arts supplies for the general art designer market. As such, articles tend to be newsbriefs of designers' work and preparation, graphic symbols and similar items.
DEPT: "Art Materials, Methods and Machinery News," "Graphics Calendar."
TYPL: "Package Design Creativity 10-15 Years Behind Times, Lubalin Tells PDC Meet," "Penn-Central Trains Eye on Corporate Identity; Couples P&C as 'Service' Mark," "Computer-Drawn Pix is 'By the Numbers.'" (3-68).
SCHL: Monthly, 35 pp.
SPAN: Aug, 1966 - Apr, 1980//
MERGED WITH
--Graphics: New York (ISSN: 0436-3264) (to form) Graphics Design, USA (ISSN: 0274-7499), May, 1980.
LC: NNC 997.A
DD: 659
ISSN: 0017-3428

✢ GRAPHIS

SUB: "International journal for graphic and applied art."
PUBL: The Graphis Press, Zurich, Switzerland.
DESC: A great deal of loving care goes into the publication of this internationally acclaimed magazine of the graphic arts. Full color printing on high quality gloss paper in three languages (English, German, French) provides a superb forum for the individual interested in all aspects of graphic layout and design. Topics range from record covers, advertising, architecture, and paper sculpture, to fine arts photography. A superb periodical for just browsing or graphic arts reference.
DEPT: None. (9-10-78).
TYPL: "The Sunday Times Magazine: News and Image," "Harlow Cattaneo--a New Line of Paper Sculpture," "The Record Cover--Still the Favorite Design Field," "Paul Peter Piech. 100 Martin Luther King Posters." (9-10-78).
SCHL: Bimonthly, 90 pp.
SPAN: Sep/Oct, 1944+
LC: N 8.G73
DD: 705
ISSN: 0017-3452
ABST: --Art Index (ISSN: 0004-3222)
--Film Literature Index (ISSN: 0093-6758)

Grassroots

? - ?//
(ISSN: 0046-3541)
SEE: GRASSROOTS EDITOR

✢ GRASSROOTS EDITOR

SUB: "A journal for newspeople."
SUB: "A bimonthly journal for editorial writers."
PUBL: International Society of Weekly Newspaper Editors, Northern Illinois University, Department of Journalism, DeKalb, IL 60115.
DESC: Serving the interests of the International Society of Weekly Newspaper Editors, *Grassroots Editor* concentrates on issues involving editors and publishers in small to medium size markets. *Grassroots Editor* has a special emphasis on the ethics of journalism as it relates to editors and publishers. Typical articles from the 1990 - 1991 time period include: "Editorial Page Critiques," "Linked to the Community," "Weeklies' German Roots," "Farewell to Progress," "Reporters Rate Press Aides," "Irish Weeklies Thriving," and "Trust People, Not Tools." Editor Brod called this serial: "Community journalism; a quarterly journal for newspeople." Highly recommended for its faithful exploration and forum for issues of import to the community newspaper field. For the sampled issues of 1982 and 1991: black ink on uncoated paper stock in stapled magazine format, limited advertising (8 ½ x 11 inches / 215 x 280 mm).
DEPT: None. (summer-84). "Page Two," editorial commentary column by Donald F. Brod; "Letters." (winter-91).
TYPL: "Watching the Environment," "Publisher's Survival Rules," "Man Who Wears Three Hats," "Good News or Bad News?," "Coverage of the Schools." (summer-84). "Ben Harris Led the Way," "Cairo Weekly in English." (winter-91).
SCHL: Quarterly (Jan, 1960 - 1966); Bimonthly (1967 - 1974); Quarterly (1975+), 16 pp.
SPAN: Jan, 1960+

VARIES
--? - ? as Grassroots (ISSN: 0046-3541).
LC: PN 4700.G72
DD: 070
ISSN: 0017-3541

Great TV Entertainment
1980 - 1982//
SEE: CABLE GUIDE, THE

✤ GREATER AMUSEMENTS
SUB: "America's first and only regional motion picture trade newspaper."
SUB: "America's foremost motion picture regional trade journal."
SUB: "America's oldest motion picture trade paper."
DESC: This slick publication concerns promotion and news of the motion picture industry. *Greater Amusement*'s focus is the Hollywood industry; production and promotion, and distribution of its product. *International Projectionist*, which was incorporated as a separate section of the magazine in July, 1965, is concerned with that small but unique group of individuals who show films in today's theaters. Like many similar motion picture publications, this one has a large number of full-color promotional pages on new releases. Many illustrations, especially those of new films.
DEPT: "Editorial," "Industry Highlights," newsbriefs; "Picture of the Month," unique in-depth section of illustrations, production stills and discussions with distributors; "Trade Tidbits," newsbriefs column by Ray Gallo; "Special Events," picture briefs of promotional events; "Reviews," paragraph-long succinct reviews; "Exploitation, Promotion, Merchandising," pictures with briefs on promotion; "Here's What They Do!" column by Spencer Hare; "Movie Capsules," one-picture, one- paragraph summaries; "News Posts," job promotions and transfers; "Books-Records," reviews; "Magazines-Newspapers," reviews; "Fashion Tie-Ups," discussion of film fashion tie-in to American consumers; "London Jottings," news column by Edward Dryhurst; "News With Pictures," exhibitor profiles; "Radio-TV," reviews re: film; "Film Row News, USA," sentence briefs on exhibition success; "Film Exchange News," briefs; "Foreign Appointments," "Theater Maintenance," "New Theaters," profile; "New Products," "Tedascope News," projectionist briefs column by Whitney Stine.
TYPL: "Are We Ready for Automation?," "Twentieth Century Fox Sets Hammer Films in U.S.," "Far From the Madding Crowd of U.S.A.," "Theater Sound Systems." (10-67).
SCHL: Monthly, 40 pp.
SPAN: 1914+

VARIES
--Jul, 1965 - Dec, 1967 as Greater Amusements and International Projectionist.
WITH SUPPLEMENT
--Jul, 1965+, International Projectionist.
ABSORBED
--International Projectionist, Jun, 1965.
LC: PN 1993.G73
ISSN: 0017-3703

Greater Amusements and International Projectionist
Jul, 1965 - Dec, 1967//
SEE: GREATER AMUSEMENTS

Grossbild-Technik
1955 - 1959//
SEE: PHOTO TECHNIQUE INTERNATIONAL

Group Discussion Guide
Feb, 1936 - Jun, 1942//
SEE: AUDIO-VISUAL GUIDE

✤ GUILD REPORTER, THE
SUB: "Official publication of the Newspaper Guild (AFL-CIO, CLC)."
PUBL: Guild Reporter, 8611 Second Ave., Silver Springs, MD 20910.
DESC: *The Guild Reporter* is a semimonthly tabloid newspaper with items of interest to Guild members. Emphasis is on the continuing relationship between newspaper management and staff; and new technology, and the general quality of life for Guild members. There is a strong emphasis on the economics of publishing and benefits of membership in the Newspaper Guild.
DEPT: "It Seems to Us," letters; "Day Book," calendar; "As They Put It," guest commentary. (6-1-84).
TYPL: "Vancouver 'OK' Brings Strike End," "Editors Tell of Pagination and Shrinking Back Shops," "Computer Cited in Upgrading Order," "Rejection Urged on NLRB Nominee," "Opposed Labor Code Gets Nod from CLC." (6-1- 84).
SCHL: Irregular (Nov 23, 1933 - Sep, 1934); Bimonthly (Oct 1, 1934 - ?); Weekly (Aug 15, 1937 - Oct 3, 1938); Semimonthly [Monthly: Jul, Dec], (? to date); 8 pp.
SPAN: Nov 23, 1933+
LC: HD 6530.N4 G8
DD: 070.5
ISSN: 0017-5404

G

Communication Serials

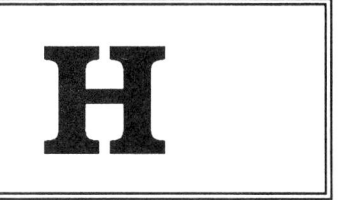

Hampton-Columbian Magazine

Oct, 1911 - Jan, 1912//
SEE: HAMPTON MAGAZINE

✣ HAMPTON MAGAZINE

SUB: "The new Broadway." (Feb, 1909 - Sep, 1911).
PUBL: ?, New York, NY.
DESC: *Broadway Magazine*, the premiere title in this series, was rather eclectic in content: articles about its namesake, fresh-water fishing, stained glass, railroad accidents, and poetry, were just a few of the sundry topics. A number of articles did supply interesting descriptions of current stage performances and profiles of the performers. Of special note were frequent full-page photographs of current stage productions, and some auxilliary activities of the theatre. Small format.
DEPT: None. (2-05).
TYPL: "The Actor and the Critic," "The Clown Speaks," "From the Church Choir to Parsifal," "Removing Six Million Cubic Yards of Snow in Manhattan Borough." (2-05).
SCHL: Monthly, 90 pp.
SPAN: Apr, 1898+?
VARIES
--Apr, 1898 - Nov, 1907 as Broadway Magazine.
--Dec, 1907 - Sep, 1908 as New Broadway Magazine.
--Oct, 1908 - Jan, 1909 as Hampton's Broadway Magazine.
--Feb, 1909 - Sep, 1911 as Hampton's Magazine.
--Oct, 1911 - Jan, 1912 as Hampton-Columbian Magazine.
ABSORBED
--Columbian Magazine, Oct, 1911?
LC: AP 2 .H152

Hampton's Broadway Magazine

Oct, 1908 - Jan, 1909//
SEE: HAMPTON MAGAZINE

Hampton's Magazine

Feb, 1909 - Sep, 1911//
SEE: HAMPTON MAGAZINE

Hands-On Electronics

Summer, 1984 - Jan, 1989//
(ISSN: 0743-2968)
SEE: POPULAR ELECTRONICS

✣ HASSELBLAD

PUBL: Victor Hasselblad Aktiebolag, Box 220, S-401 23 Goteborg, Sweden.
DESC: This promotional magazine for Hasselblad users and owners said, "One of the aims of our magazine is to illustrate the capabilities of Hasselblad cameras and the Hasselblad system, not merely in aesthetic terms, but even in technical respects in severe external conditions." In this quality, small-format magazine that is filled with full page color photos submitted by Hasselblad owners, most photos and issues involve a unique theme. It is Issued in four language editions: English, German, Swedish and Japanese.
DEPT: None. (#3-78).
TYPL: "Five Pictures From Southwestern U.S.A.," "The Canadian Arctic," "Swans in Northern Japan," "From the Swedish Forest," "Tips From Our Service Manager." (#3-78).
SCHL: Quarterly, 35 pp.
SPAN: ?+
EDITION
--English.
ISSN: 0345-4533
LC: TR 1.H

✣ HASTINGS COMMUNICATIONS AND ENTERTAINMENT LAW JOURNAL

SUB: "A journal of communications and entertainment law."
PUBL: University of California, Hastings College of the Law, 200 McAllister St., San Francisco, CA 94102-4978.
DESC: "*Comm/Ent* addresses a variety of legal issues, including the first amendment, defamation, obscenity, the print media, film, radio, musical recordings, television, cable television, satellite communications, telecommunications, computer and other high technology, intellectual property, entertainment and sports." It is an excellent journal which addresses issues of current legal importance in the communication field. The original journal title, *Comm/Ent*, was changed in 1983 to include the law school name, and finally (in 1988) to reflect the full publisher title of the Hastings College of the Law at the University of California. It remains an important journal and resource for the changing field of communication law. For the sampled issues of 1977 and 1991: perfect-bound journal format, black ink on uncoated paper stock, limited advertising in later issues (6 ¾ x 9 ¾ inches / 175 x 245 mm).

DEPT: "Commentaries," "Notes." (fall-77). "Notes." (winter-91).
TYPL: "The 'Unfairness Doctrine': Balance and Response Over the Airwaves," "The Equal Opportunities and Fairness Doctrines in Broadcasting: Should They be Retained?," "Newsmen's Shield Laws and Subpoenas: California's Farr and the Fresno Four." (fall-77). "From Satirical to Satyrical: When is a Joke Actionable?," "Alternatives to Copyright Law Protection of Graphic Characters: The Lanham Act and Antidilution Statutes," "Scarcity of the Airwaves: Allocating and Assigning the Spectrum for High Definition Television (HDTV)," "California v. FCC: A Victory for the States," "U.S. Communications Policymaking: Who & Where." (winter-91).
SCHL: Quarterly, 240 pp.
SPAN: 1977+
VARIES
--Fall, 1977 - Summer, 1983 as Comm/Ent, A Journal of Communications and Entertainment Law.
--Fall, 1983 - Summer, 1988 as Comm/Ent, Hastings Journal of Communications and Entertainment Law.
ISSN: 0193-8398

✦ HD PRODUCTION

SUB: "An HDTV 1125/60 Group Publication."
PUBL: CRN, Inc., 8 Bond St., Great Neck, NY 11021.
DESC: Discussing "Real Standards for a Real World," contributing writer Larry Thorpe, Sony Advanced Systems, authoritatively wrote in one issue, "In HDTV, images are reproductions of the real world about us---caputured in real time. The scene content is unlimited, the lighting ranges are vast, the subject motion unpredictable, and the creative expectations are highly individualistic and subjective. Perhaps most important is the vast legacy of one hundred years of image creation: a now highly-skilled, creative, artistically temperamental, profit-oriented and gigantic body of international program producers whose demands on image excellence ever escalates. HDTV standards must never lose sight of these realities. They must allow HDTV equipment to be developed and manufactured that the end-user will, in fact, purchase and use." That is also the form and function of *HD Production*, a contemporary publication of High Definition Television (the Japanese prefer the name Hi-Vision), which in this case, is based upon the technical format of the 1125/60 Group. The 1125 refers to the number of lines of horizontal definition, while the 60 refers to the electrical system frequency (60 Hertz or Hz.) used in this system. The majority of the issue is devoted to HDTV productions planned, or finished in this technical format; the problems, the experiences, and the exhilaration of a new visual medium are explored to their fullest. A continuing thread through all HDTV publications is the ongoing comparison of 35mm motion picture film to High Definition Television. Dynamic layout design in full color on coated paper stock, magazine size with advertising (8 ⅛ x 10 ⅞ inches / 205 x 275 mm).
DEPT: "In Production," HDTV production news; "In Development," projects planned; "Definitions," commentary. (spring-91).
TYPL: "Stalking Lost Animals," "At the Movies," "HD Production Buyer's Guide," "HDTV 1125/60 Member Directory." (spring-91).
SCHL: Quarterly, 35 pp.
SPAN: Spring, 1991+
DD: 338
ISSN: 1059-9614

✦ HD SYSTEMS WORLD REVIEW

SUB: "The journal for high definition and advanced television technology."
PUBL: Meckler Corporation, 11 Ferry Lane West, Westport, CT 06880.
DESC: In a sister publication, publisher Meckler described the contents of this important magazine as containing "...papers on the most challenging topics facing the continued evolution of HDTV. Not news, rather, in-depth observations and opinions from the people who make the industry move. People and opinions you need to know about." Indeed, few would dispute the importance of the developing High Definition Television field, as well as the need to keep abreast of developments. *HD Systems World Review* is an excellent means of sorting out competing systems, technological kinks, political ramifications, and the cultural/economic impact of HDTV, both on society as well as on the visual systems of motion pictures and standard broadcast television. Articles are written by industry professionals, and any given issue will provide a wealth of information about this emerging form of communication. Some articles assume some technical understanding. Very highly recommended! Stapled magazine format, black/white editorial content, two-color cover design, minimal advertising, graphics (8 ½ x 11 inches / 215 x 280 mm).
DEPT: "From the Editor." (spring-90).
TYPL: "HDTV: How Many Lines?," "The Role of Technology in the Future of HDTV Broadcasting Systems," "HDTV and the European Economic Community," "HDTV Studio Standards: Understanding the Debates," "HDTV: An Historical Perspective, Part 2: 1940 to the Present." (spring-90).
SCHL: Quarterly, 60 pp.
SPAN: Winter, 1989/1990+
VARIES
--Winter, 1990 - ? as HDTV World Review (ISSN: 1044-9507).
ISSN: 1055-6931

✤ HDTV NEWSLETTER

SUB: "The preeminent source of worldwide HDTV reporting."
SUB: "Essential reading in the future of television and motion picture."
PUBL: Advanced Television Publishing, Inc., 901 SW King, #402, PO Box 5247, Portland, OR 97208-5247.
DESC: "The *Newsletter* works to bring together people and issues focused upon HDTV and technically Advanced Television systems. Our aim is to track with you and participate in leading ideas that bring High Quality television applications to the studio, business, motion pictures and the home." *HDTV Newsletter* discusses both the ideological and technical aspects of what television system will supersede the current NTSC (National Television Standards Committee), 525-line system in the United States. "Besides providing the finest, most up-to-date information on all HDTV related issues, *HDTV Newsletter* also hosts the only monthly forum for open discussion of the industry's most pressing concerns, and an industry undergoing this much change has many you need to know about. When all is said and done this *Newsletter* is very readable. Not some dry, technical data that must be waded through (there are enough of those), but rather an interesting open look at the future." These are issues of paramount importance to anyone in the film or video industry, and a publication (along with sister serial, *HDTV World Review*, which contains observations and opinions rather than news) which is "must" reading for anyone in the entertainment industry planning to be in the forefront of communications for the decade of the nineties and beyond. Two-column-page layout design; magazine size (8 ½ x 11 inches / 215 x 280 mm).
DEPT: "Snapshots," 'monthly short news reports'; "Sign Off," commentary. (3-87). "Aspect," "Industry Notes," "Industry Events," "Washington Beat," "New Technology," "Sign Off." (6/7-90).
TYPL: "The Status of Simulcast," "Vision 1250," "Medical Videoconference," "Japanese Electronics," "Computers Come to the Party." (6/7-90).
SPAN: Jun?, 1986+
DD: 384 11
ISSN: 0892-5771

✤ HDTV REPORT

SUB: "HDTV Report is a publication of the Eureka EU95 HDTV Directorate."
PUBL: Eureka EU95 HDTV Directorate, PO Box 523, NL 5600 AM Eindhoven, the Netherlands.
DESC: "Eureka EU95 is a project in which major electronics companies including Philips, BTS, Thomson and Nokia, and several organizations and institutions are working to develop a compatible world standard for High Definition Television--HDTV. The most striking improvements on present television standards are the number of picture lines being doubled from 625 to 1250, the screen ration changing from 4:3 to 16:9, the greater information density with 1,400,000 pixels on the screen, compared to the original 120,000, and CD-quality sound and multilingual transmission, thanks to eight sound channels." The primary function of *HDTV Report* is to help promote the 1250/50 European-based standard of High Definition television. This is an important technological race, made more complex by the tremendous political/economic stakes, a point not lost on the editors of this publication: "In 1996 the second generation of TV-satellites for Europe will become operational. Before that date the battle about HDTV standards and formats must have been decided. Will the Japanese again wipe out their European competitors and dominate the world market, as they did with the VCR? Or will European HD-MAC set the standard?" That indeed, remains the multi- billion dollar question, and one which this publication would like to see answered with the 1250/50 system format. Articles describe technical developments for this system, applications and projects in development for same, and the continuing question of "how does HDTV compare with motion picture film?" Stapled tabloid format in two-color on coated paper stock with numerous technical photographs (10 ⅝ x 15 inches / 270 x 380 mm).
DEPT: "Vision 1250 Production Projects." (3-91).
TYPL: "Vision 1250--A Growing Concept," "BTS, One of the Leading Architects of Tomorrow's Television World," "Thomson Sees D2-MAC as an Important Stepping Stone for HDTV Introduction," "The Press on HDTV--Towards the New-Shape Television Screen," "High Definition From the Point of View of a Film Director." (3-91).
SCHL: Biweekly, 12 pp.
SPAN: Dec, 1990?+
ISSN: 1055-9280

HDTV World Review

Winter, 1990 - ?//
(ISSN: 1044-9507)
SEE: HD SYSTEMS WORLD REVIEW

✤ HEALTH COMMUNICATION

PUBL: Lawrence Erlbaum Associates, Inc., 365 Broadway, Hillsdale, NJ 07642.
DESC: "*Health Communication* is a quarterly journal devoted to the publication of scholarly research on the relationship between communication processes and health." The "Instructions for Contributors" says, "*Health Communication* is dedicated to publishing scientific articles on the relationship between communication and health. Submissions are welcomed from scholars and practitioners in communication, psychology, sociology, and the other social sciences as well as those in medicine, nursing, dentisry, physical therapy, dietetics, pharmacy, and the allied health professions. Although most of the published articles are data based, we also welcome pedagogical, meth-

odological, theoretical, and applied submissions as well as reviews and policy pieces. Both qualitative and quantitative methods are appropriate. Areas to be addressed in the journal include, but are not limited to, provider- patient (or -family) interaction, communication and cooperation, health information, health promotion, interviewing, health public relations, and gerontological concerns. An important consideration for the judging of articles is the extent to which they focus on actual communicative behavior." This is another in the excellent series of Lawrence Erlbaum Associates journals and publications in the communication field. For sampled issue of 1990: perfect-bound journal format, editorial content consisting of black ink on uncoated paper stock, cover being blue ink on coated paper stock, limited advertising (6 x 9 inches / 150 x 230 mm).
DEPT: "Book Review." (#4-90).
TYPL: "The Role of Informative Television Programs in the Battle Against Aids," "Physician-Patient Communication as Interpersonal Rhetoric: A Narrative Approach," "The Relationships Among Maternal Health Locus of Control Beliefs and Expectations, Pediatrician-Mother Communication, and Maternal Satisfaction With Well-Infant Care," "Coping Strategies of Cancer Patients: Actual Communication and Imagined Interactions," "Meeting the Communication/Persuasion Challenge of AIDS in Workplaces, Neighborhoods, and Schools: A Comment on AIDS and Public Policy." (#4-90).
SCHL: Quarterly, 80 pp.
SPAN: #1, 1989+
ISSN: 1041-0236

✢ HEALTH COMMUNICATION NEWSLETTER

PUBL: International Communication Association, Health Communication Division, PO Box 9589, Austin, TX 78766.
DESC: This newsletter for health communication professionals, members of the International Communication Association, includes "...people in Communication, Public Health, Nursing, Medicine, the Allied Health Professions, Psychology, Political Science, and the other social sciences." It informs division membership on a variety of topics, including member promotions, research projects, publications and other items of import to this community. For the sampled issue of 1991: single sheet stapled typewritten newsletter on uncoated paper stock, no advertising (8 ½ x 11 inches / 215 x 280 mm).
DEPT: "From the Chair," editorial and commentary column by Gary Kreps; "People In the News," personnel newsbriefs; "Calls," for papers, projects, awards; "Publications," of members. (10-91).
TYPL: "Journal Health Communication Thriving!," "Health Communication Hotline Proposed!," "New Video on Community Living for PWA." (10-91).
SCHL: Semiyearly, 6 pp.

SPAN: Oct, 1990+

✢ HERO HOBBY

PUBL: Hero Hobby magazine, Route 1, Box 371, Clarksburg, WV 26301.
DESC: *Hero Hobby* is a nostalgia magazine covering four main areas: broadcasting, motion pictures, cartoon art, and magic. Its pages are filled with motion picture stills, reprints of radio logs (primarily 1940s), reprints of cartoons from that same era, and general commentary; leading one to believe that things have never been as good in the media since that time. Most articles appear to be written by editor John Cooper and range from typeset to typed to mimeographed. The reader will find much pleasant reading in editor Cooper's breezy style and enthusiasm for the "good old days."
DEPT: "Premium Parade," hand-drawn reproductions of original radio premiums.
TYPL: "Tarzan Revisited, or Finding Johnny Weissmuller at Home," "Captain Celluloid and the Film Pirates," "Roy Barcroft, Villain to the Stars." (summer-70).
SCHL: Quarterly, 30 pp.
SPAN: 1966+?

Hi Fi & Music Review
Feb, 1958 - Nov, 1958//
SEE: STEREO REVIEW

✢ HI-FI ANSWERS

SUB: "The technical magazine that solves your hi-fi queries and problems." (? - Mar, 1984).
SUB: "Defines the state of the art." (Apr, 1984 - ?).
PUBL: Haymarket Publishing, Regent House, 54-62 Regent St., London W1A 4YJ, England.
DESC: *Hi-Fi Answers* is a consumer publication designed to furnish news of new technology and music releases to the British general public. The second subtitle, therefore, is a much clearer indication of the scope and depth of this quality consumer serial. Equipment reviews offer in-depth analysis of new equipment. Articles concerning music releases, artists, and other aspects of the "software" side of the high fidelity industry are thoroughly researched and well-written. The emphasis is definitely on technology; how to choose, evaluate, purchase, set up, tweek, and enjoy stereophonic audio in the home. Large magazine format (9 x 11 ⅝ inches / 230 x 295 mm); coated cover stock with editorial content on newsprint.
DEPT: "Letters," "News," briefs; "Comment," "Earsay," "Pot Pourri," "Rock Releases," "Masterwork," "Classical Releases," "Q&A," "The Hit List," "Reviews," of equipment; "Comeback," unique manufacturers retort. (12-86).

TYPL:	"All the Way Back from Memphis." (Remainder of serial consists of regular departmental features, and equipment reviews.) (12-86).
SCHL:	Monthly, 80 pp.
SPAN:	?+?
LC:	TK 7881.7 .H47
DD:	621.389/33

✤ HI-FI CHOICE

SUB:	"The world's number one guide to buying hi-fi."
SUB:	"Voted favourite hi-fi magazine by hi-fi shops nationwide."
PUBL:	Dennis Publishing, Ltd., 14 Rathbone Place, London WIP IDE, England.
DESC:	"Every month *Hi-Fi Choice* tests more products than any other hi-fi magazine and awards 'Best Buy' and 'Recommended' accolades. A must for hi-fi buyers and enthusiasts, *Hi-Fi Choice* is packed with news, reviews, features and an extensive buyer's guide containing test summaries on over 900 hi-fi products. At *Hi-Fi Choice* the only corners we cut are on our tags -- so if you're serious about hi-fi you can't afford to miss it." Hi-fi/stereo enthusiasts serious about their avocations will want to add this excellent monthly publication to their reading lists. It focuses on entertaining and informative columns concerning new audio (and some video) equipment for the home. These excellent columns are "The Front End," "Separate Systems," and "Choice Matters;" and appear to explore everything from the latest trade show technologies to loud speakers, system configurations, and the role of accessories for the serious audiophile. Of special note are the extensive testbench reviews of new equipment, each one placed on its own page, with "Lab Report," "Sound Quality" and "Test Results" specifications in well-written, detailed reviews of new products. While there were only two feature articles in the sampled 1991 issue, they were significant. In one, readers were treated to a Japanese house visit of Pioneer's chief designer; and in the other visited a major Japanese "ear-speaker" manufacturer; both articles providing a wealth of information and full-color pictures. *Hi-Fi Choice* goes the full distance with readers, not only providing intelligent articles concerning equipment, but in a major section entitled, "The Directory," provides a very detailed listing of equipment by application, price in £, comments from reviews, features, and value of the technology. This 30-page section alone is well worth the cover price to anyone shopping for new audio equipment. Another classified section, "The Choice Dealer Directory," lists a British geographic directory of quality audio dealers, many of whom display the BADA symbol (British Audio Dealers Association). All of this is wrapped in a dynamic layout design. It is little wonder that *Hi-Fi Choice* was "Voted favourite hi-fi magazine by hi-fi shops nationwide." It well deserves the accolade. Perfect-bound magazine format, mixture of black/white and full-color editorial content, with full-color cover, all on heavy coated paper stock (8 ¼ x 11 ¾ inches / 210 x 295 mm).
DEPT:	"Menu," editorial column by Andy Benham; "Update," new products and newsbriefs; "Choice Sessions," "Statements," "21st Century Fox," column by Barry Fox; "Readers Write," 'Choice answers' letters; "Tech Talk," excellent technical column by Paul Miller; "Conclusions, Best Buys and Recommendations," based upon this issue's listening tests; "Personal Messages," commentary column by Paul Messenger. (7-91).
TYPL:	"Like Father," "It's a Family Affair." (7-91).
SCHL:	Monthly, 145 pp.
SPAN:	?+ WITH SUPPLEMENT --Driving Ambition, ?+
ISSN:	0955-1115

✤ HI-FI HERETIC

PUBL:	Mine Shaft Gap Publicatiooons, PO Box 2019, Yorba Linda, CA 92686.
DESC:	Editor and Publisher Kent Bransford described his publication this way: "As I hope you've noticed, *Hi-Fi Heretic* is different. Its subject matter is music, and the high-quality audio products that enable us to enjoy it in the home. That's it. No video, no car stereo, no bullshit. *Hi-Fi Heretic* is published solely for the benefit of its readers--*HFH* is not an advocate for the audio industry. The fundamental goal of this magazine is to help excellence flourish, and mediocrity perish." All of the featured articles in the sampled 1991 issue pertained to full-fidelity capable audio equipment. Equipment reviews were crisp explorations into performance, price, and acoustic considerations. One interesting feature of *Hi-Fi Heretic* is the departmental "Argybargy," a retort forum used by equipment manufacturers to respond to prior equipment reviews in the magazine. This is an excellent publication for high-end quality audio equipment for the home consumer. For the sampled 1991 issue: stapled magazine format, black ink with color advertisement pages on coated paper stock, cover is full-color, laminated on heavy coated paper stock (8 x 10 ½ inches / 205 x 270 mm).
DEPT:	"Introduction," commentary column by Kent S. Bransford; "Editorial," column by Kent S. Bransford; "Letters to the Editor," "Argybargy," equipment manufacturer retort to earlier reviews. (#14-91).
TYPL:	"The Ten Best Buys in Audio," "Budget Box Bingo," "Integrateds Again???," "Solitary Mien," "Meaty Beaty Big and Bouncy." (#14-91).
SCHL:	Quarterly, 60 pp.
SPAN:	?, 1990?+
ISSN:	1042-3451

✧ HI-FI NEWS AND RECORD REVIEW

SUB: "Incorporating Record News, Audio News, and Tape Recorders."
SUB: "Incorporating Audio News, Stereo News, Tape News, Tape Recorders."
PUBL: Link House Publications, Link House, Dingwall Ave., Croydon, England.
DESC: It is doubtful that anyone would accuse the editors of *Hi-Fi News and Record Review* of shirking from their public duty of providing sharp comment on music releases and new equipment for the stereophonic field. Its articles are lucid and authoritative, and contribute to its fine reputation. This serial strikes a good balance between serious critical analyses and lighter articles on the stereophonic field in general, and is an excellent consumer serial which should be in every library. For the 1990 sampled issue: black/white and full-color editorial content with full-color cover on coated paper stock in dynamic layout design, perfect-bound magazine format (8 1/4 x 11 3/4 inches / 210 x 300 mm).
DEPT: "Hi-Fi for Beginners," "Readers' Letters," "Audio News," newsbriefs; "Microphone Balance," "Stereo News," "Record Reproduction," "Details of New Products." (3-58). "Comment," "Views," "News," "Technology," "Radio," "Accessories Club," "Classical Wax," "Notes," "Books," "Compact Disc Monitor," "Back Door," comment; "Records of the Month," "Record Review Index," "Classical Issues & Reissues." (9-85). "Comment," "Views," 'Letters to the editor'; "News," 'Products, people and events'; "Sidelines," column by John Crabbe; "Technology," column by Barry Fox; "Radio," column by Trevor Butler; "Headroom," column by Ken Kessler; "Record Review Index," 'Lists all discs reviewed this month'; "Record of the Month," "Classical Reviews," "Rock/Pop/Jazz Reviews," "Capsules," 'Short rock reviews'; "Rock Reissues," 'Recycled rock, pop and jazz'; "Back Door." (3-90).
TYPL: "Building a Stereo Pre-amp," "Styli for Stereo," "Semi-fi." (3-58). "How Hi the Fi?," "George Butterworth," "Eliahu Inbal, Conductor." (9-85). "A State-of-the Art Pre-Amplifier: AMP 02," "More Than a Mirage," "Christopher Hogwood." (3-90).
SCHL: Monthly, 130 pp.
SPAN: Oct, 1970+.
VARIES
--Oct, 1970 - Dec, 1970 as Hi-Fi News incorporating Record Review.
ABSORBED
--Record News, Sep, 1959.
LC: TK 7881.7 H5
ISSN: 0018-1226

Hi-Fi News incorporating Record Review

Oct, 1970 - Dec, 1970//
SEE: HI-FI NEWS AND RECORD REVIEW

Hi Fi Review

Dec, 1958 - Jan, 1960//
SEE: STEREO REVIEW

HI-FI SOUND

SUB: "The Sound Monthly."
SUB: "Stereo, disc, tape." (Nov, 1967 - ?).
PUBL: Haymarket Publishing, Gillow House, 54-62 Regent St., London W1, England.
DESC: [*Amateur Tape Recording & Hi-Fi*]: In the February, 1961 issue the editors informed subscribers that *Amateur Tape Recording* had absorbed Popular Hi-Fi to form this new serial concerning the three home media. The editorial focus remained the same, that of articles concerning home recording and playback of voice and music. Some articles provided technical "know-how," but the major focus resided on new consumer equipment and techniques.
DESC: "A new arrival on the hi-fi scene--a magazine which caters for those who appreciate good music, well reproduced, but know little of technical ways and means. Hi-Fi Sound will reflect what is going on in audio and, above all, give close attention to the needs of the beginner who requires a complete home music system (Nov, 1967)." This consumer stereophile publication (which incorporated *Amateur Tape Recording*), continued to simplify the technology of home audio up through its January, 1977 issue. In February of that year, the publication changed title, layout, and purpose, with *Popular Hi-Fi & Sound* providing an extensive test section of new equipment, criticism and comment.
DEPT: "World of Sound," newsbriefs; "Inter-Tape Directory," for 'Tapespondents'; "Dear Sir," letters; "Tape and Disc Review," "Monthly Record Guide," "Tape Club News," "Strictly for Women." (8-61). "Hi-Fi Postbag," letters; "Q&A--Technical Queries Examined," "Sound Scene," "Odds and Ends," "Shop Window," new products; "On Test," new product evaluations. (12-67). "Questions and Answers," "Soundwaves," letters; "On Record," reviews; "Hi-Fi Guide." (1-77).
TYPL: "Fire-Fighting and Honolulu," "Further Modification for the Clarion," "My Kind of Music." (8-61). "Hi-Fi From Discs," "Tape Recorders and Hi-Fi," "Plain Man's Guide to Loudspeakers," "Into the Transistor Era." (12-67). "A Delicate Balance," "Quality Costs," "Turn on--Tune In," "Conflicting Trends." (1-77).
SCHL: Monthly, 110 pp.
SPAN: 1959 - Jan, 1977//
VARIES
--1959 - ? as Amateur Tape Recording.
--Feb, 1961 - 1963 as Amateur Tape Recording & Hi-Fi.
--1963? - Nov, 1967 as Amateur Tape Recording, Video & Hi-Fi.
ABSORBED
--Popular Hi-Fi, Feb, 1961.

MERGED WITH
--Popular Hi-Fi (to form) Popular Hi-Fi & Sound, Feb, 1977
LC: TK 7881.7 .H52
ISSN: 0018-1234

Hi Fi/Stereo Review
Feb, 1960 - Oct, 1968//
SEE: STEREO REVIEW

Hi-Fi Tape Recording
Dec, 1956 - Mar, 1960//
SEE: TAPE RECORDING

✣ HI-FI WORLD
PUBL: Audio Publishing, Ltd., 64 Castellain Rd., Maida Vale, London W9 1EX, England.
DESC: "When you consider the plethora of hi-fi products on offer to the public, the cliff-like racks chock full of uniformly black boxes, is it surprising that the man in the street ends up confused? What does a phono stage do and does he need one? What about an equaliser and one of those dohickies with fins all over it? That, of course, is why magazines exist, and why they in turn promote the ideal of specialist dealers. People want answers, the more straightforward the better. Faced with a quagmire of purchases, they want advice they can treat with confidence, a map which shows the quicksand in the right place." These lucid comments by *Hi-Fi World* columnist Roy Gregory, very nicely demonstrate the substance of this outstanding "high-end" publication for the British audio enthusiast. Editor Noel Keywood has assembled an excellent combination of the technical, the aesthetic, and the new technologies to please readers. The layout design is a pleasing combination of spot and full-color graphics. Numerous technical specifications are found concerning "test-bench" reviews, and explanations of technologies, yet articles are readable by less-experienced audio consumers. *Hi-Fi World* also sells audio accessories to its readers, noting, "Don't bother to waste time searching for specialist audio accessories. We are looking carefully for you and, where necessary, are even having them made to fulfill our quality requirements." That, plus promotion of dealers within the British Audio Dealers Association demonstrates attention to readers' interests in *Hi-Fi World*. For the sampled 1991 issue: perfect-bound magazine format, editorial content and cover consisting of spot- and full-color pages on coated paper stock (8 ¼ x 11 ¾ inches / 210 x 295 mm).
DEPT: "Trade Winds," 'Hi-Fi World brings you all the latest news from the hi-fi industry'; "In Brief," newsbriefs; "Readers' Reply," letters; "Kaleidoscope," column by Noel Keywood; "Desparate Dan," column by Danny Haikin; "Sircom's Circuits," column by Alan Sircom; "Recorded Message," column by Richard Brice; "R. G. Bargy," column by Roy Gregory; "Tweaky Corner," "Kelly's Corner," 'Richard Kelly's monthly look at budget hi-fi - old, new, borrowed or blue' column by Richard Kelly; "Readers' Queries," 'Write in with your problems' reader submitted Q&A; "Record of the Month," review. (7-91).
TYPL: "SONY Announce Recordable Mini-Disc," "On the Receiving End," "Transmission Power," "The TDL Story," "Going for Gold." (7-91).
SCHL: Monthly, 100 pp.
SPAN: ?+

HIGH FIDELITY
SUB: "The magazine for music listeners."
PUBL: ABC Consumer Magazines, Inc., 825 Seventh Ave., New York, NY 10019.
DESC: This magazine of sound provided a consumer viewpoint for new releases in music and spoken word media, along with in-depth test reports of new equipment, and general trends in the consumer audio field. Basic understanding of audio technology is assumed, as some articles focus on speaker design, technological advances, and other equipment-oriented issues. The relationship between *High Fidelity* and *Musical America* remains in doubt. Some sources claim that *Musical America* was a supplement (having been absorbed by) *High Fidelity* from February, 1965 through 1986, and then was issued under its own title from 1987 on. Other sources believe that the two publications merged in 1951, resulting in a dual-issue publication, but with *High Fidelity* on the magazine masthead. Diamandis Communications purchased *High Fidelity* magazine in fall of 1989 and absorbed it into *Stereo Review*. Sampled issue for 1980 (8 ⅛ x 10 ¾ inches / 210 x 275 mm), black/white editorial content with color and spot-color advertisements on coated paper stock.
DEPT: "CrossTalk," Technical Q&A; "High Fidelity News," newsbriefs; "Equipment Reports," "Culshaw at Large," column by John Culshaw; "Classical Records," review; "Critics' Choice," 'The most noteworthy releases reviewed recently'; "The Tape Deck," column by R.D. Darrell; "Recording Studio Design," "Input Output," 'Instruments and Accessories'; "Pop Records," review; "Jazz Records," review; "Music in Print," review; "HiFi-Crostic," puzzle column by William Peterson; "Letters." (7-80). "Letters," "Currents," equipment; "The CD Spread," reviews; "Classicial Reviews," "Front Lines," editorial; "Crosstalk," technical column by Larry Klein; "Scan Lines," visual technical column by David Ranada; "Tape Tracks," audio tape column by Robert Long; "The Autophile," equipment review column by Christopher Esse; "Medley," commentary; "Test Reports," in-depth audio equipment reviews. (10-88).
TYPL: "Tape Tests: How the New Cassettes, Including Metals, Measure Up," "Record Cleaners and the Real World," "The All-American Voice," "Recording Studio Design: Sugarloaf's View is Big and Bright,"

"Sinatra's 'Trilogy': Past, Present, and Poppycock." (7-80). "Audio Fetishes," "The Overselling of Oversampling," "The Victor Opera Series," "Special Report: All CDs Great and Small." (10-88).
SCHL: Monthly, 100 pp.
SPAN: Dec, 1958 - ?, 1989//
FROM MERGER OF
--High Fidelity (and) Audiocraft for the Hi-Fi Hobbyist.
VARIES
--Dec, 1958 - Mar, 1959 as High Fidelity & Audiocraft.
ABSORBED
--Hi Fi Music at Home, Jun, 1959.
SUPPLEMENT TO
--High Fidelity Incorporating Musical America (ISSN: 0018-1463), Feb, 1965 - 1969.
--High Fidelity and Musical America (ISSN: 0018-1463), 1970 - Jun, 1979.
--High Fidelity [Musical America Edition], Jul, 1979 - Sep, 1979.
--High Fidelity & Musical America (ISSN: 0735-9268), Oct, 1979 - Jul, 1980.
--High Fidelity [Musical America Edition] (ISSN: 0735-777x), Aug, 1980 - 1986.
ABSORBED BY
--Stereo Review (ISSN: 0039-1220), ?, 1989.
LC: ML 1.H45
ISSN: 0018-1455
ABST: --Abridged Readers' Guide to Periodical Literature (ISSN: 0001-334x)
--Book Review Index (ISSN: 0524-0581)
--Consumers Index to Product Evaluations and Information Sources (ISSN: 0094-0534)
--Film Literature Index (ISSN: 0093-6758)
--Magazine Index
--Music Index (ISSN: 0027-4348)
--Popular Magazine Review (ISSN: 0740-3763)
--Readers Guide to Periodical Literature (ISSN: 0034-0464)

High Fidelity & Audiocraft

Dec, 1958 - Mar, 1959//
SEE: HIGH FIDELITY

✥ HIGH FIDELITY/MUSICAL AMERICA

PUBL: ABC Leisure Magazines, Inc., 825 Seventh Ave., New York, NY 10019.
DESC: Aimed at the American lay public, *High Fidelity/Musical America* publishes articles conerning the technological and performance side of music-oriented media. Coverage includes laboratory tests, explanations of new technology, and reviews of new music releases. Numerous graphics.
DEPT: "About This Issue," "Letters," "Video Lab Test," "Reviews," music; "Critics' Choice," "The Tape Deck," "Jazz Reviews," "Pop Reviews." (10-84).
TYPL: "Basically Speaking," "Refinements for the Road," "Sample and Hold," "CD Players--How They Compare," "Odd Man Out--or In?" (10-84).
SCHL: Monthly, 120 pp.
SPAN: Apr, 1959+?
FROM MERGER OF
--High Fidelity (ISSN: 0018-1455), (and) Musical America, Apr, 1959.
LC: ML 1.H
ISSN: 0735-777x

High Fidelity Trade News

1957 - Jun?, 1983//
(ISSN: 0046-7367)
SEE: PERSONAL ELECTRONICS

✥ HIGH PERFORMANCE

SUB: "A quarterly magazine for the new arts audience."
SUB: "The performance art quarterly."
SUB: "Art that matters."
PUBL: Astro Artz, 240 South Broadway, 5th Fl., Los Angeles, CA 90012.
DESC: *High Performance* is the antithesis of the traditional still-life fruitbowl carefully positioned on oil painted canvas. It is more a contemporary marriage between technology and art, with technology allowing the artistic. The publication showcases live performance, video, film, exhibition, and other media of artistic expression; much of which has been missed or ignored by main-stream media. Lengthy articles supported by interesting graphics delve into artistic philosophies and reasoning behind projects, oftentimes accompanyied by critical reviews of those projects. Of special note is the umbrella-title series, "Viewpoint," which in the sampled issue reported on various projects from sundry cities (Los Angeles, San Francisco Bay Area, New York, Rochester, San Diego, Washington DC, Miami, Chicago, Seattle, Portland); and selected countries (Germany, France): It also presented unique applications of media (video, installations, books, holography, and recordings). Previous issues covered the Olympic Arts Festival, a performance in England and Ireland, visual theatre, women performance poets, and experimental music and theatre. There is a dynamic spirit about *High Performance* that makes not only for informative reading, but which stimulates and expands the sense of the artistic in public performance. For those interested in this field, *High Performance* is required reading. Perfect bound magazine format, black/white editorial content on uncoated paper stock with full-color covers. Numerous advertisements enhance the editorial content (8 ⅜ x 11 inches / 215 x 280 mm).
DEPT: "Colloquium," essay and editorial; "Letters," "Editor Speak," "Artist Books," "New Music," "Film," "Running Commentary," column by Linda Burnham; "Hot

TYPL: "High-Tech TV: Low-Level Content/Fast-Moving Ads," "Video Art: An Historical Sketch," "A Few Arguments for the Appropriation of Television," "Body Heat: Interactive Media and Human Response," "Musings on an Interactive Postmodern Metaphor." (vol 10, #1-87).
Shorts," 'News and notes from the world of live art plus a special section on video'; "Quick Sketches," "The Crowd," "Tacit." (vol 10, #1-87).
SCHL: Quarterly, 105 pp.
SPAN: Feb, 1978+
LC: NX 600.P47 H53
ISSN: 0160-9769
ABST: --Abstrax
--Art Bibliographies Modern (ISSN: 0300-466x)
--Art Index (ISSN: 0004-3222)

High School Thespian
Oct, 1929 - May, 1944//
SEE: DRAMATICS

✧ HIGH TECH LIFESTYLES
SUB: "The magazine for experienced technical professionals."
PUBL: BPI Publishing Co., 2985 Multifoods Tower, 33 South Sixth St., Minneapolis, MN 55402.
DESC: "*High Tech Lifestyles* is about the personal components of a high-technology career -- working for a balanced lifestyle, productivity, creativity, health and even trivial pursuits." A very unusual tabloid publication, *High Tech Lifestyles* is targeted to the "...personal components of a high-technology career -- profiles of people in the industry, companies that are hot, useful information about dual-career marriages, health issues, tips on achieving career objectives, recreation and a lot more." This magazine seeks a very broad subscriber base (certainly beyond just communication), and is concerned with people, rather than with product. Tabloid format; color graphics. Note: issued in two editions, "New England," and "Mid-Atlantic."
DEPT: None. (6-89).
TYPL: "In the Driver's Seat," "Wing Walker," "Advocate for Change," "A Challenging Career Path." (6-89).
SCHL: Quarterly, 35 pp.
SPAN: ?, 1988+
DD: 650 11
ISSN: 1047-0034

✧ HIGH VOLUME PRINTING
SUB: "Prepress, sheetfed, web, postpress."
PUBL: Innes Publishing Co., 425 Huehl Rd., Bldg. 11, Northbrook, IL 60062-2319.
DESC: Editor Catherine M. Stanulis summed up the purpose of *High Volume Printing* in this commentary: "Whether it's a question of what coating to use, which filter response to use or how to comply with government regulations, we can't make the decisions for you, nor do we believe that there is always one easy, clean-cut answer or solution. We can, however, provide you with several viewpoints (opinions with facts to back them) that can assist you in your information-gathering process. It is our intent to do the groundwork for you: to make you aware of what technologies, materials and equipment are available, and how they have been used, how they are being used and potential future uses for them. ... Every article in *HVP* is fair-game; open for rebuttal and discussion. If you are decidedly in support of or in opposition to any topic discussed in any issue, I'd like to hear from you." And readers respond to the invitation with a diversity of topics, issues and trends that provides a lively, spirited letters forum within this publication. The art, technique, and craft of printing is the focus of *High Volume Printing*; from prepress to postpress; from color to black/white; from the knowledgable   itical eye of an industry professional, to the high technology of computerized applications in the press room. *High Volume Printing* is the place where all of these elements come together, and shows the strong dynamics in this very important arena of communication. For the 1990 sampled issue: magazine format (8 1/4 x 10 7/8 inches / 210 x 275 mm), full color graphics throughout, printed on clay-coated paper.
DEPT: "Letters," "Personnel," newsbriefs; "Trends and Ideas," newsbriefs; "Installations & Expansions," equipment installed; "Management," "Product Information," "Product Watch," "HVP Ad/Editorial," "Literature Directory." (10/11-90).
TYPL: "Good News: Printing Shipments Up, Bad News: Slow Growth Rates," "Custom Publishing Enables Up-to-Date Textbooks," "Standardizing Color Communication: A Status Update," "The Sheetfed Press: The Race for Automation of Color Control," "Financing Equipment: How the Lender Evaluates You," "Coating and Drying on Sheetfed Litho Presses." (10/11- 90).
SCHL: Bimonthly, 100 pp.
SPAN: ?+
VARIES
--? - Sep/Oct?, 1980 as Book Production Industry & Magazine Production (ISSN: 0192-2874).
--Nov/Dec, 1980 - May, 1982 as Book and Magazine Production (ISSN: 0273-8724).
LC: Z 119 .H54
DD: 070.5/05
ISSN: 0737-1020
ABST: --Predicasts
--Printing Abstracts (ISSN: 0031-109x)

Highlights
Jan, 1975 - ?//
SEE: NAB HIGHLIGHTS

✥ HISTORICAL JOURNAL OF FILM, RADIO & TELEVISION

PUBL: Carfax Publishing Co., (in association with the International Association for Audio-Visual Media in Historical Research and Education), Haddon House, Dorchester-on-Thames, Oxford OX9 8JZ, England.

DESC: "The *Historical Journal of Film, Radio & Television* is an interdisciplinary journal concerned with the evidence provided by the mass media for historians and social scientists, and with the impact of mass communications on the political and social history of the twentieth century. The needs of those engaged in research and teaching are served by scholarly articles, book reviews and by archival reports concerned with the preservation and availability of records. The journal also reviews films, television and radio programmes of historical or educational importance. In addition, it aims to provide a survey of developments in the teaching of history and social science courses which involve the use of film and broadcast materials. It is the official journal of the International Association for Audio-Visual Media in Historical Research and Education (IAMHIST)." An excellent resource for the study of the role of film, radio and television in society. Journal format (6 7/8 x 9 3/4 inches / 175 x 245 mm).

DEPT: "Documents/Interview," "Comments/News/Notices," "Book Reviews." (#1- 83). "Comment/News/Notices," excellent review of historical exhibits and other news items of interest to media historians. (#3-88).

TYPL: "Hollywood Propaganda for World Peace," "John Grierson and the G.P.O. Film Unit, 1933-1939," "Charlie Chaplin's Early Life: Fact and Fiction," "The Intimate Voice of Australian Radio." (#1-83). "The BBC Television Newsreel and the Korean War," "'Any Resemblance to Persons Living or Dead': Film and the Challenge of Authenticity," "The British Colonial Film Uited and Sub-Saharan Africa, 1939 - 1945." (#3-88).

SCHL: Semiannual (1981 - 1986); Three issues per year (1987+), 86 pp.
SPAN: Mar, 1981+
LC: PN 1993.5.A1 H54
DD: 791.4/05
ISSN: 0143-9685
ABST: --America, History and Life (ISSN: 0002-7065)
--Film Literature Index (ISSN: 0093-6758)
--Historical Abstracts. Part A. Modern History Abstracts. (ISSN: 0363-2712)
--Historical Abstracts. Part B. Twentieth Century Abstracts. (ISSN: 0363-2725)
--Media Review Digest (ISSN: 0363-7778)
--Writings on American History (ISSN: 0364-2887)

✥ HISTORY OF PHOTOGRAPHY

SUB: "An international quarterly."
PUBL: Taylor & Francis, Inc., 10-14 Macklin St., London WC2B 5NF, England.

DESC: "*History of Photography* is devoted to the publication of original findings and the assessment of their significance. It is addressed to readers who have a serious interest in this field, to art historians and art teachers, photographers and collectors, librarians and archivists, teachers and students of journalism, and social historians. It will encourage the systematic preservation of photographic source material and will emphasize its value to sociology and art history. One of the principle purposes of the journal is to promote an understanding of the subtle relationships between photography and the other graphic arts." The Outline of Scope includes the following: "The camera obscura and related instruments; discovery of photo-chemical processes; the invention of photography in its various forms; reaction of artists and lay public to the new invention; lives of notable inventors and practitioners; the spread of photographic knowledge and practice to distant lands; earliest uses of photography in exploration, education, science and war; professional studio practice in the 19th and early 20th century; relationship between photographic technique and photographic style; growth of photographic industry and literature; development of cameras; other technical inventions and discoveries related to photography; the photography of movement and origins of the cinema; influence of painting on photographic style; influence of photography on painting and sculpture; history of photo-mechanical reproduction; influence of photography on the development of the press; history of photo-journalism; 19th and 20th century masters; the entry of photographic themes into fine literature; influence of photography on advertising; 20th century style trends; the preservation and restoration of old photographs; items of interest to photographic collectors; international gallery news; the teaching of photographic history." An outstanding publication by Taylor & Francis of London. For the sampled issues of 1977 and 1991: black/white graphics on heavy coated paper stock, cover consisting of black/white graphic with spot- ink color on heavy coated paper, limited advertising (8 1/4 x 11 3/4 inches / 210 x 300 mm).

DEPT: "Book Reviews." (#4-83). "Notes & Queries," "Recent Publications," review. (winter-91).

TYPL: "Early Photography in Iran," "Paul S. Taylor and the Origins of Documentary Photography in California," "Photograph Marriage Certificates," "Early Cineradiography and Cinefluorography," "Major Robert Gill." (#4-83). "The Department of Photographs at the Getty Museum," "Problematic Low-Sheen Salt and Albumen Prints," "Early British Patents in Photography," "Dissertations: Calotype and Daguerreotype," "Early Photography in Samoa." (winter-91).

SCHL: Quarterly, 90 pp.
SPAN: Jan, 1977+
LC: TR 15.H57
DD: 770/.9
ISSN: 0308-7298
ABST: --Abstrax
--Art Bibliographies Modern (ISSN: 0300-466x)
--Art Index (ISSN: 0004-3222)

--Repetoire International de la Litterature de l'Art (ISSN: 0145-5982)

HIT PARADER

SUB: "Top Tunes."
PUBL: Charlton Publishing Corporation, Charlton Building, Derby, CT.
DESC: In an era of live musical performance there was scant opportunity for anyone to write down the lyrics to a popular piece of music: *Hit Parader* did so. Each issue was packed with song lyrics, with over 115 in the sampled 1943 publication alone, all of which were alphabetically listed at the front of the magazine masthead. Song lyrics were identified by author and association to Broadway, motion picture, or other musical showcases. One very nice feature of *Hit Parader* was the presentation of motion picture songs, along with pictures of the stars, production stills, and brief plot information. In the wartime sampled issue, Universal Picture's new release, "Mister Big," starring Donald O'Connor, was showcased with associated production stills and featured music. The wartime theme was carried over in such popular songs as "Arise Guerillas, Arise," "Comin' In on a Wing and a Prayer," "Don't Try to Steal the Sweetheart of a Soldier," "Fighting Sons of the Navy Blue," "The Flag with a Permanent Wave," "Mr. President, I Want to Go Home," "Send Our Regards to the Boys Over There," "We Used to Call Them Dead End Kids," and "When the Dove of Peace Flies Again." A studio picture of Kitty Carlisle graced the front cover of the monthly. A wonderful historical guide to the popular musical tastes of America. For sampled issue of 1943: stapled magazine format, editorial content consisted of dark-green ink on newsprint, with two-color black/red ink cover on coated paper stock (8 7/8 x 11 3/4 inches / 225 x 300 mm).
DEPT: "To the Editor," popular bandleader comment; "The Hit Parader Band Wagon of Top Tunes," full text without music; "Facts About the Famous," cartoon profile of current singer or bandleader; "Hit Parader Gives You the Song of the Month," showcased; "Playback," new recordings, column by Bruce Gerald; "Hollywood Heart Beat," music in the movies column by Joanne Linder; "Tin Pan Alleying," humor and commentary column by Frances Bern. (9-43).
TYPL: "The Old Gray Mare is Back Where She Used to Be," "Featuring the Songs that Tommy Dorsey Helped Make Famous: It's Tommy Dorsey Time," "Fighting Songs of Fighting Nations," "Mister Big," "Down Memory Lane with Songs that Never Grow Old." (9-43).
SCHL: Monthly, 35 pp.
SPAN: Nov, 1942 - ?//

Holly Leaves

1913 - 1924//
SEE: HOLLYWOOD

HOLLYWOOD

PUBL: Fawcett Publications, Inc., 8555 Sunset Blvd., Hollywood, CA.
DESC: One of the classics of Hollywood film aficionados, *Hollywood* magazine for 32 years provided a steady stream of newspulp stories of the famed and not-so-famous of the silver screen. Here in popular duotone pages are off-screen happenings, weddings, divorces, new talent, catty fights and children's rights, secret Hollywood makeup tips, and new Hollywood film releases. In April, 1943, *Hollywood* merged with *Motion Picture* to become *Motion Picture combined with Hollywood*. Published on newsprint.
DEPT: "Movie Romance," "Fashions and Beauty," "What's New on the Screen," reviews; "The Editor's Mailbag," "The Publisher's Page," editorial; "With the News Sleuth," 'Current events in Hollywood and doings of your favorite stars;' "Cross-Examining the Stars," Q&A. (1-34). "Hollywood Newsreel," "Win the War," homefront news; "Movie Memos," "For Lovelier Hands," beauty; "Starred for Success," fashions; "Clues on Clothes," fashions; "Wartime Winners," cooking; "Movie Crossword," "Important Pictures," reviews. (2-43).
TYPL: "Why Love is Doomed in Hollywood," "Mae West's Personal Maid Tells All," "Groucho Marx Time," "Christmas Comes to Hollywood." (1-34). "Can the Rooney Marriage Survive?," "Ann Sheridan: We Didn't Part Friends," "Dorothy Lamour: Liberty Belle." (2-43).
SCHL: Monthly, 50 pp.
SPAN: 1913 - Mar, 1943//
VARIES
--1913 - 1924 as Holly Leaves.
--1925 - Jun, 1928 as Hollywood Magazine.
--Jun, 1933 - Aug, 1933 as Hollywood Movie Novels.
--Feb, 1939 - Feb, 1940 as Hollywood Screen Life.
ABSORBED BY
--Motion Picture Magazine, Apr, 1943.
LC: PN 1993.H43
DD: 791.43/05

HOLLYWOOD

SUB: "Official organ of the Hollywood Foreign Press Correspondents Association."
PUBL: N. Massaad, 6715 Hollywood Blvd., Hollywood, CA.
DESC: This was one of the most unusual serials of Hollywood, containing stories on film, the foreign press corps, local Arabic news, world developments of Lebanon, religion, and other subjects that one might not expect in a "Hollywood" magazine. Text was in English and Arabic on black/white coated stock, the official publication of the Hollywood Foreign Press Correspondents Association. But oftentimes that was the only link between *Hollywood* magazine and the "film capital of the world." In some issues the editor had merely clipped American newspaper articles concerning American-Arabic activities; at other times film publicity stills appeared without any explanation.

A typical issue (March, 1950) included articles on: Oliva de Havilland receiving the Golden Globe award, Arabic news from Jacksonville, Florida; Hollywood weddings of non-film couples; news that the Egyptians had invented an H-Bomb; film celebrities at a Peruvian reception; how to have good vision without glasses, drugs or surgery; and a personal interview (reprinted from the 1947 original) of an interview with Father Divine! This was a serial (in Arabic, English, and sometimes Spanish) that defies categorization.
SCHL: Monthly, 40 pp.
SPAN: Jan, 1950 - ?//
LC: PN 1993.H426

Hollywood

Jul, 1980 - Jan, 1983//
(ISSN: 0199-7866)
SEE: SCREEN ACTOR HOLLYWOOD

Hollywood Close Up

Mar, 1980 - May/Jun?, 1980//
(ISSN: 0199-7866)
SEE: SCREEN ACTOR HOLLYWOOD

HOLLYWOOD FILMOGRAPH

SUB: "The world's only real motion picture newspaper."
PUBL: Hollywood Filmograph, 1606 Cahuenga, Suite 213-214, Los Angeles, CA.
DESC: Here was an inside publication for the Hollywood film community. Some segments of this large magazine format weekly provided film fan information and local schedules of entertainment, but the majority of each issue dealt with industry news (with an emphasis on local news), especially as it related to talent, and new picture product ready to cast or to go into production. That this publication had a local readership was apparent from a variety of ads for local services from valets seeking positions, to fancy milk-fed poultry available in Southern California supermarkets. The clean layout style, and current industry news made this a favorite of the Hollywood community during its publication lifetime.
DEPT: "General News," "Editorials," "Diversion: Where and When," event schedule; "Reviews and Previews," "Theatre, Vaudeville and Melody," newsbriefs; "Camera Shots," column by Neil Brant; "Who's Who," column by Harry Burns; "New York News," "Bulletin Board," film production schedule; "The Passing Week," newsbriefs; "Film-o Graphs," newsbriefs; "Movietunes," column by Al Kingston; "Buzzing Around with Vic Enyart," "Talking Up," newsbriefs; "The Moving Movie Throng," column by John Hall; "About Town with Connie." (6-28-29).
TYPL: "Equity-Producers Deadlock May Last Several Weeks," "Attacks 'Bigoted, Foolish' Censors," "Special Theatre Uses of Sound," "Complete Talking Picture Contract and Rules Submitted to Producers This Week by Equity," "Sid Grauman Quits Exhibitor Ranks to Produce." (6-28-29).
SCHL: Daily [except Monday] (Apr, 1922 - May, 1923); Weekly (May?, 1923+), 35 pp.
SPAN: Apr, 1922 - Oct 27, 1934//
VARIES
--Apr, 1922 - May?, 1923 as Morning Filmograph.
--May?, 1923 - 1929 as Filmograph.
LC: PN 1993.H45

✦ HOLLYWOOD MAGAZINE

SUB: "It's not L.A."
PUBL: Aviation News Corporation, 3 Burroughs, Irvine, Ca 92718.
DESC: The subtitle says it clearly: this is a magazine ABOUT Hollywood, for the citizenry (and other interested parties), of that fabled town, which possesses no interest in (and therefore no coverage) of anything south of the Los Angeles/Hollywood city line. *Hollywood Magazine* is witty, informative, articulate, and VERY hard to put aside: articles go beyond standard supermarket fare, treating the reader and subject matter alike with respect. It is a wonderful adventure into the motion picture/television field (both past and present), which heightens understanding and appreciation of this industry of make-believe. One sample issue provided historical insight into literary giants coming to grips with the reality of the Hollywood film, a profile of the Danish film studio Nordisk, a past/present look at the home of Jayne Mansfield, automobiles of Hollywood movers and shakers, a wonderful piece of humor on who qualifies to be a "Hollywood Dude," and places around town where gourmet picnickers could stock up for their Hollywood Bowl travels. Typical of the unpredictable nature of this publication was an article recounting a German UFA cameraman nearly killing a pedestrian in the middle of a darkened highway in the 1920s: the pedestrian was Adolph Hitler. Witty, urbane, and wonderfully entertaining, *Hollywood Magazine* is for anyone who has an interest in that "state of mind" called Hollywood. Magazine format (8 x 10 ⅞ inches / 205 x 275 mm); color and black/white graphics. Volume/issue numbering, unfortunately, not utilized.
DEPT: "Newsreel," observations; "Mail Pouch," 'Words, some kind' letters; "Fade In," calendar and comment; "Point of View," editorial; "Callsheet," bios and pictures of contributors; "Hollywood High Tech," column by I. M. Hacker; "Where Hollywood Plays," column by Abby Hirsch; "The Stars' Stars," 'Bonfire of the vanities' horoscope' column by Jeremiah Sullivan; "Where Hollywood Lives," column by Mike Szymanski; "Dept. of Nip 'N' Tuck," column by Arcona; "How Hollywood Flies," column by Jane Hershey; "Diary of a D-Girl," column by Alexis Blair; "Beyond the Stars," column by Beatrice Rich; "Be-

yond the Commissary," column by Ingrid Wilmot; "Fade Out," commentary column by Andrew Marx. (9-90).
TYPL: "Fitzgerald Fizzled and Huxley Humped," "Hollywood Gone Literary," "Rosencrantz & Guildenstern are Dead, Abbott & Costello Aren't," "Babette Feasted Here," "No Man is an Island. There are Exceptions," "Queen of the Lot: Norma Shearer was Really Norma Desmond. Believe It." (9-90).
SCHL: Bimonthly, 70 pp.
SPAN: 1988+
DD: 791 11
ISSN: 1045-361x

Hollywood Magazine
1925 - Jun, 1928//
SEE: HOLLYWOOD

Hollywood Movie Novels
Jun, 1933 - Aug, 1933//
SEE: HOLLYWOOD

HOLLYWOOD NOW
SUB: "A journal in defense of American democracy."
PUBL: Hollywood Anti-Nazi League for the Defense of American Democracy, 6513 Hollywood Blvd., Los Angeles, CA.
DESC: *Hollywood Now* was developed as a very strong voice of Hollywood citizens concerned about the rise of Nazism in Europe during the 1930s. While it focused on Nazism rather and the role of media, its writers and readers were at the center of Hollywood life. Special emphasis in stories concerned Hollywood stars and producers who donated time, talent and films to raise money and the consciousness of Americans.
DEPT: None.
TYPL: "Hollywood Stars Hold Giant 'Save Spain' Rally Sunday," "New Hitler Propagandist Due In U.S.," "Money from Nazi Film Sent to Loyalist," "Nazi Angle for Powerful Radio Station in S.A.," "Legion AFL-CIO Join Hollywood Fight on Nazism." (2-3-39).
SCHL: Semimonthly (Mar 20, 1937 - ?); Weekly (?+), 4 pp.
SPAN: Oct, 1936 - Feb, 1940//
VARIES
--1936 - Mar, 1937 as Anti-Nazi News.
--Mar 20, 1937 - Nov, 1937 as News of the World.
LC: DD 253 A1H72

Hollywood Quarterly
Oct, 1945 - Summer, 1951//
SEE: FILM QUARTERLY

✤ HOLLYWOOD REPORTER
SUB: "Over fifty years of service to the industry."
SUB: "World entertainment news daily."
PUBL: Hollywood Reporter Corporation, 6715 Sunset Blvd., Hollywood, CA 90028.
DESC: For almost 60 years *The Hollywood Reporter* has ranked as "must" reading activity for the "movers and shakers" of Hollywood and the New York environs. Treating show business as business is a hallmark of this publication, with articles providing news of deals made and broken; proposed productions, economic growth of the industry, budgets, distribution, exhibition, and anything else pertinent to the business of entertainment. In one sampled issue for 1991 were such articles as European financial institutions turning from American funding to that of the expanding European production community, the changing area of network television children's programming, and an article which provided a barometer of the entertainment business via stocks, bonds, and other corporate decisions. Of special note in each issue are quality film and television program reviews, often written with information about the above-the-line team. The "Calendar" section is one of the most detailed of upcoming events calendars in the entertainment industry. There are many publications available for different aspects of the entertainment field, but none quite like the *Hollywood Reporter*, the "world entertainment news daily." For sampled issue of 1991: stapled magazine format, editorial content is primarily black ink with red spot color, and some advertising in full-color, all on coated paper stock (8 3/8 x 11 inches / 210 x 280 mm).
DEPT: "Rambling Reporter," personality news bits; "TeleVisions," video news briefs; "This Week at the Boxoffice," gross L.A. and N.Y. receipts; "The Business of Entertainment," yesterday's stock reports; "The Great Life," personality news of Hollywood and west coast; "Travel Log," whereabouts of major media individuals. (10-31-83). "Rambling Reporter," column by Robert Osborne; "Film Review," "TV Review," "Hollywood Report," column by Martin Grove; "Financial," "Entertainment Stocks," "People on the Move," personnel briefs; "Legal Notes," newsbriefs; "Stage Review," "Off the Cuff," column by Hank Grant; "Stage Notes," newsbriefs; "TeleVisions," column by Richard Hack; "Choice Real Estate Sales," unusual section of Hollywood area homes for sale; "The Great Life," column by George Christy. (3-27-87).
TYPL: "German Tax Shelter Spurs $37.5 Million in Israeli Films," "WCI Reports Record Profits Led by Music Group Gains," "Incoming FCC Chief Vows Renewed Network Inquiry." (9-77); "NATO Goes International," "Massive Ad Budget Set to Lure Holiday Gift-Givers," "Senate Support of Syndie Stall Bodes Well for Producers," (10-31-83). "UACI Unwraps Realignment of Exhibition, Entertainment," "RSO Films Signs Prod'n, Distrib'n Pact at Weintraub," "AFI Pays Tribute to Arthur Cohn," "Exhibition on a Roll," "New Tax Laws: Difficult Times Ahead." (3-27-87).

SCHL: Daily (except Saturday, Sunday and legal holidays with special editions the first week in September and last week in November), 65 pp.
SPAN: Sep 3, 1930+
LC: PN 1993.H5
DD: 791
ISSN: 0018-3660

Hollywood Screen Life

Feb, 1939 - Feb, 1940//
SEE: HOLLYWOOD

HOLLYWOOD SPECTATOR

PUBL: Hollywood Spectator, 6513 Hollywood Blvd., Hollywood, CA.
DESC: This biweekly 15-page periodical provided reviews and data on new film releases. Editor Welford Beaton preceded those reviews with a three-page commentary on what was happening in the glitter capitol. His viewpoint covered subjects ranging from the color of tablecloths in motion pictures, to the promotion of films. The magazine consisted primarily of editor Beaton's commentary and reviews, with occasional outside articles.
DEPT: "From the Editor's Easy Chair," large viewpoint column by Welford Beaton; "What Late Ones Look Like," long reviews and cast-crew data on new films; "Film Music and its Makers," concerning film scores and music. (4-15-39).
TYPL: None.
SCHL: Biweekly, 15 pp.
SPAN: Mar, 1926 - Jul, 1941//
 VARIES
 --Mar, 1926 - Jun 13, 1931 as Film Spectator, The.
 --Jun, 1931 - Mar, 1932 as Hollywood Spectator.
 --Apr, 1932 as Hollywood Star and the Hollywood Spectator.
 --Jun, 1933 - Mar, 1934 as Welford Beaton's Hollywood Spectator.
 SUSPENDED
 --May, 1932 - May, 1933.
 --Jun, 1940 - Feb, 1941.
 SUPPLEMENT TO
 --Los Angeles Spectator, Apr, 1934 - Oct, 1935.
 ABSORBED
 --Books and Films, Oct, 1938.
LC: PN 1993.H

Hollywood Spectator

Jun, 1931 - Mar, 1932//
SEE: HOLLYWOOD SPECTATOR

Hollywood Star and the Hollywood Spectator

Apr, 1932//
SEE: HOLLYWOOD SPECTATOR

✤ HOLLYWOOD STUDIO MAGAZINE

SUB: "Every issue a collector's item."
SUB: "For nostalgia & video collectors."
SUB: "The national film & collectors' magazine."
PUBL: Hollywood Studio Magazine, 3960 Laurel Canyon Blvd., Suite 450, Studio City, CA 91614-3791.
DESC: *Hollywood Studio Magazine* is a classy nostalgia piece focusing on the studio era of motion pictures, reprinting stills of that time; including a number of which have not been seen before; and articles concerning stars, especially short treatments on life stories. Feature articles on stars and starlets are well detailed, and provide interesting informational elements not seen in other magazines of this nature. Care is shown in layout and printing of studio stills. Here is a love affair with Hollywood as it was. For the 1990 sampled issue: black/white editorial content with full-color pull-out section, and full-color cover on coated paper stock in stapled magazine format (8 x 10 ¾ inches / 205 x 275 mm).
DEPT: "Movie Reel," newsbriefs; "Key Hole Portraits," unique one-line biographies of stars, column by Harry F. Parsons; "Lee Graham's Scrapbook," 'collection of unpublished candid-camera photos;' "Interesting New Books," review; "Lee Graham. . .Man About Town," current newsbriefs; "Celebrity Dining," thinly disguised reviews to promote dining spots in L.A. area; "Collectors," readers write about their own movie memorabilia. (3-79). "Letters," "Collector's Corner," pictures of individual readers and their movie memorabilia; "Man About Town," column by Lee Graham. (1-90).
TYPL: "He Followed the Yellow Brick Road," "Hollywood's Great Singing Stars," "Julie Andrews: Beneath the Veil," "The Enchanting Alice Faye," "A Pilgrimage to the Carmen Miranda Museum." (3-79). "Bette Davis," "Christmas Cards From the Stars," "I Went to the Emmys," "How to Write the Stars." (1-90).
SCHL: Monthly [except Jan or Jul] (? - May, 1987); Monthly (Jun, 1987+), 45 pp.
SPAN: May, 1953+
LC: PN 1993.H54
DD: 791.43/0973
ISSN: 0894-2188

✤ HOME & STUDIO RECORDING

SUB: "The magazine for the recording musician."
PUBL: Music Maker Publications, Inc., 22024 Lassen St., Suite 118, Chatsworth, CA 91311.

DESC: As recording technology has developed, progressing through the rigours of computerization, and made more verstatile in the process, a new interest in "home studios" has been fostered for musician and recording engineer alike. *Home & Studio Recording* provides the home and commercial worlds with information, news, technology, and trends concerning this "compact" studio field. Technological developments have made this magazine possible, and it is no surprise that its primary emphasis is on the equipment side of the industry, showcasing new products, their application, and "real-world" operation of such equipment. New emerging talent, in the form of recording engineers and producers, also receive their due, providing insight about breaking into this interesting field. Articles inform without requiring a degree in acoustical or recording engineering. Some issues feature special topics such as microphones. For the 1990 sampled issue: stapled magazine format, spot and full-color graphics and editorial content throughout on coated paper stock, including cover (8 ¼ x 10 ⅞ inches / 210 x 275 mm).
DEPT: "Fade In," editorial; "Feedback," letters; "Fast Forward," new product review; "Readers' Tapes," unique section about demo tapes; "Fade Out," comment. (7-90).
TYPL: "Stretching the Boundaries," "Studio Microphone Roundup," "Roland S-770," "Microphone Techniques for Sampling," "On the Beat." (7-90).
SCHL: Monthly, 80 pp.
SPAN: Nov, 1987+
ABSORBED
--Music Technology (ISSN: 0896-2480), ?
LC: TK 7881.4 .H65
DD: 621.389/3 19
ISSN: 0896-7172

✢ HOME ENTERTAINMENT

SUB: "The electronics lifestyle magazine."
SUB: "For today's connoisseur of tomorrow's lifestyle."
SUB: "The new way to entertain, communicate, relax and learn."
PUBL: Home Entertainment Publications, Inc., 25 Willowdale Ave., Port Washington, NY 11050.
DESC: "*Home Entertainment* is the first and only consumer electronics fashion, design, and lifestyle magazine. It is an articulate, colorful, innovative look at today's new products and technologies. Now for the first time, the world's best writers and most famous interior designers editorially and pictorially explore the elegant, exciting ways electronic products fit into life, lifestyle, and home." Full-color graphics in a dynamic layout design highlight the interaction between home consumer, new entertainment technologies, and the "coming together" of those entities within the home environment. This is an "upscale." Articles are well-written, providing detailed information on new products, and charting the trends for future electronic entertainment media. Perfect-bound magazine format, full-color throughout on coated paper stock (8 ⅜ x 10 ⅞ inches / 210 x 275 mm).
DEPT: "Letter From the Editor," editorial preview column by Judith Morrison; "From Our Readers," letters to the editor; "Sense and Nonsense," computers and the home column by Dawn Gordon; "Design Dynamics," home entertainment center design column by Dora Antler; "From Where You Sit," column by Steve Birchall; "Spirits and Snacks," food to accompany home entertainment; "Sources & Resources," new product review; "Entertainment Environments," "When You're Buying," technology guide; "Home Entertainment Visits," home profiles; "Tomorrow Things," technology to come. (winter-88).
TYPL: "How High the Tune?," "Planning the Perfect Audio-Video System," "Showcase: The Rack Becomes a Home," "A Visit with Wil Shriner, Bill Maher, Jimmy Brogan," "The CD Family Expands." (winter-88).
SCHL: Bimonthly, (Jul/Aug, 1983 - ?); Eight issues per year (Jan/Feb, 1986+), 95 pp.
SPAN: Fall, 1983+
VARIES
--? - ? as Home Entertainment Quarterly (ISSN: 0746-2719).
DD: 749
ISSN: 0746-2727

Home Entertainment Quarterly

? - ?//
(ISSN: 0746-2719)
SEE: HOME ENTERTAINMENT

✢ HOME MOVIES

SUB: "Hollywood's magazine for the amateur."
SUB: "Hollywood's magazine for the 8 mm and 16 mm amateur and professional cine photographer."
PUBL: Ver Halen Publications, 6327 Santa Monica Blvd., Hollywood, CA.
DESC: In the Hollywood tradition of motion picture promotion, Ver Halen Publications trumpeted the about to be released new version of its popular magazine: "Stupendous! Colossal! Gigantic! Big words--yet inadequate to describe the New, Bigger, More Important *Home Movies* Magazine that will make its debut... You'll want to read every one of the inspiring articles of those enthusiastic amateurs who are 'going places'; the timely contributions being gathered from amateurs and professionals the country over; and you'll like those swell title backgrounds which will continue to be a big feature of the new *Home Movies*. ... Yes! You'll agree, the new *Home Movies* is tops...stupendous, colossal, and gigantic!" These accolades could easily have been assigned to the current issues of the 1930s as well, for *Home Movies* packed a significant amount of enthusiasm in everything presented for amateur moviemaker-readers. Articles covered both the technical and aesthetic aspects of home movies,

with greater emphasis on the former. Technical subjects often contained schematic drawings and explanatory photographs or production stills. One article concerning movie animated titles even provided the title blanks for readers to cut out and use. Two feature articles of note in the sampled issue consisted of a report on a very active "Amateur Cine Club" shooting a Long Island "feature," and "Tell Me How I Can Improve My Film," provided critical analyses of three reader submitted films, two on 16mm and one on 8mm film stock. For sampled issue of 1939: stapled magazine format, editorial content consisting of black/white on coated paper stock, cover was two-color blue and black ink on coated paper stock (9 x 12 inches / 230 x 305 mm).

DEPT: "The Reader Speaks," letters; "I've Got a Problem," reader submitted Q&A technical problems; "Backyard Movies," 'Ideas for random filming and short continuities' reader submitted; "Cine Quiz," skill test; "It's New to Me," new product review column by Cinebug Shopper; "The Experimental Cine Workshop," 'Gadgets, tricks and short cuts contributed by cinebugs'; "Movie of the Month," critiqued reader-submitted projects; "Title Troubles," Q&A technical column by George Cushman. (11-39).

TYPL: "Don't Junk Your Under or Over-Exposed Shots," "How Would You Light This Scene?," "There's Magic in a Telephoto Lens," "Hollywood or Home--Good Editing Makes 'Em 'Box Office'!," "Records Provide Sound, Plot, for Home Movies." (11-39).

SCHL: Monthly, 40 pp.
SPAN: 1934+
VARIES
--1934 - 1936 as Home Movies Magazine.

Home Movies Magazine
1934 - 1936//
SEE: HOME MOVIES

✜ HOME VIDEO
PUBL: United Business Publications, 475 Park Ave. South, New York, NY 10016.
DESC: A publication which is aimed at the quickly growing field of consumer home video, most articles concentrate on two primary areas; new video technology, and new programming software available on the market. Also, it profiles stars, and gives newsbriefs of the home video industry. Of special note is an excellent "Questions & Answers" column, which provides detailed information on the NTSC television system, and other mysteries of the visual medium. Questions are submitted by readers, and responded to with clear, understandable explanations; often with charts, graphs and schematics. Also of note is a great "Preview" section, providing detailed information concerning upcoming pay-cable, network and cable television, video disk and tape product. Numerous graphics. For sampled issue of 1982: stapled magazine format with mixture of black/white and full-color pages on coated paper stock (8 ¼ x 10 ⅞ inches / 210 x 275 mm).

DEPT: "Fast Forward," editorial; "Videotimes," newsbriefs; "Videopeople," "Videocast Previews," upcoming broadcasts on TV and cable; "Video Vigilante," "Reader Comment," "Videotapes/Discs," Reviews; "Videowares," equipment reviews; "Questions & Answers," from readers; "Final Thoughts." (1/81).

TYPL: "Inside Marilyn Chambers," "How the Mob Controls Video Piracy and Pornograhy," "I Have Seen the Video Future...and It is Sex." (1/81).

SCHL: Monthly, 75 pp.
SPAN: Fall, 1979+?
LC: TK 6655.V5 H65
DD: 778.59/9/05
ISSN: 0194-2484

✜ HOME VIDEO PUBLISHER
PUBL: Knowledge Industry Publications, Inc., 701 Westchester Ave., White Plains, NY 10604.
DESC: This weekly typewritten newsletter informs television program executives, producers, suppliers, and distributors about events and trends in the home videocassette sale/rental field. Articles concern various aspects of home video product, including new releases, pricing structure, marketing concepts, corporate trends, duplication throughput, profit margins, technology and regulation. Emphasis is on production/distribution, rather than on issues faced at the retail level. A very nice resource for those contemplating or actively involved in the home video market. Subscription cost (as of Mar, 1990) was $315 per year. For the sampled issue of 1990: loose-leaf, typewritten newsletter format in black ink with spot-color on cover, no advertising (8 ½ x 11 inches / 215 x 280 mm).

DEPT: None. (3-19-90).
TYPL: "Nontheatrical Sellthrough Market Emerging Overseas, Media Says," "Duplicators Cite Tough Competition, Slim Margins, Despite a Boom Year," "MGM/UA Home Video Expanding Sales and Marketing Departments." (3-19-90).
SCHL: Biweekly (Jul 16, 1984? - ?); Weekly (?+), 8 pp.
SPAN: Jul 16, 1984+
DD: 381
ISSN: 0748-0822

✜ HOME VIEWER
SUB: "The VCR guide."
PUBL: Home Viewer Publications, 11 North 2nd St., Philadelphia, PA 19106.
DESC: "If you like the videos you'll love the magazine. Enjoy renting movies? *Home Viewer* magazine has you covered like nobody else. All your favorite blockbuster films. Rock videos. Classics and specials. Entertainment updates, VCR equipment news and more. Plus, our exclusive 'Guide' section that reviews 300 new releases each month. The picks and pans, in the most

complete video listing anywhere. So you can read about it, before you rent it. Or buy it. ...*Home Viewer* treats you to insightful interviews. Witty editorials. And provocative style. It's all you need to know about home video, in one indispensable magazine." This promotional in-magazine advertisement sums up this monthly guide to home video entertainment. Using spot and full-color pages throughout, *Home Viewer* provides a detailed index to what's hot in video store rentals and purchases. Auxiliary articles inform about current releases, Hollywood personalities, and equipment reviews; but the primary emphasis remains current videotape fare. A very helpful guide to what's available in North American release. Stapled magazine format, full-color throughout on coated paper stock (8 ⅛ x 10 ⅞ inches / 205 x 275 mm).

DEPT: "Point of View," editorial; "Viewer Mail," letters; "Video Illustrated," news items; "Video Hit Parade," 'The best of what's new this month for your VCR' colorful review section; "Top 25 Hot Picks," 'Now playing in your store'; "Home Viewer Guide," 'Every new video release'; "Video First," direct-to-tape releases; "TVCR Highlights," broadcast review; "Laser Entertainer," review of new releases; "Index to New Releases," 'The A to Z guide to every new video title available this month'; "New Releases," "This Month's New Releases," 'The only complete guide that lists and describes every new video release every month'; "Ask Mr. Movie," reader Q&A column by Steve Friedman; "Star View," profile; "Music View," and videotapes; "Modern Living," new products; "TV Diner," tube-viewing recipes; "Hollywood Hit Line," personality and production news column by Steven Rea; "Previewer," upcoming video releases, column by Krys Longan. (8-87).

TYPL: "Get That Ol' Time Baseball Feeling!," "Couch Sprouts," "CD Video Singles: Short and Sweet," "A Fairy Tale Romance," "Eddie Murphy: Hollywood's Golden Child or Beverly Hills Cop-Out?" (8-87).

SCHL: Monthly, 35 pp.
SPAN: Apr, 1981+

✢ HOMILETIC

SUB: "A review of publications in religious communication."
SUB: "For professionals in preaching."
PUBL: Academy of Homiletics and the Religious Speech Communication Association, Lutheran Theological Seminary, 61 West Confederate Avenue, Gettysburg, PA 17325.
DESC: A subscription advertisement in *Homiletic* calls attention to its three primary attributes: "INFORMATIVE: Reviews include useful ideas in new books and guide your purchases. Each issue contains articles by noted persons in the field; COMPREHENSIVE: All important publications in preaching and religious communication are reviewed; INTERDISCIPLINARY: Special sections on disciplines which inform preaching and religious communication -- Biblical Interpretation, Theology, Worship, Art & Media, Human Sciences & Culture, and Communication Theory." *Homiletic* is published by the Lutheran Theological Seminary, and is sponsored by the Academy of Homiletics and the Religious Speech Communication Association. Articles cover a broad range of theological training. Authors in one sampled issue were associated with The National Center for Christian Preaching at The Southern Baptist Theological Seminary in Louisville, Kentucky, and The Divinity School of Duke University, Durham, North Carolina. Note: volume 1, #1 was preceeded by a pilot issue dated October, 1975 and published by the Homiletic Information Project. For the sampled issues of 1976, 1977, and 1978: stapled journal format, black ink on uncoated paper with uncoated tinted paper cover in black ink, no advertising (7 x 10 ¾ inches / 175 x 275 mm). Note: height and width dimensions varied slightly for the early years of this publication. For the sampled issues of 1990: journal format (6 ½ x 10 inches / 165 x 255 mm), with minimal advertising.

DEPT: "Reviews." (78). "Preaching," reviews; "Sermons," reviews; "History of Preaching," reviews; "Biblical Interpretation," reviews; "Theology," reviews; "Worship," reviews; "Communication Theory," reviews; "Art & Media," reviews; "Human Sciences & Culture," reviews; "Dissertations," reviews; "Conferences." (summer-90).

TYPL: "Preaching as a Theological Discipline," "What is Religious Communication?" (78). "Whatever Happened to Intellectual Honesty in the Sermon?," "Theology, Vestments, and Women's Nonverbal Communication." (summer-90).

SCHL: Annual (1976 - 1979); Semiannual [Jun & Dec] (1980+), 50 pp.
SPAN: Summer, 1976+
DD: 251
ISSN: 0738-0534

✢ HORIZON

SUB: "The newsletter for satellite and television professionals."
PUBL: Satellite Communications, 6311 North O'Connor, Suite 112, Irving, TX 75039.
DESC: A promotional newsletter for Horizon Satellite Communications, a Dallas-based firm specializing in "...C and Ku-band transponder time, portable and fixed uplinks, videoconference production, video and data network planning and management, and consulting on special projects." Articles highlight services offered by the corporation.
DEPT: None.
TYPL: "'88 Political Season--Ready or Not?," "'We Interrupt This Program,'" "Teleconference Connections." (spring-87).
SCHL: Quarterly, 4 pp.
SPAN: Summer?, 1986?+?

✤ HORRORFAN

PUBL: GCR Publishing Group, Inc., 888 Seventh Ave., New York, NY 10106.
DESC: Editor Bruce J. Schoengood, on the first anniversary of his publication: "It's my belief that horror fans are easily the most underrated of all magazine consumers. They are very loyal readers who possess a great deal of knowledge about their favorite subject--horror. My goal is to give our fans their money's worth. ...*Horrorfan* will continue to be jam-packed with color previews, comprehensive retrospectives, guest columnists, exclusive interviews and a delicate balance of what is old and new in horror film and video." *Horrorfan* is unique among similar publications in devoting significant space to old horror feature films now available on videocassette. As Schoengood stated, "The born-again fan has just opened up an entire spectrum of horror film entertainment that, due to the advent of video, is now easily available to him or her." Publication is an interesting mixture of black/white and full-color pages, with sufficient news and information on movies of the past, present, and forthcoming to please any aficionado of this motion picture and video entertainment format. Numerous production stills and production shots, most in "gorious" color; magazine format (8 x 10 7/8 inches / 205 x 275 mm).
DEPT: "Letter From the Editor," column by Bruce J. Schoengood; "Letters to the Editor," 'Readers respond to Horrorfan'; "Watch the Skies," 'Films from other galaxies are landing at a theater near you'; "Guest Columnist," "Video Sleeper," "Shelf Life," 'A quick look at the delights--and the dregs--available in your local video store'. (winter-89).
TYPL: "Retrospective: Bugs--Beware!," "The Phantom of the Opera," "Interview: Bob Clark," "Communion," "Retrospective: Claude Rains." (winter-89).
SCHL: Quarterly, 70 pp.
SPAN: Winter, 1988+

✤ HOT PICKS

SUB: "In mass market and trade paper."
PUBL: Baker & Taylor Books, a GRACE Distribution company, 652 East Main St., PO Box 6920, Bridgewater, NJ 08807-0920.
DESC: *Hot Picks* is described as "...a monthly newsletter featuring the latest mass-market paperbacks and spoken-word audio cassettes for adults, young adults, and children." With only two articles, this is more catalog than newsletter. The purpose is to alert retail stores, acquisitions librarians, and others of new releases in the mass-market paperback and spoken-word audio cassette field currently available through distributor Baker & Taylor Books. Numerous advertisements by publishing concerns. For the 1990 sampled issue: stapled magazine format, black ink editorial content with full-color cover on coated paper stock (8 1/4 x 10 3/4 inches / 210 x 275 mm).
DEPT: "Buyer's Choice," editorial; "Author of the Month," profile; "Adult Books," list; "Author Index," for paperbacks and audio cassettes; "Trade Paper Releases," list; "YA & Children's Books," list of young adult and childrens releases; "Roundup," topical listing; "Audio Listings," new audio cassette releases. (8-90).
TYPL: None. (8-90).
SCHL: Monthly, 45 pp.
SPAN: Jan, 1988+

✤ HOW

SUB: "Ideas & techniques in graphic design."
PUBL: F&W Publishing Co., 1507 Dana Ave., Cincinnati, OH 45207.
DESC: "*HOW* is the magazine of ideas and techniques in graphic design that takes you to the studios of the best art directors, production designers and computer graphics professionals in the world. *HOW* explores the world of graphic design, including the latest in publication design. ...See how the world's top designers design award-winning publications. Watch as they tackle an assignment from original concept and thumbnails, through roughs and mechanicals to the finished piece." Add to that this letter to *HOW*: "In a world filled with self-proclaimed design gurus and elitist artists, I find it refreshing for a design magazine to commit space to something that actually pertains to the business of design instead of decoration. As designer and businesspeople we constantly teeter back and forth between our desire to create and our fiduciary duties to increase the bottom line for ourselves and our clients. Once you have found that equilibrium you begin to progress as an artist and businessperson. Hopefully we have found that equilibrium." This hefty magazine (due to great amounts of unique paper stock inserts by various advertisers) provides a creative forum for today's graphic designer: it presents new ideas for design, unique paper stocks and printing processes, technology as applied to artistic media, and strong recognition for the business side of profit, without which graphic design would be mere artistic expression instead of an occupation. As might be assumed, layout design, color graphics, and printing are of the highest quality, and showcase the technological/artistic level of graphic design and production today. An excellent resource. Magazine format (8 x 10 7/8 inches / 205 x 275 mm).
DEPT: "Production," "Marketplace," "Bottomline," the business of graphic design; "Gallery," showcase; "Target Tactics," Sales and promotion strategies for the graphic designer; "Annotations," editorial; "Letters," "Specs," 'People, places and things from the world of design'; "Books," review; "Who's Where," resources keyed to articles; "Coming Up," next issue topics. (7/8-90).
TYPL: "Handmade Paper: Handmade Character," "Paper Promotion: Batting 1,000," "Recycled Paper: Recycled Rhetoric," "Paper Promotion: Tubular, Rad, Real Gone," "Catalog: Paris on Paper." (7/8-90).
SCHL: Bimonthly, 140 pp.

SPAN: Nov/Dec, 1985+
LC: NC 1000 .H68
DD: 741.6 19
ISSN: 0886-0483

✤ HOWARD JOURNAL OF COMMUNICATIONS, THE

PUBL: Howard School of Communications, Center for Communications Research, Howard University Press, PO Box 1233, Howard University, Washington, DC 20059.
DESC: "The *Howard Journal of Communications* is an independent, peer-reviewed, quarterly journal designed to foster exchange among scholars of all communications disciplines on theory, application, policy, and pathology, especially from a cultural perspective." Robust, challenging, informative and always interesting, this Howard University publication is an excellent forum for the discussion of communication issues from a unique cultural perspective. Individual issues are theme-oriented, such as "The Client Across Culture," and "The Caribbean and South American Press." Each issue consists of a wide variety of communication topics, all explored within a cultural perspective. A sampling of articles from one issue included "Twenty Years After Kerner: The Portrayal of African Americans on Prime-Time Television," "A Theoretical Framework for the Investigation of the Role and Significance of Communication in the Development of the Sense of Community Among English-Speaking Caribbean Immigrants," "A Comparison of Arab and American Conceptions of 'Effective' Persuasion," and "Domestic and Foreign Language News Reliance Among Chinese and American Students." This quarterly journal is a wonderful resource which studies the interaction between, and the impact of communication media upon culture and society. Of special note are extensive notations and references provided for each article. Journal format, black/white editorial content on uncoated paper stock with full-color cover, graphics, minimal advertising (7 x 10 inches / 175 x 255 mm).
DEPT: None. (fall-90).
TYPL: "State-Press Relations in Grenada, 1955 - 1983," "The Alternative Press in Bolivia and Ecuador: The examples of 'Aquí and Punto de Vista'," "The effects of Disconfirming Information on Stereotype Change," "Communication Strategies and Agricultural Development in 1950s China: The Early Years of the People's Republic of China," "Black Elected Officeholders Find White Press Coverage Insensitive, Incomplete, and Inappropriate." (fall-90).
SCHL: Quarterly, 90 pp.
SPAN: Spring, 1988+

✤ HUENEFELD REPORT, THE

SUB: "For managers and planners in modest-sized book publishing houses."
PUBL: Huenefeld Company, Inc., PO Box 665, Bedford, MA 01730.
DESC: John Huenefeld, senior publishing consultant, and author of the respected book, "The Huenefeld Guide to Book Publishing," generates this fortnightly newsletter "for managers and planners in modest-sized book publishing houses." A one-year (Fall, 1990) subscription rate of $88 for 26 issues is a judicious means of securing topnotch information and advice about book publishing. Huenefeld states that some 26,000 North American publishers have, in the past several decades, obtained ISBN (International Standard Book Numbers) registrations, which makes for a highly competitive business. The extremely volatile marketplace has seen numerous book publishers face bankruptcy, mergers, and financial takeovers in the past five years. *The Huenefeld Report* is designed to help "modest-sized book publishing houses" by instructing publishing managers on current trade practices, technologies, tricks of the trade, and trends in North American book publishing. Each issue contains two major articles. One sampled issue had the topics, "Selling Professional/Vocational Books Directly to Readers," and "Should You Offer Free Freight to Bookstores?" This is an articulate, information-packed newsletter that can easily be classified as "required reading" for North American book publishers. Typewritten newsletter format, with occasional typewritten graphics.
DEPT: None. (10-1-90).
TYPL: "Creating an Effective Editorial Planning Model," "What Discounts do Various Types of Publishers Offer?" (10-1-90).
SCHL: Biweekly, 4 pp.
SPAN: ?+

HUMAN COMMUNICATION

SUB: "A journal of the Canadian Speech and Hearing Association."
PUBL: School of Rehabilitation Medicine, Corbett Hall, University of Alberta, Edmonton, Alberta, Canada.
DESC: The focus of *Human Communication* (French title: *Communication Humaine*), was on the physiological side of speech and hearing. Articles explored spontaneous speech patterns in mentally retarded adolescents, use of volunteer speech aides in rural Manitoba, the expanding role of language specialists, pitch patterns in children's voices, and the language utilized by children with their mothers and an unfamiliar listener. Of special note was an interesting series of article abstract "cards" scored and bound into each issue. For the issue of 1979 these cards consisted of black ink on stiff index cardstock, ready to be cut and filed for future reference. Latter issues maintained the same format, but printed these abstracts on uncoated paper stock, with a dotted line to indicate the cut point. Note: text for the publication was in English and French from 1973 to 1980; in English only from 1981+. For the sampled issues of 1979: stapled journal

format, black ink on uncoated paper stock with two-color cover on uncoated textured cover stock (5 ¾ x 8 ½ inches / 145 x 215 mm).
DEPT: "Book Reviews." (summer-79).
TYPL: "A Correlational Study of Listening Rate Preference and Oral Reading Rates of Second Language Speakers," "An Interdisciplinary Approach to Voice Management Following a Tracheal Resection: A Case Study," "General vs. Specific Nonverbal Sensitivity and Clinical Training," "Parent Training: A Means of Implementing Pragmatics in Early Language Remediation," "Further Examination of the Regression Hypothesis." (summer-79).
SCHL: Three issues per year [spring, summer, fall], 40 pp.
SPAN: Spring, 1973 - Spring, 1981//
FOREIGN TITLE
--Communication Humaine.
SUSPENDED
--Winter, 1975.
MERGED WITH
--Hear Here (to form) Human Communication Canada (ISSN: 0822-5486).
DD: 618.9/2/855005
ISSN: 0319-1419

✤ HUMAN COMMUNICATION CANADA

PUBL: Canadian Speech and Hearing Association, Department of Speech Pathology and Audiology, 305 Corbett Hall, University of Alberta, Edmonton, Alberta T6G 2G4 Canada.
DESC: "*Human Communication Canada*, while the official journal of the Canadian Association of Speech Language Pathologists and Audiologists, seeks to foster the exchange of information along the international professional community as well as among Canadians. ... The scope of *Human Communication Canada* is broadly defined. It includes information pertaining to the processes and disorders of speech, hearing and language, as well as issues relating to human communication in general. Studies addressing the etiology, assessment and treatment of persons with communicative handicaps and the applications of new technologies for the communicatively impaired are also included in the journal." Some typical articles for 1985 included "Articulation and Phonology: Inextricable Constructions in Speech Pathology," "Prevalence of Communication Disorders in Canada: A Need for a Reliable Canadian Data Base," and "Auditory Brainstem Responses from Neonates: Special Considerations." For the sampled issues of 1985: black ink on coated paper stock with one-ink color cover, advertising, in stapled magazine format (8 ⅛ x 10 ¾ inches / 205 x 275 mm). Some issues contained text in French.
DEPT: "Books," review; "Products and Materials," review; "Commentary," "Letters to the Editor," "Announcements and Professional Development," "Calendar," "Career Opportunities." (7-85).
TYPL: "Perception of Rhythm in Speech," "Worldsign: A New Multi-Sensory Language Orientation to Cued Speech," "Audiological Management of the Hearing Impaired," "Augmentative Communication Project," "Implications of Kindergarten Language Delay." (7-85).
SCHL: Eight issues per year, 50 pp.
SPAN: Jan/Feb, 1983+
FOREIGN TITLE
--Communication Humaine Canada.
FROM MERGER OF
--Hear Here (and) Human Communication (ISSN: 0319-1419).
DD: 618.92/855/055
ISSN: 0822-5486

✤ HUMAN COMMUNICATION RESEARCH

SUB: "An official journal of the International Communication Association."
PUBL: Sage Publications, Inc., 2111 West Hillcrest Dr., Newbury Park, CA 91320.
DESC: "*Human Communication Research* is devoted to advancing knowledge and understanding about human symbolic transactions. Manuscripts dealing with reports of original research, descriptions of specific pathological approaches, critical syntheses of research literature, and theoretical perspectives for the conduct of human research are encouraged. The journal maintains a broad behavioral and social scientific focus but reflects no particular methodological or substantive biases." Journal articles tend to be a mixture of descriptive and quantitative research covering the broad field of the human communication experience. During the 1990/1991 time period articles ranged from "Memory Representations of Compliance-Gaining Strategies and Tactics," to "The Relationship Between Distress and Delight in Males' and Females' Reactions to Frightening Films;" and from "The Bridging Role of Television in Immigrant Political Socialization" to "The Influence of Relationship Beliefs and Problem-Solving Responses on Satisfaction in Romantic Relationships." This is an excellent journal of considered thought, research, and debate under the direction of the International Communication Association. For the sampled issue of 1991: perfect-bound journal format, black ink on uncoated paper stock with dark-blue ink cover on coated paper stock (5 ⅜ x 8 ½ inches / 135 x 215 mm), with charts and graphs, limited advertising.
DEPT: "Book Review Essay." (fall-74). None. (fall-82). None. (winter-85). None. (6-91).
TYPL: "Affection and Reciprocity in Self-Disclosing Communication," "An Exploration of Deception as a Communication Construct," "The Mediation of Resistance to Persuasion Strategies by Language Variables and Active-Passive Participation," "Role-Taking and Role-Playing in Human Communication." (fall-74). "A Rules Approach to the Study of Television and

Society," "Testing Basil Bernstein's Sociolinguistic Theories," "Factors Involved in Generating Suspense," "Changes in Language Behavior as a Function of Verasity," (fall-82). "Loneliness, Parasocial Interaction, and Local Television News Viewing," "Deception and Arousal: Isolating the Behavioral Correlates of Deception," "Discussion Procedures and Decision-Making Performance: A Test of a Functional Perspective," "The 'Competent Communicator' as a Cognitive Prototype," "Anticipated Interaction and Information Seeking." (winter-85). "Conversations with Able-Bodied and Visibly Disabled Strangers: An Adversarial Test of Predicted Outcome Value and Uncertainty Reduction Theories," "Relational and Content Differences Between Elites and Outsiders in Innovation Networks," "The Linearity Assumption in Cultivation Research." (6-91).
SCHL: Quarterly, 140 pp.
SPAN: Fall, 1974+
LC: P 91.3 .H85
DD: 301.2/1
ISSN: 0360-3989
ABST: --Current Index to Journals in Education (ISSN: 0011-3565)
--Film Literature Index (ISSN: 0093-6758)
--Language and Language Behavior Abstracts (ISSN: 0023-8295)
--Psychological Abstracts (ISSN: 0033-0202)
--Social Welfare, Social Planning / Policy and Social Development (ISSN: 0195-7988)

✤ HUNGAROFILM BULLETIN
PUBL: Hungarofilm, Bathory u. 10; Budapest 5, Hungary.
DESC: Primary function of *Hungarofilm Bulletin* is to alert individuals about the status of production projects in Hungarian film and television industries. As such, it is typically split into three sections: 1) new films; 2) films in production; and 3) television films. Each new cinema or video production announcement is accompanied by production stills, credits, and a one-page story synopsis. Occasional articles serve to introduce Hungarian directors and new creative talents. Text in each issue consists of English, French and German.
DEPT: None.
TYPL: No Article Titles.
SCHL: Quarterly, 35 pp.
SPAN: 1965+
ISSN: 0018-7798
ABST: --Film Literature Index (ISSN: 0093-6758)

✤ HYPERMEDIA
SUB: "The guide to interactive media production."
PUBL: Mix Publications, Inc., 6400 Hollis St., #12, Emeryville, CA 94608.
DESC: "This is a guide to the creative vision and technical application of hypermedia production in the fields of education, entertainment and business. It is intended for those who have some experience with media production, computers and interactivity; preferably those who have seen those elements converge, and who nurture a vision of the hypermedia landscape. It is a forum for prominent thinkers, producers and writers to describe the vision and the realities of hypermedia production. Integrating the complex threads of interactive electronic communication requires an emphasis on the relationship between the designer/producers and their reader/listener/user/viewers. New access paths to source material and new procedures for protection and licensing must be developed. Industry standards must emerge to facilitate diversity and universal connectivity. Hypermedia shaping tools must help us share knowledge, express emotion and explore truth." It is an outstanding publication in its area. For the 1988 premiere issue: perfect-bound magazine format, full color graphics and cover on coated paper stock (8 ¼ x 10 ⅞ inches / 210 x 275 mm).
DEPT: "Computers," "Publishing," "Audio," "Audio-Visual," "Film," "Interactivity," "AEC," architecture, engineering and construction; "Management," "Communications," "3-D Graphics," "Video," "Music," "International Update." (summer-88).
TYPL: "A Paradigm for Standards," "The Digital Revolution," "Artificial Intelligence & Expert Systems," "Alan Kay on Hypermusic." (summer-88).
SCHL: ?, 90 pp.
SPAN: Summer, 1988+?

IABC Journal

Spring, 1973 - Winter, 1974//
(ISSN: 0092-7384)
SEE: JOURNAL OF COMMUNICATION MANAGEMENT

IABC News

Winter?, 1971/1972 - May?, 1982//
(ISSN: 0744-7612)
SEE: COMMUNICATION WORLD

IAM

May, 1964 - Fall, 1975//
SEE: AM

✤ IAMHIST NEWSLETTER

PUBL: International Association of Audio-Visual Media in Historical Research and Education, c/o Jan-Christopher Horak, editor, George Eastman House, 900 East Ave., Rochester, NY 14607.

DESC: Those interested in the research, study, preservation and collection of mass media should join this excellent organization: this typewritten newsletter contains a capacious amount of information concerning access, preservation efforts, location, and current status of international media collections available for research. As befits the name of the organization, it provides news and information of world media collections not often found in any other publication. One sample issue dedicated half of its editorial content to an English summary reprint of the *Newsletter of the Association History, Image and Sound* (GBG-NIEUWS), published in the Netherlands. Note: the IAMHIST is associated with the *Historical Journal of Film, Radio & Television*, an excellent journal in this same field. For sampled issue of 1990: single-sheet typewritten newsletter stapled and photo-reduced, no graphics: (8 ½ x 11 inches / 215 x 280 mm).

DEPT: None. (1-90).

TYPL: "UCLA Television Archive Opened to Public," "Conference of German Society for Film and Television Research," "Film and Propaganda in America," "Desmet Collection at Nederlands Filmmuseum." (1-90).

SCHL: Quarterly, 16 pp.
SPAN: ?+
VARIES
--? - Autumn, 1985 as Newsletter.
LC: PN 1995.2 .N48
DD: 791.43/09/09358 19

✤ IBE

SUB: "International Broadcast Engineer."
PUBL: Whitton Press, 50 High St., Eton Berks SL4 6BL, England.
DESC: "*International Broadcast Engineer* is an independent journal devoted to the design, manufacture and operation of professional television and radio broadcast, and video equipment." This highly acclaimed British publication lives up to its *International* title with a world-wide engineering approach to the operation, maintenance, and purchase of broadcast equipment. Articles are technical, with outstanding color graphics, schematics and layout design. *IBE* has become "the" magazine resource for international broadcast engineering, and for very good reasons. Articles are succinct, with detailed information presented that the production-oriented lay reader can understand. Schematics are truly outstanding in their clarity and logical portrayal of signal processing and routing. The last in this triology of accolades is the color graphics, obviously shot by professionals, and printed with the same care demonstrated throughout this magazine. In this era of international communication and broadcast equipment imports, *IBE* ranks as "must" reading for all interested in broadcast engineering, design, and application. Highly recommended. For sampled issue of 1991: perfect-bound magazine format, full-color pages throughout on heavy coated paper stock (8 ¼ x 11 ⅝ inches / 210 x 295 mm).

DEPT: "IBE Worldwide," studio profile; "News," briefs; (3-80). "Correspondence," letters; "Calendar," "New Equipment," review; "Headnotes," guest column. (3-87). "Tutorial," 'Tutorials at various levels and on various aspects of broadcast engineering and operation'; "Test Equipment," extensive outstanding reviews of new technologies; "Headnotes," "Calendar," "News." (3-91).

TYPL: "Broadcast Camera Tubes," "Bit by Bit; a Digital Television Primer," "The BBC's 'Transparent' Standards Converter," "The Coverage by Radio Telefis Eireann of the Papal Visit to Ireland," "Electronic Still Storage Devices," (3-80). "Newsroom Automation Systems," "Remote Control: The Total Studio Package," "Digital Audio Disc Recorders," "Digital Television Production: 2." (3-87). "Computer Routed Graphics and Animation," "Montreux International Televison Symposium," "Maintaining Maintenance," "CRT Display Resolution," "Video Measurements: Analogue or Digital?" (3-91).

SCHL: Bimonthly (Jan, 1981 - ?); Seven issues per year (Jul, 1988+), 85 pp.
SPAN: Oct, 1964+

FROM MERGER OF
--International TV Technical Review (and) International Sound Engineer (ISSN: 0535-269x).
LC: TK 6630.A1I57
ISSN: 0020-6229
ABST: --Computer & Control Abstracts (ISSN: 0036-8113)
--Electrical & Electronics Abstracts (ISSN: 0036-8105)
--Physics Abstracts. Science Abstracts. Series A. (ISSN: 0036-8091)

✣ IBEW JOURNAL

SUB: "Official publication of the International Brotherhood of Electrical Workers.
SUB: "The union of hearts and minds."
PUBL: International Brotherhood of Electrical Workers, 1125 15th St., NW, Washington, DC 20005.
DESC: The *Journal* is the major news vehicle of the IBEW (International Brotherhood of Electrical Workers), a primary union in the entertainment labor field. Articles explore the changing relationship between labor, management, and the electrical/electronics industry, and more specifically the role of both union and union member in this ever transitional field. Liberal use of full color graphics are used throughout the publication. The vast majority of the monthly is dedicated to news of American IBEW locals. Printed full color on coated paper stock; magazine format (8 ¼ x 10 ⅞ inches / 210 x 275 mm).
DEPT: "Editorial Comment," "Research and Education," "With the Ladies," "Local Lines," an average 40 pages of IBEW local news; "Death Claims." (12-78). "Editorial," "Local Lines," extensive ten-page coverage of IBEW local chapter news; "Tech Talk," electrical instruction; "IBEW Members in the News," color pictures and newsbriefs; "In Memoriam," obituaries; "A Monthly IBEW Safety and Health Reminder," back cover poster. (7-89).
TYPL: "AFL-CIO Statement on Controls," "Productivity, the American Worker, and the Economy." (12-78). "Out From Behind the Desk; Women Make the Grade in Nontraditional Jobs," "Keystones for the Future: Communication, Participation, Education," "Staffers Continue Proud Tradition of Humanitarianism," "Challenging Future Awaits Utility Branch," "Telecommunications Growth Hurls Challenges at Workers." (7-89).
SCHL: Monthly, 50 pp.
SPAN: 1902+
VARIES
--1902? - Jul, 1914 as Electrical Worker, The.
--Aug, 1914 - Dec, 1947? as Journal of Electrical Workers and Operators.
--Jan?, 1948 - Dec, 1971 as Electrical Workers' Journal, The.
--Jan, 1972 - Mar, 1987 as Journal.
LC: HD 6350.E3 J7
DD: 331.88/213/05
ISSN: 0897-2826

IBI Newsletter

? - ?//
SEE: INTERMEDIA

IBS Bulletin

1941 - 1955//
SEE: JOURNAL OF COLLEGE RADIO

IBS Newsletter

1955 - 1964//
SEE: JOURNAL OF COLLEGE RADIO

✣ ICA NEWSLETTER

PUBL: International Cassette Association, 216 Montego Key, Bel Marin Keys, Novato, CA 94947.
DESC: This newsletter of the International Cassette Association, a trade organization devoted to the manufacturing, development, recording and marketing of audio cassette tapes, has articles that tend to cover subject matter concerning tape cassette duplication and marketing. Some technical articles are written for a lay audience.
DEPT: "Editors Column," "Classified Ads," "Book Review," (Fall-81).
TYPL: "An Introduction to Bias," "Slide/Sound Production Workshop are Held Using New Sunier Book," "Make Perfect Fit Cartons for Shipping Small Objects," "Two-Station Cassette Loader Table Plans," (Fall-81).
SCHL: Quarterly, 16 pp.
SPAN: Spring, 1980+?

✣ ICA NEWSLETTER

PUBL: International Communication Association, Balcones Research Center, 10,100 Burnet Rd., Austin, TX 78758.
DESC: A membership newsletter of the International Communication Association, the quarterly publication presents general and division news items, personnel changes, news of academic advancement and new positions, research papers, upcoming conventions, and other news of interest to the communication academic community. In the sampled issue, articles ranged from workshop descriptions of an upcoming convention to a variety of division news items such as the Popular Communication Interest Group announcement of student paper competition winners. Two departments are of note: 1) The "International Column," providing a significant amount of information not readily found in other publications (in the sampled issue, for instance, was a listing of 28 international communication meetings, conventions and workshops scheduled for the following six month time period), and 2) the always-popular directory of

faculty positions available at various North American colleges and universities. For sampled issue of 1989: black ink on tinted, uncoated paper stock, stapled newsletter format, limited advertising (8 ½ x 11 inches / 215 x 280 mm).
DEPT: None. (spring-78). "President's Column," "International Column," "News of People in the Profession," academic awards and rewards; "Positions Available," extensive college faculty employment section. (spring-89).
TYPL: "New ICA's Deputy Director to Speak at Chicago," "FSCA Sponsors Film Competition," "Saral Seeks Input for Overview; Ethics, Education to be Covered," "ICA Division Will Sponsor Berlin Scholar," "Multidimensional Scaling Topic at Workshop." (spring-78). "Comparatively Speaking... Theme for 39th Conference," "New Journal Editor Names Book Review Editor; Seven Member Advisory Board," "Philosophy of Communication Members to Highlight Intellectual Role," "Mass Communication Submissions Reflect Breadth of Interests," "Feminist Interest Group Sponsoring Different Meeting Formats." (spring-89).
SCHL: Quarterly, 16 pp.
SPAN: 1973+
VARIES
--? - ? as NSSC Newsletter.
ISSN: 0018-876x

IDEAL KINEMA, THE
SUB: "A record of modern practice in architecture and technics."
PUBL: Kinematograph Publications, 93, Long Acre, London WC2, England.
DESC: This supplement to *Kinematograph Weekly* provided information on the technical side of film exhibition and theatre management; from acoustics to curtains; heating systems to pipe organs; and film projectors, safes, screens, seating, electric signs and usher uniforms. A number of articles included electronic schematics and discussions detailing ways in which the local theatre technician could improve building structure and equipment. In the sample issue reviewed, a surprising amount of editorial copy reflected the new medium of television, and what it might have meant to the local film exhibitor, including coverage of new video projectors, and technical explanations of the workings of the medium. Numerous graphics, especially of a technical nature; some schematics.
DEPT: "Observations," newsbriefs; "Kinema Technique and Equipment," reviews; "Editor's Letter Bag." (2-12-48).
TYPL: "Safety of Ceilings in Places of Public Entertainment," "Record Conversion for Stage Shows," "Fads and Fashions of Dance Devotees," "Television Sweep Circuits," "When the Film Found its Voice." (2-12-48).
SCHL: Weekly, 32 pp.
SPAN: 1938 - Apr, 1957//

SUPPLEMENT TO
--Kinematograph Weekly (ISSN: 0023-155x), 1938 - Apr, 1957.
ABSORBED BY
--Kine Weekly, May, 1957.
LC: NA 6845 .I3

✛ IEEE SPECTRUM
PUBL: Institute of Electrical and Electronics Engineers, 345 East 47th St., New York, NY 10017.
DESC: "There's good reason for calling our magazine *SPECTRUM*. Because in today's integrated high technology world, you need international coverage of all the issues and technological advances. That's what *SPECTRUM* delivers. Each issue brings you illuminating articles on communications, medicine, energy, politics, business and industry, aerospace, careers, education, everything you'll want to know about the world of electronics and computers." Designed for the professional scientific and engineering professional, the monthly publication details news, information, trends, and potential in electronics technologies and their developmental relationship with regulatory powers, the commercial marketplace, and society in general. The coverage is broad, and often encompasses such diverse entities as chemistry, mathematics, engineering and physics. Articles, while technical in nature, are very readable by the lay audience, and provide succinct descriptions of developing technologies and the socio-economic interaction to those emerging processes and products. For almost 30 years *IEEE Spectrum* has been "the source" for accurate, understandable information about developing technologies and society, and remains an outstanding resource for study in that area. For sampled issue of 1975: some departmental features in typewritten format on uncoated paper stock, the remainder of the issue contain black/white and color pages on coated paper stock (8 ¼ x 11 ¼ inches / 205 x 285 mm). For sampled 1991 issue: fully typeset, full-color printing on coated paper stock (8 ⅛ x 10 ⅞ inches / 205 x 275 mm).
DEPT: "Meetings," "News From Washington," "Energy Report," "News From Industry," "Regional News," "Calendar," "Focal Points," "Inside IEEE," "Forum," "Scanning the Issues," "IEEE Standards," "Book Reviews," "People." (4-75). "Newslog," newsbriefs by date; "Books," review; "Calendar," 'Meetings, conferences and conventions'; "Speakout," commentary; "Managing Technology," "Program Notes," computer-oriented news items; "Forum," letters; "EEs' Tools & Toys," new items for workplace and home; "Scanning the Institute," news items. (6-91).
TYPL: "Time and Technology: Looking Ahead in Electronics," "IEEE Spectrum's Key Area Forecasts," "Ways Around the Cash Crunch," "Mauchly on the Trials of Building ENIAC." (4-75). "East Asia's Power Crescent," "Automation: Extending Electronics in Manufacturing," "Telecommunications: Attracting Players

to a Global Market," "Medical Electronics: Emphasizing Practical, Low-Cost Equipment," "Transportation: Maglev, Rail, Subways." (6-91).
SCHL: Monthly, 120 pp.
SPAN: Jan, 1964+
VARIES
--? - ? as Journal of the AIEE (ISSN: 0095-9804).
--Jan, 1931 - Dec, 1963 as Electrical Engineering (ISSN: 0095-9197).
LC: TK1.I15
DD: 621.3/05
ISSN: 0018-9235

IEEE Transactions on Broadcast and Television Receivers

May, 1963 - Nov, 1974//
(ISSN: 0018-9308)
SEE: IEEE TRANSACTIONS ON CONSUMER ELECTRONICS

✢ IEEE TRANSACTIONS ON BROADCASTING

PUBL: Broadcast Cable and Consumer Electronics Society, IEEE, 345 East 47th St., New York, NY 10017.
DESC: This publication in the highly technical field of communication electronics is designed for the laboratory and applied electronics engneer, and concentrates on broadcast spectrum problems and technology. Articles cover a range of topics, (including from one sampled year): AM transmitter antennas, companding, dipole arrays, frequency conversion, HDTV, ionosphere, MF radio propagation, moment methods, quadrature amplitude modulation, solar radiation, TV distortion and interference, transmitter antennas, VHF radio transmitters, and video recording. Significant technical knowledge of electronic communications is assumed. For sampled issue of 1989: stapled magazine format, mixture of typeset and typewritten articles printed black ink on coated paper stock, cover consisting of two-color black/orange ink on coated paper stock, no advertising (8 ¼ x 11 inches / 210 x 280 mm).
DEPT: None. (3-82). None. (12-89).
TYPL: "The Relative Effects of Deemphasis and Noise Weighting Networks on Stereophonic and Monophonic signal to noise measurements," "A Human Factors Research Program for Videotex Technology," "Digital TV Reciever for NTSC Color TV Signals with Dual-WordLength DPCM Coding," "Quality Measurement of Television Picture by Eye Simulation." (3-82). "Stub Detuners for Free-Standing Towers," "Development of a Ghost Cancel Reference Signal for TV Broadcasting," "1/2-Inch Cassette VTR for Baseband HDTV Signal Recording," "New Chroma-key Imaging Technique with Hi-Vision Background," "Evaluation and Measurement of Airplane Flutter Interference." (12-89).
SCHL: Quarterly, 70 pp.
SPAN: Mar, 1955+
VARIES
--Mar, 1955 - Dec, 1958 as IRE Transactions on Broadcast Transmission Systems (ISSN: 0099-6866).
--Feb, 1959 - Mar, 1962 as IRE Transactions on Broadcasting (ISSN: 0096-1663).
SUSPENDED
--Jan, 1959.
LC: TK 6561.I2
DD: 384
ISSN: 0018-9316
ABST: --Communication Abstracts
--Computer & Control Abstracts (ISSN: 0036-8113)
--Electrical & Electronics Abstracts (ISSN: 0036-8105)
--Engineering Index Annual (ISSN: 0360-8557)
--Engineering Index Bioengineering Abstracts (ISSN: 0736-6213)
--Engineering Index Energy Abstracts (ISSN: 0093-8408)
--Engineering Index Monthly (1984) (ISSN: 0742-1974)
--Engineering Index Monthly (ISSN: 0013-7960)
--Index to IEEE Publications (ISSN: 0099-1368)
--International Aerospace Abstracts (ISSN: 0020-5842)
--Nuclear Science Abstracts (ISSN: 0029-5612)
--Physics Abstracts. Science Abstracts. Series A. (ISSN: 0036-8091)

IEEE TRANSACTIONS ON CABLE TELEVISION

SUB: "A publication of the IEEE Broadcast, Cable, and Consumer Electronics Society."
PUBL: IEEE Broadcast, Cable and Consumer Electronics Society, 445 Hoes Lane, Piscataway, NJ 08854.
DESC: This is another of the IEEE publications concerning specific facets of electronics technology in communications. The focus here is on cable television technology. Electronic technical knowledge is assumed. Articles range from typeset to typewritten, with graphics.
DEPT: None. (4-78).
TYPL: "Feeder-Line Shielding Revisited," "A Reliable and Reproducable Technique for Evaluating the Shielding Effectiveness of CATV Apparatus," "A Time Compression Multiplex System for Multiple Video and Data Distribution using Existing Satellite Channel.s" (4-78).
SCHL: Bimonthly (? - ?); Quarterly (?+), 80 pp.
SPAN: Oct, 1976 - Oct, 1980//
LC: TK 6675.I14a
DD: 681.388
ISSN: 0147-3204
ABST: --Computer & Control Abstracts (ISSN: 0036-8113)
--Electrical & Electronics Abstracts (ISSN: 0036-8105)
--Physics Abstracts. Science Abstracts. Series A. (ISSN: 0036-8091)

IEEE Transactions on Communication Technology

Sep, 1964 - Dec, 1971//
(ISSN: 0018-9332)
SEE: IEEE TRANSACTIONS ON COMMUNICATIONS

✣ IEEE TRANSACTIONS ON COMMUNICATIONS

SUB: "A publication of the IEEE Communications Society."
PUBL: Institute of Electrical and Electronics Engineers, 345 East 47th St., New York, NY 10017.
DESC: "The field of interest of the IEEE Communications Society consists of all telecommunications including telephone, telegraphy, facsimile, and point-to-point television, by electromagnetic propagation including radio; wire; aerial, underground, coaxial, and submarine cables; waveguides, communication satellites, and lasers; in marine, aeronautical, space and fixed stqtion services; repeaters, radio relaying, signal storage, and regeneration; telecommunication error detection and correction; multiplexing and carrier techniques; communication switching systems; data communications; and communication theory. In addition to the above, this TRANSACTIONS contains papers pertaining to analog and digital signal processing and modulation, audio and video encoding techniques, the theory and design of transmitters, receivers and repeaters for communications via optical and sonic media, the design and analysis of computer communication systems, and the development of communication software. Contributions of theory enhancing the understanding of communication systems and techniques are included, as are discussions of the social implications of the development of communication technology." Significant communication engineering knowledge is assumed. As in all IEEE publications, numerous graphs, charts, and schematics accompany each article. For 1991 sampled issue: perfect-bound magazine format, black/white editorial content on coated paper stock, two-color cover on coated paper stock, numerous graphs, charts and schematics (8 ¼ x 11 inches / 210 x 280 mm).
DEPT: "Abstracts of Forthcoming Manuscripts." (3-91).
TYPL: "An Improved Transmission Protocol for Two Interfering Queues in Packet Radio Networks," "Improved Computation Method for Radio Systems Single-Tone Spurious Prohibited Frequencies List," "Distributed Protocols for Access Arbitration in Tree-Structured Communication Channels," "The Wave Expansion Approach to Broadcasting in Multihop Radio Networks," "Performance of Equalization Techniques in a Radio Interference Environment." (3-91).
SCHL: Bimonthly (Sep, 1964 - Dec, 1971); Monthly (Feb, 1972+), 115 pp.
SPAN: 1953+
VARIES
--? - ? as IRE Transactions on Communications Systems (ISSN: 0096-2244).
--1963 - Jun, 1964 as IEEE Transactions on Communications Systems (ISSN: 0096-1965).
--Sep, 1964 - Dec, 1971 as IEEE Transactions on Communication Technology (ISSN: 0018-9332).
ABSORBED
--IEEE Transactions on Communication and Electronics, Jan 1, 1965.
LC: TK 5101.A1 I2
DD: 621.38/05
ISSN: 0090-6778

IEEE Transactions on Communications Systems

1963 - Jun, 1964//
(ISSN: 0096-1965)
SEE: IEEE TRANSACTIONS ON COMMUNICATIONS

✣ IEEE TRANSACTIONS ON CONSUMER ELECTRONICS

PUBL: The IEEE Consumer Electronics Group of the Broadcast, Cable, and Consumer Electronics Society, 345 East 47th St., New York, NY 10017.
DESC: [*IEEE Transactions on Broadcast and Television Receivers*]: This is a highly technical publication by the Institute of Electrical and Electronics Engineers concerning broadcast and video receivers. Significant electronic technical knowledge is assumed. Numerous charts, schematics, and graphics accompany submitted papers.
DESC: In this highly technical series of proposed standards and discoveries concerning consumer electronics, considerable technical knowledge of electronics is assumed. Numerous charts, graphs and schematics.
DEPT: None.
TYPL: "An AC/DC Line-Operated Transistorized TV Reciever," "Computer Aided Circuit Design," "A New Video and Noise-Immune-Sync Tube And Circuit," "A Comparison of SolidState and Electron-Tube Devices for TV-Receiver RF and IF Stages." (4-67). "Optimum Utilization of the Radio Frequency Channel for Color Television," "Color Signal Distortions in Envelope type of Second Detectors," "A Second Generation Color Tube Providing More than Twice the Brightness and Improved Contrast." (2-82).
SCHL: Bimonthly (May, 1963 - Nov, 1974); Quarterly (Feb, 1976 - ?, 1979); Five issues per year (Jul, 1979+), 130 pp.
SPAN: Jul, 1952+
VARIES
--Jul, 1952 - Oct, 1954 as Transactions of the IRE Professional Group on Broadcast and Television Receivers.
--Jan, 1955 - Nov, 1962 as IRE Transactions on Broadcast and Television Receivers (ISSN: 0096-1655).
--May, 1963 - Nov, 1974 as IEEE Transactions on Broadcast and Television Receivers (ISSN: 0018-9308).

```
         SUSPENDED
         -- Nov, 1954 - Dec, 1954.
LC:      TK 6563.I2
DD:      621.38
ISSN:    0098-3063
ABST:    --Computer & Control Abstracts (ISSN: 0036-8113)
         --Electrical & Electronics Abstracts (ISSN: 0036-8105)
         --Engineering Index Annual (ISSN: 0360-8557)
         --Engineering Index Bioengineering Abstracts (ISSN: 0736-6213)
         --Engineering Index Energy Abstracts (ISSN: 0093-8408)
         --Engineering Index Monthly (1984) (ISSN: 0742-1974)
         --Engineering Index Monthly (ISSN: 0013-7960)
         --Index to IEEE Publications (ISSN: 0099-1368)
         --Physics Abstracts. Science Abstracts. Series A. (ISSN: 0036-8091)
```

✤ IEEE TRANSACTIONS ON INFORMATION THEORY

SUB: "A journal devoted to the theoretical and experimental aspects of information transmission, processing and utilization."
PUBL: Institute of Electrical and Electronics Engineers, 345 East 47th St., New York, NY 10017-2394.
DESC: "The *IEEE Transactions on Information Theory* is a bimonthly journal that publishes theoretical and experimental papers concerned with the transmission, processing and utilization of information. The boundaries of acceptable subject matter are intentionally not sharply delimited. Rather, it is hoped that as the focus of research activity changes, a flexible policy will permit this *TRANSACTIONS* to follow suit." This highly technical journal concentrates on the theoretical side of information and signal processing, routing, transmission, reception, and error checking. Application of same is left for other IEEE publications, and there are many which explore the practical utilization of theory in the communication field. Like other quality IEEE publications, *IEEE Transactions on Information Theory* assumes the reader possesses a significant background in communications theory and design engineering. Each article contains charts, graphs and schematics to aid understanding and foster discussion of the ideas expressed in the issue. For sampled 1991 issue: perfect-bound magazine format, editorial content consisting of black ink, with numerous graphs, charts and schematics on uncoated paper stock, with one-color green cover on coated paper stock (8 ¼ x 11 inches / 210 x 280 mm).
DEPT: "Books Received," "Contributors." (5-91).
TYPL: "Capacity of Root-Mean-Square Bandlimited Gaussian Multiuser Channels," "A New Outlook on Shannon's Information Measures," "Asymptoically Efficient Estimation of Prior Probabilities in Multiclass Finite Mixtures," "Dithering and Its Effects on Sigma-Delta and Multistage Sigma-Delta Modulation," "Direct-Sequence Spread-Spectrum Multiple-Access Communications with Random Signature Sequences: A Large Deviations Analysis." (5-91).
SCHL: Irregular (1953 - Mar, 1955); Quarterly (Sep, 1955+), 255 pp.
SPAN: Feb, 1953+
         VARIES
         --1953 - 1954 as Transactions.
         --1955 - 1962 as IRE Transactions on Information Theory (ISSN: 0096-1000).
LC: Q 350.I2
DD: 001.53/9
ISSN: 0018-9448

✤ IFJ INFORMATION

SUB: "Published by the International Federation of Journalists."
PUBL: International Federation of Journalists, Bd Charlemagne 1, 1041 Brussels, Belgium.
DESC: This is a a small format publication in English, German and French covering organizational activities of the International Federation of Journalists (IFJ). There are no article titles: contents are primarily transcripts of IFJ conferences, proposals, and seminars. Note: issues from July, 1952 through January/April, 1958 are in English language only.
DEPT: None.
TYPL: No Article Titles.
SCHL: Irregular (1952 - 1969); Annual (1970+).
SPAN: Jul, 1952+
LC: PN 4699.I5

✤ ILFORD PHOTO INSTRUCTOR NEWSLETTER

PUBL: Ilford Photo Corporation, West 70 Century Rd., Paramus, NJ 07653.
DESC: Designed for the photo instructor at American colleges and universities, this semiyearly promotional serial provides an interesting resource for the teaching of photographic skills. In the sampled issue for fall, 1990, six out of 16 pages were in full color, with articles discussing the elements of color printmaking, how to teach color photography, a contemporary, non-traditional view of different color media and presentations, the theory of color, an interesting article on the historical development of the Dufaycolor process by Louis Dufay, the proper fixing of fiber based papers, and a wonderful set of "Color Assignments" for the classroom. Beyond the promotional merits of Ilford photographic film, this is a valuable idea book for today's college faculty member for the teaching of photographic skills at the undergraduate or graduate level. Magazine format, three-hole punched, center stapled, limited advertising for Ilford products (8 ½ x 11 inches / 215 x 280 mm).
DEPT: "From the Editor," editorial column by Wendy Erickson; "Product News," "New Technical Publications." (#4-90).

TYPL: "In the Light," "Non-Traditional Contemporary Illustration," "Color Theory and the Teaching of Color Photography," "Color History: Dufaycolor/Transparency Film," "LE: New Guidelines for the Proper Fixing of Fiber Base Papers." (#4-90).
SCHL: Semiannual, 16 pp.
SPAN: Spring, 1989+

✤ IMAGE

SUB: "Journal of photography of the George Eastman House."
SUB: "Journal of photography and motion pictures."
SUB: "Journal of photography and motion pictures of the George Eastman House."
PUBL: George Eastman House, 900 East Ave., Rochester, NY.
DESC: "In barely more than a century, photography has become recognized as the most facile means of communication known to man. Looking back on the early beginnings of this new art, it is at once remarkable how far we have been able to push the scope of the camera, and how excellent, within its limitations, was the work of the pioneers. The purpose of the George Eastman House...is to show the progress of the art and science of photography. Our primary method of fulfilling this mission is to exhibit apparatus, photographs and moving pictures. But much of the story of photography can be told only in words, and it is the aim of *Image* to publish articles which will reinforce our exhibitions and which will reach a larger audience than those thousands who visit us in Rochester." Another in the line of quality Kodak publications, *Image* provided superb reproductions of historical pictures, patents, letters, and other materials important to the development of photography. Well recommended.
DEPT: None. (1/2-53).
TYPL: "The Presidential Inauguration of 1865," "Centenary of the R.P.S.," "Amateur Albums," "The Hurter and Driffield Actinograph," "A Barrymore Gallery." (1/2-53).
SCHL: Monthly, [except Jun-Aug], (1952 - 1955); Monthly, [except Jul - Aug], (1956), 8 pp.
SPAN: Jan, 1952+
　　　SUSPENDED
　　　--1964.
　　　--1966 - 1970.
LC: TR 1.I47
DD: 770.974789
ISSN: 0536-5465
ABST: --Art Index (ISSN: 0004-3222)
　　　--Energy Research Abstracts (ISSN: 0160-3604)
　　　--Film Literature Index (ISSN: 0093-6758)
　　　--Repetoire International de la Litterature de l'Art (ISSN: 0145-5982)

✤ IMAGE

SUB: "The magazine of the Association of Fashion Advertising and Editorial Photographers."
PUBL: Association of Fashion and Editorial Photographers, Ltd., 9/10 Domingo St., London EC1Y 0TA, England.
DESC: Official publication of the Association of Fashion Advertising and Editorial Photographers, *Image* is a mixture of association news, and artist/portfolio showcase. Printed black/white on heavy clay stock, it stresses the creative photographic work of its members, and the maintenance of an information medium by which associates can continue to improve their professional craft. Utmost care is taken in the printing of selected photographs, oftentimes presenting only one picture per page with no other editorial content surrounding it. A quality serial. For the 1989 sampled issue: stapled magazine format, black/white and full-color graphics with full-color cover on very heavy coated paper stock (8 ¼ x 11 ¾ inches / 210 x 300 mm).
DEPT: "Openings," photographic exhibitions; "Newsflash," newsbriefs; "Services," provided by the association; "College News," column by Jackie Kelley; "Letters," "Valerie's Gallery News," awards, competitions, galleries; "On the Move," member newsbriefs; "Items," trends and product newsbriefs. (3-89).
TYPL: "Visible Roles," "With Thanks to Nancy," "Christa Peters," "Susan Griggs on Photographic Copyright." (3-89).
SCHL: Monthly, 35 pp.
SPAN: Aug, 1976+

✤ IMAGE 11

PUBL: National Press Photographers Association, Region 11, c/o Seattle Post-Intelligencer, 101 Elliott Avenue West, Seattle, WA 98119.
DESC: Similar to other regional publications of the National Press Photographers Association, *Image 11* showcases photographic works from Region 11 members, and the stories that accompany the images. Judges award points to the submitted entries, and provide commentary about the judging process. Black/white editorial copy throughout; magazine format (8 ¼ x 10 ⅝ inches / 210 x 270 mm), with minimal advertising.
DEPT: "Editor's Notes," "Clip Standings," "TV Quarterly Standings." (spring-89).
TYPL: "Anchorage Daily News Wins Pulitizer," "KOMO 1988 Television Station of the Year." (spring-89).
SCHL: Quarterly, 40 pp.
SPAN: ?+

✤ IMAGE NEWS

SUB: "Film and video news, views and ideas for the professional."
PUBL: Alan Gordon Enterprises, Inc., 1430 Cahuenga Blvd., Hollywood, CA 90028.
DESC: This is a promotional newsletter for Alan Gordon Enterprises, a Hollywood institution for the sale and rental of film, video, audio equipment for the California production industry; primary functions are to extol services, new technology, and advances in the art and technique of production. For the sampled issue of

1990: folded newsletter format, two-color blue/black ink editorial content with numerous product and production graphics (8 ½ x 11 inches / 215 x 280 mm).
DEPT: "Book Review." (spring-90).
TYPL: "More Car Support for Riggers," "How to Make a Latin American Film Connection," "Focus on Production Sound," "Image 300 Shoots Big Chrysler Crash+." (spring-90).
SCHL: Quarterly, 4 pp.
SPAN: Spring, 1988+

✤ IMAGE TECHNOLOGY

SUB: "Film, Sound, Television, Audio-Visual."
SUB: "Journal of the BKSTS."
PUBL: British Kinematograph Sound and Television Society, 547-549 Victoria House, Vernon Place, London WC1B 4DJ, England.
DESC: This official journal of the British Kinematograph, Sound and Television Society has been dispensing sound professional information and technical event coverage of the film and television fields for over 40 years. It is a journal of distinct quality, both in editorial content and print quality. Editorially speaking, there are few world publications to match its clearly explained, well-thought-out articles on the technical side of film and television. Editors and writers alike deserve praise for clearly delineating the oftentimes complex aspects of new technology, and its relationship to current standards and preferences. In terms of layout design and execution, it is the standard by which other technical journals must be compared. Outstanding color separations, heavy clay stock, clean layout design and numerous black/white schematic graphics come together as a delight for the reader. A number of articles feature background stories on shooting educational and video programs, and the production of AV presentations. General interest stories concerning motion pictures, audio and film areas are also presented, making this a publication for varied readers. Earlier issues (from 1948 - 1950) concentrated on motion picture production. It is an outstanding publication for any professional interested in the technical side of film, television, sound, and audio visual arts. For the sampled issue of 1990: stapled magazine format, outstanding color and black/white graphics with full-color laminated cover on coated paper stock (8 ¼ x 11 ¾ inches / 210 x 300 mm).
DEPT: "Society News and Views," briefs of BKSTS; "Standards page," BSI-ANSI-ISO release standards; "Question and Answer Service," Q&A; "Equipment and Services," newsbriefs. (2-76). "Update," news of film and video industry; "Letters," "Diary," upcoming events; "Bookshelf," review; "Sound News," news items; "First Reference," '...a guide to the organizations offering products and services in the film, sound, television, audio-visual and video industries'. (2-90).
TYPL: "Color Vision and the Film Industry," "The Film in Colonial Development," "From Silent to Sound," (7-48); "Wildlife Film-making--a Complete Way of Life," "Seventy Stereoscopic Films in the USSR," "Wildlife Film-making in Pictures." (2-76). "Optical Cortex - Fly by Wire Manipulation of Film and Video Cameras," "BKSTS Meeting on Professional S-VHS Equipment," "VTR Procurement, a Pragmatic View of the Choice," "Sound: Future Prospects in Video and Film Post-Synchronisation." (2-90).
SCHL: Monthly, 80 pp.
SPAN: 194u+
VARIES
--194u - Dec, 1965 as British Kinematography (ISSN: 0007-1358).
--Jan, 1966 - Dec, 1973 as British Kinematography, Sound and Television (ISSN: 0373-109x).
--Jan, 1974 - Jun, 1986 as BKSTS Journal, The (ISSN: 0305-6996).
LC: TR 845.B75
DD: 778.5/05
ISSN: 0950-2114
ABST: --Computer & Control Abstracts (ISSN: 0036-8113)
--Electrical & Electronics Abstracts (ISSN: 0036-8105)
--Physics Abstracts. Science Abstracts. Series A. (ISSN: 0036-8091)

✤ IMAGEMAKER

SUB: "The magazine of tomorrow's video and motion picture techniques."
PUBL: 2001 Publishing International, P.O. Box 610606, Miami, FL 33181.
DESC: This is a promotional device by Image Devices, a rental-service-sales house in Miami and Atlanta. Beyond promoting specific equipment carried by the firm, "Imagemaker" includes articles detailing interesting technical innovations in equipment usage.
DEPT: None. (8-81).
TYPL: "The Making of an Underwater Film," "Update on ACL-4 Housing," "Bats About HMI Lights." (8-81).
SCHL: Irregular, 30 pp.
SPAN: Aug, 1981+
ISSN: 0730-482x

✤ IMAGES & IDEAS BY PHOTOMETHODS

PUBL: Ziff-Davis Publishing Company, One Park Ave., New York, NY 10016.
DESC: Reflecting on the success of the first issue published in 1982, Editorial Director Fred Schmidt told readers; "We are convinced that the format for this coffee table/work table magazine is right. It was designed to be a medium of exchange for ideas among working photographers. ... *Images & Ideas* was also designed as a companion publication to *Photomethods*, the monthly magazine for visual communications management. The two magazines are published to complement each other." *Images & Ideas by Photomethods* is a visual feast for the eyes, a showcase for what is best in professional photography. In one sampled issue, the magazine format consisted almost entirely of submitted work, one photographer

profile per page; with discussion, philosophy, and technical information concerning the submitted works. The often stunning photographs combined with the artistic commentary make for a very pleasing reading experience. Text is kept to a minimum in order to showcase individual photography. Magazine format, full color throughout on coated paper stock (8 x 10 ¾ inches / 205 x 270 mm).
DEPT: "Cover," technical details and information concerning the cover photo on the magazine. (#1-83).
TYPL: "Professional vs Fine Arts Photography," "Music's Special Dispersion," "Dichotomy of Drvol's World," "Attractive High Tech," "Fistful of Power." (#1-83).
SCHL: Irregular, 60 pp.
SPAN: Jul, 1982+
LC: TR 1 .I48
DD: 770/.5
ISSN: 0732-7870
ABST: --Abstrax
--Art Bibliographies Modern (ISSN: 0300-466x)

Implet

Jan 20, 1912 - Jun 8, 1912//
SEE: UNIVERSAL WEEKLY

✧ IMPRINT

SUB: "The magazine of specialty advertising ideas."
PUBL: America Specialty Information Network, 2nd and Clearview Avenues, Trevose, PA 19047.
DESC: *Imprint* is primarily an advertising vehicle for firms with specialty products such as ballpoint pens, tennis bags, thermometers, coffee cups, and other items used in promotion.
DEPT: "Newsmakers," new items; "Bits and Pieces," newsbriefs of available products; "Impressions," guest column.
TYPL: "The Sharing of the Green," "Metrics: the Official System," "Establishing an Identity." (spring-76).
SCHL: 3 issues per year, 60 pp.
SPAN: Jan, 1968+

IN BLACK AND WHITE

SUB: "The eclectic newsletter for those who write and edit for the print media."
SUB: "The biweekly guide for those who write, report, and edit for publication."
PUBL: Associated Editorial Consultants, P.O. Box 2107, La Jolla, CA 92038.
DESC: *In Black and White* stands out as a most valuable publication for the print editor, reporter or layout person. It emphasizes writing skills, and critical analyses of layout and editorial design. The four to eight-page newsletter provides numerous examples on typographical errors, layout problems, and "tips-of-the-trade;" providing techniques on use of white space, indents, quotes and other kinds of print considerations.
DEPT: None. (9-6-76).
TYPL: "Copy Editor's Lament," "Unskilled Writers," "Gotchas Are a Mixed Metaphor," (Unknown); "Functional Makeup, Readable Makeup; Making It Easier on the Reader's Eye," "How Long Should a Line of Type Be?," "Bilingual Publication Show that Someone Cares," (9-6-76).
SCHL: Biweekly, 8 pp.
SPAN: Mar, 1975 - Sep, 1978//
ABSORBED BY
--Freelancers' Newsletter (ISSN: 0016-0636), Sep, 1978.

✧ IN CINEMA

PUBL: In Cinema, Ltd., 801 Second Avenue, New York, NY 10017.
DESC: This small-magazine format publication for New York City cinema patrons, provides informative, pre-feature reading material on current and past motion picture product, profiles of stars, and other interesting personality/promotional articles. The sampled 1981 issue consisted of stapled small magazine format with numerous full-color graphics and cover on coated paper stock and significant advertising targeted to cinema attendees (5 ⅛ x 8 ¼ inches / 130 x 210 mm).
DEPT: "NY/NY," filmmaking news in greater New York area; "Popcorn," 'Kernels of information'; "Close-Up," star profile; "Cuisine, Cuisine," New York city dining; "Coming Soon," upcoming motion picture releases; "Final Cut," '...a column for prominent people in the motion picture industry to have their final say about any topic that ails them'. (6-81).
TYPL: "The New Comedy of Heirs," "Soundtrack," "Film Vault." (6-81).
SCHL: Ten issues per year, 35 pp.
SPAN: ?, 1980+
ISSN: 0271-261x

✧ IN CONCERT PRESENTS

SUB: "The front row concert experience!"
PUBL: SCV USA, Inc., 19 West 44th St., Suite 812, New York, NY 10036.
DESC: This showcase magazine had its debut in July/August, 1990, featuring the New Kids on the Block. Each bimonthly issue profiles a single artist or, group of artists who perform in American live stage shows. Articles describe upcoming tours, back-stage stories, record and video reviews, quizzes and other material for fans of featured artists. Magazine format (8 ½ x 11 inches / 215 x 280 mm); full color throughout; no advertising.
DEPT: None. (7/8-90).
TYPL: "The New Kids in Concert!," "Up Close & Personal," "Backstage Access," "Fashion Passion!," "Friends of the New Kids." (7/8-90).
SCHL: Bimonthly, 65 pp.

SPAN: Jul/Aug, 1990+

✤ IN HOUSE GRAPHICS

SUB: "Where to turn for design ideas & techniques... on a desktop or not."
PUBL: In House Graphics, Inc., 342 East Third St., Loveland, CO 80537.
DESC: "Whether it's the eleventh hour and your job is on the line... or just a typical Tuesday and you're looking for a bright idea to spark up a sales brochure... *IN HOUSE GRAPHICS* is the lively monthly newsletter that brings you dozens of innovative, budget-stretching, ground-breaking design ideas. It's packed with workable touches that you can adapt and use right away-- whether you work on a desktop rig, or prepare artwork the traditional way. In every issue you get fresh ideas to provide inspiration and get your own creative juices flowing." For the employee whose work activities include producing the company newsletter, promotion materials for the upcoming open house, employee materials, and a whole host of other print-related items, *IN HOUSE GRAPHICS* is welcome indeed. This three-hole punched newsletter provides succinct suggestions and advice on preparation of artwork; which camera format to utilize, the impact of color upon the finished piece of work, and many other items one never learned (or has since forgotten) in the classroom. A clear writing style enhances this newsletter, and reflects the publishers statement that "*IN HOUSE GRAPHICS* is dedicated to the harried managers and artists who create the nation's print communications." For the 1990 sampled issue: three-hole punched stapled newsletter format, with bright two color printing on beige uncoated paper stock and excellent graphics reproduction (8 ½ x 11 inches / 215 x 280 mm).
DEPT: None. (3-86). "Finds," graphic resources; "Back to Basics," graphic tips. (1-90).
TYPL: "Letterhead Design," "Medium Format Photography: The Compromising Alternative," "Marketing with Color." (3-86). "Welcome to 'The Neon Nineties?'," "Beyond Grip & Grin," "Newsletter Spruce-Up." (1-90).
SCHL: Monthly, 16 pp.
SPAN: Jul, 1984?+
DD: 760 11
ISSN: 0883-6973

✤ IN MOTION FILM & VIDEO PRODUCTION MAGAZINE

SUB: "Film & video production magazine."
PUBL: Motion Publishing Co., 421 4th St., Annapolis, MD 21403.
DESC: "[*In Motion*]...is for professionals working in film/video production and related imaging media." This is a publication about, by, and for production professionals concerning the business side of film and video operations. It appears to be primarily East Coast oriented, roughly from New York to Florida. Typical articles profile facilities, working professionals, client relationships, equipment and production news. Of special note is a large number of display advertisments by vendors, rental companies, and production facilities; providing in some measure a mini-production directory for East Coast producers. This is a quality production publication, famed for informative stories on current projects by various creative companies, as well as for thoughtful analyses of the impact of certain elements (war, economy, international markets) on the business side of production. Well recommended. For the sampled 1991 issue: stapled magazine format, full color throughout in a dynamic layout design, all on coated paper stock (8 ¼ x 10 ⅞ inches / 210 x 275 mm).
DEPT: "Letters to the Editor," "Video News," "Television," "Motion Pictures," "Videographics," "Trade Shows," "Women in Film & Video," "The Directors Chair," "Media Moves," "Teleconferencing News," "Production News," "SE Production News," of the Southeastern states; "Facility Update," "Film Commission Report," "ITVA News," International Television Association news; "User Friendly," "Music Production News." (10-88).
TYPL: "Can Technical People Sell?," "Graphics Outsizzle Democrats in Atlanta," "Business Television is a Growing Industry." (10-88).
SCHL: Ten issues per year (? - ?); Monthly (Dec, 1987+), 80 pp.
SPAN: Jan, 1982+
        VARIES
        --? - ? as Maryland in Motion Film & Video Production Directory.
DD: 778
ISSN: 0889-6208

In-Plant Offset Printer

Feb, 1961 - ?//
SEE: IN-PLANT PRINTER & ELECTRONIC PUBLISHER

In-Plant Printer

? - Aug, 1986//
(ISSN: 0019-3232)
SEE: IN-PLANT PRINTER & ELECTRONIC PUBLISHER

✤ IN-PLANT PRINTER & ELECTRONIC PUBLISHER

PUBL: Innes Publishing Co., 425 Huehl Rd., Bldg. 11, Northbrook, IL 60065- 2319.
DESC: Designed with print management in mind, *In-Plant Printer & Electronic Publisher* provides a pragmatic approach to supplies, equipment, and various unusual needs of clients. The serial deals with traditional print-issues, while a monthly supplement, *Electronic Publisher*, "...covers typesetting, text and graphic processing, electronic printing and paste-up." This is

a "real-world" approach to the best of both types of publication printing. Of special note are paper and press advertisements printed with unique inks, foils, embossing, paper, or a combination of the above to display new techniques to the trade. See: *Electronic Publisher* for separate description of this supplement. Numerous color graphics. Sampled issue for 1990: magazine format (8 ⅛ x 10 ¾ inches / 210 x 275 mm), full color throughout on coated paper stock.

DEPT: "Editor's Note," "Letters," "News," "Management," commentary; "Calendar," "Products," "Literature." (6-87). "Editor's Note," editorial column by Andrea D. Cody; "Fast Read," newsbriefs; "Klasnic's Consultant's Corner," column by Jack Klasnic; "Calendar," "Products," new items arriving on the marketplace; "Literature," product information; "Training." (10-90).

TYPL: "More Paper Options for Any Occasion," "Printing Carbonless on a Sheetfed Press," "Cost Accounting: Make Your Budget Fit Your Company's Lifestyle," "Bindery Gaining New Status In-Plant." (6-87). "Ink Jet Systems," "The Publishing Gateway to the Future," "Manufacturer's Perspective," "Quality and High-Tech Capabilities Attract External Customers." (10-90).

SCHL: Bimonthly, 70 pp.
SPAN: Feb, 1961+
VARIES
--Feb, 1961 - ? as In-Plant Offset Printer.
--? - Aug, 1986 as In-Plant Printer (ISSN: 0019-3232).
WITH SUPPLEMENT
--Electronic Publisher, ?+.
LC: Z 119.I58
DD: 070.5/0285
ISSN: 0891-8996

✤ IN-PLANT REPRODUCTIONS

SUB: "For in-plant printing and communications."
SUB: "Electronic publishing, prepress, printing, bindery."
PUBL: North American Publishing Co., 401 North Broad St., Philadelphia, PA 19108.
DESC: Targeted to printing-plant managers, *In-Plant Reproductions* covers a myriad of printed-materials themes; including new paper stock, binding operations, photocopying, desktop publishing, shipping, computers, customer satisfaction, the bottom line, and virtually any other activity that results in a fixed image upon paper. Celebrating its 40th year of publication in 1991, *In-Plant Reproductions* provides publishing management with information and tool skills necessary to "get the job done." A sampling of articles from that issues demonstrates this theme. "Estimating the Costs of Desktop Publishing" was aptly subtitled, "How much should you charge back for a job?," detailing elements typically found within such tasks, and providing a production schedule for ready application. "Manufacturers Adapt to New Kinds of Printing" explored copy and laser papers, and the role of recycled paper. "Management Mistakes to Avoid" charted the unsuccessful steps taken by one print manager in the quest to save his printshop. A significant amount of advertising is targeting to the printing trade. This is a resource for print operations managers, be they corporate or self-employed. Stapled magazine format for sampled issue of 1991; full-color pages throughout on coated paper stock, with some specialty paper inserts (8 ⅛ x 10 ⅞ inches / 205 x 275 mm).

DEPT: "Resources for In-Plant Managers," "Editor's Note," editorial column by Judy Bocklage; "New Products," review; "Across the Nation," printing industry news listed by state; "Calendar," upcoming seminars, meetings, and trade shows. (7-91).

TYPL: "High Hopes for Hospital In-Plant," "Estimating the Costs of Desktop Publishing," "Manufacturers Adapt to New Kinds of Printing," "Environment Tops IP's Agenda," "Take the Offense in the Electronic Revolution." (7-91).

SCHL: Monthly, 60 pp.
SPAN: 1951+
VARIES
--1951 - Nov, 1979 as Reproductions Review & Methods (ISSN: 0164-4327).
--Dec, 1979 - 198u as In-Plant Reproductions (ISSN: 0198-9065).
--198u - ? as In-Plant Reproductions & Electronic Publishing (ISSN: 0886-3121).
ISSN: 1043-1942

In-Plant Reproductions

Dec, 1979 - 198u//
(ISSN: 0198-9065)
SEE: IN-PLANT REPRODUCTIONS

In-Plant Reproductions & Electronic Publishing

198u - ?//
(ISSN: 0886-3121)
SEE: IN-PLANT REPRODUCTIONS

IN SEARCH

SUB: "The Canadian communications quarterly."
SUB: "Revue canadienne de la telecommunication."
PUBL: Information Services, Department of Communications, Ottawa, Ontario K1A 0C8, Canada.
DESC: "*In Search*, a magazine of information and opinion, offers a selection of articles touching on different fields of communication. Its purpose is to provide fresh viewpoints, to add to the reader's general knowledge and to generate an increased awareness of telecommunications." The focus is on the impact of modern communications; what it means to the individual, the culture, and society. This is a serial concerned as much with the process of how humans communicate, as it is an exploration of the impact of new media within society. Text in English and French.

Typical articles for latter issues included, "The Great Hunt for Computer Communications Specialists," "The Light Wave and Glass Race," "The New Humanism Aims to Make Conscious a Different Mind Set," and "Are Satellites the Pyramids of the 20th Century?" For the sampled issues of 1979: mixture of black/white and full-color pages and cover on coated paper stock, no advertising, stapled magazine format (8 ½ x 11 inches / 215 x 280 mm).
DEPT: None. (fall-75).
TYPL: "Don't Come--Call," "The Computer: a Primer," "The Caisse 'Pop' Goes Electronic," "Rekindling the Shared Experience," "Eye in the Sky." (fall-75).
SCHL: Quarterly, 34 pp.
SPAN: Winter, 1974 - #4, 1981?//
FOREIGN EDITION
--En Quete.
LC: P 92.C3 I5
DD: 001.5/05
ISSN: 0317-4514
ABST: --Canadian Periodical Index (ISSN: 0008-4719)

Incorporation and Bylaws
Jul, 1916//
SEE: SMPTE JOURNAL

✧ INDEPENDENT, THE
SUB: "Film & Video Monthly."
PUBL: The Foundation for Independent Video and Film, 625 Broadway, 9th Floor, New York, NY 10012.
DESC: The Foundation for Independent Video and Film is "...a non-profit tax-exempt educational foundation dedicated to the promotion of independent video and film, and by the Association of Independent Video and Filmmakers, Inc., (AIVF), the national trade association of independent producers and individuals involved in independent video and film." This is a no-nonsense black/white periodical concerned exclusively with issues involving the independent film/videomaker, such as, funding, festivals, opportunities, and frustrations. The articles, all written by AIVF members, are noteworthy for the attention to detail, whether it be new coding systems for film, government censorship, or the process of raising funds for a planned project. The majority of the publication is devoted to departmental columns with several feature articles per issue. Numerous graphics. Magazine format (8 ½ x 11 inches / 215 x 280 mm).
DEPT: "Media Clips," newsbriefs; "Works in Progress Sessions," "Conference Beat," "In Focus," specific issues; "Super Eight," "Summary of AIVF Minutes," "Festivals," notices; (9-83). "Letters," "Media Clips," newsbriefs; "Field Reports," "In Focus," "Legal Briefs," excellent legal column; "Festivals," held and upcoming; "In and Out of Production," column by Renee Tajima; "Memoranda." (8/9-88). "Media Clips," "In Focus," "Legal Brief," excellent resource column by Robert L. Seigel; "Festivals," "In and Out of Production," projects in progress; "Notices," "Memoranda," AIVF/FIVF Board of Directors Meeting; "Program Notes," newsbriefs. (12-89).
TYPL: "Building an Alternative Movement," "Conjuring the Spirit of '78,'" "Tough and True Feedback at Rough-Cut Shows," "The Trouble With Time Code," (9-83). "Le PAF: The Changing French Audio-Visual Landscape," "Showdown in Kansas City: KKK vs American Cablevision," "Union Mergers on the Table," "Like a Rolling Stone: Memories of TVTV," "Home Video Case Jolts the Motion Picture Industry." (8/9-88). "Setting Standards for Fiscal Agents," "TV Diversity: Not in Name Only," "Planning Ahead: Innovations in Postproduction Sound Design." (12-89).
SCHL: Ten issues per year, 40 pp.
SPAN: Jan, 1978+
LC: PN 1993.I617
DD: 791.43/0973
ISSN: 0731-5198

Independent Broadcasting
Aug, 1974 - Nov, 1984//
(ISSN: 0305-6104)
SEE: AIRWAVES

Independent Film Journal
1937 - Nov, 1979//
(ISSN: 0019-3712)
SEE: FILM JOURNAL, THE

✧ INDEPENDENT MEDIA
PUBL: Documentary Video Associates, Ltd., 7 Campbell Court, Bramley, Basingstoke, Hants RG26 5EG, England.
DESC: *Independent Media* mirrors well the audience it seeks to serve, the British independent producer/director/artist whose work is considered to be outside the broadbased philosophy of British media. Readers will typically find features concerning social trends, oral history, works of art, projects of developing nations, and minority issues of all kinds. One sample issue (February, 1990) explored the oral history work of the British Video History Trust & The Television History Workshop; the role of film and video in the ever-changing events in East Europe; funding for women's film and video sectors; student films, video art, British cable television, and video art. This serial accurately reflects the fiercely independent nature of this unique brand of media producer in Britain, an individual whose strong artistic expression may find a sympathetic eye and ear through independent media. Sampled issue of 1990 consisted of stapled magazine format, black/white editorial and cover content on coated paper stock, with advertisements (8 ¼ x 11 ¾ inches / 210 x 295 mm).

DEPT: "News Media," late-breaking news stories of independent media; "Media Check," independent media events, showings, and workshops; "Media Mail," letters; "Shorts," calendar of upcoming events. (2-90).
TYPL: "Empires of the Senseless," "Backs to the Future," "Revenge of the Art Rockers," "Culture in Revolution." (2-90).
SCHL: Monthly, 25 pp.
SPAN: Mar, 1983?+

Independent Publisher, The
Jun, 1980 - Feb, 1981//
SEE: COSMEP NEWSLETTER

✛ INDEPENDENT PUBLISHERS TRADE REPORT
SUB: "The monthly newsletter of markets and management for the growing publisher."
PUBL: Greenfield Press, PO Box 176, Southport, CT 06490.
DESC: *Independent Publishers Trade Report* "...includes timely brief articles on emerging markets; developments in mature markets; promotional practices and ideas; trends in publishing affecting independent publishing field; technology; directions for growth; latest business practices for productivity and efficiency; acquisitions activity in the field. Henry Berry, the Editor/Publisher is exposed to the latest marketing strategies, growing areas of publishing activity, book design, promotional ideas, and other activities in the independent publishing field: This position and more than twenty years' experience in the book trade provide the basis of the information, perspectives, and advice in the *Trade Report*." Mr. Berry also is editor/publisher of *The Small Press Book Review*, a bimonthly review of new books from independent and smaller presses. Typeset newsletter format (8 ½ x 11 inches / 215 x 280 mm); no graphics.
DEPT: "Trade News," newsbriefs; "Miscellany." (1-90).
TYPL: "A New Ripple in the Baby-Boom Market," "User-Friendly Book Design." (1-90).
SCHL: Monthly, 4 pp.
SPAN: Jul, 1988+
DD: 070 11
ISSN: 0898-784x

Index
Spring, 1972 - ?//
SEE: INDEX ON CENSORSHIP

✛ INDEX ON CENSORSHIP
SUB: "The international magazine for free expression."
PUBL: Writers & Scholars International, Ltd., 39C Highbury Pl., London N5 1QP, England.
DESC: *Index on Censorship* publishes an excellent overview of the relative freedom of the press vis a vis world governments. The British publication places a special emphasis on reporting press freedom in those nations where political struggles are active, but there are sufficient incidents of censorship in all nations to easily fill a given issue. Articles are often by working journalists, and provide a rare, first-person insight into the governments, the agencies of government, and others who may fear the power of a free press in their communities. At times, due to the incarceration (or worse) of the original journalist, a colleague or associate will report the details of censorship. This publication is at times entertaining, at times brutal in its reporting of outrages perpetrated against the call for free speech, but always fascinating and informative in its role of bringing such developments to world consciousness. Of special note is the departmental section, "Index Index," which the editor refers to as, "A record of censorship, incorporating information from Amnesty International, Article 19, Interights, Campaign for Press and Broadcasting Freedom, International PEN Writers in Prison Committee (UK), Reporters Sans Frontièrs (France), and the Committee to Protect Journalists (US)." Six pages, four-columns are devoted to capsule listings of individual acts of censorship, noted by country, names, dates, and actions taken against the journalist. Also listed here is the status of press and speech freedom, and any late-breaking developments which may affect that status. Well recommended for information concerning freedom of expression issues and reporting of same. For the sampled issues of 1972: black ink on uncoated paper; with departmental section "INDEX Index" on tinted, textured uncoated paper stock, no advertising, in stapled journal format (6 ¼ x 9 ¾ inches / 170 x 235 mm), with some slight variation in dimensions during early issues. Sampled issue for 1991: stapled magazine format, black/white editorial content and graphics on uncoated paper stock, two-color cover with minimal advertising (8 ¼ x 11 inches / 210 x 275 mm).
DEPT: "Literature," "Organizations," "Reviews," "Letters to the Editor." (summer-72). "Opinion." (10-84). "Opinion," "Book Reviews," very extensive reviews; "Index Index," 'A record of censorship'. (6-91).
TYPL: "Television Coverage of Northern Ireland," "Four Years of 'Normalisation': The Academic Purge in Czechoslovakia," "Press Censorship in Spain and Portugal," "Cuba: Revolution and the Intellectual--The Strange Case of Heberto Padilla," "Greece: Banned Books." (summer-72). "Turkish Writers on Trial," "Book Boom in Tehran," "Spreading the Word in Chile," "Nightmare Country (Uganda)," "How I Became a Non-Conformist (USSR)." (10-84). "Dorfman: a Case of Conscience," "Tongue-Tied in Uganda," "Zimbabwe: One State, One Faith, One Lord," "Nigerian Journalists Missing in Liberia," "The Cost of Free Speech." (6-91).
SCHL: Quarterly (1972 - 1976); Bimonthly (1977 - ?); Ten issues per year (1988+), 45 pp.
SPAN: Spring, 1972+

VARIES
--Spring, 1972 - ? as Index.
LC: K 9.N3
DD: 344.05/31/05
ISSN: 0306-4220
ABST: --MLA International Bibliography of Books & Articles on the Modern Languages and Literatures (ISSN: 0024-8215)
--Public Affairs Information Service Bulletin (ISSN: 0033-3409)

Indian Listener

? - ?//
SEE: AKASHVANI

Industrial and Commercial Photographer

May, 1961 - Feb, 1980//
SEE: PROFESSIONAL PHOTOGRAPHER, THE

INDUSTRIAL ELECTRONICS

SUB: "A journal of radio research and progress."
PUBL: Iliffe Electrical Publications, London, England.
DESC: [*Electronic Technology*]: In its early years, wireless radio was the only topic of discussion as articles explored principles and theories of wave propagation, measurements, standarization, new equipment developments and applications (techniques) of same. Radio was still in its "wonderment" stage as new technologies seemed to develop just in time for each new issue. Latter sample issues (1961) show a preference for electronic technology, no matter what application might be intended. Throughout all issues, a large number of schematics and electronic notation are used, and significant knowledge of electronics is assumed.
DEPT: "Editorial Views," "Correspondence," "From the World's Wireless Journals," abstract briefs; "Some Recent Patents." (2-1925). "Editorial," "Correspondence," "New Books," "New Products." (12-61).
TYPL: "The Arrangement of Wireless Books and Information," "The Inter-Electrode Capacities of Thermionic Valves," "Power Amplification for Loud-Speakers Used at Wembley," "KDKA Short-Wave Station." (2-25). "Ferrite Cores as Logical Elements," "Rectifier Modulators," "Computer Magnetic Tape Unit," "Optimal Lumped Loading." (12-61).
SCHL: Monthly, 50 pp.
SPAN: Oct, 1923 - Jan, 1969//
VARIES
--Oct, 1923 - Aug, 1924 as Experimental Wireless.
--Sep, 1924 - Aug, 1931 as Experimental Wireless & the Wireless Engineer.
--Sep, 1931 - Dec, 1935 as Wireless Engineer and Experimental Wireless.
--Jan, 1936 - Dec, 1956 as Wireless Engineer.
--Jan, 1957 - Dec, 1959 as Electronic & Radio Engineer.
--Jan, 1960 - Sep, 1962 as Electronic Technology.
ABSORBED
--Wireless Engineer, Sep, 1924.
--British Communications and Electronics (ISSN: 0524-5753), Aug, 1965.
--Measurement and Control (ISSN: 0465-4366), 1964.
ABSORBED BY
--Electronics Weekly (ISSN: 0013-5224).
LC: TK 7800.I254
ISSN: 0537-5185
ABST: --Computer & Control Abstracts (ISSN: 0036-8113)
--Electrical & Electronics Abstracts (ISSN: 0036-8105)
--Electronic Publishing Abstracts (ISSN: 0739-2907)
--International Aerospace Abstracts (ISSN: 0020-5842)
--Physics Abstracts. Science Abstracts. Series A. (ISSN: 0036-8091)

Industrial Film and Audio-Visual Annual [NF]

May, 1961//
SEE: AVC

Industrial Marketing

Jun, 1935 - Mar, 1983//
(ISSN: 0019-8498)
SEE: BUSINESS MARKETING

✜ INDUSTRIAL PHOTOGRAPHY

PUBL: Media Horizons, Inc., 50 W. 23rd St., New York, NY 10010.
DESC: This is a periodical for the professional photographer who works either in a corporate or free-lance position, and whose primary work is industrial (i.e., non-commercial) photography. It also addresses areas such as company publications, multi-media presentations and other similar applications. Of special note is the application of new technology to industrial applications, such as fiber optics to photograph equipment interiors. For the sampled issue of 1990: black ink, spot and full-color editorial content with full-color cover all on coated paper stock in stapled magazine format (8 x 10 ¾ inches / 200 x 275 mm).
DEPT: "European Newsletter," continental news; "Light in the Darkroom," technique and operation; "Manilla in Motion," news column by James Manilla; "A-V Profiles," "Editor's Notebook," newsbriefs. (10-77). "AV Screen," column by William J. Staples; "European Newsletter," column by Michael J. Langford; "Video Film Scene," column by Jack Behrend; "Industry Notebook," "From the Lab," column by Martin Hershenson; "Bits and Bytes," column by Jack Neubart; "Newswire," "Product Lineup," "The Answer Man," column by Leo Lukowsky. (4-89).

TYPL:	"Photo Department Management: Training the Photographic Staff," "Rebirth of a National Monument: The Renovation of Yankee Stadium," "Why Didn't I Think of That?" (10-77). "Lighting for Studio and Location," "Anatomy of a Shoot," "Executive Portraiture." (4-90).
SCHL:	Quarterly (Fall, 1952 - Oct, 1953); Bimonthly (Jan, 1954 - ?); Monthly (?+); 55 pp.
SPAN:	Fall, 1952+
LC:	TR 1.I5
ISSN:	0019-8595
ABST:	--Applied Science and Technology Index (ISSN: 0003-6986) --Communication Abstracts --Computer & Control Abstracts (ISSN: 0036-8113) --Electrical & Electronics Abstracts (ISSN: 0036-8105) --Engineering Index Annual (ISSN: 0360-8557) --Engineering Index Monthly (ISSN: 0013-7960) --Physics Abstracts. Science Abstracts. Series A. (ISSN: 0036-8091) --Selected Water Resources Abstracts (ISSN: 0037-136x)

INDUSTRIAL TELEVISION NEWS

SUB:	"A member service of the International Industrial Television Association."
PUBL:	National Industrial Television Association, Communications Office, 15 Madison Ave., Summit, NJ 07901.
DESC:	A ten-page, typewritten newsletter concerning national activities of the International Industrial Television Association, "The *Industrial Television News* is intended to be a two-way line of communications for the members of ITVA. Since our members are distributed over a very large area, the ITN is our monthly medium of exchange for information and ideas." Covers membership news, chapter information, upcoming events, reports and new equipment.
DEPT:	"News/Notes from the President," "Chapters," news; "Cue Track," upcoming shows and events; "People," newsbriefs; "Scan Lines," personnel briefs; (3-76).
TYPL:	"Watch Television at the Office? Heaven Forbid, (3-76).
SCHL:	Monthly, 8 pp.
SPAN:	1970 - ?//. VARIES --? - ? as NITA News.
ISSN:	0300-7685

Infinity

Feb, 1952 - Mar, 1973//
(ISSN: 0019-9583)
SEE: ASMP BULLETIN

✤ INFORMATION TODAY

SUB:	"The newspaper for users and producers of electronic information services."
PUBL:	Learned Information, Inc., 143 Old Marlton Pike, Medford, NJ 08055.
DESC:	"Explosive growth" describes the information industry for the decade of the 1990s. This field of "information-on-demand" has grown in two distinct areas: on-line database and CD-ROM. These two technologies, combined with corporate "need-to-know-now" has provided the fuel for this incredible information demand and expansion. *Information Today*, aptly subtitled "The newspaper for users and producers of electronic information services," keeps readers apprised of new technologies, products, vendors, and the ongoing evolution of turning libraries (corporate, public, academic, and private) into efficient information resources. Issues of standardization, copyright, regulation, usages, vendor development, marketing, international import/export, text retrieval, and hardcopy printouts are present among a myriad of themes in each issue. Anyone wishing to remain informed about electronic information services would be well advised to subscribe to *Information Today*. Note: volume 1, #1 was preceeded by Volume 0, #0 in November, 1983 and designated "Premiere issue." For 1991 sampled issue: tabloid stapled newspaper format, black/white, spot and full color pages on uncoated paper stock (10 ⅞ x 15 inches / 275 x 380 mm).
DEPT:	"Letters," "From the Editor's Desk," editorial column by Patricia Lane; "In Brief," "CD-ROM Today," extensive news section; "News Briefs," concerning CD-ROM; "New Products," "Calendar," "Free," 'Seminars, training, workshops' upcoming events; "People Line," 'People on the move within the industry'; "Database Review," "Commentary," "Focus on Imaging," "Legal Line," "Library Technology," "Software Review," "Viewpoint." (6-91).
TYPL:	"ABI/Inform Celebrates 20th Anniversary, Adds Full Text," "Dialog Offers Assistance for Career Transitions," "Electronic Publishing: The Library and Scholarly Activity," "Conversion to Image Storage and Display: Problems and Solutions," "CD-ROM Industry Shows Steady Growth in Canada." (6-91).
SCHL:	Monthly [combined Jul/Aug & Nov/Dec issues], 75 pp.
SPAN:	Jan, 1984+
DD:	001
ISSN:	8755-6286
ABST:	--Predicasts

Inkline Journal

Jan/Feb, 1980? - Nov/Dec, 1986?//
SEE: WRITERS' JOURNAL

Inland and American Printer and Lithographer, The

Nov, 1958 - Jul, 1961//
(ISSN: 0096-2562)
SEE: AMERICAN PRINTER

Inland Printer, American Lithographer

Aug, 1961 - Dec, 1978//
(ISSN: 0020-1502)
SEE: AMERICAN PRINTER

✤ INSIDE ENTERTAINMENT

PUBL: World Perspective Communications, Inc., 3443 Parkway Center Court, Orlando, FL 32808.
DESC: "*Inside Entertainment* is a regular supplement designed to provide you, the *Entertainment Revue* reader, with up-to-date news on current and upcoming film and television productions and other events in Florida. The magazine's editors do their best, tapping all possible sources of information, to collect news that is useful and valuable to you." Supplemental "newsletter" of current projects in progress, studio/production company news, planned projects, call for talent, upcoming events, and even a rumor mill of potential film/video projects coming to Florida in the near future. Contains small advertisements by Florida firms interested in reaching state production personnel. Typeset, graphics in advertisements (8 ½ x 11 inches / 215 x 280 mm).
DEPT: "Film," "Television," "Video," "Commercials," "Theater," "Print," "People," "Miscellaneous," "Rumors." (10-89).
TYPL: None. (10-89).
SCHL: Monthly, 6 pp.
SPAN: ?+
SUPPLEMENT TO
--Entertainment Revue, ?+

✤ INSIDE HOLLYWOOD

PUBL: World Publishing Co., 990 Grove St., Evanston, IL 60201-4370.
DESC: Covering the "good, the bad, and the ugly" of Hollywood motion pictures, *Inside Hollywood* provides a thoroughly entertaining romp through the personalities and projects that make up "Tinsletown." *Inside Hollywood* is fascinating personality profiles and interviews with top film stars such as Andy Garcia, Julia Roberts, Christian Slater, Michelle Pfeiffer, Rob Lowe, John Travolta, Spike Lee, Sylvester Stallone, Patrick Swayze, Julia Roberts, Cher, Bob Hoskins, Tom Hanks, Kevin Costner, Tom Cruise, Meryl Streep, Demi Moore, and Arnold Schwarzenegger. Of special note is the "Hollywood Diary," where the stories and stars of historical Hollywood once again are placed before the readers and fans of motion pictures. In the premiere issue the two articles concerned Howard Hughes and Ginger Rogers. Magazine format (8 x 10 7/8 inches / 205 x 275 mm), with full color graphics throughout.
DEPT: "Letters," "Just for Openers," "Now Playing," 'Popular pics worthy of a view'; "Hollywood Insider," 'Squeals 'n' squabbles, rumours 'n' rumbles'; "Short Takes," 'Upcomings and shoots'; "Birthday Bash!," 'Cake cuttings'; "In Memoriam," obituaries; "Star Temps," 'Who's hot ... Who's Not'; "Movie Calendar," 'Upcoming new movie releases plus movies in production'; "Movie of the Month," "Star Words," crossword puzzle column by Daniel Bubbeco; "Star of the Month," "Hollywood Diary," stars and stories of yesteryear; "Parting Shots," commentary. (2/3-91).
TYPL: "Andy Garcia: Hollywood's 'Next Big Thing' Just Wants to Make a Living", "Yo! Rocky... We Loved Ya!," "The Real Ghosts in Patrick's Past," "On the Dark Side," "Christian Slater: Wise Guy." (2/3-91).
SCHL: Bimonthly, 70 pp.
SPAN: Jan/Feb, 1991+
DD: 791
ISSN: 1054-2825

✤ INSIDE MEDIA

SUB: "The voice of print advertising."
SUB: "For advertisers and agencies."
SUB: "Bringing advertiser and agency management inside print."
PUBL: Hanson Publishing Group, Inc., Six River Bend, PO Box 4272, Stamford, CT 06907.
DESC: [*Inside Print*]: Advertising is the lifeblood of any commercial medium: *Inside Print* functions to help media professionals stimulate that income through exploration and reporting on trends in print advertising. The emphasis here is on the print media of magazines and newspapers; with thoughtful reports on advertising strategies, successful case studies, targeting readers, and unique publication opportunities for national advertisers and their agencies. Print/media agency buyers, and in-house advertising/marketing directors will find this publication a great resource. Magazine format (8 1/8 x 10 7/8 inches / 205 x 275 mm); numerous examples of print advertisements.
DESC: [*Inside Media*]: "The first magazine exclusively written for and about today's media department," is how *Inside Media* bills itself. This large-tabloid publication provides excellent coverage of current advertising vehicles, costs, trends, and commentary; packaged in a contemporary layout design with liberal use of color, especially in reproducing front-page covers of selected periodicals and photographic stills of television broadcasts. Professional and thorough, *Inside Media* will quickly become must reading for buyers of media; and in the process strengthen the role and image of the media department. Highly recommended reading for those in the advertising and marketing field. Large tabloid magazine format (11 x 14 ½ inches / 280 x 370 mm); prominent use of color and numerous graphics.

DEPT: "Letters," "Hogan," column by Robert W. Hogan; "Ellenthal," column by Ira Ellenthal; "Johnstone," column by Lammy Johnstone; "Editors," "Gallup & Robinson," column; "International Portfolio," "Problem/Solution," "Creative Critique," column; "Opinion," "Resources/," resource material; "Changes," "Quote/Unquote," statements made concerning advertising; "Scrapbook," comment. (2-85). "Update," 'News & Notes'; "Upfront," issue column by Rachel Kaplan; "Ad Libs," 'Items of Interest'; "Who's News," 'A collection of industry movers'; "Facts," 'A collection of useful, interesting and/or unusual data'; "Creative Critique," 'Inside Print's monthly look at some ads worth noting'; "Viewpoint," guest column. (4-89). "Media Avails," special feature topics upcoming in print publications; "Market Profile," outstanding regional media/advertising opportunity profile; "Stats," ratings and reading statistic of selected media; "Calendar," 'a guide to meetings, events, seminars and parties'; "Horoscope," two week schedule; "People," personnel newsbriefs; "Newspapers," "Magazines," "Broadcast TV," "Cable TV," "Media Bytes," newsbriefs; "Media Strategies," unique section profiling one agency's approach to advertising planning and purchase. (10-25-89).

TYPL: "Fame by Association Marketing," "Nobody Reads Body Copy," "Redbook Goes for the Jugular," "What's the Payoff for Business Advertising?," "CPMs Don't Count." (2-85). "We'll Take Manhattan," "The Big Cheese," "Sears Towers," "Buying the Sizzle," "The Media Doctors Are In." (4-89). "Rival Shops to Merge Spot Buys," "Americans Buy into European TV-Production Deals," "CBS Sports Revs Up to Barnstorm Malls," "North Jersey Papers in War to Capture Upscale Readers," "Unwired Networks Try Some New Twists," "The Comedy Channel isn't Just Clowning Around." (10- 25-89).

SCHL: Monthly (1980 - ?); Monthly [plus extra issue in May] (Spring, 1982 - ?); Fourteen issues per year (Jan, 1984 - Mar, 1988); Twelve issues per year (Apr, 1988 - Jul, 1989); Semimonthly (Sep 14, 1989+), 55 pp.

SPAN: 1980+
VARIES
--Jan, 1980 - Dec, 1985 as Magazine Age (ISSN: 0194-2506).
--Jan, 1986 - Jul, 1989 as Inside Print (ISSN: 0886-9928).

SPAN: Sep 13, 1989+
LC: HF 5801 .M14
DD: 659.13/2/05 20
ISSN: 1046-5316
ABST: --Predicasts

Inside Print

Jan, 1986 - Jul, 1989//
(ISSN: 0886-9928)
SEE: INSIDE MEDIA

✤ INSIDE RADIO

SUB: "The hot news in ratings and sales."
SUB: "The radio publication you're reading the most."
SUB: "Up-to-the-minute weekly management news for radio executives."
SUB: "A confidential newsweekly for radio executives, programmers and syndicators."
PUBL: Inside Radio, Inc., 1930 E. Marlton Pike, Suite S-93, Cherry Hill, NJ 08003.
DESC: Commercial radio station managers and owners need *Inside Radio*, a magazine that seeks to provide the leading edge in a very competitive industry. This eight-page weekly newsletter details station sales, format changes, ratings trends, creative promotions and other news of interest to radio station management. Indeed, in one sample issue (Apr, 1990) *Inside Radio* listed over 200 articles categorically labled as "Hot News," "Sales Tips," "Ratings Tips," and "Management Tips," all from the previous three month time period! Of special note is a two-page ratings sheet showing competitive station status in over 20 American markets. Even at a yearly subscription rate of $190 (Spring, 1990), this is inexpensive advice indeed for today's commercial radio station manager/owner. Well recommended for insightful comment, and timliness of issues discussed. For the sampled issues of 1991: three hole-punched newsletter format, black ink on goldenrod tinted paper, no advertising (8 ½ x 11 inches / 215 x 280 mm).
DEPT: None. (7-4-83). "Inside the Birch Monthlies." (4-2-90).
TYPL: "Satellite Music Network Prepares for Major Growth," "Arbitron Signs Cluster Plus Research Service," "Pick Advertisers with Care,"."Making Employees Problems Productive," "Cuban Radio Interference Update: Negotiations Likely." (7-4-83). "Arbitron Tells Armitron to 'Stay Out of Our Industry'," "New Way to Get Free Interactive Phone Service," "Sales Incentive Plan that Billed $100,000 Last Week," "Latest Attention-Getter to Grab Media Coverage." (4-2-90).
SCHL: Weekly, 8 pp.
SPAN: Jan 1, 1976+
ISSN: 0731-9312

Instructional Innovator

Jan, 1980 - Jan, 1985//
(ISSN: 0196-6979)
SEE: TECHTRENDS

Instructional Materials

Feb, 1956 - Jun, 1956//
SEE: TECHTRENDS

✢ INTELLIGENCER

PUBL: American Journalism Historians Association, Indiana State University, Department of Communication, 430 Reeve Hall, Terre Haute, IN 47809.
DESC: This newsletter is published by the American Journalism Historians Association, which also publishes the excellent scholarly journal, *American Journalism*. Function of the *Intelligencer* is to provide news and information about AJHA members, the status of organization publications, and to briefly note organization activities. For the sampled issue of 1991: black ink on tinted uncoated paper stock in folded newsletter style, no advertising (8 ½ x 11 inches / 215 x 280 mm).
DEPT: "The President's Desk," editorial column by Leonard Teel; "Personals," "News and Notes." (2-91).
TYPL: "Research Committee Issues Paper Call," "Committee Examines AJHA's Operations," "Journal Returning to Normal Schedule." (2-91).
SCHL: ?, 4 pp.
SPAN: 1983?+

✢ INTELLIGENT DECISIONS

SUB: "Your guide to audio and video entertainment."
PUBL: Columbia Audio/Video, 1741 Second St., Highland Park, IL 60035.
DESC: New audio/video consumer products and their application to "high-tech" homes is the focus of this quality quarterly publication. One sampled issue explored the wide varieties of audio/video tape, new enclosures and packaging for home audio speakers, multi-function remote controls, the myth versus the reality of "surround sound," the dawning era of digital communication, and new means of performing equipment maintenance at home. A special emphasis of this periodical is the expensive but exciting trend toward "home theatres," concerning planning, construction, technology, and costs involved. Full-color graphics throughout show equipment installation and design in a variety of home settings. Magazine format (8 ¼ x 10 ¾ inches / 210 x 275 mm).
DEPT: "As We See It," editorial; "What's New, What's Hot." (winter-90).
TYPL: "The Gourmet of Tape," "For Your Eyes Only," "10 Unique Home Entertainment Systems," "Control at Your Fingertips," "Space Age Computing." (winter-90).
SCHL: Quarterly, 115 pp.
SPAN: ?+
ISSN: 1049-5576

Inter/View
1969 - Nov, 1972//
SEE: INTERVIEW

✢ INTERCOMM
SUB: "News/feature magazine."
PUBL: California State University at Fullerton, Department of Communications, Fullerton, CA.
DESC: *InterComm* "...encourages interaction between organizations, professionals and other universities interested in encouraging the advancement of the communications field." Part public relations vehicle, part class project, and part showcase for individual student talent, *InterComm* provides a classy forum for the activities of California State University at Fullerton's Department of Communications. The graphics, writing, and layout style are professional. Articles explore the curriculum, activities, and accomplishments of CSUF communication students. One of the better laboratory publications. Magazine format; numerous graphics.
DEPT: "Mini Mag," newsbriefs; "Alumni Profiles." (fall-79).
TYPL: "Tune in Station CSUF-TV," "Technical-Business: an Endangered Sequence," "A Day in the Life of a PR Professional," "Truth and Comm Sequences." (fall-79).
SCHL: Semiyearly, 32 pp.
SPAN: Fall, 1977?+

✢ INTERCULTURAL & DEVELOPMENT COMMUNICATION NEWSLETTER

PUBL: International Communication Association, Intercultural and Development Communication Division, PO Box 9589, Austin, TX 78766.
DESC: "This newsletter is published twice a year, Fall and Spring, to facillitate communication and coordination among our division members. Generally, the Fall issue features guidelines for upcoming conference program/paper submissions. The Spring issue outlines preliminary conference programs pertinent to our division." This newsletter serves an informational function for the Intercultural and Development Communication Division of the International Communication Association. The sampled publication provided news of membership and listed the top three academic papers in three major fields. A sampling of those paper titles included for Intercultural: "Uncertainty Reduction Among Ethnicities in the United States"; for Development: "A Pragmastist Account for Participatory Communication Research for National Development"; and for International: "Mass Media Effects on Knowledge and Attitudes: A Chinese Case in Reform." For the sampled issue of 1991: single sheet stapled newsletter format, typeset, no advertising (8 ½ x 11 inches / 215 x 280 mm).
DEPT: "Report From the Chair," editorial column by Young Y. Kim. (spring-91).
TYPL: "Inter-Divisional," "Paper/Proposal Review Process," "Intercultural Dinner," "Call for Nominations," "Overseas Intercultural Workshops." (spring-91).
SCHL: Semiyearly, 6 pp.
SPAN: ?+

Interim Drama
Nov, 1945 - Spring?, 1946//
SEE: DRAMA

✣ INTERLIT
PUBL: David C. Cook Foundation, Cook Square, Elgin, IL 60120.
DESC: The David C. Cook Foundation, "...a nonprofit institution dedicated to Christian communication," publishes this quarterly magazine on the process, art and technique of publishing printed materials for worldwide distribution. It has well-informed, pragmatic information on marketing, writing, printing, cultural barriers, language problems, and just plain production problems facing publishers of printed works. It features Christian publications, although ideas and concepts of the articles could apply to secular communication as well. Well recommended. For the sampled issues of 1991: black ink with numerous spot-ink color pages and cover on coated paper stock, no advertising, stapled magazine format (8 ¼ x 10 ¾ inches / 210 x 275 mm).
DEPT: "Editorial," "Etcetera," a potpourri of common-sense advice. (12-87).
TYPL: "Do Kenyans Want Books in English?," "What Your Translator Wishes You Knew," "Sell Your Foreign Rights," "The Making of a Magazine." (12-87).
SCHL: Quarterly, 24 pp.
SPAN: ?+

✣ INTERMEDIA
PUBL: International Institute of Communications, Tavistock House, East, Tavistock Square, London WC1H 9LG, England.
DESC: This quality publication from the International Institute of Communications covers news and reports on developing communication technologies as they relate to societies and national norms. A typical issue will include authors from a half-dozen countries writing about developments, news, and communication trends in their own nation. There are many articles to commend to readers. Of special note was an excellent comparison of production costs and estimates for television production in Germany, France, the UK, Spain, and Italy in the May/June, 1991 issue; and a wonderful discussion on "What Future for Communications Studies?" in the Aug/Sep, 1991 issue. For the sampled issues of 1977: black ink with spot-color on cover, all on uncoated paper stock in stapled magazine format, no advertising (8 ¼ x 11 ¼ inches / 210 x 285 mm). For the 1991 sampled issues: black ink with two-color cover on coated paper stock, stapled magazine format, no advertising, same dimensions as listed above.
DEPT: "Resource Material," "International Coordination." (4-77). "Editorial," "Dissent," "Books," "Intermediary," commentary. (#4-91).
TYPL: "Indonesia's Satellite Experiences," "Joint IBM/Comsat Satellite," "The Chinese Way of Broadcasting," "West Germany's Communication Policy," "New Zealand Goes Back to the Corporation." (4-77). "The Developing Countries Data and Modems Standardization," "Packet Switching's Early Days," "Inter-Media Discussion: The Future of Communications Studies," "Developing Human Resources Through Teletechnology," "World VCR Survey: One in Three TV Homes." (#4-91).
SCHL: Bimonthly, 55 pp.
SPAN: Mar/Apr, 1973+.
VARIES
--? - ? as IBI Newsletter.
LC: HE 8689.I55
DD: 384.54/05
ISSN: 0309-118x

✣ INTERMISSION
SUB: "Performing arts news magazine."
PUBL: Intermission, 6205 Redwood Lane, Alexandria, VA 22310.
DESC: This newsprint monthly covers the performing arts of the Washington, DC area (with some observations on noteworthy productions elsewhere), providing a handy reference to the performing arts pulse of the nation's capital. Advertising concerns local dining establishments and other services of interest to the arts-attending public. This same publisher produces *Intermission* for the St. Louis area as well. The 1990 sampled issue consisted of stapled magazine format on newsprint, with black ink editorial content (8 ⅛ x 10 ⅞ inches / 205 x 275 mm).
DEPT: "Calendar," performances, theatre and telephone listing; "Cinema," review. (6-90).
TYPL: "Travels with Rick Cluchey," "Grand Teton Music Festival," "West End Dinner Theatre," "Source Theatre Co." (6-90).
SCHL: Monthly, 25 pp.
SPAN: ?+

INTERNATIONAL ADVERTISER
SUB: "Incorporating International Marketing Report."
PUBL: Roth International, 615 W. 22nd St., Oak Brook, IL 60521.
DESC: *International Advertiser*, which began in July, 1980, served the needs of international advertisers and their agencies in the global market. Its emphasis was the American corporate approach to world advertising, providing workshop discussions of the means to break into specific international markets, matching the techniques of advertising to the unique cultural characteristics of a nation. Mini-cultural lessons provided advice on the interactive communication process of successfully working with other nationalities. Publisher Robert Roth showed in a commissioned survey for September, 1981 that 51% of the global advertising community preferred *International Advertiser* to

a 35% preference for *Advertising World*. The editorial content of *International Advertiser* for the next few years declined in number and scope down to the last sampled issue (Nov/Dec, 1983), which contained five articles in 30 pages. Numerous graphics, especially of print advertising examples.
DEPT: "Perspective," "Scan," newsbriefs; (9/10-81). "Scan," newsbriefs; "Perspective," editorial. (7/8-83).
TYPL: "Your Latin-American Roundtable," "The Media Scene in Greece," "New Technologies Fracture Canada's TV Market," "How Kodak breathes Fire into International Trade Shows." (9/10-81). "Foreign Product Images in Saudia Arabia," "Advertising in Malaysia," "Prime Rises Above the Clutter with Special Events," "Advertising in Eastern Europe." (7/8-83).
SCHL: Monthly (Jul, 1976 - Jun, 1980); Bimonthly (Jul/Aug, 1980+), 35 pp.
SPAN: Jul, 1976 - Nov/Dec, 1983//
VARIES
--Jul, 1976 - Jun, 1980 as International Marketing Report (ISSN: 0193-9661).
ABSORBED BY
--Advertising World (ISSN: 0163-9412).
DD: 659
ISSN: 0198-6228
ABST: --Predicasts

✢ INTERNATIONAL ADVERTISER

SUB: "The magazine for multi-national advertising."
SUB: "The magazine for international advertising."
PUBL: International Advertiser, 150 Fifth Ave., Suite 610, New York, NY 10011.
DESC: This serial was designed for those individuals whose job it was to plan, schedule, and place international advertising for their corporate or in-house clients. *Advertising World* provided up-to-date information on the changing political, social, and economic norms of nations, and the relative health of advertising media and markets within those countries. Also featured were ongoing articles concerning the changing status of global marketing/advertising. Early issues of this quarterly were typewritten, moving to typesetting by the end of its publication span. In May, 1985, *Advertising World* incorporated *International Advertiser*, and in a turnabout situation, in September, 1985, itself took on the title of *International Advertiser* (with SUB:) "Incorporating *Advertising World*." The serial was a membership publication of the International Advertising Association
DEPT: "Media Notes & Quotes," "Our Readers Write," letters; "Update Section," media briefs; "Editorial." (spring-76). "Media Notes & Quotes," "On View," 'visitors and presentations'; "Hot on the Press," 'publication news'; "Guess Who!," 'trivia persuassion'; "After 5 o'Clock," interview; "Representative Appointments," "Letters," "Research News." (2-85).

TYPL: "Bank of America is with You," "International Real Estate Advertising," "Busling Brazil Baffling Buyers?" "Arab Media Snap Back as Lebanon Problems Ease." (spring-76). "Can a Corporation Advertise a Personality?" "North American Computer/Telecommunications Advertising in Europe," "How International Computer Magazines Serve Their Market," "What is Happening in Scandinavia." (2-85).
SCHL: Quarterly (? - Summer, 1979); Bimonthly (Oct/Nov, 1979+).
SPAN: ?+
VARIES
--1974? - Jun, 1985 as Advertising World (ISSN: 0163-9412).
ABSORBED
--Twentieth Century Advertising, Jul, 1924.
--International Advertiser (ISSN: 0198-6228).
DD: 659
ISSN: 0885-3353
ABST: --Business Periodical Index (ISSN: 0007-6961)
--Management Contents

✢ INTERNATIONAL ADVERTISER, THE

SUB: "The magazine for international marketing executives."
PUBL: International Advertising Association, 342 Madison Ave., New York, NY 10017.
DESC: In this official publication of the International Advertising Association, reporters world-wide provide news stories on trends, topics and campaigns on advertisers and their products. It provides good coverage on the general status of advertising throughout the world.
DEPT: "Notes on New Publications," briefs concerning international publications; "International Advertisers," briefs; "International Agencies," briefs; "International Media," briefs; "IAA Chapter News," briefs.
TYPL: "The Changing Faces of International Advertising," "International Campaigns--A Falacy?," "International media Planning." (spring-72).
SCHL: Monthly (Jun, 1960 - ?); Quarterly (? - Spring, 1972); Bimonthly (Mar/Apr, 1988+), 6 pp.
SPAN: Jun, 1960+
SUSPENDED
--Summer, 1973 - Winter?, 1987.
VARIES
--? - ? as International Marketing Report (ISSN: 0198-6228).
LC: HF 5801.I533
ISSN: 0020-5834

✢ INTERNATIONAL BROADCASTING

SUB: "Systems and Operation."
SUB: "The equipment industry magazine."
SUB: "The broadcast technology magazine."

PUBL: BSO Publications, 13 Great James St., London WC1N 3DP, England.
DESC: "News and information for Chief Engineers and Managers of radio and television stations on all aspects of sound and television broadcast engineering worldwide--from management to support services--from operational concepts to equipment design." This is a showcase publication for international manufacturers of broadcast equipment, and technological, political, and economic trends affecting same, and provides a splendid international point-of-view on worldwide communication. For the sampled issues of 1991: full-color graphics, pages and cover on coated paper stock throughout, in stapled magazine format, advertising (8 ¼ x 11 ¾ inches / 210 x 295 mm).
DEPT: "News," multi-page section of new equipment news; "Technology," new equipment; "Comment," editorial; "Links & Patches," newsbriefs. (4-82). "Industry News," "News," newsbriefs. (4-89).
TYPL: "The Digital Dilemma--Part I Analogue to Digital Conversion," "TV Transmission Distortion; Automatic Correction," "ENG Transmission Considerations," "Can TV ever be a Sound Proposition?" (4-80); "Satellite Broadcasting in Europe: We Have the Technology, But Is There a Need?," "Norway: Public Broadcasting Challenged," "German Broadcasting: A Difficult Future," "Full of Western Promise: Korea Ch 2 Goes for Pye Transmitters," (4-82). "Automation Frontier - Closed Captioning," "Monitoring TV Stereo," "Converting HDTV Problems Into Solutions," "Powering UHF in the US." (4-89).
SCHL: Monthly, 85 pp.
SPAN: 1978+
 VARIES
 --1978 - Mar, 1980 as Broadcasting Systems & Operations.
LC: TK 6540.I562
DD: 621.3841/05
ISSN: 0141-1748
ABST: --Computer & Control Abstracts (ISSN: 0036-8113)
 --Electrical & Electronics Abstracts (ISSN: 0036-8105)
 --Electronic Publishing Abstracts (ISSN: 0739-2907)
 --Physics Abstracts. Science Abstracts. Series A. (ISSN: 0036-8091)

✤ INTERNATIONAL CABLE

SUB: "From the publishers of Communications Technology and CableFAX."
SUB: "Incorporating the official journal of the U.K. SCTE."
PUBL: Communications Technology Publications Corporation, 50 South Steel St., Suite 500, Denver, CO 80209.
DESC: This international bimonthly publication covers news, trends, technologies and various developments in the international cable television field. Topics include cable penetration, developments in the world government regulatory area, cable television company profiles, the economics of operating CATV, and a wide variety of new technologies, especially as they relate to local application and engineering acceptance. If there is a primary emphasis, it would have to be the application of technology within a managerial framework. Articles explore operating and economic climates for a given system to provide insight, information, and profitable application of those technologies to the world marketplace. Many issues are themed around a particular nation. For the 1991 sampled issue, the Canadian cable television industry was profiled. Of special note is a "magazine-within-a-magazine" supplement, *Cable Television Engineering*, for the Society of Cable Television Engineers of the United Kingdom. This separately-paged section concerns technological issues for cable television engineers, using charts, graphs and schematics for emphasis. Note: some sources indicate that *International Cable* is issued as a companion publication to *Communications Technology* (ISSN: 0884-2272) and *MSO* (ISSN: 1046-3321). Stapled magazine format, full-color pages throughout on coated paper stock (8 ⅜ x 10 ⅞ inches / 215 x 275 mm).
DEPT: "From the Editor," "News," newsbriefs concerning international cable television industry; "Product News," review. (7/8-91).
TYPL: "A Comprehensive Backbone System," "Canada: A Cabled Nation," "Economic MDU Service," "Multiple Dwelling Units," "How to Select a CAD System." (7/8-91).
SCHL: Bimonthly, 80 pp.
SPAN: Jan/Feb, 1990+
 WITH SUPPLEMENT
 --Cable Television Engineering (ISSN: 0048-718x), ?+
LC: HE 8700 .I56
DD: 384.55/5/068

✤ INTERNATIONAL DOCUMENTARY

SUB: "The journal of non-fiction film and video."
SUB: "A publication of the International Documentary Association."
SUB: "The newsletter of the International Documentary Association."
PUBL: International Documentary Association, 1551 South Robertson Blvd., Los Angeles, CA 90035.
DESC: From a promotional flyer: "Explore the reel world -- *International Documentary* provides a unique focus on non-fiction film and video--from Latin American Cinema to Women's rights, Visual Anthropology, Censorship, History on Television, and much more. *International Documentary*--informative and provocative reading. *International Documentary* features: interviews with leading film and video makers; worldwide festival coverage; profiles of new filmmakers and their work; the latest technological developments. Find out through the pages of *International Documentary* essential information on: funding sources; production techniques; marketing and distribution opportunities." Dynamic in form and content, *International Documentary* provides a forum for discussion of the documentary form, as well as a showcase for member (International Documentary

Association) productions. Critiques are refreshingly frank, as are discussions of philosophical approaches to the documentary film/video form, and its impact on society. It is an excellent resource, stapled magazine format on coated paper stock, black/white editorial content with significant graphics and advertisements of importance to the documentary community, two-color cover (8 ½ x 11 inches / 215 x 280 mm).
DEPT: "Newsbrief," "Technology," "Festival Reports," "Member News," "Festival Listings," "Announcements." (spring-91).
TYPL: "Burning Voices," "Something to Do with Ross McElwee," "Screening the War," "Docudrama: The Form of Last Resort?," "Shooting From the Hip." (spring-91).
SCHL: Quarterly, 45 pp.
SPAN: Summer, 1989?+
ISSN: 0742-5333

INTERNATIONAL EDUCATIONAL AND CULTURAL EXCHANGE

PUBL: United States Commission on International Educational and Cultural Affairs, Department of State, Washington, DC 20520.
DESC: The Advisory Commission on International Educational and Cultural Affairs was created by an act of Congress in 1961, the purpose of which was "to increase mutual understanding between people of the United States and people of other countries by means of educational and cultural exchange." World mass media are a viable segment of that educational and cultural program, and *Exchange* readers will find articles covering everything from broadcast satellites to book publishing.
DEPT: "Commission Comments," notes on commission activities; "Facts on Funding," newsbriefs; "International Affairs," conference dates.
TYPL: "The Mass Media and Cultural Exchange," "Satellite Communications; Hopes and Fears," "A Western Perspective of the Free Flow of World Information," "The Art and Business of Film," "Training Journalists for International Communication." (winter-78).
SCHL: Quarterly, 55 pp.
SPAN: Summer, 1965 - Summer, 1978//
LC: L 11.I585
DD: 370.19/6/05
ISSN: 0020-6601

✣ INTERNATIONAL FILM BUFF

PUBL: International Film Buff, 2309 Van Ness Ave., San Francisco, CA 94109.
DESC: What's in a title? Publishers Nancy Pisicchio and Gerald Gwathney said they named their new periodical *International Film Buff*, for several reasons. It was called *International* "...because we deal with films from all over the world...*Film*...[because] we're not snobs about films and will look at all kinds of film...[and] *Buff* [which implies that the reader is] one with more than passing interest." With an emphasis on the historical, this serial brings a fresh approach to consumer interaction with the motion picture. There are no academic theses, Hollywood gossip, or discussion of the impact of television on film; these are not subjects of interest to the readers of *International Film Buff*. This is, as the publisher says, "...something really different." Numerous production and publicity stills.
DEPT: "Letters," "Books," "Soundtracks." (2-76).
TYPL: "Men are Such Beasts! or the Monster as Sex Symbol," "Interview with Herbie Hancock," "The Art of Gene Kelly," "Philosophical Pronography," "The Effect of Violence." (2-76).
SCHL: Monthly, 25 pp.
SPAN: Dec, 1975+
LC: PN 1993.I6426
DD: 791.43/05
ISSN: 0361-4131

✣ INTERNATIONAL JOURNAL OF ADVERTISING

SUB: "The quarterly review of marketing communications."
PUBL: The Advertising Association and the CAM Foundation, Eastbourne, East Sussex, England.
DESC: "The *International Journal of Advertising* is the leading journal covering all aspects of marketing communications. Produced in association with the Advertising Association, it is a forum for serious, in-depth discussion of important contemporary issues from the practitioner, academic and public policy viewpoint. ...The journal focuses on topical issues of relevance to all marketing functions. Well-known academics and practitioners analyse recent developments and current best practice in these areas and predict future trends." Recent issues have explored topics such as alcohol advertising, brands and valuations, awareness advertising, management of creativity, and sales response to advertising. Special reports, such as acohol advertising, or "The Impact of Tobacco Advertising" are issued from time to time. Other typical articles include, "Promotion in the Illicit Drug Industry," "Drink and Women," "The Single European Market," and "Television Media Planning." An excellent publication for the considered study of the role of advertising in business, marketing, and society.
DEPT: "Editorial." (#1-90?).
TYPL: "The Role of Advertising in the Life of the Child," "The Effect of Marketing Communication on the Initiation of Juvenile Smoking," "Advertising and Smoking Maintenance," "Advertising and Tobacco Consumption," "Government Paternalism and Citizen Rationality. The Justifiability of Banning Tobacco Advertising." (#1-90?).
SCHL: Quarterly.
SPAN: Jan, 1982+?

VARIES
--Jan, 1982 - Mar, 1982 as Journal of Advertising (ISSN: 0261-9903).
ISSN: 0265-0487

International Journal of Communication Research
1974 - ?//
(ISSN: 0340-0158)
SEE: COMMUNICATIONS

✤ INTERNATIONAL JOURNAL OF INFORMATION MANAGEMENT

PUBL: Butterworth-Heinemann Limited, Westbury House, Bury Street, PO Box 63, Guildford GU2 5BH, England.

DESC: "*International Journal of Information Management* is the quarterly publication for senior managers in business and industry, managers and administrators in government and public service agencies, partners in professional organizations, teachers and trainers in management, public administration and related fields, information technology suppliers, service providers, information consultants, information scientists, systems analysts and researchers in business and information studies. It provides a focus and source of up-to-date information on the developing field of information management. Papers are welcomed in the areas of information systems, organizations, management, decision making, long term planning, information overload, computer and telecommunication technologies, human communication and people in systems and organizations." This is another in the excellent series of informative journals from Butterworth-Heinemann, with a truly international editorial board. As a promotional flyer stated, "The *International Journal of Information Management* aims to bring its readers the very best analysis and discussion. The journal is international in both scope and outlook. Papers originate from a wide range of countries and are rigorously refereed. Additionally, there is an international Editorial Board, whose members are themselves practitioners of information management in either business or academic environments. [The journal] keeps you fully briefed with major papers, reports and reviews. Their emphasis is not on information technology itself, but on the organizational, planning and management aspects, in particular the way in which individuals and groups react to, and use, information systems." An excellent journal and resource for the demanding field of information management. A significant number of graphs, charts and schematics accompany each article. Annual subscription cost, according to the December, 1990 issue, was £95 for the UK, £100 for Europe, and £105 for the rest of the world. Perfect-bound large journal format, black ink on uncoated paper stock for editorial content, while cover is two-color on coated paper stock, limited advertising (7 ⅞ x 10 ⅞ inches / 200 x 275 mm).

DEPT: "Editorial," "Viewpoint," guest commentary; "Book Reviews," "Software Reviews," "Calendar," international list of forthcoming information management events. (12-90).

TYPL: "Computer Disaster: Systematic Problems and Their Management," "Laptops and the Marketing Information Chain," "Information Systems Development in Developing Countries: An Evaluation and Recommendations," "Document Image Processing--New Light on an Old Problem," "Computerization of the Betting Industry." (12-90).

SCHL: Quarterly, 85 pp.
SPAN: ?+
VARIES
--? - Feb?, 1986 as Social Science Information Studies (ISSN: 0143-6236).
LC: H 61.9 .S65
DD: 025/.063
ISSN: 0268-4012
ABST: --Computer & Control Abstracts (ISSN: 0036-8113)
--Electrical & Electronics Abstracts (ISSN: 0036-8105)
--Library Information Science Abstracts (ISSN: 0024-2179)
--Physics Abstracts. Science Abstracts. Series A. (ISSN: 0036-8091)
--PAIS Foreign Language Index (ISSN: 0896-792x)
--Public Affairs Information Service Bulletin (ISSN: 0033-3409)
--Sociological Abstracts (ISSN: 0038-0202)
--Sociology of Education Abstracts
--Technical Education Abstracts

International Journal of Instructional Media
Fall, 1973 - Summer, 1983/84////
(ISSN: 0092-1815)
SEE: INTERNATIONAL JOURNAL OF INSTRUCTIONAL MEDIA AND TECHNOLOGY

INTERNATIONAL JOURNAL OF INSTRUCTIONAL MEDIA AND TECHNOLOGY

PUBL: Westwood Press, Inc., 251 Park Ave., South, New York, NY 10010.

DESC: [*International Journal of Instructional Media*]: "The *Journal* will focus on quality research, and present articles of on-going programs in instructional media education that deal with curricula, personnel, practices and materials (software and hardware, with emphasis on software). As the needs for research, assessment, and validation of our educational systems and its components become increasingly urgent (with the mounting pressure to account for time and monies spent on the entire education market); the *Journal* will

help to provide a basis for authoritative evaluation of the complex factors which comprise the present and future 'instructional media system' and the effects of these factors on the ultimate benefactor--the learner." Scholarly journal approach and format; no graphics.
DEPT: None.
TYPL: "Let's Start Using Overhead Transperencies Effectively," "Using Visual and Haiku Poetry to Awaken Hibernating Bears," "Programmed Television: Its Role in Foreign Language Instruction." (spring-74). "Pac Man and Theory Z," "The Role of Field Independence in Visual Information," "Interactive and Intelligent Environments." (winter-83/84).
SCHL: Quarterly, 90 pp.
SPAN: Fall, 1973 - Summer, 1983/84//
VARIES
--Fall, 1973 - Summer, 1983/84// as International Journal of Instructional Media (ISSN: 0092-1815).
LC: LB 1043 .I574
DD: 371.3/078
ISSN: 0092-1815
ABST: --Engineering Index

International Marketing Report

Jul, 1976 - Jun, 1980//
(ISSN: 0193-9661)
SEE: INTERNATIONAL ADVERTISER

International Marketing Report

? - ?//
(ISSN: 0198-6228)
SEE: INTERNATIONAL ADVERTISER, THE

International Photo Technik

1960 - May, 1983//
(ISSN: 0020-8280)
SEE: PHOTO TECHNIQUE INTERNATIONAL

International Photo Technique

Aug, 1983 - Nov, 1983//
SEE: PHOTO TECHNIQUE INTERNATIONAL

✢ INTERNATIONAL PHOTOGRAPHER

SUB: "A monthly journal dedicated to the advancement of the motion picture industry in all its branches."
SUB: "A journal of motion picture arts and crafts."
SUB: "The magazine of cinematography and video techniques written by professionals for professionals."
SUB: "The magazine of motion picture arts and sciences (devoted to the professional photographer."

PUBL: International Alliance of Theatrical Stage Employees and Moving Picture Machine Operators of the United States and Canada, Local 659, 7715 Sunset Blvd., Hollywood, CA 90046.
DESC: "A monthly journal dedicated to the advancement of the motion picture industry in all its branches: cinematography, professional and amateur; photography, lighting, process, sets and decor., laboratory and processing, film editing, sound recording and the allied arts and crafts of theatre projection and operation. The *International Photographer*, as the official publication of the International Photographers, Local 659, a part of the International Alliance of Theatrical Stage Employees and Motion Picture Machine Operators of the United States and Canada, not only represents the entire personnel of photographers now engaged in professional production of motion pictures in the United States and Canada, but also serves other technicians in the studios and theatres, who also are members of the International Alliance, as well as executives and creative artists of the industry" (from a 1937 masthead statement). In the 1937 sampled issue there were few feature articles, most news items being placed under a departmental subject heading such as "Camera," "Process," "Sound," "Lighting Sets," "Laboratory," "Projection," or "Radio." For that 1937 sampled issue: stapled magazine format, numerous graphics and black ink on coated paper stock, cover consisting of two-color black/purple ink on coated paper stock (9 x 12 inches / 230 x 305 mm). Some 30 years later (circa 1970), *International Photographer* had a much different function, becoming a shorter, 25-page publication serving informational needs of its union membership. By 1983, *International Photographer* had expanded its coverage once again to include news of new products, literature, production information; and news of local guilds and unions involved in motion picture and television production. The expanded editorial coverage was a welcome development for this 50+ year publication, one which has faithfully reported on current developments, new technologies, and potential trends in the entertainment industry.
DEPT: "Tradewinds," production activities; "Camera," from manufacturer to user; "Process," news items; "Sound," news items; "Lighting-Sets," how-to and news items; "Laboratory," news items; "Projection," news items; "Radio," news items; "Close-Ups," 'Notes and comment on photographer contributors and policy'; "Mail Bag," letters. (8-37). "Previews of," newsbriefs of equipment and services; "They Say--," detailed list of productions and positions held by local 659 members. (7-70). "Previews," 'Equipment-Services-Industry news'; "Production Report," in-progress productions; "Tools of the Trade," technical review. (11-83).
TYPL: "Stereophonic: Sound Counterpart of Stereo-Scopic Effect in Picture is Visioned by Technicians as Springing from Push-Pull Recording Technique," "Makeup and Lens," "Mobile Sound," "Duplex Spreads," "Mirrophonic: Western Electric Strides in

Past Ten Years; Pantages Booth." (8-37). "Film System is Key to Successful CATV," "Cinemobile Systems; a Revolution," "Torra! Torra! Torra!," "The Creative Cinematographer." (7-70). "SMPTE Lighting Seminar," "Jack Cardiff," "Historical Review of Motion Picture Standards," "Reverse or Negative Bluescreen." (11- 83).
SCHL: Monthly, 36 pp.
SPAN: Feb, 1929+
ISSN: 0020-8299
LC: TR 1.I65

✥ INTERNATIONAL PHOTOGRAPHER MAGAZINE

SUB: "The make money with your camera magazine."
PUBL: American Image, Inc., 8700 Concord Church Rd., Lewisville, NC 27023.
DESC: *International Photographer* is the authoritative voice on making money with your camera and getting the photographer into action. We want to guarantee that every person who owns a camera has the opportunity to pursue the dream of making money with his camera if he chooses. We are the reliable source for recognized affiliation, an ally for the globe trotting freelancer, indispensable to the photographer on assignment who needs back up and support. Our intention is for this to be the magazine that camera enthusiasts read for pleasure, information and inspiration. We think it should appeal to readers with an uncommon curiosity about making money, inspiring them to try new ideas and strive for success without sacrificing the pleasure of photography." This publication is affiliated with the International Freelance Photographers Organization, which, through this magazine, inspires people to venture out and take commercially viable photographs for lease or sale. Most articles are written by IFPO members, and detail how they were able to commercially profit from their photographic activities and their affiliation with the International Freelance Photographers Organization. The "Mail Bag," letters to the editor, gushes forth praise for the benefits of belonging to IFPO. Many black/white photographs, along with numerous instructional videotapes and books for the benefit of the membership. Full color cover with black/white editorial content on coated paper stock (8 ¼ x 10 ⅞ inches / 210 x 275 mm).
DEPT: "Straight From the Editor," editorial column by Vonda H. Blackburn; "Mail Bag," 'Letters from readers'; "On Assignment," "Tech Tips," "Product Picks," "Photo Tours & Workshops." (spring-91).
TYPL: "Opportunity Strikes," "How to Really Get Published," "How to Build Your Own Photographic Equipment," "How to Shoot Great Travel Photography at Home!," "How to Turn Your Vacation into a Tax Deduction." (spring-91).
SCHL: Quarterly, 65 pp.
SPAN: Spring, 1986+

INTERNATIONAL PRESS REVIEW

SUB: "A monthly devoted to the activity of the periodical press throughout the world."
PUBL: International Press Cutting Bureau, 38 Oakfield Rd., London, England.
DESC: The purpose of this short-lived serial was "...to report and to illustrate journalistic life and activity in every country, to acquaint the journalists of one land with the activities of the journalists elsewhere." The small journal format serial reported on press developments in various nations with an eye to economic, social, and governmental conditions in those nations. No graphics; newsprint.
DEPT: "New Periodical Publications," "New Reference Books." (4-24).
TYPL: "The Engineering Press of Great Britain," "Press Problems in the Latin Countries," "American Magazines in Canada," "Notes on the French Press." (4-24).
SCHL: Monthly, 50 pp.
SPAN: Mar, 1924 - Apr, 1924//
LC: PN 4701.I6

INTERNATIONAL PROJECTIONIST

PUBL: International Projectionist Publishing Co., 19 W. 44th St., New York, NY.
DESC: Debuting in 1931, *International Projectionist* was filled with information on the relatively new art of film projection for theatrical entertainment. New equipment or attachments were being developed and new media (specifically television) were also exploring the use of theaters for projection. *International Projectionist* enjoyed a heyday era once again in the mid-1950s with a variety of newly introduced film formats. It ended in July, 1965 as film equipment became simplified and Cinemascope-width screens became the norm for the American exhibitor. It has a wealth of information concerning early film equipment as well as developments in allied fields of audio, film stock; and includes "showmanship" techniques.
DEPT: "Monthly Chat," publishers comments; "In the Spotlight," newsbriefs; "IA Obituaries."
TYPL: "AC Projection Arcs Having H.I. Characteristics," "The What, Why, and How of Electron Emission," Apathy Within the Craft--and Why," "Some Unoccupied Motion Picture Fields," (1-34); "Lamp Manufacturer Assays Screen Surfaces," "This Matter of Balanced Lenses," "The VistaVision Horizontal Projector," "An Evaluation of Optical Sound," (10-54).
SCHL: Monthly, 35 pp.
SPAN: Oct, 1931 - Jun, 1965//
SUPPLEMENT TO
--Greater Amusements and International Projectionist, Jul, 1965 - ?
ABSORBED
--Projection Engineering, Apr, 1933.

ABSORBED BY
--Greater Amusements (ISSN: 0017-3703).
LC: TR 845.I

✤ INTERNATIONAL RADIO REPORT, THE

SUB: "Voice of National Academy of Radio Arts & Sciences."
SUB: "The most accurate charts in the world."
PUBL: CHRR Corp., 7011 Sunset Blvd., Hollywood, CA 90028.
DESC: This is a weekly publication "by, of, and about outstanding authorities in radio and music." *The International Radio Report* by Claude Hall is a medium of information for the professional radio personality, providing him/her with news of new record releases, entertainers, and the general state of the radio personality profession. Majority of publication is devoted to playlists at major radio stations in the United States.
DEPT: "Claude Hall's Radio Confidential," news and gossip; "Radio Insight: Sales and Programming Checklist," "Music Confidential," record news; "Letters," "New Music Showcase," profiles; "AiRwaves," news; "Leading Album Rock Songs," playlist; "Album Rock," playlist; "Starter Stations," "MASSurvey," playlist; "A/C This Week," "Adult Contemporary," playlist; "Corky's Country Corner," news; "Country Songs," playlist; "Disco," news; "Disco Stations," playlist; "Radio Profile," "Red Hots," employment wantads. (9-6-79).
TYPL: "Deregulation Top NAB Priority," "A/C Attracts 25-Plus with Total Package," "Would You Like to Know why AM Ratings are Really Falling?," "The Price You Have to Pay to be a King in Atlanta." (9-6-79).
SCHL: Weekly, 40 pp.
SPAN: 1978+
ISSN: 0160-8908

International Television

Jun, 1983 - Jul, 1986//
(ISSN: 0737-3929)
SEE: CORPORATE TELEVISION

✤ INTERNATIONAL VIDEOTEXT TELETEXT NEWS

PUBL: Arlen Communications, Inc., PO Box 40771, Washington, DC 20016.
DESC: This monthly newsletter covering the latest news in the field of videotext and teletext communication covers programming, governmental regulation, economic, system, and consumer factors which impact videotext and teletext information systems. Three-hole punched; typewritten; no graphics.
DEPT: "BoxScore," 'a monthly report on the number of users (experimental and commercial) of teletext, videotext, electronic publishing, captioning and related technologies'; (6-28-82).
TYPL: "Waiting for Their Chips to Come In: Industry Wavers, But Progress is Being Made," "Impending US Teletext Boom: Sets Due Soon, Tests Abound," "Consumer Electronics: De Facto Standards, Computers Hot, But Software Questions." (6-28-82).
SCHL: Monthly, 10 pp.
SPAN: Jul, 1980+
ISSN: 0197-677x
ABST: --Electronic Publishing Abstracts (ISSN: 0739-2907)

✤ INTERSPACE

SUB: "Weekly European satellite & space business newsletter."
SUB: "Interspace, the only weekly in the business."
PUBL: European Satellite & Space News, 32B, High Street, Alton, Hampshire GU34 1BD, England.
DESC: "*Interspace* provides the best and most frequent news and information source on Europe's emerging satellite communications markets. It provides very high quality and original news and analysis to help professionals understand their markets. *Interspace* is not a rehash of press releases; its news is original, in depth and critical" (promotional flyer). Published since 1983, this weekly newsletter has consistently dispensed important news of the European satellite market in a concise format to its numerous subscribers in Europe and elsewhere. Of special note are unique subscriber services for further information about trends, services, corporations, and topics. This service alone is well worth the £250 annual subscription fee (for 1990). Perhaps the most compelling reason to subscribe is found in the same promotional flyer: "If you do not read it, the chances are high that your competitors will and therefore have a competitive advantage over you." For the sampled 1990 issue: typeset stapled single-sheet newsletter format with two-color cover page on uncoated paper stock, no advertising (8 ¼ x 11 ½ inches / 210 x 300 mm).
DEPT: "General--Around the Industry," news; "News in Brief." (3-9-90).
TYPL: "The Dth Market 'Stabilises'," "The Significance of New Digital Audio," "Revival of Satellites Over Fibre," "New Forecasts on Satellite TV." (3-9-90).
SCHL: Weekly, 10 pp.
SPAN: 1983+

✤ INTERVIEW

SUB: "Andy Warhol's movie magazine."
PUBL: Interview, Inc., 575 Broadway, New York, NY 10012.
DESC: *Interview*, in spite of its overly large size, unfolds like an old friend each month, highlighting interviews with media personalities within a decidedly artistic landscape of creative photography, typography, and lay-

out design. Begun as *Andy Warhol's Interview*, the publication still bears the creative genius of this man, tossing aside normal conventions of magazine layout design. Articles sometimes appear identical to the trendy advertisements on facing pages, while other articles lack traditional headlines and thus seem to have no apparent beginning or ending. This latter condition requires interaction from the reader, and may be partly responsible for the success of the monthly magazine. Media personalities and artistic photography are the stars here, bearing in one month alone the likes of South African playwright Athol Fugard, Jack Nicholson, Harvey Keitel, Audrey Hepburn, the Neville Brothers, and Siegfried & Roy. Large magazine format (10 7/8 x 14 1/2 inches / 270 x 365 mm); numerous graphics, some full page size; trendy advertisements.

DEPT: "The Month," observations; "Art," "Movies," "Fashion," "Music," "Comics," "TV," "Night Life," "Dance," "Media," "Tomorrow," "Books." (8-90).
TYPL: "Athol Fugard Gives the Impression that Doing the Right Thing is Easy, that Doing the Right Thing Makes You Feel Alive, that It is as Easy as Breathing to Know the Right Way From the Wrong Way," "Salute to Summer," "Jake Jake," "That Girl With the Eyes," "Siegfried & Roy." (8-90).
SCHL: Monthly, 135 pp.
SPAN: 1969+
VARIES
--1969 - Nov, 1972 as Inter/View.
--1972 - Feb, 1977 as Andy Warhol's Interview (ISSN: 0020-5109).
ISSN: 0149-8932
ABST: --Film Literature Index (ISSN: 0093-6758)

✣ INVIEW

SUB: "Professional video from the inside out."
PUBL: Midwest Communications Corporation, 920 Broadway, New York, NY 10010.
DESC: "Each quarter *InView* will delve into the innovations, equipment and applications that are current in our industry. As in any high tech field, being up to date on the products can often make a significant difference when making a purchasing decision. We have divided the publication into five departments [Video/Audio, Graphics, Mobile Commuications, RF, Cable], each featuring new and current product descriptions along with informative articles on how end users are using the particular technology." A unique corporate promotion by one of the largest audio/video vendors in America, *InView* packages an excellent publication that any video facility owner/manager will want. Emphasis is on the technical side of video, with articles providing detailed information easily applicable by any production organization. In one sampled issue articles featured new video installations in public, private, and corporate settings, a discussion on purchasing wireless microphones, broadcast quality desktop video, a sophisticated 40-foot video truck, and cable insertion equipment. Not coincidentally articles feature equipment and services furnished by the Midwest Communications Corporation. Magazine format with numerous color graphics and spritely format (8 1/8 x 10 7/8 inches / 205 x 275 mm).

DEPT: "Video/Audio," "Graphics," "Mobile Communications," "RF," "Cable," "Editors Page," "News In-View," industry newsbriefs; "Trade Show Calendar," "Ask the Experts," technical questions; "Regional Reports," Equipment installations and sales. (spring-89). "Editor's Page," 'Comments and thoughts from the editor'; "News, People and Facilities Invew," 'A brief look at what's going on in the industry'; "Technical Tips," "Regional Report," 'A potpourri of what's going on in the world of Midwest Communications'. (fall-90).
TYPL: "NAB Show Comes of Age," "The ABC's of TBC's," "Fiber Optic Technology," "Satellite Links," "Frequency Agile Modulators," "Spreading the Word Religiously." (spring-89). "Video in Education--The 3 Rs Will Never Be the Same," "Video Covers All the Angles in University Testing Lab," "Cincinnati Music Hall's New Sound System--Not a Bad Seat in the House," "Vertex Antenna Brings CNN One Step Closer to Global Network," "MII, the Alternative Component Format--Users Speak Out on How and Why They Use It." (fall-90).
SCHL: Quarterly, 95 pp.
SPAN: Spring, 1989+

✣ INVISION

PUBL: Invision, International Thomson Publishing Ltd., 100 Avenue Rd., London NW3 3TP, England.
DESC: Distributed free with copies of *Broadcast*, the business weekly tabloid, *Invision* provides a complimentary, full-color magazine format for lengthy interviews, profiles, analyses, and color graphics; elements which are outside the function of the parent publication, *Broadcast*. The emphasis is video. Articles are categorized into unique industry segments, ranging from profiles of communication executives to editing techniques; from digital paintbox artwork to new technologies arriving on the broadcast scene.
DEPT: "Stop Frame," "Monitor," "Profile," "Technology," "Graphics," "Television," commentary; "Animation," "Effects," "Editing," "Products." (9-88).
TYPL: "Chart Hits for Super 8 Super Duo," "Virgin Visionary," "The Mast Ball," "Animated Dispatch," "MTV--A Fad Gone Bad." (9-88).
SCHL: Monthly, 60 pp.
SPAN: ?+

IOWA JOURNALIST

SUB: "Published by the School of Journalism of the University of Iowa."
PUBL: The University of Iowa, School of Journalism, Iowa City, IA 52240.

DESC: [*Iowa Journalist*]: Published by the Journalism School at the University of Iowa, *Iowa Journalist* strove to: 1) report on state-wide journalism, and 2) be a forum for discussion of professional journalism issues. Articles ranged from state newspaper conventions, to journalism offerings at the University, to news of small state newspapers. Articles of journalism style and content gleaned from out-of-state newspapers were also included. In its last issue, the editorial staff noted that, "The January number will appear as *The Iowa Publisher and Bulletin of the Iowa Press Association*. It will represent a consolidation of effort of the School of Journalism, the Iowa Press Association, and the Department of Technical Journalism of Iowa State College." Journal format; occasional graphics.

DESC: [*Iowa Publisher*]: From its January, 1930 merger, this serial moved forward to vigorous coverage of Iowa newspapers, and the role of journalists. Articles instructed, informed, and served as a forum for discussion of state issues of the press. The *Iowa Publisher* of 1961 had eliminated news items from its editorial content, and concentrated on broader issues such as "Careers in Journalism."

DESC: [*Iowa Journalist*]: A 16-page publication concentrating on issues of journalism and the School of Journalism at the University of Iowa. Magazine format; graphics.

DEPT: "For the Correspondent," advice to stringers. (7-27). "The Editor's Bookshelf." (5-30). None. (5-69).

TYPL: "Advice on Writing--and Living," "They Start It But Never Stop It," "Newspapers Also Welcomed Lindbergh," "Boy Makes a Wooden Printing Press." (7-27). "Can We Have a Cavalcade to N.E.A. Convention at Milwaukee?," "Best Spot News Story of the Month Found in the Rockwell City Advocate," "Have We Reached the End of the Latest Burlesque Period in Typography?" (5-30). "Henry Africa, Iowa Journalism's Loss," "MacDonald Answers Student Questions," "Editors Show Conflict Not *The* Value." (5-69).

SCHL: Monthly (Jan, 1925 - Mar, 1960); Eight issues per year (?, 1960+), 16 pp.

SPAN: Jan, 1925 - Jul, 1969//
VARIES
--Jan, 1925 - Dec, 1928 as Iowa Journalist, The.
--Jan, 1929 - Mar, 1960 as Iowa Publisher and the Bulletin of the Iowa Press Association, The.
--Apr?, 1960 - Oct, 1967 as Iowa Publisher, The.
SUSPENDED
--Nov, 1967 - Dec, 1967.

LC: PN 4700.I6

Iowa Journalist, The

Jan, 1925 - Dec, 1928//
SEE: IOWA JOURNALIST

Iowa Publisher, The

Apr?, 1960 - Oct, 1967//
SEE: IOWA JOURNALIST

Iowa Publisher and the Bulletin of the Iowa Press Association, The

Jan, 1929 - Mar, 1960//
SEE: IOWA JOURNALIST

✤ IPI REPORT

SUB: "Monthly bulletin of the International Press Institute."
PUBL: International Press Institute, City University, 280 St. John St., London EC1V 4PB, England.
DESC: This statement of purpose of the International Press Institute was printed as a promotional Unesco cartoon in 1979: "To improve the mass media; to promote a balanced flow of information; to preserve the freedom of information; to prserve peace through the mass media. ...Through its members--nearly 2,000 of them--in more than 60 nations, IPI is working for these same objectives. We run training courses in the third world to the specification of people on the spot...We fight for journalists' freedom to work...And we foster goodwill among nations and a sense of media responsibility." The purpose of this monthly is to report on the state of the world press, vis a vis press freedom. Of note are ongoing reports regarding the status of imprisoned or missing newsmen and women. Reports do not mince words, but provide in succinct style a description of press freedom, and lack of same in countries around the world (including the United States). While each issue is excellent, special note must be made of the end of year issue which is always devoted to the "World Press Freedom Review," a nation-by-nation scorecard of press freedom. Well recommended. For the sampled issues of 1979: black ink on uncoated paper stock, no advertising (8 ¼ x 11 ¾ inches / 210 x 300 mm). For the sampled issues of 1991: black ink on coated paper in stapled newsletter format, no advertising (8 ¼ x 8 ⅝ inches / 210 x 295 mm).

DEPT: "Review." (2-79). "Review," book reviews; "Opinion." (3-84). "Around the Globe," news items; "Obituaries." (11-91).

TYPL: "In the Small Towns and Villages of Asia and Africa, the Press Must Learn to Grow," "'Cheap Rates for All' Plea at Talks on Asia Agency," "Help Us Plead for Jailed Journalist," "The Magic Van." (2-79). "Hate Attack Hits Expose Newspaper," "Another SA Journalist Flees; Editor Queries 'Duty' of the Press," "Bringing Newspapers to Africa's Villagers," "The Crucial Role of Third World Agencies." (3-84). "Journalists Die in Yugoslavia," "Romania Still Waiting for True Democracy," "Italian Press 'Facing Big Squeeze'," "Pakistani Daily Under Threat," "Threat of Clampdown in Tanzania." (11-91).

SCHL: Monthly, 24 pp.
SPAN: May, 1952+

LC: PN 4712.I552
ISSN: 0019-0314

IPI SURVEY
PUBL: International Press Institute, Zuerich, Switzerland.
DESC: "A basic objective of the International Press Institute is a broadening and strengthening of the flow of news among people. Only by having access to an unobstructed flow of news, the Institute's founders believed, could human beings in various parts of the earth ever hope to arrive at the mutual understanding which is essential to peace." This publication determines its single-issue topics on the basis of on-going surveys of IPI members, and it is this policy which is the title of this periodical. Although generally published on an annual basis, the serial has (at least on one occasion) been published on a semiannual basis. In essence, this is a scholarly, international treatment of freedom of the press issues. Journal format; occasional graphics.
DEPT: None.
TYPL: (Single Issue Themes:) "Improvement of Information," "The News from Russia," "The Flow of the News," "The News from the Middle East," "Government Pressures on the Press."
SPAN: 1952 - 1962//
LC: PN 4784.F6 I55
ISSN: 0085-2198

✤ IRB
SUB: "Campus membership of National Religious Broadcasters."
PUBL: Intercollegiate Religious Broadcasters, Morristown, New Jersey, 07960.
DESC: This is a four-page newsletter produced by Editor Andrew Quicke, and produced by the academic arm of National Religious Broadcasters. It serves to provide news items, information on job services, and audio-video awards competitions for IRB student members. In a sampled issue for 1990, articles included an update from the IRB chairman, Andrew Quicke, information about national student achievement awards, a communication seminar, local college chapter news, and a feature article concerning the previous convention. For the sampled issue of 1990: folded newsletter format, typeset black ink on uncoated paper stock, no advertising (8 ½ x 11 inches / 215 x 280 mm).
DEPT: "Letters to the Editor." (3/4-82). None. (fall/winter-88).
TYPL: "NRB Convention: Inspiration and Power," "New Officers for 1982." (3/4-82). "Update From the IRB Chairman," "The IRB Summer Institute of Media Studies," "Why IRB?" (fall/winter-88).
SCHL: Bimonthly (? - ?); Semiyearly (? - ?); Irregular (?+), 4 pp.
SPAN: ?+

SUSPENDED
--?, 1991+?

IRE Transactions on Broadcast and Television Receivers
Jan, 1955 - Nov, 1962//
(ISSN: 0096-1655)
SEE: IEEE TRANSACTIONS ON CONSUMER ELECTRONICS

IRE Transactions on Broadcast Transmission Systems
Mar, 1955 - Dec, 1958//
(ISSN: 0099-6866)
SEE: IEEE TRANSACTIONS ON BROADCASTING

IRE Transactions on Broadcasting
Feb, 1959 - Mar, 1962//
(ISSN: 0096-1663)
SEE: IEEE TRANSACTIONS ON BROADCASTING

IRE Transactions on Communications Systems
? - ?//
(ISSN: 0096-2244)
SEE: IEEE TRANSACTIONS ON COMMUNICATIONS

IRE Transactions on Information Theory
1955 - 1962//
(ISSN: 0096-1000)
SEE: IEEE TRANSACTIONS ON INFORMATION THEORY

IREE Monitor
Oct, 1979 - Jun, 1980//
SEE: MONITOR

✤ IRIS
SUB: "A journal of theory on image and sound."
PUBL: Institute for Cinema and Culture, 162 Communications Studies Bldg., University of Iowa, Iowa City, IA 52242.
DESC: "*IRIS* is a biannual [semiannual] publication that presents current scholarship in film theory and the relation of image to sound. Begun in 1983, *IRIS* devotes each issue to a different aspect of film theory or history. The *IRIS* fall issue is produced in France, the spring issue in the United States at the University of Iowa's Institute for Cinema and Culture." This is a fascinating journal of cinema with a half-European,

half-North American approach to the theory of film and its relationship to history and society. Each issue is themed, such as: "For a Theory of the History of Cinema" from October, 1984; "Cinema and Narration," from the October, 1986 and March, 1988 issues; "Cinema and Cognitive Psychology," July, 1989; "Cinema & Architecture," of November, 1990; "Latin American Cinema," from July, 1991; and the planned "The Analysis of Images" for the November, 1992 issue. Publication schedule at times has been somewhat erratic. The first 11 issues were released as follows: #1-March, 1983; #2-October, 1983; #3-March, 1984; #4-October, 1984; #5-March, 1985; #6-March, 1986; #7-October, 1986; #8-March, 1988; #9-July, 1989; #10-May, 1990; and #11-Summer, 1990. For the sampled issue of 1990: perfect bound journal format, black ink on uncoated paper stock, limited advertising (6 x 8 ¼ inches / 150 x 210 mm).
DEPT: "Editorial," "Commentary," "Book Reviews." (summer-90).
TYPL: "Class, Ethnicity, and Gender: Explaining the Development of Early American Film Narrative," "The 'Blank Screen of Reception' in Early French Cinema," "The Urban Spectator and the Crowd in Early American Train Films," "The Story of Uncle Josh Told: Spectatorship and Apparatus in Early Cinema," "Through the Keyhole: Spectators and Matte Shots in Early Cinema." (summer-90).
SCHL: Semiyearly, 130 pp.
SPAN: Mar, 1983+
SUSPENDED
--fall, 1985.
--spring and fall, 1987.
--fall, 1988.
--fall, 1989.
ISSN: 0751-7033

✛ ITA NEWS DIGEST

SUB: "The world's largest international audio-video trade association."
PUBL: International Tape Association, 10 Columbus Circle, Suite 2270, New York, NY 10019.
DESC: This trade magazine of the dynamic International Tape Association, an organization comprised of audio/video tape manufacturers and users has few graphics, but a large number of informational articles ranging from legal aspects of recording to education to duplicating and storage of magnetic tape.
DEPT: "ITA Audio News," briefs; "ITA Video News," briefs; "ITA International News."
TYPL: "Anti-Piracy News," "Sound Recordings and the New Copyright Law," "Care and Handling of Magnetic Tape," "Understandable Over-Simplification of Complex Video Technology." (3-77).
SCHL: Bimonthly, 35 pp.
SPAN: 1973+
VARIES
--? - ? as ITA Newsletter.
LC: TK 7881.6 .I57a
DD: 384
ISSN: 0146-4647

ITA Newsletter

? - ?//
SEE: ITA NEWS DIGEST

ITC Desktop

Mar/Apr, 1989 - Mar/Apr, 1990?//
(ISSN: 1042-3923)
SEE: DESKTOP COMMUNICATIONS

Jason Rogers' Advertisers' Weekly
Jan 3, 1925 - Sep 26, 1925//
SEE: ADVERTISERS' WEEKLY

JEA NEWSWIRE
PUBL: Journalism Education Association, Tacoma, WA.
DESC: This brief, but nicely designed, newsletter was published by the Journalism Education Association for its academic membership. It targeted high school and college faculty charged with teaching journalism to undergraduates, and described both internal activities of the organization, as well as external events and news trends which could impact the journalism field and/or the academic arena. For the sampled issues of 1978 through 1980: loose-leaf newsletter format, black ink on uncoated paper, no advertising (8 ½ x 11 inches / 215 x 280 mm).
DEPT: None. (2-78).
TYPL: "California Enacts Press Rights Law," "Fund Support Continues," "KC Awards Recognize Top Students," "Keefe Dies in Iowa," "Suit Threatens JEA Treasury." (2-78).
SCHL: Monthly, 16 pp.
SPAN: Jan, 1974? - ?//
ISSN: 0270-9783

JEE
?, 1964 - Aug, 1974//
(ISSN: 0021-3608)
SEE: JEE, JOURNAL OF ELECTRONIC ENGINEERING

✤ JEE, JOURNAL OF ELECTRONIC ENGINEERING
SUB: "Journal of electronic engineering."
PUBL: Dempa Publications, 1-11-15, Higashi-Gotanda, Shinagawa-ku, Tokyo 141 Japan.
DESC: On the December, 1991 occasion of publishing its 300th issue, an editorial noted; "In 27 years of publication, *JEE* has focused consistently on introducing Japanese electronic technology to the world. The history of *JEE* follows the meteoric rise of Japanese electronics industries to their position today, where they command the top levels of technology and development capacities." That special 300th anniversary issue provided a unique article, "Predictions for the 21st Century," an exploration of advanced electronics application in business, government, and society for the coming century. "*Journal of Electronic Engineering (JEE)* each month provides a 'nuts and bolts' look at the technological breakthroughs, from submicron lithography to ultra-large scale circuitry. Feature articles describe market trends, technologies and products." Aimed specifically at the American design engineer, *JEE* provides a forum of new technology and new products for the electronic communication profession. Articles are technical in nature and feature numerous high-quality graphics and schematics which showcase new Japanese developments. Some electronic technical knowledge is assumed. Masthead page displays latest American dollar to Japanese yen conversion rate for reviewed products and technologies, which are usually quoted in Japanese currency. For the sampled issue of 1991: perfect-bound magazine format, editorial content being mixture of black/white, spot- and full-color pages and cover on coated paper stock, significant electronics trade advertising (8 ¼ x 11 $E1/4 inches / 210 x 285 mm).
DEPT: "As We See It," editorial; "JEE Newsletter," newsbriefs; "Exhibitions/Conferences," "News Spotlight," "Market Trends," "Product News," "Company Profiles," "Product Profiles." (7-84). "Broadcasting News and Report," newsbriefs. (3-87).
TYPL: "Superconductivity and Electronics Moving from Theory to Practice," "Ultrasonic Aids in Medical Diagnosis," "Micromotor Technology Advancing Rapidly with Use of Microprocessor Control," "Minifloppy Disc Drives Package High Capacity in Low Profile," "Putting Technologies Together to Improve Data Recording." (7-84). "Spotlight: Broadcasting Technology," "Display Devices: Today and Tomorrow," "Self-Propelled Submarine Cable Burier." (3-87).
SCHL: Monthly, 110 pp.
SPAN: 1964+
VARIES
--?, 1964 - Aug, 1974 as JEE (ISSN: 0021-3608).
LC: TK 7800.J2
DD: 621.381/05
ISSN: 0385-4507
ABST: --Communication Abstracts
--Computer & Control Abstracts (ISSN: 0036-8113)
--Electrical & Electronics Abstracts (ISSN: 0036-8105)
--Physics Abstracts. Science Abstracts. Series A. (ISSN: 0036-8091)
--Predicasts

✤ JMR, JOURNAL OF MARKETING RESEARCH
PUBL: American Marketing Association, 250 South Wacker Drive, Suite 200, Chicago, IL 60606.

DESC: The *Journal of Marketing Research* resembles *The Journal of Marketing,* but with an emphasis on empirical, quantitative research. Articles in both publications are well authored and oftentimes provide significant data for the mass media area of marketing. *JMR* assumes the reader has a research background. A sampling of article titles from November, 1991 issue included, "A Clusterwise Regression Method for Simultaneous Fuzzy Market Structuring and Benefit Segmentation," "Pulsing in a Discrete Model of Advertising Competition," "Effects of Repeating Varied Ad Executions on Brand Name Memory," "Investigating Heterogeneity in Brand Preferences in Logit Models for Panel Data," and "Effects of Omitting Conclusions in Advertisements to Involved and Uninvolved Audiences." An "Annotated Subject Index and Author/Title Index" is provided in the year-end issue. Excellent graphics. For the sampled issues of 1991: black ink on uncoated paper stock in perfect-bound magazine format, limited advertising, cover consisting of black and red ink on coated paper stock (8 ½ x 11 inches / 215 x 280 mm).
DEPT: "Research Notes and Communications," critical comment; "New Books in Review." (02-86).
TYPL: "Consumer Response to Television Commercials: The Impact of Involvement and Background Music on Brand Attitude Formation," "Effects of Television Commercial Repetition, Receiver Knowledge, and Commercial Length: A Test of the Two-Factor Model." (02-86).
SCHL: Quarterly.
SPAN: Feb, 1964+
LC: HF 5415.2 .J66
DD: 658.83/05
ISSN: 0022-2437
ABST: --ABI/Informer
--Accountants' Index. Supplement. (ISSN: 0748-7975)
--Business Periodical Index (ISSN: 0007-6961)
--Index of Economic Articles in Journals and Collected Volumes (ISSN: 0536-647x)
--InfoBank
--Journal of Economic Literature (ISSN: 0022-0515)
--Management Contents
--Psychological Abstracts (ISSN: 0033-0202)

✤ JOB LEADS

SUB: "The weekly media employment newsletter."
PUBL: Media Service Group, 1680 Vine St., Hollywood, CA 90028.
DESC: *Job Leads* has a single-minded purpose: to publish employment opportunities and positions desired in the radio-television industry. Format of this four-page weekly newsletter is "want-ad" style, with sufficient space remaining for a column on job advisement.
DEPT: "Job Leads Adviser," a Q&A format on typical questions concerning R-TV employment. (12-26-76).
TYPL: None.
SCHL: 50 times per year, 4 pp.
SPAN: 1972+

✤ JOE FRANKLIN'S NOSTALGIA

SUB: "It's About Time."
PUBL: Joe Franklin's Nostalgia Publications, Inc., 185 Madison Ave., Suite 1105, New York, NY 10016.
DESC: The March, 1990 premiere issue of *Joe Franklin's Nostalgia* contains this warm welcome to new readers: "In this age of NOW and HIGH TECH, it is nice to find a publication devoted to the simpler life. A magazine that lets you relax, put your feet up and remember the good old days of yesteryear. *Joe Franklin's Nostalgia* is just such a companion; a welcome friend to bring back those times that we all treasure from our past." "It's about time," is more than a subtitle; it's a feeling about this quality historical journal of American media. Founder Joe Franklin, whose name and picture is on the cover of this bi-monthly publication, has founded a serial which, it is hoped, will have many decades of successful publication; providing superb color and black/white picture reproduction on heavy glossy paper stock. Articles in the premiere issue covered such diverse topics as door-to-door salesmen, Lucille Ball, the premiere flight of the Pan American Clipper, the marketing of movie thrillers, television personality Garry Moore, rise of the Wurlizter jukebox, and the Sears-Roebuck catalog of 1908. Of special note is the regular feature, "As Time Goes By," a national calendar of upcoming shows (listed by state) where items of a nostalgic nature will be displayed, traded, and sold. This is an excellent resource for the historical study of mass communication. For sampled issue of 1990: full-color pages throughout on coated paper stock in perfect-bound magazine format, reader-friendly layout design: (8 ⅛ x 10 ⅞ inches / 205 x 275 mm).
DEPT: "Second Thoughts," 'Suggested sidetrips on a time travel itinerary'; "Memory Lane," "Stock in Trade," nostalgic items available for purchase; "Flash Back," "As Time Goes By," 'Where to go, what to buy, when to sell'; "Happy Returns," 'Sarah Shankman on books, Mike Barlow on video, Chip Stern on classic cuts'; "Back Order," new nostalgic products on today's market; "Deja Vu," column by Studs Terkel. (3-90).
TYPL: "Knock, Knock," "Night Flight," "Wheeere's Garry?," "Memory Machines." (3-90).
SCHL: Bimonthly, 100 pp.
SPAN: March, 1990+
DD: 051 11
ISSN: 1047-0476

✤ JOURNAL

SUB: "Recording the electrical era."
SUB: "Official publication of the International Brotherhood of Electrical Workers."
PUBL: Official Publications, International Brotherhood of Electrical Workers, Springfield, IL.
DESC: [*The Journal of Electrical Workers and Operators*]: Functioning to serve the interests of its membership, this journal of the International Electrical Workers

and Operators provided an interesting mixture of world news events, political issues and instruction (especially of radio communication). It primarily provided detailed news of local chapter activities and members. One sampled issue included articles on Robert Montgomery and the Screen Actors Guild, a radio company which had "just gone union," a new publication, *The Radio and Electrical Union News*, for "workers in radio, sound and electrical manufacturing industries;" and how union members as radio amateurs aided authorities during times of natural disasters, this latter article including complete schematics on construction of a portable radio transmitter. One article reported on a Hollywood motion picture hiring union electrical workers for electrical construction, placing them in such a position that they were included in the motion picture itself. The union representative demanded and received "stand-in" payment of $32 per day for the three individuals. Magazine format (9 x 12 inches / 230 x 305 mm), black/white photographs, printed on coated paper stock.

DEPT: "Magazine Chat," editor's column by George Bugniazet; "Woman's Work," IBEW auxiliary news; "Cooperating Manufacturers," subscribing to union rules and regulations; "Correspondence," lengthy column of letters on a variety of union issues; "Fraternity of the Air," 'Boys, here is our growing list of I.B.E.W amateur radio stations'; "In Memoriam," obituaries; "Your Washington Reporter," column by Budd McKillips; "On Every Job There's a Laugh or Two," humor. (9-37).
TYPL: "Milk is Food for Babies," "Confessions of a C.I.O. Organizer," "Linemen Go Out to Work and Shine as Stars," "National Electric Products Company is Union," "Amateurs Perform Service During Disasters." (9-37).
SCHL: Monthly (1948 - Dec, 1971), 50 pp.
SPAN: ?, 1893+
VARIES
--?, 1893 - Apr, 1901 as Electrical Workers' Journal, The.
--May, 1901? - Jul, 1914 as Electrical Worker, The.
--Aug, 1914 - 1948? as Journal of Electrical Workers and Operators, The.
--1948 - Dec, 1971 as Electrical Workers' Journal, The.
LC: HD 6350.E3 J7
DD: 331.881213

Journal
Winter, 1967/1968 - 1985?//
(ISSN: 0004-5438)
SEE: ARSC JOURNAL

Journal
Jan, 1972 - Mar, 1987//
SEE: IBEW JOURNAL

Journal
Jan, 1954 - Dec, 1954//
SEE: SMPTE JOURNAL

Journal des Telecommunications
? - ?//
SEE: TELECOMMUNICATION JOURNAL

✢ JOURNAL OF ADVERTISING

SUB: "Official publication of the American Academy of Advertising."
PUBL: American Academy of Advertising, P.O. Box 3275, University Station, University of Wyoming, Laramie, WY 82071.
DESC: The *Journal of Advertising* began publication on an annual basis for the first year of 1972. In 1973, two issues were published, and then commenced publication on a quarterly basis to date. Early issues (prior to 1987), noted that the *Journal of Advertising*, "...aims to encourage the discovery and development of (A) valid theory and relevant facts regarding the psychological and philosophical aspects of communication, and (B) the relationship between these and other components of the advertising process." In late, 1987 the stated purpose read, "The *Journal of Advertising* is published to contribute to the development of advertising theory and its relationship to advertising practices and processes. To this end, the *Journal* accepts original manuscripts of a theoretical, empirical, methodological, or philosophical nature which advance advertising knowledge." Of special note are excellent citations, and the use of an abstract prefacing each article. For the sampled issues of 1979 and 1991: black ink on coated paper stock in perfect-bound magazine format, advertising (8 ½ x 11 inches / 215 x 280 mm); cover for the 1979 sampled issues consisted of black ink with orange and blue spot-color, while covers for 1991 issues were screened black ink with spot-color, both on heavy coated paper.
DEPT: "Editorial," "Book Commentary," "Advertising Profiles," outstanding individuals in advertising. (fall-77). None (#3-88).
TYPL: "The Newspaper as a Source of Consumer Information for Young Adults," "The 'Decorative' Female Model: Sexual Stimuli and the Recognition of Advertisements," "Comparative Television Advertising: Examining its Nature and Frequency." (fall-77). "Cognitive Response to Advertising and Trial: Belief Strength, Belief Confidence and Product Curiosity," "Determinants of International Media Purchasing: a Survey of Media Buyers," "Emotional Feelings and Attitude Toward the Advertisement: The Roles of Brand Familiarity and Repetition." (#3-88).
SCHL: Annual (1972); Semiannual (1973); Quarterly (1974+), 45 pp.
SPAN: 1972+
LC: HF 5801.J59

DD: 659.1/05
ISSN: 0091-3367
ABST: --ABI/Informer
--Business Periodical Index (ISSN: 0007-6961)
--InfoBank
--Management Contents
--Psychological Abstracts (ISSN: 0033-0202)
--Public Affairs Information Service Bulletin (ISSN: 0033-3409)

Journal of Advertising

Jan, 1982 - Mar, 1982//
(ISSN: 0261-9903)
SEE: INTERNATIONAL JOURNAL OF ADVERTISING

✦ JOURNAL OF ADVERTISING RESEARCH

PUBL: Advertising Research Foundation, 3 E. 54th St., New York, NY 10022.
DESC: The *Journal of Advertising Research* "...is intended for practitoners and users of advertising research; [it] ...is published bimonthly by the Advertising Research Foundation and is sent to individuals in member companies as part of membership fees." Practical findings are emphasized over theoretical ideation. A gauge of the importance of this serial to the advertising community can be found in the large number of advertisements by major research and testing firms within the journal. Some issues include the supplement, *Research Currents*, which is subtitled, "Current comment and opinion as expressed at ARF conferences and workshops or from the research community at large." The December, 1991 supplement contained two articles, "How Children Use Media and Influence Purchases," and "The Effectiveness of Print Advertising." Statistical knowledge is assumed. For the sampled issue of 1979 and 1991: black ink on coated paper stock in stapled magazine format, cover consisting of rotated spot-color and black ink on coated paper stock, significant trade advertising (8 ½ x 11 inches / 215 x 280 mm).
DEPT: "Feedback," advertising articles in response to current topics; "Point of View," guest commentary. (10-77). "Editorial," column by William A. Cook. (12-91).
TYPL: "How to Set Advertising Budgets," "Match the Concept and the Product," "Product Sampling and Word of Mouth." (10-77). "Copy Tests in FTC Deception Cases: Guidelines for Researchers," "The Effect of Advertising on Heirarchical Stages in Vacation Destination Choice," "Direct-Response Advertising Information: Profiling Heavy, Light, and Nonusers," "Viewers' Reactions to Racial Cues in Advertising Stimuli," "How Direct Comparative Ads and Market Share Affect Brand Choice." (12-91).
SCHL: Quarterly (1960 - Sep, 1961); Bimonthly, (Jun, 1975+), 85 pp.
SPAN: Sep, 1960+
LC: HF 5801.J6

DD: 659.1/07/2
ISSN: 0021-8499
ABST: --ABI/Informer
--Business Periodical Index (ISSN: 0007-6961)
--InfoBank
--Management and Marketing Abstracts (ISSN: 0308-2172)
--Management Contents
--Psychological Abstracts (ISSN: 0033-0202)
--Social Welfare, Social Planning / Policy and Social Development (ISSN: 0195-7988)

✦ JOURNAL OF APPLIED COMMUNICATION RESEARCH

PUBL: Speech Communication Association, 5105 Backlick Rd., #E, Annandale, VA 22003.
DESC: "The *Journal of Applied Communication Research* publishes articles focusing on questions and problems regarding pragmatic social phenomena addressed through the analysis of human communication. It is the intent of the publication board that the articles not be characterised by any particular context, setting, methodology, epistemology, or conclusions." The Speech Communication Association assumed publication of the journal beginning with a combined issue (Nos. 1 & 2) in July, 1991, and new editor William F. Eadie issued these instructions to authors: "*JACR* solicits research reports, articles reviewing exisiting communication literature and showing how the field's findings can be applied, and commentary on applied communication issues. Research reports should thoroughly explore a problem or situation and provide significant insights from a communication perspective into the solution to the problem or the inner workings of the situation. Research published by the journal will be securely grounded in theory but will not have theory-building as the primary goal. The journal welcomes all theoretical and methodological perspectives and is particularly interested in publishing work on contemporary social issues. Articles submitted for *JACR*'s 'Applications' section should synthesize a body of theory and/or research and should demonstrate clearly how practitioners can use the information contained in the article to improve communication in a specific setting." This is an outstanding research journal, now under Speech Communication Association control, and sporting a very dynamic layout design making effective use of spot color throughout. This journal is certain to be on every communication researcher's list of "must" reading in the months and years to come. For sampled issue of 1991: perfect-bound journal format, editorial content consisting of black ink with red spot-color ink throughout, cover consisting of three-color red, blue, green ink on heavy coated paper stock, limited advertising, pictures of authors accompany most articles (6 ¾ x 10 inches / 170 x 255 mm).
DEPT: None. (fall-83). "Applications," "Commentary." (6-91).

TYPL: "The Meaning of 'Power,'" "Identifying Job Stress in a Human Service Organization," "Differences in Communication Competence Among Administrative Social Styles," "Media Effects on Information Sharing: a Field Experiment," "Reconsidering Communication Consulting." (fall-83). "Fixing With the Voice: A Research Agenda for Applied Communication," "Organizational Consultants and Organizational Research," "Style, Process, Surface, Context: Consulting as Postmodern Art," "Understanding Applied Communication Inquiry: Researcher as Organizational Consultant," "Communication Strategies for Managing Sexual Harassment in Organizations: Understanding Message Options and Their Effects." (6-91).
SCHL: Semiannual, 130 pp.
SPAN: Winter/Spring, 1973+
VARIES
--Winter/Spring, 1973 - Summer/Fall?, 1972? as Journal of Applied Communications Research (ISSN: 0090-9882).
LC: HM 258.J67
DD: 302.2/05
ISSN: 0090-9882
ABST: --Current Index to Journals in Education (ISSN: 0011-3565)
--Language and Language Behavior Abstracts (ISSN: 0023-8295)
--Resources in Education
--Speech Index

Journal of Applied Communications Research

Winter/Spring, 1973 - Summer/Fall?, 1972?//
(ISSN: 0090-9882)
SEE: JOURNAL OF APPLIED COMMUNICATION RESEARCH

✦ JOURNAL OF ARTS MANAGEMENT AND LAW, THE

SUB: "The journal of management and law of the arts."
SUB: "A publication of the entertainment law institute of the law center of the University of Southern California."
PUBL: Heldref Publishing, 4000 Albermarle St., NW, Washington, DC 20016.
DESC: "Only within the last twenty years has arts management become a formal academic discipline. And only one professional journal focuses exclusively on arts management and arts law concerns--*The Journal of Arts Management and Law.* In one source this journal brings together the information that every professional needs in this increasingly complex field. The *Journal* publishes in-depth articles on today's problems including marketing, policy, advocacy, taxation, labor relations, and technology in the arts. The *Journal* supports and informs managers who must respond creatively to the tension between the increased demand for the arts and dwindling sources of financial support. To this end, the *Journal* prints original articles, interviews, legal interpretations, and book reviews--as well as reprints of important material. Once each year the *Journal* devotes a complete issue to a timely subject of interest to our readers. Recent themed issues included, "Public Policy and the Arts," "Labor Relations and the Arts," and "Consumer Behavior and the Arts." Future special issues will address volunteers and minorities. In short, the *Journal* provides a forum for the intelligent discourse and thoughtful analysis that will strengthen the arts' most basic resource--its artists." For the sampled issues of 1991: perfect-bound journal format, black ink on uncoated paper stock with two-color cover on uncoated paper stock, limited advertising (6 x 9 inches / 150 x 230 mm).
DEPT: "Introduction," "Point," "Counterpoint," "Book Reviews." (spring-91).
TYPL: "The Public Interest in Public Culture," "The National Endowment for the Arts: Misusing Taxpayers' Money," "The National Endowment for the Arts: Fostering America's Artistic Expression," "The Culture Wars." (spring-91).
SCHL: Quarterly 100 pp.
SPAN: Winter, 1969+
VARIES
--Winter, 1969 - 1981 as Performing Arts Review (ISSN: 0031-5249).
LC: PN 2000.P47
DD: 790.2/0973
ISSN: 0733-5113

Journal of Broadcasting

Winter, 1956/1957 - Fall, 1984//
(ISSN: 0021-938x)
SEE: JOURNAL OF BROADCASTING & ELECTRONIC MEDIA

✦ JOURNAL OF BROADCASTING & ELECTRONIC MEDIA

PUBL: Broadcast Education Association, 1771 N St., NW, Washington, DC 20036.
DESC: The *Journal of Broadcasting & Electronic Media* is the official publication of the Broadcast Education Association, the pedagogical arm of the National Association of Broadcasters, but a strong organization in its own right. This quarterly journal of professional research has faithfully provided a forum for serious discussion of pedagogical and industry issues since its founding in 1956. With the issuance of *Feedback* in the 1970s, a new BEA publication devoted to the academic side of broadcasting, the *Journal of Broadcasting & Electronic Media*, moved its editorial function to that of exploring issues (historical and current) in professional broadcast and electronic media. It covers a wide variety of broadcast topics, with a growing emphasis on international topics and quantitative research. In a 35th anniversary issue for winter,

1991, current editor Alison Alexander observed, "The *Journal of Broadcasting & Electronic Media* as a journal for the dissemination of research in the field of communication studies evinces in its historical development a perceptible shift from one serving primarily as an outlet for tentative and circumscribed research articles to one wherein the research articles are characterized by rigorous application of proven methodologies and a tone of academic confidence reflective of professional surety. This shift no doubt represents a coming of age for the discipline in general and the arrival of clear-sighted purpose for the *Journal* in particular. The *Journal* has quite definitely found its niche in the world of burgeoning media studies as a vehicle for scholars who see in the consistently fine quality of the work presented in the pages of the *Journal* a confirmation of the cogency of their own efforts to advance research in the field." Most articles are authored by members of the academic community. This is a superior publication for the study of American and world electronic media. Journal format (6 x 9 inches / 150 x 230 mm) on uncoated paper stock. No advertising.

DEPT: "Books," in-depth reviews. (spring-77). "Books in Brief." (spring-89). "Review and Criticism," "Books in Brief." (winter-91).

TYPL: "Television Interview Shows: The Politics of Visibility," "Reporting Factor Analyses in Mass Media Research," "Pacific Islands Mass Communications: Selected Information Sources." (spring-77). "The Counter-Propaganda of Radio RSA: The Voice of South Africa," "The Image of Education in Primetime Network Television Series 1948 - 1988," "Source and Geographic Bias in Network Television News 1982 - 1984," "Gender Stereotypes in Italian Television Advertisements," "Gender in Canadian Local Television News: Anchors and Reporters." (spring-89). "The Impact of Television Formats on Social Policy," "The Qualitative Study of Media Audiences," "Imaginary Social Relationships with Celebrities Appearing in Television Commercials," "Analyzing Meaning in Form: Soap Opera's Compositional Construction of 'Realness'," "A Comparative Analysis of Australian, US, and British Telecasts of the Seoul Olympic Opening Ceremony." (winter-91).

SCHL: Quarterly, 135 pp.
SPAN: Winter 1956/1957+
VARIES
--Winter, 1956/1957 - Fall, 1984 as Journal of Broadcasting (ISSN: 0021-938x).
LC: PN 1991.J6
DD: 384.54/05
ISSN: 0883-8151
ABST: --Communication Abstracts
--Current Contents
--Current Index to Journals in Education (ISSN: 0011-3565)
--Humanities Index (ISSN: 0095-5981)
--Index to Journals in Communication Studies
--Legal Resource Index
--Public Affairs Information Service Bulletin (ISSN: 0033-3409)
--Social Science Citation Index (ISSN: 0091-2887)

✤ JOURNAL OF BUSINESS COMMUNICATION, THE

PUBL: Association for Business Communication, Department of Management, College of Business Administration, University of North Texas, Denton, TX 76203.

DESC: The winter, 1991 issue described the function of the organization: "the Association for Business Communication (ABC) is the association for all who teach, study, and practice business communication whether in universities, community colleges and high schools, or in business, industry, government, and nonprofit organizations. The objectives of the ABC are: to foster research and education in the communications of business, industry, government, and nonprofit organizations; to contribute to the improvement of the teaching and practice of communication by encouraging study, discussion, and experimentation; and to disseminate information by serving as a clearing house for research projects, by publishing a scholarly journal, bulletins, monographs, and book-length special publications. ... The ever-increasing demands for better business communication create needs for research and education. For those engaged in this work--indeed for all who are seriously interested in business communication, written, oral, graphic--ABC is the primary organization." The *Journal* seeks out articles of original research that "...develops, tests, or advances business, managerial, or organizational communication theory or knowledge. All types of rigorous methods--quantitative, qualitative, or combinations--are acceptable." For the sampled issues of 1978 and 1991: perfect-bound journal format, black ink on uncoated paper stock, limited advertising; cover for 1978 was black ink on tinted uncoated paper; cover for 1991 consisted of black and spot-color ink on coated paper (6 x 9 inches / 150 x 230 mm).

DEPT: "Book Reviews," "News and Notes." (fall-78). "Editorial," column by Lamar Reinsch; "News and Notes." (winter-91).

TYPL: "An Investigation of the Relationship Between Organization Climate and Communication Climate," "Worker Responses to Supervisory Communication Inequity: An Exploratory Study," "Structuring a Group's Communication for Improved Problem Solving," "Four Problems Relating to Awareness of Metacommunication in Business Correspondence," "An Examination of the Ideal Immediate Supervisor and Subordinate." (fall-78). "Brevity Versus Clarity: The Comprehensibility of Nominal Compounds in Business and Technical Prose," "Techno-Sense: Making Sense of Computer-Mediated Communication Systems," "The Impact of Nonverbal Communication in

Organizations: A Survey of Perceptions," "Focus Groups: A Qualitative Opportunity for Researchers." (winter-91).
SCHL: Quarterly, 95 pp.
SPAN: Oct, 1963+
VARIES
--Oct, 1963 - Summer, 1969 as Journal of Business Communication (ISSN: 0885-2456).
--Fall, 1969 - Summer, 1973 as ABCA Journal of Business Communication (ISSN: 0886-7216).
LC: HF 5718.J6
DD: 658
ISSN: 0021-9436
ABST: --Current Index to Journals in Education (ISSN: 0011-3565)

Journal of Business Communication

Oct, 1963 - Summer, 1969//
(ISSN: 0885-2456)
SEE: JOURNAL OF BUSINESS COMMUNICATION, THE

Journal of C4I Countermeasures [NC]

//
SEE: MILITARY ELECTRONICS / COUNTERMEASURES

JOURNAL OF COLLEGE RADIO

PUBL: Intercollegiate Broadcasting System, University of Oklahoma, Norman, OK 73069.
DESC: This is a specialized publication for those working in the area of closed circuit (carrier current), low-power radio stations on college campuses. College students acting as management, engineering, and air personalities comprise the primary audience for this publication. Articles reflect this rather narrow field of communication.
DEPT: "Publishers Report," "Music Industry Department," interesting section discussing hot albums, singles and break outs, with record reviews and short column; "Engineering," technical advice.
TYPL: "The Cross and the Microphone," "Class 'D' FM Facilities Survey," "An Interview with the Honorable Robert E. Lee." (2-74).
SCHL: Seven per year, 30 pp.
SPAN: 1941 to date.
VARIES
--1941 - 1955 as IBS Bulletin.
--1955 - 1964 as IBS Newsletter.
--1964 - 1969 as College Radio.
LC: PN 1991.J
ISSN: 0010-1133

✦ JOURNAL OF COMMUNICATION

SUB: "A publication devoted to communication in human relations."
PUBL: Oxford University Press, 200 Madison Ave., New York, NY 10016.
DESC: "The *Journal of Communication* is concerned with the study of communication theory, practice and policy. It is addressed to those in every field who are interested in research and policy developments and in the public impact of communications studies." Published by Oxford University Press in cooperation with the University of Pennsylvania, the *Journal of Communication* explores the relationship between communication and human relations, with research and applications forming the bulk of lay-readable articles. Oftentimes *Journal of Communication* clusters issues around a specific issue theme, such as "Covering the Political Campaign," "Western European Broadcasting in Transition," or "Teleconferencing: a Status Report." Publication of the journal is a joint effort between the Annenberg School Press and the International Communication Association. For the sampled issues of 1957: black ink on uncoated paper in stapled journal format, limited advertising, cover was black ink on tinted uncoated paper stock (5 ½ x 8 ¾ inches / 145 x 225 mm). For the 1990 sampled issues: black ink on coated paper in perfect-bound journal format, limited advertising, cover consisting of black ink with two-spot colors on coated paper stock (6 ½ x 9 ½ inches / 165 x 245 mm).
DEPT: "Notes, Quotes and Anecdotes," "Research Notes," "Reviews," "The President's Letter." (spring-57). "Intercom," newsbriefs; "Books," reviews. (fall-78). "Intercom," "Books." (autumn-90).
TYPL: "Measuring Point of View as a Barrier to Communication," "What Teen-Agers Can't Tell Parents and Why," "The Problems of Verifiability," "Colonel Blunderbuss' Battle Cry," "The Communicative Behavior of the Executive." (spring-57). "Casting for TV Parts: the Anatomy of Social Typing," "Government and the Press: the Question of Subsidies," "Television Economic news and the Social Construction of Economic Reality," "The Flow of News: An Assessment of the Non-Alligned News Agency's Pool." (fall-78). "When Media Use Can't Be Observed: Some Problems and Tactics of Collaborative Audience Research," "The Battle for the U.S. Airwaves, 1928 - 1935," "the Audience for Foreign Film in the United States," "Prospects for Creativity in the New Television Marketplace: Evidence from Program-Makers," "A Question of Accuracy: How Journalists and Scientists Report Research on Hazards." (autumn-90).
SCHL: Semiannual (1951 - 1953); Quarterly (1954+), 190 pp.
SPAN: May, 1951+
LC: P 87.J6
DD: 001.5/05
ISSN: 0021-9916
ABST: --ABI/Informer
--America, History and Life (ISSN: 0002-7065)

--Annual Bibliography of English Language and Literature (ISSN: 0066-3786)
--Book Review Index (ISSN: 0524-0581)
--Current Index to Journals in Education (ISSN: 0011-3565)
--Education Index (ISSN: 0013-1385)
--Energy Information Abstracts (ISSN: 0147-6521)
--Environment Abstracts (ISSN: 0093-3287)
--Film Literature Index (ISSN: 0093-6758)
--Historical Abstracts (ISSN: 0018-2435)
--InfoBank
--Language and Language Behavior Abstracts (ISSN: 0023-8295)
--MLA International Bibliography of Books & Articles on the Modern Languages and Literatures (ISSN: 0024-8215)
--Psychological Abstracts (ISSN: 0033-0202)
--Social Sciences Index (ISSN: 0094-4920)
--Social Welfare, Social Planning / Policy and Social Development (ISSN: 0195-7988)
--Women Studies Abstracts (ISSN: 0049-7835)
--Writings on American History (ISSN: 0364-2887)

✢ JOURNAL OF COMMUNICATION AND RELIGION, THE

PUBL: Religious Speech Communication Association, Manhattan Christian College, Manhattan, KS 66502.
DESC: "*The Journal of Communication and Religion* welcomes articles on any aspect of religious speech communication, no matter what the persuasion. Although the major part of each issue is devoted to scholarly articles, a resources section may report on materials and methods useful to carrying out the work of religious groups and professionals. Therefore, both research articles and resource reports are invited." This is an excellent scholarly journal for the field of religion and communication in both its interpersonal and mass media forms. The editorial philosophy can perhaps best be seen in an "Editor's Note" preceeding a special issue of religious rhetorics: "The articles offer political, philosophical, and dramatic analysis of significant religious rhetorical themes. Religious rhetoric comes bound with tradition, emotion, and perspective. The interpretive process permits exploration of possibilities that might go unnoticed in everyday examination. The enclosed articles provide an analysis of the hermenutical process, as well as reveal it in practice in political and religious contexts." For sampled issue of 1989: stapled journal format, black ink on uncoated paper stock, cover was black ink on uncoated tinted paper stock, no advertising (6 ¼ x 10 inches / 160 x 255 mm).
DEPT: None. (9-89).
TYPL: "Moving the Mercy Seat into the White House, An Exegesis of the Carter/Reagan Religious Rhetoric," "Homiletic and Hermeneutic: Buttrick and Gadamer in Dialogue," "How Rhetoric Becomes Real: Religious Sources of Gender Identity," "Finding Common Ground: Drama, Liturgy, and Preaching Intersect at Candler School of Theology," "'God and Country' in Ronald Reagan's Addresses to the National Religious Broadcasters: A 'Faith' That Backslides or Perseveres?" (9-89).
SCHL: Annual (Sep, 1978 - 1986?); Semiannual, 45 pp.
SPAN: Sep, 1978+
VARIES
--Sep, 1978 - 1986? as Religious Communication Today [NA].
DD: 251
ISSN: 0894-2838

✢ JOURNAL OF COMMUNICATION INQUIRY, THE

PUBL: Iowa Center for Communication Study, School of Journalism and Mass Communication, University of Iowa, Iowa City, IA 52242.
DESC: "*The Journal of Communication Inquiry* is concerned primarily with theoretical issues of communication. The *Journal* serves as a forum for humanistically-oriented research into the philosophical, historical, cultural, legal and ethical dimensions of communication." A serial of scholarly research; journal format; no graphics.
DEPT: None.
TYPL: "The Embeddedness of Communication in the Slime of History: Themes Leading to the Thesis of a Communication Crisis," "Superseding Instrumental Reason in Journalism Education," "Freedom of Expression and the Marketplace of Ideas Concept from Milton to Jefferson." (summer-81).
SCHL: Semiannual [summer and winter], 75 pp.
SPAN: Spring, 1974+
LC: P 87.J62
DD: 302.2/05
ISSN: 0196-8599

JOURNAL OF COMMUNICATION MANAGEMENT

PUBL: International Association of Business Communicators, 870 Market St., Suite 940, San Francisco, CA 94102.
DESC: [*Journal of Organizational Communications*]: The emphasis in this journal is internal communication, i.e., corporate newspapers and magazines, interpersonal communications processes, presentations, and structure for good communications practices. No advertising; well- illustrated. Each issue contains French and Spanish summaries of a given serial's articles for IABC members whose primary language is French or Spanish.
DEPT: None (fall-77).

TYPL: "Mirror Image for British Leyland," "Meeting Bias Face to Face," "How New U.S. Copyright Laws Affect the Communicator," "Society, Technology and Communication: a Conversation on the State of the Art." (fall-77).
SCHL: Quarterly.
SPAN: Fall, 1971 - May, 1983//
SPLIT OFF WITH
--IABC News (ISSN: 0744-7612) (from parent) IABC Notebook.
VARIES
--Fall, 1971 - Winter, 1972/1973 as Journal of Organizational Communications (ISSN: 0047-2646).
--Spring, 1973 - Winter, 1974 as IABC Journal (ISSN: 0092-7384).
--Spring, 1975? - ?, 1981 as Journal of Organizational Communication (ISSN: 0162-5659).
LC: HF 5718.J63
DD: 658.4/5/05
ISSN: 0745-1822
ABST: --ABI/Informer
--Management Contents

Journal of Educational Communication

Jul/Aug, 1975 - Dec, 1983//
(ISSN: 0745-4058)
SEE: JOURNAL OF EDUCATIONAL PUBLIC RELATIONS

✤ JOURNAL OF EDUCATIONAL PUBLIC RELATIONS

SUB: "The school PR magazine."
SUB: "School / people / public relations."
PUBL: Educational Communication Center, PO Box 657, Camp Hill, PA 17011.
DESC: The *Journal of Educational Public Relations* deals with the technique of fostering good public relations at the primary and secondary school level. It solicits "...contributions on topics relating to public relations, school-community relations, audiovisuals, management and human relations." It is a case study approach to public relations, with some graphics and charts. Some typical articles from the 1990-1991 time period include, "A Hostile Press," "A newspaper begins a vendetta against a new superintendent;" "On Air Blues for Wilson High," "Antagonism arises over programming on a new high school radio station;" and "A Major Adjustment in Focus of School-Community-Human Relationships," "in the National School Public Relations Association--Student achievement linked to PR." For the sampled issues of 1979 and 1991: black ink on coated paper stock in stapled magazine format with two-color cover on coated paper, limited advertising (8 ⅜ x 11 inches / 210 x 280 mm).
DEPT: "Research," "Book Reviews." (6-84). "Case Study and Response," "Research," "Book Reviews." (#1-91).
TYPL: "School-Business Partnership: Why Not?," "Start a Liaison Network to Promote Balanced Newspaper Coverage," "How to Deal with Angry People," "Recruit Retirees as Instructional Volunteers," "Creating a Positive School Environment." (6-84). "Home-School-Community Relationships and Superior Student Achievement--the Ingredients of a Science Mentorship Program," "Wisconsin's Families in Education Program Strengthens Home-School Communication," "Preserving the Dignity of the Child," "An Involvement Program for Parents of Prekindergarten Students." (#1-91).
SCHL: Quarterly [irregular at times] (Jul/Aug, 1975 - ?); Quarterly (? - Date) 45 pp.
SPAN: Jul/Aug, 1975+
VARIES
--Jul/Aug, 1975 - Dec, 1983 as Journal of Educational Communication (ISSN: 0745-4058).
ISSN: 0741-3653
ABST: --Current Index to Journals in Education (ISSN: 0011-3565)

✤ JOURNAL OF EDUCATIONAL TELEVISION

SUB: "A journal of the Educational Television Association."
SUB: "A publication of the National Educational Closed-Circuit Television Association."
PUBL: Carfax Publishing Co., PO Box 25, Abingdon, Oxfordshire OX14 3UE England.
DESC: "The *Journal of Educational Television*, the official journal of the Educational Television Association, is an international forum for discussion and reports on developments in the increasingly important and rapidly expanding field of the use of television and related media in teaching, learning and training. The journal welcomes contributions in the form of academic articles, technical and research reports, reviews, comments and news from those involved in and using educational television and the related communication media throughout the world." This publication's primary scope is British video programming, exploring areas of broadcast and instructional media, and the impact of such programming upon its audiences. For the sampled 1991 i ues: black ink on uncoated paper in perfect-bound journal format with two-color cover on coated paper, no advertising (6 ⅞ x 9 ⅞ inches / 175 x 250 mm).
DEPT: "Letters to the Editor," "Book and Videotape," reviews. (#1-84). "Editorial," column by Paul Kelley; "Broadcasting Notes," column by I. Reid; "Book Reviews," "ETV in Print." (#2-91).
TYPL: "New Technologies--New Opportunities?," "Time to Get Off the Shelf: Educational Television and Public Libraries Cooperation in Continuing Education," "Challenging Traditional Sex Roles Stereotypes in Careers, Education and Broadcasts," "Why and How We Made a Problem-Oriented AV Teaching Unit for Chemistry Students." (#1-84). "Adult Education, So-

cial Action and the IBA: the Sixties to the Eighties," "Television Police Dramas and Children's Beliefs About the Police," "Light and Heavy Television Viewers: Their Pictures in the Public Mind," "Teachers Using Television." (#2-91).
SCHL: Quarterly (Mar, 1975 - 1977); Three issues per year [Mar, Jul, Oct] (1978+), 60 pp.
SPAN: Mar, 1975+
VARIES
--Mar, 1975 - Nov, 1975 as Journal of Educational Television.
--Spring, 1976 - Winter, 1981 as Journal of Educational Television and Other Media.
LC: LB 1044.7 .J68
DD: 371.3/358
ISSN: 0260-7417
ABST: --Current Index to Journals in Education (ISSN: 0011-3565)

Journal of Educational Television

Mar, 1975 - Nov, 1975//
SEE: JOURNAL OF EDUCATIONAL TELEVISION

Journal of Educational Television and Other Media

Spring, 1976 - Winter, 1981//
SEE: JOURNAL OF EDUCATIONAL TELEVISION

Journal of Electrical Workers and Operators

Aug, 1914 - Dec, 1947?//
SEE: IBEW JOURNAL

Journal of Electrical Workers and Operators, The

Aug, 1914 - 1948?//
SEE: JOURNAL

✤ JOURNAL OF FILM AND VIDEO

PUBL: Rosary College, Department of Communication Arts and Sciences, 7900 W. Division St., River Forest, IL 60305.
DESC: "The *Journal of Film and Video* focuses on scholarship in the fields of film and video production, history, theory, criticism, and aesthetics. It is receptive to articles...about film and related media, problems of education in these fields, and the function of film and video in society. The *Journal* does not ascribe to any specific method as long as the article sheds light on the way we view and teach the production and study of film and video." The emphasis within the journal is on "...the way we view and teach the production and study of film in university and college curricula." Each quarterly issue publishes articles within a unique theme such as: "Japanese Cinema," "Advertising and Promotion," "Spectatorship, Narrativity, and Feminist Revison," "The Role of the Reader," "Considering Theory," and "Close Studies of Television: Encoding Research." Sampled issue for 1976 is journal format (7 x 10 inches / 175 x 255 mm). Sampled issue for 1989 is journal format (6 x 9 inches / 150 x 230 mm); occasional graphics.
DEPT: "Reviews," book reviews. (summer-82). None. (summer-89).
TYPL: "Some Thoughts on the Value of Film Education," "The Teaching of Film in English Departments," "A Survey: Use of Classic and Contemporary Documentary Films in Colleges and Universities." (fall-75). "Motion Pictures and Television, 1930 - 1945: A Pre-History of the Relations Between the Two Media," "Public Television, Indepenedent Documentary Producer and Public Policy," "Defamiliarization in Television Viewing: Aesthetic and Rhetorical Modes of Experiencing Television." (summer- 82). "Evolving Production Strategies for High-Definition Television: A Study of Julia and Julia," "The Videotape Editor as Sculptor: Paul Simon's Graceland in Africa, a Post-Production Case Study," "TV News Narration and Common Sense: Updating the Soviet Threat," "Kodak's 'America': Images from the American Eden." (summer-89).
SCHL: Semiannual (Mar, 1949 - Jan, 1950); Quarterly (Jul, 1950+), 75 pp.
SPAN: Mar, 1949+
VARIES
--Mar, 1949 - ?, 1967 as Journal of the University Film Producers Association.
--Jan, 1951 as UFPA Journal.
--1968 - ? as Journal of the University Film Association (ISSN: 0041-9311).
--Winter, 1982 - Fall, 1983 as Journal of the University Film and Video Association (ISSN: 0734-919x).
LC: PN 1993.U63
DD: 791
ISSN: 0742-4671
ABST: --Abstracts of Popular Culture (ISSN: 0147-2615)
--Arts and Humanities Citation Index (ISSN: 0162-8445)
--Current Index to Journals in Education (ISSN: 0011-3565)
--Film Literature Index (ISSN: 0093-6758)
--International Index to Film Periodicals (ISSN: 0000-0038)

Journal of Frankenstein, The

?, 1959 - Dec?, 1961//
SEE: CASTLE OF FRANKENSTEIN

JOURNAL OF LAW & TECHNOLOGY, THE

SUB: "The legal implications of a technological age."
PUBL: Georgetown University Law Center, 600 New Jersey Ave., NW, Washington, DC 20001.
DESC: This rather short-lived, student-edited publication was produced in cooperation with the Georgetown Univesity Law Center. Topics concerning regulatory trends, litigation, and international law were covered in a variety of areas. The last issue of the journal described speeches and forums of the "Second Annual Symposium on the Law and Outer Space." For the sampled issue of 1990: black ink on uncoated paper stock, with one-color ink on front cover, no advertising (6 ¾ x 9 ⅞ inches / 170 x 250 mm).
DEPT: None. (winter-90).
TYPL: "Satellite Service Business and Legal," "Telecommunications in the Soviet Union," "Aspects of Satellite Applications in Canada," "Transnational Issues Introduction," "Legislative and Regulatory Issues." (winter-90).
SCHL: Annual (1986); Semiannual (1987); Annual (1988 - 1989); Semiannual (1990+), 50 pp.
SPAN: 1986 - Winter, 1990//
ISSN: 0887-0160

✦ JOURNAL OF MARKETING

SUB: "A journal for the advancement of science in marketing."
SUB: "A quarterly publication of the American Marketing Association."
PUBL: American Marketing Association, 250 South Wacker Drive, Suite 200, Chicago, IL 60606.
DESC: A companion publication to the *Journal of Marketing Research*, the *Journal of Marketing* in earlier issues took a pragmatic applications approach to research in marketing. But in a 1979 editorial, then Editor Yoram Wind told readers, "According to the official 1978 AMA statement of objectives, the *Journal of Marketing* is to serve 'as a bridge between the scholarly and the practical'. Recent years have witnessed, however, a tendency to narrowly interpret this as a one-way bridge which focuses only on the needs of the practitioner, turning *JM* into a 'practitioner's journal'. This has to be changed. *JM* should serve as the leading marketing publication for the benefit and enhancement of members of the business and academic communities." Noting the AMA publication policy, Wind stated, "To achieve these objectives and serve the diverse needs of the various AMA segments, the *Journal of Marketing*'s editorial goal should be the advancement of the science and practice of marketing." This has resulted in a unique journal which is comfortable both in the theoretical constructs of academic consideration, and the business/consumer application of such theories and inquiry. Excellent graphics are throughout each issue. Also of note are the continuing lists of resources, and bibliographies in marketing. For the sampled issues of 1979 and 1991: perfect-bound magazine format, black ink on uncoated paper with dark-blue ink cover on coated stock, trade advertising (8 ½ x 11 inches / 215 x 280 mm).
DEPT: "Legal Developments in Marketing," "Marketing Literature Review," "Book Reviews." (01-86).
TYPL: "The Generalizability of Psychographic Market Segments Across Geographic Locations," "Characteristics of Radio Commercials and Their Recall Effectiveness," "The Politics of Marketing: Analyzing the Parallel Political Marketplace." (01-86).
SCHL: Quarterly, 140 pp.
SPAN: Jul, 1936+
FROM MERGER OF
--American Marketing Journal (ISSN: 0193-1806), (and) National Marketing Review (ISSN: 0190-9505), Jul, 1936.
LC: HF 5415.A2 J6
DD: 658.805
ISSN: 0022-2429
ABST: --ABI/Informer
--Accountants' Index. Supplement. (ISSN: 0748-7975)
--Biography Index (ISSN: 0006-3053)
--Book Review Index (ISSN: 0524-0581)
--Business Periodical Index (ISSN: 0007-6961)
--InfoBank
--Management and Marketing Abstracts (ISSN: 0308-2172)
--Management Contents
--Predicasts
--Psychological Abstracts (ISSN: 0033-0202)
--Women Studies Abstracts (ISSN: 0049-7835)

✦ JOURNAL OF MARKETING EDUCATION

PUBL: University of Colorado, Business Research Division, Campus PO Box 420, Boulder, CO 80309-0420.
DESC: "A forum for the exchange of ideas, information, and experiences related to the process of educating students in marketing, *JME* expects to deliver in a timely and compact package: (1) experiences in conveying innovative course content and methods applicable to the classroom/seminar environment, (2) ways to increase teaching effectiveness, (3) ways to improve student ratings, (4) information on new courses and course content, (5) information on new instructional techniques, and (6) articles dealing with general issues such as testing and evaluation." The *Journal of Marketing Education* is cosponsored by the Western Marketing Educators Association and the Business Research Division of the University of Colorado at Boulder. For the sampled issues of 1983 and 1991: black ink on uncoated paper, cover consisting of spot-color on uncoated stock, no advertising (8 ⅜ x 10 ⅞ inches / 215 x 275 mm).
DEPT: "From the Editor," "Professional Meetings." (spring-83). "Letter From the Editor," "Professional Meetings." (summer-91).

TYPL: "The BBA-MBA Combination: Pierson, Gordon and Howell Revisited," "A Curriculum for Personal Sales Training in an Academic Setting," "A Classroom Experiential Exercise for Studying Materials Management Decision-Making," "The Competitive Case Presentation and Critique Training Method," "The Mystery Shopper Technique as an Experiential Exercise to Teach Undergraduate Marketing Principles." (spring-83). "Master Teaching Revisited: Pursuing Excellence from the Students' Perspective," "The Marketing Concept as the Foundation of Marketing in the Classroom: An Educational Dilemma," "the Revival and Growth of Marketing Education in China," "Establishing Cross-Disciplinary Marketing Education." (summer-91).
SCHL: Semiannual, (? - 1982); Three issues per year (summer, 83+), 90 pp.
SPAN: ?+
ISSN: 0273-4753

✦ JOURNAL OF MASS MEDIA ETHICS

SUB: "Devoted to issues in mass media ethics."
SUB: "Exploring questions of media morality."
SUB: "The Journal of Mass Media Ethics is devoted to explorations of ethics problems and issues in the various fields of mass communication."
PUBL: Brigham Young University, Department of Communications, E-509 HFAC, Provo, UT 84602.
DESC: The *Journal of Mass Media Ethics* publishes scientific articles and essays that will both stimulate and contribute to reasoned discussions of mass media ethics and morality among academic and professional groups in the various branches and subdisciplines of communication and ethics. ... Important in the reviewing process is the inclusion of models, justification, and the reasoning behind moral judgments." Fulfilling a long-felt need among the working press and the academic community is this quality serial of thought and research into the area of mass communication ethics. Although the journal theoretically covers the broad range of communication topics, it focuses most often on the area of journalism ethics in broadcast and print media. Issues tend to be topical in nature, the sample issue viewed (Volume 3, #1) pertaining to "Journalism Moral Philosophy." Other topics proposed for the series were public relations ethics, advertising ethics, and international mass communications ethics. It is an important journal for today's media practitioner, and for those who teach mass communication. A sampling of 1991 articles included: "Where Morality and Law Diverge: Ethical Alternatives in the Soldier of Fortune Cases," "Ethical Problems of Advertising to Children," "Technologizing of the Word: Toward a Theoretical and Ethical Understanding," and "Of Crime and Consequence: Should Newspapers Report Rape Complainants' Names?" For sampled issue of 1988: perfect-bound journal format, editorial content consisting of black ink on coated paper stock, cover is black ink on orange color uncoated paper stock, no advertising (7 x 10 inches / 180 x 255 mm). A change in journal dimensions took place with the first issue of 1989, in conjunction with a new association with Lawrence Erlbaum Associates: (6 x 9 inches / 150 x 230 mm).
DEPT: "Foreword," "Book Reviews." (vol 3-#1-88).
TYPL: "'The Allied Controversy' and the Ethics of Journalism Education in the Pacific Northwest," "All is Not Relative: Essential Shared Values and the Press," "Power--The Key to Press Freedom: A Four-Tiered Social Model," "What Should We Teach About Formal Codes of Communication Ethics?" (vol 3-#1-88).
SCHL: Semiannual (1985 - 1989); Quarterly (1990+), 110 pp.
SPAN: Fall/Winter, 1985/1986+
LC: P 94 .J68
DD: 175/.1/05 19
ISSN: 0890-0523

✦ JOURNAL OF MEDIA ECONOMICS

PUBL: California State University at Fullerton, Department of Communications, Fullerton, CA 92634.
DESC: In its "Guidelines for Submission of Manuscripts," Editor Robert Picard tells readers, "The *Journal of Media Economics* seeks article manuscripts on economic aspects of mass media and on economic policy issues affecting media worldwide. The journal focuses on the structure, conduct, and performance of the newspaper, magazine, film, radio, television, cable, and other mass media industries. The journal seeks cross-industry and specific industry studies and individual medium case studies, as well as manuscripts devoted to social and political policy and financial and regulatory aspects of media economics." This is a long-awaited journal of the business/economics side of world communication. A serious journal of thought, research and commentary, the *Journal of Media Economics* explores various issues which are integral to the continuing evolution of these international media. Past article subjects have included advertising, cable television, media concentration, content of media, demand, integration, magazines, motion pictures, newspapers, ownership and control, public policy, radio, satellites, television, and theoretical approaches. It is a wonderful journal published by the Department of Communications at California State University, Fullerton. Journal format, black/white editorial content on uncoated paper stock with some graphics; two-color cover on coated paper stock, no advertising (5 ⅜ x 8 ⅜ inches / 135 x 210 mm).
DEPT: "Book Reviews." (fall-90).
TYPL: "Measuring and Analyzing Diversification of Corporations Involved in Pay Cable," "The Promise and Performance of Low Power Television," "Interactive Monopoly Power in the Daily Newspaper Industry," "Cable's Economic Impact on Over-the-Air Broadcasting." (fall-90).

SCHL: Semiannual (spring, 1988 - fall, 1990); Three issues per year (spring, 1991+), 65 pp.
SPAN: Spring, 1988+
DD: 380
ISSN: 0899-7764

Journal of Organizational Communications

Fall, 1971 - Winter, 1972/1973//
(ISSN: 0047-2646)
SEE: JOURNAL OF COMMUNICATION MANAGEMENT

Journal of Organizational Communication

Spring, 1975? - ?, 1981//
(ISSN: 0162-5659)
SEE: JOURNAL OF COMMUNICATION MANAGEMENT

Journal of Photographic Society of America

Mar, 1935 - Dec, 1946//
(ISSN: 0096-5812)
SEE: PSA JOURNAL

✚ JOURNAL OF POPULAR CULTURE

SUB: "Official publication of the Popular Literature Section of the Modern Language Association of America."
PUBL: Popular Culture Association, Bowling Green State University, Bowling Green, OH 43403.
DESC: An advertisement for sister publication, *Abstracts of Popular Culture*, helps define this valuable publication: "By 'Popular Culture' we mean all aspects of life which are not academic or creative in the narrowest and most esoteric sense. ... Important topics such as film, television, radio, popular literature, fairs, parades, theater, amusements, music, circuses, carnivals, urban and rural life, ethnic and women's studies, folklore, the family, sports, leisure, work, and all other aspects of the 'New Humanities'." For over 25 years the *Journal of Popular Culture* has examined the cultural norms and eccentricities of the American public, and international society. The journal explores a very wide range of cultural phenomena, from the the sawdust circus to a Texas Chili Cookoff; from degrading pornography to side-splitting cartoons; from animated billboards to the six o'clock television news, weather, and sports. An excellent journal for "the way we were and are." For the sampled issues of 1977 and 1991: black ink on uncoated paper in perfect-bound journal format, advertising, cover consisting of two-color ink on laminated paper stock (5 ¾ x 8 ⅞ inches / 145 x 225 mm).
DEPT: None. (winter-83). "Book Reviews." (spring-91).
TYPL: "Psychology and Popular Culture: Psychological Reflections on M*A*S*H," "The Texas Chili Cook-Off: An Emergent Foodway Festival," "The Extraordinary Being: Death and the Mermaid in Baroque Literature," "The Fotonovela as a Cultural Bridge for Hispanic Women in the United States," "A Profile of Antique Collectors." (winter-83). "Theatrical Antecedents of the Mall that Ate Downtown," "Roseanne-- How Did You Get Inside My House?: A Case Study of a Hit Blue-Collar Situation Comedy," "H.M.S. Pinafore and the Theater Season in Boston 1878 - 1879," "Audience Preference of Chinese Television: A Content Analysis of Letters to the Editor in the Chinese Television Broadcasting Magazine, 1983 - 1986," "Antidote to Dominance: Women's Laughter as Counteraction," "An Australian Ingredient in American Soap: The Thorn Birds." (spring-91).
SCHL: Quarterly, 150 pp.
SPAN: Summer, 1967+
LC: AP 2.J8325
ISSN: 0022-3840
ABST: --Abstract of English Studies (ISSN: 0001-3560)
--America, History and Life (ISSN: 0002-7065)
--Book Review Index (ISSN: 0524-0581)
--Historical Abstracts. Part A. Modern History Abstracts. (ISSN: 0363-2712)
--Historical Abstracts. Part B. Twentieth Century Abstracts. (ISSN: 0363-2725)
--Humanities Index (ISSN: 0095-5981)
--Index of American Periodical Verse (ISSN: 0090-9130)
--MLA International Bibliography of Books & Articles on the Modern Languages and Literatures (ISSN: 0024-8215)
--Music Index (ISSN: 0027-4348)
--Reference Sources (ISSN: 0163-3546)
--Repetoire International de la Litterature de l'Art (ISSN: 0145-5982)
--Women Studies Abstracts (ISSN: 0049-7835)

Journal of Popular Film

Winter, 1972 - 1978//
(ISSN: 0047-2719)
SEE: JOURNAL OF POPULAR FILM AND TELEVISION

✚ JOURNAL OF POPULAR FILM AND TELEVISION

SUB: "Official organ of the Popular Culture Association."
PUBL: Heldref Publications, 4000 Albemarle St., NW, Washington, DC 20016.
DESC: The *Journal of Popular Film and Television* "...is dedicated to popular film and television in the broadest sense. Concentration is upon commercial cinema and television: stars, directors, producers, studios, networks, genres, series, the audience, etc. Articles on film and television theory/criticism are invited as well as interviews, filmographies and bibliographies. There are no esoteric distinctions between 'motion

pictures,' 'film,' 'cinema,' and 'movies,' nor between 'television,' 'video,' 'network television,' or 'public television' controlling the editorial policies of the *Journal of Popular Film and Television*." *JPF&T* tends to be a periodical of widely varying articles and interests, with primary emphasis on commercial media. Some issues are themed, such as "The Catholic Imagination in Popular Film and Television," for summer, 1991. An excellent resource for the study of film and television. For the sampled issue of 1977: black ink on uncoated paper with black ink or spot-color ink on coated stock for cover, no advertising (5 ⅝ x 8 ¾ inches / 140 x 220 mm). A change in journal dimensions took place with the spring, 1980 issue (volume 8, number 1). Sampled issue for 1981 printed on uncoated paper stock, black/white editorial content with one-color cover. Sampled issue for 1988 printed on coated paper stock, black/white editorial content with two-color cover. Both sampled issues magazine format (8 ½ x 11 inches / 215 x 280 mm).
- DEPT: "Readers Forum," letters; "Reviews." (winter-81). None. (winter-88).
- TYPL: "The Shining: Ted Kramer Has a Nightmare," "If You Can't Get'em Into the Tent, You'll Never Have a Circus: an Interview with Len Hill," "When the Lights Went Out--Hollywood, the Depression and the Thirties," "The Criminal Psychopath as Hollywood Hero," "A Review of the Australian Film Industry--Past and Present," "Film Audience Research, 1960 - 1980: An Update." (winter-81). "Crocodile Dundee: Apotheosis of the Ocker," "Fifty Years of Snow White," "FEMBO: Aliens' Intentions," "Arbuckle Escapes: The Pattern of Fatty Arbuckle's Comedy," "The Premises of Comedy: Function of Dramatic Space in an Ancient and Modern Form." (winter-88).
- SCHL: Quarterly, 100 pp.
- SPAN: Winter, 1972+
  VARIES
  --Winter, 1972 - 1978 as Journal of Popular Film (ISSN: 0047-2719).
  --1978 - Winter, 1984/1985 as JPF&T.
- LC: PN 1993.J66
- DD: 791.43/05
- ISSN: 0195-6051
- ABST: --Abstracts of Popular Culture (ISSN: 0147-2615)
  --America, History and Life (ISSN: 0002-7065)
  --Art Index (ISSN: 0004-3222)
  --Book Review Index (ISSN: 0524-0581)
  --Communication Abstracts
  --Explicator, The
  --Film Literature Index (ISSN: 0093-6758)
  --Historical Abstracts. Part A. Modern History Abstracts. (ISSN: 0363-2712)
  --Historical Abstracts. Part B. Twentieth Century Abstracts. (ISSN: 0363-2725)
  --International Index to Film Periodicals (ISSN: 0000-0038)
  --International Index to Television Periodicals
  --Media Review Digest (ISSN: 0363-7778)
  --MLA International Bibliography of Books & Articles on the Modern Languages and Literatures (ISSN: 0024-8215)
  --Reference Sources (ISSN: 0163-3546)
  --Writings on American History (ISSN: 0364-2887)

JOURNAL OF RADIO LAW
- PUBL: Northwestern University Law School, Chicago, IL.
- DESC: Edited by the law schools of Northwestern University and University of Southern California in conjunction with Air Law Institute, the *Journal of Radio Law* had a short, but important publication span. The first issue for April, 1931 covered both aeronautical and radio law, a common practice in journals of the day; but commencing with the July, 1931 issue, the publication was devoted only to radio, and its immediate family, "...which includes telegraph, cable and telephone systems." Editor Louis G. Caldwell noted: "The term 'radio law' is, in itself, slightly misleading, especially if it be construed to imply the actual or threatened existence of a new and separate branch of jurisprudence. There is some justification for the implication if it be confined to governmental and international regulation of radio communication, i.e., the determination as between the nations, and as between the individuals within each nation, as to how radio facilities shall be allocated and as to how their use shall be regulated. The advent of radio, however, has introduced new problems in a number of established branches of law among which may be mentioned copyright, patents, trusts and monopolies, defamation, nuisance, unfair competition, and many others. The custom has developed of regarding all such problems as falling under the description of 'radio law', and this custom will be followed in this *Journal*." Of special importance were an extensive set of departmental columns. In the 1931 and 1932 sampled issues, "Foreign Radio Decisions" discussed radio litigation in Buenos Aires, Argentina, Lyon, France, Germany, and Italy; and "Foreign Radio Legislation" in Australia, Canada, Great Britain, Luxemburg, New Zealand, Norway, and Switzerland. In many ways the *Journal of Radio Law* was actually a journal of international radio law, an important publication which succumbed to the economic realities of the American "Great Depression." For the sampled issues of 1931 and 1932: black ink on uncoated paper stock in journal format, no advertising (6 ¼ x 9 ⅜ inches / 160 x 240 mm).
- DEPT: "General Orders of the Federal Radio Commission," column by Arthur W. Scharfeld; "Digest of Examiners' Reports and Decisions of the Federal Radio Commission," column by Howard W. Vesey; "Pending Radio Litigation in the United States," column by Arthur W. Scharfeld; "Radio Decisions in the United States," column by John W. Guider; "Radio Legislation in the United States," column by Philip G. Loucks; "Trend of Radio Regulation," column by Paul M. Segal; "Foreign Radio Decisions," column by Carl Zollmann; "Foreign Radio Legislation," column by Carl Zollmann; "International Radio Chronicle," col-

umn by Louis G. Caldwell; "Bibliography of Radio Law," column by Robert Kingsley; "Book Reviews," column by Robert Kingsley. (7-31). "Regulations of the Federal Radio Commission," column by Arthur W. Scharfeld; "Decisions of the Federal Radio Commission," column by Howard W. Vesey; "Radio Cases in the United States," column by John W. Guider; "Radio Legislation in the United States," column by Philip G. Loucks; "Foreign Radio Decisions," column by Carl Zollmann; "Foreign Radio Legislation," column by Carl Zollmann; "International Radio Chronicle," column by Louis G. Caldwell; "Bibliography of Radio Law," column by Robert Kingsley; "Book Reviews," column by Robert Kingsley. (10-32).
TYPL: "The Mexican Broadcasting Situation," "The Next World Conference at Madrid and the International Regulation of Electric and Radio Electric Transmissions," "Report of the Mixed Juridical and Technical Committee of the International Broadcasting Union." (7-31). "Protection Against the Unauthorized Use of a Broadcast in Canada," "Defamation by Radio," "Liability for Defamation in Political Broadcasts," "Protection of German Radio Listeners Against Electrical Interference." (10-32).
SCHL: Quarterly, 95 pp.
SPAN: Apr, 1931 - Oct, 1932//

JOURNAL OF SPEECH AND HEARING DISORDERS

PUBL: American Speech-Language-Hearing Association, 10801 Rockville Pike, Rockville, MD 20852.
DESC: "The *Journal of Speech and Hearing Disorders* is intended for those interested in disordered speech, language, and hearing, particularly clinicians who provide services to persons with communicative handicaps and researchers who study the etiology, assessment, and treatment of communicatively handicapping conditions." Following the November, 1990 issue, this publication *was* absorbed by the *Journal of Speech and Hearing Research. JSHR* was described as "...an archival research journal that publishes papers pertaining to the processes and disorders of hearing, language, and speech, and to the diagnosis and treatment of such disorders." For the sampled issues of 1981 and 1991: black ink on coated paper stock, with cover consisting of black and spot-color ink on coated stock, limited advertising (8 x 10 ¾ inches / 205 x 275 mm).
DEPT: "Letters to the Editor." (#1-81). "Letters to the Editor." (11-90).
TYPL: "Auditory Perceptual Impairments in Children with Specific Language Disorders: A Review of the Literature," "Earmold Options for Wideband Hearing Aids," "Psychological Considerations in Vocal Rehabilitation," "The Effect of Context on Verbal Elicited Imitation." (#1-81). "Taxonomies in Biology, Phonetics, Phonology, and Speech Motor Control," "Who Shall Be Called Language Disordered? Some Reflections and One Perspective," "Effects of Repair Strategies on Visual Identification of Sentences," "Spoken and Written English Errors of Postsecondary Students With Severe Hearing Impairment," "Tabletop Versus Microcomputer-Assisted Speech Management: Response Evocation Phase." (11-90).
SCHL: Quarterly, 130 pp.
SPAN: ? - Nov, 1990//
VARIES
--? - Jan, 1948? as Journal of Speech Disorders.
ISSN: 0022-4677

Journal of Speech Disorders

? - Jan, 1948?//
SEE: JOURNAL OF SPEECH AND HEARING DISORDERS

✢ JOURNAL OF TECHNICAL WRITING AND COMMUNICATION

PUBL: Baywood Publishing, 120 Marine St., Farmingdale, NY 11735.
DESC: "*The Journal of Technical Writing and Communication* has served, for well over a decade, as a major professional and scholarly journal for practitioners and teachers of most functional forms of communication--excluding fiction and poetry. As such, it has published, and will continue to publish, articles on professional writing, pedagogy, communication theory, technical journalism, organizational communication, rhetoric, business communication, communication for managers, intercultural communication, visual communication, user documentation, communication management, hardware and software documentation, engineering and scientific communication, and on a variety of subjects drawn from fields related to technical communication." Journal format; occasional graphics.
DEPT: "Announcements." (4-71). "Commentary," "Book Reviews," "Announcements." (#4-87).
TYPL: "Methods of Measuring Communication Results," "Some Shibboleths in the Teaching of Technical Writing," "First Things Last: Composition for Seniors, Not Freshmen," "A Different Method of Preparing Scientific and Technical Material." (4-71). "Designing Ethnographic Research in Technical Communication: Case Study Theory Into Application," "Designing Field Research in Technical Communication: Usability Testing for In-House User Documentation," "The Problem of Synonymy: Bacon's Third Idol Expanded," "The Literature of Enlightenment: Technical Periodicals and Proceedings in the 17th and 18th Centuries." (#4-87).
SCHL: Quarterly, 125 pp.
SPAN: Jan, 1971+
LC: T 11.J66
DD: 808/.066/602105
ISSN: 0047-2816
ABST: --Engineering Index Annual (ISSN: 0360-8557)

--Engineering Index Bioengineering Abstracts (ISSN: 0736-6213)
--Engineering Index Energy Abstracts (ISSN: 0093-8408)
--Engineering Index Monthly (ISSN: 0013-7960)
--Language and Language Behavior Abstracts (ISSN: 0023-8295)

Journal of the AER

Sep, 1941 - May, 1953//
SEE: PUBLIC TELECOMMUNICATIONS REVIEW

Journal of the AERT

Oct, 1953 - May, 1956//
SEE: PUBLIC TELECOMMUNICATIONS REVIEW

Journal of the AIEE

? - ?//
(ISSN: 0095-9804)
SEE: IEEE SPECTRUM

Journal of the American Institute of Graphic Arts

1965 - ?//
(ISSN: 0065-8820)
SEE: AIGA JOURNAL OF GRAPHIC DESIGN

Journal of the Audio Engineering Society

Jan, 1953 - Dec, 1985//
SEE: AES

JOURNAL OF THE BRITISH FILM ACADEMY

PUBL: British Film Academy, 3 Soho Square, London W1, England.
DESC: Only 17 issues of this publication were printed before editorship was transferred to the Society of Film and Television Arts in Great Britain. Those 17 issues varied greatly in content, quality, and even in the paper used. The periodical was issued at a time in which the motion picture industry world-wide was at a low point, which helps to explain both the size and demise of this journal in 1959. Issues concerned British film production; generally one topical issue per quarter. No illustrations.
DEPT: "New Books." (spring-58).
TYPL: "The British Film Abroad," "What is a British film?" (spring-59).
SCHL: Quarterly, 20 pp.
SPAN: ? - Spring, 1959//
LC: PN 1993.B

Journal of the Institution of Electronic and Radio Engineers, The

Jan, 1985 - Dec?, 1988//
(ISSN: 0267-1689)
SEE: ELECTRONICS & COMMUNICATIONS ENGINEERING JOURNAL

✤ JOURNAL OF THE PRODUCERS GUILD OF AMERICA, THE

PUBL: 8201 Beverly Blvd., Los Angeles, CA 90048.
DESC: This is a magazine of diverse opinion, with subjects ranging from motion picture tax shelters to film musicals, from poetry to critical essays on the role of film in society. The lineup of authors is diverse also, being such personages as: Norman Corwin, Ray Bradbury, David Gordon, Don Carle Gillette, and Jean-Paul Sartre. This is a publication of news items, trends, and Hollywood community news of interest to those who produce motion picture and television product. Articles explore regulatory, economic, and philosophical factors which enter into the process of producing for the consumer public. Articles are not lengthy in nature, but are entertaining and often informative. No graphics.
DEPT: "Book Reviews." (#3-76).
TYPL: "The Decline and Fall of the Motion Picture Tax Shelter," "The Journal Looks at a Profile of Violence," "Tough Guys," "British National Pictures Rides Again," "Whatever Happened to Filmusicals?" (#3-76).
SCHL: Quarterly, 30 pp.
SPAN: Apr, 1952+
VARIES
--Apr, 1952 - Dec, 1966 as Journal of the Screen Producers Guild.
LC: PN 1993.S
ISSN: 0032-9703

Journal of the Screen Producers Guild

Apr, 1952 - Dec, 1966//
SEE: JOURNAL OF THE PRODUCERS GUILD OF AMERICA, THE

Journal of the SMPTE

Jan, 1956 - Dec, 1975//
(ISSN: 0361-4573)
SEE: SMPTE JOURNAL

Journal of the Society of Motion Picture Engineers

1930 - 1949//
SEE: SMPTE JOURNAL

Journal of the Society of Motion Picture and Television Engineers

1950 - 1953//
SEE: SMPTE JOURNAL

Journal of the Television Society

Jun, 1928 - Autumn, 1966//
SEE: TELEVISION

Journal of the University Film and Video Association

Winter, 1982 - Fall, 1983//
(ISSN: 0734-919x)
SEE: JOURNAL OF FILM AND VIDEO

Journal of the University Film Association

1968 - ?//
(ISSN: 0041-9311)
SEE: JOURNAL OF FILM AND VIDEO

Journal of the University Film Producers Association

Mar, 1949 - ?, 1967//
SEE: JOURNAL OF FILM AND VIDEO

Journal of Typographic Research, The

Jan, 1967 - Autumn, 1970//
(ISSN: 0449-329x)
SEE: VISIBLE LANGUAGE

Journal Telegraphique [NE?]

? - ?//
SEE: TELECOMMUNICATION JOURNAL

Journal UIT

Jan, 1953 - Dec, 1961//
SEE: TELECOMMUNICATION JOURNAL

Journalism Bulletin, The

Mar, 1924 - Nov, 1927//
(ISSN: 0197-2448)
SEE: JQ. JOURNALISM QUARTERLY.

✤ JOURNALISM EDUCATOR, THE

SUB: "Devoted to research and commentary in journalism and mass communication education."

SUB: "A journal devoted to research and commentary on instruction, curriculum, and educational leadership in journalism and mass communication."

PUBL: Association for Education in Journalism and Mass Communication, University of South Carolina, Columbia, SC 29208-0251.

DESC: "*Journalism Educator* is a quarterly journal published by the Association for Education in Journalism and Mass Communication in cooperation with the Association of Schools of Journalism and Mass Communication. The publication first appeared in 1945 as *The Bulletin* of the American Society of Journalism School Administrators and changed to its current name in 1958. The focus of the journal is instruction, curriculum, and leadership in education for journalism and mass communication in American and international universities. It publishes research reports and interpretive articles refereed by a panel of peers. The journal's content also includes opinion pieces and critical reviews of books and teaching materials evaluated by the editors. *Journalism Educator* provides a forum in which scholars working in any of the subspecialties of journalism and mass communication can address a broad cross-section of the profession. All areas of inquiry are welcome, especially those represented by a division or committee of the sponsoring organizations. Contributions should add new knowledge, challenge current opinion, or inform a larger readership about scholarship and research than would otherwise be known only to communication specialists. This journal is interested in articles that explore objectives and outcomes of teaching philosophy and methods. Discussions of the role of faculty and administrators in curriculum design and professional leadership are encouraged." Several departmental features merit mention. There is an excellent "Review" section for both books and computer software, and the "Gazette" section, which provides newsbriefs of journalism education and educators. Within "Gazette," the "Faculty News" has several newsworthy subsections reporting on "New Administrators," "Promotions, Degrees, Leaves, Retirements," "Faculty Appointments," "Deaths," and "New Programs, Schools, Departments Colleges." These subdivisions are rather unique and are immeasurably informative. Also of note (in the 1991 sampled issue), was "Accrediting Council on Education in Journalism and Mass Communications 1991 Decisions," an academic orchids and onions listing of those journalism programs which received "Accreditation," "Re-Accredi-

tation," or "Provisional Re-Accreditation." *Journalism Educator* continues to stand out as a rich source of information. Well recommended for all involved in the field of education. For sampled issue of 1991: perfect bound journal format, editorial and cover printed black ink on uncoated paper stock, graphics and advertising (6 x 9 inches / 150 x 225 mm).
DEPT: "News of Journalism Education," newsbriefs. (10-77). "Commentary," "Reviews," "Book Reviews," "Software &," software reviews; "Gazette," "Faculty News." (summer-91).
TYPL: "Missouri Economics Course is Specifically for J-Majors," "Journalism Career Patterns of Women are Changing," "Eight Tips on Using Press Conferences as Final Examination," "Sixteen Point Checklist Unifies Broadcast Internship Program." (10-77). "A Theoretical Framework for Media Law Courses," "Industry's Team Approach to Classroom Projects," "Teaching Free Speech Issues in the Advertising Classroom," "Cross-Cultural Film Studies: Seeing Inside Out," "Parody as Free Expression: A Unit for Magazine Classes." (summer-91).
SCHL: Quarterly, 100 pp.
SPAN: 1945+
VARIES
--1945? - Dec?, 1957? as Bulletin.
LC: PN 4788.J63
ISSN: 0022-5517
ABST: --Current Index to Journals in Education (ISSN: 0011-3565)
--Education Index (ISSN: 0013-1385)

✤ JOURNALISM HISTORY

PUBL: California State University, Northridge Foundation, Department of Journalism, Darby Annex 103, Northridge, CA 91324.
DESC: In its call for manuscripts, *Journalism History* notes that it "...continues to evaluate and publish articles related to the full scope of journalism-mass communications history. The journal is especially concerned to find manuscripts that are focused on specific questions and hypotheses in the history of journalism and communications. ... Articles may discuss individuals, institutions or events; manuscripts which provide fresh approaches and new understanding about a topic in its broader context are especially sought." Although not all articles are historical in nature, they are of historical interest. An emphasis on primary research resources, good footnotes and pictures enhance this publication. For the sampled 1989 issue: black ink on uncoated stock for editorial content and cover in stapled magazine format, limited advertising (8 ½ x 11 inches / 215 x 280 mm).
DEPT: "Books," reviews of current books. (spring-77). "Book Reviews," column by Barbara Cloud. (spring/summer-89).
TYPL: "A Conversation with Alfred McClung Lee," "First Steps Towards a Theory of Press Control," "What You See is What You Get: Dorothea Lange and Ansel Adams at Mansanar." (spring-77). "Sixties Survivors: The Persistence of Countercultural Values in the Lives of Underground Journalists," "'The World is Ruled by Those Who Holler the Loudest': The Third-Person Effect in American Journalism History," "Storming and Defending the Color Barrier at the University of Missouri School of Journalism: The Lucile Bluford Case," "William W. Price: First White House Correspondent and Emblem of an Era." (spring/summer-89).
SCHL: Quarterly, 45 pp.
SPAN: Spring, 1974+
LC: PN 4700.J65
DD: 071/.3
ISSN: 0094-7679
ABST: --America, History and Life (ISSN: 0002-7065)
--Historical Abstracts. Part A. Modern History Abstracts. (ISSN: 0363-2712)
--Historical Abstracts. Part B. Twentieth Century Abstracts. (ISSN: 0363-2725)
--Humanities Index (ISSN: 0095-5981)
--Reference Sources (ISSN: 0163-3546)
--Writings on American History (ISSN: 0364-2887)

Journalism Quarterly

Jan, 1928 - Spring, 1971//
(ISSN: 0022-5533)
SEE: JQ. JOURNALISM QUARTERLY.

✤ JOURNALIST

SUB: "Organ of the National Union of Journalists."
PUBL: National Union of Journalists, Acorn House, 314 Grays Inn Road, London, WC1X 8DP England.
DESC: *Journalist* is a highly critical newspaper which serves two primary functions: 1) critical comment on British journalism, and 2) a communications forum for the NEC, England's journalistic union. A large number of articles and photographs indicate broad support from NEC members. It's an "activist" periodical.
DEPT: "Obituary," "Bookshelf," reviews; "People," profiles and reviews; "Around the Branches," unusually long segments detailing union journalism activities in Great Britain; "Last Words," editorial. (8-77).
TYPL: "Peace Bid as Print Workers Join Strike," "Pay Offer Sparks Radio Fury," "United Front is Key to Pay Battle," "Five-Point Press Freedom Pact," (8-77).
SCHL: Monthly, 12 pp.
SPAN: 1908+
LC: PN 4701.J
ISSN: 0022-5541

JOURNALIST, THE

SUB: "A weekly publication devoted to newspaper men and publishers." (Mar 22, 1884 - ?).
SUB: "Official journal of the International League of Press Clubs." (Apr, 1892 - 1895).

SUB: "A magazine for all who read and write." (? - Jan, 1907).
PUBL: Alan Forman, 41 Liberty St., New York, NY.
DESC: *The Journalist* in the 1800s was a decidedly different publication from that of the early 1900s. The early issues, in small tabloid format, were designed for publisher and reporter alike; with current news items regarding the price of paper, new printing press developments, subscription bases, and a host of articles profiling regional and local newspapers across the nation. It went into considerable depth on the status of individual newspapers. *The Journalist* of the early 1900s moved to journal format, and a much broader definition of journalism encompassing newspapers, magazines, books and prose. This was still a trade periodical, but one that had lost much of its bite by the end of its publication span in 1907.
DEPT: "Personals," "Notes and News," "To Correspondents," letters; "Bad Language," examples; "Dead Beat Advertisers," no bills paid. (6-21-1884). "Frontispiece," "Financial and Industrial," "Suggestions and Shop Talk," "Plain Talks on Advertising," "With the Boys and Girls," column by Uncle Dudley; "Publishers, Periodicals and Personals," newsbriefs; "Among the Amateur Journalists," newsbriefs. (11-06).
TYPL: "The Decline of the Herald," "Libel in Ireland," "Telegraph Companies at the Convention." (6-21-1884). "Cluff Vs. Carney," "Hearst and the Stock Market," "How to Get Into Print," "Matters Different and Indifferent." (11-06).
SCHL: Weekly (1884 - Jun 16, 1906); Monthly (Aug, 1906 - 1907), 12 pp.
SPAN: Mar 22, 1884 - Jan, 1907//
SUSPENDED
--Mar 23, 1895 - Apr 17, 1897.
--Jul, 1906
ABSORBED BY
--Editor and Publisher, Jan 26, 1907.
LC: PN 4700 .J8

Journalist

Fall, 1981 - Spring, 1983//
SEE: COMMUNITY COLLEGE JOURNAL

JOURNALISTS' AFFAIRS

PUBL: International Organization of Journalists, Parizka 9, 110 01 Prague 1, Czechoslovakia.
DESC: It is interesting to note that this serial promoting a "Soviet Bloc" point of view was printed totally in English. The first issue (combined issues #1, 2, and 3) was a chronology of the Vietnam war in which the editors stated: "We present this documentation to all honest journalists who want to write the truth about imperialist aggression towards the peoples of Indochina." Published in Prague, Czechoslovakia, *Journalists' Affairs* articles briefly described member activities, and the struggle of a "free" press against imperialistic nations and their actions. Typically, one article per issue was published. Journal format; no graphics.
DEPT: "Activities of the IOJ and Member Unions," "The Function and Role of the Student Press," "From the World of the Press, Radio and Television." (#11-73). "Books." (#5/6-80).
TYPL: "An Active Balance for the Organization of African Unity." (#11-73). "Dialogue Between Arab and European Journalists," "2nd International Biennial of Humour and Militant Graphic, Cuba - 81." (#5/6-80).
SCHL: Biweekly, 24 pp.
SPAN: #1, 1973 - 1980?//
LC: PN 4712.I54 J67
DD: 070/.05

JOURNALIST'S WORLD

SUB: "A periodical of the International Federation of Journalists."
PUBL: IFJ, Maison de la Presse, 4, Petite Rue au Beurre, Brussels 1, Belgium.
DESC: This periodical "is the voice of the International Federation of Journalists, an international organization of national trade unions and professional organizations of journalists in the press, radio and television fields. It is the voice for defense of press freedom, the voice for support of the moral and material interests of journalists and the voice for dedication to raising professional standards." Only 100 pages were published yearly. Text is in English, French, and Spanish.
DEPT: None. (#4-65).
TYPL: "How the Communist Press Works," "The Lesson of Dallas," "What is a Responsible Press for Emergent Nations." (#4-65).
SCHL: Quarterly, 25 pp.
SPAN: Jan/Mar, 1963 - 1968//
LC: PN 4700.J

JPF&T

1978 - Winter, 1984/1985//
SEE: JOURNAL OF POPULAR FILM AND TELEVISION

✤ JQ. JOURNALISM QUARTERLY.

SUB: "A quarterly magazine." (Mar, 1924 - Nov, 1927).
SUB: "Containing the Journalism Bulletin." (Jan, 1928 - Nov, 1929).
SUB: "Devoted to investigative studies in the field of journalism." (Mar, 1930).
SUB: "Devoted to research in journalism and mass communication."
PUBL: Association for Education in Journalism and Mass Communication, in cooperation with the Association of Schools of Journalism and Mass Communication,

and the American Society of Journalism School Administrators, University of South Carolina, Columbia, SC 29208.
DESC: Starting in 1924, *Journalism Quarterly*, (now titled simply *JQ*), has been recognized as a primary means of scholarly exploration on the form and function of mass communications in society. The emphasis in early issues was on print media, changing to the broader concept of mass communication in latter issues. What has remained constant is the focus on quality, scholarly research. Most issues are themed, such as the double issue for spring/summer, 1991 devoted to "News and Diversity." Editor Donald L. Shaw said of the issue: "Influenced by John Milton, communication scholars are interested in discovering if news diversity is helped or hurt by group newspaper ownership... Other studies in this section seek to learn if diversity in political news or in news emerging from newspaper competition has much influence on audience learning or in diversity of community public opinion." In the autumn, 1991 issue, the emphasis was "A Look at Advertising." Editor Shaw noted, "In many journalism and mass communication programs, many students have become interested in advertising or public relations in the past ten years. This issue groups three articles that examine how advertising is priced in weeklies, how effective nostalgic themes can be in television advertising, and how some advertising professionals feel about the sometimes-proposed ban on all tobacco advertising." Other articles are placed under subtitles of "Processes of Communication," "Audiences, Effects of Communication," "Professional Issues and Concerns," "International Communication," and "History and Law." Of special note is the marvelous departmental feature, "Articles on Mass Communication in U.S. and Foreign Journals," edited by Ronald E. Ostman and Dennis W. Jeffers. This quarterly bibliography of selected articles includes designations by geographic region and subject matter. This publication remains an outstanding scholarly work, which reflects quality standards by the editorial staff of *JQ* and the executive staff of the Association for Education in Journalism and Mass Communication. For the sampled issues of 1991: perfect-bound journal format, black ink on coated paper stock, cover consisting of dark-blue ink on light-blue tinted uncoated paper cover, advertising (6 x 9 inches / 150 x 230 mm).
DEPT: "Book Reviews," "Articles on Mass Communication in U.S. and Foreign Journals." (spring-84). "An Editorial Comment," column by Donald L. Shaw; "Book Reviews," "Articles on Mass Communication in U.S. and Foreign Journals," excellent ongoing bibliography column by Ronald E. Ostman and Dennis W. Jeffers. (autumn-91).
TYPL: "The Effects of Bad News and Good News on Newspaper's Image," "Developed and Developing Nation News in U.S. Wire Service Files to Asia," "The Origins of NBC's Project XX in Compilation Documentaries," "Ethical Values, the Flow of Journalistic Information and Public Relations Persons," "Television's Living Room War in Print: Vietnam in the News Magazines." (spring-84). "Advertising Practitioners Look at a Ban on Tobacco Advertising," "Cable Access: Market Concerns Amidst the Marketplace of Ideas," "Format Effects on Comprehension of Television News," "Colorization and Moral Rights: Should the United States Adopt Unified Protection for Artists," "Civil Rights Vanguard in the Deep South: Newspaper Portrayal of Fannie Lou Hamer, 1964 - 1977." (autumn-91).
SCHL: Quarterly, 275 pp.
SPAN: 1924+
VARIES
--? - ? as Monthly News Letter, American Association of Teachers of Journalism.
--Mar, 1924 - Nov, 1927 as Journalism Bulletin, The (ISSN: 0197-2448).
--Jan, 1928 - Spring, 1971 as Journalism Quarterly (ISSN: 0022-5533).
ISSN: 0022-5533
ABST: --ABI/Informer
--America, History and Life (ISSN: 0002-7065)
--Annual Bibliography of English Language and Literature (ISSN: 0066-3786)
--Book Review Index (ISSN: 0524-0581)
--Current Index to Journals in Education (ISSN: 0011-3565)
--Historical Abstracts. Part A. Modern History Abstracts. (ISSN: 0363-2712)
--Historical Abstracts. Part B. Twentieth Century Abstracts. (ISSN: 0363-2725)
--Humanities Index (ISSN: 0095-5981)
--Language and Language Behavior Abstracts (ISSN: 0023-8295)
--MLA International Bibliography of Books & Articles on the Modern Languages and Literatures (ISSN: 0024-8215)
--Public Affairs Information Service Bulletin (ISSN: 0033-3409)
--Reference Sources (ISSN: 0163-3546)
--World Surface Coating Abstracts (ISSN: 0043-9088)
--Writings on American History (ISSN: 0364-2887)

✤ JUMP CUT

SUB: "A review of contemporary cinema."
SUB: "A review of contemporary media."
PUBL: Jump Cut Associates, Box 865, Berkeley, CA 94701.
DESC: This valuable publication provides an alternative viewpoint (leftist and feminist critique, for example) on film and video content and aesthetics. Filled with highly-detailed, thoughtfully-written reviews and comment, *Jump Cut* is an aesthetic review of independent and major motion pictures. Co-editors John Hess, Chuck Kleinhans and Julia Lesage provide a dynamic variety of issue-themed articles concerning visual media. Some issues are themed, such as the sampled 1991 issue, with a dozen articles under the subhead, "African and Black Diaspora Film and Video." While those on the conservative side of the aesthetics/political fence may not share the views of

Jump Cut authors, there is no denying the import of the publication. Articles are well-researched, thought out, and endowed with a certain passion in presenting issues. A number of advertisements for like-minded publications are included. Considering the importance of this publication "...published about two times a year," one might wish that the paper stock consisted of a type that had greater durability. For the sampled issue for 1991: stapled magazine format, black/white editorial content on uncoated paper stock, cover consisted of two-color red and black ink on coated paper stock (8 ⅜ x 10 ⅞ inches / 210 x 275 mm).

DEPT: "News and Notes," newsbriefs; "In Print," book reviews; "Critical Dialogue," letters; "Report," "The Last Word," editorial. (#15-77). "The Last Word." (8-91).

TYPL: "The Subversive Charm of Alain Taner," "Women Oppressed," "Sour American Dream," (July, 77). "The Documentary Form," "Re-Evaluating Rossellini," "Revisionism Made Simple." (#15-77). "One Born Every Minute: House of Cards," "Hollywood and Low-Budget Alternatives," "South African Film History: Come Back Africa," "The U.S. Black Family Film: Take a Giant Step and Raisin in the Sun," "Mainstreams and Margins: Ethnic Notions and Tongues United." (8-91).

SCHL: Quarterly (? - ?); Semiannual (?+), 130 pp.
SPAN: May/Jun, 1974+
ISSN: 0146-5546
ABST: --Abstracts of Popular Culture (ISSN: 0147-2615)
--Alternative Press Index (ISSN: 0002-662x)
--Film Literature Index (ISSN: 0093-6758)
--International Index to Film Periodicals (ISSN: 0000-0038)
--Media Review Digest (ISSN: 0363-7778)

Junior College Journalist

Summer, 1972 - Spring/Summer, 1974 //
SEE: COMMUNITY COLLEGE JOURNALIST

K

✣ KAGAN MEDIA INDEX, THE

PUBL: Paul Kagan Associates, Inc., 126 Clock Tower Place, Carmel, CA 93923-8734.
DESC: One of an outstanding series of Kagan media publications, *The Kagan Media Index* consists primarily of charts that provide a clear economic picture of American mass media. It is a monthly typewriten newsletter that is a wonderful resource for the study and application of industry trends, and which helps elucidate understanding of the relationship between profit and loss in the media. Typical media covered in one sample issue included home video, theatrical, foreign TV/video, pay TV, network TV, satellite, broadcast, syndication, newspaper, magazine, book publishing, cellular telephone, home shopping and network television ratings. This is "MUST" reading for today's corporate media office.
DEPT: None. (10-25-89).
TYPL: "Motion Picture Studio Private Market Valuation," "1989's Boffo Box Office: Trend or Fluke?." (10-25-89).
SCHL: Monthly, 12 pp.
SPAN: Mar 10, 1987+
DD: 338 11
ISSN: 0893-2700

Kine Weekly

Sep 25, 1919 - ?//
SEE: KINEMATOGRAPH WEEKLY

Kinematograph and Lantern Weekly, The

May 16, 1907 - Sep 18, 1919//
SEE: KINEMATOGRAPH WEEKLY

KINEMATOGRAPH WEEKLY

SUB: "A magazine of popular science for the lecture-room, and the domestic circle." (Oct, 1896 - ?)
SUB: "With which is incorporated 'The Lantern World.'" (Feb, 1897 - ?)
SUB: "Established May 16, 1907."
SUB: "Incorporating the Optical Magic Lantern Journal & Photographic Enlarger, The Lantern World, and Kinematograph Chronicle."
PUBL: Odhams Press Ltd., 189 High Holborn, London WC1, England.
DESC: [*Optical Magic Lantern Journal and Photographic Enlarger, The*]: "This journal is intended to fill a void in our serial literature devoted to popular science. The magic or optical lantern, so long a mere toy, has, during late years, and since the application of photography to the preparation of the slides, gradually been assuming a higher phase; until at last it has become one of the best recognized agencies in education, and an instructive instrument in applied science. . .It will be our aim to keep our readers *au courant* with all that transpires in the world of lanternists and supply useful, practical information regarding every one of its numerous phases and applications, its mechanics, its optics, and its illumination." Latter issues (circa 1899+) contained some graphics, primarily schematics for technical matters. Of special interest are letters to the editors by pioneers in the field of magic lantern cinematic work, detailing frustrations, experiments, and success stories of developments in these fields. By 1894, illustrations were numerous, including halftones. The November, 1896 issue marked a major changeover in the serial, significantly increasing number and length of articles, with a beginning series on "Prominent Men in the Lantern World;" and in that same issue launched a new series entitled, "The Lanternist's Practical Cyclopaedia," by Charles E. Rendle. Issues beginning with Oct, 1902 were under new editorship, and an enlarged format.
DESC: [*Optical Lantern and Kinematograph Journal*]: "To the trade a monthly journal should be invaluable. New slides, recent films, special attachments, improved mechanism and new lamps come along with bewildering rapidity, and the busy lantern user can only decide their advantage to his particular outfit from the oftimes too brief description found in the maker's list. We shall assist him with an impartial and thorough review of new goods, as samples are submitted and demonstrations given. Our advertisers should remember the advantages to be gained by a change, now and again, in the wording of their announcements, which are read by those actually interested." *Optical Lantern and Kinematograph Journal* continued the fine tradition of reporting on early cinematic developments in Britain. Format was single-column, standard magazine size, with few illustrations in early issues. Of special note was a new series of special articles entitled, "Chats with Trade Leaders," commencing with the November, 1904 issue. A series of political cartoon commentaries were initiated with early 1905 issues, including topics such as the struggle between Pathe and British filmmakers. Latter issues also provide still pictures from motion picture products by Edison, Gaumont, Warwick, Pathe, and others. Of additional interest are patents with complete drawings which began to appear with the October, 1906 issue. NOTE: although the "C" in *Cinematograph* had al-

ways been pronounced as a hard "K" sound, apparently many readers were confused, and thus the publishers changed the serial title to *Kinematograph* beginning with the May, 1906 issue.
DEPT: "Applications for Patents," "General Wants and Sales," "Exchange Column," "Notes and Queries," "Selections," newsbriefs; (6-15-1889). "Editorial Table," correspondence; "Notes and Queries," notices; (8-1-1892). "Mere Mention," newsbriefs; "Prominent Men in the Lantern World," "Our Reference Shelf," "Correspondence," "Replies to Correspondents," "Patent Intelligence," (10-02). "From the Editor's Pen," "Stereoscopic Notes," newsbriefs; "Notices," "A Word of Praise," "Queries," "Review of Apparati," new equipment reviews; "New Films," motion picture product reviews; "Our Suggestion Bureau," "Tidbits," newsbriefs; "Applications for Patents," "Catalogues and Books Received," (11-04). "From the Editor's Pen," "New Films," "New Slides," "Round and About," newsbriefs; "Chats with Trade Leaders," "Heard on the 'Phone," trade rumours; "Reflections," editorial; "Catalogues and Books Received," "Round the Trade," trade news; "Patents," "Queries," (10-06).
TYPL: "The Magic Lantern: Its Construction, Illumination, Optics & Uses," "Various Names by Which the Lantern is Known," "The Smell of Oil in the Lantern," "Enlarging on Permanent Bromide Paper," (6-15-1889). "Stereoscopic Effect with the Lantern," "Hand Cameras for Obtaining Slides for the Lantern," "Ether Saturators Fourteen Years Ago," "Strength of Cylinders for Compressed Gas," (8-1-1892). "The Effect of Varying Intensity of Light on the Merit of Slides," "The Optical Lantern and the Human Mind," "Exhibition of Scientific Devices in Paris," (10-1902). "Hints on Cinematograph Work," "The Photography of Microscopic Objects," "Some Notes on Slide Making," "Illuminants or Optical Lanterns," (11-04). "Fire at the Gaumont Works," (10-06).
SCHL: Monthly (Jun 15, 1889 - Jul, 1903?); Weekly (?+), 38 pp.
SPAN: Jun 15, 1889 - Sep, 1971//
VARIES
--Jun 15, 1889 - Jun, 1903 as Optical Magic Lantern Journal and Photographic Enlarger, The.
--Nov, 1904 - May, 1906 as Optical Lantern and Cinematograph Journal.
--Jun, 1906 - Apr, 1907 as Optical Lantern and Kinematograph Journal.
--May 16, 1907 - Sep 18, 1919 as Kinematograph and Lantern Weekly, The.
--Sep 25, 1919 - ? as Kine Weekly.
WITH SUPPLEMENT
--Sub-Standard Film, Sep, 1952 - ?
--Ideal Kinema, The, ? - ?
ABSORBED
--Lantern World, The, Feb, 1897.
--Studio Review, Apr, 1957.
--Ideal Kinema, The, Apr, 1957.
SUSPENDED
--Aug, 1903 - Nov, 1904.
ABSORBED BY
--Today's Cinema, Sep, 1971.
LC: TR 845.K47
DD: 791.405
ISSN: 0023-155x

KINETRADOGRAM, THE
SUB: "A weekly record of offers and announcements."
SUB: "A weekly record of offers and announcements by the Kinematograph Trading Co., Ltd."
PUBL: Kincmatograph Trading Co., Ltd., 55-59 Shaftesbury Ave., London, England.
DESC: "The objects of this weekly record are to bring you each week clear, concise particulars of all the feature and exclusive films which we have to offer, with their vacant dates; brief reviews of all the films we add to our list; and particulars about novelties which we are able to offer from time to time." This short-lived, short-paged, small-format circular provided listings of available film product; and particulars concerning title, length, release date, and available dates for exhibition. Reviews were very brief. Some graphics in latter issues.
DEPT: None.
TYPL: Short film reviews.
SCHL: Weekly, 8 pp.
SPAN: Jan, 1913 - Jun, 1913//

✤ KNIGHT-RIDDER NEWS
PUBL: Knight-Ridder, Inc., 1 Herald Plaza, Miami, FL 33132-1693.
DESC: This quality, internal house organ showcases the activities of the formidable Knight-Ridder communications group, which as of this writing consisted of some 28 newspapers, eight television stations, business information services and cable systems. This quarterly demonstrates a real concern for quality in promoting the activities of the 20,000+ employees of the Knight-Ridder organization. For the 1989 sampled issue: stapled magazine-style format, beautiful full-color graphics and dynamic layout design throughout on heavy coated paper stock, an excellent in-house promotional publication (8 ½ x 11 inches / 215 x 280 mm).
DEPT: "Briefly," newsbriefs; "On the Move," personnel changes. (summer-86). "At a Glance," a wonderful section showcasing a Knight-Ridder division; "Briefly," news items of the Knight-Ridder organization; "On the Move," personnel changes. (fall-89).
TYPL: "The Making of a Pulitzer," "People to People Television," "Special Delivery: From Detroit, with Love," "Corporate Ad Campaign: A Symbol of Quality Journalism." (summer-86). "Everything Old is New Again," "Knight-Ridder's New Leaders," "Greetings From Key West." (fall-89).
SCHL: Quarterly, 35 pp.
SPAN: Spring, 1986+

KODAK

SUB: "A magazine for Eastman employees."
SUB: "The magazine from Eastman Employees."
PUBL: Eastman Kodak Company, Rochester, New York.
DESC: The tradition of Kodak quality is as apparent in public materials as it is in this unique house organ for Eastman employees. *Kodak* takes readers on a pictorial journey of current Kodak activities world-wide, new products, explanations of technologies, photographic galleries, employee hobbies, public use of Kodak products, and a number of other topics of interest to Eastman employees. Of interest is its detailed corporate look at the American employee.
DEPT: "The Editor's Page," "Out of the Hat," employee hobbies; "Panorama," newsbriefs; "Activities Calendar." (3-39).
TYPL: "Kodak in the 'World of Tomorrow,'" "The Story of Kodak Cubana, Limited," "How We Handle Customers' Orders," "With a Camera in Alaska," "Keeping Kodak Out Front in India." (3-39).
SCHL: Monthly (Jun, 1920 - ?); Bimonthly (? - Dec, 1938); Monthly (Jan, 1939 - ?); 20 pp.
SPAN: Jun, 1920 - Sep, 1944?//?
VARIES
--Jun, 1920 - ? as Kodak Magazine, The.
LC: TR 1.K57

Kodak Magazine, The

Jun, 1920 - ?//
SEE: KODAK

✤ KODAK PROFESSIONAL FORUM

PUBL: Eastman Kodak Company, Motion Picture and Audiovisual Markets Division, Department 640, 343 State St., Rochester, NY 14650.
DESC: Each issue of this professional serial is dedicated to a single visual medium. In one sampled issue, the chosen theme was "Film for Freedom of Imagination," or as Editor Richard F. Crowley expressed it, "Bold contrasts, subtle textures. Film catches it all. It responds to the artist's vision. What it records is limited only by light. It sets free yet captures the artist's imagination." Articles in that issue covered a television producer, motion picture cinematographer, TV commercial director, a loan company for filmmakers; and two wonderful articles concerning animator Grim Natwick, and June Foray, the voices behind Rocky the Squirrel and Natasha Fatale of the Bullwinkle Show. A very nice promotional vehicle with minimal advertising by Eastman Kodak. Magazine format (8 1/4 x 10 7/8 inches / 210 x 275 mm); uncoated paper stock cover with coated stock editorial pages; black/white graphics with selected duotones.
DEPT: "Tools of the Trade," newsbriefs; "Filmmakers' Bookshelf." (Vol 6, # 1-83).
TYPL: "The Producer Behind the Camera: A Conversation with 60 Minutes' Greg Cooke," "Richard Edlund, ASC, Talks About Magic," "A Director Who Knows What He Wants," "A Guide to What's in the Can," "A Loan Company for Filmmakers." (Vol 6, # 1-83).
SCHL: Quarterly?, 18 pp.
SPAN: ?, 1978+?

✤ KORKIS AND CAWLEY'S CARTOON QUARTERLY

PUBL: Gladstone Publishing, Ltd., 212 South Montezuma, Prescott, AZ 86303.
DESC: "Though it is easy to state that everyone loves animation, that statement cannot be taken much further. Animation encompasses so much, that to begin to divide it into its separate parts is to guarantee a debate. Whether you break it down by creator, style, time period, budget, subject, character or other sub-factor, there will be little agreement. The greatest division today is between the 'independents' and the 'studios'. Independents receive funding or grants and create what they wish. Their works test the boundaries of animation, but are often only found in festivals. Studios create product to sell to consumers (or advertisers). Their work, seen easily on TV and in theaters, is the introduction of the artform to a general public. They strive merely for entertainment and profit, but on occasion rise to more. This is what breeds the new generations of animators. Animation is a rare medium that is art, business and an elusive sprite called entertainment. It's an uneasy relationship at best. That it has survived through the years of critics, saviors, enthusiasts and economic changes shows a great strength. As the business and art of animation continue to change, that strength will inspire still new creators and critics." Any fan or professional interested in animation should have this premiere serial. It is outstanding in editorial content and for the reprinting of cartoon panels and and pictures of the animators. Articles are both authoritative and fascinating, which makes *CQ* one of the very finest serials on current and historical cartoons. In the premiere issue (winter, 1988), co-editor Jim Korkis stated: "...many of those ancient, and not-so-ancient, wizards who toiled so long in seclusion to share with us their special magic have never received recognition. Those secret chants that conjured up those cartoon characters that became such an important part of our lives are in danger of being lost forever in the mists of time. It is one of the intentions of this magazine to focus our spotlight on those names and secrets and by so doing, try to freeze for one brief moment of time that magic lantern show we call animation." Full of wit, stories, profiles, and, of course, plenty of examples of the cartoonists' art, it is published on better-quality newsprint to replicate typical comic book product. Magazine format on newsprint with numerous color graphics.

DEPT: "Editorials," "News," cartoon newsbriefs; "Leonard Maltin's Cartoon Column," "Animation Profile," "Cartoon Quarterly's Question and Answer," animation Q&A column by Jim Davis; "Cartoon Biography," "Drawing the Line," column by Will Finn; "Animation Answers," Q&A on animation. (winter-88).

TYPL: "Mickey at 60: A Birthday Party Animal," "New Zeal (Land) in Animation--Footrot Flats," "The Three (Animated) Faces of Superman," "The Bedrock Chronicles: The Evolution of the Flintstones." (winter-88).

SCHL: Quarterly, 50 pp.

SPAN: Winter, 1988+

✜ KTA NEWSLETTER

SUB: "National society honoring scholarship in journalism."

PUBL: Kappa Tau Alpha, University of Missouri, School of Journalism, PO Box 838, Columbia, MO 65202.

DESC: This four-page newsletter is designed for the membership of Kappa Tau Alpha, a "national society honoring scholarship in journalism." Articles describe activities of the organization, especially activities at the local college chapter level. Given particular focus are publications of KTA members, new books which have added insight to the process and historical development of journalism and communication. For the sampled issue of 1991: folded newsletter format, black ink on uncoated paper stock, no advertising (8 ½ x 11 inches / 215 x 280 mm).

DEPT: None. (fall-91).

TYPL: "Taft to Step Down After 30 Years on Job," "National President Calls Advisers to Meet in Boston," "Tucker Provides Support for KTA at Tennessee," "KTA Lecture Program Held at Winthrop College," "National KTA Prexy Addresses Alabama Group." (fall-91).

SCHL: Quarterly, 4 pp.

SPAN: Fall, 1983+

L

✤ LANGUAGE & COMMUNICATION

SUB: "An interdisciplinary journal." (Vol 1, #1 - ?).
PUBL: Pergamon Press, Inc., Maxwell House, Fairview Park, Elmsford, NY 10523.
DESC: "The primary aim of the journal is to fill the need for a publicational forum devoted to the discussion of topics and issues in communication which are of interdisciplinary significance. It will publish contributions from researchers in all fields relevant to the study of verbal and non-verbal communication. The investigation of language and its communicational functions will be treated as a concern shared in common by those working in: anthropology, the arts, artificial intelligence, education, ethology, linguistics, philosophy, physiology, psychology, [and] the social sciences. Emphasis [is] placed on the implications of current research for establishing common theoretical frameworks within which findings from different areas of study may be accommodated and interrelated. By focusing attention on the many ways in which language is integrated with other forms of communicational activity and interactional behaviour, it is intended to explore ways of developing a science of communication which is not restricted by existing disciplinary boundaries." Square journal format; some graphics. For the sampled issues of 1981 and 1991: black ink on uncoated paper in perfect-bound, square journal format, limited advertising. Dimensions for 1981 issues: (6 7/8 x 9 3/8 inches / 175 x 240 mm); and for sampled 1991 issues: (7 1/4 x 9 3/4 inches / 185 x 245 mm).
DEPT: "Calendar." (#1-1982). "Calendar." (#3-91).
TYPL: "Evaluation of Noncontent Speech Accommodation," "The Future Machine: a Study of the Span of Speakers' Anticipations in Conversation," "Language Acquisition, Data Compression and Generalization," "What We Might Learn from Acquired Disorders of Reading." (#1-1982). "The Acquisition of Japanese 'Gender' Particles," "Declaratives as Suggestions," "Why is There No 'True' Philosophy of Linguistics?," "Plato's Anti-Mechanistic Account of Communication," "Paralinguistic Qualifiers: Our Many Voices." (#3-91).
SCHL: Three issues per year (1981 - 1983); Quarterly (1984+), 130 pp.
SPAN: 1981+

LC: P 87.L36
DD: 001.51/05
ISSN: 0271-5309
ABST: --Communication Abstracts
--Computer & Control Abstracts (ISSN: 0036-8113)
--Current Contents
--Current Contents. Social and Behavioral Sciences. (ISSN: 0092-6361)
--Current Index to Journals in Education (ISSN: 0011-3565)
--Electrical & Electronics Abstracts (ISSN: 0036-8105)
--Language and Language Behavior Abstracts (ISSN: 0023-8295)
--Language Teaching (ISSN: 0261-4448)
--Linguistics & Language Behavior Abstracts
--MLA International Bibliography of Books & Articles on the Modern Languages and Literatures (ISSN: 0024-8215)
--Physics Abstracts. Science Abstracts. Series A. (ISSN: 0036-8091)
--Psychological Abstracts (ISSN: 0033-0202)
--Social Science Citation Index (ISSN: 0091-2887)
--Sociological Abstracts (ISSN: 0038-0202)

Law Enforcement Communications

1974? - Jan/Feb, 1984//
(ISSN: 0193-0540)
SEE: LAW ENFORCEMENT TECHNOLOGY

✤ LAW ENFORCEMENT TECHNOLOGY

PUBL: United Business Publications, 210 Crossways Park Dr., Woodbury, NY 11797.
DESC: The technological tools of mass communication are experiencing increased usage by law enforcement agencies, providing the raison d'etre for this publication; which focuses on the application of such media for crime analysis, instructional sessions, and preventive law enforcement. *Law Enforcement Technology* is an instructive periodical, one which demonstrates new techniques applied through new technologies. In a field where information detail is critical, this magazine provides real-life situations whereby law enforcement officials were able to utilize communication technologies to enhance processing of various cases from shoplifting to accident reporting to homicide. For the law enforcement communication specialist this is an excellent resource.
DEPT: "The Rap Sheet," newsbriefs; "All Points Bulletin," production advice.
TYPL: "Getting Loaded," "What You Should Know about Aircraft Accident Photography," "Captain Video Rides Again." (12-77).
SCHL: Six issues per year (1974 - Jan/Feb, 1983); Quarterly (Mar/Apr, 1983 - ?); Bimonthly (Mar/Apr, 1984 - ?); Monthly [bimonthly Jul/Aug, and Nov/Dec] (Jan, 1989+), 50 pp.
SPAN: 1974+

VARIES
--1974? - Jan/Feb, 1984 as Law Enforcement Communications (ISSN: 0193-0540).
DD: 363
ISSN: 0747-3680

✤ LEARNED PUBLISHING

SUB: "Journal of the Association of Learned and Professional Society Publishers."
PUBL: Association of Learned and Professional Society Publishers, 139 The Ryde, Hatfield, Herts AL9 5DP England.
DESC: "The Association of Learned and Professional Society Publishers (ALPSP) was founded in 1972 and is a non-profit organization comprising over a hundred British learned societies and professional institutions. Each society is engaged in publishing, either independently or with the services of a publishing house, or is on the point of doing so. Publishing houses rendering services to societies may also join. ALPSP exists to promote the development of publishing and the flow of publications of its members, representatives of which meet to discuss mutual problems and to elaborate common solutions to these questions." Not since the advent of the linotype machine have so many dynamic regulatory, distributory and technological changes seemed poised to challenge the scholarly publisher's concept of what constitutes learned publishing. The introduction of computer-modem submitted articles, desktop publishing, CD-ROM, on-line databases, style-checker software, publishing on floppy disks, and a host of other developments are presented in this dynamic, quarterly publication for the 100-plus members of the Association of Learned and Professional Society Publishers. Editor Hazel K. Bell and the Association are to be commended for a most informative, succinct review of important developments in this important field of publishing. Of special note are several department sections. "Copyright Corner" looks at news of a regulatory and legal nature, such as (in the sampled issue for 1991) a licensed copying agreement with the British Library; periodical publishers being urged to utilize both ISSN numbers and front cover barcodes; and a new guide concerning photocopying from books and journals. The "Seminars and Meetings" department provides informative abstracts of papers and talks in the scholarly publishing area. In the sampled issue appeared titles such as "Copy into Print: The Shape of the Next Twenty Years," "NVQs: Editorial Training for Freelancers and Publishers," and "What Makes a Good Journal?" Finally, "Overseas Affairs" provides capsule information concerning learned publishing developments in other parts of the world. For publishers of scholarly journals, textbooks, or reference works, membership in the Association of Learned and Professional Society Publishers (and a subsequent subscription to *Learned Publishing*) is an investment in this important industry dedicated to information dissemination. Well recommended. For sampled issue of 1991: stapled journal format, black/white editorial content on uncoated paper stock, cover consisting of two-color black/green ink on coated paper stock (5 ⅞ x 8 ¼ inches / 150 x 210 mm).
DEPT: "Copyright Corner," informative column by John Saint Aubyn; "Seminars and Meetings," condensed reports from recent events of interest to publishers; "Overseas Affairs," "Information Organization," news items; "Book Reviews," edited column by Michele Benjamin; "Publications Noted," "Coming Events," 'Conferences, meetings, fairs, exhibitions'. (4-91).
TYPL: "Scientific Information: the Views of a Learned Society and Publisher," "Electronic Advances in Scientific Information: The Commercial Angle," "Subscriptions by Deed of Covenant: Is This Charity?," "The Refereeing of Papers for Learned Journals," "Training in Journal Publishing." (4-91).
SCHL: Quarterly, 65 pp.
SPAN: 1977+
VARIES
--1977 - ? as Bulletin of ALPSP (ISSN: 0260-9428).
LC: Z 286.S37 L4
DD: 070.5/94/05
ISSN: 0953-1513

LEARNING RESOURCES

SUB: "For tomorrows teaching today."
PUBL: Association for Educational Communications and Technology, 1201 16th St., NW, Washington, DC 20036.
DESC: *Learning Resources* is a short periodical designed to provide quick tool skills in instructional media. Concentration is on use of inexpensive materials for audio-visual application, and the instruction of new techniques for old equipment. Articles have good graphics, but tend to be rather short.
DEPT: "Reader Resources," readers sharing sources of materials.
TYPL: "Putting Podunk in the Projector," "Using Visual Materials in the Foreign Language Classroom," "Super Super 8," "An Experiment in Media Equipment Instruction," "Syncronizing Hand-Drawn Film to Music." (2-75).
SCHL: Five issues per year, 30 pp.
SPAN: Apr, 1973 - May, 1975//
SUPPLEMENT TO
--AudioVisual Instruction, Apr, 1973 - Oct, 1974.
SUSPENDED
--Nov, 1974.
LC: LB 1043.A
ISSN: 0190-1974

Leica Fotografie

Jan?, 1951 - ?, 1989//
(ISSN: 0024-0621)
SEE: LEICA FOTOGRAFIE INTERNATIONAL

✣ LEICA FOTOGRAFIE INTERNATIONAL

SUB: "International magazine for 35mm photography."
PUBL: Umschau Verlag Breidenstein, GmbH, 18-24 Stuttgarter Strasse, D-6000, Frankfurt-on-Main, Germany.
DESC: This "English Edition" (also published in French and German editions) is remarkable both for sumptuous photographs in black/white and color, and for the amazing breadth of topics covered; from commercial to scientific photography, or historical reviews to modern laboratory processes; all of which bring forth a new dimension in this realm of the visual. One sampled issue explored fashion photography, black/white mountain-oriented subjects, bands of color found in agricultural crops, stop-action nature studies, and an intriguing review of a Basel trade fair in 1936. The writing is thoughtful, crisp, and interwoven with rich descriptors designed to delineate the technique and technology of photography. For example: "Normally, photography is said to concern the subjective documentation of reality. But, is it always, when one considers all those variable technical factors? These are so manifold and numerous that, in effect, objectivity remains nothing, perhaps, but a desired theoretical notion." One looks forward to each issue for exploration of photography as art form, medium of expression, and means of communication. Very highly recommended. For the sampled issues of 1986: small magazine format, full-color throughout on coated paper stock, stapled, with minimal advertising (7 x 9 ½ inches / 180 x 240 mm).
DEPT: "News from Wetzlar," newsbriefs; "Recent Books," international review; "Projection," equipment review; "Lab," technical aspects; "Product Report," review. (3-86).
TYPL: "Typical St. Christoph," "With a Lash of the Tongue," "Fifty Years Ago," "Back to Old Virginia," "Beauty and Fashion." (3-86).
SCHL: Eight issues per year, 50 pp.
SPAN: Jan, 1951+
VARIES
--Jan?, 1951 - ?, 1989 as Leica Fotografie (ISSN: 0024-0621).
EDITION
--English.
LC: TR 1 .L416
DD: 771.3/1
ISSN: 0174-0253

LEICA PHOTOGRAPHY

SUB: "The magazine for the 35mm specialist."
PUBL: Leica Photography, E. Leitz Inc., Rockleigh, NJ 07647.
DESC: This promotional periodical showcases talents of Leica owners and dealers within the United States. Some articles featured photographs around a common theme and the stories behind those photographs, such as series on flowers, or the circus. Other articles focused on the beginning photographer, with articles detailing an introduction to color photography, or the philosophical "whys and wherefores" of taking pictures. Still other articles showcased professional work, providing technical detail for the Leica camera product line. Photographs from the sampled issue for 1961 were both color and black/white photographs from the sampled issue for 1976 were in black and white. Primary emphasis is on Leica cameras and accessories. For the sampled 1948 issues: black ink editorial content, with duotone, spot- and full-color pages and full-color cover on coated paper stock in stapled magazine format, advertising for Leica products (8 ½ x 11 inches / 215 x 280 mm). For the sampled issues of 1961: small magazine format (7 ⅛ x 9 ½ inches / 180 x 240 mm), full color cover on coated paper stock. Note: some confusion exists over lineage of this publication. Most sources indicate that *Leica Photography* was first published from December, 1932 until September, 1939, and recommenced publication with the spring, 1948 issue until cessation in 1977. While later issues indicate a publication address of the United States, early issues during the 1960s had "English Edition" on the masthead, indicating both English language and the place of issuance as London, England.
DEPT: "Editorial," column by Thomas H. Elwell; "Notes and Tips," letters and other photographic information; "Leica News," product information. (fall-48). "Masters of the Leica," master photographer profile; "Practical Notes on the Leicina," technical column; "Marginal Notes," technical column by Walther Benser; "At Random," new products; "International Exhibitions," calendar; "New Books," review. (#3-61). "Showcase," one photographer photo gallery each issue; "New Products." (1-76).
TYPL: "Nature Photography as a Hobby," "Strob Flash and the Leica," "City Slickers," "Three-Dimensional Color Reproduction," "This Miniature Question." (fall-48). "In Memoriam Dr. Paul Wolff," "Why Do We Photograph?," "Darmstadt's Successful VDAV," "Experiences with Adox Developers," "A Visit to Pascal." (#3-61). "My Way with the Focomat," "Minox 35 EL," "50 mm Noctilux F/1." (#1-76).
SCHL: Monthly (Dec, 1932 - Sep, 1939); Quarterly (1948 - ?); Bimonthly (? - ?); Quarterly (? - 1976); Irregular (1976 - 1977), 25 pp.
SPAN: Dec, 1932 - ?, 1977//
SUSPENDED
--Oct, 1939 - 1947
LC: TR 1.L422
DD: 770.5
ISSN: 0024-063x

✣ LENS MAGAZINE

PUBL: United Technical Publications, 645 Stewart Ave., Garden City, NY 11530.
DESC: *Lens Magazine* is a publication which explores the spectrum of the art and technique of photography, naturally focusing on the impact of the lens within that process. It is significant that articles are much more than just discussions of which lens to choose for a

given shot. Articles delve into the aesthetics, framing, philosophy, and technical merits of a given photographic opportunity; resulting in an interesting publication. Stapled magazine format, full-color throughout on coated paper stock, advertising (8 ¼ x 11 inches / 210 x 280 mm).
DEPT: "Hollywood Comes Home," 'A column on home movies' column by George Yost; "News & Notes," product newsbriefs; "Time & Temp," 'A column on home darkroom' column by Jay Eisen; "New Products," review. (5/6-79).
TYPL: "What Went Wrong? Solving Common Problems," "Circus! Photographing the Greatest Show," "Using Color ... Selectively." (5/6-79).
SCHL: Bimonthly, 35 pp.
SPAN: Sep/Oct, 1975+?
LC: TR 1.L45
DD: 2452343
ISSN: 0363-2636

✤ LEONARDO

SUB: "The journal of the International Society for the Arts, Sciences and Technology."
SUB: "International journal of contemporary visual artists."
SUB: "International journal of the contemporary artist."
PUBL: International Society for the Arts, Sciences and Technology, 2030 Addison St., Suite 400, Berkeley, CA 94704.
DESC: "*Leonardo* is an international journal for artists and others interested in the contemporary arts. It features illustrated articles written by artists about their own work and is particularly concerned with issues related to the interaction of the arts, sciences and technology. The Journal focuses on the visual arts and also addresses music, video, performance, language, environmental and conceptual arts--especially as they relate to the visual arts or make use of the tools, materials and ideas of contemporary science and technology. New concepts, materials and techniques and other subjects of general artistic interest are treated, as are legal, economic and political aspects of art." *Leonardo* may arrive for the first-time reader poised as a wonderful enigma, on the one hand demonstrating pleasurable, insightful, thoughtful writing about contemporary arts; while at the same time being somewhat perplexing in including topics about art, science, and technology. It functions at its very best within this fascinating mixture of artistic and theoretical concepts within an applied technology framework. In the sampled issue for 1991 were articles which explored three-dimensional stereoscopic drawings, a computer-controlled video-switching system placed within the chrome helmets of three women's hairstyling chairs, "Transportable Neon Equipment for the Light Sculptor," a means of drawing with sound technologies, a comparative analysis of the dual nature of pictures with representational and abstract imagery, and "Art on a Two-Dimensional Flame Table." Of special note are a number of valued departmental features. "Gateway" was introduced in the first issue of 1991 as a "...portal through which the reader can pass, accumulating information about the events, people, places and developments that are shaping the art of tomorrow." "Words on Works" concern new artists and their projects. "Current Literature," reviews books, periodicals, audio and videotapes. "Commentaries," is considered thoughtful responses to previous articles. "Directory of Art / Science / Technology Organizations" is another excellent departmental feature. The value of this unique publication emerges after a single reading. It succeeds with clarity, insight, and informative discussion where many before it have failed. It has a 1991 subscription price of $65 (institutional: $295). Note: beginning in 1991, *Leonardo* moved to a bimonthly publication schedule, one issue of which was to be a new publication, *Leonardo Music Journal*, scheduled to include a compact disk (audio CD). For the sampled issue of 1991: perfect-bound, large journal format, editorial content with numerous graphs, charts, and pictures are black/white on coated paper stock; cover is two-color red and black on heavy cover stock (8 ¼ x 11 ¼ inches / 210 x 285 mm).
DEPT: "Editorial," "Gateway," news items; "Artist's Article," "Artists' Notes," "Sound, Music, Science and Technology," "Theoretical Perspectives on the Arts, Sciences and Technology," "Art/Science Forum," "Abstracts," "Words on Works," 'Short statements about new artworks in which art and technology coexist or merge'; "Current Literature," extensive considered reviews of books, periodicals, audio and videotapes; "Commentaries," 'Readers' comments offering substantial theoretical and practical contributions to issues that have been raised in texts published in Leonardo'. (#1-91).
TYPL: "Influences and Motivations in the Work of a Palestinian Artists/Inventor," "Hair Salon T.V.: A Computer-Controlled Video Installation," "Drawing with Sound," "Patterns in Pictures for Art and Science," "Science and Beauty: Aesthetic Structuring of Knowledge." (#1-91).
SCHL: Quarterly (? - ?); Bimonthly (Jan/Feb, 1991+), 115 pp.
SPAN: Jan, 1968+
LC: N 6490 .L42
DD: 705
ISSN: 0024-094x
ABST: --Abstrax
--Art and Archaeology Technical Abstracts (ISSN: 0004-2994)
--Art Bibliographies Modern (ISSN: 0300-466x)
--Art Index (ISSN: 0004-3222)
--Arts and Humanities Citation Index (ISSN: 0162-8445)
--Computer & Control Abstracts (ISSN: 0036-8113)
--Electrical & Electronics Abstracts (ISSN: 0036-8105)
--Mathematical Reviews (ISSN: 0025-5629)
--Physics Abstracts. Science Abstracts. Series A. (ISSN: 0036-8091)
--Repetoire International de la Litterature de l'Art (ISSN: 0145-5982)
--RILM Abstracts (ISSN: 0033-6955)

Leypoldt & Holt's Literary Bulletin
Feb, 1869 - Jun, 1869//
SEE: PUBLISHER'S WEEKLY

Liberty
Summer, 1971 - Spring?, 1973//
(ISSN: 0024-208x)
SEE: LIBERTY, THEN AND NOW

✤ LIBERTY, THEN AND NOW
SUB: "The nostalgia magazine."
PUBL: Liberty Library Corporation, 250 W. 57th St., New York, NY 10019.
DESC: *Liberty Magazine* consists of reprinted articles from the original *Liberty Magazine* of the 1920s, 30s and 40s. Each quarterly issue features a particular topic, with many issues devoted to the radio and motion picture industries. For the 1972 sampled issue, article reprints included college morals, the real romance of Fred Astaire, the loves of Lana Turner, the making of Tarzan, the Ginger Rogers voice, numerous up-close and personal interviews of Hollywood stars and starlets; and finally, "Will Hollywood Spoil Freddie Bartholomew?" from the 1936 *Liberty* magazine issue. It is enjoyable reading for the media historian. For the sampled issue of 1972: stapled magazine format with black/white editorial content and color advertising pages on coated paper stock with full-color cover (8 ¼ x 11 inches / 210 x 280 mm).
DEPT: "News of the World," "Vox Pop," letters. (spring-72).
TYPL: "The Real Romance in the Life of Fred Astaire (1936)," "The Voice of Ginger Rogers (1937)," "Tarzan and the Man Who Made Him (1945)," "Will Hollywood Spoil Freddie Bartholomew? (1936)," "Mystery of Sacco-Vanzetti, Part Two (1930)." (spring-72).
SCHL: Quarterly, 85 pp.
SPAN: Summer, 1971+?
VARIES
--Summer, 1971 - Spring?, 1973 as Liberty (ISSN: 0024-208x).
LC: AP 2.L5412
DD: 051
ISSN: 0360-3342

Library Journal/School Library Journal Previews
? - Nov?, 1973//
SEE: PREVIEWS

✤ LIES OF OUR TIMES
SUB: "A journal to correct the record."
SUB: "A magazine to correct the record."
PUBL: Institute for Media Analysis, Inc., Sheridan Square Press, Inc., 145 West 4th St., New York, NY 10012.
DESC: *"Lies of Our Times* is a magazine of media criticism. 'Our Times' are the times we live in but also the words of the *New York Times*, the most cited news medium in the U.S., our paper of record. Our 'Lies' are more than literal falsehoods; they encompass subjects that have been ignored, hypocrisies, misleading emphases, and hidden premises--the biases which systematically shape reporting. We can address only a sampling of the universe of media lies and distortions. But, we hope *LOOT* will go a long way toward correcting the record." A promotional flyer added that *"Lies of Our Times*, a monthly journal, will scrutinize the mainstream media--especially the influential *New York Times*--and analyze the ways in which they present the events of our day. We have assembled a board of contributors of more than 150 distinguished scholars and experts from many fields, including leading media critics, to review the most influential newspapers, magazines, and television programs, and to expose the misinformation, disinformation, and propaganda which all too often impede the accurate flow of information." Articles are well-written by a variety of individuals, with credentials and numerous source citations included within each. Most articles include relevant graphics. Of special note is an outstanding subject index for each issue. For the sampled issue of June, 1991 there were 400+ name and subject listings keyed to the 16 articles contained in that issue, and represented a most interesting publication. Stapled magazine format with black/white editorial content and spot color employed on the cover on coated paper stock (8 ⅜ x 11 inches / 210 x 280 mm).
DEPT: "Short Takes," short news items. (6-91).
TYPL: "The CUNY Takeover," "Politics, the Media, and the LAPD," "Covering Peace in Angola," "Of Strikes and Scabs and Workers," "School of the Americas: a Well-Kept Secret." (6-91).
SCHL: Monthly [except Aug], 24 pp.
SPAN: Jan, 1990+
DD: 302
ISSN: 1046-7912

✤ LIGHTING DIMENSIONS
SUB: "Magazine of the creative and entertainment lighting profession."
SUB: "For the entertainment lighting industry."
SUB: "The magazine for the lighting professional."
PUBL: Lighting Dimensions Associates, 135 Fifth Ave., New York, NY 10010- 7193.
DESC: "For unique coverage of lighting design and technology, turn to *Lighting Dimensions*. The only magazine that covers the entire spectrum of lighting today. Stage and studio. Architecture and interior design. If lighting is important to you -- professionally important -- *Lighting Dimensions* will keep you in touch with the best. The best work from the best designers. The best of the new products. No matter what your specialty, *Lighting Dimensions* interdisciplinary approach will

broaden your horizons." This quality publication for any professional in the lighting design and application field, is an excellent trade magazine for individuals involved with lighting operations for motion pictures, television, and other entertainment media. The emphasis is on application, with lighting director interviews, problem solving, and discussions of the state of lighting art in international locations. Full-color pictures add to understanding unique lighting applications. For the 1991 sampled issue: magazine format (8 1/8 x 10 7/8 inches / 205 x 275 mm), full color throughout on heavy coated paper stock.
DEPT: "Scenes and Events," Calendar and news briefs; "Product Update," new equiment briefs. (9/10-81). "From the Editor," "Letters," "Dates," calendar; "News," "Product News." (11-86). "From the Editor," "Letters," "Dates," "Spotlight," "News," "Product News." (1/2-91).
TYPL: "A Conversation with Bill Klages," "Beeb Salzer / From the Balcony Rail," "Television Lighting in Britain," "Lighting the Inaugural Balls," "The Future of Entertainment Lighting." (9/10-81). "Atelier International: Lighting Pioneer," "Lighting up 'The Cosby Show'," "Contracts and Letters of Agreement," "Illuminance Photometers," "IES Celebrates 80 Light Years." (11-86). "Different Strokes," "Common Bonds," "Industrial Strength Illumination," "Cinema Paradiso," "Lighting Legislation." (1/2-91).
SCHL: Monthly (Jan, 1977 - ?); Seven issues per year (1987+), 120 pp.
SPAN: Jan, 1977+
LC: PN 2091.E4L54
DD: 792/.025/05
ISSN: 0191-541x

✣ LIGHTS!

SUB: "The journal of lighting for entertainment & architecture."
PUBL: Strand Lighting, Ltd., Grant Way, Syon Lane, Isleworth, Middlesex TW7 5QD, England.
DESC: In the premiere issue for January, 1990 the publisher stated that, "In some ways *Lights* is very much the 'son of *Strandlight*'. We are still the official publication of Strand Lighting and we are still aimed particularly at you, as a lighting expert, no matter whether you are a seasoned professional lighting engineer or an enthusiastic amateur. We at Strand are still the same people, interested in your news and views as users of our products, and on hand with help and advice." Beside articles concerning new Strand equipment, and applications of same; "We will also be bringing you the views of the people who matter--the lighting designers from the worlds of film, stage, TV and music--to learn how they set about their work; and also the stars themselves, to find out how lighting influences their performance." This informative serial is printed in full color on heavy stock, and provides an excellent promotional platform for the Strand Lighting company. For the 1990 premiere issue: stapled magazine format with full-color editorial content (including cover) on heavy coated paper stock (8 1/4 x 11 5/8 inches / 210 x 295 mm).
DEPT: "News in Brief," concerning Strand lighting equipment; "New Products," for lighting applications. (1-90).
TYPL: "Black is Golden," "Galaxy Control for Berlin's Spaceship," "Toyah, Carrying Emotion With Light." (1-90).
SCHL: ?, 16 pp.
SPAN: Jan, 1990+
VARIES
--? - ? as Strandlight.
ISSN: 0958-7217

✣ LINE MONITOR, THE

SUB: "A weekly review and analysis of important regulatory and court decisions affecting broadcasters."
PUBL: Reunion Press, Inc., 5721 Magazine St., Suite 199, New Orleans, LA 70115.
DESC: As reflected in its subtitle, *The Line Monitor* provides a valuable weekly reporting service concerning broadcast regulatory developments: "Our goal is to provide the broadcast industry with timely reports on FCC and other regulatory and court decisions affecting broadcasters. Moreover, we want to provide not just a report--not just highlights, a summary, or a digest--but to provide in-depth review and analysis. We want broadcasters to know not only that the FCC has adopted a new rule, but also why it did so, how the rule will affect stations, and what stations must do to comply." The $250 yearly subscription fee may seem a bit steep to some general managers, but as editor James Popham, taking a line from the play, *Filthy Rich*, reminded his readers; "The only free cheese is in the mousetrap." It is difficult to imagine a broadcast operation that would not benefit from a subscription to this valuable publication. Newsletter format, three- hole punched; some line graphics.
DEPT: "New Construction Permits," "Proposed New FM Channels," "TV Line," newsbriefs; "Comparative Case Notes," "Broadcasters Calendar," of legal and governmental deadlines; "Quotes of the Week," "Sidelines," mini-facts. (Vol 88, # 830).
TYPL: "Main Studio Rule Clarified," "The Next Tidal Wave? FM Directional Antennas and Short Spaced Sites," "Foreign AM Channels." (Vol 88, # 830).
SCHL: Weekly (48 weeks per year), 8 pp.
SPAN: ?+

✣ LINK

SUB: "The magazine of the yellow pages medium."
PUBL: Yellow Pages Publishers Association, 340 East Big Beaver Road, Troy, MI 48083.
DESC: The official publication of the Yellow Pages Publishers Association, *Link* serves to inform, challenge, and encourage those in the Yellow Pages and advertising communities. The quality of this publication is evi-

dent in thorough editorial coverage, as well as in the dynamic layout design, utilizing color pictures throughout. Topics in two consecutive issues (Jan/Feb, 1990 & Mar/Apr, 1990) discussed directory promotions to advertisers, finding the right heading for off-beat products, the role of ASRs (Authorized Selling Representatives), trademarks/logs, and special audience Yellow Pages, such as one designed for the West Coast Asian community. Note: Volume 1, #1 was preceeded by a special issue designated "Prototype." Magazine format (8 x 10 7/8 inches / 205 x 275 mm); dynamic format design.
- DEPT: "Direct Response," letters; "Synergy," 'The media mix'; "Fine Print," 'Legal points'; "New Links," 'Expanding markets'; "Faces," 'Professional profiles'; "Progressions," 'People in the news'; "Deadlines," 'Calendar of events'; "Related Headings," 'Point of view'. (3/4-90).
- TYPL: "Holy Logos, Batman!," "Just What's So Special 'Bout Specialty Directories?," "ASRs: Who's Doing a Sell Job?" (3/4-90).
- SCHL: Bimonthly, 50 pp.
- SPAN: Nov/Dec, 1989+
- DD: 659
- ISSN: 1045-9723

✤ LINK-UP

- SUB: "The newsmagazine for users of online services: business, educational, personal."
- PUBL: Learned Information, Inc., 143 Old Marlton Pike, Medford, NJ 08055-8750.
- DESC: Notes an in-magazine subscription promotion: "If you own a modem and want to use online services more effectively, subscribe to Link-Up today! Receive the most complete coverage of the exploding online industry. Don't miss out on the most important news and articles: How-to articles, the newest online services and options, the latest databases, the most current software, electronic mail, bulletin boards, [and] educational updates." Designed for the users of these online services, Link-Up is a wonderful resource for what's new, revised, upgraded, merged, indexed and compiled in the world of information online. Articles review current electronic information services, especially new features of same, how to navigate online menus, costs involved and plans for future development. Of special note are book and software reviews of new products designed to make online database searching and retrieval even easier for new as well as seasoned information brokers. Sampled issue for 1991: stapled tabloid newspaper format, black/white editorial content with some spot color on uncoated paper stock (10 7/8 x 15 inches / 275 x 380 mm).
- DEPT: "Readers Link," letters; "Keyboard Komments," 'Thoughts and opinions on online services and computer communications' column by Don Picard; "NewsLink," late-breaking news items; "Software Review," "Book Review," "The PC Pipeline," column by Mick O'Leary; "SIG Spotlight," 'Timely briefings on special interest groups' column by Joseph A. Webb; "New Lines," 'Products and services of interest to our readers'. (5/6-91).
- TYPL: "Telebase Launches Clipping Service," "AccuWeather Brings Graphic Forecasts Online," "Switch Automatically Powers Up Micro," "NativeNet Teaches About Indigenous Cultures," "Dialog Blends Innovation with Tradition." (5/6-91).
- SCHL: Bimonthly, 40 pp.
- SPAN: Sep, 1983+
- LC: TK 5105 .L57
- DD: 004.6/16/05
- ISSN: 0739-988x
- ABST: --Computer & Control Abstracts (ISSN: 0036-8113)
  --Electrical & Electronics Abstracts (ISSN: 0036-8105)
  --Physics Abstracts. Science Abstracts. Series A. (ISSN: 0036-8091)

LISTENER

- PUBL: British Broadcasting Corporation, 35 Marylebone High St., London W1M 4AA, England.
- DESC: This spritly 35-plus page tabloid newspaper published articles of opinion, political thought, poetry, current issues, historical items, and, of course, a very complete programming section on upcoming BBC radio programs. It addressed both current issues and opinion, as well described BBC programs. An excellent program section detailed upcoming broadcasts, dramas, films, music, and special events programming. Numerous graphics.
- DEPT: "Letters to the Editor," "Master Game," chess; "Langham Diary," guest column; "Out of the Air," current events; "Books," lengthy reviews; "Television," reviews; "Radio," reviews; "Music", reviews; "Research," programming statistics; "Drama," program guide; "Music," guide; "Features," guide; "New Waves," new technology; "End Piece," editorial. (2-18-82).
- TYPL: "Race Relations: 'It's the Government, They Only Pay Lip-Service,'" "Not Regular and OTT--Nice Ideas, Shame About the Words," "Beyond the Threshold," "Why Did So Many Go to Spain 45 Years Ago to Fight?," "The Percy Out of Northumberland." (2-18-82).
- SCHL: Weekly, 35 pp.
- SPAN: Jan 16, 1929 - Jan 3, 1991//
  VARIES
  --Jan 16, 1929 - Dec 31, 1959 as Listener, The.
  --Jan 7, 1960 - Jul 27, 1967 as Listener and BBC Television Review, The.
- LC: AP 4.L4165
- ISSN: 0024-4392
- ABST: --Book Review Index (ISSN: 0524-0581)
  --Index to Book Reviews in the Humanities (ISSN: 0073-5892)

Listener, The
Jan 16, 1929 - Dec 31, 1959//
SEE: LISTENER

Listener and BBC Television Review, The
Jan 7, 1960 - Jul 27, 1967//
SEE: LISTENER

Literary Bulletin, The
Jul, 1869 - Aug, 1869//
SEE: PUBLISHER'S WEEKLY

✤ LITERATURE/FILM QUARTERLY

PUBL: Salisbury State College, Salisbury, MD 21801.
DESC: In its call to authors, the editors of *Literature/Film Quarterly* defined the structure of their scholarly journal soliciting, "Articles on individual movies, on different cinematic adaptations of a single literary work, on a director's style of adaptation, on theories of film adaptation, on the 'cinematic' qualities of authors or works, on the reciprocal influences between film and literature, on authors' attitudes toward film and film adaptations, on the role of the screen writer, and on the teaching of film." This is a serial concerning the literature of the entertainment film medium; the development, philosophy, interpretation, and especially the manner in which transformation from script to screen takes place. Published by Salisbury State College, contributing editors to the quarterly are likewise from institutions of higher learning, and articles reflect that scholarly/historical approach to literature and the screen. It provides a thoughtful approach to the dynamics of motion picture and drama. For sampled issue of 1985: stapled journal format, cover consisting of brown ink on heavy uncoated paper stock, editorial content brown ink on uncoated paper stock, no advertising, some graphics in the form of production stills at the head of each article (6 x 9 inches / 150 x 230 mm).
DEPT: "Film Review," "Book Review," "Film Notes and Queries," letters. (7-73). "Periodically Yours," editorial. (4-85).
TYPL: "Andrew Sarris Interview," "The Evolution of *Cabaret*," "Faulkner and the Film: The Two Versions of *Sanctuary*," "*Dante's Inferno:* Seeing Ken Russell Through Dante Gabriel Rossetti." (7-73). "His Girl Friday in the Cell: A Case Study of Theatre-to-Film Adaptation," "Ozmandias Melancholia: The Nature of Parody in Woody Allen's Stardus Memories," "Pictorial Imagery in Kozintsev's King Lear," "The Idea Fused in the Fact: Bergman and The Seventh Seal," "Whatever Happened to Film Noir? The Postman Always Rings Twice." (4-85).
SCHL: Quarterly, 70 pp.
SPAN: Winter, 1973+
LC: PN 1995.3 L57
DD: 791.43/05
ISSN: 0090-4260
ABST: --Abstract of English Studies (ISSN: 0001-3560)
--Film Literature Index (ISSN: 0093-6758)
--Humanities Index (ISSN: 0095-5981)
--Media Review Digest (ISSN: 0363-7778)

Literature in Performance
? - Oct, 1988?//
(ISSN: 0734-0796)
SEE: TPQ

✤ LITTLE SHOPPE OF HORRORS

PUBL: Elmer Valo Appreciation Society, c/o Richard Klemensen, PO Box 3107, Des Moines, IA 50316.
DESC: For fans of Hammer Film Productions, the *Little Shoppe of Horrors* is a warm, friendly family reunion via the medium of the printed page. Double issue numbers 10/11 for 1990 contained 170 pages of packed details, pictures, interviews, filmographies, extensive letters, video reviews; and biographies on cast, crew, production studio, distribution, exhibition and seeminly all other personnel connected with a Hammer film project. Still relatively unknown in the United States, Hammer Film Productions, Ltd., produced a rather amazing library of over 260 titles, averaging six feature films per year over a 40 year time period, covering everything from what editor Richard Klemensen calls "...comedy to thrillers; from crime to science fiction." A sampling of such titles would include "Women Without Men," "Abominable Snowman of the Himalayas," "Death of an Angel," "Dr. Jekyll and Sister Hyde," "One Million Years B.C.," and "Sword of Sherwood Forest." Equally interesting in the sampled issue were titles of Hammer films never made, including "The Black Hole of Calcutta," "Give Me Back My Body," "Jack the Ripper Goes West," "Nessie: The Loch Ness Monster," and "Wolfshead: The Legend of Robin Hood." The amount of information in a single issue is really quite incredible. It is typeset two-column 8-point with some film listings in 6-point type. This is indeed a labor of love by Editor Klemensen and the numerous volunteers who assemble this large publication. For the Hammer film fan there is no better magazine to "come home to" than *Little Shoppe of Horrors*. NOTE: neither back issues nor subscriptions are available. For sampled issue of 1990, black ink on uncoated paper stock with numerous graphics, cover consisting of full-color on heavy coated paper stock, no advertising (8 ⅜ x 11 inches / 215 x 280 mm).
DEPT: "Letters to LSoH," "Ralph's One-and-Only Traveling Fanzine Company," fanzine review; "Hammer News," news items concerning Hammer Film Produc-

TYPL: "New Blood: Second Thoughts on Hammer," "The Making of Kiss of the Vampire," "Music for Hammer Horror: An In-Depth Examination," "The Unfilmed Hammer: An A to Z Guide," "Two Titans of Animation and Their Work for Hammer: Ray Harryhausen and Jim Danforth." (7-90).
  tions, Ltd; "The Viewable Hammer," Hammer film video review column by Gary Smith; "The Keith Dudley Report," 'And other tidbits of Hammer lore' column by Keith Dudley. (7-90).
SCHL: Irregular, 170 pp.
SPAN: ?+?

Liverpool and Manchester Photographic Journal

Jan, 1857 - Dec?, 1858//
SEE: BRITISH JOURNAL OF PHOTOGRAPHY

Liverpool Photographic Journal

Jan, 1854 - Dec?, 1856//
SEE: BRITISH JOURNAL OF PHOTOGRAPHY

LOC

? - ?//
SEE: COMIC FANDOM'S FORUM

✣ LOCATION UPDATE

SUB: "The world of location filming."
SUB: "The magazine for film and video production."
SUB: "The magazine of film and video production."
PUBL: Location Update, Inc., 6922 Hollywood Blvd., Suite 612, Hollywood, CA 90028.
DESC: From an in-magazine promotion: "If you're not subscribing to *Location Update* you are missing out on what 30,000 of your colleagues are getting--the latest technical, business and location information for the entertainment industry. *Location Update*, the magazine of film and video production, gives industry professionals like you more than any other entertainment trade magazine. *Location Update*, the fastest growing entertainment trade publication, addresses the issues that concern the production community--unions, safety standards, location services, new electronic applications and much, much more." *Location Update* provides a professional approach to the broad subject of on-location scouting and production faced by a growing group of location scouts, producers and directors. This bi-monthly serial has quickly become a standard reference for on-location issues ranging from security to catering firms. A typical issue (Sep/Oct, 1988) included articles on Western "movie-towns," use of helicopters, issues in the utilization of stock footage libraries, unique Canadian locations, and commercial properties available for on-location production. A sampled issue for 1991 discussed airport location shooting, the "news or entertainment" nature of television magazine-style shows, self-regulation and state control on location services and interviews with a production designer and a group of video photographers. With a news-oriented editorial stance and liberal use of graphics, this serial is a "must" publication for film/video producers and their staffs. For sampled issue of 1991: stapled magazine format, full color throughout on coated paper stock (8 ½ x 10 ⅞ inches / 215 x 275 mm).
DEPT: "Location Forum," 'letters, opinions, stories'; "Spotlight on:," geographic profiles; "International Update," "International Cities Permit Fact Sheet," insurance and permit requirements; "California Update," "Production on Location," films shooting on-location. (9/10- 88). "Spotlight," excellent regional roundup of facilities and services; "Newsreel," news items; "Supporting Roles," locations and equipment; "Technical," "International Intrigue," "Electronic Applications," "Business," "Production Notes." (3/4-91).
TYPL: "Westerns Saddle Up for the Comeback Trail," "The Ups and Downs of Helicopters on Location," "The Virtues of 'Vice' in Miami," "Florida's Studio Development is in Full Bloom," "When the Stars are Out, Security is High." (9/10-88). "Profiles: Video Shooters," "Filming at Airports," "News or Entertainment," "The Locations Controversey," "Location Contracts--Words that Bind?" (3/4-91).
SCHL: Bimonthly, 85 pp.
SPAN: Jul/Aug, 1985+

London Calling

Sep 24, 1939 - Mar 23, 1963//
(ISSN: 0024-600x)
SEE: BBC WORLD SERVICE LONDON CALLING

Look, Listen, Learn

? - 1966//
SEE: AUDIO VISUAL JOURNAL

✣ LOS ANGELES TECHNOGRAPH

PUBL: Technograph 11251 Stagg St., Sun Valley, CA 91352.
DESC: *Technograph* is the official publication of the Los Angeles Chapter, Society of Technical Communication. Emphasis in this 12-page newsletter is on technical communications; individuals involved with the preparation, writing, and production of such items as writing technical specs, engineering projects, data communications and other areas. Many of *Technograph*'s readers are employed in the aerospace industry.
DEPT: "On the Move," personnel briefs.

TYPL: "Carol Hare Tells All How to Make a Presentation," "April Meeting Focuses on Automated Graphics," "A Logical Approach to Editing Proposals, Reports, and Manuals." (3-75).
SCHL: Bimonthly?, 12 pp.
SPAN: 1959+?

LOWBROW CINEMA

SUB: "The underbelly of film history."
PUBL: Lowbrow Cinema, PO Box 310, Bronx, NY 10473.
DESC: In the premiere issue for summer, 1982, Editor/Writer Brian Camp noted, "As the major film magazines get sucked deeper and deeper into the muddled mainstream of American critical thought, the need for an alternate voice becomes more pressing. We feel it's time to expand the mass awareness of movies to include a wider range of films and personalities. We want to acknowledge the unheralded artistry in the unlikeliest films and in the work of numerous actors, writers, directors, producers, composers, and animators who have been previously underrated, underappreciated, and unsung. We want to break down the cultural barriers that prevent large segments of the Movie/TV audience from knowing and discovering existing entertainment that is ready-made for their needs. We want to encourage creative programming on TV, creative booking in theaters and creative viewing by the audience. We want to puncture the pretensions of the critical and academic establishments and have fun doing it. ... *Lowbrow Cinema* brings impassioned writing, insightful commentary, and a sense of fun to film criticism. Where else would you find such an offbeat approach to the study of film history as 'Keeping Up With the Jones'? What other publications took the time and space to pay tribute to Vic Morrow? Join us as we seek out the unknown, the unsung, the underated and the obscure from the past, present and future of movie history. Come along for the ride as we boldly go where no film critics have gone before." It may have been typewritten, single-column format, with rub-on lettering, and paste-on pictures, but Editor Camp was forthright in his premise that *Lowbrow Cinema* was "...muscling in on the critical establishment with a fresh alternative to the star-struck mentality of mainstream movie criticism and the pretentious posturing of the film school academics." It appears to have ceased publication effective with the double issue (volume 1, #3/4) for 1985/1986. For the sampled issues of 1982 through 1986: folded newsletter style, 3-hole punched, typewritten black ink on uncoated paper, no advertising (8 ½ x 11 inches / 215 x 280 mm).
DEPT: None. (summer-82).
TYPL: "What is Lowbrow Cinema," "The Three Stooges: Clowns of the Revolution," "The Revival Scene," "Clarence Muse: Dignity on Poverty Row," "The Return of the Spectacles." (summer-82).
SCHL: Irregular, 8 pp.
SPAN: Summer, 1982 - #3/4, 1986//?

✦ LOYOLA ENTERTAINMENT JOURNAL

PUBL: Loyola of Los Angeles Entertainment Law Journal, 1441 West Olympic Blvd., Los Angeles, CA 90015.
DESC: This publication "...prints submitted articles and student notes and comments deemed worthy of publication ...on issues of Entertainment Law. Our goal is to establish a continuing dialogue between the legal community and the entertainment industry." This exceptional journal of entertainment law provides good coverage of trends, issues, and recent litigation in the fields of performing arts, mass communication, and sports. Typical articles from the first issue of 1991 included, "Proprietary Interests in Television Shows: A Production Company's View," "The Interplay of Collective Bargaining Agreements and Personal Service Contracts," and "Net Profit Participations in the Motion Picture Industry." Of special note is the departmental feature "Entertainment Law Directory," a valuable resource guide to American lawyers practising law in this specialized area. Earlier issues carried a California listing for entertainment law firms. For the sampled issues of 1983 and 1991: perfect-bound journal format, black ink on uncoated paper, with two-color cover on coated paper stock, no advertising (6 ¾ x 10 inches / 170 x 255 mm).
DEPT: "Notes and Comments." (#?-83). "Entertainment Law Directory." (#2-91).
TYPL: "The Music Business and the Sherman Act: An Analysis of the 'Economic Realities' of Blanket Licensing," "A Legal and Statistical Analysis of the National Football League Scheduling Format: Most Teams Can't Win for Losin'," "The Right of a Recording Company to Enjoin an Artist from Recording for Others," "Works Made for Hire in International Copyright Law," "The Section 110(5) Exemption for Radio Play in Commercial Establishments: A Narrowly Construed Music Copyright Haven." (#?-83). "Television and the Law in the Soviet Union," "The Changing Face of British Broadcasting," "Agents and Managers: California's Split Personality," "Copyright Transaction with Soviet Authors: The Role of VAAP," "Current and Suggested Business Practices for the Licensing of Digital Samples." (#2-91).
SCHL: Semiannual, 200 pp.
SPAN: Apr, 1981+
VARIES
--Apr, 1981 - ? as Loyola of Los Angeles Entertainment Law Journal (ISSN: 0273-4249).
LC: K 5.N8
DD: 344.73/099
ISSN: 0740-9370

Loyola of Los Angeles Entertainment Law Journal

Apr, 1981 - ?//
(ISSN: 0273-4249)
SEE: LOYOLA ENTERTAINMENT JOURNAL

✣ LPTV REPORT, THE

SUB: "News and Strategies for Community Television Broadcasting."
SUB: "Official information channel of the Community Broadcasters Association."
PUBL: Kompas/Biel & Associates, Inc., 5235 North 124th St., Suite 22, Butler, WI 53007.
DESC: "Our television--Community Television--is the natural and inevitable product of television's history. Thanks to our full power brothers, we do not have to satisfy millions of people at the same time. We are not limited by the need to speak only to widely common beliefs and attitudes. Instead, we can concentrate on the needs of the few. We can serve the interests of the small and personal. We are flexible and quick on our feet. We are the new television entrepeneurs. We deliver the community to itself." This statement in a spring, 1989 editorial reflects the essence of the Community Broadcasters Association; and *The LPTV Report*, the official publication of that organization. Whether it is referred to as "community television," or "LPTV--Low Power Television," it is a relatively new segment of the television medium whose time has come. For sampled issue of 1991: stapled magazine format, editorial content is black ink with cover in full-color, mixture of black/white, spot and full-color advertising all on coated paper stock (8 ⅜ x 10 ⅞ inches / 215 x 275 mm).
DEPT: "In Our View," editorial; "Our Readers' Comments," "LPTV and the Law," legal column by Peter Tannenwald; "The News in Community Broadcasting," column by Bob Horner; "Technical Talks," column by John H. Battison; "Supplier Side," available programming; "Supplier Solo," single product review; "At the FCC," legal developments. (4-89).
TYPL: "An NAB Walk-Through," "Baton Rouge's WKG-TV: The Little Station That Can!," "806 LPTV Applications Filed in March Window," "Cables Cited for EEO Violations." (4-89).
SCHL: Monthly, 40 pp.
SPAN: Jan, 1986+
ISSN: 0892-5585

✣ LUCASFILM FAN CLUB, THE

PUBL: Lucasfilm Fan Club, Inc., 537 Olathe St., Unit C, Aurora, CO 80011.
DESC: Loving editorial care and design craftmanship are evident in a sample issue of *The Lucasfilm Fan Club*. This fanzine has "class," with full-color pictures, clean layout design, spot-color enhancements, and a good writing style. Articles discuss new projects, and the status of current productions. Several interviews with feature actors are presented, and a general sense of Lucasfilm activities is conveyed. For the sampled issue of 1988: stapled magazine format, black/white and color graphics on coated paper stock, limited advertising pertaining to Lucasfilm motion picture collectibles (8 ⅜ x 10 ⅞ inches / 215 x 275 mm).
DEPT: "The Fan Forum," letters; "Collections," collectable Lucasfilm items; "Lucasfilm Games," product review; "Inside ILM," news of Industrial Light and Magic. (fall-88).
TYPL: "Foreign Star Wars Collectibles," "Is it Real or a Replicar? Behind the Scenes of 'Tucker: The Man & His Dream'," "Joanne Whalley, Revealing the Secrets of Sorsha," "Sneak Preview: Indiana Jones and the Last Crusade," "The Land Before Time: A Preview of a New Animation Masterpiece Presented by George Lucas and Steven Spielberg." (fall-88).
SCHL: Quarterly, 14 pp.
SPAN: Fall, 1987+
DD: 791
ISSN: 1041-5122

✣ LÜRZER'S INTERNATIONAL ARCHIVE

SUB: "Ads, TV and posters world-wide."
PUBL: American Showcase, Inc., 724 Fifth Avenue, New York, NY 10019.
DESC: "Your international spy, bringing the world's best creative thinking to your desk six times a year. Look, we all know it's a jungle out there. From Minneapolis to Milan, advertising creatives are doing battle in the war for innovative ideas. Some of them have a secret weapon. A worldwide overview of the most current trends. The newest and most innovative print, television and poster advertising. Span the globe without leaving your desk! Stimulate your creativity, feast your eyes and spark your imagination with *Archive*. The only magazine for advertising executives that's devoted exclusively to ads worldwide." This full-color, 130 page resource on heavy coated paper stock is packed with creative ideas for the advertising/marketing of products and services world-wide. Foreign language ad campaigns are translated into English, with full credit given to the advertising agency, art director, copywriter, photographer, illustrator, production company, director, and camera operator. Interestingly, all editorial pages (including front cover) have a small scissors and dotted line along the length of the page, encouraging readers to clip and save items for future reference. For today's competitive advertising community, this is one of the better creative resources. Note: this serial is published in various languages, including the original German edition, known as Lüurzer's Archiv (ISSN: 0175-3436). For the sampled 1990 issue: magazine format (8 ⅛ x 11 ¼ inches / 205 x 285 mm).
DEPT: "Interview," "Accessories," "Ad Agencies," "Audio & Video," "Automotive," "Banking, Insurance," "Beverages: Alcoholic," "Beverages: Non-alcoholic," "Children," "Computers," "Corporate Identity," "Cosmetics," "Spot Check," 'Who's producing the latest TV spots'; "Fashion," "Food," "House & Garden," "Future Events," "Miscellaneous," "Office Equip-

ment," "Pharmaceuticals," "Photo," "Public Events," "Retailers," "Sports," "Travel & Leisure," "Music Beat," 'Who's composing the latest jingles'. (6-90).
TYPL: "I am an Antenna." (6-90).

SCHL: Six issues per year, 130 pp.
SPAN: Feb, 1989+
DD: 659 11
ISSN: 0893-0260

M

MAC
Jul 17, 1967 - Dec 21, 1967//
SEE: ADWEEK

MAC/WA
Jul 13, 1967//
SEE: ADWEEK

MAC/WA
Dec 28, 1967? - Jan 4, 1970?//
SEE: ADWEEK

MAC/Western Advertising
Jan 12, 1970 - Mar 2, 1970//
SEE: ADWEEK

MAC/Western Advertising News
Mar 9, 1970 - Nov 17, 1980//
(ISSN: 0194-4789)
SEE: ADWEEK

✣ MADISON AVENUE
SUB: "The magazine of New York advertising."
SUB: "The advertising magazine."
PUBL: Madison Avenue Magazine, 369 Lexington Ave., New York, NY 10017.
DESC: As the subhead implies, *Madison Avenue* is the trade vehicle for news of the New York advertising community. The magazine is renowned for its in-depth analyses of advertising campaigns that were both successful and unsuccessful. Strategies, budgets, problems and other elements connected with those campaigns are evaluated and discussed. Of special note are published segments on media buying, industry product features, discussions of creative campaigns, and features on advertising in other selected cities besides New York City.
DEPT: "Newsletter," briefs; "Review Board," panel discussion of advertising issues; "Agency Creative Campaign," spotlighting one agency's work; "Afterword," editorial and comment. (9-76).
TYPL: "Media Buying Services and the Fine Art of Negotiating," "Why Advertising People in Glass Houses Should Throw Stones," "Television: All You Need to Know About Program practices," "How to Succeed in Radio Buying, Without Numbers." (9-76).
SCHL: Monthly, 80 pp.
SPAN: Apr, 1958+
LC: HF 5801.M13
DD: 659.1/05
ISSN: 0024-9483
ABST: --ABI/Informer
--Business Periodical Index (ISSN: 0007-6961)
--InfoBank
--Management Contents

✣ MAG TRACKS
SUB: "A newsletter for A/V professionals published by 3M's Magnetic Media Division."
PUBL: Magnetic Media Division, 3M Corporation, ?, MN.
DESC: This brief, four-page newsletter provides instruction and information on various magnetic media products used by audio and video professionals. *Mag Tracks* showcases 3M products and its talented staff. Articles in the sampled issue included a very informative item describing the basics of digital audio tape recording; another concerned the adoption of digital audio by a major Midwest recording studio; and an article by the Business Manager, 3M Professional Audio/Video Products of the Magnetic Media Division, concerned the slow but steady growth of digital audio recording in the American market. For the sampled issue of 1988: black ink with red spot-color ink and numerous graphics on coated paper stock in folded newsletter format (8 ½ x 11 inches / 215 x 280 mm).
DEPT: None. (spring-88).
TYPL: "The Basics of Digital Audio Recording," "Digital Then, Now & Forever," "Digital Audio Growing Slowly but Steadily to 50% of Pro Market." (spring-88).
SCHL: Quarterly, 4 pp.
SPAN: Winter, 1987+

✣ MAGAZINE, THE
PUBL: The Film and Television Study Center, 6233 Hollywood Blvd., Suite 203, Hollywood, CA 90028.
DESC: This publication for the non-trade events in film, radio, and television occurring in Southern California is amply illustrated, with emphasis on archival acquisitions and center activities. It is published by the Film and Television Center, a non-profit cultural organization.
DEPT: "Archival Acquisitions," new arrivals at the center; "Calendar," Film-Radio-TV cultural events in southern California. (11-75).

TYPL: "USC Cinema Library Spans Years," "History Criticism Program Grows and Blossoms," "Films for Children." (11-75).
SCHL: Bimonthly, except Jul/Aug, 8 pp.
SPAN: 1976+
LC: PN 1993.M

Magazine Age

Jan, 1980 - Dec, 1985//
(ISSN: 0194-2506)
SEE: INSIDE MEDIA

✧ MAGAZINE & BOOKSELLER

SUB: "The business paper of independent distribution."
SUB: "The sales journal of periodical distribution." (? - Sep, 1960).
SUB: "Monthly directory and sales guide for retailers." (Oct, 1960+).
PUBL: North American Publishing Co., 401 North Broad St., Philadelphia, PA 19108.
DESC: [Bestsellers]: Beginning as *Newsdealer*, and later *Bestsellers*, the purpose of this serial was to serve the retail merchant, the "exhibitor" of printed materials, including magazines, newspapers, comics, childrens books, records, and other related products. In 1960, almost a third of those merchants were drugstores; another third consisted of grocery stores, and *Bestsellers* aimed its editorial content to that audience, discussing techniques of display, the realities of distribution, and new printed product available for public consumption and store profit. Numerous graphics, especially of display items, and showcase retail stores.
DEPT: "Sound Off," letters; "Editorial," "Bestseller Sampler," "The Box Score," distribution stats; "New Paperbacks," "Magazine Directory," "Children's Books." (1-61).
TYPL: "A Hard Look at Soft Sales," "Avon's 20th Anniversary Year," "What's the Score?" (1-61).
SCHL: Monthly, 35 pp.
SPAN: 1945+
VARIES
--1945? - ? as Newsdealers' Bestsellers.
--Mar, 1946 - Sep, 1960 as Newsdealer.
--Oct, 1960 - ? as Bestsellers (ISSN: 0005-9730).
--Mar, 1972 - ? as Bestseller Business.
--? - Jan, 1982 as Marketing Bestsellers (ISSN: 0164-9876).
ABSORBED
--IPDA Profit Ways (ISSN: 0194-6668), ?
LC: Z 284.M27
DD: 338.8/260705
ISSN: 0744-3102

✧ MAGAZINE BUSINESS

SUB: "The how-to newsletter for members of the Successful Magazine Publishers Group."
PUBL: Randall Publishing Co., PO Box 2029, Tuscaloosa, AL 35403.
DESC: *Magazine Business* is the monthly "how-to" newsletter of the 3,000 plus member Successful Magazine Publishers Group, a trade association whose function it is to improve the "bottom line" by improved circulation, layout design, advertising, and editorial content. The newsletter compliments parent bimonthly publication, *Successful Magazine Publishing*, by providing helpful advice on all aspects of magazine publishing. Articles tend to be issue or problem oriented, and make the price of annual membership dues a worthwhile investment. Two-color newsletter format; graphics.
DEPT: "Publine: Our Members Call for Answers," Q&A on magazine publishing; "Magazine Business Notebook," 'Update of news and trends in publishing'; "On Members' Minds," commentary of Don Fowler, SMPG Membership Director; "The Suppliers' Side," commentary column by Bob Scroggins; "People & Publications," "PubNet," 'The publishing industry's network for: jobs (wanted or available), announcements & items for sale'. (10-89).
TYPL: "Avoiding Toll-Free Traps," "Giving Classifieds a Boost," "The Successful Follow-up Call." (10-89).
SCHL: Monthly, 8 pp.
SPAN: Apr, 1989+

✧ MAGAZINE DESIGN & PRODUCTION

SUB: "From concept through distribution."
SUB: "The authority on production technology."
PUBL: South Wind Publishing Co., 8340 Mission Rd., Suite 106, Praire Village, KS 66206.
DESC: A trade serial for press management, *Magazine Design & Production* probes problems of design, clients, supplies, new technology, circulation, paper, desktop publishing, and anything else "from concept through distribution." Publisher South Wind approaches magazine publication as one of the most exciting areas of communication available today, maintaining a considered perspective that it is a business, and therefore one which must be balanced between the artistic and "bottom-line" success. Each monthly issue is thematic. A sampling of cover themes for 1990 included "Magazines and the Environment," a discussion of the debate between plastic or paper wrapping, and the use of recycled paper in the printing process; and "Color in Magazines;" "Are Machines Taking Over?" with the subtitle, "Maintaining the Balance Between Experience and Technology." Other issues covered new technologies in the field of electronic publishing. An entire issue was on publication paper and emerging technologies in the area of binding. Of special note are a valuable yearly series of special issues. These include "The Annual Production Issue," "The Annual

Buyer's Guide," and "The Ozzie Awards for Publication Design Excellence," a wonderful showcase for the best in cover and editorial design for the past year. Readers will find a wealth of pragmatic advice and color graphics within the covers of *Magazine Design & Production*, a publication deserving of its own "Ozzie." Note: while the December, 1991 cover displayed a new publication title of *MD&P*, the publisher's statement indicated that the official title for this publication remains *Magazine Design & Production* (ISSN: 0882-049x). For the sampled issue of 1991: magazine format (8 x 10¾ inches / 205 x 275 mm), full color throughout on coated paper stock.
DEPT: "First Edition," commentary; "Art Direction," "On Management," "Electronic Prepress," "Datebook," "News Clips," "Desktop Design," "Portfolio," "Goods & Services," "Supplier Showcase," "Job Bank." (4-88). "Datebook," "Letters," "News Clips," "Portfolio," "Magazine Notes," "On Paper," "Goods & Services," "Supplier Showcase," "Job Bank," "First Edition," column by Michael Scheibach; "In Production," column by Constance Sidles; "Fifth Wave," column by Maureen Waters. (8-89). "First Edition," editorial column by Michael Scheibach; "Letters," "News Clips," "Magazine Notes," "Calendar," "Earth Notes," interesting departmental feature regarding recycling and other Earth-friendly issues in magazine publishing; "On Paper," "Technology Update," "Production Services," "Paper Trends," column by Eric O. Edelmann; "Tips for the Trade," column by Jonathan Kaplan. (3-91).
TYPL: "Guide to CAP Systems," "Playing the match Game," "Desktop or Bust!," "Micros and the Graphic Designer," "Magazine Distribution: The Private Delivery Alternative." (4-88). "Quality and Art Direction," "Color Proofs: All Roles for All Players," "The Prepress Operation," "Centralized Postage Payment System," "The ABCs of Paper Grades." (8-89). "Color in Magazines," "The Emergence of Desktop Color," "Color Proofing," "The Match Game." (3-91).
SCHL: Monthly, 55 pp.
SPAN: May, 1985+
WITH SUPPLEMENT
--For Advertisers, ?+
LC: Z 253.5 .M26
DD: 686
ISSN: 0882-049x

Magazine Industry Newsletter
Nov, 1947 - Sep 24, 1970//
SEE: MEDIA INDUSTRY NEWSLETTER

✤ MAGAZINE MATTER
SUB: "Newsletter of the Magazine Division -- AEJMC."
PUBL: Association for Education in Journalism and Mass Communication, Department of Journalism, Southwest Texas State University, San Marcos, TX 78666.
DESC: Magazine Division Head, Sammye Johnson, writing in the February, 1989 issue of this newsletter made this observation: "Research about magazines, whether involving magazine journalism or the magazine publishing industry, has been slim. ... I believe we need more systematic studies of magazine journalism and the magazine publishing industry. Unfortunately, the vastness of the field in general has made it difficult to study. We have tended to be fragmented. As educators and researchers, we need to develop methodological definitions that will allow us to build on various studies and to provide linkages." *Magazine Matter* seeks to encourage the academic/research community to move from the study of magazine descriptive content analysis to the study of process and effect in the commercial magazine industry. For the sampled issue of 1989: newsletter format, three-hole punched, black ink editorial content on uncoated paper stock (8 ½ x 11 inches / 215 x 280 mm).
DEPT: None. (2-89).
TYPL: "Annual Magazine Educator Seminar," "Thoughts After ASME's Seminar." (2-89).
SCHL: ?, 4 pp.
SPAN: ?+

Magazine of the Oxford Film Society
May, 1946 - ?, 1946//
SEE: SEQUENCE

✤ MAGAZINES IN DEPTH
SUB: "The research publication of the Magazine Division, AEJMC."
PUBL: Assocation for Education in Journalism and Mass Communication, Magazine Division, Division of Journalism, Florida A&M University, Tallahassee, FL 32307.
DESC: James Autry, President, Magazine Group, Meredith Corporatiion, made this comment concerning the explosive growth of periodicals in North America during the decade of the 1980s: "Today there are some 16,000 magazines in the United States, with 3,100 in the consumer category. And you wonder why the newsstands and the mails are crowded!" The comment is appropriate both to the commercial magazine field, and the need for academic programs to fully prepare journalism majors for this rapidly developing employment arena. *Magazines in Depth*, a publication of the Association for Education in Journalism and Mass Communication, links together the reality of commercial magazine publishing with the academic desire to prepare men and women with the necessary toolskills to enter that field. It is a fascinating and informative newsletter for the print publication medium. For the sampled issue of 1989: three-hole punched, folded newsletter format, no graphics, editorial content consisting of black ink on uncoated paper stock (8 ⅜ x 11 inches / 215 x 280 mm).
DEPT: None. (1-89).

TYPL: "The Golden Age of Magazines," "Service Journalism Today," "Implications for Teaching." (1-89).
SCHL: ?, 6 pp.
SPAN: ?+

✢ MAGAZINEWEEK

SUB: "The weekly publication of record for the magazine industry."
PUBL: Lighthouse Business Publications, 16 South Wesley, Mount Morris, IL 61054.
DESC: It is difficult imagaining a magazine publisher who is not also an avid reader of *MagazineWeek*, a tabloid news magazine filled with late- breaking news of the serial publication industry. Thorough, authoritative coverage is provided in the areas of advertising, design and layout, production, circulation, mailing lists, and other aspects of magazine publishing. Each news issue is divided into logical sections entitled, "Advertising News," "Edit & Design News," "Production News," "Circulation News," and "List News." Among a number of outstanding departmental features are a vibrant "Letters" column, filled with sharp-tongued comments and loving tributes, and a healthy dose of "common-sense" management; "Jack Edmonston on Magazine Marketing," discussing the realities of reaching the "target market"; "Alex Brown on Magazine Production," discussing problems, successes, and trends in production plant management; "Linda Ruth on Single-Copy Sales," who covers the difficult strategies connected with single-copy salesmanship; and "Stuart Jordan on Direct Marketing," on list buying, management and execution. Each issue includes an in-depth profile of a current successful publication, providing complete details from circulation to cost-per-thousand (CPM), revenues, direct costs, marginal contribution, fixed expenses, and the all-important net profit margin. This is a "must-read" for serial publishing management. Purchase of *Successful Magazine Publishing* in fall, 1989 brought about the special bimonthly section, *MagazineWeek*, which had its debut in the January 29, 1990 issue. For the sampled issue of 1991: large tabloid stapled magazine format, editorial content consisting of black ink with spot color on coated paper stock and full-color advertisements (10 ¾ x 14 ½ inches / 275 x 370 mm).
DEPT: "Shorts," newsbriefs; "People," personnel newsbriefs; "Editor's Notebook," column by Byron Freney; "Advertising News," large second section concerning magazine advertising; "Jack Edmonston on Magazine Marketing," advertisement critique column by Jack Edmonston; "Edit & Design News," large second section concerning magazine layout and design; "Don Nicholas on Magazine Trends," design critique column by Don Nicholas; "Production News," large second section on magazine production; "Circulation News," large second section for magazine publishing; "Pete Savage on Subscription Marketing," magazine subscription critique column by Pete Savage; "List News," magazine mailing lists; "Profit Profile," informative magazine profile and critique column by Jeff Marcus; "Noted & Quoted," gleanings from recent publications. (10-30-89).
TYPL: "Rizzoli Plans Push into U.S. Market," "Mailers Resist New Delivery Standards," "Advertisers Take Publishers to Task," "Iacocca to America: 'Toughen Up or Lose International Market War Forever'," "GATF Finds Causes and Solutions for Plate Blinding," "Exec Urges Discounts for Frequent Users of Subscription Agencies." (10-30-89).
SCHL: Weekly [50 issues per year], 40 pp.
SPAN: Nov 8?, 1987+
ABSORBED
--Successful Magazine Publishing (ISSN: 0892-6581), Jan 29, 1990.
DD: 070 11
ISSN: 0895-2124

Magnetic Film and Tape Recording

Feb, 1954 - Oct, 1956//
SEE: TAPE RECORDING

MAHINS MAGAZINE

PUBL: John Mahin, Number 200, Monroe St., Chicago, IL.
DESC: "It is not the purpose of *Mahin's Magazine* to supplant any other publication devoted to advertising interests. The special field of bringing the truths of psychology and advertising into closer harmony will be given the largest attention. It is the hope of the publishers to do something efficient toward reducing advertising to an exact science." Providing a mixture of home-spun humor/stories and the new field of advertising psychology, *Mahin's Magazine* attempted an ongoing definition of the role of print advertising to the American consumer. Numerous graphic reprints of newspaper and magazine advertisements.
DEPT: "Editorial." (8-02).
TYPL: "The Psychological Value of Fusion in its Relation to the Association of Advertisements," "The Barnum Principle in Advertising," "Who Pays the Publisher: Subscriber or Advertiser?," "Wholesale Clothing Advertisements." (8-02).
SCHL: Monthly, 40 pp.
SPAN: Apr, 1902 - Jun, 1904//
ABSORBED BY
--Judicious Advertising and Advertising Experience, Jun, 1904.
LC: HF 5801.M2

Mail Order Connection

? - ?//
SEE: DIRECT RESPONSE SPECIALIST, THE

✤ MAIL ORDER DIGEST

SUB: "Official newsletter of National Mail Order Association."
PUBL: National Mail Order Association, 5818 Venice Blvd., Los Angeles, CA 90019.
DESC: As the official newsletter of the National Mail Order Association, this monthly serial details trends, reports on regulatory actions in Washington, D.C., and comments on numerous success stories by direct mail marketers. Articles are forthright in their approach to this much maligned industry, reporting on the "good, the bad, and the ugly." Typical topics for one sampled issue included: the advantage of mailing direct into Canada, new twists in mailing lists, the problems of fax fraud, and the Federal Trade Commission acting to protect charities. Information in many cases is very applicable to readers' own projects in development. For sampled issue of 1989: three-hole punched, loose-leaf newsletter format, black ink, typewritten on light-beige uncoated paper stock, no graphics or advertising (8 ½ x 11 inches / 215 x 280 mm).
DEPT: "International Market Place," 'Listings of products from world-wide sources considered suitable for mail order promotion'; "Washington Newsletter," 'Rulings, regulations, reports of federal, state and local government agencies of concern to mail marketers'. (10-89).
TYPL: "Enclosed Please Find Check for $5 Million," "Telemarketing Customers -- How to Listen to Them," "Over Half of Households Find Catalogs Useful," "How Much Can One Cent Buy," "17 Common Direct Mail Mistakes -- And How to Avoid Them." (10-89).
SCHL: Monthly, 8 pp.
SPAN: ?+

Mail Order Journal

1897 - Mar, 1916//
SEE: NATIONAL ADVERTISING

MAILBAG, THE

SUB: "A journal of direct mail advertising."
SUB: "All about direct-mail advertising." (? - Mar, 1927).
SUB: "The magazine of efficiency in advertising and selling." (Apr, 1927 - Aug, 1927).
PUBL: The Mailbag Publishing Co., 510 Caxton Bldg., Cleveland, OH.
DESC: "A publication before its time," might describe this short-lived serial of direct mail advertising. With an average 15 pages of advertisements and editorial content in a small-journal format size, the subscriber market for direct-mail advertising did not appear to be sufficiently large enough to sustain publication. Most issues consisted of one to three articles, and a number of brief "idea" items. Small square format in early issues, moving to journal format in latter series. Numerous graphics, mostly by advertisers.
DEPT: None. (7-18). "The Very Idea," various direct-mail ideas. (7-27).
TYPL: "A Marshall Field Classic," "Direct Advertising for Conventions," "From Armor Plate to Razor Blades." (7-18). "On Writing to Sell," "Selling the Specialty by Mail," "Good Will Via the Routine Letter," "Coupons in Magazine Ads." (7-27).
SCHL: Monthly, 50 pp.
SPAN: Apr, 1917 - Aug, 1927//
MERGED WITH
--Postage (to form) Postage and the Mailbag, Sep, 1927.
LC: HF 5801.M3

MAKING FILMS

SUB: "The magazine for the professional filmmaker."
SUB: "The magazine for the Eastern professional filmmaker."
PUBL: R-E-M Publications, 285 Madison Ave., New York, NY 10017.
DESC: [Making Films in New York]: This magazine was concerned with "technical developments, new equipment information and comprehensive appraisals of the industry." Primarily for the professional filmmaker in New York and the Eastern region of the nation, special emphasis was placed upon important filmmakers.
DEPT: "Newsreels," news of major films ad commercials shooting in New York area; "Multi-Media," new multiple-media shows and development; "Labs and Stock," new information about eastern film labs or film stock.
TYPL: "Feature Filmmaking Returns to Astoria," "A and B Equals Problem Solved," "Lew Gifford on animation."
SCHL: Eight issues per year, 55 pp.
SPAN: Mar, 1967 - Dec, 1975/Jan, 1976//
VARIES
--Mar, 1967 - Oct/Nov, 1975 as Making Films in New York.
LC: TR 845 .M34
DD: 778.5/3/0973

Making Films in New York

Mar, 1967 - Oct/Nov, 1975//
SEE: MAKING FILMS

✤ MANAGEMENT AND SALES DIVISION NEWSLETTER

PUBL: Broadcast Education Association, Management and Sales Committee, Washington, DC.
DESC: This brief, four-page newsletter for the Management and Sales Division group of the Broadcast Education Association, a pedagogical organization for college and university broadcast educators, serves two primary functions: to provide news concerning current

professorial and professional activities; and to provide a continuing forum on the evolving nature of broadcast management/sales and its application to the college classroom. The newsletter is an excellent membership benefit of the Broadcast Education Association. Glued magazine format (8 ½ x 11 inches / 215 x 280 mm), printed black ink on light grey paper stock.
DEPT: None. (1-90). None. (3-90).
TYPL: "Competition for Cable: Is the System the Solution?," "Management and Economic Implications of Bundling and Block Booking of Television and Cable Programming." (1-90). "Convention Activities," "BEA Management and Sales Committee Regional Mini-Conference." (3-90).
SCHL: Quarterly, 4 pp.
SPAN: ?+

✦ MANAGEMENT COMMUNICATION QUARTERLY

SUB: "An international journal."
PUBL: Sage Publications, PO Box 5084, Newbury Park, CA 91359-9924.
DESC: In the premiere issue for August, 1987, Editors JoAnne Yates, Christine Kelly, and Paul C. Feingold told readers, "With this first issue, we introduce a journal that we hope will soon become a familiar friend. *McQ* grew out of and reflects the accelerating coverage of traditionally distinct fields of communication. Within the management school curriculum, at least five different communication areas--management writing and speaking, and interpersonal, organizational, and corporate communication--have a common focus on managerial and organizational effectiveness. This managerial focus creates a need for a journal that will foster research, discussion, and criticism among the many academicians and practitioners involved in communication research. *McQ* was founded for sharing research and for shaping an interdisciplinary approach to management communication." Later issues put this philosophy into this statement of purpose: "*Management Communication Quarterly* is devoted to the advancement of both theory and practice in the field of management communication. Authors are encouraged to submit original theoretical and empirical manuscripts from a wide variety of methodological perspectives covering a range of topics related to management communication in such areas as managerial writing, managerial presentation, interpersonal communication in organizations, organizational communication, and external communication. Criteria for publication include relevance to management, originality, methodological rigor, and potential significance to management communication. *McQ* also features a Communication Forum section that will include refereed book reviews, guest commentaries, notes from professionals in the field, and other nonresearch pieces. Items for this section will be selected by the editors." This publishers' statement describes the purpose, scope, and flavor of the quarterly journal. *Management Communication Quarterly* provides a nice balance between academic theory and corporate application of ideas and structure. The sampled issue for February, 1988 was the first themed- issue for the journal and focused on "Communication and Conflict Styles in Organizations." A latter issue for May, 1990 was devoted to "Written Management Communication." For the sampled issue of 1988: perfect-bound journal format, black ink on uncoated paper stock, cover consists of red ink on coated paper stock, limited advertising (5 ¼ x 8 ½ inches / 135 x 215 mm).
DEPT: "Communication Forum," umbrella title for commentary and research departments; "Commentary," "Research Instrument." (2-88).
TYPL: "Communication and Interpersonal Conflict in Organizations," "Assessing the Hall Conflict Management Survey," "Assessing the Thomas-Kilmann Conflict MODE Survey," "Assessing the Putnam-Wilson Organizational Communication Conflict Instrument (OCCI)," "Measuring Interpersonal Conflict in Organizations." (2-88).
SCHL: Quarterly, 150 pp.
SPAN: Aug, 1987+
DD: 658
ISSN: 0893-3189

Many Worlds of Music, The

Nov, 1964 - Fall, 1987//
(ISSN: 0045-317x)
SEE: BMI: MUSICWORLD

MARCONI REVIEW, THE

PUBL: GEC-Marconi Electronics, Ltd., St. Mary's House, Victoria Road, Chelmsford, Essex, England.
DESC: In the initial issue of October, 1928, Senatore G. Marconi set the tone of this publication: "One of the principal objects of this new *Review* is to make known what is being achieved by the combination of Industrial and Scientific Research, and to endeavour to show that swiftly moving scientific progress and rapid technical advance, which together can bring about achievements useful to mankind, demand industrial flexibility rather than industrial stabilization." It is a highly technical series of electronics developments by staff of the Marconi Company (later: GEC-Marconi Electronics Limited). Numerous graphics and schematics; no advertising.
DEPT: "Marconi News and Notes." (10-28). "Book Review." (1st Qtr-83).
TYPL: "A Chapter in the History of the Marconi Beam," "Portable Short Wave Military Transmitter and Receiver," "Discussion on Short Wave Fading." (10-28). "Height Measurement by Quadrilateration," "An Approximate Method of Estimating the Detection Performance of a Scanning Radar," "New Developments in Optical Shaft-Angle Encoder Design." (1st Qtr-83).

SCHL: Monthly (Oct, 1928 - Dec, 1930); Bimonthly (Jan, 1931 - Apr, 1937); Quarterly [Irregular at times] (May, 1937+), 45 pp.
SPAN: Oct, 1928 - 1st Quarter?, 1983//
SUSPENDED
--Oct, 1939 - Sep, 1944.
ABSORBED BY
--GEC Journal of Research, 1983.
LC: TK 5700.M3
DD: 621.38405
ISSN: 0025-2883
ABST: --Communication Abstracts
--Computer & Control Abstracts (ISSN: 0036-8113)
--Electrical & Electronics Abstracts (ISSN: 0036-8105)
--Electronics and Communications Abstracts Journal (ISSN: 0361-3313)
--Engineering Index Annual (ISSN: 0360-8557)
--Engineering Index Bioengineering Abstracts (ISSN: 0736-6213)
--Engineering Index Energy Abstracts (ISSN: 0093-8408)
--Engineering Index Monthly (1984) (ISSN: 0742-1974)
--Engineering Index Monthly (ISSN: 0013-7960)
--Exceptional Child Abstracts
--Excerpta Medica
--ISMEC Bulletin (ISSN: 0306-0039)
--International Aerospace Abstracts (ISSN: 0020-5842)
--Nuclear Science Abstracts (ISSN: 0029-5612)
--Physics Abstracts. Science Abstracts. Series A. (ISSN: 0036-8091)
--Pollution Abstracts with Indexes (ISSN: 0032-3624)
--Safety Science Abstracts Journal (ISSN: 0160-1342)

Marconigraph

Oct, 1912 - Mar, 1913//
SEE: WIRELESS AGE, THE

Margaret Wentworth's Sign Post

Oct 30, 1930 - May, 1948//
SEE: BROADWAY SIGN POST

✣ MARKEE

SUB: "The Southeast film & video news magazine."
SUB: "Film & video news magazine."
SUB: "Communicating the latest in film & video news."
SUB: "For the Southeast and Southwest."
PUBL: HJK Publications, Inc., 655 Fulton St., Suite 9, Sanford, FL 32771.
DESC: *Markee* "...magazine has been designed to facilitate the distribution of information about the film and video industry of the Southeastern United States and all it encompasses." The Southeast, the so-called "Third Coast," is emerging as a major segment of the audio, video, and film industry. This is partly due to the diversity in the area; ranging from independent production companies and free-lancers located in the Blue Ridge Mountains, all the way through to full traditional corporate film and video production studios and assorted sound stages in Orlando, Florida. Each issue highlights two specific production locations. In the November, 1991 issue: Tennessee and Arizona; in the December, 1991 issue: "Shooting the Islands," and New Mexico. *Markee* celebrates the excitement of this growing Southeastern industry, while recognizing that "Show Business," is indeed "business" in today's society. Well recommended for those engaged in film, video, or audio in the Southeastern United States. For sampled issue of 1991: stapled magazine format, editorial content consisting of mixture of black ink, spot and full color pages, cover being full-color all on coated paper stock (8 ⅜ x 10 ⅞ inches / 215 x 275 mm).
DEPT: "Cutaways," production newsbriefs; "Commercial Production," "Feature Filming," "Facility News," "Eye on Orlando," "Teleproduction," "Corporate Production," "Audio." (9-89).
TYPL: "Every Frame a Cameo," "Cinematography for Commercials," "Moving-Frame Cinematography Using Dollies, Cranes and Aerial Mounts," "The Man Who Trains Fish," "Cinematography-A Touch of the Dutch." (9-89).
SCHL: Monthly, 65 pp.
SPAN: Feb, 1986+

Marketing & Media Decisions

May, 1979 - Dec, 1990//
(ISSN: 0195-4296)
SEE: MEDIAWEEK

Marketing Bestsellers

? - Jan, 1982//
(ISSN: 0164-9876)
SEE: MAGAZINE & BOOKSELLER

MARKETING / COMMUNICATIONS

SUB: "The magazine of marketing/communications management."
SUB: "Journal for advertisers."
SUB: "The weekly magazine of advertising, marketing, and sales."
PUBL: Decker Communications, 501 Madison Ave., New York, NY 10022.
DESC: "Marketing-Communications" is published for those working in the advertising and marketing fields: "Their work and their interests are not quite the same as everyone elses. They live with competition, change, and innovation. They are strongly oriented toward people, their emotions and their motivations. Their opinions carry weight in marketing, advertising,

media, packaging decisions." A glossy serial providing news of advertising and marketing campaigns, strategy and philosophy. Numerous graphics.
DESC: [Printers' Ink]: This long-published weekly periodical provided a much needed service to the advertising and marketing industry, even though its title would lead one to believe that it serviced only the printing industry. *Printers Ink* during the 1930s period was a small format serial with approximately 10-12 articles per issue concerning advertising and marketing techniques. In January, 1942, *Printers Ink* became a full-sized periodical with greater emphasis on graphic layout and advertising strategies/campaigns and remained so until its decline in the 1960s and eventual demise in 1968. It was continued by *Marketing/Communications*, for a one year period before its ultimate cessation in 1968.
DEPT: "The Week's News," "Editorials," "The Little Schoolmaster's Class," (1-5-40). "Letters to the Editor," "Advertising Parade," "Newsreel Picture Spread," "Which Ad Pulled Best?," "New Ideas," "Washington," "Industrial Advertising," "Newspapers," "Newsmakers," "Account Changes," "Dates," "Notes on New Books," "Helpful Information," "Editors Page," (10-7-55). "Publisher's View," "Which Ad Pulled Best?," "David North's Column," "Marketing Trendletter," "Jerry dela Femina's Column," "New Products and Packaging," "Alen Dodd's Column," "Around the World Trendletter," "Dates of Conventions and Meetings," "Letters," "Walter Joyce's Note," "After Hours," (10-67).
TYPL: "Things to Salesman About His Firm's Advertising," "Half-Page for Broccoli: How Two Immigrants Built Big Business," "Analysis of War Picture Shows Ways Open for Jump in U.S. 1940 Exports," "Novelty Direct Mail Brings Customers to Dealers," (1-5-40). "Will New Competition Revive Private Food Brands?," "Deals Can Deal You Out of Business," "FTC Rebuffed in Farm Journal Merger Case," "How to Sell Ad Agency Stock," "Industrial Advertisers Want More Agency, Research Help," (10-7-55). "The Odd Couple: Marx and Marketing," "Harper's Happy Hippies," "The Terrible Twelve Clients," (10-67).
SCHL: Semimonthly (1888 - 1889); Weekly (1890 - 1964); Semimonthly (1965 - Sep, 1967); Monthly (Oct, 1967+), 120 pp.
SPAN: Jul 15, 1888 - Jan, 1972//
FROM MERGER OF
--Advertisers' Gazette (and) Newspaper Reporter, 1888.
ABSORBED
--Printers Ink Monthly (ISSN: 0738-6133), Dec, 1942
--Tide, Mar, 1959.
--Consumer Advertising (ISSN: 0589-4891), Oct, 1967.
VARIES
--Jul 15, 1888 - Sep 8, 1967 as Printers' Ink (ISSN: 0196-1160).
LC: HF 5801.P7
DD: 659
ISSN: 0025-3685
ABST: --ABI/Informer

--Bulletin of the Public Affairs Information Service (ISSN: 0731-0110)
--Business Periodical Index (ISSN: 0007-6961)
--InfoBank
--Predicasts

MARKETING COMMUNICATIONS
PUBL: Lakewood Publications, Inc., 50 South 9th St., Minneapolis, MN 55402.
DESC: Celebrated here was the technique and art of marketing products for retail consumption, with an emphasis on the unique and innovative. New technologies, as applied to new channels of marketing and sales, were explored; with many articles detailing successful marketing campaigns. Earlier issues focused on premiums and print advertising, but this gave way to a much broader approach to the field of marketing with new publisher, Media Horizons. For the sampled issues of 1979: stapled magazine format; editorial content consisting of black ink with full-color advertisements on coated paper; cover was full-color on coated stock (7 ⅞ x 10 ⅝ inches / 200 x 270 mm).
DEPT: "Marketwatch," new marketing ideas; "Association Notes," newsbriefs concerning trade and professional groups; "Promotion Questions and Answers," an interesting section providing answers to marketing problems sent in via readers; "Legalities," legal information forum; "Innovations," new promotion items. (11-77). "A Sample of One," editorial; "Chairman's Corner," commentary column by Joel Harnett; "Marketing Notes," "Personal Marketing," "People on the Move." (10-88).
TYPL: "The Changing Role of Print Media," "Marketing in the Middle East," "Aramis Brings Back the Baby Face." (11-77). "Mavens of the Malls: Revolutionizing the Retail Landscape," "The Fax Market Comes of Age," "Hyundai Taps into a 'Hidden Sales Force'," "Nailing Down the Home Improvement Market." (10-88).
SCHL: Nine issues per year (? - ?); Monthly (? to date), 60 pp.
SPAN: 1976 - May, 1989//
ABSORBED BY
--Potentials in Marketing (ISSN: 0032-5619), May, 1989.
LC: HF 5801.M
ISSN: 0164-4343

✤ MARKETING NEW MEDIA
PUBL: Paul Kagan Associates, Inc., 126 Clock Tower Place, Carmel, CA 93923-8734.
DESC: Another in the series of outstanding Kagan newsletters, *Marketing New Media* explores and reports on the emergence of new forms of mass media in the United States. The focus is on the marketing of these media, with an eye to their potential/actual acceptance; which, of course, is a major determinant of profit. The newsletter is broad-based, covering cable television to digital radio; HDTV and its variations;

and the ever-changing face of consumer electronics. For anyone in the marketing side of media, this is a "must" subscription. For the sampled issue of 1990: typewritten newsletter with computer generated charts and graphs. Size of newsletter bound within *Cable World* magazine is (8 ⅛ x 10 ¾ inches / 210 x 275 mm).
DEPT: "Media Marketing Index," excellent status of American consumer society. (6-30-89). "Media Marketing Index." (9-17-90).
TYPL: "Basic: Stronger Than Ever," "Top 50 MSOs New Home Conversion Ratio," "Lenfest Takes Nustar," "DARPA Awards for HDTV." (6-30-89). "Cable TV: Recession-Proof?," "Cable's Sensitivity to Sharp Rate Hikes and High Basic Rates," "Staffing for the Long Term: Fewer Subs Per Employee," "Target Marketing: Cable's New Challenge." (9-17-90).
SCHL: Semimonthly, 8 pp.
SPAN: Mar 7, 1984+
SUPPLEMENT TO
--Cable World (ISSN: 1042-7228), ?+
ISSN: 0743-2178

✧ MARKETING NEWS

SUB: "Reporting on the marketing profession."
SUB: "Reporting on the marketing profession and its association."
PUBL: American Marketing Association, Suite 200, 250 South Wacker Dr., Chicago, IL 60606-5819.
DESC: The official publication of the American Marketing Association, *Marketing News* does, as the subtitle suggests, cover both Association news, and news of the profession on a biweekly basis. The large magazine format with numerous color graphics enhances discussions of different approaches to the marketing of product to the end user. In one sampled 1991 issue, articles ranged from interactive television to vending machines dispensing hot meals on demand; marketing via fax machines to high-tech means employed by a retailer to stage a sales comeback; timekeeping software for agencies to new developments in life-stage marketing. This continues to be an excellent resource and "must" reading by individuals responsible for marketing and advertising activities in the corporate arena. For the sampled 1991 issue: stapled large magazine format, spot- and full-color pages on coated paper stock, with significant trade advertising (11 x 15 inches / 280 x 385 mm).
DEPT: "Letters," "Viewpoint," "Reader Poll," "Pricing," "Trade Shows," "Packaging & Design," "Technology Today," "Software Directory Update," "AMA Chapter News," of American Marketing Association; "AMA National News," of American Marketing Association; "The Marketplace," "Names in the News," newsbriefs; "Conference Calendar." (11-7-88).
TYPL: "Fax to the Max: How Marketers are Finding Ways to Use Facsimile," "Data-Base Marketing Alters Landscape," "Desktop Publishing: Powerful Marketing Communications Aid," "On-Line Files Offer Better Sales Leads," "Selection of Retail Site Suffers When Technology is Used Too Late." (11-7-88).
SCHL: Biweekly, 35 pp.
SPAN: Oct, 1967+
LC: HF 5415.M
DD: 658
ISSN: 0025-3790
ABST: --ABI/Informer
--Business Periodical Index (ISSN: 0007-6961)
--InfoBank
--Management Contents
--Predicasts

✧ MARKETING PULSE, THE

SUB: "Entertainment & Marketing."
SUB: "The big picture."
PUBL: Unlimited Positive Communications, Inc., PO Box 1173, Woodstock, NY 12498.
DESC: Industry readers have called *The Marketing Pulse* "extremely perceptive," "oftentimes visonary," and "has the answers before others know the questions;" all testimonials to the thorough coverage and considerable insight brought to this monthly publication. A sample list of subscribers reads like a "who's who" of the entertainment industry's front offices, as corporate entities compete in the insatiable quest of "what will happen next" in the mass media. This is a newsletter (with an emphasis on video and television), for marketing directors, advertising agencies, corporate media executives, reps, producers, distributors and any others whose daily job it is to extract a profit based on the fickle opinion of the American public. The $300 per year (for 1989) subscription fee may pay for itself many times over in the course of a year. The sampled issue of 1989 consisted of loose-leaf newsletter format, numerous charts and graphs in black ink on colored uncoated paper stock (8 ½ x 11 inches / 215 x 280 mm).
DEPT: None.
TYPL: "The Search for the Elusive Quality Program," "Bozell Sets the Stage for the 90's," "RSC Prepares to Scale the Heights of Quality." (10-89).
SCHL: Monthly, 10 pp.
SPAN: Sep, 1980?+

✧ MARQUEE

SUB: "The journal of the Theatre Historical Society."
PUBL: Theatre Historical Society, PO Box 767, San Francisco, CA 94101.
DESC: *Marquee* is a loving historical look at American theatrical construction; buildings that housed, showcased, and elegantly promoted the performing arts, from Vaudeville to legitimite stage; "Opry House" to opera center; or other forms of entertainment which stimulated the construction and operation of a "theatre" complex. It is published by the Theatre Historical Society, which explores construction details, and op-

eration and preservation of such structures in the United States; with a certain emphasis on current restoration work and archiving of materials which aid the restoration process. Numerous photographs, especially of theatre construction and finished interiors.
DEPT: "West Coast," newsbriefs; "Publications," reviews; "Newsreel," newsbriefs; "Midwest," newsbriefs. (3-83).
TYPL: "Oscar Hammerstein I: The Man Who Invented Time Square," "Harrigan's Theatre," "Fourteenth Street, Cradle of American Vaudeville." (3-83).
SCHL: Bimonthly (1969 - 1970); Quarterly (1971 - ?); Bimonthly (Aug/Sep, 1981+); 25 pp.
SPAN: Feb, 1969+
WITH SUPPLEMENT
--THS Newsletter (ISSN: 0735-5734), Jul, 1979+.
ISSN: 0025-3928
ABST: --Avery Index to Architectual Periodicals (ISSN: 0196-0008)

Martial Arts Movies

Jan, 1981 - Oct, 1982//
(ISSN: 0744-8430)
SEE: ACTION FILMS

Maryland in Motion Film & Video Production Directory

? - ?//
SEE: IN MOTION FILM & VIDEO PRODUCTION MAGAZINE

✤ MASS COMM REVIEW

PUBL: Association for Education in Journalism, Mass Comm and Society Division, Temple University, Philadelphia, PA 19122.
DESC: *Mass Comm Review* provides a scholary treatment of events and phenomena falling within the parameters of "mass communications and society," with an emphasis (at times) on print journalism. Articles are concerned with the interaction between medium and consumer, the regulator and the regulated as it pertains to the process of mass communication in the community. A sampling of articles from various issues include: "Comparative Media Systems: A Societal Approach," "Chicago Journalists and Ethical Principles," "Research in Staff-Publisher Tensions," "On the Verbing of Nouns and the Nouning of Verbs," "Newspaper Reader Feedback and Editor Implementation: An Approach," and "The Fairness Doctrine: Some Student Views." Publication averages three to five articles per issue. For the sampled issues of 1978 and 1979: stapled square magazine format; black ink on uncoated paper with spot-color on uncoated stock for cover; limited advertising (8 x 10 inches / 205 x 255 mm).
DEPT: None. (winter-78/79). None. (fall-85).
TYPL: "Patterns of Ethical Decisions Among Investigative Reporters," "Private Images Gatekeepers Bring to News of Public Women," "Mass Comm/Philosophy Courses: Some Antics with Semantics," "Job Satisfaction in Selected U.S. Daily Newspapers: A Study of Male and Female Top-Level Managers." (winter-78/79). "A Content Analysis of the Darts and Laurels Column in *Columbia Journalism Review*," "The Growing Power of the I.O.J.," "What do Communication Researchers Really Mean by 'Ethnicity?,'" "Newpaper Gimmickry Coverage in Florida Elections." (fall-85).
SCHL: Three issues per year, 35 pp.
SPAN: Aug, 1973+
ISSN: 0193-7707
ABST: --Management Contents

✤ MASS COMMUNICATION BIBLIOGRAPHERS' NEWSLETTER

PUBL: Mass Communication Bibliographers, Dolores C. Jenkins, editor, 142 Library West, University of Flordia, Gainesville, FL 32611.
DESC: Communication researchers and librarians have long awaited this publication of the Mass Communication Bibliographers Interest Group of the Association for Education in Journalism and Mass Communication (AEJMC). This typeset newsletter provides information on new bibliographic publications in the mass communication area; and profiles communication collections at public and private libraries. In the November, 1989 issue were articles concerning major reference works in communication history, underground newspaper collections, and profiles on the Eugene Patterson Library, the American Advertising Museum and Library, and the Broadcast Pioneers Library in Washington, DC. An excellent resource for this growing field of information management. Newsletter style; no graphics.
DEPT: None. (11-89).
TYPL: "Publications," "New Librarian to the Field," "Free to Good Home," "Death and Taxes Department." (11-89).
SCHL: Quarterly?, 10 pp.
SPAN: Nov, 1987?+

Mass Media Bi-Weekly Newsletter

Apr 3, 1972 - Apr 28, 1975//
(ISSN: 0163-4968)
SEE: MASS MEDIA NEWSLETTER

Mass Media Booknotes

Sep, 1973 - Jan, 1982//
(ISSN: 0740-6479)
SEE: COMMUNICATION BOOKNOTES

Mass Media Ministries Bi-Weekly Newsletter

1964? - Mar 20, 1972//
(ISSN: 0025-472x)
SEE: MASS MEDIA NEWSLETTER

MASS MEDIA NEWSLETTER

PUBL: Mass Media Ministries, Inc., 2116 North Charles St., Baltimore, MD 21218.
DESC: A subscription promotion stated that the *Mass Media Newsletter* provided: "Education Film Critiques; Current Cinema Reviews; Articles on Media Hardware; Updates on State-of-the-Art Technology; Television Previews; Book Reviews and Recommendations; Modern Music Surveys and Samples; [and] Sharing Ideas About Teaching With Media." After 16-plus years of publication, *Mass Media Newsletter* folded with the December 14, 1981 issue. Editor Edward McNulty wrote, "In a sense the passing of this *Newsletter* is somewhat like saying goodbye to an era, an era when the church came to a new awareness of the importance of media both as a channel for communication and as a shaper of our culture's values and beliefs." It provided a unique religious overview of the mass communication market, especially in the area of new film, radio, and television product. Of special interest was a feature, "Highlights for...," detailing upcoming television programs of a family-entertainment nature. For the sampled issue of 1981: folded newsletter format, black ink on uncoated paper, no advertising (8 ½ x 11 inches / 215 x 280 mm).
DEPT: "Highlights for...". (12-14-81).
TYPL: "Positive Perspectives on TV," "Gripping Drama Seen as Profound Parable," "Are Words Against Images?" (12-14-81).
SCHL: Biweekly (1964 - Apr 28, 1975); Semimonthly [Monthly during Aug, and Dec] (1975 - Apr 24, 1978); Semimonthly [Monthly during Jun - Aug, and Dec] (May 8, 1978+), 6 pp.
SPAN: 1964? - Dec 14, 1981//
VARIES
--1964? - Mar 20, 1972 as Mass Media Ministries Bi-Weekly Newsletter (ISSN: 0025-472x).
--Apr 3, 1972 - Apr 28, 1975 as Mass Media Bi-Weekly Newsletter (ISSN: 0163-4968).
ISSN: 0361-865x
ABST: --Media Review Digest (ISSN: 0363-7778)

✣ MAST

SUB: "For mailing and shipping professionals."
SUB: "Journal for the mailing & shipping professional."
PUBL: RB Publishing Company, 6000 Gisholt Drive, Suite 201, Madison, WI 53713-4816.
DESC: In business, the arrival of letters, documents, and packages is a matter of serious concern, as communication is the lifeblood of a corporation. Significant time and effort is applied to the efficiency, cost, and quality of delivery. For mail and shipping professionals *mast* is an excellent resource. Subscribers and advertisers alike attest to the need for this serial, which covers a variety of technological, governmental, and service-related issues. Typical articles might include detailed schematics on software to produce barcodes for labeling and addressing, elements in the decision-making process for the purchase of a manifest system, how to manage a small mail/shipping center, employee evaluations, wide area bar code readers, advances in envelope design, the process of training, numerous article profiles on professionals, and corporate mailroom operations. Of special note are unique departmental features, such as "Sam & Sally," which poses a problem-of-the-month with solution; a "Shop Talk" column by Dan O'Rourke, filled with easily applied suggestions for efficiency and profitability; and "$$$$$$," subtitled "Fiscal Control," for the all-important bottom-line of business operation. Deserving of commendation was a "Special Edition" supplement to the January, 1991 issue for "The New Postage Rates and Regulations," for both domestic and international mailing. Every corporate mailroom, direct marketing firm, advertising agency, and other communication areas that rely on mailing and shipping services needs a subscription to this excellent periodical. Magazine format (8 ⅜ x 10 ⅞ inches / 210 x 275 mm), full color throughout on coated paper stock. Note: the serial title *mast* is represented in all lower-case letters.
DEPT: "From Our Readers," letters; "From the Editor," editorial column by Ronald C. Brent; "Industry News," "New Products," "Calendar of Events," "Sam & Sally," problem/solution column; "Shop Talk," column by Dan O'Rourke; "Professionals," profile; "FYI Charts," "$$$$$$$," 'Fiscal control' departmental feature; "Company Profile," "International," "Tech Highlights," "Association Speaks." (10-90).
TYPL: "Contracting for Optimum Service," "Delivery Via Pneumatic Tubes," "USPS Appeal Procedures," "Packaging for the Environmentally Concerned," "The Evolution of Sorters." (10-90).
SCHL: Quarterly (? - Oct, 1990); Bimonthly (Jan, 1991+), 70 pp.
SPAN: Jan, 1988+

Master Printer

May, 1903 - Apr, 1905//
SEE: NEWSPAPER WORLD AND ADVERTISING REVIEW

MASTHEAD

SUB: "A journal for teaching history with old newspapers."
PUBL: The Masthead Society, P.O. Box 1009, Marblehead, MA 01945.
DESC: "The Masthead Society consists of an international following of educators, genealogists and historians seeking to promote world-wide appreciation of the historical data found in early newspapers. The Mast-

head Society emphasizes the enrichment of journalism and printing history, the systematic processing of genealogical data, and the development of classroom techniques involving the use of historical newspapers." This valuable newsprint publication is for individuals working in historical research. Edited by students at Salem State College, Salem MA, readers will find numerous wood cuts and photos from early journalism eras. It is truly unfortunate, therefore, that like its predecessors, Masthead is also printed on newsprint.

DEPT: "The Book Review," concerning newspaper histories; "Historic Resources Marketplace," an interesting 'want-ad' section offering old newspapers, magazines, letters and other printed items for sale. (10-77).
TYPL: "The Abuse of a President," "Historic Newspapers for Collector and Classroom," "Samuel Pike, America's Peripatetic Journalist." (10-77).
SCHL: Nine times per year (except Jun, Jul, Aug), 25 pp.
SPAN: Jan, 1977 - Sep, 1978//
LC: PN 4700.M
ISSN: 0025-5084

✤ MASTHEAD

SUB: "The quarterly publication of the National Conference of Editorial Writers."
PUBL: National Conference of Editorial Writers, Box 34928, Washington, DC 20034.
DESC: In the NCEW's basic statement of principles, it is noted that, "Editorial writing is more than another way of making money. It is a profession devoted to the public welfare and to public service. The chief duty of its practitioners is to provide the information and guidance toward sound judgments that are essential to the healthy functioning of a democracy." Articles provide background on issues; news of membership; and (of special interest), editorial product from a variety of print publications. It is an interesting serial with numerous editorial graphics and salient discussion of issues facing the editorial staff of newspapers.
DEPT: "Books," reviews; "What NCEW Members are Doing," briefs; "The Presidents Corner," column. (summer-76). "President's Letter," "Symposium," comment; "Designing the Editorial Page," "Editorial Clinic," "Book Review," "Letters to the *Masthead*." (summer-87).
TYPL: "The Daily Editorial Conflicts: Why Bother?," "Country Editor: Dream Come Nightmare?," "Press Needs to Shake the Lead Out," "Journalism Curriculum Debate Continues." (summer-76). "There's Something Besides Politics Out There," "Ain't Science Articles Fascinating?," "Canada: Press Freedom Without a First Amendment." (summer-87).
SCHL: Quarterly, 40 pp.
SPAN: Spring, 1949+
LC: PN 4700.M3
ISSN: 0025-5122
ABST: --ABI/Informer

✤ MATRIX

SUB: "A magazine for all women who write."
SUB: "Official publication of Theta Sigma Phi."
SUB: "A magazine for women in communications."
SUB: "A magazine for women in journalism & communications."
PUBL: Women in Communications, National Headquarters, Box 9561, Austin, TX 78766.
DESC: As the official publication of WICI, the emphasis is on the role of women in media. Main emphasis is on internal WICI communications.
DEPT: "Deadline Data," events calendar. (spring-77).
TYPL: "Liz Carpenters Grass Roots," "How to Make WICI Work for You," "Women, Communications, and Congress." (spring-77).
SCHL: Bimonthly (Oct/Nov, 1942 - Aug/Sep, 1946); Quarterly (Summer, 1978+), 30 pp.
SPAN: 1916+
LC: LJ 121.T5M3
DD: 371.85407
ISSN: 0025-598x

✤ MB NEWS

SUB: "The Museum of Broadcasting newsletter."
PUBL: Museum of Broadcasting, 1 East 53rd St., New York, NY 10022.
DESC: "The best of over sixty years of radio and television programming can be found at the Museum of Broadcasting. Choose from over 25,000 programs and you will be able to relive an event in history, study some of the greatest moments in the performing arts, or simply enjoy an episode of a favorite radio or television series. From Toscanini to Lucille Ball to coverage of man's first steps on the moon, there's something for everyone in the Museum's collection." Despite the subtitle labeling this serial as a newsletter, it is more a distinguished record of Museum events, seminars, and celebrations of 60 years of broadcast history. Each issue, even with its irregular publication schedule, provides a wealth of historical materials, photographs, anecdotes, and other items treasured by broadcast historians. Large format magazine (9 x 12 inches / 230 x 305 mm), many rare photographs.
DEPT: None. (winter-88).
TYPL: "The Vision of Ernie Kovacs," "The Metropolitan Opera: The Radio and Television Legacy," "BBC Television: Fifty Years," "An Evening with Alan Alda," "Carnegie Hall: The Radio and Television Concerts," "Rocky and Bullwinkle and Friends: a Tribute to Jay Ward," "The Star Trek Pilot," "Barbra Streisand: The Television Work." (winter-88).
SCHL: Irregular, 95 pp.
SPAN: Winter, 1977?+
LC: PN 1990 .M33
DD: 384.54/06/07471 19
ISSN: 0743-1279

✣ MC&S NEWSLETTER

SUB: "Association for Education in Journalism and Mass Communication."
PUBL: Association for Education in Journalism and Mass Communication, c/o Leonard Ray Teel, Department of Communication, Georgia State University, Atlanta, GA 30303.
DESC: This newsletter for the Mass Communication & Society division of the Association for Education in Journalism and Mass Communication, is concerned with "...media institutions and organizations. From these roots have sprung the work in ethics and management." Division Head, Patrick Parsons, writing in the fall, 1989 issue of the newsletter, stated that among the goals for the upcoming years would be: "...a reemphasis of the study of media organizations, specifically the interaction between individuals--their values and backgrounds--and industrial-organizational forces. We will further try to expand the sociology of media organizations beyond its more common journalistic and public relations applications to the study of advertising, telecommunications and other cultural industries as well." Typeset newsletter format; no graphics.
DEPT: None. (fall-89).
TYPL: "Spring Conference Set for Alabama," "MC&S Proposes Five Interdisciplinary Mini-Plenary Sessions," "Call for Papers." (fall-89).
SCHL: Quarterly?, 4 pp.
SPAN: ?+

Media, Agencies, Clients

Dec 19, 1951 - Jul 10, 1967//
SEE: ADWEEK

MEDIA & CONSUMER

PUBL: Media and Consumer Foundation, P.O. Box 850, Norwalk, CT 06852.
DESC: In this small-format tabloid concerned with the role of consumer purchase of products advertised by businesses through the mass media, much attention is devoted to "shady" practices of businesses in their advertising ploys with consumers. The newspaper covers national informational news with numerous reprints of ads. It is a journalistic enterprise that takes illicit advertisers to task.
DEPT: "Clip Service," newsbriefs; "Notes from Here and There," "They Said It," quotes; "Journalism Review," opinion on news media; "Commentary," (2-73).
TYPL: "What New York Banks Could Learn About Customer Service," "Foot Rashes from Water Buffalo Sandals," "Why a TV Repairman Law Doesn't Work," "How Used Car Dealers Work," "Congressional Study Laudes Food Firms," (2-73).
SCHL: Monthly, 20 pp.
SPAN: Apr, 1972 - Aug, 1975//
LC: TX 335.A1M43

DD: 640.73/05
ISSN: 0047-6439

✣ MEDIA & METHODS

SUB: "An expansion of School Paperback Journal."
SUB: "Exploration in Education."
SUB: "Educational products, technologies & programs for schools & universities."
PUBL: American Society of Educators, 1429 Walnut St., Philadelphia, PA 19102.
DESC: Editor Frank McLaughlin, in the tenth anniversary issue of 1974 told readers, "In October, 1964, a frail 7 x 10 inch, 32-page magazine called *School Paperback Journal* was launched. Its audience was primarily high school English teachers; its goal was to offer an alternative to textbook instruction by promoting individualized learning through the use of paperback books. Two years later, *SPJ* became *Media & Methods*. Its philosophy widened to encompass all media that would effectively stimulate student learning and expressiveness. Today, each issue of *M&M* is still committed to building a bridge between humanistic learning and media usage." Current issues display this statement of purpose: "*Media & Methods* is published as a non-profit, educational service to foster the exchange of information about the creative use of technologies serving media arts in education today." This is a review of mass media hardware and software for the classroom, library, and other educational settings within schools, colleges and universities. Articles are renowned for introducing new technologies, and applications of same in American educational institutions. Suggestions, new products, and especially new programs for educational application make this serial a trusted resource of educational media specialists everywhere. For the 1990 sampled issue: stapled magazine format, editorial content consisting of mixture of black/white, spot- and full-color pages (and cover) on coated paper stock (8 ⅛ x 10 ⅞ inches / 205 x 275 mm).
DESC: [Educators Guide to Media & Methods]: Aimed at primary and secondary school teachers, this digest provided a forum for discussion, and a programming preview of book, radio, television, and film materials available to teachers. Some articles discussed the role of media within the classroom, while others provided "how-to" lessons on using such items to their fullest potential with students. Small magazine format; numerous graphics.
DEPT: "Editorial," "Feedback," letters; "Essentially Couth," 'Contemporary culture commentator', column by Barry Robinson; "M & M Visits," how cities use media; "A-V Answer Man," column by Abraham Cohen; "16mm In-Sights," reviews column by William Sloan. (3-67). "Recommended," educational media review by a Media and Methods test panel; "A Room with Class," feature on the classroom; "Mediabag," newsbriefs; "Prime Time School Television," unique section with previews of upcoming network television programs and specials. (5-77). "Short

Takes," newsbriefs; "Videodisc Update," "Media Reviews," "Product Premieres," new items recently introduced; "Products in Action," review. (5/6-90).
TYPL: "The Medium is McLuhan," "James Bond: Exploits of a Culture Hero," "The Multi-Media Approach to Frost," "TV, Science--and the Slow Learner." (3-67). "VTR: a Tool, Not a Tent Show," "Poets and Poetry on Film," "Film and Video." (May-77). "CD ROM and Information Literacy: Across the Curriculum," "The Video Yearbook," "Excitement in the Library Media Center: One School's Experience," "Technology Reaching Out to Special Education Students." (5/6-90).
SCHL: Nine issues per year (Nov, 1967 - May, 1969); Five issues per year [Sep - May] (Sep, 1969+), 85 pp.
SPAN: Sep, 1969+
VARIES
--Oct, 1964 - May, 1966 as School Paperback Journal.
--Sep, 1966 - Oct, 1967 as Teacher's Guide to Media and Methods.
--Nov, 1967 - May, 1969 as Educators Guide to Media & Methods (ISSN: 0013-2063).
LC: LB 1043.M357
DD: 371.33/5
ISSN: 0025-6897
ABST: --Consumers Index to Product Evaluations and Information Sources (ISSN: 0094-0534)
--Education Index (ISSN: 0013-1385)
--Media Review Digest (ISSN: 0363-7778)
--Micro Computer Index (ISSN: 8756-7040)

✤ MEDIA & VALUES

SUB: "A quarterly resource for media literacy."
SUB: "A quarterly review of media issues and trends."
SUB: "A quarterly look at modern communications and its impact on religious values."
SUB: "A resource newsletter of the National Sisters Communications Service."
PUBL: Center for Media and Values, 1962 South Shenandoah, Los Angeles, CA 90034.
DESC: *Media & Values* is published quarterly by the Center for Media and Values, an educational not-for-profit membership organization which empowers the public by providing resources for critical awareness about media. The Center believes that a concern for values in today's media age is not so much knowing all the answers as asking the right questions." Forthright and informative, *Media & Values* has developed a very credible "...forum to stimulate creative thinking about values in the Media Age" through careful, critical essays and authoritative articles. The emphasis is on evaluating moral and ethical community standards as they apply to current forms of mass media. Each issue revolves around a theme, such as the sampled Spring/Summer, 1991 issue, "Fatal Attraction: The Selling of Addiction." Of special note are "tear-out-and-copy" discussion and group activity pages subtitled, "Reflection Resource." Each issue has the departmental "Watch, Read, Listen," with "Resources for follow-up" in the areas of print, sight/sound, and organizations. This is an excellent publication for the critical analysis of the form, function, and medium/message of contemporary society. For the representative issues of 1980: stapled newsletter format; black ink on uncoated paper in typewritten format. Issue for fall, 1981: typewritten black ink editorial content on coated paper stock. Dimensions for 1980 and 1981 issues: (8 ½ x 11 inches / 215 x 280 mm). For the sampled issue of 1991: stapled magazine format, editorial content and cover are two-color ink on uncoated and coated paper stock respectively, no advertising (8 ⅜ x 10 ⅞ inches / 215 x 275 mm).
DEPT: "Pastoring," "Family Life," "Youth," "Women," "International," "Ethnic Music," "Social Justice," "Getting Involved." (winter-86). "Reflection/Action Forum," "Reflection Resource," "Watch, Read, Listen," 'Resources for follow-up'. (spring/summer-91).
TYPL: "Looking for God in Today's Music," "Teaching Teens to Tune for Values," "Lost Listeners Anoint Musical Messiahs," "How Hits are Made: Radio's Rating Game." (winter-86). "Culture of Addiction," "How Free is Commercial Speech?," "Alcohol and Television," "How Advertisers Sell Addiction," "Learning From Television: Commercials Influence Kids." (spring/summer-91).
SCHL: Quarterly, 35 pp.
SPAN: 1977+
LC: P 94 .M35
DD: 302.2/34/05
ISSN: 0149-6980

✤ MEDIA ANTHROPOLOGIST NEWSLETTER

PUBL: Prince George's Community College, Largo, MD 20870.
DESC: "Media Anthropology, as we the editors of this newsletter envision it, is based upon three premises: 1) the American public is interested in the information that social scientists explore; 2) the media has attempted to provide this information, with varying degrees of success; 3) up to this time the media specialist and social scientist had only infrequently come together to provide the public with more coherent, substantive, yet interesting programs. With this in mind, *Media Anthropologist* has set out to become a liaison between the media specialists and the anthropologists." This is a typewritten newsletter format with numerous newsbriefs on media specials, programs and materials. No graphics.
DEPT: "Publications," books and magazines; "The Clearing House," news of media anthropologists; "Catalogs," "Audio Tools," "AV Tools," "Movies," "News in Brief," "Journals," "Opportunities," newsbriefs of openings and grants; "Calendar," "Film Review."
TYPL: "Super 8 Films for the Classroom," "The Art of Making Salvage Films," (Feb-75).
SCHL: Quarterly, 25 pp.
SPAN: Fall, 1972+
LC: PN 1995.M

ISSN: 0160-8983

✜ MEDIA ARTS
SUB: "A publication of film art fun."
SUB: "Monthly newsletter of the National Alliance of Media Arts Centers."
PUBL: National Alliance of Media Arts Centers, 8949 Wilshire Blvd., Beverly Hills, CA 90211.
DESC: This typewritten newsletter is composed primarily of reprinted articles concerning media arts centers, and very little news in the form of interviews or news items. The primary focus concerns screenings of current or potential motion pictures at these centers. No graphics.
SCHL: Bimonthly, 12 pp.
SPAN: 1980+?
DEPT: "News from Members of the Alliance," newsbriefs. (10-81).
TYPL: "Karen Cooper's Film Forum Reopens at New Home in Lower Manhattan," "Arts/Humanities Task Force Completes Deliberations and Readies Report for President Reagan," "NAMAC Writes to Senator Hatfield About the Twelve Percent Proposed Cut in the Budget of the National Endowments," (10-81).
ISSN: 0889-8928

✜ MEDIA ASIA
SUB: "An Asian mass communication quarterly."
PUBL: Asian Mass Communications Research and Information Centre, 39 Newton Rd., Singapore 11, Singapore.
DESC: "AMIC [Asian Mass Communication Research and Information Centre], is a non-profit mass communication organization serving Asia from its headquarters in Singapore. It is jointly sponsored by the Government of Singapore and the Friedrich-Ebert-Stiftung, an independent foundation in the Federal Republic of Germany. AMIC is one of several regional documentation centres around the world working in cooperation with UNESCO to promote the dissemination of information pertaining to mass communication." Among that work is the publication of *Media Asia*, a magazine of considerable editorial content, referred to as a "newsletter" in AMIC terms. This is a serial of news, reports of ongoing research, workshops, and other issues of mass communication as they are utilized and shaped by Asian cultures. This is a very good resource for the current status of communication issues in Asian-Pacific nations. Magazine format.
DEPT: "Feedback," letters; "Cues," newsbriefs; "Findings," research summaries; "Reviews." (vol 2, #3-75). "AMICINFO." (vol 7, #4-80).
TYPL: "Forty Years of Broadcasting in Papua New Guinea," "Participation in Mass Communication," "Some Research Problems in Rural Sri Lanka." (vol 2, #3-75). "A presentation of multinational advertising objectives, strategies and creative execution by Singapore Airlines," "Social Research in Asia Using Focus Group Discussions: a Case Study," "Development Journalism: a New Dimension in the Information Process," "Two Hundred Years of the Indian Press: a Case of Lopsided Growth." (vol 7, #4-80).
SCHL: Quarterly, 55 pp.
SPAN: 1974+
VARIES
--Jan, 1972 - Jul/Oct, 1973 as Documentation List [NS].
LC: P 92.A7M43
DD: 301.16
ISSN: 0377-1210

✜ MEDIA BUSINESS
SUB: "Publishing, programming, broadcasting/cable TV, radio."
PUBL: Summit Media International, Inc., 603 Park Point Drive, Suite 275, Golden, CO 80401.
DESC: [*Media Business News*]: Monitors financial changes, the status quo, and trends in the media of publishing, broadcast, cable television, and radio. It is a newsletter of clearly presented graphic charts, succinct news summaries, and excellent layout designs. This is the perfect publication for the busy corporate officer, whose position requires quality, current information on American mass media. Three-hole punched newsletter format; numerous financial charts and diagrams.
DEPT: "Publishing," "Programming," "Broadcasting & Cable TV," "Radio," "Other Media," "Analyst's Report," media corporation economic profile; "Media Trends," "Politics," "Media Finance," "Media Transactions," "Earnings," "Insider Trading," "Follow the Money," column by Paul S. Maxwell; "Media Mogul," CEO profile; "At Deadline." (12-12-88).
TYPL: "A Bona Fide 'Buy'?," "Shearson Plan Not Made for Media," "Wall Street Gorby-ized," "One Moment, Please," "A New Cable Penny Stock." (12-12-88).
SCHL: Weekly, 20 pp.
SPAN: Jan, 1987+
VARIES
--Jan, 1987 - ?, 1988? as Media Business News (ISSN: 0898-283x).
WITH SUPPLEMENT
--Media Business Markets.
DD: 380 11
ISSN: 1045-716x

✜ MEDIA BUSINESS MARKETS
PUBL: Summit Media International, Inc., 603 Park Point Drive, Suite 275, Golden, CO 80401.
DESC: This monthly supplement to *Media Business News* provides newsbriefs of financial developments, specifically status of stocks, offerings, sales, and other stock market trends concerning media corporations. Six of the eight pages consist of stock listings, called "Media Business Markets." Three-hole punched newsletter format.
DEPT: "Media Business Markets." (10-10-88).
TYPL: "Media Joins in Market Rebound." (10-10-88).

SCHL: Monthly, 8 pp.
SPAN: ?+
SUPPLEMENT TO
--Media Business News.

Media Business News

Jan, 1987 - ?, 1988?//
(ISSN: 0898-283x)
SEE: MEDIA BUSINESS

✣ MEDIA, CULTURE, AND SOCIETY

PUBL: Sage Publications, 28 Banner St., London EC1Y 8QE, England.
DESC: From Notes to Authors: "*Media, Culture & Society* provides an important international forum for the presentation of research and discussion across the whole field of cultural practice. To date, the main focus has been on the mass media (television, radio, journalism) within their political, cultural and historical contexts. But a developing additional focus is a critical engagement with the concept of the Information Society and with those issues raised by the convergence of the mass media with systems of cultural production and diffusion based upon telecommunications and computing. We are also increasingly interested in the social role of various categories of intellectual in the full range of cultural practice. The relationship of all these systems and concerns to literature, the visual and performing arts, photography, publishing and to more general artistic and cultural practices is of central reference. The journal seeks to relate academic work to contemporary cultural practice, particularly with regard to mass media and communication policy. As we are an interdisciplinary journal, contributions from people in any relevant areas are welcome. The journal is also committed to making available the work of foreign scholars and practitioners (via translation and specifically commissioned articles) as well as of American and other English-speaking countries. Contributions to the journal are externally refereed." *Media, Culture & Society* remains an excellent, authoritative, and thorough examination of the role of mass media, the perception of culture, and the interaction of the two. Another in the quality lineup of Sage Publications, this highly recommended for study, information, and considered thought. Volume two onward features one theme per issue, such as (in the sampled journal), "Boundaries and Identities." Several changes in format and dimensions have been executed during the publication span. For the sampled issues of 1979: editorial was black ink on uncoated paper, with cover consisting of two-spot color inks on coated stock (6 ¾ x 9 ⅝ inches 170 x 245 mm). Change next occured with the January, 1985 issue, primary difference being one spot-color ink employed for the cover (5 ⅛ x 8 ⅛ inches / 130 x 205 mm). Dimensions of the publication changed in January, 1990 as: (5 ⅞ x 9 inches / 150 x 230 mm). For sampled issue of 1991: black ink on uncoated paper stock, cover is green ink on coated paper stock, limited advertising (6 ⅛ x 9 ¼ inches / 155 x 235 mm). All sampled issues for 1979, 1985, 1990 and 1991 were: perfect-bound journal format.
DEPT: "Book Reviews." (4-80). "Editorial," "Review Essay," "Debate," "Commentary," "Book Reviews." (7-91).
TYPL: "Information in Health: Subsidized News," "Labour Power and Esthetic Labour in Film and Television in Britain," "Mass Communications in the 'SPD-State:' Some Issues of Media Politics in the Federal Republic of Germany 1970 - 1978," "Creativity and Control: The Journalist Betwixt His Readers and Editors." (4-80). "Media, the Political Order and National Identity," "Notes on the Emerging Global Language System: Regional, National and Supranational," "Competing Patterns of National Identity in Post-Communist Hungary," "On German Identity," "The Holocaust: Historical Memories and Contemporary Identities." (7-91).
SCHL: Quarterly, 90 pp.
SPAN: Jan, 1979+
LC: HM 258.M373
DD: 302.2/34/05
ISSN: 0163-4437

Media Decisions

Sep, 1966 - Apr, 1979//
(ISSN: 0025-6900)
SEE: MEDIAWEEK

✣ MEDIA DEVELOPMENT

SUB: "Journal of the World Association for Christian Education."
SUB: "Journal of the World Association for Christian Communication."
SUB: "World Association for Christian Communication.
PUBL: World Association for Christian Communication, 122 Kings Road, London SW3 4TR, England.
DESC: "The World Association for Christian Communication (WACC) is an organisation of corporate and personal members who wish to give high priority to Christian values in the world's communication and development needs. It is not a council or federation of churches. The majority of members are communication professionals from all walks of life. Others include partners in different communication activities and representatives of churches and church agencies." This very unique British periodical is a forum for discussions concerning the relationship between Christianity, the mass media, and interpersonal communication on an international basis. The publication describes the purpose as: "Analysis of communication theory and practice from a Christian perspective, with particular emphasis on socio-economic development." *Media Development* provides a very scholarly

treatment of important communication, political and social issues. Of special note is the printing of foreign articles in the original language of their authors. A sample issue included articles in German, Spanish, Dutch and French, with English translations promised in later issues. Many issues are themed, including the fourth issue for 1991, "Images and the Disappearing Word," and the first issue for 1992, "Language Policies and Politics." A special issue for October, 1991, "Reporting the Gulf War," included 14 articles ranging from "The Gulf War, the Media and Human Rights," to "Ethics of War Reporting," to "Iran's Press Loses Sight of Truth." For the sampled issues of 1980: stapled, magazine format; editorial content was black ink with spot-color ink on masthead printed on uncoated paper; no advertising (8 1/8 x 11 3/8 inches / 205 x 290 mm). For the 1991 sampled issues: stapled, magazine format; black ink on coated paper; cover consisting of spot-color ink on uncoated paper; limited advertising (8 1/4 x 10 3/4 inches / 210 x 275 mm).

DEPT: "Books." (#1-83); "Editorial," "Books," (an international review). (#4-85). "Book Reviews." (#4-91).

TYPL: "Philosophical Approaches to the Study of Communication," "Religion, Politics and Cultural Identity," "On the Interpretation of Language and Idiology," "Messengers of the Gods: Hermeneutics and Communication in Latin America," "Communication and the Cultural Tradition of India," "Chinese Philosophy and Recent Communication Theory." (#1-83); "Conflict in Space: Communication Satellites for What?," "Mobilising African Resources for National Communication Strategies," "Blacks in British Television Drama: the Underlying Tensions." (#4-85). "Words and Images in the Age of Technology," "Image Industry Erodes Political Space," "How Vulnerable are Children to Electronic Images?," "Brazil's Real-Life Images of Street Children," "Communicating Indian Faiths in the Video Age." (#4-91).

SCHL: Quarterly, 50 pp.
SPAN: Winter, 1953+
VARIES
--Oct, 1953 - Apr, 1968? as Christian Broadcaster (ISSN: 0577-9960).
--1970 - 1979 as WACC Journal (ISSN: 0092-7821).
LC: BV 4319.W63a
DD: 201/.41
ISSN: 0143-5558

✤ MEDIA DIGEST

SUB: "Exploring media in education and industry."
PUBL: National Educational Film Center, NEFC Bldg., 4321 Sykesville Rd., Finksburg, MD 21048.
DESC: The function of this monthly tabloid newsprint is twofold: 1) bring together (via reprint) articles of media utilization within the field of education; and 2) review new and available product (filmstrips, audio cassette, film and videotape) for the classroom. Some articles are published for the first time in *Media Digest*. Newsprint tabloid newspaper format with graphics.

DEPT: "Letters to the Editor," "Media News," newsbriefs; "Film & Video Review," "Film & Video Express," film and video rental/sales; "Filmstrip Review," "Media Techniques," "Hardware," equipment reviews; "Coming Events," "Freeloaders," free information for media in education. (winter-80).

TYPL: "Television Enters the 80's," "VCR's: Vanguard of the Video Revolution," "What Can Television Teach," "Responsibility for What's On the Tube," "Videodiscussion: The Videodisc Revolution in Film Education." (winter-80).

SCHL: Quarterly, 35 pp.
SPAN: 1972+
ISSN: 0146-2091

✤ MEDIA ETHICS UPDATE

SUB: "A service newsletter about mass communication ethics."
PUBL: Emerson College, Division of Mass Communication, 100 Beacon St., Boston, MA 02116.
DESC: "The [semiannually]-published newsletter *Media Ethics Update*, is partly a service publication, providing news about forthcoming events such as conferences, people, publications, and funding and other opportunities in the field of media ethics. It also is partly an outlet for expressions of opinion, such as (but not limited to) case studies and comments, philosophical investigations and discourses, exhortations, professional codes, policies and procedures affecting or practiced by media professionals, and the academic study of such phenomena. *Media Ethics Update* features commentary, sometimes in debate format, by active professionals, professors, lay persons and students in fields such as journalism, broadcasting, propaganda, government and education. *Media Ethics Update* had its genesis at a brainstorming session during the Media Ethics Summit Conference co-sponsored by Times-Mirror and Emerson College in 1987 that brought together representatives of many professional and academic organizations in the mass media. Intended to fulfill the need of better publicity and coordination of activities, publications and issues in the field to and for academic and professional participants in the conference and their constituencies, the first issue was published in the Spring of 1988." This is an impressive publication for the always fascinating study of ethics within various forms of mass communication. Kudos to co-editors Eric Fenn Elbot and John Michael Kittross for a stylish, authoritative and always informative newsletter. At a subscription price (for 1991) of $6 US, ($10 outside US), this publication is for those who have an interest in the entertainment or news function of mass communication systems. Highly recommended. Stapled magazine format, black ink on uncoated paper stock, no advertising (8 1/2 x 11 inches / 215 x 280 mm).

DEPT: "Upcoming Events," "Opportunities," "Publications," excellent review of current media-ethics publications; "News," news items. (spring-91).

TYPL: "Press Responsibilities and Lessons From the Gulf," "Red Light/Green Light...Green Light/Red Light," "The Unchallenged Tyranny of Sanctimony," "From a Distance: Notes on Television War Coverage," "Gannett Foundation Surveys Media Needs in Eastern Europe." (spring-91).
SCHL: Semiyearly, 16 pp.
SPAN: Spring, 1988+

✤ MEDIA HISTORY DIGEST

SUB: "A magazine of journalism heritage."
PUBL: Media History Digest, 11 West 19th St., New York, NY 10011.
DESC: An in-magazine promotion asks readers: "Are you aware of the rich heritage of journalism--its drama, humor, romance? Do you know the great media heroes and heroines of the past--in depth? Can you find these stories anywhere else? Subscribe now to *Media History Digest*--the twice annual digest filled with imaginative and intruiging stories of the history of media." A resounding Bravo! to Publisher Ferdinand C. Teubner and Editor Hiley H. Ward for producing an enlightening, informative digest of media history; one written with wit, verve, and considered thought. *Media History Digest* emphasizes printed communication. Special note must be made of the care and clarity devoted to the reprinting of accompanying pictures, graphs, charts, drawings, cartoons and other visual resources. This is a truly excellent resource for the study (especially of print) of the historical development of the mass media in North America. For the sampled issue of 1991: stapled, digest-sized magazine format, editorial content consisting of black ink on uncoated paper stock, cover is two-color black/gold ink on heavy coated paper stock, limited advertising (5 ⅜ x 8 ⅜ inches / 135 x 215 mm).
DEPT: "Media Hysteria," editorial cartoons; "Quiz." (spring/summer-91).
TYPL: "Greeley's Fledgling Paper Developed a Healthy Cry: 150 Years Ago," "Greeley's Strange Ties with the Phalanx Movement," "Karl Marx: Greeley's Ace Foreign Correspondent," "When Greeley Went West to Meet Native Americans," "Greeley's Milestone Rap With Brigham Young: First Interview?" (spring/summer-91).
SCHL: Quarterly (fall, 1980 - ?); Semiannual (1986+), 65 pp.
SPAN: Fall, 1980+
LC: P 87 .M36
DD: 001.51/0973
ISSN: 0195-6779

MEDIA IN EDUCATION AND DEVELOPMENT

SUB: "A journal of the British Council."
PUBL: Media Department, British Council, 10 Spring Gardens, London SW1A 2BN, England.
DESC: The target audience of *Media In Education and Development* was primary and secondary grade school teachers. Articles presented different forms of educational media available; how to utilize them properly; and how to guage their success in a learning environment. Articles had a world-wide education scope. Approximately one-half of each issue was devoted to a specific media theme. Since March, 1983 there had been an increased emphasis on the use of computers within the classroom. A sampling of article titles from 1981 and 1982 included: "Broadcasting and Literacy: Recent BBC Contributions," "The Newfoundland Schools Broadcasts," "A Multi-Media Strategy for a Breast-Feeding Campaign in Colombia," "Local Radio in Ireland: Commercial or Public Enterprise?," "Learning at a Distance: A World Perspective," and "English by TV in Mauritius." Subject headings for the 1982 annual index included: "Computers in Schools," "Distance Education," "General," "Health and Safety," "Information Technology," "Language Teaching," "Local Radio," "Research," "Teacher Training," and "Tertiary Education." For the sampled issues of 1982: perfect-bound magazine format; black ink for editorial content, with two spot-color ink design for the cover, both on coated paper stock, with advertising (8 x 11 ⅜ inches / 205 x 290 mm).
DEPT: "Book Reviews." (12-83).
TYPL: "Distance Education in Universities in Asia," "The TV University in China," "Continuing Education in Zambia," "Media and Mental Health," "Training with the BBC," "New Forms for a New Nicaragua," "One Year On In Channel Four." (12-83).
SCHL: Quarterly, 58 pp.
SPAN: Mar, 1971 - 1989//
VARIES
--Oct?, 1963? - Jan, 1967? as CETO News.
--Mar, 1967 - Dec, 1970 as Educational Television International.
--Mar, 1971 - Sep, 1981 as Educational Broadcasting International (ISSN: 0013-1970).
LC: LB 1044.7 .A2 E4
DD: 371.3/358
ISSN: 0262-0251
ABST: --Computer & Control Abstracts (ISSN: 0036-8113)
--Current Index to Journals in Education (ISSN: 0011-3565)
--Education Index (ISSN: 0013-1385)
--Electrical & Electronics Abstracts (ISSN: 0036-8105)
--Language Teaching (ISSN: 0261-4448)
--Physics Abstracts. Science Abstracts. Series A. (ISSN: 0036-8091)

✤ MEDIA INDUSTRY NEWSLETTER

SUB: "Weekly report to management."
SUB: "The oldest continuously published media/marketing newsletter."
PUBL: MIN Publishing, Inc., 18 East 53rd St., New York, NY 10022.

DESC: [MIN]: *"Media Industry Newsletter* specializes in what will happen, why it happened. What it will mean to you. We have a real passion for getting the story first. The reader will find no pictures, but true to the publisher's word, news 'written with a bit of humor, a dash of style, and a keen cutting edge.'" Typewritten to facilitate fast- breaking news.
DEPT: "Media Stock Averages," "Media Earnings Report," "MIN's Weekly Box Score," "Pages Sold." (8-77).
TYPL: "McGraw-Hill/Reader's Digest Deal Ready for Ink," "NY Timesers Unvail Mag-Movie Tie-In," "Book Publishers Go Hollywood? Critics Carp." (8- 77).
SCHL: Weekly.
SPAN: Nov, 1947+
VARIES
--Nov, 1947 - Sep 24, 1970 as Magazine Industry Newsletter.
DD: 338
ISSN: 0024-9793
ABST: --InfoBank

✤ MEDIA INFORMATION AUSTRALIA

SUB: "The quarterly journal of media research and resources."
SUB: "Who's doing what, when, how, why, what for, in media?"
PUBL: The Research and Survey Unit of the Australian Film and Television School, Box 305, North Ryde, NSW 2113, Australia.
DESC: When *Media Information Australia* began publication in 1976, it was a natural outgrowth of MIRE, the Media Information Research Exchange, "...a co-ordinating body of representatives from research departments in non-commercial organizations working in the media." Those organizations included: Australian Broadcasting Commission, Australian Broadcasting Control Board, Australia Council, Australian Film Commission, Australian Film Institute, Department of Government at Sydney University, Film Censorship Board, Telecom Australia (National Telecommunication Planning Branch), Film and Television School, and the Postal and Telecommunication Department (Broadcasting division). Editor and Professor Henry Mayer at the University of Sydney told readers in the second issue of 1976, "*MIA* attempts ...to counteract the fragmentation of interest in and information about the media, information, communication scene in Australia." That it accomplished the publication on "very scanty resources" was quite remarkable, and Editor Mayer pledged to make the publication "less rough and uneven." Fifteen years later, *Media Information Australia*, now published by the Australian Film, Television & Radio School, remains a marvelous resource of media information, but with the "rough, uneven edges" removed and replaced by a quality, typeset journal. Current issues are supported by the Australian Film, Television & Radio School, the Australian Broadcasting Corporation, the Australian Film Commission, the Australian Broadcasting Tribunal, and Telecom Australia. *MIA* is unique as a scholary journal of research, comment and opinion concerning mass media within Australia, and as a review of international media resources (especially publications). This quarterly publication covers a wide variety of topics with several one-themed issues throughout the year. For the sampled issues from 1976: typewritten, black ink on uncoated paper in perfect-bound magazine format; no advertising. The sampled issues for 1991: limited advertising; black ink editorial content, and multiple full-color and spot-color inks on coated stock for cover, in perfect-bound magazine format. Both sampled issues: (6 ⅞ x 9 ⅞ inches / 175 x 250 mm).
DEPT: "Media Books, Tapes A/V," reviews; "Research in Progress," "Surveys," "New Research Resources," "Media Briefs." (10-76). "Books," review; "International Notes," "Research in Progress," "Media Briefs." (5-83). "Directions," column by John O'Hara; "Reviews," "Read and Noted," column by Henry Mayer; "Media Briefs," column by Debra Mayrhofer. (5-91).
TYPL: "Australian Political Leadership in Sound & Film," "Brisbane, Video & Radio," "Inquiry Into Australian Broadcasting System," "Advertising Agencies: Media and Party Accounts," "Daytime TV: Research Project." (10-76). "Media Analysis and the Study of Discourse," "Issues in Radio Training," "Seseme Street and Playschool Revisited," "Teleconferencing Research at Telcom Australia," "Government Policy and the Information Economy." (5-83). "Ideological Spectacles: Reporting the Rat Pack," "Heard the News? Banning Broadcasting Sound," "Televangelism Reconsidered," "Domestic Telephone Research," "Racism and the Dominant Ideology: Aborigines, Television News and the Bicentenary." (5-91).
SCHL: Quarterly, 125 pp.
SPAN: Dec, 1975+
VARIES
--Dec, 1975 as Australian Media Notes.
ISSN: 0312-9616
ABST: --Australian Public Affairs Information Service (ISSN: 0005-0075)

✤ MEDIA INTERNATIONAL

SUB: "The European journal for international advertising."
SUB: "The international advertising & marketing magazine."
PUBL: Alain Charles Publishing, 27 Wilfred St., London SW1E 6PR, England.
DESC: A quality, large tabloid monthly serial, *Media International* covers advertising industry news around the world, with an emphasis on England and the European continent. Articles are succinct, timely, and oftentimes accompanied by supporting graphics. This is an excellent resource for individuals and corporations engaged in international marketing/advertising campaigns. Earlier editions had a front page billboard providing a short list of major article titles in English,

German, French, and Spanish. Of special note are excellent feature articles examining the status of advertising in particular nations. A separate *Media International America Edition* (Apr, 1989 sample copy indicates this separate edition shares the same ISSN number as the parent publication) is published bimonthly, containing some 15 pages of advertising news of interest to Canadian and American readers. It is an splendid publication for current status, and future trends in global marketing and advertising. For the sampled issues of 1991: editorial content consisting of mixture black ink, spot- and full-color pages on coated paper stock in stapled, tabloid-style format; significant advertising aimed at the trade (11 5/8 x 16 inches / 295 x 405 mm).

DEPT: "In Brief," paragraph-length news briefs; "Media Release," agency news. (4-77). "World News in Brief," advertising newsbriefs; "European News," "Nordic News," "Canadian/US News," "Media News in Brief," "Agency News in Brief," "Data...Data...," print publication newsbriefs; "Asia News in Brief," "Rendezvous," Back cover pictures of advertising personnel in the news. (4-89).
TYPL: "Management Recruitment Advertising and Media in Europe," "How to Advertise in Africa," "The Japanese Media Scene," "The Media Owners: IPC, United Kingdom." (4-77). "RSCG: Next Step to Global Network," "Fortune in Spain," "German Publishers Find New Niches," "Time-Warner Offers Prime Packages," "The Seven Paradoxes of Euro-TV," "Adasia Proves to be a Prize Draw," "Dentsu Sets High Targets Overseas." (4- 89).
SCHL: Monthly [except Jul/Aug] (Dec, 1985 - ?); Monthly (Aug, 1987+), 50 pp.
SPAN: 1973+
ISSN: 0266-8688

✤ MEDIA LAW NOTES

SUB: "Newsletter for the Law Division of AEJ & the Mass Communications Law Section of AALS."
PUBL: Law Division of the Association for Education in Journalism and Mass Communication, Communications Media Center, New York Law School, 57 Worth St., New York, NY 10013.
DESC: This 12-page newsletter on legal issues in the mass media serves primarily as an informational forum for Law Division members of the Association for Education in Journalism and Mass Communication (AEJMC), and secondarily to provide a publication medium for articles of interest to AEJMC Law Division readers. It is an excellent resource for the ever-changing relationship between American systems of communication and legal/regulatory authority within society. For the sampled issue of 1990: magazine format (8 1/2 x 11 inches / 215 x 280 mm), stapled and printed black/white on uncoated paper stock. Some graphics, no advertising.

DEPT: "Headnotes," comment. (winter-88). "Headnotes," commentary; "Directions in Research," "In Legal Journals," article bibliography; "In Non-Legal Journals," article bibliography; "Endnotes," newsbriefs. (spring-90).
TYPL: "Study: Media Lose Before High Court," "Supreme Court will Split on Flynt Case Attorney Predicts at PLI Conference," "Articles on Media Law: An Annotated Bibliography." (winter-88). "Minneapolis Convention Approaches," "Quantitative Studies Provide Insights," "'Company Line' Raises Ethical Dilemma." (spring-90).
SCHL: Quarterly, 12 pp.
SPAN: Fall, 1973?+
VARIES
--? - ? as Tortfeasor.
LC: KF 2750.A15 M4
DD: 343.73/099/05
ISSN: 0736-1750
ABST: --Legal Resource Index

Media Management Monographs

? - Dec, 1990?//
(ISSN: 0192-7663)
SEE: PUBLISHING TRENDS & TRENDSETTERS

✤ MEDIA MATTERS

SUB: "The newsletter."
SUB: "A monthly newsletter for the media and advertising industries."
PUBL: Media Dynamics, Inc., 322 East 50th St., New York, NY 10022.
DESC: With a breadth that covers the entire mass media industry, editor/publisher Edward Papazian provides a unique perspective that is both brash and refreshing. Issues are dealt with in a thorough, professional manner. Analysis is backed by solid statistics, whether the discussion concerns ratings, finances, attendence, or circulation. Subscription (for 1989) price is $175 per year. Its value to the corporate media executive should not be underestimated. *Media Matters* is another in the select group of "must read" publications for todays communication industry executives. Newsletter format; graphics.
DEPT: "In Brief," newsbriefs. (7-89).
TYPL: "Are Commercial Recall Scores Declining?," "Magazine Ad Page Exposure Timing Patterns," "Advertisers Shift Media Spending," "Coming Soon: The Passive Peoplemeter," "Channel Sampling Propensities: a New Nielsen Analysis." (7-89).
SCHL: Monthly, 12 pp.
SPAN: ?+

MEDIA MIX

SUB: "Ideas and resources for media and communication."

PUBL: Claretian Publications, 221 West Madison St., Chicago, Il 60606.
DESC: The subtitle, "Ideas and resources for media and communication," is an apt phrase for this spritely eight-page newsletter which brings new films, videos, and printed materials to the reader's attention. Noteworthy are new books and reviews of major media issues.
DEPT: "New Films," "Videosphere," news items, article-length book reviews on television; "Film Study," similar treatment pertaining to film; "Media Study," broad study of mass media. (4-77).
TYPL: Too brief for inclusion.
SCHL: Monthly (except Jul, Aug, Sep, Dec), 8 pp.
SPAN: Oct, 1969 - Jun, 1979//
ISSN: 0047-6447

✤ MEDIA MONITOR

PUBL: Center for Media and Public Affairs, 2101 L St., NW, Suite 405, Washington, DC 20037.
DESC: *Media Monitor* "...is published ten times a year by the Center for Media and Public Affairs, a nonpartisan and non-profit research organization. The Center conducts scientific studies of how the media treat social and political issues." The issue for November, 1991 covered treatment of the American presidency by various news and entertainment media. Editors Dr. S. Robert Lichter, and Dr. Linda S. Lichter, provide a succinct news publication with numerous, creative graphics to highlight and document information within the publication. This is information about the current relationship of media to government and society that simply is not found anywhere else. For the sampled issues of 1991: unique three-fold panel newsletter; black ink with spot-color on coated paper; no advertising; three-hole punched. Dimensions when folded: (8 ½ x 11 inches / 215 x 280 mm).
DEPT: None. (11-91).
TYPL: "The Postwar President: TV News Coverage of the Bush Administration, 1989 - 1991," "Finding the Spotlight," "Quayle's Comeback," "Media Momentum," "Punchlines." (11-91).
SCHL: Ten issues per year, 6 pp.
SPAN: Jan, 1987+

Media Probe

Mar, 1974 - Summer, 1977//
(ISSN: 0384-1618)
SEE: CANADIAN JOURNAL OF COMMUNICATION

Media Report

? - ?//
SEE: MEDIA REPORTER, THE

✤ MEDIA REPORT TO WOMEN

SUB: "What women are doing and thinking about the communications media."
PUBL: Communication Research Associates, Inc., 10606 Mantz Rd., Silver Spring, MD 20903-1228.
DESC: Here is a newsletter with zest, a bimonthly report to women about their relationship to American mass media. Specifically, *Media Report to Women* discusses the manner (through print articles and broadcast programming) by which the mass media define the role of women in American society. Special emphasis is given to articles and programs which display sexist tendencies.
DEPT: None. (11-76).
TYPL: "BPW Convention Votes for Curbs on Pornography and Radio-TV Sex Emphasis," "Woman Fired for Resisting Sex Assault by Station Manager Wins Out of Court Settlement," "Why Advertising Women are Needed in the Decision-Making Positions." (11-76).
SCHL: Monthly (Jun, 1972 - 1984); Bimonthly (1985+), 12 pp.
SPAN: Jun, 1972+
LC: HQ 1402.M44
DD: 302.2/3
ISSN: 0145-9651
ABST: --Film Literature Index (ISSN: 0093-6758)
--World Surface Coating Abstracts (ISSN: 0043-9088)

✤ MEDIA REPORTER, THE

PUBL: Bouverie Publishing Co., Ltd., 244-249 Temple Chambers, Temple Ave., London EC4Y 0DT, England.
DESC: "In its ten years as Britain's only quarterly review covering the world of journalism, *The Media Reporter* has established an enviable reputation for serious examination of the issues that concern journalists. Its wide ranging articles have provided an intelligent and independent commentary on current controversies in journalism, on questions of professional standards and ethics and in particular on the training of the next generation of journalists." *The Media Reporter* was incorporated into *UK Press Gazette* commencing with the April 28, 1986 issue, and thenceforth issued as a quarterly supplement to that serial in January, April, July, and October of each year.
DEPT: "Media Books," "Media Diary." (4-28-86).
TYPL: "Training--the Next Step," "Learning from the Pioneers," "Critic of the Classroom," "Slow Progress for Watchdogs," "British Journalism in Low Esteem." (4-28-86).
SCHL: Quarterly, 8 pp.
SPAN: 1976+
VARIES
--? - ? as Media Report.
SUPPLEMENT TO
--UK Press Gazette (ISSN: 0041-5170), Apr 28, 1986 to date.
LC: PN 4701 .M43
DD: 072/.91

ISSN: 0309-0256

✤ MEDIA SIGHT

SUB: "The magazine of popular culture."
PUBL: Media Sight Publications, PO Box 2630, Athens, OH 45701.
DESC: "*Media Sight* is a publication which offers a trip back into yesteryear; the world of the Saturday afternoon matinee and the dime comic book. It offers all of the excitement of a cliffhanger and all of the thrills of a detective pulp. Join us for this voyage to the land of nostalgia and down the forgotten avenues of America's past." An interesting mixture of current and past media culture, *Media Sight* reports on a wide variety of communication and cultural topics; including comic strips, film comedians, Saturday motion picture serials, science fiction, television programs ("Land of the Giants," "I Dream of Jeannie," "Leave It to Beaver"), and other items of a nostalgic value. As noted in a back-of-issue subscription page: "Each exciting issue of *Media Sight* features numerous articles, features, profiles, interviews, spotlights, and previews. Each exciting issue of *Media Sight* features clear investigative reporting. Each issue of *Media Sight* includes entertainment so intense that it is difficult to put the magazine down." For the sampled issue of 1983: stapled magazine format, black/white graphics and editorial content on newsprint (8 3/8 x 10 5/8 inches / 215 x 270 mm).
DEPT: "Editorial," column by Geoffrey Schutt; "Mailsack," letters; "Firsts," historical items and cartoon column by C. L. Crist. (winter-83).
TYPL: "Kerry Gammill Interview: Marvel's Hot Young Artist," "Buckwheat: The Myth, the Legend, the Reality," "L. Ron Hubbard: The Truth Behind the Prolific Author," "E. C. Comics: Gone But Not Forgotten." (winter-83).
SCHL: Quarterly, 60 pp.
SPAN: Winter, 1982+?

✤ MEDIA SPOTLIGHT

SUB: "A Christian review of entertainment."
PUBL: Media Spotlight Ministries, 1102 E. Chestnut Ave., Santa Ana, CA 92701.
DESC: "It is the purpose of this publication to present a Christian perspective in the review of mass communication media and entertainment including, but not limited to, motion pictures, television and radio programming, music and the theatre. Emphasis is placed upon the content of productions as they stand or fall in the light of biblical truth as well as how they affect the morals and attitudes of those who view them." Articles tend primarily to be of a critical, negative nature and aimed at such media events as Norman Vincent Peale lauding Mormon President Spencer Kimbal; Dungeons & Dragons; "The Empire Strikes Back;" and books or music concerning Christianity. Well-written with a theologically conservative viewpoint.
DEPT: "Editorial," "Books," review; "Movie Guide," a large section devoted to specific objections of recently released motion pictures; "The Media in Scripture."
TYPL: "Dungeons & Dragons, A Look at Fantasy Role-Playing Games," "What's Wrong with this Ad?." (4/6-80); "Oh God! Book II," "The Media in Scripture," "Do Unbelievers' prayers 'Falwell' on God's Ears?" (Aug/Dec-80).
SCHL: Uncertain, 16 pp.
SPAN: 1978?+?

✤ MEDIA WATCH

SUB: "Newsletter of the National Citizens Committee for Broadcasting."
PUBL: National Citizens Committee for Broadcasting, 1028 Connecticut Ave., N.W., Washington, DC 20036.
DESC: "Media Watch" is a publication for media reform in America. Begun by citizen-reformer Ralph Nader, it looks after the ethical and social impact of developments in the mass media and common carrier fields. The information contained is important, even though there was somewhat less news content (in sampled issues for 1980) than one might have expected.
DEPT: "Feedback," letters. (fall-80).
TYPL: "Reagan Election Good News for Broadcasters," "Neighborhood TV is Coming," "Results of 1980 TV Violence Monitoring." (fall-80).
SCHL: Quarterly, 6 pp.
SPAN: ?+?

✤ MEDIA WEEK

PUBL: Media Week, Ltd., City Cloisters, 188-196 Old St., London EC1V 9NP, England.
DESC: This is a news tabloid for the media buying/selling publics of Britain, packaged in a clean-cut, no-nonsense layout that enhances the media news of the week. Thorough, considered coverage is provided for such diverse media as radio, television, magazines, newspapers, and billboards, (as they pertain to advertising sale and purchase). *Media Week* is concerned more with the people, business, and news of media, rather than the numbers field of demographics, time and print purchases. For that reason, it has become an important weekly in the always competitive quest of agencies to secure new business, while holding on to current clients. *Media Week* joins in this competitive race by reporting who has gained and lost each week, and what potential media are just coming into view. How many other publications award a bottle of champagne to the writer of the best "Letters" to the editor column each week? For the 1990 sampled issue: small, stapled tabloid format, crisp graphics and layout format, printed black ink with spot-color red ink on coated paper stock with significant number of full-color advertisements (9 3/8 x 13 inches / 240 x 330 mm).

DEPT: "News," "ITV Marketplace," 'Buyers' estimates of ITV revenue (£m)'; "City Watch," London media column by William Arnold; "Advertising," "Broadcast," "International," "Print," "Business," "Comment," "Issues," "People," "Moves," personnel changes; "Letters," "Bookings," "Masterwind Up," media observations and comment column by Richard Gold. (2-23-90).
TYPL: "BSB Signs Up Top Agencies for Long-Term Packages," "Furious IPA Calls for Change in BARB Structure After Decision on Contract," "IPC Considers Further Moves in Europe with Me and Essentials," "Regional Sundays Feel the Pinch as Nationals do Battle." (2-23-90).
SCHL: Weekly, 45 pp.
SPAN: Apr 12, 1985+

✤ MEDIABRIEFS

SUB: "The quarterly newsletter for media, advertising, and public relations professionals."
PUBL: Dialog Information Services, Inc., 3460 Hillview Ave., Palo Alto, CA 94304.
DESC: Designed as a promotional publication to stimulate DIALOG database usage, *MediaBriefs* brings to the reader's attention new and overlooked aspects of this huge online service. The quarterly is targeted to "media, advertising, and public relations professionals." One article in the sampled issue for 1991 detailed how television news researchers used DIALOG for background, and provided other information concerning current news items. Another article explored the wealth of demographic information available within the service, and how such data might be applied to advertising and public relations campaigns. It is a very useful resource for those using or contemplating using Dialog Information Services. Large newsletter format, black ink (with spot color) on coated paper stock, no advertising (11 x 14 inches / 280 x 355 mm).
DEPT: "Quick Hits," database newsitems; "Search Tips," database search highlight. (summer-91).
TYPL: "Japanese Files Provide Eastern Insight," "Demographic Data Adds Depth to Stories and Direction to Ad or PR Campaigns," "Jerry Bornstein of NBC is on Top of the News with DIALOG," "Spice Up Your Speech with DIALOG," "Hot Topics Found in New PAPERS Files." (summer-91).
SCHL: Quarterly, 4 pp.
SPAN: Spring, 1991+

Mediascene

Nov/Dec, 1973 - May/Jun, 1980//
SEE: PREVUE

Mediascene Prevue

Jul/Aug, 1980 - ?, 1987//
(ISSN: 0199-9257)
SEE: PREVUE

✤ MEDIAWATCH

SUB: "A monthly report from the Media Research Center."
PUBL: Media Research Center, 113 South West St., Alexandria, VA 22314.
DESC: *MediaWatch* subscribers give strong praise to this monthly publication: "Where most conservatives complain vaguely about media bias, *MediaWatch* gives names, dates, and incriminating quotes. It reports the prejudices of the press in action, and pounces." And, "Every month when I receive *MediaWatch*, I can just see and hear the leftwingers in the major media gnashing their teeth. Bravo to *MediaWatch* for exposing the hypocrisy in so much of what's going on among the 'news' business in our time." Both praise and editorial content of this monthly eight-page newsletter is strongly placed in the conservative political camp in America. This is a no-nonsense publication, that "...will give you examples, quotes, studies and analysis exposing the liberal bias of the media, especially the TV networks." No graphics, save for an always interesting political cartoon reprint concerning alleged liberal media bias. Media Research Center also publishes the bimonthly newsletter, *TV, etc.*, a "...review of the entertainment industry and the Hollywood Left." For the sampled issue of 1990: loose-leaf newsletter format, printed blue ink on beige uncoated paper stock, no advertising (8 ½ x 10 ⅞ inches / 215 x 275 mm).
DEPT: "Newsbites," newsbriefs; "Revolving Door," monthly politics vs. media tally. (1-90).
TYPL: "Panama Canards," "NBC's Gorby Love Letter," "The 1980's: Those Evil Reagan Years," "Economy Soars, Coverage Dives." (1-90).
SCHL: Monthly, 8 pp.
SPAN: Jan, 1987+

✤ MEDIAWEEK

SUB: "The new weekly magazine for media decision-makers."
SUB: "Where marketing and media meet."
SUB: "Incorporating Marketing & Media Decisions."
PUBL: A/S/M Communications, 1515 Broadway, New York, NY 10036.
DESC: Continuing the fine reputation developed under the previous banners of *Media Decisions* and *Marketing & Media Decisions*, *MediaWeek* continues to provide detailed news, interviews, and commentaries on the changing fields of media buying and market positioning for advertising and in-house agencies. One of the elements which sets this publication apart from other trade serials is that there is a stronger emphasis on media planning and purchasing. This is for the media

buyer in advertising agencies or in-house staff, with intelligent discussions on demographics, changing societal buying patterns, new media bargains, and marketing strategies. One brand market is featured each issue. Of note are monthly "brand reports" which take an indepth look at marketing, research, and subsequent media purchases for a particular segment of the retail market. The January 14, 1991 issue contained *TV Programming*, billed as a "Supplement to *Adweek / Adweek's Marketing Week / Mediaweek*" publications. An impressive resource for the advertising marketing area, *Marketing & Media Decisions* was an Act III Publishing product, which when sold to BPI Publishing in December, 1990 assumed its current title, and moved from monthly to weekly publication status. For the sampled issues of 1979 under the title of *Marketing & Media Decisions*: editorial content was black ink with full-color advertising and cover on coated stock, in stapled magazine format, with significant advertising to the trade (7 7/8 x 10 5/8 inches / 200 x 270 mm). For the sampled issues of 1991: stapled magazine format; editorial content is full-color pages on coated paper stock; significant trade advertising (8 1/4 x 10 5/8 inches / 210 x 270 mm). Note: as of the January 14, 1991 issue, *MediaWeek* was still indicating the same ISSN (0195-4296), as previously assigned to *Marketing & Media Decisions*.

DEPT: "Focus on Marketing," "New Electronic Media" "Campaigns," "Print Beat," "Newsmakers," "DC," "Update," "New in Media," "Direct Marketing," "Homework," "Futures," "Calendar," "Broadcast Beat," "Cost Trends," "As We See It," "Mediology," "Consumer Magazines," "Marketing," "Radio," "Business Publications," "Television," "Research," "Outdoor." (9-84). "Letters," "Pro Files," profile; "Print Beat," "Direct Marketing," "Debut," new and noteworthy; "Update," "Creative Concepts," "Freeze Frame," "Tools of the Trade," "Sales Promotion," "Broadcast Beat," "Point/Counterpoint/Poll," "On the Docket," regulatory news; "Economic Eye," "Last Word," "Mediology," commentary; "Television," commentary; "Cable," commentary; "Magazines," commentary; "Planning," commentary. (12-88). "Notes From Space & Time," editorial column by Craig Reiss; "Media Dish," personality column by Kathy Kalafut; "People Meter," personnel newsbriefs; "Psycho G's," offbeat items; "Trendicators," 'For the brokers of popular culture'." (1-14-91).

TYPL: "A Day in the Life of Alec Gerster," "The VCR Phenomenon," "Seagram Pours Wine Profits," "Indies Come of Age," "What's in a Name?," "Fashion for a Penney," "Marketers Take License." (9-84). "The 1988 Media All Stars." (12-88). "Bail-Out: Clients Seek Relief as War Looms, Recession Hits," "Networks Brace for $50 Mil Withdrawal," "Daily Losses on Crisis Could Hit $27 Million," "It's Out: Time Warner Will Test Weekly Life," "Daily News Steps Up Talks With Striking Drivers Union." (1-14-91).

SCHL: Monthly (? - ?); Fifteen issues per year (? - Dec, 1990); Weekly [except first week of Jan] (Jan 14, 1991+), 55 pp.
SPAN: Sep, 1966+
VARIES
--Sep, 1966 - Apr, 1979 as Media Decisions (ISSN: 0025-6900).
--May, 1979 - Dec, 1990 as Marketing & Media Decisions (ISSN: 0195-4296).
WITH SUPPLEMENT
--TV Programming.
LC: HF 5801.M43
DD: 659
ISSN: 1055-176x
ABST: --ABI/Informer
--Business Periodical Index (ISSN: 0007-6961)
--InfoBank
--Management Contents
--Predicasts
--Trade and Industry Index

MEDIUM
PUBL: Filmage Inc., 180 Centre St., New York, NY 10013.
DESC: With the rise of film consciousness in the mid-1960s, *Medium* became one of a number of serials of aesthetic film criticism to arrive on the American scene. Like others of the genre, *Medium* took a critical look at motion picture film as art form, surveying international product and developments within the avant-garde and independent (underground) movement. Square serial format; numerous graphics; clean layout design.
DEPT: None. (summer-67).
TYPL: "Interview with Leopoldo Torre Nilsson," "Fellini's Mystery," "Canadian Cinema: A Brief Perspective," "Pornography and the Film." (summer-67).
SCHL: Quarterly, 60 pp.
SPAN: Summer, 1967 - Winter, 1968//
ISSN: 0025-8369

Memo - Corporation for Public Broadcasting
Aug 30, 1974? - ?//
SEE: REPORT

✦ MEMO TO MAILERS
PUBL: United States Postal Service Communications Department, US Postal Service, Room 5300, 475 L'Enfant Plaza SW, Washington, DC 20260-3122.
DESC: With an eye to new ideas in automation, economy of scale, and efficiency/productivity in service, *Memo to Mailers* describes a vast array of United States Postal Service activities important to the corporate media world. This is especially important for those print media which rely on the Postal Service for their distribution; and, of course, for the direct mail/marketing

field for which mail service is the life blood of the industry. *Memo to Mailers* discusses a variety of issues in each monthly newsletter, but is probably most valuable for its discussion of distribution techniques, and means by which large bulk mailers can significantly curb their postal costs. *Memo to Mailers* accomplishes much in demystifying the mailing process. From a business that handles (during 1990) 41 percent of the world's mail volume, *Memo to Mailers* is a welcome informational vehicle for the print, publishing, and direct mail fields. For the sampled issue of 1990: newsletter format; black/white graphics.

DEPT: "Postal Customer Council," "News Briefs." (2-90).
TYPL: "USPS Sets New Schedule for Service Standard Changes," "REDI System Tracks Mail Sent by Rail," "Bulk Mail Centers to Receive Sack Label Bar Code Scanners." (2-90).
SCHL: Monthly, 8 pp.
SPAN: Jan, 1966?+

✚ MEMORIES

SUB: "The magazine of then and now."
SUB: "Everything old is news again."
PUBL: Diamandis Communications, Inc., 1633 Broadway, New York, NY 10019.
DESC: "From the shows that filled our screens, to the events that shaped our lives, *Memories* illuminates our past. And puts it into perspective. *Memories* is more than read. It's remembered." "Quality" described this full-color bimonthly dedicated to "rememberance of things past." Although not exclusively mass media content, the majority of articles concerned aspects of American mass communication, presented in an interesting visual design with quality writing. One interesting aspect to this publication (especially for those interested in advertising and copywriting) was the two to five double-page spreads of a product advertisement from 15-50 years ago, and a current advertisement for the same product on the facing page. For the mass communication researcher/historian, this was one publication which could be read for work as well as pleasure. It was a dissapointment when the October, 1990 issue contained this message: "We are truly sorry to inform you that this is the last issue of *Memories* you will receive. Unfortunately, despite everyone's best efforts, and your support, the economics of publishing a magazine as unique as *Memories* has forced us to suspend publication." Despite this public cessation notice, a trade magazine reported in September, 1990 that *Memories* would NOT cease publication but rather would remain suspended, with plans to publish the magazine on a semiyearly basis. Square magazine format (9 x 10 ⅞ inches / 230 x 275 mm); numerous graphics printed on quality paper. Highly recommended.
DEPT: "From the Editor," "Letters," "Album," full page historical photo; "Yearbook," famous people's high-school yearbook pictures; "Indelible Images," Photographer profiles and the story behind the historical pictures they took; "I Remember," rememberence of news events past via eyewitnesses to those events;

"Markings," updates to historical events; "Film Festival," "Gallery," images of time past; "Perspective," commentary; "Taking Issue," commentary; "Photo Finish," picture collage. (12-89/1-90).
TYPL: "Vintage Hollywood," "The Brinks Heist," "The Trials of 'Tokyo Rose'," "Whither the TV Western?," "Winston Churchill." (12-89/1-90).
SCHL: Bimonthly (Spring, 1988 - Oct, 1990); Semiyearly (?+), 120 pp.
SPAN: Spring, 1988+
SUSPENDED
--Oct, 1990+
DD: 973 11
ISSN: 0898-9184

METRO-GOLDWYN-MAYER SHORT STORY

PUBL: Metro-Goldwyn-Mayer, 1540 Broadway, New York, NY.
DESC: This glossy, multi-colored, large format serial had one function: to promote MGM short subjects. Each issue contained a lineup of new releases, and educational articles pertaining to that short subject film. Target audience was the local film exhibitor. Each issue included the special feature, "Exploitation," which offered advice on "showmanship" for the upcoming MGM "short story" films; and a cartoon that poked fun at the length of the longer-running double-feature format. Quality printing on glossy stock.
DEPT: "Leo Jr's Lion-Up," listing of new MGM short films; "Short Waves of Response," letters; "A Few Short Words," comment. (11/12-39).
TYPL: "A Door Will Open," "Romance of the Potato," "Adventures of Stuffie," "See Your Doctor," "Alfalfa's Double." (11/12-39).
SCHL: Monthly (? - Feb, 1939); Bimonthly (Mar/Apr, 1939 - Jul/Aug, 1941).
SPAN: 1938? - Jul/Aug, 1941//
VARIES
--? - Jan, 1939 as MGM Short Story.
ABSORBED BY
--Lion's Roar, The, Sep, 1941.
LC: PN 1993.M315

✚ MGF

SUB: "Men's guide to fashion."
SUB: "Movies."
SUB: "Men's guide to fashion & entertainment."
PUBL: MGF Publications Corporation, 3 West 18th St., New York, NY 10011.
DESC: The word, "unique," applies to this quarterly publication, which blends the world of men's fashion, and the latest motion picture product; with special emphasis on male stars. The departmental regulars concentrate primarily on issues of grooming, fashion, exercise, entertainment and sex. Feature articles, on the other hand, are primarily devoted to male stars and their roles in current motion pictures, with typical inter-

views with Matthew Broderick, Jack Nicholson, Harrison Ford, Mel Gibson, Robert Downey, Jr., Randy Quaid, and Jeff Bridges. With a minimum of advertising, it is for the male reader for whom appearance, manner, physique, and the movies are of prime value. Color graphics, often full-page pictures of film production stills, grace each issue. In short, this is a magazine for and about men; their entertainment and their fashion in the decade of the 1990s. For the sampled issue of 1990: magazine format (8 ⅛ x 10 ⅞ inches / 210 x 275 mm); color graphics.

DEPT: "Letters," "Fashion News," column by Elizabeth Stewart; "Grooming," column by Alex Press; "Fitness," column by Norman Zeitchick; "Feeling Great," column by Steven Slon; "Fashion Q & A," column by Elizabeth Stewart; "Movie News," column by Alan Mirabella; "Bravos & Boos," 'A gentleman's guide to who and what's heating up and cooling off' column by Gerald Rothberg; "Mister Manners," column by Edward D. Gottlieb; "Movies on Cable," 'A guide to small screen highlights' column by Alex Press; "Sex Advisor," column by Marty Klein; "For Men Only," column by Glenn Plaskin; "MGF Quiz," column by Perry Buffington; "Pssst!," 'Reveling in the glitter and the glory' picture page column by Aubrey Reuben. (9/10-90).
TYPL: "Brando is Back in 'The Freshman'," "Is 'Two Jakes' Better Than One?," "Harrison Ford in 'Presumed Innocent'," "The Aids Report," "'Air America': Drugs and Daring Over Vietnam." (9/10-90).
SCHL: Quarterly, 65 pp.
SPAN: Feb, 1985+
DD: 646 11
ISSN: 0887-5219

MGM Short Story

? - Jan, 1939//
SEE: METRO-GOLDWYN-MAYER SHORT STORY

✧ MID-ATLANTIC GRAPHIC ARTS REVIEW

SUB: "Reviewing the graphic arts in the tri-state Philadelphia area."
PUBL: MAL Publishing Company, Philadelphia, PA.
DESC: This was a somewhat small-size publication for Philadelphia area print shop personnel and management concerned with the mechanical side of publication. Articles covered paper mills, engraving, fonts, paper coatings, and other aspects of the trade. Other serials of this type existed in various communities throughout America: one element which set the *Mid-Atlantic Graphic Arts Review* apart from the rest was the editorial policy to print sample graphic designs or advertisements into its pages. The standard was simply to bind those special printed items as inserts into the publication.
DEPT: "Among the Craftsmen," newsbriefs; "Typothatae Topics," "Junior Executives Jottings," "Job of the Month," "Notes of the Agencies," "Out in the Shop," "Items of Interest." (2-41).
TYPL: "Training Deaf Boys to be Printers," "Wesley H. Shirtk, Engineer-- Publisher." (2-41).
SCHL: Monthly, 35 pp.
SPAN: Jan, 1938+?
VARIES
--Jan, 1938 - ? as Graphic Arts Review.
ABSORBED
--Printing Impressions [Delaware Valley edition], Apr, 1963.

✧ MIDWEEK MOTION PICTURE NEWS

PUBL: Motion Picture News, Inc., 729 7th Ave., New York, NY.
DESC: Utilizing a publishing principle common to the times, some 50-plus pages of full-page advertising precedes the editorial content of this publication devoted to the motion picture exhibition industry. Advertisements were primarily for forthcoming motion picture product, and tied to the impact of *Midweek Motion Picture News*. This was an exhibitor's trade publication. Articles discussed studio, artist, and production news, but especially the operation and profitability of the local cinema theatre. Therefore, the magazine featured news reports of cinema managers throughout North America, new branch managers, declared dividends, theatres lost to fires, boxoffice holdups, new theatre chains, local censorship problems, Blue laws against motion picture exhibition on Sundays, distribution, and how to make the best of a bad film showing. Several departmental features merit attention. One was "Exhibitors Box-Office Reports," a chart noting "Title of Picture," "Population of Town," "Location," "Class of Patronage," "Weather," "Box Office Value," and "Check-Up Percentage From Other Reports," which were "...from theatre owners who reside in the smaller towns [with preference given to] exhibitors located in towns of less than 5,000 population." Another valuable department was "Theatre Management," which included subsections on theatre construction, house organs for patrons, generating community good-will, the technique of projection; music; and new developments in theatrical technology. Magazine format (235 cm wide x 310 cm high); numerous black/white photographs and production stills on coated paper stock; three-color covers.
DEPT: "Speaking Editorially," "Pictures and People," picture commentary and artists at leisure; "Production News," newsbriefs of upcoming projects; "Ideas You Can Use," exploitation concepts; "Consensus of Opinion," film commentary; "Feature Reviews," "Press Notice and Screen Service," advertising and promotion suggestions; "Exhibitors Box-Office Reports," smaller town reports; "Theatre Management," "Equipment Construction Operation," "Projection," 'Optics, elec-

tricity, practical ideas & advice'; "Feature Release Chart," "Newspaper Opinions on New Pictures." (12-30-25).
TYPL: "Designing and Publishing the Theatre House Organ," "To Bar 'Red' Grange Picture," "Federal Censorship Threatens," "German Production Falls Off," "Fabian Launches Finest Theatre in Circuit in Paterson, N.J." (12-30-25).
SCHL: Weekly, 95 pp.
SPAN: Jul 15, 1925+?

✦ MILITARY ELECTRONICS / COUNTERMEASURES

PUBL: ICDM of North America, Inc., 2065 Martin Ave., Suite 104, Santa Clara, CA 95050.
DESC: Communication is a major key in the mobilization of any armed forces, and *Military Electronics/Countermeasurers* provides a monthly update of the developments in the electronics field for military application. Issues under discussion include voice/data communication, radar, computer/information display technologies, and communication problems under specific wartime conditions. Of special importance is the operation of such communication and electronics equipment under battle/environmental conditions, from desert warfare to nuclear blast. The serial is divided into topical sections: Forum, Computer Peripherals, Countermeasures, Radiation Effects, Antisubmarine Warfare, Combat Systems, Display Systems, IC Technology, Missle Electronics, and Military Science & Technology. For the sampled issue of 1983: magazine format (8 x 10 ¾ inches / 200 x 275 mm); graphics, schematics and charts.
DEPT: "International Intelligence," "Washington Perspective," "New Hardware," "Editorial." (3-83).
TYPL: "Militarized Peripherals Accommodate Expanding Requirements," "Radiation Threshold Levels Can Be Calculated for Photodiode Noise Degradation," "Task Force Survival Relies on Early Detection," "Plasma Displays Offer Advantages for Many Tactical Applications," "Robotics Finds Applications in Ground Warfare." (3-83).
SCHL: Monthly, 105 pp.
SPAN: Jan, 1975+
VARIES
--? - Apr?, 1977 as Electronic, Electro-Optic and Infrared Countermeasures (ISSN: 0148-6373).
CONTINUED BY
--Journal of C4I Countermeasures [NC].
LC: UG 485 .E43
DD: 623/.043/05
ISSN: 0164-4076
ABST: --Computer & Control Abstracts (ISSN: 0036-8113)
--Electrical & Electronics Abstracts (ISSN: 0036-8105)
--International Aerospace Abstracts (ISSN: 0020-5842)
--Physics Abstracts. Science Abstracts. Series A. (ISSN: 0036-8091)

✦ MILLECANALI INTERNATIONAL

SUB: "Television, radio, communication."
PUBL: Gruppo Editoriale JCE srl., via Ferri, 6 - 20092 Cinisello, Balsamo (MI), Italy.
DESC: Representing the Associazione Broadcast Italiana, the Italian Broadcasting Association, and other Italian communication interests, this supplement to *Millecanali* promotes, describes, and showcases Italian communication equipment manufacturers to the English-speaking world. *Millecanali* Publisher Jacopo Castelfranchi, in an editorial preface to the sampled issue, explains to readers that from 1976 to recent times Italian broadcasting experienced an "...almost totally unregulated freedom to broadcast, both in the FM radio and the television fields. This brought about, among other things, the birth of a young and flexible domestic industry, mainly devoted to the manufacturing of transmitting equipment and station automation systems." Castelfranchi states that a recently enacted media law has "...applied an unwelcome brake to the continuous development of this wild market. As a consequence, the Italian manufacturing industry of broadcasting equipment, which over the years has come to characterize itself for an extremely high level of the performance-to-price ratio of its equipment, is now seeking new marketing channels on the international arena," which is why an international version of this famous magazine is now being issued. The majority of articles are in Italian, taken from the parent periodical, *Millecanali*, with English titles and summaries preceding each article. Departmental features also contain English-language summaries. For the sampled 1991 issue: stapled magazine format with full-color pages throughout on coated paper stock (8 ¼ x 11 inches / 210 x 280 mm).
DEPT: "News Broadcast - Business," 'News items on especially significant supplies, marketing agreements and other business deals in the fields of video, audio, computer-graphics and transmitting equipment'; "News PP-CG," 'News and reports on companies and events in the worlds of video and audio production and post-production'; "News Broadcast - Personaggi," 'The moves, change of responsibilities and other important activities of selected people in the broadcast industry'; "Notizie SMPTE," 'Frequent news items on the world-wide activity of SMPTE, with a special emphasis on the Italian section'. (4-4-91).
TYPL: "It's Las Vegas Again," "In Monte Carlo, Fantasy Celebrates Its Triumph," "More and More CCD." (4-4-91).
SCHL: Eleven issues per year, 75 pp.
SPAN: ?+
SUPPLEMENT TO
--Millecanali [NE].

✤ MILLENNIUM FILM JOURNAL

PUBL: Millenium Film Workshop, 66 East 4th St., New York, NY 10003.

DESC: "*Millenium Film Journal* is a tri-annual publication dedicated to avant-garde film theory and practice which provides a forum for discussion and debate in this country and abroad." Individual issues have focused on topics such as "Politics and Landscape," "Feminism, Dreams and Animation," or "Interviews, Rediscoveries, and the Third World." This quality journal provides a forum for the intellectual discussion of motion picture film as art, as political statement, and as dream factory. Note: volume numbering was discontinued after the first issue; some issues are double numbers, such as #23/24 issued for winter 1989/1990. Of special consideration are numerous black/white graphics used to illustrate articles. For the sampled issues of 1990 and 1991: editorial content in perfect-bound journal format consisting of black ink on uncoated paper; cover is black with blue-spot color ink on coated paper stock, advertising (7 x 10 inches / 175 x 255 mm).

DEPT: "Reviews," lengthy section. (summer/fall-79). "Interviews," "Artist Pages," "Book Reviews." (winter-90/91).

TYPL: "German Worker's Films 1919 - 1932: Some Thoughts About the Red Front in Film," "Brazilian Avant-Garde Cinema from Limite to Red Light Bandit," "The Gay Sensibility in American Avant-Garde Film," "Towards a Radical, Popular Cinema: Two Recent Films by John Jost." (summer/fall-79). "Out of Context: Some Thoughts on 'Independence'," "The Psychotechnology of Everyday Life," "Safe But Not Sound: The Toronto International Experimental Film Congress," "The Art of Programming: An Interview with Alf Bold, July, 1989," "Three Aspects of French Experimental Film: Interviews with Yann Beauvais and Rose Lowder and Alain-Alcide Sudre." (winter-90/91).

SCHL: Three issues per year, 200 pp.
SPAN: Winter, 1977/1978+

✤ MILLER'S COPYRIGHT NEWSLETTER

PUBL: Harbor View Publications Group, Copyright Information Services Division, 440 Tucker Ave., P.O. Box 1460-M, Friday Harbor, WA 98250-1460.

DESC: Based upon a "sample copy" of September, 1988, this irregularly published newsletter is designed primarily for clients of Dr. Jerome Miller, a copyright expert based in Washington state. The three articles in this issue covered the important issues of who holds copyright on creative works, deposit and registration requirements, and exemptions for business meetings. Single issues are $10 each, or $25 per year. Newsletter format; no graphics.

DEPT: "Reviewers Comments." (9-88).

TYPL: "Copyright Ownership and Rights," "Ninety-Day Registration and Deposit Deadline," "The Business-Meeting Exemption." (9-88).

SCHL: Irregular, 4 pp.
SPAN: 1988+
DD: 346
ISSN: 1043-1438

✤ MILLIMETER

SUB: "The magazine of the motion picture and television production industries."

SUB: "The magazine for and about film and videotape people."

PUBL: Penton Publishing, Inc., 1100 Superior, Cleveland, OH 44114.

DESC: With over 200 pages of articles and advertisements, this publication is for the professional video and filmmaker. Behind-the-scenes interviews, techniques, current activities, and future possibilities highlight *Millimeter*. Early issues (published in New York) had an understandable emphasis on New York City film and video activities. Now published in Cleveland, Ohio, editorial scope is national and provides a suprisingly thorough coverage of today's film and video industries. This is "must" reading for the film/video professional, especially one working in music videos, television commercial spot production, post production, or independent production companies. Of special note are ongoing "Production Guides," detailing production companies and activities at state and regional levels. This is one of a handful of video and film periodicals that provides a genuine forum where professionals come together to celebrate, explore, and debate the elements that comprise the motion picture and television production field. Magazine format (7 ¾ x 10 ⅞ inches / 200 x 275 mm), on coated paper stock.

DEPT: "Trim Bin," newsbriefs; "Close-Up," three profiles; "Chicago Loop," video-film news; "Documentary Explorations," new developments in this often overlooked area; "Cut-a-ways," new products; "Books." (10-81). "Letters," "Editor's Notes," "The Front Page," unique feature detailing film/video production or equipment in the news; "Teleproduction," "Commercials," "Motion Pictures," "Corporate Television," "Top Tracks," music videos; "Hot Spots," recent spot productions; "Graphics & Effects," "Facility Planning Achievements," new production studio profiles; "Imaging Technology," "Audio Technology," "Equipment Preview," "Close-Ups," profiles; "In Production," current listing; "Newmedia," new media technologies; "Production Guide," outstanding state or regional production profile. (10-89).

TYPL: "Will Success Spoil Dick Richards?," "Space: 1999, Son-of-Star Trek Blasts Off," "Robert Wise and 'The Hindenburg.'" (11-75); "Coppola's Electronic Cinema Process," "TV Studios on Wheels," "Rights, Restraints, Restrictions: Where Commercial Directors Stand," "Strategies for Commercial Production Survival." (10-81). "The Global Warming Trend: Can American Commercial Directors Make New Fortunes

Overseas?," "Dateline, Prime Time: Monsters," "Ambience Chasers," "Cutting a Deal: Drawing the Line," "Inside a Top Agency: Scandals, Rumors, and Rock 'n' Roll." (10-89).
SCHL: Monthly, [except Jul-Aug], 150 pp.
SPAN: 1973+
LC: TR 845.M54
DD: 778.5/05
ISSN: 0164-9655
ABST: --Film Literature Index (ISSN: 0093-6758)
--Media Review Digest (ISSN: 0363-7778)

Miniature Camera World
Dec?, 1936? - May, 1955//
SEE: 35MM PHOTOGRAPHY

Minicam
Sep, 1937 - Jan, 1940//
SEE: MODERN PHOTOGRAPHY

Minicam Photography
Feb, 1940 - Aug, 1949//
(ISSN: 0096-5863)
SEE: MODERN PHOTOGRAPHY

✤ MINORITIES IN THE NEWSPAPER BUSINESS
PUBL: ANPA Foundation, American Newspaper Publishers Association, The Newspaper Center, PO Box 17407 Dulles Airport, Washington, DC 20041.
DESC: *Minorities in the Newspaper Business* is "a publication of the American Newspaper Publishers Association Foundation, in conjunction with participating organizations of the Task Force on Minorities in the Newspaper Business." The quarterly serial brings together publishers, plant workers, and community minorities in an educational forum designed to break down myths and stereotypes; to demonstrate through examples, the benefits of a successful minorities program for newspaper owners. Two-color newsletter format; no advertising.
DEPT: None. (fall-89).
TYPL: "Thriving on Diversity," "Task Force Considers Retention Issue," "NABJ Convention Draws Largest Crowd Ever," "Name Bias: What's in a Byline?" (fall-89).
SCHL: Quarterly, 8 pp.
SPAN: Sep, 1985+

MIRROR OF TASTE, AND DRAMATIC CENSOR, THE
PUBL: Bradford and Inskeep, Philadelphia, PA.
DESC: In the premiere issue for January, 1810, Publishers Bradford and Inskeep provided readers a literate preface relating to both the form and function of this new publication devoted to the theatre: "The first and by far the larger share will be alloted to the stage, and dramatic productions. The residue to miscellaneous articles, most of them connected with the fashionable amusements, and designed to correct the abuses, which intemperate ignorance, and Licentiousness, running riot for want of critical control, have introduced into the public diversions of this opulent and luxurious city. In the composition of the several parts of this work, care will be taken to furnish the public with new and interesting matter, and to select from the current productions of the British metropolis such topics as will best tend to promote the cultivation of an elegant taste for knowledge and letters, and, at the same time, repay the reader for the trouble of perusal, with amusement and delight. Abstracts from the most popular publications will be given, accompanied with short critical remarks upon them, and, whatever appears most interesting in the periodical productions of Great Britain will be transferred into this; pruned if they be prolix, and illustrated by explanatory notes, whenever they may be found obscured by local or personal allusion." At a yearly 1810 subscription rate of eight dollars per year, this was by no means an inexpensive publication for the era, but the publishers promised 12 full monthly issues plus "To each number will be added, by way of appendix, an entire play or after-piece, printed in a small elegant type, and paged so as to be collected, at the end of each year, into a separate volume. The work will be embellished with elegant engravings by the first artists." The lead-off article in the premiere issue consisted of a "History of the Stage--Chapter One," subtitled "Objections to the Stage Considered and Refuted." This historical, departmental column was featured in every issue and ranged from North American to European and early Grecian theatrical origins. A very lengthy series of detailed biographies followed, including one of Dr. Samuel Johnson; a deceased Mr. Hallam, which the publisher referred to as "The father of the American stage;" British actor Edward Alleyn; and Thomas Abthorpe Cooper, player extraordinaire. The 48 pages consisting of the above named articles completed the whole of the *Mirror of Taste*. The second section entitled, *The Dramatic Censor*, was introduced by the publishers as thus: "The establishment of a regular and permanent work of dramatic criticism and of censorship upon the public amusements of this city has often been attempted. The uniform failure of these efforts renders it natural to apprehend that the proposition now submitted to the public will incur the charge of presumption, and perhaps experience, for a time, the coldness and discouragement with which the majority of mankind are always inclined to treat even laudable exertions, if they in any degree militate against the dictates of common prudence, and are not recommended by a certainty of public approbation." The lead article in the premiere section of *The Dramatic*

Censor was a critique of "A Cure For the Heart-Ach," which had opened at the Philadelphia Theatre on Monday, November 20, 1809. "Of the quality of this production," the magazine's critic noted, "it would be difficult for criticism to speak candidly, without adverting to the present miserable state of dramatic poetry in England, which from the days of Sam Foote has been gradually descending to its present deplorable condition. The body of dramatic writers of the last thirty years first corrupted the public taste, and now thrive by that corruption." Other critiqued works included "Pizarro," "Town and Country," "Wags of Windsor," "Village Lawyer," "Ella Rozenberg," a melo-drame, "Reconciliation, or Fraternal Discord," "False and True," "Abaellino, or the Great Bandit," "Lady of the Rock," "Road to Ruin," "Speed the Plough," "The Foundling of the Forest," and "Of Age Tomorrow," which merited this one-line critique: "Every character tolerably well played." Several items deserve special mention. "Sporting Intelligence" provided lengthy news items of fox hunts, horse racing, rabbit-breeding, and boxing, most of which originated in British publications. "Miscellany" consisted of much poetry and prose. "Music" described current American and British fare. The letters column consisted of several submissions all attesting to the vulgar behavior of theatre-goers. Noted one citizen, commenting on the noise eminating from a group of young troublemakers: "If any of you was there, gentlemen, you must have noticed it; if not, I can't write such filthy words as was spoken the whole evening. ...It is not the players you ought to criticise, they behave themselves--but it is those vagabonds that think they have a right to disturb the house because they pay their half dollar a piece." The premiere issue was rounded out with full text of the play "The F

DEPT: "History of the Stage," "Biographies," "Music," "Sporting Intelligence," "Miscellany," "Correspondence," letters. (1-1810).
TYPL: None. (1-1810).
SCHL: Monthly, 100 pp.
SPAN: Jan, 1810 - Dec, 1811//
LC: PN 1601 .M5

✦ MIX

SUB: "The recording industry magazine."
SUB: "Professional recording."
SUB: "Sound and music production."
PUBL: Act III Publishing, 6400 Hollis St., #12, Emeryville, CA 94608.
DESC: *Mix* is dedicated to the art and technique of studio recording for all media, with an emphasis on producing audio product and new technology. It is for the audio professional, providing a forum for discussion of major issues of the day; such as the "civil war," as *Mix* (Sep, 1989) described the ongoing battle between private studios (home based) and commercial recording operations. Each issue features a cluster of articles around a special topic, such as "Focus on Digital," "Studio Design," or "International Focus." Of special note is the directory function of *Mix*, providing vendor or studio lists; each issue pertaining to unique characteristics of audio recording. This serial is both authoritative and thorough in its coverage of the art and business of audio recording. Magazine format (8 x 10 ⅞ inches / 205 x 275 mm); numerous graphics.
DEPT: "Current," newsbriefs; "Committee Report," association news; "Progressions," column; "Sound Advice: Special Report," technical column; "Playback," consumer audio; "Other Side of the Tracks," column; "Classifieds," "Feedback," letters. (11-80). "Current," "Industry Notes," "Sessions/Studio News," "From the Editor," "Juxtapositions," column by Mel Lambert; "The Fast Lane," column by Stephen St. Croix; "Insider Audio," column by Ken Pohlmann; "After-Mix," column by Philip De Lancie; "Sound Reinforcement News/Tour Update," column by Mark Herman; "Preview/Hot Off the Shelf," "Field Test," new equipment; "Lunching with Bonzai," column by Mr. Bonzai; "Music & Recording Notes," "M.I. Update," Midis and music. (9-89).
TYPL: "Studer Opening," "Wally Heider." (11-80). "Production Music Libraries," "Radio and Digital Audio," "The Digitization of Australia," "Lace & Filligree: The Search for Transparency and Detail." (9-89).
SCHL: Quarterly (Sep, 1978 - ?); Monthly (Apr, 1987+), 195 pp..
SPAN: Jan, 1977+
LC: HD 9697.P563 U55
DD: 338.4/76213893/0973
ISSN: 0164-9957

✦ MOBILE SATELLITE NEWS

SUB: "The executive report on land mobile, maritime and aeronautical communications."
PUBL: Phillips Publishing, Inc., 7811 Montrose Rd., Potomac, MD 20854.
DESC: Technological, regulatory, and economic events can create a major impact on the relatively new, dynamic and volatile field of mobile/satellite communication. *Mobile Satellite News* helps to cut through the blizzard of news stories by publishing this concise monthly report of latest trends, issues, developments and forecasts in the mobile communication arena. One sampled issue provided major coverage concerning recent Federal Communications Commission actions on mobile satellite operations in the Washington, DC area; developments in "vehicular data processing and communications systems," an exclusive interview with the general manager of COMSAT; and a detailed description of a new mobile communication satellite. Developments in this field happen quickly, and the communication executive who wishes to maintain a competitive edge should subscribe to this quality Phillips publication. For those subscribers who simply cannot wait for postal service delivery, *Mobile Satellite News* is also available via NewsNet and Predicasts services. Note: the first issue for November, 1989 was preceeded by a pilot "premiere" issue for October,

1989. Published black ink (with dark blue spot coverage) on yellow uncoated paper stock with limited graphics (8 ½ x 11 inches / 215 x 280 mm).
DEPT: "Circuits," newsbriefs; "Aeronautical." (4-91).
TYPL: "US Court of Appeals Drops Bomb on Mobile Satellite Community," "Launch Plans for AMSC Still Unclear," "NASA's Support Viewed as Unfair Competition by Some," "Rockwell to Combine Mobile Satellite and Auto Divisions," "Cruisephone Combines Cellular/Satellite for Communications." (4-91).
SCHL: Monthly, 12 pp.
SPAN: Nov, 1989+
DD: 384
ISSN: 1046-5286

✤ MODERN DRAMA

PUBL: University of Toronto, Graduate Centre for Study of Drama, Toronto, Ontario M5S 2E1 Canada.
DESC: *Modern Drama* examines the status of international dramatics. Although each issue has relatively few articles, readers will find this publication a good resource for the study of theatre. It features one special themed issue per year. For 1991, the special issue was "Drama and the Novel," exploring the process of transferring dramatic works of personalized reading to the stage. In 1992, the planned special issue was to be "Drama East and West," "'...intended to encompass a wide range of topics, not only influences in either direction and cross-fertilization; but also theory and the images of the East on Western stages, as well as vice-versa." The June, 1991 issue marked the end of "Modern Drama Studies: An Annual Bibliography," under the editorship of Charles A. Carpenter, who began the annual compilation in 1973. Linda Corman, head Librarian of Trinity College, University of Toronto, assumes those bibliographic duties starting with the 1992 compilation. For the sampled issues of 1979 and 1991: black ink on uncoated paper stock; cover consisting of spot-color on coated paper; in perfect-bound journal format (6 x 9 inches / 150 x 230 mm).
DEPT: "Book Reviews." (3-79). "Book Reviews." (6-84). None. (3-91).
TYPL: "Singing in the Wilderness: The Dark Vision of O'Neill's Only Mature Comedy," "Toward a Third Stream Theatre: Lawrence Ferlinghetti's Plays," "Sam Shepard's 'Angle City': A Movie for the Stage," "Time and Harold Pinter's Possible Realities: Art as Life, and Vice Versa," "Alejandro Casona and Nikolai Evreinov: Life as Theater." (3-79). "Ambiguity, Discontinuity and Overlapping in 'Peer Gynt,'" "Modern Drama Studies: An Annual Bibliography." (6-84). "A Novelist Finds the Bar Bones of a Play," "Reading as Theatre: Understanding Defamiliarization in Beckett's Art," "'Our Country's Good': Theatre, Colony and Nation in Wertenbaker's Adaptation of 'The Playmaker'," "'What's It Going To Be Then, Eh?': The Stage Odyssey of Anthony Burgess's 'A Clockwork Orange'," "Sicilian Themes and the Restructured Stage: The Dialectic of Fiction and Drama in the Work of Luigi Pirandello." (3-91).
SCHL: Quarterly, 50 pp.
SPAN: May, 1958+
LC: PN 1861.M55
DD: 809.2/005
ISSN: 0026-7694
ABST: --Abstract of English Studies (ISSN: 0001-3560)
--Annual Bibliography of English Language and Literature (ISSN: 0066-3786)
--Film Literature Index (ISSN: 0093-6758)
--Humanities Index (ISSN: 0095-5981)
--Index to Book Reviews in the Humanities (ISSN: 0073-5892)
--MLA International Bibliography of Books & Articles on the Modern Languages and Literatures (ISSN: 0024-8215)
--Reference Sources (ISSN: 0163-3546)
--Social Science and Humanities Index (ISSN: 0037-7899)

MODERN PHOTOGRAPHY

SUB: "The miniature camera monthly."
SUB: "Combined with Minicam Photography."
PUBL: ABC Leisure Magazines, 825 Seventh Ave., New York, NY 10019.
DESC: "*Modern Photography*, your best bet for the best in cameras, equipment, processing and photo techniques. Each and every month *Modern Photography* provides its readers with detailed reports and information on new cameras, new lenses, new color films, new equipment, net techniques, new accessories, and more. What to buy and where. It's all in *Modern Photography*." For over 50 years, *Modern Photography* and its predecessors have described, questioned, debated, and introduced numerous elements of photography to the American lay audience. Some latter articles also covered visual elements of other media, especially video. With the July, 1989 issue, *Modern Photography* ceased publication, and its subscriber base was absorbed by *Popular Photography*. Articles assumed some knowledge of the photographic field. Many graphics; some in color. Large section of mail-order advertising at back of magazine. Sample issue for 1988: (7 ⅞ x 10 ½ inches / 200 x 265 mm).
DEPT: "Air Bells," comment; "Being Critical," on reader-submitted photographs; "Book Review," "Camera Club News," 'News and ideas'; "Contest Calendar," with participation information; "Exhibits to See," "Gadgets, Kinks, and Shortcuts," ideas to clip; "Inside Hollywood," "More Fact than Fancy," information column by Paul Hopkins; "Movies Photographers Should See," feature film review column by Joseph Wechsberg; "New Products," review; "Out of the Lab," hints; "Photo Data Sheets," 'Minicam Photography clip sheet for permanent reference'; "Salons," "Superpan Panning," humor column by J. H. Sammis; "The Last Word," letters. (9-42). "What's What," newsbriefs; "Too Hot to Handle," Q&A; "How to,"

technique; "Modern Tests," equipment profiles; "Letters to the Editor," "The Camera Collector," "Phototronics," "Techniques Tomorrow," "Kepler's SLR Notebook," "Color in Your Darkroom," "Sint's View," column; "Video Movies." (10-84). "Casual Observer," column by Peter Moore; "Video Journal," column by Tony Galluzzo; "Color Today," column by Martin Hershenson; "Seeing Pictures," column by Julia Scully; "First Person," column by Paul Bereswill; "On the Money," column by Fred Rosen; "Point and Shoot," column by Mason Resnick; "Well-Traveled Camera," column by David L. Miller; "Sint's View," column by Steve Sint; "Editor's Note," "Letters," "What's What," news items; "SLR Notebook," "Too Hot to Handle," Q&A; "Grabshot," as in 'grabbed any good shots?'. (6-89).
- TYPL: "Afga Ansco Celebrates its 100th Birthday," "Wartime Photo-Economy," "Sparkling Arcs," "Rumor Spiked: Take Snapshots or Make Salon Prints..This is Still the U.S.A.!," "Headlight Pictures." (9-42). "Pictures by Post: The Photographs Behind the Stamps," "Hard Knocks," "Flashy Flowers," "Processes: the New Toners." (10-84). "Inside the EOS System," "Sports Special: That was Then," "Lens Roundup." (6-89).
- SCHL: Monthly, 145 pp.
- SPAN: Sep, 1937 - Jul, 1989//
  VARIES
  --Sep, 1937 - Jan, 1940 as Minicam.
  --Feb, 1940 - Aug, 1949 as Minicam Photography (ISSN: 0096-5863).
  ABSORBED
  --Photographic Digest, Jan, 1938?
  ABSORBED BY
  --Popular Photography (ISSN: 0032-4582), Aug, 1989.
- LC: TR 1.M54
- DD: 770.5
- ISSN: 0026-8240
- ABST: --Art and Archaeology Technical Abstracts (ISSN: 0004-2994)
  --Biography Index (ISSN: 0006-3053)
  --Book Review Index (ISSN: 0524-0581)
  --Consumers Index to Product Evaluations and Information Sources (ISSN: 0094-0534)
  --Film Literature Index (ISSN: 0093-6758)
  --Magazine Index
  --Popular Magazine Review (ISSN: 0740-3763)
  --Readers Guide to Periodical Literature (ISSN: 0034-0464)

MODERN RADIO

- PUBL: Modern Radio Co., 127 Ann St., Hartford, CT.
- DESC: A publication for the radio amateur / experimenter, *Modern Radio* provided technical schematics, discussions of construction techniques, and new developments in the field of radio AND television. The serial succumbed to economic conditions of the Depression years, and for its last hurrah managed to publish a "Half-Portion Scrip Issue in Honor of the Bank Closing," for the last serial dated April, 1933. Numerous technical graphics and schematics.
- DEPT: "Short Circuits," letters and comment. (3-32).
- TYPL: "500 Watts from a Crystal Oscillator," "Results of Empire State Television," "A Tester for Electrolytic Condensers," "It isn't the Coil that's Wrong." (3-32).
- SCHL: Monthly, 30 pp.
- SPAN: Jul, 1931 - Apr, 1933//
  ABSORBED BY
  --Radio, Jul, 1933.
- LC: TK 6540.M63

Modern Recording

Oct/Nov, 1975 - Jun, 1980//
(ISSN: 0361-0004)
SEE: MODERN RECORDING & MUSIC

MODERN RECORDING & MUSIC

- PUBL: Cowan Publishing Corp., Port Washington, NY.
- DESC: This is a consumer-oriented publication aimed at amateur and semi-professional musicians. Excellent articles provide a "how-to" approach to entering the music industry, explaining both the technology and politics of the music field. Numerous articles profile recording artists and their work.
- DEPT: "Letters to the Editor," "Talkback," technical Q&A; "The Product Scene," reviews; "Musical Newsicals," newsbriefs; "Ambient Sound," column; "Notes," column; "Lab Reports," "Groove Views," album reviews. (6-82).
- TYPL: "An Overview of Synthesizers," "Recording With Stevie Nicks," "Studio Notebook," "Profile: The Tubes." (6-82).
- SCHL: Bimonthly (Oct/Nov, 1975 - ?); Monthly (?+), 84 pp.
- SPAN: Oct/Nov, 1975 - ?, 1986//
  VARIES
  --Oct/Nov, 1975 - Jun, 1980 as Modern Recording (ISSN: 0361-0004).
- LC: ML 1.M1795
- DD: 621.389/3
- ISSN: 0273-8511
- ABST: --Popular Magazine Review (ISSN: 0740-3763)

MODERN SCREEN

- SUB: "More gossip, photos, features than ever before!"
- SUB: "America's greatest movie magazine."
- PUBL: Dell Publishing Co., 1 Dag Hammarskjold Plaza, New York, NY 10017.
- DESC: *Modern Screen* is an institution that has dispensed the hottest news, gossip and stories of radio-TV-film stars since its creation in 1930. Like a host of competitors on the scene since, *Modern Screen* revels in photographically catching Hollywood's stars at parties and other events, both public and not so-public, and announcing the latest scandals and happenings. It is a

format which has worked well for some 50 years in a publishing field considered to be rather short-lived. Magazine format (8 ½ x 10 ⅞ inches / 215 x 275 mm), published on newsprint.
DEPT: "Instant Interview," "Scene Stealers of the Month," "Louella Parsons," 'Modern Screen's 8 page gossip extra by Hollywood's greatest columnist' column by Louella Parsons; "New Movies," guide column by Beverly Linet; "Music Maker of the Month," profile column by Joey Sasso. (7-62). "Ron Galella Catches the Stars Off-Guard," Hollywood photographer candid shots column by Ron Galella; "Heavenly Stars," personal horoscopes; "Close-Ups," special newsbriefs; "Hollywood Evesdropper," 'Off-the record and ultra- private quotes from your favorite stars!'; "Headline Happenings," briefs with photos; "Turn-table Tidbits," 'The inside track on the music makers!;' "Don't Breath a Word of It!" more secret information column by Paul Ravin; "Straight Talk," Q&A format column by Randi Walseth; "Daytime Dialings," news of soaps column by Marvin Bevans. (3-79).
TYPL: "The Mystery of Elvis Presley," "Is Success Destroying Vincent Edwards?," "I Predict ... Liz Has Met Her Match in Richard Burton," "Darling, Don't Make the Same Mistakes I Made in Marriage," "I Can't Live Without Michael!" (7-62). "Penny Marshall: The Day She Cried 'Don't Take Away My Little Girl," "John Travolta-Olivia Newton-John: Our Love is Forever!," "Tony Danza: the Teenage Marriage and Son He Can't Forget." (3-79).
SCHL: Monthly, 75 pp.
SPAN: Nov, 1930 - ?//
VARIES
--Nov, 1930 - ? as Modern Screen Magazine, The.
ABSORBED
--Radio Stars, Dec, 1938.
LC: PN 1993.M334
ISSN: 0026-8429

Modern Screen Magazine, The

Nov, 1930 - ?//
SEE: MODERN SCREEN

✤ MONDAY MORNING REPLAY

PUBL: Mediabase Research Corporation, 28530 Orchard Lake Rd., Suite 102, Farmington Hills, MI 48334.
DESC: Mediabase Research Corporation made this statement to prospective subscribers in one sampled issue for 1991: "With Mediabase, you get the whole story. Every oldie played, not just an occasional one. Every song played, not just selected titles. Every mix played, even those re-mixed by radio stations. Every edit of every song, regardless of length. Mediabase accurately identifies and reports to you EVERYTHING played. Anything less just doesn't cut it. Don't be left in the dark. Stick with the first and the best." Few readers would quarrel with that premise. *Monday Morning Replay* is an outstanding weekly reference work that accurately and comprehensively covers "what's hot and what's not" in the radio music programming field for American audiences. There are no articles, but numerous columns within specific music formats which describe the latest news in the industry. Of special note in these descriptive columns is "City Tracks," and "Foreplay," written by a number of individuals knowledgeable in a variety of unique radio formats. *Monday Morning Replay* is a versatile database of information; comprehensive in its over 50 pages of detailed charts, listings, and profiles of current hit music and their artists; and also noteworthy for its easy-to-use format. Radio station programmers can quickly move to their specific radio formats, and see comprehensive descriptions of programming trends and artists in the categories of hit radio, rock radio, urban radio, and adult contemporary. The 1991 subscription rate of $295 per year provides valuable information for today's radio programmer. For the sampled 1991 issue: printed tabloid magazine format (10¾ x 14 inches / 275 x 355 mm), two color editorial content throughout with full color cover and some advertising pages.
DEPT: "Tracer Tracks," The top 40 most played songs, 'Breakouts provided include the total number of plays, reach index (gross impressions), increase percentages, along with the leaders in airplay and most added stations'; "Newcomers," '1 - 40, number of plays, increase percentages and progress'; "Recordwatch," "Foreplay," 'What's up 'n' coming, Foreplay takes a look at new releases, with fresh, unique and informative profiles', column by Cathy Down; "The Inside Edge," "Mainstream," 'MMR's Mainstream chart calculates the rotations monitored on major market mainstream [format] stations'; "Rhythm/Dance Chart," 'Based on airplay on more than 30 rhythm/dance leaning stations'; "Heaviest Saturation," 'Tracer Tracks 1-40, and Newcomers, with a song-by-song analysis of those stations reaching the most audience with its airplay'; "QPI/Hottest Recurrents Chart," 'Quality Play Index figures ranked by average weekly plays per station. The hottest recurrent titles'; "Majors/Secondaries/Daypart Chart," 'MMR breaks out [format] airplay in the top 25 markets, and markets #25 and down for a better guage of major and secondary market airplay'; "MMR Fact File," 'An overview and historical look at individuals leading the industry'; "City Tracks," 'a potpourri of promotional, positioning, market news and information'; "Sample Hours," 'A unique section that provides one-hour capsules of actual music mixes'; "Tuned In," 'Every week, a station from each of the formats is featured. Tuned In breaks out music, promotional activity, positioning and account information'; "National Crossover Index," 'Charts that offer an overview of those tracks crossing format boundaries'; "Sign Off," "Back Stage," photo column by Paul Kenedy; "One-On-One," programmer interview column by Lisa Coleman; "Most Upward Movement," "Most Added Stations." (4-15-91).
TYPL: None. (4-15-91).

SCHL: Weekly [except last two weeks of December], 55 pp.
SPAN: Jan 1, 1988+
DD: 384
ISSN: 1043-4860

✤ MONITOR

SUB: "A publication of The Institution of Radio and Electronics Engineers Australia."
PUBL: ?, Australia.
DESC: Typically non-technical in nature, *Monitor* provides general news information concerning IREE members in Australia. For a period of time, *Monitor* was combined with *Proceedings of the IREE Australia*, and then split off again as the less-technical news magazine; graphics.
DEPT: "Book Review," "News from the IREE Divisions." (12-80).
TYPL: "Automation Holds Key to Success for Solar Industry Says Scientist," "Government to Issue Information Document on Plans for UHF TV," "The Reliability of Plastic Encapsulated Devices." (12-80).
SCHL: Monthly, 12 pp.
SPAN: Mar, 1979+
SPLIT INTO
--Proceedings of the IREE Australia (ISSN: 0158-0736), Mar, 1979.
VARIES
--Oct, 1979 - Jun, 1980 as IREE Monitor.
LC: TK 6540 .M67
DD: 621.38/06/094

✤ MONITOR

PUBL: Alpha Epsilon Rho, 340 Moore Hall, Central Michigan University, Mt. Pleasant, MI 48859.
DESC: This quarterly publication is designed for AERho (the National Honorary Broadcasting Society) membership, and thus is written with the interests of current college communication majors in mind. Articles tend to emphasize current college broadcast/closed circuit operations, and employment opportunities in the communications industry.
DEPT: None. (fall-80).
TYPL: "Frequency Coordination of an Earth Station," "Psychic Programming is Popular," "Exercise for Executives," "T-Shirts for Radio Promotion," "InHouse Research for a College Radio Station." (fall-80).
SCHL: Quarterly, 15 pp.
SPAN: ?+?

Monitor

Jan/Feb, 1976 - Dec, 1979//
(ISSN: 0314-4321)
SEE: PROCEEDINGS OF THE IREE AUSTRALIA

✤ MONITOR INTERNATIONAL

SUB: "Radio television video broadcasting."
SUB: "Field-production, post-production."
SUB: "Broadcasting international review."
SUB: "Quarterly supplement of Monitor Magazine audio video broadcasting."
PUBL: Media Age srl Publishing, via Stefano Jacini 4 - 20121 Milano, Italy.
DESC: "*Monitor International* was born as a magazine designed to make that which gets written and said in the lively sector of Italian broadcasting understandable to a larger public. The 'domestic' version has been informing and updating technicians for 14 years, in addition to being present in every trade show of the sector. For the international edition, too, the aim is to be a discussion forum on technical themes in all the component places." This international English edition (with a 15 page Spanish language middle section), is a quarterly supplement to the monthly Italian-language parent *Monitor Magazine*, "Audio video broadcasting," (ISSN: 0394-0896), and provides a digest of selected articles from that monthly serial. Technology is the focus, with articles often showcasing Italian applications of same. Editorial content is a pleasing mixture of both black/white and color, with a number of pictures in full color. Magazine format (8 ¼ x 11 inches / 210 x 280 mm).
DEPT: "High Frequency," "Lighting Equipment," "New Technologies," "Professional Audio," "Machine of the Month," "Spanish Language Section," 'The text of the magazine in Spanish'. (4-91).
TYPL: "Computer Analysis of Radio Broadcast," "Lighting in the TV Studio," "Clean PAL; or in other words, PAL washed clean of the artifacts which limits its quality'; "FM Stereo: What's New," "RAI Audio on Wheels: Three Brand New OB Vans." (4-91).
SCHL: Quarterly, 70 pp.
SPAN: ?+
EDITION
--International.
SUPPLEMENT TO
--Monitor Magazine (ISSN: 0394-0896) [NE], ?+.

✤ MONITORING TIMES

PUBL: Grove Enterprises, Inc., PO Box 98, 140 Dog Branch Rd., Brasstown, NC 28902.
DESC: For those interested in the fascinating hobby of monitoring radio and television signals (broadcast or satellite) worldwide, there is no finer monthly publication than *Monitoring Times*, with over 100 pages dedicated to the latest news, technology, and trends in communication monitoring. Over 25 departmental features keep track of everything from local scanners to shortwave radio, from communication on the high seas to satellite television, from new technical equipment to legal developments in the monitoring field. There is a significant amount of international communication available to monitors, and this serial provides very satisfactory coverage of stations, their frequen-

cies, programming efforts, and any changes in these. For the sampled issue of 1989: published on newsprint in stapled magazine format (8 ⅜ x 10 ⅞ inches / 215 x 280 mm).
DEPT: "Letters," "Communications," newsbriefs; "Shortwave Broadcasting," news column by Glenn Hauser; "Utility World," Utility news column by Larry Van Horn; "The Scanning Report," column by Bob Kay; "What's New?," "Uncle Skip's Corner," column by TJ 'Skip' Arey; "Federal File," column by Dave Jones; "High Seas," Ocean communication column by James R. Hay; "On the Ham Bands," column by Ike Kerschner; "The QSL Report," column by Gayle Van Horn; "Reading RTTY," column by Jack Albert; "Satellite TV," 'Adventures in the Clarke Belt' column by Ken Reitz; "American Bandscan," column by Karl Zuk; "Outer Limits," column by Dr. John Santosuosso; "Below 500 kHz," column by Joe Woodlock; "Program Guide," shortwave guide for upcoming month; "Frequency Section," station listings; "Magne Tests," column by Lawrence Magne; "Scanner Equipment," review column by Bob Grove; "Consumer Electronics," "DeMaw's Workbench," engineering column by Doug DeMaw; "Experimenter's Workshop," column by Rich Arland; "Antenna Topics," column by W Clem Small; "Ask Bob," Reader Q&A column by Bob Grove; "Convention Calendar," "Closing Comments," editorial. (9-89).
TYPL: "WJG Memphis Calling," "DXing Peru," "Glenn Hauser on SW Broadcasting," "Ham Bands Intro," "Urban Survival Tool." (9-89).
SCHL: Monthly, 110 pp.
SPAN: Jan, 1982+
ABSORBED
--International Radio, Jul, 1986.
LC: TK 6553 .M636
DD: 621.384/151
ISSN: 0889-5341

MONOGRAM
PUBL: Brighton Film Review, 63 Old Compton St., London W1V 5PN, England.
DESC: "Besides reviews of current releases and individual films of the past, auteur-analyses and features of a general nature, *Monogram* will regularly include some detail consideration of the expanding literature on the cinema, not only in the form of book-reviews, but also articles on other film-magazines. In particular, we shall keep our readers informed about developments in film-criticism abroad, notably France, Italy and Germany, and draw attention to important issues of individual magazines." This was a journal of film analysis, a studied look at the impact (especially of American films), upon society, and, in turn, society's input to the film production process. *Monogram* explored with a critical eye the import of film in everyday life, and its potential to go beyond that of a mass-consumer product to an art-form level. Magazine format; graphics.
DEPT: "Book Review." (10-75).

TYPL: "Pageants of Violence," "Is There Life on Earth?," "Dodge City and the Development of the Western," "The Case of Edgar G. Ulmer." (10-75).
SCHL: Bimonthly [irregular at times], (? - ?); Quarterly [irregular at times]; 50 pp.
SPAN: Apr, 1971 - 1978//
LC: PN 1993.M755

Monthly Bulletin
Apr, 1916//
SEE: DRAMA LEAGUE MONTHLY

MONTHLY FILM BULLETIN
PUBL: British Film Institute, 127 Charing Cross Rd., London WC2H 0EA, England.
DESC: This was almost exclusively a film review periodical with some 40 international motion picture releases reviewed each month by British Film Institute members. Each film review was meticulous in detail, from an exhaustive listing of all active cast and crew, to thorough examinations of the more esoteric elements of film psychology and sociology. Reviews were not confined to current year product, especially in the case of foreign films, which might have just recently been dubbed or subtitled in English. Produced in a magazine format with black/white production stills accompanying some reviews, it was an excellent resource for international film. In February, 1991 the Governors of the British Film Institute decided, due to significant overlap of material, that *Monthly Film Bulletin* would be absorbed into BFI's *Sight & Sound* publication; a process which would include a redesign and move from quarterly to monthly publication status. Editor Philip Dodd told subscribers: "The new 'S&S' will retain the comprehensive reviewing policy of 'MFB', offering you each month a review, synopsis and full credits of all films released in London. They will appear in an attractive, substantial, self-contained section. This review coverage will be extended to video, selected films for British television, books published on cinema and broadcasting and festivals and conferences." Indeed, the newly combined *Sight & Sound* plus *Monthly Film Bulletin* has gone through a substantial change in form, but the function remains faithful to what readers have come to expect for over 50 years. For the sampled issue of 1989: stapled magazine format, black/white editorial content with two-color cover on coated paper stock (8 ¼ x 11 ¾ inches / 210 x 300 mm).
DEPT: "Retrospective," review of a film previously reviewed; "New Short Films," listed via title, distributor and length. (11-78). "Back Page," comment. (11-89).
TYPL: Lola Montez-Her Life," "A Kuchar Quickie." (11-78). "The End of Papa & the Lost Position: Demy, Godard and the New Wave, Then and Now." (11- 89).
SCHL: Monthly, 30 pp.
SPAN: Feb, 1934 - Apr, 1991//

WITH SUPPLEMENT
--Contrast, 1961 - 1966.
ABSORBED
--Monthly Film Strip Review, 1949.
ABSORBED BY
--Sight & Sound (ISSN: 0037-4806), May, 1991.
LC: LB 1044.B66
DD: 371.335230838
ISSN: 0027-0407
ABST: --Film Literature Index (ISSN: 0093-6758)
--Media Review Digest (ISSN: 0363-7778)

Monthly Filmstrip Review
? - Jan, 1950//
SEE: VISUAL EDUCATION

Monthly News Letter, American Association of Teachers of Journalism
? - ?//
SEE: JQ. JOURNALISM QUARTERLY.

MORE
SUB: "A journalism review."
PUBL: Rosebud Associates, 750 Third Ave., New York, Ny 10017.
DESC: One of the early journalism reviews in the United States, this monthly provided critical analyses of both news and entertainment media, focusing on editorial content and programming in all media. This journalism review took reporters, producers, and talent to task for less-than-great reporting and production values. Printed on newsprint.
DEPT: "Rosebuds," plaudits for extraordinary journalism; "Hellbox," some not so applaudable journalistic efforts; "The Big Apple," New York media news.
TYPL: "When the Sword is Mightier than the Pen," "The Washington Post," "Question: the President is Coming to Your City on Friday."
SCHL: Monthly, 30 pp.
SPAN: Jun, 1971 - Jun, 1978//
ABSORBED BY
--Columbia Journalism Review (ISSN: 0010-194x).
DD: 071.471
ISSN: 0047-8091
ABST: --ABI/Informer

MORE BUSINESS
SUB: "The voice of letterpress printing and photoengraving."
PUBL: American Photo-Engravers Association, 166 West Van Buren St., Chicago.
DESC: "The aim of *MORE BUSINESS* is to co-operate with American industry, commerce and trade in the production of printing that will stimulate consumption of this nation's products. ...Advertising men everywhere are finding *MORE BUSINESS* a source of ideas and inspirations, capable of wide application and use. ...*MORE BUSINESS* is dedicated to the promotion of letterpress printing and photo-engraving, the most efficient, most flexible and most faithful methods of reproduction known to the graphic arts. Letterpress printing from photo-engraved plates permits printed presentation with strict fidelity to the original." The function of *MORE BUSINESS* was explicitly stated within the title: to serve as an advertising/promotion vehicle among potential clients, to extol the virtues and technological capabilities of this medium of marketing/packaging expression among American consumer-oriented industries. Copies were "...sold to engravers, printers and advertising agencies at the rate of 15 cents per copy for free distribution among their customers, prospects and clients." This showcase publication presented in a large magazine format utilized full and spot color throughout its pages. Most articles demonstrated a successful application of letterpress or photo-engraving technology, with a strong emphasis on product packaging. Of special note was the monthly supplement, *Glossary*, a four page leaflet which provided technical details on *MORE BUSINESS* articles. Specifically, this section detailed the "how-to" of who produced the plates, packaging materials, and accompanying materials seen within the article. For example, concerning one feature of package inserts, the *Glossary* article noted in part: "They were mounted as shown, and a panchromatic negative and print made to give the wide variety of colors proportionate relationship to one another. Then a 133-screen combination line and halftone was made for the back plate and a Ben Day zinc etching for the color plate." The *Glossary*, in conjunction with *MORE BUSINESS*, provided a very valuable showcase for both form and function in advertising and marketing promotion/packaging, and certainly boosted the net-profit lines of contributing photo-engravers and letterpress corporations. Large magazine stapled format (11 x 14 inches / 280 x 355 mm).
DEPT: "Little Lessons in Photo-Engraving." (5-37).
TYPL: "Child of the Depression," "Women Won't Climb Shelves," "Double in Brass," "A Story of Modern Merchandising," "Package Inserts." (5-37).
SCHL: Monthly, 16 pp.
SPAN: Jan, 1936 - Apr, 1942//
WITH SUPPLEMENT
--Glossary.

Morning Filmograph
Apr, 1922 - May?, 1923//
SEE: HOLLYWOOD FILMOGRAPH

✤ MOTION PICTURE
SUB: "First and best."

SUB:	"Incorporating Screen Life, Hollywood and Movie Story Magazines."
PUBL:	Macfadden Women's Media, 205 E. 42nd St., New York, NY 10017.
DESC:	For over 75 years, *Motion Picture* and its predecessors have been a source of enjoyment, information, and profiles concerning favorite film personalities and motion picture product. Indicative of *Motion Picture*'s mostly supportive role of the film industry is the number of advertisements for upcoming film releases placed in each issue of this monthly periodical. Also notable are advertisements by major vendors of health and beauty products. While *Motion Picture* certainly has its share of celebrity exposes, in the sampled issues such articles were balanced by positive role model profiles, and upbeat stories of Hollywood lifestyles, resulting in the kind of publication that major advertisers could rally around. Of special note are "Interesting Letters," in which readers speak their minds and emotions over favorite stars. Magazine format (8 ⅜ x 10 ⅞ inches / 215 x 275 mm), sampled issues published on mixture of coated stock (some color graphics), and newsprint. Dimensions of sampled issue from 1952 was (8 ⅜ x 11 ¼ inches / 215 x 285 mm); for 1962 sampled issue (8 ½ x 11 inches / 215 x 280 mm).
DEPT:	"Under Hedda's Hat," column by Hedda Hopper; "Coast to Coast With Dorothy Kilgallen," column by Dorothy Kilgallen; "The Answer Man," Q&A of the stars column by Gene Samuels; "Bulletin Board," marriages, births, splits and deaths column by Mary Callahan; "Picture Parade," reviews; "Overheard in Hollywood," column by Erskine Johnson; "My Star Twin," reader submissions column by Jo Ann Buckner. (12-54). "Your Motion Picture Shopping Section," product review; "Hollywood Today," gossip column by Snooper; "Young Hollywood," gossip column by Rona Barrett; "Interesting Letters," 'From readers everywhere'; "Hollywood Triangle," 'We never let a rumor go unfounded'. (5-62).
TYPL:	"This is It!," "I'm on My Own Now," "Escape from Fear," "Dance!," "Every Girl Should Receive Such a Love Letter." (12-54). "Doris Day's Son comes Out of Hiding!," "Anna Kashfi's Own Story: 'I Won't Be Walked On!'," "The Child Marlon Brando Brought Back From Tahiti," "What's Really Behind the Liz--Eddie Bustup Story?," "The Gypsy Life of George Maharis." (5-62).
SCHL:	Monthly, 75 pp.
SPAN:	Feb, 1911+ VARIES --Feb?, 1911 as Moving Picture Story Magazine. --Mar?, 1911 - Feb, 1914 as Motion Picture Story Magazine, The. --Mar, 1914 - Nov, 1926 as Motion Picture Magazine. --Dec, 1926 as Motion Picture. --Jan, 1927 - Aug, 1951 as Motion Picture Magazine. --Sep, 1951 - Sep, 1954 as Motion Picture and Television Magazine. ABSORBED --Movie Classic, Mar, 1937. --Screen Life, Feb, 1942. --Hollywood, Apr, 1943. --Movie Story Magazine, Aug, 1951.
LC:	PN 1993.M5
ISSN:	0027-1624

✤ MOTION PICTURE

PUBL:	Collective for Living Cinema, PO Box 39, White St., #114, New York, NY 10013.
DESC:	Editors Paul Arthur and Ivone Margulies have assembled an excellent publication of non-mainstream cinema in *Motion Picture*, a three-times-a year magazine published by the Collective for Living Cinema in New York City. Articles for the sampled 1991 issue included a discussion of films produced by Antony Balch and William Burroughs; eight mm home movies of the Vietnam war; a fascinating point/counterpoint discussion of the validity concerning the single conspirator theory on the Kennedy assassination; and development of documentary aesthetics. The layout design is excellent. Some issues include an update of films and videotapes added to the Film-maker's Cooperative Collection. For the sampled issues of 1991: black ink cover and editorial content on coated paper in stapled magazine format, with limited advertising (8 ½ x 11 inches / 215 x 280 mm).
DEPT:	"Filmakers Cooperative," 'New acquisitions'; "Drift," 'New films and videos'. (summer-91).
TYPL:	"'I Wrote Your Fading Movie': The Films of Anthony Balch and William Burroughs," "Vietnam! The Home Movie!," "The Tailored Image: Notes on the Zapruder Film," "Gilding the Ashes: Toward a Documentary Aesthetics of Failure," "Against the Grain: Politics and Postmodernism in Al Razutis' 'Amerika'." (summer-91).
SCHL:	Three issues per year, 50 pp.
SPAN:	Spring/Summer, 1986+
DD:	791
ISSN:	0892-4929

Motion Picture

Dec, 1926//
SEE: MOTION PICTURE

Motion Picture, The

Sep, 1925 - Jul, 1930//
SEE: SELECTED MOTION PICTURES

✤ MOTION PICTURE ALBUM

SUB:	"Devoted to the interests of the scenario writer." (Apr, 1912 - Dec, 1912).
PUBL:	The Photoplay Enterprise Association, Boonville, IN.
DESC:	[*Photo Playwright, The*]: This was a marvelous, if short-lived serial on the technique of writing for the motion pictures or "photo plays," which was the phrase in vogue at the time. According to the editor,

"Its purpose is to assist the scenario writer and promote his welfare, being devoted to the best interests of picture playwrights. It gives such information as is desired and needed by students of the photoplay." Discussions of what studios wanted in a photoplay, how some successful playwrights had "made it," pay rates, plot development, and other aspects of the trade were addressed. It is especially interesting to note that all of this took place in Boonville, Indiana, and not New York or the newly discovered Hollywood. Small magazine format; no graphics.

DEPT: "Brass Tack Talks," comment and advice; "The Clearing House," news and advice; "Random Notes," newsbriefs; "The Photoplay Mart," Current studio needs. (7-12).
TYPL: "Optimism vs. Realism," "Ten Things I Would Tell a Beginner," "About the Universal," "Originality," "What Moving Pictures Add to Life." (7-12).
SCHL: Monthly, 30 pp.
SPAN: Apr, 1912+?
VARIES
--Apr, 1912 - Dec, 1912 as Photo Playwright, The.

Motion Picture and Television Magazine

Sep, 1951 - Sep, 1954//
SEE: MOTION PICTURE

MOTION PICTURE AND THE FAMILY, THE

SUB: "A bulletin for all who are interested in better motion pictures."
SUB: "Comment on current films by teachers, educators, community leaders."
PUBL: Motion Picture and Distributors of America, 28 W. 44th St., New York, NY.
DESC: This tabloid-sized newspaper was produced with the blessing of Will Haye's office, and was designed to promote the use of and acceptance of Hollywood motion pictures into the American way of life. To that extent, articles dwell on use of films within school classrooms, review of films and liaison with community groups, and stories detailing Hollywood's efforts to improve the image of the motion picture industry. Of special note is the reprinting of ads and public service materials designed to be used by community groups and exhibitors to promote image building.
DEPT: "What's Next in Hollywood?," column concerning Hollywood efforts and upcoming 'family-type' films; "Who's Who in Better Films," profiles of individuals, film committees and review boards; "Films for the Pupil and Teacher," application of film to the classroom; "Selected Film Reading of the Current Month," an unusual section detailing periodical articles which put films best foot forward; "Lessons From the Movies," issues of a moral and family nature to be learned from current releases; "A Club Woman Chats on Films for the Family," regular feature discussing community interaction.
TYPL: "Animated Cartoons Have Come to be Regarded as an Important Phase of Screen Art; This Exhibit Shows How They are Made," "YWCA Girls Start a New Movie Class," "Scarsdale Conducts a Film Survey," "Libraries Afford Generous Space to Film Exhibits." (3-15-37).
SCHL: Monthly [except during summer months], 8 pp.
SPAN: Oct, 15, 1934 - May, 15, 1938//
LC: PN 1993.M36
DD: 791.405

Motion Picture Classic

Dec, 1915 - Aug, 1922//
SEE: MOVIE CLASSIC

Motion Picture Classic

Sep, 1924 - Aug, 1931//
SEE: MOVIE CLASSIC

MOTION PICTURE HERALD

PUBL: Quigley Publishing Co., Rockefeller Center, New York, NY.
DESC: *Motion Picture Herald* was a reliable trade publication for the motion picture industry, valued for its international reporting, local exhibition concerns, and trends on the business-side of film. The regard in which major film studios held this publication was evident in the numerous full-color and spot-color advertisements placed in this "issued every Saturday" weekly. It was renowned for its exhaustive listings of shooting schedules, plot descriptions, and release dates. Of special aid to the exhibitor was the splendid, "What the Picture Did For Me," department. As Motion Picture Herald described it: "The original exhibitors' reports department, established October 14, 1916. In it theatremen serve one another with information about the box-office performance of product--providing a service of the exhibitor for the exhibitor." Listed by studio, and picture title, this two-page service reprinted exhibitor comments on specific films that played at their theatres. Their remarks included type of patronage, dates of play, and forthright commentary on the value of the film to their financial ledgersheet. The "Managers' Round Table" also merits attention for its helpful sections on picture promotion (exploitation), local advertising approaches, and other aspects of local theatre management. Also of note were regular supplements, "Product Digest," with detailed film release information, and "Better Theatres," devoted to the technology, architecture, and improvement of the motion picture experience.

Magazine format (240 cm wide x 310 high); liberal use of two-color throughout, with a number of advertisements in full-color; published on coated paper stock.
DEPT: "This Week in the News," "This Week the Camera Reports:," photographic news developments; "The Hollywood Scene," started, shooting, and completed film projects listed via studio; "In Newsreels," contents listing for this week's releases; "What the Picture Did For Me," 'The original exhibitors' reports department, established October 14, 1916. In it theatremen serve one another with information about the box-office performance of product--providing a service of the exhibitor for the exhibitor'; "Short Product Playing Broadway," "Picture Grosses," 'A statistical compilation and comparison of box-office performance in first-run theatres'; "Managers' Round Table," 'An international association of showmen meeting weekly in Motion Picture Herald for mutual aid and progress'; "Displays and Ballyhoo," photographic section of successful exploitations; "Exploiting the New Films," 'How the recent pictures are being sold at the first run and pre-release date showings'; "The Selling Approach," 'On new product'; "Showmen Personals," "Attractive Showmen Ads," various advertising samples. (8-26-44).
TYPL: "Nation's Showmen Elect the Stars of Tomorrow," "Companies Have 236 Films Finished or Now Shooting," "Studio Activity Increases with 55 Films in Work," "Gross $1,363,250,000 in 1943, U.S. Reports," "20th-Fox Will Release 27 Features in 1944-45." (8-26-44).
SCHL: Weekly (Jan 3, 1931 - Jun 27?, 1962); Biweekly (Jul 11, 1962 - Jan 5, 1966); Weekly (Jan 19, 1966 - May 6, 1970); Biweekly (May 20, 1970 - Jan 27, 1971); Monthly (Feb 24, 1971+), 75 pp.
SPAN: Jan 3, 1931 - Dec, 1972//
FROM MERGER OF
--Motion Picture News (ISSN: 0748-5921) (and) Exhibitors Herald World.
WITH SUPPLEMENT
--Product Digest, ? - ?
--Better Theatres, ? - ?
MERGED WITH
--Motion Picture Daily (ISSN: 0027-1594) (to form) QP Herald (ISSN: 0090-2136).
LC: PN 1993.M854
ISSN: 0027-1616

Motion Picture Magazine
Mar, 1914 - Nov, 1926//
SEE: MOTION PICTURE

Motion Picture Magazine
Jan, 1927 - Aug, 1951//
SEE: MOTION PICTURE

Motion Picture Monthly, The
Aug, 1930 - Dec, 1931//
SEE: SELECTED MOTION PICTURES

✢ MOTION PICTURE PRODUCT DIGEST
PUBL: Quigley Publishing Co., 159 W. 53 St., New York, NY 10019.
DESC: This 12-20 page publication aimed at the American film exhibitor, is not what it once was in its former glory days as *Motion Picture Herald*. It remains, nonetheless, bullish on the state of the American film industry, as publisher Martin Quigly Jr. always has been. Although it includes *Television-Radio Today*, there is no doubt that this is a periodical whose primary concern is American film product. Of note are an wonderful group of specialized columns and departmental features. "Film Buyers Ratings," is renowned for a ratings system determined by film circuit buyers; while "Paris Scene," and "London Scene" continue to dispense timely information about film exhibition in those European locations. Continuing a tradition begun under earlier banners is the "Reviews of New Pictures," an extraordinary section detailing all conceivable elements contained in a major motion picture release. Some illustrations.
DEPT: "This Week in Brief," small brief reviews; "The Film Scene," newsbriefs; "Exhibition," newsbriefs; "Personnel," changes and appointments; "Film Buyers Rating," ratings via film circuit buyers; "Reviews of New Pictures," continuing a tradition of review excellence in the Motion Picture Herald; "Box Office Champions," current hits; "On the TV Screen," video program reviews; "Personnel," radio-TV changes; "Paris Scene," film news; "London Scene," film news.
TYPL: "Gavin Urges Government Support Film Industry," "Seek to Stem Press 'Hostility' to Film Industry," "The Effect of England on American TV-- and Vice Versa," "Strong Theatre Business Boosts General Cinema." (3- 17-73).
SCHL: Weekly (Jan 6, 1973 - May 5, 1973); Biweekly (Jun 6, 1973 - May 22, 1974); Semimonthly (Jun, 1974+), 16 pp.
SPAN: Jan 6, 1973+
FROM MERGER OF
--Motion Picture Daily (ISSN: 0027-1594) (and) Motion Picture Herald (ISSN: 0027-1616).
VARIES
--Jan 6, 1973 - May 5, 1973 as QP Herald (ISSN: 0090-2136).
--Jun 6, 1973 - May 22, 1974 as Product Digest (ISSN: 0093-2132).
LC: PN 1993.Q
ISSN: 0146-5023

MOTION PICTURE PROJECTION
PUBL: Mancall Publishing, 45 West 45th St., New York, NY.

DESC: [Motion Picture Projectionist]: *MP Projectionist* was published during a time when a great number of technological changes were occurring within the motion picture exhibition house. The projectionist not only had silent film to contend with, but also sound film, sound discs, sky projectors, follow spotlights, and even the promised coming of theatre television. With that as a basis, it is understandable that the majority of articles was technical in nature, explaining new proposed standards and acting as a forum for a wealth of companies vying for equipment sales and installations. A large number of graphics and technical diagrams.
DEPT: "As the Editor Sees It," commentary; "In the Laboratory," new technical innovations column by Samuel Wein; "New Equipment and Appliances," product briefs; "Review," Eastman Kodak Company technical review. (12-30).
TYPL: "Some Sound-on-Film Problems, and Their Relation to Continuous Projection," "Wide Film Standardization," "Some Facts on Carbon Jaws," "What is the Multi-Color Process?," "Operation of Projection Arcs from Motor Generator Sets," "Opinions on Standard Release Prints." (12-30).
SCHL: Monthly, 50 pp.
SPAN: Oct, 1927 - May, 1933//
VARIES
--Oct, 1927 - Nov, 1927 as Motion Picture Projectionist of the United States and Canada, The.
--Jan, 1928 - Jan, 1933 as Motion Picture Projectionist.
SUSPENDED
--Dec, 1927
--Aug, 1929
--Feb, 1933 - Apr, 1933
LC: TR 890.M65

Motion Picture Projectionist

Jan, 1928 - Jan, 1933//
SEE: MOTION PICTURE PROJECTION

Motion Picture Projectionist of the United States and Canada, The

Oct, 1927 - Nov, 1927//
SEE: MOTION PICTURE PROJECTION

MOTION PICTURE REVIEW DIGEST

SUB: "Devoted to the valuation of current motion pictures."
PUBL: H. W. Wilson Co., 950 University Ave., New York, NY.
DESC: This was a comprehensive, weekly digest review of motion pictures in general release. Three resources were used for the digest: 1) audience suitability ratings by special reviewing organizations (womens' clubs, religious groups, etc.); 2) general newspapers and magazines; 3) trade papers. "The purpose of the audience suitability ratings by the special reviewing organizations is chiefly to pass on questions of morality and propriety and to report on suitability for children of various ages. The purpose of the reviews in general magazines and newspapers is to inform the adult patron of artistic and entertainment qualities. The purpose of the trade paper reviews is to inform the exhibitor of probable commercial value." No graphics.
DEPT: "Directory of Producers."
TYPL: None.
SCHL: Weekly, 110 pp.
SPAN: Dec, 1935 - Jan 22, 1940//
LC: PN 1993.M67
DD: 791.43/75/05

Motion Picture Story Magazine, The

Mar?, 1911 - Feb, 1914//
SEE: MOTION PICTURE

Motion Picture Supplement

Sep, 1915 - Nov, 1915//
SEE: MOVIE CLASSIC

MOVIE

PUBL: Movie Magazine, Ltd., 25 Lloyd Baker St., London WC1X 9AT, England.
DESC: "*Movie* aims to help remedy the unhealthy lack of reasoned disagreement about films in Britain. It will embody an approach to the cinema which is not represented by any existing magazine... We are likely to be labelled as 'uncommitted', which we are only in not sharing the superficially 'committed' approach. But we are not politically opposed to other critics; it is mainly on grounds of critical method that we differ from them. ...We would like films to be the subject of enthusiastic argument in which our approach would only be one of many." Although possessing an irregular format and publication schedule at times, *Movie* maintained its original premise of considering only great movies, their producers and directors. This was a serial of thought and analysis; of the visual, social, and psychological impact of the medium. International films, especially those of American or Eastern Europe origin, were also given their due. Magazine format with numerous graphics and advertising, moving to a slightly smaller magazine format and a no-advertising policy upon resumption of publication in Spring, 1975.
SCHL: Monthly (1962 - ?); Quarterly (1964+); 65 pp.
SPAN: Jun, 1962 - Summer, 1982//
SUSPENDED
--Spring, 1972 - Winter 1974/1975.
LC: PN 1993.M74516
ISSN: 0027-268x

ABST: --Film Literature Index (ISSN: 0093-6758)

✤ MOVIE

PUBL: Ian Cameron, PO Box 1, Moffat, Dumfriesshire DG10 9SU, England.
DESC: This critical review of motion picture cinema began as a descendant of an undergraduate publication at Oxford University. Descriptive in its criticism, and less academic than other journals of a similar purpose, *Movie* has gathered a loyal audience of readers who appreciate the cinema. Most issues cover a number of motion pictures, such as "Blonde Venus," "Secret Beyond the Door," "All I Desire," "Forbidden Planet," "Home From the Hill," "Peeping Tom," "Demon a.k.a. God Told Me To," "News From Home," "Toute une nuit," and "Paris, Texas" (winter, 1990 issue). Numerous black/white graphics, most production stills from motion pictures featured in articles are published in each issue. For the sampled issues of 1990: black ink on coated paper stock in perfect-bound journal format; cover consisting of black ink with spot-color on coated paper stock; no advertising (6 5/8 x 9 3/4 inches / 170 x 250 mm).
DEPT: None. (winter-90).
TYPL: "Must We Say What They Mean? Film Criticism and Interpretation," "All That Heaven Allowed--Another Look at Sirkian Irony," "The Adventures of Rafe Hunnicut--The Bourgeois Family in 'Home from the Hill'," "Separations--Chantal Akerman's 'News From Home' and 'Toute une nuit'," "The American Trauma--'Paris, Texas'." (winter-90).
SCHL: Irregular, 130 pp.
SPAN: June, 1962+

MOVIE ACTION MAGAZINE

PUBL: Street & Smith Publications, Inc., 79-89 Seventh Ave., New York, NY.
DESC: This interesting monthly serial provided "fictionalization" synopses and "scenarios" of recently released Hollywood motion pictures. Some nine to ten "complete stories" were included in each issue, along with publicity stills from the newly released film. On newsprint; small magazine format.
DEPT: None. (6-36).
TYPL: "The Walking Dead," "The Leathernecks Have Landed," "Silver Spurs," "Here Comes Trouble." (6-36).
SCHL: Monthly, 130 pp.
SPAN: Nov, 1935 - Jun, 1936//
SUSPENDED
--Apr, 1936 - May, 1936.
LC: PN 1993.M743

Movie and Radio Guide
Feb 23, 1940 - Sep 21, 1940//
SEE: MOVIE-RADIO GUIDE

MOVIE CLASSIC

SUB: "The newsreel of the newstands." (Sep, 1931).
SUB: "The tabloid magazine of the screen." (Oct, 1931 - ?).
PUBL: Motion Picture Publications, Inc., Mount Morris, IL.
DESC: A typical fan magazine of the Hollywood motion picture industry during the 1930s, articles tended to concentrate on actors, both on and off screen, and some articles concerned assorted production services to the motion picture industry. Comparable to many other such fanzines of the era, this one also published articles which were often supportive of the Hollywood system, stars, and product; and even when not totally supportive, articles rarely delved into the true private lives of stars or star system. There were numerous advertisements, as seen in other similar magazines, for toothpaste, laxatives, blackheads, foot itch, dress remnants, and free cigarettes. Many graphics were featured, some of which were duotone.
DEPT: "Now You're Talking," readers page; "Hollywood Highlights," gossip by The Boulevardier; "Aids to Romance," column by Alison Alden. (10-36).
TYPL: "Fred MacMurray's Honeymoon Diary," "The Real Reason Why Harlow Hated Her Hair," "Merle Oberon's 20 Dangerous Days," "Nelson Eddy's Rescue Mission," "Joan Blondell's Covered Wagon Days." (10-36).
SCHL: Monthly, 90 pp.
SPAN: Sep, 1915 - Feb, 1937//
VARIES
--Sep, 1915 - Nov, 1915 as Motion Picture Supplement.
--Dec, 1915 - Aug, 1922 as Motion Picture Classic.
--Sep, 1922 - Jan, 1924 as Classic.
--Feb, 1924 - Aug, 1924 as Classic Pictorial of Screen and Stage.
--Sep, 1924 - Aug, 1931 as Motion Picture Classic.
ABSORBED
--Shadowland, Nov, 1923.
--Beauty Guide to Health-Charm-Popularity [NC], Apr, 1925.
--Screen Star Stories, Nov, 1934.
ABSORBED BY
--Motion Picture, Mar, 1937.
LC: PN 1993.M744

MOVIE DIGEST

PUBL: Star Guidance, Inc., 315 Park Ave. South, New York, NY 10010.
DESC: One of a number of "film-fan" magazines, *Movie Digest* provided a current and historical review of Hollywood motion pictures with a decided emphasis upon top-name stars. Printed on newsprint with numerous graphics, *Movie Digest* provided an interesting blend of news and gossip of Hollywood's great and ingrate. Part and parcel of each issue were back-section ads for curing baldness, putting weight on and taking it off, bosom enlargements, career schools,

lucky numbers, and false teeth by mail! Small digest format (Jan, 1972 - Nov, 1972), moving to magazine format (Jan, 1973+).
DEPT: "Dialog," letters, "Nostalgia," "Puzzle," crossword; "Lost Stars," where is?; "Found Stars," here is; "Today's Movies," reviews; "Recent Movies," reviews; "Show Biz Books," reviews; "Show Biz Records," reviews. (1-73).
TYPL: "Jennifer O'Neill: The Price She Paid for Saying 'No Nudity!,'" "Jon Voight: a Choirboy Becomes a Movie Champ--Despite Himself," "Rita Hayworth: This was My Favorite Role," "Ben Johnson: The Good Deed that Changed His Life Forever." (1-73).
SCHL: Monthly, 90 pp.
SPAN: Jan, 1972 to date?
LC: PN 1993.M69

MOVIE DREAM GUYS

PUBL: Movie Dream Guys, PO Box 215, Malibu, CA.
DESC: From the premiere issue: "This is a different kind of movie magazine. It's not only about your particular idols--but it's about YOU, and how you figure in their lives. ...We aren't telling you their life stories all over again, because you, being ardent fans, already know these by heart. But we're showing you what each guy is really like, underneath the publicity veneer, so that you can see him as clearly and sharply as though he rang your doorbell this Saturday night, and you met him in your prettiest gown and took him in to introduce to your folks. And, most intriguing of all, we graphically take you out on a date with him." This was an interesting film and television fanzine of male stars. For the four to five stars profiled per issue, each was first described in a feature article, such as "Elvis May Re-Enlist," followed by "The Things You Love About Elvis;" and in the second column, "The Things Elvis Loves About You." Finally, each star profile was wrapped up with a several page "date," article such as "Dream Date With Elvis," and a full two-page portrait of the named star. In the sampled premiere issue for January, 1960, Edd "Don't Call Me Kookie!" Byrnes not only was showcased on the double-page portrait, but also graced the front and back covers plus there was a full-coated paper portrait stretching from inside front to inside back cover. For the sampled 1960 issue: stapled magazine format, black/white editorial content on newsprint, no advertising, cover is full-color on coated paper stock (8 ¼ x 10 ¾ inches / 210 x 275 mm).
DEPT: "The Things You Love About [star]," "The Things [star] Loves About You," "Dream Date With [star]." (1-60).
TYPL: "Elvis May Re-Enlist," "'Don't Call Me Kookie!'," "Who Says Fabian Can't Sing?," "What Happened to the Boy Next Door?," "Does Frankie Avalon Have No Time for Romance?" (1-60).
SCHL: ?, 50 pp.
SPAN: Jan, 1960 - ?//

MOVIE FAN

SUB: "The favorite magazine of every movie fan," (Jan, 1954 - Nov, 1954).
PUBL: Skye Publishing Co., 270 Park Ave., New York, NY.
DESC: *Movie Fan* was one of a genre of consumer motion picture magazines published during the 1930s through the 1950s. The emphasis was on the stars themselves: at work on the stage, and at play in their homes and social gatherings common to Hollywood during this era. For the sampled 1954 issue: magazine format on newsprint.
DEPT: "On the Sound Track," column by Charlie Applewhite; "Going Hollywood," column by May Mann. (7-54).
TYPL: "Can Joe Share Marilyn with the World?," "The Inside Story of Hollywood's Divorce Epidemic," "She Has What She Wants," "I'm Still Looking for the Right Man." (7-54).
SCHL: Quarterly (Winter, 1946 - Oct/Dec, 1948); Bimonthly (Mar/Apr, 1949+); 65 pp.
SPAN: Winter, 1946 to date?
LC: PN 1993.M7452

✤ MOVIE FLASH

SUB: "The best."
PUBL: Graphic Arts Service, Inc., No. 70 - 18th Ave., Murphy, Quezon City, Phillipines.
DESC: *Movie Flash* is published in the Phillipines, and covers film, television, and recording stars in that country and the surrounding region. In the sampled issue for 1986, articles are written in a curious mixture of Tagalog and English languages. At times, only one language, at other times a mixture of Tagalog and English are employed, such as: "You ask their director, si Eddie Garcia, kung sino ang tingin niya ay mas magaling sa dalawa and he would be noncommittal: 'Both of them are very good actresses, both very sensitive, both very competent. Pareho naman silang magkakaroon ng magagandang...'" Most of the featured stars are in their teen-years or twenties, with articles providing a large number of color pictures. Of special note is a full-color centerfold poster on newsprint of a selected entertainment star. Editorial content for the sampled 1986 issue was full-color and black/white graphics on newsprint, with full-color cover on coated paper stock; no advertising within a stapled magazine format (11 x 12 ⅞ inches / 275 x 325 mm).
DEPT: "It's Me, Richard," personality column by Richard Gomez; "Lotlot and Friends," personality column by Lotlot DeLeon; "Movie Flash Reports,' 'As compiled by the Flash reportorial team' provides newsbriefs concerning activities of the famous; "Flashes," very brief news items; "Paragraphs," column by George Vail Kabristante; "Industry Report," trade news and comment column by Danny Villanueva; "Movie Review," column by Mario E. Bautista; "The GMA Record Guide," an independent review service pro-

vided by Goldwyn Morales Azul; "Anatomy of a Bold Star," column by Edgar Reyes; "TV Connection." (9-25-86).
TYPL: "Dina Versus Jacklyn: sino ang magdurusa?," "Tagumpay na Tagumpay ang Sharon Cuneta Show!," "Long Shot," "The Rebirth of Susan," "Snooky-Richard: pwedeng pang-fans, pwedeng seryosohin." (9-25-86).
SCHL: Weekly, 35 pp.
SPAN: ?+

✤ MOVIE GEEK

PUBL: University of California at San Diego, Visual Arts Department, Lajolla, CA 92037.
DESC: This university-based publication covers motion picture reviews, retorts, short stories, and scripts. It is small format, typewritten, with graphics that strive to tie together the diverse material found in any particular issue (i.e., in one sampled issue, a man wearing a snorkel mask who takes a bath while a woman plays violin).
SCHL: Quarterly, 72 pp.
SPAN: Fall, 1971+
DEPT: "Reviews," a succinct review of current motion pictures; "Retorts," letters retorting earlier reviews; "Stories and Scripts," short stories and shooting scripts via guest authors.
TYPL: None.
LC: PN 1993.M

MOVIE HUMOR

SUB: "Hollywood girls and gags!"
PUBL: ?, New York, NY?
DESC: Awash in duotone green and black ink, this serial's subtitle said it all: "Hollywood girls and gags," with the emphasis on the former, preferably in fashionable swimsuit or sans most attire. Pictures of the female form dominate each issue, much of which is presented in photo-album style with brief attribution and a witty cutline below each entry. Editorial content is almost exclusively contained within the special departmental features of the serial, and is equally split between Hollywood celebrity news and a myriad of "one-liners" that could have been penned by Mae West. Several items made this a unique serial. There was the very popular department (at least according to male readers' letters) entitled, "The Silk Stocking Section," wherein a bevy of young women displayed silk stockings in a variety of settings. Also unique was "Foto Fiddling," with the presentation of two male and two female stars. Instructions were: "Take the four pictures of familiar stars heading these pages, and with the aid of pencil, charcoal, paints, or whatever medium you like, make them look like any other famous person. It does not have to be another star -- it can be politician, poet, parson, or poet, male or female, American or foreigner, just so long as it's someone in the public eye." In between all of the saucy pictures were a number of motion picture production stills and editorial content. For its time, it was indeed spicy, undoubtedly giving a commercial boost to the American swimsuit and lingerie industries. For the sampled issue of 1938: stapled magazine format, entire editorial contents printed green/black duotone on coated paper stock (8 ⅝ x 11 ⅝ inches / 220 x 295 mm).
DEPT: "Flash," 'Straight from Hollywood and Cathrine Daly'; "What the Stars Say!," a myriad of witty/saucy statements; "The Silk Stocking Section," self-explanatory photo section; "Selection of Amateur Stars," readers home pictures; "Foto Fiddling," drawing mustaches and beards on celebrity pictures; "The Line-Up," celebrity news column by A. Lee Stewart; "From Our Readers," letters; "Betty Clewis Says," one-line humorous statements; "Reviews and Previews," upcoming films. (3-38).
TYPL: "A Blanket Check." (3-38).
SCHL: Monthly, 70 pp.
SPAN: Sep, 1935 - ?//

Movie Life

Jan, 1938 - 197u//
(ISSN: 0027-2698)
SEE: TONI HOLT'S MOVIE LIFE

✤ MOVIE MAGAZINE, THE

PUBL: Alan Weston Publishing, 1680 North Vine, Suite 900, Hollywood, CA 90028.
DESC: This publication succeeds the earlier *Movie Magazine* as both a much smaller serial and as an advertising supplement to major newspapers. Little advertising is seen. Primarily, this is a publicity vehicle for newly released motion pictures, providing "behind-the-scenes," star, production and synopsis information for readers. Full color layout.
DEPT: "Letters," "Previews." (spring-83).
TYPL: "Monty Python's The Meaning of Life," "E.T. Speaks in Many Languages," "Psycho II," "Doctor Detroit." (spring-83).
SCHL: Three issues per year, 18 pp.
SPAN: Winter, 1983+

MOVIE MAKERS

SUB: "Magazine of the Amateur Cinema League, Inc."
SUB: "To see ourselves as others see us." (Dec, 1926 - ?).
SUB: "The magazine for 8mm & 16mm filmers."
PUBL: Amateur Cinema League, Inc., New York, NY.
DESC: The Amateur Cinema League was interested solely in amateur movie-making, and even stated that the professional couldn't begin to have as much fun as the amateur, since the amateur could develop a film geared to a very specific topic and audience. Typical of amateur serials of the time, it provided numerous

articles on the "how-to" of cinematography, new equipment, and articles concerning other amateur films. Many graphics.
DEPT: "Editorials," "Clinic," 'edited by Dr. Kinema;' "Swaps," 'film loan exchange;' "Closeups," 'amateur activities.' (4-27). "Closeups," 'what filmers are doing;' "The Reader Writes," "News of the Industry," "The Clinic," 'Aids for Your Filming;' "Clubs," 'people, plans and programs;' "Editorial." (12-53).
TYPL: "The New Beacon at the Crossroads of the World," "How to Form a Movie Club," "Making Limited Appeal Pictures Pay." (4-27). "Festive Filming," "A and B Roll Editing," "A Synchronized Tape Recorder," "A Title Fader." (12-53).
SCHL: Monthly, 35 pp.
SPAN: Dec, 1926 - Nov, 1954//
VARIES
--Dec, 1926 - May, 1928 as Amateur Movie Makers.
LC: TR 845.M862

Movie Marketing
Feb, 1962 - Jan, 1966//
SEE: MOVIE/TV MARKETING

✦ MOVIE MARKETPLACE
SUB: "Recent release, classics, TV-nostalgia, special interest."
SUB: "Your shop-at-home source for 1000's of video subjects."
SUB: "Movies, sports, music, travel."
PUBL: World Publishing Co., 990 Grove St., Evanston, IL 60201-4370.
DESC: "Each issue of *Movie Marketplace* will include hundreds of new video listings. We do not have other catalogs of additional listings. See each new issue for new videos." This publication was a catalog of available videocassettes for purchase, plus fascinating profiles and reviews of selected subjects. Beginning life as *Video Marketplace*, publisher Norman Jacobs realized that the vast majority of product sold was motion picture releases, and therefore instituted the title change commencing with the July/August, 1990 issue. While the primary function of the periodical is to provide a catalog of videocassettes for sale, the articles provide lucid and interesting information about favorite stars, subject matter, and classic/new releases. Layout design is well executed, with numerous production stills, and creative use of the color videocassette covers. For the collector of motion picture entertainment, this is an excellent resource. For the 1990 sampled issue: magazine format (8 x 10 7/8 inches / 205 x 275 mm); color and black/white graphics; some editorial content (primarily catalog section) published on uncoated paper stock; minimal advertising.
DEPT: "Letters," "Video Views," comment; "Movies on Video," 'New and recent release reviews' column by James Turano; "Producer's Showcase," 'Producer video listings featuring the latest selections and variety of special interest subjects'. (8-90).
TYPL: "Sleepers--Little Films That Grow on You," "True Stories are Stranger than Fiction," "The Rapid-Fire Performances of Robin Williams," "The Best of the Courtroom Classics," "Meg Ryan--The Next Superstar." (8-90).
SCHL: Bimonthly, 70 pp.
SPAN: Oct/Nov, 1987+
VARIES
--Oct/Nov, 1987 - Jun/Jul, 1990 as Video Marketplace (ISSN: 0895-2892).
DD: 016 11
ISSN: 1051-5488

✦ MOVIE MIRROR
PUBL: Sterling's Magazines, 355 Lexington Ave., New York, NY 10017.
DESC: *Movie Mirror*'s function is to "reflect" the joys and woes of Hollywood celebrities; their battles against vice; their successful, failing, or failed marriages; or their status in the pecking order of Hollywood stardom. Articles in the 1960s concerned engagements, marriages, and divorces, with a number of articles about fabled Hollywood hearthrobs (Frank Sinatra, Bobby Rydell, Cary Grant, Troy Donahue, Vince Edwards, and Mike Landon); especially detailing how the reader might have the chance to date and marry the man she loved. By the mid-1970s, the articles provided a more realistic, though not more flattering, look at Hollywood life: drugs, broken marraiges, death threats, rape, and continuing battles over money-filled estates which were now part and parcel of the Hollywood scene. Issues contained numerous advertisements for bust developers, weight reduction methods, selling shoes in one's spare time, wigs, teeth whiteners, baldness remedies, nail lengtheners, pep pills, high school diplomas, and a wide variety of marital devices for the home. Magazine format (8 1/8 x 10 7/8 inches / 210 x 275 mm). Full color covers with black/white editorial content; published on newsprint.
DEPT: "Cindy Says," 'Cindy's sparkling column is filled with inside news on show business and show people' column by Cindy Adams; "Gossip--Hollywood is Talking About," "America's Greatest Disk Jockeys," "Readers and Writers," letters. (11-62). "Army Archerd's Hollywood," "Behind the TV Scene with Army Archerd," "Find-the-Word Puzzle." (2-75).
TYPL: "What Debbie Reynolds Tells Her Children About Liz and Eddie," "Marilyn Monroe's Last Interview: How Hollywood Did Her Wrong," "I Lived at Troy Donahue's House," "Fabian's Fun Date," "How You Can Get Into the Movies and Date the Top Stars." (11-62). "'Chico' Star Freddie Prinze and Sweetheart Saved From Drug Addiction!," "Why Robert Redford Fears for His Life," "Elvis and Priscilla: Her Surprise Wedding! Heartbroken, He Tries to Stop Secret Cere-

mony!," "Lee Majors: The Secret Friend Who Made Him a Star!," "Jean Stapleton: Every Woman on TV Can't be Liberated!" (2-75).
SCHL: Monthly (? - 1978); Bimonthly (1979+), 75 pp.
SPAN: Jun, 1946+
SPLIT OFF WITH
--Photoplay (ISSN: 0031-885x) (from parent) Photoplay Combined With Movie Mirror (ISSN: 0733-2734).
ISSN: 0027-271x

MOVIE-RADIO GUIDE

PUBL: Triangle Publications, Chicago, IL.
DESC: [Movie and Radio Guide]: *Movie and Radio Guide*, a large-format weekly guide to the latest and best entertainment in motion picture theatres and major radio networks, focused on the network radio programs, and the talented artists in these programs. Here was a somewhat rare opportunity for the American public to glimpse what their aural heroes and heroines looked like. Articles take the reader back-stage to view programs in progress, and the work required to produce a weekly network radio program. Complementing the articles was a large section detailing "This Week's Programs" on the NBC Red, NBC Blue, CBS, and Mutual Broadcasting System networks. Regional programming (via regional edition inserts) provided programming coverage for multiple state regions. Each day featured the special section, "Good Listening Guide," to outstanding programs that day. Movies, although a part of the serial's title, were less emphasized. A new, special feature, "Brief Reviews," provided capsule comments on plot and quality of the week's motion pictures. Typical articles in one issue ran the gamut from Tyrone Power to the *Movie and Radio Guide* award for distinguished acting; from a former baseball player's critical commentary on radio play-by-play announcers, to the original story, "Brother Orchid;" and features on Edward G. Robinson and Ann Southern. *Movie and Radio Guide* was dedicated to promoting radio programming and motion picture product via this showcase publication; a combination which did not disappoint. Some issues feature duotone color photographs; large magazine format (345 cm high x 270 cm wide).
DEPT: "This Week in Hollywood, " the lowdown on who's doing what, or would like to; "Movie and Radio Guide Picture of the Week," publicity stills of a newly released motion picture; "This Week on the Screen," short synopses of just-released films; "Coming Radio Events," briefs of unique radio programs; "The March of Music," radio musical highlights for the week; "Musician of the Week," musical artist profile; "On Short Waves," interesting highlights of international radio service on short-wave frequencies; "This Week Along the Airialtos," more inside information concerning New York, Hollywood, and Chicago production centers; "On the Bandwagon," aptly subtitled 'Romance, Rumors, Record Reviews, and Gossip of Your Favorite Melody Men'; "Mr. Fairfax Replies," to program-artist questions; "You Asked for Them and Here They Are," readers requests to see pictures of a particular program cast or star.
TYPL: "The Show They Couldn't Kill," "Award for Distinguished Acting," "Get Ready for Radio's Moving Day." (5-40).
SCHL: Weekly (Oct 20, 1931 - Feb 13, 1943); Monthly (Mar, 1943+), 60 pp.
SPAN: Oct 20, 1931 - Nov, 1943//
VARIES
--Oct, 1931 - Dec, 1931 as Radio Guide.
--Jan 7, 1932 - ? as Radio and Amusement Guide.
--? - Feb 16, 1940 as Radio Guide.
--Feb 23, 1940 - Sep 21, 1940 as Movie and Radio Guide.
LC: HE 8690.M6

MOVIE SHOW

PUBL: Liberty Magazine, Inc., 37 West 57th St., New York, NY.
DESC: *Movie Show* was a different kind of film-fan magazine, unique (in early issues) for its film-synopsis (via caption balloon) approach to new releases. Each new release was profiled in a series of five to ten production stills and scene descriptions, some of which also had added caption balloons with witty and humorous comments. Latter issues dropped the large format size, the scene-by-scene film descriptions, and balloon captions, moving to standard magazine size and editorial content typical of other Hollywood motion picture serials. Numerous graphics; on newsprint.
DEPT: "Personal Appearances," stars night out; "Newsreel," newsbriefs with pictures; "John Robert Powers' School for Beauty," "Gossip in the Lobby," "Reviews." (12-42).
TYPL: "Once Upon a Honeymoon," "I Married a Witch," "In Honor of Monty," "Meet Marine Private Power," "A Mud Bath for Claudette." (12-42).
SCHL: Monthly, 70 pp.
SPAN: Sep, 1942 - ?//?
LC: PN 1993.M747

MOVIE STARS

SUB: "The magazine for smart young moviegoers."
PUBL: Ideal Publishing Co., 2 Park Ave., New York, NY 10016.
DESC: Here was a "fanzine" that went for the jugular: *Movie Stars* was not afraid of exposing family-held secrets for the benefit of its considerable reader base. Articles in sampled issues discussed all sorts of love/marriage, love/hate, personality, family, and career issues concerning the likes of Paul Newman, Lawrence Welk, Bonnie Franklin, Elliott Gould, James Garner, Sophia Loren, Wolfman Jack, and others from the film and television communities of Hollywood, New York City, and elsewhere. Typical advertisements featured everything from calendar banks to wart compounds, tummy trimmers, skin lighteners, Japanese magnetic

bracelets, and help for "Childless Wives Who Want Babies." Magazine format (8 ⅛ x 10 ⅞ inches / 205 x 275 mm), numerous black/white graphics on newsprint.
DEPT: "The Naked Truth," 'Hot gossip' column by Ron Scott; "Newsmakers," "Your Star Life," 'Horoscope' column by Doris Kaye; "Celebrity Talk," 'Inside info' column by Marcia Borie; "In Tune With," 'Pop scene' column by James Carlson; "Do Your Own Thing," star suggestions column by Lorraine Sciurca. (5-76).
TYPL: "Burt's Special 'Love Powers' Make Their Dreams Come True! Dinah Reveals Baby Plans!," "As Sonny Returns, Cher's Mother Confides--At Last Her Daughter Can Do 'Normal Things' with a Man! Why Cher Was Forced to Break All the Rules of Love," "Richard's Plea: Liz, Please Don't Hurt Me Again," "Is Marriage Going Out of Style? Six Young Stars of 'Search for Tomorrow' Give Their Very Personal Views!," "The Operation that Made Nancy a New Woman." (5-76).
SCHL: Quarterly (Fall, 1940 - Winter, 1940/1941); Monthly (Feb, 1941 - 1978); Bimonthly (1979+), 80 pp.
SPAN: Fall, 1940 - 198u//
VARIES
--Fall, 1940 - Dec, 1958 as Movie Stars Parade.
--? - ? as Movie Stars. TV Close-Ups.
LC: PN 1993.M748
ISSN: 0027-2744

Movie Stars Parade
Fall, 1940 - Dec, 1958//
SEE: MOVIE STARS

Movie Stars. TV Close-Ups
? - ?//
SEE: MOVIE STARS

MOVIE TEEN
PUBL: Screen-Teen Company, 114 East 32nd St., New York, NY.
DESC: "With every issue, *Movie Teen* will bring you the top people in their fields to give you beauty, glamour and charm secrets used by the stars themselves." Although this statement was made on behalf of *Movie Teen's* departmental, "Ask the Experts!," it could also apply to the overall form and function of the bimonthly serial: that of providing Hollywood's secrets for female teenagers. The beauty, health, and happiness secrets were always presented within the context of a host of Hollywood's young stars and starlets. For example, an article entitled "You Can Marry a Movie Star," was accompanied by a number of publicity stills showing happy Hollywood couples. An article on teenagers participating in a bowling party featured a young Hugh O'Brian, Darryl Hickman, Sunny Vickers and Gloria Grey on the lanes. This was a serial for the young, and especially those that dreamed of Hollywood. For the sampled issue of 1951: stapled magazine format, numerous graphics and editorial content black ink on newsprint (8 ½ x 11 inches / 215 x 280 mm).
DEPT: "Young Hollywood," column by May Mann; "Fashion Tips for Your Figure Problems," column by Janis Carter; "Ask the Experts!," 'Movie Teen's exciting and instructive new series of articles to help you top the date lists'; "Movie Teen Mail," letters. (2/3-51).
TYPL: "Got a Crush on Curtis?," "Bachelors at Work," "Do Your Hair the Hollywood Way!," "You Can Marry a Movie Star," "Become a Hairdresser for the Stars," "Fun on a Bowling Party." (2/3-51).
SCHL: Bimonthly, 75 pp.
SPAN: Dec, 1947 - ?//

✦ MOVIE TEEN ILLUSTRATED
PUBL: Movie Teen Illustrated, PO Box 215, Malibu, CA.
DESC: Dreams of dates with Sal Mineo, Elvis, Tab Hunter, Frankie Avalon, Ricky/Dave Nelson and Tommy Sands filled the pages of this "fanzine" for American female teens. Unabashed star worship could be seen in articles such as: "Maybe You Would Like to Know How You Rate as Rick's Best Girl?;" "Purple Dreams of Elvis," (as interpreted by readers aged 13 - 17); reporting on the the issue of "Debbie vs. Liz;" or telling about parties at Molly Bee's home in Hollywood. Numerous pictures supported the premise that nobody had more fun in life than Hollywood's young. Of special note in the issue for April, 1959 was a back cover of "Elvis Stickers," ten non-stick items to be cut out and applied as the reader wished. The magazine title was something of a misnomer. The word *Teen* refered more to the reader than to the (mostly male) film stars portrayed. For the sampled issue of 1959: stapled magazine format, color covers with black/white editorial content published on uncoated paper stock, no advertising (8 ⅜ x 11 inches / 210 x 280 mm).
DEPT: "Platter Chatter," "Dear Audrey, What'll I Do?," personal problem column by Audrey Olson. (4-59).
TYPL: "A Doctor Tells Why You Love Elvis," "Pat Boone Speaks of Marrying Too Young," "Are You the Girl for Ricky?," "Dick Clark's Last Birthday?," "My Crazy Wacky Wonderful Date With Sal," "Tommy Sands Saved My Life!" (4-59).
SCHL: Eight issues per year, 50 pp.
SPAN: Apr, 1958+?

✦ MOVIE - THE VIDEO MAGAZINE
PUBL: Movie, Ltd., Research House, Fraser Rd., Perivale, Middlesex UB6 7AQ England.
DESC: "*Movie the Video Magazine* is an essential guide to your enjoyment of films on video," asserts a subscription form in the publication. It is a statement backed up by an excellent layout format and editorial content on the transfer and release of major/minor motion picture product onto videocassette. Articles provide in-depth information about each new videotape re-

lease, including preview audience reaction, marketing, distribution, star-power, and potential for the home videotape market, which in this case is Great Britain. One sampled issue traced the career and family life of Arnold Schwarzenegger, featured actress Barbara Hershey, and provided a profile on the "new era of sex-free cinema," and its historical legacy. For biographical fans of cinema, the same issue presented an interesting article on Errol Flynn, his private/public lives and the wonderful screen gems available for viewing. With full-color throughout, and a very dynamic layout design, this can indeed be considered an "...essential guide to ...enjoyment of films on video." For the sampled issue of 1989: perfect-bound magazine format (8 ¼ x 11 ¾ inches / 210 x 300 mm).

DEPT: "Write On," fascinating letters to the editor column; "News," large section detailing latest entertainment news; "London Diary," commentary column by Neil Murray; "Hollywood," news items; "Buy Video Music," 'Movie's quarterly guide to the latest music video releases'; "Double Takes," column by Allan Bryce; "Cinema Box Office Top 20," MRIB supplied data; "Reviews," extensive selection of current releases; "Video Rental Top 50," "Sales Reviews," "Book Reviews," "Released," 'new video releases, both rental and sales titles'; "Off-Screen," news and profiles of film and television industry; "Wrap-Up," back-cover comment. (3-89).

TYPL: "The Thinking Man's Beefcake," "Hershey Power," "Last Tango in Tinseltown," "King of the Hellraisers," "Crocodile Cheers." (3-89).

SCHL: Monthly, 85 pp.
SPAN: Oct, 1988?+
ISSN: 0954-8610

✜ MOVIE/TV MARKETING

SUB: "Covering the Asian markets weekly."
PUBL: Movie-TV Marketing, Box 30, Central Post Office, Tokyo 100-91, Japan.
DESC: This is an unusual international publication for those interested in the promotion or exhibition of motion picture and television product. The first section deals with motion pictures. The second section, printed upside-down, to be read from the other direction, deals with television. Many of the features of the early *Far East Film News* are continued, but with some marked alterations; a change to high-gloss coated paper stock and an increase in the number and size of graphics. It is a notable resource for international film-TV activities, especially news of Asian nations. By late 1982, the serial contained all specialized departments, with no feature articles.
DESC: [*Far East Film News*]: This is a *Motion Picture Herald* with a Far Eastern focus. It is aimed at the exhibitor, and thus features new releases, developments at major production studios (predominantly American), and reviews of films and promotional activities. Printed in blue ink; it is tabloid size, with most articles slugged "U.S." Numerous illustrations, especially exhibitor promotions are included.

DEPT: "Honolulu," film news of the islands; "Hollywood," news briefs; "Report from Europe," briefs; "Broadway," current running New York films; "Reviews," short reviews of new releases; "Product Promotion," studio activities; "Far East P.O. Scoreboard," exhibitor grosses, duration and other exhibition data; "India," briefs; "Pakistan," briefs; "Japan," extra large section of news briefs; "Amusement Stock Quotations," weekly data on both Tokyo and New York exchanges; "Singapore," briefs; "Korea," briefs; "Hong Kong," briefs; "Equipment," new products; "Export Directory," ad briefs. (6-29-56). "Too Late to Classify," late newsbriefs; "Dateline Digest," remainder of film section with news on the following: USA, Canada, United Kingdom, Italy, FRG, Austria, France, USSR, South East Asia, Australia, and Japan; "Asian Box Office Scoreboard of Completed First-Runs," "Worldwide News and New Product," remainder of television section with news on: the Americas, Europe, Africa, Asia, and peripheral areas, New zealand, and Australia; "Communications Now," two-page news section on non-broadcast hardware and software; "Calendar," upcoming TV and film festivals. (?).

TYPL: "Taiwan B.O. Plagued with Ticket and Tax Problems," "U.S. Labor Protests Indian Ban," "CinemaScope 55 Demonstration in Bankok." (6- 29- 56). "Comedy-Game Show Being Offered by Twentieth-Fox TV," "Report-Comment on Recent-Upcoming CBC TV Shows," "Embargo on Finnish Theatricals Now Only Three Years," "Background-Current Details on Bangladesh TV." (?).

SCHL: Weekly, 25 pp.
SPAN: May, 1953+
VARIES
--May, 1953 as Far East Film News and TViews.
--Jun, 1953 - May, 1959 as Far East Film News.
--Jun, 1959 as Rengo Film News.
--Jul, 1959 - Dec, 1961 as Far East Film News.
--Jan, 1962 as Global Movie Marketing.
--Feb, 1962 - Jan, 1966 as Movie Marketing.
LC: PN 1993.M749

✜ MOVIE TV SECRETS

PUBL: Country Wide Publications, Inc., Room 1400, 2 West 45th St., New York, NY.
DESC: "We were shocked at a recent Hollywood cocktail party to hear a very influential producer say, 'Actors? Actors are just cattle. To hell with actors!' Well, Pal, I say to hell with you! It's the actors who have made Hollywood what it is and have made American movies the most exciting in the world. Actors are mistreated by you big producers who consider them just so much meat. You producers better wise up. It's the stars who attract the customers and you'd better know it! It's time you stopped treating them like work horses. They're people and to their fans, they're pretty important people. Take good care of them." This editorial by *Movie TV Secret's* Jack Crandell characterises the approach of this monthly orchid/onion

serial. The media celebrity/personality was the primary focus, including: Ann-Margret, Richard Burton, Frank Sinatra, Janet Leigh, Elizabeth Taylor, Tony Perkins, Glenn Ford, Sean Flynn, Warren Beatty, and the Kennedy's, Jack and Jackie. Numerous black/white pictures, editorial copy published on newsprint with full color coated paper covers (8 1/4 x 10 7/8 inches / 210 x 275 mm).
DEPT: "Editor's Column," column by Jack Crandell; "The Midnight Beat," 'Inside Hollywood - Revealing - Tip-Offs - Predictions - News!' column by Bonnie Lori; "Movie TV Secret Report," 'Hot Gossip - Top Secret - Right off the ticker - Uncensored - Confidential - Tip-Offs - Hush-Hush!' column by Stan Blane; "My Biggest Gripe," of the stars; "Advice to the Stars," column by Anthony Cirella; "You Ask the Stars." (8-62).
TYPL: "What Debbie Will Do to Liz Since Eddie's Breakdown," "What Happened When Max Schell Tried to Make Love to Natalie's Little Sister!," "Marilyn Tells Marilyn Leave Rock Alone," "What Makes Richard Burton Sexy," "Six Ways Jack and Jackie Share Their Love." (8-62).
SCHL: Monthly, 70 pp.
SPAN: Oct, 1959+?

MOVIE WORLD
SUB: "Hollywood's intimate all-picture magazine."
PUBL: Magazine Management Co., 575 Madison Ave., New York, NY 10022.
DESC: *Movie World* was typical of the film-fan genre magazine, filled with the latest news and gossip of the inner workings and lives of various film personalities in the movie capital of the world. Articles capitalized on the latest activities of the stars and starlets of the West Coast, with numerous advertisements for everything from wigs to bust developer hormone cream, beauty kits, teeth whiteners, elevator shoes, diamond rings, pellet firing target pistols, blackhead removers and marital devices/guides. Editorially speaking, it was the stars who were the focus of this "fanzine," with an emphasis on their off-camera activities. For the sampled issue of 1976: stapled magazine format with an abundant portfolio of black/white graphics, black ink editorial content on newsprint, with full-color cover on coated paper stock (8 1/8 x 10 3/4 inches / 210 x 275 mm).
DEPT: "Starfront," celebrity column by Patrick Agan; "Fan Fare," celebrity gossip column; "The Music Box," newsbriefs column by Robbin Schneider; "Daytime Roundup," news of daytime soaps column by Nora Astor; "Blind Items," news items too hot for attribution; "Nostalgia," "On the Spot," one-page interviews; "Pinup," double-page celebrity picture; "Crossword," "Preview," upcoming entertainment; "Between You and Me," Q&A on celebrities. (11-76).
TYPL: "Elvis Weds in Quickie Ceremony! Only We Have All the Details," "Will My Son Be Normal? The Question CHER's Doctors Wouldn't Answer!," "Angie Dickinson Confesses: I'm a Wife and Mother -- But Deep Down Inside, I'm a Swinger!," "Paul Michael Glaser Attacked By Hoods! Can Police Stop Them Before They Strike Again?" (11-76).
SCHL: Monthly, 75 pp.
SPAN: 1952 - ?//
ISSN: 0027-2779

MOVIEGOER
PUBL: ?, Box 128, Stuyvesant Station, New York, NY.
DESC: Editor James Stoller set out to produce a forum for critical discussion of the "rather wonderful" films produced by the international motion picture industry. "The attempt, then, is to gather the good writers on film in, or in some cases out of, the country, and surround them with none of the waste matter or foolishness that would seem obligatory in the other film journals; to provide them in this way, with an intelligent and humane frame for their work." Response to the first issue was encouraging, but only two issues were published and the spring, 1964 issue was skipped. Journal format; some production stills.
DEPT: "Letters," "Books." (summer/autumn-64).
TYPL: "On Godard's 'Vivre Sa Vie,'" "Individual Combat," "Pop Go the Movies," "Toward Liberty Valance," "The Director Vanishes." (summer/autumn-64).
SCHL: Quarterly, 70 pp.
SPAN: Winter, 1964 - Summer/Autumn, 1966//
SUSPENDED
--Spring, 1964.
LC: PN 1993.M7518
ISSN: 0047-8296

✤ MOVIEGOER
SUB: "The feature film magazine."
PUBL: 13-30 Corporation, 505 Mark St., Knoxville, TN 37902.
DESC: Subscriptions are not taken for this monthly motion picture promotional, which, it is assumed, is given to movie-going patrons in selected theatres. Full color throughout, each issue contains three primary features: Hollywood stars; directors/writers/producers; and a feature film. Articles are not designed to be critical in nature, but rather to explore and describe new motion picture product appearing in theatres for the upcoming month. Letters to the editor indicate widespread pleasure with the magazine, and generally laude the service it provides. For the sampled issue of 1985: magazine format (8 1/4 x 10 7/8 inches / 210 x 275 mm), full color graphics throughout. Advertising in sampled issues was for major cigarette brands.
DEPT: "Letters," "Film Clips," motion pictures opening this month; "Behind the Scenes," stories behind the pictures; "Newsreel," newsbriefs; "Screen Test," quiz. (10-85).
TYPL: "Polaroids From the Brain of Steve Tesich," "A Chorus Lineup," "Kevin Kline." (10-85).
SCHL: Monthly, 24 pp.
SPAN: Jan, 1982+?

✤ MOVIEGUIDE
SUB: "A Biblical look at movies and entertainment."™
PUBL: Good News Communications, Inc., PO Box 9952, Atlanta, GA 30319.
DESC: "Christians claim to want family films, but they support the same films, often 'R' rated, that the general public supports. *MOVIEGUIDE* helps Christians develop their own discernment by looking at every aspect of a movie from a biblical worldview. And *MOVIEGUIDE* gives Christians the ability to defend themselves against the media hype of secular reviews and advertisements." The majority of each issue is devoted to reviews of motion pictures, both box office and videocassette releases, with some production stills included. Early issues were typewritten with few graphics, moving in later issues to typeset format with a considerable number of graphics. Stapled newsletter format, black ink on uncoated paper stock (8 3/8 x 10 3/4 inches / 215 x 275 mm).
DEPT: "Film Classics," review; "Christian Video," review; "Travel Guide," videocassette review. (1-20-89). None. (Vol 4, #23).
TYPL: "The Ten Best Films of 1988," "PG Films Bounce Back in 1988." (1-20-89). "Whatever Happened to Freedom of the Press or Weren't Woodward & Bernstein Heroes?," "Just As We Predicted: A Double Standard." (Vol 4, #23).
SCHL: Biweekly, 8 pp.
SPAN: ?, 1985+

Movieland
Feb, 1943 - Apr, 1958//
SEE: MOVIELAND AND TV TIME

✤ MOVIELAND AND TV TIME
PUBL: Movieland, Inc., 1476 Broadway, New York, NY.
DESC: This "movie-fan" magazine launched during World War II provided the usual grouping of stories concerning the stars, and supporting cast members of Hollywood, but with a strong emphasis on wartime film activities during the first two years of the serial's existence. Magazine format on newsprint. Sampled issue for 1960: perfect-bound magazine format, primarily black/white editorial content with some spot color and full-color pages on uncoated paper stock, with full-color cover on coated paper stock (8 5/8 x 10 7/8 inches / 220 x 275 mm).
DESC: (10/10/90) BETTER DESC FROM LC !!!!
DEPT: "Inside Hollywood," column by Ruth Waterbury, "Movieland's Movie Reviews." (4-43).
TYPL: "Tyrone Power's Experiences in Marine Boot Camp," "Judy Garland Says Good-Bye to Marriage," "Favorites of the Fleet," "Hutton, the Howling Success." (4-43).
SCHL: Monthly, 70 pp.
SPAN: Feb, 1943+?

VARIES
--Feb, 1943 - Apr, 1958 as Movieland.
LC: PN 1993.M752

✤ MOVIELINE
SUB: "Movies as a way of life."
PUBL: Movieline, Inc., 1141 South Beverly Dr., Los Angeles, CA 90035.
DESC: *Movieline* began publication as a Southern California semi-monthly regional in 1985, with primary distribution through motion picture theatres, video stores and record outlets. The magazine went national in September, 1989 with an editorial content that Associate Publisher John Molinari calls "a cross between *Spy* and *Vanity Fair*." It is a well-designed publication with trendy graphics (full color throughout), and news of the Hollywood community. It is concerned not so much with film product itself as it is with the stars/personalities, who are presented in a tasteful, thoughtful manner. For the individual who is fascinated with the stars of filmdom, and desires a publication of quality and pizazz, *Movieline* provides a fascinating forum of the great and not-so-great of the film capitol of the world. Magazine format (8 1/4 x 10 7/8 inches / 210 x 275 mm); numerous color graphics.
DEPT: "Hollywood Ink," Hollywood chatter column by Ignatz; "Letters," "The Hollywood Kids," Hollywood chatter; "Players," stars and events; "Tribal Rites," the stars out together; "L.A. Obsessions," column by Ben Kallen; "Moving Lips," column by Grover Lewis; "Premieres," column by Richard Natale; "Trivia Game," "Edge of the Apocalypse," column by Christopher H. Hunt; "Buzz," news about the hottest stars; "Inside Story:," in-depth profile; "Style," profile; "Fashion," "Reservations," "Video," new releases and current talk. (12-89). "Letters," "Buzz," Hollywood news; "Moving Lips," column by Luc Sante; "Hollywood Kids," "L.A. Obsessions," column by Ben Kallen; "Premieres," column by Stephen Farber; "The Look," "Video," reviews; "The Commissary," column by Jeff Lantos; "Players," "Edge of the Apocalypse," column by Christopher H. Hunt. (1-91).
TYPL: "Cut to the Chase," "Meg o' the Wild," "The Charge of the Warhorses." (12-89). "Believe Me This," "Nic at Noon," "The Battle Cry of Aldo Ray," "Who is that Lady?," "All About Eves." (1-91).
SCHL: Biweekly (Sep, 1989 - ?); Monthly (?+), 100 pp.
SPAN: Sep, 1989+
DD: 791
ISSN: 1055-0917

MOVIES, THE
PUBL: The Movies, 310 Madison Ave., New York, NY 10017.
DESC: This short-lived serial celebrated American motion picture product, the creative forces behind them, the audiences that viewed them, and the relationship between the film and American culture in general. *The*

Movies looked at the "why" of filmmaking; such as why a scriptwriter approached a subject in a particular manner, what led a Hollywood producer to pursue a pet project, or a star's interpretation of screen characterization. Integral to the publication was current industry news; costs of filmmaking, distribution deals, the fate of studios, and the status of Hollywood stars and personalities. Articles from one sampled issue covered a possible film based on the life of Jim Morrison, left-over props on movie backlots, film star agents who audit the box office, an interview with Kurt Russell, and an essay on one alien creature's motion picture. It was unfortunate that the serial did not continue beyond its initial five issues. Magazine format (8 1/8 x 10 7/8 inches / 205 x 275 mm); color graphics throughout.
DEPT: "Editor's Page," editorial; "Correspondence," letters; "Newsfront," news of films and the motion picture industry; "Book Reviews," "Horse Feathers," guest column; "Balcony," column by Mark Jacobson; "Brief Notices." (11-83).
TYPL: "The Way We Were: A Photo Essay From 'Still Life'," "Conspiracy Madness: the Movies After JFK," "Kiss 'N' Kill: 'Star 80' and the Playboy Ethic," "Night Moves: Fleshdancing in L.A.," "The Lion Speaks: An Interview with Frank Yablans." (11-83).
SCHL: Monthly, 85 pp.
SPAN: Jul, 1983 - Nov, 1983//
LC: PN 1993 .M7525
DD: 791.43/05
ISSN: 0742-4116

MOVIES AND MINISTRY
SUB: "A journal of the cinema and religion."
PUBL: Seminary Film Society of Southern Baptist Theological Society, Louisville, KY 40206.
DESC: "Our purpose is two-fold: to provide a medium through which we can express our beliefs concerning the relation of cinema and religion, and to provide for our readers materials which they can use effectively in their ministry." An interesting, if short-lived critical examination of the role of theology in major Hollywood film product from the point-of-view of a Baptist seminary. Format began as small booklet size (May, 1983 - July, 1973), moving to full newsletter size (September, 1973 - November, 1973), and once again back to booklet size (December, 1973 - July, 1974). Some issues dealt with single themes, such as "Using Film with Young People in Your Church," "Death in the Cinema," "The Devil You Say," or "Sex in Movies." Typewritten; no graphics.
DEPT: "Comments," "Book Review," "Film Reviews." (2-74).
TYPL: "Death in the Cinema," "A Six-Way Plan for Death," "Death in *Cries and Whispers*." (2-74).
SCHL: Monthly [except August], 28 pp.
SPAN: May, 1973 - Jul, 1974//
LC: PN 1995.5 .M68
DD: 791.43/05
ISSN: 0161-3995

MOVIES AND THE PEOPLE WHO MAKE THEM, THE
SUB: "A continuing survey of the motion picture in America."
PUBL: Elm City Review Service, 108 State St., New Haven, CT.
DESC: "*The Movies*...is an independent and impartial information service; is designed to serve as a current guide to the new films and a permanent record of the motion picture in America; Presents a cross-section of reasoned opinion on the new films, based upon personal reports of experienced movie-goers and checked against all available independent sources of information." Each issue consisted of a series of motion picture reviews: cast and crew credits, synopses, and oftentimes a small production still. In 1939, *The Movies* consisted of a magazine format, moving to a small journal format by early 1941.
DEPT: None.
TYPL: No Article Titles.
SCHL: Weekly (1939 - 1940); Biweekly (1941); 25 pp.
SPAN: Jan 4, 1939 - Apr 18, 1941//
SUSPENDED
--Jan, 1941 - Mar, 1941.
LC: PN 1993.M753
DD: 791.4

MOVIES NOW
PUBL: Flowers & Kovach Publications, Inc., 8899 Beverly Blvd., Suite 102, Los Angeles, CA 90048.
DESC: "Officially sponsored by the National Association of Theatre Owners," this bimonthly Hollywood film promotional showcased some one dozen current films in American distribution. The magazine, sold in the film theatres (and also available by subscription), devoted several pages and many production stills to each film release. Articles were short on editorial content, as the function of the magazine was to stimulate the reader's interest in attending more motion pictures, not to be analytical. The subscription price in 1971 was $5.00 for six issues, but the sample issue viewed sold for only twenty-five cents at a "special theater price." For the 1971 sampled issue: stapled magazine format, primary black ink editorial content with numerous full-color pages and full-color cover all on coated paper stock (8 3/8 x 10 7/8 inches / 210 x 275 mm).
DEPT: "Kicks From the Flicks," upcoming motion picture product; "Capsule Film Listings," descriptions and ratings of upcoming films; "Star Signs," Hollywood horoscope. (vol 1, #2-71).
TYPL: "Dennis Hopper: Triple Threat Talent," "Sally Kellerman: Star Ascending," "William Tepper: Complete Film-Maker Searches for Place," "David L. Wolper: Into the Tomorrow World of a Producer," "Sight and Sound of Drug Lyrics." (vol 1, #2-71).
SCHL: Bimonthly, 75 pp.
SPAN: ?, 1971 - ?//?

✣ MOVIES USA

SUB: "Official magazine of the Movietime Network."
PUBL: Enterex Industries, 82 Roswell Rd., #370, Atlanta GA 30350.
DESC: Unabashedly enthusiastic about today's motion picture product, this free publication (at selected participating theatres) provides a public relation's/moviegoer's dream of what the "movies" are all about, great entertainment at reasonable cost. With full color pages throughout, *MOVIES USA* showcases talent and film product currently being shown, coming soon to a neighborhood theatre. Yes, it's show business hype, but it is also quality writing, good layout design, and full color stills of favorite films for free. A nicely executed publication. For the sampled issue of 1989: full-color graphics and editorial content throughout on coated paper stock in stapled magazine format with advertising (8 ¼ x 10 ⅞ inches / 210 x 275 mm).
DEPT: "Double Exposure," 'The movies glitterati make the scene'; "Faces," 'The ones to watch'; "Take 2," closer look at current film fare; "Now Playing," 'A guide to fine flicks playing at your local movie palace'; "Videofile," 'In case you missed it on the big screen'. (12-89).
TYPL: "Captivating Crooks," "DeVito Goes for the Roses," "We're No Angels." (12-89).
SCHL: Monthly, 30 pp.
SPAN: Nov, 1987?+
DD: 791 11
ISSN: 1044-1336

MOVING IMAGE

SUB: "The magazine for film & videomakers"
PUBL: PMS Publishing Company, 609 Mission St., San Francisco, CA 94105.
DESC: It used to be "home movies" that American consumers were enthralled with, but now the "in" thing is "home video," and PMS Publishing, reflecting that change in taste, has renamed and redirected its former magazine, *Super-8 Filmaker*, to explore the new electronic medium. Indeed, *Moving Images* is a mixture of both film and video media for the American consumer market.
DEPT: "Quick Takes," newsbriefs; "Letters," "Reader's Tips," "Hot shots," people making news; "Q&A," "Items of Interest," equipment; "Basics: All About Videotape," column by Charles Bensinger; "Product Probe," reviews column by Marc Wielage; "Making Money," column by Janis Bultman; "Marketplace," "Latest Attractions," home videotapes. (9/10-81).
TYPL: "Fiesta! A Super-8 to Video Odyssey," "How to Choose a Portable Videocassette Recorder," "Simple But Spectacular Special Effects," "The Moving Image Interview: Michael Kahn--film Editor at the Top." (9/10- 81).
SCHL: Quarterly (Winter, 1971/1973 - Fall, 1973); Bimonthly (Nov/Dec, 1973 - Nov/Dec, 1976); Eight issues per year (Jan/Feb, 1977+), 72 pp.

SPAN: Winter, 1972/1973 - Jun, 1982//
VARIES
--Winter, 1972/1973 - Jul/Aug, 1981 as Super 8 Filmaker (ISSN: 0049- 2574).
LC: TR 845 .M68
DD: 778.5/05
ISSN: 0276-3494
ABST: --Film Literature Index (ISSN: 0093-6758)

MOVING PICTURE AGE

SUB: "A monthly magazine--to make the screen a greater power in education and business." (Mar, 1918 - May/Jun, 1918).
SUB: "To make the screen a greater power in education and business." (Jul, 1918 - ?).
SUB: "The only independent magazine in the field of visual instruction." (? - Apr, 1922).
SUB: "The only independent magazine in the general field of visual instruction." (May, 1922).
SUB: "A monthly publication devoted to the interests of visual instruction."
PUBL: Class Publications, Inc., 418 South Market St., Chicago, IL.
DESC: *Moving Picture Age* had absolutely no interest in large budget Hollywood motion pictures, but was a serial for the instructional and educational film where the exhibitor was the classroom teacher, or company manager. Articles were by educators, evangelists, sales managers, distributors, government officials and others who had experienced firsthand the success of utilizing motion picture films in their professions. Besides success stories, *Moving Picture Age* also described new exhibition technology and trends in educational film. Of special note in early issues (Mar, 1918 - Aug, 1918) was a separate section of the serial entitled "Industrial Film." Numerous graphics, especially of on-location film usage.
DEPT: "Editorials," "With the Reel Observor," column by Henry MacMahon; "Projection," "Educationals," "Ask Us," "Slides," "The Other Fellow's Idea." (7-18). "A Chat with the Editor," "Editorials," "The National Academy of Visual Instruction," news; "Highlights," film reviews; "Mechanics of Visualization," "Better Films," standard raising; "Gossip-Gathering on Film Boulevard," "Approved Films and Their Sources," reviews. (4-22).
TYPL: "Screen to Teach Life and Customs," "Aquatic Life Taught by Films," "Cleveland Takes Movies to Home." (7-18). "Entertainment in the Church," "Fact and Fable in Visual Education," "Small-Town Problems," "Rural Exhibitions in Montana." (4-22).
SCHL: Monthly, 35 pp.
SPAN: Mar, 1918 - Dec, 1922//
VARIES
--Mar, 1918 - Dec, 1919 as Reel and Slide Magazine.
WITH SUPPLEMENT
--Industrial Film, Mar, 1918 - Aug, 1918.
ABSORBED BY
--Educational Screen, Dec, 1922.
LC: PN 1993.M755

Moving Picture Story Magazine
Feb?, 1911//
SEE: MOTION PICTURE

Moving Picture Weekly
1915 - May, 1922//
SEE: UNIVERSAL WEEKLY

✣ MOVING PICTURES INTERNATIONAL

SUB: "Worldwide coverage of television, film, video and cable."
PUBL: Moving Pictures International, Ltd., 26, Soho Square, London W1V 5FJ, England.
DESC: This is an excellent resource for a weekly international review of events, trends, new product releases; and the economic box office status of motion pictures, broadcast and cable television, and associated video services. Articles are succinct and authoritative, and address the business-side of entertainment, appealing to the majority of entertainment managers who emphasize "business" within "show business." The London locale for publication provides an emphasis on UK advertising, but editorial content covers numerous international cities and production locations. The "Box Office Guide" section alone is easily worth the newsstand cover price of £1.50 / $3.00 (spring-91): this information-packed section is "...designed to provide a worldwide view of film performance." The first page lists "The US and UK Weekend" boxoffice gross receipts. The following four-page section provides extensive "...worldwide grosses for major film releases," the information being assembled under subtitles, "Film with Country of Origin," "Distributor," "Weeks on Release," "This Week [and] Last Week Box Office $, Admissions, Screens [and] Average Per Screen," "% Rise & Fall," and finally "Total Box Office / Admissions." This informational service compiled in the sampled spring issue by Tina McFarling and Sara Squire is an outstanding reference for a quick-read of international motion picture exhibition. Also of importance in the "Box Office Guide" is "Box Office News," which provides wonderful capsule news reports on box office receipts and film exhibition news (in the sampled issue) for Los Angeles, London, Bucharest, Munich, Sydney, and Paris. A major classified section (four out of 16 pages) is devoted to production services and resources under headings of "Financial Services," "Insurance," "For License," "Situations Vacant," "Transport," "Courses," "Festival," "Scripts," "Agencies," "For Rent," "Co-Production," "Locations," and "Facilities." For sampled issue of 1991: stapled magazine format, black/white editorial content with spot color on various pages, cover is full-color all on coated paper stock (9 ¼ x 12 ⅛ inches / 235 x 310 mm).
DEPT: "This Week," upcoming events of major importance; "News Round-Up," newsbriefs listed by international city; "Production Notes," current projects column by Mark Adams; "In Production," current projects listed by title, production company, country; "New Starts," new projects underway listed with pertinent information; "Box Office Guide," detailed financial information; "Box Office Worldwide," extensive center-page pull-out guide to international box office receipts; "Box Office News," information from variety of international cities. (5-9-91).
TYPL: "Cartel in $30m French/US Deal," "MGM-Pathe Faces 40% Sale Threat," "$76 Million Purchase Price Puts Off Packer," "Palme d'or Wide Open for 'Adult' Films," "Muppet 'Misunderstanding' Settled Out of Court." (5-9-91).
SCHL: Weekly, 20 pp.
SPAN: Sep 13, 1990?+
ISSN: 0959-6992

MSO
Sep?, 1989 - Aug, 1990//
(ISSN: 1046-3321)
SEE: MSO'S CABLE MARKETING

✣ MSO'S CABLE MARKETING

SUB: "The magazine for cable system operations."
SUB: "The operations and marketing journal of the cable television industry."
SUB: "Programming for profit."
PUBL: Communications Technology Publications Corporation, a subsidiary of Transmedia Partners, 12200 East Briarwood Ave., Suite 250, Englewood, CO 80112.
DESC: *Cable Strategies* was concerned with the continuing battle of winning subscribers and advertisers to cable television. For the consumer of cable, those strategies included new subscriber hook-ups, retention, and servicing; using promotional, technological, and marketing means. For the potential advertiser, the discussion forum included competitive media (especially network television), new programming product, and the advertising twosome: reach and frequency. September, 1989 brought a new title, *MSO*, with a new emphasis on the business of multiple system cable television operations. A merger with ailing *Cable Marketing* created the current title, *MSO's Cable MARKETING* in September/October, 1990. *MSO's Cable MARKETING* is direct, brash, thorough and timely in its coverage of events and trends affecting the multiple system operator. This is a business periodical concerned with the profit side of cable operation, and is well recommended. Magazine format and size identical for all titles: (8 ⅜ x 10 ⅞ inches / 215 x 275 mm).
DEPT: "From the Publisher," editorial; "NewsCap," newsbriefs; "Programmer Focus," cable network profile; "CAB Fare," Cabletelevision Advertising Bureau news; "CTAM Rocky Mountain Chapter Newsletter,"

"Business Dynamics," "Career Advances," personnel briefs; "Marketing Dynamics." (4-89). "Frontline," indepth look at specific aspect of cable television operation; "Portfolio," stocks & bonds; "CYA," accroynm for protect thyself, interprets impact of non-cable events on cable television; "FYI," newsbriefs; "Specs," technical side of cable; "Local Spots," local spot avails news; "Hot Takes," promotion ideas; "Done Deals," cable subscriptions; "Politics," the politics of cable; "Random Notes," commentary column by Patrick J. Gushman. (9-89).
TYPL: "Segmented Special Events: The Next Generation of Pay-Per-View," "Cable Television Advertising: More Than Just a Cute Idea," "Television Advertising: Big Stakes for Big Bucks," "Communicating with Your Customers." (4-89). "Politics is Going to Get Us--or Will It?," "Is This Any Way to Run for President?," "Cable is Still a Bargain," "You Really Want These Guys?," "Should Cable Sell Its Soul (again)?" (9-89).
SCHL: Monthly, 65 pp.
SPAN: Oct, 1987+
VARIES
--Oct, 1987 - Aug?, 1989 as Cable Strategies (ISSN: 1044-2820).
--Sep?, 1989 - Aug, 1990 as MSO (ISSN: 1046-3321).
FROM MERGER OF
--Cable Marketing (ISSN: 0279-8891) (and) MSO (ISSN: 1046-3321), Sep/Oct, 1990.
DD: 384 11

Multi-Images

1974? - Jan/Feb, 1986//
SEE: MULTI IMAGES JOURNAL

✤ MULTI IMAGES JOURNAL

SUB: "The journal of the Association for Multi-Image."
SUB: "The journal of the Association for Multi-Image International."
PUBL: Association for Multi-Image, 8019 North Himes Ave., Suite 401, Tampa, FL 33614.
DESC: [*Multi-Images*]: A quarterly publication devoted to the rapidly growing field of multiple-image presentations to mass audiences. The three primary media in this field--slides, film, and audio--form the basis for articles concerning technique, presentation sites, technical development, graphics, photography, multi-tracking and; of course, multi-image presentations.
DEPT: "Footnotes," upcoming events; "Speaking of New Products," news briefs.
TYPL: "The AV House: Teamwork and Quality Equal Success," "Multi-image and the Copyright Law," "Pin Registration Slide Mount," "Kent State Gives Multi-Media Tour." (summer-77).
SCHL: Quarterly, 30 pp.
SPAN: 1974+
VARIES
--1974? - Jan/Feb, 1986 as Multi-Images.
LC: TR 505 .M85

DD: 778.2 20
ISSN: 0893-5440

✤ MULTICHANNEL NEWS

PUBL: CNC Group/Diversified Publishing, 825 7th Ave., New York, NY 10019.
DESC: An in-magazine promotional says: "Old news is no news. You need to know what's happening now--not last week or last month. That's why you read *Multichannel News*." Covering the business side of cable television, *Multichannel News* provides a quality vehicle for disseminating the latest news events in the cable television industry. The large tabloid-size format works in conjunction with multicolor printing to bring an immediacy to the news events covered, information which is often at the cutting edge of cable television development. The large editorial content allows for indepth stories of individual companies, cable systems, conventions, and regulatory actions. An unusually large employment section, coupled with numerous advertisements, attests to subscriber loyalty and the importance of this publication. This is "must reading" for cable television management. For sampled issue of 1991: staped magazine format, full color throughout on coated paper stock (10 $E7/8 x 14 ¾ inches / 275 x 375 mm).
DEPT: "Calendar," "Finance," large section devoted to cable economics; "Facts & Figures," charts and graphs on cable; "International," "People," personnel newsbriefs; "Programming," "Stocks," "Technical & Product Development." (4-24-89).
TYPL: "Cable Ratings Climbing; Network Ratings Dipping," "Baby Bell Buys Majority Interest Option in Chicago," "Metzenbaum Puts Cable-Regulation Bills on Table," "Viacom to Seek Franchise Modifications," "Pay Nets Announce Purchases, Sales, Productions." (4-24-89).
SCHL: Weekly, 60 pp.
SPAN: 1980+
ISSN: 0276-8593

✤ MURPHY REPORTER

PUBL: University of Minnesota, School of Journalism and Mass Communication, 111 Murphy Hall, Minneapolis, MN 55455.
DESC: This in-house publication covers news of faculty, students and alumni in the School of Journalism and Mass Communications at the University of Minnesota. Student activities and faculty research and publications are noted, along with other campus developments as it impacts the School of Journalism and Mass Communication. The Reporter assumed a new newsprint format with the November, 1979 issue.
DEPT: None.
TYPL: "Library Gets Poor Grades," "Faculty Members Add Volumes to Bookshelves," "National News Council to Hold Hearings on Campus," "Alumni Garner AP Honors." (11-78).

Music & Sound Output
Nov/Dec, 1980 - Dec, 1988//
(ISSN: 0273-8902)
SEE: STAGE & STUDIO

✤ MUSIC LINE
SUB: "The CCM music report."
SUB: "The Magazine for Christian Music Ministries."
PUBL: Music Line, P.O. Box 6300, Laguna Hills, CA 92653.
DESC: "We believe music is a creative gift from God intended to bring honor to Him through artistic expressions that are consistent with a biblically based world view regardless of the musical style. By publishing news, information, features, and commentary, MusiCline seeks to provide practical helps to the various music ministries which coexist for evangelism, edification, worship, and entertainment." MusicLine is the "Billboard" of the Christian media community, with an emphasis on the musical artist and the media of radio and concerts.
DEPT: "Album Reviews," "Changes," personnel; "Charts," "Christian Musician," "Concert Promoter," "New Equipment," "Radio," "Retail," "Songwriter," "Visual Music," "Worship Leader," "Your Turn," letters. (02-86).
TYPL: "A Visible Means of Support," "Jack-of-All-Formats, Master of None," "Is Visul Music Selling?" (02-86).
SCHL: Monthly, 40 pp.
SPAN: May, 1983+
ISSN: 0746-7656

MUSICAL AMERICA
PUBL: Musical America Corporation, 113 West 57th St., New York, NY.
DESC: The denizens of "Tin Pan Alley" would find little to amuse or entertain themselves in *Musical America*, a publication dedicated to the loftier side of musical performance. This New York City-based serial covered and promoted the activities within the general spheres of opera, orchestra, and vocal endeavors in theatrical recital and concert-hall surroundings. Letterpress printed, 9 point type in four column format, allowed for a significant quantity of editorial copy to be contained in a single issue. Articles were a mixture between New York City performing arts activities, and national/international news. Black/white pictures of artists, or concerts/recitals in progress accompany most articles. One hallmark of *Musical America* was its unusual schedule of publication. There were 17 issues per year, seven of which were issued monthly (on the 15th) during the months of February, May, June, July, August, September, and October. Intermixed with this was a semimonthly publication schedule (on the 10th and 25th) during the months of November, December, January, March, and April. Large magazine format (340 cm high x 255 cm wide); two-color cover with black/white editorial content; numerous advertisements placed by teachers of singing, talent agencies, instrumental and vocal artists.
DEPT: "Mephisto's Musings," observations and comment; "Opera," "Concerts," "Musical Americana," column by Harry Marlatt; "What They Read 20 Years Ago," in Musical America; "News of the Nation's Orchestras," "New Music," 'From leading publishers'; "Obituary," extensive section; "Radio," music on the air; "Musical America's Educational Department," instruction and comment; "Music Schools and Teachers," "Around the Studios," newsbriefs; "The Party Line," backcover photographs. (1-25-46).
TYPL: "Salzburg Festivals to be Re-Established," "Madama Butterfly Returns," "Guatemala Government Fosters Musical Renaissance," "Fort Wayne Tells Success Story," "Provincial Orchestra Visits Mexico City." (1-25-46).
SCHL: Seventeen issues per year, 40 pp.
SPAN: 1898 - 1964//
SUSPENDED
--? - Oct, 1905.
MERGED WITH
--High Fidelity (to form) High Fidelity and Musical America.

✤ MUSICAL AMERICA
SUB: "The journal of classical music."
PUBL: ABC Consumer Magazines, Inc., 825 Seventh Ave., New York, NY 10019.
DESC: Continuing the fine tradition of performing arts coverage, *Musical America* takes a thorough, informative look at the artistic fields of orchestral/vocal concert, opera, dance, recording, and recital. In essence, this is a serial of classical music live performance. Oftentimes, new artists receive their first national notice in this publication. Other articles expand knowledge of current favorites, and give their concert and recording schedules. As always, numerous photographs of the artists themselves are featured throughout. An excellent publication for the pulse of live classical music performance. Magazine format.
DEPT: "Editors' Page," "OPUS Record Reviews," "Letters," "The Dance," review; "Book Reviews," "Debuts & Reappearances," in the performing arts. (9-89).
TYPL: "The Cliburn Prize," "Beyond the Gold," "Sarasota: Apprentices at Work," "More Than a Subway Token," "Great Britten." (9-89).
SCHL: Bimonthly, 100 pp.
SPAN: ?+
ABSORBED
--Opus, ?
ISSN: 1042-3443

SCHL: ?, 12 pp.

✣ NAB HIGHLIGHTS

PUBL: Station Services Department, National Association of Broadcasters, 1771 N. St., N.W., Washington, DC 20036.
DESC: [*Highlights*]: A weekly newsletter designed to keep members abreast of current political and legal issues, it emphasizes current NAB lobbying efforts. Articles describe regulatory trends, proposed legislation, current items of interest before the Federal Communications Commission, and other subjects of interest to radio and television station managers in the United States.
DEPT: None. (10-77).
TYPL: "Census Reform and the Role of Broadcasters," "FCC Inquiry on TV Program Exclusivity Contracts Halted," "NAB Asks FEC not to Discourage Broadcast Debates." (10-77).
SCHL: Weekly, 4 pp.
SPAN: Jan, 1975+?
VARIES
--Jan, 1975 - ? as Highlights.

NAB Member Service
Mar, 1949 - 195u//
SEE: NARTB MEMBER SERVICE

NAB Reports
Mar 11, 1933 - Feb 28, 1949//
SEE: NARTB MEMBER SERVICE

NAB Today [Television Edition]
? - ?//
SEE: TV TODAY

✣ NABET NEWS
SUB: "For radio, TV and film workers in the United States and Canada."
PUBL: National Association of Broadcast Employees and Technicians, AFL-CIO, 7101 Wisconsin Ave., Suite 800, Bethesda, MD 20814.
DESC: This large-format publication serves as a communication forum for members of NABET, providing information on member activities, elections, anti-NABET forces, and other labor news of interest. Issues in the early 1980s also carried the statement: "International Edition." No advertising.
DEPT: "Letters and Comment," "Flashes," newsbriefs. (12-84).
TYPL: "RKO Story: Strikebreakers ... and Solidarity," "Not Even Fire Can Stop the Music at PBS," "It was NABET Over AFTRA, 14-0," "New Agreements Wrapped Up at NBC; Retro Money Awaited." (12-84).
SCHL: Ten issues per year (Nov, 1962 - Jun, 1969); Bimonthly (Aug, 1969 - ?); Monthly (? - Feb, 1987); Bimonthly (Oct, 1987+), 4 pp.
SPAN: Nov, 1962?+
EDITION
--International Edition.
SUSPENDED
--Feb, 1987 - Oct, 1987.
LC: HD 6350.B86N18
ISSN: 0027-5697

NAEB Journal
Oct, 1957 - Jul/Aug, 1967//
SEE: PUBLIC TELECOMMUNICATIONS REVIEW

NAEB Letter
1964 - Mar, 1979//
SEE: CURRENT

NAFBRAT Quarterly
Summer, 1960 - Summer, 1963//
SEE: BETTER RADIO AND TELEVISION

NARND Bulletin
Jan, 1947? - Nov, 1952//
SEE: COMMUNICATOR

✣ NARTB MEMBER SERVICE
PUBL: National Association of Broadcasters, National Press Bldg., Washington, DC.
DESC: [*Broadcasters News Bulletin*]: This 20-page (unbound) mimeographed publication furnished local radio station managers information about NAB activities, developments of NAB member stations, and federal government intelligence, especially activities of the Federal Radio Commission. No graphics; stapled mimeographed sheets.
DEPT: "Hearing Calendar," "Miscellaneous Commission Action," "Applications Set for Hearing," "Applications Granted," "Applications Returned." (3-4-33).

TYPL: "Baldwin Joins NAB Staff," "North American Meetings Continue," "Georgia Would Sanction Athletic Broadcasts," "Bills that Died with Congress." (3-4-33).
SCHL: Irregular (? - Mar 4, 1933); Weekly (Mar 11, 1933+), 20 pp.
SPAN: ?+
VARIES
--? - Mar 4, 1933 as Broadcasters News Bulletin.
--Mar 11, 1933 - Feb 28, 1949 as NAB Reports.
--Mar, 1949 - 195u as NAB Member Service.

NATIONAL ADVERTISING

SUB: "Let there be light."
SUB: "A journal for mail-order advertisers."
SUB: "The national magazine of business promotion and sales by mail."
PUBL: 115 Dearborn St., Chicago, IL.
DESC: Devoted to the advertiser of mail-order merchandise, the *Mail Order Journal* provided timely advice on newspaper rates, ad layout, copy writing, and other techniques vital to the mail-order company. It gave basic instruction on what newspapers would accept within their columns; types of copy and graphics that had proven "pulling power" with the consumer; and general information on the state of mail-order advertising. Small format with some graphics; moving to 16-page magazine-size with no graphics in 1950, and printed in all-blue ink on white stock.
DEPT: "Among the Monthlies," newsbriefs; "The Farmer and His Favorite Medium," agricultural press news; "Personal," column by John Jones; "Among the Dailies and Weeklies," "Department of Suggestion," opinion; "Publishers' Rates Alphabetically Index." (11-20-01). "Editorial," "Timely Topics," "Advertising Agencies." (11-50).
TYPL: "A New Plan to Push a Remedy," "Fleeced Suckers Out of a Million," "Advertising Fables in Slang," "Financial Advertising." (11-20-01). "Additional Highway Post Office Routes," "Federal Trade Commission Recent Proceedings," "Printing Ink." (11-50).
SCHL: Monthly; 80, 16 pp.
SPAN: 1897? - May, 1925//
VARIES
--1897 - Mar, 1916 as Mail Order Journal.
--Apr, 1916 - Aug, 1921 as Advertising Age and Mail Order Journal, The.
LC: HF 5466.A22

✤ NATIONAL AMATEUR

SUB: "Official organ of National Amateur Press Association."
PUBL: National Amateur Press Association, 1326 W. 400 South, Salt Lake City, UT 84104.
DESC: "The National Amateur Press Association is a hobby organization founded in Philadelphia on July 4, 1876 by a group of boy printers and editors, many of whom later became nationally famous." Amateur journalism was defined as "The hobby of writing poetry, stories, and essays, which other amateurs print free in their papers; and of editing papers that publish what you wish, which you print on your press or have someone print." This was a "can-do" group of semi-journalists ranging (in 1940) from 14 to 87 years of age who published and printed their own newspapers. Issues contained official reports, poetry, journalism aids, and other assorted news items. Each member was on a free mailing list to receive some 20+ amateur publications. Journal format; graphics.
DEPT: "Official Reports," "Membership List." (12-42). "New Personalities," "Transitions," "Membership List," "President's Message." (6-54).
TYPL: "Notes in Blue--And Khaki," "'Tryout' Smith Observes 90th Birthday," "A Critic Quotes Scripture," "Historian's Report of the Trainer Administration." (12-42). "Rain Refreshes," "Portland Pageant," "Typographic Counsel." (6-54).
SCHL: Quarterly, 20 pp.
SPAN: 1878+
LC: PN 4826.N2A3
ISSN: 0027-8521

National Association of Educational Broadcasters Newsletter

19uu - 1964//
(ISSN: 0027-8610)
SEE: CURRENT

National Board of Review Magazine

Feb, 1926 - Jan, 1942//
SEE: FILMS IN REVIEW

✤ NATIONAL BROADCAST EDITORIAL ASSOCIATION NEWSLETTER

PUBL: National Broadcast Editorial Association, WDBJ-TV, Roanoke, VA 24002.
DESC: This eight-page newsletter served individuals in radio, TV, and CATV who ". . .are actively involved in preparing and presenting broadcast editorials and-or formulating editorial policies." Articles provide information on what other member stations are presenting on-air, trends in broadcast editorials, and other news items pertaining to the process of selecting issues, preparing copy, and on-air delivery.
DEPT: None. (10-75).
TYPL: "Editorials in Ford's Hometown," "Kent State," "U.S. Senate Bill No. 1." (10-75).
SCHL: Monnthly, 8 pp.
SPAN: ?+?

National Broadcast Reporter
Nov, 1931 - Oct 8, 1932//
SEE: BROADCAST REPORTER

National Cinema Workshop and Appreciation League Bulletin
Dec, 1935 - Jul, 1936//
SEE: CINEMA PROGRESS

✣ NATIONAL ENQUIRER
SUB: "Largest circulation of any paper in America."
PUBL: National Enquirer, Inc., Lantana, FL 33464.
DESC: Long a mainstay of American grocery store check-out counters, *National Enquirer* continues to publish its weekly glimpses into American society, morals, fashion, wealth, science and mayhem. The emphasis is on media celebrities; stories of who did what to whom, when, where and why. These items, along with articles detailing the incredible, the bizarre, and just plain weird of American culture, makes this favorite reading for numerous readers. For the sampled issue of 1990: square newspaper magazine format (9 ¾ x 11 ⅞ inches / 245 x 300 mm), with mixture of black/white and color graphics throughout on coated paper stock.
DEPT: "Pizzazz on Parade," fashion page; "TV--Behind the Screens," celebrity news; "Soap Opera Confidential," "Soap Suds," soap opera newsbriefs; "Next Week on Your Favorite Soaps," sneak preview; "Best Food Buys," monthly guide column by Richard A. Edwards. (9-4-90).
TYPL: "Delta's Hubby on Warpath," "'Married With Children' Gal Stranded in Busy Mall -- In Her Undies," "Docs Warn Liz: Give Up Diet or Die!," "Funnyman Milton Berle's Shocking Secret," "Top Female Stars Shine in Movies Made for Networks." (9-4-90).
SCHL: Weekly, 60 pp.
SPAN: 1926+

✣ NATIONAL EXAMINER
SUB: "America's favorite family weekly."
PUBL: Globe International, Inc., 5401 North West, Broken Sound Blvd., Boca Raton, FL 33487.
DESC: The *National Examiner* provides an interesting mixture of celebrity news (American motion pictures and television primarily), and the strange, weird, and off-the-wall of American culture. Like other grocery store check-out newsweeklies, the *National Examiner* provides detailed stories about celebrities in and out of the boudoir, the courts, and public favor. Unlike other newsweeklies, this publication also showcases the unusual in everyday life, with articles such as, "Mom Trades Her Baby Boy for a Buick," "Unborn Babies Being Snatched by Aliens," "Terror Cat! Vicious Tomcat Stalked Woman for Three Years -- Then Killed Her," and "Lose 15 Pounds in 10 Days on the Incredible Vinegar, Macaroni and Yogurt Diet." For the sampled issue of 1990: large square magazine format (10 ⅜ x 11 ¾ inches / 265 x 300 mm).
DEPT: "Hollywood Focus," column by Linda Moss; "Soap Spot," soap opera news; "This Wacky World," the world in pictures edited column by Heather Gale; "Dear Tony," Q&A advice column by Anthony Leggett; "Health Beat," column by Stephen Langer (MD); "Ring Talk," 'America's biggest and brightest wrestling column every week'; "Bruce Honick's Country Capers," music column; "The Stars and You," horoscope column by Wendy Hawks; "Sheela Wood," 'Advice for you from the heart'. (9-4-90).
TYPL: "An American Nightmare: Oprah Wants to Run for President--and Superwimp Phil Donahue will be Her VP," "Beam Me Outta Here, Scotty," "'Get Me the Ghostbusters!': Desperate Dan Aykroyd Wants to Rid His House of S-s-spooks," "Dolly Fury Over Nude Photos: 'It's a Real Slap in the Face to My Family'," "Child's Footprint Found on Moon." (9-4-90).
SCHL: Weekly, 40 pp.
SPAN: Jan, 1964+

NATIONAL EXHIBITOR, THE
SUB: "Voice of the nation's capital."
SUB: "On the fifth and twentieth."
PUBL: Barrist & Goodwin, NE Corner of 13th and Vine Sts., Philadelphia, PA.
DESC: Serving Maryland, the District of Columbia, Virginia, Eastern West Virginia and Delaware, *The National Exhibitor* championed the profession and cause of motion picture exhibitors in the East Coast region of the United States. The threat to independent exhibitors was a recurring theme through the serial as articles detailed numerous instances of powerful film interests (producers, studios, distributors) attempting to, or succeeding in taking advantage of the weaker, independent distributor. These were articles about powerful chains attempting to take over Richmond and Norfolk, Virginia theatres; a report that Paramount was forcing film shorts on exhibitors, and another article stating that Warner Brothers had substituted an inferior picture for "A Million Bid." The growing strength of unions was another common topic. One article described a Maryland projectionist school being utilized by the exhibitors as an anti-union measure. Another news item detailed new musician scales for live music, the top scale for three shows-a-day vaudeville and motion pictures being $75 per man per week. Other articles delineated union strike actions, and their effect on exhibition in various cities. Of special note were the detailed sections about the exhibitors themselves. In one sampled issue, Hagerstown, Baltimore, Frederick, Cumberland, and Lonaconing in Maryland; Luray, Petersburg, Richmond, New Market, and Norfolk in Virginia; and Delaware all had designated columns of local exhibitor developments. Perhaps most indicative of *The National Exhibitor* was an editorial comment regarding the independent exhibitor's struggle against the "big interests." Leading that

battle was Pete Harrison, a gadfly of growing renown, who was appearing before a number of exhibitor conventions, and placing the ills of the trade at the feet of the powerful film organizations. *The National Exhibitor* noted: "...his popularity with the independent theatremen throughout the nation is a sorry reflection on the long-existing policy of the producers to control opinion in the trade journals by means of the advertising they dole out. You can lead an exhibitor to trade journals, but he'll read what he wants." Magazine format (240 cm wide x 310 cm high) on coated paper stock with two-color cover.

DEPT: "Editorial Comment," "New Theatres," listing; "Alterations," theatre remodeling; "Personals," exhibitor news; "Changes," exhibitor news; "Film Row Visitors," exhibitor travel; "Newspaper Criticisms," regional newspaper reviews of current film fare; "The Box Office Barometer," 'Key city reports on first run pictures'; "Better Management," 'A clearing house for effective exploitation and admission sales ideas'; "The National Digest," 'The most important motion picture news events of the fortnight condensed for quick reading'; "What the Trade Journals Say," "Music and Musicians," column by R. R. Edwards; "Foreign Trade Notes," "European News Briefs on the Movie Industry." (9-20-27).

TYPL: "Baltimore Exhibitor Attacks Right of Film Exchange to Require Deposit," "Pathe Reduces Washington Office Force and Plans One Manager for Each Branch," "Local Theatres Sign New Wage Scale for Three Years; Boost Musicians Pay," "Campaign to Repeal Sunday Blue Laws in Maryland is Under Way in Earnest," "Dutton, Seeing Fault, Makes Apology to Exhibitor Accused of Ruining Print." (9-20-27).

SCHL: Semimonthly, 30 pp.
SPAN: Jan 5, 1923 - ?//
VARIES
--? - ? as Film News.

National Federation for Decency Newsletter

Aug, 1979//
SEE: AFA JOURNAL

✢ NATIONAL FORUM, THE

SUB: "Over 100 cartoons from America's leading cartoonist."
PUBL: Associated Features, Inc., 9501 Harrowhill Ln., Burke, VA 22015.
DESC: This unique tabloid weekly reprints over 100 editorial cartoons from the previous week's American newspapers. Grouped into topical sections, the cartoons provide a witty overview of world developments, and a sense of the American conscience. For the sampled issue of 1990: tabloid newspaper format (11 x 13 ¾ inches / 280 x 350 mm); published on newsprint.

DEPT: "Who's Who," brain teaser column by Rachael Leigh; "What's What," brain teaser column by Rachael Leigh; "Gene Owens' Political Crossword," "Larry White's Cosmic College," horoscope. (8-13-90).
TYPL: None [all editorial cartoons]. (8-13-90).
SCHL: Weekly, 20 pp.
SPAN: Jan, 1989+
DD: 051 11
ISSN: 1049-0132

✢ NATIONAL HIGH SCHOOL BROADCASTERS NEWSLETTER

PUBL: University of South Carolina College of Journalism and the South Carolina Scholastic Broadcasters Association, College of Journalism, University of South Carolina, Columbia, SC 29208.
DESC: Growing interest in broadcasting at the high school level is certainly evident in this newsletter. It is a quarterly aimed at the secondary communications teacher and functions as a news forum for those high schools having their own radio-television facilities, as well as related areas of closed circuit, cable and recording.
DEPT: None.
TYPL: "High School Radio Stations: With Whom Do They Work?," "Internship Programs: A Necessity," "State Wide High School Broadcast Associations." (12-77).
SCHL: Quarterly, 10 pp.
SPAN: Dec, 1977+

NATIONAL PHOTOGRAPHER, THE

PUBL: Photographers Association of America, 152 West Wisconsin Ave., Milwaukee, WI.
DESC: Organization President, Robert L. Ball, noted in a 1960 editorial, "Never in history has the world depended so much on the professional photographer. Never have his skill and talent been so appreciated or needed. In the field of science and industry, photography is probably the deciding factor in the tremendous progress of accelerated production. ... In the field of advertising in this highly competitive era, photography in its many aspects is a must. It would be difficult to estimate its effect on the merchandising of all products, but it is safe to say that our ever-increasing gross national product would be materially retarded if photography were suddenly eliminated and the consumer was dependent upon language description of new products introduced from day to day. ... Today it is a greater privilege than ever before to be a professional photographer, but with that privilege he must also assume a greater responsibility to a more discriminating market." Official publication of the Professional Photographers of America, this serial provided a conduit of news, membership information, business advice, and a showcase for "best" photo-

graphs to be shared among readers. This was a practical magazine with an emphasis on the technical side of photography, and included articles with suggestions on how to increase business. For the sampled issues of 1960: stapled magazine format; editorial content and cover being black ink with spot-color on coated paper stock, with advertising to the trade (8 ⅜ x 11 inches / 215 x 280 mm).
DEPT: "News and Notes," "What's Doing," "Book Briefs," "From the Mailbag," letters; "7 Ages News," "Among the Affiliates," "Local, State and Regional News," "The Commercial Corner," "The Industrial Page." (7-61).
TYPL: "Public Relations," "Now What But Who," "Bold Step in Atlanta," "Direct Mail, the Silent Salesman," "A Trouble Kit to Prevent Trouble," "Photographing Bright Metal Objects." (7-61).
SCHL: Monthly, 50 pp.
SPAN: 1949 - ?//
MERGED WITH
--Professional Photographer (ISSN: 0749-0119) (to form) National Professional Photographer (ISSN: 0734-7529).
LC: TR 1.P712

National Press Photographer

Apr, 1946 - Aug, 1974//
(ISSN: 0027-9935)
SEE: NEWS PHOTOGRAPHER

National Professional Photographer, The

Sep, 1961 - Dec, 1963//
(ISSN: 0734-7529)
SEE: PROFESSIONAL PHOTOGRAPHER, THE

NATIONAL STATIONER, THE

SUB: "A monthly magazine for dealers in stationery, post cards, fancy goods, novelties and five and ten cent goods."
PUBL: Ad-Service Publishing Co., 154 Nassau St., New York, NY.
DESC: This was a retail promotional catalog and serial for the sale of stationery, post cards, and other "five and dime" items to be found in stationery establishments. Of interest to researchers were frequent articles on new post card lines, and other printed items designed for retail sale.
DEPT: "Retail Advertising," "Trade News." (9-08).
TYPL: "The Manufacture of Writing Ink," "Post Card Suggestions," "Perfect Post Card Projector," "An Important Post Office Decision." (9-08).
SCHL: Monthly, 35 pp.
SPAN: Jan, 1908 - ?//
ABSORBED
--Post Card and Novelty Trade, The.

--Post Card and National Stationer, The.
LC: TS 1228.N3

✤ NATPE PROGRAMMER

SUB: "Official publication of the National Association of Television Program Executives."
PUBL: National Association of Television Program Executives, 740 13th St., Suite 220, San Diego, CA 92101.
DESC: This official publication of the National Association of Television Program Executives provides timely advice on the management, purchase, positioning, and promotion of television broadcast programming. Acknowledged for authoritative articles on specific programming formats, *NATPE Programmer* provides a thorough evaluation of program quality, production values, trends, and especially costs, an issue of vital importance to any television program director. In addition, special features are run throughout the year. During 1988, those special features included the topics of talk, children's, holiday, first-run, speciality, motion picture, and prime time special programming. An excellent resource for todays volatile television programming market.
DEPT: "Management," 'skills and advice for improving your job performance'; "Local Scenes," programming ideas for the local market; "Membership," list of new members; "NATPE News," organization news. (4-89).
TYPL: "How to Get a Better Job in Broadcast & Cable Programming," "NATPE*NET Opening Draws Near," "Hiring Practices Okay?" (4-89).
SCHL: Monthly [Bimonthly Mag-Aug], 25 pp.
SPAN: Jan, 1974+
VARIES
--? - ? as PD Cue (ISSN: 0193-0141).
ISSN: 0745-3094

NAVA News

1946 - Aug, 1983//
SEE: COMMUNICATIONS INDUSTRIES REPORT, THE

NBC DIGEST

SUB: "Discussion, comment, drama, humor." (Oct, 1946 - Oct, 1948).
SUB: "Published quarterly by the National Broadcasting Company." (Oct, 1946 - Oct, 1947).
SUB: "Literature of the spoken word." (Jan, 1948 - ?).
PUBL: National Broadcasting Company, 30 Rockefeller Plaza, New York, NY.
DESC: Similar in nature to the digest of talks published by the Columbia Broadcasting System in the late 1930s, this post-war NBC version added humorous radio scripts (from the likes of Fibber McGee and Molly), and other lighter programming material concerning

NBC radio and television network offerings. Small journal format; some pictures of NBC entertainment and news personalities.
DEPT: None. (1-47).
TYPL: "Welcome United Nations," by Harry S. Truman; "Freedom of Radio," by Thomas E. Dewey; "Jinx Interviews Bob Hope," "Wartime Lessons for Peacetime Psychiatry," "How Station WEAF Got Its Start," by Fred Allen; "The Pinkerton Man," a drama from 'Cavalcade of America.' (1-47).
SCHL: Quarterly; 75 pp.
SPAN: Oct, 1946 - Oct, 1948//
LC: AP 2.N125

✤ NBC NEWSLINE

PUBL: National Broadcasting Company, 3000 W. Alameda Ave., Burbank, CA 91523.
DESC: This is a sprightly employee publication with large sections concerning new NBC employees, changes in departments, new policies and other in-house interests. A noteworthy in-house publication.
DEPT: None. (8-77).
TYPL: "West Coast Programming Department Reorganized." (8-77).
SCHL: Monthly, 8 pp.
SPAN: ?+?
LC: None.

NCCT Forum

Winter, 1978 - Spring?, 1980//
SEE: TELEVISION & FAMILIES

✤ NEGRO ACTORS GUILD OF AMERICA. NEWSLETTER.

PUBL: Negro Actors Guild of America, Inc., 1674 Broadway, New York, NY.
DESC: The New York based Negro Actors Guild began publication of a quarterly newsletter, *Negro Actor*, in 1939, which had a lifespan of only two issues. In May, 1940, the Guild once again mounted a newsletter with much greater success. This mimeographed serial provided news of Guild activities, specifically: membership drives, employment, news of job discrimination, social events, and other Guild developments. This was a publication that covered problems (numerous social events going "wrong," and discrimination), and provided encouragement (prime acting roles being filled by black actors). Mimeographed; no graphics.
DEPT: None.
TYPL: No Article Titles.
SCHL: Monthly (Irregular at times), 4 pp.
SPAN: May, 1940+?
LC: PN 2000.N43

✤ NEMO

SUB: "The classic comics library."
PUBL: Fantagraphics Books, Inc., 4359 Cornell Rd., Agoura, CA 91301.
DESC: In a September, 1987 editorial, editor Richard Marschall was championing a Pulitzer prize for the comic strip form and stated: "It would be simple justice and logic -- and a move long overdue -- to recognize that the comic strip is one of America's few native art forms, and that excellence of individual expression should be noted in the same spirit that playwrights and poets and novelists and newspapermen are recognized. To those who say, or think, that comics are mostly ephemeral trivialities, we will have to sigh and patiently agree, and point out again that most plays and poems and novels and material in most newspapers are likewise junk; and why must comics, alone amongst even the popular arts, be judged by its lowest exponents?" Marschall continued: "The comic strip is a valid, proud, independent form of expression, with an incredibly rich heritage and virtually unlimited boundaries of potential -- dramatic, comedic, satiric. It deserves to be both recognized and encouraged..." This lucid editorial well represents the function and form of *Nemo*, the serious study of the classic American comic strip. Loving care is evident in the reproduction of past comic art, and accompanying articles concerning their creators. Feature articles have included the birth of Superman, cartoonist Christmas cards, cartoonists who fought in World War II, a retrospective of the comic-strip adaptations of Huckleberry Finn, political cartoonists, a complete issue devoted to Rube Goldberg, and numerous loving tributes to past cartoonists and their works. This is an excellent serial and highly recommended for the student/researcher of classic comic and illustrative art, and serves well the memory of its namesake cartoon strip. For the sampled issue of 1987: stapled magazine format; excellent reproduction of cartoon work and editorial content being black ink on uncoated paper stock, with full-color cover on coated paper stock with minimal advertising (8 3/8 x 10 3/4 inches / 215 x 275 mm).
DEPT: None. (8-86). "Editorial." (9-87).
TYPL: "Oyez! A Classic Intellectual Strip!," "Orphans of the West," "Percy Crosby's Slum Kids." (8-86). "Those Cartooning Contests," "A Classic Who's Zoo," "Silents, Please!" (9-87).
SCHL: Bimonthly, 70 pp.
SPAN: Jun, 1983+
DD: 741 11
ISSN: 0746-9438

Network News

1982 - ?//
SEE: AP BROADCASTER

✤ NETWORK WORLD

SUB: "The weekly for leading users of communications products & services."
PUBL: CW Communications, Inc., 375 Cochituate Rd., Framingham, MA 01701-9171.
DESC: The "communications" in the subtitle refers primarily to point-to-point communication services, and is sent to "...management or professionals who specify and maintain communications equipment and systems, including voice, data and video, as well as to common carriers, consultants, systems houses and manufacturers of communications equipment." Editorially split into separate sections of "Telecom Trends," "Data Delivery," "Factory Communications," and "Communications Manager," *Network World* provides a legal, financial, and technological clearing house of information for the corporate communications manager, and industries. This is an impressive resource for late-breaking news.
DEPT: "Top News," "Industry Update," "Telecom Trends," "Data Delivery," "Factory Communications," "Communications Manager," "New Products and Services." (8-4-86).
TYPL: "Network Nirvana Escapes PC Users," "French Government OKs Union of ITT and CGE," "Comsat Enters Pilot Vsat Net Venture in UK," "Satellite Rates Pared." (8-4-86).
SCHL: Monthly (Nov, 1984 - Mar, 1986); Weekly [with combined two-week issue at end of December] (1986+), 44 pp.
SPAN: Nov, 1984+
VARIES
--Nov, 1984 - Mar, 1986 as On Communications (ISSN: 8750-7854).
LC: QA 76 .C5816
DD: 004.6/05
ISSN: 0887-7661

New Broadway Magazine

Dec, 1907 - Sep, 1908//
SEE: HAMPTON MAGAZINE

✤ NEW CAPTAIN GEORGE'S WHIZZBANG, THE

PUBL: Memory Lane Publications, 594 Markham St., Toronto, Ontario, Canada.
DESC: Established in 1968, *Captain George's Whizzbang*, a popular culture nostalgia review, moved from its initial tabloid-size format to a newsprint magazine format commencing with issue number seven (volume 2, number 1) in 1970. In so doing, editor Peter Harris stated: "From an esthetic and editorial standpoint, the magazine format fits in with our intention to place more emphasis on movies, past and present, in the *Whizzbang*. We will not ignore such other areas of the popular arts as comic strips, old advertisements, the radio, pulp magazines, Big Little Books and so on. But, because we feel that many existing film magazines are not giving sufficient attention to certain facets of the movies or ignoring them altogether, we are going to devote more space in the *Whizzbang* to such topics." This Canadian serial provides a refreshing approach to popular media, including neglected cartoon strips, "B"-movies, Saturday film serials, radio celebrities from the "Golden Age," historic advertisements, etc. For the sampled issue of volume 2, #7: black ink editorial content on uncoated paper stock, with black-ink cover on coated paper with numerous black/white graphics, no advertising (8 ¼ x 10 ½ inches / 210 x 265 mm).
DEPT: "Checklist," review of movies, books, periodicals; "Comment," column by Peter Harris; "SF Readout," science fiction review column by Peter Gill; "The Collector," "The Comics," news and review; "The Radio," news and review; "And On Our Screen," historic motion picture newspaper advertisements; "Yesterday's Ads," advertisements of yesteryear; "The Whizzbang Gallery," inside back cover celebrity photo. (vol 2-# 7).
TYPL: "Roy Barcroft--Best of the Badmen," "A Hal Foster Portfolio," "My Favorite Role--Chester Morris," "World War I Flying Lives On," "Terry and the Serials." (vol 2-# 7).
SCHL: Six issues per year, 35 pp.
SPAN: Nov/Dec, 1968+
VARIES
--Nov/Dec, 1968? - Vol 1, #6? as Captain George's Whizzbang.
ISSN: 0028-4408

New Developments for the Photographic Dealer and Photo Finisher

? - ?//
SEE: PHOTO MARKETING

NEW MOVIE MAGAZINE, THE

SUB: "On sale the 15th of each month in Woolworth stores."
SUB: "One of the Tower Group of magazines."
PUBL: Tower Magazines, Incorporated, 184-10 Jamaica Ave., Jamaica, NY.
DESC: Filled from cover to cover with 130+ pages of Hollywood legend, lore, current film releases and lives of the Hollywood famous, *The New Movie Magazine* certainly mirrored the dynamic Hollywood community of the 1930s in fine style. Articles seemed to be evenly divided between the motion picture industry (including filmmaking, publicity, behind-the-scenes production) and the stars themselves (before the camera, and especially entertaining or relaxing at home). In a sampled issue for 1930, Dolores Del Rio explained why "I Want to Be Happy;" an article described the real estate boom in Beverly Hills; still another concerned Dick Arlen, "The Third Musket-

eer." In "Big Moments in Screen History," famous stars selected their favorite scenes. Among a bevy of fascinating articles were Grace Moore recounting how she almost became a missionary to China; and "What Will Hollywood Do to Amos 'n' Andy," subtitled "The golden town holds a menace for the famous radio team." *The New Movie Magazine* was delightful to read. Each issue held a number of full-page star pictures and a very extensive "Gossip" section with news from the studios. Perfect-bound magazine format, black/white editorial content with some duotone black/brown ink graphics and black/green duotone pictures on coated paper stock, cover is full-color on coated paper stock (8 ½ x 11 ¾ inches / 215 x 295 mm).

DEPT: "The Hollywood Boulevardier," 'Mr. Howe writes from Paris on film people and events' column by Herb Howe; "Reviews of the New Films," 'Concise and accurate comments upon the important new photoplays' column by Frederick James Smith; "First Aids to Beauty," 'Advice and rules for charm and attractiveness' column by Ann Boyd; "Music of the Sound Screen," 'The New Movie's service department, reviewing the newest phonograph records of film musical hits'; "Guide to the Best Films," 'Brief comments upon the leading motion pictures of the last six months'; "Gallery of Famous Film Folk," duotone green of Hollywood's famous; "Gossip of the Studios," 'All the news of the famous motion picture stars and their Hollywood activities' [and] 'The Hollywood Who's Who--and What the film famous are doing in the movie capital'; "Evangeline Adams Reads the Stars," 'The world's most famous astrologer interprets the stars and their influences' astrology column by Evangeline Adams; "Laughs of the Films," cartoon cutups from current feature films; "Home Town Stories of the Stars," star roots; "Dollar Thoughts," 'The New Movie Magazine readers express their opinions of film plays and players--and this monthly'; "How Hollywood Entertains," column by Evelyn Gray; "What the Stars Are Doing," current feature films in production. (10-30).

TYPL: "A Matinée Idol's Wife," "There's Gold in Them Thar Beverly Hills," "Big Moments of Screen History," "What Will Hollywood Do to Amos 'n' Andy," "Hazards of the Talkies." (10-30).
SCHL: Monthly, 135 pp.
SPAN: Dec, 1929 - Sep, 1935//
LC: PN 1993.N4

New Movies, The
Feb, 1942 - Jan/Feb, 1949//
SEE: FILMS IN REVIEW

NEW PHOTO-MINIATURE
SUB: "A monthly magazine of photographic information." (Apr, 1899 - Jun, 1932).
PUBL: Tennant and Ward, 287 Fourth Ave., New York, NY.

DESC: [*The Photo-Miniature*]: A most unique periodical; actually a photographic encyclopedia in monthly installments from 1899 through 1930. Printed in a small format magazine style, each monthly installment of some 30 pages explored one distinct aspect of photography. Few photos were in early issues, with a substantial number of graphics and photographs in latter issues. The sampled issue for 1901 contained a blue-paper cover with line drawing. Editorial content for that issue concerned "Flashlight Photography," and was the only article in the issue, running from page 191 through page 237. This lengthy discussion of the art and technology of lighting contained numerous subheadings for ease of finding topics. Five coated pages contained nine photographic examples of flash photography application. In addition, many pages contained hand-drawn line schematics of camera, light, and talent placement for various effects. The writing was in a warm, chatty-style For example: "The story of flashlight photography tells how the photographer, chafing under the limitations of an art largely dependent on sunlight for its successful working, devised a means of bottling the sunlight, so that he might be free to use his camera when and where he pleased--as at night, in dark interiors, in underground places, or wherever the light of day proved insufficient for his purposes. It is an interesting story, but we will here concern ourselves with it only sufficiently to get an intelligent grasp of the usefulness and convenience of the flashlight, as a means of adding to our pleasure in photography, and as a help in the work of the world." Two items are worth additional mention. The first was a departmental feature labeled "Notes," which included a variety of newsworthy items for the average photographer. Among the topics included in that 1901 issue were a recent Photographers Association convention, a new exposure scale, new interest in Gum Ozotype, information on restoring faded gelatine chloride prints, common approaches to developing film, information on using Hoechheimer's gum-bichromate papers, and other sundry items. A second feature was an Eastman Kodak sponsored news section with article titles such as "Complacency Upset," "For Unusual Wants," and "Interest the Young Folks." Small magazine format, stitched and gluebound method, editorial content on uncoated paperstock, with some photographic reproductions on coated paper stock, cover consisting of black ink on uncoated blue paper with line drawing (5 x 8 inches / 125 x 205 mm).

DEPT: "Notes," detailed information concerning the photographic field. (8-01). None. (#1-7, 1924).
TYPL: "Flashlight Photography." (8-01). "Enlarging on Gaslight Papers," "Photography for the Press," "All About Color Photography," "Bromide Printing and Enlarging," "Vacation Photography," "Seashore Photography," "Lantern Slides." (#1-7, 1924).
SCHL: Monthly, 30 pp.
SPAN: Apr, 1899 - Oct, 1936?//
VARIES
--Apr, 1899 - Jan, 1932 as Photo-Miniature, The.

SUSPENDED
--Jul, 1932 - May, 1936.

New Review of Books and Religion, The

Sep, 1976 - Jun, 1980//
(ISSN: 0146-0609)
SEE: BOOKS & RELIGION

New Show, The

Mar/Apr, 1966 - ?//
SEE: SHOW

NEW THEATRE

PUBL: New Theatre Publications, 374, Gray's Inn Road, London WC1, England.
DESC: *New Theatre* is a serial about the dramatic arts, treating "theatre" in the larger context of legitimate stage, musical, opera, radio, television, and other modes of dramatic expression. The emphasis is on current offerings within British legitimate theatres, providing an interesting mixture of players before the footlights, and the behind-the-scenes business side of dramatic arts. The square format periodical, which was suspended "for the duration," came back stronger than ever in 1946, with a recommitment to vibrant British drama. Numerous graphics, especially of production stills.
DEPT: "Ballet," reviews; "Opera," reviews; "Books," reviews. (2-49).
TYPL: "Which Way for British Musicals?," "Manchester's Team of Players," "Opera and Money," "The Art Theatre in France." (2-49).
SCHL: Monthly, 25 pp.
SPAN: Aug, 1939 - Jul, 1949//
SUSPENDED
--Sep, 1939 - Jan, 1946.
LC: PN 2001.N48

NEW THEATRE MAGAZINE

PUBL: The Green Room Society of Bristol University, Bristol, England.
DESC: This joint effort between Manchester University and Bristol University resulted in a quarterly publication of dramatic news and events concerning the dynamics and development of regional theatre. In the sampled issue for 1964, articles described current facilities and expansion of same, the development of theatre in Israel, a report on Manchester University Drama Group production at Zagreb, Yugoslavia, and a fascinating essay entitled "We Have the Right to Fail," which explored the fine line between experimental success and artistic failure. Each issue contained a number of black/white photos of stage productions. For the sampled issue of 1964: stapled square magazine format, black ink editorial content, with full-color cover, all on coated paper stock, some advertising (7 1/4 x 9 5/8 inches / 185 x 245 mm).
DEPT: "Editorial," "The Writer in the Provinces," column by Alan Plater; "Letter to the Editor," "Book Reviews." (10-64).
TYPL: "A Professional Theatre for Chester," "Sunderland Civic Theatre," "Letter to a Ratepayer," "How Big Should Our New Theatre Be?," "We Have the Right to Fail." (10-64).
SCHL: Quarterly, 40 pp.
SPAN: Oct, 1959 - 1972//
MERGED WITH
--Theatre Research (ISSN: 0040-5566) (to form) Theatre Research International (ISSN: 0307-8833).
LC: PN 2001.N485
ISSN: 0028-6893

✤ NEW THEATRE QUARTERLY

PUBL: Cambridge University Press, The Edinburgh Bldg., Shaftesbury Rd, Cambridge CB2 2RU, England.
DESC: "*Theatre Quarterly* will be a practical rather than a polemical magazine -- its concern to break down the barriers that separate critic from theatre worker, academic from creative artists, even one kind of theatre practitioner from another. We shall be concerned to emphasize and examine contemporary achievements, but also to look at the achievements of the past in ways that will reassert their potential value to the present. Though based in Britain, we shall offer an increasingly international coverage, particularly of those countries and styles of theatre that receive too little attention here. Equally, the problems of radio and television drama, and of theatre in the regions, the universities, the streets -- in short, all those kinds of living performance that presently lack an adequate voice -- will be aired, analyzed, defined." The primary difference between *Theatre Quarterly* and the *New Theatre Quarterly* is one of scope, due to the increasing diversity of the dramatic art form in the intervening ten years since the previous serial's demise. This is a quality acamdemic journal with a decidedly pedagogical approach. As one advertisement put it, "*New Theatre Quarterly* is a journal combining theatrical scholarship and practice. *NTQ*'s articles are hard hitting. They question prevailing assumptions in the theatre world. *NTQ* follows four independent premises: *Theatre needs a philosophy, *Theatre studies need methodology, *Criticism needs a language, *Theatre history has a contemporary relevance." Journal format, with graphics.
DEPT: "New Theatre Portfolio," "Theatresurvey," "Place and Performance," "Production Casebook," "Theatrefacts." (1/3-71). "NTQ Notes and Reviews." (5-86).
TYPL: "The Absurd in Greek Tragedy," "The Role of the Television Dramatist," "Silent Censorship in Britain," "The Material and the Models," "Theatre in Education." (1/3-71). "Acting With the Berliner Ensemble,"

"A Pictorial Retrospetive, 1949 - 1984," "The Employment of Children in the Victorian Theatre," "Computer Databases for Theatre Studies." (5-86).
SCHL: Quarterly, 100 pp.
SPAN: Jan/Mar, 1971+
VARIES
--Jan/Mar, 1971 - Oct/Dec, 1981 as Theatre Quarterly (ISSN: 0049-3600).
LC: PN 2001 .T435
DD: 792/.05
ISSN: 0266-464x
ABST: --Abstract of English Studies (ISSN: 0001-3560)
--Humanities Index (ISSN: 0095-5981)

New York Dramatic Mirror, The

Jan 26, 1889 - Feb 10, 1917//
SEE: DRAMATIC MIRROR, THE

New York Mirror

1879? - ?//
SEE: DRAMATIC MIRROR, THE

New York Printing News

1928 - Jan, 1931//
SEE: PRINTINGNEWS

New York State Community Theatre Journal

Dec, 1960 - Winter/Spring, 1970//
(ISSN: 0548-8974)
SEE: THEATRE JOURNAL

✤ NEW ZEALAND FILM

SUB: "News from the New Zealand Film Commission."
PUBL: New Zealand Film Commission, PO Box 11-546, Wellington, New Zealand.
DESC: This newsletter-type publication serves both to promote and provide news of motion pictures and filmmakers of New Zealand. Almost half of the editorial content of any given issue is devoted to describing recent New Zealand film product through information related to reviews, exhibitions, and distribution, with a variety of production stills. Indeed, of special note are the size and variety of production still photographs from recent and forthcoming releases. It is a notable resource for the status of New Zealand film industry. For the 1987 sampled issue: black/white editorial content and cover in stapled magazine typewritten format with a significant number of production graphics (8 ¼ x 11 ¾ inches / 210 x 300 mm).
DEPT: None. (5-87).

TYPL: "Three New Features at Cannes," "Canadian Plans," "Film Bank," "MOMA Selection," "New Corporation." (5-87).
SCHL: Three issues per year?, 12 pp.
SPAN: May, 1977?+?

News - Action for Children's Television

? - Summer, 1977//
(ISSN: 0145-6822)
SEE: RE:ACT

✤ NEWS & VIEWS

PUBL: Virginia Instructional Technology Association in Higher Education (VITA), Central Virginia Community College, 3506 Wards Rd., Lynchburg, VA 24502.
DESC: This 12-page, small format newsletter is designed to inform VITA (Virginia Instructional Technology Association in Higher Education) members about association events and news concerning use of instructional technology in Virginia schools and colleges. Approximately one-half of the sample issue viewed (winter 1989/1990) consisted of article reprints from various trade publications and invited authors. Typewritten and typeset format; some graphics.
DEPT: None. (winter-89/90).
TYPL: "Number of Videodiscs Keeps Growing," "Interactive Illusions." (winter-89/90).
SCHL: Three issues per year, 12 pp.
SPAN: ?+

News & Views

? - ?//
SEE: AWRT NEWS AND VIEWS

✤ NEWS COMPUTING JOURNAL

SUB: "A quarterly journal on microcomputer use in journalism and mass communication."
PUBL: News Computing, Duquesne University, Department of Communication, 208 DPCC, Pittsburgh, PA 15282.
DESC: A flyer for *NCJ* noted the announcement of the publication's editorial schedule for 1991-1992: "In *NCJ*'s seventh year, the editorial focus will span 10 areas of interest. These are: Technology and media ethics; Gender, race and technology use; PC use and the disabled: workplace and educational solutions; Technology and competition: newspaper and broadcast; Public relations and advertising use of PCs and PC technology; Communication theory modelling for the PC; Development of presentation materials using PCs, graphic software and peripherals; Creative approaches to writing training; Creating, using and teaching with infographics; [and] On-line research methods for scholars and students." This is a publica-

tion that seeks information, applications and trends of computer usage in the journalism and mass communication fields. A sampling of articles from prior publications include, "TV News Video Tape Morgue Program," "When Journalists Become Consultants," "A Mexican Newspaper Editor at Work," "An Electronic Chalkboard System," "Valenced Dictionary Content Analysis," "Monte Carlo Methods in Research," "The Effects of PCs On Communication," and "Corporate Publishing." It is a valuable resource for research, education, and commercial applications of data processing within the mass communication field.
DEPT: None. (#4-90).
TYPL: "Status of DTP in Journalism," "Setting Up a DTP Lab," "Classroom Networks," "Criteria for Selecting Paper," "Desktop Publishers BBS." (#4-90).
SCHL: Quarterly, 70 pp.
SPAN: 1964?+
ISSN: 0889-1596

✦ NEWS FROM APB

PUBL: Associated Press Broadcasters, 50 Rockefeller Plaza, New York, NY 10020.
DESC: This eight-page newsletter for members of the Associated Press Broadcasters Association emphasizes association news, station personnel changes and similar items. Articles describe individual station activities, especially related to newsgathering and reporting for the APB network, trends in broadcast news, and general information concerning the Associated Press Broadcasters.
DEPT: None. (2-77).
TYPL: "Morgan Beatty Memorabilia to University of Wyoming," "Thirteen NIS Stations Opt for AP Radio," "Inaugural Day Was So Cold the Telephone Froze." (2-77).
SCHL: Monthly, 8 pp.
SPAN: ?+

News From the American Film Center, Inc.

Dec, 1939 - Apr, 1940//
SEE: FILM & VIDEO NEWS

✦ NEWS LEADS

PUBL: Investigative Journalism Program, Urban Policy Research Institute, 321 South Beverly Drive, Suite W, Beverly Hills, CA 90212.
DESC: A no-nonsense magazine devoted to the cause of investigative journalism, it reprints major investigative articles. The publisher notes that "Our purpose is to put journalists in touch with each other's work by reprinting excerpts of investigative pieces and by telling the story behind the story--the methods, sources, and pitfalls--so that other journalists can save costly time and effort."
DEPT: None.
TYPL: "L.A. Health Plan is Told: Open Books," "The Fair Game: Three Named in Fair Board Probe," "An Educational Windfall."
SCHL: Bimonthly, 25 pp.
SPAN: Apr/May, 1976+

✦ NEWS MEDIA & THE LAW, THE

SUB: "Published by the Reporters Committee for Freedom of the Press."
PUBL: Reporters Committee for Freedom of the Press, 1750 Pennsylvania Ave., Washington, DC 20006.
DESC: This is an outstanding publication not only of legal decisions concerning news media and the law, but also of scholarly comment on interpreting court decisions in the United States. Each bimonthly issue contains some 60+ reports on recent court actions and their potential impact on the news-gathering process. Articles (and corresponding court cases) in issues fall under headings of "Secret Courts," "Libel & Privacy," "State-Federal FOI Act," "Prior Restraints," "Confidentiallity," "Broadcasting," and "Press at Home & Abroad." Within those headings, cases are conveniently listed by geographic state or region. Of special note is the section, "Sources & Citations," providing legal citations for each court case. A sampling of issues from 1978 included "U.S. Supreme Court Lets stand Ohio News Interview Ban; Rejects South Carolina Broadcasters-Publishers Association Gag Order Appeal," "Justice Department Asks U.S. Supreme Court to Permit Surprise Police Searches of Newsrooms," "American Bar Association Report Favors TV Coverage of Trials; Asks End to State Bans," " and "Press Asks Constitutional Shield Law." It is a unique and excellent resource by Editor Jane E. Kirtley, and Assistant Managing Editor, Rebecca Daugherty. The sampled issues of 1978 were comprised of black ink editorial content on uncoated paper stock, while 1991 issues utilized spot ink color on editorial pages. Both sampled issues were in stapled magazine format; no advertising (8 ⅛ x 10 ⅞ inches / 205 x 275 mm).
DEPT: "Sources & Citations." (9/10-83). "Roundup," news items; "Sources & Citations." (fall-91).
TYPL: "Pretrial Hearings May be Closed," "Constitution Doesn't Guarantee Access, But Pretrial Hearings Open Court Rules," "Justices Plan Major Review of Libel," "Dismissal of Golfer's Libel Suit Against UPI Allowed to Stand," "Battle Over FOIA Resumes in Senate." (9/10-83). "Judge Quashes Subpoena for The Dallas Times Herald Phone Records," "Books Aren't Subject to Products Liability Laws; Publishers Have No Duty to Investigate Accuracy," "Order Giving Officials Broad Discretion to Withhold Public Records Violates First Amendment," "Newspapers Can't Have Second Hearing on Right to Review Ju-

dicial Documents from a Closed Proceeding," "Denver Television Reporter Convicted of Staging Pit Bull Fight." (fall-91).
SCHL: Three issues per year (Mar/Apr, 1973 - Sep/Oct, 1976); Bimonthly (? - ?); Five issues per year (? - ?); Quarterly (?+), 70 pp.
SPAN: Mar/Apr, 1973+
VARIES
--Mar/Apr, 1973 - Sep/Oct, 1976 as Press Censorship Newsletter.
LC: KF 2750.A15 N48
DD: 343/.73/0998
ISSN: 0149-0737
ABST: --Legal Resource Index

News of the World
Mar 20, 1937 - Nov, 1937//
SEE: HOLLYWOOD NOW

✣ NEWS PHOTOGRAPHER
SUB: "Official publication of the National Press Photographers Association."
SUB: "National Press Photographers Association for Still and Television News."
SUB: "Dedicated to the service and advancement of news photography."
PUBL: National Press Photographers Association, 3200 Croasdaile Drive, Suite 306, Durham, NC 27705-9905.
DESC: The rigors of press photography cover many issues: freedom of the press, new technology, travel between nations, and the art/technique of printing pictures for general public readership are some of them. This serial thoroughly covers those issues and more as the official publication for the National Press Photographers Association, a group whose prime interest is professional photojournalism in both still and television news formats. The current title, *News Photographer*, emerged in mid-1974 as replacement for the earlier publication, *National Press Photographer*, which met its demise in mid-1974. For the sampled issues of 1971: stapled magazine format; editorial content and cover comprised of black ink on coated paper stock (8 ¼ x 10 ⅞ inches / 210 x 275 mm). Under the current title of *News Photographer*, sampled issues for 1975 were: black ink on coated stock, with full-color cover, and advertising (8 x 10 ⅝ inches / 200 x 275 mm). The sampled issues for 1991 were a mixture of black, spot- and full-color ink pages, with full-color cover all on coated paper with advertising (8 ¼ x 11 inches / 210 x 280 mm). Issues for 1971, 1975, and 1991 consisted of stapled magazine format.
DEPT: "The Photojournalist: Photography as Communication," column by Phil Douglis; "MNC Winners," monthly newspaper photo competition winners. (8-74). "News Views," member briefs; "MNCC Pictures of the Month," judging for monthly news photos; "Letters," unusually lively replies of members on current issues. (11-77). "Newsviews," photographs and/or photographers in the news; "President's Message," "TV Topics," covering television news; "Pictures of the Month." (7-89).
TYPL: "Rare and Rewarding: That One Touch of Genius," "Young Photographers: Frustration and Hope," "He Testifies, Then He's Fired." (8-74). "Photojournalism Stands Trial with Ronnie Zamora in Florida," "NPPA President Gary Settle Pleads for Decorum," "The Pack; Political Drama and Excitement are Plus Factors in Washington." (11-77). "Pick of the Judges," "Loneliest Experience of My Life," "Photographer Involved with Drama of Life." (7-89).
SCHL: Monthly (Apr, 1946 - Oct, 1980); Eleven issues per year (Nov, 1980 - ?); Monthly [except semi-monthly in Dec] (Jun, 1984+), 65 pp.
SPAN: Apr, 1946+
VARIES
--Apr, 1946 - Aug, 1974 as National Press Photographer (ISSN: 0027-9935).
LC: TR 820.N272
ISSN: 0199-2422

News Research Bulletin
? - 1976//
(ISSN: 0734-9238)
SEE: ANPA NEWS RESEARCH REPORT

✣ NEWSCASTER, THE
SUB: "The newsletter of the Broadcast News Committee, Broadcast Education Association."
PUBL: Broadcast News Committee, Broadcast Education Association, 1771 N St., NW, Washington, DC 20036-2891.
DESC: This short typewritten newsletter of news items is from the Broadcast News Committee of the Broadcast Education Association, the pedagogical organization which fosters liaison between college communication faculty, and the broadcast industry.
DEPT: None.
TYPL: "Agenda Set for BEA News Division in Vegas," "Utsler Outlines Goals for BEA News Committee to Consider," "TV News Directors to Discuss Video Ethics." (3-89).
SCHL: Irregular, 2 pp.
SPAN: ?, 1987+

Newsdealer
Mar, 1946 - Sep, 1960//
SEE: MAGAZINE & BOOKSELLER

Newsdealers' Bestsellers
1945? - ?//
SEE: MAGAZINE & BOOKSELLER

tion that seeks information, applications and trends of computer usage in the journalism and mass communication fields. A sampling of articles from prior publications include, "TV News Video Tape Morgue Program," "When Journalists Become Consultants," "A Mexican Newspaper Editor at Work," "An Electronic Chalkboard System," "Valenced Dictionary Content Analysis," "Monte Carlo Methods in Research," "The Effects of PCs On Communication," and "Corporate Publishing." It is a valuable resource for research, education, and commercial applications of data processing within the mass communication field.
DEPT: None. (#4-90).
TYPL: "Status of DTP in Journalism," "Setting Up a DTP Lab," "Classroom Networks," "Criteria for Selecting Paper," "Desktop Publishers BBS." (#4-90).
SCHL: Quarterly, 70 pp.
SPAN: 1964?+
ISSN: 0889-1596

✣ NEWS FROM APB

PUBL: Associated Press Broadcasters, 50 Rockefeller Plaza, New York, NY 10020.
DESC: This eight-page newsletter for members of the Associated Press Broadcasters Association emphasizes association news, station personnel changes and similar items. Articles describe individual station activities, especially related to newsgathering and reporting for the APB network, trends in broadcast news, and general information concerning the Associated Press Broadcasters.
DEPT: None. (2-77).
TYPL: "Morgan Beatty Memorabilia to University of Wyoming," "Thirteen NIS Stations Opt for AP Radio," "Inaugural Day Was So Cold the Telephone Froze." (2-77).
SCHL: Monthly, 8 pp.
SPAN: ?+

News From the American Film Center, Inc.

Dec, 1939 - Apr, 1940//
SEE: FILM & VIDEO NEWS

✣ NEWS LEADS

PUBL: Investigative Journalism Program, Urban Policy Research Institute, 321 South Beverly Drive, Suite W, Beverly Hills, CA 90212.
DESC: A no-nonsense magazine devoted to the cause of investigative journalism, it reprints major investigative articles. The publisher notes that "Our purpose is to put journalists in touch with each other's work by reprinting excerpts of investigative pieces and by telling the story behind the story--the methods, sources, and pitfalls- -so that other journalists can save costly time and effort."
DEPT: None.
TYPL: "L.A. Health Plan is Told: Open Books," "The Fair Game: Three Named in Fair Board Probe," "An Educational Windfall."
SCHL: Bimonthly, 25 pp.
SPAN: Apr/May, 1976+

✣ NEWS MEDIA & THE LAW, THE

SUB: "Published by the Reporters Committee for Freedom of the Press."
PUBL: Reporters Committee for Freedom of the Press, 1750 Pennsylvania Ave., Washington, DC 20006.
DESC: This is an outstanding publication not only of legal decisions concerning news media and the law, but also of scholarly comment on interpreting court decisions in the United States. Each bimonthly issue contains some 60+ reports on recent court actions and their potential impact on the news-gathering process. Articles (and corresponding court cases) in issues fall under headings of "Secret Courts," "Libel & Privacy," "State-Federal FOI Act," "Prior Restraints," "Confidentiallity," "Broadcasting," and "Press at Home & Abroad." Within those headings, cases are conveniently listed by geographic state or region. Of special note is the section, "Sources & Citations," providing legal citations for each court case. A sampling of issues from 1978 included "U.S. Supreme Court Lets stand Ohio News Interview Ban; Rejects South Carolina Broadcasters-Publishers Association Gag Order Appeal," "Justice Department Asks U.S. Supreme Court to Permit Surprise Police Searches of Newsrooms," "American Bar Association Report Favors TV Coverage of Trials; Asks End to State Bans," " and "Press Asks Constitutional Shield Law." It is a unique and excellent resource by Editor Jane E. Kirtley, and Assistant Managing Editor, Rebecca Daugherty. The sampled issues of 1978 were comprised of black ink editorial content on uncoated paper stock, while 1991 issues utilized spot ink color on editorial pages. Both sampled issues were in stapled magazine format; no advertising (8 ⅛ x 10 ⅞ inches / 205 x 275 mm).
DEPT: "Sources & Citations." (9/10-83). "Roundup," news items; "Sources & Citations." (fall-91).
TYPL: "Pretrial Hearings May be Closed," "Constitution Doesn't Guarantee Access, But Pretrial Hearings Open Court Rules," "Justices Plan Major Review of Libel," "Dismissal of Golfer's Libel Suit Against UPI Allowed to Stand," "Battle Over FOIA Resumes in Senate." (9/10-83). "Judge Quashes Subpoena for The Dallas Times Herald Phone Records," "Books Aren't Subject to Products Liability Laws; Publishers Have No Duty to Investigate Accuracy," "Order Giving Officials Broad Discretion to Withhold Public Records Violates First Amendment," "Newspapers Can't Have Second Hearing on Right to Review Ju-

dicial Documents from a Closed Proceeding," "Denver Television Reporter Convicted of Staging Pit Bull Fight." (fall-91).
SCHL: Three issues per year (Mar/Apr, 1973 - Sep/Oct, 1976); Bimonthly (? - ?); Five issues per year (? - ?); Quarterly (?+), 70 pp.
SPAN: Mar/Apr, 1973+
VARIES
--Mar/Apr, 1973 - Sep/Oct, 1976 as Press Censorship Newsletter.
LC: KF 2750.A15 N48
DD: 343/.73/0998
ISSN: 0149-0737
ABST: --Legal Resource Index

News of the World
Mar 20, 1937 - Nov, 1937//
SEE: HOLLYWOOD NOW

✜ NEWS PHOTOGRAPHER
SUB: "Official publication of the National Press Photographers Association."
SUB: "National Press Photographers Association for Still and Television News."
SUB: "Dedicated to the service and advancement of news photography."
PUBL: National Press Photographers Association, 3200 Croasdaile Drive, Suite 306, Durham, NC 27705-9905.
DESC: The rigors of press photography cover many issues: freedom of the press, new technology, travel between nations, and the art/technique of printing pictures for general public readership are some of them. This serial thoroughly covers those issues and more as the official publication for the National Press Photographers Association, a group whose prime interest is professional photojournalism in both still and television news formats. The current title, *News Photographer*, emerged in mid-1974 as replacement for the earlier publication, *National Press Photographer*, which met its demise in mid-1974. For the sampled issues of 1971: stapled magazine format; editorial content and cover comprised of black ink on coated paper stock (8 ¼ x 10 ⅞ inches / 210 x 275 mm). Under the current title of *News Photographer*, sampled issues for 1975 were: black ink on coated stock, with full-color cover, and advertising (8 x 10 ⅝ inches / 200 x 275 mm). The sampled issues for 1991 were a mixture of black, spot- and full-color ink pages, with full-color cover all on coated paper with advertising (8 ¼ x 11 inches / 210 x 280 mm). Issues for 1971, 1975, and 1991 consisted of stapled magazine format.
DEPT: "The Photojournalist: Photography as Communication," column by Phil Douglis; "MNC Winners," monthly newspaper photo competition winners. (8-74). "News Views," member briefs; "MNCC Pictures of the Month," judging for monthly news photos; "Letters," unusually lively replies of members on current issues. (11-77). "Newsviews," photographs and/or photographers in the news; "President's Message," "TV Topics," covering television news; "Pictures of the Month." (7-89).
TYPL: "Rare and Rewarding: That One Touch of Genius," "Young Photographers: Frustration and Hope," "He Testifies, Then He's Fired." (8-74). "Photojournalism Stands Trial with Ronnie Zamora in Florida," "NPPA President Gary Settle Pleads for Decorum," "The Pack; Political Drama and Excitement are Plus Factors in Washington." (11-77). "Pick of the Judges," "Loneliest Experience of My Life," "Photographer Involved with Drama of Life." (7-89).
SCHL: Monthly (Apr, 1946 - Oct, 1980); Eleven issues per year (Nov, 1980 - ?); Monthly [except semi-monthly in Dec] (Jun, 1984+), 65 pp.
SPAN: Apr, 1946+
VARIES
--Apr, 1946 - Aug, 1974 as National Press Photographer (ISSN: 0027-9935).
LC: TR 820.N272
ISSN: 0199-2422

News Research Bulletin
? - 1976//
(ISSN: 0734-9238)
SEE: ANPA NEWS RESEARCH REPORT

✜ NEWSCASTER, THE
SUB: "The newsletter of the Broadcast News Committee, Broadcast Education Association."
PUBL: Broadcast News Committee, Broadcast Education Association, 1771 N St., NW, Washington, DC 20036-2891.
DESC: This short typewritten newsletter of news items is from the Broadcast News Committee of the Broadcast Education Association, the pedagogical organization which fosters liaison between college communication faculty, and the broadcast industry.
DEPT: None.
TYPL: "Agenda Set for BEA News Division in Vegas," "Utsler Outlines Goals for BEA News Committee to Consider," "TV News Directors to Discuss Video Ethics." (3-89).
SCHL: Irregular, 2 pp.
SPAN: ?, 1987+

Newsdealer
Mar, 1946 - Sep, 1960//
SEE: MAGAZINE & BOOKSELLER

Newsdealers' Bestsellers
1945? - ?//
SEE: MAGAZINE & BOOKSELLER

✥ NEWSINC.

SUB: "The business of newspapers."
PUBL: NewsInc., 49 East 21st St., New York, NY 10010.
DESC: In its premiere issue, the publisher stated: "*NewsInc.* is the first magazine dedicated to the business of running newspapers. It's written for and about top newspaper executives. And it contains the latest news about the newspaper industry." In a promotional flyer in early 1990, the publisher called it "...the monthly magazine that provides the latest news about the people and strategies that make newspapers work. Each month we take a behind-the-scenes look at a newspaper industry that is being swept by change--newspaper wars that have been won and lost, profiles of the people running big city and small town papers, and practical articles on how newspapers should be run." This publication believes in the power of newsprint, and will quickly become required reading for today's newspaper manager concerned with publishing for profit. Published bimonthly during 1989, and monthly from January, 1990; becoming more timely in reporting as the changing nature of the newspaper medium. Magazine format (8 ¼ x 10 ⅞ inches / 210 x 275 mm); numerous graphics.
DEPT: "Hot Type," newsbriefs; "Marketing," newspaper advertising; "Production," "The Newsroom," "The Conference Room," financial and investment strategies; "By Design," graphic and layout critique; "The Numbers," statistics concerning newspaper management; "The Lede," commentary; "Them," commentary. (5/6-89). "Letters," "Hot Type," late breaking news; "Production," "Commentary," "Datebook," "Marketing," "Newsroom," "Clips," 'The way things used to be'; "Boardroom," "Stockwatch," of major corporate news media; "Them," 'What the competition is up to'; "--30--," 'From the editor's desk'. (3-90).
TYPL: "Home Grown," "The Sears Showdown," "The JOA Two-Step." (5/6-89). "Management Missionary," "Provincial Profits," "Employment Report." (3-90).
SCHL: Bimonthly (May/Jun, 1989 - Nov/Dec, 1989); Monthly (Jan, 1990+), 60 pp.
SPAN: May/Jun, 1989+
LC: PN 4899.N42 N556
DD: 070.5/722/097305 20
ISSN: 1043-7452

✥ NEWSLETTER

PUBL: Writers Guild of America--West, 8955 Beverly Blvd., Los Angeles, CA 90048.
DESC: *Newsletter* is a true newsletter, providing detailed news activities of members of the Writers Guild of America-West, and is filled with articles concerning member activities, workshops, and the current status of writing for the mass media. A sampled issue from 1985 is wonderfully reflective of the diverse nature of the Writers Guild-West membership. One article in that issue described a new social gathering place: "Writing, at best, is a lonely profession. Even lonelier when you're not working. ...So all of us, let's get behind this clubhouse and get to know each other. We can eat and drink and rap. We can even kick around the auteur theory and director Theophiles Q. Auteur who invented it and died broke and homeless for lack of a script." Of special consideration was the "F.Y.I." telephone number column "for accurate information in your script writing;" and an excellent resource, "TV Market List," noting production company, series title, length, network, submission information, and name/telephone number of the contact person. Perhaps most informative and entertaining of all are the letters column. Here are found letters of passion, wit, and prose; one letter described the benefits of unionism for the writing profession; another corrected writing credits for a radio dramatic series and motion picture; and another praised the wisdom and experience of "older writers," and noted; "Writers, like fine wine and women, don't get older, they get better." Numerous gems connected with writing and the entertainment media are interspersed throughout the issue, one of which was said by agent Leonard Hanzer: "The writers are the bank, the producers are the robbers and the agent is the police." For the 1983 through 1985 sampled issues: black ink on uncoated paper stock; stapled newsletter format, with advertising (8 ½ x 11 inches / 215 x 280 mm).
DEPT: "Board Actions," "Letters," "Women's Committee," "Social Committee," "Agents-Writers Committee," "VSOW," "News from Committees," "Who's Doing What?," "So They Say," "In Memoriam," "FYI." (4-84).
TYPL: "New Boardroom Dedicated," "Adapting Novels to Film: Workshop Hears Gidding," "Theme at Arrowhead: Love," "Profile: The T.J. Hooker Show," "Wise Words on Wordprocessing." (4-84).
SCHL: Monthly, 24 pp.
SPAN: 1983?+
ISSN: 0043-9533
ABST: --Media Review Digest (ISSN: 0363-7778)

✥ NEWSLETTER, THE

SUB: "The official publication of the Professional Film and Video Equipment Association."
PUBL: Professional Film and Video Equipment Association, PO Box 9436, Silver Spring, MD 20906-0436.
DESC: The Professional Film and Video Equipment Association was begun in 1973 as a manufacturer-dealer-distributor trade group whose purpose was to "...further industry understanding and foster good relations between its members." Since then, the association has developed a working relationship with SMPTE for industry standardization, an equitable system for exhibitor space at trade conventions, establishment of a security committee for SMPTE conventions, and publication (through *The Newsletter*) of the "Equipment of Questionable Origin" list, which many PFVEA members believe is worth many times the cost of membership. This listing (one-half of the content of a given issue) consists of production equipment descriptions and serial numbers of "questionable ori-

gin," and has been responsible for recovering a considerable amount of equipment for the owner. Magazine format; graphics.
DEPT: "Letter From the President," "Equipment of Questionable Origin," excellent resource listing reported stolen production equipment with serial numbers; "Association Newsline," news of the Professional Film and Video Equipment Association; "PFVEA Membership List," members of the Professional Film and Video Equipment Association. (fall-86). "Equipment of Questionable Origin List," "Membership List." (summer-88).
TYPL: "The ABC's of Rentals," "Industry Bloopers & Practical Jokes," "Considerations for Time-Coded Production Audio." (fall-86). "Close Up Lens Attachments," "Camera Lights," "65mm Cinematography: An Interview with Ed DiGiulio." (summer-88).
SCHL: Semiyearly, 35 pp.
SPAN: ?+?

✣ NEWSLETTER

PUBL: Broadcast Education Association, Gender Issues Division, c/o Jannette Dates, editor, School of Communication, Howard University, Washington, DC 20059.
DESC: This brief, two-page newsletter of the Gender Issues Division of the Broadcast Education Association, a pedagogical group alligned with the National Association of Broadcasters; explores issues of both gender and color; and more specifically the historical record, contemporary contributions, and future trends of same. For the sampled issue of 1990: stapled single-sheet newsletter format, typewritten, no graphics, black ink on uncoated paper stock (8 ½ x 11 inches / 215 x 280 mm).
DEPT: None. (6-90).
TYPL: "Call for Papers." (6-90).
SCHL: Semiyearly?, 2 pp.
SPAN: Jun, 1988+

Newsletter
? - ?//
SEE: BETTER RADIO AND TELEVISION

Newsletter
? - ?//
SEE: CMA NEWSLETTER

Newsletter
? - ?//
SEE: FOLLOW FOCUS

Newsletter
? - Autumn, 1985//
SEE: IAMHIST NEWSLETTER

Newsletter
? - 1970?//
SEE: REPORT

Newsletter / Broadcasters Promotion Association
? - ?//
SEE: BPME IMAGE MAGAZINE

Newsletter - Historians Film Committee
Mar, 1971 - Dec, 1971//
SEE: FILM & HISTORY

Newsletter - Media Institute
Fall, 1979//
(ISSN: 0270-3564)
SEE: BUSINESS AND THE MEDIA

Newsletter of the National Federation for Decency
May?, 1979//
SEE: AFA JOURNAL

Newsletter: Rhetoric Society of America
1968 - 1975//
SEE: RHETORIC SOCIETY QUARTERLY

Newspaper Fund Newsletter
Spring, 1960? - Nov, 1982//
SEE: DOW JONES NEWSPAPER FUND NEWSLETTER

Newspaper News and Advertising News?
? - ?//
SEE: ADVERTISING NEWS

Newspaper Owner and Manager
1898 - May, 1903//
SEE: NEWSPAPER WORLD AND ADVERTISING REVIEW

Newspaper Owner and World
Apr 8, 1905 - Jul 28, 1913//
SEE: NEWSPAPER WORLD AND ADVERTISING REVIEW

Newspaper Production
Nov, 1972 - Aug, 1976//
(ISSN: 0148-9631)
SEE: WEB

Newspaper Production for North and South America
Sep, 1976 - Sep, 1978//
(ISSN: 0148-964x)
SEE: WEB

✣ NEWSPAPER RESEARCH JOURNAL

PUBL: Association for Education in Journalism and Mass Communications, Newspaper Division, Department of Journalism, Memphis State University, Memphis, TN 38152.

DESC: In the premiere issue for fall, 1979, Editor Gerald C. Stone told readers, "*NRJ* is the only publication that offers original research of a practical value to the newspaper industry, and can get it into print while the findings are still fresh. Studies are presented in enough detail to let the reader evaluate their worth, but an effort is always made to stress useable outcomes. That doesn't mean every article will deliver for every reader, but if just one article per issue helps you solve a problem or stay current on newspaper topics, we'll be satisfied to provide it." *Newspaper Research Journal* emphasizes practical descriptive and quantitative research for the professional newspaper field. Herein is information on circulation, freedom of press issues, cartooning, editorials, advertising, sports, features; indeed most facets of newspaper publishing. Quantitative research is most evident in the area of graphic design, typography, and reader comprehension. An article sampler for 1991 would include, "The Pentagon & the Press: The War Continues," "The U.S. Press Corps Abroad Rebounds: A 7th World Survey of Foreign Correspondents," "Reporters' Use of Defamatory Source Material in Qualified Privilege Contexts," "Turnover and Mobility at Small Daily Newspapers," and "A Study of Civil Disorder: The Effect of News Values and Competition on Coverage by Two Competing Daily Newspapers." For the sampled issues of 1979 and 1991: black ink on uncoated paper, with two-spot ink colors on coated paper stock for cover; no advertising; in perfect-bound journal format. Dimensions of the 1979 sampled issues: (5 ¼ x 8 ⅜ inches / 135 x 215 mm). Dimensions for the sampled issues of 1991: (6 x 8 ⅞ inches / 150 x 225 mm).

DEPT: None. (fall-79). "Book Reviews." (spring-84).

TYPL: "Readability of Newspapers and magazines Over Time," "Life Style and the Daily Paper: A Psychographic Profile of Midwestern Readers," "Economics and Management: The Real Influence of Newspaper Groups," "News-Gathering Behaviors of Specialty Reporters: A Two-Level Comparison of Mass Media Decision-Making," "Social Class and Perceived Utility of Newspaper Advertising." (fall-79). "Newspaper Language and Reader's Perceptions of News Events," The 'Tort of Outrage': a New Legal Problem for the Press," "A Comparison of Legislative Sources in Newspaper and Wire Service Stories," (spring- 84). "School-Press Relations and Freedom of Access," "Do Dual Subscribers Differ from Single Subscribers," "Ethics in Editorial Cartooning: Cartoonist and Editor Views." (spring-88).

SCHL: Quarterly, 120 pp.
SPAN: Nov, 1979+
LC: PN 4700 .N515
DD: 070/.05
ISSN: 0739-5329

✣ NEWSPAPER TECHNIQUES

SUB: "The monthly publication of the INCA-FIEJ Research Association."

PUBL: IFRA, Washingtonplatz, D-6100 Darmstadt, Federal Republic of Germany.

DESC: This international monthly publication is targeted at production management, and is concerned with the "technique" of newspaper production. Articles detail problems and solutions at publishing plants worldwide in everything from handling of paper supplies to advertising strategies, color scanners, the mailroom, telecommunications and newspaper design and layout. This is a "how-to" approach to print management. Some issues feature single-themed editorial content, and many issues consist of over one-half reviews of new technology. Magazine format; numerous graphics.

DEPT: "News from the Manufacturers," new equipment; "Coming IFRA Events," calendar. (3-76). "New IFRA Members," "Letter to the Editor." (5-86).

TYPL: "Direct-Litho on the Up and Up," "Managing the Change-Over in Glasgow," "NSDG Pilot Installation for Minneapolis," "More Loss of Newspaper Circulation in North America." (3-76). "Applications to Telecommunications in Newspapers," "'The Independent,' a New U.K. Daily, Scheduled for October," "Trends in the In-House Communications Sector." (5-86).

SCHL: Monthly, 80 pp.
SPAN: 1956+
LC: Z 119.N44
DD: 070.5/72/05
ISSN: 0545-8846
ABST: --Printing Abstracts (ISSN: 0031-109x)

Newspaper World
Aug, 1913 - 1936?//
SEE: NEWSPAPER WORLD AND ADVERTISING REVIEW

NEWSPAPER WORLD AND ADVERTISING REVIEW
PUBL: Bouverie House, Fleet St., London EC4, England.
DESC: This venerable institution (since 1898) covers newspaper news within the British Isles. Although it is a smaller format than most periodicals, a large amount of news is found in the four-column 8-point type format. Information on staff members, individual newspapers, advertising and other related newspaper publishing activities is emphasized. There are some photos, although its primary function is news.
DEPT: "Briefly Personal," personnel briefs; "Features and Promotions," briefs of special sections and features; "Notes on News," undocumented information concerning the gossipy side of publishing; "PG Allen's Ad Commentary," comment concerning print advertising; "National Press Space Barometer," weekly publication data; "Periodicals' Space Barometer," weekly publication data; "Advertising Personalities," newsbriefs; "In the City," stock averages of major publications; "Radio and TV Roundup," broadcast briefs. (2-12-53).
TYPL: "MPA Meets Union's on 'Unofficial Stoppages'," "No Cut in Newsprint Ration Despite Stock Losses," "Newnes Group Launches British Edition of American Magazine," "New Irish Movement Wants to Ban British Press," "Agency Director's Views on Measurement on Readership of Advertisements." (2-12-53).
SCHL: Weekly, 70 pp.
SPAN: Jul, 1913 - 1953//
VARIES
--1898 - May, 1903 as Newspaper Owner and Manager.
--May, 1903 - Apr, 1905 as Master Printer.
--Apr 8, 1905 - Jul 28, 1913 as Newspaper Owner and World.
--Aug, 1913 - 1936? as Newspaper World.
LC: PN 4700.N

Newspaperdom
Vol 1-40, No. 5//
SEE: ADVERTISING

NFD Informer
? - Sep, 1983//
SEE: AFA JOURNAL

NFD Journal
? - ?//
SEE: AFA JOURNAL

NFD Newsletter
Jun, 1979 - Jul, 1979//
SEE: AFA JOURNAL

NFD Newsletter
Sep, 1979 - ?//
SEE: AFA JOURNAL

✣ NIE JOURNAL
PUBL: Manager of Publications, National Institute of Audio-Visual Education, New Delhi, India.
DESC: [*Audio-Visual Education*]: This monthly publication emphasized new advances in teaching and technology in conjunction with the use of audio-visual aids in the classrooms of India. Topics included photography, radio, museums, television, films and other media. Issues for 1964 demonstrated a robust publication health, which dwindled over time to few articles and poor quality printing by the time of its demise in Jan/Mar, 1966. Some issues published in English and Hindi.
DEPT: None. (6/7-64).
TYPL: "School Television--Its Scope and Future in India," "Educational Films and Separate Cinema Houses for Children," "Problem of Shortage of A.V. Aids in Schools and Some Suggestions to get Over It." (6/7-64).
SCHL: Quarterly (Apr, 1957 - Jan/Mar, 1966); Bimonthly (Sep, 1966+).
SPAN: Apr, 1957+
SUSPENDED
--Apr, 1966 - Aug, 1966.
VARIES
--Apr, 1957 - Jan/Mar, 1966 as Audio-Visual Education.
LC: L 61.D44
ISSN: 0027-6634
DD: 370

✣ NIELSEN MEDIA NEWS
PUBL: Nielsen Media Research, Nielsen Plaza, Northbrook, IL 60062.
DESC: A four-page monthly newsletter designed to explain, explore, and showcase new systems of Nielsen research concerning the areas of cable, videocassette, and broadcast television, its succinct articles discuss markets, new approaches to market analysis, and general trends in the three named video industries. Well designed graphs and charts supplement.
DEPT: None. (8-89).

TYPL: "Hispanic Networks and Nielsen Sign Measurement Agreement," "NTI Introduces Commercial Placement Report," "Daily Household TV Usage Inches Upward," "Nielsen's International Presence." (8-89).
SCHL: Monthly, 4 pp.
SPAN: ?+

❖ NIELSEN NEWSCAST, THE

PUBL: AC Nielsen Co., Media Research Division, Nielsen Plaza, Northbrook, IL 60062.
DESC: This booklet-sized publication encapsulates current ratings data on programs and audiences. Excellent charts and graphs make up the bulk of this 12-page quarterly report. Articles discuss current trends in ratings research, and the ever-changing relationship between American consumers and television programming vehicles.
DEPT: None.
TYPL: "Top Sports Events of the 1974-75 TV Season," "Nielsen All-Time Top 25 Programs," "TV Usage Greater Among Non-Whites." (#2-75).
SCHL: Quarterly, 20 pp.
SPAN: 1951+
ISSN: 0468-1835

❖ NIEMAN REPORTS

SUB: "Published quarterly by the Nieman Foundation for Journalism at Harvard University."
SUB: "The Nieman Foundation at Harvard University."
PUBL: Nieman Foundation for Journalism, Harvard University, One Francis Ave., Cambridge, MA 02138.
DESC: "Politics and the Press" is one way of describing *Nieman Reports*, a quarterly publication of journalistic articles written by Nieman Fellows. These well-written and informative articles fall into the areas of commentary, social criticism, journalistic ethics and government operation. The sampled issue of 1991, under the themed title of "1992 Presidential Election," and subtitled "A How-to on Covering the Campaign," included articles providing a coverage plan for newspapers and television, the role of press czars, issues, polls, combating apathy in news reports, and the ways and means for journalists to have "Fun on the Trail -- Despite the Image Makers." An excellent journal of considered thought and substance, *Nieman Reports* continues its long tradition of bringing "truth to light." Well recommended. For the sampled issue of 1991: stapled magazine format, black ink on quality uncoated paper stock, no advertising (8 ½ x 11 inches / 215 x 280 mm).
DEPT: "Books," "Nieman Notes," newsbriefs of Nieman Fellows. (autumn-84). "The Curator's Corner," editorial and comment; "Response," to previously published articles; "Books," extensive reviews; "Nieman Notes," newsbriefs of Nieman Fellows. (spring-91).
TYPL: "The Power and the Press," "Hazards on the Way to Glitter," "South Africa: Modernizing the Apartheid State," "New Times, Old Values," "Conflicts of Interests: a Matter of Journalistic Ethics," "South Korea and a Sentimental Journey." (autumn-84). "A Plan for Newspapers--Setting the Agenda," "A Press Czar's First Ukases, With Flogging a Penalty," "Swearing Off Polls--They Lead Press and Public Astray," "Making Voters Believers--10 Ways to Combat Apathy," "Hope and Pain in Magazine Staffs in Eastern Europe." (spring-91).
SCHL: Quarterly, 55 pp.
SPAN: Feb, 1947+
LC: PN 4700.N57
ISSN: 0028-9817
ABST: --ABI/Informer

❖ NIGHTTIME TV

SUB: "The entertainment magazine for the whole family."
SUB: "From the publishers of Daytime TV."
PUBL: Sterling's Magazines, Inc., 355 Lexington Ave., New York, NY 10017.
DESC: In an early issue, a reader wrote: "...How nice to find a TV magazine devoted to television people! Your editorial position about the face-to-face interviews is very sound--who believes what some writer says someone else thought?" Other readers echoed the opinion that a magazine devoted to nightime television shows and their personalities was long overdue for network television viewers. Publisher Sterling Magazines transfered the already successful formula from its *Daytime TV* serial to this nightime version, with editorial content neatly split into three separate sections: 1) feature articles, which tended to be upbeat, promotional items concerning entire shows, or star profiles; 2) "NTV's Personal Side," which delved into the more personal and private lives of stars; and 3) "Especially For You," the departmental features in each issue. One unique item of the publication endearing it to a number of readers, was the policy of allowing the stars/celebrities to express themselves as much as possible through direct quotes, rather than through the second-person medium. This editorial philosophy was praised through a number of readers' letters. Also worthy of recognition was a personal Q&A column by Loretta Swit, dispensing advice on everything from daughter-in-laws to teen peer pressure, to answering one West Virginia reader's request to know if Alan Alda was as handsome in person as he was on television. Ms. Swit responded "...It's a pleasure to inform you that Alan Alda is one of the nicest people I've ever met..." Also unique to this serial was the "Nashville Scene: News, Views and the Gospel Truth According to Hazel Smith," a down-home column with a very unique Nashville twang. Magazine format (8 x 10 ⅞ inches / 205 x 275 mm); published on newsprint.
DEPT: "And Now... a Word From Your Editor," "Zooming In," 'TV Superstar Gossip' column by Anton Dubrow; "Letters to Loretta," Personal Q&A column by Loretta Swit; "Beauty & Health Hints From TV's Top Stars," "Astrology Goes to Hollywood to Find Your Perfect Mate Among the Stars," column by Art Gatti;

"Celebrity Solund-Off," Television personalities speak their mind; "TV Puzzlers," puzzles; "Quick Cuts," personality news briefs; "Nashville Scene," 'News, views and the Gospel truth according to Hazel Smith', column by Hazel Smith; "Letters to the Editor." (9-75).
TYPL: "TV's Newest Superstars: The Simple Lives They Left--The Sweethearts Who Want Them Back," "M*A*S*H--The World's Wackiest Army Unit; The Stars of This Successful Show Reveal Why They Love It," "Richard Thomas: The Honeymoon's Over," "Ann-Margret: Kinky New Sex Sets Hollywood on Fire," "Doris Day: Lady on the Look-out for Love--Again." (9-75).
SCHL: Bimonthly (Mar/Apr, 1975 - Jul/Aug, 1975); Monthly (Sep, 1975+), 75 pp.
SPAN: Mar/Apr, 1975+?

✤ NIKON WORLD
PUBL: Nikon, Inc., PO Box 520, Garden City, NY 11530.
DESC: In the premiere issue for spring, 1967, Director Jerry Yrisarry noted, "Wherever there is photographic activity in the world, you'll find Nikon cameras in the thick of it. In news, photojournalism, advertising, industry, science, fashion, amateur photography...no matter what the photographic requirements may be, the vast comprehensive Nikon system is able to meet the needs. ... *NIKON WORLD* will publish outstanding photographs made by members of this 'family' as well as technical and useful information, helpful to all engaged in photography as a hobby, profession or as an aid in their work." This is a well-executed promotional publication of technology and its application for Nikon owners. The focus of the three-times-per-year publication is on showcasing the work of media professionals, in which application of different Nikon photographic equipment is demonstrated. For the sampled issues of 1967 and 1978: editorial content and cover were comprised of a mixture of black ink and full-color graphics on coated paper stock, in stapled magazine format, with limited advertising for Nikon products (8 ¼ x 11 ¼ inches / 210 x 285 mm).
DEPT: "You Asked," informational forum; "New Products," review; "News / Notes," information. (spring-68).
TYPL: "Photo-Psycho World of Alfred Gescheidt," "Eddie Adams Tries Harder," "Pictures Beat the Bulldozer," "Portfolio--Robert Pastner," "My Nikon & I." (fall-68).
SCHL: Three issues per year [spring, summer, and fall], 35 pp.
SPAN: Spring, 1967+?

NITA News
? - ?//
SEE: INDUSTRIAL TELEVISION NEWS

Norton's Literary Advertiser
May, 1851 - Jan, 1852//
SEE: AMERICAN LITERARY GAZETTE AND PUBLISHERS' CIRCULAR

Norton's Literary Gazette and Publishers' Circular
Jan, 1852 - Sep 1, 1855//
SEE: AMERICAN LITERARY GAZETTE AND PUBLISHERS' CIRCULAR

✤ NOSTALGIA ILLUSTRATED
SUB: "The pleasures of the past." (Nov, 1974 - ?).
PUBL: Magazine Management Co., 575 Madison Ave., New York, NY 10022.
DESC: For those interested in the development of American Communications, one would be hard pressed to find a more fascinating magazine than *Nostalgia Illustrated*. It reprints all: cartoons, production stills, interviews, color brochures, sheet music, advertisements, and numerous other forms of popular culture. Although there are occasional non-media articles (architecture, sports, and hobbies for example), the majority of each issue is the communication events of yesteryear. It is well recommended for historical research, especially for article reprints which are not readily available today. Magazine format; numerous graphics, some on newsprint.
DEPT: "Nostalgia Is," letters; "Nostalgia News," newsbriefs. (8-75).
TYPL: "Meet Me in St. Louis," "The Year was 1959," "If It Isn't an Eastman," "Katherine Hepburn: Spirited Lady," "Bud & Lou: We're Still Laughing," "The Soap Opera Strips," "A Night with Lana." (8-75).
SCHL: Monthly, 75 pp.
SPAN: Nov, 1974+
LC: AP 2.N87
DD: 051
ISSN: 0149-9327

Nostalgia Journal
Jun?, 1974 - Dec, 1976//
SEE: COMICS JOURNAL, THE

Novum
1972? - 1974?//
SEE: NOVUM GEBRAUCHSGRAPHIK

Novum
1980? - ?//
SEE: NOVUM GEBRAUCHSGRAPHIK

✣ NOVUM GEBRAUCHSGRAPHIK

- PUBL: Verlag F. Bruckmann KG, Nymphenburger Strasse 86, 8000 Munich 20, Federal Republic of Germany.
- DESC: This periodical of international art design is printed in four languages; German, French, Spanish and English. Numerous graphic designs (national campaigns, primarily) grace this journal, with very brief text. Emphasis often is on abstract art used with advertisements, with some discussion of typography and layout. All advertising is in German.
- DEPT: None. (1-62).
- TYPL: "Juan Carlos Distefano, an Argentinian Graphic Designer," "Hans Jurgen Rau, Graphic Advertising Art," "German Youth-Magazine," "Woodinlays from the 16th Century," "Artists Team in Uruguay," "Structural Photos by the Painter-Photographer Otto Weinthaler." (1-62).
- SCHL: Monthly, 70 pp.
- SPAN: 1972+
  VARIES
  --1972? - 1974? as Novum.
  --1974 - 1979 as Novum Gebrauchsgraphik (ISSN: 0302-9794).
  --1980? - ? as Novum.
- LC: NC 997.A
- ISSN: 0016-5743
- ABST: --Abstrax
  --Art Bibliographies Modern (ISSN: 0300-466x)
  --Art Index (ISSN: 0004-3222)

Novum Gebrauchsgraphik

1974 - 1979//
(ISSN: 0302-9794)
SEE: NOVUM GEBRAUCHSGRAPHIK

NSSC Newsletter

? - ?//
SEE: ICA NEWSLETTER

NY Filmmakers Newsletter

Nov, 1967 - Mar, 1968//
SEE: FILMMAKERS FILM & VIDEO MONTHLY

Official Doctor Who Magazine, The

1985? - ?//
SEE: DOCTOR WHO MAGAZINE

ODDFELLOW, THE

SUB: "Or 'Boz' in the boxes."
SUB: "A plague on both your houses."
PUBL: H. Hetherington, 126 Strand, London, England.
DESC: A similar publication to *Actors by Daylight*, this serial began publication only two months later, and included many of the same items. Interestingly, the publisher saw this as a "throw-away" serial, advising its readers in the first issue: "Our advice to all friends, is similar to the advice given by Dr. Nares. . .'If they should happen to like my book, they will have the goodness to render it scarce by burning it as soon as they have read it,' to which we add, say to every body you meet 'have you seen *Actors by Gaslight*, with a very strong emphasis on the word 'have'." Articles tended to be slightly more detailed than in *Actors by Daylight*, but the same small format and front-cover woodcuts were employed. And like *Actors by Daylight*, this serial is very well recommended to theatre historians for its wit and descriptive articles concerning British dramatical fare in the early 1800s.
DEPT: "The Theatrical World," theatre newsbriefs; "Dramatic Gems," anecdotes; "To Correspondents," letters. (5-26-1838); "The Stage," theatre newsbriefs; "To Correspondents," letters. (9-22-1838).
TYPL: "Mademoiselle Celeste," "Liston in School," "A Parody on Glo'ster's Opening Soliloquy, (5-26-1838); "Mr. G. Wieland," "Lays and Legends of the Queen's Theatre," "Green Room Loungers." (9-22-1838).
SCHL: Weekly, 6 pp.
SPAN: Apr 21, 1838 - ?//?
VARIES
--Apr 21, 1838 - Dec 29, 1838 as Actors by Gaslight.
LC: PN 2001 A4

✤ OF SPECIAL INTEREST

SUB: "A periodical of fact and opinion from NBC corporate and media relations."
PUBL: NBC Corporate Communications, Rm. 2561, 30 Rockefeller Plaza, New York, NY 10112.
DESC: This six-page newsletter is a mixture of programming and corporate news, all designed as a positive news vehicle for the National Broadcasting Company (NBC). It provides a promotional platform for the internal and broadcast activities of that organization, highlighting corporate, employee, and programming developments.
DEPT: None. (9-89).
TYPL: "Minorities at NBC," "Upcoming," "President Bush Adds His Voice to NBC Education Campaign." (9-89).
SCHL: Monthly?
SPAN: ?+

✤ OFF-HOLLYWOOD REPORT

SUB: "The magazine of the independent feature project."
PUBL: Independent Feature Project, 132 West 21st St., 6th Floor, New York, NY 10011.
DESC: The *Off-Hollywood Report* is a quarterly membership publication produced by The Independent Feature Project, "...a not-for-profit organization dedicated to the support and promotion of independent filmmaking." Subject matter and writing are in the bold manner of an independent (sometimes viewed as "underground"), producer/director fighting against the established norms of how a motion picture is created, produced and distributed. It is an informative publication, especially with "how-to" articles of creating film product, and the "real-life" experiences of those who have gone before. It is an excellent benefit of membership in the Independent Feature Project, and well recommended. For sampled issue of 1991: stapled magazine format, editorial content is black ink on uncoated paper stock, with full-color cover on coated paper stock (8 ½ x 11 inches / 215 x 280 mm).
DEPT: "Shorts," news items; "Production Update," "Guest Essay," "Words," review; "Announcements." (summer-91).
TYPL: "Indies, Unions, and the 90's," "The Lost Picture Show: Errors and Omissions Insurance," "Gay Cinema, Queer Flicks," "On the Beach: Stars, Indies, and the Croisette Noire," "Kiss or Sell?" (summer-91).
SCHL: Ten issues per year (1985 - ?); Quarterly (?+), 50 pp.
SPAN: 1985+
ISSN: 1045-1706

✣ OFFICIAL BULLETIN OF THE INTERNATIONAL ALLIANCE OF THEATRICAL STAGE EMPLOYEES AND MOVING PICTURE MACHINE OPERATORS OF THE UNITED STATES AND CANADA.

PUBL: International Alliance of Theatrical Stage Employees and Moving Picture Machine Operators of the United States and Canada, Suite 601, 1515 Broadway, New York, NY 10036.
DESC: With the winter 1978/1979 issue, the *IATSE Newsletter* combined with the *IATSE Bulletin* to become the *Official Bulletin of IATSE*, a quarterly designed to furnish news of other craft members and the union. Similar in nature to other craft publications, it focuses on news of the membership, obituaries, new technology, and legal issues. The IATSE craft covers many areas of the performing arts and its publication reflects this.
DEPT: "Theater Crafts," "Legitimate Theater," newsbriefs; "West Coast Notes," "East Coast Notes," "Canadian Scene," newsbriefs; "Radio and Television," newsbriefs; "Here and There," personnel items; "President's Newsletter," lengthy craft-oriented issues and news; "Obituary," lengthy segment; "Names and Addresses of Local Secretaries and Business Agents," 12-page section serving craft members.
TYPL: "Automation," "The Upcoming Hollywood Negotiations," "New York Piers to Become Studios." (winter-78/79).
SCHL: Quarterly, 30 pp.
SPAN: ?+
ISSN: 0020-5885

✣ OFFICIAL VIDEO JOURNAL, THE

PUBL: Kartes Video Communications, Inc., 10 East 106th St., Indianapolis, IN 46280.
DESC: This color newsprint tabloid is aimed at the burgeoning home videocassette market. With an editorial eye to showcasing advertiser products, each issue illustrates how new videotape products were created, or discusses the programming content of same. Some news reports are included. Of special note is the publisher's offer to sell a preview videocassette of each videotape advertiser within the journal.
DEPT: None. (4-84).
TYPL: "TV Usage Sets New Record in 1983," "GE Star Search," "Zenith Drops Beta," "The Good, the Bad, the Ugly," "New Game in Town for Instructional Video." (4-84).
SCHL: ?, 30 pp.
SPAN: ?+

✣ OHIO JOURNALIST, THE

SUB: "News from the E. W. Scripps School of Journalism, Ohio University, Athens, Ohio 45701."
PUBL: E.W. Scripps School of Journalism, Ohio University, Athens, OH 45701.
DESC: This eight to 16-page publication for alumni of the E.W. Scripps School of Journalism at Ohio University features success stories of alumni from the school; along with other articles detailing accomplishments of resident faculty and students in this well-known journalism program. Typical articles include educational opportunities for commercial media staff, faculty activities, trends in journalism education, and a large alumni news section detailing news item changes for a host of graduates dating back (in the sampled issue), to the class of 1929. For the sampled issue of 1989: black/white editorial content in a stapled magazine format on uncoated paper stock with graphics (8 3/8 x 10 3/4 inches / 210 x 270 mm).
DEPT: "Flashes From Classes," alumni newsbriefs. (spring-89).
TYPL: "Ailes Talks of Success," "Gaillimore Finds Athens 'Fertile'," "Educating the Media Generation." (spring-89).
SCHL: Three issues per year, 16 pp.
SPAN: Winter, 1976+

✣ OHIO NEWSPAPER

SUB: "Devoted to the interests of newspaper-making."
PUBL: Ohio State University, School of Journalism, Columbus, OH.
DESC: This journal covered publication activities and developments within the state of Ohio, and was published by the School of Journalism of the Ohio State University at Columbus. Editorial content in the 1920s averaged 16 pages, decreasing to eight pages by the early 1960s. As was true of other state journalism serials, great emphasis was placed on news of individual publishing organizations within the state. Magazine format; some graphics in early issues.
DEPT: "Shop Talk of Ohio Editors and Publishers." (10-21). None. (summer-61).
TYPL: "Ohioan Who Shone in Journalism Recalled," "Handling Your Corps of Correspondents," "Substantial Rewards Not All in Cities," "What It Now Means to be a Good Reporter." (10-21). "Farm News Play Varies in Ohio Press." (summer-61).
SCHL: Monthly (? - ?); Monthly [except Jul, Aug, and Sep], (? - Oct, 1958); Quarterly (Jan, 1959 - ?); 8 pp.
SPAN: Nov, 1919+
SUSPENDED
--Nov, 1958 - Dec, 1958.
LC: PN 4700.O5

OIR Information

? - ?//
SEE: OIRT INFORMATION

OIRT INFORMATION

PUBL: International Radio and Television Organization, U Mrazovky 15, 151 13 Prague 5, Czechoslovakia.
DESC: This was an information vehicle for the International Radio and Television Organization, an association of Soviet bloc broadcasters. Its mimeographed typewritten pages had no working titles or graphics, as this publication was primarily an information medium for members. It appeared that each individual nation's broadcast service submitted its own articles, leading to a variety of topics; including new exchange agreements between Bulgarian television and Mexico; prizes awarded in a young musicians' competition on Czechoslovakian radio; Polish radio and television announcing a new color television receiver; Soviet television launching a new television program called "Today in the World;" and news of competitions and contests throughout the entire OIRT network. A fascinating reference for Soviet bloc media. Text was in English, French, Russian, and German.
DEPT: None.
TYPL: No Article Titles.
SCHL: Monthly, 20 pp.
SPAN: 1956 - ?//
VARIES
--? - ? as OIR Information.
LC: PN 1991.I53
ISSN: 0029-7097

✤ OLD NEWS

PUBL: Susquehanna Times & Magazine, Inc., Route 1, Box 75a, Marietta, PA 17547.
DESC: Headlines and news stories in this newspaper are those of the past, as with interesting articles from both published and nonpublished sources. It also features articles which were part and parcel of communication history. The sampled issue of 1989 had two front-page articles, one was about the probable causes of the Johnstown Flood of 1889, devoting some two and one-half tabloid pages to the events of that catastrophe, with a number of pictures, etchings and descriptive material. The second front-page article profiled the Marquis de Lafayette in a four-page section. Other articles included Benjamin Franklin's comments and observations about women; and a final, three-page article profiling entertainment star, John Barrymore. *Old News* is an historian's delight. For the sampled issue of 1989: tabloid newspaper format on uncoated paper stock, very nicely printed, no advertising (11 ½ x 17 inches / 290 x 430 mm).
DEPT: None. (?-89).
TYPL: "Whose Fault was the Johnstown Flood?," "The Marquis de Lafayette," "Franklin on Women," "John Barrymore." (?-89).
SCHL: Monthly [Except August], 12 pp.
SPAN: Sep, 1989+
DD: 909 11
ISSN: 1047-3068

✤ OLD TIMER'S BULLETIN, THE

SUB: "Published for the old time wireless operator, historian, and collector."
SUB: "Official journal of the Antique Wireless Association."
PUBL: Antique Wireless Association, Holcomb, NY.
DESC: "An amateur organization devoted to the history of wireless," the Antique Wireless Association provides a marvelous forum for historical review and discussion within its official organ, the *Old Timer's Bulletin*. Here are news and photographs of rare equipment items; notable communication professionals and their contributions to wireless history; current news of communication museums; making old equipment work; and activities of the association. It is a splendid resource for communication historians. Small journal format; early issues were typewritten, moving to typeset format in later publications.
DEPT: "Valuation list," of equipment; "Old Time Ham-Ads." (midyear-61). "Association News," "The Auction," "The Broadcast Receiver," "The Communication Receiver," "Identification and Value," of equipment items; "Junior Wireless Club," 'devoted to early wireless'; "The Book Collector's Corner," "Key and Telegraph," "The Television Receiver," "The Loudspeaker," "Historical Artifacts," for sale; "The Vacuum Tube," "In-House," newsbriefs and comment; "On Review," "Hints and Kinks for the Experimenter," "Recent Radio and Entertainer Obituaries," "Silent Key," obituaries; "Editor's Notes," "The Museum," news of the Antique Wireless Association museum. (2-88).
TYPL: "Lee DeForest Passes and an Era is Ended," "Amateur Radio in the NYC Area Pre-WW1." (midyear-61). "Report on Annual Conference," "Collecting Early Radio Batteries," "Alan Douglas: Radio Historian." (2-88).
SCHL: Quarterly, 45 pp.
SPAN: ?+
LC: TK 6540.O54
DD: 621.3841/05

On Communications

Nov, 1984 - Mar, 1986//
(ISSN: 8750-7854)
SEE: NETWORK WORLD

✤ ON!

SUB: "For work and play."
SUB: "Video, audio & computers."
PUBL: IDG Communications, Peterborough, Inc., 80 Elm St., Peterborough, NH 03458.
DESC: In the premiere issue of *ON!* for December, 1990, editor Martin Levine noted: "Each issue of *ON!* invites you to become acquainted with the latest products and happenings in the fast-changing worlds of video, audio and computing. In short, we aim to give you the

inside story, the same advice and tips we'd pass on to friends and relatives. If it's not worth taking home, if it won't make a difference in how you work work and play at home, if it's not somehow better than what came before-- we'll let you know, and tell you why. We won't be content with mediocrity, and we don't expect you will either." This home consumer publication features the best products, applications, and software available in the three primary areas of audio, video and computers for the home market; with full color graphics, and a dynamic layout design. "*ON!* explores emerging trends and exciting breakthroughs. You'll find out what's hot and what's not--the products you'll enjoy for years and those that are merely passing fads. With each monthly issue you'll become a more savvy consumer. *ON!* gives you advice from the experts without confusing technical jargon. ... *ON!* is filled with important tips and helpful hints on how to get the most out of all the home electronics equipment you already own." Magazine format (8 x 10 ⅝ inches / 200 x 270 mm), stapled, full color throughout on coated paper stock.

DEPT: "On! This...," editorial column by Martin Levine; "Newsbreaks," 'A look at industry trends, products and developments' compiled column by Dennis Brisson; "On! Video," column by K. C. Pepper; "On! Audio," column by Joe Wiesenfelder; "On! Computers," column by David Essex; "Field Tests," new product review; "On! Shopping," column by Martin Brochstein; "On! Software," "On the disk," review column by Lafe Low; "On the Record," review column by Mike Mettler; "On the Screen," review column by Gregory Fagan; "On! Second Thought," commentary column by David Lachenbruch. (12-90).
TYPL: "The Next Picture Show," "Sound Out of Sight," "Behind the Lens," "The Remedy is Remote," "Multimedia Mania." (12-90).
SCHL: Monthly, 100 pp.
SPAN: Dec, 1990+
DD: 384
ISSN: 1052-438x

ON CABLE

PUBL: On Cable Publications, 25 Van Zant St., Norwalk, CT 06855.
DESC: This publication provided a month of daily listings of cable and pay-television programming available in the United States. Lists of programs were very complete, with descriptions tending to be somewhat brief. Each issue included numerous publicity photos of upcoming programs and several articles. Cox Communications of Atlanta, owner of *On Cable*, brought publication of the monthly serial to a halt with the December, 1985 issue. For the sampled issue of 1985: stapled magazine format, with primarily black/white editorial content concerning program schedules with full-color front and end sections showcasing feature stories and full-color cover all on coated paper stock (8 ¼ x 10 ¾ inches / 210 x 275 mm).

DEPT: "Up Front," "Hollywood," newsbriefs; "Movies," reviews; "Home Electronics," "Crossword," "Sports," "Cablegrams," cable newsbriefs; "Letters." (12-83). "PF Flyer," editorial; "Movies," "Hollywood," "Highlights," "Home Electronics," "Sports," "Cablegrams," programming newsbriefs. (12-85).
TYPL: "'SCTV' Proves There's Life After NBC," "Voight at 45," "What I Learned About Pay TV's Men at the Top," "Finding the Next Kathy Smith." (12-83). "2 New Series Hope Faerie Tales Can Come True," "Smiles and Frowns." (12-85).
SCHL: Monthly, 120 pp.
SPAN: Oct, 1980 - Dec, 1985//
ISSN: 0273-5636

✤ ON FILM

PUBL: Film Society of Santa Barbara, Film Studies, University of California, Santa Barbara, CA 93106.
DESC: With a scholarly approach to film history and psychology, and the interaction of film with society; *On Film* will please both supporters and critics of any given subject in film presented. In the sampled issue for 1983, the publication utilized a one-column typewritten format, (placing magazine content above that of design layout form). Black/white graphics are included for visual support of some articles, with care being taken both in their selection and reproduction. Although primary emphasis is on the motion picture, especially that of foreign directors and producers, some articles also apply to the sister medium of video, as in a discussion of the demise of the "Lou Grant" television series (from the sampled issue). It is an interesting publication about the theory, purpose, and importance of motion picture (and television) programming, both historical and contemporary. For the sampled issue of 1983: stapled magazine format, black/white editorial content on uncoated paper stock, cover consisting of black/white with spot color on coated paper stock, no advertising (8 ½ x 11 inches / 215 x 280 mm).
DEPT: "Conferences," review; "Books," review. (summer-83).
TYPL: "The Cabinet of Dr. Caligari: History / Psychoanalysis / Cinema," "The 'Secret' in Hitchcock's The Thirty-Nine Steps," "Who Killed Lou Grant? or the Implications of Liberal Politics in the Conservative 80s," "Marguerite Duras: Barrages Against the Pacific," "Profile of Kenneth Anger." (summer-83).
SCHL: Quarterly, 55 pp.
SPAN: Winter?, 1976+
ISSN: 0161-1585

✤ ON LINE

SUB: "At the movies."
PUBL: Michaelson Entertainment, Suite 357, 1040 1st Ave., New York, NY 10022.

DESC: A small format promotional for motion picture theatre exhibitors, provided on a complimentary basis with paid admission at participating theatres; this full-color monthly provides just the right amount of reading for pre-film education, extolling the virtues and value of upcoming exhibitor product. For the sampled issue of 1989: Full color graphics throughout on coated paper stock in small stapled digest format with advertising (5 ⅛ x 7 ⅜ inches / 130 x 185 mm).
DEPT: "Movie Calendar," expected theatre release/exhibition of coming product; "Line-On Hollywood," movie star newsbriefs; "Movie Line-Up," reviews of upcoming motion pictures; "Crossword Puzzle." (9-89).
TYPL: "On Location: Osaka, Japan," "Gene Hackman Trivia." (9-89).
SCHL: Monthly, 20 pp.
SPAN: Feb, 1989+

ON LOCATION

SUB: "The film and videotape production magazine."
SUB: "The only film & videotape production magazine."
PUBL: On Location Publishing, 6311 Romaine St., Hollywood, CA 90038.
DESC: This first-class publication covered film and videotape production in the sub-areas of "film, video, cable, special effects, animation, commercials, production, post production, and music video." This was a magazine of independent production companies, and not just those of New York City, Los Angeles, and Chicago. *On Location* had a special monthly section on production activities of a particular state, and regularly ran quality feature articles on special effects and filming/taping of special commercial projects. It also featured two monthly supplements, "On Commercials," concerning current spot TV production; and "On MusicVideo." It was an exceptional publication for the state of independent and studio production. For the sampled issues of 1981 and 1986: perfect-bound magazine format; editorial content comprised of a mixture of black ink with full-color pages on heavy coated paper stock; significant advertising targeted to the trade (8 x 10 ½ inches / 205 x 270 mm).
DEPT: "Dialogue," newsbriefs; "In Focus," manufacturer profile; "Video Takes," news of independent producers; "Video Post," technical information; "Commercial Breaks," spot TV news; "Spot Checks," new spot productions; "Jingle$," commercial music; "Head Shot," profile; "Captured Live," Newsbriefs on music tapings; "On Canada," Canadian production news; "The Big Apple," New York production newsbriefs; "Hero Takes," newsbriefs on special effects and animation; "New Products," reviews (8-82). "Dialogue," on production; "State of the States," production status report; "On Canada," media production news; "Video News," "Equipment Watch," new products; "Data-Based News," for computer imaging and effects; "EFX News," computer graphics; "Film News," "Facilities News," studio production and post production; "Equipment Watch," new product; "Audio News," "Commercial Breaks," newsbriefs; "Captured Live," music videos. (3-86).
TYPL: "'Pippin,' Sheehan-Tele-Scenes $3 million Pay TV Production Has Elaborate Distribution Plans," "Controversial HMI-type lighting grows in acceptance," "The Magic of Movie Miniatures," (8-82). "ZM Productions," "NAB Convention Theme Focuses on Broadcasters' Relationships with Community," "International Management Communication," "'St. Elsewhere' Doesn't Go 'Elsewhere' but Accomplishes 'Location' Effect in Studio Surroundings," "Commercial Budgeting Software." (3-86).
SCHL: Monthly (Oct, 1977 - Dec, 1977); Bimonthly (Jan/Feb, 1978 - Mar,Apr, 1983); Monthly (Jun, 1983+), 119 pp.
SPAN: Oct, 1977 - Mar, 1986?//?
LC: PN 1993.5 .U6O5
DD: 791.43/0973
ISSN: 0149-7014

✤ ON TRACK

SUB: "A newsletter for audio/visual professionals published by 3M's Magnetic Media Division."
PUBL: 3M Corporation, St. Paul, MN.
DESC: "3M would like *On Track* to become a forum for discussion on digital video and other crucial topics. More importantly, we would like it to help A/V professionals run their businesses even more effectively, and to further expand the channels of communication between 3M and the industry." An excellent promotional newsletter more interested in "the channel of communication between 3M and the industry," than in self-hype and product marketing. It provides an interesting forum for the discussion of magnetic media issues in the audio, film and video industries.
DEPT: None.
TYPL: "Digital Video Offers Numerous Advantages," "Digital Meets Client Demands," "What Video Equipment Best Suits User Needs?" (summer-87).
SCHL: ?, 4 pp.
SPAN: Summer, 1987+?

✤ ONSAT

SUB: "America's weekly guide to satellite TV."
PUBL: Triple D Publishing, Inc., PO Box 2384, Shelby, NC 28151-9901.
DESC: An advertisement in sister publication, *Satellite Retailer*, states that *OnSat* is "The innovative leader in magazine format programming guides, *OnSat* gives more features and more accurate information than any other guide." Information abounds concerning satellite television services within this weekly publication; information on programming, information on satellite services, information on changes and new developments. Several pages feature articles about stars, regulatory agencies, and other news or feature items; but the majority of each issue is about programming,

which is what readers/subscribers want from *OnSat*. Program listings are clear, concise, and informative. Departmental columns are interesting, and invite subscriber input and comments. This is "must" reading for producers, suppliers, and especially end-users of satellite-fed audio and video programming. In the sampled issue for June 23, 1991, 16 pages of the stapled magazine format were in full-color on coated paper stock, with the vast majority of the programming information [Eastern edition] published black/white on newsprint, minimal advertising, numerous graphics and programming charts (8 x 10 ¾ inches / 205 x 270 mm).

DEPT: "In the News," newsbriefs; "Fast Feeds," network newsbriefs column by Mark Jeffers; "Sports," "Mailbag," letters; "Dr. Dish," satellite receiver questions and answer column by Richard Maddox; "Notes & Comments," on upcoming weeks programming, column by Bill Britton; "Dolby Surround," very helpful listing of motion pictures airing this week in Dolby Stereo; "Movies," listing; "French Movies," listing; "Pay-Per-View Viewing This Week," listing; "Soap Opera Week," Q&A column by Kimberly Redmond; "Backstage," column by Marilyn Beck and Stacy Jenel Smith; "Celebrity Profile," column by Cheryl Lavin; "Ask Me About TV," Q&A column by Toni D'Amato; "Satellite Audio," guide to audio-only programming; "Transponder Service Watch," services listed by satellite; "Ku & Other Satellites," guide; "Text & Data," satellite services; "Satellite Log," program review column by Kirk Nicewonger; "TV Circles," word list puzzle column by Gayle Discoe; "TV Crossword," "Hollywood Scene," column by Marilyn Beck and Stacy Jenel Smith; "Specialty Programming for [month]," listed by subject matter; "Special Feeds Update," satellite guide column by Bill Britton; "Religious Programming," program guide; "News & Weather Programming," program guide; "Music Video Programming," guide; "French & Spanish Programming," listing; "Specials," annotated guide; "Sports," annotated program guide; "How to Subscribe," to a variety of satellite services. (6-23-91).
TYPL: "NRTC Wins First Round in Pricing Discrimination Case," "Satellite Sports: Superstation Shoot-Out," "The Fable of the Merry Merger," "John Wayne in 3-D," "The 'New' Learning Channel." (6-23-91).
SCHL: Weekly, 130 pp.
SPAN: ?+
EDITION
--Eastern.
ISSN: 0747-4059

Optic Music
Feb, 1984 - May, 1987//
(ISSN: 0889-5651)
SEE: FILM & VIDEO

✣ OPTICAL INFORMATION SYSTEMS

PUBL: Meckler Publishing, 11 Ferry Lane West, Westport, CT 06880.
DESC: [*Videodisc, Videotex*]: "*Videodisc/Videotex* magazine is devoted to the reporting and critical analysis of research and developments in videodisc, optical disk, videotex and related video technologies. International in scope it reports on activities throughout the world." A subscription to "Videodisc/Videotex" also provides a monthly subscription to the companion newsletter, "Videodisc Update."
DESC: [*Videodisc and Optical Disk*]: "*Videodisc and Optical Disk* is a bimonthly journal devoted to the reporting and critical analysis of research and practical applications of videodisc, optical disk, compact disc as a read-only memory, videotex and related technologies...Emphasis is on practical applications and case studies of existing projects and products." This publication had important applications to the quickly expanding digital audio-video fields. Numerous graphics; small format.
DEPT: "Editorial," "News and Notes," "Publication Announcements," "Book Reviews." (9/10-85).
TYPL: "Evaluation of 'Introduction to Computer Literacy' and 'DiscWriter' Authoring System," "Document Image Processing in Management Information Systems." (9/10-85).
SCHL: Quarterly (Winter, 1981 - 1983); Bimonthly (1983+), 70 pp.
SPAN: Winter, 1981+
VARIES
--Winter, 1981 - Spring, 1981 as Videodisc/Teletext (ISSN: 0198-9456).
--Summer, 1981 - Jan/Feb, 1984 as Videodisc, Videotex (ISSN: 0278-9183).
--Mar/Apr, 1984 - Nov/Dec, 1985 as Videodisc and Optical Disk (ISSN: 0742-5740).
WITH SUPPLEMENT
--Optical Information Systems Update (ISSN: 0887-5162), ?+.
ISSN: 0886-5809

Optical Information Systems Update / Library & Information Center Applications
? - Dec, 1986//
(ISSN: 0886-019x)
SEE: CD-ROM LIBRARIAN

Optical Lantern and Cinematograph Journal
Nov, 1904 - May, 1906//
SEE: KINEMATOGRAPH WEEKLY

Optical Lantern and Kinematograph Journal

Jun, 1906 - Apr, 1907//
SEE: KINEMATOGRAPH WEEKLY

Optical Magic Lantern Journal and Photographic Enlarger, The

Jun 15, 1889 - Jun, 1903//
SEE: KINEMATOGRAPH WEEKLY

✛ OPTICAL MEMORY NEWS

SUB: "Including Interactive Videodisks."
PUBL: Rothchild Consultants, P.O. Box 14817, San Francisco, CA 94114-0817.
DESC: A fascinating bimonthly newsletter concentrating on the optical field of interactive communications, the typewritten format (no graphics) allows quick perusal of news. A strong comment-critique of emerging trends is present. Much hard information is packed into the 16-page format. Well recommended for those interested in the interactive video (read optical) disk area.
DEPT: "Prime Evil," consumer advocate column; "Draw Developments," direct-read-after-write trends; "Interactive Developments," "Image Storage News," "Books Reviews," "Conference Reports," "Conference Calendar," "Canadian Developments." (9/10-82).
TYPL: "Library of Congress Installs Xerox Disk System," "Pioneer Renovates Former DVA Carson Plant," "Omex Shows 20 Million Page On-Line System," "Interactive Video Simulations and Their Production." (9/10-82).
SCHL: Bimonthly, 16 pp.
SPAN: Jan/Feb, 1982+
VARIES
--Jan, 1982 - Sep/Oct, 1983 as Optical memory Newsletter Including Interactive Videodisks (ISSN: 0731-9452).
ISSN: 0741-5869

Optical memory Newsletter Including Interactive Videodisks

Jan, 1982 - Sep/Oct, 1983//
(ISSN: 0731-9452)
SEE: OPTICAL MEMORY NEWS

Opticmusic's Film & Video Production

Jun, 1987 - Oct, 1988//
(ISSN: 0894-4423)
SEE: FILM & VIDEO

✛ ORBIT VIDEO

SUB: "The magazine of videotape entertainment."
PUBL: CommTek Publishing, Division of CommTek, Inc., 8330 Boone Blvd., Suite 600, Vienna VA 22180.
DESC: Writing in the premiere issue for January, 1989 CEO/Executive Publisher David G. Wolford and Executive Editor Michael Doan said, "Here it is, at last--the magazine you've been waiting for! We're *Orbit Video*, the magazine designed for the millions of families that shop in video stores. Let's say you've gone into a video store with a specific tape in mind. The store has run out and now you have to figure out what to watch. Let us help you make your selection. Thumb through our magazine to choose another video. And next time, before you even get to the store, you can pick the video you want or make alternative choices." A subscription page in the same issue told potential subscribers that "In each issue of *Orbit Video* you will receive: *More than 100 concise reviews and ratings of the latest releases, *Alternatives to "rented out" top new releases, *A handy pull-out reader reference card which you can take to your video store as a shopping guide in selecting video entertainment, *Tips on how to make the best use of video products and services, *Great ideas for planning special occasions using video entertainment...birthdays, anniversaries, events for the kids, *Features on famous personalities." It contains a tear-out selection card for in-store decision-making, and extensive reviews of entertainment product not making the top-ten listing. The inside back cover is reserved for a title index facilitating that last minute search for a film title before heading off to the video store. The layout is dynamic with liberal use of full-color throughout. Approximately one-half of editorial content (and all advertisements) is on coated paper stock, the remaining half on newsprint. This magazine delivers information, service, and just plain entertaining reading about the motion picture, film and video industries. Premiere issue for January, 1989: perfect-bound magazine format (8 x 10 ¾ inches / 205 x 270 mm).
DEPT: "Editor's Page," editorial commentary column by David G. Wolford and Michael Doan; "Tape Talk," review of new releases column by Laura M. Fries; "Orbit Video's Top 10," 'These are the new releases to get before the other customers clear them from the shelves'; "Spotlight," actor profile with filmography; "Laser," information and reviews; "Lifestyles," 'How to entertain with your VCR' column by Nao Hauser; "Children's Corner," review column by David Gritten; "Hardware," review column by Telka Perry and Owen R. Rubin; "Video Room," new technology info column by Jill MacNeice; "Videodical," trends and technoligies; "After the Top 10," videotape reviews; "People's Choice," 'Here are favorite releases from previous months that keep customers rushing to their video stores'; "Action / Adventure," reviews; "Children's," review; "Classics," review; "Comedy," review; "Documentaries," review; "Drama," review; "Foreign," review; "Horror," review; "Music," review; "Sports," review; "Oscar Looks Back," 'Acad-

emy award blasts from the past'; "Classics Corner," review; "Q and A," reader-submitted questions. (1-89).
TYPL: "Why Kevin Costner's Hot," "Arnold!," "The Top 100 Videos of All Time," "The Exercise Queens," "Taping Your Big Affair." (1-89).
SCHL: Monthly, 115 pp.
SPAN: Jan, 1989+
DD: 791
ISSN: 1042-1149

✦ ORGANIZATIONAL COMMUNICATION NEWSLETTER

PUBL: International Communication Association, Organizational Communication Division, PO Box 9589, Austin, TX 78766.
DESC: This membership newsletter of the Organizational Communication Division of the International Communication Association serves to alert members to upcoming events; including conventions, paper competitions, workshops and consortium meetings; plus inform the membership about promotions, publications, and other news. For the sampled issue of 1991: two-column newsletter format, black ink on uncoated paper stock, no advertising (8 ½ x 11 inches / 215 x 280 mm).
DEPT: "Members in the News," news items; "Books From Members," new publications; "Journal News," "Spotlight on the Chair," profile. (spring-91).
TYPL: "A Doctorial Student Consortium: Organizations of the Future." (spring-91).
SCHL: Semiyearly, 4 pp.
SPAN: Fall, 1980+

Our Player's Gallery

Oct, 1900 - Jan, 1901//
(ISSN: 0748-6634)
SEE: THEATRE MAGAZINE

✦ OUTDOOR & TRAVEL PHOTOGRAPHY

PUBL: Harris Publications, Inc., 1115 Broadway, New York, New York 10010.
DESC: Photographers whose interests include the world's people and places will be interested in *Outdoor & Travel Photography*, a distinctive quarterly publication for outdoor photography. Articles are a mixture of travel and technical advice, new products for outdoor photography, and exciting places to explore for adventurer and camera alike. This is a magazine for the outdoor enthusiast, but armchair photographers will also appreciate it. For the sampled issue of 1990: magazine format (8 x 10 ⅞ inches / 205 x 275 mm); full color graphics on coated paper stock.
DEPT: "Meet the Contributors," 'An introduction to our writers and photographers'; "Cover Story," 'Find out how our cover was shot'; "Letters," "Flash," 'News and notes from around the globe'; "McRae's Wildlife," column by Bill McRae; "Outdoor Videographer," column by Jerry Chiappetta; "Rothschild Reviews," column by Norman Rothschild; "Outdoor Classroom," column by Tom Boyden; "Reviewed," new products; "Readers' Portfolio," 'Our readers' images are displayed and discussed'; "New Products," 'Novel equipment for the outdoor and travel photographer'; "Book Reviews," 'Publications and videos of interest'; "Passport: Trips, Tours & Workshops," 'A directory to what's available'; "Nikon's Photo Finish." (summer-90).
TYPL: "Lens Riot! The Complete Guide to Lenses," "Shooting Ship to Shore," "Kangaroo Island," "Close-Ups in a Macro Flash," "Kids & Kameras." (summer-90).
SCHL: Quarterly, 100 pp.
SPAN: Fall, 1988+

✦ OUTDOOR PHOTOGRAPHER

SUB: "Scenic, travel, wildlife, sports."
PUBL: Werner Publishing Corporation, 16000 Ventura Blvd., Suite 800, Encino, CA 91436.
DESC: Majestic mountain peaks wrapped in a veil of new snow; Big Horn sheep; Monarch butterflies; the Purple Galinule in a field of wild flowers; or the dynamics of a white-water rafting trip among geysers of water, and multicolored waterfowl; are just some of the elements that make up each issue of *Outdoor Photographer*; a magazine with a zest for life and photography. Arm-chair adventurers will appreciate the extraordinary pictures of world scenery. The targeted reader is the real-life photographic adventurer who is willing to trek for hours or days before finding the ideal photographic situation. Numerous advertisements for camping equipment and state travel commissions attest to the success in reaching this rugged individual. It is a well-designed, exciting publication. For the sampled issue of 1990: perfect-bound magazine format with mixture of black/white and color graphics and full-color cover on coated paper stock (8 x 10 ¾ inches / 200 x 275 mm).
DEPT: "In This Issue," overview column by Steve Werner; "New Products," "Photo Adventure," column by Galen Rowell; "Basic Jones," column by Dewitt Jones; "Cover Shot," how accomplished; "Tech Tips," column by George Lepp; "Wild Side," column by Leonard Lee Rue III; "Gadget Bag," column by George Lepp; "Travel and Workshops," upcoming events calendar; "Last Frame," picture showcase. (4-90).
TYPL: "Nature's Big 10," "Eye On the Roof of the World," "Bird Man of the Blue Lagoon," "The Magellan of Quiet Light," "Mail Order Sharp Shooter." (4-90).
SCHL: Bimonthly (Feb, 1985 - Dec/Jan, 1985/1986); Nine Issues Per Year (Feb, 1986 - Apr, 1989); Monthly [except bimonthly in Jan/Feb and Jul/Aug] (May, 1989+), 90 pp.
SPAN: Feb, 1985+

DD: 778 11
ISSN: 0890-5304

✣ OVERSET

SUB: "A review of Newspaper Journalism."
PUBL: 1728 Evergreen St., Walla Walla, WA 99362.
DESC: *Overset* is one of a number of critical journalism reviews which surfaced during the 1970s. The tabloid newspaper concentrates on newspaper media in the United States, with some side comment retained for journalism schools and similar areas. Newsprint with line graphics.
DEPT: "Letters to the Editor," "Once Over Lightly," newsbriefs; "Classified," "Inside Stuff," current comment; "Cheers & Jeers," Orchid and Onion awards for newspapers. (7-79).
TYPL: "Who Does Gannett Think It's Kidding?," "Communicologists are Ruining Our Journalism Schools," "...and They Got Away With It." (7-79).
SCHL: Monthly, 16 pp.
SPAN: Jun, 1978+?

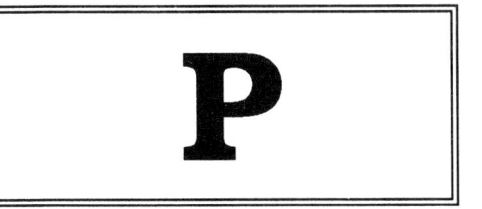

Pacific Radio News

Jan, 1917 - Oct, 1921//
SEE: AUDIO

✤ PACTSHEET

SUB: "People and careers in telecommunications."
PUBL: National Association of Educational Broadcasters, 1346 Connecticut Ave., N.W., Washington, DC 20006.
DESC: *Pactsheet* is an employment bulletin designed to serve those working, or desiring to work within the public broadcast community. The PACT in *Pactsheet* stands for "People and Careers in Telecommunications."
DEPT: None.
TYPL: No article titles. Each issue consists of positions open, or desired.
SCHL: Monthly, 4 pp.
SPAN: Dec, 1977+

PANORAMA

SUB: "Television today & tomorrow."
SUB: "The television magazine."
PUBL: Triangle Communications, 850 Third Ave., New York, NY 10022.
DESC: In the premiere issue of February, 1980, Editor Roger Youman quoted Walter Annenberg, President of Triangle Publications, on the form and function of this new publication: "The TV screen influences nearly every aspect of our society and its mores, as well as public attitudes on foreign affairs, social issues and government. We live in a time of rapid and significant changes. On network and public TV, programming is changing; movies and miniseries are creating an opportunity to develop characters and make social statements. And there is a technological revolution going on that by greatly increasing program sources for the home screen will drastically affect the viewing habits of the public, with cable, pay-cable and subscription television, satellite transmission, and videocassettes and discs growing in importance. *PANORAMA* will offer its readers an authoritative perspective on programming, new and future uses of the home screen, developments in governmental regulation and the changes in society that the 'television revolution' is causing." Editor Youman noting the subtitle of "Television today and tomorrow," added that it would "...be edited for the selective television viewer, the person who watches television about half as much as the national average, but who is concerned about the impact the home screen is having on his or her life and values, and on society in general." This was a consumer magazine that served as a critical forum of the television medium. Published by veteran publisher, Triangle Publications (*TV Guide*), and staffed by knowledgeable writers in the field; this dynamic magazine should have had a long and profitable publishing life. Unfortunately, *Panorama* succumbed in June, 1981 to the fortunes of a fickle reading public. Articles were well-written, with a wide range of interests from cable TV to new satellite technology; from debunking programming myths, to the survival of PBS. The premiere issue for February, 1980 was preceded by a "prototype" issue dated July, 1979. For the sampled issue for 1980: stapled magazine format, full-color pages throughout on coated paper stock (8 1/8 x 10 7/8 inches / 205 x 275 mm).
DEPT: "This Month," "Perspective," column by Richard Reeves; "Cable and Pay-TV," column by Seth Goldstein; "Q&A," "Sports," column by Kenneth Turan; "Panoramic View," "Surveys and Studies," column by Dick Friedman; "Videocassettes and Discs," column by David Lachenbruch; "Yesterdays," "Rear View," column by Harry Stein. (2-80). "Letters," "Impressions," comment on programming and industry; "Perspective," comment; "Cassettes in Review," review; "This Month," late-breaking newsbriefs; "Cable and Pay-TV," news; "Q&A," interview with TV actor or actress; "Panoramic View," programming newsbriefs; "Videocassettes and Discs," reviews; "Sports," TV news; "Yesterdays," programming 25, 15, 5 years ago; "Rear View," comment. (3-81).
TYPL: "The Active Viewer's Declaration of Independence," "The Road to the Stars," "Waiting for Uncle Miltie," "Is America Ready for 'United States'?," "Destination: Television." (2-80). "Someone Had to Pay for the Debacle," "Masterpiece Theatre's Most Memorable Moments," "Will Dan Rather Make It as Cronkite's Replacement?," "Inside Pay-Cable's Most Savage War," "I Discovered Early On--Get a Tough Director" (3-81).
SCHL: Monthly, 104 pp.
SPAN: Feb, 1980 - Jun, 1981//
LC: PN 1992.P36
DD: 384.55/0973
ISSN: 0191-8591

✤ PARAMOUNT WORLD

PUBL: Paramount Pictures Corporation, 1501 Broadway, New York, NY 10036.
DESC: "Issued by and for the members of the Paramount organization around the world who believe in the entertainment appeal of their motion pictures, their television enterprises and allied products, and in the

business future of their company," this periodical is unabashedly positive. *Paramount World* extolls the excitement surrounding Paramount Studios, its personnel, and especially its distributed product. The format consists of "teleprompter" headlines, typewritten articles, one-hundred-plus pictures, and a layout design philosophy that calls for as little "white space" as possible. It brings a newsworthy excitement to people and productions at Paramount. Interestingly, some articles (without explanation) simply appear in foreign languages of French, Spanish, German, or Japanese. No table of contents.
DEPT: "News from the Branches," "Business in Britain," "Europe," "Interesting Paramount Events in the U.S. & Canada," "International Personalities in Paramount Cinema Events," "Home Office News Items," "Paramount Events in Latin America," "News of the Paramount Subsidiaries," "There is No Substitute for Showmanship," "Window on the World," "Cables." (8-66).
TYPL: "Accentuating the Positive," "'Nevada Smith' Sets All-Time Record in Japan," "International Idea Session in Paris," "U.S. Showmanship for 'Is Paris Burning?' Covers an Important Event in Pittsburgh." (8-66).
SCHL: Monthly, 40 pp.
SPAN: 1955+?
FROM MERGER OF
--Paramount International News (and) The Paramounteer, 1955.
LC: PN 1993.P25

✦ PAS GRAPHIC ARTS NEWS

PUBL: CAE Productions, 3950 Campus Drive, Newport Beach, CA 92660.
DESC: A newspaper format targeted toward graphic artists and allied trades in Southern California; information on graphics programs, new books, displays, awards for outstanding design, etc. are typical of its monthly contents.
DEPT: "Free Classified," free listing of artists and their services.
TYPL: "Stone Rubbing?," "Newsletter Design Workshop Scheduled," "East Los Angeles Occupational Center." (1-78).
SCHL: Monthly, 12 pp.
SPAN: 1977+

PC Publishing

Jan, 1986 - Mar, 1991//
(ISSN: 0896-8209)
SEE: PC PUBLISHING AND PRESENTATIONS

✦ PC PUBLISHING AND PRESENTATIONS

SUB: "Desktop publishing/presentation graphics for IBM and compatible PC users."
PUBL: PC Publishing and Presentations, PO Box 941909, Atlanta, GA 30341.
DESC: "*PC Publishing and Presentations* is the definitive 'How to' guide to improving your business skills on the PC and compatibles. Information in every issue will allow you to make maximum use of the publishing and graphic tools available to get the most out of your specific publishing activity." A change in publisher commencing with the April/May, 1991 issue made a great magazine into an even better one. New publisher/editor Pauline Ores has assembled a publication not just about desktop publishing, but actually showcasing what can be accomplished in this evolving field. It is a very nice bimonthly resource for the continually changing technologies and techniques of desktop publishing. Stapled magazine format, full-color throughout on coated paper stock. For 1990 sampled issue (8 x 10 ¾ inches / 205 x 275 mm); for 1991 sampled issue (8 x 10 ⅞ inches / 205 x 275 mm).
DEPT: "Letters," "From the Desktop," editorial column by Robert Mueller; "Looking Ahead," news items; "Corporate Communications," column by Maryann Keblusek; "Hands-On Graphics," column by Ron LaFon; "Hands-On Fonts," column by David Dean; "Hands-On Pagemaker," column by Keith Thompson; "Hands-On Ventura," column by Rick Altman; "Hands-On Postscript," column by Ross Smith; "Hands-On Reviews," "New Products," "How Did They Do That?," fascinating how-to feature; "Calendar of Events. (7-90). "Typestyle," column by Daniel Will-Harris; "Graphics," column by Ron LaFon; "Showpage," column by Ross Smith; "Presentations," column by Keith Thompson," "Budget DTP," desktop publishing column by James Bell; "Editorial," column by Pauline Ores; "On Line," 'The latest tools for your desktop' column by Liz Horton; "Reviews," extensive new product section. (6/7-91).
TYPL: "Beyond VGA," "DTP Tools, Special Plotter, Update Signmaker's Craft," "Using a Slide Service Bureau," "Windows 3.0: The Beginning of Something Great," "A Question of Speed." (7-90). "Just the Fax, Please," "Optical Alternatives," "Upgrading Your PC for DTP," "Expand Your Design Versatility with Display Type," "Incorporating 3-D Images into Layouts." (6/7-91).
SCHL: Monthly (Jan, 1986 - Mar, 1991); Bimonthly (Apr/May, 1991+), 60 pp.
SPAN: Jan, 1986+
VARIES
--Jan, 1986 - Mar, 1991 as PC Publishing (ISSN: 0896-8209).
LC: Z 286.D47 P37
DD: 004
ISSN: 1056-540x

PCS, THE POPULAR CULTURE SCHOLAR

SUB: "The popular culture scholar."
SUB: "A journal of theory and analysis."
PUBL: Frostburg State College, Frostburg, MD 21532.
DESC: "The Journal is interdisciplinary and devoted to making a homogenous whole of experience by identifying similarities as well as differences between each stratum of life and art in terms of a comprehensive philosophical and aesthetic structure. Articles submitted [are to] explore the connections, influences, and relationships among the various strata of literature, history, communications, arts, and sciences." This is a scholary, typewritten journal for the study of popular culture. No graphics.
DEPT: None. (winter-77).
TYPL: "The Criticism of Detective Fiction," "Suspense Fiction: The Problem of Definition," "The Law of the Mystery Writers V. the Law of the Courts," "Doing, Knowing and Mystery: a Study of Religious Types in Detective Fiction." (winter-77).
SCHL: Quarterly, 85 pp.
SPAN: Winter, 1977//?
LC: NX 1.P2
DD: 700/.5
ISSN: 0147-4286

PD Cue

? - ?//
(ISSN: 0193-0141)
SEE: NATPE PROGRAMMER

✧ PD REPORT

PUBL: Production Division, Broadcast Education Association, 1771 N St., NW, Washington, DC 20036-2891.
DESC: This brief newsletter is for members of the Broadcast Education Association, a pedagogical organization designed to foster instruction, resources, and liaisons between the college community and the broadcast industry. It serves the needs of those interested in teaching audio and video production, through news and discussion of issues such as equipment budgets, trends in technology, and opportunities for students and faculty members in the production field. Sampled issue for 1989: photocopied, stapled newsletter (8 ½ x 11 inches / 215 x 280 mm). For sampled issue of 1991: loose-leaf newsletter style, typeset, black ink on color uncoated paper stock with limited advertising (8 ½ x 11 inches / 215 x 280 mm).
DEPT: None. (2-89). "Editorial," column by Joseph Bridges; "Letters to the Editor," "Chair Chatter," division chairperson commentary column by Suzanne Williams. (6-91).
TYPL: "Las Vegas Here We Come!," "Production Committee Events," "Production Studies." (2-89). "First Faculty Production Competition Plays to SRO Crowd at '91 Convention," "Division Business Meeting Covers Important Topics," "Tech Session Features Evaluation Reports on Sony's Hi-8 Video," "Production Challenges for Students Were Main Topics at Showcase," "Teaching Video Production with Interactive Multimedia." (6-91).
SCHL: Several issues per year, 2 pp.
SPAN: ?, 1988?+
VARIES
--? - ? as Production Committee Newsletter.

✧ PEGBAR

PUBL: VSIA, The Vancouver Society of Independent Animators, PO Box 3014, Vancouver, British Columbia, V6B 3X5 Canada.
DESC: This lively publication of the Vancouver Society of Independent Animators provides news of animation activity on a local, national, and international basis; with interesting reports of animator activities, conventions, trade fairs, technique developments, and products in production or recent release. Square journal format with numerous (fabulous) animation graphics.
DEPT: "Editorial," "Update," animation newsbriefs; "Mumbleypeg," animator newsbriefs; "New Films," animation releases. (fall-86).
TYPL: "Portland Animators," "Zagreb Review," "Contemporary Japanese Animators," "Tony de Peltrie: 100% Emotion," "Ghost of Animations Past," "Quickdraw Animation Society." (fall-86).
SCHL: Semiyearly, 30 pp.
SPAN: ?+

✧ PEIRCE-PHELPS, INC. AUDIO/VIDEO NEWSLETTER

PUBL: Peirce-Phelps, Inc., 7-7 Metropolitan Court, Gaithersburg, MD 20878.
DESC: Peirce-Phelps, a vendor of audio/video equipment, expanded into the "turnkey" realm of corporate teleconferencing facilities in the mid 1980s. This newsletter provides quality technical advice on teleconferencing design, new developments in technology, and information about the operation of such a facility. Of special note are excellent graphics depicting technical processes. Newsletter format.
DEPT: "Q & A." (5-88). "Q & A." (5-89).
TYPL: "Chips Ahoy...Solid State Technology Comes to Video," "Freedom from Assembly." (5-88). "Video Monitors: The Windows to Your Work," "Improved Definition Television: It's Not HDTV, But...," "Overheads...A Format from the Forties Moves into the Nineties." (5-89).
SCHL: Bimonthly?, 4 pp.
SPAN: May, 1988+

✧ PENCIL TEST

SUB: "The monthly bulletin of ASIFA Washington/International Animated Film Association."

PUBL:	ASIFA-Washington, 716-B Church St., Alexandria, VA 22314.
DESC:	"With the initiation of *Frame By Frame*, ASIFA Washington's newsletter and mouthpiece, we have several goals and purposes. *Frame By Frame* will fulfill the needs of the Washington area animation community along specific lines. It provides a much needed source on who's doing what, where, with whom and when. *Frame By Frame* will highlight members (professional and non-professional), news, works in progress, animation screenings, classes, seminars, critiques, jobs, plus many other items," This is the newsletter of the Washington, D.C. chapter of ASIFA (International Animated Film Association). The premiere issue was 12 pages with half-tone graphics. Later issues (samples for 1-85, 7-85, 2- 86), under banner of *Pencil Test*, were two to four pages in length, with line graphics.
DEPT:	"Calendar of Animated Events." (12-82). "Animation News," newsbriefs. (2-86).
TYPL:	"Walter Lantz Visits D.C.," "Cartoon Buff's Wish List," "Futuropolis Plays to SRO at Hirshhorn." (12-82). "The March Event." (2-86).
SCHL:	Monthly, 2 pp.
SPAN:	Dec, 1982+ VARIES --Dec, 1982 - ? as Frame By Frame.

✦ PENTAX FAMILY

SUB:	"Published by Pentax Family, Asahi Optical Company, Ltd."
PUBL:	Asahi Optical Company, Ltd., CPO 895, Tokyo 100-91, Japan.
DESC:	From an editorial: "The history of photography is much shorter than that of art but in a short period of time, photography has achieved tremendous advances. Today, photography has become very much part of our daily lives and modern life would be inconceivable without photography. Photography is now indispensable in every field of human activity. It covers not only the arts but has broad applications in journalism, industry, science and military affairs. As one form of artistic expression in photography, the use of pictorial composition borrowed from art is still much used today." This description of photographic art and application form the basis by which this lovingly-constructed publication extolls the virtues of the visual arts, both color and black/white. The emphasis within *Pentax Family* (at least for the sampled issue) was Japanese photographers and subject matter; but includes a generous sampling of art and craft from photographers worldwide. The layout design and care in reproduction are marvelous, demonstrating a sensitivity to reader and photographer alike. The wonderful array of black/white and full-color pictures is quite stunning, all of which makes *Pentax Family* well recommended. For the 1981? sampled copy: stapled magazine format, no advertising, full-color throughout (except in the printing of black/white photographic images, all on heavy coated paper (8 ¼ x 11 inches / 210 x 275 mm).
DEPT:	"Editor's Notes," "Pentax Family Gallery," reader-submitted photographs; "Pentax Journal," column by Takao Kajiwara. (#25-81?).
TYPL:	"Accessories by Hiroki Hayashi," "The Blue Impulse by Kiyoo Takakura," "City of Water--Suzhou by Yukichi Watabe," "Shoji Ueda: The Man and His Photography," "More Effective Lens System with a Minimum Number of Lenses." (#25-81?).
SCHL:	?, 70 pp.
SPAN:	?+

PEP

PUBL:	Newspaper Enterprise Association, West Third and Lakeside, Cleveland, OH.
DESC:	Within the glossy pages of this quarterly publication was a positive call to the excitement of working with the newspaper industry. Articles might include a description on how reporters could ferret out stories, aggressive reporting techniques that paid off, problems of handling issues, censorship, cartooning, subscriptions, size limits, advertising, and virtually all other aspects of newspaper operation. Articles were decidedly upbeat, even when dealing with issues of concern, and often were accompanied by photographs or drawings.
DEPT:	"Puns & Fun," "War Hunches," "Just Hunches," "Things They Tell--A Page of 'Em," "Just Among Ourselves." (5-17). "Pepitorials," "Hunches," "Ventures in Advertising," "Pepigrams," newspaper sayings. (6-19).
TYPL:	"Trapped in Riot Battle," "Suicide by Telephone," "War Censorship, Best When Least," "The Newspaper Man in Magazine Work," "Why Cynicism Tempts Newspaper Men." (5-17). "What I Think of Newspapermen (by Mary Pickford)," "Taxi-Chasing His Hunship, von Bernstorff," "The Foes of the City Desk," "The Newspaper Feud that Was and Still Is," "Do Mysterious Tipsters Ever Phone You?" (6-19).
SCHL:	Monthly, 18 pp.
SPAN:	Jan, 1916 - Nov, 1919//
LC:	PN 4700.P4

✦ PERFECT VISION, THE

SUB:	"The high end video journal."
PUBL:	Perfect Vision, PO Box 63842, Syracuse, NY 13217.
DESC:	*The Perfect Vision* is an incredible find for the serious videophile interested in acquiring, maintaining, and using the finest video hardware and software available. There are few publications that even begin to match *The Perfect Vision*. The "Letters" to the editor column itself ran 13 pages in one sampled issue! These passionate letters addressed hardware, video software products, and the editorial content of the publication itself. Letters are articulate, with reasoned judgment, and reflect an ernest desire to educate,

share, and improve the lot of home video consumers. Virtually each letter has a response, oftentimes several responses, by individuals or companies named in the letter. This section says much about the enlightened editorial stance of publisher and editor, Harry Pearson. As the subtitle implies, this is a publication for the "high-end" video user: Reviews are only of middle to high-end features and technological advances. Equipment reviews are very thorough, concerning technology, aesthetics, maintenance, and performance criteria. A very unusual feature of most reviews is a "rebuttal" column for the equipment manufacturer, which often clear up misconceptions, or clarify changes/additions to the product since the review was written. Software reviews are topical in nature. Like other video publications, much goes into discussion of the genre; actors, directors, and entertainment value. Unlike many video publications, *The Perfect Vision* provides very specific commentary on technical considerations, such as discussions of the development of a stereo soundtrack from the original mono, or the image quality of an film-to- video transfer process (which might have resulted in visual degradation or improvement compared to the original film release). In winter, 1990/1991 the subscription cost was $22 for four issues. This publication is important for any serious videophile interested in the best hardware/software for home entertainment. Concerning the sampled issue for 1990/1991: journal format (6 ¾ x 10 inches / 170 x 255 mm) printed on heavy coated paper and uncoated paper stock combination.

DEPT: "Viewpoints," 'Editorial notes'; "Letters," outstanding section containing letters of considered comment and criticism; "Editor's Choice," unusual section of equipment recommendations; "Collector's Corner." (winter-90/91).
TYPL: "The Sound of Theaters, Part the Second," "Cinema Digital Sound--Come the Revolution?," "How to Get the Most Out of Your Video System," "Horror on Laser," "Chaplin's Early Years--The Keystone Films." (winter-90/91).
SCHL: Quarterly, 160 pp.
SPAN: 1986+
DD: 384
ISSN: 0895-4143

✤ PERFORMANCE

SUB: "The touring talent weekly."
PUBL: Performance, 1020 Currie St., Ft. Worth, TX 76107.
DESC: "*Performance* is the touring talent market's weekly newspaper, showing when and where the top touring acts will be available, charting the relative drawing power of acts, and giving box office figures. *Performance* also reviews concert and club appearances from a business viewpoint as well as critically." This weekly mainly lists current tours, with articles about the media stars of the day.
DEPT: "Directory," of booking contracts; "Talent Tours Availabilities," the majority of the magazine which details who is playing where; "Box-Office Roundup," quick tabulation of gate receipts for the week.
TYPL: "Jerry Jeff Jams," "ECM Artists Tour," "Performance Equipment Field Test." (10-77).
SCHL: Weekly [except first and last weeks of each calendar year] (? - ?); Weekly [except for first two weeks of each calendar year] (?+).
SPAN: ?+
 VARIES
 --? - ? as Performance Newspaper (ISSN: 0746-9772).
DD: 790 11
ISSN: 0882-9314

✤ PERFORMANCE

PUBL: New York Performance Foundation, Inc., 249 West 13th St., New York, NY 10011.
DESC: Publisher Joseph Papp stated in the premiere issue that "The publication of *Performance* and its companion monthly *Scripts* is part of a great expansion of our work at the New York Shakespeare Festival Public Theater: two independent-spirited international magazines, one of ideas and one of texts, feeding the development of a national theater. The magazines will bring into the mainstream of American theater texts and ideas from other countries, experimental techniques and perceptions, and above all a continuing examination of the place of performance in society." Due to a lack of subsidy, *Performance* changed publishers after the fourth issue of Sep/Oct, 1972, and recommenced publication with issue number five as of March/April, 1973. It is an important journal on the impact and importance of theatre in America. Journal format; numerous production stills.
DEPT: "P/S Comment," "Letters." (4-72).
TYPL: "The Seven Levels of the Theater," "Music and Theater," "Notes for a Definition of the Japanese Film." (4-72).
SCHL: Quarterly (Dec, 1971 - Apr, 1972); Bimonthly (Jul/Aug, 1972+).
SPAN: Dec, 1971+
LC: PN 1560 .P47
DD: 790/.05
ISSN: 0006-1883

Performance Newspaper

? - ?//
(ISSN: 0746-9772)
SEE: PERFORMANCE

✤ PERFORMER, THE

SUB: "The international magazine for stage and screen."
PUBL: Franklin Productions, 6518 Whitman Ave, Van Nuys, CA 91406.

DESC: This semiannual publication is for very unique readers; travelogue film lecturers who are members of IMPALA (the International Motion Picture and Lecturers Association). The vast majority of editorial content consists of member news from the IMPALA, INTRAFILM (International Travel-Adventure Film Guild), and TAP (Travelfilm Artists and Producers) organizations. *The Performer* is concerned with the current status of travelfilms, techniques for increasing program audiences, and field techniques for production. The publication assumes all travel films are being produced with 16mm film cameras.
DEPT: "Dear Coop," humorous personality column by Don Cooper; "Letters to the Editor," "The Final Curtain," obits; "Classified Ads of Film Speakers and Subjects," "Managers and Agents of Film Artists," "Travel and Adventure Block Bookers." (spring-80).
TYPL: "TV or Not TV? That is the Question," "'Inflation Dragon' Spurs Unity at INTRAFILM Convention," "The Only Sound System You'll Ever Need," "Benefits and Problems of Historical Footage." (spring-80).
SCHL: Semiyearly, 50 pp.
SPAN: Spring, 1978+

✤ PERFORMING ARTS IN CANADA, THE

PUBL: Canadian Stage, 263 Adelaide St., West, 5th Floor, Toronto, ON M5H 1Y2 Canada.
DESC: *The Performing Arts in Canada* is a celebration of current performances, artists, and artistic endeavors in Canadian theatre, dance, music, opera and film. Numerous pictures of current productions, and profiles provide thorough coverage of the artists and performers. A marvelous resource for a sense of the state of performing arts in Canada. Magazine format; numerous graphics.
DEPT: "What's Going On in Theatre," "What's Going On in Dance," "What's Going On in Music," "What's Going On in Pop." (Spring-80).
TYPL: "Sneezy Waters Scores Again with the Show Hank Never Gave," "The Changing Images of Dance for Sale," "Training Arts Administrators for a Perilous Profession," "Alexander Hausvater's Theatre of Political Shock." (spring-80).
SCHL: Monthly (Sep, 1961 - ?); Semiyearly (? - Spring/Summer, 1962); Quarterly (Winter, 1963+); 60 pp.
SPAN: Mar, 1961+
ABSORBED
--Balletopics (ISSN: 0522-0661), Summer, 1971.
LC: PN 1582.C3P47
DD: 790.2/0971
ISSN: 0031-5230
ABST: --Canadian Periodical Index (ISSN: 0008-4719)
--Magazine Index
--Music Index (ISSN: 0027-4348)

✤ PERFORMING ARTS JOURNAL

PUBL: Performing Arts Journal, 325 Spring St., Room 318, New York, NY 10013.
DESC: "*PAJ* is the only American magazine covering all the performing arts. It offers timely, international coverage of contemporary theatre, dance, music, and drama. Don Shewey of *The Village Voice* calls the journal 'passionate in its defense of critical writing as a creative act...*PAJ* is American theatre's foremost vehicle for thinking out loud'." This subscription page quote confirms what current readers already know; that this is a critical journal of the international performing arts; which includes theatre, dance, music, drama, opera, mime, street drama, and other related forms of performance. Some issues are themed, such as the May, 1991 issue devoted to Polish theatre. Editors Bonnie Marranca and Gautam Dasgupta have placed photographs with significant white space, and all advertising has been located at the back of the issue. "*PAJ*, devoted to the contemporary spirit in drama and theatre, publishes plays, critical essays, interviews, dialogues between artists, and book reviews in every issue. As a research tool it is beneficial to students and professionals in theatre and all aspects of the humanities." For the sampled issue of 1991: perfect-bound journal format, editorial content is black/white on uncoated paper stock, cover is two-color on coated paper stock (6 x 8 ¾ inches / 150 x 220 mm).
DEPT: None. (5-91).
TYPL: "The Eyes of War," "Kaloprosopia: The Art of Personality, the Theatricalization of Discourse in Avant-Garde Theatre," "The Eve of the Great October Revolution, Chronicle of a Happening in Wroclaw," "Germany's Fourth Wall," "My Middle Europe." (5-91).
SCHL: Three issues per year, 115 pp.
SPAN: Spring, 1976+
LC: PN 1561
DD: 790.2/05
ISSN: 0735-8393
ABST: --American Humanities Index
--Book Review Index (ISSN: 0524-0581)
--Humanities Index (ISSN: 0095-5981)
--Quarterly Index to Scholarly Critical and Creative Journals

Performing Arts Review

Winter, 1969 - 1981//
(ISSN: 0031-5249)
SEE: JOURNAL OF ARTS MANAGEMENT AND LAW, THE

Perry's Broadcasting and the Law

1971 - Dec 1, 1984//
(ISSN: 0161-5823)
SEE: BROADCASTING AND THE LAW

✤ PERSONAL ELECTRONICS

PUBL: Communication Channels, Inc., 6255 Barfield Rd., Atlanta, GA 30328.
DESC: [*High Fidelity Trade News*]: In 1983, with a change of owner, publisher Gerald Sweeney felt it was time once again to restate the editorial policy of this publication: "...for more than a quarter of a century, *HFTN*'s prime function has been to help specialty dealers make a better profit by offering technical evaluations of new products and merchandising assistance on the sell-through and by examining marketing trends as they relate to product mix--all key ingredients for retail success." That formula remains intact, providing clear reviews of equipment and retail potential for audio and video store managers.
DEPT: "Letters to the Editor," "Sound Lines," comment; "As We Go to Press," newsbriefs; "News Round-Up," "Tape Recorders: Dollars & Sense," "Book Review," "New on the Market," "Rep News." (1-61). "Advertising & Promotion," "As We Go to Press," "Audio/Video Salesman," advice; "Corporate Strategies," news; "From the Editor's Desk," editorial; "Hi-Fi Video Library," literature; "Hi-Fi Video News," "Industry Update," "Technically Speaking," "Trends & Technology," "Wavemakers," personnel briefs. (4-83).
TYPL: "What's Happening to Audio Sales?," "Musicians Help Sell Components," "The Audio Dealer and His P-R Program." (1-61). "Effective P.O.P. Displays Move More Merchandise," "The Cigar Store Indian Awards," "Tracking Video's Elusive Profit," "Is There a Sell-Through Market for Video Software?" (4-83).
SCHL: Monthly, 50 pp.
SPAN: 1957+
VARIES
--1957 - Jun?, 1983 as High Fidelity Trade News (ISSN: 0046-7367).
LC: TK 7882.H5 H53
DD: 621.381/068/8
ISSN: 0739-8123

✤ PERSONAL PUBLISHING

SUB: "The magazine for desktop publishers."
PUBL: Hitchcock Publishing Co., 191 South Gary Ave., Carol Stream, IL 60188.
DESC: Dramatic developments in computer architecture, software design, and escalating charges for traditional design/pasteup practices have brought desktop publishing into its own. Developments are occuring so quickly, *Personal Publishing* remains busy just reporting on new trends, products, and techniques. Issues tend to be theme-oriented, often focusing on such elements of desktop publishing as printing quality, art graphics software, type fonts, layout design, editing, printing, or color separations. It is a valuable resource for personal publishing layout, design, and technology. The publication is in magazine format with numerous color graphics on coated paper stock. Sampled issue for 1988: (8 ½ x 10 ⅞ inches / 215 x 275 mm). Sampled issue for 1990: (8 x 10 ¾ inches / 205 x 275 mm).
DEPT: "Editor's Report," column by Daniel Brogan; "Letters," "Hot Type," new type fonts; "Thumbnails," new product reviews; "Updates," newsbriefs concerning new product updates; "Using Type," "Type Drawer," "Gallery," new graphic products; "Service Bureau," desktop publishing tips; "Casting Off," contributor profiles. (11-89).
TYPL: "Off to the Traces," "Re:Design," "Book Shelf." (11-89).
SCHL: Monthly, 80 pp.
SPAN: Oct, 1985+
VARIES
--? - Sep?, 1985 as Professional Publishing (ISSN: 0736-7457).
DD: 070 11
ISSN: 0884-951x

PERSPECTIVE

SUB: "Quarterly review of progress."
SUB: "Photography, Cinematography, Sound & Image Recording."
PUBL: Focal Press, 31 Fitzroy Square, London W1, England.
DESC: "Perspective sets out to serve members of the photographic and ancillary industries, the technologists, scientists, administrators, business men and specialist photographers whose job it is to devise or use new tools in new ways and for new ends." This was a quarterly of technological progress in the use of photography, cinematography, and sound and image recording media. Articles were highly technical, providing innovative means of applying visual and aural media to scientific thought and experimentation.
DEPT: None. (#3-66).
TYPL: "Transmitting Visual Information," "Recording Galactic Explosions," "Galaxies and Their Light," "The Radiographic Flash," "Ballistic Radiography." (#3-66).
SCHL: Quarterly, 30 pp.
SPAN: Autumn, 1958 - 1966//
VARIES
--1949/1950? - ? as Progress in Photography.
LC: TR 1.P45
ISSN: 0480-1008

✤ PERSPECTIVES ON FILM

SUB: "Ethnographic film."
PUBL: The Pennsylvania State University Audio Visual Services, Special Services Building, University Park, PA 16802.
DESC: This is both a film rental catalogue, and a collection of fascinating articles concerning documentary/instructional filmmaking. Articles in most cases are written by the filmmakers themselves and reveal an interesting insight into the collaborative effort involving producing a motion picture film for the secondary

and college classroom. Numerous graphics of the filmmaking process and production stills augment the articles. Magazine format; no advertising.
DEPT: None. (8-79).
TYPL: "Making a Film Record of the Yanomamo Indians of Southern Venezuela," "Producing Ethnographic Films: An Interview with Filmmaker Gei Zantzinger," "Nonverbal Communication: A Communicative Perspective," "Endangered Societies and Threatened Customs: Visual Preservation of the Present for the Future." (8-79).
SCHL: ?, 60 pp.
SPAN: ?+?
LC: PN 1995.9.D6 P47
DD: 791.43/05
ISSN: 0196-3007

✥ PETERSEN'S PHOTOGRAPHIC

SUB: "Petersen's Photographic shows you how..."
PUBL: Petersen Publishing Co., 6725 Sunset Blvd., Los Angeles, CA 90028.
DESC: One satisfied reader wrote to say "...Congratulations on a job well done with your magazine's format. I've just recently subscribed, and compared you to 'the other photo magazine' (which I've been reading for five years). Your magazine is head and shoulders above them." This is a dynamic magazine with a professional approach to photography, treating it both as a science and an art. Great care is evident in the placement and reprinting of submitted pictures to the serial; quite often resulting in a stunning display of the power of this medium. A pleasing balance is struck between technology, instruction, and critical review. One sampled issue included "something for everyone;" from best pictures of the year to photographing a hot-air balloon event; from automatic slide imprinters to a good article detailing the basics of photographic composition. This is a wonderful resource for photographers who strive to perfect their talents. Quality image reproduction and layout in a magazine format (7 7/8 x 10 1/2 inches / 200 x 270 mm).
DEPT: None. (fall-71). "On the Scene," the editors; "Other Voices," letters; "Guide Lines," review; "In Sight," technique; "Tools of the Trade," equipment; "Far East Journal," photographic news and review; "Club Close-Ups," column; "Where the Action Is," column; "Self-Assignment," column; "In Just Seconds," "Product Proof Sheet," new equipment; "Seminars & Workshops Calendar," "Vintage Viewfinder," historical; "Camera on Campus," column; "One to One," Reader Q&A. (3-78). "Reader's Letters," "Viewfinder," 'Photo news & events' column by Franklin Cameron; "Proof Sheet," 'New product news'; "Pro Talk," column by Gary Bernstein; "Tools of the Trade," column by Karen Geller-Shinn; "One to One," 'Your questions answered' column by Bill Hurter; "Photo Tours & Workshops," calendar. (10-90).
TYPL: "Glamour Through the Eyes of Three Top New York Photographers," "Underwater Photography," "Josef Muench Talks About Scenics," "What a Picture Editor Wants to See," "The Way-Out World of Lenses." (fall-71). "How to Find Models," "Techniques for Multiple Printing," "Multiple-Image Photography," "Image Enhancement," "Tips for Printing Color Slides," (3-78). "Understanding the Zone System," "Soft & Dreamy Imagemaking," "Starbursts Without Filters," "A Professional Profile: Against All Odds," "The Basics of Photographic Composition." (10-90).
SCHL: Quarterly (Fall, 1971 - Winter, 1971); Monthly (May, 1972+), 120 pp.
SPAN: Fall, 1971+
VARIES
--Fall, 1971 - Winter, 1971 as Photographic Quarterly.
--May, 1972 - Oct, 1979 as Petersen's Photographic Magazine (ISSN: 0048-3583).
LC: TR 1.P
ISSN: 0199-4913
ABST: --Abridged Readers' Guide to Periodical Literature (ISSN: 0001-334x)
--Book Review Index (ISSN: 0524-0581)
--Consumers Index to Product Evaluations and Information Sources (ISSN: 0094-0534)
--Magazine Index
--Popular Magazine Review (ISSN: 0740-3763)
--Readers Guide to Periodical Literature (ISSN: 0034-0464)

Petersen's Photographic Magazine

May, 1972 - Oct, 1979//
(ISSN: 0048-3583)
SEE: PETERSEN'S PHOTOGRAPHIC

✥ PHILOSOPHY AND RHETORIC

PUBL: Pennsylvania State University Press, 215 Wagner Bldg., University Park, PA 16802.
DESC: *"Philosophy and Rhetoric* publishes papers on theoretical issues involving the relationship between philosophy and rhetoric (including the relationship between formal or informal logic and rhetoric); articles on philosophical aspects of argumentation (including argumentation in philosophy itself); studies of philosophical views on the nature of rhetoric of historical figures and during historical periods; philosophical analyses of the relationship to rhetoric of other areas of human culture and thought; and psychological and sociological studies of rhetoric with a strong philosophical emphasis." Each issue contains two departmental features, "Discussion Notes;" and an extensive section of "Book Reviews." For sampled issue of 1990: perfect-bound journal format, black ink on uncoated paper stock, cover is black/yellow ink on uncoated paper stock, limited advertising (6 x 9 inches / 155 x 230 mm).
DEPT: "Discussion Notes," "Book Reviews." (#3-90).

TYPL:	"Hamblin on the Standard Treatment," "Morally Untenable Beliefs," "The Death of the Author (as Producer)," "Neo-Sophistic Rhetorical Criticism or the Historical Reconstruction of Sophistic Doctrines?," "Irreducible Dualisms and the Residue of Commonsense: On the Inevitability of Cartesian Anxiety." (#3-90).
SCHL:	Quarterly, 105 pp.
SPAN:	Jan, 1968+
LC:	B1 .P572
DD:	105
ISSN:	0031-8213

✤ PHOTIQUE

SUB:	"A buy-sell-trade magazine for antique, classic, used photographic equipment & images."
PUBL:	Photique Magazine, One Magnolia Hill, West Hartford, CT 06117.
DESC:	For the buyer or seller of vintage photographic equipment, *Photique* is a great resource for cameras, darkroom equipment, images, magic lanterns, movies, subminiatures, studio equipment or stereo image equipment and prints. Indeed, everything from "Accessories for Sale" to "Zeiss" items ca be found. Primarily a sell/buy/trade medium, each issue includes several pages of articles of historical, association or collector interest. The Photographic Historical Society of New England received special attention within the sampled issue. Stapled magazine format, black/white editorial and advertising content throughout on uncoated paper stock (8 ½ x 11 inches / 215 x 280 mm).
DEPT:	None. (10-88).
TYPL:	"Jacob Schaub and His Cameras," "Unusual Show & Tell at September PHSNE Meeting," "A Visit with Matt Isenburg." (10-88).
SCHL:	Ten issues per year, 16 pp.
SPAN:	Sep?, 1988+?

✤ PHOTO ANSWERS

SUB:	"All your photo questions answered."
SUB:	"Every page packed with photo ideas!"
PUBL:	EMAP National Publications, Ltd., Bushfield House, Orton Centre, Peterborough PE2 0UW, England.
DESC:	"Whether features, test or answers pages, *Photo Answers* is strikingly visual. It has a style that puts it out on its own, and that It has a style that puts it out on its own, and that is not just in the way it looks. *Photo Answers* prides itself on its accessiblity and the way that each and every month it offers more to its readers -- your questions answered, your portfolios featured, competitions for you to enter, practical advice on your pictures and suggestions for the month ahead. No magazine is better in touch with a photographer's needs." A more colorful, strikingly beautiful publication for the field of photography would be hard to find. It has a four-column format with insert boxes, sidebars, and pictures that stimulate the senses. This is the definitive photographic publication, with lucid descriptions, fascinating features, and a dynamic layout design. For the sampled issue of 1990: Stapled magazine format with showcase use of color, graphics, and pictures all on coated paper stock (8 ¼ x 11 ¾ inches / 210 x 295 mm).
DEPT:	"Photoworld," 'News, views and reviews from the world of photography, edited column by Colin Leftley'; "Photo Ideas," 'A scintillating selection of sumptuous snaps to set your shutters sizzling, column by Lee Frost'; "People Answers," photographic Q&A; "Talkback," letters; "Creative Answers," creative Q&A applications; "Picture of the Month," competition; "Photo Clinic," column by Lee Frost; "Camera Answers," equipment Q&A; "On Test," "Buyers Guide," "Last Word," commentary column by Philip Thomas. (3-90).
TYPL:	"Kids Masterclass," "Instant Response," "Selling Yourself," "Shoot Patterns and Textures." (3-90).
SCHL:	Monthly, 85 pp.
SPAN:	Apr, 1989+
	ABSORBED
	--SLR Photography, ?
ISSN:	0956-8719

PHOTO-BEACON, THE

SUB:	"A journal devoted to photography in all its phases." (1889 - 1892).
SUB:	"An illustrated photographic journal."
PUBL:	Photo-Beacon Co., 409 Security Bldg., Chicago, IL.
DESC:	Like other photography magazines of the era, *Photo-Beacon* had its share of introductory information for the amateur; which included chemical formulas for the development of still photography. Unique in its variety and number of pictures, the specimen issue was printed on uncoated paper stock (Feb, 1903). Although the quality of photographic printing left much to be desired, it was indeed far more advanced than other photo publications of this time. Published in Chicago, a number of articles emanated from there, especially letters to the editor describing photo train trips to Seattle, Los Angeles, and Washington, DC; and how photo work differed in those locations. Printed on coated paper stock.
DEPT:	None.
TYPL:	"Stereo Work," "Brief Criticism of the Pictures in Chicago Salon," "Silvering Mirrors," "A Jurors Opinion of the Third Chicago Salon," "The Developer and its Constituents," "Advertising and Pictorial Photography, the Key to Success." (2-1903).
SCHL:	Monthly, 30 pp.
SPAN:	1887 - Jun, 1907//
	VARIES
	--1889? - 1892? as Beacon.
	MERGED WITH
	--American Amateur Photographer and Camera & Darkroom (to form) American Photography (ISSN: 0097-577x), Jun, 1907.
LC:	TR 1.P6

✣ PHOTO/DESIGN

SUB: "For the creative team."
PUBL: BPI Communications, a subsidiary of Affiliated Publications, Inc., 1515 Broadway, New York, NY 10036.
DESC: Lakewood Publications publisher, Jerry R. Landon, in the premiere issue for August/September, 1984 told readers, "...*Photo/Design* is the first publication to acknowledge you as a talented individual who combines creativity and technical skills to give birth to the ads, brochures, catalogs, magazines and hundreds of other forms of marketing messages that motivate, inspire and inform the world. Our primary purposes is, with this magazine, to promote photography as the most creative and versatile art option, and, at the same time, to recognize that no one person is responsible for success of an ad, annual report or catalog. That's why we refer to you as 'The Creative Team'." A later statement added, "*Photo/Design* magazine addresses the informational and inspirational needs of creative professionals who commission and produce photography for advertising, editorial and corporate communications. The unique editorial approach of *Photo/Design* acknowledges the relationship between the creative executive, art director, graphic designer and photographer and is devoted to elevating the professional stature of all. The common threads throughout *Photo/Design* are graphic excellence and the promotion of photography as the most versatile art option." Lush, creative, dynamic, and readily applicable, *Photo/Design* showcases the very best in imaginative photographic art and design; with a professional approach to advertising, promotion, television, film, and other visual media that require stunning imagry. A sampling of article titles include: "Photojournalism's Colorful Reality," "Putting the Client in the Forefront," "The Predicaments of Producing a Poster," "Visual Jewels for a Jewelry Campaign," "Movement in Still Life," "The Role of Hair and Makeup Artists," "Clients Who Steal Ideas from Photographers," and "Trends in Food Photography." Marketing directors, advertising executives, graphic artists, professional photographers and others will find *Photo/Design* valuable. Magazine format (8 ½ x 10 ⅞ inches / 215 x 275 mm), full color throughout, outstanding color printing on heavy coated paper stock.
DEPT: "FYI," 'National news, quotes and comments'; "Images + Ideas." (4-85). "Editor's Note," editorial column by Steve Pollock; "FYI Shows," column by Jonathan Barkey; "FYI Books," column by Jonathan Barkey; "Legal Eye," "Consultant," "View Finder," "Ideas and Images," fascinating showcase for imaginative photography, column by Jonathan Barkey; "Portfolio," showcase. (1/2-91).
TYPL: "Studio Sampler," "Estimate/Bid Roundtable," "Generra Project," "Concept: Calendar," "Vintage Slims." (4-85). "Full Frontal Exposure," "Liquid Light & Crystal Magic," "Anatomy of a Rush Job," "Creating the Team," "A Pixel Primer." (1/2-91).
SCHL: Bimonthly, 80 pp.
SPAN: Aug/Sep, 1984+

DD: 770
ISSN: 0888-5680

Photo Developments

? - Apr?, 1964?//
SEE: PHOTO MARKETING

✣ PHOTO DISTRICT NEWS

SUB: "The international publication for the professional photographer."
PUBL: Visions Unlimited, 49 East 21st St., New York, NY 10010.
DESC: "*Photo District News* is dedicated to bringing professional photographers all the information they need to stay on top." It is done with flair, enthusiasm, and a thoroughly professional approach. This large, tabloid-sized, monthly caters to the working professional, providing wonderful "how-to" stories of shooting assignments of everything from international location paradise hotels, to a Christmas table-top shoot; from news shots to promotionals. One quickly appreciates the quality editorial content. Publisher Jeffrey Roberts said in a promotional flyer: "Success in photography doesn't come easy. Along with a superabundance of talent, today's shooters need business savvy like never before. Each month, one photography publication dedicates itself to helping you achieve success--both creatively and financially. *Photo District News* is edited specifically to satisfy the informational needs of today's professional photographers. *PDN* contains information on: technical innovations; new techniques; how to negotiate photographic fees; the right business software; getting paid on time; protecting your rights; plus: interviews with top photographers. And because *PDN* is published in three regional editions, you also receive vital information about: your local market; suppliers and support services in your area; local news of professional organizations--and more." This is an noteworthy resource for general reading; and quality news/advice for the working photographer. For sampled issue of 1991: large tabloid stapled format, full color throughout on coated paper stock (10 ¾ x 14 ½ inches / 275 x 370 mm).
DEPT: "PDNews," photography news; "AD Spotlight," advertisement shoot; "Hot Shots," pictures; "Eye on Advertising," "Magazine Rack," serial photos; "The Right Stuff," creative photographic ideas; "Unusual Assignment." (4-88).
TYPL: "Working with Children: What You Should Know," "Covering the Cuban Prisoner Crisis," "How to Get-- and Keep--a Corporate Client," "Photog Sues Police Over Press Access," "Location Photographers: This is Your First Resort," "How to Improve Color Quality in Print," "Bourke-White Remembered." (4-88).
SCHL: Monthly [except for extra issue in May and Oct], 120 pp.
SPAN: Dec, 1984?+

EDITION
--Midwestern.
SPLIT INTO
--Photo District News (ISSN: 0883-766x) (along with) Photo District News [Eastern edition] (ISSN: 1045-8158), (and) Photo District News [Southern edition] (ISSN: 1048-0153), (and) Photo District News [Western edition] (ISSN: 1048-0145), ?
DD: 650 11
ISSN: 1048-0161

Photo-Era
May, 1898 - Dec, 1920//
SEE: PHOTO-ERA MAGAZINE

PHOTO-ERA MAGAZINE
SUB: "The American journal of photography." (May, 1898 - Dec, 1920).
SUB: "An illustrated monthly of photography and allied arts."
PUBL: American Federation of Photographic Societies, Wolfeboro, NH.
DESC: Designed for the advanced amateur and professional photographer, this periodical is filled with professional photographs; some to accompany articles, others for open reader criticism. Instructional articles are definitely for the advanced student of photography, detailing items such as retouching negatives, fine points of entering competitions, and new technical developments from abroad. Occasional technical articles with blueprints are printed for construction of home-made enlargers and other types of equipment.
DEPT: "Editorial," "Advanced Competition," monthly contest; "Beginners Competition," monthly contest; "The Crucible," 'a monthly digest of photo-technical facts'; "Our Contributing Critics," a unique section printing one photo, and inviting readers to criticize from standpoint of lighting, composition, exposure, etc.; "Our Illustrations," different section discussing large number of portraits and photos which are found throughout the periodical; "On the Groundglass," column by Wilfred French; "Answers to Queries," Q&A format on technical issues; "Events of the Month," 'Announcements of club and association meetings exhibitions and conventions solicited for publication'; "Book-Review," "London Letter," interesting British photo news column by Corrine Cadby and Will Cadby; "With the Trade," trade news. (10-20).
TYPL: "Hand-Camera with Ray-Filters," "Photograph Exhibitions in Germany," "Intensifying with Chromium," "Push-the-Button Retouching," "Sky and Air--Printing in of Clouds." (10-20).
SCHL: Monthly, 50 pp.
SPAN: May, 1898 - Mar, 1932//
VARIES
--May, 1898 - Dec, 1920 as Photo-Era.
ABSORBED
--American Journal of Photography, The, Dec, 1900.
ABSORBED BY
--American Photography (ISSN: 0097-577x), Apr, 1932.
LC: TR 1.P
ISSN: 0097-5885

✦ PHOTO LAB MANAGEMENT
SUB: "The magazine for photo lab management personnel."
PUBL: PLM Publishing, Inc., PO Box 1700, 1312 Lincoln Blvd., Santa Monica, CA 90406.
DESC: *Photo Lab Management* is a monthly publication designed for lab managers, personnel and technicians. Timely articles cover process chemistries, equipment maintenance and selection, industry developments and effective marketing and management techniques." This management serial covers the photo lab field very effectively, from calculating the current worth of a business, to the management of chemicals (both production and disposal), and, of course, to the technology which constitutes the heart of the industry. PLM Publishing has created a very useful publication for the photo lab professional. Magazine format (8 ½ x 11 inches / 215 x 280 mm), with color graphics.
DEPT: "Viewpoint," editorial; "Minilab Notebook," "In the News," "New Products." (8-85).
TYPL: "Quality Control Personnel: Interviewing and Hiring," "Securing a Bank Loan: The Battle Plan," "Evaluating Lab Resources," "Silver--Our Precious Commodity," "Photofinishing is Not a Commodity Item." (8-85).
SCHL: Bimonthly (Mar/Apr, 1979 - Nov/Dec, 1984); Monthly (Jan, 1985+), 55 pp.
SPAN: Mar/Apr, 1979+
LC: TR 287 .P46
DD: 771/.1
ISSN: 0164-4769

✦ PHOTO MARKETING
SUB: "New developments for the photographic dealer and photofinisher."
SUB: "Official publication of Photo Marketing Association International."
PUBL: Photo Marketing Association International, 3000 Picture Pl., Jackson, MI 49201.
DESC: Retail sales is a tough, competitive field, especially in the photo industry, where many retail stores have a "camera" department, and offer discount prices. *Photo Marketing* targets what is profitable at present, and predicts what may be profitable in the future. The "Ideas" department offers unique marketing concepts. One sampled issue presented a special section on diversification; whether photo retailers should contemplate adding video, telephone, fax, and computers to their sales arsenal. This is one serial (and the organization behind it) that works hard for the commercial success of its members. Magazine format (8 ¼ x 11 inches / 210 x 275 mm); spot color throughout.

DEPT:	"Ideas," new marketing concepts; "CES Report," what's new at the Consumer Electronics Show; "On the Market," equipment review; "Industry News," "Association News," of Photo Marketing Association International; "Comment." (2-85).
TYPL:	"Promotion Ploys Perk Up Business," "Winter CES Stages Video Format Fight," "PMA 85 Preview," "Blueprint for Diversification." (2-85).
SCHL:	Monthly, 55 pp.
SPAN:	Jun, 1924+ VARIES --? - ? as New Developments for the Photographic Dealer and Photo Finisher. --? - Apr?, 1964? as Photo Developments.
DD:	338
ISSN:	0031-8531
ABST:	--InfoBank --Predicasts

Photo-Miniature, The

Apr, 1899 - Jan, 1932//
SEE: NEW PHOTO-MINIATURE

Photo Playwright, The

Apr, 1912 - Dec, 1912//
SEE: MOTION PICTURE ALBUM

✦ PHOTO SCREEN

SUB:	"The magazine the stars read."
PUBL:	Sterling's Magazines, 355 Lexington Ave., New York, NY 10017.
DESC:	Celebrities of Hollywood film screen, network television, legitimate stage, and New York City are featured in *Photo Screen*, "the magazine the stars read." The emphasis is on the unusual: one sampled issue covered Jackie Onassis' visit to a plastic surgeon, ESP experiences, Dean Martin and marriage, Jack Nicholson, Elvis, Connie Francis, Michael Landon, Cher, Sonny, Lee Majors, and Lindsay Wagner: "I'm Just an Old-Fashioned Girl!" Advertisements include various remedies, clothing; and health and happiness items for home, marriage, and career. Editorial content published on newsprint; magazine format (8 1/8 x 10 7/8 inches / 205 x 275 mm).
DEPT:	"From the Editor," column by Marsha Daly; "TV & Movie Scoops," "Hollywood Insider," "Overheard in Hollywood," 'What the stars are saying -- unguarded moments when they didn't know we were there!'; "Daytime Hotline," "Hollywood Beauty Hints," "Sounds of the '70s," music review; "Tattle Tales," "Just Look at Them Now," "Manhattan Party Line." (11-76).
TYPL:	"Michael Landon: His Strange ESP Experience with His Daughter!," "Cher: Heartbroken Over Baby Switch! Hospital Blamed!," "Raped Star's Agony!: 'I Couldn't Have Sex with My Husband!," "Hollywood's Two Most Sensuous Couples: How Lee Majors and Farrah Give Love Lessons to Angie Dickinson and Burt!," "Elvis: He's Shocked! Pris and Burt Reynolds Reveal Baby Plans!" (11-76).
SCHL:	Monthly (Dec, 1965? - ?); Bimonthly (?+), 75 pp.
SPAN:	Dec, 1965+
ISSN:	0031-8566

✦ PHOTO TECHNIQUE INTERNATIONAL

SUB:	"A magazine in English, German and French for applied medium and large format photography."
SUB:	"The magazine for medium and large format photography."
SUB:	"The magazine of medium and large-format photography in colour and monochrome."
SUB:	"The German magazine of medium and large format photography."
PUBL:	Photo Technique International, Rupert-Mayer-Strasse 45, D-8000, Munich 70, Federal Republic of Germany.
DESC:	[*International Photo Technik*]: "*International Photo Technik (Grossbild Technik)* is the authentic Quarterly on large-format photography. It contains more full-page colour reproductions than any other photographic magazine. Each issue brings you competent answers to problems of top quality camera technique with particular emphasis on modern colour photography. *International Photo Technik* offers you expert advice on industrial, architectural, medical, advertising, sports, news, wild life, and other special fields of photography." It has wonderful large-format still photography that is applied to the commercial advertising, promotion and marketing fields. One sampled issue for 1960 had a half-dozen articles concerning the utilization of large-format visual work in the field of advertising, all with schematics and setup descriptions. For sampled issue of 1960: perfect-bound magazine format, black/white and full-color pages on coated paper stock, cover was full-color on heavy coated paper stock (9 x 11 1/4 inches / 230 x 285 mm).
DESC:	[*International Photo Technique*]: "*International Photo Technik* appears in German, English and French; and it is the largest and leading professional photographic magazine in several languages." This is a superbly produced magazine. Extremely thick, high-gloss paper is used throughout, and the reader will marvel both at the printing and the photographs. Information on photography in specialized areas is very thorough. A recent article on mushrooms, for instance, provided a list of equipment required for the photographic session; addressing problems with light, heat, and other elements which influence an effective, quality project. Well recommended. Sampled issue for 1960: perfect-bound magazine format, editorial and advertising content was mixture of black/white, spot color, and full-color printing, all on heavy coated paper stock (9 x 11 1/4 inches / 230 x 285 mm).

DEPT: "Photokina Novelties For Our Readers," new products; "Notes From the Editor," column by J. Giebelhausen. (winter-60). "Technical News," new product briefs. (#4-77).
TYPL: "Soft Focus and Colour Film," "With the Large Format 2000 Feet Below the Earth's Surface," "Multiple Printing and Enlarging," "Electronically Controlled Transparency Projection," "Champagne in Red Rock Canyon." (#4-60). "Architecture and Cityscape," "Hunting Mushrooms with a Camera," "Effective Presentation of Jewelry," "Technology and the Right Perspective." (#4-77).
SCHL: Quarterly, 75 pp.
SPAN: 1954?+
EDITION
--English.
VARIES
--1955 - 1959 as Grossbild-Technik.
--1960 - May, 1983 as International Photo Technik (ISSN: 0020-8280).
--Aug, 1983 - Nov, 1983 as International Photo Technique.
LC: TR 1 .I64
DD: 770/.5 19

PHOTODRAMATIST, THE

SUB: "A magazine for photoplay writers." (? - May, 1921).
SUB: "The magazine for writers."
SUB: "Official organ of the Screen Writer's Guild of the Authors' League of America (Jul, 1921 - Nov, 1921).
SUB: "The scenario writer's magazine." (Dec, 1921 - ?).
SUB: "Official organ of the Screen Writers' Guild." (Dec, 1921 - Jan, 1922).
PUBL: Photodramatist Publishing Co., I. W. Hellman Bldg., 124 West Fourth St., Los Angeles, CA.
DESC: With Hollywood firmly anchored as the "Movie Capitol of the World," there was probably no better place to publish a serial on screenwriting than Southern California in the late 1910s. *The Photodramatist* took advantage of the sheer number of writers who were living there at the time to publish a fascinating publication on screenplay writing. Within its 40-odd monthly pages were articles by leading playwrights of the day on plot development, studio needs, case stories, working with stars, receiving payment in full and other bits of wisdom. This was an agressive periodical, believing that screenwriting was a profession: it was no surprise that the Screen Writers' Guild made this its official publication. Indeed, a monthly feature, "The Guild Forum," provided a meeting place for Guild members. An interesting publication; line-drawing graphics of individual authors.
DEPT: "The Guild Forum," news of the Screen Writers' Guild; "In the Foreground," 'Being a department of brief chats on topics within the camera's range'; "Gossip Street," 'From Hollywood boulevard to Times Square'; "Comment from Student Writers," 'A monthly department to which students are invited to contribute'; "Photoplays in Review," "Questions Answered," 'Concerning the writing of photoplays'; "Little Hints to Screenwriters." (2-22).
TYPL: "The Screen Drama League," "'Action' in the Photoplay," "The Trend of Production," "Writing for the Producer," "The New Art in Motion Pictures," "Characterization in Screen Drama." (2-22).
SCHL: Monthly, 40 pp.
SPAN: May?, 1919 - Aug, 1923//
ABSORBED BY
--Story World and Photodramatist, The, Aug, 1923.
LC: PN 1993.P45

✤ PHOTOEDUCATION

SUB: "A newsletter for teachers of photography."
PUBL: Polaroid Corporation, 575 Technology Square-9P, Cambridge, MA 02139.
DESC: A well-designed, color publication that functions to inform, instruct, and encourage the pedagogical art and science sides of photography; articles explain how various photographic artists achieve expression in their work, new elements of technology, exhibitions sponsored by Polaroid, and the technique of professional photography. As would be expected, excellent care has been taken in the layout design, printing, and paper in this quarterly serial for "teachers of photography." For the sampled issue of 1990: stapled magazine format employing a versatile "loop" staple procedure which allows the magazine to be filed in a three-ring binder, full-color graphics throughout on coated paper stock (8 ½ x 11 inches / 215 x 280 mm).
DEPT: "Commentary," "Polaroid Traveling Exhibitions." (spring-90).
TYPL: "Artist Profile: Thomas Barrow: Material Evidence," "A Teacher's Notes: Making Color Separations with Polaroid Type 57 Film," "Direct Screen Photography of Electronic Images." (spring-90).
SCHL: Quarterly, 16 pp.
SPAN: Winter, 1983+
VARIES
--Winter, 1983 - Spring/Summer, 1988 as Polaroid Newsletter for Photographic Education, The.

✤ PHOTOGRAPHER'S FORUM

SUB: "Magazine for the emerging professional."
PUBL: Serbin Communications, Inc., 511 Olive St., Santa Barbara, CA 93101.
DESC: *Photographer's Forum* is dedicated to quality reproduction of photography in the United States and Canada. Each issue strives to facillitate communication and publication experience among young photographers." Toward those goals, *Photographer's Forum* provides interviews with established professional photographers, and a quality forum for the display of photographic work by young photographers. The publication is associated with three noteworthy organizations: the Society for Photographic Education; the National Photography Instructors Association;

and the Western Publications Association. Articles are unique for their explanatory-style of describing events leading up to showcased pictures, the photographer's objective, and the resulting product. Photographs are placed one or two to a page, with full title, and geographic location signified. This is a unique, and valuable publication; instructional and informative about the process of becoming a professional photographer. For the sampled issues of 1981 and 1991: stapled magazine format; editorial content being a mixture of black/white and full-color graphics pages on coated paper stock, with advertising (8 ¼ x 10 ¾ inches / 210 x 275 mm).

- DEPT: "Noted," "Letters," "Book Review," column by James Kaufmann; "Darkroom," "Calendar," "Interview." (5-81). "Noted," "Book Review," column by James Kaufman; "Calendar." (11-91).
- TYPL: "Infrared Photography," "School Profile: Yale University," "Historical: Russell Lee, Photographic Communicator," "Darkroom: Columbia College," "Conversation with Jay Maisel." (5-81). "Craig Lovell," "Greg Kraus," "James Natchwey," "Galen Rowell," "11th Annual Spring Contest Winners." (11-91).
- SCHL: Quarterly, 60 pp.
- SPAN: Nov, 1978+
    VARIES
    --Nov, 1978 - ?, 1978 as Student Forum (ISSN: 0148-589x).
- ISSN: 0194-5467

PHOTOGRAPHER'S FRIEND, THE

- SUB: "A practical, independent magazine, devoted to the photographic art."
- SUB: "A compendium of valuable formulas and general information relating to the art, with a reduced price list of photographic materials and stereoscopic goods." (Oct, 1872).
- PUBL: Richard Walzl, Baltimore, MD.
- DESC: Richard Walzl was a manufacturer of photographic chemicals, and determined that there was no better way to promote the sale and use of his product than with a serial. Both the amateur and the commercial photographer was well served by this serious journal, with articles devoted to camera/darkroom technique, and the continuing philosophical discussion of how the general public might come to regard photography as art. Commercial photographers also received *The Commercial Photographic News*, a supplement designed to provide additional professional news, and especially Walzl's chemical catalogue. Each issue contained at least one fine photographic print mounted on heavy cardboard. In October, 1872 publisher Walzl decided to enlarge this serial and moved to a bimonthly schedule, and in so doing dropped publication of his supplement. This move was preceeded by an unnumbered issue called "*The Photographer's Friend*; a compendium of valuable formulas and general information relating to the art, with a reduced price list of photographic materials and stereoscopic goods." Small format.
- SCHL: Quarterly (Jan, 1871 - Oct, 1872); Bimonthly (Nov?, 1872+), 30 pp.
- SPAN: Jan, 1871 - Nov, 1874//
    ABSORBED BY
    --Philadelphia Photographer, The, 1875.
    WITH SUPPLEMENT
    --Commercial Photographic News, The, Jan, 1872 - Oct, 1872.

✦ PHOTOGRAPHER'S MARKET NEWSLETTER

- SUB: "By the editors of Photographer's Market."
- PUBL: F&W Publishing Co., 9933 Alliance Rd., Cincinnati, OH 45242.
- DESC: In the premiere issue of 1981, Editor Robert D. Lutz told readers, "*Photographer's Market Newsletter* (*PMN* for short), like our annual directory, *Photographer's Market*, has been created to serve those photographers who are eager to join in the adventure of selling their work. ... We have something in common, you and I. Photography means something to us. It's more than an album full of snapshots or a bag full of fancy hardware. It's more than just taking good pictures. Photography is much more than that. ... So what does *Photographer's Market Newsletter* have to do with all of this? It's a meeting ground, a focal point, a common voice for those photographers for whom snapping pix isn't enough. We're here to help you make your photography mean something, to make it worthwhile, to share your vision with the world, and to make your photography as rewarding as it is meaningful. In short, to help you sell your work." Designed for the commercial photographer, "Photographer's Market Newsletter" keeps readers informed about commercial opportunities; including books, galleries, paper products, periodicals and other potential commercial work. Edito Lutz: "How can *PMN* help you as you enter and explore the world of freelance photography? By acting as a kind of 'town hall' where photographers from all over can come to learn new skills and share their experiences with their peers. By bringing you the firsthand accounts of some of the world's top-selling photographers. But most of all, by giving you the markets--the people and organizations who need and use photography to communicate with the world. And pay for it." For the sampled issues of 1981: black ink with spot-blue color on masthead printed on uncoated paper. The sampled issues for 1986 were all black ink on uncoated stock. Both sampled issues were stapled, newsletter format (8 ½ x 11 inches / 215 x 280 mm).
- DEPT: "Wide Angle," 'Fresh perspectives on the world of freelance photo marketing'; "Photo Market Update," 'The latest developments and changes in the photography marketplace'; "Workshops," upcoping; "Changes," photographic buyer update; "View-

finder," profile. (11-81). "The Scorecard," changes in the photographic marketplace; "Photo Market Update." (9-84)
TYPL: "Paper Products," "Sold," "Stock Photo Agencies," "Tallon: Shooting and Selling Wildlife Photography." (11-81). "Cashing in on Free Publicity," "New Directions in Photo Marketing." (9-84).
SCHL: Monthly, 8 pp.
SPAN: Nov, 1982+
ISSN: 0278-2790

Photographic Applications in Science and Technology

Winter, 1966/1967 - Spring, 1968//
(ISSN: 0031-871x)
SEE: FUNCTIONAL PHOTOGRAPHY

Photographic Applications in Science, Technology and Medicine

Summer, 1968 - Jul, 1975//
(ISSN: 0098-8227)
SEE: FUNCTIONAL PHOTOGRAPHY

Photographic Business and Product News

Jan, 1968 - Jun?, 1975//
SEE: STUDIO PHOTOGRAPHY

Photographic Journal

Jan, 1859 - Dec, 1859//
SEE: BRITISH JOURNAL OF PHOTOGRAPHY

✧ PHOTOGRAPHIC PROCESSING

PUBL: PTN Publishing 210 Crossways Park Drive, Woodbury, NY 11797.
DESC: This publication is targeted to professional processors and photofinishing suppliers in North America, and provides details on the business, regulation, marketing, operation, and profit elements which make up the photographic processing field. Articles provide a dual emphasis on both new and improved technology as well as on business concepts in marketing and management. For sampled issue of 1989: stapled magazine format on coated paper stock, with a mixture of black/white, spot color, and full color pages throughout (8 x 10 ¾ inches / 200 x 275 mm).
DEPT: "News Highlights," "New Products," "People in the News," "On the Business Side," column by Martin Hershenson; "The Washington Scene," column by Peter Nagan; "In the Observation Post," column by Duane Gibbons; "Bottom Line," column by Allen Fishman. (11-89).
TYPL: "The Serious Amateur and You," "Drugs and Photos Can Live Together; The Law and Electronic Imaging," "Dameron: A Lab of Many Talents," "Light Valve Technology and Transparencies," "Protection Through Credit Insurance." (11-89).
SCHL: Bimonthly (? - Nov, 1977); Nine issues per year (? - Nov/Dec, 1978); Monthly (Jan, 1979+), 55 pp.
SPAN: 1964+
ISSN: 0031-8744

Photographic Product News

196u - Dec?, 1967?//
SEE: STUDIO PHOTOGRAPHY

Photographic Quarterly

Fall, 1971 - Winter, 1971//
SEE: PETERSEN'S PHOTOGRAPHIC

PHOTOGRAPHIC TIMES, THE

SUB: "An illustrated monthly magazine." (1895 - Apr, 1902).
SUB: "An illustrated monthly magazine devoted to the interests of artistic and scientific photography."
DESC: This early photography magazine (first issue: 1869), serves several purposes: to provide a forum for artistic photographic work; keep professional and amateur photographers apprised of new technical patents and developments; and provide a discussion forum for new chemical mixtures and equipment. As expected, the periodical contains a number of photographic illustrations, improving in quality and number as half tone printing processes improved. Issues in 1899 always carried one quality artistic photograph with two-color effect for the reader. As printing quality was improved this feature was dropped, and the magazine went from standard page to small format size.
DEPT: None. (9-15).
TYPL: "An Experience in Photographing War Machinery," "Kromskop Color Photography," "Some Micro-Photographic Studies in the Art of Recording and Reproducing Sounds," (4-1899); "The Camera in Treeland," "Another Method for Developing and Printing for the Amateur," "Harbor Subjects," "Some Motion Picture Entertainments as a Source of Pleasure and Profit." (9-15).
SCHL: Monthly (1871 - 1884?); Weekly (1885 - 1894); Monthly (1895 - 1915); 40 pp.
SPAN: Jan, 1871 - Dec, 1915//
VARIES
--1871 - 1880 as Photographic Times, The.
--1881 - 1894 as Photographic Times and American Photographer, The.
--1895 - Apr, 1902 as Photographic Times, The.

--May, 1902 - Dec, 1904 as Photographic Times-Bulletin, The.
ABSORBED
--Anthony's Photographic Bulletin, May, 1902.
--American Photographer, The, Feb, 1913.
ABSORBED BY
--Popular Photography [Boston],.
LC: TR 1.P

Photographic Times, The
1871 - 1880//
SEE: PHOTOGRAPHIC TIMES, THE

Photographic Times, The
1895 - Apr, 1902//
SEE: PHOTOGRAPHIC TIMES, THE

Photographic Times and American Photographer, The
1881 - 1894//
SEE: PHOTOGRAPHIC TIMES, THE

Photographic Times-Bulletin, The
May, 1902 - Dec, 1904//
SEE: PHOTOGRAPHIC TIMES, THE

✣ PHOTOGRAPHY
PUBL: Argus Specialist Publications, Argus House, Boundary Way, Hemel Hempstead HP2 7ST, England.
DESC: In this monthly British publication, a delight for the eyes, and a banquet for the intellect; one will not find pages of photo vendor/mailorder house advertisements but a place where the pictures and the photographers share equal attention. An innovative layout design adds to the reader's pleasure as each page brings new feelings, insight, and knowledge. Interestingly, all feature articles are listed under monthly special departmental headings. In one sampled issue, an article on Buddhism was headed by the departmental title, "Assignment;" a black/white portfolio of Cleveland, Ohio was under the special department title of "Profile;" and a 40th anniversary Magnum Agency article was found under "Review." A class act in stapled magazine format (for the sampled issue of 1990), with black/white and color graphics pages, including cover all on coated paper stock (8 ¼ x 11 ¾ inches / 210 x 300 mm).
DEPT: "Newsdesk," news of exhibitions; "Assignment," "Profile," "Review," "Mugshot," "Interview," "Portfolio," "Monitor," 'Your letters, our replies'. (3-90).
TYPL: "Living Buddhism," "A Town Called Cleveland," "In Our Time," "Arnold Genthe." (3-90).
SCHL: Monthly, 70 pp.

SPAN: Oct, 1965+
FROM MERGER OF
--Photography, (and) Colour Photography, (and) 35mm Photography, (and) Good Photography.
VARIES
--Oct, 1965 - Jul?, 1983 as Photography (ISSN: 0031-8809).
--Aug, 1983 - Sep, 1986? as 35mm Photography (ISSN: 0265-7198).
LC: TR 1.P88119
DD: 770
ISSN: 0950-2009

Photography
Oct, 1965 - Jul?, 1983//
(ISSN: 0031-8809)
SEE: PHOTOGRAPHY

Photography
Jan, 1952 - May, 1952//
SEE: POPULAR PHOTOGRAPHY

Photography
Aug, 1952 - Jan, 1955//
SEE: POPULAR PHOTOGRAPHY

Photography Magazine
Jun, 1952 - Jul, 1952//
SEE: POPULAR PHOTOGRAPHY

✣ PHOTOLETTER
SUB: "Serving the nations photo editors & photo illustrators."
SUB: "The newsletter serving the nation's photo editors and photo illustrators."
PUBL: Photo Source International, Osceola, WI 54020.
DESC: This brief, four-page biweekly newletter informs photo editors and illustrators of new photo resources available for sale. Issues since the premiere for 1976 have been, and continue to be typewritten, one-column style. Articles describe current needs and wants of photo editors of newspapers, magazines, school textbooks, advertising agencies, and other print media requiring graphic illustration. Each article supplies information according to specific illustrations desired, submission format and deadline, payment schedule, address, telephone number, and contact person. One sample issue had the following categories: personalities, government, thoroughbreds, children, Sunday School, native missionaries, Wisconsin, greenhouse gardening, and fishing. Each issue also contains newsbriefs concerning photo contests and other opportunities to sell photographic imagry. The sampled

issues for 1976 were stapled, single-sheet newsletter, three-hole punched; black ink on tinted uncoated paper; no advertising. For the sampled issues of 1988 through 1989: black ink on tinted uncoated beige stock with green spot-color ink. The format changed with the April 1, 1989 issue to black ink on uncoated white paper stock; maintaining the single-sheet, three-hole punched format. The dimensions of all issues (8 ½ x 11 inches / 215 x 280 mm).
DEPT: None. (10-76).
TYPL: "How's Your Supply of 'People' Pictures?," "Speaking of Time." (10-76).
SCHL: Twenty-two issues per year (except Aug 1, Jan 1), 4 pp.
SPAN: 1976+
ISSN: 0190-1400

Photolith
1950 - May, 1975//
(ISSN: 0031-8825)
SEE: PHOTOLITH, SCM

✤ PHOTOLITH, SCM
SUB: "The national magazine for school yearbooks staffs."
SUB: "The journal for scholastic media."
PUBL: National School Yearbook-Newspaper Association, Department of Mass Communications, Texas Tech University, P.O. Box 4080, Lubbock, TX 79409.
DESC: *Photolith ScM* provides "trade" information for those engaged in the production of high school newspapers and yearbooks; and functions to reproduce school publications, with a background on particular layouts, articles and stories. Other articles teach the high school journalism student writing, and aim to provide motivation on producing a quality newspaper or yearbook. Numerous photos of rather poor reproductive quality.
DEPT: "Directions," editorial; "Dates 'n Data," newsbriefs; "Authors," photos and biographies of authors.
TYPL: "Overcoming the Universal Problems Facing the new Writer," "The Seven Sins of the Writer as Rhetorical Reprobate," "Tinkering Around with High school Journalism." (2-77).
SCHL: Monthly, [except Jun - Aug], 25 pp.
SPAN: 1950+
VARIES
--1950 - May, 1975 as Photolith (ISSN: 0031-8825).

✤ PHOTOMETHODS
PUBL: Lakewood Publications, Inc., One Park Ave., New York, NY 10016.
DESC: "*Photomethods* serves industry and business; science, research, medical, education, institutions, consultants, libraries, government and military; and independent photo servies." In the late 1970s, primary emphasis was still photography, with special reports on motion picture and video activities. *Photomethods* currently is concerned almost exclusively with professional photography, and is obligatory reading for the professional. For the sampled issues of 1977: stapled, magazine format; black in on coated paper; cover comprised of full-color graphics on coated stock; advertising (8 x 11 inches / 205 x 280 mm).
DEPT: "Imaging Update," newsbriefs; "Lights and Lighting," feature; "Scientific Instrumentation," how to set up and shoot under varying circumstances; "Video Methods," feature; "In Process," inside the darkroom; "Sign and Sound," the AV viewpoint; "New Products." (2-78). "Editorial," "Scan Lines," electronic cinematography; "Images and Answers," "Tech Talk," "Perspectives," "Lighting Gallery," "Between Shot," "Supply Line," literature; "New Products." (4-88).
TYPL: "Effective Visual Presentation of Engineering Proposals," "Some Tips on Videotape Editing," "Roman Polanski on Wide Angles and Long Shots," "Photomicrography of Colorless Objects in Color." (2-78). "Dedicated Flash: A Professional Tool?," "The HDF Macro System," "Kodak's Technet System," "Beating the Deadbeats." (4-88).
SCHL: Monthly, 70 pp.
SPAN: 1958+
VARIES
--Jan, 1958 - Aug, 1974 as PMI, Photo Methods for Industry (ISSN: 0030-8110).
LC: TR 1.P2
DD: 770
ISSN: 0146-0153
ABST: --Art and Archaeology Technical Abstracts (ISSN: 0004-2994)
--Biological Abstracts (ISSN: 0006-3169)
--Predicasts

PHOTOPLAY
SUB: "Favorite of America's 'first million' movie-goers for thirty-six years."
PUBL: Macfadden-Bartell Corporation, 205 E. 42nd St., New York, NY 10017.
DESC: "For over fifty years, *Photoplay* magazine has focused on the world of entertainment and the stars and personalities that make up this fascinating world. Every month *Photoplay* features behind-the-scenes stories, interviews, timely news and photographs of the most popular performers from Hollywood, TV, and recording studios. From stories about long-time favorites to articles on upcoming starlets, *Photoplay* offers the most comprehensive and exclusive reporting available in a movie magazine today. In *Photoplay* you'll meet such stars as Liz Taylor, Connie Stevens, Troy Donahue, Natalie Wood, Warren Beatty, and Debbie Reynolds. For drama, excitement and entertainment at its best, *Photoplay*, the first and finest publication in its field." Although librarians indicate a June, 1946 startup date for this particular series, there are indications that this is a continuing publication all the way back to 1931, and with the same successful formula;

to provide readers with what they want to know about their favorite film, radio and television stars. Past and present issues are quite similar, with printing technology and paper being the primary variables. Issues for 1948 and 1961 published on newsprint. For 1961 sampled issue: (8 ½ x 10 ¾ inches / 215 x 275 mm). For sampled issue of 1976: perfect-bound magazine format, editorial content was black and spot-color ink on uncoated paper stock, with advertising content often in full-color (along with cover) on coated paper stock (8 ⅛ x 10 ⅞ inches / 205 x 275 mm).
DEPT: "What Should I Do?," 'Your problems answered' column by Claudette Colbert; "Inside Stuff," Hollywood gossip column by Cal York; "Beauty Spots," "Shadow Stage," film reviews; "Hollywood Fashion Vane," "Photoplay Fashions," full page color fashion photos; "Laughing Stock," comedy column by Erskine Johnson. (12-48). "Remember You Read It First in Photoplay," '4-page gossip section' column by Cal York; "Sidney Sounds Off," gossip column by Sidney Skolsky; "Under Hedda's Hat," gossip column by Hedda Hopper; "Readers Inc.," letters and pen pals; "Go Out to a Movie," guide; "Becoming Attractions," product review; "Your Monthly Ballot," the readers vote; "Needlework," patterns. (11-61). "Remember! You Read It First in Photoplay," personality column by Cal York; "Photoplay in Focus," editorial column by Lynne Dorsey; "Parent & Child," celebrity column; "It Happened This Way," personality column by John J. Miller; "Star-Trekking," 'Facts and Fotos' column by Tony Rizzo; "What's Cooking," celebrity meals; "Just Released," motion picture and book reviews. (6-76).
TYPL: "The Truth About Dope in Hollywood," "New Life, New Love--Greer Garson," "Swing Your Partner as the Sunny Tuftses' Barndance," "Home is the Sailor--Errol Flynn." (12-48). "They Tried to Murder Eddie," "Why I'm Afraid to Have Another Baby," "Troy Beats Up Lili Kardell!," "The Tragedy that Haunts Hollywood," "Is This Mrs. Elvis Presley?" (11-61). "Top Stars Pick Their Favorite Stars," "Lindsay Wagner: The 40 Days That Changed Her Life," "Pat Boone: Is He the New Billy Graham?," "Gail Fisher: Sun and Fun South of the Border," "Dottie West: Finding Love With a Younger Man." (6-76).
SCHL: Monthly, 50 pp.
SPAN: Jun, 1946 - Aug, 1977//
MERGED WITH
--TV Mirror (to form) Photoplay With TV Mirror (ISSN: 0163-5115).
LC: PN 1993.P
ISSN: 0031-885x

Photoplay
Jan, 1986 - Mar, 1989//
SEE: FILM MONTHLY

Photoplay
Jun, 1944 - ?, 1946//
SEE: PHOTOPLAY COMBINED WITH MOVIE MIRROR

PHOTOPLAY COMBINED WITH MOVIE MIRROR
SUB: "Two great magazines for the price of one."
PUBL: Macfadden Publications, Chanin Building, 122 East 42nd St., New York, NY.
DESC: It only lasted five years, but what a vibrant period of glamour, and excitement in motion picture product existed during that turbulent war-torn period of Hollywood history! This magazine was filled with a significant amount of editorial material concerning the motion picture personalities of that era, showcasing an interesting mixture of new film promotions, home lifestyles and public appearances. The sampled issue for 1941 included the likes of Ann Rutherford, Deanna Durbin, Myran Loy, Rosalind Russell, Clark Gable, Linda Darnell, Ellen Drew, Miriam Hopkins, Olivia de Havilland, Fred MacMurray, Betty Grable, Jackie Cooper, Helen Parrish, Gene Tierney, Jane Russell, Bonita Granville, Carole Lombard, Ann Sheridan, Claudette Colbert, Hedy Lamarr and James Stewart. Articles ranged from how to speak like a movie star to the transformation of "Tobacco Road" from Broadway to motion pictures; from an article on how to do the tango to how Ellen Drew was able to break into the movies. *Photoplay Combined with Movie Mirror* was thorough in its coverage. Articles from the sampled issue included, "The Best Figure in Hollywood" (Betty Grable got top honors just edging out Claudette Colbert); and a complete informational chart on everything from glove size down to shoe size for ten major stars. New York City Broadway productions were profiled when they were in the process of transferring to the silver screen. Perfect-bound magazine format, editorial content and cover is mixture of black/white, spot color, and full-color on coated paper stock (8 ½ x 11 ¼ inches / 215 x 285 mm).
DEPT: "Frame for Fame," full-color portraits of the stars; "Close Ups and Long Shots," motion picture star column by Ruth Waterbury; "The Shadow Stage," 'Reviewing movies of the month - A reliable guide to recent pictures'; "Inside Stuff," movie personalities column by Cal York; "Speak for Yourself," letters; "Spring Fashions," column by Gwenn Walters; "Photoplay-Movie Mirror Dancing School," how-to column by Howard Sharpe; "It's All in Your Name," column by Marian Quinn; "Movie Mirror Junior," information for the younger set; "Smart Headwork," beauty column by Gloria Mack; "Casts of Current Pictures," detailed listing of current fare. (4-41).
TYPL: "To Three Girls Facing Life," "Brenda Defies the Rule," "Gable--on the Spot," "The Best Figure in Hollywood," "The Boy Linda Darnell Loves." (4-41).
SCHL: Monthly, 125 pp.
SPAN: Jan, 1941 - May, 1946//

FROM MERGER OF
--Photoplay (ISSN: 0732-538x) (and) Movie Mirror.
VARIES
--Jun, 1944 - ?, 1946 as Photoplay.
SPLIT INTO
--Photoplay (ISSN: 0031-885x) (and) Movie Mirror (ISSN: 0027-271x).
ISSN: 0733-2734

Photoplay Movies & Video
Jan, 1950? - Dec, 1985?//
SEE: FILM MONTHLY

PHOTOPLAY STUDIES
SUB: "A magazine devoted to photoplay appreciation."
PUBL: Educational and Recreational Guides, Inc., 1501 Broadway, New York, NY.
DESC: *Photoplay Studies* was a study guide to great (and some not so great) literature that had been transformed to motion pictures. Early issues included lengthy synopses, along with suggestions for classroom projects, essays, discussion, and suggested reading lists. The journal format gave way to a magazine-sized format, where production pictures dominated each four to six-page issue. This remains an interesting promotional piece for the motion picture industry. Magazine format; numerous production stills.
DEPT: None.
TYPL: One motion picture per issue.
SCHL: Monthly, 4 pp.
SPAN: Apr, 1935 - 1940//
ABSORBED BY
--Group Discussion Guide, 1940.
LC: PN 1993.P53
DD: 792

✦ PHOTOPRO
SUB: "The magazine for working professionals."
PUBL: PhotoPro of Titusville, Inc., 5211 South Washington Ave., Titusville, FL 32780.
DESC: A promotional advertisement calls "...*PhotoPro* the bimonthly magazine written by professional photographers for professional photographers. *PhotoPro* covers the technical, practical and unusual elements of photography to benefit the working professional. Six times a year *PhotoPro* publishes tips, techniques and advice to help the professional become more successful." This is backed up by a wide variety of letters by reader-subscribers who attest to the excellence of the publication, including comments such as: "Bravo, for a fine publication;" "My congratulations to the editors and staff of *PhotoPro* for consistently maintaining the highest standards of professionalism;" and "The magazine looks terrific and the writing is extremely good. And that's a rare thing. What is even rarer is a photographic magazine designed for adults." Topics range from commercial photography, fine art, portrait, corporate, darkroom, to marketing/sales applications of the art and technique of photography. Editor David Brooks successfully walks a thin line in pleasing a most vocal and demanding subscriber audience. Pictures are reproduced with care. Editorial content is an interesting mixture of business and pleasure, artistic and commercial elements, and technology and beauty associated with photography. This is a wonderful resource for photographic professionals of varying interest. For the sampled issue of 1990: full-color and black/white pages throughout in perfect-bound magazine format, extensive advertising for products of importance to the photographic trade, on coated paper stock (8 ⅛ x 10 ⅞ inches / 205 x 275 mm).
DEPT: "Letters," "New Products," "Business," column by Loyd Searle; "Studio Casebook," column by Michael Chiusano and Tony L. Corbell; "Software Review," column by Rory Lyaght; "Photographer's Assistant," column by Dennis Miller; "Photojournalism," column by John Durniak; "Darkroom & Lab," column by James N. Burke; "40th Frame," column by Jim Elder; "Controversy," column by John Durniak; "PhotoPro Data," 'useful optical information from standard reference sources'. (winter-90).
TYPL: "Plumbing for the Studio Darkroom," "Rick Bostick Goes Back to Basics for Special Effects," "On Location: Day in the Life Series," "How to Build a Lightstand Rollaway," "Corporate Identity: The Key to Effective Promotions." (winter-90).
SCHL: Quarterly (spring, 1990 - winter, 1990); Bimonthly (Jan/Feb, 1991+), 90 pp.
SPAN: Spring, 1990+
DD: 770
ISSN: 1049-8974

✦ PHOTOSTAR
PUBL: Rockafeller, Issacs & Lambert, Inc., 2395 SW College Rd., Ocala, FL 32675.
DESC: This new magazine is photographs of the stars at work and at play. Editorial content was minimal in the premiere issue for October/November, 1990, with an even mixture of black/white and color pages throughout. A year-by-year picture profile of Madonna from 1983 to 1990 was presented. Other stars covered in the first issue were Tom Cruise, New Kids on the Block, Cher, Milli Vanilli, Richard Grieco, Patrick Swayze, and Johnny Depp. Magazine format (8 ⅜ x 10 ⅞ inches / 210 x 275 mm); color and black/white editorial graphics; no advertising.
DEPT: None. (10/11-90).
TYPL: "Madonna, Breathless Mahoney in 'Dick Tracy'," "Patrick Swayze, Dream Machine," "Paula Abdul, Hurricane Force," "Tom Cruise, Top Gun on Wheels," "Janet Jackson, RN/1814." (10/11-90).
SCHL: Bimonthly, 70 pp.
SPAN: Oct/Nov, 1990+

✣ PIC

SUB: "The only magazine for image-makers and their subjects."
SUB: "People in Camera."
PUBL: PIC International Promotions, Ltd., Lingley House, Commissioners Rd, Strood, Rochester, Kent ME2 4EU, England.
DESC: *People in Camera*, or *PIC*, is a photographic periodical of world-class stature: vibrant, full-color photographs, interesting profiles of professional photographers, and authoritative articles on technique and technology are present in a printing/layout design that makes each issue a joy to read. There is a sense of excitement which does not allow the discussions of new cameras, film stock, and other consumer items to detract from its primary function; the presentation of intimate, conversational interviews with photographers; the philosophies and thoughts that interest, motivate, and capture the imaginations of these professionals. Color separations and printing are outstanding, making this an excellent resource for the professional photographer. For the sampled issue of 1990: stapled magazine format with stunning full-color pages throughout and full-color cover, all on heavy coated paper stock (8 1/4 x 11 3/4 inches / 210 x 295 mm).
DEPT: "Focal Point," equipment review column by Chris Lees; "Books," reviews column by Dave Saunders; "Amateur Eight," 'Each month, PIC publishes eight photographs by amateur photographers'; "Lighting School," column by Laurie Haynes; "PiXword," photographic crossword puzzle; "Ask a Pro," Q&A column by Dave Saunders. (3-90).
TYPL: "Doug Marke, the View From Over There," "The Amish of Minnesota," "Edward Parker, Expedition Photographer," "Robert Quinn, Life's Meant to be Enjoyed." (3-90).
ISSN: 0956-2281

PIC

SUB: "Three magazines in one covering the entire field of entertainment."
SUB: "Sport, Broadway, Hollywood."
PUBL: Street & Smith Publications, Inc., 79 Seventh Ave., New York, NY.
DESC: *PIC* covers the three distinct sections of "Hollywood," "Broadway," and "Sports," each with its own internal, distinctive "covers." *PIC* stood for picture, and the vast majority of each issue was devoted to graphics covering popular events in the three subject areas. One sampled issue for July, 1939 showed how costume designers worked behind the scenes for major Hollywood films. Another article showed motion picture frames of Little Egypt, Lillian Russell, the Prince of Wales, the San Francisco Earthquake, Enrico Caruso, and the formation of United Artists. In the Broadway section for the same sampled 1939 issue was a section showing the "Crystal Palace" at the New York Worlds Fair and the stage acts playing there. Another article detailed the artistic craft of creating masks for Broadway and Hollywood productions. A third Broadway article showed the back-stage activities of the Billy Rose Aquacade at the New York World's Fair, starring Johnny Weissmuller and Eleanor Holm. This was a general-audience publication, with plenty of pictures, little text, and surprisingly little advertising. Stapled magazine format, black/white editorial content with some spot color, cover in full cover, all on coated paper stock (10 1/4 x 13 5/8 inches / 260 x 345 mm).
DEPT: "Speak Up," letters to the editor; "What are They Doing Now?," locating the stars; "You Asked For It," reader's picture requests; "Stellargram," horoscope for specific athletes; "Fortnightly Reading," horoscope; "The Reader's Camera Clicks," event photos submitted by readers; "The 'Pic' Album of Notorious American Murders," photos and more. (7-11-39).
TYPL: "Jean Parker Designs and Models for Athena Parker and Yolanda," "The Screen's Greatest Actress," "Billy Rose Aquacade Smash Hit of the Fair," "G-Dog Gets His Man," "Up From Paradise." (7-11-39).
SCHL: Biweekly, 50 pp.
SPAN: Jul 11, 1934 - ?//

PICTURE PLAY MAGAZINE

PUBL: Street & Smith Publications, Inc., 79 - 89 Seventh Ave., New York, NY.
DESC: With an editorial eye dedicated to the American public's ever-increasing interest in the products, producers, and stars of Hollywood, it is little wonder that *Picture Play Magazine* by Street & Smith dominated American newstands for a number of decades. Articles were inquiring and bold in examining the denizens of Hollywood. In the sampled issue for 1931, articles included a discussion of mortality among the younger screen stars, how the stars react to seeing critiques in print, where the fashionable shop for fashions, and there was an interesting piece debating the merits of "home-grown versus foreign sheiks." Each issue's frontispiece showcased a new film release. In the sampled issue were Edmund Lowe, Warner Baxter and Conchita Montenegro in "The Cisco Kid." A departmental feature found in most issues was "Art Gallery," full-page rotogravure pictures of stars such as Sylvia Sidney, Anita Page, Lois Moran, Edmund Lowe, Phillips Holmes, Miriam Hopkins, Ann Harding, Janet Gaynor and James Dunn. Also of note was the departmental feature, "They Say in New York," subtitled, "Spicy comment about the stars and films," which reviewed Broadway theatre, and Hollywood stars who made New York City their second homes. This was a view through the looking-glass of Hollywood. For the sampled issue of 1931: stapled magazine format, editorial content was primarily black ink, with duotone green and duotone brown pictures of stars throughout publication all on coated paper stock. Cover was full-color on coated paper stock (8 3/8 x 11 1/2 inches / 215 x 290 mm).
DEPT: "What the Fans Think," letters section 'Wherein our readers express opinions good and bad'; "Information, Please," 'Careful answers to questions about the

stars and films' column by Oracle; "They Say in New York," 'Spicy comment about stars in New York' column by Karen Hollis; "Art Gallery," full-page rotogravure portraits of selected stars; "Hollywood High Lights," 'Peaks of interest in news of the studios' column by Edwin Schallert and Elza Schallert; "The Screen in Review," 'Checking off the new films for what they are worth' column by Norbert Lusk; "Our Private Wire," 'Special correspondence from inside the movie colony'; "Previews," 'A look at future films'. (12-31).
TYPL: "Clark Gable's Story," "The Good Die Young," "Home Sheiks Versus Foreign," "Do Writers Dare Tell the Truth?," "Let's Go Shopping." (12-31).
SCHL: Weekly (Apr, 1915 - Nov, 1915); Semimonthly (Dec, 1915 - Mar, 1916); Monthly (Apr, 1916+), 80 pp.
SPAN: Apr 10, 1915 - ?//
VARIES
--Apr, 1915 - Nov, 1915 as Picture-Play Weekly.
LC: PN 1993.P6

Picture-Play Weekly
Apr, 1915 - Nov, 1915//
SEE: PICTURE PLAY MAGAZINE

PICTURE REPORTS
SUB: "The voice of the box office."
PUBL: Picture Reports, 6303 Yucca St., Hollywood, CA.
DESC: This short, eight-page tabloid functioned to report on new motion picture releases. With few illustrations or articles, it primarily published film reviews for theatre management consideration.
DEPT: "This Industry," commentary column by Frank Pope; "New York Highlights," newsbriefs; "Previewed," largest section of periodical; "Current Releases," box office business on A products; "Opening Performance Chart," graph detailing first run successes; "Current Releases," number of theater showing B product; "New York Reviews," reprints of New York newspaper film critics reports.
TYPL: "U.A. Pact Up for Revision," "Originals Dominate in Year's Story Buys," "Warners 'Brother Rat' does 41% Over Average Business." (11-14-38).
SCHL: Weekly, 8 pp.
SPAN: ? - ?//
LC: PN 1993.P

✤ PICTURES MAGAZINE, THE
SUB: "Published every week."
PUBL: Metro Pictures Magazine, 1476 Broadway, New York, NY.
DESC: Less than one year old in 1916, and with a claimed readership of five million Americans (based upon one million circulation), this weekly of film stars and film entertainment product struck a responsive chord in the American movie-going public. At a newsstand cost of five cents, readers could explore the off-screen lives of favorite stars (silent star great Francis X. Bushman, for example); and short stories adapted from motion picture releases. Articles respected the film colony, oftentimes referring to stars as Mr. or Mrs., and were careful not to invade stars' privacy. Eight of 20 pages were editorial, the remainder being advertisements offering such items as a full carat diamond for $97.50, portrait enlargements, books, typewriters, eye-lashes, and correspondence courses for anything from a beauty culturist to a doctor of chiropractic. It was published by Metro Pictures Magazine for the benefit and promotion of Metro picture product. For the sampled issue of 1916: stapled magazine format, editorial content consisting of black ink with many black/white graphics published on coated paper stock, with inside and outside cover consisting of black/orange spot-color inks on coated paper stock, advertising (8 ½ x 11 ½ inches / 215 x 290 mm).
DEPT: "Editorial," "In and Out of the Studios," 'News and notes of plays and players everywhere'; "Correspondence," 'Answers to queries about film talk'. (vol 2, #11-16).
TYPL: "The Home of the Great Bushman," "My Own Story," "Views of Bushmanor." (vol 2, #11-16).
SCHL: Weekly, 20 pp.
SPAN: ?, 1916+?

✤ PLAY-BOOK, THE
PUBL: Wisconsin Dramatic Society, Madison, WI.
DESC: Published by the Wisconsin Dramatic Society, *The Play-Book* "...is not primarily the voice of the theatre as an institution. The goings-on in things dramatic to-day have a much broader reference than merely to the stage." Rather, the editors felt that this was a serial designed to discuss "midland drama," "our villages," "our people," leisure, playgrounds, school plays, festivals, pageantry, dancing, and, of course, the stage. *The Play-Book* provided a relaxed forum for discussion of issues of the theatre. "We covenant not always to be interesting, but to be interested." Some issues include complete texts of plays. Journal format; line drawings and occasional graphics pages.
DEPT: None. (8-14).
TYPL: "An Address to Motion Picture Producers of America," "The Plan of a Laboratory Theatre," "Acoustics of Theatres," "Recent Tendencies in Theatre Building." (8-14).
SCHL: Monthly, 35 pp.
SPAN: Apr, 1913+
LC: PN 2000.P6

✤ PLAY SHOP, THE
SUB: "A magazine for the amateur producer and actor." (? - Mar, 1938).
SUB: "A magazine for the amateur producer, actor, and technician." (May, 1938 - ?).

PUBL:	The Division of Dramatics of the Pennsylvania State College, State College, PA.
DESC:	Issued in mimeographed form, *The Play Shop* provided a basically instructional forum for those interested in amateur theatre; furnishing information on stage lighting, rehearsals, techniques of directing, reviews of new plays, puppetry and costumes. Most issues contained a one-act play. Mimeographed; occasional graphics.
DEPT:	"Play Reviews," "On the Boards." (3-38). "The New Plays," 'Brief reviews'; "Announcements of Interest." (#2-51).
TYPL:	"If You're Doing a Musical," "Choosing the Actor," "Notes on Puppetry, choosing the Marionette Play," "Dramatics in the High School." (3-38). "The Commedia dell'Arte," "Program of the Third Annual Institute of the Pennsylvania Theatre Conference." (#2-51).
SCHL:	Quarterly, 40 pp.
SPAN:	?+?
LC:	PN 2000.P64
DD:	792.05

✦ PLAYBACK

PUBL:	Professional Video Division, JVC Company of America, 41 Slater Drive, Elmwood Park, NJ 07407.
DESC:	"*Playback* is a quarterly newsletter from the Professional Video Communications Division of JVC COMPANY OF AMERICA. Every issue of *Playback* contains application stories, product profiles and video tidbits as well as one in-depth 2-page study of a corporate use of video, called 'Casebook'." It is a promotional newsletter for the JVC Company of America. Newsletter format, three-hole punched with graphics.
DEPT:	"Case Book," corporate applications with JVC video equipment. (fall- 85).
TYPL:	"JVC Opens 1985 Professional Video Competition, Emphasizes Objectivity of Judging," "Portrait of the Video Teacher," "Arthroscopic Surgeons Depend on Video," "Professional Video Transfer System Uses JVC Units." (fall-85).
SCHL:	Quarterly, 8 pp.
SPAN:	Winter, 1982?+?

✦ PLAYBILL

SUB:	"The national theatre magazine."
SUB:	"The national magazine of the theatre."
PUBL:	Playbill, Inc., 71 Vanderbilt Ave., New York, NY 10169.
DESC:	In a promotional advertisement within a 1991 sampled issue, publisher Playbill, Incorporated extolled the virtues of its publication: "The theatre season is bursting with excitement and if you want to be among the first to hear about it all, have *PLAYBILL*'s subscriptioiin edition delivered straight to your door. Each month the subscription edition of *PLAYBILL* brings you the inside information about what's coming up on Broadway, Off-Broadway and around the nation -- often far in advance of official announcement. You'll read the behind-the-scene news of stars, scripts and productions, as well as a monthly London newsletter and some of the most sophisticated commentary on fashion, food, music, style and restaurants to be found anywhere." *PLAYBILL* delivers on all which is stated above, and does so in style. The small journal format size is perfect for home, theatre, or commuter reading for New York City patrons, and remains a wonderful barometer of Broadway productions past, present and future for theatre aficionados elsewhere. Of special note are excellent columns for Broadway, Off-Broadway and London theatre, as well as a separately paginated section for excerpts from past plays. Each issue is filled with advertisements for restaurants featuring pre and post-theatre dining. Note: the "Subscription Edition" includes all material found in the New York Theatre edition, with the exception of play programs. Stapled small journal format, printed on coated paper stock with black/white editorial content and some color advertising pages, full color cover (5 ¾ x 8 ½ inches / 145 x 215 mm).
DEPT:	"Theatre Scenes," 'Some of the outstanding productions currently playing on B'way'; "Fashion Forecast," column by Bernadine Morris; "Celebrity Choice," favorite star dining establishments; "After Theatre," post-show places to dine, column by Bob Edison; "Dear Playbill," letters concerning theatre productions of current and past times; "Broadway News," 'What's happening, coming, and playing' column by Harry Haun; "Off-B'Way News," "Now Playing," current New York City theatrical fare; "On B'Way," current productions; "Wine of Choice," column by Peter J. Morrell; "Notes From the League," information of the League of American Theatres and Producers; "A Theatregoer's Notebook," detailed description of theatre and New York City life column by Kathy Henderson; "Dining and Entertainment," New York City guide; "London News," news of London theatre, column by Sheridan Morley. (3-31-91).
TYPL:	"Simon Lost and Found," "The Sound of Kander and Ebb," "The Joffrey Ballet." (3-31-91).
SCHL:	Monthly, 60 pp.
SPAN:	Oct 31, 1982+
	EDITION
	--Subscription.
ISSN:	0745-9076

PLAYERS

SUB:	"Official publication of National Collegiate Players."
SUB:	"The magazine of American theeatre."
SUB:	"Serving theatre across America."
PUBL:	National Collegiate Players, N.I.U. Theatre, DeKalb, IL 60115.
DESC:	By 1977, the editor could refer to *Players Magazine* as "The longest lived theatre journal in the history of the English-speaking stage." This is a journal that has served the needs of its membership well. In the 1930s, articles concerned the basics of collegiate drama: cos-

tumes, publicity, touring groups, and the ever-present problem of mounting any play during the Depression years. In the sampled issue for 1964, there was a growing sense of academic-associated theatre operations, as well as a number of articles recognizing similar theatrical projects in other nations. By 1977, the serial had taken on a more business-oriented approach to college dramatic arts, with articles concerning boxoffice operation, Broadway career opportunities, and profiles of professional and collegiate drama groups, providing in the process an interesting status report on the health of community drama nationwide. Sampled issue from 1964 was stapled, magazine format, black ink on coated paper stock; and had a special "Theatre Books of the Year" section on newsprint (8 ⅝ x 11 inches / 220 x 280 mm); contained advertising.

DEPT: "Editorial," "Concerning the Theatre," newsbriefs; "Players Programs," "With the Chapters of NCP," "With the Players," "Activities," "Puppet and Marionette News Notes," "Helps and Hints for the Director," "With the Periodicals," "The New Books and Plays." (9/10-33). "Letters," "Notes," newsbriefs; "Theatre Across America," extensive state listing of current productions; "Books in Review." (3-64). None. (10/11/-77).

TYPL: "Wanted--Directors Who Can Direct," "How to Wear Costumes," "Publicity for Your Play," "Values in the four Week Rehearsal Schedule." (9/10-33). "Theatre Istanbul 1961-63," "Off-Broadway Musicals," "A Brief Visit to Theatre in Finland," "Gleanings From a Reviewer's Notebook," "What New Scenery?" (3-64). "Stratford Shakespearean Festival, Canada," "Orpheus Descending," "The Honeymoon," "The Business of Directing on Broadway." (10/11-77).

SCHL: Quarterly (1924 - ?); Bimonthly [Irregular at times], (? - Jun, 1939); Monthly [During the school year], (Oct, 1939+); 25 pp.

SPAN: 1924 - Oct/Nov, 1977?//?
VARIES
--1924 - Dec/Jan, 1967/1968 as *Players Magazine* (ISSN: 0162-394x).

LC: PN 2001.P55
ISSN: 0032-1486
ABST: --Abstract of English Studies (ISSN: 0001-3560)

Players Magazine
1924 - Dec/Jan, 1967/1968//
(ISSN: 0162-394x)
SEE: PLAYERS

✤ PLAYS
SUB: "The drama magazine for young people."
PUBL: Plays, Inc., 8 Arlington St., Boston MA 02110.
DESC: *Plays* is a compendium of short, simple, one-act plays designed for primary and secondary school drama students. Each issue provides plays in a variety of categories such as: monologue, choral reading, musical program, group reading, skits, puppet, holiday, and dramatized classics. For the sampled issues of 1980 through 1987: black ink on uncoated paper; cover consisting of spot color ink on index stock; limited advertising; in stapled journal format (5 ⅜ x 8 ⅜ inches / 135 x 210 mm).

DEPT: None. (10-84).
TYPL: "Nellie's Fishy Fate," "The Broomstick Beauty," "The Big Top Murder," "The Statue Speaks," "The Pumpkin Patch," "The Tail of Peter Rabbit." (10-84).
SCHL: Monthly (Oct-May with combined Jan/Feb issue), 60 pp.
SPAN: Sep, 1941+
ABSORBED
--One Act Play Magazine and Radio-Drama Review, Oct, 1942.
LC: PN 1601.P6
DD: 371.8952
ISSN: 0032-1540
ABST: --Children's Magazine Guide (ISSN: 0743-9873)
--Magazine Index
--Readers Guide to Periodical Literature (ISSN: 0034-0464)
--Subject Index to Children's Magazines (ISSN: 0039-4351)

✤ PLAYS AND PLAYERS
SUB: "Exclusively devoted to straight plays and musicals."
PUBL: Hansom Books, P.O. Box 294, 2&4 Old Pye St., Westminster, London SW1P 2LR, England.
DESC: This serial has remained a favorite of many London-based actors and actresses. It is a profile and celebration of the process of stage acting: it is also about people within the theatre community. Articles describe stars and their current projects, upcoming theatrical productions; and generally profiles (through pictures) current London-based productions. Latter issues showed a dramatic increase in editorial content, especially in play reviews. Magazine format; numerous graphics.

DEPT: "Personality of the Month," profile; "Play of the Month," review; "New Plays," "Green Room," newsbriefs; "Honoured Names," pictures; "Coming to Town," newsbriefs; "Plays and Players Abroad," "Plays and Players in New York," "Plays and Players at Home," "London Playguide." (2-56). "London Playguide," "Cues," newsbriefs; "Reviews," lengthy section of reviewed plays. (7-80).

TYPL: "Longing for a Cigarette," "Trying So Hard to Go Straight." (2-56). "Enterprise in Search of Financial Support," "The Life & Adventures of Nicholas Nickleby," "Who is Freddie?," "Student Jamboree." (7-80).

SCHL: Bimonthly (? - ?); Monthly (? - ?); 45 pp.
SPAN: 1953+?
ABSORBED
--Plays, Jul, 1985?
--Theatre World, 1965.
--Encore (ISSN: 0424-9658), Nov?, 1965.
LC: PN 2001.P57

DD: 792/.0941
ISSN: 0032-1559
ABST: --Humanities Index (ISSN: 0095-5981)

✧ PLAYS INTERNATIONAL
PUBL: Plays International, Ltd., F6 Greenwood Court, Harlescott, Shrewsbury, Shropshire SY1 3TB, England.
DESC: *Plays International* is an enthusiastic publication of the art and craft of the theatre, be it London stage, British regional, European, North American, or either radio or television. There are numerous listings of current productions, and extensive reviews of selected dramatic works in the above named categories. Black/white photographs of stage work provide visual accompaniment to the thorough, well-written articles and reviews. Of special note is the inclusion of a "Playtext" in each monthly issue, showcasing a current dramatic work. It is a remarkable resource for the theatre community.
DEPT: "London Shows," play directory for greater London; "Fringe," other theatre offerings and commentary column by Lyn Gardner; "Preview," "Openings," upcoming theatrical fare; "London Notices," interesting actor profiles of current stage shows; "Opera," reviews; "Stratford," reviews; "Regions," theatrical reviews; "Europe," theatrical offerings and review; "North America," theatrical offerings and review; "TV," review and commentary column by Frank Marcus; "Radio," review and commentary column by Michael Mangan; "Playtext," monthly playtext of current British offering. (12-89).
TYPL: "When an Actor Writes," "Avonside Dance," "Whale of a Man." (12-89).
SCHL: Monthly, 50 pp.
SPAN: Aug, 1985+
ISSN: 0268-2028

✧ PLAYTIME
PUBL: Johannesburg Reportory Players, Alexander Theatre, Johannesburg, South Africa.
DESC: *Playtime* is the theatre guide for productions of the Johannesburg Reportory Players, and like others of its genre, contains brief descriptions of the play, several articles concerning theatre, and numerous advertisements by sponsors of the dramatic art. Journal format.
DEPT: None. (10-62).
TYPL: "Light in the Park." (10-62).
SCHL: Irregular, 16 pp.
SPAN: ?+?
LC: PN 2980.S8P6

PM
Sep, 1934 - May, 1940//
SEE: A-D

✧ PMA NEWSLETTER
SUB: "The international newsletter of Publishers Marketing Association."
PUBL: Publishers Marketing Association, 2401 Pacific Coast Highway, Suite 109, Hermosa Beach, CA 90254.
DESC: "The *PMA Newsletter* is published monthly by Publishers Marketing Association, a nonprofit association of book, audio and video publishers. PMA is a cooperative marketing organization which provides marketing information and combined advertising programs for a variety of small to medium-sized publishers nationally." A very interesting newsletter for small independent publishers (especially desktop), it is a beneficial forum for topics that include discussions of trends in book publishing, marketing, distribution, printing, legal, governmental, and economic factors. The PMA cooperative programs are designed to place small to medium-sized publishers on a marketing/publicity par with larger entities. This is an impressive resource for small publishers. Printed two-color, magazine format with graphics.
DEPT: "Letters," "Affiliates," listing of regional publishers associations; "Marketing Programs," upcoming by Publishers Marketing Association; "Member News," "Publishing Potpourri," newsbriefs column by Jan Nathan; "Welcome to New Members." (1-90).
TYPL: "Revolution in Print," "Benjamin Franklin Corrections and Books for Review Program Explained," "Don't Overlook Trade Magazine Serial Rights." (1-90).
SCHL: Monthly, 24 pp.
SPAN: Jan, 1983+

PMI, Photo Methods for Industry
Jan, 1958 - Aug, 1974//
(ISSN: 0030-8110)
SEE: PHOTOMETHODS

Polaroid Newsletter for Photographic Education, The
Winter, 1983 - Spring/Summer, 1988//
SEE: PHOTOEDUCATION

✧ POLITICAL COMMUNICATION AND PERSUASION
SUB: "An international journal."
PUBL: Taylor & Francis, Ltd., 4 John St., London, WC1N 2ET, England.
DESC: In the premiere issue of 1980, Ray S. Cline, Chairman of the International Advisory Board for the publication wrote, "The endemic international crises at the beginning of the 1980s are so diverse and complex that even scholars and regional experts find it hard to sort out the signals from the noise in political communications and efforts at persuasion. What used to be

called psychological warfare has become virtually the standard mode of relaying information about one part of the world to another. National leaders and private opinion-makers say less and less about their true beliefs and more about what the polls or their own biases tell them will play in Peoria, Perugia, or Pretoria. Popular journalism and investigative reporting are designed to persuade rather than to enlighten. Television has become the dominant, instant- gratification news medium in the United States and most urban societies. Opinion is shaped to a greater extent by the pictures in the living room than by all the other instruments of communication. Yet everyone recognizes that in democratic countries television entertains rather than informs. It titillates conventional public emotions without too scrupulous a concern for facts, and it trivializes ideas so as to broadcast them in bursts of thirty seconds each. ... It is surely appropriate and timely to examine in an objective and scholarly way what is happening to international channels of communication and persuasion in this disorderly and violent climate. Understanding these phenomena better is the purpose to which this new journal is dedicated." Professor Yonah Alexander, editor-in-chief of the publication since its inception, is a faculty member of the Institute for Studies in International Terrorism, at the State University of New York and the Elliott School of International Affairs at The George Washington University. For the sampled issues of 1980: black ink on uncoated paper; cover comprised of black ink on tinted index stock; limited advertising (5 ¾ x 8 ⅝ inches / 145 x 220). The sampled issues for 1990: black ink on coated stock; cover consisting of red ink on white coated paper stock with limited advertising (6 ⅜ x 9 ¾ inches / 150 x 245 mm). Both sampled issues were in perfect-bound journal format.

DEPT: "Remarks," "Editor's Note," "Comments." (#1-80). None. (#4-90).
TYPL: "Transforming International Communications Strategies," "Crisis Leadership and Non-Communication: Marcos of the Philippines." (#1-80). "Setting Political Priorities: What Role for the Press?," "Evolution of Presidential News Coverage," "Presidential Roles and Rhetoric," "Glasnost and the Emotional Climate in Eastern Europe," "Understanding the Media/Terrorism Relationship: An Analysis of Ideology and the News in Time Magazine." (#4-90).
SCHL: Semiannual (? - ?); Quarterly (?+), 75 pp.
SPAN: 1980+
LC: JF 1525 .P8 P64
DD: 306/.2
ISSN: 0195-7473
ABST: --ABC Political Science (ISSN: 0001-0456)
--Communication Abstracts
--Current Military and Political Literature
--International Political Science Abstracts
--Political Science Abstracts
--Public Affairs Information Service Bulletin (ISSN: 0033-3409)
--Sociological Abstracts (ISSN: 0038-0202)
--United States Political Science Documents (ISSN: 0148-6063)
--United States State Department Documents

✤ POLITICAL COMMUNICATION NEWSLETTER

PUBL: International Communication Association, Political Communication Division, PO Box 9589, Austin, TX 78766.
DESC: This newsletter serves the membership of the Political Communication Division of the International Communication Association. Editor Susan A. Hellweg, in a spring, 1990 issue described the interests of this division in profiling panel discussions and papers about to be presented at an upcoming Dublin, Ireland conference: "Growing interest in news and politics will be represented by a half-dozen panels that span a range of theoretical and policy concerns to consider such subjects as political power and 'marginalized' news, qualitative audience studies of news reception, and news coverage of social and public policy issues, political institutions, and foreign affairs. Campaign studies will be featured in panels devoted to public opinion processes and agendas, voter decision-making, political images and advertising, debates in the 1988 U.S. campaigns, and campaign media use. Rhetorical perspectives will be presented, as will research from political cognition and communication." The newsletter contains information about members, both individually and organizationally; as well as information about upcoming events, paper competitions, and conventions. For the sampled issue of 1990: two-column typewritten newsletter format, black ink on uncoated paper stock, loose-leaf style, no advertising (8 ½ x 11 inches / 215 x 280 mm).
DEPT: "People In the News," member newsbriefs; "From the Division Chair," divisional chair column by Robert L. Savage. (spring-90).
TYPL: "Political Communication Panels at the 1990 Conference," "A New Book Merging Polcomm and Popcomm Interests," "George Washington University News." (spring-90).
SCHL: Semiyearly, 6 pp.
SPAN: Spring, 1986+

✤ POLYGRAPH INTERNATIONAL

SUB: "Magazine for the printing industry and communication technology."
PUBL: Polygraph Verlag, GMBH, Schaumainkai 85, Postfach 700854, D-6000 Frankfurt am Main 70, Germany.
DESC: "*Polygraph International* is published six times per annum in English with summaries and abridged versions in French and Spanish. Every issue covers a series of focal subjects complemented by the product information offered in the advertisements. Thus the readers also profit from the advertisers' news on ma-

chinery, materials and processes. Worldwide, specialists update their knowledge of the printing industry with the information given in *Polygraph International*. In fact, this is the only way to keep up with the latest professional requirements. With increasingly merging markets it is becoming more and more important to have all-round information. *Polygraph International* has a broad international stock of readers in the printing industry: it especially reaches offset printing houses with typesetting, reproduction, platemaking, printing and bookbinding/converting departments, but also flexographic printing houses, gravure and special printing houses, commercial printers, newspaper printing plants as well as packaging and business forms printers. But the list of regular readers also includes technical instructors as well as the staff of research institutes and consultancies." This excellent publication for the printing industry emphasizes German-made printing technologies, services, and supplies, long-held to be among the finest quality available world-wide. Except for an opening French and Spanish-language summary page, the publication and its advertisements are in English. Numerous photos and schematics accompany articles concerning new technologies and international printing developments. Publisher Ulrike Schulz said in her "Editor's Notebook" column: "One of the secrets of successful businesses is to recognize the latest trends in the industry at an early stage, and to use them to their advantage. Trade magazines can be of valuable assistance here. Therefore you should read *Polygraph International* regularly. It gives you facts you can trust, opinions you will respect, and ideas you will want to use." Perfect-bound magazine format, black/white editorial content with some advertising in full-color on coated paper stock (8 1/4 x 11 3/4 inches / 210 x 295 mm).
- DEPT: "Editor's Notebook," editorial column by Ulrike Schulz; "Typesetting," new technologies and processes; "Page-Make Up," new technologies and processes; "Reproduction," news and developments; "Pre-Press," review of technologies and processes; "Small-Offset," news and developments; "Security Printing," news and developments; "Waterless Offset," news and information; "Mailroom," fulfillment news; "Screenprinting," news and processes; "News & Notes," extensive newsbrief section. (2-91).
- TYPL: "100 Years of Bobst: From Dealer to World Concern," "Berthold Imports 'Electronic Layouts and Manuscripts' From PCs and EDP Systems," "New Offset Printing Plates, Equipment, and Systems Increase Productivity and Quality in Platemaking," "Denmark has State-of-theArt Ferag Mailroom Technology," "The Offset Printer Discovers Screen Printing." (2-91).
- SCHL: Bimonthly, 50 pp.
- SPAN: ?+
- ISSN: 0937-9924

✤ POPULAR COMMUNICATIONS

- PUBL: CQ Communications, Inc., 76 North Broadway, Hicksville, NY 11801-2953.
- DESC: "*Popular Communications*: The world's largest, most authoritative monthly magazine for short wave listing and scanner monitoring. Read by more active listeners than all other listening publications combined! If you enjoy radio communications you'll love *Popular Communications*." This serial fully covers the field of radio communication, from short wave monitoring of clandestine radio stations to new trends in radar detection; from radioteletype to historical broadcasting, to the latest technology in paging devices. Attention to layout design and quality of printing is obvious in the reproduction of current and historical graphics. It is a pronounced resource for today's shortwave and communication enthusiast. Magazine format (8 1/8 x 10 7/8 inches / 205 x 275 mm); printed black/white with some advertisements and covers in color.
- DEPT: "Emergency," 'Communications for survival'; "You Should Know," 'Interesting thoughts and ideas for enjoying the hobby'; "Broadcast Dx'ing," 'Dx, news and views of am and fm broadcasting'; "Satellite View," 'Inside the world of satellite communications'; "Listening Post," 'What's happening: international shortwave broadcasting bands'; "Clandestine Communique," 'What's new with the clandestines'; "Scanning VHF/UHF," 'Monitoring the 30 to 900 Mhz action bands'; "RTTY," 'The exciting world of radioteletype monitoring'; "Pirates Den," 'Focus on free radio broadcasting'; "Telephones Enroute," 'What's happening with cellular, marine & mobile phones'; "The Ham Column," 'Getting started as a radio amateur'; "Communications Confidential," 'Your guide to shortwave utility stations'; "Washington Pulse," 'FCC actions affecting communications'; "How I Got Started," in the communications hobby; "CB Scene," '27 MHz communications activities'; "Radar Reflections," 'Radar detectors and their use'; "Beaming In," 'An editorial'; "Mailbag," 'Letters to the editor'; "New Products," 'Review of new and interesting products'; "Pop'Comm's World Band Tuning Tips," 'When and where to tune to hear a wide variety of local and international broadcasters on shortwave'. (6-90).
- TYPL: "Hear Them Chasing Drug Smugglers!," "Reducing Cable Leaks," "Remembrance of Radio Past," "Irritatin' Stations." (6-90).
- SCHL: Monthly, 85 pp.
- SPAN: Sep, 1982+
- LC: TK 9956 .P59
- DD: 621.3841/51/05 19
- ISSN: 0733-3315

✤ POPULAR ELECTRONICS

- SUB: "The magazine for the electronics activist!"
- SUB: "The magazine for the electronics activist and the consumer electronics enthusiast!"

PUBL: Gernsback Publications, Inc., 500-B BiCounty Blvd., Farmingdale, NY 11735.
DESC: "*Popular Electronics* ... [features] timely and informative articles that help you get the most from your hobby. Each issue ... includes: exciting construction projects for the beginning and advanced builder; news and reviews on the hottest new consumer and hobby gear; helpful hints and circuits that are an experimenter's delight; technology articles that entertain while they teach; stories and columns that cover every important part of our hobby from antique radio to computers." This is another in the series of excellent Hugo Gernsback publications, which are dedicated to the public's participation in electronics since the early days of wireless communication. Articles clearly explain complex technical subjects through lucid writing, schematics, and illustrative graphics. Perhaps the greatest value of this monthly is the practicality of the articles. Magazine format with portion of magazine printed on coated paper stock, other sections printed on quality uncoated paper stock. Sampled issue for 1990: (8 x 10 ¾ inches / 205 x 270 mm).
DEPT: "Think Tank," column by Bryon G. Weis; "Antique Radio," column by Marc Ellis; "Circuit Circus," column by Charles D. Rakes; "Computer Bits," column by Jeff Holtzman; "DX Listening," column by Don Jensen; "Ham Radio," column by Joseph J. Carr; "Scanner Scene," column by Marc Saxon; "Editorial," "Letters," "Electronics Library," book reviews; "New Products." (10-90).
TYPL: "IR-Triggered Sound-Effects Generator," "200,000-Volt Van De Graaff Generator," "Build a Car-Radio Silencer," "Tune in the Radio Pirates," "The Automated Home." (10-90).
SCHL: Quarterly (? - ?); Bimonthly (? - Dec, 1986); Monthly (Jan, 1987+), 105 pp.
SPAN: Summer, 1984+
VARIES
--? - ? as Radio-Electronics Special Projects (ISSN: 0730-7616).
--Summer, 1984 - Jan, 1989 as Hands-On Electronics (ISSN: 0743-2968).
WITH SUPPLEMENT
--Gizmo, ?+
LC: TK 7800 .P65
DD: 621.381/05 20
ISSN: 1042-170x

Popular Electronics

Oct, 1954 - Dec, 1971//
(ISSN: 0032-4485)
SEE: COMPUTERS & ELECTRONICS

Popular Electronics

Jan, 1972 - Oct, 1982//
(ISSN: 0032-4485)
SEE: COMPUTERS & ELECTRONICS

Popular Electronics, Including Electronics World

Jan, 1972 - Dec, 1973//
SEE: COMPUTERS & ELECTRONICS

✤ POPULAR PHOTOGRAPHY

SUB: "World's largest photo magazine."
SUB: "The world's largest circulation photography magazine."
SUB: "The magazine of popular photography." (Jan, 1952 - May, 1952).
PUBL: Hachette Magazines, Inc., 1533 Broadway, New York, NY 10019.
DESC: One mark of a magazine "classic" is the ability of publisher and editorial staff alike not only to meet the needs of readers in any given decade, but to be able to grow with that audience as the technology, theory, and application of that field evolves. *Popular Photography* is certainly one of those classics, a publication concentrating on the popular application of photography for the serious user. *Popular Photography* has always been renowned for excellent technical articles, new product reviews, instruction, and technique. Certain milestones in the 50-year publishing span mark unique editorial viewpoints. For the sampled issue of 1941, the articles, and photography (which was in black/white), emphasized equipment, and the home-centered photographer. The post-war sampled issue of 1953 featured a number of pages showcasing color photography, and (relatively new) stereography. Feature articles were split into topical sub-headings; "Color," "Picture," "How It's Done," "For the Beginner," "In the Darkroom," "Careers," and an interesting section for the home movie enthusiast providing information on how the Hollywood cinematographers achieved a certain shot. The sampled issues for 1978 and 1991 showed an increased emphasis on new technologies, color photography, and technique. *Popular Photography*, and its other various titles, continues to meet the needs and expectations of the 35 mm camera enthusiast and advertiser alike. For sampled issue of 1941: perfect-bound magazine format, black/white editorial content with spot color in some advertisements, and full-color cover (8 ⅝ x 11 ½ inches / 220 x 290 mm). For sampled issue of 1953: perfect-bound magazine format, predominently black/white editorial with full-color pages and cover (8 ½ x 11 ⅛ inches / 215 x 285 mm). For sampled issue of 1991: full-color throughout in a perfect-bound magazine format (8 x 10 ½ inches / 200 x 265 mm). All sampled issues were printed on coated paper stock.
DEPT: "Candid Shots," editorial newsitem column by B. G. Davis; "Questions and Answers," technical submissions; "Letters to the Editor," "Pictures From Our Readers," "New Tricks for Camera Owners," 'A monthly list of valuable kinks and hints for the amateur'; "Print Criticisms," from reader-submitted photos; "Trade Notes and News," "Calendar of Photographic Exhibitions," "What the Camera Clubs

are Doing," "New Books," review; "Picture of the Month." (1-41). "Letters to the Editor," "Tools and Techniques," 'A round-up of recent developments and significant trends' column by Norman C. Lipton; "PSA," 'News and notes about the Photographic Society of America'; "Candid Shots," editorial newsitem column by Bruce Downes; "Calendar of Photographic Exhibitions," "Hollywood Report," column by Louis Hochman; "New Books," review; "Stereo Today," Stereographic photography column by Robert L. McIntyre; "Camera Clubs," column by Whit Hillyer; "Photo Tips," "Trade Notes and News." (7-53). "Letters to the Editor," "Editorial," "Cricial Focus," "Offbeat," "Viewpoint," "Movie Methods," "Help!," "Nuts & Bolts," "Pop Photo Snapshots," "Time Exposure," "Markets & Careers," "Shop Talk," "Kids & Kameras," "Shows We've Seen," "As I See It," "Schwalberg at Large," "Color Darkroom," "Tools & Techniques," "Protechniques," "Photo- Electronics," "Workshops," "I Want to Buy..." "Aids to Better Photography," "Just Out." (1-78). "Snapshots," news items; "Point and Shoot Follies," 'For serious photographers who secretly admire point & shoot cameras' column by Dan Richards; "Nature," column by B. Peterson; "SLR Notebook," column by Herbert Keppler; "The Camera Collector," column by Eaton S. Lothrop; "Letters," "Help," reader-submitted technical Q&A. (7-91).
TYPL: "First--Get a Good Subject," "Uncle Sam's Flying Camera," "1940--A Year of Progress," "Portable Lights for Your Movies," "For Variety Try Tabletops." (1-41). "A New Market for Color Slides," "Can Picture Quality Be Measured?," "Invitation to Color," "Double-Take Portraits," "So You Want to Be a Press Photographer?" (7-53). "What Lens Works With What 35," "The Sky Was the Limit," "Adventures with Night 'Illuminations,'" "The Dreamscapes of Jim Farber," "Build Your Own Lightbox." (1-78). "Your Best Shot," "Inside Flowers," "Retouching for Duffers," "Shooting Stars." (7-91).
SCHL: Monthly, 170 pp.
SPAN: May, 1937+.
VARIES
--May, 1937 - Dec, 1951 as Popular Photography : sf82-7025.
--Jan, 1952 - May, 1952 as Photography : sf82- 7026.
--Jun, 1952 - Jul, 1952 as Photography Magazine.
--Aug, 1952 - Jan, 1955 as Photography : sf82-7028.
ABSORBED
--Prize Photography, Dec, 1941.
--Photo Arts, Jul, 1948.
--American Photography (ISSN: 0097-577x), Aug, 1953.
--Camera Magazine (ISSN: 0097-5818), Aug, 1953.
--Modern Photography (ISSN: 0026-8240), Aug, 1989.
LC: TR 1.P8845
DD: 770/.5
ISSN: 0032-4582
ABST: --Consumers Index to Product Evaluations and Information Sources (ISSN: 0094-0534)
--Film Literature Index (ISSN: 0093-6758)
--Magazine Index
--Popular Magazine Review (ISSN: 0740-3763)
--Readers Guide to Periodical Literature (ISSN: 0034-0464)

Popular Photography

May, 1937 - Dec, 1951//
SEE: POPULAR PHOTOGRAPHY

Popular Radio

May, 1922 - Mar, 1928//
SEE: POPULAR RADIO AND TELEVISION

POPULAR RADIO AND TELEVISION

PUBL: Popular Radio, 627 W. 43d St., New York, NY.
DESC: This splendid resource for the development of radio and television followed in the footsteps of *Wireless Age*; *Popular Radio*, continued a mix of hard technical advice with blueprint schematics, and substantial information concerning broadcast programming. Unlike *Wireless Age*, however, *Popular Radio* did not dwell on radio program stars and cast members, but on new technical items which would shape the medium for years to come. Authors were oftentimes major broadcast figures.
DEPT: "In the World's Laboratories," latest radio developments from world scientists; "Star Program Features of the Month," upcoming broadcasts with pictorial artist inserts; "With the Experimenters," chatty technical column; "Listening In," 'Practical pointers from experimenters and broadcast listeners'; "Broadcast Listener," 'comments on radio programs, methods and technique--from the point of view of the average fan'.
TYPL: "The Coming of the 'Radio University,'" "Three Prize-Winning Ideas for Improving Broadcast Programs," "How to Build and Use a Portable Test-Board," "is Radio Broadcasting Killing the Wild Savageries of Jazz/," "How to Assemble the All-Amax Senior Three-Tube Reflex Receiver." (2-27).
SCHL: Monthly, 100 pp.
SPAN: May, 1922 - May, 1928//
VARIES
--May, 1922 - Mar, 1928 as Popular Radio.
ABSORBED
--Wireless Age, Sep, 1925.
LC: TK 6540.P6

POSITIVE IMAGE, THE

SUB: "The newspaper for communicators in business, education, government, industry, medicine."
PUBL: Eastman Kodak Company, 343 State St., Rochester, NY 14651.

DESC: Unabashedly promoting Kodak equipment and supplies, *The Positive Image* mixes helpful hints, technical solutions, and lots of promotional information on Kodak publications in its three-fold broadsheet.
DEPT: None. (2-82).
TYPL: "Multi-image Equipment: Buy or Rent?," "Animation: How it Adds Life to Your TV Spots, PR Efforts, and Training Films," "Caring for Your Slides," (2-82).
SCHL: Quarterly, 6 pp.
SPAN: Jan, 1981 - Feb, 1982//

✤ POST

SUB: "The magazine for post production professionals."
SUB: "The magazine for animation, audio, film & video professionals."
PUBL: Post Pro Publishing, Inc., 25 Willowdale Ave., Port Washington, NY 11050.
DESC: An excellent publication for the post-production video facility, *Post* provides pragmatic advice on post house management, technology, media trends, client relationships, and numerous case stories of successful post productions. Technological concepts are clearly explained from both engineering and management viewpoints, providing helpful information in purchasing or maintaining equipment at peak performance levels. *Post* is especially valuable to the post house owner, addressing trends (both technological and aesthetic); and the fickle nature of the post house client. Highly recommended. Many color graphics; large, square magazine format (10 ⅛ x 12 inches / 260 x 305 mm). Note: *Producers Quarterly*, a supplement to *Post* for a period of one year, emerged as its own publication commencing with the Spring, 1990 issue.
DEPT: "Letters," "News," "Open House," post facility profile; "Postings," "People," "Prime Time Cuts," post centers for prime-time television; "Visible Videos," music videos; "Regional Roundup," newsbriefs; "Special Effects," "Spot Check," production; "Corporate Post," "Post Pro Products." (1-87). "Letters," "News," "Postings," projects in progress; "Post Pro Products," reviews; "Postscript," post house owner profiles; "Open House," post facility profile; "Audio Today, Tomorrow...," audio trends; "Graphics & Animation," "Signposts," trends in post production; "Corporate Post," "Music & Pictures," "Spot Check," Commercial television spot production. (7-89). "Audio Today & Tomorrow," "Open House," "Listening Post," "Agency Relations," "News," "Postings." (1-8-91).
TYPL: "Component, Keeping Luminance and Chrominance on Separate Paths," "Taking the Chances Out of Live TV," "Commercial Breaks: Saving Dollars in Post," "The End of the Compositing Blues?" (1-87). "Trade Secrets: Post Surveys the Salaries of Post," "Serious Business: Expanding an In-House Corporate Facility," "Hearing Things: Audio Plays an Important Part in Successful Commercials." (7-89). "Cutting Feature Films," "Video Tape's Higher End," "Numbers Reveal Good News at ITA," "Million Dollar Upgrade," "Broadcast Looks on a Budget." (1-8-91).

SCHL: Monthly, 90 pp.
SPAN: Mar, 1986+
WITH SUPPLEMENT
--Producers Quarterly, Mar, 1989 - Feb?, 1990//.
DD: 384 11
ISSN: 0891-5628

✤ POST OFFICE MAGAZINE

PUBL: Telegraph and Telephone Journal, G.P.O. North, London EC1, England.
DESC: [*Telegraph and Telephone Journal, The*]: Begun in Oct, 1914, *The Telegraph and Telephone Journal* was designed to be a forum for discussion of events and technologies affecting the British telegraph and telephone fields. It was the first attempt to bring together what had been diverse forces up to this point. The serial covered news of communication in wartime, new technological developments, and much news concerning company personnel. Numerous photographs detailed working conditions and new pieces of equipment. There were also articles of a lighter side, such as those about company picnics. The *Telegraph and Telephone Journal* ceased as a new serial, *The Post Office Magazine*, emerged to cover all fields under that governmental organization.
DEPT: "Editorial," "Personalia." (10-14). "Editorial," "Hic et Ubique," "Reviews." (12-33).
SCHL: Monthly.
SPAN: Oct, 1914+?
VARIES
--Oct, 1914 - Dec, 1933 as Telegraph and Telephone Journal, The.
ABSORBED
--Telegraph and Telephone Journal, 1933.

✤ POST SCRIPT

SUB: "Essays in film and the humanities."
PUBL: Post Script, Literature and Languages Department, East Texas State University, Commerce, TX 75429.
DESC: "*Post Script* welcomes manuscripts on film as language and literature (narrative, character, imagery); ensemble acting, the actor as auteur; film music; film as visual art (painting and cinematic style, set design, costuming); film and photography; film history; aesthetics and ontology; the response of film and the humanities to technology; interdisciplinary studies in theme and genre; film and American Studies; reappraisals of seminal essays; book reviews and interviews; responses to articles appearing in *Post Script*." A further description of the publication is found in a 1990 "Call for Papers" for "...a special issue on contemporary Directions in Film Theory. Contributors are invited to assess the relationships between existing psychoanalytic, Marxist, feminist or de-constructionist models and emerging paradigms drawn from research in cognitive psychology, perception, or other areas that have until recently fallen outside the purview of film studies. Topics might include, but are not

limited to: explorations of the compatibility of older and newer models; evaluations of their strengths, limitations, and relevance for particular kinds of film research; advocacy of particular paradigms, whether existing or emerging; explorations of the historical, pedagogical, or institutional conditions in the field which are eliciting new paradigms; explorations of the relationship of film studies with other disciplines (e.g., literature, the social sciences) inherent in the differing paradigms and the resulting implications for research; other theoretical / methodological issues." Of special interest is the "Annual Bibliography of Film Studies," the ninth such survey published in the summer, 1990 issue of *Post Script*. Film studies articles and periodicals are noted, as well as developing fields of film/video criticism and sociological research. This is a notable publication for the professional and academic community. For the sampled issues of 1981 and 1991: stapled, journal format; with editorial content incorporating black ink on uncoated stock (issues for 1981 and 1982 were typewritten); cover design remains the same for each issue with different background color inks employed. The cover stock for 1981 was uncoated; and for 1991: coated (6 x 9 inches / 150 x 230 mm).
- DEPT: "Book Reviews," "Forum." (spring/summer-82). "Book Review." (summer-91).
- TYPL: "Don Bluth: An Interview," "The Road to Xanadu," "Film Genre: A Dialogue; The Thirties, The Forties," "Film Genre: A Dialogue; The Eighties," "The End of Screwball Comedy: The Lady Eve and The Palm Beach Story." (spring/summer-82). "Horton Foote: An Interview," "Canadian Preserve for an Endangered Species: The Free Animator," "Hitchcock and the Transcendence of Tragedy: 'I Confess' as Speculative Art," "Alfred Hitchcock: Misogynist or Feminist?," "Annual Bibliography of Film Studies--1990." (summer-90).
- SCHL: Three issues per year, 100 pp.
- SPAN: Fall, 1981+
- ISSN: 0277-9897
- ABST: --Book Review Index (ISSN: 0524-0581)
  --Film Literature Index (ISSN: 0093-6758)
  --International Index to Film Periodicals (ISSN: 0000-0038)
  --MLA International Bibliography of Books & Articles on the Modern Languages and Literatures (ISSN: 0024-8215)

Postage and the Mailbag

Sep, 1927 - Nov, 1937//
SEE: DIRECT MARKETING

✣ POSTAL WATCH

- SUB: "The national newsletter dedicated to helping mailers make better business decisions."
- PUBL: Intertec Publishing Co., PO Box 12901, Overland Park, KS 66212-0901.
- DESC: In a promotional flyer, Publisher Sandra J. Stewart noted the myriad of changes taking place in the United States Postal system and asked potential subscribers: "With all this information floating around, I've been asked repeatedly: How does all this relate to real business situations?; How do you get postage discounts?; Why does the success of the postal automation plan hinge on mailers' changing the way they do business?; How do you use the Domestic Mail Manual effectively? That's where *POSTAL WATCH* comes in. Twice a month, *POSTAL WATCH* brings the swirling pool of information into a 'user-friendly' newsletter. ... Simply, *POSTAL WATCH* shows you how to work with the system to get what you want." Articles examine proposed postage rate increases and how to implement discount rates within the new rates, new postal regulations, adapting USPS automation goals, improving corporate mail centers, using Advanced Barcode systems, and other items crucial to the economics of a corporate mailroom. The 1990 subscription price was $183 for one year. Newsletter size (8 ½ x 11 inches / 215 x 280 mm), two color printing, three-hole-punched format on coated paper stock.
- DEPT: "Washington Watch," "PW Helpline," reader Q&A; "Resource Review," publications review. (10-5-90).
- TYPL: "Minimizing the Impact of Higher Rates," "U.S. Postal Service Wants Mailer Input on Rate Implementation," "Business-to-Business Address Standards Under Debate," "Low-Cost Methods for Developing Good Prospect Files," "Americans Love Red and Green Envelopes." (10-5-90).
- SCHL: Semimonthly, 6 pp.
- SPAN: Aug 3, 1990+
- DD: 383
- ISSN: 1052-3944

✣ POSTCARD COLLECTOR

- PUBL: Krause Publications, 121 North Main, PO Box 337, Iola, WI 54945.
- DESC: A postcard collector is termed a "deltiologist," thousands of whom form the subscription backbone of this wonderful monthly magazine on the art and technique of postcard collecting. A recent promotional advertisement stated: "*Postcard Collector* is the hobby's leading, most informative postcard publication! Each monthly issue is packed with tips and ideas from experts on how to buy, sell, display, preserve and enjoy your postcards. You'll stay on top of the newest releases and the latest finds. Plus you'll find thousands of postcards for sale in the hobby's largest, most widely-read marketplace!" Published in Iola, Wisconsin, the magazine covers a wide variety of the estimated 100 million different postcards printed since the 1860s, from countries all over the world and subjects covering historical sites, advertising products, hotels, railroads, automobiles, and a host of other subjects both in picture and cartoon form. In the sampled issue for August, 1991, articles covered the historical background and sample cards of early automobile postcards used in advertising campaigns; tour-

ist and historical site advertisement cards; postcards produced by California Napa Valley vintners; Cape May, New Jersey postcards; Toledo, Ohio postcards celebrating the King Wamba Carnival; Mississippi wharfboat picture postcards; advertisement cards for American kitchen cabinets from the 1910 - 1915 era; and postcards celebrating the 30th anniversary of Project Mercury, America's first men in space. *Postcard Collector* is an interesting mixture of descriptive articles and advertisements listing postcards for sale, or desired for purchase. It is published on newsprint. *Postcard Collector* is a proven resource for deltiologists worldwide, especially for notices of collections for sale, historical background of postcards, and notices of upcoming postcard shows in the United States. Majority of editorial content is printed black ink on newsprint stock, with two pages plus cover in the sampled issue printed in two-color red/black ink on uncoated paper stock, numerous illustrations, stapled magazine format (8 x 10 ¾ inches / 205 x 275 mm).
DEPT: "Greetings From Iola," editorial commentary column by Deb Lengkeek; "Signs of the Times," postcard sampling column by Andreas Brown; "Rare and Unusual," unique postcards column by Andreas Brown; "Small Talk," column by Dave Long; "Food for Thought," Culinary postcards column by Jennifer Henderson; "Having a Fine Time In," travel postcards column by Tom Range; "Pursuing the Marvelous," postcard column by Susan Nicholson; "Convention Coverage," "PC's Mailbag," new postcard items; "Club Notes," various association events; "Show Calendar," "Deltiology Spotlight," collector profile. (8-91).
TYPL: "Raging Chariots," "Down at the Riverfront: The Wharfboat," "America's First Men Into Space," "The Evolution of the American Kitchen," "Library Liberates Its Load of Postcards." (xx-xx).
SCHL: Monthly, 75 pp.
SPAN: Jan, 1983+
ISSN: 0746-6102

Poster, The
1910 - Jan, 1930//
SEE: ADVERTISING OUTDOORS

PR
Oct, 1955 - Summer, 1960//
SEE: PUBLIC RELATIONS QUARTERLY

✛ PR WEEK
SUB: "The newspaper for the PR profession."
PUBL: PR Week, Inc., 330 West 34th St., New York, NY 10001.
DESC: The public relations professional is oftentimes caught between the whims of corporate clients and the press for information by the journalistic corps. What makes *PR WEEK* so valuable to the public relations professional is the numerous late-breaking news items of a public relations nature, demonstrating by example how difficult issues were resolved, and even how non-issues can become news items in their own right. The large-tabloid size newspaper packs a great amount of editorial content into each weekly edition. A wonderful resource for news and status of public relations in North America. For the sampled issue of 1988: loose-leaf, tabloid newspaper format with black ink editorial content and black ink with blue spot-color ink cover on uncoated paper stock (11 ⅜ x 14 ⅞ inches / 290 x 375 mm).
DEPT: "Washington News," "Wall Street News," "Editorial," "Opinion," "News Analysis," "Diary," PR news items of the strange, funny, and bizzare kind; "Carousel," personnel changes. (3-21-88).
TYPL: "Tobacco Industry Agencies Blasted in Anti-Smoke Case," "LA Labor Union Launches 'Illegal Aliens' Campaign," "Third Class Mail Lobby to Mount New Campaign," "Managing the Asbestos Crisis," "Suffering from the Figures Problem?" (3-21-88).
SCHL: Weekly, 16 pp.
SPAN: 1988+

Practical and Amateur Wireless
? - Aug 19, 1939//
SEE: PRACTICAL WIRELESS

Practical Newsletter on Agency Management
? - ?//
SEE: YELLOW SHEET, THE

PRACTICAL PHOTOGRAPHER, THE
SUB: "An illustrated monthly of technical photography."
PUBL: Photo Era Publishing Co., Boston, MA.
DESC: Renowned for both the quality and quantity of information conveyed, *The Practical Photographer*, published simultaneously in Boston and London; provided a well-crafted showcase for the artistic and technical components of photography. Each lengthy issue was filled with a variety of schematics, chemical equations, and discussions of the artistic merits of the medium. Of special note was the quality of printed photographs, oftentimes providing graphic evidence of the differences in printing papers, and other darkroom techniques. This was a practical magazine that somehow failed to rally a subscription base sufficient to sustain publication after November, 1905. Small journal format; no table of contents.
DEPT: "Notes and News," newsbriefs. (8-05).

TYPL: "The Pictorial Work of Harold Baker," "Introduction to Orthochromatic Photography," "Orthochromatism in Pictorial Work," "Preparation of the Negative for Printing." (8-05).
SCHL: Monthly, 75 pp.
SPAN: Apr, 1904 - Nov, 1905//
LC: TR 1.P9

✣ PRACTICAL PHOTOGRAPHY

SUB: "Helping you take better pictures."
SUB: "The British how-to-do-it photo magazine."
PUBL: EMAP National Publications Ltd., Bushfield House, Orton Centre, Peterborough PE2 0UW, Cambs, England.
DESC: The publishers of *Practical Photography* called it "...Britain's biggest, brightest and best-selling photo magazine." One can certainly agree about the size and sparkling format design of this monthly magazine, the purpose of which is "helping you take better pictures." An abundance of color graces this monthly. While some profiles of professional photographers do appear, the emphasis of *Practical Photography* is on the amateur photographer, a title which remains (in Britain, at least), a badge of honor. Great care is taken in color separations, placement, and printing of same; showcasing some outstanding examples of reader efforts. Vibrant, thorough, and exciting, *Practical Photography* is an excellent resource for anyone interested in the art and science of still photography. It contains numerous advertisements for British photographic vendors. For the sampled issues of 1960 through 1962: black ink on coated paper; cover comprised of full-color graphics on coated stock, in stapled magazine format (8 ⅛ x 11 inches / 210 x 280 mm). The sampled issues of 1990: magazine format (8 ⅜ x 11 ¼ inches / 210 x 295 mm).
DEPT: "Editor's Snapshots," "Between Ourselves," "Photographic Good Buys." (4-60). "Opening Shot," full-page color offering; "Up-Date," 'People and products in the news' column by Sally Whiddett; "Any Questions?," Q&A photography column by William Cheung; "Video Update," column by George Cole; "Nocon," 'Gene Nocon prints readers pictures'; "Photo Critique," 'Lynne Barbers personal photo improvement critique' column by Lynne Barbers; "Brainstorm," photo contest; "On Test," new product profile; "Beginners Corner," "Photo School," instructional series; "Photo Assignment," assignment challenge to readers; "Back Chat," letters and more column by Martyn Moore; "Prize Crossword," "Mini Tests," "Camera Mart Data Guide," "Comparison Test." (3-90).
TYPL: "How to Use Your Exposure Meter," "Get Blemish-Free Negatives," "Transformation--How to Use Photographic Make-Up," "The Right Film for the Job," "10 Ways to Sharper Pictures." (4-60). "Magnum," "Canon Ion," "A Quick Kip," "How to Shoot Stately Homes." (3-90).
SCHL: Monthly, 155.
SPAN: ?+

ABSORBED
--Practical Video Photography, ?
--Which Camcorder, ?
ISSN: 0032-6445

PRACTICAL PRINTER, THE

SUB: "A journal devoted to the printing art." (Jan, 1899 - Jul, 1899).
SUB: "A journal devoted to the art preservative." (Aug, 1899).
SUB: "A journal devoted to the interests of art printing." (Sep, 1899).
SUB: "A journal for fine printers." (Oct, 1899).
SUB: "A progressive magazine for up-to-date printers." (Nov, 1899).
SUB: "A journal devoted to the interests of art printing." (Jan, 1900).
SUB: "A journal devoted to the promotion of typographical art." (Oct, 1900), (Feb, 1901).
SUB: "A magazine devoted to the promotion of art in printing." (Mar, 1901).
SUB: "A magazine devoted to the promotion of profitable printing." (May, 1901 - Jun, 1901).
SUB: "A monthly journal devoted to the promotion of high art in every-day printing." (Oct, 1901).
SUB: "Published monthly and devoted to promoting highest excellence in every-day typography." (Feb, 1902), (Jun, 1902).
SUB: "For art and profit in the practice of typography." (Aug, 1902).
SUB: "For the benefit of printerdom." (Sep, 1902).
SUB: "Being a monthly magazine published for printers." (Aug, 1911).
PUBL: Inland Type Foundry, St. Louis, MO.
DESC: Admitting that a number of other serials about printing were already on the market, the editors of *The Practical Printer*, nonetheless, felt there was a manifest need for a serial of this stature, noting; "It is the intention to give a large part of the space to technical articles by experienced men, on printing, engraving, stereotyping, electrotyping and bookbinding. New methods of doing work and new material and machinery for producing it will always have special attention." As befits the title, this was a journal of practical hints, discussion and news, especially in the showcasing of new typefaces and other products produced and sold by the Inland Type Foundry of St. Louis. Journal format; graphics.
DEPT: None (7-1899). None (8-10).
TYPL: "Printing Tints with a Frisket," "Some Leaks I Have Observed," "Type Versus Linotype." (7-1899). "The Rush Job," "Display Type in Advertising," "Perforating, Scoring and Printing at One Operation," "Ideas to Help the Printer." (7-10).
SCHL: Monthly, 10 pp.
SPAN: Jan, 1899 - Sep, 1911//
LC: Z119.P8

Practical Television

Sep, 1934 - May, 1935//
SEE: PRACTICAL TELEVISION AND SHORT-WAVE REVIEW

PRACTICAL TELEVISION AND SHORT-WAVE REVIEW

PUBL: George Newnes, Ltd., Southampton St., Strand, London WC2, England.
DESC: Beginning and ending as a supplement, *Practical Television* began a short, independent lifespan when television moved from experimental to operational status in late, 1934 Britain. A fascinating serial, *Practical Television*'s emphasis was on international technical and programming developments of the time. The focus of early articles on mechanical television systems gave way in latter issues to discussions of "electron beam" systems in America and Germany. Discussion of short-wave developments was added to the serial commencing with the June, 1935 issue. An excellent resource for television history, especially due to the large number of photographs printed in each issue.
DEPT: "Televiews," comment; "Telenews," 'Topical reflections from the radio screen'; "Tested in Our Laboratory," 'A review of the latest television apparatus'; "ABC of Television," 'A dictionary of definitions of the more important television terms'; "Anglo-American Radio and Television Society," newsbriefs. (2-35).
TYPL: "All About the Cathode-Ray Tube," "Television Receiving Circuits," "Varied Scanning Methods," "Building a Portable Television Receiver," "Colour-Vision Possibilities." (2-35).
SCHL: Monthly, 25 pp.
SPAN: Sep, 1934 - Nov, 1935//
SUPPLEMENT TO
--Practical Wireless, ? - Aug, 1934.
--Practical & Amateur Wireless, Nov 2 - ?
VARIES
--Sep, 1934 - May, 1935 as Practical Television.
LC: TK 6630.A1P7

✤ PRACTICAL WIRELESS

SUB: "The radio magazine."
PUBL: IPC Magazines, Practical Group, Westover House, West Quay Rd., Poole, Dorset BH15 1JG, England.
DESC: A hallmark publication for the British radio amateur, *Practical Wireless* and its variety of varying titles provided late-breaking technological news, features, and test results of new equipment for the amateur radio operator. This serial was especially well-known for its liberal use of schematics, drawings, and graphics to detail the building, improvement, or repair of electronic apparatus. Commencing with the January 26, 1935 issue, the varying title of this serial was *Practical and Amateur Wireless*, from a merger of *Practical Wireless* and *Amateur Wireless* magazines. Numerous graphics, schematics, and drawings. Some pages consisted of newsprint paper stock.
DEPT: "Round the World of Wireless," international newsbriefs; "Solve This!," problem solving; "Half-Hour Experiments," "Here and There," newsbriefs; "Progressive Home Construction," "Television for All," explanation; "On Your Wavelength," column by Thermion; "Notes from the Test Bench," "Readers Wrinkles," reader submissions; "Short Wave Section," "Leaves from a Short-Wave Log," column by E. Thurway; "The Beginner's Supplement," "Radio Clubs and Societies," newsbriefs; "Replies in Brief," to letters; "Practical Letters from Readers," "Facts & Figures," test results; "Replies to Queries and Enquiries." (3-16-35). "PW Preview," new items; "Practically Yours," construction; "Names from the Past," review; "Computing Corner," "Kitchen Konstruktion," "News Desk," "On the Air," newsbriefs; "Write On," letters. (11-87).
TYPL: "Bringing Your Loud-Speaker to Life," "The Pick-Up and Instability," "The Hall-Mark Cadet." (3-16-35). "Variable Power for the IC-251E," "RTTY Tuning Indicator," "Valved Communications Receivers," "Confessions of a Radio Officer." (11-87).
SCHL: Weekly (? - ?); Monthly (?+); 60 pp.
SPAN: 1932+
VARIES
--? - ? as Practical Wireless.
--? - Aug 19, 1939 as Practical and Amateur Wireless.
--? - ? as Practical Wireless and Practical Television.
ABSORBED
--Amateur Wireless and Radiovision, Jan, 1935.
LC: TK 6540.P7
ISSN: 0141-0857

Practical Wireless

? - ?//
SEE: PRACTICAL WIRELESS

Practical Wireless and Practical Television

? - ?//
SEE: PRACTICAL WIRELESS

✤ PRE-

SUB: "The leading publication for buyers of publishing, design, and prepress products and services."
SUB: "The authority on prepress technology."
PUBL: South Wind Publishing Co., 8340 Mission Rd., Suite 106, Prairie Village, KS 66206.
DESC: "Every publisher believes in his publication, his great idea. In this case, however, *Pre-* is not a great idea. Rather, it's a practical one. A timely one. The major technical changes taking place in the print industry are occurring at the front end--at the prepress stage. What

all these technologies have in common is the prepress link. Whether you work for a commercial publisher, newspaper, corporation, educational institution, government agency, design studio, ad agency, printer, or prepress facility, you have one thing in common: the preparation of materials for print--the prepress process. A composition system or gaphics software program is used for the preparation of materials for print. An electronic color-imaging system prepares images for final output to print. Very simply, electronic design, publishing, and prepress systems and software share a common purpose. And *Pre-* is designed to address this technological commonality." An outstanding resource for prepress processes, this full-color newsmagazine reports on the techniques and technology of preparing materials for printing. Typical articles in past issues included "HDTV and the Graphic Arts," "Direct Digital Color Proofing," "Image-Processing Software," and "DTP vs. EPP." Articles are thorough, fully illustrated, and informative. After the first successful year of tabloid-size publication, *PRE-* moved to standard magazine format (8 x 10 ¾ inches / 205 x 275 mm), and a bimonthly publishing schedule commencing in Jan/Feb, 1990.
DEPT: "Up Front," commentary; "Scan Lines," technology column by Phil Kurz; "From the Desktop," desktop publishing column by Gary Olsen; "Systems," new product announcement section; "Multimedia," newsbriefs; "Software," computer and non-computer supplies and resources; "Services," "Peripherals," "News/Trends," prepress newsbriefs; "Datebook," calendar. (10-89). "Prepress Frontier," "IPA Report," International Prepress Association news column by Henry Hatch; "The New Service Bureau," column by Thad McIlroy; "Commentary," "Letters," "Up Front," "News," "Prepress Notes," "Gallery." (1/2-91).
TYPL: "Developing Skills for the Desktop Environment," "Shape, Rattle 'n' Roll," "Desktop Color is Making News," "The High-End Connection," "Print Production 1990." (10-89). "Process Integration," "Producing Catalogs On-Line," "Transforming Video into Print," "Densitometer: A Partner in Success," "Type in the '90s." (1/2-91).
SCHL: Quarterly (Jan, 1989 - Oct, 1989); Bimonthly (Jan/Feb, 1990+), 85 pp.
SPAN: Jan, 1989+
DD: 070 11
ISSN: 1042-0304

✤ PREMIERE

SUB: "The movie magazine."
PUBL: Murdoch Magazines, 2 Park Ave., New York, NY 10016.
DESC: "*Premiere* springs from a French magazine of the same name that, during the last decade, developed an approach to covering movies and moviemakers that has made it one of the most successful monthlies in France. It is aimed at that generation of filmgoers that has come to think of movies as its art form of choice. An American version of *Premiere* was inevitable: The technology of film may have been launched in Europe, but it hit the ground running when it crossed the Atlantic, and no one's caught up to us since. Today, millions of Americans have a sophisticated interest in the movies that goes well beyond the traditional fascination with stars. *Premiere* won't ignore stars--how could we? But we think our audience wants to know how movies actually get made: how a film is conceived, who contributes to its development; how it is financed, why it costs so much; how it is cast, why a certain actress lands the role; how the director is tapped, why he makes the choices he does." This is the "hot" film magazine of the '90s, with a realistic view of the entire film industry covering profit, prestige, promotion, and production of American film product. *Premiere* is a grand celebration of filmmaking. Large magazine format with full color graphics.
SCHL: Monthly, 110.
SPAN: Jun, 1987+
       SUSPENDED
       --Sep, 1987.
LC: PN 1993.P72
DD: 791.43/05
ISSN: 0894-9263

Premi'ere

Sep, 1980 - Mar, 1981//
(ISSN: 0274-7766)
SEE: AMERICAN PREMIERE

Premium Channels

? - ?//
(ISSN: 0273-561x)
SEE: PREMIUM CHANNELS TV BLUEPRINT

✤ PREMIUM CHANNELS TV BLUEPRINT

PUBL: Premium Channels Publishing Co., 1265 Sunrise Highway, Bay Shore, NY 11706.
DESC: *Premium Channels* is primarily a monthly listing of video programming available on the major cable and pay-cable channels. Short descriptions accompany highlighted programming by each cable service. No articles. Numerous promotion pictures. Newsprint.
DEPT: "The Mainly Movie Crossword." (12-83).
TYPL: None. (12-83).
SCHL: Monthly, 40 pp.
SPAN: Jan, 1980+
      VARIES
      --? - ? as Premium Channels (ISSN: 0273-561x).
ISSN: 1040-5534

✤ PRESENTATION PRODUCTS MAGAZINE

SUB: "Creating, producing, delivering."
PUBL: Pacific Magazine Group, Inc., 513 Wilshire Blvd., Suite 344, Santa Monica, CA 90401.
DESC: After only two years of publication, advertisers sing the praises of this audio-visual production publication: "*Presentation Products Magazine* is the only publication addressing the emerging presentations market. It addresses the needs of the audio visual and computer markets," and, "It seems that *Presentation Products Magazine* is quickly becoming a 'must read'." This is a publication of optimism; of brand-new technologies and means for the business world to present corporate ideas, strategies, and new product designs on a large-scale forum. The emphasis is on showcasing new products and their applications, rather than providing head-to-head critiques of these AV products, prices and merits/shortcomings. In this competitive corporate world, the method of presentation (mode, style, clarity, and a touch of "pizzazz") is oftentimes as important as the product itself. To that end, *Presentation Products Magazine* provides an excellent resource for the corporate media manager. Magazine format; numerous color graphics.
DEPT: "Publisher's Memo," "Newsworthy," late breaking news items; "New Products," "Product Spotlight." (5-90).
TYPL: "Tech 2000: A Showcase of Interactivity," "AV Specialists Propel Aircraft Exhibits," "Multi-Image Presentations," "Buyer's Guide: Computer-to-Video Connectivity." (5-90).
SCHL: Quarterly, 95 pp.
SPAN: Jan, 1988+
DD: 658 11
ISSN: 1041-9780

✤ PRESS, THE

SUB: "Reporting how the media work."
PUBL: Tone Arm Publications, 112 East 19th St., New York, NY 10003.
DESC: *The Press* is a trade publication for the journalism community. Editor Anthony King notes: "Our readers include staff members of newspapers, magazines and TV stations across the country. And we are read by scores of informed people who are not in the media business but who are concerned about how the news is reported." Articles are written by working press members and include journalists from *The Observer* of London, to the *Maine Times*, *Boston Globe*, *Chicago Sun Times*, and the *Standford University News Service*. Each issue is segmented into special departments containing one to ten articles each. A marvelous resource (some 25+ articles per issue) for understanding the working press. Magazine format.
DEPT: "Every Picture Tells," "News," "Sources and Resources," "On the Scene," "The Might of the Media," "Inside," "Issue," "Watch," "Comment." (8-82).
TYPL: "Why Meat Doesn't Advertise," "Seven Men Against Children's TV," "How Zip Codes Sell America," "The Best Loved Myths About TV," "Katherine Whitehorn Sends a Message." (8-82).
SCHL: Bimonthly, 50 pp.
SPAN: Jan/Feb, 1973?+?

Press Censorship Newsletter

Mar/Apr, 1973 - Sep/Oct, 1976//
SEE: NEWS MEDIA & THE LAW, THE

PRESS STATISTICAL REVIEW

PUBL: Legion Information Services, 25 Bream's Bldg., London EC4A 1EX, England.
DESC: [*Advertising Statistical Review*]: Identical to previous *Advertising Statistical Review of Press and Television Expenditures*, with the following format changes: smaller format, typewritten, with no between-cover advertising and absence of articles. This is first and foremost a monthly reference source of advertising expenditures in Great Britain. Contains monthly listings for over 6,000 products.
DESC: [*Advertising Statistical Review of Press and Television Expenditures*]: Monthly listings of advertising expenditures in Great Britain. Primary function is as a reference tool for the advertising agency marketing and advertising director. One or two short articles per issue, typically reflecting current trends.
DEPT: "The Month in Advertising," "Long-Range Planning and Marketing," "Promotions," "New Products and Services," "Account Changes," "Personnel Appointments," "Individual Product Expenditures," "Revisions," "Agency Abbreviations Index." (1-69). "About Legion Estimates," "Selected Media Group Expenditures," "Selected Product Category Expenditures," "New Products and Services," "Field Promotions," "Selected Top Advertisers," "Selected Top Product Groups," "Selected Account Changes by Agency," "Selected Account Changes by Product," "Product Groups Within Categories," "Grand Analysis," "Individual Product Expenditures," "Ammendments to Previous Month," "Alphabetic Product Groups Index," (9-70).
TYPL: None.
SCHL: Monthly, 100 pp.
SPAN: ? - 1975//
FROM MERGER OF
--Stat Review (and) Advertising.
VARIES
--? - 1972 as Advertising Statistical Review of Press and Television Expenditures.
--1972 - 1975 as Advertising Statistical Review (ISSN: 0065-3640).
LC: HF 6105.G

✣ PRESSTIME

SUB: "The journal of the American Newspaper Publishers Association."
PUBL: American Newspaper Publishers Association, 11600 Sunrise Valley Drive, Reston, VA 22091.
DESC: *Presstime* is a trade news magazine for the American Newspaper Publishers Association that serves its constituency well through succinct news articles, lucid commentaries on the state and trend of the newspaper business; with a quality layout design and dynamic graphics. Articles concentrate on issues of importance to publishers, employee relations, new technology, circulation, government regulation, and the cost of operation. Doomsayers will find no respite here; the newspaper world is alive, well, and profitable, thanks in no small part to the American Newspaper Publishers Association, and this excellent business publication for today's newspaper management team. An ANPA calendar of events is listed in each issue. For the sampled issue of 1990: stapled magazine format with a large variety of graphics in a dynamic layout design, printed with full-color pages throughout on coated paper stock (8 ½ x 11 inches / 215 x 280 mm). Required reading for today's print manager.
DEPT: "Courts," legal actions, "Court Briefs," newsbriefs; "Legislation," "Regulations," "World Press," "Postal Affairs," "State and Local," "Telecommunications," "Profile," "Essay," "News-Editorial," "Circulation," "Advertising," "Education," "Training," "Employee Relations," "Technology," "Newsprint," (4-80). "Chairman's Corner," "Advertising," "ANPA Calendar," "ANPA News," "Books," "Circulation," "Education," "Employee Relations," "Government Affairs," "Minority Affairs," "News-Editorial," "Newspaper Business," "Newsprint," "Overset," "Speeches," "Syndicates," "Technology," "Telecommunications," "Transportation," "World Press." (12-87). "Chairman's Corner," "Advertising," "ANPA News," "ANPA Calendar," "Circulation," "Education," "Employee Relations," "Government Affairs," "Letters," "Minority Affairs," "News-Editorial," "Newspaper Business," "Newsprint," "Overset," "Postal," "Speeches," "Technology," "Telecommunications," "World Press." (5-90).
TYPL: "Gauging World Press Freedom," "Justice Policy will Support Open Courts, Civiletti Says," "Foreign Correspondents are Staging a Comeback," "Working Women: a Newspaper Selling Point that Counts," "Lighting Changes Enhance VDT usage," (4-80). "Boom-Town Publishing," "The Urge to Merge," "Contingency Budgeting," "Affirmative Action at J-Schools." (12-87). "Grading J-Schools," "How Publishers Can Calm Angry Readers," "Moving Beyond Lip Service," "Direct-Mail Advertising Enjoys Unfair Pricing Advantage." (5-90).
SCHL: Monthly, 100 pp.
SPAN: Oct, 1979+
LC: PN 4700.P74
DD: 070/.05
ISSN: 0194-3243

ABST: --Abstract Bulletin of the Institute of Paper Chemistry (ISSN: 0020-3033)
--Electronic Publishing Abstracts (ISSN: 0739-2907)
--Printing Abstracts (ISSN: 0031-109x)

✣ PREVIEW

SUB: "The family cable magazine."
PUBL: Preview Magazine Corporation, 201 King St., Chappaqua, NY 10514.
DESC: This national cable-television programming guide has a middle newsprint section detailing local cable television offerings for the upcoming month. Published for specific cable television systems and their subscribers, it is unique for its considerable local advertising space. Magazine format; full-color national section; newsprint black/white local programming section.
DEPT: "Request TV," Pay television offerings; "Restaurant Section," advertisements; "Premium Line-Up," premium cable-television program offerings; "Sports Picks," programming guide. (12-88).
TYPL: "The Christmas Wife," "Brothers Breaks the Century Mark," "The Human Rights Now Tour." (12-88).
SCHL: Monthly, 60 pp.
SPAN: Feb, 1982+

PREVIEW

SUB: "Television, parties, movies."
PUBL: Laufer Company, 7060 Hollywood Blvd., Suite 800, Hollywood, CA 90028.
DESC: "*PreVIEW* is a ... celebrity magazine with a difference. Yes, you'll get all the news on your favorite Hollywood personalities--but much, much MORE! Each issue of *preVIEW* will focus on places as well as people ... the chic Beverly Hills haunts of the famous, what really goes on over lunch at Hollywood's most select dining spots, the celebrity boutique scene, the 'shampoo' Set, and how much they really DO know about their star-studded clientele. In addition, we turn the spotlight on new faces as well as keep you up-to-date on the music and TV fronts." The focus was on Hollywood gossip and news of current and past stars for a trendy readership. Covers were full-color pictures, with color inserts within the magazine. Fast breaking news of the Hollywood set with unattributable sources. Magazine format.
DEPT: "Hollywood, Hollywood," gossip; "Pairs and Repairs," 'Who's Going With Whom--and Who's Going Back to Whom;' "Shorts," newsbriefs; "After Hours," pictures and information on stars after dark; "New York, New York," gossip in the Big Apple; "Music, Music," music scene newsbriefs; "Station Breaks," TV Gossip; "Around the World," global gossip; "New Faces," a bevy of rising stars; "You Said It," reader sound-off; "Hollywood Classifieds," readers offer star items for trade or sale; "Lights, Camera, Action," shots of stars on the set; "Speakeasy," men- women

on-street interviews; "Name Droppers," what the stars are saying about each other; "Parting Shots," columnist Bill Royce with back-cover news briefs. (4-79).
TYPL: "Are They Too Good to be Real?," "Disco Dazzle '79." (4-79)
SCHL: Monthly, 85 pp.
SPAN: Sep, 1976? - ?//

PREVIEWS
SUB: "Audiovisual software reviews."
PUBL: R. R. Bowker Company, 1180 Avenue of the Americas, New York, NY 10036.
DESC: This is a cover-to-cover review of educational 16 mm films, videotapes, filmstrips, slides, print and word releases. Each new release is critically and thoroughly analyzed in a 200+ word review by an identified media specialist, library science specialist or educator.
DEPT: None.
TYPL: No Article Titles.
SCHL: Nine issues per year [Sep - May], 25 pp.
SPAN: ? - Dec, 1980//
VARIES
--? - Nov?, 1973 as Library Journal/School Library Journal Previews.
LC: Z 689 .L53
DD: 028.1
ISSN: 0000-0051
ABST: --Media Review Digest (ISSN: 0363-7778)

✤ PREVUE
SUB: "Dedicated to the world of entertainment."
SUB: "The magazine of tomorrow's entertainment." (Jul/Aug, 1980+).
PUBL: Prevue, PO Box 4489, Reading, PA 19606-4489.
DESC: This is a publication "...devoted to popular culture in multi-media, from the cinema to comics," which includes topics from comic book art to Hollywood motion picture musicals, from science fiction to the newest Halloween thriller. From its initial publication as *Comixscene*, through *Mediascene*, *Prevue*, and currently *Mediascene Prevue*, this remains an outstanding serial of popular culture. The emphasis is on fantasy, science fiction, and other kinds of popular culture elements. Publisher, editor, and designer James Steranko made this color-filled publication an exciting periodical, with everything from full-page foldout movie posters, to a gallery of graphic art from Star Wars, to new artist creations for comic book distribution. Note: some pages contain adult material. Numerous graphics. Issued for a period of time in tabloid format, and currently standard magazine format.
DEPT: "Editorial," "Graphic Review," "Comixscene," 'News/Views/Reviews from the world of comics.' (11/12-78). "Editorial," "Mediamail," letters; "Fast Forward," future tech; "Book Marks," reviews; "Inside Tracks," music; "Coming Attractions," previews. (11/12-81). "Editorial," "Mediamail," letters; "Shooting Stars," 'Todays top filmmakers with tomorrows hottest projects'; "Coming Attractions," 'Who's doing what and where in which productions'. (1-90).
TYPL: "Meteor: Pictorial Preview of a New Science-Fiction Spectacular," "The Making of Buck Rogers." (11/12-78). "Annie: Can an Orphan and Her Dog Find Happiness in a 35-Million Dollar Hollywood Musical?," "Blade Runner: On the Set with Harrison Ford in a Hard-Boiled Futuristic Detective Thriller," "Steven Spielberg: A Candid Conversation on Raiders of the Lost Ark and His Future Films." (11/12-81). "Sean Connery Sees Red in a White-Hot Career Conversation!," "Clint Eastwood Journeys to the Dark Continent to Relive the Legend of the African Queen!," "...They're Mean! ...They're Green! ...They're on the Screen! Teenage Mutant Ninja Turtles!" (1-90).
SCHL: Bimonthly [irregular at times] (Aug/Sep, 1982 - Jul/Aug, 1984); Five issues per year [Jan, Apr, Jul, Sep, Nov] (Nov/Dec, 1984+), 70 pp.
SPAN: Nov/Dec, 1972+
VARIES
--Nov/Dec, 1972 - Sep/Oct, 1973 as Comixscene.
--Nov/Dec, 1973 - May/Jun, 1980 as Mediascene.
--Jul/Aug, 1980 - ?, 1987 as Mediascene Prevue (ISSN: 0199-9257).
LC: P 92 .U5 M46
DD: 001.51/0973
ISSN: 1045-1234

Pride
Jan, 1957 - Jun, 1961//
(ISSN: 0032-8197)
SEE: COLLEGE & UNIVERSITY JOURNAL

✤ PRIG
PUBL: International Communication Association, Public Relations Interest Group, PO Box 9589, Austin, TX 78766.
DESC: This newsletter is an informational medium for the Public Relations Interest Group of the International Communication Association. News covers upcoming events, conventions, papers, conferences, and other news of interest to the members of this ICA interest group. For the sampled issue of 1991: typeset, two-column, newsletter format, black ink on uncoated paper stock, no advertising (8 ½ x 11 inches / 215 x 280 mm).
DEPT: "PRIG Chair's Column," editorial column by Elizabeth Toth. (fall-91).
TYPL: "Thesis/Dissertation Nominations Sought," "New Member Drive," "Annual Conferences." (fall-91).
SCHL: Semiyearly, 4 pp.
SPAN: Fall, 1987+

✤ PRINT
SUB: "A quarterly journal of the graphic arts."

SUB: "All the means of reproducing ideas in visual form by graphic symbols."
SUB: "America's graphic design magazine."
PUBL: RC Publications, 3200 Tower Oaks Blvd., Rockville, MD 20852.
DESC: Dynamic, professional, and instructive, *Print* reigns supreme in the field of graphic design and application. The care applied to graphic reproduction on a variety of paper media culminates in a stunning portfolio of design ideas and opportunities, some supplied by the editorial publisher, others supplied by paper and media vendors desiring to showcase their products in new and innovative ways. This publication for contemporary graphics design has full color lithographs, experimental papers, printing techniques and explorations of graphic layouts. Woodcuts, reprints, color tests, duotones and experimentation with typography are hallmarks of this applied technologies journal. Within the decade of the 50s, issues used fewer color pages, and fewer experimental articles, but the high quality of publication remained. By the 1980s, *Print* solidified its excellent reputation for showcasing the very best in American graphic design. A sampling of articles from that latter decade include, "Japan: Defining the Art Director's Role," "Jim McMullan: My Life in the Theatre," "Rethinking Exhibitions," "The Type Craftsman in the Computer Era," and "Tabloids: The art of Sensationalism." It is vibrant, authoritative, with a zest for exploration and a wonderment for why things are. For the sampled issue of 1991: perfect-bound magazine format (8 ⅞ x 12 inches / 225 x 305 mm), full color throughout on heavy coated paper stock, with numerous paper manufacturer inserts.
DEPT: "Book Reviews," "Top Drawer--News from the Whole Field of the Graphic Arts," newsbriefs; "Calendar of Events," "Production Notes," information on paper and illustration. (winter-50/51). "Top Drawer," graphic review of new printed materials; "Paper and Design," available aids from paper companies; "Letterhead Design," "Materials and Methods," "Letters to Print," "Books in Print." (11/12-61). "A Cold Eye," 'critical commentary on the institutions, practices, and controversies of the graphic design field'; "Intro-Spectives," 'reflective, very personal commentaries on a wide range of subjects by individuals in the design field'; "New Developments in Media Techniques," "Visual Commentary." (5/6-91).
TYPL: "Propaganda and the Graphic Arts," "Know your Colors," "Since Gutenburg," "Seeing the Unseen," "Woodcuts and Wood Engravings." (9-40). "Carl Ernst Poeschel," "The Groom Bewitched," "The Woodcuts of Antonio Frasconi," "De Druckkunst; Aen Balthasar Moerentorf." (winter 50/51). "New Direction for Designers?," "The Search for Corporate Identity: Seven Case Histories," "Eric Gill," "Experiments in Design," "Bank Checks with Character." (11/12-61). "The Death of Eros," "The Curse and Challenge of CD Packaging," "In the Land of the Aborigines," "Walking the Wall," "The Knave of Hearts." (5/6-91).
SCHL: Bimonthly (? - ?); Quarterly (? - ?), 160 pp.
SPAN: Jun, 1940+
ABSORBED
--Printing Art, Summer, 1942.
--Print Collectors Quarterly [NC], Winter, 1950/1951.
WITH SUPPLEMENT
--Rare Book Market, The, ? - ?
--Book Reviews, ? - ?
LC: Z 119.P8985
DD: 070.5/068
ISSN: 0032-8510
ABST: --Abstrax
--Art Bibliographies Modern (ISSN: 0300-466x)
--Art Index (ISSN: 0004-3222)
--Film Literature Index (ISSN: 0093-6758)
--Index to Book Reviews in the Humanities (ISSN: 0073-5892)
--Printing Abstracts (ISSN: 0031-109x)

✢ PRINT BUYERS REVIEW

PUBL: PPC Publications and Pre-Press Co., Inc., 356 South Ave., Whitman, MA 02382.
DESC: Editor-in-chief, Charlotte W. Vayo, in the premiere winter, 1989 issue stated; "Our industry is expanding very rapidly, and I welcome the opportunity to make the print buyers for books, magazines, periodicals, and catalogs aware of whatever is new in technology and equipment along with expansions of existing plants that will be offering new services. *Print Buyers Review* will contain an Economic Review, a Personal Insight, a Technology Update, and a Manufacturer's Spotlight, as well as other pertinent articles in each issue. These articles will inform both you, the print buyer, and the manufacturing community about the latest technology, effects of current economics on pricing, trends in purchasing, and any change in manufacturers' offerings." This is a splendid publication, long needed by the many independent publishers in search of information concerning the printing process. Magazine format (8 ⅛ x 10 ⅞ inches / 205 x 275 mm), with numerous color graphics.
DEPT: "Manufacturer's Spotlight," "Personal Insight," "Technology Update," "Economic Review," "Questions Answered." (Winter-89).
TYPL: "New England Book Components--Hands-On Management Works," "Gearing Up for Desktop Publishing," "Independent Representatives." (Winter-89).
SCHL: Quarterly, 45 pp.
SPAN: Winter, 1989+

✢ PRINT EDUCATION MAGAZINE

PUBL: Westana Publications, 298 Harbour Drive, P.O. Drawer G, Sausalito, CA 94965.
DESC: This serial for those interested in graphic arts printing "...is devoted to those in industry who want to learn or review; to students...and, to all the educators and counselors who have the incredible task of trying to

keep up with the demands of both students and industry at the same time!" Articles are of a "how-to" nature explaining the process, the technique, and the technology of today's graphic arts printing. Magazine format; graphics; no advertising.
DEPT: "I Would Like to Know," "Photo Essay," "Classroom Review," "Letters." (10-76).
TYPL: "Labor Needs in the Print Industry," "Rolling Stone: Print Buyer," "A Tour: Starship--or Printing Plant?," "The Independent Graphic Artist." (10-76).
SCHL: Monthly [except Jul, Aug].
SPAN: Oct, 1976+
LC: Z 119.P8987

✤ PRINT-EQUIP NEWS

SUB: "The only graphic arts newspaper serving the western United States."
PUBL: P-EN Publications, 215 Allen Ave., PO Box 5540, Glendale, CA 91221-5540.
DESC: This tabloid-size newspaper concentrates on equipment and equipment applications for the technique and profit of printing in 19 western states. Advertisements for new and used equipment and services are featured throughout the publication. Over the years, a number of departmental columns have been added, a number of which bear mentioning. "Ink Stains" describes new advances in printing inks and their application. "Desktop Publishing" provides authoritative information for print shops contemplating the move into electronic pre-press operations. "Training & Education" concerns education maintenance for staff and executive alike in a rapidly changing marketplace. "International Museum of Graphic Communication" provides an historical review of the art and technique of printing through the ages. "Kaleidoscope" notes news events and developments of interest to members of the PIA-SC, the Printing Industries Association of Southern California. And finally, "Keeping It!" provides readily applicable information for maintaining a competitive edge in the marketplace. A timely news source for the status of printing in the Western United States. Tabloid size (11 ½ x 14 ⅞ inches / 290 x 380 mm), published on newsprint with spot color throughout.
DEPT: "Kaleidoscope," news of the Printing Industries Association of Southern California; "Ink Stains," personality column; "Personnel," newsbriefs. (12-77). "Calendar," "Chemicals & the Graphic Arts," application to the printing arts column by Don Nix; "Desktop Publishing," column by Richard Brock; "Ink Stains," column by Robert J. Gans; "International Museum of Graphic Communication," museum curator column by Mark Barbour; "Kaleidoscope," 'of PIA-SC Happenings' column by Bob Lindgren; "Keeping It," 'How to generate, accumulate and conserve business wealth' column by Daniel B. Lewis; "New Products," review; "Strictly PERSONnel," personnel newsbriefs. (10-89).
TYPL: "NAPL Publishes Forms Control Program for Accurate Estimation," "Need for Sound Credit Policy was Factor in Forming PICE," "NAPL Bulletin Editor Rejects Sans Serif Typefaces for Books." (12-77). "Screen Printers Simplify Scholarship Procedures," "Houston Firm Named Manufacturer of Year," "Dealers Group Announces New Officers." (5-84). "Philip Battaglia Honored by NALC for Quarter-Century of Service," "DRUPA, World's Biggest Printing Show will Draw From the West," "Heidelberg West's Branch in Southern California Completes Move to New Printing Technical Center." (10-89).
SCHL: Monthly, 55 pp.
SPAN: 1964+
ISSN: 0048-5314

✤ PRINTED MATTER

PUBL: The Media Project, PO Box 2008, Portland, OR 97208.
DESC: "The Media Project: 13 thrilling years serving Northwest film video artists through nationwide distribution of regional films, challenging workshops and classes, exciting screenings of American independent film and video, informative publications, friendly and knowledgeable technical assistance, and the occasional Big Bash." Independent filmmakers (film and video) have a wonderful resource in this organization and its publication, *Printed Matter*; which promotes, and reports on film and video activities of its members in the greater Pacific Northwest region of the United States. It bristles with excitement over opportunities and awards earned by its members, new production opportunities for which production groups can submit bids, and the current status of film and video production. Of special note is the encouragement exhibited by the Media Project for new independent producers and their film/video products; and informative articles concerning the status of professional production work in the Pacific Northwest. Magazine format (8 ½ x 10 ⅝ inches / 215 x 270 mm); black/white editorial content on uncoated paper stock; minimal advertising.
DEPT: "Book Reviews," "Local Update," Pacific northwest production news; "Festivals," calendar; "Opportunities," Announced productions. (fall-88).
TYPL: "An Interview with Makeup Wizard E. Larry Day," "Other Voices: An Interview with Jose Araujo, Chris Spotted Eagle, Karen Ishizuka & Bob Nakamura," "Action! Oregon--The Plan for Film & Video," "Oregon's Crews: What Lies Ahead," "Freedom Productions Sends Staff to Rockport." (fall-88).
SCHL: Quarterly, 24 pp.
SPAN: ?, 1974+
ISSN: 0738-9558

Printer & Publisher

? - ?//
(ISSN: 0317-1213)
SEE: CANADIAN PRINTER

Printers' Ink

Jul 15, 1888 - Sep 8, 1967//
(ISSN: 0196-1160)
SEE: MARKETING / COMMUNICATIONS

✤ PRINTING HISTORY

SUB: "The journal of the American Printing History Association."
PUBL: American Printing History Association, 516 Butler Library, Columbia University, New York, NY.
DESC: Published by the American Printing History Association (founded 1974), *Printing History*'s "...scope is the same as that of its parent organization, American only in that it is based in the United States, and with 'printing' taken to mean the book arts in general. Undoubtedly, there will be some bias toward American subjects...but *Printing History* is open to scholarly work on all aspects of graphic communication, from cave paintings to holography, from Texas to Timbuctoo." *Printing History* is a treasure-trove of information and education. Typographical design is critical to good communication design, and this serial should be required reading for all communication theory students. Indeed, it should be on every journalist's and historian's shelf. Small magazine format; excellent reproduction of historical graphics.
DEPT: "Editorial," "Book Reviews," "Letter to the Editor." (# 7/8-82).
TYPL: "The Lost Years of the Golden Cockerel Press," "The Convivial Printer: Dining, Wining, and Marching, 1825 - 1860," "Vignettes of the Past: American Historical Broadsides Through the War of 1812," "Ephemera in the STC Revision: A Housekeeper's View." (#7/8-82).
SCHL: Semiannual, 50 pp.
SPAN: 1979+
LC: Z 124 .A2 P74
DD: 686.2/09
ISSN: 0192-9275
ABST: --Library Information Science Abstracts (ISSN: 0024-2179)
--Library Literature (ISSN: 0024-2373)
--Recently Published Articles (ISSN: 0145-5311)
--Writings on American History (ISSN: 0364-2887)

✤ PRINTING IMPRESSIONS

SUB: "America's most influential journal for the printing and allied industries."
PUBL: North American Publishing Co., 401 N. Broad St., Philadelphia, PA 19108.
DESC: With a February, 1991 qualified circulation of 95,215 readers, *Printing Impressions* certainly qualifies to post its subtitle. "America's most influential journal for the printing and allied industries." The large size format of this trade publication lends itself well to larger graphics; schematics; and numerous examples of the art and technique of paper and printing which are inserted throughout the magazine. Focus is on technology and pressroom operations. Articles typically cover new equipment, increasing profits, and information on the technology and technique of printing. Typical articles in past issues included topics of corporate image, computer software, color applications, foil and other specialty printing, sales management, and the legal side of the printing trade. Numerous photos, graphics and equipment promotional reviews. Large format size (10 ¾ x 14 inches / 275 x 355 mm), full color throughout on coated paper stock.
DEPT: "Estimating Clinic," "Financial Management," "Getting Employees Involved," "Government Printing," "Graphics Arts Securities," "Legal Labyrinths," "Management Measures," "Professionalism in Management," "Puck's Tour," "Purchase Decision Making," "Sales Presentation," "Selling Composition," "Stock Market Report," "Tax Clinic," "Age of the Pressroom," "Equipment and Supply Review," "Calendar of Meetings and Trade Exhibits," "Lithotips," "NAPL," "Otto's Night Watch," "PIA," "Postal Pointers," "Printers Library," "Supplier News," "Washington Report," (6-79). "Editor's Notebook," editorial column by Mark T. Michelson; "People, Places and Issues," "New Products," "Newspaper Production," "Printer News," "Supplier News," "Calendar," "Quick Printer / Job Printer," "Printer to Printer," "Entrepreneur to Entrepreneur." (2-91).
TYPL: "Why We're Entering 'The Age of the Pressroom,'" "What Federal Age Discrimination Rules Mean to You," "If You Want Higher Productivity, Involve Everyone!," "Profit Lies in Cost/Price Discipline, Not Markups!," "Join a Type-Swapping Pool; Make Variety a Sales Pitch," (6-79). "Catching the Brass Ring with CEPS," "Market Stabilizes Despite Economy," "The Times Journal Hits the Bulls-Eye," "Small Shop Makes Careful Purchases," "Changes in UV are A-1." (2-91).
SCHL: Monthly (Jun, 1958 - ?); Monthly [except semimonthly in May] (? - ?); Monthly (?+), 105 pp.
SPAN: June, 1958+
ABSORBED
--Web, Newspaper and Magazine Production (ISSN: 0191-4634), Aug, 1979.
WITH SUPPLEMENT
--Web, Newspaper and Magazine Production, Aug, 1979 - ?
DD: 338
ISSN: 0032-860x
ABST: --ABI/Informer
--Abstract Bulletin of the Institute of Paper Chemistry (ISSN: 0020-3033)
--Printing Abstracts (ISSN: 0031-109x)

Printing News

Jan, 1931 - Sep 30, 1989//
(ISSN: 0032-8626)
SEE: PRINTINGNEWS

PRINTING PAPER

SUB: "The paper quarterly for the graphic arts."
PUBL: Paper Makers Advertising Association, 90 Elm St., Westfield, MA 01085.
DESC: A promotional vehicle for printing papers produced by the Paper Makers Advertising Association, and aimed at print managers and buyers, this publication featured quality articles on specific themes. Each issue was printed on a variety of paper stock, with multicolored inks and other advertising techniques such as pop-ups and die-cuts. This was an innovative publication for the showcasing of unique paper and inks, and should provide graphic artists with a number of new ways to enliven their printed materials.
DEPT: "Editorial," "About the Cover Designer."
TYPL: "Insights Into the American Way," "The In-Flight Magazines," "The Printing and Paper Required to Keep United Flying." (#3-77).
SCHL: Quarterly, 50 pp.
SPAN: 1911 - 1982//
VARIES
--1911 - Winter, 1934 as Direct Advertising and Sample Book of Mill Brand Papers (ISSN: 0740-9249).
--Spring, 1935 - Jan, 1943 as Direct Advertising (ISSN: 0740-9265).
--Jan, 1943? - #3, 1977 as DA (ISSN: 0011-4693).
--? - ? as Printing Paper Quarterly.
LC: HF 5801.D2
DD: 338.4/7/676205
ISSN: 0161-5785

Printing Paper Quarterly

? - ?//
SEE: PRINTING PAPER

✤ PRINTINGNEWS

SUB: "The authoritative weekly newspaper of the printing industry."
SUB: "First with the news in the world of graphic arts."
SUB: "The only weekly trade publication in the graphic arts industry."
PUBL: Printing News, Inc., 468 Park Avenue South, New York, NY 10016.
DESC: For over 3,000 successive issues, *Printing News* has provided late-breaking graphics news in a spritely tabloid format on the management, production, technology, trends, and people in that industry. Numerous graphics and advertisements offering services and materials to those "in the trade" are featured.
DEPT: "Calendar," events; "Pi A La Mode," newsbriefs; "Services for the Trade." (4-26-86).
TYPL: "Five Steps are Offered for Improving Production Levels in the Workplace," "Frank Romano Gives Update to WIP on the Status of Desktop Publishing," "SAGA Given Practical Tips by Buyers on Who Will Get Their Printing Jobs." (4-26-86).
SCHL: Weekly [except last week in Dec], 50 pp.

SPAN: 1928+
EDITION
--East.
VARIES
--1928 - Jan, 1931 as New York Printing News.
--Jan, 1931 - Sep 30, 1989 as Printing News (ISSN: 0032-8626).
LC: Z 119 .P9562
DD: 686 11
ISSN: 1046-8595
ABST: --Abstract Bulletin of the Institute of Paper Chemistry (ISSN: 0020-3033)

✤ PRIVATE CABLE

SUB: "The SMATV, MATV, MDS & DBS systems magazine."
PUBL: National Satellite Publishing, Inc., 1909 Avenue G, PO Box 1460, Rosenberg, TX 77471.
DESC: [*Satellite TV*]: Begun in the midst of the satellite television boom in the United States, *Satellite TV* serves as a news and issues forum for a wide array of communications media, all using the stationary satellite, and then distributed via cable. Emphasis is on technology, profiles, and legal issues.
DEPT: "Editorial," "News," newsbriefs; "People," newsbriefs; "New Products." (7/8-82).
TYPL: "The NSCA: Who? What? Why?," "Eight-Channel MDS for Salt Lake City?," "Inverted Carrier Block Converters Provide 'Soft' Security for SMA-TV," "The Changing Complexion of SMATV Regulations." (7/8-82).
SCHL: Bimonthly (? - ?); Monthly (? - ?); Bimonthly [except monthly during May, Oct, Nov, Dec] (?+), 48 pp.
SPAN: Jul/Aug, 1982+
VARIES
--Jul/Aug, 1982 - ? as Satellite TV (ISSN: 0744-9739).
DD: 621
ISSN: 0745-8711

✤ PRO SOUND NEWS

SUB: "The international newsmagazine for the professional recording & sound industry."
SUB: "The international newsmagazine for the professional sound production industry."
PUBL: PSN Publications, Inc., 2 Park Ave., Suite 1820, New York, NY 10016.
DESC: *Pro Sound News* is a large format trade journal for individuals connected with professional audio for stage, sound studio, or broadcast stations. It is primarily concerned with new state-of-the-art technology and its application to current production situations. Coverage of the professional audio industry is thorough and timely, and is informative about the status of the industry. Both an international and a European edition of the serial are published. In the international version for which sample issues were available, articles covered the broad spectrum of audio recording, production, promotion, technology, and business. Of

special consideration is the detailed coverage afforded trade conventions, shows, exhibitions, and new product introductions. *Pro Sound News* enables its readers to savor the sights and sounds of these events vicariously. Beginning in fall, 1990 *Pro Sound News* carried an advertising supplement for Lexicon, entitled *Digital Domain Digest*. This (8 ½ x 11 inch) black/white insert is attached by rubber cement and is easily removed from the publication. The supplement covers new Lexicon products and their applications. Large tabloid format (11 x 14 ½ inches / 280 x 370 mm), with numerous color graphics printed on coated paper stock.

DEPT: "View From the Top," guest commentary; "The Client Tells," Q&A with clients; "Directions," for new technology; "Pro Video News," Personnel and company newsbriefs; "Mixdown," international recording studio news; "Center Stage," news of professional touring sound reinforcement companies; "Sound on Film," credits; "People," personnel briefs; "Upfront," album engineering list. (4-4-82). "Editorial," "Business Barometer," concerning sound production; "Calendar," "Pro-Briefs," equipment newsbriefs; "Digital Update," newsbriefs; "Studio News," production news; "LP Session Report," production news; "Directions," technology trends; "Pro Video News," sound production news in video production; "Broadcast Briefs," "View From the Top," audio management commentary; "Duplication News," audio tape duplication newsbriefs; "Product Preview," "Products Plus," reviews; "Sound Contracting News," "Concert Sound News," column by David Scheirman; "Pro Sound Profile," "Center Stage," 'highlights the work of professional touring sound reinforcement companies'; "Up Front," new album releases; "International Mixdown," production house news; "London Calling," British sound news column by Terri Anderson & Jim Evans; "Pro People," personnel changes; "Rep/Wrap Up." (4-1-87). "General News," "Sounding Off," "News Briefs," "Business Barometer," "Recording," "Producer Profile," "Interview," "Product Focus," "Studio Pro," 'A survey of current records and the professionals who made them'; "Music Production," "View From the Top," "NAMM Briefs," newsbriefs concerning the National Association of Music Merchants; "Audio Post Production," "Audio Edits," newsbriefs; "Product Review," "Innovations in Sound," "Tape Duplication," "Sound Reinforcement," "Sound Installation," "Sound Contracting News," "Centerstage," 'Top 10 tours of the month'; "Reinforcement Roundup," 'Regional touring highlights'; "Pro Sound Mixdown," "Spotcheck," reader Q&A. (2-91).

TYPL: "Getting More Sound on the Air," "New Look at Crystal Sound," "Sound Contractors Ready for New Orleans Convention," "Here Come the Stereo VCR's," "Selling Audio to Broadcasters," (4-4-82). "Digital Post Awaiting Full Chain," "A Special Report on Stereo TV," "Strong London AES Convention," "An Increased Acoustic Awareness," "Heightened TV Audio Spurs Sales." (4-1-87). "Used Studio Equipment Brings Affordable Quality to Upgrades," "Hostilities, Unrest Overseas Demand Caution in Export Biz," "DAT: Industry's Small Miracle," "Excitement at NAMM Confab," "Size of SR Company Determines a Differing Financial Profile." (2-91).

SCHL: Monthly, 70 pp.
SPAN: Nov, 1978+
EDITION
--International.
WITH SUPPLEMENT
--Digital Domain Digest, Fall, 1990+
DD: 338
ISSN: 0164-6338

✦ PRO VIDEOGRAM

SUB: "The newsletter of the Society of Professional Videographers."
PUBL: Society of Professional Videographers, PO Box 1933, Huntsville, AL 35807.
DESC: A membership information and application form provides benefits of joining the organization and receiving its newsletter: "The Society of Professional Videographers is a professional enrichment association primarily for professional event videographers. The need for this international professional association is a direct result of the home video revolution. Broadcasters have their professional associations, corporate producers have theirs, and professional photographers have theirs. The time has come for an association dedicated to event videographers. SPV is designed for the serious professional. Anyone involved in video production for financial gain is eligible to join. There is neither an initial category nor current plans for the novice or hobbyist. All individuals, firms, organizations and educational institutions directly or indirectly sharing an interest in the field of professional videography stand to gain from membership in the SPV." The Society of Professional Videographers and its bimonthly publication, *Pro Videogram*, is designed for individuals in commercial videography in areas as diverse as weddings, real estate, seminars, and festivals. *Pro Videogram* provides a meeting place whereby ideas, concepts, and new technologies can be shared among members. Of special interest is the "How-To" column on videographic techniques for event-videographers, and an unnamed (for 11/12-90 issue) department which profiles "accomplished event videographers." Stapled newsletter format on heavy coated paper stock, two-color editorial copy throughout, no advertising, graphics (8 ½ x 11 inches / 215 x 280 mm).

DEPT: "How-To," 'articles on techniques and marketing to address the needs of the event-type videographer'; "Soap Box," reader submitted pet peeves. (11/12-90).

TYPL: "Chapter Development Program Announcement," "JVC Introduces New Portable S-VHS Recorder for Professional Cameras," "The Single-Camera, Unedited Video Shoot," "Journal for Amiga Video Users," "Mississippi Photographer Focuses on Video Success." (11/12-90).

SCHL: Bimonthly, 16 pp.
SPAN: Nov/Dec, 1989+

Proceedings, The
Oct, 1926 - 1939//
SEE: ELECTRONICS & COMMUNICATIONS ENGINEERING JOURNAL

Proceedings - Institution of Radio and Electronics Engineers Australia
Jan, 1964 - Dec, 1971//
(ISSN: 0020-3521)
SEE: PROCEEDINGS OF THE IREE AUSTRALIA

Proceedings - Institution of Radio Engineers
1937 - 1963//
(ISSN: 0020-3521)
SEE: PROCEEDINGS OF THE IREE AUSTRALIA

✣ PROCEEDINGS OF THE IEEE
SUB: "The journal with vision."
PUBL: Institute of Electrical and Electronics Engineers, IEEE Service Center, 445 Hoes Ln., Piscataway, NJ 08854.
DESC: A highly-technical, esteemed publication, *Proceedings of the IEEE* "...welcomes for consideration 1) contributed tutorial-review papers in all areas of electrical engineering, and 2) contributed research papers on subjects of broad interest to IEEE members." For almost 80 years, the *Proceedings of the IEEE* has provided an important forum for new developments in electronic design, theory, and applications. The list of contributors reads like a "Who's Who" of the electronic design world, participants from all parts of the world, with varied scientific backgrounds. Numerous graphs, charts, and scientific notations abound within each issue. Of special note is "Scanning the Past," a delightful historical look at electronics and electrical engineering of the past. It brings a satisfying balance to the publication, demonstrating that all which is wonderful is not restricted in time. Beginning in early 1991, *Proceedings of the IEEE* began running one themed "Special Section" per issue. Among the themed topics for publication were "Future of CAD," "ISDN," "Massively Parallel Computers," "Multideimensional Signal Processing," "Nanoelectronics Technology," "Neural Networks," "Progress in Electromagnetics," "Superconductivity," and "Satellite Communications." For sampled issues of 1975 and 1991: perfect-bound magazine format, black/white editorial content with full-color cover, minimal IEEE organizational advertising, all on coated paper stock (8 ¼ x 10 ⅞ inches / 210 x 275 mm).

DEPT: "Scanning the Issue," editorial overview. (5-75). "Scanning the Issue," "Scanning the Past," excellent historical review. (3-91).
TYPL: "Physical Limits in Digital Electronics," "A Back-Matched Delay-Line Clipping Technique for Use with Fast Amplifiers," "Optimum Schottky-Barrier Height for High-Efficiency Microwave Transferred-Electron Diodes," "A Brief Review of Some Applications of Coherent Optical Processing to Image Improvement," "A High-Efficiency Granule Microphone Using Se-Te Alloys." (5-75). "Recent Advances in Long-Wavelength Semiconductor Lasers for Opitcal Fiber Communication," "Tutorial on Higher-Order Statistics (Spectra) in Signal Processing and System Theory: Theoretical Results and Some Applications," "Transmit/Receive Module Technology for X-Band Active Array Radar," "Multifunction W-Band MMIC Receiver Technology," "Advanced Channelization Technology for RF, Microwave, and Millimeterwave Applications." (3-91).
SCHL: Monthly, 140 pp.
SPAN: Jan, 1913?+
VARIES
--? - ? as Proceedings of the Institute of Radio Engineers (ISSN: 0731-5996).
--Jan, 1939 - Dec, 1962 as Proceedings of the IRE (ISSN: 0096-8390).
ISSN: 0018-9219

Proceedings of the Institute of Radio Engineers
? - ?//
(ISSN: 0731-5996)
SEE: PROCEEDINGS OF THE IEEE

Proceedings of the IRE
Jan, 1939 - Dec, 1962//
(ISSN: 0096-8390)
SEE: PROCEEDINGS OF THE IEEE

Proceedings of the IREE
Jan, 1972 - Dec, 1975//
(ISSN: 0314-4313)
SEE: PROCEEDINGS OF THE IREE AUSTRALIA

PROCEEDINGS OF THE IREE AUSTRALIA
SUB: "Proceedings of the Institution of Radio and Electronics Engineers, Australia.
PUBL: Institution of Radio and Electronics Engineers Australia, Science Center, 35-43 Clarence St., Sydney, N.S.W. 2000, Australia.

DESC: This highly technical series publishes inventions and discoveries to advance the science of electronics. Some articles were typeset; others typewritten. All contain schematics and formulas necessary for comprehension. A high level of electronics engineering knowledge was assumed. Changes in the serial took place in March, 1981: "The December issue (vol 41, #4) will be the last issue of *The Proceedings of the IREE Australia* as a separate journal. Starting in March, 1981, it will be replaced by a joint publication of the IREE Australia and the Electrical Engineering College of the IE Australia. Entitled *Journal of Electrical and Electronics Engineering, Australia,* the joint publication's cover page will state that it incorporates *Proceedings of the IREE Australia* and *Electrical Engineering Transactions of the IE Australia.*"
DEPT: None.
TYPL: "A Photomultiplier Photon counter," "A Class-AB Amplifier Technique with Low Level Crossover and Reduced Thermal Cycling," "A Device for Travel Time Monitoring." (12-80).
SCHL: Monthly (1937 - 1979); Quarterly (Jan/Feb, 1979+), 50 pp.
SPAN: 1937 - Dec?, 1980?//
VARIES
--1937 - 1963 as Proceedings - Institution of Radio Engineers (ISSN: 0020-3521).
--Jan, 1964 - Dec, 1971 as Proceedings - Institution of Radio and Electronics Engineers Australia (ISSN: 0020-3521).
--Jan, 1972 - Dec, 1975 as Proceedings of the IREE (ISSN: 0314-4313).
--Jan/Feb, 1976 - Dec, 1979 as Monitor (ISSN: 0314-4321).
SPLIT INTO
--Monitor, Mar, 1979.
MERGED WITH
--Transactions of the Institution of Engineers, Australia. Electrical Engineering (to form) Journal of Electrical and Electronics Engineering, Australia (ISSN: 0725-2986).
LC: TK 6540.I45
DD: 621.38/05
ISSN: 0158-0736
ABST: --Communication Abstracts
--Computer & Control Abstracts (ISSN: 0036-8113)
--Electrical & Electronics Abstracts (ISSN: 0036-8105)
--International Aerospace Abstracts (ISSN: 0020-5842)
--Physics Abstracts. Science Abstracts. Series A. (ISSN: 0036-8091)

Producci on [NE]

Oct/Nov, 1989 - Volume 1, #2, 1990//
(ISSN: 1048-1869)
SEE: PRODUCCIÓN Y DISTRIBUCIÓN

✢ PRODUCCIÓN Y DISTRIBUCIÓN

SUB: "The TV & film production, distribution & manufacturing marketplace of the Spanish-speaking world & Brazil."
PUBL: Izarra Media Communications, Inc., 6602 SW 112 Place, Miami, FL 33173.
DESC: A Spanish-language monthly (with English-language summaries for most articles), *Producción y Distribución* provides an all-too-rare news summary of broadcast television production and distribution in Spain and South American nations. A sampled issue for May, 1991 spoke of plans for HDTV television production; Argentinian television distribution; production trends for the Chilean television industry; a production profile of "Christina," the number one talk show of Hispanic broadcast television in the United States; a new private television channel in Spain; and a large section spotlighting manufacturing and new technologies for the Spanish-language television production industry. The format is handsome, with liberal use of spot and full-color pages throughout, all on coated paper stock in a stapled magazine format. Many American advertisements for media product and equipment are found, both in English and Spanish languages, attesting to the importance of this global television market. (8 ½ x 11 inches / 215 x 280 mm).
DEPT: "Brasil," production newsbriefs; "Argentina," production newsbriefs; "Chile," production newsbriefs; "USA," production newsbriefs; "Espana," production newsbriefs; "Dubbing," newsbriefs; "News," "Produccion," newsbriefs; "Manufacturers," newsbriefs; "Opinion," "Fabricantes," "Distribucion," newsbriefs. (5-91).
TYPL: "En el 92 arranca HDTV en México y en el 93 en USA," "Más de 60 Expositores en el IV Tele Expo Show," "Chilefilms instala Rank Cintel y co-produce con Soyus," "Christina Saralegui: Dos años ganando los ratings en TV," "Antena 3 TV, innovando la noticia y ganando audiencia." (5-91).
SCHL: Bimonthly, 55 pp.
SPAN: Oct/Nov, 1989+
VARIES
--Oct/Nov, 1989 - Volume 1, #2, 1990 as Producci on [NE] (ISSN: 1048-1869).
DD: 791
ISSN: 1048-1877

✢ PRODUCERS QUARTERLY

PUBL: Producers Quarterly Publications, 25 Willowdale Ave., Port Washington, NY 11050.
DESC: In the premiere issue for spring, 1990, President/Publisher Vincent Testa stated: "Since its inception it was our hope to create a magazine that would attempt to satisfy the needs of the plurality of markets and the varied definitions of the creative people in 'production'. So to begin with we dispensed with the market 'categories'. We don't care whether you are currently working on a full length feature film or a corporate

training tape. We believe that when asked, you simply respond by saying ...'I'm a videographer', or 'I'm a lighting director' or a recording engineer, music composer, cameraman, field producer, etc. We decided that we would pay attention to all creative 'frontline' people. The term 'producers' in this magazine's case is deliberately plural. Unlike the image of a person 'with a check book' who has little to do or say about what goes on in a project, we have created this magazine for the producers who are the doers, the active participants, the makers of the project...and all aspects of the project." Very few current publications exist with a primary focus on the audio, film, or video producer. *Producers Quarterly*, therefore, is a much needed and welcome member of this community. As a quarterly supplement to *Post* magazine, it necessarily lacked the editorial quantity desired to cover the major issues facing producers. As a stand-alone publication, it possesses both the editorial space and staff to serve this unique group of professionals, long overdue for their own trade serial. Premiere issue for spring, 1990 had 14 articles ranging across such diverse topics as Nickelodeon's new multimedia kidshow, corporate video, spot production, high school television via satellite, and film scores. *Post*, and *Producers Quarterly* are renowned publications for the radio-television-film field. Magazine format (9 x 10 ⅞ inches / 230 x 275 mm); full color throughout, printed on heavy coated paper stock.

DEPT: None. (6-89). "Concept," idea development column by Debra Kaufman; "Pre-Pro," column by Bill Intemann; "Production," column by Jon Pickow; "After Hours." (spring-90).
TYPL: "The Big Broadcast of 1989," "Transcending Sports," "The Flood of New Technologies." (6-89). "Making Sitcoms Look Like Movies," "Humor Helps Hawk Hardware," "Innovative Classics," "Reaching Around the Deaf World." (spring-90).
SCHL: Quarterly, 90 pp.
SPAN: Mar, 1989+
SUPPLEMENT TO
--Post (ISSN: 0891-5628), Mar, 1989 - Feb?, 1990//

PRODUCT DIGEST

PUBL: Quigley Publishing Co., Rockefeller Center, New York, NY.
DESC: This invaluable supplement to *Motion Picture Herald* provided the local exhibitor or film business executive with virtually any information desired concerning film releases in the United States. Issued weekly, with its own pagination, and distinct red ink boarder, *Product Digest* offered its data in unique sections. "Showmen's Reviews" furnished outstanding descriptions of feature product from the exhibitor's point-of-view. Among the evaluated elements were selection of cast, screenplay, plot, audience appeal, promotion possibilities, and the reaction of preview audiences and reviewer alike. "Short Subjects" provided short reviews. "Short Subjects Chart," provided detailed listings by studio, group title, production number, release date, and *Product Digest* page number for review. The "Release Chart" indicated dates of release for specific titles listed by studio. "Advance Synopses" offered one-paragraph descriptions of upcoming product. "Service Data" registered feature titles with 1) audience classification, 2) Legion of Decency Rating, 3) Picture Gross percentage, and 4) Round Table Exploitation articles. "The Release Chart" was an extensive "Index to reviews, advance synopses and service data in *Product Digest* section." Outstanding for its then-contemporary application for local exhibition, and for historical research today regarding detailed summaries of Hollywood film product. No graphics or advertising.
DEPT: "Showmen's Reviews," "Short Subjects," 'Reviews and synopses'; "Short Subjects Chart," 'Index to reviews, synopses'; "Release Chart," 'By companies'; "Advance Synopses," 'And information'; "Service Data," 'On features'; "The Release Chart," 'Index to reviews, advance synopses and service data in Product Digest section'. (8-26-44).
TYPL: No Article Titles. (8-26-44).
SCHL: Weekly, 15 pp.
SPAN: ? - ?//
SUPPLEMENT TO
--Motion Picture Herald (ISSN: 0027-1616).

Product Digest

Jun 6, 1973 - May 22, 1974 //
(ISSN: 0093-2132)
SEE: MOTION PICTURE PRODUCT DIGEST

Production Committee Newsletter

? - ?//
SEE: PD REPORT

Production Prospects

? - ?//
SEE: SHOW BUSINESS

✤ PRODUCTION SOUND REPORT

SUB: "The journal of production sound equipment and techniques."
PUBL: Audio Services Corporation, 10639 Riverside Dr., North Hollywood, CA 91602.
DESC: First published as something of an in-house newsletter for ASC employees, *Sound Blast* evolved into a more public means of discussing issues of importance to sound professionals in the entertainment recording industry. Now, as *Production Sound Report*, the bimonthly newsletter is described as a "unique and informative newsletter...available free to all parties interested in production sound recording for motion

pictures and video." This is not merely a promotional product brochure (although equipment brand names are mentioned), but rather a sincere attempt at providing what ASC hopes will evolve into a professional trade journal for audio mixers working in the motion picture and video entertainment industry. Of special note is the bimonthly section providing news of "the Cinema Audio Society, founded in 1964, ...a non-profit association dedicated to the advancement and recognition of sound in motion pictures and television," the function of which is to "...educate and inform the industry regarding the artistic use of sound, to achieve recognition for sound's artistry, and to foster a sense of camaraderie among sound mixers." For the sampled 1989 issue: six-page, three-fold newsletter format, black ink on coated paper stock (8 ½ x 11 inches / 215 x 280 mm).
DEPT: "A Message From Dick," editorial; "Sound Blast," personnel newsbriefs; "News From the Cinema Audio Society," organization news; "From the Technical Bench," technology. (4-89).
TYPL: "Production Sound Hints & Tips," "New Products at ASC," "Time Code Questions and Answers," "Sennheiser UHF Diversity Wireless Systems." (4-89).
SCHL: Bimonthly, 6 pp.
SPAN: ?+
VARIES
--? - Feb?, 1989 as Sound Blast.

✦ PROFESSIONAL FILM PRODUCTION
SUB: "The business magazine of film and tape."
PUBL: American Filmakers Magazine, 250 Fulton Ave., Hempstead, NY 11550.
DESC: "Conceived, planned and published for the professional film producer, *Pro Film* is totally business-oriented; a service to the producer, bringing you the information you need to make your film work successful and profitable. *Pro Film* will bring you proven marketing and management techniques, hard business facts, industry news, technical developments and applications--all the information the man in charge must be aware of and familiar with." This is a unique business-approach serial for the major and independent producer, providing insight on issues of business rarely found in other "trades." Magazine format; graphics.
DEPT: "Briefs," newsbriefs; "Murphy's Law," "Pieces of Eight," "Cross Country," 'Production notes from *Pro Film*'s Correspondents.' (8-75).
TYPL: "The Economy Takes Its Toll," "How to Package Your Independent Production," "Videotape Brings 'Instant Replay' to the Film Set," "Publicity: The Name Game," "Plan Distribution for Your Client's Film." (8-75).
SCHL: Bimonthly, 40 pp.
SPAN: Jun, 1975+
LC: PN 1995.9 .P7 P76
DD: 791.43/023/05

ISSN: 0362-5974

PROFESSIONAL PHOTOGRAPHER, THE
SUB: "Official publication of the Photographers' Association of America."
SUB: "The oldest exclusively professional photographic publication in the Western hemisphere."
PUBL: Charles Abel, Inc., 552 Fifth St., Lorain, OH.
DESC: For the professional commercial photographer, there were few publications to equal the information, interest or value to be found in *The Professional Photographer*, a publication which traced its lineage back to 1907. While editor-in-chief and publisher Charles Abel assembled a dynamic grouping of interesting articles and departments which found favor among commericial photographers, it was the departmental features which set the Abel publications apart from others in the field. Within the some dozen reguarly scheduled departments were a wealth of experience on successfully operating (read "profitability") a commercial photographic business. These departments kept readers apprised of new technologies, gave analyses of submitted photographs, discussed the fields of color and stereo photography, and announced coming conventions and other commercial opportunities. For the sampled issue of 1959: stapled magazine format, editorial content being black/white with spot color employed throughout on coated paper stock, covers in full color (7 ⅜ x 10 ⅜ inches / 185 x 265 mm).
DEPT: "Straight Talk for Professionals," continuing series of advice; "Color and You!," color photography column by Charles Smith; "'Tis Here, Maybe!," 'The gossip column of professional photography'; "Professional Stereo," stereo photography column by Branislav Denitch; "Photography in Industry," column by Robert G. Hoffman; "The Editor's Commentary," column by Charles Abel; "A Critical Analysis," of submitted photographs; "Make the Subject Interesting," column by Harry M. Nelson; "A Commercial Man's Scrap Book," 'The past, present and future of photography' column by James M. Caufield; "Press Photography," column by Robert D. Piante; "The Idea Exchange," 'Stunts, gadgets, formulae, short-cuts, just so long as they are original'; "The Marketplace," new products; "Book Reviews," "Schedule of Coming Conventions." (3-59).
TYPL: "How Bachrach Studios Sell Frames," "Nearby Store Owners Will Cooperate," "Why Feel Fatigued Every Day?," "Price Lists of Rob Paris and Helmer Brandell," "A Field Offering Many Inducements." (3-59).
SCHL: Weekly (Dec 7, 1907 - Jan, 1934); Semimonthly (Feb, 1934 - Mar, 1942); Monthly (Apr, 1942+), 75 pp.
SPAN: Dec 7, 1907 - Aug, 1961//
VARIES
--Dec 7, 1907 - Jan, 1934 as Abels Photographic Weekly.
--Feb, 1934 - ? as Professional Photographer, The.

SUSPENDED
--Jan 5, 1918.
ABSORBED
--Professional and Amateur Photographer, The, Jan 6, 1912.
--St. Louis and Canadian Photographer, ?
--Commercial Photographer, The, Apr, 1950?
MERGED WITH
--National Photographer, The (to form) National Professional Photographer (ISSN: 0734-7529), Aug, 1961.
LC: TR 1.A2
DD: 770/.565
ISSN: 0749-0119

✢ PROFESSIONAL PHOTOGRAPHER, THE

PUBL: Professional Photographers of America, PPA Publications and Events, 1090 Executive Way, Des Plaines, IL 60018.
DESC: Writing in the August, 1961 issue of *The National Professional Photographer*, Madison Geddes, the organization's past president noted, "It will be interesting to both the readers of *The Professional Photographer* and the members of the Professional Photographers of America, to learn that the next issue of *The National Photographer* will be combined with *The Professional Photographer*... It has been the wish of Mr. Abel and the Association for many years to combine these two magazines... This now makes the lineage of the Official Publication of the Association, which was founded in 1880, continuous since 1884, when it was first published as *Abel's Photographic Weekly*." The first new combined issue was dated September, 1961; bore volume number 88, issue # 1,792; and the subtitle; "*The Professional Photographer*, official journal of the Professional Photographers of America, Inc., is the oldest exclusively professional photographic publication in the western hemisphere (founded 1907 by Charles Abel)." This monthly is packed with detailed articles and lighting diagrams concerning the professional approach to commercial photography. Topics include technical, aesthetic, legal and marketing facets of photography and range from Christmas catalogs to motion picture stills; wedding albums to table top commercial product photography. There is quality reproduction of color photos. Sampled issues under the title of *National Professional Photographer* for 1961: black with spot-color ink on coated paper stock in stapled magazine format. Dimensions for September, 1961: (8 ½ x 11 inches / 215 x 280 mm). A slight change in dimensions was noted for the October, 1961 issue: (8 ½ x 11 ¼ inches / 215 x 285 mm).
DEPT: "News and Notes," "Tis Here, Maybe!," "President's Message," column by Lawton E. Osborn; "New Products," "What's Doing," "Local, State and Regional News," "Color and You," column by Charles Smith. (9-61). "Datelines," upcoming special events; "Behind the Covers," backgrounds on new pictorial works; "News," briefs; "Suppliers," newsbriefs; "Trade Talk," newsbriefs; "Contests-Exhibitions," "Deaths," "Book Briefs," "AV Perspectives," column by John Bethune; "Portrait Photographer's Clipsheet," short how-done column; "Industrial Techniques," "Education," "Schools, Seminars, and Conferences," "Photographic Impressions," technique; "Legally Speaking," column by sidney Kleinman; "Commercial Analysis," technique; "New products," "Advertising Basics," column by Hall Betancourt; "Professional Feedback," column by Ed Becker. (12-78). "President's Message," "Editorially Speaking," "Behind the Cover," production of this magazine cover; "People Photography," "Your Bottom Line," photography for profit; "In the Studio," "Practical Pointers," "Datelines," "Letters," "News," "In Depth," "State of the Art," "Viewpoint," "New Products." (4-87).
TYPL: "USDA Searches for 300 Photographs," "Jelly Bean Counting Contests," "Photography--The Research Eye," "How to Construct a Spider Box for Expendable Flashlamps," "The Photo Colorist." (9-61). "Christmas in July," "Shooting Stars; Making Stills for the Movies," "The Nuts and Bolts of Industrial Photography," "Retouching Ektachrome." (12-78). "Brides Around the World," "Environmental Wedding Portraiture," "Pro Video Tips," "New York City Style." (4-87).
SCHL: Monthly, 90 pp.
SPAN: Sep, 1961+
VARIES
--Sep, 1961 - Dec, 1963 as National Professional Photographer, The (ISSN: 0734-7529).
FROM MERGER OF
--National Photographer (and) Professional Photographer (ISSN: 0749-0119).
LC: TR 690.N3
DD: 770
ISSN: 0033-0167

✢ PROFESSIONAL PHOTOGRAPHER, THE

PUBL: EMAP Vision, Ltd., PO Box 109, Maclaren House, Scarbrook Rd., Croydon CR9 1QH England.
DESC: This is a publication for the working British professional photographer, encompassing information, technology, and technique necessary to thrive in this highly competitive field. *Professional Photographer* subtitles its feature articles under departmental names, the titles of which indicate the diversity of the serial: "Brochure," "Large Format," "Film," "Education," "Assignment," and "Photo Call." This primarily black/white monthly is neither flashy, nor imposing but provides a solid, professional approach to the business of British photography, which makes it worthy of subscription. For the sampled issue of 1990: perfect-bound magazine format, black ink editorial

content with outstanding color graphics reproductions, including full-color cover all on coated paper stock (8 ¼ x 11 ⅞ inches / 210 x 295 mm).
DEPT: "News," extensive photographic news section, including reader letters; "Product Update." (2-90).
TYPL: "Banking on Image," "Pinnacle of Perfection," "Good for Starters," "Business Matters." (2-90).
SCHL: Monthly, 50 pp.
SPAN: May, 1961+
VARIES
--May, 1961 - Feb, 1980 as Industrial and Commercial Photographer.
LC: TK 690.A1I5
DD: 770/.5
ISSN: 0019-784x

Professional Photographer, The

Feb, 1934 - ?//
SEE: PROFESSIONAL PHOTOGRAPHER, THE

Professional Publishing

? - Sep?, 1985//
(ISSN: 0736-7457)
SEE: PERSONAL PUBLISHING

Professional Video

1982? - 198u//
(ISSN: 0264-1321)
SEE: BROADCAST SYSTEMS ENGINEERING

✤ PROFIT MARKETING HOTLINE

PUBL: High Impact Marketing, 3960 Laurel Canyon Blvd., Suite 380, Studio City, CA 91614-3791.
DESC: "*Profit Marketing Hotline* is Bob Serling's quarterly newsletter of high impact marketing. The kind of marketing where the true purpose is not to be 'creative', but to create more sales. You'll find that these tips and techniques are powerful, practical, and dedicated to getting results." This rather short, but informative quarterly newsletter provides some very helpful hints to the complex world of direct mail marketing, from envelope design to writing the ideal direct mail letter. Bob Serling, publisher, works as a free-lance consultant for direct mail projects: this newsletter promotes those activities and talents of this firm. For sampled issues of 1990: single sheet black/white newsletter on uncoated paper stock, no graphics (8 ½ x 11 inches / 215 x 280 mm).
DEPT: None. (spring-90).
TYPL: "Power Preparation--How This Key Ingredient Can Radically Improve Your Leads, Sales, and Profits!," "What Causes Misdirection--the Ugly Truth!," "Bob Bly Shows You How to Increase Your Results Through Power Preparation!" (spring-90).
SCHL: Quarterly, 2 pp.

SPAN: Winter, 1988/1989+

PROFITABLE ADVERTISING

SUB: "A monthly journal devoted exclusively to advertisers." (Jun, 1891 - ?).
SUB: "We show you how to do it." (Jun, 1891 - Oct 15, 1892 [and] Jan 15, 1893 - ?).
SUB: "Illustrated monthly magazine for advertisers." (Jun 15, 1892 - ?).
SUB: "The magazine of publicity." (? - May, 1909).
SUB: "Devoted exclusively to the interests of advertisers and publishers." (? - May, 1909).
PUBL: Kate E. Griswold, 140 Boylston St., Boston, MA.
DESC: With a mixture of serious issue-oriented articles, and light-hearted cartoon sketches, publisher Kate E. Griswold maintained sanity in an ever-changing world of advertising. Admittedly, the lighter side of advertising oftentimes constituted the bulk of editorial content; with issue-oriented articles relegated to small newsbriefs. The subhead, "We show you how to do it," probably best describes the articles leading the advertising novice through the welter of advertising techniques. This is a print-medium journal that has a humorous sketch on every page, such as "Adjustable Whiskers" (Jun 15, 1892), a light-hearted look at facial hair on prominent men of advertising. Numerous graphics, especially cartoons, caricatures, and other sketches.
DEPT: "Editorials," (6-15-1892). "From PA's Point of View," opinion. (2-09).
TYPL: "Don't Monkey with the Buzz Saw," "Something About Some Railroads," "Comfort's New Press," "A Newspaper Man Gone Right." (6-15-1892). "Some All-'Round Pretty Poor Advertisements," "Some Tests of Psychology in Advertising," "Making the Big Ads Attractive and Interesting," "Coming Home to Papers and Magazines." (2-09).
SCHL: Monthly, 100 pp.
SPAN: Jun, 1891 - May, 1909//
ABSORBED
--Current Advertising, Jan, 1903.
--Returns, Feb, 1903.
MERGED WITH
--Selling Magazine, (to form) Advertising & Selling.
LC: HF 5801.A

Progress in Photography

1949/1950? - ?//
SEE: PERSPECTIVE

PROJECTION, LANTERN AND CINEMATOGRAPH

PUBL: John Wrench & Son, 50, Gray's Inn Rd., London WC, England.

DESC: In its initial issue for April, 1906, the editor noted: "It is somewhat difficult to trace the genesis of the trade circular: some so-called authorities affirm that it is of American extraction, whilst others hold that it is a natural evolution of the multi price list. Be this as it may, we have come to the conclusion that it provides an excellent means of communication between buyer and seller, and must of necessity bring the one into closer relationship with the other." See *Cinematography and Bioscope* magazine for an almost identical opening paragraph, due to the fact that Warwick Trading Company, and John Wrench & Son were actually in business together. John Wrench & Son was an optics manufacturer of long standing, who happened to move into the projection equipment field by the early 1900s. This weekly trade circular was designed to promote Wrench projectors, using graphics to extole the individual virtues of this line of cinematic equipment. The final issue of September, 1907 announced that Mr. Wrench had dissolved the business partnership with the Warwick Trading Company, which may have lead to the serial's demise.
DEPT: "Notes from All Sources," newsbriefs; (6-06).
TYPL: "The Making of Cinematograph Film at Whetstone," (6-06).
SCHL: Weekly, 8 pp.
SPAN: Apr, 1906 - Sep, 1907//

PROMOTION
PUBL: Crain Communications, Inc., 740 Rush St., Chicago, IL 60611.
DESC: Sales promotion techniques and products was the primary focus of *Promotion* magazine, a biweekly publication. The large-format serial provided new product information, late-breaking news items, and significant advertisements for promotional products. In its final issue (May 13, 1974), Crain Communications editors noted that promotion had "come of age," and therefore deserved its own place within the pages of Advertising Age, another Crain publication. Numerous graphics; many advertisements in color.
DEPT: "News Line," "Books," "Editorial," "Info for Buyers," "Letters," "Logos," "Meetings," "People," "Question Line," "Special Report," "Viewpoint," "Washington Line." (1-21-74).
TYPL: "Retailers Stress Promotion as Economic Key," "Video Cassettes Win OK from Major Companies at Audio-Visual Show," "Incentive Offers Abound for Savings Depositers," "Workshop to Discuss Overseas Techniques." (1-21-74).
SCHL: Monthly (Feb, 1953 - Apr, 1961); Weekly (May, 1961 - Dec 24, 1973); Biweekly (Jan 7, 1974+), 30 pp.
SPAN: Feb, 1953 - May 13, 1974//
VARIES
--Feb, 1953 - Apr, 1961 as Advertising Requirements.
--May, 1961 - Dec, 24, 1973 as Advertising & Sales Promotion (ISSN: 0001-8937).
ABSORBED BY
--Advertising Age.
LC: HF 5801.A345
DD: 659.1/05
ISSN: 0093-335x
ABST: --ABI/Informer

✣ PSA
SUB: "The magazine of public service advertising."
PUBL: Doug Wyles Productions, Inc., 49 West 76th St., New York, NY 10023.
DESC: Here is a long-awaited publication dealing specifically with the advertising-promotional process of public service agencies. *PSA* covers campaigns, advertising agency strategies, selection of media, and displays of currently available campaigns. Target audience of this periodical appears to be public service agencies, advertising personnel, and the media. Numerous graphics in a well-designed layout.
DEPT: "Great Ideas," "Back to Basics," "Partners," corporate and agency ties; "PSApages," listing of latest available campaigns; "Interview," "Information Please," resources. (fall-83).
TYPL: "Transit Advertising," "PSAs for Kids," "Public Service Directors," "Combined Federal Campaign." (fall-83).
SCHL: Quarterly, 50 pp.
SPAN: Fall, 1982+
ISSN: 0734-9130

✣ PSA JOURNAL
SUB: "Official publication of the Photographic Society of America."
PUBL: Photographic Society of America, 3000 United Founders Blvd., #103, Oklahoma City, OK 73112.
DESC: This membership publication provides a wide variety of information on the process, technique, and aesthetics of photography. Articles are written by association members, and cover various topics, from the darkroom to "color movies" (circa 1950s), slide show presentations, and family involvement. It provides news of chapter activities, new membership, services, and upcoming events of interest to the membership at large. A sampled issue for 1958 was in stapled magazine format, with a very clean and dynamic layout design; and editorial content and covers in black/white on coated paper stock (several advertisements in full color). Numerous graphics (8 3/8 x 11 1/8 inches / 210 x 280 mm).
DEPT: "The President Reports," "The Diffuser," letters to the editor; "The Editors Corner," "Canadiana," Canadian news; "Eastern Zone," "Central Zone," "Western Zone News," "Recorded Lectures Program," "International," "PSA News," "New Members," "New Products," "Trading Post," "Exhibitions & Competitions," "Clubs," activities and events. (1-58).
TYPL: "Corrective Retouching for Color Slides," "Travel Pictures in the Darkroom," "Photographing Bats in Action," "RIT, the Rochester Institute of Technology," "The Family and its Cameras." (1-58).

SCHL: Quarterly (Mar, 1935 - Oct, 1941); Monthly [Irregular at times], (Jan, 1942+), 60 pp.
SPAN: Mar, 1935+
VARIES
--Mar, 1935 - Dec, 1946 as Journal of Photographic Society of America (ISSN: 0096-5812).
WITH SUPPLEMENT
--Photographic Science and Technique, Jan, 1950 - Feb, 1957//
LC: TR 1.P7955
DD: 770
ISSN: 0030-8277

✤ PUBLIC BROADCASTING REPORT, THE

SUB: "The authoritative news service for public broadcasting and allied fields."
PUBL: Warren Publishing, Inc., 2115 Ward Court, NW, Washington, DC 20037.
DESC: This was from the premiere issue of October 27, 1978: "This new bi-weekly newsletter, devoted entirely to public broadcasting, is intended to open the field to broader understanding of its functions, policies, personnel and problems." At that time this newsletter indicated that "Editor & Publisher" was Albert Warren, and that it was published by *Television Digest*. Current masthead indicates "Published by Warren Publishing," with Mr. Warren remaining "Editor & Publisher." This is a splendid publication service for the American public broadcasting industry. The 16-page, small-format publication covers late-breaking news in all aspects of public radio and television; from regulation to programming; from personnel changes to public telethons. Pending legislation and regulatory policies are explained fully. Of special note is the significant amount of news concerning individual public radio and television outlets. Production plans; changes in management; grants announced and awarded; personals; and awards presented demonstrate the richness and diversity of public broadcasting. The departmental feature, "PBR Notes," provides national and international news developments under subcategories of "National Affairs / Developments," "Regulation," "International," "Education," "Commercial Media," "Station Activities," and "Miscellaneous." This remarkable news resource is well recommended to public broadcast management. As noted in the January 3, 1992 issue, *Public Broadcasting Report* is also available electronically through Newsnet, and Predicasts. It may also be received via facsimile. For the sampled issues of 1978 and 1991: folded newsletter format; three-hole punched; black in on uncoated paper with spot-color used in masthead; no advertising (8 ⅜ x 11 inches / 215 x 280 mm).
DEPT: "Personals," "FCC New Station Activity." (10-27-78). "Obituaries," "Personals." (8-24-84). "PBR Notes," "Grants," "Awards," "Personals." (1-3-92).

TYPL: "Fund-Raising Under FCC Scrutiny," "How Nixon Attacked PTV 'Liberal Bias'," "Turner Not Going to CPB," "Public Bcstg. Likes New Bill," "NPR's Ambitious Growth Plans." (10-27-78). "PBS & Stereo Broadcasts Separated by Money," "NPR Plus Service to be Dropped October 31st," "CPB Gets Increased FY 1987-89 Budget but Extra 1984 Money is Cut," "NPR Program Production Contracts Could Grow by 21.8%," "Households Tuning to PTV Up Slightly in May." (8-24-84). "Hold on CPB Reauthorization in Senate Apparently Came From GOP Leadership," "Preset Base CSG/NPPAG Grants are Part of Radio Grant Modification Plan," "PBS's Soper Sees Expedited Movement on Cooperative Fund-Raising Proposals," "ITVS Announces 25 Charter Grantees and 4 Funding Initiatives," "Southern Public Radio to be Formed as Independent Representation-Orientation Unit." (1-3-92).
SCHL: Biweekly (? - ?); Weekly (? to date), (except for last week of Aug to third week of Sep), 12 pp.
SPAN: 1978+
LC: PN 1990.9 .P82P82
DD: 384.54/43
ISSN: 0193-3663

✤ PUBLIC OPINION QUARTERLY

PUBL: Columbia University Press, Journalism Bldg., 116th St., New York, NY 10027.
DESC: As the official organ of the American Association for Public Opinion Research, *Public Opinion Quarterly* "...is hospitable to all points of view, provided that the material presented will help to illuminate problems of communication and public opinion." An excellent journal for cross-disciplinary research, herein is a "little bit of everything;" from television news to international advertising; from public debate to public opinion polls. Current issues are divided into several sub-categories. Articles are followed by "The Polls," which in the sampled issue included "Review: A Critique of the Kinsey Institute/Roper Organization National Sex Knowledge Survey," and "Intent and Purpose of the Kinsey Institute/Roper Organization Sex Knowledge Survey: A Rejoinder." The "Book Reviews" section provides highly detailed critiques of new publications in the field of information research. For the sampled issues of 1978 and 1991: perfect-bound journal format (6 x 9 inches / 150 x 225 mm). Editorial content in the 1978 issues was black ink on uncoated paper with a tinted index stock cover; for the 1991 issues, it was black ink on coated stock, the cover consisting of black or blue inks on coated index stock.
DEPT: "Comments and Letters," extended reader response; "Polls," dealing with specific topics; "News and Notes," newsbriefs concerning public opinion and individuals. (fall-77). "Book Reviews." (fall-91).
TYPL: "TV Violence and Viewer Aggression: A Cumulation of Study Results 1956 - 1976," "Rumors of Mass Poisoning in Biafra," "Bias in Random Digit Dialed

Surveys." (fall-77). "Race-of-Interviewer Effects in a Preelection Poll: Virginia 1989," "Response-Time Measurement in Survey Research: A Method for CATI and a New Look at Nonattitudes," "Work and Leisure: On the Reporting of Poll Results," "Do Open-ended Questions Measure 'Salient' Issues?," "Hardly Ever or Constantly? Group Comparisons Using Vague Quantifiers." (fall-91).
SCHL: Quarterly, 130 pp.
SPAN: Jan, 1937+
LC: HM 261.A1P8
DD: 301.15
ISSN: 0033-362x
ABST: --ABC Political Science (ISSN: 0001-0456)
--ABI/Informer
--Book Review Index (ISSN: 0524-0581)
--Combined Retrospective Index Sets
--Hospital Literature Index (ISSN: 0018-5736)
--InfoBank
--Magazine Index
--Psychological Abstracts (ISSN: 0033-0202)
--Public Affairs Information Service Bulletin (ISSN: 0033-3409)
--Social Science and Humanities Index (ISSN: 0037-7899)
--Social Sciences Index (ISSN: 0094-4920)
--Social Welfare, Social Planning / Policy and Social Development (ISSN: 0195-7988)
--United States Political Science Documents (ISSN: 0148-6063)

PUBLIC RELATIONS IDEAS

PUBL: American Association of Colleges of Teacher Education, 1201 16th St., N.W. Washington, DC 20036.
DESC: The target of this monthly is university or college public relations departments. It provides a monthly, four-page newsletter of ideas to publicize educational institutions. Articles are in a newsletter-style format with no titles. Typewritten; no illustrations.
DEPT: None. (2-65).
TYPL: None. (2-65).
SCHL: Monthly, 4 pp.
SPAN: 1951 - Dec, 1965//?
LC: LB 2846.P

✤ PUBLIC RELATIONS JOURNAL, THE

SUB: "A journal of opinion in the field of public relations practice."
SUB: "Serving public relations practitioners and educators and management."
PUBL: Public Relations Society of America, 33 Irving Place, New York, NY 10003-2376.
DESC: "The Public Relations Society of America (PRSA) is an individual membership professional society of 15,357 public relations practitioners. Its major services to members include programs of Professional Development and Accreditation, an Information Center, publications, tracking of issues of national concern, and promotion of ethical practice through adherence to PRSA's 'Code of Professional Standards'. PRSA's mission is 'To serve the public need for understanding and cooperation among its diverse interests by fostering high professional and ethical standards for all those practicing public relations." *The Public Relations Journal* functions as an information medium to carry out the purposes and mission of the Society, "Serving public relations practitioners and educators and management." Articles are of a multinational nature, reflecting the wide range of activities supervised by corporate public relations officers: advertisements reflect services and companies attempting to reach and influence these individuals. Of special note is the "hands-on" information provided the PR professional for hiring potential employees and/or services, including graphic designers, printer, videotape duplicator, legal counsel, etc. A sampling of articles from the December, 1991 issue included "Will Europe Be the Next Frontier for VNRs?," "Getting a Slice of the 'Europie'," "Opening Doors in Latin America," and "Reunification Paves Way for Business Expansion." For the sampled issues of 1979: editorial content was a mixture of black ink, and spot-color on coated and uncoated tinted stock; cover comprised of two spot-color inks on coated stock (8 x 10 ⅝ inches / 200 x 270 mm). For the sampled issues of 1991: editorial content here was also mixture of black ink, spot- and full-color pages on coated stock; cover is full-color graphics on coated stock (8 ¼ x 11 inches / 210 x 280 mm). For both sampled issues: stapled magazine format, with significant trade advertising.
DEPT: "Washington Focus," DC PR briefs; "New Media," PR utilization of new outlets such as CATV, AV; "Professional Reader," PR book reviews; "Consumerism Update," consumer development news. (9-77). "Inside Track," editorial; "Feedback," letters; "Briefings," issues of public relations in the news; "Resources," information and contacts; "Workshop," idea column for the public relations professional; "People," personnel changes; "Literature Showcase," "Technology Update," "Executive Forum," commentary. (8-89).
TYPL: "Trends in Annual Reports," "Sensitizing your Management," "Q & A Can Spice It Up," "PR's Role in Good Report Photos," "Mandating Economic Education," (9-77). "Minorities 2000: The Shape of Things to Come," "Thinking Like a Brand Manager." (8-89).
SCHL: Monthly (Oct, 1945 - ?); Monthly [except Jul] (? - ?); Monthly (?+), 40 pp.
SPAN: Oct, 1945+
LC: HM 263.A1P83
DD: 301.154
ISSN: 0033-3670
ABST: --ABI/Informer
--Business Periodical Index (ISSN: 0007-6961)
--InfoBank
--Management and Marketing Abstracts (ISSN: 0308-2172)

--Management Contents
--Predicasts

✢ PUBLIC RELATIONS NEWS

SUB: "The international weekly for public relations, public affairs, and communications executives."
PUBL: Public Relations Information Service, 127 E. 80th St., New York, NY 10021.
DESC: Since the first issue of July 17, 1944, founder and editor Denny Griswold has made *Public Relations News* "the" weekly newsletter of late-breaking events for the public relations professional. Editorial content is typewritten concisely in the (average) four-page issue. Of special note are some 2,000+ case studies published over the 40-year span of the serial, which informs about public relations. The $237 yearly subscription rate (for 1987) is well worth the price!
DEPT: "Case Study." (2-12-45). "Case Study." (7-13-87).
TYPL: "Public Relations has Gone Far in Wartime Toward Professional Recognition...," "Planners of South American Campaigns...," "Hundreds of Public Relations Programs are Jeopardized..." (2-12-45). "An Ethics Code Has Been Adopted...," "TV News Directors Want...," "The PR Field is Providing a Candidate..." (7-13-87).
SCHL: Weekly, 4 pp.
SPAN: Jan 17, 1944+
ABSORBED
--Planning for Business, Mar 25, 1946.
LC: HM 263.A1P84
DD: 301.154
ISSN: 0033-3697

✢ PUBLIC RELATIONS QUARTERLY

SUB: "The quarterly review of public relations." (Oct, 1955 - ?).
PUBL: Public Relations Quarterly, 44 West Market St., Rhinebeck, NY 12572.
DESC: Early 1950s issues of *PR* were found lacking in many ways, with only two to three articles of comment in the 30-odd pages. Thirty years later, *Public Relations Quarterly*, has evolved into a scholarly, professional approach to public relations as both art and science. Many articles provide "real-life" experiences with both thoughtful commentary, and case studies. It is a good publication for the working public relations professional. Magazine format; graphics.
DEPT: "Letters," "Books," reviews; "Writer's Notebook." (winter-1985/86).
TYPL: "Public Relations Vs. Private Enterprise," "Does Your Management Know the Language of Takeover?," "Marketing Communications is Not Hucksterism," "The Women are Coming, The Women are Coming," "Managing a Successful Public Affairs Response to an Initiative Attack." (winter-1985/86).
SCHL: Quarterly, 32 pp.
SPAN: Oct, 1955+

ABSORBED
--International Public Relations Review (ISSN: 0020-8434), Fall, 1975.
VARIES
--Oct, 1955 - Summer, 1960 as PR.
--Fall, 1960 - Winter, 1963 as Quarterly Review of Public Relations.
LC: HM 263.P766
DD: 659.2/05
ISSN: 0033-3700
ABST: --ABI/Informer
--Accountants' Index. Supplement. (ISSN: 0748-7975)
--Business Periodical Index (ISSN: 0007-6961)

✢ PUBLIC RELATIONS REVIEW

SUB: "A journal of research and comment."
PUBL: JAI Press, Inc., 55 Old Post Road #2, PO Box 1678, Greenwich, CT 06836.
DESC: In its notice to contributors, *Public Relations Review* notes that it "...is primarily devoted to original research and comment on existing research or needs for future research." A promotional flyer continues, "The review is the only quarterly journal devoted to articles that examine public relations in depth. Most of the articles are based on empirical research undertaken by professionals and academics in the field. Each issue contains half-a-dozen major articles, notes on research in brief, book reviews, and precis of new books in the fields of public relations, mass communications, organizational communications, public opinion formation social science research and evaluation, marketing, management and public policy formation." *Public Relations Review* also focuses on issues such as current professional standards within the public relations field, legal cases affecting daily operations, and book reviews on the art and craft of public relations work. It takes a broad view of public relations and its varied sub-activities. For sampled issues 1982 through 1985: black ink on uncoated paper; cover being black ink on tinted uncoated stock in perfect-bound journal format (6 x 8 ¾ inches / 150 x 220 mm). For the sampled issue of 1991: perfect-bound journal format, black ink on uncoated paper stock with a nicely designed two-color cover on heavy coated paper stock. Limited advertising (6 ⅞ x 10 inches / 175 x 255 mm).
DEPT: "Book Reviews," very substantial section of critical reviews. (spring-77). "Book Reviews," "Software Reviews," valuable information section. (summer-91).
TYPL: "Right of Privacy, Right to Know: Which Prevails?," "Apollo-Soyuz: Duel in the Sky," "Good Future Forecast for British PR," "PR Faculty: What are Their Qualifications?," "Public Relations Definitions Through the Years," (spring-77). "Public Relations as a Weapon of Modern Warfare," "How 'Bad' PR Decisions Get Made: A Roster of Faculty Judgment Heuristics," "Public Relations News Releases and Libel: Extending First Amendment Protections," "PRSA Members' Perceptions of Public Relations

Ethics," "Public Relations Practitioner Attitudes Toward Gender Issues: A Benchmark Study." (summer-91).
SCHL: Quarterly, 110 pp.
SPAN: Summer, 1975+
LC: HM 263.P767
DD: 659.2/05
ISSN: 0363-8111
ABST: --ABI/Informer
--Business Index
--Business Periodical Index (ISSN: 0007-6961)
--Communication Abstracts
--Current Index to Journals in Education (ISSN: 0011-3565)
--InfoBank
--Management Contents
--Public Affairs Information Service Bulletin (ISSN: 0033-3409)
--Reference Sources (ISSN: 0163-3546)

Public Telecommunications Letter

Apr/May, 1979 - Jan/Feb, 1980//
SEE: CURRENT

PUBLIC TELECOMMUNICATIONS REVIEW

SUB: "Public Telecommunications Review."
SUB: "A publication of the National Association of Educational Broadcasters."
PUBL: National Association of Educational Broadcasters, 1346 Conneticut Ave., N.W., Washington, DC 20036.
DESC: This was an noteworthy publication for news and issues concerning public television. Subjects ranged from station management to programming; from governmental politics to public acceptance of PBS programs. A sample of articles from the 1978 publication year included "Independents and PTV: Touching Base on the Issues," "University Broadcast Licensees: Rx for Progress," "Engineers & Electronic Technicians: Why Do We Train Them and Lose Them?," "Cameras in the Courtroom: Another Chance," "TV Ontario: From Dostoyevsky to Donald Duck," and "Commercial Television is Alive and Well and Public in Britain." It is a well-designed periodical enhanced by graphics and photos. For the sampled issues of 1978: stapled, magazine format; editorial content being black ink on coated stock; cover consisting of two spot-color inks on coated paper; advertising directed to the trade (7 7/8 x 10 3/4 inches / 205 x 275 mm).
DESC: [*AERT Journal*]: This important scholarly serial had weathered various formats, name changes, and editorial styles since its 1941 inception. Wartime issues were sparse, 14-page editions (due to newsprint shortage) that emphasized the role of education by radio. This magazine-sized journal gave way to a small format publication and name change by the early 1950s. The letter "T" was added to the title to represent the new role of television in the American educational process, and articles for that medium quickly outnumbered those of radio. By the mid-1950s, radio was virtually forgotten. In December, 1956, the journal announced that a merger had taken place between the National Association of Educational Broadcasters (NAEB), and the Association for Education by Radio-Television (AERT), with the new organization to be known as the NAEB. Articles in all of these serials emphasized education. Latter issues had numerous graphics.
DEPT: "AER Reviews." (9-42). "Editorial," "Who, What, Where, When," newsbriefs; "Book Review." (10-56). "Letters to the Editor," "NAEB Research Fact Sheets," (1/2-62). "PTR Comments," unusually large editorial page on several issues; "Professional Emphasis," use of commercial media-ideas for public broadcasters; "Letter from London," current European television fare and thoughts. (1-77).
TYPL: "Educational Radio in the United States," "School of the Air of the Americas," "Mother Goose to the Battle of Books." (9-42). "Teaching by Television," "We Have a Public Relations Problem," "St. Louis Slants Show for Senior Citizens." (10-56). "Our Common Goal: A Nationwide ETV System," "School Television and In-Service Teacher Training," "A View of Radio-Television Textbooks," "New Techniques in Radio Production," (1/2-62). "Management by Objectives: And How to Implement It," "Alternatives in Pay Programming," "Telecommunications Policy in the Executive Branch: The OTP and Reorganized Alternatives." (1-77).
SCHL: Monthly [except Jun-Aug], (Sep, 1941 - May, 1953); Monthly [except Jun-Sep], (Oct, 1953 - ?); Bimonthly (? - ?); Bimonthly (Aug, 1973+), 70 pp.
SPAN: Sep, 1941 - Nov/Dec, 1980//
VARIES
--Sep, 1941 - May, 1953 as Journal of the AER.
--Oct, 1953 - May, 1956 as Journal of the AERT.
--Oct, 1956 - May, 1957 as AERT Journal.
--Oct, 1957 - Jul/Aug, 1967 as NAEB Journal.
--Oct, 1967 - Jun, 1973 as Educational Broadcasting Review (ISSN: 0013-1660).
ISSN: 0093-8149
LC: P 87.P78
DD: 301.16/1

Publicity Problems

Sep, 1942 - May/Jun, 1946//
SEE: COLLEGE & UNIVERSITY JOURNAL

✧ PUBLISH!

SUB: "Desktop publishing."
SUB: "The magazine for desktop publishers."
PUBL: PCW Communications, Inc., 501 Second St., San Francisco, CA 94107.

DESC: "Even the best desktop publishers can use regular professional advice--with typography and graphic design...new software applications and computer technologies...and more. So why not consult with the best? Put *Publish!* to work for you...it's the magazine for desktop publishers that's produced by desktop publishers. *Publish!* is your source of professional solutions for all sorts of desktop publishing problems. No matter what you publish on your personal computer, we'll help you get higher quality for less time and money." *Publish!* is about the art, technique, and technologies connected with the burgeoning field of computer-based desktop publishing. Part of the strength of *Publish!* is that it is not wed to a given computer platform, i.e., either Macintosh or PC, but rather covers what is best across both platforms in the wider field of electronic publishing. Articles are informative, and interesting. For 1990 sampled issue: perfect-bound magazine format, full-color throughout on coated paper stock (8 1/4 x 10 7/8 inches / 210 x 275 mm).
DEPT: "Keeping Tabs," editorial column by Susan Gubernat; "Letters," "News Beat," news item column by James A. Martin; "First Look," 'A preview of future products and trends'; "About Faces," type column by Clifford Burke; "Design Basics," column by John Miles; "Showtime," presentations column by Michael Callery and Roberta Schwartz; "Q&A," 'Practical hints, tips, and advice for desktop publishers' column by Robert C. Eckhardt and Ted Nace; "Product Watch," 'Your monthly listing of the latest hardware and software'; "Tips!," 'Readers share their tricks and techniques'. (2-90).
TYPL: "Wake Up the Boardroom," "Page Makeover," "From Memo to Demo," "The Main Event," "A Moving Report." (2-90).
SCHL: Bimonthly (Sep/Oct, 1986 - Jan/Feb, 1987); Monthly (Mar, 1987+), 120 pp.
SPAN: Sep/Oct, 1986+
LC: Z 286.D47 P83
DD: 070.5/028/5
ISSN: 0897-6007

Publishers' and Stationers' Weekly Trade Circular

Jan 18, 1872 - Dec 26, 1872//
SEE: PUBLISHER'S WEEKLY

✢ PUBLISHER'S AUXILIARY

SUB: "The newspaper industry's oldest newspaper."
SUB: "Published by and responsible to the National Newspaper Association."
PUBL: National Newspaper Association, 1627 K St. N.W., Suite 400, Washington, DC 20006.
DESC: This semi-monthly publication for newspaper management emphasizes management related areas covering advertising, circulation, labor, reporting, and new technology. Articles are reflective of the vibrant nature of the National Newspaper Association, an organization dedicated to the advancement, enrichment, and continuing development of American newspapers. Of special consideration are the impressive departmental features found in most issues. Bob Brinkmann provides late-breaking information on regulatory matters from Washington, DC in the "NNA Washington Report." Donald Q. Smith hosts the "Editor's Notebook," commentary section. In the "Page of the Week," Edmund C. Arnold provides a critical eye to submitted newspaper pages in layout design, typography, masthead and other design elements. Sara Brown writes "Managing Newspaper People," a splendid column of insight and information on the managerial function for newspapers. In one sampled issue she began her column with, "Have you ever noticed that the technical wizard often has the social skills of Conan the Barbarian? It would be fine if we could be content to leave the wizard in the company of inanimate objects, but frequently the wizard comes in contact with people. And when that happens, in the words of one unlucky manager, 'our eyebrows get scorched'." The "Libel Clinic," by Barbara Dill, provides litigation-saving information for newspaper management. "Classified Advice," by Daniel Lionel, describes the means to improve the "bottom line" via increased advertising lineage. These salient departmental columns combined with late-breaking relevant news make for an extraordinarily beneficial combination for today's newspaper management team. Well recommended. For the sampled issues of 1985 through 1991: folded, tabloid newspaper format; black ink with spot color on newsprint stock, significant trade advertising (11 3/8 x 15 inches / 290 x 380 mm).
DEPT: "Ideas for Publishers," new concepts in typography and formats; "Marketplace," sale and purchase of newspaper properties; "Washington Report," DC news briefs; "The Byliner," unique section devoted to unusual AP stories, campaigns and developments. (10-77). "New Flags," newspaper premieres; "Forum," commentary; "Editor's Notebook," column by Donald Q. Smith; "Transition," personnel changes by geographic location; "News Media Update," "Managing Newspaper People," column by Sara Brown; "Page of the Week," column by Edmund C. Arnold; "NNA Washington Report," column by Bob Brinkmann; "Libel Clinic," column by Barbara Dill; "Classified Advice," column by Daniel Lionel. (12-9-91).
TYPL: "The Community Press: Health is Good," "Undecided About Six-Column Format? News Encouraging," "Gazette Staff One Jump Ahead on Blast Story." (10-77). "Reporters Jailed 10 Hours for Contempt," "Missouri Seen Allowing Cameras in Court," "ANR Reports 7.8 Percent Increase in Gross Ad Revenues," "Save Money and Headaches by Writing Clear Contracts," "Newsprint Seen as Having Great Potential as Mulch." (12-9-91).
SCHL: Weekly (1923 - 1964); Biweekly (1965 - ?); Weekly (Dec 24, 1979+), 20 pp.
SPAN: 1865+
ABSORBED
--National Publisher, 1968.

LC: PN 4700.P8
ISSN: 0048-5942
ABST: --ABI/Informer

Publishers' Guide, The
1893 - Jul 28, 1916//
SEE: ADVERTISING NEWS

Publishers' Guide and the Advertising News
Aug 4, 1916 - Aug 11, 1916//
SEE: ADVERTISING NEWS

✤ PUBLISHER'S WEEKLY

SUB: "The international news magazine of book publishing."
SUB: "A monthly record of current literature." (Jul, 1869 - Aug, 1869).
SUB: "A special medium of inter-communication for publishers, booksellers, and stationers." (Sep, 1869 - Aug 18, 1870).
SUB: "A journal devoted to the interests of the publishing ... trades, and associated branches." (Jan 18, 1872 - Dec 26, 1872).
PUBL: R.R. Bowker Co., 249 West 17th St., New York, NY 10011.
DESC: A 1991 advertisement notes that subscribers to *Publisher's Weekly* will be able to: "Keep tabs on the most recent trends in both fiction and nonfiction publishing--from novels, mysteries, and science fiction to biographies, history, self-help books, and even audio and video cassettes; Preview forthcoming titles before they are published--by referring to *PW*'s spring, summer, and fall announcement issues, along with two comprehensive spring and fall children's announcement issues; Learn what's happening in pricing, book design and manufacturing, retailing, rights and permissions, and other topics essential for an in-depth grasp of publishing as it exists today; Explore the global scene with *PW International*, a monthly magazine-within-a-magazine, that fills you in on publishing abroad, including details of major book shows all over the world; [and] Spot the bestsellers through acclaimed weekly hardcover and paperback lists, as well as new lists that cover such specialized areas as children's books, religious books, and computer and business guides, as well as cookbooks, travel books, science fiction, gardening and every other field your clients are likely to be interested in." *Publishers Weekly* is a news magazine for the book publishing industry. As such, it deals with such topics as the economics of printing, copyright law, marketing research, development of new authors and other topics. Publisher Bowker is a major force in the information and reference book field, and this publication reflects that. As of January 1, 1992, several changes in the publication were instituted. Where before *Publisher's Weekly* would be issued on a Friday, with a cover date reflecting the following Friday, the new publication schedule has *Publisher's Weekly* appearing (with same cover date) on Monday of each week. Also, the *PW International* supplement was incorporated into the magazine as of the January 1, 1992 date, along with additional departmental features and more editorial color. It is well recommended for information on the status of the American and international publishing field. For the sampled issues of 1991: black ink with spot- and full-color graphics pages and cover on coated stock; stapled magazine format; significant advertising to the trade (8 x 11 inches / 205 x 280 mm).
DEPT: "PW Interviews," major publisher personalities; "Calendar," extended upcoming events; "Rights and Permissions," fascinating department concerning current copyright laws and publishing acquisition; "The Week," newsbriefs; "People," newsbriefs; "Trade News," newsbriefs; "PW Forecasts," synopses of books about to be published; "Best Sellers," compiled from across the United States; (10-28-74). "Highlights," late breaking news items; "The Open Letter," editorial column by Fred Ciporen; "News of the Week," "Bookselling," "Children's Book Scene," "Trade News," "Audio/Video Plus," "Audio Reviews," "Book Design & Manufacturing," "Rights," column by Paul Nathan; "Transpacific," column by Sally Taylor; "PW Interviews," "Forecasts." (11-1-91).
TYPL: "Third Quarter Analysis Shows Hardcover Prices," "The Struggle to Publish 'Animal Farm,'" "International Scene: The Dutch are Still Strong on the Printing Scene," (10-28-74). "Best Books of 1991," "Frankfurt: Quarrelsome but Quiet," "The Importance of First Impressions: A Look at How Book Jackets Influence Prospective Readers," "R.R. Donnelley: Printing Books Around the World, All at Once," "Magazines Make the Move to Audio Format." (11-1-91).
SCHL: Weekly (Jan 18, 1872 - Oct 19, 1976); Weekly [except Dec] (Oct 25, 1976 - Dec, 1982); Weekly [except two issues in Dec] (Dec 17, 1982+), 50 pp.
SPAN: Feb, 1869+
VARIES
--Feb, 1869 - Jun, 1869 as Leypoldt & Holt's Literary Bulletin.
--Jul, 1869 - Aug, 1869 as Literary Bulletin, The.
--Sep, 1869 - Aug 18, 1870 as Trade Circular and Literary Bulletin, The.
--Sep 18, 1870 - Dec 26, 1871 as Trade Circular and Publishers' Bulletin, The.
--Jan 18, 1872 - Dec 26, 1872 as Publishers' and Stationers' Weekly Trade Circular.
ABSORBED
--American Literary Gazette and Publishers' Circular, Jan, 1872.
WITH SUPPLEMENT
--Weekly Record, Sep 2, 1974 - ?, (ISSN: 0094-257x).
LC: Z 1219.P98
DD: 070

ISSN: 0000-0019
ABST: --ABI/Informer
--Book Review Index (ISSN: 0524-0581)
--Business Periodical Index (ISSN: 0007-6961)
--Library Information Science Abstracts (ISSN: 0024-2179)
--Library Literature (ISSN: 0024-2373)
--Magazine Index
--Popular Magazine Review (ISSN: 0740-3763)
--Public Affairs Information Service Bulletin (ISSN: 0033-3409)
--Readers Guide to Periodical Literature (ISSN: 0034-0464)
--Reference Sources (ISSN: 0163-3546)

✤ PUBLISHING & PRODUCTION EXECUTIVE

SUB: "For buyers of printing, prepress, paper & publishing systems for magazines, catalogs, books, agency & corporate communications."
PUBL: North American Publishing Co., 401 North Broad St., Philadelphia, PA 19108.
DESC: "Superior editorial content has made *Publishing & Production Executive* the industry's #1 publication:" This is the only promotional statement in this serial, but it bespeaks industry acceptance, trust, and readership. As noted in the subtitle, this nine-issues-per-year publication is for buyers of printing supplies, equipment, and services in the field of print. Each issue places feature articles under a variety of different banners, including "Posters," "Photography," "Inserts," "Color Proofing," "Books," "Ink-Jet Printing," "Technical Publishing," "Distribution," "Associations," "Color Prepress," "Web Publications," and "The Environment." Articles are authoritative and pragmatic, and address topics such as building color files on the computer, the means of sprucing up corporate image via print, breakthroughs in mechanical-less catalogs, hologram inserts, digital halftones, novelty electronic books for children, and a host of other topics. It is fair to say that within the span of a few issues, there is something for every segment of the print industry and profession in *Publishing & Production Executive*. This is a valuable resource for all print buyers. Magazine format (8 ⅛ x 10 ⅞ inches / 205 x 275 mm), full color throughout with numerous print and paper sample inserts on heavy coated paper stock, perfect bound.
DEPT: "Editorial," column by Rose Blessing; "Your Turn," letters; "In Brief," "EnviroNotes," publishing, printing and the environment; "What's in a Print?," column by Kathy Miller; "The Production Advisor," column by Kathy Reilly," "New Products & Services," "EP New Products," new productions for electronic publishing; "Datebook," calendar; "Tech Tips," column by Kathy Miller; "Finishing Touches," reader ideas. (3-91).

TYPL: "The Postal Rate Case: Rates Soar, Hopes Fall," "Salable Image," "Minimizing Flats, Maximizing Savings," "Leap of Faith," "'Magapapers' to Mailings." (3-91).
SCHL: Seven issues per year (1989 - ?, 1990); Nine issues per year [Jan/Feb, Mar, Apr, May, Jun/Jul, Aug/Sep, Oct, Nov, and Dec] (Mar, 1990+), 75 pp.
SPAN: Jan, 1987+
VARIES
--Jan, 1987? - Oct?, 1989 as Publishing Technology (ISSN: 1040-9440).
LC: Z 284 .P86
DD: 380
ISSN: 1048-3055

✤ PUBLISHING RESEARCH QUARTERLY

PUBL: Transaction Periodicals Consortium, Department 4010, Rutgers University, New Brunswick, NJ 08903.
DESC: [*Book Research Quarterly*]: "*Book Research Quarterly* publishes scholarly articles, reports of significant research, and essays that contribute to knowledge about books; the publishing and book distribution process; and the social, historical, political, economic, legal, and technological conditions that help to shape this process throughout the world. Readership of the journal includes participants and observers in all aspects of the publishing process." A summary glance at its articles provided strong testimony to its value. One could have stated that if this review of academic media did not exist, some other means of communication and debate concerning this critical area of publishing would have had to be created. It provided a forum for considered thought on the content, value, and processes required for publishing books of academic merit. The Transaction Periodicals Consortium is to be commended for the means by which the issues of academic publishing could be explored, critiqued, and debated, issues which were of an often-clouded nature behind the hallowed "halls of ivy." Authors were individuals working professionally in the field of academic publishing. For the sampled issue of 1989: perfect-bound journal format, cover is blue ink on heavy coated paper stock, editorial content consists of black ink on uncoated paper stock, limited advertising (6 ¾ x 9 ⅞ inches / 170 x 250 mm).
DEPT: None. (winter-88/89).
TYPL: "The United States as a Market for International Scholarly Publications," "Changes in the Academic Environment: Threat or Opportunity?," "The More Things Change, the More They Stay the Same, and Other Clichées About Intermediaries in Publishing," "Beyond Plagiarism: Ethical Misconduct in Scientific and Technical Publishing," "New Technology Products: How to Separate Opportunities from Potential Disasters." (winter-88/89).
SCHL: Quarterly, 100 pp.
SPAN: Spring, 1985+

	VARIES --Spring, 1985 - Winter, 1990/1991 as Book Research Quarterly (ISSN: 0741-6148).
LC:	Z 284 .B634
DD:	070
ISSN:	1053-8801
ABST:	--MLA International Bibliography of Books & Articles on the Modern Languages and Literatures (ISSN: 0024-8215) --Public Affairs Information Service Bulletin (ISSN: 0033-3409) --Social Welfare, Social Planning / Policy and Social Development (ISSN: 0195-7988) --Sociological Abstracts (ISSN: 0038-0202)

Publishing Technology

Jan, 1987? - Oct?, 1989//
(ISSN: 1040-9440)
SEE: PUBLISHING & PRODUCTION EXECUTIVE

✤ PUBLISHING TRENDS & TRENDSETTERS

PUBL:	Oxbridge Communications, Inc., 150 Fifth Ave., New York, NY 10011.
DESC:	"*Publishing Trends & Trendsetters* is published to make it easier for the executive on the policy-making level to study fundamental and pervasive problems of periodical publishing in a systematic, different and, we hope, illuminating manner." This is an outstanding monograph series for today's competitive publisher of periodicals. The writing is concise, authoritative, and informative under the able editorial direction of Jim Mann. Typical monograph titles from 1989/1990 include "Are You Underpricing Your Editorial Product?," "The Significance of the So-Called Single-Copy Slump," "Coordinating Magazine Management with Market Lifestages," "Balancing Cashflow From Advertising and Circulation," "Increasing the Value of Value-Added Advertising Sales," "What Makes a Magazine a Superior Advertising Medium?," and "Finding and Maintaining a Magazine's Niche." This series is well recommended. The 1991 subscription price is $177 a year. For periodical publishers it may rank as a "best-buy" not only for its timeliness, but also for its readily applicable information. *Publishing Trends & Trendsetters* is published by Oxbridge Communications, a firm renowned for excellent directories on newsletters, magazines, mailing lists and the *Standard Periodical Directory*. Sampled issue for 1991: small stapled journal format, black ink editorial content with spot-color on cover, all on uncoated paper stock, no advertising or graphics (5 ½ x 8 ½ inches / 140 x 215 mm).
DEPT:	None. (6/7-91).

TYPL:	"Media Packaging and the New Marketing," "Interview with D. Claeys Bahrenburg," "New Marketing--A Major Opportunity," "Savings on a 6-Page Network Buy," "Checklist for the New Marketing." (6/7-91).
SCHL:	Ten issues per year, 16 pp.
SPAN:	?+ VARIES --? - Dec, 1990? as Media Management Monographs (ISSN: 0192-7663).

✤ PULP & PAPER CANADA

SUB:	"A Southam business publication."
SUB:	"A journal of record, technical section, CPPA."
SUB:	"Serving the industry since 1903."
PUBL:	Southam Business Communications, Inc., 1450 Don Mills Rd., Don Mills, Ontario M3B 2X7 Canada.
DESC:	A masthead quote describes *Pulp & Paper Canada* perfectly: "News of pulp and paper people and their innovations in research, technology, management and financing; reports of the application of these innovations, and forecasts of future trends." The emphasis is on the form and function of papermaking in Canada, and provides one of the world's most complete reviews of new developments in that field. Of special mention in the 1991 sample issue was a "Technical Section" detailing results of the 77th annual meeting of the Canadian Pulp and Paper Association, which included, among a number of interesting articles, the prizewinning technical papers from that convention. *Pulp & Paper Canada* is published by Southam Business Communications "...which serves business, industry, the professions and government in Canada with more than 60 publications, 63 business and consumer shows and a diversified group of communication and information services (direct mail/marketing, construction data, marketing communications, sales management systems, books)." For the sampled 1991 issue: perfect-bound, magazine format; full-color pages and cover on coated paper stock, with some specialty paper inserts (8 ⅛ x 10 ⅞ inches / 205 x 280 mm).
DEPT:	"Industry News," "Feedback," letters; "Calendar of Meetings," "Industry People," personnel newsbriefs; "Occupational Health and Safety," column by Susan Stevenson; "Input/Output," column by Neil McCubbin; "Technology News," "R&D News," new developments for pulp and paper manufacturing. (3-91).
TYPL:	"Alcell Pulping: World Class Research Right Here in Canada," "The Outlook for the Canadian Pulp and Paper Industry in 1991," "Refiner Capacity Worldwide Reached 89.5 kt/d in 1990," "A New Web Transfer System for Closing the Draw Between the Last Press and the Dryer Section," "Factors Affecting the Plane Wave Propagation of Pressure Waves in Approach Piping Systems." (3-91).
SCHL:	Thirteen issues per year (Sep, 1974 - Apr, 1985); Monthly (May, 1985+), 105 pp.
SPAN:	1903?+

VARIES
--? - ? as Pulp & Paper Magazine of Canada (ISSN: 0033-4103).
LC: TS 1080 .P85
DD: 338.4/7/6760971
ISSN: 0316-4004
ABST: --Abstract Bulletin of the Institute of Paper Chemistry (ISSN: 0020-3033)
--Bibliography of Agriculture (ISSN: 0006-1530)
--Canadian Business Index (ISSN: 0227-8669)
--Canadian Environment
--Chemical Industry Notes (ISSN: 0045-639x)
--Electrical & Electronics Abstracts (ISSN: 0036-8105)
--Energy Information Abstracts (ISSN: 0147-6521)
--Selected Water Resources Abstracts (ISSN: 0037-136x)

Pulp & Paper Magazine of Canada

? - ?//
(ISSN: 0033-4103)
SEE: PULP & PAPER CANADA

Pulse of Broadcasting, The

Jan 1, 1986? - Jan 20, 1989//
SEE: PULSE OF RADIO

✧ PULSE

SUB: "The national synopsis of editorial opinion on important issues."
PUBL: Drama Press, P.O. Box 6178, Toledo, OH 43614.
DESC: "When a newspaper writes an editorial offering its opinion on a public issue, the editorial becomes part of the public debate on that issue. When a newspaper attempts through the force of its opinion to influence the course of public affairs, the people have a right to know the opinion and the reasoning behind it." This well-edited newsprint gathers a fair and accurate sampling of the nation's newspaper editorials and matches those editorials against a factual scoreboard. It is a fascinating publication in a breezy format with numerous graphics.
DEPT: None. (4-79).
TYPL: "The Farmers in Washington, D.C.," "Iran's Unending Turmoil," "Carter, a Presidential Critique," "Energy: Another Crisis," (4-79).
SCHL: Monthly, 30 pp.
SPAN: Feb, 1979+

✧ PULSE OF RADIO

SUB: "Radio's management weekly."
SUB: "The life blood of radio."
PUBL: The Pulse Publications, 150 East 58th St., New York, NY 10022.
DESC: [*Pulse of Broadcasting, The*]: "*The Pulse of Broadcasting*--The only weekly journal by and for radio. No Television ... Never pages and pages of syndication hype ... We're *The Pulse of Broadcasting*--The life blood of radio..." The publisher might have added, "We believe in contemporary format radio," for this weekly publication unabashedly promotes this medium. It is a marvelous publication dedicated to reporting on the current status and future prospects of profitably managing and operating contemporary radio format stations. The magazine is broken into individualized departments; "General News," "Management & Marketing," "Pulse Maker Interview," "Programming," "Music," "Pulstations," "Pulse Beat," "Contemporary Radio Hit Activity Chart," "Engineering," "Tech Talk," "The Pulse of Programmers," "Guest Column," "Pulse Think Tank," and "Transfusions." For the contemporary radio general manager, this is must reading. For sampled issue of 1991: stapled magazine format, mixture of black and spot color inks, and full-color on coated paper stock, dynamic layout design (8 1/8 x 10 7/8 inches / 205 x 275 mm).
DEPT: "Pulse Maker Interview," "Pulstations," extensive listing of top weekly music at selected stations; "Pulse Beat," Listing of selected radio stations playing top-rated weekly music; "Contemporary Radio Hit Activity Chart," top-rated music in chart form; "The Pulse of Programmers," unique issue response forum for radio management; "Guest Column," commentary; "Pulse Think Tank," issue commentary; "Transfusions," personnel newsbriefs. (3-30-87).
TYPL: "Sales Management For the 1980s; Some Ideas That Really Work," "Radio Seen as 'People-Intensive' in Sillerman-Magee Seminar," "Troubleshooting the Management/Engineering Interface," "AM Stereo: Critical, but Saveable," "Understanding, Demanding Full Value For Our Product." (3-30-87).
SCHL: Weekly, 55 pp.
SPAN: Jan 1, 1986?+
VARIES
--Jan 1, 1986? - Jan 20, 1989 as Pulse of Broadcasting, The.
DD: 384 11
ISSN: 1044-1603

✤ QEX

SUB: "The ARRL experimenters' exchange."
PUBL: American Radio Relay League, 225 Main St., Newington, CT 06111.
DESC: The purpose of *QEX* is to: "1) provide a medium for the exchange of ideas and information between Amateur Radio experimenters; 2) document advanced technical work in the Amateur Radio field; and 3) support efforts to advance the state of the Amateur Radio art." It is published monthly by the American Radio Relay League, Inc., "...a noncommercial association of radio amateurs, organized for the promotion of interest in Amateur Radio communication and experimentation, for the establishment of networks to provide communications in the event of disasters or other emergencies, for the advancement of the radio art and of the public welfare, for the representation of the radio amateur in legislative matters, and for the maintenance of fraternalism and a high standard of conduct." Articles contain schematics and other electronics diagrams, and assume basic radio electronics knowledge. Magazine format (8 ¼ x 10 ⅞ inches / 210 x 275 mm); black/white graphics on uncoated paper stock.
DEPT: "VHF + Technology," column by Geoff Krauss; "Gateway," column by Stan Horzepa; "Empirically Speaking," editorial; "Bits," radio newsbriefs. (8-90).
TYPL: "Calibrating Diode Detectors," "Small Aperture IR Optical Links Using LED Light Sources." (8-90).
SCHL: Monthly, 30 pp.
SPAN: ?+
DD: 621 11
ISSN: 0886-8093

QP Herald

Jan 6, 1973 - May 5, 1973//
(ISSN: 0090-2136)
SEE: MOTION PICTURE PRODUCT DIGEST

✤ QST

SUB: "A magazine devoted exclusively to the wireless amateur."
SUB: "Devoted entirely to amateur radio."
PUBL: American Radio Relay League, 225 Main St., Newington, CT 06111.
DESC: The masthead of the American Radio Relay League's *QST* sums up both form and function of the 75-plus year old association and publication: "The American Radio Relay League, Inc., is a noncommercial association of radio amateurs, organized for the promotion of interest in Amateur Radio communication and experimentation, for the establishment of networks to provide communications in the event of disasters or other emergencies, for the advancement of the radio art and of the public welfare, for the representation of the radio amateur in legislative matters, and for the maintenance of fraternalism and a high standard of conduct. 'Of, by, and for the radio amateur', ARRL numbers within its ranks the vast majority of active amateurs in the nation and has a proud history of achievement as the standard-bearer in amateur affairs." Since 1915 *QST* has accomplished the admirable task of assembling for publication a significant amount of news events, technological developments, and especially news of ARRL and IARU membership. Each issue is packed with details concerning international amateur radio service, and news of numerous clubs, outings, conventions, and other happenings affecting the field. Today's *QST*, like earlier issues, provides a vigorous forum for new short-wave equipment, operating schedules of major stations, and international DX contests. For the amateur radio enthusiast serious about this exciting field, membership and subscription to *QST* is simply a "must." For the sampled issue of 1936: stapled magazine format, black ink with red/black ink cover on coated paper stock (6 ½ x 9 ⅜ inches / 165 x 240 mm). For the sampled issue of 1989: perfect-bound magazine format, full-color throughout on coated paper stock (8 ¼ x 10 ¾ inches / 210 x 275 mm). Significant amount of advertising exists in all issues.
DEPT: "The Editor's Mill," editorial; "What the League is Doing," 'League activities, Washington notes, board actions--for your information'; "Strays," newsbriefs; "For the Experimenter," "IARU News," 'Devoted to the interests and activities of the International Amateur Radio Union'; "Operating News," 'Conducted by the Communications Department' column by F. E. Handy and E. L. Battey; "Correspondence," letters; "Book Review." (3-36). "It Seems to Us," editorial; "League Lines," newsbriefs of ARRL; "Strays," newsbriefs and photos; "Hints and Kinks," technical trouble-shooting; "Happenings," current issues column by W. Clift; "Canadian News Fronts," column by Ron Hessler; "Washington Mailbox," legal information column by Michele Bartlett; "International News," column by Bruce Johnson; "Correspondence," very informational letters from readers; "YL News and Views," women's league news column by Louise Morreau; "The World Above 50 Megahertz," column by William Tynan; "How's DX?," column by Clarke Greene; "Public Service," "Silent Keys," obituaries; "Club Notes," "Coming Conventions," "Hamfest Calendar," "Operating news," "Operating

Events," "Station Activities." (2-79). "It Seems to Us," editorial; "Novice Notes," "Happenings," column by Phillip Sager; "Public Service," column by Luck Hurder; "IARU News," column by Richard L. Baldwin; "Amateur Satellite Communications," column by Vern Riportella; "The New Frontier," column by Bob Atkins; "Club Spectrum," column by Rick Palm; "On Line," column by Stan Horzepa; "Coming Conventions," "Hamfest Calendar," column by Bernice Dunn; "Contest Corral," column by Billy Lunt; "Special Events," column by Billy Lunt; "Correspondence," "DX Century Club Awards," column by Don Search; "New Books," "Exam Info," "Section News," column by Steven Ewald; "Feedback," corrections; "Technical Correspondence," column by Paul K. Pagel; "Hints and Kinks," column by David Newkirk; "How's DX?," column by Ellen White; "League Lines," "QSL Corner," column by Joanna Hushin; "Silent Keys," obituary column by Nancy Slipski; "The World Above 50 MHz," column by Bill Tynan; "YL News and Views," column by Joan Gibson. (5-89).

TYPL: "Pointers on Noise Silencing Circuits," "A Low Cost Crystal Transmitter," "An Improved Speech Preamplifier," "Oakland Radio Club Announces Cairo Plaque," "The Canada-USA Contact Contest, 1935." (3-36). "A First-Class Touch-Tone Encoder," "Digitized Speech," "QRN Communication--Myth or History?," "Good News and Disappointments in FCC WARC Proposals." (2-79). "A Practical Direct-Sequence Spread-Spectrum UFH Link," "A Practical Time-Domain Reflectometer," "Committee Releases Report for Comment on Possible Code-Free Amateur License," "How to Interest Significant Others in Amateur Radio Without Losing Them Forever," "Canada's Proposed Deregulation Addressed." (5-89).

SCHL: Monthly, 200 pp.
SPAN: Dec, 1915+
SUSPENDED
--Oct, 1917 - May, 1919.
LC: TK 1.Q2
DD: 621.3841/66/05
ISSN: 0033-4812
ABST: --Applied Science and Technology Index (ISSN: 0003-6986)
--Consumers Index to Product Evaluations and Information Sources (ISSN: 0094-0534)
--Reference Sources (ISSN: 0163-3546)

Quarterly Journal of Public Speaking, The

Apr, 1915 - Oct, 1917//
SEE: QUARTERLY JOURNAL OF SPEECH, THE

❖ QUARTERLY JOURNAL OF SPEECH, THE

SUB: "The official organ of the National Association of Academic Teachers of Public Speaking."

PUBL: Speech Communicaton Association, 5105 Backlick Rd., Annandale, VA 22003.
DESC: "The *Quarterly Journal of Speech* invites submissions of essays that advance an understanding of human communication regardless of its form or forum--oral or writen, informal or formal, direct or mediated, private or public, historical or contemporary. Essays may be philosophical, historical, critical or empirical in orientation." This remains one of a group of major publications long recognized as a forum for communication research, debate, issues, and trends in the communication field. The emphasis in this 75+ year-old publication is on research. Articles are as diverse as the membership of the organization it represents, the Speech Communication Association. In one sampled issue for 1991 articles included "Schismogenesis and Community: Pericles' Funeral Oration," "Public Memorializing in Postmodernity: The Vietnam Veterans Memorial as Prototype," "Telling the Famers' Story: Competing Responses to Soil Conservation Rhetoric," and "A Machiavellian Perspective on the Rhetorical Criticism of Political Discourse." A wonderful feature of the *Quarterly* is a short article abstract placed on the title page under each published article title, providing a quick-scan method for locating subjects of interest. Also of note is an excellent and extensive book review section, well-known for constructive critique and informative reviews. Articles for 1991 included, "Integrating Ideology and Archetype in Rhetorical Criticism," "The Role of the Convert in 'Eclipse of Reason' and 'The Silent Scream'," "'Levellers': The Economic Reduction of Political Equality in the Putney Debates, 1647," and "Rethinking 'the Public': The Role of Emotion in Being-With-Others." Statistics on the sampled 1972 issues: black ink on uncoated paper; cover comprised of spot ink on uncoated index stock, with advertising in perfect-bound journal format (6 3/8 x 9 3/4 inches / 160 x 250 mm). For the sampled issues of 1991: perfect-bound journal format, no graphics, black ink on uncoated paper stock, cover consists of two-color ink on coated paper stock (6 3/8 x 10 inches / 170 x 255 mm).
DEPT: "The Forum," "New Books in Review." (2-72). "Book Reviews." (5-84). "Book Reviews." (8-88).
TYPL: "The Diatribe: Last Resort for Protest," "The concept of the Paramessage in Persuasive Communication," "The New Politics Meets the Old Rhetoric: New Directions in Campaign Communication Research," "Non-Verbal Communication and the Overlooked Action in Pinter's 'The Caretaker'," "Reading Emerson for the Structures: The Coherence of the Essays." (2-72). "When Dreams Collide: Rhetorical Trajectories in the Assasination of President Kennedy," "Kenneth Burke's Break With Formalism," "Ideological Justifications," "Genre as Social Action," "The Enthymeme in Perspective," "The New Rhetoric and the Rhetoricians: Rememberences and Comments." (5-84). "KAL 007 and the Superpowers: An International Argument," "The Play as Novel: Reappropriating

Brecht's 'Drums in the Night'," "Limitations on the Comic Frame: Some Witty American Women of the Nineteenth Century." (8-88).
SCHL: Quarterly, 120 pp.
SPAN: Apr, 1915+
VARIES
--Apr, 1915 - Oct, 1917 as Quarterly Journal of Public Speaking, The.
--Jan, 1918 - Nov, 1927 as Quarterly Journal of Speech Education, The.
LC: PN 4071.Q3
DD: 808.5
ISSN: 0033-5630
ABST: --Abstract of English Studies (ISSN: 0001-3560)
--America, History and Life (ISSN: 0002-7065)
--Annual Bibliography of English Language and Literature (ISSN: 0066-3786)
--Biography Index (ISSN: 0006-3053)
--Book Review Index (ISSN: 0524-0581)
--Consumers Index to Product Evaluations and Information Sources (ISSN: 0094-0534)
--Education Index (ISSN: 0013-1385)
--Historical Abstracts. Part A. Modern History Abstracts. (ISSN: 0363-2712)
--Historical Abstracts. Part B. Twentieth Century Abstracts. (ISSN: 0363-2725)
--Humanities Index (ISSN: 0095-5981)
--Language Teaching (ISSN: 0261-4448)
--MLA International Bibliography of Books & Articles on the Modern Languages and Literatures (ISSN: 0024-8215)
--Psychological Abstracts (ISSN: 0033-0202)
--Recently Published Articles (ISSN: 0145-5311)
--Social Welfare, Social Planning / Policy and Social Development (ISSN: 0195-7988)
--Women Studies Abstracts (ISSN: 0049-7835)
--Writings on American History (ISSN: 0364-2887)

Quarterly Journal of Speech Education, The

Jan, 1918 - Nov, 1927//
SEE: QUARTERLY JOURNAL OF SPEECH, THE

Quarterly of Film, Radio, and Television, The

Fall, 1951 - Summer, 1957//
SEE: FILM QUARTERLY

✤ QUARTERLY REVIEW OF FILM AND VIDEO

PUBL: Harwood Academic Publishers, GmbH, PO Box 786, Cooper Station, New York, NY 10276.
DESC: "*Quarterly Review of Film and Video* offers in-depth articles and review essays exploring historical, theoretical, and critical issues relevant to film and television/video studies. In addition to publishing work on Hollywood film and network television, the journal also emphasizes technology and the apparatus, pedagogy, third cinema, popular culture, issues of class, feminism and sexual politics, and avant-garde and independent film and video. The word 'video' thus designates the electronic medium in its broadest terms, encompassing the study of broadcast television and artists' video as well as emerging technologies. Our scope is international, we regularly feature articles assessing developments in theory and practice from around the world. We frequently offer special issues that highlight single topics--a particular national cinema or a research area of compelling interest." This academically-aligned quarterly review covers the full spectrum of film production and criticism. Typical articles are on Italian cinema, documentaries, silent films and biographies concerning noted filmmakers. Additionally, a fair number of articles are devoted to film analysis and criticism. Of special note is a most unique and important department labeled "Archives," which lists major radio, television, and film archive acquisitions in the United States. Editorial management and offices for the *Quarterly Review of Film and Video* is the University of Southern California, School of Cinema-Television, Los Angeles, California. The sampled issues for 1976: stapled journal format; black ink on uncoated paper; cover being two spot-color inks on coated index stock, with limited advertising (5 ¼ x 8 ¼ inches / 135 x 210 mm). For the sampled issues from 1982 to 1989: black ink on coated paper, with laminated spot-ink cover (6 ⅞ x 8 ⅜ inches / 175 x 210 mm). The sampled issues of 1991 were also black ink on coated paper; cover changing to black and blue spot inks on coated index stock; no advertising (6 ¾ x 9 ⅝ inches / 170 x 245 mm). Issues for 1989 and 1991 were perfect-bound journal format. Note: although a title change appears to have taken place, the publication as of volume 13, number 4 of December, 1991, maintained the same ISSN from the previous title, *Quarterly Review of Film Studies*.
DEPT: None. (11-71). "Archives." (fall-83). None. (12-91).
TYPL: "Theory and Praxis in Pasolini's Trilogy of Life: Dacameron," "Leni Riefenstahl: a Selected Annotated Bibliography," "So Much and Yet so Little: a Survey of Books on Chaplain." (11-77). "Through the Looking Sign," "The Image and the Voice in the Film With Spoken Narration," "'Tame' Authors and the Corporate Laboratory: Stories, Writers and Scenarios in Hollywood," "The New Cinema in India." (fall-83). "Remapping the PostFranco Cinema: An Overview of the Terrain," "A Woman Without a Piano, A Book Without a Mark," "The Plain in Spain: Geography and National Identity in Spanish Cinema," "A Ms-take in the Making?: Transsexualism PostFranco, Post-Modern, Post-Haste," "'Art and a Lack of Money': The Crises of the Spanish Film Industry, 1977 - 1990." (12- 91).
SCHL: Quarterly, 130 pp.
SPAN: Feb, 1976+

VARIES
--Feb, 1976 - Feb, 1989 as Quarterly Review of Film Studies (ISSN: 0146-0013).
LC: PN 1994.Q34
DD: 791.43/05
ISSN: 0146-0013
ABST: --Book Review Index (ISSN: 0524-0581)
--Film Literature Index (ISSN: 0093-6758)
--Humanities Index (ISSN: 0095-5981)
--International Index to Film Periodicals (ISSN: 0000-0038)
--Media Review Digest (ISSN: 0363-7778)

Quarterly Review of Film Studies

Feb, 1976 - Feb, 1989//
(ISSN: 0146-0013)
SEE: QUARTERLY REVIEW OF FILM AND VIDEO

Quarterly Review of Public Relations

Fall, 1960 - Winter, 1963//
SEE: PUBLIC RELATIONS QUARTERLY

✣ QUILL, THE

SUB: "A magazine for journalists."
PUBL: Society of Professional Journalists, Sigma Delta Chi, 35 East Wacker Drive, Chicago, IL 60601.
DESC: Since 1912, the *Quill* has provided critical comment on the American journalistic media. Published primarily for members of the Society of Professional Journalists (Sigma Delta Chi), the *Quill* provides information on tool skills, techniques, and emerging issues that new journalists face. SPJ executive director, Vivian E. Vahlberg, stated that at SPJ "We nurture good journalists. Everything we do is directed at making each journalist the best he or she can be by inspiring them, rewarding them, providing perspective, training them, involving them, and nurturing a commitment to the job that goes beyond the 9-to-5. We battle to preserve and protect the climate in which American journalism has thrived--something we can do together that we can't do alone. ... We provide a common ground where journalists of all stripes can celebrate similarities, tackle common problems, and map solutions. Fraternal ties are important. They keep us motivated, tide us over rough times, make us feel we're part of something bigger. Fraternal ties help keep good people in the business." Magazine format, black/white with color covers; Numerous graphics. Sampled issue for 1989: (8 ¼ x 10 ⅞ inches / 210 x 270 mm).
DEPT: "Letters," "Day in the Life," profile; "Digest," newsbriefs; "The Ombudsman," "Report." (9-84). "President's Column," "Letters," "The Ombudsmen," column by Richard P. Cunningham; "FOI Report," a report on freedom of information; "Roundup," "Report." (6-89).
TYPL: "Critical Mass," "The SEC Power-Grab," "Most Favored Newspaper," "Rolecall." (9-84). "Perils on the Medical Beat," "Right in Conflict: Access Vs. Privacy," "LDF Awards Grants to Free-Access Groups in California and Texas," "Journalism's Best." (6-89).
SCHL: Monthly [with combined Jul/Aug issue], 60 pp.
SPAN: 1912+
VARIES
--1912 - Feb, 1930 as Quill of Sigma Delta Chi, The.
LC: PN 4700.Q5
DD: 070.5
ISSN: 0033-6475
ABST: --Humanities Index (ISSN: 0095-5981)

✣ QUILL AND SCROLL

SUB: "Official magazine of the international honorary society for highschool journalists."
PUBL: Quill and Scroll Society, School of Journalism, University of Iowa, Iowa City, IA 52242.
DESC: The official publication of the International Honorary Society for high school journalists, it provides a critical forum for secondary education journalism and offers insights about professional journalistic standards. The publication furnishes information about high school journalism classes, student achievements, the basics of layout and publication design, and developing a journalistic approach to publishing.
DEPT: "CSPAA Notes," newsbriefs of the Columbia Scholastic Press Advisers Association, "The Newest Books in Journalism," "JEA Notes," newsbriefs of the Journalism Education Association.
TYPL: "Company 'House Organs' Offer Treasure Chest of Journalistic Ideas," "Be Alert! Establish Ad Policy," "Study Reveals Nature of Mass Media Courses." (10-76).
SCHL: Bimonthly [During the school year] (? - ?); Quarterly (?+), 35 pp.
SPAN: Oct, 1926+
LC: PN 4700.Q
ISSN: 0033-6505
ABST: --Current Index to Journals in Education (ISSN: 0011-3565)

Quill of Sigma Delta Chi, The

1912 - Feb, 1930//
SEE: QUILL, THE

✣ R & R

SUB: "Radio & Records."
SUB: "The industry's newspaper."
PUBL: Radio & Records, Inc., 1930 Century Park West, Los Angeles, CA 90067.
DESC: Even with an annual subscription rate of $279 (for 1991), most commercial radio stations subscribe to this weekly, tabloid newspaper; which appears to provide ALL the information anyone would want to know about the radio and recording fields. The 100+ pages provide an excellent resource on the status of radio and records and the symbiotic relationship between them. *R & R* is especially well known for its outstanding playlist compilation covering popular American radio formats, and is well recommended to all interested in the competitive field of radio broadcasting and record production/promotion. For sampled issue of 1988: black, spot-color, and color pages on uncoated paper stock in stapled tabloid newspaper format (11 x 14 ⅜ inches / 280 x 365 mm).
DEPT: "Washington Report," "What's New," newsbriefs; "Street Talk," gossip; "Gary Owens," column; "TV News," newsbriefs concerning television; "Ratings & Research," radio research; "Brad Messer," column; "Media Marketing," research; "Picture Page," "News/Talk," "Top 40," "Black Radio," "AOR," "Country," "Pop/Adult." (4-11-80). "CHR," contemporary hit radio format column by Joel Denver; "Urban Contemporary," radio format column by Walt Love; "AOR," Album oriented rock radio column by Harvey Kojan; "AC," Adult contemporary radio format column by Mike Kinosian; "Country," radio format column by Lon Helton; "Nashville This Week," radio format news; "World Music Overview," international pops chart; "Video Music," music video hit list; "Urban Contemporary," hit list; "Country," hit list; "Adult Contemporary," hit list; "Full-Service AC," Adult contemporary hit list; "Gold-Based AC," Adult contemporary hit list; "NAC," New adult contemporary hit list; "Contemporary Jazz," hit list; "AOR Albums," Album oriented rock hit list; "AOR Tracks," Album oriented rock; "CHR," Contemporary hit radio format playlist; "The Back Page," contemporary, adult contemporary, aor, urban contemporary playlist. (8-26-88).
TYPL: "Radio Keeps Big Apple Moving," "AM Stereo Approved," "Six New Arbitron Advisory Council Members Elected," Free Rides for Citizens' Groups?," "New Lottery Law in the Works." (4-11-80). "Teller to MCA Records as President/COO," "Judges Order Inquiry Into Minority Hiring at Texas Combo," "Battling the Boss: a Blueprint," "Whither Goest the Car of the Future," "Talk on FM: Mining the 'New' Frontier." (8-26-88).
SCHL: Weekly, 105 pp.
SPAN: 1971?+
WITH SUPPLEMENT
--Radio & Records Ratings Report (ISSN: 0276-1831) [NA], 1979 - 198u//.
--Radio & Records Ratings Report & Directory [NA], 198u+.
LC: PN 1991.67 .P67 R33
DD: 384.54/0973
ISSN: 0277-4860

Radio
Nov, 1921 - Feb/Mar, 1947//
SEE: AUDIO

RADIO AGE

SUB: "The magazine of the hour."
SUB: "Official news medium for National Broadcasters' League."
SUB: "Everyday mechanics, current science."
PUBL: Radio Age, Boyce Bldg., 500 N. Dearborn St., Chicago, IL.
DESC: M.B. Smith (publisher), and Frederick Smith (editor) set the tone for *Radio Age* in the first issue: "Our special circulation: Boy beginners particularly, and amateurs generally. *Radio Age* will write Radio so that boys can understand it. There will be technical articles for the advanced students of Radio but the departments for beginners will not be written over the readers heads." This Chicago, magazine-style serial remains a very special source of detailed news on the amateur and commercial radio fields. Some schematics are provided, but the real value is in the detailed news articles with major leaders. It covers what the average boy was accomplishing with his one-tube radio set. Well-recommended for history of American radio industry. Numerous photographs.
DEPT: "Thought Waves from the Editorial Tower," "Questions and Answers," (9-22). "Amateur Radio," "Everyday Mechanics," "Current Science," "Corrected List of Broadcast Stations," (10-27).
TYPL: "Novice Gets Good Results with Armstrong Super-Regenerative Circuit," "Bank Uses Radio to Serve Public," "First National Radio Congress," "Marconi Discusses Short Waves," (9-22). "Current Radio Wisdom in Tabloids," "Bringing the Old Super Up to Date," "Independents Start Battle," (10-27).
SCHL: Monthly, 30 - 40 pp.
SPAN: May, 1922 - Jan, 1928//

ABSORBED
--Radio Topics, Jul, 1924.
LC: TK 6540 .R2

Radio Age
Oct, 1941 - ?, 1957//
SEE: ELECTRONIC AGE

Radio Album
Summer, 1948//
SEE: RADIO ALBUM MAGAZINE

✤ RADIO ALBUM MAGAZINE
PUBL: Dell Publishing Co., 261 Fifth Ave., New York, NY.
DESC: With titles such as "Radio's Number One Mugger," and "So You Want to Lead a Band," there is no doubt that *Radio Album* is a high energy fan magazine. Typical articles concerning radio artists, outside activities, and program reviews make up the bulk of the serial. Of special note are marvelous photographs of early television in the first issues. Magazine format.
DEPT: "Radio Album Reports," "Spotlight Review," "Video Review," "Tonight on Broadway," "Soap Suds Alley," "Gallery," artist profiles; (fall-48).
TYPL: "People are Funny," "Fifteen Years with Lux Radio Theater," "Life of the Party," "Meet Beulah," "Inside Durante," (fall-48).
SCHL: Quarterly, 100 pp.
SPAN: Summer, 1948+?
VARIES
--Summer, 1948 as Radio Album.
LC: HE 8690 .R14

Radio Amateur News
Jul, 1919 - Jun, 1920//
SEE: ELECTRONICS WORLD

Radio and Amusement Guide
Jan 7, 1932 - ?//
SEE: MOVIE-RADIO GUIDE

Radio & Electrical Appliance Dealer
Feb, 1944 - Apr, 1944//
SEE: ELECTRONIC SERVICING & TECHNOLOGY

Radio and Electrical Review
May 1, 1954 - Apr 1, 1964//
SEE: ELECTRONICS AND COMMUNICATIONS

Radio and Electronic Engineer, The
1963 - Nov/Dec, 1984//
(ISSN: 0033-7722)
SEE: ELECTRONICS & COMMUNICATIONS ENGINEERING JOURNAL

Radio and Electronics
Apr, 1946 - Apr, 1954//
SEE: ELECTRONICS AND COMMUNICATIONS

✤ RADIO & ELECTRONICS CONSTRUCTOR
SUB: "Incorporating the Radio Amateur."
PUBL: Data Publications, Ltd., 57 Maida Vale, W9 1SN England.
DESC: A small format serial whose narrow focus is the construction of electronics, especially as it relates to the field of short-wave amateur radio. Numerous schematics.
DEPT: "Can Anyone Help?," "In Your Workshop," "Radio Topics," (8-69).
TYPL: "Inertia Switching Circuit," "Transitor Amplifier for Battery or Mains," "Mobiling and Mobileers," (8-69).
SCHL: Monthly, 60 pp.
SPAN: ?+
VARIES
--? - ? as Radio Constructor.
ABSORBED
--Radio Amateur, Jan, 1954?
LC: TK 9956 .R17
DD: 621.38/05

RADIO & TELEVISION
PUBL: Popular Book, Inc., 99 Hudson St., New York, NY.
DESC: Another in the series of Hugo Gernsback publications, *Short Wave Craft* and its successors appealed to the ham and amateur inventor interested in electronics. Articles provided specific details on new advances in radio or television technology, with numerous graphics and schematics for construction purposes. The inclusion of *Foto-Craft*, a Gernsback photography magazine, was a strange development in the serial's history. Of special note were articles detailing world short-wave systems prior to the outbreak of World War Two.
DEPT: "Short Waves for the Broadcast Listener," "The Short Wave Experimenter," "Short Wave Stations of the World," "Ultra-Short Waves," "Short Wave Question Box," "Swappers," (8/9-30).
TYPL: "The Television Theatre is Here," "My Short Wave Experiments in Carlsbad Cavern," "Artificial Fever and Other Effects in the Human Body Produced by Short Waves," (8/9-30).
SCHL: Bimonthly (Jun/Jul, 1930 - Mar, 1932); Monthly (Apr, 1932 - Sep, 1941); 50 pp.

SPAN: Jun/Jul, 1930 - Sep, 1941//
VARIES
--Jun/Jul, 1930 - Dec, 1936 as Short Wave Craft.
--Jan, 1937 - Sep, 1938 as Short Wave & Television.
--Dec, 1939 - ? as Radio & Television Incorporating Foto-Craft.
ABSORBED
--Foto-Craft, Dec, 1939.
ABSORBED BY
--Radio-Craft (ISSN: 0033-7862), Nov/Dec, 1941.
LC: TK 6540 .R27

✣ RADIO AND TELEVISION

SUB: "Review of the International Radio and Television Organization."
PUBL: International Radio and Television Organization, Prague, Czechoslovakia.
DESC: "The OIRT is a voluntary, non-commercial association of television and radio organizations pursuing the aim of exchanging programmes as well as information concerning programme production and technical development. It promotes the exchange of truthful information and cultural values among the countries of the world." With articles in French and English (no translations), it provides a forum for the exchange of programming information between member nations of the OIRT. Early issues consisted of all-English language articles. The majority of articles in this serial are written by and about member nations in the so-called "Soviet Bloc." Issues for period 1960 - May, 1966 were in English; issues for Jul, 1966+ are in English or French. Some graphics.
DEPT: "Bibliography." (#4-60). None. (#6-84).
TYPL: "Soviet Radio and Television in the Service of Progress and Peace," "Wired Broadcasting Networks Automatization," "Technical Experience Gained in the Operation of the Bucharest Television Studio." (#4-60). "A Reportage on Lenin," "Sociological Research at Czechoslovak Television," "Restoration of Old Sound Recordings and Their Conversion to Stereo." (#6-84).
SCHL: Bimonthly, 45 pp.
SPAN: Feb, 1960?+
VARIES
--Feb, 1960? - ? as Documentation and Information Bulletin of the International Broadcasting Organization.
--1960 - May, 1966 as Radio & Television.
--Jul/Aug, 1966? - 1981 as Radio Television (ISSN: 0033-7676).
--1982 - 1984 as Radio Television International Review (ISSN: 1015-8596).
LC: PN 1991 .I52
DD: 384.54/0947
ABST: --Computer & Control Abstracts (ISSN: 0036-8113)
--Electrical & Electronics Abstracts (ISSN: 0036-8105)
--Physics Abstracts. Science Abstracts. Series A. (ISSN: 0036-8091)

Radio & Television
1960 - May, 1966//
SEE: RADIO AND TELEVISION

Radio and Television Best
Oct, 1949 - Aug, 1950//
SEE: TV SCREEN

Radio & Television Incorporating Foto-Craft
Dec, 1939 - ?//
SEE: RADIO & TELEVISION

Radio and Television Mirror
Aug, 1939 - Oct, 1942//
SEE: TV RADIO MIRROR

Radio and Television Mirror
Apr, 1948 - Feb, 1951//
SEE: TV RADIO MIRROR

Radio & Television News
Aug, 1948 - Mar, 1957//
SEE: ELECTRONICS WORLD

Radio and Television Retailing
Apr, 1939 - Dec, 1941//
SEE: TELEVISION RETAILING

Radio & Television Retailing
Apr, 1944 - Jun, 1952//
SEE: TELEVISION RETAILING

Radio and TV News
Apr, 1957 - Apr, 1959//
(ISSN: 0097-6660)
SEE: ELECTRONICS WORLD

Radio Best
Nov, 1947 - ?//
SEE: TV SCREEN

Radio Best & Television Magazine
Oct, 1950 - Dec, 1950//
SEE: TV SCREEN

RADIO BROADCAST
SUB: "Radio for every place and purpose."
SUB: "Published for the Radio Industry."
PUBL: Doubleday, Doran and Co., Garden City, NY.
DESC: Primarily dedicated to the retail engineering end of the broadcast industry, *Radio Broadcast* concentrated on new engineering developments, existing radio manufacturers' testing and research facilities, and unique means of retail advertising by radio receiver stores. Numerous graphs, charts, and photos.
DEPT: "Review," newsbriefs concerning receiver manufacturing and sales; "The March of Radio," general industry briefs; "Strays from the Laboratory," technical briefs; "Professionaly Speaking," editorial comment on recent developments; "The Serviceman's Corner," new techniques; "Book Review," "News of the Radio Industry," newsbriefs; "In the Radio Marketplace," 'News, Useful Data and Information on the Offerings of the Manufacturer'.
TYPL: "What Everyone Should Know About Radio History," "An Evening with Dr. Alexander Graham Bell," "Increasing the Selection Power of a Radio Circuit," "A Church with a Mighty Congregation," (7-22). "Characteristics of Pentode Tubes," "Automobiles with Radio," "Volume Control in Broadcasting," "High-Frequency Measuring Equipment." (3-30).
SCHL: Monthly, 50 pp.
SPAN: May, 1922 - Apr, 1930//
ABSORBED BY
--Radio Digest, Sep, 1930.
LC: TK 6540 .R3
ABST: --Engineering Index
--Readers Guide to Periodical Literature (ISSN: 0034-0464)

✤ RADIO BUSINESS REPORT
SUB: "Voice of the radio broadcasting industry."
SUB: "The breaking news of the radio industry."
SUB: "The fast read for the fast track."
PUBL: Radio Business Report, Inc., 7820 Painted Daisy Drive, Springfield, VA 22152.
DESC: Editor and publisher, Jim Carnegle, publishes this excellent weekly concerning news developments, trends, research, advertising ideas, regulatory news, and issues of general radio station management. Information is concise, to the point, and provides a quick, but informative read for today's busy media executive. As a promotional card stated, "You need to keep informed on ALL the latest news in the radio business: not just music, not just management and not just promotions and sales. But as a busy radio executive you don't need press release rewrites, you need professionals who know the hottest news and can tailor your reading for your needs. *RBR* does it for you every week!" A host of outstanding departmental features covers it all, from station trading to radio news, from FCC and politics to broadcast investments, from promotion sales and marketing to media markets and contractual law. *Radio Business Report* will demonstrate its value to the radio executive many times over in any given issue. At a 1991 subscription rate of $215, it may be out of range for most libraries, but certainly will rank as one of the smartest subscription orders a radio station general manager could ever make. This publication lives up to its varied list of subtitles. "Subscribe today and find out what your competitor already knows!!," says one promotional advertisement. Well recommended. For sampled issue of 1991: stapled magazine format, use of three spot color inks (black, red, blue) on uncoated paper stock (8 ½ x 11 inches / 215 x 280 mm).
DEPT: "Media Trends," 'News and views from the editors of RBR'; "Radio News," 'The breaking news of the radio industry'; "Radio Wars," news items; "Competing Media," news items; "Media Trends," "Media Markets & Money," 'The authoritative business and transaction digest'; "Contract Close-Up," "Question of the Week," 'The legal angle on local marketing agreements'. (4-15-91).
TYPL: "Gannett, CBS, Group W Ally for In-Band DAB," "Split-Rep Deals," "NAB Fires Volley at White House," "Local Efforts Displace RAB's Pro-Radio Campaign," "TV Networks Are Facing Big-Time Staff Cuts." (4-15-91).
SCHL: Monthly, 16 pp.
SPAN: Jan, 1984+
ISSN: 0741-8469

RADIO CITY NEWS
SUB: "Show Place of the Nation." (Apr 3, 1933 - Nov 2, 1933).
PUBL: Radio City Theatres, Music Hall, Radio City, New York, NY.
DESC: This short-lived promotional magazine was produced by master showman, S. L. Rothafel (Roxy), and concerned the activities of New York City's Radio City Music Hall. Articles showcased Radio City activities, especially those of the renowned Music Hall, and the "Roxy" radio broadcasts from same. Many backstage photos show the process of mounting various productions. Published in large magazine format with spot color April 3, 1933 - June 12, 1933. Thereafter, *Radio City News* was published with duotone color (and advertising) on newsprint; through the last issue of November, 1933.
DEPT: "Radio City Town Crier," comment. (6-12-33).
TYPL: "Colorful Shows is Roxy's Plan for Summer," "Get a Kick Out of This Story on Roxyettes?," "Outstanding Film Fare for Patrons of Music Hall," "First Wedding for Radio City." (6-12-33).
SCHL: Biweekly, 8 pp..
SPAN: Apr 3, 1933 - Nov 2, 1933//
LC: PN 2000.R25

✣ RADIO COMMUNICATION

SUB: "Journal of the Radio Society of Great Britain."
PUBL: Radio Society of Great Britain, 35 Doughty St., London WC1N 2AE, England.
DESC: "For the advancement of Amateur Radio" has been the focus of the Radio Society of Great Britain since its founding in the early 1920s. This serial is a highly technical (at times) approach to radio, with special emphasis on developing technology, and electronics. It provides interesting historical insight into the use of short-wave broadcasts by governments and other interested parties. Small magazine format.
TYPL: "A Voltage Controlled Stabilized Variable Current Overload Protected Power Unit," "Heat-Dissipating Valve Shields," (8-68). "An introduction to Data Communication," "Design of L-Networks for Matching Antennas to Transmitters," (8-64).
SCHL: Monthly, 60 pp.
SPAN: 1925+
VARIES
--1925? - ? as T & R Bulletin.
--194u - Dec, 1967 as RSGB Bulletin.
LC: TK 6540.T15
DD: 621.3841/05
ISSN: 0033-7803
ABST: --Computer & Control Abstracts (ISSN: 0036-8113)
--Electrical & Electronics Abstracts (ISSN: 0036-8105)
--Physics Abstracts. Science Abstracts. Series A. (ISSN: 0036-8091)

Radio Constructor

? - ?//
SEE: RADIO & ELECTRONICS CONSTRUCTOR

Radio-Craft

Jul, 1929 - Oct, 1941//
SEE: RADIO-ELECTRONICS

Radio-Craft

May, 1943 - Jun, 1948//
SEE: RADIO-ELECTRONICS

Radio-Craft Incorporating Radio and Television

Nov, 1941 - Apr, 1943//
SEE: RADIO-ELECTRONICS

Radio-Craft, Radio-Electronics

Jul, 1948 - Sep, 1948//
SEE: RADIO-ELECTRONICS

Radio Daily

Feb 9, 1936 - Sep 6, 1950//
SEE: RTD

Radio Daily-Television Daily

Sep 7, 1950 - Jan 5, 1962//
SEE: RTD

RADIO DEALER, THE

SUB: "For the radio retailer." (Apr, 1922 - ?).
SUB: "The radio trade journal for the radio retailer." (May, 1922 - ?).
SUB: "The radio trade journal for the radio business man." (? - Oct, 1928).
SUB: "The pioneer radio trade journal." (? - Oct, 1928).
PUBL: H.M. Konwiser, 1133 Broadway, New York, NY.
DESC: "*The Radio Dealer* introduces itself to the business men of the wireless field in this unostentatious manner, paralleling the introduction of the radio industry--so to speak. This paper is not to be the organ of any of the varied 'wireless interests.' This paper has no axe to grind. This paper has only one policy--service to the retailer, jobber and manufactuer." Thus, *The Radio Dealer* began its six-year publishing span, providing manufacturing and marketing news of radio apparatus to the general radio retailer. It was very much a business news magazine with few pictures, except for advertisements and occasional graphics showing new equipment. The phenomenal growth of radio can be seen in the editorial and advertising content, moving from 32 pages in Apr, 1922 to 138 pages in September, 1922.
DEPT: "Editorial," "Ideas for Live Wire Retailers," "Philadelphia Pointers," news of Pennsylvania radio manufacturers; "Questions and Answers," "Radio Securities," "Trade Mark Department," new radio trade-marks accepted by the Patent Office; "What the Manufacturers are Doing." (9-22). "Activities of the Jobbing Trade," "Among the Traveling Men," "Broadcasting Station Activities," "Dollar Pullers," "From the Editorial Viewpoint," "Industrial Progress," "In the Realm of Radio Shows," "Letters to the Editor," "Radio Personalities," "Radio Trade Pictures," "Sales Appeal in Trade Displays," "The Service Corner," "With the Trade Associations." (4-28).
TYPL: "A Valuable form of Advertising," "Concerning Canned Music Now Broadcasted," "German Radio Apparatus Industry," "Radio Trade Unaffected by Inventions, "The Future of Radio," "Victra-Phone Console Cabinets for Radio," "What is a Jobber?" (9-22). "Country Cousins Again Show Sales," "Customers That Forget to Remember," "Stocks in Hands of Radio Dealers," "The Members of the New Radio Commission." (4-28).
SCHL: Monthly, 138 pp.
SPAN: Apr, 1922 - Oct, 1928//

WITH SUPPLEMENT
--The Radio Manufacturer, ? - Oct, 1928//
LC: TK 6540.R35

RADIO DIAL

PUBL: Radio Dial Publishing Co., 22 East 12th St., Cincinnati, OH.
DESC: "More than 500,000 persons in Cincinnati and vicinity are radio listeners. Every one of them wants to know exactly what program is available now, later today, or tomorrow. *Radio Dial* is designed to give Greater Cincinnati dial twisters exactly what they want. Each weekly issue will present to you the official complete programs of Greater Cincinnati radio stations, as well as features on the prominent radio chains." Tabloid format; numerous graphics.
DEPT: "Around the Dial," program notes; "Our Daily Dozen," column by Don Becker; "Letter Box," "The Editor Gossips," "Program Jottings," "Network Programs," large listing. (9-18-31).
TYPL: "Marconi to Speak on Beginning of Wireless," "Kentucky Vocal Trials Thursday," "International Reception is Easy with New Gadget," "Lung Power Steam Calliope is Next Philco Radio Act." (9-18-31).
SCHL: Weekly, 8 pp.
SPAN: May 23, 1931 - May, 1939//
LC: TK 6540.R38

Radio Digest Illustrated
Apr, 1922 - Feb, 1924//
SEE: RADIO FAN-FARE

Radio Digest Programs Illustrated
? - ?, 1933//
SEE: RADIO FAN-FARE

✦ RADIO-ELECTRONICS

SUB: "Technology - video - stereo - computers - service."
SUB: "The magazine for new ideas in electronics."
SUB: "Radio-electronics in all its phases."
SUB: "Electronics publishers since 1908."
PUBL: Gernsback Publications, 200 Park Ave. South, New York, NY 10003.
DESC: By 1929, when entrepreneur Hugo Gernsback decided to begin *Radio-Craft* magazine (forerunner of *Radio-Electronics*), he had already published *Modern Electrics* (1908 - 1912), *The Electrical Experimenter* (1912 - 1922), and *Radio News* (1919 - 1929) magazines. Gernsback, who owned a successful import business and radio stations (and was among the first to broadcast television pictures in 1925), said his new magazine would be different: there would be "no pictures of the latest radio mast in Timbuktu, no stories of how Roxy killed a fly on the mike, no radio announcers flanked by goggle-eyed sopranos, and no radio mathematics that would be swell food for Einstein, but useless to the practical experimenter." Gernsback said his new magazine would deal with "every new article and apparatus brought out, radio construction galore, servicing data, short-wave dope, blueprint articles and a real section of questions and answers." Sixty years later, it is a formula that still works; with schematics and electronics at the lay level; electronic projects for home-builders; news of new technology and technique; and back pages devoted to mail-order electronics supply houses. For the sampled issue of 1946: stapled magazine format, black ink on mixture of newsprint and coated paper stock, full-color cover on coated paper, with advertising (8 3/8 x 11 3/8 inches / 215 x 290 mm). For sampled issue of 1989: perfect-bound black/white and full-color throughout on coated paper stock, significant amount of advertised electronic products and services (8 x 10 3/4 inches / 205 x 275 mm).
DEPT: "Editorial," column by Hugo Gernsback; "Radio-Electronics Monthly Review," 'Items interesting to the technician'; "World-Wide Station List," geographic listing column by Elmer R. Fuller; "Radio-Electronic Circuits," new and original electronic schematics; "New Radio-Electronic Devices," new product review; "Try This One!," 'original kinks' from readers; "The Question Box," reader-submitted Q&A; "New Radio Patents," column by I. Queen; "Technotes," model-specific defects and repair strategies; "Communications," letters; "Book Reviews." (1-46). "What's News," newsbriefs; "Editorial," "Letters," "Radio Products," review; "Computer Products," review; "Stereo Products," review; "New Products," review; "New Lit," "Books." (10-79). "What's News," technology newsbriefs; "Video News," 'What's new in this fast-changing field' column by David Lachenbruch; "Ask R-E," questions answered; "Letters," "Equipment Reports," review; "New Products," review; "Hardware Hacker," Fascinating comment column by Don Lancaster; "Shortwave Radio," column by Stanley Leinwoll; "Audio Update," column by Larry Klein; "Antique Radio," column by Richard D. Fitch. (2-89).
TYPL: "Loran-Radio Navigation Aid," "Shortwave Diathermy," "Service Sans Instruments," "Signal Generator Covers All Bands," "Portable Phono-Radio." (1-46). "Automate Your Home," "Automotive Radiator Monitor," "Home Reception Via Satellite," "Digital Logic in Videocassette Recorders," "All About Microphones," "State of Solid State." (10-79). "High Definition Tele- Vision," "Down-Counter Cookbook." (2-89).
SCHL: Monthly, 135 pp.
SPAN: Jul, 1929+
VARIES
--Jul, 1929 - Oct, 1941 as Radio-Craft.
--Nov, 1941 - Apr, 1943 as Radio-Craft Incorporating Radio and Television.
--May, 1943 - Jun, 1948 as Radio-Craft.
--Jul, 1948 - Sep, 1948 as Radio-Craft, Radio-Electronics.

ABSORBED
--Radio Review and Television News, Mar, 1933.
--Radio & Television, Nov/Dec, 1941.
LC: TK 6540.R34
ISSN: 0033-7862
ABST: --Applied Science and Technology Index (ISSN: 0003-6986)
--Computer & Control Abstracts (ISSN: 0036-8113)
--Consumers Index to Product Evaluations and Information Sources (ISSN: 0094-0534)
--Electrical & Electronics Abstracts (ISSN: 0036-8105)
--Magazine Index
--Physics Abstracts. Science Abstracts. Series A. (ISSN: 0036-8091)
--Popular Magazine Review (ISSN: 0740-3763)
--Predicasts
--Readers Guide to Periodical Literature (ISSN: 0034-0464)

Radio, Electronics and Communications

May 1, 1964 - Dec 1, 1971//
SEE: ELECTRONICS AND COMMUNICATIONS

Radio-Electronics Special Projects

? - ?//
(ISSN: 0730-7616)
SEE: POPULAR ELECTRONICS

RADIO FAN-FARE

SUB: "The national broadcast authority."
PUBL: Radio Digest Publishing Co., 420 Lexington Ave., New York, NY.
DESC: [*Radio Digest*]: Published first in Chicago, and later in New York city, *Radio Digest* fulfilled two functions. In the early 1920s issues, it explained to the general public the broadcast industry as a whole (radio receivers, programming material, and technical developments). In latter 1930s issues, the purpose was modified to profile stars and programming vehicles, and provide some general entertainment features. This is a marvelous resource for broadcast historians. Printed tabloid newsprint format in the 1920s, giving way to standard magazine format in the 1930s.
DEPT: "Book Reviews," "Radio Receiving Sets," review; "Radiophone Broadcasting Stations," 'Corrected every week'; "Radio Indi-gest," letters; "Questions and Answers." (1-20-23). "Coming and Going," 'Observations on events and incidents in the broadcasts of the month'; "Tuneful Topics," Hit radio songs column by Rudy Vallee; "Voice of the Listener," letters; "Station Parade," profile; "Professionally Speaking," business newsbriefs; "Chatter," comment; "Chain and Local Features," programming; "Western Radio News and Comment," column by W. L. Gleeson. (5-32).
TYPL: "Radio Joins Crime War," "Air Waves Help Spread Gospel," "Improve Check on Weather by Radio," "Navy will Fight Licensing: Denby," "Rectifier for Charging B Batteries." (1-20-23). "Why Not Prohibit Vocal Atrocities?," "Moonshine and Honeysuckle," "Buddy Rogers," "What's Wrong with Air Drama?," "Tell it to the Movies." (5-32).
SCHL: Weekly (? - ?); Monthly (?+), 45 pp.
SPAN: Apr, 1922 - Oct, 1933//
VARIES
--Apr, 1922 - Feb, 1924 as Radio Digest Illustrated.
--? - ?, 1933 as Radio Digest Programs Illustrated.
ABSORBED
--Radio Revue for the Listener, Sep, 1930.
--Radio-Broadcast, Sep, 1930.

✦ RADIO GUIDE

SUB: "Radio's technology magazine."
PUBL: Radio Press Group, Inc., 511 18th St., SE, Rochester, MN 55904.
DESC: This monthly publication is written by radio engineers for radio engineers. The sampled issue consisted of all-departmental segments providing information on a variety of engineering topics, including maintenance, equipment purchase, problems of a regulatory or repair nature, computer programming, and networking (through an extensive BBS listing) with other radio engineers for the sharing and exchange of information. Of special note (among many great departmental features) is the "Radio Guide Forum;" an interesting "Letters, questions, help & parts wanted from *Radio Guide* Readers" segment which hosts a wide variety of topics including, "Tech Manuals Needed," "Parts Needed," "Equipment Needed;" and "Jobs Wanted." The *Radio Guide Forum* alone is well worth the effort to subscribe. Publisher and editor Ray Topp produces a valuable publication and service for the radio engineering community, one not to be missed by engineering personnel in the field. Stapled magazine format, black/white editorial content with black/white or full-color advertisements on coated paper stock with full-color cover (8 1/8 x 10 7/8 inches / 205 x 275 mm).
DEPT: "More After This!," 'Editorial comments' column by Ray Topp; "Radio Guide Forum," 'Letters, questions, help & parts wanted from Radio Guide readers'; "State of the Art," technology newsbriefs column by Chip Morgan; "DA Systems," distribution/amplifier systems column by W. C. Alexander; "Soldering Tips," column by Richard Majestic; "Studio Site," column by Gordon Carter; "Computer Connection," column by Kelly Klaas; "Station Automation," column by Steve Walker; "BBS Listing," fascinating list of computer bulletin boards with a broadcast orientation; "Radio Programs," computer software column by Steve Walker. (3-91).
TYPL: "Spring Cleaning at AM Site," "Un-Balanced Audio Switcher," "Analog Tape Recorder Maintenance," "'Live' Automation," "Schematic Drawing Program." (3-91).

SCHL: Monthly, 45 pp.
SPAN: Jan, 1988+

Radio Guide
Oct, 1931 - Dec, 1931//
SEE: MOVIE-RADIO GUIDE

Radio Guide
? - Feb 16, 1940//
SEE: MOVIE-RADIO GUIDE

✤ RADIO HIT SONGS
SUB: "Words and music."
SUB: "Latest popular radio hit songs."
PUBL: Charlton Publishing Corporation, 49 Hawkins St., Derby, CT.
DESC: It was one thing to hear the latest song hits being played over the network radio programs, and quite another to remember the lyrics to those same tunes: *Radio Song Hits* provided the lyrics to old and new songs, some destined to be classics, and others bound for other directions. Each magazine cover featured a radio song-star, along with the titles of the music contained inside. There was an occasional small news column, or advertising mixed within the pages. Typical song titles for the sampled wartime issue for August, 1943 included "In the Blue of the Evening," "That Canteen Waltz," "Mr. President, I Want to Go Home," "You're Irish and You're Beautiful," "Send Our Regards to the Boys Over There," "We're the Army Air Force," "Picture on My Bureau," "Fighting Sons of the Navy Blue" (as featured by Rudy Vallee), "When My Daddy Comes Marching Home," "We'll Be Singing Hallelujah Marching Through Berlin," "Velvet Moon," and "Cookin' With Gas." Indeed, the lyrics to over 150 popular songs were within that single sampled issue for 1943. Each issue included complete sheet music to two selected pieces: in the sampled issue, these were "Something About You," and "Love Blossom Lane." Of special note was a complete song title and feature index at the back of the publication. This wonderful publication was, unfortunately, published on newsprint. Stapled magazine format, black/white editorial and advertising content, plus covers on wartime-mandated newsprint (9 x 12 inches / 230 x 305 mm).
DEPT: "On the Radio Hit Circuit," delightful newsbriefs concerning radio network stars; "The Moore the Merrier," radio personality news column by Garry Moore; "Guest Gag Bag," guest-submitted jokes and puns; "Radio News From the Networks," programming news from the CBS, NBC, and Mutual radio networks. (8-43).
TYPL: "Patriotic Song Contest Extended to October 31 by Fed. of Music Clubs and NBC," "Star Reporter," "In Their Spare Time," "Teach School to Learn Radio," "Song Hints by Vera Barton." (8-43).
SCHL: Monthly, 30 pp.
SPAN: Nov, 1941?+?

RADIO HOME, THE
SUB: "Something of interest for every member of the radio family." (Apr, 1926).
SUB: "A home magazine for the radio family." (May, 1926 - ?).
PUBL: Consolidated Publishers, Produce Exchange Bldg., Third and Walnut Sts., Philadelphia, PA.
DESC: *Radio in the Home* was a large format, newsprint magazine (30 pages), printed in brown ink, that served the American radio consumer in the mid-1920s. It featured the purchase of radio receivers, new technical developments, broadcast programming, and a large number of advertisements for mail-order radio equipment items. Commencing with the April, 1926 issue, *The Radio Home* (a continuation and enlargement to 70+ pages) called itself "Two Complete Radio Magazines in One," subdividing articles into the "Broadcasting Section," which concerned program activities; and the "Technical and Hook-Up" section, which emphasized new construction techniques and equipment. This "new" serial retained its large magazine format, but added a slightly improved paper quality for better halftone reproductions. Of special note was the reproduction of radio station broadcasting photographs.
DEPT: "Editorially Speaking --and still-- Editorially Speaking." (7-23). "Editorially Speaking --and still-- Editorially Speaking," "Notes From the Lab." (5-26).
TYPL: "How the Scouts Use Radio," "Radio Drama: a New Art," "A Good Crystal Hook-Up," "Take Radio on Your Hike," "Do You Know what 'Neutrodyne' Means?" (7-23). "The Junior Order of Radio Gardeners," "Those Radio Candy Recipes," "How to Hunt Interference," "Power for Your Loudspeakers," "How to Understand Radio," "This Set Needs No Batteries," "Trouble Shooting in the Powertone." (5-26).
SCHL: Monthly, 70 pp.
SPAN: Jun, 1922 - ?//?
VARIES
--Jun, 1922 - Mar, 1926 as Radio in the Home.

Radio in the Home
Jun, 1922 - Mar, 1926//
SEE: RADIO HOME, THE

RADIO INDUSTRIES
SUB: "With which is incorporated Radio Manufacturers' Monthly." (Nov, 1929 - ?).

SUB: "The only publication exclusively for the radio manufacturer." (May, 1926 - ?).
SUB: "The radio manufacturers' monthly." (? - Oct/Nov, 1934).
SUB: "Production, engineering, distribution, radio, television, sound projection." (? - Oct/Nov, 1934).
PUBL: Radio Industries, 35 East Wacker Dr., Chicago, IL.
DESC: Designed for the manufacturer of radio and television apparatus, this industrial serial showcased new receiver elements, and discussed technological advancements in the American broadcast industry. Some articles provided suggestions on improving radio equipment retail sales to the public, while others discussed patent struggles, and practical applications for radio equipment. It emphasized broadcast radio receivers and related apparatus. Numerous graphics.
DEPT: "Radio Editorials," "The Marketing of Radio." (6-26). "Bulletins from the R.M.A.," "News of the Industry," "New developments," equipment. (1-34).
TYPL: "Condenser Tissue May Answer Your Fixed Condenser Difficulty," "What Importance Does Radio Hold in the Electrical Business?," "Dept. of Commerce May Take a Hand in Radio Squabble," "All-Radio Store to Pass, Says Griffin." (6-26). "The Electric Eye and Television," "Plastics in Cabinet Design," "Role of Phototubes in Talkies." (1-34).
SPAN: May, 1926 - Oct/Nov, 1934//
VARIES
--May, 1926 - Oct, 1929 as Radio Manufacturers Monthly.
SUSPENDED
--Jul, 1926.
LC: TK 6540.R52

RADIO MANUFACTURER, THE

SUB: "A section of the *Radio Dealer* for radio manufacturers and engineers." (? - Oct, 1928).
PUBL: Radio Dealer Publishing Co., 10 East 39th St., New York, NY.
DESC: This was a short supplement to *The Radio Dealer*, and appeared to be more a departmental feature than a separate section/supplement to the parent periodical. Articles stressed the technical side of radio operation, with an emphasis on manufacturing. Some graphics.
DEPT: None. (4-28).
TYPL: "Suggested Symbols for New Tubes," "Acoustical Couplings Built-In Speakers," "The Gang Control Problem." (4-28).
SCHL: Monthly, 8 pp.
SPAN: ? - Oct, 1928//
SUPPLEMENT TO
--Radio Dealer, ? - Oct, 1928.
LC: TK 6540.R35

Radio Manufacturers Monthly
May, 1926 - Oct, 1929//
SEE: RADIO INDUSTRIES

Radio Mirror
Nov, 1933 - Jul, 1939//
SEE: TV RADIO MIRROR

Radio Mirror
Nov, 1942 - Mar, 1945//
SEE: TV RADIO MIRROR

Radio Mirror
Dec, 1945 - Mar, 1948//
SEE: TV RADIO MIRROR

Radio News
Jul, 1920 - Jul, 1948//
SEE: ELECTRONICS WORLD

✣ RADIO ONLY

SUB: "The monthly management tool."
PUBL: Inside Radio, Inc., 1930 E. Marlton Pike, Suite S-93, Cherry Hill, NJ 08003-4210.
DESC: "What you are about to read is the very first magazine ever written for the radio industry only. It's hard to believe that an industry as illustrious as ours has been so overshadowed by television, the record industry and now cable that it has constantly taken a back seat or at least shared the front seat with some other competing interest. Now, we're asking the others to move over. Starting with this...[issue], radio executives can turn to a publication that unabashedly claims to be for radio only." Thus began this "for your ears only" periodical designed for radio management, sales members and staff. *Radio Only* leaves few issues uncovered, providing interesting, thorough coverage of sales, management, women in radio, advertising, motivation, formats, technical innovations for profit, retailers, rating services and regulatory matters. A large volume of advertising indicates that this magazine is reaching its intended audience. With good layout design and intelligent writing, *Radio Only* should be "MUST" reading for every general manager in American radio, and deserves commendation not only for filling in a gaping hole for assertive radio sales and management; but also for recognizing radio today as a vibrant and exciting medium. For the sampled issues of 1991: editorial content is spot- and full-color graphics on coated stock, and likewise for the cover; significant advertising for the trade, in a stapled magazine format (8 ⅛ x 11 inches / 205 x 280 mm).
DEPT: "Data Bank," a large section detailing upcoming activities, FCC activities; "News," newsbriefs; "People," news profiles. (4-82). "Letters," "Power Sales Tools," unique calendar for upcoming selling opportunities; "Thought Starters," short items for competitive radio management; "Radio Across-The-USA,"

outstanding Birch Monthly ratings reports for the top 100 American radio markets; "Future Trends," potential trends affecting radio management. (4-89).
TYPL: "Can Pro Sports Still Boost Ratings?," "How to Know the Numbers are Real," "How to Profit from the Decline of Newspapers," "Straight Talk About Consultants," "The Broadcast Connection--it Really is who You Know." (4-82). "Hints on Hiring, Firing and Managing," "Rating Arbitron's New Diary," "How to Get in On the Subcarrier Leasing Boom," "How Interactive Phones Will Revolutionize Your Station." (4-89).
SCHL: Monthly, 55 pp.
SPAN: Apr, 1982+
LC: HE 8698 .R32
DD: 384.54/0973
ISSN: 0731-8294

✥ RADIO*PHILES

SUB: "A monthly journal of information and opinion for radio professionals, students, archivists and others interested in the modern radio broadcasting industry."
PUBL: RadioPhiles, Inc., Box 16353, Alexandria, VA 22302.
DESC: A typewritten, newsprint, journal format provides current information about radio station changes in ownership, call letters, formats, and other items of interest to radio management and personalities. Of special note is the monthly departmental column, "Forum," providing fascinating discussion of current radio issues. Subscriber comments are printed as received, providing frank and argumentative points of view. This publication (sample issue for March, 1987) may not be as slick as other industry trades, but for anyone in the radio industry, *RADIO*PHILES* is worth its subscription cost. No advertising; some graphics including monthly cartoon.
DEPT: "FCC Actions," large listing of recent regulatory actions; "Book Review," "Evolution," 'The column that chronicles the changes and developments of radio each month'; "Market Profile," monthly profile of a specific radio market; "Forum," always a fascinating no-holds-barred discussion of a current radio issue; "Aircheck Central," subscriber aircheck exchange; "Announcements." (3-87).
TYPL: "How to Make a Neo-Traditionalist in One Easy Rule-Making Proposal," "Radio and the Law: Calls as Property," "Say Hello, Wave Goodbye." (3-87).
SCHL: Monthly, 25 pp.
SPAN: Nov, 1981?+?

Radio Retailing

1925 - Mar, 1939//
SEE: TELEVISION RETAILING

Radio Retailing Combined with Radio Today

Jan, 1942 - Jul, 1942//
SEE: TELEVISION RETAILING

Radio Retailing Today

Aug, 1942 - Mar, 1944//
SEE: TELEVISION RETAILING

RADIO REVIEW AND TELEVISION NEWS

PUBL: Radio Review and Television News, 96-98 Park Place, New York, NY.
DESC: Hugo Gernsback, well-known New York publisher and electronics fan, began *Television News* in Mar, 1931 and told his readers; "Up to the present time, there has been no regular periodical in this country to describe accurately from month to month the advances in television. It will be the mission of the new magazine to portray television from each and every angle and to show the reader what work has been done, not only in this country, but the world over." Mr. Gernsback's enthusiasm influenced the editorial pages. Numerous articles, schematics, and pictures detailed the pioneering work of mechanical and electronic television. Most articles were written by television pioneers (Merlin Aylesworth, David Sarnoff, Dr. Herbert Ives, E. F. W. Alexanderson, Dr. Alfred Goldsmith, C. Francis Jenkins, and Philo T. Farnsworth), and include rare photographs of experiments and transmissions. The American Great Depression took its toll of readership, and Gernsback, to broaden his subscription base, was forced to change the title and content of his magazine in November, 1932 to include more radio than television articles. The magazine ceased publication with the January/February, 1933 issue, but remains an exceptional reference source for early 1930s television.
DEPT: "Television Gossip," "Television Question and Answer Box," (3/4-31). "Radio Kinks from Abroad," equipment newsbriefs; "Digest of Radio Patents," "List of Television Stations," (1/2-33).
TYPL: "Radio-Controlled Television Plane," "How to Build a Home Televisor," "Scanning with an Electric Pencil," "The Latest Ideas in Transmitting Television Images," (3/4-31). "A Band Bass Filter that can be Added to Any Receiver," "Rome Television is Europe's Latest," "Nipkow Still Lives!," "A New Principle Applied to Television Superheterodynes," (1/2-33).
SCHL: Bimonthly, 70 pp.
SPAN: Mar/Apr, 1931 - Jan/Feb, 1933//
VARIES
--Mar/Apr, 1931 - Sep/Oct, 1932 as Television News.
ABSORBED BY
--Radio-Craft, Mar, 1933.

Radio Romances
Apr, 1945 - Nov, 1945//
SEE: TV RADIO MIRROR

Radio Service Dealer
Apr, 1940 - Jan, 1944//
SEE: ELECTRONIC SERVICING & TECHNOLOGY

Radio Service Dealer
May, 1944 - Jul, 1950//
SEE: ELECTRONIC SERVICING & TECHNOLOGY

Radio Television
Jul/Aug, 1966? - 1981//
(ISSN: 0033-7676)
SEE: RADIO AND TELEVISION

Radio-Television Daily
Jan 12, 1962 - Aug 31, 1965//
SEE: RTD

Radio Television International Review
1982 - 1984//
(ISSN: 1015-8596)
SEE: RADIO AND TELEVISION

Radio Television Mirror
Mar, 1951 - Sep, 1951//
SEE: TV RADIO MIRROR

Radio-Television Service Dealer
195u - 195u//
SEE: ELECTRONIC SERVICING & TECHNOLOGY

✤ RADIO TIMES
SUB: "Official organ of the B.B.C." (Sep 28, 1923 - Dec, 24, 1926).
SUB: "The journal of the British Broadcasting Corporation." (Dec 31, 1926+).
PUBL: BBC Publications, 35 Marylebone High St., London W1M 4AA, England.
DESC: *Radio Times*, in a magazine-newsprint format, provides capsule comments of upcoming BBC 1 and 2 video programming, as well as BBC radio programs 1, 2, 3, and 4 to the general public. This is a BBC publication, and therefore, other commercial video and radio fare are not listed. Readers will be pleasantly surprised by unusually long program descriptions. One unusual practice is that television crew members names are often listed.
DEPT: "Preview," rotating columnists describe upcoming fare; "Review," of current series.
TYPL: "Faces of America," "New Year Season on BBC 2," "The Brotherhood of Ruralists." (1-78).
SCHL: Weekly, 70 pp.
SPAN: Sep 28, 1923+
WITH SUPPLEMENT
--World-Radio, 1925 - Sep 8, 1939//
LC: TK 6540.B78
DD: 791.4
ISSN: 0033-8060

Radio-TV Mirror
Oct, 1951 - Jul, 1954//
SEE: TV RADIO MIRROR

✤ RADIO WORLD
SUB: "Serving the Communications Industry Worldwide."
SUB: "Radio's best read newspaper."
PUBL: Industrial Marketing Advisory Services, Inc., 5827 Columbia Pike, Suite 310, Falls Church, VA 22041.
DESC: Under the earlier banner of *Broadcast Equipment Exchange*, this was a newsprint tabloid for broadcast engineering personnel dealing primarily with (new and used) equipment, and had numerous articles on equipment performance and operation (with graphics and/or schematics). With a change of title to *Radio World*, it moved away from the used equipment scenario to an emphasis on new technology, and radio station engineering management, with a wide range of articles on the practical application of both technique and technology. A very unique *Broadcast Equipment Exchange* supplement is worth the price of subscription alone. This is primarily a publication of technology, with an editorial philosophy of bringing together the diverse elements of radio management. Toward that end, *Radio World* places at the end of each article the name of an individual, organization name, and telephone number for further information. A remarkable publication for radio engineering and station management. Stapled tabloid newspaper format (10 ¾ x 14 ½ inches / 270 x 370 mm), with numerous graphics and schematics.
DEPT: "Winn Schwartau on Recording," "Readers Forum," "FCC Developments," "Bill Sacks and 'The Audio Process,'" "The Exchange," large section detailing needs and desire to sell equipment. (3-80). None. (3-82). "News Briefs," "Readers Forum," extensive letters column; "Consultants Corner," "From the Trenches," column by Alan Peterson; "Eclectic Engineer," "Bottomline Broadcaster," "Producer's File," "Facilities Showcase," "Great Idea," reader's tech ideas. (11-22-89). "News Briefs," "Readers Forum," "Cue and Review," technical column by John Gatski; "Eclectic Engineer," column by Barry Mishkind;

"Digital Domain," trends and breakthroughs on digital radio broadcasting, column by Mel Lambert; "Line Out," "Felker's Forum," radio regulation column by Lex Felker; "Workbench," an excellent technical section for day-to-day engineering solutions, column by John Bisset; "Q-Tips," column by John Q. Shepler; "Old Timer," a wonderful retrospective on the way things were in radio, column by George Riggins; "Insight on Rules," application of Federal Communication Commission rulings, column by Harold Hallikainen; "Offbeat Radio," column by Dee McVicker. (3-13-91).
TYPL: "CKLW Tests Harris AM Stereo System," "The Production Console," "dbx and the Broadcast Market," "Motor Drive Power Amps for the TR-22." (3-80). "AM Stereo Goes Marketplace," "Multi-Site Remote Control," "Mic Basics for Broadcasters," "Radio Broadcasting From Satellites." (3-82). "Hill Holds Radio Hearings," "Citations Dropped in Fatal Tower Crash," "KABL Stays On Air Despite Earthquake," "NRSC Meets on AM 'Mark'." (11-22-89). "Avionics Specs Urged," "In-Band DAB Pushed," "Translator Curb Eyed," "ROC Withholds Eureka Support," "Mulling a DAB Future, Poolside." (3-13-91).
SCHL: Monthly (Jul, 1977 - Dec, 1985); Semimonthly (Dec 15, 1985+), 40 pp.
SPAN: Jul, 1977+
VARIES
--Jul, 1977 - Jun, 1980 as Broadcast Equipment Exchange (ISSN: 0194-2190).
--Dec 15, 1985 - ? as Radio World Newspaper.
WITH SUPPLEMENT
--Buyers Guide, ?+.
--Satellite Times, ?+.
DD: 384
ISSN: 0274-8541

Radio World Newspaper
Dec 15, 1985 - ?//
SEE: RADIO WORLD

RADIOACTIVE
SUB: "For the radio members of NAB."
PUBL: Public Relations Department, National Association of Broadcasters, 1771 N St., N.W., Washington, DC 20036.
DESC: *Radioactive* is designed to interpret current problems in radio, and present imaginative ways of solving them. Typical topics include creating exciting editorials, putting life into recruiting announcements, great copywriting and new ideas for promotion. Of special interest are reprinted editorials, letters and other items from member stations.
DEPT: "State Scope," news about state broadcast organizations; "Shoptalk," items on successful promotion and programming campaigns; "Points of Law," Q-A format on broadcast law. (9-76); "Dollars and $ense," "Station Identification," "Small Talk," "Matter of Opinion," "Comment." (3-81).
TYPL: "Investigative Reporting is News," "Recruiting with Radio," "Guidelines for Better Copy." (9-76); "Steer Clear of Lotteries," "Sheridan Broadcasting Network," "Promoting Radio on Radio." (3-81).
SCHL: Monthly (? - ?); Monthly [except combined Jul/Aug issue] (? - ?); Bimonthly (?+), 20 pp.
SPAN: ? - 1988//
MERGED WITH
--Radio Today (to form) RadioWeek.
DD: 384
ISSN: 0747-4032

RADIOLAND
PUBL: Fawcett Publications, Inc., 1100 West Broadway, Louisville, KY.
DESC: Network radio programming needed this monthly "fanzine" partly to "keep up" with the professional and private lives of favorite performers, and partly to show what these performers looked like, both on and off mike. Editor Roscoe Fawcett provided articles that covered the gamut of radio programming and personalities. One sampled issue included an article on how to break into network radio; production pictures of Sigmund Romberg, Dorothy Lamour, Yogi Yorgesson, and Claudette Colbert; an article on how radio stars had turned their "handicaps into fame;" and another on how women radio stars had "won their men." One endearing feature of *Radioland* was numerous pictures of favorite radio personalities; like one with Edward G. Robinson sitting on Kate Smith's lap as she sang "Rock-a-bye Baby." Printed in black/white or duotone green, pictures of these radio stars generated many requests to "Questions and Answers," wanting to know eye and hair color of favorite personalities. *Radioland* was a splendid guide to the lives, loves, and radio performances of network radio stars and staff. Published on newsprint, magazine format, with some pages in duotone green.
DEPT: "Letters From the Stars," unique letters twist with signatures; "Flashes From the News," newsbriefs; "The Editor's Opinion," editorial; "Rudy Vallee's Music Notebook," column by Rudy Vallee; "The Radio Revue," duotone pictorial section of favorite radio personalities; "Peeking In at the Broadcasts with the Camera Snooper," pictures of network radio shows in progress; "Mike Says:," 'Sparkling news notes straight from glamorous radio row' column by Arthur J. Kellar; "They Never Told Till Now," 'Untold Stories of the Stars' column by Mary Jacobs; "Reviews of the New Programs," "Recommended Programs," "Cleanliness for Beauty," column by Wynne McKay; "Questions and Answers," Radio Q&A from readers. (1-35).

TYPL:	"Radio Secrets Winchell won't Tell!," "Love Problems of the Voice of Experience," "Radio Kids Like Christmas, Too!," "Edgar Guest Says Happiness Begins at Home," "Choose America's Favorite Radio Program." (1-35).
SCHL:	Monthly, 70 pp.
SPAN:	Sep, 1932 - ?//?

✤ RADIOTRENDS

SUB:	"The journal of radio marketing."
SUB:	"A monthly summary of critical trends in radio marketing and finance."
PUBL:	Bolton Research Corporation, 250 West Lancaster Ave., Paoli, PA 19301.
DESC:	Articles are brief, to the point, and concentrate on how radio station management can take advantage of emerging trends in broadcast marketing; which is why station management subscribes (subscription for 1991: $95 per year) to *RadioTrends*. Bolton Research Corporation has created a very nice "idea letter" for today's busy radio management team, the end result being that stations are enabled to more effectively compete within their broadcast markets. Of special interest are quotes by radio station managers from across the United States pertaining to their own experiences and opinions on a given marketing topic. The eight-page publication has information that is concise, fresh, and above all, applicable to station operation the day it is received; which is the true test of a periodical's worth. Three-hole punched, stapled newsletter format on uncoated paper stock with spot color, graphics throughout (no advertising) (8 ½ x 11 inches / 215 x 280 mm).
DEPT:	"Marketing Spotlight," broadcast manager input; "Trendicators," 'Influential ideas in brief' marketing newsbriefs; "The Radio Marketing Think Tank," "Hot Marketing IdeaStarters," "The Marketing Forum." (4-91).
TYPL:	"Selling is Out, Marketing is In," "Self-Liquidating Promotions," "WAR. Huahh. Good God Y'all. What is It Good For? ...Not Necessarily Marketing," "Don't Doubt the Database," "Marketing to the Youth of America: How Are They Different?" (4-91).
SCHL:	Monthly, 8 pp.
SPAN:	Jan, 1985+

✤ RADIOWEEK

SUB:	"A weekly resource for radio managers."
SUB:	"A resource for managers."
PUBL:	National Association of Broadcasters, 1771 N St., NW, Washington, DC 20036-2891.
DESC:	*RadioWeek* is a weekly newsletter for broadcast radio general managers and their staffs. It concerns National Association of Broadcaster news, and other items of interest connected with radio station management and operation. Almost half of the sampled issue consisted of advertisements for related radio products and services. For sampled issue of 1990: three-hole punched loose-leaf newsletter format with spot-color (color of ink changes each issue) throughout on uncoated paper stock, limited advertising (8 ½ x 10 ¾ inches / 215 x 275 mm).
DEPT:	"Stateline," state radio news items; "Actionline," NAB actions and newsbriefs; "Newsflashes," "Points of Law." (3-26-90).
TYPL:	"NAB '90, Engineering Conference Begin This Week!," "Six Peabody Awards Go to Radio," "Simulcasts Used for Urgent News." (3-26-90).
SCHL:	Weekly, 8 pp.
SPAN:	May 30, 1988+ FROM MERGER OF --RadioActive (and) Radio Today.

✤ RANGEFINDER, THE

SUB:	"A national publication for professional photographers."
SUB:	"The magazine for professional photographers."
SUB:	"A national publication for career photographers."
PUBL:	The Rangefinder Publishing Co., 1312 Lincoln Blvd., P.O. Box 1703, Santa Monica, CA 90406.
DESC:	"A monthly publication dedicated to the advancement of professional photographers both quality-wise and business-wise. Features encompass all phases of professional photography--solutions to technical problems, business practices, handling assignments, equipment test reports, processing techniques, reader's open forum, future trends." *The Rangefinder* truly serves the professional photographer through a number of quality departments and articles. From one sampled issue of 1980 came a description of fashion photography, studio investments, the legal side of photography, preparing for the Winter Olympics; and a variety of reports, columns, and other departmental fare all designed to increase the profit line for any photographic business. The informative articles are written by photographic professionals, and are written for immediate application by individuals in the field. For the 1970 sampled issues: black ink with spot-color on coated paper; cover comprised of full-color graphics on coated stock; significant trade advertising, in stapled magazine format (8 ½ x 11 inches / 215 x 280 mm). For the sampled issue of 1980: perfect-bound magazine format, black ink, spot and full-color cover and editorial content on coated paper stock with various advertising inserts consisting of different paper stock and inks (8 ⅜ x 11 inches / 215 x 280 mm).
DEPT:	"Editor's Note," "Problems and Solutions," column by Jim Stewart, "Off the Press," review column by Jim Stewart; "Capsulated Comments," "Names Make the News," "New Products and Processes," column by Joe Mather; "Competitions & Exhibitions," "Suppliers' News," "Association News," "Photographic Instruction," "School Photography Digest," column by Bill Smith; "Books for the Professional," "Tried, Tested, Approved." (4-70). "Photographers Making the News," newsbriefs; "Photography in the News," international news items concerning photography; "Association News," unique section publicizing indi-

vidual professional trade organizations; "Photographic Instruction," courses offered; "Competitions and Exhibitions," details. (7-77).
TYPL: "How the Studio Brings in the Kids," "Don't Overlook the Domestic Pet," "Make-Up for Dark Skin Types," "Informals for Profit," "You, Too, Can Have Fun at a Wedding." (4-70). "Skylight the Keylight," "Giant Dye Transfer Prints Portray Early U.S. Scenes," "Overview of Industrial Photography." (7-77).
SCHL: Monthly, 100 pp.
SPAN: Jun, 1952+
ABSORBED
--School Photographers Digest, ?
ISSN: 0033-9202

✤ RANGEFINDER, THE
SUB: "News of NPPA's region 9."
PUBL: National Press Photographers Association, Region 9, c/o Department of Communications, UMC 4605, Utah State University, Logan, UT 84322-4605.
DESC: At 60 pages, *The Rangefinder* ranks as having one of the larger number of editorial pages concerning professional photojournalism graphic work. This regional publication of the National Press Photographers Association provides a forum whereby members can submit monthly work for judging in quarterly and yearly "Photographer of the Year" competitions. Approximately one-half of one issue profiled the top ten photographers of the year and their work. The remaining editorial content detailed quarterly competition, and departmental features. Magazine format (8 ½ x 10 ⅞ inches / 215 x 275 mm); black/white graphics on uncoated paper stock; minimal advertising.
DEPT: "From the Director," "From the Editor," "Clip Results," "Grapevine," newsbriefs. (winter-90).
TYPL: "Debate in the US Warms Up on Documentary Versus Illustrative Philosophy of Photojournalism," "Region 9 NPPA 1989 Photographer of the Year, Robert Pope, is a Self-Described 'Late Bloomer'," "Chris Young Takes Eighth Place and Has Some Advice for Anyone Who is Moving and Owns a Pet," "Photojournalism '90 to Feature Faculty From Many Parts of Region 9 and the U.S." (winter-90).
SCHL: Quarterly, 60 pp.
SPAN: ?+

✤ RCA BROADCAST NEWS
PUBL: Radio Corporation of America Broadcast Systems, Bldg 2-2A, Camden, NJ 08102.
DESC: [*Broadcast News*]: "To those who are responsible for the present success of the Broadcasting Art,--to those who devote their time and attention to the advancement of this fascinating and highly useful triumph of radio service, we modestly present this publication in the hope that it will provide a pleasant and convenient medium for the exchange of ideas and information..." Thus began this interesting promotional vehicle for RCA equipment and activities. Every edition maintained a positive outlook toward the variety of broadcast activities both at home and abroad. Of special note were quality reproductions of photos accompanying articles, all printed on heavy, coated paper stock. A rich resource for historical broadcast development.
DEPT: "Broadcasting Personalities." (2-34).
TYPL: "A Visit to the New WLW," "Program Amplifier--1934 Design," "Byrd Antartic Expedition to Originate Weekly Programs from South Pole," "Solution of Vacuum Tube Problems by the Isocline Method," "The Importance of the Field Strength Survey," "Air Conditioning at the Radio City Studios of NBC." (2-34).
SCHL: Quarterly, 56 pp.
SPAN: 1931+
VARIES
--Oct, 1931 - Feb, 1954 as Broadcast News.
--Mar, 1954 - Apr, 1954 as AM-FM Television.
--May, 1954 - Feb, 1968 as Broadcast News.
LC: TK 6630.A 1B78
ISSN: 0096-7785
ABST: --Computer & Control Abstracts (ISSN: 0036-8113)
--Electrical & Electronics Abstracts (ISSN: 0036-8105)
--Physics Abstracts. Science Abstracts. Series A. (ISSN: 0036-8091)

✤ RE:ACT
SUB: "Action for Childrens Television Newsletter."
SUB: "Action for Children's Television news magazine."
PUBL: Action for Children's Television, 46 Austin St., Newtonville, MA 02160.
DESC: "Action for Children's Television (ACT) is a national nonprofit organization working to encourage diversity in children's television and to eliminate commercial abuses targeted to children. ACT initiates legal reform and promotes public awareness of issues relating to children's television through public education campaigns, publications, national conferences, and speaking engagements." *Re:Act* functions to provide the 20,000+ ACT members with information on new developments in the television field affecting children. Note: the fall, 1978 issue bears ISSN: 0145-6822 under the title of *re:act*, although most sources indicate that this ISSN number was assigned to earlier title *News - Action for Children's Television*. For the sampled issues of 1978: stapled magazine format; black with spot-color ink on coated stock; cover likewise; no advertising (8 ⅜ x 10 ¾ inches / 215 x 275 mm).
DEPT: None. (spring-78). "Short Circuit," newsbriefs; "Bookends." (spring/summer-82).
TYPL: "FTC Paves the Way to Restrict Children's Ads," "Heroes, Hamburgs, and Hard Rock: Scrimmages with TV Images for Young Teens," "PBS Softens Kids' Attitudes; Networks Respond with Predictable Platitudes." (spring-78). "In Defense of the Young," "Washington Welches on Children," "The Envelope, Please..." (spring/summer-82).
SCHL: Quarterly (? - ?); Semiannual (?+), 24 pp.

SPAN: 1970+
VARIES
--? - Summer, 1977 as News - Action for Children's Television (ISSN: 0145-6822).
DD: 791
ISSN: 0163-7908

✦ REAL LIFE/DAYTIMERS

SUB: "The inside channel to daytime TV."
PUBL: DS Magazines, Inc., 105 Union Ave., Cresskill, NJ 07626.
DESC: [*Rona Barrett's Daytimers*]: "Tuning-in MORE columns and features written by the stars themselves ... MORE full color shots of all your favorites ... and MORE pages of current news from actual interviews, *Rona Barrett's Daytimers* offers the BEST coverage of Daytime TV happenings--and the STARS that make it happen! Every issue of *DAYTIMERS* is filled with star-written features, fascinating interviews, up-to-date news on all daytimers (past and present), and comments and questions from TV viewers--YOU!" This information-packed monthly magazine that covered virtually everything happening in the world of daytime television emphasized soap operas, with occasional articles on other daytime personalities (such as gameshow host Gene Rayburn). This publication was typical of the Rona Barrett series of entertainment serials, in which readers were provided ample stories, profiles, descriptions, and gossip of their favorite stars and entertainment product. For the consumer-fan of daytime television, this was one publication well worth its price. Magazine format; full color cover, editorial content on newsprint with some full color pages on clay- coated paper stock; minimal advertising (8 ⅛ x 10 ⅞ inches / 205 x 275 mm).
DESC: [*Real Life/Daytimers*]: This unusual entertainment magazine profiles the "real lives" of the talented artists that make up the film and television industry in America. Current projects, gossip, horoscopes, and even a column on pets will be found here, but the focus is on celebrities as real people; their training as professionals, their off-screen activities (business and personal), and the characters they play on the screen. One sampled issue explored a New York City food emporium owned and operated by Dino DeLaurentiis; Liberace's favorite recipe; a historical look at "Hollywood Hunks;" and an unusual duo of an American priest living in South Korea and a Florida-based flight attendant, who worked together to provide hundreds of orphans and abandoned children a new life in the United States. It contains many graphics, celebrity photos, and production stills in both black/white and color. Printed on coated paper stock in magazine format. (8 x 10 ⅞ inches / 205 x 275 mm).
DEPT: "One Shots," 'Closeups on some of the headliners'; "Second Take," 'Quotable quotes from our daytimers'; "One Minute Interview," "It's Your Turn," 'Readers' Survey'; "Collectors' Corner," 'A special classified section'; "Birthday Bulletin Board," 'Send a card to your favorite'; "Flashbacks," 'A look down memory lane'; "Comings & Goings," 'Cast changes to keep track of!'; "Rona's Daytimers," 'What East, West, North, and South are saying!'; "Editor's Page," 'An insider's point of view'; "The New Yorkers," 'Who's doing what, with whom, in Gotham!'; "Dear Rona," 'Your chance to talk to our Ms. Rona!'; "Just Asking," 'We answer all your questions!'; "Fans & Favorites," 'The latest on fan clubbing!'; "One Man's Opinion," 'Follow the bouncing actor'; "Station Breaks," 'What daytimers do between soaps!'; "No Soap," column by Eileen Fulton; "Last Take," 'Up-to-the-minute inside cover news'. (12- 78). "Editor's Page," "Fast Features," newsbriefs; "Malcolm Boyes' Real Life Show Biz Column," column by Malcolm Boye; "Body & Mind," 'Health news'; "Celebrity Recipes," "Your November Starcast," horoscope column by Stephanie; "Pets," of the celebrities; "Flash!," 'Star Shots'; "Daytimer," daytime television-oriented; "Dr. Z's Hollywood," 'Satire'; "Flashbacks," historical celebrities; "How They've Changed," star profile; "Quotes," via celebrities; "Day's End," inside back-cover photo. (11-83).
TYPL: "Car Crash Hospitalizes Jacquie Courtney!," "If You've Got It, Flaunt It!," "Can This Doctor Mend His Own Heart?," "Vicky's Not Afraid of Her Fans Anymore!," "Has Ilene Had Her Last Tantrum?" (12-78). "Talking (and Joking) with Paul Williams & Pat McCormick," "James Bond? Superman? Indiana Jones? No, It's Stuntman Vic Armstrong, Fall Guy for the Stars," "The Triumph of Lee Grant," "Remembering Natalie," "Gere in Gear: Richard and the Women He's Loved." (11-83).
SCHL: Monthly, 70 pp.
SPAN: Apr, 1977+?
VARIES
--Apr, 1977? - ?, 198u as Rona Barrett's Daytimers (ISSN: 0199-1817).
--198u - 198u as Daytimers (ISSN: 0744-3935).
ISSN: 0746-0244

✦ REALLY, A FREE NEWSLETTER

SUB: "Mary Bold's favorite publishing tips."
PUBL: Bold Productions, PO Box 152281, Arlington, TX 76015.
DESC: This short, two-page (legal size paper) quarterly is free, and packed with information for today's electronic desktop publisher (DTP). Mary Bold produces seminars on book publishing/marketing, as well as written guides to desktop publishing available for purchase. A five dollar ($5.00) contribution helps defray postage costs. Printed on one legal- sized sheet of paper, with graphics.
DEPT: "It's Easy to Recommend," new books, organizations for desktop publishers. (spring-90).
TYPL: "Just Say No Way Can I Do Absolutely Everything for You," "An Honest Printer!," "Tips From a Desktop Publisher." (spring-90).
SCHL: Quarterly, 2 pp.

SPAN: Winter, 1988/1989+

Record [Bell Laboratories]
Jul/Aug, 1983//
(ISSN: 0743-0205)
SEE: AT&T TECHNOLOGY

Record [AT&T Bell Laboratories]
Sep, 1983 - Mar, 1986//
(ISSN: 0749-8152)
SEE: AT&T TECHNOLOGY

✦ RECORD RESEARCH
SUB: "The magazine of record statistics and information."
PUBL: Record Research, 65 Grand Ave., Brooklyn, NY 11205.
DESC: This interesting montage of typewritten, hand-lined, material breaks all rules of layout design and paste-up skills; yet is valuable in providing details concerning record releases of yesteryear. Articles describe recording artists, publishers, and recording studios and trends; but the focus is (small-type) listings of records available for sale.
DEPT: None.
TYPL: None.
SCHL: Bimonthly, 25 pp.
SPAN: Feb, 1955+
LC: ML 1 .R293
DD: 789.9/12/05
ISSN: 0034-1592
ABST: --Jazz Index (ISSN: 0344-5399)
--Music Index (ISSN: 0027-4348)

Record Review
? - ?//
(ISSN: 0198-8573)
SEE: FRESH!

Recording Engineer/Producer
Apr/May, 1970 - May, 1990//
(ISSN: 0034-1673)
SEE: REP: RECORDING ENGINEERING PRODUCTION

Reel and Slide Magazine
Mar, 1918 - Dec, 1919//
SEE: MOVING PICTURE AGE

REEL LIFE
SUB: "A weekly magazine of kinetic drama and literature."
SUB: "The Mutual Film Magazine."
SUB: "A magazine of moving pictures."
PUBL: Mutual Film Corporation, 71 West 23rd St., New York, NY.
DESC: Aimed at the motion picture exhibitor, *Reel Life* was a promotional showcasing upcoming Mutual film releases; providing release dates, running times, cast members, story synopses and other pertinent data. The majority of each issue was thus devoted to a description (many with production pictures) of a forthcoming release. Interestingly, advertising concerned theatre equipment, and upcoming releases by other film production companies. Magazine format; graphics.
DEPT: "The New Plays," synopses; "Mutual Releases," "Mutual Exchanges," "Mutual Program." (9-20-13). "Plain Talks to Exhibitors," "Stories of the New Photoplays," "The Exhibitor's End of It," promotion; "Mutual Releases," "Mutual Exchanges," "Mutual Program," "Regular Mutual Program Features," "News of the Trade," "Little Stories of Reel Life." (7-10-15).
TYPL: "Mechanical and Optical Illusions with the Motion Picture Film," "Two Men," "A Highland Romance." (9-20-13). "When All the World Seemed Mockers," "The Film Hero--His Prerequisites." (7-10-15).
SCHL: Weekly, 40 pp.
SPAN: 1912 - Jun 9, 1917//
SUSPENDED
--Aug 21, 1915
LC: PN 1993.R4

✦ REEL LIFE
SUB: "A publication of the Virginia Production Services Association."
PUBL: Virginia Production Services Association, PO Box 7419, Richmond, VA 23221-0419.
DESC: This dynamic newsletter informs members of the Virginia Production Services Association about news items, events, workshops, and other business news of interest to the membership. A special focus is announcements, profiles, and interviews with member producers in a wide variety of film and video production fields. In one sampled issue articles described Richmond, Virginia's quest for film business; a review of student projects at the Virginia Film Festival in Charlottesville; a new Norfolk animation house; and an interesting article on "Doing Business with the Government." For sampled issue of 1990: loose-leaf newsletter format, black ink on uncoated paper stock, some inserts on tinted paper stock (8 ½ x 11 inches / 215 x 280 mm).
DEPT: "Sound Bites/Short Ends," production newsbriefs. (2-90).
TYPL: "Tom Logan Talks About Agents," "Banner Year in Film Production Revenue for Virginia," "'Stonehouse' Wins Honors at ITVA," "'Scared Silly' Shoots at AFS." (2-90).
SCHL: Monthly, 10 pp.
SPAN: ?, 1989+

Relay Engineer

? - ?//
SEE: CABLE TELEVISION ENGINEERING

✤ RELIGIOUS BROADCASTING

PUBL: National Religious Broadcasters, Box 2254R, Morristown, NJ 07960.
DESC: In the past ten years, there has been a tremendous increase in media usage by religious organizations in the United States. Specifically, the growth of Christian radio and television stations has been quite phenomonal, and *Religious Broadcasting* magazine reflects this having become a dynamic periodical. This monthly receives an abundance of advertising from religious stations in their efforts to reach organizations desiring to be on the air. The focus is on programming, production organizations, and stations; not technology. Numerous graphics.
DEPT: "NRB News," newsbriefs; "Washington Report," "Broadcasters," profile newsbriefs; "Interview." (9-80); "Speaking Out," "Press-Time Reports," "Washington Watch," "Media World," "Tech Tips," "Broadcast Books," "Airing Our View." (2-84).
TYPL: "Christian Television: The Great Alternative," "Standards for Religious TV," "Communicating with Children Through TV." (8-75). "Communications Group to Sponsor New Research on Religious TV," "Training Church Members for the TV Industry," "Can Christian Stations Make a Difference?," "A Primer for New Programmers." (9-80). "Media Miracle in Central Europe," "Ford Philpot: Religion's Color TV Pioneer." (2-84).
SCHL: Bimonthly (1969 - Feb, 1982); Ten issues per year (Mar, 1982 - Nov, 1982); Eleven issues per year (Dec, 82 to date), 135 pp.
SPAN: 1969+
LC: BV 655 .R45
DD: 260
ISSN: 0034-4079

Religious Communication Today

Sep, 1978 - 1986?//
SEE: JOURNAL OF COMMUNICATION AND RELIGION, THE

RELIGIOUS MEDIA TODAY

SUB: "A timely, critical review of communications resources." (Apr, 1976 - ?).
SUB: "A critical review of communications resources for religious educators." (Apr, 1976 - ?).
PUBL: Christian Interfaith Media Evaluation Center, 432 Park Ave., South, New York, NY 10016.
DESC: This was a quarterly of thoughtful review concerning both religious and secular media as they applied to religious settings, especially those of church and school. The majority of the editorial content concerned book, film, cassette, filmstrip, and record reviews. Magazine format; graphics.
DEPT: "What They are Saying and Doing in Religious Communications," 'A news review of the religious communications field'; "Letters to the Editor," "Reviews of Books, Cassettes, Films, Filmstrips and Records." (8-76).
TYPL: "The Religious Elements in the Play Equus," "Publishers Weakly," "Resources for the Religious Education of the Retarded." (8-76).
SCHL: Quarterly, 60 pp.
SPAN: Apr, 1976 - 1982//
LC: BV 652.95 .R44
DD: 207/.2
ISSN: 0145-5427

Rengo Film News

Jun, 1959//
SEE: MOVIE/TV MARKETING

✤ REP: RECORDING ENGINEERING PRODUCTION

SUB: "Producing audio for tape, records, film, live performance, video & broadcast."
SUB: "The applications magazine for audio professionals."
SUB: "The pro audio applications magazine."
SUB: "Relating recording science to recording art to recording equipment."
PUBL: Recording and Broadcast Publications, 1850 Whitley Ave., Hollywood, CA 90028.
DESC: [*Recording Engineer/Producer*]: "*Recording Engineer/Producer* is edited to relate recording science to recording art to recording equipment, as these subjects, and their relationship to one another, may be of value and interest to those working in the field of commercially marketable recordings and live audio presentation. The editorial content includes: descriptions of sound recording techniques, uses of sound recording equipment, audio environment design, audio equipment maintenance, new products." Long considered one of the primary trade serials of the audio field, *Recording Engineer/Producer* publishes quality articles which fully explore the dynamics of producing, engineering, talent; and the technical, creative and business sides of the industry. *Recording Engineer/Producer* is also an ardant supporter of SPARS, the Society of Professional Audio Recording Services, whose members are frequent contributors to this serial. It is a remarkable publication for anyone involved with professional (commercial and technical) recording studio operation. Magazine format (8 x 10 ⅞ inches / 205 x 275 mm).
DESC: [*REP: Recording, Engineering, Production*]: With the completion of 20 years of publishing (note: an excellent overview of 20 years of this serial and the audio industry is to be found in the May, 1990 "20th Anniversary Issue."), publisher Dennis Milan an-

nounced in the June, 1990 issue: "It's the 1990s, and we're the first to admit that our 20-year-old title--*Recording Engineer/Producer*--doesn't begin to describe what today's working audio professional does on a daily basis. From this day on, we're *R•E•P*--the Pro Audio Applications Magazine for Recording, Engineering and Production. It's too limiting to say that this magazine exists only for recording engineers and record producers. *R•E•P* also addresses audio pros involved in post-production; digital recording, assembly and editing; music creation; sound reinforcement, radio and TV broadcasting; commercial spot production; industrial multimedia; mastering and duplication; and studio design." It utilizes full color throughout on coated paper stock (8 x 10 7/8 inches / 205 x 275 mm). Note to users: although the serial changed titles in June, 1990, the publication continued to use the former ISSN number 0034-1673 as late as the February, 1991 issue.

DEPT: "Letters and Late News," letters. (10-77); "Exposing Audio Mythology," "News," "The Creative Interface," "Soundman's Notes from the Road," "Studio Update," "On the Studio Trail," "New Products," "Industry Inventiveness in the Eighties," "News Notes," "Classified," "People on the Move." (2-84). "Editorial," "Guest Editorial," "News," "Managing MIDI," column by Paul D. Lehrman; "SPARS On-Line," Association news concerning the Society of Professional Audio Recording Services; "Understanding Computers," column by Jeff Burger; "Engineer/Producer Index," unique worklist of working professionals; "Tracks," facility listing; "Studio Update," newsbriefs; "The Cutting Edge," new equipment review column by Laurel Cash; "New Products," "Letters." (9-89). "From the Top," editorial; "Letters," "Random Access," "Trend Watch," "Studio Update," studio newsbriefs; "Roadwork," column by Mark Herman; "Fresh Tracks," new recordings, comments and engineering credits; "Focus:," recording profile; "Sound Business: SPARS Perspectives," via The Society of Professional Audio Recording Services; "Digital Domain," column by Rick Schwartz; "Five Questions," interesting technical column by Mack Clark and Mike Joseph; "Live & Direct," column by David Scheirman; "All Access," unique column listing audio equipment utilized by entertainment groups, column by Mark Herman; "First Look," new equipment column by Laurel Cash-Jones; "Cutting Edge," equipment profile. (2-91).

TYPL: "Location Recording--A Modified 'MS' Recording Technique," "Signal Processing--Where, Oh Where Did My Presence Go? (What Every Engineer Should Know About Noise Reduction)," "Concert Sound--In Search of the Lost Cord! (The State of the Wireless Microphone Art)." (10-77); "Carlo Sound System for the Oak Ridge Boys," "The Computer as a Circuit Design Tool," "Multitrack Mobile Recording," "The Tact Factor," "Recording Vocal and Harmony Sections." (2-84). "Electronic Editing: States of the Art," "The Marriage of SMPTE and MIDI," "Sonic Restoration Through NoNOISE," "Outdoor Sound Rein-

forcement for the Pacific Symphony Orchestra." (9-89). "Developments in Analog Tape Recorder Technology," "Stalking the Magnesaurus," "The Large Console Commitment," "Sound Image: A Big-Time Success Story." (2-91).

SCHL: Bimonthly (Apr/May, 1970 - ?, 1987); Monthly (?, 1987+), 85 pp.
SPAN: Apr/May, 1970+
VARIES
--Apr/May, 1970 - May, 1990 as Recording Engineer/Producer (ISSN: 0034-1673).
LC: TK 7881.6 .R4
DD: 621.389/32/05

✣ REPORT

SUB: "The newsletter of the Corporation for Public Broadcasting."
SUB: "Announcmcnts/information from the Corporation for Public Broadcasting."
PUBL: Corporation for Public Broadcasting, 1111 16th St., N.W., Washington, DC 20036.
DESC: This one-page, weekly newsletter provides information on CPB activities, especially in the areas of regulation, finance and programming. Typewritten. No graphics.
DEPT: None. (9-10-84).
TYPL: "CPB Files Reply Comments in FM Allocations Proceedings," "PTFP Appropriated $24 Million in FY 1985," "PTV Wins 19 Emmys for News and Documentaries," "SECA Conference," "Live from Lincoln Center Premieres September 12th." (9-10-84).
SCHL: Weekly (? - May 9, 1977); Biweekly (May 23, 1977 - ?); Weekly (May 17, 1982+), 2 pp.
SPAN: ?+
VARIES
--? - 1970? as Newsletter.
--1970? - Aug 23, 1974 as CPB Memo.
--Aug 30, 1974? - ? as Memo - Corporation for Public Broadcasting.
--? - May 10, 1982 as CPB Report

Reporter of Direct Mail Advertising, The

May, 1938 - Apr, 1968//
SEE: DIRECT MARKETING

Reports

Spring, 1975 - ?, 1987?//
SEE: BROADCAST PIONEERS LIBRARY REPORTS

Reproductions Review & Methods

1951 - Nov, 1979//
(ISSN: 0164-4327)
SEE: IN-PLANT REPRODUCTIONS

✤ RESTORATION AND 18TH CENTURY THEATRE RESEARCH

PUBL: Loyola University, Chicago, IL.
DESC: Even the best planned research can be hindered for lack of a guide to historical resources. Fortunately, researchers pursuing dramatic projects of the 17th and 18th centuries have a marvelous aid in *Restoration and 18th Century Theatre Research*. This publication abounds with information about theatre projects under way, new museum/library finds, and the process of making materials more available to scholars. One article in the 1963 sampled issue described a number of opportunities for research projects in late 17th century drama. Another article examined R. W. Lowe's, "A Bibliographical Account of English Theatrical Literature," published in 1888; while a third examined comparative 17th century drama; and a fourth presented a bibliography of restoration sources. This is a wonderful resource, guide, and reference series for all scholars in historical theatre research. Note: publication was suspended from 1977 - 1986, and recommenced in July, 1986 with new series Volume 1, #1. For sampled issue of 1963: stapled journal format, black ink on coated cream-color paper stock, typewritten; no advertising (6 x 9 inches / 155 x 230 mm).
DEPT: "Editorial," "News and Notes." (5-63).
TYPL: "Research Opportunities in Late 17th Century Drama," "Revision of Lowe's Bibliography," "Comparative Drama in the 17th Century," "Bibliography of Restoration and 18th Century Theatre." (5-63).
SCHL: Semiannual, 40 pp.
SPAN: May, 1962+
VARIES
--May, 1962 - Nov, 1962 as 17th and 18th Century Theatre Research.
SUSPENDED
--1977 - 1986.
DD: 822
ISSN: 0034-5822
ABST: --Abstract of English Studies (ISSN: 0001-3560)
--America, History and Life (ISSN: 0002-7065)
--Annual Bibliography of English Language and Literature (ISSN: 0066-3786)
--Historical Abstracts. Part A. Modern History Abstracts. (ISSN: 0363-2712)
--Historical Abstracts. Part B. Twentieth Century Abstracts. (ISSN: 0363-2725)
--MLA International Bibliography of Books & Articles on the Modern Languages and Literatures (ISSN: 0024-8215)

Retail Equipment

? - ?//
SEE: RETAIL EQUIPMENT AND MERCHANDISE

✤ RETAIL EQUIPMENT AND MERCHANDISE

SUB: "The retailer and advertiser."
SUB: "The national and international weekly for retailers, bankers, and other advertisers."
PUBL: Outing Press of Detroit, Detroit, MI.
DESC: [*Brains*]: *Brains--The Retailer and Advertiser*, provided a marvelous weekly sourcebook of ideas on retail advertising. Each weekly issue of some 30 pages consisted entirely of sample copy, and reproduced sample newspaper advertisements from throughout the United States and Canada. There was no criticism offered, but there were numerous examples of what the editor felt were "examples of good advertising." Numerous graphics; small magazine format.
DEPT: None.
TYPL: None.
SCHL: Weekly, 30 pp.
SPAN: 1892+?
VARIES
--Oct 19, 1901 - Dec, 1904 as Retailer and Advertiser, The.
--Jan, 1905 - Aug 28, 1912 as Brains.
--? - ? as Retail Equipment.
ABSORBED
--Bank Advertiser, May, 1910.
--Show Card Writer, The, Feb, 1911.

Retailer and Advertiser, The

Oct 19, 1901 - Dec, 1904//
SEE: RETAIL EQUIPMENT AND MERCHANDISE

✤ RETROFOCUS

PUBL: National Press Photographers Association, Region 8, c/o Photo Department, San Antonio Express-News, PO Box 2171, San Antonio, TX 78297-2171.
DESC: This regional publication showcases the activities and competitive submissions of professional newsphotographers of Region 8, National Press Photographers Association. The majority of editorial content is "Clips," photographs submitted for competition in categories of Feature/Multiple, News, Feature/Single, Sports, and Illustration categories. Magazine format (8 ½ x 11 inches / 215 x 280 mm); black/white editorial content on coated paper stock; minimal advertising.
DEPT: "Regional News," "Still Life," column by Louis DeLuca; "Clips" photographer's submissions for competition. (12-89).
TYPL: None. (12-89).
SCHL: Quarterly, 30 pp.
SPAN: ?+

Review of Books and Religion, The

Sep, 1981 - Sep/Oct, 1984//
(ISSN: 0732-5800)
SEE: BOOKS & RELIGION

✤ REVIEW OF INTERNATIONAL BROADCASTING

PUBL: Review of International Broadcasting, Glenn Hauser, editor, Box 6287, Knoxville, TN 37914.
DESC: This fascinating, small-format periodical devoted to the field of international broadcasting (shortwave radio), features governmental radio service broadcasts aimed at the English speaking world. Its purpose is "to provide program information, and an open forum for the discussion of programming on short-wave, and secondarily on other media; and for the discussion of related topics. Please do not ask the editor for personal advice on receivers or other equipment." Editor Hauser brings together newspaper article reprints, interviews and an invaluable summary of English-language broadcasts. It is for anyone interested in political science and communication. Of special note is the printing of short-wave broadcast schedules, especially those of the BBC World Service. Some segments of each issue are typewritten. For the sampled issues of 1980: cover and editorial content was black ink on uncoated paper; no advertising; stapled journal format (6 ½ x 8 ½ inches / 165 x 215 mm); majority of publication was typewritten content.
DEPT: None. (9-80). "Radio Equipment Forum," used and new equipment. (6-84).
TYPL: "Shortwave Radar Update," "Listener Insights on Programming," "Shows We Like," "GH's 'DX' News for RCI DX Digest." (9-80). "Newkirk on Truth," "In Defense of VOA," "VOA Seeking Major Expansion," "A Visit to Singapore Broadcasting," "DX Censorship in the Benelux," "Private Broadcasting in an Italian Town," "Short Wave Radio Through Italian Ears," "Listener Insight on Programming." (7-84).
SCHL: Monthly, 40 pp.
SPAN: Mar, 1977+
VARIES
--Mar, 1977? - ? as Glenn Hauser's Independent Publication.
ISSN: 0149-9971

✤ REWIND

SUB: "Newsletter of the History Committee of the Broadcast Education Association."
PUBL: Broadcast Education Association, History Committee, National Association of Broadcasters, Washington, DC.
DESC: This is a short newsletter of interest to members of the History Committee, Broadcast Education Association; the pedagogical broadcast organization affiliated with National Association of Broadcasters. Typewritten; no graphics (8 ½ x 11 inches / 215 x 280 mm).
DEPT: None. (fall-88). None. (summer/fall-90).
TYPL: "Call for Papers For 1989 Convention," "Historic Negative TV Political Ads Available," "TV Script Archives Available." (fall-88). "Call for Panels and Papers for 1991 Convention," "Sequel," "1990 Conference Report." (summer/fall-90).
SCHL: Quarterly [irregular at times], 2 pp.
SPAN: Summer, 1988+

✤ RF DESIGN

SUB: "Engineering principles and practices."
PUBL: Cardiff Publishing Co., 6300 South Syracuse Way, Suite 650, Englewood, CO 80111.
DESC: RF (Radio Frequency) engineering, electronic design, and applicative technologies constitute the focus of *RF Design* magazine. This monthly publication is for the working professional with an extensive electronics background. Articles describe new technologies, trends, and design strategies; and their applications to the signal transmission field. Numerous schematics and electronic formulas enhance the discussions. Extensive advertiser support provides strong testimony to the readership of each issue. The sampled issue for February, 1991 placed articles into several categories; "Featured Technology," "Cover Story," "EMC Corner," and "Design Awards." Of special note is the use of an "About the Authors" box, short biographies of the authors, with their addresses and telephone numbers included. This makes for an interactive publication, and in so doing, further enhances an already valuable magazine for the engineering electronics field. Perfect bound magazine format, full-color throughout on coated paper stock (8 ⅛ x 10 ⅞ inches / 205 x 275 mm).
DEPT: "Editorial," commentary column by Gary A. Breed; "Calendar," upcoming events; "Courses," unique calendar of upcoming instruction in various electronic and engineering fields; "News," newsbriefs; "Industry Insight," trends and analysis column by Liane Pomfret; "Product Report," technology review column by Gary A. Breed; "Products," review; "Software," review of computer programs designed for engineering and electronics applications. (2-91).
TYPL: "A Simple Two-Channel Receiver for 8-PSK," "Practical Performance Prediction Techniques for Spectrally Efficient Digital Systems," "New CAE Software Brings Design Automation to the RF Engineer," "A Novel, Wide Band, Crystal Controlled FM Transmitter," "VSWR Protection of Solid State RF Power Amplifiers." (2-91).
SCHL: Bimonthly (1978 - ?); Monthly (1980 - ?); Bimonthly (Mar/Apr, 1981 - ?); Monthly [plus extra issue in Sep] (Mar, 1986+), 145 pp.
SPAN: Nov/Dec, 1978+
LC: TK 6540 .R123
DD: 621.3841/05
ISSN: 0163-321x
ABST: --Computer & Control Abstracts (ISSN: 0036-8113)
--Electrical & Electronics Abstracts (ISSN: 0036-8105)
--Physics Abstracts. Science Abstracts. Series A. (ISSN: 0036-8091)

✤ RHETORIC SOCIETY QUARTERLY

PUBL: Rhetoric Society of America. Department of Philosophy, St. Cloud University, St. Cloud, MN 56301.

DESC: The *Rhetoric Society Quarterly* is published by the Rhetoric Society of America, "organized in 1968 for the advancement of the study of rhetoric. The purpose of this Society shall be to gather from all relevant fields of study, and to disseminate among its members, current knowledge of rhetoric, broadly construed; to identify new areas within the subject of rhetoric in which research is especially needed, and to stimulate such research; to encourage experimentation in the teaching of rhetoric; to facilitate professional cooperation among its members; to organize meetings at which members may exchange findings and ideas; and to sponsor the publication of newsletters and reports concerning all aspects of rhetoric. ... The editors [of *Rhetoric Society Quarterly*] invite manuscripts on rhetorical theory, rhetorical criticism, history of rhetoric, rhetorical pedagogy, and rhetorical research. The editors also welcome bibliographies, notes and information on rhetorical programs and conferences, reports on new developments in rhetoric, and requests and suggestions about reviews." For the sampled issues of 1978 through 1989: single-column, black ink on uncoated paper, with cover consisting of black ink on uncoated index stock; no advertising; stapled magazine format (8 ½ x 11 inches / 215 x 280 mm). For the sampled issues of 1991: perfect-bound journal format; editorial content being black ink on uncoated stock; cover comprised of spot-color on tinted uncoated index stock; no advertising (6 x 9 inches / 150 x 230 mm).

DEPT: None. (fall-78). "Notes and Information." (winter-91).

TYPL: "'The Philosophy of Composition': A Note on Psycholinguistics," "An Essay: William E. Coles, Jr. and His 1978 Summer Seminar," "Bibliography: 'Rhetoric and Moral Philosophy: A Selected Inventory of Lecture Notes and Dictates in Scottish Archives, 1700 - 1900'," "Bibliography: 'Resources for the Study of Transcendentalist Rhetoric: Emerson and Thoreau'." (fall-78). "Teaching the Topics: Character, Rhetoric, and Liberal Education," "Inventing Rhetorical Culture: Some Issues of Theory and Practice," "Reforms of Style: St. Augustine and the Seventeenth Century," "Rhetoric in Praise of Silence: The Ideology of Carlyle's Paradox," "Aristotle and the Stasis Theory: A Re-examination." (winter-91).

SCHL: Quarterly, 110 pp.
SPAN: 1968+
VARIES
--1968 - 1975 as Newsletter: Rhetoric Society of America.
LC: PN 171.4 .R46
DD: 808/.005
ISSN: 0277-3945

✤ RHETORICAL & COMMUNICATION THEORY NEWSLETTER

PUBL: Speech Communication Association, Rhetorical & Communication Theory Division, 5105 Backlick Rd., Annandale, VA 22003.

DESC: The function of this typewritten, single-sheet newsletter is to keep Rhetorical and Communication Theory Division members of the Speech Communication Association fully appraised of developments within the division. Articles serve to recap previous division meetings, list current projects in development, and detail forthcoming meetings. For sampled issue of 1990: single-sheet stapled newsletter format, typewritten, black ink on light-yellow uncoated paper stock, no advertising or graphics (8 ½ x 11 inches / 215 x 280 mm).

DEPT: None. (fall-90).
TYPL: "R&CT Chair's Address to Membership," "R&CT Convention Programs Update," "R&CT Convention Programs Selected!," "R&CT Task Force Formulates Questions," "Zeltzer Wins Student Award!" (fall-90).
SCHL: Quarterly, 6 pp.
SPAN: ?+

✤ RIGHTING WORDS

SUB: "The journal of language and editing."
PUBL: Feredonna, Inc., 252 Peters Road North, Suite 204, Knoxville, TN 37923.

DESC: From a 1991 advertisement: "Start winning the paper chase! If words are your work or prosaic patter your play, you need this refreshing approach to the English language! *Righting Words*, the journal of language and editing [is] ...a must-have reference for copy editors, writers, language professionals, libraries, [and] language students." Here is a wonderfully entertaining and enlightening serial on the grandeur and foibles of the English language. The emphasis is on print journalism, with most authors being working professionals. Articles tend to concentrate within the areas of the art and technique of print editing, and language usage. There are many remarkable departmental features in the publication. One is "Heads You Win," in which readers are invited to submit their own favorite published headline. Readers are told, "These headlines can be clever or catchy, funny or punning, a page one banner or even a tight-count masterpiece written over a brief. What matters is that you're proud of your work." Another wonderful departmental feature is "Media Watch," where new "words" are added to our daily vocabulary by various media. Among these new words, or new meanings attached to established verbage are: "Detox-retox," "Dingleberry," "Ecopoiesis," "Feebates," and "Bibliotherapy." This is an exceptional publication for those whose livlihood depends on the words they write. For the sampled 1991 issues: black ink on uncoated paper; cover

comprised of spot-color on coated index stock; perfect-bound journal format; advertising (6 ¾ x 9 ½ inches / 170 x 240 mm).
DEPT: "Noted Briefly," "Book Reviews," "A Reply," "Post Scripts," letters. (11/12-87). "From the Copy Desk," "Lingua Fractured," "Heads You Win," "Word Ways," "Media Watch," column by Louis Phillips; "Words on Books on Words," "Double Acrostic," "Noted Briefly," "The Last Word." (vol 4-#4).
TYPL: "Silent Apostrophe Makes Commotion," "Running Aground in a Galley of Type," "'Gosh, That's NOT in the Picture!,'" "Extras, Extras--Read All About'em." (11/12-87). "How to Come Up With Article Ideas," "Dancing in the Dark," "Save It on Tape," "The Birth of Punctuation," "The Joy of Writing." (vol 4-#4).
SCHL: Bimonthly, 36 pp.
SPAN: Jan/Feb, 1987+
DD: 808
ISSN: 0892-581x

RMA ENGINEER

PUBL: Radio Manufacturers Association, Engineering Division, Washington, DC.
DESC: "The *RMA Engineer* marks a new step in the direction of increased service to the radio industry by the Engineering Division of the Radio Manufacturers Association. It is the purpose of this publication to provide practical, up-to-the-minute articles on design and allied problems for the engineers of the member companies of the Association," this highly technical series has schematics and other graphics.
DEPT: "Member Companies of the RMA." (6-38).
TYPL: "Measurements of Characteristics of automobile Receivers," "Preliminary Discussion of the Underwriter's Laboratories on Television Receivers," "Oscillator Stabilization for Mechanically Tuned Household Receivers." (6-38).
SCHL: Semiannual, 25 pp.
SPAN: Nov, 1936 - May, 1940//
LC: TK 6540.R125

✢ ROMANTIC TIMES

SUB: "For readers of romantic fiction."
PUBL: The Romantic Times Publishing Group, 55 Bergen St., Brooklyn Heights, NY 11201.
DESC: *Romantic Times*, according to an advertisement, is "The bi-monthly magazine for readers of romantic fiction. Known as 'the Bible of Romantic Fiction,' according to USA Today. Over 100 ratings and reviews of series romances, historicals, regencies, romantic suspense--plus author profiles, publishers, previews & gossip!" Romance novel literature has a large and loyal following, attested to by 100-plus pages of articles, interviews, publisher's lists, ratings, and promotional campaigns found in every issue. Of special note are fascinating letters to the editor in which every topic is fair game; from explicit covers to favorite authors, from critiques of grammar to the search for a favorite lost book. The reader, bookseller, and publisher all benefit by this serial's promotion and examination of this field of literature. As one reader put it: "Let's face it--we read romances for escapism and because they are truly fantasy (better than Science Fiction in my opinion). ... I enjoy your magazine. For one thing, it saves me time in that I can usually tell from your synopsis what books I will like." For the sampled issue of 1990: stapled magazine format with numerous pictures of authors and book cover art, editorial content consisting of black ink on newsprint stock, with full-color cover on coated paper stock (8 x 10 ½ inches / 200 x 265 mm).
DEPT: "Historical Romance Ratings," "History Romance Reviews," "Series Romance Ratings," "Series Romance Reviews," "Contemporary Romance Reviews," "Regency Romance Reviews," "Under the Covers," column by Flavia Knightsbridge; "Romance Readers Letters," "Publishers Previews," of new romance novels. (6/7-90).
TYPL: "Heather Graham Pozzessere, a.k.a. Shannon Drake and Heather Graham, and Baby Makes Seven," "Jo Ann Wendt, Talks About HEROES--The Men We Love to Love," "Patricia Rice Fulfills a Childhood Dream and Creates Her Very Own Fairy Tale: Love Forever After," "Katharine Kincaid Returns to the Amazon--But This Time Safely in Wildly, My Love." (6/7-90).
SCHL: Bimonthly, 110 pp.
SPAN: Jul/Aug, 1981+
ISSN: 0747-3370

Rona Barrett's Daytimers

Apr, 1977? - ?, 198u//
(ISSN: 0199-1817)
SEE: REAL LIFE/DAYTIMERS

Rona Barrett's Gossip

May, 1972? - Dec, 1980//
(ISSN: 0199-1590)
SEE: GOSSIP

✢ RONA BARRETT'S HOLLYWOOD

PUBL: Laufer Publishing Co., 7060 Hollywood Blvd., Hollywood, CA 90028.
DESC: "Suppose YOU gave a Party and Robert Redford, Barbra, Marion, and the Entire Cast of 'That's Entertainment' showed up? Sound exciting? That's what subscribing to *Rona Barrett's Hollywood* is like--a big monthly Hollywood bash with all your favorite stars, kleig lights, color, drama, humor, and no after party clean-up." Rona Barrett's name is on one of the classier magazines of the Hollywood gossip genre. There are full-color photos throughout, including a

color-insert visit to a star's home. Ms. Barrett may use the magazine to defend a star from false rumours at times. Magazine format; numerous graphics.
DEPT: "Editors Page," gossip briefs; "Rona Barett's Hollywood," the primary portion of the magazine with many pages of photos; "Collectors," unusual section where readers offer trades of photos and other star-related items; "Rona's Hot and Cold Flashes," half-page stories of stars; "One-Minute Interview," half-page Q&A format interview; "Winners and Losers--Telling It Like It Is," stars are assigned to winner or loser columns; "Dick Maurices Las Vegas," news briefs; "The Way They Were," early star backgrounds; "Televisionary," TV briefs; "The Cats' Meow," Q&A on specific stars; "Dear Rona," readers express what they want to read; "International Jet Set," more gossip; "Show and Tell," paragraph-length items of stars; "Rona's Would You Believe?," more gossip; "At Home With," color photos of star homes; "For the Record," briefs on music; "Tell and Tell," more Q&A on stars. (5-79).
TYPL: "Priscilla and Elvis: If She Had to Do It Over, Would She Leave Him?," "Stockard Channing: Can Greases' Rizzo Rate on the Tube?," "Chris Reeve and margo T. Kidder: Fly High at Supermans' Tinsel Debut." (5-79).
SCHL: Monthly, 85 pp.
SPAN: 1971+
ISSN: 0199-2201

✤ ROSS REPORTS TELEVISION
SUB: "Casting, scripts, production."
PUBL: Television Index, Inc., 40-29 27th St., Long Island City, NY 11101.
DESC: Published by *Television Index*, *Ross Reports Television* is a pocket-sized compendium of talent opportunities and existing production/program teams in network broadcast television. One news item-style article per issue is featured under the title of "TV Pro-Log Digest," which lists new program opportunities, casting, and other production information. The vast majority of each issue (as seen in the sampled issue for 1991), is extensive New York listings under these subheadings: "Advertising Agencies," "Independent Casting Directors," "Special Talent Groups--Not Union," "Producers of TV Commercials," "Television Talent Agencies," "Musical & Variety Shows," "Literary Agencies," "Non-Television Talent Unions," "Television Talent Unions," "Network Office and Studios," "Dramatic Serials," "and "Primetime Programs." Listings also include "Los Angeles Dramatic Serials," "West Coast Program Production Studios," "Network Primetime Programs for 1990-91 Season," and "Network Program Packagers." The extensive data contained in a single pocket-sized issue of *Ross Reports Television*, is information vital to anyone working, seeking work, or contemplating a change in employment in this dynamic field. For the sampled issue of 1991: small stapled journal format, black ink on uncoated paper stock, with two separate covers consisting of black ink on salmon-colored and light pink uncoated paper stock representing the outer cover and editorial pages respectively. No graphics or advertising (4 ⅛ x 6 ½ inches / 105 x 165 mm).
DEPT: "TV Pro-Log Digest," "Television programs and production news'; "Television Talent Report." (8-91).
TYPL: None. (8-91).
SPAN: ?+
WITH SUPPLEMENT
--TV Pro-Log Digest.
LC: PN 1992.3 .U5R67
DD: 384.55/025/73

✤ ROSTRUM
SUB: "Official publication of the National Forensic League."
PUBL: National Forensic League, PO Box 38, Ripon, WI 54971.
DESC: This dynamic publication matches the vibrancy of the organization which publishes it, the National Forensic League. With a concentration in forensics and debate, *Rostrum* accomplishes several tasks. Firstly it is a news medium for information on member activities, organizational recognition, competitions, tournaments, and resource reviews. On a different level, it is an interesting informational resource, presenting current research, publications, commentary, and background material pertinent to this competitive area of the speech field. Of special note is the recognition given to outstanding individuals in the field, complete with their (black/white) photos. For the sampled issue of 1991: stapled magazine format, editorial content consisting of black ink on uncoated paper stock, cover in full-color on coated paper, advertising (8 ⅜ x 10 ⅞ inches / 215 x 275 mm).
DEPT: "The Bookshelf," review column by James Copeland. (12-91).
TYPL: "Rare Sixth Diamond to Donus Roberts," "Television Changed the Rules," "Colleague Calamity," "L/D Topic Report: Human Genetic Engineering," "Nominations in Order for Prestigious Pelham Award." (12-91).
SCHL: Monthly [except Jun, Jul, Aug], 25 pp.
SPAN: ?+

✤ ROTKIN REVIEW, THE
SUB: "A unique reporting service on photography, art & communications books for libraries and book users."
SUB: "A unique reporting service to libraries for photography, art, communications, and other visually-oriented books."
PUBL: Photography for Industry Books, 1697 Broadway, New York, NY 10019.
DESC: In the December, 1990 issue, publisher and editor, Charles E. Rotkin wrote this open letter to all subscribers: "*The Rotkin Review* has been in publication now for almost four years. Over these years we have enjoyed what we are doing, and are proud that several

authors have told us that without our reviews their books would have long been directed to the remainder tables. Let's face it. It's not easy to create a book (or a photograph or painting). As a writer/photographer it breaks my heart to see so many books which do not 'make it'. Quality or content is probably the least controlling factor in their fate. Awareness of the existence of a book by librarians or media professionals is often the make or break element in the life or death of an author's output. This was why *The Rotkin Review* was conceived." This is a remarkable review service for libraries, containing lucid, authoritative descriptions of photographic, art and visual communications books; and is well recommended. For the sampled issues of 1986 through 1990: stapled, newsletter format; three-hole punched; black ink on uncoated paper stock; limited advertising (8 ½ x 11 inches / 215 x 280 mm).
DEPT: None. (winter-86). "Commentary," column by Charles E. Rotkin; "Late Comments." (winter-90).
TYPL: "Our Expanding (and Narrowing) Horizons," "Again, What Books?," "Who's on First?," "On Getting Our Ducks in a Row." (winter-86). "New Books, Old Thoughts, Fresh Thinking." (winter-90).
SCHL: Quarterly, 8 pp.
SPAN: Summer, 1985+
DD: 770
ISSN: 0883-735x

Roundup, The

Apr, 1953 - Jun, 1988//
(ISSN: 0035-855x)
SEE: ROUNDUP QUARTERLY

✤ ROUNDUP QUARTERLY

SUB: "Official organ of the Western Writers of America."
PUBL: Western Writers of America, 1753 Victoria, Sheridan, WY 82801.
DESC: This is a very unique publication designed for members of the Western Writers of America (authors of adult and juvenile fiction or nonfiction; magazine and TV writers; and publishers, agents and critics in the West). Articles demystify the "Old West" and provide information about earlier times for the benefit of today's authors. Journal format; some graphics.
DEPT: "Our Members," profile; "The President's Page," "What's Cookin'?," newsbriefs. (3-54). "The President's Page," "The Wide Loop," 'Membership'; "Howlin'," 'Letters to Roundup'; "Bookmarks," reviews; "News Clips," 'The media on westerns'; "Along Publisher's Row," "Agent's Corner," "The West in Print." (10-85).
TYPL: "Who Shall We Write For?," "Blowing Them Up. (3-54). "Home on the Range," "The Charm of the West," "Conventional Conventions," "You Won't Believe This, but." (10-85).
SCHL: Monthly [except Jul/Aug] (Apr, 1953 - Jun, 1988); Quarterly (Sep, 1988+), 30 pp.

SPAN: Apr, 1953+
VARIES
--Apr, 1953 - Jun, 1988 as Roundup, The (ISSN: 0035-855x).
LC: PS 374.W4R67
DD: 810 11
ISSN: 1041-5289

ROXY THEATRE WEEKLY REVIEW

SUB: "The cathedral of the motion picture."
SUB: "An illustrated weekly mnagazine with program insert for the information and enjoyment of the patrons of the Roxy Theatre, New York."
SUB: "Published as the official organ of the Roxy Theatre."
PUBL: Franklin W. Lee Publishing Co., 45 West 45th St., New York, NY.
DESC: A letter written to master showman, S. L. "Roxy" Rothafel, in the October 15, 1927 issue said, "I arrived in your city a few weeks ago. Taken by and at large, including its small- town street cars, sophisticated four flushers, etc., I wasn't and still am not greatly impressed by its size or general greatness. One object of interest has stood out over and above this mess, something I regard as the most wonderful thing I've seen--it is the Roxy Theatre. It has no rival. I hesitate to use the word 'compare' when speaking of other theatres, for it seems somewhat of a degradation of a thing of beauty to 'compare' it with the gaudy, would-be art galleries so many of the newer theatres attempt to turn themselves into." Theatregoers attending performances at the Roxy Theatre modestly proclaimed it "the cathedral of the motion picture." The Roxy Theatre not only showcased major motion pictures of the day, but also full length classical music concerts with the Roxy Symphony Orchestra; plus full-length plays and other musical presentations. The *Roxy Theatre Weekly Review* provided a weekly listing of the upcoming events, detailing musical, aural and visual elements to be experienced; along with a full listing of performers in productions. Many pictures accompanied articles showcasing current talent. The public and press alike referred to Rothafel as "The Master Showman," a title put into application in virtually all areas of the Roxy empire. Typical of his employees' attitudes was a small article in the sampled issue written by the head usher which stated, "We, the attachés of the Roxy Theatre, earnestly request our patrons to kindly refrain from offering gratuities for any services rendered. We have pledged Mr. S. L. Rothafel, 'Roxy' that we will under no circumstances accept payment from his patrons for courtesies we enjoy extending to them. We regard the Roxy Theatre as a university and place ourselves in the position of students seeking better understanding and appreciation of theatre arts. Patrons of the theatre are our guests and we place ourselves in the position of hosts. ... Being associated with Mr. Rothafel is a distinct privilege and pleasure that we feel is sufficient remunera-

tion." Such was the unique attitude and pride of showmanship evident in the Roxy organization. The *Roxy Theatre Weekly Review* provided printed testimony to the "empire that was." Stapled magazine format, black ink on uncoated paper stock for editorial section, cover consisted of full- color on coated paper stock (6 ½ x 9 ½ inches / 165 x 240 mm).
DEPT: "From Our Mailbag," letters to S. L. Rothafel 'Roxy'; "Adventuring in Hollywood," motion picture news column by Rita Douglas; "Around New York with Cecile," 'Follow her suggestions about these reliable shops and places of interest' shopping column by Cecile (10-15-27).
TYPL: "Radio Season Starts in a Blaze of Glory," "The Art of Smartness," "Your Neighbor's Business in the Heart of Camera News," "Where Men are Men in the Realm of Sport," "My Theory of Dress Both on the Screen and Off." (10-15-27).
SCHL: Weekly, 25 pp.
SPAN: Aug, 1926 - ?//

Royal Television Society Journal, The

Winter 1966/1967 - Nov/Dec, 1975//
(ISSN: 0035-9270)
SEE: TELEVISION

✤ RSAP NEWSLETTER

SUB: "Research Society for American Periodicals."
PUBL: Research Society for American Periodicals, Dept. of English, University of North Texas, PO Box 5096, UNT Station, Denton, TX 76203-5096.
DESC: From the state of organization purpose of May, 1991: "The Research Society for American Periodicals is organized to offer scholars in American literature and culture, and all interested persons, an opportunity to share in the study and appreciation of American periodicals. A non-profit organization, the Research Society for American Periodicals--through such outlets as annual meetings, scholarly panels, special symposia, miscellaneous publications, and a newsletter--provides a medium of communication among interested scholars and expands the possibilities of scholarly and critical study of an important part of American literary and cultural history." The *RSAP Newsletter* reports on developments in this newly formed organization, and spotlights upcoming events, especially conventions, workshops, publication opportunities, and other items of interest to the membership. The *Research Society for American Periodicals* is also responsible for the annual journal, *American Periodicals*, of which the first impressive issue was published in fall, 1991. This is an organization for those who have an interest in the historical development of the American periodical field. Sampled issue for 1991: stapled, single-sheet newsletter; typeset format; black ink on uncoated paper stock; no advertising. Single sheets are: (8 ½ x 11 inches / 215 x 280 mm).
DEPT: None. (summer-91).

TYPL: "Formation of the Research Society for American Periodicals," "RSAP Advisory Board Selected," "Scholarly Papers at 1991 American Literature Association Meeting." (summer-91).
SCHL: Semiyearly, 8 pp.
SPAN: Winter, 1990+

RSGB Bulletin

194u - Dec, 1967//
SEE: RADIO COMMUNICATION

RTD

SUB: "The national daily newspaper of commercial radio and television."
SUB: "Journal of communications."
PUBL: Radio-Television Daily, 1501 Broadway, New York, NY 10036.
DESC: [*Radio-Television Daily*]: This daily publication provides late-breaking news of radio-television programming, ratings, and other developments of interest to the broadcast trade. Short news items predominate. Existing as a four-page periodical in 1949, with a separate television section, it became an eight-page publication devoted primarily to television by the mid-1960s. Large number of photos; tabloid format.
DEPT: "Coming and Going," personnel briefs; "Ten Years Ago," from the files of Radio Daily; "Main Street," comment and gossip; "Network Song Favorites," top thirty songs of the week; (1-26-49). "RTD Reviews," new TV series; "RTD Radio Report," audio news; "See-Saw-Seen," comment and gossip; (9-20-65).
TYPL: "Senate Group Would Limit AM Power," Sees Air Advertising Equaling Newspapers," "Get Into TV Now--It Pays, GF Official Tells AMA Meet," "Says Broadcasters Will Drop Radio in TVs Favor," (1-26-49). "Radio Talking Itself to Life," "July Goes Through Roof, Ditto Seven-Month Web Sales." (9-20-65).
SCHL: Daily [Mon - Fri], 8 pp.
SPAN: Feb 9, 1937 - Jul 22, 1966//
VARIES
--Feb 9, 1936 - Sep 6, 1950 as Radio Daily.
--Sep 7, 1950 - Jan 5, 1962 as Radio Daily-Television Daily.
--Jan 12, 1962 - Aug 31, 1965 as Radio-Television Daily.
LC: HE 8690.R35

RTNDA Bulletin

Dec, 1952? - Dec, 1970//
SEE: COMMUNICATOR

RTNDA Communicator

1971 - Jul, 1988//
(ISSN: 0033-7153)
SEE: COMMUNICATOR

✛ RUNDOWN, THE

PUBL: The Rundown, PO Box 335, Ardmore, PA 19003.
DESC: Commercial television news directors said it best: "Once a year we get together at RTNDA. But once a week, I can pick up *The Rundown* and get a good overview of the problems every news director is facing and how they're solving them;" and *"The Rundown* is a must for any newsroom that wants to keep up on current story ideas and for news management that wants to keep up on what's going on in the industry." There was no advertising or graphics in the reviewed issues, but each typewritten issue contained succinct articles on current happenings, trends, and suggestions for television news management. Of special note is the extensive use of television news survey data, which helps bring clarity to news management. Three hole punched; typewritten with no advertising or graphics.
DEPT: "Recent Series," recent news series running in American television markets; "What's Ahead," calendar and suggestions for news series. (8- 25-86).
TYPL: "1986 News Executives Survey: Financial Pressures Intense, But, Total Newscast Time Increases," "Staffing Levels: Ups and Downs," "Most Important Purchase: Audience Research," "Ku-Band: Is It Worth It?" (8- 25-86).
SCHL: Weekly?, 12 pp.
SPAN: Jan 1, 1981?+?

✛ RURAL RADIO

SUB: "The only magazine published exclusively for rural listeners!"
PUBL: Rural Radio, Inc., Nashville, TN.
DESC: Letters to the editor heap praise on *Rural Radio*, such as this one from Kentucky: "I think it is the grandest little magazine I ever saw. It gets bigger and better every month." Or this letter from Alabama; "Just a word of praise to the publisher and editor of *Rural Radio*. It is the most entertaining magazine that I have had the pleasure to read and I for one wish it long years of success;" and this Georgia letterwriter who stated, "I enjoy the magazine very much for it contains more of the pictures of my favorite entertainers and not so much Hollywood stuff. Keep it that way!" There was concern that *Rural Radio* might lose its country charm, warmth and personality. Editor E. Kirby, along with publisher E. M. Allen, maintained that *Rural Radio* was not about to "go Hollywood," preferring instead to showcase the talented artists who worked local radio stations primarily in the Midwest, the South, and East Coast regions of the United States. *Rural Radio* programming meant farm news, agricultural innovations, price reports for farm products, and especially radio entertainment. Radio stars were often in country-style clothing, with names such as "The Golden West Cowboys," "Aunt Idy and Little Clifford," "The Coon Creek Gals," "Lightcrust Doughboys," "Smiling Jack and His Missouri Mountaineers," "Jolly Joe Kelly," the "DeFord Bailey," "Duke of Paducah, "Kentucky Girls," and the "Voices of the South." This was true personality radio, with an appreciative audience that subscribed and wrote to *Rural Radio*. It is an excellent resource for radio development, history, and the successful interaction between radio stars and the public. One New York woman wrote: "I like *Rural Radio* because it gives the pictures of my favorite radio entertainers which I have been unable to find in any other magazine. Here's my dollar for a year's subscription. Believe me, nobody sold me on *Rural Radio*--after reading one copy, it sells itself." Stapled magazine format, black/white editorial content with spot color throughout (including cover) on coated paper stock (8 ¼ x 10 ¾ inches / 210 x 275 mm).
DEPT: "Editorial," editorial comment column by E. M. Kirby; "Along the Way with Lambdin Kay," humorous commentary column by Lambdin Kay; "Rural Radio Picture Roundup," favorite radio stars; "Over the Cracker Barrel," radio programming newsbriefs; "Farm Radio Highlights," schedule; "From the Technical Service Editor," technical Q&A on radio reception and setup; "Livestock Markets," program guide; "Farm News and Views," program guide; "Grain Reports," program guide; "Weather Broadcasts," program guide; "Program Highlights of Interest to Women," program guide; "Family Gossip," personality news from reader submitted questions, column by Peggy Stewart; "The Party Line," fashion and cooking column by Marjorie Arnold; "Rural Radio's Daddy Gander," 'A page for children'; "Strictly Personal," by 'The Solemn Old Judge', column by George Dewey Hay; "Spring Whittlin's," humor column by Pat Buttram; "RFD," 'Radio Farm Digest' letters. (6-38).
TYPL: "Lum 'n Abner: Promoters of Better Understanding Between Rural and City Folk," "She's Sweet Sixteen--in Radio: Mary Tucker," "WSB Star is a Ham," "Lost Sheep Find Their Way Through an Inspiring Radio Program," "W. Lee O'Daniel: 54,900 People Asked Him to Run for Governor of Texas!" (6-38).
SCHL: Monthly, 25 pp.
SPAN: Feb, 1938+?

✤ SALES & MARKETING MANAGEMENT

SUB: "The marketing magazine."
PUBL: Bill Communications, Inc., 633 3rd Ave., New York, NY 10017.
DESC: "*Sales & Marketing Management* is the only magazine edited for executives who manage the sales and marketing functions in their organizations." *Sales & Marketing Management* has provided over 60 years of quality advice, suggestions, and discussion of important issues to the sales community. Articles concern staff management, incentives, sales expenses, transportation, and the ongoing fitting together of corporate goals with the reality of the marketplace. One issue covered such various issues as, "How Do Managers Effectively Manage Their Time?;" "Keeping Travel Costs Down;" an article on recruitment entitled, "If You Thought Turnover Was Bad in Sales...;" and an article on demographics: "Growing Concerns: Eight Years of Metro-Area Expansion." A marvelous resource for the business professional. For the sampled issues of 1983: (8 x 10 ¾ inches / 200 x 270 mm). For the sampled issues of 1990: (8 x 10 ⅞ inches / 205 x 275 mm). Both sampled years: stapled, magazine format; black ink with spot-color and full-color graphics on coated paper; cover consisting of full-color graphics on coated stock; significant trade advertising.
DEPT: "Editor's Side Pocket," editorial; "Letters," "Viewpoint," guest commentary; "Demographics in Action," unique issue page in demographics display; "Travelers' Network," food favorites across America; "People," profile; "Short Takes," newsbriefs; "Business-to-Business," industry newsbriefs; "Marketers, Etc.," newsbriefs; "Computers In Sales & Marketing," "Sales Force Management," "Second Thoughts," commentary; "Books," review; "Trade Shows," "Significant Trends." (6-88). "The Race," editorial; "Letters," "Sales Force Management," "Travelers' Network," newsbriefs re sales travel; "You Said It," Q&A; "Short Takes," newsbriefs; "Computers," "Significant Trends," "Meetings," "Direct Marketing," "Sales Tools," "Fleets," "Motivation," "Hiring & Training," "Offbeat Marketing," "Sales Mart," "Product/Service Showcase," "Worth Writing For." (7-90).
TYPL: "America's Best Sales Forces," "Ten Ways to Screw Up a Sales Meeting," "On the Road: Cheap or Suite?," "Was This Firing Fair--Or a Dirty Trick?" (6-88). "Shell-Shocked on the Battlefield of Selling," "DEC Gets Its House in Order," "Getting into Golf," "Presentations: How to Do It Wrong," "Expanding Your Sales Operation? Just Dial 1-800." (7-90).
SCHL: Weekly (May 26, 1928 - Mar 16, 1929); Semimonthly [except Jun, Sep, and Dec] (Apr 6, 1929 - Nov 3, 1975); Semimonthly [irregular at times] (Nov 17, 1975 - Dec 1, 1976); Monthly [except semimonthly in Feb, Apr, Jul, and Oct] (Dec 13, 1976+), 115 pp.
SPAN: May 26, 1928+
VARIES
--May 26, 1928 - Mar 16, 1929 as Sales Management and Advertisers' Weekly.
--Apr 6, 1929 - Nov 3, 1975 as Sales Management (ISSN: 0885-9019).
FROM MERGER OF
--Advertisers' Weekly (and) Sales Management.
LC: HF 5438.A34
DD: 658.8/005
ISSN: 0163-7517
ABST: --ABI/Informer
--Accountants' Index. Supplement. (ISSN: 0748-7975)
--Business Periodical Index (ISSN: 0007-6961)
--InfoBank
--Magazine Index
--Management Contents
--Predicasts
--Reference Sources (ISSN: 0163-3546)
--Trade and Industry Index

Sales Management

Apr 6, 1929 - Nov 3, 1975//
(ISSN: 0885-9019)
SEE: SALES & MARKETING MANAGEMENT

Sales Management and Advertisers' Weekly

May 26, 1928 - Mar 16, 1929//
SEE: SALES & MARKETING MANAGEMENT

✤ SALES NEWS

SUB: "To generate more television sales."
PUBL: Television Bureau of Advertising, Inc., 477 Madison Ave., New York, NY 10022.
DESC: The Television Bureau of Advertising is a television station membership group functioning to increase television spot commercial sales via education, promotional materials, seasonal factors, and strategies against competing commercial media. For the busy television station sales manager, this monthly newsletter brings fresh ideas, news of commercial tie-ins, proposed advertising campaigns, and ways to win retail advertising dollars. For the sampled issue of

1985: Folded newsletter format with graphics, black ink on uncoated paper stock (8 ½ x 11 inches / 215 x 280 mm).
DEPT: "Territory News," TBA member news events. (8-85).
TYPL: "New Local Television Dollars Linked to Drug Store Chains," "The Automotive Industry: An Overview From TvB's Man in Detroit," "Don't Shut Your Eyes to New Ideas," "Vendor Fund: What, How, and Why!" (8-85).
SCHL: Monthly, 4 pp.
SPAN: ?+?

✦ SATELLITE COMMUNICATIONS

SUB: "The international magazine of satellite news, applications and technology."
SUB: "The international magazine for the satellite communications industry since 1977."
PUBL: Cardiff Publishing Company, 6430 South Yosemite St., Englewood, CO 80111.
DESC: With numerous full color pages to match the upbeat nature of the communications satellite field, *Satellite Communications* covers all facets of this relatively young industry; programming, legal challenges, promotions, technological developments, and trade news. Of special note is its international point-of-view in reporting events and trends in the satellite communication field. Typical articles for early 1992 included, "ATS-1 Celebrates 15th Birthday: A Milestone for the Pacific," "Space-Age Technology for Age-Old Needs," "The Pacific Telecommunications Council: A New International Organization," "China Watching," and "PSSC Study: Satellite Communications for Pacific Islands." This publication has a dynamic layout with numerous graphics. For the sampled issues of 1982: editorial content and cover being mixture of black ink with spot-, and full-color graphics on coated paper stock; significant advertising to the trade; stapled magazine format (8 x 10 ½ inches / 205 x 270 mm).
DEPT: "Publisher's Forum," "Washington Report," "Satellite Notebook," "Calendar," "Trade News," "Business," "Space Transportation News," "Teleconferencing," "Sources," "Technology," "Industry Moves." (9-84). "Publisher's Forum," "Editorial Desk," "Calendar," "News," 'Industry events, satellite information, launches and teleconferencing'; "Industry Watch," "People," 'Spotlight on key personnel changes'; "Products," review; "Business," 'Industry transactions, including contracts, mergers, new locations and corporate changes'; "Taking Stock," 'A comparison of the stock performance of publicly held corporations in satellite communications'. (4-87).
TYPL: "Bringing It All Together," "Legal Challenges and Opportunities," "Going Private," "Spreading the Word," "Communicating in Luxury," "Far Beyond the Artic Circle." (9-84). "Plumbing Europe's Television Market," "The Business of Teleports," "Sidestepping Interference," "Europe's DBS Race." (4-87).
SCHL: Monthly, 50 pp.
SPAN: Oct, 1977+
LC: TK 5104 .S3636
DD: 621.38/0422
ISSN: 0147-7439
ABST: --ABI/Informer
--Computer & Control Abstracts (ISSN: 0036-8113)
--Electrical & Electronics Abstracts (ISSN: 0036-8105)
--International Aerospace Abstracts (ISSN: 0020-5842)
--Physics Abstracts. Science Abstracts. Series A. (ISSN: 0036-8091)
--Predicasts

✦ SATELLITE NEWS

SUB: "Incorporating DBS News."
SUB: "Covering management, marketing, technology and regulation."
PUBL: Phillips Publishing, 7811 Montrose Rd., Potomac, MD 20854.
DESC: The right information at the right time can spell the difference between success and failure in as young and volatile a field as satellite communications; where issues of technology, international diplomacy, and the demands of the national marketplace can change the rules of the game almost daily. It is for corporate executives in the satellite communication field who need information quickly that *Satellite News* is published. The yearly subscription rate is $597 (for 1990). Speed of delivery is such a critical factor that Phillips also provides electronic delivery of *Satellite News* via NewsNet, ensuring that news is still "new" upon delivery. This typewritten newsletter is well recommended. For the 1990 sampled issue: Loose-leaf typewritten newsletter format with some graphics employing black ink on color uncoated paper stock (8 ½ x 11 inches / 215 x 280 mm).
DEPT: "Business Developments," "NASA," "Shuttle," "Quarterly Reports," Corporate developments; "International," "Satellite Circuit," "Space Station," "DBS," News of direct broadcast satellite. (1-23-89). "Launches," "White House," "International," "Annual Reports," "Satellite Circuit," "Teleports." (1-15-90).
TYPL: "Hughes Galaxy Petitions FCC to Drop Requirement for DBS East/West Orbital Slots," "GE Signs 5-Year Deal With GE to Provide Transponder Uplink Service," "Talks With French Could Yield Cooperation in Remote Sensing," "Satellite, Fiber, New Technologies Compete at PTC '89." (1- 23-89). "Shuttle Launches Successfully; Arianespace Liftoff Delayed," "Special Report--FCC Chairman Sikes Speaks Out on Satellites." (1-15- 90).
SCHL: Monthly (?-?); Weekly (?+), 10 pp.
SPAN: May, 1978+
ISSN: 0161-3448

✦ SATELLITE ORBIT

SUB: "World's most complete home satellite TV listings."
SUB: "Your No. 1 guide to TV entertainment."

PUBL: CommTek Publishing, Division of CommTek, Inc., 8330 Boone Blvd., Suite 600, Vienna, VA 22180.
DESC: For today's home satellite owner, *Satellite Orbit* may be the only programming guide needed. A tremendous amount of programming information and satellite schedules are contained within this 250-plus page publication. Special programming sections graphically display C-Band and KU-Band programming; listing of satellite TV services by program name; sports programming by category; favorite television programs listed by topic and name; satellite radio feeds; monthly movie listings by individual service; subscription service listing; wild feed listings; an extensively annotated movie guide; and program listings for the Armed Forces Radio and TV Service. Daily programs are listed by time, satellite, vertical/horizontal polarization, programming service name, and whether subscription service, closed captioned, repeat showing, black/white, or pay per view service is available. Magazine format; program listings on newsprint (8 x 10 ¾ inches / 205 x 275 mm).
DEPT: "Getting More From Your Dish," "Our Readers Write," "Family Fare," upcoming satellite program of a family nature; "Tuning In," upcoming program fare; "Sports," "Videos," new videos for sale or rental; "Lifestyle Products," consumer gift product review; "Programming Guide," Huge 240 page section detailing national satellite transmissions for upcoming month. (12-88). "Getting More From Your Dish," "Letters," "Tuning In," "Home Theater," 'Your guide to the hottest item in consumer electronics'; "What's New," 'Here's the latest viewing news for the month'; "Subscription Services Chart," 'Extra services you can buy--and where to call to get them'; "Your Favorite Shows--By Interest," 'The top 30 programs, children's shows and other categories'; "Sports," 'A thorough list of hundreds of live sports events'; "Specials," 'Highlighted programs, children's shows and other categories'; "What's on Movie Services," 'Look for your favorite program services--and find what's on'; "Wild Feeds," 'More shows than you can possibly watch'; "Movies," 'Complete listings and descriptions of thousands of films'; "Spanish Section," 'Extensive listings of all Spanish-language programming'; "Daily Listings." (6-90).
TYPL: "Movietime: The Quickest Hour on TV," "A Classic Christmas," "Bowling 'Em Over." (12-88). "The New Country," "Randy Travis," "'Country Classics' Contest," "World Cup Soccer." (6-90).
SCHL: Monthly, 270 pp.
SPAN: Jul, 1982+
LC: PN 1992 .S28
DD: 791.45/75/05 19
ISSN: 0732-7668

✢ SATELLITE RETAILER

SUB: "The only magazine for the serious dealer."
PUBL: Triple D Publishing, Inc., 1300 South DeKalb St., Shelby, NC 28150.
DESC: "Trade publications come and go, but *Satellite Retailer* continues to be a stable force in the world of satellite TV. *Satellite Retailer* is designed to give the retailer helpful hints and guidelines for operating an efficient business." For both the novice and the experienced dealer, *Satellite Retailer* provides good coverage of events, trends, and retail strategies in this growth-oriented field. Articles tend to be evenly split between features on the industry (conventions, promotion, or sales and technical articles); and setup, servicing, and new technological trends. There is also a good editorial balance between articles concerning the basics of retail/satellite television, and advanced industry issues and technology. One innovative concept seen (May, 1989 issue) was a tear-out chart of industry fax telephone numbers on one side, and toll-free telephone numbers on the other side. Good graphics enhance technical product reviews. Magazine format.
DEPT: "Editorial," "Terrestrial Links," '...is an editorial look at the news as it crosses our desk'; "News," "Financial News," "Letters," "Dealer Association News," news of regional and state satellite dealer associations; "Calendar," "New Products." (5-89).
TYPL: "SBCA/STTI Las Vegas '89," "A Crystal Ball to the Satellite Industry," "Creating Your Own Literature," "Screening Out Terrestrial Interference." (5-89).
SCHL: Monthly, 75 pp.
SPAN: Apr, 1985+
DD: 338 11
ISSN: 0890-1252

✢ SATELLITE TIMES

SUB: "The monthly programme guide for satellite & cable TV."
PUBL: The Satellite Organisation, Ltd., 85 & 89 Church Rd., Crystal Palace, London SE19 2TA, England.
DESC: At 140+ pages, this monthly guide to European satellite services for British consumers is as lively and diverse as the programming it covers, emanating from some eight satellite systems. Program services include such varied offerings as Eurosport, MTV Europe, Screensport, Sky News, TV3 (for Scandinavian viewers), SAT 1 (German language programming), TV5 (French), One World (programming of Third World Nations), BBC TV Europe, CNN International, The Discovery Channel, Bravo, Home Video Channel, and Indra Dhnush (Asian programming; motion pictures, series, music and Bhangra specials). This programming diversity is handled well within 100+ pages of color schedules each month. There are some articles in each issue, but the emphasis is upcoming programming. The sampled 1990 issue consisted of creative usage of spot- and full-color graphics in dynamic layout design with full-color cover on coated paper stock in stapled square magazine format (9 ⅛ x 11 ¾ inches / 230 x 300 mm). Numerous graphics, including some production stills; rich use of color in graphics and layout design.

DEPT: "What's Going On," news items and comment column by John Bryant; "In Focus," 'Your guide to this months films'; "FilmNet," upcoming films; "BBC TV Europe," viewing schedule; "The Lighter Side," of satellite television programs; "Sportseen," 'A round-up of this months sports on TV' column by Colin Jarman; "Big Noise," 'The Music Seen'; "PPV," pay-per-view schedule; "The Channels," European television and radio programming listed by satellite; "The Programme Guide," extensive European satellite programming guide of 100+ pages; "Joystick," 'Computer entertainment'; "The Wine Rack," wines viewed and reviewed; "The Green Diary," 'The monthly happenings of a suburban maintenance gardener'; "Dish of the Month," recipes; "Viewpoint," 'Readers letters'. (3-90).
TYPL: "Donna Mills, the Spice of Knots Landing," "The Oscars," "The Oxford and Cambridge Boat Race," "BSB Special Preview." (3-90).
SCHL: Monthly, 140 pp.
SPAN: ?+
ISSN: 0955-4602

Satellite TV

Jul/Aug, 1982 - ?//
(ISSN: 0744-9739)
SEE: PRIVATE CABLE

✦ SATELLITE TV WEEK

SUB: "Satellite TV Week is America's most accurate and up-to-date listing of satellite TV programming."
PUBL: Fortuna Communications Corporation, PO Box 308, Fortuna, CA 95540-0308.
DESC: *Satellite TV Week* is an excellent, large-format programming guide to North American satellite television services. The program section is black ink with spot color on newsprint, with a green-tinted sports section on newsprint, and end pages in full-color (including covers) on coated paper stock. Among a number of innovative features are program listings by "Hobbies," for the arts and crafts enthusiast; "Education" programs; and an informative section on television sports. A worthwhile guide for any satellite television owner. For the sampled issue of 1991: stapled large-format magazine (11 x 14 ½ inches / 280 x 370 mm).
DEPT: "Winners," Satellite TV Week's capsule summary of upcoming television programming; "Only on Satellite," 'For dish owners eyes only' column by Wendy Williams; "The Big Picture," guest opinion; "Industry News," "Movie Finder," 'Rated moving listings'; "Open Transponder," 'Letters from our readers'; "Pay Per View," 'The latest movies'; "Specials This Week," 'A list of program specials'; "Ask the Tech Editor," reader-submitted Q&A; "Services Directory," 'Addressing programmers'; "Hobbies," very unique listing of hobby-related television programs; "Wavelengths," 'The latest in satellite TV technology'; "Education," 'Learn by satellite'; "Channel Choice Services," excellent 'Guide to satellite audio & video'; "Recurring Feeds," column by Bob Stubbs; "Lottery Feeds," fascinating programming guide on 'Where to find the winners'; "Call Letters," 'Network abbreviations'; "Subscription Information," 'Programmers and services'; "Telephone Directory," 'Programmer listings'; "Satellite Sports," column by Fred Hoffman; "This Week in Sports," 'Sports listings'. (6-23-91).
TYPL: "Bravo for the Independents," "Tagliabue on PPV," "Top 10 Reasons Why Letterman will Not Replace Carson," "The Trivializing of America," "SBCA Challenges S.12." (6-23-91).
SCHL: Weekly, 70 pp.
SPAN: ?, 1981+
EDITION
--Eastern.
ISSN: 0744-7841

✦ SATELLITE WEEK

SUB: "The authoritative news service for satellite communications and allied fields."
PUBL: Television Digest, 1836 Jefferson Place, N.W., Washington, DC 20036.
DESC: Like its sister publications (*Television Digest*, *Video Week*, etc), *Satellite Week* is an impressively no-nonsense newsletter which functions to get out the latest news on satellite communications each week in an authoritative, compact manner. Articles explore development plans for future satellite launches, governmental and other regulatory trends and legislation, changes in the world communication community, and the application of future technologies to satellite systems. A typical sampling of articles for late, 1985 included, "AT&T Teams With Harris for Ku-Band Service Offerings," "TCI Announces Backyard Package that Includes Most Basic and Pay Programmers," "Separate Systems Aren't Intelsat's Biggest Challenge, Leahy Says," and "ABC and Affiliates to Establish Mobile Satellite News Facility." This is an extraordinary resource for this fast-breaking field of communications. The sampled issues for 1984 were: (7 ½ x 10 inches / 190 x 255 mm). A change in publication dimensions took place effective with the January 7, 1985 issue: (8 ½ x 11 inches / 215 x 280 mm). Both sampled years were: folded, newsletter format; three-hole punched; black ink on uncoated paper stock, with spot-color utilized in the masthead. Issues for 1984 were typewritten; issues for 1985+ were typeset.
DEPT: "Satellite Notes," newsbriefs; "Personals," newsbriefs. (4-14-80). "Satellite Personals," personnel changes; "Satellite TV," newsbriefs; "Earth Stations," newsbriefs; "Space Systems," "Satellite Diary," newsbriefs. (12-2-85).
TYPL: "Sears Pulls Out of Comsat Deal," "Direct Broadcasting Seminar," "Charyk Outlines Comsat Future." (4-14-80). "Leasat 3 is 'Fully Operational'," "French Select 3 Programmers for TDF-1 DBS Services," "Availability of Arianespace Insurance Proposal

Would be Limited," "Proposed Changes to Intelsat Satellites Opposed by Competitors," "Shuttle Successfully Deploys Communications Satellites." (12-2-85).
SCHL: Weekly, 8 pp.
SPAN: Jul 30, 1979+
ISSN: 0193-2861

✤ SCA WOMEN'S CAUCUS AND FEMINIST & WOMEN STUDIES DIVISION NEWSLETTER

PUBL: Speech Communication Association, c/o Communication and Theatre Department, PO Box 8259, Idaho State University, Pocatello, ID 83209.
DESC: A draft version mission statement from the sampled issue stated, "The SCA Women's Caucus is dedicated to advocacy for women in order to improve our status, voice and opportunities in the discipline of speech-communication. In doing so, the Caucus is acutely aware of common ground and shared goals which we share with other underrepresented and marginalized groups, so that we carry out our activities honoring the diversities which these groups represent. In order to fulfill our mission, the Caucus will serve a monitoring and advocacy role within the Speech-Communication Association and its associated activities. We will also conduct programs, articulate issues and advocate changes that will give fuller partnership to underrepresented groups. In particular, we will work collaboratively with the Feminist and Women Studies Division and other Caucuses of SCA to carry out our mission." For sampled issue of 1991: stapled journal format, mixture of typewritten and typeset editorial content black ink on uncoated paper stock, cover consisting of black ink on color uncoated paper stock (5 ½ x 8 ½ inches / 140 x 215 mm).
DEPT: "Notes From the Women's Caucus Editor." (9/10-91).
TYPL: "Women's Caucus -- 1990-91 Report to SCA Legislative Council," "Women at ThirtySomething: Paradoxes of Attainment," ." (9/10-91).
SCHL: Semiyearly?, 26 pp.
SPAN: ?+

✤ SCARLET STREET

SUB: "The magazine of mystery and horror."
PUBL: RH Enterprises, PO Box 604, Glen Rock, NJ 07452.
DESC: Celebrating the change in title of January, 1991, Editor Richard Valley asked readers, "How does a newsletter, originally devoted exclusively to the films of Mr. Sherlock Holmes, acquire the name of a dark fable of the 40s in its transition to magazine status? Simple, really. All it requires is a list of all the Sherlock Holmes associations that spring feverishly to mind. The first, naturally, should be Baker Street; the second, with any luck, will be 'A Study in Scarlet'. Providing you don't want to name your magazine *Baker Study*, you have your new title, one that subtly points to your founding inspiration, but paves the way for countless Highways and Byways of Mystery and Horror that *Scarlet Street* will surely explore." Among the residents of the *Street* which will be explored in future issues include Perry Mason, Hercule Poirot, Barnabas Collins, Norman Bates, Nick and Nora Charles, Charlie Chan, Philip Marlowe, Miss Marple, Count Dracula, Nero Wolfe, Tarzan the Ape Man, and She Who Must Be Obeyed. Publisher Jessie Lilley has assembled a quality, quarterly magazine that showcases productions and stars in half-page and full-page layouts on better-quality paper stock. Articles are well-written, with supporting pictures and graphics. For example, one article recounting the 90 year history of "The Hound of the Baskervilles" reprints an 1891 letter from Sir Arthur Conan Doyle to his mother, announcing his intention to eliminate Sherlock Holmes. Another extensive article details the updated look of the costume for Robin, the Boy Wonder, and faithful companion to Batman: pictures show the evolution of the character, along with a full technical schematic of the new outfit. This is a wonderful resource for all fans and students of the mystery genre. Stapled magazine format, all content in black/white, editorial on better-quality uncoated paper stock, with cover on coated paper stock, minimal advertising (8 ½ x 11 inches / 215 x 280 mm).
DEPT: "Frankly Scarlet," editorial; "Scarlet Letters," letters to the editor; "Small Screen Line-Up," upcoming television fare; "Guest Shots," review; "The News Hound," coming attractions; "Final Curtains," obituaries; "Parting Shot," essay. (1-91).
TYPL: "Music to Suck Blood By," "Baker Street Regular," "Hounded by Holmes," "Robin Takes Wing," "Universal Horrors." (1-91).
SCHL: Quarterly, 50 pp.
SPAN: Jan, 1991+
VARIES
--? - ? as Mystery Newsletter, The.
DD: 813
ISSN: 1058-8612

✤ SCENE AT THE MOVIES

PUBL: Scene at the Movies, 930 Fifth Ave., New York, NY 10021.
DESC: "Complimentary with admission" describes how most readers obtain this spritely, 24-page description of what's current in American motion picture exhibition. Printed in full color, small digest size, each issue provides interesting commentary on current film fare. It is a "quick-read" for those boring minutes before the feature presentation: *Scene at the Movies* entertains, informs, and encourages the reader to return to the theatre in the near future. It is a "preview of coming attractions" in printed form, available to be taken home and referenced for the next trip to the movies. Small journal format (5 ⅜ x 8 ⅜ inches / 135 x 215 mm), full color printing on coated paper stock.

DEPT: "The Insider," movie trends and developments column by Susan Peters; "Fast Forward," "CloseUp," profile; "Preview," motion pictures in current release; "Flashback," Hollywood product of the past; "Deep Focus," star profile with major credits. (11-90).
TYPL: "Andie MacDowell," "Tim Robbins," "Kevin Costner: The Last American Hero," "Problem Child." (11-90).
SCHL: Monthly, 24 pp.
SPAN: ?+

✦ SCHEMER, THE

SUB: "A Business Bringer."
PUBL: L.V. Patterson, Corner of Liberty Avenue and Simpson St., Alliance, OH.
DESC: Writing in the April, 1908 issue of *The Schemer*, Robert H. Gerke gave this advice on becoming a direct-mail order advertiser: "To the one who has an honest desire to lift himself out of the salary rut, I say venture, by all means. You will never get out unless you do. You will find that the satisfaction of being your master, will act as a balm to the wounds that you are bound to receive in the battle for dollars." Eighty-five years later that remains sound advice. At the turn of the century an American schemer was what one would today call an entrepreneur, an individual willing to leave the workaday world and move into the role of businessperson. *The Schemer* extolled the virtues of many different avenues of entrepreneurship, from toiletries to small home printing presses, from straw hat cleaning compounds to mail order businesses and ventures which would lead to established retail operations. One article gave formulas for over a dozen toiletry items to be sold to the public, the difference between them only a slight change in the formula. Of import to today's business operator was the large number of advertising/marketing suggestions promoting products to the public. Articles gave advice on creating advertisements and choosing media, how to assemble mail order catalogs, design tips on advertising posters and placards, and numerous other items. In this publication, the word "scheme" was seen in a very positive sense, as a creative (and hopefully profitable) way to the promotion and sale of products to the American home consumer. For its time *The Schemer* was a fount of creative, innovative ideas. It remains so even today, with the added value to historians concerning the advertising, promotion, and marketing side of a small business operation. Small stapled magazine format, no cover, black/white editorial and advertising content on uncoated paper stock (5 ¾ x 8 ¾ inches / 145 x 220 mm).
DEPT: "Agents Corner," manufacturing and promotion column by J. L. Brister; "Reliable Formulas," how to make almost anything column by E. Voltaire Boyes; "Business Starters," column by Robert H. Gerke; "Mail Order and Advertising Pointers," column by T. R. McKeown; "Distributing," column by Ray S. Loose; "General Miscellany," column by Frank J. Bachman; "Names and Addresses," reader submitted indicating interest in money-making schemes. (4-08).
TYPL: "The Preparatioon of Follow-Ups--Their Use," "A Winning Agency Scheme," "An Old But Good Scheme for This Presidential Campaign Year," "Making Money with the Hand Printing Press," "A Good Leader for Spring Mail Trade." (4-08).
SCHL: Monthly, 45 pp.
SPAN: Jan, 1898+?

✦ SCHOLARLY PUBLISHING

SUB: "A journal for authors & publishers."
PUBL: University of Toronto Press, 10 St. Mary St., Suite 700, Toronto, Canada M4Y 2W8.
DESC: This journal published by the University of Toronto Press is one of a number of benefits emanating from membership in the Society for Scholarly Publishing, a Colorado-based association of publishers, librarians, scholars and other professionals involved in the field of scholarly communication. The focus is on the publishing process, required to bring a scholarly publication to fruition, a process that includes manuscript acquisitions, marketing, editing, pre-press, promotion, distribution and production issues. Journal articles are well-crafted pieces with a considered, thoughtful look into the elements that constitute this field of publishing. A sampling of titles from 1991 included: "Humanities Journals Ten Years Later: Practices in 1989," "Caribbean Publishing, 1711 - 1900: a Preliminary Subject Analysis," "The Structure of the Association of American University Presses," "The Responsibilities of Scientific Authorship," and "Research and Publishing in China and Abroad." For late-breaking news and information of the society, readers should refer to the sister publication, the *SSP Letter*, published by the Society for Scholarly Publishing on a bimonthly basis. Journal format (6 x 9 inches / 155 x 230 mm), minimal advertising, published on uncoated paper stock.
DEPT: None (1-91).
TYPL: "The Idea of an Academic Press at the Fin de Siècle," "Publishing on a Rawhide Shoestring," "Processing Electronic Manuscripts on the PC," "European Science Editors Come Together," "Recognizing the Wrong Word, Finding the Right One." (1-91).
SCHL: Quarterly, 65 pp.
SPAN: Oct, 1969+
LC: Z 286.S37 S33
DD: 655.4
ISSN: 0036-634x
ABST: --Abstract of English Studies (ISSN: 0001-3560)
--America, History and Life (ISSN: 0002-7065)
--Historical Abstracts. Part A. Modern History Abstracts. (ISSN: 0363-2712)
--Historical Abstracts. Part B. Twentieth Century Abstracts. (ISSN: 0363-2725)
--Library Information Science Abstracts (ISSN: 0024-2179)
--Library Literature (ISSN: 0024-2373)

Scholastic Editor

1923 - Mar, 1968//
SEE: SCHOLASTIC EDITOR'S TRENDS IN PUBLICATIONS

Scholastic Editor

Sep, 1975 - May, 1982//
(ISSN: 0279-8980)
SEE: SCHOLASTIC EDITOR'S TRENDS IN PUBLICATIONS

Scholastic Editor Graphics/Communications

Apr, 1968 - May, 1975//
(ISSN: 0036-6390)
SEE: SCHOLASTIC EDITOR'S TRENDS IN PUBLICATIONS

✤ SCHOLASTIC EDITOR'S TRENDS IN PUBLICATIONS

PUBL: National Scholastic Press Association and the Associated Collegiate Press, 620 Rarig Center, 330 21st Ave., South; University of Minnesota, Minneapolis, MN 55455.
DESC: Begun in 1923 and aimed at high school and community college journalists, *Scholastic Editor* in its earlier years of publication provided interesting articles on improving school publications, with an emphasis on new techniques and styles. In latter years, its primary focus has become the highschool yearbook, with less emphasis on school magazines, videoyearbooks, etc. Articles provide "how-to" instruction, examples from school publications, and discussion of new techniques and technology. Although different issues varied greatly in page count, layout style, and use of spot color, the sampled issue of 1987 was folded tabloid-style loose-leaf newspaper with black and green spot-ink colors on uncoated paper stock (11 ⅜ x 17 ⅝ inches / 290 x 445 mm).
DEPT: "People, Products, Et.," newsbriefs. (11-77). "Trends Line," newsbriefs; "News to Use," "All American Newspaper," "TechWatch," "Today's Photographer," "All American Yearbook," "Book Update." (4-87).
TYPL: "What's News and What Isn't in the High School Newspaper," "Start in Your Own School to Explore Broadcasting Careers," "The Yearbook as an Annual Report." (11-77). "Four High Schools Win Portland Best of Show," "Eight Videos Win First All Americans," "Five College, Four High School Magazines Win 1986 Pacemakers." (4-87).

--MLA International Bibliography of Books & Articles on the Modern Languages and Literatures (ISSN: 0024-8215)
--Reference Sources (ISSN: 0163-3546)

SCHL: Six times per year [combined Nov/Dec, Jan/Feb, and Apr/May issues] (? - ?); Seven issues per year [Sep, Oct, Nov/Dec, Jan/Feb, Mar, Apr, May] (? - ?); Eight issues per year (Sep, 1975 - May, 1977); Bimonthly (Sep, 1977 - ?); Five issues per year (? - ?); Eight issues per year (? - ?); Seven issues per year (Oct, 1984+), 8 pp.
SPAN: 1923+
VARIES
--1923 - Mar, 1968 as Scholastic Editor.
--Apr, 1968 - May, 1975 as Scholastic Editor Graphics/Communications (ISSN: 0036-6390).
--Sep, 1975 - May, 1982 as Scholastic Editor (ISSN: 0279-8980).
LC: LB 3620 .S36
DD: 371.8/974/0973
ISSN: 0745-2357
ABST: --Current Index to Journals in Education (ISSN: 0011-3565)

School Paperback Journal

Oct, 1964 - May, 1966//
SEE: MEDIA & METHODS

✤ SCHOOL PRESS REVIEW, THE

PUBL: Columbia Scholastic Press Advisers Association, Box 11, Central Mail Room, Columbia University, New York, NY 10027.
DESC: For secondary school advisors of student newspapers, magazines, and yearbooks, *School Press Review* provides a meeting place for new ideas, production problems, layout techniques, and general issues of high school journalism. Numerous graphics and print examples from secondary schools nationwide. Magazine format.
DEPT: "Overview," newsbriefs. (spring-87).
TYPL: "Try a Summer Journalism Workshop," "Recruitment can Double Staff Applications," "Hazelwood School District v. Kuhlmeier," "Witness to Apartheid." (spring-87).
SCHL: Monthly [Oct - May] (? - ?); Quarterly (Winter, 1982+), 36 pp.
SPAN: Apr, 1925+
ABSORBED
--School Journalist, Jan?, 1927.
LC: LB 3621 .A2C65
DD: 371.805
ISSN: 0036-6730

Science & Electronics

Mar/Apr, 1981 - May/Jun, 1981//
(ISSN: 0279-585x)
SEE: COMMUNICATIONS WORLD

SCIENCE AND FILM

PUBL: International Scientific Film Association, Brookside Broadway Rd., Windlesham Surrey, England.
DESC: The purpose of this small format magazine is to report on uses and applications of motion picture and still film to international science. In this official journal of the International Scientific Film Association, the reader is treated to a world-wide breadth of articles concerning film application to cultural application. The names of this periodical's authors attest to its world-wide readership. Some illustrations.
DEPT: None.
TYPL: "The Presentation of Research Films Simultaneously in Different Languages," "Cine Film emulsions and Processing for Use in Research," "Time-Lapse Studies and Survey of Time Distortion as Used in Research." (9-59).
SCHL: Quarterly, 90 pp.
SPAN: Feb, 1952 - Apr, 1960//
MERGED WITH
--Scientific Film Review (to form) Scientific Film (ISSN: 0582-2475), Jun, 1960.
LC: PN 1993.S23

✢ SCIENCE-FICTION VIDEO MAGAZINE

SUB: "The SF experts tell you what to rent & what to own!!"
PUBL: Starlog Communications International, Inc., 475 Park Avenue South, New York, NY 10016.
DESC: Here is a straightforward guide to what's great and what's not in science-fiction product on videocassette. The publisher, Starlog Communications International, has extensive publishing experience in this field, with serials such as *Star Trek--The Next Generation, CineMagic, Comics Scene, Gorezone, Toxic Horror, Fangoria,* and *Starlog--The Science Fiction Universe.* The majority of a sample issue contained extensive reviews and ratings for a wide variety of product, everything from "Abbott & Costello Meet Dr. Jekyll & Mr. Hyde," through the end of the alphabet; "Zombies of the Stratosphere." In between are reviews of classics and near-classics of the science-fiction genre. Magazine format with numerous black/white and color graphics consisting of lobby posters, production stills, and publicity shots.
DEPT: "SF & Fantasy Films on Video," extensive reviews. (spring-90).
TYPL: "The Animated Star Trek," "The Battlestar Galactica Saga," "The Adventures of Buck Rogers." (spring-90).
SCHL: Semiyearly?, 85 pp.
SPAN: Fall, 1989?+

SCIENTIFIC FILM

SUB: "Journal of the International Scientific Film Association."
PUBL: International Scientific Film Association, 55A Welback St., London W1, England.
DESC: "The Scientific Film Association is the British member of the ISFA, and responsible for the production of this journal. It exists to study, discuss, publicize and encourage the use of scientific and industrial films, and promote a wider understanding of science and scientific outlook. It acts as an information center, and as a means of bringing together those who are interested in the film as the servant of science, industry and medicine." A good source of international information on the educational-industrial film in scientific circles
DEPT: "Notes and News," newsbriefs of scientific films and organizations; "Chemistry Film Appraisals," unique reviews prepared by Royal Institute of Chemistry and Scientific Film Association; "Books," specifically mass media related to science.
TYPL: "The Social Anthropological Film and Its Problems," "The Use of 8mm Film in Scientific Education and Research," "The Science of Science Foundation," "The Editing of Educational Films For Universities." (2- 65).
SCHL: Bimonthly, 25 pp.
SPAN: Jun, 1960 - Dec, 1965//
FROM MERGER OF
--Science and Film (and) Scientific Film Review.
LC: Q 192.S32
ISSN: 0582-2475

Scintillation

Winter, 1975? - 1978?//
(ISSN: 0147-5789)
SEE: CINEMONKEY

SCREEN

SUB: "Journal of the Society of Film Teachers."
SUB: "Journal of the Society for Education in Film and Television." (Sep, 1959 - Mar/Apr, 1965).
PUBL: Society for Education in Film and Television, 29 Old Compton St., London W1V 5PL, England.
DESC: "*Screen* contains articles of film and television criticism--as well as extended book and film reviews by teachers, lecturers, film makers and television practioners." An intellectual journal of commentary and thought concerning the artistic role of mass media in society, it is published by the Society for Educational in Film and Television, and goes beyond the narrow definition of film and television, expanding into other areas such as still photography, prints, framing, color and content. Some typical articles from the 1980-1981 time period included, "Taste of the Past--Cinema History on Television," "Photography, Phantasy, Function," "Commercial Film Distribution and Exhibition in the UK," "Hollywood Strikes Back--Special Effects in Recent American Cinema," "A Discussion Between Marc Karlin and Claire Johnston, Mark Nash and Paul Willemen: Problems of Independent Cin-

ema," and "British TV Today: Channel four and Innovation." For the sampled issues of 1980 and 1981: editorial content was black ink on coated paper; cover consisted of spot-color on coated index stock; limited advertising; in perfect-bound journal format (6 ½ x 9 ¼ inches / 165 x 235 mm).
DESC: [*Screen Education*]: *Screen Education* began as a supplement entitled *Education Notes* to *Screen* Magazine. Beginning with Autumn, 1971, it was separate publication entitled *Screen Education Notes*, dropping *Notes* from the title in the Spring/Summer 1974 issue. *Screen Education*'s primary function is to serve as a critical and informative journal for inclusion of film and television in education. While it has typical course syllabi, and news of film and video study programs, it is probably more regarded for its thoughtful essays of the role of media in education. Highly recommended for the academic community.
DEPT: "Syllabus Proposals," "Editorial," "Book Reviews." (spring/summer-74). "Editorial." (winter-78/79).
TYPL: "The Myth of Transparency in Film Study: An Analysis of the Ways Film has been Incorporated into CSE Examinations in English," "Culture, Codes and Curriculum: Film Teaching and the CSE Pupil," "Problems Over Practice: Relating Film Making to Film Study." (spring/summer-74). "Photography and Aesthetics," "The Discursive and the Ideological in Film-Notes on the Conditions of Political Intervention," "Television, Football, the World," "Television Situation Comedy," "Porter, or Ambivalence." (winter-78-79).
SCHL: Bimonthly (Summer, 1952 - ?); Quarterly (Oct, 1959 - Jan, 1961); Bimonthly (Mar/Apr, 1961 - Sep/Oct, 1968); Quarterly (Jan/Feb, 1969+), 110 pp.
SPAN: ? - Spring, 1982//
VARIES
--? - ? as Society of Film Teachers. Bulletin.
--Summer, 1952 - ? as Film Teacher.
--Winter, 1971 - Winter, 1973/1974 as Screen Education Notes.
--Oct, 1959 - Sep/Oct, 1968 as Screen Education (ISSN: 0306-0691).
SUPPLEMENT TO
--Screen, Autumn, 1971 - 1974.
SUSPENDED
--Nov, 1968 - Summer, 1971.
WITH SUPPLEMENT
--Education Notes, Autumn, 1971 - 1974.
MERGED WITH
--Screen Education (ISSN: 0306-0691) (to form) Screen Incorporating Screen Education (ISSN: 0036-9543), May/Jun, 1982.
LC: PN 1993.S2372
ISSN: 0036-9543
ABST: --Film Literature Index (ISSN: 0093-6758)
--Media Review Digest (ISSN: 0363-7778)

Screen, The
? - Jun 29, 1951//
SEE: SCREEN WEEKLY, THE

Screen Actor
Aug, 1959 - Nov/Dec, 1966?//
(ISSN: 0036-956x)
SEE: SCREEN ACTOR HOLLYWOOD

✤ SCREEN ACTOR HOLLYWOOD
SUB: "Official publication of the Screen Actors' Guild."
PUBL: Screen Actors Guild, 7065 Hollywood Blvd., Los Angeles 90028-7594.
DESC: Howard Keel was President of the Screen Actors Guild when *Screen Actor* was launched in August, 1959. Its purpose was to inform SAG members of developments in the acting field, new technologies, collective bargaining negotiations, and other news of interest to its readers. Much of the editorial content of this publication centered on members active in the Guild, and progress made by the Guild on behalf of SAG actors and actresses. A membership publication; graphics.
DEPT: "Editorial," "Notes and Comment," "Letters," "Books," "Bulletin Board," newsbriefs; "Residual Checks Await Claimants," listing. (10-59). "Editorial," "Memo from the National Executive Secretary," "New York Report," "Activity in Florida," "Boston Comment," "San Francisco Notes," "Books," "Letters," "Residual Checks Await Claimants." (11/12-66).
TYPL: "Reagan is Nominated for Guild Presidency," "Actors are Born, Not Made," "Another View on Merger and Board's Position," "From Hot Air to Hardware." (10-59). "Guild Asks TV Commercial Raises in Crucial Negotiations at N.Y.," "Nationwide Pay Television Requested," "Is There a Place for Sex on TV?" (11/12-66).
SCHL: Monthly (1959 - Mar, 1960); Bimonthly (Apr/May, 1960 - Apr/May, 1979); Quarterly (Summer, 1979 to date).
SPAN: Aug, 1959+
VARIES
--Aug, 1959 - Nov/Dec, 1966? as Screen Actor (ISSN: 0036-956x).
--Mar, 1980 - May/Jun?, 1980 as Hollywood Close Up (ISSN: 0199-7866).
--Jul, 1980 - Jan, 1983 as Hollywood (ISSN: 0199-7866).
--Mar, 1983 - Jan, 1986 as Screen Actor News (ISSN: 0746-9225).
--? - ? as Screen Actor Newsletter (ISSN: 0195-2684).
--? - ? as Screen Actor News (ISSN: 0745-7243).
ISSN: 0890-5266

Screen Actor News
Mar, 1983 - Jan, 1986//
(ISSN: 0746-9225)
SEE: SCREEN ACTOR HOLLYWOOD

Screen Actor News
? - ?//
(ISSN: 0745-7243)
SEE: SCREEN ACTOR HOLLYWOOD

Screen Actor Newsletter
? - ?//
(ISSN: 0195-2684)
SEE: SCREEN ACTOR HOLLYWOOD

✤ SCREEN ALBUM MAGAZINE
SUB: "Published since 1935."
PUBL: Dell Publishing Co., Inc., Dunellen, NJ.
DESC: A "Screen Album" is exactly what this famous Dell magazine of Hollywood stars and starlets is. Similar to an album, there are a minimum of article titles, most of which seemingly flow from one page to the next. Pictures are oftentimes full page size, and virtually every picture bears the signature of its star. Of special note was the 11-installment feature, "Charting the Stars," a chart of 50 stars' professional and personal lives. Among the data charted was "Name and Studio;" where and when "Born," "Height and Weight," "Eyes and Hair," "Nuts About...," number of "Kids," "Love Life," "Used to Be...," "Last Four Pictures," and "Believe It or Not." Articles in a sampled issue were very supportive of studio and star alike, and in rofiling the lives of the stars, respected their privacy. One postwar issue covered 40-plus stars including June Allyson, Dana Andrews, Lauren Bacall, Bing Crosby, Bette Davis, Gloria De Haven, Alice Faye, Errol Flynn, Clark Gable, Judy Garland, Van Johnson, Alan Ladd, Peter Lawford, along with a host of others. Magazine size (8 ½ x 10 ¾ inches / 215 x 270 mm), numerous photographs published on newsprint.
DEPT: "Charting the Stars," unique lifestyles chart of Hollywood stars. (winter-46).
TYPL: "Welcome Back!," "Esther Williams," "Screen Album Oscar to." (winter-46).
SCHL: Quarterly, 55 pp.
SPAN: 1935+?

Screen and Television Guide
Jul, 1948 - Nov, 1949//
SEE: TELEVISION AND SCREEN GUIDE

Screen Education
Oct, 1959 - Sep/Oct, 1968//
(ISSN: 0306-0691)
SEE: SCREEN

Screen Education Notes
Winter, 1971 - Winter, 1973/1974//
SEE: SCREEN

✤ SCREEN FACTS
SUB: "The magazine of Hollywood's past."
PUBL: Screen Facts Press, Box 154, Kew Gardens, NY 11415.
DESC: *Screen Facts* is devoted to Hollywood's past. It began as a small publication in 1963, but moved in later years to a larger format with numerous pictorial graphics. Many production stills from historical films are featured. A good pictorial resource for the early Hollywood film industry.
DEPT: "Movie of the Month," production stills; "Recommended Films," "Book Reviews," "Letters," "Recordings." (#21).
TYPL: "The Silent Serial," "The Saga of Frankenstein," "The Serials of Republic." (#1-63). "Esther Williams: Matched Sets." (#21).
SCHL: Bimonthly, 40 pp.
SPAN: 1963+
LC: PN 1993.S242
ISSN: 0036-9578

✤ SCREEN GREATS
SUB: "Hollywood nostalgia."
PUBL: Starlog Communications International, Inc., 475 Park Avenue South, New York, NY 10016.
DESC: "Now comes a magazine to give you... vintage gossip; all-time favorite stars; intimate biographies; now-it-can-be-told stories; behind-the-scenes reports; most-loved movies PLUS: glorious color, fold-out photos of screen favorites." It is printed in duotone color on better-quality newsprint. Of special note are four triple-fold-out color posters featuring Hollywood stars of current or past fame, plus full-color lobby cards, and other treatments that demand full color. Layout design is well-thought out, and provides a strong showcase for the dozen-plus articles in categories such as "The Way They Were," "The Way They Are," "Hollywood Gothic," "Life Story," "Interview," and "Movie Madness." Magazine format, stapled, with liberal use of spot and full color on coated and uncoated paper stock. Of interest to fans of Hollywood talent is the inclusion of several full fold-out pages featuring full-color pictures of major Hollywood stars (8 ¼ x 10 ⅞ inches / 205 x 275 mm).
DEPT: "Movie Madness," crossword puzzle. (5-90).
TYPL: "Garbo in Color! Worth a 53-Year Wait!," "Barbara Stanwyck: 'A Tough Old Dame From Brooklyn'," "Lucille Ball Before TV," "Tom Cruise--Hollywood's New King," "Dustin Hoffman's First Interview." (5-90).
SCHL: Quarterly, 65 pp.
SPAN: May, 1990+

Screen Guide

May, 1936 - Jun, 1948//
SEE: TELEVISION AND SCREEN GUIDE

Screen Guide

Oct, 1949//
SEE: TELEVISION AND SCREEN GUIDE

Screen Guide

Dec, 1949 - Apr, 1951//
SEE: TELEVISION AND SCREEN GUIDE

✣ SCREEN INTERNATIONAL

SUB:	"The paper of the entertainment industry."
SUB:	"The only film newspaper."
PUBL:	King Publications, 7 Swallow Place, 249-259 Regent St., London W1R 7AA, England.
DESC:	This British motion picture trade weekly is packed with information on new products and film developments for the British motion picture exhibitor. Articles discuss box office attendance, status of new productions, the film and exhibition trade as a whole, and how new film releases are rated. This is an international motion picture trade serial that covers world film activities, with an emphasis on the United Kingdom. Sixteen world-wide correspondents report on film developments each issue. Its chatty style and large assortment of photos makes for an interesting periodical, and one which remains required reading for professionals in the British film industry. For the sampled issue of 1990: Stapled large magazine format, editorial content consisting of mixture of black ink, spot and full-color pages on coated paper stock with significant amount of trade advertising (9 ⅝ x 13 ⅛ inches / 245 x 330 mm).
DEPT:	"We've Heard," success stories of film exhibitions; "People," personality column by Brenda Barton; "News in Brief," "In Production-- Home and Abroad," studio production slate; "Quentin Falk's Production Scene," news; "Around the Cinema," personnel news of exhibitors; "In Confidence," newsbreakers column by Peter Noble; "Theater," legitimate stage review; "The National Figures," TV ratings for the week; "The New Films," reviewed column by Marjorie Bilbow. (3-29-75). "Box Office," the economics of this week's London box offices; "In Confidence," Peter Noble's Insider's Report; "Festival Round-Up," upcoming film festivals; "World News Desk--Australia," down-under film news; "World News Desk--New York," ditto from the Big Apple; "Inside Hollywood," insiders report; "The New Films," in-depth reviews; "Talking Technology," studio and equipment developments in audio; "Peter Noble's Bookshelf," extra- large section on new film books. (1-78). "News," "In Confidence," column by Peter Noble; "News Analysis," "Indie Survivors Guide," "Appointments," "News Digest," "Opinion," "Production Report," "Reviews," "Hollywood Cinefile," column by Leonard Klady; "Production," extensive film status section; "US Box Office," report; "UK Box Office," report; "International Box Office," report. (1-27-90).
TYPL:	"Admissions Figures Up a Million," "Don't Lose Interest Say Those U.S. Video Disc Makers," "The Start of Wiping out Discrimination," "Nine-Hundred to Meet for World-Wide Kids Charity," "Sadoff Puts Flattery into Film Practice." (3-29-75). "New Deal Averts Director's Strike," "The Coup Behind 'The Wild Geese,'" "The Numbers Game." (1-78). "Pathe Cinemas for Sale," "Italian Courts Pull Plug on Berlusconi Via TV Legislation," "Yen May Back Latin American Production." (1-27-90).
SCHL:	Daily [except Sat & Sun], (? - ?); Weekly, 75 pp.
SPAN:	1911+
	VARIES
	--1911 - Jul, 1921 as Cinema News and Property Gazette.
	--May, 1923 - Feb, 1928 as Cinema News and Property Gazette, The.
	--Jul, 1921 - Nov, 1922 as Cinema.
	--Feb, 1928 - 1930? as Today's Cinema News and Property Gazette.
	--1930? - Nov, 1971 as Today's Cinema.
	--Nov 13, 1971 - Aug, 1975 as Cinema TV Today.
	--Sep 6, 1975 - ? as Screen International & Cinema TV Today.
	ABSORBED
	--Kinematograph Weekly (ISSN: 0023-155x), Sep, 1971.
LC:	PN 1993.5 .G7C5
DD:	338.4/7/791430941
ISSN:	0307-4617

Screen International & Cinema TV Today

Sep 6, 1975 - ?//
SEE: SCREEN INTERNATIONAL

SCREEN LEGENDS

SUB:	"The great stars--then and now."
PUBL:	Associated Professional Services, Inc., 7046 Hollywood Blvd., Hollywood, CA 90028.
DESC:	"*Screen Legends* is a specialized magazine which you will want to keep in your permanent home library. Each issue of *Screen Legends* presents complete, factual and exciting accounts, in story and pictures, of Hollywood's greatest stars and events." Each issue was composed of two major articles and one smaller one profiling Hollywood film stars of the past and present. In one sampled issue covering Rudolph Valentino, Ann-Margret and Robert Mitchum; 30 pages were devoted to Valentino, 28 to Margret, and four to Mitchum. A full color pull-out defines the editorial color section of the serial, while numerous black/white pictures (many of which are printed full-page), grace the remaining editorial pages. Each major

profile includes film credits by chronological release. Interestingly, this serial not only provides the phrase, "Collector's Copy" on the front cover, but also a library name-plate on the masthead page; where the owner/subscriber may complete the process of adding this bimonthly publication to his/her library collection. "So again we say, no other screen magazine, anywhere in the world, offers so much entertainment for such a modest price. ... Reader reaction to our last issue was tremendous. Although we are unable to print your letters we can tell you this: you, the readers, dictate our policy. We present the personalities you want to read about." Magazine format (8 ¾ x 10 ⅞ inches / 210 x 275 mm), full color covers and center-section pull-out, minimal advertising.
DEPT: None. (10-65).
TYPL: "Rudolph Valentino: Legend with Feet of Clay?," "Ann-Margret: Sex Legend on a Tightrope," "Big Tame Tough Guy." (10-65).
SCHL: Bimonthly, 70 pp.
SPAN: May, 1965 - ?//

✦ SCREEN LIFE

PUBL: Actual Publishing Co., Inc., 880 Third Ave., New York, NY 10022.
DESC: *Screen Life* is a bimonthly, the title of which is a bit of a misnomer. "Off-Screen-Life" might provide a better description, as the vast majority of articles in this "fanzine" consists of the lives, problems, and successes of entertainment industry stars and starlets. One sampled issue covered one star's medical problems "...that threatens her beauty," two young men's competition for a "...Swedish beauty," why Eddie Fisher "...went into hiding," an article concerning Connie Stevens-Tommy Sands as "Losers but not weepers," and a three article "cover scoop" about rumours that John and Bobby Kennedy were still alive. Numerous black/white graphics. Editorial content published on newsprint (8 ¼ x 10 ⅞ inches / 210 x 275 mm).
DEPT: "Meet Your Editor," column by Andrea Guelis; "Hollywood After Dark," Hollywood star activities column by Joey Sasso; "Have You Heard?," Hollywood star activities column by Joyce Becker. (11-69).
TYPL: "Behind the Incredible Rumors JFK & Bobby are Alive," "Dean Martin-Frank Sinatra--How 'Secret Agents' Brought Them Together," "Lawrence Welk's Heartbreak: The Women He Loves are Turning Away from God," "The Heart Transplant Doctor and the Star Who Wrecked His Marriage," "Audrey & Kate: What Those Hepburn Girls Know About Love and the Younger Man." (11-69).
SCHL: Bimonthly, 75 pp.
SPAN: Nov, 1962?+?

✦ SCREEN STARS

SUB: "The magazine for young moderns."
PUBL: Magazine Management Co., Inc., 575 Madison Avenue, New York, NY 10022.
DESC: "...Read about all the latest Hollywood scoops and juicy gossip as soon as it happens." Information, rumours and realities about personalities and their activities in film, television, and off-stage provides a hefty editorial content to this well-known publication of Hollywood, USA. One sampled issue described such diverse stars as Charles Bronson, Bea Arthur, Warren Beatty, Michael Landon, Robert Blake, Barbra Streisand, James Caan, Valerie Harper, Robert Redford, Mac Davis and Richard Thomas; even a featured story of Elvis tracking down and catching a common thief. Of special note is a photo index at the front of the issue. Published on newsprint with numerous personal articles available for purchase by mail. (8 ⅛ x 10 ⅞ inches / 205 x 275 mm).
DEPT: "Hollywood Chatter," "Star Gazing," column by Patrick Agan. (8-75).
TYPL: "Boyfriend Sets Streisand Up with Elvis!," "Charles Bronson's Tearful Mission of Mercy to Save Two Vietnamese Orphans!," "Doctors Warn Dean Martin: You're on the Verge of a Heart Attack! Cathy's Constant Care is Keeping Him Alive!," "Rob Reiner Trying to Break Up All in the Family! And He Wants Sally Struthers to Help Him Do It!," "The Shocking Truth! Richard Thomas Had to Get Married! A Baby's On the Way!" (8-75).
SCHL: Monthly, 75 pp.
SPAN: Apr, 1944+
LC: PN 1993.S26
DD: 791.405

SCREEN STORIES

SUB: "All you want to know about the movies."
PUBL: Ideal Publishing Co., 2 Park Ave., New York, NY 10016.
DESC: Supportive of the Hollywood motion picture industry, *Screen Stories* focused on promoting current film fare. Articles dealt exclusively with motion pictures, featuring plot and production details, and the lives of the film artists. Issues in the late 1950s maintained a separate 16-page section for departmental items; gossip, Q&A, crossword puzzles, and other elements not specifically tied to motion picture releases. One sampled issue focused on why Rock Hudson was Hollywood's most eligible bachelor. Articles presented numerous production stills, and information on the plot and characters. Magazine format (8 ½ x 10 ¾ inches / 215 x 275 mm). Published on newsprint.
DEPT: "Mike Connolly's Exclusive Report From Hollywood," column by Mike Connolly; "It's Your Screen," letters; "Movies to Remember," "Star of the Month," "Screen Stories Previews," "What's Playing?," 'This month in your home-town theater'; "The Question Box," reader Q&A about the stars; "Screen Picture Quiz," "Screen Crossword Puzzle," "Behind the Scenes With," on location with a film production

crew;" "To Tell the Truth," 'Do you want the real inside story?'; "Fifteen Years Ago," 'What the stars said--and did!'; "Then and Now." (7-59).
TYPL: "The Last Angry Man," "North By North West," "The Man Who Understood Women," "Holiday for Lovers," "This Earth is Mine." (7-59).
SCHL: Monthly (? - 1979); Bimonthly (1979+), 95 pp.
SPAN: 1929 - ?//
ISSN: 0036-9608

SCREEN THRILLS ILLUSTRATED

PUBL: Warren Publishing Co., 1426 East Washington Lane, Philadelphia, PA.
DESC: A sampling of readers' letters included these points of praise: "*Screen Thrills Illustrated* is a milestone in the history of American literature and movie magazines," or "It is more than a magazine; in fact it is an encyclopedia of motion picture history and I would like to say that the people responsible for its production are to be congratulated. Addicts and students of the glorious era of great movies have been waiting a long time for such a journal and *STI* fulfills their wish." Although the publishers described this serial as "Covering all aspects of exciting screen entertainment past & present...," the emphasis was on the past. In one issue, topics covered everything from the 1938 version of "The Spider;" to a filmography of the zany Marx Brothers; a re-release of the 1934 "Scarlet Letter;" the 1937 release of "The Thief of Bagdad;" and assorted other features and serials from the pre-1950s era. Of special note was "Private Screening," a column by Pa Jector, which fulfilled readers' requests for pictures of their favorite past motion picture stars, oftentimes in rare publicity or production stills. For the sampled issue of 1964: Stapled magazine format, numerous graphics from motion pictures and editorial content in black ink on newsprint, with full-color cover on coated paper stock (8 ¼ x 10 ⅞ inches / 210 x 275 mm).
DEPT: "Matinee Mail," letters; "Private Screening," picture column by Pa Jector. (5-64).
TYPL: "Nemesis of the Underworld," "The Harp, the Piano and the Mustache," "TV Honors Six-Gun Heroes," "A Hero of Modern Arabian Nights," "Western Hall of Fame." (5-64).
SCHL: Quarterly, 70 pp.
SPAN: Jun, 1962 - ?//

✤ SCREEN WEEKLY, THE

PUBL: Screen Weekly, The, Abbey Bldg., Middle Abbey St., Dublin, Ireland.
DESC: This is a British film fan magazine and celebrity guide. The small format is filled with publicity articles on upcoming motion pictures, studio gossip, and "exclusives." A middle section in the magazine provides an up-to-date listing of motion pictures currently showing in the Dublin area.

DEPT: "Studio Flashes," gossip newsbriefs; "What's On," listing of theatrical fare; "General Releases," film description briefs.
TYPL: "Virginia Mayo--She Dances--But Not on the Screen," "King Solomons' Mines," "Shaw on Chaplin," "Hollywoods Secret Weapon--Good Pictures," "The 'Bad' Women of Motion Pictures." (8-51).
SCHL: Weekly, 20 pp.
SPAN: ?+?
VARIES
--? - Jun 29, 1951 as Screen, The.
LC: PN 1993.S

Screenland

1920 - Aug, 1952//
SEE: SCREENLAND PLUS TV-LAND

✤ SCREENLAND PLUS TV-LAND

SUB: "First with all your favorites."
PUBL: Affiliated Magazines, 10 East 40th St., New York, NY.
DESC: [*Screenland*]: This era of publication presided over by J. Fred Henry provided a promotional showcase of Hollywood film stars, and, beginning in the 1930s, Hollywood/New York network radio stars. Stars' lives were considered glamorous, and all articles/pictures mirrored this glamor. Pictures were carefully staged, and star information well filtered before arriving in text form. *Screenland* in the late 1940s was split into four distinct sections, labeled "First Run Features," "Exclusive Color Photos," "The Hollywood Scene," and "For Femmes Only." Three or four stars each issue were showcased in a full page color photo in the section, "Exclusive Color Photos." In the sampled issue those stars included Ann Blyth, Van Johnson, and Patricia Neal. "For Femmes Only," provided beauty hints, fashion displays, and guides to glamour. Notably, numerous advertising pages were utilized by the studios for recent film releases. Each issue was filled with numerous black/white photos of artists at work, at play, and before the public. Magazine format (8 ½ x 11 ¼ inches / 220 x 225 mm); published on coated paper stock.
DESC: [*Screenland Plus TV-Land*]: A distinct change in editorial philosophy is evident in *Screenland Plus TV-Land* of 1970s vintage. Under new publisher, Macfadden-Bartell, the magazine reflected both the changed status of Hollywood stardom and the lost gullibility of the American public. The staged publicity photos of artists were replaced with pictures of the artists in public places, photos that often did not flatter the star. Like other such "fanzines" of the period, there was an ongoing fascinating with individuals in politics, especially Lord Snowdon, Princess Margaret, and Jackie Onassis. Love, relationships, marriage, divorce, and pregnancies all received their due in each issue. The film studio reaction to the new editorial

style of this magazine may best be seen in the absence of advertising for upcoming motion picture releases. Magazine format published on newsprint (8 ¼ x 10 ⅞ inches / 210 x 275 mm).
DEPT: "Cobina Wright's Party Gossip," column by Cobina Wright; "Your Guide to Current Films," column by Helen Hendricks; "Newsreel," star-studded picture page; "What Hollywood Itself is Talking About!," 'The stars themselves enjoy the gossip as much as you do' column by Lynn Bowers; "Right Off the Record," recording review column by Fred Robbins; "Guide to Glamour." (5-49). "Hollywood Hot Line," column by Evan Grant; "Scoops From Scottie," column by Scottie. (4-71).
TYPL: "No Pretense About Bob," "What a Girl Needs Most," "Jolson Sings Again," "Look Who's Playing Bits!," "Hobbies Come, Hobbies Go." (5-49). "An Intimate Look at Jeanne Martin's Love Life," "Innocent Doris Day Dragged into Drug & Sex Orgy!," "Elvis Presley: How Much Longer Can Priscilla Stand By Elvis?," "Liz and Burton: How Do You Say Goodbye to Someone You Love?," "All About Ali MacGraw's Dangerous Pregnancy--Her Greatest Performance was Keeping Everyone from Knowing How Sick She Really Was." (4-71).
SCHL: Monthly, 75 pp.
SPAN: 1920+
VARIES
--1920 - Aug, 1952 as Screenland.
LC: PN 1993.S35

✤ SCRIPPS HOWARD NEWS

PUBL: Scripps Howard News, 1100 Central Trust Tower, Box 5380, Cincinnati, OH 45201.
DESC: This is the promotional house organ of the Scripps Howard organization, representing (Apr, 1988) some 70-plus media operations in newspapers, publishing, syndication, radio, television, cable television and manufacturing areas. *Scripps Howard News* pulls together these diverse media organizations through profiles of employees, projects, and reports on events and happenings at selected owned-and-operated facilities each issue. For the sampled issue of 1988: Stapled magazine format with black/white editorial content and full-color cover on coated paper stock (8 ½ x 10 ⅞ inches / 215 x 275 mm).
DEPT: "Shop Talk," "Viewpoint," "Update," newsbriefs; "Idea Exchange," promotion ideas; "Newsmakers," personnel items. (4-88).
TYPL: "Hats Off to Jim Tabor," "Next Century's Newspapers," "High Performance Photographers," "Commercial Appeal Brings Political Process to Classroom," "Birmingham Papers Extend, Exchange in Joint Agreement." (4-88).
SCHL: Monthly (? - ?); Ten issues per year (?+), 32 pp.
SPAN: ?+

✤ SCRIPT NEWSLETTER

PUBL: William Miller, Director, SCRIPT, School of Telecommunications, Ohio University, Athens, OH 45701.
DESC: "SCRIPT, Screenwriting Coalition foR [the capitalized 'R' in foR is intentional] Industry Professionals and Teachers, is an organization committed to the teaching and practice of screenwriting for film, video and television. Our members are largely college and university writing teachers but also include many industry professionals." This one-page newsletter was included as part of the *Digest of the University Film and Video Association*.
DEPT: None.
TYPL: No Article Titles.
SCHL: Quarterly?, 1 pp.
SPAN: 1988?+?
SUPPLEMENT TO
--Digest of the University Film and Video Association, 1988?+?

ScriptWriter

Jan, 1980 - May, 1980//
(ISSN: 0197-9388)
SEE: SCRIPTWRITER NEWS

SCRIPTWRITER NEWS

SUB: "The working writer's newsletter."
SUB: "The creative voice of the entertainment industry."
SUB: "The most widely-read newsletter in the entertainment industry!"
PUBL: ScriptWriter News, 250 W. 57th St., Suite 219, New York, NY 10019.
DESC: A no-nonsense, eight-page, newsletter concentrating on the art and technique of entertainment writing, there are no graphics but are plenty of short articles to inform, prod, and inspire. The articles are both timely and informative. In the June, 1981 issues, for example was a salient feature, "The Care and Feeding of Agents: How to Get One, How to Keep One, and How to Get Rid of One That's Not Working." This article alone was worth the price of a year's subscription. In that same issue was a second feature, "The Art and Craft of Adaptation: Overlooked Opportunities for the Clever Script Writer." Within the article were provided the steps of adapting a story line for another medium; when a scriptwriter might run afoul of copyright restrictions; and some insights to how other scriptwriters have adapted story plotlines for other media. The information is direct from industry professionals, and written in such a fashion that a scriptwriter on the American East Coast can feel fully informed to the developments and trends of the Hollywood production community. This is an extraordinary publication, and well recommended to those who write for "a living." Some emphasis on new writing

opportunities. For the sampled issues of 1981: black ink on uncoated paper stock; folded, newsletter format; no advertising (8 ½ x 11 inches / 215 x 280 mm).
DEPT: "Short Takes," newsbriefs; "Looking," Media producers looking for new writers or material; "Q&A," technique of writing; "Local Stages," media profile; "Classifieds." (9-7-81).
TYPL: "Writing Soap Operas," "The Revival of 'A Taste of Honey' Reminds Us How Powerful a 19-Year-Old Playwright Can Be." (9-7-81).
SCHL: Twenty issues per year, 8 pp.
SPAN: Jan, 1980 - 1982?//
VARIES
--Jan, 1980 - May, 1980 as ScriptWriter (ISSN: 0197-9388).
LC: PN 1996.S38
ISSN: 0279-9596

SCSC XEROX PIPELINE
SUB: "A newsletter for registered Xerox Ventura Publisher users."
SUB: "A newsletter for Xerox Desktop Software SCSC Agreement Customers."
PUBL: Xerox Corporation, Systems Customer Support Center, MS319, PO Box 660512, Dallas, TX 75266-0512.
DESC: This very helpful information newsletter was designed for users of Xerox Ventura Publisher software for desktop publishing. It was provided free to registered users, and provided tips on applications as well as news of new Xerox products, upgrades, and known program "bugs." Numerous graphics accompanied each issue to demonstrate the versatility of the popular software package. *SCSC Xerox Ventura Pipeline* changed its name to *SCSC Xerox Pipeline* for one issue as it was being absorbed in July, 1989 (under the *Xerox Pipeline* name) within the pages of *Ventura Publisher* magazine, published by the Ventura Publisher Users Group. For the 1988 sampled issue under the title of *The Fifth Mode*: Folded newsletter format, spot blue and black ink on coated paper stock (8 ½ x 11 inches / 215 x 280 mm). For the 1989 sampled issue under the title of *SCSC Xerox Pipeline*: Stapled newsletter format, black ink with red spot color throughout on uncoated paper stock (8 ½ x 11 inches / 215 x 280 mm).
DEPT: "Ventura Pipeline User Tips," "Questions and Answers," "Applications." (Vol 2, #2-89).
TYPL: "Xerox Ventura Publisher Moves Text to Electronic Printer," "Endnotes and Footnote Numbers," "LaserMaster LX-6 Professional." (Vol 2, #2-89).
SCHL: Quarterly [irregular at times], 20 pp.
SPAN: 198u - Jul, 1989//
VARIES
--198u - 1988? as Fifth Mode, The.
--1988? - Vol 2, #1 as Xerox Ventura Pipeline.
ABSORBED BY
--Ventura Professional, Jul, 1989.

SEE; World Film News
Sep, 1938 - Nov, 1938//
SEE: DOCUMENTARY FILM NEWS

SELECTED MOTION PICTURES
PUBL: Motion Picture Producers and Distributors of America, Inc., 469 Fifth Ave., New York, NY.
DESC: With Will H. Hayes as President, the Motion Picture Producers and Distributors of America began this public relations serial to encourage the American public to participate in the motion picture industry, both by comment and box office attendance. In this eight-page monthly, the motion picture produced only good for the world at large, leaving negative news items and comment on the editorial floor. This serial also served as a means by which the MPPDA was able to list various codes of ethics and moral guidelines for the motion picture industry, showing strong support for self-regulation by this organization. Many articles pertained to newspaper items concerning the positive role of motion pictures in American society. Square format, printed on coated paper through Volume 6, #7. Beginning in August, 1930, printed on cheaper newsprint.
DEPT: "As Others See It," newspaper reports; "List of Previewed Pictures." (8/9-31).
TYPL: "Department of Public Relations with Open Door Policy Formed After Three Years Work by Committee," "Practical Ideas for Motion Picture Programs by Better Films Chairman in Pennsylvania," "A Little Piece of Blue, Glazed Glass Enables Costumers to Determine What will Look Good on the Screen," "Movies are Greatest Pastime says 85-Year-Old Woman Who hasn't Missed a Night in Eight Years." (Vol 4, #3).
SCHL: Monthly [except Jul/Aug], 12 pp.
SPAN: Sep, 1925 - Nov, 1939//
VARIES
--Sep, 1925 - Jul, 1930 as Motion Picture, The.
--Aug, 1930 - Dec, 1931 as Motion Picture Monthly, The.
LC: PN 1993.M35

Selection of Recent Books Published in Great Britain
Mar, 1940 - Apr, 1941//
SEE: BRITISH BOOK NEWS

SEMINAR
SUB: "A quarterly review for newspapermen."
PUBL: Copley Newspapers, 7776 Ivanhoe Ave., La Jolla, CA 92037.

DESC: *Seminar* was designed to be used by journalism students at both high school and college levels. Articles concerned the field of journalism, and oftentimes featured aspects of the Copley newspaper organization.
DEPT: None.
TYPL: "The Media Revolution," "Change Comes to Detroit," "Newsprint Price will Zoom." (3-74).
SCHL: Quarterly, 30 pp.
SPAN: 1968 - 1974//
LC: PN 4700

SEQUENCE

SUB: "Magazine of the Oxford University Film Society."
PUBL: Oxford University Film Society, London, England.
DESC: To mark a fresh start one year following the war, the Oxford University Film Society changed the title of its film periodical, *Film Society Magazine* to *Sequence*. It is a small size publication reflecting postwar Britain's slow return to full motion picture production. It has well-written essays, with few graphics.
DEPT: "Book Reviews," "Stills," a selection of stills to support earlier articles; "Cartoon," contemporary cartoon on films or filmmaking.
TYPL: "Film Among the Arts," "Some French Films--and a Forecast," "The Cinema of Marcel Carne," "The Czechoslovak Film Industry." (summer-46).
SCHL: ?, 25 pp.
SPAN: May, 1946 - 1952//
VARIES
--May, 1946 - ?, 1946 as Magazine of the Oxford Film Society.
LC: PN 1993.S

✤ SERIALS REVIEW

PUBL: Pierian Press, Inc., 5000 Washtenaw Ave., Ann Arbor, MI 48108.
DESC: *Serials Review* provides a librarian's perspective on the changing process of serials acquisition, cataloging, and evaluation. The decade of the nineties is a difficult time for all parties; with staff and serial order reductions on the library side, and increasing costs, decreasing advertising revenue for the serials publisher. *Serials Review* remains an island of sanity in a sea of ever-changing ideas, publications, publishers, acquisition budgets and formats. The publication is written by information professionals interested in new innovations and/or standardized processes which enhance the serials' acquisitions, cataloging and access fields. Those areas include new methods of evaluating the worth of current subscriptions, innovative means of interfacing with public inquiries for unique publications, the growing problem of cataloging and acquisitions processing, and the never-ending educational program of instructing serial publishers on proper ISSN usage. While this magazine primarily targets the serial's librarian, serial publishers would gain much simply by reading what these information professionals require in order for them to more efficiently process and make available serials to their constituent publics. Articles are not written in theoretical terms, but appropriately reflect the successes, failures, problems and solutions experienced by serial librarians on a variety of issues. Well recommended to both information professionals and serial publishers. Black/white editorial content on uncoated paper stock in stapled magazine format with two-color cover on coated paper stock, some graphics and advertising (8 ½ x 11 inches / 215 x 280 mm).
DEPT: "Editorial," commentary column by Cindy Hepfer; "Contributors," author listing; "The Balance Point," pro and con on current issues. (summer-91).
TYPL: "A Cost-Per-Use Method for Evaluating the Cost-Effectiveness of Serials: A Detailed Discussion of Methodology," "The Use of Citation Data to Evaluate Serials Subscriptions in an Academic Library," "The SISAC Bar Code Symbol," "Serials Prices," "The Future of Serials Librarianship Revisited." (summer-91).
SCHL: Three issues per year (1975); Quarterly (1976+), 95 pp.
SPAN: Jan/Jun, 1975+
LC: PN 4832 .S47
DD: 016.05
ISSN: 0098-7913
ABST: --Abstract of English Studies (ISSN: 0001-3560)
--Book Review Index (ISSN: 0524-0581)
--Library Information Science Abstracts (ISSN: 0024-2179)
--Library Literature (ISSN: 0024-2373)
--Reference Sources (ISSN: 0163-3546)

✤ SERVICE FOR COMPANY COMMUNNICATORS

PUBL: National Association of Manufacturers, 1776 F St., NW, Washington, DC 20006.
DESC: One of the more unusual periodicals in the communication field, this one is designed to be cut up and reprinted in individual company in-house publications. It consists of three sections: 1) news and editorials from other company publications; 2) article reprints from in-house organs to be used as guidelines, or reprinted in entirety with secured permission; 3) news tidbits and articles printed on one side only, ready to be cut up and pasted into company publications.
DEPT: "Editorials," "Cartoons, Shorts, Fillers."
TYPL: "Insurance Benefits: Who Needs Them? You Do: (Ask Willy Norman)," "Students Do Their Summer Thing at Machine Shop in Record Clip," "Yes Anita, We're Doing Something." (11-72).
SCHL: Monthly, 25 pp.
SPAN: Sep, 1949+
VARIES
--Sep, 1949 - Jun, 1955 as Service for Employee Publications.

--Jul, 1955 - Feb, 1974 as Service for Company Publications.
ISSN: 0361-5081

Service for Company Publications
Jul, 1955 - Feb, 1974//
SEE: SERVICE FOR COMPANY COMMUNNICATORS

Service for Employee Publications
Sep, 1949 - Jun, 1955//
SEE: SERVICE FOR COMPANY COMMUNNICATORS

✤ 73 AMATEUR RADIO
PUBL: 80 Pine St., Peterborough, NH 03458.
DESC: *73 Amateur Radio* is a technical publication for amateur radio enthusiasts, many of whom are also members of the Amateur Radio Relay League. Articles from the sampled issue were primarily of a technical nature, providing schematics, construction information, application notes, and pictures of the assembled equipment. Some editorial pages addressed organizational and on-air activities. For the sampled issue of 1964: stapled journal format, editorial content consisting of black and spot-color ink on coated paper stock with two-color cover on coated paper stock as well (6 ½ x 9 ½ inches / 165 x 240 mm).
DEPT: "New Products," review; "RTTY Docket," "Propagation Charts." (3-64).
TYPL: "The Little Punch on VHF," "Transistorized RTTY Converter," "Modulation Measurement," "144mc Transistorized Converter," "Biasing Tubes." (3-64).
SCHL: Monthly, 95 pp.
SPAN: Oct, 1960+
VARIES
--Oct, 1960 - Jul, 1982 as 73 (ISSN: 0037-3036).
--Aug, 1982 - Feb, 1985 as 73 Amateur Radio's Technical Journal (ISSN: 0745-080x).
--Mar, 1985 - Apr, 1986 as 73 for Radio Amateurs (ISSN: 0883-234x).
LC: TK 9956.S46
DD: 621.3841/66/05
ISSN: 0889-5309

✤ SF MOVIELAND
SUB: "Get the news first - direct from Hollywood."
PUBL: New Media Publishing, Inc., 8399 Topanga Canyon Blvd., Suite 210, Canoga Park, CA 91304.
DESC: "Blasting off from Hollywood, *SF MOVIELAND*, the only science fiction movie magazine produced in the home of film and television, takes you to exciting new worlds every month. With in-depth coverage, full-color special reports, exclusive interviews and revealing profiles of the actors, directors, writers and effects experts who make the magic happen, *SF MOVIELAND* brings the universes of imagination to your door..." Letters to the Editor support these statements as subscribers sing the praises of this serial of science fiction film and television product. This wonderful publication showcases the talent of production crew and actors alike. The sample issue viewed (August, 1985) was an interesting mixture of black/white and color graphics, newsprint and glossly clay paper stock. Note: running title and all editorial references refer to magazine title as being *SF Movieland*, although publisher's statement stakes claim to title of *Enterprise Incidents*, believed to be in error as this latter title is promoted in an advertisement within the sample issue. Magazine format (8 ½ x 10 ⅞ inches / 215 x 275 mm).
DEPT: "Direct From Hollywood," "News From Earth," "Preview:," "News Items," film science fiction newsbriefs; "SF Movie Books," review; "Amazing Video," review; "Tomorrow's World," comment; "Hailing Frequencies," letters; "Inside SF Movieland," "Editorial," column by Hal Schuster. (8-85).
TYPL: "Matthew Broderick: Ladyhawke's Mouse," "Beyond Thunderdome with Mad Max," "Meet the Goonies," "Dykstra Breathes Life into Space Vampires." (8-85).
SCHL: Monthly, 70 pp.
SPAN: Jan, 1983?+?

✤ SH-BOOM
SUB: "The best of then and now."
PUBL: LFP, Inc., 9171 Wilshire Blvd., Suite 300, Beverly Hills, CA 90210.
DESC: "Introducing *SH-BOOM*. The first magazine that remembers you! The music you grew up with, the stars you fell in love with. YOUR ERA--The '50s and '60s, when America was COOL and pop culture really POPPED! *SH-BOOM* takes you back then and shows you what's happening now! Each issue brings you photos and outrageous interviews that'll bring back all those memories of your favorite film, TV and rock 'n' roll stars. Plus we'll tell you what they're up to today! We'll also keep you up on revivals and concert tours. Even give you the inside scoop on which of your old favorites are out on CD and videotape!" Here is a delightful time capsule of mid-century America, a celebration of what was "in" at the time. Buddy Holly, Annette & Frankie, George Fenneman and Groucho Marx, Pat Boone, Little Richard, Frank Zappa, the "Motown Sound," the Beatles, Elvis, Connie Francis, Dick Dale, Otis Young, Steve Allen, the Flintstones, Sonny & Cher, Johnnie Ray, Tom Ewell, Marilyn Monroe, Jayne Mansfield, Wanda Jackson, Big Joe Turner, and hundreds of others appeared in just the first six issues of this very readable magazine. Memories will be jogged with visions of frosty mugs of drive-in rootbeer; Saturday morning television with Roy Rogers; UFO scares; trends in popular music; and the latest news from the petticoated citizens of the fabled village of Hooterville. For the fans of Dobie Gillis, Maynard G. Krebs, Gilligan's Island, The Beaver, Marcus Welby, and Mr. Greenjeans of the 1950s

and 60s; this publication shows you can "come home again." As Gomer might have said, "Gollllyyy." (8 1/8 x 10 7/8 inches / 205 x 275 mm).
DEPT: "And Now a Word From Our Editor," editorial; "Good Rockin' Tonight," 'Sh-Boom reviews the heart & sould of rock 'n roll'; "Please Mr. Postman," letters; "Tube Talk," column by Robin Keats; "Rewind," 'The best of then is on video today!', column by Scott Mallory; "What Happened to," personality update; "Country Corner!," 'Country Corner is a new monthly feature covering traditional country music today', column by Linda Cauthen; "Fan Clubs," extensive listing; "Rock 'n' Roll Trivia Quiz," "Sh-Boom Calendar," 'A day-by-day history of the hits and the hitmakers'; "One Step Beyond," 'Sh-Boom remembers the early heroes of rock 'n' roll!'; "Solid Gold Radio," 'North America's megawatt jukeboxes are still pumping out those hits'; "Radiowaves," oldies music on current stations. (7-90).
TYPL: "The Flying Graceland," "Cher Doesn't Hurt Me Anymore!," "Yabba Dabba Doo!," "'I Made Love to Marilyn Monroe & Jayne Mansfield'," "Revenge of the Finned Fantasies!" (7-90).
SCHL: Monthly, 75 pp.
SPAN: Jan, 1990+

✤ SHAKESPEARE QUARTERLY
SUB: "Published by the Folger Shakespeare Library."
PUBL: Folger Shakespeare Library, 201 East Capitol St., Washington, DC 20003.
DESC: A promotional advertisement asked, "Is Shakespeare Our Contemporary? How does one account for the fact that now, more than 350 years after his death, in every part of the globe, in virtually every language and culture, Shakespeare is still read, studied, and performed as a living playwright? This is the kind of question you will find addressed in the pages of *Shakespeare Quarterly*. Fore more than a quarter of a century, *Shakespeare Quarterly* has been read and depended upon by Shakespeareans the world over for such features as: articles interpreting the works in light of the intellectual, social, and artistic contexts in which they were produced; wide-ranging surveys of the full cultural impact of Shakespeare in today's world; informative reviews of the latest books and articles about Shakespeare and his age; an annual performance issue highlighting and evaluating the most important contemporary productions of Shakespeare; the unique, comprehensive, annotated World Shakespeare Bibliography; [and] announcements and advertisements reflecting the most recent trends and developments in Shakespearean activity." Sampled issues from the 1989 volume included a fascinating stage review section entitled, "Shakespeare on Stage." For the sampled issues of 1979 and 1989: black ink on coated paper; cover consisting of black ink on coated index stock; no advertising; perfect-bound journal format (6 5/8 x 9 3/4 inches / 170 x 250 mm).
DEPT: "Notes," "From the Editor," editorial column by John F. Andrews; "Announcements," "Book Reviews," extensive section. (winter-79). "Notes," "Book Reviews." (spring-89).
TYPL: "Ladies, Gentlemen, and Skulls: 'Hamlet' and the Iconographic," "'The Tempest' and the New World," "Othello, Thorello, and the Problem of the Foolish Hero," "'As Marriage Binds, and Blood Breaks': English Marriage and Shakespeare," "Sir John Davies and the Question of Topical Reference in Shakespeare's Sonnet 107." (winter-79). "Shakespeare's Hand in 'The Second Maiden's Tragedy'," "The Sonnet's Body and the Body Sonnetized in 'Romeo and Juliet'," "Discourse and the Individual: The Case of Colonialism in 'The Tempest'," "They Were Not Such Good Years," "Shakespeare at the 1988 Edinburgh Festival." (spring-89).
SCHL: Quarterly [with additional issue in December], 130 pp.
SPAN: 1950+
ISSN: 0037-3222
ABST: --Humanities Index (ISSN: 0095-5981)
--MLA International Bibliography of Books & Articles on the Modern Languages and Literatures (ISSN: 0024-8215)

✤ SHOOTING COMMERCIALS
SUB: "The magazine for creators and producers of television commercials."
PUBL: Shooting Commercials, 6407 Moore Dr., Los Angeles, CA 90048.
DESC: *Shooting Commercials* has adopted the same publishing format as in its video products; short, detailed articles (primarily on commercials in production), with very few lengthy articles on the business of commercials. This is a periodical for the producer-director whose primary function is the development or production of television commercials for advertising agencies and clients. The majority of articles come under regional report columns. A majority of advertisements are by equipment sales/rental agencies and state film/video offices whose primary job it is to lure filmmakers to their state. Tabloid, coated paper stock in newspaper format.
DEPT: "News/Views," newsbriefs; "Spotlight: New York," production briefs; "SC Middle Atlantic," same; "SC Southeast," "SC Midwest," "SC Southwest," "SC West," "Ad-Supported Cable Networks," listing. (4-82). "SC Commercial of the Month," Description and story boards; "Editorial Out Takes," guest editorial; "SC Letters," "SC West," production news column by Beverley Van Der Trim; "SC Southwest," production news column by Jan Stenza; "SC Southeast," production news column by Linda Duffy; "SC Midwest," production news column by Elizabeth Cunningham; "SC Equipment," product reviews column by Susan Sammon; "SC East," production news column by Peter Brown; "SC Music," column by Doris Elliott. (8-84).

TYPL: "Protect the Shoot With Insurance," "High-Speed Color Negative Film: New Options From an Old Medium," "Via Video Bows System One: Low Cost Computer Graphics." (4-82). "Music, Music, Music," "Washington...The State of the Art," "Some Award Winners' Reactions." (8-84).
SCHL: Biweekly (1978 - 1979); Every three weeks (1979 - 1980); Monthly (1980+), 28 pp.
SPAN: 1978+
VARIES
--1978 - 1979 as Shooting Commercials (ISSN: 0163-3236).
--1979 - 1980 as Shooting Commercials & Industrials (ISSN: 0199-0497).
ISSN: 0273-2246

Shooting Commercials
1978 - 1979//
(ISSN: 0163-3236)
SEE: SHOOTING COMMERCIALS

Shooting Commercials & Industrials
1979 - 1980//
(ISSN: 0199-0497)
SEE: SHOOTING COMMERCIALS

Short Wave & Television
Jan, 1937 - Sep, 1938//
SEE: RADIO & TELEVISION

Short Wave Craft
Jun/Jul, 1930 - Dec, 1936//
SEE: RADIO & TELEVISION

SHOW
SUB: "The magazine of entertainment."
PUBL: Show Magazine, Inc., 535 Fifth Ave., New York, NY.
DESC: Packed into a four by six inch mini-magazine format was over 60 pages of entertainment news and features concerning stars, celebrities and other interesting people from the field of entertainment. With an emphasis on pictures, *Show* provided brief, but succinct portraits of a variety of entertainment productions and occasions. For the sampled issue from 1955, there was a feature on what the censors took out from a movie or TV production before it reached the audience; and another profiled a master whipsman whose act went beyond the usual flicking of cigarette ashes from an assistant's mouth. Another article demonstrated how actors got ready to "die" in a scene from "Helen of Troy;" while another profiled boxer Henry Armstrong, a man whom *Show* called "...the greatest fighter of all time." If there was a pictorial emphasis, it would probably have been the female form, numerous examples of which appeared on outside and inside front and back covers. For the sampled issue of 1955: mini-size stapled magazine, editorial content consisting of black ink on uncoated paper stock, with full color covers on heavy coated paper, minimal advertising (4 ⅛ x 5 ⅞ inches / 105 x 150 mm).
DEPT: "Show Stoppers," personality column by Paul Steiner; "Readers Write," letters. (9-55).
TYPL: "What the Censors Censor," "Whip Strip," "Death on a Movie Lot," "24 Hours With a Beauty Queen," "Show Stoppers." (9-55).
SCHL: Monthly, 65 pp.
SPAN: Sep, 1952? - ?//

✤ SHOW
SUB: "The magazine of the arts."
SUB: "The magazine of the performing arts." (Oct, 1961 - Mar, 1962).
SUB: "Incorporating USA*1."
PUBL: Hartford Publications, Inc., 140 East 57th St., New York, NY.
DESC: Big format, dynamic design, and an overview of ALL the arts made *Show* a coffee-table centerpiece, and a favorite topic of discussion for readers interested in the full arts spectrum. The topics were as varied as they were interesting; "Tennessee Williams' Mother Tells a Stormy, Pathetic Tale;" "Jeritza, the 20th Century's Most Bewitching Diva;" "What Makes Remick Walk?;" and "Screen Test: Doing It With Mirrors-- The Dracula Bit." Among a number of special features commendend to the reader would be "This Month: The Arts," and "This Month: Datelines." The former, printed on its own green tinted uncoated paper stock, brought forth a wide assortment of reviews, profiles, critiques and showcases for multi-talents, new productions, just released or upcoming motion pictures, radio and television productions. In many ways, "This Month: The Arts" could have easily existed on its own: its presence within *Show* heightened what was already a quality magazine. "This Month: Deadlines" took a realistic view of world events: for the sampled issue of 1963 it consisted of four articles: "Washington: On the Docket;" "Peking: The Proletarianization of Poetry;" "Johannesburg: Ugly, Brutal and Dangerous;" and "Berlin: The TV Channel War." *Show* articles were written by major personalities, such as Max Lerner, C. S. Lewis, James M. Gavin and Edwin Diamond who were commissioned to write essays for "The Newest Frontier: Four Views of the Space Age." It is a wonderful review of the arts. For sampled issue of 1963: large, perfect-bound magazine format, mixture of black/white, spot and full-color pages on coated paper stock. Some specialty sections were black ink on tinted newsprint (10 ¼ x 11 ⅞ inches / 260 x 325 mm).
DEPT: "From the Publisher," editorial column by Huntington Hartford; "Letters," "Sideshow," "Television," upcoming programs; "FM Programs of Special Interest," "Documentary Show of the Month," "Drama Show of

the Month," "Personality of the Month," "Music Show of the Month," "Variety Show of the Month," "Movies," review of current releases; "Theatre," current productions of Broadway and region; "Art," review of exhibitions and talent; "Music," review; "Books," review; "Editorial," column by Robert M. Wool; "What They Are Doing Now," star update; "Datelines," wonderful news summary from world cities. (2-63).
TYPL: "Off Broadway: Slick and Not So Slick," "The Newest Frontier: Four Views of the Space Age," "Who Isn't Afraid of Edward Albee?," "Children of the Famous," "Singing Valentines." (2-63).
SCHL: Monthly, 135 pp.
SPAN: Oct, 1961+?
VARIES
--Oct, 1961 - May, 1965 as Show; The Magazine of the Arts (ISSN: 0037-4296).
--Mar/Apr, 1966 - ? as New Show, The.
ABSORBED
--Show Business Illustrated (ISSN: 0559-9210), May, 1962.
--USA #1 [NC], Oct, 1962.
LC: PN 2001.S5
ISSN: 0583-1318

SHOW

SUB: "The magazine of films and the arts."
SUB: "The magazine of entertainment and the arts."
PUBL: H & R Publications, Inc., 866 United Nations Plaza, New York, NY 10017.
DESC: From an in-magazine promotion: "*Show* offers you the best seat in the house, right in the comfort of your own living-room. And the liveliest cast--Glenda Jackson, Dustin Hoffman, David Hemmings, Ann-Margret, Elizabeth Taylor, Dick Cavett, Ed Sullivan, Ingmar Bergman, Joseph Losey, Robert Altman, Tom Courtenay, Lenny Bruce, Jane Fonda, Donald Sutherland, Jack Nicholson, John Garfield, Gloria Swanson, Jules Feiffer, Karen Black, Anthony Quinn, Pablo Picasso and Joan Miro. They're all currently appearing in *Show*." Numerous stars, starlets, playwrights, producers, designers, and other denisens of the entertainment world regularly appeared in *Show*. With a strong emphasis on New York City entertainment, *Show* was a thorough roundup of news, critiques, reviews, and new talent within the "Big Apple." Indeed, *Show* completed the entertainment scene with numerous pages of advertisements and guides to fine dining within the city; listings of Broadway and Off-Broadway productions; and a basic guide to personalities living, visiting, or working current city productions. This was a dynamic publication which lasted all too short a time. For the 1972 sampled issue: stapled magazine format, primarily black/white editorial content with some full-color pages and cover on coated paper stock (8 ½ x 11 inches / 215 x 275 mm).
DEPT: "TV Spotlight," review; "Movie Previews," "Movie Reviews," 'A roundup of current film attractions'; "Music & Recording," review; "Books," review; "Theatre U.S.A.," review; "Theatre Abroad," review; "Dining," New York City column by Sheldon Landwehr; "Fashion Show," "Videosphere," "Your Bag," letters; "Coming Attractions," in selected US cities; "Showing Up in New York," personality column by Liz Smith; "Showing Up in Hollywood," personality column by Sidney Skolsky; "The Editors Bless," orchid awards for best; "The Editors Blast," onion awards for the not so good. (5-72).
TYPL: "Xavier Hollander: From Call Girl to Madam to Best-Selling Novelist," "Sophia Loren: The Last of the Love Goddesses," "Tennessee Williams: The Revitalization of a Great Dramatist," "Alan Bates: An Actor Who Prefers to Be Anonymous," "'All in the Family's' Success Proves That We've Been Underestimating the Sophistication of the TV Audience, Says Jean Stapleton." (5-72).
SCHL: Monthly [Irregular at times] (Jan, 1970 - May, 1970); Biweekly (Jun, 1970 - Sep, 1970); Monthly (Oct, 1970+), 70 pp.
SPAN: Jan, 1970 - Nov, 1973//
ABSORBED
--Status, May, 1970.
--Entertainment World (ISSN: 0531-7991), Jun, 1970.
LC: PN 1560.S48
DD: 791.43/05
ISSN: 0037-4296

✤ SHOW BIZ WEST

SUB: "The first and last word in entertainment."
PUBL: Show Biz West, Inc., 6331 Hollywood Blvd., Suite 803, Hollywood, CA 90028.
DESC: *Show Biz West* is about entertainment, and especially the entertainer. Articles in the magazine-style format look at acting styles, new opportunities in the media, current productions, and educational opportunities for improvement. Each item concerning a new play, film or video program provides full details on auditions, plot, producer, director and writer.
DEPT: "Legit Reviews," "Film Reviews," "Casting Calls," "Film Production Chart," "Tinseltown," Hollywood news; "Vegas Tracks," news; "This is New York," news. (2-21-80).
TYPL: "Al Pacino and 'Cruising,'" "Up and Coming: Candi and Randi." (2-21-80).
SCHL: Biweekly, 32 pp.
SPAN: 1979+
ISSN: 0199-4387

✤ SHOW BUSINESS

SUB: "The entertainment weekly."
SUB: "Production Prospects."
PUBL: Leo Shull Publications, 1501 Broadway, #2900, New York, NY 10036.
DESC: The primary audience of this tabloid weekly newspaper is performers in the New York City area. Although all major entertainment media are covered, there is an emphasis on the legitimate stage production. It has a breezy format with numerous graphics.

Timely casting news and lists of upcoming productions makes this important for the entertainment community.
DEPT: "Closeup on Cable TV," news stories concerning programming; "Photography," photo services for performers; "Letters to Show Business," "New York Reviews," legitimate stage; "Casting," "Workshops," "Still Casting," "SAG Talent Agents Franchise," "Equity Industrial Producers," listing; "Equity Dinner Theatres," listing; "Equity Talent Agents," listing; "OOBA Member Theatres," listing; "Producers," listing; "ATPAM Members," listing; "Independent N.Y.C. Casting Directors," listing; "Unions and Guilds," information on joining; "Films Shooting in New York," "Off-B'way Theatres," listing; "Broadway Theatres," listing; "Broadway Shows," listing; "AFTRA Talent Agents," listing; "Hollywood Filmmakers: Who's Who," listing.
TYPL: "Jobs for Performers: Showcasing Your Talent," "Kid Agency Expands; Now Handling Adults," "SAG President Asner Says Strike Rumour 'Monstrous,'" "Cable TV and Reagonomics Worry Arts Administrators." (12-21-81).
SCHL: Daily [except Saturday and Sunday] (Sep 30, 1941 - 1948); Weekly (1949+), 50 pp.
SPAN: 1941+
VARIES
--? - ? as Production Prospects.
--Sep 30, 1941 - 1948 as Actor's Cues (ISSN: 7800-0081).
SUSPENDED
--Dec 24, 1941 - Jan 4, 1942.
ISSN: 0037-4318

SHOW BUSINESS ILLUSTRATED

PUBL: HMH Publishing Co., Playboy Building, 232 Ohio St., Chicago, IL.
DESC: Whether one called it *Show Business Illustrated*, or simply *SBI*, this was a classy publication under editor and publisher, Hugh M. Hefner; and deserved to have acquired a sufficient audience and advertising base to have lasted longer than six months. It was remarkable for several reasons, not the least of which was the fact that this 80-plus page magazine was issued every two weeks. Articles and departments fairly sparkled with wit and interesting information about some of the biggest and brightest stars to grace not only the silver screen; but television, dance, theater, and music as well. Typical of any given issue might be a profile of the Fonda family, a painter's concept of scenes from "Flower Drum Song," the Kirov Ballet on American tour, a new theatrical production of Martin Luther, a fond rememberence of the big band era, wit and wisdom from Tallulah Bankhead, Allen Ginsberg at Cannes, and "Why W.C. Fields Hated Christmas." An inside, back-cover promotion to potential advertisers said it well: "You Couldn't Ask for a Better Audience. Fashionable people at home on the town, *SBI* readers actively seek out the best in entertainment. Dinner and 'two on the aisle' to a hit are as commonplace to them as curry, caviar, La Dolce Vita or La Boheme. And after the show you're apt to find them applauding the most 'in' nightclub act in town. Affluent, active, interested and responsive--these are the men and women who buy, read--and respond to *Show Business Illustrated*. You couldn't ask for a better audience." For the sampled issue of 1961: stapled magazine format, black ink, spot and full color throughout on coated paper stock (8 ⅜ x 11 ⅛ inches / 215 x 280 mm).
DEPT: "Showbill," 'Backstage With Our Contributors'; "From the Audience," 'Letters to the editor'; "News and Reviews," 'Commentary and criticism'; "Our Man in Hollywood," column by Joe Hyams; "Listings and Ratings," 'What's on, where, and how good is it?'; "Anything For a Laugh," 'A distillation of current wit'; "Show Business Beauties," "Showbiz Quiz." (11-28-61).
TYPL: "Toll-TV: You Pays Your Money," "Candid Conversation," "Censorship," "Old Leningrad Flies High on the Road," "Three Faces of Fonda." (11-28-61).
SCHL: Biweekly [irregular at times], 85 pp.
SPAN: Sep 5, 1961 - Apr, 1962//
ABSORBED BY
--Show; The Magazine of the Arts (ISSN: 0037-4296), May, 1962.
LC: PN 1560.S5
ISSN: 0559-9210

Show; The Magazine of the Arts

Oct, 1961 - May, 1965//
(ISSN: 0037-4296)
SEE: SHOW

✣ SHOWCASE WORLD

SUB: "Where stars of tomorrow shine today!"
PUBL: Showcase World, PO Box 9236, North Hollywood, CA 91609.
DESC: Showcasing tomorrow's stars is the publishing niche for this North Hollywood-based publication. Whereas other "casting" magazines provide an interesting look at those who have "made it," *Showcase World* provides an even more interesting look at those who are still "climbing the ladder." With an emphasis on black entertainers (but not exclusive to them), *Showcase World* provides a showcase of promising talent, exploring past and present work, and (importantly for producers), where they can currently be located. Of special note was a segment of the sampled issue entitled "At Your Service," which included these articles; "Getting Your Child in Showbusiness," "Tips to Help Promote Yourself," "How to Produce Low-Budget Films," and "How to Save on Your Music Copyrights." The layout design is nicely accomplished with creative use of white-space, spot color, and well-positioned graphics. Stapled magazine format on coated paper stock (8 ½ x 11 inches / 215 x 280 mm).
DEPT: "Comedy: Laughter in the Rafters," column by Donna Y. Caldwell; "The Rap Corner," column by Doug Deutsch; "Lights On," column by Teal Marchande;

"T.V. News & Views," column by Doug Deutsch; "At Your Service," departmental banner for useful 'how-to' information; "Record Reviews," column by Lumumba T. Khann and Doug Deutsch; "Movie Review," column by Donna Y. Caldwell; "Casting Information," critical information on Hollywood-area television and film productions. (4/5-91).
TYPL: "Oleta Adams," "Sam Harris: A Voice for All Seasons," "Keenen Ivory Wayans: Color Him Real," "Dr. George Hill: The Communicator's Communicator," "Cable Networks Promise Exciting Viewing During TCA Forum." (4/5-91).
SCHL: Bimonthly, 25 pp.
SPAN: ?+

Showmen's Motion Picture Trade Review

May 27, 1933 - Feb 10, 1940//
SEE: SHOWMEN'S TRADE REVIEW

SHOWMEN'S TRADE REVIEW

SUB: "The service paper of the motion picture industry."
PUBL: Showmen's Trade Review, Inc., 1501 Broadway, New York, NY.
DESC: Editor and Publisher Charles E. "Chick" Lewis termed his publication a "Service Paper" for the motion picture industry; providing service to the distribution, promotion, and exhibition of film product in America. Thus, while a good portion of editorial content was industry news, the focus was on film distribution and exhibition, news of importance to the local film entrepreneur. In a sampled issue for 1953, news items included a new Massachusetts' minimum wage law requiring ticket sellers to be paid $.70 per hour; lobby exhibits for motion picture promotion; boxoffice decline caused by television; and the deluge of new technology for stereo sound, three-dimensional effect, panoramic wide screen; and various film formats. The issue cover contained a list of motion pictures reviewed in the current publication. Magazine format (235 cm wide x 310 cm high) on coated paper stock; two-color covers and certain advertisements.
DEPT: "The Editorial Page," column by Chick Lewis; "What's News," 'In the film industry this week'; "News Bulletins," "Film Row," exhibitor-distributor news in various cities; "Film Family Album," engaged, wedded and born to newsbriefs; "Film Events Calendar," "Selling the Picture," 'News and items concerning profitable advertising, publicity and exploitation'; "Exploitorials," promotion suggestions; "Selling Angles," exhibitor successful promotions; "Money Dates for August," anniversary dates for local promotion and tie-ins; "The Box-Office Slant," 'Current and forthcoming feature product reviewed from the theatreman's standpoint'; "Theatre Management," 'Guide to modern methods in the administrative and executive phases of theatre operation'; "Show Sense," column by Jack Jackson; "London Observations," column by Jock MacGregor; "Show Business," 'Coast to coast'; "Variety Club Notes," "Hollywood Newsreel," "Production Parade," column by George Pardon; "Feature Booking Guide," extensive listing of current and forthcoming films; "Views of the New Short Subjects," "Short Subjects Booking Guide," "Pictures Started Last Week." (7-11-53).
TYPL: "Stanley-Warner Cinerama Deal Hinges on U.S. OK in 30 Days," "Keep It 10 Degrees Cooler--and Dry, Medicos Advise," "Thanks Industry for Good May-June Films; Warns on Phoney Stereo Sound," "Flicker Blade-Fixing Increases Light for Drive-In Projection," "Fantastic But True! 3D for $152." (7-11-53).
SCHL: Weekly, 40 pp.
SPAN: May 27, 1933 - Oct 26, 1957//
VARIES
--May 27, 1933 - Feb 10, 1940 as Showmen's Motion Picture Trade Review.
WITH SUPPLEMENT
--Motion Picture Theater, [issued on irregular basis].
ABSORBED BY
--Motion Picture Exhibitor, Nov 6, 1957.
LC: PN 1993.S55

✤ SHUTTERBUG

SUB: "The nationwide marketplace for anything photographic: professional, amateur, antique."
PUBL: Coastal Associates Publishing, 5211 South Washington Ave., PO Box F, Titusville, FL 32781.
DESC: [*Shutterbug Ads*]: This 160-page newsprint tabloid consists almost entirely of advertisements to sell, buy, or trade photographic and video equipment. Approximately one-third of the publication is devoted to display advertising and some articles, with the remainder consisting of individual "want-ads."
DEPT: "Collectors' Corner," "Trade Fair Report," "Minolta Mania," "The Collectable 35," "A Photographic Collectors' Book Space," "Pentax and SLR Notes," "Medium Format Notes and Ideas," "Leica Chatter," "Coming Events," "Ask Video Dave," "What's New." (9-84).
TYPL: None. (9-84).
SCHL: Monthly, 160 pp.
SPAN: 1971+
VARIES
--? - Oct?, 1984 as Shutterbug Ads.

Shutterbug Ads

? - Oct?, 1984//
SEE: SHUTTERBUG

✤ SIDEBAR

PUBL: St. Cloud State University, Department of Mass Communications, Stewert Hall, Room 134, St. Cloud, MN 56301.

DESC: A laboratory publication for students enrolled in journalism classes at St. Cloud State University, this spritely 20-page tabloid speaks of a small, but most vigorous communications program at the university. Articles describe student activities, faculty publications, and general news developments of the department.
DEPT: "Alumni Update." (5-80).
TYPL: "Future Objectives, Departmental Plans Set," "Executive Editor Probes Politics, Press Relationship," "KVSC Seeking Power Increase," "SCSU Students Transmit News to Campus Via Ink, Air Waves." (5-80).
SCHL: Semiyearly, 20 pp.
SPAN: May, 1978+

Sidney Miller's Black Radio Exclusive

Jan 1, 1976? - ?//
(ISSN: 0161-1526)
SEE: BLACK RADIO EXCLUSIVE

✧ SIGHT & SOUND

SUB: "International film quarterly."
SUB: "The film quarterly."
SUB: "Every new film and video reviewed inside."
SUB: "A quarterly review of modern aids to learning."
PUBL: British Film Institute, 21 Stephen St., London W1P 1PL, England.
DESC: For more than 50 years, *Sight & Sound* has retained its position as one of the most literary journals of serious discussion, research and historiography concerning the motion picture medium. Film, and now television and video, have received their due as major entertainment (and, when warranted, as artistic) media. Articles are consistently informative, and display considered thought by writer and editor alike. The publisher fiercely defends the unrestrained nature of editorial content with this statement: "*Sight and Sound* is an independent critical magazine sponsored and published by the British Film Institute." This remains a superb publication covering the international motion picture scene, providing readers with well- written, carefully-considered articles on the "software" side of motion pictures; world commercial, documentary, and experimental/avant-garde product. Lengthy reviews and articles cover historical, psychological, and sociological aspects of film; with a decidedly international flavor. Issues from Spring, 1932 - Autumn, 1933 were published under the auspices of the British Institute of Adult Education. In February, 1991 Editor Philip Dodd announced that sister publication, *Monthly Film Review*, would be absorbed into a newly redesigned monthly *Sight & Sound* "...combining authoritative information and debate on cinema and broadcasting." In May, 1991 the debut issue of the merger was published. The new *Sight & Sound* had the same meticulous, informative critiques of film and television product, but in a creative, updated layout design that uses expanses of white space, with spot and full-color graphics all dressed up in a glossy full-color cover design that is simply stunning. The merging of these two fifty-year-plus publications is certain not to please all readers, but the current result is bound to attract a host of new subscribers to these two classic film and video magazines. For the sampled issue of 1991: stapled magazine format, black ink, spot and full-color page editorial content with full-color cover on coated paper stock (8 ¼ x 11 ¾ inches / 210 x 300 mm).
DEPT: "In the Picture," "Film Reviews," "Book Reviews," "Letters," "Film Guide," current showings. (summer-76). "In the Picture," new international film releases with the publics' and critics' reactions; "Letters" unique for international participation; "Film Guide," new film briefs. (summer-77). "In the Picture," films and filmmakers in the news; "Framed," profile; "Double Takes," review; "Film Reviews," "Book Reviews," "Letters," "On Now," films in current release. (springt-90).
TYPL: "Beauties and the Beast: 'Seven Beauties' and 'Taxi Driver'," "In the American Grain: an Interview With Robert Getchell," "In Latin America They Shoot Film-makers." (summer-76). "I Remember When It was a Cinema," "The Left Bank Revisited," "1930s Newsreels: Censorship and Controversy," "Roots and Angeles: U.S. Television 1976 - 1977." (summer-77). "Fog in the Channel," "A Clockwork Orange," "Altman in Kansas City," "The Worlds of Hou Hsiao-hsien." (spring-90).
SCHL: Quarterly, 65 pp.
SPAN: Spring, 1932+
LC: PN 1993.S56
DD: 791.43/05
ISSN: 0037-4806
ABST: --Art Index (ISSN: 0004-3222)
--Book Review Index (ISSN: 0524-0581)
--Film Literature Index (ISSN: 0093-6758)
--Humanities Index (ISSN: 0095-5981)
--Index to Book Reviews in the Humanities (ISSN: 0073-5892)
--Media Review Digest (ISSN: 0363-7778)

✧ SIGHT AND SOUND MARKETING

SUB: "The magazine of the home entertainment industry." (Jun, 1965 - ?).
PUBL: Drorbaugh Publications, 51 East 42nd St., New York, NY 10017.
DESC: This serial for distributors and retailers of consumer electronics provided descriptions of new products, and discussion of potential trends in consumer sales. What began as a somewhat slim editorial content in 1965 (seven articles in a 30+ page issue), dwindled to four articles in 25+ pages by November, 1971.
DEPT: "Scope," trends; "Sight & Sound Products," reviews; "Tape Recording," new products; "People," newsbriefs. (11-71).

TYPL: "Four-Channel Helps Discs Stage a Comeback," "How will four-Channel Sell?," "Southern Dealers Report," "3M Guides Writers Through High Energy Tape Facilities." (11-71).
SCHL: Eleven issues per year [with combined Nov/Dec issue], 25 pp.
SPAN: Jun, 1965+
LC: HD 9999 .R15 S5
DD: 658.8/09/62138
ISSN: 0037-4814

Sightlines

Sep/Oct, 1967 - Summer?, 1987?//
(ISSN: 0037-4830)
SEE: AFVA BULLETIN

✢ SIGNAL, THE

PUBL: Society of Broadcast Engineers, P.O. Box 50844, Indianapolis, IN 46250.
DESC: This well-designed, eight-page letter serves the members of the Society of Broadcast Engineers. The two-tone color layout uses few graphics, allowing a large amount of engineering news concerning broadcast engineering to be featured.
DEPT: "The Director's Chair," comment; "What's Your C.Q.?," quiz; "Patch Panel," personel briefs; "Sustaining Spotlight," profile; "SBE Sustaining Members," list. (4- 80).
TYPL: "Goodbye, Harold," "Needed: More Training," "FCC Proposes New FM Class and Offers Directional Tips," "New ECYA Rating Book is Good for One Trip to Shangri-la." (4-80).
SCHL: Bimonthly, 8 pp.
SPAN: Jan, 1975+

✢ SIGNALS

PUBL: Alpha Epsilon Rho, 341 Moore Hall, Central Michigan University, Mt. Pleasant, MI 48859.
DESC: *Signals* serves as a national communications vehicle for Alpha Epsilon Rho, the national honorary broadcasting society. With chapters on most large college campuses, it focuses on chapter activity, awards competition, and interviews with industry leaders.
DEPT: "Opening Theme," comment; "Chapter Edits," large segment detailing individual chapter activities, "Outcue," column of commentary by the Alpha Epsilon Rho national secretary. (11-80).
TYPL: "Historical Date Being Sought," "PR is Fine, but Honesty is Better," "Advisory Board Focus," "A Professional With Integrity (11-80).
SCHL: Monthly, 12 pp.
SPAN: ?+

✢ SIGNS OF THE TIMES

SUB: "A journal of advertising, devoted to the interests of the advertiser, the agency and the purveyor of publicity."
SUB: "The national journal of advertising displays."
SUB: "Advertising creates demand."
SUB: "Demand is the very life of commerce."
PUBL: Signs of the Times Publishing Co., 407 Gilbert Ave., Cincinnati, OH 45202.
DESC: "Plain talk, pictures and push are the ammunition for many a successful advertising campaign." This editorial snippet from a 1909 sampled issue very nicely describes the breadth, and vigor of this excellent resource for the advertising community. Catalogues, booklets, folders, mailing devices, blotters, labels, show cards, display devices, interior displays, fixtures, outlining, billposting, bulletins, wall signs, distributing, electrically operated advertising devices, electric outlining and all varied forms of accessories were presented in this monthly serial. New technology and new advertising techniques were hallmarks of each issue. Of special note was the departmental feature, "What Inventors are Doing," concerning mechanical and electrical devices with application to the advertising and retail store trade. *Signs of the Times* provided a wonderful forum for advertising opportunity, and news of the trade. Numerous graphics and equipment schematics. Large magazine format (10 ¼ x 14 ½ inches / 260 x 370 mm).
DEPT: "What the Live Ad Clubs are Doing," "Editorial Announcements," "Printed Novelties and Utility Advertising Helps," 'Embracing catalogues, booklets, folders, mailing devices, blotters, labels, and other supplementary advertising'; "Window Attractions and Show Window Displays," 'Including show cards, display devices, interior displays, fixtures, outline, etc.'; "Outdoor Advertising," 'Embracing billposting, bulletins, wall signs, distributing, etc.'; "Electric Signs," 'Embracing also electrically operated advertising devices, electric outlining and accessories'; "Commercial Signs," "What Inventors are Doing," "Publications," 'The ones worth while, the ones that count, the pick of the pile from an advertising standpoint' selected publications by frequency and geographic location. (3-09).
TYPL: "Direct to the Consumer by Mail," "Some Observations on Automobile Advertising," "Importance of Window Displays," "Department Store Advertising," "Oakland--City of Opportunity." (3-09).
SCHL: Monthly, 40 pp.
SPAN: May, 1906+
LC: TT 360.A4 S6
ISSN: 0037-5063

SILENT PICTURE, THE

SUB: "The only serious quarterly devoted entirely to the art and history of the silent motion picture."
PUBL: First Media Press, 6 East 39th St., New York, NY 10016.

DESC: *The Silent Picture* was an historical narrative on the art, technique and development of the silent motion picture in the United States and England. From its first issue, published in England (1968), to its last issues, published in New York City; the publication strongly fought for copyright release and exhibition of major silent films on 35 mm film stock. *Silent Picture* championed film festivals, catering to its unique audience; and reviewed specific actors, actresses, directors, and genre of the silent film era.
DEPT: "Publisher's Page," editorial; "Correspondence."
TYPL: "Nihilists and Bolsheviks," "Shattered Dreams," "Miriam Cooper, an Interview," "The Gish Pictorial." (#19-74).
SCHL: Quarterly, 50 pp.
SPAN: Winter 1968/69 - 1974//
LC: PN 1993 .S567
DD: 791.43
ISSN: 0037-5209
ABST: --America, History and Life (ISSN: 0002-7065)
--Historical Abstracts. Part A. Modern History Abstracts. (ISSN: 0363-2712)
--Historical Abstracts. Part B. Twentieth Century Abstracts. (ISSN: 0363-2725)

✣ SILVER SCREEN

SUB: "Reflecting the magic of Hollywood."
PUBL: Macfadden Women's Media, 205 E. 42nd St., New York, NY 10017.
DESC: One of the "fanzine" staples of American readers, *Silver Screen* has compiled and published the "latest news" of Hollywood motion picture stars and starlets since its inception in 1930. One sampled issue for 1945 was published on coated paper stock with a variety of duotones, and full color portraits of Hollywood stars Betty Grable, Laraine Day, and Joseph Cotten. Although special departmental articles covered the gossip of the film community, most published pictures were publicity release-oriented, and included a fair number of production stills from current motion pictures. Of note were numerous advertisements for films in current release by major motion picture studios, and full- page, full-color portraits of favorite stars. Thirty years later, in 1976, the sampled issue maintained the color cover, but major changes had been instituted. Editorial content was now black/white, published on newsprint. Some pictures appear to be studio-released, but most are "slice-of-life" pictures, some flattering to the star, and some decidedly unflattering. Typical of "fanzines" articles also feature the stars of television, society and politics and other newsworthy personalities in the public eye. Magazine format, issue for 1945: (8 ⅜ x 11 ¼ inches / 215 x 285 mm), issue for 1976 (8 ⅛ x 10 ⅝ inches / 210 x 270 mm).
DEPT: "Hollywood Earfuls," Hollywood gossip column by Bee Bangs; "Reviews," 'Direct From Hollywood'; "Pictures on the Fire," studio films in production column by Dick Mook; "Topics for Gossip," "We Point With Pride," new motion picture releases; "Data on Discs," record review column by Barry Larkin. (7-45). "Screen Scene," 'The highs and lows of tinseltown' column by Hank Laine; "Stardust," 'Candid interviews with the stars' column by Sheilah Graham; "Filmland Flashes," 'Inside news before it happens'; "Uncensored," 'Straight from the lips of the stars'; "Silverscope," 'What's in the stars for you?', horoscope; "Dear Ms," 'The answers to all your questions'; "Who? What? When? Where?," photo page; "Hot Flashes," 'Caught at the deadline'. (5-76).
TYPL: "Quite a Change for Our Jennifer," "Putting Men Under a Microscope," "Young Man with a Message," "Really the Pigtail Type at Heart!," "Hollywood's Small Fry." (7-45). "Jane Fonda to Lead U.S. Revolution! Nixon Marked for Death!!!," "The Mass Murder of Judy Garland--is Liza Safe?," "Introducing Rene Simard," "Marlon the Magician! How He Brought Hollywood to its Wounded Knees," "An Ultimatum to Cher From Her Fans: 'Go Back to Sonny and be a Good Mother!'." (5-76).
SCHL: Monthly (? - ?); Bimonthly (? - ?); Monthly (?+), 75 pp.
SPAN: Nov, 1930+
LC: PN 1993 .S57
DD: 791.43/05
ISSN: 0037-5365

✣ SIMPSONS ILLUSTRATED

SUB: "Our motto: No refunds."
PUBL: Welsh Publishing Group, Inc., 300 Madison Ave., New York, NY 10017.
DESC: In the premiere issue for Spring, 1991 was the following: "This full-color, glossy magazine appears quarterly and includes: Original comic strips starring your favorite Simpsons; Hidden mysteries behind the making of The Simpsons; Investigative reports probing the soft underbelly of Springfield, USA; Insightful profiles of The Simpsons characters revealing their most hideous secrets, profound thoughts, and possibly recipes; Jokes, advice, weird facts, poetry; And of course, much, much more." For fans of the popular Fox Television Network prime-time series, this is a publication to proudly display on the coffee table. Publisher Welsh obviously has fun with this "fanzine," especially (in the premiere issue) with two wonderful items. The first was "The Simpsons Simplified: A Handy, E-Z-to-Read Guide to the Denizens of Springfield," which linked each character by data lines (such as "Mutual Irritation," or "Fellow Cogs in a Mind-Numbing Bureaucracy"). The second was the "Springfield Shopper," a newsprint tabloid insert subtitled, "Serving Springfield for several years," with assorted news items and advertisements for various Springfield establishments. Suffice to say, if you like the creative, animated television series, you're "gonna love" this magazine. Stapled magazine format, full-color throughout on coated paper stock, and "shopper" insert on newsprint (8 ⅛ x 10 ⅞ inches / 205 x 275 mm).

DEPT: "Junk Mail," letters to the editor; "In the News," 'Our motto: truth is weirder than fiction'; "Behind the Scenes." (spring-91).
TYPL: "Up Close and Personal: On the Fridge," "Bart's Bedtime Story," "The Simpsons Simplified," "Insiders Reveal the Secret to Simpsons' Success: 'They Never Think Evil Thoughts'," "Simpsons Brain-Bustin' Trivia Quiz." (spring-91).
SCHL: Quarterly, 45 pp.
SPAN: Spring, 1991+
ISSN: 1054-8491

✦ SIXSHOOTERS

PUBL: National Press Photographers Association, Region 6, c/o Beverly Bethune, 1050 West Canyon Creek Court, Watkinsville, GA 30677.
DESC: "*SixShooters* is a bimonthly newsletter for photojournalists in Region Six of the National Press Photographers Association." It provides news articles about members' work and experience, with the majority of the editorial content devoted to "Clips," photographs submitted for peer judgement and evaluation for Photographer of the Year competition. Magazine format (8 ½ x 11 inches / 215 x 280 mm); black/white editorial content.
DEPT: "Director's Column," "Tech Talk," column by Ken Hawkins; "Clips," competition. (1/2-90).
TYPL: "And the Wall Came Tumbling Down," "Gary Allen is North Carolina POY," "Chasing Hugo." (1/2-90).
SCHL: Bimonthly, 40 pp.
SPAN: ?+

✦ 60 SECONDS

SUB: "Magazine of the television commercial industry."
PUBL: 60 Seconds, 6610 West Sixth St., Los Angeles, CA 90048.
DESC: In this fascinating publication for the narrow, but dynamic field of television spot production, articles provide interviews and production profiles; with a focus on current spots in production. It contains numerous advertisements by available production houses and companies. Many graphics; some in color.
DEPT: "Short Takes," 'a compilation of current commercial productions;' "Update," newsbriefs; "Equipment," review; "Music," 'survey of current compositions;' "Animation," "Golden Moments." (4-81).
TYPL: "Grooming 'Beautiful People' for Advertising," "Making Heads & Tails & Profits Out of Advertising and Publicity," "Rhinestone's are Marions Best Friend," "Special Effects Creates New Commercial Image for Pontiac." (4-81).
SCHL: Monthly, 40 pp.
SPAN: Dec, 1980+
ISSN: 0273-9291

✦ SMALL PRESS

SUB: "The magazine for independent / in-home / desktop publishing."
SUB: "The magazine of independent book publishing."
SUB: "The magazine & book review of independent publishing."
PUBL: Meckler Corporation, 11 Ferry Lane West, Westport, CT 06880.
DESC: For the independent publisher, *Small Press* provides a fount of information, news, and advice for the successful publishing operation. Articles detail issues of pragmatic concern: how many copies should one order on the first press run; understanding the relationship between publisher and distributor; or the basics of book covers, bindings and marketing. In an extensive book review section outside reviewers critique independent publications. This is foremost a resource for the independent publisher, supporting the process of small book runs in today's competitive market. It is highly recommended. For the sampled issue of 1989: Black/white editorial content with two-color cover all on coated paper stock in stapled magazine format (8 ¼ x 11 inches / 210 x 280 mm).
DEPT: "Noteworthy," newsbriefs; "Rights Marketplace," column by Rosemary Pettit; "Books For the Trade," column by John Kremer; "On the Desktop," column by Richard D. Johnson; "Continuations," column by Richard R. Centing; "Book Review," very large section of recent publications from independent publishers; "Book Review Directory," publishers from books reviewed; "Margins," column by George Myers. (12-89).
TYPL: "Performance Arts Publishers: A Sampling From an Unorthodox Community," "A Primer for Small-Press Journal Editors," "Bottom Lines: Calculating the Number of Copies in the First Print Order." (12-89).
SCHL: Bimonthly, 70 pp.
SPAN: Sep/Oct, 1983+
LC: Z 231.5 .L5 S58
DD: 070.5
ISSN: 0000-0485
ABST: --Book Review Index (ISSN: 0524-0581)

✦ SMALL PRESS BOOK REVIEW, THE

SUB: "A review of books from independent and smaller presses."
PUBL: Greenfield Press, PO Box 176, Southport, CT 06490.
DESC: *The Small Press Book Review* brings to the attention of librarians, booksellers, and the reading public noteworthy books, audiocassettes, videocassettes, and periodicals from small presses. Material reviewed is selected not only for its merit in its respective field, but for the standard of writing, editing, design, and production which is relevant to it. Except for a few cases, books reviewed are from presses publishing fewer than thirty titles per year, although most publish fewer than ten. Books from smaller university presses that are not overly specialized or academic are also

reviewed. Similarly, other material is from small, independent publishers." This is primarily a book review service for small press publishers, who oftentimes cannot match the marketing budgets of larger, more powerful publishing concerns. Magazine format; stapled and typeset on creme-color paper stock; some advertising with graphics.

DEPT: "Editor's Letter," "News Notes." (1/2-90).
TYPL: [No articles--primarily book reviews]. (1/2-90).
SCHL: Bimonthly, 25 pp.
SPAN: Jul/Aug, 1985+
LC: Z 1215 .S6
DD: 015.73/034
ISSN: 8756-7202
ABST: --Book Review Index (ISSN: 0524-0581)
--New Periodicals Index

✥ SMASH HITS

SUB: "Gorgeous guys, sizzling secrets!"
PUBL: Pilot Communications, Inc., 25 West 39th St., New York, NY 10018.
DESC: "Everyone agrees! *HOT!* has it all!! All the best stories! All the latest gossip! All the greatest color pinups! And all your Number One faves: New Kids on the Block, Johnny Depp, Neil Patrick Harris and many more!" This "teenzine" is aimed at female teen readers, providing "inside" news, information, biographies and publicity of several dozen (mostly male) young film/television stars. There is a minimum of advertising, with over 18 full-page color "pinups" of favorite stars, including front inside cover, and inside/back cover. Articles are trendy, providing information on these young stars' favorite food, recreation, and motion picture or television program plans for the future. Magazine format; printed two-color throughout on newsprint; pinup pictures are full color on coated stock. NOTE: Although both cover and masthead show title *HOT Magazine*, most bibliographic resources associate ISSN: 0899-9392 with the title *Smash Hits* by the same publisher.
DEPT: "Hot Stuff," letters; "Hot Gossip," column by Simone; "Letter Connection," pen pal listing; "Dear Kristi," Q&A on young stars column by Kristi; "Star Link," reader's messages to young stars; "Star Guide," young star addresses; "The Hot! Charts," hottest young film and television stars; "Artists Corner!," reader submissions of favorite stars; "Music Round Up!," 'Here's the latest in the world of rock n' roll!'; "Superstars," 'Your planetary predictions by Alexandria!'; "Lou's Views!," 'It's the pictures the stars begged us not to print!' column by Lou Palu. (summer-90).
TYPL: "Mark-Paul Gosselaar Speaks!," "The Newest Kid on the Block!," "The Real Truth About Johnny Depp!," "Kirk Cameron, You Know What He Likes!!," "Paula Abdul's a Workaholic!" (summer-90).
SCHL: Ten issues per year [None published in Apr or Sep], 85 pp.
SPAN: 198u+
VARIES
--? - ? as Star Hits (ISSN: 8750-7234).

DD: 784
ISSN: 0899-9392

✥ SMPTE JOURNAL

SUB: "Published by the Society of Motion Picture and Television Engineers, Inc."
SUB: "Publication of the Society of Motion Picture and Television Engineers."
PUBL: Society of Motion Picture and Television Engineers, 595 West Hartsdale Ave., White Plains, NY 10607.
DESC: "The *SMPTE Journal* publishes papers on technological, engineering, and scientific developments in motion pictures, television and related fields. ...The *Journal*'s primary objective is to follow the progress of motion-picture and television engineering and developments in allied fields." For the area of technolgical developments in the motion picture and television industry, *SMPTE Journal* is the preeminent publication. Articles are consistently informative, authoritative, and visually explanatory of whatever new technology is under discussion. The layout design of this journal is dynamic. One can discard the notion that all scientific/academic journals are stuffy, text-like publications when reading the *SMPTE Journal*. Articles contain a pleasing mixture of schematics, charts and graphic illustrations. In the sampled issue for 1991 there was a delightful surprise in the reprinting of a December, 1938 article on "Technicolor Adventures in Cinemaland," providing a very detailed developmental history of the process and its acceptance by the motion picture community. A 1975 *Journal* statement said: "The society today is the result of over fifty- eight years of achievement and leadership. Its members are engineers, scientists and technicians skilled in every branch of motion pictures, television, instrumentation, and high-speed photography." That remains so today, and makes this journal "must" reading for those following technological developments in American mass communications. Among a number of notable departmental features is "Abstracts of Papers from Other Journals," a wonderful overview of other work in progress or presented in other fields or countries relevant to the work of this journal. Of special consideration is the fact that most American technical standards are proposed/published here. It assumes some technical knowledge, but is very highly recommended to all whose livlihood depends upon technologically-based media. For the sampled issue of 1991: perfect-bound magazine format; black ink editorial content (with some full- color advertisements), with two-color ink cover all on coated paper stock (8 $\frac{1}{8}$ x 10 $\frac{7}{8}$ inches / 205 x 275 mm).
DEPT: "Education, Industry News," newsbriefs of upcoming seminars; "Books, Booklets and Brochures," available on technical issues; "New Products and Developments," briefs. (8-75). "Calendar," "Highlights," article synopses; "Section Meetings," concerning international meetings; "News," news items; "Obituar-

ies," "Engineering News," "Abstracts of Papers From Other Journals," excellent overview of other work; "New Products." (3-91).
TYPL: "ST 8: a New Agfa-Gevaert Sound Negative Film Especially Suitable for Super-8," "A Simple, Low-Cost Zero-G Cloud-Physics Camera and Optics System," "The Use of Metal Hallide Lamps on Exteriors." (8-75). "High-Resolution Electronic Intermediate System for Motion-Picture Film," "A Real-Time Video Mapping and Manipulation System," "The Accordion Charge-Transfer Mechanism: A New Development of the Frame-Transfer CCD Image Sensor," "A Hi-Vision VTR for Industrial Applications Using a ½-Inch Videocassette," "Digital Keyers in Video Switchers and Effects Systems." (3-91).
SCHL: Monthly, 110 pp.
SPAN: Jul, 1916+
VARIES
--Jul, 1916 as Incorporation and Bylaws.
--Oct, 1916 - May, 1929 as Transactions.
--1930 - 1949 as Journal of the Society of Motion Picture Engineers.
--1950 - 1953 as Journal of the Society of Motion Picture and Television Engineers.
--Jan, 1954 - Dec, 1954 as Journal.
--Jan, 1955 - Dec, 1955 as SMPTE Journal (ISSN: 0898-0438).
--Jan, 1956 - Dec, 1975 as Journal of the SMPTE (ISSN: 0361-4573).
LC: TR 845.S6
DD: 778.5/05
ISSN: 0036-1682
ABST: --Applied Science and Technology Index (ISSN: 0003-6986)
--Communication Abstracts
--Computer & Control Abstracts (ISSN: 0036-8113)
--Electrical & Electronics Abstracts (ISSN: 0036-8105)
--Engineering Index Annual (ISSN: 0360-8557)
--Engineering Index Bioengineering Abstracts (ISSN: 0736-6213)
--Engineering Index Energy Abstracts (ISSN: 0093-8408)
--Engineering Index Monthly (ISSN: 0013-7960)
--Excerpta Medica
--Film Literature Index (ISSN: 0093-6758)
--International Aerospace Abstracts (ISSN: 0020-5842)
--Physics Abstracts. Science Abstracts. Series A. (ISSN: 0036-8091)
--Reference Sources (ISSN: 0163-3546)

SMPTE Journal
Jan, 1955 - Dec, 1955//
(ISSN: 0898-0438)
SEE: SMPTE JOURNAL

✣ SOAP OPERA DIGEST
SUB: "All the stories from all the shows."
PUBL: S.O.D. Publishing, 420 Lexington Ave, New York, NY 10017.
DESC: "Here's the sensational monthly digest magazine with all the stories from all 14 day-time serials. Every issue brings you right up to date with all the events and happenings of every major show. In easy to read digest form, you get the day-by-day details ...the suspense ...the humor ...the thrills and heart-trobs of these true-to-life dramas." This 140-page monthly publication is filled with stories concerning soap stars, program story abstracts, additional articles of interest. The small format periodical's greatest value probably lies in monthly story synopses of 14 popular television soaps; a list that begins with, "All My Children" and ends with, "The Young and the Restless." For the sampled issue of 1991: stapled small-digest size magazine, black ink, spot and full-color pages on coated paper stock, with selected pages on uncoated paper stock (5 ⅛ x 7 ½ inches / 130 x 190 mm).
DEPT: "Hollywood Happenings," column by Billie Singer; "New York News," column by Sue Facter; "Veleka Advises," love-and-life advice; "Fan Club News," briefs; "Soaps and the Issues," fascinating continuing series on serious issues explored in current soap opera programs; "All My Children," program abstract; "Another World," abstract; "Another World," abstract; "As the World Turns," abstract; "Days of Our Lives," abstract; "The Doctors," abstract; "Edge of Night," abstract; "For Richer, for Poorer," abstract; "General Hospital," abstract; "Guiding Light," abstract; "Love of Life," abstract; "One Life to Live," abstract; "Ryans Hope," abstract; "Search for tomorrow," abstract; "The Young and the Restless," abstract. (5-78). "Late-Breaking News," "VCR Alert," 'A handy guide to must-see episodes'; "Comings and Goings," "New York Notebook," personality column by Jason Bonderoff; "Prime Time Update," commentary column by Roy Soleil; "Status Chart of On-Screen Happenings," 'Want to know what's been going on with whom lately? We've tallied up the statistics from all the shows'; "Editor's Note," commentary column by Meredith Berlin; "For the Record," "Trivia Questions," "Synopses Section," extensive section on 'What happened, what's happening, what will happen'; "Thumbs Up! Thumbs Down!," 'Our resident critic hands out her latest blue ribbons and booby prizes for the best and worst achievements on soaps'; "Crossword," "Network Addresses," "Behind the Scene," 'we give you backstage accounts of how soaps' most intriguing scenes come to life' column by Kate Forsyth; "Ask Us," reader submitted Q&A; "Sound Off," letters; "How Much Does It Really Cost?," the price of props; "Last Licks," portrait; "Classic Lines," 'Witty repartees, comical comebacks and sarcastic backbiting contribute to soaps' best dialogue'. (4-30-91).
TYPL: "Josh Taylor: He's Not Only an Actor, He7s a Lawyer," "She's Not Afraid of Challenges," "Jacquie Cortney Goes Antiquing." (5-78). "Why Actors Re-

ally Left Their Shows," "Family Tree," "Star Looks," "Where Are Those Characters Now?," "Facing Life." (4-30-91).
SCHL: Monthly (1975 - 1978); Biweekly (1978 - 1979); Triweekly (1979 - Jul 15, 1980); Biweekly (Aug 5, 1980+), 140 pp.
SPAN: Dec, 1975+
DD: 791
ISSN: 0164-3584

✤ SOAP OPERA PEOPLE

PUBL: Tempo Publishing Company, Inc., 475 Park Avenue South, Suite 2201, New York, NY 10016.
DESC: "Want to find out everything about your favorite stars? Read the magazine that has more exclusive interviews than any of the others!" *Soap Opera People* is about the stars and personalities of this television genre in an interview format. Indeed, what emerges from the ten-plus features per issue, is a group of bright, articulate actors and actresses who are in control of their craft, who can provide a detached analysis of their favorite characterizations, and who show an appreciation of their fans. This publication provides a common meeting ground for those who work in, and watch television soap opera programs. Magazine format (7 ⅞ x 10 ¾ inches / 200 x 275 mm); spot color. Full color covers on coated paper stock, editorial content on uncoated paper stock.
DEPT: "From the Editor's Desk," "Soaping It Up!," 'Behind the scenes from coast-to-coast!' column by Lillian Smith (and Sheila Steinbach); "Fans Who Have Met Their Favorite Stars Tell All About It!," letters; "It's Your Turn," questionaire; "Post Office," 'Where every letter is a special delivery'. (10-90).
TYPL: "Peter Reckell: On His Life, Marriage & Days," "The Guiding Light Super Puzzle," "Rena Sofer: I'm Much Happier Where I am Now," "Brad Lockerman: Lightning has Struck Twice in My Life," "GH's Kristina Malandro & Jack Wagner: She's the Lady of His Heart!" (10-90).
SCHL: Bimonthly, 80 pp.
SPAN: Dec?, 1984+

✤ SOAP OPERA STARS

PUBL: Sterlings Magazines, Inc., 355 Lexington Ave., New York, NY 10017.
DESC: "Every issue jam-packed with these exciting features: All the Stars, All the Shows, Behind-the-scene-news, Fan club info, Storyline up-date- -who'll stay & who'll go, Real-life interviews, New York & Hollywood gossip, Latest cast lists, Viewer poll--vote for your favorites, Exclusive photos--at home, backstage, on set & partying!" Daytime television, and the "soaps" in particular, have loyal viewer support, but especially in the decades of the eighties and nineties. *Soap Opera Stars* provides what fans want: news of the artists, both on and off stage; and details of their lives. Typical articles were, "Fifty Facts About Stephen Nichols & Mary Beth Evans," or "White Knights and Their Damsels in Distress." Soap opera staples ("One Life to Live," "Days of Our Lives," "All My Children," "Guiding Light," "Loving," "General Hospital," "As the World Turns," and "Generations"), each had an artist interview/profile in the sampled issue. This publication had no advertising on any of the four cover pages, instead devoting two of those pages to full page color pictures of television stars. Editorial content published on newsprint; magazine format (8 x 10 ⅞ inches / 205 x 275 mm).
DEPT: "Have You Heard?," 'The word from NY and LA'; "Who's News in Hollywood," column by Dick McInnes; "New York Notes," column by Peter J. Black; "What's Cookin'?," 'Four daytime stars share their favorite recipes with you'; "Letter box," letters; "Fan Club File," address list; "Showstoppers," latebreaking newsbriefs. (7-90).
TYPL: "Passionate Partners," "Susan Seaforth Hayes: 'I'm Back Where I Belong'," "Soap Life Can be a Drag!!," "Torn Between Two Brothers," "Hell-Bent on Happiness." (7-90).
SCHL: Monthly (? - ?); Bimonthly (Jul, 1984+), 75 pp.
SPAN: Jan, 1976+
ISSN: 0199-3003

✤ SOAP OPERA TIME

SUB: "Stars, stories, gossip."
PUBL: Swank Magazine Corporation, 888 Seventh Ave., New York, NY 10019.
DESC: *Soap Opera Time*, like several other publications of daytime television, is supportive of the artists and programs that constitute soap opera television on the American networks. Typical of the questions asked in the "Information Please" department of the serial was: "Do daytime stars enjoy signing autographs for their fans?" "Is it true that nighttime television newcomer Richard Hatch got his start on 'All My Children'?" "How many times has Kim Dixon been married on 'As the World Turns'?," or 'The character relationships on 'Another World' are so complex that it's difficult to keep track of everyone. How, for example, is Aunt Liz related to the rest of the Matthews family?" There are many pictures of soap opera stars signing autographs for their fans, and seeming to enjoy their contact with their public. One interesting departmental feature is "Soap Opera Family Series," wherein the historical plotlines unfolded to show the developmental relationship between two families on a given soap opera series. In one sampled issue, the Cory and Carrington families were profiled on "Another World." Published on newsprint, magazine format (8 ⅛ x 10 ⅞ inches / 205 x 270 mm).
DEPT: "Looking Back," daytime stars moved to nighttime television programs; "Information Please," reader Q&A column; "The Hot Spot," news of soap opera stars; "News in a Nutshell," soap artist newsbriefs. (2-77).

TYPL: "Brenda Dickson Talks About Her Broken Engagement," "A Mary Hartman Special: Loretta in Concert!," "Who's Who on All My Children," "I Don't Believe in Worrying About the Future," "Clothes Make the Man!" (2-77).
SCHL: Bimonthly, 70 pp.
SPAN: Oct/Nov, 1976+?

✢ SOAP OPERA UPDATE

SUB: "The magazine of the stars & stories."
PUBL: Soap Opera Update Magazine, Inc., 158 Linwood Plaza, Fort Lee, NJ 07024.
DESC: "Do you want to know the latest news and gossip about the shows you watch? Do you want an insider's sneak peek into the future storylines from those in the know? Do you look for exclusive in-depth interviews and photos? Do you want to know more about the characters and the stars who play them? Do you want an upscale, full-color magazine that's your hotline to every soap opera?" If the answer to all of these questions is "yes," then *Soap Opera Update* offers itself as a beautiful full-color publication dedicated to "...today's sophisticated soap fan." *Soap Opera Update* is the only full-sized, full-color magazine in its field. Our editors work diligently to give you the most in-depth interviews, exclusive photos, backstage info, special sneak previews and the hottest news on all the stars and shows. Each and every story is verified at its source, so you'll get straight facts you can count on, NOT simply rumors or tabloid teasers. Each issue of *Soap Opera Update* is packed with what you've missed and what lies ahead on every soap, intimate dialogue with the stars and headwriters, exclusive centerfolds and so much more!" Breezy layout style and full-color printing enhances the editorial content of this biweekly publication. Magazine format (8 x 10 ⅞ inches / 205 x 275 mm).
DEPT: "What's On Your Mind?," letters; "Scene Around Town," soap opera stars off stage; "Keepin' an Eye On," profile; "In & Out," 'Who's in and who's out'; "Sneak Peek," 'The inside scoop on What Lies Ahead!'; "The Big Picture," center photo layout; "On the Couch," 'A psychotherapist analyzes the soaps'; "What You Missed!," 'Complete story summaries from all the shows!'; "It's a Question of Character," 'A chance to ask whatever you wish!'; "Update... Update...," newsbriefs; "Trade Secrets," 'Tidbits and tales from behind the scenes!'. (10-9-89).
TYPL: "Observations of a Young & Restless Cover Shoot," "Master Manipulator," "It's All Greek to B&B," "The Torment and Trauma of Sarah." (10-9-89).
SCHL: Eighteen issues per year, 65 pp.
SPAN: Apr 11, 1988+
DD: 791 11
ISSN: 0898-1485

✢ SOAP OPERA WEEKLY

PUBL: News America Publishing Incorporated, 1211 Avenue of the Americas, New York, NY 10036.
DESC: This K.R. Murdoch publication is a favorite among soap opera fans. The full-color, newsprint tabloid has a number of departmental features; latest gossip, capsule summaries of upcoming (and past) soap opera plots, and numerous color pictures of favorite stars. Good marketing techniques are evident in the very unusual mix of articles. For the youthful audience, there are "typical" articles of contemporary programs: for the older audience segment, there is the very atypical approach of publishing articles of historical soap operas, some of these harkening back to the 1930s era. This publication knows its audiences, and advertisers should follow shortly. For the sampled 1990 issue: Stapled tabloid magazine format with full-color graphics and cover on uncoated paper stock (9 ⅞ x 11 ¾ inches / 250 x 295 mm).
DEPT: "The News," "Speaking My Mind," editorial; "Sneak Peeks," 'Previews of all your favorite shows'; "Last Week," plot capsules; "Public Opinion," 'Our readers tell us what's on their minds'; "The Gossip," east coast column by Pat Sellers; "The Gossip," west coast column by Janet Di Lauro; "Life Story of a Soap," historical profile; "A Reader's View," reader guest commentary; "Viewers' Voice," 'Who's hot & who's not?'; "Critical Condition," column by Marlena de Lacroix; "Any Questions?," 'You ask the questions, we get the answers'; "Moonlighting," 'Where your favorite stars are shining after work'; "Who's New," new soap opera faces; "Afterlife," life after acting in soap operas; "Pet Patter," pets of the soap opera stars; "Dressed For Success," 'Celebrities offscreen--the bad, the bold, the beautiful!'; "This Week in Soap History," unique look back at historical plots; "Hit or Miss," 'On the mark or off the track, our editors make the call'; "Soap Scramblers," crossword puzzle; "Your Lucky Stars," horoscope; "Photo Finish," pictorial themed layout. (3-20-90).
TYPL: "Up Close And Personal: Bob Woods is Loving Life," "The Daytime Dream Machine: Soap Opera Casting," "When the Soaps Went to War. . .And Then Came Home Again," "Melody Thomas Scott: TV Star Mom." (3-20-90).
SCHL: Weekly, 50 pp.
SPAN: Nov 21, 1989+
DD: 791 11
ISSN: 1047-7128

Social Science Information Studies

? - Feb?, 1986//
(ISSN: 0143-6236)
SEE: INTERNATIONAL JOURNAL OF INFORMATION MANAGEMENT

✢ SOCIAL SCIENCE MONITOR

SUB: "For public relations and advertising executives."

PUBL: Communication Research Associates, Suite 500, 7100 Baltimore Blvd., College Park, MD 20740.
DESC: *Social Science Monitor* is a four-page, monthly, typewritten newsletter aimed at the advertising executive; although it is also helpful to those outside the advertising/public relations field. Each issue tends to bring together a cluster of ideas in a particular field, such as; "Role of the Source in News Communications," "The Effectiveness of Advertising," "Communicating to Ethnic Minorities," or "Life in the Twenty-First Century." Editor Ray Hiebert brings a bright, witty style to his compilation of articles culled from numerous publications.
DEPT: None. (7-84).
TYPL: "Advertising is Not Perceived as Being Informative," "Humor May Aid Advertising Effectiveness, but Only in Specific Conditions," "Sexually Suggestive Ads May Increase Attention, but Decrease Recall," "Advertising Can Affect the Drinking Habits of Teenagers." (7-84).
SCHL: Monthly, 4 pp.
SPAN: Jan, 1979+
ISSN: 0195-7791

✤ SOCIETY FOR ANIMATION STUDIES NEWSLETTER, THE

PUBL: Society for Animation Studies, American Animation Institute, 4729 Lankershim Blvd., North Hollywood, CA 91602-1864.
DESC: This is the membership newsletter for the Society for Animation Studies, an organization concerned with the broad-based approach to animation on an international basis. A listing of paper categories for an upcoming conference may best describe the breadth and depth of this society: National Cinemas, The Globalization of Animation, Canon Formation, Modes of Production, Commerce and Art, Theories of Animation, Fleischer Studios, Inc., Canadian Animation, Television, Prehistory, Regionalism, Gender Issues, Narrative, East European Animation, Melodrama and Musicals, Fine Arts (and) Movie and Television Animated Commercials. The book and film reviews on the broad field of animation enhance, and expand the editorial content of an already interesting and serious approach to the art and technique of animation. Typeset newsletter format; no graphics.
DEPT: "Member Notes," personnel newsbriefs. (1/2-90).
TYPL: "2nd Conference Set for October 5-7, 1990," "Looking Ahead to Ottawa: What Makes a Good Conference Paper?," "Canemaker Animation Collection Opens at NYU." (1/2-90).
SCHL: Five issues per year, 4 pp.
SPAN: Jan/Feb, 1988+

Society of Cinematologists. Journal.
? - ?//
SEE: CINEMA JOURNAL

Society of Film Teachers. Bulletin
? - ?//
SEE: SCREEN

✤ SOSYAL! MAGAZINE

SUB: "Showbiz magazine."
PUBL: Pretiprint Press, 54 Montreal St., Cubao, Quezon City, Phillipines.
DESC: Similar in scope, format and editorial content to other Phillipine fan publications, *Sosyal! Magazine* covers young stars and starlets within the fields of motion pictures, television, and recording; with a specific focus on Phillipine artists. Editorial content is a mixture of Tagalog and English, but with a greater emphasis on English than other, similar Phillipine fan publications. *Sosyal! Magazine* also uses more English language for article titles. Of special note are two back-page departmental features for subscribers. The first, "Getting to Know You," is a reader forum for exchanging pen pal information; while the second, "An Affair to Remember," is a reader-submitted column of poetry. Subscribers are asked: "If you have an affair to remember and you're the one who's got the words and the touch, mail to us your poems or songs and let the world share that feeling." For sampled issue of September, 1986: editorial content is black/white with spot color on newsprint, full-color covers on coated paper stock; no advertising (11 x 12 ⅞ inches / 280 x 325 mm).
DEPT: "Maskara," personality news and comment column by Inday Badiday; "Sosyal Chatterbox," personality news column by Chito P. Alcid; "Sounds Familiar," audio recording news column by Celso A. Sabinano; "Women & the Home," food menues and recipes; "Prime Time," television programming review and commentary column by Tonee Coraza; "Dear Sosyal," letters to the editor; "Getting to Know You," penpal listing column by Mhalou Gutierrez; "An Affair to Remember," reader-submitted poetry. (9-23-86).
TYPL: "Marami ka ngang pera, wala ka namang love, wala ring kuwenta, di ba Janice?," "Dolphy & Panchito: Natural Comedians at A-1 Actors!," "Hongkong Holiday for Richard and Snooky," "Nora Aunor Talks About Lotlot," "Susan Roces: From Comedy to Drama." (9-23-86).
SCHL: Weekly, 35 pp.
SPAN: Feb 4, 1986+
ISSN: 0116-2446

Sound
Oct, 1970 - Oct, 1973//
(ISSN: 0703-6930)
SEE: SOUND & VISION

✣ SOUND & IMAGE

SUB: "From the editors of Stereo Review."
PUBL: Diamandis Communications, Inc., 1633 Broadway, New York, NY 10019.
DESC: *Stereo Review* publisher, Winston (Troy) Johnson, described this new publication: "*Stereo Review* deals with components--the latest CD player or the latest speaker. It is for people who already understand the terminology. *Sound & Image* will be for people who want quality but who don't want to spend as much time with the technical side. *Sound & Image* will put together entire systems. The photographs will be very important. We'll photograph so people will know how it looks in an upscale home." This classy serial showcases not only new technology for the upscale home consumer, but also the home settings architecturally designed and constructed for best application of that technology. Equipment utilized is top-of-the-line, with the latest electronic developments. *Sound & Image* reflects the same care and thoughtful consideration of its sister publication, *Stereo Review*, and therefore should find a ready audience for future issues. Indicative of its readership, prices are rarely mentioned: after all, "if you have to ask...". For the sampled issue of 1990: full color graphics throughout on coated paper stock in a perfect-bound magazine format (7 ⅞ x 10 ½ inches / 200 x 265 mm).
DEPT: "A/V," newsbriefs; "Sports on Video," review; "Showroom," new technology; "Life Styles," "Inside Story," "Hands On," equipment review. (summer-90).
TYPL: "The War at Home," "Haven in the Hamptons," "Working with a Custom Installer," "New York City Chic." (summer-90).
SCHL: Quarterly, 180 pp.
SPAN: Summer, 1990+
DD: 790 11
ISSN: 1050-2777

Sound & Picture Tape Recording Magazine

Apr, 1971 - Sep/Oct, 1973//
SEE: TAPE

✣ SOUND & VISION

SUB: "Canada's electronic lifestyle magazine."
SUB: "Canada's electronic entertainment magazine."
PUBL: 846342 Ontario, Ltd., 99 Atlantic Ave., Suite 302, Toronto, Ontario M6K 3J8 Canada.
DESC: An in-magazine promotion asked: "Why not have a representative of the Canadian government deliver *Sound & Vision* right to your home? *Sound & Vision Magazine* will keep you abreast of the latest developments in Home Entertainment. Whether you're shopping for hi-fi or video equipment or simply want maximum enjoyment from your existing home entertainment center, *Sound & Vision* will deliver. ...Whether you're shopping for new equipment or simply want to fine-tune your existing system, our experts can help. How-to articles, new product information, test reports, and the latest record, CD and video movie reviews make sure you get the most for your home entertainment dollar." This publication is Canadian, but the superb, articulate reviews, critique and discussions would make it welcomed in any home where the reader takes his/her audio/video system seriously. The credentials of the editorial review staff are outstanding, from acoustical authorities to recording engineers; electronic designers to audio/video producers. This is one publication that is sure to please any serious student of the art and technique of audio/video equipment for the home. Of special note is an annual "Audio/Video Preview" issue each fall which provides a succinct features list of equipment currently on the market. Magazine format with full-color advertising throughout; published on coated paper stock (8 ⅛ x 10 ⅞ inches / 205 x 275 mm).
DEPT: "Audio Tape," "Cartridges, Phono," "Cassette & DAT Decks," "CD Players, Changers, Portables, D/A Converters," "Equalizers," "Headphones," "Integrated Amplifiers," "Loudspeakers," "Microphones," "Miscellaneous Audio Products," "One-Brand Rack/Mini Component Systems," "Open Reel (Reel-to-Reel) Tape Decks," "Power Amplifiers," "Preamplifiers," "Receivers," "Record, CD & Tape Care Products," "Surround Sound/Ambience Processors," "Tonearms," "Tuners," "Turntables," "Videodisc (Laservision) Combi Players," "Camcorders," "Projection TVs," "Surround Sound/Ambience Processors," "TV Consoles (floor-standing)," "TV Monitor/Receivers, Portable TV," "Video Accessories," "VCRs (Videocassette Recorders)," "Vide Tape." (9/10-90).
TYPL: "A Thinking Man's Guide to Buying a CD Player," "CD Listening Fatigue: Real or Imaginary?," "Amplifier Damping Factor: Is it Important?," "New Tests for Low-Level Linearity: How Good are the New 18-Bit Players?" (8-88). None. (9/10-90).
SCHL: Monthly, 140 pp.
SPAN: Oct, 1970+
VARIES
--Oct, 1970 - Oct, 1973 as Sound (ISSN: 0703-6930).
--Nov, 1973 - Nov/Dec, 1984 as Sound Canada (ISSN: 0383-6908).
ABSORBED
--Audio Video Canada (ISSN: 0710-4413).
DD: 338.4/762138/0971
ISSN: 0829-3678

SOUND AND VISION BROADCASTING

SUB: "Information, practice, technique."
PUBL: Marconi Communication Systems, Broadcasting Division, Chelmsford, England.
DESC: This is a promotional organ for the purpose of showcasing Marconi Communication Systems radio and television equipment in use world-wide. Approxi-

mately one-half the articles pertain to British broadcasting, and half to world and international broadcasting; all of which, of course, are utilizing Marconi equipment in some fashion. Some articles on programming are also included. Printed in English with summaries in French, German, and Spanish. Magazine format; graphics.
DEPT: "On the Air," comment. (spring-61).
TYPL: "TV Western Series Produced on Tape," "Technical Facilities for Sound Effects," "Colour Medical Television in Australia," "The Operation of Transmitters in Parallel," "A Survey of Simplified Image Orthicon Operation." (spring-61).
SCHL: Four issues per year (1970 - 1971); Three issues per year (1971 - ?)
SPAN: Spring, 1960 - 1973//
MERGED WITH
--Point to Point Communication (ISSN: 0032-2334) (and) Communication Systems (to form) Communication & Broadcasting (ISSN: 0305-3601), 1974.
LC: TK6570 .B7S65
ISSN: 0038-1829

Sound Blast

? - Feb?, 1989//
SEE: PRODUCTION SOUND REPORT

Sound Canada

Nov, 1973 - Nov/Dec, 1984//
(ISSN: 0383-6908)
SEE: SOUND & VISION

✤ SOUND MANAGEMENT

SUB: "Published for RAB Members."
SUB: "How retailers sell items and images on radio."
PUBL: Radio Advertising Bureau, 304 Park Avenue South, New York, NY 10010.
DESC: [*Ear*]: This four-page newsletter is published by the Radio Advertising Bureau with one thought in mind; to reprint success stories of retail merchants' usage of radio as a sales medium. Full script and production pictures accompany most stories. For the sampled issues of 1977: black ink on coated paper stock.
DESC: [*Sound Management*]: Since advertising sales is at the profit-making heart of every commercial radio station, *Sound Management* should be obligatory reading for the commercial radio station manager, sales manager, and staff. No matter what size radio market, Radio Advertising Bureau's *Sound Management* has a host of marketing and promotional ideas that will enhance, promote, and foster greater sales of radio operations. This is a magazine of ideas; on how to be competitive in an increasingly competitive media world. Articles provide case histories, interviews with major radio advertisers, and ways to get a larger market share of the advertising dollar. It is difficult to consider a commercial radio station who is not a member of RAB, and therefore a subscriber to *Sound Management*. Magazine format; numerous graphics.
DEPT: None. (10-77). "Publisher's Letter," "Radio Voices," letters; "Middle Market Manager," "Large Market Manager," "Small Market Manager," "On the Street," marketing and consumer news of interest to radio sales; "On the Books," reviews; "Data Bank," useful statistics for radio promotion/sales in pie chart/bar graph format. (7/8-89).
TYPL: "Napoleon Nash...Sales Up 60 Per Cent with Radio," "Realtor Converted to Year 'Round Radio after 'Uncanny' Results," "Belk Matthews Ups Radio After Filling Up Drapery Clinic." (10-77). "Dealers Claim: Automakers Hold the High Cards," "Better Performance Reviews," "Copywriting Teamwork," "The Brave New Media World," "Killing Pirate Radio Sales," "Selling Promotions That Sell." (7/8-89).
SCHL: Monthly [bimonthly Jul/Aug and Dec/Jan], 35 pp.
SPAN: Nov, 1984+
VARIES
--? - ? as Ear.
DD: 384 11
ISSN: 8755-0555

SOUND STAGE

PUBL: Sound Stage, 7046 Hollywood Blvd., Hollywood, CA 90028.
DESC: In the fourth issue of this magazine, Publisher Marvin Miller noted: "This bigger and better June issue of *Sound Stage* is presented with pride, and we deem it justifiable pride. The justification comes from the magnificent mail response by you--our readers-- which has proved *Sound Stage* speaks for the majority of moviegoers in its challenging approach--an adult, objective approach, untainted by scandal-mongering- -to the movie industry. This issue is a graphic re-statement of that approach. It includes a revealing interview with Ann-Margret (the star columnists said wouldn't talk!) presented in a fresh and entertaining manner. It embraces nostalgia and whimsy in the fine feature on the 'celluloid cops'. It brings a crisp focus on Frank Sinatra that penetrates far beneath the poses this talented but moody star assumes in his life off the screen. It has, of course, all the features and departments to which you have given your hearty approval. ...There'll be more of the same in forthcoming issues to pinpoint the people, the films, and the events that are headlining Hollywood's sensational return to its status as 'The Magic City'." Readers' letters added compliments such as "How nice it is to have an 'adult' edition to enjoy rather than stooping to the level of what teenagers go for," or "This is definitely the magazine we young adults--and old ones, too--have been waiting for," and "Eureka! A magazine reflecting culture and refinement in the reporting of the Hollywood screen and its wonderful people." Full color and black/white pictures of stars both on and off-stage graced numerous well-written articles in each issue. From the golden silent days of Charlie

Chaplin or the Keystone Cops to the current hit of the 1960s television season, the Munsters; readers discovered a wealth of positive information about their favorite film and video stars. Of special note in one sampled issue was one article which disapprovingly described the breadth of Hollywood fan magazines, and their publishing philosophies. A very nice resource for the serious fan of Hollywood film and television. (8 3/8 x 10 7/8 inches / 210 x 275 mm).

DEPT: "Our Address is Hollywood!," letters; "Sound Stage on Stage," column by Lorraine Gauguin; "Quiet on the Set!," editorial; "Pen and Personality," column by Larry Jaekle; "Previews," upcoming motion picture releases; "Films," review column by Gene Ringgold; "Books," review column by Staunton Ross; "Records," review column by Chris Patrick; "Watch the Stars Come Out," emerging personalities in profile. (6-65).
TYPL: "Tsk, Tsk From Televisionland," "Monsters I Have Loved," "Ann-Margret: Cinderella Speaks," "Mama, What's a Frank Sinatra?," "An Art Director Sets the Mood." (6-65).
SCHL: Every 40 Days, 100 pp.
SPAN: Feb?, 1965 - ?//

✤ SOUTHERN COMMUNICATION JOURNAL, THE

PUBL: Southern Speech Communication Association, Department of Communication, Appalachian State University, Boone, NC 28608.
DESC: [*The Southern Speech Journal*]: In the fall, 1969 issue, new editor, Dwight L. Freshley, told readers, "We invite contributions from all areas in the Speech field. It is true that over one half of the manuscripts submitted are in Rhetoric and Public Address. We continue to welcome them. We urge contributions from communicative disorders, radio-TV-film, interpretation, theatre, speech education, and generally, those of a quantitative or behavioral approach. As in the past, other things being equal, preference will be given to Southern authors and/or topics." For the sampled 1969 issue: perfect-bound journal format; editorial content was comprised of black ink on uncoated paper; cover consisting of black ink on uncoated index stock; limited advertising (5 5/8 x 8 5/8 inches / 145 x 220 mm).
DESC: "*The Southern Communication Journal* publishes studies of human communication research that make a significant contribution to knowledge." One of a number of regional speech organization publications, *The Southern Speech Communication Journal* provides a scholarly approach to the broadly defined areas of interpersonal communication and theatre; featuring authors from among the 27 institutional members of Southern Speech Communication colleges and universities. For one sampled issue articles included critique of a Ronald Reagan political film, woman's suffrage rhetoric, an examination of a Martin Luther King Jr. speech, elements of forensics in letter writing and other areas as regards the expansive field of communication. Of special note are quality book reviews and a "Briefly Noted" section of other research. For sampled issue of 1991: Perfect-bound journal format, editorial content consisting of black ink on uncoated paper stock, with red-ink cover on index cover stock (7 x 10 inches / 180 x 255 mm).
DEPT: "Presidential Message," column by Marguerite Metcalf; "News and Notions," "Book Reviews." (fall-69). "Book Reviews." (summer-84). "Briefly Noted," additional research; "Book Reviews." (summer-91).
TYPL: "An Investigation of Improvement in Bodily Action as a Result of the Basic Course in Speech," "Negro Actors: The Added Dimensions of Color," "Palmer's Century Sermon, New Orleans, January 1, 1901," "The Ethics of Democratic Persuasion and the Birmingham Crisis," "The Confederate Invasion of Boston." (fall-69). "The Anti-Humanist Rhetoric of the New Religious Right," "The Impact of Aesthetic and Professionally-Related Objects on Credibility in the Office Setting," "Gender and Geography: Sex Differences in Spatial Pattern Preferences," "Leadership Behavior and Sex Role Socialization: Two Sides of the Same Coin." (summer-84). "Frontierism and the Materialization of the Psyche: The Rhetoric of 'Innerspace'," "Reason and Religion in 'Rerum Novarum'," "Common Law Reflections of a Forensic 'Urge' in the Art of Letter Writing," "The Rhetorical Construction of Time in Martin Luther King, Jr.'s 'Letter From Birmingham Jail'," "Symbolic Martyrdom: The Ultimate Apology." (summer-91).
SCHL: Quarterly, 100 pp.
SPAN: Oct, 1935+
VARIES
--Oct, 1935 - Mar, 1942 as Southern Speech Bulletin.
--Sep, 1942 - Summer, 1971 as Southern Speech Journal, The (ISSN: 0038-4585).
--Fall, 1971 - Summer, 1988 as Southern Speech Communication Journal, The (ISSN: 0361-8269).
LC: PN 4071.S
DD: 808
ISSN: 1041-794x

Southern Speech Bulletin
Oct, 1935 - Mar, 1942//
SEE: SOUTHERN COMMUNICATION JOURNAL, THE

Southern Speech Communication Journal, The
Fall, 1971 - Summer, 1988//
(ISSN: 0361-8269)
SEE: SOUTHERN COMMUNICATION JOURNAL, THE

Southern Speech Journal, The
Sep, 1942 - Summer, 1971//
(ISSN: 0038-4585)
SEE: SOUTHERN COMMUNICATION JOURNAL, THE

✥ SOUTHERN THEATRE
SUB: "Quarterly magazine of the Southeastern Theatre Conference."
PUBL: Southeastern Theatre Conference, Inc., UNC Greensboro, 506 Sterling St., Greensboro, NC 27412-5001.
DESC: In this quarterly publication, one sees that Southeastern United States theatre is not only alive and well; but creative, dynamic, and progressive. *Southern Theatre* both mirrors and stimulates the creative process that results in a quality theatre experience through articles which cover the process of acting, scriptwriting, stage design, directing, producing, and promotion. The use of coated paper stock enhances the crisp black/white graphics of productions and artists. Of special note is the departmental feature, "In Consideration of Design Possibilities," a forum of theatrical creativity. In one sampled issue, this departmental feature was devoted to "Sound Design for Dramatic Literature." A generous degree of advertising by academic programs, and theatre vendors attests to the loyal readership and support of the quarterly magazine. *Southern Theatre* is first-rate, and a valuable resource for the status of theatre in America's Southeast region. Magazine format, spot color on cover (8 ½ x 11 inches / 215 x 280 mm).
DEPT: "Letters," "Theatre Survey," compiled column by Marian A. Smith; "Playwriting Callboard," theatrical opportunities compiled column by Jeffery Elwell; "In Consideration of Design Possiblities." (winter-91).
TYPL: "Theatre in the Triad: Piedmont North Carolina is Coming Together as Strong Theatre and Arts Programs Thrive," "Submitting a Play: Hopes for Acceptance Often Go Unrequited; But Playwrights Must Labor to Find Stagings," "Timothy Busfield: Returning for More," "Doing It All: Artistry of a Different Sort Required to Market and Manage One-Person Show." (winter-91).
SCHL: Quarterly, 35 pp.
SPAN: 1956+
VARIES
--1956 - Summer, 1962 as Southern Theatre News.
SUSPENDED
--Fall, 1962 - Summer, 1963.
ISSN: 0584-4738

Southern Theatre News
1956 - Summer, 1962//
SEE: SOUTHERN THEATRE

✥ SPAGHETTI CINEMA
PUBL: William Connolly, 6635 DeLongpre #4, Hollywood, CA 90028.
DESC: The focus of this publication is the Italian cinema, and its significant output; including international co-op financed productions. Editor and Publisher William Connolly assembles an always interesting group of articles. From the sampled issue, these subtitles informed readers what was in store for them: "Compilation of Italian cinema reportage from a favorite out-of-print fantasy film magazine," "The Italian films of Donald Pleasence," and "Cinematic highlights from the career of the late French actor Serge Gainsbourg." Of special note is the fascinating department, "Spaghetti Mail & Cinema to Come," an extensive letter section with appropriate editorial commentary; much of which addresses "what's out there," "how is it available: film, videotape, etc.," and "how true is the copy to the original screen version?" These discussions are delightful and informative as to the whereabouts, the value, and the condition of a myriad of Italian productions. This publication focuses on Italian westerns, and uses this genre as the "jumping off" point to explore a much wider range of film categories, all tied to the Italian film industry. For the sampled issue of 1991: stapled photocopied magazine format; typewritten; limited advertising (8 ½ x 11 inches / 215 x 280 mm).
DEPT: "Hello," editorial column by William Connolly; "Spaghetti Mail & Cinema to Come," combination letters, review, and preview. (4-91).
TYPL: "Spaghetti Cinema in the Castle of Frankenstein 3," "An Englishman Abroad," "Serge Forever." (4-91).
SCHL: Five issues per year, 50 pp.
SPAN: Jan?, 1984+

✥ SPARKS
SUB: "Newsletter of the Broadcast Pioneers."
SUB: "A society of broadcast professionals contributing to the past, present and future of broadcasting."
PUBL: Broadcast Pioneers, 320 West 57th St., New York, NY 10019.
DESC: *Sparks* is the newsletter of the Broadcast Pioneers, an outstanding organization for "...all sections of the radio, television or cable industry; legal, programming, artists, owners and managers, public relations and publicity, advertising, engineering, finance and government." It provides pictures and news items of events, developments, and meetings of the Broadcast Pioneers. The sampled issue for 1991 included articles concerning an annual breakfast meeting, awarding of a "Golden Mike Award" to a pioneer broadcaster, a new collection of antique wireless equipment, and a description on the formation of the ABC radio and television network. For the sampled issue of 1991: black ink on coated paper stock, no advertising (8 ½ x 11 inches / 215 x 280 mm).
DEPT: "Fifty Years Ago," historical listing. (4-91).

TYPL: "Really Big Gong Shoe!," "Golden Mike Award to San Antonio's WOAI-AM," "Bonneville Gives Antique Radio Collection to BYU," "A Goldmine!," "More Americans Get Their News From Lifesavers." (4-91).
SCHL: Monthly?, 8 pp.
SPAN: ?+

✤ SPECIALTY ADVERTISING BUSINESS

SUB: "Official voice of the specialty advertising industry's one and only trade association."
PUBL: Specialty Advertising Association International, 1404 Walnut Hill Lane, Irving, TX 75038.
DESC: As the official publication of the Specialty Advertising Association, the primary function of this periodical is to keep its members apprised of changing events in the specialty advertising field. More than an organizational news magazine, there are also articles, graphics and thought pieces concerning this unique advertising field. A wide range of specialty advertising products (pen holders to bumper stickers to binders) are also featured.
DEPT: "Washington Report," legal viewpoint of Washington DC developments toward specialty advertising; "Looking Back," historical feature; "Membership Report," additions, changes; "Business-Wise," newsbriefs of members.
TYPL: "Warning: New Antitrust Laws Apply to SA Industry," "Challenge to YESSA: Dare to Be Different," "How It was Years Ago in Specialty Advertising," "Association Gets Postal Ruling; Saves Big $ in Calendar Mailing." (4-77).
SCHL: Monthly, 35 pp.
SPAN: 1976+
ISSN: 0195-0495

✤ SPECTATOR, THE

PUBL: Critical Studies, School of Cinema-Television, University of Southern California, University Park, Los Angeles, CA 90089-0111
DESC: [*USC Spectator, The*]: The Critical Studies discipline of the School of Cinema-Television publishes *The USC Spectator*, an essay-review-type newspaper which primarily concentrates on motion pictures (a sample issue had no articles concerning television). The newspaper tabloid format presents four to seven articles concerning the art of motion pictures; with interviews, reviews, and essays. Newsprint with graphics.
DEPT: "USC CineVision News," newsbriefs concerning USC campus. (fall-83).
TYPL: "Indian Cinema at the Crossroads," "'I'm Ready to be the Girl Wonder': An Interview with Lina Shanklin," "The Warner Brothers Collection," "Altman on Art," "Trumbull on Technology," "Australia and the Western: Beating a Dead Horse?" (fall, 83).
SCHL: Semiannual, 12 pp.
SPAN: Spring, 1982+
VARIES
--Spring, 1982 - Spring, 1987 as USC Spectator, The.
DD: 791 11
ISSN: 1051-0230

✤ SPECTRA

SUB: "To promote study, criticism, research, teaching, and applications of the principles of communications."
SUB: "Sciences, public address, education, communication, theatre, radio-TV- film, arts."
SUB: "A publication of the Speech Communication Association."
PUBL: Speech Communication Association, 5105 Backlick Rd., Suite E, Annandale, VA 22003.
DESC: "*Spectra* is the official newsletter of the Speech Communication Association. It is published monthly (except July) and mailed to all SCA members. *Spectra* supports the Association's mission of promoting the study, criticism, research, teaching, and application of communication. It does so by disseminating information, ideas and notification of events concerning the communication discipline." This eight-page printed newsletter is designed to provide information about SCA members and their colleges/universities in the areas of the sciences, public address, education, communication, theatre, radio-TV-film, and the arts. A significant portion of the sample issues reviewed (Sep, 1988 & May, 1990), was devoted to faculty vacancies at participating SCA institutions. For the sampled issue of 1991: stapled newsletter format, blue ink on uncoated paper stock, no advertising (8 ½ x 11 inches / 215 x 280 mm).
DEPT: "News and Notes," "Convention Calendar," "Appointments," faculty; "Promotions," of faculty; "On Leave," faculty; "Grants," received and work in-progress; "Personals," "Conferences/Seminars," "Necrology," "Positions Available," large section for open faculty positions. (9- 88). "Letters to the Editor," "News and Notes," extensive newsbrief section; "Conferences and Conventions," "Appointments," academic; "Grants," "Personal," "Calls for Papers," "SCA Publications," "Of Interest," "Classifieds," 2+ pages of faculty vacancies. (5-90).
TYPL: "Rostow to Keynote at New Orlean's Convention," "Greeley Named Director of Educational Services," "Celebrate the Mind," "Teachers on Teaching." (9-88). "SCA Members to Vote on Constitutional Changes," "SCA and ASCD to Assist Academically At-Risk Youth," "Rhetorical and Comm Theory Division Issue Minutes." (5-90).
SCHL: Bimonthly (1965 - 1981); Monthly [except Jul] (1982+), 8 pp.
SPAN: Oct, 1965+
ISSN: 0584-8512

✤ SPEECH AND DRAMA

SUB: "Published by the Society of Teachers of Speech and Drama."
PUBL: Speech and Drama, 14 Florence Rd., Brighton, East Sussex BN1 6DJ, England.
DESC: "The Society of Teachers of Speech and Drama was founded in 1951 by the amalgamation of two much older societies with origins going back to the early part of the century. The Society exists 'to promote the advancement of knowledge, study and practice of speech and dramatic arts, in every form, and to protect the professional interest of members.'" This small format journal places a strong emphasis on the examination of dramatic arts from a theoretical and critical viewpoint, setting aside a large segment of each issue devoted to reviews of current plays and books in the dramatic arts. Some typical articles from early, 1991 included, "Seminars with Sondheim," "BP Speak a Poem Competition," and "Byron Through an Actor's Eyes." Some graphics. For the sampled issues of 1991: (5 ½ x 8 ⅛ inches / 140 x 205 mm).
DEPT: "Reviews," "Notice Board." (spring-84). "Editorial," column by Paul Ranger; "Festivals," "Letters to the Editor," "Theatre Reviews," "Video Review," "Book Reviews," "Notice Board." (autumn-91).
TYPL: "The Rise of Elocution," "'P'--a Play," "A Structure for Drama," "Drama Students and Language Study." (spring-84). "The Polka, a Unique Children's Theatre," "The Sound of My Own Voice," "It was a Friday," "Examination News: The National Board of Speech and Drama Studies," "Grass Roots: Reading a Scene." (autumn-91).
SCHL: Three issues per year (? - ?); Semiannual (?+), 60 pp.
SPAN: 1951+
LC: PN 4071.S73
DD: 001.54

✤ SPEECH COMMUNICATION TEACHER, THE

SUB: "Ideas & strategies for classrooms and activities."
PUBL: Speech Communication Association, 5105 Backlick Rd., Bldg. E, Annandale, VA 22003.
DESC: Each article in this idea-packed publication is prefaced by a goal statement, several of which help explain the form and function of *The Speech Communication Teacher*: "To have students apply argument analysis beyond traditional public speeches and attempt to develop theories of argumentation; To expose students to the use of space as communication and the unspoken rules that guide our behavior within a given context; To describe an oral communication course for academically gifted high school students; To demonstrate that determining an author's intended meaning in a piece of literature necessitates analysis; [or] To have students develop a greater awareness of the 'frame of reference' concept." The 16 pages of this quarterly publication fulfills the subtitle of "Ideas & strategies for classrooms and activities." Faculty from elementary school to university level will find concepts which are readily applicable to their particular pedagogical settings. Every instructor of speech should subscribe to *The Speech Communication Teacher* for ideas, concepts, applications for the classroom, and the sense of collegiate dynamism evident within this educational field. Bravo to the Speech Communication Association for their support, and to Editor Mary Bozik, and Associate Editors Lois Leubitz, Nancy Oft Rose, and Thomas Kaye for their editorial skills. For sampled issue of 1991: loose-leaf; three-hole-punched newsletter format; dark blue ink on coated paper stock; no advertising (8 ½ x 11 inches / 215 x 280 mm).
DEPT: "Reviews," column by Sharon Ratliffe; "To Speak of Many Things," newsbriefs. (spring-91).
TYPL: "Group Project in Rhetorical Criticism," "The Game of Twister--An Exercise in Proxemic Interaction," "Creating an Extra and 'Real Life' Public Speaking Assignment," "Join the Breakfast Club," "The Gift of Oration for the Gifted and Talented." (spring-91).
SCHL: Quarterly, 16 pp.
SPAN: Fall, 1986+

Speech Monographs

1934 - Winter?, 1975//
(ISSN: 0038-7169)
SEE: COMMUNICATION MONOGRAPHS

Speech Teacher, The

Jan, 1952 - Nov, 1975//
(ISSN: 0038-7177)
SEE: COMMUNICATION EDUCATION

✤ SPERDVAC

PUBL: Society to Preserve and Encourage Radio Drama, Variety, and Comedy, P.O. Box 1587, Hollywood, CA 90028.
DESC: A radio-nostalgia magazine, *SPERDVAC* consists primarily of article reprints from 1930s and 1940s magazines concerning radio drama, variety, and comedy. *SPERDVAC* may also reprint an article from a current periodical which describes some facet of radio production or programming during the "golden days" of network radio. A number of old press photos and advertisements compliment this publication.
DEPT: None.
TYPL: "NBC on Its Toes," "The Promise of Television," "KFI: 50 Years of Turning On," "Next Stop: Golden Age Two," "Taking the Pulse of Heartbeat Theater." (winter-76).
SCHL: Semiyearly, 32 pp.
SPAN: Winter, 1976+?

SPLC Report

Spring, 1986 - ?//
SEE: STUDENT PRESS LAW CENTER REPORT

✤ SPOTLIGHT CASTING MAGAZINE

SUB: "Hollywood's #1 casting trade magazine."
SUB: "Film, TV/video, modeling, theatre, tech."
PUBL: Spotlight Casting Magazine, 1605 North Cahuenga Blvd., #207, Los Angeles, CA 90028.
DESC: This actor's magazine for the greater Los Angeles area showcases new talent and casting opportunities in a variety of media. *Spotlight Casting Magazine* is published every Wednesday in order to provide fresh information about new productions about to begin. Of special note is the "Casting Board" section, which details opportunities under a number of subheadings: "Film--Non Union;" "Film--Grad/Student;" "TV/Video--Non Union;" "Theatre--Equity;" "Theatre--AEA 99 Seat Plan;" "Theatre--Non Union;" "Models;" "Singers;" "Musicians;" "Dancers;" "Writers;" "Tech;" and "Variety." Each issue contains a number of service-oriented advertisements from hair styling to head shots, schools for training to agents. For sampled issue of 1991: stapled magazine format, black ink and spot color on uncoated paper stock (8 x 10 ¾ inches / 205 x 270 mm).
DEPT: "L.A. Theatre Life," column by Steve Zall; "Theatre Parties," picture page; "Marilyn Beck's Hollywood," personality column by Marilyn Beck; "On the Scene With Selene," personality column by Selene Walters; "Turning Point," column by Glenn Plaskin; "Theatre Reviews," of Los Angeles theatre; "The Fast Track with Cheryl Lavin," actor profile column by Cheryl Lavin; "The Casting Board," casting information. (5-8-91).
TYPL: "Will Smith," "Andy Garcia Receives 'El Angel' Award." (5-8-91).
SCHL: Weekly, 25 pp.
SPAN: ?+

✤ SPOTLIGHT ON VIDEO

PUBL: West Coast Video, PO Box 13350, Portland, OR 97213.
DESC: "*Spotlight on Video* is an exclusive guide to home video viewing published for the customers of West Coast Video and National Video Stores. ... Join *Spotlight* monthly for up-to-date information about video, what's happening in Hollywood, and details on why your West Coast/National Video store is *the* place to shop." This slick monthly, printed full color on coated paper stock, provides informative reading on new videocassette releases from this video rental company. Magazine size (8 ⅛ x 10 ⅞ inches / 205 x 275 mm).
DEPT: "Heard About Hollywood," 'Hollywood Hotline'™ column by Eliot Stein; "Coming Soon," 'New on Video'; "Child's Play," kid section; "In the Spotlight,"
'Critic's choice' column by Michael Medved; "Bargains & Best Buys," "Trivia," "Top of the Charts," top rentals. (5-89).
TYPL: "Guttenberg Gets His Revenge," "Benson's Back," "The King of Comedy," "Love Scenes in the Movies." (5-89).
SCHL: Monthly, 35 pp.
SPAN: Jan, 1985+

✤ SQUEEKY WHEEL, THE

SUB: "A newsletter for professionals in the communications industry."
PUBL: Martin's Words, P.O. Box 14584, Richmond, VA 23221.
DESC: "...*The Squeeky Wheel* is a newsletter for professionals in the communications industry. That is, actors, writers, printers, producers, cameramen, artists, designers, in and out of agencies. In short, anyone who is or would be professionally involved with the communications industry in this area." *The Squeeky Wheel* began in June, 1985 to expand its audience from the previous "freelancers only" category to a much broader category of "media professionals working in the Richmond, Virginia area." Concentration is on regional media activities, with some trade advertising. Magazine format.
DEPT: "Editorial," "The Center Fold," "The Financial Advisory," "Classified." (Jan/Feb-85).
TYPL: "Self Promotion, Everyone?", "Professional Mailers Aims to Do it Right," "Writers in Demand." (Jan/Feb-85).
SCHL: Bimonthly, 8 pp.
SPAN: Jan/Feb, 1984+

✤ SRDS REPORT, THE

SUB: "For the professional buyer and planner of media."
PUBL: Standard Rate and Data Service, 3004 Glenview Rd., Wilmette, IL 60091.
DESC: Designed "For the professional buyer and planner of media," and "...provided as a service to SRDS subscribers," this lively newsletter is welcome reading in the competitive field of media buying. Articles are written by media professionals, and seek to explain the complexities (and in some cases, the mysteries) of comparing media; and evaluating the value of those media for the desired targeted audiences. Numerous examples of buys in selected media, the reasons for same, and the overall strategies applied to the purchase are given. The newsletter is a wonderful supporting aid used in conjunction with other well-reknowned SRDS resource materials concerning time and space purchases in contemporary media. For the sampled issue of 1990: stapled three-hole punched newsletter format; black ink with green spot-color on heavy coated paper stock; limited promotional advertising (8 ½ x 11 inches / 215 x 280 mm).
DEPT: None. (9-90).

TYPL: "Can National Advertisers Find Love, Truth and Customers in the 'Yellow Pages'?," "What to Consider When Planning/Buying Local and Regional Media," "This Town Isn't Big Enough For Both of Us...Or, Can You Still Choose Between Competing Daily Newspapers?," "'Yellow Pages' vs. 'Yellow Pages': You Can't Keep Track of the Players Without a Scorecard." (9-90).
SCHL: Monthly, 8 pp.
SPAN: Jan, 1987+

✤ SSP LETTER

PUBL: Society for Scholarly Publishing, 10200 West 44th Ave., Suite 304, Wheat Ridge, CO 80033.
DESC: "The Society for Scholarly Publishing (SSP) was founded in 1978. It was begun, in part, to continue and expand the activities of two groups that had been dissolved--The Association for Scientific Journals and the NSF-sponsored Innovation Guide Project. Both of these groups were concerned with only a portion of the types and forms of scholarly publication. When the organizations ceased to exist, people involved with them sought to continue and broaden the exchange of information by organizing an association geared toward the interests of the scholarly and professional publishing community as a whole. A major Society objective is to enhance the general level of professionalism in scholarly publishing by informing members of the concerns and activities of their counterparts and colleagues. This activity, as well as the potential for collaborative research, makes it easier to find solutions to common problems. Thus, the Society is building on the past to formulate solutions for the present and future well-being of scholarly publication." The Society for Scholarly Publishing is a Colorado-based organization dedicated to the unique, important area of scholarly serials, books and other academic product. Membership ranges from special research librarians to scholarly press publishers; as well and includes journalists, vendors, and academic authors, as well as others. Although only two to four articles constitute the editorial content of each issue, they provide an in-depth, authoritative approach to issues in this unique area of publishing and research. The sample issue of March/April, 1990, questioned whether non-American publishers should be required to deposit copies in the Library of Congress; and covered the annual meeting of the Association of American Publishers' Professional and Scholarly Publishing Division. Stapled newsletter format; black ink on uncoated beige-color paper stock; some issues are two-color red and black ink; no graphics or advertising (8 ½ x 11 inches / 215 x 280 mm).
DEPT: "Book Review." (3/4-90).
TYPL: "Should Non-US Publishers Provide Deposit Copies to the Library of Congress?," "Employee Compensation in Scholarly Publishing." (3/4-90).
SCHL: Bimonthly, 8 pp.
SPAN: Jan/Feb, 1989+
DD: 070 11

ISSN: 1043-8246

ST. LOUIS AND CANADIAN PHOTOGRAPHER

SUB: "An illustrated monthly journal, devoted to the elevation and improvement of the photographic art."
SUB: "Westward the star of empire takes its way."
SUB: "An illustrated monthly."
SUB: "Devoted to Photography."
SUB: "A journal devoted to the elevation and improvement of photography."
SUB: "A monthly magazine devoted to photography and kindred sciences."
SUB: "The sparkling young journal, free and independent, was born to shine for all."
PUBL: St. Louis Photographic Publishing Co., 3210 Lucas Ave., St. Louis, MO.
DESC: [*The St. Louis Practical Photographer*]: In a back-page, promotional advertisement for January, 1882, publisher J. H. Fitzgibbon made this following statement: "It is beautifully illustrated every month with fine specimens of our Art, and filled with new and practical ideas from our best artists, for only $3.00 a year. The rapid strides the *St. Louis Practical Photographer* has made in the past five years has not only interested its best friends, but terrified its mean enemies. We have made arrangements to procure foreign correspondence that will be interesting and of a practical nature of things that may be brought to light the coming year. Our old and many new correspondents, will shine forth in the *Practical Photographer* for the benefit of the whole fraternity on subjects of general interest. Free discussion (but not personal) is invited on art subjects for the benefit of our readers; the same will be criticized according to our ability. We shall chronicle all new inventions and processes brought forward, and endeavor to speak of them as their merit deserves. *The St. Louis Practical Photographer* is the only journal in the United States that obtains its suport from the fraternity and dealers at large, on its own merits; all other journals are issued by stock, manufacturing and publishing houses principally to advertise their own goods and for their own individual benefit." Fiercely independent, the magazine took great pains to provide a friendly meeting place whereby amateur and professional photographer alike could discuss the art, technique, and technology of the photographic craft. Many black/white advertisements for chemicals and other equipment were present at the front and back of the issue, as was commonplace in the editorial design of the 19th century. The sampled issue for 1882 displayed a fair number of line drawings, especially as they pertained to the construction of photographic equipment, darkrooms, and camera placement for unique effects. Of special note were a number of chemical formulas submitted by reader and publisher alike for application in the field. The sampled issue for 1882 was glue-bound magazine format; black/white content on uncoated paper stock; cover

DESC: was black/white (with a line drawing of Daguerre in the 1882 sampled issue) on uncoated blue paper stock (6 ¾ x 9 ⅞ inches / 170 x 250 mm).

DESC: [*The St. Louis and Canadian Photographer*]: A number of editorial changes are evident in the new publication, including a new publisher, Mrs. Fitzgibbon-Clark (whose picture graced most issue covers); and the widespread usage of photographs in editorial content and advertisements alike. Advertising was still restricted to the front and back sections of the publication, but now virtually every commerical promotion was printed in two-color black and red ink; except for the cover advertisements, which were printed in dark blue ink, and a small section of advertisements in green ink on cream-colored paper stock. Mrs. Fitzgibbon-Clark's influence was seen in many areas of the publication, including interesting jokes and commentary on male photographers, such as one joke entitled, "The Ignorance of Men." The chemical formulas were still to be found, albeit in fewer number, as commercial establishments took over the difficult and often dangerous practice of mixing one's own darkroom concoctions. Of special consideration was the excellent departmental feature, "Convention Notes," which detailed news of recent photographic expositions, conventions, and association gatherings. The sampled issue of 1903 that included the Photographers' Association of Wisconsin, the Photographers' Association of Missouri, the Indiana Association of Photography, the Photographers' Association of Kansas, the Ohio-Michigan Association, the Photographers' Association of Kentucky and Tennessee, and the Photographers' Association of Illinois. No letters-to-the-editor column existed, all correspondence being filtered through Editor/Publisher Fitzgibbons-Clark and placed in conversational style in the column, "Editorial Chats." Perfect-bound magazine format; editorial content utilized black ink; advertisements used black; green, or two-color black/red inks; all on coated paper stock. (6 ⅞ x 10 ⅛ inches / 175 x 255 mm).

DEPT: "Our Patrons," descriptions of selected vendors advertising in the magazine; "Bureau of Information," newsbrief information concerning patents, processes, and reader comment; "Editorial Chit-Chat," editorial column by J. H. Fitzgibbon; "Special Notices," unique advertising and want section. (1-1882). "Echoes From Europe," news from the continent, column by Robert Benecke; "Convention Notes," extensive report section detailing state, regional and association convention events; "With the Amateur," advice and instruction column by Fayette J. Clute; "Items of Interest," newsbriefs concerning photographic professionals; "Latest Importations," international news of technological and business developments; "Criticism of Illustrations," critique of reader-submitted photographs, column by G. Hanmer Croughton; "Editorial Chit-Chat," editorial column by Mrs. Fitzgibbon-Clark; "Special Notices," variety of for sale and wanted photographic items; "Employment Bureau," current opportunities; "Conventions for [year]," upcoming events calendar; "Clipper," items of interest reprinted from other photographic publications. (6-03).

TYPL: "Gelatine for Dry Plates," "Address to the Chicago Photographers," "Reoutching by Artificial Light," "Sensitizing Drying and Fuming Albumenized Paper for Printing," "The Photo Art Poser." (1-1882). "Fashion Plates," "More Light in Negative Making," "Spots and Pinholes," "Using a Slow Plate," "The Earliest Photographic Studio in Vienna." (6-03).
SCHL: Monthly, 80 pp.
SPAN: Jan, 1877 - Jan, 1910//
VARIES
--Jan, 1877 - Dec?, 1882 as St. Louis Practical Photographer.
--Jan, 1883 - Dec, 1887 as St. Louis Photographer (ISSN: 0735-5629).
ABSORBED BY
--Bulletin of Photography.
LC: TR 1.S2
DD: 770/.5

✢ ST. LOUIS JOURNALISM REVIEW

SUB: "A critique of metropolitan media and events."
PUBL: St. Louis Journalism Review, 8380 Olive Blvd., St. Louis, MO 63132.
DESC: Thorough, brash, professional, and compassionate are some of the adjectives one might employ to describe the *St. Louis Journalism Review*, an outstanding critical review of St. Louis journalistic media. Here is a pragmatic, state-of-journalism report on the metropolitan St. Louis media, and it is fascinating reading. Articles thoroughly address the issues at heart, providing insight into the politics, economics, personalities, and function of area mass media. The only regret might be that there is not a *St. Louis Journalism Review* for every major city in America. Tabloid format; display-stand folded: (8 ½ x 11 ½ inches / 215 x 290 mm); and unfolded for reading: (11 ⅛ x 17 inches / 285 x 430 mm), published on newsprint with graphics.
DEPT: "Here," commentary; "There," commentary; "Every Where," commentary; "Of Note," newsbriefs; "AM/FM," commentary on St. Louis radio; "AD/PR Notes," commentary and news on St. Louis advertising; "People," personnel briefs; "Awards." (11-89).
TYPL: "Sun International Coverage Offers less of the Same," "Traditional Ad Profit Ratios Outdated, Says Sun Publisher," "Missouri Arts Council Cuts Off City Players," "Press Law Score: Mixed Results So Far." (11- 89).
SCHL: Irregular (1970 - 1979); Bimonthly (1980 - Jun, 1983); Monthly (Aug, 1983+), 25 pp.
SPAN: Oct/Nov, 1970+
ABSORBED
--Focus Midwest (ISSN: 0015-508x), ?, 1984.
LC: PN 4899.S25 S25
DD: 071/.78/66
ISSN: 0036-2972

ABST: --ABI/Informer

St. Louis Photographer

Jan, 1883 - Dec, 1887//
(ISSN: 0735-5629)
SEE: ST. LOUIS AND CANADIAN PHOTOGRAPHER

St. Louis Practical Photographer

Jan, 1877 - Dec?, 1882//
SEE: ST. LOUIS AND CANADIAN PHOTOGRAPHER

STAGE

SUB: "The magazine of after-dark entertainment."
SUB: "The world of after-dark entertainment."
PUBL: Stage Publishing Co., 50 East 42nd St., New York, NY.
DESC: "STAGE is a national publication which aims impartially to record and interpret the most significant and interesting events in the field of the theatre and its cognate arts--including motion pictures, music, radio, the dance, and the entire field of after-dark entertainment--here and abroad." Dynamic and delightful, *STAGE* proclaimed each month's issue with an unique blend of bravado and élan, reflecting the robust spectrum of entertainment media available to the primarily New York readership. It was a succinct guide to all that was good and worthy of time, viewing, and/or listening. Descriptions consisting of constructive commentary, minced no words in their appraisal of everything from Broadway theatrical fare, to W.C. Fields appearing on the Edgar Bergan and Charlie McCarthy Show over network radio. For those outside the New York City area, it was a barometer of major media trends and popular culture; or, as the masthead so aptly put it, "*STAGE* has the honor to present ...a store of articles, lantern slides, petite comic pieces, divertissements and assorted pas de deux anent the musical, dramatic, and gastronomic novelties of the world of after-dark entertainment." Articles from one sampled issue in late 1937 included a review of the new Disney cartoon, "Snow White and the Seven Dwarfs;" Ed Wynn's new musical on Broadway; a review of a new Samuel Goldwyn picture; a profile of Charles Boyer; a pictorial showcase of the new NBC Radio Orchestra leader Toscanini; what college students like to do in New York City; and the gala opening of "I'd Rather Be Right," with an all-star ensemble. Of special note was the departmental feature, "On Other Broadways," detailing (in one sampled issue), the theatrical activities in Louisiana, New Jersey, Ohio, Indiana, Utah, California, and Connecticut. Each issue was a treasure trove of pictures of current media stars and happenings, presented in a dynamic layout style with spot and full-color pages. This wonderful publication was probably best described by an in-magazine promotion outlining reasons why a current subscriber would wish to present a friend with a gift subscription: "*Stage*, the Magazine of After-Dark Entertainment, serves the lovers of metropolitan After-Dark pleasure. It enriches their enjoyment of the play, the opera, the concert, the picture, the recital, the supper club, and the rest of the rounds of life in the evening." Large magazine format (10 x 14 inches / 255 x 355 mm).
DEPT: "The Show is On," 'Being our concise and critical commendations or condemnations of that which is now on Broadway'; "Pictures Now Showing," 'Being hosannahs or hisses for the latest consignment from Hollywood'; "Dining and Dancing 'Round the Town," 'If you indulge in either, in either of the captivating worlds of New York or Hollywood, this is your guide', column by Domino Jr.; "From G-106-107," 'The output of plays during the last thirty days, with a looking forward to the next thirty' column by Ruth Woodbury Sedgwick; "Seen in the Spotlight," 'A report on the derring-do in the mythical kingdom of Hollywood' column by Katharine Best; "Records of the Month," "Radio Highlights," "On Other Broadways," 'Happenings in the byways of Broadway, North, South, East, and West' column by Albert McCleery. (12- 37).
TYPL: "Hooray for Hooray for What," "Nostalgia with Wormwood and Gall," "All-Star Orchestra," "Secrets of Our Present-Day Savarins," "Fair is Foul and Foul is Fair." (12-37).
SCHL: Monthly (Dec, 1923 - ?); Eight issues per year (? - Oct, 1929); Monthly (Nov?, 1929+), 125 pp.
SPAN: Dec, 1923 - Jun, 1939//
VARIES
--Dec, 1923 - Nov, 1925 as Theatre Guild Bulletin.
--Dec, 1925 - Sep, 1928 as Theatre Guild Quarterly.
--Oct, 1928 - Apr, 1932 as Theatre Guild Magazine.
LC: PN 2000.T7

Stage, The

1880 - Feb 12, 1959//
SEE: STAGE AND TELEVISION TODAY, THE

STAGE AND SPORT

SUB: "Illustrated." (May 5, 1906 - ?).
PUBL: Stage and Sport, 6 Adams St., Strand, London WC, England.
DESC: This unique periodical consisted of one-half sports news, and one-half news of the London stage. Each weekly issue of some 25 pages provided latest news and photographs concerning London stage events, actors and actresses, producers, and the off-stage lives of same. *Stage and Sport* covered both daylight and limelight events and was probably interesting to both male and female readers. Numerous graphics pertaining to actors, actresses, and stage performances.
DEPT: "Our Stage Causerie," 'By the Idler'; "The Variety Stage," 'by Box and Cox'; "What's On?," 'A guide to the principal theatres and music halls'. (6-2-06).

TYPL: None.
SCHL: Weekly, 25 pp.
SPAN: May 5, 1906 - Jun 30, 1906?//?

✤ STAGE & STUDIO

SUB: "The magazine for performers and producers." (? - Dec, 1988).
SUB: "Music & sound for performers & producers." (Jan, 1989+).
PUBL: Output International Publications, 25 Willowdale Ave., Port Washington, NY 11050.
DESC: [*Music & Sound Output*]: An interesting mixture of producer and production exists in this publication. Some articles discuss the role of the producer vis a vis the musician, and the creative road taken to arrive at a certain sound, an album cover, and a marketing strategy. Other articles explore the technical side of recording, providing intereviews with engineers, reviews of equipment, and the technique of production. It all comes together in the "Perspectives" department where these elements are discussed and analyzed as a final product for the home consumer. Each issue has three distinct sections: 1) Features, 2) Departments, and 3) Recording Today, which is subdivided into producing, engineering, and soundmixing. Magazine format (8 ¼ x 11 inches / 210 x 275 mm); black/white & color graphics; printed on coated paper stock.
DEPT: "Interface," letters; "Talkback," 'provides a channel of communication between the readers of *Stage & Studio* and manufacturers of music and sound equipment'; "Outfront," musicians and their product; "Business," "Output Test," equipment review; "Soft Test," music business computer software; "Product News," "Perspectives," music product reviews; "Producing," "Engineering," "Soundmixing." (12-88).
TYPL: "Ears Don't Always Correlate with Specs," "The Memphis Horns; Celebrating 25 Years," "Bill Dashiell: Recording the Horns," "Clive Martin's Recording Repertoire," "Mixing Film and the BB's." (12-88).
SCHL: Monthly, 80 pp.
SPAN: Dec, 1980+
VARIES
--Nov/Dec, 1980 - Dec, 1988 as Music & Sound Output (ISSN: 0273-8902).
LC: ML 3469 .M89
DD: 780
ISSN: 1042-9409

✤ STAGE AND TELEVISION TODAY, THE

PUBL: The Stage and Television Today, 47 Bermondsey St., London SE1 3XT, England.
DESC: *The Stage and Television Today* is a multifaceted publication concerned with the health and well-being of British, legitimate stage. The newsprint tabloid contains articles of shows that are opening or closing, auditions for a variety of artists, the on-going saga of government support for the arts, reviews of upcoming talent, rosters of where artists are currently engaged, and a wide variety of support services advertised to *Stage and Television Today* readers. Although government regulation, the economics of event staging, and the profit side of theatrical management are important factors, the emphasis here remains the artist and the ever-changing status of the shows themselves. For the sampled issue of 1990: Tabloid newsprint format with numerous black/white production stills and artist publicity pictures with black ink on newsprint (12 ⅜ x 17 ½ inches / 315 x 445 mm).
DEPT: "Theatre News," "Light Entertainment," "Seen At," "Show People," "Letters," "John Mills Showcase," "Theatre Week," "Production News," "Play Reviews," "Chit Chat and Leader," "Opera and Dance," "Regional Reviews," "Television Today," "Suppliers," "Backstage," "On Next Week," "Hamlet," "Tour News," "Television Diary," "BARB Ratings." (2-22-90).
TYPL: "Kids' Show Scrapped in ROH Cash Crisis," "Investigation After Tenor Collapses," "Hypnotists Look to Equity," "'Charity is No Short Cut'." (2-22-90).
SCHL: Weekly, 40 pp.
SPAN: 1880+
VARIES
--1880 as Stage Directory.
--1880 - Feb 12, 1959 as Stage, The.
WITH SUPPLEMENT
--Television Today, Feb 19, 1959+.
LC: PN 2000.S 775
ISSN: 0038-9099

Stage Directory

1880//
SEE: STAGE AND TELEVISION TODAY, THE

✤ STAGE PICTORIAL

SUB: "A monthly magazine devoted to the theater."
SUB: "One Hundred Pictures for Ten Cents."
PUBL: New York Star Company, 1493 Broadway, New York, NY.
DESC: In the premiere issue for March, 1912, the publisher placed the following in the inside front cover: "1000 Pictures for $1.00 - This is what the *Stage Pictorial* aims to give its readers during the coming year--one thousand pictures for one hundred cents. It required 111 separate pictures to make up the illustratioins in this copy in your hand. This makes the *Stage Pictorial* the most profusely illustrated periodical offered to the American public. Subscribe for *Stage Pictorial*, and bring the New York theaters to your home every month. *Stage Pictorial* is now and will be--MOSTLY NEWS PICTURES." And so it was for the premiere issue of 1912, a myriad of stage pictures in black/white and duotone purple ink, verbiage kept to a minimum. At times that meant as little as a cut line below the picture identifying it. All the major Broad-

way stars were represented, including, John Drew, Ethel Barrymore, Weber & Fields, Marie Dressler, David Warfield, Blanche Ring, Frances Starr, Thomas A. Wise, Donald Brian, George M. Cohan, and Billy Burke. Aspiring stars and starlets also received their due, with cut lines describing their current Broadway roles. Virtually all pictures were of actual theatre productions, or studio publicity shots, with several showing interiors of artists' homes; and one portraying the theatre marquee at night. While the monthly may appear to be a publicist's dream, the publisher could deliver a bit of sharp comment concerning entertainers as in the following: "...the prima donna in John Cort's production of 'The Rose of Panama,' is playing her first engagement on Broadway. She isn't very pretty, but is clever and has a way about her." Historians and researchers will appreciate the care which was taken with the quality and size of photographic reproductions. Black/white editorial content; no advertising; lavish use of pictures on coated paper stock in stapled magazine format (8 x 11 ¼ inches / 205 x 285 mm).
DEPT: "It's a Fact," Broadway newsbriefs. (3-12).
TYPL: "That Weber and Fields Jubilee Company," "The Irish Players that Caused the Trouble," "Love Scenes in some of the Musical Comedies Seen on Broadway this Season," "Miss Ethel Barrymore at the Empire, New York," "Burlesque Also has its Beauties." (3-12).
SCHL: Monthly, 35 pp.
SPAN: Mar, 1912+?

STAGE PICTORIAL
PUBL: Stage Pictorial Publishing Co., 1501 Broadway, New York, NY.
DESC: With an emphasis on New York City Broadway theatre, *Stage Pictorial* covered the dynamics of plays, artists, and the play-going public. True to its title, it provided pictures portraying the diversity of New York City performing arts. Articles covered current fare and new stage debuts; backgrounds on artists and their play vehicles; other live theatrical formats, such as ice shows, playwright and actor profiles; and issues/trends currently under discussion by the New York theatrical community. In one sampled issue for 1945, numerous articles were devoted to the "war boom" in theatre attendance; and there was a fascinating look at the "Hollywood Raiders" of Broadway talent and scripts. *Stage Pictorial* provided a large number of "stage stills," photographs of current Broadway hits and their casts, to complement lengthy articles about those Broadway-based events. Magazine format, full-color cover with black/white editorial content; published on newsprint (8 ½ x 11 ¼ inches / 215 x 285 mm).
DEPT: "Laughs From the Shows," humorous lines from current Broadway hits; "Hit Parade," 'An alphabetical listing of the Broadway shows, some old, some new'. (winter-45).
TYPL: "Beatrice Lillie: Here on Furlough From Troops, England's Greatest Comedienne Shows Us How to Laugh Again," "War Time Theatre Boom," "Hollywood Raiders: The Play Producer Risks His Fortune on New Discoveries, but Film Scouts Snatch 'Em When They Make Good," "John P. Marquand: America's Foremost Novelist Brings Literary Lustre to the Stage," "The Late George Apley: Prize Winning Novel is Converted into a Brilliant Dramatic Hit." (winter-45).
SCHL: Quarterly (Winter, 1944); Monthly (Feb, 1945+).
SPAN: Winter, 1944 - Jul, 1946//
SUSPENDED
--Jun, 1946.
LC: PN 2000.S65

STAGE SOUVENIR, THE
SUB: "An illustrated monthly journal."
PUBL: The Stage Souvenir, Effingham House, Arundel St., London WC, England.
DESC: "In presenting an illustrated record of productions on the London stage, we believe we are stepping into a vacant place, where we are wanted. If not, we shall soon fall out. All theatre goers know that the successful London play of to-day, and more especially the light musical piece, lives to quite a ripe old age. A year is a mere nothing for its run in London alone, whilst numerous touring companies keep it alive at all the best theatres in the kingdom for several years. It is impossible to calculate the actual number of London and provincial playgoers, who, during its lifetime, go to see one particular successful play. It is in the interest of this vast multitude that *The Stage Souvenir* begins its existence, and because our theatrical contemporaries are unable to cope with all the many excellent plays which ought to be permanently illustrated and recorded." This was indeed a souvenir of the London stage, each monthly issue consisting of a hand-mounted photograph of a theatrical star, and numerous handsome duotones of specific scenes. Layout design of the 30+ page serial was spritely and imaginative, with a variety of photoscenes and printed dialogue. Of special note was the superb quality of printed photographs, making this a unique historical record of the London theatre.
DEPT: None.
TYPL: None.
SCHL: Monthly, 25 pp.
SPAN: Jul 20, 1903? - Oct 20, 1903?//?

✧ STAR
PUBL: Star Editorial, Inc., 600 South East Coast Ave., Lantana, FL 33464.
DESC: With over 500,000 subscribers, *Star* ranks as one of the higher circulation publications in celebrity-watching news and trends. Articles cover human interest stories, fashions, home entertainment, motion picture and television news; but the focus is the media celebrity, the "Star" of stage and screen; with more

color pictures than other similar celebrity grocery store weeklies, and a dynamic color layout design that also works well for advertisements. Square newsprint design (9 ⅞ x 12 ¾ inches / 250 x 320 mm), with stapled midsection.
DEPT: "Star People," Hollywood column by Janet Charlton; "Ask the Insider," Q&A on celebrities; "Soaps," soap opera news; "Have You Heard?," Soap opera newsbriefs; "Star File," soap opera star profile; "Starscope," horoscope column by Laurie Brady; "Star Health," health and beauty; "Your Word," letters; "Your Family Doctor," column by Dr. Norton Luger (MD); "Star Whirly Words," puzzle; "Laugh Yourself Well," column by Joey Adams; "Dear Meg," 'Every week the column with a heart'; "What People are Wearing," "Star Crossword," puzzle; "Star Videos," review of what's new on videocassette. (9-4-90).
TYPL: "Elton John Secretly Checks into Clinic with Mystery Eating Disorder," "'Baby' Tony Danza Blasts Connie Sellecca for Quitting New Show," "The Woman Who Knows Dolly Parton Better Than Dolly's Husband," "Greedy Hagman's Outrageous Demands Kill Off Dallas," "New Kids on the Block Heartthrob Hits Back at Gay Smear Campaign." (9-4-90).
SCHL: Weekly, 50 pp.
SPAN: Jan 4, 1974+

Star Hits

? - ?//
(ISSN: 8750-7234)
SEE: SMASH HITS

✢ STAR SIGNALS

SUB: "Business news of the private satellite marketplace."
SUB: "The magazine for the earth-station receive industry."
PUBL: Interstar Satellite Systems, 21708 Marilla St., Chatsworth, CA 91331.
DESC: The business and technology of satellite communications is rapidly growing. *Star Signals* was begun as a response to that growth. Publisher Dick Pelletier, in the premiere issue noted; "A direct communication link such as *Star Signals* is urgently needed between manufacturers, distributors, installers and customers in our specialized, receive-only branch of the booming satellite-TV industry. *Star Signals* will help show you how to put it all together, from basic equipment to accounting systems to marketing plans." The emphasis is on "receive-only" satellite dish systems.
DEPT: "Industry News," newsbriefs.
TYPL: "World Peace Through Telecommunications," "ESA Breaks Superpower Space Monopolies," "Markets and Legalities Examined During Satellite Seminars," "What the Satellite Pioneer Should Know About Accounting." (9-81).
SCHL: Monthly?, 32 pp.
SPAN: Sep, 1981+

✢ STAR TREK: THE NEXT GENERATION

SUB: "The official magazine."
PUBL: Starlog Communications International, 475 Park Avenue south, 8th Floor, New York, New York 10016.
DESC: "Each volume is all-slick, all-color and packaged with exclusive interviews, detailed episode guides, behind-the-scenes photos, art and blueprints, actual scenes from the shows--PLUS spectacular pull-out posters!" This serial, based on the continuing saga of the Enterprise, and its crew, is quite obviously a fan-magazine. It is presented in a quality layout design, with numerous color photographs of television episodes, and character profiles. Interestingly, virtually every page has some color tint to it, making this one of the more colorful "fanzines" available. Of note are large pull-out color posters, and a minimum of advertising that compliments a well-done publication. Full-color publication; stapled magazine format; on coated paper stock (8 x 10 ⅞ inches / 205 x 275 mm).
DEPT: None. (5-90).
TYPL: "Marina Sirtis, Counselor Deanna Troi," "The Special Effects," "Gates McFadden, Dr. Beverly Crusher," "The Romulans." (5-90).
SCHL: Quarterly, 70 pp.
SPAN: Dec, 1987+

✢ STAR TREK: THE OFFICIAL FAN CLUB MAGAZINE

PUBL: Official Fan Club, Inc., 537 Olathe St., Suite C, Aurora, CO 80011.
DESC: As the official publication of the *Star Trek* and *Star Trek: The Next Generation* series, much is expected, and indeed much is provided members for a very reasonable (for 1991) subscription rate of only $11.95 per year. Articles are accurate, fair, and informative in examining series characters, plots, marketing, and behind-the-scenes craftsmanship exhibited by a host of talented production teams. Layout design is quite dynamic, with liberal use of full-color and spot-color throughout. A six-page "Star Trek Merchandise Catalog" provides every conceivable momento from the television and motion picture series, some items which are only available through club membership. Stapled magazine format; full and spot-color throughout on coated paper stock; advertising related to Star Trek items of interest (8 ½ x 11 inches / 215 x 275 mm).
DEPT: "Reader's Comments," letters; "Where No Man," review column by Salman Nensi; "Convention Listing," extensive two-month convention calendar. (4/5-91).
TYPL: "Whoopi Goldberg: Guinan's Guide to the Galaxy," "Gene Roddenberry: Creating Guinan," "To Boldly Go: From Fan to Professional," "Star Trek VI: Exclusive Update." (4/5-91).
SCHL: Bimonthly, 14 pp.
SPAN: ?+
ISSN: 0883-3125

✧ STARBURST

SUB: "The magazine of cinema & television fantasy."
SUB: "The fantastic media magazine."
SUB: "Britain's premiere science fiction magazine."
PUBL: Visual Imagination, Ltd., PO Box 371, London SW14 8JL, England.
DESC: "Wherever there is Science-Fiction or Fantasy, *Starburst* is there to give you the latest news and insights. Genre movies are previewed in advance of their cinema releases. There are in-depth interviews with the big name stars, as well as writers, directors and the legions of technical people who make Fantasy a reality on both large and small screens. We turn the spotlight on radio, stage productions, comics and books. There's a regular Videofile to keep you up to date with the ever increasing number of fantastic, horrific and unusual video releases...plus the near legendary 'It's Only a Movie' column from the wickedly witty John Brosnan. There's no better magazine for keeping abreast of the Fantasy world." This wonderful British publication is for the science fiction/fanatasy consumer of film and television product. With a mixture of black/white and color graphics, *Starburst* covers the breadth of fantasy television series and motion pictures. Past features have included a werewolf issue, "Star Trek" television and film series, the making of "Dragonslayer," a special issue on the making of "Krull," "The Avengers," "Sleeping Beauty," "Blade Runner," "Escape from New York, the "James Bond" film series; plus interviews with actors, directors, special effects technicians, makeup wizards, and others involved in the process of film/video- making. Of special note are interesting historical reviews of past fantasy projects, and unique issues devoted to single topics such as aliens, fantasy females, comic heroes on screen, and zombies. For the sampled issue of 1990: stapled magazine format with mixture of black ink; spot and full-color pages on coated paper stock (8 ¼ x 11 ⅝ inches / 210 x 295 mm)..
DEPT: "Starburst Letters," 'Our readers write...'; "Flickers," cartoon strip column by Tim Quinn and Dicky Howett; "Things to Come," 'All the news that's fit to print...and a few items that aren't, courtesy of our globetrotting newshound Tony Crawley' column by Tony Crawley; "TV Zone," column by Richard Holliss; "Video File," column by Barry Forshaw; "It's Only a Movie," column by John Brosnan; "Book World," review column by Chris Charles. (6-83). "Things to Come," 'The latest news of fantasy in both film and television' column by Michael Courtland; "Bookshelf," 'The latest from the science fiction, fantasy and horror worlds'; "Preview," of upcoming movies; "Comic Store," review of current releases column by Gary Russell; "Feedback," 'Some more of your comments and views in our lively monthly letters column'; "Soundtracks," record review column by Richard Sayer; "TV Zone," column by Paul Mount; "Videofile," 'A round-up of the latest releases of the unusual, fantastic, horrific and probably out of this world'; "It's Only a Movie," witty film commentary column by John Brosnan. (5-90).
TYPL: "The Jedi Interview," "Things That Go Bump in the Night," "Preview: The Keep," "Friday 13th." (6-83). "An Excellent Review with Stephen Herek, the Most Triumphant 'Bill and Ted' Director," "Daniel Rhodes," "Another Spell of Meddings Magic," "A Quantum Leap Into the Unknown: Dean Stockwell." (5-90).
SCHL: Monthly, 50 pp.
SPAN: Sep, 1978?+
ABSORBED
--Video Now, ?
ISSN: 0955-114x

Starlog Presents Comics Scene

Jan/Feb, 1981 - ?, 1982//
(ISSN: 0732-5622)
SEE: COMICS SCENE

✧ STARZ

PUBL: Craigle Publications, PO Box 57497, Sherman Oaks, CA 91413.
DESC: This teenage fan magazine with a mid-1990 debut has a decided emphasis on male teen stars of motion pictures, television, and music fields. Each issue contains some 25+ articles on favorite stars, contests that offer prizes such as beach towels, or trips to Hollywood to meet music stars, and some 15 "Fabulous Knock-Out Pin-Ups!" in full color, including two large folded posters. The first ten personalities featured in articles for the sampled issue were: Mark-Paul Gosselaar, Taylor Dayne, Tommy Page, Richard Greico, Young M.C., Jay Ferguson, Glenn Medeiros, Sinead O'Connor, Mark Slaughter, and Lisa Stansfield. The issue for October, 1990 also included a large section entitled "New Stuff on New Kids!," concerning the New Kids on the Block group. Magazine format (8 x 10 ¾ inches / 200 x 275 mm); numerous black/white and full-color graphics; editorial content on uncoated paper stock.
DEPT: "Starz in Your Eyes!," "Editor Meg tells all!" column by Meg Howard; "Shout It Out!," 'Your turn to speak up!' letters; "About the Starz," 'Your questions answered'; "That's Show Biz!," 'What's happening in Hollywood'; "Rock 'N' Rolling Along!," 'The music scene'; "Stuck on Starz," 'Write your favorites'. (10-90).
TYPL: "Someone is Protecting Me--So Says Madonna!," "Mark-Paul Gosselaar: 'If I Weren't an Actor'," "Tommy Page: Friendship is a Two-Way Street," "Is Richard as Tough as He Looks?," "Music Time with Tommy!" (10-90).
SCHL: Monthly, 90 pp.
SPAN: Sep, 1990+

✧ STATIC

PUBL: Association for Education in Journalism and Mass Communication, Radio-Television Journalism Division, School of Journalism, University of Wisconsin, Madison, WI 53706.
DESC: This is a four to six-page mimeographed newsletter of the Radio-Television Journalism Division of AEJ, containing R-TV journalism news of interest to AEJ members. Articles report on student and faculty activities, journalism program development, and issues of importance to academic institutions.
DEPT: None. (3-76).
TYPL: "ENG in Broadcast Journalism Education: Indiana's Ready to Go," "Indiana has RTNDA ENG Session Videocassette Available," "Division Announces Broadcast Journalism Research Consortium." (3-76).
SCHL: Quarterly?
SPAN: ?+?

✧ STEP-BY-STEP ELECTRONIC DESIGN

SUB: "The how-to newsletter for desktop designers."
PUBL: "Dynamic Graphics, Inc., 6000 North Forest Park Dr., Peoria, IL 61614-3592.
DESC: Dynamic Graphics has been "the" source for outstanding clip-art graphics for the graphic design industry for many years. Now, in association with sister publication *Step-By-Step Graphics*, Dynamic Graphics is publishing this excellent guide to quality design via desktop publishing. As befits the title, readers are walked through each design step on their way to a finished product, whether the project be accomplished by full color, black/white, scanned or hand-drawn technology. No advertising means that every page contains a solid amount of information. In an industry where multiple forms of software programs and equipment coexist, it is a difficult task indeed to satisfy everyone, but *Step-By-Step Electronic Design* comes very close via the wide variety of media utilized in each issue. For the graphic designer committed to electronic design, this publication is required reading, and one which will receive continued use over time. Full color magazine format; three-hole punched for filing; full color graphics.
DEPT: "In the Trenches," practical application; "The Graphic Eye," "Resources," 'Brief reviews of products and services of interest to electronic designers'; "Q&A," 'Solutions to problems about desktop production'; "Design Workshop," graphic design, step-by-step; "Calendar." (4-90).
TYPL: "Time-Saving Drawing Techniques," "Textured Scans for a Recipe Book," "Page Layout Productivity Tips." (4-90).
SCHL: Monthly, 16 pp.
SPAN: Jan, 1989+
DD: 621
ISSN: 1055-2774

✧ STEP-BY-STEP GRAPHICS

SUB: "The how-to reference magazine for visual communicators."
PUBL: Dynamic Graphics, Inc., 6000 N. Forest Park Drive, Peoria, IL 61615-9979.
DESC: *Step-By-Step Graphics* is in a class by itself; distinctive, authoritative, instructional, and au courant, this remains "the" publication for the graphics professional. Over 150 pages of ideas, concepts, interviews, and news of graphic trends comprise each issue. Reflecting its name, a number of articles demonstrate "step-by-step" techniques in a variety of areas including metallic inks, animation, photo retouching, and various applications of graphic design and production. Many issues include full color inserts of the final product, demonstrating the processes and techniques described in that issue. Magazine format (8 ¼ x 10 ⅞ inches / 210 x 275 mm), numerous full-color graphics.
DEPT: "Editor's Note," "Letters," "Career Tips," 'Helpful hints covering a variety of practical professional development issues'; "Solutions," 'Experts provide practical answers to help you solve your visual communications problems'; "Business Side," column by Ellen Opat-Inkeles; "ABCs of Type," column by Allan Haley; "Freelancing," "Methods of the Masters," "Shortcuts," 'These timesaving tricks and tips will help you get the job out the door' reader submissions; "Reference Shelf," 'Book reviews of the latest and standard titles imparting how-to and career aid information'; "Calendar," 'Upcoming seminars, trade shows, exhibitions, deadlines and other events in visual communications'; "Viewpoint," "Looking Ahead," 'A sampling of upcoming articles'. (7/8-90).
TYPL: "Stimulating New Thinking with Type," "The Magic of Metallic Inks," "Restoring a Legacy Through Identity," "3-D Realism Meets the Surreal," "Retouching Color Photos on Screen." (7/8-90).
SCHL: Seven issues per year, 150 pp.
SPAN: Nov/Dec, 1985+
DD: 760
ISSN: 0886-7682

✧ STEREO REVIEW

SUB: "The magazine for people who listen."
SUB: "Incorporating High Fidelity."
SUB: "Formerly Hi Fi/Stereo Review."
PUBL: Diamandis Communications, Inc., 1633 Broadway, New York, NY 10019.
DESC: Authoritative, thorough, reliable; for over 30 years, *Stereo Review* and its predecessors have produced a publication of uncompromising quality on the current status and future trends of consumer audio. With the upsurge of video in the decade of the nineties, *Stereo Review* includes reviews of new visual technology, but does so in a manner that does not compromise its basic focus, of stereo audio for the home consumer. The publication has two basic sections; hardware and software. The "Equipment" segment provides outstanding reviews of new technology understandable

both to the engineer and the lay reader. "Music" features articles concerning the artistic side of the medium, with interviews, artist profiles, and reviews of current releases. Of special note is the professional, courteous manner in which letters to the editor are written and responded to by the magazine's contributing staff. One would be hard-pressed to surpass *Stereo Review*. For the sampled issue of 1991: full and spot-color throughout on coated paper stock in a stapled magazine format (8 x 10 ½ inches / 200 x 265 mm).

DEPT: "New Products," 'Roundup of the latest audio equipment and accessories'; "Audio Questions and Answers," reader-submitted Q&A column by Larry Klein; "Car Stereo," column by Ivan Berger; "Tape Talk," column by Craig Stark; "Technical Talk," column by Julian D. Hirsch; "Equipment Test Reports," column by Julian D. Hirsch; Signal Processors," 'A buyer's guide to equalizers, imagers, noise reducers, and the like' column by Ivan Berger; "Bulletin," late-breaking news column by William Livingstone; "Speaking of Music," editorial commentary column by William Anderson; "Best Recordings of the Month," "Letters to the Editor," "Going on Record," column by James Goodfriend. (1-82). "Bulletin," newsbriefs; "Letters," "New Products," review; "Audio Q & A," column by Ian G. Masters; "Signals," trends column by Ken C. Pohlmann; "Technical Talk," column by Julian Hirsch; "Popular Music," reviews of new releases; "Classical Music," reviews; "Going on Record," column by William Livingstone; "The High End," commentary column by Ralph Hodges; "Record Makers," newsbrief column by Christie Barter and Steve Simels. (4-90).

TYPL: "Audiophile Discs," "Interview: The Gatlin Brothers." (1-82). "CES Show Stoppers," "Video for the Nineties," "Roots of Rock-And-Roll," "Yo-Yo Ma." (4-90).

SCHL: Monthly, 115 pp.
SPAN: Feb, 1958+
VARIES
--Feb, 1958 - Nov, 1958 as Hi Fi & Music Review.
--Dec, 1958 - Jan, 1960 as Hi Fi Review.
--Feb, 1960 - Oct, 1968 as Hi Fi/Stereo Review.
ABSORBED
--High Fidelity (ISSN: 0018-1455), ?, 1989.
LC: ML 1 .H43
DD: 780/.5
ISSN: 0039-1220
ABST: --Book Review Index (ISSN: 0524-0581)
--Consumers Index to Product Evaluations and Information Sources (ISSN: 0094-0534)
--Music Article Guide
--Music Index (ISSN: 0027-4348)
--Popular Magazine Review (ISSN: 0740-3763)
--Readers Guide to Periodical Literature (ISSN: 0034-0464)
--RILM Abstracts (ISSN: 0033-6955)

✦ STEREOPHILE

PUBL: Stereophile, 208 Delgado, Santa Fe, NM 87501.

DESC: *Stereophile* is a gathering place, a forum for the literate stereophile who is passionate about the quality of music emanating from today's stereophonic audio system. In one sampled issue for 1988, nine full pages were devoted to letters from readers and subscribers. These were letters of passion and spoke highly of this monthly publication: "*Stereophile*, where have you been all my life? Reading your magazine was almost like viewing the Grand Canyon for the first time. Your opinions exhibit considerable dynamic range with excellent mental imaging and good focus on the detail. Humor is slightly dry and crisp in the upper registers, but with fine overall transparency (especially in the bass). Sonic integrity is well-defined and presented with depth and resolution across the entire soundpage. Highly recommended." Another reader comments; "I don't usually write to publications, but I do feel it is a privilege to be one of your subscribers. *Stereophile* is the most informative and well-written publication on the market today, and this comes from a person who has sold audio and enjoyed music for 15 years." These accolades have been well-earned, for great care is evident in each month's editorial content, from a review of a new record/CD release, to scrutinizing testbench results of a new stereo product recently arriving on the home market. The publication targets (and gets) discerning stereophiles, those for whom cost is (almost) no object, who insist on the highest quality of construction or artistic performance for the money invested. Equipment reviews and reviews of reviews ("Follow Up") demonstrate not only a meticulous quest for accurate information, but also a sense of fairness toward the manufacturer and the upper limits of what contemporary technology is capable of achieving. This latter philosophy is echoed in the wonderful "Manufacturers' Comments," department where stereo equipment manufacturers and vendors have an opportunity to respond to reviews of their equipment, to clarify evaluations, or simply to comment on the volatile nature of an industry dependent upon consumer tastes and trends. For those individuals for whom stereo audio is an experience rather than just background sound, *Stereophile* is MUST reading! Perfect bound, journal format with a mixture of black/white editorial content and advertisements throughout on coated paper stock (5 ½ x 8 ⅜ inches / 140 x 215 mm).

DEPT: "As We See It," Founder and Chief Tester commentary column by J. Gordon Holt; "Letters," unusually large and literate letters to the editor column; "Industry Update," 'High-end news from the USA and UK'; "Equipment Reports," extensive testbench product reviews; "Follow Up," stereo equipment review updates; "Pure Gold," column by Alvin Gold; "Building a Library," column by Christopher Breunig; "Record Reviews," "Manufacturers' Comments," an opportunity for stereo equipment manufacturers to speak out; "The Final Word," 'Publisher Larry Archibald muses in print on the state of the industry' column by Larry Archibald. (1-88).

TYPL: "A New York State of Mind," "New York, New York," "In Search of Black Diamonds," "Back on Black Vinyl." (1-88).
SCHL: Monthly, 230 pp.
SPAN: Jan, 1978+
ISSN: 0585-2544

STORY WORLD AND PHOTODRAMATIST, THE

SUB: "A magazine for the cultivation of self-expression through creative writing." (? - Aug, 1923).
PUBL: Photodramatist Publishing Co., 6411 Hollywood Blvd., Hollywood, CA.
DESC: A publication for the professional screenwriter, *The Story World and Photodramatist* provided first-hand information on the creative side of scriptwriting through the use of example. Articles discussed characterization, what producers wanted in their scripts, how to write for a major screen star, the problem of censorship, receiving payment (in full), and other issues. Authors were professionals themselves, Charlie Chaplain writing on directing his first drama and his concept of the perfect script. Also appearing regularly was a column by Frederick Palmer, a well-known advertiser, which offered correspondence school script-writing lessons. Journal format; occasional graphics; newsprint.
DEPT: "Facts about Fiction," instructional column by George Allan England; "Today and Tomorrow," comment; "In the Foreground," editorial; "Good English and Its Use," instructional column by Hazel Spencer; "H. H. Van Loan's Own Corner," comment; "The Service Bureau," "For Your Bookshelf," reviews. (7-23).
TYPL: "The Screen Story of the Future," "The Government Agent in Fiction," "Adaptations--or Screen Plays?," "Are Americans People?" (7-23).
SCHL: Monthly, 90 pp.
SPAN: Jul?, 1919 - Aug, 1925//
ABSORBED
--Photodramatist, The, Aug, 1923.
LC: PN 1993.P45

✤ STORYBOARD / THE ART OF LAUGHTER

SUB: "The journal of animation art."
SUB: "Your journal of animation art and Disneyana collecting."
SUB: "The art of laughter."
PUBL: Laughter Publicatioiins, Inc., 80 Main St., Nashua, NH 03060.
DESC: "Are you tired of not getting the latest information on animation art, movies and television shows? Are you confused about the value of that cel you purchased on your last visit to Disneyland or the Universal Tour? Have you ever wondered why it costs so much for a cel of your favorite cartoon character? How much is that old Mickey Mouse doll worth? What about your upcoming vacation, just what Theme Park should you visit, and indeed, just what is a Theme Park? The answer to all these questions and hundreds more are all found on the pages of *StoryboarD/The Art of Laughter*, the only magazine of its type in the world." For anyone interested in the burgeoning field of animation art, theme parks and collectibles, a subscription to *StoryboarD/The Art of Laughter* is an absolute MUST! This publication is first-class from full-color pages on heavy coated paper stock; to the wonderful, informative articles about theme parks, collectibles and animation artists and their work. Indeed, one may never see better reproductions of animation cells than in this publication. While the emphasis is on Walt Disney Company animation, theme parks, and collectibles, Publisher Stephen E. Fiott and Editor Peter Primrose are quick to point out (to one reader's question) that they are neither exclusively devoted to Disney nor do they maintain a "blind critical eye" to Disney or to any other animation organization. "To be sure, we ARE NOT a 'fanzine', and we will continue with this unbiased reporting on major theme park and animation art events. However, we will also report both sides of any issue. We are not out to get anyone or any company. Our job will be to report ALL the news, and to make suitable editorial comments on these issues within the confines of fairness, decency and our own opinions." Stapled magazine format; full-color throughout on heavy coated paper stock. Many advertisements also in full color (8 ½ x 11 inches / 215 x 280 mm).
DEPT: "In This Issue," editorial description; "Readers Forum," letters; "Animated Trends," excellent commentary column by Dave Wirbal; "Cheers and Jeers," thumbs up/down on a variety of animation news items; "Collecting Disneyana," informative column by Tom Tumbusch; "California Dreamin'," column by Van Arsdale France; "Restoration," animation art column by Stephen Worth and Lew Stude; "Reviews," animation productions reviewed; "The Last Word," publisher commentary column by Steve Fiott. (1/2-91).
TYPL: "Mickey Mouse: Fifty Years and Back to the Future," "An Interview with Virgil Ross," "The Making of a Collectible." (1/2-91).
SCHL: Bimonthly, 50 pp.
SPAN: Fall, 1990+
ISSN: 1040-3167

Strandlight

? - ?//
SEE: LIGHTS!

✤ STRANGE ADVENTURES

SUB: "Paving the way for the future."
SUB: "The fanzine of science fiction, fantasy and horror -- in cinema, books, video, comics, art & television."
PUBL: Tony Lee, 13 Hazely Combe, Arreton, Isle of Wight P030 EAJ, England.

DESC: With stark black/white layout design, graphics, and drawings *Strange Adventures* explores the world of "...science fiction, fantasy and horror -- in cinema, books, video, comics, art & television." Articles are typewritten, but display a knowledgeable manner about the media and these genres. Typical of the innovative fetures in the sampled issue was "The Great Apes," an A - Z listing of motion pictures featuring all the cinema simians from Bonzo to Kong and then some. Of special note are excellent reviews of films, books, and video releases all with extensive critiques, a very expressive letters columnn "The Empire Writes Back," and a detailed "Megazine Scene," describing the form, function and style of a number of similar fanzines. Editor and Publisher Tony Lee has created an informative, and always fascinating publication for this genre. One small note of caution: some readers may find an occasional drawing or graphic to be too violent or suggestive of violence, but that after all is the essence of any *Strange Adventure*. For the sampled issue of 1991: Stapled magazine format, black ink on uncoated paper stock, numerous graphics, no advertising (8 ⅜ x 11 ¾ inches / 210 x 295 mm).
DEPT: "Intro," editorial column by Tony Lee; "Reel People," column by Tony Lee; "Megazine Scene," review of other fanzines; "Print Out," book review; "On the Box," film and television review; "Pulp Culture," book review; "The Empire Writes Back," letters; "Videozone," reviews; "Department of Reality," news items. (6-91).
TYPL: "The Great Apes," "The Martians are Coming," "Predators." (6-91).
SCHL: Monthly, 24 pp.
SPAN: Feb, 1989+

Student Forum

Nov, 1978 - ?, 1978//
(ISSN: 0148-589x)
SEE: PHOTOGRAPHER'S FORUM

✢ STUDENT PRESS LAW CENTER REPORT

PUBL: Student Press Law Center, 800 18th St., NW, Suite 300, Washington, DC 20006.
DESC: "The Student Press Law Center is the only national organization devoted exclusively to protecting the First Amendment rights of this nation's high school and college journalists. The Center serves as a national legal aid agency providing legal assistance and information to students and faculty advisers experiencing censorship or other legal problems. Three times a year (Winter, Spring and Fall), the Center publishes a comprehensive Report summarizing current controversies over student press rights. In addition, the Reports explain and analyze complex legal issues most often confronted by student journalists. Major court and legislative actions are highlighted." Some 20-30 articles per issue are presented. This is "must" reading for any journalism advisor. Magazine format.
DEPT: None. (spring-85). None. (spring-86).
TYPL: "Georgia Supreme Court Rebuffs Dogged Editors," "Class Project Produces Libel Judgement," "Comic Situation Becomes Court Battle," "Homophobia in Nebraska?" (spring-85). "Twisted Times Editor Still Shouts Dispute Not Moot," "Court Orders High School to Run Story," "Editors Win Settlement in Cut-and-Dried Case," "No Settlement in Sight so Adviser Sues School." (spring-86).
SCHL: Three issues per year, 40 pp.
SPAN: Winter, 1978+
VARIES
--Spring, 1986 - ? as SPLC Report.
LC: KF 4165.A15 S8
DD: 344/.73/0793
ISSN: 0160-3825

Studies in the Anthropology of Visual Communication

Fall, 1974 - 1979//
(ISSN: 0192-6918)
SEE: STUDIES IN VISUAL COMMUNICATION

STUDIES IN VISUAL COMMUNICATION

PUBL: Annenberg School Press, Annenberg School of Communications, Box 13358, Philadelphia, PA 19101.
DESC: "*Studies in Visual Communication* continues *Studies in the Anthropology of Visual Communication* (Volumes 1 - 5), founded in 1974 by Sol Worth. *Studies in Visual Communication* is a multidisciplinary journal drawing on the many areas of scholarship that focus upon aspects of visual communication. The editors welcome theoretical and empirical contributions devoted to signficant problems and issues in the study of visual communication." The publication offered a mixture of historical review and current photographic/visual works. Visuals were printed black/white on high-quality paper. For the sampled issues of 1985: black ink on coated paper; cover comprised of black ink with spot-color on coated index stock; in perfect-bound magazine format; no advertising (8 ¼ x 10 ¾ inches / 210 x 275 mm).
DEPT: "Briefly Noted," newsbriefs; "Reviews and Discussion," large section of book reviews. (fall-83). "Editor's Note." (spring-85).
TYPL: "The Photographic Work of E. J. Marey," "Clarence H. White Reconsidered: An Alternative to the Modernist Aesthetic of Straight Photography," "The United States View Company of Richfield, Pennsylvania," "Filmmaking by 'Young Filmmakers.'" (fall-83). "Emil Otto Hoppé, 1878 - 1972," "Forming a Profession," "Harald Lechenperg, Photojournalist," "Bernd Lohse, Photojournalist." (spring-85).

SCHL: Three issues per year [irregular at times] (Fall, 1974 - ?); Three issues per year (Spring, 1980 - Fall, 1983); Quarterly (Fall, 1983 - 1985//), 100 pp.
SPAN: Fall, 1974 - Fall, 1985//
VARIES
--Fall, 1974 - 1979 as Studies in the Anthropology of Visual Communication (ISSN: 0192-6918).
LC: BF 241 .S84
DD: 302.2
ISSN: 0276-6558
ABST: --Abstrax
--Art Bibliographies Modern (ISSN: 0300-466x)
--Film Literature Index (ISSN: 0093-6758)

Studio News
Winter, 1942 - Jun, 1950//
SEE: ART DIRECTION

✦ STUDIO PHOTOGRAPHY
SUB: "The business magazine for the professional portrait and commercial photographer."
PUBL: PTN Publishing Co., 210 Crossways Park West, Woodbury, NY 11797.
DESC: "*Studio Photography* is the business magazine of professional photography, providing the portrait, commercial and wedding photographer with the information one needs to operate a profitable, successful studio." It provides articles on making a profit, new darkroom applications, emerging opportunities, notable trends, and new techniques in the art and craft of commercial photography. Monthly columns address many of the business aspects of this industry, providing the owner-operator with "state-of-the-art" technology and business acumen required for successful operation. For the trade; excellent resource for numerous color graphic examples of commercial photography. Stapled magazine format, black/white and full-color pages throughout on coated paper stock (8 x 10 ¾ inches / 205 x 275 mm).
DEPT: "Letters to the Editor," "New Products," "Light and Lighting," column by Peter Nicastro; "Viewpoint." (10-72). "Pro Talk," "Legal Photographer," "Videography," "Bulletin Board," "New Products," "Market Page," "Book Reviews." (2-88). "Under the Cover," editorial; "Bulletin Board," "New Products," "Industry News," "F-Stop," production stories; "Videography," column by David Fox; "Computers in the Studio," column by Joel Sampson; "Point Sources," techniques and technologies column by Mike Ballai; "Legal Photographer," column by Larry Shavelson; "Dollars and Sense," column by Sharon Cohen. (1-89).
TYPL: "Photography and the Law," "Bank Credit Cards and the Portrait Studio," "Students and Cameras Abroad," "Nothing Succeeds Like Publicity." (10-72). "Dream Job," "Selling Wedding Albums," "James B. Wood's Hollywood Americana," "The Craft of Portraiture."

(2-88). "An Editorial Style in Advertising," "Studio of the Year: Bruce Andre," "Shedding Light on Barebulb," "X-Rays and Film: An Update." (1-89).
SCHL: Bimonthly (196u - ?); Monthly (?+), 60 pp.
SPAN: Jan, 1965+
EDITION
--Professional Photographers Edition.
VARIES
--196u - Dec?, 1967? as Photographic Product News.
--Jan, 1968 - Jun?, 1975 as Photographic Business and Product News.
ISSN: 0746-0996

Studio Sound
May, 1973 - ?//
SEE: STUDIO SOUND AND BROADCAST ENGINEERING

✦ STUDIO SOUND AND BROADCAST ENGINEERING
PUBL: Link House Publications, Ltd., Dingwall Ave., Croydon CR9 2TA, England.
DESC: In 1959, when this publication began, the title, *The Tape Recorder*, was an appropriate banner for both the exciting new realm of studio recording and the home consumer. The serial then commenced a variety of changes, including the spinning off of *Video and Audio-Visual Review* (now called *Professional Video*), and *Broadcast Sound* in September, 1982. Some 30 years of evolution has made *Studio Sound and Broadcast Engineering* a world-class publication today, showcasing studio recording facilities, trends, technology, and the profit side of the art and technique of studio sound. Articles contain a good balance between issues of a technological or business nature, and information about the status of studio recording in the United Kingdom, and to some extent the United States. Of special interest are ongoing columns, "Business," by Barry Fox; and "Perspective," by Martin Polon. A quality publication for the studio recording industry. Magazine format (8 ¼ x 11 ¾ inches / 210 x 300 mm), full color throughout on coated paper stock.
DEPT: "News," "Studio Diary," production news; "Survey," equipment; "Business," "Review," equipment. (6-81). "Editorial," "News," 'Events, news, moves and comment from inside and outside the industry'; "Products," 'Information on new products, developments, upgrades and software updates'; "Music News," 'Product updates and developments from another side of the business'; "Business," column by Barry Fox; "Perspective," column by Martin Polon. (12-89). "Editorial," 'Studio Sound's viewpoint on events and trends, and their implications'; "News," 'Events, news, moves and comment from inside and outside the recording industry'; "Products," 'Information on new products, developments, upgrades and software updates'; "Music News," 'Product updates and developments from another side of the business', compiled column by Zenon Schoepe; "Live Sound," 'Keeping

abreast of live sound news and equipment'; "Business," column by Barry Fox; "Perspective," column by Martin Polon; "Monitor Systems," column by Philip Newell. (2-91).
TYPL: "AES 68th Convention, Hamburg--A Report," "Glyn Johns," "Designing a Mixing Console." (6-81). "MADI Interface--An Overview," "The Loudspeaker Connector Debate," "Digital Audio Monitoring." (12-89). "Maintaining Digital Audio Quality," "AES Preview," "Conversation with Quincy Jones," "Sounding Out D-2," "VCAs Revisited." (2-91).
SCHL: Monthly, 90 pp.
SPAN: Jan?, 1959+
VARIES
--Jan?, 1959 - ? as Tape Recorder, The.
--? - Apr, 1973? as Tape Recorder.
--May, 1973 - ? as Studio Sound.
ISSN: 0144-5944

STV

Jan, 1983 - 198u//
(ISSN: 0885-6745)
SEE: STV GUIDE

STV GUIDE

SUB: "The home satellite television magazine™".
SUB: "The most complete guide to satellite TV."
PUBL: Triple D Publishing, Inc., 1300 South DeKalb St., Shelby, NC 28150.
DESC: In satellite television, events occurred quickly, and home consumers without the benefit of a publication such as *STV* may have become lost. Fortunately, *STV* provided a monthly update on the home satellite television industry, serving up a pleasant mix of feature, technical, and satellite programming articles. Other sister publications provided in-depth programming services. *STV Guide* had programming schedules by transponder, but concentrated primarily on news of the home satellite industry as it related to the home consumer. Magazine format.
DEPT: "Editor's Corner," "The Canadian Scene," column by Bill Barr; "And Now a Few Words About...," 'Editorial comment column by Mike L. Gustafson'; "Spacewatch," column by Jeffrey Manber; "New Products," "The Feed Finders," news of satellite feeds column by Bill Britton; "News," "Uplink Downlink," letters to editor; "Consumer Problems," home consumer satellite television; "Transponder Service Watch," programming schedule by transponder; "Video/Audio Services," satellite programming in alphabetical order. (9-86).
TYPL: "SPOT: The New French Remote Sensing Satellite," "Purchasing a Satellite System," "Hanging By a Thread: The Tethered Satellite Program," "Is Your Receiver Videocipher Compatible?" (9-86).
SCHL: Monthly, 80 pp.
SPAN: Jan, 1983 - Jun, 1990//

VARIES
--Jan, 1983 - 198u as STV (ISSN: 0885-6745).
DD: 384 11
ISSN: 1040-631x

SUCCESSFUL MAGAZINE PUBLISHING

SUB: "The magazine for growing magazines."
SUB: "Official journal of the Successful Magazine Publishers Group."
SUB: "The journal of the Small Magazine Publishers Group."
PUBL: Randall Publishing Co., PO Box 2029, Tuscaloosa, AL 35403.
DESC: This was the official publication of the Successful Magazine Publishers Group, a trade association dedicated to the premise that publication success could be attained through quality management of circulation, layout design, advertising, editorial content, printing, and other managerial aspects critical to the publishing process. Articles were positive, providing practical information, case studies, and discussion of trends in the industry. The approximate $100 annual membership fee was inexpensive for the kind of professional information and advice contained in *Successful Magazine Publishing* and companion monthly newsletter, *Magazine Business*. The publication was purchased by Lighthouse Communications in fall, 1989, and absorbed into its weekly serial, *MagazineWeek*, as of January 29, 1990; where it now appears as a bimonthly special section. Well recommended for any serial publisher. For the 1989 sampled issue: Perfect-bound magazine format with mixture of black ink, spot and full-color pages with full-color cover on coated paper stock (8 1/8 x 10 7/8 inches / 210 x 275 mm).
DEPT: "Editor's Journal," "Letters to the Editor," "For Your Information," newsbriefs; "Members Make the News," members of the Successful Magazine Publishers Group; "Coming Up," calendar; "Publishing Law," "Print & Production," "Circulation," "Design." (9/10-89).
TYPL: "For Love of Country," "Expanding the Editor's Role," "Advertorials," "Buying and Selling Magazines." (9/10-89).
SCHL: Bimonthly, 70 pp.
SPAN: Jan/Feb, 1984 - Nov/Dec, 1989//
ABSORBED BY
--MagazineWeek (ISSN: 0895-2124), Jan 29, 1990.
DD: 070 11
ISSN: 0892-6581

Successful Writing

Dec, 1920 - Feb, 1921//
SEE: WRITER'S DIGEST

Super 8 Filmaker

Winter, 1972/1973 - Jul/Aug, 1981//
(ISSN: 0049-2574)
SEE: MOVING IMAGE

✣ SUPER TEEN

SUB: "Your #1 NKOTB spot!"
PUBL: Sterling's Magazines, Inc., 355 Lexington Ave., New York, NY 10017.
DESC: The latest news, biographies, publicity shots, and production stills of current teenage stars of motion pictures, television, and music fields can be found in this monthly publication. The emphasis is on male artists in the film and television field, with numerous pictures of same, almost all of which are "off-stage, off-screen." In one sample issue, the music group, New Kids on the Block, secured both the cover picture and a significant portion of editorial copy within the magazine. Each issue contains full-color, full-page pinups, including a large centerfold poster. For the 1990 sampled issue: Stapled magazine format; editorial content being black ink with spot color on uncoated paper stock; cover, and pull-out poster section on coated paper stock (8 1/8 x 10 7/8 inches / 205 x 275 mm).
DEPT: "Super Teen Tattler!," color pictures of favorite teen stars; "Super Teen Stuff!," 'The juiciest juice from East to West' column by Diana; "Behind-the-Scenes at Super Teen," 'The inside scoops behind the stories inside!'; "The Total Truth!," Q&A on teenage stars; "Jodi's Hollywood Hotline!," 'What's happening out in La La Land, where the stars work and play all day?'; "Super Teen on the Scene!," 'Gettin' up close & personal with...'; "Video Views!," new film/video releases column by Bob Schartoff; "NKOTB Klub!," letters for the New Kids on the Block; "Hot Picks!," "Go Go Girls!," female artist news; "Q&A With...," interview; "Lettin' Loose!," reader comment on teen stars; "Super Teen Mailbox!," addresses of teen stars; "Super Teen USA!," letters; "Super Teen's All-Star Advice Pages!," teenage stars Q&A advice column. (10- 90).
TYPL: "Tommy Page: Why This Babe Says 'I Truly Try to Respond to My Fans'," "All Those Adorable Linear Babes!," "Go on a 'Blue Lagoon 2' Cattle Call!," "A Day in the Big Apple with ANA!," "Jerry O'Connell's European Vacation Scrapbook!" (10-90).
SCHL: Ten issues per year, 120 pp.
SPAN: Oct, 1978+
ISSN: 8750-1767

Super Television

Jan, 1985? - Mar, 1989?//
SEE: CAMCORDER

✣ SYN-AUD-CON NEWSLETTER

SUB: "Synergetic audio concepts."
PUBL: Synergetic Audio Concepts, PO Box 669, San Juan Capistrano, CA 92693.
DESC: "The modern diffusion of misinformation deserves no mercy, and the technical writers who do not hesitate to spread lies for the sake of money should be punished just as one punishes the purveyors of adulterated food. One poisons the body, the other the mind." This anonymous quote in the Summer, 1989 issue of *Syn-Aud-Con Newsletter* succinctly describes this salient publication for professional sound engineers. Don & Carolyn Davis, who moved from California to a southern Indiana farm, developed a series of workshops where novice and professional alike could come together for the purpose of exploring audio engineering concepts. Their dynamic forum provides for both manufacturer and audio engineer a place (either on the farm for audio workshops, or via two excellent publications), whereby concepts can be considered, discussed and added, or deleted from accepted engineering practices. The editors give credit (oftentimes overdue) to those that deserve it, and admonish copy and article writers who might lack professional knowledge of their crafts. This is a publication for all audio technical personnel, especially for those involved in acoustic and audio design, development, and application. Black/white magazine format; numerous graphs, charts, pictures, and schematics; Audio engineering expertise is assumed.
DEPT: "Tech Topics." (summer-89).
TYPL: "Study of Microsecond Signal Delay," "Concert Sound Reinforcement Information Picture's Worth a Thousand Words," "Do Digital Filters Ring?," "PA-70 Loudspeaker Study." (summer-89).
SCHL: Quarterly, 30 pp.
SPAN: Fall, 1973+
ISSN: 0739-750x

✣ SYSTEMSLETTER

SUB: "A publication of the Information Systems Division of the International Communication Association."
PUBL: International Communication Association, Information Systems Division, PO Box 9589, Austin, TX 78766.
DESC: This newsletter serves the needs of members within the Information Systems Division of the International Communication Association. One author, Mike Allen, of the University of Wisconsin--Milwaukee, well described the form and function of this division in an article for the publication: "Consider three popular areas within the division: cognition, organizational technology, and methodology. All three appear to be types of information systems: Cognitive structures allow a person to organize and make sense of the world; organizations can be popularly thought of as systems and technological means of information transmission seem a logical topic of study; methodologies represent systems of generating and evaluating information generated by research experiences. Rather than seek a core for existence (one may be possible though the probability low), the goal of our

division should be to promote the examination of phenomena with a view toward generating knowledge & descriptions (often in the form of theories). Let philosophers, theologians, and romantics seek the meaning of life and the center of existence. As scientists, let us examine those things we call information systems, in whatever form, and at whatever level of analysis, in an effort to generate understanding." For the sampled issue of 1990: newsletter format; black ink on tinted uncoated paper stock; no advertising (8 ½ x 11 inches / 215 x 280 mm).

DEPT: None. (winter-90).
TYPL: "Network Conference Held at Suny-Buffalo," "Sunbelt Social Network Conference to Be Held Feb. 15-18," "ISSS Cybernetics Conference Held in Britain This Summer," "1989 Annual Meeting of the American Society for Cybernetics," "Sound Off: Does Information Systems Really Need an Identity?" (winter-90).
SCHL: Quarterly?, 6 pp.
SPAN: ?+

T

T & R Bulletin
1925? - ?//
SEE: RADIO COMMUNICATION

✢ TABS
PUBL: Rank Strand Electric, Ltd., 29 King St., Covent Garden, London WC2E 8JH, England.
DESC: This delightful, small journal is devoted to the promotion, maintenance, installation, and operation of lighting instruments for various theatrical situations. Since publication is by the Rank Strand Electric firm of London, it should be anticipated that it is their fine line of lighting instruments which will take center stage. Articles are informative, and cope with a wide range of lighting applications, often providing theatre construction schematics; and illustrating how a given problem was resolved. For example, one article in the sampled issue described a theatrical production which required both quality scene projection upstage, while providing full lighting capabilities for the actors downstage. Several items are noteworthy in the sampled issue, from the large number of black/white and color photographs which add to understandability and pleasure; to the lively "Correspondence" section, whereby lighting professionals debate the merits of new technologies, application, and lighting design techniques. Also of note is a French and German language summary page of the editorial content. For the sampled issue of 1971: stapled small, journal format; editorial content consisting of black ink (with a number of full-color pictures) on coated paper stock; no advertising (5 ⅞ x 8 ¼ inches / 150 x 210 mm).
DEPT: "Editorial," "Correspondence," letters; "Synopsis," issue article summaries in French and German. (3-71).
TYPL: "Pantomime at the Theatre Royal, Norwich," "After Strange Gods," "Madame Tussaud in Amsterdam," "Only Preset Controls Will Do," "Super Projection in the Garden at the Garden." (3-71).
SCHL: ?, 40 pp.
SPAN: ?+?

TAKE ONE
SUB: "The film magazine."
PUBL: Unicorn Publishing, Box 1778, Station B, Montreal, Quebec H3B 3L3, Canada.
DESC: With an interesting circulation policy that placed only every other issue on the newstand, *Take One* was a fascinating combination of Hollywood, Canadian, European and third-world motion picture news. One sampled issue dealt with new Hollywood producers, discussed the traffic in pirated films, presented a historical piece on Pola Negri, and discussed a female producer/director of pornographic films. This was, in essence, a Canadian publication with a world film viewpoint. Articles were well-written and struck a harmonious balance between esoteric film criticism and popular film reaction. Magazine format (8 ⅜ x 11 inches / 210 x 280 mm); black/white production stills.
DEPT: "The News Page," 'The truth 24 times per second'; "Letters," "Notes From the New Cinema," column by Bob Cowan; "Letter From Switzerland," column by Fred Barron; "Holding Pattern," column by James Monaco; "Film as Business," column by Michael F. Mayer; "Coffee, Brandy and Cigars," column by Herman G. Weinberg; "Book News," "Book Reviews," column by Glen Hunter and Harold Weaver; "Books on Film: A Checklist," column by George L. George; "Conferences & Competitions," "Booker's Guide to 16mm Films," "16mm News," "Misc," newsbriefs. (9-20-75). "Letters," "Dish Night," "At the Movies," "Film Books," "Pundents." (1-79).
TYPL: "Of Mice & Cats," "So You Wanna Be a Star," "A Hollywood Survival Handbook," "Why We (Should Not) Fight," "Mother and Me and the Kiddie Business." (9-20-75). "Working His Way Through College," "Stars Behind the Lens," "The Write-a-Script-for DePalma Contest," "Blind Bidding," "Celluloid Classroom." (1-79).
SCHL: Monthly, 55 pp.
SPAN: Sep/Oct, 1966 - Nov, 1979//
LC: PN 1993.T
ISSN: 0039-9132

TALKING PICTURE MAGAZINE
SUB: "Only publication devoted to talking pictures and television." (Oct, 1929).
SUB: "All ways interesting." (Dec, 1929 - Jul, 1934).
PUBL: Daniel O'Malley Co., 20 West 60th St., New York, NY.
DESC: *Talking Picture Magazine* began as a public offering of articles, advertisements, and story synopses targeted to producers, writers, and playgoers; and included the new medium of television in the first issue. References to television were reduced by the second issue, and removed from the serial altogether by the fourth issue, of January, 1930. In February, 1930 the serial settled into its final format of reproducing story synopses (after copyright) for its intended producer and writer audience. Each of these latter issues reproduced some 100+ story synopses available to motion picture (and perhaps television) producers. Latter issues were typeset in 8-point type with no graphics.

DEPT: "Current Copyrights," script synopses; "Sound Effects," newsbriefs. (11-29).
TYPL: "Fast Life," "From Convent to Screen is Mary Nolan's Career." (11-29).
SCHL: Monthly (Oct, 1929 - May, 1930); Bimonthly [irregular at times], (Jul, 1930+), 18 pp.
SPAN: Oct, 1929 - Jul, 1934//
LC: PN 1993.T25

TALKING SCREEN
PUBL: Dell Publishing Co., 100 Fifth Ave., New York, NY.
DESC: A film-fan magazine, this serial was only concerned with "talking" motion pictures, and especially their stars. Uniquely printed in dark green duotones, the articles discussed actors' backgrounds, their current projects, and their leisure activities. Magazine format; numerous graphics.
DEPT: "Press Time Topics," newsbriefs; "Brief Guide," 'To give you a line or so on current talkie offerings'; "Just Your Style--and Hollywood's," column by Dorothea Hawley Cartwright; "In Reply Would Say," Q&A; "Editorial," "Tidings from Talkie Town," gossip; "Affairs of the Heart," 'Film folk who are saying We Will-- We do!-- We're through'; "Tips from Types," personality pointers from Crosby Frank; "Talking Screen Reviews," "Lest We Forget," trivia; "Role Call," 'Who's doing what and where.' (7-30).
TYPL: "Hollywood's Bad Actors," "So You're from Hollywood," "Their Business is Looking Up," "What Love Means to Me," "Victor McLaglen Interviews Victor McLaglen." (7-30).
SCHL: Bimonthly (Jan, 1930 - May, 1930); Monthly (Jun, 1930+), 95 pp.
SPAN: Jan, 1930 - Oct, 1930//
LC: PN 1993.T3

TALKS
SUB: "A quarterly digest of addresses of diversified interest broadcast over the Columbia network." (Jan, 1936 - ?).
SUB: "A quarterly digest of addresses presented in the public interest by the Columbia network."
PUBL: Columbia Broadcasting System, Inc., New York, NY.
DESC: With a foreword by William S. Paley, the Columbia Broadcasting System in January, 1936 launched this quarterly digest of radio talks broadcast over its radio network. "The growing vitality of American radio as an instrument for the swift exchange of significant thought is assuming increasing importance in our national growth. The Columbia Broadcasting System presents this magazine as a cross-section of some of these interesting contemporary ideas."
DEPT: None.
TYPL: "The Future of Ethiopia," "Fish and Their Management," "Labor Speaks of Security," "Religion and the Modern Mind." (4-36).
SCHL: Quarterly, 65 pp.
SPAN: Jan, 1936 - Jul, 1949//

WITH SUPPLEMENT
--Special Supreme Court Edition, Apr, 1937.
LC: AP 2 .T16
DD: 051

Tan
Nov, 1952 - Oct, 1971//
(ISSN: 0039-9345)
SEE: BLACK STARS

Tan Confessions
Nov, 1950 - Sep, 1952//
SEE: BLACK STARS

TAPE
PUBL: Conde Nast Publications, Ltd., Belmont Rd., London W4, England.
DESC: This was a consumer-oriented serial for tape recorded home entertainment. Articles covered stereo equipment, use of tape by broadcasters, and technological developments. The majority of this publication was reviews of new tape recorded product. Magazine format; graphics.
DEPT: "Tapenews," newsbriefs; "Tapecraft," uses for tape; "Hellyer's Clinic," problem solving; "Taperecorded," reviews; "Wildlife Recording," "Local Radio," "Hospitals Radio," "Tape Trends," "Tapeproducts," review. (12-73).
TYPL: "You have Only to Point a Mike," "Hire a Studio by the Hour," "Higher-Fi or Lower Cost?," "Push-Button Pleasure." (12-73).
SCHL: Monthly (1957 - Nov, 1959); Biweekly (Nov 4, 1959 - 1961); Monthly (1962+), 170 pp.
SPAN: Nov, 1972? - ?//?
VARIES
--Feb, 1957 - Nov, 1957 as Tape Recording and Reproduction Magazine.
--Dec, 1957 - Nov, 1958 as Tape Recording & High Fidelity Reproduction Magazine.
--Aug, 1958 - Aug 10, 1960 as Tape Recording and Hi-Fi Magazine.
--Aug 24, 1960 - 1961 as Tape Recording Fortnightly.
--1961 - Mar, 1971 as Tape Recording Magazine (ISSN: 0039-9558).
--Apr, 1971 - Sep/Oct, 1973 as Sound & Picture Tape Recording Magazine.
LC: TK 7881.6 .T29
DD: 621.389/32/05

Tape and Film Recording
Nov/Dec, 1953//
SEE: TAPE RECORDING

Tape Business

May/Jun, 1987 - ?//
SEE: TAPE/DISC BUSINESS

✣ TAPE DECK QUARTERLY

PUBL: ?, Box 1592, 20 Hampton Rd., Southampton, NY 11968.
DESC: *Tape Deck Quarterly* is a highly specialized publication in an era where pre-recorded audio tape sales have stablized or dropped in popularity. It does a credible job of detailing new cassette and tape products, and techniques of tape recording and editing, with the emphasis on reviewing of new audio tape releases.
DEPT: "Letters," "New Tape Products," "Feldman Lab Reports," "Classical Tape Reviews," "The Jazz Page," "Country Tape Reviews," "MOR Tape Reviews," "Rock Tape Reviews," "New Recorded Tape Releases." (winter-75).
TYPL: "Up the Hamateur," "FTC Power Rule," "Editing Tape." (winter-75).
SCHL: Quarterly, 65 pp.
SPAN: 1974+

✣ TAPE/DISC BUSINESS

SUB: "The newspublication for manufacturers, dealers, and duplicators of videotape and audiotape."
PUBL: Knowledge Industry Publications, Inc., 701 Westchester Ave., White Plains, NY 10604.
DESC: "*Tape/Disc Business* is the monthly news source that duplicators, replicators, manufacturers, dealers and major purchasers of audio and video tape count on for keeping them informed of rapid technological changes, regulation and legislation, imports and exports, major and subtle trends, and industry news." Of special note is a monthly editorial newsletter on light yellow uncoated paperstock that provides late-breaking news of the tape and disc industry. For the 1988 sampled issue: stapled magazine format with black ink editorial content and full-color cover on coated paper stock, with a special "Tape Business" section printed black ink on beige uncoated paper stock (8 ½ x 11 inches / 215 x 280 mm).
DEPT: "The Business of Tape," column by Harry Paney; "Report From Japan," column by Mitch Taura; "Industry News," unique late-breaking news section in newsletter format; "The Nature of Business," column by Neil Heller. (1-88).
TYPL: "Maintenance and Quality Are Synonyms," "Five Duplicators Dominate U.S. Movie Duplication Market," "DAT Legislation Drags Into New Year," "Copy Protection, Common Sense?" (1-88).
SCHL: Bimonthly (May/Jun, 1987? - ?); Monthly (?+), 16 pp.
SPAN: May/Jun, 1987+
VARIES
--May/Jun, 1987 - ? as Tape Business.

Tape Recorder, The

Jan?, 1959 - ?//
SEE: STUDIO SOUND AND BROADCAST ENGINEERING

Tape Recorder

? - Apr, 1973?//
SEE: STUDIO SOUND AND BROADCAST ENGINEERING

TAPE RECORDING

PUBL: A-TR Publications, 145 E. 52nd St., New York, NY 10022.
DESC: This magazine was devoted to the interests of individuals within the magnetic tape field, ranging from audio and film stock to electronic video recording. Articles described the recording session process in divergent locations of home, studio, and concert hall; providing problems and solutions for recording sessions in each of those places. Other articles described new technologies emerging in the audio tape field and their application to home consumer and commercial projects. Also, issues contained quality reviews of prerecorded audio tapes coming to the home consumer market, and other items of interest to the reader. Target audience was the American home consumer.
DEPT: "Tape Notes," newsbriefs; "Tape Reviews," prominent tape review section during 1960s heyday of reel-to-reel tape releases.
TYPL: "Acoustics in the Concert Hall," "Here's a Magic Genie for Your Recorder," "Recording Vocals with Piano," "Cometh the Cartridge." (5-69).
SCHL: Bimonthly (Nov/Dec, 1953 - Sep/Oct, 1956); Monthly (Dec, 1956 - ?); Seven times per year (?+), 35 pp.
SPAN: Nov/Dec, 1953 - Nov/Dec, 1970//
VARIES
--Nov/Dec, 1953 as Tape and Film Recording.
--Feb, 1954 - Oct, 1956 as Magnetic Film and Tape Recording.
--Dec, 1956 - Mar, 1960 as Hi-Fi Tape Recording.
--May, 1960 - ? as Tape Recording.
ABSORBED BY
--Tape Recording Magazine, Jan, 1971.
LC: TK 5981.H
ISSN: 0496-8816

Tape Recording

May, 1960 - ?//
SEE: TAPE RECORDING

Tape Recording and Hi-Fi Magazine

Aug, 1958 - Aug 10, 1960//
SEE: TAPE

Tape Recording & High Fidelity Reproduction Magazine

Dec, 1957 - Nov, 1958//
SEE: TAPE

Tape Recording and Reproduction Magazine

Feb, 1957 - Nov, 1957//
SEE: TAPE

Tape Recording Fortnightly

Aug 24, 1960 - 1961//
SEE: TAPE

Tape Recording Magazine

1961 - Mar, 1971//
(ISSN: 0039-9558)
SEE: TAPE

TARGET

SUB: "The political cartoon quarterly."
PUBL: Target, 461 Sharon Drive, Wayne, PA 19087.
DESC: In the autumn, 1981 premiere issue, editor Richard Samuel West noted, "American political cartooning has never been as healthy as it is now. Even though the number of newspapers in America is shrinking, the number of cartoonists is growing. This is because many papers, previously without cartoonists, are awakening to the special advantage that having a cartoonist of their own provides. ... Finally, the art is more lively and the artists more ambitious than ever before. *Target* is here to celebrate political cartooning. Because there are some things that can't be communicated through pictures, *Target* hopes to supplement the flood of graphic images with some words about what cartoonists are thinking about the nation, their profession, the daily challenge of cartooning, and their own work. To learn this, *Target* will talk to and listen to cartoonists from all over North America. We'll also explore the history of cartooning to unearth important stories and excellent artists that time has passed by. These tasks will contribute to a more knowledgeable assessment, primarily through book reviews and editorials, of the present state of the art." *Target* was the trade journal for American political cartoonists in the news editorial room. Each issue was a fascinating array of political cartoons, profiles of individual cartoonists, and the state of political cartooning in the North American journalism field. The quarterly ceased publication with the summer, 1987 issue in which editor West reflected; "...I simply hope that cartoonists have been strengthened, enlightened, or redirected in some manner by the 600-plus pages of criticism, opinion, and interviews that we have published over the years." This remains a noteworthy resource for the philosophies, backgrounds, and profiles of professional newspaper cartoonists. The sampled issues of 1981 and 1982 consisted of black ink on uncoated paper, in a stapled magazine format (8 ¼ x 10 ⅝ inches / 210 x 270). Note: the dimensions for the premiere issue of autumn, 1981 were slightly different (8 x 10 ⅛ inches / 205 x 255 mm).
DEPT: "On Target," editorial; "Books in Review," "Portfolio," sample cartoons; "American Drawing Board," newsbriefs; "British Drawing Board," newsbriefs; "Canadian Drawing Board," newsbriefs. (autumn-81). "Books in Review," "Portfolio," "American Drawing Board," "Canadian Drawing Board." (summer-87).
TYPL: "Don Wright, Cartooning Journalist," "A Responsibility to Fairness," "Post-War Apologia: The Nast-Grant Partnership." (autumn-81). "Cartooning as Sport--Keefe on the Inside Track," "The Pulitzer War," "The Rauch Treatment," "Cartoonists on Trial." (summer-87).
SCHL: Quarterly, 35 pp.
SPAN: Autumn, 1981 - Summer, 1987//
ISSN: 8756-1808

✢ TARGET MARKETING

SUB: "Dedicated to database marketing."
SUB: "Dedicated to direct marketing excellence."
PUBL: North American Publishing Co., 401 North Broad St., Philadelphia, PA 19108.
DESC: Direct mail product marketing is a highly competitive field in which the dynamics of reaching the target consumer are always evolving. Charting those changes, and marking future trends is *Target Marketing*, a monthly serial about direct marketing. New ideas are the lifeblood of direct marketing, and this publication provides thorough coverage of same, along with discussions on the elements of direct marketing; including envelope design, list management, postage, brochures, reply mail, and package inserts. Magazine format (8 ¼ x 10 ⅞ inches / 205 x 275 mm), with numerous advertisements by direct marketing suppliers.
DEPT: "Editor's Notebook," "On Target," newsbriefs; "Wavemaker," successful direct marketing profiles; "Hit or Miss," new direct mail projects; "Exclusive Gallup Survey," monthly feature; "Coming Events," calendar; "Hotline Names," personnel newsbriefs; "List Management," "Finish Line," newsbriefs; "Columnists," guest columnists on direct marketing issues. (5-88). "Editor's Notebook," "On Target," "TM Gallery," pix; "Misleading Mail," 'Misleading Mail of the Month Award'; "TM at Large," invited commentary on direct marketing issues; "Newswatch," newsbriefs; "Buyer's Guide," new product review; "Hotline Names," personnel newsbriefs; "Coming Events," calendar; "Finish Line," new ideas in direct marketing; "On Catalogs," column by Jack Schmid; "On Creative," column by Joan Harris; "Columnist," col-

umn by Richard Armstrong; "60- Second Seminar," column by 'Rocket' Ray Jutkins; "List News," '...for and about the list business'; "Broker Forum," "Catalog News." (3-90).
TYPL: "Polishing Mail Order's Tarnished Image," "List Abuse: The Non-Issue That Won't Go Away," "Risky Business: Choosing a Direct Marketing Agency," "Package Inserts: Where Do They Fit in Your Media Mix?" (5-88). "Addicted to Sweepstakes," "Can We Make DM Higher Ed High Brow?," "There's Money in Lists for Telemarketing," "Overseas Carriers Do It All." (3-90).
SCHL: Monthly, 105 pp.
SPAN: Jan, 1978+
VARIES
--Jan, 1978? - Jul, 1986? as ZIP Target Marketing (ISSN: 0739-6953).
LC: HF 5410 .Z56
DD: 658.8/4 19
ISSN: 0889-5333
ABST: --ABI/Informer
--Predicasts

✧ TAYLORTALK

SUB: "What's happening in yearbooks."
PUBL: Taylor Publishing Co., P.O. Box 597, Dallas, TX 75221.
DESC: "*TaylorTalk* is produced four times a year--September through May--for yearbook advisers and staffs..." A more professionally produced serial for assembling yearbooks would be hard to find. This quarterly is a showcase of "how-to" articles on publishing, presenting the variety of print capabilities available through the Taylor Publishing firm. Articles provide valuable instruction on layout design, editorial content, staff and publication management, information of value to the first-time or veteran yearbook manager. Many college textbooks on layout design, typography, graphics, and color don't equal this publication. For the sampled issue of 1988: black ink, spot and full-color graphics and pages on coated paper stock with full-color cover on heavy coated paper stock in stapled magazine format (9 x 12 inches / 230 x 305 mm).
DEPT: None. (1-88).
TYPL: "Get Real," "Sensible Diplomacy," "Claiming Your Turf," "The Presentation is Half the Fun." (#1-88).
SCHL: Quarterly (Sep - May); 34 pp.
SPAN: ?+

✧ TBI

SUB: "Television Business International."
PUBL: 21st Century Publishing, London, England.
DESC: There is no finer means of charting the political, economic and communication trends within a global market than *TBI*. It is truly international in scope, providing in one sampled issue television news items from over 25 nations. Of special note are feature article summaries in six languages, including English, German, and Japanese. This is television from a business point of view, with articles that are both thorough and authoritative. *TBI* is MUST reading for today's executive interested in the international broadcast, cable and satellite television market. Act III Publishing sold the title to 21st Century Publishing of London in January, 1991. For sampled issue of 1990: stapled magazine format; spot and full-color on coated paper stock (8 ¼ x 10 ⅞ inches / 210 x 275 mm).
DEPT: "Monitor," 'The television business, by TBI correspondents worldwide'; "Perspective," column by Les Brown and Bill Grantham; "Letter from London," column by Barrie Heads; "People to Watch," "Focus," large feature section concerning different television issue each month; "Finance," column by William Phillips; "Technology," column by George Jarrett; "Advertising," column by Toby Syfret; "Forecasts," 'Television scans its own future'. (1-89).
TYPL: "Ole! Here's Latin Power," "What Makes Programs Work?," "The Hottest Place in Europe," "White Paper Shows Up Ideological Goulash," "Tide Turns in Family Feud Over Media." (1-89).
SCHL: Ten issues per year [combined Jul/Aug, Nov/Dec issues], 65 pp.
SPAN: Feb, 1988+
ISSN: 0953-6841

TC, Theatre Crafts

Mar/Apr, 1967 - ?//
SEE: THEATRE CRAFTS

✧ TDR

SUB: "A journal of performance studies."
SUB: "The drama review."
PUBL: Tisch School of the Arts/New York University, MIT Press, 55 Hayward St., Cambridge, MA 02142.
DESC: "*TDR* is a scholarly, lively journal examining and debating the whole range of performance: theatre, dance rituals, politics, performance art, sports. Contributors are anthropologists, sociologists, performance scholars, and artists from all over the world. Each issue presents information from many different perspectives with beautifully illustrated photos and figures." *The Drama Review* serves as an international review of dramatic theatre. Some issues are devoted to a single topic. Typical of the articles from the 1991 volume are: "Bums on Seats: Parties, Art, and Politics in London's East End," "Teatro Festival: The Latino Festival Theatre," "The Thinker as Playwright: An Interview with Eric Bentley," "Whither Avant-Garde Radio Art?," "Theatre in Transition: The Cultural Struggle in South Africa," "Reality and Fantasy: The Performing Body in an Australian Noh Play," and "The Radicality of the Puppet Theatre." A promotional advertisement aptly put it, "Scholarly, yet readable, *TDR*'s pages contain politics, anthropology and performance theory. From Yoruba masked performance to the post modern dancing of Pina Bausch--no

other journal can bring you the excitement, the innovation, and the milieu of today's provocative performances." For the 1991 sampled issues: (7 x 10 inches / 175 x 250 mm).
DEPT: "Theatre Reports," "New Books." (summer-84). "Letters, Etc.," "Currents," news items. (summer-91).
TYPL: "American Scenography," "Richard Foreman's Scenography: Examples from His Work in France," "Aspects of Central European Design," "Scenography of Outdoor Performances in Japan," "West German Scenography." (summer-84). "To Put One's Fingers in the Bleeding Wound: Palestinian Theatre Under Israeli Censorship," "Stepping, Saluting, Cracking, and Freaking: The Cultural Politics of African-American Step Shows," "Crossing the Corpus Callosum: An Interview with Joan Schenkar," "The Role of the Raksasa: An Interview with Pak Asep Sunanda, Dalang of Wayang Golek Purwa," "Dispossessing the Spectator: Performance, Environment, and Subjectivity in Theatre of the Homeless." (summer-91).
SCHL: Quarterly, 190 pp.
SPAN: 1955?+
VARIES
--1955? - May?, 1957 as Carleton Drama Review (ISSN: 0161-3936).
--Jun, 1957 - Summer, 1967 as Tulane Drama Review (ISSN: 0886-800x).
--Fall, 1967 - Winter, 1968 as TDR (ISSN: 0273-4354).
--Spring, 1968 - Winter, 1987 as Drama Review, The (ISSN: 0012-5962).
LC: PN 2000 .D68
DD: 792/.05
ISSN: 0012-5962
ABST: --Abstract of English Studies (ISSN: 0001-3560)
--American Humanities Index
--Annual Bibliography of English Language and Literature (ISSN: 0066-3786)
--Arts and Humanities Citation Index (ISSN: 0162-8445)
--Book Review Index (ISSN: 0524-0581)
--International Index
--Magazine Index
--MLA International Bibliography of Books & Articles on the Modern Languages and Literatures (ISSN: 0024-8215)
--Social Science and Humanities Index (ISSN: 0037-7899)

TDR
Fall, 1967 - Winter, 1968//
(ISSN: 0273-4354)
SEE: TDR

Teacher's Guide to Media and Methods
Sep, 1966 - Oct, 1967//
SEE: MEDIA & METHODS

✤ TEACHER'S GUIDE TO TELEVISION
SUB: "Using television to lead families to museums and libraries."
PUBL: 225 West Ord Valley Dr., Tucson, AZ 85704.
DESC: An exceptional publication for teachers designed to incorporate current television fare into classroom instruction, each issue has 10-12 well written reviews which probe issues found within television programs and TV specials. Each article is subdivided into "Aim," "Teaching Suggestions Before Viewing," "Synopsis," and "For Further Exploration." Numerous publicity stills from the programs are featured. This is a publication aimed at teachers, but one which reaches beyond the pedagogical profession. For the sampled issues of 1978 through 1983: editorial content consisted of black ink with spot-color on uncoated paper stock; no advertising; stapled magazine format (8 ¼ x 10 ¾ inches / 210 x 275 mm).
DEPT: "Specially Selected Programs of Educational Value," programming guide to American network television; "Learning Resources," available films and videotapes. (spring-78). "Learning Resources." (spring-84).
TYPL: None. (spring-78). "TV News and Public Affairs Program--Up-to-the-Minute Teaching Resources." (spring-84).
SCHL: Semiannual, 35 pp.
SPAN: Nov, 1968+
DD: 371.3
ISSN: 0496-9960

Tech Photo Pro Imaging Systems
Jun, 1988 - Sep?, 1988//
(ISSN: 1040-0141)
SEE: ADVANCED IMAGING

TECHNICAL PHOTOGRAPHY
SUB: "For industrial, military and government still, cine and AV professionals."
PUBL: PTN Publishing Co., 101 Crossways Park West, Woodbury, NY 11797.
DESC: The focus here is photography concerning small mechanical items, product shoots, microscopic items and other subjects of interest to a technical-industrial photography department. Abundant information is provided on the technique of the film image, from the camera through the lab; including the corporate presentation.
DEPT: "New Products," "Film Talk," motion picture feature; "AV News amd Reviews," briefs; "From the Lab," information feature; "Jim's Scrapbook," technical advice from Jim Gupton; "News Notes," briefs; "Looking Ahead," upcoming events; "News Makers," profiles.

TYPL: "Profile; Fenwal's Photo Department," "AFP Holds First Photo Competition," "Techniques: Getting Good B/W from Color." (1-78). "NAVA Review," "N.Y. State Department of Commerce's Photo Unit," "Disc Photography," "The Large Format View Camera." (3-82).
SCHL: Bimonthly (Dec, 1968/Jan, 1969 - Apr/May, 1977); Monthly (Jun, 1977+), 60 pp.
SPAN: Dec, 1968/Jan, 1969 - May, 1988//
MERGED WITH
--Functional Photography (ISSN: 0360-7216) (to form) Tech Photo Pro Imaging Systems (ISSN: 1040-0141), Jun, 1988.
LC: TR 1.T38
DD: 770/.5
ISSN: 0040-0971
ABST: --Abstract Bulletin of the Institute of Paper Chemistry (ISSN: 0020-3033)

Technician
Sep, 1953 - Dec, 1953//
SEE: ELECTRONIC TECHNICAN/DEALER

Technician
Aug, 1956 - Oct, 1956//
SEE: ELECTRONIC TECHNICAN/DEALER

Technician & Circuit Digests
Jan, 1954 - Jul, 1956//
SEE: ELECTRONIC TECHNICAN/DEALER

✢ TECHNOLOGY AND CULTURE

SUB: "The international quarterly of the Society for the History of Technology."
PUBL: Society for the History of Technology, University of Chicago Press, 5801 Ellis Ave., Chicago, IL 60637.
DESC: "The title of our publication, *Technology and Culture*, was not lightly chosen. It reveals the breadth of our definition of culture and indicates our awareness of the complex and intricate interrelationships of all aspects of technology. We use 'culture' in the broad anthropological sense defined by Edward B. Tylor almost a century ago: 'Culture is that complex whole which includes knowledge, belief, art, morals, laws, custom, and any other capabilities and habits acquired by man as a member of society.' Technology itself is one of the most distinctive and significant of man's capabilities, and it is essential that we learn how it developed in order to analyze its relations with the other elements of culture." This serial provides important information on the relationship between society and technology, and in so doing, promotes understanding of communication technology development. Excellent historical resource; journal format; no graphics.
DEPT: "Book Reviews," "Communications," "Notes." (summer-60). "Research Note," "Exhibit Reviews," "Book Reviews." (10-86).
TYPL: "An Attempt to Measure the Rise of American Inventing and the Decline of Patenting," "The Legend of Eli Whitney and Interchangeable Parts." (summer-60). "Engineering in the 20th Century," "Engineering Knowledge in the Laser Field." (10-86).
SCHL: Quarterly, 150 pp.
SPAN: Winter, 1959+
LC: T 1.T27
ISSN: 0040-165x
ABST: --America, History and Life (ISSN: 0002-7065)
--Energy Information Abstracts (ISSN: 0147-6521)
--Excerpta Medica
--Historical Abstracts. Part A. Modern History Abstracts. (ISSN: 0363-2712)
--Historical Abstracts. Part B. Twentieth Century Abstracts. (ISSN: 0363-2725)
--International Aerospace Abstracts (ISSN: 0020-5842)
--Social Sciences Index (ISSN: 0094-4920)
--Social Welfare, Social Planning / Policy and Social Development (ISSN: 0195-7988)
--Writings on American History (ISSN: 0364-2887)

✢ TECHTRENDS

SUB: "To help improve instruction through the more effective use of materials." (Feb, 1956 - ?).
SUB: "For leaders in education and training."
SUB: "The official publication of the Association for Educational Communications and Technology." (Jan, 1980 - Jan, 1985).
PUBL: Association for Educational Communications & Technology, 1105 Vermont Ave., NW, Suite 820, Washington, DC 20005.
DESC: [*Audio-Visual Instruction*]: The National Education Association had established a Department of Visual Instruction (DAVI) in 1923, one year after founding *Educational Screen*. By 1954, however, DAVI had outgrown that serial's focus, and the decision was made to launch *Instructional Materials*, later renamed *Audio-Visual Instruction*. This was a serial of the classroom, where the best theories of audio-visual instruction met their test. It explored new equipment, and techniques of using audio-visual equipment in the classroom, confronting the tendency in the late 1950s of teachers to be threatened by the very media designed to aid them. Numerous graphics; magazine format.
DESC: [*Instructional Innovator*]: The official publication of the Association for Educational Communications and Technology, *Instructional Innovator* was for the elementary and high school teacher, as well as others who functioned within audiovisual learning centers. Articles, therefore, tended to operate on two levels; 1) management oriented features; and 2) "how-to" articles for classroom use. Articles tended to be short, but numerous.

DESC: *"TechTrends* welcomes submissions on any aspect of new technology in education and training in schools, colleges, and private industry." Articles range from personal networking to media management, distant learning courses, electronic clearinghouses, use of robotics in education, interactive cable television for rural schools, an evaluation of computer gradebook software, and other issues developing in the field of technology and instruction. Typical articles from 1991 include, "Linking Education and Industry: Reasons for Mutual Cooperation," "Tune-In and Turn On! Videos in the Classroom," " Teaching a Non-Relevant Curriculum," and "What Does Higher Ed Think About Educational Technology Services? A Study of Differing Perceptions." This is a splendid publication for educators who recognize the increasing role of technology in the classroom, library, and home environment. For the sampled issues of 1986 and 1991: editorial content consisted of black ink on coated paper; cover comprised of full-color graphics on coated stock; advertising; in stapled magazine format (8 ¼ x 11 inches / 210 x 280 mm).

DEPT: "Editorial Comment," "Editor's Notebook," "Within the DAVI Family," "News and Views," "Materials and Equipment," "Looking at New Literature." (12-56). "Teacher's Guides to Television," lengthy guidelines for upcoming specials and series; "Clips," publisher briefs; "New Products," "AECT Archives Software Collection," a listing of software gathered by AECT and available to members; "Literature," review; "Division Forum," news concerning AECT; "ERIC," developments in data base operations; "Media Q and A," how-to Q&A. (4-78). "The Leading Edge," "New Products," "According to informed sources," comment. (11/12-85).

TYPL: "Save Your Treasures--Put Them on Tape," "A New Way to Introduce Library Films," "Teacher Education--Our Best Investment." (12-56). "Why Media Budges Get Cut," "The Cost of Renting Films," "The Shifting Base of Public Financing," "Rediscover Radio." (4-78). "VCRs Silently Take Over the Classroom," "Unique Techniques for Special Effects on Color Slides," "How to Make Computer Literacy Cost-Effective." (11/12-85).

SCHL: Monthly [except Jul - Sep], (Feb, 1956 - Jun, 1958); Monthly [except Jul - Aug], (Sep, 1958 - ?); Eight issues per year [combined issues Feb/Mar, May/Jun, Jul/Aug, Nov/Dec] (? - ?); Monthly [except Jun-Aug] (Jan, 1980 - Dec, 1981); Monthly [except Jun-Aug, and Dec] (Jan, 1982+), 30 pp.

SPAN: Feb, 1956+
VARIES
--Feb, 1956 - Jun, 1956 as Instructional Materials.
--Oct, 1956 - May, 1978 as Audiovisual Instruction (ISSN: 0004-7635).
--Sep, 1978 - Dec, 1979 as Audiovisual Instruction with/Instructional Resources (ISSN: 0191-3417).
--Jan, 1980 - Jan, 1985 as Instructional Innovator (ISSN: 0196-6979).
WITH SUPPLEMENT
--Learning Resources, ?, 1973 - Nov?, 1974.

LC: LB 1043.A815
DD: 371.3/07/8
ISSN: 8756-3894
ABST: --Biography Index (ISSN: 0006-3053)
--Computer & Control Abstracts (ISSN: 0036-8113)
--Current Contents
--Current Index to Journals in Education (ISSN: 0011-3565)
--Education Index (ISSN: 0013-1385)
--Electrical & Electronics Abstracts (ISSN: 0036-8105)
--Electronics and Communications Abstracts Journal (ISSN: 0361-3313)
--Exceptional Child Abstracts
--INSPEC Science Abstracts
--International Index to Multi-Media Information (ISSN: 0094-6818)
--Media Review Digest (ISSN: 0363-7778)
--Micro Computer Index (ISSN: 8756-7040)
--Physics Abstracts. Science Abstracts. Series A. (ISSN: 0036-8091)

✤ TEEN DREAM

PUBL: Starline Publications, Inc., 63 Grand Avenue, Suite #230, River Edge, NJ 07661.

DESC: "...All the info and pin-ups you'll ever need on those ultra-tough New Kids, along with lots of scoops on all your other musical and Hollywood faves. There will be features on Paula Abdul, Fred Savage and Neil Patrick Harris just to name a few! Published by Starline Publications, Inc., this is one teen mag you won't want to be without ... *Teen Dream* is a teen entertainment fantasy, 64 solid pages of fun 'n' fotos you'll never forget!" Articles, profiles, gossip, and lots of full color "pin-up" pictures make up this bimonthly publication. The stars are primarly from motion pictures, television, and music fame. Note: confusion exists over Main Title entry. The title on the front cover reads *Starline Presents Teen Dream*, while the title on the publisher page reads *Starline Presents # 25*. Elsewhere, in self-promotion pages within the issue, the publication is referred to as *Teen Dream*. Sample issue was numbered, and contained no publication date. Magazine format (8 x 10 ¾ inches / 205 x 275 mm); color pages and graphics on coated and uncoated paper.

DEPT: "Letter From the Editor," "All-Star Teen Word Search," puzzle; "Hollywood Hotline," 'All the freshest gossip -- fresh from our tinseltown snoop'; "Ask Ian," Q&A advice column by Ian Bonner; "Rock Around the Clock," 'Where you can rock, rock, rock to the latest music biz talk, talk talk!' column by Elianne Halbersberg. (#25-90).

TYPL: "Jonathan Knight: He's Not Afraid of Being Shy!," "New Kids Rumor Mill: What's True and False!," "Bringing Teenage Mutant Ninja Turtles to Life," "Paula Abdul: Many Faces, Many Talents," "Tommy Page: Dreaming of You." (#25-90).

SCHL: Quarterly, 70 pp.
SPAN: 198u+
DD: 051 11

✤ TEL-COMS

SUB: "News monthly for interactive telecommunications."
PUBL: Parker Communications Corporation, 2801 International Lane, Suite 205, Madison, WI 53704.
DESC: "*TEL-COMS* is distributed free of charge in the U.S. only to qualified management or professionals who use, manage, maintain telecommunications or teleconferencing equipment and systems, including audio, audio graphics, video and computer teleconferencing, as well as to domestic companies that manufacture and market teleconferencing products, services and systems." This is a tabloid newspaper on standards, equipment, facilities, and the general business status of telecommunications.
DEPT: "Publishers Forum," "Business Notes," "Calendar." (11-88).
TYPL: "Chrysler Unveils World's Largest Private Satellite Network," "Bellcore Creates Video Window, a Sizable Advance for Video Conferencing," "CCITT Takes Big Step Toward Video Conferencing Standard." (11-88).
SCHL: Monthly, 8 pp.
SPAN: Jun, 1988+
ISSN: 1048-1702

✤ TELCO REPORT, THE

SUB: "The only weekly publication of international television programming."
SUB: "The world's foremost source for television program information."
PUBL: Telco Productions, 2730 Wilshire Blvd., Suite 404, Santa Monica, CA 90403.
DESC: Published since 1969, this succinct weekly publication consists of some eight pages of new program syndication sandwiched between approximately four pages of advertisements by leading world television producers and syndicators. Each listing (arranged by subject area) provides program synopses, running times, and sales contact information. No graphics or feature articles.
DEPT: "Telco Talk," newsbriefs. (1-27-89).
SCHL: Weekly (except first week of July, and last week of December), 12 pp.
SPAN: 1969+.
ISSN: 0142-730X

Tele-Screen Century Series

1942 - 1943//
SEE: TELESCREEN

✤ TELECAST

SUB: "The national television picture magazine." (Nov, 1949 - ?).
PUBL: G & E Publishing Co., 475 Fifth Ave., New York, NY.
DESC: "Along with more than 2,000,000 other people who own television sets today, we think TV is just about the most important thing that's happening in America right now. We think it's so important, in fact, that a national magazine devoted exclusively to the new entertainment medium is needed." *Telecast* was a very upbeat consumer magazine about the new medium, its current programming and technology (primarily home receivers), and its potential for growth. Many articles explained back-stage aspects of the new medium. This is a marvelous historical resource for the early days of network television. Magazine format; graphics.
DEPT: "Letters to the Editor," "Your Receiver," "Telecast Talks It Over," newsbriefs; "Editorial," "Telecast Peeks at New Shows," "We Nominate for Stardom," profile. (1-50).
TYPL: "Introducing Bill Lawrence," "My Life With Milton Berle," "TV's Blonde Bombshell," "Yankee Doodle Dandies." (1-50).
SCHL: Monthly, 55 pp.
SPAN: Nov, 1949+
LC: HE 8690.T35

✤ TELECOM JAPAN, THE

PUBL: Dempa Times, Inc., 23-12 Nishi-shim-bashi, 3-chome, Minato-ku, Tokyo, 105 Japan.
DESC: This tabloid newspaper is designed to promote, discuss, and inform about Japanese video, audio and television broadcast activities; and new technologies. Primary emphasis is on "Hi-Vision," the Japanese name for what North Americans call "HDTV" or "High-Definition Television." Many articles pertaining to Hi-Vision demonstrate practical applications for public education, advertising, information and entertainment consideration. A number of schematic drawings explain the Japanese system and new technological developments, especially as they relate to the North American marketplace. Full-color cover with black/white editorial content on coated paper stock; tabloid newspaper format (10 ½ x 14 inches / 265 x 355 mm) unfolded.
DEPT: "Activities of NHK," news roundup. (4-15-91).
TYPL: "Tasks in Japan's Broadcasting Policy and Future Measures," "Hi-Vision Today," "What is Radio Japan?," "Sony's Broadcasting System Strongly Highlights the Digital Era [of Industry] with its [Advanced] Skill and Integrity," "Toshiba Assertive About Tackling HDTV." (4-15-91).
SCHL: Monthly?, 30 pp.
SPAN: ?+

✤ TELECOMMUNICATION JOURNAL

SUB: "Official organ of the International Telecommunication Union."
SUB: "Monthly magazine of the International Telecommunication Union."

PUBL: International Telecommunication Union, Union Internationale des Telecommunications, Place des Nations, 1211 Geneva 20, Switzerland.
DESC: Published in three separate editions of English, French and Spanish, *Telecommunication Journal* provides news and general information concerning the International Telecommunication Union and its member nations. There are two emphases present in this serial; 1) technical, and 2) member nation facilities. The former provides detailed technical information on new international standards and agreements. The member nation articles provide a positive look at telecommunication developments (especially new facilities) within various countries. Whereas issues of the 1960s were primarily concerned with broadcasting, telephone and telegraph; issues of the 1980s are at times exclusively devoted to the role of satellites in world and international communication. Numerous graphics.
DEPT: "Editorial," "News Section," "Books," "Review Review," articles in other technical serials; "The Journal Fifty Years Ago," "Official Announcements," "Smoothed Monthly Sunspot Numbers." (2-62). "Editorial," "Union Activities," "Official Announcements," "ITU Publications," "Conferences or Meetings External to the ITU," "The Journal One Hundred Years Ago," "News," "New Products," "Books," "Review of Reviews," "Basic Indices for Ionospheric Propagation." (5-87).
TYPL: "Space Communications of the Next Generation," "Fishing vs. Cables," "Administrative Radio Conferences--Time for a Change?" (2-62). "The User and the ISDN," "ISDN: the Case for Satellites," "Bringing the Benefits of Telecommunications to Developing Economies." (5-87).
SCHL: Monthly, 70 pp.
SPAN: 1934+
FOREIGN EDITION
--Journal des Telecommunications.
--Boletin de Telecomunicaciones.
VARIES
--? - ? as Journal Telegraphique [NE?].
--? - ? as Journal des Telecommunications [NE].
--1948 - 1952 as Telecommunication Journal.
--Jan, 1953 - Dec, 1961 as Journal UIT.
LC: HE 7601.J63
DD: 384/.05
ISSN: 0497-137x
ABST: --Applied Science and Technology Index (ISSN: 0003-6986)
--Computer & Control Abstracts (ISSN: 0036-8113)
--Electrical & Electronics Abstracts (ISSN: 0036-8105)
--Engineering Index Annual (ISSN: 0360-8557)
--Engineering Index Bioengineering Abstracts (ISSN: 0736-6213)
--Engineering Index Energy Abstracts (ISSN: 0093-8408)
--Engineering Index Monthly (ISSN: 0013-7960)
--International Aerospace Abstracts (ISSN: 0020-5842)
--Physics Abstracts. Science Abstracts. Series A. (ISSN: 0036-8091)

Telecommunication Journal
1948 - 1952//
SEE: TELECOMMUNICATION JOURNAL

✦ TELECOMMUNICATION JOURNAL OF AUSTRALIA, THE

PUBL: Telecommunication Society of Australia, Box 1802Q, Melbourne, Victoria 3001, Australia.
DESC: This is a journal of Australian engineering progress, produced by the Postal Electrical Society of Victoria. Articles from the sampled issues of the 1930s were technical in nature, but readable by lay persons interested in telecommunications. Articles explored new technologies, especially in terms of application to home and industry, and served to disseminate information about new apparatus and trends in the telecommunication industry. Some schematics and graphics; magazine format.
DEPT: "Answers to Examination Papers." (6-37).
TYPL: "Transmission Improvements in Exchange and Subscribers' Equipment," "Post Office Publicity," "Signal Distortion on Teleprinter Circuits," "Broadcast in Australia of the British Broadcasting Corporation Coronation Programme." (6-37).
SCHL: Three issues per year, 50 pp.
SPAN: Jun, 1935+
LC: TK 5101.A1T36
ISSN: 0040-2486
ABST: --Computer & Control Abstracts (ISSN: 0036-8113)
--Electrical & Electronics Abstracts (ISSN: 0036-8105)
--Engineering Index Annual (ISSN: 0360-8557)
--Engineering Index Bioengineering Abstracts (ISSN: 0736-6213)
--Engineering Index Energy Abstracts (ISSN: 0093-8408)
--Engineering Index Monthly (ISSN: 0013-7960)
--International Aerospace Abstracts (ISSN: 0020-5842)
--Physics Abstracts. Science Abstracts. Series A. (ISSN: 0036-8091)

✦ TELECOMMUNICATIONS

SUB: "Directed to technical management personnel involved with transmission, reception, processing and display of information."
SUB: "Datacommunications, teleprocessing, transmission."
PUBL: Horizon House Publications, 685 Canton St., Norwood, MA 02062.
DESC: The emphasis here is in point-to-point data and communications transmission. For the sampled issues of 1982, the focus was on new technologies, their potential application in the telecommunication field (telephone, telegraph, closed-circuit television, satellite communication, data transfer), and acceptence of these new technologies into the communication field. This is a technical journal for the operating engineer in the field, and the reader is expected to have a basic

understanding of electronics. Articles are placed under one of four typical subdivisions: "Feature Section," "Industry Segments," "Telecommunications Business," or "Data Communications." This is a noteworthy publication for ascertaining the status of point-to-point communication (telecommunication) in the world today. For the sampled issues of 1982 and 1991: stapled, magazine format; editorial content comprised of black ink with spot-color on coated paper; cover was full-color graphics on coated stock (8 x 10 ⅝ inches / 205 x 270).
DEPT: "Telecom News," "Calendar," "Telecom Products." (12-82). "Commentary," column by Tom Valovic; "Bulletin," "Global News," "News Briefs," "Standards Update," "Data Communications Products," "Application Note," "Industry Segments," "Telecommunications Business," "Data Communications," "Show Preview," "Product Feature," "New Products." (3-91).
TYPL: "The Fiber Optic Revolution Spreads," "Applications of Fiber Optics to Local Area Networks," "Equalizing/Conditioning Lines for Data Transmission," "Fiber Optics in Europe," "Optical-Fiber Development and Application in Japan," "An Uncommon Satellite Carrier." (12-82). "The Growing Importance of Network Management Systems and Equipment," "Managing DEC's Enterprise-Wide Terminal Connectivity Strategy," "An ISDN Desktop Central Office Switch for Rural and Remote Area Communications," "Business Watch on Communication," "Thoroughly Modern Modems: Still the Workhorse of Today's Networks." (3-91).
SCHL: Monthly [except semimonthly in April], 85 pp.
SPAN: Sep, 1981+
EDITION
--North American.
FROM SPLIT OF
--Telecommunications [International Edition] (ISSN: 0040-2494) (into) Telecommunications [Euro-global Edition] (ISSN: 0192-6209) and Telecommunications [North American Edition] (ISSN: 0278-4831).
VARIES
--Sep, 1981? - ? as Telecommunications [Euro-global Edition] (ISSN: 0192-6209).
--? - Mar, 1986 as Telecommunications [Global Edition] (ISSN: 0278-484x).
LC: TK 5101.A1T32
DD: 621
ISSN: 0278-4831
ABST: --ABI/Informer
--Business Periodical Index (ISSN: 0007-6961)
--Engineering Index Annual (ISSN: 0360-8557)
--Engineering Index Monthly (ISSN: 0013-7960)
--Predicasts
--Ship Abstracts (ISSN: 0346-1025)

Telecommunications [Euro-global Edition]

Sep, 1981? - ?//
(ISSN: 0192-6209)
SEE: TELECOMMUNICATIONS

Telecommunications [Global Edition]

? - Mar, 1986//
(ISSN: 0278-484x)
SEE: TELECOMMUNICATIONS

✤ TELECOMMUNICATIONS ALERT

SUB: "An overview of telecommunications news."
SUB: "A digest of telecommunications news."
PUBL: United Communications Group, 11300 Rockville Pike, Suite 1100, Rockville, MD 20852-3030.
DESC: Serving the needs of point-to-point data, voice, and other users of telecommunications services, *Telecommunications Alert* provides brief summaries of major news items occurring each month. This is a newsletter for executives and technical personnel within the data transmission field; and one which provides numerous succinct, late-breaking news items of the industry. In the 1991 sampled issues, articles were subdivided under headings of: "Telecom Business," "Telcos," "Long Distance," "Regulation & Legislation," "Marketing," "Customer Premises Equipment," "Telecom Management," "International," "Technology," and "Network Products." Some 95 articles were in a single (December, 1991) issue. Of note are two departmental sections which help to discern each issue's news. The first is a "Company Index," a listing of all communication corporations named in articles within the issue. The second is an "Index of Publications," a wonderful "direction finder" for additional information. As each article provides complete documentation of article title, date, page number, and publication name, follow-up research becomes easier. Electronic editions of *Telecommunications Alert* are available via News-Net and Predicasts online information services. In December, 1991, in response to a desire for more frequent telecommunications information, publisher Dave Douglass announced the startup of *The CCMI Industry News Summary By Fax*, a daily facsimile newsletter service in conjunction with sister group, CCMI. Annual subscription rate for *Telecommunications Alert* in 1991 was $198. For the sampled issues of 1983 and 1991: stapled, newsletter format; black ink with spot-color on uncoated paper; no advertising (8 ½ x 11 inches / 215 x 280 mm). Sampled issues for 1983 were typewritten; those for 1991 were typeset.
DEPT: "Key Telecommunications Stocks," "Index of Publications," as cited in each monthly report. (8-84). "Company Index," as cited in articles; "Index of Publications," as cited in articles (12-91).

TYPL: "Interconnect," "Companies to Sell Centrex," "Rebuilt Horizons to be Made Widely Available," "New England PBX Users Can Buy AIOD Service from Telco." (8-84). "Telesphere to Sell Assets to CEO," "GTE Introduces 100-mbps Service," "Retail Group to Sign Contract with MCI," "Sears Tries Interactive Fax Service," "Silent Monitoring of Calls Spreading." (12-91).
SCHL: Monthly, 16 pp.
SPAN: Oct, 1983+
DD: 384
ISSN: 0742-5384

✦ TELECOMMUNICATIONS POLICY

PUBL: Butterworth-Heinemann, Ltd., Linacre House, Jordan Hill, Oxford, OX2 8DP, England.
DESC: "*Telecommunications Policy* is an international quarterly journal [which] invites contributions on any aspect of the assessment, control, and management of development in telecommunications and information systems. ... Articles for *Telecommunications Policy* should refer principally to the political, economic and social aspects of telecommunications." The emphasis is on international communication, with a subsidiary focus on the relationship between governments and their media. A strong, international editorial board sets the tone for this scholarly journal on telecommunication policy developments. It is an exceptional publication for trends, news, and analyses on developing telecommunications technologies and their application. For the sampled 1980 issues: black ink on uncoated paper; cover comprised of spot-color on coated index stock; perfect-bound, journal format (7 ⅞ x 10 ⅞ inches / 200 x 275 mm). Subscription costs in 1991 were: £152 in UK; £160 in Europe; £168 in the rest of the world.
DEPT: "Rejoinders," letters; "Book Review," "Publications," "Calendar." (6-84). None. (10-91).
TYPL: "Telecommunications for Development: Findings of the ITU-OECD Project," "Doctrine, Decision and Development in International Telecommunications," "Regulation of the Canadian Cable Industry: a Comparative Analysis," "Telecommunications Policymaking in New Zealand During the Last Two Decades." (6-84). "Open Network Architecture: Journey to an Unknown Destination?," "Competition for 800 Service: An Economic Evaluation," "An Analysis of Policy Options for High-Definition Television," "Local Telecommunications Competitors: Strategy and Policy," "Value-Added Services: Regulation and Reality in the Federal Republic of Germany." (10-91).
SCHL: Quarterly (? - ?); Bimonthly [Feb, Apr, Jun, Aug, Oct, Dec] (?+), 80 pp.
SPAN: Dec, 1976+
LC: HE 7601.T44
DD: 384/.05
ISSN: 0308-5961
ABST: --ABI/Informer

--Computer & Control Abstracts (ISSN: 0036-8113)
--Electrical & Electronics Abstracts (ISSN: 0036-8105)
--Engineering Index Annual (ISSN: 0360-8557)
--Engineering Index Bioengineering Abstracts (ISSN: 0736-6213)
--Engineering Index Energy Abstracts (ISSN: 0093-8408)
--Engineering Index Monthly (ISSN: 0013-7960)
--International Aerospace Abstracts (ISSN: 0020-5842)
--Physics Abstracts. Science Abstracts. Series A. (ISSN: 0036-8091)

✦ TELECOMMUNICATIONS REPORTS

SUB: "A confidential Washington news letter covering the telephone, telegraph and radio communications fields and containing a complete and authentic record of the activities of the Federal Communications Commission and Congress." (Aug 9, 1934 - ?).
PUBL: Broadcasting Publications, Inc., 1293 National Press Bldg., Washington, DC 20045.
DESC: In conjunction with the newly created Federal Communications Commission, this weekly provided Commission news in two distinct ways; "Trends and Developments," in which the editors made comment on recent FCC actions and the general state of the communications industry; and a section of varying lengths listing those actions. It began as a printed 12 page newsletter, moving to mimeograph style commencing with the September 6, 1934 issue. No graphics during the time of the mimeographed format.
DEPT: None. (1-10-35).
TYPL: "Telephone Industry Not Cited by White House," "FCC Now Ready to Grow," "Telegraph Division Waives Time for Western Union Market News Rates," "Commission Sets New Hearing for Western Radio Applications." (1-10-35).
SCHL: Weekly, 12 pp.
SPAN: Aug 9, 1934+?
LC: HE 7775.T36

✦ TELECOMMUNICATIONS WEEK

PUBL: Business Research Publications, Inc., 817 Broadway, New York, NY 10003.
DESC: An "off-spring" of *Telecommunications Report*, *Telecommunications Week* provides via weekly newsletter format a condensation of the week's news in the telecommunications field. The focus is on late-breaking news and emerging trends in the industry; covering events in the regulatory, commercial, litigation, and economic fields. Articles provide a succinct means of maintaining understanding of the growth, and direction of that growth in the telecommunication industry.
DEPT: "Moves and Changes," "Financing and Earnings," "State Rates," "Calendar," "Editor's Notes." (4-28-82).

TYPL: "Citicorp Takes Banking into Outer Space," "AT&T Agrees to New Divestiture Amendments," "The Shape of Things to Come at MCI," "Congress Explores Reasonable Phone Rates." (4-83).
SCHL: Weekly, 8 pp.
SPAN: 1982+
DD: 384
ISSN: 1040-418x

✧ TELECONFERENCE MAGAZINE

SUB: "The business communications magazine."
PUBL: Applied Business Communications, Inc., 2401 Crow Canyon Rd., Suite 310, San Ramon, CA 94583.
DESC: New media technologies of the past 20 years have created a myriad of new application resources, and often have redefined the process of how unique segments of education, business, and society accomplish their necessary tasks. Certainly this is true at the corporate level for education, training, and inter-branch communication. Teleconferencing has demonstrated itself to be a cost-effective medium where everyone benefits, at a fraction of the cost and time necessary for previously required cross-country travel. *TeleConference Magazine* reports on this medium at several different levels. First, there are reports about ever-changing technology, explained in laymen's terms, with schematics. Second, the publication reports on industry news, both of vendor and end-user. Third, and probably most important of all, *TeleConference Magazine* provides detailed applications of teleconferencing by a variety of corporations. These articles show corporate managers personal applications, problems, costs, and successes in using the medium and are a very good resource for anyone contemplating use of teleconferencing for organizational applications. Of special note is a well-planned layout design. A banner-slug appears at the top of each article page, with labels such as "Lead Article," "Medical Application," "Financial Industry Application," "Training by Audio," "Technical Article," and so forth; clearly identifying the nature of the article/departmental segment for future reference. Stapled magazine format; black/white editorial content with full-color advertisement pages in front and back sections and full-color covers; all on coated paper stock (8 ½ x 11 inches / 215 x 280 mm).
DEPT: "Telenews," teleconferncing newsbriefs; "People in Teleconferencing," people newsbriefs. (5/6-90).
TYPL: "ASTD's Phenomenal Growth in Corporate Training Teleconferences," "High Definition Medicine--HSN Introduces HDTV to Health Care Training," "Business Television Opens New Channels of Communication," "Satellite Technology Brings Wall Street to Main Street," "Atlantic Video Beams Interactive Teleconference Series." (5/6-90).
SCHL: Bimonthly, 45 pp.
SPAN: 1981+
ISSN: 0739-7208

✧ TELECONNECT

SUB: "The telecom industry's favorite magazine."
SUB: "The voice of the telephone interconnect industry."
PUBL: Teleconnect Magazine, 12 West 21 St., New York, NY 10010.
DESC: Point-to-point or telecommunications is the focus of this publication; which provides practical advice on advanced development of the corporate communication structure; from facsimile to PBX telephone systems, from voice mail to paging concepts. Each issue is packed with product comparisons, corporate applications, and new trends in telecommunication technology. It is helpful for managers of communication systems. Magazine format; numerous graphics.
DEPT: "Scouting," newsbriefs; "Dollar Saving Tips," "To the Industry," "Tutorial," how-to column; "Sales Seminar," advice; "Innovations," new product review; "Puzzle," crossword; "Insiders," personnel changes; "Calendar." (9-89).
TYPL: "Round Up the Usual Suspects," "Maintaining the Private Network," "Good Times for Voice Processing," "Teleconnect's Most Wanted," "Seeing the Future that Works." (9-89).
SCHL: Monthly, 150 pp.
SPAN: Mar, 1983+
LC: TK 6001 .T43
ISSN: 0740-9354

Telefilm International

? - ?//
SEE: TELEVISION INTERNATIONAL

Telefilm Magazine

Nov, 1958 - Jun/Jul, 1963//
SEE: TELEVISION INTERNATIONAL

Telegraph Age

1883 - Dec 16, 1909//
SEE: WIRE & RADIO COMMUNICATIONS

Telegraph and Telephone Age

Jan, 1910 - Jun, 1953//
SEE: WIRE & RADIO COMMUNICATIONS

Telegraph and Telephone Journal, The

Oct, 1914 - Dec, 1933//
SEE: POST OFFICE MAGAZINE

✧ TELEGRAPH WORLD

SUB: "Organ of Association Western Union Employees."

PUBL: Association of Western Union Employees, 404 N. Wesley Ave., Mount Morris, IL.
DESC: In this official trade organ of the Association of Western Union Employees, issues concentrated on labor issues, and news of various locals. There were some graphics, especially of local activities and conventions. The small format newsprint in early issues gave way to a standard magazine format by the 1940s.
DEPT: "Things About Testing and Regulating Work," technical series; "Under the Crossarm," news of locals; (3-19). "Things to Think About," newsbriefs; "Obituaries," (6-40).
TYPL: "'A.W.E.' Success Involves Revolution," "The New Order in Human Relations," "Loyalty to the Company Demanded," "The Development of Automatic and Printing Telegraph Systems in America," (3-19). "AWUE Beats ACA 278 to 135 in Pittsburgh, Pa., NLRB Election," "In What Group do You Happen to Be?," (6-40).
SCHL: Monthly, 12 - 25 pp.
SPAN: Jan, 1919+?
VARIES
--Jan, 1919 - ? as Telegraph World, The.
LC: TK1 .T2

Telegraph World, The

Jan, 1919 - ?//
SEE: TELEGRAPH WORLD

TELEGRAPHER, THE

SUB: "Devoted principally to the interests of the National Telegraphic Union, and to telegraphers and telegraphing in general."
SUB: "A journal of electrical progress."
PUBL: The Telegrapher, 20 Cortlandt St., Room 5, New York, NY.
DESC: *The Telegrapher* began in a burst of enthusiasm, telling readers it would contain "... besides all matters pertaining to the 'Union,' everything of telegraphic interest to telegraphers. Correspondence, scientific articles, extracts from works on telegraphy; articles upon electricity and magnetism; statistics; improvements in telegraphing; telegraph instruments and materials; promotions, removals, resignations, withdrawals, marriages and deaths of telegraphers."
In its prime, the serial did all this and more, providing a unique perspective on the role of telegraphy and the telegrapher for a period of ten years following the Civil War. Latter issues, especially those of 1877 (the last year of publication) degenerated to a four page advertising flyer with no editorial content. Of special note were lengthy articles detailing local and regional meetings of N.T.U. members, and the state of telegraphy in those areas. Early issues had few graphics; latter issues were replete with graphics as part of paid advertisements. An editor's note in the first issue mentions that this is the second attempt to publish a "successful" telegraphic journal in America, without providing any other information on the initial effort.
DEPT: "Married," "Died," "Quotations of Telegraph Stock," (12-26-1864).
TYPL: "Origin of Atmospheric Electricity," "The Telegraphic Repeater," "A Chapter About Insulators," "Apparatus for Measuring the Velocity of Projectiles," (12-26-1864).
SCHL: Monthly (Sep 26, 1864 - Sep 25, 1865); Semimonthly (Oct 16, 1865 - ?); Weekly (? - Feb 3, 1877), 4 - 30 pp.
SPAN: Sep 26, 1864 - Feb 3, 1877//
ABSORBED BY
--Journal of the Telegraph, Feb, 1877.
LC: T1T1.T3

Telegraphic Journal and Electrical Review

Jan, 1873 - Dec, 1891//
SEE: ELECTRICAL REVIEW

Telegraphic Journal and Monthly Illustrated Review of Electrical Science

Nov 15, 1872 - Dec, 1872//
SEE: ELECTRICAL REVIEW

✤ TELEMARKETING

SUB: "The magazine of business telecommunications."
SUB: "Bridging the gap between telecommunications suppliers and end users."
SUB: "The voice of the industry since 1982."
PUBL: Technology Marketing Corporation, 1 Technology Plaza, Norwalk, CT 06854.
DESC: Designed as a news vehicle for the corporate marketing manager, *Telemarketing* concentrates primarily on new and innovative technology in the burgeoning telecommunications field. Articles explore the technology so critical to this marketing form, and the personal touch (technique) required to follow through to successful completion. Also included are extensive equipment reviews, and articles on assembling an effective sales team. Of special interest are numerous successful telemarketing stories utilizing new media technology. Feature articles are subdivided into categories of: "Sales and Closing Methods," "Eye on Service Agencies," "Banking and Financial Applications," and "Technology." Note: issue for June/July, 1982 was also called the Premiere Issue. Magazine format (8 ¼ x 11 inches / 210 x 280 mm).
DEPT: "Publisher's Outlook," "TeleNews," briefs; "Telecommunications and the Law," "Letters to the Editor," "TeleFocus," "Classified." (8-85). "Publisher's Outlook," "TeleNews," 'New products'; "Industry Law,"

"Telemarketing's Corpus Juris," "Q&A," reader submitted questions; "Square One," the basics of telemarketing. (7-90).
TYPL: "The Video Teleconferencing Panorama," "Overcoming Management Objections to Videoconferencing," "The Next Generation of Telemarketing Systems." (8-85). "How Blue Cross and Blue Shield of Virginia Turned a $250,000 Systems Investment into a MULTIMILLION DOLLAR Corporate Revenue Contribution," "Telemarketing in Mexico: A Story of Success," "Generating Sales Leads with Telemarketing," "Telemarketing for Financial Institutions--Moving Beyond the Debate," "Voice Messaging Improves Telemarketing Management and Coordination." (7-90).
SCHL: Bimonthly (Jun/Jul, 1982 - Jun, 1983); Monthly (Jul, 1983+), 95 pp.
SPAN: Jun/Jul, 1982+
LC: HF 5415 .1265 .T43
DD: 658.8/5
ISSN: 0730-6156
ABST: --Predicasts

✤ TELEMATICS AND INFORMATICS

SUB: "An international journal on telecommunications & information technology."
SUB: "An international journal."
PUBL: Pergamon Press, Inc., Fairview Park, Elmsford, NY 10523.
DESC: *Telematics and Informatics*...is neither purely academic nor trade oriented. It represents an extraordinary alliance of business and industry, academia and governmental organizations. It seeks to bridge the communication gap between these three distinct institutions whose communities have been separated intellectually for years. Thus, it is a uniquely designed publication that has created its own path and will follow its own course. *Telematics and Informatics* will, through its four pertinent sub-sections, i.e., feature articles, legislative and policy focus, literature review and patent search, serve its readers in private and public sectors with neutrallity and scholarly values. Under the guidance of an able body of international advisors, it will cover state-of-the-art technology and will report on emerging issues. The articles are written to serve readers with either technical or non-technical backgrounds." This is a journal concerned with emerging technologies and their impact on international government and society. This is an exceptional publication filled with thought-provoking articles, research, and essays concerning the form and function of communication in today's international marketplace. Various special issues are published during the course of a year, such as "Europe 1992: Impacts on the Communications Environment," numbered #3 of volume 8 during 1991. That special issue included articles such as, "Growing Convergence Between Broadcasting and Telecommunication: Policy Problems at the Level of the Commission of the European Communities," "HDTV as a Spearhead of European Industrial Policy," "Restructuring Irish Media for an Integrated Europe: A View From the Celtic Periphery," and "European Integration and National Elites: British Media and the Triumph of Federalism?" Other special issue topics have included, "Space Applications of Artificial Intelligence," "Telecom Policies in the Bush Administration, "Telecommunications for the Developing World: Innovative Stragegies," and "Expert Systems and Expert Support Systems." It is highly recommended. For the sampled issues of 1984 and 1991: editorial content consists of black ink on uncoated paper; cover is spot-color ink on coated index stock; perfect-bound journal format (6 ⅝ x 10 inches / 170 x 255 mm).
DEPT: "Editorial," "Literature Review," "NTIS Section," available publications; "PATSEARCH," available information. (#1-84). "NTIS Section," "PATSEARCH." (#1/2-91).
TYPL: "Development of the Information and Telecommunications Systems," "The Emerging Data Policy in Japan," "Third World Entry into the Electronic Age," "Making Information Useful: Computer Communications Architecture," "Telematics and the ITU." (#1-84). "HDTV: Technology and Strategic Positioning," "High-Definition Television: A Survey of Potential Adopters in Belgium," "Universal Service Policies in Korea: Past and Future," "Information Engineering Methodology: A Tool for Competitive Advantage," "Estimating the Demand for Backyard Satellite Dishes: The U.S. Experience." (#1/2-91).
SCHL: Quarterly, 125 pp.
SPAN: 1984+
LC: TK 5101 .A1 T43
DD: 384
ISSN: 0736-5853
ABST: --Artificial Intelligence Abstracts
--Communication Abstracts
--Computer & Control Abstracts (ISSN: 0036-8113)
--Electrical & Electronics Abstracts (ISSN: 0036-8105)
--Information Science Abstracts
--International Aerospace Abstracts (ISSN: 0020-5842)
--Library Information Science Abstracts (ISSN: 0024-2179)
--Physics Abstracts. Science Abstracts. Series A. (ISSN: 0036-8091)

✤ TELEMEMO

PUBL: Western Educational Society for Telecommunications, 2001 Associated Rd., Fullerton, CA 92631.
DESC: A small-format newsletter of the Western Educational Society for Telecommunications, this 12-page publication covers member news from 13 western states in the area of public and educational communications.
DEPT: "From the States," individual state member news items.
TYPL: "Documentary Production Grants Offered," "New West Members," "Presidents Message." (8-76).

SCHL: Bimonthly, 12 pp.
SPAN: ?+

TELEPHONE MAGAZINE

SUB: "An illustrated monthly magazine." (Jan, 1893 - ?).
SUB: "Devoted to the electrical and allied mechanical interests at the World's Columbian Exposition." (Jan, 1893 - ?).
PUBL: ?, Chicago, IL.
DESC: [*Electrical Engineering and Telephone Magazine*]: Without a doubt, one of the most impressive buildings among a host of impressive structures at the Chicago World's Fair (Columbian Exposition) in 1893 was the "Electricity building." How fitting it was, therefore, that a new periodical would describe the wonders of this building, the electrical requirements of the exposition in general, and provide a detailed analysis of the apparatus displayed for the general public. The serial also provided interesting coverage of telegraph displays, patents granted, and obituaries of famous electrical engineers or inventors of the day. Numerous graphics. A fascinating and valuable reference for development of electrical communication systems.
DEPT: "A Synoptical Index of Current Electrical Literature," large listing; "Titles of Recent Publications," "New Publications Received," "Comment and Clippings," "Electrical Patents." (5-1893).
TYPL: "The Electric Power Circuits at the World's Fair," "Thirty-Three Millions Expended." (5-1893).
SCHL: Monthly (Jan, 1893 - ?); Semimonthly (Apr, 1897 - Jun, 1898).
SPAN: Jan, 1893 - Aug, 1905//
VARIES
--Jan, 1893 - May, 1893 as World's Fair Electrical Engineering.
--Jun, 1893 - Jul, 1898 as Electrical Engingeering.
--Aug, 1898 - Dec, 1899 as Electrical Engineering and Telephone Magazine.
ABSORBED BY
--Telephony (ISSN: 0040-2656), Sep, 1905.
LC: TK 1.T35
ABST: --Applied Science and Technology Index (ISSN: 0003-6986)
--Industrial Arts Index

✤ TELEPHONE NEWS, THE

SUB: "Published in the interests of employees of the Bell Telephone Company of Pennsylvania and the Diamond State Telephone Company."
PUBL: Bell Telephone Company, Philadelphia, PA.
DESC: *The Telephone News* existed as an in-house publication for the employees (for the sampled issue of 1939) of the Bell Telephone Company of Pennsylvania and the Diamond State Telephone Company. Articles honored various employees, explained the importance of key functions, and proclaimed the technological and business advances accomplished by the two telephone entities. Numerous photographs show employees both at work and at play, attending an annual picnic or workshop, for example. The emphasis is on people. For the sampled issue for 1939: small stapled-magazine format; black/white editorial content and cover on coated paper with limited institutional advertising (7 ½ x 10 ⅝ inches / 190 x 270 mm).
DEPT: "Have You Heard About," employee profiles; "Nellie Kellie's Kolumn," employee news column by Nellie Kellie; "Anniversarians," employment anniversaries of selected workers; "Honor Roll Notes," "The Hang Up Page," humorous column by Bell Boy. (8-39).
TYPL: "Twenty-Fifth Anniversary of Transcontinental Telephone Service," "More Cable for Sleet Sector," "New Pioneer Officers," "Accent on Accuracy," "Among the Girls." (8-39).
SCHL: Monthly, 50 pp.
SPAN: Aug, 1905+
VARIES
--Bell Telephone Company of Pennsylvania News, The.

Telephone Worker

May, 1941 - Jun, 1947//
SEE: CWA NEWS

✤ TELEPROFESSIONAL

SUB: "The guide to effective inside sales & support." (? - Nov/Dec, 1990).
SUB: "Effective marketing through telecommunications." (Jan, 1991+).
PUBL: Teleprofessional, Inc., 209 West Fifth St., suite N, Waterloo, IA 50701-5420
DESC: *TeleProfessional* is a newsworthy, informative publication concerning the high-tech arena of telemarketing services by American firms to the home consumer public. In a creative editorial mode, articles (labeled with icons) fall into one of three distinct subject areas: 1) "indicates that this feature article addresses issues of importance to executive-level management... strategic and tactical issues affecting overall business plans; 2) indicates that this feature article addresses issues of importance to sales and marketing management... ideas relating to the structure and implementation of sales programs; 3) indicates that this feature article addresses issues of importance to tele-management and TSRs... ideas for improving the telebusiness functions of your company." Advertisers offer technology, and/or services for profitably utilizing this field of marketing/sales. Magazine format (8 ¼ x 10 ⅞ inches / 210 x 275 mm); color used throughout on coated paper stock.
DEPT: "Insides & Insights," comment; "Telecom Communique," "Toward More Successful Selling," "The Controversy Arena," "On-Line to Profits," "What's Happening," calendar; "Who's New(s)," personnel newsbriefs; "Close-Up," product information; "Tips For Successful Selling," column by Stan Billue; "Re-

views," "What's New(s)," new products and services; "Words For Thought," commentary column by Robert E. Van-Voorhis. (7-8/90).
TYPL: "Adding Computer Automation to Your Center," "Don't Mistake Autodialing for Robot Dialing," "The Route to Greater Sales," "Don't Give Up on Outbound," "Voice Response... Future Technology with a Past." (7/8-90).
SCHL: Quarterly (? - ?); Bimonthly (? - Nov/Dec, 1990); Monthly (Jan, 1991+), 65 pp.
SPAN: Spring, 1986+
LC: HF 5415 .1265 .T47
DD: 658.8/5
ISSN: 0886-9642

TELESCAN

SUB: "The digest of the Center for Learning and Telecommunications."
PUBL: Center for Learning and Telecommunications, AAHE Suite 780, One Dupont Circle, Washington, DC 20036.
DESC: "The Center for Learning and Telecommunications was established at the American Association for Higher Education under a grant from the Carnegie Corporation of New York. Bi-monthly issues of *Telescan* serve as a central source of information on ways higher education can use new telecommunications technologies to reach students in off-campus settings. ... *Telescan* keeps you updated on all the technologies--broadcast and cable television and radio, ITFS, teletext, videotext, telephone and satellite teleconferencing, direct broadcast satellites, dial access, computers, audio and videotapes, and videodiscs." The eight-page newsletter provides capsule information on media resources, programs, and publications. For the sampled issues of 1981 through 1985: stapled, newsletter format; black ink with spot-color on tinted, uncoated paper; no advertising (8 ½ x 11 inches / 215 x 280 mm).
DEPT: "Capitol Scan," 'devoted to national initiatives involving applications of technology-based instruction in higher education;' "Print Scan," print media capsules; "Source Scan," 'a review of a variety of books, research reports, and occasional papers;' "Macro Scan," conferences, workshops, seminars upcoming. (9/10-81). "Audio Scan," "Macro Scan," "Compu Scan," 'Articles, books, programs, and projects involving the uses of computer technologies'. (6-85).
TYPL: "PBS Launches New Adult Learning Program Service," "AERA and USC Form Two New Units on Adult Learning," "Dartmouth Receives $200,000 for Videodisc Project," "Computer Conference Held in Texas." (9/10-81). "Focus On: Resources in Educational Telecommunications." (6-85).
SCHL: Bimonthly, 16 pp.
SPAN: Sep/Oct, 1981 - Jun, 1985//
DD: 378
ISSN: 8755-5867

TELESCREEN

SUB: "For the arts of television."
SUB: "The magazine dedicated to the cultural aspect of television."
PUBL: Telescreen Century Magazine, 371 South Orange Ave., Newark, NJ.
DESC: Here was a serial dedicated to the "possibilities" of television. During the war years, with television "on hold," *Telescreen* postulated the probable demise of motion pictures, and what the entertainment arts might be like in post-war America. By late 1945, with television activities gaining momentum, the serial emphasized programming, with many behind-the-scenes pictures of productions, comment by television directors and producers on transferring a cultural product to the small black/white screen, and an increasing number of articles on the art and technique of production. It had no articles concerning television technology, but is historically valuable for the view of the potential of the medium seen from the formative period of the 1940s.
DEPT: "Editorial," "Stars on the Horizon," "The New York Scene," "Chicago Video Vignettes," "Chicago Program Notes," "Hollywood Tele-views." (4-46).
TYPL: "Television Drama," "Acting in Television is Tough--and Exciting," "Stanislavsky Comes to Television," "Preparing Teen-Agers for Television," "The Television Director and His Audience." (4-46).
SCHL: Quarterly, 30 pp.
SPAN: 1942 - Jul, 1948//
VARIES
--1942 - 1943 as Tele-Screen Century Series.
--1944 - Spring, 1945 as Telescreen Century.
LC: HE 8690.T39

Telescreen Century
1944 - Spring, 1945//
SEE: TELESCREEN

Telespan's BusinessTV
1986 - Jul/Aug, 1990//
(ISSN: 0896-3142)
SEE: TELESPAN'S BUSINESSTV GUIDE

✤ TELESPAN'S BUSINESSTV GUIDE

SUB: "The magazine of television for business use."
PUBL: Telespan Publishing Corp., P.O. Box 6250, Altadena, CA 91001.
DESC: [*Telespan's BusinessTV*]: If letters to the editor are any indicator, then *Telespan's BusinessTV* was a resounding success for the corporate television manager. Within the 50-odd pages of this bimonthly serial were pragmatic approaches to the continuing problems of training, teleconferencing, and promotional

projects that face corporate video staff members; issues significant at the business level, but which ofttimes get short shrift in the normal video production periodicals. A supplement, *BusinessTV Video 8 Guide*, began publication with the March/April, 1990 issue of *Telespan's BusinessTV*. Of special note within the parent serial was a unique section entitled "Program Charts," which provided a quarterly listing of upcoming corporate televised events, and their scheduled cable/satellite networks. Some confusion existed over publication schedule, with the serial's publication statement showing quarterly, but all other indications pointing to a bimonthly itinerary. For the sampled 1990 issue: full color pages on coated paper stock (8 ⅜ x 11 inches / 210 x 280 mm).

DEPT: "Publisher's Note," "Letters," "Getting the Most Out of Business Television," column by Gwenn Kelly; "The Brush Report," column by Judith Brush and Douglas Brush; "Program Charts," satellite listing. (Summer-87). "Publisher's Note," "Letters," "BusinessTV Guide," 'programming-at-a-glance'; "BusinessTV Guide Alaphabetical Listings," 'Listed by title'; "Business Videos," "Ike Ink," column by Ike Pappas; "Looking In On Business Television," column by David W. Shively. (7/8-89).

TYPL: "Buying by Television," "AIDS: Informing Corporate America," "Video Networks Become Sine Qua Non for Lawyers," "How It Works: A Tutorial on Business Television." (Summer-87). "Business Television Service and Product Suppliers," "New Networks: Westcott Launches Law Enforcement Network." (7/8-89).

SCHL: Quarterly (1986 - Jul/Aug, 1990); Monthly (Sep, 1990+), 48 pp.
SPAN: 1986+
VARIES
--1986 - Jul/Aug, 1990 as Telespan's BusinessTV (ISSN: 0896-3142).
WITH SUPPLEMENT
--BusinessTV Video 8 Guide, Mar/Apr, 1990 - Jul/Aug, 1990//.
DD: 650

TELEVISER

SUB: "The journal of television."
SUB: "The journal of video production, advertising & operation."
PUBL: Television Publications, 1780 Broadway, New York, NY.
DESC: The six-year span of this publication focused on television, and appeared during what might be called a critical time in the development of the medium. What *Televiser* lacked in pages, it more than made up for with relevant commentary, news articles, and photographs. Emphasis was on programming, advertising, and trade news, although occasional articles surfaced on new technical developments, and studio profiles.

DEPT: "Effectivisions," commentary column by John DeMott; "Commercials of the Month," 'An advertising directory of film commercials;' "Film Facts," video and film comment column by Jerry Albert.
TYPL: "Movies vs. Television," "The Television Casting Director," "TV Reports on Crime," "Electrical Ventriloquism," "TV Station Revenues Top 100 Million." (4-51).
SCHL: Quarterly (fall, 1944 - summer, 1945); Bimonthly (Sep/Oct, 1945 - Dec, 1951); 25 pp.
SPAN: Fall, 1944 - Dec, 1951//
LC: HE 8690.T

TELEVISION

SUB: "The magazine of video facts." (1944 - May, 1955).
SUB: "The magazine of video fact." (fall, 1944 - ?).
SUB: "The business magazine of the industry."
PUBL: Television, 1735 DeSales St., N.W., Washington, DC 20036.
DESC: The spring of 1944 was an auspicious time to begin a new serial for television. Post-war planning had already begun, and experimental television broadcasts had dramatically increased schedules in New York, Philadelphia, Chicago, and Los Angeles. *Television* covered the business of the industry, encompassing articles of legal, marketing, programming, sales, and technical value to broadcast executives. Early war issues (published by the Frederick Kugel Company of New York) were small journal format, with numerous graphics. Sampled issues from mid-1960s indicated a move to a standard magazine format.
DESC: [*Television Magazine*]: *Television Magazine* covered American television in the areas of economics, commercial production, programming, and regulation. Many of its features were later incorporated into Broadcasting Magazine. Tabloid-size with good graphics. The March issue was entitled, "Annual Data Book."
DEPT: "Television in Review," "One Man's Reflections," column by Dr. Alfred N. Goldsmith; "Programming," production problem analysis; "Editorial." (fall-44). "Focus on Finance," index of 66 television-associated stocks; "Focus on News," briefs; "Focus on People," newsbriefs with pictures; "Focus on Television," background on articles within this issue; "Telestatus," video statistics. (10-64). "Television on Location," newsbriefs; "Letters," "Closeup," profiles; "Focus on Finance," "Playback," 'A monthly measure of comment and criticism about television'; "Focus on Commercials," "Editorials." (9-68).
TYPL: "Advertising Agencies Tackle Television," "Color in the Air," "Television for Theaters," "Why Television for a Newspaper?," "Is a 'Hays Office' Necessary for Television?" (fall-44). "The Perils and Promise of Going Public," "The Optimum TV Schedule," "How This Commercial was Made." (10-64). "Network Program Costs Still on the Up Escalator," "Hidden Tension in Network-Affiliate Relationship," "The Big Local Boom in the Not-So-Big Television Markets." (9-68).

SCHL: Quarterly, (spring, 1944 - ?); Monthly (irregular at times), 60 pp.
SPAN: Spring, 1944 - Sep, 1968//
VARIES
--Spring, 1944 - Jan, 1949 as Television.
--Feb, 1949 - Apr, 1955 as Television Magazine.
ABSORBED BY
--Broadcasting (ISSN: 0007-2028), Oct, 1968.
LC: HE 8690.T4
ABST: --Communication Abstracts
--Computer & Control Abstracts (ISSN: 0036-8113)
--Electrical & Electronics Abstracts (ISSN: 0036-8105)
--Engineering Index Annual (ISSN: 0360-8557)
--Engineering Index Bioengineering Abstracts (ISSN: 0736-6213)
--Engineering Index Energy Abstracts (ISSN: 0093-8408)
--Engineering Index Monthly (ISSN: 0013-7960)
--Physics Abstracts. Science Abstracts. Series A. (ISSN: 0036-8091)

✣ TELEVISION

SUB: "The world's first television journal."
SUB: "Official organ of the Television Society."
PUBL: Royal Television Society, Tavistock House East, Tavistock Square, London WC1H 9HR, England.
DESC: With Sir Ambrose Fleming as president (circa 1944), and John Logie Baird and Joseph J. Denton as honorary fellows, the Television Society of London quickly established itself as the premiere organization of television development in Great Britain. The Television Society began in 1927, with its serial begining publication shortly thereafter, in June of 1928. The publication was suspended for the "duration" of World War Two, and recommenced with the March, 1944 issue (volume 4, number 1). Articles in that first resumed issue covered what television "might" be like in the expected post-war era. By 1945, articles became much more technically oriented, a format development keyed to then-current issues. It has numerous graphics, and schmatics, which assume technical knowledge.
DEPT: "Television Notes," "Abstracts," (6-44). "Society Affairs," "Book Reviews," (10/12-61).
TYPL: "The Signal Converter and its Application to Television," "Picture Definition," "Electron Bombardment in Television Tubes," (6-44). "Measurement Techniques for Television Broadcasting," "Mass Production of Printed Circuits," "A Wide Range Standards Converter," (10/12-61).
SCHL: Three issues per year (1928 - 1943); Quarterly (1944 - 1969); Six issues per year (1970 - 1975); Bimonthly [irregular at times] (1976+), 50 pp.
SPAN: Jun, 1928+
SUSPENDED
--Dec, 1930.
VARIES
--Jun, 1928 - Autumn, 1966 as Journal of the Television Society.

--Winter 1966/1967 - Nov/Dec, 1975 as Royal Television Society Journal, The (ISSN: 0035-9270).
LC: TK 6630.A1T425
DD: 621.388/005
ISSN: 0308-454x
ABST: --Computer & Control Abstracts (ISSN: 0036-8113)
--Electrical & Electronics Abstracts (ISSN: 0036-8105)
--Physics Abstracts. Science Abstracts. Series A. (ISSN: 0036-8091)

TELEVISION

SUB: "All about television."
PUBL: Experimenter Publishing Co., 230 Fifth Ave, New York, NY.
DESC: Only two issues of this Hugo Gernsback serial were published, for despite an editorial entitled, "Television is Here," the general public did not respond in kind at the newstand. The first issue was a stand-alone publication, "All About Television," providing a detailed explanation of the technical development of mechanical video up to July, 1927. The second issue was designed to be the start of a continuing series covering technical developments in this new technology, and encouraging readers to construct their own television receivers at home. Gernsback's *Television* ceased publication after this second issue. As in all Gernsback publications, there was a wealth of pictures, schematics, and enthusiasm concerning this new visual medium.
DEPT: None. (7-27). None. (7-28).
TYPL: "Experimental Information for Building a Baird Television Machine," "Technique for Building Mechanisms for Transmitting Photographs," "Television, Historical and Futuristic," (7-27). "Special Details on Jenkins Radio Movies," "How to Build a Television Receiver," "New Belin Photo-Transmitter," "Quartz Crystals Synchronize Television Sets," "Campbell Swinton Television System," (7-28).
SCHL: Irregular, 35 - 100 pp.
SPAN: Summer, 1927 - Jul, 1928//
VARIES
--Summer, 1927 as All About Television.
LC: TK 6630.A1T4

TELEVISION

SUB: "America's first television journal."
SUB: "Official organ of the Television Society of America."
PUBL: The Television Publishing Co., 417 Fifth Ave., New York, NY.
DESC: "*Television*, America's first magazine devoted to this new science, is planned to tell the story of Television plainly and concisely. The mission of this magazine will be to interest the experimenter as well as the scientist and professional man and to promote and assist in the perfection of this, the world's newest wireless development, and particular pains will be taken to preserve lucidity so that the youngest amateur may derive knowledge from each and every article."

Television encouraged the radio amateur to enter the exciting new field of television, at a time when video technology was such that the radio amateur could indeed contribute to the growing body of technical knowledge in this new medium. The Television Society's claim to be "America's first television journal," is at first confusing, since Hugo Gernsback's serial, *Television*, predated this publication by one year. The answer lies in Gernsback's own admission that his first issue was designed not to be a serial at all, but rather a "stand-alone" publication. Anticipated demand led to the second issue, one year later in July, 1928, one month after the publication start of this serial by the Television Society of America. Like the Gernsback publication, *Television* also concentrated on technical articles, with numerous pictures, graphics, and schematics. Note that only four issues were published, including a special "Preview" issue in June, 1928.
DEPT: None. (11-28). None. (1/2-29).
TYPL: "Can You Solve These Television Problems?," "Jenkins Invents the Scanning Drum," "What Experimenters Should Know About Optical Projections," "Chicago Goes on the Air with Pictures," (11-28). "New Realism with the Television Stereoscope," "What Causes Photo-Electric Cell Fatigue?," "Dr. Alexanderson Puts Television Pictures on the Wall," "Fourteen-Year-Old Genius Makes Own Television Receiver," "Marconi Predicted Television," (1/2-29).
SCHL: Irregular (Jun, 1928; Nov, 1928; Jan/Feb, 1929; Mar/Apr, 1929), 35 pp.
SPAN: Jun, 1928 - Mar/Apr, 1929//
LC: TK 6630 .A1T43

Television

Mar, 1928 - Jan, 1935//
SEE: ELECTRONIC ENGINEERING

Television

Spring, 1944 - Jan, 1949//
SEE: TELEVISION

Television Age

Aug, 1953 - Dec, 1969//
SEE: TELEVISION/RADIO AGE

Television Age International

Apr, 1984 - Jul?, 1985//
SEE: TELEVISION / RADIO AGE INTERNATIONAL

Television & Children

Summer, 1980 - Summer/Fall, 1984//
(ISSN: 0276-7309)
SEE: TELEVISION & FAMILIES

TELEVISION & FAMILIES

SUB: "A forum for information, research and opinion published quarterly by the National Council for Children and Television."
SUB: "Quarterly journal of the National Council for Children and Television."
PUBL: National Council for Children and Television, 20 Nassau St., Suite 200, Princeton, NJ 08542.
DESC: This was a long-awaited, scholarly journal concerning television and children. A wide variety of authors from broadcasting, pedagogical, and psychological fields contribute articles to this quarterly periodical. Issues, programs, and learning concepts are typical themes in this 50-page publication. For the sampled issues of 1979 and 1980: stapled, newsletter format; brown ink on uncoated paper stock; no advertising (8 ½ x 11 inches / 215 x 280 mm).
DEPT: "Letters." (spring-79). None.
TYPL: "The Promise of Television's Second Generation," "Three Cheers for Parents (When They're Parents)," "The Future of Network Programming." (spring-79). "Welcome to the Revolution," "Good Guys Make Good Shows: A Conversation with Vanessa," "In Conversation with Gary David Goldberg," "Family Ties: Sex at Sixteen?," "TV Violence: What's All the Fuss About?," "Prime Time from a Post-Liberal Perspective." (spring-84).
SCHL: Quaterly, 50 pp.
SPAN: Winter, 1978 - Winter, 1988//
  VARIES
  --Winter, 1978 - Spring?, 1980 as NCCT Forum.
  --Summer, 1980 - Summer/Fall, 1984 as Television & Children (ISSN: 0276-7309).
  SUSPENDED
  --Winter, 1980.
LC: HQ 784 .T4 N35a
DD: 305.2/3
ISSN: 0894-6248
ABST: --Current Index to Journals in Education (ISSN: 0011-3565)

✤ TELEVISION AND SCREEN GUIDE

SUB: "The only indispensable movie monthly."
SUB: "Hollywood's picture news magazine."
PUBL: Triangle Publications, 400 N. Broad St., Philadelphia, PA.
DESC: This is a typical consumer publication of the film sound era, dedicated to the premise that life in Hollywood, whether before the radio microphone or film cameras, is glamorous, fun-filled, and just sufficiently sinful that every reader would wish to live there. The

magazine format serial was printed on newsprint, with numerous graphics, some of which were in color. Interviews fill the pages of this weekly monument to the studio publicity office, and the American fan's insatiable appetite to know everything that's fit to print about their favorite stars of Hollywood motion pictures and television programming.

DEPT: "Gossip Guide," "Coloreviews," new movie ratings; "Brief Guide," movie ratings; "Your Home," "Your Beauty," "Your Happiness," "Fashions for You," (6-36). "Hollywood Life," column by Carl Schroeder; "Fashions in Full Color," "Beauty," "Screen Guide Reviews," "Letters to the Editor," (11-45).

TYPL: "Behind the Scenes of the Bartholomew Feud," "Exclusive! Mae West Explains Herself," "Talent Scouts are Searching for You," "Fred Astaire as His Best Friends Know Him," (6-36). "Esther Williams' Family Party," "Play Golf with Crosby," "Four Million Dollars Worth of Picture," "Sinatra's Big Job," (11-45).

SCHL: Monthly, 40 - 70 pp.

SPAN: May, 1936+?
VARIES
--May, 1936 - Jun, 1948 as Screen Guide.
--Oct, 1949 as Screen Guide.
--Dec, 1949 - Apr, 1951 as Screen Guide.
--Jul, 1948 - Nov, 1949 as Screen and Television Guide.

LC: PN 1993 .S247

Television and Short-Wave World

Feb, 1935 - Sep, 1939//
SEE: ELECTRONIC ENGINEERING

✦ TELEVISION BROADCAST

SUB: "The leading magazine for the television industry."
SUB: "The international journal of broadcast technology."
SUB: "Applying television technology."
SUB: "Covering television equipment, news, applications and technology."

PUBL: PSN Publications, Inc., 2 Park Ave., New York, NY 10016.

DESC: "...Our mission [is] to report new, interesting, or unique applications of television technology at the station and in the teleproduction environment." This statement from the initial issue of this new serial shows its focus as the technology of broadcasting. Earlier issues, under the banner of *Broadcast Communications*, and several other title variations, had a somewhat broader scope; with departmental articles on broadcast programming, the FCC, and a very unique continuing column on the elusive duties of the promotion director. Early *Broadcast Communications* issues covered news of RTNDA, SBE chapters; and contained a supplement, "Access to Cable Communications." In many ways, the new *Television Broadcast* is a much stronger publication, and one which has found its niche in "Covering television equipment, news, applications and technology." It is an excellent resource for those in television production, management or engineering. Tabloid format, with numerous color graphics. Sampled issue for 1983: (8 ⅛ x 10 ⅞ inches / 205 x 275 mm). Sampled issue for 1991: (10 ¾ x 14 ½ inches / 275 x 365 mm).

DEPT: "Cable/View," "Interactive File," new equipment; "World Update," newsbriefs; "RTNDA Newsline," "Newsmakers," profiles; "Product Premier," "On-The-Air," FCC newsbriefs; "Radio Loud & Clear," developments; "Stay Tuned," promotion; "Program Guide," programming; "News Directions," newsroom developments. (4-82). "General News," "Opinion," "International News," "Post," news of post production; "Graphics," "Station Breaks," station promotionals of merit. (4-89). "Opinion," column by Martin Polon; "News Briefs," "Spotlight," equipment profile; "Broadcast Management/Engineering," technical and managerial issues; "Downlink," Question response; "Strictly Business," column by Bob Paulson; "Guest Column," "ENG/News Technology," "Michael Murrie," news operation column by Michael Murrie; "Post Production," "Glen Pensinger," post production column by Glen Pensinger; "Bits & Pieces," newsbriefs; "Teleproduction," "Mel Lambert," audio-for-video column by Mel Lambert; "Howard Fields," trends and regulation column by Howard Fields; "Graphics," "Claire Doyle," graphics trends and issues column by Claire Doyle; "Transmission," "Ron Merrell," broadcast transmission column by Ron Merrell; "New Products," "People & Places," personnel newsbriefs at facilities, stations, and manufacturers; "Station Breaks," newsbriefs under subject headings of community service, plant improvements, and station awards. (2-91).

TYPL: "Wireless Mikes Put You on the Scene...Anywhere," "Here's How to Figure DA Metric Conversion," "Rental Vans Can Snare Your Critical Remotes," "Superstation Economics," "Getting Started in Local Ad Sales," "Beyond the Cable Myth." (4-82). "Engineers Are Fixin' to Buy," "Fiber Captures Shuttle on ATV," "Audio Quality Improves as Field Miking is Taken More Seriously," "Local Stations Seeing the Rewards of Closed Captioning Programming." (4-89). "TVB Survey Shows Bigger Spending on Equipment in Smallest Markets," "Hi8 Serves with Honor as Networks Cover Gulf," "Post Problems: Shrunken Ad Budgets, Too Many Houses," "HDTV's Hidden Agenda: Heavy Shackles on ENG Operations," "Broadcast Contribution to Gulf War Could Come in Form of Spectrum Fee." (2-91).

SCHL: Monthly, 65 pp.

SPAN: Jan, 1978+
VARIES
--? - Sep, 1983 as Broadcast Communications (ISSN: 0164-999x).
--Oct, 1983 - Dec, 1983 as Television/Broadcast Communications (ISSN: 0746-5777).
--Jan, 1984 - Dec, 1984 as TV Broadcast Communications.

WITH SUPPLEMENT
--Access to Cable Communications, ? - ?.
ABSORBED
--BME's Television Engineering (ISSN: 1049-4588), Oct, 1990.
LC: TK 6540.B8432
DD: 621.3841/05
ISSN: 0898-767x

Television/Broadcast Communications
Oct, 1983 - Dec, 1983//
(ISSN: 0746-5777)
SEE: TELEVISION BROADCAST

TELEVISION BULLETIN
PUBL: Carroll O'Toole and Co., 225 Broadway, New York, NY.
DESC: "Every so often science gives to the world some new and startling discovery which catches, almost instantly, the imagination of the public. The latest scientific marvel which falls into this classification is TELEVISION." So began the first issue of this financial advisory by Carroll O'Toole & Company of New York City. Even in 1931, during the midst of the Depression, the O'Toole staff informed readers: "We strongly advise the purchase of good TELEVISION stocks at the present time in anticipation of the sharp up-swing in prices which inevitably follows the awakening of public interest in a new industry of this kind." This newsletter provided information of technological developments, and especially economic opportunities for those wishing to purchase stock. Baird Television, Ltd., U. A. Sanabria of Chicago, May Radio & Television Company, Canadian and German television operations, among others, were analyzed and discussed in investment terms. Newsletter format; some graphics.
DEPT: None. (11-10-32).
TYPL: "Profits in Progress," "Baird Stock Adapted to American Market," "Canadian Television Limited," "Transmission and Reception of Television." (11-10-32).
SCHL: Irregular, 6 pp.
SPAN: Jul 25, 1931 - Dec 19, 1932//
LC: TK 6630 .A1T453

✤ TELEVISION DIGEST WITH CONSUMER ELECTRONICS
SUB: "Martin Codel's authoritative news service of the visual broadcasting and frequency modulation arts and industry."
SUB: "The authoritative service for broadcasting, consumer electronics and allied fields."
PUBL: Television Digest, 1836 Jefferson Place, N.W., Washington, DC 20036.
DESC: This weekly newsletter, covering trends and developments in all phases of broadcasting and consumer electronic industries, contains much information on the business side of industry. Articles describe late-breaking news events of a regulatory, commercial, and technological variety; providing succinct reports of how these emerging technologies might impact the broadcast or home consumer markets. This is an impressive resource for broadcast and home consumer electronics managers. There are numerous charts and graphs to accompany articles. Three-hole punched for ready reference.
DEPT: "Summary," index of weeks news; "Personals," "Trade Personals," "Financial Reports of TV-Electronic Companies," stock and financial reports on 10-15 firms.
TYPL: "No Main Theme for NAB Convention," "Influencing Ferris--Who, How & Why," "Sears Out of Direct Broadcasting Deal," "PSTV Test in LA Proposed," "FCC Chooses Magnavox AM Stereo System," "US Color Quota Impact Worldwide." (4- 14-80).
SCHL: Weekly, 4 - 15 pp.
SPAN: 1961+
VARIES
--1961 - ? as Television Digest with Consumer Electronics (ISSN: 0897-4632).
--? - May 21, 1984 as Weekly Television Digest with Consumer Electronics (ISSN: 0897-5620).
LC: TK 6540 .T45
DD: 384
ISSN: 0497-1515

Television Digest with Consumer Electronics
1961 - ?//
(ISSN: 0897-4632)
SEE: TELEVISION DIGEST WITH CONSUMER ELECTRONICS

TELEVISION ENGINEERING
SUB: "A magazine for the experimenter who builds his own equipment." (Dec, 1922 - Jan, 1924).
SUB: "A magazine of technical accuracy for the radio engineer, dealer and manufacturer." (Feb, 1924 - ?).
PUBL: Bryan Davis Publishing Co., New York, NY.
DESC: [*Communications*]: In the beginning, *Radio and Model Engineering* editors noted that their publication would be a "...trade magazine for Experimenters who build their own apparatus and do experimental work in their own homes. The publishers believe that the substantial part of experimental work is not done by cranks, but by serious-minded men, and for them the articles in *R* and *M* will be written." The focus of this publication moved from the home experimenter to the professional broadcast engineer, but the premise always remained that of experimentation and construction of communication equipment. Articles were of a highly technical nature, with complete schematics; and earlier issues included parts lists for the

convenience of its reader / experimentors. Of note was a special issue on Super-Heterodyne receivers, with first construction data published in the United States (Feb, 1924). Small magazine format.
DEPT: "Editorial." (9-24). "News and Views," "Veteran Wireless Operators' Association News," "The Industry Offers," new products. (11-49).
TYPL: "R-D-X Reflex," "How to Assemble the Haynes Tuner," "Ware Type T Neutrodyne." (9-24). "A Chart for Resonant-Circuit Calculations," "Iron-Core Interstage and Output 3-kw MF Transmitter Design," "Audio Measurements in AM, FM and TV," "Simplified Remote Amplifier." (11-49).
SCHL: Monthly, 35 pp.
SPAN: Sep, 1937? - Apr, 1952//
FROM MERGER OF
--Broadcast Engineer (and) Radio Engineering (and) Communication and Broadcast Engineering, Sep, 1937.
VARIES
--Sep, 1937 - Dec, 1949 as Communications (ISSN: 0161-374x).
ABSORBED BY
--Communication Engineering (ISSN: 0414-1121), May, 1952.
LC: TK 6630 .A1T4535
ISSN: 0495-0372

✤ TELEVISION HISTORY

PUBL: William J. Felchner, 700 East Macoupin St., Staunton, IL 62088.
DESC: The Monkees, The Girl From UNCLE, The Wild, Wild West, The Munsters, The Addams Family, Voyage to the Bottom of the Sea, Superman, Batman, Gidget, Lost in Space, and even Davy Crockett are all here in *Television History* nee *TV Search*, a one-man publication dedicated to the history behind American television programming. Publisher/editor, William J. Felchner, fills in many information gaps concerning program series and characters; and oftentimes gives an episode-by-episode guide to the featured series. Of note is the attention paid to premiums and collectable items from that golden era, oftentimes with graphics (photocopied) of those items, some of which are available for sale to collectors. *Television History* provides a wonderful service to those interested in the "early days" of American television and its associated products. Typewritten and photocopied in booklet form (5 ⅜ x 8 ½ inches / 140 x 215 mm).
DEPT: "TV Auction," television memorabilia for sale; "TV Checklist," 'For collectors and researchers'; "Q&A," reader submitted questions on television history; "Collector's Showcase," premiums and other items connected with historic television programs; "Quiz." (1/2-90).
TYPL: "The Lucille Ball-Desi Arnaz Show," "Dramatic Television Debuts: James Dean." (1/2-90).
SCHL: Bimonthly, 60 pp.
SPAN: Jan, 1983+
VARIES
--Jan/Feb, 1983 - Nov/Dec, 1989 as TV Search.

✤ TELEVISION INTERNATIONAL

PUBL: Television International, P.O. Box 2430, Hollywood, CA 90028 (and) 52, Rue de Moillebeau, 1202 Geneva, Switzerland.
DESC: *Television International* bills itself as the publication "read by television program executives in 142 countries." The focus is on American video program development, trends, sales and other factors affecting television programming in the United States. There are approximately five to seven articles per issue.
DEPT: None. (1-77).
TYPL: "Movies Rebound as Programming Staple," "The FCC Wants to Know: Have the Networks Grown Too Big for the Industrys' Good,?" "Congress Listens; Hollywood Talks Under Oath; But Does Washington Listen?" (1-77).
SCHL: One issue every six weeks (1956 - Oct, 1958); Monthly (Nov, 1958+); 40 pp.
SPAN: 1956+
VARIES
--Nov, 1958 - Jun/Jul, 1963 as Telefilm Magazine.
--? - ? as Telefilm International.

Television Magazine
Feb, 1949 - Apr, 1955//
SEE: TELEVISION

Television Mail
? - ?//
SEE: BROADCAST

Television News
Mar/Apr, 1931 - Sep/Oct, 1932//
SEE: RADIO REVIEW AND TELEVISION NEWS

TELEVISION OPPORTUNITIES

SUB: "In the development of a new industry--TV."
PUBL: Television Opportunities, 256 W. 55th St., New York, NY.
DESC: "*Television Opportunities Newsletter* is the only publication in the world to report vital news--basic information--on what is happening and going to happen when global telecommunications, including television, becomes a reality." Toward that goal, this eight-page bimonthly concentrates on corporate developments, regulatory issues and major addresses by industry leaders concerning the future of the visual electronic medium. Articles are written by industry professionals at the request of *Television Opportunities Newsletters*, or are extracts of previously publish-

ed materials. It is a notable publication for trend watchers. Originally published on newsprint, the newsletter moved to coated paper stock in 1953.
DEPT: "New Books on TV," reviews; "Books You Need," being sold by Television Opportunities. (7/8-53).
TYPL: "Democracy and Freedom Can be Promoted Via Global TV Says Senator A. Wiley," "US Senator Hickenlooper Cites Facts in Support of Global Television Commission," "Facsimile--An Aid to Global TV," "A Review of Television Abroad," "Economy of Projection Units Stressed," "Television in East and West Germany." (7/8-53).
SCHL: Monthly (Nov, 1948 - Dec, 1952); Bimonthly (Jan/Feb, 1953 - Sep/Oct, 1956), 8 pp.
SPAN: Nov, 1948 - Sep/Oct, 1956//?
LC: HE 8700.8 .T42
DD: 384.55/4/0973
ISSN: 0093-1594

✦ TELEVISION PERSONALITIES

SUB: "Who's who in television."
PUBL: Television Times, Ltd., 39a Bartholomew Close, London EC1, England.
DESC: *Television Personalities* is the first of a series that Television Times, Ltd., will publish at intervals. In future numbers the biographies of many other television stars will be given, as well as those of the unseen but important 'backroom boys.'" It is a small format publication consisting entirely of profiles (with pictures) of various BBC (British Broadcasting Corporation), video artists.
DEPT: None.
TYPL: None.
SCHL: Irregular, 40 pp.
SPAN: Oct, 1953+?
LC: PN 1992.4 .A2T4

✦ TELEVISION PROGRAMMER, THE

SUB: "Covering the entire international programming marketplace--syndication, network, cable, public broadcasting, home video, foreign markets."
PUBL: Communications Research Institute, 25 Central Park West, Suite 1B, New York, NY 10023.
DESC: The sampled issues of 1979 demonstrated this to be a publication of great breadth, concerning media programming. A sample issue addressed network television, government regulation, syndication, subscription TV, public television, and foreign markets. Articles described new technologies and their introduction to the world communication market; the content and availability of programming material to communication media; and news of the international television marketplace in terms of regulatory, commercial, and programming trends.
DEPT: "People/Places/Things," newsbriefs. (11-12-79).
TYPL: "Network Ratings Race Tightens--ABC Leads," "FCC Says More Kidvid Programming Needed," "Tulsa Independent Goes with Westar III," "ACPTS Funding Production of Documentary Series," "France and West Germany to Launch Direct-to-Home Satellite." (11-12-79).
SCHL: Weekly?, 8 pp.
SPAN: 1979+?

✦ TELEVISION QUARTERLY

SUB: "The journal of the National Academy of Television Arts and Sciences."
PUBL: The National Academy of Television Arts and Sciences, 111 West 57th St., New York, NY 10019.
DESC: In the premiere issue of February, 1962 the Editorial Board made this statement of purpose: "Those who are associated with the planning of this Journal believe it is time for a penetrating, provocative and continuing examination of television as an art, a science, an industry, and a social force. Accordingly, our purpose is to be both independent and critical. We hold that the function of this Journal is to generate currents of new ideas about television, and we will therefore try to assure publication of all material which stimulates thought and has editorial merit. This Journal has only one aim--to take a serious look at television." *Television Quarterly* is a scholarly study of issues current in American television, and is published by the National Academy of Television Arts and Sciences, the primary association representing the broadcast television industry. Importantly, authors are oftentimes broadcast executives, or individuals in the midst of current controversy, ensuring that each issue provides fascinating reading on the issues, trends and philosophies concerning the medium. For the sampled issues from 1962: black ink on uncoated paper; cover consisting of spot-color on uncoated index stock; advertising; perfect-bound journal format (6 x 9 inches / 150 x 225 mm). For the 1991 sampled issues: perfect-bound, journal format; black ink on coated paper; cover comprised of spot-color on laminated index stock; significant trade advertising (6 ¼ x 9 ⅜ inches / 160 x 240 mm).
DEPT: "Books in Review," "Comment." (2-62). None. (spring-77). "Review and Comment." (#3-88).
TYPL: "Government's Role in the American System of Broadcasting," "The Active Eyebrow--A Changing Style for Censorship," "The Documentary Heritage," "The Dilemma of the TV Advertiser," "On the Reliability of Ratings." (2-62). "'Star Trek,' and the Bubble-Gum Fallacy," "Off-Camera Intrigue in Mississippi," "The Adams Family: a Metaphor of American Morality," "A Scientist in Television-Land." (spring-77). "The Shrinking TV Foreign Correspondent--Or What's Wrong with the System," "Global TV: The Myth of 'Wall-to-Wall Dallas'," "It's Howdy Doody Time!," "News as Drama: Mystery and Adventure in '60 Minutes'," "'Did They Ever Catch the Criminals Who Committed the Armed Robbery on People's Drive? Hill Street Blues' Remembered." (#3-88).

SCHL: Quarterly, 100 pp.
SPAN: Feb, 1962+
LC: PN 1992.T45
ISSN: 0040-2796

✦ TELEVISION/RADIO AGE

PUBL: Television Editorial Co., 1270 Avenue of the Americas, New York, NY 10020.
DESC: "No business on the American scene has advanced so rapidly in so short a time as television. Similarly, no business has been faced so early with so many pressures and problems. Out of these pressures and with a consciousness of those problems, this magazine has been conceived. Its name *Television Age*, expresses our view of the magnitude and destiny of the medium." This excellent biweekly periodical covers broadcast developments in a slightly different fashion than other business trade serials, being more issue oriented than reactive to weekly news developments. It is a very good reference news source for major developments in the broadcast industry. Magazine format; numerous graphics.
DEPT: "Publishers Letter," editorial; "Viewpoints," guest articles by major broadcast executives; "Commercials," short, descriptive paragraphs about newy produced spots; "Spot Report," spot radio-TV news; "Wall Street Report," excellent series on current financial news. (9-76). "Publisher's Letter," "Letters," "Sidelights," "Tele-Scope," "TV Business Barometer," "International Report," "Cable Report," "Radio Report," "Radio Business Barometer," "Spot Report," "Retail Report," "Buyer's Opinion," "Media Professionals," "Viewpoints," "Programming Production," "Commercials," "Wall Street Report," "In the Picture," "Inside the FCC." (11-24-86).
TYPL: "Computer Systems Offer Stations Negotiating Edge," "Evolution of Agency Fee System Tied to Cost Control," "Progress Due on Quad Radio Standard." (9-76). "Stations Stress Local Sales Development," "Arbitron and Birch Compared," "Weekly Sitcoms Command Station Attention," "Radio Seen as Direct Response Growth Area," "What Can Revive Network TV Documentaries?" (11-24-86).
SCHL: Monthly (Aug, 1953 - Dec, 1969); Biweekly (Jan 12, 1970+); 65 pp.
SPAN: Aug, 1953+
VARIES
--Aug, 1953 - Dec, 1969 as Television Age.
LC: HE 8690.T42
DD: 384.54/05
ISSN: 0040-277x
ABST: --Business Periodical Index (ISSN: 0007-6961)
--Computer & Control Abstracts (ISSN: 0036-8113)
--Electrical & Electronics Abstracts (ISSN: 0036-8105)
--InfoBank
--Physics Abstracts. Science Abstracts. Series A. (ISSN: 0036-8091)
--Trade and Industry Index

✦ TELEVISION / RADIO AGE INTERNATIONAL

PUBL: Television Editorial Corp., 1270 Avenue of the Americas, New York, NY 10020.
DESC: Published quarterly as a supplement to *Television/Radio Age*, this publication focuses, quite naturally, on broadcast production, programming, and legal and financial issues from the viewpoint of world broadcasters. It provides a good vantage point from which to evaluate world competition, and technological development.
DEPT: "Publisher's Letter," "International Scope," newsbriefs; "International Profile," "Meetings," "Top TV Programs," ratings survey; "World TV Set Count." (4-80).
TYPL: "MIP-TV Faces Marketplace Expanded by Needs of New Technologies," "Intra-European Cooperation Critical in Direct-to-Home Satellite Development," "Scandinavian Broadcast Growth Hinges on Nordsat, Financing, Reorganization," "United Nations Broadcast Arms Fight to Maintain Neutrality Despite 152 Bosses." (4-80).
SCHL: Quarterly, 142 pp.
SPAN: ?+
VARIES
--? - Feb, 1984 as Television/Radio Age International.
--Apr, 1984 - Jul?, 1985 as Television Age International.
SUPPLEMENT TO
--Television/Radio Age, ?+.

Television/Radio Age International

? - Feb, 1984//
SEE: TELEVISION / RADIO AGE INTERNATIONAL

TELEVISION RETAILING

SUB: "The business magazine of the radio industry." (Jan, 1925 - ?).
PUBL: Caldwell-Clements, 480 Lexington Ave., New York, NY.
DESC: Beginning in January, 1925 as *Radio Retailing*, and ending in August, 1953 as *Television Retailing*, this serial for over 25 years provided the promotional "knowhow" of retailing radio and television apparatus to the American public. Issues were a mixture of retail promotional hints, and technical information on circuitry for the in-house repair technician. Over the years, various magazines were absorbed; such as *Radio & Television*, *Radio & Television Today*, *TV Technician*, and *Appliance Retailing* to form this one umbrella publication with two monthly supplements. It is an interesting look at retailing strategies for radio and television equipment. *Television Retailing* and supplement, *TV-Electronic Technician*, were magazine format; graphics. Supplement, *TV & Appliance Mart*, was in a tabloid format with graphics.

DEPT: "The Editors Have This to Say--," editorial; "New Merchandise for the Dealer to Sell," "What the Trade is Talking About." (4-25). "Latest Television, Radio Sets on the Market," "Sales Reports From All Over USA," "State of the Market," "Phono Market News and Trends," "Activities in the Electrical Appliance Industry," "New Products for Services." (5-53).
TYPL: "Why You Should Sell Radio on Time Payments--and How," "Ways to Interest the Women in Radio," "Are You Selling to the Farmer?," "How Music Dealers are Selling Radio." (4-25). "Diversified Dealer Gets Big Share of Sales," "Keep Your customers Coming Back to Buy," "Selling the Hi-Fi Prospect." (5-53).
SCHL: Monthly, 130 pp.
SPAN: Jan, 1925 - Aug, 1953//
VARIES
--1925 - Mar, 1939 as Radio Retailing.
--Apr, 1939 - Dec, 1941 as Radio and Television Retailing.
--Jan, 1942 - Jul, 1942 as Radio Retailing Combined with Radio Today.
--Aug, 1942 - Mar, 1944 as Radio Retailing Today.
--Apr, 1944 - Jun, 1952 as Radio & Television Retailing.
WITH SUPPLEMENT
--TV & Appliance Mart (ISSN: 0025-4061), ? - ?
--TV-Electronic Technician, ? - ?
ABSORBED
--Electrical Retailing, Feb, 1925.
--Radio and Television Today, Jan, 1942.
SPLIT INTO
--Mart (ISSN: 0025-4061) (and) Technician.
LC: TK 6540.R7

✤ TELEVISION WEEK

PUBL: MEED House, 21 John St., London WC1N 2BP, England.
DESC: *Television Week* is sent weekly throughout the United Kingdom on a strictly controlled circulation basis "...to executive and technical staff involved in the conception, planning, acquisition, production and post-production of television and video programmes and commercials," and also in Europe to program planners and buyers. It is an excellent tabloid of the events, issues, and trends of British television; and to a lesser extent of other nations, most notably the United States. It provides a succinct summary of the events of British television in a well-designed, tabloid format.
DEPT: "Scanners," newsbriefs; "Focus," editorial; "National Top Tens," ratings for week ending; "International Top Tens," top television shows from selected nations; "Out-Takes," programming and observations via 'Groucho'; "Comment," column by Peter Lloyd; "Feedback," technology column by Mitch Mitchell; "Techscan," technology; "On Location," production companies and projects in the areas of corporate, arts, quiz, TV films/drama and factual; "Viewpoint," column by Richard Brooks; "Letters," "Revolving Door," personnel newsbriefs; "Dateline," calendar; "Spy," the lighter side of the television industry. (1-19-89).
TYPL: "US Public Stations Fight for TV Worth Watching," "ITC is Likely to Rule Out a Maxwell Bid For Central," "TV2 Set to Join EBU in March," "BSB to Pitch For IBA's Two New Satellite Channels," "Bringing C5 to Scotland." (1-19-89).
SCHL: Weekly, 40 pp.
SPAN: Oct 27, 1988+
ISSN: 0955-1344

TELEVISION WEEKLY NEWS

PUBL: Television Weekly News, 6368 Hollywood Blvd., Hollywood, CA.
DESC: Publisher Harry Ray believed in Hollywood, and believed in the coming of television: "We are preparing for the immediate future, in which the firmly established talking motion picture, of course, remains supreme; for the talking motion picture is the present vital motivating force behind television. The broadcasting of talking motion pictures will be the big job of the broadcasting stations. In all matters related to the two industries *Television Weekly News* will supply the latest news." Here was a West-Coast serial dedicated to the premise that radio, television and film would, in the near future, go hand-in-hand, much in the same way as sound fit the previously silent mode of motion picture film. The serial encouraged television development, at the same time exposing video racketeers; and it charted the general development of the medium in Hollywood. It contained numerous graphics, especially of film artists who had appeared or were to appear on television programs. It remains a remarkable resource for the relationship between film and video during these early, critical years.
DEPT: "Tele-Visions," editorial; "Radio Entertainment," "Motion Pictures," "Stage Amusements," "Television Stations Now in Operation," (5-2-31).
TYPL: "K.F.W.B. to Have Television," "Television History," (5-2-31).
SCHL: Weekly, 20 pp.
SPAN: Apr 18, 1931 - Aug 8, 1931//?
LC: TK 6630 .A1T5

✤ TELEVISIONS

PUBL: Washington Community Video Center, P.O. Box 21068, Washington, DC 20009.
DESC: *Televisions* is a high-quality tabloid which includes: "video and art, hardware, citizen action, regulation, social services satellites, education, public television, cable and public access." Commercial broadcasting and home software areas are NOT emphasized in this publication. Articles explore citizen responsibility toward media usage and access to programming channels; also the role of media in society, and the relationship between government, media, and the consumer public. It is well-illustrated. Typical articles for

1980 and 1981 included, "The Sitcoms of Garry Marshall," "Live From the Kitchen," "TV Acting: Is the BBC the Best?," "Television Images, Codes and Messages," and a "Primer on Satellite Access." For the sampled issues of 1979 through 1981: stapled, newsletter format; editorial content being black ink on tinted uncoated paper; advertising (8 ½ x 11 inches / 215 x 280 mm).

DEPT: "The 526th Line," viewpoint on the state of communication arts; "Media Gratees," who got what and when; "Calendar," upcoming video events; "Art," the state of video as an art form; "Regulation," "Education," reviews of unusual current video projects; "Citizen Action," current activities. (7-78).

TYPL: "Vietnam Video," "TV as the Liberals Scapegoat," "CETA Staffs Video Groups Across the Country: Background and Five Profiles," "Banning TV Advertising for Kids: Pros and Nos Muster Forces for Hearing," "Broadcast Management Text: What Makes a Good Case Study?" (7-78).

SCHL: Four issues per year, 20 pp.
SPAN: Summer, 1973+
VARIES
--Summer, 1973 - Autumn, 1974 as Community Video Report.

✤ TGIF

SUB: "Casting news."
SUB: "Entertainment, views, reviews."
PUBL: TGIF Enterprises, PO Box 1683, Hollywood, CA 90078.
DESC: "*TGIF* is published every other Friday as a service to the entertainment industry and single people in general." It lists new stage shows and commercials for crew calls. Published on newsprint.
DEPT: "TGIF Openings for Acting Talent," "TGIF Openings for Entertainers," "TGIF Openings for Musicians," "TGIF Openings for Writers," "TGIF Openings for Models." (10-77).
TYPL: "Mr. Whipple, Just Squeezing By," "The True Story of 'Julia,'" "From Silver Screen to Golden Stage." (10-77).
SCHL: Bimonthly, 16 pp.
SPAN: ?+?
ISSN: 0274-7693

The Advisers Bulletin
? - ?//
SEE: CSPAA BULLETIN

✤ THE JOURNAL

SUB: "Technological Horizons in Education."
PUBL: THE Journal, 150 El Camino Real, Suite 112, Tustin, CA 92680-3615.
DESC: The integration of computers, mass media, and education into academia is a relatively recent development, and receives the focus of *T.H.E. Journal*; subtitled "Technological Horizons in Education." It reports new developments in technology and education in the United States, with ample articles on Computer Assisted Instruction (CAI), and Interactive Video applications; including the media of video, slides, filmstrips, and motion pictures. It is a unique forum for discussion of academic issues, with continuing insight into the integration of computers and media in education; and is a good publication for charting the changing role of technology in education. Magazine format (8 ⅛ x 10 ⅞ inches / 205 x 275 mm), with numerous graphics, especially off-screen stills of software programs. Also of note is a unique editorial layout style that places most departmental articles at the front, and feature articles at the back of each issue.

DEPT: "Editorial," "Calendar," "News," "New Publications," "Books," reviews; "Software/Courseware," review; "Applications," educational; "New Products." (9-82). "Editorial," "Technology Update," "News," "Software & Courseware," new products; "Applications," "Multimedia," "Calendar." (12/1-90).

TYPL: "Computers and the Schools," "CDI: It Teaches," "The Search for New Intellectual Technologies," "Adding Apples and Oranges: Telecourses Are Both Different and Important," "Interactive Video in the Pacific Northwest." (9-82). "Toward the Development of a Worldwide Model for Teenage Education," "Signs of Change in the Soviet Union," "The Feedback Classroom: Teaching's Silent Friend." (12/1-90).

SCHL: Six issues per year (May, 1974 - Nov, 1986); Monthly [except Jul, Dec] (Dec, 1986 to date), 90 pp.
SPAN: May, 1974+
LC: LB 1028.3 .J69
DD: 371.3/07/8
ISSN: 0192-592x
ABST: --Computer & Control Abstracts (ISSN: 0036-8113)
--Current Index to Journals in Education (ISSN: 0011-3565)
--Education Index (ISSN: 0013-1385)
--Electrical & Electronics Abstracts (ISSN: 0036-8105)
--Micro Computer Index (ISSN: 8756-7040)
--Physics Abstracts. Science Abstracts. Series A. (ISSN: 0036-8091)

✤ THEATER

PUBL: Yale School of Drama, Yale Repretory Theater, 222 York St., New Haven, CT 06520.
DESC: On the occasion of change of title and editorial content in fall, 1977, the editors noted, "*Theater* began in 1968 as *Yale/Theatre*, its declared purpose being to examine contemporary American theater through the facilities of the Yale School of Drama--to 'communicate the pulse of this place and this time' in 'theatre, thought, discussion, dream, art, people'. The magazine's focus, however has rarely been limited to theater events in either New Haven or New York; since

1968 the scope of *Yale/Theatre* has broadened to encompass work throughout America and abroad. We are acknowledging this fact through our change in title. *Theater* will continue to publish writing on diverse theater subjects--particularly on groups, playwrights, and plays which we regard as exemplary and deserving of attention. At present there are far too few American theater magazines that locate theatrical events in a greater cultural, social, or aesthetic context. We wish to print essays, interviews, and retrospectives that reflect these larger concerns, and not simply documentation that is time-bound to particular productions." *Theater* is a high-quality review of drama, with special emphasis on performance. "Each issue contains: a play, essays, interviews with noted theater artists and photos of production from around the world." For the sampled issues of 1977 and 1978: perfect-bound, journal format; black ink on tinted uncoated paper; cover consisting of spot-color on tinted uncoated stock (9 ⅛ x 9 ⅛ inches / 235 x 235 mm).

DEPT: "Theater in Washington," column by Mohammad Kowsar; "Theater in New York," column by Eileen Blumenthal. (summer-78). "Books Recently Received." (spring-84).

TYPL: "The Theater of Cruelty and the Closure of Representation," "Andrei Serban on Artaud: An Interview," "Eclecticism, Oriental Theater and Artaud," "The Alfred Jarry Theater: A Portfolio of Photographs," "Artaud and Ibsen." (summer-78). "Ten Directors in Search of a Theater," "My Life as Chopin: an Interview with Philip Bosakowski." (spring-84).

SCHL: Three issues per year, 100 pp.
SPAN: Spring, 1968+
VARIES
--Spring, 1968 - Spring, 1977 as Yale/Theatre (ISSN: 0044-0167).
LC: PN 2000.Y34
DD: 792/.05
ISSN: 0161-0775
ABST: --Film Literature Index (ISSN: 0093-6758)
--Humanities Index (ISSN: 0095-5981)
--Index to Book Reviews in the Humanities (ISSN: 0073-5892)
--MLA International Bibliography of Books & Articles on the Modern Languages and Literatures (ISSN: 0024-8215)

✣ THEATER NOW

PUBL: Southern Players, Southern Illinois University, Carbondale, IL 62901.
DESC: A short, wide format serial designed to promote the dramatic arts, editor Jay Raphael stated in the first issue that he would "...publish anything that will encourage an individual to be *of* the theater rather than about it." Emphasis is on Southern Illinois drama activities, with some news of other university drama centers. Most articles are relatively short; no graphics.
DEPT: "Notes and Queries," "Playbills." (spring-72).

TYPL: "Riding the Spanish New Wave," "An Interview with Marcel Marceau," "Upstaging Language Barriers," "Crisis in the Berliner Ensemble." (spring-72).
SCHL: Semiannual, 35 pp.
SPAN: Spring, 1972+
LC: PN 2000.T3

✣ THEATERWEEK

PUBL: That New Magazine, Inc., 28 West 25th St., 4th Fl., New York, NY 10010.
DESC: Designed for the professional theatre community, *TheaterWeek* charts the status of current theatrical offerings, upcoming projects, just opened productions; and the issues, trends and controversies current in the field. Crisp black/white editorial content and a generous number of graphics on white uncoated paper stock support the "now" approach of this weekly periodical. Reviews and listings of live stage in New York City is the focus; with current fare listings concentrating on this always-important center of live stage performance in the United States. The importance of this publication to artists is evident in the numerous advertisements for auditions, new projects and companies being formed, calls for scripts, and other stage craft positions. *TheaterWeek* is an important serial for those on, off, and way-off Broadway whose professions and passions reside in live stage performance. Magazine format (8 x 10 ½ inches / 200 x 265 mm), full color covers, with black/white editorial content on a brilliant-white uncoated paper stock.
DEPT: "The Critics," wonderful sampling of critical reviews for current stage productions; "Theater News," newsbriefs column by Ken Mandelbaum; "Stagestruck," theatrical commentary column by Peter Filichia; "Reviews," extensive play critiques column by Richard Sneerwell and Guy Leslie; "Beyond Broadway," "Cabaret," listing of cabaret reviews at various locations; "TheaterWeek Listings," extensive listing of current theatrical fare; "Off Broadway," listing of current offerings; "Off-Off Broadway," current offerings far from the Great White Way. (1-21-91).
TYPL: "Peter Brook as Prospero," "A Theater of Cruelty," "Letter From Paris," "Musical Comedy Divorce." (1-21-91).
SCHL: Weekly, 50 pp.
SPAN: Aug 13, 1987+
DD: 792
ISSN: 0896-1956

THEATRE

PUBL: ?, 77 Dean St., London W1, England.
DESC: This was a newsletter (later in booklet format) concerned with current play productions of the London regional theatre community and designed for the public. Early issues provided eight pages of newsletter information with no graphics. Latter issues moved to a spot color, small journal format with increased edi-

torial content. There was some critical analysis of London stage productions, but primarily this was a serial of current information.
DEPT: "News Round-Up," "The London Theatre," playlist; "Stage Door," column by Robert Muller; "Round the Provinces," theatre in the UK; "Theatre Diary," playtimes and offerings. (4-3-48). "Theatre Diary," "London Theatre." (11-52).
TYPL: "National Theatre Assured," "Instructors Instructed," "Bankruptcy in West End?" (4-3-48). "State Aid for Stage Arts," "History on the Air," "New Ballets," "High Balcony." (11-52).
SCHL: Semimonthly (Jul 15, 1946 - Jan 19, 1952); Weekly (? - ?); Monthly (? - ?); 25 pp.
SPAN: Jul 15, 1946 - Feb 14, 1953//
VARIES
--Jul 15, 1946 - Jan 19, 1952 as Theatre Newsletter.
LC: PN 2001.T39

THEATRE, THE
SUB: "A monthly review and magazine."
SUB: "A monthly review of the drama, music, and the fine arts." (Jan, 1880 - Aug, 1894).
PUBL: Wyman & Sons, 81 Great Queen St., Lincoln's-Inn Fields, London WC, England.
DESC: This journal of British theatre brought to the playgoer each month several articles dealing with theatre as art, history, and social comment. Included monthly were two or three hand-mounted photographs of well-known actors and actresses of the day, under the special departmental feature of "Portraits," which included biographical profiles. It oftentimes discussed the health of theatre world-wide, and new innovations in directing, or technology for the stage. Journal format. Of special note was the departmental feature, "At the Play," which discoursed about theatre news in London, the Provinces, Paris, Berlin, Vienna, Italian cities, Madrid, and New York. Later issues included woodcuts and poetry.
DEPT: "The Watch Tower," comment; "Portraits," "The Round Table," "En Passant," detailed obituaries; "At the Play," current fare; "Echoes from the Green Room," newsbriefs; "Literature." (2-1879). "Our Portraits and Biographies," "Reviews," "Our Play-box," reviews; "Our Amateurs' Play-Box," reviews; "Art Notes," "Musical Notes," "Our Omnibus-Box," newsbriefs; "New Plays," listing. (7-1892).
TYPL: "Competent Dramatists," "Dramatic Criticism of the Day," "Social Responsibilities of the Actor." (2-1879). "Playbills, Past and Present," "How to Enjoy the Theatre." (7-1892).
SCHL: Weekly (Jan, 1877 - Jul, 1878); Monthly (Aug, 1878+).
SPAN: Jan, 1877 - Dec, 1897//
LC: PN 2001.T4

THEATRE, THE
SUB: "A magazine of drama, comedy and music." (Jan, 1959 - Sep, 1960).
SUB: "Drama, comedy, music." (Oct, 1960+).
PUBL: Atlas Publishing Co., 425 West 25th St., New York, NY.
DESC: "The public is becoming more theatre conscious. It is the aim of the publishers of The Theatre to stimulate this interest by making the people of the theatre as interesting to the public as they are to their colleagues--and to eventually turn the interested reader into the active theatre-goer." The emphasis was on people within the theatre, their lives, acting styles, interests, and other facets of the acting community in the New York City area, with some articles concerning actors in other cities or even other nations. In some ways, The Theatre functioned as a public relations magazine of "the Great White Way," by providing articles on new plays, theatre schedules, and general events, information, and stories of the Broadway theatre community. Latter issues also provided sections concerning nightclub activities, musical recordings, and other events that augmented the Broadway scene.
DEPT: "New York," column by Cindy Adams; "Fashion a la carte," fashion news; "Manhattan Tips," 'And Adventures in Eating'; "New York Life," column by Baron Theo von Roth; "Dateline: London," column by Neil Stevens; "Theatre Crossword," "Theatre Calendar," "Letters to the Editor," "Daily Events," "Theatre Dining," "Drama Blackboard," upcoming national plays; "Books and Records," review. (12-60).
TYPL: "Lucille Ball in 'Wildcat,'" "Confessions of a First-Nighter," "At Home with Maurice Evans," "Opening Night," "The Art of Acting." (12-60).
SCHL: Monthly, 50 pp.
SPAN: Jan, 1959 - Sep, 1961//
MERGED WITH
--New York Guide (to form) New York Guide and Theatre Magazine (ISSN: 0545-6142).

THEATRE, THE
SUB: "A weekly record of the stage." (Mar 20, 1886 - Apr 27, 1893).
SUB: "An illustrated weekly magazine; drama, music, art."
PUBL: Theatre Publishing Co., Number 33, West 23rd St., New York, NY.
DESC: "The publisher of The Theatre has asked the Editor to make no long-winded 'salutatory' about what the 'policy of this paper' shall be, or draw a mortgage on the future by extravagant promises. The motive is exactly what the title-page indicates: a record of the stage." Early issues (1880s) were just that, a record of the stage with a very unusual section of New York city theatres; their bills of fare, seating diagrams, and short descriptions of current fare. These issues were filled with numerous caricatures of well-known Broadway stars, and other commentary on the New York stage. Latter issues (1893) moved to normal magazine format, with a more concise theatre section. Typical flavor of

this periodical could be seen in an editorial (Mar 11, 1893) which ranted against the popular ballet/drama/musical, "The Black Crook," noting that: "The females in this lift their legs to their heads and hold them pointed to heaven as indicators of their virtue. The disgusting gyrations of these females are applauded by respectable looking women." A brief notice appeared in the last issue of April 27, 1893: "A new magazine devoted to the stage is announced to appear in this city next month. I hope the proprietors of it will be happy. Simultaneously *The Theatre* will publish a magazine too, and that will be nice."
DEPT: "Entre Nous," comment; "Notes and News," "Good Words," published reviews. (4-26-1886). "Entre Nous," comment; "Literary Chatter," newsbriefs. (3-11-1893).
TYPL: "Portrait of John Gilbert," "Barnum," "Our Managers," "A Famous French Actor." (4-26-1886). "The Marmozets of the Stage," "Scenery in Shakespeare's Time." (3-11-1893).
SCHL: Weekly (Sep - May); Monthly (Jun - Aug), 12 pp.
SPAN: Mar 20, 1886 - Apr 27, 1893//
LC: PN 2000.T4

Theatre, The

May, 1901 - Jul, 1917//
(ISSN: 0891-6861)
SEE: THEATRE MAGAZINE

THEATRE AND SCHOOL

SUB: "Quarterly of the Drama Teachers Association."
PUBL: Drama Teachers Association, Berkeley, CA.
DESC: Originally published by the Drama Teachers Association of California, and later by the national Drama Teachers Association, *Theatre and School* provided an exchange of information about the role and development of dramatic arts within secondary schools in the nation. The Association was "...composed of men and women throughout the United States who have a special interest in drama with its allied arts as a great educational force in modern society." Some early issues printed on color paper. Journal format; few graphics.
DEPT: "Field Notes." (3-26). "Book and News Notes," "Play Calendar." (5-36).
TYPL: "Annual Spring Conference and Shakespearean Festival," "Producing a Community Pageant." (3-26). "Twenty Years of Speech and Drama at Mills," "Radio as a Career," "The Federal Theatre Project," "Is the Movie Greater Than the Book?" (5-36).
SCHL: Monthly [Oct - Jun], (? - ?); Quarterly (? - ?); 30 pp.
SPAN: 1922 - May, 1937//
LC: PN 3175.A1T5

THEATRE ARTS

PUBL: Theatre Arts, Inc., New York, NY.
DESC: [*Theatre Arts Monthly*]: Celebrating the vitality and professionalism of American and European theatre, this monthly serial noted all that was well and good in that field. Various auxiliary areas of college theatre and ballet were featured in some articles. In one sampled issue from 1937 were discussions concerning the craft of good acting, the process of apprenticeship as recalled by John Gielgud, how Sweden's National Theatre successfully "organized" their audiences, the transition of Fred and Adele Astaire from Broadway to Hollywood silver screen, the rise of tragedy in London theatre, and "African Sculpture and Plays as Ritual." The format was as interesting as the editorial content itself. The issue for 1937 was printed black/white on cream-color paper. Pages containing advertisement graphics, and editorial content picture pages were on coated paper stock: editorial content with line drawings was printed letterpress fashion on uncoated paper stock. Editorial content consisted primarily of one column, five-inch-wide format; with occasional use of two-column, one wide, one narrow format in opening editorial section. Pagination was utilized only for editorial content, and all illustrations are clearly labeled with pagination on the contents page. For the sampled issue of 1937: magazine format (8 1/4 x 11 inches / 210 x 280 mm).
DESC: [*Theatre Arts*]: The year 1954 is considered by some to have been the height of the so-called "Golden Age" of television, and one of the low points both for Hollywood and New York's "Great White Way," but one certainly did not see any such gloom in *Theatre Arts* magazine. Continuing the premise that good theatre was alive, well and thriving, the magazine continued the fine tradition of reprinting the texts of current productions, interviewing and profiling theatrical talent, and exploring the general status of American and international theatre. In the sampled issue for 1954 there was a special section on Japanese theatre which showcased a wide variety of Japanese theatrical formats. Sampled issue for 1954: stapled magazine format, primarily black/white editorial content, with spot color employed throughout and on the cover on coated paper stock (8 5/8 x 11 1/2 inches / 220 x 290 mm).
DEPT: "The World and the Theatre," newsbriefs; "Broadway in Review," column by Edith J. Isaacs; "The English Scene," British theatre column by Ashley Dukes; "Theatre Arts Bookshelf," book reviews; "See For Yourself," 'Attractions current in New York, some to look forward to, and a list of those that have closed since the last recording'. (5-37). "Letters," "Broadway," extensive 'Reviews of Broadway productions'; "Calendar," "Theatre on the Disc," music review column by Sigmund Spaeth; "Theatre Arts Gallery," profile. (3-54).
TYPL: "The Pleasure in Good Acting," "An Artist's Apprenticeship," "Fred Astaire: The Actor-Dancer Attacks His Part," "Answers to Prayers," "A Lyric Theatre," "Organizing an Audience." (5-37). "Boys Will Be Boys," "Tale of Two Cities--Jealousy, Illinois and

Underground, New York," "Gin and Smpathy," "Saroyan Speaks Up," Kabuki Is a Must for America." (3-54).
SCHL: Quarterly (Nov, 1916 - Oct, 1923); Monthly (Jan, 1924+), 95 pp.
SPAN: Nov, 1916 - Jan, 1964//
VARIES
--Nov, 1916 - Oct, 1923 as Theatre Arts Magazine.
--Jan, 1924 - Oct, 1939 as Theatre Arts Monthly.
SUSPENDED
--Nov, 1948 - Dec, 1948.
ABSORBED
--Stage Magazine, May, 1950.
LC: PN 2000.T45

Theatre Arts Magazine

Nov, 1916 - Oct, 1923//
SEE: THEATRE ARTS

Theatre Arts Monthly

Jan, 1924 - Oct, 1939//
SEE: THEATRE ARTS

Theatre Communications

Apr, 1979 - Mar, 1984//
(ISSN: 0275-5971)
SEE: AMERICAN THEATRE

Theatre Communications Group Newsletter

Jan, 1973 - Mar, 1979//
(ISSN: 0163-9137)
SEE: AMERICAN THEATRE

THEATRE-CRAFT

SUB: "A book of the new spirit in the theatre."
PUBL: 71 Great Russell St., London, WC1, England.
DESC: The raison d'etre of *Theatre-Craft* was a recognition that by 1919 the stagnation of wartime British theatre was over and a theatrical rebirth was happening throughout Britain, especially within community groups, leagues and societies, what the Americans called theatre playhouses, small non-commercial groups interested in fostering the theatre arts. It was for this group of people that this serial was published, to provide a unique forum for discussion of community theatre, and the rebirth of British theatre art. This short-lived serial discussed Czech drama, new dance techniques, management of American playhouses, and other exciting international developments which might be readily adapted by British community theatre groups. Small square format; letterpress with some illustrations on coated paper stock. It would appear that only four issues were published during the two-year lifespan.
DEPT: "Editorial," "Notes," book reviews; "Correspondence." (#4, summer-20).
TYPL: "Dramatic Art and the Voice," "The Doom of the Drama," "The Aesthetic Basis of Stage-Craft," "A Note on the Irish Theatre," "The Folk-Music Play." (#4, summer-20).
SCHL: Semiyearly, 60 pp.
SPAN: 1919 - 1921//
ABSORBED BY
--English Review.

THEATRE CRAFT

PUBL: A. C. Sanucci, 1513 Randall St., Glendale, CA.
DESC: *Theatre Craft* was "...a new publication devoted primarily to the activities of the Little Theatre, and including in its pages a sprinkling of screen, television, radio, music and the legitimate stage." First and foremost, this was a promotional serial for the "little theatres" of Glendale, the "Valley," and Pasadena, California. It discussed current area projects, profiled emerging stars, and generally promoted the cause of small theatre in Southern California. Journal format; numerous graphics.
DEPT: "Listen For a Minute," editorial; "Here It Is," 'Pocket reviews'; "Recommendations of the Month," plays; "Tots and Teens Dramatics," "Musically Speaking," "Around Hollywood," "Golden Gate Glitters," "Playtime Schedule," "Talent Roster," profiles. (1-48).
TYPL: "Fans Make Stars," "The Canfield Studio Theatre." (1-48).
SCHL: Monthly, 20 pp.
SPAN: Jan, 1947 - May, 1948?//
LC: PN 2000.T47
DD: 792.05

✦ THEATRE CRAFTS

SUB: "The magazine for professionals in theatre, film, video, and the performing arts."
PUBL: Theatre Crafts, 135 Fifth Ave., New York, NY 10010-7193.
DESC: This is an excellent publication for the professional working in craft services, the below-the-line personnel, without which the show would never be. Early issues concentrated on legitimate theatre: current issues came to include television, motion pictures, and the performing arts as well. This is one serial where technology and the creative side of crafts have indeed come together. Highly recommended, especially for case studies in problem solving. Sampled issue for 1990: magazine format (8 x 10 ¾ inches / 205 x 275 mm); numerous graphics, many in color.
DEPT: "Editor's Page," "From the Greenroom," author profiles; "New Products," "Books & Records," "Letters," "Conventions/Meetings." (5/6-67). "Letters," "News," "How-To," "In Production," profiles; "Prod-

TYPL: "An Opera Company Grows in Brooklyn," "Repertory Theatre: The Problems of a Complete Concept in Lighting and Sound," "Costumes for Children of All Ages." (5/6-67). "The Speed of Lighting," "Making Your Theatre Accessible," "Aiming for the Mind's Eye," "Missing Link." (4-87). "A New Spike Lee Joint," "Summer Opera Sampler," "Letting Nature Lead the Way." (7/8-90).

uct News," "Callboard," ads. (4-87). "Editorial," "News," newsbriefs; "Lighting," column by Karl Ruling; "Resource," for theatre equipment and supplies; "Show Report," column by Ellen Lampert; "Books," reviews. (8/9-90).

SCHL: Bimonthly (? - ?); Nine issues per year (? - ?); Ten issues per year [combined Jun/Jul and Aug/Sep issues] (Dec, 1985+), 100 pp.
SPAN: Mar/Apr, 1967+
VARIES
--Mar/Apr, 1967 - ? as TC, Theatre Crafts.
LC: PN 2000.T48
DD: 792/.05
ISSN: 0040-5469
ABST: --Book Review Index (ISSN: 0524-0581)
--Magazine Index
--Popular Magazine Review (ISSN: 0740-3763)
--Readers Guide to Periodical Literature (ISSN: 0034-0464)

✦ THEATRE DESIGN & TECHNOLOGY

SUB: "Journal of the United States Institute for Theatre Technology."
SUB: "The journal for design & production professionals in the performing arts."
PUBL: USITT, 10 West 19th St., Suite 5A, New York, NY 10011-4206.
DESC: With an emphasis on the technical side of theatre, *Theatre Design & Technology* provides a comprehensive review of new technology, theatre design and application of technology to stage construction and operation. This is a wonderful resource for the working professional in performing arts. One sampled issue held articles on the uses of drama in the commercial arena of marketing presentations, courtyard philosophy of theatre architecture, and the issue of function versus "The Horizon" in contemporary Czechoslovak design. The always excellent series of departmental features focused on "Engineering," "Lighting," and "Architecture" in each issue. Membership in the United States Institute for Theatre Technology is represented by all major technical theatre vendors. The purpose of USITT is "...to disseminate information and facilitate communication for the professional development of its members. ... Encourage research and investigations in the field of theatre planning and design, construction, equipment, aesthetics, presentation and operations; Combine and conserve the records of such studies and investigations...," to publish study information, provide contact between members, provide representation at national and international conferences, and "Encourage good practices in the field of theatre planning and design, construction, equipment, aesthetics, presentation and operation, based on the experience of those engaged in the theatre on all levels as developed by studies in those fields." USITT is the United States Center for the international organization, OISTAT (Organisation Internationale des Scénographes, Techniciens et Architectes de Théâtre). Typical articles for 1991 include, "The International Jury Process," "Of Garbage & Gold: Great Britain at PQ'91," "Designs for a Theatre in Transition," "Contemporary American Designers: George Tsypin," and "Postmodern Issues in Action Design 5." Magazine format (8 ¼ x 11 inches / 210 x 280mm), with black/white and color graphics throughout.

DEPT: "Theatre Architecture," "Research," "Sound," "Computers," "Book Reviews," "New Products," "OISTT," periodical and book review. (summer-84). "Editors' Note," "Engineering," "Lighting," "Architecture," "Readers' Response," letters; "New Products," review; "International Journal Report," excellent international theatre journal/magazine review column by Norma Adler. (summer-90).
TYPL: "Orange County Performing Arts Center: a Design Report," "The Permanent Adaptable Stage Setting of Sam Hume," "Steel-Framed Stock Platforming," "Using Time Manager," "TRS-80 Model III Light Plot Using Profile Three Plus." (summer-84). "Passion, Poison and Profession," "Marketing as Theatre," "The Courtyard Theatre: Philosophies and Practicalities," "Postmodern Issues in Action," "The Minotaurus: Svoboda Directs." (summer-90).
SCHL: Quarterly, 80 pp.
SPAN: May, 1965+
VARIES
--May, 1965 - Feb, 1968 as Theatre Design & Technology (ISSN: 0040-5477).
--May, 1968 - Winter, 1977 as Theatre Design and Technology (ISSN: 0040-5477).
LC: NA 1.T45
DD: 792
ISSN: 0040-5477
ABST: --Architectural Periodicals Index (ISSN: 0033-6912)
--Avery Index to Architectual Periodicals (ISSN: 0196-0008)

Theatre Design & Technology
May, 1965 - Feb, 1968//
(ISSN: 0040-5477)
SEE: THEATRE DESIGN & TECHNOLOGY

Theatre Design and Technology
May, 1968 - Winter, 1977//
(ISSN: 0040-5477)
SEE: THEATRE DESIGN & TECHNOLOGY

Underground, New York," "Gin and Smpathy," "Saroyan Speaks Up," Kabuki Is a Must for America." (3-54).
SCHL: Quarterly (Nov, 1916 - Oct, 1923); Monthly (Jan, 1924+), 95 pp.
SPAN: Nov, 1916 - Jan, 1964//
VARIES
--Nov, 1916 - Oct, 1923 as Theatre Arts Magazine.
--Jan, 1924 - Oct, 1939 as Theatre Arts Monthly.
SUSPENDED
--Nov, 1948 - Dec, 1948.
ABSORBED
--Stage Magazine, May, 1950.
LC: PN 2000.T45

Theatre Arts Magazine

Nov, 1916 - Oct, 1923//
SEE: THEATRE ARTS

Theatre Arts Monthly

Jan, 1924 - Oct, 1939//
SEE: THEATRE ARTS

Theatre Communications

Apr, 1979 - Mar, 1984//
(ISSN: 0275-5971)
SEE: AMERICAN THEATRE

Theatre Communications Group Newsletter

Jan, 1973 - Mar, 1979//
(ISSN: 0163-9137)
SEE: AMERICAN THEATRE

THEATRE-CRAFT

SUB: "A book of the new spirit in the theatre."
PUBL: 71 Great Russell St., London, WC1, England.
DESC: The raison d'etre of *Theatre-Craft* was a recognition that by 1919 the stagnation of wartime British theatre was over and a theatrical rebirth was happening throughout Britain, especially within community groups, leagues and societies, what the Americans called theatre playhouses, small non-commercial groups interested in fostering the theatre arts. It was for this group of people that this serial was published, to provide a unique forum for discussion of community theatre, and the rebirth of British theatre art. This short-lived serial discussed Czech drama, new dance techniques, management of American playhouses, and other exciting international developments which might be readily adapted by British community theatre groups. Small square format; letterpress with some illustrations on coated paper stock. It would appear that only four issues were published during the two-year lifespan.
DEPT: "Editorial," "Notes," book reviews; "Correspondence." (#4, summer-20).
TYPL: "Dramatic Art and the Voice," "The Doom of the Drama," "The Aesthetic Basis of Stage-Craft," "A Note on the Irish Theatre," "The Folk-Music Play." (#4, summer-20).
SCHL: Semiyearly, 60 pp.
SPAN: 1919 - 1921//
ABSORBED BY
--English Review.

THEATRE CRAFT

PUBL: A. C. Sanucci, 1513 Randall St., Glendale, CA.
DESC: *Theatre Craft* was "...a new publication devoted primarily to the activities of the Little Theatre, and including in its pages a sprinkling of screen, television, radio, music and the legitimate stage." First and foremost, this was a promotional serial for the "little theatres" of Glendale, the "Valley," and Pasadena, California. It discussed current area projects, profiled emerging stars, and generally promoted the cause of small theatre in Southern California. Journal format; numerous graphics.
DEPT: "Listen For a Minute," editorial; "Here It Is," 'Pocket reviews'; "Recommendations of the Month," plays; "Tots and Teens Dramatics," "Musically Speaking," "Around Hollywood," "Golden Gate Glitters," "Playtime Schedule," "Talent Roster," profiles. (1-48).
TYPL: "Fans Make Stars," "The Canfield Studio Theatre." (1-48).
SCHL: Monthly, 20 pp.
SPAN: Jan, 1947 - May, 1948?//
LC: PN 2000.T47
DD: 792.05

✤ THEATRE CRAFTS

SUB: "The magazine for professionals in theatre, film, video, and the performing arts."
PUBL: Theatre Crafts, 135 Fifth Ave., New York, NY 10010-7193.
DESC: This is an excellent publication for the professional working in craft services, the below-the-line personnel, without which the show would never be. Early issues concentrated on legitimate theatre: current issues came to include television, motion pictures, and the performing arts as well. This is one serial where technology and the creative side of crafts have indeed come together. Highly recommended, especially for case studies in problem solving. Sampled issue for 1990: magazine format (8 x 10 ¾ inches / 205 x 275 mm); numerous graphics, many in color.
DEPT: "Editor's Page," "From the Greenroom," author profiles; "New Products," "Books & Records," "Letters," "Conventions/Meetings." (5/6-67). "Letters," "News," "How-To," "In Production," profiles; "Prod-

uct News," "Callboard," ads. (4-87). "Editorial," "News," newsbriefs; "Lighting," column by Karl Ruling; "Resource," for theatre equipment and supplies; "Show Report," column by Ellen Lampert; "Books," reviews. (8/9-90).
TYPL: "An Opera Company Grows in Brooklyn," "Repertory Theatre: The Problems of a Complete Concept in Lighting and Sound," "Costumes for Children of All Ages." (5/6-67). "The Speed of Lighting," "Making Your Theatre Accessible," "Aiming for the Mind's Eye," "Missing Link." (4-87). "A New Spike Lee Joint," "Summer Opera Sampler," "Letting Nature Lead the Way." (7/8-90).
SCHL: Bimonthly (? - ?); Nine issues per year (? - ?); Ten issues per year [combined Jun/Jul and Aug/Sep issues] (Dec, 1985+), 100 pp.
SPAN: Mar/Apr, 1967+
VARIES
--Mar/Apr, 1967 - ? as TC, Theatre Crafts.
LC: PN 2000.T48
DD: 792/.05
ISSN: 0040-5469
ABST: --Book Review Index (ISSN: 0524-0581)
--Magazine Index
--Popular Magazine Review (ISSN: 0740-3763)
--Readers Guide to Periodical Literature (ISSN: 0034-0464)

✦ THEATRE DESIGN & TECHNOLOGY

SUB: "Journal of the United States Institute for Theatre Technology."
SUB: "The journal for design & production professionals in the performing arts." •
PUBL: USITT, 10 West 19th St., Suite 5A, New York, NY 10011-4206.
DESC: With an emphasis on the technical side of theatre, *Theatre Design & Technology* provides a comprehensive review of new technology, theatre design and application of technology to stage construction and operation. This is a wonderful resource for the working professional in performing arts. One sampled issue held articles on the uses of drama in the commercial arena of marketing presentations, courtyard philosophy of theatre architecture, and the issue of function versus "The Horizon" in contemporary Czechoslovak design. The always excellent series of departmental features focused on "Engineering," "Lighting," and "Architecture" in each issue. Membership in the United States Institute for Theatre Technology is represented by all major technical theatre vendors. The purpose of USITT is "...to disseminate information and facilitate communication for the professional development of its members. ... Encourage research and investigations in the field of theatre planning and design, construction, equipment, aesthetics, presentation and operations; Combine and conserve the records of such studies and investigations...," to publish study information, provide contact between members, provide representation at national and international conferences, and "Encourage good practices in the field of theatre planning and design, construction, equipment, aesthetics, presentation and operation, based on the experience of those engaged in the theatre on all levels as developed by studies in those fields." USITT is the United States Center for the international organization, OISTAT (Organisation Internationale des Scénographes, Techniciens et Architectes de Théâtre). Typical articles for 1991 include, "The International Jury Process," "Of Garbage & Gold: Great Britain at PQ'91," "Designs for a Theatre in Transition," "Contemporary American Designers: George Tsypin," and "Postmodern Issues in Action Design 5." Magazine format (8 ¼ x 11 inches / 210 x 280mm), with black/white and color graphics throughout.
DEPT: "Theatre Architecture," "Research," "Sound," "Computers," "Book Reviews," "New Products," "OISTT," periodical and book review. (summer-84). "Editors' Note," "Engineering," "Lighting," "Architecture," "Readers' Response," letters; "New Products," review; "International Journal Report," excellent international theatre journal/magazine review column by Norma Adler. (summer-90).
TYPL: "Orange County Performing Arts Center: a Design Report," "The Permanent Adaptable Stage Setting of Sam Hume," "Steel-Framed Stock Platforming," "Using Time Manager," "TRS-80 Model III Light Plot Using Profile Three Plus." (summer-84). "Passion, Poison and Profession," "Marketing as Theatre," "The Courtyard Theatre: Philosophies and Practicalities," "Postmodern Issues in Action," "The Minotaurus: Svoboda Directs." (summer-90).
SCHL: Quarterly, 80 pp.
SPAN: May, 1965+
VARIES
--May, 1965 - Feb, 1968 as Theatre Design & Technology (ISSN: 0040-5477).
--May, 1968 - Winter, 1977 as Theatre Design and Technology (ISSN: 0040-5477).
LC: NA 1.T45
DD: 792
ISSN: 0040-5477
ABST: --Architectural Periodicals Index (ISSN: 0033-6912)
--Avery Index to Architectual Periodicals (ISSN: 0196-0008)

Theatre Design & Technology
May, 1965 - Feb, 1968//
(ISSN: 0040-5477)
SEE: THEATRE DESIGN & TECHNOLOGY

Theatre Design and Technology
May, 1968 - Winter, 1977//
(ISSN: 0040-5477)
SEE: THEATRE DESIGN & TECHNOLOGY

THEATRE DOCUMENTATION

PUBL: University of Sao Paulo, School of Communications and Arts, Sao Paulo, Brazil.
DESC: "*Theatre Documentation* is an international medium of communication between theatre scholars and theatre collection curators, and a reference tool for everyone interested in the performing arts." A most versitile serial, *Theatre Documentation* had three specific topics: 1) bibliography, classification and collections (for the development of indexes, listings, and library holdings); 2) theatre practice and education (for systems of dance notation, instructional materials, etc); and 3) news of international theatre scholarship (to report on developments of theatre societies, exhibitions, new publications, and the activities of the International Section of Libraries and Museums of the Performing Arts). Each article, in a sense, was its own reference work, ready to be placed into other resource files to enrich the study and practice of theatre. Journal format.
DEPT: "Expositions," listing; "Theatre Library Association News," "Footnotes in the Theatre Library World," news items; "Scholarly Works in Progress," "New Publications," review. (fall-68).
TYPL: "Pigeonholing Pinter: a Bibliography," "The Dance Classification System of the Juilliard School Library," "Translations of Spanish Golden Age Drama in Tsarist Russia," "An Index to: *A Record of the Boston Stage*," "Bibliotheques et Musees des arts du spectacle dans le monde." (fall-68).
SCHL: Semiannual, 100 pp.
SPAN: Fall, 1968 - 1971/1972//
LC: PN 1560.T398
ISSN: 0040-5485

Theatre Guild Bulletin
Dec, 1923 - Nov, 1925//
SEE: STAGE

Theatre Guild Magazine
Oct, 1928 - Apr, 1932//
SEE: STAGE

Theatre Guild Quarterly
Dec, 1925 - Sep, 1928//
SEE: STAGE

THEATRE JOURNAL

PUBL: New York State Community Theatre Association, 917 Vrooman Ave., Schenectday, NY 12309.
DESC: [*Community Theatre Bulletin*]: This mimeographed serial provided a forum of news, viewpoints, and activities of the New York State Community Theatre Association. Early issues centered on community theatre at Ithica. Later editions encompassed community theatre throughout the state. Publication schedule was quite irregular; no graphics.
DEPT: "News of the Theatres," "Across the Editor's Desk," "Calendar." (9-58).
TYPL: "Renaissance?." (9-58).
SCHL: Quarterly [Irregular at times] (Mar, 1955? - Winter/Spring, 1970?); Semiannual (1971?+); 36 pp.
SPAN: Mar, 1955 - Fall, 1973//
VARIES
--Mar, 1955? - Sep, 1960 as Community Theatre Bulletin (ISSN: 0414-1520).
--Dec, 1960 - Winter/Spring, 1970 as New York State Community Theatre Journal (ISSN: 0548-8974).

✣ THEATRE JOURNAL

SUB: "The journal of the University and College Theatre Association."
PUBL: The Johns Hopkins University Press in cooperation with the Association for Theatre in Higher Education, Journals Division, 701 West 40th St., Suite 275, Baltimore, MD 21211.
DESC: [*Theatre Journal*]: "The primary aim of *TJ* is to provide an outlet for scholarship and criticism in the theatre arts." First appearing in 1949 under the title, *Educational Theatre Journal*, this periodical was primarily a collection of newsbriefs and minutes from AETA business meetings. Illustrations and research-oriented articles were added in the 1960s, and later (January, 1979) the word, *Educational*, was dropped from the masthead. A promotional advertisement for the publication said: "*Theatre Journal*'s wide-ranging scholarly articles and timely reviews have made it one of the most authoritative and useful journals of theatre studies available today. Drawing contributions from practitioners as well as scholars, *Theatre Journal* publishes articles on a broad range of topics, presenting social and historical studies, production reviews, and theoretical inquiries that illuminate dramatic text and production." Each issue is based upon a specific topic, such as one sampled issue entitled "Women and/in Drama." The October, 1991 issue was devoted to radio drama, with articles such as, "Radio and the Theater: A British Perspective," "The Contours of Acoustic Art," "Listening to the Radio," "Fundamental Sounds: Recording Samuel Beckett's Radio Plays," and "Directing a Radio Production of Eugene O'Neill's 'The Hairy Ape, edited by Travis C. Bogard'." It is a scholarly journal of current theatre and historical theatre development and well recommended. For the sampled issues of 1979 and 1991: perfect-bound, journal format; black ink on coated paper; cover consisting of black ink on coated index stock (6 ¾ x 10 inches / 175 x 255 mm).
DESC: [*Educational Theatre Journal*]: This is a quality journal concerned with university/college theatre. Articles are evenly divided into discussions of the mechanics of mounting a theatrical presentation, and discussions of using audio-visual aids to teach theatre crafts and history to college-level students. In its transformation

from *Educational Theatre Journal* into *Theatre Journal*, the pedagogical articles were dropped, and the editorial content became a forum for an often philosophical or historical discussion of the role and function of theatre. In either form, this is an excellent reference. No graphics; journal format.
DEPT: "Books in Review," "Official Notices," "News." (5-50). "Theatre in Review," commentary; "Books in Review." (12-78). "Theatre Review," "Book Review." (5-84). "Theatre Review," edited column by Kate Davy; "Book Review," edited column by Katherine E. Kelly; "Books Received." (10-90).
TYPL: "Children's Theatre in the Round," "Drama in the Church, 1949," "Creative Use of the Motion Picture," "The Need for Production Organization." (5-50). "An Alchemical Brew: From Separatio to Coagulatio in Yeate's 'The Only Jealousy of Emer,'" "Legend Focusing Legend in Yeate's 'Deirdre,'" "Katherine of Sutton: the First Flish Playwright," "Toward the Performance of Troubadour Poetry: Speaker and the Voice in 'Peire Vidal." (12-78). "The Search for New Endings: The Theatre in Search of a Fix," "Some Versions of Performance Art," "The Gist of the Breath," "Creativity in the Theatre: Robert Edmond Jones and C.G. Jung." (5-84). "Wordscapes of the Body: Performative Language as Gestus in Maria Irene Fornes's Plays," "Karl Marx's Youngest Daughter and 'A Doll's House'," "The Politics of the Body: Pina Bausch's 'Tanztheater'." (10-90).
SCHL: Quarterly, 125 pp.
SPAN: Oct, 1949+
VARIES
--Oct, 1949 - Dec, 1978 as Educational Theatre Journal (ISSN: 0013-1989).
LC: PN 3171.E38
DD: 792/.05
ISSN: 0192-2882
ABST: --Abstract of English Studies (ISSN: 0001-3560)
--Book Review Index (ISSN: 0524-0581)
--Current Contents. Social and Behavioral Sciences. (ISSN: 0092-6361)
--Current Index to Journals in Education (ISSN: 0011-3565)
--Education Index (ISSN: 0013-1385)
--Humanities Index (ISSN: 0095-5981)
--Index to Book Reviews in the Humanities (ISSN: 0073-5892)
--MLA International Bibliography of Books & Articles on the Modern Languages and Literatures (ISSN: 0024-8215)

THEATRE MAGAZINE

PUBL: Theatre Magazine Co., 2 West 45th St., New York, NY.
DESC: This lavishly produced monthly extolled the joys of theatre, and New York City theatre in particular. A large magazine format, (coated paper stock, with type and layout styles keyed to the times), combined articles of people, plays, and parties about which the public wished to read. Pictures oftentimes were placed one to a page, and treated with special care in layout. Each issue had considerable advertising, much of which was in full color. Articles from one sampled issue for 1927 were a treasure trove of reading concerning the wonders of the "talkies." Al Jolson talked about his first day in motion pictures. David Wark Griffith discussed the motion pictures of "to-day and to-morrow." Lon Chaney explained his preference for "grotesque" characters. Roi Henri Fricken provided details on an experiment in play production, while Mr. First Nighter discussed the pageantry of Broadway. Articles described motion picture set design, Hollywood gossip, what author Elinor Glyn meant by "IT;" and there were 15 full-page portraits, including Greta Garbo, Basil Rathbone, Colleen Moore, Lon Chaney, Emil Jannings; and front cover girl, Clara Bow. As publishers Paul and Louis Meyer said: "*THEATRE MAGAZINE* is growing fast and no one interested in the drama or the films can really keep abreast of the times through any other channel than the pages of this publication. This is not a boast; it is a statement of widely recognized and acknowledged fact." This marvelous serial believed in and promoted the vitality of drama in New York City, as well as the developing medium of the motion picture in Hollywood. Magazine format (9 ¾ x 12 ¾ inches / 250 x 325 mm); full-color cover and advertisements with black/white editorial content.
DEPT: "Editorial," "Heard on Broadway," 'The tattle and trivia of the nation's theatrical main street' column by Ward Morehouse; "Biographical Page," "Theatre Magazine's Court of Appeal," forum for play review; "The Amateur's Green Room," upcoming actors; "The Promenades of Angelina," "Mr. Hornblow Goes to the Play," review; "Cinema," review; "Vaudeville," review; "Music," review, "The New Plays," reviews; "The Amateur Stage," "Fashions," "The Vanity Box," column by Anne Archbald. (1-24). "What's On the Bords," current theatre schedule; "The Theatre Between Covers," column by Ralph Bailey; "Travel Sketch," "The Tributary Theatre," "Fashions," "Gifts of Fragrance," "Heard on Broadway," "The Editor Goes to the Play." (12-29).
TYPL: "Are You Safe in the Theatre?," "Charles Chaplin--Poet and Dramatist," "The World's Premier Theatre." (1-24). "The Power Behind the Showshop Thrones," "Speed It Up, Slow It Down, or Take It Off," "There's Youth Behind Those Footlights." (12-29).
SCHL: Quarterly (Oct, 1900 - Jan, 1901); Monthly (May, 1901 - Apr, 1931), 65 pp.
SPAN: Oct, 1900 - Apr, 1931//
VARIES
--Oct, 1900 - Jan, 1901 as Our Player's Gallery (ISSN: 0748-6634).
--May, 1901 - Jul, 1917 as Theatre, The (ISSN: 0891-6861).
LC: PN 2000.T5
DD: 792 11
ISSN: 0749-8829

THEATRE NEWS
PUBL: American Theatre Association, 1029 Vermont Ave., NW, Washington, DC 20005.
DESC: Published nine times each year, *Theatre News* provides news items and non-research-oriented articles to the membership of the American Theatre Association. The sampled issue contained articles on the American College Theatre Festival, the ways and means of auditioning for theatrical producers; and a special supplement on the "Theatre Movement Program," about theatre movement specialists. Special note should be made of the "News" department, informative newsbriefs under subtitles of "People in the News," "Publications," "Conferences," "Playwrights," "Schools," and "Miscellaneous." For the sampled issue of 1978: stapled magazine format; black ink on coated paper stock; some advertising (8 ½ x 11 inches / 215 x 280 mm).
DEPT: "Washington Routine," editorial column by Jack Morrison; "CTAA," column by Lucille M. Paolillo; "ACTA," column by Twink Lynch; "News," assorted news item column by Elena Nierman. (11-78).
TYPL: "Auditions--Preparing, Using Your First 15 Seconds, Surviving," "On the Training of Movement Teachers and Related Problems," "The Personal Neutral Mask," "Some Experiences at the Vakhtangov," "Group Creation: A Search for a Resonant Language of Movement." (11-78).
SCHL: Nine issues per year, 20 pp.
SPAN: Oct, 1968 - 1986//
ISSN: 0563-4040

Theatre Newsletter
Jul 15, 1946 - Jan 19, 1952//
SEE: THEATRE

✤ THEATRE NOTEBOOK
SUB: "A quarterly of notes and research." (Oct, 1945 - ?).
SUB: "A journal of the history and technique of the British Theatre."
PUBL: The Society for Theatre Research, c/o The Theatre Museum, Tavistock St., Covent Garden, London WC2E 7PA, England.
DESC: In the beginning, *Theatre Notebook* was very much a "quarterly of notes and research," moving between current developments and historical reviews of British theatre. Articles varied from juvenile drama publishers, to puppetry, pantomime, theatrical photography, theatre construction; and historical theatrical theses and dissertations in progress. The current serial has maintained its initial focus. This is a most enjoyable publication, especially valuable for theatre historians. Journal format; graphics.
DEPT: "Editorial," "Queries," "Answers to Queries." (7/9-48). "Editorial," "Notes and Queries," "Book Reviews." (#3-86).
TYPL: "Welsh Interlude Players of the 18th Century," "Pictorial Records of Provincial Theatres," "Theodore de Banville and the Hanlon Lees Troupe." (7/9-48). "The Theatre Royal, Leicester," "An English Influence on Russian Revolutionary Festivals," "Thespis's Poorest Children: Penny Theatres and the Law," "A North of England Marionette Theatre in the 1860s." (#3-86).
SCHL: Quarterly (? - ?); Three issues per year (?+), 40 pp.
SPAN: Oct, 1945+
LC: PN 2001.T43
ISSN: 0040-5523
ABST: --Abstract of English Studies (ISSN: 0001-3560)
--Annual Bibliography of English Language and Literature (ISSN: 0066-3786)
--Architectural Periodicals Index (ISSN: 0033-6912)
--Humanities Index (ISSN: 0095-5981)
--MLA International Bibliography of Books & Articles on the Modern Languages and Literatures (ISSN: 0024-8215)

Theatre Quarterly
Jan/Mar, 1971 - Oct/Dec, 1981//
(ISSN: 0049-3600)
SEE: NEW THEATRE QUARTERLY

THEATRE RESEARCH
SUB: "Journal of the International Federation for Theatre Research."
PUBL: International Federation for Theatre Research, 14 Woronzow Rd., London NW8, England.
DESC: The International Federation for Theatre Research was founded in 1955. "Its essential task is to make itself an efficient centre of communication between research workers in all countries -- a centre from which may grow friendly exchanges of information and knowledge, mutual encouragement and assistance, and every useful form of international co-operation in theatrical history and research." Published in English and French, the journal (without translation) held true to its task. Articles covered all aspects of theatre, and were of special import in that they reflected cultural diversity. The last issue appeared as Number 4, 1974, with an announcement of a new journal, *Theatre Research International*, to be published three times per year. In the new journal, bilingualism was replaced by English with French summaries. Journal format; graphics.
DEPT: "Correspondence." (6-58). "Book Reviews." (#1-72).
TYPL: "The Puppet Theatre of Cardinal Ottoboni," "American Theatre and Drama in the XVIII Century," "We Need Theatre HIstory Iconographies." (6-58). "An Acting Tradition from Homer to Aeschylus," "The Genesis of Gas Lights," "Tavernier's Account of the Theatre in Tongking." (#1-72).
SCHL: Three issues per year (Mar, 1958 - ?); Semiyearly (? - #2, 1974), 110 pp.
SPAN: Mar, 1958 - #4, 1974//

MERGED WITH
--New Theatre Magazine (ISSN: 0028-6893) (to form) Theatre Research International (ISSN: 0307-8833).
LC: PN 2000.A1T5
ISSN: 0040-5566
ABST: --Annual Bibliography of English Language and Literature (ISSN: 0066-3786)

THEATRE TIME

PUBL: Theatre Publications, P.O. Box 959, Grand Central Station, New York, NY.
DESC: *Theatre Time* was a small magazine of dramatic thought and comment. Editorial content (some four to five articles per issue) centered on New York City theatre, with analyses of trends, genres, and the works of playwrights. Photographs appeared full page and were production stills of actors and actresses during on-stage production. Magazine format; no advertising.
DEPT: "One Minute Interviews." (summer- 49).
TYPL: "A Future for the 'Social Theatre?,'" "The Drama in the Dell," "The Little Man and Arthur Miller," "The Blue Hand of Censorship." (summer- 49).
SCHL: Quarterly, 25 pp.
SPAN: Spring, 1949 - Winter, 1952//
LC: PN 2000.T72
DD: 792.05

Theatre Today
#1 - 7//
SEE: FILM AND THEATRE TODAY

✢ THEATRE TOPICS

SUB: "Dramaturgy, performance studies, pedagogy."
PUBL: Johns Hopkins University Press, 701 West 40th St., Suite 275, Baltimore, MD 21211-2190.
DESC: In the premiere issue, editor, Beverley Byers-Pevitts, stated; "*Theatre Topics* is committed to publishing articles in the areas of Dramaturgy, Performance Studies, and Theatre Pedagogy. We will not be publishing theatre reviews or book reviews. Realizing that established ways of performing, studying and presenting our creative work must be re-examined, we will publish three types of articles: 'Subject Articles'...; 'Comments on Process', a section reserved for description of practical applications in the various aspects of theatre...; and 'Responses' intended to promote a dialogue between universities and practitioners... We ask our colleagues and readers to utilize this journal as a tool for establishing an on-going dialogue among theatre practitioners/artists/teachers. *Theatre Topics* will serve as a vehicle for discussion and comment on our art, our teaching and our past, present, and future creative activities." Journal, perfect-bound format (6¾ x 10 inches / 170 x 255 mm); graphics and minimal advertising; printed on uncoated acid-free paper.
DEPT: "Editor's Comment." (3-91).
TYPL: "Traditional Alaskan Eskimo Theatre: Performing the Spirits of the Earth," "Quiet Revolution: Feminist Considerations in Adapting Literature for Children's Theatre," "A 'Way' for Actors: Asian Martial Arts," "Decor or Space: Architectural Stage Design and the Contemporary Theatre," "The Sounds of Violence: Vocal Training in Stage Combat." (3-91).
SCHL: Semiannual, 100 pp.
SPAN: Mar, 1991+
DD: 792
ISSN: 1054-8378

THEATRE WORKSHOP

SUB: "A quarterly journal of the theatre and film arts." (Oct, 1936 - Sep/Oct, 1937).
SUB: "An official publication of the New Theatre League." (Oct, 1936 - Sep/Oct, 1937).
SUB: "A journal of the theatre and film arts published by the New Theatre League." (Apr/Jun, 1938).
PUBL: New Theatre League (now incorporated as Peoples Theatre, Inc.), 132 west 43rd St., New York, NY.
DESC: This small, square-format serial published during the depths of the American Depression was a theatrical workshop for actor, stage technician and manager alike, with each issue being devoted to a specific workshop topic. Specific issues featured some of the greatest names of American theatre who provided their expertise. It was, unfortunately, short-lived due to the American Great Depression. Some advertising and occasional graphics.
DEPT: "Notes," book reviews. (1/3-37).
TYPL: "The Actor's Creative Work," "Body Training for Actors," "Advice to the Players," "Four Directors and the Actor," "Founders of the Modern Theatre." (1/3-37).
SCHL: Quarterly, 85 pp.
SPAN: Oct, 1936 - Apr/Jun, 1938//
LC: PN 2000 .T73

35MM PHOTOGRAPHY

SUB: "Largest net sale of any journal soley devoted to the miniature camera."
PUBL: Photographic Bulletin, London, England.
DESC: [*Camera World*] The field of 35mm photography, or miniature photography as many preferred to call it, was in its infancy in the 1930s when this British serial began. Some 50 pages of the small, square-format magazine were devoted to the art and technical side of 35 mm cameras. Articles showcased readers' pictures, provided news of film societies, dark room techniques, and latest technical improvements in the field.
DEPT: "New Apparatus," "News from the Societies." (9-37).

TYPL:	"Determining Exposures for Agfacolor," "Control of Contrast by Filters," "Agricultural Photography," "Calculating Exposure by Mental Arithmetic." (9-37).
SCHL:	Monthly, 50 pp.
SPAN:	May, 1958 - Sep, 1965// VARIES
	--Dec?, 1936? - May, 1955 as Miniature Camera World.
	--Jun, 1955 - Apr, 1958 as Camera World. MERGED WITH
	--Photography, (and) Colour Photography, (and) Good Photography (to form) Photography.
LC:	TR 1.T47

✣ TIFFEN PROFESSIONAL NEWSLETTER

PUBL:	Tiffen Manufacturing Corporation, 90 Oser Ave., Hauppauge, NY 11788.
DESC:	An interesting corporate, promotional newsletter that provides good technical and applied information regarding Tiffen professional filter products, this quarterly newsletter "...is distributed to professional dealers, cinematographers, videographers, and people associated with the image-making industries." Of special note are extensive graphics showing comparative applications of these filters in a variety of motion picture productions. For sampled issue of 1990: full-color newsletter format on coated paper stock, extensive number of full-color graphics (8 ½ x 11 inches / 215 x 280 mm).
DEPT:	"The Nat Tiffen Column," "Products," new filter items; "People," "Insight," on filter usage; "On Location," productions using Tiffen filters; "Shows," industry trade shows. (fall-88).
TYPL:	"A Change in the Air," "Shedding Some Light on Fog Filters," "A Coral Sunset Over Canada." (fall-88).
SCHL:	Quarterly, 4 pp.
SPAN:	Spring?, 1987+

✣ TIME SCREEN

SUB:	"The magazine of British telefantasy."
PUBL:	Time Screen, 574 Manchester Rd., Stocksbridge, Sheffield S30 5DX, England.
DESC:	This fanzine is dedicated to British "telefantasy," video programs of "fantasy" appearing on various British television outlets. The sampled issue of winter, 1987/1988 included "Star Cops," "The Survivors," "Space: 1999," "Ace of Wands," "Shadows," and "The Owl Service." Articles are informative, and writers are knowledgable. Accompanying some articles are very detailed "Episode Guides," listing broadcast date, title, playwright and other "above-the-line" members, short plot synopsis, and time of broadcast. Also of note are a large number of production stills from featured productions. The sampled issue was photo-reduced, typeset copy in two-column layout format. Those interested in this television genre would be well advised to seek out copies of the publication,

both for the excellent reviews and for the sheer pleasure of reading about favorite and new programs. For the sampled issue of 1987/1988: stapled magazine format; black ink on coated paper stock with full-color covers also on coated paper stock; limited advertising (8 ¼ x 11 ¾ inches / 210 x 295 mm).

DEPT:	"Mindbender," quiz; "Editorial," column by Anthony McKay; "Letters," extensive section with responses. (winter-87/88).
TYPL:	"Seven Serpents, Sulphur and Salt," "A Horseman Riding By," "Survivors," "Reach Across the Stars," "The Legend Unravelled." (winter-87/88).
SCHL:	Quarterly, 40 pp.
SPAN:	Summer, 1985+?

TM

? - ?//
(ISSN: 8755-3104)
SEE: TS

Today's Cinema

1930? - Nov, 1971//
SEE: SCREEN INTERNATIONAL

Today's Cinema News and Property Gazette

Feb, 1928 - 1930?//
SEE: SCREEN INTERNATIONAL

Today's Speech

Apr, 1953 - Fall, 1975//
(ISSN: 0040-8573)
SEE: COMMUNICATION QUARTERLY

✣ TONI HOLT'S MOVIE LIFE

SUB:	"Hollywood's only all-picture magazine."
SUB:	"An Ideal magazine."
PUBL:	Ideal Publishing Co., 2 Park Ave., New York, NY 10016.
DESC:	[*Movie Life*]: A "movie-fan" publication, *Movie Life* published over 40 years of articles detailing beauty secrets, tennis matches, and pictorial albums on behalf of the stars. What set this serial apart from the large number of others of this genre was the tremendous number of photographs printed in each issue, often reducing articles to cutline status. The emphasis was on the stars; their home life, their work before the camera, and what they did in their leisure time, which at times appeared to be most of the day. One sampled issue from 1978 included articles on Kristy McNichol, Sylvester Stallone, Linda Ronstadt, John Forsythe, Marthe Keller, Richard Dreyfuss, Robert Blake, Cheryl Ladd; and Parker Stevenson, the latter in an article

entitled, "Mystery Girl Tells His Mother: 'I Must Marry Your Son'." Magazine format; newsprint. Sampled issue for 1953: stapled magazine format, editorial content on newsprint, mostly black/white, with some spot color, and (surprisingly) several full-color pages on newsprint, cover consisting of full-color on coated paper stock (8 ⅝ x 11 inches / 220 x 280 mm). Sampled issue for March, 1978: (8 ⅛ x 10 ¾ inches / 205 x 275 mm).
DEPT: "Off Stage Shots," "Candid Close-Ups," pictures; "Coming and Going," activities of the stars; "Flash News Views." (3-38). "Hollywood Turns On With Toni Holt," "Film Section," "International Star Track-Gossip," "Jacquie Eastlund Predicts," horoscopes for the stars; "Rock Follies with Dave Jenkins." (9-79).
TYPL: "Hollywood Home Girl," "Tennis Matches," "Movie Life in Hollywood," "The Movie Life of Myrna Loy," "A Colossal Production." (3-38). "The Battle of the Blonds," "Eric Roberts: Why He's Drawn to the Dark Side of Gypsy Life," "Ted Kennedy: Will His Hollywood Past Hurt His Political Future?" (9-79).
SCHL: Bimonthly (? - ?); Monthly (197u - 197u); Bimonthly (197u+), 55 pp.
SPAN: Jan, 1938+
VARIES
--Jan, 1938 - 197u as Movie Life (ISSN: 0027-2698).
LC: PN 1993.M746
DD: 791.4
ISSN: 0199-199x

✥ TOP SECRET
SUB: "The magazine for secret agent connoisseurs."
PUBL: Caruba Enterprises, PO Box 1146, Maplewood, NJ 07040.
DESC: For the secret-agent enthusiast, *Top Secret* is an interesting look at the actors, producers, plots, and finished product of motion pictures and television series in Great Britain and the United States. Bowing to numerous requests, the featured article in the third issue was an interview with David McCallum concerning his role in the "U.N.C.L.E." television series. Also featured were an interview with Sam Rolfe, creator of that television program; the developmental history of "Wild, Wild West;" a "James Bond" simulation game, and an examination of the Emma Peel character in "The Avengers." For the sampled 1986 issue: stapled magazine format, editorial content being black ink, with full-color cover all on coated paper stock, limited advertising (8 ⅛ x 10 ¾ inches / 205 x 275 mm).
DEPT: "From the Green Dome," editorial column by David Caruba; "The Positive / Negative Clan," letters; "Role Playing," column by Alec Billyou; "Deadline," 'The Avengers column' information column by Dave Rogers; "Poetry Behind the Typewriter," column by Brooks Cook. (4-86).
TYPL: "The McCallum Interview," "Sam Rolfe Interviewed," "On Her Majesty's Secret Service," "Where the Sun Always Sets: It's Home, Home on the Range as Top Secret Explores the Wild, Wild West." (4-86).
SCHL: Bimonthly, 35 pp.

SPAN: Dec/Jan, 1985/1986+?

Tortfeasor
? - ?//
SEE: MEDIA LAW NOTES

✥ TPQ
PUBL: Speech Communication Association, 5105 Backlick Rd., Bldg. E, Annandale, VA 22004.
DESC: An advertisement for *TPQ* called this publication "A major new journal devoted to the history, theory, and criticism of any type of Text realized in and presented through Performance. Includes: traditional literary studies in drama, poetry, short stories, novels, and nonfiction; intercultural studies of oral and written texts; [and] studies of speeches and scripts--television, radio, and film--delivered or performed in a variety of social contexts. Cross- disciplinary in scope, *Text and Performance* draws on a wide range of disciplines--communication (rhetoric, interpretation, mass media), theatre, the classics, English, aesthetics, linguistics, religion, anthropology, psychology, cultural history, and sociology." In the July, 1991 issue, editor-elect, Kristin Langellier, noted that "*Text and Performance Quarterly* publishes scholarship addressing the constitutive elements of text, performers, and audiences as they advance the understanding of performance within the communication process. The performance of texts participates in personal, social, and cultural relations as well as aesthetic experience. Manuscripts addressing aesthetic, historical, psychological, sociocultural, and political dimensions of performance are welcome from scholars of a variety of disciplines." Typical articles for late, 1991 included, "The Body-in-Writing: Miniatures in Mary Norton's 'Borrowers'," "In Process: Leonardo Shapiro, the Shaliko Company, and 'Strangers'," "Two Essays on Simone Benmussa's Adaptation of a Story by George Moore," and "Postmodernism, Symbolicity, and the Rhetoric of the Hyperreal: Kenneth Burke, Fredric Jameson, and Jean Baudrillard." Journal format with editorial content consisting of black ink on uncoated paper stock; and two-color cover on coated paper stock (6 ¾ x 10 inches / 170 x 255 mm). Note: while *TPQ* indicates ISSN 0033-5630, some sources report the ISSN as being 1046-2937.
DEPT: "Books in Review." (1-90).
TYPL: "Tracing Connections Between Women's Personal Narratives and the Short Stories of Grace Paley," "Search for the Final Syllable: Cirilo Bautista," "Mishima's Seppuku Speech: A Critical-Cultural Analysis." (1-90).
SCHL: Quarterly, 90 pp.
SPAN: Jan, 1981?+
VARIES
--? - Oct, 1988? as Literature in Performance (ISSN: 0734-0796).
DD: 809 11

ISSN: 0033-5630

Trade Circular and Literary Bulletin, The

Sep, 1869 - Aug 18, 1870//
SEE: PUBLISHER'S WEEKLY

Trade Circular and Publishers' Bulletin, The

Sep 18, 1870 - Dec 26, 1871//
SEE: PUBLISHER'S WEEKLY

Transactions

1953 - 1954//
SEE: IEEE TRANSACTIONS ON INFORMATION THEORY

Transactions

Oct, 1916 - May, 1929//
SEE: SMPTE JOURNAL

Transactions of the IRE Professional Group on Broadcast and Television Receivers

Jul, 1952 - Oct, 1954//
SEE: IEEE TRANSACTIONS ON CONSUMER ELECTRONICS

Travel & Camera

Feb, 1969 - Dec/Jan, 1970/1971//
(ISSN: 0049-4542)
SEE: TRAVEL & LEISURE

✢ TRAVEL & LEISURE

SUB: "The international magazine of travel and photography."

PUBL: U.S. Camera Publishing Corporation, 132 West 31st St., New York, NY 10001.

DESC: [*U.S. Camera*]: Although the cover for 1948 is labeled, "combined with *Travel and Camera*," there was little to do with travel in the sampled issue. The focus was on photography. November, 1948 marked a change in editorial philosophy: "*U.S. Camera* magazine is out to do a better job in photography than any general or photographic publication in the United States. ... From experience, we feel that this is the magazine for which you have been waiting. We know many have asked for it--pointedly. We believe we are giving you, the camera users of America, the simple, sound, entertaining, instructive, universal photographic magazine you want." This was a magazine for everyone's interests. One sampled issue included a step-by-step explanation of how Norman Rockwell used photography for a magazine cover, the means to build a cold light enlarger, the technique of animal photography, the use of photographs in clothes design, and a large number of departments covering narrower aspects of the field. Cover and some advertisements in color, editorial content in black/white on coated paper stock (8 3/8 x 11 1/8 inches / 215 x 285 mm).

DESC: [*U.S. Camera and Travel*]: By the mid-1960s, the word "travel" was firmly entrenched within the title of this evolving publication, and pointed to a growing emphasis on travel photography. In the sampled issue for 1967, articles addressed the technical, and aesthetic aspects of photography, as well as techniques of both. The "build-it-yourself" articles were now gone, with an increased emphasis on 35mm, slides, equipment, and the new medium of "home movies." Advertisements provided strong testimony to increased buying patterns of new equipment from local dealers, and articles provided "test bench" results of same, along with accessories and application of the equipment. Editorial content was a mixture of color and black/white pages, all on coated paper stock with full-color cover (8 3/8 x 11 1/8 inches / 210 x 285 mm).

DESC: [*Travel & Camera*]: This is a magazine for those who love travel, new adventures; and taking quality photographs of them. For the sampled issue for 1970, most articles looked at several domestic and international destinations, providing consideration of travel, lodging, sightseeing, dining, and other aspects of travel. Of special note is the "Photographer's Guide," specific information on photography, camera stores, film processing, customs, and other issues of using a camera while on vacation. Many graphics were in full color, and professionally shot, enhancing one's desire to travel to a given location. The publication is both a travel guide, and a guide to photography; and has a zest for both. For the sampled issue of 1970: magazine format with mixture of color and black/white editorial content on coated paper stock; with exception of special travel guide section printed black/white on newsprint (8 3/8 x 11 1/8 inches / 210 x 280 mm).

DEPT: "Letters to the Editor," "Camera and Travel Shopper," product review column by Rudy Maschke; "Press Photography," column by Paul Threlfall; "Magazine Photography," column by Roy Pinney; "Editorial," "News and Notes of Women in Photography," unusual department column by Mildred Stagg; "Tomorrow's Photographers," youth column by Norris Harkness; "Technique Technicalities," Q&A column by Will Connell; "Movie and Slide News," new releases reviewed; "Photo Previews," 'Here's the latest news of the photographic world'; "New Products," "New Books," "Trade News," "Salons and Contests," "Markets," "Camera Clubs," "Readers' Picture Page," reader submissions; "Helpful Hints." (11-48). "Reader's Page," reader submissions; "Letters," "Between the Lines," news behind the articles; "Creative Color," column by Arthur Rothstein; "New Cameras, Lenses, Meters, Accessories," 'A wrap-up of some of

the more exciting products available right now'; "35mm Techniques," column by Peter Stackpole; "Answers by Arnold," Q&A technical column by Rus Arnold; "Travel & Camera," one-page travel section; "Foto Facts," column by Paul Farber; "Sound," column by Jerry Wesson; "Lens Lines," column by Willard Clark; "Movie Q's and A's," Q&A moviemaking column by John R. Gregory; "Books in Review," "Contests Exhibits," upcoming; "Worth Knowing," photographic news items. (9-67). "Travel Guide," unusual photography-oriented section; "In Focus," photographer profiles; "Letters," "Calendar," "Readers' Gallery," reader submissions. (10-70).
TYPL: "Norman Rockwell 'Shoots' a Cover," "Using Photoelectric Exposure Meters," "Build This Cold Light Enlarger," "Photography at the Art Center School," "Movie Careers in the Air Force." (11-48). "Woman on the Run," "Camera Collectors and Why They Grow," "Offbeat Corsica," "Use an Exposure Meter for Flash?," "Kodak Goes Ektagraphic." (9-67). "The Rhine River," "The Greek Isles," "The Daytona 200," "Movies: Standard Features," "Preserving the Prairie." (10-70).
SCHL: Quarterly (? - ?); Monthly [except Jul/Aug, and Dec/Jan combined issues], 80 pp.
SPAN: 1935+
VARIES
--1935 - ? as U.S. Camera.
--? - Jul, 1941 as U.S. Camera Magazine.
--Aug, 1941 - 1949? as U.S. Camera.
--1950 - 1952 as U.S. Camera Annual (ISSN: 0749-0275).
--1952? - Dec, 1963 as U.S. Camera.
--Jan?, 1964 - Jan, 1969? as U.S. Camera & Travel.
--Feb, 1969 - Dec/Jan, 1970/1971 as Travel & Camera (ISSN: 0049-4542).
LC: TR 1.U5
DD: 770.5
ISSN: 0041-2007

✦ TRI-S SPOT/LIGHT
SUB: "A magazine about buying and selling Christian Radio."
PUBL: Soma Communications, Inc., 2227 Meadow Dr., Carrollton, TX 75007.
DESC: "Dynamic, informative, supportive," are adjectives that describe the quality of TRI-S Spot/Light, a magazine dedicated to the concept of Christian radio as contemporary radio; and that general managers of Christian radio can successfully compete in advertising sales no matter what mix of formats their individual markets might be. Utilizing latest demographic information available, editor and publisher Gary Crossland translates this data into a practical workshop for the Christian general manager. With a magazine format, numerous black/white charts and graphs provide clear indications of trends and target advertisers in the radio marketplace. Well recommended for religious radio broadcasters.
DEPT: None. (2-89).
TYPL: "Christian Radio: #1 For Auto Sales," "Good News for America's Travel Agents," "New Advertising Potential For Real Estate," "The Push Approach to Advertising." (2-89).
SCHL: Monthly, 30 pp.
SPAN: ?+
LC: HE 8697.25.U6 T74
DD: 384.54/43 19

✦ TS
SUB: "The poster magazine of teen stars."
PUBL: Starlog Telecommunications, Inc., 475 Park Avenue South, New York, NY 10016.
DESC: This quarterly magazine functions primarily as a publication of posters of teen stars bound in magazine format for newstand sale. The majority of stars are young, male actors of motion pictures and television, with several posters devoted to teen music. One sampled issue contained articles and posters on Fred Savage, Michael J. Fox, Wil Wheaton, Kiefer Sutherland & Lou Diamond Phillips, Patrick Swayze, River Phoenix, Ralph Macchio, Jon Bon Jovi, Bangles, Tiffany, Rob Stone, Kirk Cameron and Jami Gertz. Magazine format (8 x 10 ⅞ inches / 205 x 275 mm); in full color.
DEPT: "Opening Shots," star pictures; "Music Teletype!," 'Chart-toppers & hip-hoppers'. (summer-89).
TYPL: "Michael J. Fox Goes to War!," "Wil Wheaton In the 20th Century!," "Kiefer Sutherland & Lou Diamond Phillips: Watch Out! They're Renegades!," "Patrick Swayze: Tapping Toes or Flying Fists?," "River Phoenix: Indiana Jones First Crusade." (summer-89).
SCHL: Quarterly, 60 pp.
SPAN: Spring, 1985+
VARIES
--? - ? as TM (ISSN: 8755-3104).
DD: 051
ISSN: 8756-3312

Tulane Drama Review
Jun, 1957 - Summer, 1967//
(ISSN: 0886-800x)
SEE: TDR

✦ TV & APPLIANCE MART
SUB: "Magazine of appliance and TV Retailing."
SUB: "Merchandising, Appliances, Radio, Records, Television."
PUBL: Caldwell-Clements, Inc., 480 Lexington Ave., New York, NY.
DESC: This small tabloid supplement features retail prices of refrigerators, washers, ranges, air conditioners, vacuum cleaners, freezers, and in the communication field; clock-radios, television receivers, and phonograph records. Half of each issue is new product descriptions with photos.

DEPT: "The Price Mart," listing of retail prices and models; "New Appliances, TV, Radios." (2-53).
TYPL: No Article Titles.
SCHL: Monthly, 8 pp.
SPAN: Sep, 1953+?
SUPPLEMENT TO
--Television Retailing, ? - ?
LC: HD 9999.H83U6
ISSN: 0025-4061

TV & Communications
Jan, 1964 - Dec, 1966//
SEE: CABLE TV BUSINESS MAGAZINE

✤ TV & RADIO FAXLETTER
SUB: "A twice-monthly analysis of federal issues affecting the cable and broadcast industries."
PUBL: Howard Fields, PO Box 33578, Washington, DC 20033.
DESC: In the decade of the 1990s, "time is money," and that the right information, received in a timely manner, is a powerful competitive weapon in the communication field. That is one major reason for subscribing ($95 per year for 1991) to the *TV & Radio FAXletter*, a biweekly compendium of the latest radio and television news delivered via the subscriber's fax machine. As publisher Howard Fields put it, "Every other Monday morning, you can have on your desk a facsimile copy of *TV & Radio FAXletter*, providing you with an up-to-date analysis of federal news important to the cable and broadcast industries. This FAXletter cuts through the dross of who said what to whom to answer: What does it mean to me?" In the sampled issue, information was segmented by medium under "Broadcast," "Broadcast and Cable," "Cable," "Broadcast TV and Radio," and "Broadcast and Cable." No advertising, single column black/white editorial content (8 ½ x 11 inches / 215 x 280 mm).
DEPT: "Coming Up!," trends and events forthcoming. (4-8-91).
TYPL: "Don't Make Any Plans Yet Based on Senate Action So Far on Campaign Spending Reform," "The FCC Move to Redefine congested Areas in the Microwave Services May be Delayed," "Conventioneers Once Again Were Misled by Those They Pay to Come and Speak to Them," "A Chorus is Building for the FCC to Short-Circuit the Federal Aviation Administration," "The U.S. Supreme Court Will be Ruling Soon on Cases Important to Each Industry." (4-8-91).
SCHL: Semimonthly, 3 pp.
SPAN: ?+

✤ TV AND SCREEN SECRETS
PUBL: Magazine Management Company, 625 Madison Ave., New York, NY 10022.
DESC: Personalities of the stage, screen, television and politics were fair game for this "fanzine," the function of which was to bring closely-held secrets to public scrutiny. Headlines and articles were designed to hold shock-value, and were exposes of stars and personalities. One sampled issue contained stories surrounding Mia Farrow, Sharon Tate, Terry Melcher, Ali MacGraw, Lawrence Welk, Liza Minelli, Dean Martin, Sally Field, and Michael Cole. The featured film of the month was "Goodbye, Mr. Chips," with Peter O'Toole & Petula Clark. Published on newsprint; with numerous advertisements targeted at women (8 ¼ x 10 ¾ inches / 210 x 275 mm).
DEPT: "Watching the Beautiful People," column by Stephen Lewis; "In With the TV Set," column by David Levine; "Star Secrets Revealed," column by Salome; "Our Pick Pic of the Month," feature film review. (3-70).
TYPL: "Uncensored Report on Hollywood's Hippie Murder Club: How Doris Day's Son Escaped Sharon Tate's Horrible Fate," "Shocking Plans Revealed at Last Kennedy Reunion: Ted to Divorce! Ethel to Remarry!," "Lawrence Welk Suffers Breakdown!," "Liza Minelli: I Won't Live My Mother's Life," "Dean Martin Walks Out on Jeanne for the Last Time!" (3-70).
SCHL: Monthly, 70 pp.
SPAN: Jan, 1969+?

TV Availabilities
? - ?//
SEE: BILLBOARD TV PROGRAM AND TIME AVAILABILITIES, THE

TV Broadcast Communications
Jan, 1984 - Dec, 1984//
SEE: TELEVISION BROADCAST

TV Communications
Jan, 1967 - Jun, 1976//
(ISSN: 0039-8519)
SEE: CABLE TV BUSINESS MAGAZINE

✤ TV DAY STARS
PUBL: Magazine Management Co., Inc., 575 Madison Ave., New York, NY 10022.
DESC: This serial promoted the artists and programs of American network television. Stars were handled with kindness, as articles detailed their home and production lives for fans. One article detailed a daytime soap actor's stage opera background; another interviewed a soap opera couple who were expecting a baby; another showed a holiday party of the cast of, "All My Children," and "One Life to Live." Magazine format; published on newsprint (8 ⅛ x 10 ¾ inches / 210 x 275 mm).

DEPT: "Across My Desk," commentary and letters to the editor; "Soap Scoops," information and gossip column by Tony Rizzo; "Channel Chatter," soap opera news column by R. Marian Rose; "Ask Adrienne," reader Q&A column by Adrienne LaRussa; "Starscope," column by J.M. Fitzmartin; "The Country Express," news column by Loudilla Johnson; "Fan Club Forum," fan news column by Lynne Abrahamson; "The Answer Man," Reader Q&A column by Dick Maurice. (4-77).
TYPL: "Every Moment is Precious When I'm With My Children," "I Couldn't Ask For a More Wonderful Life!," "I'm Living My Childhood Fantasies!," "Looking Back on Somerset!," "Every Day is Beautiful When I Wake Up in My Husband's Arms!" (4-77).
SCHL: Monthly, 80 pp.
SPAN: Jan, 1972+?

TV-ELECTRONIC TECHNICIAN
PUBL: Caldwell-Clements, Inc., 480 Lexington Ave., New York, NY.
DESC: Each issue supplement consisted of ciruit diagrams for television repair technicians. Some five or six different television models were featured each issue.
DEPT: None.
TYPL: None.
SCHL: Monthly, 25 pp.
SPAN: ? - ?
SUPPLEMENT TO
--Television Retailing, ? - ?

✢ TV ENTERTAINMENT
PUBL: TVSM, Inc., 309 Lakeside Drive, Horsham, PA 19044.
DESC: This well-executed guide to cable television programming in the United States has articles about stars, program highlights; and an extensive daily guide to television programming. *TV Entertainment* was born out of a merger of three separate publications in 1989; *Cable Time*, *Choice*, and *Cable Choice*. During mid-1990, publisher Crosby Vandenburgh Group of Boston merged this serial with TVSM's *Cable Guide*, maintaining separate publication titles, but placing both programming guides under the TVSM corporate roof. It is for these reasons, it is assumed, that two separate ISSN numbers have been assigned to what appears to be a single continuing title. Magazine format; editorial content full color on coated paper stock; daily programming guide black/white on newsprint middle section.
DEPT: "Feedback," 'Readers sound off'; "Talk Show," 'Behind-the-screen scene'; "Highlights," 'Tops on the tube'; "Now Showing," movies and specials on cable this month; "Premium Services," program listing; "Daily Listings," program guide; "Video View," "Word for Word," quotes remembered; "Teleplay," crossword puzzle and trivia; "Guest Star," commentary. (8-90).
TYPL: "The Lip Runneth Over," "This is Not Steve Martin," "Three From the Heart," "Riots of Passage," "Rivers' Edge." (8-90).
SCHL: Monthly, 30 pp.
SPAN: ?, 1989+
FROM MERGER OF
--Cable Time, (and) Choice (and) Cable Choice, ?, 1989.
VARIES
--198u - 198u as TV Entertainment Monthly (ISSN: 1044-0682).
ISSN: 1049-1163

TV Entertainment Monthly
198u - 198u//
(ISSN: 1044-0682)
SEE: TV ENTERTAINMENT

✢ TV, ETC.
SUB: "The Media Research Center's bi-monthly review of the entertainment industry and the Hollywood Left."
PUBL: Media Research Center, 111 South Columbus St., Alexandria, VA 22414.
DESC: "The makers of *MediaWatch* introduce *TV, etc.*, the Media Research Center's bimonthly review of the entertainment industry and the Hollywood Left. Through *TV, etc.* you'll learn: Which rock stars donate concert proceeds to the far-left Christic Institute; Which far-left (and pro-communist) groups supported Hollywood's *Housing Now!* march; Which popular television shows consistently slam conservatives; How much money the entertainment community has poured into the campaign warchests of liberal Congressmen and Senators." Media Research Center also publishes monthly *MediaWatch*, which comments and reports on American news media. For the sampled issue of 1990: loose-leaf, two-color, newsletter format on uncoated paper stock (8 ½ x 10 ⅞ inches / 215 x 275 mm).
DEPT: "Profile," media artist profiles; "Sound Bites," 'And Now, a Word From the Stars'; "The Music Industry," newsbriefs; "Networks," newsbriefs; "Cable," newsbriefs. (1/2-90).
TYPL: "Mid-Season Report Card," "An A+ For Liberalism," "Liberal Themes, Holiday $$$," "MTV's Liberal Look at the '80s." (1/2-90).
SCHL: Bimonthly, 8 pp.
SPAN: Jan/Feb, 1989+
DD: 384
ISSN: 1054-2329

✢ TV GOLD
SUB: "The magazine for the television generation."
PUBL: Movieland Publishing, Inc., 8399 Topanga Canyon Blvd., Suite 208, Canoga Park, CA 91304.
DESC: The letters to the editor column is filled with praise for this serial that is a nostalgic look at television's finest: "What can I say except that in *TV Gold* you've

got yourself a class act, and a winner, to be sure," "I feel as if I should tell you that *TV Gold* is an outstanding work of art and features. Truely a one of a kind magazine," and "I can't tell you how I felt when I went to the local newsstand and saw *TV Gold*! Finally, I thought, a magazine for couch potatoes." Publisher and editor Hal Schuster, nicknamed "Happy Hal, the TV Addict," mirrors that enthusiasm. Among the television programs profiled in two sample issues were: "Laredo," "M*A*S*H," "Bullwinkle," "Strike Force," "Andy Griffith," "Shari Lewis," "The Fugitive," "The Outer Limits," "Gilligan's Island," "Wanted: Dead or Alive," "Ozzie and Harriet," "The Mickey Mouse Club," "Adam Twelve," "Jim Nabors," and "The Monkees." *TV Gold* appears is an entertainment publication that delights those who remember television's earlier days; and facillitates a current generation's discovery of the best that earlier television was. *TV Gold* is to be savored and appreciated for what it is; pure entertainment for television series aficionados. For the sampled issue of 1987: stapled magazine format, editorial content consisting of black ink on uncoated paper stock; cover and center-poster pull-out section in full-color on coated paper stock; limited advertising (8 1/8 x 10 3/4 inches / 205 x 270 mm).

DEPT: "Test Patterns," editorial column by Hal Schuster; "TV Talk," 'Missives from the TV Generation' letters; "Reruns," 'The latest news of the nostalgia world' column by Hal Schuster; "TV Trivia Quiz," "Sci Fi," program review; "Sitcom," program review; "Oaters," western program review; "Sitcom History," historical program review; "Do You Remember?," "TV Gallery," pictorial section. (1-87).
TYPL: "How Well Do You Know Your TV Indians?," "The Outer Limits," "Gilligan's Island," "The Mickey Mouse Club," "Wanted: Dead or Alive." (1-87).
SCHL: Monthly (Jun, 1986 - Jan, 1987); Quarterly (spring, 1987+), 55 pp.
SPAN: Jun, 1986+?

✤ TV GUIDE

SUB: "America's television magazine."
PUBL: News America Publications, Inc., 100 Matsonford Rd., Radnor, PA 19088.
DESC: At the beginning of the "Golden Age" of live television, *TV Guide* was there to explain the medium, extole its virtues, and help Americans be selective in their viewing habits. *TV Guide*, under new publisher and president Joseph Cece, is continuing that tradition as the largest circulation magazine entering the 1990s; resulting in more regional editions, some of which contain listings for more than 40 cable channels, more editorial content, and bolder critiques of the medium, its participants and product. Indeed, special cable editions of *TV Guide* were launched in 1986 for Brooklyn, Staten Island and Queens, and in fall, 1990 for cable subscribers in Manhattan. It is *TV Guide* that has led the way in examining the relationship of television to society; its impact, importance, entertainment and informational qualities. With the explosive growth in the cable television industry, this seems sure to be one publication which will chart its development. For the sampled 1990 issue: perfect-bound, small magazine format, editorial content full-color, including cover on coated paper stock, (5 x 7 3/8 inches / 125 x 185 mm); weekly listing section on newsprint.

DEPT: "TV Guide Insider," 'What's happening, who's hot in television today'; "Grapevine," column by Marilyn Beck; "Soaps," column by Michael Logan; "Sports View," column by Jim Baker; "Video Cassette Report," column by Myles Callum; "Cheers 'N' Jeers," "TV Guide Plus," late breaking news; "Letters," "The Collins Report," programming column by Monica Collins; "This Week," upcoming program column by Paul Droesch; "This Week's Movies," upcoming on broadcast and cable channels column by Art Durbano; "Four-Star Movies," top rated motion pictures; "Soap Opera Guide," column by Susie Wetmore and Tom Mitchell; "This Week's Sports," "Pay TV Movie Guide," "Television Crossword," "Horoscope," column by Patric Walker. (7-14-90).
TYPL: "The Goodwill Games: Seattle's Global Showdown," "Larry King Tries on a New Crown," "Jonathon Brandmeier Comes to Late-Night TV," "For TV's Morning Viewers: It's Bryant vs. Greg Gumbel." (7-14-90).
SCHL: Weekly, 195 pp.
SPAN: Apr 3, 1953+
EDITION
--Denver Edition.
--Los Angeles Metro Edition.
--Michigan State Edition.
--Nebraska Edition.
--North Carolina Edition.
--Philadelphia Edition.
--South Georgia Edition.
--South Texas Edition.
--Southern Michigan Edition.
--St. Louis Edition.
--Television Guide.
--Virginia Edition.
--Virginia-Carolina Edition.
--Washington-Baltimore Edition.
ISSN: 0039-8543
ABST: --Magazine Index
--Popular Magazine Review (ISSN: 0740-3763)
--Predicasts

✤ TV GUIDE

SUB: "ITV, BBC & satellite."
PUBL: Murdoch Magazines, 2nd Floor, 214 Gray's Inn Road, London WC1X 8EZ, England.
DESC: For the British television consumer, one need look no further for complete video programming schedules and articles about British media stars than Murdoch's *TV Guide*. Complete in every fashion, this weekly, 70+ page serial is a bevy of color from front to back, every page filled with color graphics, production stills, and other format items that bring a dynamic

thrust to what could have been a rather stodgy presentation. There is a certain excitement to the international mixture of television programming available to British consumers, which the Murdoch organization promotes through publication of *TV Guide*, a serial which no connoisseur of British television should be without. For the sampled issue of 1990: stapled magazine format, lively use of color pages throughout on coated paper stock (8 1/4 x 10 7/8 inches / 210 x 275 mm) with minimal advertising.
DEPT: "News," video newsbriefs; "Hollywood Hotline," 'Gossip, scandal, news-- read it here first' column by Kevin Wilson; "Films on Satellite," 'Kevin Wilson reviews the movies showing on satellite this week'; "Your 28-Page 12-Channel TV And Satellite Guide," "TV Pen Pals," 'Make TV friends through *TV Guide*'; "You Ask Us," 'We have the solutions to your TV queries'; "Video," 'Fast forward or rewind? We review this weeks releases'; "TV Teasers," crossword. (2-24-90).
TYPL: "Streets Ahead!," "Fast Cars, Big Money," "The Men Behind Wiseguy," "The Eat is On!" (2-24-90).
SCHL: Weekly, 65 pp.
SPAN: Apr 1, 1989+

✤ TV HITS

SUB: "Posters, prizes, interviews, gossip."
PUBL: K2 Publications, 277 Liverpool Road, London N1 1LX, England.
DESC: Vibrant color, sizzling gossip, interviews, readers' poll results, and numerous color pictures of primarily young male television and film stars (or would-be stars) grace this monthly which appeals to the British teenage female audience. With some articles as "Jason has a heart-to-heart with *TV Hits*," "'The Wonder Years' Kevin on girls, football and stardom," or "Maddonna's not just a pop star--she makes films too!;" *TV Hits* becomes a publicist's "dream-come-true," dispensing the latest inside news on what young TV/film stars are doing, thinking, and saying about their lives, their projects, and their fans. Each issue includes a "*TV Hits* Minibook," a folded poster sheet ready for hanging. For the sampled issue of 1990: stapled magazine format, full-color pages throughout in dynamic layout design on coated paper stock with minimal advertising (8 3/8 x 11 3/4 inches / 210 x 300 mm).
DEPT: "Bits & Pieces," news items of TV/Film stars; "Face to Face," Young TV star interviews; "Penpals," "Vidfile," star profile with film/video credits; "20 Questions," to a profiled star; "Mailbag," letters; "Hollywood Hotline," 'Every month, Howie Weiss--friend of the stars--brings us all the latest news from Hollywood: sneak previews, new faces, tips for the top, whos talking to whom and, of course, all the gossip we're allowed to print'; "Stickybeak," 'Nosing out some strange facts from the worlds of TV, film and pop'; "Songfile," pop song lyrics. (3-90).
TYPL: "'Sometimes It All Gets Too Much'," "Mega-Fit," "'We All Date Fans'." (3-90).
SCHL: Monthly, 40 pp.

SPAN: Sep, 1989?+
ISSN: 0958-2363

TV MIRROR

PUBL: TV Mirror, New York City, NY.
DESC: No matter what title this serial was published under, and there were many, the purpose was always the same; to provide entertaining and informative articles concerning top radio and television artists of the period. Like other similar publications, this one has a large pictorial content, and articles are a publicist's "dream come true." Most issues (up to 1953 at least) carried national broadcast schedules, but this was more of a convenience to the reader; the real purpose being to bring the reader backstage to the fun of show business. Magazine format.
DEPT: "Editorial," "Radio Mirror's Gallery of Stars," "We Have With Us," program previews; "Gilding a Radio Lily," fashions; "Radio Mirror Homemaking Department," "Our Public Broadcasting," letters; "Radio Mirror Crossword Puzzle." (1-34). "What's New from Coast to Coast," column by Jill Warren; "Information Booth," Q&A; "New Patterns for You," fashion; "New Designs for Living," needlecraft; "Inside Radio," program listings; "TV Program Highlights," "Daytime Diary." (12-53).
TYPL: "What's Wrong with Radio--According to Roxy," "Vass You Dere Sharlie?," "How I Keep Bing Straight," (1-34). "Arthur Godfrey's Songstress--Marion Marlowe," "My Friend, Red Buttons," "Big-Hearted Jackie Gleason," (12-53).
SCHL: Monthly, 120 pp.
SPAN: 1933 - Aug, 1977//
MERGED WITH
--Photoplay (ISSN: 0031-885x) (to form) Photoplay With TV Mirror (ISSN: 0163-5115), Aug, 1977.
LC: HE 8690 .R

TV People

? - ?//
(ISSN: 0492-0538)
SEE: TV PEOPLE AND PICTURES

TV PEOPLE AND PICTURES

PUBL: Non-Pareil Publishing Corporation, New York, NY.
DESC: [*TV People*]: Within the pages of this monthly and then bimonthly publication were the biggest names in network television in the United States. Stars such as Julius La Rosa, Betty White, Liberace, Frank Parker, Eddie Fisher, Martin & Lewis, Arlene McQuade, Perry Como, Arlene Francis, Gale Storm, Art Carney, Doug Edwards, Joan Caulfield, Donald O'Conner, and Charlie Farrell, among a host of other top-name talent, were featured at work and at play; at home and before the camera, leading lives that their television fans always imagined. Like other fanzines, this one

also took readers behind the scenes. Of special note were two personality columns. "TV Tattler," by Joe Cal Cagno, was the place "Wherein your favorite TV stars confide in Joe on matters pertaining to love, marriage, career and other items of a highly personal nature." The second column of note was "Studio Secrets," by Paul Denis: "for the absolute inside, the hush-hush gossip in the lives and loves of TV personalities you absolutely positively can't beat Paul's prize patter." For the sampled issue of 1955: perfect-bound magazine format, editorial content was black/white on newsprint, with full-color cover on coated paper stock (8 ⅜ x 10 ⅞ inches / 215 x 275 mm).

DEPT: "Hello, Friends," editorial column by Bessie Little; "TV Mail Bag," letters; "TV Tattler," 'Wherein your favorite TV stars confide in Joe on matters pertaining to love, marriage, career and other items of a highly personal nature' column by Joe Cal Cagno; "Studio Secrets," 'For the absolute inside, the hush-hush gossip in the lives and loves of TV personalities you absolutely positively can't beat Paul's prize patter' column by Paul Denis. (1-55).
TYPL: "Has the Kid Made Good?," "The Saga of Young Bess," "Liberace--Too Busy for Romance?," "Two Sleepy People," "A Girl Named Fuzzy." (1-55).
SCHL: Monthly (? - ?); Bimonthly (?+), 75 pp.
SPAN: Sep, 1953 - ?//
VARIES
--? - ? as TV People (ISSN: 0492-0538).

✦ TV PICTURE LIFE

SUB: "Combined with TV Stage."
PUBL: Sanford Schwarz, 355 Lexington Ave., New York, NY 10017.
DESC: Network television personalities come under scrutiny in the pages of *TV Picture Life*, a monthly publication dedicated to exploring the private lives of television stars of both daytime and nighttime shows. One sampled issue included Lawrence Welk, James Brolin, Sandy Duncan, Sally Struthers, Kristie Floren, Bobby Burgess, Robert Young, Susan St. James, Mike Landon, and Bobby Sherman. It is similar to other publications that cover media personalities. A 1972 issue had a very unique, four-page, full-color section in the middle of the issue of star pictures and advertisements. Magazine format (8 ⅛ x 10 ⅞ inches / 205 x 275 mm), published on newsprint, with covers and four-page middle section consisting of full color on coated paper stock.
DEPT: "Horoscope For the Stars and For You," column by Leigh Gregory; "Andy Taylor's Hollywood Beat," column by Andy Taylor; "TV Close-Ups With Polly Wright," column by Polly Wright; "Daytime TV Gossip," column by Helen Martin; "TV Picture Life's Personality of the Month," Artist profile; "Book Parade," fiction and non-fiction book reviews. (3-72).
TYPL: "Tanya's New Baby Threatens Her Marriage!," "We Peek in on Mr. and Mrs. James Brolin: One Step Ahead of the Stork!," "Sandy Duncan Faces Blindness Again! Her Last Chance to Save Her Sight!," "Sally Struthers' Pre-Nuptial Honeymoon! We Find Her Hidden Love Nest!," "'Love Means Being Together Even When You're All Alone!' Kristie Floren's Own Story About Her Life With Bobby Burgess!!!" (3-72).
SCHL: Monthly (? - ?); Bimonthly (?+), 85 pp.
SPAN: 1953+
ABSORBED
--TV Stage.

✦ TV PROGRAM INVESTOR

PUBL: Paul Kagan Associates, Inc., 126 Clock Tower Place, Carmel, CA 93923-8734.
DESC: The area of television program development and syndication has been highly volatile ever since the late 1950s, when networks gave up their strong control of the program development-network-syndication process. This is due in part to the changing nature of the television networks in the United States, but also due to the fickle tastes of the American television public. A television investor, therefore, must be armed with credible information concerning any investment made. *TV Program Investor*, another excellent Paul Kagan Associates newsletter, dispenses the kind and quality of data required for such investment/development purposes. It provides lucid, fact-filled paragraphs about television programming; its development, network/cable first-run, or syndication. Articles range from discussions of comparative network ratings to syndication prices, from the alternative channel of barter to new programs currently in development. Major conventions, international markets, the issue of reruns, network stocks, signal piracy, writers' strikes, program financing and changes in viewing habits are all in *TV Program Investor*. It is credible, useful information for those who absolutely need to know what is happening in the television programming field. Typewritten newsletter format with computer generated graphs and charts.
SCHL: Semimonthly, 8 pp.
SPAN: Sep 13, 1985+
DD: 332 11
ISSN: 0885-2340

✦ TV RADIO MIRROR

PUBL: Macfadden Publications, 205 East 42nd St., New York, NY.
DESC: With the first great surge of full time network radio programming in the early 1930s came this serial, aimed at the American housewife, and filled with news of her favorite radio stars; latest decorating, cooking, beauty hints; and continuing peeks into the emerging medium of television. Issues during that first decade of publication introduced readers to the faces behind the radio microphone, and demonstrated that radio/television celebrities could have lives just as exciting as their Hollywood film counterparts. Home life also received attention. In the sample issue for July, 1940, articles ranged from "a famous an-

nouncer's wife helps you to better housekeeping (Mrs. Harry Von Zell)," to "With complete frankness, Bette Davis, our most vibrant and vital star, tells from her own surprising experience how any woman can apply the secrets that will change plainness into fascination." Of special note was the very extensive section detailing network radio programming across all three time zones, with monthly radio highlights showcased in a separate column. By the 1960s, when television was king, articles were covering television personalities; such as Danny Thomas, Gertrude Berg, Connie Francis, Donna Reed, Allen Ludden, Joey Bishop, Dick Clark, Bobby Darin, Vincent Edwards, and the Lennon Sisters. This serial, and others to follow, are testimony to the well-designed editorial content by Macfadden Publications that continues to have readers returning for more. Sampled issue for 1945: perfect-bound magazine format; mixture of black/white, spot color and full-color pages on coated paper stock (8 5/8 x 11 1/4 inches / 220 x 285 mm). For sample issue of 1962: magazine format (8 1/2 x 10 7/8 inches / 215 x 275 mm). One-half of sample issue for 1940 printed duotone; numerous graphics.

DEPT: "What Do You Want to Say?," reader opinion page; "What's New From Coast to Coast," news of radio-television celebrities; "Radio's Photo Mirror," radio personality pictures; "Song of the Month," sheetmusic; "Hollywood Radio Whispers," gossip column by George Fisher; "The Cooking Corner," celebrity recipes column by Kate Smith; "Facing the Music," radio music program news column by Ken Alden; "Inside Radio," extensive weekly radio program listing; "What Do You Want to Know?," fan club questions; "Frame for Beauty," hints column by Dr. Grace Gregory. (7-40). "New Patterns For You," dress-making; "Information Booth," letters; "What's New From Coast to Coast," gossip column by Eunice Field; "New Designs for Living," handcraft patterns; "Johnny Carson's Corner," column by Johnny Carson; "Record Care," "Tops in Singles," chart; "Your Monthly On Record Guide," "The Wonderful World of Ed Sullivan," column by Ed Sullivan. (6-62).

TYPL: "How to Be Beautiful--Though Otherwise," "Kate Hopkins, Angel of Mercy," "How to Sing for Money," "The Romance of Helen Trent," "Should Television's Progress be Slowed Up?" (7-40). "Edd Byrnes and the Girl who Wouldn't Say Yes," "A Minister, Priest and Rabbi Discuss: Is the Twist Immoral?," "How Vince Edwards Treats His Mother," "What Dick Clark Says About the Girl He Wants to Marry," "An Insider's Guide to the White House; What You Didn't See on TV." (6-62).

SCHL: Monthly, 100 pp.
SPAN: Nov, 1933+
VARIES
--Nov, 1933 - Jul, 1939 as Radio Mirror.
--Aug, 1939 - Oct, 1942 as Radio and Television Mirror.
--Nov, 1942 - Mar, 1945 as Radio Mirror.
--Apr, 1945 - Nov, 1945 as Radio Romances.
--Dec, 1945 - Mar, 1948 as Radio Mirror.
--Apr, 1948 - Feb, 1951 as Radio and Television Mirror.
--Mar, 1951 - Sep, 1951 as Radio Television Mirror.
--Oct, 1951 - Jul, 1954 as Radio-TV Mirror.
EDITION
--Atlantic.
--Keystone.
--North Atlantic.
LC: HE 8690.R16

✦ TV RADIO SHOW

PUBL: Star Guidance, Inc., 315 Park Avenue South, New York, NY 10010.
DESC: With a focus on American network television personalities, this serial looks (sometimes kindly) at the lives, loves, and careers of a bevy of video entertainers. One sampled issue included Dean Martin, Carol Burnett, Frank Sinatra, Ben Murphy, Flip Wilson, Sandi Jensen, Glenn Ford, Sandy Duncan, Don Adams, Nancy Barrett, Ron Harper, Eileen Fulton, and Andy Griffith. Some daytime network television personalities are also featured. One article per issue provides a profile of a radio personality. Magazine format (8 1/8 x 10 7/8 inches / 210 x 275 mm); published on newsprint.
DEPT: "TV Scoops & Secrets," 'Inside gossip and exclusive photos of your favorite stars' via Cleo; "What's Happening!," 'Hollywood, New York, London, Paris, Rome' column by Bernice McGeehan; "Daytime TV World," 'TV Radio Show's daytime gossip newspaper' column by Bob Lardine; "TV Radio Show's Personality of the Month," "I'd Like to See More of...," reader poll of favorite star. (1-72).
TYPL: "The Secret Frank Sinatra's Children are Keeping From Him," "Ben Murphy: Like a Kid in a Candy Store," "Funny Man, Sad Man: The Flip wilson Nobody Knows... After Years of Silence--He Talks About Himself," "Sandi Jensen Makes a Woman's Hardest Decision: 'No More Children'," "The Night Glenn Ford Saved Judy Garland From Suicide." (1-72).
SCHL: Monthly, 85 pp.
SPAN: Oct, 1966+?

✦ TV RADIO TALK

SUB: "Tune in to TV Radio Talk for the top stories first!"
PUBL: Ideal Publishing Co., 750 Third Ave., New York, NY 10017.
DESC: The emphasis in *TV Radio Talk* is on network television personalities, their private and professional lives both coming under scrutiny. Articles detail the "good," the "bad," and the gossip of the stars of daytime/nightime American television. One sampled issue included Peggy Lennon, Tanya Welk, Tom Jones, Paul McCartney, Leslie Uggams, Michael Parks, Lucille Ball, Huntely & Brinkley, Anne Baxter, Robert & Betty Young, Sally Flynn, and New York City's "Cousin Brucie" Morrow. Magazine format (8 1/2 x 10 7/8 inches / 215 x 275 mm); published on newsprint.

DEPT:	"Army Archerd Makes TV Radio Talk," 'The latest hottest gossip! Read it here first!' column by Army Archerd; "Out For a Spin," 'Latest releases and gossip of your favorite recording stars' column by Bob Lardine; "TV Radio Talk Goes to the Movies," column by Marjorie Rosen; "Dateline: Daytime," 'It's what's happening' column by Maggie Glick; "TV Radio Talk," celebrity profile. (1-70).
TYPL:	"Lennon Killer's Last Obscene Message to Her!," "Hurt by the Lennons, Snubbed by Welk Girls, She Nears Collapse After Baby Shower!," "The Stars' Prayers for the New Year," "Wife Cries in Shame as Police Accuse Him of Indecent Behavior," "Is the Real Paul Dead?" (1-70).
SCHL:	Monthly (? - 1978); Bimonthly (1979+), 75 pp.
SPAN:	?+?
ISSN:	0194-4266

✤ TV SCREEN

SUB:	"Magazine for the millions."
PUBL:	Radio Best, Inc., 452 Fifth Ave., New York, NY.
DESC:	*Radio Best* and its television successor were consumer magazines at their finest, providing an exciting behind-the-scenes look at the art, artists, and technique of broadcasting. Typical articles concerning fashion, artists' popularity, and program reviews are also evident. Early issues of *Radio Best* were published on newsprint, switching in June, 1948 to a coated paper stock.
DEPT:	"Letters and Pictures to the Editor," "Hollywood on the Air," column by Favius Friedman; "Seat on the Dial," review; "Silver Mike Award," "Report to the Listeners," column by Saul Carson; "Microfun," best radio jokes of month; "Evening Guide to Listening," "Records of the Month," "This Month's Disc Jockey," (3-48).
TYPL:	"The Double Life of Jack Benny," "Those Amusing Nelsons," "Seven League Boots Has Lowell Thomas," "Who is the Nation's Favorite Radio Comedian?," (3-48).
SCHL:	Monthly (Nov, 1947 - Nov, 1949); Bimonthly (Jan, 1950+); 70 pp.
SPAN:	Nov, 1947+? VARIES --Nov, 1947 - ? as Radio Best. --Oct, 1949 - Aug, 1950 as Radio and Television Best. --Oct, 1950 - Dec, 1950 as Radio Best & Television Magazine.
LC:	HE 8690.T8

TV Search

Jan/Feb, 1983 - Nov/Dec, 1989//
SEE: TELEVISION HISTORY

TV SHOW

PUBL:	Picture Magazines, Inc., 105 East 35th St., New York, NY.
DESC:	Publisher Adrian Lopez and editor Lawrence Sanders set the stage for their premiere publication in this 1951 editorial: "Television is America's youngest industry, with a world of confidence, a breathtaking energy and a limitless future. We want *TV Show* to speak for this fabulous new medium of communication, and we want *TV Show* to speak for you, so that you may feel a part of this eighth wonder of the world. *TV Show* is interested in people, and our aim is to bring you intimate, inside stories and pictures of the people of TV. In addition, each issue of *TV Show* will present television columns by the nation's top-flight fashion, theatre and sports experts. We hope to serve as your guide to the wonderful world of video." Indeed, the first issue for May, 1951 was a wonderful collection of all that was good, new, and innovative in the medium. Several articles provided behind-the-scenes pictures of "Your Show of Shows," "Broadway Open House," "Molly Goldberg," "Queen for a Day," and the "Gabby Hayes Show." One article pertained to the censored "plunging neckline" for television's women stars. Another asked when the American West Coast would enjoy live network television from the East, while another picture page displayed a number of "television firsts" from the 1930s and 40s. Of note was a special featuring the comments of four major newspaper columnists on the status and potential for the new commercial medium. Robert Sylvester, Eileen Ford, Max Kase and Dorothy Kilgallen each took their turns in exploring and commenting on progress and innovations present in 1951 television programming. This was a wonderful resource and photographic adventure into before-the-camera entertainment and behind-the-scenes television production. Stapled magazine format, editorial content black/white on newsprint, cover on coated paper stock with spot color (10 x 13 ⅛ inches / 255 x 335 mm).
DEPT:	"From the Editors," editorial comment; "Cover Girl," background on cover picture. (5-51).
TYPL:	"Sid Caesar in Your Show of Shows," "Oh, Those TV Necklines!," "What Keeps Winchell Off TV?," "A Candid Look at Broadway Open House," "TV Show Presents the Inside Story of Television by America's Top Columnists." (5-51).
SCHL:	Monthly, 45 pp.
SPAN:	May, 1951 - ?//?

TV STAR PARADE

SUB:	"First and best in today's TV magazines!"
PUBL:	Ideal Publishing, 575 Madison Ave., New York, NY 10022.
DESC:	Mirroring the successes of Hollywood screen publications, *TV Star Parade* captured a loyal audience interested in who in "television land" was doing what to whom, in what manner, and the consequences of those actions. Cover article titles span the gamut of

off-stage activities, with a combination of publicity and celebrity snapshots certain to pique curiosity. Like all fanzines, this one contains numerous advertisements for everything from "24 Color Wallet Photos," to "Childless Wives Who Want Babies;" and including high school finishing courses, luxury jewelry, bust developers, weight-reduction, shopping calculators, pellet firing target pistols (with silencer), and a wide variety of marital devices and instruction for improving one's love life. The 30-plus year publication span for *TV Star Parade* provided strong testimony to the popularity and longevity of this publication. Magazine format (8 1/8 x 10 7/8 inches / 205 x 275 mm), full color cover with editorial content on newsprint.

DEPT: "Between Commercials," 'A chat with the editor' column by Kathy Loy; "Talk Around Town," celebrity news and gossip column by Jennifer Tobin; "Daytime Television," "The Tattletale Tribune," 'Gossip hot off the presses'; "Nostalgia Bonus," 'What were you watching twenty years ago?'; "Records," 'Best buys of the month'. (4-76).

TYPL: "Sonny & Cher Start 'New Family' Together! How They Told Chastity About the Baby!," "Burt Makes New Love Deal with Dinah!," "Tony Orlando & Freddie Prinze," "The Truth About Valerie Harper's Marriage," "Sally Struthers Confesses: 'I Wish Doctors Could Come Up with a Cure for Heartache!'." (4-76).

SCHL: Irregular (Fall, 1951 - May, 1953); Monthly (Jul, 1953 - Feb, 1959); ? (Mar, 1959 - Oct, 1979); Bimonthly (Nov, 1979 - ?//), 75 pp.

SPAN: Fall, 1951 - ?//
LC: PN 1992.T2
ISSN: 0041-4530

✢ TV STARS

PUBL: Lorelei Publishing, 2 Park Ave., New York, NY 10016.

DESC: This is part of the growing family of consumer publications which focuses on media stars, their private lives and secrets. Full color studio photos grace the inside and back covers; with newsprint center pages. *TV Stars*, owing either to its quarterly status or reduced advertising, has a much larger amount of editorial and photo pages than many of its counterparts. Printing quality is also better than many other magazines in this field.

DEPT: "Star Static," six pages of gossip and photos.

TYPL: "Laughter is Healing," "Ed Asner- the unlikely Sex Symbol," "How to do Everything Wrong--and be a Success," "Debbi Morgan Lived a Lifetime in 'Roots,'" "Tony Danza: Stardom Took Him by Surprise." (5-79).

SCHL: Quarterly, 70 pp.
SPAN: May, 1978+

✢ TV TECHNOLOGY

PUBL: Industrial Marketing Advisory Services, Inc., 5827 Columbia Pike, Suite 310, Falls Church, VA 22041.

DESC: Of the multitude of publications concerning broadcast equipment, *TV Technology* certainly ranks at the top. Designed for radio/television production and engineering staffs, it maintains a balance between authoritative technical information, and a warm editorial style that makes it welcome reading. Articles are technical and pragmatic, providing practical information for the technical side of station operation. The "Readers Forum" is lengthy letters to the editor about a wide variety of issues, and is fascinating reading. Probably its best testimony of quality is that articles are written by authors who "work in the trenches" of station operation. This is a refreshing approach, and speaks much to the popularity of this outstanding publication. Of special note: each monthly issue is split into three major sections; Engineering, Production, and Buyers Guide. Tabloid magazine format (10 7/8 x 14 5/8 inches / 275 x 375 mm), with color pages throughout on coated paper stock.

DEPT: "Readers' Forum," "Opinion," "Tech Tip." (10-83). "Newswatch," newsbriefs; "Readers Forum," excellent letters to editor column; "Latebreak," late breaking news; "Inside View," newsmaker profile; "Business Watch," "FYI," people, equipment, production, and company newsbriefs; "Union Quarterly," broadcast union news items; "Focus on Audio," engineering column by Randy Hoffner; "Masked Engineer," engineering column by Mario Orazio; "Focus on Quality," engineering column by Warner W. Johnston; "News From the Back Porch," engineering column by David Ostmo; "News Technology," "Focus on Graphics," column by Carla Breeden-Conrad; "Focus on Editing," column by Jay Ankeney; "Production Manager," column by Craig Johnston; "Industry Roundup," Buyers Guide column by Richard Farrell; "User Report," "Technology Update." (11-89).

TYPL: "SMPTE Will Test 1/4 Inch Video," "Talks Resume at NBC, NABET Strike Averted," "Cable Carriage of Teletext?," "Comments on ITFS Stress Interference," "Group Works to Set Limits on Radiation." (10-83). "Computers Hot at RTNDA," "Ritter Speaks Out on HDTV," "Audio for HD Under SMPTE Scrutiny," "An Introduction to MIDI Technology." (11-89).

SCHL: Monthly [except semimonthly in May and October], 50 pp.

SPAN: Sep, 1983+
WITH SUPPLEMENT
--Buyers Guide, Sep, 1983+.

DD: 384
ISSN: 0887-1701

✢ TV TIMES

PUBL: Australian Broadcasting Commission, 145 Elizabeth St., Sydney, Australia.

DESC: This popular guide to Australian Television, published in a magazine-sized format, has the usual behind-the-scenes articles concerning video stars, production stories, and, of course, an extensive listing of the upcoming week's television programming. There are numerous advertisements for consumer products and services.
DEPT: "James Bradford in Hollywood," news from stateside; "FC Kennedy," commentary; "You Were Asking," a readers mailbag; "Telesnack."
TYPL: "Experts Get the Goods on Starsky and Hutch," "Call for More TV Shows for Migrants," "Writings Not just One Long Picnic." (1-22-77).
SCHL: Weekly, 65 pp.
SPAN: 1958+
ISSN: 0039-8608

✤ TV TODAY

PUBL: National Association of Broadcasters, 1771 N St., NW, Washington, DC 20036-2891.
DESC: Receiving this serial is one excellent reason for American television broadcasters to become members of the National Association of Broadcasters. *TV Today* is a member advocacy newsletter which not only details the work of this excellent organization, but also alerts television owners and operators to governmental regulation, national business trends, and other problems/developments, both current and potential. News of television station operation is included as well, especially in the area of television station management seminars, resources, and materials. In the sampled issue for April, 1991 an "Agreement Form for Political Broadcasts," subtitled "Interim Form to be Used Until New FCC Disclosure Requirements Adopted" was enclosed for station application. An eight-page newsletter published on a weekly schedule, it is an excellent asset for any television station manager. Loose-leaf newsletter format on uncoated paper stock, three-hole punched, spot color employed, with advertising (8 ½ x 10 ⅞ inches / 215 x 275 mm).
DEPT: None. (4/15/-91).
TYPL: "NAB Issues Interim Political Broadcast Agreement Form," "FCC Rules on Kidvid Legislation," "Divided Commissioin Eases Fin-Syn Restrictions," "Advertising Tax Battle Possible in California," "Preparing for a Crisis--Before It Happens." (4-15-91).
SCHL: Weekly [except for the first week of each month], 8 pp.
SPAN: 1933+
VARIES
--? - ? as NAB Today [Television Edition].

TV WORLD

SUB: "Pictures and stories."
PUBL: Official Magazine Corporation, 655 Madison Ave., New York, NY.
DESC: With the likes of Gale Storm, George Burns & Gracie Allen, Clint Walker, Hugh O'Brian, and James Arness on the cover of a sampled 1957 issue, *TV World* couldn't help but sell copies at the newsstand. All of the major, minor, and newcomer stars or starlets of television received their "time in the sun" within this monthly. The sampled issue also had a feature on television stars and their faiths; Private Doberman telling about Sergeant Bilko; a birthday party for a child star; what Betty White will tell her future husband; and the rise from poverty to Disney stardom for television host, Jimmie Dodd. *TV World* was promotional in nature, always showing the best side of television celebrities. Magazine format (8 ⅝ x 10 ¾ inches / 220 x 275 mm), full color cover, editorial content is black/white on newsprint.
DEPT: "Hello, Friends," commentary column by Bessie Little; "Tele-Tales," television news and gossip column by Joe Cal Cagno; "Channel Gossip," column by Paul Denis; "TV Letters," 'What do you like in TV World? What are your gripes?'. (12-57).
TYPL: "TV's Purest Stars," "For Adults Only: Cowboy Madness," "Law and Order at Home," "What Keeps Gracie so Young?," "Sentimental Sergeant." (12-57).
SCHL: Monthly, 75 pp.
SPAN: Aug, 1953 - ?//

✤ TV WORLD

SUB: "International business magazine for television."
SUB: "International business magazine for television and video."
PUBL: International Thomson Business Publishing, Ltd., 7 Swallow Place, London W1, England.
DESC: This British publication provides an excellent overview of international and world television programming from the various points of view of the producer and the audience. At times, there is a discussion on the potential for international syndication. Other articles discuss audience appeal and production case stories and promotion. Some issues cover international conventions (such as VIDCOM, NATPE or MIFED), government regulation, or the changing viewing habits in world television. Of special note is "Focus On," a regular segment profiling television programming within a given nation. Some discussion of technological developments is provided, but the accent is on programming. As the publisher notes in the masthead: "*TV World* is published for personnel in executive and management positions in TV broadcasting and video production and distribution companies, governmental organizations and educational institutions concerned with TV and video." Typical subject topics from 1991 issues included, "A guide to Scandinavia for would-be co-producers," "Making use of tax incentives and low cost locations to help meet the cost of drama production," "A look at the world's most popular soaps," "Inside Japan...a guide to new areas opening up in the world of Japanese broadcasting," and "Distribution: Agents of Change. Is there still room for middle-men in this cost-conscious industry?" It is an excellent

resource for the status of world television broadcasting. For sampled issues of 1983 and 1991: stapled, magazine format; editorial content consisting of black ink with spot- and full-color graphics on coated paper, and cover in full color on coated stock. Dimensions for the 1983 issues: (8 x 10 ½ inches / 205 x 270 mm); and for the 1991 issues: (8 x 10 ⅝ inches / 205 x 270 mm).
DEPT: "World Round-Up," newsbriefs; "Focus On," world television program profile; "Hollywood Notebook," "Ratings," program ratings. (11-80). "World Round-Up," "In Production," newsbriefs; "International Ratings," "Focus On," "Events Diary," "The Editor's Letter," "People on the Move," newsbriefs, "New Deals...New Deals." (1-89).
TYPL: "Video Comes of Age in Cannes," "Shadow Boxing With the Law," "Broadcasters Membership Battle," "Parkinson's Private Gold Rush," "All's Well that Sells Well," "New Black Shows for Syndication." (11- 80). "ITV Enters a Fight for its Rights," "The Art of Comedy," "Shopping at Home--the French Way," "TV Soccer Strikes Back," "The Gentle Art of Marathons." (1-89).
SCHL: Monthly (1977 - Nov, 1984); Ten issues per year (Dec, 1984 / Jan, 1985 to date), 40 pp.
SPAN: 1977+
LC: HE 8700.T18
DD: 384.55/05
ISSN: 0142-7466

✤ 20/20

SUB: "Entertainment, the arts & much more."
PUBL: Time Out 20/20 Limited, Tower House, Southampton St., London WC2E 7HD, England.
DESC: With a dynamic mixture of entertainment personalities, newsmakers, and what's new in the arts, *20/20* always makes for interesting reading of the unique and unusual of the world. A typical issue for January, 1990 featured Spanish film director Pedro Almodovar, actor Al Pacino, a photo essay of Hollywood, a Paul Newman profile, and Green activists of the western United States. A large monthly "In View" section includes reviews of current and new fare in the lively arts of Great Britain. The large, square format contains numerous color photographs in accompaniment to well-written articles. The focus is on current, not past, entertainment and the arts. For the sampled issue of 1990: full-color, spot-color and black ink editorial content with full-color cover on coated paper stock (9 ⅛ x 11 ⅞ inches / 230 x 300 mm).
DEPT: "Letters," "Film," review column by Geoff Andrew; "Video," review column by Rupert Smith; "Music," review column by Rupert Smith; "Classical & Opera," review column by Martin Hoyle; "Theatre," review column by Jane Edwardes; "Art," review column by Sarah Kent; "Television," review column by Alkarim Jivani; "Books," review column by Maria Lexton; "Free Offers," monthly giveaway via 20/20. (1-90).
TYPL: "Tour de Farce," "Return Match," "Remote Control," "Slaying Power." (1- 90).
SCHL: Monthly, 130 pp.
SPAN: Apr, 1989+

TVC

Jul, 1976 - Oct?, 1982//
(ISSN: 0164-8489)
SEE: CABLE TV BUSINESS MAGAZINE

✤ TWIN CITIES JOURNALISM REVIEW

PUBL: Twin Cities Media Project, P.O. Box 17113, St. Paul, MN 55117.
DESC: This is a Northern journalistic review of broadcast and print news journalism operations in the Minneapolis-St. Paul area. Articles and letters to the editor show strong support by working press.
DEPT: "Letters to the Editor," unique due to flavor and content.
TYPL: "The UNcoverage of Women's Sports," "News Consultants Heat Up the WCCO-KSTP Battle," "Inside the Sun--Low Quality, Morale, and Pay."
SCHL: Bimonthly, 25 pp.
SPAN: Feb, 1972+

✤ TWR

PUBL: Trans World Radio, 700 Shunpike Rd., PO Box 98, Chatham, NJ 07928.
DESC: This is the promotional quarterly magazine of Trans World Radio, a worldwide Christian evangelical organization which operates radio transmitters in a number of nations. Articles provide some interesting insights into the problems and joys of operating radio transmitters in these nations, and the ever-changing relationship between organizations such as TWR and the host governments. Magazine format; numerous color graphics.
DEPT: "President's Corner," "Editorial." (1-89).
TYPL: "Tangier...Birthplace of TWR's Worldwide Outreach," "Slavic Gospel Association Reaches Behind the Iron Curtain," "Radio in Russia." (1-89).
SCHL: Monthly [except Jul/Aug] (? - ?); Quarterly (winter, 1988+), 25 pp.
SPAN: Sep/Oct, 1980+
DD: 384
ISSN: 0274-9831

U

✤ U & LC
SUB: "The international journal of typographics."
PUBL: The International Typeface Corporation, 216 E. 45th St., New York, NY 10017.
DESC: *U & LC* (*Upper and Lower Case*) is both a promotional and informational publication. Its primary function is to promote the use of its licensed fonts, which include everything from metal letters for letterpress to coldtype to rub-on lettering. The newsprint tabloid devotes a full page to each new typestyle, with accompanying notes on its development. The remainder of the publication is lengthy articles with superb graphics detailing some aspect of typography in mass communications. It is a unique and valuable publication for anyone working with typography. Tabloid newsprint.
DEPT: "Thanks!," letters. (#2-74). "Editorial," "Book Shelf." (8-87).
TYPL: "A Proposition for Education in Letterforms & Handwriting," "The Interdependence of Technique and Typography," "Technical Training for Technicians and Typographers," (#2-74). "Deltiology: the New Old Craze," "Windmills & Weights," "The Brothers Grimm & ITC Benguiat." (8-87).
SCHL: Quarterly, 75 pp.
SPAN: 1974+
LC: Z 119.U
ISSN: 0362-6245

UFPA Journal
Jan, 1951//
SEE: JOURNAL OF FILM AND VIDEO

✤ UK PRESS GAZETTE
SUB: "Journalism's newspaper."
SUB: "Every Monday--for journalists and all who work with them."
SUB: "Journalism's independent newspaper."
PUBL: Bouverie Publishing Co., Ltd., 244-249 Temple Chambers, Temple Ave., London EC4Y 0DT, England.
DESC: "Every Monday, *UK Press Gazette* gives an insight into the turbulent media world via its incisive news, its balanced comment and its penetrating features." It is a weekly trade magazine for the professional journalist, providing late-breaking news on legal, financial, readership, promotional, and regulatory changes. Articles are authoritative, with a lucid eye to the business of newspaper, print, and broadcast journalism. This is "must" reading for the British journalism community. As of the April 28, 1986 issue, *The Media Reporter* was absorbed by *UK Press Gazette*, and issued as a quarterly supplement in January, April, July, and October of each year. For the sampled issue of 1990: stapled, tall magazine format; editorial content consisting of black ink on uncoated paper stock with black/red spot ink cover on coated paper stock with numerous black/white graphics of newsmakers (9 ¼ x 13 inches / 235 x 330 mm).
DEPT: "Opinion," "Dog Watches Dog," 'A weekly appreciation of what is not always appreciated'; "Changing Faces and Places," "Obituary," "Letters," "News Contact Directory," very valuable resource; "The Week Ahead," "Dateline America," newsbriefs. (4-28-86). "Magazines," "Broadcasting," "In Brief," "Obituaries," "Opinion," "Press Pack," cartoon commentary; "Freelances," "Profile," "Dog Watches Dog," column by Steve Platt; "Letters," "Changing Faces and Places," personnel newsbriefs; "Diary," upcoming events of journalistic merit. (2-19-90).
TYPL: "Wapping--Libya: NUJ in Turmoil," "Mail Chapels Sound a Warning on Conditions," "Observer Cleared in Bribery Case after Exposea," "The Rambo of No. 10--Made by Maggie in Her Own Image." (4-28-86). "New Libel Reforms Mauled by Critics," "Scottish Universal Puts Ban on 'Moonlighting'," "Award Winner Fired Over Freelance Work," "Targets for Local Radio Will Bolster Journalism." (2-19-90).
SCHL: Weekly, 40 pp.
SPAN: 1965+
WITH SUPPLEMENT
--Media Reporter, The (ISSN: 0309-0256), Apr 28, 1986+.
ISSN: 0041-5170

UNION LABOR SUN
PUBL: Union Labor Sun, 3620 W. Pico Blvd., Los Angeles, CA.
DESC: Union labor news within the major motion picture studios was the focus of the *Union Labor Sun*, the word *Sun* being an acronym for Studio Union News. Articles feature suspected or proven anti-union forces within film management. This tabloid offers fascinating insight into the development of film, radio and television.
DEPT: "Hollywood Diary," chatty gossip of studio inside happenings; "Recommended Radio," programs which SUN readers have voted to be their favorites; "On Through the Years," interesting historical comments on a current day labor issue; "New York Vignette," New York gossip column by John Skinner.

TYPL: "'NLRB's Commie If It Rules Against Us' Says Brewer," "Electricians Who Respected Pickets Put Out of H'wood," "2nd Biggest Profit Called MGM's 'Dip,'" "AFL Chiefs Urged to Halt Flouting by Prods, IATSE," "Extras Re-Elect All Incumbants." (5-28-47).
SCHL: Weekly, 4 pp.
SPAN: ? - ?//
LC: HD 6515.M

Union Tabloid

Feb, 1978 - Jun 30, 1983//
(ISSN: 0275-8342)
SEE: GRAPHIC COMMUNICATOR

UNIQUE

SUB: "The magazine of popular culture."
PUBL: Hugh M. Cook, PO Box 1224, Bridgeview, IL 60455.
DESC: In the premiere issue for July/August, 1990, editor and publisher Hugh M. Cook told readers; "Welcome to *UNIQUE* magazine. If you're expecting a life-style magazine filled with articles on where to eat, what to wear and how to spend your money, you're bound to be disappointed. What you will find in *UNIQUE* is a rich assortment of fact, fiction, humor and photography devoted to chronicling the popular culture that surrounds us. *UNIQUE* will reflect the changes in popular culture--without the damning, the criticism, the holier-than-thou attitude that one finds in other magazines. We'll be looking at the horizon of popular culture through a wide-angle lens. Therefore, you'll see coverage of the good, the bad and the weird aspects of the society that we live in." Continuing on in "Editor's Notes," Cook promised a minimum of three new short stories per issue (reflecting the 90s boom in short story fiction), with a mixture of mystery, science fiction, horror and fantasy. The premiere issue covered fiction, music, cinema, television, pictorial essays, rock 'n roll, satirical prose and even a cartoon strip on "All Creatures Small and Fuzzy." One-fourth of each issue's editorial content was to be fiction. As a mid-issue promotion put it: "*UNIQUE*'s editorial mix is lighter, cooler, looser, hipper. More fiction and humor. Less nonfiction. Dynamic graphics and spectacular photography. A magazine that you can relax with. Have fun with it. Escape with. A magazine that's not for everyone, but is for everyone who enjoys the pleasure of reading." Lack of public support caused cessation of this promising publication after only two issues. Magazine format (8 1/8 x 10 7/8 inches / 205 x 275 mm); black/white and color graphics.
DEPT: "Editor's Notes," "Review: Literature," column by James Sallis; "Review: Music," column by Sean Colbert; "Review: Cinema," column by David Morgan; "Pictorial," photo essay; "Rock Record," column by Elyse Glickman; "Satire." (7/8-90).

TYPL: "The Church Lady Goes Hollywood," "Sea Crusader," "She Pulled Legs Off Spiders," "Amoeba Politics," "All Creatures Small and Fuzzy." (7/8-90).
SCHL: Bimonthly, 70 pp.
SPAN: Jul/Aug, 1990 - Sep/Oct, 1990//
DD: 051 11
ISSN: 1046-8439

UNIVERSAL WEEKLY

SUB: "A magazine for motion picture exhibitors."
SUB: "Universal has the pictures."
SUB: "The pleasure is all yours."
PUBL: Moving Picture Weekly Publishing Co., 1600 Broadway, New York, NY.
DESC: In "Straight From the Shoulder Talk" number 339, Carl Laemmle, President of the Universal Pictures Corporation, told motion picture exhibitors: "Once in a while one of the other companies in this business pokes its head up over its rut, lets out a peep of delight, then ducks back and goes paddling along in its rut again. You then sit up, lift your eyebrows and exclaim: 'Well, I declare, this fellow is coming to life. I though he was dead.' But you're never surprised when the Universal comes out with something big and new, because we're doing it ALL THE TIME. We have no rut. A rut is the worst thing in the world for the entertainment business. It is deadly. You don't want schemes. You don't want tricks. You want something new and something different for your people all the time. And there never was a time when you could not get exactly that very thing from the Universal." This weekly, square-shaped magazine promoted Universal motion picture product among American exhibitors. Advertising and editorial content alike praised current Universal motion pictures (through pictures and stories of successful exhibitors); and soon-to-be released films, with a number of suggestions for local "exploitation." One sampled issue showcased a promotional tie-in with *Collier's* magazine for the Universal film, "The Leather Pushers." Another detailed how New York City's Rivoli Theatre handed out over one-million flyers emblazoned with a "Must Do" list, which included attendance at the Universal motion picture, "Merry Go Round." Newspaper promotions, advertisements running in national publications, parades, walking sandwich signs, radio music programs, children's petitions, and a New York City float devoted to "The Abysmal Brute" (Jack London story), all received their due in the pages of *Universal Weekly*. Each weekly issue included the special section, "Additional Publicity and Exploitation for..," which provided the local exhibitor with numerous ideas and "stunts" for promoting an upcoming Universal release. This special feature contained subsections; "At a Glance," production statistics; "Cast," credits; "Notes," suggested promotional copy for local advertising and press releases; and "Exploitation," providing various suggestions for promotions. Also of note are news items concerning the health and welfare of Universal exhibitors in New York, Los Angeles, Kan-

sas City, Tennessee, Connecticut, and Texas. Each weekly issue contains story synopses of new films. This was a medium of pure publicity. Carl Laemmle told readers, "Variety, variety and more variety is Universal's slogan. You can't get in a rut with Universal pictures because there ain't no such animile in Universal policy. The me-too boys have always tried to cash in on Universal's enterprising novelties by copying them, but, like the cow's tail, the copyist is always in one certain place and that is-- BEHIND!" Square magazine format (205 cm wide x 265 cm high); black/white graphics and printing on coated paper stock.
DEPT: "Straight From the Shoulder Talk," column by Carl Laemmle; "Universal Moviegrams," newsbriefs as regards Universal releases; "At a Glance," production data; "Notes," suggested news release elements; "Exploitation," publicity ideas; "The Data Throwaway," 'A series of inexpensive, practical exploitation suggestions'; "Los Angeles Notes," Southern California exhibitor newsbriefs column by H.D. McBride; "Gotham Bugle," 'Happenings in the little village of New York and there-abouts' column by Joe Weil; "Kansas City Notes," exhibitor newsbriefs column by L.D. Balsly; "In Tennessee," exhibitor newsbriefs column by Harry Williams; "Texas Northers," Texas exhibitor newsbriefs column by Jack Meredith. (7-14-23).
TYPL: "'Merry Go Round' Premiere at Rivoli Theatre an Ovation," "Carl Laemmle Sails for Europe," "Four Hours a Day Needed for Chaney to Make Up," "'Trifling With Honor' Opens Braves Ball Park at Boston," "Tie-Ups Galore Planned for Baby Peggy." (7-14-23).
SCHL: Weekly, 45 pp.
SPAN: Jan 20, 1912 - May 9, 1936//
VARIES
--Jan 20, 1912 - Jun 8, 1912 as Implet.
--Jun 22, 1912 - Jun, 1915 as Universal Weekly.
--1915 - May, 1922 as Moving Picture Weekly.
LC: PN 1993.U6

Universal Weekly

Jun 22, 1912 - Jun, 1915//
SEE: UNIVERSAL WEEKLY

University Film Journal

? - ?, 1968//
SEE: UNIVERSITY VISION

✤ UNIVERSITY FILM STUDY CENTER. NEWSLETTER.

PUBL: University Film Study Center, Box 275, Cambridge, MA 02138.
DESC: The University Film Study Center is a consortium of 12 universities in the New England area. This newsletter provides a medium for news exchange, film festivals, new archive acquisitions, grants, publications, and other items of interest to the 12 member group.
DEPT: "Film Information," news briefs; "Calendar," upcoming film-related events, contests, and festivals.
TYPL: "Center Screen Series: Animation and Special Effects," "Sixth Annual Summer Institute," "Independent Film: Artists on Artists." (2-76).
SCHL: Bimonthly, 10 pp.
SPAN: 1971+

UNIVERSITY VISION

SUB: "The journal of the British Universities Film Council."
PUBL: British Universities Film Council, Royalty House, 72 Dean St., London W1V 5HB, England.
DESC: This small format journal for the study of mass communications, promotes the use of films in university education. Primarily a journal of descriptive research, authors evaluate the impact of mass media on culture and societal relationships for entertainment, instruction and research. It provides thoughtful commentary. Few graphics.
DEPT: "Forward," editorial; "Reviews."
TYPL: "A Biologist Looks at 'Communication,'" "Film and Television Techniques in Communications Research," "Communication and Language," "Impact of Film on the University," "Film and the Historian." (10-68).
SCHL: Three issues per year (?-?); Semiyearly, 50 pp.
SPAN: ? - 1976//
VARIES
--? - ?, 1968 as University Film Journal.
LC: LB 1044.U
ISSN: 0042-0395

✤ UPDATE

SUB: "A multimedia ministry to reach the multitudes in Latin America."
PUBL: STAR (Spanish Television and Radio) Productions, 627 Hemlock Lane, Lakeland, FL 33805.
DESC: In this four-page newsletter concerning the activities of STAR Productions, a religious organization engaged in the production of radio and television programs for South America; articles detail programs in progress, audience statistics, and profiles of individual artists. STAR Productions is affiliated with the Assemblies of God.
DEPT: None. (fall-81).
TYPL: "STAR Hustles to Keep Up With Latin American TV Boom," "Antennas Await Gospel Message," "'Lugar Secreto' Has Weekly Audience in the Millions." (fall-81).
SCHL: Quarterly, 4 pp.
SPAN: ?+

✢ UPI ADVANCE

PUBL: United Press International Corporate Affairs, 1400 I St., NW, Washington, DC 20005.
DESC: This monthly newsletter, in a two-color magazine format, showcases the corporate and news gathering activities of United Press International and its worldwide staff. It has numerous black/white photos of UPI staff on location, at work, and in the media. Commencing with the March, 1990 issue was the "...the first of what is envisioned as a 'periodic' newsletter for the onetime employees of United Press, United Press International and Acme Newspictures." This supplement, *The Downholder*, appeared as a two-page, two-column report on the activities and status of former UPI employees. For the sampled issue of 1990: stapled newsletter format, editorial content consisting of black ink with red spot-color ink on coated paper stock (8 ½ x 11 inches / 215 x 280 mm).
DEPT: "The UPI Newsroom," 'Editorial staff promotions, new assignments, new hires'; "UPI Radio Roundup," newsbriefs; "FYI," commentary. (3-90).
TYPL: "UPI to Expand International News Coverage," "UPI Profitable, Steinle Plans New Venture," "UPI Photographer Keeps Capturing the Moments." (3- 90).
SCHL: Monthly, 8 pp.
SPAN: Jan, 1989+
WITH SUPPLEMENT
--Downholder, The, Mar, 1990+.

URBAN TELECOMMUNICATIONS FORUM

PUBL: Urban Telecommunications Forum, 276 Riverside Drive, New York, NY 10025.
DESC: "The *Urban Telecommunications Forum* is published by the non-profit Urban Telecommunications Workshop in association with the Urban Communications Teaching and Research Center of Rutgers University (Livingston College), as a monthly review of the current research and practical state of the art and science of using broadband cable communications for the purpose of government, institutions, private and public organizations, businesses and individuals in urban areas generally and municipalities in particular, with emphasis on exploring and shaping the potential public benefits. And, as a forum for reviewing the resulting implications for urban interaction and urban forum." Typed format.
DEPT: "Publications," new cable periodicals and research; "Conferences," upcoming.
TYPL: "User Planned Cable Communications Systems," "Program of Apprenticeships in Cable TV," "Baltimore Citizens Ask FCC to Void County Cable Franchise." (8-73).
SCHL: Monthly, 12 pp.
SPAN: Aug, 1972 - Nov, 1975//
ISSN: 0092-9441

U.S. Camera

1935 - ?//
SEE: TRAVEL & LEISURE

U.S. Camera

Aug, 1941 - 1949?//
SEE: TRAVEL & LEISURE

U.S. Camera

1952? - Dec, 1963//
SEE: TRAVEL & LEISURE

U.S. Camera & Travel

Jan?, 1964 - Jan, 1969?//
SEE: TRAVEL & LEISURE

U.S. Camera Annual

1950 - 1952//
(ISSN: 0749-0275)
SEE: TRAVEL & LEISURE

U.S. Camera Magazine

? - Jul, 1941//
SEE: TRAVEL & LEISURE

✢ US MAGAZINE

SUB: "The entertainment magazine."
PUBL: Straight Arrow Publishers, Inc., 745 Fifth Ave., New York, NY 10151.
DESC: This wonderful consumer magazine of stars, celebrities and personalities has developed a loyal audience in its ten-plus years of publication. *US* is about people; personalities prominent in the entertainment industry, and more specifically motion pictures, music, and television. One sampled issue covered Tom Cruise, Ingrid Chavez, Joie Lee, Molly Ringwald, Emilio Estevez, Kiefer Sutherland, Lou Diamond Phillips, Andrew Dice Clay, and Louie Louie. *US* dispenses articles on a personal and informative level. The editorial philosophy is supportive of the entertainment industry and its stars and personalities. Note: an "introductory" issue labeled volume 0, #1 was published November 30, 1976. Magazine format (8 x 10 ½ inches / 205 x 270 mm); many color graphics on coated paper stock.
DEPT: "Letters," "Loose Talk," interesting quotes column by Lisa Bernhard; "Faces & Places," event photos and stars; "Reviews," movies, music, television, and videos; "Biz Buzz," entertainment news items column by Lisa Bernhard. (8-6-90).

TYPL:	"Tom Cruise and His Movie Machine," "Joie de Vivre," "Breaking Away," "Hollywood Witch-Hunt: A Special Report," "Horseplay," "Andrew Dice Clay." (8-6-90).
SCHL:	Weekly (1985 - ?); Biweekly [with combined end of Jul, end of year issues] (Feb, 1991+), 70 pp.
SPAN:	May 3, 1977+
LC:	AP 2 .U844
DD:	051

ISSN: 0147-510x

USC Spectator, The

Spring, 1982 - Spring, 1987//
SEE: SPECTATOR, THE

V

✧ V

SUB: "The magazine of videocassettes."
SUB: "The guide to home movies."
SUB: "Guide to home videos."
PUBL: Fairfield Publishing Co., Inc., 104 Fifth Ave., New York, NY 10011.
DESC: A wonderful companion to the home VCR and television viewer is the magazine *V*, an upbeat compendium of what is good, great, bad or just plain ugly in current and about-to-be released videocassettes for the American home market. This bimonthly features interesting filmmaker/star interviews and profiles, appropriately accompanied by filmographies and videocassette availabilities. But the primary reason for reading/subscribing to *V* is the informative, critical reviews of current videocassette releases. The reviews cover a broad range of viewing tastes, all the way from an excellent "Children & Parenting" review section; to instructional cooking videotapes, professional wrestling, music, concerts, health, fitness; and a myriad of Hollywood entertainment products for the viewer. Full color throughout with a dynamic layout design on coated paper stock (8 ⅜ x 10 ⅞ inches / 210 x 275 mm).
DEPT: "Editor's View," editorial column by Richard Wien; "Video Vibes," column by Amy Appleton; "New Movies," 'In your video stores now' review column by Tony Chiu; "Film Classics," 'First time on home video'; "Video Tracking," 'Fast forwarding the stars'; "Star Finder," where to locate videocassettes of favorite stars; "Video Equipment," column by Henry B. Cohen; "New Products," review; "Reviews," 'New & noteworthy this issue'; "Children & Parenting," videocassette review; "Health & Fitness," videocassette review; "Music & Concerts," videocassette review; "How-To & Education," videocassette review; "Documentaries & Travel," videocassette review; "Sports & Recreation," videocassette review; "Mixed Bag," videocassette review; "Under $20," videocassettes for sale; "Spot Light," single videocassette of merit review. (9-88).
TYPL: "Michael Douglas and the Wall Street Payoff," "The World According to Belinda Carlisle," "Paul Newman: Shooting Straight," "Kids Rate the Classics," "RoboDirector or CineMagician." (9-88).
SCHL: Monthly (Oct, 1987 - ?); Bimonthly (Oct/Nov, 1988+), 90 pp.

SPAN: Oct, 1987+
LC: PN 1992.93 .V15
DD: 016.79143/75
ISSN: 1041-1402

✧ VARIETY

SUB: "A variety paper for variety people."
SUB: "The international entertainment weekly."
PUBL: Cahners Publishing Co., 475 Park Avenue South, New York, NY 10016.
DESC: For over 70 years, *Variety* has been the bible of vaudeville, films, video, television, radio, music, and the legitimate stage: it still is. Its own unique style of *Variety*-ese and exhaustive news coverage make it foremost in the trade news publication field for hard news and "hearsay" of the vast entertainment field. Its departments are especially renowned, and are well-recommended to the reader/researcher. The only shortcoming of this famous publication was that for most of its publication history that it was printed on newsprint stock; but happily that problem was resolved in 1991, and the new coated paper stock is a welcome change. *Variety* has been, remains, and will probably continue to be "the" publication for the American entertainment industry. It is very highly recommended for all who work, study, or are affiliated with any segment of the entertainment field. For the sampled issue of 1990: (10 ¾ x 14 ¼ inches / 270 x 360 mm). Sampled issue for 1991: stapled tabloid format with spot and full color pages on coated paper stock (10 ¾ x 14 ½ inches / 270 x 370 mm).
DEPT: "50 Top-Grossing Films," complete financial data for United States exhibition; "Film Reviews," famed critical analyses; "Amusement Stock Quotations," weekly listing of 75+ stocks; "New York Sound Track," New York based newsbriefs; "Inside Stuff-Pictures," the lowdown on...; "International Sound Track," newsbriefs from London, Paris, Rome, Berlin, and Madrid Variety offices; "Television Reviews," weekly review of series and specials; "And Now a Word From...," human interest column by Carroll Carroll; "Notes from Broadcast Markets in the U.S. and Abroad," newsbriefs; "Concert Reviews," current events; "50 Top Selling LPs and Tapes," activity on the national retail level; "50 Best-Selling Pop Singles," from top 25 markets; "What's Up in the Music Business," newsbriefs; "New Acts," legitimate stage-cabaret reviews; "Night Club Reviews," reviews; "Shows Out of Town," reviews; "Shows on Broadway," reviews; "Casting News," newsbriefs; "Shows Abroad," overseas legitimate stage reviews; "Literati," book reviews; "Obituaries," *Variety*'s obit column, famed for its thoroughness. (12-77). "Newslines," film newsbriefs; "Executive Shuffle," changed positions; "Production Pulse," status; "Weekend Boxoffice Report," for USA and Canada; "Film Production," extensive project status section; "NY & LA Grosses," box office receipts; "NY Showcases," box office receipts; "Future Films," announced projects; "Vintage Variety," headlines of yesteryear; "Soundtrack," "Homevideo,"

"Variety Top 50 Video Titles," 'Variety's survey of rental transactions'; "Television, Cable & Radio," "Cable Roundup," "Broadcast Markets," "International," "Roundup," international news; "International Film Grosses," "International Update," newsbriefs by country; "Film Reviews," extensive detailed section; "New York Critics' Opinions," films; "London Critics' Opinions," films; "Washington, DC Critics' Opinions," films; "MPAA Ratings," for new releases; "Chi Critics' Opinions," Chicago film reviews; "Los Angeles Critics' Opinions," films; "Homevideo Review," "Television Reviews," network and cable; "Looking & Booking," live show status; "Night Club Reviews," "Legit," "Resident Legit Reviews," "Chatter in the Wings," stage news; "Broadway Grosses," "Season Boxoffice Totals," "Times Square Ticket Sales," "Road Grosses," "Broadway Legit Grosses," "London Shows," "Resident Legit Grosses," "Off-B'Way Schedule," Off-Broadway, New York; "Broadway Schedule," "Obituaries," reknowned rememberence section; "Literati," "Bookshelf," reviews; "Finance," excellent segment on entertainment monies; "Marketing," "Variety Buzz," news, rumors and rumblings column by Michael Fleming; "Letters." (8-8-90).
TYPL: "TV Short-Flights May Kill Off Pilots," "Fox Mum, Nite Not, on Hub Subpoenas," "No Strike Vs. cinemas, Hike in Film Credit Cheer Italo Industry," "ABC Radio Reppery to do El Foldo Act." (12-77). "Bond Bombshell: 007 Goes on the Block," "Newcomers Turn Completion Game into Risky Business," "Shelved Theatricals Find TV Life After Death," "Indies Labels Band Together for Anti-Counterfeit Unit," "The Bond Game: Vying For a Piece of the Risk." (8-8-90).
SCHL: Weekly, 75 pp.
SPAN: Dec 16, 1905+
LC: PN 2000.V3
DD: 790.2/05
ISSN: 0042-2738
ABST: --Film Literature Index (ISSN: 0093-6758)
--InfoBank
--Magazine Index
--Media Review Digest (ISSN: 0363-7778)
--Popular Magazine Review (ISSN: 0740-3763)

VE-Time Drama
May, 1945 - Jul, 1945//
SEE: DRAMA

✤ VELVET LIGHT TRAP
SUB: "Review of Cinema."
PUBL: University of Texas Press, 2100 Comal, Austin, TX 78722.
DESC: "The *Velvet Light Trap* is a journal devoted to investigating historical questions that illuminate the understanding of film. It publishes articles and interviews written with the highest scholarly standards yet accessible to a broad range of readers. The journal draws on a variety of theoretical and historiographic approaches from the humanities and social sciences. The journal welcomes any effort that will help foster the ongoing process of evaluation and negotiation in film history. The *Velvet Light Trap* will maintain its traditional commitment to the study of American film, occasionally expanding its scope to adjacent institutions, related media, and other national cinemas. The journal encourages both approaches and objects of study that have been neglected or excluded in past scholarship." This wonderful, theme-oriented film serial has issues such as, "The Fifties," "The Western," "Sex and Violence," "Rereading Hollywood," "RKO Radio Pictures," and "Hollywood Independents." Articles maintain high standards of scholarship and research, while remaining entertaining, and readable. Typical articles from 1991 include: "Film History in the 1980s," "Film, Politics, and Ideology: Reflections on Hollywood Film in the Age of Reagan," "'After It Happened...': The Battle to Present AIDS in Television Drama," "The Same Old Others: The Western, 'Lonesome Dove', and the Lingering Difficulty of Difference," "Retrospective Narratives in Hungarian Cinema: The 1980s 'Diary' Trilogy of Marta Meszaros," and "Woman Teaching Women: Teaching Film to Co-ed Classes in the 1980s." Numerous black/white graphics, primarily film product and production stills, grace this excellent survey of the cinema. Magazine format, two-color cover, glue-bound.
DEPT: None. (fall-89).
TYPL: "Working at the Fleischer Studio: An Annotated Interview with Myron Waldman," "The Reforming Fantasy: Recurrent Theme and Structure in American Studio Cartoons," "An Interview with Paul Glabicki," "Animation, Postmodernism, and MTV." (fall-89).
SCHL: Bimonthly (? - ?); Quarterly (? - ?); Semiannually (?+), 115 pp.
SPAN: Jun, 1971+
LC: PN 1993.V44
DD: 791.43/05
ISSN: 0149-1830
ABST: --Film Literature Index (ISSN: 0093-6758)

VENTURA LETTER, THE
SUB: "The newsletter for Ventura Users of North America."
SUB: "The magazine for Ventura Users of North America."
SUB: "The newspaper for Ventura Users of North America."
PUBL: Ventura Users of North America, 1 Heath Street West, Toronto, Ontario, Canada, M4V 1T2.
DESC: Ventura Users of North America (VUNA) was an association of destop publishers, graphic artists, and others who had purchased and were utilizing Xerox Ventura Publisher software. *The Ventura Letter* was the official publication of this group. "In this publication, produced by John and Daniel Wilson the founders of VUNA, topics will range from detailed discussions of techniques for using Ventura, to layout and design, typography, training, usage; and hard-

ware, software, and book reviews that Ventura users will find useful," For more than a year, *The Ventura Letter* was published as a newsletter, stapled magazine format using black ink on uncoated paper stock (8 x 10 ⅝ inches / 205 x 270 mm). Commencing with the August, 1988 issue, *The Ventura Letter* was published on coated paper, multicolor cover, in stapled magazine format on coated paper stock (8 ⅜ x 10 ¾ inches / 210 x 275 mm). Finally, in January of 1989, VUNA co-founder John Wilson announced that VUNA would become part of VPUG (The Ventura Publisher Users Group) and *The Ventura Letter* was absorbed by that group's publication, *Ventura Professional!*. Articles in both newsletter and magazine format were highly applicable to projects and problems at hand, providing clear examples of layout designs and graphic shortcuts.

DEPT: "Products," review; "Fonts," new product review; "Ventura-ing," product hints; "Users' Forum," BBS letters; "Chapter File Templates," available for purchase by Ventura software users. (8-88).

TYPL: "Instant Publishing," "Ventura Makeover," "Eight Ways to Convert Spreadsheets," "Video and Audio Based Training." (8-88).

SCHL: Bimonthly (Apr/May, 1987 - Jun/Jul, 1988); Monthly (Aug, 1988+), 30 pp.

SPAN: Apr/May, 1987 - Dec, 1988//
ABSORBED BY
--Ventura Professional!, Jan, 1989.

✦ VENTURA PROFESSIONAL!

SUB: "The how to magazine for Xerox Ventura Publisher professionals."

SUB: "Official newsletter of the Xerox Ventura Publisher User's Group."

PUBL: Ventura Publisher Users Group (VPUG), 7502 Aaron Place, San Jose, CA 95139.

DESC: User groups for specific computer hardware and/or software applications have become a necessity today. The Ventura Publisher Users Group is certainly one of the better self-help organizations, with an outstanding monthly that educates about, and encourages use of the desktop publishing software product known as Ventura Publisher. Articles are always accompanied by distinct graphic examples, at times designed to walk the user through the necessary steps, at times showing a variety of applications for a given mode. Absorption of the *Ventura Letter* from a similar Canadian group, Ventura Users of North America, boosted circulation in summer, 1989. In April, 1989, Xerox Corporation, publishers of Ventura Publisher software, merged their Systems Customer Support Center newsletter, *Xerox Pipeline*, with *Ventura Professional*, commencing with the July, 1989 issue. For those in desktop publishing who work with Ventura Publisher software, this is MUST reading, providing fresh ideas, insights, and applications of this popular software package. Also of note is the operation of an electronic bulletin board (BBS) by the VPUG, available to subscribers of the magazine. For sampled issue of 1990: stapled magazine format, black/white and full-color pages on coated paper stock (8 x 10 ½ inches / 205 x 265 mm).

DEPT: "Publisher Info," editorial; "Edit Mode," column by Lynn Walterick; "Graphics Mode," column by Toni Will-Harris and Daniel Will-Harris; "Show Column Guides," contributor profiles; "Dialog Box," letters; "Shelf Help," new publications reviewed column by Luther Sperberg; "INS Special Item," newsbrief IN-Serts column by Michael Copeland; "Options Menu," new product review; "Facing Pages View," column by George Sheldon; "Desk Menu," column by Harold Sims; "Help Menu," Q&A help; "Multi-Chapter," VPUG chapter listing. (11-89).

TYPL: "Ventura Publisher Compatibility Guide," "Workshop: Creating Table Templates." (11-89).

SCHL: Monthly, 70 pp.

SPAN: ?+
VARIES
--? - 1988 as Ventura Publishes.
ABSORBED
--Ventura Letter, The, Jan, 1989.
--Xerox Pipeline, Jul, 1989.

DD: 686 11

ISSN: 1046-9885

Ventura Publishes

? - 1988//
SEE: VENTURA PROFESSIONAL!

✦ VERBATIM

SUB: "The language quarterly."

PUBL: Verbatim, 5845 West 82nd St., #110, Indianapolis, IN 46278.

DESC: Talleyrand supposedly said that "Speech was given to man to disguise his thoughts." In *Verbatim*, the opposite is true. Here words are explored, examined and dissected down to their original root meanings, in the quest for clearer speech, writing, and understanding of the communication process. Issues are a cornucopia of ideas, and insights; and literate debate over the meaning, origination, and application of words. Editor Laurence Urdang clarified why *Verbatim* does not identify authors beyond name, and city of residence: "...we think it unfair to intimidate readers with short biographies that, in effect, are often likely to set forth authors either as unassailable authorities or as commentators who are unqualified to utter opinions about anything outside their fields. It is our position that the language is everyone's 'property', hence fair game for comment by anyone. We receive articles from all kinds of writers--academics, amateur and professional free-lance writers, people who are interested in language and concerned about it but who might never before have written anything for publication, casual critics, assiduous critics, carping critics, etc." It is this refreshing editorial stance which allows a current Texas prisoner to write about prison slang; to be followed by a discussion of "charisma," American geographic place names, and a passionate debate over "mistranslation" of certain Biblical words. The articles are a delight, but equally fascinating are the letters to the Editor, which are wisely interspersed between articles. Here are letters of passion; letters that joyfully announce discoveries of printed faux pas; of misapplication of words and their unintended meanings. For the professional writer, the dedicated researcher, the casual speaker, and all those who treasure the value of well-chosen words and application, *Verbatim* is a "must-read" publication. Highly recommended. Subscription cost for 1991 was $16.50 (£11.50) per year in the United States and Canada; $20.00 (£11.50) per year elsewhere. For the sampled issues of 1982 through 1991: brown ink on uncoated paper stock; with advertising; in stapled newsletter format (8 ½ x 11 inches / 215 x 280 mm).

DEPT: "Obiter Dicta," opinion and commentary; "Nota Bene," "Sic! Sic! Sic!," "Bibliographia," book reviews; "Epistolae," "Pairing Pairs," "Anglo-American Crossword Puzzle," "Miscellanea." (summer-82). "Sic! Sic! Sic!," faux pas of the mighty and famous; "Epistolae," letters to the editor; "Bibliographia," book reviews; "Obiter Dicta," opinion and commentary; "Miscellanea," miscellaneous news items. (autumn-91).

TYPL: "Holy Water, Jeans and Trade Unionists," "The Christening," "Who Needs Enemies...?," "The Misplaced Stop," "698 Japanese Loanwords in English." (summer-82). "Speaking of the Unmentionables," "Wrenches in the Gorse and Bracken," "Cross-Talk," "Texas Prison Slang," "Unraveling the American Place-Name Cover." (autumn-91).

SCHL: Quarterly, 35 pp.
SPAN: 1974+
ISSN: 0162-0932

✤ VIA SATELLITE

SUB: "The magazine of satellite broadcasting."
PUBL: Phillips Publishing, Inc., 7811 Montrose Rd., Rockville, MD 20850.
DESC: Satellites have become an integral part of the technology, language, process and profit of mass communication services. *Via Satellite* provides an interesting forum whereby new technology is explored, but it is especially important for its articles on the applications of satellite service technology. It is in the applications side of satellite usage that the reader is treated to the diversity of communication satellites, and the quickly evolving state of the industry. Early issues contained two to three articles per issue, evolving to a current seven to ten articles per issue. *Via Satellite* is an excellent resource (especially for international developments) for any organization working in the field of satellite communication. Magazine format with color graphics (8 ⅜ x 10 ⅞ inches / 210 x 275 mm).
DEPT: "Viewpoint," "Calendar," "Letter to the Editor," "News," "Contracts," signed for satellite services; "Programming," "People," "Technology," "Services,"
"Publications," books of note on satellite services. (4-87). "Editor's Note," "News," "International," "Calendar," "Contracts," "Technology." (12-89). "Editor's Note," editorial column by Scott Chase; "Calendar," "News," "Focus on Europe," "International," "Transmissions," "Services," "Satellite Circuit," 'A round-up of firms making news in the satellite industry' column by David Bross; "Contracts," "People," "Technology." (2-91).

TYPL: "Interview With RCA Americom Prsident, Andrew T. Hospodor," "Distant Television Signals and Copyright." (4-87). "Top Gun Meets Broadcast News: A New Horizon in SNG," "The VNR Revolution: Satellite-Delivered Public Relations Gains Acceptance," "Evolving Technology: Spar Aerospace--Canada's Satellite Pioneer." (12-89). "The European VSAT Scene: Working Through Familiar Problems," "Electron Tubes Serving KU-Band Space Communications," "History Lesson: Even After 25 Years, Pioneer 6 Keeps on Ticking," "Euromergermania: Keeping a Flow Chart on Competition," "Lost in Space: International Satellite Communications Policy." (2-91).

SCHL: Monthly, 90 pp.
SPAN: Jan, 1986+
DD: 384 11
ISSN: 1041-0643

Victorian Periodicals Newsletter

Jan, 1968 - Winter, 1978//
(ISSN: 0049-6189)
SEE: VICTORIAN PERIODICALS REVIEW

✤ VICTORIAN PERIODICALS REVIEW

PUBL: Research Society for Victorian Periodicals, Southern Illinoise University at Edwardsville, English Dept., Box 43, Edwardsville, IL 62026-1001.
DESC: "The editors of *VPR* invite articles or notes with a historical, critical, or bibliographical emphasis dealing with the editorial and publishing history of Victorian periodicals (newspapers, magazines or reviews) or with the importance of periodicals for an understanding of the history and culture of Victorian Britain. While the central focus is on Great Britain and Ireland during the Victorian era, *VPR* is also interested in work dealing with the press in other parts of the Empire and in material relating to the earlier decades of the nineteenth century and to the Edwardian period." This is a fascinating typewritten periodical; limited graphics.
DEPT: "Letter to the Editor," "Book Reviews," "Announcements." (winter-85).
TYPL: "Thackeray in Australia: The Periodical Press," "Class vs. Gender Identification in the 'Englishwomans Review' of the 1880s," "The Fate of a Young Churchillian Conceit: 'The War on the Nile' Letters and the 'Morning Post.'" (winter-85).
SCHL: Quarterly, 30 pp.

SPAN: Jan, 1968+
VARIES
--Jan, 1968 - Winter, 1978 as Victorian Periodicals Newsletter (ISSN: 0049-6189).
LC: PN 5124.P4V52
DD: 052
ISSN: 0709-4698
ABST: --America, History and Life (ISSN: 0002-7065)
--Historical Abstracts. Part A. Modern History Abstracts. (ISSN: 0363-2712)
--Historical Abstracts. Part B. Twentieth Century Abstracts. (ISSN: 0363-2725)
--Index to Book Reviews in the Humanities (ISSN: 0073-5892)
--MLA International Bibliography of Books & Articles on the Modern Languages and Literatures (ISSN: 0024-8215)
--Recently Published Articles (ISSN: 0145-5311)
--Reference Sources (ISSN: 0163-3546)

✤ VIDEO

PUBL: Link House Magazines, Robert Rogers House, New Orchard Poole, Dorset BH15 1LU, England.
DESC: [*Video and Audio-Visual Review*]: This 50-page British publication (primarily devoted to advertising) has several good articles per issue about television and related AV development. It also reviews BBC productions and films scheduled for broadcast. Of special note is a continuing survey of video equipment lines (manufacturers, prices, and specifications).
DESC: This British periodical emphasizing the non-broadcast side of video production has numerous news and feature articles concerning independent production work, studios, and new technology in Great Britain. Because the focus remains the non-broadcast production video, there is a lack of material concerning television operations. Good news reports on industry trends.
DEPT: "Perspective," newsbriefs; "Publications," video programs and films reviewed with data for rental or sale; "Performance," technical review; "Planner," upcoming video events; "Periscope," world video newsbriefs; "Products," reviews. (7-76). "Diary," "News," "Equipment," "Statistics," "Industry," "Around the Studios," "Broadcasting." (4-81).
TYPL: "Television Lighting Techniques," "Video Statistics: Vital or Not,?" "TV Camera Pick-Up Tubes," "Television Projectors Surveyed." (7-76). "Is Colour Film Stable?," "Rank Phicom Video--The Inside Story," "The Making of VLP '79," "Videotext--A Service in Search of an Audience." (4-81).
SCHL: Monthly, 50 pp.
SPAN: Nov, 1974+
VARIES
--Nov, 1974 - May, 1978 as Video and Audio-Visual Review.
ISSN: 0141-9013

Video
1980 - 1983?//
(ISSN: 0276-0835)
SEE: VIDEO EIGHTIES MAGAZINE

Video
Winter, 1978 - Aug?, 1987//
(ISSN: 0147-8907)
SEE: VIDEO MAGAZINE

✤ VIDEO AGE INTERNATIONAL

SUB: "The business journal of television."
SUB: "The business journal of television: broadcasting, cable-TV, pay-TV, home video."
PUBL: TV Trade Media Inc., 216 E. 75th St., NY 10021.
DESC: This is a first-class publication for the business of developing programming material for the international television market. While *Video Age International* does provide some articles on developing technology, the emphasis is the program producer and new product available for international use. Articles on technology explore ways that current or future programming might adapt to the new communications media. Of special interest is a listing each issue of "People In the News," listing names of individuals appearing in this issue, and is a most helpful guide.
DEPT: "People in the News," name list; "Editors' Letter," "International Update," newsbriefs; "International Profile," "International Viewpoint," guest column; "International Meetings," "International Forum," letters. (4-82).
TYPL: "Bernard Chevry's Success Linked with Television Market," "U.S. TV Season, Coproduction Deals at MIP-TV," "West German Television Struggles Over the Old Order," "Cable Television Boosts Teleproduction Growth," "Common Standard for Satellite Broadcast Sought." (4-82). "Fall Receptive to Home Video," "Basic Business is Western Cable Show's Theme," "Thirty Firms Vie for Private TV in Spain," "Far East TV Marked by Expansion." (10-83).
SCHL: Seven issues per year (Jan, Mar, Apr, May, Aug, Sep, Oct), 70 pp.
SPAN: Jan, 1981+
WITH SUPPLEMENT
--Video Licensing (ISSN: 0882-2638), ? - ?
LC: PN 1992.V53
DD: 384.55/4/05
ISSN: 0278-5013

✤ VIDEO ALERT

PUBL: Baker & Taylor Books, a Grace Company, 8140 North Lehigh Ave., Morton Grove, IL 60053.

DESC: *Video Alert* is "...a monthly announcement newsletter featuring music audio and videos in entertainment and instructional categories, for adults and children." Printed in duotone magazine format, this serial showcases audio and video material distributed by the Baker & Taylor Company for sale to libraries and retail establishments. Although primarily a catalog of current releases, readers will discover a host of accompanying articles which are witty and thoughtful pieces on available video product. For the 1990 sampled issue: stapled magazine format, numerous black/white and duotone graphics with full-color cover, all on coated paper stock (8 ½ x 11 inches / 215 x 280 mm).
DEPT: "Baker & Taylor's New Video Beat," "Editor's Picks," "Instructional New Releases," "Collector's Corner," "Recent Reviews and Awards," "Special Order," unique video titles; "New Releases," "Family Features," "Family New Releases," "New Audio Releases," "Video and Audio Bestsellers." (6/7-90).
TYPL: "Roger is Everything You Want in a Documentary... and 'Moore'," "Steven Spielberg's Soaring Romantic Fantasy Takes Flight on Video," "Michael Caine on the Art and Heart of Movie Acting." (6/7-90).
SCHL: Twelve issues per year, 70 pp.
SPAN: Jan, 1987+

Video and Audio-Visual Review
Nov, 1974 - May, 1978//
SEE: VIDEO

✢ VIDEO ANSWERS
SUB: "What to buy; How to use it."
PUBL: Bushfield House, Orton Centre, Peterborough PE2 0UW, England.
DESC: From the publishers of *Practical Photography* magazine comes this home video consumer publication, "...the magazine that answers all your buying and technique questions." It compares a wide variety of consumer video equipment, with considered thought given to application by the home videographer. Products are often showcased in large, full-color displays, with additional insets for hidden features. "Likes" and "Dislikes" boxes provide bottom-line evaluations. Other feature articles discuss various video techniques; from shooting video of children's events to lens converters to future trends. The ongoing "Buyer's Directory" provides detailed technical listing of certain video equipment. For sampled issue of 1990: editorial content consisted of mixture of black ink, spot- and full-color pages (including full-color cover) on coated paper stock (8 ¼ x 11 ¾ inches / 210 x 300 mm).
DEPT: "Newsline," 'The latest hot gossip from the world of video'; "Group Test," video testbench; "Buying Answers," video buyers guide; "Helpline," Q&A column by Eugene Trundle; "Picture Search," new videotape releases; "Jargon Answers," 'Our regular layperson's guide to things technical in the video world'; "Reader's Playback," letters. (1/2-90).
TYPL: "Fast Forward," "Get Converted!," "Child's Play," "Three-Legged Land." (1/2-90).
SCHL: Bimonthly, 85 pp.
SPAN: ?+
ISSN: 0957-9273

✢ VIDEO BUSINESS
PUBL: International Thomson Retail Press, Inc., 345 Park Avenue South, New York, NY 10010.
DESC: For retailers and distributors of home videos, *Video Business* reports on the status of the video cassette sale and rental industry each month. It is a dynamic market in an almost constant state of flux, and this periodical provides good coverage of store operation, industry trends, and the changing tastes of the American public. The majority of each issue is devoted to the numerous videocassettes coming into the market each month from motion picture exhibition, independent productions, and foreign distribution. As no retailer could possibly stock all of the new releases, *Video Business* provides an excellent service in listing what is available, to individual owner/operator. This is an important serial for the videocassette industry, and especially so for the independent video businessman or woman. Magazine format with numerous color advertisements. Sample issue for 1989: (8 ⅛ x 10 ⅞ inches / 205 x 275 mm).
DEPT: "Our View," comment; "Offscreen," commentary column by Seth Goldstein; "The Scoop," commentary column by Robert Gerson; "Vidbits," newsbriefs column by Glenn Kenny; "Screenplay," latebreaking news; "New Gear," hardware; "Moving Up," what's hot in videocassette titles; "New Releases," "Power Broker," video store management column by Marc Berman and John Gaffney; "Issues & Answers," "Accessories," "The Tape Scene," "Profile," corporate profile; "Publicity," column by Richard Ziff; "Music Video Business," "Video Briefs," newsbriefs. (2-86). "Opening Shots," editorial; "News Wire," newsbriefs; "Late Breaks," newsbriefs; "People," "Box Office," "Chronicle," "Retail Roundup," column by Anne S. Torpey; "Retailer of the Week," "The Informer," upcoming releases column by James Mitchell; "Budgeting," "Substitutes," creative retailing; "Buyer's Corner," "Tipsheet," reviews; "New Releases," chart; "Promo Tips," "Forecaster," column by Paul Sweeting; "Profile," "Marketing," "Shop Talk," "Back Page," comment. (1-22-89).
TYPL: "Standing in the Shadows," "An Earful of Video," "Serials," "Walking the X-Rated Tightrope." (2-86). "LIVE Execs Move to Calm Wall St. Fears," "Batman Scrambles Year-End Picture," "Two Settle in Paramount Local Ad Suit," "Vestron: No Deal on Store," "Land Before It's Time," "Nestle Sponsors Children's Video." (1-22-89).
SCHL: Monthly, 50 pp.
SPAN: Jan, 1981+

LC: HD 9697.V543 U546
DD: 621.388/33
ISSN: 0279-571x

✤ VIDEO BUYER
SUB: "The guide to collectable films on video."
PUBL: Focus Magazines, Greencoat House, Francis St., London SW1P 1DG England.
DESC: Publisher and editor, Chris Adam-Smith, has produced a very up-beat magazine/catalog of recent videos for the British market. With full-color pages, *Video Buyer* combines three resources into one bimonthly publication. At the start of each issue are a half-dozen articles concerning film stars and theme videos: next are color-coded pages for new video releases in Music, Comedy, Children's Films, Drama Action & Adventure, Sci-Fi & Horror, and Sport & General Interest categories. Finally, a large 25 page section lists some 500 current and past releases available to the home consumer. Full color pages allow for printing sample videotape covers, or production stills. Of special note is the "Top 30 Sell-through Video Chart," providing data on sales movement of individual titles in the UK. For the sampled issue of 1990: beautiful layout design with dynamic full-color pages throughout on coated paper stock (8 ¼ x 11 ¾ inches / 210 x 300 mm).
DEPT: "Letters," 'Your say, your way!'; "New Releases," full color section of new videos in music, comedy, children's films, drama, action and adventure, sci fi and horror, and sport and general interest; "Children's Competition," contest; "Features Competition," contest; "Blob Competition," contest; "Readers Survey," "Competition Winners," from previous contests; "Callanetics Competition," contest; "Video Buyer," large 25 page section on current and older releases. (3/4-90).
TYPL: "King of Terror," "Do the Right Swing," "Harrison Ford," "Beware the Blob." (3/4-90).
SCHL: Bimonthly, 100 pp.
SPAN: Nov/Dec, 1989+
ISSN: 0957-8552

✤ VIDEO CAMERA
PUBL: Reed Prospect Magazines, Prospect House, 9-13 Ewell Rd., Cheam, Surrey SM1 4QQ, England.
DESC: Many home consumer video publications contain four to six feature articles in a given issue: *Video Camera* published twenty-two feature articles in a single bimonthly issue (Mar/Apr, 1990). There is probably a feature article of interest to any reader in a given issue. In the sample issue reviewed, topics ranged from still video cameras to wireless radio microphones, how to utilize professional editing suites, latest video tube technology, new 3D video camcorders, techniques of animation, miniature TV monitors, producing comedies, and evaluating videotape. Of special note is "Picturesque Parade," a calendar of upcoming British events for videographers. This is a quality video consumer publication from the publishers of *Amateur Photographer* and *What Camera?* For the sampled issue of 1990: perfect-bound magazine format with editorial mixture of black ink, spot- and full-color pages (including cover) on coated paper stock (8 ¼ x 11 ¾ inches / 210 x 300 mm).
DEPT: "News," extensive section on latest video newsbriefs and products; "Test," new video product. (3/4-90).
TYPL: "ION Points to the Future," "Waiting for 3D," "Interviewing and Getting Your Message Across," "Going Public." (3/4-90).
SCHL: Bimonthly, 90 pp.
SPAN: May/Jun, 1989?+

✤ VIDEO CAPSULE
PUBL: The Salvation Army, Office of Media Ministries, PO Box 2608, Dallas, TX 75221.
DESC: This is a short descriptive newsletter of activities of the Office of Media Ministries for The Salvation Army, Southern Territory. It describes video shoots, and staff news, but primarily reviews new videocassettes received and available to those within the ministry. Sampled issue of 1988 consisted of newsletter format, black ink editorial content with spot blue and red-color ink cover on uncoated paper stock (8 ½ x 11 inches / 215 x 280 mm).
DEPT: "From the Director's Chair," commentary; "New Videos," reviews; "Comments From the Field," users comment on videotapes. (Vol 6, #2-88).
TYPL: "Visions of Zimbabwe," "Faraway Places," "Through the Eyes of a Star." (Vol 6, #2-88).
SCHL: Quarterly?, 4 pp.
SPAN: ?+?

Video Cassettes Newsletter
Mar, 1971 - Feb, 1972//
SEE: VIDEOCASSETTE AND CATV NEWSLETTER

Video Cassettes; the Systems, the Market, the Future
? - ?//
SEE: VIDEOCASSETTE AND CATV NEWSLETTER

✤ VIDEO CHOICE
SUB: "The leading review magazine for the video enthusiast."
PUBL: Connell Communications, Inc., 331 Jaffrey Rd., Peterborough, NH 03458.
DESC: A promotional advertisement stated: "In the next year, you are going to buy or rent lots of videotapes. And most of the tapes you buy will cost you more than $20, some as much as $75. That's why you need *Video Choice*. *Video Choice* reviews and rates hundreds of

videotapes, letting you know which tapes are worth buying or renting. Avoid one bad buy through *Video Choice*, and you've paid for your subscription." This delightful publication focuses on only one item; new videocassettes on the market in either rental or purchase availability. Reviews cover a broad range of topics, with very detailed information about each new release. In the sampled issue for 1988, some 60-plus reviews were published under the following categories: "Business," "Children's," "Classics," "Documentary," "Education," "Exercise & Health," "Fine Arts," "Food & Wine," "Games," "Hobby," "Home," "Nature," "New Age," "Parenting," "Sports," and "Travel." As a different promotional put it, "*Video Choice* reviews and rates these hard-to-find tapes that are guaranteed to delight, amuse, instruct, inspire, teach, and illuminate." For the sampled issue of 1988: perfect-bound magazine format, full-color throughout on coated paper stock (8 x 10 ¾ inches / 205 x 270 mm).
DEPT: "Input/Output," 'Our video expert will answer any question in his crusade to wipe out video intimidation' column by Jim Teates; "Video Hotline," 'All the latest on the video front' column by Dorothy Rosa; "Collector's Classics," column by Tracey McIntire; "The Video Photographer," column by Taumas Jacobs; "Industry Insight," column by Paul Taublieb; "The Video Enthusiast," commentary column by Jeff Edmonds; "Watch Word," editorial column by Deborah Navas. (4-88).
TYPL: "Sybervision: The Method," "Monitor TVs: The New Wave," "Can Yoga Make You Fit?," "The Art of Fly Fishing," "Building a Classic Film Collection." (4-88).
SCHL: Monthly, 105 pp.
SPAN: Mar, 1988+?
ISSN: 0896-2871

✦ VIDEO EIGHTIES MAGAZINE
SUB: "Art & communications."
PUBL: Video 80, 299 Cortland St., San Francisco, CA 94110.
DESC: *Video 80* magazine is difficult to describe. It is published quarterly under a license from the San Francisco International Video Festival, and concentrates on the "art" in the video medium. Articles and newsbriefs also deal with computers, computer animation, 3-D, the origins of life, stock market options in the video field, laser weaponry used by the Department of Defense, and a legal column concerning video technology and programming. It's a fascinating periodical for anyone interested in the non-broadcast side of video production and programming. In fall, 1982 *Video 80* went from a tri-annual to a quarterly publication, and from large tabloid to magazine format size.
DEPT: "Dr. Telecom," knows all and covers all in the video and non-video field; "Field Report," special news report; "Video Lawyer," comment; "For Immediate Release," newsbriefs; "Art Related News," newsbriefs. (spring-82). "For Immediate Release," "New Media," "Field Report," "Viewed," "Image Access," "Suite Talk," "Art Related Notes." (fall-82).
TYPL: "Noreshi Towai," "Artificial Metabolism," "Ronald Reagan: The Politics of Image," "The Romantic Image," "Bay Area Video Showcase," "Post-Production Techniques," "An Introduction to Computer Animation," "The Optical Videodisc and New Media Forms." (spring-82). "Erotic Amateurs," "Fassbinder," "Will There be Condominiums in Data Space?." (fall-82).
SCHL: Triannual (1980 - spring, 1982), Quarterly (fall, 1982+), 46 pp.
SPAN: 1980+?
VARIES
--1980 - 1983? as Video (ISSN: 0276-0835).
--? - ? as Video 80.

Video 80
? - ?//
SEE: VIDEO EIGHTIES MAGAZINE

✦ VIDEO INFO
SUB: "The newsletter that links professional and consumer video."
PUBL: Popular Video, Inc., P.O. Box 2269, G.P.O., New York, NY 10001.
DESC: This is an eight-page typewritten newsletter designed to keep subscribers up to date with fast-breaking news in the professional and home video industry. The sample issue had fewer news items than other newsletters in its field. *Video Info* has clearly defined sections of "News & Views," (2 pp), "Software Sources," (2 pp), and a "Hardware Report" (2 pp).
DEPT: "News & Views," newsbriefs; "Software Sources," new videotape releases; "Hardware Report," equipment briefs; "Back Page," misc. (6-79).
TYPL: "Video Evolution and Revolution Felt at Summer CES; LVR and New Disc Appear," "Sony Betascan System: A Threat to VHS?," "Public Television Library Sales are Up." (6-79).
SCHL: Monthly, 8 pp.
SPAN: Jun, 1979?+?

✦ VIDEO INSIDER
SUB: "Confidential weekly news for the video retailer, distributor and supplier."
PUBL: Video Insider, 223 Conestoga Rd., Wayne, PA 19087.
DESC: For the videocassette retailer, *Video Insider* is "must" reading to stay informed about new releases, trends in retail operation, regulation, distribution, marketing, and ascertaining the fickle taste of the American videocassette rental market. The newsweekly provides a host of news items, retailer/distributor news, and extensive reviews and charts for videocassette sales and rentals in categories of Original Programming, Children's, Music, and Adult video. In one sampled issue, topics ranged from the Consumer Electronics Show, to the anticipated summer avalanche of videocassette

releases and a new development in double-coated videotape, to a reader's forum on the question of how theatrical hits affect videostore rentals. Of special note are excellent analyses accompanying the "Top 30" charts for best rentals and sales. These one-column evaluations provide the video store owner with a second opinion of the videocassettes' potential with the store's particular clientele. Included are prices, cut-off dates for ordering, street date (first day availability to public), and informed analysis as to market suitability. Magazine format (8 ½ x 10 ⅞ inches / 215 x 275 mm); coated paper stock.
DEPT: "Overview," editorial; "Flashmakers," late breaking news; "Breaking News," "Marketing Tip," "New Product Merchandiser," "Calendar," "Insider Pix," 'A summary of titles of merit listed by order cut-off date'; "New Releases," reviews; "National Top Thirty," week's sale and rental chart; "Analysis," of weeks best selling/renting videos; "Original Programming," column by Cindy Spielvogel; "Children's Video," column by Loretta MacAlpine; "Video Music," column by Barry Gutman; "Adult Video," column by Charles Sands; "Promotion Indicator," marketing ideas; "Speak Out," survey; "Movers & Shakers," personnel newsbriefs. (6-4-90).
TYPL: "Prerecorded Video Scarce at CES," "MGM/UA Tries Lower Prices for Rental and Sell-Through," "Double Coating Sets New Blank Tape Standard," "Are You Ready for Summer?," "Cool Cat Comes to CBS/Fox Video." (6-4-90).
SCHL: Weekly, 40 pp.
SPAN: 1983+
ISSN: 1046-0837

✤ VIDEO MAGAZINE

SUB: "The #1 magazine of home video."
SUB: "World's biggest video publication."
PUBL: Reese Publishing Co., 460 West 34th St., New York, NY 10001.
DESC: Designed for the booming home video market, *Video* magazine covers the breadth of consumer video equipment, trends, and techniques in a spritely, full-color layout design. In a spring, 1991 trade press interview, publisher Eric C. Schwartz said of his magazine; "It's very important that we have a clear sense of the video buyer and where he is in the marketplace. We want to be recognized as the publication that spots the trends, and be ready to report on the trends. Our readership has a love affair with the technology. Just like *Car & Driver* readers are passionate about reading about the newest Porsche 911, our readers are passionate about the new video technology." Equipment tops the list of feature articles, with new technology and equipment comparisons being among the most popular topics. Creative graphics enhance sometimes difficult technical concepts, and a crisp, clear writing style certainly aids understanding. Considerable attention is also paid to new and current videotapes available to the home consumer, providing reviews, evaluations, and production stills from selected tapes. Extensive film advertising points to the impact of this publication in the video community. For 1988 sampled issue: full-color layout magazine format, all on coated paper stock (8 x 10 ½ inches / 200 x 265 mm).
DEPT: "News & Views," newsbriefs; "Top 15 Bestselling Titles," "Directory," of new cassette releases; "Reviews," longer reviews of new cassettes; "VideoTests," very detailed comparisons; "Channel One," editorial; "Feedback," letters; "New Products," "Videogram," newsbriefs; "Video Programmer," comment; "TV Den," understanding equipment; "Arcade Alley," review; "Videology," 'Exploring the science of video;' "Fine Tuning," 'Your video questions answered.' (4-82). "Reviews," new videotape product; "Kidvid," videotape review; "Directory," 'The latest releases on tape and disc'; "Videotests," extensive lab/consumer reviews; "Channel One," editorial; "Feedback," 'Letters from readers'; "Late News," column by Stan Pinkwas; "Gazette," column by Ira Robbins; "New Products," column by Lou Kesten; "Technically Speaking," "West Coast Notes," column by Wolf Schneider; "Audio Input," "Q&A," column by Roderick Woodcock; "Off the Air," commentary. (6-88).
TYPL: "Rock Around the Clock," "How to Tape Stereo and Simulcast Cable Programs," "Is Video Dangerous?," "Secrets of the New Anti-Piracy Technology," "Putting More Pay Into Pay-TV," "Oscar Winners Revisited." (4-82). "Timeshifting by Telephone," "Pint-Size Pictures," "The Steadycam." (6-88).
SCHL: Quarterly (Winter, 1978 - ?); Monthly (Aug, 1982+), 135 pp.
SPAN: Winter, 1978+
VARIES
--Winter, 1978 - Aug?, 1987 as Video (ISSN: 0147-8907).
LC: TK 6630.A1V49
DD: 778.59/9/05
ISSN: 1044-7288

VIDEO MANAGEMENT

SUB: "The bi-weekly newsletter for users and producers of video hardware, programs, and services." (May, 1979 - Jul, 1980).
SUB: "The bi-weekly newspaper for users and producers of video hardware, programs and services."
SUB: "The news magazine for the professional video manager."
SUB: "The newsmonthly for organizational television."
SUB: "Management insights for the decision maker." (? - Aug, 1989).
SUB: "Strategies, applications and solutions." (Sep, 1989+).
PUBL: Knowledge Industry Publications, 701 Westchester Ave., White Plains, NY 10604.
DESC: This serial went through a number of transformations during its 12 year publication life. In the late 1970s (as *VU Marketplace*), this periodical was primarily a 14-page newsletter emphasizing the home and corporate video field. By the early 1980s (as *Video Users Marketplace*), there was a decided shift to the corpo-

rate field, with an emphasis on technical and business developments. Within a short time, *Video Users Marketplace* became simply *Video User*, and in April, 1984 experienced another title change to *Video Manager*. This latter title more clearly defined the function of this tabloid-size newspaper; that of serving the needs of corporate, studio, and professional video management. Later, the publication was redesigned to standard magazine size and format, with imaginative use of color and graphics. In recognition of the expanding role of outside services, one last title change (September, 1989) was made to *Video Management*, but changes within the field occurred too quickly and cessation took place in December, 1989, with a merger into sister publication, *AV Video*. Group Publisher Dan Boucher, in shutting down the serial, noted: "We've watched the pure video manager enter the realm of endangered species. Today, video managers call themselves corporate communicators, working in video, slides, audio, multimedia and computer graphics. We've found that the video department is not immune to the downsizing going on in corporate America. We've seen the identification of video departments in the minds of many upper-level managers transformed from 'critical communications hub' to 'capital-intensive, non-revenue-generating drain.'" Final format was magazine size, numerous graphics.

DEPT: "Classified," "Hardware," reviews; "Services," reviews; "Video Resources," software reviews; "Financials," newsbriefs; "People in Video," briefs; "Shoots and Edits," work in progress at different shops; "Meetings and Events," upcoming. (4-30-79). "VU Video Scans," "People," "Facilities," "Shoots," "Events," "ITVA News," "Programs," "Videoconferencing," "Resources," "Changing Channels," "Marketplace." (4-84). "Penstripes," editorial; "News & Views," newsbriefs; "Keeping Posted," upcoming events; "Kaleidoscope," column by Ken Jurek; "Corporate Perspectives," column by Richard Van Deusen; "Off the Shelf," first look at new equipment; "Final Cut," commentary. (9-89).

TYPL: "Matsushita Introduces Disc System at ITA," "Video Bidders List in Preparation," "Users Like One-Inch Ampex VTR; Complain About Reverse Slo-Mo," "Looking Hard at Hardware: Cameras." (4-30-79). "Broadcast- Industrial Gap Narrowing as Money Frees Up for Corporate Video," "Many Problems, Few Answers Generated by Equipment Failure, Managers Agree," "Closing the Loop: Evaluating Programs for Survival." (4-84). "Transcoding: The Format Connection," "The Free-Lancer's Bill of Rights," "Catering to Corporate." (9-89).

SCHL: Biweekly (? - ?); Monthly [except combined Jul/Aug issue] (? - ?); Monthly (? - Dec, 1989), 70 pp.

SPAN: 1978 - Dec, 1989//
VARIES
--1978 - ? as Video Users Marketplace.
--May, 1979 - Jul, 1980 as VU Marketplace (ISSN: 0149-6832).
--Aug, 1980 - Mar, 1984 as Video User (ISSN: 0273-7817).
--Apr, 1984 - Aug, 1989 as Video Manager (ISSN: 0747-3745).
ABSORBED BY
--AV Video (ISSN: 0747-1335), Dec, 1989.

DD: 658 11
ISSN: 1047-7713

Video Manager

Apr, 1984 - Aug, 1989//
(ISSN: 0747-3745)
SEE: VIDEO MANAGEMENT

Video Marketplace

Oct/Nov, 1987 - Jun/Jul, 1990//
(ISSN: 0895-2892)
SEE: MOVIE MARKETPLACE

✤ VIDEO MONTHLY

SUB: "The new video magazine with free 32 page video catalogue."
PUBL: Odhams Leisure Group, Denington Road, Wellinborough, Northamptonshire NN8 2PY, England.
DESC: Debuting in March of 1990, this British monthly serial showcases recent motion picture product presently being released on videocassette for the British consumer public. This new publication has the typical features of a number of other magazines of this type, but reviews are commendable for their clarity, plot synopses, and thoughtful consideration of what the motion picture means in terms of entertainment for the reader. Of special note is the subsection, "It's a Wrap," that gives the "bottom line" evaluation of the motion picture release. For the sampled issue of 1990: full-color pages and cover throughout in a dynamic layout design on coated paper stock in stapled magazine format (8 ¼ x 11 ¾ inches / 210 x 300 mm).
DEPT: "Video Views," 'A selection of the very latest movies on video viewed and reviewed for content, style and value for money!'; "Film Talk," 'Ken Ferguson with all of the latest news and gossip from Hollywood to Pinewood'; "New Releases," 'The new videos in your rental store together with the latest and best on sell-through'; "Interview." (3-90).
TYPL: "A Quiet Life in The 'Burbs," "No Fly Like an Old Fly!," "Far Away in a Land of Dreams...". (3-90).
SCHL: Monthly, 45 pp.
SPAN: Mar, 1990+
ISSN: 0958-1766

Video Movies

Mar, 1984 - ?, 1984//
(ISSN: 0742-8111)
SEE: VIDEO TIMES

✧ VIDEO NEWS AND USED

SUB: "A monthly magazine for professional video equipment users."
PUBL: Castlestone Publishing Ltd., 3214 Wharton Way, Mississauga, Ontario L4X 2C1 Canada.
DESC: At the front of the April, 1990 issue was this publisher's statement concerning the objective of this serial: "To share knowledge with professional video equipment users. To provide a medium for instructing, advising, announcing and advertising. To generally provide a communication tool at the grass roots level of the professional video equipment industry. To maintain an easy to read format, filled with quality and useful information. To always place the readers' needs first by listening to their requests for knowledge and endeavoring to fulfill them accordingly." This year-old publication for the Canadian video industry shows great promise as it moves through the inevitable stages of growth in advertisers, and thus in editorial content. The monthly is primarily for producers and production houses interested in emerging trends in equipment, and maintenance of same. For the sampled issue of 1990: stapled magazine format, editorial content consisting of black ink with blue spot-color application on coated paper stock, with certain special sections on color uncoated paper stock in black ink (8 ¼ x 11 inches / 210 x 280 mm).
DEPT: "Publisher's Page," "Profile," Canadian production facility. (4-90).
TYPL: "NAB Product Report," "JVC Discontinues 3/4," "Timebase Correctors and Frame Synchronizers," "Hi Fidelity Audio on Videotape." (4-90).
SCHL: Monthly, 35 pp.
SPAN: May, 1989?+
ISSN: 0847-4990

✧ VIDEO PROPHILES

SUB: "The magazine for serious video users."
PUBL: IDG Communications, 80 Elm St., Peterborough, NH 03458.
DESC: Publisher/editorial director, Marjorie Costello, in the June, 1991 issue told readers; "Welcome to the premiere issue of *Video PROphiles*, the magazine for serious video users. *Video PROphiles* is the first publication specifically designed to answer the needs of up-and-coming video professionals and dedicated hobbyists. ... We intend to provide you with information on equipment that's right for your needs--both professional and consumer products. *Video PROphiles* will offer hands-on tips to improve your technique, as well as objective evaluations of the latest gear. That means camcorders, VCRs, editing devices, computer equipment, sound gear and all the accessories that set you apart from the mass-market consumer. Not only will *Video PROphiles* bridge the gap between the worlds of consumer and professional video, it will also cover the merging technologies of video and computers--on all platforms. Together, we'll make our way through the multimedia maze. On the business side, we'll seek out inspirational success stories of video entrepreneurs who've made it big. We'll show how their efforts can help your business prosper." Published by IDG Communications/Peterborough, Inc., a successful publisher of over 145 varied publications, *Video PROphiles* has the quality elements required to become a reading staple of this emerging group of "video professionals and dedicated hobbyists." The premiere issue displayed a dynamic layout design with many full-color photographs throughout. Stapled magazine format on coated paper stock (8 x 10 ¾ inches / 200 x 275 mm).
DEPT: "From the PROphiles," editorial/publisher column by Marjorie Costello; "PRO Bono," column by Nolan K. Bushnell; "News PROphiles," 'Reports and updates from around the globe'; "Product PROphiles," 'A roundup of the latest noteworthy gear'; "Producer PROphiles," column by Judith Morrison; "Screening PROphiles," column by Gregory P. Fagan; "Future Tech," column by David Ranada; "Close Focus," column by Michael Heiss; "Editing Suite," column by Christin Hardman; "The Five-Minute Videographer," column by Marjorie Costello; "Field Tests," testbench reviews. (6-91).
TYPL: "Camcorder Buyer's Guide," "Why Multimedia?," "Ca$h-cording: Money for Something," "Videodisc Wizardry," "Speaker, Speaker, on the Wall." (6-91).
SCHL: Bimonthly, 90 pp.
SPAN: Jun, 1991+
ISSN: 1055-6060

✧ VIDEO REVIEW

SUB: "The world authority on home video."
SUB: "The world authority on consumer video."
SUB: "The world authority on home entertainment."
PUBL: Viare Publishing, 902 Broadway, New York, NY 10010.
DESC: Among the plethora of magazines aimed at the home video market, *Video Review* ranks among the best. The large, obligatory sections on new video cassette releases are there, of course, but the magazine is superior in providing information on the consumer field. *Video Reviews*' primary forte is its equipment reviews, thoroughly tested by Leonard Feldman of the CBS Technology Center. Reviews include waveform, vectorscope, and oscilloscope test pictures to allow the more sophisticated consumer to choose between equipment items. "Fill" articles are kept to a minimum. This is a magazine that desires to provide as many hard facts to its audience as possible. Typical articles for late 1991 included, "The Buzz About Cable," "Videogames at Hyperspeed," "Stocking Stuffers," and "Critic's Choice: Eyes on the Prize." It is well recommended for the home consumer field. Magazine format; numerous color and black/white graphics (8 x 10 ½ inches / 205 x 270 mm).
DEPT: "Viewpoints," editorial; "Letters," "Newsbreaks," newsbriefs; "Freeze-Frames," newsbriefs; "Questions," Q&A from readers; "New Products," reviews; "Test Reports," excellent section on equipment test-

ing; "Video Picks," new cassette releases; "Previews," scheduled for release; "Coming on TV," upcoming cable and broadcast programs; "Video Views," column; "Looking Ahead," column; "Backspace," guest column. (4-82). "Collectibles," "Rentals," "Cheap Thrills," "Kid Vid," "Laser Discs," "Lab Test Reports," "Viewpoint," "Letters," "High-Tech Q&A," "Freeze-Frames," "Newsbreaks," "Soundwave," "Camcorder College," "Video Hunter." (1-92).
TYPL: "Beating the Best Video Games," "Video Warranties: What They Cover-and Cover Up," "The Video Equipment Rental Revolution." (4-82). "High Def: Tomorrow's Television, Today?," "Caution: This Tape May be Hazardous to Your VCR," "Special Report: New Products at the Consumer Electronics Show." (3-88). "Special Report: Tokyo Tech," "High Honors," "Critic's Choice: Unforgettable!," "Star Trek: a 25th Anniversary Episode Guide." (1-92).
SCHL: Monthly, 110 pp.
SPAN: Apr, 1980+
ISSN: 0196-8793

Video Software Dealer

Sep, 1985 - ?, 1989//
(ISSN: 0894-3001)
SEE: VIDEO SOFTWARE MAGAZINE

✦ VIDEO SOFTWARE MAGAZINE

SUB: "The industry monthly."
PUBL: VSD Publications, Inc., 6750 Centinela Ave., Suite 300, Culver City, CA 90230.
DESC: The sale and rental of videocassettes to the general public has experienced explosive growth, from a few cassettes located "behind the counter" to a multi-million dollar service industry. For many segments of the public, it is the local video dealer who is the primary source for entertainment. *Video Software Dealer*, and now *Video Software Magazine* are two fine examples of trade publications distributed to video store managers which are designed to inform, promote, and enhance the sale/rental of videocassette product on the market. Within both magazines are a number of star interviews, profiles of producers, directors, and film subject trend analyses. These articles are interesting, and informative, and include a variety of supporting graphics. It specialty is information on new releases, and gaining/maintaining a competitive edge in the marketplace. An amazing amount of information is gathered each month on distributor information of cost, preorder date, street date, box office gross, supplier information on new releases, in-depth critiques and evaluations of current/old releases, business strategies on building sales, advertising, marketing, and profit-analysis. Of special note is the "Retailing to Win" column by Brooks Jensen, a wonderful series providing a number of very useful suggestions for building local-store sales and rental. *Video Software Magazine* issues contain "EDI's Box Office Advisor," a pull-out poster prepared by Entertainment Data, Inc., which lists domestic box office grosses for current theatrical releases, number of weeks that the film grossed $1 million, number of theatrical screens at release, when released, theatrical distributor, and "Projected Home Video Release Date." Both publications have full-color pages throughout on coated paper stock. *Video Software Dealer* was in stapled magazine format, while *Video Software Magazine* is in perfect-bound magazine format (8 ⅛ x 10 ⅞ inches / 205 x 275 mm).
DEPT: "Speaking Out," "News Flashes," 'News bits and short takes'; "Reader Feedback," letters; "Studio Promotions," "Industry Associations," "Hot Pre-Orders," "Video for Kids," "Music on Video," "Video Horror," "New Releases," "Pre-Order Calendar," "Street Date Calendar," "National Top Titles," "After the Blockbusters," lesser-known film review column by J. Martin Chitwood; "Retailing to Win," business strategy column by Brooks Jensen; "Scanning the Regions," "Sleepers," 'A title that becomes an unexpected hit, or an obscure title that does much better than anticipated'; "Hardware & Accessories," "On the Move," personnel newsbriefs; "The Final Page," photo page. (1-88). "Perspective," publisher commentary column by David Rowe; "Production Notes," issue detail column by Barbara Wexler; "Retailing to Win," column by Brooks Jensen; "The Mail Room," letters; "Dailies," newsbriefs; "Case Study," fascinating research department; "Sleepers," "Laser Chart," laserdisc releases; "Music Chart," "Products & Services," "Spotlight Marketing." (1-91).
TYPL: "Spotlight: La Bamba," "Promoting Valentine's Day," "Telemarketing," "Dealer Profile." (1-88). "Global Village," "One-on-One," "Goodman's Web," "Passion Play," "Children's Video." (1-91).
SCHL: Monthly (Sep, 1985 - Jun, 1990); Monthly [with extra issue in Jul and Dec] (Jul, 1990+), 90 pp.
SPAN: Sep, 1985+
VARIES
--Sep, 1985 - ?, 1989 as Video Software Dealer (ISSN: 0894-3001).
DD: 791
ISSN: 1046-607x

✦ VIDEO STORE

SUB: "The journal for the specialty video retailer and video department."
SUB: "Entertainment merchandising."
PUBL: Edgell Communications, Inc., 7500 Old Oak Blvd., Cleveland, OH 44130.
DESC: The development of local video stores for the sale/rental of cassettes and laser discs has been nothing short of phenomenal. Where-as in the 1920s, 30s and 40s motion picture theatres were "the place to be" to experience imaginative lobby displays, promotions, and wonderful elements of "Show Biz;" today those same creative elements can be seen in the pages of *Video Store* and the many thousands of local video

store operations around the world. These owners/managers carry on this exhibitor tradition through advertising promotions, video monitors playing sample segments of current releases, coupons, "two-for-ones," and other marketing techniques; elements which are discussed, advertised, and analyzed in each issue of *Video Store*. The focus of each monthly issue is information and analysis of current releases, distribution/release plans; and suggestions for store stocking, promotion and marketing to the public. Industry problems and trends are also featured, especially as they affect the "bottom line" of profitability. Of special note is the departmental segment, "Entertainment Merchandising," which includes "EM News," "EM Shopper," and other news of interest to store managers. The 204 page-issue provides strong testimony to the amount of news and information generated in the video cassette sale/rental industry in the decade of the 1990s. Perfect-bound magazine format with full-color throughout on coated paper stock, numerous creative advertisements with pull-out posters and advertising supplements (8 x 10 7/8 inches / 205 x 275 mm).

DEPT: "Focus," editorial column by Frank Moldstad; "Communique," publisher commentary column by David Allen Shaw; "Letters," "Reporter," news items; "Marquee," "Shorts," newsbriefs column by Jack Sweet; "Video Stories," commentary column by Van Wallach; "Surveys," interesting research and statistics column by Bart Story; "Box Office 100," 'Due from the theatre to thee'; "Tapetrack," 'Ranking the month's biggest titles by units shipped'; "Regions," regional business activity column by Rachel S. Meltzer; "Promotions," applications column by Charles Wesley Orton; "People," "Rushes," 'The all-new, all-blue, redesigned rental and sellthrough new release listings'; "Guidelines," column by Frank Barnako. (8-90).
TYPL: "If I Owned a Video Store," "Rainy Day Blues...er, Greens," "Opening Up the Closed Caption Market." (8-90).
SCHL: Monthly, 195 pp.
SPAN: Aug, 1979+
LC: HD 9697.V543U55
DD: 381/.4562138833
ISSN: 0195-1750

✢ VIDEO SYSTEMS

SUB: "The journal of close-circuit communications."
SUB: "The magazine for video professionals."
SUB: "The journal of production management."
SUB: "The official magazine of the International Television Association." (Oct, 1990+).
PUBL: Intertec Publishing Co., 9221 Quivira Rd., PO Box 12901, Overland Park, KS 66212.
DESC: Bridging the gap between industrial television and broadcast television, *Video Systems* in earlier years had served its readers a varied selection of articles on technology, technique, and programming in the industrial (corporate) television area. Current editorial content has moved more toward the independent production field, providing a strong forum for news of video production, be it corporate, field, or independent. Part of the unique approach of this publication consists of articles which show production techniques of top production houses. Of special note are photographic layouts profiling a corporate or independent television production center. In October, 1990 several changes took place within this serial. A new logo was unveiled for the first time; the International Television Association began its own magazine-within-a-magazine; and publisher, Intertec, began a series of authoritative supplements to various issues of the serial. The supplement for November, 1990 was "Videoconferencing," and for January, 1991 was "Computers & Video." *Video Systems* is well known for excellent articles on how programs are produced, edited, and packaged, and remains one of a handful of leading publications for video technology, management and operation. Magazine format (8 x 10 7/8 inches / 205 x 275 mm), full color throughout on coated paper stock.

DEPT: "Preview," editorial; "News," newsbriefs; "Business," newsbriefs; "Shoots," on-location and studio newsbriefs; "Question & Answer," from readers; "New Products," reviews; "Spotlight," one product profile; "Viewfinder," a forum for comment. (8-82). "Editorial," "News & Business," "Leading Edge," new technology column by Michael Heiss; "Management," column by Brad Dick; "Video2," television lighting column by Bill Holshevnikoff; "Sound Ideas," column by Roy Rising; "Question & Answer," Q&A column by Rick Lehtinen; "New Products," "People," "Shoots," production activities. (10-89). "Editorial," "News & Business," "Leading Edge," column by Michael Heiss; "Management," column by Brad Dick; "ITVA Today," 'News and views from the International Television Association'; "Video2," column by Bill Holshevnikoff; "Sound Ideas," column by Roy W. Rising; "Computer Scan," column by Rick Lehtinen; "Question & Answer," column by Ned Soseman; "New Products." (2-91).
TYPL: "Music and Video," "Tune Trips on MTV, Etc.," "Making a Rock Video," "Digital Music--Direct," "The New Wave Nerve," "Audio for Today's Video," "Facility Profile: Pacific Arts Video Records." (8-82). "Recipe For Quality," "On the Road Again: Location Audio," "Fun With Electricity," "Still Video Systems in the Video Environment." (10-89). "The Heart of Video Production," "From Idea to Program," "Instant Creativity," "Management Solutions." (2-91).
SCHL: Bimonthly (Nov/Dec, 1975 - Jan/Feb, 1981); Monthly (Mar, 1981+); 90 pp.
SPAN: Nov/Dec, 1975+
LC: TK 6680.V53
DD: 384.55/5/05
ISSN: 0361-0942

✦ VIDEO TECHNOLOGY NEWS

SUB: "Broadcast, cable, computer video, consumer electronics, HDTV, fiber, new media, satellites, telecommunications, training."

PUBL: Phillips Publishing, Inc., 7811 Montrose Rd., Potomac, MD 20854.

DESC: In the field of visual communication, nothing drives the regulatory, economic, and corporate arena more than technology. Major corporate and national fortunes are continually at stake, and maintaining a competitive edge in this volatile industry may rely on efficient receipt of the lastest news concerning developments, issues, and problems. That is the raison d'être of *Video Technology News*, a publication of excellent repute, that presents a concise compilation of the important trends, issues, and forecasts affecting this field. In one sampled issue for 1991, articles described the costs of HDTV to broadcasters, CD-ROM video products for the home market, the threat of computer video to post production video houses, the resurgence of 16mm film in place of videotape, and the future of direct broadcast satellite. This is another excellent publication from the Phillips family of communication newsletters. The subscription cost for this biweekly is $495 per year (1991), and is also available electronically via NewsNet and Predicasts services. Printed black ink (front cover spot color) on yellow uncoated paper stock (8 ½ x 11 inches / 215 x 280 mm).

DEPT: "Broadcasting," "Technology," "Video-Conferencing," "CD-ROM," "Legislation," "Production," "Competing Media," "Videonews," "DBS." (4-15-91).

TYPL: "Broadcast Industry's Big Show for 1991 is in High-Definition," "NHK Shows Advanced Technology Never Seen Outside Japan," "Low-Bandwidth Systems Expected to Dominate Videoconferencing Market," "Cable Regulation Update," "Quick and Dirty: Computer Video Threatens High-end Production." (4-15-91).

SCHL: Semimonthly, 8 pp.
SPAN: Sep 26, 1988+
DD: 384
ISSN: 1040-2772

✦ VIDEO--THE MAGAZINE

PUBL: Selwood Press, Ltd., Suite C, Elsinore House, 43 Buckingham St., Aylesbury, Bucks HP20 2NQ, England.

DESC: *Video--The Magazine* thoroughly covers the field of recent motion picture and original video production releases on videocassette for the British home consumer. The emphasis is on reviews; providing story synopsis, critique, British film ratings, and distributor. Feature articles focus on selected stars, with one sample issue showcasing such stars as Eric Stoltz, Sarah Douglas, Burt Reynolds and Rob Lowe. Some articles/departments provide information on video equipment and Hollywood gossip, but the raison d'etre for *Video--The Magazine* is the dynamic home videotape market itself. For the sampled 1990 issue: stapled magazine format with mixture of black ink, spot- and full-color editorial content and full-color cover on coated paper stock (8 ⅜ x 11 ¾ inches / 210 x 295 mm).

DEPT: "News," extensive section; "To Buy," current product; "To Rent," available videotapes; "Reviews," of films on videotape; "Music," news and reviews on music videos; "Gossip." (2-90).

TYPL: "High Flyer!," "Forever in Thigh High Boots!," "Story of the Blues," "The Lowe Down." (2-90).

SCHL: Monthly, 50 pp.
SPAN: ?+
ISSN: 0263-5003

✦ VIDEO TIMES

SUB: "New products, trends and people in video today." (? - spring, 1988).

SUB: "The #1 source for the video pro." (Summer, 1988 - ?).

SUB: "The news magazine of the video industry (Winter, 1990?+).

PUBL: Video Times, MPCS Video Center Building, 4100 North 28th Terrace, Hollywood, FL 33020.

DESC: First and foremost, this is a video products catalog for the MPCS corporation, with the unusual twist of a quarterly publication schedule and magazine-type articles on various aspects of production and technology. Products are showcased either by themselves, or as part of well-written articles describing "real-life" production situations. It is unique in its field, and free to qualified personnel in the industrial, professional, educational, cable and broadcast video industries. Magazine format (8 ⅛ x 10 ⅞ inches / 210 x 275 mm), with numerous graphics.

DEPT: "Editor's Page," "Technically Speaking," "Troubleshooting," "News Briefs," "IPC People and Projects," "MPCS Briefs," "Buylines," used/demo equipment for sale; "New Products," "Manufacturer's Showcase," product briefs. (fall-88). "Editor's Note," "News & Business Report," "Technology Update," "Upcoming Events Calendar," "Letters," "Engineering Tips," "Products Showcase," "Final Word," commentary. (winter-90).

TYPL: "Video in Litigation," "Unconventional Coverage," "The Audio-for-Video Explosion," "A Studio Perspective: Tips from the Trade, for the Trade." (fall-88). "Happy Birthday U-matic," "HDTV--The Even Playing Field Gets Muddy," "Future Vision--A Look at the Best in Digital Video Effects," "Lightweight Video Steadicam." (winter-90).

SCHL: Quarterly, 90 pp.
SPAN: Winter, 1982+
SUPPLEMENT TO
--Backstage, ? - ?.

✦ VIDEO TIMES

SUB: "For home viewing on tape & disc."

SUB: "The monthly magazine of video entertainment."
SUB: "The best guide to videotapes."
PUBL: Publications International, Ltd., 3841 West Oakton St., Skokie, IL 60076.
DESC: "*Video Times* is packed with color, entertainment and information: * 300 reviews of the latest and hottest video releases--each month! *Special, in-depth coverage of comedy, adventure, horror, music, fine arts, children's video, and much more. *Timely and entertaining cover stories. *Exclusive interviews with your favorite stars and directors. *Behind-the-scenes coverage of your favorite movies. *Page after page of delightful, full-color photos. If you own a VCR--or if you just love movies--you'll love *Video Times*." This monthly publication packs a lot of information and pictures about new film and video production releases on videocassette and laserdiscs. It describes productions; providing storyline, and a four-star rating system to evaluate the quality of each release. Of special note is the segment "[month] Video Releases" which details new cassettes on the marketplace, along with news of price reductions on previously-released product. The layout design is innovative and adds excitement to an already dynamic publication. Perfect-bound magazine format, full color pages throughout each issue on coated paper stock (8 x 10 ⅞ inches / 205 x 275 mm).
DEPT: "Letters," "Video Beat," column by Jim McCullaugh; "Popcorn," news items; "Celebrity Corner," wonderful star interviews column by Steve Dale; "2nd Take," oldies but goodies in review; "Programming Guide," reviews; "Keynote Reviews," cassette spotlight; "Short Takes," shorter videocassette reviews; "Calendar." (4-87).
TYPL: "Through the Years with the Academy Awards," "The Best of the Last 12 Months," "Bankable Bonds: The 007's That Might Have Been." (4-87).
SCHL: Monthly, 85 pp.
SPAN: Jan, 1985+
VARIES
--Mar, 1984 - ?, 1984 as Video Movies (ISSN: 0742-8111).
LC: PN 1992.95 .V495
DD: 791.45/05
ISSN: 0742-8111

✦ VIDEO TIMES

SUB: "Your complete guide to video."
PUBL: Nashwood, Ltd., 143 Mare St., London E8 3RH, England.
DESC: Bold imaginative color and layout design is strikingly evident in each issue of this British publication concerning recent motion pictures released for the home videocassette market. Film aficionados may chaff a bit at the relatively short length of feature articles. There is a full-color presentation of production stills, and other materials connected with these motion picture products. There is no doubt (considering a 20-page 'videos for sale' section at the end of the serial) that the emphasis here is on videocassette sale and rental; providing information, critique, and evaluation of current releases. Indeed, for the British home videocassette consumer, this may be the only video magazine needed, and a good one it is. The sampled issue for 1990 consisted of full-color stapled magazine format, with numerous production stills on coated paper stock (8 ¼ x 11 ¾ inches / 210 x 300 mm).
DEPT: "Editorial," "Competition," monthly video contest; "Charts," 'For rent and for sale'; "Rent Reviews," detailed, entertaining reviews of current film-on-videocassette releases; "Video Clips," 'The best of the rest of this month's videos reviewed by Sarah Lewis' column by Sarah Lewis; "Movie News," 'Big screen gossip and info'; "For Sale," 'Vids to buy and keep'; "Music For Sale," videotape review. (3-90).
TYPL: "Mel Gibson--Lethal Weaponeer," "May the Schwarz Be With You," "Ryan's Daughter," "Love, Revenge and Cappuccino." (3-90).
SCHL: Monthly, 40 pp.
SPAN: ?+
ISSN: 0954-6871

✦ VIDEO TODAY

SUB: "The top selling video entertainment magazine."
PUBL: Argus Publications, Ltd., Argus House, Boundary Way, Hemel Hempstead, Herts, HP2 7ST England.
DESC: This British home consumer publication is designed to showcase the best of recent motion pictures releases on videocassette, and provides news items, trends, and other entertainment developments that impact this volatile field. The focus is on reviews, accomplished in a thorough manner, with principle cast, producer, running time, certificate and critic rating attached to each release. Production stills, some in color, accompany most reviews. For the sampled issue of 1990: stapled magazine format featuring black/white and full-color editorial content on coated paper stock (8 ¼ x 11 ¾ inches / 210 x 300 mm).
DEPT: "News," "Editorial," "Letters to the Editor," "Caption Competition," reader contest; "Comedy Reviews," "Action Reviews," "Drama Reviews," "Competition," reader contest; "Horror Reviews," "In Store," recent motion pictures now available on videocassette; "Music," music video video column by Darrin Williamson; "Movie Scene," "Video Tomorrow," '*Video Today* looking at tomorrows video'; "In Production," 'Out and about with Ken Ferguson'. (3-90).
TYPL: "Steve Martin Talks Dirty," "Oscars," "Wildlife," "Sarah Douglas." (3-90).
SCHL: Monthly, 55 pp.
SPAN: ?+
ISSN: 0144-6010

Video User

Aug, 1980 - Mar, 1984//
(ISSN: 0273-7817)
SEE: VIDEO MANAGEMENT

Video Users Marketplace

1978 - ?//
SEE: VIDEO MANAGEMENT

✤ VIDEO WATCHDOG

SUB: "The perfectionist's guide to fantastic video."
SUB: "The truth about uncut fantastic video."
SUB: "Rarities, retitlings, restorations."
PUBL: Tim Lucas, Video Watchdog, PO Box 5283, Department M, Cincinnati, OH 45205-0283.
DESC: A promotional advertisement had this to say about *Video Watchdog*: "Restores missing and/or censored scenes from new and classic Horror, Science Fiction and Fantasy films on video! Unveils ground-breaking videographies and essays (not time-killing articles, but true additions to the literature about fantasy filmmaking)! Unmasks sneaky video retitlings and poor transfer quality! Presents for the first time authorized, English-language translations of important interviews from those gorgeous foreign filmzines you could never read!" All this and more is true for this first-class publication by Publisher and Editor Tim Lucas. The layout design demonstrates great care, both in actual composition as well as in reproduction of graphics, posters, and star/film pictures. That same quality is evident in the editorial content. *Video Watchdog* subscribers are film purists, willing to spend time and money to track down original, released, uncut versions of their favorite entertainment fare. Indeed, many letters to the editor are concerned with discrepancies in running time and inquires as to cut scenes in different distributor versions. Reviews are international in scope, covering in one sampled 1991 issue; the United States, Asia, France, Germany, and Venezuela. Each reviewed film notes presence of "Closed Captioned," "Digital," "Digital Stereo," "Hi-Fi," "Letterboxed," "Stereo," or "Surround Sound Stereo" elements. This is an excellent resource for those serious about their film/videocassette purchases or rentals. As another fanzine editor observed: "Frankly I'm jealous. I wish that I had the money and the writing experience to put out a magazine like this. 1st class all the way." For sampled issue of 1991: stapled journal format, editorial content consisting of black ink on coated paper stock with two-color black/yellow ink cover on coated paper stock (6 x 8 ¼ inches / 155 x 210 mm).
DEPT: "Kennel," author profile; "The Watchdog Barks," editorial column by Tim Lucas; "Watchdog News," "Video Around the World," reviews; "The Letterbox," letters. (9/10-91).
TYPL: "The Trouble with TITIAN," "Five Graves For a Medium," "Who is Ralph Zucker?," "Barbara Steele Videography," "The Barbara Steele Interview." (9/10-91).
SCHL: Bimonthly, 65 pp.
SPAN: Sep/Oct, 1990+

✤ VIDEO WEEK

SUB: "Devoted to the business of program sales & distribution for videocassettes, disc, pay TV & allied new media."
PUBL: Television Digest, 1836 Jefferson Place, N.W., Washington, DC 20036.
DESC: The subtitle says it all: this is a small tabloid format newsletter which has one emphasis; program sales and distribution. Utilizing the talented staff of Television Digest, *Video Week* is able to provide fast-breaking news, not on the programs themselves, but on the media that will purchase or lease those programs. It is an excellent resource for individuals whose work involves program syndication and sales. Three-hole punched. No graphics.
DEPT: "Summary-Index of Week's News," "Video Notes," newsbriefs; "Personnals," newsbriefs; "Programming Report," newsbriefs. (4-14-80).
TYPL: "Playcable 5-City Test Begins," "Schein Moves to Polygram," "Time-Life Video's Foreign Look," "From Las Vegas by Satellite," "PTV Programming for Pay TV?," "VCR Sales at 893,000 Annual Rate." (4-14-80).
SCHL: Weekly, 8 pp.
SPAN: Feb 4, 1980+
ISSN: 0196-5905

✤ VIDEO WORLD

SUB: "Britain's fastest growing magazine."
PUBL: Northern & Shell, Northern & Shell Building, PO Box 381, Mill Harbour, London E14 9TW, England.
DESC: *Video World* is dedicated to the popular, adult-oriented motion picture videotape release in Britain. Its 100+ pages are filled with reviews, interviews, and production stills from horror films to science fiction; from funky comedies to intense dramas; and a large advertisement section on adult films available on videocassette. *Video World* makes no pretense about serving everyone's tastes. Some of the pictorial features, and adult film advertisements are adults-only fare. *Video World* presents the best of adult-themed motion pictures on video for the British home consumer, a task it performs well, and for which it has become, as the subtitle plainly states; "Britain's fastest growing magazine." For the sampled issue of 1990: stapled magazine format, editorial content consisting of mixture of black ink, spot- and full-color pages (including cover) on coated paper stock (8 ⅜ x 11 ⅝ inches / 215 x 295 mm).
DEPT: "Ed-Lines," editorial; "Video Classic," classic films on tape; "Bryce is Right," fan question column by Allan Bryce; "Reviews," "Bargain Basement," inexpensive videos; "Competition Winners," "Cutting Room," "Video World Wordsearch," "Equipment News," "Re-Make," what-if pictorial. (3-90).
TYPL: "Gore Blimey (Something Slimey)," "The Funky Gibson," "Creature Feature," "Showman Shostrom." (3-90).
SCHL: Monthly, 100 pp.

SPAN: ?+
ISSN: 0265-1297

VIDEOCASSETTE AND CATV NEWSLETTER
SUB: "The systems, the market, the future."
PUBL: Martin Roberts and Associates, Box 5254X, Beverly Hills, CA 90210.
DESC: This well-researched publication deals with news of video cassette and cable operations. Emphasis is on the application of both media on instructional and home fronts. Stories feature reports on new innovations and prospects for future entries into the field. Occasional graphics; typed format; three-hole punched for filing.
DEPT: None. (3-73).
TYPL: "Digital Recording--a Definition and a Status Report," "Pocket Sized Tv Receivers to be Marketed Later this Year," "Film Exhibitors Offered Equipment to Extend Box Office Reach," "Hilton to Wire 40,000 Rooms for Pay TV." (3-73).
SCHL: Monthly.
SPAN: Jun, 1971 - ?, 1981?//
VARIES
--? - ? as Video Cassettes; the Systems, the Market, the Future.
--Mar, 1971 - Feb, 1972 as Video Cassettes Newsletter.
ISSN: 0049-6243

Videodisc and Optical Disk
Mar/Apr, 1984 - Nov/Dec, 1985//
(ISSN: 0742-5740)
SEE: OPTICAL INFORMATION SYSTEMS

✧ VIDEODISC DESIGN / PRODUCTION GROUP. NEWS.
PUBL: Nebraska Videodisc Design/Production Group, KUON-TV, University of Nebraska-Lincoln, P.O. Box 83111, Lincoln, NE 68501.
DESC: "The Nebraska Videodisc Design/Production Group consists of designers and producers specifically concerned with the development and production of programs that exploit the unique capabilities of the videodisc. The group was formed in 1978 under a grant from the Corporation for Public Broadcasting to investigate the applications of videodisc technology on behalf of public and instructional television, to design and produce videodiscs for a wide range of educational aplications, to develop production methods for premastering, and to disseminate research on videodisc formats, design/production, and potential educational, industrial, commercial markets for videodisc technology." An excellent newsletter for new developments in this new communications field.
DEPT: None. (9/10-81). None. (2-84).
TYPL: "Videodisc/Personal Computer 'Overlay' Interface Updated by Nebraska Videodisc Group," "Preparation for Premastering," "How to Ship a Videodisc," "The Nebraska Group's Microcomputer Game Project." (9/10-81). "Annenberg Update: Interactive Videodisc Science Instruction," "Nebraska Group Embarks on Indonesian Project," "Jumping Into the Future." (2-84).
SCHL: Bimonthly, 6 pp.
SPAN: 1979+

✧ VIDEODISC MONITOR, THE
SUB: "Your eye on the industry."
PUBL: The Videodisc Monitor, PO Box 26, Falls Church, VA 22046.
DESC: This monthly newsletter provides news of developments in the videodisc industry for corporate managers, producers, and educators.
DEPT: "Newsline," "Barometer," stocks; "Grapevine," "Personals," "Tech Talk," "Media Watch," "Reviews," "Editorial," "Letters," "Calendar."
TYPL: "The Next Generation," "Pioneer and Sony Join Fray," "Conferences Highlight Autumn," "Laser Fever at AMOA."
SCHL: Monthly, 20 pp.
SPAN: Sep, 1983+
ISSN: 0739-7089

Videodisc/Teletext
Winter, 1981 - Spring, 1981//
(ISSN: 0198-9456)
SEE: OPTICAL INFORMATION SYSTEMS

Videodisc, Videotex
Summer, 1981 - Jan/Feb, 1984//
(ISSN: 0278-9183)
SEE: OPTICAL INFORMATION SYSTEMS

✧ VIDEOGRAPHY
SUB: "The magazine of professional video production, technology, and applications."
PUBL: PSN Publications, Two Park Avenue, Suite 1820, New York, NY 10016.
DESC: *Videography* covers both programming innovations and applications of new video technology for home, corporate, and broadcast video, with an emphasis on the corporate area. It is a publication for the trade, and in a 1987 reader survey ranked first and second in professional trade publications most read by video professionals. Articles provide useful information and applications for production, and intelligent discussion of industry trends. It covers the video professional industry in a thorough and competent manner. Of note are special issues, inserts and supplements throughout the year, such as "*Videography* Presents The Profes-

sional Special-Event Videographer's Handbook" (January, 1991), a 22 page special insert for new professionals in the field; or an annual "Production Directory," a very thorough guide to "facilities and services" in postproduction, videographics, and rental services. Magazine format (8 ⅛ x 10 ⅞ inches / 205 x 275 mm), numerous graphics, full color throughout on coated paper stock.
DEPT: "News and Comment," newsbriefs; "Corporate Video," news column; "Washington View," TV rules and regs; "The Home Screen," new developments; "Video Art," using video as a paintbrush; "Software Review," "Hardware Review." (12-77). "Video Research," "Washington View," "Hands On," "The Cutting Edge," "Product Perspectives." (4-83). "Latebreak," news; "Industry News," "Facilities," new equipment at production houses; "Production," newsbriefs; "People," personnel newsbriefs; "Meetings & Shows," upcoming; "Editor's Page," "Letters," "Research & Developments," column by Mark Schubin; "More to Follow," column by David Allen; "Production Technique," column by Jim St. Lawrence; "Product Perspectives," column by Michael Heiss; "Closing Comment," commentary. (3-87). "Latebreak," "Headline News," "Editor's Corner," "Points of View," column by John Rice; "People," "Meetings & Shows," "Research & Developments," column by Mark Schubin; "Technology," "Corporate Video Decisions," "Production," "Production Technique," column by Jim St. Lawrence; "Producer to Producer," column by Michael Wiese; "Multimedia," "Audio-For-Video," "Conversation," profile; "Product Introductions," "Products," "Closing Comment." (1-91).
TYPL: "Video and Dance," "Special Report: Time Base Correctors," "Conversation with Larry Finley." (12-77). "The One-Piece Takes on the World," "Getting the Right Stuff," "Guide to Videodisc Systems," "Getting Film to Disc." (4-83). "NAB Preview: Business Old and New," "New on Nickelodeon," "A Problem-Solving Program." (3-87). "S-VHS and Hi-8: Perfect in Post?," "The New Wave in Wireless Mics," "The Professional Approach to Profitability," "Video in a Window." (1-91).
SCHL: Monthly, 100 pp.
SPAN: Apr, 1976+
ABSORBED
--Corporate Video Decisions (ISSN: 1050-8287), Sep, 1990.
LC: TK 6630 .A1V53
DD: 621.388/005
ISSN: 0363-1001
ABST: --Film Literature Index (ISSN: 0093-6758)

✦ VIDEOMAKER

SUB: "The video Camera user's magazine."
PUBL: Videomaker, Inc., 1166 East Lassen Ave., Chico, CA 95926.
DESC: A promotional advertisement noted, "Enter Videomaker--the original magazine for video camera users. . .about creating videos. This is the magazine geared especially for you--the creative enthusiast or the seasoned professional. Finally, your videos can match the highest quality attainable anywhere, using readily available, affordable equipment. Videomaker's readers get expert advice on camera technique, editing, special effects, sound recording and lighting--as well as scripting, casting, set design, and production management. Videomaker offers you valuable resource information, tools and tips, technical data, buyer's guides and much, much more!" Dynamic graphics, hard information, and an excellent layout format makes Videomaker an outstanding resource for video camcorder enthusiasts. Contained within 115 color pages are a host of articles detailing new products, novel ideas for shooting video, and reader profiles. This is a publication where the reader/subscriber is an active participant, whether providing his/her own "tricks of the trade," discussing the creation of special effects, or sharing concepts for commercial opportunities whereby the videomaker's hobby can turn into a part-time profit center. Numerous advertisements for mail order camcorders and accessories attest to the readership and loyalty paid to this publication. A quality serial for the home consumer. Magazine format (8 x 10 ⅞ inches / 205 x 275 mm).
DEPT: "Viewfinder," editorial column by Matthew York; "Sound Reasoning," audio column by Cliff Roth; "Videocrafts," column by Hal Burke; "Video For Hire," column by Kristin Tucker; "Desktop Video," column by Mark Swain; "Special FX," special video effects column by John Hoglin; "Profile," videomaker profile column by Erica Shames; "Letters," "Quick Focus," newsbriefs column by Natasha Cole; "Video Q+A," column by Stuart Sweetow; "Product Scene," new product profile; "Tools and Tips," ideas for videographers; "Calendar," upcoming video events and contests. (1-90).
TYPL: "Buyers Guide to Camcorders: Hi8," "Start 'Em Young, Like an Old Pro," "Make Fiction Videos a Reality!," "Give Your Video Character, From A to Z." (1-90).
SCHL: Bimonthly (Jun/Jul, 1986 - Dec, 1989); Nine issues per year (Jan, 1990+).
SPAN: Jun/Jul, 1986+
DD: 384
ISSN: 0889-4973

✦ VIDEOPLAY MAGAZINE

SUB: "The how-to magazine for home video."
PUBL: C. S. Tepfer Publishing Co., 51 Sugar Hollow Rd., Danbury, CT 06810.
DESC: Videoplay Magazine is a home consumer magazine with an emphasis on videocassette releases. Started as a section in the parent magazine, Educational & Industrial Television, in October, 1972, Videoplay Magazine made its own publishing debut in December, 1979. In its premiere issue the publisher noted: "Whether you want to use a videocassette recorder to get more enjoyment from your television set, or whether you are part of that growing circle of video

enthusiasts, we intend to interest, entertain, inform and sometimes excite you." One sampled issue for 1982 included articles on lighting apparatus, camera picture tubes, satellite earth stations, new videotape releases of Western genre productions, a "Do-It-Yourself Guide to VCR Repair," and a number of equipment testbench reviews for the home video enthusiast. A promotional advertisement promised readers: "Keep on top of video equipment and new programming by reading *Videoplay* throughout the year. Along with buyer's guides, you'll find each issue packed with *Videoplay's* unique how-to hints on improving your video shoots; news of the latest in low-cost gadgets; camera and portable video tips; and advanced looks at what's coming in video games and computer video; and more." For 1981 issue: stapled magazine format, black/white and full-color throughout on coated paper stock (8 1/4 x 10 7/8 inches / 210 x 275 mm).

DEPT: "VideoplayPourri," newsbriefs. (12-79). "Reviews," "Previews," "Questions and Answers," "Video Response," "Videofun," puzzle. (4/5-81).
TYPL: "Shoppers' Guide to VCRs & Cameras," "Science Fiction Films," "Videoplay Test Reports," "Fun with Home Video," "Finding the Programs." (12-79). "Film-to-Tape Transfer," "Creating Video Graphics," "Swashbucklers--Where Swords Play and Chivalry Reigns," "Swashbucklers on Cassette," "Something for Everyone--Programming Services Available Via Satellite." (4/5-81).
SCHL: Monthly (Dec, 1979 - ?), Bimonthly (?+), 100 pp.
SPAN: Dec, 1979+
LC: TK 9960 .V54
DD: 621.388/332/05
ISSN: 0273-9828

✤ VIDEOPRO

SUB: "Voice of the industry professional."
SUB: "For the business of production."
PUBL: VidPro Publishing, Inc., 902 Broadway, New York, NY 10010.
DESC: In its premiere issue, editor Alice Wolf noted: "We are a magazine about professional video production geared to professionals involved in production and management. Basically non-broadcast in nature, *VideoPro* will keep you informed of those broadcast decisions that can have an effect on your own work." *VideoPro* is geared toward production, including technology, freelancing, trends, maintenance, post-production, budgeting, and production company profiles. Long a favorite with production company staff members, *Videopro* provides an intelligent array of stories encompassing the current status and future trends of this visual art. Magazine format, with numerous graphics.
DEPT: "Editor's Note," "Low Power Television Report," "The Legal Angle," "The Brush Report," "Studio Management," "Thinking Ahead," "Newsbreaks," newsbriefs; "Facilities/Production Services," profile; "People," "Pro Products," review. (4-84).

TYPL: "Lighting: A Look at the Latest Equipment," "Sellers Beware: The New Breed of NAB Buyer," "Shopping for Video Projectors: Finding your Personal Best," "Group Think: Audio Recording." (4-84).
SCHL: Monthly (Nov, 1982 - ?); Monthly [except Aug] (1984+), 72 pp.
SPAN: Nov, 1982+
LC: TK 6630 .A1 V54
DD: 384.55/05
ISSN: 0746-3286

✤ VIDEOTOOLS

PUBL: C.T.L. Electronics, 86 West Broadway, New York, NY 10007.
DESC: This underground-video newspaper introduces technical concepts to readers, and brings interesting video developments to their attention. It is aimed at the beginning videofile.
DEPT: None. (8-75).
TYPL: "Video in London," "Sarnoff on the Future of T.V.," "Making Video in Color and Black and White." (8-75).
SCHL: "Published regularly," 8 pp.
SPAN: ?+?

✤ VIEW

SUB: "The magazine of television programming."
PUBL: View Communications Corporation, 80 Fifth Ave., New York, NY 10011.
DESC: "*View* has grown and prospered. It has done so because it was founded on an idea--that software, the engine that drives the television business--is of such critical importance to executives at all levels of the industry, that it deserves its own, first class publication. *View* will distinguish itself by offering unequaled insight into the issues and trends affecting the industry. Be it network, cable, syndication, local TV, local cable, or, perhaps someday, DBS, it is all television, and *View* is the magazine of its program industry." This is a superb independent publication for the video programming field, consisting of thorough, contemplative articles for immediate applications, and is an exellent resource for any executive in the realm of video programming. Numerous graphics, charts.
DEPT: "Production Notes," "Current," "Churn Chart," "Ratings Review," "Software Marketplace," "Corner Office," "Our View," editorial; "Promotion View," "Washington View," "Your View." (9-84). "Our View," "Monitor," newsbriefs; "Station Strategy," "Cable Connections," "News Desk," "Sports Page," "Promotion View," "Minds Behind the Media," "Eye on Access," "Last Words." (4-17-89).
TYPL: "TV Sports: Can the Nets Hold the Line?," "The Made-for-Pay Push: Is it Reel?," "Gold Medallion Awards: the BPA Winners' Circle," "Roundtable:

Cablevision's Chuck Dolan." (9-84). "Something in Common," "Prime Time for News," "Hour by Hour." (4-17-89).
SCHL: Monthly (? - ?); Semimonthly [except monthly in Mar, Jul and Aug] (Feb, 1988 - Mar, 1990); Weekly (Mar ?, 1990+), 45 pp.
SPAN: 1980+
SUSPENDED
--Apr 2, 1990+?
DD: 384
ISSN: 0273-8392

View

Aug, 1965 - Jun/Jul, 1967//
SEE: E-ITV

✤ VIEWCAMERA

SUB: "The journal of large format photography."
PUBL: Steve Simmons Photography, 3045 65th St., Suite 4, Sacramento, CA 95820.
DESC: In the March/April, 1991 issue, author Gerry Tsuruda explains in part why he moved up to large format photography: "The mention of view-camera photography to the uninitiated conjures up the image of an ominous black hood from which a mass of legs, both human and mechanical, descend. My initial reaction to this sight was instantaneous, I thought 'That guy is crazy'. My opinion was reinforced when I saw the same guy hoist the mass of equipment over his shoulder and stumble up the side of a steep hill. To a seasoned 35mm photographer, this was insanity. Somehow, between then and now, I too wandered off the proverbial deep-end. My plunge into insanity did not happen all at one time. However, as I started to realize the advantages the larger format afforded me, I was drawn-in and eventually hooked." These are sentiments which could be echoed by thousands of professional photographers. Publisher/editor, Steve Simmons, produces a quality magazine designed not only to inform about new products and applications in the field, but also to showcase the artistic work of large format photographers. Great care is taken in the reproduction of those photographs, a full-half page being provided for each one. Technical information and philosophical approaches by the photographer/artistan accompany many such reproductions, and are probably sufficient, as author Tsuruda noted, "hook one" on this wonderful viewcamera format. Stapled magazine format, color and black/white editorial content on coated paper stock, advertising (8 ½ x 11 inches / 215 x 280 mm).
DEPT: "Notes and News," newsbriefs; "New Products," review. (3/4-91).
TYPL: "Gay Outlaw: Solarized Polaroid Images," "Cay Lang: 16 x 20 Polaroid Images of Figures," "Recommended Exposure Indices for Infrared Film," "Peter LeGrand: Infrared Studies of the Figure," "Orthochromatic Film for Portraits, Figures, and Architecture." (3/4-91).
SCHL: Bimonthly, 65 pp.
SPAN: Jan/Feb, 1988+

✤ VIEWS

SUB: "The journal of photography in New England."
SUB: "A publication of the Photographic Resource Center at Boston University."
PUBL: Photographic Resource Center, 602 Commonwealth Ave., Boston, MA 02215.
DESC: *Views*, an aptly titled publication, showcases current photography, disseminates alternative viewpoints, and provides an instructive classroom for creative means of utilizing the photographic form to present, structure, and package a message. The large magazine format contributes to a dynamic layout design. Articles are informative, and seek to explore/explain different methods and philosophies of each issue's featured photographers. In the reviewed sample issue, the theme of war was seen from a number of differing views, including those of war correspondents, and press censorship issues. There was a very unique three-artist showcase of responses to the 1991 war in the Persian Gulf. While the publication is subtitled "The journal of photography in New England," this is a magazine of interest to anyone in the journalistic and photographic fields who takes both message and medium seriously. For the 1991 sampled issue: stapled large magazine format, black ink on uncoated paper stock, limited advertising (10 ⅞ x 15 ¼ inches / 275 x 390 mm).
DEPT: "Books," reviews; "Editorial," editorial column by Daniel P. Younger; "Letters to the Editor," "Exhibitions," review. (summer-91).
TYPL: "Burrowing in the Sand: Notes on Post War Media," "War Stories: Narrative Reporting in the Gulf War," "Press Censorship in the Persian Gulf: An Interview With Jonathan L. Wiggs, Boston Globe Photographer," "Artists Respond to the War," "First World War Photographers." (summer-91).
SCHL: Three issues per year, 25 pp.
SPAN: ?+
ISSN: 0743-8044

✤ VISIBLE LANGUAGE

SUB: "The journal for research on the visual media of language expression."
SUB: "The research journal concerned with all that is involved with our being literate."
PUBL: Visible Language, Wayne State University Press, The Leonard Simmons Bldg., 5959 Woodward, Detroit, MI 48202.
DESC: *Visible Language* is concerned with research and ideas that help define the unique role and properties of written language. It is a basic premise of the journal that writing/reading form a distinct system of lan-

guage expression which must be defined and developed on its own terms." This is a scholary journal that explores typography, writing style, graphics, and the printing process. Occasional experimental articles on typography, color and style appear.

DESC: [*Journal of Typographic Research*]: "The objectives of the *Journal of Typographic Research* are quite simply stated: to report and to encourage scientific investigation of our alphabetic and related symbols." It oftentimes ventured into areas of communication theory, application of type legibility, and the artistic application of experimental typographic design. Journal format; with graphics.

DEPT: "Research in Progress," "Book Reviews," "Abstracts of Journal Articles in French and German." (10-67). "Abstracts of Articles in French, German, and Spanish," "Authors," profile. (#3-80). None (autumn-86).

TYPL: "Three Fonts of Computer-Drawn Letters," "The Development of CBS News 36," "Typography: Evolution and Revolution," "Vertical Group Exercises in Graphic Design." (10-67). "Visible Language: Freud's Imprint," "Killer Bees: an Ontology in Abeyance," "Defoe's Daydream: Becoming Moll Flanders," "The Contract: a Stele for Rowland Barthes." (#3-80). "Instructional Text: the Transition from Page to Screen," "Italian Sixteenth-Century Italian Writing Books and the Scribal Reality in Verona," "Variations in Spelling and the Special Case of Colloquial Contractions." (autumn-86).

SCHL: Quarterly, 100 pp.
SPAN: Jan, 1967+
VARIES
--Jan, 1967 - Autumn, 1970 as Journal of Typographic Research, The (ISSN: 0449-329x).
LC: Z 119.J88
DD: 001.5/52/05
ISSN: 0022-2224
ABST: --Annual Bibliography of English Language and Literature (ISSN: 0066-3786)
--Computer & Control Abstracts (ISSN: 0036-8113)
--Electrical & Electronics Abstracts (ISSN: 0036-8105)
--Electronic Publishing Abstracts (ISSN: 0739-2907)
--Language and Language Behavior Abstracts (ISSN: 0023-8295)
--Mathematical Reviews (ISSN: 0025-5629)
--MLA International Bibliography of Books & Articles on the Modern Languages and Literatures (ISSN: 0024-8215)
--Physics Abstracts. Science Abstracts. Series A. (ISSN: 0036-8091)
--Printing Abstracts (ISSN: 0031-109x)

✤ VISIO

SUB: "Electronics, high-technology, recreation."
PUBL: LFP, Inc., 9100 Wilshire Blvd., West Tower, 6th Fl., Beverly Hills, CA 90210.
DESC: "Just as the industrial revolution transformed the world in the 18th century, so has the electronic revolution of the 20th century changed the face of modern society. Innovations in electronics technology have permeated virtually every aspect of life today, forever altering the worlds of business, communications, transportation, home entertainment and recreation. Today's consumer is hard-pressed to keep up with the myriad advances occuring each day, resulting in a vast information gap between manufacturers and the general public. Enter *VISIO*, a new monthly magazine devoted exclusively to bridging that gap, to bringing the new technology directly into consumers' lives and catering to their needs and interests in a manner unique among electronics publications. Charting this rapidly expanding technology, explaining how it works and how it affects our readers, will be the goal and focus of each issue." *VISIO* is a "consumer's electronics show" providing descriptions on the newest technology in the fields of audio, video, automotive, computer, home office, and recreation. For the 1990 sampled issue: full-color pages throughout on heavy coated paper stock in stapled magazine format (8 x 10 ¾ inches / 205 x 275 mm).

DEPT: "Editorial," "Off the Drawing Board," 'Inventions and dimensions on your retailers' shelves'; "Freeze Frame," video column by Cliff Roth; "Sound Advice," audio column by Bruce Avery; "Have Power, Will Travel," portable electronics column by David Miller; "Programming the Future," software column by Jerry Kindela; "The Electronic Mind," computer column by Craig Patchett; "The Home Office," column by Janet Endrijonas. (5-90).

TYPL: "What's New in Communications?," "Zooming In on Camcorders," "Video Dream Machines, a Connoisseur's Guide." (5-90).

SCHL: Monthly, 85 pp.
SPAN: May, 1990+

Vision

Spring, 1962 - Summer, 1962//
SEE: FILM COMMENT

✤ VISUAL COMMUNICATION NEWSLETTER, THE

SUB: "A division of the Association for Education in Journalism and Mass Communication."
PUBL: Association for Education in Journalism and Mass Communication, Visual Communication Division, 1621 College St., University of South Carolina, Columbia, SC 29208-0251.
DESC: This is a publication for the Visual Communication Division membership of the Association for Education in Journalism and Mass Communication. Articles cover events, convention sessions, creative teaching strategies, visual layout designs, visual literacy, documentary photojournalism, and a host of other pedagogical issues of interest to the academic membership division. For sampled issue of 1991: loose-leaf newsletter format, blue ink on light-grey uncoated paper stock, no advertising (8 ½ x 11 inches / 215 x 280 mm).
DEPT: "Personals." (7-91).

TYPL: "16 Sessions! Are We Growing or What!," "VisCom Goal is to Increase Visability Within AEJMC," "NPPA Proposes VisCom-NPPA Juried Academic Journal," "Evansville Mac Lab to Open in Fall," "South Carolina Students Try Knight-Ridder 'Hot Buttons'." (7-91).
SCHL: Monthly, 12 pp.
SPAN: ?+

✦ VISUAL EDUCATION

SUB: "The magazine of the National Committee for Audio-Visual Aids in Education."
SUB: "Developed from the National Committee's bulletin."
PUBL: National Committee for Audio-Visual Aids in Education, 254 Belsize Rd., London NW6 4BY, England.
DESC: This quality periodical details new software and hardware for the instructional educational fields. Over a span of several decades it has developed many excellent departmental features which make up the majority of the magazine, and which reflect the status of instructional education in Great Britain today. Well detailed with numerous graphics.
DEPT: "Roving Report," multipage newsbriefs; "Letters," "Technical News and Comment," 'Technical information service national audio-visual aids centre;' "Educational Broadcasting," BBC materials; "News from the Open University," ITV news; "A-V Workshop," new techniques; "Review Section," film, multimedia, filmstrip, audio, video, learning pack reviews.
TYPL: "Pre-School Children's Television and Language Development: a Study," "Leaving Home: Planning a Teaching Pack to Demonstrate the Facts," "CCTV at the Cheyene Spastics Centre," "Feminist Filmmakers Forever!," "Teaching the Visual Language of Film." (12- 79).
SCHL: Monthly, 45 pp.
SPAN: ?+
VARIES
--? - Jan, 1950 as Monthly Filmstrip Review.
WITH SUPPLEMENT
--Visual Aids, Films and Filmstrips, Jun, 1951 - ?
LC: LB 1043.5 .V57
DD: 371.33505
ISSN: 0042-7152
ABST: --Film Literature Index (ISSN: 0093-6758)

✦ VIZIONS

SUB: "The magazine of total multimedia."
PUBL: Vizions Publishing Corporation, 21 Elm St., PO Box 1328, Camden, ME 04843.
DESC: In the second issue of *Vizions*, Bruce A. Taylor, president of Camden New Media (parent firm) enters a fascinating discussion of what exactly multimedia is, the core-issue at the heart of *Vizions*: "Discovering what 'great multimedia' means will be one of this decade's most challenging quests. It will be a heuristic journey that we all will take--whether consciously or not. Figuring it out has a lot to do (we think) with understanding how the mind works--how we integrate information received through our senses, pass it through the screens and filters of our own existence and experience, massage it with our native intellect, and come up with 'new' knowledge that we can truly 'own' because of the individualized ways in which we gained it." *Vizions* is a wonderful new resource, poised on the threshold of the new visual technologies it reports about, explaining in studied terms to the lay audience, and boldly theorizing applications to the classroom, corporate office, and home living room. Mr. Taylor continues: "We'll explore with you the ways personal computing is integrating multimedia--everything from video compression to virtual reality. We'll get a close look at the work of leading developers in many fields. We'll tell you who's doing it. We'll let them explain to us the 'whys' and 'hows' of the technology tools use. In every issue, we'll look at how these technologies are being applied in education and training, art and entertainment, games and simulation, exhibit and public-access information, archives and libraries, medicine and science, commerce and industry, publishing and communications." This is an excellent publication for those in education, information systems, and the business world, enlightening readers about the impact, importance, and cost relationship of these new multimedia in the learning and information-seeking processes. Stapled magazine format, full-color throughout on coated paper stock (8 1/8 x 10 7/8 inches / 205 x 275 mm).
DEPT: "Editorial," "Market View," "Profile," "Tech Trends," "Opinion." (spring-91).
TYPL: "A Champion for Technology in Education," "Science Comes to School on CD-ROM," "The Seven Stages of Multimedia," "CD-ROM Enters the Computing Mainstream," "Interactive TV Casts Viewers as Directors." (spring-91).
SCHL: Quarterly, 35 pp.
SPAN: Winter, 1990/1991+
DD: 006
ISSN: 1053-6256

VJ-Time Drama

Oct, 1945//
SEE: DRAMA

✦ VTA PLAYBACK

SUB: "A quarterly newsletter published for the creators, writers, art directors, sponsors and broadcasters of programs, commercials, corporate films and special events."
PUBL: Video Tape Associates, 1575 Sheridan Rd., NE, Atlanta, GA 30324.
DESC: This is the promotional newsletter for Video Tape Associates, a production and post-production facility in Atlanta, Georgia. It is filled with news of client

projects, staff profiles, and commentary on industry trends by VTA officers. Three-fold newsletter format, spot color with black/white graphics.
DEPT: None. (3/4-89).
TYPL: "VTA Answers Client Questions About D-2 Format," "Clients Applaud Talents of Dave 'Zippy' Wheeler," "Successful Edit Depends On Open Communication." (3/4-89).
SCHL: Quarterly, 6 pp.
SPAN: ?+

VU Marketplace

May, 1979 - Jul, 1980//
(ISSN: 0149-6832)
SEE: VIDEO MANAGEMENT

VUE

SUB: "News magazine of CATV and pay-cable."
SUB: "Newsweekly of cable television."
SUB: "The weekly news service of TV and communications magazine."
PUBL: Cardiff Publishing, 6430 South Yosemite St., Englewood, CO 80111.
DESC: CATV's growth in the 70's was well documented by this brief, biweekly news magazine. Continuing many departments and columns by its predecessor (*CATV magazine*), *Vue* has expanded coverage with greater depth and special reports on this quick growth industry.
DESC: [*CATV*]: CATV was still not "big" business in 1967 when *CATV* began publishing. Even by 1971 there was no significant amount of news to report within the cable industry, as evidenced by the average 20-page issues. Software, being a relatively recent area, required *CATV* to report primarily on legal issues and technical developments.
DEPT: "CATV Week," newsbriefs; "CATV Headliners," personnel briefs; "CATV Viewpoint," editorial; "Point of Interest," Washington politics column by Jacqueline Morse; "CATV System News," national systems; "CATV Finance," economic and stock quotes; "CATV Profile," profile. (8-23- 71). "Insight," heard around town; "News Vue," current news items; "Careers," personnel briefs; "Systems Circuit," news of individual CATV systems; "The Market," economic and manufacturing newsbriefs; "Finance," "Stocks," "Programming," software--availability and acceptance; "Upcoming," calendar; "Profile," one catv executive profiled. (7-10-78).
TYPL: "Public Utility for Cable Systems Looms Larger on Eastern Horizon," "Cypress Invites CATV Use by Minorities," "NYC Sports Will be Shown on Continental Cablevision." (8-23-71). "Satellite Transmission--Everybody Loves a Winner," "How to Borrow Cable Dollars," "UPI Delivers Newstime Via RCA Satellite," "Warner Versus ABC at Ohio State." (7-10-78).
SCHL: Weekly (Mar, 1965 - Oct 18, 1976); Biweekly [except Dec], (? - ?); Weekly (? - 1978//), 30 pp.
SPAN: Mar, 1965 - Sep, 11, 1978//
VARIES
--Mar, 1965 - Aug, 1967 as Cable Television Review.
--Aug 14, 1967 - Oct 18, 1976 as CATV (ISSN: 0574-9204).
ABSORBED BY
--TVC (ISSN: 0164-8489), Oct 1, 1978.
LC: HE 8690.C

V
Communication Serials

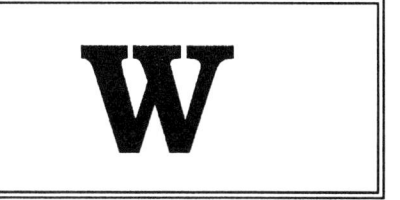

WACC Journal

1970 - 1979//
(ISSN: 0092-7821)
SEE: MEDIA DEVELOPMENT

War-Time Drama

Winter?, 1939/1940? - Apr?, 1945//
SEE: DRAMA

✣ WASHINGTON JOURNALISM REVIEW

SUB: "The national media magazine from Washington."
PUBL: Washington Journalism Review, 2233 Wisconsin Ave., NW, Washington, DC 20007.
DESC: "Newspapers, television, news magazines...a vast assortment of information brought to you 24 hours a day to shed light on events both large and small. Yet, who is left to sort through and illuminate the huge communication industry itself? The *Washington Journalism Review* is the authoritative source of information on one of the most profound influences in your life. We cannot avoid being bombarded by print and broadcast news, so take the time to read the one magazine that analyzes this news and gives you special insights. The *Washington Journalism Review* highlights the best in the business and tells the plain truth about why they are best. Regular features examine the business of journalism, profile people in the trade, look at legal issues, review books on the press, and give you technological updates." This brightly written, well-illustrated journalism review published in Washington, DC has articles which have both "bark and bite," and are well documented in their charges. It is an excellent addition to the growing list of regional journalism critiques. Stapled magazine format, color and black/white printing on coated paper stock throughout (8 3/8 x 11 inches / 210 x 280 mm).
DEPT: "Clippings," newsbriefs of the DC area; "Calendar," media conferences-expos to be held; "Boldface," profiles of 2-3 DC area newspeople; "Books," reviews; "Penpoint," editorial-commentary. (10-77). "Top of the Review," "Letters," "Movers & Shakers," "Clippings," "Books," "Take 2". (5-88).
TYPL: "ABC's Captain Success: Welcome to Roone's Wide World of News," "Newsletters: The Fourth and a half Estate," "J-Schools Held Captive in Bell-Shaped Curve," (10-77). "Owning Your Own Weekly," "Answering Hart & Kennedy," "Larry Flynt, Freedom Fighter," "CBS Eye on the Op-Ed Sparrow." (5-88).
SCHL: Monthly (? - ?); Ten issues per year (Jan/Feb, 1980+), 45 pp.
SPAN: Oct, 1977+
VARIES
--Oct, 1977 - 1980 as Washington Journalism Review (ISSN: 0149-1172).
--Jan/Feb, 1981 - Dec, 1982 as WJR (ISSN: 0743-9881).
LC: AP 2.W18
ISSN: 0741-8876
ABST: --Book Review Index (ISSN: 0524-0581)

Washington Journalism Review

Oct, 1977 - 1980//
(ISSN: 0149-1172)
SEE: WASHINGTON JOURNALISM REVIEW

✣ WASHINGTON NEWSPAPER, THE

SUB: "The journal of the Washington Newspaper Publishers Association."
SUB: "A publication dedicated to the study and improvement of journalism in Washington."
SUB: "Official publication, Washington Newspaper Publishers Association."
PUBL: Washington Newspaper Publishers Association, 3838 Stone Way North, Seattle, WA 98103.
DESC: The December, 1991 issue contains this quote by renowned newspaper reporter, Helen Thomas of UPI: "the newspaper delivers more public service for less money than any other institution." These words echo in the pages of *The Washington Newspaper*, the official publication of the Washington Newspaper Publishers Association. Emphasis is upon member news, reviews of photo pages, and new ideas in newspaper management and reporting. Articles report changes in local and regional newspaper ownership, innovative applications of newspaper promotion within the community, and the general status of newspaper operations in Washington state. The October/November, 1991 issue featured a story on examples of Washington state newspapers reaching out to the youth market; WNPA member winners of the Better Newspaper Contest; the purchase and sale of various newspaper operations; and news of editorial staff changes at state newspapers. Note: although the masthead reports publication to be monthly, the October, and November, 1991 issues were combined as volume 77, #3. For the sampled issues of 1991: folded, tabloid newspaper-style format; black ink with spot-color on newsprint; limited advertising to the trade (11 3/8 x 17 3/8 inches / 290 x 440 mm).

DEPT: "Gerry-Meandering," written by the WNPA manager; "WNPA Magazine memories," time-capsules; "Briefly," member newsbriefs; "The Copy Hook," news of Washington State press women. (12-78). "Opinion," "Publishers' Calendar," upcoming events; "People in the News," "--30--," obituaries; "Out of Our Minds," 'A collection of editorial excerpts from Washington community newspapers'. (12-91).
TYPL: "How to Handle the 'Big Story,'" "Problem: Public Records Vs Privacy," "Avoid 'Showdown' With Your News Sources on Public Records Issue." (12-78). "Should Newspapers Inform the Public?," "Nationwide Decline Hits Women Execs Hardest," "Dixie Lee Bradley Has Helped Community Newspapers Succeed," "Jennifer Simms is New Owner of the North Beach Beacon," "Chelan's Mirror Marks Centennial, 54 Years Under Gavin Ownership." (12-91).
SCHL: Monthly, 8 pp.
SPAN: 1914+
LC: PN 4700.W3
ISSN: 0043-0684

WATCH
SUB: "Television in the Eighties."
PUBL: Titsch Publishig Co., 1139 Delaware St., Box 4305, Denver, CO 80204.
DESC: *Watch* was a product of the tremendous technological breakthroughs experienced in the late seventies and anticipated for the decade of the eighties. In its initial issue, editor Paul FitzPatrick said: "*WATCH*, Television in the Eighties' principal purpose is to tie together all the threads of existing and emerging software and technological developments into a cohesive package of feature and analytical articles. The magazine, consequently, has no master other than the broad-based television business." *Watch* saw itself as a trade magazine to the newly emerging technological industries of satellites, cable, and interactive television. Colorful, dynamic layout design added to the overall impression of a burgeoning medium.
DEPT: "Behind the Lines," editorial; "New York Watch," "Letters," "Short Takes," newsbriefs; "People to Watch," "Los Angeles Watch," (5-80).
TYPL: "Programming Soars North of the Border," "The 'Premiere' of a New Pay TV Network," "A Circle of Critical Children," "Everyman's On-Line Information Resource," "Offbeat Programming: Videowest Storms the Bay," (5-80).
SCHL: Monthly, 60 pp.
SPAN: Dec, 1979 - May, 1980?//?
SUSPENDED
--Jan, 1980.
ABSORBED BY
--Cablevision, Oct, 1980.
LC: PN 1992 .W37
DD: 384.55/0973
ISSN: 0195-7961

✤ W • B
SUB: "Waldenbooks' news, reviews & exclusive interviews with today's hottest authors."
PUBL: The Walden Book Company, Inc., 201 High Ridge Rd., Stamford, CT 06904.
DESC: The purpose of this large-square format bimonthly is to promote merchandise, a mission well-accomplished through interesting interviews with major authors, side stories concerning new publications, and an extensive review of new books currently in Walden bookstores. Articles are witty, and accompanied by contemporary graphics and layout designs. This serial benefits the serious reader who does not subscribe to major literary reviews, as well as the profit side of the Walden Book Company, and book publishing in general. Note: although *W•B* is indeed a serial (being issued bimonthly), the front cover (sample issue Volume 1, Number 6, Mar/Apr, 1990), possesses an ISBN number rather than ISSN number assignment. Large square format design with numerous color graphics.
DEPT: "Letters," "Keeping Up With the Authors," author activities column by Jane Heller; "Inside Romance," "Grapevine," romance author activity column by Jennifer McCord; "The Acid Test," Science Fiction column by Peter Heck; "Quizmaster," Science Fiction quiz; "Deep Waters," mystery novel quiz; "New & Current," extensive new book review section feature full-color book covers. (3/4-90).
TYPL: "Master Storyteller Arthur Hailey Goes Behind the Scenes of the Evening News," "America's Hottest Christian Novelist, Frank Peretti, Says the New Age Movement May be Hazardous to Your Spiritual Health," "Jerry Baker, America's Best-Known Gardener, Maintains that Flowering Plants are Worth Their Care and Feeding." (3/4-90).
SCHL: Bimonthly, 65 pp.
SPAN: May/Jun, 1989+

✤ WCA NEWSLETTER
SUB: "World Communication Association."
PUBL: World Communication Association, c/o Dr. Ronald L. Applbaum, President, Westfield State College, Westfield, MA 01086.
DESC: In his presidential acceptance speech of July, 1991, President-elect Ronald L. Applbaum noted; "We are in the midst of an Information Age and a Communication Revolution. ... It is communication that provides the vehicle for dealing with the problems and complexities of our future--for spreading the ideas of different peoples. And the technologies of communication provide us the opportunity to pursue individuality to a degree not previously possible. They also allow us to share and access the experience and knowledge of others. Most importantly, they provide the analytical resource capable of dealing with the incredible environmental, economic and other structural interdependencies of the world. ... The World Communication Association also has a dream. A dream that maintaining peace throughout this globe

can be achieved through mutual understanding and more effective communication among and between people." The *WCA Newsletter* functions to disseminate information concerning the membership and the World Communication Association organization. Articles in the sampled issue detailed the entering presidential acceptance speech; described a communication program at the University of South Africa; presented a revised constitution and by-laws; and described the recently completed convention at the University of Jyväskylä, Finland. For the sampled issues of 1991: folded, newsletter format; black ink on uncoated paper (8 ½ x 11 inches / 215 x 280 mm).
DEPT: None. (fall-91).
TYPL: "Thinking in Different Terms," "The Communication Program: University of South Africa," "Revision of the WCA Constituion and By-Laws," "Convention News: Letter from Finland." (fall-91).
SCHL: Quarterly, 16 pp.
SPAN: ?+

✤ WEB
SUB: "The production management magazine of newspapers."
SUB: "Newspaper and magazine production."
PUBL: North American Publishing Co., Philadelphia, PA.
DESC: [*Newspaper Production*]: "Selectively distributed without charge to management personnel only in newspaper printing plants and trade service companies in the newspaper industry." In this trade publication with emphasis on the technical aspects of print operation, articles discuss cost factors, color, labor, and other issues of importance to print management.
DEPT: "Scanning the Industry," newsbriefs; "National News," briefs; "Installations," unique feature department detailing production plants receiving new print equipment; "Financial," newsbriefs; "Personnel," briefs; "Coming Events."
TYPL: "What's Wrong with ROP Color?," "Small Daily Does Big Job in Color Reproduction," "Industry Update: Survey of Typesetting Keyboards." (4-75).
SCHL: Monthly (Nov, 1972 - Oct, 1978); Bimonthly (Nov/Dec, 1978+), 50 pp.
SPAN: Nov, 1972+
FROM MERGER OF
--American Press (ISSN: 0003-0600) (and) Printing Management [Newspaper Industry edition].
VARIES
--Nov, 1972 - Aug, 1976 as Newspaper Production (ISSN: 0148-9631).
--Sep, 1976 - Sep, 1978 as Newspaper Production for North and South America (ISSN: 0148-964x).
LC: Z 119 .N42
DD: 658.8/09/070572
ISSN: 0191-4634
ABST: --ABI/Informer

Weekly Television Digest with Consumer Electronics
? - May 21, 1984//
(ISSN: 0897-5620)
SEE: TELEVISION DIGEST WITH CONSUMER ELECTRONICS

Welford Beaton's Hollywood Spectator
Jun, 1933 - Mar, 1934//
SEE: HOLLYWOOD SPECTATOR

✤ WESTERN JOURNAL OF SPEECH COMMUNICATION
SUB: "The official journal of the Western States Communication Association."
PUBL: Western States Communication Association, Executive Secretary-WSCA, Communication Department, University of Utah, Salt Lake City, UT 84112.
DESC: "The *Western Journal of Speech Communication* is the scholarly journal of the Western States Communication Association. It is dedicated to the publication of manuscripts that advance the learned public's understanding of any aspect of human speech communication. *WJSC* encourages contributions from scholars in rhetorical and communication theory, interpersonal communication, public address, philosophy of communication, language behavior, intercultural communication, argumentation, organizational communication, oral interpretation, group communication, free speech, and applied communication. All theoretical and methodological perspectives are welcome..." Other typical articles from 1991 included: "Perceiving Nonverbal Messages: Effects of Immediacy and Encoded Intent on Receiver Judgments," "'Just How Much Did That Wheelchair Cost?': Management of Privacy Boundaries by Persons with Disabilities," "Organizational Commitment and Identification: An Examination of Conceptual and Operational Convergence," and "How Employees See the Boss: Test of an Argumentative and Affirming Model of Supervisors' Communicative Behavior." For the sampled issues of 1969 through 1977: black ink on uncoated stock; cover consisting of black ink on tinted uncoated index stock. For the 1991 sampled issues: black ink on coated paper; cover comprised of spot-color ink on coated index stock. For all sampled issues: perfect-bound, journal format (6 x 9 inches / 155 x 230 mm).
DEPT: "News and Notes." (winter-69). "News and Notes." (winter-77). None. (fall-91).
TYPL: "Ours Just to Reason Why," "The Play Was Not the Thing," "Effects of Group Information upon Word Replacement," "The Shortest Treatise on the Art of Reading," "Symptomatic Signals in Speaking and Writing." (winter-69). "Symposium: What Criteria Should be Used to Judge the Admissibility of Evidence to Support Theoretical Propositions in Communication Research?" (winter-77). "Public Opinion and

the Nuclear Freeze: The Rhetoric of Popular Sovereignty in Foreign Policy Debate," "'Places in the Heart': The Rhetorical Force of an Open Text," "A Postmodern Look at Traditional Communication Postulates," "Cognitive Processing of One- and Two-sided Persuasive Messages," "Meta-Analysis Comparing the Persuasiveness of One-sided and Two-sided Messages." (fall-91).
SCHL: Quarterly, 90 pp.
SPAN: 1937+
VARIES
--1937 - 1975 as Western Speech (ISSN: 0043-4205).
--Spring, 1975 - Fall, 1976 as Western Speech Communication (ISSN: 0147-2216).
LC: PN 4071 .W45
DD: 001.54/2/05
ISSN: 0193-6700
ABST: --Communication Abstracts
--Current Index to Journals in Education (ISSN: 0011-3565)
--Historical Abstracts (ISSN: 0018-2435)
--Human Resources Abstracts
--Linguistics & Language Behavior Abstracts
--Psychological Abstracts (ISSN: 0033-0202)
--Sociological Abstracts (ISSN: 0038-0202)

Western Monthly [Kansas City]
1902 - Sep, 1907//
SEE: ADVERTISING ADVOCATE

✧ WESTERN PHOTOGRAPHER MAGAZINE
SUB: "The magazine for the serious photographer."
PUBL: BKY Publications, PO Box 19269, San Diego, CA 92159.
DESC: *Western Photographer* is a unique magazine devoted to the activities of Serious Photographers throughout the U.S.A. It is written for serious photographers and about serious photographers including our future models. We are concerned with the activities, events, contests and photographic opportunities which are or will become available to all photographers and models. ... As the only publication of its kind, in its 31st year, *Western Photographer* provides inter-council communication; conducts photo contests; assists and advises those who wish to sponsor or promote photo events." This magazine packs information and pictures into an 80-page format on a wide variety of topics. Interestingly, many advertisements are placed in side-columns. Articles are written by professionals, and reflect their commitment to their work and helping others. This is a wonderful resource for today's commercial photographer. Regretfully, it is published on newsprint. Stapled magazine format, black/white editorial content with multi-color cover, numerous advertisements for photographic equipment and services (8 x 10 ½ inches / 205 x 265 mm).
DEPT: "The Bear Facts," 'From the Editor's Desk' editorial column by S. T. Bear; "The Feminine Eye," column by Joyce E. Widoff; "Calendar of Events," "Photo Traveler Tours," "The View From Arizona," column by Ron Wilhelm; "Book and Video Reviews," column by Jack Qualman; "The Video Invasion," column by Bob Keller; "The Photo Bug," column by M. R. Dolliver; "Stokes' Notes From the Darkroom," column by Orvil Stokes; "Modeling Plus," column by Joi Ashli; "Marketing Your Photographs," column by Rohn Engh; "Snapshots," photographic newsbriefs column by Shutter Speed; "Trade Shows," upcoming; "Art/Exhibits/Seminars," upcoming; "Classes, Workshops & Tours," upcoming; "Model of the Month." (5-91).
TYPL: "Why I Build Cameras," "Photographing Tennis," "Girls of Winter, Australia," "Photo Marketing," "Right of Privacy." (5-91).
SCHL: Monthly, 80 pp.
SPAN: Jan, 1961+

Western Speech
1937 - 1975//
(ISSN: 0043-4205)
SEE: WESTERN JOURNAL OF SPEECH COMMUNICATION

Western Speech Communication
Spring, 1975 - Fall, 1976//
(ISSN: 0147-2216)
SEE: WESTERN JOURNAL OF SPEECH COMMUNICATION

✧ WHAT EDITORS WANT
SUB: "A monthly special report for writers, literary agents, publicists, artists, cartoonists, and photographers."
PUBL: The Writers Institute, 70 5th Ave., New York, NY.
DESC: *What Editors Want* is a succinct title for this serial published by the Writers Institute of New York City. The typewritten format covers different aspects of the writing process, and submission guidelines of several different periodicals. Information is very thorough, and should help authors achieve successful sales.
DEPT: "History," a short description of the publication; "The Editor," profile; "Articles," large section detailing specific articles purchased; "Style," "Payment and Length," "Questions to the Editor," interesting section in which Q&A inquiries are made of the profiled editor; "Save Your Stamps," Articles not accepted; "Art and Photography," "Summary." (1-64).
TYPL: None.
SCHL: Monthly, 60 pp.
SPAN: ?+?
LC: PN 101.W

✧ WHAT SATELLITE
SUB: "Buying & using satellite."

SUB: "Day by day satellite programmes."
SUB: "What to buy and what to watch."
SUB: "From the publishers of *What Video*."
PUBL: WV Publications, Ltd., 57/59 Rochester Place, London NW1 9JU, England.
DESC: Satellite television programming, technological trends, and legal developments for the British video consumer make *What Satellite* sparkle. Each month the 140+ page publication packs some 25-plus departmental and feature segments on the satellite television industry into its editorial content, with a strong emphasis on new technology, and legal/legislative developments which will affect the British home consumer. Articles are authoritative, and well-detailed. It is a good resource for this British entertainment medium. For the sampled 1990 issue: stapled magazine format, numerous black/white and color graphics, editorial content consisting of black ink, spot and full-color pages, including full-color cover on coated paper stock (8 3/8 x 11 3/4 inches / 215 x 300 mm).
DEPT: "What's News," varied British satellite news; "Your Letters," 'Praise and scorn, rantings and ravings'; "Viewpoint," commentary column by Barry Fox; "Dish Doctor," Q&A column by Andy Demetriou; "Dish Owner's Guide to Europe," 'Our regular run-down of all the satellite channels available to UK dish owners'; "Satellite Search," 'Get the most out of your system with our guide to TV from space'; "Test Report," equipment profile; "Buyers Guide," 'Equipment run-down--prices, features and form'; "Programming," "No Holds Barred," 'The first of our regular columns for wrestling fans'; "Sparklies," '*What Satellite's* quick fax on what's happening in satellite TV technology'. (3-90).
TYPL: "Sky or BSB?, Time to Choose," "Ten Tips for the Perfect Dish," "Sort Out This Scrambling Mess," "When BBC and ITV Signals Interfere with Satellite TV." (3-90).
SCHL: Monthly, 140 pp.
SPAN: ?+

✤ WHAT VIDEO

SUB: "Britain's best selling video magazine."
PUBL: WV Publications, Ltd., 57-59 Rochester Place, London NW1 9JU, England.
DESC: "*What Video* is the comprehensive guide to the world of video technology, offering a mix of in-depth hardware tests together with a variety of features, articles and news." Another advertisement refers to it as "...the definitive guide to new VCRs, camcorders, bargain prices and every possible exciting development in video technology." *What Video*, with 170+ pages each month, keeps the British video consumer abreast of what's new on the technological and software fronts. Of special note are some half-dozen notable "Equipment Tests" used to profile and critique new video products. It is an excellent resource on British consumer video. For the sampled issue of 1990: perfect-bound magazine format with mixture of black ink, spot- and full-color pages on coated paper stock (8 1/4 x 11 3/4 inches / 210 x 300 mm).
DEPT: "Hi-Tech News," newsbriefs; "Electronic Mail," letters; "Video Clinic," 'Paul Richards ponders your problems'; "Britain," video comment and news column by Barry Fox; "America," video comment and news stateside column by Robert Angus; "Japan," video comment and news column by Allan Shriver; "21st Century Emporia," 'We highlight the latest diversions in advanced home entertainment'; "Movies on Tape," 'Paul Andrews looks at the latest releases on tape for sale or rental' column by Paul Andrews; "Buyers Guide," "Last Lines," 'Small talk and hot wax from the flip side of *What Video*'. (3-90).
TYPL: "The Pros and Cons of Budget Nicam," "Genlocks Explained," "BSB--A Credible Alternative to Sky TV," "Cross-Colour Killers." (3-90).
SCHL: Monthly, 170 pp.
SPAN: ?+
ISSN: 0956-2354

✤ WHAT'S WORKING

SUB: "In DM and fulfillment."
PUBL: JPL Publications, United Communications Group, 4550 Montgomery Ave., Suite 700N, Bethesda, MD 20814.
DESC: Direct mail pieces must be exemplary to stand out among the 2,000+ items mailed every month in the United States. That means creative quality control from copy design to envelope printing; multi-color layout to die-cut pop-up attention-grabbing media that will hold the attention of the recipient long enough to buy, subscribe, or initiate a telephone order. Editor Patricia Cody provides a goldmine of information to the direct mail specialist, as she details prime examples of what worked and didn't work with consumers. *What's Working* even provided the results of their own direct mail test with two unique envelope appeals using the phrase, "This is a Test," on one and, "Wait! Don't Drop that Mailing" on the other. The ideas contained in reviewed samples are fresh and unique, and provide a springboard for subscriber's own direct mail projects. Of special note is the name, company, mailing address and telephone number for the designers of these successful promotions. It is an excellent resource (even at 1990 yearly subscription price of $182) for advertising agencies, in-house corporate marketing centers, and direct mail specialists. For sampled issue of 1990: typewritten copy, printed black/white, three-hole punched newsletter format with graphics on uncoated paper stock (8 1/2 x 11 inches / 215 x 280 mm).
DEPT: None. (1-15-90).
TYPL: "Check Out These Response Builders," "Natural History Museum Uses Member Interests to Lure Birds of a Feather," "Nothing Looks Special About This Fund-Raising Appeal Except Results." (1-15-90).
SCHL: Biweekly, 6 pp.
SPAN: ?+

❖ WHO'S MAILING WHAT!

SUB: "The monthly newsletter, analysis and record of the Direct Marketing Archive."
PUBL: Who's Mailing What!, Inc., 210 Red Fox Rd., Stamford, CT 06903.
DESC: "The 1,000 to 1,500 mailings listed in each issue of *WHO'S MAILING WHAT!* represent a single month of mail. When these mailings come in, they become part of the finest collection of direct mail in the world. The Direct Marketing Archive can make you an instant expert (overnight if need be) on what's in the mail in more than 175 business and consumer categories." This most unusual publication catalogs, reviews, and archives a variety of printed direct mail pieces aimed at the American public. Editor and publisher Denison Hatch throws out "roses and onions" at the reviewed packages in a fresh and direct manner; with a considered use of print quality, graphics, layout design, copy and color. Some four pages of 5-6 point type at the back of each issue lists direct mail pieces received by the publication during the previous month. It is this latter service which easily justifies the $168 yearly fee, providing overnight or fax service of sample items to subscribers only. This is an excellent resource for any publisher, advertising agency, or marketing specialist wanting to know *WHO'S MAILING WHAT!* For the sampled issue of 1989: typewriten copy in stapled magazine format; two-color covers with graphics of sample direct mail pieces all on uncoated paper stock (8 ⅜ x 10 ⅞ inches / 215 x 275 mm).
DEPT: "Direct Responses," letters; "Reviews," of items connected with direct mail; "Trends," in direct mail; "Offshore Data Entry," direct mail trends and news outside the States; "This Month in the Archive," new direct mail items added to the Direct Marketing Archive; "The Monthly Record," incredible monthly listing of direct mail items received at the Direct Marketing Archive. (11-89).
TYPL: "The Top Seven," "Catalogs on Demand," "The Business of Faxing." (11- 89).
SCHL: Monthly, 16 pp.
SPAN: Oct, 1984+
DD: 659 11
ISSN: 8755-2671

❖ WHO'S WHO IN MOVIES AND TV

PUBL: Sterling's Magazines, 355 Lexington Ave., New York, NY 10017.
DESC: *Who's Who* attempts to cover everything and everybody that's "hot" in motion pictures and television. A quick glance at any cover may make it hard to believe that they have missed anyone. Like its counterparts, the emphasis is on gossip, photos, and little known information about Hollywood's great and not-so-great. Although publicity shots of stars at public events make up a significant portion of this publication, there are interesting pictorial surveys of newly breaking motion pictures as well. Of special note is the "Star Index," an alphabetical listing of all stars mentioned in that issue.
DEPT: "Star Index," alphabetical listing; "Celebrity Party Line," 'Latest, hottest gossip burning up the wires...'; "The Stars' Addresses," for those wishing to write; "Heavenly Stars," a horoscope for stars and their readers.
TYPL: "Farrah, Cher, and--Margret and Others Share Clothes, Hair, Make-Up, Diet, Exercise and Plastic Surgery Secrets," "Elvis 'Life Story' in Clip'n Save Photo Album!," "Twenty Bedroom Scandals! Twenty Superstar Couples and Those Hollywood Schockers the Town Can't Forget!," "Celebrities Who Sample California Love Cults," "Macho Men Who Make Their Women Suffer." (3-79).
SCHL: ?, 75 pp.
SPAN: ?+

❖ WIDE ANGLE

SUB: "A film quarterly of theory, criticism and practice."
SUB: "A quarterly journal of film history, theory & criticism."
SUB: "A quarterly journal of film history, theory, criticism and practice."
PUBL: Ohio University, Department of Film, College of Fine Arts and the Athens International Film Festival, Box 388, Athens, OH 45701.
DESC: *Wide Angle* was born in the best of circumstances as a set of elaborate program notes for the 1976 Athens International Film Festival. Both the Festival and *Wide Angle* magazine are doing well. Layout of this magazine is similar to other film critiques, covering far ranging topics from comedy to special effects, from avant-garde films to nickelodeons. It is notable for its fine layout, and love for film. Each issue focuses on a single theme, i.e., "Independent Filmmakers," "John Ford," "Film Aesthetics," and "Modern European Cinema." A promotional advertisement characterized the publication: "*Wide Angle* presents today's best scholarship in film studies and examines a wide range of topics from international cinema to the history and aesthetics of film." Of special note is Wide Angle's reporting on films and filmmakers within the Midwest, an area seldom addressed. Some typical articles from 1991 included "The Perils of Pleasure? Fan Magazine Discourse as Women's Commodified Culture in the 1920s;" "'O, Lubitsch, Where Wert Thou?', 'Passion', the German Invasion and the Emergence of the Name 'Lubitsch';" "'A Host of Others': Toward a Nonlinear History of Poverty Row and the Coming of Sound;" and "The Dream of Disruption: Melodrama and Gag Structure in Keaton's 'Sherlock Junior'." Sampled issue from 1991: perfect-bound wide-journal format, black ink on uncoated paper, cover is two-color ink on coated paper stock (8 ⅝ x 7 ⅞ inches / 220 x 200 mm).
DEPT: "Books," thoughtful reviews. (4-91).

TYPL: "Snap!thology and Other Discursive Practices in Tongues Untied," "Through Brazilian Eyes: America," "Something Borrowed, Something Taped: Video Nuptials," "The Mirror Framed: A Case for Expression in Documentary," "Point of View and Spectator Position in 'Meat and Primate'." (4-91).
SCHL: Quarterly, 75 pp.
SPAN: Spring, 1976+
LC: PN 1993.W48
DD: 791.43/05
ISSN: 0160-6840
ABST: --Film Literature Index (ISSN: 0093-6758)
--Media Review Digest (ISSN: 0363-7778)

Wid's

Jun 1, 1916 - May 2, 1918//
SEE: FILM TV DAILY

Wid's Daily

May 8, 1918 - Dec, 31, 1921//
SEE: FILM TV DAILY

Wid's Films and Film Folk

Oct 14, 1915 - May 25, 1916//
SEE: FILM TV DAILY

WIRE & RADIO COMMUNICATIONS

SUB: "A semi-monthly journal devoted to land-line telegraphs, submarine cable interests, radio-telegraphy and allied industries." (1883 - 1909).
SUB: "Published since 1883 to further the advancement of communications techniques." (Jan, 1965 - Feb, 1965).
PUBL: Communications Publishing Corporation, P.O. Box 50, Verona, NJ.
DESC: During the heyday of the land telegraph line, no member of the Order of Commercial Telegraphers of North America would be without his official organ; *The Telegraph Age* (or its successive non-union titles), a trade journal of technical information and news. During the 1890s, the Commercial Telegraphers group came under suspicion by the major land telegraph corporations, and this magazine primarily addressed news concerning such treatment; as well as adressing work place issues. The last issues of this serial was as a general business publication for land and radio operated communication firms. The new serial title of *Wire & Radio Communications* only lasted two issues before succumbing to a lack of interest from readers. There were few graphics in early issues, with most space devoted to news items, especially anecdotes and newsbriefs of local operations, and some schematics as they applied to system development. Latter issues in 1909 contained more advertising than editorial content.
DEPT: "Editorial." (1-1-1893). "Some Points on Electricity," "Editorial," "New Books," "Educational," (1-1-1899). "Reviews & Books," "Financial News." (1-65).
TYPL: "Reinstated O.R.T. Strikers," "Typewriters at the World's Fair," "One by One They Pass Away." (1-1-1893). "A Direct-Reading Ohmmeter," "Got Even with the News' Thief," "Shortest Telegraph Line," "The Telegraph in Porto Rico and Cuba," (1-1-1899). "Interesting Subjects Treated in Back Issues," "Some Valuable Telegraph Books," "Maver and Davis' Quadruplex," (12-16-1909). "Uncrowded UHF Communications," "New Problems in Interference," "Cable Coast-to-Coast." (1-65).
SCHL: Semimonthly (? - ?); Monthly (Jul, 1953+), 35 pp.
SPAN: 1883 - Feb, 1965//
VARIES
--1883 - Dec 16, 1909 as Telegraph Age.
--Jan, 1910 - Jun, 1953 as Telegraph and Telephone Age.
--Jul, 1953 - Jan, 1959 as Wire and Radio Communications.
ABSORBED BY
--Communication News (ISSN: 0010-3632), Mar, 1965.
LC: TK 1.T4

Wire and Radio Communications

Jul, 1953 - Jan, 1959//
SEE: WIRE & RADIO COMMUNICATIONS

WIRELESS AGE, THE

SUB: "An illustrated monthly magazine of radio communication."
SUB: "The radio magazine."
PUBL: Wireless Press, 326 Broadway, New York, NY.
DESC: *Wireless Age* was an information-packed magazine for the radio novice, amateur operator, program listener, and audio professional. Articles, as befitted that exciting developmental period of radio history, concentrated on new equipment for purchase or building, and the thrill of being able to pick up long-distance radio stations. The viewpoint that radio would be an uplifting experience to American education and culture can be seen within regular feature stories on voice diction, and cultural programming. Many articles were written by broadcast pioneer manufacturers; such as Crosby, Voorhees, and Bradley. One indication of the turbulant times was a disclaimer for items deleted due to "Controversy in scientific circles and in the courts, either now or in the future," a reference to the patent struggles of the era.
DEPT: "Editorial Chat," "Broadcast Impressions," an unique page of cartoons showing readers what popular radio broadcasters looked like; "Cross- word Contest," related to radio terminology; "World-Wide News," international radio briefs via Wireless Age managing

	editor; "Appliances and Devices," newsbriefs of new products; "Broadcasting Station Directory," useful feature listing call letters, frequencies and owner of individual stations.
TYPL:	"Continental Re-Broadcasts," "Rural Life Modernized--Radio Broadcasting is Turning the Wanderlust Spirit of Youth Away from the Big Cities Back to the Country and Great Open Spaces," "The Wampas Baby Stars of 1925," "The Women's Hour," "The Funmaker of Roxies Gang," "Meet Some of the Atlantic Coasts Popular Broadcasters," "Tube Transmitter Design." (3-25).
SCHL:	Monthly, 100 pp.
SPAN:	Oct, 1912 - Aug, 1925// VARIES --Oct, 1912 - Mar, 1913 as Marconigraph. SUSPENDED --Apr, 1913 - Sep, 1913. ABSORBED BY --Popular Radio, Sep, 1925.
LC:	TK 5700.W4

Wireless Engineer

Jan, 1936 - Dec, 1956//
SEE: INDUSTRIAL ELECTRONICS

Wireless Engineer and Experimental Wireless

Sep, 1931 - Dec, 1935//
SEE: INDUSTRIAL ELECTRONICS

Wireless World, The

Jul, 1932 - Sep, 1983//
(ISSN: 0043-6062)
SEE: ELECTRONICS WORLD + WIRELESS WORLD

Wireless World and Radio Review, The

Apr, 1922 - Jun, 1932//
SEE: ELECTRONICS WORLD + WIRELESS WORLD

✦ WISCONSIN PHOTOGRAPHER

SUB:	"Wisconsin's new photo monthly--a publication serving the photo-graphic enthusiast."
PUBL:	Wisconsin Photographer, 771 N. Water St., Milwaukee, WI 53202.
DESC:	This tabloid-sized publication provides publicity and is a means of state-wide communications for "badger" photographers and members of allied fields. Articles range from academic coursework to professional photo-journalism; from photo galleries to sports photography. Interesting interviews with professional photographers compliment the liberal use of photos in each issue. Printed on quality paper stock.
DEPT:	"Coming Into Focus," news briefs of exhibits and camera clubs; "Collectables," 'a column exploring the world of photographica;' "Technicalities," 'Advice on technical matters for all photographers;' "Photographic Profiles," "Stock and Trade," 'focusing on Wisconsin photo dealers and manufacturers;' "Sell and Swap," "The Back Page," 'a photographic statement.'
TYPL:	"A Place for Photography," "Moon Flight Soared Around the World," "A City's Family Album." (11-78).
SCHL:	Monthly, 30 pp.
SPAN:	Oct, 1978+ SUSPENDED --Dec, 1978.
ISSN:	0164-4122

✦ WITTYWORLD

SUB:	"International cartoon magazine."
PUBL:	WittyWorld Publications, PO Box 1458, North Wales, PA 19454.
DESC:	"*WittyWorld* is published quarterly for professionals in related fields of graphics, advertising, illustration, animation and commercial arts; students and academicians; art communication and cultural programs and cartoon fans and collectors." This publication delights the eye, while providing scholarly historical insight into the art and technique of cartooning. The art of cartooning is oftentimes in the midst of politics, and much editorial content is given over to the consequent current or historical plight of international cartoonists and their works. This is a treasure-trove of information concerning film, legal rights, comic books, political cartooning, syndication, exhibits, festivals; in short, world-wide developments in cartooning. Editorial content is segmented into "Comics," "Editorial/Political," "General Gag," and "Museum." Well recommended. Numerous graphic reprints of cartoons.
DEPT:	"Letters," "Witty Wire," newsbriefs; "Law," legal aspects; "Reviews," "Cartoon Laboratory," profile; "Syndicate," "Calendar." (fall-87).
TYPL:	"Spain's Unknown Cartoonist," "The Francisco V. Coching Art Exhibit," "Poison Penmen," "Editor Jailed Over a Cartoon in India," "Polish Contemporary Cartoon," "Switzerland, Satire and Serious People." (fall-87).
SCHL:	Quarterly, 50 pp.
SPAN:	Summer, 1987+
DD:	741
ISSN:	0892-9807

WJR

Jan/Feb, 1981 - Dec, 1982//
(ISSN: 0743-9881)
SEE: WASHINGTON JOURNALISM REVIEW

WOMEN & FILM
PUBL: Women and Film, Box 4501, Berkeley, CA 94704.
DESC: This is an excellent publication exploring the role of women and film; which for the sampled issues of 1975, unfortunately were published on newsprint. Articles cover a variety of subjects in style, creating a great resource for film studies. Good layout and graphics.
DEPT: "Third World Perspectives," fascinating section concerning development of film and relationship to women in new nations; "Independent Women's Cinema," "Ideological Massage," reviews; "Movie Channel," reviews; "Super 8 News," "San Francisco Filmex," "Book Reviews," "Feedback/Feedforward," letters. (summer-75).
TYPL: "Report from Knokke: Exprimental-5," "Interview with Jill Godmilow," "Interview with Eleanor Perry," "Documentary, Realism & Women's Cinema," "New Day Films: an Alternative in Distribution." (summer-75).
SCHL: Three times per year, 130 pp.
SPAN: 1972 - Aug, 1976//
LC: PN 1993.W
DD: 396
ISSN: 0049-7797

✤ WOMEN & LANGUAGE
PUBL: Women & Language, Communication Department, George Mason University, Fairfax, VA 22030.
DESC: "*Women and Language* is an interdisciplinary research periodical affiliated with the Organization for the Study of Communication Language and Gender and currently published by the Communication Department at George Mason University, Fairfax, Virginia. The mission of *Women and Language* is to provide a feminist forum for those interested in communication, language and gender. It seeks to stimulate dialogue and inquiry centering the questions of how gender is constructed and how the processes of difference, dichotomy and hierarchy are involved in such gender constructions. It aims to uncover the interconnections among sex, gender, race, class, and heterosexual hegemony, examining the role of symbolic communication, verbal and nonverbal, in those processes and connections, attending especially to the impacts of masculinist paradigms in communication. *Women and Language*, a periodical that is both newsletter and journal, provides an outlet for descriptive research and theoretical speculation and welcomes submissions of completed research, essays, personal narratives, poetry, information about work in progress, bibliographical materials, and news. It seeks to share information from conferences, magazines, newspapers, scholarly publications and correspondence from around the world." For the sampled issue of 1991: black ink on uncoated paper; cover consisting of black ink with spot-color on uncoated index stock; no advertising; stapled magazine format (8 ¼ x 11 inches / 210 x 280 mm).
DEPT: "Report from Media Watch," "Book Reviews," "Journals and Periodicals," review; "Films and Videos," review. (spring-91).
TYPL: "Lesbian Pornography: Cultural Transgression and Sexual Demystification," "The Silenced Majority: Women in Israel's 1988 Television Election Campaign," "Strategies and Tactics: Teenagers' Readings of an Australian Soap Opera," "Television's Realist Portrayal of African-American Women and the Case of 'L.A. Law'." (spring-91).
SCHL: Quarterly (Jan, 1976 - Winter, 1977); Three issues per year (Spring, 1978 - Winter, 1978); Semiannual (Spring, 1979 - Fall, 1979); Annual (Winter, 1980 - Spring, 1982); Semiyearly (Winter, 1983+), 60 pp.
SPAN: Jan, 1976+

WOODCOCK'S PRINTERS' AND LITHOGRAPHERS' WEEKLY GAZETTE AND NEWSPAPER REPORTER
SUB: "Only authoritative weekly typographical paper published." (Jan 6, 1879? - Mar 24, 1879).
SUB: "The only weekly journal published treating on typography, lithography, bookbinding and stationery." (Mar 31, 1879 - ?).
PUBL: W.H. Woodcock, American Printers' Warehouse, 78 - 80 Murray St., New York, NY.
DESC: This small-format serial was a valuable resource of second-hand type, equipment, inks, and helpful trade news for the newspaper publisher. Issues from 1875 dwelt primarily on circulation figures, news of management changes, and other eclectic articles. The February 22, 1875 issue devoted a page and one-half to "Rules for Playing Draw Poker." By 1879, issues focused on specific news developments of circulation, and press, and took on a greater degree of seriousness; with a few notable exceptions, such as an article for December 29, 1879 entitled "The Stomachaphone," and subtitled "Edison Outdone--a Machine that will, by wire, Distribute Hash and Beer." Few illustrations.
DEPT: "Newspaper Intelligence," newsbriefs concerning changes; "Personals," "Press and Printer," newsbriefs concerning; "State of Trade," one-line status quos in American cities; "Tramps," status report of hoboes showing up at various newspaper offices; "News Items," "Correspondence," "Questions & Answers," "Circulations," "Trade Notices," "Miscellaneous." (1-4-1875). "Tidings from the Craft." (12-29-1879).
TYPL: "The Newspaper of the Future," "Setting and Distributing." (1-4-1875). "Impersonality in Newspapers," "The Stomachaphone," "Police Court Scene in a Western City." (12-29-1879).
SCHL: Weekly, 12 pp.
SPAN: Jan, 1871 - 1884?//
VARIES
--? - ? as American Newspapers and Printers Gazette.
LC: PN 4700.A5

✤ WORLD BROADCAST NEWS

SUB: "News of technology for international broadcasters."
PUBL: World Broadcast News, 888 7th Ave., 38th Floor, New York, NY 10106.
DESC: *World Broadcast News* is an international magazine of broadcast technology, providing a forum for information on emerging technical equipment, comparing existing world facilities, and serving as an advertising vehicle to reach international broadcast executives. This is one of a very few American publications with an almost exclusive international television editorial content, and provides a needed advertising forum for American television equipment manufacturers and distributors. There is some emphasis on American broadcast news. It is sent on a complimentary basis only to those individuals responsible for broadcast operations outside the United States and Canada. Typical articles from 1991 included, "Versatile Generator for D2-MAC," "3-D, Why and How," "NAB Radio '91: Grappling with a Digital Future," "Satellites: Local Coverage from the Skies," and "InterBEE 91: Bigger than ever at Makurhari Messe." Additional reports included Moscow, London, Vienna, Jakarta, Budapest, New York, Auckland, Tokyo, Sydney, Dar Es Salaam, Buenos Aires, Columbo, Port of Spain, Ndola, Geneva, Amsterdam, Beijing, Manama, Dublin, Milan, Kuala Lumpur, and Basingstoke. An exceptional publication for the world of commercial and public broadcasting. For sampled issue of 1988: stapled magazine format; with mixture of black/white, spot- and full-color pages on coated paper stock (8 x 11 inches / 205 x 280 mm).
DEPT: "World Watch," newsbriefs; "UN Perspective," United Nations activities in film and video; "International Product Review," "Global Marketplace." (6-84). "Late News Roundup," "Letter From America," column by Gerald Walker; "World Watch," broadcast newsbriefs listed via nation; "Products," review; "Global Marketplace," "On Air," '...an open channel to air comments, observations, gossip, and the unconventional about the international broadcast scene'. (1-88).
TYPL: "West Germany Moves Towards Private Television," "Canada Widens Program Choice with New Special Service Channels," "NAB Exhibit is Tour de Force of Technology," "MIP-TV Hints at Programming Revolution in the Wings," "Digital Still Stores Becoming More Versital and Affordable," "Many Ways to Read Audio Levels." (6-84). "Satellite News Gathering, HDTV Systems Spark Busy InterBEE," "Irish Pirates Turn Legitimate Local Stations," "The Era of Change--Italy." (1-88).
SCHL: Eleven issues per year (with combined Jul/Aug Directory of World Broadcast Equipment), 50 pp.
SPAN: Jan, 1978+
VARIES
--Jan, 1978 - Jan, 1990 as BM/E's World Broadcast News.
DD: 384 11
ISSN: 1050-012x

✤ WORLD COMMUNICATION

SUB: "The journal of the Communication Association of the Pacific."
SUB: "A journal of the World Communication Association."
PUBL: World Communication Association, Ronald Applbaum, Secretary General, Pan American University, AB 320, Edinburg, TX 78539.
DESC: [*Communication*]: This small-format, typewritten journal served as a forum for submitted papers, with an emphasis on interpersonal speech communication for the Communication Association of the Pacific. There were no graphics. Published on a somewhat erratic schedule, *Communication* ceased publication in September, 1984 and was continued by the annual, *Communication Reports*, which appeared in December, 1984 by the World Communication Association before cessation. For the sampled issues of 1983 and 1984: stapled journal format; typewritten black ink on uncoated paper; cover consisting of spot-color on beige uncoated index stock; no advertising (7 x 9 ⅛ inches / 180 x 230 mm).
DESC: [*World Communication*] "*World Communication* is committed to publishing articles of ten pages or more of text that (1) report findings related to human communication; (2) discuss methodological issues; (3) review literature; and (4) provide synthesis and analysis of significant contemporary communication issues." The spring, 1988 issue detailed editorial policies, among them being a listing of "...the range of human communication forms and functions, and areas of study, that may be within the purview of this journal: aging, business and professional, children's speech, diffusion of innovations, ethics, executive and management development, family, forensics, gender-related, health services, instructional, interpersonal, intercultural, international, legal, linguistic symbolization, listening, mass media, nonverbal, organizational, political, rhetoric and culture, small group, and technological communication: computers, electronic mail, and message systems." This is a splendid journal for the study of the form and function of communication in international fields of application. Note: the July, 1991 issue of *World Communication* still maintains ISSN: 0882-4088, assigned (according to some sources) to the earlier *Communication*. For the sampled issues of 1985 through 1991: perfect-bound, journal format; no advertising (7 x 9 ⅛ inches / 180 x 230 mm). Commencing with the July, 1991 issue, editorial content was black ink on coated paper; cover consisting of blue ink on coated index stock.
DEPT: None. (12-83). None. (7-91).
TYPL: "The intercultural Perspective on Human Communication," "Racial Perceptions of Communicator Style," "A Cross-Cultural Comparison of Personal Characteristics and Skills Attributed to Communicatively Competent Persons Within Organizations," "Management as Communication: Performance Evaluation and Employee Self- Worth." (12-83). "Politics and Communication in a New World Age," "Herbert Matthews and Castro's Revolution: A Lapse in Discretion

at 'The New York Times'," "Three Pioneers of Cuban Television," "Principal's Use of Power, Behavior Alteration Strategies and Affinity-Seeking Strategies: Effects on Teacher Job Satisfaction," "Cultural Differences in Public Speaking." (7-91).
SCHL: Three issues per year [irregular at times] (Jul, 1972 - Sep, 1984); Annually (Dec, 1984); Semiannual (Spring, 1985+), 140 pp.
SPAN: Jul, 1972+
VARIES
--Jul, 1972 - Sep, 1984 as Communication (ISSN: 0882-4088).
--Dec, 1984 as Communication Reports.
ABST: --Language and Language Behavior Abstracts (ISSN: 0023-8295)

World Film News

Apr, 1936 - ?//
SEE: DOCUMENTARY FILM NEWS

World Film News

Feb, 1937 - Aug, 1938//
SEE: DOCUMENTARY FILM NEWS

World Film News and Television Progress

?, 1936 - Jan, 1937//
SEE: DOCUMENTARY FILM NEWS

✦ WORLD MEDIA REPORT

SUB: "Quarterly journal of the World Media Study Group."
SUB: "A global survey of trends and developments in print & electronic media."
PUBL: World Media Report, Box 519, Baldwin Pl., New York, NY 10505-0519.
DESC: This relatively new quarterly publishes news columns on the status of mass media on the international scene. As authors are identified only by name, it is unknown whether these news articles are based upon visitation, or observation; or if they are residents of the individual nations about which they are writing. Special emphasis is on the political status of mass media activities within reported nations. No graphics.
DEPT: "Book Reviews." (5-83).
TYPL: "Development Journalism: Another Perspective," "Some Impressions of the Cuban Mass Media," "Media Report from South Africa," "Unions & a Free Press in Great Britain," "Media Report from Australia." (5-83).
SCHL: Quarterly, 12 pp.
SPAN: Feb, 1983+
LC: P 87.W63
DD: 001.51/05
ISSN: 0887-4182

✦ WORLD OF FANDOM, THE

SUB: "The important magazine."
PUBL: Allen Shevy and Chris Mygrant, 3118 Sandspur Drive, Tampa, FL 33618.
DESC: With an emphasis on science fiction, fantasy, and horror, *World of Fandom* covers current entertainment product in the motion picture, television, and comic art fields. In addition, there are a variety of articles concerning current music personalities, and other elements of popular culture. For the sampled issue of 1989: stapled magazine format, minimal advertising, with black/white graphics and black ink editorial and cover on uncoated paper stock (8 ¼ x 10 ¾ inches / 210 x 270 mm).
DEPT: "Editorial," column by Allen Shevy; "Critical Comments," commentary on comic books, magazines, music, television, and the movies. (vol 2, #5- 89).
TYPL: "Star Trek: The Next Generation Second Season," "Freddy's Nightmares," "Tim Burton Discusses The Batman Movie," "Interview with Roger Pedersen." (vol 2, #5-89).
SCHL: Quarterly, 50 pp.
SPAN: Jul, 1985+

✦ WORLD PRESS REVIEW

SUB: "News and views from around the world."
SUB: "News and views from the foreign press."
SUB: "The magazine of world press."
PUBL: Stanley Foundation, 230 Park Ave., New York, NY 10169.
DESC: "*World Press Review* (formerly *Atlas World Press Review*) is published as a nonprofit educational service to foster international information exchange. The magazine is composed entirely of material from the press outside the U.S. or by journalists affiliated with foreign press organizations." For many years, *World Press Review* has provided an engrossing review of international news, commentary and wit. It continues that tradition today by reporting on what the world press has to say about social, economic, military, and legislative developments about newsworthy developments and events. Importantly, these are local reports by local media publications, speaking with nationalistic voices. A reading of any issue of *World Press Review* places international developments on a more literate footing, allowing the reader a time to reflect and provide consideration of local voices from a different cultural, social, and governmental perspective. For the professional journalist, the publication provides a fascinating insight into the workings of the international press. Both entertaining and informative, *World Press Review* is highly recommended. For the sampled issues of 1991: stapled, magazine format; black ink with spot-color on coated paper; cover comprised of full-color graphics on coated stock; advertising (8 ⅛ x 10 ⅞ inches / 210 x 275 mm).
DESC: [*Atlas World Press Review*]: This well-known digest of foreign newspaper articles about major world events and problems prides itself on preserving the

original intent of articles through verbatim translations. *Atlas World Press Review* has long been a unique publication.
DEPT: "Letters," "Editor's Corner," "Early Warning," "Global Culture," "Calendar," "Vox Populi," "The World in Cartoons," "People," "Business Briefs," "The World Economy," "Travel Briefs." (10-84). "Regional Reports," "Mirror on the U.S.," "Business," "Science," "Military Affairs," "Education," "Press," "Art," "Theater," "Sports," "Travel," "Commentary," "Other." (1-92).
TYPL: "Starting Over," "The Gulf States Regroup," "Preventing Disasters." (10-84). "Separatism: Western Europe Discovers Its 'Baltics'," "Japan: A Country Governed by Lack of Interest," "The Soviet Union: The Secret Business of the Communist Party," "Music: The World Dances to a New Beat," "Parenthood: My Kids, the Con Artists." (1-92).
SCHL: Monthly, 70 pp.
SPAN: ?+
VARIES
--Mar, 1961 - Apr, 1972 as Atlas (ISSN: 0004-6930) : 63-24771.
--May, 1974 - Feb, 1980 as Atlas World Press Review (ISSN: 0161-6528).
LC: AP 2.A833
DD: 051
ISSN: 0195-8895
ABST: --Energy Information Abstracts (ISSN: 0147-6521)
--Environment Abstracts (ISSN: 0093-3287)
--InfoBank
--Magazine Index
--Popular Magazine Review (ISSN: 0740-3763)
--Public Affairs Information Service Bulletin (ISSN: 0033-3409)
--Readers Guide to Periodical Literature (ISSN: 0034-0464)

✢ WORLD SCREEN

SUB: "Bulletin of the International Film and Television Council."
PUBL: International Film and Television Council, Via Santa Susanna, 17, Rome, Italy.
DESC: The IFTC was created by resolution of a UNESCO general conference in New Delhi in 1956. It "...is an international non-governmental organization, independent, non-profit-making, and open to representative international federations or associations whose work lies in the field of the film and television." The IFTC serves primarily as a clearing house for information and ideas on a world film-television basis. As such, it attempts to report on new developments in various nations, and their impact upon those nations' media. Issued in English and French. No illustrations.
DEPT: "Editorial," "Activities," conference information on IFTC seminars; "Publications," a most valuable listing of house organs and newsletters via IFTC members.

TYPL: "Technical Problems Arising in Preservation of Cine Films," "Papers From the UNESCO Conference on the Information Media in Africa," "Exchanging Information on Good Television Programs," "The Role of the International Federation of Film Archives," "A Report on Intervision." (spring/summer-62).
SCHL: Semiyearly, 110 pp.
SPAN: Dec, 1959+?
WITH SUPPLEMENT
--Calendar of International Film and Television Events, ? to date?
LC: PN 1993.W92
ISSN: 0512-3658

WORLD THEATRE

SUB: "A bi-monthly review."
PUBL: International Theatre Institute, with assistance of UNESCO, Brussels, Belgium.
DESC: "In the present struggle of all men of good will towards international understanding and co-operation, the efforts of the diplomatists are not sufficient. Each and every one of us must do all in our power to weave a strong fabric of common interests uniting us to our fellows in other countries. *World Theatre* is, above all, the occasion for a friendly conversation over the frontiers and across the seas. In the long run there is no reason why it should not introduce and bring together, actors, authors, designers, directors, producers, critics, architects, and in short, all those who are concerned with the theatre throughout the world." *World Theatre* is a means by which theatrical companies could share their stories of development with others. Each issue included some ten feature articles, plus newsbriefs from a dozen nations. By the mid-1960s, *World Theatre* moved from a normal magazine format to a tall, narrow format. Some issues were devoted to single topics, such as "The Public (Vol 2, #2)," or double issues, such as "Piscator and the Documentary Theatre (Vol 17, #5 and 6)." Note: volume 1, #1 was preceded by an unnumbered and undated issue in English; Volume 1, #1 and 2 were published in French language only; and published in English and French languages commencing with volume 1, #3 to date.
DEPT: "World Information," newsbriefs. (Vol 2, #2). "Editorial," "Bibliography," "International Theatre," newsbriefs; "Technical Data," specific play information. (Vol 17, #3+4-68).
TYPL: "The Public," "Propaganda; How to Launch a Play," "The American Barter Theatre," "The French National Popular Theatre," "Audience Organizations in Switzerland." (Vol 2, #2). "Operas of Recent Years," "Opera Houses?--Blow Them Up!," "Is Musical Theatre Improvable?," "After an Inquiry in Lyric Art." (Vol 17, #3+4-68).
SCHL: Quarterly (1950 - 1964); Bimonthly (1965 - 1968); 70 pp.
SPAN: 1950 - 1968//
FOREIGN TITLE
--Theatre dans le Monde.

ABSORBED
--ITI Technical Data, Jan, 1965.
LC: PN 2001.W6
ISSN: 0512-3704
ABST: --International Index
--Social Science and Humanities Index (ISSN: 0037-7899)

World's Fair Electrical Engineering

Jan, 1893 - May, 1893//
SEE: TELEPHONE MAGAZINE

World's Press News

1929 - Oct, 1935//
SEE: CAMPAIGN

World's Press News and Advertiser's Review

1944 - Nov 13, 1964//
SEE: CAMPAIGN

World's Press News and Advertising

Nov, 1935 - Aug, 19, 1937//
SEE: CAMPAIGN

✦ WOW! MAGAZINE

SUB: "#1 Pinup Magazine! All-color! All-stars!"
SUB: "Exclusive pinups! Giant centerfold!"
PUBL: Pilot Communications, Inc., 25 West 39th St., New York, NY 10018.
DESC: "*WOW!* has the latest and greatest pinups, pix and news! You'll find more EXCLUSIVE PINUPS and GREAT STORIES on New Kids on the Block, Neil Patrick Harris, Jay Ferguson, Johnny Depp and all your faves!" This teen "fanzine" for females covers all current and upcoming young, male teen stars, with an emphasis on motion picture and television. Articles detail likes and dislikes on a variety of lifestyle issues, current production activities, and future plans for film and television projects. Like sister publication, *HOT! Magazine*, this publication also has a minimum of advertising; more than a dozen full-color, full-page pinups of favorite teen stars on coated paper stock. Editorial content is in two-color creative design layouts on uncoated paper stock; stapled magazine format (8 x 10 ⅞ inches / 205 x 275 mm).
DEPT: "Post Marx," letters; "Tattle Tales," 'The latest update from the gossip grape vine with your WOW! reporter, Dominique Cordova!'; "Soap Dish," 'What's happening in the world of daytime dramas' column by Bubbles LaFleur; "WOW! Art Gallery," reader submissions; "Fan Notes," reader submitted personal messages to young stars; "Fansville," young star addresses; "Pen Friends," pen pal listing; "Rock Report," 'Featuring that rumor-mongering Rockin' Robin!'; "Dear Crystal," Q&A on young stars; "Ask Kathy!," Q&A on health, beauty, fashion or fitness; "Star Scope," 'Horoscope by Roxanne!'; "The WOW! Readers' Poll," 'All your faves! Based on your votes!'. (9-90).
TYPL: "Hunks in Trunks," "The Many Faces of Johnny Depp!," "The New Kids Concert Experience," "How to Win Danny Wood's Heart!," "Can You Handle Having a Boyfriend?" (9-90).
SCHL: Monthly (1987 - ?, 1989); Monthly [except Jan, Apr and Sep, plus two issues in Dec] (Jun, 1989+), 85 pp.
SPAN: Oct, 1987+
DD: 791 11
ISSN: 0897-4721

WPN and Advertisers' Review

Nov 20, 1964 - Sep 4, 1968?//
SEE: CAMPAIGN

✦ WRAP

SUB: "The magazine of television production & postproduction."
PUBL: View Communications, 49 East 21st St., New York, NY 10010.
DESC: "Cover to cover, issue after issue, *Wrap* is: the only publication edited exclusively for television production & postproduction executives at TV stations, broadcast networks, TV/cable/home video production companies and postproduction facilities; The only publication 100 percent devoted to the needs of the TV production & postproduction community; *Wrap* combines coverage of TV technology and equipment applications with indepth looks at actual works in progress, interviews with leading producers, surveys of equipment buying trends plus departments and columns that cover the latest developments in equipment, technology, production and postproduction. *Wrap* is must reading for television producers, directors, general managers, engineers and production executives." Dedicated solely to production/postproduction, *Wrap* provides succinct coverage of news and trends in the video production field; news most useful to production managers. One sampled issue covered new lighting for studio applications, the reality of HDTV, how one local television station used stereosurround sound to enhance baseball telecasts, invasion of CCD video cameras into the studio, and an informative essay on the speed of technological change in the production field. According to industry trade publications (July, 1990), *Wrap* parent publisher A/S/M has temporarily suspended publication, effective summer, 1990. Magazine format (8 ⅜ x 10 ⅞ inches / 215 x 275 mm); color graphics on coated paper stock.

DEPT: "Wrap Up," editorial; "Monitor," extensive section on current TV production; "Postscript," 'Postproduction notes'; "Music Box," music videos; "Credits," profile; "Station Circuit," television station production; "On Location," "Teleproduction," "Technology," "Convention," report; "Fade Out," historical. (9/10-89).
TYPL: "Horsing Around with Beta," "High-Def Marriage: Film & Video," "Art Schneider: A Veteran Editor a Cut Above the Rest," "Home Fun: Stereosurround Helps WGN-TV Chicago Make Viewers Feel Like Part of the Game," "Playing the Field." (9/10-89).
SCHL: Bimonthly (Oct/Nov, 1987 - Apr/May, 1989); Monthly [bimonthly in Jun/Jul, Aug/Sep] (May, 1989 - Dec, 1989); Bimonthly (Jan/Feb, 1990+), 40 pp.
SPAN: Oct/Nov, 1987+
SUSPENDED
--Jul/Aug, 1990+
DD: 384
ISSN: 0896-1697

✤ WRITER, THE

SUB: "The oldest magazine for literary workers--founded in Boston 1887."
SUB: "The oldest magazine for literary workers."
PUBL: Writer, Inc., 120 Boylston St., Boston, MA 02116.
DESC: This publication for the professional working writer, has an editorial board that speaks for itself: Isaac Asimov, Marjorie Holmes, Lowell Thomas, Irving Wallace, and Sloan Wilson. No graphics, or splashy layout design, or color pages (beyond the coated stock covers) but plenty of encouragement and sage advice for writing in all media is given. Articles tend to be short, authoritative, and to the point. It is a format which has worked successfully for over 100 years of publication. Some typical articles from 1992, include: "Why I Write Novels," "Dialogue that Works," "Writing the Newspaper Travel Article," "Put Your Characters to Work in Juvenile Mysteries," and "The Shape of Poetry." The February, 1992 issue also included articles on "The Professional Response," "Mastering the Craft of Craft Writing," and "Markets for Business and Trade Articles." Sampled issue for 1990: magazine format (7 ½ x 10 ½ inches / 190 x 265 mm); editorial content on uncoated paper stock; minimal graphics; advertising.
DEPT: "They Say...," quotable quotes for writers; "Roving Editor," amusing anecdotes and newsbriefs; "Off the Cuff," observations; "Market News," particulars on specific publications; "Writers Conferences," upcoming; "This Month's Special Market Lists," reviews of magazines in specific demographic or speciality areas; "Prize Offers," literary prizes now available in contests; "The Writer's Library," new books; "Market Newsletter," late-breaking news in writing field. (6-78). "Letters to the editor," "They Say," 'Quotes for writers'; "Roving Editor," "Off the Cuff," advice on authorship; "The Professional Response," 'Answers to questions writers ask' column by Sidney Sheldon; "The Rostrum," "Where to Sell Manuscripts," large literary market section; "Prize Offers," literary competition; "The Writer's Library," book reviews; "Market Newsletter," late breaking news. (8-90).
TYPL: "Television Techniques for Novel Writing," "Of Necessity, Major Events, and Boxcars," "Emotional Value in Fiction." (6-78). "Writing the Pro/Con Article," "The Short Way to Crime," "Making Coincidence Convincing," "Historical Detection, Unlimited," "A Science Fiction Editor Looks at Writers." (8-90).
SCHL: Monthly, 50 pp.
SPAN: Apr, 1887+
LC: PN 101.W7
DD: 808/.025/05
ISSN: 0043-9517
ABST: --Magazine Index
--Popular Magazine Review (ISSN: 0740-3763)
--Readers Guide to Periodical Literature (ISSN: 0034-0464)

✤ WRITER'S DIGEST

SUB: "A monthly journal of information on writing photoplays, short stories, verse, news stories, publicity, advertising, etc." (Dec, 1920 - Feb, 1921).
SUB: "A monthly journal on writing photoplays, short stories, poems, popular songs, etc." (Mar, 1921 - Aug, 1921).
SUB: "The world's leading magazine for writers."
SUB: "Your monthly guide to getting published."
PUBL: F&W Publishing Co., 1507 Dana Ave., Cincinnati, OH 45207.
DESC: "Since 1920 *Writer's Digest* has provided plenty of 'how-to' instruction, information and inspiration for people who love to write. Each issue is packed with advice from bestselling authors, dozens of tips and techniques for creating better manuscripts, and the most up-to-date information available on how and where to sell fiction, nonfiction, poetry and scripts. *Writer's Digest* is required reading for both published and aspiring writers." This is the magazine for writers desirous of earning money from publication of their articles in periodicals and other media. Authors whose publishing credits are conspicuously noted write for the magazine, providing readers with guidelines on selling their projects. Magazine format (8 x 10 ⅞ inches / 205 x 275 mm).
DEPT: "Forum," letters; "Just Paging," column by Hal Goldberg; "Radio and TV," column by Lee Otis; "Writer's Market," submission information; "Broadway," column by Leo Shull; "Cartoonist Cues," column by Pat Fulford; "An Idea a Day," fascinating day-by-day listing of article possibilities, column by Frank A. Dickson. (11-51). "Letters," with long inquiries and responses; "The Writing Life," paragraph-length items concerning the writing process; "Nonfiction," writing advice; "Pictures," advice; "Poetry," advice; "Markets," particulars on what a periodical publisher is looking for, payments, and publication schedules. (4-78). "Poetry," column by Judson Jerome; "Nonfiction," column by Art Spikol; "The Electronic Writer,"

column by Ronald John Donovan; "Fiction," column by Lawrence Block; "Letters," "The Writing Life," "The Markets," "Tip Sheet." (5-90).
TYPL: "Hollywood TV Producers Buying From Inland Writers," "Book Publishers Pass the Buck," "I Remember This Story," "The Slicks Are Killing Their Taboos," "Who'll Help Burn Down Greenwich Village?" (11-51). "Making Editors Pay as You Go," "How to Turn Book Research into Magazine Sales," "On the Warpath with John Toland." (4-78). "Sell Your Novel," "A Sign of Good Nonfiction Writing: The Billboard Paragraph," "The Strange Case of the English Language," "'Staging' Your Fiction," "Chronicle: Magic of the Mesa." (5-90).
SCHL: Monthly, 90 pp.
SPAN: 1920+
VARIES
--Dec, 1920 - Feb, 1921 as Successful Writing.
--Mar, 1921 - Aug, 1921 as Writer's Digest, The.
ABSORBED
--Author and Composer, 1934.
LC: PN 101.W82
ISSN: 0043-9525
ABST: --Magazine Index
--Readers Guide to Periodical Literature (ISSN: 0034-0464)

Writer's Digest, The

Mar, 1921 - Aug, 1921//
SEE: WRITER'S DIGEST

✧ WRITERS' JOURNAL

PUBL: Minnesota Ink, Inc., PO Box 9148 North St. Paul, MN 55109.
DESC: This is a wonderful publication for the freelance writer, whether just beginning to collect rejection slips; or for the professional intent on maintaining the competitive edge in writing. Advice is practical and useful. One sample issue contained articles that varied from poetic rhythm in advertising copy designed to catch the readers' senses, to the technique of travel writing, to tips for the weekend writer to improve his/her craft. Sampled issue for 1990: magazine format (8 ½ x 11 inches / 215 x 280 mm); printed black/white on uncoated paper stock.
DEPT: "Mailbox," "Book Reviews," "Hot Off the Desktop," "On the Technical Side," "Every Day with Poetry," "Esther Comments," "Words...Tools of Our Trade." (7/8-90).
TYPL: "Poetic Methods That Move Prospects," "Most Every Place is 'Great'--a Look at Travel Writing," "Weekend Writer," "Twelve Steps to Successful Freelancing in Direct Marketing," "Dan Sullivan Speaks Out." (7/8-90).
SCHL: Bimonthly, 40 pp.
SPAN: Jan/Feb, 1980+
VARIES
--Jan/Feb, 1980? - Nov/Dec, 1986? as Inkline Journal.

DD: 808 11
ISSN: 0891-8759

Writer's Northwest Handbook Newsletter

? - ?//
(ISSN: 0895-8971)
SEE: WRITER'S NW

Writer's Northwest Newsletter

Winter, 1987 - Winter, 1988//
(ISSN: 0895-898x)
SEE: WRITER'S NW

✧ WRITER'S NW

SUB: "News & reviews for the community of the printed word."
PUBL: Media Weavers, Blue Heron Publishing, Inc., Route 3, PO Box 376, Hillsboro, OR 97124.
DESC: Blue Heron Publishing provides a wonderful, journalistic quarterly with *Writer's NW*. Here is a dynamic serial that believes in, and seeks to encourage writing and publishing activities in the Pacific Northwest. Articles cover authors who have "made it," or are in the process of preparing their manuscripts for a potential publisher. Writing skills, writing opportunities, and the general state of authorship in the Northwestern states all receive their due. Of special note are extensive book listings of all new product, and a similarly large section detailing writing opportunities for serials, contests, and other fields. It is an asset for writer and publisher alike. Published in tabloid newsprint format (11 ½ x 17 ½ inches / 290 x 445 mm); black/white graphics.
DEPT: "Northwest New Releases," book reviews; "Updates," 'Writer's Northwest Handbook' publication opportunities; "Reviews," selected new books; "News & Notes," newsbriefs; "Letters to the Editor," "Calendar," upcoming events for writers and publishers. (summer-90).
TYPL: "Of Love Stories and Baseball: An Interview with W.P. Kinsella," "Bordering on Prodigious: Book Publishing in British Columbia," "BookMarx: Northwest Reviews," "ISBN Agency Policies Discriminate," "Attending Writers' Conferences Tips for Success." (summer-90).
SCHL: Quarterly, 12 pp.
SPAN: ?+
VARIES
--? - ? as Writer's Northwest Handbook Newsletter (ISSN: 0895-8971).
--Winter, 1987 - Winter, 1988 as Writer's Northwest Newsletter (ISSN: 0895-898x).
DD: 070
ISSN: 1053-833x

WRITERS ON WRITING

SUB: "A literary commentary."
PUBL: Spindrift Press, PO Box 2222, Cocoa, FL 32922-2222.
DESC: "*Writers on Writing* is dedicated to providing a forum for writers who have something meaningful to say about writing and American letters. What kind of writing? Serious writing. Not slick writing. Not pimped writing. Writing with profound intent, intelligence, integrity. Writing that says something thought-provoking about ourselves and our times. And what kind of writers? Rebel writers. Writers who like to rock the boat, who have something exciting and honest to say about fiction or non-fiction or poetry, or the state of writing and writers in this country. This kind of writing and these kinds of writers sometimes are to be found in 'little' magazines and in the products of small presses, as contrasted to commercial ad-dependent magazines and conglomerated publishers. The world of letters in America today is in a state of shock. It is constantly being squeezed and crowded and compressed. A lot of printed matter is pure schlock, fudge, Establishment-Disney oriented. ... WOW wants to set the record straight and to help place the writer where he rightfully belongs: ahead of everyone and everything in the literary world--ahead of editors, of publishers, of critics, of readers. The entire publishing establishment seems to have forgotten that it is the writer who lays every one of those golden literary eggs." For the sampled issues of 1982 through 1987: folded, newsletter format; 3-hole punched; black ink on tinted uncoated paper; early issues consisted of typewritten editorial content; limited advertising (8 ½ x 11 inches / 215 x 280 mm).
DEPT: None. (10-82). None. (7-91).
TYPL: "Why Writers on Writing?," "Starting Out," "Discovering One's Own Voice," "Writing as a Career." (10-82). "Keeping the Faith," "One Writer's Dilemma," "Ode to Truth," "Elegant Writing." (7-91).
SCHL: Quarterly?, 4 pp.
SPAN: Jul, 1982 - Jul, 1991//

✤ WRITING CONCEPTS

SUB: "The newsletter on writing & editing."
PUBL: Communications Concepts, Inc., 2100 National Press Bldg., Suite 202, Washington, DC 20045.
DESC: Editor and publisher, Bill Londino, along with managing editor, Carolyn Mulford, wrote in the premiere issue, "Welcome to the first issue of *Writing Concepts*, a national monthly newsletter for writers, editors and others who strive to improve their own and their colleagues' writing. We're not talking about poetry and novels (although we assume some of our readers write these after hours). This newsletter focuses on the skills, knowledge and creativity needed to produce high-quality qrticles, brochures, annual reports, speeches, direct mail, videos and almost anything else that comes through your office. This new monthly exists because many readers of our flagship periodical, *Communications Concepts*, praised the Writing and Editing department in that newsletter and asked us to expand it. Those readers also told us they like receiving pragmatic advice from their peers--other successful writers and editors from around the country. We go straight to the sources for our material. Most articles in *Writing Concepts* will be based on interviews with or presentations by respected practitioners." Professional writers in various fields will profit from subscribing to this remarkable new publication which is filled with pragmatic information readily applicable to the workplace. Well recommended. For the sampled issue of 1991: folded; newsletter format; black ink with spot color on uncoated paper; no advertising (8 ½ x 11 inches / 215 x 280 mm).
DEPT: "Writing Techniques," "Style Matters," "Managing Publications," "Editorial Consulting," "Electronic Editing," "Editorial Resources," "Editor's Desk," column by Bill Londino. (?-91).
TYPL: "Get New Ammunition for the War of the Words," "Stimulate, Not Stifle, Your Creativity," "Improve Business Writing with Six Keys to Clarity," "Editors Give Usage Preferences in Annual Survey," "Watch For and Prevent Burnout." (?-91).
SCHL: Monthly, 8 pp.
SPAN: ?, 1991+
ISSN: 1050-4788

✤ WRITTEN COMMUNICATION

SUB: "A quarterly journal of research, theory and application."
PUBL: Sage Publications, 275 South Beverly Dr., Beverly Hills, CA 90212.
DESC: "*Written Communication* is devoted to advancing knowledge of writing through theoretical, historical and empirical research. It is a cross-disciplinary journal that addresses substantive issues in writing from perspectives such as rhetoric, discourse analysis, pragmatics, sociolinguistics, psychology, linguistics, journalism, and anthropology. Among topics of interest are the nature of writing ability, the assessment of writing, the impact of technology on writing, social and political consequences of writing and writing instruction, nonacademic writing, literacy, social construction of knowledge, cognition and composing, structure of written text, gender and writing, and connections among writing, reading, speaking, and listening. No worthy topic in writing is beyond the scope of the journal. Published articles will collectively represent a wide range of methodologies, but the methodology of each study must be handled expertly." Another in the excellent line of research journals, *Written Communication* provides a quality platform for the dissemination of theoretical frameworks, trends in the communication process, and debate over any and all issues that comprise this form of communication. Some issues are theme oriented, such as the sampled January, 1991 issue, which focused on "Computers, Language, and Writing." A new departmental feature also began in that sampled issue, "On

the Other Hand," providing a lively forum for reader responses to published articles. Perfect-bound journal format, black ink on uncoated paper stock for editorial section, coated paper stock for cover, limited advertising (5 ⅜ x 8 ½ inches / 135 x 215 mm).
DEPT: None. (1-85). "Editors' Comments," "Reviewer Acknowledgments," "On the Other Hand," pro and con article commentary. (1-91).
TYPL: "Physicists Reading Physics: Schema-Laden Purposes and Purpose-Laden Schema," "Are Social-Cognitive Ability and Narrative Writing Skill Related?," "The Rhetoric of Explanation: Explanatory Rhetoric from 1850 to the Present," "Some Effects of Varying the Structure of a Topic on College Students' Writing," "Cognitive Components of Blocking." (1-85). "Interactive Written Discourse as an Emergent Register," "The Composing Process for Computer Conversation," "Computer Talk: Long Distance Conversations by Computer," "Patterns of Social Interaction and Learning to Write: Some Effects of Network Technologies." (1-91).
SCHL: Quarterly, 130 pp.
SPAN: Jan, 1984+
ISSN: 0741-0883
ABST: --Automatic Subject Citation Alert
--Communication Abstracts
--Current Contents
--Current Index to Journals in Education (ISSN: 0011-3565)
--Human Resources Abstracts
--Linguistics & Language Behavior Abstracts
--Social Planning / Planning & Development Abstracts
--Social Science Citation Index (ISSN: 0091-2887)
--Sociological Abstracts (ISSN: 0038-0202)

✤ WSCA NEWS

SUB: "A newsletter of the Western Speech Communication Association."
PUBL: Western Speech Communication Association, Dept. of Human Communication Studies, California State University, Chico, CA 95929.
DESC: This thrice-yearly newsletter of the Western Speech Communication Association, now called Western States Communication Association, is published for its membership, to inform of late-breaking news, changes, and upcoming events. Typical articles from 1991 issues included news of an upcoming convention; publications by the academic membership; and several awards programs slated for the year. For the sampled issues of 1991: newsletter format (8 ½ x 11 inches / 215 x 280 mm). One issue was printed in brown ink on buff-color paper; another issue for 1991 was dark-blue ink on tinted-grey uncoated paper stock; no advertising.
DEPT: "From the President," "News and Nuggets," newsbriefs. (1-91).
TYPL: "Sunny and Warm," "Phoenix in February," "Journal Name Change," "K-12 Model Program," "Call for Distinguished Service Award Nominees." (1-91).
SCHL: Three issues per year, 4 pp.
SPAN: Jan, 1984+

Xerox Ventura Pipeline
1988? - Vol 2, #1//
SEE: SCSC XEROX PIPELINE

X   Communication Serials

Yale/Theatre

Spring, 1968 - Spring, 1977//
(ISSN: 0044-0167)
SEE: THEATER

✤ YELLOW PAGES UPDATE

SUB: "Industry news, views and trends."
PUBL: American Association of Yellow Pages Publishers, 500 Chesterfield Center, Suite 250, Chesterfield, MO 63017.
DESC: "The American Association of Yellow Pages Publishers (AAYPP), formed in 1984, is a not-for-profit association representing the interests of Yellow Pages publishers, advertisers and consumers. Member publishers of the AAYPP produce over 85 percent of all the Yellow Pages directories published across the nation." The function of this quarterly serial and the association was expressed in this manner: "The future of our industry ...is bright. As we progress, we understand more fully the Yellow Pages and its potential, how our medium functions, what its unique capabilities are and how it can be made better. This, in turn, enables us to help others outside the industry understand and appreciate to a greater degree the many benefits of the Yellow Pages." This is an issues-oriented publication. For the sampled issue of 1987: wonderful usage of black/red/yellow inks on coated paper stock in excellent layout design (8 ½ x 11 inches / 215 x 280 mm).
DEPT: "From the AAYPP Executive Director," "Industry News and Developments." (12-87).
TYPL: "Right to Compete or Threat of Monopoly?," "How Many Fingers are Walking?," "Find Us Fast," "All Rights Reserved." (12-87).
SCHL: Quarterly, 12 pp.
SPAN: Summer, 1986+
DD: 381 11
ISSN: 0888-6695

✤ YELLOW SHEET, THE

SUB: "The practical newsletter on agency management."
PUBL: Communications Management, Inc., suite 220, 763 New Ballas Road South, St. Louis, MO 63141-8704.
DESC: Business periodicals concerned with the field of advertising often focus on new and current business; who's shooting what commercials, or designing product materials, and moving between which agencies. Something these business trade publications often overlook is the business of advertising itself. In *The Yellow Sheet*, in capsule newsletter format, publisher Jabet Wilkins and editor George Johnson discuss agency ownership, and management and efficient operation; all designed to improve agency profits. This is the kind of information one does not receive in the classroom, and certainly will not learn from the competition. Articles discuss how to gain clients, and how to retain them. There are also discussions of efficiency, quality appraisal, trends, and an excellent departmental feature: "In each issue of *The Yellow Sheet* we include a section called 'Case Study.' One month, we present a real, live problem or situation that one of our agency friends was faced with. Then in the following issue, we tell what action the agency took to rectify the situation, what the results were from that action and what the agency owner learned from the experience." This is truly "hands-on" management with the typical "crises" agencies face each day; and often justifies the subscription cost. This is a marvelous resource that will aid and improve the management and operation status of any advertising agency. Newsletter format, three-hole-punched, black ink on yellow uncoated paper stock (8 ½ x 11 inches / 215 x 280 mm), no advertising.
DEPT: "Case Study," excellent first-hand report of problem resolvement. (2-91).
TYPL: "Close, Detailed Communication: The Third Key to Client Satisfaction," "Take a Vacation and Improve Your Agency at the Same Time!," "What is Your Agency's Scrap Rate? What Can You Do to Reduce It?," "Why Across-the-Board Budget Cuts Always are a Mistake," "How to Recognize an Entrepreneur at the Track and in the Office." (2-91).
SCHL: Monthly, 6 pp.
SPAN: 1984?+
VARIES
--? - ? as Practical Newsletter on Agency Management.
DD: 658
ISSN: 1043-4933

YOUNG VIEWERS

PUBL: Center for Children's Media, 451 West Broadway, New York, NY 10012-3156.
DESC: *"Young Viewers Magazine/Film Review* is a quarterly publication on children's non-print media. Short 16mm films are reviewed, in depth, with children; their responses are indicated along with helpful suggestions for using and introducing each film. The publication includes interviews with filmmakers and reports on how people use film and video with children and young adolescents in libraries, schools, museums, and community organizations." It was published by the Center for Children's Media, later

called the Media Center for Children. "MCC works to encourage the participatory use of media and promotes the development of media for children as an art form. To do this, MCC tests films and videos with children and disseminates the results in this publication and in an ongoing series of books. In addition, MCC offers consultation services, workshops, and seminars." MCC founder, Maureen Gaffney, announced cessation of the publication as the MCC moved in a new direction of children and media; "Several factors were involved in this decision, two of which had to do with changes introduced in the educational media market by the appearance of home video. One was a diminished interest in purchasing media for use with groups. The second was an increase in volume, coupled with a generally diminished quality, of film/video productions. But the third and perhaps most important factor was a growing awareness of both the need for and lack of an effective critical viewing curriculum for junior-high school students. It finally dawned on us that there would be no significant change in children's media in this country unless it happened in the schools. Thus, we have decided to devote a major part of the next decade to developing and implementing such a curriculum." For the sampled issues of 1980 through 1988: stapled, newsletter format; black ink on uncoated paper; no advertising (8 ½ x 11 inches / 215 x 280 mm).

DEPT: None. (spring-80).
TYPL: "Story, Synthesis, Sequencing: A Picture Storybook Model," "Hispanic Films, Hispanic Kids: A Report From Chicago," "Playing with Film: An Approach to Programming," "Museum Film Programs, A Proper Balance," "Something for Everyone--Family Films and Children's Programming." (spring-80).
SCHL: Quarterly, 40 pp.
SPAN: Fall, 1977 - ?, 1988//
LC: P 94.5 .C55 Y68
DD: 001.51/088054
ISSN: 0886-4802

✤ ZEISS INFORMATION

PUBL: Carl Zeiss, Oberkochen, Germany.
DESC: *Zeiss Information* provides a highly-technical review of Zeiss lens applications to the fields of science and technology. Articles are well-written, detailing the application of Zeiss technologies to a given segment of research or industry. Most articles are accompanied by a large number of photographs, some of which are in color. Technical knowledge concerning lens optics is assumed. Stapled magazine format on coated paper stock (8 ¼ x 11 ¾ inches / 210 x 295 mm). Note: ISSN for German edition of *Zeiss Information* is 0376-012x.
DEPT: "What's New at ZEISS," product review and news. (#77/78-71).
TYPL: "Zeiss Phocosin, a New Photoelectric Digitization System for Length Measurement with Digital Increments of 0.1 Micron," "A Visit to the Manned Spacecraft Center Houston," "Color Television Microscopy," "Photomacrography, When Luminars, When Tessovar?," "The Use of Phase-Contrast and Interference-Contrast Microscopy for the Study of Living Cells in Gynecology." (#77/78-71).
SCHL: Quarterly (1963 - ?); Irregular [2-3 issues per year] (Sep, 1983+), 45 pp.
SPAN: 1963+
VARIES
--? - ? as Zeiss Werkzeitschrift [English Edition].
ISSN: 0044-2054
ABST: --Energy Research Abstracts (ISSN: 0160-3604)
--Metals Abstracts (ISSN: 0026-0924)
--World Aluminum Abstracts (ISSN: 0002-6697)

Zeiss Werkzeitschrift [English Edition]

? - ?//
SEE: ZEISS INFORMATION

ZIP Target Marketing

Jan, 1978? - Jul, 1986?//
(ISSN: 0739-6953)
SEE: TARGET MARKETING

✤ ZOOM

SUB: "The international image magazine."
SUB: "The image magazine."
PUBL: ZAO, 2, rue du Faubourg Poissonniere, 75010 Paris, France.
DESC: A visual feast for the eyes, *ZOOM* delights with the possibilities of photographic art (and secondarily the art of printing and layout design) in a large format magazine (9 ½ x 12 ¾ inches / 240 x 325 mm). This Paris-based publication is issued in French, with US/UK English editions published in the same caring manner. Editorial content is at a minimum in order to properly showcase the photography of international artists, oftentimes printing color photographs on black backgrounds, and black/white work on white backgrounds in order not to interfere with the photographer's philosophy and intent. One 1990 issue was singularly devoted to "Women in Photography." This is an outstanding resource; a serial that professional and layman alike will appreciate. Large magazine format, quality printing and layout design with minimal advertising.
DEPT: None. (#48-90).
TYPL: "Genevieve Naylor," "Women in Photography," "Beverly Parker, Kenda North," "Elaine Mayes." (#48-90).
SCHL: Five issues per year, 95 pp.
SPAN: ?+
LC: TR 640 .Z66
DD: 770/.5

Z

Serial Indices

Abstracts & Indexes

The abstracting and indexing sources listed below are identified by their unique ISSN number (when available). Abstracting and Indexing services which changed names (and, it is assumed, ISSN numbers), may be listed more than once. Serial ISSN numbers, (when known), are listed following the main entry title.

Researchers should refer to individual abstracting and indexing sources to ascertain inclusive dates for those services.

A

ABC Political Science
(ISSN: 0001-0456)
- POLITICAL COMMUNICATION AND PERSUASION - ISSN: 0195-7473
- PUBLIC OPINION QUARTERLY - ISSN: 0033-362x

ABI/Informer
- ADVERTISING AGE - ISSN: 0001-8899
- ADWEEK'S MARKETING WEEK - ISSN: 0892-8274
- AMERICAN DEMOGRAPHICS - ISSN: 0163-4089
- AT&T TECHNOLOGY - ISSN: 0889-8979
- BROADCASTING - ISSN: 0007-2028
- BUSINESS COMMUNICATIONS REVIEW - ISSN: 0162-3885
- BUSINESS MARKETING - ISSN: 0745-5933
- CALIFORNIA PUBLISHER - ISSN: 0008-1434
- CHICAGO JOURNALISM REVIEW - ISSN: 0009-3580
- COLUMBIA JOURNALISM REVIEW - ISSN: 0010-194x
- COMMUNICATION WORLD - ISSN: 0744-7612
- COMMUNICATIONS - ISSN: 0341-2059
- COMMUNICATIONS AND THE LAW - ISSN: 0162-9093
- DIRECT MARKETING - ISSN: 0012-3188
- EDITOR AND PUBLISHER - ISSN: 0013-094x
- GRAPHIC ARTS MONTHLY - ISSN: 0017-3274
- JMR, JOURNAL OF MARKETING RESEARCH - ISSN: 0022-2437
- JOURNAL OF ADVERTISING - ISSN: 0091-3367
- JOURNAL OF ADVERTISING RESEARCH - ISSN: 0021-8499
- JOURNAL OF COMMUNICATION - ISSN: 0021-9916
- JOURNAL OF COMMUNICATION MANAGEMENT - ISSN: 0745-1822
- JOURNAL OF MARKETING - ISSN: 0022-2429
- JQ. JOURNALISM QUARTERLY. - ISSN: 0022-5533
- MADISON AVENUE - ISSN: 0024-9483
- MARKETING / COMMUNICATIONS - ISSN: 0025-3685
- MARKETING NEWS - ISSN: 0025-3790
- MASTHEAD - ISSN: 0025-5122
- MEDIAWEEK - ISSN: 1055-176x
- MORE - ISSN: 0047-8091
- NIEMAN REPORTS - ISSN: 0028-9817
- PRINTING IMPRESSIONS - ISSN: 0032-860x
- PROMOTION - ISSN: 0093-335x
- PUBLIC OPINION QUARTERLY - ISSN: 0033-362x
- PUBLIC RELATIONS JOURNAL, THE - ISSN: 0033-3670
- PUBLIC RELATIONS QUARTERLY - ISSN: 0033-3700
- PUBLIC RELATIONS REVIEW - ISSN: 0363-8111
- PUBLISHER'S AUXILIARY - ISSN: 0048-5942
- PUBLISHER'S WEEKLY - ISSN: 0000-0019
- SALES & MARKETING MANAGEMENT - ISSN: 0163-7517
- SATELLITE COMMUNICATIONS - ISSN: 0147-7439
- ST. LOUIS JOURNALISM REVIEW - ISSN: 0036-2972
- TARGET MARKETING - ISSN: 0889-5333
- TELECOMMUNICATIONS - ISSN: 0278-4831
- TELECOMMUNICATIONS POLICY - ISSN: 0308-5961
- WEB - ISSN: 0191-4634

Abridged Readers' Guide to Periodical Literature
(ISSN: 0001-334x)
- COMPUTERS & ELECTRONICS - ISSN: 0745-1458
- HIGH FIDELITY - ISSN: 0018-1455
- PETERSEN'S PHOTOGRAPHIC - ISSN: 0199-4913

Abstract Bulletin of the Institute of Paper Chemistry
(ISSN: 0020-3033)
- AMERICAN PRINTER - ISSN: 0744-6616
- BRITISH PRINTER - ISSN: 0007-1684
- CANADIAN PRINTER - ISSN: 0849-0767
- ELECTRONICS - ISSN: 0883-4989

Abstracts & Indexes INDEX

GRAPHIC ARTS MONTHLY - ISSN: 0017-3274

PRESSTIME - ISSN: 0194-3243

PRINTING IMPRESSIONS - ISSN: 0032-860x

PRINTINGNEWS - ISSN: 1046-8595

PULP & PAPER CANADA - ISSN: 0316-4004

TECHNICAL PHOTOGRAPHY - ISSN: 0040-0971

Abstract of English Studies
(ISSN: 0001-3560)

DRAMA - ISSN: 0012-5946

JOURNAL OF POPULAR CULTURE - ISSN: 0022-3840

LITERATURE/FILM QUARTERLY - ISSN: 0090-4260

MODERN DRAMA - ISSN: 0026-7694

NEW THEATRE QUARTERLY - ISSN: 0266-464x

PLAYERS - ISSN: 0032-1486

QUARTERLY JOURNAL OF SPEECH, THE - ISSN: 0033-5630

RESTORATION AND 18TH CENTURY THEATRE RESEARCH - ISSN: 0034-5822

SCHOLARLY PUBLISHING - ISSN: 0036-634x

SERIALS REVIEW - ISSN: 0098-7913

TDR - ISSN: 0012-5962

THEATRE JOURNAL - ISSN: 0192-2882

THEATRE NOTEBOOK - ISSN: 0040-5523

Abstracts of Popular Culture
(ISSN: 0147-2615)

JOURNAL OF FILM AND VIDEO - ISSN: 0742-4671

JOURNAL OF POPULAR FILM AND TELEVISION - ISSN: 0195-6051

JUMP CUT - ISSN: 0146-5546

Abstrax

ART PAPERS - ISSN: 0278-1441

HIGH PERFORMANCE - ISSN: 0160-9769

HISTORY OF PHOTOGRAPHY - ISSN: 0308-7298

IMAGES & IDEAS BY PHOTOMETHODS - ISSN: 0732-7870

JOURNAL OF POPULAR CULTURE - ISSN: 0022-3840

LEONARDO - ISSN: 0024-094x

NOVUM GEBRAUCHSGRAPHIK - ISSN: 0016-5743

PRINT - ISSN: 0032-8510

STUDIES IN VISUAL COMMUNICATION - ISSN: 0276-6558

Access

Accountants' Index. Supplement.
(ISSN: 0748-7975)

BUSINESS MARKETING - ISSN: 0745-5933

JMR, JOURNAL OF MARKETING RESEARCH - ISSN: 0022-2437

JOURNAL OF MARKETING - ISSN: 0022-2429

PUBLIC OPINION QUARTERLY - ISSN: 0033-362x

PUBLIC RELATIONS QUARTERLY - ISSN: 0033-3700

SALES & MARKETING MANAGEMENT - ISSN: 0163-7517

Alternative Press Index
(ISSN: 0002-662x)

CAMERA OBSCURA - ISSN: 0270-5346

CINEASTE - ISSN: 0009-7004

JUMP CUT - ISSN: 0146-5546

America, History and Life
(ISSN: 0002-7065)

FILM & HISTORY - ISSN: 0360-3695

HISTORICAL JOURNAL OF FILM, RADIO & TELEVISION - ISSN: 0143-9685

JOURNAL OF COMMUNICATION - ISSN: 0021-9916

JOURNAL OF POPULAR CULTURE - ISSN: 0022-3840

JOURNAL OF POPULAR FILM AND TELEVISION - ISSN: 0195-6051

JOURNALISM HISTORY - ISSN: 0094-7679

JQ. JOURNALISM QUARTERLY. - ISSN: 0022-5533

QUARTERLY JOURNAL OF SPEECH, THE - ISSN: 0033-5630

RESTORATION AND 18TH CENTURY THEATRE RESEARCH - ISSN: 0034-5822

SCHOLARLY PUBLISHING - ISSN: 0036-634x

SILENT PICTURE, THE - ISSN: 0037-5209

TECHNOLOGY AND CULTURE - ISSN: 0040-165x

VICTORIAN PERIODICALS REVIEW - ISSN: 0709-4698

American Humanities Index

PERFORMING ARTS JOURNAL - ISSN: 0735-8393

TDR - ISSN: 0012-5962

Annual Bibliography of English Language and Literature
(ISSN: 0066-3786)

DRAMA & THEATRE - ISSN: 0012-5954

DRAMA SURVEY - ISSN: 0419-7127

JOURNAL OF COMMUNICATION - ISSN: 0021-9916

JQ. JOURNALISM QUARTERLY. - ISSN: 0022-5533

MODERN DRAMA - ISSN: 0026-7694

QUARTERLY JOURNAL OF SPEECH, THE - ISSN: 0033-5630

RESTORATION AND 18TH CENTURY THEATRE RESEARCH - ISSN: 0034-5822

TDR - ISSN: 0012-5962

THEATRE NOTEBOOK - ISSN: 0040-5523

THEATRE RESEARCH - ISSN: 0040-5566

VISIBLE LANGUAGE - ISSN: 0022-2224

Applied Science and Technology Index
(ISSN: 0003-6986)

AES - ISSN: 0747-8909

AT&T TECHNICAL JOURNAL - ISSN: 8756-2324

AT&T TECHNOLOGY - ISSN: 0889-8979

AUDIO - ISSN: 0004-752x

DB - ISSN: 0011-7145

ELECTRONIC ENGINEERING - ISSN: 0013-4902

ELECTRONICS - ISSN: 0883-4989

ELECTRONICS WORLD + WIRELESS WORLD - ISSN: 0959-8332

INDUSTRIAL PHOTOGRAPHY - ISSN: 0019-8595

QST - ISSN: 0033-4812

RADIO-ELECTRONICS - ISSN: 0033-7862

SMPTE JOURNAL - ISSN: 0036-1682

TELECOMMUNICATION JOURNAL - ISSN: 0497-137x

TELEPHONE MAGAZINE - ISSN: 0736-5853

Architectural Periodicals Index
(ISSN: 0033-6912)

THEATRE DESIGN & TECHNOLOGY - ISSN: 0040-5477

THEATRE NOTEBOOK - ISSN: 0040-5523

Art and Archaeology Technical Abstracts
(ISSN: 0004-2994)
- GRAPHIC ARTS MONTHLY - ISSN: 0017-3274
- LEONARDO - ISSN: 0024-094x
- MODERN PHOTOGRAPHY - ISSN: 0026-8240
- PHOTOMETHODS - ISSN: 0146-0153
- TECHNOLOGY AND CULTURE - ISSN: 0040-165x

Art Bibliographies Modern
(ISSN: 0300-466x)
- ART PAPERS - ISSN: 0278-1441
- HIGH PERFORMANCE - ISSN: 0160-9769
- HISTORY OF PHOTOGRAPHY - ISSN: 0308-7298
- IMAGES & IDEAS BY PHOTOMETHODS - ISSN: 0732-7870
- JOURNAL OF POPULAR CULTURE - ISSN: 0022-3840
- LEONARDO - ISSN: 0024-094x
- NOVUM GEBRAUCHSGRAPHIK - ISSN: 0016-5743
- PRINT - ISSN: 0032-8510
- STUDIES IN VISUAL COMMUNICATION - ISSN: 0276-6558

Art Index
(ISSN: 0004-3222)
- AFTERIMAGE - ISSN: 0300-7472
- AMERICAN CINEMATOGRAPHER - ISSN: 0002-7928
- AMERICAN FILM - ISSN: 0361-4751
- APERTURE - ISSN: 0003-6420
- ART DIRECTION - ISSN: 0004-3109
- BRITISH JOURNAL OF PHOTOGRAPHY - ISSN: 0007-1196
- CINEMA JOURNAL - ISSN: 0009-7101
- COMMUNICATION ARTS - ISSN: 0010-3519
- CREATIVE CAMERA - ISSN: 0011-0876
- FILM COMMENT - ISSN: 0015-119x
- FILM CULTURE - ISSN: 0015-1211
- FILM QUARTERLY - ISSN: 0015-1386
- FILMS IN REVIEW - ISSN: 0015-1688
- GRAPHIS - ISSN: 0017-3452
- HIGH PERFORMANCE - ISSN: 0160-9769
- HISTORY OF PHOTOGRAPHY - ISSN: 0308-7298
- IMAGE - ISSN: 0536-5465
- JOURNAL OF POPULAR FILM AND TELEVISION - ISSN: 0195-6051
- LEONARDO - ISSN: 0024-094x
- NOVUM GEBRAUCHSGRAPHIK - ISSN: 0016-5743
- PRINT - ISSN: 0032-8510
- SIGHT & SOUND - ISSN: 0037-4806

Artificial Intelligence Abstracts
- TELEMATICS AND INFORMATICS - ISSN: 0736-5853

Arts and Humanities Citation Index
(ISSN: 0162-8445)
- CAMERA OBSCURA - ISSN: 0270-5346
- CINEMA JOURNAL - ISSN: 0009-7101
- JOURNAL OF FILM AND VIDEO - ISSN: 0742-4671
- LEONARDO - ISSN: 0024-094x
- TDR - ISSN: 0012-5962

Australian Public Affairs Information Service
(ISSN: 0005-0075)
- AUSTRALIAN JOURNAL OF SCREEN THEORY - ISSN: 0313-4059
- CINEMA PAPERS - ISSN: 0311-3639
- MEDIA INFORMATION AUSTRALIA - ISSN: 0312-9616

Automatic Subject Citation Alert
- WRITTEN COMMUNICATION - ISSN: 0741-0883

Avery Index to Architectual Periodicals
(ISSN: 0196-0008)
- MARQUEE - ISSN: 0025-3928
- THEATRE DESIGN & TECHNOLOGY - ISSN: 0040-5477

B

Bibliography of Agriculture
(ISSN: 0006-1530)
- PULP & PAPER CANADA - ISSN: 0316-4004

Biography Index
(ISSN: 0006-3053)
- BROADCASTING - ISSN: 0007-2028
- FILM QUARTERLY - ISSN: 0015-1386
- JOURNAL OF MARKETING - ISSN: 0022-2429
- MODERN PHOTOGRAPHY - ISSN: 0026-8240
- QUARTERLY JOURNAL OF SPEECH, THE - ISSN: 0033-5630
- TECHTRENDS - ISSN: 8756-3894

Biological Abstracts
(ISSN: 0006-3169)
- ACUSTICA - ISSN: 0001-7884
- PHOTOMETHODS - ISSN: 0146-0153

Book Review Digest
(ISSN: 0006-7326)
- COLUMBIA JOURNALISM REVIEW - ISSN: 0010-194x

Book Review Index
(ISSN: 0524-0581)
- AB BOOKMAN'S WEEKLY - ISSN: 0001-0340
- AFTERIMAGE - ISSN: 0300-7472
- AMERICAN FILM - ISSN: 0361-4751
- ART DIRECTION - ISSN: 0004-3109
- BRITISH BOOK NEWS - ISSN: 0007-0343
- COLUMBIA JOURNALISM REVIEW - ISSN: 0010-194x
- DOWN BEAT - ISSN: 0012-5768
- DRAMA - ISSN: 0012-5946
- FILM COMMENT - ISSN: 0015-119x
- FILM CRITICISM - ISSN: 0163-5069
- FILM QUARTERLY - ISSN: 0015-1386
- FILMS IN REVIEW - ISSN: 0015-1688
- HIGH FIDELITY - ISSN: 0018-1455
- JOURNAL OF COMMUNICATION - ISSN: 0021-9916
- JOURNAL OF MARKETING - ISSN: 0022-2429
- JOURNAL OF POPULAR CULTURE - ISSN: 0022-3840
- JOURNAL OF POPULAR FILM AND TELEVISION - ISSN: 0195-6051
- JQ. JOURNALISM QUARTERLY. - ISSN: 0022-5533
- LISTENER - ISSN: 0024-4392
- MODERN PHOTOGRAPHY - ISSN: 0026-8240
- PERFORMING ARTS JOURNAL - ISSN: 0735-8393

Abstracts & Indexes

PETERSEN'S PHOTOGRAPHIC - ISSN: 0199-4913

POST SCRIPT - ISSN: 0277-9897

PUBLIC OPINION QUARTERLY - ISSN: 0033-362x

PUBLISHER'S WEEKLY - ISSN: 0000-0019

QUARTERLY JOURNAL OF SPEECH, THE - ISSN: 0033-5630

QUARTERLY REVIEW OF FILM AND VIDEO - ISSN: 0146-0013

SERIALS REVIEW - ISSN: 0098-7913

SIGHT & SOUND - ISSN: 0037-4806

SMALL PRESS - ISSN: 0000-0485

SMALL PRESS BOOK REVIEW, THE - ISSN: 8756-7202

STEREO REVIEW - ISSN: 0039-1220

TDR - ISSN: 0012-5962

THEATRE CRAFTS - ISSN: 0040-5469

THEATRE JOURNAL - ISSN: 0192-2882

WASHINGTON JOURNALISM REVIEW - ISSN: 0741-8876

British Technology Index
(ISSN: 0007-1889)

ELECTRONIC ENGINEERING - ISSN: 0013-4902

Bulletin of the Public Affairs Information Service
(ISSN: 0731-0110)

MARKETING / COMMUNICATIONS - ISSN: 0025-3685

Business Index

PUBLIC RELATIONS REVIEW - ISSN: 0363-8111

Business Periodical Index
(ISSN: 0007-6961)

ADVERTISING AGE - ISSN: 0001-8899

ADWEEK'S MARKETING WEEK - ISSN: 0892-8274

AMERICAN DEMOGRAPHICS - ISSN: 0163-4089

AMERICAN PRINTER - ISSN: 0744-6616

AVC - ISSN: 1045-6910

BROADCASTING - ISSN: 0007-2028

BUSINESS MARKETING - ISSN: 0745-5933

COMMUNICATIONS NEWS - ISSN: 0010-3632

DIRECT MARKETING - ISSN: 0012-3188

EDITOR AND PUBLISHER - ISSN: 0013-094x

GRAPHIC ARTS MONTHLY - ISSN: 0017-3274

INTERNATIONAL ADVERTISER - ISSN: 0000-0000

JMR, JOURNAL OF MARKETING RESEARCH - ISSN: 0022-2437

JOURNAL OF ADVERTISING - ISSN: 0091-3367

JOURNAL OF ADVERTISING RESEARCH - ISSN: 0021-8499

JOURNAL OF MARKETING - ISSN: 0022-2429

MADISON AVENUE - ISSN: 0024-9483

MARKETING / COMMUNICATIONS - ISSN: 0025-3685

MARKETING NEWS - ISSN: 0025-3790

MEDIAWEEK - ISSN: 1055-176x

PUBLIC RELATIONS JOURNAL, THE - ISSN: 0033-3670

PUBLIC RELATIONS QUARTERLY - ISSN: 0033-3700

PUBLIC RELATIONS REVIEW - ISSN: 0363-8111

PUBLISHER'S WEEKLY - ISSN: 0000-0019

SALES & MARKETING MANAGEMENT - ISSN: 0163-7517

TELECOMMUNICATIONS - ISSN: 0278-4831

TELEVISION/RADIO AGE - ISSN: 0040-277x

C

Canadian Business Index
(ISSN: 0227-8669)

BROADCASTER - ISSN: 0008-3038

CANADIAN JOURNAL OF COMMUNICATION - ISSN: 0705-3657

CANADIAN PRINTER - ISSN: 0849-0767

ELECTRONICS & COMMUNICATIONS - ISSN: 0013-5100

PULP & PAPER CANADA - ISSN: 0316-4004

Canadian Environment

PULP & PAPER CANADA - ISSN: 0316-4004

Canadian Periodical Index
(ISSN: 0008-4719)

APPLIED ARTS QUARTERLY - ISSN: 0829-9242

CINEMA/CANADA - ISSN: 0009-7071

IN SEARCH - ISSN: 0317-4514

PERFORMING ARTS IN CANADA, THE - ISSN: 0031-5230

Chemical Abstracts
(ISSN: 0009-2258)

ELECTRONICS LETTERS - ISSN: 0013-5194

SMPTE JOURNAL - ISSN: 0036-1682

Chemical Industry Notes
(ISSN: 0045-639x)

PULP & PAPER CANADA - ISSN: 0316-4004

Children's Magazine Guide
(ISSN: 0743-9873)

PLAYS - ISSN: 0032-1540

CIS Abstracts
(ISSN: 0302-7651)

ACUSTICA - ISSN: 0001-7884

AUSTRALASIAN PRINTER - ISSN: 0004-8453

ELECTRICAL REVIEW - ISSN: 0013-4384

ELECTRONIC ENGINEERING - ISSN: 0013-4902

Communication Abstracts

ACUSTICA - ISSN: 0001-7884

AEG-TELEFUNKEN PROGRESS - ISSN: 0001-107x

AMERICAN PRINTER - ISSN: 0744-6616

COMSAT TECHNICAL REVIEW - ISSN: 0095-9669

ELECTRONIC ENGINEERING - ISSN: 0013-4902

GRAPHIC ARTS MONTHLY - ISSN: 0017-3274

IEEE TRANSACTIONS ON BROADCASTING - ISSN: 0018-9316

INDUSTRIAL PHOTOGRAPHY - ISSN: 0019-8595

JEE, JOURNAL OF ELECTRONIC ENGINEERING - ISSN: 0385-4507

JOURNAL OF BROADCASTING & ELECTRONIC MEDIA - ISSN: 0883-8151

JOURNAL OF POPULAR FILM AND TELEVISION - ISSN: 0195-6051

LANGUAGE & COMMUNICATION - ISSN: 0271-5309

MARCONI REVIEW, THE - ISSN: 0025-2883

POLITICAL COMMUNICATION AND PERSUASION - ISSN: 0195-7473

PROCEEDINGS OF THE IREE AUSTRALIA - ISSN: 0158-0736

PUBLIC RELATIONS REVIEW - ISSN: 0363-8111

SMPTE JOURNAL - ISSN: 0036-1682

TELEMATICS AND INFORMATICS - ISSN: 0736-5853

TELEVISION - ISSN: 8755-5867

WESTERN JOURNAL OF SPEECH COMMUNICATION - ISSN: 0193-6700

WRITTEN COMMUNICATION - ISSN: 0741-0883

Coal Abstracts
(ISSN: 0309-4979)

AEG-TELEFUNKEN PROGRESS - ISSN: 0001-107x

CONGRESSIONAL QUARTERLY'S EDITORIAL RESEARCH REPORTS - ISSN: 0013-0958

ELECTRICAL REVIEW - ISSN: 0013-4384

Combined Retrospective Index Sets

PUBLIC OPINION QUARTERLY - ISSN: 0033-362x

Computer & Control Abstracts
(ISSN: 0036-8113)

ABU TECHNICAL REVIEW - ISSN: 0126-6209

ACUSTICA - ISSN: 0001-7884

AES - ISSN: 0747-8909

AT&T TECHNOLOGY - ISSN: 0889-8979

ATR - ISSN: 0001-2777

BRITISH JOURNAL OF PHOTOGRAPHY - ISSN: 0007-1196

CD-ROM LIBRARIAN - ISSN: 0893-9934

COMMUNICATIONS - ISSN: 0341-2059

COMMUNICATIONS AND THE LAW - ISSN: 0162-9093

COMPUTERS & ELECTRONICS - ISSN: 0745-1458

COMSAT TECHNICAL REVIEW - ISSN: 0095-9669

CQ - ISSN: 0007-893x

DB - ISSN: 0011-7145

EBU REVIEW. TECHNICAL. - ISSN: 0012-7493

ELECTRICAL COMMUNICATION - ISSN: 0013-4252

ELECTRICAL REVIEW - ISSN: 0013-4384

ELECTRONIC ENGINEERING - ISSN: 0013-4902

ELECTRONICS - ISSN: 0883-4989

ELECTRONICS & COMMUNICATIONS - ISSN: 0013-5100

ELECTRONICS LETTERS - ISSN: 0013-5194

FUNCTIONAL PHOTOGRAPHY - ISSN: 0360-7216

IBE - ISSN: 0020-6229

IEEE TRANSACTIONS ON BROADCASTING - ISSN: 0018-9316

IEEE TRANSACTIONS ON CABLE TELEVISION - ISSN: 0147-3204

IEEE TRANSACTIONS ON CONSUMER ELECTRONICS - ISSN: 0098-3063

IMAGE TECHNOLOGY - ISSN: 0950-2114

INDUSTRIAL ELECTRONICS - ISSN: 0537-5185

INDUSTRIAL PHOTOGRAPHY - ISSN: 0019-8595

INTERNATIONAL BROADCASTING - ISSN: 0141-1748

INTERNATIONAL JOURNAL OF INFORMATION MANAGEMENT - ISSN: 0268-4012

JEE, JOURNAL OF ELECTRONIC ENGINEERING - ISSN: 0385-4507

LANGUAGE & COMMUNICATION - ISSN: 0271-5309

LEONARDO - ISSN: 0024-094x

LINK-UP - ISSN: 0739-988x

MARCONI REVIEW, THE - ISSN: 0025-2883

MEDIA IN EDUCATION AND DEVELOPMENT - ISSN: 0262-0251

MILITARY ELECTRONICS / COUNTER-MEASURES - ISSN: 0164-4076

PROCEEDINGS OF THE IREE AUSTRALIA - ISSN: 0158-0736

RADIO AND TELEVISION - ISSN: 0277-4860

RADIO COMMUNICATION - ISSN: 0033-7803

RADIO-ELECTRONICS - ISSN: 0033-7862

RCA BROADCAST NEWS - ISSN: 0096-7785

RF DESIGN - ISSN: 0163-321x

SATELLITE COMMUNICATIONS - ISSN: 0147-7439

SMPTE JOURNAL - ISSN: 0036-1682

TECHTRENDS - ISSN: 8756-3894

TELECOMMUNICATION JOURNAL - ISSN: 0497-137x

TELECOMMUNICATION JOURNAL OF AUSTRALIA, THE - ISSN: 0040-2486

TELECOMMUNICATIONS POLICY - ISSN: 0308-5961

TELEMATICS AND INFORMATICS - ISSN: 0736-5853

TELEVISION - ISSN: 8755-5867

TELEVISION - ISSN: 0308-454x

TELEVISION/RADIO AGE - ISSN: 0040-277x

THE JOURNAL - ISSN: 0192-592x

VISIBLE LANGUAGE - ISSN: 0022-2224

Consumers Index to Product Evaluations and Information Sources
(ISSN: 0094-0534)

AUDIO - ISSN: 0004-752x

CAMERA 35 INCORPORATING PHOTO WORLD - ISSN: 0008-2171

COMPUTERS & ELECTRONICS - ISSN: 0745-1458

EPIEGRAM - ISSN: 0531-7991

HIGH FIDELITY - ISSN: 0018-1455

MEDIA & METHODS - ISSN: 0025-6897

MODERN PHOTOGRAPHY - ISSN: 0026-8240

PETERSEN'S PHOTOGRAPHIC - ISSN: 0199-4913

POPULAR PHOTOGRAPHY - ISSN: 0032-4582

QST - ISSN: 0033-4812

QUARTERLY JOURNAL OF SPEECH, THE - ISSN: 0033-5630

RADIO-ELECTRONICS - ISSN: 0033-7862

STEREO REVIEW - ISSN: 0039-1220

Cumulative Monthly Periodical Index

Current Contents

JOURNAL OF BROADCASTING & ELECTRONIC MEDIA - ISSN: 0883-8151

LANGUAGE & COMMUNICATION - ISSN: 0271-5309

TECHTRENDS - ISSN: 8756-3894

WRITTEN COMMUNICATION - ISSN: 0741-0883

Current Contents. Social and Behavioral Sciences.
(ISSN: 0092-6361)

    LANGUAGE & COMMUNICATION - ISSN: 0271-5309

    THEATRE JOURNAL - ISSN: 0192-2882

Current Index to Journals in Education
(ISSN: 0011-3565)

    ACA BULLETIN - ISSN: 0360-0939

    COMMUNICATION EDUCATION - ISSN: 0363-4523

    COMMUNICATION QUARTERLY - ISSN: 0146-3373

    COMMUNICATION RESEARCH - ISSN: 0093-6502

    COMMUNICATION STUDIES - ISSN: 1051-0974

    CSPAA BULLETIN - ISSN: 0010-1990

    EDUCATIONAL COMMUNICATION AND TECHNOLOGY - ISSN: 0148-5806

    HUMAN COMMUNICATION RESEARCH - ISSN: 0360-3989

    JOURNAL OF APPLIED COMMUNICATION RESEARCH - ISSN: 0090-9882

    JOURNAL OF BROADCASTING & ELECTRONIC MEDIA - ISSN: 0883-8151

    JOURNAL OF BUSINESS COMMUNICATION, THE - ISSN: 0021-9436

    JOURNAL OF COMMUNICATION - ISSN: 0021-9916

    JOURNAL OF EDUCATIONAL PUBLIC RELATIONS - ISSN: 0741-3653

    JOURNAL OF EDUCATIONAL TELEVISION - ISSN: 0260-7417

    JOURNAL OF FILM AND VIDEO - ISSN: 0742-4671

    JOURNALISM EDUCATOR, THE - ISSN: 0022-5517

    JQ. JOURNALISM QUARTERLY. - ISSN: 0022-5533

    LANGUAGE & COMMUNICATION - ISSN: 0271-5309

    MEDIA IN EDUCATION AND DEVELOPMENT - ISSN: 0262-0251

    PUBLIC RELATIONS REVIEW - ISSN: 0363-8111

    QUILL AND SCROLL - ISSN: 0033-6505

    SCHOLASTIC EDITOR'S TRENDS IN PUBLICATIONS - ISSN: 0745-2357

    TECHTRENDS - ISSN: 8756-3894

    TELEVISION & FAMILIES - ISSN: 0894-6248

    THE JOURNAL - ISSN: 0192-592x

    THEATRE JOURNAL - ISSN: 0192-2882

    WESTERN JOURNAL OF SPEECH COMMUNICATION - ISSN: 0193-6700

    WRITTEN COMMUNICATION - ISSN: 0741-0883

Current Military and Political Literature

    POLITICAL COMMUNICATION AND PERSUASION - ISSN: 0195-7473

E

Education Index
(ISSN: 0013-1385)

    AV GUIDE - ISSN: 0091-360x

    COMMUNICATION QUARTERLY - ISSN: 0146-3373

    E-ITV - ISSN: 0743-7773

    EDUCATIONAL BROADCASTING - ISSN: 0046-1474

    EDUCATIONAL COMMUNICATION AND TECHNOLOGY - ISSN: 0148-5806

    EDUCATIONAL MEDIA INTERNATIONAL - ISSN: 0004-7597

    EDUCATIONAL SCREEN - ISSN: 0013-1946

    EPIEGRAM - ISSN: 0531-7991

    JOURNAL OF COMMUNICATION - ISSN: 0021-9916

    JOURNALISM EDUCATOR, THE - ISSN: 0022-5517

    MEDIA & METHODS - ISSN: 0025-6897

    MEDIA IN EDUCATION AND DEVELOPMENT - ISSN: 0262-0251

    QUARTERLY JOURNAL OF SPEECH, THE - ISSN: 0033-5630

    TECHTRENDS - ISSN: 8756-3894

    THE JOURNAL - ISSN: 0192-592x

    THEATRE JOURNAL - ISSN: 0192-2882

Electrical & Electronics Abstracts
(ISSN: 0036-8105)

    ABU TECHNICAL REVIEW - ISSN: 0126-6209

    ACUSTICA - ISSN: 0001-7884

    AES - ISSN: 0747-8909

    AT&T TECHNOLOGY - ISSN: 0889-8979

    ATR - ISSN: 0001-2777

    BRITISH JOURNAL OF PHOTOGRAPHY - ISSN: 0007-1196

    CD-ROM LIBRARIAN - ISSN: 0893-9934

    COMMUNICATIONS - ISSN: 0341-2059

    COMMUNICATIONS AND THE LAW - ISSN: 0162-9093

    COMPUTERS & ELECTRONICS - ISSN: 0745-1458

    COMSAT TECHNICAL REVIEW - ISSN: 0095-9669

    CQ - ISSN: 0007-893x

    DB - ISSN: 0011-7145

    EBU REVIEW. TECHNICAL. - ISSN: 0012-7493

    ELECTRICAL COMMUNICATION - ISSN: 0013-4252

    ELECTRICAL REVIEW - ISSN: 0013-4384

    ELECTRONIC ENGINEERING - ISSN: 0013-4902

    ELECTRONICS - ISSN: 0883-4989

    ELECTRONICS & COMMUNICATIONS - ISSN: 0013-5100

    ELECTRONICS LETTERS - ISSN: 0013-5194

    FUNCTIONAL PHOTOGRAPHY - ISSN: 0360-7216

    IBE - ISSN: 0020-6229

    IEEE TRANSACTIONS ON BROADCASTING - ISSN: 0018-9316

    IEEE TRANSACTIONS ON CABLE TELEVISION - ISSN: 0147-3204

    IEEE TRANSACTIONS ON CONSUMER ELECTRONICS - ISSN: 0098-3063

    IMAGE TECHNOLOGY - ISSN: 0950-2114

    INDUSTRIAL ELECTRONICS - ISSN: 0537-5185

    INDUSTRIAL PHOTOGRAPHY - ISSN: 0019-8595

    INTERNATIONAL BROADCASTING - ISSN: 0141-1748

    INTERNATIONAL JOURNAL OF INFORMATION MANAGEMENT - ISSN: 0268-4012

    JEE, JOURNAL OF ELECTRONIC ENGINEERING - ISSN: 0385-4507

    LANGUAGE & COMMUNICATION - ISSN: 0271-5309

    LEONARDO - ISSN: 0024-094x

    LINK-UP - ISSN: 0739-988x

    MARCONI REVIEW, THE - ISSN: 0025-2883

    MEDIA IN EDUCATION AND DEVELOPMENT - ISSN: 0262-0251

    MILITARY ELECTRONICS / COUNTERMEASURES - ISSN: 0164-4076

    PROCEEDINGS OF THE IREE AUSTRALIA - ISSN: 0158-0736

    PULP & PAPER CANADA - ISSN: 0316-4004

    RADIO AND TELEVISION - ISSN: 0277-4860

Abstracts & Indexes INDEX

QUARTERLY JOURNAL OF SPEECH, THE - ISSN: 0033-5630

RESTORATION AND 18TH CENTURY THEATRE RESEARCH - ISSN: 0034-5822

SCHOLARLY PUBLISHING - ISSN: 0036-634x

SILENT PICTURE, THE - ISSN: 0037-5209

TECHNOLOGY AND CULTURE - ISSN: 0040-165x

VICTORIAN PERIODICALS REVIEW - ISSN: 0709-4698

Hospital Literature Index
(ISSN: 0018-5736)

BIOMEDICAL COMMUNICATIONS - ISSN: 0092-8607

E-ITV - ISSN: 0743-7773

PUBLIC OPINION QUARTERLY - ISSN: 0033-362x

PUBLIC RELATIONS JOURNAL, THE - ISSN: 0033-3670

Human Resources Abstracts

WESTERN JOURNAL OF SPEECH COMMUNICATION - ISSN: 0193-6700

WRITTEN COMMUNICATION - ISSN: 0741-0883

Humanities Index
(ISSN: 0095-5981)

AMERICAN FILM - ISSN: 0361-4751

COMMUNICATION QUARTERLY - ISSN: 0146-3373

COMMUNICATION RESEARCH - ISSN: 0093-6502

FILM COMMENT - ISSN: 0015-119x

FILM QUARTERLY - ISSN: 0015-1386

JOURNAL OF BROADCASTING & ELECTRONIC MEDIA - ISSN: 0883-8151

JOURNAL OF POPULAR CULTURE - ISSN: 0022-3840

JOURNALISM HISTORY - ISSN: 0094-7679

JQ. JOURNALISM QUARTERLY. - ISSN: 0022-5533

LITERATURE/FILM QUARTERLY - ISSN: 0090-4260

MODERN DRAMA - ISSN: 0026-7694

NEW THEATRE QUARTERLY - ISSN: 0266-464x

PERFORMING ARTS JOURNAL - ISSN: 0735-8393

PLAYS AND PLAYERS - ISSN: 0032-1559

QUARTERLY JOURNAL OF SPEECH, THE - ISSN: 0033-5630

QUARTERLY REVIEW OF FILM AND VIDEO - ISSN: 0146-0013

QUILL, THE - ISSN: 0033-6475

SHAKESPEARE QUARTERLY - ISSN: 0037-3222

SIGHT & SOUND - ISSN: 0037-4806

TDR - ISSN: 0012-5962

THEATER - ISSN: 0161-0775

THEATRE JOURNAL - ISSN: 0192-2882

THEATRE NOTEBOOK - ISSN: 0040-5523

I

Index of American Periodical Verse
(ISSN: 0090-9130)

JOURNAL OF POPULAR CULTURE - ISSN: 0022-3840

Index of Economic Articles in Journals and Collected Volumes
(ISSN: 0536-647x)

JMR, JOURNAL OF MARKETING RESEARCH - ISSN: 0022-2437

Index to Book Reviews in the Humanities
(ISSN: 0073-5892)

AMERICAN FILM - ISSN: 0361-4751

DRAMA - ISSN: 0012-5946

FILMS IN REVIEW - ISSN: 0015-1688

LISTENER - ISSN: 0024-4392

MODERN DRAMA - ISSN: 0026-7694

PRINT - ISSN: 0032-8510

SIGHT & SOUND - ISSN: 0037-4806

THEATER - ISSN: 0161-0775

THEATRE JOURNAL - ISSN: 0192-2882

VICTORIAN PERIODICALS REVIEW - ISSN: 0709-4698

Index to IEEE Publications
(ISSN: 0099-1368)

IEEE TRANSACTIONS ON BROADCASTING - ISSN: 0018-9316

IEEE TRANSACTIONS ON CONSUMER ELECTRONICS - ISSN: 0098-3063

Index to Journals in Communication Studies

JOURNAL OF BROADCASTING & ELECTRONIC MEDIA - ISSN: 0883-8151

Index to Legal Periodicals
(ISSN: 0019-4077)

COMMUNICATIONS AND THE LAW - ISSN: 0162-9093

FEDERAL COMMUNICATIONS LAW JOURNAL - ISSN: 0163-7606

Index to Religious Periodical Literature
(ISSN: 0019-4107)

BOOKS & RELIGION - ISSN: 0890-0841

Industrial Arts Index

ADVERTISING AGENCY - ISSN: 0001-8899

BUSINESS MARKETING - ISSN: 0745-5933

ELECTRONICS - ISSN: 0883-4989

GENERAL ELECTRIC REVIEW - ISSN: 0095-9480

TELEPHONE MAGAZINE - ISSN: 0736-5853

InfoBank

ADVERTISING AGE - ISSN: 0001-8899

ADVERTISING AND GRAPHIC ARTS TECHNIQUES - ISSN: 0747-3168

ADWEEK - ISSN: 0199-4743

AMERICAN DEMOGRAPHICS - ISSN: 0163-4089

ART DIRECTION - ISSN: 0004-3109

BILLBOARD - ISSN: 0006-2510

BOX OFFICE - ISSN: 0006-8527

BROADCASTING - ISSN: 0007-2028

BUSINESS MARKETING - ISSN: 0745-5933

DIRECT MARKETING - ISSN: 0012-3188

EDITOR AND PUBLISHER - ISSN: 0013-094x

JMR, JOURNAL OF MARKETING RESEARCH - ISSN: 0022-2437

JOURNAL OF ADVERTISING - ISSN: 0091-3367

JOURNAL OF ADVERTISING RESEARCH - ISSN: 0021-8499

JOURNAL OF COMMUNICATION - ISSN: 0021-9916

JOURNAL OF MARKETING - ISSN: 0022-2429

RADIO COMMUNICATION - ISSN: 0033-7803

RADIO-ELECTRONICS - ISSN: 0033-7862

RCA BROADCAST NEWS - ISSN: 0096-7785

RF DESIGN - ISSN: 0163-321x

SATELLITE COMMUNICATIONS - ISSN: 0147-7439

SMPTE JOURNAL - ISSN: 0036-1682

TECHTRENDS - ISSN: 8756-3894

TELECOMMUNICATION JOURNAL - ISSN: 0497-137x

TELECOMMUNICATION JOURNAL OF AUSTRALIA, THE - ISSN: 0040-2486

TELECOMMUNICATIONS POLICY - ISSN: 0308-5961

TELEMATICS AND INFORMATICS - ISSN: 0736-5853

TELEVISION - ISSN: 8755-5867

TELEVISION - ISSN: 0308-454x

TELEVISION/RADIO AGE - ISSN: 0040-277x

THE JOURNAL - ISSN: 0192-592x

VISIBLE LANGUAGE - ISSN: 0022-2224

Electronic Publishing Abstracts
(ISSN: 0739-2907)

COMMUNICATIONS NEWS - ISSN: 0010-3632

ELECTRONIC ENGINEERING - ISSN: 0013-4902

INDUSTRIAL ELECTRONICS - ISSN: 0537-5185

INTERNATIONAL BROADCASTING - ISSN: 0141-1748

INTERNATIONAL VIDEOTEXT TELETEXT NEWS - ISSN: 0197-677x

PRESSTIME - ISSN: 0194-3243

VISIBLE LANGUAGE - ISSN: 0022-2224

Electronics and Communications Abstracts Journal
(ISSN: 0361-3313)

AV VIDEO - ISSN: 0747-1335

MARCONI REVIEW, THE - ISSN: 0025-2883

TECHTRENDS - ISSN: 8756-3894

Energy Information Abstracts
(ISSN: 0147-6521)

ACUSTICA - ISSN: 0001-7884

AMERICAN DEMOGRAPHICS - ISSN: 0163-4089

COLUMBIA JOURNALISM REVIEW - ISSN: 0010-194x

ELECTRONIC ENGINEERING - ISSN: 0013-4902

JOURNAL OF COMMUNICATION - ISSN: 0021-9916

PULP & PAPER CANADA - ISSN: 0316-4004

TECHNOLOGY AND CULTURE - ISSN: 0040-165x

WORLD PRESS REVIEW - ISSN: 0195-8895

Energy Research Abstracts
(ISSN: 0160-3604)

ACUSTICA - ISSN: 0001-7884

AEG-TELEFUNKEN PROGRESS - ISSN: 0001-107x

AEU - ISSN: 0001-1096

CONGRESSIONAL QUARTERLY'S EDITORIAL RESEARCH REPORTS - ISSN: 0013-0958

ELECTRICAL COMMUNICATION - ISSN: 0013-4252

ELECTRICAL REVIEW - ISSN: 0013-4384

IMAGE - ISSN: 0536-5465

ZEISS INFORMATION - ISSN: 0044-2054

Engineering Index

COMMUNICATION EDUCATION - ISSN: 0363-4523

ELECTRONIC ENGINEERING - ISSN: 0013-4902

GENERAL ELECTRIC REVIEW - ISSN: 0095-9480

INTERNATIONAL JOURNAL OF INSTRUCTIONAL MEDIA AND TECHNOLOGY - ISSN: 0092-1815

RADIO BROADCAST - ISSN: 0277-4860

Engineering Index Annual
(ISSN: 0360-8557)

ACUSTICA - ISSN: 0001-7884

AEG-TELEFUNKEN PROGRESS - ISSN: 0001-107x

AES - ISSN: 0747-8909

AEU - ISSN: 0001-1096

AT&T TECHNOLOGY - ISSN: 0889-8979

AWA TECHNICAL REVIEW - ISSN: 0001-2920

COMSAT TECHNICAL REVIEW - ISSN: 0095-9669

EBU REVIEW. TECHNICAL. - ISSN: 0012-7493

ELECTRICAL COMMUNICATION - ISSN: 0013-4252

ELECTRONICS - ISSN: 0883-4989

IEEE TRANSACTIONS ON BROADCASTING - ISSN: 0018-9316

IEEE TRANSACTIONS ON CONSUMER ELECTRONICS - ISSN: 0098-3063

INDUSTRIAL PHOTOGRAPHY - ISSN: 0019-8595

JOURNAL OF TECHNICAL WRITING AND COMMUNICATION - ISSN: 0047-2816

MARCONI REVIEW, THE - ISSN: 0025-2883

SMPTE JOURNAL - ISSN: 0036-1682

TELECOMMUNICATION JOURNAL - ISSN: 0497-137x

TELECOMMUNICATION JOURNAL OF AUSTRALIA, THE - ISSN: 0040-2486

TELECOMMUNICATIONS - ISSN: 0278-4831

TELECOMMUNICATIONS POLICY - ISSN: 0308-5961

TELEVISION - ISSN: 8755-5867

Engineering Index Bioengineering Abstracts
(ISSN: 0736-6213)

ACUSTICA - ISSN: 0001-7884

AES - ISSN: 0747-8909

AEU - ISSN: 0001-1096

AT&T TECHNOLOGY - ISSN: 0889-8979

ATR - ISSN: 0001-2777

COMSAT TECHNICAL REVIEW - ISSN: 0095-9669

EBU REVIEW. TECHNICAL. - ISSN: 0012-7493

ELECTRICAL COMMUNICATION - ISSN: 0013-4252

ELECTRONIC ENGINEERING - ISSN: 0013-4902

ELECTRONICS - ISSN: 0883-4989

ELECTRONICS LETTERS - ISSN: 0013-5194

IEEE TRANSACTIONS ON BROADCASTING - ISSN: 0018-9316

IEEE TRANSACTIONS ON CONSUMER ELECTRONICS - ISSN: 0098-3063

JOURNAL OF TECHNICAL WRITING AND COMMUNICATION - ISSN: 0047-2816

MARCONI REVIEW, THE - ISSN: 0025-2883

SMPTE JOURNAL - ISSN: 0036-1682

TELECOMMUNICATION JOURNAL - ISSN: 0497-137x

TELECOMMUNICATION JOURNAL OF AUSTRALIA, THE - ISSN: 0040-2486

TELECOMMUNICATIONS POLICY - ISSN: 0308-5961

TELEVISION - ISSN: 8755-5867

Engineering Index Energy Abstracts
(ISSN: 0093-8408)

ACUSTICA - ISSN: 0001-7884

AEG-TELEFUNKEN PROGRESS - ISSN: 0001-107x

AES - ISSN: 0747-8909

AEU - ISSN: 0001-1096

AT&T TECHNOLOGY - ISSN: 0889-8979

ATR - ISSN: 0001-2777

COMSAT TECHNICAL REVIEW - ISSN: 0095-9669

EBU REVIEW. TECHNICAL. - ISSN: 0012-7493

ELECTRICAL COMMUNICATION - ISSN: 0013-4252

ELECTRONIC ENGINEERING - ISSN: 0013-4902

ELECTRONICS - ISSN: 0883-4989

ELECTRONICS LETTERS - ISSN: 0013-5194

IEEE TRANSACTIONS ON BROADCASTING - ISSN: 0018-9316

IEEE TRANSACTIONS ON CONSUMER ELECTRONICS - ISSN: 0098-3063

JOURNAL OF TECHNICAL WRITING AND COMMUNICATION - ISSN: 0047-2816

MARCONI REVIEW, THE - ISSN: 0025-2883

SMPTE JOURNAL - ISSN: 0036-1682

TELECOMMUNICATION JOURNAL - ISSN: 0497-137x

TELECOMMUNICATION JOURNAL OF AUSTRALIA, THE - ISSN: 0040-2486

TELECOMMUNICATIONS POLICY - ISSN: 0308-5961

TELEVISION - ISSN: 8755-5867

Engineering Index Monthly (1984)
(ISSN: 0742-1974)

ACUSTICA - ISSN: 0001-7884

AES - ISSN: 0747-8909

AEU - ISSN: 0001-1096

AT&T TECHNOLOGY - ISSN: 0889-8979

ATR - ISSN: 0001-2777

COMSAT TECHNICAL REVIEW - ISSN: 0095-9669

EBU REVIEW. TECHNICAL. - ISSN: 0012-7493

ELECTRICAL COMMUNICATION - ISSN: 0013-4252

ELECTRONICS LETTERS - ISSN: 0013-5194

IEEE TRANSACTIONS ON BROADCASTING - ISSN: 0018-9316

IEEE TRANSACTIONS ON CONSUMER ELECTRONICS - ISSN: 0098-3063

MARCONI REVIEW, THE - ISSN: 0025-2883

Engineering Index Monthly
(ISSN: 0013-7960)

ACUSTICA - ISSN: 0001-7884

AEG-TELEFUNKEN PROGRESS - ISSN: 0001-107x

AES - ISSN: 0747-8909

AEU - ISSN: 0001-1096

AT&T TECHNOLOGY - ISSN: 0889-8979

ATR - ISSN: 0001-2777

AWA TECHNICAL REVIEW - ISSN: 0001-2920

COMSAT TECHNICAL REVIEW - ISSN: 0095-9669

EBU REVIEW. TECHNICAL. - ISSN: 0012-7493

ELECTRICAL COMMUNICATION - ISSN: 0013-4252

ELECTRONIC ENGINEERING - ISSN: 0013-4902

ELECTRONICS - ISSN: 0883-4989

ELECTRONICS LETTERS - ISSN: 0013-5194

IEEE TRANSACTIONS ON BROADCASTING - ISSN: 0018-9316

IEEE TRANSACTIONS ON CONSUMER ELECTRONICS - ISSN: 0098-3063

INDUSTRIAL PHOTOGRAPHY - ISSN: 0019-8595

JOURNAL OF TECHNICAL WRITING AND COMMUNICATION - ISSN: 0047-2816

MARCONI REVIEW, THE - ISSN: 0025-2883

SMPTE JOURNAL - ISSN: 0036-1682

TELECOMMUNICATION JOURNAL - ISSN: 0497-137x

TELECOMMUNICATION JOURNAL OF AUSTRALIA, THE - ISSN: 0040-2486

TELECOMMUNICATIONS - ISSN: 0278-4831

TELECOMMUNICATIONS POLICY - ISSN: 0308-5961

TELEVISION - ISSN: 8755-5867

Engineering Index Annual
(ISSN: 0360-8557)

ELECTRONICS LETTERS - ISSN: 0013-5194

Environment Abstracts
(ISSN: 0093-3287)

ACUSTICA - ISSN: 0001-7884

AMERICAN DEMOGRAPHICS - ISSN: 0163-4089

AT&T TECHNOLOGY - ISSN: 0889-8979

COLUMBIA JOURNALISM REVIEW - ISSN: 0010-194x

JOURNAL OF COMMUNICATION - ISSN: 0021-9916

PULP & PAPER CANADA - ISSN: 0316-4004

WORLD PRESS REVIEW - ISSN: 0195-8895

Exceptional Child Abstracts

AV VIDEO - ISSN: 0747-1335

MARCONI REVIEW, THE - ISSN: 0025-2883

TECHTRENDS - ISSN: 8756-3894

Excerpta Medica

ACUSTICA - ISSN: 0001-7884

AEU - ISSN: 0001-1096

AT&T TECHNOLOGY - ISSN: 0889-8979

EDUCATIONAL MEDIA INTERNATIONAL - ISSN: 0004-7597

ELECTRONICS - ISSN: 0883-4989

MARCONI REVIEW, THE - ISSN: 0025-2883

SMPTE JOURNAL - ISSN: 0036-1682

TECHNOLOGY AND CULTURE - ISSN: 0040-165x

Explicator, The

JOURNAL OF POPULAR FILM AND TELEVISION - ISSN: 0195-6051

F

Film Literature Index
(ISSN: 0093-6758)

- AFI EDUCATION NEWSLETTER - ISSN: 0883-6213
- AFTERIMAGE - ISSN: 0300-7472
- AFVA BULLETIN - ISSN: 0164-6508
- AMERICAN CINEMATOGRAPHER - ISSN: 0002-7928
- AMERICAN CLASSIC SCREEN - ISSN: 0195-8267
- AMERICAN FILM - ISSN: 0361-4751
- AUSTRALIAN JOURNAL OF SCREEN THEORY - ISSN: 0313-4059
- BOX OFFICE - ISSN: 0006-8527
- BRIGHT LIGHTS - ISSN: 0147-4049
- CAMERA OBSCURA - ISSN: 0270-5346
- CANTRILLS FILMNOTES - ISSN: 0158-4154
- CINEASTE - ISSN: 0009-7004
- CINEFANTASTIQUE - ISSN: 0145-6032
- CINEFEX - ISSN: 0198-1056
- CINEMA/CANADA - ISSN: 0009-7071
- CINEMA JOURNAL - ISSN: 0009-7101
- CINEMA PAPERS - ISSN: 0311-3639
- CINEMAGIC - ISSN: 0090-3000
- CINEMONKEY - ISSN: 0162-0126
- COLUMBIA JOURNALISM REVIEW - ISSN: 0010-194x
- COMMUNICATION RESEARCH TRENDS - ISSN: 0144-4646
- FILM - ISSN: 0015-1025
- FILM & VIDEO NEWS - ISSN: 8750-068x
- FILM BULLETIN - ISSN: 0015-1122
- FILM COMMENT - ISSN: 0015-119x
- FILM CRITICISM - ISSN: 0163-5069
- FILM CULTURE - ISSN: 0015-1211
- FILM JOURNAL, THE - ISSN: 0046-3787
- FILM LIBRARY QUARTERLY - ISSN: 0015-1327
- FILM MAKING - ISSN: 0013-2543
- FILM QUARTERLY - ISSN: 0015-1386
- FILMS ILLUSTRATED - ISSN: 0015-167x
- FILMS IN REVIEW - ISSN: 0015-1688
- FOCUS ON FILM - ISSN: 0015-5128
- FUNNYWORLD - ISSN: 0071-9943
- GRAPHIS - ISSN: 0017-3452
- HIGH FIDELITY - ISSN: 0018-1455
- HISTORICAL JOURNAL OF FILM, RADIO & TELEVISION - ISSN: 0143-9685
- HUMAN COMMUNICATION RESEARCH - ISSN: 0360-3989
- HUNGAROFILM BULLETIN - ISSN: 0018-7798
- IMAGE - ISSN: 0536-5465
- INTERVIEW - ISSN: 0149-8932
- JOURNAL OF COMMUNICATION - ISSN: 0021-9916
- JOURNAL OF FILM AND VIDEO - ISSN: 0742-4671
- JOURNAL OF POPULAR FILM AND TELEVISION - ISSN: 0195-6051
- JUMP CUT - ISSN: 0146-5546
- LITERATURE/FILM QUARTERLY - ISSN: 0090-4260
- MEDIA REPORT TO WOMEN - ISSN: 0145-9651
- MILLIMETER - ISSN: 0164-9655
- MODERN DRAMA - ISSN: 0026-7694
- MODERN PHOTOGRAPHY - ISSN: 0026-8240
- MONTHLY FILM BULLETIN - ISSN: 0027-0407
- MOVIE - ISSN: 0027-268x
- MOVING IMAGE - ISSN: 0276-3494
- POPULAR PHOTOGRAPHY - ISSN: 0032-4582
- POST SCRIPT - ISSN: 0277-9897
- PRINT - ISSN: 0032-8510
- QUARTERLY REVIEW OF FILM AND VIDEO - ISSN: 0146-0013
- SCREEN - ISSN: 0036-9543
- SIGHT & SOUND - ISSN: 0037-4806
- SMPTE JOURNAL - ISSN: 0036-1682
- STUDIES IN VISUAL COMMUNICATION - ISSN: 0276-6558
- THEATER - ISSN: 0161-0775
- VARIETY - ISSN: 0042-2738
- VELVET LIGHT TRAP - ISSN: 0149-1830
- VIDEOGRAPHY - ISSN: 0363-1001
- VISUAL EDUCATION - ISSN: 0042-7152
- WIDE ANGLE - ISSN: 0160-6840

Fluidex

- ELECTRONICS - ISSN: 0883-4989

G

GeoRef

- FUNCTIONAL PHOTOGRAPHY - ISSN: 0360-7216

H

Historical Abstracts
(ISSN: 0018-2435)

- JOURNAL OF COMMUNICATION - ISSN: 0021-9916
- WESTERN JOURNAL OF SPEECH COMMUNICATION - ISSN: 0193-6700

Historical Abstracts. Part A. Modern History Abstracts.
(ISSN: 0363-2712)

- FILM & HISTORY - ISSN: 0360-3695
- HISTORICAL JOURNAL OF FILM, RADIO & TELEVISION - ISSN: 0143-9685
- JOURNAL OF POPULAR CULTURE - ISSN: 0022-3840
- JOURNAL OF POPULAR FILM AND TELEVISION - ISSN: 0195-6051
- JOURNALISM HISTORY - ISSN: 0094-7679
- JQ. JOURNALISM QUARTERLY. - ISSN: 0022-5533
- QUARTERLY JOURNAL OF SPEECH, THE - ISSN: 0033-5630
- RESTORATION AND 18TH CENTURY THEATRE RESEARCH - ISSN: 0034-5822
- SCHOLARLY PUBLISHING - ISSN: 0036-634x
- SILENT PICTURE, THE - ISSN: 0037-5209
- TECHNOLOGY AND CULTURE - ISSN: 0040-165x
- VICTORIAN PERIODICALS REVIEW - ISSN: 0709-4698

Historical Abstracts. Part B. Twentieth Century Abstracts.
(ISSN: 0363-2725)

- FILM & HISTORY - ISSN: 0360-3695
- FILM HERITAGE - ISSN: 0015-1270
- HISTORICAL JOURNAL OF FILM, RADIO & TELEVISION - ISSN: 0143-9685
- JOURNAL OF POPULAR CULTURE - ISSN: 0022-3840
- JOURNAL OF POPULAR FILM AND TELEVISION - ISSN: 0195-6051
- JOURNALISM HISTORY - ISSN: 0094-7679
- JQ. JOURNALISM QUARTERLY. - ISSN: 0022-5533

MADISON AVENUE - ISSN: 0024-9483

MARKETING / COMMUNICATIONS - ISSN: 0025-3685

MARKETING NEWS - ISSN: 0025-3790

MEDIA INDUSTRY NEWSLETTER - ISSN: 0024-9793

MEDIAWEEK - ISSN: 1055-176x

PHOTO MARKETING - ISSN: 0031-8531

PUBLIC OPINION QUARTERLY - ISSN: 0033-362x

PUBLIC RELATIONS JOURNAL, THE - ISSN: 0033-3670

PUBLIC RELATIONS REVIEW - ISSN: 0363-8111

SALES & MARKETING MANAGEMENT - ISSN: 0163-7517

TELEVISION/RADIO AGE - ISSN: 0040-277x

VARIETY - ISSN: 0042-2738

WORLD PRESS REVIEW - ISSN: 0195-8895

Information Science Abstracts

LANGUAGE & COMMUNICATION - ISSN: 0271-5309

TELEMATICS AND INFORMATICS - ISSN: 0736-5853

INSPEC Science Abstracts

TECHTRENDS - ISSN: 8756-3894

International Aerospace Abstracts
(ISSN: 0020-5842)

ACUSTICA - ISSN: 0001-7884

AEU - ISSN: 0001-1096

AT&T TECHNOLOGY - ISSN: 0889-8979

ATR - ISSN: 0001-2777

COMSAT TECHNICAL REVIEW - ISSN: 0095-9669

ELECTRICAL COMMUNICATION - ISSN: 0013-4252

ELECTRONIC AGE - ISSN: 0013-4783

ELECTRONIC ENGINEERING - ISSN: 0013-4902

ELECTRONICS - ISSN: 0883-4989

ELECTRONICS LETTERS - ISSN: 0013-5194

FUNCTIONAL PHOTOGRAPHY - ISSN: 0360-7216

IEEE TRANSACTIONS ON BROADCASTING - ISSN: 0018-9316

INDUSTRIAL ELECTRONICS - ISSN: 0537-5185

MARCONI REVIEW, THE - ISSN: 0025-2883

MILITARY ELECTRONICS / COUNTERMEASURES - ISSN: 0164-4076

PROCEEDINGS OF THE IREE AUSTRALIA - ISSN: 0158-0736

SATELLITE COMMUNICATIONS - ISSN: 0147-7439

SMPTE JOURNAL - ISSN: 0036-1682

TECHNOLOGY AND CULTURE - ISSN: 0040-165x

TELECOMMUNICATION JOURNAL - ISSN: 0497-137x

TELECOMMUNICATION JOURNAL OF AUSTRALIA, THE - ISSN: 0040-2486

TELECOMMUNICATIONS POLICY - ISSN: 0308-5961

TELEMATICS AND INFORMATICS - ISSN: 0736-5853

International Index

TDR - ISSN: 0012-5962

WORLD THEATRE - ISSN: 0512-3704

International Index to Film Periodicals
(ISSN: 0000-0038)

CAMERA OBSCURA - ISSN: 0270-5346

CINEMA JOURNAL - ISSN: 0009-7101

FILM JOURNAL, THE - ISSN: 0046-3787

FILM LIBRARY QUARTERLY - ISSN: 0015-1327

JOURNAL OF FILM AND VIDEO - ISSN: 0742-4671

JOURNAL OF POPULAR FILM AND TELEVISION - ISSN: 0195-6051

JUMP CUT - ISSN: 0146-5546

POST SCRIPT - ISSN: 0277-9897

QUARTERLY REVIEW OF FILM AND VIDEO - ISSN: 0146-0013

International Index to Multi-Media Information
(ISSN: 0094-6818)

TECHTRENDS - ISSN: 8756-3894

International Index to Periodicals

DRAMA - ISSN: 0012-5946

International Index to Television Periodicals

JOURNAL OF POPULAR FILM AND TELEVISION - ISSN: 0195-6051

International Political Science Abstracts

POLITICAL COMMUNICATION AND PERSUASION - ISSN: 0195-7473

ISMEC Bulletin
(ISSN: 0306-0039)

AEU - ISSN: 0001-1096

AV VIDEO - ISSN: 0747-1335

BIOMEDICAL COMMUNICATIONS - ISSN: 0092-8607

ELECTRICAL COMMUNICATION - ISSN: 0013-4252

MARCONI REVIEW, THE - ISSN: 0025-2883

J

Jazz Index
(ISSN: 0344-5399)

DOWN BEAT - ISSN: 0012-5768

RECORD RESEARCH - ISSN: 0034-1592

Journal of Economic Literature
(ISSN: 0022-0515)

JMR, JOURNAL OF MARKETING RESEARCH - ISSN: 0022-2437

L

Language and Language Behavior Abstracts
(ISSN: 0023-8295)

COMMUNICATION - ISSN: 0305-4233

COMMUNICATION EDUCATION - ISSN: 0363-4523

COMMUNICATION QUARTERLY - ISSN: 0146-3373

COMMUNICATION STUDIES - ISSN: 1051-0974

COMMUNICATIONS - ISSN: 0341-2059

HUMAN COMMUNICATION RESEARCH - ISSN: 0360-3989

JOURNAL OF APPLIED COMMUNICATION RESEARCH - ISSN: 0090-9882

JOURNAL OF COMMUNICATION - ISSN: 0021-9916

JOURNAL OF TECHNICAL WRITING AND COMMUNICATION - ISSN: 0047-2816

JQ. JOURNALISM QUARTERLY. - ISSN: 0022-5533

LANGUAGE & COMMUNICATION - ISSN: 0271-5309

VISIBLE LANGUAGE - ISSN: 0022-2224

WORLD COMMUNICATION - ISSN: 1050-012x

Language Teaching
(ISSN: 0261-4448)

LANGUAGE & COMMUNICATION - ISSN: 0271-5309

MEDIA IN EDUCATION AND DEVELOPMENT - ISSN: 0262-0251

QUARTERLY JOURNAL OF SPEECH, THE - ISSN: 0033-5630

Legal Resource Index

CARDOZO ARTS & ENTERTAINMENT LAW JOURNAL - ISSN: 0736-7694

COMMUNICATIONS AND THE LAW - ISSN: 0162-9093

FEDERAL COMMUNICATIONS LAW JOURNAL - ISSN: 0163-7606

JOURNAL OF BROADCASTING & ELECTRONIC MEDIA - ISSN: 0883-8151

MEDIA LAW NOTES - ISSN: 0736-1750

NEWS MEDIA & THE LAW, THE - ISSN: 0149-0737

Library Information Science Abstracts
(ISSN: 0024-2179)

AUTHOR, THE - ISSN: 0005-0628

BRITISH BOOK NEWS - ISSN: 0007-0343

INTERNATIONAL JOURNAL OF INFORMATION MANAGEMENT - ISSN: 0268-4012

PRINTING HISTORY - ISSN: 0192-9275

PUBLISHER'S WEEKLY - ISSN: 0000-0019

SCHOLARLY PUBLISHING - ISSN: 0036-634x

SERIALS REVIEW - ISSN: 0098-7913

TELEMATICS AND INFORMATICS - ISSN: 0736-5853

Library Literature
(ISSN: 0024-2373)

AB BOOKMAN'S WEEKLY - ISSN: 0001-0340

AFVA BULLETIN - ISSN: 0164-6508

FILM LIBRARY QUARTERLY - ISSN: 0015-1327

PRINTING HISTORY - ISSN: 0192-9275

PUBLISHER'S WEEKLY - ISSN: 0000-0019

SCHOLARLY PUBLISHING - ISSN: 0036-634x

SERIALS REVIEW - ISSN: 0098-7913

Life Sciences Collection

ACUSTICA - ISSN: 0001-7884

Linguistics & Language Behavior Abstracts

LANGUAGE & COMMUNICATION - ISSN: 0271-5309

WESTERN JOURNAL OF SPEECH COMMUNICATION - ISSN: 0193-6700

WRITTEN COMMUNICATION - ISSN: 0741-0883

M

Magazine Index

AMERICAN FILM - ISSN: 0361-4751

AUDIO - ISSN: 0004-752x

CAMERA 35 INCORPORATING PHOTO WORLD - ISSN: 0008-2171

CINEMA/CANADA - ISSN: 0009-7071

COMPUTERS & ELECTRONICS - ISSN: 0745-1458

DOWN BEAT - ISSN: 0012-5768

ELECTRONICS - ISSN: 0883-4989

FILM COMMENT - ISSN: 0015-119x

FILM QUARTERLY - ISSN: 0015-1386

HIGH FIDELITY - ISSN: 0018-1455

MODERN PHOTOGRAPHY - ISSN: 0026-8240

PERFORMING ARTS IN CANADA, THE - ISSN: 0031-5230

PETERSEN'S PHOTOGRAPHIC - ISSN: 0199-4913

PLAYS - ISSN: 0032-1540

POPULAR PHOTOGRAPHY - ISSN: 0032-4582

PUBLIC OPINION QUARTERLY - ISSN: 0033-362x

PUBLISHER'S WEEKLY - ISSN: 0000-0019

RADIO-ELECTRONICS - ISSN: 0033-7862

SALES & MARKETING MANAGEMENT - ISSN: 0163-7517

TDR - ISSN: 0012-5962

THEATRE CRAFTS - ISSN: 0040-5469

TV GUIDE - ISSN: 0039-8543

VARIETY - ISSN: 0042-2738

WORLD PRESS REVIEW - ISSN: 0195-8895

WRITER, THE - ISSN: 0043-9517

WRITER'S DIGEST - ISSN: 0043-9525

Management and Marketing Abstracts
(ISSN: 0308-2172)

BUSINESS MARKETING - ISSN: 0745-5933

CAMPAIGN - ISSN: 0008-2309

COMMUNICATIONS NEWS - ISSN: 0010-3632

JOURNAL OF ADVERTISING RESEARCH - ISSN: 0021-8499

JOURNAL OF MARKETING - ISSN: 0022-2429

PUBLIC RELATIONS JOURNAL, THE - ISSN: 0033-3670

Management Contents

ADWEEK'S MARKETING WEEK - ISSN: 0892-8274

AMERICAN DEMOGRAPHICS - ISSN: 0163-4089

CAMPAIGN - ISSN: 0008-2309

COMMUNICATION WORLD - ISSN: 0744-7612

DIRECT MARKETING - ISSN: 0012-3188

FEDERAL COMMUNICATIONS LAW JOURNAL - ISSN: 0163-7606

INTERNATIONAL ADVERTISER - ISSN: 0885-3353

JMR, JOURNAL OF MARKETING RESEARCH - ISSN: 0022-2437

JOURNAL OF ADVERTISING - ISSN: 0091-3367

JOURNAL OF ADVERTISING RESEARCH - ISSN: 0021-8499

JOURNAL OF COMMUNICATION MANAGEMENT - ISSN: 0745-1822

JOURNAL OF MARKETING - ISSN: 0022-2429

MADISON AVENUE - ISSN: 0024-9483

MARKETING NEWS - ISSN: 0025-3790

MASS COMM REVIEW - ISSN: 0193-7707

MEDIAWEEK - ISSN: 1055-176x
PUBLIC RELATIONS JOURNAL, THE - ISSN: 0033-3670
PUBLIC RELATIONS REVIEW - ISSN: 0363-8111
SALES & MARKETING MANAGEMENT - ISSN: 0163-7517

Mathematical Reviews
(ISSN: 0025-5629)

ACUSTICA - ISSN: 0001-7884
AT&T TECHNICAL JOURNAL - ISSN: 8756-2324
ELECTRONICS LETTERS - ISSN: 0013-5194
LEONARDO - ISSN: 0024-094x
VISIBLE LANGUAGE - ISSN: 0022-2224

Media Review Digest
(ISSN: 0363-7778)

AFTER DARK - ISSN: 0002-0702
AFVA BULLETIN - ISSN: 0164-6508
AMERICAN FILM - ISSN: 0361-4751
CINEASTE - ISSN: 0009-7004
CINEFANTASTIQUE - ISSN: 0145-6032
CINEMA/CANADA - ISSN: 0009-7071
CINEMA PAPERS - ISSN: 0311-3639
COMMUNICATION BOOKNOTES - ISSN: 0748-657x
COMMUNICATION EDUCATION - ISSN: 0363-4523
COMPUTER PICTURES - ISSN: 0883-5683
E-ITV - ISSN: 0743-7773
FILM - ISSN: 0015-1025
FILM & VIDEO NEWS - ISSN: 8750-068x
FILM BULLETIN - ISSN: 0015-1122
FILM COMMENT - ISSN: 0015-119x
FILM CULTURE - ISSN: 0015-1211
FILM LIBRARY QUARTERLY - ISSN: 0015-1327
FILM QUARTERLY - ISSN: 0015-1386
FILMS IN REVIEW - ISSN: 0015-1688
HISTORICAL JOURNAL OF FILM, RADIO & TELEVISION - ISSN: 0143-9685
JOURNAL OF POPULAR FILM AND TELEVISION - ISSN: 0195-6051
JUMP CUT - ISSN: 0146-5546
LITERATURE/FILM QUARTERLY - ISSN: 0090-4260
MASS MEDIA NEWSLETTER - ISSN: 0361-865x
MEDIA & METHODS - ISSN: 0025-6897
MILLIMETER - ISSN: 0164-9655
MONTHLY FILM BULLETIN - ISSN: 0027-0407
NEWSLETTER - ISSN: 0043-9533
PREVIEWS - ISSN: 0000-0051
QUARTERLY REVIEW OF FILM AND VIDEO - ISSN: 0146-0013
SCREEN - ISSN: 0036-9543
SIGHT & SOUND - ISSN: 0037-4806
TECHTRENDS - ISSN: 8756-3894
VARIETY - ISSN: 0042-2738
WIDE ANGLE - ISSN: 0160-6840

Metals Abstracts
(ISSN: 0026-0924)

ELECTRICAL REVIEW - ISSN: 0013-4384
ELECTRONIC ENGINEERING - ISSN: 0013-4902
ELECTRONICS LETTERS - ISSN: 0013-5194
ZEISS INFORMATION - ISSN: 0044-2054

Micro Computer Index
(ISSN: 8756-7040)

COMPUTERS & ELECTRONICS - ISSN: 0745-1458
MEDIA & METHODS - ISSN: 0025-6897
TECHTRENDS - ISSN: 8756-3894
THE JOURNAL - ISSN: 0192-592x

MLA International Bibliography of Books & Articles on the Modern Languages and Literatures
(ISSN: 0024-8215)

ARSC JOURNAL - ISSN: 0004-5438
CINEMA JOURNAL - ISSN: 0009-7101
COMMUNICATION EDUCATION - ISSN: 0363-4523
FILM CRITICISM - ISSN: 0163-5069
INDEX ON CENSORSHIP - ISSN: 0306-4220
JOURNAL OF COMMUNICATION - ISSN: 0021-9916
JOURNAL OF POPULAR CULTURE - ISSN: 0022-3840
JOURNAL OF POPULAR FILM AND TELEVISION - ISSN: 0195-6051
JQ. JOURNALISM QUARTERLY. - ISSN: 0022-5533
LANGUAGE & COMMUNICATION - ISSN: 0271-5309
MODERN DRAMA - ISSN: 0026-7694
POST SCRIPT - ISSN: 0277-9897
PUBLISHING RESEARCH QUARTERLY - ISSN: 1053-8801
QUARTERLY JOURNAL OF SPEECH, THE - ISSN: 0033-5630
RESTORATION AND 18TH CENTURY THEATRE RESEARCH - ISSN: 0034-5822
SCHOLARLY PUBLISHING - ISSN: 0036-634x
SHAKESPEARE QUARTERLY - ISSN: 0037-3222
TDR - ISSN: 0012-5962
THEATER - ISSN: 0161-0775
THEATRE JOURNAL - ISSN: 0192-2882
THEATRE NOTEBOOK - ISSN: 0040-5523
VICTORIAN PERIODICALS REVIEW - ISSN: 0709-4698
VISIBLE LANGUAGE - ISSN: 0022-2224

Music Article Guide

STEREO REVIEW - ISSN: 0039-1220

Music Index
(ISSN: 0027-4348)

ARSC JOURNAL - ISSN: 0004-5438
BILLBOARD - ISSN: 0006-2510
DOWN BEAT - ISSN: 0012-5768
FRESH! - ISSN: 0886-9596
GRAMOPHONE - ISSN: 0017-310x
HIGH FIDELITY - ISSN: 0018-1455
JOURNAL OF POPULAR CULTURE - ISSN: 0022-3840
PERFORMING ARTS IN CANADA, THE - ISSN: 0031-5230
RECORD RESEARCH - ISSN: 0034-1592
STEREO REVIEW - ISSN: 0039-1220

N

New Periodicals Index

SMALL PRESS BOOK REVIEW, THE - ISSN: 8756-7202

Nexis

CONGRESSIONAL QUARTERLY'S EDITORIAL RESEARCH REPORTS - ISSN: 0013-0958
ELECTRONICS - ISSN: 0883-4989

Nuclear Science Abstracts
(ISSN: 0029-5612)

ACUSTICA - ISSN: 0001-7884

Abstracts & Indexes

AES - ISSN: 0747-8909

ELECTRONICS LETTERS - ISSN: 0013-5194

IEEE TRANSACTIONS ON BROADCASTING - ISSN: 0018-9316

MARCONI REVIEW, THE - ISSN: 0025-2883

P

Paper & Board Abstracts
(ISSN: 0307-0778)

PULP & PAPER CANADA - ISSN: 0316-4004

Physics Abstracts. Science Abstracts. Series A.
(ISSN: 0036-8091)

ABU TECHNICAL REVIEW - ISSN: 0126-6209

ACUSTICA - ISSN: 0001-7884

AT&T TECHNOLOGY - ISSN: 0889-8979

ATR - ISSN: 0001-2777

BRITISH JOURNAL OF PHOTOGRAPHY - ISSN: 0007-1196

CD-ROM LIBRARIAN - ISSN: 0893-9934

COMMUNICATIONS - ISSN: 0341-2059

COMMUNICATIONS AND THE LAW - ISSN: 0162-9093

COMPUTERS & ELECTRONICS - ISSN: 0745-1458

COMSAT TECHNICAL REVIEW - ISSN: 0095-9669

CQ - ISSN: 0007-893x

DB - ISSN: 0011-7145

EBU REVIEW. TECHNICAL. - ISSN: 0012-7493

ELECTRICAL COMMUNICATION - ISSN: 0013-4252

ELECTRICAL REVIEW - ISSN: 0013-4384

ELECTRONIC ENGINEERING - ISSN: 0013-4902

ELECTRONICS - ISSN: 0883-4989

ELECTRONICS & COMMUNICATIONS - ISSN: 0013-5100

ELECTRONICS LETTERS - ISSN: 0013-5194

FUNCTIONAL PHOTOGRAPHY - ISSN: 0360-7216

IBE - ISSN: 0020-6229

IEEE TRANSACTIONS ON BROADCASTING - ISSN: 0018-9316

IEEE TRANSACTIONS ON CABLE TELEVISION - ISSN: 0147-3204

IEEE TRANSACTIONS ON CONSUMER ELECTRONICS - ISSN: 0098-3063

IMAGE TECHNOLOGY - ISSN: 0950-2114

INDUSTRIAL ELECTRONICS - ISSN: 0537-5185

INDUSTRIAL PHOTOGRAPHY - ISSN: 0019-8595

INTERNATIONAL BROADCASTING - ISSN: 0141-1748

INTERNATIONAL JOURNAL OF INFORMATION MANAGEMENT - ISSN: 0268-4012

JEE, JOURNAL OF ELECTRONIC ENGINEERING - ISSN: 0385-4507

LANGUAGE & COMMUNICATION - ISSN: 0271-5309

LEONARDO - ISSN: 0024-094x

LINK-UP - ISSN: 0739-988x

MARCONI REVIEW, THE - ISSN: 0025-2883

MEDIA IN EDUCATION AND DEVELOPMENT - ISSN: 0262-0251

MILITARY ELECTRONICS / COUNTERMEASURES - ISSN: 0164-4076

PROCEEDINGS OF THE IREE AUSTRALIA - ISSN: 0158-0736

RADIO AND TELEVISION - ISSN: 0277-4860

RADIO COMMUNICATION - ISSN: 0033-7803

RADIO-ELECTRONICS - ISSN: 0033-7862

RCA BROADCAST NEWS - ISSN: 0096-7785

RF DESIGN - ISSN: 0163-321x

SATELLITE COMMUNICATIONS - ISSN: 0147-7439

SMPTE JOURNAL - ISSN: 0036-1682

TECHTRENDS - ISSN: 8756-3894

TELECOMMUNICATION JOURNAL - ISSN: 0497-137x

TELECOMMUNICATION JOURNAL OF AUSTRALIA, THE - ISSN: 0040-2486

TELECOMMUNICATIONS POLICY - ISSN: 0308-5961

TELEMATICS AND INFORMATICS - ISSN: 0736-5853

TELEVISION - ISSN: 8755-5867

TELEVISION - ISSN: 0308-454x

TELEVISION/RADIO AGE - ISSN: 0040-277x

THE JOURNAL - ISSN: 0192-592x

VISIBLE LANGUAGE - ISSN: 0022-2224

Pollution Abstracts with Indexes
(ISSN: 0032-3624)

AEU - ISSN: 0001-1096

AV VIDEO - ISSN: 0747-1335

BIOMEDICAL COMMUNICATIONS - ISSN: 0092-8607

ELECTRICAL COMMUNICATION - ISSN: 0013-4252

MARCONI REVIEW, THE - ISSN: 0025-2883

Popular Magazine Review
(ISSN: 0740-3763)

AMERICAN FILM - ISSN: 0361-4751

AUDIO - ISSN: 0004-752x

COMPUTERS & ELECTRONICS - ISSN: 0745-1458

DOWN BEAT - ISSN: 0012-5768

FILM COMMENT - ISSN: 0015-119x

HIGH FIDELITY - ISSN: 0018-1455

MODERN PHOTOGRAPHY - ISSN: 0026-8240

MODERN RECORDING & MUSIC - ISSN: 0273-8511

PETERSEN'S PHOTOGRAPHIC - ISSN: 0199-4913

POPULAR PHOTOGRAPHY - ISSN: 0032-4582

PUBLISHER'S WEEKLY - ISSN: 0000-0019

RADIO-ELECTRONICS - ISSN: 0033-7862

STEREO REVIEW - ISSN: 0039-1220

THEATRE CRAFTS - ISSN: 0040-5469

TV GUIDE - ISSN: 0039-8543

VARIETY - ISSN: 0042-2738

WORLD PRESS REVIEW - ISSN: 0195-8895

WRITER, THE - ISSN: 0043-9517

Population Index
(ISSN: 0032-4701)

AMERICAN DEMOGRAPHICS - ISSN: 0163-4089

Predicasts

ADVERTISING AGE - ISSN: 0001-8899

AMERICAN DEMOGRAPHICS - ISSN: 0163-4089

AMERICAN PRINTER - ISSN: 0744-6616

BROADCASTING - ISSN: 0007-2028

BUSINESS MARKETING - ISSN: 0745-5933

CABLE TV ADVERTISING - ISSN: 0270-885x

CABLE TV PROGRAMMING - ISSN: 0278-503x
CAMPAIGN - ISSN: 0008-2309
COMMUNICATIONS NEWS - ISSN: 0010-3632
DBS NEWS - ISSN: 0733-9739
DIRECT MARKETING - ISSN: 0012-3188
E-ITV - ISSN: 0743-7773
EDUCATIONAL COMMUNICATION AND TECHNOLOGY - ISSN: 0148-5806
ELECTRICAL REVIEW - ISSN: 0013-4384
ELECTRONIC ENGINEERING - ISSN: 0013-4902
ELECTRONIC PRODUCTS - ISSN: 0013-4953
ELECTRONICS - ISSN: 0883-4989
ELECTRONICS & COMMUNICATIONS - ISSN: 0013-5100
FOCUS - ISSN: 1046-0489
HIGH VOLUME PRINTING - ISSN: 0737-1020
INFORMATION TODAY - ISSN: 8755-6286
INSIDE MEDIA - ISSN: 1046-5316
INTERNATIONAL ADVERTISER - ISSN: 0198-6228
JEE, JOURNAL OF ELECTRONIC ENGINEERING - ISSN: 0385-4507
JOURNAL OF MARKETING - ISSN: 0022-2429
MARKETING / COMMUNICATIONS - ISSN: 0025-3685
MARKETING NEWS - ISSN: 0025-3790
MEDIAWEEK - ISSN: 1055-176x
PHOTO MARKETING - ISSN: 0031-8531
PHOTOMETHODS - ISSN: 0146-0153
PUBLIC RELATIONS JOURNAL, THE - ISSN: 0033-3670
RADIO-ELECTRONICS - ISSN: 0033-7862
SALES & MARKETING MANAGEMENT - ISSN: 0163-7517
SATELLITE COMMUNICATIONS - ISSN: 0147-7439
TARGET MARKETING - ISSN: 0889-5333
TELECOMMUNICATIONS - ISSN: 0278-4831
TELEMARKETING - ISSN: 0730-6156
TV GUIDE - ISSN: 0039-8543

Printing Abstracts
(ISSN: 0031-109x)

AMERICAN PRINTER - ISSN: 0744-6616
AUSTRALASIAN PRINTER - ISSN: 0004-8453
BRITISH JOURNAL OF PHOTOGRAPHY - ISSN: 0007-1196
BRITISH PRINTER - ISSN: 0007-1684
CAMPAIGN - ISSN: 0008-2309

CANADIAN PRINTER - ISSN: 0849-0767
EDITOR AND PUBLISHER - ISSN: 0013-094x
FIEJ-BULLETIN - ISSN: 0046-3531
GRAPHIC ARTS MONTHLY - ISSN: 0017-3274
HIGH VOLUME PRINTING - ISSN: 0737-1020
NEWSPAPER TECHNIQUES - ISSN: 0545-8846
PRESSTIME - ISSN: 0194-3243
PRINT - ISSN: 0032-8510
PRINTING IMPRESSIONS - ISSN: 0032-860x
VISIBLE LANGUAGE - ISSN: 0022-2224

Psychological Abstracts
(ISSN: 0033-0202)

COMMUNICATION - ISSN: 0305-4233
COMMUNICATION RESEARCH - ISSN: 0093-6502
COMMUNICATION STUDIES - ISSN: 1051-0974
COMMUNICATIONS - ISSN: 0341-2059
EDUCATIONAL COMMUNICATION AND TECHNOLOGY - ISSN: 0148-5806
HUMAN COMMUNICATION RESEARCH - ISSN: 0360-3989
JMR, JOURNAL OF MARKETING RESEARCH - ISSN: 0022-2437
JOURNAL OF ADVERTISING - ISSN: 0091-3367
JOURNAL OF ADVERTISING RESEARCH - ISSN: 0021-8499
JOURNAL OF COMMUNICATION - ISSN: 0021-9916
JOURNAL OF MARKETING - ISSN: 0022-2429
LANGUAGE & COMMUNICATION - ISSN: 0271-5309
PUBLIC OPINION QUARTERLY - ISSN: 0033-362x
QUARTERLY JOURNAL OF SPEECH, THE - ISSN: 0033-5630
WESTERN JOURNAL OF SPEECH COMMUNICATION - ISSN: 0193-6700

PAIS Foreign Language Index
(ISSN: 0896-792x)

INTERNATIONAL JOURNAL OF INFORMATION MANAGEMENT - ISSN: 0268-4012

Political Science Abstracts

POLITICAL COMMUNICATION AND PERSUASION - ISSN: 0195-7473

Public Affairs Information Service Bulletin
(ISSN: 0033-3409)

ADVERTISING - ISSN: 1042-0711
ADVERTISING MAGAZINE - ISSN: 0001-8961
AMERICAN DEMOGRAPHICS - ISSN: 0163-4089
BROADCASTING - ISSN: 0007-2028
CONGRESSIONAL QUARTERLY'S EDITORIAL RESEARCH REPORTS - ISSN: 0013-0958
FOLIO: - ISSN: 0046-4333
GANNETT CENTER JOURNAL - ISSN: 0893-8342
INDEX ON CENSORSHIP - ISSN: 0306-4220
INTERNATIONAL JOURNAL OF INFORMATION MANAGEMENT - ISSN: 0268-4012
JOURNAL OF ADVERTISING - ISSN: 0091-3367
JOURNAL OF BROADCASTING & ELECTRONIC MEDIA - ISSN: 0883-8151
JQ. JOURNALISM QUARTERLY. - ISSN: 0022-5533
MARKETING / COMMUNICATIONS - ISSN: 0025-3685
POLITICAL COMMUNICATION AND PERSUASION - ISSN: 0195-7473
PUBLIC OPINION QUARTERLY - ISSN: 0033-362x
PUBLIC RELATIONS REVIEW - ISSN: 0363-8111
PUBLISHER'S WEEKLY - ISSN: 0000-0019
PUBLISHING RESEARCH QUARTERLY - ISSN: 1053-8801
WORLD PRESS REVIEW - ISSN: 0195-8895

Q

Quarterly Index to Scholarly Critical and Creative Journals

PERFORMING ARTS JOURNAL - ISSN: 0735-8393

Abstracts & Indexes INDEX 714

R

Readers Guide Abstracts
(ISSN: 0886-0092)

CHANNELS - ISSN: 0895-643x
DOWN BEAT - ISSN: 0012-5768

Readers Guide to Periodical Literature
(ISSN: 0034-0464)

CHANNELS - ISSN: 0895-643x
COMPUTERS & ELECTRONICS - ISSN: 0745-1458
DOWN BEAT - ISSN: 0012-5768
ELECTRONICS WORLD - ISSN: 0013-5232
FILM COMMENT - ISSN: 0015-119x
FILM QUARTERLY - ISSN: 0015-1386
HIGH FIDELITY - ISSN: 0018-1455
MODERN PHOTOGRAPHY - ISSN: 0026-8240
PETERSEN'S PHOTOGRAPHIC - ISSN: 0199-4913
PLAYS - ISSN: 0032-1540
POPULAR PHOTOGRAPHY - ISSN: 0032-4582
PUBLISHER'S WEEKLY - ISSN: 0000-0019
RADIO BROADCAST - ISSN: 0277-4860
RADIO-ELECTRONICS - ISSN: 0033-7862
STEREO REVIEW - ISSN: 0039-1220
THEATRE CRAFTS - ISSN: 0040-5469
WORLD PRESS REVIEW - ISSN: 0195-8895
WRITER, THE - ISSN: 0043-9517
WRITER'S DIGEST - ISSN: 0043-9525

Recently Published Articles
(ISSN: 0145-5311)

COMBROAD - ISSN: 0951-0826
FILM & HISTORY - ISSN: 0360-3695
PRINTING HISTORY - ISSN: 0192-9275
QUARTERLY JOURNAL OF SPEECH, THE - ISSN: 0033-5630
VICTORIAN PERIODICALS REVIEW - ISSN: 0709-4698

Reference Sources
(ISSN: 0163-3546)

AB BOOKMAN'S WEEKLY - ISSN: 0001-0340
AMERICAN FILM - ISSN: 0361-4751
AVC - ISSN: 1045-6910
BRITISH BOOK NEWS - ISSN: 0007-0343
COLLEGE MEDIA REVIEW - ISSN: 0739-1056
COMMUNICATION EDUCATION - ISSN: 0363-4523
EDUCATIONAL COMMUNICATION AND TECHNOLOGY - ISSN: 0148-5806
FILMS IN REVIEW - ISSN: 0015-1688
JOURNAL OF POPULAR CULTURE - ISSN: 0022-3840
JOURNAL OF POPULAR FILM AND TELEVISION - ISSN: 0195-6051
JOURNALISM HISTORY - ISSN: 0094-7679
JQ. JOURNALISM QUARTERLY. - ISSN: 0022-5533
MODERN DRAMA - ISSN: 0026-7694
PUBLIC RELATIONS REVIEW - ISSN: 0363-8111
PUBLISHER'S WEEKLY - ISSN: 0000-0019
QST - ISSN: 0033-4812
SALES & MARKETING MANAGEMENT - ISSN: 0163-7517
SCHOLARLY PUBLISHING - ISSN: 0036-634x
SERIALS REVIEW - ISSN: 0098-7913
SMPTE JOURNAL - ISSN: 0036-1682
VICTORIAN PERIODICALS REVIEW - ISSN: 0709-4698

Religion Index One
(ISSN: 0149-8428)

BOOKS & RELIGION - ISSN: 0890-0841

Repetoire International de la Litterature de l'Art
(ISSN: 0145-5982)

AFTERIMAGE - ISSN: 0300-7472
HISTORY OF PHOTOGRAPHY - ISSN: 0308-7298
IMAGE - ISSN: 0536-5465
JOURNAL OF POPULAR CULTURE - ISSN: 0022-3840
LEONARDO - ISSN: 0024-094x

Resources in Education

JOURNAL OF APPLIED COMMUNICATION RESEARCH - ISSN: 0090-9882

RILM Abstracts
(ISSN: 0033-6955)

ACUSTICA - ISSN: 0001-7884
ARSC JOURNAL - ISSN: 0004-5438
DOWN BEAT - ISSN: 0012-5768
LEONARDO - ISSN: 0024-094x
STEREO REVIEW - ISSN: 0039-1220

S

Safety Science Abstracts Journal
(ISSN: 0160-1342)

AEU - ISSN: 0001-1096
AV VIDEO - ISSN: 0747-1335
BIOMEDICAL COMMUNICATIONS - ISSN: 0092-8607
ELECTRICAL COMMUNICATION - ISSN: 0013-4252
MARCONI REVIEW, THE - ISSN: 0025-2883

Science Abstracts

Selected Water Resources Abstracts
(ISSN: 0037-136x)

INDUSTRIAL PHOTOGRAPHY - ISSN: 0019-8595
PULP & PAPER CANADA - ISSN: 0316-4004

Ship Abstracts
(ISSN: 0346-1025)

ELECTRICAL REVIEW - ISSN: 0013-4384
ELECTRONIC ENGINEERING - ISSN: 0013-4902
TELECOMMUNICATIONS - ISSN: 0278-4831

Social Planning / Planning & Development Abstracts

WRITTEN COMMUNICATION - ISSN: 0741-0883

Social Science and Humanities Index
(ISSN: 0037-7899)

DRAMA SURVEY - ISSN: 0419-7127

MODERN DRAMA - ISSN: 0026-7694
PUBLIC OPINION QUARTERLY - ISSN: 0033-362x
TDR - ISSN: 0012-5962
WORLD THEATRE - ISSN: 0512-3704

Social Science Citation Index
(ISSN: 0091-2887)

COMMUNICATION STUDIES - ISSN: 1051-0974
JOURNAL OF BROADCASTING & ELECTRONIC MEDIA - ISSN: 0883-8151
LANGUAGE & COMMUNICATION - ISSN: 0271-5309
WRITTEN COMMUNICATION - ISSN: 0741-0883

Social Sciences Index
(ISSN: 0094-4920)

COMMUNICATION RESEARCH - ISSN: 0093-6502
JOURNAL OF COMMUNICATION - ISSN: 0021-9916
PUBLIC OPINION QUARTERLY - ISSN: 0033-362x
TECHNOLOGY AND CULTURE - ISSN: 0040-165x

Social Welfare, Social Planning / Policy and Social Development
(ISSN: 0195-7988)

COMMUNICATION - ISSN: 0305-4233
COMMUNICATIONS - ISSN: 0341-2059
HUMAN COMMUNICATION RESEARCH - ISSN: 0360-3989
JOURNAL OF ADVERTISING RESEARCH - ISSN: 0021-8499
JOURNAL OF COMMUNICATION - ISSN: 0021-9916
PUBLIC OPINION QUARTERLY - ISSN: 0033-362x
PUBLISHING RESEARCH QUARTERLY - ISSN: 1053-8801
QUARTERLY JOURNAL OF SPEECH, THE - ISSN: 0033-5630
TECHNOLOGY AND CULTURE - ISSN: 0040-165x

Sociological Abstracts
(ISSN: 0038-0202)

AT&T TECHNOLOGY - ISSN: 0889-8979
COMMUNICATION - ISSN: 0305-4233
COMMUNICATION EDUCATION - ISSN: 0363-4523

COMMUNICATION QUARTERLY - ISSN: 0146-3373
COMMUNICATIONS - ISSN: 0341-2059
EDUCATIONAL COMMUNICATION AND TECHNOLOGY - ISSN: 0148-5806
GENERAL ELECTRIC REVIEW - ISSN: 0095-9480
HUMAN COMMUNICATION RESEARCH - ISSN: 0360-3989
INDEX ON CENSORSHIP - ISSN: 0306-4220
INTERNATIONAL JOURNAL OF INFORMATION MANAGEMENT - ISSN: 0268-4012
JOURNAL OF ADVERTISING - ISSN: 0091-3367
JOURNAL OF APPLIED COMMUNICATION RESEARCH - ISSN: 0090-9882
JOURNAL OF BROADCASTING & ELECTRONIC MEDIA - ISSN: 0883-8151
JOURNAL OF COMMUNICATION - ISSN: 0021-9916
JQ. JOURNALISM QUARTERLY. - ISSN: 0022-5533
LANGUAGE & COMMUNICATION - ISSN: 0271-5309
MANAGEMENT COMMUNICATION QUARTERLY - ISSN: 0893-3189
POLITICAL COMMUNICATION AND PERSUASION - ISSN: 0195-7473
PUBLIC OPINION QUARTERLY - ISSN: 0033-362x
PUBLISHING RESEARCH QUARTERLY - ISSN: 1053-8801
QUARTERLY JOURNAL OF SPEECH, THE - ISSN: 0033-5630
TECHNOLOGY AND CULTURE - ISSN: 0040-165x
WESTERN JOURNAL OF SPEECH COMMUNICATION - ISSN: 0193-6700
WRITTEN COMMUNICATION - ISSN: 0741-0883

Sociology of Education Abstracts

INTERNATIONAL JOURNAL OF INFORMATION MANAGEMENT - ISSN: 0268-4012

Speech Index

JOURNAL OF APPLIED COMMUNICATION RESEARCH - ISSN: 0090-9882

Subject Index to Children's Magazines
(ISSN: 0039-4351)

PLAYS - ISSN: 0032-1540

Subject Index to Periodicals

DRAMA - ISSN: 0012-5946

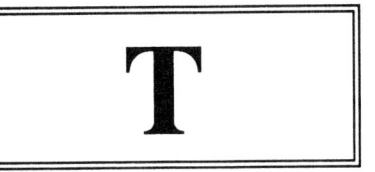

T

Technical Education Abstracts

INTERNATIONAL JOURNAL OF INFORMATION MANAGEMENT - ISSN: 0268-4012

Trade and Industry Index

ADVERTISING AGE - ISSN: 0001-8899
AMERICAN PRINTER - ISSN: 0744-6616
AVC - ISSN: 1045-6910
BILLBOARD - ISSN: 0006-2510
BROADCASTING - ISSN: 0007-2028
COMMUNICATIONS NEWS - ISSN: 0010-3632
COMPUTER PICTURES - ISSN: 0883-5683
EDITOR AND PUBLISHER - ISSN: 0013-094x
ELECTRONICS - ISSN: 0883-4989
GRAPHIC ARTS MONTHLY - ISSN: 0017-3274
MEDIAWEEK - ISSN: 1055-176x
SALES & MARKETING MANAGEMENT - ISSN: 0163-7517
TELEVISION/RADIO AGE - ISSN: 0040-277x

U

United States Political Science Documents
(ISSN: 0148-6063)

POLITICAL COMMUNICATION AND PERSUASION - ISSN: 0195-7473

Abstracts & Indexes — INDEX

PUBLIC OPINION QUARTERLY - ISSN: 0033-362x

United States State Department Documents

POLITICAL COMMUNICATION AND PERSUASION - ISSN: 0195-7473

W

Women Studies Abstracts
(ISSN: 0049-7835)

JOURNAL OF COMMUNICATION - ISSN: 0021-9916

JOURNAL OF MARKETING - ISSN: 0022-2429

JOURNAL OF POPULAR CULTURE - ISSN: 0022-3840

QUARTERLY JOURNAL OF SPEECH, THE - ISSN: 0033-5630

World Aluminum Abstracts
(ISSN: 0002-6697)

ELECTRICAL REVIEW - ISSN: 0013-4384

ELECTRONICS LETTERS - ISSN: 0013-5194

ZEISS INFORMATION - ISSN: 0044-2054

World Surface Coating Abstracts
(ISSN: 0043-9088)

BRITISH JOURNAL OF PHOTOGRAPHY - ISSN: 0007-1196

JQ. JOURNALISM QUARTERLY. - ISSN: 0022-5533

MEDIA REPORT TO WOMEN - ISSN: 0145-9651

Writings on American History
(ISSN: 0364-2887)

CINEMA JOURNAL - ISSN: 0009-7101

FILM & HISTORY - ISSN: 0360-3695

HISTORICAL JOURNAL OF FILM, RADIO & TELEVISION - ISSN: 0143-9685

JOURNAL OF COMMUNICATION - ISSN: 0021-9916

JOURNAL OF POPULAR FILM AND TELEVISION - ISSN: 0195-6051

JOURNALISM HISTORY - ISSN: 0094-7679

JQ. JOURNALISM QUARTERLY. - ISSN: 0022-5533

PRINTING HISTORY - ISSN: 0192-9275

QUARTERLY JOURNAL OF SPEECH, THE - ISSN: 0033-5630

TECHNOLOGY AND CULTURE - ISSN: 0040-165x

Associations

Organizations affiliated with serials are listed in this index. An "Association" is any organization supported by membership, which functions for the common good of all. An association may be the publisher of record, the location of editorial offices, or may be affiliated with the publication via a regularly published listing of association events and news. Both current and past association titles are listed when known.

The term "Association" generally INCLUDES the following: Academy, Alliance, Amalgamation, Association, Bureau, Center, Club, Coalition, Collective, Committee, Conference, Consortium, Council, Enthusiasts, Federation, Fraternity, Group, Guild, Institute, Institution, League, Organization, Quorom, Society, Sorority, and Union. In general, this listing EXCLUDES terms such as Associates, College, School, Services, University, and Workshop, as well as commercial entities whose primary function is the publication of this serial.

A

Academy of Homiletics
HOMILETIC

Academy of Motion Picture Arts and Sciences
Academy of Motion Picture Arts and Sciences. Bulletin *which varied under* BULLETIN
AMERICAN PREMIERE
BULLETIN
Premi'ere *which varied under* AMERICAN PREMIERE

Academy of Television Arts & Sciences
DEBUT
EMMY

Action for Childrens Television
News - Action for Children's Television *which varied under* RE:ACT
RE:ACT

Actors Forum Group
ACTORS FORUM

Advertising Association
Advertising *which varied under* ADVERTISING MAGAZINE
ADVERTISING MAGAZINE
Advertising Quarterly *which varied under* ADVERTISING MAGAZINE
INTERNATIONAL JOURNAL OF ADVERTISING
Journal of Advertising *which varied under* INTERNATIONAL JOURNAL OF ADVERTISING

Advertising Managers Association
ADVERTISING AND MARKETING MANAGEMENT
Advertising Management *which varied under* ADVERTISING AND MARKETING MANAGEMENT

Advertising Research Foundation
JOURNAL OF ADVERTISING RESEARCH

AFL-CIO
GUILD REPORTER, THE

Air Law Institute
JOURNAL OF RADIO LAW

Alaska Professional Photographers of America
NATIONAL PHOTOGRAPHER, THE

Alpha Epsilon Rho
MONITOR
SIGNALS

Alpha Phi Gamma
COLLEGIATE JOURNALIST

Amateur Cinema League
Amateur Movie Makers *which varied under* MOVIE MAKERS
MOVIE MAKERS

Amateur Radio Defense Association
AMATEUR RADIO DEFENSE

American Academy of Advertising
JOURNAL OF ADVERTISING

American Academy of Air Law
AIR LAW REVIEW

American Academy of Homiletics
HOMILETIC

American Animation Institute
SOCIETY FOR ANIMATION STUDIES NEWSLETTER, THE

American Association for Public Opinion Research
PUBLIC OPINION QUARTERLY

American Association of Advertising Agencies
4A'S WASHINGTON NEWSLETTER, THE
AGENCY
FOUR A NEWSLETTER

American Association of Colleges of Teacher Education
PUBLIC RELATIONS IDEAS

American Association of Yellow Pages Publishers
YELLOW PAGES UPDATE

American Bar Association
COMMUNICATIONS LAWYER
ENTERTAINMENT AND SPORTS LAWYER, THE

American Book Trade Association
Leypoldt & Holt's Literary Bulletin *which varied under* PUBLISHER'S WEEKLY
Literary Bulletin, The *which varied under* PUBLISHER'S WEEKLY
PUBLISHER'S WEEKLY
Publishers' and Stationers' Weekly Trade Circular *which varied under* PUBLISHER'S WEEKLY
Trade Circular and Literary Bulletin, The *which varied under* PUBLISHER'S WEEKLY
Trade Circular and Publishers' Bulletin, The *which varied under* PUBLISHER'S WEEKLY

American Book Trade Union
Leypoldt & Holt's Literary Bulletin *which varied under* PUBLISHER'S WEEKLY
Literary Bulletin, The *which varied under* PUBLISHER'S WEEKLY
PUBLISHER'S WEEKLY
Publishers' and Stationers' Weekly Trade Circular *which varied under* PUBLISHER'S WEEKLY
Trade Circular and Literary Bulletin, The *which varied under* PUBLISHER'S WEEKLY
Trade Circular and Publishers' Bulletin, The *which varied under* PUBLISHER'S WEEKLY

American Business Communication Association
ABCA Bulletin, The *which varied under* BULLETIN OF THE ASSOCIATION FOR BUSINESS COMMUNICATION, THE
ABWA Bulletin *which varied under* BULLETIN OF THE ASSOCIATION FOR BUSINESS COMMUNICATION, THE
BULLETIN OF THE ASSOCIATION FOR BUSINESS COMMUNICATION, THE

American Business Writing Association
ABCA Journal of Business Communication *which varied under* JOURNAL OF BUSINESS COMMUNICATION, THE
Journal of Business Communication *which varied under* JOURNAL OF BUSINESS COMMUNICATION, THE
JOURNAL OF BUSINESS COMMUNICATION, THE

American Cinema Editors
AMERICAN CINEMEDITOR
Cinemeditor *which varied under* AMERICAN CINEMEDITOR

American College Public Relations Association
COLLEGE & UNIVERSITY JOURNAL
College Public Relations *which varied under* COLLEGE & UNIVERSITY JOURNAL
College Public Relations Quarterly *which varied under* COLLEGE & UNIVERSITY JOURNAL
College Publicity Digest, The *which varied under* COLLEGE & UNIVERSITY JOURNAL
Pride *which varied under* COLLEGE & UNIVERSITY JOURNAL
Publicity Problems *which varied under* COLLEGE & UNIVERSITY JOURNAL

American College Publicity Association
COLLEGE & UNIVERSITY JOURNAL
College Public Relations *which varied under* COLLEGE & UNIVERSITY JOURNAL
College Public Relations Quarterly *which varied under* COLLEGE & UNIVERSITY JOURNAL
College Publicity Digest, The *which varied under* COLLEGE & UNIVERSITY JOURNAL
Pride *which varied under* COLLEGE & UNIVERSITY JOURNAL
Publicity Problems *which varied under* COLLEGE & UNIVERSITY JOURNAL

American Council for Better Broadcasts
BETTER BROADCASTS NEWS
Better Broadcasts Newsletter *which varied under* BETTER BROADCASTS NEWS

American Family Association
AFA JOURNAL
National Federation for Decency Newsletter *which varied under* AFA JOURNAL
Newsletter of the National Federation for Decency *which varied under* AFA JOURNAL
NFD Informer *which varied under* AFA JOURNAL
NFD Journal *which varied under* AFA JOURNAL

NFD Newsletter *which varied under* AFA JOURNAL

NFD Newsletter *which varied under* AFA JOURNAL

American Federation of Film Societies

AFFS Newsletter *which varied under* CRITIC

American Federation of Film Societies. Newsletter *which varied under* CRITIC

CRITIC

Film Society Newsletter *which varied under* CRITIC

Film Society Review *which varied under* CRITIC

For Film *which varied under* CRITIC

American Federation of Photographic Societies

Photo-Era *which varied under* PHOTO-ERA MAGAZINE

PHOTO-ERA MAGAZINE

American Film and Video Association

AFVA BULLETIN

Sightlines *which varied under* AFVA BULLETIN

American Film Institute

AFI EDUCATION NEWSLETTER

AFI Report *which varied under* AMERICAN FILM INSTITUTE. QUARTERLY.

AMERICAN FILM

American Film Institute Report *which varied under* AMERICAN FILM INSTITUTE. QUARTERLY.

AMERICAN FILM INSTITUTE. QUARTERLY.

CLOSE-UP

DIALOGUE ON FILM

American Institute of Cinematography

CINEMA PROGRESS

National Cinema Workshop and Appreciation League Bulletin *which varied under* CINEMA PROGRESS

American Institute of Graphic Arts

AIGA Journal *which varied under* AIGA JOURNAL OF GRAPHIC DESIGN

AIGA JOURNAL OF GRAPHIC DESIGN

Journal of the American Institute of Graphic Arts *which varied under* AIGA JOURNAL OF GRAPHIC DESIGN

American Journalism Historians Association

AMERICAN JOURNALISM

INTELLIGENCER

American League of Amateur Photographers, The

DEVELOPER, THE

American Marketing Association

JMR, JOURNAL OF MARKETING RESEARCH

JOURNAL OF MARKETING

MARKETING NEWS

American Newspaper Publishers Association

ANPA NEWS RESEARCH REPORT

ANPA Newspaper Information Service Newsletter *which varied under* ANPA PUBLIC AFFAIRS NEWSLETTER

ANPA PUBLIC AFFAIRS NEWSLETTER

MINORITIES IN THE NEWSPAPER BUSINESS

News Research Bulletin *which varied under* ANPA NEWS RESEARCH REPORT

NEWSINC.

PRESSTIME

American Newspaper Publishers Association Foundation

MINORITIES IN THE NEWSPAPER BUSINESS

American Photo-Engravers Association

MORE BUSINESS

American Printing History Association

PRINTING HISTORY

American Radio Relay League

QEX

QST

American Society for Information Service

CABLE LIBRARIES

American Society of Cinematographers

AMERICAN CINEMATOGRAPHER

American Society of Composers, Authors and Publishers

ASCAP IN ACTION

ASCAP News *which varied under* ASCAP IN ACTION

ASCAP Today *which varied under* ASCAP IN ACTION

American Society of Educators

Educators Guide to Media & Methods *which varied under* MEDIA & METHODS

MEDIA & METHODS

School Paperback Journal *which varied under* MEDIA & METHODS

Teacher's Guide to Media and Methods *which varied under* MEDIA & METHODS

American Society of Journalism School Administrators

Bulletin *which varied under* JOURNALISM EDUCATOR, THE

JOURNALISM EDUCATOR, THE

Associations

American Society of Magazine Photographers

American Society of Magazine Photographers Newsletter *which varied under* ASMP BULLETIN

American Society of Magazine Photographers. News *which varied under* ASMP BULLETIN

ASMP BULLETIN

ASMP News *which varied under* ASMP BULLETIN

Bulletin. ASMP *which varied under* ASMP BULLETIN

Infinity *which varied under* ASMP BULLETIN

American Society of Newspaper Editors

BULLETIN OF THE AMERICAN SOCIETY OF NEWSPAPER EDITORS, THE

American Speech-Language-Hearing Association

JOURNAL OF SPEECH AND HEARING DISORDERS

Journal of Speech Disorders *which varied under* JOURNAL OF SPEECH AND HEARING DISORDERS

American Theatre Association

Educational Theatre Journal *which varied under* THEATRE JOURNAL

THEATRE JOURNAL

THEATRE NEWS

American Women in Radio and Television

AWRT NEWS AND VIEWS

News & Views *which varied under* AWRT NEWS AND VIEWS

Amnesty International

Index *which varied under* INDEX ON CENSORSHIP

INDEX ON CENSORSHIP

Ann Arbor Film Cooperative

CINEGRAM

Antique Wireless Association

OLD TIMER'S BULLETIN, THE

Article 19

Index *which varied under* INDEX ON CENSORSHIP

INDEX ON CENSORSHIP

Arts Council of Northern Ireland

FILM DIRECTIONS

Asia-Pacific Broadcasting Union

ABU NEWSLETTER

ABU TECHNICAL REVIEW

Asian Mass Communication Research and Information Centre

ASIAN JOURNAL OF COMMUNICATION

Documentation List *which varied under* MEDIA ASIA

MEDIA ASIA

Asociación Electrotécnica y Electrónica Española

EUROPEAN TRANSACTIONS ON TELECOMMUNICATIONS AND RELATED TECHNOLOGIES

Associated Advertising Clubs of America

Advertisers Magazine *which varied under* ADVERTISING ADVOCATE

ADVERTISING ADVOCATE

Western Monthly [Kansas City] *which varied under* ADVERTISING ADVOCATE

Associated Collegiate Press

Scholastic Editor *which varied under* SCHOLASTIC EDITOR'S TRENDS IN PUBLICATIONS

Scholastic Editor *which varied under* SCHOLASTIC EDITOR'S TRENDS IN PUBLICATIONS

Scholastic Editor Graphics/Communications *which varied under* SCHOLASTIC EDITOR'S TRENDS IN PUBLICATIONS

SCHOLASTIC EDITOR'S TRENDS IN PUBLICATIONS

Associated Press

AP BROADCASTER

Network News *which varied under* AP BROADCASTER

Associated Press Broadcasters

NEWS FROM APB

Association des Ingénieurs Electriciens sortis de l'Institut Montefiore

EUROPEAN TRANSACTIONS ON TELECOMMUNICATIONS AND RELATED TECHNOLOGIES

Association for Business Communication

ABCA Journal of Business Communication *which varied under* JOURNAL OF BUSINESS COMMUNICATION, THE

Journal of Business Communication *which varied under* JOURNAL OF BUSINESS COMMUNICATION, THE

JOURNAL OF BUSINESS COMMUNICATION, THE

Association for Communication Administration

ACA BULLETIN

Bulletin of the Association of Departments & Administrators in Speech Communication *which varied under* ACA BULLETIN

Association for Education by Radio

AERT Journal *which varied under* PUBLIC TELECOMMUNICATIONS REVIEW

QUARTERLY JOURNAL OF SPEECH, THE - ISSN: 0033-5630

RESTORATION AND 18TH CENTURY THEATRE RESEARCH - ISSN: 0034-5822

SCHOLARLY PUBLISHING - ISSN: 0036-634x

SILENT PICTURE, THE - ISSN: 0037-5209

TECHNOLOGY AND CULTURE - ISSN: 0040-165x

VICTORIAN PERIODICALS REVIEW - ISSN: 0709-4698

Hospital Literature Index
(ISSN: 0018-5736)

BIOMEDICAL COMMUNICATIONS - ISSN: 0092-8607

E-ITV - ISSN: 0743-7773

PUBLIC OPINION QUARTERLY - ISSN: 0033-362x

PUBLIC RELATIONS JOURNAL, THE - ISSN: 0033-3670

Human Resources Abstracts

WESTERN JOURNAL OF SPEECH COMMUNICATION - ISSN: 0193-6700

WRITTEN COMMUNICATION - ISSN: 0741-0883

Humanities Index
(ISSN: 0095-5981)

AMERICAN FILM - ISSN: 0361-4751

COMMUNICATION QUARTERLY - ISSN: 0146-3373

COMMUNICATION RESEARCH - ISSN: 0093-6502

FILM COMMENT - ISSN: 0015-119x

FILM QUARTERLY - ISSN: 0015-1386

JOURNAL OF BROADCASTING & ELECTRONIC MEDIA - ISSN: 0883-8151

JOURNAL OF POPULAR CULTURE - ISSN: 0022-3840

JOURNALISM HISTORY - ISSN: 0094-7679

JQ. JOURNALISM QUARTERLY. - ISSN: 0022-5533

LITERATURE/FILM QUARTERLY - ISSN: 0090-4260

MODERN DRAMA - ISSN: 0026-7694

NEW THEATRE QUARTERLY - ISSN: 0266-464x

PERFORMING ARTS JOURNAL - ISSN: 0735-8393

PLAYS AND PLAYERS - ISSN: 0032-1559

QUARTERLY JOURNAL OF SPEECH, THE - ISSN: 0033-5630

QUARTERLY REVIEW OF FILM AND VIDEO - ISSN: 0146-0013

QUILL, THE - ISSN: 0033-6475

SHAKESPEARE QUARTERLY - ISSN: 0037-3222

SIGHT & SOUND - ISSN: 0037-4806

TDR - ISSN: 0012-5962

THEATER - ISSN: 0161-0775

THEATRE JOURNAL - ISSN: 0192-2882

THEATRE NOTEBOOK - ISSN: 0040-5523

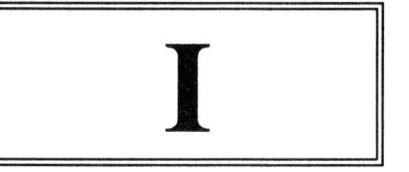

I

Index of American Periodical Verse
(ISSN: 0090-9130)

JOURNAL OF POPULAR CULTURE - ISSN: 0022-3840

Index of Economic Articles in Journals and Collected Volumes
(ISSN: 0536-647x)

JMR, JOURNAL OF MARKETING RESEARCH - ISSN: 0022-2437

Index to Book Reviews in the Humanities
(ISSN: 0073-5892)

AMERICAN FILM - ISSN: 0361-4751

DRAMA - ISSN: 0012-5946

FILMS IN REVIEW - ISSN: 0015-1688

LISTENER - ISSN: 0024-4392

MODERN DRAMA - ISSN: 0026-7694

PRINT - ISSN: 0032-8510

SIGHT & SOUND - ISSN: 0037-4806

THEATER - ISSN: 0161-0775

THEATRE JOURNAL - ISSN: 0192-2882

VICTORIAN PERIODICALS REVIEW - ISSN: 0709-4698

Index to IEEE Publications
(ISSN: 0099-1368)

IEEE TRANSACTIONS ON BROADCASTING - ISSN: 0018-9316

IEEE TRANSACTIONS ON CONSUMER ELECTRONICS - ISSN: 0098-3063

Index to Journals in Communication Studies

JOURNAL OF BROADCASTING & ELECTRONIC MEDIA - ISSN: 0883-8151

Index to Legal Periodicals
(ISSN: 0019-4077)

COMMUNICATIONS AND THE LAW - ISSN: 0162-9093

FEDERAL COMMUNICATIONS LAW JOURNAL - ISSN: 0163-7606

Index to Religious Periodical Literature
(ISSN: 0019-4107)

BOOKS & RELIGION - ISSN: 0890-0841

Industrial Arts Index

ADVERTISING AGENCY - ISSN: 0001-8899

BUSINESS MARKETING - ISSN: 0745-5933

ELECTRONICS - ISSN: 0883-4989

GENERAL ELECTRIC REVIEW - ISSN: 0095-9480

TELEPHONE MAGAZINE - ISSN: 0736-5853

InfoBank

ADVERTISING AGE - ISSN: 0001-8899

ADVERTISING AND GRAPHIC ARTS TECHNIQUES - ISSN: 0747-3168

ADWEEK - ISSN: 0199-4743

AMERICAN DEMOGRAPHICS - ISSN: 0163-4089

ART DIRECTION - ISSN: 0004-3109

BILLBOARD - ISSN: 0006-2510

BOX OFFICE - ISSN: 0006-8527

BROADCASTING - ISSN: 0007-2028

BUSINESS MARKETING - ISSN: 0745-5933

DIRECT MARKETING - ISSN: 0012-3188

EDITOR AND PUBLISHER - ISSN: 0013-094x

JMR, JOURNAL OF MARKETING RESEARCH - ISSN: 0022-2437

JOURNAL OF ADVERTISING - ISSN: 0091-3367

JOURNAL OF ADVERTISING RESEARCH - ISSN: 0021-8499

JOURNAL OF COMMUNICATION - ISSN: 0021-9916

JOURNAL OF MARKETING - ISSN: 0022-2429

F

Film Literature Index
(ISSN: 0093-6758)

- AFI EDUCATION NEWSLETTER - ISSN: 0883-6213
- AFTERIMAGE - ISSN: 0300-7472
- AFVA BULLETIN - ISSN: 0164-6508
- AMERICAN CINEMATOGRAPHER - ISSN: 0002-7928
- AMERICAN CLASSIC SCREEN - ISSN: 0195-8267
- AMERICAN FILM - ISSN: 0361-4751
- AUSTRALIAN JOURNAL OF SCREEN THEORY - ISSN: 0313-4059
- BOX OFFICE - ISSN: 0006-8527
- BRIGHT LIGHTS - ISSN: 0147-4049
- CAMERA OBSCURA - ISSN: 0270-5346
- CANTRILLS FILMNOTES - ISSN: 0158-4154
- CINEASTE - ISSN: 0009-7004
- CINEFANTASTIQUE - ISSN: 0145-6032
- CINEFEX - ISSN: 0198-1056
- CINEMA/CANADA - ISSN: 0009-7071
- CINEMA JOURNAL - ISSN: 0009-7101
- CINEMA PAPERS - ISSN: 0311-3639
- CINEMAGIC - ISSN: 0090-3000
- CINEMONKEY - ISSN: 0162-0126
- COLUMBIA JOURNALISM REVIEW - ISSN: 0010-194x
- COMMUNICATION RESEARCH TRENDS - ISSN: 0144-4646
- FILM - ISSN: 0015-1025
- FILM & VIDEO NEWS - ISSN: 8750-068x
- FILM BULLETIN - ISSN: 0015-1122
- FILM COMMENT - ISSN: 0015-119x
- FILM CRITICISM - ISSN: 0163-5069
- FILM CULTURE - ISSN: 0015-1211
- FILM JOURNAL, THE - ISSN: 0046-3787
- FILM LIBRARY QUARTERLY - ISSN: 0015-1327
- FILM MAKING - ISSN: 0013-2543
- FILM QUARTERLY - ISSN: 0015-1386
- FILMS ILLUSTRATED - ISSN: 0015-167x
- FILMS IN REVIEW - ISSN: 0015-1688
- FOCUS ON FILM - ISSN: 0015-5128
- FUNNYWORLD - ISSN: 0071-9943
- GRAPHIS - ISSN: 0017-3452
- HIGH FIDELITY - ISSN: 0018-1455
- HISTORICAL JOURNAL OF FILM, RADIO & TELEVISION - ISSN: 0143-9685
- HUMAN COMMUNICATION RESEARCH - ISSN: 0360-3989
- HUNGAROFILM BULLETIN - ISSN: 0018-7798
- IMAGE - ISSN: 0536-5465
- INTERVIEW - ISSN: 0149-8932
- JOURNAL OF COMMUNICATION - ISSN: 0021-9916
- JOURNAL OF FILM AND VIDEO - ISSN: 0742-4671
- JOURNAL OF POPULAR FILM AND TELEVISION - ISSN: 0195-6051
- JUMP CUT - ISSN: 0146-5546
- LITERATURE/FILM QUARTERLY - ISSN: 0090-4260
- MEDIA REPORT TO WOMEN - ISSN: 0145-9651
- MILLIMETER - ISSN: 0164-9655
- MODERN DRAMA - ISSN: 0026-7694
- MODERN PHOTOGRAPHY - ISSN: 0026-8240
- MONTHLY FILM BULLETIN - ISSN: 0027-0407
- MOVIE - ISSN: 0027-268x
- MOVING IMAGE - ISSN: 0276-3494
- POPULAR PHOTOGRAPHY - ISSN: 0032-4582
- POST SCRIPT - ISSN: 0277-9897
- PRINT - ISSN: 0032-8510
- QUARTERLY REVIEW OF FILM AND VIDEO - ISSN: 0146-0013
- SCREEN - ISSN: 0036-9543
- SIGHT & SOUND - ISSN: 0037-4806
- SMPTE JOURNAL - ISSN: 0036-1682
- STUDIES IN VISUAL COMMUNICATION - ISSN: 0276-6558
- THEATER - ISSN: 0161-0775
- VARIETY - ISSN: 0042-2738
- VELVET LIGHT TRAP - ISSN: 0149-1830
- VIDEOGRAPHY - ISSN: 0363-1001
- VISUAL EDUCATION - ISSN: 0042-7152
- WIDE ANGLE - ISSN: 0160-6840

Fluidex
- ELECTRONICS - ISSN: 0883-4989

G

GeoRef
- FUNCTIONAL PHOTOGRAPHY - ISSN: 0360-7216

H

Historical Abstracts
(ISSN: 0018-2435)

- JOURNAL OF COMMUNICATION - ISSN: 0021-9916
- WESTERN JOURNAL OF SPEECH COMMUNICATION - ISSN: 0193-6700

Historical Abstracts. Part A. Modern History Abstracts.
(ISSN: 0363-2712)

- FILM & HISTORY - ISSN: 0360-3695
- HISTORICAL JOURNAL OF FILM, RADIO & TELEVISION - ISSN: 0143-9685
- JOURNAL OF POPULAR CULTURE - ISSN: 0022-3840
- JOURNAL OF POPULAR FILM AND TELEVISION - ISSN: 0195-6051
- JOURNALISM HISTORY - ISSN: 0094-7679
- JQ. JOURNALISM QUARTERLY. - ISSN: 0022-5533
- QUARTERLY JOURNAL OF SPEECH, THE - ISSN: 0033-5630
- RESTORATION AND 18TH CENTURY THEATRE RESEARCH - ISSN: 0034-5822
- SCHOLARLY PUBLISHING - ISSN: 0036-634x
- SILENT PICTURE, THE - ISSN: 0037-5209
- TECHNOLOGY AND CULTURE - ISSN: 0040-165x
- VICTORIAN PERIODICALS REVIEW - ISSN: 0709-4698

Historical Abstracts. Part B. Twentieth Century Abstracts.
(ISSN: 0363-2725)

- FILM & HISTORY - ISSN: 0360-3695
- FILM HERITAGE - ISSN: 0015-1270
- HISTORICAL JOURNAL OF FILM, RADIO & TELEVISION - ISSN: 0143-9685
- JOURNAL OF POPULAR CULTURE - ISSN: 0022-3840
- JOURNAL OF POPULAR FILM AND TELEVISION - ISSN: 0195-6051
- JOURNALISM HISTORY - ISSN: 0094-7679
- JQ. JOURNALISM QUARTERLY. - ISSN: 0022-5533

Abstracts & Indexes

TELECOMMUNICATIONS POLICY - ISSN: 0308-5961

TELEVISION - ISSN: 8755-5867

Engineering Index Energy Abstracts
(ISSN: 0093-8408)

ACUSTICA - ISSN: 0001-7884

AEG-TELEFUNKEN PROGRESS - ISSN: 0001-107x

AES - ISSN: 0747-8909

AEU - ISSN: 0001-1096

AT&T TECHNOLOGY - ISSN: 0889-8979

ATR - ISSN: 0001-2777

COMSAT TECHNICAL REVIEW - ISSN: 0095-9669

EBU REVIEW. TECHNICAL. - ISSN: 0012-7493

ELECTRICAL COMMUNICATION - ISSN: 0013-4252

ELECTRONIC ENGINEERING - ISSN: 0013-4902

ELECTRONICS - ISSN: 0883-4989

ELECTRONICS LETTERS - ISSN: 0013-5194

IEEE TRANSACTIONS ON BROADCASTING - ISSN: 0018-9316

IEEE TRANSACTIONS ON CONSUMER ELECTRONICS - ISSN: 0098-3063

JOURNAL OF TECHNICAL WRITING AND COMMUNICATION - ISSN: 0047-2816

MARCONI REVIEW, THE - ISSN: 0025-2883

SMPTE JOURNAL - ISSN: 0036-1682

TELECOMMUNICATION JOURNAL - ISSN: 0497-137x

TELECOMMUNICATION JOURNAL OF AUSTRALIA, THE - ISSN: 0040-2486

TELECOMMUNICATIONS POLICY - ISSN: 0308-5961

TELEVISION - ISSN: 8755-5867

Engineering Index Monthly (1984)
(ISSN: 0742-1974)

ACUSTICA - ISSN: 0001-7884

AES - ISSN: 0747-8909

AEU - ISSN: 0001-1096

AT&T TECHNOLOGY - ISSN: 0889-8979

ATR - ISSN: 0001-2777

COMSAT TECHNICAL REVIEW - ISSN: 0095-9669

EBU REVIEW. TECHNICAL. - ISSN: 0012-7493

ELECTRICAL COMMUNICATION - ISSN: 0013-4252

ELECTRONICS LETTERS - ISSN: 0013-5194

IEEE TRANSACTIONS ON BROADCASTING - ISSN: 0018-9316

IEEE TRANSACTIONS ON CONSUMER ELECTRONICS - ISSN: 0098-3063

MARCONI REVIEW, THE - ISSN: 0025-2883

Engineering Index Monthly
(ISSN: 0013-7960)

ACUSTICA - ISSN: 0001-7884

AEG-TELEFUNKEN PROGRESS - ISSN: 0001-107x

AES - ISSN: 0747-8909

AEU - ISSN: 0001-1096

AT&T TECHNOLOGY - ISSN: 0889-8979

ATR - ISSN: 0001-2777

AWA TECHNICAL REVIEW - ISSN: 0001-2920

COMSAT TECHNICAL REVIEW - ISSN: 0095-9669

EBU REVIEW. TECHNICAL. - ISSN: 0012-7493

ELECTRICAL COMMUNICATION - ISSN: 0013-4252

ELECTRONIC ENGINEERING - ISSN: 0013-4902

ELECTRONICS - ISSN: 0883-4989

ELECTRONICS LETTERS - ISSN: 0013-5194

IEEE TRANSACTIONS ON BROADCASTING - ISSN: 0018-9316

IEEE TRANSACTIONS ON CONSUMER ELECTRONICS - ISSN: 0098-3063

INDUSTRIAL PHOTOGRAPHY - ISSN: 0019-8595

JOURNAL OF TECHNICAL WRITING AND COMMUNICATION - ISSN: 0047-2816

MARCONI REVIEW, THE - ISSN: 0025-2883

SMPTE JOURNAL - ISSN: 0036-1682

TELECOMMUNICATION JOURNAL - ISSN: 0497-137x

TELECOMMUNICATION JOURNAL OF AUSTRALIA, THE - ISSN: 0040-2486

TELECOMMUNICATIONS - ISSN: 0278-4831

TELECOMMUNICATIONS POLICY - ISSN: 0308-5961

TELEVISION - ISSN: 8755-5867

Engineering Index Annual
(ISSN: 0360-8557)

ELECTRONICS LETTERS - ISSN: 0013-5194

Environment Abstracts
(ISSN: 0093-3287)

ACUSTICA - ISSN: 0001-7884

AMERICAN DEMOGRAPHICS - ISSN: 0163-4089

AT&T TECHNOLOGY - ISSN: 0889-8979

COLUMBIA JOURNALISM REVIEW - ISSN: 0010-194x

JOURNAL OF COMMUNICATION - ISSN: 0021-9916

PULP & PAPER CANADA - ISSN: 0316-4004

WORLD PRESS REVIEW - ISSN: 0195-8895

Exceptional Child Abstracts

AV VIDEO - ISSN: 0747-1335

MARCONI REVIEW, THE - ISSN: 0025-2883

TECHTRENDS - ISSN: 8756-3894

Excerpta Medica

ACUSTICA - ISSN: 0001-7884

AEU - ISSN: 0001-1096

AT&T TECHNOLOGY - ISSN: 0889-8979

EDUCATIONAL MEDIA INTERNATIONAL - ISSN: 0004-7597

ELECTRONICS - ISSN: 0883-4989

MARCONI REVIEW, THE - ISSN: 0025-2883

SMPTE JOURNAL - ISSN: 0036-1682

TECHNOLOGY AND CULTURE - ISSN: 0040-165x

Explicator, The

JOURNAL OF POPULAR FILM AND TELEVISION - ISSN: 0195-6051

RADIO COMMUNICATION - ISSN: 0033-7803

RADIO-ELECTRONICS - ISSN: 0033-7862

RCA BROADCAST NEWS - ISSN: 0096-7785

RF DESIGN - ISSN: 0163-321x

SATELLITE COMMUNICATIONS - ISSN: 0147-7439

SMPTE JOURNAL - ISSN: 0036-1682

TECHTRENDS - ISSN: 8756-3894

TELECOMMUNICATION JOURNAL - ISSN: 0497-137x

TELECOMMUNICATION JOURNAL OF AUSTRALIA, THE - ISSN: 0040-2486

TELECOMMUNICATIONS POLICY - ISSN: 0308-5961

TELEMATICS AND INFORMATICS - ISSN: 0736-5853

TELEVISION - ISSN: 8755-5867

TELEVISION - ISSN: 0308-454x

TELEVISION/RADIO AGE - ISSN: 0040-277x

THE JOURNAL - ISSN: 0192-592x

VISIBLE LANGUAGE - ISSN: 0022-2224

Electronic Publishing Abstracts
(ISSN: 0739-2907)

COMMUNICATIONS NEWS - ISSN: 0010-3632

ELECTRONIC ENGINEERING - ISSN: 0013-4902

INDUSTRIAL ELECTRONICS - ISSN: 0537-5185

INTERNATIONAL BROADCASTING - ISSN: 0141-1748

INTERNATIONAL VIDEOTEXT TELETEXT NEWS - ISSN: 0197-677x

PRESSTIME - ISSN: 0194-3243

VISIBLE LANGUAGE - ISSN: 0022-2224

Electronics and Communications Abstracts Journal
(ISSN: 0361-3313)

AV VIDEO - ISSN: 0747-1335

MARCONI REVIEW, THE - ISSN: 0025-2883

TECHTRENDS - ISSN: 8756-3894

Energy Information Abstracts
(ISSN: 0147-6521)

ACUSTICA - ISSN: 0001-7884

AMERICAN DEMOGRAPHICS - ISSN: 0163-4089

COLUMBIA JOURNALISM REVIEW - ISSN: 0010-194x

ELECTRONIC ENGINEERING - ISSN: 0013-4902

JOURNAL OF COMMUNICATION - ISSN: 0021-9916

PULP & PAPER CANADA - ISSN: 0316-4004

TECHNOLOGY AND CULTURE - ISSN: 0040-165x

WORLD PRESS REVIEW - ISSN: 0195-8895

Energy Research Abstracts
(ISSN: 0160-3604)

ACUSTICA - ISSN: 0001-7884

AEG-TELEFUNKEN PROGRESS - ISSN: 0001-107x

AEU - ISSN: 0001-1096

CONGRESSIONAL QUARTERLY'S EDITORIAL RESEARCH REPORTS - ISSN: 0013-0958

ELECTRICAL COMMUNICATION - ISSN: 0013-4252

ELECTRICAL REVIEW - ISSN: 0013-4384

IMAGE - ISSN: 0536-5465

ZEISS INFORMATION - ISSN: 0044-2054

Engineering Index

COMMUNICATION EDUCATION - ISSN: 0363-4523

ELECTRONIC ENGINEERING - ISSN: 0013-4902

GENERAL ELECTRIC REVIEW - ISSN: 0095-9480

INTERNATIONAL JOURNAL OF INSTRUCTIONAL MEDIA AND TECHNOLOGY - ISSN: 0092-1815

RADIO BROADCAST - ISSN: 0277-4860

Engineering Index Annual
(ISSN: 0360-8557)

ACUSTICA - ISSN: 0001-7884

AEG-TELEFUNKEN PROGRESS - ISSN: 0001-107x

AES - ISSN: 0747-8909

AEU - ISSN: 0001-1096

AT&T TECHNOLOGY - ISSN: 0889-8979

AWA TECHNICAL REVIEW - ISSN: 0001-2920

COMSAT TECHNICAL REVIEW - ISSN: 0095-9669

EBU REVIEW. TECHNICAL. - ISSN: 0012-7493

ELECTRICAL COMMUNICATION - ISSN: 0013-4252

ELECTRONICS - ISSN: 0883-4989

IEEE TRANSACTIONS ON BROADCASTING - ISSN: 0018-9316

IEEE TRANSACTIONS ON CONSUMER ELECTRONICS - ISSN: 0098-3063

INDUSTRIAL PHOTOGRAPHY - ISSN: 0019-8595

JOURNAL OF TECHNICAL WRITING AND COMMUNICATION - ISSN: 0047-2816

MARCONI REVIEW, THE - ISSN: 0025-2883

SMPTE JOURNAL - ISSN: 0036-1682

TELECOMMUNICATION JOURNAL - ISSN: 0497-137x

TELECOMMUNICATION JOURNAL OF AUSTRALIA, THE - ISSN: 0040-2486

TELECOMMUNICATIONS - ISSN: 0278-4831

TELECOMMUNICATIONS POLICY - ISSN: 0308-5961

TELEVISION - ISSN: 8755-5867

Engineering Index Bioengineering Abstracts
(ISSN: 0736-6213)

ACUSTICA - ISSN: 0001-7884

AES - ISSN: 0747-8909

AEU - ISSN: 0001-1096

AT&T TECHNOLOGY - ISSN: 0889-8979

ATR - ISSN: 0001-2777

COMSAT TECHNICAL REVIEW - ISSN: 0095-9669

EBU REVIEW. TECHNICAL. - ISSN: 0012-7493

ELECTRICAL COMMUNICATION - ISSN: 0013-4252

ELECTRONIC ENGINEERING - ISSN: 0013-4902

ELECTRONICS - ISSN: 0883-4989

ELECTRONICS LETTERS - ISSN: 0013-5194

IEEE TRANSACTIONS ON BROADCASTING - ISSN: 0018-9316

IEEE TRANSACTIONS ON CONSUMER ELECTRONICS - ISSN: 0098-3063

JOURNAL OF TECHNICAL WRITING AND COMMUNICATION - ISSN: 0047-2816

MARCONI REVIEW, THE - ISSN: 0025-2883

SMPTE JOURNAL - ISSN: 0036-1682

TELECOMMUNICATION JOURNAL - ISSN: 0497-137x

TELECOMMUNICATION JOURNAL OF AUSTRALIA, THE - ISSN: 0040-2486

Educational Broadcasting Review *which varied under* PUBLIC TELECOMMUNICATIONS REVIEW

Journal of the AER *which varied under* PUBLIC TELECOMMUNICATIONS REVIEW

Journal of the AERT *which varied under* PUBLIC TELECOMMUNICATIONS REVIEW

NAEB Journal *which varied under* PUBLIC TELECOMMUNICATIONS REVIEW

PUBLIC TELECOMMUNICATIONS REVIEW

Association for Education by Radio-Television

AERT Journal *which varied under* PUBLIC TELECOMMUNICATIONS REVIEW

Educational Broadcasting Review *which varied under* PUBLIC TELECOMMUNICATIONS REVIEW

Journal of the AER *which varied under* PUBLIC TELECOMMUNICATIONS REVIEW

Journal of the AERT *which varied under* PUBLIC TELECOMMUNICATIONS REVIEW

NAEB Journal *which varied under* PUBLIC TELECOMMUNICATIONS REVIEW

PUBLIC TELECOMMUNICATIONS REVIEW

Association for Education in Journalism and Mass Communication

AEJ Newsletter, The *which varied under* AEJMC NEWS

AEJMC NEWS

AEJMC Newsletter, The *which varied under* AEJMC NEWS

Bulletin *which varied under* JOURNALISM EDUCATOR, THE

CLIO AMONG THE MEDIA

COMMUNICATIONS TECHNOLOGY & POLICY NEWS

JOURNALISM EDUCATOR, THE

JOURNALISM HISTORY

MAGAZINE MATTER

MAGAZINES IN DEPTH

MC&S NEWSLETTER

MEDIA LAW NOTES

NEWSPAPER RESEARCH JOURNAL

Tortfeasor *which varied under* MEDIA LAW NOTES

VISUAL COMMUNICATION NEWSLETTER, THE

Association for Education in Journalism

MASS COMM REVIEW

STATIC

Association for Educational Communications and Technology

Audio-Visual Communication Review *which varied under* EDUCATIONAL COMMUNICATION AND TECHNOLOGY

AV Communication Review *which varied under* EDUCATIONAL COMMUNICATION AND TECHNOLOGY

EDUCATIONAL COMMUNICATION AND TECHNOLOGY

FILM & VIDEO NEWS

Film News *which varied under* FILM & VIDEO NEWS

Film News *which varied under* FILM & VIDEO NEWS

Film/AV News *which varied under* FILM & VIDEO NEWS

LEARNING RESOURCES

News From the American Film Center, Inc. *which varied under* FILM & VIDEO NEWS

Association for Educational Communications & Technology

Audiovisual Instruction *which varied under* TECHTRENDS

Audiovisual Instruction with/Instructional Resources *which varied under* TECHTRENDS

Instructional Innovator *which varied under* TECHTRENDS

Instructional Materials *which varied under* TECHTRENDS

TECHTRENDS

Association for Imaging Service Bureaus

PRE-

Association for Multi-Image

MULTI IMAGES JOURNAL

Multi-Images *which varied under* MULTI IMAGES JOURNAL

Association for Multi-Image International

MULTI IMAGES JOURNAL

Multi-Images *which varied under* MULTI IMAGES JOURNAL

Association for Professional Broadcast Education

Journal of Broadcasting *which varied under* JOURNAL OF BROADCASTING & ELECTRONIC MEDIA

JOURNAL OF BROADCASTING & ELECTRONIC MEDIA

Association for Recorded Sound Collections

ARSC JOURNAL

Journal *which varied under* ARSC JOURNAL

Association for Theatre in Higher Education

Educational Theatre Journal *which varied under* THEATRE JOURNAL

THEATRE JOURNAL

THEATRE TOPICS

Association of American Publishers

AAP MONTHLY REPORT

Association of Fashion and Editorial Photographers

IMAGE

Association of Learned and Professional Society Publishers

Bulletin of ALPSP *which varied under* LEARNED PUBLISHING

LEARNED PUBLISHING

Associations

Association of Schools of Journalism and Mass Communication
Bulletin *which varied under* JOURNALISM EDUCATOR, THE
JOURNALISM EDUCATOR, THE

Association of Visual Communicators
COMMUNICATOR, THE

Association of Working Press
CHICAGO JOURNALISM REVIEW

Association Professional Photographers, Province of Quebec
NATIONAL PHOTOGRAPHER, THE

Association Western Union Employees
TELEGRAPH WORLD

Telegraph World, The *which varied under* TELEGRAPH WORLD

Associazione Broadcast Italiana
MILLECANALI INTERNATIONAL

Associazione Elettrotecnica ed Elettronica Italiana
EUROPEAN TRANSACTIONS ON TELECOMMUNICATIONS AND RELATED TECHNOLOGIES

Audio Engineering Society
AES

Journal of the Audio Engineering Society *which varied under* AES

Audio League, The
AUDIO LEAGUE. REPORT.

Australian Broadcasting Commission
Australian Media Notes *which varied under* MEDIA INFORMATION AUSTRALIA
MEDIA INFORMATION AUSTRALIA

Australian Broadcasting Control Board
Australian Media Notes *which varied under* MEDIA INFORMATION AUSTRALIA
MEDIA INFORMATION AUSTRALIA

Australian Broadcasting Tribunal
Australian Media Notes *which varied under* MEDIA INFORMATION AUSTRALIA
MEDIA INFORMATION AUSTRALIA

Australian Film Commission
Australian Media Notes *which varied under* MEDIA INFORMATION AUSTRALIA
MEDIA INFORMATION AUSTRALIA

Authors League of America
PHOTODRAMATIST, THE

B

Bijou Society
AMERICAN CLASSIC SCREEN

Bolingbroke Society, The
DRAMA SURVEY

Book Trade Association of Philadelphia
Leypoldt & Holt's Literary Bulletin *which varied under* PUBLISHER'S WEEKLY

Literary Bulletin, The *which varied under* PUBLISHER'S WEEKLY
PUBLISHER'S WEEKLY

Publishers' and Stationers' Weekly Trade Circular *which varied under* PUBLISHER'S WEEKLY

Trade Circular and Literary Bulletin, The *which varied under* PUBLISHER'S WEEKLY

Trade Circular and Publishers' Bulletin, The *which varied under* PUBLISHER'S WEEKLY

Booksellers Association of Great Britain and Ireland
BRITISH BOOK NEWS

Selection of Recent Books Published in Great Britain *which varied under* BRITISH BOOK NEWS

Boston Photo Clan
AMATEUR PHOTOGRAPHER'S WEEKLY, THE

Boston University
VIEWS

Bristol University
NEW THEATRE MAGAZINE

British Council
BRITISH BOOK NEWS

Selection of Recent Books Published in Great Britain *which varied under* BRITISH BOOK NEWS

British Federation of Film Societies
FILM

British Film Academy
JOURNAL OF THE BRITISH FILM ACADEMY

British Film Institute
CONTRAST
MONTHLY FILM BULLETIN
SIGHT & SOUND

British Institution of Radio Engineers

British Institution of Radio Engineers. Journal *which varied under* ELECTRONICS & COMMUNICATIONS ENGINEERING JOURNAL

ELECTRONICS & COMMUNICATIONS ENGINEERING JOURNAL

Journal of the Institution of Electronic and Radio Engineers, The *which varied under* ELECTRONICS & COMMUNICATIONS ENGINEERING JOURNAL

Proceedings, The *which varied under* ELECTRONICS & COMMUNICATIONS ENGINEERING JOURNAL

Radio and Electronic Engineer, The *which varied under* ELECTRONICS & COMMUNICATIONS ENGINEERING JOURNAL

British Kinematograph Sound and Television Society

BKSTS Journal, The *which varied under* IMAGE TECHNOLOGY

British Kinematography *which varied under* IMAGE TECHNOLOGY

British Kinematography, Sound and Television *which varied under* IMAGE TECHNOLOGY

IMAGE TECHNOLOGY

British Theatre Association

DRAMA

Drama *which varied under* DRAMA

Interim Drama *which varied under* DRAMA

VE-Time Drama *which varied under* DRAMA

VJ-Time Drama *which varied under* DRAMA

War-Time Drama *which varied under* DRAMA

Broadcast Cable Financial Management Association

BROADCAST CABLE FINANCIAL JOURNAL

Broadcast Financial Journal *which varied under* BROADCAST CABLE FINANCIAL JOURNAL

Broadcast Credit Association

BROADCAST CABLE FINANCIAL JOURNAL

Broadcast Financial Journal *which varied under* BROADCAST CABLE FINANCIAL JOURNAL

Broadcast Education Association

BEA NEWSLETTER

FEEDBACK

Journal of Broadcasting *which varied under* JOURNAL OF BROADCASTING & ELECTRONIC MEDIA

JOURNAL OF BROADCASTING & ELECTRONIC MEDIA

MANAGEMENT AND SALES DIVISION NEWSLETTER

NEWSCASTER, THE

NEWSLETTER

PD REPORT

Production Committee Newsletter *which varied under* PD REPORT

REWIND

Broadcast Financial Management Association

BROADCAST CABLE FINANCIAL JOURNAL

Broadcast Financial Journal *which varied under* BROADCAST CABLE FINANCIAL JOURNAL

Broadcast Pioneers

SPARKS

Broadcast Pioneers Library

BROADCAST PIONEERS LIBRARY REPORTS

Reports *which varied under* BROADCAST PIONEERS LIBRARY REPORTS

Broadcast Promotion & Marketing Executives

BPME IMAGE MAGAZINE

Newsletter / Broadcasters Promotion Association *which varied under* BPME IMAGE MAGAZINE

Broadcast, Cable, and Consumer Electronics Society, The

IEEE TRANSACTIONS ON BROADCASTING

IEEE TRANSACTIONS ON CABLE TELEVISION

IRE Transactions on Broadcast Transmission Systems *which varied under* IEEE TRANSACTIONS ON BROADCASTING

IRE Transactions on Broadcasting *which varied under* IEEE TRANSACTIONS ON BROADCASTING

C

California Intercollegiate Press Association

CIPA NEWS

California Newspaper Publishers Association

CALIFORNIA PUBLISHER

CAM Foundation, The

INTERNATIONAL JOURNAL OF ADVERTISING

Journal of Advertising *which varied under* INTERNATIONAL JOURNAL OF ADVERTISING

Camera Club of New York

AMATEUR PHOTOGRAPHER'S WEEKLY, THE

Campaign for Press and Broadcasting Freedom

Index *which varied under* INDEX ON CENSORSHIP

INDEX ON CENSORSHIP

Canadian Institute for Theatre Technology

BROADCAST + TECHNOLOGY

Associations INDEX

Broadcast Equipment Today *which varied under* BROADCAST + TECHNOLOGY

Broadcast Technology *which varied under* BROADCAST + TECHNOLOGY

Canadian Pulp and Paper Association

PULP & PAPER CANADA

Pulp & Paper Magazine of Canada *which varied under* PULP & PAPER CANADA

Canadian Society of Cinematographers

Canadian Cinematography *which varied under* CINEMA/CANADA

CINEMA/CANADA

Canadian Speech and Hearing Association

HUMAN COMMUNICATION

HUMAN COMMUNICATION CANADA

Catholic Press Association

CATHOLIC JOURNALIST

Catholic Journalist Newsletter *which varied under* CATHOLIC JOURNALIST

Catholic School Press Association

CATHOLIC SCHOOL EDITOR

Caucus for Producers, Writers & Directors, The

CAUCUS QUARTERLY, THE

Center for Advanced Study in Telecommunications

Broadcast Bibliophile Booknotes *which varied under* COMMUNICATION BOOKNOTES

COMMUNICATION BOOKNOTES

Mass Media Booknotes *which varied under* COMMUNICATION BOOKNOTES

Center for Educational Public Relations Committee-at-Large

Journal of Educational Communication *which varied under* JOURNAL OF EDUCATIONAL PUBLIC RELATIONS

JOURNAL OF EDUCATIONAL PUBLIC RELATIONS

Center for Learning and Telecommunications

TELESCAN

Center for Media and Public Affairs

MEDIA MONITOR

Center for Media and Values

MEDIA & VALUES

Central Canada Association of Broadcast Engineers

BROADCAST + TECHNOLOGY

Broadcast Equipment Today *which varied under* BROADCAST + TECHNOLOGY

Broadcast Technology *which varied under* BROADCAST + TECHNOLOGY

Central States Communication Association

Central States Speech Journal *which varied under* COMMUNICATION STUDIES

COMMUNICATION STUDIES

Central States Speech Association

Central States Speech Journal *which varied under* COMMUNICATION STUDIES

COMMUNICATION STUDIES

Centre for the Study of Communication and Culture

COMMUNICATION RESEARCH TRENDS

CSCC Newsletter *which varied under* COMMUNICATION RESEARCH TRENDS

Centro Internazionale per il Cinema di Animazione

ANIMAFILM

Christian Booksellers Association

BOOKSTORE JOURNAL

Christians in the Arts Networking

CANEWS

Cincinnati Industrial Photographers

NATIONAL PHOTOGRAPHER, THE

Cinema Appreciation League

CINEMA PROGRESS

National Cinema Workshop and Appreciation League Bulletin *which varied under* CINEMA PROGRESS

Collective for Living Cinema

MOTION PICTURE

College Media Advisers

CMA NEWSLETTER

COLLEGE MEDIA REVIEW

College Press Review *which varied under* COLLEGE MEDIA REVIEW

Newsletter *which varied under* CMA NEWSLETTER

College of Preachers

HOMILETIC

Colorado Editorial Association

COLORADO EDITOR

Colorado Editor and the Intermountain Press *which varied under* COLORADO EDITOR

Colorado Press Association

COLORADO EDITOR

Colorado Editor and the Intermountain Press *which varied under* COLORADO EDITOR

Columbia Photographic Society

Camera *which varied under* CAMERA MAGAZINE

CAMERA MAGAZINE

Columbia Scholastic Press Advisers Association

Bulletin *which varied under* CSPAA BULLETIN

Bulletin of the Columbia Scholastic Press Advisors Association *which varied under* CSPAA BULLETIN

CSPAA BULLETIN

SCHOOL PRESS REVIEW, THE

The Advisers Bulletin *which varied under* CSPAA BULLETIN

Commission of the European Communities

EUROPEAN TRANSACTIONS ON TELECOMMUNICATIONS AND RELATED TECHNOLOGIES

Commission on Freedom of Speech

FREE SPEECH

Committee of Small Magazine Editors and Publishers

COSMEP NEWSLETTER

COSMEP Newsletter *which varied under* COSMEP NEWSLETTER

Independent Publisher, The *which varied under* COSMEP NEWSLETTER

Committee to Protect Journalists

Index *which varied under* INDEX ON CENSORSHIP

INDEX ON CENSORSHIP

Communication Association of the Pacific

Communication *which varied under* WORLD COMMUNICATION

Communication Reports *which varied under* WORLD COMMUNICATION

WORLD COMMUNICATION

Communications Workers of America

CWA NEWS

Telephone Worker *which varied under* CWA NEWS

Community College Journalism Association

CCJA Journalist *which varied under* COMMUNITY COLLEGE JOURNALIST

COMMUNITY COLLEGE JOURNALIST

Community College Journalist *which varied under* COMMUNITY COLLEGE JOURNALIST

Journalist *which varied under* COMMUNITY COLLEGE JOURNALIST

Junior College Journalist *which varied under* COMMUNITY COLLEGE JOURNALIST

Consulting Committee of the Professional Electroengineers' Organizations in Finland

EUROPEAN TRANSACTIONS ON TELECOMMUNICATIONS AND RELATED TECHNOLOGIES

Consumer Electronics Group of the Broadcast, Cable, and Consumer Electronics Society, The

IEEE Transactions on Broadcast and Television Receivers *which varied under* IEEE TRANSACTIONS ON CONSUMER ELECTRONICS

IEEE TRANSACTIONS ON CONSUMER ELECTRONICS

IRE Transactions on Broadcast and Television Receivers *which varied under* IEEE TRANSACTIONS ON CONSUMER ELECTRONICS

Transactions of the IRE Professional Group on Broadcast and Television Receivers *which varied under* IEEE TRANSACTIONS ON CONSUMER ELECTRONICS

Council on Church and Media

FORUM

Council on International Nontheatrical Events

CINE NEWS

D

David C. Cook Foundation

INTERLIT

Directors Guild of America

ACTION!

Documentary Film Group

FOCUS!

Donald McGannon Communication Research Center

MEDIA ETHICS UPDATE

Dow Jones Newspaper Fund

ALUMNI NEWSLINE

Drama League of America, The

DRAMA LEAGUE MONTHLY

Monthly Bulletin *which varied under* DRAMA LEAGUE MONTHLY

Drama Teachers Association

THEATRE AND SCHOOL

E

Eastern Communication Association

COMMUNICATION QUARTERLY

Today's Speech *which varied under* COMMUNICATION QUARTERLY

Associations

Ed Press Association of America
Journal of Educational Communication *which varied under* JOURNAL OF EDUCATIONAL PUBLIC RELATIONS

JOURNAL OF EDUCATIONAL PUBLIC RELATIONS

Educational Communication Center
Journal of Educational Communication *which varied under* JOURNAL OF EDUCATIONAL PUBLIC RELATIONS

JOURNAL OF EDUCATIONAL PUBLIC RELATIONS

Educational Film Library Association
AFVA BULLETIN

EFLA BULLETIN

FILM & VIDEO NEWS

Film News *which varied under* FILM & VIDEO NEWS

Film News *which varied under* FILM & VIDEO NEWS

Film/AV News *which varied under* FILM & VIDEO NEWS

News From the American Film Center, Inc. *which varied under* FILM & VIDEO NEWS

Sightlines *which varied under* AFVA BULLETIN

Educational Television Association
JOURNAL OF EDUCATIONAL TELEVISION

Journal of Educational Television *which varied under* JOURNAL OF EDUCATIONAL TELEVISION

Journal of Educational Television and Other Media *which varied under* JOURNAL OF EDUCATIONAL TELEVISION

Educational Theatre Association
Curtain *which varied under* DRAMATICS

DRAMATICS

Dramatics *which varied under* DRAMATICS

Dramatics' Curtain *which varied under* DRAMATICS

High School Thespian *which varied under* DRAMATICS

Elmer Valo Appreciation Society
LITTLE SHOPPE OF HORRORS

Emerson College
MEDIA ETHICS UPDATE

Emerson College Film Society
GRAND ILLUSIONS

Entertainment Law Institute
JOURNAL OF ARTS MANAGEMENT AND LAW, THE

Performing Arts Review *which varied under* JOURNAL OF ARTS MANAGEMENT AND LAW, THE

EPIE Institute
EPIEGRAM

Eureka EU95 HDTV Directorate
HDTV REPORT

European Broadcasting Union
EBU Bulletin *which varied under* EBU REVIEW. TECHNICAL.

EBU Documentation and Information Bulletin *which varied under* EBU REVIEW. TECHNICAL.

EBU Review. Part A: Technical *which varied under* EBU REVIEW. TECHNICAL.

EBU Review. Part B: General and Legal *which varied under* EBU REVIEW. PROGRAMMES, ADMINISTRATION, LAW.

EBU REVIEW. PROGRAMMES, ADMINISTRATION, LAW.

EBU Review. Radio and Television Programmes, Administration, Law *which varied under* EBU REVIEW. PROGRAMMES, ADMINISTRATION, LAW.

EBU REVIEW. TECHNICAL.

F

Facets Multimedia
FACETS FEATURES

Focus: Chicago *which varied under* FACETS FEATURES

Federal Communications Bar Association
Federal Communications Bar Journal *which varied under* FEDERAL COMMUNICATIONS LAW JOURNAL

FEDERAL COMMUNICATIONS LAW JOURNAL

Federation Internationale des Editeurs de Journaux et Publications
Bulletin d'Informations *which varied under* FIEJ-BULLETIN

FIEJ-BULLETIN

Federation of Film Societies, The
FILM

Film and Television Study Center
MAGAZINE, THE

Film Artistes' Association
FILM ARTISTE

Film Library Information Council
FILM LIBRARY QUARTERLY

Film Library Quarterly *which varied under* FILM LIBRARY QUARTERLY

FLQ *which varied under* FILM LIBRARY QUARTERLY

Film Society of Lincoln Center
FILM COMMENT

Vision *which varied under* FILM COMMENT

Film Society of Santa Barbara
    ON FILM

Finnish Film Foundation
    FACTS ABOUT FILM FINLAND
    Finland Filmland *which varied under* FINNISH FILMS
    FINNISH FILMS

Forum Committee on the Entertainment and Sports Industries
    ENTERTAINMENT AND SPORTS LAWYER, THE

Foundation for Art in Cinema
    Canyon Cinemanews *which varied under* CINEMANEWS, THE
    CINEMANEWS, THE

Foundation for Independent Video and Film, The
    INDEPENDENT, THE

Freedom of Information Center
    FOI DIGEST
    Freedom of Information News Digest *which varied under* FOI DIGEST

G

Gannett Foundation
    GF MAGAZINE

Graphic Arts Association of Michigan
    GRAPHIC

Graphic Arts International Union
    Graphic Arts Unionist *which varied under* GRAPHIC COMMUNICATOR
    GRAPHIC COMMUNICATOR
    Union Tabloid *which varied under* GRAPHIC COMMUNICATOR

Graphic Communications Union
    Graphic Arts Unionist *which varied under* GRAPHIC COMMUNICATOR
    GRAPHIC COMMUNICATOR
    Union Tabloid *which varied under* GRAPHIC COMMUNICATOR

Greater Lima Industrial Photographers Association
    NATIONAL PHOTOGRAPHER, THE

Green Room Society of Bristol University
    NEW THEATRE MAGAZINE

Group for Film Study
    CINEMAGES
    Film Study *which varied under* CINEMAGES

H

Harvard University
    NIEMAN REPORTS

HDTV 1125/60 Group
    HD PRODUCTION

Historians Film Committee
    FILM & HISTORY
    Newsletter - Historians Film Committee *which varied under* FILM & HISTORY

Hollywood Anti-Nazi League for the Defense of American Democracy
    Anti-Nazi News *which varied under* HOLLYWOOD NOW
    HOLLYWOOD NOW
    News of the World *which varied under* HOLLYWOOD NOW

Hollywood Foreign Press Correspondents Association
    HOLLYWOOD

Hollywood Stuntmen's Hall of Fame
    FALLING FOR STARS
    Falling for Stars News *which varied under* FALLING FOR STARS

I

IEEE Communications Society
    IEEE TRANSACTIONS ON COMMUNICATIONS
    IEEE Transactions on Communications Systems *which varied under* IEEE TRANSACTIONS ON COMMUNICATIONS
    IEEE Transactions on Communication Technology *which varied under* IEEE TRANSACTIONS ON COMMUNICATIONS
    IRE Transactions on Communications Systems *which varied under* IEEE TRANSACTIONS ON COMMUNICATIONS

INCA-FIEJ Research Association
    NEWSPAPER TECHNIQUES

Independent Broadcasting Authority
    AIRWAVES
    Independent Broadcasting *which varied under* AIRWAVES

Associations INDEX

Independent California Canyon Cinema News Co-op

Canyon Cinemanews *which varied under* CINEMANEWS, THE

CINEMANEWS, THE

Independent Feature Project

OFF-HOLLYWOOD REPORT

Industrial Photographers of Southern California

NATIONAL PHOTOGRAPHER, THE

Institute for Cinema and Culture

IRIS

Institute for Media Analysis

LIES OF OUR TIMES

Institute of Electrical and Electronics Engineers

Electrical Engineering *which varied under* IEEE SPECTRUM

IEEE SPECTRUM

IEEE Transactions on Broadcast and Television Receivers *which varied under* IEEE TRANSACTIONS ON CONSUMER ELECTRONICS

IEEE TRANSACTIONS ON BROADCASTING

IEEE TRANSACTIONS ON CABLE TELEVISION

IEEE TRANSACTIONS ON COMMUNICATIONS

IEEE Transactions on Communications Systems *which varied under* IEEE TRANSACTIONS ON COMMUNICATIONS

IEEE Transactions on Communication Technology *which varied under* IEEE TRANSACTIONS ON COMMUNICATIONS

IEEE TRANSACTIONS ON CONSUMER ELECTRONICS

IEEE TRANSACTIONS ON INFORMATION THEORY

IRE Transactions on Broadcast and Television Receivers *which varied under* IEEE TRANSACTIONS ON CONSUMER ELECTRONICS

IRE Transactions on Broadcast Transmission Systems *which varied under* IEEE TRANSACTIONS ON BROADCASTING

IRE Transactions on Broadcasting *which varied under* IEEE TRANSACTIONS ON BROADCASTING

IRE Transactions on Communications Systems *which varied under* IEEE TRANSACTIONS ON COMMUNICATIONS

IRE Transactions on Information Theory *which varied under* IEEE TRANSACTIONS ON INFORMATION THEORY

Journal of the AIEE *which varied under* IEEE SPECTRUM

PROCEEDINGS OF THE IEEE

Proceedings of the Institute of Radio Engineers *which varied under* PROCEEDINGS OF THE IEEE

Proceedings of the IRE *which varied under* PROCEEDINGS OF THE IEEE

Transactions *which varied under* IEEE TRANSACTIONS ON INFORMATION THEORY

Transactions of the IRE Professional Group on Broadcast and Television Receivers *which varied under* IEEE TRANSACTIONS ON CONSUMER ELECTRONICS

Institute of the Science of the Press

GAZETTE

Institution of Electrical Engineers

British Institution of Radio Engineers. Journal *which varied under* ELECTRONICS & COMMUNICATIONS ENGINEERING JOURNAL

ELECTRONICS & COMMUNICATIONS ENGINEERING JOURNAL

ELECTRONICS LETTERS

Journal of the Institution of Electronic and Radio Engineers, The *which varied under* ELECTRONICS & COMMUNICATIONS ENGINEERING JOURNAL

Proceedings, The *which varied under* ELECTRONICS & COMMUNICATIONS ENGINEERING JOURNAL

Radio and Electronic Engineer, The *which varied under* ELECTRONICS & COMMUNICATIONS ENGINEERING JOURNAL

Institution of Radio and Electronics Engineers Australia

IREE Monitor *which varied under* MONITOR

MONITOR

Monitor *which varied under* PROCEEDINGS OF THE IREE AUSTRALIA

Proceedings - Institution of Radio Engineers *which varied under* PROCEEDINGS OF THE IREE AUSTRALIA

Proceedings - Institution of Radio and Electronics Engineers Australia *which varied under* PROCEEDINGS OF THE IREE AUSTRALIA

Proceedings of the IREE *which varied under* PROCEEDINGS OF THE IREE AUSTRALIA

PROCEEDINGS OF THE IREE AUSTRALIA

Intercollegiate Broadcasting System

College Radio *which varied under* JOURNAL OF COLLEGE RADIO

IBS Bulletin *which varied under* JOURNAL OF COLLEGE RADIO

IBS Newsletter *which varied under* JOURNAL OF COLLEGE RADIO

JOURNAL OF COLLEGE RADIO

Intercollegiate Religious Broadcasters

CAMPUS BROADCASTERS

IRB

Interights

Index *which varied under* INDEX ON CENSORSHIP

INDEX ON CENSORSHIP

International Advertising Association

INTERNATIONAL ADVERTISER, THE

International Marketing Report *which varied under* INTERNATIONAL ADVERTISER, THE

International Alliance of Theatrical Stage Employees and Moving Picture Machine Operators of the United States and Canada

INTERNATIONAL PHOTOGRAPHER

OFFICIAL BULLETIN OF THE INTERNATIONAL ALLIANCE OF THEATRICAL STAGE EMPLOYEES AND MOVING PICTURE MACHINE OPERATORS OF THE UNITED STATES AND CANADA.

International Amateur Radio Union

QST

International Animated Film Association

Animation Newsletter *which varied under* ANIMATOR

ANIMATOR

ASIFA NOUVELLES

Frame By Frame *which varied under* PENCIL TEST

PENCIL TEST

International Animated Film Society-East

ANYMATOR

International Animated Film Society

GRAFFITI

International Association for Audio-Visual Media in Historical Research and Education

HISTORICAL JOURNAL OF FILM, RADIO & TELEVISION

IAMHIST NEWSLETTER

Newsletter *which varied under* IAMHIST NEWSLETTER

International Association of Business Communicators

COMMUNICATION WORLD

IABC Journal *which varied under* JOURNAL OF COMMUNICATION MANAGEMENT

IABC News *which varied under* COMMUNICATION WORLD

JOURNAL OF COMMUNICATION MANAGEMENT

Journal of Organizational Communications *which varied under* JOURNAL OF COMMUNICATION MANAGEMENT

Journal of Organizational Communication *which varied under* JOURNAL OF COMMUNICATION MANAGEMENT

International Brotherhood of Electrical Workers

Electrical Worker, The *which varied under* IBEW JOURNAL

Electrical Worker, The *which varied under* JOURNAL

Electrical Workers' Journal, The *which varied under* IBEW JOURNAL

Electrical Workers' Journal, The *which varied under* JOURNAL

Electrical Workers' Journal, The *which varied under* JOURNAL

IBEW JOURNAL

JOURNAL

Journal *which varied under* IBEW JOURNAL

Journal of Electrical Workers and Operators *which varied under* IBEW JOURNAL

Journal of Electrical Workers and Operators, The *which varied under* JOURNAL

International Cassette Association

ICA NEWSLETTER

International Committee on Communications, American Section

AIR LAW REVIEW

International Committee on Radio of the American Academy of Air Law

AIR LAW REVIEW

International Committee on Wireless Telegraphy, American Section

AIR LAW REVIEW

International Communication Association

CAT NEWS

COMMUNICATION LAW & POLICY NEWSLETTER

COMMUNICATION THEORY

COMMUNIQUÉ

FEMINIST SCHOLARSHIP INTEREST GROUP NEWSLETTER OF THE INTERNATIONAL COMMUNICATION ASSOCIATION

FORUM

HEALTH COMMUNICATION NEWSLETTER

HUMAN COMMUNICATION RESEARCH

ICA NEWSLETTER

INTERCULTURAL & DEVELOPMENT COMMUNICATION NEWSLETTER

NSSC Newsletter *which varied under* ICA NEWSLETTER

ORGANIZATIONAL COMMUNICATION NEWSLETTER

POLITICAL COMMUNICATION NEWSLETTER

PRIG

SYSTEMSLETTER

International Communication Projects

CHRONICLE OF INTERNATIONAL COMMUNICATION

International Communications Industries Association

COMMUNICATIONS INDUSTRIES REPORT, THE

NAVA News *which varied under* COMMUNICATIONS INDUSTRIES REPORT, THE

International Council for Educational Media

Audio-Visual Media *which varied under* EDUCATIONAL MEDIA INTERNATIONAL

EDUCATIONAL MEDIA INTERNATIONAL

International Council for Educational Films

Audio-Visual Media *which varied under* EDUCATIONAL MEDIA INTERNATIONAL

EDUCATIONAL MEDIA INTERNATIONAL

International Council for the Advancement of Audio-Visual Media

Audio-Visual Media *which varied under* EDUCATIONAL MEDIA INTERNATIONAL

EDUCATIONAL MEDIA INTERNATIONAL

International Documentary Association

INTERNATIONAL DOCUMENTARY

International Electrical Workers and Operators

Electrical Worker, The *which varied under* JOURNAL

Electrical Workers' Journal, The *which varied under* JOURNAL

Electrical Workers' Journal, The *which varied under* JOURNAL

JOURNAL

Journal of Electrical Workers and Operators, The *which varied under* JOURNAL

International Federation for Theatre Research

THEATRE RESEARCH

International Federation of Journalists

IFJ INFORMATION

JOURNALIST'S WORLD

International Federation of Newspaper Publishers

Bulletin d'Informations *which varied under* FIEJ-BULLETIN

FIEJ-BULLETIN

International Federation of Photographic Art

CAMERA

International Film and Television Council

WORLD SCREEN

International Freelance Photographers Organization

INTERNATIONAL PHOTOGRAPHER MAGAZINE

International Institute of Communications

IBI Newsletter *which varied under* INTERMEDIA

INTERMEDIA

International League of Press Clubs

JOURNALIST, THE

International Motion Picture and Lecturers Association

PERFORMER, THE

International Organization of Journalists

DEMOCRATIC JOURNALIST

JOURNALISTS' AFFAIRS

International PEN Writers in Prison Committee

Index *which varied under* INDEX ON CENSORSHIP

INDEX ON CENSORSHIP

International Prepress Association

PRE-

International Press Institute

IPI REPORT

IPI SURVEY

International Radio and Television Organization

Documentation and Information Bulletin of the International Broadcasting Organization *which varied under* RADIO AND TELEVISION

OIR Information *which varied under* OIRT INFORMATION

OIRT INFORMATION

Radio & Television *which varied under* RADIO AND TELEVISION

RADIO AND TELEVISION

Radio Television *which varied under* RADIO AND TELEVISION

Radio Television International Review *which varied under* RADIO AND TELEVISION

International Scientific Film Association

SCIENCE AND FILM

SCIENTIFIC FILM

International Society for the Arts, Sciences and Technology.

LEONARDO

International Society of Weekly Newspaper Editors

Grassroots *which varied under* GRASSROOTS EDITOR

GRASSROOTS EDITOR

International Tape Association

ITA NEWS DIGEST

ITA Newsletter *which varied under* ITA NEWS DIGEST

International Telecommunication Union

Journal des Telecommunications *which varied under* TELECOMMUNICATION JOURNAL

Journal Telegraphique [NE?] *which varied under* TELECOMMUNICATION JOURNAL

Journal UIT *which varied under* TELECOMMUNICATION JOURNAL

TELECOMMUNICATION JOURNAL

International Television Association
CORPORATE TELEVISION
International Television *which varied under* CORPORATE TELEVISION
VIDEO SYSTEMS

International Theatre Institute
WORLD THEATRE

International Thespian Society, The
Curtain *which varied under* DRAMATICS
DRAMATICS
Dramatics *which varied under* DRAMATICS
Dramatics' Curtain *which varied under* DRAMATICS
High School Thespian *which varied under* DRAMATICS

International Tournee of Animation
ANIMATION MAGAZINE
Animation News *which varied under* ANIMATION MAGAZINE

International Travel-Adventure Film Guild
PERFORMER, THE

Iowa Center for Communication Study
JOURNAL OF COMMUNICATION INQUIRY, THE

Italian Broadcasting Association
MILLECANALI INTERNATIONAL

J

James Bond 007 Fan Club
BONDAGE

Johannesburg Reportory Players
PLAYTIME

Journalism Education Association
JEA NEWSWIRE

Journalism Education Association of the United States
C: JET
Communication: Journalism Education Today *which varied under* C: JET

K

Kappa Tau Alpha
KTA NEWSLETTER

Koninklijk Instituut van Ingenieurs Afd elektrotechniek
EUROPEAN TRANSACTIONS ON TELECOMMUNICATIONS AND RELATED TECHNOLOGIES

Koninklijke Belgische Vereniging der Elektrotechnici
EUROPEAN TRANSACTIONS ON TELECOMMUNICATIONS AND RELATED TECHNOLOGIES

L

League of American Theatres and Producers
PLAYBILL

Lithographers and Photoengravers International Union
Graphic Arts Unionist *which varied under* GRAPHIC COMMUNICATOR
GRAPHIC COMMUNICATOR
Union Tabloid *which varied under* GRAPHIC COMMUNICATOR

M

Manchester University
NEW THEATRE MAGAZINE

Mass Communication Bibliographers
MASS COMMUNICATION BIBLIOGRAPHERS' NEWSLETTER

Masthead Society
MASTHEAD

Media Action Research Center
MEDIA & VALUES

Media and Consumer Foundation
MEDIA & CONSUMER

Media Center for Children
YOUNG VIEWERS

Telecommunication Journal *which varied under* TELECOMMUNICATION JOURNAL

Associations INDEX 732

Media Research Center
    TV, ETC.

Mid-States Industrial Photographers Association
    NATIONAL PHOTOGRAPHER, THE

Modern Language Association
    JOURNAL OF POPULAR CULTURE

Motion Picture Producers and Distributors of America
    Motion Picture Monthly, The *which varied under* SELECTED MOTION PICTURES
    Motion Picture, The *which varied under* SELECTED MOTION PICTURES
    SELECTED MOTION PICTURES

Museum of Broadcasting
    MB NEWS

Museum of Cartoon Art
    CARTOONIST PROFILES

N

National Academy of Television Arts and Sciences
    TELEVISION QUARTERLY

National Alliance of Media Arts Centers
    MEDIA ARTS

National Amateur Press Association
    NATIONAL AMATEUR

National Association for Better Broadcasting
    BETTER RADIO AND TELEVISION
    NAFBRAT Quarterly *which varied under* BETTER RADIO AND TELEVISION
    Newsletter *which varied under* BETTER RADIO AND TELEVISION

National Association for Better Radio and Television
    BETTER RADIO AND TELEVISION
    NAFBRAT Quarterly *which varied under* BETTER RADIO AND TELEVISION
    Newsletter *which varied under* BETTER RADIO AND TELEVISION

National Association of Academic Teachers of Public Speaking
    Quarterly Journal of Public Speaking, The *which varied under* QUARTERLY JOURNAL OF SPEECH, THE
    Quarterly Journal of Speech Education, The *which varied under* QUARTERLY JOURNAL OF SPEECH, THE
    QUARTERLY JOURNAL OF SPEECH, THE

National Association of Art Directors
    ART DIRECTION
    Art Director & Studio News *which varied under* ART DIRECTION
    Studio News *which varied under* ART DIRECTION

National Association of Broadcast Engineers and Technicians
    BROADCAST ENGINEERS' JOURNAL, THE

National Association of Broadcast Employees and Technicians
    NABET NEWS

National Association of Broadcasters
    AIR TIME
    Broadcasters News Bulletin *which varied under* NARTB MEMBER SERVICE
    CODE NEWS
    Highlights *which varied under* NAB HIGHLIGHTS
    NAB HIGHLIGHTS
    NAB Member Service *which varied under* NARTB MEMBER SERVICE
    NAB Reports *which varied under* NARTB MEMBER SERVICE
    NAB Today [Television Edition] *which varied under* TV TODAY
    NARTB MEMBER SERVICE
    RADIOACTIVE
    RADIOWEEK
    REWIND
    TV TODAY

National Association of College Broadcasters
    COLLEGE BROADCASTER

National Association of Educational Broadcasters
    AERT Journal *which varied under* PUBLIC TELECOMMUNICATIONS REVIEW
    Educational Broadcasting Review *which varied under* PUBLIC TELECOMMUNICATIONS REVIEW
    Journal of the AER *which varied under* PUBLIC TELECOMMUNICATIONS REVIEW
    Journal of the AERT *which varied under* PUBLIC TELECOMMUNICATIONS REVIEW
    NAEB Journal *which varied under* PUBLIC TELECOMMUNICATIONS REVIEW
    PACTSHEET
    PUBLIC TELECOMMUNICATIONS REVIEW

National Association of Manufacturers
    SERVICE FOR COMPANY COMMUNNICATORS

Service for Company Publications *which varied under* SERVICE FOR COMPANY COMMUNNICATORS

Service for Employee Publications *which varied under* SERVICE FOR COMPANY COMMUNNICATORS

National Association of Music Merchants

PRO SOUND NEWS

National Association of Television Program Executives

NATPE PROGRAMMER

PD Cue *which varied under* NATPE PROGRAMMER

National Association of Theatre Owners

MOVIES NOW

National Board of Review of Motion Pictures

FILMS IN REVIEW

National Board of Review Magazine *which varied under* FILMS IN REVIEW

New Movies, The *which varied under* FILMS IN REVIEW

National Book Council

BRITISH BOOK NEWS

Selection of Recent Books Published in Great Britain *which varied under* BRITISH BOOK NEWS

National Book League

BRITISH BOOK NEWS

Selection of Recent Books Published in Great Britain *which varied under* BRITISH BOOK NEWS

National Broadcast Editorial Association

EDITORIALIST, THE

NATIONAL BROADCAST EDITORIAL ASSOCIATION NEWSLETTER

National Broadcasters League

RADIO AGE

National Brotherhood of Electrical Workers

Electrical Worker, The *which varied under* JOURNAL

Electrical Workers' Journal, The *which varied under* JOURNAL

Electrical Workers' Journal, The *which varied under* JOURNAL

JOURNAL

Journal of Electrical Workers and Operators, The *which varied under* JOURNAL

National Cinema Workshop and Cinema League

CINEMA PROGRESS

National Cinema Workshop and Appreciation League Bulletin *which varied under* CINEMA PROGRESS

National Citizens Committee for Broadcasting

ACCESS

MEDIA WATCH

National Coalition Against Censorship

CENSORSHIP NEWS

National Collegiate Players

PLAYERS

Players Magazine *which varied under* PLAYERS

National Committee for Audio-Visual Aids in Education

Monthly Filmstrip Review *which varied under* VISUAL EDUCATION

VISUAL EDUCATION

National Committee of Film Forums

FILM FORUM REVIEW

National Conference of Editorial Writers

MASTHEAD

National Council for Children and Television

NCCT Forum *which varied under* TELEVISION & FAMILIES

Television & Children *which varied under* TELEVISION & FAMILIES

TELEVISION & FAMILIES

National Editorial Association

FOI DIGEST

Freedom of Information News Digest *which varied under* FOI DIGEST

National Educational Closed-Circuit Television Association

JOURNAL OF EDUCATIONAL TELEVISION

Journal of Educational Television *which varied under* JOURNAL OF EDUCATIONAL TELEVISION

Journal of Educational Television and Other Media *which varied under* JOURNAL OF EDUCATIONAL TELEVISION

National Federation for Decency

AFA JOURNAL

National Federation for Decency Newsletter *which varied under* AFA JOURNAL

Newsletter of the National Federation for Decency *which varied under* AFA JOURNAL

NFD Informer *which varied under* AFA JOURNAL

NFD Journal *which varied under* AFA JOURNAL

NFD Newsletter *which varied under* AFA JOURNAL

NFD Newsletter *which varied under* AFA JOURNAL

National Film Society

AMERICAN CLASSIC SCREEN

Associations — INDEX

National Forensic League
ROSTRUM

National Industrial Television Association
INDUSTRIAL TELEVISION NEWS

NITA News *which varied under* INDUSTRIAL TELEVISION NEWS

National Institute of Audio-Visual Education
Audio-Visual Education *which varied under* NIE JOURNAL

NIE JOURNAL

National Mail Order Association
MAIL ORDER DIGEST

National Newspaper Association
PUBLISHER'S AUXILIARY

National Photography Instructors Association
PHOTOGRAPHER'S FORUM

Student Forum *which varied under* PHOTOGRAPHER'S FORUM

National Press Photographers Association
4SIGHT MAGAZINE

DARKSLIDE

IMAGE 11

National Press Photographer *which varied under* NEWS PHOTOGRAPHER

NEWS PHOTOGRAPHER

RANGEFINDER, THE

RETROFOCUS

SIXSHOOTERS

National Press Photographers Association for Still and Television News
National Press Photographer *which varied under* NEWS PHOTOGRAPHER

NEWS PHOTOGRAPHER

National Religious Broadcasters
CAMPUS BROADCASTERS

RELIGIOUS BROADCASTING

National Scholastic Press Association
Scholastic Editor *which varied under* SCHOLASTIC EDITOR'S TRENDS IN PUBLICATIONS

Scholastic Editor *which varied under* SCHOLASTIC EDITOR'S TRENDS IN PUBLICATIONS

Scholastic Editor Graphics/Communications *which varied under* SCHOLASTIC EDITOR'S TRENDS IN PUBLICATIONS

SCHOLASTIC EDITOR'S TRENDS IN PUBLICATIONS

National School Public Relations Association
Journal of Educational Communication *which varied under* JOURNAL OF EDUCATIONAL PUBLIC RELATIONS

JOURNAL OF EDUCATIONAL PUBLIC RELATIONS

National School Yearbook-Newspaper Association
Photolith *which varied under* PHOTOLITH, SCM

PHOTOLITH, SCM

National Sisters Communications Service
MEDIA & VALUES

National Society for the Study of Communication
JOURNAL OF COMMUNICATION

National Society of Art Directors
ART DIRECTION

Art Director & Studio News *which varied under* ART DIRECTION

Studio News *which varied under* ART DIRECTION

National Telegraphic Union
TELEGRAPHER, THE

National Union of Journalists
JOURNALIST

National University of Singapore, Department of Mass Communication
ASIAN JOURNAL OF COMMUNICATION

Negro Actors Guild of America
NEGRO ACTORS GUILD OF AMERICA. NEWSLETTER.

New Theatre League
THEATRE WORKSHOP

New York Performance Foundation
PERFORMANCE

New York Society of Amateur Photographers
CAMERA AND DARK ROOM

New York State Community Theatre Association
Community Theatre Bulletin *which varied under* THEATRE JOURNAL

New York State Community Theatre Journal *which varied under* THEATRE JOURNAL

THEATRE JOURNAL

New Zealand Electronics Institute
ELECTRONICS AND COMMUNICATIONS

Radio and Electrical Review *which varied under* ELECTRONICS AND COMMUNICATIONS

Radio and Electronics *which varied under* ELECTRONICS AND COMMUNICATIONS

Radio, Electronics and Communications *which varied under*

ELECTRONICS AND COMMUNICATIONS

New Zealand Radio and Electrical Traders' Federation
ELECTRONICS AND COMMUNICATIONS
Radio and Electrical Review *which varied under* ELECTRONICS AND COMMUNICATIONS
Radio and Electronics *which varied under* ELECTRONICS AND COMMUNICATIONS
Radio, Electronics and Communications *which varied under* ELECTRONICS AND COMMUNICATIONS

New Zealand Radio and Television Manufacturers' Federation
ELECTRONICS AND COMMUNICATIONS
Radio and Electrical Review *which varied under* ELECTRONICS AND COMMUNICATIONS
Radio and Electronics *which varied under* ELECTRONICS AND COMMUNICATIONS
Radio, Electronics and Communications *which varied under* ELECTRONICS AND COMMUNICATIONS

New Zealand Radio, TV and Electrical Association
ELECTRONICS AND COMMUNICATIONS
Radio and Electrical Review *which varied under* ELECTRONICS AND COMMUNICATIONS
Radio and Electronics *which varied under* ELECTRONICS AND COMMUNICATIONS
Radio, Electronics and Communications *which varied under* ELECTRONICS AND COMMUNICATIONS

Newspaper Enterprise Association
PEP

Newspaper Guild
GUILD REPORTER, THE

Nieman Foundation for Journalism
NIEMAN REPORTS

North American Short Wave Association
FRENDX

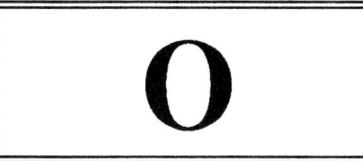

O

Ohio State University
Broadcast Bibliophile Booknotes *which varied under* COMMUNICATION BOOKNOTES
COMMUNICATION BOOKNOTES
Mass Media Booknotes *which varied under* COMMUNICATION BOOKNOTES

Ohio University
WIDE ANGLE

Organization for the Study of Communication Language and Gender
WOMEN & LANGUAGE

Oxford University Film Society
Magazine of the Oxford Film Society *which varied under* SEQUENCE
SEQUENCE

P

Paper Makers Advertising Association
DA *which varied under* PRINTING PAPER
Direct Advertising *which varied under* PRINTING PAPER
Direct Advertising and Sample Book of Mill Brand Papers *which varied under* PRINTING PAPER
PRINTING PAPER
Printing Paper Quarterly *which varied under* PRINTING PAPER

Peoples Theatre
THEATRE WORKSHOP

Photo Marketing Association International
New Developments for the Photographic Dealer and Photo Finisher *which varied under* PHOTO MARKETING
Photo Developments *which varied under* PHOTO MARKETING
PHOTO MARKETING

Photo Pictorialists of Buffalo
AMATEUR PHOTOGRAPHER'S WEEKLY, THE

Photographers Association of America
Abels Photographic Weekly *which varied under* PROFESSIONAL PHOTOGRAPHER, THE
COMMERCIAL PHOTOGRAPHER, THE
NATIONAL PHOTOGRAPHER, THE
PROFESSIONAL PHOTOGRAPHER, THE
Professional Photographer, The *which varied under* PROFESSIONAL PHOTOGRAPHER, THE

Photographers' Association of California
CAMERA CRAFT

Photographic Historical Society of New England
PHOTIQUE

Photographic Resource Center
VIEWS

Associations   INDEX   736

Photographic Society of America
Journal of Photographic Society of America *which varied under* PSA JOURNAL
PSA JOURNAL

Photography Instructors Association
CAMERA & DARKROOM PHOTOGRAPHY

Darkroom Photography *which varied under* CAMERA & DARKROOM PHOTOGRAPHY

Pi Delta Epsilon
COLLEGIATE JOURNALIST

Polish Film Makers' Association
ANIMAFILM

Popular Culture Association
JOURNAL OF POPULAR CULTURE

Journal of Popular Film *which varied under* JOURNAL OF POPULAR FILM AND TELEVISION

JOURNAL OF POPULAR FILM AND TELEVISION

JPF&T *which varied under* JOURNAL OF POPULAR FILM AND TELEVISION

Postal Electrical Society of Victoria
TELECOMMUNICATION JOURNAL OF AUSTRALIA, THE

Printing Industries Association
PRINT-EQUIP NEWS

Producers Guild of America
JOURNAL OF THE PRODUCERS GUILD OF AMERICA, THE

Journal of the Screen Producers Guild *which varied under* JOURNAL OF THE PRODUCERS GUILD OF AMERICA, THE

Professional Film and Video Equipment Association
FOLLOW FOCUS

Newsletter *which varied under* FOLLOW FOCUS
NEWSLETTER, THE

Professional Photographers of America
NATIONAL PHOTOGRAPHER, THE

National Professional Photographer, The *which varied under* PROFESSIONAL PHOTOGRAPHER, THE

PHOTOMETHODS

PMI, Photo Methods for Industry *which varied under* PHOTOMETHODS

PROFESSIONAL PHOTOGRAPHER, THE

Public Relations Society of America
PUBLIC RELATIONS JOURNAL, THE

Public Relations Student Society of America
FORUM

Publishers Board of Trade
Leypoldt & Holt's Literary Bulletin *which varied under* PUBLISHER'S WEEKLY

Literary Bulletin, The *which varied under* PUBLISHER'S WEEKLY

PUBLISHER'S WEEKLY

Publishers' and Stationers' Weekly Trade Circular *which varied under* PUBLISHER'S WEEKLY

Trade Circular and Literary Bulletin, The *which varied under* PUBLISHER'S WEEKLY

Trade Circular and Publishers' Bulletin, The *which varied under* PUBLISHER'S WEEKLY

Publishers Marketing Association
PMA NEWSLETTER

Q

Quill and Scroll Society
QUILL AND SCROLL

R

Radio Advertising Bureau
Ear *which varied under* SOUND MANAGEMENT
SOUND MANAGEMENT

Radio Manufacturers Association
RMA ENGINEER

Radio Signal Survey League
ALL-WAVE RADIO

Radio Society of Great Britain
RADIO COMMUNICATION

RSGB Bulletin *which varied under* RADIO COMMUNICATION

T & R Bulletin *which varied under* RADIO COMMUNICATION

Radio-Television News Directors Association
Broadcast Communications *which varied under* TELEVISION BROADCAST
COMMUNICATOR

NARND Bulletin *which varied under* COMMUNICATOR

RTNDA Bulletin *which varied under* COMMUNICATOR

RTNDA Communicator *which varied under* COMMUNICATOR

TELEVISION BROADCAST

Television/Broadcast Communications *which varied under* TELEVISION BROADCAST

TV Broadcast Communications *which varied under* TELEVISION BROADCAST

Religious Speech Communication Association

HOMILETIC

JOURNAL OF COMMUNICATION AND RELIGION, THE

Religious Communication Today *which varied under* JOURNAL OF COMMUNICATION AND RELIGION, THE

Reporters Committee for Freedom of the Press

NEWS MEDIA & THE LAW, THE

Press Censorship Newsletter *which varied under* NEWS MEDIA & THE LAW, THE

Reporters Sans Frontièrs

Index *which varied under* INDEX ON CENSORSHIP

INDEX ON CENSORSHIP

Research Society for American Periodicals

RSAP NEWSLETTER

Research Society for Victorian Periodicals

Victorian Periodicals Newsletter *which varied under* VICTORIAN PERIODICALS REVIEW

VICTORIAN PERIODICALS REVIEW

Rhetoric Society of America

Newsletter: Rhetoric Society of America *which varied under* RHETORIC SOCIETY QUARTERLY

RHETORIC SOCIETY QUARTERLY

Royal Television Society

Journal of the Television Society *which varied under* TELEVISION

Royal Television Society Journal, The *which varied under* TELEVISION

TELEVISION

Rutgers University

Book Research Quarterly *which varied under* PUBLISHING RESEARCH QUARTERLY

PUBLISHING RESEARCH QUARTERLY

S

Schweizerischer Elektrotechnischer Verein

EUROPEAN TRANSACTIONS ON TELECOMMUNICATIONS AND RELATED TECHNOLOGIES

Screen Actors Guild

Hollywood *which varied under* SCREEN ACTOR HOLLYWOOD

Hollywood Close Up *which varied under* SCREEN ACTOR HOLLYWOOD

Screen Actor *which varied under* SCREEN ACTOR HOLLYWOOD

SCREEN ACTOR HOLLYWOOD

Screen Actor News *which varied under* SCREEN ACTOR HOLLYWOOD

Screen Actor News *which varied under* SCREEN ACTOR HOLLYWOOD

Screen Actor Newsletter *which varied under* SCREEN ACTOR HOLLYWOOD

Screen Writers Guild

PHOTODRAMATIST, THE

Screenwriting Coalition foR Industry Professionals and Teachers

SCRIPT NEWSLETTER

Seminary Film Society of Southern Baptist Theological Society

MOVIES AND MINISTRY

Shakespeare Association of America

SHAKESPEARE QUARTERLY

Sigma Delta Chi

Quill of Sigma Delta Chi, The *which varied under* QUILL, THE

QUILL, THE

Silha Center for the Study of Media Ethics

MEDIA ETHICS UPDATE

Société Royale Belge des Electriciens

EUROPEAN TRANSACTIONS ON TELECOMMUNICATIONS AND RELATED TECHNOLOGIES

Society for Animation Studies

SOCIETY FOR ANIMATION STUDIES NEWSLETTER, THE

Society for Cinema Studies

CINEMA JOURNAL

Society of Cinematologists. Journal. *which varied under* CINEMA JOURNAL

Society for Collegiate Journalists

COLLEGIATE JOURNALIST

Society for Education in Film and Television

Film Teacher *which varied under* SCREEN

SCREEN

Screen Education *which varied under* SCREEN

Associations

Screen Education Notes *which varied under* SCREEN

Society of Film Teachers. Bulletin *which varied under* SCREEN

Society for Film History Research
CINEMA STUDIES

Society for Photographic Education
EXPOSURE

PHOTOGRAPHER'S FORUM

Student Forum *which varied under* PHOTOGRAPHER'S FORUM

Society for Scholarly Publishing
SCHOLARLY PUBLISHING

SSP LETTER

Society for the History of Technology
TECHNOLOGY AND CULTURE

Society for Theatre Research
THEATRE NOTEBOOK

Society of Authors, The
Author, Playwright and Composer *which varied under* AUTHOR, THE

AUTHOR, THE

Author, The *which varied under* AUTHOR, THE

Society of Broadcast Engineers
Broadcast Communications *which varied under* TELEVISION BROADCAST

SIGNAL, THE

TELEVISION BROADCAST

Television/Broadcast Communications *which varied under* TELEVISION BROADCAST

TV Broadcast Communications *which varied under* TELEVISION BROADCAST

Society of Cable Television Engineers
CABLE TELEVISION ENGINEERING

COMMUNICATIONS ENGINEERING & DESIGN

Communications/Engineering Digest *which varied under* COMMUNICATIONS ENGINEERING & DESIGN

INTERNATIONAL CABLE

Relay Engineer *which varied under* CABLE TELEVISION ENGINEERING

Society of Cinematologists
CINEMA JOURNAL

Society of Cinematologists. Journal. *which varied under* CINEMA JOURNAL

Society of Film Teachers
Film Teacher *which varied under* SCREEN

SCREEN

Screen Education *which varied under* SCREEN

Screen Education Notes *which varied under* SCREEN

Society of Film Teachers. Bulletin *which varied under* SCREEN

Society of Motion Picture and Television Engineers
Incorporation and Bylaws *which varied under* SMPTE JOURNAL

Journal *which varied under* SMPTE JOURNAL

Journal of the SMPTE *which varied under* SMPTE JOURNAL

Journal of the Society of Motion Picture Engineers *which varied under* SMPTE JOURNAL

Journal of the Society of Motion Picture and Television Engineers *which varied under* SMPTE JOURNAL

SMPTE JOURNAL

SMPTE Journal *which varied under* SMPTE JOURNAL

Transactions *which varied under* SMPTE JOURNAL

Society of Newspaper Design
DESIGN

Society of Photographers in Communications, The
American Society of Magazine Photographers Newsletter *which varied under* ASMP BULLETIN

American Society of Magazine Photographers. News *which varied under* ASMP BULLETIN

ASMP BULLETIN

ASMP News *which varied under* ASMP BULLETIN

Bulletin. ASMP *which varied under* ASMP BULLETIN

Infinity *which varied under* ASMP BULLETIN

Society of Professional Journalists
Quill of Sigma Delta Chi, The *which varied under* QUILL, THE

QUILL, THE

Society of Professional Videographers.
PRO VIDEOGRAM

Society of Teachers of Speech and Drama
SPEECH AND DRAMA

Society of Technical Communication
LOS ANGELES TECHNOGRAPH

Society to Preserve and Encourage Radio Drama, Variety, and Comedy
SPERDVAC

South Carolina Scholastic Broadcasters Association
NATIONAL HIGH SCHOOL BROADCASTERS NEWSLETTER

Southeastern Theatre Conference
SOUTHERN THEATRE

Southern Theatre News *which varied under* SOUTHERN THEATRE

Southern Speech Communication Association

SOUTHERN COMMUNICATION JOURNAL, THE

Southern Speech Bulletin *which varied under* SOUTHERN COMMUNICATION JOURNAL, THE

Southern Speech Communication Journal, The *which varied under* SOUTHERN COMMUNICATION JOURNAL, THE

Southern Speech Journal, The *which varied under* SOUTHERN COMMUNICATION JOURNAL, THE

Southern States Communication Association

C-O-N-N-E-C-T-I-O-N-S

Southern States Speech Association

C-O-N-N-E-C-T-I-O-N-S

Specialty Advertising Association International

SPECIALTY ADVERTISING BUSINESS

Speech Communication Association

COMMUNICATION EDUCATION

COMMUNICATION MONOGRAPHS

CRITICAL STUDIES IN MASS COMMUNICATION

JOURNAL OF APPLIED COMMUNICATION RESEARCH

Journal of Applied Communications Research *which varied under* JOURNAL OF APPLIED COMMUNICATION RESEARCH

Literature in Performance *which varied under* TPQ

Quarterly Journal of Public Speaking, The *which varied under* QUARTERLY JOURNAL OF SPEECH, THE

Quarterly Journal of Speech Education, The *which varied under* QUARTERLY JOURNAL OF SPEECH, THE

QUARTERLY JOURNAL OF SPEECH, THE

RHETORICAL & COMMUNICATION THEORY NEWSLETTER

SCA WOMEN'S CAUCUS AND FEMINIST & WOMEN STUDIES DIVISION NEWSLETTER

SPECTRA

SPEECH COMMUNICATION TEACHER, THE

Speech Monographs *which varied under* COMMUNICATION MONOGRAPHS

Speech Teacher, The *which varied under* COMMUNICATION EDUCATION

TPQ

States Consortium for Improving Software Selection

EPIEGRAM

Successful Magazine Publishers Group

MAGAZINE BUSINESS

SUCCESSFUL MAGAZINE PUBLISHING

T

Telecom Australia

Australian Media Notes *which varied under* MEDIA INFORMATION AUSTRALIA

MEDIA INFORMATION AUSTRALIA

Telecommunication Society of Australia

ATR

TELECOMMUNICATION JOURNAL OF AUSTRALIA, THE

Telecommunications Research and Action Center

ACCESS

Television Bureau of Advertising

SALES NEWS

Television Society

ELECTRONIC ENGINEERING

Electronics and Television & Short-Wave World *which varied under* ELECTRONIC ENGINEERING

Journal of the Television Society *which varied under* TELEVISION

Royal Television Society Journal, The *which varied under* TELEVISION

TELEVISION

Television *which varied under* ELECTRONIC ENGINEERING

Television and Short-Wave World *which varied under* ELECTRONIC ENGINEERING

Television Society of America

TELEVISION

Theatre Communications Group

AMERICAN THEATRE

Theatre Communications *which varied under* AMERICAN THEATRE

Theatre Communications Group Newsletter *which varied under* AMERICAN THEATRE

Theatre Education Association

Curtain *which varied under* DRAMATICS

DRAMATICS

Dramatics *which varied under* DRAMATICS

Dramatics' Curtain *which varied under* DRAMATICS

High School Thespian *which varied under* DRAMATICS

Theatre Historical Society

MARQUEE

Theatre Library Association

BROADSIDE

Theta Sigma Phi

MATRIX

Tisch School of the Arts
Carleton Drama Review *which varied under* TDR

Drama Review, The *which varied under* TDR

TDR

TDR *which varied under* TDR

Tulane Drama Review *which varied under* TDR

Transaction Periodicals Consortium
Book Research Quarterly *which varied under* PUBLISHING RESEARCH QUARTERLY

PUBLISHING RESEARCH QUARTERLY

Travelfilm Artists and Producers
PERFORMER, THE

Twin Cities Media Project
TWIN CITIES JOURNALISM REVIEW

U

United Kingdom Society of Cable Television Engineers
INTERNATIONAL CABLE

United States Institute for Theatre Technology
THEATRE DESIGN & TECHNOLOGY

Theatre Design & Technology *which varied under* THEATRE DESIGN & TECHNOLOGY

Theatre Design and Technology *which varied under* THEATRE DESIGN & TECHNOLOGY

University and College Theatre Association
Educational Theatre Journal *which varied under* THEATRE JOURNAL

THEATRE JOURNAL

University Film and Video Association
DIGEST OF THE UNIVERSITY FILM AND VIDEO ASSOCIATION

Digest of the University Film Association *which varied under* DIGEST OF THE UNIVERSITY FILM AND VIDEO ASSOCIATION

University Film Association
DIGEST

University Film Study Center
UNIVERSITY FILM STUDY CENTER. NEWSLETTER.

University of California
Comm/Ent, A Journal of Communications and Entertainment Law *which varied under* HASTINGS COMMUNICATIONS AND ENTERTAINMENT LAW JOURNAL

Comm/Ent, Hastings Journal of Communications and Entertainment Law *which varied under* HASTINGS COMMUNICATIONS AND ENTERTAINMENT LAW JOURNAL

HASTINGS COMMUNICATIONS AND ENTERTAINMENT LAW JOURNAL

University of Rochester
CAMERA OBSCURA

University of South Carolina
Bulletin *which varied under* JOURNALISM EDUCATOR, THE

JOURNALISM EDUCATOR, THE

University of South Carolina College of Journalism
NATIONAL HIGH SCHOOL BROADCASTERS NEWSLETTER

University of Wyoming
COMMUNIQUÉ

Urban Telecommunications Forum
URBAN TELECOMMUNICATIONS FORUM

V

Vancouver Society of Independent Animators
PEGBAR

Ventura Publisher Users Group
VENTURA PROFESSIONAL!

Ventura Publishes *which varied under* VENTURA PROFESSIONAL!

Ventura Users of North America
VENTURA LETTER, THE

Verband Deutscher Elektrotechniker
EUROPEAN TRANSACTIONS ON TELECOMMUNICATIONS AND RELATED TECHNOLOGIES

Video Software Dealers Association
VIDEO STORE

Virginia Instructional Technology Association in Higher Education
NEWS & VIEWS

W

Washington Newspaper Publishers Association
WASHINGTON NEWSPAPER, THE

Western Educational Society for Telecommunications
TELEMEMO

Western Marketing Educators Association
JOURNAL OF MARKETING EDUCATION

Western Publications Association
PHOTOGRAPHER'S FORUM

Student Forum *which varied under* PHOTOGRAPHER'S FORUM

Western Speech Association
WESTERN JOURNAL OF SPEECH COMMUNICATION

Western Speech *which varied under* WESTERN JOURNAL OF SPEECH COMMUNICATION

Western Speech Communication *which varied under* WESTERN JOURNAL OF SPEECH COMMUNICATION

Western Speech Communication Association
COMMUNICATION REPORTS

WSCA NEWS

Western States Communication Association
WESTERN JOURNAL OF SPEECH COMMUNICATION

Western Speech *which varied under* WESTERN JOURNAL OF SPEECH COMMUNICATION

Western Speech Communication *which varied under* WESTERN JOURNAL OF SPEECH COMMUNICATION

WSCA NEWS

Western Writers of America
ROUNDUP QUARTERLY

Roundup, The *which varied under* ROUNDUP QUARTERLY

Wisconsin Dramatic Society
PLAY-BOOK, THE

Women in Communications
MATRIX

World Association for Christian Communication
ACTION

Christian Broadcaster *which varied under* MEDIA DEVELOPMENT

MEDIA DEVELOPMENT

WACC Journal *which varied under* MEDIA DEVELOPMENT

World Association for Christian Education
Christian Broadcaster *which varied under* MEDIA DEVELOPMENT

MEDIA DEVELOPMENT

WACC Journal *which varied under* MEDIA DEVELOPMENT

World Communication Association
Communication *which varied under* WORLD COMMUNICATION

Communication Reports *which varied under* WORLD COMMUNICATION

COMMUNICATION RESEARCH REPORTS

WCA NEWSLETTER

WORLD COMMUNICATION

Writers & Scholars International
Index *which varied under* INDEX ON CENSORSHIP

INDEX ON CENSORSHIP

Writers Guild of America, West
NEWSLETTER

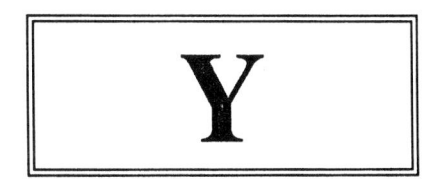

Y

Yellow Pages Publishers Association
LINK

Columnists

The names of columnists with their associated columns and publication title(s) are listed here. This is not an inclusive listing due to two factors: 1) Only those columnist names which appeared in sampled issues appear here; and 2) Attribution is by published name. It is therefore possible that two unique columnists sharing the same first and last names will share multiple listings. The occasional use of a "Nom de Plume" is considered to be a valid columnist name for the purposes of this listing. When doubt existed concerning authorship no attribution was provided.

A

Abbott, Denise
AMERICAN CINEMEDITOR: "Scene and Heard," editors in the news,

Abbott, William
FOLIO:: "William Abbott on Ad Marketing."

Abel, Charles
PROFESSIONAL PHOTOGRAPHER, THE: "The Editor's Commentary."

Abrahamson, Lynne
TV DAY STARS: "Fan Club Forum," fan news.

Ackner, Anni
FACTSHEET FIVE: "Stars on One," media commentary.

Adams, Bob
CMA NEWSLETTER: "Newspaper."

Adams, Bobby
DARKROOM PHOTOGRAPHY: "Larger Formats."

Adams, Cindy
CELEBRITY: "Cindy Says," newsbriefs.
MOVIE MIRROR: "Cindy Says," 'Cindy's sparkling column is filled with inside news on show business and show people'
THEATRE, THE: "New York."

Adams, Danny E.
4TH MEDIA JOURNAL, THE: "Washington Line," regulatory news and information.

Adams, Evangeline
NEW MOVIE MAGAZINE, THE: "Evangeline Adams Reads the Stars," 'The world's most famous astrologer interprets the stars and their influences' astrology.

Adams, Joey
STAR: "Laugh Yourself Well."

Adams, Mark
MOVING PICTURES INTERNATIONAL: "Production Notes," current projects.

Adebayo, Dotun
BLACK RADIO EXCLUSIVE: "The British Invasion," newsbriefs about British black artists.

Adler, Norma
THEATRE DESIGN & TECHNOLOGY: "International Journal Report," excellent international theatre journal/magazine review.

Agan, Patrick
MOVIE WORLD: "Starfront," celebrity.
SCREEN STARS: "Star Gazing."

Agudelo, Carlos
BILLBOARD: "Latin Notas."

Alane, Breena
CASTING CALL: "Palm Springs," 'Show Biz'

Albert, Jack
MONITORING TIMES: "Reading RTTY."

Albert, Jerry
TELEVISER: "Film Facts," video and film comment.

Alcid, Chito P.
SOSYAL! MAGAZINE: "Sosyal Chatterbox," personality news.

Alden, Alison
MOVIE CLASSIC: "Aids to Romance."

Alden, Ken
TV RADIO MIRROR: "Facing the Music," radio music program news.

Alexander, W. C.
RADIO GUIDE: "DA Systems," distribution/amplifier systems.

Allen, Ben
BACK STAGE: "Allen on the Avenue," personality.
BACK STAGE/SHOOT: "Allen Asks."

Allen, Casey
CAMERA 35 INCORPORATING PHOTO WORLD: "Behind the Scenes."

Allen, David
VIDEOGRAPHY: "More to Follow."

Allocca, Anne Marie
DAYTIME TV: "Latest News."

Altman, Larry
ELECTRONIC DESIGN: "Editorial."

Altman, Rick
PC PUBLISHING AND PRESENTATIONS: "Hands-On Ventura."

Anchors, Bill
EPI-LOG: "Editorial."

Anderson, Theo
DESKTOP COMMUNICATIONS: "Network Publishing."

Anderson, William
STEREO REVIEW: "Speaking of Music," editorial commentary.

Andrew, Geoff
20/20: "Film," review.

Columnists

Andrews, John F.
SHAKESPEARE QUARTERLY: "From the Editor," editorial.

Andrews, Paul
WHAT VIDEO: "Movies on Tape," 'Paul Andrews looks at the latest releases on tape for sale or rental'

Andrews, Sir Linton
CAMPAIGN: "Press."

Androw, Mark
FLASH: "Film and Video Views."

Angus, Robert
WHAT VIDEO: "America," video comment and news stateside.

Ankeney, Jay
TV TECHNOLOGY: "Focus on Editing."

Antler, Dora
HOME ENTERTAINMENT: "Design Dynamics," home entertainment center design.

Anzalone, Frank
CQ: "Contest Calendar."

Appleton, Amy
V: "Video Vibes."

Applewhite, Charlie
MOVIE FAN: "On the Sound Track."

Archbald, Anne
THEATRE MAGAZINE: "The Vanity Box."

Archerd, Army
TV RADIO TALK: "Army Archerd Makes TV Radio Talk," 'The latest hottest gossip! Read it here first!'

Archibald, Larry
STEREOPHILE: "The Final Word," 'Publisher Larry Archibald muses in print on the state of the industry'

Arcona
HOLLYWOOD MAGAZINE: "Dept. of Nip 'N' Tuck."

Arey, TJ 'Skip'
MONITORING TIMES: "Uncle Skip's Corner."

Arland, Rich
MONITORING TIMES: "Experimenter's Workshop."

Armstrong, James
AFTER DARK: "San Francisco," city review.

Armstrong, Richard
TARGET MARKETING: "Columnist."

Arnold, Ed
EDITOR'S WORKSHOP: "Short Spots," design.

Arnold, Edmund C.
PUBLISHER'S AUXILIARY: "Page of the Week."

Arnold, Marjorie
RURAL RADIO: "The Party Line," fashion and cooking.

Arnold, Rus
TRAVEL & LEISURE: "Answers by Arnold," Q&A technical.

Arnold, William
MEDIA WEEK: "City Watch," London media.

Ashford, Rod
CAMERA & CAMCORDER MONTHLY: "Photo Clinic," Q&A.

Ashli, Joi
WESTERN PHOTOGRAPHER MAGAZINE: "Modeling Plus."

Astor, Nora
MOVIE WORLD: "Daytime Roundup," news of daytime soaps.

Atkins, Bob
QST: "The New Frontier."

Aubyn, John Saint
LEARNED PUBLISHING: "Copyright Corner," informative.

Avery, Bruce
VISIO: "Sound Advice," audio.

B

Bachman, Frank J.
SCHEMER, THE: "General Miscellany."

Badiday, Inday
SOSYAL! MAGAZINE: "Maskara," personality news and comment.

Bailey, Ralph
THEATRE MAGAZINE: "The Theatre Between Covers."

Baird, Thomas
DOCUMENTARY FILM NEWS: "Television," new feature beginning in Aug, 1938

Baker, Jim
TV GUIDE: "Sports View."

Baker, Rob
AFTER DARK: "Off Off and Away," theatre review.

Baker, Vic
DIRECT MARKETING: "Canadian Memo."

Baldwin, Richard L.
QST: "IARU News."

Ballai, Mike
STUDIO PHOTOGRAPHY: "Point Sources," techniques and technologies.

Balsly, L.D.
UNIVERSAL WEEKLY: "Kansas City Notes," exhibitor newsbriefs.

Balun, Charles
DEEP RED: "News Slashes," horror film newsbriefs.

Bangs, Bee
SILVER SCREEN: "Hollywood Earfuls," Hollywood gossip.

Barbers, Lynne
PRACTICAL PHOTOGRAPHY: "Photo Critique," 'Lynne Barbers personal photo improvement critique'

Barbour, Alan G.
FILMS IN REVIEW: "Video-Syncrasy."

Barbour, Mark
PRINT-EQUIP NEWS: "International Museum of Graphic Communication," museum currator.

Barkey, Jonathan
PHOTO/DESIGN: "Ideas and Images," fascinating showcase for imaginative photography,
PHOTO/DESIGN: "FYI Books."
PHOTO/DESIGN: "FYI Shows."

Barnako, Frank
VIDEO STORE: "Guidelines."

Barnett, Casey
AMERICAN PREMIERE: "Location Shooting: Who's Shooting Where."

Barnhorst, Donald E.
ENTERTAINMENT REVUE: "Eye on Film."

Baron, Ron
AFTER DARK: "Rock," review.

Barr, Bill
STV GUIDE: "The Canadian Scene."

Barrett, Rona
GOSSIP: "Rona's Bonus Scrapbook," 'Nostalgic photos from Rona's own album'
GOSSIP: "Dear Rona," 'What you have to say to our Ms. Rona!'
GOSSIP: "Rona's Would You Believe?," 'Unbelieveable tidbits from Rona!'
GOSSIP: "Rona Barrett's Gossip," 'Our Ms. Rona with the latest--and the best!'
MOTION PICTURE: "Young Hollywood," gossip.

Barron, Fred
TAKE ONE: "Letter From Switzerland."

Barry, Dave
COMIC RELIEF: "Dave Barry," humor.

Barter, Christie
STEREO REVIEW: "Record Makers," newsbrief.

Bartlett, Michele
QST: "Washington Mailbox," legal information.

Barton, Brenda
SCREEN INTERNATIONAL: "People," personality.

Bates, Brent
CMA NEWSLETTER: "Newspaper."

Battey, E. L.
QST: "Operating News," 'Conducted by the Communications Department'

Battison, John H.
LPTV REPORT, THE: "Technical Talks."

Baumann, Keith
DESKTOP COMMUNICATIONS: "From the Font."

Bautista, Mario E.
MOVIE FLASH: "Movie Review."

Bear, S. T.
WESTERN PHOTOGRAPHER MAGAZINE: "The Bear Facts," 'From the Editor's Desk' editorial.

Beaton, Welford
HOLLYWOOD SPECTATOR: "From the Editor's Easy Chair," large viewpoint.

Beaumont-Craggs, Ray
AMATEUR PHOTOGRAPHER: "Sound and Picture."

Beck, Jerry
GET ANIMATED! UPDATE.: "Notes From New York," animation news.

Beck, Marilyn
ONSAT: "Hollywood Scene."
ONSAT: "Backstage."
SPOTLIGHT CASTING MAGAZINE: "Marilyn Beck's Hollywood," personality.
TV GUIDE: "Grapevine."

Becker, Don
RADIO DIAL: "Our Daily Dozen."

Becker, Ed
PROFESSIONAL PHOTOGRAPHER, THE: "Professional Feedback."

Becker, Joyce
DAYTIME TV: "Soap Opera Festival."
SCREEN LIFE: "Have You Heard?," Hollywood star activities.

Beckerman, Howard
BACK STAGE: "Animation Spot."

FILMMAKERS FILM & VIDEO MONTHLY: "Animation Kit."

Beeman, Renee
EXHIBITORS TRADE REVIEW: "Live News of the West Coast," Hollywood trade news.

Behrend, Jack
INDUSTRIAL PHOTOGRAPHY: "Video Film Scene."

Bell, James
PC PUBLISHING AND PRESENTATIONS: "Budget DTP," desktop publishing.

Belton, John
FILMMAKERS FILM & VIDEO MONTHLY: "New Books," review.

Benecke, Robert
ST. LOUIS AND CANADIAN PHOTOGRAPHER: "Echoes From Europe," news from the continent,

Benham, Andy
HI-FI CHOICE: "Menu," editorial.

Benjamin, Michele
LEARNED PUBLISHING: "Book Reviews," edited.

Bennett, Dianne
GOSSIP: "Lowdown on the music scene'

Benser, Walther
LEICA PHOTOGRAPHY: "Marginal Notes," technical.

Bensinger, Charles
MOVING IMAGE: "Basics: All About Videotape."

Bereswill, Paul
MODERN PHOTOGRAPHY: "First Person."

Berger, Ivan
AUDIO: "Spectrum."
STEREO REVIEW: "Car Stereo."

Berger, Myron
CINEMA, VIDEO & CABLE MOVIE DIGEST: "Ask the Expert," video Q&A.

Berlin, Meredith
SOAP OPERA DIGEST: "Editor's Note," commentary.

Berman, Marc
VIDEO BUSINESS: "Power Broker," video store management.

Bermann, Sid
EXHIBITORS HERALD WORLD: "Sid Says About Songs," best selling sheet music and comment.

Bern, Frances
HIT PARADER: "Tin Pan Alleying," humor and commentary.

Bernhard, Lisa
US MAGAZINE: "Biz Buzz," entertainment news items.
US MAGAZINE: "Loose Talk," interesting quotes.

Bernsley, Joseph
ELECTRONICS WORLD: "I Want to Know," technical Q&A.

Bernstein, Gary
PETERSEN'S PHOTOGRAPHIC: "Pro Talk."

Bernstein, Sid
ADVERTISING AGE: "Con-Sid-erations."

Berstein, Herman
AUDIO: "Tape Guide," specific tape Q&A.

Best, Katharine
STAGE: "Seen in the Spotlight," 'A report on the derring-do in the mythical kingdom of Hollywood'

Betancourt, Hall
PROFESSIONAL PHOTOGRAPHER, THE: "Advertising Basics."

Bethune, John
PROFESSIONAL PHOTOGRAPHER, THE: "AV Perspectives."

Betker, Mike
COMIC INFORMER: "The Voided Snoid," 'Video.

Bevans, Marvin
MODERN SCREEN: "Daytime Dialings," news of soaps.

Bilbow, Marjorie
SCREEN INTERNATIONAL: "The New Films," reviewed.

Billue, Stan
TELEPROFESSIONAL: "Tips For Successful Selling."

Billyou, Alec
TOP SECRET: "Role Playing."

Biner, Tony
CELLULOID NIGHTMARE: "Editorial," 'Editor/Publisher Dude'

Birchall, Steve
HOME ENTERTAINMENT: "From Where You Sit."

Birnbaum, Hugh
CAMERA 35 INCORPORATING PHOTO WORLD: "Positives & Negatives."

Columnists

Bisset, John
RADIO WORLD: "Workbench," an excellent technical section for day-to-day engineering solutions,

Black, Peter
CONTRAST: "Editorial."

Black, Peter J.
SOAP OPERA STARS: "New York Notes."

Blackburn, Vonda H.
INTERNATIONAL PHOTOGRAPHER MAGAZINE: "Straight From the Editor," editorial.

Blackman, Victor
AMATEUR PHOTOGRAPHER: "Cameravaria," photographic potpourri.

Blair, Alexis
HOLLYWOOD MAGAZINE: "Diary of a D-Girl."

Blake, Larry
EQ: "Film & Video Sound," Visual Media.

Blane, Stan
MOVIE TV SECRETS: "Movie TV Secret Report," 'Hot Gossip - Top Secret - Right off the ticker - Uncensored - Confidential - Tip-Offs - Hush-Hush!'

Blessing, Rose
PUBLISHING & PRODUCTION EXECUTIVE: "Editorial."

Block, Lawrence
WRITER'S DIGEST: "Fiction."

Blumenthal, Eileen
THEATER: "Theater in New York."

Bocklage, Judy
IN-PLANT REPRODUCTIONS: "Editor's Note," editorial.

Bodart, Joni
BOOKTALKER, THE: "From the Editor," editorial.

Bodkins, Odds
ADVERTISING AGENCY: "The 8-pt Page."

Bonderoff, Jason
SOAP OPERA DIGEST: "New York Notebook," personality.

Bonner, Ian
TEEN DREAM: "Ask Ian," Q&A advice.

Bonzai, Mr.
MIX: "Lunching with Bonzai."

Boord, Kenneth R.
ELECTRONICS WORLD: "Short-Wave."

Borie, Marcia
MOVIE STARS: "Celebrity Talk," 'Inside info'

Bossin, Hye
CANADIAN FILM DIGEST: "On the Square," comment.

Bourn, Mary Kate
CD REVIEW: "Worth a Look," new equipment.

Bowers, Lynn
SCREENLAND PLUS TV-LAND: "What Hollywood Itself is Talking About!," 'The stars themselves enjoy the gossip as much as you do'

Boy, Bell
TELEPHONE NEWS, THE: "The Hang Up Page," humorous.

Boyd, Ann
NEW MOVIE MAGAZINE, THE: "First Aids to Beauty," 'Advice and rules for charm and attractiveness'

Boyden, Tom
OUTDOOR & TRAVEL PHOTOGRAPHY: "Outdoor Classroom."

Boye, Malcolm
REAL LIFE/DAYTIMERS: "Malcolm Boyes' Real Life Show Biz Column."

Boyes, E. Voltaire
SCHEMER, THE: "Reliable Formulas," how to make almost anything.

Boyes, Malcolm
CELEBRITY PLUS: "Spice," celebrity.

Bradford-Wilson, Perry
COMIC RELIEF: "Funny Stuff," editorial.

Brady, James
ADVERTISING AGE: "Brady."

Brady, Laurie
STAR: "Starscope," horoscope.

Brambert, Dave
COMPUTER PUBLISHING: "Software Corner."

Bransford, Kent S.
HI-FI HERETIC: "Editorial."
HI-FI HERETIC: "Introduction," commentary.

Brant, Neil
HOLLYWOOD FILMOGRAPH: "Camera Shots."

Breed, Gary A.
RF DESIGN: "Product Report," technology review.
RF DESIGN: "Editorial," commentary.

Breeden-Conrad, Carla
TV TECHNOLOGY: "Focus on Graphics."

Brent, Ronald C.
MAST: "From the Editor," editorial.

Breunig, Christopher
STEREOPHILE: "Building a Library."

Brewer, Bryan
CD REVIEW: "CD & Beyond."

Brice, Richard
HI-FI WORLD: "Recorded Message."

Bridges, Joseph
PD REPORT: "Editorial."

Briggs, Joe Bob
COMIC RELIEF: "Joe Bob Briggs," humor.

Bring, Bob
AMERICAN CINEMEDITOR: "Trim Bin," who is editing what listing,

Bringe, Paul
DIRECT MARKETING: "Upgrading Letter Copy," advice.

Brinkmann, Bob
PUBLISHER'S AUXILIARY: "NNA Washington Report."

Brisson, Dennis
ON!: "Newsbreaks," 'A look at industry trends, products and developments' compiled.

Brister, J. L.
SCHEMER, THE: "Agents Corner," manufacturing and promotion.

Brittain, David
CREATIVE CAMERA: "Talkback," editorial.

Britton, Bill
ONSAT: "Special Feeds Update," satellite guide.
ONSAT: "Notes & Comments," on upcoming weeks programming,
STV GUIDE: "The Feed Finders," news of satellite feeds.

Brochstein, Martin
ON!: "On! Shopping."

Brock, Luther
DIRECT MARKETING: "Marketing Viewpoint International."
DIRECT MARKETING: "Marketing Viewpoints," advice.

Brock, Richard
PRINT-EQUIP NEWS: "Desktop Publishing."

Brod, Donald F.
GRASSROOTS EDITOR: "Page Two," editorial commentary.

Brogan, Daniel
PERSONAL PUBLISHING: "Editor's Report."

Brooks, Richard
TELEVISION WEEK: "Viewpoint."

Brosnan, John
STARBURST: "It's Only a Movie," witty film commentary.

Bross, David
VIA SATELLITE: "Satellite Circuit," 'A round-up of firms making news in the satellite industry'

Brown, Andreas
POSTCARD COLLECTOR: "Rare and Unusual," unique postcards.
POSTCARD COLLECTOR: "Signs of the Times," postcard sampling.

Brown, Curtis F.
BIJOU: "Movies Then/Movies Now," fascinating dual look at movies past and present,
BIJOU: "Sparklers and Fizzlers," orchids and onions survey.

Brown, Les
TBI: "Perspective."

Brown, Peter
SHOOTING COMMERCIALS: "SC East," production news.

Brown, Sara
PUBLISHER'S AUXILIARY: "Managing Newspaper People."

Brownlee, Barry
DRAMA-LOGUE: "The Underground Astrologer."

Bruce, Robert R.
CABLE TV AND NEW MEDIA LAW & FINANCE: "F.C.C. Watch," commission developments.

Brueggeman, Peter
CD-ROM LIBRARIAN: "Optical Product Review."

Brush, Douglas
TELESPAN'S BUSINESSTV GUIDE: "The Brush Report."

Brush, Judith
TELESPAN'S BUSINESSTV GUIDE: "The Brush Report."

Brush, Stephanie
COMIC RELIEF: "Stephanie Brush," humor.

Bryant, John
SATELLITE TIMES: "What's Going On," news items and comment.

Bryce, Allan
MOVIE - THE VIDEO MAGAZINE: "Double Takes."
VIDEO WORLD: "Bryce is Right," fan question.

Bubbeco, Daniel
INSIDE HOLLYWOOD: "Star Words," crossword puzzle.

Buchman, Chris
FILMS IN REVIEW: "The Television Scene."

Buchwald, Mel
CONSUMER ELECTRONICS: "The Last Word," comment.

Buck, Rinker
ADWEEK'S MARKETING WEEK: "Editor's Note," editorial.

Buckner, Jo Ann
MOTION PICTURE: "My Star Twin," reader submissions.

Buckwalter, Len
ELECTRONICS ILLUSTRATED: "CB Corner."

Buffington, Perry
MGF: "MGF Quiz."

Bugniazet, George
JOURNAL: "Magazine Chat," editor's.

Bultman, Janis
MOVING IMAGE: "Making Money."

Burbage
GAMBIT: "Theatre Diary," news and happenings.

Burchell, Sam
AUDIO/VIDEO INTERIORS: "Designers," audio/video designer profile.

Bureau, William
GRAPHIC ARTS MONTHLY: "Paper."

Burger, Jeff
REP: RECORDING ENGINEERING PRODUCTION: "Understanding Computers."

Burgi, Michael
CHANNELS: "Database," communication industry facts and figures.

Burke, Clifford
PUBLISH!: "About Faces," type.

Burke, Hal
VIDEOMAKER: "Videocrafts."

Burke, James N.
PHOTOPRO: "Darkroom & Lab."

Burnham, Linda
HIGH PERFORMANCE: "Running Commentary."

Burns, Harry
HOLLYWOOD FILMOGRAPH: "Who's Who."

Burstein, Herman
AUDIO: "Tape Guide."

Bushnell, Nolan K.
VIDEO PROPHILES: "PRO Bono."

Butler, Trevor
HI-FI NEWS AND RECORD REVIEW: "Radio."

Buttram, Pat
RURAL RADIO: "Spring Whittlin's," humor.

C

Cadby, Corrine
PHOTO-ERA MAGAZINE: "London Letter," interesting British photo news.

Cadby, Will
PHOTO-ERA MAGAZINE: "London Letter," interesting British photo news.

Cagno, Joe Cal
TV PEOPLE AND PICTURES: "TV Tattler," 'Wherein your favorite TV stars confide in Joe on matters pertaining to love, marriage, career and other items of a highly personal nature'
TV WORLD: "Tele-Tales," television news and gossip.

Caldwell, Donna Y.
SHOWCASE WORLD: "Movie Review."
SHOWCASE WORLD: "Comedy: Laughter in the Rafters."

Caldwell, Louis G.
JOURNAL OF RADIO LAW: "International Radio Chronicle."

Callahan, Mary
MOTION PICTURE: "Bulletin Board," marriages, births, splits and deaths.

Callery, Michael
PUBLISH!: "Showtime," presentations.

Callum, Myles
TV GUIDE: "Video Cassette Report."

Cameron, Franklin
PETERSEN'S PHOTOGRAPHIC: "Viewfinder," 'Photo news & events'

Canale, Larry
CD REVIEW: "Capsule Critiques," music review.
CD REVIEW: "The First Word," editorial.

Canby, Edward Tatnall
AUDIO: "Audio Etc."
AUDIO: "Audio, Etc.."

Caples, John
DIRECT MARKETING: "Direct Response," advice.

Carlson, James
MOVIE STARS: "In Tune With," 'Pop scene'

Carnemolla, John
AUSTRALIAN PHOTOGRAPHY: "Talkabout."

Carr, Joseph J.
POPULAR ELECTRONICS: "Ham Radio."

Carroll, Carroll
VARIETY: "And Now a Word From...," human interest.

Carson, Johnny
TV RADIO MIRROR: "Johnny Carson's Corner."

Carson, Saul
TV SCREEN: "Report to the Listeners."

Carter, Gordon
RADIO GUIDE: "Studio Site."

Carter, Janis
MOVIE TEEN: "Fashion Tips for Your Figure Problems."

Cartwright, Dorothea Hawley
TALKING SCREEN: "Just Your Style--and Hollywood's."

Cartwright, Tim
ELECTRONICS ILLUSTRATED: "Good Reading," 'Books, pamphlets, booklets, flyers, bulletins and application notes'

Caruba, David
TOP SECRET: "From the Green Dome," editorial.

Cash, Laurel
REP: RECORDING ENGINEERING PRODUCTION: "The Cutting Edge," new equipment review.

Cash-Jones, Laurel
REP: RECORDING ENGINEERING PRODUCTION: "First Look," new equipment.

Castiglione, Dennis J.
FLASH: "Printing Forum."

Catalano, Debbie
CASTING NEWS: "Local Pop Music," review.

Caufield, James M.
PROFESSIONAL PHOTOGRAPHER, THE: "A Commercial Man's Scrap Book," 'The past, present and future of photography'

Cauthen, Linda
SH-BOOM: "Country Corner!," 'Country Corner is a new monthly feature covering traditional country music today',

Cavuoto, James
COMPUTER PUBLISHING: "The Last Desktop," back cover commentary.

Cawley, John
GET ANIMATED! UPDATE.: "Checking," commentary.

Cecile
ROXY THEATRE WEEKLY REVIEW: "Around New York with Cecile," 'Follow her suggestions about these reliable shops and places of interest' shopping.

Centing, Richard R.
SMALL PRESS: "Continuations."

Chalmers, Robin
CD REVIEW: "Current Samples," news items.

Chambers, Frank V.
CAMERA, THE: "Just Between You and Me," editorial.

Chapman, Robert
DARKROOM AND CREATIVE CAMERA TECHNIQUES: "Photochemistry Question and Answer," technical.

Charles, Chris
STARBURST: "Book World," review.

Charlton, Janet
STAR: "Star People," Hollywood.

Chase, Scott
VIA SATELLITE: "Editor's Note," editorial.

Chatterton, John
CASTING NEWS: "Curtain Calls."

Chernofsky, Jacob L.
AB BOOKMAN'S WEEKLY: "Editor's Corner."

Cheung, William
PRACTICAL PHOTOGRAPHY: "Any Questions?," Q&A photography.

Chiappetta, Jerry
OUTDOOR & TRAVEL PHOTOGRAPHY: "Outdoor Videographer."

Chitwood, J. Martin
VIDEO SOFTWARE MAGAZINE: "After the Blockbusters," lesser-known film review.

Chiu, Tony
V: "New Movies," 'In your video stores now' review.

Chiusano, Michael
PHOTOPRO: "Studio Casebook."

Christensen, Howard
BROADCAST + TECHNOLOGY: "Howard Christensen."

Christy, George
HOLLYWOOD REPORTER: "The Great Life."

Ciporen, Fred
PUBLISHER'S WEEKLY: "The Open Letter," editorial.

Cirella, Anthony
MOVIE TV SECRETS: "Advice to the Stars."

Clark, Mack
REP: RECORDING ENGINEERING PRODUCTION: "Five Questions," interesting technical.

Clark, Mrs. Fitzgibbon-
ST. LOUIS AND CANADIAN PHOTOGRAPHER: "Editorial Chit-Chat," editorial.

Clark, Willard
TRAVEL & LEISURE: "Lens Lines."

Clarke, Coleene
BILLBOARD: "Nashville Scene," news.

Clavering, Basil
DOCUMENTARY FILM NEWS: "Movie Theater Management," problems and opportunities of the exhibitor, a.

Clee, Nicholas
BRITISH BOOK NEWS: "Notes and News from the Book Trade in Britain," current events.

Clifford, Tony
FILM FAN MONTHLY: "Odds and Ends."

Clift, W.
QST: "Happenings," current issues.

Cloud, Barbara
JOURNALISM HISTORY: "Book Reviews."

Clute, Fayette J.
ST. LOUIS AND CANADIAN PHOTOGRAPHER: "With the Amateur," advice and instruction.

Cody, Andrea D.
IN-PLANT PRINTER & ELECTRONIC PUBLISHER: "Editor's Note," editorial.

Coelln, Ott
COMPUTER PICTURES: "Camera Eye," comment.

Cohen, Abraham
MEDIA & METHODS: "A-V Answer Man."

Cohen, Henry B.
V: "Video Equipment."

Cohen, Michael
CASTING NEWS: "Local Pop Music," review.

Cohen, Sharon
STUDIO PHOTOGRAPHY: "Dollars and Sense."

Colbert, Claudette
PHOTOPLAY: "What Should I Do?," 'Your problems answered'

Colbert, Sean
UNIQUE: "Review: Music."

Cole, George
PRACTICAL PHOTOGRAPHY: "Video Update."

Cole, Natasha
VIDEOMAKER: "Quick Focus," newsbriefs.

Coleman, A. D.
CAMERA 35 INCORPORATING PHOTO WORLD: "Light Readings."

Coleman, Lisa
MONDAY MORNING REPLAY: "One-On-One," programmer interview.

Collins, Monica
TV GUIDE: "The Collins Report," programming.

Collins, Nancy
AMAZING HEROES: "Video Views."

Colucci, D. M.
CASTING NEWS: "Curtain Calls."

Compton, Ted
BACK STAGE: "On the Un-Coast."

Connell, Will
TRAVEL & LEISURE: "Technique Technicalities," Q&A.

Connolly, Mike
SCREEN STORIES: "Mike Connolly's Exclusive Report From Hollywood."

Connolly, William
SPAGHETTI CINEMA: "Hello," editorial.

Cook, Brooks
TOP SECRET: "Poetry Behind the Typewriter."

Cook, Page
FILMS IN REVIEW: "The Sound Track."

Cook, William A.
JOURNAL OF ADVERTISING RESEARCH: "Editorial."

Cooper, Don
PERFORMER, THE: "Dear Coop," humorous personality.

Copeland, James
ROSTRUM: "The Bookshelf," review.

Copeland, Michael
VENTURA PROFESSIONAL!: "INS Special Item," newsbrief INSerts.

Coraza, Tonee
SOSYAL! MAGAZINE: "Prime Time," television programming review and commentary.

Corbell, Tony L.
PHOTOPRO: "Studio Casebook."

Corrigan, Timothy R.
COMICS BUYER'S GUIDE: "Fanzine Guide."

Costello, Marjorie
VIDEO PROPHILES: "The Five-Minute Videographer."
VIDEO PROPHILES: "From the PROphiles," editorial/publisher.

Court, Paul
BROADCAST + TECHNOLOGY: "Theatre Technology," CITT news of the Canadian Institute for Theatre Technology,

Courtland, Michael
STARBURST: "Things to Come," 'The latest news of fantasy in both film and television'

Cowan, Bob
TAKE ONE: "Notes From the New Cinema."

Cowan, S. R.
ELECTRONIC SERVICING & TECHNOLOGY: "Editorial."

Coyne, Patrick
COMMUNICATION ARTS: "Editor's Column," editorial comment.

Crabbe, John
HI-FI NEWS AND RECORD REVIEW: "Sidelines."

Craig, Robert T.
COMMUNICATION THEORY: "Editorial."

Cramer, Konrad
CAMERA, THE: "Pictorial Print Analysis."

Crandell, Jack
MOVIE TV SECRETS: "Editor's Column."

Crawley, John
ANIMATOR: "The USA Scene," animation news from the States.

Crawley, Tony
STARBURST: "Things to Come," 'All the news that's fit to print...and a few items that aren't, courtesy of our globetrotting newshound Tony Crawley'

Crist, C. L.
MEDIA SIGHT: "Firsts," historical items and cartoon.

Croix, Stephen St.
MIX: "The Fast Lane."

Croughton, G. Hanmer
ST. LOUIS AND CANADIAN PHOTOGRAPHER: "Criticism of Illustrations," critique of reader-submitted photographs,

Cruse, Howard
COMICS SCENE: "Loose Cruse."

Cullinan, Fiona
FILM REVIEW: "Who's Dating Who," 'All this month's celebrity clinching, partner pinching and relationship lynching'

Culshaw, John
HIGH FIDELITY: "Culshaw at Large."

Cunningham, Elizabeth
SHOOTING COMMERCIALS: "SC Midwest," production news.

Cunningham, Richard P.
QUILL, THE: "The Ombudsmen."

Cushman, George
HOME MOVIES: "Title Troubles," Q&A technical.

D

D'Amato, Toni
ONSAT: "Ask Me About TV," Q&A.

Dale, Steve
VIDEO TIMES: "Celebrity Corner," wonderful star interviews.

Daly, Marsha
PHOTO SCREEN: "From the Editor."

Daly, Phil M.
FILM TV DAILY: "Along the Rialto."

Dare, Michael
BILLBOARD: "2nd Features," 'This weekly column is provided as a guide through the wilderness of unfamiliar feature video titles'

Dargan, Bob
ELECTRONIC SERVICING & TECHNOLOGY: "Answer Man," technical fixit.

Darrell, R.D.
HIGH FIDELITY: "The Tape Deck."

David, Peter
COMICS BUYER'S GUIDE: "But I Digress," commentary.

Davies, Jim
DIRECTION: "Adwatch."

Davis, B. G.
POPULAR PHOTOGRAPHY: "Candid Shots," editorial newsitem.

Columnists

Davis, James M.
EXHIBITORS TRADE REVIEW: "Illustrated Screen Reports," edited.

Davis, Jim
KORKIS AND CAWLEY'S CARTOON QUARTERLY: "Cartoon Quarterly's Question and Answer," animation Q&A.

Davis, Ted
BROADCASTER: "Editorial."

Davy, Daryl
FILM FAN MONTHLY: "Davy on 16 MM."

Davy, Kate
THEATRE JOURNAL: "Theatre Review," edited.

Dawson, E.T.
EXHIBITORS HERALD WORLD: "Up and Down the Alley," music news and personalities.

Dawson, Jan
FILM COMMENT: "Journals--Australia."

DeLeon, Lotlot
MOVIE FLASH: "Lotlot and Friends," personality.

DeLuca, Louis
RETROFOCUS: "Still Life."

DeMaw, Doug
MONITORING TIMES: "DeMaw's Workbench," engineering.

DeMott, John
TELEVISER: "Effectivisions," commentary.

Dean, David
PC PUBLISHING AND PRESENTATIONS: "Hands-On Fonts."

Dean, Peter
AMATEUR PHOTOGRAPHER: "Make Mine Movies," 'A series of help and advice for the non-expert film-maker'

Decker, Dwight R.
AMAZING HEROES: "Doc's Bookshelf."

Demetriou, Andy
WHAT SATELLITE: "Dish Doctor," Q&A.

Denis, Paul
TV PEOPLE AND PICTURES: "Studio Secrets," 'For the absolute inside, the hush-hush gossip in the lives and loves of TV personalities you absolutely positively can't beat Paul's prize patter'
TV WORLD: "Channel Gossip."

Denitch, Branislav
PROFESSIONAL PHOTOGRAPHER, THE: "Professional Stereo," stereo photography.

Denver, Joel
R & R: "CHR," contemporary hit radio format.

Desmarais, Norman
CD-ROM LIBRARIAN: "Supplement to CD-ROMS in Print," update compiled.
CD-ROM LIBRARIAN: "Editorial."

Deusen, Richard Van
VIDEO MANAGEMENT: "Corporate Perspectives."

Deutsch, Doug
SHOWCASE WORLD: "Record Reviews."
SHOWCASE WORLD: "T.V. News & Views."
SHOWCASE WORLD: "The Rap Corner."

Deva, Jeannie
CASTING NEWS: "The Voice Doctor."

Dewey, Lucia
DRAMA-LOGUE: "Dance Spectrum."
DRAMA-LOGUE: "Performance Art."

DiLauro, Janet
DAYTIME TV: "Inside Hollywood," 'Daytime TV's West coast woman in the know!'

Diallist
ELECTRONICS WORLD + WIRELESS WORLD: "Random Radiations."

Diana
SUPER TEEN: "Super Teen Stuff!," 'The juiciest juice from East to West'

Dick, Brad
VIDEO SYSTEMS: "Management."

Dickson, Frank A.
WRITER'S DIGEST: "An Idea a Day," fascinating day-by-day listing of article possibilities,

Dill, Barbara
PUBLISHER'S AUXILIARY: "Libel Clinic."

Discoe, Gayle
ONSAT: "TV Circles," word list puzzle.

Dizard, Wilson
COMPUTER PUBLISHING: "Washington Update."

Doan, Michael
ORBIT VIDEO: "Editor's Page," editorial commentary.

Dobbs, G. Michael
ANIMATO!: "Koko Komments."

Dobrin, Ron
AFTER DARK: "Vienna," city review.

Dolliver, M. R.
WESTERN PHOTOGRAPHER MAGAZINE: "The Photo Bug."

Donovan, Ronald John
WRITER'S DIGEST: "The Electronic Writer."

Doran, Jean
CASTING CALL: "Hollywood Reporting."

Dorr, John
CQ: "Contest Calendar," 'News/views of on-the-air competition'

Dorr, Kevin
CABLE MARKETING: "Sales Management."

Dorsey, Lynne
PHOTOPLAY: "Photoplay in Focus," editorial.

Douglas, Rita
ROXY THEATRE WEEKLY REVIEW: "Adventuring in Hollywood," motion picture news.

Douglis, Phil
NEWS PHOTOGRAPHER: "The Photojournalist: Photography as Communication."

Down, Cathy
MONDAY MORNING REPLAY: "Foreplay," 'What's up 'n' coming, Foreplay takes a look at new releases, with fresh, unique and informative profiles',

Downes, Bruce
POPULAR PHOTOGRAPHY: "Candid Shots," editorial newsitem.

Doyle, Billy H.
FILMS IN REVIEW: "Obituaries."

Doyle, Claire
TELEVISION BROADCAST: "Claire Doyle," graphics trends and issues.

Drabick, Matt
AV VIDEO: "Amiga Niches."

Droesch, Paul
TV GUIDE: "This Week," upcoming program.

Dryhurst, Edward
GREATER AMUSEMENTS: "London Jottings," news.

Dubrow, Anton
NIGHTTIME TV: "Zooming In," 'TV Superstar Gossip'

Dudley, Keith
LITTLE SHOPPE OF HORRORS: "The Keith Dudley Report," 'And other tidbits of Hammer lore'

Dudley, Uncle
JOURNALIST, THE: "With the Boys and Girls."

Duffy, Ben
ADVERTISER MAGAZINE, THE: "AD-Lib."

Duffy, Linda
SHOOTING COMMERCIALS: "SC Southeast," production news.

Duffy, Thom
BILLBOARD: "The Beat."

Dukes, Ashley
THEATRE ARTS: "The English Scene," British theatre.

Dunn, Bernice
QST: "Hamfest Calendar."

Durbano, Art
TV GUIDE: "This Week's Movies," upcoming on broadcast and cable channels.

Durniak, John
PHOTOPRO: "Controversy."
PHOTOPRO: "Photojournalism."

Dutter, Barry
FOUR COLOR: "On the Racks," new comic product reviewes.

Dyk, Timothy
COMMUNICATIONS LAWYER: "Courtside," recent communication legal decisions,

E

Earl, Linda
CINEMA/CANADA: "Shoot Alberta."

Eckhardt, Robert C.
PUBLISH!: "Q&A," 'Practical hints, tips, and advice for desktop publishers'

Edelmann, Eric O.
MAGAZINE DESIGN & PRODUCTION: "Paper Trends."

Edelson, Michael
CAMERA 35: "Critic's Corner."

Edison, Bob
PLAYBILL: "After Theatre," post-show places to dine,

Edmonds, Jeff
VIDEO CHOICE: "The Video Enthusiast," commentary.

Edmondson, Brad
AMERICAN DEMOGRAPHICS: "Editor's Note."

Edmonston, David B.
CAMERA, THE: "Print Analysis Department."

Edmonston, Jack
MAGAZINEWEEK: "Jack Edmonston on Magazine Marketing," advertisement critique.

Edwardes, Jane
20/20: "Theatre," review.

Edwards, Norma
CAMERA & DARKROOM PHOTOGRAPHY: "Grab Shots."

Edwards, R. R.
NATIONAL EXHIBITOR, THE: "Music and Musicians."

Edwards, Richard A.
NATIONAL ENQUIRER: "Best Food Buys," monthly guide.

Eisen, Jay
LENS MAGAZINE: "Time & Temp," 'A column on home darkroom'

Elder, Jim
CAMERA 35: "Tips from a Pro."
CAMERA 35 INCORPORATING PHOTO WORLD: "The 40th Frame."
PHOTOPRO: "40th Frame."

Ellenthal, Ira
INSIDE MEDIA: "Ellenthal."

Elliott, Doris
SHOOTING COMMERCIALS: "SC Music."

Ellis, Julie
BLACK STARS: "Let's Talk--Music."

Ellis, Marc
POPULAR ELECTRONICS: "Antique Radio."

Ellis, Michael
BILLBOARD: "Hot 100 Singles Spotlight."

Elwell, Jeffery
SOUTHERN THEATRE: "Playwriting Callboard," theatrical opportunities compiled.

Elwell, Thomas H.
LEICA PHOTOGRAPHY: "Editorial."

Endrijonas, Janet
VISIO: "The Home Office."

Engh, Rohn
WESTERN PHOTOGRAPHER MAGAZINE: "Marketing Your Photographs."

England, George Allan
STORY WORLD AND PHOTODRAMATIST, THE: "Facts about Fiction," instructional.

English, Howard
BROADCAST + TECHNOLOGY: "Discover."

BROADCAST + TECHNOLOGY: "Programming."

Ephland, John
DOWN BEAT: "On the Beat."

Ericksenn, Lief
CAMERA 35: "The Third Eye."
CAMERA 35 INCORPORATING PHOTO WORLD: "The Third Eye."
CAMERA 35 INCORPORATING PHOTO WORLD: "Editor's Notebook," editorial.

Erickson, Wendy
ILFORD PHOTO INSTRUCTOR NEWSLETTER: "From the Editor," editorial.

Esse, Christopher
HIGH FIDELITY: "The Autophile," equipment review.

Esse, Christopher J.
AUDIO/VIDEO INTERIORS: "Editorial Perspective."

Essex, David
ON!: "On! Computers."

Evans, Lindley
ABC WEEKLY: "Interval."

Evans, Terri Anderson & Jim
PRO SOUND NEWS: "London Calling," British sound news.

Everson, William K.
FILMS IN REVIEW: "Book Reviews."

Ewald, Steven
QST: "Section News."

Exter, Thomas
AMERICAN DEMOGRAPHICS: "Demographic Forecasts."
AMERICAN DEMOGRAPHICS: "Spending Money."

F

Facter, Sue
SOAP OPERA DIGEST: "New York News."

Fagan, Gregory
ON!: "On the Screen," review.

Fagan, Gregory P.
VIDEO PROPHILES: "Screening PROphiles."

Fagel, Barnet C.
CAR AUDIO AND ELECTRONICS: "Street Security."

Columnists

Fairbridge, Jerry
BROADCAST + TECHNOLOGY: "Jerry Fairbridge."

Fairman, Leroy
ADVERTISING & SELLING: "Clay Feet," current ad critiques.

Farber, Paul
TRAVEL & LEISURE: "Foto Facts."

Farber, Stephen
MOVIELINE: "Premieres."

Farrell, Richard
TV TECHNOLOGY: "Industry Roundup," Buyers Guide.

Fashion, Hy
CASTING CALL: "Wardrobe."

Fayre, Dave
BAND LEADERS: "Waxing Wise," musical commentary.

Fee, Debi
FRESH!: "Hollywood Now," news and information.

Feld, Bruce
DRAMA-LOGUE: "Theatre Beat."

Felder, Raoul Lionel
FAME: "Love and the Law."

Felker, Lex
RADIO WORLD: "Felker's Forum," radio regulation.

Ferguson, Ken
FILM MONTHLY: "Scene & Heard," film news.

Field, Eunice
TV RADIO MIRROR: "What's New From Coast to Coast," gossip.

Fields, Howard
TELEVISION BROADCAST: "Howard Fields," trends and regulation.

Filichia, Peter
THEATERWEEK: "Stagestruck," theatrical commentary.

Findlay, Bob
BROADCAST + TECHNOLOGY: "CCBE Newsletter," news of the Central Canada Association of Broadcast Engineers.

Finn, Will
KORKIS AND CAWLEY'S CARTOON QUARTERLY: "Drawing the Line."

Finnigan, Joseph
EMMY: "Finnigan's File."

Flott, Steve
STORYBOARD / THE ART OF LAUGHTER: "The Last Word," publisher commentary.

Fisher, George
TV RADIO MIRROR: "Hollywood Radio Whispers," gossip.

Fisher, Joe
EXHIBITORS HERALD WORLD: "Chicago Personalities," Chicago exhibition.

Fishman, Allen
PHOTOGRAPHIC PROCESSING: "Bottom Line."

Fitch, Richard D.
RADIO-ELECTRONICS: "Antique Radio."

Fitzgibbon, J. H.
ST. LOUIS AND CANADIAN PHOTOGRAPHER: "Editorial Chit-Chat," editorial.

Fitzmartin, J.M.
TV DAY STARS: "Starscope."

Fleischmann, Mark
AUDIO/VIDEO INTERIORS: "Home Theater."

Fleming, Michael
VARIETY: "Variety Buzz," news, rumors and rumblings.

Fletcher, Peter
ELECTRONICS: "Letter From London."

Flick, Larry
BILLBOARD: "Dance Trax."

Flores, LarriAnn
BLACK RADIO EXCLUSIVE: "Rappin' It Up," rap records.
BLACK RADIO EXCLUSIVE: "On Stage," black artists in live performance.

Forshaw, Barry
STARBURST: "Video File."

Forsyth, Kate
SOAP OPERA DIGEST: "Behind the Scene," 'we give you backstage accounts of how soaps' most intriguing scenes come to life'

Fox, Barry
BROADCAST SYSTEMS INTERNATIONAL: "The Barry Fox Column."
HI-FI CHOICE: "21st Century Fox."
HI-FI NEWS AND RECORD REVIEW: "Technology."
STUDIO SOUND AND BROADCAST ENGINEERING: "Business."
WHAT SATELLITE: "Viewpoint," commentary.
WHAT VIDEO: "Britain," video comment and news.

Fox, David
STUDIO PHOTOGRAPHY: "Videography."

Fox, Douglas
EXHIBITORS HERALD WORLD: "What's in a Name," marvelous personal.

Fox, Tom
EDUCATIONAL MEDIA INTERNATIONAL: "Editorial."

France, Van Arsdale
STORYBOARD / THE ART OF LAUGHTER: "California Dreamin'."

French, Ken
AVC: "Audio."

French, Wilfred
PHOTO-ERA MAGAZINE: "On the Groundglass."

Freney, Byron
MAGAZINEWEEK: "Editor's Notebook."

Freudenberger, Herbert J.
FAME: "Surviving Success."

Friedman, Dick
PANORAMA: "Surveys and Studies."

Friedman, Favius
TV SCREEN: "Hollywood on the Air."

Friedman, Steve
HOME VIEWER: "Ask Mr. Movie," reader Q&A.

Fries, Laura M.
ORBIT VIDEO: "Tape Talk," review of new releases.

Frost, Lee
PHOTO ANSWERS: "Photo Clinic."
PHOTO ANSWERS: "Photo Ideas," 'A scintillating selection of sumptuous snaps to set your shutters sizzling,

Frye, John
ELECTRONICS WORLD: "Antennas and Grounds."

Frye, John T.
ELECTRONICS WORLD: "Mac's Service Shop," technical.

Fulford, Pat
WRITER'S DIGEST: "Cartoonist Cues."

Fuller, Elmer R.
RADIO-ELECTRONICS: "World-Wide Station List," geographic listing.

Fulton, Eileen
REAL LIFE/DAYTIMERS: "No Soap."

G

Gaffney, John
VIDEO BUSINESS: "Power Broker," video store management.

Gale, Heather
NATIONAL EXAMINER: "This Wacky World," the world in pictures edited.

Galella, Ron
MODERN SCREEN: "Ron Galella Catches the Stars Off-Guard," Hollywood photographer candid shots.

Gallo, Ray
GREATER AMUSEMENTS: "Trade Tidbits," newsbriefs.

Galluzzo, Tony
MODERN PHOTOGRAPHY: "Video Journal."

Gans, Robert J.
PRINT-EQUIP NEWS: "Ink Stains."

Gardner, Lyn
PLAYS INTERNATIONAL: "Fringe," other theatre offerings and commentary.

Garfield, Bob
ADVERTISING AGE: "Garfield," comment.

Garner, Kenneth
GRAPHIC ARTS MONTHLY: "Selling."

Garner, Lou
COMPUTERS & ELECTRONICS: "Solid State," technical.

Gartner, Michael
ADVERTISING AGE: "Words."

Gatski, John
RADIO WORLD: "Cue and Review," technical.

Gatti, Art
NIGHTTIME TV: "Astrology Goes to Hollywood to Find Your Perfect Mate Among the Stars."

Gauguin, Lorraine
SOUND STAGE: "Sound Stage on Stage."

Gavin, Robert
CAMPAIGN: "PR Affairs."

Gayer, Dixon
BAND LEADERS: "Behind the Midwest Baton," 'News of the band world out Chicago way',

Geerdes, Clay
COMICS FANDOM EXAMINER: "Comix Wavola."

Geller-Shinn, Karen
PETERSEN'S PHOTOGRAPHIC: "Tools of the Trade."

George, George L.
AMERICAN CINEMATOGRAPHER: "The Bookshelf," book review.
BACK STAGE: "Book News."
CINEMA/CANADA: "Bookshelf," review.
TAKE ONE: "Books on Film: A Checklist."

Gerald, Bruce
HIT PARADER: "Playback," new recordings,

Gerke, Robert H.
SCHEMER, THE: "Business Starters."

Gernsback, Hugo
ELECTRONICS WORLD: "The DX Listener," editorial.
RADIO-ELECTRONICS: "Editorial."

Gerson, Bob
CONSUMER ELECTRONICS: "Fast Forward," comment.

Gerson, Robert
VIDEO BUSINESS: "The Scoop," commentary.

Giancola, Chris
CAR STEREO REVIEW: "Car Tunes," Music review.

Gibbons, Duane
PHOTOGRAPHIC PROCESSING: "In the Observation Post."

Gibson, Joan
QST: "YL News and Views."

Gibson, Martin L. 'Red'
CMA NEWSLETTER: "Black and White and Red All Over."

Giebelhausen, J.
PHOTO TECHNIQUE INTERNATIONAL: "Notes From the Editor."

Gill, Peter
NEW CAPTAIN GEORGE'S WHIZZBANG, THE: "SF Readout," science fiction review.

Gillespie, Noel
AFTER DARK: "D.C.," city review.

Gillick, Karen
DIRECT MARKETING: "Career Directions."

Gillman, Bob
AV VIDEO: "TGA SIG," computer.

Giovanelli, Joseph
AUDIO: "Audioclinic."
AUDIO: "Audio Clinic," technical Q&A.

Given, David M.
ENTERTAINMENT AND SPORTS LAWYER, THE: "Editor's Column."

Gleeson, W. L.
RADIO FAN-FARE: "Western Radio News and Comment."

Gleiberman, Owen
ENTERTAINMENT WEEKLY: "Movie Reviews."

Glick, Maggie
TV RADIO TALK: "Dateline: Daytime," 'It's what's happening'

Glickman, Elyse
UNIQUE: "Rock Record."

Gold, Alvin
STEREOPHILE: "Pure Gold."

Gold, Richard
MEDIA WEEK: "Masterwind Up," media observations and comment.

Goldberg, Hal
WRITER'S DIGEST: "Just Paging."

Goldberg, Paul
ELECTRONIC SERVICING & TECHNOLOGY: "The Work Bench."

Goldfind, Norman
BIJOU: "Publisher's Page," editorial.

Goldner, Diane
FAME: "FAME Says It All About Society."

Goldsmith, Dr. Alfred N.
TELEVISION: "One Man's Reflections."

Goldstein, Howard
AV VIDEO: "Under the Covers," computer graphics.

Goldstein, Seth
CONSUMER ELECTRONICS: "Outtakes," comment.
PANORAMA: "Cable and Pay-TV."
VIDEO BUSINESS: "Offscreen," commentary.

Gomez, Richard
MOVIE FLASH: "It's Me, Richard," personality.

Goodfriend, James
STEREO REVIEW: "Going on Record."

Goodman, Dean
DRAMA-LOGUE: "San Francisco Scene."

Gordon, Barbara
COMMUNICATION ARTS: "Free-Lance."

Gordon, Dawn
HOME ENTERTAINMENT: "Sense and Nonsense," computers and the home.

Gore, Christian
FILM THREAT: "Editorial."

Gottlieb, Edward D.
MGF: "Mister Manners."

Gould, Morton
ASCAP IN ACTION: "President's Page," editorial.

Graham, Lee
HOLLYWOOD STUDIO MAGAZINE: "Man About Town."

Columnists

Graham, Sheilah
SILVER SCREEN: "Stardust," 'Candid interviews with the stars'

Grant, Evan
SCREENLAND PLUS TV-LAND: "Hollywood Hot Line."

Grant, Hank
HOLLYWOOD REPORTER: "Off the Cuff."

Grantham, Bill
TBI: "Perspective."

Gray, Evelyn
NEW MOVIE MAGAZINE, THE: "How Hollywood Entertains."

Green, Hugh
ADVANCED IMAGING: "What's in Store."

Green, Ted
BACK STAGE: "Main Street."

Green, Wayne
CD REVIEW: "The Last Word," editorial.
ELECTRONICS ILLUSTRATED: "The Ham Shack."

Greenberger, Robert
COMICS SCENE: "Word Balloons," editorial.

Greene, Clarke
QST: "How's DX?."

Gregory, Dr. Grace
TV RADIO MIRROR: "Frame for Beauty," hints.

Gregory, John R.
TRAVEL & LEISURE: "Movie Q's and A's," Q&A moviemaking.

Gregory, Leigh
TV PICTURE LIFE: "Horoscope For the Stars and For You."

Gregory, Roy
HI-FI WORLD: "R. G. Bargy."

Grein, Paul
BILLBOARD: "Chart Beat."

Grid, Free
ELECTRONICS WORLD + WIRELESS WORLD: "Unbiased," personality.

Griffin, George
GRAPHIC ARTS MONTHLY: "Hows Your Advertising?."

Griffin, William J.
ELECTRONICS WORLD: "New Developments in Radio Apparatus."

Gritten, David
ORBIT VIDEO: "Children's Corner," review.

Grove, Bob
MONITORING TIMES: "Ask Bob," Reader Q&A.
MONITORING TIMES: "Scanner Equipment," review.

Grove, Martin
HOLLYWOOD REPORTER: "Hollywood Report."

Grumman, Bob
FACTSHEET FIVE: "Experioddica."

Gubernat, Susan
PUBLISH!: "Keeping Tabs," editorial.

Guelis, Andrea
SCREEN LIFE: "Meet Your Editor."

Guider, John W.
JOURNAL OF RADIO LAW: "Radio Cases in the United States."
JOURNAL OF RADIO LAW: "Radio Decisions in the United States."

Gushman, Patrick J.
MSO'S CABLE MARKETING: "Random Notes," commentary.

Gustafson, Mike L.
STV GUIDE: "And Now a Few Words About...," 'Editorial comment.

Gutierrez, Mhalou
SOSYAL! MAGAZINE: "Getting to Know You," penpal listing.

Gutman, Barry
VIDEO INSIDER: "Video Music."

Gwynn, Edith
FILMLAND: "Hollywood Secrets," 'Here's the inside on all the gossip'

H

Hack, Richard
HOLLYWOOD REPORTER: "TeleVisions."

Hacker, I. M.
HOLLYWOOD MAGAZINE: "Hollywood High Tech."

Hagen, Jerry
CQ: "DX," news of international radio amateurs,

Hager, Hal
FORECAST: "What's New," commentary.

Haikin, Danny
HI-FI WORLD: "Desparate Dan."

Halbersberg, Elianne
TEEN DREAM: "Rock Around the Clock," 'Where you can rock, rock, rock to the latest music biz talk, talk talk!'

Haley, Allan
STEP-BY-STEP GRAPHICS: "ABCs of Type."

Hall, John
HOLLYWOOD FILMOGRAPH: "The Moving Movie Throng."

Hall, Tom
CABLE TELEVISION ENGINEERING: "Random Reflections," news item.

Hallikainen, Harold
RADIO WORLD: "Insight on Rules," application of Federal Communication Commission rulings,

Hamlin, Fred
ELECTRONICS WORLD: "Spot Radio News," 'Presenting latest information on the radio industry'

Handy, F. E.
QST: "Operating News," 'Conducted by the Communications Department'

Hansford, M. M.
DRAMATIC MIRROR, THE: "Broadway Picture Programs and Music," very unique and extensive information on music and programs accompanying motion pictures,

Hanson, J. J.
FOLIO:: "Hanson on Magazines."

Hardman, Christin
VIDEO PROPHILES: "Editing Suite."

Hare, Spencer
GREATER AMUSEMENTS: "Here's What They Do."

Harkness, Norris
TRAVEL & LEISURE: "Tomorrow's Photographers," youth.

Harkness, Norris W.
CAMERA, THE: "Diminutive Camera Technique and Practice," commentary and technique.

Harlan, Steve
EQ: "In the Pocket," Down to Business.

Harnett, Joel
MARKETING COMMUNICATIONS: "Chairman's Corner," commentary.

Harris, Bob
BACK STAGE: "The Reel West."
COMPUTER PICTURES: "Offscreen," production profile.

Harris, Chod
CQ: "DX," 'News of communication around the world'

Harris, Joan
TARGET MARKETING: "On Creative."

Harris, Peter
NEW CAPTAIN GEORGE'S WHIZZBANG, THE: "Comment."

Harris, Wayne
CAR STEREO REVIEW: "Wire Service," electronic wiring.

Hart, Ruyssell
AMERICAN PHOTO: "Photofile," 'A roundup of new and noteworthy products'

Hartford, Huntington
SHOW: "From the Publisher," editorial.

Hartgrave, Lee
CASTING CALL: "Lee Hartgrave's Show Buzz."

Hastings, Douglas Macdonald
BBC WORLD SERVICE LONDON CALLING: "London Letter."

Hatch, Henry
PRE-: "IPA Report," International Prepress Association news.

Haun, Harry
PLAYBILL: "Broadway News," 'What's happening, coming, and playing'

Hauser, Glenn
MONITORING TIMES: "Shortwave Broadcasting," news.

Hauser, Nao
ORBIT VIDEO: "Lifestyles," 'How to entertain with your VCR'

Hawkins, Ken
SIXSHOOTERS: "Tech Talk."

Hawks, Wendy
NATIONAL EXAMINER: "The Stars and You," horoscope.

Hay, George Dewey
RURAL RADIO: "Strictly Personal," by 'The Solemn Old Judge',

Hay, James R.
MONITORING TIMES: "High Seas," Ocean communication.

Haynes, Laurie
PIC: "Lighting School."

Heads, Barrie
TBI: "Letter from London."

Heck, Peter
W•B: "The Acid Test," Science Fiction.

Heiserman, David L.
COMPUTERS & ELECTRONICS: "Opportunity Awareness," 'Thoughtful reflections on your future'

Heiss, Michael
VIDEO PROPHILES: "Close Focus."
VIDEO SYSTEMS: "Leading Edge."
VIDEOGRAPHY: "Product Perspectives."

Heller, Jane
W•B: "Keeping Up With the Authors," author activities.

Heller, Neil
TAPE/DISC BUSINESS: "The Nature of Business."

Helton, Lon
R & R: "Country," radio format.

Hemmen, Joyce
4TH MEDIA JOURNAL, THE: "Editor's Letter," editorial.

Henderson, Jennifer
POSTCARD COLLECTOR: "Food for Thought," Culinary postcards.

Henderson, Kathy
PLAYBILL: "A Theatregoer's Notebook," detailed description of theatre and New York City life.

Hendricks, Helen
SCREENLAND PLUS TV-LAND: "Your Guide to Current Films."

Henninger, Edward F.
COMPUTER PUBLISHING: "Type Style," typography.

Hepfer, Cindy
SERIALS REVIEW: "Editorial," commentary.

Herman, James
BUSINESS COMMUNICATIONS REVIEW: "Net Management Directions."

Herman, Mark
MIX: "Sound Reinforcement News/Tour Update."
REP: RECORDING ENGINEERING PRODUCTION: "All Access," unique column listing audio equipment utilized by entertainment groups,
REP: RECORDING ENGINEERING PRODUCTION: "Roadwork."

Herron, R. Patricia
FLASH: "First Draft," editorial.

Hershenson, Martin
INDUSTRIAL PHOTOGRAPHY: "From the Lab."
MODERN PHOTOGRAPHY: "Color Today."
PHOTOGRAPHIC PROCESSING: "On the Business Side."

Hershey, Jane
HOLLYWOOD MAGAZINE: "How Hollywood Flies."

Hessler, Ron
QST: "Canadian News Fronts."

Heuring, David
AMERICAN CINEMATOGRAPHER: "Ask ASC," questions and comments.

Heyden, Terry Vander
CMA NEWSLETTER: "From the Vice President for Member Services."

Higgason, Frank
GRAPHIC ARTS MONTHLY: "Composing Room."

Hillyer, Whit
POPULAR PHOTOGRAPHY: "Camera Clubs."

Hirsch, Abby
HOLLYWOOD MAGAZINE: "Where Hollywood Plays."

Hirsch, Foster
BIJOU: "Bijou Books," review.

Hirsch, Julian
STEREO REVIEW: "Technical Talk."

Hirsch, Julian D.
STEREO REVIEW: "Technical Talk."

Hobbs, Nicole
ENTERTAINMENT CONNECTION MAGAZINE: "On the Scene."

Hobson, Charles
BLACK STARS: "Following the Stars."

Hochman, Louis
POPULAR PHOTOGRAPHY: "Hollywood Report."

Hocura, Ed
CANADIAN FILM DIGEST: "Its My Bag," personality.

Hodges, Ralph
CAR STEREO REVIEW: "The Fast Lane."
STEREO REVIEW: "The High End," commentary.

Hoffman, Fred
SATELLITE TV WEEK: "Satellite Sports."

Hoffman, Neil
DRAMA-LOGUE: "Las Vegas Desert Spiel."

Hoffman, Robert G.
PROFESSIONAL PHOTOGRAPHER, THE: "Photography in Industry."

Hoffman-Keating, Lynn
BACK STAGE: "AICP/Atlanta Report."

Hoffner, Randy
TV TECHNOLOGY: "Focus on Audio," engineering.

Hogan, Robert W.
INSIDE MEDIA: "Hogan."

Columnists

Hoglin, John
VIDEOMAKER: "Special FX," special video effects.

Holden, Larry
AFTER DARK: "Dallas-Ft. Worth," city review.

Holland, Bill
BILLBOARD: "Washington Roundup," radio news.

Hollis, Karen
PICTURE PLAY MAGAZINE: "They Say in New York," 'Spicy comment about stars in New York'

Holliss, Richard
STARBURST: "TV Zone."

Holman, L. Bruce
FILMMAKERS FILM & VIDEO MONTHLY: "Building Cine Stuff."

Holshevnikoff, Bill
VIDEO SYSTEMS: "Video2."

Holt, J. Gordon
COMPUTERS & ELECTRONICS: "Stereo Scene."
STEREOPHILE: "As We See It," Founder and Chief Tester commentary.

Holtzman, Jeff
POPULAR ELECTRONICS: "Computer Bits."

Holtzman, Will
BIJOU: "Movies Then/Movies Now," fascinating dual look at movies past and present,

Hooper, Terry
COMICS FANDOM EXAMINER: "Tel's From the Crypt."

Hopkins, Paul
MODERN PHOTOGRAPHY: "More Fact than Fancy," information.

Hopper, Ed
CQ: "The Awards Program."

Hopper, Hedda
MOTION PICTURE: "Under Hedda's Hat."
PHOTOPLAY: "Under Hedda's Hat," gossip.

Horn, Gayle Van
MONITORING TIMES: "The QSL Report."

Horn, Larry Van
MONITORING TIMES: "Utility World," Utility news.

Horner, Bob
LPTV REPORT, THE: "The News in Community Broadcasting."

Horowitz, David B.
ENTERTAINMENT REVUE: "Eye on Television."

Horowitz, Is
BILLBOARD: "Classical Keeping Score."

Horowitz, Marc
AUDIOVIDEO INTERNATIONAL: "Point of Sale," retail strategies and commentary.

Horton, Liz
PC PUBLISHING AND PRESENTATIONS: "On Line," 'The latest tools for your desktop'

Horzepa, Stan
QEX: "Gateway."
QST: "On Line."

Hosansky, David
CORPORATE TELEVISION: "FYI."

Howard, Meg
STARZ: "Starz in Your Eyes!," 'Editor Meg tells all!'

Howe, Herb
NEW MOVIE MAGAZINE, THE: "The Hollywood Boulevardier," 'Mr. Howe writes from Paris on film people and events'

Howett, Dicky
STARBURST: "Flickers," cartoon strip.

Hoyle, Martin
20/20: "Classical & Opera," review.

Huffman, John L.
COMMUNICATION LAW & POLICY NEWSLETTER: "From the Chair," chair's.

Huizenga, Chris
AFTER DARK: "Book Bits," review.
AFTER DARK: "Pop," music review.

Hunt, Christopher H.
MOVIELINE: "Edge of the Apocalypse."

Hunter, Alf
BROADCAST + TECHNOLOGY: "Lighting Technology," STLD information.

Hunter, Glen
TAKE ONE: "Book Reviews."

Hurder, Luck
QST: "Public Service."

Hurter, Bill
PETERSEN'S PHOTOGRAPHIC: "One to One," 'Your questions answered'

Hurtig, Brent
EQ: "Editor's Notes."

Hushin, Joanna
QST: "QSL Corner."

Hyams, Joe
SHOW BUSINESS ILLUSTRATED: "Our Man in Hollywood."

I

Ignatz
MOVIELINE: "Hollywood Ink," Hollywood chatter.

Iley, Chrissy
DIRECTION: "Vidbeat."

Ingelhart, Louis
CMA NEWSLETTER: "Press Law."

Insider, The
FILMLAND: "Hollywood Tattletale," personality.

Intemann, Bill
PRODUCERS QUARTERLY: "Pre-Pro."

Irvine, Reed
AIM REPORT: "Notes From the Editor's Cuff," editorial.

Isaacs, Edith J.
THEATRE ARTS: "Broadway in Review."

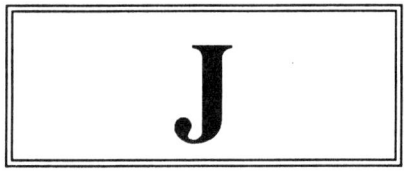

J

Jackson, Al
BEST OF FILM & VIDEO: "Hot From Hollywood," gossip.

Jackson, Jack
SHOWMEN'S TRADE REVIEW: "Show Sense."

Jacobs, George
CQ: "Propagation," 'The science of predicting radio conditions'

Jacobs, Mary
RADIOLAND: "They Never Told Till Now," 'Untold Stories of the Stars'

Jacobs, Taumas
VIDEO CHOICE: "The Video Photographer."

Jacobson, Linda
EQ: "Future Watch."

Jacobson, Mark
MOVIES, THE: "Balcony."

Jae-Ha-Kim
CELEBRITY PLUS: "Rave and Grave Reviews," concerning books, records and videos,

Jaekle, Larry
SOUND STAGE: "Pen and Personality."

James, Terry
CAMCORDER USER: "Helpline," Q&A.

Jameson, Richard T.
FILM COMMENT: "Book Marks," comment.

Jarman, Colin
SATELLITE TIMES: "Sportseen," 'A round-up of this months sports on TV'

Jarrett, George
TBI: "Technology."

Jarvis, Jeff
ENTERTAINMENT WEEKLY: "Critic on the Loose," comment.

Jector, Pa
SCREEN THRILLS ILLUSTRATED: "Private Screening," picture.

Jeffers, Dennis W.
JQ. JOURNALISM QUARTERLY.: "Articles on Mass Communication in U.S. and Foreign Journals," excellent ongoing bibliography.

Jeffers, Mark
ONSAT: "Fast Feeds," network newsbriefs.

Jegerings, Ron
DARKROOM AND CREATIVE CAMERA TECHNIQUES: "Questions on Photography."

Jenkins, J. C.
EXHIBITORS HERALD WORLD: "J.C. Jenkins--His Colyum," traveling film commentary.

Jensen, Brooks
VIDEO SOFTWARE MAGAZINE: "Retailing to Win."

Jensen, Don
POPULAR ELECTRONICS: "DX Listening."

Jerome, Judson
WRITER'S DIGEST: "Poetry."

Jivani, Alkarim
20/20: "Television," review.

Johnson, Bruce
QST: "International News."

Johnson, Erskine
MOTION PICTURE: "Overheard in Hollywood."
PHOTOPLAY: "Laughing Stock," comedy.

Johnson, Loudilla
TV DAY STARS: "The Country Express," news.

Johnson, Richard D.
SMALL PRESS: "On the Desktop."

Johnston, Craig
TV TECHNOLOGY: "Production Manager."

Johnston, Warner W.
TV TECHNOLOGY: "Focus on Quality," engineering.

Johnstone, Lammy
INSIDE MEDIA: "Johnstone."

Jones, Dave
MONITORING TIMES: "Federal File."

Jones, Dewitt
OUTDOOR PHOTOGRAPHER: "Basic Jones."

Jones, John
NATIONAL ADVERTISING: "Personal."

Jones, R. A.
COMICS WEEK: "Random Samplings."

Joseph, Mike
REP: RECORDING ENGINEERING PRODUCTION: "Five Questions," interesting technical.

Jr, Domino
STAGE: "Dining and Dancing 'Round the Town," 'If you indulge in either, in either of the captivating worlds of New York or Hollywood, this is your guide',

Jurek, Ken
AVC: "Video."
VIDEO MANAGEMENT: "Kaleidoscope."

Jutkins, 'Rocket' Ray
TARGET MARKETING: "60- Second Seminar."

K

Kabristante, George Vail
MOVIE FLASH: "Paragraphs."

Kajiwara, Takao
PENTAX FAMILY: "Pentax Journal."

Kalafut, Kathy
MEDIAWEEK: "Media Dish," personality.

Kallen, Ben
MOVIELINE: "L.A. Obsessions."

Kalp, Gayla
CABLE MARKETING: "Employee Dynamics."

Kamin, Vince
FLASH: "Tangents."

Kaminsky, James
CORPORATE VIDEO DECISIONS: "Editor's Notes," editorial.

Kapalka, Jeff
COMICS WEEK: "Reviews," critique of new releases.

Kaplan, Jonathan
MAGAZINE DESIGN & PRODUCTION: "Tips for the Trade."

Kaplan, Rachel
INSIDE MEDIA: "Upfront," issue.

Kaufman, Debra
PRODUCERS QUARTERLY: "Concept," idea development.

Kaufman, James
PHOTOGRAPHER'S FORUM: "Book Review."

Kaufmann, James
PHOTOGRAPHER'S FORUM: "Book Review."

Kay, Bob
MONITORING TIMES: "The Scanning Report."

Kay, Lambdin
RURAL RADIO: "Along the Way with Lambdin Kay," humorous commentary.

Kaye, Doris
MOVIE STARS: "Your Star Life," 'Horoscope'

Kaye, Gordon D.
GRAPHIC DESIGN: USA: "Graphics Update," newsbriefs.

Keats, Robin
SH-BOOM: "Tube Talk."

Keblusek, Maryann
PC PUBLISHING AND PRESENTATIONS: "Corporate Communications."

Kellar, Arthur J.
RADIOLAND: "Mike Says:," 'Sparkling news notes straight from glamorous radio row'

Keller, Bob
WESTERN PHOTOGRAPHER MAGAZINE: "The Video Invasion."

Kelley, Carol
CD-ROM LIBRARIAN: "Optical News," extensive news.

Kelley, Jackie
IMAGE: "College News."

Columnists

Kelley, Paul
JOURNAL OF EDUCATIONAL TELEVISION: "Editorial."

Kellie, Nellie
TELEPHONE NEWS, THE: "Nellie Kellie's Kolumn," employee news.

Kelly, Gwenn
TELESPAN'S BUSINESSTV GUIDE: "Getting the Most Out of Business Television."

Kelly, Katherine E.
THEATRE JOURNAL: "Book Review," edited.

Kelly, Richard
HI-FI WORLD: "Kelly's Corner," 'Richard Kelly's monthly look at budget hi-fi - old, new, borrowed or blue'

Kenedy, Paul
MONDAY MORNING REPLAY: "Back Stage," photo.

Kennedy, Dana
FAME: "FAME Says It All About Hollywood."

Kennedy, Tom
EXHIBITORS TRADE REVIEW: "Exploitorials," newsbriefs regarding exhibitor promotion.

Kenny, Glenn
VIDEO BUSINESS: "Vidbits," newsbriefs.

Kent, Sarah
20/20: "Art," review.

Keppler, Herbert
POPULAR PHOTOGRAPHY: "SLR Notebook."

Kerr, Kevin
ADWEEK'S MARKETING WEEK: "Corridor Talk," marketing, media and advertising tidbits.

Kerschner, Ike
MONITORING TIMES: "On the Ham Bands."

Kessler, Ken
HI-FI NEWS AND RECORD REVIEW: "Headroom."

Kesten, Lou
VIDEO MAGAZINE: "New Products."

Keywood, Noel
HI-FI WORLD: "Kaleidoscope."

Khann, Lumumba T.
SHOWCASE WORLD: "Record Reviews."

Kilgallen, Dorothy
MOTION PICTURE: "Coast to Coast With Dorothy Kilgallen."

Kim, Young Y.
INTERCULTURAL & DEVELOPMENT COMMUNICATION NEWSLETTER: "Report From the Chair," editorial.

Kindela, Jerry
VISIO: "Programming the Future," software.

Kingsley, Robert
JOURNAL OF RADIO LAW: "Book Reviews."
JOURNAL OF RADIO LAW: "Bibliography of Radio Law."

Kingston, Al
HOLLYWOOD FILMOGRAPH: "Movietunes."

Kinosian, Mike
R & R: "AC," Adult contemporary radio format.

Kirby, E. M.
RURAL RADIO: "Editorial," editorial comment.

Kirby, Kathryn
FILM REVIEW: "Worldwide Movie Making," 'Who's making what, with who and where', excellent production status.
FILMS AND FILMING: "World Wide Movie Making," excellent current projects and prospects.

Kirsch, Bob
BILLBOARD: "Studio Track," studio.

Kitt, Priscilla
FANTASTIC FILMS: "Cinemasneak," 'Advance production information and first photos from forthcoming attractions'

Klaas, Kelly
RADIO GUIDE: "Computer Connection."

Klady, Leonard
SCREEN INTERNATIONAL: "Hollywood Cinefile."

Klasnic, Jack
IN-PLANT PRINTER & ELECTRONIC PUBLISHER: "Klasnic's Consultant's Corner."

Klein, Larry
HIGH FIDELITY: "Crosstalk," technical.
RADIO-ELECTRONICS: "Audio Update."
STEREO REVIEW: "Audio Questions and Answers," reader-submitted Q&A.

Klein, Marty
MGF: "Sex Advisor."

Kleinman, Sidney
PROFESSIONAL PHOTOGRAPHER, THE: "Legally Speaking."

Kling, Bob
GRAPHIC ARTS MONTHLY: "Washington Newsletter."

Klymkiw, Greg
CINEMA/CANADA: "Prairie Pulse," commentary.

Kneitel, Tom
ELECTRONICS ILLUSTRATED: "Uncle Tom's Corner," technical Q&A.

Knickerbocker, Father
AGRICULTURAL ADVERTISING: "The New York Listening Post."

Knightsbridge, Flavia
ROMANTIC TIMES: "Under the Covers."

Knox, Mary
BACK STAGE/SHOOT: "Ad Nauseam," editorial.

Koegler, Horst
AFTER DARK: "Germany West," city review.

Kohorst, Ed
DESIGN: "Editor's Note," editorial.

Kojan, Harvey
R & R: "AOR," Album oriented rock radio.

Korkis, Jim
ANIMATO!: "Harlequin," trivia.
GET ANIMATED! UPDATE.: "The Wayback Machine," historical newsnotes.

Kostyu, Paul E.
COMMUNICATION LAW & POLICY NEWSLETTER: "From the Editor," editorial.

Kowsar, Mohammad
THEATER: "Theater in Washington."

Kraft, David Anthony
COMICS INTERVIEW: "Up Front," editorial.

Kramer, Arthur
CAMERA 35: "Technical Topics."

Krauss, Geoff
QEX: "VHF + Technology."

Kremer, John
SMALL PRESS: "Books For the Trade."

Kreps, Gary
HEALTH COMMUNICATION NEWSLETTER: "From the Chair," editorial and commentary.

Kristi
SMASH HITS: "Dear Kristi," Q&A on young stars.

Kuehn, Richard A.
BUSINESS COMMUNICATIONS REVIEW: "Consultant's Corner."

Kuman, Peg
DIRECT MARKETING: "Telemarketing."

Kumin, Daniel
CD REVIEW: "The 17th Bit."
CD REVIEW: "Worth a Look."

Kunin, Howard
AMERICAN CINEMEDITOR: "From the Editor," editorial.

Kunz, Michael
COMIC RELIEF: "Funny Stuff," editorial.

Kurz, Phil
PRE-: "Scan Lines," technology.

Kyle, Andrew J.
COMICS FANDOM EXAMINER: "Kyle."

L

LaFleur, Bubbles
WOW! MAGAZINE: "Soap Dish," 'What's happening in the world of daytime dramas'

LaFon, Ron
PC PUBLISHING AND PRESENTATIONS: "Graphics."
PC PUBLISHING AND PRESENTATIONS: "Hands-On Graphics."

LaRussa, Adrienne
TV DAY STARS: "Ask Adrienne," reader Q&A.

Lachenbruch, David
ON!: "On! Second Thought," commentary.
PANORAMA: "Videocassettes and Discs."
RADIO-ELECTRONICS: "Video News," 'What's new in this fast-changing field'

Lacroix, Marlena de
SOAP OPERA WEEKLY: "Critical Condition."

Ladybug
CB LIFE: "Seatcovers."

Laemmle, Carl
UNIVERSAL WEEKLY: "Straight From the Shoulder Talk."

Laine, Hank
SILVER SCREEN: "Screen Scene," 'The highs and lows of tinseltown'

Lake, Don
ADVANCED IMAGING: "Getting the Picture."

Lambert, Mel
MIX: "Juxtapositions."
RADIO WORLD: "Digital Domain," trends and breakthroughs on digital radio broadcasting,
TELEVISION BROADCAST: "Mel Lambert," audio-for-video.

Lampert, Ellen
THEATRE CRAFTS: "Show Report."

Lanan, Adele
CMA NEWSLETTER: "Electronic Media."

Lancaster, Don
RADIO-ELECTRONICS: "Hardware Hacker," Fascinating comment.

Lancie, Philip De
MIX: "After-Mix."

Landen, Richard
DOCTOR WHO MAGAZINE: "Controversy Corner."

Landwehr, Sheldon
SHOW: "Dining," New York City.

Lane, Joe
FACTSHEET FIVE: "The Fishing Hole," publishing.

Lane, Patricia
INFORMATION TODAY: "From the Editor's Desk," editorial.

Langer, Stephen
NATIONAL EXAMINER: "Health Beat."

Langford, Michael J.
INDUSTRIAL PHOTOGRAPHY: "European Newsletter."

Lantos, Jeff
MOVIELINE: "The Commissary."

Lardine, Bob
TV RADIO SHOW: "Daytime TV World," 'TV Radio Show's daytime gossip newspaper'
TV RADIO TALK: "Out For a Spin," 'Latest releases and gossip of your favorite recording stars'

Larkin, Barry
SILVER SCREEN: "Data on Discs," record review.

Lauro, Janet Di
SOAP OPERA WEEKLY: "The Gossip," west coast.

Lavin, Cheryl
ONSAT: "Celebrity Profile."
SPOTLIGHT CASTING MAGAZINE: "The Fast Track with Cheryl Lavin," actor profile.

Lawrence, Jim St.
VIDEOGRAPHY: "Production Technique."

Leadbetter, DG
AUTO SOUND & SECURITY: "Sound Off."

Lee, Tony
STRANGE ADVENTURES: "Reel People."
STRANGE ADVENTURES: "Intro," editorial.

Leech, Michael
AFTER DARK: "London," city review.

Lees, Chris
PIC: "Focal Point," equipment review.

Leftley, Colin
PHOTO ANSWERS: "Photoworld," 'News, views and reviews from the world of photography, edited.

Leggett, Anthony
NATIONAL EXAMINER: "Dear Tony," Q&A advice.

Lehman, Ernest
AMERICAN FILM: "Lehman at Large," commentary.

Lehrman, Paul D.
REP: RECORDING ENGINEERING PRODUCTION: "Managing MIDI."

Lehtinen, Rick
VIDEO SYSTEMS: "Computer Scan."
VIDEO SYSTEMS: "Question & Answer," Q&A.

Leifert, Don
AMAZING CINEMA: "Classic Film Salute."

Leigh, Alan
BLACK RADIO EXCLUSIVE: "In Other Media," black news item.

Leigh, Rachael
NATIONAL FORUM, THE: "What's What," brain teaser.
NATIONAL FORUM, THE: "Who's Who," brain teaser.

Leinwoll, Stanley
RADIO-ELECTRONICS: "Shortwave Radio."

Lengkeek, Deb
POSTCARD COLLECTOR: "Greetings From Iola," editorial commentary.

Leonian, Phillip
CAMERA 35: "Comments on Color."

Lepp, George
OUTDOOR PHOTOGRAPHER: "Gadget Bag."
OUTDOOR PHOTOGRAPHER: "Tech Tips."

Columnists

Leslie, Guy
THEATERWEEK: "Reviews," extensive play critiques.

Levenson, Jeff
BILLBOARD: "Jazz Blue Notes."

Levesque, Jim
CINEMA/CANADA: "Production Guide."

Levine, David
TV AND SCREEN SECRETS: "In With the TV Set."

Levine, Martin
ONI: "On! This...," editorial.

Lewis, Chick
SHOWMEN'S TRADE REVIEW: "The Editorial Page."

Lewis, Daniel B.
PRINT-EQUIP NEWS: "Keeping It," 'How to generate, accumulate and conserve business wealth'

Lewis, Grover
MOVIELINE: "Moving Lips."

Lewis, Sarah
VIDEO TIMES: "Video Clips," 'The best of the rest of this month's videos reviewed by Sarah Lewis'

Lewis, Sean Day-
BROADCAST: "Notebook."

Lewis, Stephen
TV AND SCREEN SECRETS: "Watching the Beautiful People."

Lexton, Maria
20/20: "Books," review.

Lichtman, Irv
BILLBOARD: "Inside Track," news and trends.
BILLBOARD: "Words & Music," talent.

Lightfoot, Chris
COMICS FANDOM EXAMINER: "The Alternative Forum."

Linder, Joanne
HIT PARADER: "Hollywood Heart Beat," music in the movies.

Lindgren, Bob
PRINT-EQUIP NEWS: "Kaleidoscope," 'of PIA-SC Happenings'

Lindvall, Terry
FILM WITNESS: "Terry Lindvall's Sprocket Holes," film commentary.

Linet, Beverly
MODERN SCREEN: "New Movies," guide.

Lionel, Daniel
PUBLISHER'S AUXILIARY: "Classified Advice."

Lipton, Norman C.
POPULAR PHOTOGRAPHY: "Tools and Techniques," 'A round-up of recent developments and significant trends'

Little, Bessie
FILMLAND: "Hello, Friends," editorial.
TV PEOPLE AND PICTURES: "Hello, Friends," editorial.
TV WORLD: "Hello, Friends," commentary.

Livingstone, William
STEREO REVIEW: "Going on Record."
STEREO REVIEW: "Bulletin," late-breaking news.

Lloyd, Peter
TELEVISION WEEK: "Comment."

Logan, Michael
TV GUIDE: "Soaps."

Londino, Bill
WRITING CONCEPTS: "Editor's Desk."

Loney, Glenn
AFTER DARK: "Other Stages," theatre review.

Loney, Jacquie
BROADCAST + TECHNOLOGY: "Ad Lib!."

Long, Dave
POSTCARD COLLECTOR: "Small Talk."

Long, Robert
HIGH FIDELITY: "Tape Tracks," audio tape.

Longan, Krys
HOME VIEWER: "Previewer," upcoming video releases,

Loose, Ray S.
SCHEMER, THE: "Distributing."

Lori, Bonnie
MOVIE TV SECRETS: "The Midnight Beat," 'Inside Hollywood - Revealing - Tip-Offs - Predictions - News!'

Lothrop, Eaton S.
POPULAR PHOTOGRAPHY: "The Camera Collector."

Loucks, Philip G.
JOURNAL OF RADIO LAW: "Radio Legislation in the United States."

Love, Gael
FAME: "Editor's Letter."

Love, Harry
GRAFFITI: "Animation Profiles."

Love, Walt
R & R: "Urban Contemporary," radio format.

Low, Lafe
ONI: "On the disk," review.

Loy, Kathy
TV STAR PARADE: "Between Commercials," 'A chat with the editor'

Lucas, Tim
GOREZONE: "Video Watchdog®," video releases.
VIDEO WATCHDOG: "The Watchdog Barks," editorial.

Lucchesi, Marianne
BACK STAGE: "AICP/SF Report."

Luchs, Kurt
COMPUTER PUBLISHING: "Behind the Desk," editorial.

Luger, Dr. Norton
STAR: "Your Family Doctor."

Lukowsky, Leo
INDUSTRIAL PHOTOGRAPHY: "The Answer Man."

Lunt, Billy
QST: "Special Events."
QST: "Contest Corral."

Lusk, Norbert
PICTURE PLAY MAGAZINE: "The Screen in Review," 'Checking off the new films for what they are worth'

Lyaght, Rory
PHOTOPRO: "Software Review."

Lynch, Joe
CQ: "VHF Plus," 'All about the world above HF',

Lynch, Twink
THEATRE NEWS: "ACTA."

Lytle, Richard
CMA NEWSLETTER: "From the Editor."

M

MacAlpine, Loretta
VIDEO INSIDER: "Children's Video."

MacGregor, Jock
SHOWMEN'S TRADE REVIEW: "London Observations."

MacMahon, Henry
MOVING PICTURE AGE: "With the Reel Observor."

MacNeice, Jill
ORBIT VIDEO: "Video Room," new technology info.

MacQuillin, Ian
CAMCORDER USER: "Eyeview."

Mack, Gloria
PHOTOPLAY COMBINED WITH MOVIE MIRROR: "Smart Headwork," beauty.

Maddox, Richard
ONSAT: "Dr. Dish," satellite receiver questions and answer.

Madsen, Axel
CAHIERS DU CINEMA IN ENGLISH: "Small Talk," current Hollywood news.

Magne, Lawrence
MONITORING TIMES: "Magne Tests."

Maia, Frederick O.
CQ: "Washington Readout," 'Regulatory happenings from the world of amateur radio',

Majestic, Richard
RADIO GUIDE: "Soldering Tips."

Majka, Chris
CINEMA/CANADA: "Eastern Wave."

Mallory, Scott
SH-BOOM: "Rewind," 'The best of then is on video today!',

Manber, Jeffrey
STV GUIDE: "Spacewatch."

Mancha, Ernestine
ENTERTAINMENT CONNECTION MAGAZINE: "Movie Notes."

Mandel, Charles
CINEMA/CANADA: "Shoot Alberta."

Mandelbaum, Ken
THEATERWEEK: "Theater News," newsbriefs.

Mangan, Michael
PLAYS INTERNATIONAL: "Radio," review and commentary.

Mangels, Andy
AMAZING HEROES: "Backstage."

Manilla, James
INDUSTRIAL PHOTOGRAPHY: "Manilla in Motion," news.

Mann, May
MOVIE FAN: "Going Hollywood."
MOVIE TEEN: "Young Hollywood."

Mannheim, L. A.
CAMERA: "Technical Round-Up," new photographic developments.

Marans, Michael
EQ: "Hands-On Production," Creative Workshop.

Marcello, Lesley
CMA NEWSLETTER: "From the President."

Marchande, Teal
SHOWCASE WORLD: "Lights On."

Marcus, Frank
PLAYS INTERNATIONAL: "TV," review and commentary.

Marcus, Jeff
MAGAZINEWEEK: "Profit Profile," informative magazine profile and critique.

Margolis, Art
ELECTRONICS ILLUSTRATED: "Service Tips."
ELECTRONICS WORLD: "Test Bench Puzzler."

Marill, Alvin H.
FILMS IN REVIEW: "The Television Scene."

Marlatt, Harry
MUSICAL AMERICA: "Musical Americana."

Martenhoff, Jim
CB LIFE: "CB Life Afloat."

Martin, Helen
TV PICTURE LIFE: "Daytime TV Gossip."

Martin, James A.
PUBLISH!: "News Beat," news item.

Marx, Andrew
HOLLYWOOD MAGAZINE: "Fade Out," commentary.

Maschke, Rudy
TRAVEL & LEISURE: "Camera and Travel Shopper," product review.

Mason, R. H.
AMATEUR PHOTOGRAPHER: "Notes for Novices."

Masters, Ian G.
STEREO REVIEW: "Audio Q & A."

Math, Irwin
CQ: "Math's Notes."

Mather, Joe
RANGEFINDER, THE: "New Products and Processes."

Maurice, Dick
TV DAY STARS: "The Answer Man," Reader Q&A.

Maxford, Howard
FILM REVIEW: "Tales From the Script," 'This month's movie books reviewed',

Maxwell, Paul S.
MEDIA BUSINESS: "Follow the Money."

Mayer, Henry
MEDIA INFORMATION AUSTRALIA: "Read and Noted."

Mayer, Martin
AMERICAN FILM: "About Television."

Mayer, Michael F.
TAKE ONE: "Film as Business."

Mayfield, Geoff
BILLBOARD: "Retail Track."

Mayrhofer, Debra
MEDIA INFORMATION AUSTRALIA: "Media Briefs."

McAdams, Janine
BILLBOARD: "The Rhythm and the Blues."

McBride, H.D.
UNIVERSAL WEEKLY: "Los Angeles Notes," Southern California exhibitor newsbriefs.

McCleery, Albert
STAGE: "On Other Broadways," 'Happenings in the byways of Broadway, North, South, East, and West'

McCloskey, Jason
DRAMA-LOGUE: "Cabaret Corner."

McCombs, Phil
FAME: "FAME Says It All About Books."

McCord, Jennifer
W•B: "Grapevine," romance author activity.

McCubbin, Neil
PULP & PAPER CANADA: "Input/Output."

McCullaugh, Jim
VIDEO TIMES: "Video Beat."

McDowell, Barbara
COMMUNICATIONS LAWYER: "Courtside," recent communication legal decisions,

McDowell, Michael
AFTER DARK: "Boston," city review.

McGeehan, Bernice
TV RADIO SHOW: "What's Happening!," 'Hollywood, New York, London, Paris, Rome'

McGillivray, David
FILM REVIEW: "Film Fax," 'Your questions answered by David McGillivray, our man with all the answers'
FILM REVIEW: "Your Questions Answered."

McGowan, Chris
BILLBOARD: "Laser Scans," home video.

Columnists

McIlroy, Thad
PRE-: "The New Service Bureau."

McInnes, Dick
SOAP OPERA STARS: "Who's News in Hollywood."

McIntire, Tracey
VIDEO CHOICE: "Collector's Classics."

McIntyre, Robert L.
POPULAR PHOTOGRAPHY: "Stereo Today," Stereographic photography.

McKay, Alice
ADWEEK: "Television."

McKay, Anthony
TIME SCREEN: "Editorial."

McKay, Herbert C.
CAMERA, THE: "Modern Color Photography," technique and technology.

McKay, Wynne
RADIOLAND: "Cleanliness for Beauty."

McKeown, T. R.
SCHEMER, THE: "Mail Order and Advertising Pointers."

McKillips, Budd
JOURNAL: "Your Washington Reporter."

McLeod, Jonah
ELECTRONICS: "Up Front," editorial.

McLeod, Marilyn
ENTERTAINMENT CONNECTION MAGAZINE: "For the Record."

McNeil, Darrell
COMICS BUYER'S GUIDE: "Animation News."

McQuillan, John
BUSINESS COMMUNICATIONS REVIEW: "Doing Business Electronically."

McRae, Bill
OUTDOOR & TRAVEL PHOTOGRAPHY: "McRae's Wildlife."

McVicker, Dee
RADIO WORLD: "Offbeat Radio."

Medved, Michael
SPOTLIGHT ON VIDEO: "In the Spotlight," 'Critic's choice'

Meggs, Philip B.
COMMUNICATION ARTS: "Opinion / Commentary."

Meilach, Dona
AVC: "Analog Presentations."

Meltzer, Rachel S.
VIDEO STORE: "Regions," regional business activity.

Meredith, Jack
UNIVERSAL WEEKLY: "Texas Northers," Texas exhibitor newsbriefs.

Merrell, Ron
TELEVISION BROADCAST: "Ron Merrell," broadcast transmission.

Messenger, Paul
HI-FI CHOICE: "Personal Messages," commentary.

Messner, Fred
BUSINESS ADVERTISING: "Messner on Business Ads," critique.

Metcalf, Marguerite
SOUTHERN COMMUNICATION JOURNAL, THE: "Presidential Message."

Mettler, Mike
CAR STEREO REVIEW: "Car Tunes," Music review.
ONI: "On the Record," review.

Mewborn, Brant
AFTER DARK: "Broadway Buzz."

Meyers, Barbara
AGAINST THE GRAIN: "The Meyers Connection."

Michelson, Mark T.
PRINTING IMPRESSIONS: "Editor's Notebook," editorial.

Miele, Louis
AFTER DARK: "Dining Out."

Miles, John
PUBLISH!: "Design Basics."

Miles, Mel
BACK STAGE: "Chicago Report."

Miller, David
VISIO: "Have Power, Will Travel," portable electronics.

Miller, David L.
MODERN PHOTOGRAPHY: "Well-Traveled Camera."

Miller, Dennis
PHOTOPRO: "Photographer's Assistant."

Miller, F. D.
AV VIDEO: "PC Plus."

Miller, John J.
PHOTOPLAY: "It Happened This Way," personality.

Miller, Kathy
PUBLISHING & PRODUCTION EXECUTIVE: "Tech Tips."
PUBLISHING & PRODUCTION EXECUTIVE: "What's in a Print?."

Miller, Paul
HI-FI CHOICE: "Tech Talk," excellent technical.

Mills, Bart
AMPERSAND'S COLLEGE ENTERTAINMENT GUIDE: "Movie Roundup," new film releases.

Mims, Forrest M.
COMPUTERS & ELECTRONICS: "Project of the Month."
COMPUTERS & ELECTRONICS: "Experimenter's Corner."
COMPUTERS & ELECTRONICS: "Solid State Developments."

Mirabella, Alan
MGF: "Movie News."

Mishkind, Barry
RADIO WORLD: "Eclectic Engineer."

Mitchell, James
VIDEO BUSINESS: "The Informer," upcoming releases.

Mitchell, Martin
AFTER DARK: "More Films," review.

Mitchell, Mitch
TELEVISION WEEK: "Feedback," technology.

Mitchell, Peter
AUDIO/VIDEO INTERIORS: "Digital By Design."

Mitchell, Tom
TV GUIDE: "Soap Opera Guide."

Moffitt, John
CINEMA HALL-MARKS: "Critic on the Hearth."

Moldstad, Frank
VIDEO STORE: "Focus," editorial.

Monaco, James
TAKE ONE: "Holding Pattern."

Mook, Dick
SILVER SCREEN: "Pictures on the Fire," studio films in production.

Moore, Garry
RADIO HIT SONGS: "The Moore the Merrier," radio personality news.

Moore, Martyn
PRACTICAL PHOTOGRAPHY: "Back Chat," letters and more.

Moore, Peter
MODERN PHOTOGRAPHY: "Casual Observer."

Moore, Richie
EQ: "Studio Clinic," Tech Support.

Morehouse, Ward
THEATRE MAGAZINE: "Heard on Broadway," 'The tattle and trivia of the nation's theatrical main street'

Morgan, Chip
RADIO GUIDE: "State of the Art," technology newsbriefs.

Morgan, David
UNIQUE: "Review: Cinema."

Morgen, Robert W.
BROADCAST PROGRAMMING AND PRODUCTION: "Broadcast Buffoonery," broadcast cartoon series noteworthy as it is created.

Morley, Sheridan
PLAYBILL: "London News," news of London theatre,

Morreau, Louise
QST: "YL News and Views," women's league news.

Morrell, Peter J.
PLAYBILL: "Wine of Choice."

Morris, Bernadine
PLAYBILL: "Fashion Forecast."

Morrison, Jack
THEATRE NEWS: "Washington Routine," editorial.

Morrison, Judith
HOME ENTERTAINMENT: "Letter From the Editor," editorial preview.
VIDEO PROPHILES: "Producer PROphiles."

Morse, Jacqueline
VUE: "Point of Interest," Washington politics.

Moss, Linda
NATIONAL EXAMINER: "Hollywood Focus."

Moulton, Tom
BILLBOARD: "Disco Mix."

Mount, Paul
STARBURST: "TV Zone."

Mueller, Robert
PC PUBLISHING AND PRESENTATIONS: "From the Desktop," editorial.

Mulder, Karen
CANEWS: "The CANdid Report: A Living Stone Collection," news.

Muller, Robert
THEATRE: "Stage Door."

Murray, Edward
CD REVIEW: "Worth a Look."

Murray, Jane
BRITISH BOOK NEWS: "Notes and News from the Book Trade in Britain," current events.

Murray, Neil
MOVIE - THE VIDEO MAGAZINE: "London Diary," commentary.

Murrie, Michael
TELEVISION BROADCAST: "Michael Murrie," news operation.

Myers, George
SMALL PRESS: "Margins."

N

Nace, Ted
PUBLISH!: "Q&A," 'Practical hints, tips, and advice for desktop publishers'

Nadler, Bob
CAMERA 35 INCORPORATING PHOTO WORLD: "Safelight."

Nagan, Peter
PHOTOGRAPHIC PROCESSING: "The Washington Scene."

Nangle, John
FILMS IN REVIEW: "Book Reviews."

Nash, James Alan
AFTER DARK: "Art Scene."

Natale, Richard
MOVIELINE: "Premieres."

Nathan, Jan
PMA NEWSLETTER: "Publishing Potpourri," newsbriefs.

Nathan, Paul
PUBLISHER'S WEEKLY: "Rights."

Navas, Deborah
VIDEO CHOICE: "Watch Word," editorial.

Navone, David
CAR AUDIO AND ELECTRONICS: "Troubleshooting."

Neff, Dick
ADVERTISING AGENCY: "The Peeled Eye."

Neill, Bill
CAR AUDIO AND ELECTRONICS: "Down the Road."

Nelson, Harry M.
PROFESSIONAL PHOTOGRAPHER, THE: "Make the Subject Interesting."

Nelson, Lee J.
ADVANCED IMAGING: "Off the Shelf."

Nensi, Salman
STAR TREK: THE OFFICIAL FAN CLUB MAGAZINE: "Where No Man," review.

Neubart, Jack
INDUSTRIAL PHOTOGRAPHY: "Bits and Bytes."

Newcomb, Doug
CAR AUDIO AND ELECTRONICS: "Tunes to Go."

Newell, Philip
STUDIO SOUND AND BROADCAST ENGINEERING: "Monitor Systems."

Newkirk, David
QST: "Hints and Kinks."

Newman, Melinda
BILLBOARD: "The Eye," music video.

Nicastro, Peter
STUDIO PHOTOGRAPHY: "Light and Lighting."

Nicewonger, Kirk
ONSAT: "Satellite Log," program review.

Nicholas, Don
MAGAZINEWEEK: "Don Nicholas on Magazine Trends," design critique.

Nichols, Roger
EQ: "Across the Board."

Nicholson, Susan
POSTCARD COLLECTOR: "Pursuing the Marvelous," postcard.

Nierman, Elena
THEATRE NEWS: "News," assorted news item.

Nikki
ENTERTAINMENT CONNECTION MAGAZINE: "Nikki's Poetry Corner."

Nix, Don
PRINT-EQUIP NEWS: "Chemicals & the Graphic Arts," application to the printing arts.

Noble, Peter
SCREEN INTERNATIONAL: "In Confidence."

Nochimson, David
ENTERTAINMENT AND SPORTS LAWYER, THE: "Editor's Column."

Norwood, Rick
COMICS REVUE: "A Letter from Rick," editorial.

Novak, Joe
CAMERA 35 INCORPORATING PHOTO WORLD: "Books in Review."

Columnists INDEX

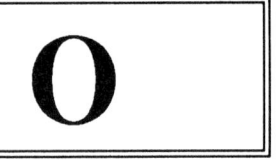

O

O'Connell, Bill
BIJOU: "Looking Ahead with Bijou," commentary.

O'Hara, John
MEDIA INFORMATION AUSTRALIA: "Directions."

O'Leary, Mick
LINK-UP: "The PC Pipeline."

O'Neill, Mark
CINEMA/CANADA: "Fronts West."

O'Rourke, Dan
MAST: "Shop Talk."

Octave, Madame
EXHIBITORS HERALD WORLD: "Hollywood Tunes," music news.

Oddie, Alan
FILMMAKERS FILM & VIDEO MONTHLY: "Film Nut News."

Oertle, V. Lee
CB LIFE: "CB Afield."

Olsen, Gary
PRE-: "From the Desktop," desktop publishing.

Olson, Audrey
MOVIE TEEN ILLUSTRATED: "Dear Audrey, What'll I Do?," personal problem.

Opat-Inkeles, Ellen
STEP-BY-STEP GRAPHICS: "Business Side."

Oracle
PICTURE PLAY MAGAZINE: "Information, Please," 'Careful answers to questions about the stars and films'

Orazio, Mario
TV TECHNOLOGY: "Masked Engineer," engineering.

Ores, Pauline
DESKTOP COMMUNICATIONS: "Corporate View."
PC PUBLISHING AND PRESENTATIONS: "Editorial."

Orr, Bill
CQ: "Radio FUNdamentals," 'Things to learn, projects to build, and gear to use',

Orton, Charles Wesley
VIDEO STORE: "Promotions," applications.

Osborn, Lawton E.
PROFESSIONAL PHOTOGRAPHER, THE: "President's Message."

Osborne, Robert
HOLLYWOOD REPORTER: "Rambling Reporter."

Ostman, Ronald E.
JQ. JOURNALISM QUARTERLY.: "Articles on Mass Communication in U.S. and Foreign Journals," excellent ongoing bibliography.

Ostmo, David
TV TECHNOLOGY: "News From the Back Porch," engineering.

Otis, Lee
WRITER'S DIGEST: "Radio and TV."

P

Pacheco, Patrick
AFTER DARK: "Reviews: Theater On Broadway and Off."

Pagel, Paul K.
QST: "Technical Correspondence."

Paige, Earl
BILLBOARD: "Store Monitor," home video.

Palenchar, Joseph
CAR STEREO REVIEW: "Security & Communications."

Palm, Rick
QST: "Club Spectrum."

Palmer, Carl
GRAPHIC ARTS MONTHLY: "Phototopography."

Palu, Lou
SMASH HITS: "Lou's Views!," 'It's the pictures the stars begged us not to print!'

Paney, Harry
TAPE/DISC BUSINESS: "The Business of Tape."

Paolillo, Lucille M.
THEATRE NEWS: "CTAA."

Pappas, Brynda
AMERICAN FILM: "AFI News," 'A newsletter about film and television activities of special interest to the American Film Institute members', edited.

Pappas, Ike
TELESPAN'S BUSINESSTV GUIDE: "Ike Ink."

Pardon, George
SHOWMEN'S TRADE REVIEW: "Production Parade."

Pardy, George T.
EXHIBITORS TRADE REVIEW: "Illustrated Screen Reports," edited.

Parker, Tom
AMERICAN DEMOGRAPHICS: "The Lincoln Sample," a cross-country odyssey.

Parnau, Jeff
FOLIO:: "Jeff Parnau on Production."

Parsons, Harry F.
HOLLYWOOD STUDIO MAGAZINE: "Key Hole Portraits," unique one-line biographies of stars,

Parsons, Louella
MODERN SCREEN: "Louella Parsons," 'Modern Screen's 8 page gossip extra by Hollywood's greatest columnist'

Patchett, Craig
VISIO: "The Electronic Mind," computer.

Patrick, Chris
SOUND STAGE: "Records," review.

Patterson, Dave
COMIC INFORMER: "Fanzine Update," fanzine reviews.

Patton, Doug
AUDIO/VIDEO INTERIORS: "Form & Function."

Paul, Billy
BLACK RADIO EXCLUSIVE: "Tech Notes," technical radio.

Paulson, Bob
TELEVISION BROADCAST: "Strictly Business."

Peluso, Polly
CASTING CALL: "Las Vegas Casting."

Pensinger, Glen
TELEVISION BROADCAST: "Glen Pensinger," post production.

Pepper, K. C.
ON!: "On! Video."

Perry, Telka
ORBIT VIDEO: "Hardware," review.

Peter, John
FOLIO:: "John Peter on Design."

Peters, Susan
SCENE AT THE MOVIES: "The Insider," movie trends and developments.

Peterson, Alan
RADIO WORLD: "From the Trenches."

Peterson, B.
POPULAR PHOTOGRAPHY: "Nature."

Peterson, William
HIGH FIDELITY: "HiFi-Crostic," puzzle.

Pettit, Rosemary
SMALL PRESS: "Rights Marketplace."

Pfeiffer, Katherine Shelly
DESKTOP COMMUNICATIONS: "Bookshelf," reviews.

Phillips, Gene
COMIC INFORMER: "The Lion's Den."

Phillips, Louis
RIGHTING WORDS: "Media Watch."

Phillips, William
TBI: "Finance."

Piante, Robert D.
PROFESSIONAL PHOTOGRAPHER, THE: "Press Photography."

Picard, Don
LINK-UP: "Keyboard Komments," 'Thoughts and opinions on online services and computer communications'

Pickow, Jon
PRODUCERS QUARTERLY: "Production."

Pierce, Dale
EUROPEAN TRASH CINEMA: "News From Spain."

Pinkwas, Stan
VIDEO MAGAZINE: "Late News."

Pinney, Roy
TRAVEL & LEISURE: "Magazine Photography."

Piscopo, Maria
DARKROOM PHOTOGRAPHY: "Making Money," in photography,

Pittaro, Ernie
AMAZING CINEMA: "Pittaro's Clinic," 'Questions & Answers on Film & Effects'

Plaskin, Glenn
MGF: "For Men Only."
SPOTLIGHT CASTING MAGAZINE: "Turning Point."

Plater, Alan
NEW THEATRE MAGAZINE: "The Writer in the Provinces."

Platt, Steve
UK PRESS GAZETTE: "Dog Watches Dog."

Pohlmann, Ken
MIX: "Insider Audio."

Pohlmann, Ken C.
STEREO REVIEW: "Signals," trends.

Pollock, Steve
PHOTO/DESIGN: "Editor's Note," editorial.

Polon, Martin
STUDIO SOUND AND BROADCAST ENGINEERING: "Perspective."
TELEVISION BROADCAST: "Opinion."

Pomfret, Liane
RF DESIGN: "Industry Insight," trends and analysis.

Pope, Frank
PICTURE REPORTS: "This Industry," commentary.

Porteous, John
BROADCASTER: "See, Hear," commentary.

Porteous, Sandra
BROADCAST + TECHNOLOGY: "Atlantic Airwaves."

Posch, Robert
DIRECT MARKETING: "Legal Outlook."

Post, George
DARKROOM PHOTOGRAPHY: "Color Corner."

Powell, Helena
AVC: "Computer Graphics."

Powell, Tom
AMUSEMENT BUSINESS: "T. P. on Amusement Business."

Press, Alex
MGF: "Movies on Cable," 'A guide to small screen highlights'
MGF: "Grooming."

Provenzano, Tom
DRAMA-LOGUE: "Screen Scene."

Puntney, Linda
CMA NEWSLETTER: "Yearbook."

Q

Qualman, Jack
WESTERN PHOTOGRAPHER MAGAZINE: "Book and Video Reviews."

Queen, I.
RADIO-ELECTRONICS: "New Radio Patents."

Quinn, Marian
PHOTOPLAY COMBINED WITH MOVIE MIRROR: "It's All in Your Name."

Quinn, Tim
STARBURST: "Flickers," cartoon strip.

R

Rakes, Charles D.
POPULAR ELECTRONICS: "Circuit Circus."

Ranada, David
HIGH FIDELITY: "Scan Lines," visual technical.
VIDEO PROPHILES: "Future Tech."

Range, Tom
POSTCARD COLLECTOR: "Having a Fine Time In," travel postcards.

Ranger, Paul
SPEECH AND DRAMA: "Editorial."

Raphel, Murray
DIRECT MARKETING: "Ideas for Retailers," advice.

Rapp, Stan
DIRECT MARKETING: "Rapp Around the World."

Raso, Anne M.
CELEBRITY PLUS: "Rave and Grave Reviews," concerning books, records and videos,

Ratliff, Marie
AMUSEMENT BUSINESS: "Boxscore," 'Top concert grosses reported' and detailed information.
BILLBOARD: "Country Corner."

Ratliffe, Sharon
SPEECH COMMUNICATION TEACHER, THE: "Reviews."

Ravin, Paul
MODERN SCREEN: "Don't Breath a Word of It!" more secret information.

Rea, Steven
HOME VIEWER: "Hollywood Hit Line," personality and production news.

Read, Oliver
ELECTRONICS WORLD: "For the Record," editorial.

Redmond, Kimberly
ONSAT: "Soap Opera Week," Q&A.

Reed, Carol
CD-ROM LIBRARIAN: "Optical Product Review."

Reeves, Richard
PANORAMA: "Perspective."

Reid, I.
JOURNAL OF EDUCATIONAL TELEVISION: "Broadcasting Notes."

Reilly, Alan
ADVERTISING & SELLING: "Advertising, [year]--and After."

Reilly, Kathy
PUBLISHING & PRODUCTION EXECUTIVE: "The Production Advisor."

Reilly, Patricia M.
COMMUNICATIONS LAWYER: "From the Chair," chair commentary.

Reinsch, Lamar
JOURNAL OF BUSINESS COMMUNICATION, THE: "Editorial."

Reiss, Craig
MEDIAWEEK: "Notes From Space & Time," editorial.

Reitz, Ken
MONITORING TIMES: "Satellite TV," 'Adventures in the Clarke Belt'

Reizner, Dick
AV VIDEO: "Tips to Clip."

Resnick, Mason
MODERN PHOTOGRAPHY: "Point and Shoot."

Reuben, Aubrey
MGF: "Pssst!," 'Reveling in the glitter and the glory' picture page.

Reyes, Edgar
MOVIE FLASH: "Anatomy of a Bold Star."

Reznicki, Jack
FLASH: "Final Copy."

Rialto, Mlle
DRAMATIC MIRROR, THE: "No Man's Land," news items concerning Broadway celebrities,

Rice, John
VIDEOGRAPHY: "Points of View."

Rich, Beatrice
HOLLYWOOD MAGAZINE: "Beyond the Stars."

Rich, Milton
ADVERTISER MAGAZINE, THE: "Lithography, Printing & Production."

Richards, Dan
POPULAR PHOTOGRAPHY: "Point and Shoot Follies," 'For serious photographers who secretly admire point & shoot cameras'

Richardson, F. H.
EXHIBITORS HERALD WORLD: "Sound Pictures," new technology.

Richardson, John David
AFTER DARK: "Recordings: Classical," review.
AFTER DARK: "Classical Scene."

Richmond, Norman
BLACK RADIO EXCLUSIVE: "Canadian Report," newsbrief column on Canadian black artists.

Richmond, Wendy
COMMUNICATION ARTS: "Design Technology."

Rickey, Carrie
FAME: "FAME Says It All About Film."

Riggins, George
RADIO WORLD: "Old Timer," a wonderful retrospective on the way things were in radio,

Riley, Tom
ACCESS REPORTS/FREEDOM OF INFORMATION: "News From Canada," freedom of information.

Ringgold, Gene
SOUND STAGE: "Films," review.

Riportella, Vern
QST: "Amateur Satellite Communications."

Rising, Roy
VIDEO SYSTEMS: "Sound Ideas."

Rising, Roy W.
VIDEO SYSTEMS: "Sound Ideas."

Rizzo, Tony
PHOTOPLAY: "Star-Trekking," 'Facts and Fotos'
TV DAY STARS: "Soap Scoops," information and gossip.

Robbins, Fred
SCREENLAND PLUS TV-LAND: "Right Off the Record," recording review.

Robbins, Ira
VIDEO MAGAZINE: "Gazette."

Robinson, Barry
MEDIA & METHODS: "Essentially Couth," 'Contemporary culture commentator',

Rodgers, Harold A.
COMPUTERS & ELECTRONICS: "Audiophile Recordings," review.
COMPUTERS & ELECTRONICS: "Entertainment Electronics."

Rogers, Dave
TOP SECRET: "Deadline," 'The Avengers column' information.

Rohleder, Charles
AMERICAN NEWSPAPER BOY, THE: "Sales," positive advice.

Romine, Damon
DEBUT: "Damon Romine Goes Behind the Scenes."

Rosa, Dorothy
VIDEOCHOICE: "Video Hotline," 'All the latest on the video front'

Rose, R. Marian
TV DAY STARS: "Channel Chatter," soap opera news.

Rosen, Craig
BILLBOARD: "Networks and Syndication."

Rosen, Fred
MODERN PHOTOGRAPHY: "On the Money."

Rosen, Marjorie
TV RADIO TALK: "TV Radio Talk Goes to the Movies."

Rosenbaum, Jonathan
AMERICAN FILM: "Focus on Education."
FILM COMMENT: "Journals--London & New York."

Ross, Sean
BILLBOARD: "Vox Jox."

Ross, Staunton
SOUND STAGE: "Books," review.

Rossi, Terri
BILLBOARD: "Terri Rossi's Rhythm Section."

Roth, Baron Theo von
THEATRE, THE: "New York Life."

Roth, Cliff
VIDEOMAKER: "Sound Reasoning," audio.
VISIO: "Freeze Frame," video.

Roth, Jill
AMERICAN PRINTER: "Editor's Desk."

Rothberg, Gerald
MGF: "Bravos & Boos," 'A gentleman's guide to who and what's heating up and cooling off'

Rothschild, Norman
OUTDOOR & TRAVEL PHOTOGRAPHY: "Rothschild Reviews."

Rothstein, Arthur
TRAVEL & LEISURE: "Creative Color."

Rotkin, Charles E.
ROTKIN REVIEW, THE: "Commentary."

Rowe, David
VIDEO SOFTWARE MAGAZINE: "Perspective," publisher commentary.

Rowell, Galen
OUTDOOR PHOTOGRAPHER: "Photo Adventure."

Rubin, Owen R.
ORBIT VIDEO: "Hardware," review.

Ruling, Karl
THEATRE CRAFTS: "Lighting."

Russell, Gary
DOCTOR WHO MAGAZINE: "Off the Shelf," video and fanzine review.
STARBURST: "Comic Store," review of current releases.

Russell, W.S.
EXHIBITORS HERALD WORLD: "Russell Says," live stage news.

S

Sabinano, Celso A.
SOSYALI MAGAZINE: "Sounds Familiar," audio recording news.

Sager, Phillip
QST: "Happenings."

Sallis, James
UNIQUE: "Review: Literature."

Salmans, Sandra
AGENCY: "Law Review."

Salome
TV AND SCREEN SECRETS: "Star Secrets Revealed."

Sammis, J. H.
MODERN PHOTOGRAPHY: "Superpan Panning," humor.

Sammon, Susan
SHOOTING COMMERCIALS: "SC Equipment," product reviews.

Sampson, Joel
STUDIO PHOTOGRAPHY: "Computers in the Studio."

Samuels, Gene
MOTION PICTURE: "The Answer Man," Q&A of the stars.

Sander, Michael
DRAMA-LOGUE: "New York, New York."

Sanders, Deborah Michelle
COSMEP NEWSLETTER: "Dear Deborah," legal Q&A on publishing.

Sandow, Greg
ENTERTAINMENT WEEKLY: "Music Reviews."

Sands, Charles
VIDEO INSIDER: "Adult Video."

Sante, Luc
MOVIELINE: "Moving Lips."

Santosuosso, Dr. John
MONITORING TIMES: "Outer Limits."

Sard, Mark D.
ARK: "Torture Garden," enlightened comment on good and not so good comic releases,

Sarna, John
CABLE TV AND NEW MEDIA LAW & FINANCE: "Video People: Recent Deals," news.

Sarris, editor Andrew
CAHIERS DU CINEMA IN ENGLISH: "Editor's Eyrie."

Sasso, Joey
MODERN SCREEN: "Music Maker of the Month," profile.
SCREEN LIFE: "Hollywood After Dark," Hollywood star activities.

Saunders, Dave
PIC: "Ask a Pro," Q&A.
PIC: "Books," reviews.

Savage, Pete
MAGAZINEWEEK: "Pete Savage on Subscription Marketing," magazine subscription critique.

Savage, Robert L.
POLITICAL COMMUNICATION NEWSLETTER: "From the Division Chair," divisional chair.

Saxon, Marc
POPULAR ELECTRONICS: "Scanner Scene."

Sayer, Richard
STARBURST: "Soundtracks," record review.

Schallert, Edwin
PICTURE PLAY MAGAZINE: "Hollywood High Lights," 'Peaks of interest in news of the studios'

Schallert, Elza
PICTURE PLAY MAGAZINE: "Hollywood High Lights," 'Peaks of interest in news of the studios'

Scharfeld, Arthur W.
JOURNAL OF RADIO LAW: "Regulations of the Federal Radio Commission."
JOURNAL OF RADIO LAW: "Pending Radio Litigation in the United States."
JOURNAL OF RADIO LAW: "General Orders of the Federal Radio Commission."

Schartoff, Bob
SUPER TEEN: "Video Views!," new film/video releases.

Schaub, George
DARKROOM PHOTOGRAPHY: "Basics," of photography.

Scheibach, Michael
MAGAZINE DESIGN & PRODUCTION: "First Edition," editorial.

Schein, Eliot
FOLIO:: "Eliot Schein on Circulation Direct Marketing."

Scheirman, David
PRO SOUND NEWS: "Concert Sound News."
REP: RECORDING ENGINEERING PRODUCTION: "Live & Direct."

Scherer, Wilfred M.
CQ: "Q&A," technical reader-submitted questions,

Schmid, Jack
TARGET MARKETING: "On Catalogs."

Schneider, Robbin
MOVIE WORLD: "The Music Box," newsbriefs.

Schneider, Wolf
VIDEO MAGAZINE: "West Coast Notes."

Schoengood, Bruce J.
HORRORFAN: "Letter From the Editor."

Schoepe, Zenon
STUDIO SOUND AND BROADCAST ENGINEERING: "Music News," 'Product updates and developments from another side of the business', compiled.

Schonauer, David
AMERICAN PHOTO: "Editor's Note."

Schroeder, Carl
TELEVISION AND SCREEN GUIDE: "Hollywood Life."

Schubin, Mark
VIDEOGRAPHY: "Research & Developments."

Schulz, Ulrike
POLYGRAPH INTERNATIONAL: "Editor's Notebook," editorial.

Schuster, Hal
SF MOVIELAND: "Editorial."
TV GOLD: "Reruns," 'The latest news of the nostalgia world'
TV GOLD: "Test Patterns," editorial.

Schutt, Geoffrey
MEDIA SIGHT: "Editorial."

Schwartz, Kevin
CMA NEWSLETTER: "Advertising/Business."

Columnists

Schwartz, Rick
  REP: RECORDING ENGINEERING PRODUCTION: "Digital Domain."

Schwartz, Roberta
  PUBLISH!: "Showtime," presentations.

Sciurca, Lorraine
  MOVIE STARS: "Do Your Own Thing," star suggestions.

Scott, Ron
  FOLIO:: "Ron Scott on Single-Copy Sales."
  MOVIE STARS: "The Naked Truth," 'Hot gossip'

Scottie
  SCREENLAND PLUS TV-LAND: "Scoops From Scottie."

Scroggins, Bob
  MAGAZINE BUSINESS: "The Suppliers' Side," com entary.

Scully, Ed
  CAMERA 35: "On Color."

Scully, Julia
  MODERN PHOTOGRAPHY: "Seeing Pictures."

Search, Don
  QST: "DX Century Club Awards."

Searle, Loyd
  PHOTOPRO: "Business."

Sedgwick, Ruth Woodbury
  STAGE: "From G-106-107," 'The output of plays during the last thirty days, with a looking forward to the next thirty'

Segal, Paul M.
  JOURNAL OF RADIO LAW: "Trend of Radio Regulation."

Seigel, Robert L.
  INDEPENDENT, THE: "Legal Brief," excellent resource.

Sellers, Pat
  SOAP OPERA WEEKLY: "The Gossip," east coast.

Sennett, Ted
  BIJOU: "Talk About Movies," discussion and commentary.
  BIJOU: "The Editor's Page," editorial.

Shames, Erica
  VIDEOMAKER: "Profile," videomaker profile.

Shane, Denny
  FILMLAND: "For the Love of Mike," personality.

Sharp, J.D.
  EQ: "The Sharp Angle."

Sharpe, Howard
  PHOTOPLAY COMBINED WITH MOVIE MIRROR: "Photoplay-Movie Mirror Dancing School," how-to.

Shavelson, Larry
  STUDIO PHOTOGRAPHY: "Legal Photographer."

Shaw, David Allen
  VIDEO STORE: "Communique," publisher commentary.

Shaw, Donald L.
  JQ. JOURNALISM QUARTERLY.: "An Editorial Comment."

Sheldon, George
  VENTURA PROFESSIONAL!: "Facing Pages View."

Sheldon, Sidney
  WRITER, THE: "The Professional Response," 'Answers to questions writers ask'

Shepler, John Q.
  RADIO WORLD: "Q-Tips."

Shevy, Allen
  WORLD OF FANDOM, THE: "Editorial."

Shively, David W.
  TELESPAN'S BUSINESSTV GUIDE: "Looking In On Business Television."

Shoales, Ian
  COMIC RELIEF: "Ian Shoales," humor.

Shopper, Cinebug
  HOME MOVIES: "It's New to Me," new product review.

Shorten, Harry
  AFTERNOON TV: "From the Editor's Desk," a reader interest.

Shriver, Allan
  AMATEUR PHOTOGRAPHER: "AP Tested," test bench review.
  WHAT VIDEO: "Japan," video comment and news.

Shull, Leo
  WRITER'S DIGEST: "Broadway."

Sidles, Constance
  MAGAZINE DESIGN & PRODUCTION: "In Production."

Sievert, Charles
  ADVERTISER MAGAZINE, THE: "Reporter's Notebook."

Silva, Raul da
  FILMMAKERS FILM & VIDEO MONTHLY: "Superserious-8."

Silver, Gerald
  GRAPHIC ARTS MONTHLY: "Estimating."

Simels, Steve
  STEREO REVIEW: "Record Makers," newsbrief.

Simone
  SMASH HITS: "Hot Gossip."

Sims, Harold
  VENTURA PROFESSIONAL!: "Desk Menu."

Singer, Billie
  SOAP OPERA DIGEST: "Hollywood Happenings."

Sint, Steve
  MODERN PHOTOGRAPHY: "Sint's View."

Sircom, Alan
  HI-FI WORLD: "Sircom's Circuits."

Skenazy, Lenore
  ADVERTISING AGE: "The Next Trend."

Skinner, John
  UNION LABOR SUN: "New York Vignette," New York gossip.

Skolsky, Sidney
  PHOTOPLAY: "Sidney Sounds Off," gossip.
  SHOW: "Showing Up in Hollywood," personality.

Slipski, Nancy
  QST: "Silent Keys," obituary.

Sloan, William
  MEDIA & METHODS: "16mm In-Sights," reviews.

Sloane, T. O'Conor
  EXHIBITORS TRADE REVIEW: "Better Screen Results," 'A department devoted to projection'

Slon, Steven
  MGF: "Feeling Great."

Slothower, John
  CMA NEWSLETTER: "Technology."

Small, W Clem
  MONITORING TIMES: "Antenna Topics."

Smith, Barry
  DIRECTION: "Computer Graphics," technology.

Smith, Bill
  RANGEFINDER, THE: "School Photography Digest."

Smith, Cecil
  AV VIDEO: "Technical Smithy."

Smith, Charles
  PROFESSIONAL PHOTOGRAPHER, THE: "Color and You!," color photography.
  PROFESSIONAL PHOTOGRAPHER, THE: "Color and You."

Smith, Donald Q.
PUBLISHER'S AUXILIARY: "Editor's Notebook."

Smith, E.B.
ADVERTISING & SELLING: "Copy Clinic."

Smith, Elliot Blair
CD REVIEW: "CD Business."

Smith, Frederick James
NEW MOVIE MAGAZINE, THE: "Reviews of the New Films," 'Concise and accurate comments upon the important new photoplays'

Smith, Gary
LITTLE SHOPPE OF HORRORS: "The Viewable Hammer," Hammer film video review.

Smith, Hazel
NIGHTTIME TV: "Nashville Scene," 'News, views and the Gospel truth according to Hazel Smith',

Smith, Kate
TV RADIO MIRROR: "The Cooking Corner," celebrity recipes.

Smith, Kenneth
COMICS JOURNAL, THE: "Dramas of the Mind."

Smith, Lillian
FILMLAND: "Filmland Reviews," motion picture review.
SOAP OPERA PEOPLE: "Soaping It Up!," 'Behind the scenes from coast-to-coast!'

Smith, Liz
SHOW: "Showing Up in New York," personality.

Smith, Marian A.
SOUTHERN THEATRE: "Theatre Survey," compiled.

Smith, Ray
CAMCORDER USER: "Ray Smith."

Smith, Ross
PC PUBLISHING AND PRESENTATIONS: "Showpage."
PC PUBLISHING AND PRESENTATIONS: "Hands-On Postscript."

Smith, Rupert
20/20: "Music," review.
20/20: "Video," review.

Smith, Stacy Jenel
ONSAT: "Hollywood Scene."
ONSAT: "Backstage."

Smith, Steven T.
FILMMAKERS FILM & VIDEO MONTHLY: "Product Report," review.

Sneerwell, Richard
THEATERWEEK: "Reviews," extensive play critiques.

Snitzer, Milton S.
COMPUTERS & ELECTRONICS: "Direct & Current," editorial.

Snooper
MOTION PICTURE: "Hollywood Today," gossip.

Sobel, Stanford
COMPUTER PICTURES: "Paradox," production comment.

Soleil, Roy
SOAP OPERA DIGEST: "Prime Time Update," commentary.

Solomon, Charles
GRAFFITI: "The Wisdom of Solomon."

Solomon, Leslie
COMPUTERS & ELECTRONICS: "Computer Sources."
COMPUTERS & ELECTRONICS: "Communications," technical.

Soseman, Ned
VIDEO SYSTEMS: "Question & Answer."

Soter, Tom
BACK STAGE/SHOOT: "On the Market."

Southwick, Thomas P.
CABLE WORLD: "And Another Thing."

Spaeth, Sigmund
THEATRE ARTS: "Theatre on the Disc," music review.

Spar, Laurie
DIRECT MARKETING: "Foundations for the Future."

Speed, Shutter
WESTERN PHOTOGRAPHER MAGAZINE: "Snapshots," photographic newsbriefs.

Spencer, Hazel
STORY WORLD AND PHOTODRAMATIST, THE: "Good English and Its Use," instructional.

Sperberg, Luther
VENTURA PROFESSIONAL!: "Shelf Help," new publications reviewed.

Spielvogel, Cindy
VIDEO INSIDER: "Original Programming."

Spikol, Art
WRITER'S DIGEST: "Nonfiction."

Spillman, Ronald
AMATEUR PHOTOGRAPHER: "Practically Speaking."

Stacey, Robert T.
DIRECT MARKETING: "Canadian Memo."

Stackpole, Peter
TRAVEL & LEISURE: "35mm Techniques."

Stagg, Mildred
TRAVEL & LEISURE: "News and Notes of Women in Photography," unusual department.

Stalter, Katharine
FILM & VIDEO: "Post Production News."
FILM & VIDEO: "Production News."

Stamas, Belka
FACTSHEET FIVE: "NTSC Cyberbeat," media.

Stanbury, C.M.
ELECTRONICS ILLUSTRATED: "The Listener."

Staples, William J.
INDUSTRIAL PHOTOGRAPHY: "AV Screen."

Stark, Craig
STEREO REVIEW: "Tape Talk."

Stark, Phyllis
BILLBOARD: "Promotions & Marketing."

Steadman, Nick
DARKROOM PHOTOGRAPHY: "Special Effects."

Steane, John
GRAMOPHONE: "A Quarterly Retrospect," 'The gramophone and the voice'

Stecker, Elinor
FILMMAKERS FILM & VIDEO MONTHLY: "Filmmakers Notebook."

Steele, Paul David
CAMERA, THE: "Along the Main Stem," commentary.

Stein, Eliot
SPOTLIGHT ON VIDEO: "Heard About Hollywood," 'Hollywood Hotline'™

Stein, Harry
PANORAMA: "Rear View."

Stein, Lisa
CABLEVISION: "From Washington."

Steiner, Paul
DRAMATICS: "Theatre Talk."
SHOW: "Show Stoppers," personality.

Stenza, Jan
SHOOTING COMMERCIALS: "SC Southwest," production news.

Stephanie
REAL LIFE/DAYTIMERS: "Your November Starcast," horoscope.

Stepter, Elaine
BLACK RADIO EXCLUSIVE: "In the Mix," studio news of black artists.

Columnists — INDEX

Stern, Laurence
EXHIBITORS HERALD WORLD: "Motion Picture Finance."

Stettner, Lou
CAMERA 35: "A Humanist View."

Stevens, Neil
THEATRE, THE: "Dateline: London."

Stevenson, Susan
PULP & PAPER CANADA: "Occupational Health and Safety."

Stewart, A. Lee
MOVIE HUMOR: "The Line-Up," celebrity news.

Stewart, Elizabeth
MGF: "Fashion Q & A."
MGF: "Fashion News."

Stewart, Jim
RANGEFINDER, THE: "Off the Press," review.
RANGEFINDER, THE: "Problems and Solutions."

Stewart, Peggy
RURAL RADIO: "Family Gossip," personality news from reader submitted questions,

Stine, Whitney
GREATER AMUSEMENTS: "Tedascope News," projectionist briefs.

Stokes, Orvil
WESTERN PHOTOGRAPHER MAGAZINE: "Stokes' Notes From the Darkroom."

Stone, Emerson
COMMUNICATOR: "News Practices."

Stone, Phil
BROADCAST + TECHNOLOGY: "The Phil Stone Report."
BROADCAST + TECHNOLOGY: "Broadcast Beat."

Stoop, Norma McLain
AFTER DARK: "TV Spotlight," review.
AFTER DARK: "Films," review.
AFTER DARK: "Behind Both Screens."

Story, Bart
VIDEO STORE: "Surveys," interesting research and statistics.

Stoutsenberger, Leo
CARTOONIST PROFILES: "Ask Leo," Q&A.

Strom, David
AMAZING HEROES: "Strom's Index."

Struhl, Warren
DESKTOP COMMUNICATIONS: "Desktop Paper."

Stubbs, Bob
SATELLITE TV WEEK: "Recurring Feeds."

Stude, Lew
STORYBOARD / THE ART OF LAUGHTER: "Restoration," animation art.

Styles, John
ANIMATIONS: "Punchlines."

Suber, Charles
DOWN BEAT: "The First Chorus."

Sullivan, Ed
TV RADIO MIRROR: "The Wonderful World of Ed Sullivan."

Sullivan, Jeremiah
HOLLYWOOD MAGAZINE: "The Stars' Stars," 'Bonfire of the vanities' horoscope'

Summers, Jimmy
AMPERSAND'S COLLEGE ENTERTAINMENT GUIDE: "Quick Takes," 'Previews of major upcoming films, groups on tour and television events, plus some inside scoop on personalities you like to watch',

Sunshine, Robert
FILM JOURNAL, THE: "In Focus," editorial.

Swain, Mark
VIDEOMAKER: "Desktop Video."

Sweet, Jack
VIDEO STORE: "Shorts," newsbriefs.

Sweeting, Paul
VIDEO BUSINESS: "Forecaster."

Sweetow, Stuart
VIDEOMAKER: "Video Q+A."

Swisher, Viola Hegyi
AFTER DARK: "Los Angeles," city review.

Swit, Loretta
NIGHTTIME TV: "Letters to Loretta," Personal Q&A.

Syfret, Toby
TBI: "Advertising."

Sylvester, David
ELECTRONICS: "Management Edge."

Szymanski, Mike
HOLLYWOOD MAGAZINE: "Where Hollywood Lives."

T

Tajima, Renee
INDEPENDENT, THE: "In and Out of Production."

Tannenwald, Peter
LPTV REPORT, THE: "LPTV and the Law," legal.

Tappan, Mel
CB LIFE: "Tappan on Sideband."

Taublieb, Paul
VIDEO CHOICE: "Industry Insight."

Taura, Mitch
TAPE/DISC BUSINESS: "Report From Japan."

Taylor, Andy
TV PICTURE LIFE: "Andy Taylor's Hollywood Beat."

Taylor, N.A.
CANADIAN FILM DIGEST: "Our Business," industry comment.

Taylor, Sally
PUBLISHER'S WEEKLY: "Transpacific."

Teates, Jim
VIDEO CHOICE: "Input/Output," 'Our video expert will answer any question in his crusade to wipe out video intimidation'

Teel, Leonard
INTELLIGENCER: "The President's Desk," editorial.

Terkel, Studs
JOE FRANKLIN'S NOSTALGIA: "Deja Vu."

Terry, Janet
CMA NEWSLETTER: "Magazine."

Thermion
PRACTICAL WIRELESS: "On Your Wavelength."

Thomas, Philip
PHOTO ANSWERS: "Last Word," commentary.

Thompson, Don
COMICS BUYER'S GUIDE: "Comics Guide."

Thompson, Keith
PC PUBLISHING AND PRESENTATIONS: "Presentations."
PC PUBLISHING AND PRESENTATIONS: "Hands-On Pagemaker."

Thompson, Pat
CINEMA/CANADA: "Mini- Reviews."

Thornley, Kerry
FACTSHEET FIVE: "Conspiracy Corner."

Threlfall, Paul
TRAVEL & LEISURE: "Press Photography."

Thurway, E.
PRACTICAL WIRELESS: "Leaves from a Short-Wave Log."

Tobin, Jennifer
TV STAR PARADE: "Talk Around Town," celebrity news and gossip.

Topp, Ray
RADIO GUIDE: "More After This!," 'Editorial comments'

Torgerson, Kimberly
DARKROOM PHOTOGRAPHY: "Editor's Page," editorial.

Torpey, Anne S.
VIDEO BUSINESS: "Retail Roundup."

Torrez, Pompano Joe
EUROPEAN TRASH CINEMA: "The View From Twin Shore," 'A biased look at European Trash Cinema',

Toth, Elizabeth
PRIG: "PRIG Chair's Column," editorial.

Toth, Victor J.
BUSINESS COMMUNICATIONS REVIEW: "Washington Perspective."

Trim, Beverley Van Der
SHOOTING COMMERCIALS: "SC West," production news.

Triplett, J. W.
AMERICAN NEWSPAPER BOY, THE: "Sparks," short positive advice on building subscribers.

Trundle, Eugene
VIDEO ANSWERS: "Helpline," Q&A.

Tucker, Ken
ENTERTAINMENT WEEKLY: "Television Reviews."

Tucker, Kristin
VIDEOMAKER: "Video For Hire."

Tumbusch, Tom
STORYBOARD / THE ART OF LAUGHTER: "Collecting Disneyana," informative.

Turan, Kenneth
PANORAMA: "Sports."

Turano, James
MOVIE MARKETPLACE: "Movies on Video," 'New and recent release reviews'

Turnmire, Pat
CAR STEREO REVIEW: "Tool Aid," 'Tools and accessories for professional installers and the do-it-yourselfer'

Tyler, James
ADVERTISING & SELLING: "Peeled Eye," newsbriefs.

Tynan, Bill
QST: "The World Above 50 MHz."

Tynan, William
QST: "The World Above 50 Megahertz."

Tyree, Dan
COMICS BUYER'S GUIDE: "Dan T's Inferno."

U

Unger, Hugh S.
CQ: "Awards," 'News of certificate and award collecting'

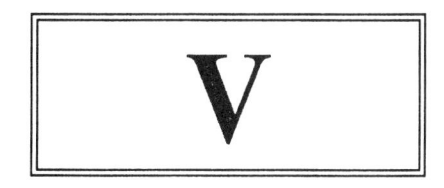

V

Vallee, Rudy
RADIO FAN-FARE: "Tuneful Topics," Hit radio songs.
RADIOLAND: "Rudy Vallee's Music Notebook."

Valovic, Tom
TELECOMMUNICATIONS: "Commentary."

Van-Voorhis, Robert E.
TELEPROFESSIONAL: "Words For Thought," commentary.

Vandervoort, Paul
BAND LEADERS: "Hollywood Bandstand," big bands and personalities in Hollywood motion pictures,

Veljkovic, Morag
AFTER DARK: "Las Vegas," city review.

Vernier, David
CD REVIEW: "New Release Spotlight."
CD REVIEW: "The First Word," editorial.

Vertlieb, Steve
CINEMACABRE: "Soundtrack."

Vesey, Howard W.
JOURNAL OF RADIO LAW: "Decisions of the Federal Radio Commission."
JOURNAL OF RADIO LAW: "Digest of Examiners' Reports and Decisions of the Federal Radio Commission."

Vick, Edd
AMAZING HEROES: "Small Talk."
COMICS FANDOM EXAMINER: "The Alternative Forum."

Vickers, Doug
ADWEEK: "Press."

Villanueva, Danny
MOVIE FLASH: "Industry Report," trade news and comment.

Vischer, Peter
EXHIBITORS HERALD WORLD: "Broadway," New York City exhibition news.

W

Waddell, Ray
AMUSEMENT BUSINESS: "Up Close & Personal," artist or business profile.

Wait, Rolbert
EQ: "The Big Picture," Visual Media.

Waldrop, Judith
AMERICAN DEMOGRAPHICS: "Seasons."

Walker, Gerald
WORLD BROADCAST NEWS: "Letter From America."

Walker, Patric
TV GUIDE: "Horoscope."

Walker, Steve
RADIO GUIDE: "Radio Programs," computer software.
RADIO GUIDE: "Station Automation."

Wall, George
ELECTRONICS WORLD: "Radio Happenings of the Month Illustrated."

Wallach, Van
VIDEO STORE: "Video Stories," commentary.

Walseth, Randi
MODERN SCREEN: "Straight Talk," Q&A format.

Walterick, Lynn
VENTURA PROFESSIONAL!: "Edit Mode."

Walters, Gwenn
PHOTOPLAY COMBINED WITH MOVIE MIRROR: "Spring Fashions."

Walters, Selene
SPOTLIGHT CASTING MAGAZINE: "On the Scene With Selene," personality.

Warech, Gene
DRAMA-LOGUE: "Community Theatre."

Warech, Lynn
DRAMA-LOGUE: "Community Theatre."

Warren, Carl
COMPUTERS & ELECTRONICS: "Computer Bits."

Warren, Jill
TV MIRROR: "What's New from Coast to Coast."

Waryncia, Lou
CD REVIEW: "What's New on CD," new releases.

Waterbury, Ruth
MOVIELAND AND TV TIME: "Inside Hollywood."
PHOTOPLAY COMBINED WITH MOVIE MIRROR: "Close Ups and Long Shots," motion picture star.

Waters, Maureen
MAGAZINE DESIGN & PRODUCTION: "Fifth Wave."

Weaver, Harold
TAKE ONE: "Book Reviews."

Webb, Joseph A.
LINK-UP: "SIG Spotlight," 'Timely briefings on special interest groups'

Wechsberg, Joseph
MODERN PHOTOGRAPHY: "Movies Photographers Should See," feature film review.

Weil, Joe
UNIVERSAL WEEKLY: "Gotham Bugle," 'Happenings in the little village of New York and there-abouts'

Wein, Samuel
MOTION PICTURE PROJECTION: "In the Laboratory," new technical innovations.

Weinberg, Herman G.
TAKE ONE: "Coffee, Brandy and Cigars."

Weinberg, Norman
EQ: "It's About Time," Creative Workshop.

Weis, Bryon G.
POPULAR ELECTRONICS: "Think Tank."

Wels, Byron G.
CB LIFE: "From My 10-20."

Welsh, Bill
CQ: "Bill's Basics," 'How-to for the newcomer to amateur radio',

Werner, Steve
OUTDOOR PHOTOGRAPHER: "In This Issue," overview.

Wesson, Jerry
TRAVEL & LEISURE: "Sound."

Wetmore, Susie
TV GUIDE: "Soap Opera Guide."

Wexler, Barbara
VIDEO SOFTWARE MAGAZINE: "Production Notes," issue detail.

Whiddett, Sally
PRACTICAL PHOTOGRAPHY: "Up-Date," 'People and products in the news'

White, Ellen
QST: "How's DX?."

White, Gordon Eliot
CQ: "Surplus Sidelights," unusual military surplus equipment.

White, Jan V.
COMPUTER PUBLISHING: "Electronic Art World," 'For the art & design professional'

Whyte, Bert
AUDIO: "Behind the Scenes."
AUDIO: "Video Scenes," comment.
ELECTRONICS WORLD: "Certified Record Revue."
ELECTRONICS WORLD: "Sound on Tape," review.

Wickes, E. M.
DRAMATIC MIRROR, THE: "In the Song Shop," music on Broadway and in Vaudeville,

Widmer, Laura
CMA NEWSLETTER: "From the Vice President."

Widoff, Joyce E.
WESTERN PHOTOGRAPHER MAGAZINE: "The Feminine Eye."

Wielage, Marc
MOVING IMAGE: "Product Probe," reviews.

Wien, Richard
V: "Editor's View," editorial.

Wiese, Michael
VIDEOGRAPHY: "Producer to Producer."

Wiesenfelder, Joe
ONI: "On! Audio."

Wilhelm, Ron
WESTERN PHOTOGRAPHER MAGAZINE: "The View From Arizona."

Will-Harris, Daniel
DESKTOP COMMUNICATIONS: "Trade Secrets."
PC PUBLISHING AND PRESENTATIONS: "Typestyle."
VENTURA PROFESSIONAL!: "Graphics Mode."

Will-Harris, Toni
VENTURA PROFESSIONAL!: "Graphics Mode."

Williams, David E.
FILM THREAT: "Underground," independent cinema review.

Williams, Harry
UNIVERSAL WEEKLY: "In Tennessee," exhibitor newsbriefs.

Williams, Sharon
FANTASTIC FILMS: "Databank," 'A look at what's happening in the world of films, theater, literature, conventions and fandom'

Williams, Suzanne
PD REPORT: "Chair Chatter," division chairperson commentary.

Williams, Wendy
SATELLITE TV WEEK: "Only on Satellite," 'For dish owners eyes only'

Williamson, Darrin
VIDEO TODAY: "Music," music video video.

Wilmot, Ingrid
HOLLYWOOD MAGAZINE: "Beyond the Commissary."

Wilson, Kevin
TV GUIDE: "Hollywood Hotline," 'Gossip, scandal, news-- read it here first'

Winkler, John
CAMPAIGN: "Marketing," comment.

Winski, Joe
ADVERTISING AGE: "Slices."

Wirbal, Dave
STORYBOARD / THE ART OF LAUGHTER: "Animated Trends," excellent commentary.

Wolf, Chuck
AP BROADCASTER: "The News Doctor," journalistic advice.

Wolff, Michael
COMIC INFORMER: "Tales of the Flying Desk," editorial.

Wolford, David G.
ORBIT VIDEO: "Editor's Page," editorial commentary.

Wood, Mayrose
   DESKTOP COMMUNICATIONS: "Vertical Markets."

Wood, Teri S.
   AMAZING HEROES: "The Cartoonist."

Woodcock, Rod
   CAMCORDER: "Camcorder Tests," test bench reviews.
   CAMCORDER: "Video Trends."

Woodcock, Roderick
   VIDEO MAGAZINE: "Q&A."

Woodlock, Joe
   MONITORING TIMES: "Below 500 kHz."

Woodruff, Peter
   ABC WEEKLY: "Show Business."

Wool, Robert M.
   SHOW: "Editorial."

Woolf, Robert G.
   ENTERTAINMENT AND SPORTS LAWYER, THE: "Chairman's Column."

Woram, John
   BILLBOARD: "Sound Waves," audio.

Worth, Stephen
   STORYBOARD / THE ART OF LAUGHTER: "Restoration," animation art.

Wright, Cobina
   SCREENLAND PLUS TV-LAND: "Cobina Wright's Party Gossip."

Wright, Polly
   TV PICTURE LIFE: "TV Close-Ups With Polly Wright."

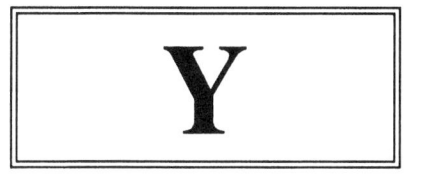

Y

Yahn, Steve
   BUSINESS MARKETING: "FrontTALK," managing editor.

Yencharis, Leonard R.
   ADVANCED IMAGING: "ROI."

York, Cal
   PHOTOPLAY: "Remember! You Read It First in Photoplay," personality.
   PHOTOPLAY: "Inside Stuff," Hollywood gossip.
   PHOTOPLAY COMBINED WITH MOVIE MIRROR: "Inside Stuff," movie personalities.

York, Matthew
   VIDEOMAKER: "Viewfinder," editorial.

Yost, George
   LENS MAGAZINE: "Hollywood Comes Home," 'A column on home movies'

Young, Garry De
   FACTSHEET FIVE: "Curmudgeon Corner."

Younger, Daniel P.
   VIEWS: "Editorial," editorial.

Z

Zall, Steve
   SPOTLIGHT CASTING MAGAZINE: "L.A. Theatre Life."

Zeitchick, Norman
   MGF: "Fitness."

Zhito, Lisa
   AMUSEMENT BUSINESS: "Nashville Notes."

Ziff, Richard
   VIDEO BUSINESS: "Publicity."

Zimmerman, Howard
   COMICS SCENE: "Ed. Notes," editorial.

Zollmann, Carl
   JOURNAL OF RADIO LAW: "Foreign Radio Legislation."
   JOURNAL OF RADIO LAW: "Foreign Radio Decisions."

Zook, Glen E.
   CQ: "F.M.."

Zuk, Karl
   MONITORING TIMES: "American Bandscan."

Zweigler, Mark
   AFTER DARK: "On the Town."

Departments

This index consists of regularly published *Special Departments* from one or more sampled issues. Excluded from this listing are classified advertisement sections. Department titles which are not self-explanatory may have an added description in italics; italicized descriptions in single quotes being from the serial.

Department listings are keyed to a single dated issue as shown in the main title entry and should not be considered as an exhaustive listing of *Departments* in the lineage of a given serial.

-$

--30-- - *obit column* - CALIFORNIA PUBLISHER
--30-- - *'From the editor's desk'* - NEWSINC.
--30-- - *obituaries* - WASHINGTON NEWSPAPER, THE
$$$$$$$ - *'Fiscal control' departmental feature* - MAST

1

16mm Film Booking Chart - FILM WORLD AND A-V NEWS MAGAZINE
16mm In-Sights - *reviews column by William Sloan* - MEDIA & METHODS
16mm News - FOCUS ON FILM
16mm News - TAKE ONE
17th Bit, The - *column by Daniel Kumin* - CD REVIEW

2

20 Questions - *to a profiled star* - TV HITS
20 Years Ago - DEALERSCOPE
21st Century Emporia - *'We highlight the latest diversions in advanced home entertainment'* - WHAT VIDEO

21st Century Fox - *column by Barry Fox* - HI-FI CHOICE
2nd Features - *'This weekly column is provided as a guide through the wilderness of unfamiliar feature video titles' column by Michael Dare* - BILLBOARD
2nd Take - *oldies but goodies in review* - VIDEO TIMES

3

35mm Techniques - *column by Peter Stackpole* - TRAVEL & LEISURE
3-D Graphics - HYPERMEDIA

4

40th Frame, The - *column by Jim Elder* - CAMERA 35 INCORPORATING PHOTO WORLD
40th Frame - *column by Jim Elder* - PHOTOPRO
4th Estate, The - *comment* - EDITOR AND PUBLISHER

5

50 and 25 Years Ago in the Record - *paragraph-long reprinted stories from 25 and 50 years ago* - AT&T TECHNOLOGY
50 Best-Selling Pop Singles - *from top 25 markets* - VARIETY
50 Top Selling LPs and Tapes - *activity on the national retail level* - VARIETY
50 Top-Grossing Films - *complete financial data for United States exhibition* - VARIETY
526th Line, The - *viewpoint on the state of communication arts* - TELEVISIONS

6

60- Second Seminar - *column by 'Rocket' Ray Jutkins* - TARGET MARKETING

7

7 Ages News - NATIONAL PHOTOGRAPHER, THE

| **Departments** | **INDEX** | 776 |

8

8-pt Page, The - *column by Odds Bodkins* - ADVERTISING AGENCY

A

AAAA Recommends, The - *'Our best bets for some new products and services'* - AGENCY
AAJA Activities - AFRO-ASIAN JOURNALIST
AB Stock Index - *selected stock activities* - AMUSEMENT BUSINESS
Abandoned Stone Quarry, The - FACTSHEET FIVE
ABC of Television - *'A dictionary of definitions of the more important television terms'* - PRACTICAL TELEVISION AND SHORT-WAVE REVIEW
ABCs of Type - *column by Allan Haley* - STEP-BY-STEP GRAPHICS
About Current Plays - DRAMATIC REVIEW, THE
About Faces - *type column by Clifford Burke* - PUBLISHI
About Legion Estimates - PRESS STATISTICAL REVIEW
About Our Members - *profiles* - COMBROAD
About People and Product - BOX OFFICE
About Stock Plays and Players in Many Cities - *selected theatre review* - DRAMATIC MIRROR, THE
About Television - *column by Martin Mayer* - AMERICAN FILM
About the Ad Women - *newsbriefs* - FOURTH ESTATE
About the Cover Designer - PRINTING PAPER
About the Magazines - ADVERTISING EXPERIENCE
About the Starz - *'Your questions answered'* - STARZ
About This Issue - HIGH FIDELITY/MUSICAL AMERICA
About Town with Connie - HOLLYWOOD FILMOGRAPH
Above the Line - ENTERTAINMENT REVUE
Abstracts - LEONARDO
Abstracts - TELEVISION
Abstracts and Reviews - EBU REVIEW. TECHNICAL.
Abstracts of Articles in French, German, and Spanish - VISIBLE LANGUAGE
Abstracts of Forthcoming Manuscripts - IEEE TRANSACTIONS ON COMMUNICATIONS
Abstracts of Journal Articles in French and German - VISIBLE LANGUAGE

Abstracts of Papers From Other Journals - *excellent overview of other work* - SMPTE JOURNAL
Abstracts, Resumes, Zusammenfassungen - *Article abstracts in author's original language* - EUROPEAN JOURNAL OF COMMUNICATION
AC - *Adult contemporary radio format column by Mike Kinosian* - R & R
A/C This Week - INTERNATIONAL RADIO REPORT, THE
Academic Openings - *employment opportunities* - C-O-N-N-E-C-T-I-O-N-S
Academy Calendar - *upcoming events* - DEBUT
Academy News - EMMY
Accessories - LÜRZER'S INTERNATIONAL ARCHIVE
Accessories - VIDEO BUSINESS
Accessories Club - HI-FI NEWS AND RECORD REVIEW
According to informed sources - *comment* - TECHTRENDS
Account Activity - *news of winning and losing agencies* - ADWEEK'S MARKETING WEEK
Account Changes - ADVERTISERS' WEEKLY
Account Changes - ADVERTISING AGENCY
Account Changes - CAMPAIGN
Account Changes - MARKETING / COMMUNICATIONS
Account Changes - PRESS STATISTICAL REVIEW
Accounts - *briefs of ads and public relations* - AD WEEKLY
Acid Test, The - *Science Fiction column by Peter Heck* - W•B
Across My Desk - *commentary and letters to the editor* - TV DAY STARS
Across the Board - *column by Roger Nichols* - EQ
Across the Editor's Desk - THEATRE JOURNAL
Across the Nation - *printing industry news listed by state* - IN-PLANT REPRODUCTIONS
ACTA - *column by Twink Lynch* - THEATRE NEWS
Action - *'Late-Breaking News'* - BACK STAGE/SHOOT
Action / Adventure - *reviews* - ORBIT VIDEO
Action Band Receivers - *equipment review* - COMMUNICATIONS WORLD
Action Forum, The - *letters* - ACTION!
Action Reviews - VIDEO TODAY
Actionline - *NAB actions and newsbriefs* - RADIOWEEK
Activities - PLAYERS
Activities - *conference information on IFTC seminars* - WORLD SCREEN
Activities Calendar - KODAK
Activities in the Electrical Appliance Industry - TELEVISION RETAILING
Activities of NHK - *news roundup* - TELECOM JAPAN, THE
Activities of the IOJ and Member Unions - JOURNALISTS' AFFAIRS
Activities of the Jobbing Trade - RADIO DEALER, THE

Activity in Florida - SCREEN ACTOR HOLLYWOOD
Actors - *extensive upcoming auditions listing* - CASTING NEWS
Actor's Diary, An - DRAMA
Ad Agencies - LÜRZER'S INTERNATIONAL ARCHIVE
Ad Agency Activities - ADVERTISER MAGAZINE, THE
Ad Agency News & Views - BACK STAGE
Ad Eye by Hermes - *personnel changes* - CAMPAIGN
Ad Glib - *comment* - FILMS IN REVIEW
Ad Impact - ADWEEK'S MARKETING WEEK
Ad Lib - CAMERA 35
Ad Lib - DOWN BEAT
Ad Lib! - *column by Jacquie Loney* - BROADCAST + TECHNOLOGY
Ad Libs - *'Items of Interest'* - INSIDE MEDIA
Ad Lines - *similar briefs concerning advertising* - BLACK JOURNALISM REVIEW
Ad Marketing - *personnel briefs* - FOLIO:
Ad Nauseam - *editorial column by Mary Knox* - BACK STAGE/SHOOT
A-D Shorts - *newsbriefs* - A-D
AD Spotlight - *advertisement shoot* - PHOTO DISTRICT NEWS
Ad Strategy - *critique* - CABLE MARKETING
Ad Watch - *critique* - CONSUMER ELECTRONICS
Ad Weekly International - *ad news* - AD WEEKLY
AdBeat - *advertising news shorts* - ADVERTISING AGE
Additional Bibliography on - *review. (#2-84).* - COMMUNICATION RESEARCH TRENDS
AD-Lib - *column by Ben Duffy* - ADVERTISER MAGAZINE, THE
Adlib - *advertising commentary* - CAMPAIGN
Ad-Lib! - *newsbriefs* - BROADCAST + TECHNOLOGY
Ad-Man's Diary - *newsbriefs* - ADVERTISING AND MARKETING MANAGEMENT
Admen's Guide to Advertising Services, The - ADWEEK
Admonitor, The - AUDIO CRITIC, THE
AD/PR Notes - *commentary and news on St. Louis advertising* - ST. LOUIS JOURNALISM REVIEW
Ad-Supported Cable Networks - *listing* - SHOOTING COMMERCIALS
Adult Books - *listing* - FORECAST
Adult Books - *list* - HOT PICKS
Adult Contemporary - *playlist* - INTERNATIONAL RADIO REPORT, THE
Adult Contemporary - *hit list* - R & R
Adult Video - *column by Charles Sands* - VIDEO INSIDER
Advance Synopses - *'And information'* - PRODUCT DIGEST
Advanced Competition - *monthly contest* - PHOTO-ERA MAGAZINE
Adventuring in Hollywood - *motion picture news column by Rita Douglas* - ROXY THEATRE WEEKLY REVIEW
Advertisements - *small display rate cards* - ADVERTISERS GAZETTE

Advertisements - *large 30-plus page of individual newspaper rate cards* - ADVERTISERS GUIDE
Advertisers - ADVERTISING & SELLING
Advertisers Interviewed - *profile* - ADVERTISERS GAZETTE
Advertisers' Round Table, The - *'Current retail advertising criticised'* - AD SENSE
Advertising - CABLE WORLD
Advertising - CABLEAGE
Advertising - CABLEVISION
Advertising - CHANNELS
Advertising - EDITOR AND PUBLISHER
Advertising - MEDIA WEEK
Advertising - PRESSTIME
Advertising - *column by Toby Syfret* - TBI
Advertising Agencies - NATIONAL ADVERTISING
Advertising & Promotion - PERSONAL ELECTRONICS
Advertising Art News - *newsbriefs* - ADVERTISER MAGAZINE, THE
Advertising Basics - *column by Hall Betancourt* - PROFESSIONAL PHOTOGRAPHER, THE
Advertising Department - ADVERTISING
Advertising Gallery, The - *sample ads* - ADVERTISERS' WEEKLY
Advertising News - CABLE WORLD
Advertising News - *large second section concerning magazine advertising* - MAGAZINEWEEK
Advertising Parade - MARKETING / COMMUNICATIONS
Advertising Personalities - *newsbriefs* - NEWSPAPER WORLD AND ADVERTISING REVIEW
Advertising Profiles - *outstanding individuals in advertising* - JOURNAL OF ADVERTISING
Advertising Research - CRC NEWSLETTER
Advertising Talk - COMMON SENSE
Advertising, [year]--and After - *column by Alan Reilly* - ADVERTISING & SELLING
Advertising/Business - *column by Kevin Schwartz* - CMA NEWSLETTER
Advertising's Month - *media comparison* - ADVERTISING & SELLING
Advice to the Stars - *column by Anthony Cirella* - MOVIE TV SECRETS
Adwatch - *column by Jim Davies* - DIRECTION
Adweek Digest - *activity by agency* - ADWEEK
Adweek Digest Top 50 - *agency facts and figures* - ADWEEK
Adweek Piggyback Register - *proposed marketing surveys* - ADWEEK
AEC - *architecture, engineering and construction* - HYPERMEDIA
AECT Archives Software Collection - *a listing of software gathered by AECT and available to members* - TECHTRENDS
AER Reviews - PUBLIC TELECOMMUNICATIONS REVIEW
Aerial Photography - COMMERCIAL PHOTOGRAPHER, THE
Aerial Safety - ASMP BULLETIN
Aeronautical - MOBILE SATELLITE NEWS

Affair to Remember, An - *reader-submitted poetry* - SOSYALI MAGAZINE
Affairs of the Heart - *'Film folk who are saying We Will-- We do!-- We're through'* - TALKING SCREEN
Affiliates - *listing of regional publishers associations* - PMA NEWSLETTER
AFI Calendar - *American Film Institute events* - AMERICAN FILM
AFI News - *'A newsletter about film and television activities of special interest to the American Film Institute members', edited column by Brynda Pappas* - AMERICAN FILM
After 5 o'Clock - *interview* - INTERNATIONAL ADVERTISER
After Hours - *guest column* - BUSINESS ADVERTISING
After Hours - MARKETING / COMMUNICATIONS
After Hours - *pictures and information on stars after dark* - PREVIEW
After Hours - PRODUCERS QUARTERLY
After the Blockbusters - *lesser-known film review column by J. Martin Chitwood* - VIDEO SOFTWARE MAGAZINE
After the Top 10 - *videotape reviews* - ORBIT VIDEO
After Theatre - *post-show places to dine, column by Bob Edison* - PLAYBILL
Afterlife - *life after acting in soap operas* - SOAP OPERA WEEKLY
After-Mix - *column by Philip De Lancie* - MIX
Afterthoughts - *commentary* - BPME IMAGE MAGAZINE
Afterword - *editorial and comment* - MADISON AVENUE
AFTRA Talent Agents - *listing* - SHOW BUSINESS
Age of the Pressroom - PRINTING IMPRESSIONS
Agencies - ADVERTISING & SELLING
Agencies Ask Us - *Q&A* - ADVERTISING AGENCY
Agency Abbreviations Index - PRESS STATISTICAL REVIEW
Agency Account Changes - FOCUS
Agency Action - *personnel newsbriefs* - DIRECT MARKETING
Agency Bookshelf - ADVERTISING AGENCY
Agency Creative Campaign - *spotlighting one agency's work* - MADISON AVENUE
Agency News in Brief - MEDIA INTERNATIONAL
Agency People on the Move - BACK STAGE/SHOOT
Agency Relations - POST
Agenda - *upcoming international photography seminars and workshops* - CAMERA
Agent's Corner - ROUNDUP QUARTERLY
Agents Corner - *manufacturing and promotion column by J. L. Brister* - SCHEMER, THE
Agents-Writers Committee - NEWSLETTER
AICP/Atlanta Report - *column by Lynn Hoffman-Keating* - BACK STAGE
AICP/SF Report - *column by Marianne Lucchesi* - BACK STAGE
Aids to Better Photography - POPULAR PHOTOGRAPHY

Aids to Help You in Photo and Video - CAMERART
Aids to Romance - *column by Alison Alden* - MOVIE CLASSIC
AIGA Calendar of Events - AIGA JOURNAL OF GRAPHIC DESIGN
Air Bells - *comment* - MODERN PHOTOGRAPHY
Air Report - AIRBRUSH ACTION
Aircheck Central - *subscriber aircheck exchange* - RADIO*PHILES
Airing Our View - RELIGIOUS BROADCASTING
AIRwaves - *news* - INTERNATIONAL RADIO REPORT, THE
Album - *full page historical photo* - MEMORIES
Album Releases - BILLBOARD
Album Reviews - BILLBOARD
Album Reviews - MUSIC LINE
Album Rock - *playlist* - INTERNATIONAL RADIO REPORT, THE
Album Rock Tracks - BILLBOARD
Album Specials - FILM ALBUM MAGAZINE
Albums Chart - *weekly black radio format listing* - BLACK RADIO EXCLUSIVE
Alen Dodd's Column - MARKETING / COMMUNICATIONS
All Access - *unique column listing audio equipment utilized by entertainment groups, column by Mark Herman* - REP: RECORDING ENGINEERING PRODUCTION
All American Newspaper - SCHOLASTIC EDITOR'S TRENDS IN PUBLICATIONS
All American Yearbook - SCHOLASTIC EDITOR'S TRENDS IN PUBLICATIONS
All My Children - *program abstract* - SOAP OPERA DIGEST
All Points Bulletin - *production advice* - LAW ENFORCEMENT TECHNOLOGY
Allen Asks - *column by Ben Allen* - BACK STAGE/SHOOT
Allen on the Avenue - *personality column by Ben Allen* - BACK STAGE
All-Star Teen Word Search - *puzzle* - TEEN DREAM
Along Publisher's Row - ROUNDUP QUARTERLY
Along Studio Street - *'program ideas for stations and advertisers'* - BROADCAST REPORTER
Along the Main Stem - *commentary column by Paul David Steele* - CAMERA, THE
Along the Rialto - *column by Phil M. Daly* - FILM TV DAILY
Along the Way with Lambdin Kay - *humorous commentary column by Lambdin Kay* - RURAL RADIO
Alphabetic Product Groups Index - PRESS STATISTICAL REVIEW
Alphabetical Listing of Pictures - *new releases* - FILM BUYER
Alphabetical Movie Listings - ENTERTAINER, THE
Alterations - *theatre remodeling* - NATIONAL EXHIBITOR, THE
Alternative Forum, The - *column by Chris Lightfoot and Edd Vick* - COMICS FANDOM EXAMINER

Alternative Theatre Directory - *extensive national workshop listing by state* - ALTERNATIVE THEATRE
Alumni News - COMMUNIQUÉ
Alumni News - *status of previous Academy interns* - DEBUT
Alumni Profiles - INTERCOMM
Alumni Update - SIDEBAR
AMA Chapter News - *of American Marketing Association* - MARKETING NEWS
AMA National News - *of American Marketing Association* - MARKETING NEWS
Amateur Eight - *'Each month, PIC publishes eight photographs by amateur photographers'* - PIC
Amateur Radio - RADIO AGE
Amateur Satellite Communications - *column by Vern Riportella* - QST
Amateur Stage, The - THEATRE MAGAZINE
Amateur's Green Room, The - *upcoming actors* - THEATRE MAGAZINE
Amazing Readers - *letters* - AMAZING HEROES
Amazing Video - *'Capsule Reviews of Current Video Fare'* - AMAZING CINEMA
Amazing Video - *review* - SF MOVIELAND
Ambient Sound - *column* - MODERN RECORDING & MUSIC
America - *video comment and news stateside column by Robert Angus* - WHAT VIDEO
American Bandscan - *column by Karl Zuk* - MONITORING TIMES
American Cinema Editors Current Assignments - AMERICAN CINEMEDITOR
American Drawing Board - *newsbriefs* - TARGET
America's Greatest Disk Jockeys - MOVIE MIRROR
AM/FM - *commentary on St. Louis radio* - ST. LOUIS JOURNALISM REVIEW
AMICINFO - MEDIA ASIA
Amiga Niches - *column by Matt Drabick* - AV VIDEO
Ammendments to Previous Month - PRESS STATISTICAL REVIEW
Among the Affiliates - NATIONAL PHOTOGRAPHER, THE
Among the Agencies - *accounts* - ADVERTISING NEWS
Among the Amateur Journalists - *newsbriefs* - JOURNALIST, THE
Among the Craftsmen - *newsbriefs* - MID-ATLANTIC GRAPHIC ARTS REVIEW
Among the Dailies and Weeklies - NATIONAL ADVERTISING
Among the Fraternity - AMERICAN PRESS
Among the Monthlies - *newsbriefs* - NATIONAL ADVERTISING
Among the Traveling Men - RADIO DEALER, THE
Amusement Stock Quotations - *weekly data on both Tokyo and New York exchanges* - MOVIE/TV MARKETING
Amusement Stock Quotations - *weekly listing of 75+ stocks* - VARIETY
Analog Presentations - *column by Dona Meilach* - AVC
Analysis - *of weeks best selling/renting videos* - VIDEO INSIDER

Analyst's Portfolio - COMMUNICATIONSWEEK
Analyst's Report - *media corporation economic profile* - MEDIA BUSINESS
Anatomy of a Bold Star - *column by Edgar Reyes* - MOVIE FLASH
And Another Thing - *column by Thomas P. Southwick* - CABLE WORLD
And Now a Few Words About... - *'Editorial comment column by Mike L. Gustafson'* - STV GUIDE
And Now a Word From... - *human interest column by Carroll Carroll* - VARIETY
And Now a Word From Our Editor - *editorial* - SH-BOOM
And Now... a Word From Your Editor - NIGHTTIME TV
And On Our Screen - *historic motion picture newspaper advertisements* - NEW CAPTAIN GEORGE'S WHIZZBANG, THE
And Selected Short Subjects - *newsbriefs* - FILMOGRAPH
Andy Taylor's Hollywood Beat - *column by Andy Taylor* - TV PICTURE LIFE
Anglo-American Crossword Puzzle - VERBATIM
Anglo-American Radio and Television Society - *newsbriefs* - PRACTICAL TELEVISION AND SHORT-WAVE REVIEW
Animated Trends - *excellent commentary column by Dave Wirbal* - STORYBOARD / THE ART OF LAUGHTER
Animation - INVISION
Animation - 60 SECONDS
Animation Answers - *Q&A on animation* - KORKIS AND CAWLEY'S CARTOON QUARTERLY
Animation Kit - *column by Howard Beckerman* - FILMMAKERS FILM & VIDEO MONTHLY
Animation News - *column by Darrell McNeil* - COMICS BUYER'S GUIDE
Animation News - *newsbriefs* - PENCIL TEST
Animation Profile - KORKIS AND CAWLEY'S CARTOON QUARTERLY
Animation Profiles - *column by Harry Love* - GRAFFITI
Animation Spot - *column by Howard Beckerman* - BACK STAGE
Animatorial/Fan Mail - ANIMATO!
Anniversarians - *employment anniversaries of selected workers* - TELEPHONE NEWS, THE
Anniversary Dates - *detailing years of services of Fox employees* - FOCUS ON FOX
Annotations - *editorial* - HOW
Announcements - *news of grants, seminars and archive acquisitions* - AFI EDUCATION NEWSLETTER
Announcements - *club notes* - CQ
Announcements - EDUCATIONAL SCREEN
Announcements - INTERNATIONAL DOCUMENTARY
Announcements - JOURNAL OF TECHNICAL WRITING AND COMMUNICATION
Announcements - OFF-HOLLYWOOD REPORT
Announcements - RADIO PHILES
Announcements - SHAKESPEARE QUARTERLY
Announcements - VICTORIAN PERIODICALS REVIEW

Announcements and Professional Development - HUMAN COMMUNICATION CANADA
Announcements From Around the World - *journalism history newsbriefs* - CLIO AMONG THE MEDIA
Announcements of Interest - PLAY SHOP, THE
Annual Reports - SATELLITE NEWS
Another World - *abstract* - SOAP OPERA DIGEST
ANPA Calendar - PRESSTIME
ANPA News - PRESSTIME
Answer Man - *technical fixit column by Bob Dargan* - ELECTRONIC SERVICING & TECHNOLOGY
Answer Man, The - *column by Leo Lukowsky* - INDUSTRIAL PHOTOGRAPHY
Answer Man, The - *Q&A of the stars column by Gene Samuels* - MOTION PICTURE
Answer Man, The - *Reader Q&A column by Dick Maurice* - TV DAY STARS
Answer Print, The - *Q&A format on editing items* - AMERICAN CINEMEDITOR
Answers - *Q&A* - FILM MAKING
Answers by Arnold - *Q&A technical column by Rus Arnold* - TRAVEL & LEISURE
Answers to Correspondence - COMMON SENSE
Answers to Correspondents - AMATEUR POINTER FOR AMATEUR PHOTOGRAPHERS, THE
Answers to Correspondents - AMERICAN AMATEUR PHOTOGRAPHER AND CAMERA & DARKROOM
Answers to Correspondents - EXHIBITORS' TIMES
Answers to Examination Papers - TELECOMMUNICATION JOURNAL OF AUSTRALIA, THE
Answers to Queries - *Q&A format on technical issues* - PHOTO-ERA MAGAZINE
Answers to Queries - THEATRE NOTEBOOK
Antenna News - ELECTRONICS WORLD
Antenna Topics - *column by W Clem Small* - MONITORING TIMES
Antennas and Grounds - *column by John Frye* - ELECTRONICS WORLD
Antiquarian Activities and Letters - GRAPHIC ANTIQUARIAN
Antique Radio - *column by Marc Ellis* - POPULAR ELECTRONICS
Antique Radio - *column by Richard D. Fitch* - RADIO-ELECTRONICS
Any Questions? - *Q&A* - AUSTRALIAN PHOTOGRAPHY
Any Questions? - *Q&A photography column by William Cheung* - PRACTICAL PHOTOGRAPHY
Any Questions? - *'You ask the questions, we get the answers'* - SOAP OPERA WEEKLY
Anything For a Laugh - *'A distillation of current wit'* - SHOW BUSINESS ILLUSTRATED
AOR - R & R
AOR Albums - *Album oriented rock hit list* - R & R
AOR Tracks - *Album oriented rock* - R & R

AP Network News - AP BROADCASTER
AP People - *personnel briefs* - AP BROADCASTER
AP Sports - AP BROADCASTER
AP Tested - *test bench review column by Allan Shriver* - AMATEUR PHOTOGRAPHER
Appearance and Manners - EXHIBITORS' TIMES
Appliances and Devices - *newsbriefs of new products* - WIRELESS AGE, THE
Application - *of 900 telephone service* - 4TH MEDIA JOURNAL, THE
Application Note - TELECOMMUNICATIONS
Applications - ELECTRONICS WORLD + WIRELESS WORLD
Applications - JOURNAL OF APPLIED COMMUNICATION RESEARCH
Applications - SCSC XEROX PIPELINE
Applications - *educational* - THE JOURNAL
Applications for Patents - KINEMATOGRAPH WEEKLY
Applications Granted - NARTB MEMBER SERVICE
Applications Returned - NARTB MEMBER SERVICE
Applications Set for Hearing - NARTB MEMBER SERVICE
Appointments - ADWEEK
Appointments - BROADCAST + TECHNOLOGY
Appointments - CABLEAGE
Appointments - CANADIAN PRINTER
Appointments - *personnel briefs* - CINEMA/CANADA
Appointments - SCREEN INTERNATIONAL
Appointments - *faculty* - SPECTRA
Approved Films and Their Sources - *reviews* - MOVING PICTURE AGE
Arbitron People - *personnel briefs* - BEYOND THE RATINGS
Arbitron People - *personnel briefs* - BEYOND THE RATINGS/RADIO
Arbitron People - *personnel newsbriefs* - BEYOND THE RATINGS/TELEVISION
ARB's Top 10 Films in 15 Key Markets - BILLBOARD TV PROGRAM AND TIME AVAILABILITIES, THE
Arcade Alley - *review* - VIDEO MAGAZINE
Architecture - THEATRE DESIGN & TECHNOLOGY
Archival Acquisitions - *new arrivals at the center* - MAGAZINE, THE
Archives - *'Disney facts, films and trivia'* - DISNEY CHANNEL MAGAZINE, THE
Archives - QUARTERLY REVIEW OF FILM AND VIDEO
Are You Watching - *'Test your soap smarts'* - EPISODES
Argentina - *production newsbriefs* - PRODUCCIÓN Y DISTRIBUCIÓN
Argybargy - *equipment manufacturer retort to earlier reviews* - HI-FI HERETIC
Army Archerd Makes TV Radio Talk - *'The latest hottest gossip! Read it here first!' column by Army Archerd* - TV RADIO TALK
Army Archerd's Hollywood - MOVIE MIRROR
Aroun Books - BRITISH BOOK NEWS

Around Filmdom - *pictures* - FILMWORLD
Around Florida - *locations of note* - ENTERTAINMENT REVUE
Around Hollywood - THEATRE CRAFT
Around New York with Cecile - *'Follow her suggestions about these reliable shops and places of interest' shopping column by Cecile (10-15-27)* - ROXY THEATRE WEEKLY REVIEW
Around the Agencies - *newsbriefs* - AM
Around the Branches - *unusually long segments detailing union journalism activities in Great Britain* - JOURNALIST
Around the Cinema - *personnel news of exhibitors* - SCREEN INTERNATIONAL
Around the Dial - *at ABC daytime television* - EPISODES
Around the Dial - *program notes* - RADIO DIAL
Around the Globe - *news items* - IPI REPORT
Around the Nation - AUDIOVIDEO INTERNATIONAL
Around the Studios - *program newsbriefs* - BBC WORLD SERVICE LONDON CALLING
Around the Studios - *newsbriefs* - MUSICAL AMERICA
Around the Studios - VIDEO
Around the World - *global gossip* - PREVIEW
Around the World Print News - *industry newsbriefs* - AUSTRALASIAN PRINTER
Around the World Trendletter - MARKETING / COMMUNICATIONS
Art - FILM & VIDEO NEWS
Art - INTERVIEW
Art - *review of exhibitions and talent* - SHOW
Art - *the state of video as an art form* - TELEVISIONS
Art - *review column by Sarah Kent* - 20/20
Art - WORLD PRESS REVIEW
Art & Media - *reviews* - HOMILETIC
Art and Photography - WHAT EDITORS WANT
Art Direction - MAGAZINE DESIGN & PRODUCTION
Art Gallery - *graphic art portfolios* - AV VIDEO
Art Gallery - *'Contributions from our talented readers'* - COMIC CELLAR, THE
Art Gallery - *full-page rotogravure portraits of selected stars* - PICTURE PLAY MAGAZINE
Art Materials, Methods and Machinery News - GRAPHICS: U.S.A.
Art Notes - THEATRE, THE
Art Related News - *newsbriefs* - VIDEO EIGHTIES MAGAZINE
Art Related Notes - VIDEO EIGHTIES MAGAZINE
Art Scene - *column by James Alan Nash* - AFTER DARK
Art/Exhibits/Seminars - *upcoming* - WESTERN PHOTOGRAPHER MAGAZINE
Articles - *large section detailing specific articles purchased* - WHAT EDITORS WANT
Articles and Books - *reviews* - FOI DIGEST
Articles Digest - FEDERAL COMMUNICATIONS LAW JOURNAL
Articles on Mass Communication in U.S. and Foreign Journals - JQ. JOURNALISM QUARTERLY.

Articles Pertinent to the Campus Press - *bibliography of current articles* - COLLEGE MEDIA REVIEW
Artifact Reviews - *'Artifacts are things that have a presence beyond being carriers of print--buttons, stickers, armbands, Moebius strips and other goodies'* - FACTSHEET FIVE
Artist Books - HIGH PERFORMANCE
Artist Developments - *dance music newsbriefs* - BILLBOARD
Artist Pages - MILLENNIUM FILM JOURNAL
Artistic Home, The - ALBUM, THE
Artist's Article - LEONARDO
Artists Corner! - *reader submissions of favorite stars* - SMASH HITS
Artists' Notes - LEONARDO
Art/Science Forum - LEONARDO
As I See It - POPULAR PHOTOGRAPHY
As Others See It - *newspaper reports* - SELECTED MOTION PICTURES
As the Editor Sees It - *commentary* - MOTION PICTURE PROJECTION
As the World Turns - *abstract* - SOAP OPERA DIGEST
As They Appear to Me - *editorial* - AD SENSE
As They Put It - *guest commentary* - GUILD REPORTER, THE
As Time Goes By - *'Where to go, what to buy, when to sell'* - JOE FRANKLIN'S NOSTALGIA
As Viewed by the Managing Editor - AD SENSE
As We Go to Press - *newsbriefs* - PERSONAL ELECTRONICS
As We See It - *editorial* - INTELLIGENT DECISIONS
As We See It - *editorial* - JEE, JOURNAL OF ELECTRONIC ENGINEERING
As We See It - MEDIAWEEK
As We See It - *Founder and Chief Tester commentary column by J. Gordon Holt* - STEREOPHILE
ASCAP Foundation - ASCAP IN ACTION
Asia News in Brief - MEDIA INTERNATIONAL
Asian Box Office Scoreboard of Completed First-Runs - MOVIE/TV MARKETING
ASIFA International - *newsbriefs* - ASIFA NOUVELLES
ASIFA News - *newsbriefs of the International Animated Film Association* - ANIMAFILM
Ask a Pro - *Q&A column by Dave Saunders* - PIC
Ask Adrienne - *reader Q&A column by Adrienne LaRussa* - TV DAY STARS
Ask ASC - *questions and comments column by David Heuring* - AMERICAN CINEMATOGRAPHER
Ask Bob - *Reader Q&A column by Bob Grove* - MONITORING TIMES
Ask Dr. Science - *wonderful Duck's Breath Mystery Theatre column concerning the mysteries of life* - COMIC RELIEF
Ask Hank - COMMUNICATIONS WORLD
Ask Hank, He Knows! - *Q&A* - COMMUNICATIONS WORLD

Departments

Ask Ian - *Q&A advice column by Ian Bonner* - TEEN DREAM
Ask Kathy! - *Q&A on health, beauty, fashion or fitness* - WOW! MAGAZINE
Ask Leo - *Q&A column by Leo Stoutsenberger* - CARTOONIST PROFILES
Ask Me About TV - *Q&A column by Toni D'Amato* - ONSAT
Ask Mr. Movie - *reader Q&A column by Steve Friedman* - HOME VIEWER
Ask R-E - *questions answered* - RADIO-ELECTRONICS
Ask the Expert - *video Q&A column by Myron Berger* - CINEMA, VIDEO & CABLE MOVIE DIGEST
Ask the Experts - *technical questions* - IN VIEW
Ask the Experts! - *'Movie Teen's exciting and instructive new series of articles to help you top the date lists'* - MOVIE TEEN
Ask the Insider - *Q&A on celebrities* - STAR
Ask the Tech Editor - *reader-submitted Q&A* - SATELLITE TV WEEK
Ask Us - MOVING PICTURE AGE
Ask Us - *reader submitted Q&A* - SOAP OPERA DIGEST
Ask Video Dave - SHUTTERBUG
Ask Video Phil - *Q&A by readers* - FAST FORWARD
Aspect - HDTV NEWSLETTER
Aspects of Advertising - *editorial* - ADVERTISING AND MARKETING MANAGEMENT
Assignment - *readers are challenged to send in photos embodying a challenge theme* - AMERICAN PHOTO
Assignment - PHOTOGRAPHY
Associate Director's Column - 4SIGHT MAGAZINE
Association Briefs - *newsbriefs* - AEJMC NEWS
Association Events - COMMUNICATIONS
Association News - ELECTRONIC SERVICING & TECHNOLOGY
Association News - FILM WORLD AND A-V NEWS MAGAZINE
Association News - OLD TIMER'S BULLETIN, THE
Association News - *of Photo Marketing Association International* - PHOTO MARKETING
Association News - RANGEFINDER, THE
Association Newsline - *news of the Professional Film and Video Equipment Association* - NEWSLETTER, THE
Association Notes - *newsbriefs concerning trade and professional groups* - MARKETING COMMUNICATIONS
Association Speaks - MAST
Association Update - *news of various media trade groups* - AVC
Association Update - *cable association news* - CABLE TV BUSINESS MAGAZINE
Associations - BROADCAST + TECHNOLOGY
Astrology & Poetry - ENTERTAINMENT CONNECTION MAGAZINE
Astrology Goes to Hollywood to Find Your Perfect Mate Among the Stars - *column by Art Gatti* - NIGHTTIME TV
At a Glance - *regular program schedule* - BBC WORLD SERVICE LONDON CALLING

At a Glance - *a wonderful section showcasing a Knight-Ridder division* - KNIGHT-RIDDER NEWS
At a Glance - *production data* - UNIVERSAL WEEKLY
At Deadline - *newsbriefs* - COMMUNIQUE
At Deadline - MEDIA BUSINESS
At Home With - *color photos of star homes* - RONA BARRETT'S HOLLYWOOD
At Issue - *editorial* - COLUMBIA JOURNALISM REVIEW
At Random - *new products* - LEICA PHOTOGRAPHY
At the FCC - *legal developments* - LPTV REPORT, THE
At the Movies - TAKE ONE
At the Play - *current fare* - THEATRE, THE
At the Theater - *large section of film and video reviews from a Christian perspective* - ALPHA AND OMEGA FILM REPORT
At the Theatres - *listing* - BROADWAY WEEKLY
At Your Service - *departmental banner for useful 'how-to' information* - SHOWCASE WORLD
AT&T Monitor - COMMUNICATIONSWEEK
Atlanta - BOX OFFICE
Atlantic Airwaves - *column by Sandra Porteous* - BROADCAST + TECHNOLOGY
ATPAM Members - *listing* - SHOW BUSINESS
Attractive Showmen Ads - *various advertising samples* - MOTION PICTURE HERALD
ATV Watch - *advanced television developments* - BME'S TELEVISION ENGINEERING
Auction, The - OLD TIMER'S BULLETIN, THE
Audio - *column by Ken French* - AVC
Audio - *product review* - GRAMOPHONE
Audio - HYPERMEDIA
Audio - MARKEE
Audio Aids - AUDIOCRAFT FOR THE HI-FI HOBBYIST
Audio & Video - LÜRZER'S INTERNATIONAL ARCHIVE
Audio Clinic - *technical Q&A column by Joseph Giovanelli* - AUDIO
Audio Edits - *newsbriefs* - PRO SOUND NEWS
Audio Equipment - *new developments* - BROADCAST SYSTEMS ENGINEERING
Audio, Etc. - *column by Edward Tatnall Canby* - AUDIO
Audio Etc - *column by Edward Tatnall Canby* - AUDIO
Audio for Video - BME'S TELEVISION ENGINEERING
Audio Glossary - AUTO SOUND & SECURITY
Audio Input - VIDEO MAGAZINE
Audio Listings - *new audio cassette releases* - HOT PICKS
Audio News - *newsbriefs* - HI-FI NEWS AND RECORD REVIEW
Audio News - ON LOCATION
Audio Post Production - PRO SOUND NEWS
Audio Q & A - *column by Ian G. Masters* - STEREO REVIEW
Audio Questions and Answers - *reader-submitted Q&A column by Larry Klein* - STEREO REVIEW
Audio Reviews - FACTSHEET FIVE

Audio Reviews - PUBLISHER'S WEEKLY
Audio Scan - TELESCAN
Audio Tape - SOUND & VISION
Audio Technology - MILLIMETER
Audio Today & Tomorrow - POST
Audio Today, Tomorrow... - *audio trends* - POST
Audio Tools - MEDIA ANTHROPOLOGIST NEWSLETTER
Audio Track - *pro audio production news by city* - BILLBOARD
Audio Update - *column by Larry Klein* - RADIO-ELECTRONICS
Audioclinic - *Q&A column by Joseph Giovanelli* - AUDIO
Audio-For-Video - VIDEOGRAPHY
Audiogenic - *guest commentary* - AUDIOPHILE WITH HI-FI ANSWERS
Audionews - AUDIOCRAFT FOR THE HI-FI HOBBYIST
Audiophile Recordings - *reissues* - ABSOLUTE SOUND, THE
Audiophile Recordings - *review column by Harold A. Rodgers* - COMPUTERS & ELECTRONICS
Audiophile Selection - *equipment guide* - AUDIOPHILE WITH HI-FI ANSWERS
Audio/Video Plus - PUBLISHER'S WEEKLY
Audio/Video Salesman - *advice* - PERSONAL ELECTRONICS
AudioVideo View, The - *editorial comment* - AUDIOVIDEO INTERNATIONAL
Audio-Visual - HYPERMEDIA
Audio-Visual News - *briefs* - AUDIO VISUAL
Audio-Visual On-Line - *production tips and comment* - FUNCTIONAL PHOTOGRAPHY
Auditions - CASTING CALL
Auditions - *'Young musicians deserving recognition'* - DOWN BEAT
Auditions - ENTERTAINMENT REVUE
Auditorium - *letters* - AUDIOPHILE WITH HI-FI ANSWERS
Auds & Arenas - *auditorium and arena news* - AMUSEMENT BUSINESS
Australia Photography Test Report - AUSTRALIAN PHOTOGRAPHY
Australian Newsletter - ADVERTISING REVIEW
Author Index - FORECAST
Author Index - *for paperbacks and audio cassettes* - HOT PICKS
Author of the Month - *profile* - HOT PICKS
Authors - *photos and biographies of authors* - PHOTOLITH, SCM
Authors - *profile* - VISIBLE LANGUAGE
Automotive - LÜRZER'S INTERNATIONAL ARCHIVE
Autophile, The - *equipment review column by Christopher Esse* - HIGH FIDELITY
Autosound - CONSUMER ELECTRONICS PRODUCT NEWS
A/V - *newsbriefs* - SOUND & IMAGE
A-V Answer Man - *column by Abraham Cohen* - MEDIA & METHODS
AV Clinic - *specific problem solving* - BIOMEDICAL COMMUNICATIONS
A-V Industry News - AUDIO-VISUAL GUIDE
AV News - AUDIO VISUAL

INDEX — Departments

AV News amd Reviews - *briefs* - TECHNICAL PHOTOGRAPHY
AV Perspectives - *column by John Bethune* - PROFESSIONAL PHOTOGRAPHER, THE
A-V Profiles - INDUSTRIAL PHOTOGRAPHY
AV Screen - *column by William J. Staples* - INDUSTRIAL PHOTOGRAPHY
AV Tools - MEDIA ANTHROPOLOGIST NEWSLETTER
A-V Workshop - *new techniques* - VISUAL EDUCATION
Awards - AMERICAN THEATRE
Awards - CLIO AMONG THE MEDIA
Awards - *'News of certificate and award collecting' column by Hugh S. Unger* - CQ
Awards - FILM
Awards - FOLIO:
Awards - PUBLIC BROADCASTING REPORT, THE
Awards - ST. LOUIS JOURNALISM REVIEW
Awards and Grants - CURRENT
Awards Program, The - *column by Ed Hopper* - CQ
Award-Winning Plays & Playwrights - BAKER'S NEWS

B

Back Chat - *letters and more column by Martyn Moore* - PRACTICAL PHOTOGRAPHY
Back Door - *comment* - HI-FI NEWS AND RECORD REVIEW
Back Order - *new nostalgic products on today's market* - JOE FRANKLIN'S NOSTALGIA
Back Page, The - *guest column* - BULLETIN OF THE AMERICAN SOCIETY OF NEWSPAPER EDITORS, THE
Back Page - *film newsbriefs* - FILM COMMENT
Back Page - *comment* - MONTHLY FILM BULLETIN
Back Page, The - *contemporary, adult contemporary, aor, urban contemporary playlist* - R & R
Back Page - *comment* - VIDEO BUSINESS
Back Page - *misc* - VIDEO INFO
Back Page, The - *'a photographic statement.'*
Back Seat - *observations* - CAR STEREO REVIEW
Back Stage - *photo column by Paul Kenedy* - MONDAY MORNING REPLAY
Back Talk - *reader response* - COMICS CAREER NEWSLETTER
Back to Basics - *graphic tips* - IN HOUSE GRAPHICS
Back to Basics - PSA
Background - *'news and views on the best of the months films'* - FILMS ILLUSTRATED
Backspace - *guest column* - VIDEO REVIEW
Backstage - *column by Andy Mangels* - AMAZING HEROES
Backstage - *column by Marilyn Beck and Stacy Jenel Smith* - ONSAT
Backstage - STAGE AND TELEVISION TODAY, THE

Backstage--Chicago and Midwest - *Windy City news* - BACK STAGE
Backstage--West - *production briefs of the west coast* - BACK STAGE
Backwash - *'Readers Forum'* - ALL-WAVE RADIO
Backyard Movies - *'Ideas for random filming and short continuities' reader submitted* - HOME MOVIES
Bad Language - *examples* - JOURNALIST, THE
Baker & Taylor's New Video Beat - VIDEO ALERT
Balance Point, The - *pro and con on current issues* - SERIALS REVIEW
Balcony - *column by Mark Jacobson* - MOVIES, THE
Ballet - *reviews* - NEW THEATRE
Baltimore - BOX OFFICE
B&R Reviews - *book reviews* - BOOKS & RELIGION
Banking, Insurance - LÜRZER'S INTERNATIONAL ARCHIVE
BAPSA: (Broadcast Advertising Producers Society of America), a Forum for Creative Exchange - *news* - ENTERTAINMENT MONTHLY
BARB Ratings - STAGE AND TELEVISION TODAY, THE
Bargain Basement - *inexpensive videos* - VIDEO WORLD
Bargains & Best Buys - SPOTLIGHT ON VIDEO
Barometer - ADVERTISING AGENCY
Barometer - *stocks* - VIDEODISC MONITOR, THE
Barry Fox Column, The - *column by Barry Fox* - BROADCAST SYSTEMS INTERNATIONAL
Basic Facts - *tables of facts* - ADVERTISERS' WEEKLY
Basic Indices for Ionospheric Propagation - TELECOMMUNICATION JOURNAL
Basic Jones - *column by Dewitt Jones* - OUTDOOR PHOTOGRAPHER
Basics - *of photography column by George Schaub* - DARKROOM PHOTOGRAPHY
Basics: All About Videotape - *column by Charles Bensinger* - MOVING IMAGE
BBC TV Europe - *viewing schedule* - SATELLITE TIMES
BBS Listing - *fascinating list of computer bulletin boards with a broadcast orientation* - RADIO GUIDE
BCA Update - *news of Broadcast Credit Association* - BROADCAST CABLE FINANCIAL JOURNAL
BCR Seminars - *upcoming* - BUSINESS COMMUNICATIONS REVIEW
Beaming In - *'An editorial'* - POPULAR COMMUNICATIONS
Bear Facts, The - *'From the Editor's Desk' editorial column by S. T. Bear* - WESTERN PHOTOGRAPHER MAGAZINE
Beat, The - *column by Thom Duffy* - BILLBOARD
Beauty - TELEVISION AND SCREEN GUIDE
Beauty & Health Hints From TV's Top Stars - NIGHTTIME TV
Beauty Spots - PHOTOPLAY
Becoming Attractions - *product review* - PHOTOPLAY

Bed and Bored - *patient education* - BIOMEDICAL COMMUNICATIONS
Beginners Competition - *monthly contest* - PHOTO-ERA MAGAZINE
Beginners Corner - PRACTICAL PHOTOGRAPHY
Beginner's Supplement, The - PRACTICAL WIRELESS
Behind Both Screens - *column by Norma McLain Stoop* - AFTER DARK
Behind the Cover - *production of this magazine cover* - PROFESSIONAL PHOTOGRAPHER, THE
Behind the Covers - *backgrounds on new pictorial works* - PROFESSIONAL PHOTOGRAPHER, THE
Behind the Desk - *editorial column by Kurt Luchs* - COMPUTER PUBLISHING
Behind the Lines - *editorial* - WATCH
Behind the Midwest Baton - *'News of the band world out Chicago way', column by Dixon Gayer* - BAND LEADERS
Behind the Scene - *'we give you backstage accounts of how soaps' most intriguing scenes come to life' column by Kate Forsyth* - SOAP OPERA DIGEST
Behind the Scenes - *production column by Bert Whyte* - AUDIO
Behind the Scenes - *column by Casey Allen* - CAMERA 35 INCORPORATING PHOTO WORLD
Behind the Scenes - DISNEY CHANNEL MAGAZINE, THE
Behind the Scenes - *stories behind the pictures* - MOVIEGOER
Behind the Scenes - SIMPSONS ILLUSTRATED
Behind the Scenes in Publishing - *editorial* - ELECTRONICS WORLD
Behind the Scenes With - *on location with a film production crew* - SCREEN STORIES
Behind the Screen - *profiles* - FILMFARE
Behind the TV Scene with Army Archerd - MOVIE MIRROR
Behind-the-Scenes at Super Teen - *'The inside scoops behind the stories inside!'* - SUPER TEEN
Being Critical - *on reader-submitted photographs* - MODERN PHOTOGRAPHY
Below 500 kHz - *column by Joe Woodlock* - MONITORING TIMES
Below the Line - EMMY
Below the Line - ENTERTAINMENT REVUE
Bender on Black-and-White - CAMERA & DARKROOM PHOTOGRAPHY
Best - *current ads of outstanding quality* - ART DIRECTION
Best Buy Guide - CAMCORDER USER
Best Buys in Network Television - BILLBOARD TV PROGRAM AND TIME AVAILABILITIES, THE
Best Cartoons on 16mm - *reviews* - FOCUS ON FILM
Best Food Buys - *monthly guide column by Richard A. Edwards* - NATIONAL ENQUIRER
Best Recordings of the Month - STEREO REVIEW

Best Sellers - *compiled from across the United States* - PUBLISHER'S WEEKLY
Best-Seller Lists - BOOKSTORE JOURNAL
Bestseller Sampler - MAGAZINE & BOOKSELLER
Best-Sellers - *list of fiction & non-fiction* - ENTERTAINMENT WEEKLY
Bet You Missed It! - *summary of recent articles of interest* - AGAINST THE GRAIN
Better Films - *standard raising* - MOVING PICTURE AGE
Better Management - *'A clearing house for effective exploitation and admission sales ideas'* - NATIONAL EXHIBITOR, THE
Better Screen Results - *'A department devoted to projection' column by T. O'Conor Sloane* - EXHIBITORS TRADE REVIEW
Betty Clewis Says - *one-line humorous statements* - MOVIE HUMOR
Between Commercials - *'A chat with the editor' column by Kathy Loy* - TV STAR PARADE
Between Ourselves - PRACTICAL PHOTOGRAPHY
Between Shot - PHOTOMETHODS
Between the Lines - *editorial* - CABLEVISION
Between the Lines - *news behind the articles* - TRAVEL & LEISURE
Between the Lines: - *profiles* - BOOKSTORE JOURNAL
Between You and Me - *Q&A on celebrities* - MOVIE WORLD
Beverages: Alcoholic - LÜRZER'S INTERNATIONAL ARCHIVE
Beverages: Non-alcoholic - LÜRZER'S INTERNATIONAL ARCHIVE
Beyond Broadway - THEATERWEEK
Beyond the Commissary - *column by Ingrid Wilmot* - HOLLYWOOD MAGAZINE
Beyond the Stars - *column by Beatrice Rich* - HOLLYWOOD MAGAZINE
BFM Member News - *news of Broadcast Financial Management Association members* - BROADCAST CABLE FINANCIAL JOURNAL
Biblical Interpretation - *reviews* - HOMILETIC
Bibliofiles - ADWEEK'S MARKETING WEEK
Bibliographia - *book reviews* - VERBATIM
Bibliography - ARSC JOURNAL
Bibliography - RADIO AND TELEVISION
Bibliography - WORLD THEATRE
Bibliography of Radio Law - *column by Robert Kingsley* - JOURNAL OF RADIO LAW
Big Apple, The - *New York media news* - MORE
Big Apple, The - *New York production newsbriefs* - ON LOCATION
Big Noise - *'The Music Seen'* - SATELLITE TIMES
Big Picture, The - *Visual Media column by Rolbert Wait* - EQ
Big Picture, The - *guest opinion* - SATELLITE TV WEEK
Big Picture, The - *center photo layout* - SOAP OPERA UPDATE
Bijou Books - *review column by Foster Hirsch* - BIJOU
Bijou Quiz Corner - *'The movie scene: from mirth to mayhem'* - BIJOU

Bill Sacks and 'The Audio Process, - RADIO WORLD
Billboard Album Radio Action - BILLBOARD
Billboard Singles Radio Action - *top moving records on regional and national basis* - BILLBOARD
Billboard Top 25 Singles - AMUSEMENT BUSINESS
Billboard's PD of the Week - *radio program director profile* - BILLBOARD
Bill's Basics - *'How-to for the newcomer to amateur radio', column by Bill Welsh* - CQ
Biographical Page - THEATRE MAGAZINE
Biographies - MIRROR OF TASTE, AND DRAMATIC CENSOR, THE
Birthday Bash! - *'Cake cuttings'* - INSIDE HOLLYWOOD
Birthday Bulletin Board - *'Send a card to your favorite'* - REAL LIFE/DAYTIMERS
Birthdays of the Stars - DAYTIME TV
Bits - *radio newsbriefs* - QEX
Bits and Bytes - *column by Jack Neubart* - INDUSTRIAL PHOTOGRAPHY
Bits and Pieces - *newsbriefs* - CONSUMER ELECTRONICS
Bits and Pieces - *newsbriefs of available products* - IMPRINT
Bits & Pieces - *newsbriefs* - TELEVISION BROADCAST
Bits & Pieces - *news items of TV/Film stars* - TV HITS
Biz Buzz - *entertainment news items column by Lisa Bernhard* - US MAGAZINE
Black and White and Red All Over - *column by Martin L. 'Red' Gibson* - CMA NEWSLETTER
Black Eyes - *Bad examples* - EDITORIAL EYE, THE
Black Radio - R & R
Black Stars Letters - *letters* - BLACK STARS
Black Theatre Notes - BLACK THEATRE
Blind Items - *news items too hot for attribution* - MOVIE WORLD
Blindfold Test - DOWN BEAT
Blob Competition - *contest* - VIDEO BUYER
Blockbuster Crossword - BLOCKBUSTER VIDEO MAGAZINE
Blockbuster Picks - *film rental suggestions* - BLOCKBUSTER VIDEO MAGAZINE
Blood and Thunder - *letters to editor* - COMICS JOURNAL, THE
Blood & Thunder - *letters* - COMICS JOURNAL, THE
Blood in the Ink - *editorial* - COLORADO EDITOR
Blooper Brigade - COMMUNICATION BRIEFINGS
Blow Hot, Blow Cold - *gossip* - FILMWORLD
Blueprint - *'Blueprint is a column intended to provide suggested answers to readers electronics design problems'* - ETI
Blues Reviews - CD REVIEW
BM/E's Program marketplace - *lengthy profile of program suppliers* - BME'S TELEVISION ENGINEERING
Board Actions - NEWSLETTER
Boardroom - NEWSINC.

BOC Monitor - COMMUNICATIONSWEEK
Body & Mind - *'Health news'* - REAL LIFE/DAYTIMERS
Boldface - *profiles of 2-3 DC area newspeople* - WASHINGTON JOURNALISM REVIEW
Bolex Showcase - *product reviews* - BOLEX REPORTER, THE
Bolex-pressions - *letters* - BOLEX REPORTER, THE
Book and News Notes - THEATRE AND SCHOOL
Book and Video Reviews - *column by Jack Qualman* - WESTERN PHOTOGRAPHER MAGAZINE
Book and Videotape - *reviews* - JOURNAL OF EDUCATIONAL TELEVISION
Book Beat - COMMUNICATOR
Book Bits - *review column by Chris Huizenga* - AFTER DARK
Book Briefs - NATIONAL PHOTOGRAPHER, THE
Book Briefs - PROFESSIONAL PHOTOGRAPHER, THE
Book Browser, The - *'Opening lines from five new books'* - ENTERTAINMENT WEEKLY
Book Collector's Corner, The - OLD TIMER'S BULLETIN, THE
Book Commentary - JOURNAL OF ADVERTISING
Book Design & Manufacturing - PUBLISHER'S WEEKLY
Book Fair Calendar - *upcoming events* - AB BOOKMAN'S WEEKLY
Book Marks - *comment column by Richard T. Jameson* - FILM COMMENT
Book Marks - *reviews* - PREVUE
Book News - *column by George L. George* - BACK STAGE
Book News - TAKE ONE
Book Notes - BOOKSTORE JOURNAL
Book Notes - BRITISH LITHOGRAPHER
Book of the Month - *best of the review group* - COMMUNICATION BOOKNOTES
Book Parade - *fiction and non-fiction book reviews* - TV PICTURE LIFE
Book Review - ABC WEEKLY
Book Review - ANIMATION MAGAZINE
Book Review - ART PAPERS
Book Review - ASIAN JOURNAL OF COMMUNICATION
Book Review - BETTER RADIO AND TELEVISION
Book Review - BRIGHT LIGHTS
Book Review - BRITISH INSTITUTE OF RECORDED SOUND. BULLETIN.
Book Review - CARDOZO ARTS & ENTERTAINMENT LAW JOURNAL
Book Review - CINEMA/CANADA
Book Review - COLLEGE BROADCASTER
Book Review - COMMUNICATIONS AND THE LAW
Book Review - COMMUNITY COLLEGE JOURNALIST
Book Review - DOCUMENTARY FILM NEWS
Book Review - EDUCATIONAL COMMUNICATION AND TECHNOLOGY
Book Review - ELECTRONICS & COMMUNICATIONS ENGINEERING JOURNAL

Book Review - FEDERAL COMMUNICATIONS LAW JOURNAL
Book Review - FEEDBACK
Book Review - GANNETT CENTER JOURNAL
Book Review - GAZETTE
Book Review - GENERAL ELECTRIC REVIEW
Book Review - HEALTH COMMUNICATION
Book Review - ICA NEWSLETTER
Book Review - IMAGE NEWS
Book Review - LINK-UP
Book Review - LITERATURE/FILM QUARTERLY
Book Review - MARCONI REVIEW, THE
Book Review, The - *concerning newspaper histories* - MASTHEAD
Book Review - MASTHEAD
Book Review - MODERN PHOTOGRAPHY
Book Review - MONITOR
Book Review - MONOGRAM
Book Review - MOVIES AND MINISTRY
Book Review - PERSONAL ELECTRONICS
Book Review - *column by James Kaufmann* - PHOTOGRAPHER'S FORUM
Book Review - POST SCRIPT
Book Review - PUBLIC TELECOMMUNICATIONS REVIEW
Book Review - QST
Book Review - RADIO BROADCAST
Book Review - RADIO*PHILES
Book Review - *very large section of recent publications from independent publishers* - SMALL PRESS
Book Review - SSP LETTER
Book Review - TELECOMMUNICATIONS POLICY
Book Review - THEATRE JOURNAL
Book Review Directory - *publishers from books reviewed* - SMALL PRESS
Book Review Essay - HUMAN COMMUNICATION RESEARCH
Book Reviews - ACUSTICA
Book Reviews - *new art techniques books* - ADVERTISING AND GRAPHIC ARTS TECHNIQUES
Book Reviews - *rather extensive critiques of internationally published books on advertising and marketing* - ADVERTISING AND MARKETING
Book Reviews - ADVERTISING AND MARKETING MANAGEMENT
Book Reviews - AEU
Book Reviews - AFVA BULLETIN
Book Reviews - AIGA JOURNAL OF GRAPHIC DESIGN
Book Reviews - AIR LAW REVIEW
Book Reviews - AMERICAN JOURNALISM
Book Reviews - ANIMATION MAGAZINE
Book Reviews - ANIMATOR
Book Reviews - ART DIRECTION
Book Reviews - AUDIOCRAFT FOR THE HI-FI HOBBYIST
Book Reviews - BIOMEDICAL COMMUNICATIONS
Book Reviews - BOOKSTORE JOURNAL
Book Reviews - BROADSIDE
Book Reviews - CELLULOID NIGHTMARE
Book Reviews - CLOSE-UP
Book Reviews - COLLEGE & UNIVERSITY JOURNAL

Book Reviews - COLLEGE BROADCASTER
Book Reviews - COLLEGE MEDIA REVIEW
Book Reviews - COMMON SENSE
Book Reviews - COMMUNICATION ARTS
Book Reviews - *major review section* - COMMUNICATION EDUCATION
Book Reviews - COMMUNICATION QUARTERLY
Book Reviews - COMMUNICATION RESEARCH TRENDS
Book Reviews - COMMUNICATION THEORY
Book Reviews - DRAMA & THEATRE
Book Reviews - DRAMA SURVEY
Book Reviews - EBU REVIEW. PROGRAMMES, ADMINISTRATION, LAW.
Book Reviews - EDUCATIONAL COMMUNICATION AND TECHNOLOGY
Book Reviews - ELECTRONICS AND COMMUNICATIONS
Book Reviews - ELECTRONICS & COMMUNICATIONS
Book Reviews - ELECTRONICS WORLD
Book Reviews - ENTERTAINMENT REVUE
Book Reviews - FACTSHEET FIVE
Book Reviews - FEDERAL COMMUNICATIONS LAW JOURNAL
Book Reviews - FEEDBACK
Book Reviews - FILM
Book Reviews - FILM & VIDEO NEWS
Book Reviews - FILM DIRECTIONS
Book Reviews - FILM FAN MONTHLY
Book Reviews - FILM LIBRARY QUARTERLY
Book Reviews - FILM QUARTERLY
Book Reviews - *'The latest film-flavoured hard- and paper-backs'* - FILM REVIEW
Book Reviews - FILMS IN REVIEW
Book Reviews - FUNCTIONAL PHOTOGRAPHY
Book Reviews - HISTORICAL JOURNAL OF FILM, RADIO & TELEVISION
Book Reviews - HISTORY OF PHOTOGRAPHY
Book Reviews - HUMAN COMMUNICATION
Book Reviews - IEEE SPECTRUM
Book Reviews - *very extensive reviews* - INDEX ON CENSORSHIP
Book Reviews - INTERNATIONAL JOURNAL OF INFORMATION MANAGEMENT
Book Reviews - IRIS
Book Reviews - JOURNAL OF ARTS MANAGEMENT AND LAW, THE
Book Reviews - JOURNAL OF BUSINESS COMMUNICATION, THE
Book Reviews - JOURNAL OF EDUCATIONAL PUBLIC RELATIONS
Book Reviews - JOURNAL OF EDUCATIONAL TELEVISION
Book Reviews - JOURNAL OF MARKETING
Book Reviews - JOURNAL OF MASS MEDIA ETHICS
Book Reviews - JOURNAL OF MEDIA ECONOMICS
Book Reviews - JOURNAL OF POPULAR CULTURE
Book Reviews - *column by Robert Kingsley* - JOURNAL OF RADIO LAW
Book Reviews - JOURNAL OF TECHNICAL WRITING AND COMMUNICATION
Book Reviews - JOURNAL OF THE PRODUCERS GUILD OF AMERICA, THE

Book Reviews - JOURNALISM EDUCATOR, THE
Book Reviews - *column by Barbara Cloud* - JOURNALISM HISTORY
Book Reviews - JQ. JOURNALISM QUARTERLY.
Book Reviews - *edited column by Michele Benjamin* - LEARNED PUBLISHING
Book Reviews - MEDIA, CULTURE, AND SOCIETY
Book Reviews - MEDIA DEVELOPMENT
Book Reviews - MEDIA IN EDUCATION AND DEVELOPMENT
Book Reviews - MILLENNIUM FILM JOURNAL
Book Reviews - MODERN DRAMA
Book Reviews - MOVIE - THE VIDEO MAGAZINE
Book Reviews - MOVIES, THE
Book Reviews - MUSICAL AMERICA
Book Reviews - NEW THEATRE MAGAZINE
Book Reviews - NEWSPAPER RESEARCH JOURNAL
Book Reviews - OPTICAL INFORMATION SYSTEMS
Book Reviews - *'Publications and videos of interest'* - OUTDOOR & TRAVEL PHOTOGRAPHY
Book Reviews - PHILOSOPHY AND RHETORIC
Book Reviews - POST SCRIPT
Book Reviews - PRINT
Book Reviews - PRINTED MATTER
Book Reviews - PRINTING HISTORY
Book Reviews - PROFESSIONAL PHOTOGRAPHER, THE
Book Reviews - PUBLIC OPINION QUARTERLY
Book Reviews - *very substantial section of critical reviews* - PUBLIC RELATIONS REVIEW
Book Reviews - QUARTERLY JOURNAL OF SPEECH, THE
Book Reviews - RADIO-ELECTRONICS
Book Reviews - RADIO FAN-FARE
Book Reviews - RIGHTING WORDS
Book Reviews - SCREEN
Book Reviews - SCREEN FACTS
Book Reviews - SEQUENCE
Book Reviews - *extensive section* - SHAKESPEARE QUARTERLY
Book Reviews - SIGHT & SOUND
Book Reviews - SOUTHERN COMMUNICATION JOURNAL, THE
Book Reviews - SPEECH AND DRAMA
Book Reviews - STUDIO PHOTOGRAPHY
Book Reviews - *column by Glen Hunter and Harold Weaver* - TAKE ONE
Book Reviews - TECHNOLOGY AND CULTURE
Book Reviews - TELEVISION
Book Reviews - THEATRE DESIGN & TECHNOLOGY
Book Reviews - THEATRE NOTEBOOK
Book Reviews - THEATRE RESEARCH
Book Reviews - VICTORIAN PERIODICALS REVIEW
Book Reviews - VISIBLE LANGUAGE
Book Reviews - WOMEN & LANGUAGE
Book Reviews - WORLD MEDIA REPORT
Book Reviews - WRITERS' JOURNAL
Book Shelf - U & LC
Book Spread - FOCUS ON FILM
Book Survey - BRITISH BOOK NEWS

Book Update - SCHOLASTIC EDITOR'S TRENDS IN PUBLICATIONS
Book World - *review column by Chris Charles* - STARBURST
Bookends - RE:ACT
Booker's Guide to 16mm Films - TAKE ONE
Bookings - MEDIA WEEK
Bookmarks - *reviews* - ROUNDUP QUARTERLY
Booknotes - *review* - C-SPAN UPDATE
Bookrack - *reviews* - CINEMACABRE
Book-Review - PHOTO-ERA MAGAZINE
Bookreviews - AEU
Books - *reviews* - AMERICAN FILM
Books - *lengthy reviews* - AMERICAN PHOTO
Books - ART & DESIGN NEWS
Books - *reviews* - AV GUIDE
Books - *reviews* - BETTER EDITING
Books - *review* - BRITISH JOURNAL OF PHOTOGRAPHY
Books - *review* - BUSINESS MARKETING
Books - *review* - CAMERA
Books - *review* - CAMERA & CAMCORDER MONTHLY
Books - CAMERA ARTS
Books - *reviews* - CINEASTE
Books - CINEMONKEY
Books - *review* - COLUMBIA JOURNALISM REVIEW
Books - COMBROAD
Books - *reviews* - COMMENT ON THE MEDIA
Books - *new releases* - COMMUNICATION ARTS
Books - *review* - COMMUNICATIONS LAWYER
Books - CRITIC
Books - CTVD
Books - DRAMA
Books - *lengthy reviews* - DRAMATICS
Books - EMMY
Books - *review* - EMPIRE
Books - FACETS FEATURES
Books - *reviews* - FANTASY ZONE
Books - *reviews* - FILM COMMENT
Books - FILM CRITICISM
Books - FILM JOURNAL, THE
Books - FILM QUARTERLY
Books - FILMS ILLUSTRATED
Books - *review* - FOI DIGEST
Books - HI-FI NEWS AND RECORD REVIEW
Books - *review* - HOW
Books - *review* - HUMAN COMMUNICATION CANADA
Books - *review* - IEEE SPECTRUM
Books - INTERMEDIA
Books - INTERNATIONAL FILM BUFF
Books - INTERVIEW
Books - *in-depth reviews* - JOURNAL OF BROADCASTING & ELECTRONIC MEDIA
Books - *reviews* - JOURNAL OF COMMUNICATION
Books - *reviews of current books* - JOURNALISM HISTORY
Books - JOURNALISTS' AFFAIRS
Books - *lengthy reviews* - LISTENER
Books - *reviews* - MASTHEAD
Books - MEDIA DEVELOPMENT
Books - *review* - MEDIA INFORMATION AUSTRALIA
Books - *review* - MEDIA SPOTLIGHT
Books - MILLIMETER

Books - MOVIEGOER
Books - *reviews* - NEW THEATRE
Books - NIEMAN REPORTS
Books - *review* - ON FILM
Books - *reviews column by Dave Saunders* - PIC
Books - PRESSTIME
Books - PROMOTION
Books - *reviews* - PUBLIC RELATIONS QUARTERLY
Books - RADIO-ELECTRONICS
Books - *review* - SALES & MARKETING MANAGEMENT
Books - *specifically mass media related to science* - SCIENTIFIC FILM
Books - SCREEN ACTOR HOLLYWOOD
Books - *review* - SHOW
Books - *review column by Staunton Ross* - SOUND STAGE
Books - TELECOMMUNICATION JOURNAL
Books - *reviews* - THE JOURNAL
Books - *reviews* - THEATRE CRAFTS
Books - *review column by Maria Lexton* - 20/20
Books - *reviews* - VIEWS
Books - *reviews* - WASHINGTON JOURNALISM REVIEW
Books - *thoughtful reviews* - WIDE ANGLE
Books / Publications / Videos - *reviews* - COMMUNICATIONS INDUSTRIES REPORT, THE
Books & Documents - *review* - CHRONICLE OF INTERNATIONAL COMMUNICATION
Books & Periodicals - *reviews* - FILMOGRAPH
Books & Pictures - *reviews* - A-D
Books and Records - *review* - THEATRE, THE
Books & Records - THEATRE CRAFTS
Books and Reviews - ANIMAFILM
Books and Speeches - *reviews* - BULLETIN OF THE AMERICAN SOCIETY OF NEWSPAPER EDITORS, THE
Books at Random - *reviews* - ELECTRONIC AGE
Books, Booklets and Brochures - *available on technical issues* - SMPTE JOURNAL
Books for Journalists - *reviews* - CATHOLIC JOURNALIST
Books for the Professional - RANGEFINDER, THE
Books For the Trade - *column by John Kremer* - SMALL PRESS
Books From Members - *new publications* - ORGANIZATIONAL COMMUNICATION NEWSLETTER
Books in Brief - CREATIVE CAMERA
Books in Brief - JOURNAL OF BROADCASTING & ELECTRONIC MEDIA
Books in Print - PRINT
Books in Review - CAMERA 35
Books in Review - *column by Joe Novak* - CAMERA 35 INCORPORATING PHOTO WORLD
Books in Review - PLAYERS
Books in Review - TARGET
Books in Review - TELEVISION QUARTERLY
Books in Review - THEATRE JOURNAL
Books in Review - TPQ
Books in Review - TRAVEL & LEISURE

Books of the Quarter - FILM ART
Books on Film: A Checklist - *column by George L. George* - TAKE ONE
Books on the Film - FILM GUIDE
Books on the Theatre - FILM AND THEATRE TODAY
Books on View - *reviews* - AMERICAN FILM INSTITUTE. QUARTERLY.
Books Received - AMERICAN LITERARY GAZETTE AND PUBLISHERS' CIRCULAR
Books Received - BROADSIDE
Books Received - CANADIAN PHOTOGRAPHIC JOURNAL, THE
Books Received - IEEE TRANSACTIONS ON INFORMATION THEORY
Books Received - THEATRE JOURNAL
Books Recently Received - THEATER
Books Reviews - OPTICAL MEMORY NEWS
Books to Come - BOOKSTORE JOURNAL
Books You Need - *being sold by Television Opportunities* - TELEVISION OPPORTUNITIES
Bookselling - PUBLISHER'S WEEKLY
Bookshelf - ADVERTISING MAGAZINE
Bookshelf - *reviews of better film and television publications* - AMERICAN CINEMATOGRAPHER
Bookshelf, The - *reviews* - AMERICAN CINEMATOGRAPHER
Bookshelf, The - AMERICAN PREMIERE
Bookshelf - *reviews* - AUTHOR, THE
Bookshelf, The - BIG REEL, THE
Bookshelf - *review column by George L. George* - CINEMA/CANADA
Bookshelf - *reviews column by Katherine Shelly Pfeiffer* - DESKTOP COMMUNICATIONS
Bookshelf - *review* - IMAGE TECHNOLOGY
Bookshelf - *reviews* - JOURNALIST
Bookshelf, The - *review column by James Copeland* - ROSTRUM
Bookshelf - *'The latest from the science fiction, fantasy and horror worlds'* - STARBURST
Bookshelf - *reviews* - VARIETY
Books-Monographs - *review* - ACTION
Books-Records - *reviews* - GREATER AMUSEMENTS
Bookworm - *book reviews* - ANIMATIONS
Boston - *city review column by Michael McDowell* - AFTER DARK
Boston - BOX OFFICE
Boston Comment - SCREEN ACTOR HOLLYWOOD
Bottom Line - *column by Allen Fishman* - PHOTOGRAPHIC PROCESSING
Bottomline - *the business of graphic design* - HOW
Bottomline Broadcaster - RADIO WORLD
Box 392: Letters to the Editor - AUDIO CRITIC, THE
Box Office - *economically speaking* - ENTERTAINMENT WEEKLY
Box Office - *the economics of this week's London box offices* - SCREEN INTERNATIONAL
Box Office - VIDEO BUSINESS

Box Office 100 - *'Due from the theatre to thee'* - VIDEO STORE
Box Office Barometer, The - *'Key city reports on first run pictures'* - NATIONAL EXHIBITOR, THE
Box Office Champions - *current hits* - MOTION PICTURE PRODUCT DIGEST
Box Office Guide - *detailed financial information* - MOVING PICTURES INTERNATIONAL
Box Office News - *information from variety of international cities* - MOVING PICTURES INTERNATIONAL
Box Office Worldwide - *extensive center-page pull-out guide to international box office receipts* - MOVING PICTURES INTERNATIONAL
Box Score, The - *distribution stats* - MAGAZINE & BOOKSELLER
Boxoffice Barometer - *economic ratings of major motion pictures in 20 cities* - BOX OFFICE
Box-Office Grosses - CINEMA PAPERS
Box-Office Roundup - *quick tabulation of gate receipts for the week* - PERFORMANCE
Box-Office Slant, The - *'Current and forthcoming feature product reviewed from the theatreman's standpoint'* - SHOWMEN'S TRADE REVIEW
Boxography - *historical cereal box lineage* - FLAKE
Boxscore - *'Top concert grosses reported' and detailed information column by Marie Ratliff* - AMUSEMENT BUSINESS
Boxscore - *'Top concert grosses' compiled by Amusement Business* - BILLBOARD
BoxScore - *'a monthly report on the number of users (experimental and commercial) of teletext, videotext, electronic publishing, captioning and related technologies'* - INTERNATIONAL VIDEOTEXT TELETEXT NEWS
BPL Helped - *Broadcast Pioneers Library users* - BROADCAST PIONEERS LIBRARY REPORTS
Brad Messer - *column* - R & R
Brady - *column by James Brady* - ADVERTISING AGE
Brady's Bunch - *personnel observations* - ADVERTISING AGE
Brainstorm - *photo contest* - PRACTICAL PHOTOGRAPHY
Brasil - *production newsbriefs* - PRODUCCIÓN Y DISTRIBUCIÓN
Brass Tack Talks - *comment and advice* - MOTION PICTURE ALBUM
Brass Tacks - *production observation and instruction* - ENTERTAINMENT REVUE
Bravo Program Guide - *cable television programming guide* - AMERICAN FILM
Bravos & Boos - *'A gentleman's guide to who and what's heating up and cooling off column by Gerald Rothberg* - MGF
BRE Music Report - *top of the weekly chart singles and albums* - BLACK RADIO EXCLUSIVE
Breaking News - VIDEO INSIDER

Breezing Along With the B's - *B movie nostalgia column* - BIG REEL, THE
BRE-Flicks - *black radio personality pictures* - BLACK RADIO EXCLUSIVE
Brief Guide - *'To give you a line or so on current talkie offerings'* - TALKING SCREEN
Brief Guide - *movie ratings* - TELEVISION AND SCREEN GUIDE
Brief Notices - MOVIES, THE
Briefing - *excellent compilation of late-breaking news in business communication* - BUSINESS COMMUNICATIONS REVIEW
Briefing - *review* - COLUMBIA JOURNALISM REVIEW
Briefing - *outstanding full-color section of recent ads* - DIRECTION
Briefings - *latebreaking news* - FOLIO:
Briefings - *issues of public relations in the news* - PUBLIC RELATIONS JOURNAL, THE
Briefly - *newsbriefs* - DWB
Briefly - *newsbriefs* - KNIGHT-RIDDER NEWS
Briefly - *member newsbriefs* - WASHINGTON NEWSPAPER, THE
Briefly Noted - ELECTRONIC MEDIA
Briefly Noted - *additional research* - SOUTHERN COMMUNICATION JOURNAL, THE
Briefly Noted - *newsbriefs* - STUDIES IN VISUAL COMMUNICATION
Briefly Personal - *personnel briefs* - NEWSPAPER WORLD AND ADVERTISING REVIEW
Briefs - AMERICAN PRESS
Briefs - COMMENT ON THE MEDIA
Briefs - *technological items* - ELECTRONIC DESIGN
Briefs - *newsbriefs* - PROFESSIONAL FILM PRODUCTION
Britain - *video comment and news column by Barry Fox* - WHAT VIDEO
British Books Abroad - *'The British Council Overseas'* - BRITISH BOOK NEWS
British Documentary Activity - DOCUMENTARY FILM NEWS
British Drawing Board - *newsbriefs* - TARGET
British Invasion, The - *newsbriefs about British black artists column by Dotun Adebayo* - BLACK RADIO EXCLUSIVE
British Top 100 - *record chart* - BROADCAST
Broadcast - *broadcast journalism review* - FEED-BACK
Broadcast - MEDIA WEEK
Broadcast Analysis - BROADCAST
Broadcast Beat - *column* - BROADCAST + TECHNOLOGY
Broadcast Beat - MEDIAWEEK
Broadcast Books - RELIGIOUS BROADCASTING
Broadcast Briefs - PRO SOUND NEWS
Broadcast Buffoonery - *broadcast cartoon series noteworthy as it is created column by Robert W. Morgen* - BROADCAST PROGRAMMING AND PRODUCTION
Broadcast Business - BROADCAST + TECHNOLOGY
Broadcast Dx'ing - *'Dx, news and views of am and fm broadcasting'* - POPULAR COMMUNICATIONS

Broadcast Equipment Design - ABU TECHNICAL REVIEW
Broadcast Impressions - *an unique page of cartoons showing readers what popular radio broadcasters looked like* - WIRELESS AGE, THE
Broadcast Industry News - *large number of industry newsbriefs* - BME'S TELEVISION ENGINEERING
Broadcast Life - AP BROADCASTER
Broadcast Listener - *'comments on radio programs, methods and technique--from the point of view of the average fan'* - POPULAR RADIO AND TELEVISION
Broadcast Management/Engineering - *technical and managerial issues* - TELEVISION BROADCAST
Broadcast Markets - VARIETY
Broadcast News - *newsbriefs* - BROADCASTER
Broadcast Receiver, The - OLD TIMER'S BULLETIN, THE
Broadcast TV - INSIDE MEDIA
Broadcasters - *profile newsbriefs* - RELIGIOUS BROADCASTING
Broadcasters Calendar - *of legal and governmental deadlines* - LINE MONITOR, THE
Broadcasting - UK PRESS GAZETTE
Broadcasting - VIDEO
Broadcasting - VIDEO TECHNOLOGY NEWS
Broadcasting & Cable TV - MEDIA BUSINESS
Broadcasting and the Public - *news* - AMATEUR WIRELESS AND RADIOVISION
Broadcasting News and Report - *newsbriefs* - JEE, JOURNAL OF ELECTRONIC ENGINEERING
Broadcasting Notes - *column by I. Reid* - JOURNAL OF EDUCATIONAL TELEVISION
Broadcasting Personalities - RCA BROADCAST NEWS
Broadcasting Research - CRC NEWSLETTER
Broadcasting Station Activities - RADIO DEALER, THE
Broadcasting Station Directory - *useful feature listing call letters, frequencies and owner of individual stations* - WIRELESS AGE, THE
Broadway - BOX OFFICE
Broadway - *New York City exhibition news column by Peter Vischer* - EXHIBITORS HERALD WORLD
Broadway - *current running New York films* - MOVIE/TV MARKETING
Broadway - *extensive 'Reviews of Broadway productions'* - THEATRE ARTS
Broadway - *column by Leo Shull* - WRITER'S DIGEST
Broadway at a Glance - *theatre listings* - BROADWAY SIGN POST
Broadway Box Office - *current show statistics* - CASTING NEWS
Broadway Buzz - *column by Brant Mewborn* - AFTER DARK
Broadway Grosses - VARIETY
Broadway in Review - *column by Edith J. Isaacs* - THEATRE ARTS
Broadway Legit Grosses - VARIETY

Departments   INDEX   786

Broadway News - *'What's happening, coming, and playing' column by Harry Haun* - PLAYBILL
Broadway Picture Programs and Music - *very unique and extensive information on music and programs accompanying motion pictures, column by M. M. Hansford* - DRAMATIC MIRROR, THE
Broadway Schedule - VARIETY
Broadway Shows - *listing* - SHOW BUSINESS
Broadway Theatres - *listing* - SHOW BUSINESS
Broadway Time Table, The - *current theatrical fare in New York City* - DRAMATIC MIRROR, THE
Brochures - ART & DESIGN NEWS
Broker Forum - TARGET MARKETING
Bruce Honick's Country Capers - *music column* - NATIONAL EXAMINER
Brush Report, The - *column by Judith Brush and Douglas Brush* - TELESPAN'S BUSINESSTV GUIDE
Brush Report, The - VIDEOPRO
Bryce is Right - *fan question column by Allan Bryce* - VIDEO WORLD
Budgeting - VIDEO BUSINESS
Buffalo - BOX OFFICE
Building a Library - *column by Christopher Breunig* - STEREOPHILE
Building Cine Stuff - *constructing your own* - FILMMAKERS FILM & VIDEO MONTHLY
Bulletin - *late-breaking news column by William Livingstone* - STEREO REVIEW
Bulletin - TELECOMMUNICATIONS
Bulletin Board, The - *letters and newsbriefs* - BULLETIN OF THE AMERICAN SOCIETY OF NEWSPAPER EDITORS, THE
Bulletin Board - BULLETIN OF THE ASSOCIATION FOR BUSINESS COMMUNICATION, THE
Bulletin Board - *current broadband news* - COMMUNICATIONS ENGINEERING & DESIGN
Bulletin Board - FILM COMMENT
Bulletin Board - *wantads* - FILMMAKERS FILM & VIDEO MONTHLY
Bulletin Board - *extensive newsbriefs on 900 telephone service trends and developments* - 4TH MEDIA JOURNAL, THE
Bulletin Board - *'Swap star stuff with other readers!'* - GOSSIP
Bulletin Board - *film production schedule* - HOLLYWOOD FILMOGRAPH
Bulletin Board - *marriages, births, splits and deaths column by Mary Callahan* - MOTION PICTURE
Bulletin Board - *newsbriefs* - SCREEN ACTOR HOLLYWOOD
Bulletin Board - STUDIO PHOTOGRAPHY
Bulletined Plays - *listings by city* - DRAMA LEAGUE MONTHLY
Bulletins from the R.M.A. - RADIO INDUSTRIES
Bunbury - *column* - ADVERTISING AND MARKETING MANAGEMENT
Bureau of Information - *newsbrief information concerning patents, processes, and reader comment* - ST. LOUIS AND CANADIAN PHOTOGRAPHER
Buses - ELECTRONICS

Business - *issues and problems* - ASMP BULLETIN
Business - BROADCAST ENGINEERING
Business - CABLEVISION
Business - LOCATION UPDATE
Business - MEDIA WEEK
Business - *column by Loyd Searle* - PHOTOPRO
Business - SATELLITE COMMUNICATIONS
Business - STAGE & STUDIO
Business - STUDIO SOUND AND BROADCAST ENGINEERING
Business - *newsbriefs* - VIDEO SYSTEMS
Business - WORLD PRESS REVIEW
Business Activities - ELECTRONICS
Business & Finance - COMMUNICATIONSWEEK
Business and Home TV Screen - *updated information to supplement Business Screen Magazine* - BACK STAGE
Business Barometer - *concerning sound production* - PRO SOUND NEWS
Business Briefly - BROADCASTING
Business Briefs - AVC
Business Briefs - BME'S TELEVISION ENGINEERING
Business Briefs - *news items* - BUSINESS OF FILM, THE
Business Briefs - WORLD PRESS REVIEW
Business Briefs & Trends - ELECTRONICS & COMMUNICATIONS
Business Developments - SATELLITE NEWS
Business Diary - *newsbriefs of film events, personnel, and developments* - BUSINESS OF FILM, THE
Business Dynamics - MSO'S CABLE MARKETING
Business File - COMMUNICATIONSWEEK
Business in Britain - PARAMOUNT WORLD
Business Media Update - *new publications* - BUSINESS MARKETING
Business News - *briefs* - ART DIRECTION
Business News - COMMUNICATIONS
Business Notes - CABLE TV BUSINESS MAGAZINE
Business Notes - GRAPHIC ARTS, THE
Business Notes - TEL-COMS
Business of Entertainment, The - *yesterday's stock reports* - HOLLYWOOD REPORTER
Business of Tape, The - *column by Harry Paney* - TAPE/DISC BUSINESS
Business Papers - ADVERTISING & SELLING
Business Publications - MEDIAWEEK
Business Report - BROADCAST + TECHNOLOGY
Business Shoot - BACK STAGE/SHOOT
Business Side, The - CHANNELS
Business Side - *column by Ellen Opat-Inkeles* - STEP-BY-STEP GRAPHICS
Business Starters - *column by Robert H. Gerke* - SCHEMER, THE
Business Videos - TELESPAN'S BUSINESSTV GUIDE
Business Watch - TV TECHNOLOGY
Business/Management Newsletter - *excellent late breaking news column* - AMERICAN PRINTER
Business-to-Business - *industry newsbriefs* - SALES & MARKETING MANAGEMENT
BusinessTV Guide - *'programming-at-a-glance'* - TELESPAN'S BUSINESSTV GUIDE

BusinessTV Guide Alaphabetical Listings - *'Listed by title'* - TELESPAN'S BUSINESSTV GUIDE
Business-Wise - *newsbriefs of members* - SPECIALTY ADVERTISING BUSINESS
But I Digress - *commentary column by Peter David* - COMICS BUYER'S GUIDE
Buy Video Music - *'Movie's quarterly guide to the latest music video releases'* - MOVIE - THE VIDEO MAGAZINE
Buyer's 10-14 - *'Regarding what's new in CB'* - CB LIFE
Buyer's Blueprint - BUSINESS COMMUNICATIONS REVIEW
Buyers Brief - *short product review* - BUYERS GUIDE
Buyer's Choice - *editorial* - HOT PICKS
Buyer's Corner - VIDEO BUSINESS
Buyers Guide - *equipment listing* - BRITISH JOURNAL OF PHOTOGRAPHY
Buyers Guide - PHOTO ANSWERS
Buyer's Guide - *new product review* - TARGET MARKETING
Buyers Guide - *'Equipment run-down-- prices, features and form'* - WHAT SATELLITE
Buyers Guide - WHAT VIDEO
Buyer's Opinion - TELEVISION/RADIO AGE
Buying and Booking Guide - *unusually detailed descriptions of current or soon to be released motion pictures* - FILM JOURNAL, THE
Buying & Selling Strategies - BEYOND THE RATINGS/RADIO
Buying Answers - *video buyers guide* - VIDEO ANSWERS
Buylines - *used/demo equipment for sale* - VIDEO TIMES
Buzz - *news about the hottest stars* - MOVIELINE
Buzzing Around with Vic Enyart - HOLLYWOOD FILMOGRAPH
By Design - *graphic and layout critique* - NEWSINC.
By Request - *printing of 'to be seen again' photos* - AMERICAN PHOTO
By the Ad Sense Man - *advertising trends* - AD SENSE
Byliner, The - *unique section devoted to unusual AP stories, campaigns and developments* - PUBLISHER'S AUXILIARY

C

CAB Fare - *Cabletelevision Advertising Bureau news* - MSO'S CABLE MARKETING
Cabaret - *listing of cabaret reviews at various locations* - THEATERWEEK
Cabaret Corner - *column by Jason McCloskey* - DRAMA-LOGUE

Cable - *newsbriefs* - BROADCASTER
Cable - INVIEW
Cable - *commentary* - MEDIAWEEK
Cable - *newsbriefs* - TV, ETC.
Cable + Satellite News - BROADCAST + TECHNOLOGY
Cable Ad-Dendums - CABLE TV ADVERTISING
Cable and Pay-TV - *column by Seth Goldstein* - PANORAMA
Cable Comments - CABLE COMMUNICATIONS MAGAZINE
Cable Connections - VIEW
Cable Movie Calendar - *'What's playing on the movie channels for each day in [month]'* - CINEMA, VIDEO & CABLE MOVIE DIGEST
Cable Movie Highlights - *'An A to Z listing with a story line for each cable movie'* - CINEMA, VIDEO & CABLE MOVIE DIGEST
Cable News Network - ENTERTAINER, THE
Cable People - CABLE MARKETING
Cable Programming - CABLE COMMUNICATIONS MAGAZINE
Cable Report - TELEVISION/RADIO AGE
Cable Roundup - VARIETY
Cable Scan - *newsbriefs* - CABLE MARKETING
Cable Stats - CABLEVISION
Cable Tech - *newsbriefs* - CABLE MARKETING
Cable Ticker - *cable management* - CABLE MARKETING
Cable TV - INSIDE MEDIA
Cable World Business Extra - *excellent 2nd section on the business of cable television operation* - CABLE WORLD
Cablegrams - *cable newsbriefs* - ON CABLE
Cables - PARAMOUNT WORLD
CableScope - *newsbriefs* - CABLEVISION
Cable/View - TELEVISION BROADCAST
Cablevision Information - *for this region* - CABLE GUIDE, THE
CableVision Plus - CABLEVISION
Calendar - ADVERTISING AGE
Calendar - ADVERTISING AGENCY
Calendar - *extensive listing of upcoming events, workshops, and seminars for advertising, marketing, and media professionals* - ADWEEK'S MARKETING WEEK
Calendar - *upcoming film and media festivals, seminars, and conventions* - AFI EDUCATION NEWSLETTER
Calendar - AFVA BULLETIN
Calendar - AGENCY
Calendar - *upcoming events* - AMUSEMENT BUSINESS
Calendar - ART & DESIGN NEWS
Calendar - ART DIRECTION
Calendar - *upcoming events* - ASIFA NOUVELLES
Calendar - AVC
Calendar - BALLETT INTERNATIONAL
Calendar - BEYOND THE RATINGS
Calendar - BILLBOARD
Calendar - BROADCAST + TECHNOLOGY
Calendar - *upcoming events of interest to special librarians* - BUSINESS INFORMATION ALERT

Calendar - *upcoming events* - C-O-N-N-E-C-T-I-O-N-S
Calendar - CABLE TV BUSINESS MAGAZINE
Calendar - CABLEVISION
Calendar - CAMERA & DARKROOM PHOTOGRAPHY
Calendar - COMMUNICATIONS INDUSTRIES REPORT, THE
Calendar - COMMUNICATOR, THE
Calendar - CURRENT
Calendar - DIRECT MARKETING
Calendar - EDITORIAL EYE, THE
Calendar - ELECTRONIC MEDIA
Calendar - *of upcoming international events and conventions* - ELECTRONICS & COMMUNICATIONS ENGINEERING JOURNAL
Calendar - FILM & VIDEO
Calendar - GRAPHIC ARTS MONTHLY
Calendar - HUMAN COMMUNICATION CANADA
Calendar - IBE
Calendar - IEEE SPECTRUM
Calendar - IN-PLANT PRINTER & ELECTRONIC PUBLISHER
Calendar - *upcoming seminars, meetings, and trade shows* - IN-PLANT REPRODUCTIONS
Calendar - INFORMATION TODAY
Calendar - *'a guide to meetings, events, seminars and parties'* - INSIDE MEDIA
Calendar - *performances, theatre and telephone listing* - INTERMISSION
Calendar - *international list of forthcoming information management events* - INTERNATIONAL JOURNAL OF INFORMATION MANAGEMENT
Calendar - LANGUAGE & COMMUNICATION
Calendar - *Film-Radio-TV cultural events in southern California* - MAGAZINE, THE
Calendar - MAGAZINE DESIGN & PRODUCTION
Calendar - MEDIA ANTHROPOLOGIST NEWSLETTER
Calendar - MEDIAWEEK
Calendar - *upcoming TV and film festivals* - MOVIE/TV MARKETING
Calendar - MULTICHANNEL NEWS
Calendar - PHOTOGRAPHER'S FORUM
Calendar - PRINT-EQUIP NEWS
Calendar - PRINTING IMPRESSIONS
Calendar - *events* - PRINTINGNEWS
Calendar - PRO SOUND NEWS
Calendar - *extended upcoming events* - PUBLISHER'S WEEKLY
Calendar - *upcoming events* - RF DESIGN
Calendar - SATELLITE COMMUNICATIONS
Calendar - SATELLITE RETAILER
Calendar - SMPTE JOURNAL
Calendar - STEP-BY-STEP ELECTRONIC DESIGN
Calendar - *'Upcoming seminars, trade shows, exhibitions, deadlines and other events in visual communications'* - STEP-BY-STEP GRAPHICS
Calendar - TEL-COMS
Calendar - TELECOMMUNICATIONS
Calendar - TELECOMMUNICATIONS POLICY
Calendar - TELECOMMUNICATIONS WEEK
Calendar - TELECONNECT

Calendar - *upcoming video events* - TELEVISIONS
Calendar - THE JOURNAL
Calendar - THEATRE ARTS
Calendar - THEATRE JOURNAL
Calendar - TRAVEL & LEISURE
Calendar - *upcoming film-related events, contests, and festivals* - UNIVERSITY FILM STUDY CENTER. NEWSLETTER.
Calendar - VIA SATELLITE
Calendar - VIDEO INSIDER
Calendar - VIDEO TIMES
Calendar - VIDEODISC MONITOR, THE
Calendar - *upcoming video events and contests* - VIDEOMAKER
Calendar - *media conferences-expos to be held* - WASHINGTON JOURNALISM REVIEW
Calendar - WITTYWORLD
Calendar - WORLD PRESS REVIEW
Calendar - *upcoming events for writers and publishers* - WRITER'S NW
Calendar of Animated Events - PENCIL TEST
Calendar of Events - ANIMAFILM
Calendar of Events - CABLE COMMUNICATIONS MAGAZINE
Calendar of Events - ELECTRONIC TECHNICAN/DEALER
Calendar of Events - ELECTRONICS WORLD
Calendar of Events - FLASH
Calendar of Events - FOUR A NEWSLETTER
Calendar of Events - MAST
Calendar of Events - PRINT
Calendar of Events - WESTERN PHOTOGRAPHER MAGAZINE
Calendar of Events. (7-90). - PC PUBLISHING AND PRESENTATIONS
Calendar of Feature Releases - *distributors and dates of their release* - FILM JOURNAL, THE
Calendar of International Technical Meetings - EBU REVIEW. TECHNICAL.
Calendar of Meetings - PULP & PAPER CANADA
Calendar of Meetings and Trade Exhibits - PRINTING IMPRESSIONS
Calendar of Photographic Exhibitions - POPULAR PHOTOGRAPHY
Calendar of the News - *newsbriefs* - EDITORIAL
Calendar of Upcoming Events - ETV NEWSLETTER
Calendar Reviews - FACTSHEET FIVE
Calendar/Associations - DIRECT MARKETING
Calgari - BOX OFFICE
California Dreamin' - *column by Van Arsdale France* - STORYBOARD / THE ART OF LAUGHTER
California Update - LOCATION UPDATE
Call for Entries - BOARD REPORT FOR GRAPHIC ARTISTS
Call Letters - *'Network abbreviations'* - SATELLITE TV WEEK
Callanetics Competition - *contest* - VIDEO BUYER
Callboard - *items of interest to DGA members* - ACTION!

Departments INDEX 788

Callboard - *ads* - THEATRE CRAFTS
Calls - *for papers, projects, awards* - HEALTH COMMUNICATION NEWSLETTER
Calls for Papers - SPECTRA
Callsheet - *bios and pictures of contributors* - HOLLYWOOD MAGAZINE
Camcorder College - VIDEO REVIEW
Camcorder Tests - *test bench reviews column by Rod Woodcock* - CAMCORDER
Camcorders - SOUND & VISION
Camera - *from manufacturer to user* - INTERNATIONAL PHOTOGRAPHER
Camera and Travel Shopper - *product review column by Rudy Maschke* - TRAVEL & LEISURE
Camera Answers - *equipment Q&A* - PHOTO ANSWERS
Camera Clinic - EIGHT MM MOVIE MAKER AND CINE CAMERA
Camera Club News, The - *various club newsbriefs* - CAMERA MAGAZINE
Camera Club News - *'News and ideas'* - MODERN PHOTOGRAPHY
Camera Clubs - *column by Whit Hillyer* - POPULAR PHOTOGRAPHY
Camera Clubs - TRAVEL & LEISURE
Camera Collector, The - MODERN PHOTOGRAPHY
Camera Collector, The - *column by Eaton S. Lothrop* - POPULAR PHOTOGRAPHY
Camera Eye - *comment column by Ott Coelln* - COMPUTER PICTURES
Camera Forum, The - *Q&A* - CAMERA MAGAZINE
Camera Mart Data Guide - PRACTICAL PHOTOGRAPHY
Camera on Campus - *column* - PETERSEN'S PHOTOGRAPHIC
Camera Shots - *column by Neil Brant* - HOLLYWOOD FILMOGRAPH
Camera: Then - *historical briefs from early Camera issues* - CAMERA
Cameravaria - *photographic potpourri column by Victor Blackman* - AMATEUR PHOTOGRAPHER
Campaign - ADWEEK'S MARKETING WEEK
Campaign Briefs - CAMPAIGN
Campaign Formula, The - *picture story of successful promotions* - EXHIBITORS TRADE REVIEW
Campaign Medals - *onions and roses for recent campaigns* - CAMPAIGN
Campaigns - *varied group of ad reprints* - ADVERTISING NEWS
Campaigns - *profile* - ASIAN ADVERTISING & MARKETING
Campaigns - MEDIAWEEK
Can Anyone Help? - RADIO & ELECTRONICS CONSTRUCTOR
CAN Opening - *performing arts opportunities* - CANEWS
Canada - *Canadian recording news* - BILLBOARD
Canadian Developments - OPTICAL MEMORY NEWS
Canadian Drawing Board - *newsbriefs* - TARGET
Canadian Film News - CINEMA/CANADA

Canadian Memo - *newsbriefs column by Vic Baker* - DIRECT MARKETING
Canadian News Fronts - *column by Ron Hessler* - QST
Canadian Report - *newsbrief column on Canadian black artists column by Norman Richmond* - BLACK RADIO EXCLUSIVE
Canadian Scene - *newsbriefs* - OFFICIAL BULLETIN OF THE INTERNATIONAL ALLIANCE OF THEATRICAL STAGE EMPLOYEES AND MOVING PICTURE MACHINE OPERATORS OF THE UNITED STATES AND CANADA.
Canadian Scene, The - *column by Bill Barr* - STV GUIDE
Canadiana - *Canadian news* - PSA JOURNAL
Canadian/US News - MEDIA INTERNATIONAL
Canbys Capsules - AUDIO
Cancelled Magazines - BOOK PROMOTION HOTLINE
Candid Close-Ups - *pictures* - TONI HOLT'S MOVIE LIFE
CANdid Report: A Living Stone Collection, The - *news column by Karen Mulder* - CANEWS
Candid Shots - *editorial newsitem column by B. G. Davis* - POPULAR PHOTOGRAPHY
Candid Shots from the Editor - *editorial* - AUSTRALIAN PHOTOGRAPHY
Capital Letter - COLUMBIA JOURNALISM REVIEW
Capitol Scan - *'devoted to national initiatives involving applications of technology-based instruction in higher education* - TELESCAN
Capsulated Comments - RANGEFINDER, THE
Capsule Critiques - *music review column by Larry Canale* - CD REVIEW
Capsule Film Listings - *descriptions and ratings of upcoming films* - MOVIES NOW
Capsules - *'Other notable programming'* - ENTERTAINMENT WEEKLY
Capsules - *'Short rock reviews'* - HI-FI NEWS AND RECORD REVIEW
Captain Video's - *TV column* - CAMPAIGN
Caption Competition - *reader contest* - VIDEO TODAY
Captured Live - *Newsbriefs on music tapings* - ON LOCATION
Car Stereo - *column by Ivan Berger* - STEREO REVIEW
Car Tunes - *Music review column by Chris Giancola and Mike Mettler* - CAR STEREO REVIEW
Career Advances - *personnel briefs* - MSO'S CABLE MARKETING
Career Directions - *column by Karen Gillick* - DIRECT MARKETING
Career Opportunities - COMMUNICATIONSWEEK
Career Opportunities - HUMAN COMMUNICATION CANADA
Career Profile - ENTERTAINMENT REVUE
Career Tips - *'Helpful hints covering a variety of practical professional development issues'* - STEP-BY-STEP GRAPHICS
Careerline - *employment opportunities* - AWRT NEWS AND VIEWS
Careers - *personnel briefs* - VUE

Carolinas Report, The - *black radio playlist* - BLACK RADIO EXCLUSIVE
Carousel - *personnel changes* - PR WEEK
Cartoon - *contemporary cartoon on films or filmmaking* - SEQUENCE
Cartoon Biography - KORKIS AND CAWLEY'S CARTOON QUARTERLY
Cartoon Comics - FILM FUN
Cartoon Laboratory - *profile* - WITTYWORLD
Cartoon Quarterly's Question and Answer - *animation Q&A column by Jim Davis* - KORKIS AND CAWLEY'S CARTOON QUARTERLY
Cartoonist, The - *column by Teri S. Wood* - AMAZING HEROES
Cartoonist Cues - *column by Pat Fulford* - WRITER'S DIGEST
Cartoons, Shorts, Fillers - SERVICE FOR COMPANY COMMUNICATORS
Cartridges, Phono - SOUND & VISION
Case Book - *corporate applications with JVC video equipment* - PLAYBACK
Case Study - ELECTRONIC PUBLISHER
Case Study - PUBLIC RELATIONS NEWS
Case Study - *fascinating research department* - VIDEO SOFTWARE MAGAZINE
Case Study - *excellent first-hand report of problem resolvement* - YELLOW SHEET, THE
Case Study and Response - JOURNAL OF EDUCATIONAL PUBLIC RELATIONS
Cassette & DAT Decks - SOUND & VISION
Cassette Reports - *an interesting section detailing new audio cassettes of speakers and workshops in direct mail* - DIRECT MARKETING
Cassettes in Review - *review* - PANORAMA
Casting - SHOW BUSINESS
Casting Board, The - *casting information* - SPOTLIGHT CASTING MAGAZINE
Casting Calls - SHOW BIZ WEST
Casting Information - *critical information on Hollywood-area television and film productions* - SHOWCASE WORLD
Casting News - *newsbriefs* - VARIETY
Casting Notices - *extensive listing* - DRAMA-LOGUE
Casting Off - *contributor profiles* - PERSONAL PUBLISHING
Casts of Current Pictures - *detailed listing of current fare* - PHOTOPLAY COMBINED WITH MOVIE MIRROR
Casual Observer - *column by Peter Moore* - MODERN PHOTOGRAPHY
Catalog News - TARGET MARKETING
Catalogs - ART & DESIGN NEWS
Catalogs - MEDIA ANTHROPOLOGIST NEWSLETTER
Catalogue - *new product review* - CABLEVISION
Catalogues and Books Received - KINEMATOGRAPH WEEKLY
Catch-Lines - *interesting news briefs concerning reporters, pressroom workers, etc.* - EDITOR AND PUBLISHER
Cats' Meow, The - *Q&A on specific stars* - RONA BARRETT'S HOLLYWOOD
CATV Finance - *economic and stock quotes* - VUE

CATV Headliners - *personnel briefs* - VUE
CATV Profile - *profile* - VUE
CATV System News - *national systems* - VUE
CATV Viewpoint - *editorial* - VUE
CATV Week - *newsbriefs* - VUE
Caught - *review* - DOWN BEAT
Caught in the Act - *live show showcase* - DOWN BEAT
CB Afield - *column by V. Lee Oertle* - CB LIFE
CB Corner - *column by Len Buckwalter* - ELECTRONICS ILLUSTRATED
CB Life Afloat - *column by Jim Martenhoff* - CB LIFE
CB Scene - *'27 MHz communications activities'* - POPULAR COMMUNICATIONS
CBA News - *news of the Christian Booksellers Association* - BOOKSTORE JOURNAL
CCBE Newsletter - *news of the Central Canada Association of Broadcast Engineers, column by Bob Findlay* - BROADCAST + TECHNOLOGY
CCI Newsletter - APERTURE, THE
CCIR Papers Reviewed - ABU TECHNICAL REVIEW
CD & Beyond - *column by Bryan Brewer* - CD REVIEW
CD Business - *column by Elliot Blair Smith* - CD REVIEW
CD Players, Changers, Portables, D/A Converters - SOUND & VISION
CD Spread, The - *reviews* - HIGH FIDELITY
CD-ROM - VIDEO TECHNOLOGY NEWS
CD-ROM Report: News - CD-ROM
CD-ROM Report: Products - CD-ROM
CD-ROM Today - *extensive news section* - INFORMATION TODAY
Celebrities I've Met - *fan close-encounters* - CELEBRITY PLUS
Celebrities of the Stage - *actor profiles* - ARTHURIAN THEATRE MAGAZINE, THE
Celebrity Choice - *favorite star dining establishments* - PLAYBILL
Celebrity Corner - *'New and familiar faces on the big screen'* - CINEMA, VIDEO & CABLE MOVIE DIGEST
Celebrity Corner - *wonderful star interviews column by Steve Dale* - VIDEO TIMES
Celebrity Crossword - *'Pencil games for the movie enthusiast'* - CINEMA, VIDEO & CABLE MOVIE DIGEST
Celebrity Dining - *thinly disguised reviews to promote dining spots in L.A. area* - HOLLYWOOD STUDIO MAGAZINE
Celebrity Horoscope - CELEBRITY
Celebrity Party Line - *'Latest, hottest gossip burning up the wires...'* - WHO'S WHO IN MOVIES AND TV
Celebrity Profile - *column by Cheryl Lavin* - ONSAT
Celebrity Profiles - CELEBRITY
Celebrity Recipes - REAL LIFE/DAYTIMERS
Celebrity Salutes - *tribute essay* - CELEBRITY
Celebrity Solund-Off - *Television personalities speak their mind* - NIGHTTIME TV
Celebrity Talk - *'Inside info' column by Marcia Borie* - MOVIE STARS
Cellular Parade - DEALERSCOPE

Centennial Exhibition--What Folks Say - ADVERTISERS GAZETTE
Center Fold, The - SQUEEKY WHEEL, THE
Center Stage - *news of professional touring sound reinforcement companies* - PRO SOUND NEWS
Center Stage: - *music and video profile* - BOOKSTORE JOURNAL
Centerstage - *'Top 10 tours of the month'* - PRO SOUND NEWS
Central Zone - PSA JOURNAL
Centrenews - *of the Puppet Centre Trust* - ANIMATIONS
Certified Record Revue - *column by Bert Whyte* - ELECTRONICS WORLD
CES Report - *what's new at the Consumer Electronics Show* - PHOTO MARKETING
CFE News - CINEMA/CANADA
Ch. Two-Four - *column by Ormel duke* - CB LIFE
Chain and Local Features - *programming* - RADIO FAN-FARE
Chair Chatter - *division chairperson commentary column by Suzanne Williams* - PD REPORT
Chairman's Column - *column by Robert G. Woolf* - ENTERTAINMENT AND SPORTS LAWYER, THE
Chairman's Corner - *commentary column by Joel Harnett* - MARKETING COMMUNICATIONS
Chairman's Corner - PRESSTIME
Changes - COMPUTER PICTURES
Changes - INSIDE MEDIA
Changes - *personnel* - MUSIC LINE
Changes - *exhibitor news* - NATIONAL EXHIBITOR, THE
Changes - *photographic buyer update* - PHOTOGRAPHER'S MARKET NEWSLETTER
Changes in Personnel - ABU NEWSLETTER
Changing Channels - VIDEO MANAGEMENT
Changing Faces and Places - UK PRESS GAZETTE
Changing Hands - *radio-TV stations sold* - BROADCASTING
Changing Roles for Gannetteers - *job promotions and changes* - GANNETTEER
Channel Chatter - *soap opera news column by R. Marian Rose* - TV DAY STARS
Channel Choice Services - *excellent 'Guide to satellite audio & video'* - SATELLITE TV WEEK
Channel Directory - *for this region* - CABLE GUIDE, THE
Channel Directory - ENTERTAINER, THE
Channel Echoes - *British news* - ALL-WAVE RADIO
Channel Gossip - *column by Paul Denis* - TV WORLD
Channel One - *editorial* - VIDEO MAGAZINE
Channel to Channel - *'What's happening behind the TV scene'* - GOSSIP
Channels, The - *European television and radio programming listed by satellite* - SATELLITE TIMES
Chapter Chatter - *individual 'letters' detailing chapter events and news* - BROADCAST ENGINEERS' JOURNAL, THE

Chapter Edits - *large segment detailing individual chapter activities* - SIGNALS
Chapter File Templates - *available for purchase by Ventura software users* - VENTURA LETTER, THE
Chapter News - DARKSLIDE
Chapters - *news* - INDUSTRIAL TELEVISION NEWS
Chart Beat - *column by Paul Grein* - BILLBOARD
Charting the Stars - *unique lifestyles chart of Hollywood stars* - SCREEN ALBUM MAGAZINE
Charts - *Box-office rankings in Los Angeles, London, Australia* - EMPIRE
Charts - MUSIC LINE
Charts - *'For rent and for sale'* - VIDEO TIMES
Chat with the Editor, A - MOVING PICTURE AGE
Chats With the Editors - *letters* - AMATEUR RADIO DEFENSE
Chats with Trade Leaders - KINEMATOGRAPH WEEKLY
Chatter - *comment* - RADIO FAN-FARE
Chatter in the Wings - *stage news* - VARIETY
Cheap Thrills - VIDEO REVIEW
Check List of Current Books and Monographs - *radio issues review* - AIR LAW REVIEW
Checking - *commentary column by John Cawley* - GET ANIMATED! UPDATE.
Checklist - *review of movies, books, periodicals* - NEW CAPTAIN GEORGE'S WHIZBANG, THE
Cheers & Jeers - *Orchid and Onion awards for newspapers* - OVERSET
Cheers and Jeers - *thumbs up/down on a variety of animation news items* - STORYBOARD / THE ART OF LAUGHTER
Cheers 'N' Jeers - TV GUIDE
Chemicals & the Graphic Arts - *application to the printing arts column by Don Nix* - PRINT-EQUIP NEWS
Chemistry Film Appraisals - *unique reviews prepared by Royal Institute of Chemistry and Scientific Film Association* - SCIENTIFIC FILM
Chi Critics' Opinions - *Chicago film reviews* - VARIETY
Chicago - BOX OFFICE
Chicago Loop - *video-film news* - MILLIMETER
Chicago Notes - EXHIBITORS' TIMES
Chicago Personalities - *Chicago exhibition column by Joe Fisher* - EXHIBITORS HERALD WORLD
Chicago Program Notes - TELESCREEN
Chicago Report - *column by Mel Miles* - BACK STAGE
Chicago Summer Attractions - DRAMATIC MAGAZINE, THE
Chicago Video Vignettes - TELESCREEN
Chief's Column, The - BULLETIN OF PHOTOGRAPHY
Children - LÜRZER'S INTERNATIONAL ARCHIVE
Children & Parenting - *videocassette review* - V
Children's - *review* - ORBIT VIDEO
Children's Book Scene - PUBLISHER'S WEEKLY

Departments INDEX

Children's Books - *listing* - FORECAST
Children's Books - MAGAZINE & BOOKSELLER
Children's Competition - *contest* - VIDEO BUYER
Children's Corner - *review column by David Gritten* - ORBIT VIDEO
Children's Film of the Month - DOCUMENTARY FILM NEWS
Children's Video - *column by Loretta MacAlpine* - VIDEO INSIDER
Child's Play - *kid section* - SPOTLIGHT ON VIDEO
Chile - *production newsbriefs* - PRODUCCIÓN Y DISTRIBUCIÓN
Chip 'n Dale Rescue Rangers - *comic section* - DISNEY ADVENTURES
Chit Chat and Leader - STAGE AND TELEVISION TODAY, THE
Choice - *favorite ad designs* - DIRECTION
Choice Real Estate Sales - *unusual section of Hollywood area homes for sale* - HOLLYWOOD REPORTER
Choice Sessions - HI-FI CHOICE
Choices - *unique applications* - CAR AUDIO AND ELECTRONICS
Chords & Discords - *'A forum for readers'* - DOWN BEAT
CHR - *contemporary hit radio format column by Joel Denver* - R & R
Christian Musician - MUSIC LINE
Christian Video - *review* - MOVIEGUIDE
Christiansen's Column - CAMPAIGN
Chronicle - *newsbriefs* - COLUMBIA JOURNALISM REVIEW
Chronicle - VIDEO BUSINESS
Churn Chart - VIEW
Cindy Says - *newsbriefs column by Cindy Adams* - CELEBRITY
Cindy Says - *'Cindy's sparkling column is filled with inside news on show business and show people' column by Cindy Adams* - MOVIE MIRROR
Cine Calendar - *upcoming festivals and competitions for nontheatrical product* - CINE NEWS
Cine Quiz - *skill test* - HOME MOVIES
Cinecapsules - *film reviews* - FILM & BROADCASTING REVIEW
Cine-Chat - *letters* - CINE-KODAK NEWS, THE
Cinema - *review* - INTERMISSION
Cinema - *review* - THEATRE MAGAZINE
Cinema Box Office Top 20 - *MRIB supplied data* - MOVIE - THE VIDEO MAGAZINE
Cinema Journal Book Reviews - *unusually long reviews* - CINEMA JOURNAL
Cinema Library, The - *book reviews* - DOCUMENTARY FILM NEWS
Cinema Scope - *highlights past production credits associated with current hit films* - BLOCKBUSTER VIDEO MAGAZINE
Cinema Sourcebook - *'The newest in film-book literature'* - FILMFAX
Cinema Workshop - *interesting production concepts* - AMERICAN CINEMATOGRAPHER
Cinemacabre Video - *reviews* - CINEMACABRE

Cinemasneak - *'Advance production information and first photos from forthcoming attractions' column by Priscilla Kitt* - FANTASTIC FILMS
Cinematography Assignments - *listing* - CINEMA/CANADA
Cinescenes - *newsbriefs* - FILMMAKERS FILM & VIDEO MONTHLY
Circuit and Service Forum - ELECTRONIC SERVICING & TECHNOLOGY
Circuit Breakers - *'The movies doing this months rounds'* - FILM REVIEW
Circuit Circus - *column by Charles D. Rakes* - POPULAR ELECTRONICS
Circuit Components - ELECTRONIC PRODUCTS
Circuit Digests - *full technical schematics of home electronic equipment* - ELECTRONIC TECHNICAN/DEALER
Circuit Ideas - ELECTRONICS WORLD + WIRELESS WORLD
Circuits - BROADCAST ENGINEERING
Circuits - *newsbriefs* - MOBILE SATELLITE NEWS
Circulation - BROADCAST PIONEERS LIBRARY REPORTS
Circulation - EDITOR AND PUBLISHER
Circulation - *personnel briefs* - FOLIO:
Circulation - PRESSTIME
Circulation - SUCCESSFUL MAGAZINE PUBLISHING
Circulation News - *large second section for magazine publishing* - MAGAZINEWEEK
Circulations - WOODCOCK'S PRINTERS' AND LITHOGRAPHERS' WEEKLY GAZETTE AND NEWSPAPER REPORTER
Citizen Action - *current activities* - TELEVISIONS
City Notes - ELECTRICAL REVIEW
City Tracks - *'a potpourri of promotional, positioning, market news and information'* - MONDAY MORNING REPLAY
City Watch - *London media column by William Arnold* - MEDIA WEEK
Claire Doyle - *graphics trends and issues column by Claire Doyle* - TELEVISION BROADCAST
Clandestine Communique - *'What's new with the clandestines'* - POPULAR COMMUNICATIONS
Class and Trade Journalism - ADVERTISING
Classes, Workshops & Tours - *upcoming* - WESTERN PHOTOGRAPHER MAGAZINE
Classic - *one-page lookback at classic films* - EMPIRE
Classic Film Salute - *column by Don Leifert* - AMAZING CINEMA
Classic Lines - *'Witty repartees, comical comebacks and sarcastic backbiting contribute to soaps' best dialogue'* - SOAP OPERA DIGEST
Classical & Opera - *review column by Martin Hoyle* - 20/20
Classical Issues & Reissues - HI-FI NEWS AND RECORD REVIEW
Classical Keeping Score - *column by Is Horowitz* - BILLBOARD
Classical Music - ABSOLUTE SOUND, THE
Classical Music - *reviews* - STEREO REVIEW

Classical Record Reviews - AUDIO
Classical Records - *review* - HIGH FIDELITY
Classical Releases - HI-FI ANSWERS
Classical Reviews - AUDIO
Classical Reviews - CD REVIEW
Classical Reviews - HI-FI NEWS AND RECORD REVIEW
Classical Scene - *column by John David Richardson* - AFTER DARK
Classical Tape Reviews - TAPE DECK QUARTERLY
Classical Wax - HI-FI NEWS AND RECORD REVIEW
Classicial Reviews - HIGH FIDELITY
Classics - *review* - ORBIT VIDEO
Classics Corner - *review* - ORBIT VIDEO
Classified - *film offerings* - FILM FAN MONTHLY
Classified - OVERSET
Classified - REP: RECORDING ENGINEERING PRODUCTION
Classified - SQUEEKY WHEEL, THE
Classified - TELEMARKETING
Classified - VIDEO MANAGEMENT
Classified Ads - CINEFAN
Classified Ads - ICA NEWSLETTER
Classified Ads of Film Speakers and Subjects - PERFORMER, THE
Classified Advice - *column by Daniel Lionel* - PUBLISHER'S AUXILIARY
Classifieds - MIX
Classifieds - SCRIPTWRITER NEWS
Classifieds - *2+ pages of faculty vacancies* - SPECTRA
Classroom & Community - FILM & VIDEO NEWS
Classroom Review - PRINT EDUCATION MAGAZINE
Claude Hall's Radio Confidential - *news and gossip* - INTERNATIONAL RADIO REPORT, THE
Clay Feet - *current ad critiques column by Leroy Fairman* - ADVERTISING & SELLING
Cleanliness for Beauty - *column by Wynne McKay* - RADIOLAND
Clear Channels - *newsbriefs of personnel changes* - COMMUNICATOR
Clearing House - *'Sells and buys equipment, theatres, services'* - BOXOFFICE
Clearing House, The - *news of media anthropologists* - MEDIA ANTHROPOLOGIST NEWSLETTER
Clearing House, The - *news and advice* - MOTION PICTURE ALBUM
Clebrity Exclusive - *interview* - CELEBRITY
Client Tells, The - *Q&A with clients* - PRO SOUND NEWS
Clinic - *'edited by Dr. Kinema* - MOVIE MAKERS
Clinic, The - *'Aids for Your Filming* - MOVIE MAKERS
Clip - *photographer's submissions for competition* - RETROFOCUS
Clip File - FOUR A NEWSLETTER
Clip List, The - BILLBOARD
Clip Results - RANGEFINDER, THE
Clip Service - *newsbriefs* - MEDIA & CONSUMER
Clip Standings - DARKSLIDE
Clip Standings - IMAGE 11

Clipper - *items of interest reprinted from other photographic publications* - ST. LOUIS AND CANADIAN PHOTOGRAPHER
Clipping Comment - GOOD NEWS: CHRISTIANS IN JOURNALISM
Clippings - *newsbriefs of the DC area* - WASHINGTON JOURNALISM REVIEW
Clips - CHRISTIAN FILM & VIDEO
Clips - DARKSLIDE
Clips - *'The way things used to be'* - NEWSINC.
Clips - *competition* - SIXSHOOTERS
Clips - *publisher briefs* - TECHTRENDS
Clips From the Cutting Room - *news of Hollywood stars and starlets* - FILM FUN
Close Focus - *column by Michael Heiss* - VIDEO PROPHILES
Close Up - *star profile* - GOSSIP
Close Ups and Long Shots - *motion picture star column by Ruth Waterbury* - PHOTOPLAY COMBINED WITH MOVIE MIRROR
Closed Circuit - *billed as 'insider report, behind the scene, before the fact* - BROADCASTING
Closer Look, A - CABLEAGE
Close-Up - A & E PROGRAM GUIDE
Close-Up - *comment and observations* - CAR STEREO REVIEW
CloseUp - COMMUNICATIONSWEEK
Close-Up - *star profile* - IN CINEMA
Close-Up - *three profiles* - MILLIMETER
CloseUp - *profile* - SCENE AT THE MOVIES
Close-Up - *product information* - TELEPROFESSIONAL
Closeup - *profiles* - TELEVISION
Closeup on Cable TV - *news stories concerning programming* - SHOW BUSINESS
CloseUps - *profiles* - AMERICAN PREMIERE
Close-Ups - *'Notes and comment on photographer contributors and policy'* - INTERNATIONAL PHOTOGRAPHER
Close-Ups - *profiles* - MILLIMETER
Close-Ups - *special newsbriefs* - MODERN SCREEN
Closeups - *'amateur activities.' (4-27).* - MOVIE MAKERS
Closing Comment - *commentary* - VIDEOGRAPHY
Closing Comments - *editorial* - MONITORING TIMES
Closing Shots - CAMCORDER USER
Club Close-Ups - *column* - PETERSEN'S PHOTOGRAPHIC
Club Contact - *'John Wright on what's happening around the country's video clubs'* - CAMCORDER USER
Club News - *ad association newsbriefs* - ADWEEK
Club News - *graphic arts organizations* - COMMUNICATION ARTS
Club News - *of regional marketing clubs* - DIRECT MARKETING
Club Notes - *extensive section discussion photo club activities in the United States* - CAMERA CRAFT
Club Notes - *various association events* - POSTCARD COLLECTOR
Club Notes - QST

Club Scene, The - FILM MAKING
Club Spectrum - *column by Rick Palm* - QST
Club Woman Chats on Films for the Family, A - *regular feature discussing community interaction* - MOTION PICTURE AND THE FAMILY, THE
Clubs - *news* - DOCTOR WHO MAGAZINE
Clubs - *'people, plans and programs* - MOVIE MAKERS
Clubs - *activities and events* - PSA JOURNAL
Clubs, Conferences, Seminars - *calendar* - COMMUNICATION ARTS
Clubs, Contests, and Exhibitions - *'Clubs, societies and associations of photographers like to know how other clubs are doing'* - CAMERA, THE
Clues on Clothes - *fashions* - HOLLYWOOD
CMA Calendar - *of upcoming events* - CMA NEWSLETTER
CMA People - *personnel newsbriefs* - CMA NEWSLETTER
CMA Shorts - *newsbriefs* - CMA NEWSLETTER
Coast to Coast With Dorothy Kilgallen - *column by Dorothy Kilgallen* - MOTION PICTURE
Cobina Wright's Party Gossip - *column by Cobina Wright* - SCREENLAND PLUS TV-LAND
Cockalorum - *pertaining to industry newsbriefs* - DOCUMENTARY FILM NEWS
Coffee, Brandy and Cigars - *column by Herman G. Weinberg* - TAKE ONE
Cold Eye, A - *'critical commentary on the institutions, practices, and controversies of the graphic design field'* - PRINT
Collectable 35, The - SHUTTERBUG
Collectables - *historical cameras* - BRITISH JOURNAL OF PHOTOGRAPHY
Collectables - *'a column exploring the world of photographica* - WISCONSIN PHOTOGRAPHER
Collectibles - VIDEO REVIEW
Collecting Disneyana - *informative column by Tom Tumbusch* - STORYBOARD / THE ART OF LAUGHTER
Collecting Scene, The - *extensive section on available motion picture product for collectors* - FILM FAN MONTHLY
Collecting Scene, The - FILMS IN REVIEW
Collections - *collectable Lucasfilm items* - LUCASFILM FAN CLUB, THE
Collector, The - NEW CAPTAIN GEORGE'S WHIZZBANG, THE
Collectors - *readers write about their own movie memorabilia* - HOLLYWOOD STUDIO MAGAZINE
Collectors - *unusual section where readers offer trades of photos and other star-related items* - RONA BARRETT'S HOLLYWOOD
Collector's Classics - *column by Tracey McIntire* - VIDEO CHOICE
Collector's Corner - *pictures of individual readers and their movie memorabilia* - HOLLYWOOD STUDIO MAGAZINE
Collector's Corner - PERFECT VISION, THE
Collectors' Corner - *'A special classified section'* - REAL LIFE/DAYTIMERS

Collectors' Corner - SHUTTERBUG
Collector's Corner - VIDEO ALERT
Collector's Showcase - *premiums and other items connected with historic television programs* - TELEVISION HISTORY
College - CHRISTIAN DRAMA
College Drama News - DRAMA MAGAZINE, THE
College News - *column by Jackie Kelley* - IMAGE
Collins Report, The - *programming column by Monica Collins* - TV GUIDE
Colloquium - *essay and editorial* - HIGH PERFORMANCE
Color and You - *column by Charles Smith* - PROFESSIONAL PHOTOGRAPHER, THE
Color and You! - *color photography column by Charles Smith* - PROFESSIONAL PHOTOGRAPHER, THE
Color Corner - CAMERA & DARKROOM PHOTOGRAPHY
Color Corner - *column by George Post* - DARKROOM PHOTOGRAPHY
Color Darkroom - POPULAR PHOTOGRAPHY
Color in Your Darkroom - MODERN PHOTOGRAPHY
Color Today - *column by Martin Hershenson* - MODERN PHOTOGRAPHY
Coloreviews - *new movie ratings* - TELEVISION AND SCREEN GUIDE
Colour Clinic - *technical advice* - AUSTRALIAN PHOTOGRAPHY
Column, The - *music* - AUDIO
Columnist - *column by Richard Armstrong* - TARGET MARKETING
Columnist and Artist Addresses - FACTSHEET FIVE
Columnists - *guest columnists on direct marketing issues* - TARGET MARKETING
Comeback - *unique manufacturers retort* - HI-FI ANSWERS
Comedy - *review* - ORBIT VIDEO
Comedy Reviews - VIDEO TODAY
Comedy: Laughter in the Rafters - *column by Donna Y. Caldwell* - SHOWCASE WORLD
Comic Store - *review of current releases column by Gary Russell* - STARBURST
Comic Strip - *unique comic strip rendition of a Dr. Who story* - DOCTOR WHO MAGAZINE
Comics - FILM THREAT
Comics - INTERVIEW
Comics, The - *news and review* - NEW CAPTAIN GEORGE'S WHIZZBANG, THE
Comics Career Portfolio - COMICS CAREER NEWSLETTER
Comics Guide - *column by Don Thompson* - COMICS BUYER'S GUIDE
Comics in Review - AMAZING HEROES
Comics Library - *review* - COMICS JOURNAL, THE
Comics Reporter - *news* - COMICS SCENE
Comics Reviews - FACTSHEET FIVE
Comics Screen - *comic characters in development for other media* - COMICS SCENE
Coming - *new film product* - CINEFANTASTIQUE

Departments INDEX

Coming and Going - *personnel briefs* - FILM TV DAILY
Coming and Going - *'Observations on events and incidents in the broadcasts of the month'* - RADIO FAN-FARE
Coming and Going - *personnel briefs* - RTD
Coming and Going - *activities of the stars* - TONI HOLT'S MOVIE LIFE
Coming Attractions - *forthcoming videocassette releases* - BEST OF FILM & VIDEO
Coming Attractions - *upcoming film product* - FILM THREAT
Coming Attractions - *previews* - PREVUE
Coming Attractions - *in selected US cities* - SHOW
Coming Cine Events - FILM MAKING
Coming Comics - *release data* - COMIC READER, THE
Coming Conventions - QST
Coming Distractions - *upcoming releases* - AMAZING HEROES
Coming Events - FACETS FEATURES
Coming Events - *'Conferences, meetings, fairs, exhibitions'* - LEARNED PUBLISHING
Coming Events - MEDIA DIGEST
Coming Events - SHUTTERBUG
Coming Events - *calendar* - TARGET MARKETING
Coming Events - WEB
Coming Events, Manuscript Calls, Deadlines - CLIO AMONG THE MEDIA
Coming IFRA Events - *calendar* - NEWSPAPER TECHNIQUES
Coming Into Focus - *news briefs of exhibits and camera clubs* - WISCONSIN PHOTOGRAPHER
Coming Next Month - ELECTRONICS WORLD
Coming on TV - *upcoming cable and broadcast programs* - VIDEO REVIEW
Coming Radio Events - *briefs of unique radio programs* - MOVIE-RADIO GUIDE
Coming Releases - BOOKS AND FILMS
Coming Soon - *upcoming motion picture releases* - IN CINEMA
Coming Soon - *'New on Video'* - SPOTLIGHT ON VIDEO
Coming to Town - *newsbriefs* - PLAYS AND PLAYERS
Coming Up - *British film society events* - FILM
Coming Up - *next issue topics* - HOW
Coming Up - *calendar* - SUCCESSFUL MAGAZINE PUBLISHING
Coming Up! - *trends and events forthcoming* - TV & RADIO FAXLETTER
Comings & Goings - *'Cast changes to keep track of!'* - REAL LIFE/DAYTIMERS
Comings and Goings - SOAP OPERA DIGEST
Comix Wavola - *column by Clay Geerdes* - COMICS FANDOM EXAMINER
Comixscene - *'News/Views/Reviews from the world of comics.' (11/12-78).* - PREVUE
Comment - *editorial* - AD WEEKLY
Comment - ADVANCED IMAGING
Comment - ALTERNATIVE THEATRE
Comment - *'A forum for diverse views on the media'* - AMERICAN FILM
Comment - BRITISH JOURNAL OF PHOTOGRAPHY

Comment - *editorial* - BROADCAST
Comment - BROADCAST SYSTEMS INTERNATIONAL
Comment - *editorial commentary by Elspeth Tavares and Lloyd Shepherd* - BUSINESS OF FILM, THE
Comment - COMIC READER, THE
Comment - *editorial* - COMMUNICATIONS
Comment - EDUCATIONAL COMMUNICATION AND TECHNOLOGY
Comment - ELECTRONICS WORLD + WIRELESS WORLD
Comment - FILM & VIDEO NEWS
Comment - *newsbriefs* - FILM ART
Comment - HI-FI ANSWERS
Comment - HI-FI NEWS AND RECORD REVIEW
Comment - *editorial* - INTERNATIONAL BROADCASTING
Comment - MEDIA WEEK
Comment - *column by Peter Harris* - NEW CAPTAIN GEORGE'S WHIZZBANG, THE
Comment - PHOTO MARKETING
Comment - PRESS, THE
Comment - RADIOACTIVE
Comment - TELEVISION QUARTERLY
Comment - *column by Peter Lloyd* - TELEVISION WEEK
Comment and Clippings - TELEPHONE MAGAZINE
Comment and Review - CLOSE-UP
Comment from Student Writers - *'A monthly department to which students are invited to contribute'* - PHOTODRAMATIST, THE
Commentaries - HASTINGS COMMUNICATIONS AND ENTERTAINMENT LAW JOURNAL
Commentaries - *'Readers' comments offering substantial theoretical and practical contributions to issues that have been raised in texts published in Leonardo'* - LEONARDO
Commentary - AMUSEMENT BUSINESS
Commentary - AT&T MAGAZINE
Commentary - AUDIO VISUAL
Commentary - AVC
Commentary - BILLBOARD
Commentary - BRITISH PRINTER
Commentary - CABLE TV BUSINESS MAGAZINE
Commentary - CRITIC
Commentary - EIGHT MM MOVIE MAKER AND CINE CAMERA
Commentary - GRAMOPHONE
Commentary - HUMAN COMMUNICATION CANADA
Commentary - INFORMATION TODAY
Commentary - IRIS
Commentary - JOURNAL OF APPLIED COMMUNICATION RESEARCH
Commentary - JOURNAL OF TECHNICAL WRITING AND COMMUNICATION
Commentary - JOURNALISM EDUCATOR, THE
Commentary - MANAGEMENT COMMUNICATION QUARTERLY
Commentary - MEDIA & CONSUMER
Commentary - MEDIA, CULTURE, AND SOCIETY
Commentary - NEWSINC.
Commentary - PHOTOEDUCATION

Commentary - PRE-
Commentary - *column by Charles E. Rotkin* - ROTKIN REVIEW, THE
Commentary - *column by Tom Valovic* - TELECOMMUNICATIONS
Commentary - WORLD PRESS REVIEW
Commentary from the Council - *ongoing dialogue between Arbitron and the Arbitron Radio Advisory Council* - BEYOND THE RATINGS
Comment/News/Notices - *excellent review of historical exhibits and other news items of interest to media historians* - HISTORICAL JOURNAL OF FILM, RADIO & TELEVISION
Comments - COMMERCIAL CAMERA
Comments - *from readers* - COMMUNICATION ENGINEERING
Comments - MOVIES AND MINISTRY
Comments - POLITICAL COMMUNICATION AND PERSUASION
Comments and Letters - *extended reader response* - PUBLIC OPINION QUARTERLY
Comments & Trends - COLLEGE & UNIVERSITY JOURNAL
Comments from Abroad - *lengthy letters* - BULGARIAN FILMS
Comments From the Field - *users comment on videotapes* - VIDEO CAPSULE
Comments of the Month - BRITISH COMMUNICATIONS AND ELECTRONICS
Comments on Color - *column by Phillip Leonian* - CAMERA 35
Comments/News/Notices - HISTORICAL JOURNAL OF FILM, RADIO & TELEVISION
Commercial Analysis - *technique* - PROFESSIONAL PHOTOGRAPHER, THE
Commercial Breaks - *spot TV news* - ON LOCATION
Commercial Corner, The - NATIONAL PHOTOGRAPHER, THE
Commercial Man's Scrap Book, A - *'The past, present and future of photography' column by James M. Caufield* - PROFESSIONAL PHOTOGRAPHER, THE
Commercial Production - MARKEE
Commercial Radio Trends - COMMUNICATION AND BROADCAST ENGINEERING
Commercial Signs - SIGNS OF THE TIMES
Commercial Talent Directory - *listing of New York, Chicago, Los Angeles agencies* - ENTERTAINMENT MONTHLY
Commercials - FILM & VIDEO
Commercials - INSIDE ENTERTAINMENT
Commercials - MILLIMETER
Commercials - *short, descriptive paragraphs about newy produced spots* - TELEVISION/RADIO AGE
Commercials of the Month - *'An advertising directory of film commercials'* - TELEVISER
Commissary, The - *column by Jeff Lantos* - MOVIELINE
Commission Comments - *notes on commission activities* - INTERNATIONAL EDUCATIONAL AND CULTURAL EXCHANGE
Commission Docket for forthcoming Month - BROADCAST REPORTER

Committee Report - *association news* - MIX
Commonwealth Press - *status* - CAMPAIGN
Communication Forum - *umbrella title for commentary and research departments* - MANAGEMENT COMMUNICATION QUARTERLY
Communication Receiver, The - OLD TIMER'S BULLETIN, THE
Communication Theory - *reviews* - HOMILETIC
Communications - *technical column by Leslie Solomon* - COMPUTERS & ELECTRONICS
Communications - HYPERMEDIA
Communications - *newsbriefs* - MONITORING TIMES
Communications - *letters* - RADIO-ELECTRONICS
Communications - TECHNOLOGY AND CULTURE
Communications Confidential - *'Your guide to shortwave utility stations'* - POPULAR COMMUNICATIONS
Communications Digest - *newsbriefs* - AVC
Communications Management - COMMUNICATIONS CONCEPTS
Communications Manager - NETWORK WORLD
Communications Now - *two-page news section on non-broadcast hardware and software* - MOVIE/TV MARKETING
Communications Review - *upcoming events* - BIOMEDICAL COMMUNICATIONS
Communique - *reprint of recent topical news speeches* - COMMUNICATOR
Communique - *CWA president's column* - CWA NEWS
Communique - *publisher commentary column by David Allen Shaw* - VIDEO STORE
Communiquotes - *quotes from RCA personnel appearing before public groups* - COMMUNICATE
Communities - GF MAGAZINE
Community Theatre - *column by Gene Warech and Lynn Warech* - DRAMA-LOGUE
Compact Disc Monitor - HI-FI NEWS AND RECORD REVIEW
Companies - GRAPHIC ARTS MONTHLY
Company Index - *as cited in articles* - TELECOMMUNICATIONS ALERT
Company News - BROADCAST SYSTEMS INTERNATIONAL
Company Profile - BRITISH BOOK NEWS
Company Profile - BROADCAST SYSTEMS INTERNATIONAL
Company Profile - MAST
Company Profiles - JEE, JOURNAL OF ELECTRONIC ENGINEERING
Comparative Case Notes - LINE MONITOR, THE
Comparison Test - PRACTICAL PHOTOGRAPHY
Competing Media - *news items* - RADIO BUSINESS REPORT
Competing Media - VIDEO TECHNOLOGY NEWS
Competition - *monthly video contest* - VIDEO TIMES
Competition - *reader contest* - VIDEO TODAY

Competition Winners - *from previous contests* - VIDEO BUYER
Competition Winners - VIDEO WORLD
Competitions - DIGEST OF THE UNIVERSITY FILM AND VIDEO ASSOCIATION
Competitions & Exhibitions - RANGEFINDER, THE
Competitions and Exhibitions - *details* - RANGEFINDER, THE
Components - *new product review* - AUDIO/VIDEO INTERIORS
Components - CONSUMER ELECTRONICS PRODUCT NEWS
Composing Room - *column by Frank Higgason* - GRAPHIC ARTS MONTHLY
Compu Scan - *'Articles, books, programs, and projects involving the uses of computer technologies'* - TELESCAN
Compute - BME'S TELEVISION ENGINEERING
Computer Audio - DB
Computer Bits - *column by Carl Warren* - COMPUTERS & ELECTRONICS
Computer Bits - *column by Jeff Holtzman* - POPULAR ELECTRONICS
Computer Connection - *column by Kelly Klaas* - RADIO GUIDE
Computer Graphics - *column by Helena Powell* - AVC
Computer Graphics - *technology column by Barry Smith* - DIRECTION
Computer Products - *review* - RADIO-ELECTRONICS
Computer Scan - *column by Rick Lehtinen* - VIDEO SYSTEMS
Computer Sources - *column by Leslie Solomon* - COMPUTERS & ELECTRONICS
Computer Systems - ELECTRONIC PRODUCTS
Computer Visuals - BACK STAGE
Computers - HYPERMEDIA
Computers - LÜRZER'S INTERNATIONAL ARCHIVE
Computers - SALES & MARKETING MANAGEMENT
Computers - THEATRE DESIGN & TECHNOLOGY
Computers In Sales & Marketing - SALES & MARKETING MANAGEMENT
Computers in the Studio - *column by Joel Sampson* - STUDIO PHOTOGRAPHY
Computing Corner - PRACTICAL WIRELESS
Concept - *idea development column by Debra Kaufman* - PRODUCERS QUARTERLY
Concerning Foreign Markets - AMERICAN ADVERTISER
Concerning the Theatre - *newsbriefs* - PLAYERS
Concert Promoter - MUSIC LINE
Concert Reviews - *current events* - VARIETY
Concert Sound News - *column by David Scheirman* - PRO SOUND NEWS
Concerts - MUSICAL AMERICA
Conclusions, Best Buys and Recommendations - *based upon this issue's listening tests* - HI-FI CHOICE
Condensed Thoughts - *humorous comment* - EDITORIAL
Conference Beat - INDEPENDENT, THE
Conference Calendar - FORECAST
Conference Calendar - MARKETING NEWS

Conference Calendar - OPTICAL MEMORY NEWS
Conference Planning - CAMPAIGN
Conference Reports - OPTICAL MEMORY NEWS
Conference Room, The - *financial and investment strategies* - NEWSINC.
Conferences - AEU
Conferences - DIGEST OF THE UNIVERSITY FILM AND VIDEO ASSOCIATION
Conferences - FOLIO:
Conferences - HOMILETIC
Conferences - *review* - ON FILM
Conferences - *upcoming* - URBAN TELECOMMUNICATIONS FORUM
Conferences & Competitions - TAKE ONE
Conferences and Conventions - SPECTRA
Conferences & Events - *calendar of upcoming events* - COLLEGE BROADCASTER
Conferences or Meetings External to the ITU - TELECOMMUNICATION JOURNAL
Conferences/Seminars - SPECTRA
Connect Locater, The - *'teaching materials and where to find them'* - CONNECT
Connect Report, The - *'programming of note'* - CONNECT
Connect Study Guide, The - CONNECT
Connect Survey, The - *comprehensive survey of upcoming cable television educational programs* - CONNECT
Consensus of Opinion - *film commentary* - MIDWEEK MOTION PICTURE NEWS
Considerations - *equipment reviews* - ABSOLUTE SOUND, THE
Con-Sid-erations - *column by Sid Bernstein* - ADVERTISING AGE
Conspiracy Corner - *column by Kerry Thornley* - FACTSHEET FIVE
Consultant - PHOTO/DESIGN
Consultants - *professional cards* - BUYERS GUIDE
Consultant's Corner - *column by Richard A. Kuehn* - BUSINESS COMMUNICATIONS REVIEW
Consultants Corner - RADIO WORLD
Consumer Data - *American consumer demographics* - ADWEEK'S MARKETING WEEK
Consumer Electronics - FUTUREHOME TECHNOLOGY NEWS
Consumer Electronics - MONITORING TIMES
Consumer Magazines - MEDIAWEEK
Consumer Problems - *home consumer satellite television* - STV GUIDE
Consumerism Update - *consumer development news* - PUBLIC RELATIONS JOURNAL, THE
Consumers Corner - CWA NEWS
Contact - *stories and contact prints* - AMERICAN PHOTO
Contact - FRENDX
Contact Numbers for Your Diary - *excellent resource listing for industry professionals* - BUSINESS OF FILM, THE
Contemporary Jazz - *hit list* - R & R
Contemporary Journalism - EDITORIAL REVIEW

Departments INDEX

Contemporary Radio Hit Activity Chart - *top-rated music in chart form* - PULSE OF RADIO
Contemporary Romance Reviews - ROMANTIC TIMES
Contest Calendar - CQ
Contest Calendar - *with participation information* - MODERN PHOTOGRAPHY
Contest Corral - *column by Billy Lunt* - QST
Contests Exhibits - *upcoming* - TRAVEL & LEISURE
Contests-Exhibitions - PROFESSIONAL PHOTOGRAPHER, THE
Continuations - *column by Richard R. Centing* - SMALL PRESS
Continuity Associates - *product newsbriefs* - COMIC READER, THE
Continuity Queries - *reader Q&A. 5-91*) - DOCTOR WHO MAGAZINE
Contract Close-Up - RADIO BUSINESS REPORT
Contracts - *signed for satellite services* - VIA SATELLITE
Contributors - *author pictures and biographies* - EUROPEAN TRANSACTIONS ON TELECOMMUNICATIONS AND RELATED TECHNOLOGIES
Contributors - *unique pictorial attribution* - FAME
Contributors - IEEE TRANSACTIONS ON INFORMATION THEORY
Contributors - *author listing* - SERIALS REVIEW
Controls, Switches, Drives - ELECTRONIC PRODUCTS
Controversies - ABSOLUTE SOUND, THE
Controversies and Letters - ABSOLUTE SOUND, THE
Controversy - *column by John Durniak* - PHOTOPRO
Controversy and Correspondence - FILM QUARTERLY
Controversy & Correspondence - *opinion and letters* - FILM QUARTERLY
Controversy Arena, The - TELEPROFESSIONAL
Controversy Corner - *column by Richard Landen* - DOCTOR WHO MAGAZINE
Convention - *report* - WRAP
Convention Calendar - MONITORING TIMES
Convention Calendar - SPECTRA
Convention Coverage - POSTCARD COLLECTOR
Convention Dates - ADVERTISING & SELLING
Convention Listing - *extensive two-month convention calendar* - STAR TREK: THE OFFICIAL FAN CLUB MAGAZINE
Convention Notes - *extensive report section detailing state, regional and association convention events* - ST. LOUIS AND CANADIAN PHOTOGRAPHER
Conventions - COMPUTER PICTURES
Conventions for [year] - *upcoming events calendar* - ST. LOUIS AND CANADIAN PHOTOGRAPHER
Conventions to Come, The - BULLETIN OF PHOTOGRAPHY
Conventions/Meetings - THEATRE CRAFTS

Convergence - *newsbriefs* - COMMUNICATIONSWEEK
Conversation - *profile* - VIDEOGRAPHY
Cooking Corner, The - *celebrity recipes column by Kate Smith* - TV RADIO MIRROR
Co-operating Manufacturers - *subscribing to union rules and regulations* - JOURNAL
Copy Chasers - *features concerning unique copy approaches* - BUSINESS MARKETING
Copy Clinic - ADVERTISING AGENCY
Copy Clinic - *column by E.B. Smith* - ADVERTISING & SELLING
Copy Clipped from Here and There - *sample copy items* - ADVERTISING IDEAS
Copy Hook, The - *news of Washington State press women* - WASHINGTON NEWSPAPER, THE
Copy Points - CLIO MAGAZINE
Copyright Corner - *informative column by John Saint Aubyn* - LEARNED PUBLISHING
Corky's Country Corner - *news* - INTERNATIONAL RADIO REPORT, THE
Corner Office - VIEW
Corporate Communications - *column by Maryann Keblusek* - PC PUBLISHING AND PRESENTATIONS
Corporate Identity - LÜRZER'S INTERNATIONAL ARCHIVE
Corporate Imagery - *animation and graphics* - CORPORATE TELEVISION
Corporate Perspectives - *column by Richard Van Deusen* - VIDEO MANAGEMENT
Corporate Post - POST
Corporate Production - MARKEE
Corporate Profile - CABLEAGE
Corporate Strategies - *news* - PERSONAL ELECTRONICS
Corporate Television - MILLIMETER
Corporate Video - *news column* - VIDEOGRAPHY
Corporate Video Decisions - VIDEOGRAPHY
Corporate View - *column by Pauline Ores* - DESKTOP COMMUNICATIONS
Corrected List of Broadcast Stations - RADIO AGE
Correspondence - *city news* - AFTERIMAGE
Correspondence - AMERICAN PHOTOGRAPHY
Correspondence - BRITISH JOURNAL OF PHOTOGRAPHY
Correspondence - CAMERA ARTS
Correspondence - ELECTRICAL REVIEW
Correspondence - FILM ART
Correspondence - FILM GUIDE
Correspondence - GOOD NEWS: CHRISTIANS IN JOURNALISM
Correspondence - GRAMOPHONE
Correspondence - *letters* - IBE
Correspondence - INDUSTRIAL ELECTRONICS
Correspondence - *lengthy column of letters on a variety of union issues* - JOURNAL
Correspondence - KINEMATOGRAPH WEEKLY
Correspondence - *letters* - MIRROR OF TASTE, AND DRAMATIC CENSOR, THE
Correspondence - *letters* - MOVIES, THE
Correspondence - *'Answers to queries about film talk'* - PICTURES MAGAZINE, THE
Correspondence - *letters* - QST

Correspondence - SILENT PICTURE, THE
Correspondence - *letters* - TABS
Correspondence - THEATRE-CRAFT
Correspondence - THEATRE RESEARCH
Correspondence - WOODCOCK'S PRINTERS' AND LITHOGRAPHERS' WEEKLY GAZETTE AND NEWSPAPER REPORTER
Correspondence From Readers - *letters* - ELECTRONICS WORLD
Correspondent's Column - CABLE TV BUSINESS MAGAZINE
Corridor Talk - *marketing, media and advertising tidbits column by Kevin Kerr* - ADWEEK'S MARKETING WEEK
Cosmetics - LÜRZER'S INTERNATIONAL ARCHIVE
Cost Trends - MEDIAWEEK
Counterpoint - JOURNAL OF ARTS MANAGEMENT AND LAW, THE
Country - R & R
Country Cooking - ENTERTAINMENT CONNECTION MAGAZINE
Country Corner - *column by Marie Ratliff* - BILLBOARD
Country Corner! - *'Country Corner is a new monthly feature covering traditional country music today', column by Linda Cauthen* - SH-BOOM
Country Express, The - *news column by Loudilla Johnson* - TV DAY STARS
Country Over, The - *individual press news* - AMERICAN ADVERTISER REPORTER
Country Reviews - CD REVIEW
Country Songs - *playlist* - INTERNATIONAL RADIO REPORT, THE
Country Store - GOOD OLD DAYS
Country Tape Reviews - TAPE DECK QUARTERLY
Country Things - *explained and remembered* - GOOD OLD DAYS
Couplings - *'Hollywood's newest twosomes-- and a few untwosomes'* - GOSSIP
Course File - *detailed model syllabi* - AFI EDUCATION NEWSLETTER
Courses - *unique calendar of upcoming instruction in various electronic and engineering fields* - RF DESIGN
Courses-Conferences - *international schedule* - ACTION
Court Briefs - *newsbriefs* - PRESSTIME
Courts - *California legislation affecting journalism* - FEED-BACK
Courts - *legal actions,* - PRESSTIME
Courtside - *recent communication legal decisions, column by Timothy Dyk and Barbara McDowell* - COMMUNICATIONS LAWYER
Cover - *technical details and information concerning the cover photo on the magazine* - IMAGES & IDEAS BY PHOTOMETHODS
Cover 2 - *personnel newsbriefs* - CAMPAIGN
Cover Girl - *background on cover picture* - TV SHOW
Cover Shot - *how accomplished* - OUTDOOR PHOTOGRAPHER
Cover Story - *'Find out how our cover was shot'* - OUTDOOR & TRAVEL PHOTOGRAPHY
CQ Showcase - *new products* - CQ

Craft at Work, The - *unique section of craft techniques* - GRAPHIC COMMUNICATOR
Creative Analysis - *unique content analysis of a newspaper* - ADVERTISERS' WEEKLY
Creative Answers - *creative Q&A applications* - PHOTO ANSWERS
Creative Color - *column by Arthur Rothstein* - TRAVEL & LEISURE
Creative Concepts - MEDIAWEEK
Creative Critique - *column* - INSIDE MEDIA
Creative Interface, The - REP: RECORDING ENGINEERING PRODUCTION
Creative Pulse - FLASH
Creative Spotlight - FLASH
Creative Techniques - CORPORATE TELEVISION
Creatively Thinking - *ideas* - CORPORATE TELEVISION
Creatives - BROADCAST
Creator Overview - *profile* - FA
Credits - *profile* - WRAP
Cricial Focus - POPULAR PHOTOGRAPHY
Critic on the Hearth - *column by John Moffitt* - CINEMA HALL-MARKS
Critic on the Loose - *comment column by Jeff Jarvis* - ENTERTAINMENT WEEKLY
Critical Analysis, A - *of submitted photographs* - PROFESSIONAL PHOTOGRAPHER, THE
Critical Comments - *commentary on comic books, magazines, music, television, and the movies* - WORLD OF FANDOM, THE
Critical Condition - *column by Marlena de Lacroix* - SOAP OPERA WEEKLY
Critical Dialogue - *letters* - JUMP CUT
Critical Mass - *'Current releases rated by reviewers across the country'* - ENTERTAINMENT WEEKLY
Critical Reviews - ANIMATIONS
Criticism and Achievement - *variety of viewpoints* - CLOSE-UP
Criticism of Illustrations - *critique of reader-submitted photographs, column by G. Hanmer Croughton* - ST. LOUIS AND CANADIAN PHOTOGRAPHER
Critics, The - *wonderful sampling of critical reviews for current stage productions* - THEATERWEEK
Critics' Choice - *'The most noteworthy releases reviewed recently'* - HIGH FIDELITY
Critics' Choice - HIGH FIDELITY/MUSICAL AMERICA
Critics' Choices - *top-rated productions* - DRAMA-LOGUE
Critic's Corner - *column by Michael Edelson* - CAMERA 35
Critics' Page - EDISON KINETROGRAM
Critiques F/X - *'Reviews'* - COMICS FANDOM EXAMINER
Cross Country - ASMP BULLETIN
Cross Country - *'Production notes from Pro Film's Correspondents.' (8-75)* - PROFESSIONAL FILM PRODUCTION
Cross- word Contest - *related to radio terminology* - WIRELESS AGE, THE
Cross-Canada News - CANADIAN PRINTER
Cross-Examining the Stars - *Q&A* - HOLLYWOOD

Crossover Radio Airplay - BILLBOARD
CrossTalk - *Technical Q&A* - HIGH FIDELITY
Crosstalk - *technical column by Larry Klein* - HIGH FIDELITY
Crosstalk: an Engineering Management Journal - BME'S TELEVISION ENGINEERING
Crossword - *puzzle* - CASTING NEWS
Crossword - MOVIE WORLD
Crossword - ON CABLE
Crossword - SOAP OPERA DIGEST
Crossword Puzzle - ON LINE
Crowd, The - HIGH PERFORMANCE
CRTC - *legal decisions from Canadian Radio and Television Commission* - BROADCAST + TECHNOLOGY
CRTC Decisions - *briefs of Canadian Radio-TV Commission* - BROADCASTER
Crucible, The - *'a monthly digest of photo-technical facts'* - PHOTO-ERA MAGAZINE
Crumbs from Other Tables - *gleaned news items* - ADVERTISING AGENCY
CSC Assignments - CINEMA/CANADA
CSMC Booknotes - CRITICAL STUDIES IN MASS COMMUNICATION
CSN Checklist - *checklist of upcoming comic book releases* - COMIC SHOP NEWS
CSPAA Notes - *newsbriefs of the Columbia Scholastic Press Advisers Association,* - QUILL AND SCROLL
C-SPAN - ENTERTAINER, THE
CTAA - *column by Lucille M. Paolillo* - THEATRE NEWS
CTAM Rocky Mountain Chapter Newsletter - MSO'S CABLE MARKETING
Cue and Review - *technical column by John Gatski* - RADIO WORLD
Cue Card - *'Our carry-along, week-at-a-glance list of what's new and avilable in film, TV, video, music, books, and for kids--plus a postcard'* - ENTERTAINMENT WEEKLY
Cue Track - *upcoming shows and events* - INDUSTRIAL TELEVISION NEWS
Cues - *newsbriefs* - MEDIA ASIA
Cues - *newsbriefs* - PLAYS AND PLAYERS
Cuisine, Cuisine - *New York city dining* - IN CINEMA
Culshaw at Large - *column by John Culshaw* - HIGH FIDELITY
Cultural Scene - *newsbriefs* - FILMWORLD
Curator's Corner, The - *editorial and comment* - NIEMAN REPORTS
Curent Opinion - *newsbriefs* - ABC WEEKLY
Curmudgeon Corner - *column by Garry De Young* - FACTSHEET FIVE
Current - *film releases* - BOOKS AND FILMS
Current - *newsbriefs* - MIX
Current - VIEW
Current Advertising - ADWEEK
Current Bibliography - *articles and books of interest* - COMMUNICATIONS LAWYER
Current Campaigns - ADVERTISING AGENCY
Current Commentary - CURRENT
Current Copyrights - *script synopses* - TALKING PICTURE MAGAZINE

Current Literature - *extensive considered reviews of books, periodicals, audio and videotapes* - LEONARDO
Current Literature Reviews - CSPAA BULLETIN
Current Monitor - CURRENT
Current People - *newsbriefs* - CURRENT
Current Releases - *box office business on A products* - PICTURE REPORTS
Current Research in the College of Communications - CRC NEWSLETTER
Current Research on - *review* - COMMUNICATION RESEARCH TRENDS
Current Samples - CD REVIEW
Current Science - RADIO AGE
Currents - *equipment* - HIGH FIDELITY
Currents - *news items* - TDR
Currents: A Guest Editorial - BME'S TELEVISION ENGINEERING
Curtain Calls - *column by John Chatterton and D. M. Colucci* - CASTING NEWS
Cutaways - *production newsbriefs* - MARKEE
Cut-a-ways - *new products* - MILLIMETER
Cutting Edge, The - *new equipment review column by Laurel Cash* - REP: RECORDING ENGINEERING PRODUCTION
Cutting Edge - *equipment profile* - REP: RECORDING ENGINEERING PRODUCTION
Cutting Edge, The - VIDEOGRAPHY
Cutting Room - VIDEO WORLD
CYA - *accroynm for protect thyself, interprets impact of non-cable events on cable television* - MSO'S CABLE MARKETING
Cyber - *'Kidtech and science'* - DISNEY ADVENTURES

D

DA Systems - *distribution/amplifier systems column by W. C. Alexander* - RADIO GUIDE
Dailies - *newsbriefs* - VIDEO SOFTWARE MAGAZINE
Daily Events - THEATRE, THE
Daily Listings - SATELLITE ORBIT
Daily Listings - *program guide* - TV ENTERTAINMENT
Daily Newspaper Notes - *newsbriefs* - ADVERTISING ADVOCATE
Dallas - BOX OFFICE
Dallas-Ft. Worth - *city review column by Larry Holden* - AFTER DARK
Damon Romine Goes Behind the Scenes - *column by Damon Romine* - DEBUT
Dan T's Inferno - *column by Dan Tyree* - COMICS BUYER'S GUIDE
Dance - INTERVIEW
Dance, The - *review* - MUSICAL AMERICA
Dance Spectrum - *column by Lucia Dewey* - DRAMA-LOGUE
Dance Trax - *column by Larry Flick* - BILLBOARD

Departments

Dancers - *auditions listing* - CASTING NEWS
Daredevil Newsbits - DAREDEVILS
Daring Comments - *letters* - DAREDEVILS
Darkroom - PHOTOGRAPHER'S FORUM
Darkroom & Lab - *column by James N. Burke* - PHOTOPRO
Darts and Laurels - *onions and orchids handed out to news media* - COLUMBIA JOURNALISM REVIEW
Data Bank - *a large section detailing upcoming activities, FCC activities* - RADIO ONLY
Data Bank - *useful statistics for radio promotion/sales in pie chart/bar graph format* - SOUND MANAGEMENT
Data Communication & Networks - COMMUNICATIONSWEEK
Data Communications - TELECOMMUNICATIONS
Data Communications Products - TELECOMMUNICATIONS
Data Delivery - NETWORK WORLD
Data Network - COMMUNICATIONSWEEK
Data on Discs - *record review column by Barry Larkin* - SILVER SCREEN
Data Throwaway, The - *'A series of inexpensive, practical exploitation suggestions'* - UNIVERSAL WEEKLY
Databank - *'A look at what's happening in the world of films, theater, literature, conventions and fandom' column by Sharon Williams* - FANTASTIC FILMS
Database - *communication industry facts and figures column by Michael Burgi* - CHANNELS
Database Report - BUSINESS INFORMATION ALERT
Database Review - INFORMATION TODAY
Data-Based News - *for computer imaging and effects* - ON LOCATION
Data...Data... - *print publication newsbriefs* - MEDIA INTERNATIONAL
Datebook - MAGAZINE DESIGN & PRODUCTION
Datebook - NEWSINC.
Datebook - *calendar* - PRE-
Datebook - *calendar* - PUBLISHING & PRODUCTION EXECUTIVE
Dateline - *advertising and marketing newsbriefs* - ASIAN ADVERTISING & MARKETING
Dateline - E-ITV
Dateline - *calendar* - TELEVISION WEEK
Dateline America - *newsbriefs* - UK PRESS GAZETTE
Dateline Digest - *remainder of film section with news on the following: USA, Canada, United Kingdom, Italy, FRG, Austria, France, USSR, South East Asia, Australia, and Japan* - MOVIE/TV MARKETING
Dateline Europe - CABLE COMMUNICATIONS MAGAZINE
Dateline U.K. - CABLE COMMUNICATIONS MAGAZINE
Dateline USA - CABLE COMMUNICATIONS MAGAZINE
Dateline: Daytime - *'It's what's happening' column by Maggie Glick* - TV RADIO TALK

Dateline: London - *column by Neil Stevens* - THEATRE, THE
Datelines - *upcoming special events* - PROFESSIONAL PHOTOGRAPHER, THE
Datelines - *wonderful news summary from world cities* - SHOW
Dates - ELECTRONICS & COMMUNICATIONS
Dates - *calendar* - LIGHTING DIMENSIONS
Dates - MARKETING / COMMUNICATIONS
Dates and Deadlines - *conference and convention information of interest to black broadcasters and journalists* - AIR TIME
Dates for Your Diary - CANADIAN PRINTER
Dates 'n Data - *newsbriefs* - PHOTOLITH, SCM
Dates of Conventions and Meetings - MARKETING / COMMUNICATIONS
Dave Barry - *humor column by Dave Barry* - COMIC RELIEF
David North's Column - MARKETING / COMMUNICATIONS
Davy on 16 MM - *column by Daryl Davy* - FILM FAN MONTHLY
Day Book - *calendar* - GUILD REPORTER, THE
Day by Day - *unique 'captains log' tracks designer day activities* - DIRECTION
Day in the Life - *profile* - QUILL, THE
Day to Day - *program schedule* - BBC WORLD SERVICE LONDON CALLING
Day's End - *inside back-cover photo* - REAL LIFE/DAYTIMERS
Days of Our Lives - *abstract* - SOAP OPERA DIGEST
Daytime Dialings - *news of soaps column by Marvin Bevans* - MODERN SCREEN
Daytime Diary - TV MIRROR
Daytime Hotline - PHOTO SCREEN
Daytime Roundup - *news of daytime soaps column by Nora Astor* - MOVIE WORLD
Daytime Television - TV STAR PARADE
Daytime TV Gossip - *column by Helen Martin* - TV PICTURE LIFE
Daytime TV World - *'TV Radio Show's daytime gossip newspaper' column by Bob Lardine* - TV RADIO SHOW
Daytimer - *daytime television-oriented* - REAL LIFE/DAYTIMERS
DBS - *News of direct broadcast satellite* - SATELLITE NEWS
DBS - VIDEO TECHNOLOGY NEWS
DBS in Brief - DBS NEWS
DBS Radio - DBS NEWS
D.C. - *city review column by Noel Gillespie* - AFTER DARK
DC - MEDIAWEEK
DC Coming Comics - COMIC READER, THE
DC News - *newsbriefs concerning DC Comic products* - COMIC READER, THE
Dead Beat Advertisers - *no bills paid* - JOURNALIST, THE
Dead Zines - *'Alas, another list of people who have recently ceased publishing'* - FACTSHEET FIVE
Deadline - *'The Avengers column' information column by Dave Rogers* - TOP SECRET
Deadline Data - *events calendar* - MATRIX
Deadlines - *'Calendar of events'* - LINK

Dealer Association News - *news of regional and state satellite dealer associations* - SATELLITE RETAILER
Dealer Visit - *unique vendor interaction with reader problems and inquiries* - AUDIOPHILE WITH HI-FI ANSWERS
Dear Audrey, What'll I Do? - *personal problem column by Audrey Olson* - MOVIE TEEN ILLUSTRATED
Dear Coop - *humorous personality column by Don Cooper* - PERFORMER, THE
Dear Crystal - *Q&A on young stars* - WOW! MAGAZINE
Dear Deborah - *legal Q&A on publishing column by Deborah Michelle Sanders* - COSMEP NEWSLETTER
Dear Editor - *letters* - AUDIO
Dear Kristi - *Q&A on young stars column by Kristi* - SMASH HITS
Dear Meg - *'Every week the column with a heart'* - STAR
Dear Ms - *'The answers to all your questions'* - SILVER SCREEN
Dear Playbill - *letters concerning theatre productions of current and past times* - PLAYBILL
Dear Rona - *'What you have to say to our Ms. Rona!' column by Rona Barrett* - GOSSIP
Dear Rona - *'Your chance to talk to our Ms. Rona!'* - REAL LIFE/DAYTIMERS
Dear Rona - *readers express what they want to read* - RONA BARRETT'S HOLLYWOOD
Dear Sir - *letters* - HI-FI SOUND
Dear Sosyal - *letters to the editor* - SOSYALI MAGAZINE
Dear Tony - *Q&A advice column by Anthony Leggett* - NATIONAL EXAMINER
Death Claims - IBEW JOURNAL
Deaths - DRAMATIC MIRROR, THE
Deaths - PROFESSIONAL PHOTOGRAPHER, THE
Debate - MEDIA, CULTURE, AND SOCIETY
Debut - *new and noteworthy* - MEDIAWEEK
Debuts & Reappearances - *in the performing arts* - MUSICAL AMERICA
Decisions of the Federal Radio Commission - *column by Howard W. Vesey* - JOURNAL OF RADIO LAW
Deep Focus - *star profile with major credits* - SCENE AT THE MOVIES
Deep Waters - *mystery novel quiz* - W•B
Definitions - *commentary* - HD PRODUCTION
Deja Vu - *column by Studs Terkel* - JOE FRANKLIN'S NOSTALGIA
Deleted Wholesalers - BOOK PROMOTION HOTLINE
Deltiology Spotlight - *collector profile* - POSTCARD COLLECTOR
DeMaw's Workbench - *engineering column by Doug DeMaw* - MONITORING TIMES
Demographic Forecasts - *column by Thomas Exter* - AMERICAN DEMOGRAPHICS
Demographics in Action - *unique issue page in demographics display* - SALES & MARKETING MANAGEMENT
Denis Gifford's Flavour of the Month - *TV releases* - FILMS AND FILMING
Denver - BOX OFFICE

Denver Journal - CABLE TV BUSINESS MAGAZINE
Department for Retailers - AMERICAN ADVERTISER
Department of Reality - *news items* - STRANGE ADVENTURES
Department of Suggestion - *opinion* - NATIONAL ADVERTISING
Depropaganda Fide - DOCUMENTARY FILM NEWS
Dept. of Nip 'N' Tuck - *column by Arcona* - HOLLYWOOD MAGAZINE
Des Moines - BOX OFFICE
Design - *graphics projects* - ART DIRECTION
Design - SUCCESSFUL MAGAZINE PUBLISHING
Design Basics - *column by John Miles* - PUBLISH!
Design Dynamics - *home entertainment center design column by Dora Antler* - HOME ENTERTAINMENT
Design Engineering - ELECTRONIC DESIGN
Design Project - *case study* - FLASH
Design Technology - *column by Wendy Richmond* - COMMUNICATION ARTS
Design Workshop - *graphic design, step-by-step* - STEP-BY-STEP ELECTRONIC DESIGN
Designers - *audio/video designer profile column by Sam Burchell* - AUDIO/VIDEO INTERIORS
Designing the Editorial Page - MASTHEAD
Desk Menu - *column by Harold Sims* - VENTURA PROFESSIONAL!
Desktop Concepts - COMMUNICATIONS CONCEPTS
Desktop Design - MAGAZINE DESIGN & PRODUCTION
Desktop Paper - *column by Warren Struhl* - DESKTOP COMMUNICATIONS
Desktop Publishing - *column by Richard Brock* - PRINT-EQUIP NEWS
Desktop Video - *column by Mark Swain* - VIDEOMAKER
Desparate Dan - *column by Danny Haikin* - HI-FI WORLD
Details of New Products - HI-FI NEWS AND RECORD REVIEW
Detroit - BOX OFFICE
Development News - *newsbriefs* - ABU TECHNICAL REVIEW
Developments - *news* - ELECTRONIC PUBLISHER
Dial Light - *publisher comment* - ALL-WAVE RADIO
Dialog - *letters,* - MOVIE DIGEST
Dialog Box - *letters* - VENTURA PROFESSIONAL!
Dialogue - *considered replies to past articles* - CINEMA JOURNAL
Dialogue - *newsbriefs* - ON LOCATION
Dialogue on Film - *unique interviews* - AMERICAN FILM
Diary - *comment* - ADWEEK
Diary - *brief summaries of major writing group meetings* - AUTHOR, THE
Diary - *event calendar* - BRITISH JOURNAL OF PHOTOGRAPHY

Diary - *'Dates, locations and addresses of the important events this year'* - BROADCAST SYSTEMS ENGINEERING
Diary - *upcoming events* - IMAGE TECHNOLOGY
Diary - *PR news items of the strange, funny, and bizzare kind* - PR WEEK
Diary - *upcoming events of journalistic merit* - UK PRESS GAZETTE
Diary - VIDEO
Diary of a D-Girl - *column by Alexis Blair* - HOLLYWOOD MAGAZINE
Dick Maurices Las Vegas - *news briefs* - RONA BARRETT'S HOLLYWOOD
Did You Know That - *personality chit-chat* - BAND LEADERS
Died - TELEGRAPHER, THE
Diffuser, The - *letters to the editor* - PSA JOURNAL
Digest - *newsbriefs* - QUILL, THE
Digest of Examiners' Reports and Decisions of the Federal Radio Commission - *column by Howard W. Vesey* - JOURNAL OF RADIO LAW
Digest of Radio Patents - RADIO REVIEW AND TELEVISION NEWS
Digital Audio - DB
Digital By Design - *column by Peter Mitchell* - AUDIO/VIDEO INTERIORS
Digital Domain - *trends and breakthroughs on digital radio broadcasting, column by Mel Lambert* - RADIO WORLD
Digital Domain - *column by Rick Schwartz* - REP: RECORDING ENGINEERING PRODUCTION
Digital Update - *newsbriefs* - PRO SOUND NEWS
Diminutive Camera Technique and Practice - *commentary and technique column by Norris W. Harkness* - CAMERA, THE
Dining - *New York City column by Sheldon Landwehr* - SHOW
Dining and Dancing 'Round the Town - *'If you indulge in either, in either of the captivating worlds of New York or Hollywood, this is your guide', column by Domino Jr.* - STAGE
Dining and Entertainment - *New York City guide* - PLAYBILL
Dining Out - *column by Louis Miele* - AFTER DARK
Direct & Current - *editorial column by Milton S. Snitzer* - COMPUTERS & ELECTRONICS
Direct Current - *Washington, DC newsbriefs* - BROADCAST ENGINEERING
Direct From Hollywood - SF MOVIELAND
Direct Intelligence - *newsbriefs* - DIRECT MARKETING
Direct Mail/Sales Promotion - *from a printer's point-of-view* - AMERICAN PRINTER
Direct Marketing - ADVERTISING AGE
Direct Marketing - MEDIAWEEK
Direct Marketing - SALES & MARKETING MANAGEMENT
Direct Marketing News - DIRECT MARKETING

Direct Response - *advice column by John Caples* - DIRECT MARKETING
Direct Response - *letters* - LINK
Direct Responses - *letters* - WHO'S MAILING WHAT!
Direct Talk - *comment and analysis* - ASIAN ADVERTISING & MARKETING
Direction - *comment* - CANADIAN PRINTER
Directions - *column by John O'Hara* - MEDIA INFORMATION AUSTRALIA
Directions - *editorial* - PHOTOLITH, SCM
Directions - *for new technology* - PRO SOUND NEWS
Directions in Research - MEDIA LAW NOTES
Directly Speaking - *commentary* - DESIGN
Directors Chair, The - IN MOTION FILM & VIDEO PRODUCTION MAGAZINE
Director's Chair, The - *comment* - SIGNAL, THE
Director's Column - 4SIGHT MAGAZINE
Director's Column - SIXSHOOTERS
Directors Guild of Canada - *newsbriefs* - CINEMA/CANADA
Director's Notes - *editorial* - EPISODES
Directory - *of booking contracts* - PERFORMANCE
Directory - *of new cassette releases* - VIDEO MAGAZINE
Directory of Producers - MOTION PICTURE REVIEW DIGEST
Disc of the Month - CD REVIEW
Disco - *news* - INTERNATIONAL RADIO REPORT, THE
Disco Action - *playlist* - BILLBOARD
Disco Mix - *column by Tom Moulton* - BILLBOARD
Disco Stations - *playlist* - INTERNATIONAL RADIO REPORT, THE
Discographies - ARSC JOURNAL
Discos - BILLBOARD
Discover - *column by Howard English* - BROADCAST + TECHNOLOGY
Discoveries - *new cereal boxes and giveaways recently found* - FLAKE
Discussion Notes - PHILOSOPHY AND RHETORIC
Dish Doctor - *Q&A column by Andy Demetriou* - WHAT SATELLITE
Dish Night - TAKE ONE
Dish of the Month - *recipes* - SATELLITE TIMES
Dish Owner's Guide to Europe - *'Our regular rundown of all the satellite channels available to UK dish owners'* - WHAT SATELLITE
Disney Beat - *Disney production-related items* - DISNEY ADVENTURES
Disney Beat - DISNEY CHANNEL MAGAZINE, THE
Disney Night Time - *highlights* - DISNEY CHANNEL MAGAZINE, THE
Display & Commercial Art - ADWEEK
Displays and Ballyhoo - *photographic section of successful exploitations* - MOTION PICTURE HERALD
Displays Subassemblies - ELECTRONIC PRODUCTS
Dissent - INTERMEDIA
Dissertations - *reviews* - HOMILETIC

Departments INDEX

Distant Signals - *newsbriefs* - BROADCASTING ABROAD
Distribucion - *newsbriefs* - PRODUCCIÓN Y DISTRIBUCIÓN
Distributing - *column by Ray S. Loose* - SCHEMER, THE
Distribution Notes - *newsbriefs* - CINEMA/CANADA
Distributor News - ELECTRONICS & COMMUNICATIONS
Diversion: Where and When - *event schedule* - HOLLYWOOD FILMOGRAPH
Division Forum - *news concerning AECT* - TECHTRENDS
Division Head Speaks - CLIO AMONG THE MEDIA
Division News - ENTERTAINMENT AND SPORTS LAWYER, THE
DM Data - *'Pieces of mail by class'* - DIRECT MARKETING
DM People - *'Promotions & Newcomers'* - DIRECT MARKETING
Do You Remember? - TV GOLD
Do Your Own Thing - *star suggestions column by Lorraine Sciurca* - MOVIE STARS
Doc's Bookshelf - *column by Dwight R. Decker* - AMAZING HEROES
Doctor Who Letters - DOCTOR WHO MAGAZINE
Doctors, The - *abstract* - SOAP OPERA DIGEST
Documentaries - *review* - ORBIT VIDEO
Documentaries & Travel - *videocassette review* - V
Documentary Explorations - *new developments in this often overlooked area* - MILLIMETER
Documentary in the United States - DOCUMENTARY FILM NEWS
Documentary Show of the Month - SHOW
Documents/Interview - HISTORICAL JOURNAL OF FILM, RADIO & TELEVISION
Dog Watches Dog - *'A weekly appreciation of what is not always appreciated'* - UK PRESS GAZETTE
Doing Business Electronically - *column by John McQuillan* - BUSINESS COMMUNICATIONS REVIEW
Doings of Those Concerned - ADVERTISING EXPERIENCE
Dolby Surround - *very helpful listing of motion pictures airing this week in Dolby Stereo* - ONSAT
Dollar Pullers - RADIO DEALER, THE
Dollar Saving Tips - TELECONNECT
Dollar Thoughts - *'The New Movie Magazine readers express their opinions of film plays and players--and this monthly'* - NEW MOVIE MAGAZINE, THE
Dollars and $ense - RADIOACTIVE
Dollars and Sense - *column by Sharon Cohen* - STUDIO PHOTOGRAPHY
Don Iddon from New York - *comment* - CAMPAIGN
Don Nicholas on Magazine Trends - *design critique column by Don Nicholas* - MAGAZINEWEEK
Done Deals - *cable subscriptions* - MSO'S CABLE MARKETING

Donors - BROADCAST PIONEERS LIBRARY REPORTS
Don't Breath a Word of It - *more secret information column by Paul Ravin* - MODERN SCREEN
Double Acrostic - RIGHTING WORDS
Double Exposure - *'The movies glitterati make the scene'* - MOVIES USA
Double Takes - *column by Allan Bryce* - MOVIE - THE VIDEO MAGAZINE
Double Takes - *review* - SIGHT & SOUND
Down the Road - *column by Bill Neill* - CAR AUDIO AND ELECTRONICS
Downlink - *Question response* - TELEVISION BROADCAST
Dr. Cyclops - *videocassette reviews* - FANGORIA
Dr. Dish - *satellite receiver questions and answer column by Richard Maddox* - ONSAT
Dr. Syntax Presents Good Writing Points - CAMPAIGN
Dr. Telecom - *knows all and covers all in the video and non-video field* - VIDEO EIGHTIES MAGAZINE
Dr. Z's Hollywood - *'Satire'* - REAL LIFE/DAY-TIMERS
Drama - BBC WORLD SERVICE LONDON CALLING
Drama - *program guide* - LISTENER
Drama - *review* - ORBIT VIDEO
Drama Blackboard - *upcoming national plays* - THEATRE, THE
Drama Forum - DRAMA & THEATRE
Drama League of America, The - *newsbriefs* - DRAMA MAGAZINE, THE
Drama Reviews - VIDEO TODAY
Drama Show of the Month - SHOW
Dramas of the Mind - *column by Kenneth Smith* - COMICS JOURNAL, THE
Dramatic Chat - DRAMATIC MAGAZINE, THE
Dramatic Gems - *anecdotes* - ODDFELLOW, THE
Dramatic Incidents and Notes Theatrical and Miscellaneous - ACTORS BY DAYLIGHT
Draw Developments - *direct-read-after-write trends* - OPTICAL MEMORY NEWS
Drawing Board - *'a forum for new and aspiring humorists'* - COMIC RELIEF
Drawing the Line - *column by Will Finn* - KORKIS AND CAWLEY'S CARTOON QUARTERLY
Dream Date With [star] - MOVIE DREAM GUYS
Dressed For Success - *'Celebrities offscreen--the bad, the bold, the beautiful!'* - SOAP OPERA WEEKLY
Drift - *'New films and videos'* - MOTION PICTURE
Dubbing - *newsbriefs* - PRODUCCIÓN Y DISTRIBUCIÓN
Ducktales - *comic section* - DISNEY ADVENTURES
Duplication News - *audio tape duplication newsbriefs* - PRO SOUND NEWS
DX - *news of international radio amateurs* - CQ
DX Century Club Awards - *column by Don Search* - QST

DX Listener, The - *editorial column by Hugo Gernsback* - ELECTRONICS WORLD
DX Listening - *column by Don Jensen* - POPULAR ELECTRONICS

E

Early Warning - WORLD PRESS REVIEW
Earnings - MEDIA BUSINESS
Earsay - HI-FI ANSWERS
Earth Notes - *interesting departmental feature regarding recycling and other Earth-friendly issues in magazine publishing* - MAGAZINE DESIGN & PRODUCTION
Earth Stations - *newsbriefs* - SATELLITE WEEK
East Coast Notes - OFFICIAL BULLETIN OF THE INTERNATIONAL ALLIANCE OF THEATRICAL STAGE EMPLOYEES AND MOVING PICTURE MACHINE OPERATORS OF THE UNITED STATES AND CANADA.
Eastern Wave - *column by Chris Majka* - CINEMA/CANADA
Eastern Zone - PSA JOURNAL
Easy Listening - *top-50 playlist* - BILLBOARD
Easy Way - *pasteup design shortcuts* - ADVERTISING AND GRAPHIC ARTS TECHNIQUES
EBU Newsreel - *upcoming events* - EBU REVIEW. PROGRAMMES, ADMINISTRATION, LAW.
EBU Technical Meetings - EBU REVIEW. TECHNICAL.
Echoes From Europe - *news from the continent, column by Robert Benecke* - ST. LOUIS AND CANADIAN PHOTOGRAPHER
Echoes from the Green Room - *newsbriefs* - THEATRE, THE
Eclectic Engineer - RADIO WORLD
Economic Eye - MEDIAWEEK
Economic Review - PRINT BUYERS REVIEW
Ed Forum - ADWEEK'S MARKETING WEEK
Ed. Notes - *editorial column by Howard Zimmerman* - COMICS SCENE
Edge of Night - *abstract* - SOAP OPERA DIGEST
Edge of the Apocalypse - *column by Christopher H. Hunt* - MOVIELINE
Edit & Design News - *large second section concerning magazine layout and design* - MAGAZINEWEEK
Edit Mode - *column by Lynn Walterick* - VENTURA PROFESSIONAL!
Editing - INVISION
Editing Room - *editorial* - AMERICAN FILM
Editing Suite - *column by Christin Hardman* - VIDEO PROPHILES
Editor, The - *profile* - WHAT EDITORS WANT
Editor Goes to the Play, The - THEATRE MAGAZINE
Editor Gossips, The - RADIO DIAL
Editor Speak - HIGH PERFORMANCE
Editorial - ABU TECHNICAL REVIEW
Editorial - ADVERTISERS GAZETTE
Editorial - ADVERTISING

Editorial - *short positive encouragements* - ADVERTISING ADVOCATE
Editorial - ADVERTISING & SELLING
Editorial - ADVERTISING DISPLAYS
Editorial - ADVERTISING EXPERIENCE
Editorial - ADVERTISING NEWS
Editorial - ADVERTISING OUTDOORS
Editorial - ADVERTISING REVIEW
Editorial - ADWEEK
Editorial - AFRO-ASIAN JOURNALIST
Editorial - AFTER DARK
Editorial - AGRICULTURAL ADVERTISING
Editorial - AM
Editorial - AMAZING HEROES
Editorial - AMERICAN THEATRE
Editorial - ANIMAFILM
Editorial - ANIMATO!
Editorial - ANIMATOR
Editorial - ASIFA NOUVELLES
Editorial - AUDIO VISUAL JOURNAL
Editorial - AUDIOCRAFT FOR THE HI-FI HOBBYIST
Editorial - BALLETT INTERNATIONAL
Editorial - BETTER RADIO AND TELEVISION
Editorial - BROADCAST ENGINEERING
Editorial - BROADCAST SYSTEMS INTERNATIONAL
Editorial - BROADCASTER
Editorial - BUSINESS COMMUNICATIONS REVIEW
Editorial - CAMERA OBSCURA
Editorial - CAVERNE COMMUNICATION, THE
Editorial - CD-ROM
Editorial - *column by Norman Desmarais* - CD-ROM LIBRARIAN
Editorial - *'Editor/Publisher Dude' column by Tony Biner* - CELLULOID NIGHTMARE
Editorial - CINEASTE
Editorial - CINEMA/CANADA
Editorial - CINEMA THE WORLD OVER
Editorial - CINEMACABRE
Editorial - CLOSE-UP
Editorial - COLLEGE BROADCASTER
Editorial - COMIC CELLAR, THE
Editorial - COMIC FANDOM'S FORUM
Editorial - COMICS BUYER'S GUIDE
Editorial - COMICS CAREER NEWSLETTER
Editorial - COMICS FEATURE
Editorial - COMICS JOURNAL, THE
Editorial - COMICS WEEK
Editorial - COMMUNICATION AND BROADCAST ENGINEERING
Editorial - *column by Robert T. Craig* - COMMUNICATION THEORY
Editorial - COMPUTER PICTURES
Editorial - COMPUTERS & ELECTRONICS
Editorial - CONTEMPORARY PHOTOGRAPHER
Editorial - *column by Peter Black* - CONTRAST
Editorial - DAREDEVILS
Editorial - DB
Editorial - DEEP RED
Editorial - DESKTOP COMMUNICATIONS
Editorial - DIRECT MARKETING
Editorial - DRAMA MAGAZINE, THE
Editorial - DWB
Editorial - EBU REVIEW. TECHNICAL.
Editorial - *column by Tom Fox* - EDUCATIONAL MEDIA INTERNATIONAL

Editorial - *column by Larry Altman* - ELECTRONIC DESIGN
Editorial - *column by S. R. Cowan* - ELECTRONIC SERVICING & TECHNOLOGY
Editorial - ELECTRONICS
Editorial - ELECTRONICS AND COMMUNICATIONS
Editorial - ELECTRONICS & COMMUNICATIONS
Editorial - EMMY
Editorial - ENTERTAINMENT MONTHLY
Editorial - *column by Bill Anchors* - EPI-LOG
Editorial - EUROPEAN JOURNAL OF COMMUNICATION
Editorial - EUROPEAN TRASH CINEMA
Editorial - FACTSHEET FIVE
Editorial - FILM AND THEATRE TODAY
Editorial - FILM FORUM REVIEW
Editorial - FILM MAKING
Editorial - FILM MEDIA
Editorial - *column by Christian Gore* - FILM THREAT
Editorial - FILM WORLD AND A-V NEWS MAGAZINE
Editorial - FILMING
Editorial - FILMS AND FILMING
Editorial - FLAKE
Editorial - *personnel briefs* - FOLIO:
Editorial - FORUM
Editorial - 4A'S WASHINGTON NEWSLETTER, THE
Editorial - GAMBIT
Editorial - GENERAL ELECTRIC REVIEW
Editorial - GRAMOPHONE
Editorial - GRAPHIC
Editorial - GRAPHIC ARTS, THE
Editorial - GREATER AMUSEMENTS
Editorial - *column by Kent S. Bransford* - HI-FI HERETIC
Editorial - IBEW JOURNAL
Editorial - INDUSTRIAL ELECTRONICS
Editorial - INTERLIT
Editorial - INTERMEDIA
Editorial - INTERNATIONAL ADVERTISER
Editorial - INTERNATIONAL JOURNAL OF ADVERTISING
Editorial - INTERNATIONAL JOURNAL OF INFORMATION MANAGEMENT
Editorial - IRIS
Editorial - JOURNAL OF ADVERTISING
Editorial - *column by William A. Cook* - JOURNAL OF ADVERTISING RESEARCH
Editorial - *column by Lamar Reinsch* - JOURNAL OF BUSINESS COMMUNICATION, THE
Editorial - *column by Paul Kelley* - JOURNAL OF EDUCATIONAL TELEVISION
Editorial - *column by Thomas H. Elwell* - LEICA PHOTOGRAPHY
Editorial - LEONARDO
Editorial - MAGAZINE & BOOKSELLER
Editorial - MAHINS MAGAZINE
Editorial - MEDIA & METHODS
Editorial - MEDIA, CULTURE, AND SOCIETY
Editorial - MEDIA DEVELOPMENT
Editorial - *column by Geoffrey Schutt* - MEDIA SIGHT
Editorial - MEDIA SPOTLIGHT
Editorial - MILITARY ELECTRONICS / COUNTERMEASURES
Editorial - MOVIE MAKERS

Editorial - NATIONAL ADVERTISING
Editorial - NEMO
Editorial - NEW THEATRE MAGAZINE
Editorial - OPTICAL INFORMATION SYSTEMS
Editorial - *column by Pauline Ores* - PC PUBLISHING AND PRESENTATIONS
Editorial - *column by Joseph Bridges* - PD REPORT
Editorial - PEGBAR
Editorial - PHOTO-ERA MAGAZINE
Editorial - PHOTOMETHODS
Editorial - PICTURES MAGAZINE, THE
Editorial - PLAYERS
Editorial - POPULAR ELECTRONICS
Editorial - POPULAR PHOTOGRAPHY
Editorial - POST OFFICE MAGAZINE
Editorial - PR WEEK
Editorial - PREVUE
Editorial - PRINTING HISTORY
Editorial - PRINTING PAPER
Editorial - PRIVATE CABLE
Editorial - PRO SOUND NEWS
Editorial - PROMOTION
Editorial - PUBLIC TELECOMMUNICATIONS REVIEW
Editorial - *column by Rose Blessing* - PUBLISHING & PRODUCTION EXECUTIVE
Editorial - RADIO DEALER, THE
Editorial - *column by Hugo Gernsback* - RADIO-ELECTRONICS
Editorial - REP: RECORDING ENGINEERING PRODUCTION
Editorial - RESTORATION AND 18TH CENTURY THEATRE RESEARCH
Editorial - *commentary column by Gary A. Breed* - RF DESIGN
Editorial - *editorial comment column by E. M. Kirby* - RURAL RADIO
Editorial - SATELLITE RETAILER
Editorial - SCREEN
Editorial - SCREEN ACTOR HOLLYWOOD
Editorial - *commentary column by Cindy Hepfer* - SERIALS REVIEW
Editorial - *column by Hal Schuster* - SF MOVIELAND
Editorial - *column by Robert M. Wool* - SHOW
Editorial - *column by Paul Ranger* - SPEECH AND DRAMA
Editorial - SQUEEKY WHEEL, THE
Editorial - STUDIO SOUND AND BROADCAST ENGINEERING
Editorial - TABS
Editorial - TALKING SCREEN
Editorial - TELECAST
Editorial - TELECOMMUNICATION JOURNAL
Editorial - TELEMATICS AND INFORMATICS
Editorial - TELESCREEN
Editorial - TELEVISION
Editorial - TELEVISION ENGINEERING
Editorial - THE JOURNAL
Editorial - THEATRE-CRAFT
Editorial - THEATRE CRAFTS
Editorial - THEATRE MAGAZINE
Editorial - THEATRE NOTEBOOK
Editorial - *column by Anthony McKay* - TIME SCREEN

Departments INDEX 800

Editorial - TRAVEL & LEISURE
Editorial - TV MIRROR
Editorial - TWR
Editorial - U & LC
Editorial - VIDEO SYSTEMS
Editorial - VIDEO TIMES
Editorial - VIDEO TODAY
Editorial - VIDEODISC MONITOR, THE
Editorial - *editorial column by Daniel P. Younger* - VIEWS
Editorial - VISIO
Editorial - VIZIONS
Editorial - WIRE & RADIO COMMUNICATIONS
Editorial - *column by Allen Shevy* - WORLD OF FANDOM, THE
Editorial - WORLD SCREEN
Editorial - WORLD THEATRE
Editorial and Letters - FUNNYWORLD
Editorial Announcements - SIGNS OF THE TIMES
Editorial Chat - WIRELESS AGE, THE
Editorial Chit-Chat - *editorial column by J. H. Fitzgibbon* - ST. LOUIS AND CANADIAN PHOTOGRAPHER
Editorial Clinic - MASTHEAD
Editorial Comment - ADVERTISING & SELLING
Editorial Comment - CABLE TV BUSINESS MAGAZINE
Editorial Comment - CAMERA MAGAZINE
Editorial Comment - ELECTRONICS WORLD + WIRELESS WORLD
Editorial Comment - IBEW JOURNAL
Editorial Comment, An - *column by Donald L. Shaw* - JQ. JOURNALISM QUARTERLY.
Editorial Comment - NATIONAL EXHIBITOR, THE
Editorial Comment - TECHTRENDS
Editorial Consulting - WRITING CONCEPTS
Editorial Desk - SATELLITE COMMUNICATIONS
Editorial Introductions - ABC WEEKLY
Editorial Note and Comment - AMERICAN PHOTOGRAPHY
Editorial Notes - AMERICAN AMATEUR PHOTOGRAPHER AND CAMERA & DARKROOM
Editorial Notes - AMERICAN PRESS
Editorial Notes - APR
Editorial Notes - CLIO AMONG THE MEDIA
Editorial Notes - GRAMOPHONE
Editorial Out Takes - *guest editorial* - SHOOTING COMMERCIALS
Editorial Page - ADVERTISER MAGAZINE, THE
Editorial Page, The - ADVERTISING AGENCY
Editorial Page, The - *column by Chick Lewis* - SHOWMEN'S TRADE REVIEW
Editorial Perspective - *column by Christopher J. Esse* - AUDIO/VIDEO INTERIORS
Editorial Point of View, The - ADVERTISING & SELLING
Editorial Resources - WRITING CONCEPTS
Editorial Siftings - AMERICAN ADVERTISER
Editorial Table - *correspondence* - KINEMATOGRAPH WEEKLY
Editorial Views - INDUSTRIAL ELECTRONICS
Editorial Workshop - EDITOR AND PUBLISHER

Editorial/Letters - CINEMA/CANADA
Editorially Speaking - FILM & VIDEO NEWS
Editorially Speaking - PROFESSIONAL PHOTOGRAPHER, THE
Editorially Speaking --and still-- Editorially Speaking - RADIO HOME, THE
Editorials - ADVERTISERS' WEEKLY
Editorials - ADVERTISING AGE
Editorials - BUSINESS ADVERTISING
Editorials - CAMERA AND DARK ROOM
Editorials - COLLEGE & UNIVERSITY JOURNAL
Editorials - COMMERCIAL PHOTOGRAPHER, THE
Editorials - COMMON SENSE
Editorials - EDUCATIONAL SCREEN
Editorials - EXPORT ADVERTISER
Editorials - FILM GUIDE
Editorials - HOLLYWOOD FILMOGRAPH
Editorials - KORKIS AND CAWLEY'S CARTOON QUARTERLY
Editorials - MARKETING / COMMUNICATIONS
Editorials - MOVIE MAKERS
Editorials - MOVING PICTURE AGE
Editorials - PROFITABLE ADVERTISING
Editorials - SERVICE FOR COMPANY COMMUNICATORS
Editorials - TELEVISION
Editors - INSIDE MEDIA
Editor's Album - CAMERART
Editors Bench - CINEMAGIC
Editors Blast, The - *onion awards for the not so good* - SHOW
Editors Bless, The - *orchid awards for best* - SHOW
Editor's Bookshelf, The - IOWA JOURNALIST
Editor's Choice - *special equipment review* - ABSOLUTE SOUND, THE
Editor's Choice - *unusual section of equipment recommendations* - PERFECT VISION, THE
Editor's Column - *editorial comment column by Patrick Coyne* - COMMUNICATION ARTS
Editor's Column - *column by David Nochimson* - ENTERTAINMENT AND SPORTS LAWYER, THE
Editors Column - ICA NEWSLETTER
Editor's Column - *column by Jack Crandell* - MOVIE TV SECRETS
Editor's Comment - THEATRE TOPICS
Editor's Commentary, The - *column by Charles Abel* - PROFESSIONAL PHOTOGRAPHER, THE
Editor's Comments - ANTIQUE RADIO CLASSIFIED
Editors' Comments - WRITTEN COMMUNICATION
Editor's Corner - *column by Jacob L. Chernofsky* - AB BOOKMAN'S WEEKLY
Editors Corner, The - PSA JOURNAL
Editor's Corner - STV GUIDE
Editor's Corner - VIDEOGRAPHY
Editor's Corner - WORLD PRESS REVIEW
Editor's CQ, The - *comment* - AMATEUR RADIO DEFENSE
Editor's Desk - *column by Jill Roth* - AMERICAN PRINTER
Editor's Desk, The - EDITOR'S WORKSHOP

Editor's Desk - FACETS FEATURES
Editor's Desk - GRAPHIC ANTIQUARIAN
Editor's Desk - *column by Bill Londino* - WRITING CONCEPTS
Editor's Essay - BROADCAST PIONEERS LIBRARY REPORTS
Editor's Eyrie - *column by editor Andrew Sarris* - CAHIERS DU CINEMA IN ENGLISH
Editors Have This to Say--, The - *editorial* - TELEVISION RETAILING
Editor's Journal - CAMERA ARTS
Editor's Journal - SUCCESSFUL MAGAZINE PUBLISHING
Editor's Letter - ELECTRONICS
Editor's Letter - *column by Gael Love* - FAME
Editor's Letter - FLORIDA REEL
Editor's Letter - *editorial column by Joyce Hemmen* - 4TH MEDIA JOURNAL, THE
Editor's Letter - SMALL PRESS BOOK REVIEW, THE
Editor's Letter, The - TV WORLD
Editors' Letter - VIDEO AGE INTERNATIONAL
Editor's Letter Bag - IDEAL KINEMA, THE
Editor's Mailbag, The - HOLLYWOOD
Editor's Mill, The - *editorial* - QST
Editor's Note - *editorial column by Rinker Buck* - ADWEEK'S MARKETING WEEK
Editor's Note - AGENCY
Editor's Note - *column by Brad Edmondson* - AMERICAN DEMOGRAPHICS
Editor's Note - *column by David Schonauer* - AMERICAN PHOTO
Editor's Note - CHANNELS
Editor's Note - COLLEGE MEDIA REVIEW
Editor's Note - COMMUNITY COLLEGE JOURNALIST
Editor's Note - CORPORATE TELEVISION
Editor's Note - *editorial column by Ed Kohorst* - DESIGN
Editor's Note - IN-PLANT PRINTER & ELECTRONIC PUBLISHER
Editor's Note - *editorial column by Judy Bocklage* - IN-PLANT REPRODUCTIONS
Editor's Note - MODERN PHOTOGRAPHY
Editor's Note - *editorial column by Steve Pollock* - PHOTO/DESIGN
Editor's Note - POLITICAL COMMUNICATION AND PERSUASION
Editor's Note - RANGEFINDER, THE
Editor's Note - *commentary column by Meredith Berlin* - SOAP OPERA DIGEST
Editor's Note - STEP-BY-STEP GRAPHICS
Editor's Note - STUDIES IN VISUAL COMMUNICATION
Editors' Note - THEATRE DESIGN & TECHNOLOGY
Editor's Note - VIA SATELLITE
Editor's Note - VIDEO TIMES
Editor's Note - VIDEOPRO
Editor's Notebook - CAMERA 35
Editor's Notebook - *editorial column by Lief Ericksenn* - CAMERA 35 INCORPORATING PHOTO WORLD
Editor's Notebook - DIRECT MARKETING
Editors Notebook - *editorial* - GRAPHIC ARTS MONTHLY

Editor's Notebook - *newsbriefs* - INDUSTRIAL PHOTOGRAPHY
Editor's Notebook - *column by Byron Freney* - MAGAZINEWEEK
Editor's Notebook - *editorial column by Ulrike Schulz* - POLYGRAPH INTERNATIONAL
Editor's Notebook - *editorial column by Mark T. Michelson* - PRINTING IMPRESSIONS
Editor's Notebook - *column by Donald Q. Smith* - PUBLISHER'S AUXILIARY
Editor's Notebook - TARGET MARKETING
Editor's Notebook - TECHTRENDS
Editor's Notes - CANTRILLS FILMNOTES
Editor's Notes - CLIO AMONG THE MEDIA
Editor's Notes - CORPORATE VIDEO DECISIONS
Editor's Notes - *column by Brent Hurtig* - EQ
Editor's Notes - FILM CRITICISM
Editor's Notes - FREE SPEECH
Editor's Notes - IMAGE 11
Editor's Notes - MILLIMETER
Editor's Notes - OLD TIMER'S BULLETIN, THE
Editor's Notes - PENTAX FAMILY
Editor's Notes - TELECOMMUNICATIONS WEEK
Editor's Notes - UNIQUE
Editor's Opinion, The - *editorial* - RADIOLAND
Editor's Page - ART & CINEMA
Editor's Page, The - *editorial column by Ted Sennett* - BIJOU
Editors Page - CAMERA & DARKROOM PHOTOGRAPHY
Editor's Page, The - CINEFAN
Editor's Page - COMMUNICATION QUARTERLY
Editor's Page - *editorial column by Kimberly Torgerson* - DARKROOM PHOTOGRAPHY
Editors Page - INVIEW
Editor's Page - *'Comments and thoughts from the editor'* - INVIEW
Editor's Page, The - KODAK
Editors Page - MARKETING / COMMUNICATIONS
Editor's Page - *editorial* - MOVIES, THE
Editors' Page - MUSICAL AMERICA
Editor's Page - *editorial commentary column by David G. Wolford and Michael Doan* - ORBIT VIDEO
Editor's Page - *'An insider's point of view'* - REAL LIFE/DAYTIMERS
Editors Page - *gossip briefs* - RONA BARRETT'S HOLLYWOOD
Editor's Page - THEATRE CRAFTS
Editor's Page - VIDEO TIMES
Editor's Page - VIDEOGRAPHY
Editor's Picks - VIDEO ALERT
Editor's Point of View, The - AMERICAN PHOTOGRAPHY
Editor's Post Box - FILM MAKING
Editor's Remarks - COMMUNICATION MONOGRAPHS
Editor's Report - *column by Daniel Brogan* - PERSONAL PUBLISHING
Editors Review - *news items* - AUDIO
Editor's Side Pocket - *editorial* - SALES & MARKETING MANAGEMENT
Editor's Snapshots - PRACTICAL PHOTOGRAPHY

Editor's Space, The - ELECTRONICS & COMMUNICATIONS
Editor's View - COMPUTER PICTURES
Editor's View - *editorial column by Richard Wien* - V
Editors Workshop, The - *commentary* - ARS TYPOGRAPHICA
Ed-Lines - *editorial* - VIDEO WORLD
Education - PRESSTIME
Education - PROFESSIONAL PHOTOGRAPHER, THE
Education - *'Learn by satellite'* - SATELLITE TV WEEK
Education - *reviews of unusual current video projects* - TELEVISIONS
Education - WORLD PRESS REVIEW
Education and Workshop - ANIMAFILM
Education, Industry News - *newsbriefs of upcoming seminars* - SMPTE JOURNAL
Educational - WIRE & RADIO COMMUNICATIONS
Educational Broadcasting - *BBC materials* - VISUAL EDUCATION
Educational Department - DRAMA LEAGUE MONTHLY
Educational Intelligence - *educational newsbriefs* - ADVERTISERS GUIDE
Educationals - MOVING PICTURE AGE
EEs' Tools & Toys - *new items for workplace and home* - IEEE SPECTRUM
Effectivisions - *commentary column by John DeMott* - TELEVISER
Effects - INVISION
EFX News - *computer graphics* - ON LOCATION
EI Kit Report - *review* - ELECTRONICS ILLUSTRATED
EI Ticker, The - *latebreaking newsbriefs* - ELECTRONICS ILLUSTRATED
Electric Signs - *'Embracing also electrically operated advertising devices, electric outlining and accessories'* - SIGNS OF THE TIMES
Electrical Patents - TELEPHONE MAGAZINE
Electrical Science in Foreign Journals - ELECTRICAL REVIEW
Electronic Applications - LOCATION UPDATE
Electronic Art World - *'For the art & design professional' column by Jan V. White* - COMPUTER PUBLISHING
Electronic Editing - WRITING CONCEPTS
Electronic Firsts - *basic electronics* - AUDIOCRAFT FOR THE HI-FI HOBBYIST
Electronic Imagery - *separate videography section* - AMERICAN CINEMATOGRAPHER
Electronic Mail - *letters* - WHAT VIDEO
Electronic Marketplace - *new products* - ELECTRONICS ILLUSTRATED
Electronic Media - *column by Adele Lanan* - CMA NEWSLETTER
Electronic Mind, The - *computer column by Craig Patchett* - VISIO
Electronic Prepress - MAGAZINE DESIGN & PRODUCTION
Electronic Special Effects - CINEMAGIC
Electronic Writer, The - *column by Ronald John Donovan* - WRITER'S DIGEST
Electronically Speaking - *RCA newsbriefs* - ELECTRONIC AGE

Electronics - ELECTRONICS
Electronics Abroad - *newsbriefs* - ELECTRONICS
Electronics Forum - *commentary* - ELECTRONIC PUBLISHER
Electronics in the News - *product applications* - ELECTRONICS ILLUSTRATED
Electronics Index - *outstanding full-color status check of the electronics industry* - ELECTRONICS
Electronics Library - *book review* - COMPUTERS & ELECTRONICS
Electronics Library - *book reviews* - POPULAR ELECTRONICS
Electronics Newsletter - *latebreaking news items* - ELECTRONICS
Electronics Review - *newsbriefs* - ELECTRONICS
Elegy - *'Assault of the killer editorial'* - FANGORIA
Eliot Schein on Circulation Direct Marketing - *column by Eliot Schein* - FOLIO:
Ellenthal - *column by Ira Ellenthal* - INSIDE MEDIA
Emergency - *'Communications for survival'* - POPULAR COMMUNICATIONS
Empire Writes Back, The - *letters* - STRANGE ADVENTURES
Empirically Speaking - *editorial* - QEX
Employee Dyamics - *advice* - CABLE MARKETING
Employee Dynamics - *column by Gayla Kalp* - CABLE MARKETING
Employee Relations - PRESSTIME
Employment Bureau - *current opportunities* - ST. LOUIS AND CANADIAN PHOTOGRAPHER
En Passant - *detailed obituaries* - THEATRE, THE
End Notes - COMICS FEATURE
End Paper - *back-page commentary* - CAMERA ARTS
End Piece - *editorial* - LISTENER
Endnotes - *newsbriefs* - MEDIA LAW NOTES
Energy Report - IEEE SPECTRUM
Engineering - COLLEGE BROADCASTER
Engineering - ELECTRONIC DESIGN
Engineering - *technical advice* - JOURNAL OF COLLEGE RADIO
Engineering - STAGE & STUDIO
Engineering - THEATRE DESIGN & TECHNOLOGY
Engineering and Equipment - BROADCASTER
Engineering Applications - AMATEUR RADIO DEFENSE
Engineering News - SMPTE JOURNAL
Engineering Reports - AES
Engineering Tips - VIDEO TIMES
Engineer/Producer Index - *unique worklist of working professionals* - REP: RECORDING ENGINEERING PRODUCTION
Engineers - ELECTRONICS
English Scene, The - *British theatre column by Ashley Dukes* - THEATRE ARTS
ENG/News Technology - TELEVISION BROADCAST

Departments INDEX

Enquiry Desk - EIGHT MM MOVIE MAKER AND CINE CAMERA
Entertainment Electronics - *column by Harold A. Rodgers* - COMPUTERS & ELECTRONICS
Entertainment Environments - HOME ENTERTAINMENT
Entertainment Law Directory - LOYOLA ENTERTAINMENT JOURNAL
Entertainment Stocks - HOLLYWOOD REPORTER
Entrances & Exits - *personnel newsbriefs* - AMERICAN THEATRE
Entre Nous - *comment* - THEATRE, THE
Entrepreneur to Entrepreneur - PRINTING IMPRESSIONS
EnviroNotes - *publishing, printing and the environment* - PUBLISHING & PRODUCTION EXECUTIVE
EOW - *observations* - ADVERTISING AGENCY
Epilogue - AMERICAN FILM
Epistolae - VERBATIM
Equalizers - SOUND & VISION
Equipment - *new products* - MOVIE/TV MARKETING
Equipment - *review* - 60 SECONDS
Equipment - VIDEO
Equipment and Materials - AVC
Equipment & Materials - *product reviews* - AVC
Equipment and Services - *newsbriefs* - IMAGE TECHNOLOGY
Equipment and Supply Review - PRINTING IMPRESSIONS
Equipment Construction Operation - MIDWEEK MOTION PICTURE NEWS
Equipment News - BACK STAGE
Equipment News - FILM & VIDEO
Equipment News - FILMMAKERS FILM & VIDEO MONTHLY
Equipment News - VIDEO WORLD
Equipment of Questionable Origin - *important section listing possible stolen items* - FOLLOW FOCUS
Equipment of Questionable Origin - *excellent resource listing reported stolen production equipment with serial numbers* - NEWSLETTER, THE
Equipment of Questionable Origin List - NEWSLETTER, THE
Equipment Preview - MILLIMETER
Equipment Profiles - *unusually long section providing full technical performance data* - AUDIO
Equipment Reports - HIGH FIDELITY
Equipment Reports - *review* - RADIO-ELECTRONICS
Equipment Reports - *extensive testbench product reviews* - STEREOPHILE
Equipment Review - COMBROAD
Equipment Reviews - COLLEGE BROADCASTER
Equipment Reviews - GRAMOPHONE
Equipment Showcase - GRAPHIC ANTIQUARIAN
Equipment Spectrum - *new technology* - EDUCATIONAL BROADCASTING

Equipment Test Reports - *column by Julian D. Hirsch* - STEREO REVIEW
Equipment Watch - *new products* - ON LOCATION
Equipment: Central Office - COMMUNICATIONSWEEK
Equipment: CPE - COMMUNICATIONSWEEK
Equipment: Transmission - COMMUNICATIONSWEEK
Equipment/Supplies - GRAPHIC ARTS MONTHLY
Equipping the Theatre - EXHIBITORS TRADE REVIEW
Equity Dinner Theatres - *listing* - SHOW BUSINESS
Equity Industrial Producers - *listing* - SHOW BUSINESS
Equity Talent Agents - *listing* - SHOW BUSINESS
ERIC - *developments in data base operations* - TECHTRENDS
ERIC Report - COMMUNICATION EDUCATION
Errata - BROADCAST PIONEERS LIBRARY REPORTS
Espana - *production newsbriefs* - PRODUCCIÓN Y DISTRIBUCIÓN
Essay - PRESSTIME
Essentially Couth - *'Contemporary culture commentator', column by Barry Robinson* - MEDIA & METHODS
Esther Comments - WRITERS' JOURNAL
Estimating - *column by Gerald Silver* - GRAPHIC ARTS MONTHLY
Estimating Clinic - PRINTING IMPRESSIONS
Et Al - *miscellaneous news items* - COMIC READER, THE
ET Viewpoint - *editorial* - ELECTRONIC TECHNICAN/DEALER
Etcetera - *a potpourri of common-sense advice* - INTERLIT
Ethnic Music - MEDIA & VALUES
ETV in Print - JOURNAL OF EDUCATIONAL TELEVISION
Europe - PARAMOUNT WORLD
Europe - *theatrical offerings and review* - PLAYS INTERNATIONAL
European News - MEDIA INTERNATIONAL
European News Briefs on the Movie Industry - NATIONAL EXHIBITOR, THE
European News Roundup - FOCUS
European Newsletter - *continental news* - INDUSTRIAL PHOTOGRAPHY
European Observer - ELECTRONICS
European Trash Comments - *letters* - EUROPEAN TRASH CINEMA
Evaluation Samples - ELECTRONIC DESIGN
Evangeline Adams Reads the Stars - *'The world's most famous astrologer interprets the stars and their influences' astrology column by Evangeline Adams* - NEW MOVIE MAGAZINE, THE
Evening Guide to Listening - TV SCREEN
Events - *calendar* - ADVANCED IMAGING
Events - *calendar* - BROADCAST
Events - CABLEVISION
Events - *upcoming items* - CINEMA/CANADA
Events - COMPUTER PICTURES

Events - *calendar of upcoming conferences, workshops, and other related gatherings* - DIGITAL MEDIA
Events - VIDEO MANAGEMENT
Events Abroad - *newsbriefs* - FOI DIGEST
Events Diary - TV WORLD
Events of the Month - *'Announcements of club and association meetings exhibitions and conventions solicited for publication'* - PHOTO-ERA MAGAZINE
Every Day with Poetry - WRITERS' JOURNAL
Every Picture Tells - PRESS, THE
Every Where - *commentary* - ST. LOUIS JOURNALISM REVIEW
Everybody's a Critic - *letters* - ENTERTAINMENT WEEKLY
Everyday Mechanics - RADIO AGE
Evolution - *'The column that chronicles the changes and developments of radio each month'* - RADIO*PHILES
EW Lab Tested - ELECTRONICS WORLD
EW List of Entertainment Stocks - ENTERTAINMENT WORLD
EW Report Card - EDITOR'S WORKSHOP
EW Reports - *newsbriefs* - ENTERTAINMENT WORLD
Exam Info - QST
Exchange, The - *large section detailing needs and desire to sell equipment* - RADIO WORLD
Exchange Column - KINEMATOGRAPH WEEKLY
Exclusive Gallup Survey - *monthly feature* - TARGET MARKETING
Exclusive Supply Release Dates - EXHIBITORS' TIMES
Exec Stats - *black radio personnel changes* - BLACK RADIO EXCLUSIVE
Executive Digest - CABLE TV BUSINESS MAGAZINE
Executive Director's Desk - ASMP BULLETIN
Executive Director's Report - COMMUNICATOR, THE
Executive Forum - *commentary* - PUBLIC RELATIONS JOURNAL, THE
Executive Outlook - *application* - CORPORATE VIDEO DECISIONS
Executive Secretary's Corner - C-O-N-N-E-C-T-I-O-N-S
Executive Shuffle - *changed positions* - VARIETY
Executive Turntable - *executive moves* - BILLBOARD
Exhibit - *communication showcase* - COMMUNICATION ARTS
Exhibit Planning - AISLE VIEW
Exhibit Reviews - TECHNOLOGY AND CULTURE
Exhibit Selling - AISLE VIEW
Exhibition - *newsbriefs* - MOTION PICTURE PRODUCT DIGEST
Exhibition Diary - AM
Exhibition Notes - *current displays related to antiquarian/specialist books* - AB BOOKMAN'S WEEKLY
Exhibitions - *detailed synopses* - AMERICAN PHOTO
Exhibitions - BROADSIDE
Exhibitions - *review* - VIEWS

Exhibitions and Announcements - CAMERA
Exhibitions & Competitions - PSA JOURNAL
Exhibitions/Conferences - JEE, JOURNAL OF ELECTRONIC ENGINEERING
Exhibitors Box-Office Reports - *smaller town reports* - MIDWEEK MOTION PICTURE NEWS
Exhibitor's End of It, The - *promotion* - REEL LIFE
Exhibits to See - MODERN PHOTOGRAPHY
Experimental Cine Workshop, The - *'Gadgets, tricks and short cuts contributed by cinebugs'* - HOME MOVIES
Experimenter's Corner - *column by Forrest M. Mims* - COMPUTERS & ELECTRONICS
Experimenter's Workshop - *column by Rich Arland* - MONITORING TIMES
Experioddica - *column by Bob Grumman* - FACTSHEET FIVE
Explitettes - *'a clearing house for tabloid exploitation ideas'* - FILM TV DAILY
Exploitation - *publicity ideas* - UNIVERSAL WEEKLY
Exploitation, Promotion, Merchandising - *pictures with briefs on promotion* - GREATER AMUSEMENTS
Exploiting the New Films - *'How the recent pictures are being sold at the first run and pre-release date showings'* - MOTION PICTURE HERALD
Exploiting the Picture - EXHIBITORS TRADE REVIEW
Exploitips - *'Suggestions for selling the picture - ad aids'* - BOXOFFICE
Exploitorials - *newsbriefs regarding exhibitor promotion column by Tom Kennedy* - EXHIBITORS TRADE REVIEW
Exploitorials - *promotion suggestions* - SHOWMEN'S TRADE REVIEW
Export Directory - *ad briefs* - MOVIE/TV MARKETING
Exposing Audio Mythology - REP: RECORDING ENGINEERING PRODUCTION
Expositions - *listing* - THEATRE DOCUMENTATION
Exposures - *full color pix and personality profile* - FAME
Extra... Extra... - ANIMATIONS
Eye, The - *music video column by Melinda Newman* - BILLBOARD
Eye on Access - VIEW
Eye on Advertising - PHOTO DISTRICT NEWS
Eye on Film - *column by Donald E. Barnhorst* - ENTERTAINMENT REVUE
Eye on Orlando - MARKEE
Eye on Television - *column by David B. Horowitz* - ENTERTAINMENT REVUE
Eye on the Press - *newsbriefs* - AM
Eyeview - *column by Ian MacQuillin* - CAMCORDER USER

F

F & F Interview - FILMS AND FILMING
Fabricantes - PRODUCCIÓN Y DISTRIBUCIÓN
Face to Face - *Young TV star interviews* - TV HITS
Faces - *'Professional profiles'* - LINK
Faces - *'The ones to watch'* - MOVIES USA
Faces and Footnotes - *personnel newsbriefs* - ADVERTISING & SELLING
Faces & Places - *event photos and stars* - US MAGAZINE
Facilities - BACK STAGE
Facilities - BROADCAST
Facilities - FILM & VIDEO
Facilities - VIDEO MANAGEMENT
Facilities - *new equipment at production houses* - VIDEOGRAPHY
Facilities News - *studio production and post production* - ON LOCATION
Facilities Showcase - RADIO WORLD
Facilities/Production Services - *profile* - VIDEOPRO
Facility Forum - CORPORATE TELEVISION
Facility News - MARKEE
Facility Planning Achievements - *new production studio profiles* - MILLIMETER
Facility Update - IN MOTION FILM & VIDEO PRODUCTION MAGAZINE
Facing Pages View - *column by George Sheldon* - VENTURA PROFESSIONAL!
Facing the Music - *radio music program news column by Ken Alden* - TV RADIO MIRROR
Factory Automation - ELECTRONICS
Factory Communications - NETWORK WORLD
Facts - *'A collection of useful, interesting and/or unusual data'* - INSIDE MEDIA
Facts about Fiction - *instructional column by George Allan England* - STORY WORLD AND PHOTODRAMATIST, THE
Facts About the Famous - *cartoon profile of current singer or bandleader* - HIT PARADER
Facts & Figures - *charts and graphs on cable* - MULTICHANNEL NEWS
Facts & Figures - *test results* - PRACTICAL WIRELESS
Facts on Funding - *newsbriefs* - INTERNATIONAL EDUCATIONAL AND CULTURAL EXCHANGE
Factsheet Five Projects - *'News of books you can buy from us, sales of our mailing list (and how to avoid getting your name sold), the FF index and t-shirts, and ways you can get pounds of zines for only the cost of postage'* - FACTSHEET FIVE
Faculty Advisor - *written by faculty advisors to college campus radio and television operations* - COLLEGE BROADCASTER
Faculty News - JOURNALISM EDUCATOR, THE

Fade In - *calendar and comment* - HOLLYWOOD MAGAZINE
Fade In - *editorial* - HOME & STUDIO RECORDING
Fade Out - *commentary column by Andrew Marx* - HOLLYWOOD MAGAZINE
Fade Out - *comment* - HOME & STUDIO RECORDING
Fade Out - *historical* - WRAP
Fairs & Expos - *news and information* - AMUSEMENT BUSINESS
FAME Says It All About Books - *column by Phil McCombs* - FAME
FAME Says It All About Film - *column by Carrie Rickey* - FAME
FAME Says It All About Hollywood - *column by Dana Kennedy* - FAME
FAME Says It All About Society - *column by Diane Goldner* - FAME
Families - DISNEY CHANNEL MAGAZINE, THE
Family - AFA JOURNAL
Family Fare - *upcoming satellite program of a family nature* - SATELLITE ORBIT
Family Features - VIDEO ALERT
Family Gossip - *personality news from reader submitted questions, column by Peggy Stewart* - RURAL RADIO
Family Life - MEDIA & VALUES
Family New Releases - VIDEO ALERT
Fan Club File - *address list* - SOAP OPERA STARS
Fan Club Forum - *fan news column by Lynne Abrahamson* - TV DAY STARS
Fan Club Listings - DAYTIME TV
Fan Club News - *briefs* - SOAP OPERA DIGEST
Fan Clubs - *extensive listing* - SH-BOOM
Fan Fare - *celebrity gossip column* - MOVIE WORLD
Fan Forum, The - *letters* - LUCASFILM FAN CLUB, THE
Fan Notes - *reader submitted personal messages to young stars* - WOWI MAGAZINE
Fan Tales - EPISODES
Fan Zone - *'Letters to the Editor'* - DEEP RED
Fandom's Forum - *extensive discourse on comics* - COMIC FANDOM'S FORUM
Fanfare Forum - *editorial and letters* - FANFARE
Fang Mail - *'Growls from the monster mail bag'* - FAMOUS MONSTERS OF FILMLAND
Fanmail From Some Flounder - *letters* - ANIMATO!
Fans & Favorites - *'The latest on fan clubbing!'* - REAL LIFE/DAYTIMERS
Fans Who Have Met Their Favorite Stars Tell All About It! - *letters* - SOAP OPERA PEOPLE
Fansville - *young star addresses* - WOWI MAGAZINE
Fanzine Guide - *column by Timothy R. Corrigan* - COMICS BUYER'S GUIDE
Fanzine Update - *fanzine reviews column by Dave Patterson* - COMIC INFORMER
Far East Journal - *photographic news and review* - PETERSEN'S PHOTOGRAPHIC
Far East P.O. Scoreboard - *exhibitor grosses, duration and other exhibition data* - MOVIE/TV MARKETING

Far Forward - *product promotion* - DEALERSCOPE
Farm News and Views - *program guide* - RURAL RADIO
Farm Radio Highlights - *schedule* - RURAL RADIO
Farmer and His Favorite Medium, The - *agricultural press news* - NATIONAL ADVERTISING
Fashion - INTERVIEW
Fashion - LÜRZER'S INTERNATIONAL ARCHIVE
Fashion - MOVIELINE
Fashion a la carte - *fashion news* - THEATRE, THE
Fashion Forecast - *column by Bernadine Morris* - PLAYBILL
Fashion News - *column by Elizabeth Stewart* - MGF
Fashion Q & A - *column by Elizabeth Stewart* - MGF
Fashion Show - SHOW
Fashion Tie-Ups - *discussion of film fashion tie-in to American consumers* - GREATER AMUSEMENTS
Fashion Tips for Your Figure Problems - *column by Janis Carter* - MOVIE TEEN
Fashions - THEATRE MAGAZINE
Fashions and Beauty - HOLLYWOOD
Fashions for You - TELEVISION AND SCREEN GUIDE
Fashions in Full Color - TELEVISION AND SCREEN GUIDE
Fast Features - *newsbriefs* - REAL LIFE/DAYTIMERS
Fast Feeds - *network newsbriefs column by Mark Jeffers* - ONSAT
Fast Forward - *comment column by Bob Gerson* - CONSUMER ELECTRONICS
Fast Forward - *new product review* - HOME & STUDIO RECORDING
Fast Forward - *editorial* - HOME VIDEO
Fast Forward - *future tech* - PREVUE
Fast Forward - SCENE AT THE MOVIES
Fast Lane, The - *column by Ralph Hodges* - CAR STEREO REVIEW
Fast Lane, The - *column by Stephen St. Croix* - MIX
Fast Read - *newsbriefs* - IN-PLANT PRINTER & ELECTRONIC PUBLISHER
Fast Track with Cheryl Lavin, The - *actor profile column by Cheryl Lavin* - SPOTLIGHT CASTING MAGAZINE
Fates and Fortunes - *personnel briefs* - BROADCASTING
Fates & Fortunes - *personnel newsbriefs* - BROADCASTING ABROAD
Favorite Film Fun Models - FILM FUN
FC Kennedy - *commentary* - TV TIMES
FCC Actions - *large listing of recent regulatory actions* - RADIO*PHILES
FCC Developments - RADIO WORLD
FCC Docket - ACCESS
FCC New Station Activity - PUBLIC BROADCASTING REPORT, THE

FCC Rules and Regulations - *superb interpretations of current rules and regulations by leading broadcast legal authorities* - BME'S TELEVISION ENGINEERING
FCC Update - BROADCAST ENGINEERING
F.C.C. Watch - *commission developments column by Robert R. Bruce* - CABLE TV AND NEW MEDIA LAW & FINANCE
Feature Booking Guide - *extensive listing of current and forthcoming films* - SHOWMEN'S TRADE REVIEW
Feature Chart - *release data by studios* - BOX OFFICE
Feature Filming - MARKEE
Feature Index - *'A check-up on current product'* - BOXOFFICE
Feature Release Chart - MIDWEEK MOTION PICTURE NEWS
Feature Reviews - *excellent lengthy reviews of current productions, with two unique subsections: 'Exploitips,' promotion information, and 'Catchlines,' slogans usable for promotion. (The following special articles are featured in the Modern Theater section of Boxoffice:)* - BOX OFFICE
Feature Reviews - MIDWEEK MOTION PICTURE NEWS
Features - *program descriptions* - BBC WORLD SERVICE LONDON CALLING
Features - *reviews* - FILM BULLETIN
Features - *guide* - LISTENER
Features and Promotions - *briefs of special sections and features* - NEWSPAPER WORLD AND ADVERTISING REVIEW
Features Competition - *contest* - VIDEO BUYER
Federal Communication Commission Reports - COMMUNICATION AND BROADCAST ENGINEERING
Federal File - *column by Dave Jones* - MONITORING TIMES
Federal Trade Commission Says - ADVERTISING AGENCY
Feed Finders, The - *news of satellite feeds column by Bill Britton* - STV GUIDE
Feedback - *letters* - ACCESS
Feedback - *letters* - AUTO SOUND & SECURITY
Feedback - *letters* - BME'S TELEVISION ENGINEERING
Feedback - *letters* - HOME & STUDIO RECORDING
Feedback - *advertising articles in response to current topics* - JOURNAL OF ADVERTISING RESEARCH
Feedback - *letters* - MEDIA & METHODS
Feedback - *letters* - MEDIA ASIA
Feedback - *letters* - MEDIA WATCH
Feedback - *letters* - MIX
Feedback - *letters* - PUBLIC RELATIONS JOURNAL, THE
Feedback - *letters* - PULP & PAPER CANADA
Feedback - *corrections* - QST
Feedback - *'Some more of your comments and views in our lively monthly letters column'* - STARBURST
Feedback - *technology column by Mitch Mitchell* - TELEVISION WEEK

Feedback - *'Readers sound off'* - TV ENTERTAINMENT
Feedback - *letters* - VIDEO MAGAZINE
Feedback From Our Readers - *letters* - ELECTRONICS ILLUSTRATED
Feedback/Feedforward - *letters* - WOMEN & FILM
Feeling Great - *column by Steven Slon* - MGF
Feldman Lab Reports - TAPE DECK QUARTERLY
Felker's Forum - *radio regulation column by Lex Felker* - RADIO WORLD
Fellowships and Grants - CLIO AMONG THE MEDIA
Feminine Eye, The - *column by Joyce E. Widoff* - WESTERN PHOTOGRAPHER MAGAZINE
Festival Highlights - *special film showings for the upcoming month* - AMERICAN MOVIE CLASSICS MAGAZINE
Festival Listings - INTERNATIONAL DOCUMENTARY
Festival Report - AMERICAN FILM
Festival Report - ANIMAFILM
Festival Reports - INTERNATIONAL DOCUMENTARY
Festival Round-Up - *upcoming film festivals* - SCREEN INTERNATIONAL
Festivals - *news of upcoming events* - ASIFA NOUVELLES
Festivals - CINEASTE
Festivals - *upcoming events and reviews of recent screenings* - CINEGRAM
Festivals - CINEMA/CANADA
Festivals - *calendar* - FILMMAKERS FILM & VIDEO MONTHLY
Festivals - *notices* - INDEPENDENT, THE
Festivals - *calendar* - PRINTED MATTER
Festivals - SPEECH AND DRAMA
Festivals and Conferences - *'A schedule of theatre festivals and conferences sanctioned by the Educational Theatre Association'* - DRAMATICS
Festivals/Calendar - ANIMATION MAGAZINE
Few Minutes With, A - *interview* - CINEFANTASTIQUE
Few Short Words, A - *comment* - METRO-GOLDWYN-MAYER SHORT STORY
Fiction - *column by Lawrence Block* - WRITER'S DIGEST
FIEJ Throughout the World - *newsbriefs* - FIEJ-BULLETIN
Field Notes - THEATRE AND SCHOOL
Field Promotions - PRESS STATISTICAL REVIEW
Field Report - BROADCAST ENGINEERING
Field Report - *special news report* - VIDEO EIGHTIES MAGAZINE
Field Reports - INDEPENDENT, THE
Field Test - AMERICAN PHOTO
Field Test - *new equipment* - MIX
Field Tests - *new product review* - ONI
Field Tests - *testbench reviews* - VIDEO PROPHILES
Fifteen Years Ago - *'What the stars said-- and did!'* - SCREEN STORIES
Fifth Wave - *column by Maureen Waters* - MAGAZINE DESIGN & PRODUCTION

Fifty Years Ago - *historical listing* - SPARKS
Figures - AGENCY
File Scene International - *letters from London* - CINEMA
Film - HIGH PERFORMANCE
Film - HYPERMEDIA
Film - INSIDE ENTERTAINMENT
Film - *review column by Geoff Andrew* - 20/20
Film and History News - FILM & HISTORY
Film and TV Press - *reviews of publications concerning media* - FILM & VIDEO NEWS
Film & Video Express - *film and video rental/sales* - MEDIA DIGEST
Film & Video Review - MEDIA DIGEST
Film & Video Sound - *Visual Media column by Larry Blake* - EQ
Film and Video Views - *column by Mark Androw* - FLASH
Film Artistes Newsreel & Production Guide - *member newsbriefs* - FILM ARTISTE
Film as Business - *column by Michael F. Mayer* - TAKE ONE
Film Books - TAKE ONE
Film Buyers Rating - *ratings via film circuit buyers* - MOTION PICTURE PRODUCT DIGEST
Film Campaign - FLASH
Film Casting - *opportunity briefs* - BACK STAGE
Film Catalogue of the Month - DOCUMENTARY FILM NEWS
Film Censorship Listings - *status* - CINEMA PAPERS
Film Classics - *review* - MOVIEGUIDE
Film Classics - *'First time on home video'* - V
Film Clips - *motion pictures opening this month* - MOVIEGOER
Film Commission News - *news of state film commission activities* - FILM & VIDEO
Film Commission Report - IN MOTION FILM & VIDEO PRODUCTION MAGAZINE
Film Company News - *extensive news section divided by major studio* - FILM JOURNAL, THE
Film Crossword - FILM REVIEW
Film Events Calendar - SHOWMEN'S TRADE REVIEW
Film Exchange News - *briefs* - GREATER AMUSEMENTS
Film Expositions & Conventions - *listing* - AMERICAN PREMIERE
Film Facts - *video and film comment column by Jerry Albert* - TELEVISER
Film Family Album - *engaged, wedded and born to newsbriefs* - SHOWMEN'S TRADE REVIEW
Film Fax - *'Your questions answered by David McGillivray, our man with all the answers' column by David McGillivray* - FILM REVIEW
Film Feedback - *a Q&A column on technique* - FILMMAKERS FILM & VIDEO MONTHLY
Film Festival - MEMORIES
Film Guide - *capsule descriptions of current film fare* - CINEASTE

Film Guide - *listing of British film theaters and current programs* - DOCUMENTARY FILM NEWS
Film Guide - FILMS ILLUSTRATED
Film Guide - *current showings* - SIGHT & SOUND
Film Information - *news briefs* - UNIVERSITY FILM STUDY CENTER. NEWSLETTER.
Film Letter from Hollywood - FILMFARE
Film Libraries - DOCUMENTARY FILM NEWS
Film Music - CINEGRAM
Film Music and its Makers - *concerning film scores and music* - HOLLYWOOD SPECTATOR
Film News - *feature film newsbriefs* - FILM
Film News - ON LOCATION
Film Notes and Queries - *letters* - LITERATURE/FILM QUARTERLY
Film Nut News - *column by Alan Oddie* - FILMMAKERS FILM & VIDEO MONTHLY
Film of the Month - DOCUMENTARY FILM NEWS
Film of the Month - FILMS AND FILMING
Film Production - *extensive project status section* - VARIETY
Film Production Chart - SHOW BIZ WEST
Film Ratings - CINEFANTASTIQUE
Film Review - ANIMATION MAGAZINE
Film Review - *Variety's famed critical review of new releases* - DAILY VARIETY
Film Review - FILM & HISTORY
Film Review - FILM ART
Film Review - HOLLYWOOD REPORTER
Film Review - LITERATURE/FILM QUARTERLY
Film Review - MEDIA ANTHROPOLOGIST NEWSLETTER
Film Reviews - *covering both domestic and international releases* - CINEASTE
Film Reviews - CINEMA/CANADA
Film Reviews - *lengthy* - CINEMA PAPERS
Film Reviews - CINEMACABRE
Film Reviews - DRAMA-LOGUE
Film Reviews - EDUCATIONAL COMMUNICATION AND TECHNOLOGY
Film Reviews - FILM & HISTORY
Film Reviews - FILM HERITAGE
Film Reviews - FILM LIBRARY QUARTERLY
Film Reviews - FILM REVIEW
Film Reviews - FILM TV DAILY
Film Reviews - MOVIES AND MINISTRY
Film Reviews - SHOW BIZ WEST
Film Reviews - SIGHT & SOUND
Film Reviews - *famed critical analyses* - VARIETY
Film Reviews Extra - FILM REVIEW
Film Row - *exhibitor-distributor news in various cities* - SHOWMEN'S TRADE REVIEW
Film Row News, USA - *sentence briefs on exhibition success* - GREATER AMUSEMENTS
Film Row Visitors - *exhibitor travel* - NATIONAL EXHIBITOR, THE
Film Scene - *paragraph-length news on the industry* - CINEMA
Film Scene, The - *newsbriefs* - MOTION PICTURE PRODUCT DIGEST
Film Section - TONI HOLT'S MOVIE LIFE

Film Societies - DOCUMENTARY FILM NEWS
Film Society News - DOCUMENTARY FILM NEWS
Film Society News - FILM
Film Society of Glasgow, The - DOCUMENTARY FILM NEWS
Film Study - *similar treatment pertaining to film* - MEDIA MIX
Film Talk - *motion picture feature* - TECHNICAL PHOTOGRAPHY
Film Talk - *'Ken Ferguson with all of the latest news and gossip from Hollywood to Pinewood'* - VIDEO MONTHLY
Filmakers Cooperative - *'New acquisitions'* - MOTION PICTURE
Filmfax - *'Interviews and information focusing on the latest developments in state-of-the-art cinema'* - FANTASTIC FILMS
Filmland Flashes - *'Inside news before it happens'* - SILVER SCREEN
Filmland Forum - *letters column* - FILMLAND
Filmland Reviews - *motion picture review column by Lillian Smith* - FILMLAND
Filmmakers' Bookshelf - KODAK PROFESSIONAL FORUM
Filmmakers Forum - CINEMAGIC
Filmmaker's Notebook - *technique instruction* - FILMMAKERS FILM & VIDEO MONTHLY
Filmmakers Notebook - *column by Elinor Stecker* - FILMMAKERS FILM & VIDEO MONTHLY
FilmNet - *upcoming films* - SATELLITE TIMES
Film-o Graphs - *newsbriefs* - HOLLYWOOD FILMOGRAPH
Films - *reviews* - ABC WEEKLY
Films - *review column by Norma McLain Stoop* - AFTER DARK
Films - *review column by Gene Ringgold* - SOUND STAGE
Films and Filming Abroad - FILMS AND FILMING
Films and Filming in Hollywood - FILMS AND FILMING
Films and Filmstrips - *new releases* - AV GUIDE
Films & Video Tapes - *distribution and festival listing* - CASTING NEWS
Films and Videos - *review* - WOMEN & LANGUAGE
Films for the Pupil and Teacher - *application of film to the classroom* - MOTION PICTURE AND THE FAMILY, THE
Films in Production - *data on Canadian product* - CANADIAN FILM DIGEST
Films in Release - *with an entertainment value system* - FILMS IN REVIEW
Films of the Quarter - *reviews* - DOCUMENTARY FILM NEWS
Films of the Quarter - FILM ART
Films on Satellite - *'Kevin Wilson reviews the movies showing on satellite this week'* - TV GUIDE
Films Reviewed - *reprint of newspaper critics reviews* - DOCUMENTARY FILM NEWS
Films Shooting in New York - SHOW BUSINESS
Films to Come - *'A sneak photo-preview of pix in the pipeline'* - FILM REVIEW

Departments INDEX

Films We See, The - *'reviews of recent reviews* - CINEMA AND THEATRE
Filmstrip Review - MEDIA DIGEST
Film/Video Reviews - FILM & VIDEO NEWS
Filter - AUDIO VISUAL
Final Copy - *column by Jack Reznicki* - FLASH
Final Curtain, The - *obits* - PERFORMER, THE
Final Curtains - *obituaries* - SCARLET STREET
Final Cut - *'...a column for prominent people in the motion picture industry to have their final say about any topic that ails them'* - IN CINEMA
Final Cut - *commentary* - VIDEO MANAGEMENT
Final Frame - CAMERA & DARKROOM PHOTOGRAPHY
Final Frame - *'reserved for images that have been altered in some way'* - DARKROOM PHOTOGRAPHY
Final Page, The - *photo page* - VIDEO SOFTWARE MAGAZINE
Final Thoughts - HOME VIDEO
Final Word, The - *'Publisher Larry Archibald muses in print on the state of the industry' column by Larry Archibald* - STEREOPHILE
Final Word - *commentary* - VIDEO TIMES
Finance - ELECTRONIC MEDIA
Finance - *large section devoted to cable economics* - MULTICHANNEL NEWS
Finance - *column by William Phillips* - TBI
Finance - *excellent segment on entertainment monies* - VARIETY
Finance - VUE
Finance Briefs - *financial news concerning motion picture production and distribution* - BUSINESS OF FILM, THE
Financial - *data* - FILM TV DAILY
Financial - HOLLYWOOD REPORTER
Financial - *newsbriefs* - WEB
Financial Advisory, The - SQUEEKY WHEEL, THE
Financial and Industrial - JOURNALIST, THE
Financial Management - PRINTING IMPRESSIONS
Financial News - CABLE WORLD
Financial News - SATELLITE RETAILER
Financial News - WIRE & RADIO COMMUNICATIONS
Financial Notes - CABLE TV BUSINESS MAGAZINE
Financial Notes - *economic news of the industry* - FILM JOURNAL, THE
Financial Reports of TV-Electronic Companies - *stock and financial reports on 10-15 firms* - TELEVISION DIGEST WITH CONSUMER ELECTRONICS
Financial Services Chart - CABLEVISION
Financials - *newsbriefs* - VIDEO MANAGEMENT
Financing and Earnings - TELECOMMUNICATIONS WEEK
Financing Films - *excellent monetary status of project financing* - ENTERTAINMENT REVUE
Findings - *research summaries* - MEDIA ASIA
Finds - *graphic resources* - IN HOUSE GRAPHICS
Find-the-Word Puzzle - MOVIE MIRROR
Fine Print - *'Legal points'* - LINK

Fine Tuning - *'Your video questions answered.' (4-82).* - VIDEO MAGAZINE
Finish Line - *newsbriefs* - TARGET MARKETING
Finishing Touches - *reader ideas* - PUBLISHING & PRODUCTION EXECUTIVE
Finnigan's File - *column by Joseph Finnigan* - EMMY
First Aids to Beauty - *'Advice and rules for charm and attractiveness' column by Ann Boyd* - NEW MOVIE MAGAZINE, THE
First Chorus, The - *column by Charles Suber* - DOWN BEAT
First Draft - *editorial column by R. Patricia Herron* - FLASH
First Edition - *commentary* - MAGAZINE DESIGN & PRODUCTION
First Impression - *new books* - BOOKS & RELIGION
First Look - *'A preview of future products and trends'* - PUBLISHI
First Look - *new equipment column by Laurel Cash-Jones* - REP: RECORDING ENGINEERING PRODUCTION
First Person - *column by Paul Bereswill* - MODERN PHOTOGRAPHY
First Reference - *'...a guide to the organizations offering products and services in the film, sound, television, audio-visual and video industries'* - IMAGE TECHNOLOGY
First Runs - *week's gross* - BOXOFFICE
First Runs on Broadway - *'Their presentation and press comments by various New York dailies'* - EXHIBITORS TRADE REVIEW
First Showings by Wire Summary of Last Two Weeks - DRAMATIC MIRROR, THE
First Word, The - *editorial column by David Vernier* - CD REVIEW
Firsts - *historical items and cartoon column by C. L. Crist* - MEDIA SIGHT
Fishing Hole, The - *publishing column by Joe Lane* - FACTSHEET FIVE
Fitness - *column by Norman Zeitchick* - MGF
Five Questions - *interesting technical column by Mack Clark and Mike Joseph* - REP: RECORDING ENGINEERING PRODUCTION
Five-Minute Videographer, The - *column by Marjorie Costello* - VIDEO PROPHILES
Flash - *unusual...* - AMERICAN PHOTO
Flash - *'Straight from Hollywood and Cathrine Daly'* - MOVIE HUMOR
Flash - *'News and notes from around the globe'* - OUTDOOR & TRAVEL PHOTOGRAPHY
Flash Back - JOE FRANKLIN'S NOSTALGIA
Flash News Views - TONI HOLT'S MOVIE LIFE
Flash! - *'Star Shots'* - REAL LIFE/DAYTIMERS
Flashback - *Hollywood product of the past* - SCENE AT THE MOVIES
Flashbacks - *'A look down memory lane'* - REAL LIFE/DAYTIMERS
Flashes - *very brief news items* - MOVIE FLASH
Flashes - *newsbriefs* - NABET NEWS
Flashes From Classes - *alumni newsbriefs* - OHIO JOURNALIST, THE

Flashes From the News - *newsbriefs* - RADIOLAND
Flashmakers - *late breaking news* - VIDEO INSIDER
Fleets - SALES & MARKETING MANAGEMENT
Flickers - *cartoon strip column by Tim Quinn and Dicky Howett* - STARBURST
Flipbooks - ANIMATOI
Florida - BACK STAGE
F.M. - *column by Glen E. Zook* - CQ
FM Programs of Special Interest - SHOW
Focal Point - *photo submissions* - CAMERA & CAMCORDER MONTHLY
Focal Point - *equipment review column by Chris Lees* - PIC
Focal Points - IEEE SPECTRUM
Focus - BROADCAST SYSTEMS INTERNATIONAL
Focus - EMMY
Focus - *'A close-up of a company'* - FLORIDA REEL
Focus - *on recently published and forthcoming titles by topic* - FORECAST
Focus - *large feature section concerning different television issue each month* - TBI
Focus - *editorial* - TELEVISION WEEK
Focus - *editorial column by Frank Moldstad* - VIDEO STORE
Focus On - FORECAST
Focus On - *world television program profile* - TV WORLD
Focus on Audio - *engineering column by Randy Hoffner* - TV TECHNOLOGY
Focus on Commercials - TELEVISION
Focus on Editing - *column by Jay Ankeney* - TV TECHNOLOGY
Focus on Education - *column by Jonathan Rosenbaum* - AMERICAN FILM
Focus on Europe - VIA SATELLITE
Focus on Finance - *index of 66 television-associated stocks* - TELEVISION
Focus on Fleet Street - CAMPAIGN
Focus on Graphics - *column by Carla Breeden-Conrad* - TV TECHNOLOGY
Focus on Imaging - INFORMATION TODAY
Focus on Marketing - MEDIAWEEK
Focus on News - *briefs* - TELEVISION
Focus on People - *newsbriefs with pictures* - TELEVISION
Focus on Quality - *engineering column by Warner W. Johnston* - TV TECHNOLOGY
Focus on Sponsored Cinema - *reviews* - FOCUS ON FILM
Focus on Television - *background on articles within this issue* - TELEVISION
Focus on the New Films - *large film review section* - FOCUS ON FILM
Focus: - *recording profile* - REP: RECORDING ENGINEERING PRODUCTION
FOI Boxscore - *newsbriefs* - COLORADO EDITOR
FOI In the States - *state news roundup* - FOI DIGEST
FOI Report - *a report on freedom of information* - QUILL, THE
Folkbag - *reviews* - AUDIO
Follow the Money - *column by Paul S. Maxwell* - MEDIA BUSINESS

Follow Up - *stereo equipment review updates* - STEREOPHILE
Following the Stars - *column by Charles Hobson* - BLACK STARS
Fonts - *new product review* - VENTURA LETTER, THE
Food - LÜRZER'S INTERNATIONAL ARCHIVE
Food & Drink - *merchandise and food preparation news* - AMUSEMENT BUSINESS
Food for Thought - *Culinary postcards column by Jennifer Henderson* - POSTCARD COLLECTOR
Foolscap - *cartoon comment* - BOOKS & RELIGION
Footloose Reporter, The - ALL-WAVE RADIO
Footnotes - *upcoming events* - MULTI IMAGES JOURNAL
Footnotes in the Theatre Library World - *news items* - THEATRE DOCUMENTATION
For Creative Men - ADVERTISING AGENCY
For Immediate Release - *newsbriefs* - VIDEO EIGHTIES MAGAZINE
For Lovelier Hands - *beauty* - HOLLYWOOD
For Men Only - *column by Glenn Plaskin* - MGF
For Richer, for Poorer - *abstract* - SOAP OPERA DIGEST
For Sale - *'Vids to buy and keep'* - VIDEO TIMES
For the Beginner - AMERICAN PHOTOGRAPHY
For the Beginner - CAMERA MAGAZINE
For the Correspondent - *advice to stringers* - IOWA JOURNALIST
For the Experimenter - QST
For the Love of Mike - *personality column by Denny Shane* - FILMLAND
For the Record - *account and trade newsbriefs* - ADVERTISING AGE
For the Record - *ommissions and corrections* - BILLBOARD
For the Record - *detailed FCC actions for the week* - BROADCASTING
For the Record - *editorial column by Oliver Read* - ELECTRONICS WORLD
For the Record - *column by Marilyn McLeod* - ENTERTAINMENT CONNECTION MAGAZINE
For the Record - GOSSIP
For the Record - *briefs on music* - RONA BARRETT'S HOLLYWOOD
For the Record - SOAP OPERA DIGEST
For the Records - *new RCA releases* - ELECTRONIC AGE
For the Serviceman - ELECTRONICS AND COMMUNICATIONS
For Your Bookshelf - *reviews* - STORY WORLD AND PHOTODRAMATIST, THE
For Your Information - BUSINESS INFORMATION ALERT
For Your Information - *newsbriefs* - SUCCESSFUL MAGAZINE PUBLISHING
Forecaster - *column by Paul Sweeting* - VIDEO BUSINESS
Forecasts - PUBLISHER'S WEEKLY
Forecasts - *'Television scans its own future'* - TBI
Foreign - *review* - ORBIT VIDEO
Foreign Appointments - GREATER AMUSEMENTS

Foreign Desk, The - *world animation news* - GET ANIMATED! UPDATE.
Foreign Radio Decisions - *column by Carl Zollmann* - JOURNAL OF RADIO LAW
Foreign Radio Legislation - *column by Carl Zollmann* - JOURNAL OF RADIO LAW
Foreign Trade Notes - NATIONAL EXHIBITOR, THE
Foreplay - *'What's up 'n' coming, Foreplay takes a look at new releases, with fresh, unique and informative profiles', column by Cathy Down* - MONDAY MORNING REPLAY
Foreword - JOURNAL OF MASS MEDIA ETHICS
Form & Function - *column by Doug Patton* - AUDIO/VIDEO INTERIORS
Forthcoming - *'A look at Four Color to come'* - FOUR COLOR
Forthcoming Books - *brief descriptions and information* - BRITISH BOOK NEWS
Fortnightly Reading - *horoscope* - PIC
Forum - *guest commentary* - ADVERTISING AGE
Forum - AVC
Forum - *guest commentary* - BUSINESS MARKETING
Forum - *letters* - C: JET
Forum - *letters* - COMMUNICATION EDUCATION
Forum - COMMUNICATION THEORY
Forum - *'Editorial, perspective, comment, letters'* - COMMUNICATIONSWEEK
Forum - IEEE SPECTRUM
Forum - POST SCRIPT
Forum - *commentary* - PUBLISHER'S AUXILIARY
Forum, The - QUARTERLY JOURNAL OF SPEECH, THE
Forum - *always a fascinating no-holds-barred discussion of a current radio issue* - RADIO·PHILES
Forum - *letters* - WRITER'S DIGEST
Forum Schedule - FACETS FEATURES
Forward - *editorial* - UNIVERSITY VISION
Foto Facts - *column by Paul Farber* - TRAVEL & LEISURE
Foto Fiddling - *drawing mustaches and beards on celebrity pictures* - MOVIE HUMOR
Fotofile - CAMERA MAGAZINE
Found Stars - *here is* - MOVIE DIGEST
Foundations for the Future - *column by Laurie Spar* - DIRECT MARKETING
Four-Star Movies - *top rated motion pictures* - TV GUIDE
Fox Report, The - *'Animation news from John Cawley'* - ANIMATO!
Fractional Currency - *homespun sayings* - ADVERTISERS GUIDE
Frame for Beauty - *hints column by Dr. Grace Gregory* - TV RADIO MIRROR
Frame for Fame - *full-color portraits of the stars* - PHOTOPLAY COMBINED WITH MOVIE MIRROR
Framed - *profile* - SIGHT & SOUND
Franchise File - *fascinating programming profile* - BROADCAST
Frankly Scarlet - *editorial* - SCARLET STREET

Fraternity of the Air - *'Boys, here is our growing list of I.B.E.W amateur radio stations'* - JOURNAL
Free - *'Seminars, training, workshops' upcoming events* - INFORMATION TODAY
Free Classified - *free listing of artists and their services* - PAS GRAPHIC ARTS NEWS
Free Offers - *monthly giveaway via 20/20* - 20/20
Free-Lance - *column by Barbara Gordon* - COMMUNICATION ARTS
Freelances - UK PRESS GAZETTE
Freelancing - STEP-BY-STEP GRAPHICS
Freeloaders - *free information for media in education* - MEDIA DIGEST
Freeze Frame - MEDIAWEEK
Freeze Frame - *video column by Cliff Roth* - VISIO
Freeze-Frames - *newsbriefs* - VIDEO REVIEW
French & Spanish Programming - *listing* - ONSAT
French Movies - *listing* - ONSAT
Frequency Section - *station listings* - MONITORING TIMES
Fresh Faces - *new artists on the applied arts scene* - APPLIED ARTS QUARTERLY
Fresh Facts - *'Here's your chance to find out everything you need to know about how to succeed in show business'* - FRESH!
Fresh Tracks - *new recordings, comments and engineering credits* - REP: RECORDING ENGINEERING PRODUCTION
Friends Forum - *news and information by Friends of Libraries, USA* - FORECAST
Fringe - *other theatre offerings and commentary column by Lyn Gardner* - PLAYS INTERNATIONAL
From a Managers Notebook - *exhibitor commentary* - CINEMA AND THEATRE
From G-106-107 - *'The output of plays during the last thirty days, with a looking forward to the next thirty' column by Ruth Woodbury Sedgwick* - STAGE
From Hollywood - *developments* - EDUCATIONAL SCREEN
From My 10-20 - *column by Byron G. Wels* - CB LIFE
From Our Colleagues - *letters* - AFRO-ASIAN JOURNALIST
From Our Letter Box - COLORADO EDITOR
From Our Mailbag - *letters to S. L. Rothafel 'Roxy'* - ROXY THEATRE WEEKLY REVIEW
From Our Readers - *letters to the editor* - HOME ENTERTAINMENT
From Our Readers - *letters* - MAST
From Our Readers - *letters* - MOVIE HUMOR
From PA's Point of View - *opinion* - PROFITABLE ADVERTISING
From the AAYPP Executive Director - YELLOW PAGES UPDATE
From the Audience - *'Letters to the editor'* - SHOW BUSINESS ILLUSTRATED
From the Bench - *readers technical suggestions* - COMMUNICATIONS
From the Chair - *chair's column by John L. Huffman* - COMMUNICATION LAW & POLICY NEWSLETTER

Departments

From the Chair - *chair commentary column by Patricia M. Reilly* - COMMUNICATIONS LAWYER
From the Chair - *PRSSA Chairman's column* - FORUM
From the Chair - *editorial and commentary column by Gary Kreps* - HEALTH COMMUNICATION NEWSLETTER
From the Chairman - COMMUNICATOR
From the Clubhouse - *newsbriefs* - AMERICAN CINEMATOGRAPHER
From the Copy Desk - RIGHTING WORDS
From the Desktop - *editorial column by Robert Mueller* - PC PUBLISHING AND PRESENTATIONS
From the Desktop - *desktop publishing column by Gary Olsen* - PRE-
From the Director - *editorial* - AMERICAN FILM
From the Director - RANGEFINDER, THE
From the Director's Chair - *commentary* - VIDEO CAPSULE
From the Division Chair - *divisional chair column by Robert L. Savage* - POLITICAL COMMUNICATION NEWSLETTER
From the Editor - ADVANCED IMAGING
From the Editor - *editorial column by Howard Kunin* - AMERICAN CINEMEDITOR
From the Editor - *editorial column by Joni Bodart* - BOOKTALKER, THE
From the Editor - BUSINESS INFORMATION ALERT
From the Editor - *column by Richard Lytle* - CMA NEWSLETTER
From the Editor - *editorial column by Paul E. Kostyu* - COMMUNICATION LAW & POLICY NEWSLETTER
From the Editor - EXPOSURE
From the Editor - *editorial* - FILM WITNESS
From the Editor - HD SYSTEMS WORLD REVIEW
From the Editor - *editorial column by Wendy Erickson* - ILFORD PHOTO INSTRUCTOR NEWSLETTER
From the Editor - INTERNATIONAL CABLE
From the Editor - JOURNAL OF MARKETING EDUCATION
From the Editor - LIGHTING DIMENSIONS
From the Editor - *editorial column by Ronald C. Brent* - MAST
From the Editor - MEMORIES
From the Editor - MIX
From the Editor - *column by Marsha Daly* - PHOTO SCREEN
From the Editor - RANGEFINDER, THE
From the Editor - *editorial column by John F. Andrews* - SHAKESPEARE QUARTERLY
From the Editor to You - FILM MONTHLY
From the Editorial Viewpoint - RADIO DEALER, THE
From the Editors - ADWEEK'S MARKETING WEEK
From the Editors - DEBUT
From the Editors - *editorial comment* - TV SHOW
From the Editor's Desk - *a reader interest column by Harry Shorten* - AFTERNOON TV
From the Editor's Desk - *editorial column by Patricia Lane* - INFORMATION TODAY
From the Editor's Desk - *editorial* - PERSONAL ELECTRONICS
From the Editor's Desk - SOAP OPERA PEOPLE
From the Editor's Easy Chair - *large viewpoint column by Welford Beaton* - HOLLYWOOD SPECTATOR
From the Editor's Pen - KINEMATOGRAPH WEEKLY
From the Field Manager's Office - COLORADO EDITOR
From the Film Centres - FILMFARE
From the Font - *column by Keith Baumann* - DESKTOP COMMUNICATIONS
From the Green Dome - *editorial column by David Caruba* - TOP SECRET
From the Greenroom - *author profiles* - THEATRE CRAFTS
From the July Magazines - DRAMATIC MAGAZINE, THE
From the Lab - *column by Martin Hershenson* - INDUSTRIAL PHOTOGRAPHY
From the Lab - *information feature* - TECHNICAL PHOTOGRAPHY
From the Mailbag - *letters* - NATIONAL PHOTOGRAPHER, THE
From the Music Capitols of the World - *briefs* - BILLBOARD
From the President - AEJMC NEWS
From the President - *column by Lesley Marcello* - CMA NEWSLETTER
From the President - COMMUNICATOR, THE
From the President - DEBUT
From the President - EDITORIALIST, THE
From the President - WSCA NEWS
From the PROphiles - *editorial/publisher column by Marjorie Costello* - VIDEO PROPHILES
From the Publisher - ADVERTISING AGENCY
From the Publisher - ART & DESIGN NEWS
From the Publisher - CINEMA THE WORLD OVER
From the Publisher - *editorial* - MSO'S CABLE MARKETING
From the Publisher - *editorial column by Huntington Hartford* - SHOW
From the States - *individual state member news items* - TELEMEMO
From the Technical Bench - *technology* - PRODUCTION SOUND REPORT
From the Technical Service Editor - *technical Q&A on radio reception and setup* - RURAL RADIO
From the Top - *editorial* - REP: RECORDING ENGINEERING PRODUCTION
From the Trenches - *column by Alan Peterson* - RADIO WORLD
From the Vice President - *column by Laura Widmer* - CMA NEWSLETTER
From the Vice President for Member Services - *column by Terry Vander Heyden* - CMA NEWSLETTER
From the World of the Press, Radio and Television - JOURNALISTS' AFFAIRS
From the World's Wireless Journals - *abstract briefs* - INDUSTRIAL ELECTRONICS
From Washington - CABLEVISION
From Washington - *regulatory news* - ELECTRONIC DESIGN
From Where You Sit - *column by Steve Birchall* - HOME ENTERTAINMENT
Front Desk, The - *'A monthly digest of news, information, stories, production details and the occasional slice of madness.'* - EMPIRE
Front End, The - *editorial* - CAR STEREO REVIEW
Front Lines - *editorial* - HIGH FIDELITY
Front Page - *news concerning black format radio* - BLACK RADIO EXCLUSIVE
Front Page, The - *unique feature detailing film/video production or equipment in the news* - MILLIMETER
Frontispiece - JOURNALIST, THE
Frontline - *indepth look at specific aspect of cable television operation* - MSO'S CABLE MARKETING
Frontlines - *guest commentary* - AMERICAN THEATRE
Fronts West - *column by Mark O'Neill* - CINEMA/CANADA
FrontTALK - *managing editor column by Steve Yahn* - BUSINESS MARKETING
F-Stop - *production stories* - STUDIO PHOTOGRAPHY
Full Reviews - ABSOLUTE SOUND, THE
Full Size Blueprints - AMATEUR WIRELESS AND RADIOVISION
Full-Service AC - *Adult contemporary hit list* - R & R
Fun and Games - CELEBRITY
Function and Role of the Student Press, The - JOURNALISTS' AFFAIRS
Funding - *grants, awards, and fund information* - CASTING NEWS
Funniest Animal: or, What Passes for *Funnyworld*'s Editorial Page, The - FUNNYWORLD
Funny Book Roulette - *detailed critiques of current releases* - COMICS JOURNAL, THE
Funny Stuff - *editorial column by Perry Bradford-Wilson and Michael Kunz* - COMIC RELIEF
Further Information - *where to write* - BASELINE
Future Events - LÜRZER'S INTERNATIONAL ARCHIVE
Future Festivals - FILMMAKERS FILM & VIDEO MONTHLY
Future Films - BOOKS AND FILMS
Future Films - *announced projects* - VARIETY
Future Shock - *upcoming articles* - GOREZONE
Future Tech - *column by David Ranada* - VIDEO PROPHILES
Future Trends - *potential trends affecting radio management* - RADIO ONLY
Future Watch - *column by Linda Jacobson* - EQ
Futurehome - FUTUREHOME TECHNOLOGY NEWS

Futures - MEDIAWEEK
F/X Comics - *a page of comics* - COMICS FANDOM EXAMINER
FYI - *artist profiles* - CD REVIEW
FYI - *newsbriefs* - COLORADO EDITOR
FYI - *upcoming events* - CORPORATE TELEVISION
FYI - *newsbriefs* - MSO'S CABLE MARKETING
FYI - NEWSLETTER
FYI - *'National news, quotes and comments'* - PHOTO/DESIGN
FYI - *people, equipment, production, and company newsbriefs* - TV TECHNOLOGY
FYI - *commentary* - UPI ADVANCE
FYI Books - *column by Jonathan Barkey* - PHOTO/DESIGN
FYI Charts - MAST
FYI Shows - *column by Jonathan Barkey* - PHOTO/DESIGN

G

GA! Feature Guide - *feature animated films in progress* - GET ANIMATED! UPDATE.
GA! Newsreel - *animation newsbriefs* - GET ANIMATED! UPDATE.
Gadget Bag - *column by George Lepp* - OUTDOOR PHOTOGRAPHER
Gadgets, Kinks, and Shortcuts - *ideas to clip* - MODERN PHOTOGRAPHY
Gallery - *photo essay* - AMERICAN PHOTO
Gallery - *'guide, products, news'* - CREATIVE CAMERA
Gallery - *reader submissions* - DESKTOP COMMUNICATIONS
Gallery - *showcase* - HOW
Gallery - *images of time past* - MEMORIES
Gallery - *new graphic products* - PERSONAL PUBLISHING
Gallery - PRE-
Gallery - *artist profiles* - RADIO ALBUM MAGAZINE
Gallery of Advertising Displays - ADVERTISING DISPLAYS
Gallery of Famous Film Folk - *duotone green of Hollywood's famous* - NEW MOVIE MAGAZINE, THE
Gallifrey Guardian - DOCTOR WHO MAGAZINE
Gallup & Robinson - *column* - INSIDE MEDIA
Game Reviews - FACTSHEET FIVE
Gannett News Highlights - *corporate news briefs* - GANNETTEER
Garfield - *comment column by Bob Garfield* - ADVERTISING AGE
Gary Owens - *column* - R & R
Gateway - *news items* - LEONARDO
Gateway - *column by Stan Horzepa* - QEX
Gazette - JOURNALISM EDUCATOR, THE
Gazette - *column by Ira Robbins* - VIDEO MAGAZINE
Gene Owens' Political Crossword - NATIONAL FORUM, THE

General Advertisements - AMERICAN ADVERTISER
General Hospital - *abstract* - SOAP OPERA DIGEST
General Miscellany - *column by Frank J. Bachman* - SCHEMER, THE
General News - CONSUMER ELECTRONICS
General News - *newsbriefs* - EDUCATIONAL MEDIA INTERNATIONAL
General News - HOLLYWOOD FILMOGRAPH
General News - PRO SOUND NEWS
General News - TELEVISION BROADCAST
General News Items - ADVERTISERS GAZETTE
General Newspaper Items - *newsbriefs* - ADVERTISERS GAZETTE
General Orders of the Federal Radio Commission - *column by Arthur W. Scharfeld* - JOURNAL OF RADIO LAW
General Releases - *film description briefs* - SCREEN WEEKLY, THE
General Wants and Sales - KINEMATOGRAPH WEEKLY
General--Around the Industry - *news* - INTERSPACE
Germany / France - *comic and artist news* - ARK
Germany West - *city review column by Horst Koegler* - AFTER DARK
Gerry-Meandering - *written by the WNPA manager* - WASHINGTON NEWSPAPER, THE
Get Involved - *letters* - DISNEY CHANNEL MAGAZINE, THE
Getting Employees Involved - PRINTING IMPRESSIONS
Getting Involved - MEDIA & VALUES
Getting More From Your Dish - SATELLITE ORBIT
Getting the Most Out of Business Television - *column by Gwenn Kelly* - TELESPAN'S BUSINESSTV GUIDE
Getting the Picture - *column by Don Lake* - ADVANCED IMAGING
Getting to Know You - *penpal listing column by Mhalou Gutierrez* - SOSYALI MAGAZINE
Ghostal Mail - *v-e-r-y unusual letters to the editor* - CASTLE OF FRANKENSTEIN
Gifts - BROADCAST PIONEERS LIBRARY REPORTS
Gifts of Fragrance - THEATRE MAGAZINE
Gilding a Radio Lily - *fashions* - TV MIRROR
Girl on the Cover, The - *picture profile* - FILM FUN
Girls Make News - *Hollywood stars and starlets in the news* - FILM FUN
Giving - GF MAGAZINE
Glamour Gallery - FILM ALBUM MAGAZINE
Glen Pensinger - *post production column by Glen Pensinger* - TELEVISION BROADCAST
Global Culture - WORLD PRESS REVIEW
Global Gallery - *'Creative advertising from around the world'* - ADVERTISING AGE
Global Gossip - *'Whether it's happening in Paris, London, or even Timbuktu, Our Man is on the scene to give you the lowdown on the swinging jetsetters!'* - GOSSIP
Global Marketplace - WORLD BROADCAST NEWS

Global News - TELECOMMUNICATIONS
Globe Girdling - ALL-WAVE RADIO
Globecasting - *news of world-international broadcast developments* - BROADCAST ENGINEERING
Glossary - *'CD-ROM buzzwords you should know'* - CD-ROM
GMA Record Guide, The - *an independent review service provided by Goldwyn Morales Azul* - MOVIE FLASH
Go Go Girls! - *female artist news* - SUPER TEEN
Go Out to a Movie - *guide* - PHOTOPLAY
Going Hollywood - *column by May Mann* - MOVIE FAN
Going on Record - *column by James Goodfriend* - STEREO REVIEW
Goings On - *gossip* - FILMWORLD
Gold Key News - *product newsbriefs* - COMIC READER, THE
Gold-Based AC - *Adult contemporary hit list* - R & R
Golden Gate Glitters - THEATRE CRAFT
Golden Moments - 60 SECONDS
Good English and Its Use - *instructional column by Hazel Spencer* - STORY WORLD AND PHOTODRAMATIST, THE
Good Ideas for Advertisers - ADWEEK
Good Old Days in the Kitchen - *recipes and rememberences* - GOOD OLD DAYS
Good Reading - *'Books, pamphlets, booklets, flyers, bulletins and application notes' column by Tim Cartwright* - ELECTRONICS ILLUSTRATED
Good Rockin' Tonight - *'Sh-Boom reviews the heart & sould of rock 'n roll'* - SH-BOOM
Good Words - *published reviews* - THEATRE, THE
Goods & Services - MAGAZINE DESIGN & PRODUCTION
Gore Scoreboard - *unique four-skull horror film rating system* - DEEP RED
Gospel Truth - ENTERTAINMENT CONNECTION MAGAZINE
Gossip - DRAMATIC REVIEW, THE
Gossip - *'Hot reviews, hot gossip from the movie scene'* - FILM REVIEW
Gossip, The - *east coast column by Pat Sellers* - SOAP OPERA WEEKLY
Gossip - VIDEO--THE MAGAZINE
Gossip Guide - TELEVISION AND SCREEN GUIDE
Gossip in the Lobby - MOVIE SHOW
Gossip of Itinerants - *'told by the nomads of journalism'* - AMERICAN JOURNALIST, THE
Gossip of the Studios - *'All the news of the famous motion picture stars and their Hollywood activities' [and] 'The Hollywood Who's Who--and What the film famous are doing in the movie capital'* - NEW MOVIE MAGAZINE, THE
Gossip Street - *'From Hollywood boulevard to Times Square'* - PHOTODRAMATIST, THE
Gossip-Gathering on Film Boulevard - MOVING PICTURE AGE
Gossip--Hollywood is Talking About - MOVIE MIRROR

Gotham Bugle - *'Happenings in the little village of New York and there-abouts' column by Joe Weil* - UNIVERSAL WEEKLY
Government - *excellent feature on government and theatre* - AMERICAN THEATRE
Government Affairs - PRESSTIME
Government & Industry News - COLLEGE BROADCASTER
Government & Law - CABLEVISION
Government News - *excellent regulatory review* - COMMUNICATIONS INDUSTRIES REPORT, THE
Government Printing - PRINTING IMPRESSIONS
Grab Shots - *column by Norma Edwards* - CAMERA & DARKROOM PHOTOGRAPHY
Grab Shots - *newsbriefs* - DARKROOM PHOTOGRAPHY
Grabshot - *as in 'grabbed any good shots?'* - MODERN PHOTOGRAPHY
Grabshots - CAMERA & DARKROOM PHOTOGRAPHY
Grain Reports - *program guide* - RURAL RADIO
Grand Analysis - PRESS STATISTICAL REVIEW
Grants - PUBLIC BROADCASTING REPORT, THE
Grants - *received and work in-progress* - SPECTRA
Grapevine - BLACK RADIO EXCLUSIVE
Grapevine, The - *gossip* - CAMPAIGN
Grapevine - *newsbriefs* - RANGEFINDER, THE
Grapevine - *column by Marilyn Beck* - TV GUIDE
Grapevine - VIDEODISC MONITOR, THE
Grapevine - *romance author activity column by Jennifer McCord* - W•B
Graphic Arts Financial - *newsbriefs* - CANADIAN PRINTER
Graphic Design People - *personnel newsbriefs* - GRAPHIC DESIGN: USA
Graphic Eye, The - STEP-BY-STEP ELECTRONIC DESIGN
Graphic Guides - *how-to via cartoons by DCR* - COMICS CAREER NEWSLETTER
Graphic Review - PREVUE
Graphics - INVIEW
Graphics - INVISION
Graphics - *column by Ron LaFon* - PC PUBLISHING AND PRESENTATIONS
Graphics - TELEVISION BROADCAST
Graphics Action - *agency account activity* - GRAPHIC DESIGN: USA
Graphics & Animation - POST
Graphics & Effects - MILLIMETER
Graphics Arts Securities - PRINTING IMPRESSIONS
Graphics Calendar - COMPUTER PICTURES
Graphics Calendar - GRAPHICS: U.S.A.
Graphics Creations - COMPUTER PICTURES
Graphics Mode - *column by Toni Will-Harris and Daniel Will-Harris* - VENTURA PROFESSIONAL!
Graphics People - *profiles* - FLASH
Graphics Update - *newsbriefs* - COMPUTER PICTURES
Graphics Update - *newsbriefs column by Gordon D. Kaye* - GRAPHIC DESIGN: USA

Grass Route - *retail news* - BILLBOARD
Great American Cinemas - *wonderful section concerning restored cinema theatres* - AMERICAN MOVIE CLASSICS MAGAZINE
Great Idea - *reader's tech ideas* - RADIO WORLD
Great Idea Contest - *the technical minded vie for prizes with new engineering concepts* - BME'S TELEVISION ENGINEERING
Great Ideas - PSA
Great Life, The - *personality news of Hollywood and west coast* - HOLLYWOOD REPORTER
Green Diary, The - *'The monthly happenings of a suburban maintenance gardener'* - SATELLITE TIMES
Green Room - *newsbriefs* - PLAYS AND PLAYERS
Greetings From Iola - *editorial commentary column by Deb Lengkeek* - POSTCARD COLLECTOR
Grooming - *column by Alex Press* - MGF
Groove Views - *album reviews* - MODERN RECORDING & MUSIC
Grounded Ear, The - *'what's new in sound reproduction* - AUDIOCRAFT FOR THE HI-FI HOBBYIST
Group Test - *video testbench* - VIDEO ANSWERS
Grumbler, The - *commentary* - DRAMATIC REVIEW, THE
Guess Who! - *'trivia persuassion'* - INTERNATIONAL ADVERTISER
Guest Column - FILM COMMENT
Guest Column - *commentary* - PULSE OF RADIO
Guest Column - TELEVISION BROADCAST
Guest Columnist - HORRORFAN
Guest Editor - ADVERTISER MAGAZINE, THE
Guest Editorial - COMIC INFORMER
Guest Editorial - CORPORATE TELEVISION
Guest Editorial - EQ
Guest Editorial - FOUR A NEWSLETTER
Guest Editorial - REP: RECORDING ENGINEERING PRODUCTION
Guest Essay - OFF-HOLLYWOOD REPORT
Guest Gag Bag - *guest-submitted jokes and puns* - RADIO HIT SONGS
Guest Shots - *review* - SCARLET STREET
Guest Spot - *guest commentary* - COMICS SCENE
Guest Star - *column* - CABLE GUIDE, THE
Guest Star - *commentary* - TV ENTERTAINMENT
Guide Lines - *review* - PETERSEN'S PHOTOGRAPHIC
Guide to... - FILM MAKING
Guide to Glamour - SCREENLAND PLUS TV-LAND
Guide to the Best Films - *'Brief comments upon the leading motion pictures of the last six months'* - NEW MOVIE MAGAZINE, THE
Guidelines - *column by Frank Barnako* - VIDEO STORE
Guiding Light - *abstract* - SOAP OPERA DIGEST

Guild Forum, The - *news of the Screen Writers' Guild* - PHOTODRAMATIST, THE
Gut Reactions - *letters* - GOREZONE

H

H. H. Van Loan's Own Corner - *comment* - STORY WORLD AND PHOTODRAMATIST, THE
Hailing Frequencies - *letters* - SF MOVIELAND
Half-Hour Experiments - PRACTICAL WIRELESS
Hall of Shame - FACTSHEET FIVE
Ham Clinic - *Q&A on equipment* - CQ
Ham Column, The - *'Getting started as a radio amateur'* - POPULAR COMMUNICATIONS
Ham Radio - *column by Joseph J. Carr* - POPULAR ELECTRONICS
Ham Shack, The - *column by Wayne Green* - ELECTRONICS ILLUSTRATED
Ham Shop - *classifieds* - CQ
Hamfest Calendar - QST
Hamlet - STAGE AND TELEVISION TODAY, THE
Hammer News - *news items concerning Hammer Film Productions, Ltd* - LITTLE SHOPPE OF HORRORS
Hands On - *equipment review* - SOUND & IMAGE
Hands On - VIDEOGRAPHY
Hands-On Fonts - *column by David Dean* - PC PUBLISHING AND PRESENTATIONS
Hands-On Graphics - *column by Ron LaFon* - PC PUBLISHING AND PRESENTATIONS
Hands-On Pagemaker - *column by Keith Thompson* - PC PUBLISHING AND PRESENTATIONS
Hands-On Postscript - *column by Ross Smith* - PC PUBLISHING AND PRESENTATIONS
Hands-On Production - *Creative Workshop column by Michael Marans* - EQ
Hands-On Reviews - PC PUBLISHING AND PRESENTATIONS
Hands-On Ventura - *column by Rick Altman* - PC PUBLISHING AND PRESENTATIONS
Hang Up Page, The - *humorous column by Bell Boy* - TELEPHONE NEWS, THE
Hanson on Magazines - *column by J. J. Hanson* - FOLIO:
Happenings - *current issues column by W. Clift* - QST
Happy Returns - *'Sarah Shankman on books, Mike Barlow on video, Chip Stern on classic cuts'* - JOE FRANKLIN'S NOSTALGIA
Hardcopy - *book reviews* - ACCESS
Hardware - COMPUTER PICTURES
Hardware - *equipment reviews* - MEDIA DIGEST

Hardware - *review column by Telka Perry and Owen R. Rubin* - ORBIT VIDEO
Hardware - *reviews* - VIDEO MANAGEMENT
Hardware & Accessories - VIDEO SOFTWARE MAGAZINE
Hardware Hacker - *Fascinating comment column by Don Lancaster* - RADIO-ELECTRONICS
Hardware Report - *equipment briefs* - VIDEO INFO
Hardware Review - VIDEOGRAPHY
Harlequin - *trivia column by Jim Korkis* - ANIMATO!
Harpoonist, The - *ad critique* - AGRICULTURAL ADVERTISING
Hartford - BOX OFFICE
Harvey Coming Comics - COMIC READER, THE
Hate Mail - *letters* - FILM THREAT
Have Power, Will Travel - *portable electronics column by David Miller* - VISIO
Have You Heard About - *employee profiles* - TELEPHONE NEWS, THE
Have You Heard? - *Hollywood star activities column by Joyce Becker* - SCREEN LIFE
Have You Heard? - *'The word from NY and LA'* - SOAP OPERA STARS
Have You Heard? - *Soap opera newsbriefs* - STAR
Having a Fine Time In - *travel postcards column by Tom Range* - POSTCARD COLLECTOR
Head Shot - *profile* - ON LOCATION
Head to Head - *competitive review* - AUDIOPHILE WITH HI-FI ANSWERS
Headline Happenings - *briefs with photos* - MODERN SCREEN
Headline News - VIDEOGRAPHY
Headliners - *profile* - BROADCAST
Headlines - COMICS FEATURE
Headlines and Phrases - *'from the pens of those who know how to pull business'* - AD SENSE
Headnotes - *guest column* - IBE
Headnotes - *comment* - MEDIA LAW NOTES
Headphones - SOUND & VISION
Headroom - *column by Ken Kessler* - HI-FI NEWS AND RECORD REVIEW
Heads You Win - RIGHTING WORDS
Health - FAME
Health & Fitness - *videocassette review* - V
Health Beat - *column by Stephen Langer (MD)* - NATIONAL EXAMINER
Heard About Hollywood - *'Hollywood Hotline' column by Eliot Stein* - SPOTLIGHT ON VIDEO
Heard Along Broadway - *gossip* - BROADWAY WEEKLY
Heard on Broadway - *'The tattle and trivia of the nation's theatrical main street' column by Ward Morehouse* - THEATRE MAGAZINE
Heard on the New York Rialto - *from the New York office* - DRAMATIC REVIEW, THE
Heard on the 'Phone - *trade rumours* - KINEMATOGRAPH WEEKLY

Hearing Calendar - NARTB MEMBER SERVICE
Hearings During Past Week - BROADCAST REPORTER
Heavenly Stars - *personal horoscopes* - MODERN SCREEN
Heavenly Stars - *a horoscope for stars and their readers* - WHO'S WHO IN MOVIES AND TV
Heaviest Saturation - *'Tracer Tracks 1-40, and Newcomers, with a song-by-song analysis of those stations reaching the most audience with its airplay'* - MONDAY MORNING REPLAY
Hellbox - *some not so applaudable journalistic efforts* - MORE
Hello - *editorial column by William Connolly* - SPAGHETTI CINEMA
Hello, Friends - *editorial column by Bessie Little* - FILMLAND
Hello, Friends - *editorial column by Bessie Little* - TV PEOPLE AND PICTURES
Hello, Friends - *commentary column by Bessie Little* - TV WORLD
Hellyer's Clinic - *problem solving* - TAPE
Help - *reader-submitted technical Q&A* - POPULAR PHOTOGRAPHY
Help Menu - *Q&A help* - VENTURA PROFESSIONAL!
Help! - POPULAR PHOTOGRAPHY
Helpful Hints - TRAVEL & LEISURE
Helpful Information - MARKETING / COMMUNICATIONS
Helpline - *Q&A column by Terry James* - CAMCORDER USER
Helpline - *Q&A column by Eugene Trundle* - VIDEO ANSWERS
Helps and Hints for the Director - PLAYERS
Here - *commentary* - ST. LOUIS JOURNALISM REVIEW
Here and There - *personnel items* - OFFICIAL BULLETIN OF THE INTERNATIONAL ALLIANCE OF THEATRICAL STAGE EMPLOYEES AND MOVING PICTURE MACHINE OPERATORS OF THE UNITED STATES AND CANADA.
Here and There - *newsbriefs* - PRACTICAL WIRELESS
Here It Is - *'Pocket reviews'* - THEATRE CRAFT
Here's How - CAMERA MAGAZINE
Here's What They Do - *column by Spencer Hare* - GREATER AMUSEMENTS
Hero Takes - *newsbriefs on special effects and animation* - ON LOCATION
Hic et Ubique - POST OFFICE MAGAZINE
Hi-Fi for Beginners - HI-FI NEWS AND RECORD REVIEW
Hi-Fi Guide - HI-FI SOUND
Hi-Fi Postbag - *letters* - HI-FI SOUND
Hi-Fi Video Library - *literature* - PERSONAL ELECTRONICS
Hi-Fi Video News - PERSONAL ELECTRONICS
HiFi-Crostic - *puzzle column by William Peterson* - HIGH FIDELITY
High End, The - *chart and products* - DIGITAL EVOLUTION MAGAZINE
High End, The - *commentary column by Ralph Hodges* - STEREO REVIEW

High Fidelity News - *newsbriefs* - HIGH FIDELITY
High Frequency - MONITOR INTERNATIONAL
High Seas - *Ocean communication column by James R. Hay* - MONITORING TIMES
Highlights - *picture and news page* - AFTER DARK
Highlights - *newsbriefs* - BRITISH COMMUNICATIONS AND ELECTRONICS
Highlights - *for the upcoming month* - CABLE GUIDE, THE
Highlights - ELECTRONICS
Highlights - *film reviews* - MOVING PICTURE AGE
Highlights - ON CABLE
Highlights - *late breaking news items* - PUBLISHER'S WEEKLY
Highlights - *article synopses* - SMPTE JOURNAL
Highlights - *'Tops on the tube'* - TV ENTERTAINMENT
Highlights for.. - MASS MEDIA NEWSLETTER
Highlights of the News - BROADCAST REPORTER
High-Tech Q&A - VIDEO REVIEW
Hints and Kinks - *technical trouble-shooting* - QST
Hints and Kinks for the Experimenter - OLD TIMER'S BULLETIN, THE
Hints to Beginners - AMERICAN PHOTOGRAPHY
Hiring & Training - SALES & MARKETING MANAGEMENT
Historic Resources Marketplace - *an interesting 'want-ad' section offering old newspapers, magazines, letters and other printed items for sale* - MASTHEAD
Historical Artifacts - *for sale* - OLD TIMER'S BULLETIN, THE
Historical Romance Ratings - ROMANTIC TIMES
History - *a short description of the publication* - WHAT EDITORS WANT
History & Current Events - FILM & VIDEO NEWS
History of Preaching - *reviews* - HOMILETIC
History of the Stage - MIRROR OF TASTE, AND DRAMATIC CENSOR, THE
History Romance Reviews - ROMANTIC TIMES
Hit List, The - HI-FI ANSWERS
Hit or Miss - *'On the mark or off the track, our editors make the call'* - SOAP OPERA WEEKLY
Hit or Miss - *new direct mail projects* - TARGET MARKETING
Hit Parade - *'An alphabetical listing of the Broadway shows, some old, some new'* - STAGE PICTORIAL
Hit Parader Band Wagon of Top Tunes, The - *full text without music* - HIT PARADER
Hit Parader Gives You the Song of the Month - *showcased* - HIT PARADER
Hi-Tech News - *newsbriefs* - WHAT VIDEO
Hither and Yon - *BMI newsbriefs* - BMI: MUSICWORLD
Hits of the World - *international playlist* - BILLBOARD

Departments INDEX

Hobbies - *very unique listing of hobby-related television programs* - SATELLITE TV WEEK

Hogan - *column by Robert W. Hogan* - INSIDE MEDIA

Holding Pattern - *column by James Monaco* - TAKE ONE

Hollywood - *'News and views of the productiooon center'* - BOXOFFICE

Hollywood - *news items* - MOVIE - THE VIDEO MAGAZINE

Hollywood - *news briefs* - MOVIE/TV MARKETING

Hollywood - *newsbriefs* - ON CABLE

Hollywood After Dark - *Hollywood star activities column by Joey Sasso* - SCREEN LIFE

Hollywood Bandstand - *big bands and personalities in Hollywood motion pictures, column by Paul Vandervoort* - BAND LEADERS

Hollywood Beauty Hints - PHOTO SCREEN

Hollywood Boulevardier, The - *'Mr. Howe writes from Paris on film people and events' column by Herb Howe* - NEW MOVIE MAGAZINE, THE

Hollywood Bulletin - *newsbriefs* - EXPERIMENTAL CINEMA

Hollywood Chatter - SCREEN STARS

Hollywood Cinefile - *column by Leonard Klady* - SCREEN INTERNATIONAL

Hollywood Classifieds - *readers offer star items for trade or sale* - PREVIEW

Hollywood Comes Home - *'A column on home movies' column by George Yost* - LENS MAGAZINE

Hollywood Diary - *stars and stories of yesteryear* - INSIDE HOLLYWOOD

Hollywood Diary - *chatty gossip of studio inside happenings* - UNION LABOR SUN

Hollywood Earfuls - *Hollywood gossip column by Bee Bangs* - SILVER SCREEN

Hollywood Evesdropper - *'Off-the record and ultra- private quotes from your favorite stars!'* - MODERN SCREEN

Hollywood Fashion Vane - PHOTOPLAY

Hollywood Filmmakers: Who's Who - *listing* - SHOW BUSINESS

Hollywood Flashes - *newsbriefs* - FILM TV DAILY

Hollywood Focus - *column by Linda Moss* - NATIONAL EXAMINER

Hollywood Happenings - *newsbriefs* - BOX OFFICE

Hollywood Happenings - *column by Billie Singer* - SOAP OPERA DIGEST

Hollywood Heart Beat - *music in the movies column by Joanne Linder* - HIT PARADER

Hollywood High Lights - *'Peaks of interest in news of the studios' column by Edwin Schallert and Elza Schallert* - PICTURE PLAY MAGAZINE

Hollywood High Tech - *column by I. M. Hacker* - HOLLYWOOD MAGAZINE

Hollywood Highlights - *gossip by The Boulevardier* - MOVIE CLASSIC

Hollywood Hit Line - *personality and production news column by Steven Rea* - HOME VIEWER

Hollywood, Hollywood - *gossip* - PREVIEW

Hollywood Hot Line - *column by Evan Grant* - SCREENLAND PLUS TV-LAND

Hollywood Hotline - *'Boze Hadleigh reports from Beverly Hills'* - FILM MONTHLY

Hollywood Hotline - *'All the freshest gossip -- fresh from our tinseltown snoop'* - TEEN DREAM

Hollywood Hotline - *'Gossip, scandal, news-- read it here first' column by Kevin Wilson* - TV GUIDE

Hollywood Hotline - *'Every month, Howie Weiss--friend of the stars--brings us all the latest news from Hollywood: sneak previews, new faces, tips for the top, whos talking to whom and, of course, all the gossip we're allowed to print'* - TV HITS

Hollywood, Inc. - CHANNELS

Hollywood Ink - *Hollywood chatter column by Ignatz* - MOVIELINE

Hollywood Insider - *'Squeals 'n' squabbles, rumours 'n' rumbles'* - INSIDE HOLLYWOOD

Hollywood Insider - PHOTO SCREEN

Hollywood Kids, The - *hot gossip, Hollywood-style* - EMPIRE

Hollywood Kids, The - *Hollywood chatter* - MOVIELINE

Hollywood Kids - MOVIELINE

Hollywood Life - *column by Carl Schroeder* - TELEVISION AND SCREEN GUIDE

Hollywood Newsreel - HOLLYWOOD

Hollywood Newsreel - SHOWMEN'S TRADE REVIEW

Hollywood Notebook - TV WORLD

Hollywood Now - *news and information column by Debi Fee* - FRESH!

Hollywood on the Air - *column by Favius Friedman* - TV SCREEN

Hollywood Radio Whispers - *gossip column by George Fisher* - TV RADIO MIRROR

Hollywood Remembered - AMERICAN PREMIERE

Hollywood Report - *news of upcoming films* - BOX OFFICE

Hollywood Report - *column by Martin Grove* - HOLLYWOOD REPORTER

Hollywood Report - *column by Louis Hochman* - POPULAR PHOTOGRAPHY

Hollywood Reporter Box Office, The - BILLBOARD

Hollywood Reporting - *column by Jean Doran* - CASTING CALL

Hollywood Scene, The - *started, shooting, and completed film projects listed via studio* - MOTION PICTURE HERALD

Hollywood Scene - *column by Marilyn Beck and Stacy Jenel Smith* - ONSAT

Hollywood Secrets - *'Here's the inside on all the gossip' column by Edith Gwynn* - FILMLAND

Hollywood Tattletale - *personality column by The Insider* - FILMLAND

Hollywood Tele-views - TELESCREEN

Hollywood Today - *gossip column by Snooper* - MOTION PICTURE

Hollywood Triangle - *'We never let a rumor go unfounded'* - MOTION PICTURE

Hollywood Tunes - *music news column by Madame Octave* - EXHIBITORS HERALD WORLD

Hollywood Turns On With Toni Holt - TONI HOLT'S MOVIE LIFE

Home Electronics - ON CABLE

Home Entertainment Visits - *home profiles* - HOME ENTERTAINMENT

Home News - *British puppet-related news* - ANIMATIONS

Home Office, The - *column by Janet Endrijonas* - VISIO

Home Office News Items - PARAMOUNT WORLD

Home Screen, The - *new developments* - VIDEOGRAPHY

Home Theater - *column by Mark Fleischmann* - AUDIO/VIDEO INTERIORS

Home Theater - *'Your guide to the hottest item in consumer electronics'* - SATELLITE ORBIT

Home Town Stories of the Stars - *star roots* - NEW MOVIE MAGAZINE, THE

Home Video - BILLBOARD

Home Video - *new product releases* - CINEASTE

Home Video Directory - *a large section detailing releases* - ANIMATION MAGAZINE

Home Viewer Guide - *'Every new video release'* - HOME VIEWER

Homescreen - *information concerning home software- hardware* - CINEGRAM

Homevideo - VARIETY

Homevideo Review - VARIETY

Homework - MEDIAWEEK

Hong Kong - *briefs* - MOVIE/TV MARKETING

Honolulu - *film news of the islands* - MOVIE/TV MARKETING

Honor Roll Notes - TELEPHONE NEWS, THE

Honoured Names - *pictures* - PLAYS AND PLAYERS

Horoscope - *two week schedule* - INSIDE MEDIA

Horoscope - *column by Patric Walker* - TV GUIDE

Horoscope For the Stars and For You - *column by Leigh Gregory* - TV PICTURE LIFE

Horoscope Highlights - CINEMA, VIDEO & CABLE MOVIE DIGEST

Horror - *review* - ORBIT VIDEO

Horror Reviews - VIDEO TODAY

HorrorScope - *what's new in horror films* - GOREZONE

Horse Feathers - *guest column* - MOVIES, THE

Hospitals Radio - TAPE

Hot 100 Sales & Airplay - BILLBOARD

Hot 100 Singles - *famed Billboard playlist compiled from retail stores, one-stop sales reports and radio playlists* - BILLBOARD

Hot 100 Singles Action - BILLBOARD

Hot 100 Singles Spotlight - *column by Michael Ellis* - BILLBOARD

Hot Adult Contemporary - BILLBOARD

INDEX — Departments

Hot & Col - *critical look at contemporary advertising* - APPLIED ARTS QUARTERLY
Hot & Cold Eye, The - *film reviews* - CTVD
Hot & Cold Eye - CTVD
Hot Country & Single Tracks - *'Compiled from a national sample of monitored country radio by Broadcast Data Systems'* - BILLBOARD
Hot Country LPs - *playlist* - BILLBOARD
Hot Country Singles - *playlist* - BILLBOARD
Hot Dance Breakouts - *chart* - BILLBOARD
Hot Dance Music - *club play and 12-inch singles sales* - BILLBOARD
Hot Dates - *'Editor's pick of top upcoming events'* - CABLE WORLD
Hot Flashes - *'Caught at the deadline'* - SILVER SCREEN
Hot From Hollywood - *gossip column by Al Jackson* - BEST OF FILM & VIDEO
Hot Gossip - *column by Simone* - SMASH HITS
Hot Latin LPs - *playlist* - BILLBOARD
Hot Latin Tracks - BILLBOARD
Hot Line - *Q&A column* - CLOSE-UP
Hot Line - *Washington, D.C. news* - COMMUNICATIONS NEWS
Hot Marketing IdeaStarters - RADIOTRENDS
Hot News - *'on car audio, security, cellular phones, or other auto electronics'* - CAR AUDIO AND ELECTRONICS
Hot Off the Desktop - WRITERS' JOURNAL
Hot Off the Press! - *unusual back-cover information page on black celebrities* - FRESH!
Hot on the Press - *'publication news'* - INTERNATIONAL ADVERTISER
Hot Picks! - SUPER TEEN
Hot Pre-Orders - VIDEO SOFTWARE MAGAZINE
Hot R&B Playlists - *'Sample playlists of the nation's largest urban radio stations'* - BILLBOARD
Hot R&B Singles - BILLBOARD
Hot R&B Singles Action - BILLBOARD
Hot R&B Singles Sales & Airplay - BILLBOARD
Hot Rap Singles - BILLBOARD
Hot Shorts - *'News and notes from the world of live art plus a special section on video'* - HIGH PERFORMANCE
Hot Shots - *outstanding photo submissions* - CAMERA & CAMCORDER MONTHLY
Hot Shots - CAMERA & DARKROOM PHOTOGRAPHY
Hot shots - *people making news* - MOVING IMAGE
Hot Shots - *pictures* - PHOTO DISTRICT NEWS
Hot Soul Singles - *playlist* - BILLBOARD
Hot Spot, The - *news of soap opera stars* - SOAP OPERA TIME
Hot Spots - *recent spot productions* - MILLIMETER
Hot Stuff - *letters* - SMASH HITS
Hot Takes - *promotion ideas* - MSO'S CABLE MARKETING
Hot Topics - COMICS CAREER NEWSLETTER
Hot Type - *guest commentary* - BOOKS & RELIGION
Hot Type - *newsbriefs* - NEWSINC.

Hot Type - *new type fonts* - PERSONAL PUBLISHING
Hot! Charts, The - *hottest young film and television stars* - SMASH HITS
Hotline Names - *personnel newsbriefs* - TARGET MARKETING
House & Garden - LÜRZER'S INTERNATIONAL ARCHIVE
House Beat - BACK STAGE/SHOOT
Houston - BOX OFFICE
How Did They Do That? - *fascinating how-to feature* - PC PUBLISHING AND PRESENTATIONS
How Hollywood Entertains - *column by Evelyn Gray* - NEW MOVIE MAGAZINE, THE
How Hollywood Flies - *column by Jane Hershey* - HOLLYWOOD MAGAZINE
How I Got Started - *in the communications hobby* - POPULAR COMMUNICATIONS
How It Works - *detailed lay explanation* - EQ
How Much Does It Really Cost? - *the price of props* - SOAP OPERA DIGEST
How the Shows are Doing on the Road - *road report* - DRAMATIC MIRROR, THE
How They've Changed - *star profile* - REAL LIFE/DAYTIMERS
How To - COMPUTER PICTURES
How to - *technique* - MODERN PHOTOGRAPHY
How to Light Commercial Photographs - COMMERCIAL PHOTOGRAPHER, THE
How to Subscribe - *to a variety of satellite services* - ONSAT
How to Write Advertisements - *'A department devoted to practical suggestions.' (5-01)* - COMMON SENSE
Howard Christensen - *column by Howard Christensen* - BROADCAST + TECHNOLOGY
Howard Fields - *trends and regulation column by Howard Fields* - TELEVISION BROADCAST
Howlin' - *'Letters to Roundup'* - ROUNDUP QUARTERLY
How's DX? - *column by Clarke Greene* - QST
Hows Your Advertising? - *column by George Griffin* - GRAPHIC ARTS MONTHLY
How-To - *'articles on techniques and marketing to address the needs of the event-type videographer'* - PRO VIDEOGRAM
How-To - THEATRE CRAFTS
How-To & Education - *videocassette review* - V
Human Sciences & Culture - *reviews* - HOMILETIC
Humanist View, A - *column by Lou Stettner* - CAMERA 35
Hunches - PEP
HVP Ad/Editorial - HIGH VOLUME PRINTING

I

I Remember - *rememberence of news events past via eyewitnesses to those events* - MEMORIES
I Want to Buy.. - POPULAR PHOTOGRAPHY
I Want to Know - *technical Q&A column by Joseph Bernsley* - ELECTRONICS WORLD
I, Witness - *fascinating first-person photographers report* - AMERICAN PHOTO
I Would Like to Know - PRINT EDUCATION MAGAZINE
IA Obituaries - INTERNATIONAL PROJECTIONIST
IAA Chapter News - *briefs* - INTERNATIONAL ADVERTISER, THE
IAMA - *presidents column* - ADVERTISING AND MARKETING MANAGEMENT
IAMA News - ADVERTISING AND MARKETING MANAGEMENT
Ian Shoales - *humor column by Ian Shoales* - COMIC RELIEF
IARU News - *'Devoted to the interests and activities of the International Amateur Radio Union'* - QST
IBE Worldwide - *studio profile* - IBE
IBEW Members in the News - *color pictures and newsbriefs* - IBEW JOURNAL
IC Update - ELECTRONIC PRODUCTS
ICEM News - *information concerning the International Council for Educational Media* - EDUCATIONAL MEDIA INTERNATIONAL
I'd Like to See More of... - *reader poll of favorite star* - TV RADIO SHOW
Idea a Day, An - *fascinating day-by-day listing of article possibilities, column by Frank A. Dickson* - WRITER'S DIGEST
Idea Exchange, The - *'Stunts, gadgets, formulae, short-cuts, just so long as they are original'* - PROFESSIONAL PHOTOGRAPHER, THE
Idea Exchange - *promotion ideas* - SCRIPPS HOWARD NEWS
Ideas - *new marketing concepts* - PHOTO MARKETING
Ideas and Images - *fascinating showcase for imaginative photography, column by Jonathan Barkey* - PHOTO/DESIGN
Ideas for Design - ELECTRONIC DESIGN
Ideas for Live Wire Retailers - RADIO DEALER, THE
Ideas for Publishers - *new concepts in typography and formats* - PUBLISHER'S AUXILIARY
Ideas for Retailers - *advice column by Murray Raphel* - DIRECT MARKETING
Ideas That Work - COMMUNICATIONS CONCEPTS
Ideas You Can Use - *exploitation concepts* - MIDWEEK MOTION PICTURE NEWS
Identification and Value - *of equipment items* - OLD TIMER'S BULLETIN, THE
Ideological Massage - *reviews* - WOMEN & FILM

Departments INDEX

IEEE Standards - IEEE SPECTRUM
If Rumors Were Horses - *newsbriefs* - AGAINST THE GRAIN
If You Ask Me - CLIO MAGAZINE
Ike Ink - *column by Ike Pappas* - TELESPAN'S BUSINESSTV GUIDE
Illuminations - *'notes and essays from around the world'* - AMERICAN FILM
Illustrated Screen Reports - *edited column by George T. Pardy and James M. Davis* - EXHIBITORS TRADE REVIEW
Image Access - VIDEO EIGHTIES MAGAZINE
Image Storage News - OPTICAL MEMORY NEWS
Images + Ideas - PHOTO/DESIGN
Images and Answers - PHOTOMETHODS
Imaging Technology - *excellent technical feature* - BRITISH JOURNAL OF PHOTOGRAPHY
Imaging Technology - MILLIMETER
Imaging Update - *newsbriefs* - PHOTOMETHODS
Important Events - FACTSHEET FIVE
Important Pictures - *reviews* - HOLLYWOOD
Impressions - *guest column* - IMPRINT
Impressions - *comment on programming and industry* - PANORAMA
Impulse - *'Action guide'* - DISNEY ADVENTURES
In * Print - *review* - DWB
In a Few Lines - *newsbriefs* - FIEJ-BULLETIN
In & Out - *extensive section detailing perceived stars rise and fall with their publics* - BEST OF FILM & VIDEO
In & Out - *'Who's in and who's out'* - SOAP OPERA UPDATE
In and Out of Production - *column by Renee Tajima* - INDEPENDENT, THE
In and Out of the Studios - *'News and notes of plays and players everywhere'* - PICTURES MAGAZINE, THE
In Brief - ACCESS REPORTS/FREEDOM OF INFORMATION
In Brief - ADWEEK
In Brief - ART DIRECTION
In Brief - BLACK RADIO EXCLUSIVE
In Brief - *legal insight to film and video production* - ENTERTAINMENT REVUE
In Brief - FCC WEEK
In Brief - *newsbriefs* - HI-FI WORLD
In Brief - INFORMATION TODAY
In Brief - *paragraph-length news briefs* - MEDIA INTERNATIONAL
In Brief - *newsbriefs* - MEDIA MATTERS
In Brief - PUBLISHING & PRODUCTION EXECUTIVE
In Brief - UK PRESS GAZETTE
In Camera - *newsbriefs together with photographs of interesting items* - AMERICAN PHOTO
In Camera - *commentary* - FILM MAKING
In Camera - *newsbriefs* - FILMS AND FILMING
In Code - *essay* - ADVERTISING AND MARKETING MANAGEMENT
In Concert - *newsbriefs* - BMI: MUSICWORLD
In Confidence - *newsbreakers column by Peter Noble* - SCREEN INTERNATIONAL
In Consideration of Design Possiblities - SOUTHERN THEATRE

In Demand - *'This list represents titles most in demand by librarians'* - FORECAST
In Depth - PROFESSIONAL PHOTOGRAPHER, THE
In Development - *projects planned* - HD PRODUCTION
In Focus - *film newsbriefs* - FILM & BROADCASTING REVIEW
In Focus - *editorial column by Robert Sunshine* - FILM JOURNAL, THE
In Focus - *specific issues* - INDEPENDENT, THE
In Focus - *manufacturer profile* - ON LOCATION
In Focus - *'Your guide to this months films'* - SATELLITE TIMES
In Focus - *photographer profiles* - TRAVEL & LEISURE
In Just Seconds - PETERSEN'S PHOTOGRAPHIC
In Legal Journals - *article bibliography* - MEDIA LAW NOTES
In Memoriam - *obituaries* - AMERICAN CINEMEDITOR
In Memoriam - AMERICAN THEATRE
In Memoriam - *obituaries* - IBEW JOURNAL
In Memoriam - *obituaries* - INSIDE HOLLYWOOD
In Memoriam - *obituaries* - JOURNAL
In Memoriam - NEWSLETTER
In Newsreels - *contents listing for this week's releases* - MOTION PICTURE HERALD
In Non-Legal Journals - *article bibliography* - MEDIA LAW NOTES
In Other Media - *black news item column by Alan Leigh* - BLACK RADIO EXCLUSIVE
In Our Opinion - ADVERTISING AGENCY
In Our View - *editorial* - LPTV REPORT, THE
In print - *new film-video publications* - AFI EDUCATION NEWSLETTER
In Print - *book reviews* - AMERICAN THEATRE
In Print - *review* - CORPORATE TELEVISION
In Print - *review* - FLORIDA REEL
In Print - *book reviews* - FOCUS ON FILM
In Print - *book reviews* - JUMP CUT
In Process - *inside the darkroom* - PHOTOMETHODS
In Production - BOOKS AND FILMS
In Production - BROADCAST
In Production - *newsbriefs* - CINEMA FRANCAIS
In Production - CINEMA PAPERS
In Production - *film project details* - EMPIRE
In Production - FILMS AND FILMING
In Production - *HDTV production news* - HD PRODUCTION
In Production - *column by Constance Sidles* - MAGAZINE DESIGN & PRODUCTION
In Production - *current listing* - MILLIMETER
In Production - *current projects listed by title, production company, country* - MOVING PICTURES INTERNATIONAL
In Production - *profiles* - THEATRE CRAFTS
In Production - *newsbriefs* - TV WORLD
In Production - *'Out and about with Ken Ferguson'* - VIDEO TODAY
In Production-- Home and Abroad - *studio production slate* - SCREEN INTERNATIONAL
In Reply Would Say - *Q&A* - TALKING SCREEN

In Sight - *technique* - PETERSEN'S PHOTOGRAPHIC
In Store - *recent motion pictures now available on videocassette* - VIDEO TODAY
In Tennessee - *exhibitor newsbriefs column by Harry Williams* - UNIVERSAL WEEKLY
In the Advertising Workshop - *ad critique by Adcraft* - AGRICULTURAL ADVERTISING
In the City - *stock averages of major publications* - NEWSPAPER WORLD AND ADVERTISING REVIEW
In the Foreground - *'Being a department of brief chats on topics within the camera's range'* - PHOTODRAMATIST, THE
In the Foreground - *editorial* - STORY WORLD AND PHOTODRAMATIST, THE
In the Kitchen - EPISODES
In the Laboratory - *new technical innovations column by Samuel Wein* - MOTION PICTURE PROJECTION
In the Margin - *commentary* - ADVERTISING MAGAZINE
In the Mix - *studio news of black artists column by Elaine Stepter* - BLACK RADIO EXCLUSIVE
In the News - CABLE TV BUSINESS MAGAZINE
In the News - *newsbriefs* - CORPORATE TELEVISION
In the News - *newsbriefs* - ONSAT
In the News - PHOTO LAB MANAGEMENT
In the News - *'Our motto: truth is weirder than fiction'* - SIMPSONS ILLUSTRATED
In The Nick of Time - *'The Movie Serial in the Sound Era* - BIG REEL, THE
In the Observation Post - *column by Duane Gibbons* - PHOTOGRAPHIC PROCESSING
In the Picture - SIGHT & SOUND
In the Picture - TELEVISION/RADIO AGE
In the Pocket - *Down to Business column by Steve Harlan* - EQ
In the Provinces - *newsbriefs* - AMATEUR ACTOR ILLUSTRATED, THE
In the Radio Marketplace - *'News, Useful Data and Information on the Offerings of the Manufacturer'* - RADIO BROADCAST
In the Realm of Radio Shows - RADIO DEALER, THE
In the Realm of the Dance - DRAMA MAGAZINE, THE
In the Song Shop - *music on Broadway and in Vaudeville, column by E. M. Wickes* - DRAMATIC MIRROR, THE
In the Spotlight - *personnel newsbriefs* - CATHOLIC JOURNALIST
In the Spotlight - *profile* - FLORIDA REEL
In the Spotlight - *newsbriefs* - INTERNATIONAL PROJECTIONIST
In the Spotlight - *'Critic's choice' column by Michael Medved* - SPOTLIGHT ON VIDEO
In the Studio - PROFESSIONAL PHOTOGRAPHER, THE
In the Trenches - *practical application* - STEP-BY-STEP ELECTRONIC DESIGN
In the World's Laboratories - *latest radio developments from world scientists* - POPULAR RADIO AND TELEVISION
In This Issue - *overview column by Steve Werner* - OUTDOOR PHOTOGRAPHER

In This Issue - *editorial description* - STORYBOARD / THE ART OF LAUGHTER
In Tune With - *'Pop scene' column by James Carlson* - MOVIE STARS
In With the TV Set - *column by David Levine* - TV AND SCREEN SECRETS
In Writing for Veries - *'Addresses of principal short-wave stations by country'* - ALL-WAVE RADIO
In Your Workshop - RADIO & ELECTRONICS CONSTRUCTOR
Indelible Images - *Photographer profiles and the story behind the historical pictures they took* - MEMORIES
Independent Cinema - *news on independent filmmakers* - GRAND ILLUSIONS
Independent Film Review - CINEMANEWS, THE
Independent Film-Maker, The - DOCUMENTARY FILM NEWS
Independent N.Y.C. Casting Directors - *listing* - SHOW BUSINESS
Independent Women's Cinema - WOMEN & FILM
Independents - AMERICAN FILM
Independents - *filmmaker profiles* - CINEASTE
Index Index - *'A record of censorship'* - INDEX ON CENSORSHIP
Index of Films - FILM FORUM REVIEW
Index of Publications - *as cited in each monthly report. (8-84).* - TELECOMMUNICATIONS ALERT
Index to New Releases - *'The A to Z guide to every new video title available this month'* - HOME VIEWER
India - *briefs* - MOVIE/TV MARKETING
Indie Survivors Guide - SCREEN INTERNATIONAL
Individual Product Expenditures - PRESS STATISTICAL REVIEW
Industrial Advertising - ADVERTISING AGENCY
Industrial Advertising - MARKETING / COMMUNICATIONS
Industrial Marketing News - *newsbriefs* - AM
Industrial Page, The - NATIONAL PHOTOGRAPHER, THE
Industrial Progress - RADIO DEALER, THE
Industrial Techniques - PROFESSIONAL PHOTOGRAPHER, THE
Industry - VIDEO
Industry Associations - VIDEO SOFTWARE MAGAZINE
Industry Beat: Cable - ELECTRONIC MEDIA
Industry Beat: Syndication - ELECTRONIC MEDIA
Industry Clips - *news items* - BROADCASTER
Industry Date Book, The - *calendar of events* - FILM TV DAILY
Industry Events - HDTV NEWSLETTER
Industry Highlights - *newsbriefs* - GREATER AMUSEMENTS
Industry Insight - *trends and analysis column by Liane Pomfret* - RF DESIGN
Industry Insight - *column by Paul Taublieb* - VIDEO CHOICE

Industry Inventiveness in the Eighties - REP: RECORDING ENGINEERING PRODUCTION
Industry Law - TELEMARKETING
Industry Moves - SATELLITE COMMUNICATIONS
Industry News - *newsbriefs* - BROADCAST + TECHNOLOGY
Industry News - *briefs* - BROADCAST ENGINEERING
Industry News - BROADCAST SYSTEMS INTERNATIONAL
Industry News - *newsbriefs* - CHRISTIAN ADVERTISING FORUM
Industry News - *personnel and corporate newsbriefs* - COMMUNICATIONS INDUSTRIES REPORT, THE
Industry News - *'New products, services, business closures, etc.'* - DIGITAL EVOLUTION MAGAZINE
Industry News - ELECTRONICS & COMMUNICATIONS
Industry News - INTERNATIONAL BROADCASTING
Industry News - MAST
Industry News - PHOTO MARKETING
Industry News - PULP & PAPER CANADA
Industry News - SATELLITE TV WEEK
Industry News - *newsbriefs* - STAR SIGNALS
Industry News - STUDIO PHOTOGRAPHY
Industry News - *unique late-breaking news section in newsletter format* - TAPE/DISC BUSINESS
Industry News - VIDEOGRAPHY
Industry News and Developments - YELLOW PAGES UPDATE
Industry News Roundup - *newsbriefs* - AMERICAN PRINTER
Industry Notebook - INDUSTRIAL PHOTOGRAPHY
Industry Notes - CABLE COMMUNICATIONS MAGAZINE
Industry Notes - HDTV NEWSLETTER
Industry Notes - MIX
Industry Offers, The - *new products* - TELEVISION ENGINEERING
Industry People - *personnel newsbriefs* - PULP & PAPER CANADA
Industry Report - *trade news and comment column by Danny Villanueva* - MOVIE FLASH
Industry Roundup - BUYERS GUIDE
Industry Roundup - *Buyers Guide column by Richard Farrell* - TV TECHNOLOGY
Industry Segments - TELECOMMUNICATIONS
Industry Update - NETWORK WORLD
Industry Update - PERSONAL ELECTRONICS
Industry Update - *'High-end news from the USA and UK'* - STEREOPHILE
Industry Watch - SATELLITE COMMUNICATIONS
Inevitable Interviewer, The - ALBUM, THE
Inexpensive - *chart and products* - DIGITAL EVOLUTION MAGAZINE
Info for Buyers - PROMOTION
Infograms - *'Late breaking news from the comics industry and related media'* - COMIC INFORMER

Informal Comics - *'Showcase for the best in fan strips'* - COMIC INFORMER
Information - *'Services for artists'* - ART PAPERS
Information - *news column* - CABLEVISION
Information Booth - *Q&A* - TV MIRROR
Information Booth - *letters* - TV RADIO MIRROR
Information Organization - *news items* - LEARNED PUBLISHING
Information Please - *requests by comic book collectors* - COMICS BUYER'S GUIDE
Information Please - *'about collector's items that aren't completely identifiable* - GRAPHIC ANTIQUARIAN
Information, Please - *'Careful answers to questions about the stars and films' column by Oracle* - PICTURE PLAY MAGAZINE
Information Please - *resources* - PSA
Information Please - *reader Q&A column* - SOAP OPERA TIME
Informer, The - *upcoming releases column by James Mitchell* - VIDEO BUSINESS
Informer Reviews - *'Critiques on all media'* - COMIC INFORMER
In-House - *newsbriefs and comment* - OLD TIMER'S BULLETIN, THE
In-House Production - CORPORATE TELEVISION
Ink Stains - *personality column* - PRINT-EQUIP NEWS
Innerviews - EMMY
Innovations - *new promotion items* - MARKETING COMMUNICATIONS
Innovations - *new product review* - TELECONNECT
Innovations in Sound - PRO SOUND NEWS
In-Plant Operations - *a special section* - AMERICAN PRINTER
Input - *comment* - CONSUMER ELECTRONICS
Input Output - *'Instruments and Accessories'* - HIGH FIDELITY
Input/Output - *column by Neil McCubbin* - PULP & PAPER CANADA
Input/Output - *'Our video expert will answer any question in his crusade to wipe out video intimidation' column by Jim Teates* - VIDEO CHOICE
INS Special Item - *newsbrief INSerts column by Michael Copeland* - VENTURA PROFESSIONAL!
Inside - PRESS, THE
Inside Advertising - *Ad projects* - AMERICAN PHOTO
Inside ASCAP - *staff profiles* - ASCAP IN ACTION
Inside C-SPAN - C-SPAN UPDATE
Inside Edge, The - MONDAY MORNING REPLAY
Inside Gossip - *inside front cover page* - GOSSIP
Inside Hollywood - *newsbriefs* - DAYTIME TV
Inside Hollywood - MODERN PHOTOGRAPHY
Inside Hollywood - *column by Ruth Waterbury,* - MOVIELAND AND TV TIME
Inside Hollywood - *insiders report* - SCREEN INTERNATIONAL
Inside IEEE - IEEE SPECTRUM

Departments INDEX 816

Inside ILM - *news of Industrial Light and Magic* - LUCASFILM FAN CLUB, THE
Inside Looking Out - *Florida production observations* - ENTERTAINMENT REVUE
Inside Moves - ENTERTAINMENT CONNECTION MAGAZINE
Inside Radio - *program listings* - TV MIRROR
Inside Radio - *extensive weekly radio program listing* - TV RADIO MIRROR
Inside Romance - W • B
Inside SF Movieland - SF MOVIELAND
Inside Story - SOUND & IMAGE
Inside Story: - *in-depth profile* - MOVIELINE
Inside Stuff - *current comment* - OVERSET
Inside Stuff - *Hollywood gossip column by Cal York* - PHOTOPLAY
Inside Stuff - *movie personalities column by Cal York* - PHOTOPLAY COMBINED WITH MOVIE MIRROR
Inside Stuff-Pictures - *the lowdown on...* - VARIETY
Inside the Agencies - *newsbriefs* - ADVERTISING AGENCY
Inside the Birch Monthlies - INSIDE RADIO
Inside the Camera - CAMERA MAGAZINE
Inside the Division - CLIO AMONG THE MEDIA
Inside the FCC - TELEVISION/RADIO AGE
Inside the Ratings - *newsbriefs about Arbitron subscribers* - BEYOND THE RATINGS/RADIO
Inside the Ratings - *news of clients and the Arbitron company* - BEYOND THE RATINGS/TELEVISION
Inside Track - *industry gossip* - BILLBOARD
Inside Track - *editorial* - PUBLIC RELATIONS JOURNAL, THE
Inside Tracks - *music* - PREVUE
Inside View - *newsmaker profile* - TV TECHNOLOGY
Insider, The - *industry topics under discussion* - ELECTRONIC MEDIA
Insider - *'Tony Crawley reports the latest screen chat'* - FILM MONTHLY
Insider, The - *movie trends and developments column by Susan Peters* - SCENE AT THE MOVIES
Insider Audio - *column by Ken Pohlmann* - MIX
Insider Pix - *'A summary of titles of merit listed by order cut-off date'* - VIDEO INSIDER
Insider Trading - MEDIA BUSINESS
Insiders - *personnel changes* - TELECONNECT
Insides & Insights - *comment* - TELEPROFESSIONAL
Insight - ETI
Insight - *on filter usage* - TIFFEN PROFESSIONAL NEWSLETTER
Insight - *heard around town* - VUE
Insight on Rules - *application of Federal Communication Commission rulings, column by Harold Hallikainen* - RADIO WORLD
Installation Directory - *pertaining to companies which installed window displays. (10-30)* - ADVERTISING DISPLAYS

Installations - *showcase* - CAR AUDIO AND ELECTRONICS
Installations - *equipment recently installed* - COMPUTER PUBLISHING
Installations - *unique feature department detailing production plants receiving new print equipment* - WEB
Installations & Expansions - *equipment installed* - HIGH VOLUME PRINTING
Instant Interview - MODERN SCREEN
Instructional New Releases - VIDEO ALERT
Integrated Amplifiers - SOUND & VISION
Interactive Developments - OPTICAL MEMORY NEWS
Interactive File - *new equipment* - TELEVISION BROADCAST
Interactivity - HYPERMEDIA
Interchange - *BPME membership news* - BPME IMAGE MAGAZINE
Intercom - *newsbriefs* - JOURNAL OF COMMUNICATION
Inter-Connection Packaging - ELECTRONIC PRODUCTS
Interesting Letters - *'From readers everywhere'* - MOTION PICTURE
Interesting New Books - *review* - HOLLYWOOD STUDIO MAGAZINE
Interesting Paramount Events in the U.S. & Canada - PARAMOUNT WORLD
Interface - *letters* - COMPUTERS & ELECTRONICS
Interface - *letters* - STAGE & STUDIO
Intermediary - *commentary* - INTERMEDIA
International - *world news* - BILLBOARD
International - CRITIC
International - DBS NEWS
International - ELECTRONICS
International - MAST
International - MEDIA & VALUES
International - MEDIA WEEK
International - MULTICHANNEL NEWS
International - PSA JOURNAL
International - SATELLITE NEWS
International - VARIETY
International - VIA SATELLITE
International Advertisers - *briefs* - INTERNATIONAL ADVERTISER, THE
International Affairs - *conference dates* - INTERNATIONAL EDUCATIONAL AND CULTURAL EXCHANGE
International Agencies - *briefs* - INTERNATIONAL ADVERTISER, THE
International Box Office - *report* - SCREEN INTERNATIONAL
International Briefs - *news items* - BUSINESS OF FILM, THE
International Cities Permit Fact Sheet - *insurance and permit requirements* - LOCATION UPDATE
International Column - ICA NEWSLETTER
International Coordination - INTERMEDIA
International Exhibitions - *calendar* - LEICA PHOTOGRAPHY
International Film Grosses - VARIETY
International Forum - *letters* - VIDEO AGE INTERNATIONAL
International Intelligence - MILITARY ELECTRONICS / COUNTERMEASURES

International Intrigue - LOCATION UPDATE
International Jet Set - *more gossip* - RONA BARRETT'S HOLLYWOOD
International Journal Report - *excellent international theatre journal/magazine review column by Norma Adler* - THEATRE DESIGN & TECHNOLOGY
International Market Place - *'Listings of products from world-wide sources considered suitable for mail order promotion'* - MAIL ORDER DIGEST
International Media - *briefs* - INTERNATIONAL ADVERTISER, THE
International Meetings - VIDEO AGE INTERNATIONAL
International Mixdown - *production house news* - PRO SOUND NEWS
International Museum of Graphic Communication - *museum currator column by Mark Barbour* - PRINT-EQUIP NEWS
International News - *of puppetry* - ANIMATIONS
International News - *extensive section of animation newsbriefs* - ANYMATOR
International News - AUDIOVIDEO INTERNATIONAL
International News - CAMPAIGN
International News - *column by Bruce Johnson* - QST
International News - TELEVISION BROADCAST
International Newsletter - *news review* - BUSINESS MARKETING
International Newswatch - COMICS JOURNAL, THE
International Notes - MEDIA INFORMATION AUSTRALIA
International Personalities in Paramount Cinema Events - PARAMOUNT WORLD
International Portfolio - INSIDE MEDIA
International Product Review - WORLD BROADCAST NEWS
International Profile - TELEVISION / RADIO AGE INTERNATIONAL
International Profile - VIDEO AGE INTERNATIONAL
International Programming - C-SPAN UPDATE
International Radio - *radio news by nation* - ELECTRONICS WORLD
International Radio Chronicle - *column by Louis G. Caldwell* - JOURNAL OF RADIO LAW
International Ratings - TV WORLD
International Report - TELEVISION/RADIO AGE
International Review - EDUCATIONAL COMMUNICATION AND TECHNOLOGY
International Scope - *newsbriefs* - TELEVISION / RADIO AGE INTERNATIONAL
International Sound Track - *newsbriefs from London, Paris, Rome, Berlin, and Madrid Variety offices* - VARIETY
International Star Track--Gossip - TONI HOLT'S MOVIE LIFE
International Theatre - *newsbriefs* - WORLD THEATRE

International Top Tens - *top television shows from selected nations* - TELEVISION WEEK
International Update - HYPERMEDIA
International Update - LOCATION UPDATE
International Update - *newsbriefs by country* - VARIETY
International Update - *newsbriefs* - VIDEO AGE INTERNATIONAL
International Viewpoint - *guest column* - VIDEO AGE INTERNATIONAL
Internationally Speaking - *ITVA world news* - CORPORATE TELEVISION
Inter-Tape Directory - *for 'Tapespondents'* - HI-FI SOUND
Interval - *column by Lindley Evans* - ABC WEEKLY
Interview - BULGARIAN FILMS
Interview - *insightful information* - CINEASTE
Interview - DWB
Interview - FA
Interview - LÜRZER'S INTERNATIONAL ARCHIVE
Interview - PHOTOGRAPHER'S FORUM
Interview - PHOTOGRAPHY
Interview - PRO SOUND NEWS
Interview - PSA
Interview - RELIGIOUS BROADCASTING
Interview - VIDEO MONTHLY
Interview With..., An - FILM BULLETIN
Interviews - MILLENNIUM FILM JOURNAL
Into the Vortex - DOCTOR WHO MAGAZINE
Intro - *editorial column by Tony Lee* - STRANGE ADVENTURES
Introduction - *commentary column by Kent S. Bransford* - HI-FI HERETIC
Introduction - JOURNAL OF ARTS MANAGEMENT AND LAW, THE
Intro-Spectives - *'reflective, very personal commentaries on a wide range of subjects by individuals in the design field'* - PRINT
I/O - *'Readers respond' with letters* - DIGITAL MEDIA
IPA Report - *International Prepress Association news column by Henry Hatch* - PRE-
IPC People and Projects - VIDEO TIMES
Is That So! - *film personnal newsbriefs* - DRAMATIC MIRROR, THE
ISDN Monitor - *newsbriefs concerning integrated services digital networks* - COMMUNICATIONSWEEK
Issue - PRESS, THE
Issues - MEDIA WEEK
Issues & Answers - VIDEO BUSINESS
Issues in Library-Vendor Relations - AGAINST THE GRAIN
Issues of Concern - COMMUNICATION REPORTS
It Happened This Way - *personality column by John J. Miller* - PHOTOPLAY
It Seems to Us - *letters* - GUILD REPORTER, THE
It Seems to Us - *editorial* - QST
It Was Rumored - *film stars of yesteryear* - AMERICAN MOVIE CLASSICS MAGAZINE
ITA Audio News - *briefs* - ITA NEWS DIGEST
ITA International News - ITA NEWS DIGEST
ITA Video News - *briefs* - ITA NEWS DIGEST

Items - *newsbriefs* - DRAMATIC MIRROR AND LITERARY COMPANION, THE
Items - *trends and product newsbriefs* - IMAGE
Items of Interest - AMERICAN PRESS
Items of Interest - *'by an old timer* - BULLETIN OF PHOTOGRAPHY
Items of Interest - MID-ATLANTIC GRAPHIC ARTS REVIEW
Items of Interest - *equipment* - MOVING IMAGE
Items of Interest - *newsbriefs concerning photographic professionals* - ST. LOUIS AND CANADIAN PHOTOGRAPHER
It's a Fact - *Broadway newsbriefs* - STAGE PICTORIAL
It's a Question of Character - *'A chance to ask whatever you wish!'* - SOAP OPERA UPDATE
It's About Time - *Creative Workshop column by Norman Weinberg* - EQ
It's All in Your Name - *column by Marian Quinn* - PHOTOPLAY COMBINED WITH MOVIE MIRROR
It's Easy to Recommend - *new books, organizations for desktop publishers* - REALLY, A FREE NEWSLETTER
It's Me, Richard - *personality column by Richard Gomez* - MOVIE FLASH
Its My Bag - *personality column by Ed Hocura* - CANADIAN FILM DIGEST
It's New to Me - *new product review column by Cinebug Shopper* - HOME MOVIES
It's Only a Movie - *column by John Brosnan* - STARBURST
It's Your Screen - *letters* - SCREEN STORIES
It's Your Turn - *'Readers' Survey'* - REAL LIFE/DAYTIMERS
It's Your Turn - *questionaire* - SOAP OPERA PEOPLE
ITU Publications - TELECOMMUNICATION JOURNAL
ITV Marketplace - *'Buyers' estimates of ITV revenue (£m)'* - MEDIA WEEK
ITVA News - *International Television Association news* - IN MOTION FILM & VIDEO PRODUCTION MAGAZINE
ITVA News - VIDEO MANAGEMENT
ITVA Report - *news concerning International Television Association* - CORPORATE TELEVISION
ITVA Today - CORPORATE TELEVISION
ITVA Today - *'News and views from the International Television Association'* - VIDEO SYSTEMS
I've Got a Problem - *reader submitted Q&A technical problems* - HOME MOVIES

J

Jack Edmonston on Magazine Marketing - *advertisement critique column by Jack Edmonston* - MAGAZINEWEEK

Jackpots - *picture page* - AMUSEMENT BUSINESS
Jacksonville - BOX OFFICE
Jacquie Eastlund Predicts - *horoscopes for the stars* - TONI HOLT'S MOVIE LIFE
James Bradford in Hollywood - *news from stateside* - TV TIMES
Jan's Potpourri - *newsbriefs* - AUDIO VISUAL JOURNAL
Japan - *extra large section of news briefs* - MOVIE/TV MARKETING
Japan - *video comment and news column by Allan Shriver* - WHAT VIDEO
Jargon Answers - *'Our regular layperson's guide to things technical in the video world'* - VIDEO ANSWERS
Jazz - BILLBOARD
Jazz Blue Notes - *column by Jeff Levenson* - BILLBOARD
Jazz Chart - *weekly radio playlist* - BLACK RADIO EXCLUSIVE
Jazz LP - *playlist* - BILLBOARD
Jazz Page, The - TAPE DECK QUARTERLY
Jazz Profile - BLACK RADIO EXCLUSIVE
Jazz Records - *review* - HIGH FIDELITY
Jazz Reviews - CD REVIEW
Jazz Reviews - HIGH FIDELITY/MUSICAL AMERICA
J.C. Jenkins--His Colyum - *traveling film commentary column by J. C. Jenkins* - EXHIBITORS HERALD WORLD
JEA Notes - *newsbriefs of the Journalism Education Association* - QUILL AND SCROLL
JEE Newsletter - *newsbriefs* - JEE, JOURNAL OF ELECTRONIC ENGINEERING
Jeff Parnau on Production - *column by Jeff Parnau* - FOLIO:
Jerry dela Femina's Column - MARKETING / COMMUNICATIONS
Jerry Fairbridge - *column by Jerry Fairbridge* - BROADCAST + TECHNOLOGY
Jim Korkis' Animation Anecdotes - ANIMATION MAGAZINE
Jim Korkis's Animation Anecdotes - *'Jim Korkis's roundup of tidbits and trivia about animation past and present'* - ANIMATO!
Jim's Scrapbook - *technical advice from Jim Gupton* - TECHNICAL PHOTOGRAPHY
Jingle$ - *commercial music* - ON LOCATION
Job Bank - MAGAZINE DESIGN & PRODUCTION
Job Leads Adviser - *a Q&A format on typical questions concerning R-TV employment* - JOB LEADS
Job of the Month - MID-ATLANTIC GRAPHIC ARTS REVIEW
Jobs - *academic marketplace* - AFI EDUCATION NEWSLETTER
Jobs - CMA NEWSLETTER
Jobs - *unusual section listing job openings and RTNDA members seeking job changes* - COMMUNICATOR
Jobs - DIGEST OF THE UNIVERSITY FILM AND VIDEO ASSOCIATION
Jobsline - *employment opportunities* - ALUMNI NEWSLINE

Departments INDEX

Jodi's Hollywood Hotline! - *'What's happening out in La La Land, where the stars work and play all day?'* - SUPER TEEN

Joe Bob Briggs - *humor column by Joe Bob Briggs* - COMIC RELIEF

John Mills Showcase - STAGE AND TELEVISION TODAY, THE

John Peter on Design - *column by John Peter* - FOLIO:

John Robert Powers' School for Beauty - MOVIE SHOW

Johnny Carson's Corner - *column by Johnny Carson* - TV RADIO MIRROR

Johnstone - *column by Lammy Johnstone* - INSIDE MEDIA

Joint Ethics - *news of the Joint Ethics Committee* - ART DIRECTION

Jokes the TV Censors Killed - BEHIND THE SCENE

Journal - *news items* - DRAMATICS

Journal Fifty Years Ago, The - TELECOMMUNICATION JOURNAL

Journal News - ORGANIZATIONAL COMMUNICATION NEWSLETTER

Journal One Hundred Years Ago, The - TELECOMMUNICATION JOURNAL

Journalism Research - CRC NEWSLETTER

Journalism Review - *opinion on news media* - MEDIA & CONSUMER

Journalistic Incidents - *very brief news items* - ADVERTISERS GUIDE

Journals - MEDIA ANTHROPOLOGIST NEWSLETTER

Journals and Periodicals - *review* - WOMEN & LANGUAGE

Journals--Australia - *column by Jan Dawson* - FILM COMMENT

Journals--London & New York - *column by Jonathan Rosenbaum* - FILM COMMENT

Joystick - *'Computer entertainment'* - SATELLITE TIMES

JS Johar's Question Box - Q&A - FILMFARE

Judgment Call - COLUMBIA JOURNALISM REVIEW

Judy's Column - *news items* - AUDIO VISUAL JOURNAL

Junior Executives Jottings - MID-ATLANTIC GRAPHIC ARTS REVIEW

Junior Wireless Club - *'devoted to early wireless'* - OLD TIMER'S BULLETIN, THE

Junk Mail - *letters to the editor* - SIMPSONS ILLUSTRATED

Just a Few Lines - *newsbriefs* - ABU NEWSLETTER

Just Among Ourselves - *newsbriefs* - COLORADO EDITOR

Just Among Ourselves - PEP

Just Asking - *questions posed to celebrities* - FRESH!

Just Asking - *'We answer all your questions!'* - REAL LIFE/DAYTIMERS

Just at Random - *newsbriefs* - COMMERCIAL PHOTOGRAPHER, THE

Just Between You and Me - *editorial column by Frank V. Chambers* - CAMERA, THE

Just Breaking - *new advertising campaigns* - ART DIRECTION

Just for Openers - INSIDE HOLLYWOOD

Just for Variety - *news bits about personalities* - DAILY VARIETY

Just Hunches - PEP

Just Look at Them Now - PHOTO SCREEN

Just Out - POPULAR PHOTOGRAPHY

Just Paging - *column by Hal Goldberg* - WRITER'S DIGEST

Just Released - *motion picture and book reviews* - PHOTOPLAY

Just Your Style--and Hollywood's - *column by Dorothea Hawley Cartwright* - TALKING SCREEN

Juxtapositions - *column by Mel Lambert* - MIX

K

Kaleidoscope - *column by Noel Keywood* - HI-FI WORLD

Kaleidoscope - *news of the Printing Industries Association of Southern California* - PRINT-EQUIP NEWS

Kaleidoscope - *column by Ken Jurek* - VIDEO MANAGEMENT

Kansas City - BOX OFFICE

Kansas City Notes - *exhibitor newsbriefs column by L.D. Balsly* - UNIVERSAL WEEKLY

Keepin' an Eye On - *profile* - SOAP OPERA UPDATE

Keeping It - *'How to generate, accumulate and conserve business wealth' column by Daniel B. Lewis* - PRINT-EQUIP NEWS

Keeping Posted - *upcoming events* - VIDEO MANAGEMENT

Keeping Tabs - *editorial column by Susan Gubernat* - PUBLISH!

Keeping Up With the Authors - *author activities column by Jane Heller* - W•B

Keith Dudley Report, The - *'And other tidbits of Hammer lore' column by Keith Dudley* - LITTLE SHOPPE OF HORRORS

Kelly's Corner - *'Richard Kelly's monthly look at budget hi-fi - old, new, borrowed or blue' column by Richard Kelly* - HI-FI WORLD

Kennel - *author profile* - VIDEO WATCHDOG

Kepler's SLR Notebook - MODERN PHOTOGRAPHY

Key and Telegraph - OLD TIMER'S BULLETIN, THE

Key Hole Portraits - *unique one-line biographies of stars, column by Harry F. Parsons* - HOLLYWOOD STUDIO MAGAZINE

Key Telecommunications Stocks - TELECOMMUNICATIONS ALERT

Keyboard Komments - *'Thoughts and opinions on online services and computer communications' column by Don Picard* - LINK-UP

Keynote Reviews - *cassette spotlight* - VIDEO TIMES

Kick Back - *an interesting section of the magazine devoted to the magazine ombudsman* - FEED-BACK

Kicks From the Flicks - *upcoming motion picture product* - MOVIES NOW

Kid Vid - VIDEO REVIEW

Kiddie Cassettes - *'Cheaper than a babysitter and twice as reliable. What's available for the under-12 set'* - CINEMA, VIDEO & CABLE MOVIE DIGEST

Kids & Kameras - POPULAR PHOTOGRAPHY

Kids' Clubhouse - *children's fare* - BLOCKBUSTER VIDEO MAGAZINE

Kids Reviews - *various media* - ENTERTAINMENT WEEKLY

Kidvid - *videotape review* - VIDEO MAGAZINE

Kinema Technique and Equipment - *reviews* - IDEAL KINEMA, THE

Kitchen Konstruktion - PRACTICAL WIRELESS

Klasnic's Consultant's Corner - *column by Jack Klasnic* - IN-PLANT PRINTER & ELECTRONIC PUBLISHER

Koko Komments - *column by G. Michael Dobbs* - ANIMATO!

Korea - *briefs* - MOVIE/TV MARKETING

Ku & Other Satellites - *guide* - ONSAT

Kudos - *awards* - BMI: MUSICWORLD

Kyle - *column by Andrew J. Kyle* - COMICS FANDOM EXAMINER

L

L.A. Obsessions - *column by Ben Kallen* - MOVIELINE

L.A. Theatre Life - *column by Steve Zall* - SPOTLIGHT CASTING MAGAZINE

Lab - *technical aspects* - LEICA FOTOGRAFIE INTERNATIONAL

Lab Report - *new developments in communications technology* - COMMUNICATIONS NEWS

Lab Reports - MODERN RECORDING & MUSIC

Lab Test Reports - VIDEO REVIEW

Laboratory - *news items* - INTERNATIONAL PHOTOGRAPHER

Labs and Stock - *new information about eastern film labs or film stock* - MAKING FILMS

Lancashire-West - CAMPAIGN

Langham Diary - *guest column* - LISTENER

Language Arts - FILM & VIDEO NEWS

Language Broadcasts - BBC WORLD SERVICE LONDON CALLING

Large Market Manager - SOUND MANAGEMENT

Large Plant Management - *'special section for plants with 10 or more employees'* - AMERICAN PRINTER

Larger Formats - CAMERA & DARKROOM PHOTOGRAPHY

International Top Tens - *top television shows from selected nations* - TELEVISION WEEK
International Update - HYPERMEDIA
International Update - LOCATION UPDATE
International Update - *newsbriefs by country* - VARIETY
International Update - *newsbriefs* - VIDEO AGE INTERNATIONAL
International Viewpoint - *guest column* - VIDEO AGE INTERNATIONAL
Internationally Speaking - *ITVA world news* - CORPORATE TELEVISION
Inter-Tape Directory - *for 'Tapespondents'* - HI-FI SOUND
Interval - *column by Lindley Evans* - ABC WEEKLY
Interview - BULGARIAN FILMS
Interview - *insightful information* - CINEASTE
Interview - DWB
Interview - FA
Interview - LÜRZER'S INTERNATIONAL ARCHIVE
Interview - PHOTOGRAPHER'S FORUM
Interview - PHOTOGRAPHY
Interview - PRO SOUND NEWS
Interview - PSA
Interview - RELIGIOUS BROADCASTING
Interview - VIDEO MONTHLY
Interview With..., An - FILM BULLETIN
Interviews - MILLENNIUM FILM JOURNAL
Into the Vortex - DOCTOR WHO MAGAZINE
Intro - *editorial column by Tony Lee* - STRANGE ADVENTURES
Introduction - *commentary column by Kent S. Bransford* - HI-FI HERETIC
Introduction - JOURNAL OF ARTS MANAGEMENT AND LAW, THE
Intro-Spectives - *'reflective, very personal commentaries on a wide range of subjects by individuals in the design field'* - PRINT
I/O - *'Readers respond' with letters* - DIGITAL MEDIA
IPA Report - *International Prepress Association news column by Henry Hatch* - PRE-
IPC People and Projects - VIDEO TIMES
Is That So! - *film personnal newsbriefs* - DRAMATIC MIRROR, THE
ISDN Monitor - *newsbriefs concerning integrated services digital networks* - COMMUNICATIONSWEEK
Issue - PRESS, THE
Issues - MEDIA WEEK
Issues & Answers - VIDEO BUSINESS
Issues in Library-Vendor Relations - AGAINST THE GRAIN
Issues of Concern - COMMUNICATION REPORTS
It Happened This Way - *personality column by John J. Miller* - PHOTOPLAY
It Seems to Us - *letters* - GUILD REPORTER, THE
It Seems to Us - *editorial* - QST
It Was Rumored - *film stars of yesteryear* - AMERICAN MOVIE CLASSICS MAGAZINE
ITA Audio News - *briefs* - ITA NEWS DIGEST
ITA International News - ITA NEWS DIGEST
ITA Video News - *briefs* - ITA NEWS DIGEST

Items - *newsbriefs* - DRAMATIC MIRROR AND LITERARY COMPANION, THE
Items - *trends and product newsbriefs* - IMAGE
Items of Interest - AMERICAN PRESS
Items of Interest - *'by an old timer'* - BULLETIN OF PHOTOGRAPHY
Items of Interest - MID-ATLANTIC GRAPHIC ARTS REVIEW
Items of Interest - *equipment* - MOVING IMAGE
Items of Interest - *newsbriefs concerning photographic professionals* - ST. LOUIS AND CANADIAN PHOTOGRAPHER
It's a Fact - *Broadway newsbriefs* - STAGE PICTORIAL
It's a Question of Character - *'A chance to ask whatever you wish!'* - SOAP OPERA UPDATE
It's About Time - *Creative Workshop column by Norman Weinberg* - EQ
It's All in Your Name - *column by Marian Quinn* - PHOTOPLAY COMBINED WITH MOVIE MIRROR
It's Easy to Recommend - *new books, organizations for desktop publishers* - REALLY, A FREE NEWSLETTER
It's Me, Richard - *personality column by Richard Gomez* - MOVIE FLASH
Its My Bag - *personality column by Ed Hocura* - CANADIAN FILM DIGEST
It's New to Me - *new product review column by Cinebug Shopper* - HOME MOVIES
It's Only a Movie - *column by John Brosnan* - STARBURST
It's Your Screen - *letters* - SCREEN STORIES
It's Your Turn - *'Readers' Survey'* - REAL LIFE/DAYTIMERS
It's Your Turn - *questionaire* - SOAP OPERA PEOPLE
ITU Publications - TELECOMMUNICATION JOURNAL
ITV Marketplace - *'Buyers' estimates of ITV revenue (£m)'* - MEDIA WEEK
ITVA News - *International Television Association news* - IN MOTION FILM & VIDEO PRODUCTION MAGAZINE
ITVA News - VIDEO MANAGEMENT
ITVA Report - *news concerning International Television Association* - CORPORATE TELEVISION
ITVA Today - CORPORATE TELEVISION
ITVA Today - *'News and views from the International Television Association'* - VIDEO SYSTEMS
I've Got a Problem - *reader submitted Q&A technical problems* - HOME MOVIES

J

Jack Edmonston on Magazine Marketing - *advertisement critique column by Jack Edmonston* - MAGAZINEWEEK

Jackpots - *picture page* - AMUSEMENT BUSINESS
Jacksonville - BOX OFFICE
Jacquie Eastlund Predicts - *horoscopes for the stars* - TONI HOLT'S MOVIE LIFE
James Bradford in Hollywood - *news from stateside* - TV TIMES
Jan's Potpourri - *newsbriefs* - AUDIO VISUAL JOURNAL
Japan - *extra large section of news briefs* - MOVIE/TV MARKETING
Japan - *video comment and news column by Allan Shriver* - WHAT VIDEO
Jargon Answers - *'Our regular layperson's guide to things technical in the video world'* - VIDEO ANSWERS
Jazz - BILLBOARD
Jazz Blue Notes - *column by Jeff Levenson* - BILLBOARD
Jazz Chart - *weekly radio playlist* - BLACK RADIO EXCLUSIVE
Jazz LP - *playlist* - BILLBOARD
Jazz Page, The - TAPE DECK QUARTERLY
Jazz Profile - BLACK RADIO EXCLUSIVE
Jazz Records - *review* - HIGH FIDELITY
Jazz Reviews - CD REVIEW
Jazz Reviews - HIGH FIDELITY/MUSICAL AMERICA
J.C. Jenkins--His Colyum - *traveling film commentary column by J. C. Jenkins* - EXHIBITORS HERALD WORLD
JEA Notes - *newsbriefs of the Journalism Education Association* - QUILL AND SCROLL
JEE Newsletter - *newsbriefs* - JEE, JOURNAL OF ELECTRONIC ENGINEERING
Jeff Parnau on Production - *column by Jeff Parnau* - FOLIO:
Jerry dela Femina's Column - MARKETING / COMMUNICATIONS
Jerry Fairbridge - *column by Jerry Fairbridge* - BROADCAST + TECHNOLOGY
Jim Korkis' Animation Anecdotes - ANIMATION MAGAZINE
Jim Korkis's Animation Anecdotes - *'Jim Korkis's roundup of tidbits and trivia about animation past and present'* - ANIMATO!
Jim's Scrapbook - *technical advice from Jim Gupton* - TECHNICAL PHOTOGRAPHY
Jingle$ - *commercial music* - ON LOCATION
Job Bank - MAGAZINE DESIGN & PRODUCTION
Job Leads Adviser - *a Q&A format on typical questions concerning R-TV employment* - JOB LEADS
Job of the Month - MID-ATLANTIC GRAPHIC ARTS REVIEW
Jobs - *academic marketplace* - AFI EDUCATION NEWSLETTER
Jobs - CMA NEWSLETTER
Jobs - *unusual section listing job openings and RTNDA members seeking job changes* - COMMUNICATOR
Jobs - DIGEST OF THE UNIVERSITY FILM AND VIDEO ASSOCIATION
Jobsline - *employment opportunities* - ALUMNI NEWSLINE

Departments INDEX 818

Jodi's Hollywood Hotline! - *'What's happening out in La La Land, where the stars work and play all day?'* - SUPER TEEN
Joe Bob Briggs - *humor column by Joe Bob Briggs* - COMIC RELIEF
John Mills Showcase - STAGE AND TELEVISION TODAY, THE
John Peter on Design - *column by John Peter* - FOLIO:
John Robert Powers' School for Beauty - MOVIE SHOW
Johnny Carson's Corner - *column by Johnny Carson* - TV RADIO MIRROR
Johnstone - *column by Lammy Johnstone* - INSIDE MEDIA
Joint Ethics - *news of the Joint Ethics Committee* - ART DIRECTION
Jokes the TV Censors Killed - BEHIND THE SCENE
Journal - *news items* - DRAMATICS
Journal Fifty Years Ago, The - TELECOMMUNICATION JOURNAL
Journal News - ORGANIZATIONAL COMMUNICATION NEWSLETTER
Journal One Hundred Years Ago, The - TELECOMMUNICATION JOURNAL
Journalism Research - CRC NEWSLETTER
Journalism Review - *opinion on news media* - MEDIA & CONSUMER
Journalistic Incidents - *very brief news items* - ADVERTISERS GUIDE
Journals - MEDIA ANTHROPOLOGIST NEWSLETTER
Journals and Periodicals - *review* - WOMEN & LANGUAGE
Journals--Australia - *column by Jan Dawson* - FILM COMMENT
Journals--London & New York - *column by Jonathan Rosenbaum* - FILM COMMENT
Joystick - *'Computer entertainment'* - SATELLITE TIMES
JS Johar's Question Box - Q&A - FILMFARE
Judgment Call - COLUMBIA JOURNALISM REVIEW
Judy's Column - *news items* - AUDIO VISUAL JOURNAL
Junior Executives Jottings - MID-ATLANTIC GRAPHIC ARTS REVIEW
Junior Wireless Club - *'devoted to early wireless'* - OLD TIMER'S BULLETIN, THE
Junk Mail - *letters to the editor* - SIMPSONS ILLUSTRATED
Just a Few Lines - *newsbriefs* - ABU NEWSLETTER
Just Among Ourselves - *newsbriefs* - COLORADO EDITOR
Just Among Ourselves - PEP
Just Asking - *questions posed to celebrities* - FRESH!
Just Asking - *'We answer all your questions!'* - REAL LIFE/DAYTIMERS
Just at Random - *newsbriefs* - COMMERCIAL PHOTOGRAPHER, THE
Just Between You and Me - *editorial column by Frank V. Chambers* - CAMERA, THE
Just Breaking - *new advertising campaigns* - ART DIRECTION
Just for Openers - INSIDE HOLLYWOOD
Just for Variety - *news bits about personalities* - DAILY VARIETY
Just Hunches - PEP
Just Look at Them Now - PHOTO SCREEN
Just Out - POPULAR PHOTOGRAPHY
Just Paging - *column by Hal Goldberg* - WRITER'S DIGEST
Just Released - *motion picture and book reviews* - PHOTOPLAY
Just Your Style--and Hollywood's - *column by Dorothea Hawley Cartwright* - TALKING SCREEN
Juxtapositions - *column by Mel Lambert* - MIX

K

Kaleidoscope - *column by Noel Keywood* - HI-FI WORLD
Kaleidoscope - *news of the Printing Industries Association of Southern California* - PRINT-EQUIP NEWS
Kaleidoscope - *column by Ken Jurek* - VIDEO MANAGEMENT
Kansas City - BOX OFFICE
Kansas City Notes - *exhibitor newsbriefs column by L.D. Balsly* - UNIVERSAL WEEKLY
Keepin' an Eye On - *profile* - SOAP OPERA UPDATE
Keeping It - *'How to generate, accumulate and conserve business wealth' column by Daniel B. Lewis* - PRINT-EQUIP NEWS
Keeping Posted - *upcoming events* - VIDEO MANAGEMENT
Keeping Tabs - *editorial column by Susan Gubernat* - PUBLISH!
Keeping Up With the Authors - *author activities column by Jane Heller* - W•B
Keith Dudley Report, The - *'And other tidbits of Hammer lore' column by Keith Dudley* - LITTLE SHOPPE OF HORRORS
Kelly's Corner - *'Richard Kelly's monthly look at budget hi-fi - old, new, borrowed or blue' column by Richard Kelly* - HI-FI WORLD
Kennel - *author profile* - VIDEO WATCHDOG
Kepler's SLR Notebook - MODERN PHOTOGRAPHY
Key and Telegraph - OLD TIMER'S BULLETIN, THE
Key Hole Portraits - *unique one-line biographies of stars, column by Harry F. Parsons* - HOLLYWOOD STUDIO MAGAZINE
Key Telecommunications Stocks - TELECOMMUNICATIONS ALERT
Keyboard Komments - *'Thoughts and opinions on online services and computer communications' column by Don Picard* - LINK-UP

Keynote Reviews - *cassette spotlight* - VIDEO TIMES
Kick Back - *an interesting section of the magazine devoted to the magazine ombudsman* - FEED-BACK
Kicks From the Flicks - *upcoming motion picture product* - MOVIES NOW
Kid Vid - VIDEO REVIEW
Kiddie Cassettes - *'Cheaper than a babysitter and twice as reliable. What's available for the under-12 set'* - CINEMA, VIDEO & CABLE MOVIE DIGEST
Kids & Kameras - POPULAR PHOTOGRAPHY
Kids' Clubhouse - *children's fare* - BLOCKBUSTER VIDEO MAGAZINE
Kids Reviews - *various media* - ENTERTAINMENT WEEKLY
Kidvid - *videotape review* - VIDEO MAGAZINE
Kinema Technique and Equipment - *reviews* - IDEAL KINEMA, THE
Kitchen Konstruktion - PRACTICAL WIRELESS
Klasnic's Consultant's Corner - *column by Jack Klasnic* - IN-PLANT PRINTER & ELECTRONIC PUBLISHER
Koko Komments - *column by G. Michael Dobbs* - ANIMATO!
Korea - *briefs* - MOVIE/TV MARKETING
Ku & Other Satellites - *guide* - ONSAT
Kudos - *awards* - BMI: MUSICWORLD
Kyle - *column by Andrew J. Kyle* - COMICS FANDOM EXAMINER

L

L.A. Obsessions - *column by Ben Kallen* - MOVIELINE
L.A. Theatre Life - *column by Steve Zall* - SPOTLIGHT CASTING MAGAZINE
Lab - *technical aspects* - LEICA FOTOGRAFIE INTERNATIONAL
Lab Report - *new developments in communications technology* - COMMUNICATIONS NEWS
Lab Reports - MODERN RECORDING & MUSIC
Lab Test Reports - VIDEO REVIEW
Laboratory - *news items* - INTERNATIONAL PHOTOGRAPHER
Labs and Stock - *new information about eastern film labs or film stock* - MAKING FILMS
Lancashire-West - CAMPAIGN
Langham Diary - *guest column* - LISTENER
Language Arts - FILM & VIDEO NEWS
Language Broadcasts - BBC WORLD SERVICE LONDON CALLING
Large Market Manager - SOUND MANAGEMENT
Large Plant Management - *'special section for plants with 10 or more employees'* - AMERICAN PRINTER
Larger Formats - CAMERA & DARKROOM PHOTOGRAPHY

INDEX — Departments

Larger Formats - *column by Bobby Adams* - DARKROOM PHOTOGRAPHY
Larry White's Cosmic College - *horoscope* - NATIONAL FORUM, THE
Las Vegas - *city review column by Morag Veljkovic* - AFTER DARK
Las Vegas Casting - *column by Polly Peluso* - CASTING CALL
Las Vegas Desert Spiel - *column by Neil Hoffman* - DRAMA-LOGUE
Laser - *information and reviews* - ORBIT VIDEO
Laser Chart - *laserdisc releases* - VIDEO SOFTWARE MAGAZINE
Laser Discs - VIDEO REVIEW
Laser Entertainer - *review of new releases* - HOME VIEWER
Laser Scans - *home video column by Chris McGowan* - BILLBOARD
Last Desktop, The - *back cover commentary column by James Cavuoto* - COMPUTER PUBLISHING
Last Frame - *picture showcase* - OUTDOOR PHOTOGRAPHER
Last Licks - *portrait* - SOAP OPERA DIGEST
Last Lines - *'Small talk and hot wax from the flip side of What Video'* - WHAT VIDEO
Last Page - *film and video newsbriefs* - ALPHA AND OMEGA FILM REPORT
Last Page, The - *commentary* - AMERICAN CINEMATOGRAPHER
Last Pages - *BRJ comments on other media* - BLACK JOURNALISM REVIEW
Last Take - *'Up-to-the-minute inside cover news'* - REAL LIFE/DAYTIMERS
Last Week - *plot capsules* - SOAP OPERA WEEKLY
Last Word, The - *newsbriefs* - ADVERTISING & SELLING
Last Word, The - *editorial column by Wayne Green* - CD REVIEW
Last Word, The - *letters* - COMICS INTERVIEW
Last Word, The - *comment column by Mel Buchwald* - CONSUMER ELECTRONICS
Last Word, The - *editorial comment* - ENTERTAINMENT REVUE
Last Word, The - *editorial. (#15-77).* - JUMP CUT
Last Word - MEDIAWEEK
Last Word, The - *letters* - MODERN PHOTOGRAPHY
Last Word - *commentary column by Philip Thomas* - PHOTO ANSWERS
Last Word, The - RIGHTING WORDS
Last Word, The - *publisher commentary column by Steve Fiott* - STORYBOARD / THE ART OF LAUGHTER
Last Words - *editorial* - JOURNALIST
Last Words - VIEW
Late Breaks - *newsbriefs* - VIDEO BUSINESS
Late Comments - ROTKIN REVIEW, THE
Late Films - FILM WORLD AND A-V NEWS MAGAZINE
Late News - *recent ad campaigns* - ART DIRECTION
Late News - *column by Stan Pinkwas* - VIDEO MAGAZINE

Late News Roundup - WORLD BROADCAST NEWS
Latebreak - *late breaking news* - TV TECHNOLOGY
Latebreak - *news* - VIDEOGRAPHY
Late-Breaking News - SOAP OPERA DIGEST
Latent Images - *fascinating feature printing some bygone photos* - AMERICAN PHOTO
Latest Attractions - *home videotapes* - MOVING IMAGE
Latest Books - FIEJ-BULLETIN
Latest Cast Lists - *of soap operas* - DAYTIME TV
Latest Films - *extensive reviews* - CINEMATOGRAPHY AND BIOSCOPE MAGAZINE
Latest Importations - *international news of technological and business developments* - ST. LOUIS AND CANADIAN PHOTOGRAPHER
Latest News - DAYTIME TV
Latest Television, Radio Sets on the Market - TELEVISION RETAILING
Latin Notas - *column by Carlos Agudelo* - BILLBOARD
Latin Scene - *briefs* - BILLBOARD
Laugh Lighters - *jokes* - AMERICAN NEWSPAPER BOY, THE
Laugh Yourself Well - *column by Joey Adams* - STAR
Laughing Stock - *comedy column by Erskine Johnson* - PHOTOPLAY
Laughs From the Shows - *humorous lines from current Broadway hits* - STAGE PICTORIAL
Laughs of the Films - *cartoon cutups from current feature films* - NEW MOVIE MAGAZINE, THE
Launches - SATELLITE NEWS
Law, The - AMERICAN TELEPHONE JOURNAL, THE
Law - *legal aspects* - WITTYWORLD
Law Reports - ADWEEK
Law Review - *column by Sandra Salmans* - AGENCY
Law Review Articles - *review* - FOI DIGEST
Leader - *editorial* - BRITISH PRINTER
Leader - *editorial* - CAMPAIGN
Leading Album Rock Songs - *playlist* - INTERNATIONAL RADIO REPORT, THE
Leading Edge, The - TECHTRENDS
Leading Edge - *new technology column by Michael Heiss* - VIDEO SYSTEMS
Leading the Week - CABLEVISION
League Lines - *newsbriefs of ARRL* - QST
Learn - *'English by radio'* - BBC WORLD SERVICE LONDON CALLING
Learning Resources - *available films and videotapes* - TEACHER'S GUIDE TO TELEVISION
Leaves from a Short-Wave Log - *column by E. Thurway* - PRACTICAL WIRELESS
Lede, The - *commentary* - NEWSINC.
Lee Graham...Man About Town - *current newsbriefs* - HOLLYWOOD STUDIO MAGAZINE
Lee Graham's Scrapbook - *'collection of unpublished candid-camera photos* - HOLLYWOOD STUDIO MAGAZINE

Lee Hartgrave's Show Buzz - *column by Lee Hartgrave* - CASTING CALL
Legal - AMERICAN ADVERTISER REPORTER
Legal - ASMP BULLETIN
Legal - COLLEGE BROADCASTER
Legal - DBS NEWS
Legal - FUTUREHOME TECHNOLOGY NEWS
Legal Angle, The - VIDEOPRO
Legal Brief - *excellent resource column by Robert L. Seigel* - INDEPENDENT, THE
Legal Briefs - *excellent legal column* - INDEPENDENT, THE
Legal Decisions - AMERICAN JOURNALIST, THE
Legal Developments in Marketing - JOURNAL OF MARKETING
Legal Eye - PHOTO/DESIGN
Legal Labyrinths - PRINTING IMPRESSIONS
Legal Line - INFORMATION TODAY
Legal Notebook - *in-depth articles on current broadcast issues* - EBU REVIEW. PROGRAMMES, ADMINISTRATION, LAW.
Legal Notes - *newsbriefs* - HOLLYWOOD REPORTER
Legal Outlook - *column by Robert Posch* - DIRECT MARKETING
Legal Photographer - STUDIO PHOTOGRAPHY
Legal Problems in Photography - CAMERA MAGAZINE
Legal Watch - ADWEEK'S MARKETING WEEK
Legal Wrap-Up - *newsbriefs* - ASCAP IN ACTION
Legalities - *legal information forum* - MARKETING COMMUNICATIONS
Legally Speaking - *column by Sidney Kleinman* - PROFESSIONAL PHOTOGRAPHER, THE
Legislation - PRESSTIME
Legislation - VIDEO TECHNOLOGY NEWS
Legislative and Administrative Activities - *comments on radio law and legislation* - AIR LAW REVIEW
Legit - VARIETY
Legit Reviews - SHOW BIZ WEST
Legitimate Theater - *newsbriefs* - OFFICIAL BULLETIN OF THE INTERNATIONAL ALLIANCE OF THEATRICAL STAGE EMPLOYEES AND MOVING PICTURE MACHINE OPERATORS OF THE UNITED STATES AND CANADA.
Lehman at Large - *commentary column by Ernest Lehman* - AMERICAN FILM
Leica Chatter - SHUTTERBUG
Leica News - *product information* - LEICA PHOTOGRAPHY
Lens Caps - *comment and observations* - FILMMAKERS FILM & VIDEO MONTHLY
Lens Lines - *'Commentary by the editors on things seen and heard'* - CAMERA 35
Lens Lines - *column by Willard Clark* - TRAVEL & LEISURE
Leo Jr's Lion-Up - *listing of new MGM short films* - METRO-GOLDWYN-MAYER SHORT STORY
Leonard Maltin's Cartoon Column - KORKIS AND CAWLEY'S CARTOON QUARTERLY

Departments INDEX

Lessons From the Movies - *issues of a moral and family nature to be learned from current releases* - MOTION PICTURE AND THE FAMILY, THE
Lest We Forget - *trivia* - TALKING SCREEN
Let's Get the Facts - *unique reader questionaire feature* - AMERICAN PRINTER
Let's Talk--Music - *column by Julie Ellis* - BLACK STARS
Letter - ACUSTICA
Letter - *excellent letters detailing the status of photography in a world city* - AMERICAN PHOTO
Letter - CINEMA/CANADA
Letter - *unique for international participation* - SIGHT & SOUND
Letter Box - RADIO DIAL
Letter box - *letters* - SOAP OPERA STARS
Letter Connection - *pen pal listing* - SMASH HITS
Letter from Abroad, A - ALBUM, THE
Letter From America - *column by Gerald Walker* - WORLD BROADCAST NEWS
Letter From London - *column by Peter Fletcher* - ELECTRONICS
Letter from London - *current European television fare and thoughts* - PUBLIC TELECOMMUNICATIONS REVIEW
Letter from London - *column by Barrie Heads* - TBI
Letter from Rick, A - *editorial column by Rick Norwood* - COMICS REVUE
Letter From Switzerland - *column by Fred Barron* - TAKE ONE
Letter From the Editor - FILMS IN REVIEW
Letter From the Editor - *editorial preview column by Judith Morrison* - HOME ENTERTAINMENT
Letter From the Editor - *column by Bruce J. Schoengood* - HORRORFAN
Letter From the Editor - JOURNAL OF MARKETING EDUCATION
Letter From the Editor - TEEN DREAM
Letter From the President - NEWSLETTER, THE
Letter Page - *'The pros speak'* - COMIC CELLAR, THE
Letter to Editor - DIRECT MARKETING
Letter to the Editor - CLIO AMONG THE MEDIA
Letter to the Editor - NEW THEATRE MAGAZINE
Letter to the Editor - NEWSPAPER TECHNIQUES
Letter to the Editor - PRINTING HISTORY
Letter to the Editor - VIA SATELLITE
Letter to the Editor - VICTORIAN PERIODICALS REVIEW
Letterbox, The - *letters* - VIDEO WATCHDOG
Letterhead Design - PRINT
Lettering - *letters* - COMICS SCENE
Letters - *large section* - AD WEEKLY
Letters - ADVERTISING AGE
Letters - ADWEEK
Letters - ADWEEK'S MARKETING WEEK
Letters - AEU
Letters - AFTER DARK
Letters - AMERICAN CINEMATOGRAPHER
Letters - AMERICAN DEMOGRAPHICS

Letters - AMERICAN FILM
Letters - *'With Bob Dorian'* - AMERICAN MOVIE CLASSICS MAGAZINE
Letters - AMUSEMENT BUSINESS
Letters - ANIMATIONS
Letters - AP BROADCASTER
Letters - APPLIED ARTS QUARTERLY
Letters - ART DIRECTION
Letters - ART PAPERS
Letters - ASIAN ADVERTISING & MARKETING
Letters - AUSTRALIAN PHOTOGRAPHY
Letters - AV VIDEO
Letters - AVC
Letters - BETTER RADIO AND TELEVISION
Letters - BRITISH JOURNAL OF PHOTOGRAPHY
Letters - BROADCAST
Letters - BROADCAST REPORTER
Letters - CABLE TV BUSINESS MAGAZINE
Letters - CAMERA 35
Letters - CANTRILLS FILMNOTES
Letters - CAR AUDIO AND ELECTRONICS
Letters - CELEBRITY PLUS
Letters - CHANNELS
Letters - *caustic, humorous and important reader viewpoints* - CHICAGO JOURNALISM REVIEW
Letters - CINEASTE
Letters - CINEFANTASTIQUE
Letters - CINEMA PAPERS
Letters - CINEMANEWS, THE
Letters - CLIO MAGAZINE
Letters - COLLEGE BROADCASTER
Letters - COLUMBIA JOURNALISM REVIEW
Letters - *extensive commentary by readers* - COMIC RELIEF
Letters - COMICS FEATURE
Letters - COMPUTER PUBLISHING
Letters - CORPORATE TELEVISION
Letters - COSMEP NEWSLETTER
Letters - CQ
Letters - CREATIVE CAMERA
Letters - CRITIC
Letters - DB
Letters - DWB
Letters - EDITOR'S WORKSHOP
Letters - EDUCATIONAL COMMUNICATION AND TECHNOLOGY
Letters - ELECTRONICS AND COMMUNICATIONS
Letters - ELECTRONICS WORLD
Letters - ELECTRONICS WORLD + WIRELESS WORLD
Letters - EMMY
Letters - EMPIRE
Letters - EXPOSURE
Letters - *very extensive section* - FA
Letters - FACETS FEATURES
Letters - *'The readers talk back, with a few pot shots from the editor'* - FACTSHEET FIVE
Letters - FALLING FOR STARS
Letters - FILM & HISTORY
Letters - FILM COMMENT
Letters - FILM MAKING
Letters - FILM WITNESS
Letters - FILMMAKERS FILM & VIDEO MONTHLY
Letters - FILMS ILLUSTRATED

Letters - FILMS IN REVIEW
Letters - FLAKE
Letters - FOLIO:
Letters - FOUR A NEWSLETTER
Letters - FOUR COLOR
Letters - FRESH!
Letters - FUNNYWORLD
Letters - GRASSROOTS EDITOR
Letters - HI-FI ANSWERS
Letters - HIGH FIDELITY
Letters - HIGH FIDELITY/MUSICAL AMERICA
Letters - HIGH PERFORMANCE
Letters - HIGH VOLUME PRINTING
Letters - HOLLYWOOD STUDIO MAGAZINE
Letters - HOW
Letters - IMAGE
Letters - IMAGE TECHNOLOGY
Letters - IN-PLANT PRINTER & ELECTRONIC PUBLISHER
Letters - INDEPENDENT, THE
Letters - INFORMATION TODAY
Letters - INSIDE HOLLYWOOD
Letters - INSIDE MEDIA
Letters - INTERNATIONAL ADVERTISER
Letters - INTERNATIONAL FILM BUFF
Letters - INTERNATIONAL RADIO REPORT, THE
Letters - LIGHTING DIMENSIONS
Letters - MAGAZINE DESIGN & PRODUCTION
Letters - MARKETING / COMMUNICATIONS
Letters - MARKETING NEWS
Letters - MEDIA WEEK
Letters - MEDIAWEEK
Letters - MEMORIES
Letters - MGF
Letters - MILLIMETER
Letters - MODERN PHOTOGRAPHY
Letters - MONITORING TIMES
Letters - MOVIE MAGAZINE, THE
Letters - MOVIE MARKETPLACE
Letters - MOVIEGOER
Letters - MOVIELINE
Letters - MOVING IMAGE
Letters - MUSICAL AMERICA
Letters - *unusually lively replies of members on current issues* - NEWS PHOTOGRAPHER
Letters - NEWSINC.
Letters - NEWSLETTER
Letters - ON CABLE
Letters - OUTDOOR & TRAVEL PHOTOGRAPHY
Letters - PANORAMA
Letters - PC PUBLISHING AND PRESENTATIONS
Letters - *outstanding section containing letters of considered comment and criticism* - PERFECT VISION, THE
Letters - PERFORMANCE
Letters - PERSONAL PUBLISHING
Letters - PHOTOGRAPHER'S FORUM
Letters - PHOTOPRO
Letters - PLAYERS
Letters - PMA NEWSLETTER
Letters - POPULAR ELECTRONICS
Letters - POPULAR PHOTOGRAPHY
Letters - POST
Letters - PRE-
Letters - PRESSTIME

Letters - PRINT EDUCATION MAGAZINE
Letters - PROFESSIONAL PHOTOGRAPHER, THE
Letters - PROMOTION
Letters - PUBLIC RELATIONS QUARTERLY
Letters - PUBLISH!
Letters - QUILL, THE
Letters - RADIO-ELECTRONICS
Letters - RADIO ONLY
Letters - REP: RECORDING ENGINEERING PRODUCTION
Letters - SALES & MARKETING MANAGEMENT
Letters - SATELLITE ORBIT
Letters - SATELLITE RETAILER
Letters - SCREEN ACTOR HOLLYWOOD
Letters - SCREEN FACTS
Letters - SHOW
Letters - SIGHT & SOUND
Letters - SOUTHERN THEATRE
Letters - STAGE AND TELEVISION TODAY, THE
Letters - STEP-BY-STEP GRAPHICS
Letters - STEREO REVIEW
Letters - *unusually large and literate letters to the editor column* - STEREOPHILE
Letters - TAKE ONE
Letters - TAPE DECK QUARTERLY
Letters - TELESPAN'S BUSINESSTV GUIDE
Letters - TELEVISION
Letters - TELEVISION & FAMILIES
Letters - TELEVISION/RADIO AGE
Letters - TELEVISION WEEK
Letters - THEATRE ARTS
Letters - THEATRE CRAFTS
Letters - *extensive section with responses* - TIME SCREEN
Letters - TRAVEL & LEISURE
Letters - TV GUIDE
Letters - 20/20
Letters - UK PRESS GAZETTE
Letters - US MAGAZINE
Letters - VARIETY
Letters - *'Your say, your way!'* - VIDEO BUYER
Letters - VIDEO REVIEW
Letters - VIDEO STORE
Letters - VIDEO TIMES
Letters - VIDEODISC MONITOR, THE
Letters - VIDEOGRAPHY
Letters - VIDEOMAKER
Letters - VISUAL EDUCATION
Letters - WASHINGTON JOURNALISM REVIEW
Letters - WATCH
Letters - W • B
Letters - WITTYWORLD
Letters - WORLD PRESS REVIEW
Letters - *with long inquiries and responses* - WRITER'S DIGEST
Letters and Comment - NABET NEWS
Letters and Late News - *letters* - REP: RECORDING ENGINEERING PRODUCTION
Letters & Notes - *letters to the editor plus newsbriefs* - COMMUNICATIONS CONCEPTS
Letters and Pictures to the Editor - TV SCREEN
Letters, Etc. - TDR

Letters From - *news of contemporary photography from Boston, New York, Japan, Minneapolis and other centers* - CONTEMPORARY PHOTOGRAPHER
Letters from Our Readers - ADWEEK
Letters From Our Readers - ELECTRONICS WORLD
Letters from Readers - ADVERTISING AGENCY
Letters From the Fringe Few! - *extensive pasionate letter section* - CELLULOID NIGHTMARE
Letters From the Stars - *unique letters twist with signatures* - RADIOLAND
Letters to Editor - DAYTIME TV
Letters to Loretta - *Personal Q&A column by Loretta Swit* - NIGHTTIME TV
Letters to LSoH - LITTLE SHOPPE OF HORRORS
Letters to Print - PRINT
Letters to Show Business - SHOW BUSINESS
Letters to the *Masthead* - MASTHEAD
Letters to the Editor - ABC WEEKLY
Letters to the Editor - ADVANCED IMAGING
Letters to the Editor - ADVERTISER MAGAZINE, THE
Letters to the Editor - ADVERTISING AND MARKETING MANAGEMENT
Letters to the Editor - ADWEEK
Letters to the Editor - AMERICAN PRINTER
Letters to the Editor - AMERICAN THEATRE
Letters to the Editor - BACK STAGE/SHOOT
Letters to the Editor - BASELINE
Letters to the Editor - BILLBOARD
Letters to the Editor - BPME IMAGE MAGAZINE
Letters to the Editor - *'Kudos, challenges, criticisms and ideas from our readers'* - CAMERA 35 INCORPORATING PHOTO WORLD
Letters to the Editor - CELEBRITY
Letters to the Editor - CINEMACABRE
Letters to the Editor - DESKTOP COMMUNICATIONS
Letters to the Editor - EDITOR AND PUBLISHER
Letters to the Editor - ELECTRONIC MEDIA
Letters to the Editor - ELECTRONIC TECHNICIAN/DEALER
Letters to the Editor - ELECTRONICS AND COMMUNICATIONS
Letters to the Editor - ELECTRONICS & COMMUNICATIONS
Letters to the Editor - ELECTRONICS WORLD + WIRELESS WORLD
Letters to the Editor - ENTERTAINMENT WORLD
Letters to the Editor - FACTS ABOUT FILM FINLAND
Letters to the Editor - FILM MEDIA
Letters to the Editor - GOOD OLD DAYS
Letters to the Editor - HI-FI HERETIC
Letters to the Editor - *'Readers respond to Horrorfan'* - HORRORFAN
Letters to the Editor - HUMAN COMMUNICATION CANADA
Letters to the Editor - IN MOTION FILM & VIDEO PRODUCTION MAGAZINE
Letters to the Editor - INDEX ON CENSORSHIP
Letters to the Editor - IRB

Letters to the Editor - JOURNAL OF EDUCATIONAL TELEVISION
Letters to the Editor - JOURNAL OF SPEECH AND HEARING DISORDERS
Letters to the Editor - LISTENER
Letters to the Editor - MARKETING / COMMUNICATIONS
Letters to the Editor - MEDIA DIGEST
Letters to the Editor - MODERN PHOTOGRAPHY
Letters to the Editor - MODERN RECORDING & MUSIC
Letters to the Editor - NIGHTTIME TV
Letters to the Editor - OVERSET
Letters to the Editor - PD REPORT
Letters to the Editor - PERFORMER, THE
Letters to the Editor - PERSONAL ELECTRONICS
Letters to the Editor - POPULAR PHOTOGRAPHY
Letters to the Editor - PUBLIC TELECOMMUNICATIONS REVIEW
Letters to the Editor - RADIO DEALER, THE
Letters to the Editor - RELIGIOUS MEDIA TODAY
Letters to the Editor - SPECTRA
Letters to the Editor - SPEECH AND DRAMA
Letters to the Editor - STEREO REVIEW
Letters to the Editor - STUDIO PHOTOGRAPHY
Letters to the Editor - SUCCESSFUL MAGAZINE PUBLISHING
Letters to the Editor - TELECAST
Letters to the Editor - TELEMARKETING
Letters to the Editor - TELEVISION AND SCREEN GUIDE
Letters to the Editor - THEATRE, THE
Letters to the Editor - TRAVEL & LEISURE
Letters to the Editor - *unique due to flavor and content* - TWIN CITIES JOURNALISM REVIEW
Letters to the Editor - VIDEO TODAY
Letters to the Editor - VIEWS
Letters to the editor - WRITER, THE
Letters to the Editor - WRITER'S NW
Letters to the Editor & to NACB - COLLEGE BROADCASTER
Letters to the Editors - AMERICAN AMATEUR PHOTOGRAPHER AND CAMERA & DARKROOM
Letter-Writers' Symposium - ADVERTISING
Lettin' Loose! - *reader comment on teen stars* - SUPER TEEN
Libel Clinic - *column by Barbara Dill* - PUBLISHER'S AUXILIARY
Library Technology - INFORMATION TODAY
Licensed Release Dates - EXHIBITORS' TIMES
Life of Childhood, The - ALBUM, THE
Life Story of a Soap - *historical profile* - SOAP OPERA WEEKLY
Life Styles - SOUND & IMAGE
Lifelines - *marriage announcements and 'Final curtains' obituaries* - AMUSEMENT BUSINESS
Lifelines - *births, marriages and deaths* - BILLBOARD
Lifestyle Products - *consumer gift product review* - SATELLITE ORBIT

Departments INDEX

Lifestyles - *'How to entertain with your VCR'* column by Nao Hauser - ORBIT VIDEO
LIFO - *new product newsbriefs* - DEALERSCOPE
Light and Lighting - *column by Peter Nicastro* - STUDIO PHOTOGRAPHY
Light Entertainment - STAGE AND TELEVISION TODAY, THE
Light in the Darkroom - *technique and operation* - INDUSTRIAL PHOTOGRAPHY
Light Readings - *column by A. D. Coleman* - CAMERA 35 INCORPORATING PHOTO WORLD
Light Topics - CAMERA AND DARK ROOM
Lighter Side, The - *of satellite television programs* - SATELLITE TIMES
Lighting - *column by Karl Ruling* - THEATRE CRAFTS
Lighting - THEATRE DESIGN & TECHNOLOGY
Lighting Angles - CAMERA MAGAZINE
Lighting Equipment - MONITOR INTERNATIONAL
Lighting Gallery - PHOTOMETHODS
Lighting School - *column by Laurie Haynes* - PIC
Lighting Technology - *STLD information column by Alf Hunter* - BROADCAST + TECHNOLOGY
Lighting-Sets - *how-to and news items* - INTERNATIONAL PHOTOGRAPHER
Lights and Lighting - *feature* - PHOTOMETHODS
Lights, Camera, Action - *shots of stars on the set* - PREVIEW
Lights On - *column by Teal Marchande* - SHOWCASE WORLD
Lincoln Sample, The - *a cross-country odyssey column by Tom Parker* - AMERICAN DEMOGRAPHICS
Line In/Line Out - *information for corresponding* - EQ
Line Out - RADIO WORLD
Line-On Hollywood - *movie star newsbriefs* - ON LINE
Lines and Splices - *editorial* - BIG REEL, THE
Line-Up, The - *celebrity news column by A. Lee Stewart* - MOVIE HUMOR
Lingua Fractured - RIGHTING WORDS
Links & Patches - *newsbriefs* - INTERNATIONAL BROADCASTING
Lion's Den, Th - *column by Gene Phillips* - COMIC INFORMER
List Management - TARGET MARKETING
List News - *direct mail list news* - DIRECT MARKETING
List News - *magazine mailing lists* - MAGAZINEWEEK
List News - *'...for and about the list business'* - TARGET MARKETING
List of Announcements - *publishers booklists* - AMERICAN LITERARY GAZETTE AND PUBLISHERS' CIRCULAR
List of Broadcast Stations in the United States - ELECTRONICS WORLD
List of Previewed Pictures - SELECTED MOTION PICTURES
List of Television Stations - RADIO REVIEW AND TELEVISION NEWS
List Watch - FOLIO:

Listen For a Minute - *editorial* - THEATRE CRAFT
Listener, The - *column by C.M. Stanbury* - ELECTRONICS ILLUSTRATED
Listeners' Letters - AMATEUR WIRELESS AND RADIOVISION
Listeners Notebook - FRENDX
Listening In - *'Practical pointers from experimenters and broadcast listeners'* - POPULAR RADIO AND TELEVISION
Listening Post - *shortwave* - ELECTRONICS AND COMMUNICATIONS
Listening Post - *'What's happening: international shortwave broadcasting bands'* - POPULAR COMMUNICATIONS
Listening Post - POST
Listings - *Gallerys and current exhibitions* - AMERICAN PHOTO
Listings - *'Comic consumer guide'* - COMICS FEATURE
Listings and Ratings - *'What's on, where, and how good is it?'* - SHOW BUSINESS ILLUSTRATED
Literacy - GF MAGAZINE
Literary Chatter - *newsbriefs* - THEATRE, THE
Literary Intelligence - *newsbriefs* - AMERICAN LITERARY GAZETTE AND PUBLISHERS' CIRCULAR
Literary News and Notes - *information concerning upcoming publications* - AUTHOR, THE
Literary Notes - EDITORIAL REVIEW
Literati - *book reviews* - VARIETY
Literature - AUDIO VISUAL
Literature - ELECTRONIC PUBLISHER
Literature - IN-PLANT PRINTER & ELECTRONIC PUBLISHER
Literature - INDEX ON CENSORSHIP
Literature - *review* - TECHTRENDS
Literature - THEATRE, THE
Literature and Supplies - *new products* - ADVERTISING AND GRAPHIC ARTS TECHNIQUES
Literature and Supplies - *new products* - ART DIRECTION
Literature & Supplies - ART DIRECTION
Literature Directory - HIGH VOLUME PRINTING
Literature Exchange - COMPUTER PUBLISHING
Literature Library - COMMUNICATIONS WORLD
Literature of Business - *new books and magazines concerning advertising* - ADVERTISING ADVOCATE
Literature Review - TELEMATICS AND INFORMATICS
Literature Showcase - PUBLIC RELATIONS JOURNAL, THE
Literature/Samples - GRAPHIC ARTS MONTHLY
Lithography, Printing & Production - *column by Milton Rich* - ADVERTISER MAGAZINE, THE
Lithotips - PRINTING IMPRESSIONS
Little Birdie Told Me, A - *'Thelma Scumm, animation's most prominent society reporter, tells all about everybody who's anybody'* - ANIMATO!

Little Cinema - *news on art, documentary, religious and educational releases* - CINEMA
Little Hints to Screenwriters - PHOTODRAMATIST, THE
Little Lessons in Photo-Engraving - MORE BUSINESS
Little Schoolmaster's Class, The - MARKETING / COMMUNICATIONS
Little Stories of Reel Life - REEL LIFE
Little Theatre in Australia, The - ABC WEEKLY
Live & Direct - *column by David Scheirman* - REP: RECORDING ENGINEERING PRODUCTION
Live News and Notes of the International Advertising Association - FOURTH ESTATE
Live News of the West Coast - *Hollywood trade news column by Renee Beeman* - EXHIBITORS TRADE REVIEW
Live Sound - *'Keeping abreast of live sound news and equipment'* - STUDIO SOUND AND BROADCAST ENGINEERING
Livestock Markets - *program guide* - RURAL RADIO
Living Legend - ENTERTAINMENT CONNECTION MAGAZINE
Local Lines - *an average 40 pages of IBEW local news* - IBEW JOURNAL
Local Manipulation - *comment* - AMATEUR PHOTOGRAPHER'S WEEKLY, THE
Local Pop Music - *review column by Michael Cohen and Debbie Catalano* - CASTING NEWS
Local Radio - TAPE
Local Releases - BOXOFFICE
Local Scenes - *programming ideas for the local market* - NATPE PROGRAMMER
Local Spots - *local spot avails news* - MSO'S CABLE MARKETING
Local Stages - *media profile* - SCRIPTWRITER NEWS
Local, State and Regional News - NATIONAL PHOTOGRAPHER, THE
Local, State and Regional News - PROFESSIONAL PHOTOGRAPHER, THE
Local Update - *Pacific northwest production news* - PRINTED MATTER
Locals - *'original and catchy write ups'* - AMERICAN ADVERTISER
Location Forum - *'letters, opinions, stories'* - LOCATION UPDATE
Location Shooting: Who's Shooting Where - *column by Casey Barnett* - AMERICAN PREMIERE
Locker Room - ENTERTAINMENT CONNECTION MAGAZINE
Log Report - FRENDX
Logos - PROMOTION
London - *city review column by Michael Leech* - AFTER DARK
London Calling - *British sound news column by Terri Anderson & Jim Evans* - PRO SOUND NEWS
London Critics' Opinions - *films* - VARIETY
London Diary - *commentary column by Neil Murray* - MOVIE - THE VIDEO MAGAZINE

London Jottings - *news column by Edward Dryhurst* - GREATER AMUSEMENTS
London Letter - *column by Douglas Macdonald Hastings* - BBC WORLD SERVICE LONDON CALLING
London Letter - CABLEAGE
London Letter - *interesting British photo news column by Corrine Cadby and Will Cadby* - PHOTO-ERA MAGAZINE
London News - *news of London theatre, column by Sheridan Morley* - PLAYBILL
London Notices - *interesting actor profiles of current stage shows* - PLAYS INTERNATIONAL
London Observations - *column by Jock MacGregor* - SHOWMEN'S TRADE REVIEW
London Playguide - PLAYS AND PLAYERS
London Report - ADVERTISER MAGAZINE, THE
London Scene - *film news* - MOTION PICTURE PRODUCT DIGEST
London Shows - *play directory for greater London* - PLAYS INTERNATIONAL
London Shows - VARIETY
London Theatre, The - *playlist* - THEATRE
London Theatre - THEATRE
London Theatres at a Glance - *playbill* - ARTHURIAN THEATRE MAGAZINE, THE
Long-Range Planning and Marketing - PRESS STATISTICAL REVIEW
Look, The - MOVIELINE
Look Ahead, A - *calendar* - CABLE WORLD
Look of the Book, The - *critique and suggestions on publication design* - COMMUNICATION WORLD
Looking - *Media producers looking for new writers or material* - SCRIPTWRITER NEWS
Looking Ahead - *new upcoming product* - CANADIAN FILM DIGEST
Looking Ahead - *news items* - PC PUBLISHING AND PRESENTATIONS
Looking Ahead - *'A sampling of upcoming articles'* - STEP-BY-STEP GRAPHICS
Looking Ahead - *upcoming events* - TECHNICAL PHOTOGRAPHY
Looking Ahead - *column* - VIDEO REVIEW
Looking Ahead with Bijou - *commentary column by Bill O'Connell* - BIJOU
Looking & Booking - *live show status* - VARIETY
Looking at New Literature - TECHTRENDS
Looking Back - *Art Direction graphics of yesteryear* - ART DIRECTION
Looking Back - *twenty-five years ago in California newspapers* - CALIFORNIA PUBLISHER
Looking Back - *daytime stars moved to nighttime television programs* - SOAP OPERA TIME
Looking Back - *historical feature* - SPECIALTY ADVERTISING BUSINESS
Looking Hollywood Way - *film entertainment of yesteryear* - GOOD OLD DAYS
Looking In On Business Television - *column by David W. Shively* - TELESPAN'S BUSINESSTV GUIDE
Loose Cruse - *column by Howard Cruse* - COMICS SCENE

Loose Talk - *interesting quotes column by Lisa Bernhard* - US MAGAZINE
Los Angeles - *city review column by Viola Hegyi Swisher* - AFTER DARK
Los Angeles Critics' Opinions - *films* - VARIETY
Los Angeles Notes - *Southern California exhibitor newsbriefs column by H.D. McBride* - UNIVERSAL WEEKLY
Los Angeles Watch - WATCH
Lost and Found - *review of overlooked films* - CINEASTE
Lost Stars - *where is?* - MOVIE DIGEST
Lotlot and Friends - *personality column by Lotlot DeLeon* - MOVIE FLASH
Lottery Feeds - *fascinating programming guide on 'Where to find the winners'* - SATELLITE TV WEEK
Loudspeaker, The - OLD TIMER'S BULLETIN, THE
Loudspeakers - SOUND & VISION
Louella Parsons - *'Modern Screen's 8 page gossip extra by Hollywood's greatest columnist' column by Louella Parsons* - MODERN SCREEN
Louisville - BOX OFFICE
Lou's Views! - *'It's the pictures the stars begged us not to print!' column by Lou Palu* - SMASH HITS
Love and the Law - *column by Raoul Lionel Felder* - FAME
Love of Life - *abstract* - SOAP OPERA DIGEST
Low Power Television Report - VIDEOPRO
Lowdown on the music scene' column by Dianne Bennett - GOSSIP
Lower Case, The - *comic comment* - COLUMBIA JOURNALISM REVIEW
LP Session Report - *production news* - PRO SOUND NEWS
LPTV and the Law - *legal column by Peter Tannenwald* - LPTV REPORT, THE
Lucasfilm Games - *product review* - LUCASFILM FAN CLUB, THE
Lunching with Bonzai - *column by Mr. Bonzai* - MIX

M

M & M Visits - *how cities use media* - MEDIA & METHODS
M Street Law - *'The law in public broadcasting'* - CURRENT
Machine of the Month - MONITOR INTERNATIONAL
Macro Scan - *conferences, workshops, seminars upcoming* - TELESCAN
Mac's Service Shop - *technical column by John T. Frye* - ELECTRONICS WORLD
Magazine - *column by Janet Terry* - CMA NEWSLETTER

Magazine Business Notebook - *'Update of news and trends in publishing'* - MAGAZINE BUSINESS
Magazine Chat - *editor's column by George Bugniazet* - JOURNAL
Magazine Comparison - *ad pages, circulation and CPM figures on 40+ Christian periodicals* - CHRISTIAN ADVERTISING FORUM
Magazine Directory - MAGAZINE & BOOKSELLER
Magazine Notes - *newsbriefs* - ADVERTISING ADVOCATE
Magazine Notes - MAGAZINE DESIGN & PRODUCTION
Magazine People - *personality profile* - FOLIO:
Magazine Photography - *column by Roy Pinney* - TRAVEL & LEISURE
Magazine Print Focus - AUSTRALASIAN PRINTER
Magazine Print Scope - *pre-press developments* - AUSTRALASIAN PRINTER
Magazine Publicity - CURRENT ADVERTISING
Magazine Rack, The - *news of new periodicals* - FILM & VIDEO NEWS
Magazine Rack - *serial photos* - PHOTO DISTRICT NEWS
Magazine Spotlight - AUSTRALASIAN PRINTER
Magazine Watch - FOLIO:
Magazines - ADVERTISING & SELLING
Magazines - INSIDE MEDIA
Magazines - *commentary* - MEDIAWEEK
Magazines - UK PRESS GAZETTE
Magazines-Newspapers - *reviews* - GREATER AMUSEMENTS
Magne Tests - *column by Lawrence Magne* - MONITORING TIMES
Mail Art Contacts - FACTSHEET FIVE
Mail Bag - *letters* - INTERNATIONAL PHOTOGRAPHER
Mail Bag - *'Letters from readers'* - INTERNATIONAL PHOTOGRAPHER MAGAZINE
Mail Box, The - *letters* - BIG REEL, THE
Mail Order and Advertising Pointers - *column by T. R. McKeown* - SCHEMER, THE
Mail Pouch - *'Words, some kind' letters* - HOLLYWOOD MAGAZINE
Mail Room, The - *letters* - VIDEO SOFTWARE MAGAZINE
Mailbag - FILM ARTISTE
Mailbag - *letters* - ONSAT
Mailbag - *'Letters to the editor'* - POPULAR COMMUNICATIONS
Mailbag - *letters* - TV HITS
Mailbox - CAMERA & DARKROOM PHOTOGRAPHY
Mailbox - *letters* - DARKROOM PHOTOGRAPHY
Mailbox - *letters* - GRAPHIC ARTS MONTHLY
Mailbox - WRITERS' JOURNAL
Mailroom - *fulfillment news* - POLYGRAPH INTERNATIONAL
Mailsack - *letters* - MEDIA SIGHT
Main Street - *personality column by Ted Green* - BACK STAGE
Main Street - *comment and gossip* - RTD
Maine - BOX OFFICE

Departments INDEX

Mainly About People in the Advertising Business - ADVERTISING NEWS
Mainly About Women - ABC WEEKLY
Mainly Movie Crossword, The - PREMIUM CHANNELS TV BLUEPRINT
Mainly Personal - ADWEEK
Mainstream - *'MMR's Mainstream chart calculates the rotations monitored on major market mainstream [format] stations'* - MONDAY MORNING REPLAY
Majors/Secondaries/Daypart Chart - *'MMR breaks out [format] airplay in the top 25 markets, and markets #25 and down for a better guage of major and secondary market airplay'* - MONDAY MORNING REPLAY
Make Mine Movies - *'A series of help and advice for the non-expert film-maker'* column by Peter Dean - AMATEUR PHOTOGRAPHER
Make the Subject Interesting - *column by Harry M. Nelson* - PROFESSIONAL PHOTOGRAPHER, THE
Makeup FX Lab - *fascinating how-to makeup series* - GOREZONE
Making $$$ in Filmmaking - FILMMAKERS FILM & VIDEO MONTHLY
Making Money - CAMERA & DARKROOM PHOTOGRAPHY
Making Money - *in photography, column by Maria Piscopo* - DARKROOM PHOTOGRAPHY
Making Money - *column by Janis Bultman* - MOVING IMAGE
Making News - *newsbriefs* - BUSINESS AND THE MEDIA
Making of the Covers - *how front cover was created* - COMPUTER PICTURES
Making Retail Advertisements - AMERICAN ADVERTISER
Making the Theatre Pay - EXHIBITORS TRADE REVIEW
Malcolm Boyes' Real Life Show Biz Column - *column by Malcolm Boye* - REAL LIFE/DAYTIMERS
Man About Town - *column by Lee Graham* - HOLLYWOOD STUDIO MAGAZINE
Man in Japan - *business newsbriefs* - CONSUMER ELECTRONICS
Man in the Cage, The - *comment* - AD SENSE
Management - *newsbriefs concerning changes or promotions* - AMUSEMENT BUSINESS
Management - CABLEVISION
Management - *personnel briefs* - FOLIO:
Management - HIGH VOLUME PRINTING
Management - HYPERMEDIA
Management - *commentary* - IN-PLANT PRINTER & ELECTRONIC PUBLISHER
Management - *'skills and advice for improving your job performance'* - NATPE PROGRAMMER
Management - *column by Brad Dick* - VIDEO SYSTEMS
Management Edge - *column by David Sylvester* - ELECTRONICS
Management for Engineers - BROADCAST ENGINEERING

Management Measures - PRINTING IMPRESSIONS
Management Moves - ADWEEK'S MARKETING WEEK
Management Strategies - CORPORATE VIDEO DECISIONS
Management Tips - BPME IMAGE MAGAZINE
Managers and Agents of Film Artists - PERFORMER, THE
Managers' Round Table - *'An international association of showmen meeting weekly in Motion Picture Herald for mutual aid and progress'* - MOTION PICTURE HERALD
Managing MIDI - *column by Paul D. Lehrman* - REP: RECORDING ENGINEERING PRODUCTION
Managing Newspaper People - *column by Sara Brown* - PUBLISHER'S AUXILIARY
Managing Publications - WRITING CONCEPTS
Managing Technology - IEEE SPECTRUM
Manhattan Party Line - PHOTO SCREEN
Manhattan Tips - *'And Adventures in Eating'* - THEATRE, THE
Manilla - BOX OFFICE
Manilla in Motion - *news column by James Manilla* - INDUSTRIAL PHOTOGRAPHY
Manufacturers - *newsbriefs* - PRODUCCIÓN Y DISTRIBUCIÓN
Manufacturers' Comments - *an opportunity for stereo equipment manufacturers to speak out* - STEREOPHILE
Manufacturer's Corner - *response* - ABSOLUTE SOUND, THE
Manufacturers' Literature - ELECTRONICS WORLD
Manufacturers Products - ELECTRONICS WORLD + WIRELESS WORLD
Manufacturer's Showcase - *product briefs* - VIDEO TIMES
Manufacturer's Spotlight - PRINT BUYERS REVIEW
Manufacturers Technical Digest - *technical information for servicing* - ELECTRONIC TECHNICAN/DEALER
Manufacturing & Supply - CANADIAN PRINTER
Maple Briefs - *Canadian newsbriefs* - BILLBOARD
March of Music, The - *radio musical highlights for the week* - MOVIE-RADIO GUIDE
March of Radio, The - *general industry briefs* - RADIO BROADCAST
Marconi News and Notes - MARCONI REVIEW, THE
Marginal Notes - *technical column by Walther Benser* - LEICA PHOTOGRAPHY
Margins - *column by George Myers* - SMALL PRESS
Marilyn Beck's Hollywood - *personality column by Marilyn Beck* - SPOTLIGHT CASTING MAGAZINE
Market, The - *economic and manufacturing newsbriefs* - VUE
Market Diary - *stock performance of selected cable television companies* - CABLE WORLD
Market Eye - CHANNELS

Market Info - *briefs* - BUSINESS MARKETING
Market Memoranda - *individual market surveys concerning a particular programming format* - BROADCAST PROGRAMMING AND PRODUCTION
Market News - *particulars on specific publications* - WRITER, THE
Market Newsletter - *late-breaking news in writing field* - WRITER, THE
Market Page - STUDIO PHOTOGRAPHY
Market Place, The - *reader equipment responses* - ABSOLUTE SOUND, THE
Market Profile - *outstanding regional media/advertising opportunity profile* - INSIDE MEDIA
Market Profile - *monthly profile of a specific radio market* - RADIO*PHILES
Market Quotations - *major music organizations* - BILLBOARD
Market Studies - ADVERTISING AGENCY
Market Trends - JEE, JOURNAL OF ELECTRONIC ENGINEERING
Market View - VIZIONS
Marketer's Economist, The - ADWEEK'S MARKETING WEEK
Marketers, Etc. - *newsbriefs* - SALES & MARKETING MANAGEMENT
Marketing - *of cable services* - CABLE COMMUNICATIONS MAGAZINE
Marketing - CABLE WORLD
Marketing - CABLEAGE
Marketing - *comment column by John Winkler* - CAMPAIGN
Marketing - MEDIAWEEK
Marketing - *newspaper advertising* - NEWSINC.
Marketing - VARIETY
Marketing - VIDEO BUSINESS
Marketing & Distribution - COMMUNICATIONSWEEK
Marketing Dynamics - MSO'S CABLE MARKETING
Marketing Forum, The - RADIOTRENDS
Marketing Literature Review - JOURNAL OF MARKETING
Marketing Mix - *media briefs* - BUSINESS MARKETING
Marketing Monitor - *newsbriefs* - BUSINESS MARKETING
Marketing News - CABLE WORLD
Marketing Notes - MARKETING COMMUNICATIONS
Marketing of Radio, The - RADIO INDUSTRIES
Marketing Pointers - *newsbriefs* - AM
Marketing Programs - *upcoming by Publishers Marketing Association* - PMA NEWSLETTER
Marketing Services - *newsbriefs* - CABLE MARKETING
Marketing Spotlight - *broadcast manager input* - RADIOTRENDS
Marketing Tip - VIDEO INSIDER
Marketing Today - ADVERTISING REVIEW
Marketing Trendletter - MARKETING / COMMUNICATIONS
Marketing Trends - ADVERTISING NEWS

Marketing Trends - AUDIOVIDEO INTERNATIONAL
Marketing Update - ADWEEK'S MARKETING WEEK
Marketing Viewpoint International - *column by Luther Brock* - DIRECT MARKETING
Marketing Viewpoints - *advice column by Luther Brock* - DIRECT MARKETING
Marketing Your Photographs - *column by Rohn Engh* - WESTERN PHOTOGRAPHER MAGAZINE
Marketplace - *cable and the stock market* - CABLE WORLD
Marketplace - HOW
Marketplace, The - MARKETING NEWS
Marketplace - MOVING IMAGE
Marketplace, The - *new products* - PROFESSIONAL PHOTOGRAPHER, THE
Marketplace - *sale and purchase of newspaper properties* - PUBLISHER'S AUXILIARY
Marketplace - VIDEO MANAGEMENT
Markets - TRAVEL & LEISURE
Markets - *particulars on what a periodical publisher is looking for, payments, and publication schedules* - WRITER'S DIGEST
Markets, The - WRITER'S DIGEST
Markets & Careers - POPULAR PHOTOGRAPHY
Marketwatch - *new technology* - AUDIOVIDEO INTERNATIONAL
Marketwatch - *new marketing ideas* - MARKETING COMMUNICATIONS
Markings - *updates to historical events* - MEMORIES
Marks Barks - *record reviews* - ABSOLUTE SOUND, THE
Marquee - VIDEO STORE
Married - TELEGRAPHER, THE
Marvel Coming Comics - COMIC READER, THE
Marvel News - *product newsbriefs* - COMIC READER, THE
Maskara - *personality news and comment column by Inday Badiday* - SOSYALI MAGAZINE
Masked Engineer - *engineering column by Mario Orazio* - TV TECHNOLOGY
MASSurvey - *playlist* - INTERNATIONAL RADIO REPORT, THE
Master Game - *chess* - LISTENER
Master Syllabi - *classroom application* - COMMUNICATION EDUCATION
Masters of the Leica - *master photographer profile* - LEICA PHOTOGRAPHY
Masterwind Up - *media observations and comment column by Richard Gold* - MEDIA WEEK
Masterwork - HI-FI ANSWERS
Materials - *product review* - COMMUNICATION ARTS
Materials and Equipment - TECHTRENDS
Materials and Methods - PRINT
Materials Handling - CANADIAN PRINTER
Math's Notes - *column by Irwin Math* - CQ
Matinee Mail - *letters* - SCREEN THRILLS ILLUSTRATED

Matrix Data Bank - *series newsbriefs* - DOCTOR WHO MAGAZINE
Matter of Opinion - RADIOACTIVE
Matters of Current Comment - ADVERTISING EXPERIENCE
McRae's Wildlife - *column by Bill McRae* - OUTDOOR & TRAVEL PHOTOGRAPHY
Mechanical Department - ADVERTISING
Mechanics of Visualization - MOVING PICTURE AGE
Media - AFA JOURNAL
Media - AUDIO VISUAL
Media - GF MAGAZINE
Media - INTERVIEW
Media Avails - *special feature topics upcoming in print publications* - INSIDE MEDIA
Media Books - MEDIA REPORTER, THE
Media Books, Tapes A/V - *reviews* - MEDIA INFORMATION AUSTRALIA
Media Briefs - MEDIA INFORMATION AUSTRALIA
Media Business Markets - MEDIA BUSINESS MARKETS
Media Buyers Bulletin - *briefs of media buyers* - ADVERTISING NEWS
Media Bytes - *newsbriefs* - INSIDE MEDIA
Media Check - *independent media events, showings, and workshops* - INDEPENDENT MEDIA
Media Clips - *newsbriefs* - INDEPENDENT, THE
Media Deals - CHANNELS
Media Diary - MEDIA REPORTER, THE
Media Dish - *personality column by Kathy Kalafut* - MEDIAWEEK
Media Earnings Report - MEDIA INDUSTRY NEWSLETTER
Media Finance - MEDIA BUSINESS
Media Gratees - *who got what and when* - TELEVISIONS
Media Hysteria - *editorial cartoons* - MEDIA HISTORY DIGEST
Media in Scripture, The - MEDIA SPOTLIGHT
Media Mail - *letters* - INDEPENDENT MEDIA
Media Management - *excellent section concerning the business of video* - AV VIDEO
Media Marketing - *research* - R & R
Media Marketing Index - *excellent status of American consumer society* - MARKETING NEW MEDIA
Media Markets & Money - *'The authoritative business and transaction digest'* - RADIO BUSINESS REPORT
Media Mix - *news and comment* - ASIAN ADVERTISING & MARKETING
Media Mogul - *CEO profile* - MEDIA BUSINESS
Media Moves - IN MOTION FILM & VIDEO PRODUCTION MAGAZINE
Media News - *newsbriefs concerning blacks in media positions* - BLACK JOURNALISM REVIEW
Media News - *newsbriefs* - COMIC READER, THE
Media News - *newsbriefs* - MEDIA DIGEST
Media News and Views - BUSINESS ADVERTISING
Media News Digest - *media campaigns* - AD WEEKLY
Media News in Brief - MEDIA INTERNATIONAL

Media Notes & Quotes - INTERNATIONAL ADVERTISER
Media Notes: Magazines - BOOK MARKETING UPDATE
Media Notes: National Television Shows - BOOK MARKETING UPDATE
Media Notes: Radio Talk Shows - BOOK MARKETING UPDATE
Media Professionals - TELEVISION/RADIO AGE
Media Q and A - *how-to Q&A* - TECHTRENDS
Media Release - *agency news* - MEDIA INTERNATIONAL
Media Report - ADVERTISING AGENCY
Media Reviews - MEDIA & METHODS
Media Space Record - ADWEEK
Media Stock Averages - MEDIA INDUSTRY NEWSLETTER
Media Strategies - *unique section profiling one agency's approach to advertising planning and purchase* - INSIDE MEDIA
Media Study - *broad study of mass media* - MEDIA MIX
Media Techniques - MEDIA DIGEST
Media Transactions - MEDIA BUSINESS
Media Trends - MEDIA BUSINESS
Media Trends - *'News and views from the editors of RBR'* - RADIO BUSINESS REPORT
Media Watch - *column by Louis Phillips* - RIGHTING WORDS
Media Watch - VIDEODISC MONITOR, THE
Media World - RELIGIOUS BROADCASTING
Media: Books - BALLETT INTERNATIONAL
Mediabag - *newsbriefs* - MEDIA & METHODS
Mediagraph - *publications data in chart form* - CAMPAIGN
Mediagraphy - *reviews* - CABLE LIBRARIES
Mediamail - *letters* - PREVUE
MediaWorks - *ratecard and editorial changes* - ADVERTISING AGE
Mediology - MEDIAWEEK
Medium Format Notes and Ideas - SHUTTERBUG
Medley - *commentary* - HIGH FIDELITY
Meet and Greet - *pictures* - ASCAP IN ACTION
Meet the Collectors - BIG REEL, THE
Meet the Collectors - GRAPHIC ANTIQUARIAN
Meet the Contributors - *'An introduction to our writers and photographers'* - OUTDOOR & TRAVEL PHOTOGRAPHY
Meet Your Editor - *column by Andrea Guelis* - SCREEN LIFE
Meeting Preview - *scheduled events and speakers at forthcoming events* - ELECTRONICS
Meetings - BUSINESS MARKETING
Meetings - *upcoming events* - CABLE LIBRARIES
Meetings - *calendar of upcoming events* - ELECTRONICS
Meetings - IEEE SPECTRUM
Meetings - PROMOTION
Meetings - SALES & MARKETING MANAGEMENT
Meetings - TELEVISION / RADIO AGE INTERNATIONAL
Meetings and Events - *upcoming. (4-30-79).* - VIDEO MANAGEMENT

Meetings & Shows - *upcoming* - VIDEOGRAPHY
Meetings/Conventions - GRAPHIC ARTS MONTHLY
Megazine Scene - *review of other fanzines* - STRANGE ADVENTURES
Mel Lambert - *audio-for-video column by Mel Lambert* - TELEVISION BROADCAST
Melting Pot, The - *reviews of amateur fantasy and monster press* - CASTLE OF FRANKENSTEIN
Member Companies of the RMA - RMA ENGINEER
Member News - INTERNATIONAL DOCUMENTARY
Member News - PMA NEWSLETTER
Member Notes - *personnel newsbriefs* - SOCIETY FOR ANIMATION STUDIES NEWSLETTER, THE
Member Update - *newsbriefs* - FOLLOW FOCUS
Members in the News - *news items* - ORGANIZATIONAL COMMUNICATION NEWSLETTER
Members Make the News - *members of the Successful Magazine Publishers Group* - SUCCESSFUL MAGAZINE PUBLISHING
Members Report - COMBROAD
Membership - BROADCAST PIONEERS LIBRARY REPORTS
Membership - *list of new members* - NATPE PROGRAMMER
Membership List - NATIONAL AMATEUR
Membership List - NEWSLETTER, THE
Membership Report - FEEDBACK
Membership Report - *additions, changes* - SPECIALTY ADVERTISING BUSINESS
Membership Reports - FEEDBACK
Memo from the National Executive Secretary - SCREEN ACTOR HOLLYWOOD
Memo From the Publisher - BUSINESS COMMUNICATIONS REVIEW
Memoranda - INDEPENDENT, THE
Memories of a Journeyman - BRITISH PRINTER
Memory Lane - JOE FRANKLIN'S NOSTALGIA
Men of Mark in Advertising - *profiles* - ADWEEK
Men Who Make Advertising - *profile* - ADVERTISING & SELLING
Menu - *editorial column by Andy Benham* - HI-FI CHOICE
Mephisto's Musings - *observations and comment* - MUSICAL AMERICA
Mere Gossip - ALBUM, THE
Mere Mention - *newsbriefs* - KINEMATOGRAPH WEEKLY
Mergers & Acquisitions - FUTUREHOME TECHNOLOGY NEWS
Mergers/Acquisitions - FOLIO:
Message From Dick, A - *editorial* - PRODUCTION SOUND REPORT
Messaging - *voice message applications and commentary* - BUSINESS COMMUNICATIONS REVIEW
Messner on Business Ads - *critique column by Fred Messner* - BUSINESS ADVERTISING

Methods of the Masters - STEP-BY-STEP GRAPHICS
Meyers Connection, The - *column by Barbara Meyers* - AGAINST THE GRAIN
MGF Quiz - *column by Perry Buffington* - MGF
M.I. Update - *Midis and music* - MIX
Miami - BOX OFFICE
Michael Jackson - *newspaper comment* - CAMPAIGN
Michael Murrie - *news operation column by Michael Murrie* - TELEVISION BROADCAST
Mickey's Just for Kids Section - DISNEY CHANNEL MAGAZINE, THE
Microfun - *best radio jokes of month* - TV SCREEN
Micro/Macro Focus - *unique photographic equipment* - FUNCTIONAL PHOTOGRAPHY
Microphone Balance - HI-FI NEWS AND RECORD REVIEW
Microphones - SOUND & VISION
Microscopic Eye, The - *for photo-micrographers* - COMMERCIAL PHOTOGRAPHER, THE
Mid Range - *chart and products* - DIGITAL EVOLUTION MAGAZINE
Mid-Atlantic Report, The - *black radio playlist* - BLACK RADIO EXCLUSIVE
Middle Market Manager - SOUND MANAGEMENT
Midnight Beat, The - *'Inside Hollywood - Revealing - Tip-Offs - Predictions - News!' column by Bonnie Lori* - MOVIE TV SECRETS
Midsection - FILM COMMENT
Mid-South Report, The - *black radio playlist* - BLACK RADIO EXCLUSIVE
Midwest - BACK STAGE
Midwest - *newsbriefs* - MARQUEE
Midwest Report, The - *black radio playlist* - BLACK RADIO EXCLUSIVE
Might of the Media, The - PRESS, THE
Mike Connolly's Exclusive Report From Hollywood - *column by Mike Connolly* - SCREEN STORIES
Mike Says: - *'Sparkling news notes straight from glamorous radio row' column by Arthur J. Kellar* - RADIOLAND
Milestones - FOLIO:
Military Affairs - WORLD PRESS REVIEW
Mindbender - *quiz* - TIME SCREEN
Minds Behind the Media - VIEW
Mini Mag - *newsbriefs* - INTERCOMM
Mini- Reviews - *column by Pat Thompson* - CINEMA/CANADA
Mini Tests - PRACTICAL PHOTOGRAPHY
Minilab Notebook - PHOTO LAB MANAGEMENT
MiniMACs - *newsbriefs* - ADWEEK
Minneapolis - BOX OFFICE
Minolta Mania - SHUTTERBUG
Minority Affairs - PRESSTIME
MIN's Weekly Box Score - MEDIA INDUSTRY NEWSLETTER
Mirror, The - *'a column of comment'* - FILM TV DAILY
Mirror on the U.S. - WORLD PRESS REVIEW
Misc - *newsbriefs* - TAKE ONE

Miscellanea - VERBATIM
Miscellaneous - *newsbriefs and errata* - ACUSTICA
Miscellaneous - AEU
Miscellaneous - INSIDE ENTERTAINMENT
Miscellaneous - LÜRZER'S INTERNATIONAL ARCHIVE
Miscellaneous - WOODCOCK'S PRINTERS' AND LITHOGRAPHERS' WEEKLY GAZETTE AND NEWSPAPER REPORTER
Miscellaneous Audio Products - SOUND & VISION
Miscellaneous Commission Action - NARTB MEMBER SERVICE
Miscellaneous News - FACTSHEET FIVE
Miscellania - *newsbriefs* - COMICS JOURNAL, THE
Miscellanies - DRAMATIC MAGAZINE, THE
Miscellany, The - *letters to the editor* - DOCUMENTARY FILM NEWS
Miscellany - DOCUMENTARY FILM NEWS
Miscellany - FOLIO:
Miscellany - INDEPENDENT PUBLISHERS TRADE REPORT
Miscellany - MIRROR OF TASTE, AND DRAMATIC CENSOR, THE
Misleading Mail - *'Misleading Mail of the Month Award'* - TARGET MARKETING
Missing Equipment - *unique feature detailing serial numbers of reported missing film equipment* - FILMO TOPICS
Missions - CHRISTIAN DRAMA
Mister Manners - *column by Edward D. Gottlieb* - MGF
Mixdown - *international recording studio news* - PRO SOUND NEWS
Mixed Bag - *videocassette review* - V
MMR Fact File - *'An overview and historical look at individuals leading the industry'* - MONDAY MORNING REPLAY
MNC Winners - *monthly newspaper photo competition winners* - NEWS PHOTOGRAPHER
MNCC Pictures of the Month - *judging for monthly news photos* - NEWS PHOTOGRAPHER
Mobile Communications - INVIEW
Model of the Month - WESTERN PHOTOGRAPHER MAGAZINE
Modeling Plus - *column by Joi Ashli* - WESTERN PHOTOGRAPHER MAGAZINE
Modern Color Methods - CAMERA MAGAZINE
Modern Color Photography - *technique and technology column by Herbert C. McKay* - CAMERA, THE
Modern Living - *new products* - HOME VIEWER
Modern Movie Methods - CAMERA MAGAZINE
Modern Rock Tracks - BILLBOARD
Modern Tests - *equipment profiles* - MODERN PHOTOGRAPHY
MOI Five Minute Films - DOCUMENTARY FILM NEWS
MOMA News - *newsbriefs from Museum of Modern Art* - DIGEST OF THE UNIVERSITY FILM AND VIDEO ASSOCIATION
Moments with the New Books - DRAMA MAGAZINE, THE

Monday Memo - *guest column on advertising* - BROADCASTING
Monday's Newcomers - *'A review of the weeks commercials'* - CAMPAIGN
Money - CABLEVISION
Money - COMPUTER PICTURES
Money Dates for August - *anniversary dates for local promotion and tie-ins* - SHOWMEN'S TRADE REVIEW
Monitor - *story behind a photojournalism project* - AMERICAN PHOTO
Monitor - INVISION
Monitor - *'Your letters, our replies'* - PHOTOGRAPHY
Monitor - *'The television business, by TBI correspondents worldwide'* - TBI
Monitor - *newsbriefs* - VIEW
Monitor - *extensive section on current TV production* - WRAP
Monitor Systems - *column by Philip Newell* - STUDIO SOUND AND BROADCAST ENGINEERING
Monster Club Members - *listing of names and hometowns of new members* - FAMOUS MONSTERS OF FILMLAND
Monster Club Section - *monster youth club news* - FAMOUS MONSTERS OF FILMLAND
Monster Invasion - *'The Fangoria fright file of up-to-the-minute newsbreaks and other horrible happenings!'* - FANGORIA
Monstorama Quiz - FAMOUS MONSTERS OF FILMLAND
Month, The - *observations* - INTERVIEW
Month in Advertising, The - PRESS STATISTICAL REVIEW
Monthly Chat - *publishers comments* - INTERNATIONAL PROJECTIONIST
Monthly Competition - CAMERA CRAFT
Monthly Guide to Local Participating Program Availabilities - BILLBOARD TV PROGRAM AND TIME AVAILABILITIES, THE
Monthly IBEW Safety and Health Reminder, A - *back cover poster* - IBEW JOURNAL
Monthly Ratings - BROADCAST
Monthly Record, The - *incredible monthly listing of direct mail items received at the Direct Marketing Archive* - WHO'S MAILING WHAT!
Monthly Record Guide - HI-FI SOUND
Montreal - *city review* - AFTER DARK
Moonlighting - *'Where your favorite stars are shining after work'* - SOAP OPERA WEEKLY
Moore the Merrier, The - *radio personality news column by Garry Moore* - RADIO HIT SONGS
MOR Tape Reviews - TAPE DECK QUARTERLY
More After This! - *'Editorial comments' column by Ray Topp* - RADIO GUIDE
More Fact than Fancy - *information column by Paul Hopkins* - MODERN PHOTOGRAPHY
More Films - *review column by Martin Mitchell* - AFTER DARK
More to Follow - *column by David Allen* - VIDEOGRAPHY

Most Added Stations - MONDAY MORNING REPLAY
Most Upward Movement - MONDAY MORNING REPLAY
Motion Picture Finance - *column by Laurence Stern* - EXHIBITORS HERALD WORLD
Motion Pictures - *reviews* - ENTERTAINMENT WORLD
Motion Pictures - FILM & VIDEO
Motion Pictures - IN MOTION FILM & VIDEO PRODUCTION MAGAZINE
Motion Pictures - MILLIMETER
Motion Pictures - TELEVISION WEEKLY NEWS
Motion Pictures in Education - *same* - FILMO TOPICS
Motion Pictures in Industry - *newsbriefs of the use of film equipment* - FILMO TOPICS
Motion Pictures Rated by the Code and Rating Administration - *assigned rating codes* - BOX OFFICE
Motivation - SALES & MARKETING MANAGEMENT
Movers & Shakers - *personnel newsbriefs* - VIDEO INSIDER
Movers & Shakers - WASHINGTON JOURNALISM REVIEW
Moves - *personnel changes* - MEDIA WEEK
Moves and Changes - TELECOMMUNICATIONS WEEK
Movie and Radio Guide Picture of the Week - *publicity stills of a newly released motion picture* - MOVIE-RADIO GUIDE
Movie and Slide News - *new releases reviewed* - TRAVEL & LEISURE
Movie Calendar - *'Upcoming new movie releases plus movies in production'* - INSIDE HOLLYWOOD
Movie Calendar - *expected theatre release/exhibition of coming product* - ON LINE
Movie Capsules - *one-picture, one-paragraph summaries* - GREATER AMUSEMENTS
Movie Channel - *reviews* - WOMEN & FILM
Movie Crossword - HOLLYWOOD
Movie Finder - *'Rated moving listings'* - SATELLITE TV WEEK
Movie Flash Reports,' 'As compiled by the Flash reportorial team' provides newsbriefs concerning activities of the famous - *MOVIE FLASH*
Movie Guide - *a large section devoted to specific objections of recently released motion pictures* - MEDIA SPOTLIGHT
Movie Line-Up - *reviews of upcoming motion pictures* - ON LINE
Movie Madness - *crossword puzzle* - SCREEN GREATS
Movie Master Class - CAMCORDER USER
Movie Memos - HOLLYWOOD
Movie Methods - POPULAR PHOTOGRAPHY
Movie Mirror Junior - *information for the younger set* - PHOTOPLAY COMBINED WITH MOVIE MIRROR
Movie Montage - *newsbriefs* - FILMFARE

Movie News - *column by Alan Mirabella* - MGF
Movie News - *'Big screen gossip and info'* - VIDEO TIMES
Movie Notes - *column by Ernestine Mancha* - ENTERTAINMENT CONNECTION MAGAZINE
Movie of the Month - *critiqued reader-submitted projects* - HOME MOVIES
Movie of the Month - INSIDE HOLLYWOOD
Movie of the Month - *production stills* - SCREEN FACTS
Movie Previews - SHOW
Movie Q's and A's - *Q&A moviemaking column by John R. Gregory* - TRAVEL & LEISURE
Movie Reel - *newsbriefs* - HOLLYWOOD STUDIO MAGAZINE
Movie Review - BLACK STARS
Movie Review - *column by Mario E. Bautista* - MOVIE FLASH
Movie Review - *column by Donna Y. Caldwell* - SHOWCASE WORLD
Movie Reviews - *column by Owen Gleiberman* - ENTERTAINMENT WEEKLY
Movie Reviews - *'A roundup of current film attractions'* - SHOW
Movie Romance - HOLLYWOOD
Movie Roundup - *new film releases column by Bart Mills* - AMPERSAND'S COLLEGE ENTERTAINMENT GUIDE
Movie Scene - VIDEO TODAY
Movie Teen Mail - *letters* - MOVIE TEEN
Movie Theater Management - *problems and opportunities of the exhibitor, a column by Basil Clavering* - DOCUMENTARY FILM NEWS
Movie Trax - *'Paul Cliff reports on the new soundtrack releases'* - FILM MONTHLY
Movie TV Secret Report - *'Hot Gossip - Top Secret - Right off the ticker - Uncensored - Confidential - Tip-Offs - Hush-Hush!' column by Stan Blane* - MOVIE TV SECRETS
Movieland's Movie Reviews - MOVIELAND AND TV TIME
Movies - AUSTRALIAN PHOTOGRAPHY
Movies - INTERVIEW
Movies - MEDIA ANTHROPOLOGIST NEWSLETTER
Movies - *reviews* - ON CABLE
Movies - *listing* - ONSAT
Movies - *'Complete listings and descriptions of thousands of films'* - SATELLITE ORBIT
Movies - *review of current releases* - SHOW
Movies on Cable - *'A guide to small screen highlights' column by Alex Press* - MGF
Movies on Tape - *'Paul Andrews looks at the latest releases on tape for sale or rental' column by Paul Andrews* - WHAT VIDEO
Movies on Video - *'New and recent release reviews' column by James Turano* - MOVIE MARKETPLACE
Movies Photographers Should See - *feature film review column by Joseph Wechsberg* - MODERN PHOTOGRAPHY

Movies Then/Movies Now - *fascinating dual look at movies past and present, column by Curtis F. Brown and Will Holtzman* - BIJOU
Movies to Remember - SCREEN STORIES
Movietunes - *column by Al Kingston* - HOLLYWOOD FILMOGRAPH
Moving Lips - *column by Grover Lewis* - MOVIELINE
Moving Movie Throng, The - *column by John Hall* - HOLLYWOOD FILMOGRAPH
Moving Up - *what's hot in videocassette titles* - VIDEO BUSINESS
MPAA Ratings - *for new releases* - VARIETY
MPCS Briefs - VIDEO TIMES
MPTOA Sidelights - FILM TV DAILY
Mr. Fairfax Replies - *to program-artist questions* - MOVIE-RADIO GUIDE
Mr. Hornblow Goes to the Play - *review* - THEATRE MAGAZINE
MTV - ENTERTAINER, THE
Mugshot - PHOTOGRAPHY
Multi-Chapter - *VPUG chapter listing* - VENTURA PROFESSIONAL!
Multi-Media - *new multiple-media shows and development* - MAKING FILMS
Multimedia - *newsbriefs* - PRE-
Multimedia - THE JOURNAL
Multimedia - VIDEOGRAPHY
Mumbleypeg - *animator newsbriefs* - PEGBAR
Murphy's Law - PROFESSIONAL FILM PRODUCTION
Museum, The - *news of the Antique Wireless Association museum* - OLD TIMER'S BULLETIN, THE
Musi - *reviews* - LISTENER
Music, The - ABSOLUTE SOUND, THE
Music - BBC WORLD SERVICE LONDON CALLING
Music - CINEMONKEY
Music - *reviews* - COMMENT ON THE MEDIA
Music - HYPERMEDIA
Music - INTERVIEW
Music - *guide* - LISTENER
Music - MIRROR OF TASTE, AND DRAMATIC CENSOR, THE
Music - *review* - ORBIT VIDEO
Music - *review* - SHOW
Music - *'survey of current compositions* - 60 SECONDS
Music - *review,* - THEATRE MAGAZINE
Music - *review column by Rupert Smith* - 20/20
Music - *news and reviews on music videos* - VIDEO--THE MAGAZINE
Music - *music video video column by Darrin Williamson* - VIDEO TODAY
Music & Concerts - *videocassette review* - V
Music and Musicians - *column by R. R. Edwards* - NATIONAL EXHIBITOR, THE
Music & Pictures - POST
Music & Recording - *reviews* - ENTERTAINMENT WORLD
Music & Recording - *review* - SHOW
Music & Recording Notes - MIX
Music & Recordings - *newsbriefs* - FILM TV DAILY
Music and Talent - *live stage elements* - EXHIBITORS HERALD WORLD

Music Beat - *'Who's composing the latest jingles'* - LÜRZER'S INTERNATIONAL ARCHIVE
Music Box, The - *newsbriefs column by Robbin Schneider* - MOVIE WORLD
Music Box - *music videos* - WRAP
Music Chart - VIDEO SOFTWARE MAGAZINE
Music Charts, The - *Top selling albums* - ENTERTAINMENT WEEKLY
Music Charts and Playlists - COLLEGE BROADCASTER
Music Charts & Reviews - COLLEGE BROADCASTER
Music Confidential - *record news* - INTERNATIONAL RADIO REPORT, THE
Music For Sale - *videotape review* - VIDEO TIMES
Music for Your Pleasure - *review* - BETTER LISTENING
Music in Print - *review* - HIGH FIDELITY
Music Industry, The - *newsbriefs* - TV, ETC.
Music Industry Department - *interesting section discussing hot albums, singles and break outs, with record reviews and short column* - JOURNAL OF COLLEGE RADIO
Music Maker of the Month - *profile column by Joey Sasso* - MODERN SCREEN
Music, Music - *music scene newsbriefs* - PREVIEW
Music News - BOOKSTORE JOURNAL
Music News - *'Product updates and developments from another side of the business'* - STUDIO SOUND AND BROADCAST ENGINEERING
Music Notes - BACK STAGE
Music of the Sound Screen - *'The New Movie's service department, reviewing the newest phonograph records of film musical hits'* - NEW MOVIE MAGAZINE, THE
Music on Video - *new releases* - BEST OF FILM & VIDEO
Music on Video - VIDEO SOFTWARE MAGAZINE
Music Page, The - ABC WEEKLY
Music People - *artist pictures and newsbriefs* - BMI: MUSICWORLD
Music Production - PRO SOUND NEWS
Music Production News - IN MOTION FILM & VIDEO PRODUCTION MAGAZINE
Music Review - AUTO SOUND & SECURITY
Music Reviews - BLACK RADIO EXCLUSIVE
Music Reviews - BOOKSTORE JOURNAL
Music Reviews - COLLEGE BROADCASTER
Music Reviews - *column by Greg Sandow* - ENTERTAINMENT WEEKLY
Music Round Up! - *'Here's the latest in the world of rock n' roll!'* - SMASH HITS
Music Schools and Teachers - MUSICAL AMERICA
Music Show of the Month - SHOW
Music Teletype! - *'Chart-toppers & hip-hoppers'* - TS
Music Video Business - VIDEO BUSINESS
Music Video Production Listings - FILM & VIDEO
Music Video Production Listings Breakdown - FILM & VIDEO

Music Video Production Listings - FILM & VIDEO
Music Video Programming - *guide* - ONSAT
Music Videos - FILM & VIDEO
Music View - *and videotapes* - HOME VIEWER
Music Workshop - DOWN BEAT
Music Zine Reviews - FACTSHEET FIVE
Musical Americana - *column by Harry Marlatt* - MUSICAL AMERICA
Musical America's Educational Department - *instruction and comment* - MUSICAL AMERICA
Musical Chat - DRAMATIC MAGAZINE, THE
Musical Newsicals - *newsbriefs* - MODERN RECORDING & MUSIC
Musical Notes - THEATRE, THE
Musically Speaking - THEATRE CRAFT
Musician of the Week - *musical artist profile* - MOVIE-RADIO GUIDE
Musicians - *needed for upcoming productions* - CASTING NEWS
Mutual Exchanges - REEL LIFE
Mutual Program - REEL LIFE
Mutual Releases - EXHIBITORS' TIMES
Mutual Releases - REEL LIFE
My Biggest Gripe - *of the stars* - MOVIE TV SECRETS
My Broadcasting Diary - AMATEUR WIRELESS AND RADIOVISION
My Star Twin - *reader submissions column by Jo Ann Buckner* - MOTION PICTURE
My Turn - *guest editorial* - BPME IMAGE MAGAZINE
Mystery Shopper - CONSUMER ELECTRONICS

N

NABET-AMC Local-700 - *newsbriefs* - CINEMA/CANADA
NAC - *New adult contemporary hit list* - R & R
NACB News - *news of National Association of College Broadcasters* - COLLEGE BROADCASTER
NAEB Research Fact Sheets - PUBLIC TELECOMMUNICATIONS REVIEW
Naked Truth, The - *'Hot gossip' column by Ron Scott* - MOVIE STARS
Name Droppers - *what the stars are saying about each other* - PREVIEW
Names and Addresses - *reader submitted indicating interest in money-making schemes* - SCHEMER, THE
Names and Addresses of Local Secretaries and Business Agents - *12-page section serving craft members* - OFFICIAL BULLETIN OF THE INTERNATIONAL ALLIANCE OF THEATRICAL STAGE EMPLOYEES AND MOVING PICTURE MACHINE OPERATORS OF THE UNITED STATES AND CANADA.
Names from the Past - *review* - PRACTICAL WIRELESS

Names in the News - *newsbriefs* - MARKETING NEWS
Names Make the News - RANGEFINDER, THE
NAMM Briefs - *newsbriefs concerning the National Association of Music Merchants* - PRO SOUND NEWS
NAPL - PRINTING IMPRESSIONS
NASA - SATELLITE NEWS
Nashville Notes - *column by Lisa Zhito* - AMUSEMENT BUSINESS
Nashville Scene - *news column by Coleene Clarke* - BILLBOARD
Nashville Scene - *'News, views and the Gospel truth according to Hazel Smith', column by Hazel Smith* - NIGHTTIME TV
Nashville This Week - *radio format news* - R & R
Nat Tiffen Column, The - TIFFEN PROFESSIONAL NEWSLETTER
National Academy of Visual Instruction, The - *news* - MOVING PICTURE AGE
National Crossover Index - *'Charts that offer an overview of those tracks crossing format boundaries'* - MONDAY MORNING REPLAY
National Digest, The - *'The most important motion picture news events of the fortnight condensed for quick reading'* - NATIONAL EXHIBITOR, THE
National Editorial Directory - *complete list of newspaper managers and primary staff members* - AMERICAN JOURNALIST, THE
National Figures, The - *TV ratings for the week* - SCREEN INTERNATIONAL
National News - *briefs* - WEB
National Press Space Barometer - *weekly publication data* - NEWSPAPER WORLD AND ADVERTISING REVIEW
National Top Tens - *ratings for week ending* - TELEVISION WEEK
National Top Thirty - *week's sale and rental chart* - VIDEO INSIDER
National Top Titles - VIDEO SOFTWARE MAGAZINE
NATPE News - *organization news* - NATPE PROGRAMMER
Nature - *column by B. Peterson* - POPULAR PHOTOGRAPHY
Nature of Business, The - *column by Neil Heller* - TAPE/DISC BUSINESS
Necrology - BULLETIN OF PHOTOGRAPHY
Necrology - SPECTRA
Nederlandesche Filmiga Bulletin - DOCUMENTARY FILM NEWS
Needlework - *patterns* - PHOTOPLAY
Nellie Kellie's Kolumn - *employee news column by Nellie Kellie* - TELEPHONE NEWS, THE
Net Management Directions - *column by James Herman* - BUSINESS COMMUNICATIONS REVIEW
Net o' Things, The - *newsbriefs* - AGRICULTURAL ADVERTISING
Network Addresses - SOAP OPERA DIGEST
Network Notes - CABLE TV PROGRAMMING
Network Programs - *large listing* - RADIO DIAL

Network Publishing - *column by Theo Anderson* - DESKTOP COMMUNICATIONS
Network Song Favorites - *top thirty songs of the week* - RTD
Networking - *similar public service minded organizations* - ACCESS
Networking - *news of productions and personnel* - CANEWS
Networks - CABLEAGE
Networks - *newsbriefs* - TV, ETC.
Networks and Syndication - *column by Craig Rosen* - BILLBOARD
New ... and the Observed, The - *'Hot flashes, fresh faces, and things you never knew you couldn't live without'* - FAME
New Acts - *legitimate stage-cabaret reviews* - VARIETY
New Advertisers - *to newspapers* - ADVERTISING NEWS
New Age Reviews - CD REVIEW
New & Current - *extensive new book review section feature full-color book covers* - W•B
New & Noteworthy - CAMERA ARTS
New Apparatus - 35MM PHOTOGRAPHY
New Appliances, TV, Radios - TV & APPLIANCE MART
New Audio Releases - VIDEO ALERT
New Audition Material - BAKER'S NEWS
New Books - *reviews* - ADVERTISING MAGAZINE
New Books - *reviews* - CANTRILLS FILMNOTES
New Books - *reviews* - COMMERCIAL PHOTOGRAPHER, THE
New Books - *most of which are Moscow published* - DEMOCRATIC JOURNALIST
New Books - DRAMATIC MAGAZINE, THE
New Books - ELECTRONICS
New Books - *review column by John Belton* - FILMMAKERS FILM & VIDEO MONTHLY
New Books - - INDUSTRIAL ELECTRONICS
New Books - JOURNAL OF THE BRITISH FILM ACADEMY
New Books - *review* - LEICA PHOTOGRAPHY
New Books - *review* - POPULAR PHOTOGRAPHY
New Books - QST
New Books - TDR
New Books - TRAVEL & LEISURE
New Books - WIRE & RADIO COMMUNICATIONS
New Books and Plays, The - PLAYERS
New Books in Review - JMR, JOURNAL OF MARKETING RESEARCH
New Books in Review - QUARTERLY JOURNAL OF SPEECH, THE
New Books on TV - *reviews* - TELEVISION OPPORTUNITIES
New Books Reviewed - ADWEEK
New Cameras, Lenses, Meters, Accessories - *'A wrap-up of some of the more exciting products available right now'* - TRAVEL & LEISURE
New Catalogues - *of antiquarian and specialist booksellers* - AB BOOKMAN'S WEEKLY
New Cinema - *'A round-up of the new cinema releases'* - CINEMA, VIDEO & CABLE MOVIE DIGEST

New Comics News - *new releases* - COMICS JOURNAL, THE
New Construction Permits - LINE MONITOR, THE
New Contributors - CONTEMPORARY PHOTOGRAPHER
New Deals...New Deals - TV WORLD
New Designs for Living - *needlecraft* - TV MIRROR
New Designs for Living - *handcraft patterns* - TV RADIO MIRROR
New developments - *equipment* - RADIO INDUSTRIES
New Developments in Media Techniques - PRINT
New Developments in Radio Apparatus - *column by William J. Griffin* - ELECTRONICS WORLD
New Documentary Films - DOCUMENTARY FILM NEWS
New Electronic Medi - MEDIAWEEK
New England - BACK STAGE
New Equipment - AMERICAN PRINTER
New Equipment - *reviews* - AV GUIDE
New Equipment - BME'S TELEVISION ENGINEERING
New Equipment - FILM & VIDEO
New Equipment - FILM MEDIA
New Equipment - *review* - IBE
New Equipment - MUSIC LINE
New Equipment and Appliances - *product briefs* - MOTION PICTURE PROJECTION
New Equipment and Developments - *new product briefs* - BOX OFFICE
New Faces - *a bevy of rising stars* - PREVIEW
New Films - CINEMANEWS, THE
New Films - EMPIRE
New Films - *motion picture product reviews* - KINEMATOGRAPH WEEKLY
New Films - MEDIA MIX
New Films - *animation releases* - PEGBAR
New Films, The - *reviewed column by Marjorie Bilbow* - SCREEN INTERNATIONAL
New Flags - *newspaper premieres* - PUBLISHER'S AUXILIARY
New For the Road - *new product review* - CAR STEREO REVIEW
New Frontier, The - *column by Bob Atkins* - QST
New Gear - *hardware* - VIDEO BUSINESS
New Hardware - MILITARY ELECTRONICS / COUNTERMEASURES
New Haven - BOX OFFICE
New Ideas - MARKETING / COMMUNICATIONS
New IFRA Members - NEWSPAPER TECHNIQUES
New in Media - MEDIAWEEK
New Lines - *'Products and services of interest to our readers'* - LINK-UP
New Links - *'Expanding markets'* - LINK
New Lit - RADIO-ELECTRONICS
New Literature - AMERICAN PRINTER
New Literature - COMPUTERS & ELECTRONICS
New Literature - *sales and other print materials* - EDUCATIONAL BROADCASTING
New Literature - ELECTRONIC DESIGN

Departments   INDEX   830

New Machinery, Equipment and Materials - BRITISH PRINTER
New Machines - *product review* - CAR AUDIO AND ELECTRONICS
New Media - *PR utilization of new outlets such as CATV, AV* - PUBLIC RELATIONS JOURNAL, THE
New Media - VIDEO EIGHTIES MAGAZINE
New Members - ASCAP IN ACTION
New Members - PSA JOURNAL
New Merchandise for the Dealer to Sell - TELEVISION RETAILING
New Movies - *guide column by Beverly Linet* - MODERN SCREEN
New Movies - *'In your video stores now' review column by Tony Chiu* - V
New Music - DRAMATIC MAGAZINE, THE
New Music - HIGH PERFORMANCE
New Music - *'From leading publishers'* - MUSICAL AMERICA
New Music Showcase - *profiles* - INTERNATIONAL RADIO REPORT, THE
New on the Market - PERSONAL ELECTRONICS
New Orleans - BOX OFFICE
New Paperbacks - MAGAZINE & BOOKSELLER
New Patents - CANADIAN PRINTER
New Patterns for You - *fashion* - TV MIRROR
New Patterns For You - *dress-making* - TV RADIO MIRROR
New Periodical Publications - INTERNATIONAL PRESS REVIEW
New Personalities - NATIONAL AMATEUR
New Pictures - *'The Exhibitors Herald-World presents in concise form information on current and forthcoming attractions'* - EXHIBITORS HERALD WORLD
New Plays, The - *'Brief reviews'* - PLAY SHOP, THE
New Plays - PLAYS AND PLAYERS
New Plays, The - *synopses* - REEL LIFE
New Plays - *listing* - THEATRE, THE
New Plays, The - *reviews* - THEATRE MAGAZINE
New Posts - *personnel newsbriefs* - FILM JOURNAL, THE
New Product Merchandiser - VIDEO INSIDER
New Product Watch - ADWEEK'S MARKETING WEEK
New Products - *review* - AIRBRUSH ACTION
New Products - AUSTRALIAN PHOTOGRAPHY
New Products - AVC
New Products - *review* - BME'S TELEVISION ENGINEERING
New Products - BROADCAST + TECHNOLOGY
New Products - BROADCASTER
New Products - BUSINESS COMMUNICATIONS REVIEW
New Products - CLOSE-UP
New Products - *review* - COMMUNICATIONS INDUSTRIES REPORT, THE
New Products - COMMUNICATIONS WORLD
New Products - *review* - COMPUTERS & ELECTRONICS
New Products - *review* - CORPORATE TELEVISION
New Products - CORPORATE VIDEO DECISIONS
New Products - DB

New Products - DEALERSCOPE
New Products - *review* - ELECTRONIC DESIGN
New Products - ELECTRONIC SERVICING & TECHNOLOGY
New Products - *showcase* - ELECTRONIC TECHNICIAN/DEALER
New Products - ELECTRONICS
New Products - ELECTRONICS AND COMMUNICATIONS
New Products - ELECTRONICS & COMMUNICATIONS
New Products - ELECTRONICS WORLD
New Products - FUNCTIONAL PHOTOGRAPHY
New Products - GRAMOPHONE
New Products - GREATER AMUSEMENTS
New Products - *review* - IN-PLANT REPRODUCTIONS
New Products - INDUSTRIAL ELECTRONICS
New Products - INFORMATION TODAY
New Products - LEICA PHOTOGRAPHY
New Products - *review* - LENS MAGAZINE
New Products - *for lighting applications* - LIGHTS!
New Products - MAST
New Products - *review* - MODERN PHOTOGRAPHY
New Products - *review* - NIKON WORLD
New Products - *reviews (8-82)*. - ON LOCATION
New Products - *'Novel equipment for the outdoor and travel photographer'* - OUTDOOR & TRAVEL PHOTOGRAPHY
New Products - OUTDOOR PHOTOGRAPHER
New Products - PC PUBLISHING AND PRESENTATIONS
New Products - PHOTO LAB MANAGEMENT
New Products - PHOTOGRAPHIC PROCESSING
New Products - PHOTOMETHODS
New Products - PHOTOPRO
New Products - *'Review of new and interesting products'* - POPULAR COMMUNICATIONS
New Products - POPULAR ELECTRONICS
New Products - PRESENTATION PRODUCTS MAGAZINE
New Products - *review* - PRINT-EQUIP NEWS
New Products - PRINTING IMPRESSIONS
New Products - PRIVATE CABLE
New Products - PROFESSIONAL PHOTOGRAPHER, THE
New products - PROFESSIONAL PHOTOGRAPHER, THE
New Products - PROFESSIONAL PHOTOGRAPHER, THE
New Products - PSA JOURNAL
New Products - *review* - RADIO-ELECTRONICS
New Products - REP: RECORDING ENGINEERING PRODUCTION
New Products - SATELLITE RETAILER
New Products - *review* - 73 AMATEUR RADIO
New Products - SMPTE JOURNAL
New Products - *'Roundup of the latest audio equipment and accessories'* - STEREO REVIEW
New Products - STUDIO PHOTOGRAPHY
New Products - STV GUIDE

New Products - TECHNICAL PHOTOGRAPHY
New Products - TECHTRENDS
New Products - TELECOMMUNICATION JOURNAL
New Products - TELECOMMUNICATIONS
New Products - TELEVISION BROADCAST
New Products - THE JOURNAL
New Products - THEATRE CRAFTS
New Products - THEATRE DESIGN & TECHNOLOGY
New Products - TRAVEL & LEISURE
New Products - *review* - V
New Products - VIDEO MAGAZINE
New Products - *reviews* - VIDEO REVIEW
New Products - *reviews* - VIDEO SYSTEMS
New Products - VIDEO TIMES
New Products - *review* - VIEWCAMERA
New Products and Developments - AES
New Products and Developments - *briefs* - SMPTE JOURNAL
New Products and Packaging - MARKETING / COMMUNICATIONS
New Products and Processes - ACTION!
New Products and Processes - *column by Joe Mather* - RANGEFINDER, THE
New Products & Services - BILLBOARD
New Products and Services - *news briefs* - BROADCAST PROGRAMMING AND PRODUCTION
New Products and Services - DB
New Products and Services - NETWORK WORLD
New Products and Services - PRESS STATISTICAL REVIEW
New Products for Services - TELEVISION RETAILING
New Products Roundup - ADVERTISING AGE
New Publications - *directories, books and periodicals* - AFVA BULLETIN
New Publications - *extensive and helpful review section* - BUSINESS INFORMATION ALERT
New Publications - THE JOURNAL
New Publications - *review* - THEATRE DOCUMENTATION
New Publications Received - TELEPHONE MAGAZINE
New Radio Patents - *column by I. Queen* - RADIO-ELECTRONICS
New Radio-Electronic Devices - *new product review* - RADIO-ELECTRONICS
New Ratings - AMERICAN ADVERTISER REPORTER
New Receivers - *product review* - ELECTRONICS WORLD
New Record Releases - BLACK RADIO EXCLUSIVE
New Recorded Tape Releases - TAPE DECK QUARTERLY
New Reference Books - INTERNATIONAL PRESS REVIEW
New Release Spotlight - *column by David Vernier* - CD REVIEW
New Releases - BLOCKBUSTER VIDEO MAGAZINE
New Releases - BULGARIAN FILMS
New Releases - *'A listing of new compact disc, cassette and LP releases scheduled to appear this month'* - GRAMOPHONE

New Releases - HOME VIEWER
New Releases - VIDEO ALERT
New Releases - VIDEO BUSINESS
New Releases - *full color section of new videos in music, comedy, children's films, drama, action and adventure, sci fi and horror, and sport and general interest* - VIDEO BUYER
New Releases - *reviews* - VIDEO INSIDER
New Releases - *'The new videos in your rental store together with the latest and best on sell-through'* - VIDEO MONTHLY
New Releases - VIDEO SOFTWARE MAGAZINE
New Research Resources - MEDIA INFORMATION AUSTRALIA
New Service Bureau, The - *column by Thad McIlroy* - PRE-
New Short Films - *listed via title, distributor and length* - MONTHLY FILM BULLETIN
New Shorts - FILM BULLETIN
New Slides - KINEMATOGRAPH WEEKLY
New Starts - *new projects underway listed with pertinent information* - MOVING PICTURES INTERNATIONAL
New Tape Products - TAPE DECK QUARTERLY
New Tech - EMMY
New Technical Publications - ILFORD PHOTO INSTRUCTOR NEWSLETTER
New Technologies - MONITOR INTERNATIONAL
New Technology - HDTV NEWSLETTER
New Theaters - *profile* - GREATER AMUSEMENTS
New Theatre Books - BAKER'S NEWS
New Theatre Portfolio - NEW THEATRE QUARTERLY
New Theatres - *listing* - NATIONAL EXHIBITOR, THE
New Tricks for Camera Owners - *'A monthly list of valuable kinks and hints for the amateur'* - POPULAR PHOTOGRAPHY
New TV Spot Campaigns - BILLBOARD TV PROGRAM AND TIME AVAILABILITIES, THE
New Video Releases - *review* - AMERICAN FILM
New Videoclips - BILLBOARD
New Videos - *'A review of the new video releases'* - CINEMA, VIDEO & CABLE MOVIE DIGEST
New Videos - *reviews* - VIDEO CAPSULE
New Waves - *new technology* - LISTENER
New York - *column by Cindy Adams* - THEATRE, THE
New York Critics' Opinions - *films* - VARIETY
New York Highlights - *newsbriefs* - PICTURE REPORTS
New York Life - *column by Baron Theo von Roth* - THEATRE, THE
New York Listening Post, The - *column by Father Knickerbocker* - AGRICULTURAL ADVERTISING
New York, New York - *column by Michael Sander* - DRAMA-LOGUE
New York, New York - *gossip in the Big Apple* - PREVIEW
New York News - HOLLYWOOD FILMOGRAPH

New York News - *column by Sue Facter* - SOAP OPERA DIGEST
New York Notebook - *personality column by Jason Bonderoff* - SOAP OPERA DIGEST
New York Notes - *column by Peter J. Black* - SOAP OPERA STARS
New York Openings - *theatre listing* - CAHIERS DU CINEMA IN ENGLISH
New York Report - SCREEN ACTOR HOLLYWOOD
New York Reviews - *reprints of New York newspaper film critics reports* - PICTURE REPORTS
New York Reviews - *legitimate stage* - SHOW BUSINESS
New York Scene, The - TELESCREEN
New York Showings - *review and comment* - EXHIBITORS HERALD WORLD
New York Sound Track - *New York based newsbriefs* - VARIETY
New York Vignette - *New York gossip column by John Skinner* - UNION LABOR SUN
New York Watch - WATCH
New Yorkers, The - *'Who's doing what, with whom, in Gotham!'* - REAL LIFE/DAYTIMERS
New Zealand News - *current products and artist news* - ARK
Newcomers - *'1 - 40, number of plays, increase percentages and progress'* - MONDAY MORNING REPLAY
Newest Additions to the Bookshelves - CAMERA, THE
Newest Books in Journalism, The - QUILL AND SCROLL
Newmedia - *new media technologies* - MILLIMETER
News - *briefs* - ADVERTISING NEWS
News - ANIMATION MAGAZINE
News - *recent ad campaigns* - ART DIRECTION
News - *world newsbriefs* - ASIFA NOUVELLES
News - *audio newsbriefs* - AUDIOPHILE WITH HI-FI ANSWERS
News - *'Creative, Production, Post Production'* - BACK STAGE/SHOOT
News - BALLETT INTERNATIONAL
News - BLACK THEATRE
News - BRITISH JOURNAL OF PHOTOGRAPHY
News - *briefs* - BROADCAST ENGINEERING
News - *briefs* - BROADCASTER
News - *newsbriefs* - CHRISTIAN REVIEW
News - CINEMA/CANADA
News - COMICS FEATURE
News - COMICS WEEK
News - *newsbriefs* - CORPORATE VIDEO DECISIONS
News - CRITIC
News - *'What's happening or shouldn't have* - CTVD
News - DEALERSCOPE
News - DOWN BEAT
News - DWB
News - *new electronic products* - ETI
News - *news items concerning fantasy and science fiction film/video product* - FANTASY ZONE
News - FILM & VIDEO

News - FOUR COLOR
News - *briefs* - HI-FI ANSWERS
News - HI-FI NEWS AND RECORD REVIEW
News - *briefs* - IBE
News - IN-PLANT PRINTER & ELECTRONIC PUBLISHER
News - *multi-page section of new equipment news* - INTERNATIONAL BROADCASTING
News - *newsbriefs concerning international cable television industry* - INTERNATIONAL CABLE
News - *cartoon newsbriefs* - KORKIS AND CAWLEY'S CARTOON QUARTERLY
News - LIGHTING DIMENSIONS
News - *news items* - MEDIA ETHICS UPDATE
News - MEDIA WEEK
News - *large section detailing latest entertainment news* - MOVIE - THE VIDEO MAGAZINE
News - POST
News - PRE-
News - PRESS, THE
News - *newsbriefs* - PRIVATE CABLE
News - PRODUCCIÓN Y DISTRIBUCIÓN
News - *briefs* - PROFESSIONAL PHOTOGRAPHER, THE
News - *newsbriefs* - RADIO ONLY
News - REP: RECORDING ENGINEERING PRODUCTION
News - *newsbriefs* - RF DESIGN
News - *'Industry events, satellite information, launches and teleconferencing'* - SATELLITE COMMUNICATIONS
News - SATELLITE RETAILER
News - SCREEN INTERNATIONAL
News - *news items* - SMPTE JOURNAL
News, The - SOAP OPERA WEEKLY
News - STUDIO SOUND AND BROADCAST ENGINEERING
News - STV GUIDE
News - TELECOMMUNICATION JOURNAL
News - THE JOURNAL
News - THEATRE CRAFTS
News - THEATRE JOURNAL
News - *assorted news item column by Elena Nierman* - THEATRE NEWS
News - *video newsbriefs* - TV GUIDE
News - VIA SATELLITE
News - VIDEO
News - *extensive section on latest video newsbriefs and products* - VIDEO CAMERA
News - *newsbriefs* - VIDEO SYSTEMS
News - *extensive section* - VIDEO--THE MAGAZINE
News - VIDEO TODAY
News / Notes - *information* - NIKON WORLD
News About Jobs - ADVERTISING AND MARKETING MANAGEMENT
News About People - *lengthy personnel segments* - AD WEEKLY
News About People - ADWEEK
News Analysis - PR WEEK
News Analysis - SCREEN INTERNATIONAL
News & Business - VIDEO SYSTEMS
News & Business Report - VIDEO TIMES
News and Comment - *newsbriefs* - VIDEOGRAPHY

Departments INDEX 832

News and Events - *from the Museum of Cartoon Art* - CARTOONIST PROFILES
News and Gossip of the Week - AMATEUR WIRELESS AND RADIOVISION
News and New Releases - CHRISTIAN FILM & VIDEO
News and Notes - BULLETIN OF PHOTOGRAPHY
News and Notes - BULLETIN OF THE ASSOCIATION FOR BUSINESS COMMUNICATION, THE
News and Notes - *photographic newsbriefs* - CAMERA, THE
News and Notes - *newsbriefs* - CINEFANTASTIQUE
News and Notes - COMMUNICATION STUDIES
News & Notes - *newsbriefs* - COMPUTER PUBLISHING
News & Notes - *television newsbriefs* - ENTERTAINMENT WEEKLY
News and Notes - INTELLIGENCER
News and Notes - JOURNAL OF BUSINESS COMMUNICATION, THE
News and Notes - *newsbriefs* - JUMP CUT
News & Notes - *product newsbriefs* - LENS MAGAZINE
News and Notes - NATIONAL PHOTOGRAPHER, THE
News and Notes - OPTICAL INFORMATION SYSTEMS
News & Notes - *extensive newsbrief section* - POLYGRAPH INTERNATIONAL
News and Notes - PROFESSIONAL PHOTOGRAPHER, THE
News and Notes - *newsbriefs concerning public opinion and individuals* - PUBLIC OPINION QUARTERLY
News and Notes - RESTORATION AND 18TH CENTURY THEATRE RESEARCH
News and Notes - SPECTRA
News and Notes - WESTERN JOURNAL OF SPEECH COMMUNICATION
News & Notes - *newsbriefs* - WRITER'S NW
News and Notes of Women in Photography - *unusual department column by Mildred Stagg* - TRAVEL & LEISURE
News & Notes: SSCA Members on the Move! - *newsbriefs* - C-O-N-N-E-C-T-I-O-N-S
News and Notions - SOUTHERN COMMUNICATION JOURNAL, THE
News and Nuggets - *newsbriefs* - WSCA NEWS
News and Reviews - *'From Around the World'* - ARK
News and Reviews - *'Commentary and criticism'* - SHOW BUSINESS ILLUSTRATED
News & Technology - ELECTRONIC DESIGN
News and Views - *newsbriefs* - AFRO-ASIAN JOURNALIST
News and Views - AUSTRALASIAN PRINTER
News and Views - *'Publications on audio-visual aids and educational technology published in member countries, other activities, exhibitions, conferences, equipment testing* - EDUCATIONAL MEDIA INTERNATIONAL
News and Views - FILM GUIDE
News & Views - GRAMOPHONE
News and Views - TECHTRENDS
News and Views - TELEVISION ENGINEERING

News & Views - *newsbriefs* - VIDEO INFO
News & Views - *newsbriefs* - VIDEO MAGAZINE
News & Views - *newsbriefs* - VIDEO MANAGEMENT
News & Weather Programming - *program guide* - ONSAT
News Beat - *news item column by James A. Martin* - PUBLISH!
News Brevities - ELECTRONIC ENGINEERING
News Briefs - ADWEEK'S MARKETING WEEK
News Briefs - AV VIDEO
News Briefs... - COMICS CAREER NEWSLETTER
News Briefs - COMPUTER PICTURES
News Briefs - FACTS ABOUT FILM FINLAND
News Briefs - *information concerning Mennonite Brethren communication developments* - FORUM
News Briefs - *concerning CD-ROM* - INFORMATION TODAY
News Briefs - MEMO TO MAILERS
News Briefs - PRO SOUND NEWS
News Briefs - RADIO WORLD
News Briefs - TELECOMMUNICATIONS
News Briefs - TELEVISION BROADCAST
News Briefs - VIDEO TIMES
News Broadcast - Business - *'News items on especially significant supplies, marketing agreements and other business deals in the fields of video, audio, computer-graphics and transmitting equipment'* - MILLECANALI INTERNATIONAL
News Broadcast - Personaggi - *'The moves, change of responsibilities and other important activities of selected people in the broadcast industry'* - MILLECANALI INTERNATIONAL
News Bulletins - SHOWMEN'S TRADE REVIEW
News Clips - *briefs* - CANADIAN FILM DIGEST
News Clips - MAGAZINE DESIGN & PRODUCTION
News Clips - *'The media on westerns'* - ROUNDUP QUARTERLY
News Contact Directory - *very valuable resource* - UK PRESS GAZETTE
News Desk - PRACTICAL WIRELESS
News Desk - VIEW
News Digest - SCREEN INTERNATIONAL
News Digest of Accounts and Personnel, The - ADVERTISING & SELLING
News Directions - *personnel changes* - COMMUNICATOR
News Directions - *newsroom developments* - TELEVISION BROADCAST
News Doctor, The - *journalistic advice column by Chuck Wolf* - AP BROADCASTER
News Extra - *late-breaking newsbriefs* - CAMPAIGN
News File - GOOD NEWS: CHRISTIANS IN JOURNALISM
News Flashes - *'News bits and short takes'* - VIDEO SOFTWARE MAGAZINE
News Focus - *commentary* - BROADCAST
News From Canada - *freedom of information column by Tom Riley* - ACCESS REPORTS/FREEDOM OF INFORMATION

News from CEC Information Technology and Telecommunications - EUROPEAN TRANSACTIONS ON TELECOMMUNICATIONS AND RELATED TECHNOLOGIES
News from Centres - DRAMA LEAGUE MONTHLY
News from Committees - NEWSLETTER
News From Earth - SF MOVIELAND
News from Here and There--and Short News Flashes - FOURTH ESTATE
News From Industry - IEEE SPECTRUM
News from Manchester - CAMPAIGN
News From Members - DIGEST OF THE UNIVERSITY FILM AND VIDEO ASSOCIATION
News from Members of the Alliance - *newsbriefs* - MEDIA ARTS
News from National - COMMUNICATOR, THE
News from North and South - DRAMA
News from Secretariat - ABU NEWSLETTER
News from SIMA - BRITISH COMMUNICATIONS AND ELECTRONICS
News From Spain - *column by Dale Pierce* - EUROPEAN TRASH CINEMA
News from Suppliers - AUSTRALASIAN PRINTER
News From the Back Porch - *engineering column by David Ostmo* - TV TECHNOLOGY
News from the Branches - PARAMOUNT WORLD
News From the Cinema Audio Society - *organization news* - PRODUCTION SOUND REPORT
News from the General Publishing Division - AAP MONTHLY REPORT
News From the Higher Education Division - AAP MONTHLY REPORT
News from the IREE Divisions - MONITOR
News from the Manufacturers - *new equipment* - NEWSPAPER TECHNIQUES
News from the Open University - *ITV news* - VISUAL EDUCATION
News From the Paperback Publishing Division - AAP MONTHLY REPORT
News from the School Division - AAP MONTHLY REPORT
News from the Societies - 35MM PHOTOGRAPHY
News from USA - DOCUMENTARY FILM NEWS
News From Washington - AAP MONTHLY REPORT
News from Washington - AMATEUR RADIO DEFENSE
News From Washington - IEEE SPECTRUM
News from Wetzlar - *newsbriefs* - LEICA FOTOGRAFIE INTERNATIONAL
News Front - ELECTRONICS
News Highlights - PHOTOGRAPHIC PROCESSING
News Hound, The - *coming attractions* - SCARLET STREET
News in a Nutshell - *soap artist newsbriefs* - SOAP OPERA TIME
News in Brief - AFRO-ASIAN JOURNALIST
News in brief - CINEMATOGRAPHY AND BIOSCOPE MAGAZINE

News in Brief - ENTERTAINMENT WORLD
News in Brief - FUTUREHOME TECHNOLOGY NEWS
News in Brief - INTERSPACE
News in Brief - *concerning Strand lighting equipment* - LIGHTS!
News in Brief - MEDIA ANTHROPOLOGIST NEWSLETTER
News in Brief - SCREEN INTERNATIONAL
News in Community Broadcasting, The - *column by Bob Horner* - LPTV REPORT, THE
News in Pix - FILMFARE
News InView - *industry newsbriefs* - INVIEW
News Items - *film science fiction newsbriefs* - SF MOVIELAND
News Items - WOODCOCK'S PRINTERS' AND LITHOGRAPHERS' WEEKLY GAZETTE AND NEWSPAPER REPORTER
News Line - PROMOTION
News Makers - *profiles* - TECHNICAL PHOTOGRAPHY
News Media - *late-breaking news stories of independent media* - INDEPENDENT MEDIA
News Media Update - PUBLISHER'S AUXILIARY
News Notes - *extensive section detailing AEJMC member individual and school activities* - AEJMC NEWS
News Notes - *briefs* - AFTERIMAGE
News Notes - *newsbriefs* - AFVA BULLETIN
News Notes - AIGA JOURNAL OF GRAPHIC DESIGN
News Notes - *briefs* - CANADIAN FILM DIGEST
News Notes - *newsbriefs from members concerning publishing* - COSMEP NEWSLETTER
News Notes - *production newsbriefs* - EXHIBITORS HERALD WORLD
News Notes - *'doings and data on the film scene'* - FILM MEDIA
News Notes - GRAPHIC ARTS MONTHLY
News Notes - REP: RECORDING ENGINEERING PRODUCTION
News Notes - SMALL PRESS BOOK REVIEW, THE
News Notes - *briefs* - TECHNICAL PHOTOGRAPHY
News of General Interest - GRAPHIC COMMUNICATOR
News of Interest - *newsbriefs* - AFA JOURNAL
News of Journalism Education - *newsbriefs* - JOURNALISM EDUCATOR, THE
News of Latest A-V Materials and Equipment - AUDIO-VISUAL GUIDE
News of Members - *from this international association of independent publishers* - COSMEP NEWSLETTER
News of People in the Profession - *academic awards and rewards* - ICA NEWSLETTER
News of Radio Broadcasting - BROADCAST REPORTER
News of Record - *FCC actions* - ELECTRONIC MEDIA
News of the Guild - *newsbriefs* - ACTION!
News of the Industry - *newsbriefs* - ELECTRONIC TECHNICAN/DEALER
News of the Industry - MOVIE MAKERS
News of the Industry - RADIO INDUSTRIES

News of the Month - EIGHT MM MOVIE MAKER AND CINE CAMERA
News of the Nation's Orchestras - MUSICAL AMERICA
News of the Paramount Subsidiaries - PARAMOUNT WORLD
News of the Radio Industry - *newsbriefs* - RADIO BROADCAST
News of the Sections - *chapter briefs* - AES
News of the Theatres - THEATRE JOURNAL
News of the Trade - REEL LIFE
News of the Week, The - *motion picture developments* - EXHIBITORS TRADE REVIEW
News of the Week - PUBLISHER'S WEEKLY
News of the World - LIBERTY, THEN AND NOW
News on the March - *newsbriefs on Chicago journalism scenes* - CHICAGO JOURNALISM REVIEW
News Page - *newsbriefs* - FUNCTIONAL PHOTOGRAPHY
News Page, The - *'The truth 24 times per second'* - TAKE ONE
News, People and Facilities Invew - *'A brief look at what's going on in the industry'* - INVIEW
News Posts - *job promotions and transfers* - GREATER AMUSEMENTS
News PP-CG - *'News and reports on companies and events in the worlds of video and audio production and post-production'* - MILLECANALI INTERNATIONAL
News Practices - *column by Emerson Stone* - COMMUNICATOR
News PROphiles - *'Reports and updates from around the globe'* - VIDEO PROPHILES
News Round-Up - *newsbriefs* - ANIMATOR
News Roundup - ELECTRONICS
News Round-Up - *newsbriefs listed by international city* - MOVING PICTURES INTERNATIONAL
News Round-Up - PERSONAL ELECTRONICS
News Round-Up - THEATRE
News Scene - CANADIAN PRINTER
News Section - TELECOMMUNICATION JOURNAL
News Slashes - *horror film newsbriefs column by Charles Balun* - DEEP RED
News Spotlight - JEE, JOURNAL OF ELECTRONIC ENGINEERING
News Summary - ELECTRONIC MEDIA
News Technology - TV TECHNOLOGY
News to Use - SCHOLASTIC EDITOR'S TRENDS IN PUBLICATIONS
News Updates - ELECTRONICS
News Views - *member briefs* - NEWS PHOTOGRAPHER
News Vue - *current news items* - VUE
News Wire - *newsbriefs* - CABLEVISION
News Wire - *newsbriefs* - VIDEO BUSINESS
News With Pictures - *exhibitor profiles* - GREATER AMUSEMENTS
Newsbeat - E-ITV
Newsbeat - FUNCTIONAL PHOTOGRAPHY
Newsbites - *newsbriefs* - MEDIAWATCH
Newsbreaks - *'A look at industry trends, products and developments' compiled column by Dennis Brisson* - ON!

Newsbreaks - *newsbriefs* - VIDEO REVIEW
Newsbreaks - *newsbriefs* - VIDEOPRO
Newsbrief - INTERNATIONAL DOCUMENTARY
Newsbriefs - AID
Newsbriefs - ART PAPERS
Newsbriefs - BUSINESS MARKETING
NewsCap - *newsbriefs* - MSO'S CABLE MARKETING
Newsdesk - *news of exhibitions* - PHOTOGRAPHY
News-Editorial - PRESSTIME
Newsflash - *newsbriefs* - IMAGE
Newsflashes - RADIOWEEK
Newsfront - *news of films and the motion picture industry* - MOVIES, THE
Newsgram - *late breaking news briefs* - FILM JOURNAL, THE
Newsletter - *briefs* - MADISON AVENUE
Newsline - AMAZING HEROES
Newsline - *TSI newsbriefs* - BASELINE
Newsline... - *newsbriefs* - BILLBOARD
Newsline - *'The latest hot gossip from the world of video'* - VIDEO ANSWERS
Newsline - VIDEODISC MONITOR, THE
Newslines - *newsbriefs* - BROADCAST
Newslines - *film newsbriefs* - VARIETY
NewsLink - *late-breaking news items* - LINK-UP
News/Listings - CREATIVE CAMERA
Newslog - *newsbriefs by date* - IEEE SPECTRUM
Newsmakers - *people, projects in the news* - ADVISER UPDATE
Newsmakers - *picture page* - BILLBOARD
Newsmakers - DIRECT MARKETING
Newsmakers - ELECTRONICS
Newsmakers - *new items* - IMPRINT
Newsmakers - MARKETING / COMMUNICATIONS
Newsmakers - MEDIAWEEK
Newsmakers - MOVIE STARS
Newsmakers - *personnel items* - SCRIPPS HOWARD NEWS
Newsmakers - *profiles* - TELEVISION BROADCAST
Newsmonth - *newsbriefs* - AMERICAN PRESS
News/Notes from the President - INDUSTRIAL TELEVISION NEWS
Newspaper - *column by Bob Adams* - CMA NEWSLETTER
Newspaper Ad Activities - ADVERTISER MAGAZINE, THE
Newspaper Ad Trends - ADVERTISING AGENCY
Newspaper Business - PRESSTIME
Newspaper Criticisms - *regional newspaper reviews of current film fare* - NATIONAL EXHIBITOR, THE
Newspaper Gossip - ADVERTISING NEWS
Newspaper Intelligence - *data on new, suspended, and ceased publications* - ADVERTISERS GAZETTE
Newspaper Intelligence - *newsbriefs concerning changes* - WOODCOCK'S PRINTERS' AND LITHOGRAPHERS' WEEKLY GAZETTE AND NEWSPAPER REPORTER
Newspaper News - *newsbriefs* - FOURTH ESTATE
Newspaper Notes - ADVERTISING ADVOCATE

Departments INDEX

Newspaper Notes - AMERICAN JOURNALIST, THE
Newspaper Operations - *a special section* - AMERICAN PRINTER
Newspaper Opinions on New Pictures - MIDWEEK MOTION PICTURE NEWS
Newspaper Production - PRINTING IMPRESSIONS
Newspapers - ADVERTISING & SELLING
Newspapers - *newsbriefs concerning changes in member publications* - CALIFORNIA PUBLISHER
Newspapers - INSIDE MEDIA
Newspapers - MARKETING / COMMUNICATIONS
Newspeople in the News - EDITOR AND PUBLISHER
Newspictures - *title and content listing* - EXHIBITORS HERALD WORLD
Newsprint - PRESSTIME
Newsreel - *newsbriefs* - AMERICAN FILM
Newsreel - *newsbriefs* - FANTASY ZONE
Newsreel - *newsbriefs* - FILM MAKING
Newsreel - *newsbriefs* - FILMS AND FILMING
Newsreel - *animation newsbriefs* - GRAFFITI
Newsreel - *observations* - HOLLYWOOD MAGAZINE
Newsreel - *news items* - LOCATION UPDATE
Newsreel - *newsbriefs* - MARQUEE
Newsreel - *newsbriefs with pictures* - MOVIE SHOW
Newsreel - *newsbriefs* - MOVIEGOER
Newsreel - *star-studded picture page* - SCREENLAND PLUS TV-LAND
Newsreel Picture Spread - MARKETING / COMMUNICATIONS
Newsreels - *news of major films ad commercials shooting in New York area* - MAKING FILMS
Newsroom, The - NEWSINC.
Newsroom - NEWSINC.
News/Talk - R & R
News/Trends - *prepress newsbriefs* - PRE-
Newsviews - *photographs and/or photographers in the news* - NEWS PHOTOGRAPHER
News/Views - *newsbriefs* - SHOOTING COMMERCIALS
Newswatch - *very large section of latebreaking news concerning comics industry* - COMICS JOURNAL, THE
Newswatch - *newsbriefs* - TARGET MARKETING
Newswatch - *newsbriefs* - TV TECHNOLOGY
Newswire - *late breaking news items* - CABLE WORLD
Newswire - INDUSTRIAL PHOTOGRAPHY
Newsworthy - *commentary* - AP BROADCASTER
Newsworthy - *late breaking news items* - PRESENTATION PRODUCTS MAGAZINE
Next Trend, The - *column by Lenore Skenazy* - ADVERTISING AGE
Next Week - *upcoming editorial content* - AMATEUR PHOTOGRAPHER
Next Week on Your Favorite Soaps - *sneak preview* - NATIONAL ENQUIRER
Nielsen Ratings - DAYTIME TV
Nieman Notes - *newsbriefs of Nieman Fellows* - NIEMAN REPORTS

Night Club Reviews - *reviews* - VARIETY
Night Life - *reviews* - ENTERTAINMENT WORLD
Night Life - INTERVIEW
Night Prowl - ENTERTAINMENT CONNECTION MAGAZINE
Nightmare Library - *book reviews* - FANGORIA
Nighttime Soap News - DAYTIME TV
Nikki's Poetry Corner - *column by Nikki* - ENTERTAINMENT CONNECTION MAGAZINE
Nikon's Photo Finish - OUTDOOR & TRAVEL PHOTOGRAPHY
Nine to Five-Thirty - *advertising comment* - CAMPAIGN
NKOTB Klub! - *letters for the New Kids on the Block* - SUPER TEEN
NMRA News - COMMUNICATIONS
NNA Washington Report - *column by Bob Brinkmann* - PUBLISHER'S AUXILIARY
No. 1 in Billboard - *front cover chart* - BILLBOARD
No Holds Barred - *'The first of our regular columns for wrestling fans'* - WHAT SATELLITE
No Man's Land - *news items concerning Broadway celebrities, column by Mlle Rialto* - DRAMATIC MIRROR, THE
No Soap - *column by Eileen Fulton* - REAL LIFE/DAYTIMERS
Nocon - *'Gene Nocon prints readers pictures'* - PRACTICAL PHOTOGRAPHY
Nonfiction - *writing advice* - WRITER'S DIGEST
Non-Theatrical Distribution in Great Britain - DOCUMENTARY FILM NEWS
Nordic News - MEDIA INTERNATIONAL
North America - *theatrical offerings and review* - PLAYS INTERNATIONAL
Northeast Report, The - *black radio playlist* - BLACK RADIO EXCLUSIVE
Northwest New Releases - *book reviews* - WRITER'S NW
Nostalgia - *'Film Monthly looks back'* - FILM MONTHLY
Nostalgia - MOVIE DIGEST
Nostalgia - MOVIE WORLD
Nostalgia Bonus - *'What were you watching twenty years ago?'* - TV STAR PARADE
Nostalgia Is - *letters* - NOSTALGIA ILLUSTRATED
Nostalgia News - *newsbriefs* - NOSTALGIA ILLUSTRATED
Nostalgia Newsfront - *sort of a 'whatever happened to' news feature* - FLASHBACK
Nostalgia Quiz - GOOD OLD DAYS
Nostalgic News - *'Excerpts from--old time newspapers across the nation--early 1900s'* - GOOD OLD DAYS
Nota Bene - VERBATIM
Note and Comment - *newsbriefs* - FOURTH ESTATE
Notebook - *column by Sean Day-Lewis* - BROADCAST
Notebook - *comment by the Secretary-General* - COMBROAD
Noted - PHOTOGRAPHER'S FORUM

Noted & Quoted - *'...a slightly irreverent look at some of the stories that beg for a less than serious tack'* - DIRECT MARKETING
Noted & Quoted - *gleanings from recent publications* - MAGAZINEWEEK
Noted Briefly - RIGHTING WORDS
Noted But Not Seen - *'Zines which sent us advertising instead of copies'* - FACTSHEET FIVE
Notes - CARDOZO ARTS & ENTERTAINMENT LAW JOURNAL
Notes - FORDHAM ENTERTAINMENT, MEDIA & INTELLECTUAL PROPERTY LAW FORUM
Notes - HASTINGS COMMUNICATIONS AND ENTERTAINMENT LAW JOURNAL
Notes - HI-FI NEWS AND RECORD REVIEW
Notes - *column* - MODERN RECORDING & MUSIC
Notes - *detailed information concerning the photographic field* - NEW PHOTO-MINIATURE
Notes - *newsbriefs* - PLAYERS
Notes - SHAKESPEARE QUARTERLY
Notes - TECHNOLOGY AND CULTURE
Notes - *book reviews* - THEATRE-CRAFT
Notes - *book reviews* - THEATRE WORKSHOP
Notes - *suggested news release elements* - UNIVERSAL WEEKLY
Notes and Comment - SCREEN ACTOR HOLLYWOOD
Notes and Comments - *newsbriefs* - CAMERA CRAFT
Notes and Comments - LOYOLA ENTERTAINMENT JOURNAL
Notes & Comments - *on upcoming weeks programming, column by Bill Britton* - ONSAT
Notes and Communications - FILM QUARTERLY
Notes and Information - RHETORIC SOCIETY QUARTERLY
Notes and News - AMERICAN PHOTOGRAPHY
Notes and News - JOURNALIST, THE
Notes and News - *newsbriefs* - PRACTICAL PHOTOGRAPHER, THE
Notes and News - *newsbriefs of scientific films and organizations* - SCIENTIFIC FILM
Notes and News - THEATRE, THE
Notes and News - *newsbriefs* - VIEWCAMERA
Notes and News from the Book Trade in Britain - *current events column by Nicholas Clee and Jane Murray* - BRITISH BOOK NEWS
Notes & Queries - HISTORY OF PHOTOGRAPHY
Notes and Queries - KINEMATOGRAPH WEEKLY
Notes and Queries - THEATER NOW
Notes and Queries - THEATRE NOTEBOOK
Notes and Tips - *letters and other photographic information* - LEICA PHOTOGRAPHY
Notes for Novices - *column by R. H. Mason* - AMATEUR PHOTOGRAPHER
Notes From Abroad - *international and world theatre news* - AMERICAN THEATRE
Notes from All Sources - *newsbriefs* - PROJECTION, LANTERN AND CINEMATOGRAPH

Notes from Broadcast Markets in the U.S. and Abroad - *newsbriefs* - VARIETY
Notes from Here and There - MEDIA & CONSUMER
Notes from Magazines - *photographic news culled from other publications* - APR
Notes From New York - *animation news column by Jerry Beck* - GET ANIMATED! UPDATE.
Notes From Space & Time - *editorial column by Craig Reiss* - MEDIAWEEK
Notes From the Editor - *column by J. Giebelhausen* - PHOTO TECHNIQUE INTERNATIONAL
Notes From the Editor's Cuff - *editorial column by Reed Irvine* - AIM REPORT
Notes From the Lab - RADIO HOME, THE
Notes From the League - *information of the League of American Theatres and Producers* - PLAYBILL
Notes from the Magazines - APR
Notes From the New Cinema - *column by Bob Cowan* - TAKE ONE
Notes from the President - ACA BULLETIN
Notes from the Test Bench - PRACTICAL WIRELESS
Notes From the Women's Caucus Editor - SCA WOMEN'S CAUCUS AND FEMINIST & WOMEN STUDIES DIVISION NEWSLETTER
Notes of a Reader - ACTORS BY DAYLIGHT
Notes of the Agencies - MID-ATLANTIC GRAPHIC ARTS REVIEW
Notes of the Month - DOCUMENTARY FILM NEWS
Notes on New Books - MARKETING / COMMUNICATIONS
Notes on New Publications - *briefs concerning international publications* - INTERNATIONAL ADVERTISER, THE
Notes on News - *undocumented information concerning the gossipy side of publishing* - NEWSPAPER WORLD AND ADVERTISING REVIEW
Notes on People - *personnel briefs* - AFVA BULLETIN
Notes, Quotes and Anecdotes - JOURNAL OF COMMUNICATION
Notes: Radio - *case notes from recent legal proceedings* - AIR LAW REVIEW
Noteworthy - *'Briefs from the applied arts'* - APPLIED ARTS QUARTERLY
Noteworthy - *newsbriefs* - SMALL PRESS
Nothing But the Truth - *'You ask it--we'll tell you the truth'* - GOSSIP
Notice Board - SPEECH AND DRAMA
Notices - *an unusually long and detailed section listing upcoming workshops and seminars* - AFTERIMAGE
Notices - INDEPENDENT, THE
Notices - KINEMATOGRAPH WEEKLY
Notices of Books - ELECTRICAL REVIEW
Notices to Correspondents - ACTORS BY DAYLIGHT

Notizie SMPTE - *'Frequent news items on the world-wide activity of SMPTE, with a special emphasis on the Italian section'* - MILLECANALI INTERNATIONAL
Novice - *news of the novice group* - CQ
Novice Notes - QST
Now Playing - *'Popular pics worthy of a view'* - INSIDE HOLLYWOOD
Now Playing - *'A guide to fine flicks playing at your local movie palace'* - MOVIES USA
Now Playing - *current New York City theatrical fare* - PLAYBILL
Now Showing - *movies and specials on cable this month* - TV ENTERTAINMENT
Now You Know - *reader Q&A* - FILMS AND FILMING
Now You're Talking - *readers page* - MOVIE CLASSIC
NRB News - *newsbriefs* - RELIGIOUS BROADCASTING
NTIS Section - *available publications* - TELEMATICS AND INFORMATICS
NTQ Notes and Reviews - NEW THEATRE QUARTERLY
NTSC Cyberbeat - *media column by Belka Stamas* - FACTSHEET FIVE
Nuggets - *publicity ideas for exhibitors* - BOXOFFICE
Numbers, The - *statistics concerning newspaper management* - NEWSINC.
Nutrition - FILM & VIDEO NEWS
Nuts & Bolts - POPULAR PHOTOGRAPHY
NY & LA Grosses - *box office receipts* - VARIETY
NY Showcases - *box office receipts* - VARIETY
NY/NY - *filmmaking news in greater New York area* - IN CINEMA

O

Oaters - *western program review* - TV GOLD
Obiter Dicta - *opinion and commentary* - VERBATIM
Obituaries - BIG REEL, THE
Obituaries - COMICS BUYER'S GUIDE
Obituaries - *also well-known section for its in-depth information usually not found elsewhere* - DAILY VARIETY
Obituaries - EDITOR AND PUBLISHER
Obituaries - *quality tributes of Hollywood artists* - EMPIRE
Obituaries - FILM TV DAILY
Obituaries - *column by Billy H. Doyle* - FILMS IN REVIEW
Obituaries - IPI REPORT
Obituaries - PUBLIC BROADCASTING REPORT, THE
Obituaries - SMPTE JOURNAL
Obituaries - TELEGRAPH WORLD
Obituaries - UK PRESS GAZETTE
Obituaries - *Variety's obit column, famed for its thoroughness* - VARIETY

Obituary - EDUCATIONAL MEDIA INTERNATIONAL
Obituary - JOURNALIST
Obituary - *extensive section* - MUSICAL AMERICA
Obituary - *lengthy segment* - OFFICIAL BULLETIN OF THE INTERNATIONAL ALLIANCE OF THEATRICAL STAGE EMPLOYEES AND MOVING PICTURE MACHINE OPERATORS OF THE UNITED STATES AND CANADA.
Obituary - UK PRESS GAZETTE
Obituary Notes - FOURTH ESTATE
Observations - *newsbriefs* - IDEAL KINEMA, THE
Observations as We Pass Along - ADVERTISING NEWS
Ocupational Health and Safety - *column by Susan Stevenson* - PULP & PAPER CANADA
Odds and Ends - *anecdotes* - ABC WEEKLY
Odds and Ends - *column by Tony Clifford* - FILM FAN MONTHLY
Odds and Ends - HI-FI SOUND
Of a Personal Nature - *personnel newsbriefs* - ADVERTISING EXPERIENCE
Of Interest - SPECTRA
Of Note - *newsbriefs* - ST. LOUIS JOURNALISM REVIEW
Off Air - *commentary* - BROADCAST
Off Broadway - *listing of current offerings* - THEATERWEEK
Off Off and Away - *theatre review column by Rob Baker* - AFTER DARK
Off Stage Shots - TONI HOLT'S MOVIE LIFE
Off the Air - *commentary* - VIDEO MAGAZINE
Off the Cuff - *latest confidential news and gossip* - AD WEEKLY
Off the Cuff - *column by Hank Grant* - HOLLYWOOD REPORTER
Off the Cuff - *observations* - WRITER, THE
Off the Drawing Board - *'Inventions and dimensions on your retailers' shelves'* - VISIO
Off the Record - EMMY
Off the Shelf - *column by Lee J. Nelson* - ADVANCED IMAGING
Off the Shelf - *video and fanzine review column by Gary Russell* - DOCTOR WHO MAGAZINE
Off the Shelf - *first look at new equipment* - VIDEO MANAGEMENT
Offbeat - POPULAR PHOTOGRAPHY
Offbeat Marketing - SALES & MARKETING MANAGEMENT
Offbeat Radio - *column by Dee McVicker* - RADIO WORLD
Off-B'Way News - PLAYBILL
Off-B'Way Schedule - *Off-Broadway, New York* - VARIETY
Off-Bway Theatres - *listing* - SHOW BUSINESS
Offguard - *pictures the celebrities wish not had been taken* - CELEBRITY
Office Equipment - LÜRZER'S INTERNATIONAL ARCHIVE
Official Announcements - TELECOMMUNICATION JOURNAL
Official Notices - THEATRE JOURNAL
Official Reports - NATIONAL AMATEUR

Departments

Off-Off Broadway - *current offerings far from the Great White Way* - THEATERWEEK
Offscreen - *production profile column by Bob Harris* - COMPUTER PICTURES
Off-Screen - *news and profiles of film and television industry* - MOVIE - THE VIDEO MAGAZINE
Offscreen - *commentary column by Seth Goldstein* - VIDEO BUSINESS
Offset - *news concerning* - AMERICAN PRESS
Offshore Data Entry - *direct mail trends and news outside the States* - WHO'S MAILING WHAT!
Oh, So? - *letters* - COMICS BUYER'S GUIDE
Ohio Valley Report, The - *black radio playlist* - BLACK RADIO EXCLUSIVE
OISTT - *periodical and book review* - THEATRE DESIGN & TECHNOLOGY
Oklahoma City - BOX OFFICE
Old Time Comic - *reprinted comic strip* - GOOD OLD DAYS
Old Time Ham-Ads - OLD TIMER'S BULLETIN, THE
Old Time Music - *reprinted sheet music* - GOOD OLD DAYS
Old Timer - *a wonderful retrospective on the way things were in radio, column by George Riggins* - RADIO WORLD
Ombudsman, The - QUILL, THE
Ombudsmen, The - *column by Richard P. Cunningham* - QUILL, THE
On (Experimental) Film - *column by Mike Hoolboom* - CINEMA/CANADA
On Air - CHANNELS
On Air - *'...an open channel to air comments, observations, gossip, and the unconventional about the international broadcast scene'* - WORLD BROADCAST NEWS
On Assignment - INTERNATIONAL PHOTOGRAPHER MAGAZINE
On B'Way - *current productions* - PLAYBILL
On Canada - *Canadian production news* - ON LOCATION
On Catalogs - *column by Jack Schmid* - TARGET MARKETING
On Color - *column by Ed Scully* - CAMERA 35
On Copyright - *column* - BMI: MUSICWORLD
On Creative - *column by Joan Harris* - TARGET MARKETING
On Developing - CAMERA AND DARK ROOM
On Every Job There's a Laugh or Two - *humor* - JOURNAL
On Leave - *faculty* - SPECTRA
On Line - *'The latest tools for your desktop' column by Liz Horton* - PC PUBLISHING AND PRESENTATIONS
On Line - *column by Stan Horzepa* - QST
On Location - *back-page photo* - AMERICAN PHOTO
On Location - *films in progress* - CINEMA/CANADA
On Location - *'Short previews of feature films in progress'* - CINEMA, VIDEO & CABLE MOVIE DIGEST
On Location - FLORIDA REEL

On Location - *production companies and projects in the areas of corporate, arts, quiz, TV films/drama and factual* - TELEVISION WEEK
On Location - *productions using Tiffen filters* - TIFFEN PROFESSIONAL NEWSLETTER
On Location - WRAP
On Management - MAGAZINE DESIGN & PRODUCTION
On Members' Minds - *commentary of Don Fowler, SMPG Membership Director* - MAGAZINE BUSINESS
On Next Week - STAGE AND TELEVISION TODAY, THE
On Now - *films in current release* - SIGHT & SOUND
On Other Broadways - *'Happenings in the byways of Broadway, North, South, East, and West' column by Albert McCleery* - STAGE
On Paper - MAGAZINE DESIGN & PRODUCTION
On Record - *interview* - AMUSEMENT BUSINESS
On Record - *reviews* - HI-FI SOUND
On Release - *analysis of current box office receipts in various international cities* - BUSINESS OF FILM, THE
On Review - OLD TIMER'S BULLETIN, THE
On Short Waves - *interesting highlights of international radio service on shortwave frequencies* - MOVIE-RADIO GUIDE
On Stage - *state-by-state listing of current theatrical fare* - AMERICAN THEATRE
On Stage - *black artists in live performance column by LarriAnn Flores* - BLACK RADIO EXCLUSIVE
On Stage - ENTERTAINMENT CONNECTION MAGAZINE
On Target - *product review* - DOCTOR WHO MAGAZINE
On Target - *editorial* - TARGET
On Target - *newsbriefs* - TARGET MARKETING
On Test - *equipment review* - CAMERA & CAMCORDER MONTHLY
On Test - *new product evaluations* - HI-FI SOUND
On Test - PHOTO ANSWERS
On Test - *new product profile* - PRACTICAL PHOTOGRAPHY
On the Air - *newsbriefs* - PRACTICAL WIRELESS
On the Air - *comment* - SOUND AND VISION BROADCASTING
On the Bandwagon - *aptly subtitled 'Romance, Rumors, Record Reviews, and Gossip of Your Favorite Melody Men'* - MOVIE-RADIO GUIDE
On the Beat - *column by John Ephland* - DOWN BEAT
On the Beat with the Editors - *newsbriefs* - ASMP BULLETIN
On the Boards - PLAY SHOP, THE
On the Books - *reviews* - SOUND MANAGEMENT
On the Box - *film and television review* - STRANGE ADVENTURES
On the Business Side - *column by Martin Hershenson* - PHOTOGRAPHIC PROCESSING
On the Couch - *'A psychotherapist analyzes the soaps'* - SOAP OPERA UPDATE

On the Desktop - *column by Richard D. Johnson* - SMALL PRESS
On the disk - *review column by Lafe Low* - ONI
On the Docket - *regulatory news* - MEDIAWEEK
On the Floor - *sales floor tactics* - DEALERSCOPE
On the Groundglass - *column by Wilfred French* - PHOTO-ERA MAGAZINE
On the Ham Bands - *column by Ike Kerschner* - MONITORING TIMES
On the Market - *column by Tom Soter* - BACK STAGE/SHOOT
On the Market - *equipment review* - PHOTO MARKETING
On the Money - *column by Fred Rosen* - MODERN PHOTOGRAPHY
On the Move - *agency change of address* - ADWEEK
On the Move - *personnel briefs* - BROADCASTER
On the Move - *appointments and promotions in the ITV world* - EDUCATIONAL BROADCASTING
On the Move - *member newsbriefs* - IMAGE
On the Move - *personnel changes* - KNIGHT-RIDDER NEWS
On the Move - *personnel briefs* - LOS ANGELES TECHNOGRAPH
On the Move - *personnel newsbriefs* - VIDEO SOFTWARE MAGAZINE
On the Other Hand - *pro and con article commentary* - WRITTEN COMMUNICATION
On the Racks - *new comic product reviewes column by Barry Dutter* - FOUR COLOR
On the Radio Hit Circuit - *delightful newsbriefs concerning radio network stars* - RADIO HIT SONGS
On the Record - *review column by Mike Mettler* - ONI
On the Road - EXHIBITORS' TIMES
On the Scene - AISLE VIEW
On the Scene - *artist profiles* - BMI: MUSICWORLD
On the Scene - *column by Nicole Hobbs* - ENTERTAINMENT CONNECTION MAGAZINE
On the Scene - *the editors* - PETERSEN'S PHOTOGRAPHIC
On the Scene - PRESS, THE
On the Scene With Selene - *personality column by Selene Walters* - SPOTLIGHT CASTING MAGAZINE
On the Screen - *review column by Gregory Fagan* - ONI
On the Side - *quarterly scrapbook of newsbriefs* - AUTHOR, THE
On the Sound Track - *column by Charlie Applewhite* - MOVIE FAN
On the Spot - *one-page interviews* - MOVIE WORLD
On the Square - *comment column by Hye Bossin* - CANADIAN FILM DIGEST
On the Street - *marketing and consumer news of interest to radio sales* - SOUND MANAGEMENT
On the Studio Trail - REP: RECORDING ENGINEERING PRODUCTION
On the Technical Side - WRITERS' JOURNAL

On the Town - *column by Mark Zweigler* - AFTER DARK
On the TV Screen - *video program reviews* - MOTION PICTURE PRODUCT DIGEST
On the Un-Coast - *column by Ted Compton* - BACK STAGE
On Through the Years - *interesting historical comments on a current day labor issue* - UNION LABOR SUN
On Video - *new videocassette releases* - ALPHA AND OMEGA FILM REPORT
On Video - *new releases* - BEST OF FILM & VIDEO
On View - *'visitors and presentations'* - INTERNATIONAL ADVERTISER
On Your Wavelength - *column by Thermion* - PRACTICAL WIRELESS
On! Audio - *column by Joe Wiesenfelder* - ONI
On! Computers - *column by David Essex* - ONI
On! Second Thought - *commentary column by David Lachenbruch* - ONI
On! Shopping - *column by Martin Brochstein* - ONI
On! Software - ONI
On! This... - *editorial column by Martin Levine* - ONI
On! Video - *column by K. C. Pepper* - ONI
Once Over Lightly - *newsbriefs* - OVERSET
One Life to Live - *abstract* - SOAP OPERA DIGEST
One Man's Opinion - *'Follow the bouncing actor'* - REAL LIFE/DAYTIMERS
One Man's Reflections - *column by Dr. Alfred N. Goldsmith* - TELEVISION
One Man's Work - *profile* - FUNCTIONAL PHOTOGRAPHY
One Minute Interview - GOSSIP
One Minute Interview - REAL LIFE/DAYTIMERS
One Minute Interviews - THEATRE TIME
One on One - *profile* - FLASH
One Shots - *'Closeups on some of the headliners'* - REAL LIFE/DAYTIMERS
One Step Beyond - *'Sh-Boom remembers the early heroes of rock 'n' roll!'* - SH-BOOM
One to One - *Reader Q&A* - PETERSEN'S PHOTOGRAPHIC
One-Brand Rack/Mini Component Systems - SOUND & VISION
One-Minute Interview - *half-page Q&A format interview* - RONA BARRETT'S HOLLYWOOD
One-On-One - *programmer interview column by Lisa Coleman* - MONDAY MORNING REPLAY
One-Shot Reviews - FACTSHEET FIVE
On-Line Services - FUTUREHOME TECHNOLOGY NEWS
On-Line to Profits - TELEPROFESSIONAL
Only on Satellite - *'For dish owners eyes only' column by Wendy Williams* - SATELLITE TV WEEK
OnScreen - *puppetry on television or film* - ANIMATIONS
On-The-Air - *FCC newsbriefs* - TELEVISION BROADCAST
OOBA Member Theatres - *listing* - SHOW BUSINESS

Oooooops! - *schematic corrections* - ETI
Op-Edd Page - *'Opinions, editorials, and your letters'* - COMICS FANDOM EXAMINER
Open Channel - *commentary* - ETI
Open Forum - *letters* - BOOKSTORE JOURNAL
Open House - *post facility profile* - POST
Open Letter, The - *editorial column by Fred Ciporen* - PUBLISHER'S WEEKLY
Open Mike - *letters column important for responses* - BROADCASTING
Open Reel (Reel-to-Reel) Tape Decks - SOUND & VISION
Open Transponder - *'Letters from our readers'* - SATELLITE TV WEEK
Opening Notes - COMICS FEATURE
Opening Performance Chart - *graph detailing first run successes* - PICTURE REPORTS
Opening Shot - *full-page color offering* - PRACTICAL PHOTOGRAPHY
Opening Shots - *comment* - COMICS JOURNAL, THE
Opening Shots - *star pictures* - TS
Opening Shots - *editorial* - VIDEO BUSINESS
Opening Theme - *comment* - SIGNALS
Openings - *photographic exhibitions* - IMAGE
Openings - *upcoming theatrical fare* - PLAYS INTERNATIONAL
Opera - MUSICAL AMERICA
Opera - *reviews* - NEW THEATRE
Opera - *reviews* - PLAYS INTERNATIONAL
Opera and Dance - STAGE AND TELEVISION TODAY, THE
Operating Events - QST
Operating News - *'Conducted by the Communications Department' column by F. E. Handy and E. L. Battey* - QST
Operating news - QST
Operations - CABLE WORLD
Operations - CABLEAGE
Operations - CABLEVISION
Operations News - CABLE WORLD
Operators Forum and Question Box, The - *Q&A* - EXHIBITORS' TIMES
Opinion - *editorial* - ADVERTISING NEWS
Opinion - APPLIED ARTS QUARTERLY
Opinion - ASIAN ADVERTISING & MARKETING
Opinion - CINEMA/CANADA
Opinion - COLUMBIA JOURNALISM REVIEW
Opinion - *editorial* - CWA NEWS
Opinion - FILM MEDIA
Opinion - INDEX ON CENSORSHIP
Opinion - INSIDE MEDIA
Opinion - IPI REPORT
Opinion - PR WEEK
Opinion - PRODUCCIÓN Y DISTRIBUCIÓN
Opinion - SCREEN INTERNATIONAL
Opinion - TELEVISION BROADCAST
Opinion - TV TECHNOLOGY
Opinion - UK PRESS GAZETTE
Opinion - VIZIONS
Opinion - WASHINGTON NEWSPAPER, THE
Opinion / Commentary - *column by Philip B. Meggs* - COMMUNICATION ARTS
Opinion and Comment - AMERICAN TELEPHONE JOURNAL, THE

Opinion & Comment - CABLE MARKETING
Opinion and Fact - *a forum for opinions concerning use of instructional media* - AID
Opinions - DARKSLIDE
Opportunities - *newsbriefs of openings and grants* - MEDIA ANTHROPOLOGIST NEWSLETTER
Opportunities - MEDIA ETHICS UPDATE
Opportunities - *Announced productions* - PRINTED MATTER
Opportunity Awareness - *'Thoughtful reflections on your future' column by David L. Heiserman* - COMPUTERS & ELECTRONICS
Optical News - *extensive news column by Carol Kelley* - CD-ROM LIBRARIAN
Optical Product Review - *column by Peter Brueggeman and Carol Reed* - CD-ROM LIBRARIAN
Options Menu - *new product review* - VENTURA PROFESSIONALI
OPUS Record Reviews - MUSICAL AMERICA
Or Bookshelves - *paragraph-length reviews* - CAMERA CRAFT
Orbit Video's Top 10 - *'These are the new releases to get before the other customers clear them from the shelves'* - ORBIT VIDEO
Organ Solos - *live stage/theatre programs* - EXHIBITORS HERALD WORLD
Organizations - INDEX ON CENSORSHIP
Original Programming - *column by Cindy Spielvogel* - VIDEO INSIDER
Oscar Looks Back - *'Academy award blasts from the past'* - ORBIT VIDEO
Other - WORLD PRESS REVIEW
Other Fellow's Idea, The - MOVING PICTURE AGE
Other Friends - BROADCAST PIONEERS LIBRARY REPORTS
Other Media - MEDIA BUSINESS
Other Meetings of Interest - CLIO AMONG THE MEDIA
Other People's Pictures - EIGHT MM MOVIE MAKER AND CINE CAMERA
Other Side of the Tracks - *column* - MIX
Other Stages - *theatre review column by Glenn Loney* - AFTER DARK
Other Voices - *letters* - PETERSEN'S PHOTOGRAPHIC
Ottawa - BOX OFFICE
Otto's Night Watch - PRINTING IMPRESSIONS
Our Address is Hollywood! - *letters* - SOUND STAGE
Our Amateurs' Play-Box - *reviews* - THEATRE, THE
Our Art Supplement - ALBUM, THE
Our Business - *industry comment column by N.A. Taylor* - CANADIAN FILM DIGEST
Our Contributing Critics - *a unique section printing one photo, and inviting readers to criticize from standpoint of lighting, composition, exposure, etc.* - PHOTO-ERA MAGAZINE
Our Daily Dozen - *column by Don Becker* - RADIO DIAL
Our Department of Criticism - *commentary* - AMERICAN ADVERTISER

Departments INDEX 838

Our Illustrations - *different section discussing large number of portraits and photos which are found throughout the periodical* - PHOTO-ERA MAGAZINE
Our Man in Hollywood - *column by Joe Hyams* - SHOW BUSINESS ILLUSTRATED
Our Members - *profile* - ROUNDUP QUARTERLY
Our Omnibus-Box - *newsbriefs* - THEATRE, THE
Our Patrons - *descriptions of selected vendors advertising in the magazine* - ST. LOUIS AND CANADIAN PHOTOGRAPHER
Our Pick Pic of the Month - *feature film review* - TV AND SCREEN SECRETS
Our Play-box - *reviews* - THEATRE, THE
Our Portfolio - AMERICAN AMATEUR PHOTOGRAPHER AND CAMERA & DARKROOM
Our Portfolio - AMERICAN PHOTOGRAPHY
Our Portraits and Biographies - THEATRE, THE
Our Private Wire - *'Special correspondence from inside the movie colony'* - PICTURE PLAY MAGAZINE
Our Public Broadcasting - *letters* - TV MIRROR
Our Readers' Comments - LPTV REPORT, THE
Our Readers Say - *letters* - CQ
Our Readers Write - *letters* - BOOK MARKETING UPDATE
Our Readers Write - *letters* - INTERNATIONAL ADVERTISER
Our Readers Write - SATELLITE ORBIT
Our Reference Shelf - KINEMATOGRAPH WEEKLY
Our Stage Causerie - *'By the Idler'* - STAGE AND SPORT
Our Suggestion Bureau - KINEMATOGRAPH WEEKLY
Our Table - *book reviews* - AMERICAN AMATEUR PHOTOGRAPHER AND CAMERA & DARKROOM
Our Table - AMERICAN PHOTOGRAPHY
Our View - *comment* - VIDEO BUSINESS
Our View - *editorial* - VIEW
Out For a Spin - *'Latest releases and gossip of your favorite recording stars' column by Bob Lardine* - TV RADIO TALK
Out in the Shop - MID-ATLANTIC GRAPHIC ARTS REVIEW
Out of Our Minds - *'A collection of editorial excerpts from Washington community newspapers'* - WASHINGTON NEWSPAPER, THE
Out of the Air - *current events* - LISTENER
Out of the Hat - *employee hobbies* - KODAK
Out of the Lab - *hints* - MODERN PHOTOGRAPHY
Outcue - *column of commentary by the Alpha Epsilon Rho national secretary* - SIGNALS
Outdoor - MEDIAWEEK
Outdoor Advertising - *'Embracing billposting, bulletins, wall signs, distributing, etc.'* - SIGNS OF THE TIMES
Outdoor Classroom - *column by Tom Boyden* - OUTDOOR & TRAVEL PHOTOGRAPHY

Outdoor Industry Abroad, The - ADVERTISING OUTDOORS
Outdoor Publicity, Etc. - ADVERTISING EXPERIENCE
Outdoor Videographer - *column by Jerry Chiappetta* - OUTDOOR & TRAVEL PHOTOGRAPHY
Outer Limits - *column by Dr. John Santosuosso* - MONITORING TIMES
Outfront - *musicians and their product* - STAGE & STUDIO
Outline - *gossip briefs* - CAMPAIGN
Outlook - ADWEEK'S MARKETING WEEK
Output Test - *equipment review* - STAGE & STUDIO
Outside Looking In - *out-of-staters survey the Florida production scene* - ENTERTAINMENT REVUE
Outside Services - *outside support suppliers* - CORPORATE VIDEO DECISIONS
Outstanding in the Week's News - *newsbriefs* - BOXOFFICE
Outtakes - *described as 'heavy and light industry gossip unavailable elsewhere'* - ACTION!
Outtakes - *comment column by Seth Goldstein* - CONSUMER ELECTRONICS
Outtakes - EMMY
Out-Takes - *programming and observations via 'Groucho'* - TELEVISION WEEK
Over the Counter - *sales tips* - COMMUNICATIONS
Over the Cracker Barrel - *radio programming newsbriefs* - RURAL RADIO
Over the Tape - *'News of the radio, telegraph and telephone industries* - COMMUNICATION AND BROADCAST ENGINEERING
Overheard in Hollywood - *column by Erskine Johnson* - MOTION PICTURE
Overheard in Hollywood - *'What the stars are saying -- unguarded moments when they didn't know we were there!'* - PHOTO SCREEN
Overseas Affairs - LEARNED PUBLISHING
Overset - PRESSTIME
Overview - *newsbriefs* - SCHOOL PRESS REVIEW, THE
Overview - *editorial* - VIDEO INSIDER

P

Packaging & Design - MARKETING NEWS
Page Five--The Late News - *newsbriefs* - ADVERTISING AGENCY
Page of Sport - ABC WEEKLY
Page of the Week - *column by Edmund C. Arnold* - PUBLISHER'S AUXILIARY
Page Two - *editorial commentary column by Donald F. Brod* - GRASSROOTS EDITOR
Page-Make Up - *new technologies and processes* - POLYGRAPH INTERNATIONAL
Pages Sold - MEDIA INDUSTRY NEWSLETTER

Pairing Pairs - VERBATIM
Pairs and Repairs - *'Who's Going With Whom--and Who's Going Back to Whom*' - PREVIEW
Pakistan - *briefs* - MOVIE/TV MARKETING
Palm Springs - *'Show Biz' column by Breena Alane* - CASTING CALL
Pamphlet Cover - *samples* - GRAPHIC ARTS, THE
Panorama - *newsbriefs* - KODAK
Panoramic View - PANORAMA
Paper - *column by William Bureau* - GRAPHIC ARTS MONTHLY
Paper and Design - *available aids from paper companies* - PRINT
Paper Trends - *column by Eric O. Edelmann* - MAGAZINE DESIGN & PRODUCTION
Papers & Conferences - *upcoming* - CLIO AMONG THE MEDIA
Papers for Junior Students - ELECTRICAL REVIEW
Pappas on Programming - FRENDX
Paradox - *production comment column by Stanford Sobel* - COMPUTER PICTURES
Paragraphs - *column by George Vail Kabristante* - MOVIE FLASH
Paramount Events in Latin America - PARAMOUNT WORLD
Parent & Child - *celebrity column* - PHOTOPLAY
Paris Scene - *film news* - MOTION PICTURE PRODUCT DIGEST
Paris Theatricals - *Theatrical activities* - ACTORS BY DAYLIGHT
Parks & Attractions - *news and information* - AMUSEMENT BUSINESS
Parting Shot, The - *comment* - ABSOLUTE SOUND, THE
Parting Shot - *inside back cover comment* - ASIAN ADVERTISING & MARKETING
Parting Shot - *essay* - SCARLET STREET
Parting Shots - *readers letters* - AMERICAN PHOTO
Parting Shots - *commentary* - INSIDE HOLLYWOOD
Parting Shots - *columnist Bill Royce with back-cover news briefs* - PREVIEW
Parting Words - CABLEVISION
Partners - *corporate and agency ties* - PSA
Party Line, The - *backcover photographs* - MUSICAL AMERICA
Party Line, The - *fashion and cooking column by Marjorie Arnold* - RURAL RADIO
Passing Parade, The - *comment* - ABSOLUTE SOUND, THE
Passing Scene, The - *celebrities remembered* - GOOD OLD DAYS
Passing Week, The - *newsbriefs* - HOLLYWOOD FILMOGRAPH
Passport: Trips, Tours & Workshops - *'A directory to what's available'* - OUTDOOR & TRAVEL PHOTOGRAPHY
Past Perfect - *enduring personality profile* - FAME
Pastoring - MEDIA & VALUES
Patch Panel - *personel briefs* - SIGNAL, THE
Patent Intelligence - KINEMATOGRAPH WEEKLY

Patents - AMERICAN TELEPHONE JOURNAL, THE
Patents - KINEMATOGRAPH WEEKLY
Patents in Prospect - BRITISH COMMUNICATIONS AND ELECTRONICS
PATSEARCH - *available information* - TELEMATICS AND INFORMATICS
Pay Per View - *'The latest movies'* - SATELLITE TV WEEK
Pay TV Movie Guide - TV GUIDE
Payment and Length - WHAT EDITORS WANT
Pay-Per-View Calendar - *upcoming broadcasts* - CABLE GUIDE, THE
Pay-Per-View Viewing This Week - *listing* - ONSAT
PBR Notes - PUBLIC BROADCASTING REPORT, THE
PC Connections - COMMUNICATIONSWEEK
PC Pipeline, The - *column by Mick O'Leary* - LINK-UP
PC Plus - *column by F. D. Miller* - AV VIDEO
PCB Foil Patterns - ETI
PC's Mailbag - *new postcard items* - POSTCARD COLLECTOR
PDNews - *photography news* - PHOTO DISTRICT NEWS
Pearson's Corner - *essay* - AUDIO VISUAL JOURNAL
Peeking In at the Broadcasts with the Camera Snooper - *pictures of network radio shows in progress* - RADIOLAND
Peeled Eye, The - *column by Dick Neff* - ADVERTISING AGENCY
Peeled Eye - *newsbriefs column by James Tyler* - ADVERTISING & SELLING
Pen and Personality - *column by Larry Jaekle* - SOUND STAGE
Pen Friends - *pen pal listing* - WOWI MAGAZINE
Pen Pals - *listing* - BONDAGE
Pen Pals - *'Find the friend you've been wanting'* - FRESH!
Pending Radio Litigation in the United States - *column by Arthur W. Scharfeld* - JOURNAL OF RADIO LAW
Penpals - TV HITS
Penpoint - *editorial-commentary* - WASHINGTON JOURNALISM REVIEW
Penstripes - *editorial* - VIDEO MANAGEMENT
Pentax and SLR Notes - SHUTTERBUG
Pentax Family Gallery - *reader-submitted photographs* - PENTAX FAMILY
Pentax Journal - *column by Takao Kajiwara* - PENTAX FAMILY
People - ABU NEWSLETTER
People - *newsbriefs* - ACTION
People - *personnel newsbriefs* - ADVANCED IMAGING
People - *newsbriefs* - ADVERTISING AGE
People - ADWEEK
People - *newsbriefs* - ADWEEK'S MARKETING WEEK
People - AMERICAN PRESS
People - *profile and newsbriefs* - AMERICAN THEATRE
People - *newsbriefs concerning changes and promotions* - ASIAN ADVERTISING & MARKETING

People - *personnel newsbriefs* - AUDIOVIDEO INTERNATIONAL
People - AUSTRALASIAN PRINTER
People - AVC
People - BROADCAST + TECHNOLOGY
People - *personnel briefs* - BROADCAST ENGINEERING
People - *personnel briefs* - BROADCASTER
People - BROADSIDE
People - CABLE TV BUSINESS MAGAZINE
People - CABLE WORLD
People - CABLEVISION
People - *newsbriefs* - CALIFORNIA PUBLISHER
People - *newsbriefs* - CINEMA AND THEATRE
People - CINEMA/CANADA
People - CONSUMER ELECTRONICS
People - DEALERSCOPE
People - *personnel newsbriefs* - ELECTRONICS
People - *newsbriefs concerning additions, retirements and other personnel notes* - FOCUS ON FOX
People - GRAPHIC ARTS MONTHLY
People - IEEE SPECTRUM
People - *newsbriefs* - INDUSTRIAL TELEVISION NEWS
People - INSIDE ENTERTAINMENT
People - *personnel newsbriefs* - INSIDE MEDIA
People - *profiles and reviews* - JOURNALIST
People - *personnel newsbriefs* - MAGAZINEWEEK
People - MEDIA WEEK
People - *personnel newsbriefs* - MULTICHANNEL NEWS
People - POST
People - *newsbriefs* - PRIVATE CABLE
People - *personnel briefs* - PRO SOUND NEWS
People - PROMOTION
People - *personnel changes* - PUBLIC RELATIONS JOURNAL, THE
People - *newsbriefs* - PUBLISHER'S WEEKLY
People - *news profiles* - RADIO ONLY
People - *profile* - SALES & MARKETING MANAGEMENT
People - *'Spotlight on key personnel changes'* - SATELLITE COMMUNICATIONS
People - *personality column by Brenda Barton* - SCREEN INTERNATIONAL
People - *newsbriefs* - SIGHT AND SOUND MARKETING
People - *personnel briefs* - ST. LOUIS JOURNALISM REVIEW
People - TIFFEN PROFESSIONAL NEWSLETTER
People - VIA SATELLITE
People - VIDEO BUSINESS
People - VIDEO MANAGEMENT
People - VIDEO STORE
People - VIDEO SYSTEMS
People - *personnel newsbriefs* - VIDEOGRAPHY
People - VIDEOPRO
People - WORLD PRESS REVIEW
People & Careers - COMMUNICATIONSWEEK
People & Ideas - APERTURE
People & Places - *personnel newsbriefs at facilities, stations, and manufacturers* - TELEVISION BROADCAST
People & Projects - CLIO AMONG THE MEDIA
People & Publications - MAGAZINE BUSINESS

People Answers - *photographic Q&A* - PHOTO ANSWERS
People Chatter - AUDIOVIDEO INTERNATIONAL
People in Publishing - CANADIAN PRINTER
People in Teleconferencing - *people newsbriefs* - TELECONFERENCE MAGAZINE
People in the News - *briefs* - BROADCAST ENGINEERING
People in the News - *personnel newsbriefs* - BUSINESS OF FILM, THE
People in the News - *personnel briefs* - ETV NEWSLETTER
People In the News - *personnel newsbriefs* - HEALTH COMMUNICATION NEWSLETTER
People in the News - PHOTOGRAPHIC PROCESSING
People In the News - *member newsbriefs* - POLITICAL COMMUNICATION NEWSLETTER
People in the News - *name list* - VIDEO AGE INTERNATIONAL
People in the News - WASHINGTON NEWSPAPER, THE
People in Video - *briefs* - VIDEO MANAGEMENT
People Line - *'People on the move within the industry'* - INFORMATION TODAY
People Meter - *personnel newsbriefs* - MEDIAWEEK
People Mix - CLIO MAGAZINE
People on the Move - *newsbriefs* - ADVERTISING AND MARKETING MANAGEMENT
People on the Move - *personnel briefs* - HOLLYWOOD REPORTER
People on the Move - MARKETING COMMUNICATIONS
People on the Move - REP: RECORDING ENGINEERING PRODUCTION
People on the Move - *newsbriefs,* - TV WORLD
People Photography - PROFESSIONAL PHOTOGRAPHER, THE
People, Places and Issues - PRINTING IMPRESSIONS
People, Places, Happenings - DB
People, Products, Et. - *newsbriefs* - SCHOLASTIC EDITOR'S TRENDS IN PUBLICATIONS
People to Watch - TBI
People to Watch - WATCH
Peopleline - *Newspaper Fund alumni newsbriefs* - ALUMNI NEWSLINE
People/Places/Things - *newsbriefs* - TELEVISION PROGRAMMER, THE
People-Promo - *briefs* - BROADCASTER
People's Choice - *'Here are favorite releases from previous months that keep customers rushing to their video stores'* - ORBIT VIDEO
Peoplescape - *personnel changes* - COMPUTER PUBLISHING
PeopleWorks - *profiles* - ADVERTISING AGE
Pepigrams - *newspaper sayings* - PEP
Pepitorials - PEP
Performance - *technical review* - VIDEO
Performance Art - *column by Lucia Dewey* - DRAMA-LOGUE
Periodical Articles - *review* - FOI DIGEST
Periodically Yours - *editorial* - LITERATURE/FILM QUARTERLY

Departments INDEX

Periodicals - *resourceful listing of current comments in various publications* - AMERICAN FILM

Periodicals and Serials - *'Reviews of new titles'* - BRITISH BOOK NEWS

Periodicals' Space Barometer - *weekly publication data* - NEWSPAPER WORLD AND ADVERTISING REVIEW

Peripherals - PRE-

Periscope - *world video newsbriefs* - VIDEO

Perplexities - *Q&A column* - AMATEUR PHOTOGRAPHER'S WEEKLY, THE

Person to Person - *advice column* - FRESH!

Personal - AMERICAN ADVERTISER REPORTER

Personal - *column by John Jones* - NATIONAL ADVERTISING

Personal - SPECTRA

Personal Appearances - *stars night out* - MOVIE SHOW

Personal Communications - *cb equipment* - CONSUMER ELECTRONICS PRODUCT NEWS

Personal Gossip About Writers - *human-interest insight into famous authors* - AUTHOR, THE

Personal Insight - PRINT BUYERS REVIEW

Personal Marketing - MARKETING COMMUNICATIONS

Personal Messages - *commentary column by Paul Messenger* - HI-FI CHOICE

Personal Notes - *academic changes, awards, grants* - FEEDBACK

Personalia - *personnel briefs* - EBU REVIEW. PROGRAMMES, ADMINISTRATION, LAW.

Personalia - POST OFFICE MAGAZINE

Personalities and Posts - ABU TECHNICAL REVIEW

Personalities of the Week - BBC WORLD SERVICE LONDON CALLING

Personality of the Month - *profile* - PLAYS AND PLAYERS

Personality of the Month - SHOW

Personals - ADVERTISING ADVOCATE

Personals - BEA NEWSLETTER

Personals - INTELLIGENCER

Personals - JOURNALIST, THE

Personals - *exhibitor news* - NATIONAL EXHIBITOR, THE

Personals - PUBLIC BROADCASTING REPORT, THE

Personals - *newsbriefs* - SATELLITE WEEK

Personals - SPECTRA

Personals - TELEVISION DIGEST WITH CONSUMER ELECTRONICS

Personals - VIDEODISC MONITOR, THE

Personals - VISUAL COMMUNICATION NEWSLETTER, THE

Personals - WOODCOCK'S PRINTERS' AND LITHOGRAPHERS' WEEKLY GAZETTE AND NEWSPAPER REPORTER

Personnals - *newsbriefs* - VIDEO WEEK

Personnel - *newsbriefs* - HIGH VOLUME PRINTING

Personnel - *changes and appointments* - MOTION PICTURE PRODUCT DIGEST

Personnel - *newsbriefs* - PRINT-EQUIP NEWS

Personnel - *briefs* - WEB

Personnel Appointments - PRESS STATISTICAL REVIEW

Personnel File - COMMUNICATIONSWEEK

Perspective - *comment* - AD WEEKLY

Perspective - AMAZING HEROES

Perspective - *commentary* - AMERICAN PRINTER

Perspective - CAMERA ARTS

Perspective - *commentary* - CORPORATE TELEVISION

Perspective - INTERNATIONAL ADVERTISER

Perspective - *commentary* - MEMORIES

Perspective - *column by Richard Reeves* - PANORAMA

Perspective - *column by Martin Polon* - STUDIO SOUND AND BROADCAST ENGINEERING

Perspective - *column by Les Brown and Bill Grantham* - TBI

Perspective - *newsbriefs* - VIDEO

Perspective - *publisher commentary column by David Rowe* - VIDEO SOFTWARE MAGAZINE

Perspectives - *column* - BUSINESS MARKETING

Perspectives - PHOTOMETHODS

Perspectives - *music product reviews* - STAGE & STUDIO

Pet Patter - *pets of the soap opera stars* - SOAP OPERA WEEKLY

Pete Savage on Subscription Marketing - *magazine subscription critique column by Pete Savage* - MAGAZINEWEEK

Peter Noble's Bookshelf - *extra-large section on new film books* - SCREEN INTERNATIONAL

Pets - *of the celebrities* - REAL LIFE/DAYTIMERS

PF Flyer - *editorial* - ON CABLE

PFVEA Membership List - *members of the Professional Film and Video Equipment Association* - NEWSLETTER, THE

PG Allen's Ad Commentary - *comment concerning print advertising* - NEWSPAPER WORLD AND ADVERTISING REVIEW

Pharmaceuticals - LÜRZER'S INTERNATIONAL ARCHIVE

Phil Klineman - *commentary on agencys* - CAMPAIGN

Phil Stone Report, The - BROADCAST + TECHNOLOGY

Philadelphia - BOX OFFICE

Philadelphia Notes - EXHIBITORS' TIMES

Philadelphia Pointers - *news of Pennsylvania radio manufacturers* - RADIO DEALER, THE

Phono Market News and Trends - TELEVISION RETAILING

Photo - LÜRZER'S INTERNATIONAL ARCHIVE

Photo Adventure - *column by Galen Rowell* - OUTDOOR PHOTOGRAPHER

Photo Assignment - *assignment challenge to readers* - PRACTICAL PHOTOGRAPHY

Photo Bug, The - *column by M. R. Dolliver* - WESTERN PHOTOGRAPHER MAGAZINE

Photo Clinic - *Q&A column by Rod Ashford* - CAMERA & CAMCORDER MONTHLY

Photo Clinic - *column by Lee Frost* - PHOTO ANSWERS

Photo Critique - *'Lynne Barbers personal photo improvement critique' column by Lynne Barbers* - PRACTICAL PHOTOGRAPHY

Photo Data Sheets - *'Minicam Photography clip sheet for permanent reference'* - MODERN PHOTOGRAPHY

Photo-Electronics - POPULAR PHOTOGRAPHY

Photo Essay - PRINT EDUCATION MAGAZINE

Photo Finish - *picture collage* - MEMORIES

Photo Finish - *pictorial themed layout* - SOAP OPERA WEEKLY

Photo Flashes - *newsbriefs* - DARKROOM AND CREATIVE CAMERA TECHNIQUES

Photo Ideas - *'A scintillating selection of sumptuous snaps to set your shutters sizzling, column by Lee Frost'* - PHOTO ANSWERS

Photo Market Update - *'The latest developments and changes in the photography marketplace'* - PHOTOGRAPHER'S MARKET NEWSLETTER

Photo News in Brief - *new product review* - CAMERA

Photo of the Month - FRESH!

Photo Previews - *'Here's the latest news of the photographic world'* - TRAVEL & LEISURE

Photo Review - ADVERTISING AGE

Photo Review - ANTIQUE RADIO CLASSIFIED

Photo Revue - *highlights of current advertising* - ADVERTISING AGE

Photo School - *instructional series* - PRACTICAL PHOTOGRAPHY

Photo Summary of Week's News for Southern Showmen - BOXOFFICE

Photo Technique - *an analysis of current photo communications* - COMMUNICATION WORLD

Photo Tips - POPULAR PHOTOGRAPHY

Photo Tours & Workshops - INTERNATIONAL PHOTOGRAPHER MAGAZINE

Photo Tours & Workshops - *calendar* - PETERSEN'S PHOTOGRAPHIC

Photo Traveler Tours - WESTERN PHOTOGRAPHER MAGAZINE

Photo: Now - *international newsbriefs of new products* - CAMERA

Photochemistry Question and Answer - *technical column by Robert Chapman* - DARKROOM AND CREATIVE CAMERA TECHNIQUES

Photofile - *'A roundup of new and noteworthy products' column by Ruyssell Hart* - AMERICAN PHOTO

Photograms - *letters* - DARKROOM AND CREATIVE CAMERA TECHNIQUES

Photographer's Assistant - *column by Dennis Miller* - PHOTOPRO

Photographers Making the News - *newsbriefs* - RANGEFINDER, THE

Photographers Marketplace - CAMERA & DARKROOM PHOTOGRAPHY

Photographic Collectors' Book Space, A - SHUTTERBUG

Photographic Exhibitions - CAMERA ARTS

Photographic Good Buys - PRACTICAL PHOTOGRAPHY

Photographic Impressions - *technique* - PROFESSIONAL PHOTOGRAPHER, THE

Photographic Instruction - RANGEFINDER, THE

Photographic Items of Interest - CAMERA AND DARK ROOM
Photographic Profiles - WISCONSIN PHOTOGRAPHER
Photographic Societies, The - *newsbriefs* - APR
Photography - *photo services for performers* - SHOW BUSINESS
Photography in Industry - *column by Robert G. Hoffman* - PROFESSIONAL PHOTOGRAPHER, THE
Photography in the News - *international news items concerning photography* - RANGEFINDER, THE
Photojournalism - *column by John Durniak* - PHOTOPRO
Photojournalist: Photography as Communication, The - *column by Phil Douglis* - NEWS PHOTOGRAPHER
Photokina Novelties For Our Readers - *new products* - PHOTO TECHNIQUE INTERNATIONAL
Photomechanical - AMERICAN PRINTER
Photoplay Fashions - *full page color fashion photos* - PHOTOPLAY
Photoplay in Focus - *editorial column by Lynne Dorsey* - PHOTOPLAY
Photoplay Mart, The - *Current studio needs* - MOTION PICTURE ALBUM
Photoplay-Movie Mirror Dancing School - *how-to column by Howard Sharpe* - PHOTOPLAY COMBINED WITH MOVIE MIRROR
Photoplays in Review - PHOTODRAMATIST, THE
PhotoPro Data - *'useful optical information from standard reference sources'* - PHOTOPRO
Phototopography - *column by Carl Palmer* - GRAPHIC ARTS MONTHLY
Phototronics - MODERN PHOTOGRAPHY
Photoworld - *'News, views and reviews from the world of photography, edited column by Colin Leftley'* - PHOTO ANSWERS
Photpourri - CAMERA 35
Pi A La Mode - *newsbriefs* - PRINTINGNEWS
PIA - PRINTING IMPRESSIONS
Pick of Books - CHRISTIAN REVIEW
Pick of the Penguin - *letters* - DOCTOR WHO MAGAZINE
Pick of the Post - *letters* - EIGHT MM MOVIE MAKER AND CINE CAMERA
Pick of the Week - AKASHVANI
Picked Up on the Air - *anecdotes* - ABC WEEKLY
Pictorial - *photo essay* - UNIQUE
Pictorial Print Analysis - *column by Konrad Cramer* - CAMERA, THE
Pictorial Salon Calendar - *upcoming exhibitions calendar* - CAMERA, THE
Pictorial Section - *'Film news in pictures* - EXHIBITORS HERALD WORLD
Picture Criticism - CAMERA AND DARK ROOM
Picture First Showings Reported by Wire - *telegraph box office reports* - DRAMATIC MIRROR, THE

Picture Grosses - *'A statistical compilation and comparison of box-office performance in first-run theatres'* - MOTION PICTURE HERALD
Picture of the Month - *unique in-depth section of illustrations, production stills and discussions with distributors* - GREATER AMUSEMENTS
Picture of the Month - *competition* - PHOTO ANSWERS
Picture of the Month - POPULAR PHOTOGRAPHY
Picture Page - R & R
Picture Parade - *lengthy reviews* - CINEMA PROGRESS
Picture Parade - *reviews* - MOTION PICTURE
Picture Preview - CINEMA PAPERS
Picture Search - *new videotape releases* - VIDEO ANSWERS
Pictures - *advice* - WRITER'S DIGEST
Pictures and People - *picture commentary and artists at leisure* - MIDWEEK MOTION PICTURE NEWS
Pictures From Our Readers - POPULAR PHOTOGRAPHY
Pictures Now Showing - *'Being hosannahs or hisses for the latest consignment from Hollywood'* - STAGE
Pictures of the Month - NEWS PHOTOGRAPHER
Pictures on the Fire - *studio films in production column by Dick Mook* - SILVER SCREEN
Pictures Started Last Week - SHOWMEN'S TRADE REVIEW
Pieces of Eight - PROFESSIONAL FILM PRODUCTION
Pilgrim's Scrip, The - *commentary* - AGAINST THE GRAIN
Pin Up of the Past - FILMS AND FILMING
Pinboard - *newsbriefs* - BRITISH JOURNAL OF PHOTOGRAPHY
Pinholes - *one sentence comments* - CAMERA MAGAZINE
Pinpoints from the ABC Talks - ABC WEEKLY
Pinup - *double-page celebrity picture* - MOVIE WORLD
Pioneers - *excellent historical profiles* - ELECTRONICS WORLD + WIRELESS WORLD
Pipeline - COMMUNICATIONSWEEK
Pirates Den - *'Focus on free radio broadcasting'* - POPULAR COMMUNICATIONS
Pittaro's Clinic - *'Questions & Answers on Film & Effects' column by Ernie Pittaro* - AMAZING CINEMA
Pittsburgh - BOX OFFICE
Pix, People, Pickups - *news of new productions just signed* - DAILY VARIETY
PiXword - *photographic crossword puzzle* - PIC
Pizzazz on Parade - *fashion page* - NATIONAL ENQUIRER
Place and Performance - NEW THEATRE QUARTERLY
Placement Service - *news of academic employment opportunities* - AEJMC NEWS

Plain Talks on Advertising - JOURNALIST, THE
Plain Talks to Exhibitors - REEL LIFE
Planner - *upcoming video events* - VIDEO
Planning - *commentary* - MEDIAWEEK
Plant and Equipment - EDITOR AND PUBLISHER
Platter Chatter - MOVIE TEEN ILLUSTRATED
Play Calendar - THEATRE AND SCHOOL
Play of the Month - *review* - PLAYS AND PLAYERS
Play Reviews - PLAY SHOP, THE
Play Reviews - STAGE AND TELEVISION TODAY, THE
Playback - *new recordings, column by Bruce Gerald* - HIT PARADER
Playback - *consumer audio* - MIX
Playback - *'A monthly measure of comment and criticism about television'* - TELEVISION
Playbills - THEATER NOW
Players - *stars and events* - MOVIELINE
Players Programs - PLAYERS
Playlist - *popular song playlist* - BROADCASTING
Plays and Players Abroad - PLAYS AND PLAYERS
Plays and Players at Home - PLAYS AND PLAYERS
Plays and Players in New York - PLAYS AND PLAYERS
Plays and Players of the Week - BROADWAY WEEKLY
Plays & Playwrights - AMERICAN THEATRE
Plays in Performance - *world-wide reviews* - DRAMA
Plays in Print - DRAMA
Playtext - *monthly playtext of current British offering* - PLAYS INTERNATIONAL
Playtime Schedule - THEATRE CRAFT
Playwriting Callboard - *theatrical opportunities compiled column by Jeffery Elwell* - SOUTHERN THEATRE
Please Mr. Postman - *letters* - SH-BOOM
Plotline Hotline - *plot developments* - DAYTIME TV
Pluggy's Letter - *column* - AMERICAN NEWSPAPER BOY, THE
Poetry - *advice* - WRITER'S DIGEST
Poetry and Songs - DRAMATIC MAGAZINE, THE
Poetry Behind the Typewriter - *column by Brooks Cook* - TOP SECRET
Poetry Reviews - FACTSHEET FIVE
Point - JOURNAL OF ARTS MANAGEMENT AND LAW, THE
Point / Counterpoint / Poll - MEDIAWEEK
Point and Shoot - *column by Mason Resnick* - MODERN PHOTOGRAPHY
Point and Shoot Follies - *'For serious photographers who secretly admire point & shoot cameras' column by Dan Richards* - POPULAR PHOTOGRAPHY
Point Blank - *'The responsibility of publishing is discussed'* - FOUR COLOR
Point of Interest - *Washington politics column by Jacqueline Morse* - VUE

Point of Sale - *retail strategies and commentary column by Marc Horowitz* - AUDIO-VIDEO INTERNATIONAL
Point of View - *commentary* - FOLIO:
Point of View, A - 4SIGHT MAGAZINE
Point of View - *editorial* - HOLLYWOOD MAGAZINE
Point of View - *editorial* - HOME VIEWER
Point of View - *guest commentary* - JOURNAL OF ADVERTISING RESEARCH
Point Sources - *techniques and technologies column by Mike Ballai* - STUDIO PHOTOGRAPHY
Pointers for Printers - AMERICAN PRINTER
Points of Law - *Q-A format on broadcast law* - RADIOACTIVE
Points of Law - RADIOWEEK
Points of View - *letters* - E-ITV
Points of View - *column by John Rice* - VIDEOGRAPHY
Polaroid Traveling Exhibitions - PHOTOEDUCATION
Politics - MEDIA BUSINESS
Politics - *the politics of cable* - MSO'S CABLE MARKETING
Polls - *dealing with specific topics* - PUBLIC OPINION QUARTERLY
Poloroid Technology - CLOSE-UP
Pop - *music review column by Chris Huizenga* - AFTER DARK
Pop Photo Snapshots - POPULAR PHOTOGRAPHY
Pop Records - *review* - HIGH FIDELITY
Pop Reviews - HIGH FIDELITY/MUSICAL AMERICA
Pop/Adult - R & R
Pop'Comm's World Band Tuning Tips - *'When and where to tune to hear a wide variety of local and international broadcasters on shortwave'* - POPULAR COMMUNICATIONS
Popcorn - *movie-connected news items* - FILM THREAT
Popcorn - *'Kernels of information'* - IN CINEMA
Popcorn - *news items* - VIDEO TIMES
Pop/Rock Reviews - CD REVIEW
Popular Music - *reviews of new releases* - STEREO REVIEW
Popular Songs - *lyrics* - DRAMATIC MIRROR AND LITERARY COMPANION, THE
Popular Study Course - DRAMA MAGAZINE, THE
Population Explosion - FILM TV DAILY
Portfolio - *artist showcase* - ART DIRECTION
Portfolio - *photographer showcase* - CAMERA & CAMCORDER MONTHLY
Portfolio - *electronic industry stocks* - DEALERSCOPE
Portfolio - MAGAZINE DESIGN & PRODUCTION
Portfolio - *stocks & bonds* - MSO'S CABLE MARKETING
Portfolio - *showcase* - PHOTO/DESIGN
Portfolio - PHOTOGRAPHY
Portfolio - *sample cartoons* - TARGET
Portrait Photographer's Clipsheet - *short how-done column* - PROFESSIONAL PHOTOGRAPHER, THE

Portraits - *profile* - ENTERTAINMENT CONNECTION MAGAZINE
Portraits - THEATRE, THE
Positions Available - *extensive college faculty employment section* - ICA NEWSLETTER
Positions Available - *large section for open faculty positions* - SPECTRA
Positions Open - *employment opportunities* - ETV NEWSLETTER
Positive / Negative Clan, The - *letters* - TOP SECRET
Positives & Negatives - *column by Hugh Birnbaum* - CAMERA 35 INCORPORATING PHOTO WORLD
Post - *most interesting letters* - FEED-BACK
Post - *news of post production* - TELEVISION BROADCAST
Post Box - FILMFARE
Post Marx - *letters* - WOW! MAGAZINE
Post Office - *'Where every letter is a special delivery'* - SOAP OPERA PEOPLE
Post Pro Products - POST
Post Production - TELEVISION BROADCAST
Post Production News - *column by Katharine Stalter* - FILM & VIDEO
Post Scripts - *letters* - RIGHTING WORDS
Postal - PRESSTIME
Postal Affairs - PRESSTIME
Postal Customer Council - MEMO TO MAILERS
Postal Pointers - PRINTING IMPRESSIONS
Postal Zone - *letters* - FANGORIA
Postcard Radio Literature - AMATEUR WIRELESS AND RADIOVISION
Postings - POST
Postscript - *post house owner profiles* - POST
Postscript - *'Postproduction notes'* - WRAP
Pot Pour Ri - *newsbriefs* - CHRISTIAN DRAMA
Pot Pourri - HI-FI ANSWERS
Power Amplifiers - SOUND & VISION
Power Broker - *video store management column by Marc Berman and John Gaffney* - VIDEO BUSINESS
Power Playlists - *'Current playlists of the nation's largest and most influential top 40 radio stations'* - BILLBOARD
Power Sales Tools - *unique calendar for upcoming selling opportunities* - RADIO ONLY
Power Sources - ELECTRONIC PRODUCTS
PPV - *pay-per-view schedule* - SATELLITE TIMES
PR Affairs - *column by Robert Gavin* - CAMPAIGN
PR Briefs - *news notes* - FORUM
Practical H nts - AMERICAN PHOTOGRAPHY
Practical Letters from Readers - PRACTICAL WIRELESS
Practical Notes on the Leicina - *technical column* - LEICA PHOTOGRAPHY
Practical Pointers - PROFESSIONAL PHOTOGRAPHER, THE
Practically Speaking - *column by Ronald Spillman* - AMATEUR PHOTOGRAPHER
Practically Yours - *construction* - PRACTICAL WIRELESS

Prairie Pulse - *commentary column by Greg Klymkiw* - CINEMA/CANADA
Praxinoscope - *'Animato's melange of news, commentary, and more'* - ANIMATO!
Preaching - *reviews* - HOMILETIC
Preamplifiers - SOUND & VISION
Precede - *late breaking media news* - FEED-BACK
Premiere Salutes - AMERICAN PREMIERE
Premieres - *column by Richard Natale* - MOVIELINE
Premium Line-Up - *premium cable-television program offerings* - PREVIEW
Premium Parade - *hand-drawn reproductions of original radio premiums* - HERO HOBBY
Premium Services - *program listing* - TV ENTERTAINMENT
Pre-Order Calendar - VIDEO SOFTWARE MAGAZINE
Pre-Press - *review of technologies and processes* - POLYGRAPH INTERNATIONAL
Prepress Connections - AMERICAN PRINTER
Prepress Frontier - PRE-
Prepress Notes - PRE-
Pre-Pro - *column by Bill Intemann* - PRODUCERS QUARTERLY
Presentation Graphics - CORPORATE VIDEO DECISIONS
Presentations - *column by Keith Thompson,* - PC PUBLISHING AND PRESENTATIONS
Presenting Management - AVC
Preservation - *of historic films* - AMERICAN FILM
Preservation - BROADCAST PIONEERS LIBRARY REPORTS
President Reports, The - PSA JOURNAL
Presidential Address - *AAAA Presidents' column* - AGENCY
Presidential Message - *column by Marguerite Metcalf* - SOUTHERN COMMUNICATION JOURNAL, THE
President's Column - ADVERTISING AND MARKETING MANAGEMENT
President's Column - ICA NEWSLETTER
President's Column - QUILL, THE
Presidents Corner, The - *column* - MASTHEAD
President's Corner - TWR
President's Desk, The - *editorial column by Leonard Teel* - INTELLIGENCER
President's Letter, The - JOURNAL OF COMMUNICATION
President's Letter - MASTHEAD
President's Message - AWRT NEWS AND VIEWS
President's Message - EMMY
President's Message - FOUR A NEWSLETTER
President's Message - NATIONAL AMATEUR
President's Message - NEWS PHOTOGRAPHER
President's Message - *column by Lawton E. Osborn* - PROFESSIONAL PHOTOGRAPHER, THE

President's Newsletter - *lengthy craft-oriented issues and news* - OFFICIAL BULLETIN OF THE INTERNATIONAL ALLIANCE OF THEATRICAL STAGE EMPLOYEES AND MOVING PICTURE MACHINE OPERATORS OF THE UNITED STATES AND CANADA.
President's Page - *editorial column by Morton Gould* - ASCAP IN ACTION
President's Page, The - ROUNDUP QUARTERLY
President's Report - ASMP BULLETIN
President's Report - CINEMA JOURNAL
Press - *column by Doug Vickers* - ADWEEK
Press - *column by Sir Linton Andrews* - CAMPAIGN
Press - CRITIC
Press - WORLD PRESS REVIEW
Press and Printer - *newsbriefs concerning* - WOODCOCK'S PRINTERS' AND LITHOGRAPHERS' WEEKLY GAZETTE AND NEWSPAPER REPORTER
Press Clubs - AMERICAN JOURNALIST, THE
Press Commentary - ABSOLUTE SOUND, THE
Press Comments on Edison Films - EDISON KINETROGRAM
Press Conference - *news briefs* - EDUCATIONAL BROADCASTING
Press Law - *column by Louis Ingelhart* - CMA NEWSLETTER
Press Notice and Screen Service - *advertising and promotion suggestions* - MIDWEEK MOTION PICTURE NEWS
Press Pack - *cartoon commentary* - UK PRESS GAZETTE
Press Photography - *column by Robert D. Piante* - PROFESSIONAL PHOTOGRAPHER, THE
Press Photography - *column by Paul Threlfall* - TRAVEL & LEISURE
Press Review - BALLETT INTERNATIONAL
Press Time Topics - *newsbriefs* - TALKING SCREEN
Press-Time Reports - RELIGIOUS BROADCASTING
Pressue Points - *'Readers find answers to some sensitive questions about the agency business'* - AGENCY
Prettiest Extra Girl of the Month - FILM FUN
Preview - *upcoming events in graphic design* - DIRECTION
Preview - DWB
Preview - *upcoming entertainment* - MOVIE WORLD
Previe - PLAYS INTERNATIONAL
Preview - *rotating columnists describe upcoming fare* - RADIO TIMES
Preview - *motion pictures in current release* - SCENE AT THE MOVIES
Preview - *of upcoming movies* - STARBURST
Preview - *editorial* - VIDEO SYSTEMS
Preview: - SF MOVIELAND
Previewed - *largest section of periodical* - PICTURE REPORTS
Previewer - *upcoming video releases, column by Krys Longan* - HOME VIEWER
Preview/Hot Off the Shelf - MIX
Previews - ELECTRONIC DESIGN

Previews - *new film/video reviews* - FANTASY ZONE
Previews - *'Equipment-Services-Industry news'* - INTERNATIONAL PHOTOGRAPHER
Previews - MOVIE MAGAZINE, THE
Previews - *'A look at future films'* - PICTURE PLAY MAGAZINE
Previews - *upcoming motion picture releases* - SOUND STAGE
Previews - *scheduled for release* - VIDEO REVIEW
Previews - VIDEOPLAY MAGAZINE
Previews and Reviews - *assorted in-depth reviews of new releases* - FILM & VIDEO NEWS
Previews of - *newsbriefs of equipment and services* - INTERNATIONAL PHOTOGRAPHER
Previews of Coming Atractions - *upcoming events* - BIG REEL, THE
Price Bulletin - *listing of photographic chemicals sold by R. Walzl* - COMMERCIAL PHOTOGRAPHIC NEWS, THE
Price Mart, The - *listing of retail prices and models* - TV & APPLIANCE MART
Pricing - MARKETING NEWS
PRIG Chair's Column - *editorial column by Elizabeth Toth* - PRIG
Prime Evil - *consumer advocate column* - OPTICAL MEMORY NEWS
Prime Time - *television programming review and commentary column by Tonee Coraza* - SOSYALI MAGAZINE
Prime Time Cuts - *post centers for prime-time television* - POST
Prime Time School Television - *unique section with previews of upcoming network television programs and specials* - MEDIA & METHODS
Prime Time Update - *commentary column by Roy Soleil* - SOAP OPERA DIGEST
Print - INSIDE ENTERTAINMENT
Print - MEDIA WEEK
Print Analysis Department - *critique* - BULLETIN OF PHOTOGRAPHY
Print Analysis Department - *column by David B. Edmonston* - CAMERA, THE
Print & Production - SUCCESSFUL MAGAZINE PUBLISHING
Print Beat - MEDIAWEEK
Print Criticism Department - *highly critical and insightful column concerning reader submitted pictures* - CAMERA, THE
Print Criticisms - *from reader-submitted photos* - POPULAR PHOTOGRAPHY
Print Happenings - *newsbriefs* - AUSTRALASIAN PRINTER
Print Out - *new product review* - AUSTRALASIAN PRINTER
Print Out - *book review* - STRANGE ADVENTURES
Print Reviews - *critique* - ENTERTAINMENT WEEKLY
Print Scan - *print media capsules* - TELESCAN
Print Scene - AUSTRALASIAN PRINTER
Print Talk - AUSTRALASIAN PRINTER

Printed Novelties and Utility Advertising Helps - *'Embracing catalogues, booklets, folders, mailing devices, blotters, labels, and other supplementary advertising'* - SIGNS OF THE TIMES
Printed Things - CURRENT ADVERTISING
Printer News - PRINTING IMPRESSIONS
Printer to Printer - PRINTING IMPRESSIONS
Printers Bookshelf - BRITISH PRINTER
Printer's Devil, The - *'Giving printers a hot time each week...printbuyer Terry Snow of Hobson, Bates* - CAMPAIGN
Printers Library - PRINTING IMPRESSIONS
Printing File - *newsbriefs* - CANADIAN PRINTER
Printing Forum - *column by Dennis J. Castiglione* - FLASH
Printing Industry News - *newsbriefs* - BRITISH PRINTER
Private Eye - CHANNELS
Private Screening - *picture column by Pa Jector* - SCREEN THRILLS ILLUSTRATED
Prize Crossword - PRACTICAL PHOTOGRAPHY
Prize Offers - *literary prizes now available in contests* - WRITER, THE
PRO Bono - *column by Nolan K. Bushnell* - VIDEO PROPHILES
Pro Files - *profile* - MEDIAWEEK
Pro People - *personnel changes* - PRO SOUND NEWS
Pro Products - *review* - VIDEOPRO
Pro Session - DOWN BEAT
Pro Shop - *product showcase* - DOWN BEAT
Pro Sound Mixdown - PRO SOUND NEWS
Pro Sound Profile - PRO SOUND NEWS
Pro Talk - *column by Gary Bernstein* - PETERSEN'S PHOTOGRAPHIC
Pro Talk - STUDIO PHOTOGRAPHY
Pro Video News - *Personnel and company newsbriefs* - PRO SOUND NEWS
Pro/Am Athletics - *news* - AMUSEMENT BUSINESS
Probe - *editorial* - CONSUMER ELECTRONICS
Probing the News - *newsbriefs* - ELECTRONICS
Problems and Solutions - *column by Jim Stewart,* - RANGEFINDER, THE
Problem/Solution - INSIDE MEDIA
Problems--Queries - AMERICAN TELEPHONE JOURNAL, THE
Pro-Briefs - *equipment newsbriefs* - PRO SOUND NEWS
Proceedings of Societies - ELECTRICAL REVIEW
Process - *news items* - INTERNATIONAL PHOTOGRAPHER
Produccion - *newsbriefs* - PRODUCCIÓN Y DISTRIBUCIÓN
Producer Profile - PRO SOUND NEWS
Producer PROphiles - *column by Judith Morrison* - VIDEO PROPHILES
Producer to Producer - *column by Michael Wiese* - VIDEOGRAPHY
Producers - *listing* - SHOW BUSINESS
Producers Bulletin Board - CINEMAGIC
Producer's File - RADIO WORLD

Departments INDEX 844

Producer's Showcase - *'Producer video listings featuring the latest selections and variety of special interest subjects'* - MOVIE MARKETPLACE
Producing - STAGE & STUDIO
Product Alert - ADWEEK'S MARKETING WEEK
Product Analysis - CLIO MAGAZINE
Product Close-Up - *brief comparison of new video products* - FAST FORWARD
Product Close-Ups - AV VIDEO
Product Feature - TELECOMMUNICATIONS
Product Feature FYI - *equipment profile* - DIGITAL EVOLUTION MAGAZINE
Product Focus - AV VIDEO
Product Focus - PRO SOUND NEWS
Product Gallery, The - *technical review* - COMPUTERS & ELECTRONICS
Product Groups Within Categories - PRESS STATISTICAL REVIEW
Product Guide - *'New Items to Aid or Entertain' books and other reviews* - AMAZING CINEMA
Product Information - HIGH VOLUME PRINTING
Product Introductions - VIDEOGRAPHY
Product Lineup - INDUSTRIAL PHOTOGRAPHY
Product Marketplace - CABLE MARKETING
Product News - COMMUNICATIONS
Product News - ILFORD PHOTO INSTRUCTOR NEWSLETTER
Product News - *review* - INTERNATIONAL CABLE
Product News - JEE, JOURNAL OF ELECTRONIC ENGINEERING
Product News - LIGHTING DIMENSIONS
Product News - STAGE & STUDIO
Product News - THEATRE CRAFTS
Product Perspectives - VIDEOGRAPHY
Product Picks - INTERNATIONAL PHOTOGRAPHER MAGAZINE
Product Premier - TELEVISION BROADCAST
Product Premieres - *new items recently introduced* - MEDIA & METHODS
Product Preview - PRO SOUND NEWS
Product Probe - CAMERA & DARKROOM PHOTOGRAPHY
Product Probe - DARKROOM PHOTOGRAPHY
Product Probe - *reviews column by Marc Wielage* - MOVING IMAGE
Product Profile - *application/review of new products* - AMERICAN PRINTER
Product Profiles - JEE, JOURNAL OF ELECTRONIC ENGINEERING
Product Promotion - *studio activities* - MOVIE/TV MARKETING
Product Proof Sheet - *new equipment* - PETERSEN'S PHOTOGRAPHIC
Product Proofs - *very detailed new product reviews* - DARKROOM AND CREATIVE CAMERA TECHNIQUES
Product PROphiles - *'A roundup of the latest noteworthy gear'* - VIDEO PROPHILES
Product Releases - COLLEGE BROADCASTER
Product Report - AMERICAN PRESS
Product Report - *review column by Steven T. Smith* - FILMMAKERS FILM & VIDEO MONTHLY

Product Report - *review* - LEICA FOTOGRAFIE INTERNATIONAL
Product Report - *technology review column by Gary A. Breed* - RF DESIGN
Product Review - CAMERA & DARKROOM PHOTOGRAPHY
Product Review - PRO SOUND NEWS
Product Review and Preview - AUDIOVIDEO INTERNATIONAL
Product Roundup - AUDIOVIDEO INTERNATIONAL
Product Scene, The - *reviews* - MODERN RECORDING & MUSIC
Product Scene - *new product profile* - VIDEOMAKER
Product Showcase - FLASH
Product Spotlight - PRESENTATION PRODUCTS MAGAZINE
Product Update - BROADCAST SYSTEMS INTERNATIONAL
Product Update - CAMERA & DARKROOM PHOTOGRAPHY
Product Update - COMPUTER PUBLISHING
Product Update - *new equiment briefs* - LIGHTING DIMENSIONS
Product Update - PROFESSIONAL PHOTOGRAPHER, THE
Product Watch - *digital radio newsbriefs* - DIGITAL RADIO NEWS
Product Watch - HIGH VOLUME PRINTING
Product Watch - *'Your monthly listing of the latest hardware and software'* - PUBLISHI
Production - CABLEAGE
Production - *personnel briefs* - FOLIO:
Production - HOW
Production - NEWSINC.
Production - *column by Jon Pickow* - PRODUCERS QUARTERLY
Production - *extensive film status section* - SCREEN INTERNATIONAL
Production - VIDEO TECHNOLOGY NEWS
Production - *newsbriefs* - VIDEOGRAPHY
Production Advisor, The - *column by Kathy Reilly,* - PUBLISHING & PRODUCTION EXECUTIVE
Production and Casting Logs - *listing* - ENTERTAINMENT WORLD
Production Casebook - NEW THEATRE QUARTERLY
Production Companies - FILM & VIDEO
Production Guide - CINEMA/CANADA
Production Guide - *outstanding state or regional production profile* - MILLIMETER
Production House News - E-ITV
Production Manager - *column by Craig Johnston* - TV TECHNOLOGY
Production News - *lengthy segment on East/West Coast activities* - ENTERTAINMENT MONTHLY
Production News - FILM & VIDEO
Production News - IN MOTION FILM & VIDEO PRODUCTION MAGAZINE
Production News - *large second section on magazine production* - MAGAZINEWEEK
Production News - *newsbriefs of upcoming projects* - MIDWEEK MOTION PICTURE NEWS

Production News - STAGE AND TELEVISION TODAY, THE
Production Notes - LOCATION UPDATE
Production Notes - *current projects column by Mark Adams* - MOVING PICTURES INTERNATIONAL
Production Notes - *information on paper and illustration* - PRINT
Production Notes - *issue detail column by Barbara Wexler* - VIDEO SOFTWARE MAGAZINE
Production Notes - VIEW
Production on Location - *films shooting on-location* - LOCATION UPDATE
Production Parade - *column by George Pardon* - SHOWMEN'S TRADE REVIEW
Production Pulse - *status* - VARIETY
Production Report - *in-progress productions* - INTERNATIONAL PHOTOGRAPHER
Production Report - SCREEN INTERNATIONAL
Production Scene - *briefs of films and shooting schedules* - CINEMA AND THEATRE
Production Services - MAGAZINE DESIGN & PRODUCTION
Production Slate - *'New Films Coming Your Way'* - AMAZING CINEMA
Production Spotlight - AVC
Production Survey - CINEMA PAPERS
Production Technique - *column by Jim St. Lawrence* - VIDEOGRAPHY
Production Update - OFF-HOLLYWOOD REPORT
Products - *review* - ADVANCED IMAGING
Products - *newsbriefs* - BRITISH JOURNAL OF PHOTOGRAPHY
Products - ELECTRONIC PUBLISHER
Products - ELECTRONICS
Products - IN-PLANT PRINTER & ELECTRONIC PUBLISHER
Products - INVISION
Products - *review* - RF DESIGN
Products - *review* - SATELLITE COMMUNICATIONS
Products - *'Information on new products, developments, upgrades and software updates'* - STUDIO SOUND AND BROADCAST ENGINEERING
Products - *new filter items* - TIFFEN PROFESSIONAL NEWSLETTER
Products - *review* - VENTURA LETTER, THE
Products - *reviews* - VIDEO
Products - VIDEOGRAPHY
Products - *review* - WORLD BROADCAST NEWS
Products and Materials - *review* - HUMAN COMMUNICATION CANADA
Products and Processes - *the one segment given to technical aspects of visual imagry* - AFTERIMAGE
Products & Services - VIDEO SOFTWARE MAGAZINE
Products in Action - *review* - MEDIA & METHODS
Products Plus - *detailed production introductions* - COMMUNICATIONS INDUSTRIES REPORT, THE
Products Plus - *reviews* - PRO SOUND NEWS
Products Showcase - COMPUTER PICTURES

Products Showcase - VIDEO TIMES
Products to Watch - ELECTRONICS
Product/Service Showcase - SALES & MARKETING MANAGEMENT
Professional Audio - MONITOR INTERNATIONAL
Professional Book Shelf, The - COLLEGE & UNIVERSITY JOURNAL
Professional Emphasis - *use of commercial media-ideas for public broadcasters* - PUBLIC TELECOMMUNICATIONS REVIEW
Professional Feedback - *column by Ed Becker* - PROFESSIONAL PHOTOGRAPHER, THE
Professional Meetings - JOURNAL OF MARKETING EDUCATION
Professional Notes - CINEMA JOURNAL
Professional Reader - *PR book reviews* - PUBLIC RELATIONS JOURNAL, THE
Professional Response, The - *'Answers to questions writers ask' column by Sidney Sheldon* - WRITER, THE
Professional Stereo - *stereo photography column by Branislav Denitch* - PROFESSIONAL PHOTOGRAPHER, THE
Professionalism in Management - PRINTING IMPRESSIONS
Professionally Speaking - *business newsbriefs* - RADIO FAN-FARE
Professionals - *profile* - MAST
Professionaly Speaking - *editorial comment on recent developments* - RADIO BROADCAST
Profile - ANIMATION MAGAZINE
Profile - BPME IMAGE MAGAZINE
Profile - EDITOR'S WORKSHOP
Profile - ELECTRONICS & COMMUNICATIONS
Profile - *of a successful 900 telephone service company* - 4TH MEDIA JOURNAL, THE
Profile - *star biography* - FRESH!
Profile - GF MAGAZINE
Profile - INVISION
Profile - PHOTOGRAPHY
Profile - PRESSTIME
Profile - *media artist profiles* - TV, ETC.
Profile - UK PRESS GAZETTE
Profile - *corporate profile* - VIDEO BUSINESS
Profile - *Canadian production facility* - VIDEO NEWS AND USED
Profile - *videomaker profile column by Erica Shames* - VIDEOMAKER
Profile - VIZIONS
Profile - *one catv executive profiled* - VUE
Profile: ASC - *profiles one outstanding ASC member* - AMERICAN CINEMATOGRAPHER
Profiles - *of a major broadcast executive* - BROADCASTING
Profiles - FILM & VIDEO NEWS
Profit Profile - *informative magazine profile and critique column by Jeff Marcus* - MAGAZINEWEEK
Program Charts - *satellite listing* - TELESPAN'S BUSINESSTV GUIDE
Program Guide - *shortwave guide for upcoming month* - MONITORING TIMES
Program Guide - *programming* - TELEVISION BROADCAST
Program Highlights - C-SPAN UPDATE

Program Highlights - DISNEY CHANNEL MAGAZINE, THE
Program Highlights of Interest to Women - *program guide* - RURAL RADIO
Program Jottings - RADIO DIAL
Program Listings - ENTERTAINER, THE
Program Note - CHANNELS
Program Notes - *computer-oriented news items* - IEEE SPECTRUM
Program Notes - *newsbriefs* - INDEPENDENT, THE
Program Pipeline - CURRENT
Programme Guide, The - *extensive European satellite programming guide of 100+ pages* - SATELLITE TIMES
Programmer Focus - *cable network profile* - MSO'S CABLE MARKETING
Programmes for the BBC's North American Transmission - BBC WORLD SERVICE LONDON CALLING
Programmes for the BBC's Pacific and Central Transmissions - BBC WORLD SERVICE LONDON CALLING
Programming - BROADCAST
Programming - *column by Howard English* - BROADCAST + TECHNOLOGY
Programming - *newsbriefs* - BROADCASTER
Programming - *listing* - C-SPAN UPDATE
Programming - CABLE WORLD
Programming - CABLEAGE
Programming - CABLEVISION
Programming - MEDIA BUSINESS
Programming - MULTICHANNEL NEWS
Programming - *production problem analysis* - TELEVISION
Programming - VIA SATELLITE
Programming - *software--availability and acceptance* - VUE
Programming - WHAT SATELLITE
Programming Clips - *newsbriefs* - CABLE MARKETING
Programming Guide - *huge 240 page section detailing national satellite transmissions for upcoming month* - SATELLITE ORBIT
Programming Guide - *reviews* - VIDEO TIMES
Programming Index - CABLE GUIDE, THE
Programming News - CABLE WORLD
Programming Production - TELEVISION/RADIO AGE
Programming Report - *newsbriefs* - VIDEO WEEK
Programming the Future - *software column by Jerry Kindela* - VISIO
Programs - VIDEO MANAGEMENT
Progress - FUNCTIONAL PHOTOGRAPHY
Progressions - *'People in the news'* - LINK
Progressions - *column* - MIX
Progressive Home Construction - PRACTICAL WIRELESS
Project of the Month - *column by Forrest M. Mims* - COMPUTERS & ELECTRONICS
Projection - *news items* - INTERNATIONAL PHOTOGRAPHER
Projection - *equipment review* - LEICA FOTOGRAFIE INTERNATIONAL

Projection - *'Optics, electricity, practical ideas & advice'* - MIDWEEK MOTION PICTURE NEWS
Projection - MOVING PICTURE AGE
Projection and Sound - BOX OFFICE
Projection TVs - SOUND & VISION
Projections - *upcoming events* - FILM LIBRARY QUARTERLY
Promenades of Angelina, The - THEATRE MAGAZINE
Prominent Men in the Lantern World - KINEMATOGRAPH WEEKLY
Promising Programs - *upcoming* - BETTER BROADCASTS NEWS
Promo Tips - VIDEO BUSINESS
Promotion - AISLE VIEW
Promotion - COMPUTER PICTURES
Promotion Indicator - *marketing ideas* - VIDEO INSIDER
Promotion Questions and Answers - *an interesting section providing answers to marketing problems sent in via readers* - MARKETING COMMUNICATIONS
Promotion View - VIEW
Promotions - AMUSEMENT BUSINESS
Promotions - PRESS STATISTICAL REVIEW
Promotions - *of faculty* - SPECTRA
Promotions - *applications column by Charles Wesley Orton* - VIDEO STORE
Promotions & Marketing - *column by Phyllis Stark* - BILLBOARD
Proof of Performance - *a how-to, when-to technical construction series* - COMMUNICATIONS ENGINEERING & DESIGN
Proof Sheet - *'New product news'* - PETERSEN'S PHOTOGRAPHIC
Propagation - *atmospheric conditions* - CQ
Propagation Charts - 73 AMATEUR RADIO
Prophet, The - *horoscope* - BLACK RADIO EXCLUSIVE
Proposed New FM Channels - LINE MONITOR, THE
Protechniques - POPULAR PHOTOGRAPHY
Provincial Intelligence - DRAMATIC MAGAZINE, THE
P/S Comment - PERFORMANCE
PSA - *'News and notes about the Photographic Society of America'* - POPULAR PHOTOGRAPHY
PSA News - PSA JOURNAL
PSApages - *listing of latest available campaigns* - PSA
Pssst! - *'Reveling in the glitter and the glory' picture page column by Aubrey Reuben* - MGF
Psycho Gs - *offbeat items* - MEDIAWEEK
PTR Comments - *unusually large editorial page on several issues* - PUBLIC TELECOMMUNICATIONS REVIEW
Public Events - LÜRZER'S INTERNATIONAL ARCHIVE
Public Eye, The - CHANNELS
Public Opinion - *'Our readers tell us what's on their minds'* - SOAP OPERA WEEKLY
Public Policy - *newsbriefs* - COMMUNICATIONSWEEK
Public Relations Beat - ADVERTISING AGE

Departments INDEX 846

Public Service - QST
Publication Announcements - OPTICAL INFORMATION SYSTEMS
Publication Design & Production - COMMUNICATIONS CONCEPTS
Publications - *of members* - HEALTH COMMUNICATION NEWSLETTER
Publications - *reviews* - MARQUEE
Publications - *books and magazines* - MEDIA ANTHROPOLOGIST NEWSLETTER
Publications - *excellent review of current media-ethics publications* - MEDIA ETHICS UPDATE
Publications - *'The ones worth while, the ones that count, the pick of the pile from an advertising standpoint' selected publications by frequency and geographic location* - SIGNS OF THE TIMES
Publications - TELECOMMUNICATIONS POLICY
Publications - *new cable periodicals and research* - URBAN TELECOMMUNICATIONS FORUM
Publications - *books of note on satellite services* - VIA SATELLITE
Publications - *video programs and films reviewed with data for rental or sale* - VIDEO
Publications - *a most valuable listing of house organs and newsletters via IFTC members* - WORLD SCREEN
Publications Noted - LEARNED PUBLISHING
Publications Received - ELECTRONICS AND COMMUNICATIONS
Publicity - *column by Richard Ziff* - VIDEO BUSINESS
Publicity News - *upcoming titles, author tours, book club sales, and media tie-ins* - FORECAST
Publine: Our Members Call for Answers - *Q&A on magazine publishing* - MAGAZINE BUSINESS
Publisher Info - *editorial* - VENTURA PROFESSIONAL!
Publisher Marketshares - *comics ordered for month* - COMICS BUYER'S GUIDE
Publishers & Publications - ADVERTISER MAGAZINE, THE
Publishers' Calendar - *upcoming events* - WASHINGTON NEWSPAPER, THE
Publishers' Choice - FACTSHEET FIVE
Publisher's Forum - SATELLITE COMMUNICATIONS
Publishers Forum - TEL-COMS
Publisher's Letter - FLORIDA REEL
Publisher's Letter - SOUND MANAGEMENT
Publishers Letter - *editorial* - TELEVISION/RADIO AGE
Publisher's Letter - TELEVISION/RADIO AGE
Publisher's Letter - TELEVISION / RADIO AGE INTERNATIONAL
Publisher's Marketplace - *a white-pages listing of services useful to magazine management* - FOLIO:
Publisher's Memo - PRESENTATION PRODUCTS MAGAZINE
Publishers Newsbriefs - CATHOLIC JOURNALIST
Publisher's Note - ENTERTAINMENT REVUE

Publisher's Note - *personal observations* - FOLIO:
Publisher's Note - TELESPAN'S BUSINESSTV GUIDE
Publisher's Outlook - TELEMARKETING
Publisher's Page - *opinion* - ADVERTISER MAGAZINE, THE
Publishers Page - *editorial combined with letters* - ARS TYPOGRAPHICA
Publisher's Page - *editorial column by Norman Goldfind* - BIJOU
Publisher's Page, The - *editorial* - HOLLYWOOD
Publisher's Page - *editorial* - SILENT PICTURE, THE
Publisher's Page - VIDEO NEWS AND USED
Publishers, Periodicals and Personals - *newsbriefs* - JOURNALIST, THE
Publishers Perspective - *editorial* - GRAPHIC ARTS MONTHLY
Publisher's Picks - *of new releases* - COMICS FEATURE
Publishers Place - *newsbriefs* - BACK STAGE
Publisher's Place - *guest editorial* - FORECAST
Publishers Previews - *of new romance novels* - ROMANTIC TIMES
Publisher's Profile - AGAINST THE GRAIN
Publishers' Rates Alphabetically Index - NATIONAL ADVERTISING
Publisher's Report - ADVERTISER MAGAZINE, THE
Publishers Report - JOURNAL OF COLLEGE RADIO
Publisher's View - BUSINESS ADVERTISING
Publisher's View - MARKETING / COMMUNICATIONS
Publishers Who Will Substantiate Their Circulation Claims - ADVERTISING EXPERIENCE
Publishing - BRITISH BOOK NEWS
Publishing - HYPERMEDIA
Publishing - MEDIA BUSINESS
Publishing Law - SUCCESSFUL MAGAZINE PUBLISHING
Publishing Potpourri - *newsbriefs column by Jan Nathan* - PMA NEWSLETTER
PubNet - *'The publishing industry's network for: jobs (wanted or available), announcements & items for sale'* - MAGAZINE BUSINESS
Puck's Tour - PRINTING IMPRESSIONS
Pulp Culture - *book review* - STRANGE ADVENTURES
Pulse Beat - *Listing of selected radio stations playing top-rated weekly music* - PULSE OF RADIO
Pulse Local Ratings - BILLBOARD TV PROGRAM AND TIME AVAILABILITIES, THE
Pulse Maker Interview - PULSE OF RADIO
Pulse of Programmers, The - *unique issue response forum for radio management* - PULSE OF RADIO
Pulse Syndicated Film Ratings - BILLBOARD TV PROGRAM AND TIME AVAILABILITIES, THE
Pulse Think Tank - *issue commentary* - PULSE OF RADIO

Pulstations - *extensive listing of top weekly music at selected stations* - PULSE OF RADIO
Punchlines - *column by John Styles* - ANIMATIONS
Pundents - TAKE ONE
Puns & Fun - PEP
Puppet and Marionette News Notes - PLAYERS
Puppet Department, The - DRAMA MAGAZINE, THE
Purchase Decision Making - PRINTING IMPRESSIONS
Pure Gold - *column by Alvin Gold* - STEREOPHILE
Purely Personal - *personal briefs* - FOURTH ESTATE
Purrs and Growls - *comment* - BULLETIN OF THE ASSOCIATION FOR BUSINESS COMMUNICATION, THE
Pursuing the Marvelous - *postcard column by Susan Nicholson* - POSTCARD COLLECTOR
Puzzle - *crossword* - MOVIE DIGEST
Puzzle - *crossword* - TELECONNECT
PW Forecasts - *synopses of books about to be published* - PUBLISHER'S WEEKLY
PW Helpline - *reader Q&A* - POSTAL WATCH
PW Interviews - *major publisher personalities* - PUBLISHER'S WEEKLY
PW Preview - *new items* - PRACTICAL WIRELESS

Q

Q and A - *reader-submitted questions* - ORBIT VIDEO
Q & A - PEIRCE-PHELPS, INC. AUDIO/VIDEO NEWSLETTER
Q&A - CAMERA & DARKROOM PHOTOGRAPHY
Q&A - CD-ROM
Q&A - *technical reader-submitted questions, column by Wilfred M. Scherer* - CQ
Q&A - *reader-submitted questions* - DARKROOM PHOTOGRAPHY
Q&A - HI-FI ANSWERS
Q&A - MOVING IMAGE
Q&A - PANORAMA
Q&A - *'Practical hints, tips, and advice for desktop publishers' column by Robert C. Eckhardt and Ted Nace* - PUBLISH!
Q&A - *technique of writing* - SCRIPTWRITER NEWS
Q&A - *'Solutions to problems about desktop production'* - STEP-BY-STEP ELECTRONIC DESIGN
Q&A - *reader submitted questions* - TELEMARKETING
Q&A - *reader submitted questions on television history* - TELEVISION HISTORY
Q&A - *column by Roderick Woodcock* - VIDEO MAGAZINE

Q&A With... - *interview* - SUPER TEEN
Q&A--Technical Queries Examined - HI-FI SOUND
QPI/Hottest Recurrents Chart - *'Quality Play Index figures ranked by average weekly plays per station. The hottest recurrent titles'* - MONDAY MORNING REPLAY
QSL Contest - CQ
QSL Corner - *column by Joanna Hushin* - QST
QSL Report, The - *column by Gayle Van Horn* - MONITORING TIMES
QSL Reports - FRENDX
Q-Tips - *column by John Q. Shepler* - RADIO WORLD
Quality Control - AMERICAN PRINTER
Quarter, The - *news of film regulation* - CINEMA PAPERS
Quarterly Reports - *Corporate developments* - SATELLITE NEWS
Quarterly Retrospect, A - *'The gramophone and the voice' column by John Steane* - GRAMOPHONE
Quarterly Review of Decisions - AIR LAW REVIEW
Quentin Falk's Production Scene - *news* - SCREEN INTERNATIONAL
Queries - *Q&A format for the neophyte writer* - AUTHOR, THE
Queries - KINEMATOGRAPH WEEKLY
Queries - THEATRE NOTEBOOK
Query Department - CAMERA AND DARK ROOM
Question & Answer - *from readers* - VIDEO SYSTEMS
Question and Answer Service - *Q&A* - IMAGE TECHNOLOGY
Question Box - ABU TECHNICAL REVIEW
Question Box, The - *reader-submitted Q&A* - RADIO-ELECTRONICS
Question Box, The - *reader Q&A about the stars* - SCREEN STORIES
Question Is, The - AGENCY
Question Line - PROMOTION
Question of the Week - *'The legal angle on local marketing agreements'* - RADIO BUSINESS REPORT
Questions - *Q&A from readers* - VIDEO REVIEW
Questions & Answers - *provides advice on professional film questions* - AMERICAN CINEMATOGRAPHER
Questions & Answers - *audio-related problems from readers* - AUDIOPHILE WITH HI-FI ANSWERS
Questions and Answers - *extensive technical Q&A section* - CAMERA, THE
Questions and Answers - CAMERA CRAFT
Questions and Answers - *concerning film technique* - CINEMA/CANADA
Questions and Answers - *letters to editor* - EDISON KINETOGRAM
Questions and Answers - *basic Q&A cinema technique format* - FILMO TOPICS
Questions and Answers - HI-FI SOUND
Questions & Answers - *from readers* - HOME VIDEO
Questions and Answers - *technical submissions* - POPULAR PHOTOGRAPHY

Questions and Answers - RADIO AGE
Questions and Answers - RADIO DEALER, THE
Questions and Answers - RADIO FAN-FARE
Questions and Answers - *Radio Q&A from readers* - RADIOLAND
Questions and Answers - SCSC XEROX PIPELINE
Questions and Answers - VIDEOPLAY MAGAZINE
Questions & Answers - WOODCOCK'S PRINTERS' AND LITHOGRAPHERS' WEEKLY GAZETTE AND NEWSPAPER REPORTER
Questions Answered - *'Concerning the writing of photoplays'* - PHOTODRAMATIST, THE
Questions Answered - PRINT BUYERS REVIEW
Questions on Photography - *column by Ron Jegerings* - DARKROOM AND CREATIVE CAMERA TECHNIQUES
Questions to the Editor - *interesting section in which Q&A inquiries are made of the profiled editor* - WHAT EDITORS WANT
Quick Cuts - *personality news briefs* - NIGHTTIME TV
Quick Focus - *newsbriefs column by Natasha Cole* - VIDEOMAKER
Quick Hits - *database newsitems* - MEDIABRIEFS
Quick Look at the Locally Edited Magazines, A - EDITORIAL NEWSLETTER
Quick Printer / Job Printer - PRINTING IMPRESSIONS
Quick Printing - AMERICAN PRINTER
Quick Reference Chart for Buyers and Bookers - *extensive listing of new feature films* - FILM BUYER
Quick Reference Picture Chart - *very extensive listing of current film releases* - EXHIBITORS HERALD WORLD
Quick Sketches - HIGH PERFORMANCE
Quick Takes - *'Previews of major upcoming films, groups on tour and television events, plus some inside scoop on personalities you like to watch', column by Jimmy Summers (with Greg Ptacek, Victor Davis and Sharon J. Pang)* - AMPERSAND'S COLLEGE ENTERTAINMENT GUIDE
Quick Takes - *short opinions* - ELECTRONIC MEDIA
Quick Takes - *newsbriefs* - MOVING IMAGE
Quiet on the Set! - *editorial* - SOUND STAGE
Quiz - MEDIA HISTORY DIGEST
Quiz - TELEVISION HISTORY
Quizmaster - *Science Fiction quiz* - W•B
Quizzical Culture - *'Film Fun's quiz of movie hits and misses'* - FILM FUN
Quotations of Telegraph Stock - TELEGRAPHER, THE
Quote of the Month - COMMUNICATION BRIEFINGS
Quote of the Week - BLACK RADIO EXCLUSIVE
Quoteables - AMERICAN PREMIERE
Quoted as Saying - *mid-speech quotes* - 4A'S WASHINGTON NEWSLETTER, THE
Quotes - *via celebrities* - REAL LIFE/DAYTIMERS
Quotes of the Week - LINE MONITOR, THE
Quote/Unquote - *statements made concerning advertising* - INSIDE MEDIA

R

R. G. Bargy - *column by Roy Gregory* - HI-FI WORLD
RAB Report - CLIO MAGAZINE
Race, The - *editorial* - SALES & MARKETING MANAGEMENT
Rack LP Best Sellers - *playlist* - BILLBOARD
Rack Singles Best Sellers - *playlist* - BILLBOARD
Radar Reflections - *'Radar detectors and their use'* - POPULAR COMMUNICATIONS
Radio - BILLBOARD
Radio - BROADCAST
Radio - HI-FI NEWS AND RECORD REVIEW
Radio - *news items* - INTERNATIONAL PHOTOGRAPHER
Radio - *reviews* - LISTENER
Radio - MEDIA BUSINESS
Radio - MEDIAWEEK
Radio - MUSIC LINE
Radio - *music on the air* - MUSICAL AMERICA
Radio, The - *news and review* - NEW CAPTAIN GEORGE'S WHIZZBANG, THE
Radio - *review and commentary column by Michael Mangan* - PLAYS INTERNATIONAL
Radio Across-The-USA - *outstanding Birch Monthly ratings reports for the top 100 American radio markets* - RADIO ONLY
Radio Album Reports - RADIO ALBUM MAGAZINE
Radio and Television - *newsbriefs* - OFFICIAL BULLETIN OF THE INTERNATIONAL ALLIANCE OF THEATRICAL STAGE EMPLOYEES AND MOVING PICTURE MACHINE OPERATORS OF THE UNITED STATES AND CANADA.
Radio and TV - *column by Lee Otis* - WRITER'S DIGEST
Radio & TV News - ELECTRONICS WORLD
Radio and TV Roundup - *broadcast briefs* - NEWSPAPER WORLD AND ADVERTISING REVIEW
Radio Business Barometer - TELEVISION/RADIO AGE
Radio Cases in the United States - *column by John W. Guider* - JOURNAL OF RADIO LAW
Radio City Town Crier - *comment* - RADIO CITY NEWS
Radio Clubs and Societies - *newsbriefs* - PRACTICAL WIRELESS
Radio Decisions in the United States - *column by John W. Guider* - JOURNAL OF RADIO LAW
Radio Design Practice - *new design newsbriefs* - COMMUNICATION ENGINEERING
Radio Developments Shown in Pictures - ELECTRONICS WORLD
Radio Dial - *radio briefs* - BACK STAGE
Radio Editorials - RADIO INDUSTRIES
Radio Entertainment - TELEVISION WEEKLY NEWS

Departments

Radio Equipment Forum - *used and new equipment* - REVIEW OF INTERNATIONAL BROADCASTING
Radio FUNdamentals - *'Things to learn, projects to build, and gear to use', column by Bill Orr* - CQ
Radio Guide Forum - *'Letters, questions, help & parts wanted from Radio Guide readers'* - RADIO GUIDE
Radio Happenings of the Month Illustrated - *column by George Wall* - ELECTRONICS WORLD
Radio Highlights - STAGE
Radio Indi-gest - *letters* - RADIO FAN-FARE
Radio Insight: Sales and Programming Checklist - INTERNATIONAL RADIO REPORT, THE
Radio Intelligence - *'Research news and knowledge you can use* - CURRENT
Radio Kinks from Abroad - *equipment newsbriefs* - RADIO REVIEW AND TELEVISION NEWS
Radio Legislation in the United States - *column by Philip G. Loucks* - JOURNAL OF RADIO LAW
Radio Loud & Clear - *developments* - TELEVISION BROADCAST
Radio Marketing Think Tank, The - RADIOTRENDS
Radio Mirror Crossword Puzzle - TV MIRROR
Radio Mirror Homemaking Department - TV MIRROR
Radio Mirror's Gallery of Stars - TV MIRROR
Radio News - BME'S TELEVISION ENGINEERING
Radio News - *'The breaking news of the radio industry'* - RADIO BUSINESS REPORT
Radio News From the Networks - *programming news from the CBS, NBC, and Mutual radio networks* - RADIO HIT SONGS
Radio News Laboratories - *new products* - ELECTRONICS WORLD
Radio Newsreel - *pictures* - ABC WEEKLY
Radio Personalities - RADIO DEALER, THE
Radio Plays for Next Week - ABC WEEKLY
Radio Products - *review* - RADIO-ELECTRONICS
Radio Profile - INTERNATIONAL RADIO REPORT, THE
Radio Programming and Production for Profit - *a valuable feature sharing successful programming items* - BME'S TELEVISION ENGINEERING
Radio Programs - *computer software column by Steve Walker* - RADIO GUIDE
Radio Proving Post - *new equipment* - ALL-WAVE RADIO
Radio Ratings - *college stations compared to other radio media in market* - COLLEGE BROADCASTER
Radio Receiving Sets - *review* - RADIO FAN-FARE
Radio Report - TELEVISION/RADIO AGE
Radio Revue, The - *duotone pictorial section of favorite radio personalities* - RADIOLAND

Radio Round & About - ABC WEEKLY
Radio Securities - RADIO DEALER, THE
Radio Set Directory - ELECTRONICS WORLD
Radio Set Owner's Information - *reader Q&A by specific model* - ELECTRONICS WORLD
Radio Talk - BEYOND THE RATINGS/TELEVISION
Radio Topics - RADIO & ELECTRONICS CONSTRUCTOR
Radio Trade Pictures - RADIO DEALER, THE
Radio Update - *information from the radio side of ratings systems* - BEYOND THE RATINGS/TELEVISION
Radio Voices - *letters* - SOUND MANAGEMENT
Radio Wars - *news items* - RADIO BUSINESS REPORT
Radio Workshop - *unique articles concerning radio engineering* - BROADCAST ENGINEERING
Radio Wrinkles - *newsbriefs* - ELECTRONICS WORLD
Radio-Electronic Circuits - *new and original electronic schematics* - RADIO-ELECTRONICS
Radio-Electronics Monthly Review - *'Items interesting to the technician'* - RADIO-ELECTRONICS
Radiophone Broadcasting Stations - *'Corrected every week'* - RADIO FAN-FARE
Radio's Photo Mirror - *radio personality pictures* - TV RADIO MIRROR
Radiotics - *humorous misprints concerning radio* - ELECTRONICS WORLD
Radio-TV - *reviews re: film* - GREATER AMUSEMENTS
Radiowaves - *oldies music on current stations* - SH-BOOM
Railroad Advertising - AGRICULTURAL ADVERTISING
Ralph's One-and-Only Traveling Fanzine Company - *fanzine review* - LITTLE SHOPPE OF HORRORS
Rambling Reporter - *personality news bits* - HOLLYWOOD REPORTER
R&D News - *new developments for pulp and paper manufacturing* - PULP & PAPER CANADA
Random Access - REP: RECORDING ENGINEERING PRODUCTION
Random Notes - ART IN ADVERTISING
Random Notes - *newsbriefs* - MOTION PICTURE ALBUM
Random Notes - *commentary column by Patrick J. Gushman* - MSO'S CABLE MARKETING
Random Radiations - *column by Diallist* - ELECTRONICS WORLD + WIRELESS WORLD
Random Reflections - *news item column by Tom Hall* - CABLE TELEVISION ENGINEERING
Random Samplings - *column by R. A. Jones* - COMICS WEEK
Rap Corner, The - *column by Doug Deutsch* - SHOWCASE WORLD
Rap Sheet, The - *newsbriefs* - LAW ENFORCEMENT TECHNOLOGY

Rapp Around the World - *column by Stan Rapp* - DIRECT MARKETING
Rappin' It Up - *rap records column by Larri-Ann Flores* - BLACK RADIO EXCLUSIVE
Rare and Unusual - *unique postcards column by Andreas Brown* - POSTCARD COLLECTOR
Rate Department - *detailed rate cards for various publications* - AD SENSE
Ratings - *detailed accounting for the preceeding week* - BROADCAST
Ratings, The - *televisions' top and bottom five* - ENTERTAINMENT WEEKLY
Ratings - *program ratings* - TV WORLD
Ratings & Research - *radio research* - R & R
Ratings Review - VIEW
Rave and Grave Reviews - *concerning books, records and videos, column by Anne M. Raso and Jae-Ha-Kim* - CELEBRITY PLUS
Ray Smith - *column by Ray Smith* - CAMCORDER USER
Re: Radio - BROADCAST ENGINEERING
Re:Edits - *'Opinions, ideas and announcements'* - FILMFAX
Read and Noted - *column by Henry Mayer* - MEDIA INFORMATION AUSTRALIA
Read 'Em and Reap - *resources* - COMMUNICATION BRIEFINGS
Reader Comment - HOME VIDEO
Reader Feedback - ELECTRONIC DESIGN
Reader Feedback - *letters* - VIDEO SOFTWARE MAGAZINE
Reader Poll - MARKETING NEWS
Reader Resources - *readers sharing sources of materials* - LEARNING RESOURCES
Reader Speaks, The - *letters* - HOME MOVIES
Reader Writes, The - MOVIE MAKERS
Readers and Writers - *letters* - MOVIE MIRROR
Reader's Camera Clicks, The - *event photos submitted by readers* - PIC
Readers' Choice - *reader poll* - BLOCKBUSTER VIDEO MAGAZINE
Readers Comment - *letters* - ELECTRONICS
Reader's Comments - AMERICAN PREMIERE
Readers Comments - ELECTRONICS
Reader's Comments - *letters* - STAR TREK: THE OFFICIAL FAN CLUB MAGAZINE
Reader's Criticism - AMATEUR PHOTOGRAPHER'S WEEKLY, THE
Readers' Forum - AUDIOCRAFT FOR THE HI-FI HOBBYIST
Readers' Forum - *letters* - CD REVIEW
Readers Forum - *letters* - JOURNAL OF POPULAR FILM AND TELEVISION
Readers Forum - RADIO WORLD
Readers Forum - *letters* - STORYBOARD / THE ART OF LAUGHTER
Readers' Forum - TV TECHNOLOGY
Readers Forum - *excellent letters to editor column* - TV TECHNOLOGY
Readers' Gallery - *reader submissions* - TRAVEL & LEISURE
Readers Inc. - *letters and pen pals* - PHOTOPLAY

Reader's Letters - EIGHT MM MOVIE MAKER AND CINE CAMERA
Readers' Letters - HI-FI NEWS AND RECORD REVIEW
Reader's Letters - PETERSEN'S PHOTOGRAPHIC
Readers Link - *letters* - LINK-UP
Reader's Page - *reader submissions* - TRAVEL & LEISURE
Readers' Picture Page - *reader submissions* - TRAVEL & LEISURE
Reader's Playback - *letters* - VIDEO ANSWERS
Readers Poll - DAYTIME TV
Readers' Poll - DAYTIME TV
Reader's Poll Results - *on current issues* - CELEBRITY PLUS
Readers' Portfolio - *'Our readers' images are displayed and discussed'* - OUTDOOR & TRAVEL PHOTOGRAPHY
Readers' Queries - *'Write in with your problems' reader submitted Q&A* - HI-FI WORLD
Readers' Reply - *letters* - HI-FI WORLD
Readers' Response - *letters* - THEATRE DESIGN & TECHNOLOGY
Readers Scene, The - *letters* - BEHIND THE SCENE
Readers Survey - VIDEO BUYER
Readers' Tapes - *unique section about demo tapes* - HOME & STUDIO RECORDING
Readers Tell Us - BROADCAST PIONEERS LIBRARY REPORTS
Readers Tips - CAMERA & DARKROOM PHOTOGRAPHY
Readers Tips - *photographic shortcuts* - DARKROOM PHOTOGRAPHY
Reader's Tips - MOVING IMAGE
Reader's View, A - *reader guest commentary* - SOAP OPERA WEEKLY
Readers Wrinkles - *reader submissions* - PRACTICAL WIRELESS
Readers Write, The - ACTORS FORUM
Readers Write - *letters to the editor* - AMATEUR PHOTOGRAPHER
Readers Write - *'Choice answers' letters* - HI-FI CHOICE
Readers Write - *letters* - SHOW
Reading RTTY - *column by Jack Albert* - MONITORING TIMES
Readout - *'Reviews of some of the newer SF literary releases'* - FANTASTIC FILMS
Rear View - *column by Harry Stein* - PANORAMA
Received and Noted - *reviews* - FILM CULTURE
Receivers - SOUND & VISION
Recent Books - DRAMA
Recent Books - *international review* - LEICA FOTOGRAFIE INTERNATIONAL
Recent Developments - ELECTRONIC ENGINEERING
Recent FCC Actions - *newsbriefs on FCC rulings concerning ETV* - ETV REPORTER
Recent Films in Review - *lengthy reviews* - CINEFAN
Recent Film/Video Releases - *software reviews* - AFVA BULLETIN

Recent Home Video Titles - GET ANIMATED! UPDATE.
Recent Movies - *reviews* - MOVIE DIGEST
Recent Photographic Patents - AMERICAN PHOTOGRAPHY
Recent Publications - *review* - HISTORY OF PHOTOGRAPHY
Recent Publications and Exhibitions - CLOSE-UP
Recent Radio and Entertainer Obituaries - OLD TIMER'S BULLETIN, THE
Recent Reviews and Awards - VIDEO ALERT
Recent Series - *recent news series running in American television markets* - RUNDOWN, THE
Recommendations of the Month - *plays* - THEATRE CRAFT
Recommended - *educational media review by a Media and Methods test panel* - MEDIA & METHODS
Recommended Films - SCREEN FACTS
Recommended New Books - AUDIO-VISUAL GUIDE
Recommended Newspaper List - ADVERTISERS' WEEKLY
Recommended Programs - RADIOLAND
Recommended Radio - *programs which SUN readers have voted to be their favorites* - UNION LABOR SUN
Recommended Radio and Television Programs - BETTER RADIO AND TELEVISION
Recommended Reading - *new materials* - ETV NEWSLETTER
Record & CD Reviews - *extensive listing* - DOWN BEAT
Record Care - TV RADIO MIRROR
Record, CD & Tape Care Products - SOUND & VISION
Record Label Servicing - COLLEGE BROADCASTER
Record Makers - *newsbrief column by Christie Barter and Steve Simels* - STEREO REVIEW
Record of the Month - HI-FI NEWS AND RECORD REVIEW
Record of the Month - *review* - HI-FI WORLD
Record Rack - *briefs* - BILLBOARD
Record Reproduction - HI-FI NEWS AND RECORD REVIEW
Record Review Index - HI-FI NEWS AND RECORD REVIEW
Record Reviews - DOWN BEAT
Record Reviews - GRAMOPHONE
Record Reviews - *column by Lumumba T. Khann and Doug Deutsch* - SHOWCASE WORLD
Record Reviews - STEREOPHILE
Recorded Lectures Program - PSA JOURNAL
Recorded Message - *column by Richard Brice* - HI-FI WORLD
Recording - PRO SOUND NEWS
Recording Studio Design - HIGH FIDELITY
Recordings - *review* - CHRISTIAN REVIEW
Recordings - SCREEN FACTS
Recordings: Classical - *review column by John David Richardson* - AFTER DARK

Records - *review column by Chris Patrick* - SOUND STAGE
Records - *'Best buys of the month'* - TV STAR PARADE
Records & Recording - AUDIO CRITIC, THE
Records and Tapes - *reviews* - ABSOLUTE SOUND, THE
Records of the Month - HI-FI NEWS AND RECORD REVIEW
Records of the Month - STAGE
Records of the Month - TV SCREEN
Recordwatch - MONDAY MORNING REPLAY
Recurring Feeds - *column by Bob Stubbs* - SATELLITE TV WEEK
Red Hots - *employment wantads* - INTERNATIONAL RADIO REPORT, THE
Reel News - *'Industry news'* - FLORIDA REEL
Reel News in Review - *newsbriefs* - FILM JOURNAL, THE
Reel People - *column by Tony Lee* - STRANGE ADVENTURES
Reel Talk - *profile* - APPLIED ARTS QUARTERLY
Reel West, The - *column by Bob Harris* - BACK STAGE
Reference File - *available publishers materials* - AVC
Reference Shelf - BOOKSTORE JOURNAL
Reference Shelf - *'Book reviews of the latest and standard titles imparting how-to and career aid information'* - STEP-BY-STEP GRAPHICS
Reflection Resource - MEDIA & VALUES
Reflection/Action Forum - MEDIA & VALUES
Reflections - *letters* - EQ
Reflections - *editorial* - KINEMATOGRAPH WEEKLY
Refreshment Service - *subtitled as 'added income opportunities for progressive exhibitors* - BOX OFFICE
Regency Romance Reviews - ROMANTIC TIMES
Regional Clips - 4SIGHT MAGAZINE
Regional News - *ad campaigns from various American cities* - ART DIRECTION
Regional News - 4SIGHT MAGAZINE
Regional News - IEEE SPECTRUM
Regional News - RETROFOCUS
Regional Report - *ITVA chapter news* - CORPORATE TELEVISION
Regional Report - *'A potpourri of what's going on in the world of Midwest Communications'* - INVIEW
Regional Reports - *Equipment installations and sales* - INVIEW
Regional Reports - WORLD PRESS REVIEW
Regional Reviews - STAGE AND TELEVISION TODAY, THE
Regional Roundup - *newsbriefs* - POST
Regions - *theatrical reviews* - PLAYS INTERNATIONAL
Regions - *regional business activity column by Rachel S. Meltzer* - VIDEO STORE
Register of Releases - *16 MM documentary, educational, factual and industrial films, 8 mm cassettes and filmstrips and entertainment guide* - AUDIO VISUAL

Regular Mutual Program Features - REEL LIFE
Regulation - DBS NEWS
Regulation - TELEVISIONS
Regulations - PRESSTIME
Regulations of the Federal Radio Commission - *column by Arthur W. Scharfeld* - JOURNAL OF RADIO LAW
Regulatory Roundup - CABLE LIBRARIES
Reinforcement Roundup - *'Regional touring highlights'* - PRO SOUND NEWS
Rejoinders - *letters* - TELECOMMUNICATIONS POLICY
Related Headings - *'Point of view'* - LINK
Relating to Advertisers - *newsbriefs* - AMERICAN ADVERTISER REPORTER
Release Chart - *'By companies'* - PRODUCT DIGEST
Release Chart, The - *'Index to reviews, advance synopses and service data in Product Digest section'* - PRODUCT DIGEST
Released - *'new video releases, both rental and sales titles'* - MOVIE - THE VIDEO MAGAZINE
Reliable Formulas - *how to make almost anything column by E. Voltaire Boyes* - SCHEMER, THE
Religious Programming - *program guide* - ONSAT
Re-Make - *what-if pictorial* - VIDEO WORLD
Remarks - POLITICAL COMMUNICATION AND PERSUASION
Remember You Read It First in Photoplay - *personality column by Cal York* - PHOTOPLAY
Remember! You Read It First in Photoplay - *personality column by Cal York* - PHOTOPLAY
Rendezvous - *Back cover pictures of advertising personnel in the news* - MEDIA INTERNATIONAL
Rent Reviews - *detailed, entertaining reviews of current film-on-videocassette releases* - VIDEO TIMES
Rentals - VIDEO REVIEW
Rep News - PERSONAL ELECTRONICS
Replies in Brief - *to letters* - PRACTICAL WIRELESS
Replies to Correspondents - KINEMATOGRAPH WEEKLY
Replies to Queries and Enquiries - PRACTICAL WIRELESS
Reply, A - RIGHTING WORDS
Report - BALLETT INTERNATIONAL
Report - JUMP CUT
Report - QUILL, THE
Report from Europe - *briefs* - MOVIE/TV MARKETING
Report From Japan - *column by Mitch Taura* - TAPE/DISC BUSINESS
Report from Media Watch - WOMEN & LANGUAGE
Report From the Chair - *editorial column by Young Y. Kim* - INTERCULTURAL & DEVELOPMENT COMMUNICATION NEWSLETTER

Report to the Listeners - *column by Saul Carson* - TV SCREEN
Report: Comics - *extensive news section concerning British/American comic publications* - FA
Reporter - *news items* - VIDEO STORE
Reporter's Notebook - *column by Charles Sievert* - ADVERTISER MAGAZINE, THE
Reporting for Radio - COMMUNICATOR
Reports - *newsbriefs* - CHANNELS
Reports from the Regions - ACTF / PAC NEWS
Representative Appointments - INTERNATIONAL ADVERTISER
Reproduction - *news and developments* - POLYGRAPH INTERNATIONAL
Rep/Wrap Up - PRO SOUND NEWS
Request TV - *Pay television offerings* - PREVIEW
Reruns - *'The latest news of the nostalgia world' column by Hal Schuster* - TV GOLD
Research - JOURNAL OF EDUCATIONAL PUBLIC RELATIONS
Research - *programming statistics* - LISTENER
Research - MEDIAWEEK
Research - THEATRE DESIGN & TECHNOLOGY
Research Abstracts - EDUCATIONAL COMMUNICATION AND TECHNOLOGY
Research & Developments - *column by Mark Schubin* - VIDEOGRAPHY
Research and Education - IBEW JOURNAL
Research & Reports - *news items* - EPIEGRAM
Research in Progress - *brief listings of known academic and commercial research projects* - DIGEST
Research in Progress - MEDIA INFORMATION AUSTRALIA
Research in Progress - VISIBLE LANGUAGE
Research Instrument - MANAGEMENT COMMUNICATION QUARTERLY
Research News - INTERNATIONAL ADVERTISER
Research Note - TECHNOLOGY AND CULTURE
Research Notes - ASIAN JOURNAL OF COMMUNICATION
Research Notes - *newsbriefs on new equipment* - BRITISH PRINTER
Research Notes - ELECTRONICS WORLD + WIRELESS WORLD
Research Notes - JOURNAL OF COMMUNICATION
Research Notes and Communications - *critical comment* - JMR, JOURNAL OF MARKETING RESEARCH
Research Report - *newsbriefs of recently published research into instructional media* - AID
Research Report - COLLEGE & UNIVERSITY JOURNAL
Research Report - CORPORATE TELEVISION
Research Reports - COMMUNICATION STUDIES
Reservations - MOVIELINE
Resident Legit Grosses - VARIETY
Resident Legit Reviews - VARIETY
Residual Checks Await Claimants - *listing* - SCREEN ACTOR HOLLYWOOD
Resource - *for theatre equipment and supplies* - THEATRE CRAFTS

Resource Guide, The - *new products and services* - AISLE VIEW
Resource Guide - *product guide* - 4TH MEDIA JOURNAL, THE
Resource Material - INTERMEDIA
Resource Review - *publications review* - POSTAL WATCH
Resources - *helpful listing of potential materials and people* - ADWEEK'S MARKETING WEEK
Resources - *available materials* - AFI EDUCATION NEWSLETTER
Resources - AMERICAN PREMIERE
Resources/ - *resource material* - INSIDE MEDIA
Resources - *information and contacts* - PUBLIC RELATIONS JOURNAL, THE
Resources - *'Brief reviews of products and services of interest to electronic designers'* - STEP-BY-STEP ELECTRONIC DESIGN
Resources - VIDEO MANAGEMENT
Resources for In-Plant Managers - IN-PLANT REPRODUCTIONS
Response - *to previously published articles* - NIEMAN REPORTS
Restaurant Section - *advertisements* - PREVIEW
Restoration - *animation art column by Stephen Worth and Lew Stude* - STORYBOARD / THE ART OF LAUGHTER
Restoration Topics - *care and cleaning of antique radios* - ANTIQUE RADIO CLASSIFIED
Retail - *marketing, promotion, and sales* - BILLBOARD
Retail - MUSIC LINE
Retail Advertising - NATIONAL STATIONER, THE
Retail Advertising and Advertising Men - ADVERTISING NEWS
Retail Report - TELEVISION/RADIO AGE
Retail Roundup - *column by Anne S. Torpey* - VIDEO BUSINESS
Retail Track - *column by Geoff Mayfield* - BILLBOARD
Retailer of the Week - VIDEO BUSINESS
Retailers - LÜRZER'S INTERNATIONAL ARCHIVE
Retailing to Win - *business strategy column by Brooks Jensen* - VIDEO SOFTWARE MAGAZINE
Retorts - *letters retorting earlier reviews* - MOVIE GEEK
Retro - *retrospective profile* - FILM REVIEW
Retro - *comment* - FILMS AND FILMING
Retrospect - *from the pages of Amusement business ten and twenty years ago* - AMUSEMENT BUSINESS
Retrospective - DWB
Retrospective - *review of a film previously reviewed* - MONTHLY FILM BULLETIN
Reverb - *letters* - CINEMA/CANADA
Review - ADVERTISING AND MARKETING MANAGEMENT
Review - ART & CINEMA
Review - *new exhibitions* - BRITISH JOURNAL OF PHOTOGRAPHY
Review - *critical reviews of current films* - CINEMA
Review - ETI

Review - *films* - FILM THREAT
Review - *large segment detailing film releases, video view, books, and film music* - FILMS AND FILMING
Review - FLAKE
Review - IPI REPORT
Review - *Eastman Kodak Company technical review* - MOTION PICTURE PROJECTION
Review - PHOTOGRAPHY
Review - *newsbriefs concerning receiver manufacturing and sales* - RADIO BROADCAST
Review - *of current series* - RADIO TIMES
Review - *equipment* - STUDIO SOUND AND BROADCAST ENGINEERING
Review and Comment - TELEVISION QUARTERLY
Review and Criticism - JOURNAL OF BROADCASTING & ELECTRONIC MEDIA
Review and Forecast - *guest commentary* - CABLE COMMUNICATIONS MAGAZINE
Review Board - *panel discussion of advertising issues* - MADISON AVENUE
Review Digest and Alphabetical Index - *superb section of all currently-released motion pictures with information and titles, types, distributors, issue reviews, and rating via the Hollywood Reporter, Box Office, Variety, Parents Magazine, and the New York Daily News* - BOX OFFICE
Review Essay - *extended communications reviews* - COMMUNICATION RESEARCH
Review Essay - MEDIA, CULTURE, AND SOCIETY
Review Essays - COMMUNICATION RESEARCH
Review of Acoustical Patents - AES
Review of Apparati - *new equipment reviews* - KINEMATOGRAPH WEEKLY
Review of Business Facts and Trends - ADVERTISERS' WEEKLY
Review of New Films - FILM GUIDE
Review of Recent Advertising, A - ART IN ADVERTISING
Review of Reviews - TELECOMMUNICATION JOURNAL
Review of Technical Publications - ABU TECHNICAL REVIEW
Review of the Month, A - ACTOR ILLUSTRATED, THE
Review Review - *articles in other technical serials* - TELECOMMUNICATION JOURNAL
Review Section - *extensive segment of current film fare* - FILM MONTHLY
Review Section - *film, multi-media, filmstrip, audio, video, learning pack reviews* - VISUAL EDUCATION
Review: Cinema - *column by David Morgan* - UNIQUE
Review: Literature - *column by James Sallis* - UNIQUE
Review: Music - *column by Sean Colbert* - UNIQUE
Reviewed - *new products* - OUTDOOR & TRAVEL PHOTOGRAPHY
Reviewer Acknowledgments - WRITTEN COMMUNICATION
Reviewers Comments - MILLER'S COPYRIGHT NEWSLETTER

Reviews - *in-depth, illustrated reviews of new books and films* - AFTERIMAGE
Reviews - ANIMATIONS
Reviews - *of current comic, strips, and graphic work* - ARK
Reviews - *extensive section* - ART PAPERS
Reviews - *books* - AT&T MAGAZINE
Reviews - BLACK THEATRE
Reviews - '*Opinions on current feature productions*' - BOXOFFICE
Reviews - CAMERA OBSCURA
Reviews - CHRISTIAN FILM & VIDEO
Reviews - CINEFANTASTIQUE
Reviews - CINEMA/CANADA
Reviews - CINEMONKEY
Reviews - CLOSE-UP
Reviews - *critique of new releases column by Jeff Kapalka* - COMICS WEEK
Reviews - *very lengthy book reviews* - COMMUNICATION QUARTERLY
Reviews - CREATIVE CAMERA
Reviews, The - *extensive audio reviews for the car* - DRIVING AMBITION
Reviews - *of current books and publications* - EUROPEAN JOURNAL OF COMMUNICATION
Reviews - EXPOSURE
Reviews - *current fantasy product* - FANTASY ZONE
Reviews - *films* - FILM QUARTERLY
Reviews - FILMFARE
Reviews - FILMS AND FILMING
Reviews - FOUR COLOR
Reviews - FUNNYWORLD
Reviews - GET ANIMATED! UPDATE.
Reviews - *paragraph-long succinct reviews* - GREATER AMUSEMENTS
Reviews - *of equipment* - HI-FI ANSWERS
Reviews - *music* - HIGH FIDELITY/MUSICAL AMERICA
Reviews - HOMILETIC
Reviews - INDEX ON CENSORSHIP
Reviews - JOURNAL OF COMMUNICATION
Reviews - *book reviews* - JOURNAL OF FILM AND VIDEO
Reviews - JOURNAL OF POPULAR FILM AND TELEVISION
Reviews - JOURNALISM EDUCATOR, THE
Reviews - MEDIA ASIA
Reviews - MEDIA INFORMATION AUSTRALIA
Reviews - *lengthy section* - MILLENNIUM FILM JOURNAL
Reviews - *a succinct review of current motion pictures* - MOVIE GEEK
Reviews - MOVIE SHOW
Reviews - *extensive selection of current releases* - MOVIE - THE VIDEO MAGAZINE
Reviews - *short reviews of new releases* - MOVIE/TV MARKETING
Reviews - *extensive new product section* - PC PUBLISHING AND PRESENTATIONS
Reviews - *lengthy section of reviewed plays* - PLAYS AND PLAYERS
Reviews - POST OFFICE MAGAZINE
Reviews - SCREEN INTERNATIONAL
Reviews - '*Direct From Hollywood*' - SILVER SCREEN

Reviews - SPEECH AND DRAMA
Reviews - *column by Sharon Ratliffe* - SPEECH COMMUNICATION TEACHER, THE
Reviews - *animation productions reviewed* - STORYBOARD / THE ART OF LAUGHTER
Reviews - TELEPROFESSIONAL
Reviews - *extensive play critiques column by Richard Sneerwell and Guy Leslie* - THEATERWEEK
Reviews - THEATRE, THE
Reviews - UNIVERSITY VISION
Reviews - *movies, music, television, and videos* - US MAGAZINE
Reviews - '*New & noteworthy this issue*' - V
Reviews - *longer reviews of new cassettes* - VIDEO MAGAZINE
Reviews - *of films on videotape* - VIDEO--THE MAGAZINE
Reviews - VIDEO WORLD
Reviews - VIDEODISC MONITOR, THE
Reviews - VIDEOPLAY MAGAZINE
Reviews - *of items connected with direct mail* - WHO'S MAILING WHAT!
Reviews - WITTYWORLD
Reviews - *selected new books* - WRITER'S NW
Reviews & Books - WIRE & RADIO COMMUNICATIONS
Reviews and Discussion - *large section of book reviews* - STUDIES IN VISUAL COMMUNICATION
Reviews and Previews - HOLLYWOOD FILMOGRAPH
Reviews and Previews - *upcoming films* - MOVIE HUMOR
Reviews of Books - GAMBIT
Reviews of Books, Cassettes, Films, Filmstrips and Records - RELIGIOUS MEDIA TODAY
Reviews of Current Short Subjects - EXHIBITORS TRADE REVIEW
Reviews of Independent Productions - *lengthy reports* - EXHIBITORS TRADE REVIEW
Reviews of New Films - FILM TV DAILY
Reviews of New Pictures - *continuing a tradition of review excellence in the Motion Picture Herald* - MOTION PICTURE PRODUCT DIGEST
Reviews of New Releases - FILM WORLD AND A-V NEWS MAGAZINE
Reviews of Opera - GAMBIT
Reviews of Plays - GAMBIT
Reviews of Records - ARSC JOURNAL
Reviews of Teaching/Learning Resources - COMMUNICATION EDUCATION
Reviews of the New Films - '*Concise and accurate comments upon the important new photoplays*' *column by Frederick James Smith* - NEW MOVIE MAGAZINE, THE
Reviews of the New Programs - RADIOLAND
Reviews: Books - FA
Reviews: Comics - FA
Reviews: Theater On Broadway and Off - *column by Patrick Pacheco* - AFTER DARK
Revisions - PRESS STATISTICAL REVIEW
Revival - FILMS AND FILMING

Departments INDEX 852

Revolving Door - *monthly politics versus media tally* - MEDIAWATCH
Revolving Door - *personnel newsbriefs* - TELEVISION WEEK
Rewind - *'The best of then is on video today!', column by Scott Mallory* - SH-BOOM
RF - INVIEW
RF Connections - ELECTRONICS WORLD + WIRELESS WORLD
RFD - *'Radio Farm Digest' letters* - RURAL RADIO
Rhode Island - BOX OFFICE
Rhythm and the Blues, The - *column by Janine McAdams* - BILLBOARD
Rhythm/Dance Chart - *'Based on airplay on more than 30 rhythm/dance leaning stations'* - MONDAY MORNING REPLAY
Rider TV Field Manual Service Data Sheets - *removable schematics* - ELECTRONIC SERVICING & TECHNOLOGY
Riffs - DOWN BEAT
Right of Reply, The - *'Readers' answers to last issue's review'* - ANIMATIONS
Right of Reply - *unique vendor replies to previous reviews* - AUDIOPHILE WITH HI-FI ANSWERS
Right Off the Record - *recording review column by Fred Robbins* - SCREENLAND PLUS TV-LAND
Right Off the Reel - EXHIBITORS' TIMES
Right Stuff, The - *creative photographic ideas* - PHOTO DISTRICT NEWS
Right Thing, The - AGENCY
Rights - *column by Paul Nathan* - PUBLISHER'S WEEKLY
Rights and Permissions - *fascinating department concerning current copyright laws and publishing acquisition* - PUBLISHER'S WEEKLY
Rights Marketplace - *column by Rosemary Pettit* - SMALL PRESS
Ring Talk - *'America's biggest and brightest wrestling column every week'* - NATIONAL EXAMINER
RN Circuit Page - *'circuit diagrams and parts lists'* - ELECTRONICS WORLD
Road Grosses - VARIETY
Roadwork - *column by Mark Herman* - REP: RECORDING ENGINEERING PRODUCTION
Rock - *review column by Ron Baron* - AFTER DARK
Rock Around the Clock - *'Where you can rock, rock, rock to the latest music biz talk, talk talk!' column by Elianne Halbersberg* - TEEN DREAM
Rock Follies with Dave Jenkins - TONI HOLT'S MOVIE LIFE
Rock 'n' Roll Trivia Quiz - SH-BOOM
Rock 'N' Rolling Along! - *'The music scene'* - STARZ
Rock Record - *column by Elyse Glickman* - UNIQUE
Rock Reissues - *'Recycled rock, pop and jazz'* - HI-FI NEWS AND RECORD REVIEW
Rock Releases - HI-FI ANSWERS
Rock Report - *'Featuring that rumor-mongering Rockin' Robin!'* - WOW! MAGAZINE
Rock Tape Reviews - TAPE DECK QUARTERLY

Rock/Pop/Jazz Reviews - HI-FI NEWS AND RECORD REVIEW
Rod Allen's Own Thing - *column* - CLIO MAGAZINE
Roger Rabbit - *comic section* - DISNEY ADVENTURES
ROI - *column by Leonard R. Yencharis* - ADVANCED IMAGING
Role Call - *'Complete cast lists of all the shows'* - DAYTIME TV
Role Call - *'Who's doing what and where.' (7-30)* - TALKING SCREEN
Role Playing - *column by Alec Billyou* - TOP SECRET
Romance in American Journalism - *publisher profile* - FOURTH ESTATE
Romance Readers Letters - ROMANTIC TIMES
Ron Galella Catches the Stars Off-Guard - *Hollywood photographer candid shots column by Ron Galella* - MODERN SCREEN
Ron Merrell - *broadcast transmission column by Ron Merrell* - TELEVISION BROADCAST
Ron Scott on Single-Copy Sales - *column by Ron Scott* - FOLIO:
Rona Barett's Hollywood - *the primary portion of the magazine with many pages of photos* - RONA BARRETT'S HOLLYWOOD
Rona Barrett's Gossip - *'Our Ms. Rona with the latest--and the best!' column by Rona Barrett* - GOSSIP
Rona's Bonus Scrapbook - *'Nostalgic photos from Rona's own album' column by Rona Barrett* - GOSSIP
Rona's Daytimers - *'What East, West, North, and South are saying!'* - REAL LIFE/DAYTIMERS
Rona's Hot and Cold Flashes - *half-page stories of stars* - RONA BARRETT'S HOLLYWOOD
Rona's Odds & Ends - *'So odd--it'll be the end of you!'* - GOSSIP
Rona's Would You Believe? - *'Unbelieveable tidbits from Rona!' column by Rona Barrett* - GOSSIP
Rona's Would You Believe? - *more gossip* - RONA BARRETT'S HOLLYWOOD
Room with Class, A - *feature on the classroom* - MEDIA & METHODS
Roper's America - ADWEEK'S MARKETING WEEK
Rosebuds - *plaudits for extraordinary journalism* - MORE
Roses and Razzberries - *critical commentary* - ALL-WAVE RADIO
Roster Changes - *personnel briefs* - BPME IMAGE MAGAZINE
Rostrum, The - WRITER, THE
Rothschild Reviews - *column by Norman Rothschild* - OUTDOOR & TRAVEL PHOTOGRAPHY
Round and About - *newsbriefs* - KINEMATOGRAPH WEEKLY
Round Table, The - THEATRE, THE
Round the Provinces - *theatre in the UK* - THEATRE

Round the Trade - *trade news* - KINEMATOGRAPH WEEKLY
Round the World of Wireless - *international newsbriefs* - PRACTICAL WIRELESS
Roundup - *station news* - BROADCASTER
Roundup - *topical listing* - HOT PICKS
Roundup - *news items* - NEWS MEDIA & THE LAW, THE
Roundup - QUILL, THE
Roundup - *international news* - VARIETY
Routes - *unique roadshow itinerary for carnivals and circuses* - AMUSEMENT BUSINESS
Roving Editor - *amusing anecdotes and newsbriefs* - WRITER, THE
Roving Report - *multipage newsbriefs* - VISUAL EDUCATION
RTD Radio Report - *audio news* - RTD
RTD Reviews - *new TV series* - RTD
RTNDA Newsline - TELEVISION BROADCAST
RTTY - CQ
RTTY - *'The exciting world of radioteletype monitoring'* - POPULAR COMMUNICATIONS
RTTY Docket - 73 AMATEUR RADIO
Rudy Vallee's Music Notebook - *column by Rudy Vallee* - RADIOLAND
Rumors - INSIDE ENTERTAINMENT
Rumour - ADWEEK
Running Commentary - *column by Linda Burnham* - HIGH PERFORMANCE
Running the Numbers - CHANNELS
Rural Radio Picture Roundup - *favorite radio stars* - RURAL RADIO
Rural Radio's Daddy Gander - *'A page for children'* - RURAL RADIO
Rushes - *'The all-new, all-blue, redesigned rental and sellthrough new release listings'* - VIDEO STORE
Russell Says - *live stage news column by W.S. Russell* - EXHIBITORS HERALD WORLD
Ryans Hope - *abstract* - SOAP OPERA DIGEST

S

Safelight - *column by Bob Nadler* - CAMERA 35 INCORPORATING PHOTO WORLD
SAG Talent Agents Franchise - SHOW BUSINESS
Sales - *positive advice column by Charles Rohleder* - AMERICAN NEWSPAPER BOY, THE
Sales & Marketing - *printing promotion* - AMERICAN PRINTER
Sales Appeal in Trade Displays - RADIO DEALER, THE
Sales Force Management - SALES & MARKETING MANAGEMENT
Sales Leaders Retail Survey - AUDIOVIDEO INTERNATIONAL
Sales Management - *column by Kevin Dorr* - CABLE MARKETING
Sales Mart - SALES & MARKETING MANAGEMENT
Sales Presentation - PRINTING IMPRESSIONS

Sales Promotion - ASIAN ADVERTISING & MARKETING
Sales Promotion - MEDIAWEEK
Sales Report - *equipment sales* - BROADCASTER
Sales Reports From All Over USA - TELEVISION RETAILING
Sales Reviews - MOVIE - THE VIDEO MAGAZINE
Sales Seminar - *advice* - TELECONNECT
Sales Tools - SALES & MARKETING MANAGEMENT
Salons - MODERN PHOTOGRAPHY
Salons and Contests - TRAVEL & LEISURE
Salt Lake City - BOX OFFICE
Salute to Blues & Jazz - ENTERTAINMENT CONNECTION MAGAZINE
Sam & Sally - *problem/solution column* - MAST
Sample Hours - *'A unique section that provides one-hour capsules of actual music mixes'* - MONDAY MORNING REPLAY
Sample of One, A - *editorial* - MARKETING COMMUNICATIONS
San Antonio - BOX OFFICE
San Francisco - *city review column by James Armstrong* - AFTER DARK
San Francisco Filmex - WOMEN & FILM
San Francisco Notes - SCREEN ACTOR HOLLYWOOD
San Francisco Scene - *column by Dean Goodman* - DRAMA-LOGUE
Satellite Audio - *guide to audio-only programming* - ONSAT
Satellite Circuit - SATELLITE NEWS
Satellite Circuit - *'A round-up of firms making news in the satellite industry' column by David Bross* - VIA SATELLITE
Satellite Diary - *newsbriefs* - SATELLITE WEEK
Satellite Log - *program review column by Kirk Nicewonger* - ONSAT
Satellite Notebook - SATELLITE COMMUNICATIONS
Satellite Notes - *newsbriefs* - SATELLITE WEEK
Satellite Personals - *personnel changes* - SATELLITE WEEK
Satellite Search - *'Get the most out of your system with our guide to TV from space'* - WHAT SATELLITE
Satellite Sports - *column by Fred Hoffman* - SATELLITE TV WEEK
Satellite Technology - BROADCAST ENGINEERING
Satellite TV - *'Adventures in the Clarke Belt' column by Ken Reitz* - MONITORING TIMES
Satellite TV - *newsbriefs* - SATELLITE WEEK
Satellite View - *'Inside the world of satellite communications'* - POPULAR COMMUNICATIONS
Satire - UNIQUE
Save Your Stamps - *Articles not accepted* - WHAT EDITORS WANT
SBE News - *communications column for members of the Society of Broadcast Engineers* - BROADCAST ENGINEERING
SBE Sustaining Members - *list* - SIGNAL, THE
SBE Update - BROADCAST ENGINEERING

SC Commercial of the Month - *Description and story boards* - SHOOTING COMMERCIALS
SC East - *production news column by Peter Brown* - SHOOTING COMMERCIALS
SC Equipment - *product reviews column by Susan Sammon* - SHOOTING COMMERCIALS
SC Letters - SHOOTING COMMERCIALS
SC Middle Atlantic - *same* - SHOOTING COMMERCIALS
SC Midwest - SHOOTING COMMERCIALS
SC Music - *column by Doris Elliott* - SHOOTING COMMERCIALS
SC Southeast - SHOOTING COMMERCIALS
SC Southwest - SHOOTING COMMERCIALS
SC West - SHOOTING COMMERCIALS
SCA Publications - SPECTRA
Scan - *'News, contracts and people from the TV and video industries'* - BROADCAST SYSTEMS ENGINEERING
Scan - *newsbriefs* - INTERNATIONAL ADVERTISER
Scan Lines - *visual technical column by David Ranada* - HIGH FIDELITY
Scan Lines - *personnel briefs* - INDUSTRIAL TELEVISION NEWS
Scan Lines - *electronic cinematography* - PHOTOMETHODS
Scan Lines - *technology column by Phil Kurz* - PRE-
Scanner Equipment - *review column by Bob Grove* - MONITORING TIMES
Scanner Scene - *column by Marc Saxon* - POPULAR ELECTRONICS
Scanners - *newsbriefs* - TELEVISION WEEK
Scanning Report, The - *column by Bob Kay* - MONITORING TIMES
Scanning the Industry - *newsbriefs* - WEB
Scanning the Institute - *news items* - IEEE SPECTRUM
Scanning the Issue - *editorial overview* - PROCEEDINGS OF THE IEEE
Scanning the Issues - IEEE SPECTRUM
Scanning the Past - *excellent historical review* - PROCEEDINGS OF THE IEEE
Scanning the Regions - VIDEO SOFTWARE MAGAZINE
Scanning VHF/UHF - *'Monitoring the 30 to 900 Mhz action bands'* - POPULAR COMMUNICATIONS
Scarlet Letters - *letters to the editor* - SCARLET STREET
Scene and Heard - *editors in the news, column by Denise Abbott* - AMERICAN CINEMEDITOR
Scene & Heard - *film news column by Ken Ferguson* - FILM MONTHLY
Scene Around Town - *soap opera stars off stage* - SOAP OPERA UPDATE
Scene Stealers of the Month - MODERN SCREEN
Scene/Agencies - CLIO MAGAZINE
Scene/and Heard - CLIO MAGAZINE
Scene/Festivals - CLIO MAGAZINE
Scene/Production - CLIO MAGAZINE
Scenes and Events - *Calendar and news briefs* - LIGHTING DIMENSIONS

Scene/Technical - CLIO MAGAZINE
Scene/World - CLIO MAGAZINE
Schedule of Coming Conventions - PROFESSIONAL PHOTOGRAPHER, THE
Schedule of Exhibitor Conventions - EXHIBITORS TRADE REVIEW
Schedule of the BBC's Foreign Language Services - BBC WORLD SERVICE LONDON CALLING
Scholarly Works in Progress - THEATRE DOCUMENTATION
School Department - *use of AV in the classroom* - EDUCATIONAL SCREEN
School Photography Digest - *column by Bill Smith* - RANGEFINDER, THE
Schools - BALLETT INTERNATIONAL
Schools, Seminars, and Conferences - PROFESSIONAL PHOTOGRAPHER, THE
Schwalberg at Large - POPULAR PHOTOGRAPHY
Sci Fi - *program review* - TV GOLD
Science - WORLD PRESS REVIEW
Science and Medicine - ABC WEEKLY
Scientific Instrumentation - *how to set up and shoot under varying circumstances* - PHOTOMETHODS
Scoop, The - *commentary column by Robert Gerson* - VIDEO BUSINESS
Scoops From Scottie - *column by Scottie* - SCREENLAND PLUS TV-LAND
Scope - *trends* - SIGHT AND SOUND MARKETING
Score, The - *music for motion pictures* - CINEFANTASTIQUE
Scoreboard - *magazine contest winners* - AUSTRALIAN PHOTOGRAPHY
Scoreboard - FRENDX
Scoreboard Competition - *details on monthly winners* - AUSTRALIAN PHOTOGRAPHY
Scorecard, The - *'In stereo where available' and 'Subtitled in Esperanto' humor newsbriefs* - COMIC RELIEF
Scorecard, The - *changes in the photographic marketplace* - PHOTOGRAPHER'S MARKET NEWSLETTER
Scouting - *newsbriefs* - TELECONNECT
Scrapbook - *comment* - INSIDE MEDIA
Screen Crossword Puzzle - SCREEN STORIES
Screen Guide Reviews - TELEVISION AND SCREEN GUIDE
Screen in Review, The - *'Checking off the new films for what they are worth' column by Norbert Lusk* - PICTURE PLAY MAGAZINE
Screen Picture Quiz - SCREEN STORIES
Screen Scene - *column by Tom Provenzano* - DRAMA-LOGUE
Screen Scene - *'The highs and lows of tinseltown' column by Hank Laine* - SILVER SCREEN
Screen Stories Previews - SCREEN STORIES
Screen Test - *quiz* - MOVIEGOER
Screening PROphiles - *column by Gregory P. Fagan* - VIDEO PROPHILES
Screening Room, The - AMERICAN PREMIERE
Screening Room - *'A critical look at the latest business videos'* - CORPORATE VIDEO DECISIONS

Departments

Screening Room, The - *reviews* - E-ITV
Screening Room - E-ITV
Screenings - *review of new film product* - AMERICAN FILM
Screenings - *upcoming animation* - ANYMATOR
Screenplay - *latebreaking news* - VIDEO BUSINESS
Screenprinting - *news and processes* - POLYGRAPH INTERNATIONAL
Scripts - *wanted, and production company contacts* - CASTING NEWS
SE Production News - *of the Southeastern states* - IN MOTION FILM & VIDEO PRODUCTION MAGAZINE
Search for tomorrow - *abstract* - SOAP OPERA DIGEST
Search Tips - *database search highlight* - MEDIABRIEFS
Season Boxoffice Totals - VARIETY
Seasons - *column by Judith Waldrop* - AMERICAN DEMOGRAPHICS
Season-to-Date Ratings - ELECTRONIC MEDIA
Season-to-Date TV Ratings - ELECTRONIC MEDIA
Seat on the Dial - *review* - TV SCREEN
Seatcovers - *column by Ladybug* - CB LIFE
Second Look, A - *reviews with the aid of the passage of time* - CINEASTE
Second Take - *'Quotable quotes from our daytimers'* - REAL LIFE/DAYTIMERS
Second Thoughts - *concerning past equipment reviews* - ABSOLUTE SOUND, THE
Second Thoughts - *'Suggested sidetrips on a time travel itinerary'* - JOE FRANKLIN'S NOSTALGIA
Second Thoughts - *commentary* - SALES & MARKETING MANAGEMENT
Secondhand Scene - *classic film cameras reviewed* - CAMERA & CAMCORDER MONTHLY
Section Meetings - *concerning international meetings* - SMPTE JOURNAL
Section News - *column by Steven Ewald* - QST
Securities Price Range - *for film organizations on Chicago and New York Stock Markets* - EXHIBITORS HERALD WORLD
Security & Communications - *column by Joseph Palenchar* - CAR STEREO REVIEW
Security Printing - *news and developments* - POLYGRAPH INTERNATIONAL
See For Yourself - *'Attractions current in New York, some to look forward to, and a list of those that have closed since the last recording'* - THEATRE ARTS
See, Hear - *commentary column by John Porteous* - BROADCASTER
Seeing Pictures - *column by Julia Scully* - MODERN PHOTOGRAPHY
Seen and Noted - *currently running ads of note* - ART DIRECTION
Seen At - STAGE AND TELEVISION TODAY, THE
Seen in the Spotlight - *'A report on the derring-do in the mythical kingdom of Hollywood' column by Katharine Best* - STAGE
See-Saw-Seen - *comment and gossip* - RTD
Selected Account Changes by Agency - PRESS STATISTICAL REVIEW

Selected Account Changes by Product - PRESS STATISTICAL REVIEW
Selected Air Programmes - AKASHVANI
Selected Books - ABC WEEKLY
Selected Doordarshan Programmes - AKASHVANI
Selected Film Reading of the Current Month - *an unusual section detailing periodical articles which put films best foot forward* - MOTION PICTURE AND THE FAMILY, THE
Selected Media Group Expenditures - PRESS STATISTICAL REVIEW
Selected Product Category Expenditures - PRESS STATISTICAL REVIEW
Selected Shorts - *'The following from news services, press releases, and newspapers reflect recent items of interest'* - COMMUNICATIONS INDUSTRIES REPORT, THE
Selected Top Advertisers - PRESS STATISTICAL REVIEW
Selected Top Product Groups - PRESS STATISTICAL REVIEW
Selection of Amateur Stars - *readers home pictures* - MOVIE HUMOR
Selections - *newsbriefs* - KINEMATOGRAPH WEEKLY
Self-Assignment - *column* - PETERSEN'S PHOTOGRAPHIC
Sell and Swap - WISCONSIN PHOTOGRAPHER
Sellers on Style - *format comment* - CAMPAIGN
Selling - *column by Kenneth Garner* - GRAPHIC ARTS MONTHLY
Selling Angles - *exhibitor successful promotions* - SHOWMEN'S TRADE REVIEW
Selling Approach, The - *'On new product'* - MOTION PICTURE HERALD
Selling Composition - PRINTING IMPRESSIONS
Selling Seats - *'Practical ideas by practical showmen'* - BOXOFFICE
Selling the Picture - *'News and items concerning profitable advertising, publicity and exploitation'* - SHOWMEN'S TRADE REVIEW
Seminars and Meetings - *condensed reports from recent events of interest to publishers* - LEARNED PUBLISHING
Seminars & Workshops Calendar - PETERSEN'S PHOTOGRAPHIC
Sense and Nonsense - *computers and the home column by Dawn Gordon* - HOME ENTERTAINMENT
Series Romance Ratings - ROMANTIC TIMES
Series Romance Reviews - ROMANTIC TIMES
Sermons - *reviews* - HOMILETIC
Service Association of the Month - ELECTRONICS WORLD
Service Bureau - *desktop publishing tips* - PERSONAL PUBLISHING
Service Bureau, The - STORY WORLD AND PHOTODRAMATIST, THE
Service Corner, The - RADIO DEALER, THE
Service Data - *'On features'* - PRODUCT DIGEST
Service Industry News - ELECTRONICS WORLD
Service Notes - ELECTRONICS WORLD

Service Talks - *'Incorporated in this department of the Herald-World, which is a department containing news, information and gossip on current productions, is the Moving Picture World department: Through the Box Office Window' by T.O. Service* - EXHIBITORS HERALD WORLD
Service Tips - *column by Art Margolis* - ELECTRONICS ILLUSTRATED
Serviceman's Corner, The - *new techniques* - RADIO BROADCAST
Services - COMPUTER PICTURES
Services - *provided by the association* - IMAGE
Services - PRE-
Services - VIA SATELLITE
Services - *reviews* - VIDEO MANAGEMENT
Services Directory - *'Addressing programmers'* - SATELLITE TV WEEK
Services for the Trade - PRINTINGNEWS
Services: Enhanced - COMMUNICATIONSWEEK
Services: Local - COMMUNICATIONSWEEK
Services: Long Distance - COMMUNICATIONSWEEK
Sessions/Studio News - MIX
Set Pieces - *'Star news from film and video'* - FILM REVIEW
Sex Advisor - *column by Marty Klein* - MGF
SF & Fantasy Films on Video - *extensive reviews* - SCIENCE-FICTION VIDEO MAGAZINE
SF Movie Books - *review* - SF MOVIELAND
SF Readout - *science fiction review column by Peter Gill* - NEW CAPTAIN GEORGE'S WHIZZBANG, THE
Shadow Stage - *film reviews* - PHOTOPLAY
Shadow Stage, The - *'Reviewing movies of the month - A reliable guide to recent pictures'* - PHOTOPLAY COMBINED WITH MOVIE MIRROR
Shape of Things to Come, The - *'As seen thru the terror tell-us-scope'* - FAMOUS MONSTERS OF FILMLAND
Sharp Angle, The - *column by J.D. Sharp* - EQ
Sh-Boom Calendar - *'A day-by-day history of the hits and the hitmakers'* - SH-BOOM
Sheela Wood - *'Advice for you from the heart'* - NATIONAL EXAMINER
Shelf Help - *new publications reviewed column by Luther Sperberg* - VENTURA PROFESSIONAL!
Shelf Life - *'A quick look at the delights--and the dregs--available in your local video store'* - HORRORFAN
Shining Star - ENTERTAINMENT CONNECTION MAGAZINE
Shoot Alberta - *column by Linda Earl and Charles Mandel* - CINEMA/CANADA
Shooting Stars - *'Todays top filmmakers with tomorrows hottest projects'* - PREVUE
Shoots - VIDEO MANAGEMENT
Shoots - *on-location and studio newsbriefs* - VIDEO SYSTEMS
Shoots and Edits - *work in progress at different shops* - VIDEO MANAGEMENT
Shop Hints - *'Tips for home and bench service'* - ELECTRONIC TECHNICIAN/DEALER

855 INDEX Departments

Shop Talk - AUSTRALASIAN PRINTER
Shop Talk - *column by Dan O'Rourke* - MAST
Shop Talk - POPULAR PHOTOGRAPHY
Shop Talk - SCRIPPS HOWARD NEWS
Shop Talk - VIDEO BUSINESS
Shop Talk at Thirty - *commentary* - EDITOR AND PUBLISHER
Shop Talk of Ohio Editors and Publishers - OHIO NEWSPAPER
Shop Window - *new products* - HI-FI SOUND
Shopping Digest - COMPUTER PICTURES
Shopping the Audio Market - *product news* - AES
Shoptalk - EDITOR'S WORKSHOP
Shoptalk - *items on successful promotion and programming campaigns* - RADIOACTIVE
Short Circuit - *newsbriefs* - RE:ACT
Short Circuits - *letters and comment* - MODERN RADIO
Short Ends - *newsbriefs* - CINEMA/CANADA
Short Feature, The - *production news of film shorts* - EXHIBITORS HERALD WORLD
Short Feature, The - *extensive section listed by producer* - FILM BUYER
Short Features With Sound - *title, plot, release date* - EXHIBITORS HERALD WORLD
Short Film Bookings for - DOCUMENTARY FILM NEWS
Short Notes - *direct mail ideas and news items* - DIRECT MARKETING
Short Notices - *upcoming films* - CINEFANTASTIQUE
Short Product Playing Broadway - MOTION PICTURE HERALD
Short Spots - *design column by Ed Arnold* - EDITOR'S WORKSHOP
Short Subject Reviews - BOXOFFICE
Short Subjects - ANIMATO!
Short Subjects - *'From here, there and everywhere'* - FANFARE
Short Subjects - *'Reviews and synopses'* - PRODUCT DIGEST
Short Subjects and Serials - *reviews* - EXHIBITORS TRADE REVIEW
Short Subjects Booking Guide - SHOWMEN'S TRADE REVIEW
Short Subjects Chart - *'Index to reviews, synopses'* - PRODUCT DIGEST
Short Takes - *newsbriefs* - BLACK RADIO EXCLUSIVE
Short Takes - *newsbriefs* - ENTERTAINMENT CONNECTION MAGAZINE
Short Takes - *newsbriefs* - FILMS AND FILMING
Short Takes - *briefs of individual Gannett newspapers* - GANNETTEER
Short Takes - *'Upcomings and shoots'* - INSIDE HOLLYWOOD
Short Takes - *short news items* - LIES OF OUR TIMES
Short Takes - *newsbriefs* - MEDIA & METHODS
Short Takes - *newsbriefs* - SALES & MARKETING MANAGEMENT
Short Takes - *newsbriefs* - SCRIPTWRITER NEWS
Short Takes - *'a compilation of current commercial productions* - 60 SECONDS

Short Takes - *shorter videocassette reviews* - VIDEO TIMES
Short Takes - *newsbriefs* - WATCH
Short Throws - *briefs* - CANADIAN FILM DIGEST
Short Wave Experimenter, The - RADIO & TELEVISION
Short Wave Question Box - RADIO & TELEVISION
Short Wave Section - PRACTICAL WIRELESS
Short Wave Stations of the World - RADIO & TELEVISION
Short Waves for the Broadcast Listener - RADIO & TELEVISION
Short Waves of Response - *letters* - METRO-GOLDWYN-MAYER SHORT STORY
Shortcuts - *'These timesaving tricks and tips will help you get the job out the door' reader submissions* - STEP-BY-STEP GRAPHICS
Shorts - *new product news* - AUDIO VISUAL
Shorts - *calendar of upcoming events* - INDEPENDENT MEDIA
Shorts - *newsbriefs* - MAGAZINEWEEK
Shorts - *news items* - OFF-HOLLYWOOD REPORT
Shorts - *newsbriefs* - PREVIEW
Shorts - *newsbriefs column by Jack Sweet* - VIDEO STORE
Short-Takes - *newsbriefs* - BROADCASTER
Short-Wave - *column by Kenneth R. Boord* - ELECTRONICS WORLD
Shortwave Broadcasting - *news column by Glenn Hauser* - MONITORING TIMES
Shortwave Center - *newsbriefs* - FRENDX
Shortwave Radio - *column by Stanley Leinwoll* - RADIO-ELECTRONICS
Short-Wave Station List - ALL-WAVE RADIO
Shot Across the Masthead, A - *opinion* - BULLETIN OF THE AMERICAN SOCIETY OF NEWSPAPER EDITORS, THE
Shout It Out! - *'Your turn to speak up!' letters* - STARZ
Show and Tell - *paragraph-length items of stars* - RONA BARRETT'S HOLLYWOOD
Show Biz Books - *reviews* - MOVIE DIGEST
Show Biz Records - *reviews* - MOVIE DIGEST
Show Business - *column by Peter Woodruff* - ABC WEEKLY
Show Business - *'Coast to coast'* - SHOWMEN'S TRADE REVIEW
Show Business Beauties - SHOW BUSINESS ILLUSTRATED
Show Calendar - AISLE VIEW
Show Calendar - POSTCARD COLLECTOR
Show Column Guides - *contributor profiles* - VENTURA PROFESSIONAL!
Show is On, The - *'Being our concise and critical commendations or condemnations of that which is now on Broadway'* - STAGE
Show People - STAGE AND TELEVISION TODAY, THE
Show Preview - TELECOMMUNICATIONS
Show Report - *column by Ellen Lampert* - THEATRE CRAFTS
Show Sense - *column by Jack Jackson* - SHOWMEN'S TRADE REVIEW

Show Stoppers - *personality column by Paul Steiner* - SHOW
Showbill - *upcoming events* - AV VIDEO
Showbill - *'Backstage With Our Contributors'* - SHOW BUSINESS ILLUSTRATED
Showbiz Quiz - SHOW BUSINESS ILLUSTRATED
Showbiz Stock Transactions - *yesterday's stock quotations* - DAILY VARIETY
Showcase - *'Stars of the month' profile* - CINEMA, VIDEO & CABLE MOVIE DIGEST
Showcase - *designer profile* - DIRECTION
Showcase - *one photographer photo gallery each issue* - LEICA PHOTOGRAPHY
Showing Up in Hollywood - *personality column by Sidney Skolsky* - SHOW
Showing Up in New York - *personality column by Liz Smith* - SHOW
Showmen Personals - MOTION PICTURE HERALD
Showmen's Reviews - PRODUCT DIGEST
Showpage - *column by Ross Smith* - PC PUBLISHING AND PRESENTATIONS
Showroom - *new technology* - SOUND & IMAGE
Shows - *industry trade shows* - TIFFEN PROFESSIONAL NEWSLETTER
Shows Abroad - *overseas legitimate stage reviews* - VARIETY
Shows on Broadway - *reviews* - VARIETY
Shows Out of Town - *reviews* - VARIETY
Shows We've Seen - POPULAR PHOTOGRAPHY
Showstoppers - *latebreaking newsbriefs* - SOAP OPERA STARS
Showtime - *presentations column by Michael Callery and Roberta Schwartz* - PUBLISH!
Shuttle - SATELLITE NEWS
Shy People - *'Firms no longer advertising, and deadbeat advertisers'* - ADVERTISING NEWS
Sic! Sic! Sic! - VERBATIM
Sid Says About Songs - *best selling sheet music and comment column by Sid Bermann* - EXHIBITORS HERALD WORLD
Side Band - CQ
Sidelights - TELEVISION/RADIO AGE
Sidelines - *column by John Crabbe* - HI-FI NEWS AND RECORD REVIEW
Sidelines - *mini-facts* - LINE MONITOR, THE
Sideshow - SHOW
Sidney Sounds Off - *gossip column by Sidney Skolsky* - PHOTOPLAY
SIG Spotlight - *'Timely briefings on special interest groups' column by Joseph A. Webb* - LINK-UP
Sight & Sound Products - *reviews* - SIGHT AND SOUND MARKETING
Sign and Sound - *the AV viewpoint* - PHOTOMETHODS
Sign Off - *commentary* - HDTV NEWSLETTER
Sign Off - MONDAY MORNING REPLAY
Signal Processors - *'A buyer's guide to equalizers, imagers, noise reducers, and the like' column by Ivan Berger* - STEREO REVIEW
Signals - *trends column by Ken C. Pohlmann* - STEREO REVIEW
Signals & Noise - *letters* - AUDIO

Departments INDEX

Signed... Sealed... Delivered! - *letters* - COMIC FANDOM'S FORUM
Significant Trends - SALES & MARKETING MANAGEMENT
Signing On - *new product marketing review* - ADWEEK'S MARKETING WEEK
Signings - *new contracts* - BILLBOARD
Signposts - *trends in post production* - POST
Signs of the Times - *postcard sampling column by Andreas Brown* - POSTCARD COLLECTOR
Silent Key - *obituaries* - OLD TIMER'S BULLETIN, THE
Silent Keys - *obituaries* - QST
Silk Stocking Section, The - *self-explanatory photo section* - MOVIE HUMOR
Silver Mike Award - TV SCREEN
Silverscope - *'What's in the stars for you?', horoscope* - SILVER SCREEN
Singapore - *briefs* - MOVIE/TV MARKETING
Single Reviews - BILLBOARD
Singles Chart - *weekly listing* - BLACK RADIO EXCLUSIVE
Sint's View - *column* - MODERN PHOTOGRAPHY
Sircom's Circuits - *column by Alan Sircom* - HI-FI WORLD
Sitcom - *program review* - TV GOLD
Sitcom History - *historical program review* - TV GOLD
Slated for Success - FILM ALBUM MAGAZINE
Sleepers - *'A title that becomes an unexpected hit, or an obscure title that does much better than anticipated'* - VIDEO SOFTWARE MAGAZINE
Slices - *column by Joe Winski* - ADVERTISING AGE
Slide Showcase - *sample portfolios* - AVC
Slides - MOVING PICTURE AGE
SLR Notebook - MODERN PHOTOGRAPHY
SLR Notebook - *column by Herbert Keppler* - POPULAR PHOTOGRAPHY
Small Market Manager - SOUND MANAGEMENT
Small Screen Line-Up - *upcoming television fare* - SCARLET STREET
Small Talk - *column by Edd Vick* - AMAZING HEROES
Small Talk - *current Hollywood news column by Axel Madsen* - CAHIERS DU CINEMA IN ENGLISH
Small Talk - *column by Dave Long* - POSTCARD COLLECTOR
Small Talk - RADIOACTIVE
Smaller Screen, The - *dealing with television* - FILM MAKING
Small-Offset - *news and developments* - POLYGRAPH INTERNATIONAL
Smart Headwork - *beauty column by Gloria Mack* - PHOTOPLAY COMBINED WITH MOVIE MIRROR
Smoothed Monthly Sunspot Numbers - TELECOMMUNICATION JOURNAL
SMPTE - *report* - BROADCAST + TECHNOLOGY
Snapshots - *'monthly short news reports'* - HDTV NEWSLETTER
Snapshots - *news items* - POPULAR PHOTOGRAPHY

Snapshots - *photographic newsbriefs column by Shutter Speed* - WESTERN PHOTOGRAPHER MAGAZINE
Snapshots: Photo News in Brief - CAMERART
Sneak Peek - *'The inside scoop on What Lies Ahead!'* - SOAP OPERA UPDATE
Sneak Peeks - *'Previews of all your favorite shows'* - SOAP OPERA WEEKLY
So. Calif. Opening Nights - *theatre listing* - DRAMA-LOGUE
So It Seems - *comment* - AMERICAN PRESS
So They Say - NEWSLETTER
Soap Box - *letters* - EPISODES
Soap Box - *reader submitted pet peeves* - PRO VIDEOGRAM
Soap Bubbles - *five pages of the hottest info on television's afternoon stars* - AFTERNOON TV
Soap Dish - *'Wit and whimsy from your favorite stars'* - EPISODES
Soap Dish - *'What's happening in the world of daytime dramas' column by Bubbles LaFleur* - WOW! MAGAZINE
Soap Doctor - *'We answer your questions'* - DAYTIME TV
Soap Opera Confidential - NATIONAL ENQUIRER
Soap Opera Festival - *meeting stars in person* - DAYTIME TV
Soap Opera Guide - *column by Susie Wetmore and Tom Mitchell* - TV GUIDE
Soap Opera Week - *Q&A column by Kimberly Redmond* - ONSAT
Soap Scoops - *information and gossip column by Tony Rizzo* - TV DAY STARS
Soap Scramblers - *crossword puzzle* - SOAP OPERA WEEKLY
Soap Snaps - *picture section* - EPISODES
Soap Spot - *soap opera news* - NATIONAL EXAMINER
Soap Suds - *soap opera newsbriefs* - NATIONAL ENQUIRER
Soap Suds Alley - RADIO ALBUM MAGAZINE
Soaping It Up! - *'Behind the scenes from coast-to-coast!' column by Lillian Smith (and Sheila Steinbach)* - SOAP OPERA PEOPLE
Soaps - *soap opera news* - STAR
Soaps - *column by Michael Logan* - TV GUIDE
Soaps and the Issues - *fascinating continuing series on serious issues explored in current soap opera programs* - SOAP OPERA DIGEST
Social Committee - NEWSLETTER
Social Justice - MEDIA & VALUES
Societies and Clubs - *'List of Radio Groups in the British Isles* - ELECTRONICS WORLD + WIRELESS WORLD
Society Affairs - TELEVISION
Society News - *concerning camera clubs* - AMERICAN AMATEUR PHOTOGRAPHER AND CAMERA & DARKROOM
Society News - AMERICAN PHOTOGRAPHY
Society News and Views - *briefs of BKSTS* - IMAGE TECHNOLOGY
Soft Test - *music business computer software* - STAGE & STUDIO

Software - *product reviews* - AVC
Software - COMPUTER PICTURES
Software - *computer and non-computer supplies and resources* - PRE-
Software - *review of computer programs designed for engineering and electronics applications* - RF DESIGN
Software & - *software reviews* - JOURNALISM EDUCATOR, THE
Software & Courseware - *new products* - THE JOURNAL
Software Corner - *column by Dave Brambert* - COMPUTER PUBLISHING
Software Directory Update - MARKETING NEWS
Software Marketplace - VIEW
Software News - *reviews* - ETV NEWSLETTER
Software Review - INFORMATION TODAY
Software Review - LINK-UP
Software Review - *column by Rory Lyaght* - PHOTOPRO
Software Review - VIDEOGRAPHY
Software Reviews - FACTSHEET FIVE
Software Reviews - INTERNATIONAL JOURNAL OF INFORMATION MANAGEMENT
Software Reviews - *valuable information section* - PUBLIC RELATIONS REVIEW
Software Sampler - DEALERSCOPE
Software Sources - *new videotape releases* - VIDEO INFO
Software/Courseware - *review* - THE JOURNAL
Soldering Tips - *column by Richard Majestic* - RADIO GUIDE
Solicitors Tale, A - *by Carew* - AGRICULTURAL ADVERTISING
Solid Gold Radio - *'North America's megawatt jukeboxes are still pumping out those hits'* - SH-BOOM
Solid State - *technical column by Lou Garner* - COMPUTERS & ELECTRONICS
Solid State - ELECTRONICS
Solid State Developments - *column by Forrest M. Mims* - COMPUTERS & ELECTRONICS
Solutions - *'Experts provide practical answers to help you solve your visual communications problems'* - STEP-BY-STEP GRAPHICS
Solve This! - *problem solving* - PRACTICAL WIRELESS
Some of Your Business - BACK STAGE/SHOOT
Some Personal Notes - ADVERTISING
Some Points on Electricity - WIRE & RADIO COMMUNICATIONS
Some Recent Patents - INDUSTRIAL ELECTRONICS
Some Successful Advertising Men - ADVERTISING
Song Hits in Current Films - *very unique index by film title, and producer* - FILM BUYER
Song of the Month - *sheetmusic* - TV RADIO MIRROR
Songfile - *pop song lyrics* - TV HITS
Songs that Scored in Vaudeville This Week - *brief listing* - DRAMATIC MIRROR, THE

857　　　　INDEX　　　　Departments

Songwriter - MUSIC LINE
Soon to be Bestsellers - FORECAST
Sosyal Chatterbox - *personality news column by Chito P. Alcid* - SOSYALI MAGAZINE
Soul LPs - *playlist* - BILLBOARD
Sound, The - *equipment review* - ABSOLUTE SOUND, THE
Sound - *news items* - INTERNATIONAL PHOTOGRAPHER
Sound - THEATRE DESIGN & TECHNOLOGY
Sound - *column by Jerry Wesson* - TRAVEL & LEISURE
Sound Advice - *audio column by Bruce Avery* - VISIO
Sound Advice: Special Report - *technical column* - MIX
Sound and Picture - *column by Ray Beaumont-Craggs* - AMATEUR PHOTOGRAPHER
Sound Bites - CHANNELS
Sound Bites - *'And Now, a Word From the Stars'* - TV, ETC.
Sound Bites/Short Ends - *production newsbriefs* - REEL LIFE
Sound Blast - *personnel newsbriefs* - PRODUCTION SOUND REPORT
Sound Business: SPARS Perspectives - *via The Society of Professional Audio Recording Services* - REP: RECORDING ENGINEERING PRODUCTION
Sound Contracting News - PRO SOUND NEWS
Sound Effects - *newsbriefs* - TALKING PICTURE MAGAZINE
Sound Ideas - *column by Roy Rising* - VIDEO SYSTEMS
Sound Installation - PRO SOUND NEWS
Sound Lines - *comment* - PERSONAL ELECTRONICS
Sound Matters - FILM MAKING
Sound, Music, Science and Technology - LEONARDO
Sound News - *news items* - IMAGE TECHNOLOGY
Sound Off - *column by DG Leadbetter* - AUTO SOUND & SECURITY
Sound Off - *letters* - CAR STEREO REVIEW
Sound Off - *letters* - MAGAZINE & BOOKSELLER
Sound Off - *letters* - SOAP OPERA DIGEST
Sound on Film - *credits* - PRO SOUND NEWS
Sound on Tape - *review column by Bert Whyte* - ELECTRONICS WORLD
Sound Pictures - *new technology column by F. H. Richardson* - EXHIBITORS HERALD WORLD
Sound Reasoning - *audio column by Cliff Roth* - VIDEOMAKER
Sound Reinforcement - DB
Sound Reinforcement - PRO SOUND NEWS
Sound Reinforcement News/Tour Update - *column by Mark Herman* - MIX
Sound Scene - HI-FI SOUND
Sound Stage on Stage - *column by Lorraine Gauguin* - SOUND STAGE
Sound Track - *news briefs* - AES
Sound Track, The - FILMS IN REVIEW
Sound Waves - *audio briefs* - BACK STAGE

Sound Waves - *audio column by John Woram* - BILLBOARD
Sound-Fancier's Guide - AUDIOCRAFT FOR THE HI-FI HOBBYIST
Sounding Off - PRO SOUND NEWS
Soundman's Notes from the Road - REP: RECORDING ENGINEERING PRODUCTION
Soundmixing - STAGE & STUDIO
Sounds Familiar - *audio recording news column by Celso A. Sabinano* - SOSYALI MAGAZINE
Sounds of the '70s - *music review* - PHOTO SCREEN
Soundtrack - *column by Steve Vertlieb* - CINEMACABRE
Soundtrack, The - *record albums with nostalgic themes* - FLASHBACK
Soundtrack - VARIETY
Soundtracks - INTERNATIONAL FILM BUFF
Soundtracks - *record review column by Richard Sayer* - STARBURST
Soundwave - VIDEO REVIEW
Soundwaves - *letters* - HI-FI SOUND
Source Notes - FILM & HISTORY
Source Scan - *'a review of a variety of books, research reports, and occasional papers* - TELESCAN
Sources - *literature and software* - AFTERIMAGE
Sources - SATELLITE COMMUNICATIONS
Sources & Citations - NEWS MEDIA & THE LAW, THE
Sources & Resources - *new product review* - HOME ENTERTAINMENT
Sources and Resources - PRESS, THE
Southeast Report, The - *black radio playlist* - BLACK RADIO EXCLUSIVE
Space Communications - CQ
Space Station - SATELLITE NEWS
Space Systems - SATELLITE WEEK
Space Transportation News - SATELLITE COMMUNICATIONS
Spacewatch - *column by Jeffrey Manber* - STV GUIDE
Spaghetti Mail & Cinema to Come - *combination letters, review, and preview* - SPAGHETTI CINEMA
Spanish Language Section - *'The text of the magazine in Spanish'* - MONITOR INTERNATIONAL
Spanish Section - *'Extensive listings of all Spanish-language programming'* - SATELLITE ORBIT
Sparklers and Fizzlers - *orchids and onions survey column by Curtis F. Brown* - BIJOU
Sparklies - *'What Satellite's quick fax on what's happening in satellite TV technology'* - WHAT SATELLITE
Sparks - *short positive advice on building subscribers column by J. W. Triplett* - AMERICAN NEWSPAPER BOY, THE
SPARS On-Line - *Association news concerning the Society of Professional Audio Recording Services* - REP: RECORDING ENGINEERING PRODUCTION
Speak for Yourself - *letters* - PHOTOPLAY COMBINED WITH MOVIE MIRROR
Speak Out - *survey* - VIDEO INSIDER

Speak Up - *letters to the editor* - PIC
Speakeasy - *men- women on-street interviews* - PREVIEW
Speaking Editorially - MIDWEEK MOTION PICTURE NEWS
Speaking My Mind - *editorial* - SOAP OPERA WEEKLY
Speaking of Music - *editorial commentary column by William Anderson* - STEREO REVIEW
Speaking of New Products - *news briefs* - MULTI IMAGES JOURNAL
Speaking Out - RELIGIOUS BROADCASTING
Speaking Out - VIDEO SOFTWARE MAGAZINE
Speakout - *commentary* - IEEE SPECTRUM
Special Effects - CAMERA & DARKROOM PHOTOGRAPHY
Special Effects - *column by Nick Steadman* - DARKROOM PHOTOGRAPHY
Special Effects - POST
Special Events - *calendar* - BROADCASTER
Special Events - *picture briefs of promotional events* - GREATER AMUSEMENTS
Special Events - *column by Billy Lunt* - QST
Special Events Calendar - BROADCASTER
Special Feature - CELEBRITY
Special Features - *book reviews* - CHRISTIAN REVIEW
Special Feeds Update - *satellite guide column by Bill Britton* - ONSAT
Special FX - *special video effects column by John Hoglin* - VIDEOMAKER
Special Notices - *unique advertising and want section* - ST. LOUIS AND CANADIAN PHOTOGRAPHER
Special Order - *unique video titles* - VIDEO ALERT
Special Report - PROMOTION
Specially Selected Programs of Educational Value - *programming guide to American network television* - TEACHER'S GUIDE TO TELEVISION
Specials - *annotated guide* - ONSAT
Specials - *'Highlighted programs, children's shows and other categories'* - SATELLITE ORBIT
Specials This Week - *'A list of program specials'* - SATELLITE TV WEEK
Specialty Programming for [month] - *listed by subject matter* - ONSAT
Specialty: - *reviewing one aspect of the print medium* - ENTERTAINMENT WEEKLY
Specs - *'People, places and things from the world of design'* - HOW
Specs - *technical side of cable* - MSO'S CABLE MARKETING
Spectrum - *column by Ivan Berger* - AUDIO
Spectrum - *radio and audio newsbriefs* - BROADCAST SYSTEMS ENGINEERING
Spectrum: the Regulatory Environment - BME'S TELEVISION ENGINEERING
Speeches - PRESSTIME
Spending Money - *column by Thomas Exter* - AMERICAN DEMOGRAPHICS
Spice - *celebrity column by Malcolm Boyes* - CELEBRITY PLUS

Departments

Spirits and Snacks - *food to accompany home entertainment* - HOME ENTERTAINMENT
Sponsored Field - *spot news* - BACK STAGE
Sponsored Films - FILM & VIDEO NEWS
Sponsored Scene - FOCUS ON FILM
Sponsors Want to Know - FILM MEDIA
Sport - ABC WEEKLY
Sport - *sports schedule* - BBC WORLD SERVICE LONDON CALLING
Sport Scene - ABU NEWSLETTER
Sporting Intelligence - MIRROR OF TASTE, AND DRAMATIC CENSOR, THE
Sports - ENTERTAINMENT WEEKLY
Sports - LÜRZER'S INTERNATIONAL ARCHIVE
Sports - ON CABLE
Sports - ONSAT
Sports - *review* - ORBIT VIDEO
Sports - *column by Kenneth Turan* - PANORAMA
Sports - SATELLITE ORBIT
Sports - WORLD PRESS REVIEW
Sports & Recreation - *videocassette review* - V
Sports on Video - *review* - SOUND & IMAGE
Sports Page - VIEW
Sports Picks - *programming guide* - PREVIEW
Sports View - *column by Jim Baker* - TV GUIDE
Sportseen - *'A round-up of this months sports on TV' column by Colin Jarman* - SATELLITE TIMES
Spot Agency News - ART DIRECTION
Spot Check - *'Who's producing the latest TV spots'* - LÜRZER'S INTERNATIONAL ARCHIVE
Spot Check - *production* - POST
Spot Checks - *new spot productions* - ON LOCATION
Spot Light - *single videocassette of merit review* - V
Spot News - COMMUNICATION ENGINEERING
Spot News - *'Latest information on the electronic industry'* - ELECTRONICS WORLD
Spot Radio News - *'Presenting latest information on the radio industry' column by Fred Hamlin* - ELECTRONICS WORLD
Spot Report - *spot radio-TV news* - TELEVISION/RADIO AGE
Spotcheck - *reader Q&A* - PRO SOUND NEWS
Spotlight - *on innovation* - ANIMATIONS
Spotlight - BACK STAGE/SHOOT
Spotlight - *Fox briefs* - FOCUS ON FOX
Spotlight - *star newsbriefs* - FRESH!
Spotlight - LIGHTING DIMENSIONS
Spotlight - *excellent regional roundup of facilities and services* - LOCATION UPDATE
Spotlight - *actor profile with filmography* - ORBIT VIDEO
Spotlight - *equipment profile* - TELEVISION BROADCAST
Spotlight - *one product profile* - VIDEO SYSTEMS
Spotlight Marketing - VIDEO SOFTWARE MAGAZINE
Spotlight on Documentary - FILM GUIDE
Spotlight on the Chair - *profile* - ORGANIZATIONAL COMMUNICATION NEWSLETTER
Spotlight on: - *geographic profiles* - LOCATION UPDATE
Spotlight Review - RADIO ALBUM MAGAZINE
Spotlight Special - *special priced rentals* - BLOCKBUSTER VIDEO MAGAZINE
Spotlight: New York - *production briefs* - SHOOTING COMMERCIALS
Spots - *'Statewide commercial production'* - FLORIDA REEL
Spring Fashions - *column by Gwenn Walters* - PHOTOPLAY COMBINED WITH MOVIE MIRROR
Spring Whittlin's - *humor column by Pat Buttram* - RURAL RADIO
Spy - *the lighter side of the television industry* - TELEVISION WEEK
Square One - *the basics of telemarketing* - TELEMARKETING
St. John - *and* - BOX OFFICE
St. Louis - BOX OFFICE
Staff - *performing arts staff positions available* - CASTING NEWS
Staff Changes - BUSINESS AND THE MEDIA
Stage, The - *theatre newsbriefs* - ODDFELLOW, THE
Stage Amusements - TELEVISION WEEKLY NEWS
Stage & Screen Reviews - CD REVIEW
Stage Chat - DRAMATIC MAGAZINE, THE
Stage Door - *column by Robert Muller* - THEATRE
Stage Notes - *newsbriefs* - HOLLYWOOD REPORTER
Stage Review - HOLLYWOOD REPORTER
Stage Shows - *extensive reviews* - EXHIBITORS HERALD WORLD
Stages - AMERICAN THEATRE
Stagestruck - *theatrical commentary column by Peter Filichia* - THEATERWEEK
Standard Hook-Ups - *how-to* - ELECTRONICS WORLD
Standards - *new proposed and accepted standards by the Acoustical Society of America* - AES
Standards and Information Documents - AES
Standards page - *BSI-ANSI-ISO release standards* - IMAGE TECHNOLOGY
Standards Update - TELECOMMUNICATIONS
Star Crossword - *puzzle* - STAR
Star File - *soap opera star profile* - STAR
Star Finder - *where to locate videocassettes of favorite stars* - V
Star Gazing - *column by Patrick Agan* - SCREEN STARS
Star Guide - *young star addresses* - SMASH HITS
Star Health - *health and beauty* - STAR
Star Index - *alphabetical listing* - WHO'S WHO IN MOVIES AND TV
Star Link - *reader's messages to young stars* - SMASH HITS
Star of the Month - INSIDE HOLLYWOOD
Star of the Month - SCREEN STORIES
Star People - *Hollywood column by Janet Charlton* - STAR
Star Program Features of the Month - *upcoming broadcasts with pictorial artist inserts* - POPULAR RADIO AND TELEVISION
Star Scope - *'Horoscope by Roxanne!'* - WOW! MAGAZINE
Star Secrets Revealed - *column by Salome* - TV AND SCREEN SECRETS
Star Signs - *Hollywood horoscope* - MOVIES NOW
Star Static - *six pages of gossip and photos* - TV STARS
Star Struck - *star birthdays and astrological signs* - FILM REVIEW
Star Temps - *'Who's hot ... Who's Not'* - INSIDE HOLLYWOOD
Star Treks - *celebrity news by Jae-Ha-Kim* - CELEBRITY PLUS
Star Videos - *review of what's new on videocassette* - STAR
Star View - *profile* - HOME VIEWER
Star Whirly Words - *puzzle* - STAR
Star Words - *crossword puzzle column by Daniel Bubbeco* - INSIDE HOLLYWOOD
Starburst Letters - *'Our readers write...'* - STARBURST
Starcast - *'What the stars hold in store this month'* - FILM REVIEW
Starch Newspaper Scores - ADVERTISING AGENCY
Stardust - *'Candid interviews with the stars' column by Sheilah Graham* - SILVER SCREEN
Starfront - *celebrity column by Patrick Agan* - MOVIE WORLD
Stargazing - CASTING CALL
Starred for Success - *fashions* - HOLLYWOOD
Stars' Addresses, The - *for those wishing to write* - WHO'S WHO IN MOVIES AND TV
Stars and You, The - *horoscope column by Wendy Hawks* - NATIONAL EXAMINER
Stars on One - *media commentary column by Anni Ackner* - FACTSHEET FIVE
Stars on the Horizon - TELESCREEN
Stars' Stars, The - *'Bonfire of the vanities' horoscope' column by Jeremiah Sullivan* - HOLLYWOOD MAGAZINE
Starscan - *'A closer look at some of your favorite film personalities'* - FANTASTIC FILMS
Starscope - *horoscope* - BLACK STARS
Starscope - *horoscope column by Laurie Brady* - STAR
Starscope - *column by J.M. Fitzmartin* - TV DAY STARS
Starter Stations - INTERNATIONAL RADIO REPORT, THE
Starting from Scratch - FILM MAKING
Star-Trekking - *'Facts and Fotos' column by Tony Rizzo* - PHOTOPLAY
Starz in Your Eyes! - *'Editor Meg tells all!' column by Meg Howard* - STARZ
State and Local - PRESSTIME
State of the Art - AMERICAN PHOTO
State of the Art - BACK STAGE/SHOOT
State of the Art - PROFESSIONAL PHOTOGRAPHER, THE

State of the Art - *technology newsbriefs column by Chip Morgan* - RADIO GUIDE
State of the Market - TELEVISION RETAILING
State of the States - *production status report* - ON LOCATION
State of Trade - *one-line status quos in American cities* - WOODCOCK'S PRINTERS' AND LITHOGRAPHERS' WEEKLY GAZETTE AND NEWSPAPER REPORTER
State Rates - TELECOMMUNICATIONS WEEK
State Rights - *'All the news of activities in the territories'* - EXHIBITORS TRADE REVIEW
State Scope - *news about state broadcast organizations* - RADIOACTIVE
Stateline - *state radio news items* - RADIOWEEK
Statements - HI-FI CHOICE
Station Activities - QST
Station Automation - *column by Steve Walker* - RADIO GUIDE
Station Breaks - *TV Gossip* - PREVIEW
Station Breaks - *'What daytimers do between soaps!'* - REAL LIFE/DAYTIMERS
Station Breaks - *station promotionals of merit* - TELEVISION BROADCAST
Station Circuit - *television station production* - WRAP
Station Identification - RADIOACTIVE
Station Parade - *profile* - RADIO FAN-FARE
Station Profiles - COLLEGE BROADCASTER
Station Strategy - VIEW
Stations in the News - BROADCAST + TECHNOLOGY
Statistics - VIDEO
Stats - *ratings and reading statistic of selected media* - INSIDE MEDIA
Status Chart of On-Screen Happenings - *'Want to know what's been going on with whom lately? We've tallied up the statistics from all the shows'* - SOAP OPERA DIGEST
StatWatch - *statistics* - DEALERSCOPE
Stay Tuned - *promotion* - TELEVISION BROADCAST
Stellargram - *horoscope for specific athletes* - PIC
Stephanie Brush - *humor column by Stephanie Brush* - COMIC RELIEF
Steppin' Out - *ASCAP events* - ASCAP IN ACTION
Stereo News - HI-FI NEWS AND RECORD REVIEW
Stereo Products - *review* - RADIO-ELECTRONICS
Stereo Scene - *column by J. Gordon Holt* - COMPUTERS & ELECTRONICS
Stereo Today - *Stereographic photography column by Robert L. McIntyre* - POPULAR PHOTOGRAPHY
Stereoscopic Notes - *newsbriefs* - KINEMATOGRAPH WEEKLY
Stickybeak - *'Nosing out some strange facts from the worlds of TV, film and pop'* - TV HITS
Still Casting - SHOW BUSINESS
Still Life - *column by Louis DeLuca* - RETROFOCUS
Still Video - *'Steve Parker investigates the latest developments'* - CAMCORDER USER

Stills - *a selection of stills to support earlier articles* - SEQUENCE
Stock and Trade - *'focusing on Wisconsin photo dealers and manufacturers* - WISCONSIN PHOTOGRAPHER
Stock in Trade - *nostalgic items available for purchase* - JOE FRANKLIN'S NOSTALGIA
Stock Index - *over 100 publicly-held companies listed* - BROADCASTING
Stock Market Report - PRINTING IMPRESSIONS
Stocks - MULTICHANNEL NEWS
Stocks - VUE
Stockwatch - *of major corporate news media* - NEWSINC.
Stokes' Notes From the Darkroom - *column by Orvil Stokes* - WESTERN PHOTOGRAPHER MAGAZINE
Stop Action - BACK STAGE
Stop Frame - INVISION
Stop Press - *late-breaking news of special importance* - ASIAN ADVERTISING & MARKETING
Stop Press - *late-breaking video releases* - FILM REVIEW
Store Monitor - *home video column by Earl Paige* - BILLBOARD
Store News - BOOKSTORE JOURNAL
Stories and Scripts - *short stories and shooting scripts via guest authors* - MOVIE GEEK
Stories of the New Photoplays - REEL LIFE
Story Film of the Month - DOCUMENTARY FILM NEWS
Story-Board - *unique production profile* - CORPORATE TELEVISION
Straight From the Editor - *editorial column by Vonda H. Blackburn* - INTERNATIONAL PHOTOGRAPHER MAGAZINE
Straight from the Shoulder - *guest commentary* - COMMUNICATOR
Straight From the Shoulder Talk - *column by Carl Laemmle* - UNIVERSAL WEEKLY
Straight Talk - *Q&A format column by Randi Walseth* - MODERN SCREEN
Straight Talk for Professionals - *continuing series of advice* - PROFESSIONAL PHOTOGRAPHER, THE
Stratford - *reviews* - PLAYS INTERNATIONAL
Strays - *newsbriefs* - QST
Strays from the Laboratory - *technical briefs* - RADIO BROADCAST
Street - *'What's happening'* - DISNEY ADVENTURES
Street Date Calendar - VIDEO SOFTWARE MAGAZINE
Street Security - *column by Barnet C. Fagel* - CAR AUDIO AND ELECTRONICS
Street Talk - BACK STAGE/SHOOT
Street Talk - *advertising agency and business news by selected cities* - FLASH
Street Talk - *gossip* - R & R
Strictly Ad Lib - *music notes from international cities* - DOWN BEAT
Strictly Business - *column by Bob Paulson* - TELEVISION BROADCAST
Strictly for Women - HI-FI SOUND

Strictly Personal - *by 'The Solemn Old Judge', column by George Dewey Hay* - RURAL RADIO
Strictly PERSONnel - *personnel newsbriefs* - PRINT-EQUIP NEWS
Strictly TV - BROADCAST ENGINEERING
Strom's Index - *column by David Strom* - AMAZING HEROES
Stuck on Starz - *'Write your favorites'* - STARZ
Student Animation Workshops - ANIMATION MAGAZINE
Students' Column - ELECTRICAL REVIEW
Studio, The - *production and business news* - EXHIBITORS HERALD WORLD
Studio Action - *production credits* - BILLBOARD
Studio Casebook - *column by Michael Chiusano and Tony L. Corbell* - PHOTOPRO
Studio Clinic - *Tech Support column by Richie Moore* - EQ
Studio Diary - *production news* - STUDIO SOUND AND BROADCAST ENGINEERING
Studio Flashes - *gossip newsbriefs* - SCREEN WEEKLY, THE
Studio Management - VIDEOPRO
Studio News - *production news* - PRO SOUND NEWS
Studio Pro - *'A survey of current records and the professionals who made them'* - PRO SOUND NEWS
Studio Promotions - VIDEO SOFTWARE MAGAZINE
Studio Reference Series - *excellent technical series* - EQ
Studio Secrets - *'For the absolute inside, the hush-hush gossip in the lives and loves of TV personalities you absolutely positively can't beat Paul's prize patter' column by Paul Denis* - TV PEOPLE AND PICTURES
Studio Site - *column by Gordon Carter* - RADIO GUIDE
Studio Strategies - *production* - CABLE MARKETING
Studio Track - *studio column by Bob Kirsch* - BILLBOARD
Studio Update - REP: RECORDING ENGINEERING PRODUCTION
Style - *profile* - MOVIELINE
Style - WHAT EDITORS WANT
Style Matters - WRITING CONCEPTS
Subscriber Status - *radio-TV code station additions and deletions* - CODE NEWS
Subscribers Corner - ENTERTAINER, THE
Subscription Information - *'Programmers and services'* - SATELLITE TV WEEK
Subscription Services Chart - *'Extra services you can buy--and where to call to get them'* - SATELLITE ORBIT
Substitutes - *creative retailing* - VIDEO BUSINESS
Sugar n Spice - *readers comments* - FILMWORLD
Suggested Reading - BETTER BROADCASTS NEWS
Suggestions and Shop Talk - JOURNALIST, THE

Departments INDEX 860

Suite Talk - VIDEO EIGHTIES MAGAZINE
Summary - *index of weeks news* - TELEVISION DIGEST WITH CONSUMER ELECTRONICS
Summary - WHAT EDITORS WANT
Summary of AIVF Minutes - INDEPENDENT, THE
Summary-Index of Week's News - VIDEO WEEK
Summer Seminars - DIGEST OF THE UNIVERSITY FILM AND VIDEO ASSOCIATION
Sunbelt Rap - *briefs on the following areas: account action, client news, ad agencies, newspapers, magazines, kudos, television, radio, promotion, associations, film/tape, and classified* - COMMUNIQUE
Super 8 News - WOMEN & FILM
Super Eight - INDEPENDENT, THE
Super Teen Mailbox! - *addresses of teen stars* - SUPER TEEN
Super Teen on the Scene! - *'Gettin' up close & personal with...'* - SUPER TEEN
Super Teen Stuff! - *'The juiciest juice from East to West' column by Diana* - SUPER TEEN
Super Teen Tattler! - *color pictures of favorite teen stars* - SUPER TEEN
Super Teen USA! - *letters* - SUPER TEEN
Super Teen's All-Star Advice Pages! - *teenage stars Q&A advice column* - SUPER TEEN
Superpan Panning - *humor column by J. H. Sammis* - MODERN PHOTOGRAPHY
Superserious-8 - *column by Raul da Silva* - FILMMAKERS FILM & VIDEO MONTHLY
Superstars - *'Your planetary predictions by Alexandria!'* - SMASH HITS
Supplement to CD-ROMS in Print - *update compiled column by Norman Desmarais* - CD-ROM LIBRARIAN
Supplier News - BOOKSTORE JOURNAL
Supplier News - PRINTING IMPRESSIONS
Supplier Showcase - MAGAZINE DESIGN & PRODUCTION
Supplier Side - *available programming* - LPTV REPORT, THE
Supplier Solo - *single product review* - LPTV REPORT, THE
Suppliers - *newsbriefs* - PROFESSIONAL PHOTOGRAPHER, THE
Suppliers - STAGE AND TELEVISION TODAY, THE
Suppliers' News - RANGEFINDER, THE
Suppliers' Side, The - *commentary column by Bob Scroggins* - MAGAZINE BUSINESS
Supply Line - *literature* - PHOTOMETHODS
Supporting Roles - *locations and equipment* - LOCATION UPDATE
Surplus Sidelights - *unusual military surplus equipment column by Gordon Eliot White* - CQ
Surround Sound/Ambience Processors - SOUND & VISION
Survey - *equipment* - STUDIO SOUND AND BROADCAST ENGINEERING
Surveys - MEDIA INFORMATION AUSTRALIA
Surveys - *interesting research and statistics column by Bart Story* - VIDEO STORE

Surveys and Studies - *column by Dick Friedman* - PANORAMA
Surviving Success - *column by Herbert J. Freudenberger* - FAME
Sustainer News - DIGEST OF THE UNIVERSITY FILM AND VIDEO ASSOCIATION
Sustaining Spotlight - *profile* - SIGNAL, THE
Swappers - RADIO & TELEVISION
Swaps - *'film loan exchange* - MOVIE MAKERS
SWC Computer Corner - FRENDX
Sweepstakes - *reader contest* - EPISODES
Swipefile - *great graphic design ideas* - ART DIRECTION
Sydney Notes - *newsbriefs* - FILM GUIDE
Syllabus Exchange - COMMUNIQUÉ
Syllabus Proposals - SCREEN
Symposium - *comment* - MASTHEAD
Syndicate - WITTYWORLD
Syndicated Columns - BOOK PROMOTION HOTLINE
Syndicates - EDITOR AND PUBLISHER
Syndicates - PRESSTIME
Syndication Standings - ELECTRONIC MEDIA
Syndication Story - *briefs about syndicated materials* - BACK STAGE
Syndicators Directory - *a continuing update on TV syndicators and their properties* - BACK STAGE
Synergy - *'The media mix'* - LINK
Synopses Section - *extensive section on 'What happened, what's happening, what will happen'* - SOAP OPERA DIGEST
Synopsis - *issue article summaries in French and German* - TABS
Synoptical Index of Current Electrical Literature, A - *large listing* - TELEPHONE MAGAZINE
Systems - ELECTRONICS
Systems - *new product announcement section* - PRE-
Systems Circuit - *news of individual CATV systems* - VUE

T

T. P. on Amusement Business - *column by Tom Powell* - AMUSEMENT BUSINESS
Table of Cases - *brief listing of legal cases 'reported, noted, commented upon or digested'* - AIR LAW REVIEW
Tacit - HIGH PERFORMANCE
Take - WASHINGTON JOURNALISM REVIEW
Take 2 - *closer look at current film fare* - MOVIES USA
Taking Issue - *commentary* - MEMORIES
Taking Stock - *'A comparison of the stock performance of publicly held corporations in satellite communications'* - SATELLITE COMMUNICATIONS
Tale Spin - *comic section* - DISNEY ADVENTURES

Talent - BILLBOARD
Talent & Celebrities - *news and publicity* - AMUSEMENT BUSINESS
Talent in Action - *talent reviews* - BILLBOARD
Talent Roster - *profiles* - THEATRE CRAFT
Talent Tours Availabilities - *the majority of the magazine which details who is playing where* - PERFORMANCE
Tales From the Script - *'This month's movie books reviewed', column by Howard Maxford* - FILM REVIEW
Tales of the Flying Desk - *editorial column by Michael Wolff* - COMIC INFORMER
Talk About Movies - *discussion and commentary column by Ted Sennett* - BIJOU
Talk Around Town - *celebrity news and gossip column by Jennifer Tobin* - TV STAR PARADE
Talk of the Week - *newsbriefs* - ADVERTISERS' WEEKLY
Talk Show - *'Behind-the-screen scene'* - TV ENTERTAINMENT
Talkabout - *column by John Carnemolla* - AUSTRALIAN PHOTOGRAPHY
Talkback - BROADCAST
Talkback - *editorial column by David Brittain* - CREATIVE CAMERA
Talkback - *technical Q&A* - MODERN RECORDING & MUSIC
Talkback - *letters* - PHOTO ANSWERS
Talkback - *'provides a channel of communication between the readers of Stage & Studio and manufacturers of music and sound equipment'* - STAGE & STUDIO
Talkie Tidbits - *picture page* - FILM FUN
Talkie Tips - *rated reviews of current film fare* - FILM FUN
Talking Screen Reviews - TALKING SCREEN
Talking Technology - *studio and equipment developments in audio* - SCREEN INTERNATIONAL
Talking Up - *newsbriefs* - HOLLYWOOD FILMOGRAPH
Tangents - *column by Vince Kamin* - FLASH
Tape and Disc Review - HI-FI SOUND
Tape Club News - HI-FI SOUND
Tape Deck, The - *column by R.D. Darrell* - HIGH FIDELITY
Tape Deck, The - HIGH FIDELITY/MUSICAL AMERICA
Tape Duplication - PRO SOUND NEWS
Tape Duplicator - *convention briefs* - BILLBOARD
Tape Guide - *specific tape Q&A column by Herman Berstein* - AUDIO
Tape News and Views - AUDIOCRAFT FOR THE HI-FI HOBBYIST
Tape Notes - *newsbriefs* - TAPE RECORDING
Tape Recorders & Tape - CONSUMER ELECTRONICS PRODUCT NEWS
Tape Recorders: Dollars & Sense - PERSONAL ELECTRONICS
Tape Recording - *new products* - SIGHT AND SOUND MARKETING
Tape Reviews - *prominent tape review section during 1960s heyday of reel-to-reel tape releases* - TAPE RECORDING
Tape Scene, The - VIDEO BUSINESS

Tape Talk - *review of new releases column by Laura M. Fries* - ORBIT VIDEO
Tape Talk - *column by Craig Stark* - STEREO REVIEW
Tape Topics - BACK STAGE
Tape Tracks - *audio tape column by Robert Long* - HIGH FIDELITY
Tape Trends - TAPE
Tape-Audio-Video - *hardware news* - BILLBOARD
Tapecraft - *uses for tape* - TAPE
Tapenews - *newsbriefs* - TAPE
Tapeproducts - *review* - TAPE
Taperecorded - *reviews* - TAPE
Tapetrack - *'Ranking the month's biggest titles by units shipped'* - VIDEO STORE
Tappan on Sideband - *column by Mel Tappan* - CB LIFE
TARGA SIG - *special interest group column* - AV VIDEO
Target Tactics - *Sales and promotion strategies for the graphic designer* - HOW
Tattle Tales - PHOTO SCREEN
Tattle Tales - *'The latest update from the gossip grape vine with your WOW! reporter, Dominique Cordova!'* - WOW! MAGAZINE
Tattletale Tribune, The - *'Gossip hot off the presses'* - TV STAR PARADE
Tax Clinic - PRINTING IMPRESSIONS
TCR Mailboat - *letters* - COMIC READER, THE
TCR Message - *editorial* - COMIC READER, THE
Teacher's Guides to Television - *lengthy guidelines for upcoming specials and series* - TECHTRENDS
Teaching Aid Reviews - COMMUNICATION EDUCATION
Tear Sheets - *samples* - FLASH
Teasers n Trailers - *comic comment* - FILMWORLD
Tech - *technical newsbriefs* - CINEGRAM
Tech Corner - AIRBRUSH ACTION
Tech Highlights - MAST
Tech Notes - AMERICAN PHOTO
Tech Notes - *technical radio column by Billy Paul* - BLACK RADIO EXCLUSIVE
Tech Talk - *newsbriefs* - BROADCASTER
Tech Talk - *excellent technical column by Paul Miller* - HI-FI CHOICE
Tech Talk - *electrical instruction* - IBEW JOURNAL
Tech Talk - PHOTOMETHODS
Tech Talk - *column by Ken Hawkins* - SIX-SHOOTERS
Tech Talk - VIDEODISC MONITOR, THE
Tech Tip - TV TECHNOLOGY
Tech Tips - *'A user's guide to know-how'* - AMERICAN PHOTO
Tech Tips - *reader ideas* - ETI
Tech Tips - INTERNATIONAL PHOTOGRAPHER MAGAZINE
Tech Tips - *column by George Lepp* - OUTDOOR PHOTOGRAPHER
Tech Tips - *column by Kathy Miller* - PUBLISHING & PRODUCTION EXECUTIVE
Tech Tips - RELIGIOUS BROADCASTING
Tech Topics - SYN-AUD-CON NEWSLETTER

Tech Trends - VIZIONS
Tech Watch - BME'S TELEVISION ENGINEERING
Technical - LOCATION UPDATE
Technical Abstracts - *from recent presentations* - ELECTRONICS
Technical & Product Development - MULTICHANNEL NEWS
Technical Books - *review* - ELECTRONICS WORLD
Technical Briefs - EDITOR AND PUBLISHER
Technical Corner - FOLLOW FOCUS
Technical Correspondence - *column by Paul K. Pagel* - QST
Technical Course - FILM MAKING
Technical Data - *specific play information* - WORLD THEATRE
Technical Management - ELECTRONIC DESIGN
Technical News - CINEMA/CANADA
Technical News - *new product briefs* - PHOTO TECHNIQUE INTERNATIONAL
Technical News and Comment - *'Technical information service national audiovisual aids centre* - VISUAL EDUCATION
Technical Round-Up - *new photographic developments column by L. A. Mannheim* - CAMERA
Technical Smithy - AV VIDEO
Technical Talk - *column by Julian D. Hirsch* - STEREO REVIEW
Technical Talks - *column by John H. Battison* - LPTV REPORT, THE
Technical Tips - INVIEW
Technical Topics - *column by Arthur Kramer* - CAMERA 35
Technical Topics - FRENDX
Technicalities - *'Advice on technical matters for all photographers* - WISCONSIN PHOTOGRAPHER
Technically Speaking - PERSONAL ELECTRONICS
Technically Speaking - VIDEO MAGAZINE
Technically Speaking - VIDEO TIMES
Technique Technicalities - *Q&A column by Will Connell* - TRAVEL & LEISURE
Techniques Tomorrow - MODERN PHOTOGRAPHY
Technitopics - *column* - BROADCAST + TECHNOLOGY
Technology - BROADCAST
Technology - CABLE WORLD
Technology - CABLEAGE
Technology - CABLEVISION
Technology - *column by John Slothower* - CMA NEWSLETTER
Technology - ELECTRONIC MEDIA
Technology - FUTUREHOME TECHNOLOGY NEWS
Technology - HI-FI NEWS AND RECORD REVIEW
Technology - *new equipment* - INTERNATIONAL BROADCASTING
Technology - INTERNATIONAL DOCUMENTARY
Technology - INVISION
Technology - PRESSTIME
Technology - SATELLITE COMMUNICATIONS
Technology - *column by George Jarrett* - TBI
Technology - VIA SATELLITE
Technology - VIDEO TECHNOLOGY NEWS

Technology - VIDEOGRAPHY
Technology - WRAP
Technology News - CABLE WORLD
Technology News - PULP & PAPER CANADA
Technology Today - MARKETING NEWS
Technology Trends - BUSINESS COMMUNICATIONS REVIEW
Technology Update - BUYERS GUIDE
Technology Update - FLASH
Technology Update - MAGAZINE DESIGN & PRODUCTION
Technology Update - PRINT BUYERS REVIEW
Technology Update - PUBLIC RELATIONS JOURNAL, THE
Technology Update - THE JOURNAL
Technology Update - TV TECHNOLOGY
Technology Update - VIDEO TIMES
Technology/Equipment - ELECTRONIC MEDIA
Technotes - *model-specific defects and repair strategies* - RADIO-ELECTRONICS
Techphoto Applications - CLOSE-UP
Techscan - *technology* - TELEVISION WEEK
TechWatch - SCHOLASTIC EDITOR'S TRENDS IN PUBLICATIONS
Tedascope News - *projectionist briefs column by Whitney Stine* - GREATER AMUSEMENTS
Telco Talk - *newsbriefs* - TELCO REPORT, THE
Telecast Peeks at New Shows - TELECAST
Telecast Talks It Over - *newsbriefs* - TELECAST
Telecom Communique - TELEPROFESSIONAL
Telecom News - TELECOMMUNICATIONS
Telecom Products - TELECOMMUNICATIONS
Telecom Trends - NETWORK WORLD
Telecommunication - *'panorama of progress in the fields of communication and broadcasting* - COMMUNICATION AND BROADCAST ENGINEERING
Telecommunications - PRESSTIME
Telecommunications and the Law - TELEMARKETING
Telecommunications Business - TELECOMMUNICATIONS
Teleconference Update - CORPORATE TELEVISION
Teleconferencing - SATELLITE COMMUNICATIONS
Teleconferencing News - IN MOTION FILM & VIDEO PRODUCTION MAGAZINE
Teleconferencing Report - E-ITV
TeleFocus - TELEMARKETING
Telemarketing - *column by Peg Kuman* - DIRECT MARKETING
Telemarketing's Corpus Juris - TELEMARKETING
Tele-News - CABLE COMMUNICATIONS MAGAZINE
Telenews - *'Topical reflections from the radio screen'* - PRACTICAL TELEVISION AND SHORT-WAVE REVIEW
Telenews - *teleconferncing newsbriefs* - TELECONFERENCE MAGAZINE
TeleNews - *briefs* - TELEMARKETING
Telephone Directory - *'Programmer listings'* - SATELLITE TV WEEK

Departments INDEX 862

Telephones Enroute - *'What's happening with cellular, marine & mobile phones'* - POPULAR COMMUNICATIONS
Teleplay - *crossword puzzle and trivia* - TV ENTERTAINMENT
Teleports - SATELLITE NEWS
Teleproduction - MARKEE
Teleproduction - MILLIMETER
Teleproduction - TELEVISION BROADCAST
Teleproduction - WRAP
Teleproduction Journal - E-ITV
Teleproductions - FILM & VIDEO
Tele-Scope - TELEVISION/RADIO AGE
Telesnack - TV TIMES
Telestatus - *video statistics* - TELEVISION
Tele-Tales - *television news and gossip column by Joe Cal Cagno* - TV WORLD
Tele-Views - *newsbriefs* - CABLE COMMUNICATIONS MAGAZINE
Televiews - *comment* - PRACTICAL TELEVISION AND SHORT-WAVE REVIEW
Television - *column by Alice McKay* - ADWEEK
Television - AMERICAN FILM
Television - CONSUMER ELECTRONICS PRODUCT NEWS
Television - CRITIC
Television - CTVD
Television - *new feature beginning in Aug, 1938 column by Thomas Baird* - DOCUMENTARY FILM NEWS
Television - *reviews* - FILM & BROADCASTING REVIEW
Television - IN MOTION FILM & VIDEO PRODUCTION MAGAZINE
Television - INSIDE ENTERTAINMENT
Television - *commentary* - INVISION
Television - *reviews* - LISTENER
Television - MEDIAWEEK
Television - *upcoming programs* - SHOW
Television - *review column by Alkarim Jivani* - 20/20
Television & Radio - *reviews* - ENTERTAINMENT WORLD
Television, Cable & Radio - VARIETY
Television Crossword - TV GUIDE
Television Diary - STAGE AND TELEVISION TODAY, THE
Television for All - *explanation* - PRACTICAL WIRELESS
Television Gossip - RADIO REVIEW AND TELEVISION NEWS
Television in Review - TELEVISION
Television Notes - TELEVISION
Television on Location - *newsbriefs* - TELEVISION
Television Question and Answer Box - RADIO REVIEW AND TELEVISION NEWS
Television Receiver, The - OLD TIMER'S BULLETIN, THE
Television Reviews - AFA JOURNAL
Television Reviews - *column by Ken Tucker* - ENTERTAINMENT WEEKLY
Television Reviews - *weekly review of series and specials* - VARIETY
Television Scene, The - FILMS IN REVIEW
Television Stations Now in Operation - TELEVISION WEEKLY NEWS

Television Talent Report - ROSS REPORTS TELEVISION
Television Today - STAGE AND TELEVISION TODAY, THE
Televisionary - *TV briefs* - RONA BARRETT'S HOLLYWOOD
TeleVisions - *video news briefs* - HOLLYWOOD REPORTER
Tele-Visions - *editorial* - TELEVISION WEEKLY NEWS
Telex - *newsbriefs* - ANIMAFILM
Tell and Tell - *more Q&A on stars* - RONA BARRETT'S HOLLYWOOD
Tel's From the Crypt - *column by Terry Hooper* - COMICS FANDOM EXAMINER
Ten Years Ago - CONSUMER ELECTRONICS
Ten Years Ago - *from the files of Radio Daily* - RTD
Terrestrial Links - *'...is an editorial look at the news as it crosses our desk'* - SATELLITE RETAILER
Terri Rossi's Rhythm Section - *column by Terri Rossi* - BILLBOARD
Territory News - *TBA member news events* - SALES NEWS
Terry Lindvall's Sprocket Holes - *film commentary column by Terry Lindvall* - FILM WITNESS
Test - *new video product* - VIDEO CAMERA
Test Bench Puzzler - *column by Art Margolis* - ELECTRONICS WORLD
Test Department - EIGHT MM MOVIE MAKER AND CINE CAMERA
Test Equipment - *extensive outstanding reviews of new technologies* - IBE
Test Equipment Product Report - ELECTRONICS WORLD
Test Measurement - ELECTRONIC PRODUCTS
Test Patterns - *editorial column by Hal Schuster* - TV GOLD
Test Report - *equipment review* - AMATEUR PHOTOGRAPHER
Test Report - *test bench report* - BROADCAST SYSTEMS ENGINEERING
Test Report - CAR AUDIO AND ELECTRONICS
Test Report - *equipment profile* - WHAT SATELLITE
Test Reports - *extensive test bench reports* - CAR STEREO REVIEW
Test Reports - *in-depth audio equipment reviews* - HIGH FIDELITY
Test Reports - *excellent section on equipment testing* - VIDEO REVIEW
Test Yourself - *unique self-exam on editing judgement* - EDITORIAL EYE, THE
Tested in Our Laboratory - *'A review of the latest television apparatus'* - PRACTICAL TELEVISION AND SHORT-WAVE REVIEW
Texas - BACK STAGE
Texas Northers - *Texas exhibitor newsbriefs column by Jack Meredith* - UNIVERSAL WEEKLY
Text & Data - *satellite services* - ONSAT
TGA SIG - *computer column by Bob Gillman* - AV VIDEO
TGIF Openings for Acting Talent - TGIF
TGIF Openings for Entertainers - TGIF
TGIF Openings for Models - TGIF

TGIF Openings for Musicians - TGIF
TGIF Openings for Writers - TGIF
Thanks! - *letters* - U & LC
That's Show Biz! - *'What's happening in Hollywood'* - STARZ
That's the Way It Was - *historical photos* - AUDIO
Theater - INSIDE ENTERTAINMENT
Theater - *legitimate stage review* - SCREEN INTERNATIONAL
Theater - WORLD PRESS REVIEW
Theater Crafts - OFFICIAL BULLETIN OF THE INTERNATIONAL ALLIANCE OF THEATRICAL STAGE EMPLOYEES AND MOVING PICTURE MACHINE OPERATORS OF THE UNITED STATES AND CANADA.
Theater in New York - *column by Eileen Blumenthal* - THEATER
Theater in Washington - *column by Mohammad Kowsar* - THEATER
Theater Maintenance - GREATER AMUSEMENTS
Theater News - *newsbriefs column by Ken Mandelbaum* - THEATERWEEK
TheaterWeek Listings - *extensive listing of current theatrical fare* - THEATERWEEK
Theatre - *reviews* - ENTERTAINMENT WORLD
Theatre, The - *new technologies and management technique* - EXHIBITORS HERALD WORLD
Theatre - *current productions of Broadway and region* - SHOW
Theatre - *review column by Jane Edwardes* - 20/20
Theatre Abroad - *review* - SHOW
Theatre Across America - *extensive state listing of current productions* - PLAYERS
Theatre Architecture - THEATRE DESIGN & TECHNOLOGY
Theatre Arts Bookshelf - *book reviews* - THEATRE ARTS
Theatre Arts Gallery - *profile* - THEATRE ARTS
Theatre Beat - *column by Bruce Feld* - DRAMA-LOGUE
Theatre Between Covers, The - *column by Ralph Bailey* - THEATRE MAGAZINE
Theatre Calendar - THEATRE, THE
Theatre Construction News - *'This department is devoted to theatre building news and publishes the earliest news obtainable concerning projected theatres, schools, etc., where motion picture equipment will be used'* - EXHIBITORS TRADE REVIEW
Theatre Crossword - THEATRE, THE
Theatre Diary - *news and happenings column by Burbage* - GAMBIT
Theatre Diary - *playtimes and offerings* - THEATRE
Theatre Dining - THEATRE, THE
Theatre in Review - *commentary* - THEATRE JOURNAL
Theatre Library Association News - THEATRE DOCUMENTATION
Theatre Magazine's Court of Appeal - *forum for play review* - THEATRE MAGAZINE

Theatre Management - MIDWEEK MOTION PICTURE NEWS
Theatre Management - *'Guide to modern methods in the administrative and executive phases of theatre operation'* - SHOWMEN'S TRADE REVIEW
Theatre News - STAGE AND TELEVISION TODAY, THE
Theatre on the Disc - *music review column by Sigmund Spaeth* - THEATRE ARTS
Theatre Parties - *picture page* - SPOTLIGHT CASTING MAGAZINE
Theatre Reports - TDR
Theatre Review - THEATRE JOURNAL
Theatre Reviews - *extensive West Coast stage productions* - DRAMA-LOGUE
Theatre Reviews - SPEECH AND DRAMA
Theatre Reviews - *of Los Angeles theatre* - SPOTLIGHT CASTING MAGAZINE
Theatre Scenes - *'Some of the outstanding productions currently playing on B'way'* - PLAYBILL
Theatre Survey - DRAMA SURVEY
Theatre Survey - *compiled column by Marian A. Smith* - SOUTHERN THEATRE
Theatre Talk - *column by Paul Steiner* - DRAMATICS
Theatre Technology - *CITT news of the Canadian Institute for Theatre Technology, column by Paul Court* - BROADCAST + TECHNOLOGY
Theatre Ticket - ENTERTAINMENT CONNECTION MAGAZINE
Theatre U.S.A. - *review* - SHOW
Theatre, Vaudeville and Melody - *newsbriefs* - HOLLYWOOD FILMOGRAPH
Theatre Week - STAGE AND TELEVISION TODAY, THE
Theatrefacts - NEW THEATRE QUARTERLY
Theatregoer's Notebook, A - *detailed description of theatre and New York City life column by Kathy Henderson* - PLAYBILL
Theatresurvey - NEW THEATRE QUARTERLY
Theatrical Film Critique - *reviews* - EDUCATIONAL SCREEN
Theatrical Journal - *detailed happenings in Drury Lane, Covent Garden, Haymarket, and minor theatres* - DRAMATIC MAGAZINE, THE
Theatrical World, The - *theatre newsbriefs* - ODDFELLOW, THE
Them - *commentary* - NEWSINC.
Then and Now - *nostalgia* - CELEBRITY
Then and Now - SCREEN STORIES
Theology - *reviews* - HOMILETIC
Theoretical Perspectives on the Arts, Sciences and Technology - LEONARDO
Theory and Practice - DB
There - *commentary* - ST. LOUIS JOURNALISM REVIEW
There is No Substitute for Showmanship - PARAMOUNT WORLD
These Struck Our Fancy - *outstanding showcase for the best in scholastic newspaper journalism* - ADVISER UPDATE

They Never Told Till Now - *'Untold Stories of the Stars' column by Mary Jacobs* - RADIOLAND
They Said It - *quotes* - MEDIA & CONSUMER
They Say-- - *detailed list of productions and positions held by local 659 members* - INTERNATIONAL PHOTOGRAPHER
They Say... - *quotable quotes for writers* - WRITER, THE
They Say - *'Quotes for writers'* - WRITER, THE
They Say in New York - *'Spicy comment about stars in New York' column by Karen Hollis* - PICTURE PLAY MAGAZINE
Things About Testing and Regulating Work - *technical series* - TELEGRAPH WORLD
Things at Hand - *comment* - AMERICAN ADVERTISER REPORTER
Things I Hear - *newsbriefs* - CANADIAN PRINTER
Things They Tell--A Page of 'Em - PEP
Things to Come - *'All the news that's fit to print...and a few items that aren't, courtesy of our globetrotting newshound Tony Crawley' column by Tony Crawley* - STARBURST
Things to Think About - *newsbriefs* - TELEGRAPH WORLD
Things Well Done - ART IN ADVERTISING
Things Worth Knowing - AMERICAN PRESS
Things You Love About [star], The - MOVIE DREAM GUYS
Things [star] Loves About You, The - MOVIE DREAM GUYS
Think Pieces - ABSOLUTE SOUND, THE
Thinking Ahead - VIDEOPRO
Third Eye, The - *column by Lief Ericksenn* - CAMERA 35
Third Eye, The - *column by Lief Ericksenn* - CAMERA 35 INCORPORATING PHOTO WORLD
Third World Perspectives - *fascinating section concerning development of film and relationship to women in new nations* - WOMEN & FILM
This Electronic Age - *cartoon comment* - ELECTRONIC AGE
This Industry - *commentary column by Frank Pope* - PICTURE REPORTS
This is New York - *news* - SHOW BIZ WEST
This Month - PANORAMA
This Month in Cartoons - *outstanding section showcasing best editorial cartoons* - COMIC RELIEF
This Month in the Archive - *new direct mail items added to the Direct Marketing Archive* - WHO'S MAILING WHAT!
This Month on AMC - *'Easy-to-read calendar and alphabetical descriptions for this month's AMC programming'* - AMERICAN MOVIE CLASSICS MAGAZINE
This Month's Disc Jockey - TV SCREEN
This Month's New Releases - *'The only complete guide that lists and describes every new video release every month'* - HOME VIEWER

This Months Releases - *one-line look at British and American releases* - DOCUMENTARY FILM NEWS
This Month's Special Market Lists - *reviews of magazines in specific demographic or speciality areas* - WRITER, THE
This Wacky World - *the world in pictures edited column by Heather Gale* - NATIONAL EXAMINER
This Week - *upcoming events of major importance* - MOVING PICTURES INTERNATIONAL
This Week - *upcoming program column by Paul Droesch* - TV GUIDE
This Week Along the Airialtos - *more inside information concerning New York, Hollywood, and Chicago production centers* - MOVIE-RADIO GUIDE
This Week at the Boxoffice - *gross L.A. and N.Y. receipts* - HOLLYWOOD REPORTER
This Week in Advertising - ADWEEK
This Week in Brief - *small brief reviews* - MOTION PICTURE PRODUCT DIGEST
This Week in Hollywood, - *the lowdown on who's doing what, or would like to* - MOVIE-RADIO GUIDE
This Week in Soap History - *unique look back at historical plots* - SOAP OPERA WEEKLY
This Week in Sports - *'Sports listings'* - SATELLITE TV WEEK
This Week in the News - MOTION PICTURE HERALD
This Week on the Screen - *short synopses of just-released films* - MOVIE-RADIO GUIDE
This Week the Camera Reports: - *photographic news developments* - MOTION PICTURE HERALD
This Week's Movies - *upcoming on broadcast and cable channels column by Art Durbano* - TV GUIDE
This Week's Sports - TV GUIDE
Those Young Pros - *a continuing feature profiling one new photographer* - ASMP BULLETIN
Thought Starters - *short items for competitive radio management* - RADIO ONLY
Thought Waves from the Editorial Tower - RADIO AGE
Thoughts For the Critical Viewer - *'A collection of notes and quotes* - BETTER BROADCASTS NEWS
Through the Enlarging Glass - *'The further adventures of Alice in Advertising-Land'* - AGRICULTURAL ADVERTISING
Thru the Grapevine - *recent projects using Fostex equipment* - ECHO BUSS
Thumbnails - *new product reviews* - PERSONAL PUBLISHING
Thumbs Up! Thumbs Down! - *'Our resident critic hands out her latest blue ribbons and booby prizes for the best and worst achievements on soaps'* - SOAP OPERA DIGEST
Tidbits - *newsbriefs* - KINEMATOGRAPH WEEKLY
Tidings from Talkie Town - *gossip* - TALKING SCREEN

Departments INDEX

Tidings from the Craft - WOODCOCK'S PRINTERS' AND LITHOGRAPHERS' WEEKLY GAZETTE AND NEWSPAPER REPORTER
Tie-In Network - *companies seeking or offering promotional opportunities* - ADWEEK'S MARKETING WEEK
Time $avers & Money Makers - COMMUNICATIONS CONCEPTS
Time & Temp - *'A column on home darkroom' column by Jay Eisen* - LENS MAGAZINE
Time Exposure - POPULAR PHOTOGRAPHY
Timely Topics - *'A digest of current opinion'* - FILM TV DAILY
Timely Topics - NATIONAL ADVERTISING
Times Square Ticket Sales - VARIETY
Timothy Seed's Letters to His Son Who Writes Advertisements - *home-spun advice* - COMMON SENSE
Tin Pan Alleying - *humor and commentary column by Frances Bern* - HIT PARADER
Tinseltown - *Hollywood news* - SHOW BIZ WEST
Tip of the Month - AISLE VIEW
Tip Sheet - WRITER'S DIGEST
Tips - ELECTRONICS ILLUSTRATED
Tips For Successful Selling - *column by Stan Billue* - TELEPROFESSIONAL
Tips for the Trade - *column by Jonathan Kaplan* - MAGAZINE DESIGN & PRODUCTION
Tips from a Pro - *column by Jim Elder* - CAMERA 35
Tips From TEA - *exhibition advice from TEA members* - FILM JOURNAL, THE
Tips from Types - *personality pointers from Crosby Frank* - TALKING SCREEN
Tips of the Month - *short communicator suggestions* - COMMUNICATION BRIEFINGS
Tips to Clip - AV VIDEO
Tips! - *'Readers share their tricks and techniques'* - PUBLISH!
Tipsheet - *reviews* - VIDEO BUSINESS
Tis Here, Maybe! - PROFESSIONAL PHOTOGRAPHER, THE
Title Index - *of television shows* - CABLE GUIDE, THE
Title Troubles - *Q&A technical column by George Cushman* - HOME MOVIES
Titles of Recent Publications - TELEPHONE MAGAZINE
TM at Large - *invited commentary on direct marketing issues* - TARGET MARKETING
TM Gallery - *pix* - TARGET MARKETING
To Buy - *current product* - VIDEO--THE MAGAZINE
To Correspondents - *letters* - JOURNALIST, THE
To Correspondents - *letters* - ODDFELLOW, THE
To Rent - *available videotapes* - VIDEO--THE MAGAZINE
To Speak of Many Things - *newsbriefs* - SPEECH COMMUNICATION TEACHER, THE
To Tell the Truth - *'Do you want the real inside story?'* - SCREEN STORIES
To the Editor - ADVERTISING & SELLING
To the Editor - *unusually long letters dealing with writers complaints* - AUTHOR, THE
To the Editor - *popular bandleader comment* - HIT PARADER
To the Industry - TELECONNECT
Today and Tomorrow - *comment* - STORY WORLD AND PHOTODRAMATIST, THE
Today's Movies - *reviews* - MOVIE DIGEST
Today's Photographer - SCHOLASTIC EDITOR'S TRENDS IN PUBLICATIONS
Tomorrow - INTERVIEW
Tomorrow Things - *technology to come* - HOME ENTERTAINMENT
Tomorrow's Photographers - *youth column by Norris Harkness* - TRAVEL & LEISURE
Tomorrow's World - *comment* - SF MOVIELAND
Tonearms - SOUND & VISION
Tonight on Broadway - RADIO ALBUM MAGAZINE
Too Hot to Handle - *Q&A* - MODERN PHOTOGRAPHY
Too Hot to Print - *adult cartoons not accepted by other publications* - BEHIND THE SCENE
Too Late to Classify - *late newsbriefs* - MOVIE/TV MARKETING
Tool Aid - *'Tools and accessories for professional installers and the do-it-yourselfer' column by Pat Turnmire* - CAR STEREO REVIEW
Tools and Techniques - *'A round-up of recent developments and significant trends' column by Norman C. Lipton* - POPULAR PHOTOGRAPHY
Tools & Techniques - POPULAR PHOTOGRAPHY
Tools and Tips - *ideas for videographers* - VIDEOMAKER
Tools of the Trade - *technical review* - INTERNATIONAL PHOTOGRAPHER
Tools of the Trade - *newsbriefs* - KODAK PROFESSIONAL FORUM
Tools of the Trade - MEDIAWEEK
Tools of the Trade - *equipment* - PETERSEN'S PHOTOGRAPHIC
Toons on Tape - *videocassette releases* - ANIMATO!
Top 10 Videos - *'Rental and sales charts'* - CINEMA, VIDEO & CABLE MOVIE DIGEST
Top 15 Bestselling Titles - VIDEO MAGAZINE
Top 20 Albums - *record statistics* - CASTING NEWS
Top 20 Films - *current statistics* - CASTING NEWS
Top 20 Video Rentals - *current statistics* - CASTING NEWS
Top 25 Hot Picks - *'Now playing in your store'* - HOME VIEWER
Top 40 - R & R
Top Album Picks - *annotated review of 50 major albums* - BILLBOARD
Top Classical Albums - BILLBOARD
Top Contemporary Jazz Albums - BILLBOARD
Top Country Albums - BILLBOARD
Top Crossover Albums - BILLBOARD
Top Drawer - *graphic review of new printed materials* - PRINT
Top Drawer--News from the Whole Field of the Graphic Arts - *newsbriefs* - PRINT
Top Jazz Albums - BILLBOARD
Top LPs and Tape - *playlist* - BILLBOARD
Top Music Videos - BILLBOARD
Top News - NETWORK WORLD
Top of Mind - *noteworthy advertising newsbriefs* - AGENCY
Top of the Charts - *top rentals* - SPOTLIGHT ON VIDEO
Top of the Pile - *record releases* - AUDIO
Top of the Review - WASHINGTON JOURNALISM REVIEW
Top Pop Albums - BILLBOARD
Top R&B Albums - BILLBOARD
Top Single Picks - *similar annotation* - BILLBOARD
Top Tapes - ENTERTAINMENT WEEKLY
Top Ten - *current hits in pop/rock, jazz, and classical categories* - CD REVIEW
Top Tracks - *music videos* - MILLIMETER
Top TV Programs - *ratings survey* - TELEVISION / RADIO AGE INTERNATIONAL
Top Video Rentals - BILLBOARD
Top Video Sales - BILLBOARD
Top Videodisc Sales - BILLBOARD
Topics for Gossip - SILVER SCREEN
Topics of Technical Interest - ABU NEWSLETTER
Tops in Singles - *chart* - TV RADIO MIRROR
Toronto - BOX OFFICE
Torture Garden - *enlightened comment on good and not so good comic releases, column by Mark D. Sard* - ARK
Total Truth!, The - *Q&A on teenage stars* - SUPER TEEN
Tots and Teens Dramatics - THEATRE CRAFT
Tour News - STAGE AND TELEVISION TODAY, THE
Toward More Successful Selling - TELEPROFESSIONAL
Tracer Tracks - *The top 40 most played songs, 'Breakouts provided include the total number of plays, reach index (gross impressions), increase percentages, along with the leaders in airplay and most added stations'* - MONDAY MORNING REPLAY
Tracks - BACK STAGE/SHOOT
Tracks - *facility listing* - REP: RECORDING ENGINEERING PRODUCTION
Trade Catalogues Received - CANADIAN PHOTOGRAPHIC JOURNAL, THE
Trade Editors Analyze Business Conditions - ADVERTISING & SELLING
Trade Fair Report - SHUTTERBUG
Trade Flashes - *new technologies newsbriefs* - ELECTRONIC SERVICING & TECHNOLOGY
Trade Mark Department - *new radio trademarks accepted by the Patent Office* - RADIO DEALER, THE
Trade News - CANADIAN PRINTER
Trade News - CINEMA/CANADA
Trade News - *newsbriefs* - INDEPENDENT PUBLISHERS TRADE REPORT

Trade News - NATIONAL STATIONER, THE
Trade News - *newsbriefs* - PUBLISHER'S WEEKLY
Trade News - SATELLITE COMMUNICATIONS
Trade News - TRAVEL & LEISURE
Trade Notes and News - POPULAR PHOTOGRAPHY
Trade Notices - WOODCOCK'S PRINTERS' AND LITHOGRAPHERS' WEEKLY GAZETTE AND NEWSPAPER REPORTER
Trade Paper Releases - *list* - HOT PICKS
Trade Papers - CURRENT ADVERTISING
Trade Personals - TELEVISION DIGEST WITH CONSUMER ELECTRONICS
Trade Reports - BRITISH LITHOGRAPHER
Trade Secrets - *column by Daniel Will-Harris* - DESKTOP COMMUNICATIONS
Trade Secrets - *'Tidbits and tales from behind the scenes!'* - SOAP OPERA UPDATE
Trade Show Calendar - INVIEW
Trade Shows - IN MOTION FILM & VIDEO PRODUCTION MAGAZINE
Trade Shows - MARKETING NEWS
Trade Shows - SALES & MARKETING MANAGEMENT
Trade Shows - *upcoming* - WESTERN PHOTOGRAPHER MAGAZINE
Trade Talk - *one-line report of personnel changes* - ART DIRECTION
Trade Talk - *newsbriefs* - PROFESSIONAL PHOTOGRAPHER, THE
Trade Tidbits - *newsbriefs column by Ray Gallo* - GREATER AMUSEMENTS
Trade Winds - ELECTRONICS AND COMMUNICATIONS
Trade Winds - *'Hi-Fi World brings you all the latest news from the hi-fi industry'* - HI-FI WORLD
Tradewinds - *production activities* - INTERNATIONAL PHOTOGRAPHER
Trading Post - PSA JOURNAL
Trailers - *films in progress* - AMERICAN FILM
Training - IN-PLANT PRINTER & ELECTRONIC PUBLISHER
Training - PRESSTIME
Tramps - *status report of hoboes showing up at various newspaper offices* - WOODCOCK'S PRINTERS' AND LITHOGRAPHERS' WEEKLY GAZETTE AND NEWSPAPER REPORTER
Transfusions - *personnel newsbriefs* - PULSE OF RADIO
Transition - *personnel changes by geographic location* - PUBLISHER'S AUXILIARY
Transitions - NATIONAL AMATEUR
Transmission - TELEVISION BROADCAST
Transmissions - VIA SATELLITE
Transpacific - *column by Sally Taylor* - PUBLISHER'S WEEKLY
Transponder Service Watch - *services listed by satellite* - ONSAT
Transponder Service Watch - *programming schedule by transponder* - STV GUIDE
Transportation - PRESSTIME
Travel - WORLD PRESS REVIEW

Travel and Adventure Block Bookers - PERFORMER, THE
Travel & Camera - *one-page travel section* - TRAVEL & LEISURE
Travel & Leisure - LÜRZER'S INTERNATIONAL ARCHIVE
Travel and Workshops - *upcoming events calendar* - OUTDOOR PHOTOGRAPHER
Travel Briefs - WORLD PRESS REVIEW
Travel Department, The - DRAMA MAGAZINE, THE
Travel Guide - *videocassette review* - MOVIEGUIDE
Travel Guide - *unusual photography-oriented section* - TRAVEL & LEISURE
Travel Log - *whereabouts of major media individuals* - HOLLYWOOD REPORTER
Travel Sketch - THEATRE MAGAZINE
Travelers' Network - *food favorites across America* - SALES & MARKETING MANAGEMENT
Traveling Shots - *newsbriefs on film and filmmakers* - AFVA BULLETIN
Trend of Radio Broadcasting - BROADCAST REPORTER
Trend of Radio Regulation - *column by Paul M. Segal* - JOURNAL OF RADIO LAW
Trend Watch - REP: RECORDING ENGINEERING PRODUCTION
Trendicators - *'For the brokers of popular culture'* - MEDIAWEEK
Trendicators - *'Influential ideas in brief marketing newsbriefs* - RADIOTRENDS
Trendletter - BUSINESS ADVERTISING
Trends - AMERICAN THEATRE
Trends - EDITOR'S WORKSHOP
Trends - *in direct mail* - WHO'S MAILING WHAT!
Trends and Ideas - *newsbriefs* - HIGH VOLUME PRINTING
Trends & Technology - PERSONAL ELECTRONICS
Trends Line - *newsbriefs* - SCHOLASTIC EDITOR'S TRENDS IN PUBLICATIONS
Tribal Rites - *the stars out together* - MOVIELINE
Tributary Theatre, The - THEATRE MAGAZINE
Tried, Tested, Approved - RANGEFINDER, THE
Trim Bin - *who is editing what listing, column by Bob Bring* - AMERICAN CINEMEDITOR
Trim Bin - *newsbriefs* - MILLIMETER
Trivia - SPOTLIGHT ON VIDEO
Trivia Game - MOVIELINE
Trivia Questions - SOAP OPERA DIGEST
Troubleshooting - BROADCAST ENGINEERING
Troubleshooting - *column by David Navone* - CAR AUDIO AND ELECTRONICS
Troubleshooting - VIDEO TIMES
Try This One! - *'original kinks' from readers* - RADIO-ELECTRONICS
T-Shirt Reviews - FACTSHEET FIVE
Tube Talk - *column by Robin Keats* - SH-BOOM
Tuned In - *corporate changes newsbriefs* - BUYERS GUIDE

Tuned In - *'Every week, a station from each of the formats is featured. Tuned In breaks out music, promotional activity, positioning and account information'* - MONDAY MORNING REPLAY
Tuneful Topics - *Hit radio songs column by Rudy Vallee* - RADIO FAN-FARE
Tuners - SOUND & VISION
Tunes to Go - *column by Doug Newcomb* - CAR AUDIO AND ELECTRONICS
Tuning In - *upcoming program fare* - SATELLITE ORBIT
Turning Point - *column by Glenn Plaskin* - SPOTLIGHT CASTING MAGAZINE
Turn-table Tidbits - *'The inside track on the music makers!* - MODERN SCREEN
Turntables - SOUND & VISION
Tuscon - BOX OFFICE
Tutorial - *'Tutorials at various levels and on various aspects of broadcast engineering and operation'* - IBE
Tutorial - *how-to column* - TELECONNECT
TV - INTERVIEW
TV - *review and commentary column by Frank Marcus* - PLAYS INTERNATIONAL
TV Advertisers - ADVERTISER MAGAZINE, THE
TV & Movie Scoops - PHOTO SCREEN
TV & Radio - ADVERTISING AGENCY
TV Auction - *television memorabilia for sale* - TELEVISION HISTORY
TV Briefs - *news items* - BUSINESS OF FILM, THE
TV Business Barometer - TELEVISION/RADIO AGE
TV Checklist - *'For collectors and researchers'* - TELEVISION HISTORY
TV Circles - *word list puzzle column by Gayle Discoe* - ONSAT
TV Close-Ups With Polly Wright - *column by Polly Wright* - TV PICTURE LIFE
TV Commercial Production - *briefs* - BACK STAGE
TV Connection - MOVIE FLASH
TV Consoles (floor-standing) - SOUND & VISION
TV Crossword - ONSAT
TV Cuts - ART DIRECTION
TV Den - *understanding equipment* - VIDEO MAGAZINE
TV Diner - *tube-viewing recipes* - HOME VIEWER
TV Direc - *television news* - AP BROADCASTER
TV Film - AMERICAN PREMIERE
TV Gallery - *pictorial section* - TV GOLD
TV Guide Insider - *'What's happening, who's hot in television today'* - TV GUIDE
TV Guide Plus - *late breaking news* - TV GUIDE
TV Letters - *'What do you like in TV World? What are your gripes?'* - TV WORLD
TV Line - *newsbriefs* - LINE MONITOR, THE
TV Mail Bag - *letters* - TV PEOPLE AND PICTURES
TV Monitor/Receivers, Portable TV - SOUND & VISION
TV News - *newsbriefs concerning television* - R & R

Departments INDEX 866

T.V. News & Views - *column by Doug Deutsch* - SHOWCASE WORLD
TV Pen Pals - *'Make TV friends through TV Guide'* - TV GUIDE
TV Picture - *news items concerning Arbitron and its rating service* - BEYOND THE RATINGS/RADIO
TV Picture Life's Personality of the Month - *Artist profile* - TV PICTURE LIFE
TV Program Highlights - TV MIRROR
TV Programming and Production for Profit - *successful video productions* - BME'S TELEVISION ENGINEERING
TV Pro-Log Digest - *'Television programs and production news'* - ROSS REPORTS TELEVISION
TV Puzzlers - *puzzles* - NIGHTTIME TV
TV Quarterly Standings - IMAGE 11
TV Radio Show's Personality of the Month - TV RADIO SHOW
TV Radio Talk - *celebrity profile* - TV RADIO TALK
TV Radio Talk Goes to the Movies - *column by Marjorie Rosen* - TV RADIO TALK
TV Ratings - *of prior weeks broadcasts* - CAMPAIGN
TV Review - HOLLYWOOD REPORTER
TV Scoops & Secrets - *'Inside gossip and exclusive photos of your favorite stars' via Cleo* - TV RADIO SHOW
TV Spotlight - *review column by Norma McLain Stoop* - AFTER DARK
TV Spotlight - *review* - SHOW
TV Station Representatives - BILLBOARD TV PROGRAM AND TIME AVAILABILITIES, THE
TV Talk - *'Missives from the TV Generation' letters* - TV GOLD
TV Tattler - *'Wherein your favorite TV stars confide in Joe on matters pertaining to love, marriage, career and other items of a highly personal nature' column by Joe Cal Cagno* - TV PEOPLE AND PICTURES
TV Teasers - *crossword* - TV GUIDE
TV Topics - *covering television news* - NEWS PHOTOGRAPHER
TV Trivia Quiz - TV GOLD
TV Zone - *column by Richard Holliss* - STARBURST
TvB Report - CLIO MAGAZINE
TV--Behind the Screens - *celebrity news* - NATIONAL ENQUIRER
TVCR Highlights - *broadcast review* - HOME VIEWER
TV/Video Corner - *newsbriefs* - AFVA BULLETIN
Tweaky Corner - HI-FI WORLD
Type Drawer - PERSONAL PUBLISHING
Type Style - *typography column by Edward F. Henninger* - COMPUTER PUBLISHING
Type-Lice - *typos and fluffs in area media* - FEED-BACK
Type-ology - *'For the advancement of technical printing knowledge among non-printer advertisers'* - AMERICAN ADVERTISER
Typesetting - *new technologies and processes* - POLYGRAPH INTERNATIONAL

Typothatae Topics - MID-ATLANTIC GRAPHIC ARTS REVIEW
Typothetae Activities - CANADIAN PRINTER

U

UK Box Office - *report* - SCREEN INTERNATIONAL
UK News - *current work by artist and corporate group* - ARK
Ultra-Short Waves - RADIO & TELEVISION
UN Perspective - *United Nations activities in film and video* - WORLD BROADCAST NEWS
Unbiased - *personality column by Free Grid* - ELECTRONICS WORLD + WIRELESS WORLD
Uncensored - *'Straight from the lips of the stars'* - SILVER SCREEN
Uncle Skip's Corner - *column by TJ 'Skip' Arey* - MONITORING TIMES
Uncle Tom's Corner - *technical Q&A column by Tom Kneitel* - ELECTRONICS ILLUSTRATED
Under $20 - *videocassettes for sale* - V
Under Hedda's Hat - *column by Hedda Hopper* - MOTION PICTURE
Under Hedda's Hat - *gossip column by Hedda Hopper* - PHOTOPLAY
Under the Cover - *editorial* - STUDIO PHOTOGRAPHY
Under the Covers - *interview* - AV VIDEO
Under the Covers - *column by Flavia Knightsbridge* - ROMANTIC TIMES
Under the Crossarm - *news of locals* - TELEGRAPH WORLD
Underground - *independent cinema review column by David E. Williams* - FILM THREAT
Underground Astrologer, The - *column by Barry Brownlee* - DRAMA-LOGUE
Understanding Computers - *column by Jeff Burger* - REP: RECORDING ENGINEERING PRODUCTION
U-Net Program Profile - COLLEGE BROADCASTER
Unfinished Business - *letters* - COLUMBIA JOURNALISM REVIEW
Union Activities - TELECOMMUNICATION JOURNAL
Union Film & TV - *now casting* - DRAMA-LOGUE
Union Quarterly - *broadcast union news items* - TV TECHNOLOGY
Unions and Guilds - *information on joining* - SHOW BUSINESS
Universal Moviegrams - *newsbriefs as regards Universal releases* - UNIVERSAL WEEKLY
Universal Release Dates - EXHIBITORS' TIMES
Unusual Assignment - PHOTO DISTRICT NEWS

Up and Down the Alley - *music news and personalities column by E.T. Dawson* - EXHIBITORS HERALD WORLD
Up Close & Personal - *artist or business profile column by Ray Waddell* - AMUSEMENT BUSINESS
Up Front - *brief review of current issue* - AMUSEMENT BUSINESS
Up Front - *commentary* - AV VIDEO
Up Front - *editorial column by David Anthony Kraft* - COMICS INTERVIEW
Up Front - *editorial column by Jonah McLeod* - ELECTRONICS
Up Front - *reviews* - FILMS ILLUSTRATED
Up Front - ON CABLE
Up Front - *commentary* - PRE-
Up Front - *new album releases* - PRO SOUND NEWS
Up the Mailbox - *'What you have to say about the stars!'* - GOSSIP
Up Through A Century - *newspaper history profiles* - FOURTH ESTATE
Upcoming - *calendar* - VUE
Upcoming Events - MEDIA ETHICS UPDATE
Upcoming Events Calendar - VIDEO TIMES
Upcoming Illustrator - *profile* - ART DIRECTION
Upcoming Meetings - AES
Upcoming Meetings - CLIO AMONG THE MEDIA
Upcoming Photographer - *profile* - ART DIRECTION
Upcoming Projects - BUSINESS AND THE MEDIA
Upcoming Seminars & Workshops - BOARD REPORT FOR GRAPHIC ARTISTS
Update - *newsbriefs* - ADVANCED IMAGING
Update - BME'S TELEVISION ENGINEERING
Update - *artist projects* - BMI: MUSICWORLD
Update - *newsbriefs* - BROADCASTER
Update - CABLEVISION
Update - ELECTRONICS WORLD + WIRELESS WORLD
Update - EMMY
Update - *'News & notes from the world of modern recording and knob twisting'* - EQ
Update - *news briefs* - FOLIO:
Update - FRENDX
Update - *new products and newsbriefs* - HI-FI CHOICE
Update - *news of film and video industry* - IMAGE TECHNOLOGY
Update - *'News & Notes'* - INSIDE MEDIA
Update - MEDIAWEEK
Update - *animation newsbriefs* - PEGBAR
Up-Date - *'People and products in the news' column by Sally Whiddett* - PRACTICAL PHOTOGRAPHY
Update - *newsbriefs* - SCRIPPS HOWARD NEWS
Update - *newsbriefs* - 60 SECONDS
Update Section - *media briefs* - INTERNATIONAL ADVERTISER
Update... Update... - *newsbriefs* - SOAP OPERA UPDATE
Updates - *'The latest imaging news in brief'* - ADVANCED IMAGING
Updates - *newsbriefs concerning new product updates* - PERSONAL PUBLISHING

Updates - *'Writer's Northwest Handbook' publication opportunities* - WRITER'S NW NEWS
Upfront - *issue column by Rachel Kaplan* - INSIDE MEDIA
Upfront - *album engineering list* - PRO SOUND NEWS
Upgrading Letter Copy - *advice column by Paul Bringe* - DIRECT MARKETING
UPI Newsroom, The - *'Editorial staff promotions, new assignments, new hires'* - UPI ADVANCE
UPI Radio Roundup - *newsbriefs* - UPI ADVANCE
Uplink Downlink - *letters to editor* - STV GUIDE
Upper Mid Range - *chart and products* - DIGITAL EVOLUTION MAGAZINE
Urban Contemporary - *radio format column by Walt Love* - R & R
US Box Office - *report* - SCREEN INTERNATIONAL
U.S. Patents Relating to Photography - *excellent resource section 'Compiled from Patent Office Gazette'* - CAMERA, THE
USA - *production newsbriefs* - PRODUCCIÓN Y DISTRIBUCIÓN
USA News - *current work by artist and corporate group* - ARK
USA Scene, The - *animation news from the States column by John Crawley* - ANIMATOR
USA-CA - CQ
Usage & Applications - COMMUNICATIONSWEEK
Usage Forum - EDITORIAL EYE, THE
USC CineVision News - *newsbriefs concerning USC campus* - SPECTATOR, THE
Used Equipment - FILMMAKERS FILM & VIDEO MONTHLY
User Friendly - IN MOTION FILM & VIDEO PRODUCTION MAGAZINE
User Profile - BROADCAST SYSTEMS INTERNATIONAL
User Report - BUYERS GUIDE
User Report - TV TECHNOLOGY
User Review - COLLEGE BROADCASTER
User's Evaluations - *unique equipment review* - CAR STEREO REVIEW
Users' Forum - *BBS letters* - VENTURA LETTER, THE
Using Type - PERSONAL PUBLISHING
Utility World - *Utility news column by Larry Van Horn* - MONITORING TIMES

V

Vacuum Tube, The - OLD TIMER'S BULLETIN, THE
Valerie's Gallery News - *awards, competitions, galleries* - IMAGE

Valuation list - *of equipment* - OLD TIMER'S BULLETIN, THE
Vancouver - BOX OFFICE
Vanity Box, The - *column by Anne Archbald* - THEATRE MAGAZINE
Vantage Point - ELECTRONIC DESIGN
Variety Artists - *auditions and needed* - CASTING NEWS
Variety Buzz - *news, rumors and rumblings column by Michael Fleming* - VARIETY
Variety Club Notes - SHOWMEN'S TRADE REVIEW
Variety Show of the Month - SHOW
Variety Stage, The - *'by Box and Cox'* - STAGE AND SPORT
Variety Top 50 Video Titles - *'Variety's survey of rental transactions'* - VARIETY
Vaudeville - *review* - THEATRE MAGAZINE
Vaudeville Volleys - *review of current vaudeville fare* - DRAMATIC MIRROR, THE
VCR Alert - *'A handy guide to must-see episodes'* - SOAP OPERA DIGEST
VCRs (Videocassette Recorders) - SOUND & VISION
Vegas Tracks - *news* - SHOW BIZ WEST
Veleka Advises - *love-and-life advice* - SOAP OPERA DIGEST
Ventura Pipeline User Tips - SCSC XEROX PIPELINE
Ventura-ing - *product hints* - VENTURA LETTER, THE
Ventures in Advertising - PEP
Vermont - BOX OFFICE
Vertical Markets - *column by Mayrose Wood* - DESKTOP COMMUNICATIONS
Very Idea, The - *various direct-mail ideas* - MAILBAG, THE
Veteran Wireless Operators Association News - COMMUNICATION AND BROADCAST ENGINEERING
Veteran Wireless Operators' Association News - TELEVISION ENGINEERING
VHF - CQ
VHF + Technology - *column by Geoff Krauss* - QEX
VHF Plus - *'All about the world above HF', column by Joe Lynch* - CQ
Victorian A.B.C. Highlights - ABC WEEKLY
Vidbeat - *column by Chrissy Iley* - DIRECTION
Vidbits - *newsbriefs column by Glenn Kenny* - VIDEO BUSINESS
Vide Tape - SOUND & VISION
Video - *column by Ken Jurek* - AVC
Video - *new product review* - DRAMATICS
Video - FOCUS ON FILM
Video - HYPERMEDIA
Video - INSIDE ENTERTAINMENT
Video - *new releases and current talk* - MOVIELINE
Video - *'Fast forward or rewind? We review this weeks releases'* - TV GUIDE
Video - *review column by Rupert Smith* - 20/20
Video 8 Programming - *large section guide to business applications video* - BUSINESSTV VIDEO 8 GUIDE
Video Accessories - SOUND & VISION
Video and Audio Bestsellers - VIDEO ALERT

Video Around the World - *reviews* - VIDEO WATCHDOG
Video Art - *using video as a paintbrush* - VIDEOGRAPHY
Video Beat - *column by Jim McCullaugh* - VIDEO TIMES
Video Briefs - *newsbriefs* - VIDEO BUSINESS
Video Buyer - *large 25 page section on current and older releases* - VIDEO BUYER
Video Cassette Report - *column by Myles Callum* - TV GUIDE
Video Classic - *classic films on tape* - VIDEO WORLD
Video Classics - *review* - AMERICAN FILM
Video Clinic - *'Paul Richards ponders your problems'* - WHAT VIDEO
Video Clips - *'The best of the rest of this month's videos reviewed by Sarah Lewis' column by Sarah Lewis* - VIDEO TIMES
Video Conferencing - CORPORATE VIDEO DECISIONS
Video Dog House - *horror films in videocassette release* - DEEP RED
Video Enthusiast, The - *commentary column by Jeff Edmonds* - VIDEO CHOICE
Video Equipment - *reviews* - BROADCAST SYSTEMS ENGINEERING
Video Equipment - *column by Henry B. Cohen* - V
Video File - *column by Barry Forshaw* - STARBURST
Video Film Scene - *column by Jack Behrend* - INDUSTRIAL PHOTOGRAPHY
Video First - *direct-to-tape releases* - HOME VIEWER
Video For Hire - *column by Kristin Tucker* - VIDEOMAKER
Video for Kids - VIDEO SOFTWARE MAGAZINE
Video Guide - *'The critical guide to this months major rental releases'* - FILM REVIEW
Video Hit Parade - *'The best of what's new this month for your VCR' colorful review section* - HOME VIEWER
Video Horror - VIDEO SOFTWARE MAGAZINE
Video Hotline - *'All the latest on the video front' column by Dorothy Rosa* - VIDEO CHOICE
Video Hunter - VIDEO REVIEW
Video Illustrated - *news items* - HOME VIEWER
Video Invasion, The - *column by Bob Keller* - WESTERN PHOTOGRAPHER MAGAZINE
Video Journal - *column by Tony Galluzzo* - MODERN PHOTOGRAPHY
Video Lab Test - HIGH FIDELITY/MUSICAL AMERICA
Video Lawyer - *comment* - VIDEO EIGHTIES MAGAZINE
Video Methods - *feature* - PHOTOMETHODS
Video Movies - MODERN PHOTOGRAPHY
Video Music - *music video hit list* - R & R
Video Music - *column by Barry Gutman* - VIDEO INSIDER
Video News - CAMERART
Video News - IN MOTION FILM & VIDEO PRODUCTION MAGAZINE
Video News - ON LOCATION

Departments INDEX 868

Video News - *'What's new in this fast-changing field'* column by David Lachenbruch - RADIO-ELECTRONICS
Video Notes - *newsbriefs* - VIDEO WEEK
deo Parade - *Films available on video cassette* - BIG REEL, THE
Video People: Recent Deals - *news column by John Sarna* - CABLE TV AND NEW MEDIA LAW & FINANCE
Video Photographer, The - *column by Taumas Jacobs* - VIDEO CHOICE
Video Picks - *new cassette releases* - VIDEO REVIEW
Video Playback - *developments in video* - AFVA BULLETIN
Video Post - *technical information* - ON LOCATION
Video Programmer - *comment* - VIDEO MAGAZINE
Video Q+A - *column by Stuart Sweetow* - VIDEOMAKER
Video Rental Top 50 - MOVIE - THE VIDEO MAGAZINE
Video Research - VIDEOGRAPHY
Video Resources - *software reviews* - VIDEO MANAGEMENT
Video Response - VIDEOPLAY MAGAZINE
Video Review - DWB
Video Review - RADIO ALBUM MAGAZINE
Video Review - SPEECH AND DRAMA
Video Reviews - BOOKSTORE JOURNAL
Video Reviews - *critique* - ENTERTAINMENT WEEKLY
Video Reviews - FACTSHEET FIVE
Video Reviews - FILM LIBRARY QUARTERLY
Video Reviews - FILM REVIEW
Video Room - *new technology info column by Jill MacNeice* - ORBIT VIDEO
Video Scenes - *comment column by Bert Whyte* - AUDIO
Video Sleeper - HORRORFAN
Video Speed Servicing Systems - ELECTRONIC SERVICING & TECHNOLOGY
Video Stories - *commentary column by Van Wallach* - VIDEO STORE
Video Takes - *news of independent producers* - ON LOCATION
Video Tomorrow - *'Video Today looking at tomorrows video'* - VIDEO TODAY
Video Track - *music video production news by city* - BILLBOARD
Video Tracking - *'Fast forwarding the stars'* - V
Video Trends - *column by Rod Woodcock* - CAMCORDER
Video Update - ADWEEK'S MARKETING WEEK
Video Update - *column by George Cole* - PRACTICAL PHOTOGRAPHY
Video Vibes - *column by Amy Appleton* - V
Video View - *'Film Monthly's guide to the latest video releases'* - FILM MONTHLY
Video View - TV ENTERTAINMENT
Video Views - *column by Nancy Collins* - AMAZING HEROES
Video Views - *comment* - MOVIE MARKETPLACE

Video Views - *'A selection of the very latest movies on video viewed and reviewed for content, style and value for money!'* - VIDEO MONTHLY
Video Views - *column* - VIDEO REVIEW
Video Views! - *new film/video releases column by Bob Schartoff* - SUPER TEEN
Video Vigilante - HOME VIDEO
Video Watchdog® - *video releases column by Tim Lucas* - GOREZONE
Video World Wordsearch - VIDEO WORLD
Video2 - *television lighting column by Bill Holshevnikoff* - VIDEO SYSTEMS
Video/Audio - INVIEW
Video/Audio Services - *satellite programming in alphabetical order* - STV GUIDE
Videocassettes and Discs - *column by David Lachenbruch* - PANORAMA
Videocast Previews - *upcoming broadcasts on TV and cable* - HOME VIDEO
Videoconferencing - VIDEO MANAGEMENT
Video-Conferencing - VIDEO TECHNOLOGY NEWS
Videocrafts - *column by Hal Burke* - VIDEOMAKER
Videodical - *trends and technoligies* - ORBIT VIDEO
Videodisc (Laservision) Combi Players - SOUND & VISION
Videodisc Update - MEDIA & METHODS
Videofile - *'In case you missed it on the big screen'* - MOVIES USA
Videofile - *'A round-up of the latest releases of the unusual, fantastic, horrific and probably out of this world'* - STARBURST
Videofun - *puzzle* - VIDEOPLAY MAGAZINE
Videogram - *newsbriefs* - VIDEO MAGAZINE
Videographics - IN MOTION FILM & VIDEO PRODUCTION MAGAZINE
Videography - STUDIO PHOTOGRAPHY
Videology - *'Exploring the science of video* - VIDEO MAGAZINE
Videonews - VIDEO TECHNOLOGY NEWS
Videopeople - HOME VIDEO
VideoplayPourri - *newsbriefs* - VIDEOPLAY MAGAZINE
Videos - *previews, new releases and best buys* - FANTASY ZONE
Videos - *new videos for sale or rental* - SATELLITE ORBIT
Videos to Buy - EMPIRE
Videos to Rent - EMPIRE
Videoscan - *'Rare and unusual video releases'* - FILMFAX
Videosphere - *news items, article-length book reviews on television* - MEDIA MIX
Videosphere - SHOW
Video-Syncrasy - *column by Alan G. Barbour* - FILMS IN REVIEW
Videotape - FILMMAKERS FILM & VIDEO MONTHLY
Videotapes - ART & DESIGN NEWS
Videotapes/Discs - *Reviews* - HOME VIDEO
Videotech Update - ELECTRONIC MEDIA
VideoTests - *very detailed comparisons* - VIDEO MAGAZINE
Videotests - *extensive lab/consumer reviews* - VIDEO MAGAZINE

Videotimes - *newsbriefs* - HOME VIDEO
Videowares - *equipment reviews* - HOME VIDEO
Videozone - *reviews* - STRANGE ADVENTURES
Vidfile - *star profile with film/video credits* - TV HITS
Vienna - *city review column by Ron Dobrin* - AFTER DARK
View Finder - PHOTO/DESIGN
View From Arizona, The - *column by Ron Wilhelm* - WESTERN PHOTOGRAPHER MAGAZINE
View From the Top - *guest commentary* - PRO SOUND NEWS
View From Twin Shore, The - *'A biased look at European Trash Cinema', column by Pompano Joe Torrez* - EUROPEAN TRASH CINEMA
Viewable Hammer, The - *Hammer film video review column by Gary Smith* - LITTLE SHOPPE OF HORRORS
Viewed - VIDEO EIGHTIES MAGAZINE
Viewer Mail - *letters* - C-SPAN UPDATE
Viewer Mail - *letters* - HOME VIEWER
Viewers' Voice - *'Who's hot & who's not?'* - SOAP OPERA WEEKLY
Viewfinder - *'Photo news & events'* column by Franklin Cameron - PETERSEN'S PHOTOGRAPHIC
Viewfinder - *profile* - PHOTOGRAPHER'S MARKET NEWSLETTER
Viewfinder - *a forum for comment* - VIDEO SYSTEMS
Viewfinder - *editorial column by Matthew York* - VIDEOMAKER
Viewing Summary - *ratings data* - BROADCAST
Viewpoint - ACCESS
Viewpoint - *editorial* - BME'S TELEVISION ENGINEERING
Viewpoint - DEALERSCOPE
Viewpoint - *letters* - DIRECTION
Viewpoint - ELECTRONIC MEDIA
Viewpoint - EMMY
Viewpoint - *commentary* - FA
Viewpoint - INFORMATION TODAY
Viewpoint - *guest column* - INSIDE MEDIA
Viewpoint - *guest commentary* - INTERNATIONAL JOURNAL OF INFORMATION MANAGEMENT
Viewpoint - MARKETING NEWS
Viewpoint - *editorial* - PHOTO LAB MANAGEMENT
Viewpoint - POPULAR PHOTOGRAPHY
Viewpoint - PROFESSIONAL PHOTOGRAPHER, THE
Viewpoint - PROMOTION
Viewpoint - *guest commentary* - SALES & MARKETING MANAGEMENT
Viewpoint - *'Readers letters'* - SATELLITE TIMES
Viewpoint - SCRIPPS HOWARD NEWS
Viewpoint - STEP-BY-STEP GRAPHICS
Viewpoint - STUDIO PHOTOGRAPHY
Viewpoint - *column by Richard Brooks* - TELEVISION WEEK
Viewpoint - VIA SATELLITE
Viewpoint - VIDEO REVIEW

INDEX — Departments

Viewpoint - *commentary column by Barry Fox* - WHAT SATELLITE
Viewpoints - *editorial* - ABSOLUTE SOUND, THE
Viewpoints - *'Editorial notes'* - PERFECT VISION, THE
Viewpoints - *guest articles by major broadcast executives* - TELEVISION/RADIO AGE
Viewpoints - *editorial* - VIDEO REVIEW
Views - *comment* - CREATIVE CAMERA
Views - HI-FI NEWS AND RECORD REVIEW
Views From the States - *state roundup of news concerning freedom of information* - ACCESS REPORTS/FREEDOM OF INFORMATION
Views of the New Short Subjects - SHOWMEN'S TRADE REVIEW
Vintage Catalog - *other mailorder items of a similar nature* - FLASHBACK
Vintage Variety - *headlines of yesteryear* - VARIETY
Vintage Video - CINEMA, VIDEO & CABLE MOVIE DIGEST
Vintage Viewfinder - *historical* - PETERSEN'S PHOTOGRAPHIC
Visible Videos - *music videos* - POST
Vision 1250 Production Projects - HDTV REPORT
Visual Commentary - PRINT
Visual Music - MUSIC LINE
Visual Publications - *product newsbriefs* - COMIC READER, THE
VO News - *briefs on voice-over work* - ENTERTAINMENT MONTHLY
Voice Doctor, The - *column by Jeannie Deva* - CASTING NEWS
Voice of the Box Office, The - *'How the latest releases are being received throughout the country'* - EXHIBITORS TRADE REVIEW
Voice of the Industry, The - *'Letters from readers'* - EXHIBITORS HERALD WORLD
Voice of the Listener - *letters* - RADIO FANFARE
Voice Over - *commentary* - AFVA BULLETIN
Voided Snoid, The - *'Video column by Mike Betker'* - COMIC INFORMER
Volunteers - BROADCAST PIONEERS LIBRARY REPORTS
Vox Jox - *column by Sean Ross* - BILLBOARD
Vox Pop - *'A collection of comments compiled from our reader CD rating cards'* - CD REVIEW
Vox Pop - *letters* - LIBERTY, THEN AND NOW
Vox Populi - *letters* - AT&T MAGAZINE
Vox Populi - WORLD PRESS REVIEW
Voyeur - *'We like to watch' a column of pictures and observations* - FAME
VSOW - NEWSLETTER
VU Video Scans - VIDEO MANAGEMENT

W

Walkin' in the Past - GOOD OLD DAYS
Wall St. Report - FILM TV DAILY
Wall Street Analysis - CABLEAGE
Wall Street News - PR WEEK
Wall Street Report - *excellent series on current financial news* - TELEVISION/RADIO AGE
Walter Joyce's Note - MARKETING / COMMUNICATIONS
Wanted: Scenerios - DOCUMENTARY FILM NEWS
War Hunches - PEP
Wardrobe - *column by Hy Fashion* - CASTING CALL
Warren Coming Comics - *product newsbriefs* - COMIC READER, THE
Wartime Winners - *cooking* - HOLLYWOOD
Was My Face Red - *reader submitted mistakes* - CAMERA MAGAZINE
Washington - BOX OFFICE
Washington - ELECTRONICS
Washington - FUTUREHOME TECHNOLOGY NEWS
Washington - MARKETING / COMMUNICATIONS
Washington Beat - HDTV NEWSLETTER
Washington, DC Critics' Opinions - *films* - VARIETY
Washington Focus - AUDIOVIDEO INTERNATIONAL
Washington Focus - *DC PR briefs* - PUBLIC RELATIONS JOURNAL, THE
Washington Line - *regulatory news and information column by Danny E. Adams* - 4TH MEDIA JOURNAL, THE
Washington Line - PROMOTION
Washington Mailbox - *legal information column by Michele Bartlett* - QST
Washington News - COMMUNICATIONS
Washington News - PR WEEK
Washington Newsletter - *latebreaking regulatory news items* - ELECTRONICS
Washington Newsletter - *column by Bob Kling* - GRAPHIC ARTS MONTHLY
Washington Newsletter - *'Rulings, regulations, reports of federal, state and local government agencies of concern to mail marketers'* - MAIL ORDER DIGEST
Washington Perspective - *column by Victor J. Toth* - BUSINESS COMMUNICATIONS REVIEW
Washington Perspective - MILITARY ELECTRONICS / COUNTERMEASURES
Washington Pulse - *'FCC actions affecting communications'* - POPULAR COMMUNICATIONS
Washington Readout - *'Regulatory happenings from the world of amateur radio', column by Frederick O. Maia* - CQ
Washington Report - PRINTING IMPRESSIONS
Washington Report - *DC news briefs* - PUBLISHER'S AUXILIARY
Washington Report - R & R
Washington Report - RELIGIOUS BROADCASTING
Washington Report - SATELLITE COMMUNICATIONS
Washington Report - *legal viewpoint of Washington DC developments toward specialty advertising* - SPECIALTY ADVERTISING BUSINESS
Washington Roundup - *radio news column by Bill Holland* - BILLBOARD
Washington Routine - *editorial column by Jack Morrison* - THEATRE NEWS
Washington Scene, The - *column by Peter Nagan* - PHOTOGRAPHIC PROCESSING
Washington Update - *column by Wilson Dizard* - COMPUTER PUBLISHING
Washington View - *TV rules and regs* - VIDEOGRAPHY
Washington View - VIEW
Washington Watch - COMMUNICATIONSWEEK
Washington Watch - POSTAL WATCH
Washington Watch - RELIGIOUS BROADCASTING
Washingtonia - *newsbriefs* - 4A'S WASHINGTON NEWSLETTER, THE
Wasteland, The - FANGORIA
Watch - PRESS, THE
Watch, Read, Listen - *'Resources for follow-up'* - MEDIA & VALUES
Watch the Skies - *'Films from other galaxies are landing at a theater near you'* - HORRORFAN
Watch the Stars Come Out - *emerging personalities in profile* - SOUND STAGE
Watch Tower, The - *comment* - THEATRE, THE
Watch Word - *editorial column by Deborah Navas* - VIDEO CHOICE
Watchdog Barks, The - *editorial column by Tim Lucas* - VIDEO WATCHDOG
Watchdog News - VIDEO WATCHDOG
Watching the Beautiful People - *column by Stephen Lewis* - TV AND SCREEN SECRETS
Waterless Offset - *news and information* - POLYGRAPH INTERNATIONAL
Watts New - *new product section* - AUTO SOUND & SECURITY
Wavelengths - *'The latest in satellite TV technology'* - SATELLITE TV WEEK
Wavemaker - *successful direct marketing profiles* - TARGET MARKETING
Wavemakers - *personnel briefs* - PERSONAL ELECTRONICS
Wax Museum - *'The latest news on record collectibles'* - FILMFAX
Waxing Wise - *musical commentary column by Dave Fayre* - BAND LEADERS
Way They Were, The - *early star backgrounds* - RONA BARRETT'S HOLLYWOOD
Wayback Machine, The - *historical newsnotes column by Jim Korkis* - GET ANIMATED! UPDATE.
Ways and Means - EMMY
We Get Letters - COLORADO EDITOR
We Have With Us - *program previews* - TV MIRROR

Departments INDEX

We Hear - ADWEEK
We Name for Fame - *prediction* - CELEBRITY
We Nominate for Stardom - *profile* - TELECAST
We Point With Pride - *new motion picture releases* - SILVER SCREEN
We Present - FILM ALBUM MAGAZINE
Weather Broadcasts - *program guide* - RURAL RADIO
Wedding Bells - FILM TV DAILY
Week, The - *newsbriefs* - PUBLISHER'S WEEKLY
Week Ahead, The - UK PRESS GAZETTE
Week in Brief, The - *news outline for the reader short on time* - BROADCASTING
Weekend Boxoffice Report - *for USA and Canada* - VARIETY
Weeks Campaigns at A-Glance, The - *excellent but brief overview of current advertising campaigns in Great Britain* - AD WEEKLY
Week's Messages, The - *newsbriefs* - AMERICAN TELEPHONE JOURNAL, THE
Week's News, The - MARKETING / COMMUNICATIONS
Weingarten Looks at. . . . - *jazz and blues reviews* - AUDIO
Weird News - *'Real news items from the mainstream press'* - COMIC RELIEF
Welcome to New Members - PMA NEWSLETTER
Well-Traveled Camera - *column by David L. Miller* - MODERN PHOTOGRAPHY
West - BACK STAGE
West Coast - *newsbriefs* - MARQUEE
West Coast Notes - OFFICIAL BULLETIN OF THE INTERNATIONAL ALLIANCE OF THEATRICAL STAGE EMPLOYEES AND MOVING PICTURE MACHINE OPERATORS OF THE UNITED STATES AND CANADA.
West Coast Notes - *column by Wolf Schneider* - VIDEO MAGAZINE
West in Print, The - ROUNDUP QUARTERLY
West Report, The - *black radio playlist* - BLACK RADIO EXCLUSIVE
Western News - *newsbriefs* - COMIC READER, THE
Western Radio News and Comment - *column by W. L. Gleeson* - RADIO FAN-FARE
Western Zone News - PSA JOURNAL
We've Heard - *success stories of film exhibitions* - SCREEN INTERNATIONAL
What are They Doing Now? - *locating the stars* - PIC
What Do You Want to Know? - *fan club questions* - TV RADIO MIRROR
What Do You Want to Say? - *reader opinion page* - TV RADIO MIRROR
What Folks Say - *Positive comments concerning the N.W. Ayer & Sons Company* - ADVERTISERS GUIDE
What Goes On - *newsbriefs* - BETTER EDITING
What Happened to - *personality update* - SH-BOOM
What Hollywood Itself is Talking About! - *'The stars themselves enjoy the gossip as much as you do' column by Lynn Bowers* - SCREENLAND PLUS TV-LAND

What Inventors are Doing - SIGNS OF THE TIMES
What Late Ones Look Like - *long reviews and cast-crew data on new films* - HOLLYWOOD SPECTATOR
What NCEW Members are Doing - *briefs* - MASTHEAD
What Other Listener's Think - *letters* - BBC WORLD SERVICE LONDON CALLING
What Our Papers Say - AFRO-ASIAN JOURNALIST
What Our Philosopher Has to Say - *comment* - COMMON SENSE
What People are Wearing - STAR
What Should I Do? - *'Your problems answered' column by Claudette Colbert* - PHOTOPLAY
What the Camera Clubs are Doing - POPULAR PHOTOGRAPHY
What the Fans Think - *letters section 'Wherein our readers express opinions good and bad'* - PICTURE PLAY MAGAZINE
What the League is Doing - *'League activities, Washington notes, board actions-- for your information'* - QST
What the Live Ad Clubs are Doing - SIGNS OF THE TIMES
What the Manufacturers are Doing - RADIO DEALER, THE
What the Picture Did For Me - *'Verdicts on films in language of exhibitor'* - EXHIBITORS HERALD WORLD
What the Picture Did For Me - *'The original exhibitors' reports department, established October 14, 1916. In it theatremen serve one another with information about the box-office performance of product--providing a service of the exhibitor for the exhibitor'* - MOTION PICTURE HERALD
What the Societies are Doing - *'News of the amateur companies in and about London'* - AMATEUR ACTOR ILLUSTRATED, THE
What the Stars Are Doing - *current feature films in production* - NEW MOVIE MAGAZINE, THE
What the Stars Say! - *a myriad of witty/saucy statements* - MOVIE HUMOR
What the Trade is Talking About - TELEVISION RETAILING
What the Trade Journals Say - NATIONAL EXHIBITOR, THE
What They Are Doing Now - *star update* - SHOW
What They are Saying and Doing in Religious Communications - *'A news review of the religious communications field'* - RELIGIOUS MEDIA TODAY
What They are Showing - *film festival calendar* - FILM & VIDEO NEWS
What They Give the Public - *exhibition program at various theatres* - EXHIBITORS TRADE REVIEW
What They Read 20 Years Ago - *in Musical America* - MUSICAL AMERICA
What We Hear About Advertisers - *newsbriefs* - ADVERTISING EXPERIENCE

What You Missed! - *'Complete story summaries from all the shows!'* - SOAP OPERA UPDATE
What's Ahead - *calendar and suggestions for news series* - RUNDOWN, THE
What's Cookin'? - *newsbriefs* - ROUNDUP QUARTERLY
What's Cookin'? - *'Four daytime stars share their favorite recipes with you'* - SOAP OPERA STARS
What's Cooking - *celebrity meals* - PHOTOPLAY
What's Doing - NATIONAL PHOTOGRAPHER, THE
What's Doing - PROFESSIONAL PHOTOGRAPHER, THE
What's Going On - *news items and comment column by John Bryant* - SATELLITE TIMES
What's Going On in Dance - PERFORMING ARTS IN CANADA, THE
What's Going On in Music - PERFORMING ARTS IN CANADA, THE
What's Going On in Pop - PERFORMING ARTS IN CANADA, THE
What's Going On in Theatre - PERFORMING ARTS IN CANADA, THE
What's Happening - *calendar of upcoming non-electronics related events* - EXECUTIVES ON THE GO
What's Happening - FILMMAKERS FILM & VIDEO MONTHLY
What's Happening - *calendar* - TELEPROFESSIONAL
What's Happening! - *'Hollywood, New York, London, Paris, Rome' column by Bernice McGeehan* - TV RADIO SHOW
Whats Hot - *upcoming projects and people* - CINEGRAM
What's in a Name - *marvelous personal column by Douglas Fox* - EXHIBITORS HERALD WORLD
What's in a Print? - *column by Kathy Miller* - PUBLISHING & PRODUCTION EXECUTIVE
What's in Store - *column by Hugh Green* - ADVANCED IMAGING
What's New - *newsbriefs* - ADVERTISING AND MARKETING MANAGEMENT
What's New - AMATEUR PHOTOGRAPHER
What's New - *products* - AMERICAN CINEMATOGRAPHER
What's New - *new products* - AUDIO
What's New - *new product information* - BOOKSTORE JOURNAL
What's New - CAMERA MAGAZINE
What's New - *comic books recently shipped to retailers* - COMICS WEEK
Whats New - *pictorial display of recent direct mail items* - DIRECT MARKETING
What's New - DIRECT MARKETING
What's New - *commentary column by Hal Hager* - FORECAST
What's New - *newsbriefs* - R & R
What's New - *'Here's the latest viewing news for the month'* - SATELLITE ORBIT
What's New - SHUTTERBUG
What's New at Lexicon - DIGITAL DOMAIN DIGEST

What's New at ZEISS - *product review and news* - ZEISS INFORMATION
What's New from Coast to Coast - *column by Jill Warren* - TV MIRROR
What's New From Coast to Coast - *news of radio-television celebrities* - TV RADIO MIRROR
Whats New in Audio - *product reviews* - AUDIO
What's New in Audio - AUDIO
What's New in Graphic Arts - GRAPHIC ARTS
What's New in Photo Products - CAMERART
What's New in Radio - *product review* - ELECTRONICS WORLD
What's New in Video - AUDIO
What's New on CD - *new releases column by Lou Waryncia* - CD REVIEW
What's New on CD? - CD REVIEW
What's New on the Screen - *reviews* - HOLLYWOOD
What's New on Videotape - AUDIO VISUAL JOURNAL
What's New, What's Hot - INTELLIGENT DECISIONS
What's New(s) - *new products and services* - TELEPROFESSIONAL
What's New? - MONITORING TIMES
What's News - *newsbriefs* - RADIO-ELECTRONICS
What's News - *'In the film industry this week'* - SHOWMEN'S TRADE REVIEW
What's News - *varied British satellite news* - WHAT SATELLITE
What's News? - *new products* - AUSTRALIAN PHOTOGRAPHY
What's Next - *following month highlights* - DISNEY CHANNEL MAGAZINE, THE
What's Next in Hollywood? - *column concerning Hollywood efforts and upcoming 'family-type' films* - MOTION PICTURE AND THE FAMILY, THE
What's On - *extensive international event calendar of puppet theatre programs* - ANIMATIONS
What's On - *'a monthly calendar'* - CHANNELS
What's On - *schedule* - DISNEY CHANNEL MAGAZINE, THE
What's On - *listing of theatrical fare* - SCREEN WEEKLY, THE
What's on Movie Services - *'Look for your favorite program services--and find what's on'* - SATELLITE ORBIT
What's On the Air - ABC WEEKLY
What's On the Bords - *current theatre schedule* - THEATRE MAGAZINE
What's On Your Mind? - *letters* - SOAP OPERA UPDATE
What's On? - *'A guide to the principal theatres and music halls'* - STAGE AND SPORT
What's Playing? - *'This month in your hometown theater'* - SCREEN STORIES
What's the Problem - CORPORATE TELEVISION
What's the Problem? - CORPORATE TELEVISION

What's Up in the Music Business - *newsbriefs* - VARIETY
What's What - *newsbriefs* - MODERN PHOTOGRAPHY
What's What - *brain teaser column by Rachael Leigh* - NATIONAL FORUM, THE
What's Wrong with this Photograph? - *analysis* - COMMERCIAL PHOTOGRAPHER, THE
What's Your C.Q.? - *quiz* - SIGNAL, THE
When You're Buying - *technology guide* - HOME ENTERTAINMENT
Where Hollywood Lives - *column by Mike Szymanski* - HOLLYWOOD MAGAZINE
Where Hollywood Plays - *column by Abby Hirsch* - HOLLYWOOD MAGAZINE
Where No Man - *review column by Salman Nensi* - STAR TREK: THE OFFICIAL FAN CLUB MAGAZINE
Where Shows Are - *short location information* - DRAMATIC MIRROR, THE
Where the Action Is - *column* - PETERSEN'S PHOTOGRAPHIC
Where the Acts are Next Week and How They Did This Week - *American vaudeville fare* - DRAMATIC MIRROR, THE
Where Things Stand - *an excellent feature billed as a 'status report on major issues in electronic communications* - BROADCASTING
Where to Sell Manuscripts - *large literary market section* - WRITER, THE
Where'll We Go? - *New York City restaurant guide* - DRAMATIC MIRROR, THE
Which Ad Pulled Best? - MARKETING / COMMUNICATIONS
White House - SATELLITE NEWS
White's Radio Log - COMMUNICATIONS WORLD
Whizzbang Gallery, The - *inside back cover celebrity photo* - NEW CAPTAIN GEORGE'S WHIZZBANG, THE
WHO News - *news of Doctor Who television series* - DWB
Who, What, Where, When - *newsbriefs* - PUBLIC TELECOMMUNICATIONS REVIEW
Who? What? When? Where? - *photo page* - SILVER SCREEN
Wholesalers - BOOK PROMOTION HOTLINE
Who's Dating Who - *'All this month's celebrity clinching, partner pinching and relationship lynching' column by Fiona Cullinan* - FILM REVIEW
Who's Doing What? - NEWSLETTER
Who's New - *new soap opera faces* - SOAP OPERA WEEKLY
Who's New(s) - *personnel newsbriefs* - TELEPROFESSIONAL
Who's News - CELEBRITY
Who's News - ELECTRONIC MEDIA
Who's News - *'A collection of industry movers'* - INSIDE MEDIA
Who's News in Hollywood - *column by Dick McInnes* - SOAP OPERA STARS
Who's Where - *resources keyed to articles* - HOW

Who's Who - *column by Harry Burns* - HOLLYWOOD FILMOGRAPH
Who's Who - *brain teaser column by Rachael Leigh* - NATIONAL FORUM, THE
Who's Who in Advertising - *profiles* - ADVERTISING RESULTS MAGAZINE
Who's Who in Better Films - *profiles of individuals, film committees and review boards* - MOTION PICTURE AND THE FAMILY, THE
Why Didn't I Think of That - *techniques and other suggestions sent in by readers* - FAST FORWARD
Why Publish - *'In which several publishers answer this curious question'* - FACTSHEET FIVE
Wide Angle - *'Fresh perspectives on the world of freelance photo marketing'* - PHOTOGRAPHER'S MARKET NEWSLETTER
Wide Angles - *Florida production news* - ENTERTAINMENT REVUE
Wide Loop, The - *'Membership'* - ROUNDUP QUARTERLY
Wild Feeds - *'More shows than you can possibly watch'* - SATELLITE ORBIT
Wild Side - *column by Leonard Lee Rue* - OUTDOOR PHOTOGRAPHER
Wildlife Recording - TAPE
William Abbott on Ad Marketing - *column by William Abbott* - FOLIO:
Win the War - *homefront news* - HOLLYWOOD
Window Attractions and Show Window Displays - *'Including show cards, display devices, interior displays, fixtures, outline, etc.'* - SIGNS OF THE TIMES
Window Dresser, The - *techniques* - AMERICAN ADVERTISER
Window on the World - PARAMOUNT WORLD
Wine of Choice - *column by Peter J. Morrell* - PLAYBILL
Wine Rack, The - *wines viewed and reviewed* - SATELLITE TIMES
Winn Schwartau on Recording - RADIO WORLD
Winners - *Satellite TV Week's capsule summary of upcoming television programming* - SATELLITE TV WEEK
Winners and Losers--Telling It Like It Is - *stars are assigned to winner or loser columns* - RONA BARRETT'S HOLLYWOOD
Winners' Corner - *Boxoffice champs* - FILM TV DAILY
Wire Service - *electronic wiring column by Wayne Harris* - CAR STEREO REVIEW
Wisdom of Solomon, The - *column by Charles Solomon* - GRAFFITI
With the Amateur - *advice and instruction column by Fayette J. Clute* - ST. LOUIS AND CANADIAN PHOTOGRAPHER
With the Boys and Girls - *column by Uncle Dudley* - JOURNALIST, THE
With the Broadcasters - ADVERTISER MAGAZINE, THE
With the Chapters of NCP - PLAYERS
With the Collectors - *antique radios held by collectors* - ANTIQUE RADIO CLASSIFIED

Departments INDEX

With the Experimenters - *chatty technical column* - POPULAR RADIO AND TELEVISION
With the Ladies - IBEW JOURNAL
With the News Sleuth - *'Current events in Hollywood and doings of your favorite stars* - HOLLYWOOD
With the Periodicals - PLAYERS
With the Players - PLAYERS
With the Reel Observer - *column by Henry MacMahon* - MOVING PICTURE AGE
With the Reps - ADVERTISER MAGAZINE, THE
With the Trade - *trade news* - PHOTO-ERA MAGAZINE
With the Trade Associations - RADIO DEALER, THE
Within the DAVI Family - TECHTRENDS
Within the Industry - *personnel newsbriefs* - ELECTRONICS WORLD
Without Fear or Favor - *'By an old exhibitor', entertainment commentary* - DRAMATIC MIRROR, THE
Witty Wire - *newsbriefs* - WITTYWORLD
WNPA Magazine memories - *time-capsules* - WASHINGTON NEWSPAPER, THE
Woman's Work - *IBEW auxiliary news* - JOURNAL
Women - MEDIA & VALUES
Women & the Home - *food menues and recipes* - SOSYALI MAGAZINE
Women in Film & Video - IN MOTION FILM & VIDEO PRODUCTION MAGAZINE
Women Working - *current status of various projects* - CAMERA OBSCURA
Women's Committee - NEWSLETTER
Wonderful World of Ed Sullivan, The - *column by Ed Sullivan* - TV RADIO MIRROR
Word Balloons - *editorial column by Robert Greenberger* - COMICS SCENE
Word for Word - *quotes remembered* - TV ENTERTAINMENT
Word of Praise, A - KINEMATOGRAPH WEEKLY
Word Puzzle - CASTING NEWS
Word to the Wise, A - ADVERTISING AGENCY
Word Ways - RIGHTING WORDS
Words - *column by Michael Gartner* - ADVERTISING AGE
Words - *review* - OFF-HOLLYWOOD REPORT
Words...Tools of Our Trade - WRITERS' JOURNAL
Words & Music - *talent column by Irv Lichtman* - BILLBOARD
Words For Thought - *commentary column by Robert E. Van-Voorhis* - TELEPROFESSIONAL
Words on Books on Words - RIGHTING WORDS
Words on Works - *'Short statements about new artworks in which art and technology coexist or merge'* - LEONARDO
WordWatching - *writing style how-to* - COMMUNICATOR
Work Bench, The - *column by Paul Goldberg* - ELECTRONIC SERVICING & TECHNOLOGY
Workbench - *an excellent technical section for day-to-day engineering solutions, column by John Bisset* - RADIO WORLD

Working Words - EDITOR'S WORKSHOP
Works in Progress - *an unusual section detailing major film studio activity as 'shooting,' 'post-production,' and 'future projects* - GRAND ILLUSIONS
Works in Progress Sessions - INDEPENDENT, THE
Works in the Press - ACTORS BY DAYLIGHT
Workshop - *idea column for the public relations professional* - PUBLIC RELATIONS JOURNAL, THE
Workshops - *upcoming* - AID
Workshops - *upcoping* - PHOTOGRAPHER'S MARKET NEWSLETTER
Workshops - POPULAR PHOTOGRAPHY
Workshops - SHOW BUSINESS
World Above 50 Megahertz, The - *column by William Tynan* - QST
World Above 50 MHz, The - *column by Bill Tynan* - QST
World and the Theatre, The - *newsbriefs* - THEATRE ARTS
World Communication - EDUCATIONAL COMMUNICATION AND TECHNOLOGY
World Economy, The - WORLD PRESS REVIEW
World in Cartoons, The - WORLD PRESS REVIEW
World Information - *newsbriefs* - WORLD THEATRE
World Music Overview - *international pops chart* - R & R
World News - AUDIOVIDEO INTERNATIONAL
World News Desk-- New York - *ditto from the Big Apple* - SCREEN INTERNATIONAL
World News Desk--Australia - *down-under film news* - SCREEN INTERNATIONAL
World News in Brief - *advertising newsbriefs* - MEDIA INTERNATIONAL
World of Science in Pictures - AMERICAN NEWSPAPER BOY, THE
World of Sound - *newsbriefs* - HI-FI SOUND
World of Wireless - *newsbriefs on international technical developments* - ELECTRONICS WORLD + WIRELESS WORLD
World Press - PRESSTIME
World Reviews - CD REVIEW
World Round-Up - *newsbriefs* - TV WORLD
World Service Frequencies - BBC WORLD SERVICE LONDON CALLING
World TV Set Count - TELEVISION / RADIO AGE INTERNATIONAL
World Update - *newsbriefs* - TELEVISION BROADCAST
World Wags - *newsbriefs* - ABC WEEKLY
World Watch - *newsbriefs* - WORLD BROADCAST NEWS
World Wide Movie Making - *excellent current projects and prospects column by Kathryn Kirby* - FILMS AND FILMING
Worldwatch - ADWEEK'S MARKETING WEEK
Worldwide Movie Making - *'Who's making what, with who and where', excellent production status column by Kathryn Kirby* - FILM REVIEW
Worldwide News - ELECTRONICS

World-Wide News - *international radio briefs via Wireless Age managing editor* - WIRELESS AGE, THE
Worldwide News and New Product - *remainder of television section with news on: the Americas, Europe, Africa, Asia, and peripheral areas, New zealand, and Australia* - MOVIE/TV MARKETING
World-Wide Station List - *geographic listing column by Elmer R. Fuller* - RADIO-ELECTRONICS
Worship - *reviews* - HOMILETIC
Worship Leader - MUSIC LINE
Worth a Look - *column by Daniel Kumin and Edward Murray* - CD REVIEW
Worth Knowing - *photographic news items* - TRAVEL & LEISURE
Worth Quoting - *newsbriefs of special interest to those in advertising and marketing* - COMMUNIQUE
Worth Reading - AMERICAN PRESS
Worth Writing For - SALES & MARKETING MANAGEMENT
WOW! Art Gallery - *reader submissions* - WOW! MAGAZINE
WOW! Readers' Poll, The - *'All your faves! Based on your votes!'* - WOW! MAGAZINE
Wrap Up - *editorial* - WRAP
Wrap-Up - *back-cover comment* - MOVIE - THE VIDEO MAGAZINE
Write On - *fascinating letters to the editor column* - MOVIE - THE VIDEO MAGAZINE
Write On - *letters* - PRACTICAL WIRELESS
Writer in the Provinces, The - *column by Alan Plater* - NEW THEATRE MAGAZINE
Writers Conferences - *upcoming* - WRITER, THE
Writer's Library, The - *new books* - WRITER, THE
Writer's Market - *submission information* - WRITER'S DIGEST
Writer's Notebook - PUBLIC RELATIONS QUARTERLY
Writing & Editing - COMMUNICATIONS CONCEPTS
Writing Life, The - *paragraph-length items concerning the writing process* - WRITER'S DIGEST
Writing Techniques - WRITING CONCEPTS
Written by Our Readers - *readers comment* - ADVERTISING AGENCY

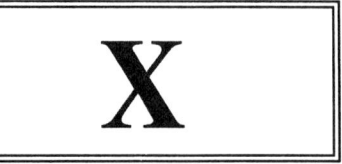

X

Xoxxox - *'Puzzles, games and activities'* - DISNEY ADVENTURES

Y

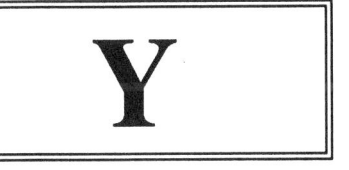

YA & Children's Books - *list of young adult and childrens releases* - HOT PICKS
Yearbook - *column by Linda Puntney* - CMA NEWSLETTER
Yearbook - *famous people's highschool yearbook pictures* - MEMORIES
Yesterdays - PANORAMA
Yesterday's Ads - *advertisements of yesteryear* - NEW CAPTAIN GEORGE'S WHIZ-ZBANG, THE
YesterHits - *'Hits from Billboard 10 and 20 Years Ago This Week'* - BILLBOARD
YL - CQ
YL News and Views - *women's league news column by Louise Morreau* - QST
You Ask the Stars - MOVIE TV SECRETS
You Ask Us - *'We have the solutions to your TV queries'* - TV GUIDE
You Asked - *informational forum* - NIKON WORLD
You Asked For It - *reader's picture requests* - PIC
You Asked for Them and Here They Are - *readers requests to see pictures of a particular program cast or star* - MOVIE-RADIO GUIDE
You Axed For It - *'An extra generous helping of extra special reader-requested fotos'* - FAMOUS MONSTERS OF FILMLAND
You Said It - *reader sound-off* - PREVIEW
You Said It - *Q&A* - SALES & MARKETING MANAGEMENT
You Should Know - *'Interesting thoughts and ideas for enjoying the hobby'* - POPULAR COMMUNICATIONS
You Tell Us - *reader input* - EPISODES
You the Viewer - *letters* - DAYTIME TV
You Were Asking - *a readers mailbag* - TV TIMES
Young and the Restless, The - *abstract* - SOAP OPERA DIGEST
Young Hollywood - *gossip column by Rona Barrett* - MOTION PICTURE
Young Hollywood - *column by May Mann* - MOVIE TEEN
Your 28-Page 12-Channel TV And Satellite Guide - TV GUIDE
Your Bug - *letters* - SHOW
Your Beauty - TELEVISION AND SCREEN GUIDE
Your Bottom Line - *photography for profit* - PROFESSIONAL PHOTOGRAPHER, THE
Your Business - CORPORATE TELEVISION
Your Family Doctor - *column by Dr. Norton Luger (MD)* - STAR
Your Favorite Shows--By Interest - *'The top 30 programs, children's shows and other categories'* - SATELLITE ORBIT
Your Guide to Current Films - *column by Helen Hendricks* - SCREENLAND PLUS TV-LAND

Your Happiness - TELEVISION AND SCREEN GUIDE
Your Home - TELEVISION AND SCREEN GUIDE
Your Letters - CAMCORDER USER
Your Letters - *'Praise and scorn, rantings and ravings'* - WHAT SATELLITE
Your Lucky Stars - *horoscope* - SOAP OPERA WEEKLY
Your Marketing Instincts - ADWEEK'S MARKETING WEEK
Your Monthly Ballot - *the readers vote* - PHOTOPLAY
Your Monthly On Record Guide - TV RADIO MIRROR
Your Motion Picture Shopping Section - *product review* - MOTION PICTURE
Your November Starcast - *horoscope column by Stephanie* - REAL LIFE/DAYTIMERS
Your Point of View - *letters* - FILMWORLD
Your Points of View - *letters* - FILM MONTHLY
Your Questions Answered - *column by David McGillivray* - FILM REVIEW
Your Receiver - TELECAST
Your Star Life - *'Horoscope' column by Doris Kaye* - MOVIE STARS
Your Turn - *guest editorial* - BROADCASTER
Your Turn - *letters. (02-86)* - MUSIC LINE
Your Turn - *letters* - PUBLISHING & PRODUCTION EXECUTIVE
Your View - VIEW
Your Washington Reporter - *column by Budd McKillips* - JOURNAL
Your Word - *letters* - STAR
You're On! - *guest commentary* - COMMUNICATOR
Youth - MEDIA & VALUES

Z

Zero Bias - *editorial* - CQ
Zine Reviews - FACTSHEET FIVE
Zip Code - *letters* - DISNEY ADVENTURES
Zooming In - *'TV Superstar Gossip' column by Anton Dubrow* - NIGHTTIME TV

Departments

International

This index is comprised of communication serials published outside the United States. These periodicals meet the criteria of publication (article summaries at minimum) in English, and published on a semiannual (twice a year), or more frequent basis.

Australia

ABC WEEKLY - Dec 2, 1939+?

ABU NEWSLETTER - Apr, 1965+?

Advertising and Newspaper News *which varied ? - ? under* ADVERTISING NEWS

ADVERTISING NEWS - 1928+

APR - 1894 - Dec, 1956//

ATR - Nov, 1967+

AUSTRALASIAN PRINTER - 1950+

Australian Film Guide *which varied* Jun, 1966 - 1967 *under* FILM INDEX

AUSTRALIAN JOURNAL OF SCREEN THEORY - 1976 - 1984//

Australian Media Notes *which varied* Dec, 1975 *under* MEDIA INFORMATION AUSTRALIA

AUSTRALIAN PHOTOGRAPHY - 1950+

AWA TECHNICAL REVIEW - Mar, 1935+?

CANTRILLS FILMNOTES - Mar, 1971+

CINEMA PAPERS - Jan, 1974+

FILM GUIDE - ?+?

FILM INDEX - Jun, 1966+?

FILM JOURNAL - 1958 - 1964//

IREE Monitor *which varied* Oct, 1979 - Jun, 1980 *under* MONITOR

MEDIA INFORMATION AUSTRALIA - Dec, 1975+

MONITOR - Mar, 1979+

Monitor *which varied* Jan/Feb, 1976 - Dec, 1979 *under* PROCEEDINGS OF THE IREE AUSTRALIA

Newspaper News and Advertising News? *which varied ? - ? under* ADVERTISING NEWS

Proceedings - Institution of Radio Engineers *which varied* 1937 - 1963 *under* PROCEEDINGS OF THE IREE AUSTRALIA

Proceedings - Institution of Radio and Electronics Engineers Australia *which varied* Jan, 1964 - Dec, 1971 *under* PROCEEDINGS OF THE IREE AUSTRALIA

PROCEEDINGS OF THE IREE AUSTRALIA - 1937 - Dec?, 1980?//

Proceedings of the IREE *which varied* Jan, 1972 - Dec, 1975 *under* PROCEEDINGS OF THE IREE AUSTRALIA

TELECOMMUNICATION JOURNAL OF AUSTRALIA, THE - Jun, 1935+

TV TIMES - 1958+

Belgium

ASIFA NOUVELLES - May, 1988+

IFJ INFORMATION - Jul, 1952+

JOURNALIST'S WORLD - Jan/Mar, 1963 - 1968//

WORLD THEATRE - 1950 - 1968//

Brazil

THEATRE DOCUMENTATION - Fall, 1968 - 1971/1972//

Bulgaria

BULGARIAN FILMS - 1960+

BULGARSKO FOTO - 1966+

Canada

APPLIED ARTS QUARTERLY - Spring, 1986+

BROADCAST + TECHNOLOGY - Sep/Oct, 1975+

Broadcast Equipment Today *which varied* Sep/Oct, 1975 - Dec, 1979 *under* BROADCAST + TECHNOLOGY

Broadcast Technology *which varied* Sep/Oct, 1979 - Sep, 1986 *under* BROADCAST + TECHNOLOGY

BROADCASTER - Jan, 1942+

CABLE COMMUNICATIONS MAGAZINE - May, 1934?+

Cable Communications *which varied* Jun/Jul, 1973 - Apr, 1979 *under* CABLE COMMUNICATIONS MAGAZINE

Canadian Broadcaster, The *which varied* Jan, 1942 - Sep, 1969 *under* BROADCASTER

Canadian Cinematography *which varied* 1961 - May/Jun, 1967 *under* CINEMA/CANADA

Canadian Film and TV Bi-Weekly *which varied* May 26, 1965 - Dec 24, 1969 *under* CANADIAN FILM DIGEST

CANADIAN FILM DIGEST - 1936 - Dec, 1976//

Canadian Film Weekly *which varied* 1936 - May 12, 1965 *under* CANADIAN FILM DIGEST

Canadian Film Weekly *which varied* Jan 14, 1970 - May 29, 1970 *under* CANADIAN FILM DIGEST

CANADIAN JOURNAL OF COMMUNICATION - Mar, 1974+

CANADIAN PHOTOGRAPHIC JOURNAL, THE - Feb, 1892+?

CANADIAN PRINTER - 1891+

Canadian Printer & Publisher *which varied ?* - Aug, 1989 *under* CANADIAN PRINTER

Canadian Telephone Journal, The *which varied* May, 1934? - Dec, 1965 *under* CABLE COMMUNICATIONS MAGAZINE

Canadian Telephone and Cable Television Journal *which varied* Spring, 1966 - Apr/May, 1973 *under* CABLE COMMUNICATIONS MAGAZINE

Captain George's Whizzbang *which varied* Nov/Dec, 1968? - Vol 1, #6? *under* NEW CAPTAIN GEORGE'S WHIZZBANG, THE

CBC TIMES - 1948 - Jan, 1970//

CINEMA/CANADA - 1961+

COMIC CELLAR, THE - 1980 - Summer, 1982//?

DIGITAL EVOLUTION MAGAZINE - Jul, 1989+

ELECTRONICS & COMMUNICATIONS - Mar/Apr 1953 - Feb, 1984//

HUMAN COMMUNICATION - Spring, 1973 - Spring, 1981//

HUMAN COMMUNICATION CANADA - Jan/Feb, 1983+

IN SEARCH - Winter, 1974 - #4, 1981?//

Media Probe *which varied* Mar, 1974 - Summer, 1977 *under* CANADIAN JOURNAL OF COMMUNICATION

MODERN DRAMA - May, 1958+

NEW CAPTAIN GEORGE'S WHIZZBANG, THE - Nov/Dec, 1968+

PEGBAR - ?+

PERFORMING ARTS IN CANADA, THE - Mar, 1961+

Printer & Publisher *which varied* ? - ? *under* CANADIAN PRINTER

PULP & PAPER CANADA - 1903?+

Pulp & Paper Magazine of Canada *which varied* ? - ? *under* PULP & PAPER CANADA

SCHOLARLY PUBLISHING - Oct, 1969+

Sound *which varied* Oct, 1970 - Oct, 1973 *under* SOUND & VISION

SOUND & VISION - Oct, 1970+

Sound Canada *which varied* Nov, 1973 - Nov/Dec, 1984 *under* SOUND & VISION

TAKE ONE - Sep/Oct, 1966 - Nov, 1979//

VENTURA LETTER, THE - Apr/May, 1987 - Dec, 1988//

VIDEO NEWS AND USED - May, 1989?+

Czechoslovakia

DEMOCRATIC JOURNALIST - Nov, 1953+

Documentation and Information Bulletin of the International Broadcasting Organization *which varied* Feb, 1960? - ? *under* RADIO AND TELEVISION

JOURNALISTS' AFFAIRS - #1, 1973 - 1980?//

OIR Information *which varied* ? - ? *under* OIRT INFORMATION

OIRT INFORMATION - 1956 - ?//

Radio & Television *which varied* 1960 - May, 1966 *under* RADIO AND TELEVISION

RADIO AND TELEVISION - Feb, 1960?+

Radio Television *which varied* Jul/Aug, 1966? - 1981 *under* RADIO AND TELEVISION

Radio Television International Review *which varied* 1982 - 1984 *under* RADIO AND TELEVISION

Finland

FACTS ABOUT FILM FINLAND - 1972? - 1978//

Finland Filmland *which varied* 1978 - ? *under* FINNISH FILMS

FINNISH FILMS - 1970?+

France

Audio-Visual Media *which varied* Spring, 1967 - Mar, 1971 *under* EDUCATIONAL MEDIA INTERNATIONAL

Bulletin d'Informations *which varied* May, 1949 - Oct, 1965 *under* FIEJ-BULLETIN

CINEMA FRANCAIS - May, 1976+

EDUCATIONAL MEDIA INTERNATIONAL - Mar, 1971+

FIEJ-BULLETIN - Mar, 1949 - Jun, 1986//

ZOOM - ?+

Germany

ACUSTICA - Jan, 1951+

AEG Progress *which varied* ? - 1967 *under* AEG-TELEFUNKEN PROGRESS

AEG-TELEFUNKEN PROGRESS - ? - #2, 1982//

AEU - Jul/Aug, 1947+

Archiv der Elektrischen Ubertragung *which varied* Jul/Aug, 1947 - Dec, 1970 *under* AEU

BALLETT INTERNATIONAL - Jan, 1978+

COMMUNICATIONS - 1974+

Grossbild-Technik *which varied* 1955 - 1959 *under* PHOTO TECHNIQUE INTERNATIONAL

International Journal of Communication Research *which varied* 1974 - ? *under* COMMUNICATIONS

International Photo Technik *which varied* 1960 - May, 1983 *under* PHOTO TECHNIQUE INTERNATIONAL

International Photo Technique *which varied* Aug, 1983 - Nov, 1983 *under* PHOTO TECHNIQUE INTERNATIONAL

LEICA FOTOGRAFIE INTERNATIONAL - Jan, 1951+

Leica Fotografie *which varied* Jan?, 1951 - ?, 1989 *under* LEICA FOTOGRAFIE INTERNATIONAL

NEWSPAPER TECHNIQUES - 1956+

Novum *which varied* 1972? - 1974? *under* NOVUM GEBRAUCHSGRAPHIK

Novum *which varied* 1980? - ? *under* NOVUM GEBRAUCHSGRAPHIK

NOVUM GEBRAUCHSGRAPHIK - 1972+

Novum Gebrauchsgraphik *which varied* 1974 - 1979 *under* NOVUM GEBRAUCHSGRAPHIK

PHOTO TECHNIQUE INTERNATIONAL - 1954?+

POLYGRAPH INTERNATIONAL - ?+

ZEISS INFORMATION - 1963+

Zeiss Werkzeitschrift [English Edition] *which varied* ? - ? *under* ZEISS INFORMATION

Hong Kong

ASIAN ADVERTISING & MARKETING - Jan, 1986+

Hungary

HUNGAROFILM BULLETIN - 1965+

India

AKASHVANI - 1936+

Audio-Visual Education *which varied* Apr, 1957 - Jan/Mar, 1966 *under* NIE JOURNAL

CINEMA VISION INDIA - Jan, 1980 - Jan, 1983//

CLOSE-UP - Jul, 1968+

Film World *which varied* 1964 - Jul, 1975? *under* FILMWORLD

FILMFARE - 1952+

FILMING - Jan, 1969//

FILMWORLD - Oct, 1964 - 1983?//

Indian Listener *which varied* ? - ? *under* AKASHVANI

NIE JOURNAL - Apr, 1957+

Indonesia

AFRO-ASIAN JOURNALIST - Mar, 1964 - 1974//?

Ireland

DRAMA, THE - Oct 23, 1821 - Dec 10, 1821//

SCREEN WEEKLY, THE - ?+?

Screen, The *which varied* ? - Jun 29, 1951 *under* SCREEN WEEKLY, THE

Italy

ANIMAFILM - 1979+

EUROPEAN TRANSACTIONS ON TELECOMMUNICATIONS AND RELATED TECHNOLOGIES - Jan/Feb, 1990+

FILMIS - ?, 1969? - ?, 1979?//

MILLECANALI INTERNATIONAL - ?+

MONITOR INTERNATIONAL - ?+

WORLD SCREEN - Dec, 1959+?

Japan

ABU TECHNICAL REVIEW - Mar, 1969+

CAMERART - Spring, 1958+

Far East Film News and TViews *which varied* May, 1953 *under* MOVIE/TV MARKETING

Far East Film News *which varied* Jun, 1953 - May, 1959 *under* MOVIE/TV MARKETING

Far East Film News *which varied* Jul, 1959 - Dec, 1961 *under* MOVIE/TV MARKETING

Global Movie Marketing *which varied* Jan, 1962 *under* MOVIE/TV MARKETING

JEE *which varied* ?, 1964 - Aug, 1974 *under* JEE, JOURNAL OF ELECTRONIC ENGINEERING

JEE, JOURNAL OF ELECTRONIC ENGINEERING - 1964+

Movie Marketing *which varied* Feb, 1962 - Jan, 1966 *under* MOVIE/TV MARKETING

MOVIE/TV MARKETING - May, 1953+

PENTAX FAMILY - ?+

Rengo Film News *which varied* Jun, 1959 *under* MOVIE/TV MARKETING

TELECOM JAPAN, THE - ?+

Netherlands

GAZETTE - Jan, 1955+

HDTV REPORT - Dec, 1990?+

New Zealand

ELECTRONICS AND COMMUNICATIONS - Apr, 1946 - Oct/Nov, 1974//

NEW ZEALAND FILM - May, 1977?+?

Radio and Electronics *which varied* Apr, 1946 - Apr, 1954 *under* ELECTRONICS AND COMMUNICATIONS

Radio and Electrical Review *which varied* May 1, 1954 - Apr 1, 1964 *under* ELECTRONICS AND COMMUNICATIONS

Radio, Electronics and Communications *which varied* May 1, 1964 - Dec 1, 1971 *under* ELECTRONICS AND COMMUNICATIONS

Pakistan

CINEMA THE WORLD OVER - Jul, 1975+

Philippines

MOVIE FLASH - ?+

SOSYAL! MAGAZINE - Feb 4, 1986+

Poland

Film *which varied* Nov, 1961 - Feb, 1962 *under* FILM BULLETIN

FILM BULLETIN - May, 1961+

Singapore

ASIAN JOURNAL OF COMMUNICATION - Sep, 1990+

Documentation List *which varied* Jan, 1972 - Jul/Oct, 1973 *under* MEDIA ASIA

MEDIA ASIA - 1974+

South Africa

PLAYTIME - ?+?

Sweden

HASSELBLAD - ?+

Switzerland

CAMERA - Jan, 1922 - Dec, 1981//

EBU Bulletin *which varied* 1954 - 1957 *under* EBU REVIEW. TECHNICAL.

EBU Documentation and Information Bulletin *which varied* 1950 - 1953 *under* EBU REVIEW. TECHNICAL.

EBU Review. Part B: General and Legal *which varied* Feb, 1958 - Nov, 1971 *under* EBU REVIEW. PROGRAMMES, ADMINISTRATION, LAW.

EBU Review. Part A: Technical *which varied* Jan, 1958 - Dec, 1971 *under* EBU REVIEW. TECHNICAL.

EBU REVIEW. PROGRAMMES, ADMINISTRATION, LAW. - Feb, 1958+

EBU Review. Radio and Television Programmes, Administration, Law *which varied* Jan, 1972 - 1982 *under* EBU REVIEW. PROGRAMMES, ADMINISTRATION, LAW.

EBU REVIEW. TECHNICAL. - 1950+

GRAPHIS - Sep/Oct, 1944+

IPI SURVEY - 1952 - 1962//

Journal des Telecommunications *which varied* ? - ? *under* TELECOMMUNICATION JOURNAL

Journal Telegraphique [NE?] *which varied* ? - ? *under* TELECOMMUNICATION JOURNAL

Journal UIT *which varied* Jan, 1953 - Dec, 1961 *under* TELECOMMUNICATION JOURNAL

TELECOMMUNICATION JOURNAL - 1934+

Telecommunication Journal *which varied* 1948 - 1952 *under* TELECOMMUNICATION JOURNAL

Telefilm International *which varied* ? - ? *under* TELEVISION INTERNATIONAL

Telefilm Magazine *which varied* Nov, 1958 - Jun/Jul, 1963 *under* TELEVISION INTERNATIONAL

TELEVISION INTERNATIONAL - 1956+

United Kingdom

16 MM Film User *which varied* Nov, 1946 - Oct, 1947 *under* AUDIO VISUAL

20/20 - Apr, 1989+

35mm Photography *which varied* Aug, 1983 - Sep, 1986? *under* PHOTOGRAPHY

35MM PHOTOGRAPHY - May, 1958 - Sep, 1965//

8 MM *which varied* May, 1969 - Aug, 1970 *under* FILM MAKING

8 MM Movie-Maker *which varied* Oct, 1957 - 1964? *under* EIGHT MM MOVIE MAKER AND CINE CAMERA

8mm Magazine *which varied* 1962? - Apr?, 1969? *under* FILM MAKING

ACES - Apr/May, 1988+

ACTION - Jul, 1975+

ACTOR ILLUSTRATED, THE - Jan, 1905 - Jan, 1906//

ACTORS BY DAYLIGHT - Mar 3, 1838 - Mar 16, 1839//

Actors by Gaslight *which varied* Apr 21, 1838 - Dec 29, 1838 *under* ODDFELLOW, THE

AD WEEKLY - ? - ?//

Ad Weekly *which varied* Jun 6, 1969 - Oct 6, 1972 *under* ADWEEK

Advertisers Weekly *which varied* 1913 - May 30, 1969 *under* ADWEEK

Advertising *which varied* Summer, 1978 - Winter, 1979/1980 *under* ADVERTISING MAGAZINE

ADVERTISING AND MARKETING - 1964+

ADVERTISING AND MARKETING MANAGEMENT - 1964 - Jul, 1970//

ADVERTISING MAGAZINE - Autumn, 1964+

Advertising Management *which varied* 1964 - Dec?, 1969 *under* ADVERTISING AND MARKETING MANAGEMENT

Advertising Quarterly *which varied* Autumn, 1964 - 1977 *under* ADVERTISING MAGAZINE

ADVERTISING REVIEW - Summer, 1954 - Nov/Dec, 1958//

Advertising Statistical Review of Press and Television Expenditures *which varied* ? - 1972 *under* PRESS STATISTICAL REVIEW

Advertising Statistical Review *which varied* 1972 - 1975 *under* PRESS STATISTICAL REVIEW

ADWEEK - 1913+

AFTERIMAGE - Apr, 1970 - Spring, 1981//

AIRWAVES - Aug, 1974+

ALBUM - Feb, 1970+

ALBUM, THE - February 4, 1895 - Mar, 1896//

ALPHABET AND IMAGE - 1946 - Dec, 1948//

AM - May, 1964+

AMATEUR ACTOR ILLUSTRATED, THE - Jan, 1905+

Amateur Movie Maker *which varied* ? - ? *under* EIGHT MM MOVIE MAKER AND CINE CAMERA

AMATEUR PHOTOGRAPHER - Jun 19, 1918+

Amateur Photographer and Photography, The *which varied* Jun 19, 1918 - Jul 27, 1927 *under* AMATEUR PHOTOGRAPHER

Amateur Photographer & Cinematographer, The *which varied* Aug 3, 1927 - Jun 13, 1945 *under* AMATEUR PHOTOGRAPHER

Amateur Tape Recording *which varied* 1959 - ? *under* HI-FI SOUND

Amateur Tape Recording & Hi-Fi *which varied* Feb, 1961 - 1963 *under* HI-FI SOUND

Amateur Tape Recording, Video & Hi-Fi *which varied* 1963? - Nov, 1967 *under* HI-FI SOUND

AMATEUR WIRELESS AND RADIOVISION - Jun 10, 1922 - Jan 19, 1935//

Amateur Wireless and Electrics *which varied* No. 1 - 331 *under* AMATEUR WIRELESS AND RADIOVISION

Animation Newsletter *which varied* Jan, 1978? - ?, 1983? *under* ANIMATOR

ANIMATIONS - Oct/Nov, 1977+

ANIMATOR - Jan, 1978?+

ARK - Sep/Oct?, 1984?+

ARTHURIAN THEATRE MAGAZINE, THE - Feb, 1905+

AUDIO VISUAL - Nov, 1946+

AUDIOPHILE WITH HI-FI ANSWERS - May, 1990?+

Author, Playwright and Composer *which varied* Oct, 1926 - Winter, 1948 *under* AUTHOR, THE

AUTHOR, THE - 1948+?

Author, The *which varied* May 15, 1890 - Sep, 1926 *under* AUTHOR, THE

BASELINE - 1981?+?

BBC Empire Broadcasting *which varied* ? - Sep 17, 1939 *under* BBC WORLD SERVICE LONDON CALLING

BBC ENGINEERING - 1955? - Jul, 1980//

BBC Engineering Monographs *which varied* 1955? - 1969 *under* BBC ENGINEERING

BBC London Calling *which varied* Apr, 1963 - Jun, 1981 *under* BBC WORLD SERVICE LONDON CALLING

BBC QUARTERLY, THE - Apr, 1946 - Autumn, 1954//

BBC WORLD SERVICE LONDON CALLING - ?+

BEST OF FILM & VIDEO - Mar/Apr, 1990+

BIOSCOPE, THE - Sep 18, 1908 - May 4, 1932//

BKSTS Journal, The *which varied* Jan, 1974 - Jun, 1986 *under* IMAGE TECHNOLOGY

BRITISH BOOK NEWS - Mar, 1940+

BRITISH COMMUNICATIONS AND ELECTRONICS - May, 1955 - Aug, 1965//

BRITISH INSTITUTE OF RECORDED SOUND. BULLETIN. - Summer, 1956+?

British Institution of Radio Engineers. Journal *which varied* 1939 - Dec, 1962 *under* ELECTRONICS & COMMUNICATIONS ENGINEERING JOURNAL

BRITISH JOURNAL OF PHOTOGRAPHY - Jan, 1854+

British Kinematography *which varied* 194u - Dec, 1965 *under* IMAGE TECHNOLOGY

British Kinematography, Sound and Television *which varied* Jan, 1966 - Dec, 1973 *under* IMAGE TECHNOLOGY

BRITISH LITHOGRAPHER - Oct/Nov, 1891 - Aug/Sep, 1895//

BRITISH PRINTER - 1888+

BROADCAST - 1973+

Broadcast Sound *which varied* 198u - Feb, 1985 *under* BROADCAST SYSTEMS ENGINEERING

BROADCAST SYSTEMS ENGINEERING - Oct, 1974?+

BROADCAST SYSTEMS INTERNATIONAL - ?+

Broadcasting Systems & Operations *which varied* 1978 - Mar, 1980 *under* INTERNATIONAL BROADCASTING

Bulletin of ALPSP *which varied* 1977 - ? *under* LEARNED PUBLISHING

BUSINESS OF FILM, THE - Nov, 1982+

CABLE TELEVISION ENGINEERING - 1971+

CAMCORDER USER - ?+

CAMERA & CAMCORDER MONTHLY - ? - Mar, 1990//

Camera Owner *which varied* 1963? - Jul, 1967 *under* CREATIVE CAMERA

Camera World *which varied* Jun, 1955 - Apr, 1958 *under* 35MM PHOTOGRAPHY

CAMPAIGN - 1929+

CETO News *which varied* Oct?, 1963? - Jan, 1967? *under* MEDIA IN EDUCATION AND DEVELOPMENT

Christian Broadcaster *which varied* Oct, 1953 - Apr, 1968? *under* MEDIA DEVELOPMENT

CINEMA - Dec, 1968 to date.

Cinema *which varied* Jul, 1921 - Nov, 1922 *under* SCREEN INTERNATIONAL

CINEMA AND THEATRE - 1932+?

Cinema News and Property Gazette *which varied* 1911 - Jul, 1921 *under* SCREEN INTERNATIONAL

Cinema News and Property Gazette, The *which varied* May, 1923 - Feb, 1928 *under* SCREEN INTERNATIONAL

Cinema Quarterly *which varied* Autumn, 1932 - Summer, 1935 *under* DOCUMENTARY FILM NEWS

CINEMA STUDIES - Mar, 1960 - Sep, 1967//

Cinema TV Today *which varied* Nov 13, 1971 - Aug, 1975 *under* SCREEN INTERNATIONAL

CINEMATOGRAPHY AND BIOSCOPE MAGAZINE - Apr, 1906 - Jan/Mar, 1907//

CLOSE-UP - Jul, 1927 - Dec, 1933//

COLOUR - ?+

COMBROAD - Jan, 1967+

Commonwealth Broadcasting Conference *which varied* Jan, 1967 - Apr/Jun, 1974 *under* COMBROAD

COMMUNICATION - Jun, 1974+

COMMUNICATION RESEARCH TRENDS - Spring, 1980+

Communications and Electronics *which varied* Oct, 1954 - Apr, 1955 *under* BRITISH COMMUNICATIONS AND ELECTRONICS

CONTRAST - Autumn, 1961 - 1966//

CREATIVE CAMERA - 1963+?

Creative Camera Owner *which varied* Aug, 1967 - Jan, 1968 *under* CREATIVE CAMERA

CSCC Newsletter *which varied* ? - ? *under* COMMUNICATION RESEARCH TRENDS

DASH WORLD - Winter, 1990+

Design & Art Direction *which varied* ? - Jan 17, 1986 *under* DIRECTION

DIRECTION - ?+

DISCOURSE & SOCIETY - Jul, 1990+

DOCTOR WHO MAGAZINE - 1985?+?

DOCUMENTARY FILM NEWS - Autumn, 1932 - Jan, 1949//

Documentary News Letter *which varied* Jan, 1940 - Nov/Dec, 1947 *under* DOCUMENTARY FILM NEWS

DRAMA - Jul, 1919+

Drama *which varied* Jul, 1919 - Jul/Sep, 1939 *under* DRAMA

DRAMATIC CENSOR, THE - Jan 4, 1800 - Jul, 1801//

DRAMATIC MAGAZINE, THE - Mar 2, 1829 - Apr, 1831//

DRIVING AMBITION - ?+

DWB - ?+

EDISON KINETROGRAM - Apr 15, 1910 - Apr 1, 1913//

Educational Broadcasting International *which varied* Mar, 1971 - Sep, 1981 *under* MEDIA IN EDUCATION AND DEVELOPMENT

Educational Television International *which varied* Mar, 1967 - Dec, 1970 *under* MEDIA IN EDUCATION AND DEVELOPMENT

EIGHT MM MOVIE MAKER AND CINE CAMERA - ? - Feb, 1967//

ELECTRICAL COMMUNICATION - Aug, 1922+

ELECTRICAL REVIEW - Nov 15, 1872+?

Electrical Review International *which varied* ? - ? *under* ELECTRICAL REVIEW

Electronic & Radio Engineer *which varied* Jan, 1957 - Dec, 1959 *under* INDUSTRIAL ELECTRONICS

ELECTRONIC ENGINEERING - Mar, 1928+?

Electronic Technology *which varied* Jan, 1960 - Sep, 1962 *under* INDUSTRIAL ELECTRONICS

ELECTRONICS & COMMUNICATIONS ENGINEERING JOURNAL - Oct, 1926+

Electronics & Wireless World *which varied* Oct, 1983 - Sep, 1989 *under* ELECTRONICS WORLD + WIRELESS WORLD

Electronics and Television & Short-Wave World *which varied* Oct, 1939 - May, 1941 *under* ELECTRONIC ENGINEERING

ELECTRONICS LETTERS - Mar, 1965+

ELECTRONICS WORLD + WIRELESS WORLD - Apr, 1922+

EMPIRE - Jul, 1989+

ETI - Jan, 1972?+

EUROPEAN JOURNAL OF COMMUNICATION - Mar, 1986+

Experimental Wireless *which varied* Oct, 1923 - Aug, 1924 *under* INDUSTRIAL ELECTRONICS

Experimental Wireless & the Wireless Engineer *which varied* Sep, 1924 - Aug, 1931 *under* INDUSTRIAL ELECTRONICS

FA - ?+

FANTASY ZONE - ?+

FILM - Oct, 1954+

Film *which varied* Spring, 1933 *under* FILM ART

FILM AND THEATRE TODAY - Mar, 1946 - 1949//

FILM ART - Spring, 1933 - Spring, 1937//

FILM ARTISTE - 1964 - 1974//

FILM DIRECTIONS - 1977+

FILM MAKING - 1962? - Oct, 1980//

FILM MONTHLY - Jan, 1950?+

FILM REVIEW - 1951+

Film Review Now *which varied* Jun, 1990 - Jul, 1990 *under* FILM REVIEW

Film Teacher *which varied* Summer, 1952 - ? *under* SCREEN

Film User *which varied* Nov, 1947 - Nov, 1971 *under* AUDIO VISUAL

Films & Filming Incorporating Focus on Film *which varied* ? - ? *under* FILMS AND FILMING

FILMS AND FILMING - Oct, 1954 - Mar, 1990//

FILMS ILLUSTRATED - Jul, 1971 - ?//

FOCUS ON FILM - Jan/Feb, 1970 - 1981//

FUNCTIONAL PHOTOGRAPHY - 1949 - Mar, 1955//

GAMBIT - ?+

GRAMOPHONE - Apr, 1923+

Gramophone *which varied* Apr, 1923 - ? *under* GRAMOPHONE

Gramophone Including Compact Disc News and Reviews *which varied* ? - ? *under* GRAMOPHONE

GRAPHIC ARTS - ?+?

HI-FI ANSWERS - ?+?

HI-FI CHOICE - ?+

HI-FI NEWS AND RECORD REVIEW - Oct, 1970+.

Hi-Fi News incorporating Record Review *which varied* Oct, 1970 - Dec, 1970 *under* HI-FI NEWS AND RECORD REVIEW

HI-FI SOUND - 1959 - Jan, 1977//

HI-FI WORLD - ?+

HISTORICAL JOURNAL OF FILM, RADIO & TELEVISION - Mar, 1981+

HISTORY OF PHOTOGRAPHY - Jan, 1977+

IAM *which varied* May, 1964 - Fall, 1975 *under* AM

IBE - Oct, 1964+

IBI Newsletter *which varied* ? - ? *under* INTERMEDIA

IDEAL KINEMA, THE - 1938 - Apr, 1957//

IMAGE - Aug, 1976+

IMAGE TECHNOLOGY - 194u+

Independent Broadcasting *which varied* Aug, 1974 - Nov, 1984 *under* AIRWAVES

INDEPENDENT MEDIA - Mar, 1983?+

Index *which varied* Spring, 1972 - ? *under* INDEX ON CENSORSHIP

INDEX ON CENSORSHIP - Spring, 1972+

Industrial and Commercial Photographer *which varied* May, 1961 - Feb, 1980 *under* PROFESSIONAL PHOTOGRAPHER, THE

INDUSTRIAL ELECTRONICS - Oct, 1923 - Jan, 1969//

Interim Drama *which varied* Nov, 1945 - Spring?, 1946 *under* DRAMA

INTERMEDIA - Mar/Apr, 1973+.

INTERNATIONAL BROADCASTING - 1978+

INTERNATIONAL JOURNAL OF ADVERTISING - Jan, 1982+?

INTERNATIONAL JOURNAL OF INFORMATION MANAGEMENT - ?+

INTERNATIONAL PRESS REVIEW - Mar, 1924 - Apr, 1924//

INTERSPACE - 1983+

INVISION - ?+

IPI REPORT - May, 1952+

Journal of Advertising *which varied* Jan, 1982 - Mar, 1982 *under* INTERNATIONAL JOURNAL OF ADVERTISING

JOURNAL OF EDUCATIONAL TELEVISION - Mar, 1975+

Journal of Educational Television *which varied* Mar, 1975 - Nov, 1975 *under* JOURNAL OF EDUCATIONAL TELEVISION

Journal of Educational Television and Other Media *which varied* Spring, 1976 - Winter, 1981 *under* JOURNAL OF EDUCATIONAL TELEVISION

Journal of the Institution of Electronic and Radio Engineers, The *which varied* Jan, 1985 - Dec?, 1988 *under* ELECTRONICS & COMMUNICATIONS ENGINEERING JOURNAL

JOURNAL OF THE BRITISH FILM ACADEMY - ? - Spring, 1959//

Journal of the Television Society *which varied* Jun, 1928 - Autumn, 1966 *under* TELEVISION

JOURNALIST - 1908+

Kine Weekly *which varied* Sep 25, 1919 - ? *under* KINEMATOGRAPH WEEKLY

Kinematograph and Lantern Weekly, The *which varied* May 16, 1907 - Sep 18, 1919 *under* KINEMATOGRAPH WEEKLY

KINEMATOGRAPH WEEKLY - Jun 15, 1889 - Sep, 1971//

KINETRADOGRAM, THE - Jan, 1913 - Jun, 1913//

LEARNED PUBLISHING - 1977+

LIGHTS! - Jan, 1990+

LISTENER - Jan 16, 1929 - Jan 3, 1991//

Listener and BBC Television Review, The *which varied* Jan 7, 1960 - Jul 27, 1967 *under* LISTENER

Listener, The *which varied* Jan 16, 1929 - Dec 31, 1959 *under* LISTENER

Liverpool and Manchester Photographic Journal *which varied* Jan, 1857 - Dec?, 1858 *under* BRITISH JOURNAL OF PHOTOGRAPHY

Liverpool Photographic Journal *which varied* Jan, 1854 - Dec?, 1856 *under* BRITISH JOURNAL OF PHOTOGRAPHY

London Calling *which varied* Sep 24, 1939 - Mar 23, 1963 *under* BBC WORLD SERVICE LONDON CALLING

Magazine of the Oxford Film Society *which varied* May, 1946 - ?, 1946 *under* SEQUENCE

MARCONI REVIEW, THE - Oct, 1928 - 1st Quarter?, 1983//

Master Printer *which varied* May, 1903 - Apr, 1905 *under* NEWSPAPER WORLD AND ADVERTISING REVIEW

MEDIA DEVELOPMENT - Winter, 1953+

MEDIA IN EDUCATION AND DEVELOPMENT - Mar, 1971 - 1989//

MEDIA INTERNATIONAL - 1973+

Media Report *which varied* ? - ? *under* MEDIA REPORTER, THE

MEDIA REPORTER, THE - 1976+

MEDIA WEEK - Apr 12, 1985+

MEDIA, CULTURE, AND SOCIETY - Jan, 1979+

Miniature Camera World *which varied* Dec?, 1936? - May, 1955 *under* 35MM PHOTOGRAPHY

MONOGRAM - Apr, 1971 - 1978//

MONTHLY FILM BULLETIN - Feb, 1934 - Apr, 1991//

Monthly Filmstrip Review *which varied* ? - Jan, 1950 *under* VISUAL EDUCATION

MOVIE - Jun, 1962 - Summer, 1982//

MOVIE - June, 1962+

MOVIE - THE VIDEO MAGAZINE - Oct, 1988?+

MOVING PICTURES INTERNATIONAL - Sep 13, 1990?+

NEW THEATRE - Aug, 1939 - Jul, 1949//

NEW THEATRE MAGAZINE - Oct, 1959 - 1972//

NEW THEATRE QUARTERLY - Jan/Mar, 1971+

Newspaper Owner and Manager *which varied* 1898 - May, 1903 *under* NEWSPAPER WORLD AND ADVERTISING REVIEW

Newspaper Owner and World *which varied* Apr 8, 1905 - Jul 28, 1913 *under* NEWSPAPER WORLD AND ADVERTISING REVIEW

NEWSPAPER WORLD AND ADVERTISING REVIEW - Jul, 1913 - 1953//

Newspaper World *which varied* Aug, 1913 - 1936? *under* NEWSPAPER WORLD AND ADVERTISING REVIEW

ODDFELLOW, THE - Apr 21, 1838 - ?//?

Official Doctor Who Magazine, The *which varied* 1985? - ? *under* DOCTOR WHO MAGAZINE

Optical Lantern and Cinematograph Journal *which varied* Nov, 1904 - May, 1906 *under* KINEMATOGRAPH WEEKLY

Optical Lantern and Kinematograph Journal *which varied* Jun, 1906 - Apr, 1907 *under* KINEMATOGRAPH WEEKLY

Optical Magic Lantern Journal and Photographic Enlarger, The *which varied* Jun 15, 1889 - Jun, 1903 *under* KINEMATOGRAPH WEEKLY

PERSPECTIVE - Autumn, 1958 - 1966//

PHOTO ANSWERS - Apr, 1989+

Photographic Journal *which varied* Jan, 1859 - Dec, 1859 *under* BRITISH JOURNAL OF PHOTOGRAPHY

PHOTOGRAPHY - Oct, 1965+

Photography *which varied* Oct, 1965 - Jul?, 1983 *under* PHOTOGRAPHY

Photoplay *which varied* Jan, 1986 - Mar, 1989 *under* FILM MONTHLY

Photoplay Movies & Video *which varied* Jan, 1950? - Dec, 1985? *under* FILM MONTHLY

PIC - ?+?

PLAYS AND PLAYERS - 1953+?

PLAYS INTERNATIONAL - Aug, 1985+

POLITICAL COMMUNICATION AND PERSUASION - 1980+

POST OFFICE MAGAZINE - Oct, 1914+?

Practical and Amateur Wireless *which varied* ? - Aug 19, 1939 *under* PRACTICAL WIRELESS

PRACTICAL PHOTOGRAPHY - ?+

PRACTICAL TELEVISION AND SHORT-WAVE REVIEW - Sep, 1934 - Nov, 1935//

Practical Television *which varied* Sep, 1934 - May, 1935 *under* PRACTICAL TELEVISION AND SHORT-WAVE REVIEW

PRACTICAL WIRELESS - 1932+

Practical Wireless *which varied* ? - ? *under* PRACTICAL WIRELESS

Practical Wireless and Practical Television *which varied* ? - ? *under* PRACTICAL WIRELESS

PRESS STATISTICAL REVIEW - ? - 1975//

Proceedings, The *which varied* Oct, 1926 - 1939 *under* ELECTRONICS & COMMUNICATIONS ENGINEERING JOURNAL

PROFESSIONAL PHOTOGRAPHER, THE - May, 1961+

Professional Video *which varied* 1982? - 198u *under* BROADCAST SYSTEMS ENGINEERING

Progress in Photography *which varied* 1949/1950? - ? *under* PERSPECTIVE

PROJECTION, LANTERN AND CINEMATOGRAPH - Apr, 1906 - Sep, 1907//

RADIO & ELECTRONICS CONSTRUCTOR - ?+

Radio and Electronic Engineer, The *which varied* 1963 - Nov/Dec, 1984 *under* ELECTRONICS & COMMUNICATIONS ENGINEERING JOURNAL

RADIO COMMUNICATION - 1925+

Radio Constructor *which varied* ? - ? *under* RADIO & ELECTRONICS CONSTRUCTOR

RADIO TIMES - Sep 28, 1923+

Relay Engineer *which varied* ? - ? *under* CABLE TELEVISION ENGINEERING

Royal Television Society Journal, The *which varied* Winter 1966/1967 - Nov/Dec, 1975 *under* TELEVISION

RSGB Bulletin *which varied* 194u - Dec, 1967 *under* RADIO COMMUNICATION

SATELLITE TIMES - ?+

SCIENCE AND FILM - Feb, 1952 - Apr, 1960//

SCIENTIFIC FILM - Jun, 1960 - Dec, 1965//

SCREEN - ? - Spring, 1982//

Screen Education Notes *which varied* Winter, 1971 - Winter, 1973/1974 *under* SCREEN

Screen Education *which varied* Oct, 1959 - Sep/Oct, 1968 *under* SCREEN

SCREEN INTERNATIONAL - 1911+

Screen International & Cinema TV Today *which varied* Sep 6, 1975 - ? *under* SCREEN INTERNATIONAL

SEE; World Film News *which varied* Sep, 1938 - Nov, 1938 *under* DOCUMENTARY FILM NEWS

Selection of Recent Books Published in Great Britain *which varied* Mar, 1940 - Apr, 1941 *under* BRITISH BOOK NEWS

SEQUENCE - May, 1946 - 1952//

SIGHT & SOUND - Spring, 1932+

Social Science Information Studies *which varied* ? - Feb?, 1986 *under* INTERNATIONAL JOURNAL OF INFORMATION MANAGEMENT

Society of Film Teachers. Bulletin *which varied* ? - ? *under* SCREEN

Sound & Picture Tape Recording Magazine *which varied* Apr, 1971 - Sep/Oct, 1973 *under* TAPE

SOUND AND VISION BROADCASTING - Spring, 1960 - 1973//

SPEECH AND DRAMA - 1951+

STAGE AND SPORT - May 5, 1906 - Jun 30, 1906?//?

STAGE AND TELEVISION TODAY, THE - 1880+

Stage Directory *which varied* 1880 *under* STAGE AND TELEVISION TODAY, THE

STAGE SOUVENIR, THE - Jul 20, 1903? - Oct 20, 1903?//?

Stage, The *which varied* 1880 - Feb 12, 1959 *under* STAGE AND TELEVISION TODAY, THE

STARBURST - Sep, 1978?+

Strandlight *which varied* ? - ? *under* LIGHTS!

STRANGE ADVENTURES - Feb, 1989+

Studio Sound *which varied* May, 1973 - ? *under* STUDIO SOUND AND BROADCAST ENGINEERING

STUDIO SOUND AND BROADCAST ENGINEERING - Jan?, 1959+

T & R Bulletin *which varied* 1925? - ? *under* RADIO COMMUNICATION

TABS - ?+?

TAPE - Nov, 1972? - ?//?

Tape Recorder *which varied* ? - Apr, 1973? *under* STUDIO SOUND AND BROADCAST ENGINEERING

Tape Recorder, The *which varied* Jan?, 1959 - ? *under* STUDIO SOUND AND BROADCAST ENGINEERING

Tape Recording and Reproduction Magazine *which varied* Feb, 1957 - Nov, 1957 *under* TAPE

Tape Recording & High Fidelity Reproduction Magazine *which varied* Dec, 1957 - Nov, 1958 *under* TAPE

Tape Recording and Hi-Fi Magazine *which varied* Aug, 1958 - Aug 10, 1960 *under* TAPE

Tape Recording Fortnightly *which varied* Aug 24, 1960 - 1961 *under* TAPE

Tape Recording Magazine *which varied* 1961 - Mar, 1971 *under* TAPE

TBI - Feb, 1988+

TELECOMMUNICATIONS POLICY - Dec, 1976+

Telegraph and Telephone Journal, The *which varied* Oct, 1914 - Dec, 1933 *under* POST OFFICE MAGAZINE

Telegraphic Journal and Monthly Illustrated Review of Electrical Science *which varied* Nov 15, 1872 - Dec, 1872 *under* ELECTRICAL REVIEW

Telegraphic Journal and Electrical Review *which varied* Jan, 1873 - Dec, 1891 *under* ELECTRICAL REVIEW

Television *which varied* Mar, 1928 - Jan, 1935 *under* ELECTRONIC ENGINEERING

TELEVISION - Jun, 1928+

Television and Short-Wave World *which varied* Feb, 1935 - Sep, 1939 *under* ELECTRONIC ENGINEERING

Television Mail *which varied* ? - ? *under* BROADCAST

TELEVISION PERSONALITIES - Oct, 1953+?

TELEVISION WEEK - Oct 27, 1988+

THEATRE - Jul 15, 1946 - Feb 14, 1953//

Theatre Newsletter *which varied* Jul 15, 1946 - Jan 19, 1952 *under* THEATRE

THEATRE NOTEBOOK - Oct, 1945+

Theatre Quarterly *which varied* Jan/Mar, 1971 - Oct/Dec, 1981 *under* NEW THEATRE QUARTERLY

THEATRE RESEARCH - Mar, 1958 - #4, 1974//

Theatre Today *which varied* #1 - 7 *under* FILM AND THEATRE TODAY

THEATRE, THE - Jan, 1877 - Dec, 1897//

THEATRE-CRAFT - 1919 - 1921//

TIME SCREEN - Summer, 1985+?

Today's Cinema *which varied* 1930? - Nov, 1971 *under* SCREEN INTERNATIONAL

Today's Cinema News and Property Gazette *which varied* Feb, 1928 - 1930? *under* SCREEN INTERNATIONAL

TV GUIDE - Apr 1, 1989+

TV HITS - Sep, 1989?+

TV WORLD - 1977+

UK PRESS GAZETTE - 1965+

University Film Journal *which varied* ? - ?, 1968 *under* UNIVERSITY VISION

UNIVERSITY VISION - ? - 1976//

VE-Time Drama *which varied* May, 1945 - Jul, 1945 *under* DRAMA

VIDEO - Nov, 1974+

Video and Audio-Visual Review *which varied* Nov, 1974 - May, 1978 *under* VIDEO

VIDEO ANSWERS - ?+

VIDEO BUYER - Nov/Dec, 1989+

VIDEO CAMERA - May/Jun, 1989?+

VIDEO MONTHLY - Mar, 1990+

VIDEO TIMES - ?+

VIDEO TODAY - ?+

VIDEO WORLD - ?+

VIDEO-THE MAGAZINE - ?+

VISUAL EDUCATION - ?+

VJ-Time Drama *which varied* Oct, 1945 *under* DRAMA

WACC Journal *which varied* 1970 - 1979 *under* MEDIA DEVELOPMENT

War-Time Drama *which varied* Winter?, 1939/1940? - Apr?, 1945 *under* DRAMA

WHAT SATELLITE - ?+

WHAT VIDEO - ?+

Wireless Engineer and Experimental Wireless *which varied* Sep, 1931 - Dec, 1935 *under* INDUSTRIAL ELECTRONICS

Wireless Engineer *which varied* Jan, 1936 - Dec, 1956 *under* INDUSTRIAL ELECTRONICS

Wireless World and Radio Review, The *which varied* Apr, 1922 - Jun, 1932 *under* ELECTRONICS WORLD + WIRELESS WORLD

Wireless World, The *which varied* Jul, 1932 - Sep, 1983 *under* ELECTRONICS WORLD + WIRELESS WORLD

World Film News *which varied* Apr, 1936 - ? *under* DOCUMENTARY FILM NEWS

World Film News and Television Progress *which varied* ?, 1936 - Jan, 1937 *under* DOCUMENTARY FILM NEWS

World Film News *which varied* Feb, 1937 - Aug, 1938 *under* DOCUMENTARY FILM NEWS

World's Press News *which varied* 1929 - Oct, 1935 *under* CAMPAIGN

World's Press News and Advertising *which varied* Nov, 1935 - Aug, 19, 1937 *under* CAMPAIGN

World's Press News and Advertiser's Review *which varied* 1944 - Nov 13, 1964 *under* CAMPAIGN

WPN and Advertisers' Review *which varied* Nov 20, 1964 - Sep 4, 1968? *under* CAMPAIGN

ISSN

Verifiable ISSN (International Standard Serial Numbering) numbers are included in this index. This international system assigns a unique eight digit group (some ISSN numbers possess an X check digit) to a unique serial title. In the listing below, serial titles in UPPER case are *Main Title* entries; those in upper and lower case are *VARIES* entries.

ISSN	Title
0001-0235	Advertising Techniques *Varied under* ADVERTISING AND GRAPHIC ARTS TECHNIQUES
0001-0340	AB BOOKMAN'S WEEKLY
0001-0383	ABCA Bulletin, The *Varied under* BULLETIN OF THE ASSOCIATION FOR BUSINESS COMMUNICATION, THE
0001-0448	ABC NEWS BULLETIN
0001-107x	AEG-TELEFUNKEN PROGRESS
0001-1096	AEU
0001-2424	ASCAP Today *Varied under* ASCAP IN ACTION
0001-2777	ATR
0001-2890	AV Communication Review *Varied under* EDUCATIONAL COMMUNICATION AND TECHNOLOGY
0001-2920	AWA TECHNICAL REVIEW
0001-7884	ACUSTICA
0001-8880	ADWEEK
0001-8899	ADVERTISING AGE
0001-8902	ADVERTISING AND MARKETING
0001-8929	Advertising and Newspaper News *Varied under* ADVERTISING NEWS
0001-8937	Advertising & Sales Promotion *Varied under* PROMOTION
0001-8961	ADVERTISING MAGAZINE
0002-0702	AFTER DARK
0002-4937	ALBUM
0002-7928	AMERICAN CINEMATOGRAPHER
0003-0600	AMERICAN PRESS
0003-1178	BULLETIN OF THE AMERICAN SOCIETY OF NEWSPAPER EDITORS, THE
0003-2344	AMUSEMENT BUSINESS
0003-6420	APERTURE
0003-6943	APPLIED PHOTOGRAPHY
0004-3109	ART DIRECTION
0004-5438	Journal *Varied under* ARSC JOURNAL
0004-5438	ARSC JOURNAL
0004-6930	Atlas *Varied under* WORLD PRESS REVIEW
0004-752x	AUDIO
0004-7546	AUDIO AMATEUR, THE
0004-7562	Audio Visual Communications *Varied under* AVC
0004-7570	AUDIO VISUAL JOURNAL
0004-7597	EDUCATIONAL MEDIA INTERNATIONAL
0004-7635	Audiovisual Instruction *Varied under* TECHTRENDS
0004-8453	AUSTRALASIAN PRINTER
0004-9964	AUSTRALIAN PHOTOGRAPHY
0005-0628	AUTHOR, THE
0005-2817	BBC Engineering Monographs *Varied under* BBC ENGINEERING
0005-3201	BM/E *Varied under* BME'S TELEVISION ENGINEERING
0005-3635	BACK STAGE
0005-8564	Bell Laboratories Record *Varied under* AT&T TECHNOLOGY
0005-8580	Bell System Technical Journal *Varied under* AT&T TECHNICAL JOURNAL
0005-9730	Bestsellers *Varied under* MAGAZINE & BOOKSELLER
0006-0054	BETTER BROADCASTS NEWS
0006-0119	BETTER EDITING
0006-0194	BETTER RADIO AND TELEVISION
0006-1883	PERFORMANCE
0006-2510	BILLBOARD
0006-4270	BLACK THEATRE
0006-6516	BOLEX REPORTER, THE
0006-7563	BOOKSTORE JOURNAL
0006-8527	BOX OFFICE
0007-0343	BRITISH BOOK NEWS
0007-1196	BRITISH JOURNAL OF PHOTOGRAPHY
0007-1358	British Kinematography *Varied under* IMAGE TECHNOLOGY
0007-1684	BRITISH PRINTER
0007-1994	BROADCAST ENGINEERING
0007-2028	BROADCASTING
0007-4012	BULGARSKO FOTO
0007-8832	COSMEP Newsletter *Varied under* COSMEP NEWSLETTER
0007-8832	COSMEP NEWSLETTER
0007-893x	CQ
0007-9219	CTVD
0007-9227	CWA NEWS
0008-1434	CALIFORNIA PUBLISHER
0008-2082	CAMERART
0008-2171	CAMERA 35
0008-2309	CAMPAIGN
0008-3038	BROADCASTER
0008-3569	CANADIAN FILM DIGEST

ISSN			
0008-4816	Canadian Printer & Publisher *Varied under* CANADIAN PRINTER	0012-5962	TDR
		0012-5989	DRAMATICS
0008-5162	Canadian Telephone and Cable Television Journal *Varied under* CABLE COMMUNICATIONS MAGAZINE	0012-7493	EBU Review. Part B: General and Legal *Varied under* EBU REVIEW. PROGRAMMES, ADMINISTRATION, LAW.
0008-5758	Canyon Cinemanews *Varied under* CINEMANEWS, THE	0012-7493	EBU REVIEW. PROGRAMMES, ADMINISTRATION, LAW.
0008-7068	CARTOONIST PROFILES	0012-8023	ETV NEWSLETTER
0008-8021	Catholic Film Newsletter *Varied under* FILM & BROADCASTING REVIEW	0013-094x	EDITOR AND PUBLISHER
		0013-0958	Editorial Research Reports *Varied under* CONGRESSIONAL QUARTERLY'S EDITORIAL RESEARCH REPORTS
0008-8129	CATHOLIC JOURNALIST		
0008-834x	CATHOLIC SCHOOL EDITOR		
0008-9575	Central States Speech Journal *Varied under* COMMUNICATION STUDIES	0013-0958	CONGRESSIONAL QUARTERLY'S EDITORIAL RESEARCH REPORTS
0009-3580	CHICAGO JOURNALISM REVIEW	0013-1660	Educational Broadcasting Review *Varied under* PUBLIC TELECOMMUNICATIONS REVIEW
0009-7004	CINEASTE		
0009-7047	CINEMA	0013-1776	Educational-Instructional Broadcasting *Varied under* EDUCATIONAL BROADCASTING
0009-7071	CINEMA/CANADA		
0009-7101	CINEMA JOURNAL		
0010-0927	COLLEGE & UNIVERSITY JOURNAL	0013-1946	EDUCATIONAL SCREEN
0010-1117	College Press Review *Varied under* COLLEGE MEDIA REVIEW	0013-1970	Educational Broadcasting International *Varied under* MEDIA IN EDUCATION AND DEVELOPMENT
0010-1133	JOURNAL OF COLLEGE RADIO		
0010-1214	COLLEGIATE JOURNALIST	0013-1989	Educational Theatre Journal *Varied under* THEATRE JOURNAL
0010-194x	COLUMBIA JOURNALISM REVIEW		
		0013-2063	Educators Guide to Media & Methods *Varied under* MEDIA & METHODS
0010-1990	CSPAA BULLETIN		
0010-3519	COMMUNICATION ARTS		
0010-3535	Communication: Journalism Education Today *Varied under* C: JET	0013-2543	FILM MAKING
		0013-4252	ELECTRICAL COMMUNICATION
		0013-4384	ELECTRICAL REVIEW
0010-356x	COMMUNICATIONS	0013-4783	ELECTRONIC AGE
0010-3632	COMMUNICATIONS NEWS	0013-4872	ELECTRONIC DESIGN
0010-7506	CONTEMPORARY PHOTOGRAPHER	0013-4902	ELECTRONIC ENGINEERING
		0013-4953	ELECTRONIC PRODUCTS
0011-0876	CREATIVE CAMERA	0013-497x	Electronic Servicing *Varied under* ELECTRONIC SERVICING & TECHNOLOGY
0011-4693	DA *Varied under* PRINTING PAPER		
0011-5509	DAILY VARIETY	0013-4988	Electronic Technican *Varied under* ELECTRONIC TECHNICAN/DEALER
0011-7129	DAYTIME TV		
0011-7145	DB		
0011-7218	DEALERSCOPE	0013-5070	Electronics *Varied under* ELECTRONICS
0011-8214	DEMOCRATIC JOURNALIST	0013-5100	ELECTRONICS & COMMUNICATIONS
0012-3188	DIRECT MARKETING		
0012-5768	DOWN BEAT	0013-5178	ELECTRONICS ILLUSTRATED
0012-5946	DRAMA	0013-5194	ELECTRONICS LETTERS
0012-5954	DRAMA & THEATRE	0013-5232	ELECTRONICS WORLD
0012-5962	Drama Review, The *Varied under* TDR		

0013-595x	Elementary Electronics *Varied under* COMMUNICATIONS WORLD	
0014-7443	FAMOUS MONSTERS OF FILMLAND	
0014-9055	Federal Communications Bar Journal *Varied under* FEDERAL COMMUNICATIONS LAW JOURNAL	
0015-1025	FILM	
0015-1122	FILM ARTISTE	
0015-119x	FILM COMMENT	
0015-1211	FILM CULTURE	
0015-1238	FILM FAN MONTHLY	
0015-1270	FILM HERITAGE	
0015-1289	FILM INDEX	
0015-1327	Film Library Quarterly *Varied under* FILM LIBRARY QUARTERLY	
0015-1327	FILM LIBRARY QUARTERLY	
0015-1343	Film News *Varied under* FILM & VIDEO NEWS	
0015-1386	FILM QUARTERLY	
0015-1408	Film Society Review *Varied under* CRITIC	
0015-1459	Film User *Varied under* AUDIO VISUAL	
0015-1475	Film World *Varied under* FILMWORLD	
0015-1548	FILMFARE	
0015-1610	Filmmakers Newsletter *Varied under* FILMMAKERS FILM & VIDEO MONTHLY	
0015-1629	FILMOGRAPH	
0015-167x	FILMS AND FILMING	
0015-1688	FILMS IN REVIEW	
0015-4180	COMMUNIQUE	
0015-5128	FOCUS ON FILM	
0015-5349	FOI DIGEST	
0016-4283	GAMBIT	
0016-5492	GAZETTE	
0016-5743	NOVUM GEBRAUCHSGRAPHIK	
0017-310x	Gramophone *Varied under* GRAMOPHONE	
0017-310x	GRAMOPHONE	
0017-3274	GRAPHIC ANTIQUARIAN	
0017-3312	Graphic Arts Monthly and the Printing Industry *Varied under* GRAPHIC ARTS MONTHLY	
0017-3363	Graphic Arts Unionist *Varied under* GRAPHIC COMMUNICATOR	
0017-3428	GRAPHICS: U.S.A.	
0017-3452	GRAPHIS	
0017-3541	GRASSROOTS EDITOR	

ISSN	Title
0017-3703	GREATER AMUSEMENTS
0017-5404	GUILD REPORTER, THE
0018-1226	HI-FI NEWS AND RECORD REVIEW
0018-1234	HI-FI SOUND
0018-1455	HIGH FIDELITY
0018-3660	HOLLYWOOD REPORTER
0018-7798	HUNGAROFILM BULLETIN
0018-876x	ICA NEWSLETTER
0018-9219	PROCEEDINGS OF THE IEEE
0018-9235	IEEE SPECTRUM
0018-9308	IEEE Transactions on Broadcast and Television Receivers *Varied under* IEEE TRANSACTIONS ON CONSUMER ELECTRONICS
0018-9316	IEEE TRANSACTIONS ON BROADCASTING
0018-9332	IEEE Transactions on Communication Technology *Varied under* IEEE TRANSACTIONS ON COMMUNICATIONS
0018-9448	IEEE TRANSACTIONS ON INFORMATION THEORY
0019-0314	IPI REPORT
0019-3232	In-Plant Printer *Varied under* IN-PLANT PRINTER & ELECTRONIC PUBLISHER
0019-3712	Independent Film Journal *Varied under* FILM JOURNAL, THE
0019-784x	PROFESSIONAL PHOTOGRAPHER, THE
0019-8498	Industrial Marketing *Varied under* BUSINESS MARKETING
0019-8595	INDUSTRIAL PHOTOGRAPHY
0019-9583	Infinity *Varied under* ASMP BULLETIN
0020-1502	Inland Printer, American Lithographer *Varied under* AMERICAN PRINTER
0020-3521	Proceedings - Institution of Radio Engineers *Varied under* PROCEEDINGS OF THE IREE AUSTRALIA
0020-3521	Proceedings - Institution of Radio and Electronics Engineers Australia *Varied under* PROCEEDINGS OF THE IREE AUSTRALIA
0020-5109	Andy Warhol's Interview *Varied under* INTERVIEW
0020-5834	INTERNATIONAL ADVERTISER, THE
0020-5885	OFFICIAL BULLETIN OF THE INTERNATIONAL ALLIANCE OF THEATRICAL STAGE EMPLOYEES AND MOVING PICTURE MACHINE OPERATORS OF THE UNITED STATES AND CANADA.
0020-6229	IBE
0020-6601	INTERNATIONAL EDUCATIONAL AND CULTURAL EXCHANGE
0020-8280	International Photo Technik *Varied under* PHOTO TECHNIQUE INTERNATIONAL
0020-8299	INTERNATIONAL PHOTOGRAPHER
0021-3608	JEE *Varied under* JEE, JOURNAL OF ELECTRONIC ENGINEERING
0021-8499	JOURNAL OF ADVERTISING RESEARCH
0021-938x	Journal of Broadcasting *Varied under* JOURNAL OF BROADCASTING & ELECTRONIC MEDIA
0021-9436	JOURNAL OF BUSINESS COMMUNICATION, THE
0021-9916	JOURNAL OF COMMUNICATION
0022-2224	VISIBLE LANGUAGE
0022-2429	JOURNAL OF MARKETING
0022-2437	JMR, JOURNAL OF MARKETING RESEARCH
0022-3840	JOURNAL OF POPULAR CULTURE
0022-4677	JOURNAL OF SPEECH AND HEARING DISORDERS
0022-5517	JOURNALISM EDUCATOR, THE
0022-5533	Journalism Quarterly *Varied under* JQ. JOURNALISM QUARTERLY.
0022-5533	JQ. JOURNALISM QUARTERLY.
0022-5541	JOURNALIST
0023-155x	KINEMATOGRAPH WEEKLY
0024-0621	Leica Fotografie *Varied under* LEICA FOTOGRAFIE INTERNATIONAL
0024-063x	LEICA PHOTOGRAPHY
0024-094x	LEONARDO
0024-208x	Liberty *Varied under* LIBERTY, THEN AND NOW
0024-4392	LISTENER
0024-600x	London Calling *Varied under* BBC WORLD SERVICE LONDON CALLING
0024-9483	MADISON AVENUE
0024-9793	MEDIA INDUSTRY NEWSLETTER
0025-2883	MARCONI REVIEW, THE
0025-3685	MARKETING / COMMUNICATIONS
0025-3790	MARKETING NEWS
0025-3928	MARQUEE
0025-4061	TV & APPLIANCE MART
0025-472x	Mass Media Ministries Bi-Weekly Newsletter *Varied under* MASS MEDIA NEWSLETTER
0025-5084	MASTHEAD
0025-5122	MASTHEAD
0025-598x	MATRIX
0025-6897	MEDIA & METHODS
0025-6900	Media Decisions *Varied under* MEDIAWEEK
0025-8369	MEDIUM
0026-7694	MODERN DRAMA
0026-8240	MODERN PHOTOGRAPHY
0026-8429	MODERN SCREEN
0027-0407	MONTHLY FILM BULLETIN
0027-1616	MOTION PICTURE HERALD
0027-1624	MOTION PICTURE
0027-268x	MOVIE
0027-2698	Movie Life *Varied under* TONI HOLT'S MOVIE LIFE
0027-271x	MOVIE MIRROR
0027-2744	MOVIE STARS
0027-2779	MOVIE WORLD
0027-5697	NABET NEWS
0027-6634	NIE JOURNAL
0027-8521	NATIONAL AMATEUR
0027-8610	National Association of Educational Broadcasters Newsletter *Varied under* CURRENT
0027-9935	National Press Photographer *Varied under* NEWS PHOTOGRAPHER
0028-4408	NEW CAPTAIN GEORGE'S WHIZZBANG, THE
0028-6893	NEW THEATRE MAGAZINE
0028-9817	NIEMAN REPORTS
0029-7097	OIRT INFORMATION
0030-8110	PMI, Photo Methods for Industry *Varied under* PHOTOMETHODS
0030-8277	PSA JOURNAL
0031-5230	PERFORMING ARTS IN CANADA, THE
0031-5249	Performing Arts Review *Varied under* JOURNAL OF ARTS MANAGEMENT AND LAW, THE
0031-8213	PHILOSOPHY AND RHETORIC
0031-8531	PHOTO MARKETING
0031-8566	PHOTO SCREEN

ISSN					
0031-871x	Photographic Applications in Science and Technology *Varied under* FUNCTIONAL PHOTOGRAPHY	0033-8060	RADIO TIMES	0038-9099	STAGE AND TELEVISION TODAY, THE
		0033-9202	RANGEFINDER, THE	0039-1220	STEREO REVIEW
		0034-1592	RECORD RESEARCH	0039-8519	TV Communications *Varied under* CABLE TV BUSINESS MAGAZINE
		0034-1673	Recording Engineer/Producer *Varied under* REP: RECORDING ENGINEERING PRODUCTION		
0031-8744	PHOTOGRAPHIC PROCESSING				
0031-8809	Photography *Varied under* PHOTOGRAPHY			0039-8543	TV GUIDE
		0034-4079	RELIGIOUS BROADCASTING	0039-8608	TV TIMES
0031-8825	Photolith *Varied under* PHOTOLITH, SCM	0034-5822	RESTORATION AND 18TH CENTURY THEATRE RESEARCH	0039-9132	TAKE ONE
				0039-9345	Tan *Varied under* BLACK STARS
0031-885x	PHOTOPLAY	0035-855x	Roundup, The *Varied under* ROUNDUP QUARTERLY		
0032-1486	PLAYERS			0039-9558	Tape Recording Magazine *Varied under* TAPE
0032-1540	PLAYS	0035-9270	Royal Television Society Journal, The *Varied under* TELEVISION		
0032-1559	PLAYS AND PLAYERS			0040-0971	TECHNICAL PHOTOGRAPHY
0032-4485	Popular Electronics *Varied under* COMPUTERS & ELECTRONICS			0040-165x	TECHNOLOGY AND CULTURE
		0036-1682	SMPTE JOURNAL	0040-2486	TELECOMMUNICATION JOURNAL OF AUSTRALIA, THE
		0036-2972	ST. LOUIS JOURNALISM REVIEW		
0032-4485	Popular Electronics *Varied under* COMPUTERS & ELECTRONICS			0040-277x	TELEVISION/RADIO AGE
	0036-634x	SCHOLARLY PUBLISHING	0040-2788	BROADCAST
		0036-6390	Scholastic Editor Graphics/Communications *Varied under* SCHOLASTIC EDITOR'S TRENDS IN PUBLICATIONS	0040-2796	TELEVISION QUARTERLY
0032-4582	POPULAR PHOTOGRAPHY			0040-5469	THEATRE CRAFTS
0032-6445	PRACTICAL PHOTOGRAPHY			0040-5477	Theatre Design & Technology *Varied under* THEATRE DESIGN & TECHNOLOGY
0032-8197	Pride *Varied under* COLLEGE & UNIVERSITY JOURNAL				
0032-8510	PRINT	0036-6730	SCHOOL PRESS REVIEW, THE		
0032-860x	PRINTING IMPRESSIONS	0036-9543	SCREEN	0040-5477	Theatre Design and Technology *Varied under* THEATRE DESIGN & TECHNOLOGY
0032-8626	Printing News *Varied under* PRINTINGNEWS	0036-956x	Screen Actor *Varied under* SCREEN ACTOR HOLLYWOOD		
		0036-9578	SCREEN FACTS	0040-5477	THEATRE DESIGN & TECHNOLOGY
0032-9703	JOURNAL OF THE PRODUCERS GUILD OF AMERICA, THE	0036-9608	SCREEN STORIES		
	0037-3036	73 *Varied under* 73 AMATEUR RADIO	0040-5485	THEATRE DOCUMENTATION
0033-0167	PROFESSIONAL PHOTOGRAPHER, THE			0040-5523	THEATRE NOTEBOOK
		0037-3222	SHAKESPEARE QUARTERLY	0040-5566	THEATRE RESEARCH
0033-362x	PUBLIC OPINION QUARTERLY	0037-4296	Show; The Magazine of the Arts *Varied under* SHOW	0040-8573	Today's Speech *Varied under* COMMUNICATION QUARTERLY
0033-3670	PUBLIC RELATIONS JOURNAL, THE				
	0037-4296	SHOW	0041-2007	TRAVEL & LEISURE
0033-3697	PUBLIC RELATIONS NEWS	0037-4318	SHOW BUSINESS	0041-4530	TV STAR PARADE
0033-3700	PUBLIC RELATIONS QUARTERLY	0037-4806	SIGHT & SOUND	0041-5170	UK PRESS GAZETTE
	0037-4814	SIGHT AND SOUND MARKETING	0041-6746	CINEMA FRANCAIS
0033-4103	Pulp & Paper Magazine of Canada *Varied under* PULP & PAPER CANADA			0041-9311	Journal of the University Film Association *Varied under* JOURNAL OF FILM AND VIDEO
	0037-4830	Sightlines *Varied under* AFVA BULLETIN		
0033-4812	QST				
0033-5630	QUARTERLY JOURNAL OF SPEECH, THE	0037-5063	SIGNS OF THE TIMES		
	0037-5209	SILENT PICTURE, THE	0042-0395	UNIVERSITY VISION
0033-5630	TPQ	0037-5365	SILVER SCREEN	0042-2738	VARIETY
0033-6475	QUILL, THE	0038-1829	SOUND AND VISION BROADCASTING	0042-7152	VISUAL EDUCATION
0033-6505	QUILL AND SCROLL			0043-0684	WASHINGTON NEWSPAPER, THE
0033-7153	RTNDA Communicator *Varied under* COMMUNICATOR	0038-4585	Southern Speech Journal, The *Varied under* SOUTHERN COMMUNICATION JOURNAL, THE		
0033-7676	Radio Television *Varied under* RADIO AND TELEVISION			0043-4205	Western Speech *Varied under* WESTERN JOURNAL OF SPEECH COMMUNICATION
0033-7722	Radio and Electronic Engineer, The *Varied under* ELECTRONICS & COMMUNICATIONS ENGINEERING JOURNAL	0038-7169	Speech Monographs *Varied under* COMMUNICATION MONOGRAPHS	0043-6062	Wireless World, The *Varied under* ELECTRONICS WORLD + WIRELESS WORLD
	0038-7177	Speech Teacher, The *Varied under* COMMUNICATION EDUCATION		
			0043-9517	WRITER, THE
0033-7803	RADIO COMMUNICATION			0043-9525	WRITER'S DIGEST
0033-7862	RADIO-ELECTRONICS			0043-9533	NEWSLETTER

ISSN	Title
0044-0167	Yale/Theatre *Varied under* THEATER
0044-2054	ZEISS INFORMATION
0044-7625	AMERICAN CINEMEDITOR
0044-7684	American Film Institute Report *Varied under* AMERICAN FILM INSTITUTE. QUARTERLY.
0045-2246	Black oracle *Varied under* CINEMACABRE
0045-317x	Many Worlds of Music, The *Varied under* BMI: MUSICWORLD
0045-3188	Broadcast Bibliophile Booknotes *Varied under* COMMUNICATION BOOKNOTES
0046-1466	Educational & Industrial Television *Varied under* E-ITV
0046-1474	EDUCATIONAL BROADCASTING
0046-3531	FIEJ-BULLETIN
0046-3541	Grassroots *Varied under* GRASSROOTS EDITOR
0046-3787	FILM JOURNAL, THE
0046-4333	FOLIO:
0046-6158	GOOD OLD DAYS
0046-7367	High Fidelity Trade News *Varied under* PERSONAL ELECTRONICS
0047-2646	Journal of Organizational Communications *Varied under* JOURNAL OF COMMUNICATION MANAGEMENT
0047-2719	Journal of Popular Film *Varied under* JOURNAL OF POPULAR FILM AND TELEVISION
0047-2816	JOURNAL OF TECHNICAL WRITING AND COMMUNICATION
0047-6439	MEDIA & CONSUMER
0047-6447	MEDIA MIX
0047-8091	MORE
0047-8296	MOVIEGOER
0048-3583	Petersen's Photographic Magazine *Varied under* PETERSEN'S PHOTOGRAPHIC
0048-5314	PRINT-EQUIP NEWS
0048-5942	PUBLISHER'S AUXILIARY
0048-718x	CABLE TELEVISION ENGINEERING
0049-2574	Super 8 Filmaker *Varied under* MOVING IMAGE
0049-3600	Theatre Quarterly *Varied under* NEW THEATRE QUARTERLY
0049-4542	Travel & Camera *Varied under* TRAVEL & LEISURE
0049-6189	Victorian Periodicals Newsletter *Varied under* VICTORIAN PERIODICALS REVIEW
0049-6243	VIDEOCASSETTE AND CATV NEWSLETTER
0049-7797	WOMEN & FILM
0065-3640	Advertising Statistical Review *Varied under* PRESS STATISTICAL REVIEW
0065-8820	Journal of the American Institute of Graphic Arts *Varied under* AIGA JOURNAL OF GRAPHIC DESIGN
0068-2748	BROADSIDE
0069-4169	Cinemeditor *Varied under* AMERICAN CINEMEDITOR
0071-9943	FUNNYWORLD
0085-2198	IPI SURVEY
0090-2136	QP Herald *Varied under* MOTION PICTURE PRODUCT DIGEST
0090-3000	CINEMAGIC
0090-4260	LITERATURE/FILM QUARTERLY
0090-6778	IEEE TRANSACTIONS ON COMMUNICATIONS
0090-9831	CRITIC
0090-9882	Journal of Applied Communications Research *Varied under* JOURNAL OF APPLIED COMMUNICATION RESEARCH
0090-9882	JOURNAL OF APPLIED COMMUNICATION RESEARCH
0091-3367	JOURNAL OF ADVERTISING
0091-360x	AUDIO-VISUAL GUIDE
0091-360x	AV GUIDE
0092-1815	International Journal of Instructional Media *Varied under* INTERNATIONAL JOURNAL OF INSTRUCTIONAL MEDIA AND TECHNOLOGY
0092-1815	INTERNATIONAL JOURNAL OF INSTRUCTIONAL MEDIA AND TECHNOLOGY
0092-7384	IABC Journal *Varied under* JOURNAL OF COMMUNICATION MANAGEMENT
0092-7821	WACC Journal *Varied under* MEDIA DEVELOPMENT
0092-8607	BIOMEDICAL COMMUNICATIONS
0092-9441	URBAN TELECOMMUNICATIONS FORUM
0093-1594	TELEVISION OPPORTUNITIES
0093-2132	Product Digest *Varied under* MOTION PICTURE PRODUCT DIGEST
0093-335x	PROMOTION
0093-6499	AudioVideo *Varied under* AUDIOVIDEO INTERNATIONAL
0093-6502	COMMUNICATION RESEARCH
0093-8149	PUBLIC TELECOMMUNICATIONS REVIEW
0094-7679	JOURNALISM HISTORY
0095-1447	CINEFAN
0095-4063	COMMUNICATIONS WORLD
0095-9197	Electrical Engineering *Varied under* IEEE SPECTRUM
0095-9480	GENERAL ELECTRIC REVIEW
0095-9499	General Radio Experimenter, The *Varied under* GR TODAY
0095-9669	COMSAT TECHNICAL REVIEW
0095-9804	Journal of the AIEE *Varied under* IEEE SPECTRUM
0096-1000	IRE Transactions on Information Theory *Varied under* IEEE TRANSACTIONS ON INFORMATION THEORY
0096-1655	IRE Transactions on Broadcast and Television Receivers *Varied under* IEEE TRANSACTIONS ON CONSUMER ELECTRONICS
0096-1663	IRE Transactions on Broadcasting *Varied under* IEEE TRANSACTIONS ON BROADCASTING
0096-1965	IEEE Transactions on Communications Systems *Varied under* IEEE TRANSACTIONS ON COMMUNICATIONS
0096-2244	IRE Transactions on Communications Systems *Varied under* IEEE TRANSACTIONS ON COMMUNICATIONS
0096-2562	Inland and American Printer and Lithographer, The *Varied under* AMERICAN PRINTER
0096-5812	Journal of Photographic Society of America *Varied under* PSA JOURNAL
0096-5863	Minicam Photography *Varied under* MODERN PHOTOGRAPHY
0096-7785	RCA BROADCAST NEWS
0096-8390	Proceedings of the IRE *Varied under* PROCEEDINGS OF THE IEEE
0096-8692	Bell Telephone Magazine *Varied under* AT&T MAGAZINE
0097-1138	ABSOLUTE SOUND, THE
0097-577x	AMATEUR PHOTOGRAPHER'S WEEKLY, THE
0097-577x	AMERICAN PHOTOGRAPHY
0097-5818	CAMERA MAGAZINE

ISSN	Title
0097-5885	PHOTO-ERA MAGAZINE
0097-6660	Radio and TV News *Varied under* ELECTRONICS WORLD
0097-8329	CONSUMER ELECTRONICS PRODUCT NEWS
0098-213x	FORECAST
0098-3063	IEEE TRANSACTIONS ON CONSUMER ELECTRONICS
0098-7913	SERIALS REVIEW
0098-8227	Photographic Applications in Science, Technology and Medicine *Varied under* FUNCTIONAL PHOTOGRAPHY
0098-8863	EXPOSURE
0099-1090	COMMUNICATOR, THE
0099-6866	IRE Transactions on Broadcast Transmission Systems *Varied under* IEEE TRANSACTIONS ON BROADCASTING
0112-9775	ELECTRONICS AND COMMUNICATIONS
0116-2446	SOSYALI MAGAZINE
0126-6209	ABU TECHNICAL REVIEW
0129-2986	ASIAN JOURNAL OF COMMUNICATION
0140-7740	ANIMATIONS
0141-0857	PRACTICAL WIRELESS
0141-1748	INTERNATIONAL BROADCASTING
0141-8920	Advertising *Varied under* ADVERTISING MAGAZINE
0141-9013	VIDEO
0142-7229	ETI
0142-730x	TELCO REPORT, THE
0142-7466	TV WORLD
0143-5558	MEDIA DEVELOPMENT
0143-6236	Social Science Information Studies *Varied under* INTERNATIONAL JOURNAL OF INFORMATION MANAGEMENT
0143-9685	HISTORICAL JOURNAL OF FILM, RADIO & TELEVISION
0144-4646	COMMUNICATION RESEARCH TRENDS
0144-5944	STUDIO SOUND AND BROADCAST ENGINEERING
0144-6010	VIDEO TODAY
0145-3483	CINEGRAM
0145-5427	RELIGIOUS MEDIA TODAY
0145-6032	CINEFANTASTIQUE
0145-6261	FEED-BACK
0145-6822	News - Action for Children's Television *Varied under* RE:ACT
0145-9651	MEDIA REPORT TO WOMEN
0146-0013	Quarterly Review of Film Studies *Varied under* QUARTERLY REVIEW OF FILM AND VIDEO
0146-0013	QUARTERLY REVIEW OF FILM AND VIDEO
0146-0153	PHOTOMETHODS
0146-0609	New Review of Books and Religion, The *Varied under* BOOKS & RELIGION
0146-2091	MEDIA DIGEST
0146-3373	COMMUNICATION QUARTERLY
0146-4647	ITA NEWS DIGEST
0146-4701	AUDIO CRITIC, THE
0146-5023	MOTION PICTURE PRODUCT DIGEST
0146-5546	JUMP CUT
0147-2216	Western Speech Communication *Varied under* WESTERN JOURNAL OF SPEECH COMMUNICATION
0147-3204	IEEE TRANSACTIONS ON CABLE TELEVISION
0147-4049	BRIGHT LIGHTS
0147-4286	PCS, THE POPULAR CULTURE SCHOLAR
0147-4871	FEEDBACK
0147-510x	US MAGAZINE
0147-5789	Scintillation *Varied under* CINEMONKEY
0147-7439	SATELLITE COMMUNICATIONS
0147-8907	Video *Varied under* VIDEO MAGAZINE
0148-5806	EDUCATIONAL COMMUNICATION AND TECHNOLOGY
0148-589x	Student Forum *Varied under* PHOTOGRAPHER'S FORUM
0148-6373	Electronic, Electro-Optic and Infrared Countermeasures *Varied under* MILITARY ELECTRONICS / COUNTERMEASURES
0148-9631	Newspaper Production *Varied under* WEB
0148-964x	Newspaper Production for North and South America *Varied under* WEB
0149-0737	NEWS MEDIA & THE LAW, THE
0149-1172	Washington Journalism Review *Varied under* WASHINGTON JOURNALISM REVIEW
0149-1830	VELVET LIGHT TRAP
0149-6832	VU Marketplace *Varied under* VIDEO MANAGEMENT
0149-6980	MEDIA & VALUES
0149-7014	ON LOCATION
0149-8932	INTERVIEW
0149-9262	ACCESS
0149-9327	NOSTALGIA ILLUSTRATED
0149-9971	REVIEW OF INTERNATIONAL BROADCASTING
0158-0736	PROCEEDINGS OF THE IREE AUSTRALIA
0158-4154	CANTRILLS FILMNOTES
0160-1989	FRENDX
0160-3825	STUDENT PRESS LAW CENTER REPORT
0160-6840	WIDE ANGLE
0160-7294	Business Screen *Varied under* COMPUTER PICTURES
0160-7316	FLQ *Varied under* FILM LIBRARY QUARTERLY
0160-8908	INTERNATIONAL RADIO REPORT, THE
0160-8983	MEDIA ANTHROPOLOGIST NEWSLETTER
0160-9769	HIGH PERFORMANCE
0161-0775	THEATER
0161-1526	Sidney Miller's Black Radio Exclusive *Varied under* BLACK RADIO EXCLUSIVE
0161-1585	ON FILM
0161-3448	SATELLITE NEWS
0161-374x	Communications *Varied under* TELEVISION ENGINEERING
0161-3936	Carleton Drama Review *Varied under* TDR
0161-3995	MOVIES AND MINISTRY
0161-5785	PRINTING PAPER
0161-5823	Perry's Broadcasting and the Law *Varied under* BROADCASTING AND THE LAW
0161-5823	BROADCASTING AND THE LAW
0161-6528	Atlas World Press Review *Varied under* WORLD PRESS REVIEW
0161-6854	American Photographer *Varied under* AMERICAN PHOTO
0161-7605	CABLE LIBRARIES
0161-9063	Broadcast Financial Journal *Varied under* BROADCAST CABLE FINANCIAL JOURNAL
0162-0010	COLORADO EDITOR
0162-0126	CINEMONKEY
0162-0932	VERBATIM
0162-3885	BUSINESS COMMUNICATIONS REVIEW
0162-394x	Players Magazine *Varied under* PLAYERS
0162-5659	Journal of Organizational Communication *Varied under* JOURNAL OF COMMUNICATION MANAGEMENT

ISSN	Title
0162-9093	COMMUNICATIONS AND THE LAW
0163-3007	BLACK STARS
0163-321x	RF DESIGN
0163-3236	Shooting Commercials *Varied under* SHOOTING COMMERCIALS
0163-4089	AMERICAN DEMOGRAPHICS
0163-4437	MEDIA, CULTURE, AND SOCIETY
0163-4968	Mass Media Bi-Weekly Newsletter *Varied under* MASS MEDIA NEWSLETTER
0163-5069	FILM CRITICISM
0163-7460	Art Product News *Varied under* ART & DESIGN NEWS
0163-7517	SALES & MARKETING MANAGEMENT
0163-7606	FEDERAL COMMUNICATIONS LAW JOURNAL
0163-7908	RE:ACT
0163-8378	CELEBRITY
0163-9137	Theatre Communications Group Newsletter *Varied under* AMERICAN THEATRE
0163-9250	Darkroom Photography *Varied under* CAMERA & DARKROOM PHOTOGRAPHY
0163-9250	DARKROOM PHOTOGRAPHY
0163-9412	Advertising World *Varied under* INTERNATIONAL ADVERTISER
0164-2111	FANGORIA
0164-3495	EMMY
0164-3584	SOAP OPERA DIGEST
0164-4076	MILITARY ELECTRONICS / COUNTERMEASURES
0164-4122	WISCONSIN PHOTOGRAPHER
0164-4327	Reproductions Review & Methods *Varied under* IN-PLANT REPRODUCTIONS
0164-4343	MARKETING COMMUNICATIONS
0164-4769	PHOTO LAB MANAGEMENT
0164-6338	PRO SOUND NEWS
0164-6508	AFTERNOON TV
0164-6834	Audio Visual Product News *Varied under* AV VIDEO
0164-8489	TVC *Varied under* CABLE TV BUSINESS MAGAZINE
0164-9655	MILLIMETER
0164-9876	Marketing Bestsellers *Varied under* MAGAZINE & BOOKSELLER
0164-9957	MIX
0164-999x	Broadcast Communications *Varied under* TELEVISION BROADCAST
0174-0253	LEICA FOTOGRAFIE INTERNATIONAL
0190-1400	PHOTOLETTER
0190-1974	LEARNING RESOURCES
0191-3417	Audiovisual Instruction with/Instructional Resources *Varied under* TECHTRENDS
0191-4634	WEB
0191-4898	BROADCAST PROGRAMMING AND PRODUCTION
0191-541x	LIGHTING DIMENSIONS
0191-5428	COMMUNICATIONS ENGINEERING & DESIGN
0191-8591	PANORAMA
0192-2874	Book Production Industry & Magazine Production *Varied under* HIGH VOLUME PRINTING
0192-2882	THEATRE JOURNAL
0192-592x	THE JOURNAL
0192-6209	Telecommunications [Euroglobal Edition] *Varied under* TELECOMMUNICATIONS
0192-6918	Studies in the Anthropology of Visual Communication *Varied under* STUDIES IN VISUAL COMMUNICATION
0192-7175	ELECTRONIC TECHNICAN/DEALER
0192-7663	Media Management Monographs *Varied under* PUBLISHING TRENDS & TRENDSETTERS
0192-9275	PRINTING HISTORY
0192-9933	American Printer and Lithographer *Varied under* AMERICAN PRINTER
0193-0141	PD Cue *Varied under* NATPE PROGRAMMER
0193-0540	Law Enforcement Communications *Varied under* LAW ENFORCEMENT TECHNOLOGY
0193-2861	SATELLITE WEEK
0193-3663	PUBLIC BROADCASTING REPORT, THE
0193-6700	WESTERN JOURNAL OF SPEECH COMMUNICATION
0193-7383	EDITORIAL EYE, THE
0193-7707	MASS COMM REVIEW
0193-8398	HASTINGS COMMUNICATIONS AND ENTERTAINMENT LAW JOURNAL
0193-9661	International Marketing Report *Varied under* INTERNATIONAL ADVERTISER
0194-2190	Broadcast Equipment Exchange *Varied under* RADIO WORLD
0194-2484	HOME VIDEO
0194-2506	Magazine Age *Varied under* INSIDE MEDIA
0194-3243	PRESSTIME
0194-3588	DM NEWS
0194-4266	TV RADIO TALK
0194-4339	Filmmakers *Varied under* FILMMAKERS FILM & VIDEO MONTHLY
0194-4339	Filmmakers *Varied under* FILMMAKERS FILM & VIDEO MONTHLY
0194-4789	MAC/Western Advertising News *Varied under* ADWEEK
0194-5114	Commercials Monthly *Varied under* ENTERTAINMENT MONTHLY
0194-5467	PHOTOGRAPHER'S FORUM
0194-7869	COMICS JOURNAL, THE
0195-0495	SPECIALTY ADVERTISING BUSINESS
0195-1017	Film News *Varied under* FILM & VIDEO NEWS
0195-1750	VIDEO STORE
0195-2684	Screen Actor Newsletter *Varied under* SCREEN ACTOR HOLLYWOOD
0195-3850	Darkroom Techniques *Varied under* DARKROOM AND CREATIVE CAMERA TECHNIQUES
0195-3850	DARKROOM AND CREATIVE CAMERA TECHNIQUES
0195-4296	Marketing & Media Decisions *Varied under* MEDIAWEEK
0195-6051	JOURNAL OF POPULAR FILM AND TELEVISION
0195-6779	MEDIA HISTORY DIGEST
0195-7473	POLITICAL COMMUNICATION AND PERSUASION
0195-7791	SOCIAL SCIENCE MONITOR
0195-7961	WATCH
0195-8267	AMERICAN CLASSIC SCREEN
0195-8585	ANPA NEWS RESEARCH REPORT
0195-8895	WORLD PRESS REVIEW
0196-1160	Printers' Ink *Varied under* MARKETING / COMMUNICATIONS
0196-3007	PERSPECTIVES ON FILM
0196-5905	VIDEO WEEK
0196-6979	Instructional Innovator *Varied under* TECHTRENDS

ISSN					
0196-8599	JOURNAL OF COMMUNICATION INQUIRY, THE	0199-9257	Mediascene Prevue *Varied under* PREVUE	0270-885x	CABLE TV ADVERTISING
0196-8793	VIDEO REVIEW	0199-9486	CLASSIC IMAGES REVIEW	0270-9783	JEA NEWSWIRE
0197-2359	Advertising Age/Europe *Varied under* FOCUS	0204-8884	BULGARIAN FILMS	0271-1583	CAMERA ARTS
		0250-6998	CINEMA VISION INDIA	0271-261x	IN CINEMA
0197-2448	Journalism Bulletin, The *Varied under* JQ. JOURNALISM QUARTERLY.	0257-893x	ASIAN ADVERTISING & MARKETING	0271-5309	LANGUAGE & COMMUNICATION
		0260-7417	JOURNAL OF EDUCATIONAL TELEVISION	0272-2720	DRAMA-LOGUE
0197-677x	INTERNATIONAL VIDEOTEXT TELETEXT NEWS			0273-2246	SHOOTING COMMERCIALS
		0260-9428	Bulletin of ALPSP *Varied under* LEARNED PUBLISHING	0273-4249	Loyola of Los Angeles Entertainment Law Journal *Varied under* LOYOLA ENTERTAINMENT JOURNAL
0197-6907	AIGA Journal *Varied under* AIGA JOURNAL OF GRAPHIC DESIGN	0261-4472	AFTERIMAGE		
		0261-9903	Journal of Advertising *Varied under* INTERNATIONAL JOURNAL OF ADVERTISING		
0197-7849	ASCAP IN ACTION			0273-4354	TDR *Varied under* TDR
0197-9388	ScriptWriter *Varied under* SCRIPTWRITER NEWS			0273-4753	JOURNAL OF MARKETING EDUCATION
		0262-0251	MEDIA IN EDUCATION AND DEVELOPMENT		
0198-1056	CINEFEX			0273-561x	Premium Channels *Varied under* PREMIUM CHANNELS TV BLUEPRINT
0198-1064	CINEMACABRE	0263-5003	VIDEO–THE MAGAZINE		
0198-6228	INTERNATIONAL ADVERTISER	0263-5682	Broadcast Sound *Varied under* BROADCAST SYSTEMS ENGINEERING		
0198-6228	International Marketing Report *Varied under* INTERNATIONAL ADVERTISER, THE			0273-5636	ON CABLE
				0273-7043	FANTASTIC FILMS
		0264-1321	Professional Video *Varied under* BROADCAST SYSTEMS ENGINEERING	0273-7493	GOSSIP
0198-6554	C: JET			0273-7817	Video User *Varied under* VIDEO MANAGEMENT
0198-7240	BETTER LISTENING				
0198-7305	CINEMANEWS, THE	0264-1755	Advertising Age's Focus *Varied under* FOCUS	0273-8392	VIEW
0198-8573	Record Review *Varied under* FRESH!			0273-8511	MODERN RECORDING & MUSIC
		0265-0487	INTERNATIONAL JOURNAL OF ADVERTISING		
0198-9065	In-Plant Reproductions *Varied under* IN-PLANT REPRODUCTIONS			0273-8724	Book and Magazine Production *Varied under* HIGH VOLUME PRINTING
		0265-1297	VIDEO WORLD		
		0265-7198	35mm Photography *Varied under* PHOTOGRAPHY		
0198-9456	Videodisc/Teletext *Varied under* OPTICAL INFORMATION SYSTEMS			0273-8902	Music & Sound Output *Varied under* STAGE & STUDIO
		0266-3244	Electronics & Wireless World *Varied under* ELECTRONICS WORLD + WIRELESS WORLD		
				0273-9291	60 SECONDS
0199-0497	Shooting Commercials & Industrials *Varied under* SHOOTING COMMERCIALS			0273-9828	VIDEOPLAY MAGAZINE
				0274-6328	Ad Forum *Varied under* ADWEEK'S MARKETING WEEK
		0266-464x	NEW THEATRE QUARTERLY		
0199-1590	Rona Barrett's Gossip *Varied under* GOSSIP	0266-8688	MEDIA INTERNATIONAL	0274-7499	Graphics Design, USA *Varied under* GRAPHIC DESIGN: USA
		0267-1689	Journal of the Institution of Electronic and Radio Engineers, The *Varied under* ELECTRONICS & COMMUNICATIONS ENGINEERING JOURNAL		
0199-1817	Rona Barrett's Daytimers *Varied under* REAL LIFE/DAYTIMERS			0274-7693	TGIF
				0274-7766	Premi'ere *Varied under* AMERICAN PREMIERE
0199-199x	TONI HOLT'S MOVIE LIFE				
0199-2201	RONA BARRETT'S HOLLYWOOD			0274-8541	RADIO WORLD
		0267-3231	EUROPEAN JOURNAL OF COMMUNICATION	0274-9831	TWR
0199-2422	NEWS PHOTOGRAPHER			0275-3804	Audio Engineering *Varied under* AUDIO
0199-3003	SOAP OPERA STARS	0267-3789	AIRWAVES		
0199-4387	SHOW BIZ WEST	0267-565x	BROADCAST SYSTEMS ENGINEERING	0275-5971	Theatre Communications *Varied under* AMERICAN THEATRE
0199-4743	ADWEEK				
0199-4913	PETERSEN'S PHOTOGRAPHIC	0268-2028	PLAYS INTERNATIONAL		
0199-7300	FILM JOURNAL, THE	0268-4012	INTERNATIONAL JOURNAL OF INFORMATION MANAGEMENT	0275-8342	Union Tabloid *Varied under* GRAPHIC COMMUNICATOR
0199-7459	COMICS FEATURE				
0199-7866	Hollywood Close Up *Varied under* SCREEN ACTOR HOLLYWOOD	0270-3564	Newsletter - Media Institute *Varied under* BUSINESS AND THE MEDIA	0276-0835	Video *Varied under* VIDEO EIGHTIES MAGAZINE
				0276-1572	Channels of Communications *Varied under* CHANNELS
0199-7866	Hollywood *Varied under* SCREEN ACTOR HOLLYWOOD	0270-3572	BUSINESS AND THE MEDIA		
		0270-5346	CAMERA OBSCURA	0276-3494	MOVING IMAGE
		0270-5869	Bell Telephone Quarterly *Varied under* AT&T MAGAZINE	0276-6558	STUDIES IN VISUAL COMMUNICATION

ISSN	Title
0276-7309	Television & Children *Varied under* TELEVISION & FAMILIES
0276-8593	MULTICHANNEL NEWS
0277-3945	RHETORIC SOCIETY QUARTERLY
0277-4860	R & R
0277-9897	POST SCRIPT
0278-0011	CHRONICLE OF INTERNATIONAL COMMUNICATION
0278-1441	ART PAPERS
0278-2790	PHOTOGRAPHER'S MARKET NEWSLETTER
0278-4831	TELECOMMUNICATIONS
0278-484x	Telecommunications [Global Edition] *Varied under* TELECOMMUNICATIONS
0278-5013	VIDEO AGE INTERNATIONAL
0278-503x	CABLE TV PROGRAMMING
0278-8179	AEJ Newsletter, The *Varied under* AEJMC NEWS
0278-9183	Videodisc, Videotex *Varied under* OPTICAL INFORMATION SYSTEMS
0278-9922	ELECTRONIC SERVICING & TECHNOLOGY
0279-0041	AMERICAN PREMIERE
0279-070x	Computers and Programming *Varied under* COMMUNICATIONS WORLD
0279-4004	CABLEAGE
0279-571x	VIDEO BUSINESS
0279-585x	Science & Electronics *Varied under* COMMUNICATIONS WORLD
0279-8891	CABLE MARKETING
0279-8980	Scholastic Editor *Varied under* SCHOLASTIC EDITOR'S TRENDS IN PUBLICATIONS
0279-9596	SCRIPTWRITER NEWS
0300-7472	AFTERIMAGE
0300-7685	INDUSTRIAL TELEVISION NEWS
0302-9794	Novum Gebrauchsgraphik *Varied under* NOVUM GEBRAUCHSGRAPHIK
0305-2249	AUDIO VISUAL
0305-4233	COMMUNICATION
0305-6104	Independent Broadcasting *Varied under* AIRWAVES
0305-6996	BKSTS Journal, The *Varied under* IMAGE TECHNOLOGY
0306-0691	Screen Education *Varied under* SCREEN
0306-4220	INDEX ON CENSORSHIP
0307-4617	SCREEN INTERNATIONAL
0308-2369	BBC ENGINEERING
0308-454x	TELEVISION
0308-5961	TELECOMMUNICATIONS POLICY
0308-7298	HISTORY OF PHOTOGRAPHY
0309-0256	MEDIA REPORTER, THE
0309-118x	INTERMEDIA
0311-3639	CINEMA PAPERS
0312-9616	MEDIA INFORMATION AUSTRALIA
0313-4059	AUSTRALIAN JOURNAL OF SCREEN THEORY
0314-4313	Proceedings of the IREE *Varied under* PROCEEDINGS OF THE IREE AUSTRALIA
0314-4321	Monitor *Varied under* PROCEEDINGS OF THE IREE AUSTRALIA
0316-4004	PULP & PAPER CANADA
0317-1213	Printer & Publisher *Varied under* CANADIAN PRINTER
0317-4514	IN SEARCH
0318-0050	Canadian Telephone Journal, The *Varied under* CABLE COMMUNICATIONS MAGAZINE
0318-0069	CABLE COMMUNICATIONS MAGAZINE
0319-1389	Canadian Broadcaster, The *Varied under* BROADCASTER
0319-1419	HUMAN COMMUNICATION
0340-0158	International Journal of Communication Research *Varied under* COMMUNICATIONS
0341-2059	COMMUNICATIONS
0345-4533	HASSELBLAD
0355-1520	FACTS ABOUT FILM FINLAND
0355-1539	Finland Filmland *Varied under* FINNISH FILMS
0360-0939	ACA BULLETIN
0360-3342	LIBERTY, THEN AND NOW
0360-3695	FILM & HISTORY
0360-3989	HUMAN COMMUNICATION RESEARCH
0360-7216	FUNCTIONAL PHOTOGRAPHY
0361-0004	Modern Recording *Varied under* MODERN RECORDING & MUSIC
0361-0942	VIDEO SYSTEMS
0361-4131	INTERNATIONAL FILM BUFF
0361-4573	Journal of the SMPTE *Varied under* SMPTE JOURNAL
0361-4751	AMERICAN FILM
0361-5081	SERVICE FOR COMPANY COMMUNNICATORS
0361-8269	Southern Speech Communication Journal, The *Varied under* SOUTHERN COMMUNICATION JOURNAL, THE
0361-8366	ALPHABET AND IMAGE
0361-8374	CABLEVISION
0361-865x	MASS MEDIA NEWSLETTER
0361-9168	American Society of Magazine Photographers. News *Varied under* ASMP BULLETIN
0361-9168	Bulletin. ASMP *Varied under* ASMP BULLETIN
0362-0875	FILM & BROADCASTING REVIEW
0362-0905	Focus: Chicago *Varied under* FACETS FEATURES
0362-1162	Audio & Video News *Varied under* AUDIOVIDEO INTERNATIONAL
0362-1162	AUDIOVIDEO INTERNATIONAL
0362-4722	CONSUMER ELECTRONICS
0362-5974	PROFESSIONAL FILM PRODUCTION
0362-6245	U & LC
0363-1001	VIDEOGRAPHY
0363-2636	LENS MAGAZINE
0363-2911	ART & CINEMA
0363-4523	COMMUNICATION EDUCATION
0363-7751	COMMUNICATION MONOGRAPHS
0363-8111	PUBLIC RELATIONS REVIEW
0364-7625	ACCESS REPORTS/FREEDOM OF INFORMATION
0366-7073	CAMERA
0373-109x	British Kinematography, Sound and Television *Varied under* IMAGE TECHNOLOGY
0374-2393	Archiv der Elektrischen Ubertragung *Varied under* AEU
0377-1210	MEDIA ASIA
0383-0225	Canadian Film Weekly *Varied under* CANADIAN FILM DIGEST
0383-0233	Canadian Film and TV Bi-Weekly *Varied under* CANADIAN FILM DIGEST
0383-6908	Sound Canada *Varied under* SOUND & VISION
0383-9338	Broadcast Equipment Today *Varied under* BROADCAST + TECHNOLOGY
0384-1618	Media Probe *Varied under* CANADIAN JOURNAL OF COMMUNICATION
0385-4507	JEE, JOURNAL OF ELECTRONIC ENGINEERING

ISSN	Title
0409-283x	Better Broadcasts Newsletter *Varied under* BETTER BROADCASTS NEWS
0412-5479	CINEMAGES
0414-0303	COMMERCIAL CAMERA
0414-1121	COMMUNICATION ENGINEERING
0414-1520	Community Theatre Bulletin *Varied under* THEATRE JOURNAL
0419-7127	DRAMA SURVEY
0422-7840	EIGHT MM MOVIE MAKER AND CINE CAMERA
0423-9865	EBU Review. Part A: Technical *Varied under* EBU REVIEW. TECHNICAL.
0424-0197	ETV REPORTER
0424-6101	Educational Television *Varied under* E-ITV
0437-163x	GANNETTEER
0449-329x	Journal of Typographic Research, The *Varied under* VISIBLE LANGUAGE
0468-1835	NIELSEN NEWSCAST, THE
0480-1008	PERSPECTIVE
0492-0538	TV People *Varied under* TV PEOPLE AND PICTURES
0495-0372	TELEVISION ENGINEERING
0496-8816	TAPE RECORDING
0496-9960	TEACHER'S GUIDE TO TELEVISION
0497-137x	TELECOMMUNICATION JOURNAL
0497-1515	TELEVISION DIGEST WITH CONSUMER ELECTRONICS
0512-3658	WORLD SCREEN
0512-3704	WORLD THEATRE
0515-491x	ADVERTISING REVIEW
0519-4229	AUDIOCRAFT FOR THE HI-FI HOBBYIST
0524-5753	BRITISH COMMUNICATIONS AND ELECTRONICS
0527-3919	CAMERA CRAFT
0531-7991	ENTERTAINMENT WORLD
0533-1056	FILMING
0536-5465	IMAGE
0537-5185	INDUSTRIAL ELECTRONICS
0545-8846	NEWSPAPER TECHNIQUES
0547-3861	CODE NEWS
0548-8974	New York State Community Theatre Journal *Varied under* THEATRE JOURNAL
0559-9210	SHOW BUSINESS ILLUSTRATED
0563-4040	THEATRE NEWS
0567-3607	AD Assistant *Varied under* ADVERTISING AND GRAPHIC ARTS TECHNIQUES
0567-8390	ACTION!
0569-6712	ANPA Newspaper Information Service Newsletter *Varied under* ANPA PUBLIC AFFAIRS NEWSLETTER
0571-8716	Audio-Visual Media *Varied under* EDUCATIONAL MEDIA INTERNATIONAL
0574-9204	CATV *Varied under* VUE
0574-9905	Cablecasting and Educational Television *Varied under* E-ITV
0575-0954	CAHIERS DU CINEMA IN ENGLISH
0576-4823	Canadian Cinematography *Varied under* CINEMA/CANADA
0577-9960	Christian Broadcaster *Varied under* MEDIA DEVELOPMENT
0582-2475	SCIENTIFIC FILM
0583-1318	SHOW
0584-4738	SOUTHERN THEATRE
0584-8512	SPECTRA
0585-2544	STEREOPHILE
0589-5758	CONTRAST
0590-7918	Canadian Film Weekly *Varied under* CANADIAN FILM DIGEST
0703-6930	Sound *Varied under* SOUND & VISION
0705-3657	CANADIAN JOURNAL OF COMMUNICATION
0709-4698	VICTORIAN PERIODICALS REVIEW
0709-9797	Broadcast Technology *Varied under* BROADCAST + TECHNOLOGY
0709-9797	BROADCAST + TECHNOLOGY
0722-6268	BALLETT INTERNATIONAL
0730-482x	IMAGEMAKER
0730-6156	TELEMARKETING
0730-7616	Radio-Electronics Special Projects *Varied under* POPULAR ELECTRONICS
0730-7799	COMMUNICATION BRIEFINGS
0731-5198	INDEPENDENT, THE
0731-5996	Proceedings of the Institute of Radio Engineers *Varied under* PROCEEDINGS OF THE IEEE
0731-8294	RADIO ONLY
0731-9312	INSIDE RADIO
0731-9452	Optical memory Newsletter Including Interactive Videodisks *Varied under* OPTICAL MEMORY NEWS
0732-1880	ENTERTAINMENT AND SPORTS LAWYER, THE
0732-5622	Starlog Presents Comics Scene *Varied under* COMICS SCENE
0732-5800	Review of Books and Religion, The *Varied under* BOOKS & RELIGION
0732-7668	SATELLITE ORBIT
0732-7870	IMAGES & IDEAS BY PHOTOMETHODS
0733-2734	PHOTOPLAY COMBINED WITH MOVIE MIRROR
0733-3315	POPULAR COMMUNICATIONS
0733-5113	JOURNAL OF ARTS MANAGEMENT AND LAW, THE
0733-9739	DBS NEWS
0734-0796	Literature in Performance *Varied under* TPQ
0734-7529	National Professional Photographer, The *Varied under* PROFESSIONAL PHOTOGRAPHER, THE
0734-9130	PSA
0734-919x	Journal of the University Film and Video Association *Varied under* JOURNAL OF FILM AND VIDEO
0734-9238	News Research Bulletin *Varied under* ANPA NEWS RESEARCH REPORT
0735-5629	St. Louis Photographer *Varied under* ST. LOUIS AND CANADIAN PHOTOGRAPHER
0735-777x	HIGH FIDELITY/MUSICAL AMERICA
0735-8393	PERFORMING ARTS JOURNAL
0736-1750	MEDIA LAW NOTES
0736-3745	FACETS FEATURES
0736-489x	CABLE TV AND NEW MEDIA LAW & FINANCE
0736-5322	AIGA JOURNAL OF GRAPHIC DESIGN
0736-5853	TELEMATICS AND INFORMATICS
0736-7457	Professional Publishing *Varied under* PERSONAL PUBLISHING
0736-7694	CARDOZO ARTS & ENTERTAINMENT LAW JOURNAL
0737--762	COMMUNICATIONS LAWYER
0737-1020	HIGH VOLUME PRINTING
0737-2582	Film/AV News *Varied under* FILM & VIDEO NEWS
0737-3929	International Television *Varied under* CORPORATE TELEVISION
0738-0534	HOMILETIC

ISSN	Title
0738-2553	Electronic Products *Varied under* ELECTRONIC PRODUCTS
0738-5714	FCC WEEK
0738-7792	AIM REPORT
0738-9558	PRINTED MATTER
0739-1056	COLLEGE MEDIA REVIEW
0739-3180	CRITICAL STUDIES IN MASS COMMUNICATION
0739-5329	NEWSPAPER RESEARCH JOURNAL
0739-6953	ZIP Target Marketing *Varied under* TARGET MARKETING
0739-7089	VIDEODISC MONITOR, THE
0739-7208	TELECONFERENCE MAGAZINE
0739-750x	SYN-AUD-CON NEWSLETTER
0739-8123	PERSONAL ELECTRONICS
0739-988x	LINK-UP
0739-991x	CURRENT
0740-5545	CLOSE-UP
0740-6479	Mass Media Booknotes *Varied under* COMMUNICATION BOOKNOTES
0740-8382	About Music and Writers *Varied under* BMI: MUSICWORLD
0740-9249	Direct Advertising and Sample Book of Mill Brand Papers *Varied under* PRINTING PAPER
0740-9265	Direct Advertising *Varied under* PRINTING PAPER
0740-9354	TELECONNECT
0740-9370	LOYOLA ENTERTAINMENT JOURNAL
0741-0069	COMMUNICATIONS CONCEPTS
0741-0883	WRITTEN COMMUNICATION
0741-3653	JOURNAL OF EDUCATIONAL PUBLIC RELATIONS
0741-5869	OPTICAL MEMORY NEWS
0741-6148	Book Research Quarterly *Varied under* PUBLISHING RESEARCH QUARTERLY
0741-8469	RADIO BUSINESS REPORT
0741-8876	WASHINGTON JOURNALISM REVIEW
0742-2105	CLOSE-UP
0742-4116	MOVIES, THE
0742-4671	JOURNAL OF FILM AND VIDEO
0742-5333	INTERNATIONAL DOCUMENTARY
0742-5384	TELECOMMUNICATIONS ALERT
0742-5740	Videodisc and Optical Disk *Varied under* OPTICAL INFORMATION SYSTEMS
0742-8111	Video Movies *Varied under* VIDEO TIMES
0742-8111	VIDEO TIMES
0743-0205	Record [Bell Laboratories] *Varied under* AT&T TECHNOLOGY
0743-1279	MB NEWS
0743-2178	MARKETING NEW MEDIA
0743-2968	Hands-On Electronics *Varied under* POPULAR ELECTRONICS
0743-3204	BOMB MAGAZINE
0743-619x	Digital Audio & Compact Disc Review *Varied under* CD REVIEW
0743-7773	E-ITV
0743-8044	VIEWS
0743-9881	WJR *Varied under* WASHINGTON JOURNALISM REVIEW
0744-3102	MAGAZINE & BOOKSELLER
0744-3935	Daytimers *Varied under* REAL LIFE/DAYTIMERS
0744-4370	CHRISTIAN ADVERTISING FORUM
0744-5784	ASMP BULLETIN
0744-6616	AMERICAN PRINTER
0744-6675	Advertising Age [Electronic Media Edition] *Varied under* ELECTRONIC MEDIA
0744-723x	BIG REEL, THE
0744-7612	IABC News *Varied under* COMMUNICATION WORLD
0744-7612	COMMUNICATION WORLD
0744-7841	SATELLITE TV WEEK
0744-8430	Martial Arts Movies *Varied under* ACTION FILMS
0744-8775	ENTERTAINMENT MONTHLY
0744-9739	Satellite TV *Varied under* PRIVATE CABLE
0745-0311	ELECTRONIC MEDIA
0745-080x	73 Amateur Radio's Technical Journal *Varied under* 73 AMATEUR RADIO
0745-1458	COMPUTERS & ELECTRONICS
0745-1822	JOURNAL OF COMMUNICATION MANAGEMENT
0745-2357	SCHOLASTIC EDITOR'S TRENDS IN PUBLICATIONS
0745-2808	Cable Television Business Magazine *Varied under* CABLE TV BUSINESS MAGAZINE
0745-3094	NATPE PROGRAMMER
0745-4058	Journal of Educational Communication *Varied under* JOURNAL OF EDUCATIONAL PUBLIC RELATIONS
0745-4570	COMICS BUYER'S GUIDE
0745-5933	BUSINESS MARKETING
0745-5992	BLACK RADIO EXCLUSIVE
0745-6506	AMAZING HEROES
0745-7243	Screen Actor News *Varied under* SCREEN ACTOR HOLLYWOOD
0745-8711	PRIVATE CABLE
0745-9076	PLAYBILL
0746-0244	REAL LIFE/DAYTIMERS
0746-0996	STUDIO PHOTOGRAPHY
0746-2719	Home Entertainment Quarterly *Varied under* HOME ENTERTAINMENT
0746-2727	HOME ENTERTAINMENT
0746-3286	VIDEOPRO
0746-3626	GRAPHIC COMMUNICATOR
0746-3812	C-SPAN UPDATE
0746-5777	Television/Broadcast Communications *Varied under* TELEVISION BROADCAST
0746-6102	POSTCARD COLLECTOR
0746-7656	MUSIC LINE
0746-8121	COMMUNICATIONSWEEK
0746-8989	Audio Visual Directions *Varied under* AV VIDEO
0746-9225	Screen Actor News *Varied under* SCREEN ACTOR HOLLYWOOD
0746-9438	NEMO
0746-9772	Performance Newspaper *Varied under* PERFORMANCE
0746-9837	4SIGHT MAGAZINE
0747-1335	AV VIDEO
0747-3168	ADVERTISING AND GRAPHIC ARTS TECHNIQUES
0747-3370	ROMANTIC TIMES
0747-3575	COMIC READER, THE
0747-3680	LAW ENFORCEMENT TECHNOLOGY
0747-3745	Video Manager *Varied under* VIDEO MANAGEMENT
0747-4032	RADIOACTIVE
0747-4059	ONSAT
0747-4644	DISNEY CHANNEL MAGAZINE, THE
0747-8909	AEJMC NEWS
0748-0822	HOME VIDEO PUBLISHER
0748-3252	ElectronicsWeek *Varied under* ELECTRONICS
0748-612x	AT&T Bell Laboratories Technical Journal *Varied under* AT&T TECHNICAL JOURNAL
0748-6324	GRAFFITI
0748-657x	COMMUNICATION BOOKNOTES

ISSN INDEX

ISSN	Title
0748-6634	Our Player's Gallery *Varied under* THEATRE MAGAZINE
0748-8173	AAP MONTHLY REPORT
0749-0119	PROFESSIONAL PHOTOGRAPHER, THE
0749-0275	U.S. Camera Annual *Varied under* TRAVEL & LEISURE
0749-6001	CENSORSHIP NEWS
0749-7466	BEYOND THE RATINGS
0749-8152	Record [AT&T Bell Laboratories] *Varied under* AT&T TECHNOLOGY
0749-8829	THEATRE MAGAZINE
0751-7033	IRIS
0822-5486	HUMAN COMMUNICATION CANADA
0824-8435	Cable Communications *Varied under* CABLE COMMUNICATIONS MAGAZINE
0829-3678	SOUND & VISION
0829-9242	APPLIED ARTS QUARTERLY
0847-4990	VIDEO NEWS AND USED
0849-0767	CANADIAN PRINTER
0882-049x	MAGAZINE DESIGN & PRODUCTION
0882-1127	AMERICAN JOURNALISM
0882-1925	FLASH
0882-4088	Communication *Varied under* WORLD COMMUNICATION
0882-4096	COMMUNICATION RESEARCH REPORTS
0882-9314	PERFORMANCE
0883-234x	73 for Radio Amateurs *Varied under* 73 AMATEUR RADIO
0883-3125	STAR TREK: THE OFFICIAL FAN CLUB MAGAZINE
0883-4989	ELECTRONICS
0883-5683	COMPUTER PICTURES
0883-6213	AFI EDUCATION NEWSLETTER
0883-6973	IN HOUSE GRAPHICS
0883-735x	ROTKIN REVIEW, THE
0883-8151	JOURNAL OF BROADCASTING & ELECTRONIC MEDIA
0884-0008	CA Magazine *Varied under* COMMUNICATION ARTS
0884-951x	PERSONAL PUBLISHING
0885-047x	First Stage *Varied under* DRAMA & THEATRE
0885-2340	TV PROGRAM INVESTOR
0885-2456	Journal of Business Communication *Varied under* JOURNAL OF BUSINESS COMMUNICATION, THE
0885-3353	INTERNATIONAL ADVERTISER
0885-6745	STV *Varied under* STV GUIDE
0885-727x	Audio-Visual Communication Review *Varied under* EDUCATIONAL COMMUNICATION AND TECHNOLOGY
0885-9019	Sales Management *Varied under* SALES & MARKETING MANAGEMENT
0886-019x	Optical Information Systems Update / Library & Information Center Applications *Varied under* CD-ROM LIBRARIAN
0886-0483	HOW
0886-3121	In-Plant Reproductions & Electronic Publishing *Varied under* IN-PLANT REPRODUCTIONS
0886-4802	YOUNG VIEWERS
0886-5809	OPTICAL INFORMATION SYSTEMS
0886-7216	ABCA Journal of Business Communication *Varied under* JOURNAL OF BUSINESS COMMUNICATION, THE
0886-7682	STEP-BY-STEP GRAPHICS
0886-800x	Tulane Drama Review *Varied under* TDR
0886-8093	QEX
0886-9596	FRESH!
0886-9642	TELEPROFESSIONAL
0886-9928	Inside Print *Varied under* INSIDE MEDIA
0887-0160	JOURNAL OF LAW & TECHNOLOGY, THE
0887-1701	TV TECHNOLOGY
0887-4182	WORLD MEDIA REPORT
0887-5219	MGF
0887-7661	NETWORK WORLD
0888-3718	Adweek [National Marketing Edition] *Varied under* ADWEEK'S MARKETING WEEK
0888-5680	PHOTO/DESIGN
0888-6695	YELLOW PAGES UPDATE
0889-1596	NEWS COMPUTING JOURNAL
0889-4523	CORPORATE TELEVISION
0889-4973	VIDEOMAKER
0889-5309	73 AMATEUR RADIO
0889-5333	TARGET MARKETING
0889-5341	MONITORING TIMES
0889-5651	Optic Music *Varied under* FILM & VIDEO
0889-6208	IN MOTION FILM & VIDEO PRODUCTION MAGAZINE
0889-8928	MEDIA ARTS
0889-8979	AT&T TECHNOLOGY
0890-0523	JOURNAL OF MASS MEDIA ETHICS
0890-0841	BOOKS & RELIGION
0890-1252	SATELLITE RETAILER
0890-3387	CHRISTIAN FILM & VIDEO
0890-5266	SCREEN ACTOR HOLLYWOOD
0890-5304	OUTDOOR PHOTOGRAPHER
0890-6823	FACTSHEET FIVE
0891-5628	POST
0891-6861	Theatre, The *Varied under* THEATRE MAGAZINE
0891-8759	WRITERS' JOURNAL
0891-8813	BOOK MARKETING UPDATE
0891-8996	IN-PLANT PRINTER & ELECTRONIC PUBLISHER
0892-4929	MOTION PICTURE
0892-5585	LPTV REPORT, THE
0892-5771	HDTV NEWSLETTER
0892-581x	RIGHTING WORDS
0892-5968	GET ANIMATED! UPDATE.
0892-6581	SUCCESSFUL MAGAZINE PUBLISHING
0892-8274	ADWEEK'S MARKETING WEEK
0892-9807	WITTYWORLD
0893-0260	LÜRZER'S INTERNATIONAL ARCHIVE
0893-2700	KAGAN MEDIA INDEX, THE
0893-3189	MANAGEMENT COMMUNICATION QUARTERLY
0893-4215	COMMUNICATION REPORTS
0893-5440	MULTI IMAGES JOURNAL
0893-8342	GANNETT CENTER JOURNAL
0893-9934	CD-ROM LIBRARIAN
0894-2188	HOLLYWOOD STUDIO MAGAZINE
0894-2838	JOURNAL OF COMMUNICATION AND RELIGION, THE
0894-3001	Video Software Dealer *Varied under* VIDEO SOFTWARE MAGAZINE
0894-3443	CAR STEREO REVIEW
0894-4423	Opticmusic's Film & Video Production *Varied under* FILM & VIDEO
0894-6248	TELEVISION & FAMILIES
0894-9263	PREMIERE
0895-0393	FILMFAX
0895-2124	MAGAZINEWEEK
0895-2310	EXTRA!
0895-2892	Video Marketplace *Varied under* MOVIE MARKETPLACE
0895-4143	PERFECT VISION, THE
0895-643x	CHANNELS
0895-8971	Writer's Northwest Handbook Newsletter *Varied under* WRITER'S NW
0895-898x	Writer's Northwest Newsletter *Varied under* WRITER'S NW
0896-1697	WRAP

ISSN	Title
0896-1956	THEATERWEEK
0896-2871	VIDEO CHOICE
0896-3142	Telespan's BusinessTV *Varied under* TELESPAN'S BUSINESSTV GUIDE
0896-4513	DEEP RED
0896-6389	FILM THREAT
0896-7172	HOME & STUDIO RECORDING
0896-8209	PC Publishing *Varied under* PC PUBLISHING AND PRESENTATIONS
0896-8225	Celebrity Focus *Varied under* CELEBRITY PLUS
0896-8802	GOREZONE
0897-2826	IBEW JOURNAL
0897-4381	CELEBRITY PLUS
0897-4632	Television Digest with Consumer Electronics *Varied under* TELEVISION DIGEST WITH CONSUMER ELECTRONICS
0897-4721	WOW! MAGAZINE
0897-5620	Weekly Television Digest with Consumer Electronics *Varied under* TELEVISION DIGEST WITH CONSUMER ELECTRONICS
0897-6007	PUBLISH!
0898-0438	SMPTE Journal *Varied under* SMPTE JOURNAL
0898-1485	SOAP OPERA UPDATE
0898-283x	Media Business News *Varied under* MEDIA BUSINESS
0898-3119	COMICS FANDOM EXAMINER
0898-3720	CAR AUDIO AND ELECTRONICS
0898-6940	FAME
0898-767x	TELEVISION BROADCAST
0898-784x	INDEPENDENT PUBLISHERS TRADE REPORT
0898-9184	MEMORIES
0899-7764	JOURNAL OF MEDIA ECONOMICS
0899-9392	SMASH HITS
0937-9924	POLYGRAPH INTERNATIONAL
0950-2009	PHOTOGRAPHY
0950-2114	IMAGE TECHNOLOGY
0951-0826	COMBROAD
0953-1513	LEARNED PUBLISHING
0953-6841	TBI
0954-0695	ELECTRONICS & COMMUNICATIONS ENGINEERING JOURNAL
0954-6871	VIDEO TIMES
0954-8610	MOVIE - THE VIDEO MAGAZINE
0955-1115	HI-FI CHOICE
0955-114x	STARBURST
0955-1344	TELEVISION WEEK
0955-4602	SATELLITE TIMES
0956-0890	FILM MONTHLY
0956-2281	PIC
0956-2354	WHAT VIDEO
0956-8719	PHOTO ANSWERS
0957-5340	FANTASY ZONE
0957-8552	VIDEO BUYER
0957-9265	DISCOURSE & SOCIETY
0957-9273	VIDEO ANSWERS
0958-1766	VIDEO MONTHLY
0958-2363	TV HITS
0958-7217	LIGHTS!
0958-9147	BEST OF FILM & VIDEO
0959-5813	BROADCAST SYSTEMS INTERNATIONAL
0959-6992	MOVING PICTURES INTERNATIONAL
0959-7697	AUDIOPHILE WITH HI-FI ANSWERS
0959-8332	ELECTRONICS WORLD + WIRELESS WORLD
1015-8596	Radio Television International Review *Varied under* RADIO AND TELEVISION
1040-0141	Tech Photo Pro Imaging Systems *Varied under* ADVANCED IMAGING
1040-2772	VIDEO TECHNOLOGY NEWS
1040-3167	STORYBOARD / THE ART OF LAUGHTER
1040-418x	TELECOMMUNICATIONS WEEK
1040-497x	AWRT NEWS AND VIEWS
1040-5534	PREMIUM CHANNELS TV BLUEPRINT
1040-631x	STV GUIDE
1040-8509	AIRBRUSH ACTION
1040-9440	Publishing Technology *Varied under* PUBLISHING & PRODUCTION EXECUTIVE
1041-0236	HEALTH COMMUNICATION
1041-0643	VIA SATELLITE
1041-1402	V
1041-1933	FILM & VIDEO
1041-5122	LUCASFILM FAN CLUB, THE
1041-5289	ROUNDUP QUARTERLY
1041-5378	AUDIO/VIDEO INTERIORS
1041-617x	ANIMATION MAGAZINE
1041-7117	COMMUNICATOR
1041-794x	SOUTHERN COMMUNICATION JOURNAL, THE
1041-8342	Digital Audio's CD Review *Varied under* CD REVIEW
1041-9780	PRESENTATION PRODUCTS MAGAZINE
1042-0304	PRE-
1042-0711	ADVANCED IMAGING
1042-0746	BUSINESS INFORMATION ALERT
1042-1149	ORBIT VIDEO
1042-1556	Comic Relief Magazine *Varied under* COMIC RELIEF
1042-170x	POPULAR ELECTRONICS
1042-3443	MUSICAL AMERICA
1042-3451	HI-FI HERETIC
1042-3923	ITC Desktop *Varied under* DESKTOP COMMUNICATIONS
1042-539x	ANIMATO!
1042-6736	BMI: MUSICWORLD
1042-7228	CABLE WORLD
1042-9409	STAGE & STUDIO
1043-1438	MILLER'S COPYRIGHT NEWSLETTER
1043-1942	IN-PLANT REPRODUCTIONS
1043-2094	AGAINST THE GRAIN
1043-3791	ASCAP News *Varied under* ASCAP IN ACTION
1043-4860	MONDAY MORNING REPLAY
1043-4933	YELLOW SHEET, THE
1043-7452	NEWSINC.
1043-7487	BME For Technical and Engineering Management *Varied under* BME'S TELEVISION ENGINEERING
1043-8246	SSP LETTER
1044-0682	TV Entertainment Monthly *Varied under* TV ENTERTAINMENT
1044-0852	Electronic Publishing & Printing *Varied under* COMPUTER PUBLISHING
1044-1336	MOVIES USA
1044-1603	PULSE OF RADIO
1044-1700	CD REVIEW
1044-2820	Cable Strategies *Varied under* MSO'S CABLE MARKETING
1044-7288	VIDEO MAGAZINE
1044-7407	FINELINE
1044-9507	HDTV World Review *Varied under* HD SYSTEMS WORLD REVIEW
1045-1234	PREVUE
1045-1706	OFF-HOLLYWOOD REPORT
1045-361x	HOLLYWOOD MAGAZINE
1045-6910	AVC
1045-716x	MEDIA BUSINESS
1045-9723	LINK
1046-0489	FLORIDA REEL
1046-0837	VIDEO INSIDER
1046-3321	MSO *Varied under* MSO'S CABLE MARKETING
1046-5286	MOBILE SATELLITE NEWS

ISSN	Title	ISSN	Title
1046-5316	INSIDE MEDIA	1053-833x	WRITER'S NW
1046-574x	Communications/Engineering Digest *Varied under* COMMUNICATIONS ENGINEERING & DESIGN	1053-8801	PUBLISHING RESEARCH QUARTERLY
		1054-0415	COMPUTER PUBLISHING
		1054-2329	TV, ETC.
1046-607x	VIDEO SOFTWARE MAGAZINE	1054-2825	INSIDE HOLLYWOOD
1046-7912	LIES OF OUR TIMES	1054-8378	THEATRE TOPICS
1046-8439	UNIQUE	1054-8491	SIMPSONS ILLUSTRATED
1046-8595	PRINTINGNEWS	1055-0917	MOVIELINE
1046-8986	AMERICAN PHOTO	1055-176x	MEDIAWEEK
1046-9885	VENTURA PROFESSIONAL!	1055-2286	ART & DESIGN NEWS
1047-0034	HIGH TECH LIFESTYLES	1055-2774	STEP-BY-STEP ELECTRONIC DESIGN
1047-0476	JOE FRANKLIN'S NOSTALGIA		
1047-3068	OLD NEWS	1055-6060	VIDEO PROPHILES
1047-7128	SOAP OPERA WEEKLY	1055-6931	HD SYSTEMS WORLD REVIEW
1047-7268	CONNECT	1055-9280	HDTV REPORT
1047-7713	VIDEO MANAGEMENT	1055-9639	COMIC RELIEF
1047-8787	Camcorder Report *Varied under* CAMCORDER	1055-9825	BACK STAGE/SHOOT
		1056-540x	PC PUBLISHING AND PRESENTATIONS
1048-0161	PHOTO DISTRICT NEWS		
1048-1702	TEEN DREAM	1056-7038	DIGITAL MEDIA
1048-1869	Producci on [NE] *Varied under* PRODUCCIÓN Y DISTRIBUCIÓN	1056-8484	CAMERA & DARKROOM PHOTOGRAPHY
		1058-8612	SCARLET STREET
		1059-9614	HD PRODUCTION
1048-1877	PRODUCCIÓN Y DISTRIBUCIÓN	1120-3862	EUROPEAN TRANSACTIONS ON TELECOMMUNICATIONS AND RELATED TECHNOLOGIES
1048-3055	PUBLISHING & PRODUCTION EXECUTIVE		
1048-8804	CAMCORDER	1181-7917	DIGITAL EVOLUTION MAGAZINE
1049-0132	NATIONAL FORUM, THE		
1049-0434	ENTERTAINMENT WEEKLY	7800-0081	Actor's Cues *Varied under* SHOW BUSINESS
1049-1163	TV ENTERTAINMENT		
1049-4456	BOOK PROMOTION HOTLINE	8750-0280	ENTERTAINER, THE
1049-4588	BME'S TELEVISION ENGINEERING	8750-068x	FILM & VIDEO NEWS
		8750-1767	SUPER TEEN
1049-5576	INTELLIGENT DECISIONS	8750-3255	AMERICAN THEATRE
1049-8974	PHOTOPRO	8750-7234	Star Hits *Varied under* SMASH HITS
1050-012x	WORLD BROADCAST NEWS		
1050-1800	DESKTOP COMMUNICATIONS	8750-7471	ANTIQUE RADIO CLASSIFIED
1050-2491	DISNEY ADVENTURES	8750-7854	On Communications *Varied under* NETWORK WORLD
1050-2777	SOUND & IMAGE		
1050-3293	COMMUNICATION THEORY	8755-0555	SOUND MANAGEMENT
1050-4788	WRITING CONCEPTS	8755-2671	WHO'S MAILING WHAT!
1050-7868	EQ	8755-3104	TM *Varied under* TS
1050-8287	CORPORATE VIDEO DECISIONS	8755-5867	TELESCAN
		8755-6286	INFORMATION TODAY
1051-0230	SPECTATOR, THE	8756-1808	TARGET
1051-0974	COMMUNICATION STUDIES	8756-1972	BULLETIN OF THE ASSOCIATION FOR BUSINESS COMMUNICATION, THE
1051-5488	MOVIE MARKETPLACE		
1051-9971	FUTUREHOME TECHNOLOGY NEWS		
		8756-2324	AT&T TECHNICAL JOURNAL
1052-3944	POSTAL WATCH	8756-3312	TS
1052-438x	ONI	8756-3894	TECHTRENDS
1053-6213	4TH MEDIA JOURNAL, THE	8756-7202	SMALL PRESS BOOK REVIEW, THE
1053-6256	VIZIONS		

Publishers

Names of publishers in this list are the current cited publisher for a sampled issue annotation, or in the case of a serial which has ceased publication, the last listed publisher at time of cessation. Some publishers may have multiple listings due to slight changes in their corporate name, or printing of same in the publication masthead.

Excluded from this listing are publisher names which are identical to the serial title.

A

A. C. Sanucci
THEATRE CRAFT

A-D Publishing Co.
A-D

A/S/M Communications
ADWEEK
ADWEEK'S MARKETING WEEK
MEDIAWEEK

A-TR Publications
TAPE RECORDING

A. W. Ayer and Son
ADVERTISERS GUIDE

AB Bookman Publications
AB BOOKMAN'S WEEKLY

ABC Consumer Magazines
HIGH FIDELITY
MUSICAL AMERICA

ABC Daytime Circle
EPISODES

ABC Leisure Magazines
HIGH FIDELITY/MUSICAL AMERICA
MODERN PHOTOGRAPHY

Absolute Sound
ABSOLUTE SOUND, THE

AC Nielsen Co.
NIELSEN NEWSCAST, THE

Academy of Homiletics and the Religious Speech Communication Association
HOMILETIC

Academy of Motion Picture Arts and Sciences
BULLETIN

Academy of Television Arts & Sciences
DEBUT

Academy of Television Arts and Sciences
EMMY

Access Reports
ACCESS REPORTS/FREEDOM OF INFORMATION

Accuracy in Media
AIM REPORT

Aceville Publications
CAMERA & CAMCORDER MONTHLY

Acme Press
ACES

Act III Publishing
AGENCY
BME'S TELEVISION ENGINEERING
CHANNELS
CORPORATE VIDEO DECISIONS
MIX

Action for Children's Television
RE:ACT

Actor Illustrated
ACTOR ILLUSTRATED, THE

Actual Publishing Co.
SCREEN LIFE

Ad-Lib Publications
BOOK MARKETING UPDATE
BOOK PROMOTION HOTLINE

Ad Sense Co.
AD SENSE

Ad-Service Publishing Co.
NATIONAL STATIONER, THE

ADA Publishing Co.
ADVERTISING AND GRAPHIC ARTS TECHNIQUES

Adobe Systems Inc.
COLOPHON

Advanced Television Publishing
HDTV NEWSLETTER

Advertiser Publishing Co.
ADVERTISER MAGAZINE, THE

Advertisers' Weekly
ADVERTISERS' WEEKLY

Advertising Abroad Publishing Co.
EXPORT ADVERTISER

Advertising and Marketing
ADVERTISING AND MARKETING

Advertising & Selling Co.
ADVERTISING & SELLING

Publishers

Advertising Association
ADVERTISING MAGAZINE

Advertising Association and the CAM Foundation
INTERNATIONAL JOURNAL OF ADVERTISING

Advertising Displays Publishing Co.
ADVERTISING DISPLAYS

Advertising Ideas
ADVERTISING IDEAS

Advertising Management
ADVERTISING AND MARKETING MANAGEMENT

Advertising News Company
ADVERTISING NEWS

Advertising Research Foundation
JOURNAL OF ADVERTISING RESEARCH

Advertising Trade Publications
ART DIRECTION

AEG Telefunken Zentralabteilung Firmenverlag
AEG-TELEFUNKEN PROGRESS

Affiliated Magazines
SCREENLAND PLUS TV-LAND

Afro-Asian Journalists Association
AFRO-ASIAN JOURNALIST

Afterimage Publishing
AFTERIMAGE

Against the Grain
AGAINST THE GRAIN

Agency Publishing Co.
ADVERTISING AGENCY

Airbrush Action
AIRBRUSH ACTION

Alain Charles Publishing
MEDIA INTERNATIONAL

Alan Forman
JOURNALIST, THE

Alan Gordon Enterprises
IMAGE NEWS

Alan Weston Communications
AMPERSAND'S COLLEGE ENTERTAINMENT GUIDE

Alan Weston Publishing
MOVIE MAGAZINE, THE

Alert Publications
BUSINESS INFORMATION ALERT

All India Radio
AKASHVANI

Allen Shevy and Chris Mygrant
WORLD OF FANDOM, THE

Alpha Epsilon Rho
MONITOR
SIGNALS

Alpha-Omega Productions
ALPHA AND OMEGA FILM REPORT

Alternative Theatre
ALTERNATIVE THEATRE

Amalgamated Wireless (A/SIA) Ltd.
AWA TECHNICAL REVIEW

Amateur Cinema League
MOVIE MAKERS

America Specialty Information Network
IMPRINT

American Academy of Advertising
JOURNAL OF ADVERTISING

American Association of Advertising Agencies
4A'S WASHINGTON NEWSLETTER, THE
FOUR A NEWSLETTER

American Association of Colleges of Teacher Education
PUBLIC RELATIONS IDEAS

American Association of Yellow Pages Publishers
YELLOW PAGES UPDATE

American Bar Association
COMMUNICATIONS LAWYER
ENTERTAINMENT AND SPORTS LAWYER, THE

American Business Communication Association
BULLETIN OF THE ASSOCIATION FOR BUSINESS COMMUNICATION, THE

American Business Press
BETTER EDITING

American Cinema Editors
AMERICAN CINEMEDITOR

American Classic Screen
AMERICAN CLASSIC SCREEN

American College Public Relations Association
COLLEGE & UNIVERSITY JOURNAL

American College Theater Festival
ACTF / PAC NEWS

American Council for Better Broadcasts
BETTER BROADCASTS NEWS

American Demographics
AMERICAN DEMOGRAPHICS

American Family Association
AFA JOURNAL

American Federation of Film Societies
CRITIC

American Federation of Photographic Societies
PHOTO-ERA MAGAZINE

American Film and Video Association
AFVA BULLETIN

American Film Institute
AFI EDUCATION NEWSLETTER
AMERICAN FILM INSTITUTE. QUARTERLY.
CLOSE-UP
DIALOGUE ON FILM

American Filmakers Magazine
PROFESSIONAL FILM PRODUCTION

American Image
INTERNATIONAL PHOTOGRAPHER MAGAZINE

American Institute of Cinematography
CINEMA PROGRESS

American Institute of Graphic Arts
AIGA JOURNAL OF GRAPHIC DESIGN

American Journalism
AMERICAN JOURNALISM

American Journalism Historians Association
INTELLIGENCER

American Journalist Printing and Publishing Co.
AMERICAN JOURNALIST, THE

American League of Amateur Photographers
DEVELOPER, THE

American Marketing Association
JMR, JOURNAL OF MARKETING RESEARCH
JOURNAL OF MARKETING
MARKETING NEWS

American Newspaper Boy Press
AMERICAN NEWSPAPER BOY, THE

American Newspaper Publishers Association
ANPA PUBLIC AFFAIRS NEWSLETTER
PRESSTIME

American Photo-Engravers Association
MORE BUSINESS

American Photographic Publishing Co.
AMERICAN AMATEUR PHOTOGRAPHER AND CAMERA & DARKROOM
AMERICAN PHOTOGRAPHY
CAMERA AND DARK ROOM

American Premiere Ltd.
AMERICAN PREMIERE

American Press Magazine
AMERICAN PRESS

American Printing History Association
PRINTING HISTORY

American Radio Relay League
QEX
QST

American Showcase
LÜRZER'S INTERNATIONAL ARCHIVE

American Society of Composers
ASCAP IN ACTION

American Society of Educators
MEDIA & METHODS

American Society of Newspaper Editors
BULLETIN OF THE AMERICAN SOCIETY OF NEWSPAPER EDITORS, THE

American Speech-Language-Hearing Association
JOURNAL OF SPEECH AND HEARING DISORDERS

American Telephone and Telegraph Co.
AT&T MAGAZINE
AT&T TECHNICAL JOURNAL

American Telephone Journal Co.
AMERICAN TELEPHONE JOURNAL, THE

American Theatre Association
THEATRE NEWS

American Women in Radio and Television
AWRT NEWS AND VIEWS

Animation Magazine
ANIMATION MAGAZINE

Animato
ANIMATO!

Annenberg School Press
STUDIES IN VISUAL COMMUNICATION

ANPA Foundation
MINORITIES IN THE NEWSPAPER BUSINESS

ANPA News Research Center
ANPA NEWS RESEARCH REPORT

Anthony & Scovill Co.
AMATEUR POINTER FOR AMATEUR PHOTOGRAPHERS, THE

Antique Wireless Association
OLD TIMER'S BULLETIN, THE

AP Broadcast News Center
AP BROADCASTER

Aperture Foundation
APERTURE

Applied Arts
APPLIED ARTS QUARTERLY

Applied Business Communications
TELECONFERENCE MAGAZINE

Arbitron Ratings Company
BEYOND THE RATINGS
BEYOND THE RATINGS/RADIO
BEYOND THE RATINGS/TELEVISION

Argus Publications
VIDEO TODAY

Argus Specialist Publications
ETI
FILM MONTHLY
PHOTOGRAPHY

Arlen Communications
INTERNATIONAL VIDEOTEXT TELETEXT NEWS

Art and Technics
ALPHABET AND IMAGE

Art Dynamo
ART DYNAMO

Art in Advertising Co.
ART IN ADVERTISING

Arthur and Corinne Cantrill
CANTRILLS FILMNOTES

Arthurian Theatre Magazine
ARTHURIAN THEATRE MAGAZINE, THE

Arts & Entertainment Network
A & E PROGRAM GUIDE

Arts Council of Northern Ireland
FILM DIRECTIONS

Asahi Optical Company
PENTAX FAMILY

ASC Holding Corporation
AMERICAN CINEMATOGRAPHER

Ashley Communications
FRESH!

Asia-Pacific Broadcasting Union
ABU NEWSLETTER
ABU TECHNICAL REVIEW

Asian Mass Communication Research and Information Centre (AMIC)
ASIAN JOURNAL OF COMMUNICATION
MEDIA ASIA

ASIFA-Washington
PENCIL TEST

Assocation for Education in Journalism and Mass Communication
MAGAZINES IN DEPTH

Associated Cable Enterprises
CABLE MARKETING

Associated Editorial Consultants
IN BLACK AND WHITE

Associated Features
NATIONAL FORUM, THE

Associated Press Broadcasters
NEWS FROM APB

Associated Professional Services
SCREEN LEGENDS

Associated Publications
BOXOFFICE

Publishers

Association for Business Communication
JOURNAL OF BUSINESS COMMUNICATION, THE

Association for Communication Administration
ACA BULLETIN

Association for Education in Journalism and Mass Communication
AEJMC NEWS
CLIO AMONG THE MEDIA
COMMUNICATIONS TECHNOLOGY & POLICY NEWS
JOURNALISM EDUCATOR, THE
JQ. JOURNALISM QUARTERLY.
MAGAZINE MATTER
MC&S NEWSLETTER
STATIC
VISUAL COMMUNICATION NEWSLETTER, THE

Association for Education in Journalism
MASS COMM REVIEW

Association for Education in Journalism and Mass Communications
NEWSPAPER RESEARCH JOURNAL

Association for Educational Communications and Technology
EDUCATIONAL COMMUNICATION AND TECHNOLOGY
LEARNING RESOURCES

Association for Educational Communications & Technology
TECHTRENDS

Association for Multi-Image
MULTI IMAGES JOURNAL

Association for Recorded Sound Collections
ARSC JOURNAL

Association of American Publishers
AAP MONTHLY REPORT

Association of Fashion and Editorial Photographers
IMAGE

Association of Learned and Professional Society Publishers
LEARNED PUBLISHING

Association of Visual Communicators (AVC)
COMMUNICATOR, THE

Association of Western Union Employees
TELEGRAPH WORLD

Association of Working Press
CHICAGO JOURNALISM REVIEW

Associazione Elettrotecnica ed Elettronica Italiana
EUROPEAN TRANSACTIONS ON TELECOMMUNICATIONS AND RELATED TECHNOLOGIES

Astro Artz
HIGH PERFORMANCE

Atlanta Art Papers
ART PAPERS

Atlas Publishing Co.
THEATRE, THE

ATV Corporation
CHANNEL ONE

Audio Amateur
AUDIO AMATEUR, THE

Audio Critic
AUDIO CRITIC, THE

Audio Engineering Society
AES

Audio League
AUDIO LEAGUE. REPORT.

Audio Publishing
HI-FI WORLD

Audio Services Corporation
PRODUCTION SOUND REPORT

Audio-Visual Bureau
AUDIO-VISUAL BULLETIN

Audiocom
AUDIOCRAFT FOR THE HI-FI HOBBYIST

Audit Bureau of Circulation
ABC NEWS BULLETIN

Australian Broadcasting Commission
ABC WEEKLY
TV TIMES

Avant Film Publications
CINEMA

Aviation News Corporation
HOLLYWOOD MAGAZINE

B

Back Stage Publications
BACK STAGE
BACK STAGE/SHOOT

Baker & Taylor Books
FORECAST
HOT PICKS
VIDEO ALERT

Baker's Plays
BAKER'S NEWS

Ballett International
BALLETT INTERNATIONAL

Baronet Publishing
BIJOU

Barrington Publications
EDUCATIONAL BROADCASTING

Barrist & Goodwin
NATIONAL EXHIBITOR, THE

Bartex Publishing Group
DEALERSCOPE

Baywood Publishing
JOURNAL OF TECHNICAL WRITING AND COMMUNICATION

BBC Publications
BBC ENGINEERING
RADIO TIMES

BBC World Service
BBC WORLD SERVICE LONDON CALLING

BCR Enterprises
BUSINESS COMMUNICATIONS REVIEW

Bell and Howell
FILMO TOPICS

Bell Telephone Company
TELEPHONE NEWS, THE

Benjamin N. Cardozo School of Law
CARDOZO ARTS & ENTERTAINMENT LAW JOURNAL

Bennett Coleman & Co.
FILMFARE

Bernard Jones Publications
AMATEUR WIRELESS AND RADIOVISION

Bill Communications
SALES & MARKETING MANAGEMENT

Billboard Publications
AMERICAN FILM

Billboard Publishing Co.
BILLBOARD TV PROGRAM AND TIME AVAILABILITIES, THE

Billy Goat Strut Publishing
FINELINE

Bioscope Publishing Company
BIOSCOPE, THE

BJR Publishing Co.
BLACK JOURNALISM REVIEW

BKY Publications
WESTERN PHOTOGRAPHER MAGAZINE

Black Radio Exclusive
BLACK RADIO EXCLUSIVE

Blake Enterprises
GRAPHIC ANTIQUARIAN

BLOCKBUSTER Entertainment Corporation
BLOCKBUSTER VIDEO MAGAZINE

Blue Pencil Club
BLUE PENCIL MAGAZINE

BMI Corporate Relations Dept.
BMI: MUSICWORLD

Board Report
BOARD REPORT FOR GRAPHIC ARTISTS

Bohlau Verlag
COMMUNICATIONS

Bold Productions
REALLY, A FREE NEWSLETTER

Bolingbroke Society
DRAMA SURVEY

Bolton Research Corporation
RADIOTRENDS

Bouverie House
NEWSPAPER WORLD AND ADVERTISING REVIEW

Bouverie Publishing Co.
MEDIA REPORTER, THE

UK PRESS GAZETTE

BPI Communications
AMUSEMENT BUSINESS
BILLBOARD
PHOTO/DESIGN

BPI Publishing Co.
HIGH TECH LIFESTYLES

Bradford and Inskeep
MIRROR OF TASTE, AND DRAMATIC CENSOR, THE

Brigham Young University
JOURNAL OF MASS MEDIA ETHICS

Brighton Film Review
MONOGRAM

British Broadcasting Corporation
BBC QUARTERLY, THE
LISTENER

British Council
BRITISH BOOK NEWS

British Federation of Film Societies
FILM

British Film Academy
JOURNAL OF THE BRITISH FILM ACADEMY

British Film Institute
CONTRAST
MONTHLY FILM BULLETIN
SIGHT & SOUND

British Institute of Recorded Sound
BRITISH INSTITUTE OF RECORDED SOUND. BULLETIN.

British Kinematograph Sound and Television Society
IMAGE TECHNOLOGY

British Theatre Association
DRAMA

British Universities Film Council
UNIVERSITY VISION

Broadband Publications
E-ITV

Broadcast Cable and Consumer Electronics Society
IEEE TRANSACTIONS ON BROADCASTING

Broadcast Cable Financial Management Association
BROADCAST CABLE FINANCIAL JOURNAL

Broadcast Education Association
BEA NEWSLETTER
BROADCAST EDUCATOR NEWS NOTES
FEEDBACK
JOURNAL OF BROADCASTING & ELECTRONIC MEDIA
MANAGEMENT AND SALES DIVISION NEWSLETTER
NEWSLETTER
REWIND

Broadcast News Committee
NEWSCASTER, THE

Broadcast Pioneers
SPARKS

Broadcast Pioneers Library
BROADCAST PIONEERS LIBRARY REPORTS

Broadcast Promotion & Marketing Executives
BPME IMAGE MAGAZINE

Broadcast Reporter
BROADCAST REPORTER

Broadcasting and the Law
BROADCASTING AND THE LAW

Broadcasting Publications
BROADCASTING
BROADCASTING ABROAD
TELECOMMUNICATIONS REPORTS

Broadway Magazine Co.
BROADWAY WEEKLY

Brook Press Ltd.
BUSINESS OF FILM, THE

Bryan Davis Publishing Co.
COMMUNICATION AND BROADCAST ENGINEERING
TELEVISION ENGINEERING

BSO Publications
INTERNATIONAL BROADCASTING

Bulgarian Cinematography State Corporation
BULGARIAN FILMS

Burr McIntosh Co.
BURR MCINTOSH MONTHLY, THE

Bushfield House
VIDEO ANSWERS

Publishers

Business Press International
ELECTRICAL REVIEW

Business Research Publications
TELECOMMUNICATIONS WEEK

BusinessTV
BUSINESSTV VIDEO 8 GUIDE

Butterworth-Heinemann
TELECOMMUNICATIONS POLICY

Butterworth-Heinemann Limited
INTERNATIONAL JOURNAL OF INFORMATION MANAGEMENT

C

C. Abel
COMMERCIAL PHOTOGRAPHER, THE

C. J. Bucher Ltd.
CAMERA

C. S. Tepfer Publishing Co.
CABLE LIBRARIES
VIDEOPLAY MAGAZINE

C-SPAN Department of Educational Services
C-SPAN IN THE CLASSROOM

C-Span Update
C-SPAN UPDATE

Cable World Associates
CABLE WORLD

CAE Productions
PAS GRAPHIC ARTS NEWS

Cahiers Publishing Co. Inc.
CAHIERS DU CINEMA IN ENGLISH

Cahners Publishing Co.
GRAPHIC ARTS MONTHLY
VARIETY

Caldwell-Clements
TELEVISION RETAILING
TV & APPLIANCE MART
TV-ELECTRONIC TECHNICIAN

California Intercollegiate Press Association
CIPA NEWS

California Newspaper Publishers Association
CALIFORNIA PUBLISHER

California State University
JOURNALISM HISTORY

California State University at Fullerton
INTERCOMM
JOURNAL OF MEDIA ECONOMICS

Calmor & Associates
AUSTRALASIAN PRINTER

Calvin Co.
APERTURE, THE

Cambridge University Press
NEW THEATRE QUARTERLY

Camera
CAMERA, THE

Camera Craft Publishing Co.
CAMERA CRAFT

Camera Magazine
CAMERA MAGAZINE

Camera Obscura
CAMERA OBSCURA

CamerArt
CAMERART

Canadian Broadcasting Corporation
CBC TIMES

Canadian Film-TV Bi-Weekly
CANADIAN FILM DIGEST

Canadian Journal of Communication
CANADIAN JOURNAL OF COMMUNICATION

Canadian Society of Cinematographers
CINEMA/CANADA

Canadian Speech and Hearing Association
HUMAN COMMUNICATION CANADA

Canadian Stage
PERFORMING ARTS IN CANADA, THE

Capital Cities/ABC
COMMUNICATIONS ENGINEERING & DESIGN

Capital Cities Media
CABLEVISION

Cardiff Publishing
CABLE TV BUSINESS MAGAZINE
COMMUNICATIONS
VUE

Cardiff Publishing Co.
RF DESIGN

Cardiff Publishing Company
SATELLITE COMMUNICATIONS

Carfax Publishing Co.
HISTORICAL JOURNAL OF FILM, RADIO & TELEVISION
JOURNAL OF EDUCATIONAL TELEVISION

Carl Zeiss
ZEISS INFORMATION

Carroll O'Toole and Co.
TELEVISION BULLETIN

Cartoonist Profiles
CARTOONIST PROFILES

Caruba Enterprises
TOP SECRET

Casting News Publications
CASTING NEWS

Castlestone Publishing
DIGITAL EVOLUTION MAGAZINE

Castlestone Publishing Ltd.
VIDEO NEWS AND USED

Catholic Press Association
CATHOLIC JOURNALIST

Catholic School Press Association
CATHOLIC SCHOOL EDITOR

Caucus for Producers
CAUCUS QUARTERLY, THE

Caverne Publishing
CAVERNE COMMUNICATION, THE

CBN Cable Network
CABLE LINES

CBS Magazines
AUDIO

Celluloid Nightmare Production
CELLULOID NIGHTMARE

Center for Advanced Study in Telecommunications (CAST)
COMMUNICATION BOOKNOTES

Center for Children's Media
YOUNG VIEWERS

Center for Learning and Telecommunications
TELESCAN

Center for Media and Public Affairs
MEDIA MONITOR

Center for Media and Values
MEDIA & VALUES

Central States Communication Association
COMMUNICATION STUDIES

Centro Internazionale per il Cinema di Animazione
ANIMAFILM

CES Publishing Corp.
CONSUMER ELECTRONICS

CFW Enterprises
ACTION FILMS

Charles Abel
PROFESSIONAL PHOTOGRAPHER, THE

Charles Austin Bates
CURRENT ADVERTISING

Charlton Publishing Corporation
HIT PARADER
RADIO HIT SONGS

Christian Booksellers Association
BOOKSTORE JOURNAL

Christian Interfaith Media Evaluation Center
RELIGIOUS MEDIA TODAY

Christians in the Arts Networking
CANEWS

CHRR Corp.
INTERNATIONAL RADIO REPORT, THE

Cineaste Publishers
CINEASTE

Cinefantastique
CINEFANTASTIQUE

Cinefex
CINEFEX

Cinegram Inc.
CINEGRAM

Cinema Enterprises
AMAZING CINEMA

Cinema Papers Pty
CINEMA PAPERS

Cinema Products Corporation
CINEMA PERSPECTIVES

Cinema Rising
CINEMA

Cinema Vision India
CINEMA VISION INDIA

Cinemonkey
CINEMONKEY

Claretian Publications
MEDIA MIX

Class Publications
MOVING PICTURE AGE

CLIO Awards Enerprises
CLIO MAGAZINE

CMP Publications
CLOSEUP
COMMUNICATIONSWEEK

CNC Group/Diversified Publishing
MULTICHANNEL NEWS

Coastal Associates Publishing
SHUTTERBUG

Code Authority
CODE NEWS

Collective for Living Cinema
MOTION PICTURE

College Media Advisers
CMA NEWSLETTER
COLLEGE MEDIA REVIEW

Colorado Press Association
COLORADO EDITOR

Columbia Audio/Video
INTELLIGENT DECISIONS

Columbia Broadcasting System
TALKS

Columbia Scholastic Press Advisers Association
CSPAA BULLETIN
SCHOOL PRESS REVIEW, THE

Columbia University Press
COLUMBIA JOURNALISM REVIEW
PUBLIC OPINION QUARTERLY

Comic Corporation of America
BAND LEADERS

Comic Informer Enterprises
COMIC INFORMER

Commission on Freedom of Speech
FREE SPEECH

Common-Sense Publishing Co.
COMMON SENSE

Commonwealth Broadcasting Association
COMBROAD

CommTek Publishing
ORBIT VIDEO
SATELLITE ORBIT

Communication Arts
COMMUNICATION ARTS

Communication Channels
PERSONAL ELECTRONICS

Communication Research Associates
MEDIA REPORT TO WOMEN
SOCIAL SCIENCE MONITOR

Communication Research Trends
COMMUNICATION RESEARCH TRENDS

Communications Concepts
COMMUNICATIONS CONCEPTS
WRITING CONCEPTS

Communications Management
YELLOW SHEET, THE

Communications Publishing Corporation
WIRE & RADIO COMMUNICATIONS

Communications Research Center
CRC NEWSLETTER

Communications Research Institute
TELEVISION PROGRAMMER, THE

Communications Satellite Corporation
COMSAT TECHNICAL REVIEW

Communications Technology Publications Corporation
INTERNATIONAL CABLE
MSO'S CABLE MARKETING

Publishers

Communications Workers of America
CWA NEWS

Community College Journalism Association
COMMUNITY COLLEGE JOURNALIST

Conde Nast Publications
TAPE

Congressional Quarterly
CONGRESSIONAL QUARTERLY'S EDITORIAL RESEARCH REPORTS

Connell Communications
VIDEO CHOICE

Consolidated Publishers
RADIO HOME, THE

Contemporary Photographer
CONTEMPORARY PHOTOGRAPHER

Copley Newspapers
SEMINAR

Corporate Communications Group
CLOSE-UP

Corporation for Public Broadcasting
REPORT

COSMEP
COSMEP NEWSLETTER

Council on Church and Media
FORUM

Council on International Nontheatrical Events
CINE NEWS

Country Wide Publications
MOVIE TV SECRETS

Cowan Publishing Corp.
MODERN RECORDING & MUSIC

CQ Communications
POPULAR COMMUNICATIONS

Craigie Publications
STARZ

Crain Communications
ADVERTISING AGE
BUSINESS MARKETING
ELECTRONIC MEDIA
FOCUS
PROMOTION

Creative Camera
CREATIVE CAMERA

Critical Studies
SPECTATOR, THE

CRN
HD PRODUCTION

Crosby Vandenburgh Group
AMERICAN MOVIE CLASSICS MAGAZINE
CONNECT

Crown Communications
GOOD NEWS: CHRISTIANS IN JOURNALISM

C.S. Tepfer Publishing Co.
ETV NEWSLETTER

C.T.L. Electronics
VIDEOTOOLS

Current Publishing Committee
CURRENT

CurtCo Publishing
AUDIO/VIDEO INTERIORS
CAR AUDIO AND ELECTRONICS

Curtis Mark Communications and the Wheaton College Graduate School of Communications
CHRISTIAN FILM & VIDEO

CW Communications
CD-ROM
NETWORK WORLD

D

Daily Variety
DAILY VARIETY

Dandad Publishing Co.
AFTER DARK

Daniel O'Malley Co.
TALKING PICTURE MAGAZINE

Data Publications
RADIO & ELECTRONICS CONSTRUCTOR

David C. Cook Foundation
INTERLIT

Davis Publications
COMMUNICATIONS WORLD

Dawson-Butwick Publishers
FCC WEEK

DCK & Associates
AD • MENTOR, THE

Decker Communications
BUSINESS ADVERTISING
MARKETING / COMMUNICATIONS

Dell Publishing Co.
MODERN SCREEN
RADIO ALBUM MAGAZINE
SCREEN ALBUM MAGAZINE
TALKING SCREEN

Dempa Publications
AUDIOVIDEO INTERNATIONAL
JEE, JOURNAL OF ELECTRONIC ENGINEERING

Dempa Times
TELECOM JAPAN, THE

Dennis Publishing
DRIVING AMBITION
HI-FI CHOICE

D.F. Mendola
BROADWAY SIGN POST

Dialog Information Services
MEDIABRIEFS

Diamandis Communications
AMERICAN PHOTO
CAR STEREO REVIEW
MEMORIES
SOUND & IMAGE
STEREO REVIEW

Dipok Dey
FILMING

Direction
DIRECTION

Directors Guild of America
ACTION!

Disney Channel
DISNEY CHANNEL MAGAZINE, THE

Distinctive Publications
GRAPHIC ARTS

Diversified Publications
BROADCAST + TECHNOLOGY

Division of Dramatics of the
Pennsylvania State College
  PLAY SHOP, THE

Documentary Film Group
  FOCUS!

Documentary Video Associates
  INDEPENDENT MEDIA

Donald Mann
  AMERICAN TELEGRAPH MAGAZINE

Doubleday
  RADIO BROADCAST

Doug Wyles Productions
  PSA

Dow Jones Newspaper Fund
  ADVISER UPDATE
  ALUMNI NEWSLINE
  DOW JONES NEWSPAPER FUND
    NEWSLETTER

Drama Corporation
  DRAMA MAGAZINE, THE

Drama League of America
  DRAMA LEAGUE MONTHLY

Drama-Logue
  DRAMA-LOGUE

Drama Press
  PULSE

Drama Teachers Association
  THEATRE AND SCHOOL

Dramatic Magazine Press
  DRAMATIC MAGAZINE, THE

Dramatic Mirror Co.
  DRAMATIC MIRROR, THE

DRN
  DIGITAL RADIO NEWS

Drorbaugh Publications
  SIGHT AND SOUND MARKETING

DS Magazines
  REAL LIFE/DAYTIMERS

Duke University
  BOOKS & RELIGION

Dynamic Graphics
  STEP-BY-STEP GRAPHICS

F

Facets Multimedia
  FACETS FEATURES

FAIR
  EXTRA!

Fairfield Publishing Co.
  V

Fame Magazine Group
  FAME

Fandom Unlimited Enterprises
  CINEFAN

F&W Publishing Co.
  HOW
  PHOTOGRAPHER'S MARKET
    NEWSLETTER
  WRITER'S DIGEST

Fanfare
  FANFARE

FantaCo Enterprises
  DEEP RED

Fantagraphics Books
  AMAZING HEROES
  COMICS JOURNAL, THE
  NEMO

Fantastic Films
  FANTASTIC FILMS

Fawcett Publications
  ELECTRONICS ILLUSTRATED
  HOLLYWOOD
  RADIOLAND

Federation Internationale des Editeurs
de Journaux et Publications
  FIEJ-BULLETIN

Feredonna
  RIGHTING WORDS

Fictioneer Books
  COMICS INTERVIEW
  COMICS REVUE

Fifer International
  COMIC CELLAR, THE

Film and Television Study Center
  MAGAZINE, THE

Film Artistes' Association
  FILM ARTISTE

Film Centre
  DOCUMENTARY FILM NEWS

Film Criticism
  FILM CRITICISM

Film Culture Non-Profit
  FILM CULTURE

Film Fan Monthly
  FILM FAN MONTHLY

Film Forum
  CLOSE-UP

Film Fun Publishing Co.
  FILM FUN

Film Library Information Council
  FILM LIBRARY QUARTERLY

Film Polski
  FILM BULLETIN

Film Society of Lincoln Center
  FILM COMMENT

Film Society of Santa Barbara
  ON FILM

Film World International Publications
  FILMWORLD

Filmage Inc.
  MEDIUM

Filmcraft Publications
  ANIMATOR

Filmfax
  FILMFAX

Finnish Film Foundation
  FACTS ABOUT FILM FINLAND

First Media Press
  SILENT PICTURE, THE

Flowers & Kovach Publications
  MOVIES NOW

Focal Press
  PERSPECTIVE

Focus Magazines
  VIDEO BUYER

Publishers

Folger Shakespeare Library
SHAKESPEARE QUARTERLY

Fordham School of Law
FORDHAM ENTERTAINMENT, MEDIA & INTELLECTUAL PROPERTY LAW FORUM

Fortuna Communications Corporation
SATELLITE TV WEEK

Fostex Corporation of America
ECHO BUSS

Foundation for Art in Cinema
CINEMANEWS, THE

Foundation for Independent Video and Film
INDEPENDENT, THE

Fountain Press
EIGHT MM MOVIE MAKER AND CINE CAMERA

Fourth Estate
FOURTH ESTATE

Franklin Productions
PERFORMER, THE

Franklin W. Lee Publishing Co.
ROXY THEATRE WEEKLY REVIEW

Frostburg State College
PCS, THE POPULAR CULTURE SCHOLAR

G

G & E Publishing Co.
TELECAST

G. Gilson
CANADIAN PHOTOGRAPHIC JOURNAL, THE

Gannett Company
GANNETTEER

Gannett Foundation
GF MAGAZINE

Gannett Foundatioon Media Center and the Gannett Foundation
GANNETT CENTER JOURNAL

Gary Leigh
DWB

Gary Morris
BRIGHT LIGHTS

GCR Publishing Group
HORRORFAN

GEC-Marconi Electronics
MARCONI REVIEW, THE

General Electric Company
GENERAL ELECTRIC REVIEW

General Gramophone Publications
GRAMOPHONE

General Radio Co.
GR TODAY

George Eastman House
IMAGE

George Newnes
PRACTICAL TELEVISION AND SHORT-WAVE REVIEW

George P. Rowell
ADVERTISERS GAZETTE

George Stover
CINEMACABRE

George W. Childs
AMERICAN LITERARY GAZETTE AND PUBLISHERS' CIRCULAR

Georgetown University Law Center
JOURNAL OF LAW & TECHNOLOGY, THE

Gernsback Publications
POPULAR ELECTRONICS
RADIO-ELECTRONICS

Gladstone Publishing
KORKIS AND CAWLEY'S CARTOON QUARTERLY

Globe Communications
CELEBRITY PLUS

Globe International
NATIONAL EXAMINER

Globe Publishing
AUSTRALIAN PHOTOGRAPHY

Good News Communications
MOVIEGUIDE

Gordon and Breach Science Publishers
COMMUNICATION

Gorez Goz Publishing Company
FILM & VIDEO NEWS

Gothic Castle Publishing
CASTLE OF FRANKENSTEIN

Grady Publishing Company
ART & DESIGN NEWS

Graphic Arts Association of Michigan
GRAPHIC

Graphic Arts Company
GRAPHIC ARTS, THE

Graphic Arts International Union
GRAPHIC COMMUNICATOR

Graphic Arts Service
MOVIE FLASH

Graphics: USA
GRAPHICS: U.S.A.

Graphis Press
GRAPHIS

Great Barrington
COMMUNICATION ENGINEERING

Green Room Society of Bristol University
NEW THEATRE MAGAZINE

Greenfield Press
INDEPENDENT PUBLISHERS TRADE REPORT
SMALL PRESS BOOK REVIEW, THE

Group for Film Study
CINEMAGES

Grove Enterprises
MONITORING TIMES

Gruppo Editoriale JCE srl.
MILLECANALI INTERNATIONAL

Guild Reporter
GUILD REPORTER, THE

H

H & R Publications
SHOW

H. Hetherington
ODDFELLOW, THE

H. W. Wilson Co.
MOTION PICTURE REVIEW DIGEST

Hachette Magazines
POPULAR PHOTOGRAPHY

Hampton Books
CTVD

Hansom Books
PLAYS AND PLAYERS

Hanson Publishing Group
FOLIO:
INSIDE MEDIA

Harbor View Publications Group
MILLER'S COPYRIGHT NEWSLETTER

Harcourt Brace Jovanovich Publications
ELECTRONIC TECHNICAN/DEALER

Harris Publications
OUTDOOR & TRAVEL PHOTOGRAPHY

Hartford Publications
SHOW

Harwood Academic Publishers
QUARTERLY REVIEW OF FILM AND VIDEO

Hayden Publishing co.
ELECTRONIC DESIGN

Haymarket Magazines
AUDIOPHILE WITH HI-FI ANSWERS

Haymarket Publishing
CAMPAIGN
HI-FI ANSWERS
HI-FI SOUND

Hearst Business Communications
ELECTRONIC PRODUCTS

Heldref Publications
JOURNAL OF POPULAR FILM AND TELEVISION

Heldref Publishing
JOURNAL OF ARTS MANAGEMENT AND LAW, THE

Henry Greenwood & Co.
BRITISH JOURNAL OF PHOTOGRAPHY

Hero Hobby magazine
HERO HOBBY

Heywood
BRITISH COMMUNICATIONS AND ELECTRONICS

High Impact Marketing
PROFIT MARKETING HOTLINE

Historians Film Committee
FILM & HISTORY

Hitchcock Publishing Co.
PERSONAL PUBLISHING

HJK Publications
MARKEE

H.M. Konwiser
RADIO DEALER, THE

HMH Publishing Co.
SHOW BUSINESS ILLUSTRATED

Hoke Communications
DIRECT MARKETING

Hollywood Anti-Nazi League for the Defense of American Democracy
HOLLYWOOD NOW

Hollywood Filmograph
HOLLYWOOD FILMOGRAPH

Hollywood Reporter Corporation
HOLLYWOOD REPORTER

Hollywood Spectator
HOLLYWOOD SPECTATOR

Hollywood Studio Magazine
HOLLYWOOD STUDIO MAGAZINE

Home Entertainment Products Department
FAST FORWARD

Home Entertainment Publications
HOME ENTERTAINMENT

Home Viewer Publications
HOME VIEWER

Horizon House Publications
TELECOMMUNICATIONS

House of White Birches
GOOD OLD DAYS

Howard Fields
TV & RADIO FAXLETTER

Howard School of Communications
HOWARD JOURNAL OF COMMUNICATIONS, THE

Hudson H. Luce
FACTSHEET FIVE

Huenefeld Company
HUENEFELD REPORT, THE

Hugh M. Cook
UNIQUE

Hulton Press
ELECTRONIC ENGINEERING

Hungarofilm
HUNGAROFILM BULLETIN

Hutchinson Co.
CINEMA AND THEATRE

HW Wilson Co.
BOOKTALKER, THE

I

Ian Cameron
MOVIE

ICDM of North America
MILITARY ELECTRONICS / COUNTERMEASURES

Ideal Publishing
TV STAR PARADE

Ideal Publishing Co.
FILM FAMILIES
MOVIE STARS
SCREEN STORIES
TONI HOLT'S MOVIE LIFE
TV RADIO TALK

IDG Communications
ON!
VIDEO PROPHILES

Publishers INDEX

IEEE Broadcast
  IEEE TRANSACTIONS ON CABLE TELEVISION

IEEE Consumer Electronics Group of the Broadcast
  IEEE TRANSACTIONS ON CONSUMER ELECTRONICS

IFJ
  JOURNALIST'S WORLD

IFRA
  NEWSPAPER TECHNIQUES

Ilford Photo Corporation
  ILFORD PHOTO INSTRUCTOR NEWSLETTER

Iliffe Electrical Publications
  INDUSTRIAL ELECTRONICS

In Cinema
  IN CINEMA

In House Graphics
  IN HOUSE GRAPHICS

Ina Roberts and Anthony Belle
  BOOKS AND FILMS

Independent Broadcasting Authority
  AIRWAVES

Independent Feature Project
  OFF-HOLLYWOOD REPORT

Independent Magazines
  FILMS ILLUSTRATED

Industrial Marketing Advisory Services
  BUYERS GUIDE
  RADIO WORLD
  TV TECHNOLOGY

Industry Reports
  ETV REPORTER

Information Services
  IN SEARCH

Ingram Brothers
  ALBUM, THE

Inland Type Foundry
  PRACTICAL PRINTER, THE

Innes Publishing Co.
  ELECTRONIC PUBLISHER
  HIGH VOLUME PRINTING
  IN-PLANT PRINTER & ELECTRONIC PUBLISHER

Inside Radio
  INSIDE RADIO
  RADIO ONLY

Institute for Cinema and Culture
  IRIS

Institute for Media Analysis
  LIES OF OUR TIMES

Institute of Adult Education
  FILM FORUM REVIEW

Institute of Electrical and Electronics Engineers
  IEEE SPECTRUM
  IEEE TRANSACTIONS ON COMMUNICATIONS
  IEEE TRANSACTIONS ON INFORMATION THEORY
  PROCEEDINGS OF THE IEEE

Institute of International Research and Development
  AID

Institute of the Science of the Press
  GAZETTE

Institution of Electrical Engineers
  ELECTRONICS & COMMUNICATIONS ENGINEERING JOURNAL
  ELECTRONICS LETTERS

Institution of Radio and Electronics Engineers Australia
  PROCEEDINGS OF THE IREE AUSTRALIA

Intercollegiate Broadcasting System
  JOURNAL OF COLLEGE RADIO

Intercollegiate Religious Broadcasters
  CAMPUS BROADCASTERS
  IRB

Intermission
  INTERMISSION

International Advertiser
  INTERNATIONAL ADVERTISER

International Advertising Association
  INTERNATIONAL ADVERTISER, THE

International Alliance of Theatrical Stage Employees and Moving Picture Machine Operators of the United States and Canada
  INTERNATIONAL PHOTOGRAPHER
  OFFICIAL BULLETIN OF THE INTERNATIONAL ALLIANCE OF THEATRICAL STAGE EMPLOYEES AND MOVING PICTURE MACHINE OPERATORS OF THE UNITED STATES AND CANADA.

International Animated Film Association
  ASIFA NOUVELLES

International Animated Film Society/ASIFA-Hollywood
  GRAFFITI

International Animated Film Society-East
  ANYMATOR

International Association of Audio-Visual Media in Historical Research and Education
  IAMHIST NEWSLETTER

International Association of Business Communicators
  COMMUNICATION WORLD
  JOURNAL OF COMMUNICATION MANAGEMENT

International Brotherhood of Electrical Workers
  IBEW JOURNAL

International Cassette Association
  ICA NEWSLETTER

International Communication Association
  CAT NEWS
  COMMUNICATION LAW & POLICY NEWSLETTER
  COMMUNICATION THEORY
  COMMUNIQUÉ
  FEMINIST SCHOLARSHIP INTEREST GROUP NEWSLETTER OF THE INTERNATIONAL COMMUNICATION ASSOCIATION
  FORUM
  HEALTH COMMUNICATION NEWSLETTER
  ICA NEWSLETTER
  INTERCULTURAL & DEVELOPMENT COMMUNICATION NEWSLETTER
  ORGANIZATIONAL COMMUNICATION NEWSLETTER
  POLITICAL COMMUNICATION NEWSLETTER
  PRIG
  SYSTEMSLETTER

International Communication Projects
  CHRONICLE OF INTERNATIONAL COMMUNICATION

International Communications Industries Association (ICIA)
  COMMUNICATIONS INDUSTRIES REPORT, THE

International Council for Educational Media
EDUCATIONAL MEDIA INTERNATIONAL

International Desktop Communications
DESKTOP COMMUNICATIONS

International Documentary Association
INTERNATIONAL DOCUMENTARY

International Federation for Theatre Research
THEATRE RESEARCH

International Federation of Journalists
IFJ INFORMATION

International Film and Television Council
WORLD SCREEN

International Film Buff
INTERNATIONAL FILM BUFF

International Institute of Communications
INTERMEDIA

International Organization of Journalists
DEMOCRATIC JOURNALIST
JOURNALISTS' AFFAIRS

International Press Cutting Bureau
INTERNATIONAL PRESS REVIEW

International Press Institute
IPI REPORT
IPI SURVEY

International Projectionist Publishing Co.
INTERNATIONAL PROJECTIONIST

International Radio and Television Organization
OIRT INFORMATION
RADIO AND TELEVISION

International Scientific Film Association
SCIENCE AND FILM
SCIENTIFIC FILM

International Society for the Arts
LEONARDO

International Society of Weekly Newspaper Editors
GRASSROOTS EDITOR

International Tape Association
ITA NEWS DIGEST

International Telecommunication Union
TELECOMMUNICATION JOURNAL

International Telephone and Telegraph Co.
ELECTRICAL COMMUNICATION

International Theatre Institute
WORLD THEATRE

International Thespian Society
DRAMATICS

International Thomson Business Publishing
BROADCAST
TV WORLD

International Thomson Retail Press
VIDEO BUSINESS

International Typeface Corporation
U & LC

Interstar Satellite Systems
STAR SIGNALS

Intertec Publishing Co.
BROADCAST ENGINEERING
POSTAL WATCH
VIDEO SYSTEMS

Intertec Publishing Corp.
ELECTRONIC SERVICING & TECHNOLOGY

Interview
INTERVIEW

Investigative Journalism Program
NEWS LEADS

Invision
INVISION

Iowa Center for Communication Study
JOURNAL OF COMMUNICATION INQUIRY, THE

IPC business Press
AMATEUR PHOTOGRAPHER

IPC Magazines
PRACTICAL WIRELESS

Izarra Media Communications
PRODUCCIÓN Y DISTRIBUCIÓN

J

J. C. Abel
AMATEUR PHOTOGRAPHER'S WEEKLY, THE

J. Patie
ACTORS BY DAYLIGHT

J. Roach and C. Chapple
DRAMATIC CENSOR, THE

Jacobs Publications
ALL-STAR ACTION HEROES

JAI Press
PUBLIC RELATIONS REVIEW

James Bond 007 Fan Club
BONDAGE

JB Publishing Corporation
BEHIND THE SCENE

Joe Franklin's Nostalgia Publications
JOE FRANKLIN'S NOSTALGIA

Johannesburg Repertory Players
PLAYTIME

John Calder
GAMBIT

John Cawley
GET ANIMATED! UPDATE.

John H. Reid
FILM INDEX

John Mahin
MAHINS MAGAZINE

John V. Terrey
ANTIQUE RADIO CLASSIFIED

John Wrench & Son
PROJECTION, LANTERN AND CINEMATOGRAPH

Johns Hopkins University Press
THEATRE TOPICS

Johns Hopkins University Press in cooperation with the Association for Theatre in Higher Education
THEATRE JOURNAL

Publishers — INDEX

Johnson Publishing Co.
BLACK STARS

Journalism Education Association
JEA NEWSWIRE

Journalism Education Association of the United States
C: JET

JPL Publications
WHAT'S WORKING

Jump Cut Associates
JUMP CUT

K

K2 Publications
TV HITS

Kamin Publishers
FILMS

Kappa Tau Alpha
KTA NEWSLETTER

Kartes Video Communications
OFFICIAL VIDEO JOURNAL, THE

Kate E. Griswold
PROFITABLE ADVERTISING

Kaye Publishing Corp.
GRAPHIC DESIGN: USA

Kinematograph Publications
IDEAL KINEMA, THE

Kinematograph Trading Co.
KINETRADOGRAM, THE

King Publications
SCREEN INTERNATIONAL

Knight-Ridder
KNIGHT-RIDDER NEWS

Knowledge Industry Publications
COMPUTER PICTURES
HOME VIDEO PUBLISHER
TAPE/DISC BUSINESS
VIDEO MANAGEMENT

Kodak (Australasia) Pty.
APR

Komitet za Izkustvo i Kultura
BULGARSKO FOTO

Kompas/Biel & Associates
LPTV REPORT, THE

Krause Publications
COMICS BUYER'S GUIDE
POSTCARD COLLECTOR

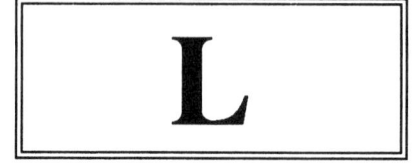

L

Lakewood Publications
MARKETING COMMUNICATIONS
PHOTOMETHODS

Laufer Company
PREVIEW

Laufer Publishing Co.
GOSSIP
RONA BARRETT'S HOLLYWOOD

Laughter Publicatioiins
STORYBOARD / THE ART OF LAUGHTER

Laurant Publishing
AFTERNOON TV

Law Division of the Association for Education in Journalism and Mass Communication
MEDIA LAW NOTES

Lawrence Erlbaum Associates
HEALTH COMMUNICATION

Lawrence Ragan Communications
EDITOR'S WORKSHOP

Leader Publications
CABLE TV AND NEW MEDIA LAW & FINANCE

Learned Information
INFORMATION TODAY
LINK-UP

Legion Information Services
PRESS STATISTICAL REVIEW

Leica Photography
LEICA PHOTOGRAPHY

Leo Shull Publications
SHOW BUSINESS

Lexicon
DIGITAL DOMAIN DIGEST

LFP
CAMERA & DARKROOM PHOTOGRAPHY
FILM THREAT
SH-BOOM
VISIO

Liberty Library Corporation
LIBERTY, THEN AND NOW

Liberty Magazine
MOVIE SHOW

Lighthouse Business Publications
MAGAZINEWEEK

Lighting Dimensions Associates
LIGHTING DIMENSIONS

Link House
BROADCAST SYSTEMS ENGINEERING
BROADCAST SYSTEMS INTERNATIONAL

Link House Magazines
VIDEO

Link House Publications
HI-FI NEWS AND RECORD REVIEW
STUDIO SOUND AND BROADCAST ENGINEERING

Location Update
LOCATION UPDATE

Long-Critchfield Publishing House
AGRICULTURAL ADVERTISING

Lorelei Publishing
TV STARS

Lowbrow Cinema
LOWBROW CINEMA

Loyola of Los Angeles Entertainment Law Journal
LOYOLA ENTERTAINMENT JOURNAL

Loyola University
RESTORATION AND 18TH CENTURY THEATRE RESEARCH

Lucasfilm Fan Club
LUCASFILM FAN CLUB, THE

L.V. Patterson
SCHEMER, THE

M

M. L. Starke
AMERICAN ADVERTISER

Macfadden-Bartell Corporation
PHOTOPLAY

Macfadden Publications
PHOTOPLAY COMBINED WITH MOVIE MIRROR
TV RADIO MIRROR

Macfadden Women's Media
MOTION PICTURE
SILVER SCREEN

Maclarens
AUDIO VISUAL

Maclean Hunter
AMERICAN PRINTER

Maclean-Hunter
BRITISH PRINTER
CANADIAN PRINTER

Macmillan Creative Services Group
FLASH

Madison Avenue Magazine
MADISON AVENUE

Magazine Management Co.
CELEBRITY
MOVIE WORLD
NOSTALGIA ILLUSTRATED
SCREEN STARS
TV DAY STARS

Magazine Management Company
TV AND SCREEN SECRETS

Magazine Press
ELECTRONICS AND COMMUNICATIONS

Magnetic Media Division
MAG TRACKS

Maher Publishing
DOWN BEAT

Mailbag Publishing Co.
MAILBAG, THE

MAL Publishing Company
MID-ATLANTIC GRAPHIC ARTS REVIEW

Malone College
CHRISTIAN DRAMA

Manager of Publications
NIE JOURNAL

Mancall Publishing
MOTION PICTURE PROJECTION

Manson Publications Corporation
ALL-WAVE RADIO

Marchbanks Press
ARS TYPOGRAPHICA

Marconi Communication Systems
SOUND AND VISION BROADCASTING

Martin Roberts and Associates
VIDEOCASSETTE AND CATV NEWSLETTER

Martin's Words
SQUEEKY WHEEL, THE

Marvel Comics
DOCTOR WHO MAGAZINE
FANTASY ZONE

Mass Communication Bibliographers
MASS COMMUNICATION BIBLIOGRAPHERS' NEWSLETTER

Mass Media Ministries
MASS MEDIA NEWSLETTER

Masthead Society
MASTHEAD

McMullen Publishing
AUTO SOUND & SECURITY

Meckler Corporation
CD-ROM LIBRARIAN
HD SYSTEMS WORLD REVIEW
SMALL PRESS

Meckler Publishing
COMMUNICATIONS AND THE LAW
OPTICAL INFORMATION SYSTEMS

Media Age srl Publishing
MONITOR INTERNATIONAL

Media and Consumer Foundation
MEDIA & CONSUMER

Media Department
MEDIA IN EDUCATION AND DEVELOPMENT

Media Dynamics
MEDIA MATTERS

Media History Digest
MEDIA HISTORY DIGEST

Media Horizons
CORPORATE TELEVISION
INDUSTRIAL PHOTOGRAPHY

Media Institute
BUSINESS AND THE MEDIA

Media Project
PRINTED MATTER

Media Research Center
MEDIAWATCH
TV, ETC.

Media Service Group
JOB LEADS

Media Sight Publications
MEDIA SIGHT

Media Spotlight Ministries
MEDIA SPOTLIGHT

Media Weavers
WRITER'S NW

Media Week
MEDIA WEEK

Mediabase Research Corporation
MONDAY MORNING REPLAY

MEED House
TELEVISION WEEK

Mel Pogue Enterprises
CASTING CALL

Memory Lane Publications
NEW CAPTAIN GEORGE'S WHIZZBANG, THE

Merchants Publishing Co.
AMERICAN ADVERTISER

Mercury House Publications
AD WEEKLY
ADWEEK
AM

Metro-Goldwyn-Mayer
METRO-GOLDWYN-MAYER SHORT STORY

Metro Pictures Magazine
PICTURES MAGAZINE, THE

Publishers INDEX

MGF Publications Corporation
MGF

Michaelson Entertainment
ON LINE

Midwest Communications Corporation
INVIEW

Mill Hollow Corporation
DM NEWS

Millenium Film Workshop
MILLENNIUM FILM JOURNAL

Miller
BROADCAST ACCOUNTING ALERT

Miller Freeman Publications
EQ

Miller Magazines
CAMCORDER

MIN Publishing
MEDIA INDUSTRY NEWSLETTER

Mine Shaft Gap Publicatiooons
HI-FI HERETIC

Minnesota Ink
WRITERS' JOURNAL

Missionary Secretariat
FILMIS

Mix Publications
HYPERMEDIA

Modern Radio Co.
MODERN RADIO

Montage Publishing
AV VIDEO

Moore Publishing Co.
ADVERTISING AGENCY

Motion Picture and Distributors of America
MOTION PICTURE AND THE FAMILY, THE

Motion Picture News
MIDWEEK MOTION PICTURE NEWS

Motion Picture Producers and Distributors of America
SELECTED MOTION PICTURES

Motion Picture Publications
MOVIE CLASSIC

Motion Publishing Co.
IN MOTION FILM & VIDEO PRODUCTION MAGAZINE

Movie
MOVIE - THE VIDEO MAGAZINE

Movie Digest
CINEMA, VIDEO & CABLE MOVIE DIGEST

Movie Dream Guys
MOVIE DREAM GUYS

Movie Magazine
MOVIE

Movie Teen Illustrated
MOVIE TEEN ILLUSTRATED

Movie-TV Marketing
MOVIE/TV MARKETING

Movieland
MOVIELAND AND TV TIME

Movieland Publishing
TV GOLD

Movieline
MOVIELINE

Movies
MOVIES, THE

Moving Picture Weekly Publishing Co.
UNIVERSAL WEEKLY

Moving Pictures International
MOVING PICTURES INTERNATIONAL

Mr. Cereal Box
FLAKE

MU Press
COMICS FANDOM EXAMINER

Murdoch Magazines
PREMIERE
TV GUIDE

Murray Summers
FILMOGRAPH

Muscatine Journal
CLASSIC IMAGES REVIEW

Museum of Broadcasting
MB NEWS

Music Line
MUSIC LINE

Music Maker Publications
HOME & STUDIO RECORDING

Musical America Corporation
MUSICAL AMERICA

Mutual Film Corporation
REEL LIFE

N

N. Massaad
HOLLYWOOD

Nashwood
VIDEO TIMES

National Academy of Television Arts and Sciences
TELEVISION QUARTERLY

National Alliance of Media Arts Centers
MEDIA ARTS

National Amateur Press Association
NATIONAL AMATEUR

National Association for Better Broadcasting
BETTER RADIO AND TELEVISION

National Association of Broadcast Employees and Technicians
NABET NEWS

National Association of Broadcast Engineers and Technicians
BROADCAST ENGINEERS' JOURNAL, THE

National Association of Broadcasters
AIR TIME
NARTB MEMBER SERVICE
RADIOWEEK
TV TODAY

National Association of College Broadcasters
COLLEGE BROADCASTER

National Association of Educational Broadcasters
PACTSHEET
PUBLIC TELECOMMUNICATIONS REVIEW

National Association of Manufacturers
SERVICE FOR COMPANY COMMUNNICATORS

National Association of Television Program Executives
NATPE PROGRAMMER

National Board of Review of Motion Pictures
FILMS IN REVIEW

National Broadcast Editorial Association
EDITORIALIST, THE
NATIONAL BROADCAST EDITORIAL ASSOCIATION NEWSLETTER

National Broadcasting Company
NBC DIGEST
NBC NEWSLINE

National Cinema Development Corporation
CINEMA THE WORLD OVER

National Citizens Committee for Broadcasting
MEDIA WATCH

National Coalition Against Censorship
CENSORSHIP NEWS

National Collegiate Players
PLAYERS

National Committee for Audio-Visual Aids in Education
VISUAL EDUCATION

National Conference of Editorial Writers
MASTHEAD

National Council for Children and Television
TELEVISION & FAMILIES

National Educational Film Center
MEDIA DIGEST

National Enquirer
NATIONAL ENQUIRER

National Forensic League
ROSTRUM

National Industrial Television Association
INDUSTRIAL TELEVISION NEWS

National Mail Order Association
MAIL ORDER DIGEST

National Newspaper Association
PUBLISHER'S AUXILIARY

National Press Photographers Association
4SIGHT MAGAZINE
DARKSLIDE
IMAGE 11
NEWS PHOTOGRAPHER
RANGEFINDER, THE
RETROFOCUS
SIXSHOOTERS

National Religious Broadcasters
RELIGIOUS BROADCASTING

National Satellite Publishing
PRIVATE CABLE

National Scholastic Press Association and the Associated Collegiate Press
SCHOLASTIC EDITOR'S TRENDS IN PUBLICATIONS

National School Yearbook-Newspaper Association
PHOTOLITH, SCM

National Union of Journalists
JOURNALIST

Navy Internal Relations Activity
DIRECTION

NBC Corporate Communications
OF SPECIAL INTEREST

Nebraska Videodisc Design/Production Group
VIDEODISC DESIGN / PRODUCTION GROUP. NEWS.

Negro Actors Guild of America
NEGRO ACTORS GUILD OF AMERICA. NEWSLETTER.

New Art Publications
BOMB MAGAZINE

New Lafayette Publications
BLACK THEATRE

New Media Publishing
COMIC FANDOM'S FORUM
COMICS FEATURE
DAREDEVILS
GOLDEN AGE OF COMICS
SF MOVIELAND

New Melbourne Film Group
FILM JOURNAL

New Theatre League (now incorporated as Peoples Theatre
THEATRE WORKSHOP

New Theatre Publications
NEW THEATRE

New York Performance Foundation
PERFORMANCE

New York Reporter Printing Co.
AMERICAN ADVERTISER REPORTER

New York Star Company
STAGE PICTORIAL

New York State Community Theatre Association
THEATRE JOURNAL

New Zealand Film Commission
NEW ZEALAND FILM

News America Publications
TV GUIDE

News America Publishing Incorporated
SOAP OPERA WEEKLY

News Computing
NEWS COMPUTING JOURNAL

NewsInc.
NEWSINC.

Newspaper Advertiser Publishing Co.
ADVERTISING

Newspaper Enterprise Association
PEP

Nielsen Media Research
NIELSEN MEDIA NEWS

Nieman Foundation for Journalism
NIEMAN REPORTS

Nikon
NIKON WORLD

Non-Pareil Publishing Corporation
TV PEOPLE AND PICTURES

North American Publishing Co.
IN-PLANT REPRODUCTIONS
MAGAZINE & BOOKSELLER
PRINTING IMPRESSIONS
PUBLISHING & PRODUCTION EXECUTIVE
TARGET MARKETING
WEB

Publishers

North American Short Wave Association
FRENDX

Northern & Shell
VIDEO WORLD

Northwestern University Law School
JOURNAL OF RADIO LAW

O

Odhams Leisure Group
VIDEO MONTHLY

Odhams Press Ltd.
KINEMATOGRAPH WEEKLY

OffBeat Productions
COMICS CAREER NEWSLETTER

Official Fan Club
STAR TREK: THE OFFICIAL FAN CLUB MAGAZINE

Official Magazine Corporation
TV WORLD

Official Publications
JOURNAL

Ohio State University
OHIO NEWSPAPER

Ohio University
WIDE ANGLE

On Cable Publications
ON CABLE

On Location Publishing
ON LOCATION

Optic Music
FILM & VIDEO

O'Quinn Studios
CINEMAGIC

Orpheus Publications
FILM REVIEW
FILMS AND FILMING

Outdoor Advertising Association of America
ADVERTISING OUTDOORS

Outing Press of Detroit
RETAIL EQUIPMENT AND MERCHANDISE

Output International Publications
STAGE & STUDIO

Oxbridge Communications
PUBLISHING TRENDS & TRENDSETTERS

Oxford University Film Society
SEQUENCE

Oxford University Press
JOURNAL OF COMMUNICATION

P

P-EN Publications
PRINT-EQUIP NEWS

Pacific Magazine Group
COMPUTER PUBLISHING
PRESENTATION PRODUCTS MAGAZINE

Pacific Radio Publishing Co.
AMATEUR RADIO DEFENSE

Page One Publishers & Bookworks
COMIC RELIEF

Paillard Products
BOLEX REPORTER, THE

Paper Makers Advertising Association
PRINTING PAPER

Paragon Q Publishing
COMICS WEEK
FOUR COLOR

ParaGraphics
COMIC SHOP NEWS

Paramount Pictures Corporation
PARAMOUNT WORLD

Parker Communications Corporation
TEL-COMS

Paul Kagan Associates
CABLE TV ADVERTISING
CABLE TV PROGRAMMING
KAGAN MEDIA INDEX, THE
MARKETING NEW MEDIA
TV PROGRAM INVESTOR

PC Publishing and Presentations
PC PUBLISHING AND PRESENTATIONS

PCW Communications
PUBLISH!

Peirce-Phelps
PEIRCE-PHELPS, INC. AUDIO/VIDEO NEWSLETTER

Penblade Publishers
FILM MAKING

Pennsylvania State University Audio Visual Services
PERSPECTIVES ON FILM

Pennsylvania State University Press
PHILOSOPHY AND RHETORIC

Penton Publishing
ELECTRONICS
EXECUTIVES ON THE GO
MILLIMETER

Pentragram Publications
FLASHBACK

Perfect Vision
PERFECT VISION, THE

Performance
PERFORMANCE

Performing Arts Journal
PERFORMING ARTS JOURNAL

Pergamon Press
LANGUAGE & COMMUNICATION
TELEMATICS AND INFORMATICS

Petersen Publishing Co.
PETERSEN'S PHOTOGRAPHIC

Phillips and Co.
ADVISOR

Phillips Publishing
DBS NEWS
FUTUREHOME TECHNOLOGY NEWS
MOBILE SATELLITE NEWS
SATELLITE NEWS
VIA SATELLITE
VIDEO TECHNOLOGY NEWS

Photique Magazine
PHOTIQUE

Photo-Beacon Co.
PHOTO-BEACON, THE

Photo Era Publishing Co.
PRACTICAL PHOTOGRAPHER, THE

Photo Marketing Association International
PHOTO MARKETING

Photo Source International
PHOTOLETTER

Photo Technique International
PHOTO TECHNIQUE INTERNATIONAL

Photodramatist Publishing Co.
PHOTODRAMATIST, THE
STORY WORLD AND PHOTODRAMATIST, THE

Photographers Association of America
NATIONAL PHOTOGRAPHER, THE

Photographic Bulletin
35MM PHOTOGRAPHY

Photographic Resource Center
VIEWS

Photographic Society of America
PSA JOURNAL

Photography for Industry Books
ROTKIN REVIEW, THE

Photography in Business
FILM MEDIA

Photoplay Enterprise Association
MOTION PICTURE ALBUM

PhotoPro of Titusville
PHOTOPRO

PIC International Promotions
PIC

Picture Magazines
TV SHOW

Picture Reports
PICTURE REPORTS

Pierian Press
SERIALS REVIEW

Pilot Communications
SMASH HITS
WOW! MAGAZINE

Playbill
PLAYBILL

Plays
PLAYS

Plays International
PLAYS INTERNATIONAL

PLM Publishing
PHOTO LAB MANAGEMENT

PMS Publishing Company
MOVING IMAGE

Polaroid Corporation
PHOTOEDUCATION

Polygraph Verlag
POLYGRAPH INTERNATIONAL

POOL
CLOSE-UP

Popular Book
RADIO & TELEVISION

Popular Culture Association
JOURNAL OF POPULAR CULTURE

Popular Publications
CAMERA 35

Popular Radio
POPULAR RADIO AND TELEVISION

Popular Video
VIDEO INFO

Post Pro Publishing
POST

Post Script
POST SCRIPT

PPC Publications and Pre-Press Co.
PRINT BUYERS REVIEW

PR Week
PR WEEK

Premium Channels Publishing Co.
PREMIUM CHANNELS TV BLUEPRINT

Press Centre Limited
FUNCTIONAL PHOTOGRAPHY

Preston Publications
DARKROOM AND CREATIVE CAMERA TECHNIQUES

Pretiprint Press
SOSYAL! MAGAZINE

Preview Magazine Corporation
PREVIEW

Prevue
PREVUE

Prince George's Community College
MEDIA ANTHROPOLOGIST NEWSLETTER

Printing News
PRINTINGNEWS

Producers Quarterly Publications
PRODUCERS QUARTERLY

Production Division
PD REPORT

Professional Film and Video Equipment Association
FOLLOW FOCUS
NEWSLETTER, THE

Professional Photographers of America
PROFESSIONAL PHOTOGRAPHER, THE

Professional Video Division
PLAYBACK

PSN Publications
PRO SOUND NEWS
TELEVISION BROADCAST
VIDEOGRAPHY

PTN Publishing 210 Crossways Park Drive
PHOTOGRAPHIC PROCESSING

PTN Publishing Co.
ADVANCED IMAGING
AVC
FUNCTIONAL PHOTOGRAPHY
STUDIO PHOTOGRAPHY
TECHNICAL PHOTOGRAPHY

Public Relations Department
RADIOACTIVE

Public Relations Information Service
PUBLIC RELATIONS NEWS

Public Relations Quarterly
PUBLIC RELATIONS QUARTERLY

Public Relations Society of America
PUBLIC RELATIONS JOURNAL, THE

Public Relations Student Society of America
FORUM

Publications International
VIDEO TIMES

Publishers

Publishers Marketing Association
PMA NEWSLETTER

Pubsun Corp.
FILM JOURNAL, THE

Pulse Publications
PULSE OF RADIO

Puppet Centre Trust
ANIMATIONS

Q

Quigley Publishing Co.
EXHIBITORS HERALD WORLD
FILM BUYER
MOTION PICTURE HERALD
MOTION PICTURE PRODUCT DIGEST
PRODUCT DIGEST

Quill and Scroll Society
QUILL AND SCROLL

R

R-E-M Publications
MAKING FILMS

R. R. Bowker Company
PREVIEWS

R. R. Lawson Co.
ADVERTISING RESULTS MAGAZINE

R. Walzl
COMMERCIAL PHOTOGRAPHIC NEWS, THE

Radio Advertising Bureau
SOUND MANAGEMENT

Radio Age
RADIO AGE

Radio & Records
R & R

Radio Best
TV SCREEN

Radio Business Report
RADIO BUSINESS REPORT

Radio City Theatres
RADIO CITY NEWS

Radio Corporation of America
COMMUNICATE
ELECTRONIC AGE

Radio Corporation of America Broadcast Systems
RCA BROADCAST NEWS

Radio Dealer Publishing Co.
RADIO MANUFACTURER, THE

Radio Dial Publishing Co.
RADIO DIAL

Radio Digest Publishing Co.
RADIO FAN-FARE

Radio Industries
RADIO INDUSTRIES

Radio Manufacturers Association
RMA ENGINEER

Radio Press Group
RADIO GUIDE

Radio Review and Television News
RADIO REVIEW AND TELEVISION NEWS

Radio Society of Great Britain
RADIO COMMUNICATION

Radio-Television Daily
RTD

Radio Television News Directors Association
COMMUNICATOR

RadioPhiles
RADIO*PHILES

Raithby
BRITISH LITHOGRAPHER

Randall Publishing Co.
MAGAZINE BUSINESS
SUCCESSFUL MAGAZINE PUBLISHING

Rangefinder Publishing Co.
RANGEFINDER, THE

Rank Strand Electric
TABS

INDEX

RB Publishing Company
MAST

RC Publications
PRINT

Record Research
RECORD RESEARCH

Recording and Broadcast Publications
BROADCAST PROGRAMMING AND PRODUCTION
REP: RECORDING ENGINEERING PRODUCTION

Recording-Engineer/Producer
AUDIO PRODUCTION FOR BROADCAST

Red Circle Magazines
FILMLAND

Reed Business Publishing
ELECTRONICS WORLD + WIRELESS WORLD

Reed Prospect Magazines
VIDEO CAMERA

Reese Publishing Co.
VIDEO MAGAZINE

Regent University
FILM WITNESS

Religious Speech Communication Association
JOURNAL OF COMMUNICATION AND RELIGION, THE

Reporters Committee for Freedom of the Press
NEWS MEDIA & THE LAW, THE

Research and Survey Unit of the Australian Film and Television School
MEDIA INFORMATION AUSTRALIA

Research Society for American Periodicals
RSAP NEWSLETTER

Research Society for Victorian Periodicals
VICTORIAN PERIODICALS REVIEW

Reunion Press
LINE MONITOR, THE

Review Company
DRAMATIC REVIEW, THE

Review of International Broadcasting
REVIEW OF INTERNATIONAL BROADCASTING

RH Enterprises
SCARLET STREET

Rhetoric Society of America. Department of Philosophy
RHETORIC SOCIETY QUARTERLY

Richard Walzl
PHOTOGRAPHER'S FRIEND, THE

Rising Sun Press
FILM GUIDE

RLD Communications
BOX OFFICE

Rockafeller
PHOTOSTAR

Romantic Times Publishing Group
ROMANTIC TIMES

Rosary College
JOURNAL OF FILM AND VIDEO

Rosebud Associates
MORE

Roth International
INTERNATIONAL ADVERTISER

Rothchild Consultants
OPTICAL MEMORY NEWS

Royal Television Society
TELEVISION

R.R. Bowker Co.
PUBLISHER'S WEEKLY

Rundown
RUNDOWN, THE

Rural Radio
RURAL RADIO

S

S. Hirzel Verlag GmbH & Co.
ACUSTICA
AEU

Sagamore Publishing Co.
DB

Sage Publications
COMMUNICATION RESEARCH
DISCOURSE & SOCIETY
EUROPEAN JOURNAL OF COMMUNICATION
HUMAN COMMUNICATION RESEARCH
MANAGEMENT COMMUNICATION QUARTERLY
MEDIA, CULTURE, AND SOCIETY
WRITTEN COMMUNICATION

Sahadi Publications
CAMERA 35 INCORPORATING PHOTO WORLD

Salisbury State College
LITERATURE/FILM QUARTERLY

Salvation Army
VIDEO CAPSULE

San Francisco State University
FEED-BACK

Sanford Schwarz
TV PICTURE LIFE

Satellite Communications
HORIZON

Satellite Organisation
SATELLITE TIMES

Saturn Press
FILM AND THEATRE TODAY

Scene at the Movies
SCENE AT THE MOVIES

School of Law
AIR LAW REVIEW

School of Rehabilitation Medicine
HUMAN COMMUNICATION

Screen Actors Guild
SCREEN ACTOR HOLLYWOOD

Screen Facts Press
SCREEN FACTS

Screen-Teen Company
MOVIE TEEN

Screen Weekly
SCREEN WEEKLY, THE

Scripps Howard News
SCRIPPS HOWARD NEWS

ScriptWriter News
SCRIPTWRITER NEWS

SCV USA
IN CONCERT PRESENTS

Select Publications
FILM ALBUM MAGAZINE

Selwood Press
BEST OF FILM & VIDEO
VIDEO--THE MAGAZINE

Seminary Film Society of Southern Baptist Theological Society
MOVIES AND MINISTRY

Serbin Communications
PHOTOGRAPHER'S FORUM

Seton Hall University
COMMENT ON THE MEDIA

Seybold Publications
DIGITAL MEDIA

Sheptow Publishing
DARKROOM PHOTOGRAPHY

Shooting Commercials
SHOOTING COMMERCIALS

Show Biz West
SHOW BIZ WEST

Show Magazine
SHOW

Showcase World
SHOWCASE WORLD

Showmen's Trade Review
SHOWMEN'S TRADE REVIEW

Signs of the Times Publishing Co.
SIGNS OF THE TIMES

Skye Publishing Co.
MOVIE FAN

Soap Opera Update Magazine
SOAP OPERA UPDATE

Society for Animation Studies
SOCIETY FOR ANIMATION STUDIES NEWSLETTER, THE

Society for Cinema Studies
CINEMA JOURNAL

Society for Collegiate Journalists
COLLEGIATE JOURNALIST

Publishers INDEX

Society for Education in Film and Television
SCREEN

Society for Film History Research
CINEMA STUDIES

Society for Photographic Education
EXPOSURE

Society for Scholarly Publishing
SSP LETTER

Society for the History of Technology
TECHNOLOGY AND CULTURE

Society for Theatre Research
THEATRE NOTEBOOK

Society of Authors
AUTHOR, THE

Society of Broadcast Engineers
SIGNAL, THE

Society of Cable Television Engineers
CABLE TELEVISION ENGINEERING

Society of Motion Picture and Television Engineers
SMPTE JOURNAL

Society of Newspaper Design
DESIGN

Society of Professional Journalists
QUILL, THE

Society of Professional Videographers
PRO VIDEOGRAM

Society to Preserve and Encourage Radio Drama
SPERDVAC

S.O.D. Publishing
SOAP OPERA DIGEST

Soma Communications
TRI-S SPOT/LIGHT

Sony Broadcast & Communications
DASH WORLD

Sound Stage
SOUND STAGE

South Wind Publishing Co.
FOR ADVERTISERS
MAGAZINE DESIGN & PRODUCTION
PRE-

Southam Business Communications
BROADCASTER
PULP & PAPER CANADA

Southam Communications Ltd.
ELECTRONICS & COMMUNICATIONS

Southeastern Theatre Conference
SOUTHERN THEATRE

Southern Players
THEATER NOW

Southern Speech Communication Association
SOUTHERN COMMUNICATION JOURNAL, THE

Southern States Communication Association
C-O-N-N-E-C-T-I-O-N-S

Specialty Advertising Association International
SPECIALTY ADVERTISING BUSINESS

Spectator International
CINEMA

Speech and Drama
SPEECH AND DRAMA

Speech Communication Association
COMMUNICATION EDUCATION
COMMUNICATION MONOGRAPHS
CRITICAL STUDIES IN MASS COMMUNICATION
JOURNAL OF APPLIED COMMUNICATION RESEARCH
QUARTERLY JOURNAL OF SPEECH, THE
RHETORICAL & COMMUNICATION THEORY NEWSLETTER
SCA WOMEN'S CAUCUS AND FEMINIST & WOMEN STUDIES DIVISION NEWSLETTER
SPECTRA
SPEECH COMMUNICATION TEACHER, THE
TPQ

Spindrift Press
WRITERS ON WRITING

Spotlight Casting Magazine
SPOTLIGHT CASTING MAGAZINE

St. Bride's Press
ADVERTISING REVIEW

St. Cloud State University
SIDEBAR

St. Louis Journalism Review
ST. LOUIS JOURNALISM REVIEW

St. Louis Photographic Publishing Co.
ST. LOUIS AND CANADIAN PHOTOGRAPHER

St. Regis Publications
BETTER LISTENING
CONSUMER ELECTRONICS PRODUCT NEWS

Stage and Sport
STAGE AND SPORT

Stage and Television Today
STAGE AND TELEVISION TODAY, THE

Stage Pictorial Publishing Co.
STAGE PICTORIAL

Stage Publishing Co.
STAGE

Stage Souvenir
STAGE SOUVENIR, THE

Standard Gravure Co.
EDITORIAL NEWSLETTER

Standard Rate and Data Service
SRDS REPORT, THE

Stanley Foundation
WORLD PRESS REVIEW

Star Editorial
STAR

Star Guidance
MOVIE DIGEST
TV RADIO SHOW

STAR (Spanish Television and Radio) Productions
UPDATE

Starline Publications
TEEN DREAM

Starlog Communications International
COMICS SCENE
FANGORIA
GOREZONE
SCIENCE-FICTION VIDEO MAGAZINE
SCREEN GREATS
STAR TREK: THE NEXT GENERATION

Starlog Telecommunications
TS

State University College
DRAMA & THEATRE

Station Services Department
NAB HIGHLIGHTS

Stereophile
STEREOPHILE

Sterling Harbor Press
EPIEGRAM

Sterling's Magazines
DAYTIME TV
MOVIE MIRROR
NIGHTTIME TV
PHOTO SCREEN
SUPER TEEN
WHO'S WHO IN MOVIES AND TV

Sterlings Magazines
SOAP OPERA STARS

Steve Simmons Photography
VIEWCAMERA

Stilson & Stilson
DIRECT RESPONSE SPECIALIST, THE

Straight Arrow Publishers
US MAGAZINE

Strand Lighting
LIGHTS!

Street & Smith Publications
MOVIE ACTION MAGAZINE
PIC
PICTURE PLAY MAGAZINE

Street Enterprises
COMIC READER, THE

Student Press Law Center
STUDENT PRESS LAW CENTER REPORT

Studios
FILM ART

Summit Media International
MEDIA BUSINESS
MEDIA BUSINESS MARKETS

Suncraft International
FILMMAKERS FILM & VIDEO MONTHLY

Susquehanna Times & Magazine
OLD NEWS

Swank Magazine Corporation
SOAP OPERA TIME

Synergetic Audio Concepts
SYN-AUD-CON NEWSLETTER

T

Take 5 Publishing
FLORIDA REEL

Tantivy Press
FOCUS ON FILM

Target
TARGET

Taylor & Francis
HISTORY OF PHOTOGRAPHY
POLITICAL COMMUNICATION AND PERSUASION

Taylor Publishing Co.
TAYLORTALK

Technograph 11251 Stagg St.
LOS ANGELES TECHNOGRAPH

Technology Marketing Corporation
TELEMARKETING

Telco Productions
TELCO REPORT, THE

Telecommunication Society of Australia
ATR
TELECOMMUNICATION JOURNAL OF AUSTRALIA, THE

Telecommunications Research and Action Center
ACCESS

Teleconnect Magazine
TELECONNECT

Telegraph and Telephone Journal
POST OFFICE MAGAZINE

Telegrapher
TELEGRAPHER, THE

Teleprofessional
TELEPROFESSIONAL

Telescreen Century Magazine
TELESCREEN

Telespan Publishing Corp.
TELESPAN'S BUSINESSTV GUIDE

Television
TELEVISION

Television Bureau of Advertising
SALES NEWS

Television Digest
SATELLITE WEEK
TELEVISION DIGEST WITH CONSUMER ELECTRONICS
VIDEO WEEK

Television Editorial Co.
CABLEAGE
TELEVISION/RADIO AGE

Television Editorial Corp.
TELEVISION / RADIO AGE INTERNATIONAL

Television Index
ROSS REPORTS TELEVISION

Television International
TELEVISION INTERNATIONAL

Television Opportunities
TELEVISION OPPORTUNITIES

Television Publications
TELEVISER

Television Publishing Co.
TELEVISION

Television Times
TELEVISION PERSONALITIES

Television Weekly News
TELEVISION WEEKLY NEWS

Tempo Publishing Company
SOAP OPERA PEOPLE

Tennant and Ward
NEW PHOTO-MINIATURE

Ter-Sat Media Publications
CABLE COMMUNICATIONS MAGAZINE

TGIF Enterprises
TGIF

That New Magazine
THEATERWEEK

THE Journal
THE JOURNAL

Theatre Arts
THEATRE ARTS

Theatre Communications Group
AMERICAN THEATRE

Publishers

Theatre Crafts
THEATRE CRAFTS

Theatre Historical Society
MARQUEE

Theatre Library Association
BROADSIDE

Theatre Magazine Co.
THEATRE MAGAZINE

Theatre Publications
THEATRE TIME

Theatre Publishing Co.
THEATRE, THE

Thomas Atkins
FILM JOURNAL, THE

Tiffen Manufacturing Corporation
TIFFEN PROFESSIONAL NEWSLETTER

Tim Lucas
VIDEO WATCHDOG

Time Out 20/20 Limited
20/20

Time Screen
TIME SCREEN

Tisch School of the Arts/New York University
TDR

Titan Books
ARK

Titsch Publishig Co.
WATCH

Tone Arm Publications
PRESS, THE

Tony Lee
STRANGE ADVENTURES

Tower Magazines
NEW MOVIE MAGAZINE, THE

Trans World Radio
TWR

Transaction Periodicals Consortium
PUBLISHING RESEARCH QUARTERLY

Travel & Trade Publishing Asia
ASIAN ADVERTISING & MARKETING

Triangle Communications
PANORAMA

Triangle Publications
MOVIE-RADIO GUIDE
TELEVISION AND SCREEN GUIDE

Trident Comics
FA

Triple D Publishing
ONSAT
SATELLITE RETAILER
STV GUIDE

TSI Ltd.
BASELINE

Turner & Fisher
DRAMATIC MIRROR AND LITERARY COMPANION, THE

TV Host
ENTERTAINER, THE

TV Mirror
TV MIRROR

TV Trade Media Inc.
VIDEO AGE INTERNATIONAL

TVSM
CABLE GUIDE, THE
TV ENTERTAINMENT

Twentieth Century-Fox Film Corporation
FOCUS ON FOX

Twentieth Century Publications
CB LIFE

Twin Cities Media Project
TWIN CITIES JOURNALISM REVIEW

U

UCLA School of Law
FEDERAL COMMUNICATIONS LAW JOURNAL

Umschau Verlag Breidenstein
LEICA FOTOGRAFIE INTERNATIONAL

Unicorn Publishing
TAKE ONE

Unifrance Film
CINEMA FRANCAIS

Union Labor Sun
UNION LABOR SUN

United Business Publications
BIOMEDICAL COMMUNICATIONS
HOME VIDEO
LAW ENFORCEMENT TECHNOLOGY

United Communications Group
TELECOMMUNICATIONS ALERT

United Press International Corporate Affairs
UPI ADVANCE

United States Catholic Conference
FILM & BROADCASTING REVIEW

United States Commission on International Educational and Cultural Affairs
INTERNATIONAL EDUCATIONAL AND CULTURAL EXCHANGE

United States Federal Trade Commission
ADVERTISING ALERT

United States Postal Service Communications Department
MEMO TO MAILERS

United Technical Publications
LENS MAGAZINE

University Film and Video Association
DIGEST OF THE UNIVERSITY FILM AND VIDEO ASSOCIATION

University Film Association
DIGEST

University Film Study Center
UNIVERSITY FILM STUDY CENTER. NEWSLETTER.

University of Alabama
ALABAMA JOURNALIST

University of California
HASTINGS COMMUNICATIONS AND ENTERTAINMENT LAW JOURNAL

University of California at San Diego
MOVIE GEEK

University of California Press
FILM QUARTERLY

University of Cincinnati
CINEMA NOW

University of Colorado
JOURNAL OF MARKETING EDUCATION

University of Dayton
FILM HERITAGE

University of Iowa
IOWA JOURNALIST

University of Minnesota
AUDIO VISUAL JOURNAL
MURPHY REPORTER

University of Missouri School of Journalism
FOI DIGEST

University of New South Wales
AUSTRALIAN JOURNAL OF SCREEN THEORY

University of Sao Paulo
THEATRE DOCUMENTATION

University of South Carolina College of Journalism and the South Carolina Scholastic Broadcasters Association
NATIONAL HIGH SCHOOL BROADCASTERS NEWSLETTER

University of Texas Press
VELVET LIGHT TRAP

University of Toronto
MODERN DRAMA

University of Toronto Press
SCHOLARLY PUBLISHING

University of Wyoming
COMMUNIQUÉ

Unlimited Positive Communications
MARKETING PULSE, THE

Urban Telecommunications Forum
URBAN TELECOMMUNICATIONS FORUM

U.S. Camera Publishing Corporation
TRAVEL & LEISURE

USITT
THEATRE DESIGN & TECHNOLOGY

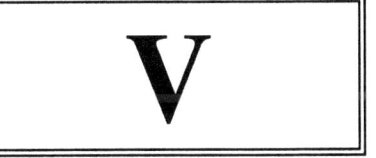

V

Ventura Publisher Users Group (VPUG)
VENTURA PROFESSIONAL!

Ventura Users of North America
VENTURA LETTER, THE

Ver Halen Publications
HOME MOVIES

Verbatim
VERBATIM

Verlag F. Bruckmann KG
NOVUM GEBRAUCHSGRAPHIK

Viare Publishing
VIDEO REVIEW

Victor Hasselblad Aktiebolag
HASSELBLAD

Video 80
VIDEO EIGHTIES MAGAZINE

Video Insider
VIDEO INSIDER

Video Tape Associates
VTA PLAYBACK

Video Times
VIDEO TIMES

Videodisc Monitor
VIDEODISC MONITOR, THE

Videomaker
VIDEOMAKER

Videosonic Arts
FANTASTIC TELEVISION!

VidPro Publishing
VIDEOPRO

View Communications
WRAP

View Communications Corporation
VIEW

Virginia Instructional Technology Association in Higher Education (VITA)
NEWS & VIEWS

Virginia Production Services Association
REEL LIFE

Virgo Publishing
4TH MEDIA JOURNAL, THE

Visible Language
VISIBLE LANGUAGE

Visions Unlimited
PHOTO DISTRICT NEWS

Visual Imagination
STARBURST

Visual Studies Workshop
AFTERIMAGE

Vizions Publishing Corporation
VIZIONS

VRI Arts Publishing
ART & CINEMA

VSD Publications
VIDEO SOFTWARE MAGAZINE

VSIA
PEGBAR

W

W. A. Johnston
EXHIBITORS' TIMES

W. Underwood
DRAMA, THE

Walden Book Company
W •B

Warren Publishing
PUBLIC BROADCASTING REPORT, THE

Warren Publishing Co.
FAMOUS MONSTERS OF FILMLAND
SCREEN THRILLS ILLUSTRATED

Warwick Trading Company
CINEMATOGRAPHY AND BIOSCOPE MAGAZINE

Washington Community Video Center
TELEVISIONS

Publishers INDEX

Washington Journalism Review
WASHINGTON JOURNALISM REVIEW

Washington Newspaper Publishers Association
WASHINGTON NEWSPAPER, THE

W.D. Publications
DISNEY ADVENTURES

Welsh Publishing Group
SIMPSONS ILLUSTRATED

Werner Publishing Corporation
OUTDOOR PHOTOGRAPHER

West Coast Video
SPOTLIGHT ON VIDEO

Westana Publications
PRINT EDUCATION MAGAZINE

Western Educational Society for Telecommunications
TELEMEMO

Western Speech Communication Association
COMMUNICATION REPORTS
WSCA NEWS

Western States Communication Association
WESTERN JOURNAL OF SPEECH COMMUNICATION

Western Writers of America
ROUNDUP QUARTERLY

Westwood Press
INTERNATIONAL JOURNAL OF INSTRUCTIONAL MEDIA AND TECHNOLOGY

W.G. Souther
ADVERTISING EXPERIENCE

WGE Publishing
CD REVIEW

W.H. Woodcock
WOODCOCK'S PRINTERS' AND LITHOGRAPHERS' WEEKLY GAZETTE AND NEWSPAPER REPORTER

Whittaker
DRAMATIC MAGAZINE, THE

Whitton Press
IBE

Who's Mailing What!
WHO'S MAILING WHAT!

Wike Associates
CHRISTIAN ADVERTISING FORUM

William Connolly
SPAGHETTI CINEMA

William H. Hills
AUTHOR, THE

William J. Felchner
TELEVISION HISTORY

William Miller
SCRIPT NEWSLETTER

Wireless Press
WIRELESS AGE, THE

Wisconsin Dramatic Society
PLAY-BOOK, THE

Wisconsin Photographer
WISCONSIN PHOTOGRAPHER

WittyWorld Publications
WITTYWORLD

Women and Film
WOMEN & FILM

Women & Language
WOMEN & LANGUAGE

Women in Communications
MATRIX

World Association for Christian Communication
ACTION
MEDIA DEVELOPMENT

World Broadcast News
WORLD BROADCAST NEWS

World Communication Association
COMMUNICATION RESEARCH REPORTS
WCA NEWSLETTER
WORLD COMMUNICATION

World Media Report
WORLD MEDIA REPORT

World Perspective Communications
ENTERTAINMENT REVUE
INSIDE ENTERTAINMENT

World Publishing Co.
INSIDE HOLLYWOOD
MOVIE MARKETPLACE

Worth International Communications
COMMUNIQUE

Writer
WRITER, THE

Writers & Scholars International
INDEX ON CENSORSHIP

Writers Guild of America--West
NEWSLETTER

Writers Institute
WHAT EDITORS WANT

WV Publications
CAMCORDER USER
WHAT SATELLITE
WHAT VIDEO

Wyman & Sons
THEATRE, THE

X

Xerox Corporation
SCSC XEROX PIPELINE

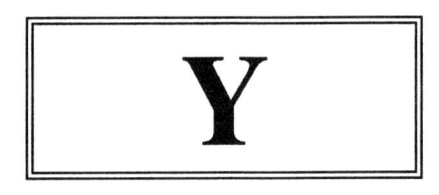

Y

Yaffa Publishing Group
ADVERTISING NEWS

Yale School of Drama
THEATER

Yellow Pages Publishers Association
LINK

Z

ZAO
ZOOM

Ziff-Davis Publishing Co.
CAMERA ARTS
COMPUTERS & ELECTRONICS
ELECTRONICS WORLD

Subject Headings

Guide

This subject heading guide contains approximately 5,400 serial title listings under some 1,300 various subject headings. Dates of publication (when known) are provided. For the sake of clarity, only *Main Title* entries are listed. Upon locating a desired serial, the reader is directed to the *Main Title* entry for detailed information.

In a field as diverse as communication and the performing arts, the task of assembling recognizable and accurate media names and subject headings has been formidable. Various academic faculty, librarians, and professionals in the communication and performing arts fields were queried in the search for a usable structure for application to these indices.

It became obvious that variations in geographic location, career fields, and time itself (which has a wonderful way of sending current terminology to the outdated phraseology dustbin), all contributed to the quest for proper descriptive terminology. The reader is enjoined to appreciate the necessarily subjective and sometimes arbitrary nature of selected subject heading terminology.

Certain media have been grouped together under umbrella provisos in order to better describe the breadth of a given serial. For example, **Broadcasting** encompassess both **Radio** and **Television** media. Other communication media are in a stand-alone mode. Structurally speaking, applications (such as *Fan, Management, Theory,* or *Legal*) may apply to any or all media, and are always subservient to that medium or media.

A guide to media structure and a subject heading listing of definitions follows.

Defined Media with Subsets

Audio	Electronics	Point-to-Point Media
Audio / Video	Film	Print
Audio	Magazines	Magazines
Video	Mail	Newspapers
Audiovisual	Mass Communication	Radio
Books	Motion Pictures	Speech
Broadcasting	Cinema	Telecommunication
Radio	Film	Television
Television	Newspapers	Theatre
Cable Television	Outdoor	Video
Cinema	Performing Arts	
Communication	Photography	

Definition of Subject Heading Terminology

Academic
Pertaining to the area of teaching, or non-commercial applications.

Access
Community access to local media forums, most often applied to local newspapers, radio, television and cable television media. Also see: *Community*.

Acting
The process of acting. Also see: *Artist*.

Action
Specific film, radio, or television genre employing strong physical action scenes.

Adult
Media applications for individuals age 18 and older.

Advocate
Public organizations that campaign for improvements in specific media.

Aesthetics
The study of the artistic, cultural and sensuous aspects of entertainment media.

Alternative Media
Non-mainstream media; sometimes referred to as "guerilla" or "underground."

Amateur
Pertaining to non-professional activities. Proud badge of honor during the late 19th and early 20th centuries, especially in photography, theatre, and radio.

Animation
The process of creating movement (stop-action cel or computer generated) in film and video media.

Archival
An organized process of preserving material for future generations, applied to the preservation of all media.

Artist
Includes actor, actress, and performer. Also see *Acting*.

Audio
Non-broadcast applications of the audio medium, including compact discs, records, technology, and the recording process in studio surroundings.

Audio / Video
Non-broadcast applications of both audio and video media. For audio applications excluding video, SEE *Audio*. For video applications excluding audio, SEE *Video*.

Audio Visual
Presentation applications including overhead projection, closed-circuit telecommunication, and audio or video as applied to the presentation forum.

Author
Creative indvidual behind written works for media.

Authorship
For the process of written works for media, see: *Writing*.

Avant-garde
Pertaining to new, oftentimes daring explorations outside the mainstream media.

Books
Printed publications of a non-periodic nature. SEE *Print*, which encompasses printed material, including magazines and newspapers.

Broadcasting
Includes both radio and television media. SEE *Audio* or *Video* for non-broadcast applications. Also SEE *Cable Television*.

Cable Television
Video in a non-broadcast medium

Carrier Current
A unique form of localized audio/radio broadcasting through electrical current lines, most often found on college campuses.

Cartoons
Drawings of a satirical nature, including editorial cartoons, comic books and strips. Also see: *Animation*.

Cassette
Pre-recorded audio or video programming material. Also see: *Stock* for blank audio or video tape stock.

Cinema
Motion Picture Exhibition. Also SEE: *Film* for non-exhibition, or *Motion Pictures*, the umbrella term for exhibition AND non-exhibition film.

Circulation
Applied to *Magazines* and *Newspapers*, the process of building and maintaining a subscriber base. Also see: *Distribution* for the treatment of distributing said publications.

Collector
A private individual or organization, which as a hobby or for financial gain, acquires, sells, and/or holds unique historical items.

College
A two or four year institution of higher learning, including Community College designations. Also see: *Education, Elementary, Highschool,* and *Instructional*.

Comics
Magazine booklets or newspaper comic strip applications. Also see: *Animation*, and the umbrella term *Cartoons* which includes both *Comics* and *Animation*.

Commercial
A business-oriented application of a medium or media. Replaces "professional." Also see: *Amateur* for non-commercial applications of media, primarily in vogue from the late 19th to the early 20th century.

Communication
General and non-mediated communication.

Community
Media applications which are community / public oriented. Also see: *Access*.

Compact Disks
See: *Records & Compact Discs*.

Concert
Live stage performance, usually of a musical nature. Also see: *Theatre* for live dramatic performance.

Construction
Buildings, studios or other structures relevant to the media.

Corporate
Media usage within corporate or business settings. Also see: *Business* for the "business of" specific media.

Cultural
Elements of media relevant to the social and intellectual growth of the community. Also see: *Intercultural* for the effect of various media upon multiple community cultures, or the impact of cultures on the media.

Dance
Any form of rhythmic movement to music or rhythmic sound, including ballet, modern, experimental, and theatrical productions.

Design
The process of assembling elements which results in an effective and pleasing style. Applicable to print layout, stage, lighting, and other creative media utilizations.

Desktop Publishing
Computerized pre-press operation for editorial, type, and layout functions output on a laser printer.

Direct Marketing
Advertising promotion distributed directly to a chosen list of consumers.

Directing
An individual responsible for the supervision of artists, and the creative interpretation of the script or score utilized by those artists.

Distribution
The fullfillment side of marketing; the physical movement of media products from source to consumer.

Documentary
Factual media presentation, most often applied to film, radio, television, and theatre productions.

Editing
The creative selective operation utilized in preparing media for public presentation. Pertinent to a variety of media including print publications, scripts, scores, advertising copy, and radio-television-film productions.

Editorial
Pertaining to sections of news journalism containing commentary and unique issue-oriented viewpoints.

Education
General learning field. Also see: *College, Highschool, Instructional, Pedagogy,* and *School.*

Electronics
Development of sophisticated electrical circuitry and devices utilized in communication field.

Emerging
Developmental aspects of established, or newly emerging media.

Employment
Aspects of employee management and working conditions within unique media.

Engineering
Professional supervision and design of technology required for the operation of specific forms of mass communication, most often radio, television, film, and telecommunication.

Ethics
The study of moral choices as applied to specific media, most often utilized in the area of journalistic "gate-keeping" functions. The discussion of ethics is frequently associated with the reporting, writing and editing functions of assembling radio/television newscasts, newspaper and magazine publications.

Exhibition
The business of motion picture theatre operation

Fan
Public interest and devotion to artists and/or programs and productions within mass communication arena. Often publications oriented to media stars and their productions.

Fantasy
Genre productions encompassing illusionary and make-believe elements on an imaginative scale, frequently associated with film or television dramatic works.

Fashion
Media application, commonly photography, for the marketing and retail sale of items of apparel.

Film
Non-exhibition form. See: *Cinema* for exhibited film, and *Motion Pictures* for both exhibted and non-exhibited formats.

Finance
The raising of capital, and other economic operatives pertaining to the profitable operation of specific media.

Graphics
Line drawings, pictures, halftones, and other visual elements as applied to various communication media.

Guide
Program guide, i.e. a guide to the programming, or available entertainment items within a specific medium. For mass communication, descriptive counsel on upcoming programming or product release. For the theatre, concert and performing arts fields, similar guidance on content and presentation of unique stage events.

Ham
The field of amateur short-wave radio.

HDTV
High Definition Television, an emerging visual medium incorporating the best elements of film and video.

Historical
Pertaining to media development, content or societal impact.

Home Consumer
Commonly media-oriented print publications designed for public home consumption.

Horror
Genre productions associated with elements of fear of the unknown usually in the radio, television, film, and print media.

House Organ
Print publications designed for "in-house" distribution to employees, staff, and other interested parties. Function is to promote the interest

Subject Headings

and well-being of the corporation and the employee community.

Independent
Producers and their projects which are independent of traditional large corporate operations. May apply to financial elements, production, marketing and distribution.

Instructional
The process of education; may be used in conjunction with education headings *Elementary, College, Highschool.*

Instrumental
Utilization of musical instruments; non-vocal.

Interactive
The technology and operation of instructional media designed for personal education. Typically found in the combination of computers with audio/video media.

Intercultural
The effect and relationship of specific media with multiple cultural settings. Also see: *Cultural* for individual media applications.

International
Publications and other forms of mass media whose scope extends beyond national borders and interests. Publications and media without this designation are considered to focus on interests of the nation of origin, with the subject heading of "World."

Interpersonal
All aspects of speech and interpersonal (non-mediated) communication.

Journalism
The creative process of writing for mass communication. Also see: *News* and *Scripts*.

Legal
Regulatory and judicial aspects of communication and the performing arts.

Libraries
Relating private and public libraries to specific communication applications.

Literature
Print publications associated with communication and the performing arts.

Location
Planning and execution of on-location production sites for radio, television, and film media.

Low Power Television
Community-oriented television operations which maintain a special low-power frequency authorization.

Magazines
Printed publications of a periodic nature. See media headings: *Books, Mail, Newspapers,* or *Outdoor*. Also see: *Print*, the umbrella heading for all of these media.

Mail
The communication medium of *Mail* includes the application of *Direct Mail*.

Management
The supervision and operation of specific media. Also see: *Business, Exhibition, Finance, House Organ,* and *Legal* for explicit elements of management.

Marketing
The promotion of products for sale, including the tradtional areas of "product, price, place, and promotion."

Mass Media
Includes mass media headings *Broadcasting, Cable Television, Cinema,* and *Print*.

Media Buying
The selection and purchase of print space and radio-television time slots for advertising purposes.

Minorities
As defined by societal structure within specific nations. Most often related to gender, racial and cultural groups.

Motion Pictures
Major media heading encompassing *Film* and *Cinema*.

Museums
Organizations and structures dedicated to the preservation and presentation of media and culture for the public.

News
Specific form of mass communication application in presenting current issues and events of importance to the general public.

Newspapers
A mass medium under general media heading *Print*.

Outdoor
A print-advertising medium most often encompassing outdoor billboard and poster advertising, found under general media heading *Print*.

Pedagogy
The process of teaching . Also see: *Education, College,* and *Highschool*.

Performance
The critical study of artist presentation on stage and media.

Performing Arts
A general media heading which encompasses *Theatre, Dance, Music,* and *Vaudeville*.

Photography
A major media heading defined as the art, technique, and technology of fixing visual elements within a given medium, commonly paper.

Popular Culture
Societal elements commonly considered not to be of an intellectual or serious nature, but which are integral to the developmental fabric of society and the community.

Pre-production
The planning, creation and mechanical assembly of components prior to the execution of a project in print publication, radio-television-film, and the performing arts.

Post-production
A specific time period for refinement of radio, television and film projects before release and distribution to the general public.

Preservation
The act of conserving specific elements of communication and the performing arts for the use and enlightenment of current and future generations.

Print
A major media heading encompassing *Books, Magazines, Mail, Newspapers,* and *Outdoor.*

Printing
The stage of publishing whereby mechanical means are employed to fix text and graphics to printed media.

Producing
The management and business side of creating and completing a project. Commonly applied to the areas of radio, television, film, and the performing arts.

Production
The creative project developed for distribution or exhibition in a specific medium.

Programming
The art and technique of selecting and scheduling programs for radio, television, and satellite media.

Programming Guide
See: *Guide.*

Projection
The science and technique of motion picture and video presentation. Most often related to motion picture exhibition during the first half of the 20th century.

Promotion
Refers to publications and other media specifically designed to promote the interests of a commercial communications firm.

Public
Designation for the area of "public broadcasting." For items of a "public" nature, see: *Community.*

Public Relations
Issue-oriented discipline which utilizes communication media for furthering the public's acceptance and understanding of corporate or organizational concerns.

Publishing
The supervision and business of creating printed documents. Most often associated with book, magazine and newspaper media.

Puppetry
Manipulated animated wooden figures, usually associated with television or theatrical productions.

Radio
Aural broadcast medium of either an AM (Amplitude Modulation) or FM (Frequency Modulation) nature. Also see: *Television,* and *Broadcasting* which includes both media.

Ratings
A system for critical assessment of a program's popularity, commonly related to radio and television.

Recording
The process of fixing an audio or video project on magnetic media (tape stock).

Records & Compact Discs
Recording medium and released product of the audio recording process.

Regulation
Governmental supervision and control of media form and function.

Religion
As applied to religious media, and varying forms of media programming or content related to man's relationship with a "higher power."

Research
The art, technique and technology associated with the quest for new knowledge and understanding of media.

Retail
Specific aspects of commercial media sales and service with the general public.

Review
General review and consideration of the status and events in communication and the performing arts.

Rhetoric
Elements connected with verbal and written communication; specifically content and style.

Sales
Explicitly oriented to the sales departments of certain media; the corporate segment responsible for selling air time or publication space to advertisers and their agencies.

Satellites
The business, technology, and operation of artificial satellites used for the purpose of communication.

Satire
A unique style of creative project designed to elicit humor by exposé or commentary on elements of society, government, and the media.

School
An institution of education including: *Elementary, Highschool,* and *College.*

Science Fiction
Productions or projects of a fictional nature, based primarily on scientific conjecture. Commonly a specific genre for books, magazines, radio, television, and film projects.

Scripts
Both the process of scriptwriting and the property itself. Applies to numerous media.

Shortwave
Shortwave radio, commonly of an international nature. Also see: *Ham* for amateur shortwave radio.

Soap Operas
Popular daytime radio and television program genre.

Soviet Bloc
A term employed to describe the pre-1990 confederation of nations within the Soviet sphere of influence, and specifically applied to several unique serials, the coverage of which was directly linked to a Soviet political philosophy.

Specialty Advertising
Advertising/promotion items (pencils, pens, letter openers, etc) designed to contain several lines of advertising, and which are often given free to current and/or potential customers.

Special Effects
Applies to extraordinary elements in any production or stage performance.

Spot
Refers to television, radio, and film spot commercial production.

Stock
  Non-recorded (blank) magnetic tape stock for use in radio, television, and film.

Studio
  A large, enclosed structure or room which has been especially equipped for the needs of production in radio, television, audio and film.

Teaching
  The art and craft of pedagogy; used here in the supportive relationship between media and teaching.

Technology
  The practical application of science into the media workplace; anything associated with "equipment" used in the creation, production, and distribution of media product.

Teleconferencing
  The process of linking together via television satellite groups of people in diverse geographic locations.

Teletext
  Any information-based system delivered into consumer homes via cable television, and which is available to the consumer on demand.

Television
  Broadcast visual medium.

Theatre
  Stage performance including such applications as *Burlesque, Comedy, Concerts, Drama, Music,* and *Vaudeville.*

Theory
  Abstract reasoning concerning the form and function of communication and the performing arts.

Typography
  The process of selecting, and utilizing type fonts and styles for print publications.

Unions & Guilds
  Media labor organizations consisting of skilled craftspeople, working together for the common good of the organization.

Vaudeville
  A unique form of musical comedy theatre popular during the late 19th, and early 20th centuries. See: *Theatre.*

Video
  Non-broadcast visual medium. See: *Audio/Video* for major media heading which includes both media; also *Television* and *Broadcasting* for mass media applications.

Videodisc
  Video recording medium, most often by means of laser technology.

Videotext
  A broadcast process by which enormous amounts of information is generated, transmitted, received, decoded, and displayed on home television receivers.

Wartime
  The role and function of media during a specific period of war.

World Media
  See: *International.*

Writing
  The act and process of authoring text material for any medium.

Youth
  A person under 18 years of age.

Subject Heading

This index consists of approximately 5,400 serial titles listed under 1,300 subject headings See the *Subject Heading Guide* for complete descriptions of media and subject headings. Publication span information, when known, is included with the Main Ttitle entry. Country of origin, when different than the United States, is present within brackets.

Audio

Artist
AMUSEMENT BUSINESS - Jan 9, 1961+
MOVIE FLASH - ?+ {Philippines}
SOSYAL! MAGAZINE - Feb 4, 1986+ {Philippines}

Automobile
AUTO SOUND & SECURITY - Jan/Feb, 1990+
CAR AUDIO AND ELECTRONICS - Jul, 1988+
CAR STEREO REVIEW - Fall, 1987+
DRIVING AMBITION - ?+ {United Kingdom}

Business
AMUSEMENT BUSINESS - Jan 9, 1961+
ICA NEWSLETTER - Spring, 1980+?

Cassettes
ICA NEWSLETTER - Spring, 1980+?

Collector
RECORD RESEARCH - Feb, 1955+

Computers
ONI - Dec, 1990+

Concert
AMUSEMENT BUSINESS - Jan 9, 1961+

Distribution
STAGE & STUDIO - Dec, 1980+

Electronics
AUDIO AMATEUR, THE - Winter, 1970+

Employment
MODERN RECORDING & MUSIC - Oct/Nov, 1975 - ?, 1986//

Engineering
ACUSTICA - Jan, 1951+ {Germany}
AES - Jan, 1953+
DB - 1967+
EQ - Mar/Apr, 1990+
MIX - Jan, 1977+
MODERN RECORDING & MUSIC - Oct/Nov, 1975 - ?, 1986//
PRO SOUND NEWS - Nov, 1978+
REP: RECORDING ENGINEERING PRODUCTION - Apr/May, 1970+
SYN-AUD-CON NEWSLETTER - Fall, 1973+

Exhibition
AMUSEMENT BUSINESS - Jan 9, 1961+

Fan
MOVIE FLASH - ?+ {Philippines}
SOSYAL! MAGAZINE - Feb 4, 1986+ {Philippines}

Guide
CD REVIEW - Sep, 1984+
CHRISTIAN REVIEW - Jan, 1973+
DRIVING AMBITION - ?+ {United Kingdom}
GRAMOPHONE - Apr, 1923+ {United Kingdom}
HI-FI CHOICE - ?+ {United Kingdom}
HI-FI HERETIC - ?, 1990?+
HI-FI NEWS AND RECORD REVIEW - Oct, 1970+. {United Kingdom}
HIGH FIDELITY/MUSICAL AMERICA - Apr, 1959+?
HIT PARADER - Nov, 1942 - ?//
HOT PICKS - Jan, 1988+
ONI - Dec, 1990+
RADIO HIT SONGS - Nov, 1941?+?
STEREOPHILE - Jan, 1978+

Home Consumer
ABSOLUTE SOUND, THE - Feb, 1973+
AUDIO - Jan, 1917+
AUDIO AMATEUR, THE - Winter, 1970+
AUDIO CRITIC, THE - Jan/Feb, 1977+?
AUDIO LEAGUE. REPORT. - Oct, 1954 - Jun, 1957.
AUDIO/VIDEO INTERIORS - Feb/Mar, 1989+
AUDIOCRAFT FOR THE HI-FI HOBBYIST - Jun, 1957 - Nov, 1958//
AUDIOPHILE WITH HI-FI ANSWERS - May, 1990?+ {United Kingdom}
BETTER LISTENING - Jul, 1955+?
CAR AUDIO AND ELECTRONICS - Jul, 1988+
CAR STEREO REVIEW - Fall, 1987+
CD REVIEW - Sep, 1984+
CONSUMER ELECTRONICS - 1972+
CONSUMER ELECTRONICS PRODUCT NEWS - Jan, 1975+
GRAMOPHONE - Apr, 1923+ {United Kingdom}
HI-FI ANSWERS - ?+? {United Kingdom}
HI-FI HERETIC - ?, 1990?+
HI-FI NEWS AND RECORD REVIEW - Oct, 1970+. {United Kingdom}
HI-FI WORLD - ?+ {United Kingdom}
HIGH FIDELITY - Dec, 1958 - ?, 1989//
HIGH FIDELITY/MUSICAL AMERICA - Apr, 1959+?
HOME & STUDIO RECORDING - Nov, 1987+
ONI - Dec, 1990+
STEREOPHILE - Jan, 1978+

Instructional
SYN-AUD-CON NEWSLETTER - Fall, 1973+

International
PRO SOUND NEWS - Nov, 1978+

Audio/Video
Subject Heading

Management
AMUSEMENT BUSINESS - Jan 9, 1961+

Marketing
AMUSEMENT BUSINESS - Jan 9, 1961+

Music
BRITISH INSTITUTE OF RECORDED SOUND. BULLETIN. - Summer, 1956+? {United Kingdom}
CD REVIEW - Sep, 1984+
EQ - Mar/Apr, 1990+
HI-FI NEWS AND RECORD REVIEW - Oct, 1970+. {United Kingdom}
HIT PARADER - Nov, 1942 - ?//
HOME & STUDIO RECORDING - Nov, 1987+
MODERN RECORDING & MUSIC - Oct/Nov, 1975 - ?, 1986//
RADIO HIT SONGS - Nov, 1941?+?
STAGE & STUDIO - Dec, 1980+

Preservation
ARSC JOURNAL - Winter, 1967/1968+

Producing
AMUSEMENT BUSINESS - Jan 9, 1961+
REP: RECORDING ENGINEERING PRODUCTION - Apr/May, 1970+
STAGE & STUDIO - Dec, 1980+

Production
AMUSEMENT BUSINESS - Jan 9, 1961+
AUDIO PRODUCTION FOR BROADCAST - Spring, 1982+
DB - 1967+
PRO SOUND NEWS - Nov, 1978+
PRODUCTION SOUND REPORT - ?+

Promotion
BETTER LISTENING - Jul, 1955+?
DASH WORLD - Winter, 1990+ {United Kingdom}
DIGITAL DOMAIN DIGEST - Fall, 1990+
ECHO BUSS - Winter, 1986?+?

Recording
EQ - Mar/Apr, 1990+
GRAMOPHONE - Apr, 1923+ {United Kingdom}
HOME & STUDIO RECORDING - Nov, 1987+
MAG TRACKS - Winter, 1987+
MIX - Jan, 1977+
MODERN RECORDING & MUSIC - Oct/Nov, 1975 - ?, 1986//
PRODUCTION SOUND REPORT - ?+
REP: RECORDING ENGINEERING PRODUCTION - Apr/May, 1970+
STAGE & STUDIO - Dec, 1980+

Records & Compact Discs
ARSC JOURNAL - Winter, 1967/1968+
BRITISH INSTITUTE OF RECORDED SOUND. BULLETIN. - Summer, 1956+? {United Kingdom}
CD REVIEW - Sep, 1984+
CHRISTIAN REVIEW - Jan, 1973+
DASH WORLD - Winter, 1990+ {United Kingdom}
DB - 1967+
HIGH FIDELITY - Dec, 1958 - ?, 1989//
HIGH FIDELITY/MUSICAL AMERICA - Apr, 1959+?
MIX - Jan, 1977+
MODERN RECORDING & MUSIC - Oct/Nov, 1975 - ?, 1986//
PRO SOUND NEWS - Nov, 1978+
RECORD RESEARCH - Feb, 1955+
REP: RECORDING ENGINEERING PRODUCTION - Apr/May, 1970+

Religion
CHRISTIAN REVIEW - Jan, 1973+

Retail
BETTER LISTENING - Jul, 1955+?
CHRISTIAN REVIEW - Jan, 1973+
CONSUMER ELECTRONICS - 1972+
CONSUMER ELECTRONICS PRODUCT NEWS - Jan, 1975+
HOT PICKS - Jan, 1988+
RECORD RESEARCH - Feb, 1955+

Review
ARSC JOURNAL - Winter, 1967/1968+
AUDIO PRODUCTION FOR BROADCAST - Spring, 1982+
HI-FI WORLD - ?+ {United Kingdom}
STEREOPHILE - Jan, 1978+

Stock
MAG TRACKS - Winter, 1987+

Technology
AES - Jan, 1953+
AUDIO - Jan, 1917+
AUDIO AMATEUR, THE - Winter, 1970+
AUDIO CRITIC, THE - Jan/Feb, 1977+?
AUDIO LEAGUE. REPORT. - Oct, 1954 - Jun, 1957.
AUDIO PRODUCTION FOR BROADCAST - Spring, 1982+
AUDIO/VIDEO INTERIORS - Feb/Mar, 1989+
AUDIOCRAFT FOR THE HI-FI HOBBYIST - Jun, 1957 - Nov, 1958//
AUDIOPHILE WITH HI-FI ANSWERS - May, 1990?+ {United Kingdom}
CAR AUDIO AND ELECTRONICS - Jul, 1988+
CAR STEREO REVIEW - Fall, 1987+
CONSUMER ELECTRONICS - 1972+
DASH WORLD - Winter, 1990+ {United Kingdom}
DIGITAL DOMAIN DIGEST - Fall, 1990+
EQ - Mar/Apr, 1990+
GRAMOPHONE - Apr, 1923+ {United Kingdom}
HI-FI ANSWERS - ?+? {United Kingdom}
HI-FI CHOICE - ?+ {United Kingdom}
HIGH FIDELITY - Dec, 1958 - ?, 1989//
HIGH FIDELITY/MUSICAL AMERICA - Apr, 1959+?
HOME & STUDIO RECORDING - Nov, 1987+
MIX - Jan, 1977+
MODERN RECORDING & MUSIC - Oct/Nov, 1975 - ?, 1986//
PRO SOUND NEWS - Nov, 1978+
PRODUCTION SOUND REPORT - ?+
REP: RECORDING ENGINEERING PRODUCTION - Apr/May, 1970+
STEREOPHILE - Jan, 1978+
SYN-AUD-CON NEWSLETTER - Fall, 1973+
TAPE - Nov, 1972? - ?//? {United Kingdom}
TAPE DECK QUARTERLY - 1974+

Audio/Video

Academic
EDUCATIONAL MEDIA INTERNATIONAL - Mar, 1971+ {France}
INTERCOMM - Fall, 1977?+
PD REPORT - ?, 1988?+
TELEMEMO - ?+

Acting
DRAMA-LOGUE - Jan, 1970?+

Actor
CELEBRITY PLUS - Jan, 1987+

Alternative Media
FACTSHEET FIVE - Jul, 1982+
INDEPENDENT MEDIA - Mar, 1983?+ {United Kingdom}

Amateur
FACTSHEET FIVE - Jul, 1982+
INDUSTRIAL ELECTRONICS - Oct, 1923 - Jan, 1969// {United Kingdom}
RADIO-ELECTRONICS - Jul, 1929+

Artist
HOLLYWOOD REPORTER - Sep 3, 1930+
SH-BOOM - Jan, 1990+
SHOWCASE WORLD - ?+

Avant-garde
HIGH PERFORMANCE - Feb, 1978+

Boston
ART DYNAMO - Summer, 1991?+

Business
- HOLLYWOOD REPORTER - Sep 3, 1930+
- PRESENTATION PRODUCTS MAGAZINE - Jan, 1988+
- TELEVISION DIGEST WITH CONSUMER ELECTRONICS - 1961+

Cd rom
- VIZIONS - Winter, 1990/1991+

Collector
- GRAPHIC ANTIQUARIAN - Jul, 1970+

Corporate
- PRESENTATION PRODUCTS MAGAZINE - Jan, 1988+

Design
- IEEE TRANSACTIONS ON COMMUNICATIONS - 1953+

Distribution
- HOLLYWOOD REPORTER - Sep 3, 1930+
- ITA NEWS DIGEST - 1973+
- SIGHT AND SOUND MARKETING - Jun, 1965+

Education
- VIZIONS - Winter, 1990/1991+

Electronics
- ELECTRONICS AND COMMUNICATIONS - Apr, 1946 - Oct/Nov, 1974// {New Zealand}
- GENERAL ELECTRIC REVIEW - Mar 2, 1903 - Nov, 1958//
- GR TODAY - Jun, 1926+?
- INDUSTRIAL ELECTRONICS - Oct, 1923 - Jan, 1969// {United Kingdom}
- JEE, JOURNAL OF ELECTRONIC ENGINEERING - 1964+ {Japan}
- MILITARY ELECTRONICS / COUNTERMEASURES - Jan, 1975+
- POPULAR ELECTRONICS - Summer, 1984+

Employment
- DRAMA-LOGUE - Jan, 1970?+

Engineering
- ART DYNAMO - Summer, 1991?+
- ELECTRONICS AND COMMUNICATIONS - Apr, 1946 - Oct/Nov, 1974// {New Zealand}
- ELECTRONICS & COMMUNICATIONS ENGINEERING JOURNAL - Oct, 1926+ {United Kingdom}
- ELECTRONICS LETTERS - Mar, 1965+ {United Kingdom}
- GR TODAY - Jun, 1926+?
- IEEE TRANSACTIONS ON COMMUNICATIONS - 1953+
- IEEE TRANSACTIONS ON CONSUMER ELECTRONICS - Jul, 1952+
- JEE, JOURNAL OF ELECTRONIC ENGINEERING - 1964+ {Japan}
- MILITARY ELECTRONICS / COUNTERMEASURES - Jan, 1975+
- STUDIO SOUND AND BROADCAST ENGINEERING - Jan?, 1959+ {United Kingdom}

Fan
- SH-BOOM - Jan, 1990+

Finance
- HOLLYWOOD REPORTER - Sep 3, 1930+
- TELEVISION DIGEST WITH CONSUMER ELECTRONICS - 1961+

Guide
- AUDIO VISUAL JOURNAL - ? - Spring, 1978//
- MASS MEDIA NEWSLETTER - 1964? - Dec 14, 1981//
- MEDIA DIGEST - 1972+
- MEDIA IN EDUCATION AND DEVELOPMENT - Mar, 1971 - 1989// {United Kingdom}
- MEDIA MIX - Oct, 1969 - Jun, 1979//
- ONSAT - ?+
- RELIGIOUS MEDIA TODAY - Apr, 1976 - 1982//
- SMALL PRESS BOOK REVIEW, THE - Jul/Aug, 1985+
- STEREO REVIEW - Feb, 1958+

Historical
- GRAPHIC ANTIQUARIAN - Jul, 1970+
- IAMHIST NEWSLETTER - ?+
- SH-BOOM - Jan, 1990+

Home Consumer
- ELECTRONICS AND COMMUNICATIONS - Apr, 1946 - Oct/Nov, 1974// {New Zealand}
- ELECTRONICS ILLUSTRATED - May, 1958 - 1972//
- FUTUREHOME TECHNOLOGY NEWS - Sep 10, 1990+
- HI-FI SOUND - 1959 - Jan, 1977// {United Kingdom}
- HOME ENTERTAINMENT - Fall, 1983+
- INTELLIGENT DECISIONS - ?+
- POPULAR ELECTRONICS - Summer, 1984+
- RADIO-ELECTRONICS - Jul, 1929+
- SOUND & VISION - Oct, 1970+ {Canada}
- TELEVISION DIGEST WITH CONSUMER ELECTRONICS - 1961+
- VISIO - May, 1990+

Information
- VIZIONS - Winter, 1990/1991+

Instructional
- AUDIO-VISUAL BULLETIN - Mar, 1948+?
- AVC - May, 1961+
- ETV REPORTER - 1967+
- LAW ENFORCEMENT TECHNOLOGY - 1974+
- MEDIA DIGEST - 1972+
- MEDIA IN EDUCATION AND DEVELOPMENT - Mar, 1971 - 1989// {United Kingdom}
- NEWS & VIEWS - ?+
- NIE JOURNAL - Apr, 1957+ {India}
- VIZIONS - Winter, 1990/1991+

International
- EDUCATIONAL MEDIA INTERNATIONAL - Mar, 1971+ {France}
- IAMHIST NEWSLETTER - ?+

Law Enforcement
- LAW ENFORCEMENT TECHNOLOGY - 1974+

Management
- AV VIDEO - Fall, 1978+

Marketing
- AUDIOVIDEO INTERNATIONAL - Jan, 1973+
- SIGHT AND SOUND MARKETING - Jun, 1965+

Military
- MILITARY ELECTRONICS / COUNTERMEASURES - Jan, 1975+

Minorities
- FACTSHEET FIVE - Jul, 1982+

Multimedia
- VIZIONS - Winter, 1990/1991+

New England
- ART DYNAMO - Summer, 1991?+

Performance
- HIGH PERFORMANCE - Feb, 1978+

Popular Culture
- SH-BOOM - Jan, 1990+

Presentation
- PRESENTATION PRODUCTS MAGAZINE - Jan, 1988+

Production
- AV VIDEO - Fall, 1978+
- FILM & VIDEO - Feb, 1984+
- IN MOTION FILM & VIDEO PRODUCTION MAGAZINE - Jan, 1982+
- INDEPENDENT MEDIA - Mar, 1983?+ {United Kingdom}
- ITA NEWS DIGEST - 1973+
- PD REPORT - ?, 1988?+
- REEL LIFE - ?, 1989+
- UPDATE - ?+

Programming
- ONSAT - ?+

Audio Visual
Subject Heading

Promotion
GENERAL ELECTRIC REVIEW - Mar 2, 1903 - Nov, 1958//
IMAGE NEWS - Spring, 1988+
INTERCOMM - Fall, 1977?+

Recording
MAG TRACKS - Winter, 1987+
STUDIO SOUND AND BROADCAST ENGINEERING - Jan?, 1959+ {United Kingdom}

Religion
MASS MEDIA NEWSLETTER - 1964? - Dec 14, 1981//
RELIGIOUS MEDIA TODAY - Apr, 1976 - 1982//
UPDATE - ?+

Research
ELECTRONICS & COMMUNICATIONS ENGINEERING JOURNAL - Oct, 1926+ {United Kingdom}
ELECTRONICS LETTERS - Mar, 1965+ {United Kingdom}
IAMHIST NEWSLETTER - ?+
LEONARDO - Jan, 1968+
TECHTRENDS - Feb, 1956+

Retail
AUDIOVIDEO INTERNATIONAL - Jan, 1973+
DEALERSCOPE - ? - Feb, 1986//
PERSONAL ELECTRONICS - 1957+
SIGHT AND SOUND MARKETING - Jun, 1965+
TELEVISION RETAILING - Jan, 1925 - Aug, 1953//
TV & APPLIANCE MART - Sep, 1953+?

Review
ART DYNAMO - Summer, 1991?+
IEEE SPECTRUM - Jan, 1964+
SHOWCASE WORLD - ?+
SMALL PRESS BOOK REVIEW, THE - Jul/Aug, 1985+
SOUND & VISION - Oct, 1970+ {Canada}
STEREO REVIEW - Feb, 1958+

Satellites
ONSAT - ?+

School
EDUCATIONAL MEDIA INTERNATIONAL - Mar, 1971+ {France}
ETV REPORTER - 1967+
MEDIA & METHODS - Sep, 1969+
MEDIA DIGEST - 1972+
NIE JOURNAL - Apr, 1957+ {India}
TECHTRENDS - Feb, 1956+
VISUAL EDUCATION - ?+ {United Kingdom}

Servicing
ELECTRONIC TECHNICAN/DEALER - Sep, 1953 - Mar, 1982//

Spanish
UPDATE - ?+

Stock
MAG TRACKS - Winter, 1987+
ON TRACK - Summer, 1987+?
TAPE/DISC BUSINESS - May/Jun, 1987+
TAPE RECORDING - Nov/Dec, 1953 - Nov/Dec, 1970//

Technology
AV VIDEO - Fall, 1978+
ELECTRONICS & COMMUNICATIONS ENGINEERING JOURNAL - Oct, 1926+ {United Kingdom}
ELECTRONICS ILLUSTRATED - May, 1958 - 1972//
ELECTRONICS LETTERS - Mar, 1965+ {United Kingdom}
FOLLOW FOCUS - 198u+
FUTUREHOME TECHNOLOGY NEWS - Sep 10, 1990+
GENERAL ELECTRIC REVIEW - Mar 2, 1903 - Nov, 1958//
HI-FI SOUND - 1959 - Jan, 1977// {United Kingdom}
IEEE SPECTRUM - Jan, 1964+
IEEE TRANSACTIONS ON CONSUMER ELECTRONICS - Jul, 1952+
IN MOTION FILM & VIDEO PRODUCTION MAGAZINE - Jan, 1982+
INDUSTRIAL ELECTRONICS - Oct, 1923 - Jan, 1969// {United Kingdom}
INTELLIGENT DECISIONS - ?+
LEONARDO - Jan, 1968+
MEDIA & METHODS - Sep, 1969+
NEWS & VIEWS - ?+
PERSPECTIVE - Autumn, 1958 - 1966// {United Kingdom}
RADIO-ELECTRONICS - Jul, 1929+
STEREO REVIEW - Feb, 1958+
STUDIO SOUND AND BROADCAST ENGINEERING - Jan?, 1959+ {United Kingdom}
TEL-COMS - Jun, 1988+
TELEVISION DIGEST WITH CONSUMER ELECTRONICS - 1961+
VISUAL EDUCATION - ?+ {United Kingdom}

Teleconferencing
TEL-COMS - Jun, 1988+
TELECONFERENCE MAGAZINE - 1981+

Virginia
REEL LIFE - ?, 1989+

Audio Visual

Animation
ADVANCED IMAGING - Jun, 1988+

Business
COMMUNICATIONS INDUSTRIES REPORT, THE - 1946+
KINEMATOGRAPH WEEKLY - Jun 15, 1889 - Sep, 1971// {United Kingdom}
PRESENTATION PRODUCTS MAGAZINE - Jan, 1988+

Cd rom
VIZIONS - Winter, 1990/1991+

Computers
COMPUTER PICTURES - Jan/Feb, 1983+

Corporate
COMMUNICATOR, THE - 1973+
PRESENTATION PRODUCTS MAGAZINE - Jan, 1988+

Distribution
COMPUTER PICTURES - Jan/Feb, 1983+

Documentary
FILM & VIDEO NEWS - Dec, 1939 - Apr, 1984//

Education
VIZIONS - Winter, 1990/1991+

Exhibition
KINEMATOGRAPH WEEKLY - Jun 15, 1889 - Sep, 1971// {United Kingdom}

Graphics
ADVANCED IMAGING - Jun, 1988+
COMPUTER PICTURES - Jan/Feb, 1983+

Guide
AUDIO VISUAL JOURNAL - ? - Spring, 1978//
EFLA BULLETIN - Summer, 1977 - #3/4, 1987//
FILM & VIDEO NEWS - Dec, 1939 - Apr, 1984//
MEDIA DIGEST - 1972+
MEDIA IN EDUCATION AND DEVELOPMENT - Mar, 1971 - 1989// {United Kingdom}

Information
VIZIONS - Winter, 1990/1991+

Instructional
AFVA BULLETIN - Sep/Oct, 1967+
AUDIO VISUAL - Nov, 1946+ {United Kingdom}
AUDIO-VISUAL BULLETIN - Mar, 1948+?
AVC - May, 1961+

EDUCATIONAL SCREEN - Jan, 1922 - Sum, 1956//
FILM & VIDEO NEWS - Dec, 1939 - Apr, 1984//
INTERNATIONAL JOURNAL OF INSTRUCTIONAL MEDIA AND TECHNOLOGY - Fall, 1973 - Summer, 1983/84//
LAW ENFORCEMENT TECHNOLOGY - 1974+
LEARNING RESOURCES - Apr, 1973 - May, 1975//
MEDIA DIGEST - 1972+
MEDIA IN EDUCATION AND DEVELOPMENT - Mar, 1971 - 1989// {United Kingdom}
NIE JOURNAL - Apr, 1957+ {India}
VIZIONS - Winter, 1990/1991+

Interactive
ADVANCED IMAGING - Jun, 1988+
COMMUNICATIONS INDUSTRIES REPORT, THE - 1946+

International
INTERNATIONAL JOURNAL OF INSTRUCTIONAL MEDIA AND TECHNOLOGY - Fall, 1973 - Summer, 1983/84//

Law Enforcement
LAW ENFORCEMENT TECHNOLOGY - 1974+

Libraries
EFLA BULLETIN - Summer, 1977 - #3/4, 1987//

Management
AV VIDEO - Fall, 1978+

Multimedia
COMMUNICATIONS INDUSTRIES REPORT, THE - 1946+
VIZIONS - Winter, 1990/1991+

Presentation
PRESENTATION PRODUCTS MAGAZINE - Jan, 1988+

Production
AV VIDEO - Fall, 1978+
COMPUTER PICTURES - Jan/Feb, 1983+
MULTI IMAGES JOURNAL - 1974+

Regulation
COMMUNICATIONS INDUSTRIES REPORT, THE - 1946+

Research
EDUCATIONAL COMMUNICATION AND TECHNOLOGY - Winter, 1953 - ?, 1988//

Review
AFVA BULLETIN - Sep/Oct, 1967+

Sales
COMMUNICATIONS INDUSTRIES REPORT, THE - 1946+

School
EDUCATIONAL SCREEN - Jan, 1922 - Sum, 1956//
EPIEGRAM - Oct, 1972 - Jun, 1977//
EPIEGRAM - 1987+
FILM & VIDEO NEWS - Dec, 1939 - Apr, 1984//
LEARNING RESOURCES - Apr, 1973 - May, 1975//
MEDIA & METHODS - Sep, 1969+
MEDIA DIGEST - 1972+
NIE JOURNAL - Apr, 1957+ {India}
VISUAL EDUCATION - ?+ {United Kingdom}

Technology
ADVANCED IMAGING - Jun, 1988+
AV GUIDE - Sep, 1956+
AV VIDEO - Fall, 1978+
COMMUNICATIONS INDUSTRIES REPORT, THE - 1946+
COMMUNICATOR, THE - 1973+
EDUCATIONAL COMMUNICATION AND TECHNOLOGY - Winter, 1953 - ?, 1988//
EDUCATIONAL SCREEN - Jan, 1922 - Sum, 1956//
EPIEGRAM - Oct, 1972 - Jun, 1977//
EPIEGRAM - 1987+
KINEMATOGRAPH WEEKLY - Jun 15, 1889 - Sep, 1971// {United Kingdom}
MEDIA & METHODS - Sep, 1969+
MULTI IMAGES JOURNAL - 1974+
VISUAL EDUCATION - ?+ {United Kingdom}

Teletext
EDUCATIONAL COMMUNICATION AND TECHNOLOGY - Winter, 1953 - ?, 1988//

Books

Academic
PUBLISHING RESEARCH QUARTERLY - Spring, 1985+
SCHOLARLY PUBLISHING - Oct, 1969+ {Canada}

Activist
AIM REPORT - Aug, 1972+

Authorship
BOOKTALKER, THE - Sep, 1989+
ROMANTIC TIMES - Jul/Aug, 1981+

Britain
BRITISH BOOK NEWS - Mar, 1940+ {United Kingdom}

Business
PUBLISHER'S WEEKLY - Feb, 1869+

Distribution
AGAINST THE GRAIN - Mar, 1989+
BOOK MARKETING UPDATE - Dec, 1986+
HUENEFELD REPORT, THE - ?+

Fan
BONDAGE - 1973+
DWB - ?+ {United Kingdom}
FANTASY ZONE - ?+ {United Kingdom}
STRANGE ADVENTURES - Feb, 1989+ {United Kingdom}

Fantasy
FANTASY ZONE - ?+ {United Kingdom}

Guide
CHRISTIAN REVIEW - Jan, 1973+
HOT PICKS - Jan, 1988+
SHOW - Jan, 1970 - Nov, 1973//

Ireland
BRITISH BOOK NEWS - Mar, 1940+ {United Kingdom}

James Bond
BONDAGE - 1973+

Management
AMERICAN LITERARY GAZETTE AND PUBLISHERS' CIRCULAR - Nov 2, 1863 - Jan 15, 1872//
HUENEFELD REPORT, THE - ?+

Marketing
AMERICAN LITERARY GAZETTE AND PUBLISHERS' CIRCULAR - Nov 2, 1863 - Jan 15, 1872//
BOOK MARKETING UPDATE - Dec, 1986+
BOOK PROMOTION HOTLINE - Jan 5, 1990+
PUBLISHER'S WEEKLY - Feb, 1869+

Mystery
SCARLET STREET - Jan, 1991+

New York City
SHOW - Jan, 1970 - Nov, 1973//

Novel
ROMANTIC TIMES - Jul/Aug, 1981+

Production
TAYLORTALK - ?+

Promotion
BOOK MARKETING UPDATE - Dec, 1986+
BOOK PROMOTION HOTLINE - Jan 5, 1990+
W • B - May/Jun, 1989+

Publishing
AGAINST THE GRAIN - Mar, 1989+
AMERICAN LITERARY GAZETTE AND PUBLISHERS' CIRCULAR - Nov 2, 1863 - Jan 15, 1872//
BRITISH BOOK NEWS - Mar, 1940+ {United Kingdom}
HUENEFELD REPORT, THE - ?+
INDEPENDENT PUBLISHERS TRADE REPORT - Jul, 1988+
PUBLISHER'S WEEKLY - Feb, 1869+
PUBLISHING RESEARCH QUARTERLY - Spring, 1985+
SCHOLARLY PUBLISHING - Oct, 1969+ {Canada}

Records & Compact Discs
CHRISTIAN REVIEW - Jan, 1973+

Religion
BOOKS & RELIGION - Jan/Feb, 1985+
BOOKSTORE JOURNAL - Jun, 1968+
CHRISTIAN REVIEW - Jan, 1973+

Retail
AB BOOKMAN'S WEEKLY - Jan 3, 1948+
BOOKSTORE JOURNAL - Jun, 1968+
CHRISTIAN REVIEW - Jan, 1973+
HOT PICKS - Jan, 1988+

Review
BOOKS & RELIGION - Jan/Feb, 1985+
BOOKTALKER, THE - Sep, 1989+
BRITISH BOOK NEWS - Mar, 1940+ {United Kingdom}
SCARLET STREET - Jan, 1991+
SHOW - Jan, 1970 - Nov, 1973//

Romantic
ROMANTIC TIMES - Jul/Aug, 1981+

School
TAYLORTALK - ?+

World
BRITISH BOOK NEWS - Mar, 1940+ {United Kingdom}

Writing
ROMANTIC TIMES - Jul/Aug, 1981+
ROUNDUP QUARTERLY - Apr, 1953+

Yearbooks
TAYLORTALK - ?+

Broadcasting

Academic
AFI EDUCATION NEWSLETTER - Mar/Apr, 1978 - Sep/Oct, 1982//
BROADCAST EDUCATOR NEWS NOTES - Sep, 1987?+
CAMPUS BROADCASTERS - ? - ?//
FEEDBACK - Fall, 1960?+
IRB - ?+
JOURNAL OF BROADCASTING & ELECTRONIC MEDIA - Winter 1956/1957+
MONITOR - ?+?
NEWSCASTER, THE - ?, 1987+
PD REPORT - ?, 1988?+
SIGNALS - ?+
STATIC - ?+?

Acting
NEW THEATRE - Aug, 1939 - Jul, 1949// {United Kingdom}

Activist
AIM REPORT - Aug, 1972+
BETTER BROADCASTS NEWS - Oct, 1955+

Actor
CELEBRITY PLUS - Jan, 1987+

Advertising
AMERICAN DEMOGRAPHICS - Jan, 1979+
BPME IMAGE MAGAZINE - ?+
CLIO MAGAZINE - Oct, 1968 - ?, 1976//?
FLAKE - ?, 1990+
JOURNALISM EDUCATOR, THE - 1945+
YELLOW SHEET, THE - 1984?+

Advocate
BETTER RADIO AND TELEVISION - Winter, 1960+

Agency
YELLOW SHEET, THE - 1984?+

Amateur
ELECTRONIC ENGINEERING - Mar, 1928+? {United Kingdom}
MODERN RADIO - Jul, 1931 - Apr, 1933//
RADIO & TELEVISION - Jun/Jul, 1930 - Sep, 1941//
RADIO REVIEW AND TELEVISION NEWS - Mar/Apr, 1931 - Jan/Feb, 1933//

Archival
MB NEWS - Winter, 1977?+

Artist
BMI: MUSICWORLD - 1962+
DRAMA - Jul, 1919+ {United Kingdom}

FRESH! - Jan 1, 1985+
HOLLYWOOD REPORTER - Sep 3, 1930+
MODERN SCREEN - Nov, 1930 - ?//
SCREENLAND PLUS TV-LAND - 1920+
SH-BOOM - Jan, 1990+
SHOWCASE WORLD - ?+
TV MIRROR - 1933 - Aug, 1977//
TV RADIO MIRROR - Nov, 1933+
TV RADIO TALK - ?+?
TV SCREEN - Nov, 1947+?
VARIETY - Dec 16, 1905+

Asia
TELECOM JAPAN, THE - ?+ {Japan}

Black
FRESH! - Jan 1, 1985+

Business
BILLBOARD - Nov, 1894+
BROADCAST - 1973+ {United Kingdom}
BROADCAST ACCOUNTING ALERT - ?+
BROADCAST CABLE FINANCIAL JOURNAL - Mar, 1972+
BROADCAST REPORTER - Nov 7, 1931 - Jun 15, 1933//
BROADCAST SYSTEMS INTERNATIONAL - ?+ {United Kingdom}
BROADCASTER - Jan, 1942+ {Canada}
BROADCASTING - Oct 15, 1931+
BROADCASTING ABROAD - Jan, 1989+
COMBROAD - Jan, 1967+ {United Kingdom}
HOLLYWOOD REPORTER - Sep 3, 1930+
JOURNAL OF MEDIA ECONOMICS - Spring, 1988+
MEDIA BUSINESS - Jan, 1987+
RTD - Feb 9, 1937 - Jul 22, 1966//
TELEVISION DIGEST WITH CONSUMER ELECTRONICS - 1961+
TELEVISION/RADIO AGE - Aug, 1953+
VARIETY - Dec 16, 1905+

Carrier Current
MONITOR - ?+?

Collector
BIG REEL, THE - Jun, 1974?+
FLAKE - ?, 1990+

College
MONITOR - ?+?
SIGNALS - ?+

Cultural
DISCOURSE & SOCIETY - Jul, 1990+ {United Kingdom}
HOWARD JOURNAL OF COMMUNICATIONS, THE - Spring, 1988+
NIEMAN REPORTS - Feb, 1947+

Demographics
AMERICAN DEMOGRAPHICS - Jan, 1979+

Design
IEEE TRANSACTIONS ON COMMUNICATIONS - 1953+
RF DESIGN - Nov/Dec, 1978+

Directing
ACTION! - Sep/Oct, 1966 - Nov/Dec, 1978//

Discourse
DISCOURSE & SOCIETY - Jul, 1990+ {United Kingdom}

Distribution
HOLLYWOOD REPORTER - Sep 3, 1930+

Economics
JOURNAL OF MEDIA ECONOMICS - Spring, 1988+

Editorial
EDITORIALIST, THE - Sep/Oct, 1974+
NATIONAL BROADCAST EDITORIAL ASSOCIATION NEWSLETTER - ?+?

Education
BEA NEWSLETTER - Dec, 1987+

Electronics
BBC ENGINEERING - 1955? - Jul, 1980// {United Kingdom}
COMMUNICATION ENGINEERING - Nov, 1940 - Mar, 1954//
ELECTRONICS AND COMMUNICATIONS - Apr, 1946 - Oct/Nov, 1974// {New Zealand}
ELECTRONICS WORLD + WIRELESS WORLD - Apr, 1922+ {United Kingdom}
GENERAL ELECTRIC REVIEW - Mar 2, 1903 - Nov, 1958//
GR TODAY - Jun, 1926+?

Employment
AIR TIME - ?+
JOB LEADS - 1972+
JOURNALISM EDUCATOR, THE - 1945+
NEWSLETTER - Jun, 1988+
PACTSHEET - Dec, 1977+

Engineering
ABU TECHNICAL REVIEW - Mar, 1969+ {Japan}
AEG-TELEFUNKEN PROGRESS - ? - #2, 1982// {Germany}
BBC ENGINEERING - 1955? - Jul, 1980// {United Kingdom}
BME'S TELEVISION ENGINEERING - Jan, 1965 - Sep, 1990//
BROADCAST + TECHNOLOGY - Sep/Oct, 1975+ {Canada}
BROADCAST ENGINEERING - May, 1959+
BROADCAST ENGINEERS' JOURNAL, THE - 1934 - Oct, 1952//
BROADCAST SYSTEMS ENGINEERING - Oct, 1974?+ {United Kingdom}
COMMUNICATION AND BROADCAST ENGINEERING - Oct, 1934 - Aug, 1937//
COMMUNICATION ENGINEERING - Nov, 1940 - Mar, 1954//
EBU REVIEW. TECHNICAL. - 1950+ {Switzerland}
ELECTRONICS AND COMMUNICATIONS - Apr, 1946 - Oct/Nov, 1974// {New Zealand}
ELECTRONICS & COMMUNICATIONS ENGINEERING JOURNAL - Oct, 1926+ {United Kingdom}
ELECTRONICS LETTERS - Mar, 1965+ {United Kingdom}
ELECTRONICS WORLD + WIRELESS WORLD - Apr, 1922+ {United Kingdom}
GR TODAY - Jun, 1926+?
IBE - Oct, 1964+ {United Kingdom}
IEEE TRANSACTIONS ON BROADCASTING - Mar, 1955+
IEEE TRANSACTIONS ON COMMUNICATIONS - 1953+
INTERNATIONAL BROADCASTING - 1978+ {United Kingdom}
MODERN RADIO - Jul, 1931 - Apr, 1933//
RADIO REVIEW AND TELEVISION NEWS - Mar/Apr, 1931 - Jan/Feb, 1933//
RADIO WORLD - Jul, 1977+
RF DESIGN - Nov/Dec, 1978+
SIGNAL, THE - Jan, 1975+
SOUND AND VISION BROADCASTING - Spring, 1960 - 1973// {United Kingdom}
STUDIO SOUND AND BROADCAST ENGINEERING - Jan?, 1959+ {United Kingdom}

Ethics
FINELINE - Apr, 1989+
GANNETT CENTER JOURNAL - Spring, 1987+
JOURNAL OF MASS MEDIA ETHICS - Fall/Winter, 1985/1986+
NIEMAN REPORTS - Feb, 1947+

Fan
FRESH! - Jan 1, 1985+
HERO HOBBY - 1966+?
MODERN SCREEN - Nov, 1930 - ?//
PHOTOPLAY - Jun, 1946 - Aug, 1977//
SCREENLAND PLUS TV-LAND - 1920+
SH-BOOM - Jan, 1990+
TV MIRROR - 1933 - Aug, 1977//
TV RADIO MIRROR - Nov, 1933+
TV RADIO TALK - ?+?
TV SCREEN - Nov, 1947+?

Finance
BROADCAST CABLE FINANCIAL JOURNAL - Mar, 1972+
HOLLYWOOD REPORTER - Sep 3, 1930+
TELEVISION DIGEST WITH CONSUMER ELECTRONICS - 1961+

Freedom of the Press
GANNETT CENTER JOURNAL - Spring, 1987+

Graphics
COMMUNICATION ARTS - Aug, 1959+

Guide
ABC WEEKLY - Dec 2, 1939+? {Australia}
AIRWAVES - Aug, 1974+ {United Kingdom}
AKASHVANI - 1936+ {India}
BETTER RADIO AND TELEVISION - Winter, 1960+
CBC TIMES - 1948 - Jan, 1970// {Canada}
DRAMA - Jul, 1919+ {United Kingdom}
MB NEWS - Winter, 1977?+
MILLECANALI INTERNATIONAL - ?+ {Italy}
RADIO TIMES - Sep 28, 1923+ {United Kingdom}
SHOW - Oct, 1961+?
TV RADIO MIRROR - Nov, 1933+
TV SCREEN - Nov, 1947+?

Historical
AMERICAN JOURNALISM - Summer, 1983+
BBC QUARTERLY, THE - Apr, 1946 - Autumn, 1954// {United Kingdom}
BIG REEL, THE - Jun, 1974?+
BROADCAST PIONEERS LIBRARY REPORTS - Spring, 1975+
HERO HOBBY - 1966+?
IAMHIST NEWSLETTER - ?+
JOURNAL OF BROADCASTING & ELECTRONIC MEDIA - Winter 1956/1957+
JOURNAL OF POPULAR FILM AND TELEVISION - Winter, 1972+
JQ. JOURNALISM QUARTERLY. - 1924+
MB NEWS - Winter, 1977?+
REWIND - Summer, 1988+
SH-BOOM - Jan, 1990+
SPARKS - ?+

Home Consumer
BIG REEL, THE - Jun, 1974?+
ELECTRONIC SERVICING & TECHNOLOGY - Apr, 1940+
ELECTRONICS AND COMMUNICATIONS - Apr, 1946 - Oct/Nov, 1974// {New Zealand}
TELEVISION DIGEST WITH CONSUMER ELECTRONICS - 1961+
TELEVISION ENGINEERING - Sep, 1937? - Apr, 1952//

House Organ
COMMUNICATE - ?+
KNIGHT-RIDDER NEWS - Spring, 1986+

Information
DISCOURSE & SOCIETY - Jul, 1990+ {United Kingdom}

Broadcasting Subject Heading — INDEX

Instructional
EDUCATIONAL BROADCASTING - Jun, 1971 - Mar/Apr, 1977//
WRITER, THE - Apr, 1887+

Intercultural
GANNETT CENTER JOURNAL - Spring, 1987+

International
ABU NEWSLETTER - Apr, 1965+? {Australia}
ABU TECHNICAL REVIEW - Mar, 1969+ {Japan}
AEG-TELEFUNKEN PROGRESS - ? - #2, 1982// {Germany}
BROADCAST SYSTEMS ENGINEERING - Oct, 1974?+ {United Kingdom}
BROADCAST SYSTEMS INTERNATIONAL - ?+ {United Kingdom}
BROADCASTING ABROAD - Jan, 1989+
COMBROAD - Jan, 1967+ {United Kingdom}
DRAMA - Jul, 1919+ {United Kingdom}
EBU REVIEW. PROGRAMMES, ADMINISTRATION, LAW. - Feb, 1958+ {Switzerland}
EBU REVIEW. TECHNICAL. - 1950+ {Switzerland}
GANNETT CENTER JOURNAL - Spring, 1987+
IAMHIST NEWSLETTER - ?+
IBE - Oct, 1964+ {United Kingdom}
INTERNATIONAL BROADCASTING - 1978+ {United Kingdom}
JOURNAL OF MEDIA ECONOMICS - Spring, 1988+
JOURNALISTS' AFFAIRS - #1, 1973 - 1980?// {Czechoslovakia}
JOURNALIST'S WORLD - Jan/Mar, 1963 - 1968// {Belgium}
JQ. JOURNALISM QUARTERLY. - 1924+
MONITOR INTERNATIONAL - ?+ {Italy}
OIRT INFORMATION - 1956 - ?// {Czechoslovakia}
RADIO AND TELEVISION - Feb, 1960?+ {Czechoslovakia}
TELECOMMUNICATION JOURNAL - 1934+ {Switzerland}
WORLD BROADCAST NEWS - Jan, 1978+

Journalism
AMERICAN JOURNALISM - Summer, 1983+
FINELINE - Apr, 1989+
GANNETT CENTER JOURNAL - Spring, 1987+
JOURNAL OF MASS MEDIA ETHICS - Fall/Winter, 1985/1986+
JOURNALISM EDUCATOR, THE - 1945+
JOURNALIST - 1908+ {United Kingdom}
JOURNALISTS' AFFAIRS - #1, 1973 - 1980?// {Czechoslovakia}
JOURNALIST'S WORLD - Jan/Mar, 1963 - 1968// {Belgium}
JQ. JOURNALISM QUARTERLY. - 1924+
NIEMAN REPORTS - Feb, 1947+

Legal
AIR LAW REVIEW - Jan, 1930 - Oct, 1941//
BROADCASTING AND THE LAW - 1971+
EBU REVIEW. PROGRAMMES, ADMINISTRATION, LAW. - Feb, 1958+ {Switzerland}
FINELINE - Apr, 1989+
LINE MONITOR, THE - ?+
NAB HIGHLIGHTS - Jan, 1975+?

Licensing
ASCAP IN ACTION - Fall, 1979+

Lighting
LIGHTING DIMENSIONS - Jan, 1977+

Literature
COMMUNICATION BOOKNOTES - Nov, 1969+

Management
AIRWAVES - Aug, 1974+ {United Kingdom}
BME'S TELEVISION ENGINEERING - Jan, 1965 - Sep, 1990//
BROADCAST ACCOUNTING ALERT - ?+
BROADCAST CABLE FINANCIAL JOURNAL - Mar, 1972+
BROADCAST REPORTER - Nov 7, 1931 - Jun 15, 1933//
BROADCAST SYSTEMS INTERNATIONAL - ?+ {United Kingdom}
BROADCASTER - Jan, 1942+ {Canada}
BROADCASTING - Oct 15, 1931+
BROADCASTING ABROAD - Jan, 1989+
COMMUNICATOR - Jan, 1947?+
EBU REVIEW. PROGRAMMES, ADMINISTRATION, LAW. - Feb, 1958+ {Switzerland}
INTERNATIONAL BROADCASTING - 1978+ {United Kingdom}
MANAGEMENT AND SALES DIVISION NEWSLETTER - ?+
OIRT INFORMATION - 1956 - ?// {Czechoslovakia}
PUBLIC BROADCASTING REPORT, THE - 1978+
PUBLIC TELECOMMUNICATIONS REVIEW - Sep, 1941 - Nov/Dec, 1980//
RELIGIOUS BROADCASTING - 1969+
RTD - Feb 9, 1937 - Jul 22, 1966//
RUNDOWN, THE - Jan 1, 1981?+?

Marketing
AMERICAN DEMOGRAPHICS - Jan, 1979+
BPME IMAGE MAGAZINE - ?+
FLAKE - ?, 1990+

Membership
IBEW JOURNAL - 1902+
MANAGEMENT AND SALES DIVISION NEWSLETTER - ?+
NAB HIGHLIGHTS - Jan, 1975+?
NEWS FROM APB - ?+
PUBLIC TELECOMMUNICATIONS REVIEW - Sep, 1941 - Nov/Dec, 1980//

Minneapolis
TWIN CITIES JOURNALISM REVIEW - Feb, 1972+

Minorities
AIR TIME - ?+
HOWARD JOURNAL OF COMMUNICATIONS, THE - Spring, 1988+
NEWSLETTER - Jun, 1988+

Music
ASCAP IN ACTION - Fall, 1979+
BILLBOARD - Nov, 1894+
BMI: MUSICWORLD - 1962+

Mystery
SCARLET STREET - Jan, 1991+

News
AP BROADCASTER - 1982+
CHICAGO JOURNALISM REVIEW - Oct, 1968 - Sep, 1975//
CIPA NEWS - ?+?
COMMUNICATOR - Jan, 1947?+
CONGRESSIONAL QUARTERLY'S EDITORIAL RESEARCH REPORTS - ?+
EDITORIALIST, THE - Sep/Oct, 1974+
FEED-BACK - Oct, 1974+
NATIONAL BROADCAST EDITORIAL ASSOCIATION NEWSLETTER - ?+?
NEWS FROM APB - ?+
NEWSCASTER, THE - ?, 1987+
RUNDOWN, THE - Jan 1, 1981?+?
ST. LOUIS JOURNALISM REVIEW - Oct/Nov, 1970+
STATIC - ?+?
TWIN CITIES JOURNALISM REVIEW - Feb, 1972+
UK PRESS GAZETTE - 1965+ {United Kingdom}
WASHINGTON JOURNALISM REVIEW - Oct, 1977+

Political
NAB HIGHLIGHTS - Jan, 1975+?

Popular Culture
JOURNAL OF POPULAR FILM AND TELEVISION - Winter, 1972+
SH-BOOM - Jan, 1990+

Preservation
BROADCAST PIONEERS LIBRARY REPORTS - Spring, 1975+

Production
ACTION! - Sep/Oct, 1966 - Nov/Dec, 1978//
AUDIO PRODUCTION FOR BROADCAST - Spring, 1982+
BROADCAST PROGRAMMING AND PRODUCTION - Apr, 1975 - ?//
DRAMA - Jul, 1919+ {United Kingdom}

EBU REVIEW. PROGRAMMES, ADMINISTRATION, LAW. - Feb, 1958+ {Switzerland}
EDUCATIONAL BROADCASTING - Jun, 1971 - Mar/Apr, 1977//
ENTERTAINMENT REVUE - Apr, 1988+
FILM & VIDEO - Feb, 1984+
LIGHTING DIMENSIONS - Jan, 1977+
NEW THEATRE - Aug, 1939 - Jul, 1949// {United Kingdom}
PD REPORT - ?, 1988?+
RUNDOWN, THE - Jan 1, 1981?+?

Programming
BBC QUARTERLY, THE - Apr, 1946 - Autumn, 1954// {United Kingdom}
BETTER BROADCASTS NEWS - Oct, 1955+
BETTER RADIO AND TELEVISION - Winter, 1960+
BILLBOARD - Nov, 1894+
BROADCAST - 1973+ {United Kingdom}
BROADCAST PROGRAMMING AND PRODUCTION - Apr, 1975 - ?//
BROADCAST REPORTER - Nov 7, 1931 - Jun 15, 1933//
BROADCAST SYSTEMS INTERNATIONAL - ?+ {United Kingdom}
BROADCASTER - Jan, 1942+ {Canada}
BROADCASTING - Oct 15, 1931+
BROADCASTING ABROAD - Jan, 1989+
EBU REVIEW. PROGRAMMES, ADMINISTRATION, LAW. - Feb, 1958+ {Switzerland}
ELECTRONIC AGE - Oct, 1941 - Fall, 1971//
NBC DIGEST - Oct, 1946 - Oct, 1948//
POPULAR RADIO AND TELEVISION - May, 1922 - May, 1928//
PUBLIC TELECOMMUNICATIONS REVIEW - Sep, 1941 - Nov/Dec, 1980//
RADIO AND TELEVISION - Feb, 1960?+ {Czechoslovakia}
RTD - Feb 9, 1937 - Jul 22, 1966//

Promotion
BMI: MUSICWORLD - 1962+
BPME IMAGE MAGAZINE - ?+
BROADCAST REPORTER - Nov 7, 1931 - Jun 15, 1933//
ELECTRONIC AGE - Oct, 1941 - Fall, 1971//
GENERAL ELECTRIC REVIEW - Mar 2, 1903 - Nov, 1958//
INVIEW - Spring, 1989+
KNIGHT-RIDDER NEWS - Spring, 1986+
RCA BROADCAST NEWS - 1931+
SOUND AND VISION BROADCASTING - Spring, 1960 - 1973// {United Kingdom}

Public
CURRENT - 19uu+
PACTSHEET - Dec, 1977+
PUBLIC BROADCASTING REPORT, THE - 1978+
PUBLIC TELECOMMUNICATIONS REVIEW - Sep, 1941 - Nov/Dec, 1980//

REPORT - ?+

Public Relations
BPME IMAGE MAGAZINE - ?+
JOURNALISM EDUCATOR, THE - 1945+

Ratings
BEYOND THE RATINGS - Mar, 1978?+?
NIELSEN MEDIA NEWS - ?+
NIELSEN NEWSCAST, THE - 1951+
RTD - Feb 9, 1937 - Jul 22, 1966//

Recording
MAG TRACKS - Winter, 1987+
STUDIO SOUND AND BROADCAST ENGINEERING - Jan?, 1959+ {United Kingdom}

Records & Compact Discs
BILLBOARD - Nov, 1894+

Regulation
AIR LAW REVIEW - Jan, 1930 - Oct, 1941//
BROADCAST SYSTEMS INTERNATIONAL - ?+ {United Kingdom}
BROADCASTING - Oct 15, 1931+
BROADCASTING ABROAD - Jan, 1989+
BROADCASTING AND THE LAW - 1971+
CODE NEWS - Mar, 1968 - ?//
FCC WEEK - 198u+
FEDERAL COMMUNICATIONS LAW JOURNAL - Mar, 1937+
JQ. JOURNALISM QUARTERLY. - 1924+
LINE MONITOR, THE - ?+
RADIO WORLD - Jul, 1977+
TELECOMMUNICATION JOURNAL - 1934+ {Switzerland}
TV & RADIO FAXLETTER - ?+

Religion
CAMPUS BROADCASTERS - ? - ?//
IRB - ?+
RELIGIOUS BROADCASTING - 1969+

Repair
ELECTRONIC SERVICING & TECHNOLOGY - Apr, 1940+

Research
AT&T TECHNICAL JOURNAL - Jul, 1922+
BEYOND THE RATINGS - Mar, 1978?+?
DISCOURSE & SOCIETY - Jul, 1990+ {United Kingdom}
ELECTRONICS & COMMUNICATIONS ENGINEERING JOURNAL - Oct, 1926+ {United Kingdom}
ELECTRONICS LETTERS - Mar, 1965+ {United Kingdom}
HOWARD JOURNAL OF COMMUNICATIONS, THE - Spring, 1988+
IAMHIST NEWSLETTER - ?+

JOURNAL OF BROADCASTING & ELECTRONIC MEDIA - Winter 1956/1957+
JQ. JOURNALISM QUARTERLY. - 1924+
NIELSEN MEDIA NEWS - ?+
NIELSEN NEWSCAST, THE - 1951+

Review
AT&T TECHNICAL JOURNAL - Jul, 1922+
AUDIO PRODUCTION FOR BROADCAST - Spring, 1982+
BBC QUARTERLY, THE - Apr, 1946 - Autumn, 1954// {United Kingdom}
BILLBOARD - Nov, 1894+
CHICAGO JOURNALISM REVIEW - Oct, 1968 - Sep, 1975//
CIPA NEWS - ?+?
COMMUNICATION ARTS - Aug, 1959+
CURRENT - 19uu+
ENTERTAINMENT REVUE - Apr, 1988+
FEED-BACK - Oct, 1974+
HOWARD JOURNAL OF COMMUNICATIONS, THE - Spring, 1988+
IEEE SPECTRUM - Jan, 1964+
JOURNAL OF BROADCASTING & ELECTRONIC MEDIA - Winter 1956/1957+
JOURNAL OF POPULAR FILM AND TELEVISION - Winter, 1972+
JOURNALISTS' AFFAIRS - #1, 1973 - 1980?// {Czechoslovakia}
JQ. JOURNALISM QUARTERLY. - 1924+
NIEMAN REPORTS - Feb, 1947+
SCARLET STREET - Jan, 1991+
SHOW - Oct, 1961+?
SHOWCASE WORLD - ?+
ST. LOUIS JOURNALISM REVIEW - Oct/Nov, 1970+
TELECOM JAPAN, THE - ?+ {Japan}
TWIN CITIES JOURNALISM REVIEW - Feb, 1972+
UK PRESS GAZETTE - 1965+ {United Kingdom}
VARIETY - Dec 16, 1905+
WASHINGTON JOURNALISM REVIEW - Oct, 1977+

Saint Louis
ST. LOUIS JOURNALISM REVIEW - Oct/Nov, 1970+

Saint Paul
TWIN CITIES JOURNALISM REVIEW - Feb, 1972+

Sales
BROADCASTER - Jan, 1942+ {Canada}
MANAGEMENT AND SALES DIVISION NEWSLETTER - ?+

Satellites
TELECOMMUNICATION JOURNAL - 1934+ {Switzerland}

Scripts
NBC DIGEST - Oct, 1946 - Oct, 1948//
NEW THEATRE - Aug, 1939 - Jul, 1949// {United Kingdom}
WRITER, THE - Apr, 1887+

Short Wave
ELECTRONIC ENGINEERING - Mar, 1928+? {United Kingdom}
MODERN RADIO - Jul, 1931 - Apr, 1933//
RADIO & TELEVISION - Jun/Jul, 1930 - Sep, 1941//

Society
GANNETT CENTER JOURNAL - Spring, 1987+

Soviet Bloc
JOURNALISTS' AFFAIRS - #1, 1973 - 1980?// {Czechoslovakia}

Stock
MAG TRACKS - Winter, 1987+

Teaching
BEA NEWSLETTER - Dec, 1987+
MANAGEMENT AND SALES DIVISION NEWSLETTER - ?+

Technology
ABU TECHNICAL REVIEW - Mar, 1969+ {Japan}
AEG-TELEFUNKEN PROGRESS - ? - #2, 1982// {Germany}
AT&T TECHNICAL JOURNAL - Jul, 1922+
AUDIO PRODUCTION FOR BROADCAST - Spring, 1982+
BBC ENGINEERING - 1955? - Jul, 1980// {United Kingdom}
BME'S TELEVISION ENGINEERING - Jan, 1965 - Sep, 1990//
BROADCAST - 1973+ {United Kingdom}
BROADCAST + TECHNOLOGY - Sep/Oct, 1975+ {Canada}
BROADCAST ENGINEERING - May, 1959+
BROADCAST SYSTEMS ENGINEERING - Oct, 1974?+ {United Kingdom}
COMMUNICATION AND BROADCAST ENGINEERING - Oct, 1934 - Aug, 1937//
COMMUNICATION ENGINEERING - Nov, 1940 - Mar, 1954//
EBU REVIEW. TECHNICAL. - 1950+ {Switzerland}
ELECTRONIC AGE - Oct, 1941 - Fall, 1971//
ELECTRONIC ENGINEERING - Mar, 1928+? {United Kingdom}
ELECTRONICS & COMMUNICATIONS ENGINEERING JOURNAL - Oct, 1926+ {United Kingdom}
ELECTRONICS LETTERS - Mar, 1965+ {United Kingdom}
FOLLOW FOCUS - 198u+
GENERAL ELECTRIC REVIEW - Mar 2, 1903 - Nov, 1958//
IBE - Oct, 1964+ {United Kingdom}

IEEE SPECTRUM - Jan, 1964+
IEEE TRANSACTIONS ON BROADCASTING - Mar, 1955+
INTERNATIONAL BROADCASTING - 1978+ {United Kingdom}
INVIEW - Spring, 1989+
LIGHTING DIMENSIONS - Jan, 1977+
MILLECANALI INTERNATIONAL - ?+ {Italy}
MODERN RADIO - Jul, 1931 - Apr, 1933//
MONITOR INTERNATIONAL - ?+ {Italy}
POPULAR RADIO AND TELEVISION - May, 1922 - May, 1928//
RADIO & TELEVISION - Jun/Jul, 1930 - Sep, 1941//
RADIO REVIEW AND TELEVISION NEWS - Mar/Apr, 1931 - Jan/Feb, 1933//
RADIO WORLD - Jul, 1977+
RF DESIGN - Nov/Dec, 1978+
SOUND AND VISION BROADCASTING - Spring, 1960 - 1973// {United Kingdom}
STUDIO SOUND AND BROADCAST ENGINEERING - Jan?, 1959+ {United Kingdom}
TELECOM JAPAN, THE - ?+ {Japan}
TELEVISION DIGEST WITH CONSUMER ELECTRONICS - 1961+
TELEVISION ENGINEERING - Sep, 1937? - Apr, 1952//
WORLD BROADCAST NEWS - Jan, 1978+

Typography
COMMUNICATION ARTS - Aug, 1959+

Unions & Guilds
BROADCAST ENGINEERS' JOURNAL, THE - 1934 - Oct, 1952//
IBEW JOURNAL - 1902+
JOURNALIST - 1908+ {United Kingdom}
NABET NEWS - Nov, 1962?+

Writing
WRITER, THE - Apr, 1887+

Cable Television

Academic
JOURNAL OF BROADCASTING & ELECTRONIC MEDIA - Winter 1956/1957+

Access
URBAN TELECOMMUNICATIONS FORUM - Aug, 1972 - Nov, 1975//

Advertising
AMERICAN DEMOGRAPHICS - Jan, 1979+
BPME IMAGE MAGAZINE - ?+
CABLE TV ADVERTISING - Jun, 1975?+

ELECTRONIC MEDIA - Aug 5, 1982+

Alternative Media
INDEPENDENT MEDIA - Mar, 1983?+ {United Kingdom}

Animation
STORYBOARD / THE ART OF LAUGHTER - Fall, 1990+

Artist
SHOWCASE WORLD - ?+

Business
BROADCAST - 1973+ {United Kingdom}
BROADCAST CABLE FINANCIAL JOURNAL - Mar, 1972+
CABLE COMMUNICATIONS MAGAZINE - May, 1934?+ {Canada}
CABLE MARKETING - Feb, 1981 - Aug?, 1990//
CABLE TV BUSINESS MAGAZINE - Jan, 1964 - Jan 4, 1991//
CABLE TV PROGRAMMING - Sep 25, 1981+
CABLE WORLD - Jan 9, 1989+
CABLEAGE - May 18, 1981+
CABLEVISION - 1975+
ELECTRONIC MEDIA - Aug 5, 1982+
JOURNAL OF MEDIA ECONOMICS - Spring, 1988+
MEDIA BUSINESS - Jan, 1987+
MOVING PICTURES INTERNATIONAL - Sep 13, 1990?+ {United Kingdom}
MSO'S CABLE MARKETING - Oct, 1987+
MULTICHANNEL NEWS - 1980+
VIDEOCASSETTE AND CATV NEWSLETTER - Jun, 1971 - ?, 1981?//
VUE - Mar, 1965 - Sep, 11, 1978//
WATCH - Dec, 1979 - May, 1980?//?

Cassettes
VIDEOCASSETTE AND CATV NEWSLETTER - Jun, 1971 - ?, 1981?//

Community
URBAN TELECOMMUNICATIONS FORUM - Aug, 1972 - Nov, 1975//

Corporate
E-ITV - Aug, 1965 - Feb/Mar, 1988//

Demographics
AMERICAN DEMOGRAPHICS - Jan, 1979+

Design
IEEE TRANSACTIONS ON COMMUNICATIONS - 1953+

Distribution
VIDEO WEEK - Feb 4, 1980+

Cable Television — Subject Heading

Economics
JOURNAL OF MEDIA ECONOMICS - Spring, 1988+

Editorial
NATIONAL BROADCAST EDITORIAL ASSOCIATION NEWSLETTER - ?+?

Education
C-SPAN IN THE CLASSROOM - Aug/Sep, 1989+

Emerging
MARKETING NEW MEDIA - Mar 7, 1984+

Engineering
COMMUNICATIONS ENGINEERING & DESIGN - Oct, 1975+
ELECTRONICS & COMMUNICATIONS ENGINEERING JOURNAL - Oct, 1926+ {United Kingdom}
IEEE TRANSACTIONS ON CABLE TELEVISION - Oct, 1976 - Oct, 1980//
IEEE TRANSACTIONS ON COMMUNICATIONS - 1953+

Finance
BROADCAST CABLE FINANCIAL JOURNAL - Mar, 1972+
MULTICHANNEL NEWS - 1980+

Government
C-SPAN IN THE CLASSROOM - Aug/Sep, 1989+

Guide
A & E PROGRAM GUIDE - Jan?, 1986+
AMERICAN MOVIE CLASSICS MAGAZINE - Jan, 1988+
CABLE GUIDE, THE - 1980?+
CINEMA, VIDEO & CABLE MOVIE DIGEST - May, 1991+
CONNECT - Oct, 1989+
DISNEY ADVENTURES - Nov 12, 1990+
DISNEY CHANNEL MAGAZINE, THE - Jan, 1983+
ENTERTAINER, THE - Sep, 1982+
ON CABLE - Oct, 1980 - Dec, 1985//
PREMIUM CHANNELS TV BLUEPRINT - Jan, 1980+
PREVIEW - Feb, 1982+
TV ENTERTAINMENT - ?, 1989+
TV GUIDE - Apr 3, 1953+
TV GUIDE - Apr 1, 1989+ {United Kingdom}

Historical
JOURNAL OF BROADCASTING & ELECTRONIC MEDIA - Winter 1956/1957+
JQ. JOURNALISM QUARTERLY. - 1924+
SPARKS - ?+

House Organ
KNIGHT-RIDDER NEWS - Spring, 1986+

International
CABLE TELEVISION ENGINEERING - 1971+ {United Kingdom}
INTERNATIONAL CABLE - Jan/Feb, 1990+
JOURNAL OF MEDIA ECONOMICS - Spring, 1988+
JQ. JOURNALISM QUARTERLY. - 1924+
MOVING PICTURES INTERNATIONAL - Sep 13, 1990?+ {United Kingdom}

Journalism
JQ. JOURNALISM QUARTERLY. - 1924+

Legislative
C-SPAN UPDATE - ?+

Libraries
CABLE LIBRARIES - May, 1973+

Management
BROADCAST CABLE FINANCIAL JOURNAL - Mar, 1972+
CABLE TELEVISION ENGINEERING - 1971+ {United Kingdom}
CABLE TV BUSINESS MAGAZINE - Jan, 1964 - Jan 4, 1991//
INTERNATIONAL CABLE - Jan/Feb, 1990+
MSO'S CABLE MARKETING - Oct, 1987+
MULTICHANNEL NEWS - 1980+

Marketing
AMERICAN DEMOGRAPHICS - Jan, 1979+
BPME IMAGE MAGAZINE - ?+
CABLE MARKETING - Feb, 1981 - Aug?, 1990//
CABLE WORLD - Jan 9, 1989+
CABLEAGE - May 18, 1981+
MSO'S CABLE MARKETING - Oct, 1987+

News
NATIONAL BROADCAST EDITORIAL ASSOCIATION NEWSLETTER - ?+?

Production
INDEPENDENT MEDIA - Mar, 1983?+ {United Kingdom}

Programming
AMERICAN MOVIE CLASSICS MAGAZINE - Jan, 1988+
BROADCAST - 1973+ {United Kingdom}
C-SPAN UPDATE - ?+
CABLE LIBRARIES - May, 1973+
CABLE TV PROGRAMMING - Sep 25, 1981+
CABLE WORLD - Jan 9, 1989+
CABLEAGE - May 18, 1981+
CINEMA, VIDEO & CABLE MOVIE DIGEST - May, 1991+
ELECTRONIC MEDIA - Aug 5, 1982+
MSO'S CABLE MARKETING - Oct, 1987+
ON CABLE - Oct, 1980 - Dec, 1985//
VIDEO WEEK - Feb 4, 1980+
WATCH - Dec, 1979 - May, 1980?//?

Promotion
BPME IMAGE MAGAZINE - ?+
CABLE LINES - Jan, 1985+
INVIEW - Spring, 1989+
KNIGHT-RIDDER NEWS - Spring, 1986+

Public
C-SPAN IN THE CLASSROOM - Aug/Sep, 1989+
C-SPAN UPDATE - ?+

Public Relations
BPME IMAGE MAGAZINE - ?+

Ratings
NIELSEN MEDIA NEWS - ?+

Regulation
CABLEVISION - 1975+
FCC WEEK - 198u+
FEDERAL COMMUNICATIONS LAW JOURNAL - Mar, 1937+
JQ. JOURNALISM QUARTERLY. - 1924+
TV & RADIO FAXLETTER - ?+

Research
CABLE TV PROGRAMMING - Sep 25, 1981+
ELECTRONICS & COMMUNICATIONS ENGINEERING JOURNAL - Oct, 1926+ {United Kingdom}
JOURNAL OF BROADCASTING & ELECTRONIC MEDIA - Winter 1956/1957+
JQ. JOURNALISM QUARTERLY. - 1924+
NIELSEN MEDIA NEWS - ?+

Review
CABLE COMMUNICATIONS MAGAZINE - May, 1934?+ {Canada}
E-ITV - Aug, 1965 - Feb/Mar, 1988//
ELECTRONIC MEDIA - Aug 5, 1982+
IEEE SPECTRUM - Jan, 1964+
JOURNAL OF BROADCASTING & ELECTRONIC MEDIA - Winter 1956/1957+
JQ. JOURNALISM QUARTERLY. - 1924+
SHOWCASE WORLD - ?+
URBAN TELECOMMUNICATIONS FORUM - Aug, 1972 - Nov, 1975//
WATCH - Dec, 1979 - May, 1980?//?

Sales
CABLE TV ADVERTISING - Jun, 1975?+
CABLE WORLD - Jan 9, 1989+
CABLEAGE - May 18, 1981+

Teaching
C-SPAN IN THE CLASSROOM - Aug/Sep, 1989+
CONNECT - Oct, 1989+

Cinema

Technology
BROADCAST - 1973+ {United Kingdom}
CABLE TELEVISION ENGINEERING - 1971+ {United Kingdom}
CABLE WORLD - Jan 9, 1989+
CABLEVISION - 1975+
COMMUNICATIONS ENGINEERING & DESIGN - Oct, 1975+
E-ITV - Aug, 1965 - Feb/Mar, 1988//
ELECTRONICS & COMMUNICATIONS ENGINEERING JOURNAL - Oct, 1926+ {United Kingdom}
IEEE SPECTRUM - Jan, 1964+
IEEE TRANSACTIONS ON CABLE TELEVISION - Oct, 1976 - Oct, 1980//
INTERNATIONAL CABLE - Jan/Feb, 1990+
INTERNATIONAL VIDEOTEXT TELETEXT NEWS - Jul, 1980+
INVIEW - Spring, 1989+
MARKETING NEW MEDIA - Mar 7, 1984+
VUE - Mar, 1965 - Sep, 11, 1978//

Theory
INTERNATIONAL VIDEOTEXT TELETEXT NEWS - Jul, 1980+

Videotext
INTERNATIONAL VIDEOTEXT TELETEXT NEWS - Jul, 1980+

World
CABLE TELEVISION ENGINEERING - 1971+ {United Kingdom}
INTERNATIONAL CABLE - Jan/Feb, 1990+

Cinema

Action
ALL-STAR ACTION HEROES - ?, 1989?+
DAREDEVILS - Nov, 1983+?

Adventure
DAREDEVILS - Nov, 1983+?

Advertising
AMERICAN DEMOGRAPHICS - Jan, 1979+

Aesthetics
ON FILM - Winter?, 1976+

Alternative Media
EUROPEAN TRASH CINEMA - ?, 1990?+

Animation
STORYBOARD / THE ART OF LAUGHTER - Fall, 1990+

Art Form
ON FILM - Winter?, 1976+

Artist
AFTER DARK - May, 1968 - Jan, 1983//
BEHIND THE SCENE - Aug, 1954 - ?//
DRAMATIC MIRROR, THE - 1879 - Apr, 1922//
FILM ALBUM MAGAZINE - Summer, 1948+?
FILM ARTISTE - 1964 - 1974// {United Kingdom}
FILM FAMILIES - 1978+
FILMFARE - 1952+ {India}
FILMS AND FILMING - Oct, 1954 - Mar, 1990// {United Kingdom}
FILMS ILLUSTRATED - Jul, 1971 - ?// {United Kingdom}
FILMS IN REVIEW - Feb, 1926+
FRESH! - Jan 1, 1985+
GOSSIP - May, 1972?+
HOLLYWOOD MAGAZINE - 1988+
HOLLYWOOD NOW - Oct, 1936 - Feb, 1940//
INSIDE HOLLYWOOD - Jan/Feb, 1991+
INTERVIEW - 1969+
MODERN SCREEN - Nov, 1930 - ?//
MOTION PICTURE - Feb, 1911+
MOVIE FLASH - ?+ {Philippines}
MOVIE MIRROR - Jun, 1946+
MOVIE-RADIO GUIDE - Oct 20, 1931 - Nov, 1943//
MOVIE STARS - Fall, 1940 - 198u//
MOVIE TEEN - Dec, 1947 - ?//
MOVIE TEEN ILLUSTRATED - Apr, 1958+?
MOVIE TV SECRETS - Oct, 1959+?
MOVIELINE - Sep, 1989+
PHOTO SCREEN - Dec, 1965+
PHOTOSTAR - Oct/Nov, 1990+
PIC - Jul 11, 1934 - ?//
PREMIERE - Jun, 1987+
PREVIEW - Sep, 1976? - ?//
RONA BARRETT'S HOLLYWOOD - 1971+
SCENE AT THE MOVIES - ?+
SCREEN ACTOR HOLLYWOOD - Aug, 1959+
SCREEN ALBUM MAGAZINE - 1935+?
SCREEN LIFE - Nov, 1962?+?
SCREEN STARS - Apr, 1944+
SCREEN STORIES - 1929 - ?//
SCREEN WEEKLY, THE - ?+? {Ireland}
SCREENLAND PLUS TV-LAND - 1920+
SH-BOOM - Jan, 1990+
SHOWCASE WORLD - ?+
SILVER SCREEN - Nov, 1930+
SOSYAL! MAGAZINE - Feb 4, 1986+ {Philippines}
SOUND STAGE - Feb?, 1965 - ?//
STARZ - Sep, 1990+
SUPER TEEN - Oct, 1978+
TALKING SCREEN - Jan, 1930 - Oct, 1930//
TEEN DREAM - 198u+
TELEVISION AND SCREEN GUIDE - May, 1936+?
TGIF - ?+?
THEATRE MAGAZINE - Oct, 1900 - Apr, 1931//
TONI HOLT'S MOVIE LIFE - Jan, 1938+
TS - Spring, 1985+
TV AND SCREEN SECRETS - Jan, 1969+?
WHO'S WHO IN MOVIES AND TV - ?+
WOW! MAGAZINE - Oct, 1987+

Avant-garde
EUROPEAN TRASH CINEMA - ?, 1990?+

Black
FRESH! - Jan 1, 1985+

Business
DAILY VARIETY - 1933+
GREATER AMUSEMENTS - 1914+
HOLLYWOOD MAGAZINE - 1988+
JOURNAL OF MEDIA ECONOMICS - Spring, 1988+
KINEMATOGRAPH WEEKLY - Jun 15, 1889 - Sep, 1971// {United Kingdom}
MOTION PICTURE HERALD - Jan 3, 1931 - Dec, 1972//

Cassettes
MOVIE - THE VIDEO MAGAZINE - Oct, 1988?+ {United Kingdom}

Collector
GRAPHIC ANTIQUARIAN - Jul, 1970+

Cultural
HOWARD JOURNAL OF COMMUNICATIONS, THE - Spring, 1988+

Dance
AFTER DARK - May, 1968 - Jan, 1983//

Demographics
AMERICAN DEMOGRAPHICS - Jan, 1979+

Distribution
BIOSCOPE, THE - Sep 18, 1908 - May 4, 1932// {United Kingdom}
BOXOFFICE - Dec 1, 1920? - 1977//
EDISON KINETOGRAM - Apr 15, 1910 - Apr 1, 1913// {United Kingdom}
EXHIBITORS HERALD WORLD - Jan 7, 1928 - Dec 27, 1930//
EXHIBITORS TRADE REVIEW - Dec 9, 1916 - Apr 17, 1926//
FILM BUYER - ? - Dec 27, 1930?//
GREATER AMUSEMENTS - 1914+
KINETRADOGRAM, THE - Jan, 1913 - Jun, 1913// {United Kingdom}
MIDWEEK MOTION PICTURE NEWS - Jul 15, 1925+?
MOTION PICTURE HERALD - Jan 3, 1931 - Dec, 1972//
NATIONAL EXHIBITOR, THE - Jan 5, 1923 - ?//
PICTURE REPORTS - ? - ?//
PRODUCT DIGEST - ? - ?//

REEL LIFE - 1912 - Jun 9, 1917//
SCREEN INTERNATIONAL - 1911+ {United Kingdom}
SHOWMEN'S TRADE REVIEW - May 27, 1933 - Oct 26, 1957//
UNIVERSAL WEEKLY - Jan 20, 1912 - May 9, 1936//

Economics
JOURNAL OF MEDIA ECONOMICS - Spring, 1988+

Employment
TGIF - ?+?

Europe
EUROPEAN TRASH CINEMA - ?, 1990?+

Exhibition
BIOSCOPE, THE - Sep 18, 1908 - May 4, 1932// {United Kingdom}
BOX OFFICE - 1920+
BOXOFFICE - Dec 1, 1920? - 1977//
DRAMATIC MIRROR, THE - 1879 - Apr, 1922//
EDISON KINETROGRAM - Apr 15, 1910 - Apr 1, 1913// {United Kingdom}
EXHIBITORS HERALD WORLD - Jan 7, 1928 - Dec 27, 1930//
EXHIBITORS' TIMES - May 17, 1913 - Sep 27, 1913//
EXHIBITORS TRADE REVIEW - Dec 9, 1916 - Apr 17, 1926//
FILM BUYER - ? - Dec 27, 1930?//
FILM JOURNAL, THE - 1937+
IDEAL KINEMA, THE - 1938 - Apr, 1957// {United Kingdom}
INTERNATIONAL PROJECTIONIST - Oct, 1931 - Jun, 1965//
KINEMATOGRAPH WEEKLY - Jun 15, 1889 - Sep, 1971// {United Kingdom}
MIDWEEK MOTION PICTURE NEWS - Jul 15, 1925+?
MOTION PICTURE HERALD - Jan 3, 1931 - Dec, 1972//
MOTION PICTURE PROJECTION - Oct, 1927 - May, 1933//
NATIONAL EXHIBITOR, THE - Jan 5, 1923 - ?//
PROJECTION, LANTERN AND CINEMATOGRAPH - Apr, 1906 - Sep, 1907// {United Kingdom}
REEL LIFE - 1912 - Jun 9, 1917//
SCREEN INTERNATIONAL - 1911+ {United Kingdom}
SHOWMEN'S TRADE REVIEW - May 27, 1933 - Oct 26, 1957//
UNIVERSAL WEEKLY - Jan 20, 1912 - May 9, 1936//

Fan
ALL-STAR ACTION HEROES - ?, 1989?+
AMPERSAND'S COLLEGE ENTERTAINMENT GUIDE - Fall, 1977+
BEHIND THE SCENE - Aug, 1954 - ?//
CINEFEX - Mar, 1980+
DAREDEVILS - Nov, 1983+?
DEEP RED - Dec, 1987+
FAMOUS MONSTERS OF FILMLAND - 1958+?
FANGORIA - 1979+
FANTASTIC FILMS - Jan, 1982+
FANTASY ZONE - ?+ {United Kingdom}
FILM ALBUM MAGAZINE - Summer, 1948+?
FILM ARTISTE - 1964 - 1974// {United Kingdom}
FILM FAMILIES - 1978+
FILM REVIEW - 1951+ {United Kingdom}
FILMWORLD - Oct, 1964 - 1983?// {India}
FRESH! - Jan 1, 1985+
GOSSIP - May, 1972?+
HERO HOBBY - 1966+?
HOLLYWOOD - 1913 - Mar, 1943//
HOLLYWOOD - Jan, 1950 - ?//
HOLLYWOOD STUDIO MAGAZINE - May, 1953+
MODERN SCREEN - Nov, 1930 - ?//
MOTION PICTURE - Feb, 1911+
MOVIE CLASSIC - Sep, 1915 - Feb, 1937//
MOVIE DIGEST - Jan, 1972 to date?
MOVIE FAN - Winter, 1946 to date?
MOVIE FLASH - ?+ {Philippines}
MOVIE HUMOR - Sep, 1935 - ?//
MOVIE MIRROR - Jun, 1946+
MOVIE STARS - Fall, 1940 - 198u//
MOVIE TEEN - Dec, 1947 - ?//
MOVIE TEEN ILLUSTRATED - Apr, 1958+?
MOVIE TV SECRETS - Oct, 1959+?
MOVIE WORLD - 1952 - ?//
MOVIELAND AND TV TIME - Feb, 1943+?
PHOTO SCREEN - Dec, 1965+
PHOTOPLAY - Jun, 1946 - Aug, 1977//
PHOTOSTAR - Oct/Nov, 1990+
PIC - Jul 11, 1934 - ?//
PICTURES MAGAZINE, THE - ?, 1916+?
PREVIEW - Sep, 1976? - ?//
RONA BARRETT'S HOLLYWOOD - 1971+
SCREEN ALBUM MAGAZINE - 1935+?
SCREEN LEGENDS - May, 1965 - ?//
SCREEN LIFE - Nov, 1962?+?
SCREEN STARS - Apr, 1944+
SCREEN STORIES - 1929 - ?//
SCREEN WEEKLY, THE - ?+? {Ireland}
SCREENLAND PLUS TV-LAND - 1920+
SH-BOOM - Jan, 1990+
SILVER SCREEN - Nov, 1930+
SMASH HITS - 198u+
SOSYAL! MAGAZINE - Feb 4, 1986+ {Philippines}
SOUND STAGE - Feb?, 1965 - ?//
STARZ - Sep, 1990+
SUPER TEEN - Oct, 1978+
TALKING SCREEN - Jan, 1930 - Oct, 1930//
TEEN DREAM - 198u+
TELEVISION AND SCREEN GUIDE - May, 1936+?
TONI HOLT'S MOVIE LIFE - Jan, 1938+
TOP SECRET - Dec/Jan, 1985/1986+?
TS - Spring, 1985+
TV AND SCREEN SECRETS - Jan, 1969+?
WHO'S WHO IN MOVIES AND TV - ?+
WOW! MAGAZINE - Oct, 1987+

Fantasy
FANTASY ZONE - ?+ {United Kingdom}

Finance
DAILY VARIETY - 1933+
GREATER AMUSEMENTS - 1914+
PREMIERE - Jun, 1987+

Guide
ALPHA AND OMEGA FILM REPORT - Jan, 1985?+
AMPERSAND'S COLLEGE ENTERTAINMENT GUIDE - Fall, 1977+
BOOKS AND FILMS - Oct, 1935 - Oct, 1938//
BROADWAY SIGN POST - Oct 30, 1930 - ?//?
BULGARIAN FILMS - 1960+ {Bulgaria}
DISNEY ADVENTURES - Nov 12, 1990+
FILM & BROADCASTING REVIEW - 1964 - Sep 1, 1980//
FILM INDEX - Jun, 1966+? {Australia}
FILM REVIEW - 1951+ {United Kingdom}
FILMFARE - 1952+ {India}
FILMS AND FILMING - Oct, 1954 - Mar, 1990// {United Kingdom}
FILMS ILLUSTRATED - Jul, 1971 - ?// {United Kingdom}
FILMS IN REVIEW - Feb, 1926+
HIT PARADER - Nov, 1942 - ?//
HOLLYWOOD SPECTATOR - Mar, 1926 - Jul, 1941//
HUNGAROFILM BULLETIN - 1965+ {Hungary}
IN CINEMA - ?, 1980+
INSIDE HOLLYWOOD - Jan/Feb, 1991+
KINETRADOGRAM, THE - Jan, 1913 - Jun, 1913// {United Kingdom}
MGF - Feb, 1985+
MOTION PICTURE - Feb, 1911+
MOTION PICTURE REVIEW DIGEST - Dec, 1935 - Jan 22, 1940//
MOVIE MAGAZINE, THE - Winter, 1983+
MOVIE-RADIO GUIDE - Oct 20, 1931 - Nov, 1943//
MOVIE SHOW - Sep, 1942 - ?//?
MOVIE - THE VIDEO MAGAZINE - Oct, 1988?+ {United Kingdom}
MOVIEGOER - Jan, 1982+?
MOVIEGUIDE - ?, 1985+
MOVIES AND THE PEOPLE WHO MAKE THEM, THE - Jan 4, 1939 - Apr 18, 1941//
MOVIES NOW - ?, 1971 - ?//?
MOVIES USA - Nov, 1987?+
ON LINE - Feb, 1989+
PIC - Jul 11, 1934 - ?//
ROXY THEATRE WEEKLY REVIEW - Aug, 1926 - ?//
SCENE AT THE MOVIES - ?+

SELECTED MOTION PICTURES - Sep, 1925 - Nov, 1939//
SF MOVIELAND - Jan, 1983?+?
STAGE - Dec, 1923 - Jun, 1939//
THEATRE MAGAZINE - Oct, 1900 - Apr, 1931//

Historical
BRIGHT LIGHTS - Fall, 1974 - #1, 1980//
CINEMA STUDIES - Mar, 1960 - Sep, 1967// {United Kingdom}
FILM JOURNAL, THE - Spring, 1971 - 1975?//
FILMFAX - Jan/Feb, 1986+
FILMOGRAPH - Spring, 1970 - Summer, 1976//
FILMS IN REVIEW - Feb, 1926+
GRAPHIC ANTIQUARIAN - Jul, 1970+
HERO HOBBY - 1966+?
HOLLYWOOD STUDIO MAGAZINE - May, 1953+
SCREEN LEGENDS - May, 1965 - ?//
SH-BOOM - Jan, 1990+

Home Consumer
INSIDE HOLLYWOOD - Jan/Feb, 1991+
MOVIE - THE VIDEO MAGAZINE - Oct, 1988?+ {United Kingdom}

Horror
DEEP RED - Dec, 1987+
FAMOUS MONSTERS OF FILMLAND - 1958+?
FANGORIA - 1979+
FANTASTIC FILMS - Jan, 1982+

House Organ
PARAMOUNT WORLD - 1955+?

International
CAHIERS DU CINEMA IN ENGLISH - Jan, 1966 - Dec, 1967//
DAILY VARIETY - 1933+
FILM QUARTERLY - Oct, 1945+
FILMWORLD - Oct, 1964 - 1983?// {India}
GREATER AMUSEMENTS - 1914+
JOURNAL OF MEDIA ECONOMICS - Spring, 1988+
MOVIEGOER - Winter, 1964 - Summer/Autumn, 1966//
SCREEN INTERNATIONAL - 1911+ {United Kingdom}
TAKE ONE - Sep/Oct, 1966 - Nov, 1979// {Canada}

Literature
FILM JOURNAL, THE - Spring, 1971 - 1975?//

Management
SHOWMEN'S TRADE REVIEW - May 27, 1933 - Oct 26, 1957//

Marketing
AMERICAN DEMOGRAPHICS - Jan, 1979+
BOX OFFICE - 1920+

Minorities
HOWARD JOURNAL OF COMMUNICATIONS, THE - Spring, 1988+

Music
AMPERSAND'S COLLEGE ENTERTAINMENT GUIDE - Fall, 1977+
HIT PARADER - Nov, 1942 - ?//
SUPER TEEN - Oct, 1978+

Mystery
SCARLET STREET - Jan, 1991+

New York City
THEATRE MAGAZINE - Oct, 1900 - Apr, 1931//

Popular Culture
SH-BOOM - Jan, 1990+

Production
CINEFEX - Mar, 1980+
DAILY VARIETY - 1933+
FACTS ABOUT FILM FINLAND - 1972? - 1978// {Finland}
FALLING FOR STARS - 1965+
FILMING - Jan, 1969// {India}
GREATER AMUSEMENTS - 1914+
HOLLYWOOD MAGAZINE - 1988+
MOTION PICTURE HERALD - Jan 3, 1931 - Dec, 1972//
MOVIES, THE - Jul, 1983 - Nov, 1983//
PREMIERE - Jun, 1987+
PRODUCT DIGEST - ? - ?//
TALKING PICTURE MAGAZINE - Oct, 1929 - Jul, 1934//
THEATRE CRAFTS - Mar/Apr, 1967+

Programming
BIOSCOPE, THE - Sep 18, 1908 - May 4, 1932// {United Kingdom}

Projection
MOTION PICTURE PROJECTION - Oct, 1927 - May, 1933//
PROJECTION, LANTERN AND CINEMATOGRAPH - Apr, 1906 - Sep, 1907// {United Kingdom}

Promotion
BULLETIN - 1928+
FACTS ABOUT FILM FINLAND - 1972? - 1978// {Finland}
HOLLYWOOD NOW - Oct, 1936 - Feb, 1940//
HUNGAROFILM BULLETIN - 1965+ {Hungary}
KINETRADOGRAM, THE - Jan, 1913 - Jun, 1913// {United Kingdom}
METRO-GOLDWYN-MAYER SHORT STORY - 1938? - Jul/Aug, 1941//
MOVIEGOER - Jan, 1982+?
MOVIES USA - Nov, 1987?+
PICTURE REPORTS - ? - ?//
PICTURES MAGAZINE, THE - ?, 1916+?
PRODUCT DIGEST - ? - ?//
REEL LIFE - 1912 - Jun 9, 1917//
SELECTED MOTION PICTURES - Sep, 1925 - Nov, 1939//

Public
HOLLYWOOD SPECTATOR - Mar, 1926 - Jul, 1941//

Regulation
MOTION PICTURE HERALD - Jan 3, 1931 - Dec, 1972//

Religion
ALPHA AND OMEGA FILM REPORT - Jan, 1985?+
FILM & BROADCASTING REVIEW - 1964 - Sep 1, 1980//
MOVIEGUIDE - ?, 1985+
MOVIES AND MINISTRY - May, 1973 - Jul, 1974//

Research
FILM JOURNAL, THE - Spring, 1971 - 1975?//
HOWARD JOURNAL OF COMMUNICATIONS, THE - Spring, 1988+

Review
ALPHA AND OMEGA FILM REPORT - Jan, 1985?+
BOOKS AND FILMS - Oct, 1935 - Oct, 1938//
BRIGHT LIGHTS - Fall, 1974 - #1, 1980//
CAHIERS DU CINEMA IN ENGLISH - Jan, 1966 - Dec, 1967//
CINEFEX - Mar, 1980+
DAILY VARIETY - 1933+
DEEP RED - Dec, 1987+
DRAMATIC MIRROR, THE - 1879 - Apr, 1922//
FILM AND THEATRE TODAY - Mar, 1946 - 1949// {United Kingdom}
FILM DIRECTIONS - 1977+ {United Kingdom}
FILM GUIDE - ?+? {Australia}
FILM JOURNAL, THE - Spring, 1971 - 1975?//
FILM JOURNAL, THE - 1937+
FILM QUARTERLY - Oct, 1945+
FILMFAX - Jan/Feb, 1986+
FILMING - Jan, 1969// {India}
FILMOGRAPH - Spring, 1970 - Summer, 1976//
FILMWORLD - Oct, 1964 - 1983?// {India}
HOLLYWOOD MAGAZINE - 1988+
HOLLYWOOD SPECTATOR - Mar, 1926 - Jul, 1941//
HOWARD JOURNAL OF COMMUNICATIONS, THE - Spring, 1988+
INTERVIEW - 1969+
MOVIE - Jun, 1962 - Summer, 1982// {United Kingdom}
MOVIEGOER - Winter, 1964 - Summer/Autumn, 1966//
MOVIELINE - Sep, 1989+
MOVIES, THE - Jul, 1983 - Nov, 1983//

MOVIES AND MINISTRY - May, 1973 - Jul, 1974//
SCARLET STREET - Jan, 1991+
SCREEN LIFE - Nov, 1962?+?
SHOWCASE WORLD - ?+
STAGE - Dec, 1923 - Jun, 1939//
TAKE ONE - Sep/Oct, 1966 - Nov, 1979// (Canada)

Scripts
BOOKS AND FILMS - Oct, 1935 - Oct, 1938//
MOTION PICTURE ALBUM - Apr, 1912+?
MOVIE ACTION MAGAZINE - Nov, 1935 - Jun, 1936//
PHOTODRAMATIST, THE - May?, 1919 - Aug, 1923//
SCRIPT NEWSLETTER - 1988?+?
STORY WORLD AND PHOTODRAMATIST, THE - Jul?, 1919 - Aug, 1925//
TALKING PICTURE MAGAZINE - Oct, 1929 - Jul, 1934//

Secret Agent
TOP SECRET - Dec/Jan, 1985/1986+?

Special Effects
FANTASTIC FILMS - Jan, 1982+

Technology
BIOSCOPE, THE - Sep 18, 1908 - May 4, 1932// (United Kingdom)
INTERNATIONAL PROJECTIONIST - Oct, 1931 - Jun, 1965//
KINEMATOGRAPH WEEKLY - Jun 15, 1889 - Sep, 1971// (United Kingdom)
PROJECTION, LANTERN AND CINEMATOGRAPH - Apr, 1906 - Sep, 1907// (United Kingdom)

Teletext
MOVIE - Jun, 1962 - Summer, 1982// (United Kingdom)
ON FILM - Winter?, 1976+

Unions & Guilds
FILM ARTISTE - 1964 - 1974// (United Kingdom)
JOURNAL - ?, 1893+
SCREEN ACTOR HOLLYWOOD - Aug, 1959+

Wartime
HOLLYWOOD NOW - Oct, 1936 - Feb, 1940//

World
BULGARIAN FILMS - 1960+ (Bulgaria)

Writing
MOTION PICTURE ALBUM - Apr, 1912+?
SCRIPT NEWSLETTER - 1988?+?
STORY WORLD AND PHOTODRAMATIST, THE - Jul?, 1919 - Aug, 1925//

Youth
MOVIE TEEN - Dec, 1947 - ?//
MOVIE TEEN ILLUSTRATED - Apr, 1958+?
TS - Spring, 1985+

Communication

Academic
ACA BULLETIN - Oct, 1972+
C-O-N-N-E-C-T-I-O-N-S - ?+
COMMENT ON THE MEDIA - ?+?
COMMUNICATION LAW & POLICY NEWSLETTER - Nov, 1990+
COMMUNICATION MONOGRAPHS - 1934+
COMMUNIQUÉ - ?+?
ICA NEWSLETTER - 1973+
PUBLIC RELATIONS IDEAS - 1951 - Dec, 1965//?
QUARTERLY JOURNAL OF SPEECH, THE - Apr, 1915+
THE JOURNAL - May, 1974+
WSCA NEWS - Jan, 1984+

Activist
SCA WOMEN'S CAUCUS AND FEMINIST & WOMEN STUDIES DIVISION NEWSLETTER - ?+

Advertising
AISLE VIEW - ? - Jul 15, 1991//
IMPRINT - Jan, 1968+
SIGNS OF THE TIMES - May, 1906+
SPECIALTY ADVERTISING BUSINESS - 1976+

Aesthetics
COMMUNICATION STUDIES - Nov, 1949+

Big Bands
BAND LEADERS - Nov, 1942 - ?//

Business
ACA BULLETIN - Oct, 1972+
BUSINESS INFORMATION ALERT - Jan, 1989+
HORIZON - Summer?, 1986?+?
INTERSPACE - 1983+ (United Kingdom)
JOURNAL OF BUSINESS COMMUNICATION, THE - Oct, 1963+
MANAGEMENT COMMUNICATION QUARTERLY - Aug, 1987+
PRIVATE CABLE - Jul/Aug, 1982+
SATELLITE COMMUNICATIONS - Oct, 1977+
STAR SIGNALS - Sep, 1981+
STV GUIDE - Jan, 1983 - Jun, 1990//
VIA SATELLITE - Jan, 1986+

CD ROM
CD-ROM - Sep?, 1986+

CD-ROM LIBRARIAN - Jan, 1987+
INFORMATION TODAY - Jan, 1984+

College
COLLEGE & UNIVERSITY JOURNAL - 1917 - May, 1974//
COMMUNIQUÉ - ?+
PUBLIC RELATIONS IDEAS - 1951 - Dec, 1965//?

Computers
CD-ROM - Sep?, 1986+
LINK-UP - Sep, 1983+
THE JOURNAL - May, 1974+

Copyright
MILLER'S COPYRIGHT NEWSLETTER - 1988+

Corporate
JOURNAL OF COMMUNICATION MANAGEMENT - Fall, 1971 - May, 1983//

Cultural
CRITICAL STUDIES IN MASS COMMUNICATION - Mar, 1984+
DISCOURSE & SOCIETY - Jul, 1990+ (United Kingdom)
HOWARD JOURNAL OF COMMUNICATIONS, THE - Spring, 1988+
IN SEARCH - Winter, 1974 - #4, 1981?// (Canada)
PCS, THE POPULAR CULTURE SCHOLAR - Winter, 1977//?
VISIBLE LANGUAGE - Jan, 1967+

Database
INFORMATION TODAY - Jan, 1984+
MEDIABRIEFS - Spring, 1991+

Design
BRITISH COMMUNICATIONS AND ELECTRONICS - May, 1955 - Aug, 1965// (United Kingdom)
IEEE TRANSACTIONS ON COMMUNICATIONS - 1953+
IEEE TRANSACTIONS ON INFORMATION THEORY - Feb, 1953+

Development
INTERCULTURAL & DEVELOPMENT COMMUNICATION NEWSLETTER - ?+

Digital
DIGITAL MEDIA - Jun, 1991+

Discourse
DISCOURSE & SOCIETY - Jul, 1990+ (United Kingdom)

Display
SIGNS OF THE TIMES - May, 1906+

Communication
Subject Heading

Editing
JOURNAL OF TECHNICAL WRITING AND COMMUNICATION - Jan, 1971+
VISIBLE LANGUAGE - Jan, 1967+

Education
ACA BULLETIN - Oct, 1972+

Electronics
BRITISH COMMUNICATIONS AND ELECTRONICS - May, 1955 - Aug, 1965// {United Kingdom}
COMPUTERS & ELECTRONICS - Oct, 1954 - Apr, 1985//
MARCONI REVIEW, THE - Oct, 1928 - 1st Quarter?, 1983// {United Kingdom}

Engineering
BRITISH COMMUNICATIONS AND ELECTRONICS - May, 1955 - Aug, 1965// {United Kingdom}
IEEE TRANSACTIONS ON COMMUNICATIONS - 1953+
IEEE TRANSACTIONS ON INFORMATION THEORY - Feb, 1953+
MARCONI REVIEW, THE - Oct, 1928 - 1st Quarter?, 1983// {United Kingdom}
MONITOR - Mar, 1979+ {Australia}

Ethics
JOURNAL OF COMMUNICATION INQUIRY, THE - Spring, 1974+

Finance
INTERSPACE - 1983+ {United Kingdom}
SATELLITE NEWS - May, 1978+
SATELLITE WEEK - Jul 30, 1979+

Gender
WOMEN & LANGUAGE - Jan, 1976+

Graphics
JOURNAL OF BUSINESS COMMUNICATION, THE - Oct, 1963+
VISUAL COMMUNICATION NEWSLETTER, THE - ?+

Guide
SATELLITE ORBIT - Jul, 1982+
SATELLITE TIMES - ?+ {United Kingdom}
WHAT SATELLITE - ?+ {United Kingdom}

Health
HEALTH COMMUNICATION - #1, 1989+
HEALTH COMMUNICATION NEWSLETTER - Oct, 1990+

Historical
JOURNAL OF COMMUNICATION INQUIRY, THE - Spring, 1974+
JOURNAL OF POPULAR CULTURE - Summer, 1967+

QUARTERLY JOURNAL OF SPEECH, THE - Apr, 1915+

Home Consumer
STAR SIGNALS - Sep, 1981+

Homiletics
HOMILETIC - Summer, 1976+

Information
BUSINESS INFORMATION ALERT - Jan, 1989+
CD-ROM - Sep?, 1986+
CD-ROM LIBRARIAN - Jan, 1987+
DISCOURSE & SOCIETY - Jul, 1990+ {United Kingdom}
IEEE TRANSACTIONS ON INFORMATION THEORY - Feb, 1953+
INFORMATION TODAY - Jan, 1984+
INTERNATIONAL JOURNAL OF INFORMATION MANAGEMENT - ?+ {United Kingdom}
LINK-UP - Sep, 1983+
MEDIABRIEFS - Spring, 1991+
SYSTEMSLETTER - ?+

Instructional
COMMUNICATION BRIEFINGS - Dec, 1981+

Intercultural
INTERCULTURAL & DEVELOPMENT COMMUNICATION NEWSLETTER - ?+

International
COMMUNICATION RESEARCH REPORTS - Dec, 1984+
ICA NEWSLETTER - 1973+
INTERSPACE - 1983+ {United Kingdom}
JOURNAL OF COMMUNICATION MANAGEMENT - Fall, 1971 - May, 1983//
WCA NEWSLETTER - ?+
WORLD COMMUNICATION - Jul, 1972+

Language
VERBATIM - 1974+
WOMEN & LANGUAGE - Jan, 1976+

Legal
CARDOZO ARTS & ENTERTAINMENT LAW JOURNAL - Spring, 1982+
COMMUNICATION LAW & POLICY NEWSLETTER - Nov, 1990+
COMMUNICATIONS LAWYER - Winter, 1983+
HASTINGS COMMUNICATIONS AND ENTERTAINMENT LAW JOURNAL - 1977+
PRIVATE CABLE - Jul/Aug, 1982+
SATELLITE COMMUNICATIONS - Oct, 1977+
SATELLITE NEWS - May, 1978+
SATELLITE WEEK - Jul 30, 1979+

Libraries
BUSINESS INFORMATION ALERT - Jan, 1989+

FORUM - Fall, 1991+

Literature
COMMUNICATION RESEARCH TRENDS - Spring, 1980+ {United Kingdom}
ROTKIN REVIEW, THE - Summer, 1985+

Management
ACA BULLETIN - Oct, 1972+
INTERNATIONAL JOURNAL OF INFORMATION MANAGEMENT - ?+ {United Kingdom}
JOURNAL OF COMMUNICATION MANAGEMENT - Fall, 1971 - May, 1983//
MANAGEMENT COMMUNICATION QUARTERLY - Aug, 1987+
SATELLITE COMMUNICATIONS - Oct, 1977+
SATELLITE NEWS - May, 1978+
SATELLITE WEEK - Jul 30, 1979+

Marketing
AISLE VIEW - ? - Jul 15, 1991//
SALES & MARKETING MANAGEMENT - May 26, 1928+

Membership
MONITOR - Mar, 1979+ {Australia}
SPECIALTY ADVERTISING BUSINESS - 1976+

Minorities
FEMINIST SCHOLARSHIP INTEREST GROUP NEWSLETTER OF THE INTERNATIONAL COMMUNICATION ASSOCIATION - ?+
HOWARD JOURNAL OF COMMUNICATIONS, THE - Spring, 1988+
SCA WOMEN'S CAUCUS AND FEMINIST & WOMEN STUDIES DIVISION NEWSLETTER - ?+
WOMEN & LANGUAGE - Jan, 1976+

Minority
FEMINIST SCHOLARSHIP INTEREST GROUP NEWSLETTER OF THE INTERNATIONAL COMMUNICATION ASSOCIATION - ?+

Music
BAND LEADERS - Nov, 1942 - ?//

Online
LINK-UP - Sep, 1983+

Philosophy
COMMUNIQUÉ - ?+?

Political
POLITICAL COMMUNICATION NEWSLETTER - Spring, 1986+

Popular Culture
JOURNAL OF POPULAR CULTURE - Summer, 1967+

PCS, THE POPULAR CULTURE SCHOLAR - Winter, 1977//?

Programming
STV GUIDE - Jan, 1983 - Jun, 1990//
WHAT SATELLITE - ?+ {United Kingdom}

Promotion
COMMUNIQUÉ - ?+
HORIZON - Summer?, 1986?+?
MARCONI REVIEW, THE - Oct, 1928 - 1st Quarter?, 1983// {United Kingdom}

Public
COMMUNICATION LAW & POLICY NEWSLETTER - Nov, 1990+

Public Relations
COLLEGE & UNIVERSITY JOURNAL - 1917 - May, 1974//
JOURNAL OF EDUCATIONAL PUBLIC RELATIONS - Jul/Aug, 1975+
PR WEEK - 1988+
PRIG - Fall, 1987+
PUBLIC RELATIONS IDEAS - 1951 - Dec, 1965//?
PUBLIC RELATIONS JOURNAL, THE - Oct, 1945+
PUBLIC RELATIONS NEWS - Jan 17, 1944+
PUBLIC RELATIONS QUARTERLY - Oct, 1955+
PUBLIC RELATIONS REVIEW - Summer, 1975+

Regulation
CARDOZO ARTS & ENTERTAINMENT LAW JOURNAL - Spring, 1982+
COMMUNICATIONS LAWYER - Winter, 1983+
HASTINGS COMMUNICATIONS AND ENTERTAINMENT LAW JOURNAL - 1977+
WHAT SATELLITE - ?+ {United Kingdom}

Religion
FORUM - Spring, 1988?+
HOMILETIC - Summer, 1976+
JOURNAL OF COMMUNICATION AND RELIGION, THE - Sep, 1978+

Research
CANADIAN JOURNAL OF COMMUNICATION - Mar, 1974+ {Canada}
COMMUNICATION MONOGRAPHS - 1934+
COMMUNICATION QUARTERLY - Apr, 1953+
COMMUNICATION REPORTS - Winter, 1988+
COMMUNICATION RESEARCH - Jan, 1974+
COMMUNICATION RESEARCH REPORTS - Dec, 1984+
COMMUNICATION RESEARCH TRENDS - Spring, 1980+ {United Kingdom}
COMMUNICATION THEORY - Feb, 1991+
CRITICAL STUDIES IN MASS COMMUNICATION - Mar, 1984+
DISCOURSE & SOCIETY - Jul, 1990+ {United Kingdom}

EDUCATIONAL COMMUNICATION AND TECHNOLOGY - Winter, 1953 - ?, 1988//
FORUM - Fall, 1991+
HOWARD JOURNAL OF COMMUNICATIONS, THE - Spring, 1988+
HUMAN COMMUNICATION RESEARCH - Fall, 1974+
JOURNAL OF APPLIED COMMUNICATION RESEARCH - Winter/Spring, 1973+
JOURNAL OF COMMUNICATION - May, 1951+
JOURNAL OF COMMUNICATION AND RELIGION, THE - Sep, 1978+
JOURNAL OF COMMUNICATION INQUIRY, THE - Spring, 1974+
LANGUAGE & COMMUNICATION - 1981+
LEONARDO - Jan, 1968+
PUBLIC OPINION QUARTERLY - Jan, 1937+
PUBLIC RELATIONS REVIEW - Summer, 1975+
QUARTERLY JOURNAL OF SPEECH, THE - Apr, 1915+
SPECTRA - Oct, 1965+
STUDIES IN VISUAL COMMUNICATION - Fall, 1974 - Fall, 1985//
VERBATIM - 1974+
WESTERN JOURNAL OF SPEECH COMMUNICATION - 1937+
WORLD COMMUNICATION - Jul, 1972+

Retail
SATELLITE RETAILER - Apr, 1985+
STAR SIGNALS - Sep, 1981+
STV GUIDE - Jan, 1983 - Jun, 1990//

Review
C-O-N-N-E-C-T-I-O-N-S - ?+
CD-ROM LIBRARIAN - Jan, 1987+
COMMENT ON THE MEDIA - ?+?
COMMUNICATION - Jun, 1974+ {United Kingdom}
COMMUNICATION WORLD - Winter?, 1971/1972?+
CRITICAL STUDIES IN MASS COMMUNICATION - Mar, 1984+
DIGITAL MEDIA - Jun, 1991+
FORUM - Spring, 1988?+
HOWARD JOURNAL OF COMMUNICATIONS, THE - Spring, 1988+
HUMAN COMMUNICATION RESEARCH - Fall, 1974+
IEEE SPECTRUM - Jan, 1964+
IN SEARCH - Winter, 1974 - #4, 1981?// {Canada}
JOURNAL OF APPLIED COMMUNICATION RESEARCH - Winter/Spring, 1973+
JOURNAL OF POPULAR CULTURE - Summer, 1967+
ORGANIZATIONAL COMMUNICATION NEWSLETTER - Fall, 1980+
PCS, THE POPULAR CULTURE SCHOLAR - Winter, 1977//?
ROTKIN REVIEW, THE - Summer, 1985+
SPECTRA - Oct, 1965+
VISUAL COMMUNICATION NEWSLETTER, THE - ?+

WCA NEWSLETTER - ?+
WORLD COMMUNICATION - Jul, 1972+

Rhetoric
COMMUNICATION STUDIES - Nov, 1949+
PHILOSOPHY AND RHETORIC - Jan, 1968+
RHETORICAL & COMMUNICATION THEORY NEWSLETTER - ?+

Sales
AISLE VIEW - ? - Jul 15, 1991//
SALES & MARKETING MANAGEMENT - May 26, 1928+

Satellites
COMSAT TECHNICAL REVIEW - Fall, 1971+
HORIZON - Summer?, 1986?+?
PRIVATE CABLE - Jul/Aug, 1982+
SATELLITE COMMUNICATIONS - Oct, 1977+
SATELLITE NEWS - May, 1978+
SATELLITE ORBIT - Jul, 1982+
SATELLITE RETAILER - Apr, 1985+
SATELLITE TIMES - ?+ {United Kingdom}
SATELLITE WEEK - Jul 30, 1979+
STAR SIGNALS - Sep, 1981+
STV GUIDE - Jan, 1983 - Jun, 1990//
VIA SATELLITE - Jan, 1986+
WHAT SATELLITE - ?+ {United Kingdom}

School
JOURNAL OF EDUCATIONAL PUBLIC RELATIONS - Jul/Aug, 1975+

Specialty
SPECIALTY ADVERTISING BUSINESS - 1976+

Speech
HOMILETIC - Summer, 1976+
JOURNAL OF BUSINESS COMMUNICATION, THE - Oct, 1963+
PHILOSOPHY AND RHETORIC - Jan, 1968+
WSCA NEWS - Jan, 1984+

Systems
SYSTEMSLETTER - ?+

Technology
CD-ROM - Sep?, 1986+
COMSAT TECHNICAL REVIEW - Fall, 1971+
CRITICAL STUDIES IN MASS COMMUNICATION - Mar, 1984+
EDUCATIONAL COMMUNICATION AND TECHNOLOGY - Winter, 1953 - ?, 1988//
IEEE SPECTRUM - Jan, 1964+
IEEE TRANSACTIONS ON INFORMATION THEORY - Feb, 1953+
LEONARDO - Jan, 1968+
LOS ANGELES TECHNOGRAPH - 1959+?
PRIVATE CABLE - Jul/Aug, 1982+

Electronics

Teletext
COMMUNICATION MONOGRAPHS - 1934+
COMMUNICATION QUARTERLY - Apr, 1953+
COMMUNICATION REPORTS - Winter, 1988+
COMMUNICATION RESEARCH - Jan, 1974+
COMMUNICATION RESEARCH REPORTS - Dec, 1984+
COMMUNICATION THEORY - Feb, 1991+
EDUCATIONAL COMMUNICATION AND TECHNOLOGY - Winter, 1953 - ?, 1988//
JOURNAL OF COMMUNICATION - May, 1951+
JOURNAL OF COMMUNICATION INQUIRY, THE - Spring, 1974+
LANGUAGE & COMMUNICATION - 1981+
RHETORICAL & COMMUNICATION THEORY NEWSLETTER - ?+
WESTERN JOURNAL OF SPEECH COMMUNICATION - 1937+

Visual
VISUAL COMMUNICATION NEWSLETTER, THE - ?+

Women
FEMINIST SCHOLARSHIP INTEREST GROUP NEWSLETTER OF THE INTERNATIONAL COMMUNICATION ASSOCIATION - ?+
SCA WOMEN'S CAUCUS AND FEMINIST & WOMEN STUDIES DIVISION NEWSLETTER - ?+
WOMEN & LANGUAGE - Jan, 1976+

World
WCA NEWSLETTER - ?+

Writing
COMMUNICATION BRIEFINGS - Dec, 1981+
JOURNAL OF BUSINESS COMMUNICATION, THE - Oct, 1963+
JOURNAL OF TECHNICAL WRITING AND COMMUNICATION - Jan, 1971+
LOS ANGELES TECHNOGRAPH - 1959+?
VISIBLE LANGUAGE - Jan, 1967+

Electronics

Amateur
RADIO-ELECTRONICS - Jul, 1929+

Components
ELECTRONIC DESIGN - Dec, 1952+

ELECTRONIC PRODUCTS - 1958+

Design
EUROPEAN TRANSACTIONS ON TELECOMMUNICATIONS AND RELATED TECHNOLOGIES - Jan/Feb, 1990+ {Italy}
IEEE TRANSACTIONS ON COMMUNICATIONS - 1953+
PROCEEDINGS OF THE IEEE - Jan, 1913?+
RF DESIGN - Nov/Dec, 1978+

Engineering
AEU - Jul/Aug, 1947+ {Germany}
ELECTRONIC PRODUCTS - 1958+
ELECTRONICS & COMMUNICATIONS ENGINEERING JOURNAL - Oct, 1926+ {United Kingdom}
ELECTRONICS LETTERS - Mar, 1965+ {United Kingdom}
IEEE TRANSACTIONS ON COMMUNICATIONS - 1953+
PROCEEDINGS OF THE IREE AUSTRALIA - 1937 - Dec?, 1980?// {Australia}
RF DESIGN - Nov/Dec, 1978+
SMPTE JOURNAL - Jul, 1916+
TELECOMMUNICATION JOURNAL OF AUSTRALIA, THE - Jun, 1935+ {Australia}

Home Consumer
ELECTRONICS ILLUSTRATED - May, 1958 - 1972//
RADIO-ELECTRONICS - Jul, 1929+

International
AEU - Jul/Aug, 1947+ {Germany}

Leisure
EXECUTIVES ON THE GO - ?+?

Management
EXECUTIVES ON THE GO - ?+?

Research
ELECTRONICS & COMMUNICATIONS ENGINEERING JOURNAL - Oct, 1926+ {United Kingdom}
ELECTRONICS LETTERS - Mar, 1965+ {United Kingdom}

Review
IEEE SPECTRUM - Jan, 1964+

Servicing
ELECTRONIC TECHNICAN/DEALER - Sep, 1953 - Mar, 1982//

Technology
AEU - Jul/Aug, 1947+ {Germany}
ELECTRONIC DESIGN - Dec, 1952+
ELECTRONIC PRODUCTS - 1958+

ELECTRONICS & COMMUNICATIONS ENGINEERING JOURNAL - Oct, 1926+ {United Kingdom}
ELECTRONICS ILLUSTRATED - May, 1958 - 1972//
ELECTRONICS LETTERS - Mar, 1965+ {United Kingdom}
EUROPEAN TRANSACTIONS ON TELECOMMUNICATIONS AND RELATED TECHNOLOGIES - Jan/Feb, 1990+ {Italy}
IEEE SPECTRUM - Jan, 1964+
PROCEEDINGS OF THE IEEE - Jan, 1913?+
PROCEEDINGS OF THE IREE AUSTRALIA - 1937 - Dec?, 1980?// {Australia}
RADIO-ELECTRONICS - Jul, 1929+
RF DESIGN - Nov/Dec, 1978+
SMPTE JOURNAL - Jul, 1916+
TELECOMMUNICATION JOURNAL OF AUSTRALIA, THE - Jun, 1935+ {Australia}

Teletext
EUROPEAN TRANSACTIONS ON TELECOMMUNICATIONS AND RELATED TECHNOLOGIES - Jan/Feb, 1990+ {Italy}

Unions & Guilds
JOURNAL - ?, 1893+

Film

Academic
DIGEST - ?+?
DIGEST OF THE UNIVERSITY FILM AND VIDEO ASSOCIATION - ?+
FILMMAKERS FILM & VIDEO MONTHLY - Nov, 1967 - Jan/Feb, 1982//
JOURNAL OF FILM AND VIDEO - Mar, 1949+

Advertising
FLASH - Jul/Aug, 1990+

Aesthetics
ART & CINEMA - Jan, 1973+
FLASH - Jul/Aug, 1990+
IRIS - Mar, 1983+
POST SCRIPT - Fall, 1981+

Alternative Media
CINEMA NOW - 1968+?
CINEMANEWS, THE - Jan, 1963 - 1980?//?
INDEPENDENT MEDIA - Mar, 1983?+ {United Kingdom}

Amateur
HOME MOVIES - 1934+

Animation
ANIMAFILM - 1979+ {Italy}

Electronics — Satellite (listing above Teletext)
SATELLITE COMMUNICATIONS - Oct, 1977+
SATELLITE NEWS - May, 1978+
SATELLITE WEEK - Jul 30, 1979+
STAR SIGNALS - Sep, 1981+
WHAT SATELLITE - ?+ {United Kingdom}

ANIMATION MAGAZINE - Jan, 1987+
ANIMATOI - 1983+
ANIMATOR - Jan, 1978?+ {United Kingdom}
ANYMATOR - ?+
ASIFA NOUVELLES - May, 1988+ {Belgium}
PEGBAR - ?+ {Canada}
WITTYWORLD - Summer, 1987+

Artist
BOMB MAGAZINE - Spring, 1981+

Avant-garde
FILMMAKERS FILM & VIDEO MONTHLY - Nov, 1967 - Jan/Feb, 1982//
HIGH PERFORMANCE - Feb, 1978+

Boston
ART DYNAMO - Summer, 1991?+

Business
ANIMATOR - Jan, 1978?+ {United Kingdom}
FILM MEDIA - Jun, 1957 - Jan/Mar, 1960//
INDEPENDENT, THE - Jan, 1978+
VIDEO SOFTWARE MAGAZINE - Sep, 1985+
VIDEO STORE - Aug, 1979+

Cartoons
WITTYWORLD - Summer, 1987+

Cassettes
PREVIEWS - ? - Dec, 1980//
V - Oct, 1987+
VIDEO SOFTWARE MAGAZINE - Sep, 1985+
VIDEO STORE - Aug, 1979+
VIDEO TIMES - Jan, 1985+
VIDEO WATCHDOG - Sep/Oct, 1990+

Collector
FILM FAN MONTHLY - 1961 - Jun, 1975//

Commercial
BACK STAGE/SHOOT - Jul 6, 1990+

Computers
COMPUTER PICTURES - Jan/Feb, 1983+

Corporate
SCIENTIFIC FILM - Jun, 1960 - Dec, 1965// {United Kingdom}

Distribution
COMPUTER PICTURES - Jan/Feb, 1983+
INDEPENDENT, THE - Jan, 1978+

Documentary
FILM & VIDEO NEWS - Dec, 1939 - Apr, 1984//
INTERNATIONAL DOCUMENTARY - Summer, 1989?+

PERSPECTIVES ON FILM - ?+?

Exhibition
PERFORMER, THE - Spring, 1978+

Finance
INDEPENDENT, THE - Jan, 1978+

Graphics
COMPUTER PICTURES - Jan/Feb, 1983+
FLASH - Jul/Aug, 1990+

Guide
AMERICAN MOVIE CLASSICS MAGAZINE - Jan, 1988+
EFLA BULLETIN - Summer, 1977 - #3/4, 1987//
FILM & VIDEO NEWS - Dec, 1939 - Apr, 1984//
FILM FORUM REVIEW - Spring, 1946 - Winter, 1948/49//
FILM MONTHLY - Jan, 1950?+ {United Kingdom}
FILMIS - ?, 1969? - ?, 1979?// {Italy}
MASS MEDIA NEWSLETTER - 1964? - Dec 14, 1981//
MEDIA ARTS - 1980+?
MOVING PICTURE AGE - Mar, 1918 - Dec, 1922//
PREVIEWS - ? - Dec, 1980//
SEQUENCE - May, 1946 - 1952// {United Kingdom}
V - Oct, 1987+
VIDEO TIMES - Jan, 1985+
VIDEO WATCHDOG - Sep/Oct, 1990+
YOUNG VIEWERS - Fall, 1977 - ?, 1988//

Historical
ANIMATOI - 1983+
FILM & HISTORY - Mar, 1971+
FILM FAN MONTHLY - 1961 - Jun, 1975//

Home Consumer
CINEMAGIC - Winter, 1972+
EIGHT MM MOVIE MAKER AND CINE CAMERA - ? - Feb, 1967// {United Kingdom}
FILM MAKING - 1962? - Oct, 1980// {United Kingdom}
MOVIE MAKERS - Dec, 1926 - Nov, 1954//
MOVING IMAGE - Winter, 1972/1973 - Jun, 1982//

Independent
CINEMANEWS, THE - Jan, 1963 - 1980?//?
FILMMAKERS FILM & VIDEO MONTHLY - Nov, 1967 - Jan/Feb, 1982//
INDEPENDENT, THE - Jan, 1978+

Instructional
AFVA BULLETIN - Sep/Oct, 1967+
AUDIO VISUAL - Nov, 1946+ {United Kingdom}
AVC - May, 1961+
EDUCATIONAL SCREEN - Jan, 1922 - Sum, 1956//
FILM & VIDEO NEWS - Dec, 1939 - Apr, 1984//

FILM FORUM REVIEW - Spring, 1946 - Winter, 1948/49//
FILM LIBRARY QUARTERLY - Winter, 1967/68 - 1985//
FILM WORLD AND A-V NEWS MAGAZINE - Feb, 1945 - Jun, 1966//

Intercultural
FILMIS - ?, 1969? - ?, 1979?// {Italy}

International
AFTERIMAGE - Apr, 1970 - Spring, 1981// {United Kingdom}
ANIMAFILM - 1979+ {Italy}
ASIFA NOUVELLES - May, 1988+ {Belgium}
INTERNATIONAL DOCUMENTARY - Summer, 1989?+
IRIS - Mar, 1983+
WORLD SCREEN - Dec, 1959+? {Italy}

Libraries
EFLA BULLETIN - Summer, 1977 - #3/4, 1987//
FILM LIBRARY QUARTERLY - Winter, 1967/68 - 1985//

Marketing
FILM MEDIA - Jun, 1957 - Jan/Mar, 1960//

Museums
MEDIA ARTS - 1980+?

New England
ART DYNAMO - Summer, 1991?+

New York City
BACK STAGE/SHOOT - Jul 6, 1990+

Performance
HIGH PERFORMANCE - Feb, 1978+

Producing
CINE NEWS - May?, 1991+
INTERNATIONAL DOCUMENTARY - Summer, 1989?+

Production
ANIMATOR - Jan, 1978?+ {United Kingdom}
BACK STAGE/SHOOT - Jul 6, 1990+
CINE-KODAK NEWS, THE - Jun, 1924+?
CINE NEWS - May?, 1991+
CINEMAGIC - Winter, 1972+
CINEMANEWS, THE - Jan, 1963 - 1980?//?
COMPUTER PICTURES - Jan/Feb, 1983+
EIGHT MM MOVIE MAKER AND CINE CAMERA - ? - Feb, 1967// {United Kingdom}
ENTERTAINMENT MONTHLY - 1977+
FILM MAKING - 1962? - Oct, 1980// {United Kingdom}
FILM WORLD AND A-V NEWS MAGAZINE - Feb, 1945 - Jun, 1966//

Magazines — Subject Heading

FILMMAKERS FILM & VIDEO MONTHLY - Nov, 1967 - Jan/Feb, 1982//
FILMO TOPICS - 1925 - ?//?
HOME MOVIES - 1934+
INDEPENDENT, THE - Jan, 1978+
INDEPENDENT MEDIA - Mar, 1983?+ (United Kingdom)
INSIDE ENTERTAINMENT - ?+
INTERNATIONAL DOCUMENTARY - Summer, 1989?+
JOURNAL OF FILM AND VIDEO - Mar, 1949+
MAKING FILMS - Mar, 1967 - Dec, 1975/Jan, 1976//
MILLIMETER - 1973+
MOVIE MAKERS - Dec, 1926 - Nov, 1954//
MOVING IMAGE - Winter, 1972/1973 - Jun, 1982//
PRINTED MATTER - ?, 1974+
REEL LIFE - ?, 1989+
SCIENCE AND FILM - Feb, 1952 - Apr, 1960// (United Kingdom)
SCIENTIFIC FILM - Jun, 1960 - Dec, 1965// (United Kingdom)
TRAVEL & LEISURE - 1935+

Programming
AMERICAN MOVIE CLASSICS MAGAZINE - Jan, 1988+

Promotion
APERTURE, THE - May, 1959+?
BOLEX REPORTER, THE - Dec, 1950 - 1974//
CINE-KODAK NEWS, THE - Jun, 1924+?
FILMO TOPICS - 1925 - ?//?
INSIDE ENTERTAINMENT - ?+
PRINTED MATTER - ?, 1974+

Puppetry
ANIMATIONS - Oct/Nov, 1977+ (United Kingdom)

Religion
FILMIS - ?, 1969? - ?, 1979?// (Italy)
MASS MEDIA NEWSLETTER - 1964? - Dec 14, 1981//

Research
FILM & HISTORY - Mar, 1971+
JOURNAL OF FILM AND VIDEO - Mar, 1949+
LEONARDO - Jan, 1968+
SCIENCE AND FILM - Feb, 1952 - Apr, 1960// (United Kingdom)
SCIENTIFIC FILM - Jun, 1960 - Dec, 1965// (United Kingdom)

Review
AFTERIMAGE - Apr, 1970 - Spring, 1981// (United Kingdom)
AFVA BULLETIN - Sep/Oct, 1967+
ANIMATION MAGAZINE - Jan, 1987+
ART & CINEMA - Jan, 1973+
ART DYNAMO - Summer, 1991?+
BOMB MAGAZINE - Spring, 1981+

CINEMA NOW - 1968+?
CINEMANEWS, THE - Jan, 1963 - 1980?//?
JOURNAL OF FILM AND VIDEO - Mar, 1949+
WORLD SCREEN - Dec, 1959+? (Italy)
YOUNG VIEWERS - Fall, 1977 - ?, 1988//

School
EDUCATIONAL SCREEN - Jan, 1922 - Sum, 1956//
FILM & VIDEO NEWS - Dec, 1939 - Apr, 1984//
FILM WORLD AND A-V NEWS MAGAZINE - Feb, 1945 - Jun, 1966//
MOVING PICTURE AGE - Mar, 1918 - Dec, 1922//

Society
POST SCRIPT - Fall, 1981+
SEQUENCE - May, 1946 - 1952// (United Kingdom)

Teaching
DIGEST OF THE UNIVERSITY FILM AND VIDEO ASSOCIATION - ?+
FILM & HISTORY - Mar, 1971+

Technology
APERTURE, THE - May, 1959+?
BOLEX REPORTER, THE - Dec, 1950 - 1974//
EDUCATIONAL SCREEN - Jan, 1922 - Sum, 1956//
LEONARDO - Jan, 1968+
MILLIMETER - 1973+
SCIENCE AND FILM - Feb, 1952 - Apr, 1960// (United Kingdom)
SCIENTIFIC FILM - Jun, 1960 - Dec, 1965// (United Kingdom)
TRAVEL & LEISURE - 1935+

Teletext
IRIS - Mar, 1983+
POST SCRIPT - Fall, 1981+

Travel
TRAVEL & LEISURE - 1935+

Virginia
REEL LIFE - ?, 1989+

Youth
YOUNG VIEWERS - Fall, 1977 - ?, 1988//

Magazines

Acting
CASTING CALL - Jan 17, 1976+

Advocate
LIES OF OUR TIMES - Jan, 1990+

Animation
KORKIS AND CAWLEY'S CARTOON QUARTERLY - Winter, 1988+

Business
COLORADO EDITOR - 1926+
FOLIO: - Jun, 1972+
MAGAZINE BUSINESS - Apr, 1989+
MAGAZINE DESIGN & PRODUCTION - May, 1985+
MAGAZINE MATTER - ?+
MAGAZINES IN DEPTH - ?+
MAGAZINEWEEK - Nov 8?, 1987+

Cartoons
KORKIS AND CAWLEY'S CARTOON QUARTERLY - Winter, 1988+

Circulation
FOLIO: - Jun, 1972+

Collector
FOUR COLOR - Nov/Dec, 1986+

Colorado
COLORADO EDITOR - 1926+

Comics
AMAZING HEROES - Jun, 1981+
COMIC READER, THE - Jul, 1978?+?
FA - ?+ (United Kingdom)
FOUR COLOR - Nov/Dec, 1986+
GOLDEN AGE OF COMICS - Jun?, 1982+

Design
EDITOR'S WORKSHOP - ?+

Distribution
ABC NEWS BULLETIN - 1914+

Employment
CASTING CALL - Jan 17, 1976+
MAGAZINES IN DEPTH - ?+

Ethics
LIES OF OUR TIMES - Jan, 1990+

Fan
DWB - ?+ (United Kingdom)

Finance
MAGAZINEWEEK - Nov 8?, 1987+

Guide
AMAZING HEROES - Jun, 1981+

RSAP NEWSLETTER - Winter, 1990+

Historical
KORKIS AND CAWLEY'S CARTOON QUARTERLY - Winter, 1988+
RSAP NEWSLETTER - Winter, 1990+

House Organ
NBC NEWSLINE - ?+?

International
PRESS, THE - Jan/Feb, 1973?+?

Journalism
LIES OF OUR TIMES - Jan, 1990+

Libraries
SERIALS REVIEW - Jan/Jun, 1975+

Management
ABC NEWS BULLETIN - 1914+
FOLIO: - Jun, 1972+

Marketing
PUBLISHING TRENDS & TRENDSETTERS - ?+

Membership
SUCCESSFUL MAGAZINE PUBLISHING - Jan/Feb, 1984 - Nov/Dec, 1989//

News
EDITOR'S WORKSHOP - ?+
LIES OF OUR TIMES - Jan, 1990+
PRESS, THE - Jan/Feb, 1973?+?

Newsletter
EDITOR'S WORKSHOP - ?+

Printing
MAGAZINE BUSINESS - Apr, 1989+
MAGAZINE DESIGN & PRODUCTION - May, 1985+

Production
MAGAZINEWEEK - Nov 8?, 1987+
PRESS, THE - Jan/Feb, 1973?+?

Promotion
FOLIO: - Jun, 1972+

Publishing
COLORADO EDITOR - 1926+
MAGAZINE BUSINESS - Apr, 1989+
MAGAZINE DESIGN & PRODUCTION - May, 1985+
MAGAZINES IN DEPTH - ?+
MAGAZINEWEEK - Nov 8?, 1987+
PUBLISHING TRENDS & TRENDSETTERS - ?+
SERIALS REVIEW - Jan/Jun, 1975+
SUCCESSFUL MAGAZINE PUBLISHING - Jan/Feb, 1984 - Nov/Dec, 1989//

Research
MAGAZINE MATTER - ?+
MAGAZINES IN DEPTH - ?+
RSAP NEWSLETTER - Winter, 1990+

Review
COMIC READER, THE - Jul, 1978?+?
FA - ?+ {United Kingdom}
FOUR COLOR - Nov/Dec, 1986+
RSAP NEWSLETTER - Winter, 1990+

Science Fiction

Typography
MAGAZINE DESIGN & PRODUCTION - May, 1985+
MAGAZINEWEEK - Nov 8?, 1987+

Mail

Advertising
DIRECT MARKETING - Sep, 1927+
DM NEWS - Sep, 1979+
MAILBAG, THE - Apr, 1917 - Aug, 1927//
MAST - Jan, 1988+
WHAT'S WORKING - ?+
WHO'S MAILING WHAT! - Oct, 1984+

Business
TARGET MARKETING - Jan, 1978+

Direct Marketing
DIRECT MARKETING - Sep, 1927+
DIRECT RESPONSE SPECIALIST, THE - Feb, 1987?+
DM NEWS - Sep, 1979+
MAIL ORDER DIGEST - ?+
MAILBAG, THE - Apr, 1917 - Aug, 1927//
MAST - Jan, 1988+
MEMO TO MAILERS - Jan, 1966?+
TARGET MARKETING - Jan, 1978+
WHAT'S WORKING - ?+
WHO'S MAILING WHAT! - Oct, 1984+

Distribution
POSTAL WATCH - Aug 3, 1990+

Guide
POSTAL WATCH - Aug 3, 1990+

Marketing
DIRECT MARKETING - Sep, 1927+
DIRECT RESPONSE SPECIALIST, THE - Feb, 1987?+
DM NEWS - Sep, 1979+

Production
TARGET MARKETING - Jan, 1978+
WHAT'S WORKING - ?+
WHO'S MAILING WHAT! - Oct, 1984+

Review
MAIL ORDER DIGEST - ?+
MAILBAG, THE - Apr, 1917 - Aug, 1927//

Technology
MAST - Jan, 1988+
POSTAL WATCH - Aug 3, 1990+

Writing
DIRECT RESPONSE SPECIALIST, THE - Feb, 1987?+

Mass Media

Academic
AEJMC NEWS - 1968?+
ASIAN JOURNAL OF COMMUNICATION - Sep, 1990+ {Singapore}
C-O-N-N-E-C-T-I-O-N-S - ?+
CAT NEWS - ?+
CMA NEWSLETTER - ?+
COLLEGE MEDIA REVIEW - Summer, 1983+
COLLEGIATE JOURNALIST - Fall, 1963+
COMMUNICATION MONOGRAPHS - 1934+
OHIO JOURNALIST, THE - Winter, 1976+
PUBLIC RELATIONS IDEAS - 1951 - Dec, 1965//?

Access
ACCESS - Jan 13, 1975 - 1985//

Acting
SHOW BIZ WEST - 1979+

Activist
AIM REPORT - Aug, 1972+
MEDIA WATCH - ?+?

Advertising
AD • MENTOR, THE - ?+
AD WEEKLY - ? - ?// {United Kingdom}
ADVERTISING - Mar, 1892 - Jul 9, 1925//
ADVERTISING AGE - 1930+
ADVERTISING AGENCY - Apr, 1923 - Aug 29, 1958//

ADVERTISING ALERT - Nov 6, 1961 - Nov 10, 1965?//?
ADVERTISING AND MARKETING MANAGEMENT - 1964 - Jul, 1970// {United Kingdom}
ADVERTISING MAGAZINE - Autumn, 1964+ {United Kingdom}
ADVERTISING NEWS - 1928+ {Australia}
ADWEEK - 1913+ {United Kingdom}
ADWEEK - Dec, 1951+
ADWEEK'S MARKETING WEEK - Jun, 1980+
AGENCY - Spring, 1990+
AM - May, 1964+ {United Kingdom}
AMERICAN DEMOGRAPHICS - Jan, 1979+
ASIAN ADVERTISING & MARKETING - Jan, 1986+ {Hong Kong}
BUSINESS MARKETING - Jan, 1915+
CAMPAIGN - 1929+ {United Kingdom}
CHRISTIAN ADVERTISING FORUM - Apr/May, 1981+
COMMUNIQUE - 1919 - ?//
DIRECTION - ?+ {United Kingdom}
EXPORT ADVERTISER - Dec, 1928 - Jun, 1932//
FOCUS - Jan, 1979 - Jul, 1987//
FOUR A NEWSLETTER - ?+
4A'S WASHINGTON NEWSLETTER, THE - ?+?
GAZETTE - Jan, 1955+ {Netherlands}
INSIDE MEDIA - Sep 13, 1989+
INTERNATIONAL ADVERTISER - Jul, 1976 - Nov/Dec, 1983//
INTERNATIONAL ADVERTISER - ?+
INTERNATIONAL ADVERTISER, THE - Jun, 1960+
INTERNATIONAL JOURNAL OF ADVERTISING - Jan, 1982+? {United Kingdom}
JOURNAL OF ADVERTISING - 1972+
JOURNAL OF ADVERTISING RESEARCH - Sep, 1960+
JOURNAL OF MARKETING - Jul, 1936+
MADISON AVENUE - Apr, 1958+
MARKETING / COMMUNICATIONS - Jul 15, 1888 - Jan, 1972//
MARKETING COMMUNICATIONS - 1976 - May, 1989//
MEDIA & VALUES - 1977+
MEDIA INTERNATIONAL - 1973+ {United Kingdom}
MEDIA WEEK - Apr 12, 1985+ {United Kingdom}
MEDIAWEEK - Sep, 1966+
PRESS STATISTICAL REVIEW - ? - 1975// {United Kingdom}
PROMOTION - Feb, 1953 - May 13, 1974//
PSA - Fall, 1982+
RETAIL EQUIPMENT AND MERCHANDISE - 1892+?
SCHEMER, THE - Jan, 1898+?
SOCIAL SCIENCE MONITOR - Jan, 1979+
YELLOW SHEET, THE - 1984?+

Advisement
CMA NEWSLETTER - ?+
COLLEGE MEDIA REVIEW - Summer, 1983+

Advocate
BUSINESS AND THE MEDIA - Fall, 1979+

Agency
AD • MENTOR, THE - ?+
AGENCY - Spring, 1990+
YELLOW SHEET, THE - 1984?+

Application
NEWS COMPUTING JOURNAL - 1964?+

Artist
BLACK STARS - Nov, 1950 - Jul, 1981//
FAME - Jun, 1988 - Dec, 1990//
INTERVIEW - 1969+
NATIONAL ENQUIRER - 1926+
NATIONAL EXAMINER - Jan, 1964+
SHOW BIZ WEST - 1979+
STAR - Jan 4, 1974+
UNIQUE - Jul/Aug, 1990 - Sep/Oct, 1990//
US MAGAZINE - May 3, 1977+

Asia
ASIAN ADVERTISING & MARKETING - Jan, 1986+ {Hong Kong}
ASIAN JOURNAL OF COMMUNICATION - Sep, 1990+ {Singapore}
MEDIA ASIA - 1974+ {Singapore}

Black
BLACK JOURNALISM REVIEW - Summer, 1976+?
BLACK STARS - Nov, 1950 - Jul, 1981//

Business
ADVERTISING - Mar, 1892 - Jul 9, 1925//
ENTERTAINMENT WORLD - Oct 3, 1969 - May 29, 1970//
ERNST & YOUNG ENTERTAINMENT BUSINESS JOURNAL - Spring, 1989?+
EUROPEAN JOURNAL OF COMMUNICATION - Mar, 1986+ {United Kingdom}
HYPERMEDIA - Summer, 1988+?
INSIDE MEDIA - Sep 13, 1989+
JOURNAL OF MEDIA ECONOMICS - Spring, 1988+
KAGAN MEDIA INDEX, THE - Mar 10, 1987+
MEDIA BUSINESS MARKETS - ?+
MEDIA INDUSTRY NEWSLETTER - Nov, 1947+
MEDIA MATTERS - ?+

College
PUBLIC RELATIONS IDEAS - 1951 - Dec, 1965//?

Community
GF MAGAZINE - Spring?, 1989+

Computers
HYPERMEDIA - Summer, 1988+?
NEWS COMPUTING JOURNAL - 1964?+

Corporate
AM - May, 1964+ {United Kingdom}
BUSINESS MARKETING - Jan, 1915+

Cultural
DISCOURSE & SOCIETY - Jul, 1990+ {United Kingdom}
FANFARE - 1964 - 1983//
HOWARD JOURNAL OF COMMUNICATIONS, THE - Spring, 1988+
MASS COMM REVIEW - Aug, 1973+
MEDIA ANTHROPOLOGIST NEWSLETTER - Fall, 1972+
MEDIA ASIA - 1974+ {Singapore}
MEDIA, CULTURE, AND SOCIETY - Jan, 1979+ {United Kingdom}
TECHNOLOGY AND CULTURE - Winter, 1959+
TELEMATICS AND INFORMATICS - 1984+
UNIQUE - Jul/Aug, 1990 - Sep/Oct, 1990//
UNIVERSITY VISION - ? - 1976// {United Kingdom}

Demographics
AMERICAN DEMOGRAPHICS - Jan, 1979+

Digital
DIGITAL MEDIA - Jun, 1991+

Discourse
DISCOURSE & SOCIETY - Jul, 1990+ {United Kingdom}

Economics
JOURNAL OF MEDIA ECONOMICS - Spring, 1988+

Electronics
ELECTRONICS - Apr, 1930+
ELECTRONICS & COMMUNICATIONS - Mar/Apr 1953 - Feb, 1984// {Canada}
ELECTRONICS WORLD - Jul, 1919 - Dec, 1971//
ELECTRONICS WORLD + WIRELESS WORLD - Apr, 1922+ {United Kingdom}
ETI - Jan, 1972?+ {United Kingdom}

Emerging
MARKETING NEW MEDIA - Mar 7, 1984+
TELEMATICS AND INFORMATICS - 1984+

Employment
CMA NEWSLETTER - ?+
COLLEGE MEDIA REVIEW - Summer, 1983+
HIGH TECH LIFESTYLES - ?, 1988+
SHOW BIZ WEST - 1979+

Engineering
AEG-TELEFUNKEN PROGRESS - ? - #2, 1982// {Germany}

ELECTRONICS - Apr, 1930+

ELECTRONICS & COMMUNICATIONS - Mar/Apr 1953 - Feb, 1984// {Canada}

ELECTRONICS LETTERS - Mar, 1965+ {United Kingdom}

ELECTRONICS WORLD - Jul, 1919 - Dec, 1971//

ELECTRONICS WORLD + WIRELESS WORLD - Apr, 1922+ {United Kingdom}

SMPTE JOURNAL - Jul, 1916+

Ethics

COLUMBIA JOURNALISM REVIEW - Fall, 1961+

EXTRA! - Jul, 1987+

GANNETT CENTER JOURNAL - Spring, 1987+

MEDIA & CONSUMER - Apr, 1972 - Aug, 1975//

MEDIA & VALUES - 1977+

MEDIA ETHICS UPDATE - Spring, 1988+

MEDIA REPORTER, THE - 1976+ {United Kingdom}

NEWS MEDIA & THE LAW, THE - Mar/Apr, 1973+

Europe

EUROPEAN JOURNAL OF COMMUNICATION - Mar, 1986+ {United Kingdom}

Fan

BLACK STARS - Nov, 1950 - Jul, 1981//

LIBERTY, THEN AND NOW - Summer, 1971+?

NATIONAL ENQUIRER - 1926+

NATIONAL EXAMINER - Jan, 1964+

SPERDVAC - Winter, 1976+?

STAR - Jan 4, 1974+

US MAGAZINE - May 3, 1977+

Finance

ERNST & YOUNG ENTERTAINMENT BUSINESS JOURNAL - Spring, 1989?+

INSIDE MEDIA - Sep 13, 1989+

KAGAN MEDIA INDEX, THE - Mar 10, 1987+

MEDIA BUSINESS MARKETS - ?+

MEDIA INDUSTRY NEWSLETTER - Nov, 1947+

Freedom of the Press

ACCESS REPORTS/FREEDOM OF INFORMATION - Jun 16, 1975+

CENSORSHIP NEWS - Spring, 1980+

COLLEGIATE JOURNALIST - Fall, 1963+

FOI DIGEST - May/June, 1959 - Nov/Dec, 1985//

GANNETT CENTER JOURNAL - Spring, 1987+

INDEX ON CENSORSHIP - Spring, 1972+ {United Kingdom}

NEWS MEDIA & THE LAW, THE - Mar/Apr, 1973+

Graphics

DIRECTION - ?+ {United Kingdom}

Guide

ENTERTAINMENT WEEKLY - Feb 16, 1990+

FAME - Jun, 1988 - Dec, 1990//

MEDIA SPOTLIGHT - 1978?+?

Historical

EUROPEAN JOURNAL OF COMMUNICATION - Mar, 1986+ {United Kingdom}

GOOD OLD DAYS - 1964+

JOE FRANKLIN'S NOSTALGIA - March, 1990+

JOURNALISM HISTORY - Spring, 1974+

LIBERTY, THEN AND NOW - Summer, 1971+?

MEDIA HISTORY DIGEST - Fall, 1980+

MEDIA SIGHT - Winter, 1982+?

MEMORIES - Spring, 1988+

NEW CAPTAIN GEORGE'S WHIZZBANG, THE - Nov/Dec, 1968+ {Canada}

NOSTALGIA ILLUSTRATED - Nov, 1974+

SPERDVAC - Winter, 1976+?

TECHNOLOGY AND CULTURE - Winter, 1959+

Home Consumer

ETI - Jan, 1972?+ {United Kingdom}

House Organ

GANNETTEER - Jan, 1955+

SCRIPPS HOWARD NEWS - ?+

UPI ADVANCE - Jan, 1989+

Information

DISCOURSE & SOCIETY - Jul, 1990+ {United Kingdom}

INTERNATIONAL JOURNAL OF INFORMATION MANAGEMENT - ?+ {United Kingdom}

SYSTEMSLETTER - ?+

Instructional

AID - 1961 - 1963//

HYPERMEDIA - Summer, 1988+?

Interactive

HYPERMEDIA - Summer, 1988+?

MEDIA ANTHROPOLOGIST NEWSLETTER - Fall, 1972+

Intercultural

ACTION - Jul, 1975+ {United Kingdom}

CHRONICLE OF INTERNATIONAL COMMUNICATION - Jan, 1980 - Sep/Oct, 1985//

GANNETT CENTER JOURNAL - Spring, 1987+

MEDIA DEVELOPMENT - Winter, 1953+ {United Kingdom}

International

ACTION - Jul, 1975+ {United Kingdom}

AD WEEKLY - ? - ?// {United Kingdom}

ADVERTISING AGE - 1930+

AEG-TELEFUNKEN PROGRESS - ? - #2, 1982// {Germany}

CHRONICLE OF INTERNATIONAL COMMUNICATION - Jan, 1980 - Sep/Oct, 1985//

COMMUNICATIONS - 1974+ {Germany}

DEMOCRATIC JOURNALIST - Nov, 1953+ {Czechoslovakia}

ELECTRONICS - Apr, 1930+

EXPORT ADVERTISER - Dec, 1928 - Jun, 1932//

FOCUS - Jan, 1979 - Jul, 1987///

GANNETT CENTER JOURNAL - Spring, 1987+

GAZETTE - Jan, 1955+ {Netherlands}

IFJ INFORMATION - Jul, 1952+ {Belgium}

INDEX ON CENSORSHIP - Spring, 1972+ {United Kingdom}

INTERNATIONAL ADVERTISER - Jul, 1976 - Nov/Dec, 1983//

INTERNATIONAL ADVERTISER - ?+

INTERNATIONAL ADVERTISER, THE - Jun, 1960+

INTERNATIONAL EDUCATIONAL AND CULTURAL EXCHANGE - Summer, 1965 - Summer, 1978//

INTERNATIONAL JOURNAL OF ADVERTISING - Jan, 1982+? {United Kingdom}

JOURNAL OF MEDIA ECONOMICS - Spring, 1988+

MEDIA ASIA - 1974+ {Singapore}

MEDIA DEVELOPMENT - Winter, 1953+ {United Kingdom}

MEDIA INTERNATIONAL - 1973+ {United Kingdom}

TELEMATICS AND INFORMATICS - 1984+

WORLD COMMUNICATION - Jul, 1972+

WORLD MEDIA REPORT - Feb, 1983+

Journalism

BLACK JOURNALISM REVIEW - Summer, 1976+?

BUSINESS AND THE MEDIA - Fall, 1979+

GANNETT CENTER JOURNAL - Spring, 1987+

GAZETTE - Jan, 1955+ {Netherlands}

JOURNALISM HISTORY - Spring, 1974+

MEDIA ETHICS UPDATE - Spring, 1988+

MEDIA REPORTER, THE - 1976+ {United Kingdom}

MEDIAWATCH - Jan, 1987+

MORE - Jun, 1971 - Jun, 1978//

NEWS MEDIA & THE LAW, THE - Mar/Apr, 1973+

OHIO JOURNALIST, THE - Winter, 1976+

QUILL, THE - 1912+

QUILL AND SCROLL - Oct, 1926+

Language

VERBATIM - 1974+

Legal

CABLE TV AND NEW MEDIA LAW & FINANCE - ?+

COMMUNICATIONS AND THE LAW - Winter, 1979+

COMMUNICATIONS LAWYER - Winter, 1983+

ENTERTAINMENT AND SPORTS LAWYER, THE - Spring, 1982+

ERNST & YOUNG ENTERTAINMENT BUSINESS JOURNAL - Spring, 1989?+

Mass Media
Subject Heading

FORDHAM ENTERTAINMENT, MEDIA & INTELLECTUAL PROPERTY LAW FORUM - Autumn, 1990+

HASTINGS COMMUNICATIONS AND ENTERTAINMENT LAW JOURNAL - 1977+

JOURNAL OF LAW & TECHNOLOGY, THE - 1986 - Winter, 1990//

LOYOLA ENTERTAINMENT JOURNAL - Apr, 1981+

MEDIA LAW NOTES - Fall, 1973?+

NEWS MEDIA & THE LAW, THE - Mar/Apr, 1973+

Libraries

FORUM - Fall, 1991+

MASS COMMUNICATION BIBLIOGRAPHERS' NEWSLETTER - Nov, 1987?+

Literature

CRC NEWSLETTER - Jan, 1975+

MASS COMMUNICATION BIBLIOGRAPHERS' NEWSLETTER - Nov, 1987?+

ROTKIN REVIEW, THE - Summer, 1985+

Management

ADVERTISING - Mar, 1892 - Jul 9, 1925//

CAMPAIGN - 1929+ {United Kingdom}

CMA NEWSLETTER - ?+

COLLEGE MEDIA REVIEW - Summer, 1983+

ERNST & YOUNG ENTERTAINMENT BUSINESS JOURNAL - Spring, 1989?+

INTERNATIONAL JOURNAL OF INFORMATION MANAGEMENT - ?+ {United Kingdom}

SOCIAL SCIENCE MONITOR - Jan, 1979+

Marketing

ADVERTISING AGE - 1930+

ADVERTISING ALERT - Nov 6, 1961 - Nov 10, 1965?//?

ADVERTISING AND MARKETING MANAGEMENT - 1964 - Jul, 1970// {United Kingdom}

ADWEEK - Dec, 1951+

ADWEEK'S MARKETING WEEK - Jun, 1980+

AM - May, 1964+ {United Kingdom}

AMERICAN DEMOGRAPHICS - Jan, 1979+

ASIAN ADVERTISING & MARKETING - Jan, 1986+ {Hong Kong}

BUSINESS MARKETING - Jan, 1915+

COMMUNIQUE - 1919 - ?//

DIRECTION - ?+ {United Kingdom}

EXPORT ADVERTISER - Dec, 1928 - Jun, 1932//

FOCUS - Jan, 1979 - Jul, 1987//

INSIDE MEDIA - Sep 13, 1989+

INTERNATIONAL ADVERTISER - Jul, 1976 - Nov/Dec, 1983//

INTERNATIONAL ADVERTISER - ?+

INTERNATIONAL ADVERTISER, THE - Jun, 1960+

JMR, JOURNAL OF MARKETING RESEARCH - Feb, 1964+

JOURNAL OF MARKETING EDUCATION - ?+

MARKETING / COMMUNICATIONS - Jul 15, 1888 - Jan, 1972//

MARKETING COMMUNICATIONS - 1976 - May, 1989//

MARKETING NEWS - Oct, 1967+

MEDIA INDUSTRY NEWSLETTER - Nov, 1947+

MEDIA INTERNATIONAL - 1973+ {United Kingdom}

MEDIAWEEK - Sep, 1966+

PROFIT MARKETING HOTLINE - Winter, 1988/1989+

PROMOTION - Feb, 1953 - May 13, 1974//

SCHEMER, THE - Jan, 1898+?

Media Buying

ADWEEK'S MARKETING WEEK - Jun, 1980+

CAMPAIGN - 1929+ {United Kingdom}

MADISON AVENUE - Apr, 1958+

MEDIA WEEK - Apr 12, 1985+ {United Kingdom}

MEDIAWEEK - Sep, 1966+

PRESS STATISTICAL REVIEW - ? - 1975// {United Kingdom}

SRDS REPORT, THE - Jan, 1987+

Membership

DIRECTION - 1965+

FORUM - 1969+

INTERNATIONAL ADVERTISER, THE - Jun, 1960+

MARKETING NEWS - Oct, 1967+

OFFICIAL BULLETIN OF THE INTERNATIONAL ALLIANCE OF THEATRICAL STAGE EMPLOYEES AND MOVING PICTURE MACHINE OPERATORS OF THE UNITED STATES AND CANADA. - ?+

QUILL, THE - 1912+

Minorities

BLACK JOURNALISM REVIEW - Summer, 1976+?

BLACK STARS - Nov, 1950 - Jul, 1981//

HOWARD JOURNAL OF COMMUNICATIONS, THE - Spring, 1988+

MATRIX - 1916+

MEDIA REPORT TO WOMEN - Jun, 1972+

News

ACCESS REPORTS/FREEDOM OF INFORMATION - Jun 16, 1975+

CENSORSHIP NEWS - Spring, 1980+

COLUMBIA JOURNALISM REVIEW - Fall, 1961+

DEMOCRATIC JOURNALIST - Nov, 1953+ {Czechoslovakia}

FOI DIGEST - May/June, 1959 - Nov/Dec, 1985//

IFJ INFORMATION - Jul, 1952+ {Belgium}

INDEX ON CENSORSHIP - Spring, 1972+ {United Kingdom}

MEDIA MONITOR - Jan, 1987+

UPI ADVANCE - Jan, 1989+

Persuasion

POLITICAL COMMUNICATION AND PERSUASION - 1980+ {United Kingdom}

Political

MEDIA MONITOR - Jan, 1987+

MEDIAWATCH - Jan, 1987+

POLITICAL COMMUNICATION AND PERSUASION - 1980+ {United Kingdom}

POLITICAL COMMUNICATION NEWSLETTER - Spring, 1986+

TV, ETC. - Jan/Feb, 1989+

Popular Culture

GOOD OLD DAYS - 1964+

MEDIA SIGHT - Winter, 1982+?

MEMORIES - Spring, 1988+

NEW CAPTAIN GEORGE'S WHIZZBANG, THE - Nov/Dec, 1968+ {Canada}

NOSTALGIA ILLUSTRATED - Nov, 1974+

PREVUE - Nov/Dec, 1972+

SPERDVAC - Winter, 1976+?

UNIQUE - Jul/Aug, 1990 - Sep/Oct, 1990//

Production

SQUEEKY WHEEL, THE - Jan/Feb, 1984+

Programming

MEDIA & VALUES - 1977+

MEDIA WATCH - ?+?

Promotion

GF MAGAZINE - Spring?, 1989+

PROMOTION - Feb, 1953 - May 13, 1974//

SQUEEKY WHEEL, THE - Jan/Feb, 1984+

Public

ENTERTAINMENT WEEKLY - Feb 16, 1990+

PSA - Fall, 1982+

Public Relations

ACCESS - Jan 13, 1975 - 1985//

DIRECTION - 1965+

FORUM - 1969+

GAZETTE - Jan, 1955+ {Netherlands}

PRIG - Fall, 1987+

PUBLIC RELATIONS IDEAS - 1951 - Dec, 1965//?

PUBLIC RELATIONS JOURNAL, THE - Oct, 1945+

PUBLIC RELATIONS NEWS - Jan 17, 1944+

PUBLIC RELATIONS QUARTERLY - Oct, 1955+

PUBLIC RELATIONS REVIEW - Summer, 1975+

Publishing

ACCESS - Jan 13, 1975 - 1985//

ADVERTISING - Mar, 1892 - Jul 9, 1925//

CAMPAIGN - 1929+ {United Kingdom}

DIRECTION - 1965+

ENTERTAINMENT WEEKLY - Feb 16, 1990+

FORUM - 1969+
GAZETTE - Jan, 1955+ {Netherlands}
PRIG - Fall, 1987+
PSA - Fall, 1982+
PUBLIC RELATIONS IDEAS - 1951 - Dec, 1965//?
PUBLIC RELATIONS JOURNAL, THE - Oct, 1945+
PUBLIC RELATIONS NEWS - Jan 17, 1944+
PUBLIC RELATIONS QUARTERLY - Oct, 1955+
PUBLIC RELATIONS REVIEW - Summer, 1975+

Regulation
ACCESS - Jan 13, 1975 - 1985//
ADVERTISING ALERT - Nov 6, 1961 - Nov 10, 1965?//?
CABLE TV AND NEW MEDIA LAW & FINANCE - ?+
COMMUNICATIONS AND THE LAW - Winter, 1979+
COMMUNICATIONS LAWYER - Winter, 1983+
ENTERTAINMENT AND SPORTS LAWYER, THE - Spring, 1982+
FORDHAM ENTERTAINMENT, MEDIA & INTELLECTUAL PROPERTY LAW FORUM - Autumn, 1990+
4A'S WASHINGTON NEWSLETTER, THE - ?+?
HASTINGS COMMUNICATIONS AND ENTERTAINMENT LAW JOURNAL - 1977+
JOURNAL OF LAW & TECHNOLOGY, THE - 1986 - Winter, 1990//
LOYOLA ENTERTAINMENT JOURNAL - Apr, 1981+

Religion
ACTION - Jul, 1975+ {United Kingdom}
CHRISTIAN ADVERTISING FORUM - Apr/May, 1981+
MEDIA DEVELOPMENT - Winter, 1953+ {United Kingdom}
MEDIA SPOTLIGHT - 1978?+?

Research
ADVERTISING MAGAZINE - Autumn, 1964+ {United Kingdom}
ASIAN JOURNAL OF COMMUNICATION - Sep, 1990+ {Singapore}
AT&T TECHNOLOGY - Sep, 1925+
ATR - Nov, 1967+ {Australia}
COMMUNICATION MONOGRAPHS - 1934+
COMMUNICATIONS - 1974+ {Germany}
CRC NEWSLETTER - Jan, 1975+
DISCOURSE & SOCIETY - Jul, 1990+ {United Kingdom}
ELECTRONICS LETTERS - Mar, 1965+ {United Kingdom}
FORUM - Fall, 1991+
HOWARD JOURNAL OF COMMUNICATIONS, THE - Spring, 1988+
JMR, JOURNAL OF MARKETING RESEARCH - Feb, 1964+
JOURNAL OF ADVERTISING - 1972+
JOURNAL OF ADVERTISING RESEARCH - Sep, 1960+

JOURNAL OF MARKETING - Jul, 1936+
MASS COMM REVIEW - Aug, 1973+
MEDIA INFORMATION AUSTRALIA - Dec, 1975+ {Australia}
NEWS COMPUTING JOURNAL - 1964?+
PUBLIC RELATIONS REVIEW - Summer, 1975+
UNIVERSITY VISION - ? - 1976// {United Kingdom}
VERBATIM - 1974+
WORLD COMMUNICATION - Jul, 1972+

Retail
ADWEEK'S MARKETING WEEK - Jun, 1980+
MEDIA & CONSUMER - Apr, 1972 - Aug, 1975//
RETAIL EQUIPMENT AND MERCHANDISE - 1892+?
SCHEMER, THE - Jan, 1898+?

Review
C-O-N-N-E-C-T-I-O-N-S - ?+
CHRONICLE OF INTERNATIONAL COMMUNICATION - Jan, 1980 - Sep/Oct, 1985//
COLUMBIA JOURNALISM REVIEW - Fall, 1961+
DEMOCRATIC JOURNALIST - Nov, 1953+ {Czechoslovakia}
DIGITAL MEDIA - Jun, 1991+
ENTERTAINMENT WEEKLY - Feb 16, 1990+
ENTERTAINMENT WORLD - Oct 3, 1969 - May 29, 1970//
EXTRA! - Jul, 1987+
FAME - Jun, 1988 - Dec, 1990//
FANFARE - 1964 - 1983//
GAZETTE - Jan, 1955+ {Netherlands}
HOWARD JOURNAL OF COMMUNICATIONS, THE - Spring, 1988+
INTERVIEW - 1969+
MC&S NEWSLETTER - ?+
MEDIA, CULTURE, AND SOCIETY - Jan, 1979+ {United Kingdom}
MEDIA INFORMATION AUSTRALIA - Dec, 1975+ {Australia}
MEDIA MATTERS - ?+
MEDIA REPORTER, THE - 1976+ {United Kingdom}
MEDIAWATCH - Jan, 1987+
MORE - Jun, 1971 - Jun, 1978//
PREVUE - Nov/Dec, 1972+
QUILL, THE - 1912+
QUILL AND SCROLL - Oct, 1926+
ROTKIN REVIEW, THE - Summer, 1985+
TV, ETC. - Jan/Feb, 1989+
UNIQUE - Jul/Aug, 1990 - Sep/Oct, 1990//
WORLD COMMUNICATION - Jul, 1972+
WORLD MEDIA REPORT - Feb, 1983+

Richmond
SQUEEKY WHEEL, THE - Jan/Feb, 1984+

Sales
AD • MENTOR, THE - ?+

PROMOTION - Feb, 1953 - May 13, 1974//

School
HYPERMEDIA - Summer, 1988+?

Scripps Howard
SCRIPPS HOWARD NEWS - ?+

Scripts
SCRIPTWRITER NEWS - Jan, 1980 - 1982?//

Society
GANNETT CENTER JOURNAL - Spring, 1987+
MEDIA, CULTURE, AND SOCIETY - Jan, 1979+ {United Kingdom}
MEDIA MONITOR - Jan, 1987+

Speech
BULLETIN OF THE ASSOCIATION FOR BUSINESS COMMUNICATION, THE - May, 1937+

Student
FORUM - 1969+

Systems
SYSTEMSLETTER - ?+

Teaching
COLLEGIATE JOURNALIST - Fall, 1963+
JOURNAL OF MARKETING EDUCATION - ?+
QUILL AND SCROLL - Oct, 1926+

Technology
AEG-TELEFUNKEN PROGRESS - ? - #2, 1982// {Germany}
AT&T TECHNOLOGY - Sep, 1925+
ATR - Nov, 1967+ {Australia}
CAT NEWS - ?+
COMMUNICATIONS TECHNOLOGY & POLICY NEWS - ?, 1988+
ELECTRONICS LETTERS - Mar, 1965+ {United Kingdom}
HIGH TECH LIFESTYLES - ?, 1988+
INTERMEDIA - Mar/Apr, 1973+. {United Kingdom}
JOURNAL OF LAW & TECHNOLOGY, THE - 1986 - Winter, 1990//
MARKETING NEW MEDIA - Mar 7, 1984+
SMPTE JOURNAL - Jul, 1916+
TECHNOLOGY AND CULTURE - Winter, 1959+
TELEMATICS AND INFORMATICS - 1984+

Teletext
COMMUNICATION MONOGRAPHS - 1934+

Unions & Guilds
NEWSLETTER - 1983?+
OFFICIAL BULLETIN OF THE INTERNATIONAL ALLIANCE OF THEATRICAL STAGE EMPLOYEES AND MOVING PIC-

Motion Pictures
Subject Heading

TURE MACHINE OPERATORS OF THE UNITED STATES AND CANADA. - ?+

Women
MATRIX - 1916+
MEDIA REPORT TO WOMEN - Jun, 1972+

World
INTERMEDIA - Mar/Apr, 1973+. {United Kingdom}

Writing
BULLETIN OF THE ASSOCIATION FOR BUSINESS COMMUNICATION, THE - May, 1937+
NEWSLETTER - 1983?+
SCRIPTWRITER NEWS - Jan, 1980 - 1982?//

Motion Pictures

Academic
AFI EDUCATION NEWSLETTER - Mar/Apr, 1978 - Sep/Oct, 1982//
CINEMA PROGRESS - Dec, 1935 - Jun/Jul, 1939//
UNIVERSITY FILM STUDY CENTER. NEWSLETTER. - 1971+

Acting
BACK STAGE - Dec 2, 1960+
CASTING CALL - Jan 17, 1976+
DRAMA-LOGUE - Jan, 1970?+
HOLLYWOOD FILMOGRAPH - Apr, 1922 - Oct 27, 1934//
SPOTLIGHT CASTING MAGAZINE - ?+

Actor
CELEBRITY PLUS - Jan, 1987+

Aesthetics
CINEMONKEY - Winter, 1975+
CLOSE-UP - Jul, 1927 - Dec, 1933// {United Kingdom}
MOTION PICTURE - Spring/Summer, 1986+
MOVIE - June, 1962+ {United Kingdom}

Alternative Media
CANTRILLS FILMNOTES - Mar, 1971+ {Australia}
CINEASTE - Summer, 1967+
CINEMA - Dec, 1968 to date. {United Kingdom}
FACETS FEATURES - 1967+
MEDIUM - Summer, 1967 - Winter, 1968//
MILLENNIUM FILM JOURNAL - Winter, 1977/1978+

Animation
GRAFFITI - ?+

PENCIL TEST - Dec, 1982+
SOCIETY FOR ANIMATION STUDIES NEWSLETTER, THE - Jan/Feb, 1988+

Archival
MAGAZINE, THE - 1976+

Artist
AMERICAN CLASSIC SCREEN - Sep/Oct, 1976 - Nov/Dec, 1984//
BIJOU - Apr/May, 1977 - 1978//
DOCUMENTARY FILM NEWS - Autumn, 1932 - Jan, 1949// {United Kingdom}
ENTERTAINMENT CONNECTION MAGAZINE - ?+
FILM FUN - ?+?
FILMLAND - 1951+?
HOLLYWOOD REPORTER - Sep 3, 1930+
MOVIE DREAM GUYS - Jan, 1960 - ?//
NEW MOVIE MAGAZINE, THE - Dec, 1929 - Sep, 1935//
PHOTOPLAY COMBINED WITH MOVIE MIRROR - Jan, 1941 - May, 1946//
PICTURE PLAY MAGAZINE - Apr 10, 1915 - ?//
SCREEN GREATS - May, 1990+
SHOW - Sep, 1952? - ?//
SHOW BUSINESS ILLUSTRATED - Sep 5, 1961 - Apr, 1962//
TV HITS - Sep, 1989?+ {United Kingdom}
20/20 - Apr, 1989+ {United Kingdom}
VARIETY - Dec 16, 1905+

Avant-garde
FILM ART - Spring, 1933 - Spring, 1937// {United Kingdom}
FILM CULTURE - Jan, 1955+
MILLENNIUM FILM JOURNAL - Winter, 1977/1978+
MOTION PICTURE - Spring/Summer, 1986+
OFF-HOLLYWOOD REPORT - 1985+

B Movies
CELLULOID NIGHTMARE - ?, 1990+?

Black
ENTERTAINMENT CONNECTION MAGAZINE - ?+

Business
AMERICAN PREMIERE - Sep, 1980+
BACK STAGE - Dec 2, 1960+
BUSINESS OF FILM, THE - Nov, 1982+ {United Kingdom}
CANADIAN FILM DIGEST - 1936 - Dec, 1976// {Canada}
CINEMA AND THEATRE - 1932+? {United Kingdom}
CINEMA/CANADA - 1961+ {Canada}
FILM TV DAILY - Oct 14, 1915+
FILMS - Nov, 1939 - Winter, 1940//
FLORIDA REEL - Oct/Nov, 1989+

HOLLYWOOD REPORTER - Sep 3, 1930+
JOURNAL OF THE PRODUCERS GUILD OF AMERICA, THE - Apr, 1952+
MARKETING PULSE, THE - Sep, 1980?+
MOVIE/TV MARKETING - May, 1953+ {Japan}
MOVING PICTURES INTERNATIONAL - Sep 13, 1990?+ {United Kingdom}
PROFESSIONAL FILM PRODUCTION - Jun, 1975+
VARIETY - Dec 16, 1905+

Cassettes
HOME VIEWER - Apr, 1981+
ORBIT VIDEO - Jan, 1989+

Casting
SPOTLIGHT CASTING MAGAZINE - ?+

Cinematography
AMERICAN CINEMATOGRAPHER - Nov 1, 1920+

Collector
BIG REEL, THE - Jun, 1974?+
CLASSIC IMAGES REVIEW - Nov, 1979 - ?, 1981//
VIDEO BUYER - Nov/Dec, 1989+ {United Kingdom}

Cultural
CINEMA - Jun, 1947 - Aug, 1947//
CINEMA - Dec, 1968 to date. {United Kingdom}
CINEMA PROGRESS - Dec, 1935 - Jun/Jul, 1939//
MOTION PICTURE AND THE FAMILY, THE - Oct, 15, 1934 - May, 15, 1938//

Directing
ACTION! - Sep/Oct, 1966 - Nov/Dec, 1978//

Distribution
BUSINESS OF FILM, THE - Nov, 1982+ {United Kingdom}
CINEMATOGRAPHY AND BIOSCOPE MAGAZINE - Apr, 1906 - Jan/Mar, 1907// {United Kingdom}
HOLLYWOOD REPORTER - Sep 3, 1930+
MARKETING PULSE, THE - Sep, 1980?+
MOVIE/TV MARKETING - May, 1953+ {Japan}

Editing
AMERICAN CINEMEDITOR - Winter, 1950+

Employment
CASTING CALL - Jan 17, 1976+
DRAMA-LOGUE - Jan, 1970?+

Engineering
CAVERNE COMMUNICATION, THE - Jun, 1987+
IMAGE TECHNOLOGY - 194u+ {United Kingdom}

Exhibition
- CANADIAN FILM DIGEST - 1936 - Dec, 1976// {Canada}
- CINEMA AND THEATRE - 1932+? {United Kingdom}
- CINEMATOGRAPHY AND BIOSCOPE MAGAZINE - Apr, 1906 - Jan/Mar, 1907// {United Kingdom}
- MOTION PICTURE PRODUCT DIGEST - Jan 6, 1973+
- SILENT PICTURE, THE - Winter 1968/69 - 1974//

Fan
- ACTION FILMS - Jan, 1981+
- AMAZING CINEMA - May, 1981+
- BIJOU - Apr/May, 1977 - 1978//
- BONDAGE - 1973+
- CASTLE OF FRANKENSTEIN - ?, 1959 - ?, 1974//
- CINEFAN - Jul, 1974+
- CINEFANTASTIQUE - Fall, 1970+
- FILM FUN - ?+?
- FILMLAND - 1951+?
- GOREZONE - May, 1988+
- HORRORFAN - Winter, 1988+
- LITTLE SHOPPE OF HORRORS - ?+?
- LUCASFILM FAN CLUB, THE - Fall, 1987+
- MOVIE DREAM GUYS - Jan, 1960 - ?//
- NEW MOVIE MAGAZINE, THE - Dec, 1929 - Sep, 1935//
- PHOTOPLAY COMBINED WITH MOVIE MIRROR - Jan, 1941 - May, 1946//
- PICTURE PLAY MAGAZINE - Apr 10, 1915 - ?//
- SCREEN GREATS - May, 1990+
- STAR TREK: THE OFFICIAL FAN CLUB MAGAZINE - ?+
- STRANGE ADVENTURES - Feb, 1989+ {United Kingdom}
- TV HITS - Sep, 1989?+ {United Kingdom}

Filters
- TIFFEN PROFESSIONAL NEWSLETTER - Spring?, 1987+

Finance
- AMERICAN PREMIERE - Sep, 1980+
- FILM TV DAILY - Oct 14, 1915+
- HOLLYWOOD REPORTER - Sep 3, 1930+
- JOURNAL OF THE PRODUCERS GUILD OF AMERICA, THE - Apr, 1952+
- MARKETING PULSE, THE - Sep, 1980?+

Guide
- ACTION FILMS - Jan, 1981+
- AUDIO-VISUAL GUIDE - Feb, 1936 - Jun, 1956//
- BEST OF FILM & VIDEO - Mar/Apr, 1990+ {United Kingdom}
- CHRISTIAN FILM & VIDEO - Jan/Feb?, 1984+
- CINEMA FRANCAIS - May, 1976+ {France}
- CINEMA THE WORLD OVER - Jul, 1975+ {Pakistan}
- CINEMA, VIDEO & CABLE MOVIE DIGEST - May, 1991+
- CLOSE-UP - Jul, 1968+ {India}
- EMPIRE - Jul, 1989+ {United Kingdom}
- FILM - Oct, 1954+ {United Kingdom}
- FILM BULLETIN - May, 1961+ {Poland}
- FILM COMMENT - Spring, 1962+
- FILM THREAT - Feb, 1985+
- FINNISH FILMS - 1970?+ {Finland}
- FOCUS I - Oct, 1969?+?
- INTERNATIONAL FILM BUFF - Dec, 1975+
- JOURNAL OF THE BRITISH FILM ACADEMY - ? - Spring, 1959// {United Kingdom}
- MEDIA MIX - Oct, 1969 - Jun, 1979//
- MONTHLY FILM BULLETIN - Feb, 1934 - Apr, 1991// {United Kingdom}
- MOVIE MARKETPLACE - Oct/Nov, 1987+
- NEW ZEALAND FILM - May, 1977?+? {New Zealand}
- ORBIT VIDEO - Jan, 1989+
- PHOTOPLAY STUDIES - Apr, 1935 - 1940//
- SCIENCE-FICTION VIDEO MAGAZINE - Fall, 1989?+
- SHOW - Oct, 1961?+?
- SHOW - Jan, 1970 - Nov, 1973//
- SIGHT & SOUND - Spring, 1932+ {United Kingdom}
- STARBURST - Sep, 1978?+ {United Kingdom}

Historical
- AMERICAN CLASSIC SCREEN - Sep/Oct, 1976 - Nov/Dec, 1984//
- AMERICAN FILM - Oct, 1975+
- AMERICAN FILM INSTITUTE. QUARTERLY. - 1967?+?
- BIG REEL, THE - Jun, 1974?+
- CINEMA VISION INDIA - Jan, 1980 - Jan, 1983// {India}
- CLASSIC IMAGES REVIEW - Nov, 1979 - ?, 1981//
- FILM CULTURE - Jan, 1955+
- FILM HERITAGE - Fall, 1965 - Spring, 1977//
- FLASHBACK - 1972+?
- GRAND ILLUSIONS - Feb, 1977 - Summer, 1980//
- HISTORICAL JOURNAL OF FILM, RADIO & TELEVISION - Mar, 1981+ {United Kingdom}
- IAMHIST NEWSLETTER - ?+
- IMAGE - Jan, 1952+
- JOURNAL OF POPULAR FILM AND TELEVISION - Winter, 1972+
- LOWBROW CINEMA - Summer, 1982 - #3/4, 1986//?
- MAGAZINE, THE - 1976+
- SCREEN FACTS - 1963+
- SCREEN GREATS - May, 1990+
- SCREEN THRILLS ILLUSTRATED - Jun, 1962 - ?//
- SILENT PICTURE, THE - Winter 1968/69 - 1974//

Home Consumer
- BIG REEL, THE - Jun, 1974?+
- CINEGRAM - Mar/Apr, 1976+

Horror
- AMAZING CINEMA - May, 1981+
- CASTLE OF FRANKENSTEIN - ?, 1959 - ?, 1974//
- CINEFAN - Jul, 1974+
- CINEFANTASTIQUE - Fall, 1970+
- CINEMACABRE - Mar, 1969+
- GOREZONE - May, 1988+
- HORRORFAN - Winter, 1988+
- LITTLE SHOPPE OF HORRORS - ?+?
- WORLD OF FANDOM, THE - Jul, 1985+

Independent
- OFF-HOLLYWOOD REPORT - 1985+

Instructional
- WRITER, THE - Apr, 1887+

International
- AUSTRALIAN JOURNAL OF SCREEN THEORY - 1976 - 1984// {Australia}
- BUSINESS OF FILM, THE - Nov, 1982+ {United Kingdom}
- CINEASTE - Summer, 1967+
- CINEMA PAPERS - Jan, 1974+ {Australia}
- CINEMA THE WORLD OVER - Jul, 1975+ {Pakistan}
- CLOSE-UP - Jul, 1927 - Dec, 1933// {United Kingdom}
- CLOSE-UP - Jul, 1968+ {India}
- CTVD - Winter, 1961/1962+
- DOCUMENTARY FILM NEWS - Autumn, 1932 - Jan, 1949// {United Kingdom}
- FILM JOURNAL - 1958 - 1964// {Australia}
- FOCUS ON FILM - Jan/Feb, 1970 - 1981// {United Kingdom}
- HISTORICAL JOURNAL OF FILM, RADIO & TELEVISION - Mar, 1981+ {United Kingdom}
- IAMHIST NEWSLETTER - ?+
- MEDIUM - Summer, 1967 - Winter, 1968//
- MONOGRAM - Apr, 1971 - 1978// {United Kingdom}
- MONTHLY FILM BULLETIN - Feb, 1934 - Apr, 1991// {United Kingdom}
- MOVIE/TV MARKETING - May, 1953+ {Japan}
- MOVING PICTURES INTERNATIONAL - Sep 13, 1990?+ {United Kingdom}
- SIGHT & SOUND - Spring, 1932+ {United Kingdom}
- SOCIETY FOR ANIMATION STUDIES NEWSLETTER, THE - Jan/Feb, 1988+

Italy
- SPAGHETTI CINEMA - Jan?, 1984+

James Bond
- BONDAGE - 1973+

Licensing
- ASCAP IN ACTION - Fall, 1979+

Motion Pictures
Subject Heading Index

Lighting
LIGHTING DIMENSIONS - Jan, 1977+
LIGHTS! - Jan, 1990+ {United Kingdom}

Literature
COMMUNICATION BOOKNOTES - Nov, 1969+
CTVD - Winter, 1961/1962+
MONOGRAM - Apr, 1971 - 1978// {United Kingdom}

Location
LOCATION UPDATE - Jul/Aug, 1985+
ON LOCATION - Oct, 1977 - Mar, 1986?//?

Management
AMERICAN PREMIERE - Sep, 1980+

Marketing
BUSINESS OF FILM, THE - Nov, 1982+ {United Kingdom}
MOVIE/TV MARKETING - May, 1953+ {Japan}
PROFESSIONAL FILM PRODUCTION - Jun, 1975+

Marxist
JUMP CUT - May/Jun, 1974+

Membership
PENCIL TEST - Dec, 1982+

Minorities
CAMERA OBSCURA - Fall, 1976+
JUMP CUT - May/Jun, 1974+
WOMEN & FILM - 1972 - Aug, 1976//

Music
ASCAP IN ACTION - Fall, 1979+

New York City
SHOW - Jan, 1970 - Nov, 1973//

Popular Culture
JOURNAL OF POPULAR FILM AND TELEVISION - Winter, 1972+

Preservation
AMERICAN FILM - Oct, 1975+
AMERICAN FILM INSTITUTE. QUARTERLY. - 1967?+?

Producing
AMAZING CINEMA - May, 1981+
JOURNAL OF THE PRODUCERS GUILD OF AMERICA, THE - Apr, 1952+
PRODUCERS QUARTERLY - Mar, 1989+

Production
ACTION! - Sep/Oct, 1966 - Nov/Dec, 1978//
AMAZING CINEMA - May, 1981+
AMERICAN CINEMATOGRAPHER - Nov 1, 1920+
AMERICAN CINEMEDITOR - Winter, 1950+
AMERICAN FILM - Oct, 1975+
BACK STAGE - Dec 2, 1960+
CAMERA OBSCURA - Fall, 1976+
CAMERART - Spring, 1958+ {Japan}
CANADIAN FILM DIGEST - 1936 - Dec, 1976// {Canada}
CAVERNE COMMUNICATION, THE - Jun, 1987+
CINEMA - 1962 - 1976//
CINEMA/CANADA - 1961+ {Canada}
DIALOGUE ON FILM - 1972 - May/Jun, 1975//
DOCUMENTARY FILM NEWS - Autumn, 1932 - Jan, 1949// {United Kingdom}
ENTERTAINMENT REVUE - Apr, 1988+
FILM & VIDEO - Feb, 1984+
FILM TV DAILY - Oct 14, 1915+
FLORIDA REEL - Oct/Nov, 1989+
HOLLYWOOD FILMOGRAPH - Apr, 1922 - Oct 27, 1934//
IMAGEMAKER - Aug, 1981+
IN MOTION FILM & VIDEO PRODUCTION MAGAZINE - Jan, 1982+
INTERNATIONAL PHOTOGRAPHER - Feb, 1929+
LIGHTING DIMENSIONS - Jan, 1977+
LIGHTS! - Jan, 1990+ {United Kingdom}
LOCATION UPDATE - Jul/Aug, 1985+
MARKEE - Feb, 1986+
ON LOCATION - Oct, 1977 - Mar, 1986?//?
PRODUCERS QUARTERLY - Mar, 1989+
PRODUCTION SOUND REPORT - ?+
PROFESSIONAL FILM PRODUCTION - Jun, 1975+
SPECTATOR, THE - Spring, 1982+
TIFFEN PROFESSIONAL NEWSLETTER - Spring?, 1987+
20/20 - Apr, 1989+ {United Kingdom}

Programming
CINEMA, VIDEO & CABLE MOVIE DIGEST - May, 1991+

Promotion
CINEMA FRANCAIS - May, 1976+ {France}
CINEMA PERSPECTIVES - ?+?
FILM BULLETIN - May, 1961+ {Poland}
FINNISH FILMS - 1970?+ {Finland}
FOCUS ON FOX - Feb, 1976+
IMAGE NEWS - Spring, 1988+
IMAGEMAKER - Aug, 1981+
MOTION PICTURE AND THE FAMILY, THE - Oct, 15, 1934 - May, 15, 1938//
NEW ZEALAND FILM - May, 1977?+? {New Zealand}

Recording
PRODUCTION SOUND REPORT - ?+

Regulation
CINEMA/CANADA - 1961+ {Canada}

Religion
CHRISTIAN FILM & VIDEO - Jan/Feb?, 1984+
FILM WITNESS - 1984?+

Research
HISTORICAL JOURNAL OF FILM, RADIO & TELEVISION - Mar, 1981+ {United Kingdom}
IAMHIST NEWSLETTER - ?+
VELVET LIGHT TRAP - Jun, 1971+

Retail
CLASSIC IMAGES REVIEW - Nov, 1979 - ?, 1981//
MOVIE MARKETPLACE - Oct/Nov, 1987+

Review
AMERICAN CLASSIC SCREEN - Sep/Oct, 1976 - Nov/Dec, 1984//
AMERICAN FILM - Oct, 1975+
AMERICAN FILM INSTITUTE. QUARTERLY. - 1967?+?
AUDIO-VISUAL GUIDE - Feb, 1936 - Jun, 1956//
AUSTRALIAN JOURNAL OF SCREEN THEORY - 1976 - 1984// {Australia}
BIJOU - Apr/May, 1977 - 1978//
CAMERART - Spring, 1958+ {Japan}
CANTRILLS FILMNOTES - Mar, 1971+ {Australia}
CAVERNE COMMUNICATION, THE - Jun, 1987+
CELLULOID NIGHTMARE - ?, 1990+?
CINEASTE - Summer, 1967+
CINEMA - Jun, 1947 - Aug, 1947//
CINEMA - 1962 - 1976//
CINEMA - Dec, 1968 to date. {United Kingdom}
CINEMA HALL-MARKS - Jul, 1933 - ?//
CINEMA JOURNAL - Fall?, 1961+
CINEMA PAPERS - Jan, 1974+ {Australia}
CINEMA PROGRESS - Dec, 1935 - Jun/Jul, 1939//
CINEMA THE WORLD OVER - Jul, 1975+ {Pakistan}
CINEMA VISION INDIA - Jan, 1980 - Jan, 1983// {India}
CINEMACABRE - Mar, 1969+
CINEMAGES - Mar, 1955 - 1958//
CINEMONKEY - Winter, 1975+
CLOSE-UP - Fall, 1982 - Spring, 1987//
CLOSE-UP - Jul, 1927 - Dec, 1933// {United Kingdom}
CRITIC - Oct, 1956?+
CTVD - Winter, 1961/1962+
DOCUMENTARY FILM NEWS - Autumn, 1932 - Jan, 1949// {United Kingdom}
EMPIRE - Jul, 1989+ {United Kingdom}
ENTERTAINMENT CONNECTION MAGAZINE - ?+
ENTERTAINMENT REVUE - Apr, 1988+

EXPERIMENTAL CINEMA - Feb, 1930 - Jun, 1934//
FACETS FEATURES - 1967+
FILM ART - Spring, 1933 - Spring, 1937// {United Kingdom}
FILM COMMENT - Spring, 1962+
FILM CRITICISM - Spring, 1976+
FILM CULTURE - Jan, 1955+
FILM FUN - ?+?
FILM HERITAGE - Fall, 1965 - Spring, 1977//
FILM JOURNAL - 1958 - 1964// {Australia}
FILM THREAT - Feb, 1985+
FILM WITNESS - 1984?+
FILMS - Nov, 1939 - Winter, 1940//
FOCUS! - Oct, 1969?+?
FOCUS ON FILM - Jan/Feb, 1970 - 1981// {United Kingdom}
GRAND ILLUSIONS - Feb, 1977 - Summer, 1980//
HISTORICAL JOURNAL OF FILM, RADIO & TELEVISION - Mar, 1981+ {United Kingdom}
INTERNATIONAL FILM BUFF - Dec, 1975+
JOURNAL OF POPULAR FILM AND TELEVISION - Winter, 1972+
JOURNAL OF THE BRITISH FILM ACADEMY - ? - Spring, 1959// {United Kingdom}
JUMP CUT - May/Jun, 1974+
KODAK PROFESSIONAL FORUM - ?, 1978+?
LITERATURE/FILM QUARTERLY - Winter, 1973+
LOWBROW CINEMA - Summer, 1982 - #3/4, 1986//?
MEDIUM - Summer, 1967 - Winter, 1968//
MILLENNIUM FILM JOURNAL - Winter, 1977/1978+
MONOGRAM - Apr, 1971 - 1978// {United Kingdom}
MOTION PICTURE - Spring/Summer, 1986+
MOVIE - June, 1962+ {United Kingdom}
MOVIE GEEK - Fall, 1971+
NEW MOVIE MAGAZINE, THE - Dec, 1929 - Sep, 1935//
OFF-HOLLYWOOD REPORT - 1985+
QUARTERLY REVIEW OF FILM AND VIDEO - Feb, 1976+
SCREEN - ? - Spring, 1982// {United Kingdom}
SHOW - Sep, 1952? - ?//
SHOW - Oct, 1961+?
SHOW - Jan, 1970 - Nov, 1973//
SHOW BUSINESS ILLUSTRATED - Sep 5, 1961 - Apr, 1962//
SPAGHETTI CINEMA - Jan?, 1984+
STARBURST - Sep, 1978?+ {United Kingdom}
UNIVERSITY FILM STUDY CENTER. NEWSLETTER. - 1971+
VARIETY - Dec 16, 1905+
VELVET LIGHT TRAP - Jun, 1971+
WIDE ANGLE - Spring, 1976+
WOMEN & FILM - 1972 - Aug, 1976//

School
PHOTOPLAY STUDIES - Apr, 1935 - 1940//

Science Fiction

Scripts
WRITER, THE - Apr, 1887+

Silent Film
SILENT PICTURE, THE - Winter 1968/69 - 1974//

Southeast United States
MARKEE - Feb, 1986+

Star Trek
STAR TREK: THE OFFICIAL FAN CLUB MAGAZINE - ?+

Studio
UNION LABOR SUN - ? - ?//

Technology
AMERICAN CINEMATOGRAPHER - Nov 1, 1920+
CAMERART - Spring, 1958+ {Japan}
CAVERNE COMMUNICATION, THE - Jun, 1987+
CINEFANTASTIQUE - Fall, 1970+
CINEGRAM - Mar/Apr, 1976+
CINEMA - 1962 - 1976//
CINEMA PERSPECTIVES - ?+?
FOLLOW FOCUS - 198u+
IMAGE TECHNOLOGY - 194u+ {United Kingdom}
IN MOTION FILM & VIDEO PRODUCTION MAGAZINE - Jan, 1982+
LIGHTING DIMENSIONS - Jan, 1977+
NEWSLETTER, THE - ?+?
PERSPECTIVE - Autumn, 1958 - 1966// {United Kingdom}
PRODUCTION SOUND REPORT - ?+

Teletext
AUSTRALIAN JOURNAL OF SCREEN THEORY - 1976 - 1984// {Australia}
EXPERIMENTAL CINEMA - Feb, 1930 - Jun, 1934//
FILM ART - Spring, 1933 - Spring, 1937// {United Kingdom}
JUMP CUT - May/Jun, 1974+
LITERATURE/FILM QUARTERLY - Winter, 1973+
MOVIE - June, 1962+ {United Kingdom}
QUARTERLY REVIEW OF FILM AND VIDEO - Feb, 1976+
WIDE ANGLE - Spring, 1976+

Third Coast
MARKEE - Feb, 1986+

Unions & Guilds
INTERNATIONAL PHOTOGRAPHER - Feb, 1929+

UNION LABOR SUN - ? - ?//

Women
CAMERA OBSCURA - Fall, 1976+
JUMP CUT - May/Jun, 1974+
WOMEN & FILM - 1972 - Aug, 1976//

World
BUSINESS OF FILM, THE - Nov, 1982+ {United Kingdom}

Writing
WRITER, THE - Apr, 1887+

Newspapers

Academic
ALABAMA JOURNALIST - ?+

Advertising
ADVERTISERS GAZETTE - Nov, 1866 - 1888//
ADVERTISERS GUIDE - Jun, 1876+?
ADVERTISERS' WEEKLY - Jan 5, 1924 - May 19, 1928//
ADVERTISING - Mar, 1892 - Jul 9, 1925//
ADVERTISING IDEAS - ? - ?//
AMERICAN ADVERTISER REPORTER - 1886 - Sep 13, 1893?//
NATIONAL ADVERTISING - 1897? - May, 1925//
NEWSPAPER WORLD AND ADVERTISING REVIEW - Jul, 1913 - 1953// {United Kingdom}

Advising
ADVISER UPDATE - ?+

Advocate
LIES OF OUR TIMES - Jan, 1990+

Animation
STORYBOARD / THE ART OF LAUGHTER - Fall, 1990+

Business
ADVERTISING - Mar, 1892 - Jul 9, 1925//
CALIFORNIA PUBLISHER - 1918+
COLORADO EDITOR - 1926+
EDITOR AND PUBLISHER - Jun 29, 1901+
FIEJ-BULLETIN - Mar, 1949 - Jun, 1986// {France}
FOURTH ESTATE - Mar 1, 1894 - Nov 26, 1927//
GRASSROOTS EDITOR - Jan, 1960+
PRESSTIME - Oct, 1979+
PUBLISHER'S AUXILIARY - 1865+

Cartoons
BLUE PENCIL MAGAZINE - Feb, 1900 - Nov, 1901//

Newspapers
Subject Heading

NATIONAL FORUM, THE - Jan, 1989+
TARGET - Autumn, 1981 - Summer, 1987//

Circulation
WOODCOCK'S PRINTERS' AND LITHOGRAPHERS' WEEKLY GAZETTE AND NEWSPAPER REPORTER - Jan, 1871 - 1884?//

Colorado
COLORADO EDITOR - 1926+

Comics
GOLDEN AGE OF COMICS - Jun?, 1982+

Design
DESIGN - Mar, 1980+

Distribution
AMERICAN NEWSPAPER BOY, THE - ?+?
NEWSINC. - May/Jun, 1989+

Editing
BULLETIN OF THE AMERICAN SOCIETY OF NEWSPAPER EDITORS, THE - 1923+
EDITORIAL NEWSLETTER - ?+?
GRASSROOTS EDITOR - Jan, 1960+
MASTHEAD - Spring, 1949+
RIGHTING WORDS - Jan/Feb, 1987+
TARGET - Autumn, 1981 - Summer, 1987//

Editorial
EDITORIAL - May 6, 1915 - Apr 14, 1917//
EDITORIAL REVIEW - Aug, 1909 - Aug, 1912//
MASTHEAD - Spring, 1949+
PULSE - Feb, 1979+
TARGET - Autumn, 1981 - Summer, 1987//

Education
ALUMNI NEWSLINE - Fall, 1988+

Employment
IOWA JOURNALIST - Jan, 1925 - Jul, 1969//
MINORITIES IN THE NEWSPAPER BUSINESS - Sep, 1985+

Ethics
GRASSROOTS EDITOR - Jan, 1960+
LIES OF OUR TIMES - Jan, 1990+

Finance
NEWSINC. - May/Jun, 1989+

Freedom of the Press
FIEJ-BULLETIN - Mar, 1949 - Jun, 1986// {France}
IPI REPORT - May, 1952+ {United Kingdom}

Graphics
WOODCOCK'S PRINTERS' AND LITHOGRAPHERS' WEEKLY GAZETTE AND NEWSPAPER REPORTER - Jan, 1871 - 1884?//

Guide
AUDIO-VISUAL GUIDE - Feb, 1936 - Jun, 1956//

High School
ADVISER UPDATE - ?+

Historical
MASTHEAD - Jan, 1977 - Sep, 1978//
OLD NEWS - Sep, 1989+

House Organ
KNIGHT-RIDDER NEWS - Spring, 1986+

International
FIEJ-BULLETIN - Mar, 1949 - Jun, 1986// {France}
IPI REPORT - May, 1952+ {United Kingdom}
IPI SURVEY - 1952 - 1962// {Switzerland}
NEWSPAPER TECHNIQUES - 1956+ {Germany}
PRESS, THE - Jan/Feb, 1973?+?
WORLD PRESS REVIEW - ?+

Journalism
ADVISER UPDATE - ?+
ALABAMA JOURNALIST - ?+
AMERICAN JOURNALIST, THE - Sep 15, 1883 - Jun, 1885//
BLUE PENCIL MAGAZINE - Feb, 1900 - Nov, 1901//
DOW JONES NEWSPAPER FUND NEWSLETTER - Spring, 1960?+
IOWA JOURNALIST - Jan, 1925 - Jul, 1969//
IPI SURVEY - 1952 - 1962// {Switzerland}
LIES OF OUR TIMES - Jan, 1990+
OVERSET - Jun, 1978+?
RIGHTING WORDS - Jan/Feb, 1987+

Management
ADVERTISING - Mar, 1892 - Jul 9, 1925//
AMERICAN ADVERTISER REPORTER - 1886 - Sep 13, 1893?//
AMERICAN PRESS - 1882 - Oct, 1972//
ANPA PUBLIC AFFAIRS NEWSLETTER - ?+
BULLETIN OF THE AMERICAN SOCIETY OF NEWSPAPER EDITORS, THE - 1923+
EDITOR AND PUBLISHER - Jun 29, 1901+
FIEJ-BULLETIN - Mar, 1949 - Jun, 1986// {France}
FOURTH ESTATE - Mar 1, 1894 - Nov 26, 1927//
NEWSINC. - May/Jun, 1989+
NEWSPAPER TECHNIQUES - 1956+ {Germany}
NEWSPAPER WORLD AND ADVERTISING REVIEW - Jul, 1913 - 1953// {United Kingdom}
PEP - Jan, 1916 - Nov, 1919//
PRESSTIME - Oct, 1979+

PUBLISHER'S AUXILIARY - 1865+
WEB - Nov, 1972+

Membership
NEWSPAPER RESEARCH JOURNAL - Nov, 1979+

Minorities
MINORITIES IN THE NEWSPAPER BUSINESS - Sep, 1985+

News
AMERICAN NEWSPAPER BOY, THE - ?+?
EDITORIAL - May 6, 1915 - Apr 14, 1917//
FIEJ-BULLETIN - Mar, 1949 - Jun, 1986// {France}
GUILD REPORTER, THE - Nov 23, 1933+
LIES OF OUR TIMES - Jan, 1990+
NATIONAL FORUM, THE - Jan, 1989+
OHIO NEWSPAPER - Nov, 1919+
PRESS, THE - Jan/Feb, 1973?+?
SEMINAR - 1968 - 1974//
WASHINGTON NEWSPAPER, THE - 1914+
WORLD PRESS REVIEW - ?+

Newsboys
AMERICAN NEWSPAPER BOY, THE - ?+?

Popular Culture
OLD NEWS - Sep, 1989+

Printing
WOODCOCK'S PRINTERS' AND LITHOGRAPHERS' WEEKLY GAZETTE AND NEWSPAPER REPORTER - Jan, 1871 - 1884?//

Production
AMERICAN PRESS - 1882 - Oct, 1972//
BULLETIN OF THE AMERICAN SOCIETY OF NEWSPAPER EDITORS, THE - 1923+
NEWSINC. - May/Jun, 1989+
NEWSPAPER TECHNIQUES - 1956+ {Germany}
PRESS, THE - Jan/Feb, 1973?+?
PRESSTIME - Oct, 1979+
WEB - Nov, 1972+

Promotion
KNIGHT-RIDDER NEWS - Spring, 1986+
PEP - Jan, 1916 - Nov, 1919//
SEMINAR - 1968 - 1974//

Publishing
ADVERTISING - Mar, 1892 - Jul 9, 1925//
CALIFORNIA PUBLISHER - 1918+
COLORADO EDITOR - 1926+
GRASSROOTS EDITOR - Jan, 1960+
PEP - Jan, 1916 - Nov, 1919//
WOODCOCK'S PRINTERS' AND LITHOGRAPHERS' WEEKLY GAZETTE AND NEWSPAPER REPORTER - Jan, 1871 - 1884?//

Research
ANPA NEWS RESEARCH REPORT - Apr 8, 1977 - Dec, 1983//
NEWSPAPER RESEARCH JOURNAL - Nov, 1979+

Retail
ADVERTISING IDEAS - ? - ?//

Review
ALUMNI NEWSLINE - Fall, 1988+
AUDIO-VISUAL GUIDE - Feb, 1936 - Jun, 1956//
EDITOR AND PUBLISHER - Jun 29, 1901+
EDITORIAL - May 6, 1915 - Apr 14, 1917//
EDITORIAL REVIEW - Aug, 1909 - Aug, 1912//
NEWSINC. - May/Jun, 1989+
OHIO NEWSPAPER - Nov, 1919+
OVERSET - Jun, 1978+?
WASHINGTON NEWSPAPER, THE - 1914+

Sales
AMERICAN ADVERTISER REPORTER - 1886 - Sep 13, 1893?//

Satire
BLUE PENCIL MAGAZINE - Feb, 1900 - Nov, 1901//

School
ADVISER UPDATE - ?+
SEMINAR - 1968 - 1974//

Teaching
DOW JONES NEWSPAPER FUND NEWSLETTER - Spring, 1960?+
MASTHEAD - Jan, 1977 - Sep, 1978//
SEMINAR - 1968 - 1974//

Unions & Guilds
FIEJ-BULLETIN - Mar, 1949 - Jun, 1986// {France}
GUILD REPORTER, THE - Nov 23, 1933+

Washington
WASHINGTON NEWSPAPER, THE - 1914+

Writing
DOW JONES NEWSPAPER FUND NEWSLETTER - Spring, 1960?+
MASTHEAD - Spring, 1949+
PULSE - Feb, 1979+
WORLD PRESS REVIEW - ?+

Outdoor

Advertising
ADVERTISING OUTDOORS - Feb 22, 1896 - Dec, 1931//
AMERICAN DEMOGRAPHICS - Jan, 1979+
SIGNS OF THE TIMES - May, 1906+

Demographics
AMERICAN DEMOGRAPHICS - Jan, 1979+

Display
SIGNS OF THE TIMES - May, 1906+

Marketing
ADVERTISING OUTDOORS - Feb 22, 1896 - Dec, 1931//
AMERICAN DEMOGRAPHICS - Jan, 1979+

Performing Arts

Acting
CASTING CALL - Jan 17, 1976+
DRAMA-LOGUE - Jan, 1970?+
NEW THEATRE - Aug, 1939 - Jul, 1949// {United Kingdom}
SHOW BIZ WEST - 1979+
SHOW BUSINESS - 1941+
SPOTLIGHT CASTING MAGAZINE - ?+

Actor
CASTING NEWS - Aug 1, 1988?+
CELEBRITY PLUS - Jan, 1987+

Advertising
AMERICAN DEMOGRAPHICS - Jan, 1979+

Animation
STORYBOARD / THE ART OF LAUGHTER - Fall, 1990+

Art Form
BALLETT INTERNATIONAL - Jan, 1978+ {Germany}

Artist
AFTER DARK - May, 1968 - Jan, 1983//
AMUSEMENT BUSINESS - Jan 9, 1961+
ART PAPERS - 1976+
CANEWS - ?+
CELEBRITY - Jun, 1975 - ?//.
DOWN BEAT - Jul, 1934+
DRAMA - Jul, 1919+ {United Kingdom}
DRAMATIC MAGAZINE, THE - Aug, 1897 - Aug, 1900//
DRAMATIC MIRROR, THE - 1879 - Apr, 1922//
ENTERTAINMENT CONNECTION MAGAZINE - ?+
FAME - Jun, 1988 - Dec, 1990//
FRESH! - Jan 1, 1985+
IN CONCERT PRESENTS - Jul/Aug, 1990+
JOURNAL OF ARTS MANAGEMENT AND LAW, THE - Winter, 1969+
NEGRO ACTORS GUILD OF AMERICA. NEWSLETTER. - May, 1940+?
PERFORMANCE - ?+
PHOTOSTAR - Oct/Nov, 1990+
PIC - Jul 11, 1934 - ?//
SH-BOOM - Jan, 1990+
SHOW - Sep, 1952? - ?//
SHOW BIZ WEST - 1979+
SHOW BUSINESS ILLUSTRATED - Sep 5, 1961 - Apr, 1962//
SHOWCASE WORLD - ?+
STAGE AND TELEVISION TODAY, THE - 1880+ {United Kingdom}
STAGE PICTORIAL - Mar, 1912+?
STAGE PICTORIAL - Winter, 1944 - Jul, 1946//
SUPER TEEN - Oct, 1978+
TGIF - ?+?
THEATRE ARTS - Nov, 1916 - Jan, 1964//
VARIETY - Dec 16, 1905+

Avant-garde
ART PAPERS - 1976+
HIGH PERFORMANCE - Feb, 1978+

Black
ENTERTAINMENT CONNECTION MAGAZINE - ?+
FRESH! - Jan 1, 1985+
NEGRO ACTORS GUILD OF AMERICA. NEWSLETTER. - May, 1940+?

Blues
DOWN BEAT - Jul, 1934+

Boston
ART DYNAMO - Summer, 1991?+
CASTING NEWS - Aug 1, 1988?+

Business
AMUSEMENT BUSINESS - Jan 9, 1961+
VARIETY - Dec 16, 1905+

Casting
SPOTLIGHT CASTING MAGAZINE - ?+

Concert
AMUSEMENT BUSINESS - Jan 9, 1961+
MUSICAL AMERICA - 1898 - 1964//

Performing Arts
Subject Heading — INDEX

Cultural
HOWARD JOURNAL OF COMMUNICATIONS, THE - Spring, 1988+

Dance
AFTER DARK - May, 1968 - Jan, 1983//
BALLETT INTERNATIONAL - Jan, 1978+ (Germany)
MUSICAL AMERICA - ?+
PERFORMING ARTS IN CANADA, THE - Mar, 1961+ (Canada)

Demographics
AMERICAN DEMOGRAPHICS - Jan, 1979+

Employment
CASTING CALL - Jan 17, 1976+
DRAMA-LOGUE - Jan, 1970?+
SHOW BIZ WEST - 1979+
SHOW BUSINESS - 1941+
STAGE AND TELEVISION TODAY, THE - 1880+ (United Kingdom)
TGIF - ?+?

Exhibition
AMUSEMENT BUSINESS - Jan 9, 1961+
DRAMATIC MIRROR, THE - 1879 - Apr, 1922//

Fan
FRESH! - Jan 1, 1985+
IN CONCERT PRESENTS - Jul/Aug, 1990+
PHOTOSTAR - Oct/Nov, 1990+
PIC - Jul 11, 1934 - ?//
SH-BOOM - Jan, 1990+
STAGE PICTORIAL - Mar, 1912+?
SUPER TEEN - Oct, 1978+

Funding
ART PAPERS - 1976+

Guide
DRAMA - Jul, 1919+ (United Kingdom)
FAME - Jun, 1988 - Dec, 1990//
HIT PARADER - Nov, 1942 - ?//
INTERMISSION - ?+
MEDIA ARTS - 1980+?
PIC - Jul 11, 1934 - ?//
RADIO CITY NEWS - Apr 3, 1933 - Nov 2, 1933//
ROXY THEATRE WEEKLY REVIEW - Aug, 1926 - ?//
SHOW - Oct, 1961+?
SHOW - Jan, 1970 - Nov, 1973//
STAGE - Dec, 1923 - Jun, 1939//
STAGE AND TELEVISION TODAY, THE - 1880+ (United Kingdom)
STAGE PICTORIAL - Winter, 1944 - Jul, 1946//

Historical
SH-BOOM - Jan, 1990+

THEATRE DOCUMENTATION - Fall, 1968 - 1971/1972// (Brazil)

Instrumental
MUSICAL AMERICA - ?+

Intercultural
PERFORMING ARTS JOURNAL - Spring, 1976+

International
DRAMA - Jul, 1919+ (United Kingdom)
THEATRE DOCUMENTATION - Fall, 1968 - 1971/1972// (Brazil)

Jazz
DOWN BEAT - Jul, 1934+

Legal
CARDOZO ARTS & ENTERTAINMENT LAW JOURNAL - Spring, 1982+
COMMUNICATIONS LAWYER - Winter, 1983+
ENTERTAINMENT AND SPORTS LAWYER, THE - Spring, 1982+
FORDHAM ENTERTAINMENT, MEDIA & INTELLECTUAL PROPERTY LAW FORUM - Autumn, 1990+
HASTINGS COMMUNICATIONS AND ENTERTAINMENT LAW JOURNAL - 1977+
JOURNAL OF ARTS MANAGEMENT AND LAW, THE - Winter, 1969+
LOYOLA ENTERTAINMENT JOURNAL - Apr, 1981+

Licensing
ASCAP IN ACTION - Fall, 1979+

Lighting
LIGHTING DIMENSIONS - Jan, 1977+
LIGHTS! - Jan, 1990+ (United Kingdom)

Literature
COMMUNICATION BOOKNOTES - Nov, 1969+

Management
AMUSEMENT BUSINESS - Jan 9, 1961+
JOURNAL OF ARTS MANAGEMENT AND LAW, THE - Winter, 1969+
STAGE AND TELEVISION TODAY, THE - 1880+ (United Kingdom)

Marketing
AMERICAN DEMOGRAPHICS - Jan, 1979+
AMUSEMENT BUSINESS - Jan 9, 1961+

Minorities
HOWARD JOURNAL OF COMMUNICATIONS, THE - Spring, 1988+
NEGRO ACTORS GUILD OF AMERICA. NEWSLETTER. - May, 1940+?

Museums
MEDIA ARTS - 1980+?

Music
ASCAP IN ACTION - Fall, 1979+
DOWN BEAT - Jul, 1934+
DRAMATIC MAGAZINE, THE - Aug, 1897 - Aug, 1900//
HIT PARADER - Nov, 1942 - ?//
MUSIC LINE - May, 1983+
MUSICAL AMERICA - 1898 - 1964//
MUSICAL AMERICA - ?+
PERFORMING ARTS IN CANADA, THE - Mar, 1961+ (Canada)
RADIO CITY NEWS - Apr 3, 1933 - Nov 2, 1933//
SUPER TEEN - Oct, 1978+

New England
ART DYNAMO - Summer, 1991?+
CASTING NEWS - Aug 1, 1988?+

New York City
SHOW - Jan, 1970 - Nov, 1973//
SHOW BUSINESS - 1941+
STAGE PICTORIAL - Winter, 1944 - Jul, 1946//

Opera
DRAMATIC MAGAZINE, THE - Aug, 1897 - Aug, 1900//
PERFORMING ARTS IN CANADA, THE - Mar, 1961+ (Canada)

Performance
HIGH PERFORMANCE - Feb, 1978+

Popular Culture
SH-BOOM - Jan, 1990+

Producing
AMUSEMENT BUSINESS - Jan 9, 1961+

Production
AMUSEMENT BUSINESS - Jan 9, 1961+
DRAMA - Jul, 1919+ (United Kingdom)
DRAMATIC MAGAZINE, THE - Aug, 1897 - Aug, 1900//
ENTERTAINMENT REVUE - Apr, 1988+
LIGHTING DIMENSIONS - Jan, 1977+
LIGHTS! - Jan, 1990+ (United Kingdom)
NEW THEATRE - Aug, 1939 - Jul, 1949// (United Kingdom)

Radio City Music Hall
RADIO CITY NEWS - Apr 3, 1933 - Nov 2, 1933//

Records & Compact Discs
DOWN BEAT - Jul, 1934+

Regulation
- CARDOZO ARTS & ENTERTAINMENT LAW JOURNAL - Spring, 1982+
- COMMUNICATIONS LAWYER - Winter, 1983+
- ENTERTAINMENT AND SPORTS LAWYER, THE - Spring, 1982+
- FORDHAM ENTERTAINMENT, MEDIA & INTELLECTUAL PROPERTY LAW FORUM - Autumn, 1990+
- HASTINGS COMMUNICATIONS AND ENTERTAINMENT LAW JOURNAL - 1977+
- JOURNAL OF ARTS MANAGEMENT AND LAW, THE - Winter, 1969+
- LOYOLA ENTERTAINMENT JOURNAL - Apr, 1981+

Religion
- CANEWS - ?+
- MUSIC LINE - May, 1983+

Research
- HOWARD JOURNAL OF COMMUNICATIONS, THE - Spring, 1988+
- LEONARDO - Jan, 1968+
- THEATRE DOCUMENTATION - Fall, 1968 - 1971/1972// {Brazil}

Review
- ART DYNAMO - Summer, 1991?+
- ART PAPERS - 1976+
- BALLETT INTERNATIONAL - Jan, 1978+ {Germany}
- DOWN BEAT - Jul, 1934+
- DRAMATIC MIRROR, THE - 1879 - Apr, 1922//
- ENTERTAINMENT CONNECTION MAGAZINE - ?+
- ENTERTAINMENT REVUE - Apr, 1988+
- FAME - Jun, 1988 - Dec, 1990//
- HOWARD JOURNAL OF COMMUNICATIONS, THE - Spring, 1988+
- MUSICAL AMERICA - ?+
- PERFORMING ARTS JOURNAL - Spring, 1976+
- SHOW - Sep, 1952? - ?//
- SHOW - Oct, 1961+?
- SHOW - Jan, 1970 - Nov, 1973//
- SHOW BUSINESS ILLUSTRATED - Sep 5, 1961 - Apr, 1962//
- SHOWCASE WORLD - ?+
- STAGE - Dec, 1923 - Jun, 1939//
- VARIETY - Dec 16, 1905+

Scripts
- NEW THEATRE - Aug, 1939 - Jul, 1949// {United Kingdom}

Technology
- LEONARDO - Jan, 1968+
- LIGHTING DIMENSIONS - Jan, 1977+

Unions & Guilds
- NEGRO ACTORS GUILD OF AMERICA. NEWSLETTER. - May, 1940+?

Vocal
- MUSICAL AMERICA - 1898 - 1964//
- MUSICAL AMERICA - ?+

World
- BALLETT INTERNATIONAL - Jan, 1978+ {Germany}
- PERFORMING ARTS JOURNAL - Spring, 1976+
- THEATRE ARTS - Nov, 1916 - Jan, 1964//

Photography

Academic
- INTERCOMM - Fall, 1977?+
- PHOTOEDUCATION - Winter, 1983+

Advertising
- AMERICAN DEMOGRAPHICS - Jan, 1979+
- APPLIED PHOTOGRAPHY - May, 1931 - 1975//
- IMAGES & IDEAS BY PHOTOMETHODS - Jul, 1982+
- PHOTO/DESIGN - Aug/Sep, 1984+

Aesthetics
- CAMERA, THE - ?+?
- CAMERA 35 INCORPORATING PHOTO WORLD - Jun, 1978 - Apr, 1982//
- LEICA FOTOGRAFIE INTERNATIONAL - Jan, 1951+ {Germany}
- PENTAX FAMILY - ?+ {Japan}
- PHOTOGRAPHER'S FRIEND, THE - Jan, 1871 - Nov, 1874//
- PHOTOPRO - Spring, 1990+

Amateur
- AMATEUR PHOTOGRAPHER - Jun 19, 1918+ {United Kingdom}
- AMATEUR PHOTOGRAPHER'S WEEKLY, THE - Jul 12, 1912 - Oct 17, 1919//
- AMATEUR POINTER FOR AMATEUR PHOTOGRAPHERS, THE - Jan, 1899 - Feb, 1902//
- AMERICAN AMATEUR PHOTOGRAPHER AND CAMERA & DARKROOM - Jan, 1907 - Jun, 1907//
- AMERICAN PHOTOGRAPHY - Jul, 1907 - Jul, 1953//
- CAMERA AND DARK ROOM - Feb, 1899 - Dec, 1906//
- DEVELOPER, THE - 1893 - Jan, 1896//

Animation
- ADVANCED IMAGING - Jun, 1988+

Art Form
- IMAGES & IDEAS BY PHOTOMETHODS - Jul, 1982+

Avant-garde
- CONTEMPORARY PHOTOGRAPHER - May/Jun, 1960 - Fall, 1971//

Business
- BULLETIN OF PHOTOGRAPHY - Aug 14, 1907 - Jun 24, 1931//
- COMMERCIAL CAMERA - May, 1931 - 1969//
- COMMERCIAL PHOTOGRAPHER, THE - Oct, 1925 - Mar, 1950//
- COMMERCIAL PHOTOGRAPHIC NEWS, THE - Jan, 1872 - Oct, 1872//
- IMAGES & IDEAS BY PHOTOMETHODS - Jul, 1982+
- PHOTOGRAPHER'S MARKET NEWSLETTER - Nov, 1982+
- PHOTOGRAPHIC PROCESSING - 1964+
- PHOTOPRO - Spring, 1990+
- PROFESSIONAL PHOTOGRAPHER, THE - Dec 7, 1907 - Aug, 1961//
- ST. LOUIS AND CANADIAN PHOTOGRAPHER - Jan, 1877 - Jan, 1910//
- STUDIO PHOTOGRAPHY - Jan, 1965+

Collector
- GRAPHIC ANTIQUARIAN - Jul, 1970+
- HISTORY OF PHOTOGRAPHY - Jan, 1977+ {United Kingdom}
- PHOTIQUE - Sep?, 1988+?

Commercial
- CAMERA CRAFT - May, 1900 - Mar, 1942//
- COMMERCIAL CAMERA - May, 1931 - 1969//
- COMMERCIAL PHOTOGRAPHER, THE - Oct, 1925 - Mar, 1950//
- IMAGES & IDEAS BY PHOTOMETHODS - Jul, 1982+
- INTERNATIONAL PHOTOGRAPHER MAGAZINE - Spring, 1986+
- LEICA FOTOGRAFIE INTERNATIONAL - Jan, 1951+ {Germany}
- NEW PHOTO-MINIATURE - Apr, 1899 - Oct, 1936?//
- PROFESSIONAL PHOTOGRAPHER, THE - Dec 7, 1907 - Aug, 1961//
- ST. LOUIS AND CANADIAN PHOTOGRAPHER - Jan, 1877 - Jan, 1910//
- WESTERN PHOTOGRAPHER MAGAZINE - Jan, 1961+

Corporate
- FUNCTIONAL PHOTOGRAPHY - 1949 - Mar, 1955// {United Kingdom}
- FUNCTIONAL PHOTOGRAPHY - Winter, 1966/1967 - May?, 1988//
- INDUSTRIAL PHOTOGRAPHY - Fall, 1952+
- TECHNICAL PHOTOGRAPHY - Dec, 1968/Jan, 1969 - May, 1988//

Darkroom
- DARKROOM PHOTOGRAPHY - Mar/Apr, 1979+?

Photography Subject Heading

Demographics
AMERICAN DEMOGRAPHICS - Jan, 1979+

Design
PHOTO/DESIGN - Aug/Sep, 1984+

Exterior
OUTDOOR & TRAVEL PHOTOGRAPHY - Fall, 1988+
OUTDOOR PHOTOGRAPHER - Feb, 1985+

Fashion
IMAGE - Aug, 1976+ {United Kingdom}

Graphics
ADVANCED IMAGING - Jun, 1988+
AFTERIMAGE - 1972+
PHOTO/DESIGN - Aug/Sep, 1984+

Historical
CAMERA ARTS - Nov/Dec, 1980 - Jul, 1983//
GRAPHIC ANTIQUARIAN - Jul, 1970+
HISTORY OF PHOTOGRAPHY - Jan, 1977+ {United Kingdom}
IMAGE - Jan, 1952+
PHOTIQUE - Sep?, 1988+?

Home Consumer
PHOTO ANSWERS - Apr, 1989+ {United Kingdom}
35MM PHOTOGRAPHY - May, 1958 - Sep, 1965// {United Kingdom}

House Organ
KODAK - Jun, 1920 - Sep, 1944?//?

Instructional
AMATEUR PHOTOGRAPHER - Jun 19, 1918+ {United Kingdom}
AMERICAN AMATEUR PHOTOGRAPHER AND CAMERA & DARKROOM - Jan, 1907 - Jun, 1907//
AMERICAN PHOTOGRAPHY - Jul, 1907 - Jul, 1953//
AUSTRALIAN PHOTOGRAPHY - 1950+ {Australia}
BIOMEDICAL COMMUNICATIONS - Jan, 1973 to date.
DARKROOM AND CREATIVE CAMERA TECHNIQUES - Jan, 1979+
ILFORD PHOTO INSTRUCTOR NEWSLETTER - Spring, 1989+

Interactive
ADVANCED IMAGING - Jun, 1988+

Intercultural
APERTURE - Apr, 1952+

International
APERTURE - Apr, 1952+
CAMERA - Jan, 1922 - Dec, 1981// {Switzerland}
HISTORY OF PHOTOGRAPHY - Jan, 1977+ {United Kingdom}
LEICA FOTOGRAFIE INTERNATIONAL - Jan, 1951+ {Germany}
OUTDOOR PHOTOGRAPHER - Feb, 1985+
PHOTO DISTRICT NEWS - Dec, 1984?+
PHOTO-ERA MAGAZINE - May, 1898 - Mar, 1932//
PHOTO TECHNIQUE INTERNATIONAL - 1954?+ {Germany}
ZOOM - ?+ {France}

Laboratory
PHOTO LAB MANAGEMENT - Mar/Apr, 1979+

Large Format
VIEWCAMERA - Jan/Feb, 1988+

Lens
LENS MAGAZINE - Sep/Oct, 1975+?
ZEISS INFORMATION - 1963+ {Germany}

Literature
COMMUNICATION BOOKNOTES - Nov, 1969+
ROTKIN REVIEW, THE - Summer, 1985+

Management
PHOTO LAB MANAGEMENT - Mar/Apr, 1979+
PHOTO MARKETING - Jun, 1924+
STUDIO PHOTOGRAPHY - Jan, 1965+

Marketing
AMERICAN DEMOGRAPHICS - Jan, 1979+
PHOTO MARKETING - Jun, 1924+
PHOTOGRAPHER'S MARKET NEWSLETTER - Nov, 1982+
PHOTOPRO - Spring, 1990+

Medical
BIOMEDICAL COMMUNICATIONS - Jan, 1973 to date.

New England
VIEWS - ?+

News
DARKSLIDE - ?+
4SIGHT MAGAZINE - Mar/Apr, 1983+
IMAGE 11 - ?+
INTERNATIONAL PHOTOGRAPHER MAGAZINE - Spring, 1986+
NEWS PHOTOGRAPHER - Apr, 1946+
RANGEFINDER, THE - ?+
RETROFOCUS - ?+
SIXSHOOTERS - ?+

Processing
PHOTOGRAPHIC PROCESSING - 1964+

Production
AMATEUR PHOTOGRAPHER'S WEEKLY, THE - Jul 12, 1912 - Oct 17, 1919//
AMATEUR POINTER FOR AMATEUR PHOTOGRAPHERS, THE - Jan, 1899 - Feb, 1902//
AMERICAN AMATEUR PHOTOGRAPHER AND CAMERA & DARKROOM - Jan, 1907 - Jun, 1907//
APPLIED PHOTOGRAPHY - May, 1931 - 1975//
APR - 1894 - Dec, 1956// {Australia}
ASMP BULLETIN - ?+
AUSTRALIAN PHOTOGRAPHY - 1950+ {Australia}
BIOMEDICAL COMMUNICATIONS - Jan, 1973 to date.
BRITISH JOURNAL OF PHOTOGRAPHY - Jan, 1854+ {United Kingdom}
CAMERA & CAMCORDER MONTHLY - ? - Mar, 1990// {United Kingdom}
CAMERA AND DARK ROOM - Feb, 1899 - Dec, 1906//
CAMERA & DARKROOM PHOTOGRAPHY - Mar/Apr, 1979+
CAMERA MAGAZINE - Mar, 1949 - Jul, 1953//
CAMERA 35 INCORPORATING PHOTO WORLD - Jun, 1978 - Apr, 1982//
CAMERART - Spring, 1958+ {Japan}
CANADIAN PHOTOGRAPHIC JOURNAL, THE - Feb, 1892+? {Canada}
COMMERCIAL PHOTOGRAPHER, THE - Oct, 1925 - Mar, 1950//
DARKROOM PHOTOGRAPHY - Mar/Apr, 1979+?
FUNCTIONAL PHOTOGRAPHY - 1949 - Mar, 1955// {United Kingdom}
INDUSTRIAL PHOTOGRAPHY - Fall, 1952+
MODERN PHOTOGRAPHY - Sep, 1937 - Jul, 1989//
NEW PHOTO-MINIATURE - Apr, 1899 - Oct, 1936?//
OUTDOOR & TRAVEL PHOTOGRAPHY - Fall, 1988+
OUTDOOR PHOTOGRAPHER - Feb, 1985+
PETERSEN'S PHOTOGRAPHIC - Fall, 1971+
PHOTO ANSWERS - Apr, 1989+ {United Kingdom}
PHOTO-BEACON, THE - 1887 - Jun, 1907//
PHOTO DISTRICT NEWS - Dec, 1984?+
PHOTO-ERA MAGAZINE - May, 1898 - Mar, 1932//
PHOTO TECHNIQUE INTERNATIONAL - 1954?+ {Germany}
PHOTOGRAPHER'S FRIEND, THE - Jan, 1871 - Nov, 1874//
PHOTOGRAPHIC TIMES, THE - Jan, 1871 - Dec, 1915//
PHOTOMETHODS - 1958+
PIC - ?+? {United Kingdom}
POPULAR PHOTOGRAPHY - May, 1937+.
PRACTICAL PHOTOGRAPHER, THE - Apr, 1904 - Nov, 1905//

PRACTICAL PHOTOGRAPHY - ?+ {United Kingdom}
PROFESSIONAL PHOTOGRAPHER, THE - Sep, 1961+
PROFESSIONAL PHOTOGRAPHER, THE - May, 1961+ {United Kingdom}
RANGEFINDER, THE - Jun, 1952+
SCIENCE AND FILM - Feb, 1952 - Apr, 1960// {United Kingdom}
ST. LOUIS AND CANADIAN PHOTOGRAPHER - Jan, 1877 - Jan, 1910//
TECHNICAL PHOTOGRAPHY - Dec, 1968/Jan, 1969 - May, 1988//
35MM PHOTOGRAPHY - May, 1958 - Sep, 1965// {United Kingdom}
TRAVEL & LEISURE - 1935+
WESTERN PHOTOGRAPHER MAGAZINE - Jan, 1961+

Promotion
APR - 1894 - Dec, 1956// {Australia}
BURR MCINTOSH MONTHLY, THE - Apr, 1903 - May, 1910//
CLOSE-UP - Sep, 1970+
HASSELBLAD - ?+ {Sweden}
INTERCOMM - Fall, 1977?+
KODAK - Jun, 1920 - Sep, 1944?//?
LEICA PHOTOGRAPHY - Dec, 1932 - ?, 1977//
PHOTOEDUCATION - Winter, 1983+
POSITIVE IMAGE, THE - Jan, 1981 - Feb, 1982//

Public
EXPOSURE - 1963+

Research
FUNCTIONAL PHOTOGRAPHY - Winter, 1966/1967 - May?, 1988//
LEONARDO - Jan, 1968+
SCIENCE AND FILM - Feb, 1952 - Apr, 1960// {United Kingdom}

Retail
BULLETIN OF PHOTOGRAPHY - Aug 14, 1907 - Jun 24, 1931//
COMMERCIAL CAMERA - May, 1931 - 1969//
PHOTO MARKETING - Jun, 1924+
PHOTOGRAPHER'S FRIEND, THE - Jan, 1871 - Nov, 1874//
PHOTOLETTER - 1976+
ST. LOUIS AND CANADIAN PHOTOGRAPHER - Jan, 1877 - Jan, 1910//

Review
AFTERIMAGE - 1972+
ALBUM - Feb, 1970+ {United Kingdom}
ALBUM, THE - February 4, 1895 - Mar, 1896// {United Kingdom}
AMERICAN PHOTO - June, 1978+
APERTURE - Apr, 1952+
ASMP BULLETIN - ?+
AUSTRALIAN PHOTOGRAPHY - 1950+ {Australia}

BULGARSKO FOTO - 1966+ {Bulgaria}
BURR MCINTOSH MONTHLY, THE - Apr, 1903 - May, 1910//
CAMERA - Jan, 1922 - Dec, 1981// {Switzerland}
CAMERA, THE - ?+?
CAMERA ARTS - Nov/Dec, 1980 - Jul, 1983//
CAMERA CRAFT - May, 1900 - Mar, 1942//
CAMERA MAGAZINE - Mar, 1949 - Jul, 1953//
CAMERA 35 - Spring, 1957 - May?, 1978//
CAMERA 35 INCORPORATING PHOTO WORLD - Jun, 1978 - Apr, 1982//
CAMERART - Spring, 1958+ {Japan}
CANADIAN PHOTOGRAPHIC JOURNAL, THE - Feb, 1892+? {Canada}
CONTEMPORARY PHOTOGRAPHER - May/Jun, 1960 - Fall, 1971//
CREATIVE CAMERA - 1963+? {United Kingdom}
EXPOSURE - 1963+
4SIGHT MAGAZINE - Mar/Apr, 1983+
IMAGE - Aug, 1976+ {United Kingdom}
IMAGE 11 - ?+
MODERN PHOTOGRAPHY - Sep, 1937 - Jul, 1989//
NATIONAL PHOTOGRAPHER, THE - 1949 - ?//
NIKON WORLD - Spring, 1967+?
PHOTO-BEACON, THE - 1887 - Jun, 1907//
PHOTO TECHNIQUE INTERNATIONAL - 1954?+ {Germany}
PHOTOGRAPHER'S FORUM - Nov, 1978+
PHOTOGRAPHY - Oct, 1965+ {United Kingdom}
PIC - ?+? {United Kingdom}
PSA JOURNAL - Mar, 1935+
RANGEFINDER, THE - ?+
ROTKIN REVIEW, THE - Summer, 1985+
SHUTTERBUG - 1971+
VIEWS - ?+
WISCONSIN PHOTOGRAPHER - Oct, 1978+
ZOOM - ?+ {France}

Studio
STUDIO PHOTOGRAPHY - Jan, 1965+

Teaching
ILFORD PHOTO INSTRUCTOR NEWSLETTER - Spring, 1989+
PHOTOEDUCATION - Winter, 1983+

Technology
ADVANCED IMAGING - Jun, 1988+
AMATEUR PHOTOGRAPHER - Jun 19, 1918+ {United Kingdom}
AMERICAN PHOTOGRAPHY - Jul, 1907 - Jul, 1953//
BRITISH JOURNAL OF PHOTOGRAPHY - Jan, 1854+ {United Kingdom}
CAMERA, THE - ?+?
CAMERA & CAMCORDER MONTHLY - ? - Mar, 1990// {United Kingdom}
CAMERA AND DARK ROOM - Feb, 1899 - Dec, 1906//
CAMERA MAGAZINE - Mar, 1949 - Jul, 1953//

CAMERA 35 - Spring, 1957 - May?, 1978//
CAMERART - Spring, 1958+ {Japan}
CANADIAN PHOTOGRAPHIC JOURNAL, THE - Feb, 1892+? {Canada}
DARKROOM AND CREATIVE CAMERA TECHNIQUES - Jan, 1979+
DEVELOPER, THE - 1893 - Jan, 1896//
FUNCTIONAL PHOTOGRAPHY - Winter, 1966/1967 - May?, 1988//
IMAGES & IDEAS BY PHOTOMETHODS - Jul, 1982+
INDUSTRIAL PHOTOGRAPHY - Fall, 1952+
LEICA PHOTOGRAPHY - Dec, 1932 - ?, 1977//
LENS MAGAZINE - Sep/Oct, 1975+?
LEONARDO - Jan, 1968+
MODERN PHOTOGRAPHY - Sep, 1937 - Jul, 1989//
NEW PHOTO-MINIATURE - Apr, 1899 - Oct, 1936?//
PERSPECTIVE - Autumn, 1958 - 1966// {United Kingdom}
PETERSEN'S PHOTOGRAPHIC - Fall, 1971+
PHOTIQUE - Sep?, 1988+?
PHOTO ANSWERS - Apr, 1989+ {United Kingdom}
PHOTO-ERA MAGAZINE - May, 1898 - Mar, 1932//
PHOTO LAB MANAGEMENT - Mar/Apr, 1979+
PHOTOGRAPHIC TIMES, THE - Jan, 1871 - Dec, 1915//
PHOTOMETHODS - 1958+
PHOTOPRO - Spring, 1990+
PIC - ?+? {United Kingdom}
POPULAR PHOTOGRAPHY - May, 1937+.
PRACTICAL PHOTOGRAPHER, THE - Apr, 1904 - Nov, 1905//
PRACTICAL PHOTOGRAPHY - ?+ {United Kingdom}
PSA JOURNAL - Mar, 1935+
RANGEFINDER, THE - Jun, 1952+
SCIENCE AND FILM - Feb, 1952 - Apr, 1960// {United Kingdom}
SHUTTERBUG - 1971+
TECHNICAL PHOTOGRAPHY - Dec, 1968/Jan, 1969 - May, 1988//
35MM PHOTOGRAPHY - May, 1958 - Sep, 1965// {United Kingdom}
TRAVEL & LEISURE - 1935+
WESTERN PHOTOGRAPHER MAGAZINE - Jan, 1961+
ZEISS INFORMATION - 1963+ {Germany}

Travel
TRAVEL & LEISURE - 1935+

Wisconsin
WISCONSIN PHOTOGRAPHER - Oct, 1978+

Point-to-Point Media

Business
AMERICAN TELEGRAPH MAGAZINE - Oct, 1852 - Jul, 1853//
AMERICAN TELEPHONE JOURNAL, THE - 1900 - Aug 29, 1908//
CABLE COMMUNICATIONS MAGAZINE - May, 1934?+ {Canada}
TELECOMMUNICATIONS - Sep, 1981+

CB
CB LIFE - ?+?

Corporate
NETWORK WORLD - Nov, 1984+

Cultural
TECHNOLOGY AND CULTURE - Winter, 1959+

Design
IEEE TRANSACTIONS ON COMMUNICATIONS - 1953+

Electronics
COMMUNICATION ENGINEERING - Nov, 1940 - Mar, 1954//
ELECTRONICS WORLD + WIRELESS WORLD - Apr, 1922+ {United Kingdom}
MILITARY ELECTRONICS / COUNTERMEASURES - Jan, 1975+

Engineering
COMMUNICATION ENGINEERING - Nov, 1940 - Mar, 1954//
ELECTRICAL COMMUNICATION - Aug, 1922+ {United Kingdom}
ELECTRONICS WORLD + WIRELESS WORLD - Apr, 1922+ {United Kingdom}
IEEE TRANSACTIONS ON COMMUNICATIONS - 1953+
MILITARY ELECTRONICS / COUNTERMEASURES - Jan, 1975+

Historical
TECHNOLOGY AND CULTURE - Winter, 1959+

House Organ
COMMUNICATE - ?+

International
TELECOMMUNICATION JOURNAL - 1934+ {Switzerland}
TELECOMMUNICATIONS - Sep, 1981+

Legal
CABLE TV AND NEW MEDIA LAW & FINANCE - ?+

Literature
COMMUNICATION BOOKNOTES - Nov, 1969+

Management
AMERICAN TELEPHONE JOURNAL, THE - 1900 - Aug 29, 1908//
BUSINESS COMMUNICATIONS REVIEW - Jan?, 1971+
NETWORK WORLD - Nov, 1984+

Military
MILITARY ELECTRONICS / COUNTERMEASURES - Jan, 1975+

Promotion
AT&T MAGAZINE - Apr, 1922 - 1985//
INVIEW - Spring, 1989+

Regulation
AMERICAN TELEGRAPH MAGAZINE - Oct, 1852 - Jul, 1853//
CABLE TV AND NEW MEDIA LAW & FINANCE - ?+
COMMUNICATIONSWEEK - Feb 1, 1984+
FCC WEEK - 198u+
FEDERAL COMMUNICATIONS LAW JOURNAL - Mar, 1937+
TELECOMMUNICATION JOURNAL - 1934+ {Switzerland}

Research
AT&T TECHNICAL JOURNAL - Jul, 1922+
AT&T TECHNOLOGY - Sep, 1925+

Review
AMERICAN TELEGRAPH MAGAZINE - Oct, 1852 - Jul, 1853//
AT&T MAGAZINE - Apr, 1922 - 1985//
AT&T TECHNICAL JOURNAL - Jul, 1922+
CABLE COMMUNICATIONS MAGAZINE - May, 1934?+ {Canada}
COMMUNICATIONS NEWS - Oct, 1964+
COMMUNICATIONSWEEK - Feb 1, 1984+

Satellites
TELECOMMUNICATION JOURNAL - 1934+ {Switzerland}
TELECOMMUNICATIONS - Sep, 1981+

Technology
AMERICAN TELEGRAPH MAGAZINE - Oct, 1852 - Jul, 1853//
AMERICAN TELEPHONE JOURNAL, THE - 1900 - Aug 29, 1908//
AT&T MAGAZINE - Apr, 1922 - 1985//
AT&T TECHNICAL JOURNAL - Jul, 1922+
AT&T TECHNOLOGY - Sep, 1925+
BUSINESS COMMUNICATIONS REVIEW - Jan?, 1971+
CB LIFE - ?+?
COMMUNICATION ENGINEERING - Nov, 1940 - Mar, 1954//
COMMUNICATIONS - 1964+
COMMUNICATIONS NEWS - Oct, 1964+
COMMUNICATIONSWEEK - Feb 1, 1984+
ELECTRICAL COMMUNICATION - Aug, 1922+ {United Kingdom}
INTERMEDIA - Mar/Apr, 1973+. {United Kingdom}
INVIEW - Spring, 1989+
NETWORK WORLD - Nov, 1984+
TECHNOLOGY AND CULTURE - Winter, 1959+
TELECOMMUNICATIONS - Sep, 1981+

Unions & Guilds
CWA NEWS - May, 1941+

World
INTERMEDIA - Mar/Apr, 1973+. {United Kingdom}

Print

Academic
AEJMC NEWS - 1968?+
CATHOLIC SCHOOL EDITOR - 1922 - Jun, 1975//
COMMUNITY COLLEGE JOURNALIST - Summer, 1972+
CSPAA BULLETIN - Summer?, 1930 - Summer, 1986//
INTELLIGENCER - 1983?+
INTERCOMM - Fall, 1977?+
JEA NEWSWIRE - Jan, 1974? - ?//
KTA NEWSLETTER - Fall, 1983+
LEARNED PUBLISHING - 1977+ {United Kingdom}
MURPHY REPORTER - ?+?
SCHOLARLY PUBLISHING - Oct, 1969+ {Canada}
SIDEBAR - May, 1978+

Activist
AIM REPORT - Aug, 1972+

Advertising
AD SENSE - 1896 - Aug, 1906//
ADVERTISER MAGAZINE, THE - Oct, 1930 - 195u//
ADVERTISER'S DIGEST - Dec, 1935 - ?//?
ADVERTISING ADVOCATE - 1902 - 1911?/?
ADVERTISING AGENCY - Sep/Oct, 1936 - Mar/Apr, 1938?//?
ADVERTISING AND MARKETING - 1964+ {United Kingdom}

Print Subject Heading

ADVERTISING & SELLING - Jun, 1909 - Apr, 1924//
ADVERTISING EXPERIENCE - 1894 - Dec, 1902//
ADVERTISING NEWS - 1893 - Sep 21, 1918//
ADVERTISING RESULTS MAGAZINE - Aug, 1909 - Sep/Oct, 1909//
ADVERTISING REVIEW - Summer, 1954 - Nov/Dec, 1958// {United Kingdom}
ADVISOR - Feb, 1899 - Dec, 1902//
AGRICULTURAL ADVERTISING - 1893 - Dec, 1918//
AMERICAN ADVERTISER - Jan, 1905 - Feb, 1906//
AMERICAN ADVERTISER - Feb, 1887+?
AMERICAN DEMOGRAPHICS - Jan, 1979+
APPLIED ARTS QUARTERLY - Spring, 1986+ {Canada}
ART DIRECTION - Winter, 1942+
ART IN ADVERTISING - Mar, 1890 - Feb, 1899?//
BOARD REPORT FOR GRAPHIC ARTISTS - ?+
BUSINESS ADVERTISING - Mar, 1964 - Aug, 1967//
COMMON SENSE - Jan, 1901 - Dec, 1910//
COMMUNICATIONS CONCEPTS - May, 1984+
CURRENT ADVERTISING - Jan, 1897 - Jan, 1903//
FLAKE - ?, 1990+
FLASH - Jul/Aug, 1990+
JOURNALISM EDUCATOR, THE - 1945+
LÜRZER'S INTERNATIONAL ARCHIVE - Feb, 1989+
MAHINS MAGAZINE - Apr, 1902 - Jun, 1904//
MORE BUSINESS - Jan, 1936 - Apr, 1942//
NOVUM GEBRAUCHSGRAPHIK - 1972+ {Germany}
PROFITABLE ADVERTISING - Jun, 1891 - May, 1909//
PUBLISHING & PRODUCTION EXECUTIVE - Jan, 1987+
YELLOW PAGES UPDATE - Summer, 1986+
YELLOW SHEET, THE - 1984?+

Aesthetics
FLASH - Jul/Aug, 1990+

Agency
YELLOW SHEET, THE - 1984?+

Alternative Media
COMIC FANDOM'S FORUM - ?+
COMICS FANDOM EXAMINER - Apr, 1988+
FACTSHEET FIVE - Jul, 1982+

Amateur
FACTSHEET FIVE - Jul, 1982+
NATIONAL AMATEUR - 1878+

Animation
CARTOONIST PROFILES - Winter, 1969+

COMICS FEATURE - Mar, 1980+
FUNNYWORLD - Oct, 1966 - Apr, 1981//
WITTYWORLD - Summer, 1987+

Britain
VICTORIAN PERIODICALS REVIEW - Jan, 1968+

Business
COMICS FANDOM EXAMINER - Apr, 1988+
COMICS WEEK - Jul 13, 1987+?
DESKTOP COMMUNICATIONS - Mar/Apr, 1989+
GRAPHIC ARTS MONTHLY - Jan, 1938+
HOW - Nov/Dec, 1985+
IN-PLANT PRINTER & ELECTRONIC PUBLISHER - Feb, 1961+
JOURNAL OF MEDIA ECONOMICS - Spring, 1988+
JOURNALIST, THE - Mar 22, 1884 - Jan, 1907//
MEDIA BUSINESS - Jan, 1987+
POLYGRAPH INTERNATIONAL - ?+ {Germany}
PRINT-EQUIP NEWS - 1964+
PRINTINGNEWS - 1928+

Cartoons
ARK - Sep/Oct?, 1984?+ {United Kingdom}
COMIC RELIEF - May, 1989+
WITTYWORLD - Summer, 1987+

Collector
FLAKE - ?, 1990+
POSTCARD COLLECTOR - Jan, 1983+

Comics
ACES - Apr/May, 1988+ {United Kingdom}
ARK - Sep/Oct?, 1984?+ {United Kingdom}
CARTOONIST PROFILES - Winter, 1969+
COMIC CELLAR, THE - 1980 - Summer, 1982//? {Canada}
COMIC FANDOM'S FORUM - ?+
COMIC INFORMER - Oct/Nov, 1981+
COMIC RELIEF - May, 1989+
COMIC SHOP NEWS - Jul 1, 1987+
COMICS BUYER'S GUIDE - 1971+
COMICS CAREER NEWSLETTER - Apr, 1988+
COMICS FANDOM EXAMINER - Apr, 1988+
COMICS FEATURE - Mar, 1980+
COMICS INTERVIEW - ?, 1983+
COMICS JOURNAL, THE - Jun?, 1974+
COMICS REVUE - 1983+
COMICS SCENE - Jan/Feb, 1981+
COMICS WEEK - Jul 13, 1987+?
FUNNYWORLD - Oct, 1966 - Apr, 1981//
GOLDEN AGE OF COMICS - Jun?, 1982+
NEMO - Jun, 1983+

Computers
COMPUTER PUBLISHING - Jan/Feb, 1986+

ELECTRONIC PUBLISHER - ?+

Corporate
BUSINESS ADVERTISING - Mar, 1964 - Aug, 1967//

Cultural
DISCOURSE & SOCIETY - Jul, 1990+ {United Kingdom}
NIEMAN REPORTS - Feb, 1947+
VICTORIAN PERIODICALS REVIEW - Jan, 1968+

Demographics
AMERICAN DEMOGRAPHICS - Jan, 1979+

Design
AIGA JOURNAL OF GRAPHIC DESIGN - 1947+
APPLIED ARTS QUARTERLY - Spring, 1986+ {Canada}
ART IN ADVERTISING - Mar, 1890 - Feb, 1899?//
COMMON SENSE - Jan, 1901 - Dec, 1910//
MORE BUSINESS - Jan, 1936 - Apr, 1942//
PRE- - Jan, 1989+
PRINT - Jun, 1940+
REALLY, A FREE NEWSLETTER - Winter, 1988/1989+
STEP-BY-STEP GRAPHICS - Nov/Dec, 1985+
WRITING CONCEPTS - ?, 1991+

Desktop Publishing
COLOPHON - ?+?
COMPUTER PUBLISHING - Jan/Feb, 1986+
COSMEP NEWSLETTER - Mar, 1981+
DESKTOP COMMUNICATIONS - Mar/Apr, 1989+
ELECTRONIC PUBLISHER - ?+
IN HOUSE GRAPHICS - Jul, 1984?+
PC PUBLISHING AND PRESENTATIONS - Jan, 1986+
PERSONAL PUBLISHING - Oct, 1985+
PUBLISH! - Sep/Oct, 1986+
PUBLISHING & PRODUCTION EXECUTIVE - Jan, 1987+
REALLY, A FREE NEWSLETTER - Winter, 1988/1989+
SCSC XEROX PIPELINE - 198u - Jul, 1989//
SERVICE FOR COMPANY COMMUNNICATORS - Sep, 1949+
SMALL PRESS - Sep/Oct, 1983+
STEP-BY-STEP ELECTRONIC DESIGN - Jan, 1989+
VENTURA LETTER, THE - Apr/May, 1987 - Dec, 1988// {Canada}
VENTURA PROFESSIONAL! - ?+

Direct Marketing
PUBLISHING & PRODUCTION EXECUTIVE - Jan, 1987+

Print
Subject Heading

Discourse
DISCOURSE & SOCIETY - Jul, 1990+ {United Kingdom}

Economics
JOURNAL OF MEDIA ECONOMICS - Spring, 1988+

Editing
BETTER EDITING - Fall, 1965 - Mar/Apr, 1974//
EDITORIAL EYE, THE - 1978+
IN BLACK AND WHITE - Mar, 1975 - Sep, 1978//
WRITING CONCEPTS - ?, 1991+

Editorial
COMIC RELIEF - May, 1989+

Employment
COMICS CAREER NEWSLETTER - Apr, 1988+
INTERNATIONAL PRESS REVIEW - Mar, 1924 - Apr, 1924// {United Kingdom}
JOURNALISM EDUCATOR, THE - 1945+

Ethics
FINELINE - Apr, 1989+
GANNETT CENTER JOURNAL - Spring, 1987+
GOOD NEWS: CHRISTIANS IN JOURNALISM - Jan, 1987+?
JOURNAL OF MASS MEDIA ETHICS - Fall/Winter, 1985/1986+
NIEMAN REPORTS - Feb, 1947+

Europe
ACES - Apr/May, 1988+ {United Kingdom}

Fan
HERO HOBBY - 1966+?

Freedom of the Press
GANNETT CENTER JOURNAL - Spring, 1987+
STUDENT PRESS LAW CENTER REPORT - Winter, 1978+

Graphics
A-D - Sep, 1934 - Apr/May, 1942//
AD SENSE - 1896 - Aug, 1906//
ADVERTISER MAGAZINE, THE - Oct, 1930 - 195u//
ADVERTISING AGENCY - Sep/Oct, 1936 - Mar/Apr, 1938?//?
ADVERTISING AND GRAPHIC ARTS TECHNIQUES - Sep, 1965+
ADVERTISING DISPLAYS - May, 1930 - 1932//
ADVERTISING EXPERIENCE - 1894 - Dec, 1902//
AIGA JOURNAL OF GRAPHIC DESIGN - 1947+
AIRBRUSH ACTION - May/Jun, 1985+
ALPHABET AND IMAGE - 1946 - Dec, 1948// {United Kingdom}
ARS TYPOGRAPHICA - Spring, 1918 - Autumn, 1934//

ART & DESIGN NEWS - Jan/Feb, 1979+
ART DIRECTION - Winter, 1942+
ART IN ADVERTISING - Mar, 1890 - Feb, 1899?//
BOARD REPORT FOR GRAPHIC ARTISTS - ?+
COMMUNICATION ARTS - Aug, 1959+
FLASH - Jul/Aug, 1990+
GRAPHIC - Summer, 1955+?
GRAPHIC ARTS, THE - Jan, 1911 - Jun, 1915//
GRAPHIC DESIGN: USA - May, 1980+
GRAPHICS: U.S.A. - Aug, 1966 - Apr, 1980//
GRAPHIS - Sep/Oct, 1944+ {Switzerland}
HOW - Nov/Dec, 1985+
LÜRZER'S INTERNATIONAL ARCHIVE - Feb, 1989+
MORE BUSINESS - Jan, 1936 - Apr, 1942//
NOVUM GEBRAUCHSGRAPHIK - 1972+ {Germany}
PAS GRAPHIC ARTS NEWS - 1977+
PRINT - Jun, 1940+
PRINT EDUCATION MAGAZINE - Oct, 1976+
PRINTING HISTORY - 1979+
PROFITABLE ADVERTISING - Jun, 1891 - May, 1909//
REALLY, A FREE NEWSLETTER - Winter, 1988/1989+
STEP-BY-STEP ELECTRONIC DESIGN - Jan, 1989+
STEP-BY-STEP GRAPHICS - Nov/Dec, 1985+

Guide
SMALL PRESS BOOK REVIEW, THE - Jul/Aug, 1985+

High School
C: JET - 1967+

Historical
ALPHABET AND IMAGE - 1946 - Dec, 1948// {United Kingdom}
AMERICAN JOURNALISM - Summer, 1983+
ARS TYPOGRAPHICA - Spring, 1918 - Autumn, 1934//
CARTOONIST PROFILES - Winter, 1969+
CLIO AMONG THE MEDIA - Fall, 1969?+
HERO HOBBY - 1966+?
INTELLIGENCER - 1983?+
JQ. JOURNALISM QUARTERLY. - 1924+
KTA NEWSLETTER - Fall, 1983+
PRINTING HISTORY - 1979+
VICTORIAN PERIODICALS REVIEW - Jan, 1968+

Horror
WORLD OF FANDOM, THE - Jul, 1985+

House Organ
MURPHY REPORTER - ?+?
SERVICE FOR COMPANY COMMUNNICATORS - Sep, 1949+

Independent
COSMEP NEWSLETTER - Mar, 1981+
PMA NEWSLETTER - Jan, 1983+

Information
DISCOURSE & SOCIETY - Jul, 1990+ {United Kingdom}

Instructional
AMERICAN ADVERTISER - Feb, 1887+?
AUTHOR, THE - 1948+? {United Kingdom}
AUTHOR, THE - Jan 15, 1889 - Jan 15, 1892//
STEP-BY-STEP ELECTRONIC DESIGN - Jan, 1989+
WRITER, THE - Apr, 1887+
WRITER'S DIGEST - 1920+
WRITERS' JOURNAL - Jan/Feb, 1980+

Intercultural
GANNETT CENTER JOURNAL - Spring, 1987+

International
AFRO-ASIAN JOURNALIST - Mar, 1964 - 1974//? {Indonesia}
AUSTRALASIAN PRINTER - 1950+ {Australia}
GANNETT CENTER JOURNAL - Spring, 1987+
GRAPHIS - Sep/Oct, 1944+ {Switzerland}
INTERLIT - ?+
INTERNATIONAL PRESS REVIEW - Mar, 1924 - Apr, 1924// {United Kingdom}
JOURNAL OF MEDIA ECONOMICS - Spring, 1988+
JOURNALISTS' AFFAIRS - #1, 1973 - 1980?// {Czechoslovakia}
JOURNALIST'S WORLD - Jan/Mar, 1963 - 1968// {Belgium}
JQ. JOURNALISM QUARTERLY. - 1924+
NOVUM GEBRAUCHSGRAPHIK - 1972+ {Germany}

Investigative
NEWS LEADS - Apr/May, 1976+

Journalism
AFRO-ASIAN JOURNALIST - Mar, 1964 - 1974//? {Indonesia}
AMERICAN JOURNALISM - Summer, 1983+
C: JET - 1967+
FINELINE - Apr, 1989+
GANNETT CENTER JOURNAL - Spring, 1987+
IN BLACK AND WHITE - Mar, 1975 - Sep, 1978//
JOURNAL OF MASS MEDIA ETHICS - Fall/Winter, 1985/1986+
JOURNALISM EDUCATOR, THE - 1945+
JOURNALIST - 1908+ {United Kingdom}
JOURNALIST, THE - Mar 22, 1884 - Jan, 1907//
JOURNALISTS' AFFAIRS - #1, 1973 - 1980?// {Czechoslovakia}
JOURNALIST'S WORLD - Jan/Mar, 1963 - 1968// {Belgium}
JQ. JOURNALISM QUARTERLY. - 1924+

NATIONAL AMATEUR - 1878+
NEWS LEADS - Apr/May, 1976+
NIEMAN REPORTS - Feb, 1947+
PHOTOLITH, SCM - 1950+

Legal
FINELINE - Apr, 1989+
STUDENT PRESS LAW CENTER REPORT - Winter, 1978+

Literature
COMMUNICATION BOOKNOTES - Nov, 1969+

Management
ADVERTISING NEWS - 1893 - Sep 21, 1918//
AMERICAN PRINTER - Nov, 1958+
AUSTRALASIAN PRINTER - 1950+ {Australia}
BRITISH PRINTER - 1888+ {United Kingdom}
CSPAA BULLETIN - Summer?, 1930 - Summer, 1986//
HIGH VOLUME PRINTING - ?+
IN-PLANT REPRODUCTIONS - 1951+
PRINTINGNEWS - 1928+

Manufacturing
PULP & PAPER CANADA - 1903?+ {Canada}

Marketing
ADVERTISING AND MARKETING - 1964+ {United Kingdom}
ADVERTISING & SELLING - Jun, 1909 - Apr, 1924//
AMERICAN DEMOGRAPHICS - Jan, 1979+
BUSINESS ADVERTISING - Mar, 1964 - Aug, 1967//
FLAKE - ?, 1990+
LÜRZER'S INTERNATIONAL ARCHIVE - Feb, 1989+
MAGAZINE & BOOKSELLER - 1945+

Membership
AAP MONTHLY REPORT - Sep, 1984+
GRAPHIC COMMUNICATOR - Nov, 1964+
PMA NEWSLETTER - Jan, 1983+
SCHOOL PRESS REVIEW, THE - Apr, 1925+

Minneapolis
TWIN CITIES JOURNALISM REVIEW - Feb, 1972+

Minorities
FACTSHEET FIVE - Jul, 1982+

News
CHICAGO JOURNALISM REVIEW - Oct, 1968 - Sep, 1975//
CIPA NEWS - ?+?
CONGRESSIONAL QUARTERLY'S EDITORIAL RESEARCH REPORTS - ?+
FEED-BACK - Oct, 1974+

INTERNATIONAL PRESS REVIEW - Mar, 1924 - Apr, 1924// {United Kingdom}
ST. LOUIS JOURNALISM REVIEW - Oct/Nov, 1970+
TWIN CITIES JOURNALISM REVIEW - Feb, 1972+
UK PRESS GAZETTE - 1965+ {United Kingdom}
WASHINGTON JOURNALISM REVIEW - Oct, 1977+

Packaging
POLYGRAPH INTERNATIONAL - ?+ {Germany}

Paper
PULP & PAPER CANADA - 1903?+ {Canada}

Philadelphia
MID-ATLANTIC GRAPHIC ARTS REVIEW - Jan, 1938+?

Popular Culture
NEMO - Jun, 1983+

Postcards
NATIONAL STATIONER, THE - Jan, 1908 - ?//
POSTCARD COLLECTOR - Jan, 1983+

Printing
ARS TYPOGRAPHICA - Spring, 1918 - Autumn, 1934//
BRITISH LITHOGRAPHER - Oct/Nov, 1891 - Aug/Sep, 1895// {United Kingdom}
BRITISH PRINTER - 1888+ {United Kingdom}
GRAPHIC - Summer, 1955+?
GRAPHIC ARTS - ?+? {United Kingdom}
GRAPHIC ARTS, THE - Jan, 1911 - Jun, 1915//
HIGH VOLUME PRINTING - ?+
IN-PLANT REPRODUCTIONS - 1951+
MID-ATLANTIC GRAPHIC ARTS REVIEW - Jan, 1938+?
POLYGRAPH INTERNATIONAL - ?+ {Germany}
PRACTICAL PRINTER, THE - Jan, 1899 - Sep, 1911//
PRINT - Jun, 1940+
PRINT BUYERS REVIEW - Winter, 1989+
PRINT EDUCATION MAGAZINE - Oct, 1976+
PRINT-EQUIP NEWS - 1964+
PRINTING HISTORY - 1979+
PRINTING IMPRESSIONS - June, 1958+
PRINTINGNEWS - 1928+
PUBLISHING & PRODUCTION EXECUTIVE - Jan, 1987+

Production
ADVERTISER MAGAZINE, THE - Oct, 1930 - 195u//
ALPHABET AND IMAGE - 1946 - Dec, 1948// {United Kingdom}
AMERICAN PRINTER - Nov, 1958+
AUSTRALASIAN PRINTER - 1950+ {Australia}

BRITISH LITHOGRAPHER - Oct/Nov, 1891 - Aug/Sep, 1895// {United Kingdom}
CANADIAN PRINTER - 1891+ {Canada}
GRAPHIC ARTS - ?+? {United Kingdom}
GRAPHIC ARTS MONTHLY - Jan, 1938+
GRAPHIC COMMUNICATOR - Nov, 1964+
IN-PLANT PRINTER & ELECTRONIC PUBLISHER - Feb, 1961+
PRE- - Jan, 1989+

Profile
CARTOONIST PROFILES - Winter, 1969+

Promotion
BOARD REPORT FOR GRAPHIC ARTISTS - ?+
COLOPHON - ?+?
INTERCOMM - Fall, 1977?+
MORE BUSINESS - Jan, 1936 - Apr, 1942//
PRINTING PAPER - 1911 - 1982//
SCSC XEROX PIPELINE - 198u - Jul, 1989//
SIDEBAR - May, 1978+

Public Relations
JOURNALISM EDUCATOR, THE - 1945+

Publishing
AAP MONTHLY REPORT - Sep, 1984+
BETTER EDITING - Fall, 1965 - Mar/Apr, 1974//
CANADIAN PRINTER - 1891+ {Canada}
CATHOLIC JOURNALIST - 1945+
CATHOLIC SCHOOL EDITOR - 1922 - Jun, 1975//
COMPUTER PUBLISHING - Jan/Feb, 1986+
COSMEP NEWSLETTER - Mar, 1981+
DESKTOP COMMUNICATIONS - Mar/Apr, 1989+
ELECTRONIC PUBLISHER - ?+
GRAPHIC - Summer, 1955+?
IN HOUSE GRAPHICS - Jul, 1984?+
INTERLIT - ?+
JOURNALISM EDUCATOR, THE - 1945+
LEARNED PUBLISHING - 1977+ {United Kingdom}
PERSONAL PUBLISHING - Oct, 1985+
PMA NEWSLETTER - Jan, 1983+
PRINT BUYERS REVIEW - Winter, 1989+
PUBLISHING & PRODUCTION EXECUTIVE - Jan, 1987+
REALLY, A FREE NEWSLETTER - Winter, 1988/1989+
SCHOLARLY PUBLISHING - Oct, 1969+ {Canada}
SCHOLASTIC EDITOR'S TRENDS IN PUBLICATIONS - 1923+
SCHOOL PRESS REVIEW, THE - Apr, 1925+
SMALL PRESS - Sep/Oct, 1983+
VENTURA LETTER, THE - Apr/May, 1987 - Dec, 1988// {Canada}
VENTURA PROFESSIONAL! - ?+
WHAT EDITORS WANT - ?+?

WRITER'S NW - ?+

Regulation
JQ. JOURNALISM QUARTERLY. - 1924+

Religion
CATHOLIC JOURNALIST - 1945+
CATHOLIC SCHOOL EDITOR - 1922 - Jun, 1975//
INTERLIT - ?+

Research
ARS TYPOGRAPHICA - Spring, 1918 - Autumn, 1934//
CLIO AMONG THE MEDIA - Fall, 1969?+
DISCOURSE & SOCIETY - Jul, 1990+ {United Kingdom}
JQ. JOURNALISM QUARTERLY. - 1924+
WRITTEN COMMUNICATION - Jan, 1984+

Retail
ADVERTISING DISPLAYS - May, 1930 - 1932//
COMIC SHOP NEWS - Jul 1, 1987+
MAGAZINE & BOOKSELLER - 1945+
NATIONAL STATIONER, THE - Jan, 1908 - ?//

Review
ADVERTISING ADVOCATE - 1902 - 1911?/?
ADVERTISING EXPERIENCE - 1894 - Dec, 1902//
AMERICAN ADVERTISER - Jan, 1905 - Feb, 1906//
ART DIRECTION - Winter, 1942+
ART IN ADVERTISING - Mar, 1890 - Feb, 1899?//
CHICAGO JOURNALISM REVIEW - Oct, 1968 - Sep, 1975//
CIPA NEWS - ?+?
COMICS JOURNAL, THE - Jun?, 1974+
COMICS WEEK - Jul 13, 1987+?
COMMUNICATION ARTS - Aug, 1959+
CURRENT ADVERTISING - Jan, 1897 - Jan, 1903//
FEED-BACK - Oct, 1974+
GOOD NEWS: CHRISTIANS IN JOURNALISM - Jan, 1987+?
JOURNALISTS' AFFAIRS - #1, 1973 - 1980?// {Czechoslovakia}
JQ. JOURNALISM QUARTERLY. - 1924+
MAHINS MAGAZINE - Apr, 1902 - Jun, 1904//
NIEMAN REPORTS - Feb, 1947+
SMALL PRESS BOOK REVIEW, THE - Jul/Aug, 1985+
ST. LOUIS JOURNALISM REVIEW - Oct/Nov, 1970+
TWIN CITIES JOURNALISM REVIEW - Feb, 1972+
UK PRESS GAZETTE - 1965+ {United Kingdom}
WASHINGTON JOURNALISM REVIEW - Oct, 1977+
WRITERS ON WRITING - Jul, 1982 - Jul, 1991//

Revolutionary
AFRO-ASIAN JOURNALIST - Mar, 1964 - 1974//? {Indonesia}

Saint Louis
ST. LOUIS JOURNALISM REVIEW - Oct/Nov, 1970+

Saint Paul
TWIN CITIES JOURNALISM REVIEW - Feb, 1972+

Sale
ADVERTISER'S DIGEST - Dec, 1935 - ?//?
WHAT EDITORS WANT - ?+?

Sales
ADVERTISER'S DIGEST - Dec, 1935 - ?//?

Scholarly
LEARNED PUBLISHING - 1977+ {United Kingdom}

School
C: JET - 1967+
PHOTOLITH, SCM - 1950+
SCHOLASTIC EDITOR'S TRENDS IN PUBLICATIONS - 1923+
SCHOOL PRESS REVIEW, THE - Apr, 1925+
STUDENT PRESS LAW CENTER REPORT - Winter, 1978+

Scripts
WRITER, THE - Apr, 1887+

Society
GANNETT CENTER JOURNAL - Spring, 1987+

Soviet Bloc
JOURNALISTS' AFFAIRS - #1, 1973 - 1980?// {Czechoslovakia}

Specification
PRINT BUYERS REVIEW - Winter, 1989+

Stock
PRINTING PAPER - 1911 - 1982//

Teaching
COMMUNITY COLLEGE JOURNALIST - Summer, 1972+
JEA NEWSWIRE - Jan, 1974? - ?//

Technology
AMERICAN PRINTER - Nov, 1958+
ART & DESIGN NEWS - Jan/Feb, 1979+
BRITISH PRINTER - 1888+ {United Kingdom}
GRAPHIC ARTS MONTHLY - Jan, 1938+
GRAPHICS: U.S.A. - Aug, 1966 - Apr, 1980//
POLYGRAPH INTERNATIONAL - ?+ {Germany}
PRACTICAL PRINTER, THE - Jan, 1899 - Sep, 1911//
PRE- - Jan, 1989+
PRINT-EQUIP NEWS - 1964+
PRINTING IMPRESSIONS - June, 1958+

Typography
ADVERTISING AGENCY - Sep/Oct, 1936 - Mar/Apr, 1938?/?
ALPHABET AND IMAGE - 1946 - Dec, 1948// {United Kingdom}
APPLIED ARTS QUARTERLY - Spring, 1986+ {Canada}
BASELINE - 1981?+? {United Kingdom}
BETTER EDITING - Fall, 1965 - Mar/Apr, 1974//
COLOPHON - ?+?
COMMON SENSE - Jan, 1901 - Dec, 1910//
COMMUNICATION ARTS - Aug, 1959+
GRAPHIC ARTS, THE - Jan, 1911 - Jun, 1915//
GRAPHIC DESIGN: USA - May, 1980+
GRAPHIS - Sep/Oct, 1944+ {Switzerland}
HOW - Nov/Dec, 1985+
IN HOUSE GRAPHICS - Jul, 1984?+
NOVUM GEBRAUCHSGRAPHIK - 1972+ {Germany}
U & LC - 1974+

Unions & Guilds
GRAPHIC COMMUNICATOR - Nov, 1964+
JOURNALIST - 1908+ {United Kingdom}

Writing
AUTHOR, THE - 1948+? {United Kingdom}
AUTHOR, THE - Jan 15, 1889 - Jan 15, 1892//
COMMUNICATIONS CONCEPTS - May, 1984+
IN HOUSE GRAPHICS - Jul, 1984?+
WHAT EDITORS WANT - ?+?
WRITER, THE - Apr, 1887+
WRITER'S DIGEST - 1920+
WRITERS' JOURNAL - Jan/Feb, 1980+
WRITER'S NW - ?+
WRITERS ON WRITING - Jul, 1982 - Jul, 1991//
WRITING CONCEPTS - ?, 1991+
WRITTEN COMMUNICATION - Jan, 1984+

Yearbook
SCHOLASTIC EDITOR'S TRENDS IN PUBLICATIONS - 1923+

Yellow Pages
YELLOW PAGES UPDATE - Summer, 1986+

Radio

Academic
COLLEGE BROADCASTER - Sep, 1988+

Advertising
ADVERTISING & SELLING - Jun, 1909 - Apr, 1924//
RADIO BUSINESS REPORT - Jan, 1984+
SOUND MANAGEMENT - Nov, 1984+

Amateur
ALL-WAVE RADIO - Sep, 1935 - Jun, 1938//
AMATEUR WIRELESS AND RADIOVISION - Jun 10, 1922 - Jan 19, 1935// {United Kingdom}
COMMUNICATIONS WORLD - 196u+?
CQ - Jan, 1945+
INDUSTRIAL ELECTRONICS - Oct, 1923 - Jan, 1969// {United Kingdom}
OLD TIMER'S BULLETIN, THE - ?+
PRACTICAL WIRELESS - 1932+ {United Kingdom}
QEX - ?+
QST - Dec, 1915+
RADIO AGE - May, 1922 - Jan, 1928//
RADIO & ELECTRONICS CONSTRUCTOR - ?+ {United Kingdom}
RADIO COMMUNICATION - 1925+ {United Kingdom}
73 AMATEUR RADIO - Oct, 1960+
WIRELESS AGE, THE - Oct, 1912 - Aug, 1925//

Artist
DRAMA MAGAZINE, THE - Feb, 1911 - Jun, 1931//
INTERNATIONAL RADIO REPORT, THE - 1978+
MOVIE-RADIO GUIDE - Oct 20, 1931 - Nov, 1943//
R & R - 1971?+
RADIO ALBUM MAGAZINE - Summer, 1948+?
RADIO FAN-FARE - Apr, 1922 - Oct, 1933//
RADIO HOME, THE - Jun, 1922 - ?//?
RADIO*PHILES - Nov, 1981?+?
RADIOLAND - Sep, 1932 - ?//?
RURAL RADIO - Feb, 1938+?
TV RADIO SHOW - Oct, 1966+?

Blacks
BLACK RADIO EXCLUSIVE - Jan 1, 1976?+

Business
PULSE OF RADIO - Jan 1, 1986?+
R & R - 1971?+
RADIO BUSINESS REPORT - Jan, 1984+
RADIO ONLY - Apr, 1982+

Carrier Current
JOURNAL OF COLLEGE RADIO - 1941 to date.

NATIONAL HIGH SCHOOL BROADCASTERS NEWSLETTER - Dec, 1977+

Cincinnati
RADIO DIAL - May 23, 1931 - May, 1939//

Collector
OLD TIMER'S BULLETIN, THE - ?+

College
JOURNAL OF COLLEGE RADIO - 1941 to date.

Digital
DIGITAL RADIO NEWS - Nov 3, 1990+

Electronics
ALL-WAVE RADIO - Sep, 1935 - Jun, 1938//
AMATEUR WIRELESS AND RADIOVISION - Jun 10, 1922 - Jan 19, 1935// {United Kingdom}
INDUSTRIAL ELECTRONICS - Oct, 1923 - Jan, 1969// {United Kingdom}

Employment
AWRT NEWS AND VIEWS - 1982?+
RADIO*PHILES - Nov, 1981?+?

Engineering
BUYERS GUIDE - ?+
PRACTICAL WIRELESS - 1932+ {United Kingdom}
RADIO GUIDE - Jan, 1988+
RMA ENGINEER - Nov, 1936 - May, 1940//
WIRELESS AGE, THE - Oct, 1912 - Aug, 1925//

Fan
RADIOLAND - Sep, 1932 - ?//?
RURAL RADIO - Feb, 1938+?
TV RADIO SHOW - Oct, 1966+?

Guide
AUDIO-VISUAL GUIDE - Feb, 1936 - Jun, 1956//
BBC WORLD SERVICE LONDON CALLING - ?+ {United Kingdom}
HIT PARADER - Nov, 1942 - ?//
LISTENER - Jan 16, 1929 - Jan 3, 1991// {United Kingdom}
MOVIE-RADIO GUIDE - Oct 20, 1931 - Nov, 1943//
RADIO ALBUM MAGAZINE - Summer, 1948+?
RADIO CITY NEWS - Apr 3, 1933 - Nov 2, 1933//
RADIO DIAL - May 23, 1931 - May, 1939//
RADIO FAN-FARE - Apr, 1922 - Oct, 1933//
RADIO HIT SONGS - Nov, 1941?+?
RADIO HOME, THE - Jun, 1922 - ?//?
RADIOLAND - Sep, 1932 - ?//?
ROXY THEATRE WEEKLY REVIEW - Aug, 1926 - ?//
RURAL RADIO - Feb, 1938+?
STAGE - Dec, 1923 - Jun, 1939//

Ham Radio
MONITORING TIMES - Jan, 1982+

Historical
ANTIQUE RADIO CLASSIFIED - Jan, 1984+

Home Consumer
ELECTRONICS ILLUSTRATED - May, 1958 - 1972//

International
FRENDX - ?+
JOURNAL OF RADIO LAW - Apr, 1931 - Oct, 1932//
POPULAR COMMUNICATIONS - Sep, 1982+
REVIEW OF INTERNATIONAL BROADCASTING - Mar, 1977+
TWR - Sep/Oct, 1980+

Legal
JOURNAL OF RADIO LAW - Apr, 1931 - Oct, 1932//

Management
INSIDE RADIO - Jan 1, 1976+
PULSE OF RADIO - Jan 1, 1986?+
RADIO BUSINESS REPORT - Jan, 1984+
RADIO ONLY - Apr, 1982+
RADIO*PHILES - Nov, 1981?+?
RADIOACTIVE - ? - 1988//
RADIOTRENDS - Jan, 1985+
RADIOWEEK - May 30, 1988+
SOUND MANAGEMENT - Nov, 1984+
TRI-S SPOT/LIGHT - ?+

Manufacturer
RADIO INDUSTRIES - May, 1926 - Oct/Nov, 1934//
RADIO MANUFACTURER, THE - ? - Oct, 1928//

Marketing
ADVERTISING & SELLING - Jun, 1909 - Apr, 1924//
RADIO BROADCAST - May, 1922 - Apr, 1930//
RADIO BUSINESS REPORT - Jan, 1984+
RADIO DEALER, THE - Apr, 1922 - Oct, 1928//
RADIOTRENDS - Jan, 1985+

Membership
NARTB MEMBER SERVICE - ?+
QEX - ?+
QST - Dec, 1915+

Military
AMATEUR RADIO DEFENSE - Nov, 1940 - Jun/Jul, 1941//

Minorities
AWRT NEWS AND VIEWS - 1982?+

Speech
Subject Heading
INDEX
970

BLACK RADIO EXCLUSIVE - Jan 1, 1976?+

Monitoring
FRENDX - ?+
MONITORING TIMES - Jan, 1982+
POPULAR COMMUNICATIONS - Sep, 1982+
REVIEW OF INTERNATIONAL BROADCASTING - Mar, 1977+

Music
HIT PARADER - Nov, 1942 - ?//
INTERNATIONAL RADIO REPORT, THE - 1978+
MONDAY MORNING REPLAY - Jan 1, 1988+
MUSIC LINE - May, 1983+
PULSE OF RADIO - Jan 1, 1986?+
R & R - 1971?+
RADIO CITY NEWS - Apr 3, 1933 - Nov 2, 1933//
RADIO HIT SONGS - Nov, 1941?+?

Production
COLLEGE BROADCASTER - Sep, 1988+
INTERNATIONAL RADIO REPORT, THE - 1978+

Programming
BLACK RADIO EXCLUSIVE - Jan 1, 1976?+
DIGITAL RADIO NEWS - Nov 3, 1990+
INSIDE RADIO - Jan 1, 1976+
INTERNATIONAL RADIO REPORT, THE - 1978+
MONDAY MORNING REPLAY - Jan 1, 1988+
MONITORING TIMES - Jan, 1982+
PULSE OF RADIO - Jan 1, 1986?+
R & R - 1971?+
RADIO ONLY - Apr, 1982+
RADIO*PHILES - Nov, 1981?+?
REVIEW OF INTERNATIONAL BROADCASTING - Mar, 1977+
RURAL RADIO - Feb, 1938+?

Promotion
RADIOTRENDS - Jan, 1985+

Radio City Music Hall
RADIO CITY NEWS - Apr 3, 1933 - Nov 2, 1933//

Ratings
BEYOND THE RATINGS/RADIO - ?+
PULSE OF RADIO - Jan 1, 1986?+
RADIO ONLY - Apr, 1982+
RADIO*PHILES - Nov, 1981?+?

Records & Compact Discs
R & R - 1971?+

Regulation
JOURNAL OF RADIO LAW - Apr, 1931 - Oct, 1932//

NARTB MEMBER SERVICE - ?+
RADIO BUSINESS REPORT - Jan, 1984+

Religion
MUSIC LINE - May, 1983+
TRI-S SPOT/LIGHT - ?+
TWR - Sep/Oct, 1980+

Research
BEYOND THE RATINGS/RADIO - ?+

Retail
RADIO BROADCAST - May, 1922 - Apr, 1930//
RADIO DEALER, THE - Apr, 1922 - Oct, 1928//

Review
AUDIO-VISUAL GUIDE - Feb, 1936 - Jun, 1956//
AWA TECHNICAL REVIEW - Mar, 1935+? (Australia)
STAGE - Dec, 1923 - Jun, 1939//

Sales
INSIDE RADIO - Jan 1, 1976+
RADIO ONLY - Apr, 1982+
SOUND MANAGEMENT - Nov, 1984+
TRI-S SPOT/LIGHT - ?+

Satellites
DIGITAL RADIO NEWS - Nov 3, 1990+

School
NATIONAL HIGH SCHOOL BROADCASTERS NEWSLETTER - Dec, 1977+

Scripts
DRAMA MAGAZINE, THE - Feb, 1911 - Jun, 1931//
TALKS - Jan, 1936 - Jul, 1949//

Short Wave
ALL-WAVE RADIO - Sep, 1935 - Jun, 1938//
AMATEUR RADIO DEFENSE - Nov, 1940 - Jun/Jul, 1941//
AMATEUR WIRELESS AND RADIOVISION - Jun 10, 1922 - Jan 19, 1935// (United Kingdom)
AWA TECHNICAL REVIEW - Mar, 1935+? (Australia)
BBC WORLD SERVICE LONDON CALLING - ?+ (United Kingdom)
COMMUNICATIONS WORLD - 196u+?
CQ - Jan, 1945+
FRENDX - ?+
LISTENER - Jan 16, 1929 - Jan 3, 1991// (United Kingdom)
MONITORING TIMES - Jan, 1982+
OLD TIMER'S BULLETIN, THE - ?+
POPULAR COMMUNICATIONS - Sep, 1982+
PRACTICAL WIRELESS - 1932+ (United Kingdom)
QEX - ?+
QST - Dec, 1915+

RADIO & ELECTRONICS CONSTRUCTOR - ?+ (United Kingdom)
RADIO COMMUNICATION - 1925+ (United Kingdom)
REVIEW OF INTERNATIONAL BROADCASTING - Mar, 1977+
73 AMATEUR RADIO - Oct, 1960+

Technology
ALL-WAVE RADIO - Sep, 1935 - Jun, 1938//
AMATEUR RADIO DEFENSE - Nov, 1940 - Jun/Jul, 1941//
AMATEUR WIRELESS AND RADIOVISION - Jun 10, 1922 - Jan 19, 1935// (United Kingdom)
ANTIQUE RADIO CLASSIFIED - Jan, 1984+
AWA TECHNICAL REVIEW - Mar, 1935+? (Australia)
BUYERS GUIDE - ?+
CQ - Jan, 1945+
DIGITAL RADIO NEWS - Nov 3, 1990+
ELECTRONICS ILLUSTRATED - May, 1958 - 1972//
INDUSTRIAL ELECTRONICS - Oct, 1923 - Jan, 1969// (United Kingdom)
OLD TIMER'S BULLETIN, THE - ?+
PRACTICAL WIRELESS - 1932+ (United Kingdom)
RADIO AGE - May, 1922 - Jan, 1928//
RADIO BROADCAST - May, 1922 - Apr, 1930//
RADIO DEALER, THE - Apr, 1922 - Oct, 1928//
RADIO FAN-FARE - Apr, 1922 - Oct, 1933//
RADIO GUIDE - Jan, 1988+
RADIO HOME, THE - Jun, 1922 - ?//?
RADIO INDUSTRIES - May, 1926 - Oct/Nov, 1934//
RADIO MANUFACTURER, THE - ? - Oct, 1928//
RMA ENGINEER - Nov, 1936 - May, 1940//
WIRELESS AGE, THE - Oct, 1912 - Aug, 1925//

Unions & Guilds
JOURNAL - ?, 1893+

Women
AWRT NEWS AND VIEWS - 1982?+

World
JOURNAL OF RADIO LAW - Apr, 1931 - Oct, 1932//

Speech

Academic
C-O-N-N-E-C-T-I-O-N-S - ?+
COMMUNICATION EDUCATION - Jan, 1952+
COMMUNICATION MONOGRAPHS - 1934+
QUARTERLY JOURNAL OF SPEECH, THE - Apr, 1915+
WSCA NEWS - Jan, 1984+

Activist
SCA WOMEN'S CAUCUS AND FEMINIST & WOMEN STUDIES DIVISION NEWSLETTER - ?+

Aesthetics
COMMUNICATION STUDIES - Nov, 1949+

Business
MANAGEMENT COMMUNICATION QUARTERLY - Aug, 1987+

Cultural
DISCOURSE & SOCIETY - Jul, 1990+ {United Kingdom}

Debate
ROSTRUM - ?+

Discourse
DISCOURSE & SOCIETY - Jul, 1990+ {United Kingdom}

Forensics
ROSTRUM - ?+

Freedom of Speech
FREE SPEECH - 1970?+?

Health
HEALTH COMMUNICATION - #1, 1989+

Historical
QUARTERLY JOURNAL OF SPEECH, THE - Apr, 1915+

Information
DISCOURSE & SOCIETY - Jul, 1990+ {United Kingdom}

Instructional
COMMUNICATION BRIEFINGS - Dec, 1981+

International
WORLD COMMUNICATION - Jul, 1972+

Management
MANAGEMENT COMMUNICATION QUARTERLY - Aug, 1987+

Minorities
SCA WOMEN'S CAUCUS AND FEMINIST & WOMEN STUDIES DIVISION NEWSLETTER - ?+

Research
COMMUNICATION EDUCATION - Jan, 1952+
COMMUNICATION MONOGRAPHS - 1934+
DISCOURSE & SOCIETY - Jul, 1990+ {United Kingdom}
QUARTERLY JOURNAL OF SPEECH, THE - Apr, 1915+
RHETORIC SOCIETY QUARTERLY - 1968+
WESTERN JOURNAL OF SPEECH COMMUNICATION - 1937+
WORLD COMMUNICATION - Jul, 1972+

Review
C-O-N-N-E-C-T-I-O-N-S - ?+
COMMUNICATION - Jun, 1974+ {United Kingdom}
COMMUNICATION WORLD - Winter?, 1971/1972?+
WORLD COMMUNICATION - Jul, 1972+

Rhetoric
COMMUNICATION STUDIES - Nov, 1949+
RHETORIC SOCIETY QUARTERLY - 1968+

Speech
BULLETIN OF THE ASSOCIATION FOR BUSINESS COMMUNICATION, THE - May, 1937+
FREE SPEECH - 1970?+?
HUMAN COMMUNICATION - Spring, 1973 - Spring, 1981// {Canada}
HUMAN COMMUNICATION CANADA - Jan/Feb, 1983+ {Canada}
JOURNAL OF SPEECH AND HEARING DISORDERS - ? - Nov, 1990//
SPEECH COMMUNICATION TEACHER, THE - Fall, 1986+
WSCA NEWS - Jan, 1984+

Teaching
COMMUNICATION EDUCATION - Jan, 1952+
SPEECH COMMUNICATION TEACHER, THE - Fall, 1986+

Teletext
COMMUNICATION MONOGRAPHS - 1934+
WESTERN JOURNAL OF SPEECH COMMUNICATION - 1937+

Women
SCA WOMEN'S CAUCUS AND FEMINIST & WOMEN STUDIES DIVISION NEWSLETTER - ?+

Writing
BULLETIN OF THE ASSOCIATION FOR BUSINESS COMMUNICATION, THE - May, 1937+
COMMUNICATION BRIEFINGS - Dec, 1981+

Telecommunication

Advertising
4TH MEDIA JOURNAL, THE - Apr, 1990+
LINK - Nov/Dec, 1989+

Business
CLOSEUP - ?+
KAGAN MEDIA INDEX, THE - Mar 10, 1987+
TELECOMMUNICATIONS ALERT - Oct, 1983+
TELECOMMUNICATIONS POLICY - Dec, 1976+ {United Kingdom}
TELECOMMUNICATIONS WEEK - 1982+
TELEGRAPH WORLD - Jan, 1919+?
VIA SATELLITE - Jan, 1986+
WIRE & RADIO COMMUNICATIONS - 1883 - Feb, 1965//

Cellular
MOBILE SATELLITE NEWS - Nov, 1989+

Cultural
TELEMATICS AND INFORMATICS - 1984+

Design
IEEE TRANSACTIONS ON COMMUNICATIONS - 1953+
RF DESIGN - Nov/Dec, 1978+

Direct Marketing
TELEPROFESSIONAL - Spring, 1986+

Emerging
TELEMATICS AND INFORMATICS - 1984+

Employment
TELEGRAPHER, THE - Sep 26, 1864 - Feb 3, 1877//

Engineering
COMMUNICATION AND BROADCAST ENGINEERING - Oct, 1934 - Aug, 1937//
IEEE TRANSACTIONS ON COMMUNICATIONS - 1953+
RF DESIGN - Nov/Dec, 1978+
WIRE & RADIO COMMUNICATIONS - 1883 - Feb, 1965//

Finance
KAGAN MEDIA INDEX, THE - Mar 10, 1987+

Home Consumer
4TH MEDIA JOURNAL, THE - Apr, 1990+

House Organ
TELEPHONE NEWS, THE - Aug, 1905+

Television

Information
4TH MEDIA JOURNAL, THE - Apr, 1990+

International
MOBILE SATELLITE NEWS - Nov, 1989+
TELECOMMUNICATIONS POLICY - Dec, 1976+ {United Kingdom}
TELEMATICS AND INFORMATICS - 1984+

Marketing
4TH MEDIA JOURNAL, THE - Apr, 1990+
LINK - Nov/Dec, 1989+
TELEMARKETING - Jun/Jul, 1982+

Production
TELEGRAPHER, THE - Sep 26, 1864 - Feb 3, 1877//

Promotion
TELEPHONE MAGAZINE - Jan, 1893 - Aug, 1905//

Regulation
MOBILE SATELLITE NEWS - Nov, 1989+
TELECOMMUNICATIONS POLICY - Dec, 1976+ {United Kingdom}
TELECOMMUNICATIONS REPORTS - Aug 9, 1934+?

Review
CLOSEUP - ?+
ELECTRICAL REVIEW - Nov 15, 1872+? {United Kingdom}

Sales
TELEMARKETING - Jun/Jul, 1982+

Satellites
MOBILE SATELLITE NEWS - Nov, 1989+
VIA SATELLITE - Jan, 1986+

School
TELESCAN - Sep/Oct, 1981 - Jun, 1985//

Teaching
TELESCAN - Sep/Oct, 1981 - Jun, 1985//

Technology
CLOSEUP - ?+
COMMUNICATION AND BROADCAST ENGINEERING - Oct, 1934 - Aug, 1937//
ELECTRICAL REVIEW - Nov 15, 1872+? {United Kingdom}
MOBILE SATELLITE NEWS - Nov, 1989+
POST OFFICE MAGAZINE - Oct, 1914+? {United Kingdom}
RF DESIGN - Nov/Dec, 1978+
TELECOMMUNICATIONS ALERT - Oct, 1983+
TELECOMMUNICATIONS WEEK - 1982+
TELEGRAPH WORLD - Jan, 1919+?

TELEGRAPHER, THE - Sep 26, 1864 - Feb 3, 1877//
TELEMATICS AND INFORMATICS - 1984+
TELEPHONE MAGAZINE - Jan, 1893 - Aug, 1905//
WIRE & RADIO COMMUNICATIONS - 1883 - Feb, 1965//

World Columbian Exposition
TELEPHONE MAGAZINE - Jan, 1893 - Aug, 1905//

Yellow Pages
LINK - Nov/Dec, 1989+

Television

Acting
BACK STAGE - Dec 2, 1960+
CASTING CALL - Jan 17, 1976+
DRAMA-LOGUE - Jan, 1970?+

Action
DAREDEVILS - Nov, 1983+?

Activist
RE:ACT - 1970+

Adventure
DAREDEVILS - Nov, 1983+?

Advertising
ADVERTISING AND MARKETING - 1964+ {United Kingdom}
BILLBOARD TV PROGRAM AND TIME AVAILABILITIES, THE - ? - Feb, 1958//
ELECTRONIC MEDIA - Aug 5, 1982+
4TH MEDIA JOURNAL, THE - Apr, 1990+
LINK - Nov/Dec, 1989+
LÜRZER'S INTERNATIONAL ARCHIVE - Feb, 1989+
SALES NEWS - ?+?
SHOOTING COMMERCIALS - 1978+
60 SECONDS - Dec, 1980+
TELEVISER - Fall, 1944 - Dec, 1951//

Advocate
AFA JOURNAL - May?, 1979+
LIES OF OUR TIMES - Jan, 1990+
TELEVISION & FAMILIES - Winter, 1978 - Winter, 1988//

Aesthetics
ON FILM - Winter?, 1976+

Amateur
AMATEUR WIRELESS AND RADIOVISION - Jun 10, 1922 - Jan 19, 1935// {United Kingdom}
TELEVISION - Jun, 1928 - Mar/Apr, 1929//

Animation
GET ANIMATED! UPDATE. - Feb, 1985+
GRAFFITI - ?+
SIMPSONS ILLUSTRATED - Spring, 1991+
SOCIETY FOR ANIMATION STUDIES NEWSLETTER, THE - Jan/Feb, 1988+
STORYBOARD / THE ART OF LAUGHTER - Fall, 1990+

Archival
MAGAZINE, THE - 1976+

Art Form
ON FILM - Winter?, 1976+

Artist
DAYTIME TV - Winter, 1970+
DOCUMENTARY FILM NEWS - Autumn, 1932 - Jan, 1949// {United Kingdom}
ENTERTAINMENT CONNECTION MAGAZINE - ?+
FANTASTIC TELEVISION! - ?+?
FILM FAMILIES - 1978+
GOSSIP - May, 1972?+
HOLLYWOOD MAGAZINE - 1988+
INTERVIEW - 1969+
MOTION PICTURE - Feb, 1911+
MOVIE DREAM GUYS - Jan, 1960 - ?//
MOVIE FLASH - ?+ {Philippines}
MOVIE MIRROR - Jun, 1946+
MOVIE STARS - Fall, 1940 - 198u//
MOVIE TV SECRETS - Oct, 1959+?
NIGHTTIME TV - Mar/Apr, 1975+?
PHOTO SCREEN - Dec, 1965+
PHOTOSTAR - Oct/Nov, 1990+
PREVIEW - Sep, 1976? - ?//
REAL LIFE/DAYTIMERS - Apr, 1977+?
RONA BARRETT'S HOLLYWOOD - 1971+
ROSS REPORTS TELEVISION - ?+
SCREEN ACTOR HOLLYWOOD - Aug, 1959+
SCREEN LIFE - Nov, 1962?+?
SCREEN STARS - Apr, 1944+
SHOW - Sep, 1952? - ?//
SHOW BUSINESS ILLUSTRATED - Sep 5, 1961 - Apr, 1962//
SOAP OPERA DIGEST - Dec, 1975+
SOAP OPERA PEOPLE - Dec?, 1984+
SOAP OPERA STARS - Jan, 1976+
SOAP OPERA TIME - Oct/Nov, 1976+?
SOAP OPERA UPDATE - Apr 11, 1988+
SOSYAL! MAGAZINE - Feb 4, 1986+ {Philippines}
SOUND STAGE - Feb?, 1965 - ?//
STARZ - Sep, 1990+
SUPER TEEN - Oct, 1978+

TEEN DREAM - 198u+
TELEVISION AND SCREEN GUIDE - May, 1936+?
TELEVISION PERSONALITIES - Oct, 1953+? (United Kingdom)
TELEVISION WEEKLY NEWS - Apr 18, 1931 - Aug 8, 1931//?
TGIF - ?+?
TS - Spring, 1985+
TV AND SCREEN SECRETS - Jan, 1969+?
TV DAY STARS - Jan, 1972+?
TV HITS - Sep, 1989?+ (United Kingdom)
TV PEOPLE AND PICTURES - Sep, 1953 - ?//
TV PICTURE LIFE - 1953+
TV RADIO SHOW - Oct, 1966+?
TV SHOW - May, 1951 - ?//?
TV STAR PARADE - Fall, 1951 - ?//
TV STARS - May, 1978+
TV WORLD - Aug, 1953 - ?//
WHO'S WHO IN MOVIES AND TV - ?+
WOW! MAGAZINE - Oct, 1987+

Black
ENTERTAINMENT CONNECTION MAGAZINE - ?+

Business
BACK STAGE - Dec 2, 1960+
CANADIAN FILM DIGEST - 1936 - Dec, 1976// (Canada)
CINEMA/CANADA - 1961+ (Canada)
CLOSEUP - ?+
DAILY VARIETY - 1933+
ELECTRONIC MEDIA - Aug 5, 1982+
FILM TV DAILY - Oct 14, 1915+
FLORIDA REEL - Oct/Nov, 1989+
HOLLYWOOD MAGAZINE - 1988+
KAGAN MEDIA INDEX, THE - Mar 10, 1987+
MARKETING PULSE, THE - Sep, 1980?+
MOVING PICTURES INTERNATIONAL - Sep 13, 1990?+ (United Kingdom)
PROFESSIONAL FILM PRODUCTION - Jun, 1975+
TELECOMMUNICATIONS ALERT - Oct, 1983+
TELECOMMUNICATIONS POLICY - Dec, 1976+ (United Kingdom)
TELECOMMUNICATIONS WEEK - 1982+
TELEGRAPH WORLD - Jan, 1919+?
TELEVISION - Spring, 1944 - Sep, 1968//
TELEVISION - Jun, 1928+ (United Kingdom)
TELEVISION BULLETIN - Jul 25, 1931 - Dec 19, 1932//
TELEVISION OPPORTUNITIES - Nov, 1948 - Sep/Oct, 1956//?
TELEVISION WEEK - Oct 27, 1988+ (United Kingdom)
TELEVISION WEEKLY NEWS - Apr 18, 1931 - Aug 8, 1931//?
TV PROGRAM INVESTOR - Sep 13, 1985+
TV WORLD - 1977+ (United Kingdom)
VIA SATELLITE - Jan, 1986+

VIDEO TECHNOLOGY NEWS - Sep 26, 1988+
WATCH - Dec, 1979 - May, 1980?//?
WIRE & RADIO COMMUNICATIONS - 1883 - Feb, 1965//

Cassettes
HOME VIEWER - Apr, 1981+
ORBIT VIDEO - Jan, 1989+
VIEW - 1980+

Cellular
MOBILE SATELLITE NEWS - Nov, 1989+

Collector
TELEVISION HISTORY - Jan, 1983+

Comics
COMICS SCENE - Jan/Feb, 1981+

Community
LPTV REPORT, THE - Jan, 1986+

Corporate
VIDEO MANAGEMENT - 1978 - Dec, 1989//

Cultural
CHANNELS - Apr/May, 1981 - Dec 17?, 1990//
TELEMATICS AND INFORMATICS - 1984+
TELESCREEN - 1942 - Jul, 1948//

Daytime
DAYTIME TV - Winter, 1970+
EPISODES - Mar/Apr, 1990+

Dbs
DBS NEWS - Sep, 1982+

Design
IEEE TRANSACTIONS ON COMMUNICATIONS - 1953+
RF DESIGN - Nov/Dec, 1978+

Digital
DIGITAL EVOLUTION MAGAZINE - Jul, 1989+ (Canada)

Direct Marketing
TELEPROFESSIONAL - Spring, 1986+

Distribution
MARKETING PULSE, THE - Sep, 1980?+
PRODUCCIÓN Y DISTRIBUCIÓN - Oct/Nov, 1989+
VIDEO WEEK - Feb 4, 1980+

Electronics
AMATEUR WIRELESS AND RADIOVISION - Jun 10, 1922 - Jan 19, 1935// (United Kingdom)

Emerging
TELEMATICS AND INFORMATICS - 1984+

Employment
AWRT NEWS AND VIEWS - 1982?+
CASTING CALL - Jan 17, 1976+
DEBUT - Spring, 1988+
DRAMA-LOGUE - Jan, 1970?+
ROSS REPORTS TELEVISION - ?+
TELEGRAPHER, THE - Sep 26, 1864 - Feb 3, 1877//
TGIF - ?+?

Engineering
CAVERNE COMMUNICATION, THE - Jun, 1987+
COLOUR - ?+ (United Kingdom)
COMMUNICATION AND BROADCAST ENGINEERING - Oct, 1934 - Aug, 1937//
HDTV NEWSLETTER - Jun?, 1986+
IEEE TRANSACTIONS ON COMMUNICATIONS - 1953+
IMAGE TECHNOLOGY - 194u+ (United Kingdom)
RF DESIGN - Nov/Dec, 1978+
TELEVISION - Jun, 1928 - Mar/Apr, 1929//
TELEVISION BROADCAST - Jan, 1978+
TV TECHNOLOGY - Sep, 1983+
WIRE & RADIO COMMUNICATIONS - 1883 - Feb, 1965//

Ethics
LIES OF OUR TIMES - Jan, 1990+

Exhibition
CANADIAN FILM DIGEST - 1936 - Dec, 1976// (Canada)

Fan
AMPERSAND'S COLLEGE ENTERTAINMENT GUIDE - Fall, 1977+
BONDAGE - 1973+
CASTLE OF FRANKENSTEIN - ?, 1959 - ?, 1974//
DAREDEVILS - Nov, 1983+?
DAYTIME TV - Winter, 1970+
DOCTOR WHO MAGAZINE - 1985?+? (United Kingdom)
DWB - ?+ (United Kingdom)
EPI-LOG - Dec, 1990+
EPISODES - Mar/Apr, 1990+
FILM FAMILIES - 1978+
GOSSIP - May, 1972?+
MOTION PICTURE - Feb, 1911+
MOVIE DREAM GUYS - Jan, 1960 - ?//
MOVIE FLASH - ?+ (Philippines)
MOVIE MIRROR - Jun, 1946+
MOVIE STARS - Fall, 1940 - 198u//
MOVIE TV SECRETS - Oct, 1959+?
NIGHTTIME TV - Mar/Apr, 1975+?
PHOTO SCREEN - Dec, 1965+

Television
Subject Heading

PHOTOSTAR - Oct/Nov, 1990+
PREVIEW - Sep, 1976? - ?//
RONA BARRETT'S HOLLYWOOD - 1971+
SCREEN LIFE - Nov, 1962?+?
SCREEN STARS - Apr, 1944+
SIMPSONS ILLUSTRATED - Spring, 1991+
SMASH HITS - 198u+
SOAP OPERA DIGEST - Dec, 1975+
SOAP OPERA PEOPLE - Dec?, 1984+
SOAP OPERA STARS - Jan, 1976+
SOAP OPERA TIME - Oct/Nov, 1976+?
SOAP OPERA UPDATE - Apr 11, 1988+
SOSYAL! MAGAZINE - Feb 4, 1986+ {Philippines}
SOUND STAGE - Feb?, 1965 - ?//
STAR TREK: THE NEXT GENERATION - Dec, 1987+
STAR TREK: THE OFFICIAL FAN CLUB MAGAZINE - ?+
STARZ - Sep, 1990+
STRANGE ADVENTURES - Feb, 1989+ {United Kingdom}
SUPER TEEN - Oct, 1978+
TEEN DREAM - 198u+
TELEVISION AND SCREEN GUIDE - May, 1936+?
TELEVISION HISTORY - Jan, 1983+
TIME SCREEN - Summer, 1985+? {United Kingdom}
TOP SECRET - Dec/Jan, 1985/1986+?
TS - Spring, 1985+
TV AND SCREEN SECRETS - Jan, 1969+?
TV DAY STARS - Jan, 1972+?
TV GOLD - Jun, 1986+?
TV HITS - Sep, 1989?+ {United Kingdom}
TV PEOPLE AND PICTURES - Sep, 1953 - ?//
TV PICTURE LIFE - 1953+
TV RADIO SHOW - Oct, 1966+?
TV STAR PARADE - Fall, 1951 - ?//
TV STARS - May, 1978+
TV WORLD - Aug, 1953 - ?//
WHO'S WHO IN MOVIES AND TV - ?+
WOW! MAGAZINE - Oct, 1987+

Fantasy
TIME SCREEN - Summer, 1985+? {United Kingdom}

Finance
DAILY VARIETY - 1933+
FILM TV DAILY - Oct 14, 1915+
KAGAN MEDIA INDEX, THE - Mar 10, 1987+
MARKETING PULSE, THE - Sep, 1980?+
TELEVISION BULLETIN - Jul 25, 1931 - Dec 19, 1932//
TV PROGRAM INVESTOR - Sep 13, 1985+

Graphics
ADVERTISING AND GRAPHIC ARTS TECHNIQUES - Sep, 1965+

LÜRZER'S INTERNATIONAL ARCHIVE - Feb, 1989+

Guide
AFTERNOON TV - 1969+
AMPERSAND'S COLLEGE ENTERTAINMENT GUIDE - Fall, 1977+
DISNEY ADVENTURES - Nov 12, 1990+
EPISODES - Mar/Apr, 1990+
JOURNAL OF THE BRITISH FILM ACADEMY - ? - Spring, 1959// {United Kingdom}
MEDIA MIX - Oct, 1969 - Jun, 1979//
MOTION PICTURE - Feb, 1911+
ONSAT - ?+
ORBIT VIDEO - Jan, 1989+
SATELLITE TV WEEK - ?, 1981+
SCIENCE-FICTION VIDEO MAGAZINE - Fall, 1989?+
SF MOVIELAND - Jan, 1983?+?
SHOW - Jan, 1970 - Nov, 1973//
STARBURST - Sep, 1978?+ {United Kingdom}
TEACHER'S GUIDE TO TELEVISION - Nov, 1968+
TELECAST - Nov, 1949+
TELEVISION & FAMILIES - Winter, 1978 - Winter, 1988//
TV GOLD - Jun, 1986+?
TV GUIDE - Apr 3, 1953+
TV GUIDE - Apr 1, 1989+ {United Kingdom}
TV SHOW - May, 1951 - ?//?
TV TIMES - 1958+ {Australia}
VIEW - 1980+

Ham Radio
MONITORING TIMES - Jan, 1982+

High Defintion TV (HDTV)
HDTV NEWSLETTER - Jun?, 1986+

Historical
AMERICAN FILM - Oct, 1975+
AMERICAN FILM INSTITUTE. QUARTERLY. - 1967?+?
EPI-LOG - Dec, 1990+
FANTASTIC TELEVISION! - ?+?
FILMFAX - Jan/Feb, 1986+
HISTORICAL JOURNAL OF FILM, RADIO & TELEVISION - Mar, 1981+ {United Kingdom}
MAGAZINE, THE - 1976+
TELEVISION HISTORY - Jan, 1983+
TV GOLD - Jun, 1986+?

Home Consumer
4TH MEDIA JOURNAL, THE - Apr, 1990+
TELECAST - Nov, 1949+
TELEVISION - Summer, 1927 - Jul, 1928//
TV SHOW - May, 1951 - ?//?

Horror
CASTLE OF FRANKENSTEIN - ?, 1959 - ?, 1974//

WORLD OF FANDOM, THE - Jul, 1985+

House Organ
TELEPHONE NEWS, THE - Aug, 1905+

Information
4TH MEDIA JOURNAL, THE - Apr, 1990+

Instructional
ETV NEWSLETTER - Dec, 1966+
JOURNAL OF EDUCATIONAL TELEVISION - Mar, 1975+ {United Kingdom}

International
CTVD - Winter, 1961/1962+
DAILY VARIETY - 1933+
DBS NEWS - Sep, 1982+
DOCUMENTARY FILM NEWS - Autumn, 1932 - Jan, 1949// {United Kingdom}
HISTORICAL JOURNAL OF FILM, RADIO & TELEVISION - Mar, 1981+ {United Kingdom}
JOURNAL OF EDUCATIONAL TELEVISION - Mar, 1975+ {United Kingdom}
MOBILE SATELLITE NEWS - Nov, 1989+
MOVING PICTURES INTERNATIONAL - Sep 13, 1990?+ {United Kingdom}
PRACTICAL TELEVISION AND SHORT-WAVE REVIEW - Sep, 1934 - Nov, 1935// {United Kingdom}
PRESS, THE - Jan/Feb, 1973?+?
SOCIETY FOR ANIMATION STUDIES NEWSLETTER, THE - Jan/Feb, 1988+
TBI - Feb, 1988+ {United Kingdom}
TELCO REPORT, THE - 1969+.
TELECOMMUNICATIONS POLICY - Dec, 1976+ {United Kingdom}
TELEMATICS AND INFORMATICS - 1984+
TELEVISION INTERNATIONAL - 1956+ {Switzerland}
TELEVISION / RADIO AGE INTERNATIONAL - ?+
TELEVISION WEEK - Oct 27, 1988+ {United Kingdom}
TV WORLD - 1977+ {United Kingdom}
VIDEQ AGE INTERNATIONAL - Jan, 1981+
VIDEO TECHNOLOGY NEWS - Sep 26, 1988+

James Bond
BONDAGE - 1973+

Journalism
LIES OF OUR TIMES - Jan, 1990+

Lighting
LIGHTS! - Jan, 1990+ {United Kingdom}

Literature
CTVD - Winter, 1961/1962+

Location
LOCATION UPDATE - Jul/Aug, 1985+

WRAP - Oct/Nov, 1987+

Low Power Television
LPTV REPORT, THE - Jan, 1986+

Management
INDUSTRIAL TELEVISION NEWS - 1970 - ?//.
NATPE PROGRAMMER - Jan, 1974+
TELEVISION - Spring, 1944 - Sep, 1968//
TELEVISION PROGRAMMER, THE - 1979+?
TV TODAY - 1933+
VIDEO MANAGEMENT - 1978 - Dec, 1989//

Marketing
ADVERTISING AND MARKETING - 1964+ {United Kingdom}
4TH MEDIA JOURNAL, THE - Apr, 1990+
LINK - Nov/Dec, 1989+
LÜRZER'S INTERNATIONAL ARCHIVE - Feb, 1989+
PROFESSIONAL FILM PRODUCTION - Jun, 1975+
TELEMARKETING - Jun/Jul, 1982+

Media Buying
BILLBOARD TV PROGRAM AND TIME AVAILABILITIES, THE - ? - Feb, 1958//

Minorities
AWRT NEWS AND VIEWS - 1982?+

Monitoring
MONITORING TIMES - Jan, 1982+

Music
AMPERSAND'S COLLEGE ENTERTAINMENT GUIDE - Fall, 1977+
SUPER TEEN - Oct, 1978+

New York City
SHOW - Jan, 1970 - Nov, 1973//

News
LIES OF OUR TIMES - Jan, 1990+
PRESS, THE - Jan/Feb, 1973?+?

Post Production
PRODUCCIÓN Y DISTRIBUCIÓN - Oct/Nov, 1989+
WRAP - Oct/Nov, 1987+

Preservation
AMERICAN FILM - Oct, 1975+
AMERICAN FILM INSTITUTE. QUARTERLY. - 1967?+?

Producing
PRODUCERS QUARTERLY - Mar, 1989+

Production
AMERICAN FILM - Oct, 1975+
BACK STAGE - Dec 2, 1960+
CANADIAN FILM DIGEST - 1936 - Dec, 1976// {Canada}
CAVERNE COMMUNICATION, THE - Jun, 1987+
CINEMA/CANADA - 1961+ {Canada}
DAILY VARIETY - 1933+
DIGITAL EVOLUTION MAGAZINE - Jul, 1989+ {Canada}
DOCUMENTARY FILM NEWS - Autumn, 1932 - Jan, 1949// {United Kingdom}
FILM TV DAILY - Oct 14, 1915+
FLORIDA REEL - Oct/Nov, 1989+
HOLLYWOOD MAGAZINE - 1988+
INDUSTRIAL TELEVISION NEWS - 1970 - ?//.
INTERNATIONAL PHOTOGRAPHER - Feb, 1929+
INVISION - ?+ {United Kingdom}
LIGHTS! - Jan, 1990+ {United Kingdom}
LOCATION UPDATE - Jul/Aug, 1985+
PRESS, THE - Jan/Feb, 1973?+?
PRODUCCIÓN Y DISTRIBUCIÓN - Oct/Nov, 1989+
PRODUCERS QUARTERLY - Mar, 1989+
PROFESSIONAL FILM PRODUCTION - Jun, 1975+
ROSS REPORTS TELEVISION - ?+
SHOOTING COMMERCIALS - 1978+
60 SECONDS - Dec, 1980+
SPECTATOR, THE - Spring, 1982+
TELEGRAPHER, THE - Sep 26, 1864 - Feb 3, 1877//
TELESCREEN - 1942 - Jul, 1948//
TELEVISION - Jun, 1928+ {United Kingdom}
TELEVISION BROADCAST - Jan, 1978+
TELEVISION / RADIO AGE INTERNATIONAL - ?+
THEATRE CRAFTS - Mar/Apr, 1967+
TV SHOW - May, 1951 - ?//?
VIDEO MANAGEMENT - 1978 - Dec, 1989//
WRAP - Oct/Nov, 1987+

Programming
AFA JOURNAL - May?, 1979+
AFTERNOON TV - 1969+
CHANNELS - Apr/May, 1981 - Dec 17?, 1990//
CONTRAST - Autumn, 1961 - 1966// {United Kingdom}
DAYTIME TV - Winter, 1970+
ELECTRONIC MEDIA - Aug 5, 1982+
EPI-LOG - Dec, 1990+
EPISODES - Mar/Apr, 1990+
FANTASTIC TELEVISION! - ?+?
MONITORING TIMES - Jan, 1982+
NATPE PROGRAMMER - Jan, 1974+
OF SPECIAL INTEREST - ?+
ONSAT - ?+
PANORAMA - Feb, 1980 - Jun, 1981//

PRACTICAL TELEVISION AND SHORT-WAVE REVIEW - Sep, 1934 - Nov, 1935// {United Kingdom}
PRODUCCIÓN Y DISTRIBUCIÓN - Oct/Nov, 1989+
RE:ACT - 1970+
REAL LIFE/DAYTIMERS - Apr, 1977+?
TBI - Feb, 1988+ {United Kingdom}
TELCO REPORT, THE - 1969+.
TELEVISER - Fall, 1944 - Dec, 1951//
TELEVISION - Spring, 1944 - Sep, 1968//
TELEVISION - Jun, 1928+ {United Kingdom}
TELEVISION & FAMILIES - Winter, 1978 - Winter, 1988//
TELEVISION INTERNATIONAL - 1956+ {Switzerland}
TELEVISION PROGRAMMER, THE - 1979+?
TELEVISION / RADIO AGE INTERNATIONAL - ?+
TELEVISION WEEK - Oct 27, 1988+ {United Kingdom}
TELEVISION WEEKLY NEWS - Apr 18, 1931 - Aug 8, 1931//?
TV PROGRAM INVESTOR - Sep 13, 1985+
TV WORLD - 1977+ {United Kingdom}
VIDEO AGE INTERNATIONAL - Jan, 1981+
VIDEO WEEK - Feb 4, 1980+
VIEW - 1980+
WATCH - Dec, 1979 - May, 1980?//?

Promotion
CHANNEL ONE - ?+?
OF SPECIAL INTEREST - ?+
TELEPHONE MAGAZINE - Jan, 1893 - Aug, 1905//

Puppetry
ANIMATIONS - Oct/Nov, 1977+ {United Kingdom}
GET ANIMATED! UPDATE. - Feb, 1985+

Ratings
BEYOND THE RATINGS/TELEVISION - ?+

Regulation
CINEMA/CANADA - 1961+ {Canada}
MOBILE SATELLITE NEWS - Nov, 1989+
TELECOMMUNICATIONS POLICY - Dec, 1976+ {United Kingdom}
TELECOMMUNICATIONS REPORTS - Aug 9, 1934+?
TELEVISION - Spring, 1944 - Sep, 1968//
TELEVISION OPPORTUNITIES - Nov, 1948 - Sep/Oct, 1956//?
TV TODAY - 1933+
VIDEO TECHNOLOGY NEWS - Sep 26, 1988+

Repair
TV-ELECTRONIC TECHNICIAN - ? - ?

Research
BEYOND THE RATINGS/TELEVISION - ?+

Television
Subject Heading

HISTORICAL JOURNAL OF FILM, RADIO & TELEVISION - Mar, 1981+ {United Kingdom}

Retail
TV-ELECTRONIC TECHNICIAN - ? - ?

Review
AMERICAN FILM - Oct, 1975+
AMERICAN FILM INSTITUTE. QUARTERLY. - 1967?+?
CAVERNE COMMUNICATION, THE - Jun, 1987+
CHANNELS - Apr/May, 1981 - Dec 17?, 1990//
CLOSEUP - ?+
CONTRAST - Autumn, 1961 - 1966// {United Kingdom}
CTVD - Winter, 1961/1962+
DAILY VARIETY - 1933+
DOCUMENTARY FILM NEWS - Autumn, 1932 - Jan, 1949// {United Kingdom}
ELECTRICAL REVIEW - Nov 15, 1872+? {United Kingdom}
ELECTRONIC MEDIA - Aug 5, 1982+
EMMY - Winter, 1979+
ENTERTAINMENT CONNECTION MAGAZINE - ?+
FILM DIRECTIONS - 1977+ {United Kingdom}
FILMFAX - Jan/Feb, 1986+
HISTORICAL JOURNAL OF FILM, RADIO & TELEVISION - Mar, 1981+ {United Kingdom}
HOLLYWOOD MAGAZINE - 1988+
INTERVIEW - 1969+
JOURNAL OF THE BRITISH FILM ACADEMY - ? - Spring, 1959// {United Kingdom}
KODAK PROFESSIONAL FORUM - ?, 1978+?
PANORAMA - Feb, 1980 - Jun, 1981//
SCREEN - ? - Spring, 1982// {United Kingdom}
SCREEN LIFE - Nov, 1962?+?
SHOW - Sep, 1952? - ?//
SHOW - Jan, 1970 - Nov, 1973//
SHOW BUSINESS ILLUSTRATED - Sep 5, 1961 - Apr, 1962//
STARBURST - Sep, 1978?+ {United Kingdom}
TELEVISION QUARTERLY - Feb, 1962+
TV WORLD - 1977+ {United Kingdom}
WATCH - Dec, 1979 - May, 1980?//?

Sales
BILLBOARD TV PROGRAM AND TIME AVAILABILITIES, THE - ? - Feb, 1958//
SALES NEWS - ?+?
TELEMARKETING - Jun/Jul, 1982+
TELEVISION WEEK - Oct 27, 1988+ {United Kingdom}

Satellites
MOBILE SATELLITE NEWS - Nov, 1989+
ONSAT - ?+
SATELLITE TV WEEK - ?, 1981+
VIA SATELLITE - Jan, 1986+

School
ETV NEWSLETTER - Dec, 1966+
JOURNAL OF EDUCATIONAL TELEVISION - Mar, 1975+ {United Kingdom}
TEACHER'S GUIDE TO TELEVISION - Nov, 1968+
TELESCAN - Sep/Oct, 1981 - Jun, 1985//

Science Fiction

Scripts
CAUCUS QUARTERLY, THE - April, 1983+
SCRIPT NEWSLETTER - 1988?+?

Secret Agent
TOP SECRET - Dec/Jan, 1985/1986+?

Short Wave
AMATEUR WIRELESS AND RADIOVISION - Jun 10, 1922 - Jan 19, 1935// {United Kingdom}
MONITORING TIMES - Jan, 1982+

Soap Operas
AFTERNOON TV - 1969+
EPISODES - Mar/Apr, 1990+
REAL LIFE/DAYTIMERS - Apr, 1977+?
SOAP OPERA DIGEST - Dec, 1975+
SOAP OPERA PEOPLE - Dec?, 1984+
SOAP OPERA STARS - Jan, 1976+
SOAP OPERA TIME - Oct/Nov, 1976+?
SOAP OPERA UPDATE - Apr 11, 1988+
TV DAY STARS - Jan, 1972+?

Spanish
PRODUCCIÓN Y DISTRIBUCIÓN - Oct/Nov, 1989+

Spot
SHOOTING COMMERCIALS - 1978+
60 SECONDS - Dec, 1980+

Star Trek
STAR TREK: THE NEXT GENERATION - Dec, 1987+
STAR TREK: THE OFFICIAL FAN CLUB MAGAZINE - ?+

Teaching
TELESCAN - Sep/Oct, 1981 - Jun, 1985//

Technology
AMATEUR WIRELESS AND RADIOVISION - Jun 10, 1922 - Jan 19, 1935// {United Kingdom}
CAVERNE COMMUNICATION, THE - Jun, 1987+
CLOSEUP - ?+
COLOUR - ?+ {United Kingdom}
COMMUNICATION AND BROADCAST ENGINEERING - Oct, 1934 - Aug, 1937//
DIGITAL EVOLUTION MAGAZINE - Jul, 1989+ {Canada}
ELECTRICAL REVIEW - Nov 15, 1872+? {United Kingdom}
HDTV NEWSLETTER - Jun?, 1986+
IMAGE TECHNOLOGY - 194u+ {United Kingdom}
MOBILE SATELLITE NEWS - Nov, 1989+
POST OFFICE MAGAZINE - Oct, 1914+? {United Kingdom}
PRACTICAL TELEVISION AND SHORT-WAVE REVIEW - Sep, 1934 - Nov, 1935// {United Kingdom}
RF DESIGN - Nov/Dec, 1978+
TELECAST - Nov, 1949+
TELECOMMUNICATIONS ALERT - Oct, 1983+
TELECOMMUNICATIONS WEEK - 1982+
TELEGRAPH WORLD - Jan, 1919+?
TELEGRAPHER, THE - Sep 26, 1864 - Feb 3, 1877//
TELEMATICS AND INFORMATICS - 1984+
TELEPHONE MAGAZINE - Jan, 1893 - Aug, 1905//
TELEVISER - Fall, 1944 - Dec, 1951//
TELEVISION - Jun, 1928+ {United Kingdom}
TELEVISION - Summer, 1927 - Jul, 1928//
TELEVISION - Jun, 1928 - Mar/Apr, 1929//
TELEVISION BROADCAST - Jan, 1978+
TELEVISION WEEKLY NEWS - Apr 18, 1931 - Aug 8, 1931//?
TV TECHNOLOGY - Sep, 1983+
VIDEO TECHNOLOGY NEWS - Sep 26, 1988+
WIRE & RADIO COMMUNICATIONS - 1883 - Feb, 1965//

Teletext
ON FILM - Winter?, 1976+

Unions & Guilds
INTERNATIONAL PHOTOGRAPHER - Feb, 1929+
SCREEN ACTOR HOLLYWOOD - Aug, 1959+

Women
AWRT NEWS AND VIEWS - 1982?+

World Columbian Exposition
TELEPHONE MAGAZINE - Jan, 1893 - Aug, 1905//

Writing
CAUCUS QUARTERLY, THE - April, 1983+
SCRIPT NEWSLETTER - 1988?+?

Yellow Pages
LINK - Nov/Dec, 1989+

Youth
RE:ACT - 1970+
TS - Spring, 1985+

Theatre

Academic
ACTF / PAC NEWS - ?+

Acting
ACTOR ILLUSTRATED, THE - Jan, 1905 - Jan, 1906// {United Kingdom}
ACTORS FORUM - Nov, 1956 - Feb, 1957?//?
AMATEUR ACTOR ILLUSTRATED, THE - Jan, 1905+ {United Kingdom}
BACK STAGE - Dec 2, 1960+
CASTING CALL - Jan 17, 1976+
GAMBIT - ?+ {United Kingdom}
NEW THEATRE - Aug, 1939 - Jul, 1949// {United Kingdom}
NEW THEATRE MAGAZINE - Oct, 1959 - 1972// {United Kingdom}
PLAYS AND PLAYERS - 1953+? {United Kingdom}
SHOW BIZ WEST - 1979+
SHOW BUSINESS - 1941+
THEATERWEEK - Aug 13, 1987+
THEATRE WORKSHOP - Oct, 1936 - Apr/Jun, 1938//

Aesthetics
ART & CINEMA - Jan, 1973+
MODERN DRAMA - May, 1958+ {Canada}

Alternative Media
ALTERNATIVE THEATRE - Sep/Oct, 1975+
BLACK THEATRE - 1968 - 1972//

Amateur
ACTOR ILLUSTRATED, THE - Jan, 1905 - Jan, 1906// {United Kingdom}
AMATEUR ACTOR ILLUSTRATED, THE - Jan, 1905+ {United Kingdom}
PLAY SHOP, THE - ?+?

Animation
GET ANIMATED! UPDATE. - Feb, 1985+

Artist
ACTOR ILLUSTRATED, THE - Jan, 1905 - Jan, 1906// {United Kingdom}
ACTORS BY DAYLIGHT - Mar 3, 1838 - Mar 16, 1839// {United Kingdom}
ACTORS FORUM - Nov, 1956 - Feb, 1957?//?
AFTER DARK - May, 1968 - Jan, 1983//
AMERICAN THEATRE - Jan, 1973+
BOMB MAGAZINE - Spring, 1981+
BROADWAY WEEKLY - Feb 18, 1903+?
DRAMA MAGAZINE, THE - Feb, 1911 - Jun, 1931//
DRAMATIC CENSOR, THE - Jan 4, 1800 - Jul, 1801// {United Kingdom}
DRAMATIC MAGAZINE, THE - Aug, 1897 - Aug, 1900//
DRAMATIC REVIEW, THE - Dec 2, 1899 - Aug 4, 1900?//
HAMPTON MAGAZINE - Apr, 1898+?
INTERVIEW - 1969+
NEGRO ACTORS GUILD OF AMERICA. NEWSLETTER. - May, 1940+?
PERFORMANCE - ?+
PLAYS AND PLAYERS - 1953+? {United Kingdom}
SHOW BIZ WEST - 1979+
SOUTHERN THEATRE - 1956+
STAGE AND TELEVISION TODAY, THE - 1880+ {United Kingdom}
STAGE PICTORIAL - Mar, 1912+?
STAGE PICTORIAL - Winter, 1944 - Jul, 1946//
TGIF - ?+?
THEATERWEEK - Aug 13, 1987+
THEATRE, THE - Jan, 1877 - Dec, 1897// {United Kingdom}
THEATRE, THE - Jan, 1959 - Sep, 1961//
THEATRE, THE - Mar 20, 1886 - Apr 27, 1893//
THEATRE ARTS - Nov, 1916 - Jan, 1964//
THEATRE MAGAZINE - Oct, 1900 - Apr, 1931//
VARIETY - Dec 16, 1905+

Avant-garde
HIGH PERFORMANCE - Feb, 1978+

Black
BLACK THEATRE - 1968 - 1972//
NEGRO ACTORS GUILD OF AMERICA. NEWSLETTER. - May, 1940+?

Business
BACK STAGE - Dec 2, 1960+
VARIETY - Dec 16, 1905+

Career
ACTORS FORUM - Nov, 1956 - Feb, 1957?//?

Community
THEATRE-CRAFT - 1919 - 1921// {United Kingdom}
THEATRE CRAFT - Jan, 1947 - May, 1948?//
THEATRE JOURNAL - Mar, 1955 - Fall, 1973//

Construction
MARQUEE - Feb, 1969+

Cultural
TECHNOLOGY AND CULTURE - Winter, 1959+
THEATRE TOPICS - Mar, 1991+

Dance
AFTER DARK - May, 1968 - Jan, 1983//

Design
THEATRE TOPICS - Mar, 1991+

Directing
THEATRE TOPICS - Mar, 1991+

Drama
TPQ - Jan, 1981?+

Education
THEATRE NEWS - Oct, 1968 - 1986//

Elementary
PLAYS - Sep, 1941+

Employment
CASTING CALL - Jan 17, 1976+
SHOW BIZ WEST - 1979+
SHOW BUSINESS - 1941+
STAGE AND TELEVISION TODAY, THE - 1880+ {United Kingdom}
TGIF - ?+?

Fan
BROADWAY WEEKLY - Feb 18, 1903+?
HERO HOBBY - 1966+?
STAGE PICTORIAL - Mar, 1912+?

Guide
ACTORS BY DAYLIGHT - Mar 3, 1838 - Mar 16, 1839// {United Kingdom}
ARTHURIAN THEATRE MAGAZINE, THE - Feb, 1905+ {United Kingdom}
AUDIO-VISUAL GUIDE - Feb, 1936 - Jun, 1956//
BROADWAY SIGN POST - Oct 30, 1930 - ?//?
DRAMA, THE - Oct 23, 1821 - Dec 10, 1821// {Ireland}
DRAMA LEAGUE MONTHLY - Apr, 1916 - May, 1919//
DRAMATIC CENSOR, THE - Jan 4, 1800 - Jul, 1801// {United Kingdom}
DRAMATIC MAGAZINE, THE - Mar 2, 1829 - Apr, 1831// {United Kingdom}
DRAMATIC MIRROR AND LITERARY COMPANION, THE - Aug 14, 1841 - May 7, 1842//
ODDFELLOW, THE - Apr 21, 1838 - ?//? {United Kingdom}
PLAYBILL - Oct 31, 1982+
PLAYTIME - ?+? {South Africa}
ROXY THEATRE WEEKLY REVIEW - Aug, 1926 - ?//
STAGE - Dec, 1923 - Jun, 1939//
STAGE AND SPORT - May 5, 1906 - Jun 30, 1906?//? {United Kingdom}
STAGE AND TELEVISION TODAY, THE - 1880+ {United Kingdom}
STAGE PICTORIAL - Winter, 1944 - Jul, 1946//
STAGE SOUVENIR, THE - Jul 20, 1903? - Oct 20, 1903?//? {United Kingdom}
THEATRE - Jul 15, 1946 - Feb 14, 1953// {United Kingdom}
THEATRE, THE - Jan, 1959 - Sep, 1961//
THEATRE, THE - Mar 20, 1886 - Apr 27, 1893//
THEATRE MAGAZINE - Oct, 1900 - Apr, 1931//

Theatre Subject Heading

Historical
- HERO HOBBY - 1966+?
- MARQUEE - Feb, 1969+
- RESTORATION AND 18TH CENTURY THEATRE RESEARCH - May, 1962+
- TECHNOLOGY AND CULTURE - Winter, 1959+
- THEATRE DOCUMENTATION - Fall, 1968 - 1971/1972// {Brazil}
- THEATRE NOTEBOOK - Oct, 1945+ {United Kingdom}
- THEATRE RESEARCH - Mar, 1958 - #4, 1974// {United Kingdom}

Instructional
- THEATRE WORKSHOP - Oct, 1936 - Apr/Jun, 1938//

International
- DRAMA SURVEY - May, 1961 - Winter, 1968/1969//
- NEW THEATRE QUARTERLY - Jan/Mar, 1971+ {United Kingdom}
- PERFORMANCE - Dec, 1971+
- PLAYS INTERNATIONAL - Aug, 1985+ {United Kingdom}
- SOUTHERN COMMUNICATION JOURNAL, THE - Oct, 1935+
- SPEECH AND DRAMA - 1951+ {United Kingdom}
- TDR - 1955?+
- THEATER - Spring, 1968+
- THEATRE, THE - Jan, 1877 - Dec, 1897// {United Kingdom}
- THEATRE DESIGN & TECHNOLOGY - May, 1965+
- THEATRE DOCUMENTATION - Fall, 1968 - 1971/1972// {Brazil}
- THEATRE RESEARCH - Mar, 1958 - #4, 1974// {United Kingdom}
- TPQ - Jan, 1981?+
- WORLD THEATRE - 1950 - 1968// {Belgium}

Johannesburg
- PLAYTIME - ?+? {South Africa}

Lighting
- TABS - ?+? {United Kingdom}

Literature
- BROADSIDE - May, 1940+
- DRAMA SURVEY - May, 1961 - Winter, 1968/1969//

London
- STAGE AND SPORT - May 5, 1906 - Jun 30, 1906?//? {United Kingdom}
- STAGE SOUVENIR, THE - Jul 20, 1903? - Oct 20, 1903?//? {United Kingdom}
- THEATRE - Jul 15, 1946 - Feb 14, 1953// {United Kingdom}

Management
- STAGE AND TELEVISION TODAY, THE - 1880+ {United Kingdom}

Minorities
- BLACK THEATRE - 1968 - 1972//
- NEGRO ACTORS GUILD OF AMERICA. NEWSLETTER. - May, 1940+?

Music
- DRAMATIC MAGAZINE, THE - Aug, 1897 - Aug, 1900//

New York City
- PLAYBILL - Oct 31, 1982+
- SHOW BUSINESS - 1941+
- STAGE PICTORIAL - Winter, 1944 - Jul, 1946//
- THEATERWEEK - Aug 13, 1987+
- THEATRE, THE - Jan, 1959 - Sep, 1961//
- THEATRE MAGAZINE - Oct, 1900 - Apr, 1931//
- THEATRE TIME - Spring, 1949 - Winter, 1952//

New York State
- THEATRE JOURNAL - Mar, 1955 - Fall, 1973//

Opera
- DRAMATIC MAGAZINE, THE - Aug, 1897 - Aug, 1900//

Performance
- HIGH PERFORMANCE - Feb, 1978+
- TPQ - Jan, 1981?+

Plays
- BAKER'S NEWS - Winter, 1989+

Playwrights
- GAMBIT - ?+ {United Kingdom}
- NEW THEATRE MAGAZINE - Oct, 1959 - 1972// {United Kingdom}

Producing
- AMERICAN THEATRE - Jan, 1973+
- SOUTHERN THEATRE - 1956+
- THEATERWEEK - Aug 13, 1987+

Production
- ACTORS FORUM - Nov, 1956 - Feb, 1957?//?
- BACK STAGE - Dec 2, 1960+
- DRAMA & THEATRE - Winter, 1961/1962 - Spring, 1975//
- DRAMATIC MAGAZINE, THE - Aug, 1897 - Aug, 1900//
- DRAMATIC MIRROR AND LITERARY COMPANION, THE - Aug 14, 1841 - May 7, 1842//
- DRAMATIC REVIEW, THE - Dec 2, 1899 - Aug 4, 1900?//
- NEW THEATRE - Aug, 1939 - Jul, 1949// {United Kingdom}
- NEW THEATRE MAGAZINE - Oct, 1959 - 1972// {United Kingdom}
- NEW THEATRE QUARTERLY - Jan/Mar, 1971+ {United Kingdom}
- PLAY SHOP, THE - ?+?
- PLAYBILL - Oct 31, 1982+
- PLAYS INTERNATIONAL - Aug, 1985+ {United Kingdom}
- SOUTHERN THEATRE - 1956+
- THEATER - Spring, 1968+
- THEATER NOW - Spring, 1972+
- THEATRE, THE - Jan, 1877 - Dec, 1897// {United Kingdom}
- THEATRE, THE - Jan, 1959 - Sep, 1961//
- THEATRE, THE - Mar 20, 1886 - Apr 27, 1893//
- THEATRE-CRAFT - 1919 - 1921// {United Kingdom}
- THEATRE CRAFT - Jan, 1947 - May, 1948?//
- THEATRE CRAFTS - Mar/Apr, 1967+
- THEATRE DESIGN & TECHNOLOGY - May, 1965+
- THEATRE NEWS - Oct, 1968 - 1986//
- THEATRE NOTEBOOK - Oct, 1945+ {United Kingdom}
- THEATRE WORKSHOP - Oct, 1936 - Apr/Jun, 1938//

Puppetry
- ANIMATIONS - Oct/Nov, 1977+ {United Kingdom}
- GET ANIMATED! UPDATE. - Feb, 1985+

Religion
- CHRISTIAN DRAMA - October, 1977 - January, 1986//?

Research
- BROADSIDE - May, 1940+
- RESTORATION AND 18TH CENTURY THEATRE RESEARCH - May, 1962+
- SOUTHERN COMMUNICATION JOURNAL, THE - Oct, 1935+
- THEATRE DOCUMENTATION - Fall, 1968 - 1971/1972// {Brazil}
- THEATRE JOURNAL - Oct, 1949+
- THEATRE NOTEBOOK - Oct, 1945+ {United Kingdom}
- THEATRE RESEARCH - Mar, 1958 - #4, 1974// {United Kingdom}

Review
- ACTORS BY DAYLIGHT - Mar 3, 1838 - Mar 16, 1839// {United Kingdom}
- ALTERNATIVE THEATRE - Sep/Oct, 1975+
- ART & CINEMA - Jan, 1973+
- AUDIO-VISUAL GUIDE - Feb, 1936 - Jun, 1956//
- BAKER'S NEWS - Winter, 1989+
- BLACK THEATRE - 1968 - 1972//
- BOMB MAGAZINE - Spring, 1981+
- DRAMA, THE - Oct 23, 1821 - Dec 10, 1821// {Ireland}
- DRAMA LEAGUE MONTHLY - Apr, 1916 - May, 1919//

DRAMA SURVEY - May, 1961 - Winter, 1968/1969//
DRAMATIC CENSOR, THE - Jan 4, 1800 - Jul, 1801// {United Kingdom}
DRAMATIC MAGAZINE, THE - Mar 2, 1829 - Apr, 1831// {United Kingdom}
DRAMATIC MIRROR AND LITERARY COMPANION, THE - Aug 14, 1841 - May 7, 1842//
DRAMATIC REVIEW, THE - Dec 2, 1899 - Aug 4, 1900?//
DRAMATICS - Jan, 1929+
FILM AND THEATRE TODAY - Mar, 1946 - 1949// {United Kingdom}
HAMPTON MAGAZINE - Apr, 1898+?
INTERVIEW - 1969+
MODERN DRAMA - May, 1958+ {Canada}
NEW THEATRE QUARTERLY - Jan/Mar, 1971+ {United Kingdom}
ODDFELLOW, THE - Apr 21, 1838 - ?//? {United Kingdom}
PERFORMANCE - Dec, 1971+
PLAY-BOOK, THE - Apr, 1913+
SHAKESPEARE QUARTERLY - 1950+
SOUTHERN COMMUNICATION JOURNAL, THE - Oct, 1935+
SPEECH AND DRAMA - 1951+ {United Kingdom}
STAGE - Dec, 1923 - Jun, 1939//
TDR - 1955?+
THEATER - Spring, 1968+
THEATER NOW - Spring, 1972+
THEATRE, THE - Jan, 1877 - Dec, 1897// {United Kingdom}
THEATRE JOURNAL - Oct, 1949+
THEATRE TIME - Spring, 1949 - Winter, 1952//
VARIETY - Dec 16, 1905+
WORLD THEATRE - 1950 - 1968// {Belgium}

School
PLAYS - Sep, 1941+
THEATRE AND SCHOOL - 1922 - May, 1937//

Scripts
AMERICAN THEATRE - Jan, 1973+
DRAMA & THEATRE - Winter, 1961/1962 - Spring, 1975//
DRAMA MAGAZINE, THE - Feb, 1911 - Jun, 1931//
NEW THEATRE - Aug, 1939 - Jul, 1949// {United Kingdom}
NEW THEATRE QUARTERLY - Jan/Mar, 1971+ {United Kingdom}
PERFORMANCE - Dec, 1971+
SCRIPTWRITER NEWS - Jan, 1980 - 1982?//

Shakespeare
SHAKESPEARE QUARTERLY - 1950+

Southern California
THEATRE CRAFT - Jan, 1947 - May, 1948?//

Teaching
THEATRE TOPICS - Mar, 1991+

Technology
SOUTHERN THEATRE - 1956+
TABS - ?+? {United Kingdom}
TECHNOLOGY AND CULTURE - Winter, 1959+

Unions & Guilds
NEGRO ACTORS GUILD OF AMERICA. NEWSLETTER. - May, 1940+?

Vaudeville
DRAMATIC REVIEW, THE - Dec 2, 1899 - Aug 4, 1900?//
MARQUEE - Feb, 1969+

World
THEATRE ARTS - Nov, 1916 - Jan, 1964//

Writing
ACTF / PAC NEWS - ?+
DRAMA & THEATRE - Winter, 1961/1962 - Spring, 1975//
SCRIPTWRITER NEWS - Jan, 1980 - 1982?//

Video

Academic
COLLEGE BROADCASTER - Sep, 1988+
DIGEST OF THE UNIVERSITY FILM AND VIDEO ASSOCIATION - ?+
FILMMAKERS FILM & VIDEO MONTHLY - Nov, 1967 - Jan/Feb, 1982//
JOURNAL OF FILM AND VIDEO - Mar, 1949+

Access
TELEVISIONS - Summer, 1973+

Acting
SPOTLIGHT CASTING MAGAZINE - ?+

Adult
VIDEO WORLD - ?+ {United Kingdom}

Advertising
ELECTRONIC MEDIA - Aug 5, 1982+
FLASH - Jul/Aug, 1990+

Aesthetics
ART & CINEMA - Jan, 1973+
FLASH - Jul/Aug, 1990+

Alternative Media
CANTRILLS FILMNOTES - Mar, 1971+ {Australia}
EUROPEAN TRASH CINEMA - ?, 1990?+

Animation
ADVANCED IMAGING - Jun, 1988+
GET ANIMATED! UPDATE. - Feb, 1985+
GRAFFITI - ?+
STORYBOARD / THE ART OF LAUGHTER - Fall, 1990+
WITTYWORLD - Summer, 1987+

Archival
MAGAZINE, THE - 1976+

Art Form
VIDEO EIGHTIES MAGAZINE - 1980+?

Asia
TELECOM JAPAN, THE - ?+ {Japan}

Avant-garde
EUROPEAN TRASH CINEMA - ?, 1990?+
FILMMAKERS FILM & VIDEO MONTHLY - Nov, 1967 - Jan/Feb, 1982//

B Movies
CELLULOID NIGHTMARE - ?, 1990+?

Business
BUSINESS OF FILM, THE - Nov, 1982+ {United Kingdom}
BUSINESSTV VIDEO 8 GUIDE - Mar/Apr, 1990 - Aug, 1990//?
COMMUNICATIONS INDUSTRIES REPORT, THE - 1946+
DAILY VARIETY - 1933+
ELECTRONIC MEDIA - Aug 5, 1982+
FILM MEDIA - Jun, 1957 - Jan/Mar, 1960//
FLORIDA REEL - Oct/Nov, 1989+
HOME VIDEO PUBLISHER - Jul 16, 1984+
INDEPENDENT, THE - Jan, 1978+
MARKETING PULSE, THE - Sep, 1980?+
MOVIE/TV MARKETING - May, 1953+ {Japan}
MOVING PICTURES INTERNATIONAL - Sep 13, 1990?+ {United Kingdom}
PROFESSIONAL FILM PRODUCTION - Jun, 1975+
VIDEO PROPHILES - Jun, 1991+
VIDEO SOFTWARE MAGAZINE - Sep, 1985+
VIDEO STORE - Aug, 1979+
VIDEO TECHNOLOGY NEWS - Sep 26, 1988+
VIDEOCASSETTE AND CATV NEWSLETTER - Jun, 1971 - ?, 1981?//
WATCH - Dec, 1979 - May, 1980?//?

Cartoons
WITTYWORLD - Summer, 1987+

Video Subject Heading

Cassettes
- BLOCKBUSTER VIDEO MAGAZINE - 1989+
- HOME VIEWER - Apr, 1981+
- MOVIE - THE VIDEO MAGAZINE - Oct, 1988?+ {United Kingdom}
- OFFICIAL VIDEO JOURNAL, THE - ?+
- PREVIEWS - ? - Dec, 1980//
- SPOTLIGHT ON VIDEO - Jan, 1985+
- V - Oct, 1987+
- VIDEO BUSINESS - Jan, 1981+
- VIDEO CHOICE - Mar, 1988+?
- VIDEO INSIDER - 1983+
- VIDEO MONTHLY - Mar, 1990+ {United Kingdom}
- VIDEO REVIEW - Apr, 1980+
- VIDEO SOFTWARE MAGAZINE - Sep, 1985+
- VIDEO STORE - Aug, 1979+
- VIDEO--THE MAGAZINE - ?+ {United Kingdom}
- VIDEO TIMES - Jan, 1985+
- VIDEO TIMES - ?+ {United Kingdom}
- VIDEO TODAY - ?+ {United Kingdom}
- VIDEO WORLD - ?+ {United Kingdom}
- VIDEOCASSETTE AND CATV NEWSLETTER - Jun, 1971 - ?, 1981?//
- VIDEOPLAY MAGAZINE - Dec, 1979+
- VIEW - 1980+

Casting
- SPOTLIGHT CASTING MAGAZINE - ?+

Classifieds
- VIDEO NEWS AND USED - May, 1989?+ {Canada}

Collector
- CLASSIC IMAGES REVIEW - Nov, 1979 - ?, 1981//
- VIDEO BUYER - Nov/Dec, 1989+ {United Kingdom}

Commercial
- BACK STAGE/SHOOT - Jul 6, 1990+
- PRO VIDEOGRAM - Nov/Dec, 1989+

Community
- TELEVISIONS - Summer, 1973+
- VIDEOTOOLS - ?+?

Computers
- COMPUTER PICTURES - Jan/Feb, 1983+
- ONI - Dec, 1990+

Corporate
- COMMUNICATOR, THE - 1973+
- E-ITV - Aug, 1965 - Feb/Mar, 1988//
- TELESPAN'S BUSINESSTV GUIDE - 1986+
- VIDEO MANAGEMENT - 1978 - Dec, 1989//
- VIDEO SYSTEMS - Nov/Dec, 1975+
- VIDEOGRAPHY - Apr, 1976+

Dbs
- DBS NEWS - Sep, 1982+

Digital
- DIGITAL EVOLUTION MAGAZINE - Jul, 1989+ {Canada}

Distribution
- BUSINESS OF FILM, THE - Nov, 1982+ {United Kingdom}
- COMPUTER PICTURES - Jan/Feb, 1983+
- HOME VIDEO PUBLISHER - Jul 16, 1984+
- INDEPENDENT, THE - Jan, 1978+
- MARKETING PULSE, THE - Sep, 1980?+
- MOVIE/TV MARKETING - May, 1953+ {Japan}
- VIDEO BUSINESS - Jan, 1981+
- VIDEO INSIDER - 1983+

Documentary
- FILM & VIDEO NEWS - Dec, 1939 - Apr, 1984//
- INTERNATIONAL DOCUMENTARY - Summer, 1989?+

Engineering
- HDTV NEWSLETTER - Jun?, 1986+
- IMAGE TECHNOLOGY - 194u+ {United Kingdom}
- TELEVISION BROADCAST - Jan, 1978+

Europe
- EUROPEAN TRASH CINEMA - ?, 1990?+

Fan
- DEEP RED - Dec, 1987+
- FANGORIA - 1979+
- FANTASY ZONE - ?+ {United Kingdom}
- GOREZONE - May, 1988+
- HORRORFAN - Winter, 1988+
- STRANGE ADVENTURES - Feb, 1989+ {United Kingdom}

Fantasy
- FANTASY ZONE - ?+ {United Kingdom}

Filters
- TIFFEN PROFESSIONAL NEWSLETTER - Spring?, 1987+

Finance
- DAILY VARIETY - 1933+
- HOME VIDEO PUBLISHER - Jul 16, 1984+
- INDEPENDENT, THE - Jan, 1978+
- MARKETING PULSE, THE - Sep, 1980?+

Graphics
- ADVANCED IMAGING - Jun, 1988+
- AFTERIMAGE - 1972+
- COMPUTER PICTURES - Jan/Feb, 1983+
- FLASH - Jul/Aug, 1990+

Guide
- ALPHA AND OMEGA FILM REPORT - Jan, 1985?+
- BEST OF FILM & VIDEO - Mar/Apr, 1990+ {United Kingdom}
- CHRISTIAN FILM & VIDEO - Jan/Feb?, 1984+
- CINEMA, VIDEO & CABLE MOVIE DIGEST - May, 1991+
- EMPIRE - Jul, 1989+ {United Kingdom}
- FILM & BROADCASTING REVIEW - 1964 - Sep 1, 1980//
- FILM & VIDEO NEWS - Dec, 1939 - Apr, 1984//
- FILM MONTHLY - Jan, 1950?+ {United Kingdom}
- HOME VIDEO - Fall, 1979+?
- HUNGAROFILM BULLETIN - 1965+ {Hungary}
- MOVIE MARKETPLACE - Oct/Nov, 1987+
- MOVIE - THE VIDEO MAGAZINE - Oct, 1988?+ {United Kingdom}
- MOVIEGUIDE - ?, 1985+
- ONI - Dec, 1990+
- PERFECT VISION, THE - 1986+
- PREVIEWS - ? - Dec, 1980//
- SCIENCE-FICTION VIDEO MAGAZINE - Fall, 1989?+
- SPOTLIGHT ON VIDEO - Jan, 1985+
- V - Oct, 1987+
- VIDEO - Nov, 1974+ {United Kingdom}
- VIDEO ALERT - Jan, 1987+
- VIDEO CHOICE - Mar, 1988+?
- VIDEO MONTHLY - Mar, 1990+ {United Kingdom}
- VIDEO REVIEW - Apr, 1980+
- VIDEO--THE MAGAZINE - ?+ {United Kingdom}
- VIDEO TIMES - Jan, 1985+
- VIDEO TIMES - ?+ {United Kingdom}
- VIDEO TODAY - ?+ {United Kingdom}
- VIDEO WORLD - ?+ {United Kingdom}
- VIDEOPLAY MAGAZINE - Dec, 1979+
- VIEW - 1980+
- YOUNG VIEWERS - Fall, 1977 - ?, 1988//

High Defintion TV (HDTV)
- HD PRODUCTION - Spring, 1991+
- HD SYSTEMS WORLD REVIEW - Winter, 1989/1990+
- HDTV NEWSLETTER - Jun?, 1986+
- HDTV REPORT - Dec, 1990?+ {Netherlands}

Historical
- CLASSIC IMAGES REVIEW - Nov, 1979 - ?, 1981//
- HISTORICAL JOURNAL OF FILM, RADIO & TELEVISION - Mar, 1981+ {United Kingdom}
- MAGAZINE, THE - 1976+

Home Consumer
- AUDIO/VIDEO INTERIORS - Feb/Mar, 1989+
- CINEGRAM - Mar/Apr, 1976+
- CONSUMER ELECTRONICS - 1972+
- CONSUMER ELECTRONICS PRODUCT NEWS - Jan, 1975+

FAST FORWARD - 1980+
FILM MAKING - 1962? - Oct, 1980// {United Kingdom}
HOME VIDEO - Fall, 1979+?
MOVIE - THE VIDEO MAGAZINE - Oct, 1988?+ {United Kingdom}
MOVING IMAGE - Winter, 1972/1973 - Jun, 1982//
ONI - Dec, 1990+
PERFECT VISION, THE - 1986+
TELEVISIONS - Summer, 1973+
VIDEO ANSWERS - ?+ {United Kingdom}
VIDEO CAMERA - May/Jun, 1989?+ {United Kingdom}
VIDEO INFO - Jun, 1979?+?
VIDEO MAGAZINE - Winter, 1978+
VIDEO REVIEW - Apr, 1980+
VIDEOGRAPHY - Apr, 1976+
VIDEOMAKER - Jun/Jul, 1986+
WHAT VIDEO - ?+ {United Kingdom}

Horror
CINEMACABRE - Mar, 1969+
DEEP RED - Dec, 1987+
FANGORIA - 1979+
GOREZONE - May, 1988+
HORRORFAN - Winter, 1988+
WORLD OF FANDOM, THE - Jul, 1985+

Independent
FILMMAKERS FILM & VIDEO MONTHLY - Nov, 1967 - Jan/Feb, 1982//
INDEPENDENT, THE - Jan, 1978+
VIDEO SYSTEMS - Nov/Dec, 1975+
VIDEOGRAPHY - Apr, 1976+
VIDEOTOOLS - ?+?

Instructional
AUDIO VISUAL - Nov, 1946+ {United Kingdom}
BIOMEDICAL COMMUNICATIONS - Jan, 1973 to date.
EDUCATIONAL SCREEN - Jan, 1922 - Sum, 1956//
ETV NEWSLETTER - Dec, 1966+
FILM & VIDEO NEWS - Dec, 1939 - Apr, 1984//
FILM LIBRARY QUARTERLY - Winter, 1967/68 - 1985//
JOURNAL OF EDUCATIONAL TELEVISION - Mar, 1975+ {United Kingdom}
TELESPAN'S BUSINESSTV GUIDE - 1986+

Interactive
ADVANCED IMAGING - Jun, 1988+
COMMUNICATIONS INDUSTRIES REPORT, THE - 1946+
OPTICAL MEMORY NEWS - Jan/Feb, 1982+

Intercultural
APERTURE - Apr, 1952+

International
APERTURE - Apr, 1952+
BUSINESS OF FILM, THE - Nov, 1982+ {United Kingdom}
CTVD - Winter, 1961/1962+
DAILY VARIETY - 1933+
DBS NEWS - Sep, 1982+
HISTORICAL JOURNAL OF FILM, RADIO & TELEVISION - Mar, 1981+ {United Kingdom}
INTERNATIONAL DOCUMENTARY - Summer, 1989?+
JOURNAL OF EDUCATIONAL TELEVISION - Mar, 1975+ {United Kingdom}
MOVIE/TV MARKETING - May, 1953+ {Japan}
MOVING PICTURES INTERNATIONAL - Sep 13, 1990?+ {United Kingdom}
VIDEO TECHNOLOGY NEWS - Sep 26, 1988+
WORLD SCREEN - Dec, 1959+? {Italy}

Lens
ZEISS INFORMATION - 1963+ {Germany}

Libraries
CABLE LIBRARIES - May, 1973+
FILM LIBRARY QUARTERLY - Winter, 1967/68 - 1985//

Lighting
LIGHTING DIMENSIONS - Jan, 1977+
LIGHTS! - Jan, 1990+ {United Kingdom}

Literature
CTVD - Winter, 1961/1962+

Location
LOCATION UPDATE - Jul/Aug, 1985+
ON LOCATION - Oct, 1977 - Mar, 1986?//?
WRAP - Oct/Nov, 1987+

Management
CORPORATE TELEVISION - Jun, 1983+
CORPORATE VIDEO DECISIONS - Sep, 1988 - Aug, 1990//
VIDEO MANAGEMENT - 1978 - Dec, 1989//
VIDEO SYSTEMS - Nov/Dec, 1975+

Marketing
BUSINESS OF FILM, THE - Nov, 1982+ {United Kingdom}
FILM MEDIA - Jun, 1957 - Jan/Mar, 1960//
MOVIE/TV MARKETING - May, 1953+ {Japan}
PROFESSIONAL FILM PRODUCTION - Jun, 1975+

Medical
BIOMEDICAL COMMUNICATIONS - Jan, 1973 to date.

Membership
CORPORATE TELEVISION - Jun, 1983+

Multimedia
COMMUNICATIONS INDUSTRIES REPORT, THE - 1946+

Mystery
SCARLET STREET - Jan, 1991+

New York City
BACK STAGE/SHOOT - Jul 6, 1990+

Post Production
POST - Mar, 1986+
WRAP - Oct/Nov, 1987+

Producing
CINE NEWS - May?, 1991+
INTERNATIONAL DOCUMENTARY - Summer, 1989?+
PRODUCERS QUARTERLY - Mar, 1989+

Production
BACK STAGE/SHOOT - Jul 6, 1990+
BIOMEDICAL COMMUNICATIONS - Jan, 1973 to date.
CAMCORDER - Jan, 1985+
CAMCORDER USER - ?+ {United Kingdom}
CAMERA & CAMCORDER MONTHLY - ? - Mar, 1990// {United Kingdom}
CAMERART - Spring, 1958+ {Japan}
CINE NEWS - May?, 1991+
COLLEGE BROADCASTER - Sep, 1988+
COMPUTER PICTURES - Jan/Feb, 1983+
CORPORATE TELEVISION - Jun, 1983+
CORPORATE VIDEO DECISIONS - Sep, 1988 - Aug, 1990//
DAILY VARIETY - 1933+
DIGITAL EVOLUTION MAGAZINE - Jul, 1989+ {Canada}
ENTERTAINMENT MONTHLY - 1977+
FILM MAKING - 1962? - Oct, 1980// {United Kingdom}
FILMMAKERS FILM & VIDEO MONTHLY - Nov, 1967 - Jan/Feb, 1982//
FLORIDA REEL - Oct/Nov, 1989+
HD PRODUCTION - Spring, 1991+
HD SYSTEMS WORLD REVIEW - Winter, 1989/1990+
HDTV REPORT - Dec, 1990?+ {Netherlands}
HOME VIDEO PUBLISHER - Jul 16, 1984+
IMAGEMAKER - Aug, 1981+
INDEPENDENT, THE - Jan, 1978+
INSIDE ENTERTAINMENT - ?+
INTERNATIONAL DOCUMENTARY - Summer, 1989?+
INVISION - ?+ {United Kingdom}
JOURNAL OF FILM AND VIDEO - Mar, 1949+
LIGHTING DIMENSIONS - Jan, 1977+
LIGHTS! - Jan, 1990+ {United Kingdom}
LOCATION UPDATE - Jul/Aug, 1985+
MARKEE - Feb, 1986+

Video
Subject Heading

MILLIMETER - 1973+
MOVING IMAGE - Winter, 1972/1973 - Jun, 1982//
ON LOCATION - Oct, 1977 - Mar, 1986?//?
PLAYBACK - Winter, 1982?+?
POST - Mar, 1986+
PRINTED MATTER - ?, 1974+
PRODUCERS QUARTERLY - Mar, 1989+
PROFESSIONAL FILM PRODUCTION - Jun, 1975+
TELEVISION BROADCAST - Jan, 1978+
TELEVISIONS - Summer, 1973+
TIFFEN PROFESSIONAL NEWSLETTER - Spring?, 1987+
VIDEO - Nov, 1974+ {United Kingdom}
VIDEO CAPSULE - ?+?
VIDEO INFO - Jun, 1979?+?
VIDEO MANAGEMENT - 1978 - Dec, 1989//
VIDEO PROPHILES - Jun, 1991+
VIDEO SYSTEMS - Nov/Dec, 1975+
VIDEODISC DESIGN / PRODUCTION GROUP. NEWS. - 1979+
VIDEODISC MONITOR, THE - Sep, 1983+
VIDEOMAKER - Jun/Jul, 1986+
VIDEOPRO - Nov, 1982+
VIDEOTOOLS - ?+?
WRAP - Oct/Nov, 1987+

Programming
BUSINESSTV VIDEO 8 GUIDE - Mar/Apr, 1990 - Aug, 1990//?
CABLE LIBRARIES - May, 1973+
CINEMA, VIDEO & CABLE MOVIE DIGEST - May, 1991+
ELECTRONIC MEDIA - Aug 5, 1982+
VIEW - 1980+
WATCH - Dec, 1979 - May, 1980?//?

Promotion
BLOCKBUSTER VIDEO MAGAZINE - 1989+
FAST FORWARD - 1980+
HUNGAROFILM BULLETIN - 1965+ {Hungary}
IMAGEMAKER - Aug, 1981+
INSIDE ENTERTAINMENT - ?+
PRINTED MATTER - ?, 1974+
SPOTLIGHT ON VIDEO - Jan, 1985+
VIDEO TIMES - Winter, 1982+
VTA PLAYBACK - ?+

Puppetry
GET ANIMATED! UPDATE. - Feb, 1985+

Regulation
COMMUNICATIONS INDUSTRIES REPORT, THE - 1946+
VIDEO TECHNOLOGY NEWS - Sep 26, 1988+

Religion
ALPHA AND OMEGA FILM REPORT - Jan, 1985?+
CHRISTIAN FILM & VIDEO - Jan/Feb?, 1984+

FILM & BROADCASTING REVIEW - 1964 - Sep 1, 1980//
MOVIEGUIDE - ?, 1985+
VIDEO CAPSULE - ?+?

Research
HISTORICAL JOURNAL OF FILM, RADIO & TELEVISION - Mar, 1981+ {United Kingdom}
JOURNAL OF FILM AND VIDEO - Mar, 1949+

Retail
BLOCKBUSTER VIDEO MAGAZINE - 1989+
CLASSIC IMAGES REVIEW - Nov, 1979 - ?, 1981//
CONSUMER ELECTRONICS - 1972+
CONSUMER ELECTRONICS PRODUCT NEWS - Jan, 1975+
MOVIE MARKETPLACE - Oct/Nov, 1987+
VIDEO BUSINESS - Jan, 1981+
VIDEO INSIDER - 1983+
VIDEO MONTHLY - Mar, 1990+ {United Kingdom}
VIDEO TODAY - ?+ {United Kingdom}

Review
AFTERIMAGE - 1972+
ALPHA AND OMEGA FILM REPORT - Jan, 1985?+
APERTURE - Apr, 1952+
ART & CINEMA - Jan, 1973+
CAMERART - Spring, 1958+ {Japan}
CANTRILLS FILMNOTES - Mar, 1971+ {Australia}
CELLULOID NIGHTMARE - ?, 1990+?
CINEMACABRE - Mar, 1969+
CTVD - Winter, 1961/1962+
DAILY VARIETY - 1933+
DEEP RED - Dec, 1987+
E-ITV - Aug, 1965 - Feb/Mar, 1988//
ELECTRONIC MEDIA - Aug 5, 1982+
EMPIRE - Jul, 1989+ {United Kingdom}
FILM DIRECTIONS - 1977+ {United Kingdom}
HISTORICAL JOURNAL OF FILM, RADIO & TELEVISION - Mar, 1981+ {United Kingdom}
JOURNAL OF FILM AND VIDEO - Mar, 1949+
KODAK PROFESSIONAL FORUM - ?, 1978+?
PERFECT VISION, THE - 1986+
PRO VIDEOGRAM - Nov/Dec, 1989+
SCARLET STREET - Jan, 1991+
SHUTTERBUG - 1971+
TELECOM JAPAN, THE - ?+ {Japan}
VIDEOGRAPHY - Apr, 1976+
WATCH - Dec, 1979 - May, 1980?//?
WORLD SCREEN - Dec, 1959+? {Italy}
YOUNG VIEWERS - Fall, 1977 - ?, 1988//

Sale
COMMUNICATIONS INDUSTRIES REPORT, THE - 1946+
VIDEO TIMES - ?+ {United Kingdom}

Sales
COMMUNICATIONS INDUSTRIES REPORT, THE - 1946+

School
EDUCATIONAL SCREEN - Jan, 1922 - Sum, 1956//
ETV NEWSLETTER - Dec, 1966+
FILM & VIDEO NEWS - Dec, 1939 - Apr, 1984//
JOURNAL OF EDUCATIONAL TELEVISION - Mar, 1975+ {United Kingdom}

Scripts
SCRIPT NEWSLETTER - 1988?+?

Southeast United States
MARKEE - Feb, 1986+

Teaching
DIGEST OF THE UNIVERSITY FILM AND VIDEO ASSOCIATION - ?+

Technology
ADVANCED IMAGING - Jun, 1988+
AUDIO/VIDEO INTERIORS - Feb/Mar, 1989+
BUSINESSTV VIDEO 8 GUIDE - Mar/Apr, 1990 - Aug, 1990//?
CAMCORDER - Jan, 1985+
CAMCORDER USER - ?+ {United Kingdom}
CAMERA & CAMCORDER MONTHLY - ? - Mar, 1990// {United Kingdom}
CAMERART - Spring, 1958+ {Japan}
CINEGRAM - Mar/Apr, 1976+
COMMUNICATIONS INDUSTRIES REPORT, THE - 1946+
COMMUNICATOR, THE - 1973+
CONSUMER ELECTRONICS - 1972+
DIGITAL EVOLUTION MAGAZINE - Jul, 1989+ {Canada}
E-ITV - Aug, 1965 - Feb/Mar, 1988//
EDUCATIONAL SCREEN - Jan, 1922 - Sum, 1956//
HD PRODUCTION - Spring, 1991+
HD SYSTEMS WORLD REVIEW - Winter, 1989/1990+
HDTV NEWSLETTER - Jun?, 1986+
HDTV REPORT - Dec, 1990?+ {Netherlands}
IMAGE TECHNOLOGY - 194u+ {United Kingdom}
LIGHTING DIMENSIONS - Jan, 1977+
MILLIMETER - 1973+
NEWSLETTER, THE - ?+?
OPTICAL INFORMATION SYSTEMS - Winter, 1981+
PEIRCE-PHELPS, INC. AUDIO/VIDEO NEWSLETTER - May, 1988+
PERFECT VISION, THE - 1986+
POST - Mar, 1986+
PRO VIDEOGRAM - Nov/Dec, 1989+
SHUTTERBUG - 1971+
TELECOM JAPAN, THE - ?+ {Japan}

TELEVISION BROADCAST - Jan, 1978+
VIDEO ANSWERS - ?+ {United Kingdom}
VIDEO CAMERA - May/Jun, 1989?+ {United Kingdom}
VIDEO NEWS AND USED - May, 1989?+ {Canada}
VIDEO PROPHILES - Jun, 1991+
VIDEO REVIEW - Apr, 1980+
VIDEO TECHNOLOGY NEWS - Sep 26, 1988+
VIDEO TIMES - Winter, 1982+
VIDEOMAKER - Jun/Jul, 1986+
VIDEOPRO - Nov, 1982+
WHAT VIDEO - ?+ {United Kingdom}
ZEISS INFORMATION - 1963+ {Germany}

Teleconferencing
PEIRCE-PHELPS, INC. AUDIO/VIDEO NEWSLETTER - May, 1988+

Third Coast
MARKEE - Feb, 1986+

Videodisc
OPTICAL INFORMATION SYSTEMS - Winter, 1981+
OPTICAL MEMORY NEWS - Jan/Feb, 1982+
PERFECT VISION, THE - 1986+
VIDEODISC DESIGN / PRODUCTION GROUP. NEWS. - 1979+
VIDEODISC MONITOR, THE - Sep, 1983+

Videotext
OPTICAL INFORMATION SYSTEMS - Winter, 1981+

World
BUSINESS OF FILM, THE - Nov, 1982+ {United Kingdom}

Writing
SCRIPT NEWSLETTER - 1988?+?

Youth
YOUNG VIEWERS - Fall, 1977 - ?, 1988//

Subtitle

Subtitles in this index include those of current and past titles (listed as *VARIES* entries under MAIN TITLES). Inclusive dates of publication for each subtitle are provided when known. Also see *VFOT* index for varying forms of title which are sometimes mistakenly labeled subtitles.

#

"#1 magazine of home video, The." - VIDEO MAGAZINE

"#1 Pinup Magazine! All-color! All-stars!" - WOW! MAGAZINE

"#1 source for the video pro, The." (Summer, 1988 - ?). - VIDEO TIMES

A

"A-V communications linking the whole community." - COMPUTER PICTURES

"Action for Children's Television news magazine." - RE:ACT

"Action for Childrens Television Newsletter." - RE:ACT

"Ads, TV and posters world-wide." - LÜRZER'S INTERNATIONAL ARCHIVE

"Adventure films and television." - DAREDEVILS

"Advertiser's magazine, An." - ADVERTISING ADVOCATE

"Advertiser's problem is the problem, The." - AMERICAN ADVERTISER

"Advertising Age's spotlight on pan-European marketing." - FOCUS

"Advertising and selling by letters, folders, booklets, blotters, house magazines, catalogs, etc." - DIRECT MARKETING

"Advertising creates demand." - SIGNS OF THE TIMES

"Advertising magazine, The." - MADISON AVENUE

"Advertising's first and only semi-weekly." (Jan 7, 1965 - ?). - ADWEEK

"All about direct-mail advertising." (? - Mar, 1927). - MAILBAG, THE

"All about television." - TELEVISION

"All-talking, all-singing, all-dancing magazine, The." - FLASHBACK

"All the means of reproducing ideas in visual form by graphic symbols." - PRINT

"All the news." - DRAMATIC MIRROR, THE

"All the news about cameras and photography." - CAMERART

"All the news that's fit to animate." - ANIMATION MAGAZINE

"All the splatter that matters!" - GOREZONE

"All the stories from all the shows." - SOAP OPERA DIGEST

"All ways interesting." (Dec, 1929 - Jul, 1934). - TALKING PICTURE MAGAZINE

"All you want to know about the movies." - SCREEN STORIES

"All your photo questions answered." - PHOTO ANSWERS

"Alternative Spaces." - ART DYNAMO

"Amateur Radio." - CQ

"American journal of photography, The." (May, 1898 - Dec, 1920). - PHOTO-ERA MAGAZINE

"America's #1 horror magazine." - GOREZONE

"America's cable magazine." - CABLE GUIDE, THE

"America's favorite family weekly." - NATIONAL EXAMINER

"America's first and only regional motion picture trade newspaper." - GREATER AMUSEMENTS

"America's first television journal." - TELEVISION

"America's foremost casting newspaper." - DRAMA-LOGUE

"America's foremost motion picture regional trade journal." - GREATER AMUSEMENTS

"America's graphic design magazine." - PRINT

"America's greatest movie magazine." - MODERN SCREEN

"America's leading magazine of the arts and politics of the cinema." - CINEASTE

"America's leading magazine on the art and politics of the cinema." - CINEASTE

"America's most influential journal for the printing and allied industries." - PRINTING IMPRESSIONS

"America's oldest motion picture trade paper." - GREATER AMUSEMENTS

"America's television magazine." - TV GUIDE

"America's weekly guide to satellite TV." - ONSAT

"And miscellany of the drama, music and literature. Containing correct memoirs of the most celebrated London performers; original tales, poetry, and criticisms" (Nov 24, 1838 - Mar 16, 1839). - ACTORS BY DAYLIGHT

"And pencilings in the pit" (Mar 3, 1838 - Nov 17, 1838). - ACTORS BY DAYLIGHT

"Andy Warhol's movie magazine." - INTERVIEW

"Animation fan's magazine, The." - ANIMATO!

"Announcments/information from the Corporation for Public Broadcasting." - REPORT

"ANPA News Research Center study, An." - ANPA NEWS RESEARCH REPORT

"Applications magazine for audio professionals, The." - REP: RECORDING ENGINEERING PRODUCTION

"Applications of today's state-of-the-audio-art in broadcasting." - AUDIO PRODUCTION FOR BROADCAST

"Applying television technology." - TELEVISION BROADCAST

"Appreciation of fantastic films, An." - CINEMACABRE

"Appreciation of the fantastic, An." - CINEMACABRE

"ARRL experimenters' exchange, The." - QEX

"Art & communications." - VIDEO EIGHTIES MAGAZINE

"Art, images, ideas." - CREATIVE CAMERA

"Art of laughter, The." - STORYBOARD / THE ART OF LAUGHTER

"Art/science of selling to consumer and business markets, The." (? - Dec, 1989). - DIRECT MARKETING

"Art that matters." - HIGH PERFORMANCE

"Artists, writers, actors, directors." - BOMB MAGAZINE

"As the name indicates, is a guide to all publishers--and the newspaper fraternity in general." - ADVERTISING NEWS

"Asian mass communication quarterly, An." - MEDIA ASIA

"ASIFA-East newsletter, The." - ANYMATOR

"ASMP journal of photography in communications." - ASMP BULLETIN

"Association for Education in Journalism and Mass Communication." - MC&S NEWSLETTER

"At the movies." - ON LINE

"Audio/Acoustics/Applications." - AES

"Audio, acoustics, applications." - AES

"Audio-visual magazine, The." - EDUCATIONAL SCREEN

"Audiovisual software reviews." - PREVIEWS

"Australasian Photo-Review, The." - APR

"Australian Telecommunication Research." - ATR

"Authoritative cable television publication covering news, views, issues & developments in North America and around the world, The." - CABLE COMMUNICATIONS MAGAZINE

"Authoritative international cable television publication, The." - CABLE COMMUNICATIONS MAGAZINE

"Authoritative magazine about high fidelity, The." - AUDIO

"Authoritative news service for public broadcasting and allied fields, The." - PUBLIC BROADCASTING REPORT, THE

"Authoritative news service for satellite communications and allied fields, The." - SATELLITE WEEK

"Authoritative service for broadcasting, consumer electronics and allied fields, The." - TELEVISION DIGEST WITH CONSUMER ELECTRONICS

"Authoritative weekly newspaper of the printing industry, The." - PRINTING-NEWS

"Authority on new products and services for commercial artists and graphic designers, The." - ART & DESIGN NEWS

"Authority on prepress technology, The." - PRE-

"Authority on production technology, The." - MAGAZINE DESIGN & PRODUCTION

B

"Back Stage Supplement." - COMPUTER PICTURES

"Basic magazine of the 16 mm. industry, The." - FILM WORLD AND A-V NEWS MAGAZINE

"BEA's individual membership newsletter published in September, December and March." - BROADCAST EDUCATOR NEWS NOTES

"Being a monthly magazine published for printers." (Aug, 1911). - PRACTICAL PRINTER, THE

"Best, The." - MOVIE FLASH

"Best guide to videotapes, The." - VIDEO TIMES

"Best ideas in print for professional communicators, The." - COMMUNICATIONS CONCEPTS

"Best of then and now, The." - SH-BOOM

"Bi-monthly review, A." - WORLD THEATRE

"Bi-weekly journal devoted to the interest of publishers and advertising managers, containing certain information respecting advertisers in the United States and Canadian Provinces, A." - AMERICAN ADVERTISER REPORTER

"Bi-weekly newsletter for users and producers of video hardware, programs, and services, The." (May, 1979 - Jul, 1980). - VIDEO MANAGEMENT

"Bi-weekly newspaper for users and producers of video hardware, programs and services, The." - VIDEO MANAGEMENT

"Biblical look at movies and entertainment, A." 191 - MOVIEGUIDE

"Big magazine for agencies and advertisers, The." - ADVERTISING NEWS

"Big picture, The." - MARKETING PULSE, THE

"Bimonthly journal for editorial writers, A." - GRASSROOTS EDITOR

"Bimonthly review & resource guide, A." - CHRISTIAN FILM & VIDEO

"Bimonthly review of film and video animation, A." - GRAFFITI

"Biweekly guide for those who write, report, and edit for publication, The." - IN BLACK AND WHITE

"Biweekly news report of educational and instructional television, The." - ETV NEWSLETTER

"Biweekly newsletter on freedom of information and privacy, A." - ACCESS REPORTS/FREEDOM OF INFORMATION

"Biweekly publication of the U.S. Catholic Conference, A." - FILM & BROADCASTING REVIEW

"Book of the new spirit in the theatre, A." - THEATRE-CRAFT

"Boston / New England area arts." - ART DYNAMO

"Bradstreet of filmdom, The." - FILM TV DAILY

"Breaking news of the radio industry, The." - RADIO BUSINESS REPORT

"Bridging the gap between telecommunications suppliers and end users." - TELEMARKETING

"Bringing advertiser and agency management inside print." - INSIDE MEDIA

"Britain's best selling movie monthly." - FILM REVIEW

"Britain's best selling video magazine." - WHAT VIDEO

"Britain's fastest growing magazine." - VIDEO WORLD

"Britain's most established screen monthly." - FILMS AND FILMING

"Britain's premier comics fanzine." - FA

"Britain's premiere science fiction magazine." - STARBURST

"British Council's monthly survey for book-buyers throughout the world, The." - BRITISH BOOK NEWS

"British how-to-do-it photo magazine, The." - PRACTICAL PHOTOGRAPHY

"British journal of telefantasy, The." - DWB

"Broadcast, cable, computer video, consumer electronics, HDTV, fiber, new media, satellites, telecommunications, training." - VIDEO TECHNOLOGY NEWS

"Broadcast technology magazine, The." - INTERNATIONAL BROADCASTING

"Broadcasting international review." - MONITOR INTERNATIONAL

"Bulletin for all who are interested in better motion pictures, A." - MOTION PICTURE AND THE FAMILY, THE

"Bulletin of the Commonwealth Broadcasting Conference, The." (Dec, 1966 - ?). - COMBROAD

"Bulletin of the Finnish Film Foundation." - FACTS ABOUT FILM FINLAND

"Bulletin of the International Film and Television Council." - WORLD SCREEN

"Bulletin of the Radio Television News Directors Association." - COMMUNICATOR

"Business Bringer, A." - SCHEMER, THE

"Business communications magazine, The." - TELECONFERENCE MAGAZINE

"Business journal of television, The." - VIDEO AGE INTERNATIONAL

"Business journal of television: broadcasting, cable-TV, pay-TV, home video, The." - VIDEO AGE INTERNATIONAL

"Business magazine for portrait, commercial and industrial photographers, The." (? - Jun 24, 1931). - BULLETIN OF PHOTOGRAPHY

"Business magazine for the professional portrait and commercial photographer, The." - STUDIO PHOTOGRAPHY

"Business magazine of film and tape, The." - PROFESSIONAL FILM PRODUCTION

"Business magazine of the industry, The." - TELEVISION

"Business magazine of the radio industry, The." (Jan, 1925 - ?). - TELEVISION RETAILING

"Business news of the private satellite marketplace." - STAR SIGNALS

"Business of communications, The." - CHANNELS

"Business of newspapers, The." - NEWSINC.

"Business paper of independent distribution, The." - MAGAZINE & BOOKSELLER

"Businessweekly of radio and television, The." - BROADCASTING

"Buy-sell-trade magazine for antique, classic, used photographic equipment & images, A." - PHOTIQUE

"Buying & using satellite." - WHAT SATELLITE

"By the editors of Photographer's Market." - PHOTOGRAPHER'S MARKET NEWSLETTER

C

"California journalism review, The." - FEEDBACK

"Campus membership of National Religious Broadcasters, The." - CAMPUS BROADCASTERS

"Campus membership of National Religious Broadcasters." - IRB

"Can you take it?" - GOREZONE

"Canada's communications magazine." - BROADCASTER

"Canada's electronic entertainment magazine." - SOUND & VISION

"Canada's electronic lifestyle magazine." - SOUND & VISION

"Canada's first magazine of motion picture cinematography." - CINEMA/CANADA

"Canadian communications quarterly, The." - IN SEARCH

"Canst thou send lightnings, that they may go and say unto thee, here we are?--Job." (Oct, 1852 - Jul 15, 1853). - AMERICAN TELEGRAPH MAGAZINE

"Cartoon reviews of bills, picture programs." - DRAMATIC MIRROR, THE

"Casting news." - TGIF

"Casting, scripts, production." - ROSS REPORTS TELEVISION

"Cathedral of the motion picture, The." - ROXY THEATRE WEEKLY REVIEW

"Caucus for producers, writers, & directors, The." - CAUCUS QUARTERLY, THE

"CCM music report, The." - MUSIC LINE

"Check it out, dude!" - ACTION FILMS

"Chicago's movie journal." - FOCUS!

"Christian review of entertainment, A." - MEDIA SPOTLIGHT

"Chronicle of advertising in the west, The." - ADWEEK

"Cinema and video environmental reference network exchange." - CAVERNE COMMUNICATION, THE

"Cinema and video environmental review news exchange." - CAVERNE COMMUNICATION, THE

"Cinema, TV digest." - CTVD

"Circulated with Campaign only in the U.K." - DIRECTION

"Circulation larger than that of any other radio publication." - ELECTRONICS WORLD

"Classic comics library, The." - NEMO

"Clearing house of advertising facts and figures, The." (Sep/Oct, 1909). - ADVERTISING RESULTS MAGAZINE

"Collector's guide to comics, science fiction, fantasy, and art, The." - COMICS JOURNAL, THE

"Combined with Minicam Photography." - MODERN PHOTOGRAPHY

"Combined with TV Stage." - TV PICTURE LIFE

"Combined with Wire & Radio Communications." - COMMUNICATIONS NEWS

"Comic news, interviews, reviews, strips." - ARK

"Comics fandom examiner, The." - COMICS FANDOM EXAMINER

"Comics magazine, The." - ARK

"Comics opinion and comics review, The." - COMIC FANDOM'S FORUM

"Comment on current films by teachers, educators, community leaders." - MOTION PICTURE AND THE FAMILY, THE

"Committee of Small Magazine Editors and Publishers." - COSMEP NEWSLETTER

"Communicating the latest in film & video news." - MARKEE

"Communications Newspaper, The." - CAMPAIGN

"Compendium of valuable formulas and general information relating to the art, with a reduced price list of photographic materials and stereoscopic goods, A." (Oct, 1872). - PHOTOGRAPHER'S FRIEND, THE

"Complete and authoritative source of information on frequency modulation, The." (Dec, 1940 - Oct, 1941). - COMMUNICATION ENGINEERING

"Complete magazine of video photography, The." - CAMCORDER

"Complete movie monthly, The." - FILMWORLD

"Complete news service for the educational TV and related industries, The." - ETV REPORTER

"Complete service weekly for the communications and entertainment industry, The." - BACK STAGE

"Concerning media reform and citizen access to telecommunications." - ACCESS

"Confidential newsweekly for radio executives, programmers and syndicators, A." - INSIDE RADIO

"Confidential Washington news letter covering the telephone, telegraph and radio communications fields and containing a complete and authentic record of the activities of the Federal Communications Commission and Congress, A." (Aug 9, 1934 - ?). - TELECOMMUNICATIONS REPORTS

"Confidential weekly news for the video retailer, distributor and supplier." - VIDEO INSIDER

"Consistently the best in hobby electronics." - ELECTRONICS ILLUSTRATED

"Consumer trends for business leaders." - AMERICAN DEMOGRAPHICS

"Containing the Journalism Bulletin." (Jan, 1928 - Nov, 1929). - JQ. JOURNALISM QUARTERLY.

"Contemporary music magazine, The." - DOWN BEAT

"Contemporary view, A." - AUSTRALIAN PHOTOGRAPHY

"Continuing publications for American professional graphic artists." - BOARD REPORT FOR GRAPHIC ARTISTS

"Continuing survey of the motion picture in America, A." - MOVIES AND THE PEOPLE WHO MAKE THEM, THE

"Council on church and media." - FORUM

"Covering every wireless interest." - ELECTRONICS WORLD + WIRELESS WORLD

"Covering management, marketing, technology and regulation." - SATELLITE NEWS

"Covering television equipment, news, applications and technology." - TELEVISION BROADCAST

"Covering the Asian markets weekly." - MOVIE/TV MARKETING

"Covering the entire international programming marketplace--syndication, network, cable, public broadcasting, home video, foreign markets." - TELEVISION PROGRAMMER, THE

"Covering the international media world: TV, radio cable and satellites." - BROADCASTING ABROAD

"Crain's international newspaper of marketing." - ADVERTISING AGE

"Creating, producing, delivering." - PRESENTATION PRODUCTS MAGAZINE

"Creative recording magazine, The." - EQ

"Creative voice of the entertainment industry, The." - SCRIPTWRITER NEWS

"Critical and professional review, A." - ADVERTISING MAGAZINE

"Critical review of communications resources for religious educators, A." (Apr, 1976 - ?). - RELIGIOUS MEDIA TODAY

"Critique of metropolitan media and events, A." - ST. LOUIS JOURNALISM REVIEW

"Current study of international films and filmfolk, A." (Oct, 1964 - ?). - FILM-WORLD

"Cutting edge of what's funny, The." - COMIC RELIEF

D

"Daily newspaper of motion pictures, The." - FILM TV DAILY

"Daily register of histrionic performances on the Dublin stage; and critical review of general dramatic literature. By two gentlemen of the Dublin University, A." - DRAMA, THE

"Datacommunications, teleprocessing, transmission." - TELECOMMUNICATIONS

"Day by day satellite programmes." - WHAT SATELLITE

"Dedicated to database marketing." - TARGET MARKETING

"Dedicated to direct marketing excellence." - TARGET MARKETING

"Dedicated to the service and advancement of news photography." - NEWS PHOTOGRAPHER

"Dedicated to the world of entertainment." - PREVUE

"Defines the state of the art." (Apr, 1984 - ?). - HI-FI ANSWERS

"Demand is the very life of commerce." - SIGNS OF THE TIMES

"Desktop publishing." - PUBLISH!

"Desktop publishing/presentation graphics for IBM and compatible PC users." - PC PUBLISHING AND PRESENTATIONS

"Developed from the National Committee's bulletin." - VISUAL EDUCATION

"Devoted entirely to amateur radio." - QST

"Devoted exclusively to the interests of advertisers and publishers." (? - May, 1909). - PROFITABLE ADVERTISING

"Devoted principally to the interests of the National Telegraphic Union, and to telegraphers and telegraphing in general." - TELEGRAPHER, THE

"Devoted to commercials." (Oct, 1968 - ?). - CLIO MAGAZINE

"Devoted to frequency modulation." (Nov, 1940). - COMMUNICATION ENGINEERING

"Devoted to investigative studies in the field of journalism." (Mar, 1930). - JQ. JOURNALISM QUARTERLY.

"Devoted to issues in mass media ethics." - JOURNAL OF MASS MEDIA ETHICS

"Devoted to opinion and research on the student communications media and related areas." - COLLEGE MEDIA REVIEW

"Devoted to Photography." - ST. LOUIS AND CANADIAN PHOTOGRAPHER

"Devoted to research and commentary in journalism and mass communication education." - JOURNALISM EDUCATOR, THE

"Devoted to research development in the field of communications." - AT&T TECHNOLOGY

"Devoted to research in journalism and mass communication." - JQ. JOURNALISM QUARTERLY.

"Devoted to the art of films." - CLOSE-UP

"Devoted to the best interests of the motion picture industry." - FILM JOURNAL, THE

"Devoted to the business of program sales & distribution for videocassettes, disc, pay TV & allied new media." - VIDEO WEEK

"Devoted to the cause of good cinema." - FILM GUIDE

"Devoted to the electrical and allied mechanical interests at the World's Columbian Exposition." (Jan, 1893 - ?). - TELEPHONE MAGAZINE

"Devoted to the interests of newspaper-making." - OHIO NEWSPAPER

"Devoted to the interests of the printers and publishers of Canada." - CANADIAN PRINTER

"Devoted to the interests of the professional and amateur photographer." (Feb, 1892 - ?). - CANADIAN PHOTOGRAPHIC JOURNAL, THE

"Devoted to the interests of the scenario writer." (Apr, 1912 - Dec, 1912). - MOTION PICTURE ALBUM

"Devoted to the problems of the advertiser in the belief that anything helpful to him is helpful to all whose line of work relates to advertising." - AMERICAN ADVERTISER

"Devoted to the professional practice of advertising." (Oct 4, 1954 - Apr 4, 1955). - ADVERTISING AGENCY

"Devoted to the scientific and engineering aspects of electrical communication." - AT&T TECHNICAL JOURNAL

"Devoted to the stage and the fine arts." - DRAMATIC MIRROR AND LITERARY COMPANION, THE

"Devoted to the use of motion pictures in adult education." - FILM FORUM REVIEW

"Devoted to the valuation of current motion pictures." - MOTION PICTURE REVIEW DIGEST

"Digest of telecommunications news, A." - TELECOMMUNICATIONS ALERT

"Digest of the Center for Learning and Telecommunications, The." - TELESCAN

"Digital audio newsletter from Lexicon Inc, A." - DIGITAL DOMAIN DIGEST

"Directed to technical management personnel involved with transmission, reception, processing and display of information." - TELECOMMUNICATIONS

"Discussion, comment, drama, humor." (Oct, 1946 - Oct, 1948). - NBC DIGEST

"Division of the Association for Education in Journalism and Mass Communication, A." - VISUAL COMMUNICATION NEWSLETTER, THE

"Doctor Who Bulletin." - DWB

"Dollars & sense of direct marketing, The." - DIRECT RESPONSE SPECIALIST, THE

"Drama, comedy, music." (Oct, 1960+). - THEATRE, THE

"Drama magazine for young people, The." - PLAYS

"Drama review, The." - TDR

"Dramaturgy, performance studies, pedagogy." - THEATRE TOPICS

E

"Easy-to-read guide to movie enjoyment, An." - CINEMA, VIDEO & CABLE MOVIE DIGEST

"Eclectic newsletter for those who write and edit for the print media, The." - IN BLACK AND WHITE

"Educational consumer's newsletter, The." - EPIEGRAM

"Educational products, technologies & programs for schools & universities." - MEDIA & METHODS

"Educational programs and services newsletter, The." - DEBUT

"Effective marketing through telecommunications." (Jan, 1991+). - TELEPROFESSIONAL

"Electricity, communications, service, sound." - ELECTRONICS AND COMMUNICATIONS

"Electronic publishing, prepress, printing, bindery." - IN-PLANT REPRODUCTIONS

"Electronics and Communication." - AEU

"Electronics, high-technology, recreation." - VISIO

"Electronics lifestyle magazine, The." - HOME ENTERTAINMENT

"Electronics publishers since 1908." - RADIO-ELECTRONICS

"Electronics, science & technology monthly, The." - ETI

"Electronics today international." - ETI

"Embellished with numerous engravings of the principal performers." - DRAMATIC MAGAZINE, THE

"Engineering journal of the Canadian electronics industry, The." - ELECTRONICS & COMMUNICATIONS

"Engineering principles and practices." - RF DESIGN

"English program journal of all India." - AKASHVANI

"Entertainment & Marketing." - MARKETING PULSE, THE

"Entertainment magazine, The." - US MAGAZINE

"Entertainment magazine for the whole family, The." - NIGHTTIME TV

"Entertainment merchandising." - VIDEO STORE

"Entertainment, the arts & much more." - 20/20

"Entertainment, views, reviews." - TGIF

"Entertainment weekly, The." - SHOW BUSINESS

"Equipment industry magazine, The." - INTERNATIONAL BROADCASTING

"Essays in film and the humanities." - POST SCRIPT

"Essential reading in the future of television and motion picture." - HDTV NEWSLETTER

"Established May 16, 1907." - KINEMATOGRAPH WEEKLY

"Ethnographic film." - PERSPECTIVES ON FILM

"European journal for international advertising, The." - MEDIA INTERNATIONAL

"European journal of advertising and marketing, The." - FOCUS

"Europe's bilingual cultural magazine." - BALLETT INTERNATIONAL

"Evangelical magazine reviewing the best in Christian books and recordings, An." - CHRISTIAN REVIEW

"Every issue a collector's item." - HOLLYWOOD STUDIO MAGAZINE

"Every Monday--for journalists and all who work with them." - UK PRESS GAZETTE

"Every new film and video reviewed inside." - SIGHT & SOUND

"Every other Thursday since 1934." - DOWN BEAT

"Every page packed with photo ideas!" - PHOTO ANSWERS

"Everyday mechanics, current science." - RADIO AGE

"Everything old is news again." - MEMORIES

"Exchange of ideas and opinions, An." - CHRISTIAN ADVERTISING FORUM

"Exciting world of film collecting, The." - BIG REEL, THE

"Exclusive from the studios of ABC." - EPISODES

"Exclusive interviews, short stories, photos, strips, art, and so much more." - COMIC CELLAR, THE

"Exclusive pinups! Giant centerfold!" - WOW! MAGAZINE

"Exclusive weekly report on the FCC, the Executive Branch, and Congress, An." - FCC WEEK

"Exclusively devoted to straight plays and musicals." - PLAYS AND PLAYERS

"Executive report on information and entertainment media, The." - FUTUREHOME TECHNOLOGY NEWS

"Executive report on land mobile, maritime and aeronautical communications, The." - MOBILE SATELLITE NEWS

"Expansion of School Paperback Journal, An." - MEDIA & METHODS

"Exploration in Education." - MEDIA & METHODS

"Exploring media in education and industry." - MEDIA DIGEST

"Exploring questions of media morality." - JOURNAL OF MASS MEDIA ETHICS

F

"Facts about film in Finland." - FINNISH FILMS

"Family cable magazine, The." - PREVIEW

"Fantastic media magazine, The." - STARBURST

"Fanzine of science fiction, fantasy and horror -- in cinema, books, video, comics, art & television, The." - STRANGE ADVENTURES

"Fast read for the fast track, The." - RADIO BUSINESS REPORT

"Favorite magazine of every movie fan, The." (Jan, 1954 - Nov, 1954). - MOVIE FAN

"Favorite of America's 'first million' moviegoers for thirty-six years." - PHOTOPLAY

"Feature film magazine, The." - MOVIEGOER

"Features of lasting value." - AKASHVANI

"Featuring office at home: the electronic workplace." - CONSUMER ELECTRONICS

"Featuring stories, photos, illustrations of the happy days gone by." - GOOD OLD DAYS

"Field-production, post-production." - MONITOR INTERNATIONAL

"Film and life, The." - CINEMA PROGRESS

"Film and video monthly." - FILMMAKERS FILM & VIDEO MONTHLY

"Film & Video Monthly." - INDEPENDENT, THE

"Film & video news magazine." - MARKEE

"Film and video news, views and ideas for the professional." - IMAGE NEWS

"Film & video production magazine." - IN MOTION FILM & VIDEO PRODUCTION MAGAZINE

"Film & video reviews--from a Christian perspective." - ALPHA AND OMEGA FILM REPORT

"Film and videotape production magazine, The." - ON LOCATION

"Film magazine, The." - TAKE ONE

"Film magazine for Ireland, A." (Dec?, 1977 - ?). - FILM DIRECTIONS

"Film quarterly, The." - SIGHT & SOUND

"Film quarterly of theory, criticism and practice, A." - WIDE ANGLE

"Film society magazine, The." - FILM

"Film, Sound, Television, Audio-Visual." - IMAGE TECHNOLOGY

"Film, television, video." - FLORIDA REEL

"Film, TV/video, modeling, theatre, tech." - SPOTLIGHT CASTING MAGAZINE

"Film, video and television arts." - AMERICAN FILM

"Finance, distribution, marketing." - BUSINESS OF FILM, THE

"First and best." - MOTION PICTURE

"First and best in today's TV magazines!" - TV STAR PARADE

"First and last word in entertainment, The." - SHOW BIZ WEST

"First in radio." - ELECTRONICS WORLD

"First in radio electronics." - ELECTRONICS WORLD

"First in radio-television-audio-electronics." - ELECTRONICS WORLD

"First television journal in the world, The." - ELECTRONIC ENGINEERING

"First with all your favorites." - SCREENLAND PLUS TV-LAND

"First with the news in the world of graphic arts." - PRINTINGNEWS

"Florida film and television." - ENTERTAINMENT REVUE

"Focusing on publications standards and practices." - EDITORIAL EYE, THE

"For advertisers and agencies." - INSIDE MEDIA

"For all engaged in the screening of information, education, and entertainment." - AUDIO VISUAL

"For all movie makers." - BOLEX REPORTER, THE

"For art and profit in the practice of typography." (Aug, 1902). - PRACTICAL PRINTER, THE

"For both 8mm and 16mm movie makers." (Mar/Apr, 1941 - ?). - CINE-KODAK NEWS, THE

"For buyers of printing, prepress, paper & publishing systems for magazines, catalogs, books, agency & corporate communications." - PUBLISHING & PRODUCTION EXECUTIVE

"For comic book connoisseurs." (Nov/Dec, 1986+). - FOUR COLOR

"For consumer marketing management." - ADWEEK'S MARKETING WEEK

"For creators and producers of graphic presentations." - COMPUTER PICTURES

"For Education and Training." - AID

"For engineers and engineering managers -- worldwide." - ELECTRONIC DESIGN

"For fairness, balance and accuracy in news reporting." - AIM REPORT

"For historians and collectors of photographic paraphernalia and images." - GRAPHIC ANTIQUARIAN

"For home viewing on tape & disc." - VIDEO TIMES

"For in-plant printing and communications." - IN-PLANT REPRODUCTIONS

"For industrial, military and government still, cine and AV professionals." - TECHNICAL PHOTOGRAPHY

"For leaders in education and training." - TECHTRENDS

"For mailing and shipping professionals." - MAST

"For managers and planners in modest-sized book publishing houses." - HUENEFELD REPORT, THE

"For nostalgia & video collectors." - HOLLYWOOD STUDIO MAGAZINE

"For people in public telecommunications." - CURRENT

"For people who like movies." - FILMOGRAPH

"For people who think." - EDITORIAL

"For printers and users of printing." (Vol 1 - 3). - GRAPHIC ARTS, THE

"For professionals in preaching." - HOMILETIC

"For public relations and advertising executives." - SOCIAL SCIENCE MONITOR

"For radio, TV and film workers in the United States and Canada." - NABET NEWS

"For readers of romantic fiction." - ROMANTIC TIMES

"For technical and engineering management." - BME'S TELEVISION ENGINEERING

"For the arts of television." - TELESCREEN

"For the benefit of printerdom." (Sep, 1902). - PRACTICAL PRINTER, THE

"For the business of advertising." - ADVERTISING & SELLING

"For the business of production." - VIDEOPRO

"For the commercial photographer." (Oct/Nov, 1947 - Aug, 1953?). - COMMERCIAL CAMERA

"For the creative team." - PHOTO/DESIGN

"For the entertainment lighting industry." - LIGHTING DIMENSIONS

"For the film director." - BRIGHT LIGHTS

"For the Hi-Fi hobbyist." (Jun, 1957 - Nov, 1958). - AUDIOCRAFT FOR THE HI-FI HOBBYIST

"For the new age of broadcasting." - BROADCAST

"For the professional buyer and planner of media." - SRDS REPORT, THE

"For the professional in land mobile radio." - COMMUNICATIONS

"For the radio members of NAB." - RADIOACTIVE

"For the radio retailer." (Apr, 1922 - ?). - RADIO DEALER, THE

"For the Southeast and Southwest." - MARKEE

"For the specialist book world." - AB BOOKMAN'S WEEKLY

"For today's connoisseur of tomorrow's lifestyle." - HOME ENTERTAINMENT

"For tomorrows teaching today." - LEARNING RESOURCES

"For work and play." - ON!

"Formerly Hi Fi/Stereo Review." - STEREO REVIEW

"Forum for information, research and opinion published quarterly by the National Council for Children and Television, A." - TELEVISION & FAMILIES

"Fourth estate, The." - EDITOR AND PUBLISHER

"From concept through distribution." - MAGAZINE DESIGN & PRODUCTION

"From the editors of Stereo Review." - CAR STEREO REVIEW

"From the editors of Stereo Review." - SOUND & IMAGE

"From the publishers of Communications Technology and CableFAX." - INTERNATIONAL CABLE

"From the publishers of Daytime TV." - NIGHTTIME TV

"From the publishers of *What Video*." - WHAT SATELLITE

"Front row concert experience, The." - IN CONCERT PRESENTS

G

"Gazing at the Stars." - DRAMATIC MIRROR, THE

"German magazine of medium and large format photography, The." - PHOTO TECHNIQUE INTERNATIONAL

"Get the news first - direct from Hollywood." - SF MOVIELAND

"Global survey of trends and developments in print & electronic media, A." - WORLD MEDIA REPORT

"Gorgeous guys, sizzling secrets!" - SMASH HITS

"Graphic arts managers magazine, The." - AMERICAN PRINTER

"Great stars--then and now, The." - SCREEN LEGENDS

"Guide to collectable films on video, The." - VIDEO BUYER

"Guide to effective inside sales & support, The." (? - Nov/Dec, 1990). - TELEPROFESSIONAL

"Guide to fantastic filmmaking, The." - CINEMAGIC

"Guide to home movies, The." - V

"Guide to home videos." - V

"Guide to interactive media production, The." - HYPERMEDIA

H

"HDTV 1125/60 Group Publication, An." - HD PRODUCTION

"HDTV Report is a publication of the Eureka EU95 HDTV Directorate." - HDTV REPORT

"Helping you take better pictures." - PRACTICAL PHOTOGRAPHY

"Hi-fi choice guide to in-car entertainment, The." - DRIVING AMBITION

"High end video journal, The." - PERFECT VISION, THE

"Hollywood girls and gags!" - MOVIE HUMOR

"Hollywood nostalgia." - SCREEN GREATS

"Hollywood's #1 casting trade magazine." - SPOTLIGHT CASTING MAGAZINE

"Hollywood's intimate all-picture magazine." - MOVIE WORLD

"Hollywood's magazine for the 8 mm and 16 mm amateur and professional cine photographer." - HOME MOVIES

"Hollywood's magazine for the amateur." - HOME MOVIES

"Hollywood's only all-picture magazine." - TONI HOLT'S MOVIE LIFE

"Hollywood's picture news magazine." - TELEVISION AND SCREEN GUIDE

"Home magazine for the radio family, A." (May, 1926 - ?). - RADIO HOME, THE

"Home satellite television magazine™, The." - STV GUIDE

"Honest, justice and an interest in the other fellow." - CINEMA HALL-MARKS

"Hooray for HollyWorld™." - ENTERTAINMENT REVUE

"Horror from Hollywood." - DEEP RED

"Horror in entertainment." - FANGORIA

"Hot news in ratings and sales, The." - INSIDE RADIO

"How retailers sell items and images on radio." - SOUND MANAGEMENT

"How to advertise a retail stock." - AMERICAN ADVERTISER

"How-to-do-it magazine of home sound reproduction, The." (Nov, 1955 - ?). - AUDIOCRAFT FOR THE HI-FI HOBBYIST

"How-to magazine for home video, The." - VIDEOPLAY MAGAZINE

"How to magazine for Xerox Ventura Publisher professionals, The." - VENTURA PROFESSIONAL!

"How-to newsletter for desktop designers, The." - STEP-BY-STEP ELECTRONIC DESIGN

"How-to newsletter for members of the Successful Magazine Publishers Group, The." - MAGAZINE BUSINESS

"How-to reference magazine for visual communicators, The." - STEP-BY-STEP GRAPHICS

"Hundreds of new and intimate pictures!" - FILMLAND

I

"Ideal magazine, An." - TONI HOLT'S MOVIE LIFE

"Ideas and resources for media and communication." - MEDIA MIX

"Ideas & strategies for classrooms and activities." - SPEECH COMMUNICATION TEACHER, THE

"Ideas & techniques in graphic design." - HOW

"Ideas that work." - COMMUNICATION BRIEFINGS

"If it's here, it plays." - BILLBOARD

"I'll put a girdle 'round the earth in forty minutes.--Shakespeare." (Oct, 1852 - Jul 15, 1853). - AMERICAN TELEGRAPH MAGAZINE

"Illustrated monthly, An." - ST. LOUIS AND CANADIAN PHOTOGRAPHER

"Illustrated monthly for business men, An." - ART IN ADVERTISING

"Illustrated monthly journal, An." - STAGE SOUVENIR, THE

"Illustrated monthly journal, devoted to the elevation and improvement of the photographic art, An." - ST. LOUIS AND CANADIAN PHOTOGRAPHER

"Illustrated monthly magazine, An." (1895 - Apr, 1902). - PHOTOGRAPHIC TIMES, THE

"Illustrated monthly magazine, An." (Jan, 1893 - ?). - TELEPHONE MAGAZINE

"Illustrated monthly magazine devoted to amateur photography in all its phases and developments, An." (Jul, 1889 - ?). - AMERICAN AMATEUR PHOTOGRAPHER AND CAMERA & DARKROOM

"Illustrated monthly magazine devoted to poster advertising and poster art, An." - ADVERTISING OUTDOORS

"Illustrated monthly magazine devoted to the interests of artistic and scientific photography, An." - PHOTOGRAPHIC TIMES, THE

"Illustrated monthly magazine for advertisers, An." - ADVERTISING EXPERIENCE

"Illustrated monthly magazine for advertisers." (Jun 15, 1892 - ?). - PROFITABLE ADVERTISING

"Illustrated monthly magazine of radio communication, An." - WIRELESS AGE, THE

"Illustrated monthly of photography and allied arts, An." - PHOTO-ERA MAGAZINE

"Illustrated monthly of technical photography, An." - PRACTICAL PHOTOGRAPHER, THE

"Illustrated photographic journal, An." - PHOTO-BEACON, THE

"Illustrated weekly magazine; drama, music, art, An." - THEATRE, THE

"Illustrated weekly mnagazine with program insert for the information and enjoyment of the patrons of the Roxy Theatre, New York, An." - ROXY THEATRE WEEKLY REVIEW

"Illustrated." (May 5, 1906 - ?). - STAGE AND SPORT

"Image magazine, The." - ZOOM

"Important magazine, The." - WORLD OF FANDOM, THE

"In combination with the Little Theatre Monthly." (Oct, 1930 - Jun, 1931). - DRAMA MAGAZINE, THE

"In DM and fulfillment." - WHAT'S WORKING

"In mass market and trade paper." - HOT PICKS

"In the development of a new industry--TV." - TELEVISION OPPORTUNITIES

"In the interests of Amateur Radio Defense Association." - AMATEUR RADIO DEFENSE

"Including DBS radio, HDTV, SMATV, and TVRO." - DBS NEWS

"Including Engineering Division monographs." - BBC ENGINEERING

"Including Interactive Videodisks." - OPTICAL MEMORY NEWS

"Including photoplay and radio studies." (1936 - 1942). - AUDIO-VISUAL GUIDE

"Including Profile." - FILM FAN MONTHLY

"Incorporating Audio News, Stereo News, Tape News, Tape Recorders." - HI-FI NEWS AND RECORD REVIEW

"Incorporating Cinema Quarterly." (Apr, 1936 - ?). - DOCUMENTARY FILM NEWS

"Incorporating DBS News." - SATELLITE NEWS

"Incorporating Film User (established 1946) and Industrial Screen." - AUDIO VISUAL

"Incorporating Focus on Film." - FILMS AND FILMING

"Incorporating High Fidelity." - STEREO REVIEW

"Incorporating International Marketing Report." - INTERNATIONAL ADVERTISER

"Incorporating Marketing & Media Decisions." - MEDIAWEEK

"Incorporating Monster World." - FAMOUS MONSTERS OF FILMLAND

"Incorporating Record News, Audio News, and Tape Recorders." - HI-FI NEWS AND RECORD REVIEW

"Incorporating Screen Life, Hollywood and Movie Story Magazines." - MOTION PICTURE

"Incorporating Television Weekly." - BROADCAST

"Incorporating the Indian Radio Times." - AKASHVANI

"Incorporating The Industrial Screen and BIFA Bulletin." - AUDIO VISUAL

"Incorporating the official journal of the U.K. SCTE." - INTERNATIONAL CABLE

"Incorporating the Optical Magic Lantern Journal & Photographic Enlarger, The Lantern World, and Kinematograph Chronicle." - KINEMATOGRAPH WEEKLY

"Incorporating the Radio Amateur." - RADIO & ELECTRONICS CONSTRUCTOR

"Incorporating USA*1." - SHOW

"Independent film trade journal, The." - EXHIBITORS HERALD WORLD

"Independent film trade paper, The." - BIOSCOPE, THE

"Independent magazine devoted to the new influence in national education, The." (Feb, 1922 - ?). - EDUCATIONAL SCREEN

"Independent quarterly devoted to the serious film, An." (Autumn, 1935 - Spring, 1937). - FILM ART

"Independent reviews of feature films." (Jun 1, 1916 - May 2, 1918). - FILM TV DAILY

"India's first professional cinema quarterly." - CINEMA VISION INDIA

"Industry magazine for appliances, consumer electronics, and home entertainment, The." - DEALERSCOPE

"Industry monthly, The." - VIDEO SOFTWARE MAGAZINE

"Industry news, views and trends." - YELLOW PAGES UPDATE

"Industry promotion quarterly, An." - GRAPHIC

"Industry's news magazine, The." - BROADCAST

"Industry's newspaper, The." - R & R

"Information and analysis for cable television management." - CABLEVISION

"Information, practice, technique." - SOUND AND VISION BROADCASTING

"Inside channel to daytime TV, The." - REAL LIFE/DAYTIMERS

"Interdisciplinary journal, An." (Vol 1, #1 - ?). - LANGUAGE & COMMUNICATION

"International advertising & marketing magazine, The." - MEDIA INTERNATIONAL

"International association of independent publishers, The." - COSMEP NEWSLETTER

"International Broadcast Engineer." - IBE

"International broadcast engineer's publication, An." - COLOUR

"International business magazine for television." - TV WORLD

"International business magazine for television and video." - TV WORLD

"International cartoon magazine." - WITTYWORLD

"International electronics review, The." (Jan, 1974+). - AUDIOVIDEO INTERNATIONAL

"International entertainment weekly, The." - VARIETY

"International film quarterly." - SIGHT & SOUND

"International image magazine, The." - ZOOM

"International in scope and interest." - AIR LAW REVIEW

"International journal, An." - MANAGEMENT COMMUNICATION QUARTERLY

"International journal, An." - POLITICAL COMMUNICATION AND PERSUASION

"International journal, An." - TELEMATICS AND INFORMATICS

"International journal for graphic and applied art." - GRAPHIS

"International journal for mass communication studies, The." - GAZETTE

"International journal for the study of discourse and communication in their social, political and cultural contexts, An." - DISCOURSE & SOCIETY

"International journal of audio and visual learning, The." - EDUCATIONAL BROADCASTING

"International journal of broadcast technology, The." - TELEVISION BROADCAST

"International journal of contemporary visual artists." - LEONARDO

"International journal of motion picture photography and production techniques." - AMERICAN CINEMATOGRAPHER

"International journal of motion picture production techniques, The." - AMERICAN CINEMATOGRAPHER

"International journal of the contemporary artist." - LEONARDO

"International journal of typographics, The." - U & LC

"International journal on acoustics." - ACUSTICA

"International journal on telecommunications & information technology, An." - TELEMATICS AND INFORMATICS

"International magazine for 35mm photography." - LEICA FOTOGRAFIE INTERNATIONAL

"International magazine for free expression, The." - INDEX ON CENSORSHIP

"International magazine for photography." - CAMERA

"International magazine for photography and cinematography." - CAMERA

"International magazine for stage and screen, The." - PERFORMER, THE

"International magazine for the satellite communications industry since 1977, The." - SATELLITE COMMUNICATIONS

"International magazine of Japanese photography, The." - CAMERART

"International magazine of satellite news, applications and technology, The." - SATELLITE COMMUNICATIONS

"International magazine of travel and photography, The." - TRAVEL & LEISURE

"International music-record-tape newsweekly, The." - BILLBOARD

"International news magazine of book publishing, The." - PUBLISHER'S WEEKLY

"International newsletter of Publishers Marketing Association, The." - PMA NEWSLETTER

"International newsmagazine for the professional recording & sound industry, The." - PRO SOUND NEWS

"International newsmagazine for the professional sound production industry, The." - PRO SOUND NEWS

"International newspaper of marketing, The." - ADVERTISING AGE

"International newspaper of marketing, The." - FOCUS

"International newspaper of motion pictures & broadcasting, The." - FILM TV DAILY

"International newsweekly for sports & mass entertainment, The." - AMUSEMENT BUSINESS

"International newsweekly of music and home entertainment, The." - BILLBOARD

"International publication, An." - ELECTRONICS LETTERS

"International publication for the professional photographer, The." - PHOTO DISTRICT NEWS

"International quarterly, An." - HISTORY OF PHOTOGRAPHY

"International quarterly of animated film, The." - ANIMAFILM

"International quarterly of the Society for the History of Technology, The." - TECHNOLOGY AND CULTURE

"International review of AV materials and equipment, The." - FILM & VIDEO NEWS

"International review of the electronics world, An." (Jan, 1973 - Oct, 1973). - AUDIOVIDEO INTERNATIONAL

"International Theatre Review." - GAMBIT

"International Typographics magazine." - BASELINE

"International weekly for public relations, public affairs, and communications executives, The." - PUBLIC RELATIONS NEWS

"Interspace, the only weekly in the business." - INTERSPACE

"Intimate in Character; international in scope; independent in thought." - FILM TV DAILY

"Intimate journal for art directors, production managers and their associates, An." - A-D

"Irregular publication in which Arthur and Corinne Cantrill print anything in cinema which interests them, An." - CANTRILLS FILMNOTES

"It's About Time." - JOE FRANKLIN'S NOSTALGIA

"It's not L.A." - HOLLYWOOD MAGAZINE

"It's the difference that makes us different." - ENTERTAINMENT CONNECTION MAGAZINE

"ITV, BBC & satellite." - TV GUIDE

J

"James Bond 007 Fan Club is dedicated to the memory of Ian Fleming and his work, The." - BONDAGE

"Jazz, blues & beyond." - DOWN BEAT

"Journal dedicated to service for the advertiser and space buyer regarding newspapers and markets, A." - ADVERTISERS' WEEKLY

"Journal designed to create and foster a desire for picture making with the camera, A." (Jul 26, 1912 - ?). - AMATEUR PHOTOGRAPHER'S WEEKLY, THE

"Journal devoted to photography in all its phases, A." (1889 - 1892). - PHOTO-BEACON, THE

"Journal devoted to research and commentary on instruction, curriculum, and educational leadership in journalism and mass communication, A." - JOURNALISM EDUCATOR, THE

"Journal devoted to the art preservative, A." (Aug, 1899). - PRACTICAL PRINTER, THE

"Journal devoted to the elevation and improvement of photography, A." - ST. LOUIS AND CANADIAN PHOTOGRAPHER

"Journal devoted to the interests of advertisers, A." - ADVERTISERS GAZETTE

"Journal devoted to the interests of American companies advertising in foreign countries, A." (Dec, 1928 - ?). - EXPORT ADVERTISER

"Journal devoted to the interests of art printing, A." (Sep, 1899). - PRACTICAL PRINTER, THE

"Journal devoted to the interests of art printing, A." (Jan, 1900). - PRACTICAL PRINTER, THE

"Journal devoted to the interests of the publishing ... trades, and associated branches, A." (Jan 18, 1872 - Dec 26, 1872). - PUBLISHER'S WEEKLY

"Journal devoted to the printing art, A." (Jan, 1899 - Jul, 1899). - PRACTICAL PRINTER, THE

"Journal devoted to the promotion of typographical art, A." (Oct, 1900), (Feb, 1901). - PRACTICAL PRINTER, THE

"Journal devoted to the theoretical and experimental aspects of information transmission, processing and utilization, A." - IEEE TRANSACTIONS ON INFORMATION THEORY

"Journal for advertisers." - MARKETING / COMMUNICATIONS

"Journal for all who advertise and all who ought to advertise at home and overseas, A." (? - Apr 4, 1919). - ADWEEK

"Journal for audiophile crafts, The." - AUDIO AMATEUR, THE

"Journal for authors & publishers, A." - SCHOLARLY PUBLISHING

"Journal for commercial industrial, press and micro-photographers and all connected with the profession, A." (Oct, 1925 - ?). - COMMERCIAL PHOTOGRAPHER, THE

"Journal for design & production professionals in the performing arts, The." - THEATRE DESIGN & TECHNOLOGY

"Journal for fine printers, A." (Oct, 1899). - PRACTICAL PRINTER, THE

"Journal for high definition and advanced television technology, The." - HD SYSTEMS WORLD REVIEW

"Journal for lithographers, artists, draughtsmen, phototypers, steel & copperplate engravers, etc, A." (Oct/Nov, 1891 - ?). - BRITISH LITHOGRAPHER

"Journal for mail-order advertisers, A." - NATIONAL ADVERTISING

"Journal for newspeople, A." - GRASSROOTS EDITOR

"Journal for research on the visual media of language expression, The." - VISIBLE LANGUAGE

"Journal for scholastic media, The." - PHOTOLITH, SCM

"Journal for teaching history with old newspapers, A." - MASTHEAD

"Journal for the advancement of science in marketing, A." - JOURNAL OF MARKETING

"Journal for the business man who advertises, A." - ADVERTISING ADVOCATE

"Journal for the film industry and the cinema trade, The." - CINEMA AND THEATRE

"Journal for the mailing & shipping professional." - MAST

"Journal for the printing trades, A." - BRITISH PRINTER

"Journal for the specialty video retailer and video department, The." - VIDEO STORE

"Journal for those interested in the art and science of broadcasting, A." - BBC QUARTERLY, THE

"Journal in defense of American democracy, A." - HOLLYWOOD NOW

"Journal in the interest of newspaper publishers and advertising managers, A." - AMERICAN ADVERTISER REPORTER

"Journal of advertising and business methods, A." - AD SENSE

"Journal of advertising and marketing, The." - ADWEEK

"Journal of advertising, devoted to the interests of the advertiser, the agency and the purveyor of publicity, A." - SIGNS OF THE TIMES

"Journal of animated film, The." - ANIMAFILM

"Journal of animation art, The." - STORYBOARD / THE ART OF LAUGHTER

"Journal of cinematic illusions, The." (Mar, 1980+). - CINEFEX

"Journal of classical music, The." - MUSICAL AMERICA

"Journal of close-circuit communications, The." - VIDEO SYSTEMS

"Journal of commercial art and design, The." - COMMUNICATION ARTS

"Journal of communications." - RTD

"Journal of communications and entertainment law, A." - HASTINGS COMMUNICATIONS AND ENTERTAINMENT LAW JOURNAL

"Journal of direct mail advertising, A." - MAILBAG, THE

"Journal of electrical progress, A." - TELEGRAPHER, THE

"Journal of electronic engineering." - JEE, JOURNAL OF ELECTRONIC ENGINEERING

"Journal of feminism and film theory, A." - CAMERA OBSCURA

"Journal of film comment, A." (Spring, 1962 - Summer, 1962). - FILM COMMENT

"Journal of Florida publications, broadcasting, advertising, public relations." - COMMUNIQUE

"Journal of information for advertisers and mail order dealers, A." - ADVERTISING ADVOCATE

"Journal of language and editing, The." - RIGHTING WORDS

"Journal of large format photography, The." - VIEWCAMERA

"Journal of lighting for entertainment & architecture, The." - LIGHTS!

"Journal of management and law of the arts, The." - JOURNAL OF ARTS MANAGEMENT AND LAW, THE

"Journal of Mass Media Ethics is devoted to explorations of ethics problems and issues in the various fields of mass communication, The." - JOURNAL OF MASS MEDIA ETHICS

"Journal of media, information and communications law, The." - COMMUNICATIONS LAWYER

"Journal of motion picture arts and crafts, A." - INTERNATIONAL PHOTOGRAPHER

"Journal of newspaper publishing, The." - ADVERTISING

"Journal of newspaper publishing and advertising, The." - ADVERTISING

"Journal of non-fiction film and video, The." - INTERNATIONAL DOCUMENTARY

"Journal of opinion in the field of public relations practice, A." - PUBLIC RELATIONS JOURNAL, THE

"Journal of performance studies, A." - TDR

"Journal of photographic art, technique, and photojournalism, A." - BULGARSKO FOTO

"Journal of photographs of men, women, and events of the day, A." - ALBUM, THE

"Journal of photography and motion pictures." - IMAGE

"Journal of photography and motion pictures of the George Eastman House." - IMAGE

"Journal of photography in New England, The." - VIEWS

"Journal of photography of the George Eastman House." - IMAGE

"Journal of production management, The." - VIDEO SYSTEMS

"Journal of production sound equipment and techniques, The." - PRODUCTION SOUND REPORT

"Journal of publicity and merchandising plans, A." - AGRICULTURAL ADVERTISING

"Journal of radio communication, The." - COMMUNICATION ENGINEERING

"Journal of radio marketing, The." - RADIOTRENDS

"Journal of radio research and progress, A." - INDUSTRIAL ELECTRONICS

"Journal of record, technical section, CPPA, A." - PULP & PAPER CANADA

"Journal of research and comment, A." - PUBLIC RELATIONS REVIEW

"Journal of telecommunications reform, The." - ACCESS

"Journal of television, The." - TELEVISER

"Journal of the American Newspaper Publishers Association, The." - PRESSTIME

"Journal of the American Printing History Association, The." - PRINTING HISTORY

"Journal of the Association for Multi-Image, The." - MULTI IMAGES JOURNAL

"Journal of the Association for Multi-Image International, The." - MULTI IMAGES JOURNAL

"Journal of the Association of Learned and Professional Society Publishers." - LEARNED PUBLISHING

"Journal of the AT&T companies, A." - AT&T TECHNICAL JOURNAL

"Journal of the Audio Engineering Society." - AES

"Journal of the BKSTS." - IMAGE TECHNOLOGY

"Journal of the British Broadcasting Corporation, The." (Dec 31, 1926+). - RADIO TIMES

"Journal of the British Council, A." - MEDIA IN EDUCATION AND DEVELOPMENT

"Journal of the British Universities Film Council, The." - UNIVERSITY VISION

"Journal of the broadcast communications industry, The." - BROADCAST ENGINEERING

"Journal of the Canadian Speech and Hearing Association, A." - HUMAN COMMUNICATION

"Journal of the cinema and religion, A." - MOVIES AND MINISTRY

"Journal of the communication arts, The." - COMMUNICATION ARTS

"Journal of the Communication Association of the Pacific, The." - WORLD COMMUNICATION

"Journal of the Eastern Communication Association." - COMMUNICATION QUARTERLY

"Journal of the Educational Television Association, A." - JOURNAL OF EDUCATIONAL TELEVISION

"Journal of the electronics industry, The." - BRITISH COMMUNICATIONS AND ELECTRONICS

"Journal of the Emerson College Film Society, The." - GRAND ILLUSIONS

"Journal of the film and television arts." (Oct, 1975 - Dec/Jan, 1979). - AMERICAN FILM

"Journal of the graphic arts." - AUSTRALASIAN PRINTER

"Journal of the history and technique of the British Theatre, A." - THEATRE NOTEBOOK

"Journal of the Institution of Electronic and Radio Engineers, The." - ELECTRONICS & COMMUNICATIONS ENGINEERING JOURNAL

"Journal of the International Federation for Theatre Research." - THEATRE RESEARCH

"Journal of the International Organization of Journalists, The." - DEMOCRATIC JOURNALIST

"Journal of the International Scientific Film Association." - SCIENTIFIC FILM

"Journal of the International Society for the Arts, Sciences and Technology, The." - LEONARDO

"Journal of the International Television Association, The." - CORPORATE TELEVISION

"Journal of the National Academy of Television Arts and Sciences, The." - TELEVISION QUARTERLY

"Journal of the National Broadcast Editorial Association." - EDITORIALIST, THE

"Journal of the Radio Society of Great Britain." - RADIO COMMUNICATION

"Journal of the Small Magazine Publishers Group, The." - SUCCESSFUL MAGAZINE PUBLISHING

"Journal of the Society for Education in Film and Television." (Sep, 1959 - Mar/Apr, 1965). - SCREEN

"Journal of the Society for Film History Research." - CINEMA STUDIES

"Journal of the Society for Photographic Education." - EXPOSURE

"Journal of the Society of Cable Television Engineers." - CABLE TELEVISION ENGINEERING

"Journal of the Society of Film Teachers." - SCREEN

"Journal of the society of newspaper design, The." - DESIGN

"Journal of the theatre and film arts published by the New Theatre League, A." (Apr/Jun, 1938). - THEATRE WORKSHOP

"Journal of the Theatre Historical Society, The." - MARQUEE

"Journal of the United States Institute for Theatre Technology." - THEATRE DESIGN & TECHNOLOGY

"Journal of the University and College Theatre Association, The." - THEATRE JOURNAL

"Journal of the Washington Newspaper Publishers Association, The." - WASHINGTON NEWSPAPER, THE

"Journal of the World Association for Christian Education." - MEDIA DEVELOPMENT

"Journal of the World Association for Christian Communication." - MEDIA DEVELOPMENT

"Journal of the World Communication Association, A." - WORLD COMMUNICATION

"Journal of theory and analysis, A." - PCS, THE POPULAR CULTURE SCHOLAR

"Journal of theory on image and sound, A." - IRIS

"Journal of theory, research and development, A." - EDUCATIONAL COMMUNICATION AND TECHNOLOGY

"Journal of video production, advertising & operation, The." - TELEVISER

"Journal of wartime radio-electronic development, engineering & manufacturing, The." (Apr, 1942). - COMMUNICATION ENGINEERING

"Journal of world communication, The." (Oct, 1934 - Mar, 1937). - COMMUNICATION AND BROADCAST ENGINEERING

"Journal of world radio, The." (Apr, 1936 - Jun, 1938). - ALL-WAVE RADIO

"Journal specially devoted to the interests of advertisers, A." (Feb, 1899 - Aug, 1899). - ADVISOR

"Journal that teaches Photography, The." (? - Oct 17, 1919). - AMATEUR PHOTOGRAPHER'S WEEKLY, THE

"Journal to correct the record, A." - LIES OF OUR TIMES

"Journal with vision, The." - PROCEEDINGS OF THE IEEE

"Journalism education today." - C: JET

"Journalism report and review for northern California, The." - FEED-BACK

"Journalism review, A." - MORE

"Journalism's independent newspaper." - UK PRESS GAZETTE

"Journalism's newspaper." - UK PRESS GAZETTE

K

"Keeping the broadcast professional informed." - BROADCAST + TECHNOLOGY

L

"Language quarterly, The." - VERBATIM

"Largest circulation of any paper in America." - NATIONAL ENQUIRER

"Largest circulation optical media review for information professionals, The." - CD-ROM LIBRARIAN

"Largest net sale of any journal soley devoted to the miniature camera." - 35MM PHOTOGRAPHY

"Latest popular radio hit songs." - RADIO HIT SONGS

"Latest releases from Broadway, Off Broadway, the West End, and the regionals." - BAKER'S NEWS

"Le journal du cinema d'animation, organe officiel de l'ASIFA." - ANIMAFILM

"Leading magazine for the television industry, The." - TELEVISION BROADCAST

"Leading publication for buyers of publishing, design, and prepress products and services, The." - PRE-

"Leading review magazine for the video enthusiast, The." - VIDEO CHOICE

"Leading technical journal of the printing industry." - BRITISH PRINTER

"Leading technical magazine in the electronics world." - ELECTRONICS WORLD

"Leading the way in secondary school journalism." - C: JET

"Leading the way in secondary school journalism and media education." - C: JET

"Learning media magazine, The." - AV GUIDE

"Learning media newsletter, The." - AV GUIDE

"Legal implications of a technological age, The." - JOURNAL OF LAW & TECHNOLOGY, THE

"Let there be light." - NATIONAL ADVERTISING

"Life blood of radio, The." - PULSE OF RADIO

"Lifestyle supplement to Penton Publications: travel, lodging, resorts, recreation, leisure, A." - EXECUTIVES ON THE GO

"Lighter side of life. Fewer calories than a newspaper. More laughs per pound, The." - COMIC RELIEF

"Literary commentary, A." - WRITERS ON WRITING

"Literature of the spoken word." (Jan, 1948 - ?). - NBC DIGEST

M

"Maclean-Hunter national monthly of the Canadian graphic arts industries." - CANADIAN PRINTER

"Mag the megastars talk to, The." - FILM REVIEW

"Magazine about buying and selling Christian Radio, A." - TRI-S SPOT/LIGHT

"Magazine & book review of independent publishing, The." - SMALL PRESS

"Magazine dedicated to the cultural aspect of television, The." - TELESCREEN

"Magazine devoted exclusively to the wireless amateur, A." - QST

"Magazine devoted to photoplay appreciation, A." - PHOTOPLAY STUDIES

"Magazine devoted to the exposition of advertising, A." (Sep, 1902 - Dec, 1902). - ADVERTISING EXPERIENCE

"Magazine devoted to the interests of advertisers and newspaper publishers, A." - ADVERTISERS GUIDE

"Magazine devoted to the interests of advertisers, A." (Sep, 1899 - Dec, 1902). - ADVISOR

"Magazine devoted to the interests of the outdoor advertiser, A." (Sep, 1930 - Dec, 1931). - ADVERTISING OUTDOORS

"Magazine devoted to the promotion of art in printing, A." (Mar, 1901). - PRACTICAL PRINTER, THE

"Magazine devoted to the promotion of profitable printing, A." (May, 1901 - Jun, 1901). - PRACTICAL PRINTER, THE

"Magazine for 8mm & 16mm filmers, The." - MOVIE MAKERS

"Magazine for all who read and write, A." (? - Jan, 1907). - JOURNALIST, THE

"Magazine for all women who write, A." - MATRIX

"Magazine for and about film and videotape people, The." - MILLIMETER

"Magazine for animation, audio, film & video professionals, The." - POST

"Magazine for business builders, A." - AD SENSE

"Magazine for business men who advertise, A." - ADVERTISING ADVOCATE

"Magazine for cable system operations, The." - MSO'S CABLE MARKETING

"Magazine for Christian Music Ministries, The." - MUSIC LINE

"Magazine for collectors of photographica, The." - GRAPHIC ANTIQUARIAN

"Magazine for communication executives, The." - ASIAN ADVERTISING & MARKETING

"Magazine for communicators, The." - BROADCASTER

"Magazine for creative information, The." - FLASH

"Magazine for creative photographers, The." - CAMERA & DARKROOM PHOTOGRAPHY

"Magazine for creative photographers, The." (? - Oct, 1984). - DARKROOM PHOTOGRAPHY

"Magazine for creators and producers of television commercials, The." - SHOOTING COMMERCIALS

"Magazine for desktop publishers, The." - PERSONAL PUBLISHING

"Magazine for desktop publishers, The." - PUBLISH!

"Magazine for discriminating movie-goers, The." - CINEMA

"Magazine for Eastman employees, A." - KODAK

"Magazine for experienced technical professionals, The." - HIGH TECH LIFESTYLES

"Magazine for film and video production, The." - LOCATION UPDATE

"Magazine for film & videomaker, The." - MOVING IMAGE

"Magazine for Ganett Group people, A." - GANNETTEER

"Magazine for growing magazines, The." - SUCCESSFUL MAGAZINE PUBLISHING

"Magazine for habitual filmmakers, The." - FILMMAKERS FILM & VIDEO MONTHLY

"Magazine for independent/in-home/desktop publishing, The." - SMALL PRESS

"Magazine for international advertising, The." - INTERNATIONAL ADVERTISER

"Magazine for international marketing executives, The." - INTERNATIONAL ADVERTISER, THE

"Magazine for journalists, A." - QUILL, THE

"Magazine for kids, The." - DISNEY ADVENTURES

"Magazine for magazine management, The." - FOLIO:

"Magazine for medium and large format photography, The." - PHOTO TECHNIQUE INTERNATIONAL

"Magazine for motion picture exhibitors, A." - UNIVERSAL WEEKLY

"Magazine for movie makers, film & Video Collectors, The." - FILM MAKING

"Magazine for multi-national advertising, The." - INTERNATIONAL ADVERTISER

"Magazine for music listeners, The." - HIGH FIDELITY

"Magazine for new ideas in electronics, The." - RADIO-ELECTRONICS

"Magazine for newspaper production, The." - AMERICAN PRESS

"Magazine for people who listen, The." - STEREO REVIEW

"Magazine for performers and producers, The." (? - Dec, 1988). - STAGE & STUDIO

"Magazine for photo lab management personnel, The." - PHOTO LAB MANAGEMENT

"Magazine for photoplay writers, A." (? - May, 1921). - PHOTODRAMATIST, THE

"Magazine for post production professionals, The." - POST

"Magazine for printers and users of printing, A." - GRAPHIC ARTS, THE

"Magazine for professional and amateur, The." - ACTOR ILLUSTRATED, THE

"Magazine for professional photographers, The." - RANGEFINDER, THE

"Magazine for professional writers, A." - AMERICAN JOURNALIST, THE

"Magazine for professionals in theatre, film, video, and the performing arts, The." - THEATRE CRAFTS

"Magazine for secret agent connoisseurs, The." - TOP SECRET

"Magazine for serious video users, The." - VIDEO PROPHILES

"Magazine for smart young moviegoers, The." - MOVIE STARS

"Magazine for sponsors of business, educational, television films, The." (? - ?). - FILM MEDIA

"Magazine for sponsors of industrial, business, television films, The." (Jun, 1957 - ?). - FILM MEDIA

"Magazine for the 35mm specialist, The." - LEICA PHOTOGRAPHY

"Magazine for the amateur producer, actor, and technician, A." (May, 1938 - ?). - PLAY SHOP, THE

"Magazine for the amateur producer and actor, A." (? - Mar, 1938). - PLAY SHOP, THE

"Magazine for the cultivation of self-expression through creative writing, A." (? - Aug, 1923). - STORY WORLD AND PHOTODRAMATIST, THE

"Magazine for the earth-station receive industry, The." - STAR SIGNALS

"Magazine for the Eastern professional filmmaker, The." - MAKING FILMS

"Magazine for the electronics activist, The." - POPULAR ELECTRONICS

"Magazine for the electronics activist and the consumer electronics enthusiast, The." - POPULAR ELECTRONICS

"Magazine for the emerging professional." - PHOTOGRAPHER'S FORUM

"Magazine for the experimenter who builds his own equipment, A." (Dec, 1922 - Jan, 1924). - TELEVISION ENGINEERING

"Magazine for the Hi-Fi hobbyist, The." (Jun, 1957 - Nov, 1958). - AUDIOCRAFT FOR THE HI-FI HOBBYIST

"Magazine for the lighting professional, The." - LIGHTING DIMENSIONS

"Magazine for the millions." - TV SCREEN

"Magazine for the printing industry and communication technology." - POLYGRAPH INTERNATIONAL

"Magazine for the professional filmmaker, The." - MAKING FILMS

"Magazine for the radio industry, A." - BEYOND THE RATINGS/RADIO

"Magazine for the recording musician, The." - HOME & STUDIO RECORDING

"Magazine for the serious photographer, The." - WESTERN PHOTOGRAPHER MAGAZINE

"Magazine for the television generation, The." - TV GOLD

"Magazine for the television industry, A." - BEYOND THE RATINGS/TELEVISION

"Magazine for Ventura Users of North America, The." - VENTURA LETTER, THE

"Magazine for video professionals, The." - VIDEO SYSTEMS

"Magazine for women in communications, A." - MATRIX

"Magazine for women in journalism & communications, A." - MATRIX

"Magazine for working professionals, The." - PHOTOPRO

"Magazine for writers, The." - PHOTODRAMATIST, THE

"Magazine for young moderns, The." - SCREEN STARS

"Magazine from Eastman Employees, The." - KODAK

"Magazine in English, German and French for applied medium and large format photography, A." - PHOTO TECHNIQUE INTERNATIONAL

"Magazine of adventure, The." - DAREDEVILS

"Magazine of after-dark entertainment, The." - STAGE

"Magazine of agency operations and management, The." (Apr 29, 1955 - Dec 20, 1957). - ADVERTISING AGENCY

"Magazine of American film, The." - BRIGHT LIGHTS

"Magazine of American theeatre, The." - PLAYERS

"Magazine of appliance and TV Retailing." - TV & APPLIANCE MART

"Magazine of British telefantasy, The." - TIME SCREEN

"Magazine of broadcast management/engineering, The." - BME'S TELEVISION ENGINEERING

"Magazine of business telecommunications, The." - TELEMARKETING

"Magazine of, by and for commercial radio operators and technicians, A." - CQ

"Magazine of cinema & television fantasy, The." - STARBURST

"Magazine of cinematography and video techniques written by professionals for professionals, The." - INTERNATIONAL PHOTOGRAPHER

"Magazine of closed-circuit and community antenna TV, The." - E-ITV

"Magazine of compact-disc data storage, The." - CD-ROM

"Magazine of competitive radio-television broadcasting, The." - BROADCAST PROGRAMMING AND PRODUCTION

"Magazine of consumer markets, The." - AMERICAN DEMOGRAPHICS

"Magazine of consumer trends and lifestyles, The." - AMERICAN DEMOGRAPHICS

"Magazine of direct mail, The." - DIRECT MARKETING

"Magazine of drama, comedy and music, A." (Jan, 1959 - Sep, 1960). - THEATRE, THE

"Magazine of efficiency in advertising and selling, The." (Apr, 1927 - Aug, 1927). - MAILBAG, THE

"Magazine of entertainment, The." - SHOW

"Magazine of entertainment and the arts, The." - SHOW

"Magazine of fantasy & science fiction in the cinema, The." - FANTASTIC FILMS

"Magazine of film and video, The." - CINEGRAM

"Magazine of film and video production, The." - LOCATION UPDATE

"Magazine of films and the arts, The." - SHOW

"Magazine of Hollywood's past, The." - SCREEN FACTS

"Magazine of imaginative media, The." - FANTASTIC FILMS

"Magazine of independent book publishing, The." - SMALL PRESS

"Magazine of journalism heritage, A." - MEDIA HISTORY DIGEST

"Magazine of marketing communications, A." - ADVERTISING AND MARKETING MANAGEMENT

"Magazine of marketing/communications management, The." - MARKETING / COMMUNICATIONS

"Magazine of medium and large-format photography in colour and monochrome, The." - PHOTO TECHNIQUE INTERNATIONAL

"Magazine of miniature photography." (spring, 1957 - ?). - CAMERA 35

"Magazine of motion picture arts and sciences (devoted to the professional photographer, The." - INTERNATIONAL PHOTOGRAPHER

"Magazine of motion picutre photography, The." - AMERICAN CINEMATOGRAPHER

"Magazine of moving pictures, A." - REEL LIFE

"Magazine of mystery and horror, The." - SCARLET STREET

"Magazine of New York advertising, The." - MADISON AVENUE

"Magazine of news & criticism, The." - COMICS JOURNAL, THE

"Magazine of noteworthy examples of photography as applied to the major problems of industrial management and market development, A." - APPLIED PHOTOGRAPHY

"Magazine of personal communications, The." - CB LIFE

"Magazine of photographic applications in science, technology & medicine, The." - FUNCTIONAL PHOTOGRAPHY

"Magazine of popular culture, The." - MEDIA SIGHT

"Magazine of popular culture, The." - UNIQUE

"Magazine of popular culture and the arts, The." - FANFARE

"Magazine of popular photography, The." (Jan, 1952 - May, 1952). - POPULAR PHOTOGRAPHY

"Magazine of popular science for the lecture-room, and the domestic circle, A." (Oct, 1896 - ?) - KINEMATOGRAPH WEEKLY

"Magazine of professional video production, technology, and applications, The." - VIDEOGRAPHY

"Magazine of public service advertising, The." - PSA

"Magazine of publicity, The." (? - May, 1909). - PROFITABLE ADVERTISING

"Magazine of RCA, The." - COMMUNICATE

"Magazine of record statistics and information, The." - RECORD RESEARCH

"Magazine of satellite broadcasting, The." - VIA SATELLITE

"Magazine of science fiction people, The." - CINEMONKEY

"Magazine of sleaze film culture, A." - CELLULOID NIGHTMARE

"Magazine of specialty advertising ideas, The." - IMPRINT

"Magazine of technical accuracy for the radio engineer, dealer and manufacturer, A." (Feb, 1924 - ?). - TELEVISION ENGINEERING

"Magazine of television for business use, The." - TELESPAN'S BUSINESSTV GUIDE

"Magazine of television production & post-production, The." - WRAP

"Magazine of television programming, The." - VIEW

"Magazine of the Academy of Television Arts and Sciences, The." - EMMY

"Magazine of the Amateur Cinema League, Inc." - MOVIE MAKERS

"Magazine of the arts, The." - SHOW

"Magazine of the Association of Fashion Advertising and Editorial Photographers, The." - IMAGE

"Magazine of the Broadcast Promotion & Marketing Executives, The." - BPME IMAGE MAGAZINE

"Magazine of the Canadian Society of Cinematographers, The." - CINEMA/CANADA

"Magazine of the creative and entertainment lighting profession." - LIGHTING DIMENSIONS

"Magazine of the Directors Guild of America, The." - ACTION!

"Magazine of The Federation of Film Societies, The." - FILM

"Magazine of the film and television arts." (Feb, 1979+). - AMERICAN FILM

"Magazine of the film forum, The." - CLOSE-UP

"Magazine of the film industry, The." - AMERICAN PREMIERE

"Magazine of the home entertainment industry, The." (Jun, 1965 - ?). - SIGHT AND SOUND MARKETING

"Magazine of the hour, The." - RADIO AGE

"Magazine of the independent feature project, The." - OFF-HOLLYWOOD REPORT

"Magazine of the motion picture and television production industries, The." - MILLIMETER

"Magazine of the movies, The." - BIJOU

"Magazine of the National Committee for Audio-Visual Aids in Education, The." - VISUAL EDUCATION

"Magazine of the Oxford University Film Society." - SEQUENCE

"Magazine of the performing arts, The." (Oct, 1961 - Mar, 1962). - SHOW

"Magazine of the printing industry, The." - GRAPHIC ARTS MONTHLY

"Magazine of the Radio-Television News Directors Association, The." - COMMUNICATOR

"Magazine of the stars & stories, The." - SOAP OPERA UPDATE

"Magazine of the television commercial industry." - 60 SECONDS

"Magazine of the yellow pages medium, The." - LINK

"Magazine of then and now, The." - MEMORIES

"Magazine of tomorrow's entertainment, The." (Jul/Aug, 1980+). - PREVUE

"Magazine of tomorrow's video and motion picture techniques, The." - IMAGEMAKER

"Magazine of total multimedia, The." - VIZIONS

"Magazine of unusual film & television, The." - FILMFAX

"Magazine of video fact, The." (fall, 1944 - ?). - TELEVISION

"Magazine of video facts, The." (1944 - May, 1955). - TELEVISION

"Magazine of videocassettes, The." - V

"Magazine of videotape entertainment, The." - ORBIT VIDEO

"Magazine of visual communication, The." - ART DIRECTION

"Magazine of visual communication, serves the field of advertising art, photography, typography and related graphic arts field, The." - ART DIRECTION

"Magazine of visual fantasy and science fiction, The." - FANTASTIC FILMS

"Magazine of world press, The." - WORLD PRESS REVIEW

"Magazine on the science of advertisin, The." (Aug, 1909). - ADVERTISING RESULTS MAGAZINE

"Magazine serving the commercial broadcast production industry, The." - ENTERTAINMENT MONTHLY

"Magazine that loves movies, The." - FILM MONTHLY

"Magazine that loves movies, The." - FILMS ILLUSTRATED

"Magazine that remembers the best, The." - GOOD OLD DAYS

"Magazine the stars read, The." - PHOTO SCREEN

"Magazine to correct the record, A." - LIES OF OUR TIMES

"Magazine with a 'sense of wonder., The." - CINEFANTASTIQUE

"Magazine you can believe in, The." - BEHIND THE SCENE

"Mail marketer's newsletter of effective response/profit techniques, The." - DIRECT RESPONSE SPECIALIST, THE

"Main motion in rock & video, The." - FRESH!

"Make money with your camera magazine, The." - INTERNATIONAL PHOTOGRAPHER MAGAZINE

"Management insights for the decision maker." (? - Aug, 1989). - VIDEO MANAGEMENT

"Marketing / Advertising / Communication." - ADWEEK

"Marketing magazine, The." - SALES & MARKETING MANAGEMENT

"Marketing/management magazine for cable television executives, The." - CABLE MARKETING

"Markets, merchandising, and media." - ADVERTISING AGENCY

"Martin Codel's authoritative news service of the visual broadcasting and frequency modulation arts and industry." - TELEVISION DIGEST WITH CONSUMER ELECTRONICS

"Mary Bold's favorite publishing tips." - REALLY, A FREE NEWSLETTER

"Media, Agencies, Clients." (Feb 2, 1959 - ?). - ADWEEK

"Media, Agencies, Clients." (Jan 7, 1965 - ?). - ADWEEK

"Media guide to fantasy and science fiction, The." - FANTASY ZONE

"Media Research Center's bi-monthly review of the entertainment industry and the Hollywood Left, The." - TV, ETC.

"Medium of suggestion and a record of progress, A." - AT&T MAGAZINE

"Member service of the International Industrial Television Association, A." - INDUSTRIAL TELEVISION NEWS

"Men's guide to fashion." - MGF

"Men's guide to fashion & entertainment." - MGF

"Merchandising, Appliances, Radio, Records, Television." - TV & APPLIANCE MART

"Miniature camera monthly, The." - MODERN PHOTOGRAPHY

"Missionary bulletin of the International Catholic Film Office." - FILMIS

"Modern guide to screen entertainment, The." - EMPIRE

"Monthly bulletin of ASIFA Washington/International Animated Film Association, The." - PENCIL TEST

"Monthly bulletin of the International Press Institute." - IPI REPORT

"Monthly devoted to the activity of the periodical press throughout the world, A." - INTERNATIONAL PRESS REVIEW

"Monthly directory and sales guide for retailers." (Oct, 1960+). - MAGAZINE & BOOKSELLER

"Monthly feature magazine for newspaper management, The." - AMERICAN PRESS

"Monthly for those who use and create art in advertising." - ADVERTISER MAGAZINE, THE

"Monthly forum devoted to business communications in selected markets, A." - DIRECT MARKETING

"Monthly idea source for decision makers, A." - COMMUNICATION BRIEFINGS

"Monthly in the interest of good advertising." - ADVERTISER MAGAZINE, THE

"Monthly journal dedicated to the advancement of the motion picture industry in all its branches, A." - INTERNATIONAL PHOTOGRAPHER

"Monthly journal devoted exclusively to advertisers, A." (Jun, 1891 - ?). - PROFITABLE ADVERTISING

"Monthly journal devoted to an era of better publicity, A." - COMMON SENSE

"Monthly journal devoted to outdoor advertising, A." - ADVERTISING OUTDOORS

"Monthly journal devoted to the interests of printers, publishers, lithographers, paper dealers, bookbinders, electrotypers, engravers & kindred trades, A." (Apr, 1889 - ?). - AMERICAN PRESS

"Monthly journal devoted to the promotion of high art in every-day printing, A." (Oct, 1901). - PRACTICAL PRINTER, THE

"Monthly journal for interactive communications, The." - 4TH MEDIA JOURNAL, THE

"Monthly journal of information and opinion for radio professionals, students, archivists and others interested in the modern radio broadcasting industry, A." - RADIO*PHILES

"Monthly journal of information on writing photoplays, short stories, verse, news stories, publicity, advertising, etc, A." (Dec, 1920 - Feb, 1921). - WRITER'S DIGEST

"Monthly journal of the BFFS." - FILM

"Monthly journal on writing photoplays, short stories, poems, popular songs, etc, A." (Mar, 1921 - Aug, 1921). - WRITER'S DIGEST

"Monthly magazine devoted to photography and kindred sciences, A." - ST. LOUIS AND CANADIAN PHOTOGRAPHER

"Monthly magazine devoted to the theater, A." - STAGE PICTORIAL

"Monthly magazine for aspiring comics professionals, The." - COMICS CAREER NEWSLETTER

"Monthly magazine for dealers in stationery, post cards, fancy goods, novelties and five and ten cent goods, A." - NATIONAL STATIONER, THE

"Monthly magazine for direct marketing professionals, The." (Jan, 1990+). - DIRECT MARKETING

"Monthly magazine for literary workers, A." - AUTHOR, THE

"Monthly magazine for national advertisers, A." - ADVERTISING DISPLAYS

"Monthly magazine for professional video equipment users, A." - VIDEO NEWS AND USED

"Monthly magazine of information for members of Bell Telephone Laboratories, Incorporated, A." - AT&T TECHNOLOGY

"Monthly magazine of photographic information, A." (Apr, 1899 - Jun, 1932). - NEW PHOTO-MINIATURE

"Monthly magazine of the craftsmanship of advertising, The." - GRAPHIC ARTS, THE

"Monthly magazine of the International Telecommunication Union." - TELECOMMUNICATION JOURNAL

"Monthly magazine of video entertainment, The." - VIDEO TIMES

"Monthly magazine read by everyone in the Canadian printing industry, The." - CANADIAN PRINTER

"Monthly magazine to interest and help all literary workers, A." - AUTHOR, THE

"Monthly magazine--to make the screen a greater power in education and business, A." (Mar, 1918 - May/Jun, 1918). - MOVING PICTURE AGE

"Monthly management tool, The." - RADIO ONLY

"Monthly newsletter, analysis and record of the Direct Marketing Archive, The." - WHO'S MAILING WHAT!

"Monthly newsletter for the media and advertising industries, A." - MEDIA MATTERS

"Monthly newsletter of markets and management for the growing publisher, The." - INDEPENDENT PUBLISHERS TRADE REPORT

"Monthly newsletter of the National Alliance of Media Arts Centers." - MEDIA ARTS

"Monthly programme guide for satellite & cable TV, The." - SATELLITE TIMES

"Monthly projecting important international film manifestations, A." - EXPERIMENTAL CINEMA

"Monthly publication devoted to library film cooperation, A." - BOOKS AND FILMS

"Monthly publication devoted to the interests of visual instruction, A." - MOVING PICTURE AGE

"Monthly publication of the INCA-FIEJ Research Association, The." - NEWSPAPER TECHNIQUES

"Monthly record of current literature, A." (Jul, 1869 - Aug, 1869). - PUBLISHER'S WEEKLY

"Monthly record of the theatre in town and country at home & abroad, A." - DRAMA

"Monthly record of works published in America, England, Germany and France; with a review of the current literature of the day; contents of leading American and English periodicals; advertisements of the trade, etc., etc, A." (Jan, 1852? - Sep 1, 1855). - AMERICAN LITERARY GAZETTE AND PUBLISHERS' CIRCULAR

"Monthly report from the Media Research Center, A." - MEDIAWATCH

"Monthly review, A." - BOOKS & RELIGION

"Monthly review and magazine, A." - THEATRE, THE

"Monthly review of amateur photography, A." (Jul, 1889 - ?). - AMERICAN AMATEUR PHOTOGRAPHER AND CAMERA & DARKROOM

"Monthly review of current plays and motion pictures, A." (Feb 5, 1949 - ?). - BROADWAY SIGN POST

"Monthly review of dramatic literature, A." (Oct, 1919 - May, 1925). - DRAMA MAGAZINE, THE

"Monthly review of new books, A." - BRITISH BOOK NEWS

"Monthly review of the drama, music, and the fine arts, A." (Jan, 1880 - Aug, 1894). - THEATRE, THE

"Monthly review of the stage, A." - ACTOR ILLUSTRATED, THE

"Monthly selection of recent books, A." - BRITISH BOOK NEWS

"Monthly special report for writers, literary agents, publicists, artists, cartoonists, and photographers, A." - WHAT EDITORS WANT

"Monthly summary of critical trends in radio marketing and finance, A." - RADIOTRENDS

"Monthly topical humor review, The." - COMIC RELIEF

"More gossip, photos, features than ever before!" - MODERN SCREEN

"Most accurate charts in the world, The." - INTERNATIONAL RADIO REPORT, THE

"Most beautiful weekly paper in the world, The." (Feb 18, 1903 - ?). - BROADWAY WEEKLY

"Most complete guide to satellite TV, The." - STV GUIDE

"Most widely-read newsletter in the entertainment industry, The." - SCRIPTWRITER NEWS

"Motion picture newspaper, The." (May 17, 1913 - Aug 30, 1913). - EXHIBITORS' TIMES

"Motion picture weekly, The." (Sep 13, 1913 - Sep 27, 1913). - EXHIBITORS' TIMES

"Movie mag that's for reel, The." - FILM REVIEW

"Movie magazine, The." - PREMIERE

"Movies." - MGF

"Movies as a way of life." - MOVIELINE

"Movies, parties, television." - GOSSIP

"Movies, sports, music, travel." - MOVIE MARKETPLACE

"Movies, theatre, music, art, fashions, travel and dining out." - AFTER DARK

"Movies your mother wouldn't take you to see, The." - DEEP RED

"Multimedia ministry to reach the multitudes in Latin America, A." - UPDATE

"Museum of Broadcasting newsletter, The." - MB NEWS

"Music & sound for performers & producers." (Jan, 1989+). - STAGE & STUDIO

"Music-phonograph merchandising, radio-TV programming, coin machine operating." - BILLBOARD

"Music, pictures, drama, vaudeville, stock." - DRAMATIC MIRROR, THE

"Mutual Film Magazine, The." - REEL LIFE

N

"National and international weekly for retailers, bankers, and other advertisers, The." - RETAIL EQUIPMENT AND MERCHANDISE

"National Board of Review Magazine, The." - FILMS IN REVIEW

"National broadcast authority, The." - RADIO FAN-FARE

"National daily newspaper of commercial radio and television, The." - RTD

"National film & collectors' magazine, The." - HOLLYWOOD STUDIO MAGAZINE

"National film weekly, The." - BOX OFFICE

"National film weekly, The." - BOXOFFICE

"National journal of advertising displays, The." - SIGNS OF THE TIMES

"National journal of modern merchandising, The." (? - Feb, 1922). - ADVERTISING & SELLING

"National journal of outdoor advertising and poster art, The." (1910? - Jan, 1930). - ADVERTISING OUTDOORS

"National journal of the advertising industry, The." (Mar, 1922 - ?). - ADVERTISING & SELLING

"National magazine for school yearbooks staffs, The." - PHOTOLITH, SCM

"National magazine of business promotion and sales by mail, The." - NATIONAL ADVERTISING

"National magazine of entertainment, The." - AFTER DARK

"National magazine of sales and business-building ideas, A." (Apr 9, 1925 - Jul 9, 1925). - ADVERTISING

"National magazine of the theatre, The." - PLAYBILL

"National media magazine from Washington, The." - WASHINGTON JOURNALISM REVIEW

"National media monitor: press, radio, TV." - COLUMBIA JOURNALISM REVIEW

"National monthly issue." - ADWEEK

"National newsletter dedicated to helping mailers make better business decisions, The." - POSTAL WATCH

"National Press Photographers Association for Still and Television News." - NEWS PHOTOGRAPHER

"National publication for buyers and sellers of old radios and related items, The." - ANTIQUE RADIO CLASSIFIED

"National publication for career photographers, A." - RANGEFINDER, THE

"National publication for professional photographers, A." - RANGEFINDER, THE

"National society honoring scholarship in journalism." - KTA NEWSLETTER

"National synopsis of editorial opinion on important issues, The." - PULSE

"National television picture magazine, The." (Nov, 1949 - ?). - TELECAST

"National theatre magazine, The." - PLAYBILL

"National weekly of the communications business embracing advertising, marketing, newspapers and magazines, film and television, The." - CAMPAIGN

"Nation's advertisers--they ALL read The Advertiser, The." - ADVERTISER MAGAZINE, THE

"Nationwide marketplace for anything photographic: professional, amateur, antique, The." - SHUTTERBUG

"Network services and equipment." - CLOSEUP

"New Broadway, The." (Feb, 1909 - Sep, 1911). - HAMPTON MAGAZINE

"New developments for the photographic dealer and photofinisher." - PHOTO MARKETING

"New directions in production and presentation technology." - AV VIDEO

"New England's most complete guide to opportunities in the performing arts." - CASTING NEWS

"New products, trends and people in video today." (? - spring, 1988). - VIDEO TIMES

"New texts on theatre performance, design, and production." - BAKER'S NEWS

"New video magazine with free 32 page video catalogue, The." - VIDEO MONTHLY

"New way to entertain, communicate, relax and learn, The." - HOME ENTERTAINMENT

"New weekly magazine for media decision-makers, The." - MEDIAWEEK

"News and features weekly of the cable television industry, The." - CABLEVISION

"News and reviews." - GRAMOPHONE

"News & reviews for the community of the printed word." - WRITER'S NW

"News and Strategies for Community Television Broadcasting." - LPTV REPORT, THE

"News and views from around the world." - WORLD PRESS REVIEW

"News and views from the foreign press." - WORLD PRESS REVIEW

"News/feature magazine." - INTERCOMM

"News for broadcast members of the Associated Press." - AP BROADCASTER

"News from the E. W. Scripps School of Journalism, Ohio University, Athens, Ohio 45701." - OHIO JOURNALIST, THE

"News from the New Zealand Film Commission." - NEW ZEALAND FILM

"News, ideas & trends for America's largest audited circulation of graphic designers and art directors." - GRAPHIC DESIGN: USA

"News magazine for the professional video manager, The." - VIDEO MANAGEMENT

"News magazine of CATV and pay-cable." - VUE

"News magazine of the fifth estate, The." - BROADCASTING

"News magazine of the video industry (Winter, 1990?+), The." - VIDEO TIMES

"News monthly for interactive telecommunications." - TEL-COMS

"News of NPPA's region 9." - RANGEFINDER, THE

"News of technology for international broadcasters." - WORLD BROADCAST NEWS

"News of the show world." - DAILY VARIETY

"News! Reviews! All new fan strips." - COMIC INFORMER

"Newsbulletin for members of the Association of American Publishers, A." - AAP MONTHLY REPORT

"Newsletter, The." - MEDIA MATTERS

"Newsletter about educational materials and technology, The." - EPIEGRAM

"Newsletter containing booktalks, news, and other information of interest to booktalkers, A." - BOOKTALKER, THE

"Newsletter for A/V professionals published by 3M's Magnetic Media Division, A." - MAG TRACKS

"Newsletter for audio/visual professionals published by 3M's Magnetic Media Division, A." - ON TRACK

"Newsletter for members and friends of AFI, A." - CLOSE-UP

"Newsletter for professionals in the communications industry, A." - SQUEEKY WHEEL, THE

"Newsletter for professors, A." - C-SPAN IN THE CLASSROOM

"Newsletter for registered Xerox Ventura Publisher users, A." - SCSC XEROX PIPELINE

"Newsletter for satellite and television professionals, The." - HORIZON

"Newsletter for teachers of photography, A." - PHOTOEDUCATION

"Newsletter for the Law Division of AEJ & the Mass Communications Law Section of AALS." - MEDIA LAW NOTES

"Newsletter for Ventura Users of North America, The." - VENTURA LETTER, THE

"Newsletter for Xerox Desktop Software SCSC Agreement Customers, A." - SCSC XEROX PIPELINE

"Newsletter of American Women in Radio and Television, Inc, The." - AWRT NEWS AND VIEWS

"Newsletter of ASIFA - Hollywood, The." - GRAFFITI

"Newsletter of FAIR (Fairness & Accuracy in Reporting), The." - EXTRA!

"Newsletter of NAVA, the International Communications Industries Association, The." - COMMUNICATIONS INDUSTRIES REPORT, THE

"Newsletter of the AEJMC history division." - CLIO AMONG THE MEDIA

"Newsletter of the Association for Education in Journalism and Mass Communication, The." - AEJMC NEWS

"Newsletter of the Broadcast News Committee, Broadcast Education Association, The." - NEWSCASTER, THE

"Newsletter of the Broadcast Pioneers." - SPARKS

"Newsletter of the Corporation for Public Broadcasting, The." - REPORT

"Newsletter of the History Committee of the Broadcast Education Association." - REWIND

"Newsletter of the International Documentary Association, The." - INTERNATIONAL DOCUMENTARY

"Newsletter of the Magazine Division -- AEJMC." - MAGAZINE MATTER

"Newsletter of the National Citizens Committee for Broadcasting." - MEDIA WATCH

"Newsletter of the National Coalition Against Censorship, A." - CENSORSHIP NEWS

"Newsletter of the Society of Professional Videographers, The." - PRO VIDEOGRAM

"Newsletter of the Theatre Library Association." - BROADSIDE

"Newsletter of the Western Speech Communication Association, A." - WSCA NEWS

"Newsletter of tips, tactics and how-tos for small exhibitors, The." - AISLE VIEW

"Newsletter on journalism ethics, The." - FINELINE

"Newsletter on writing & editing, The." - WRITING CONCEPTS

"Newsletter serving the nation's photo editors and photo illustrators, The." - PHOTOLETTER

"Newsletter that links professional and consumer video, The." - VIDEO INFO

"Newsletter that's guaranteed to improve your publication, The." - EDITOR'S WORKSHOP

"Newsletter to help you improve your publication, The." - EDITOR'S WORKSHOP

"Newsmagazine for users of online services: business, educational, personal, The." - LINK-UP

"Newsmagazine of films, filmstrips, television, recordings, The." - FILM & VIDEO NEWS

"Newsmonthly for organizational television, The." - VIDEO MANAGEMENT

"Newsmonthly of advertising and selling to business, industry and the professions, The." - BUSINESS MARKETING

"Newspaper and magazine production." - WEB

"Newspaper for communicators in business, education, government, industry, medicine, The." - POSITIVE IMAGE, THE

"Newspaper for the communications industr, The." - COMMUNICATIONSWEEK

"Newspaper for the PR profession, The." - PR WEEK

"Newspaper for users and producers of electronic information services, The." - INFORMATION TODAY

"Newspaper for Ventura Users of North America, The." - VENTURA LETTER, THE

"Newspaper industry's oldest newspaper, The." - PUBLISHER'S AUXILIARY

"Newspaper, magazine, mail order, street car, and outdoor advertising." - AGRICULTURAL ADVERTISING

"Newspaper of America's network, The." - C-SPAN UPDATE

"Newspaper of direct marketing, The." - DM NEWS

"Newspaper of the Graphic Communications Union, The." - GRAPHIC COMMUNICATOR

"Newspaper of the International Communications Industries Association, The." - COMMUNICATIONS INDUSTRIES REPORT, THE

"Newspublication for manufacturers, dealers, and duplicators of videotape and audiotape, The." - TAPE/DISC BUSINESS

"Newsreel of the newstands, The." (Sep, 1931). - MOVIE CLASSIC

"Newsweekly of broadcasting and allied arts, The." - BROADCASTING

"Newsweekly of cable television." - VUE

"Nieman Foundation at Harvard University, The." - NIEMAN REPORTS

"Non theatrical 16mm film magazine." (Feb, 1945 - ?). - FILM WORLD AND A-V NEWS MAGAZINE

"North America's most informative professional video equipment magazine." - DIGITAL EVOLUTION MAGAZINE

"Nostalgia magazine, The." - LIBERTY, THEN AND NOW

"Number one authority on photography, The." - CAMERA 35

O

"Occasional newsletter, An." - BROADCAST PIONEERS LIBRARY REPORTS

"Occasional publication promoting information exchange, An." - FORUM

"Of, for, and by the motion picture exhibitor." - EXHIBITORS TRADE REVIEW

"Official guide to AM, FM, TV and worldwide SW." - COMMUNICATIONS WORLD

"Official information channel of the Community Broadcasters Association." - LPTV REPORT, THE

"Official journal of the American section of the International Committee on Wireless Telegraphy." (Jan, 1930 - Apr, 1930). - AIR LAW REVIEW

"Official journal of the American section of the International Committee on radio of the American Academy of Air Law." (Apr, 1931 - 1941). - AIR LAW REVIEW

"Official journal of the Antique Wireless Association." - OLD TIMER'S BULLETIN, THE

"Official journal of the British Typographia." (Vol 1 - 4). - BRITISH PRINTER

"Official journal of the incorporated Advertising Managers Association." - ADVERTISING AND MARKETING MANAGEMENT

"Official journal of the International Communication Association, An." - HUMAN COMMUNICATION RESEARCH

"Official journal of the International Council for Educational Media." - EDUCATIONAL MEDIA INTERNATIONAL

"Official journal of the International League of Press Clubs." (Apr, 1892 - 1895). - JOURNALIST, THE

"Official journal of the New Zealand Electronics Institute." - ELECTRONICS AND COMMUNICATIONS

"Official journal of the Successful Magazine Publishers Group." - SUCCESSFUL MAGAZINE PUBLISHING

"Official journal of the Western States Communication Association, The." - WESTERN JOURNAL OF SPEECH COMMUNICATION

"Official journal the Photographers' Association of America." - COMMERCIAL PHOTOGRAPHER, THE

"Official magazine, The." - STAR TREK: THE NEXT GENERATION

"Official magazine of the international honorary society for highschool journalists." - QUILL AND SCROLL

"Official magazine of the International Television Association, The." - CORPORATE TELEVISION

"Official magazine of the International Television Association, The." (Oct, 1990+). - VIDEO SYSTEMS

"Official magazine of the Movietime Network." - MOVIES USA

"Official monthly publication of the American College Publicity Association." - COLLEGE & UNIVERSITY JOURNAL

"Official news medium for National Broadcasters' League." - RADIO AGE

"Official newsletter of National Mail Order Association." - MAIL ORDER DIGEST

"Official newsletter of the Xerox Ventura Publisher User's Group." - VENTURA PROFESSIONAL!

"Official organ of Columbia Photographic Society." (Jul, 1897 - Feb, 1900). - CAMERA MAGAZINE

"Official organ of FIAP (International Federation of Photographic Art)." - CAMERA

"Official organ of Lithographers and Photoengravers International Union." - GRAPHIC COMMUNICATOR

"Official organ of National Amateur Press Association." - NATIONAL AMATEUR

"Official organ of the ASIFA." - ANIMAFILM

"Official organ of the B.B.C." (Sep 28, 1923 - Dec, 24, 1926). - RADIO TIMES

"Official organ of the Boston Photo Clan." - AMATEUR PHOTOGRAPHER'S WEEKLY, THE

"Official organ of the British Institution of Radio Engineers." - ELECTRONICS & COMMUNICATIONS ENGINEERING JOURNAL

"Official organ of the Camera Club of New York." - AMATEUR PHOTOGRAPHER'S WEEKLY, THE

"Official organ of the Catholic Press Association of the United States, The." - CATHOLIC JOURNALIST

"Official organ of the Educational Film Library Association." - FILM & VIDEO NEWS

"Official organ of the Hollywood Foreign Press Correspondents Association." - HOLLYWOOD

"Official organ of the International Telecommunication Union." - TELECOMMUNICATION JOURNAL

"Official organ of the National Association of Academic Teachers of Public Speaking, The." - QUARTERLY JOURNAL OF SPEECH, THE

"Official organ of the New York Society of Amateur Photographers." (Feb, 1899 - ?). - CAMERA AND DARK ROOM

"Official organ of the Photo Pictorialists of Buffalo." - AMATEUR PHOTOGRAPHER'S WEEKLY, THE

"Official organ of the Photographers' Association of California." (Nov, 1922 - Jan, 1925). - CAMERA CRAFT

"Official organ of the Popular Culture Association." - JOURNAL OF POPULAR FILM AND TELEVISION

"Official organ of the Radio Signal Survey League." (Feb, 1937 - Jun, 1938). - ALL-WAVE RADIO

"Official organ of the Screen Writer's Guild of the Authors' League of America (Jul, 1921 - Nov, 1921). - PHOTODRAMATIST, THE

"Official organ of the Screen Writers' Guild." (Dec, 1921 - Jan, 1922). - PHOTODRAMATIST, THE

"Official organ of the Television Society." (1928 - May, 1932). - ELECTRONIC ENGINEERING

"Official organ of the Television Society." - TELEVISION

"Official organ of the Television Society of America." - TELEVISION

"Official organ of the Western Writers of America." - ROUNDUP QUARTERLY

"Official periodical of the Educational Film Library Association, Inc." - AFVA BULLETIN

"Official publication of American Cinema Editors, Inc." - AMERICAN CINEMEDITOR

"Official publication of Christian Booksellers Association." - BOOKSTORE JOURNAL

"Official publication of National Collegiate Players." - PLAYERS

"Official publication of Photo Marketing Association International." - PHOTO MARKETING

"Official publication of the American Academy of Advertising." - JOURNAL OF ADVERTISING

"Official publication of the Association for Educational Communications and Technology, The." (Jan, 1980 - Jan, 1985). - TECHTRENDS

"Official publication of the Broadcast Financial Management Association, The." - BROADCAST CABLE FINANCIAL JOURNAL

"Official publication of the Catholic School Press Association." - CATHOLIC SCHOOL EDITOR

"Official publication of the Colorado Editorial Association, issued for, and devoted to the best interests of Colorado editors and the dissemination of news of interest to the publishers of the Centennial State." - COLORADO EDITOR

"Official publication of the Community College Journalism Association, The." - COMMUNITY COLLEGE JOURNALIST

"Official publication of the Institute of Broadcasting Financial management, The." - BROADCAST CABLE FINANCIAL JOURNAL

"Official publication of the International Brotherhood of Electrical Workers. - IBEW JOURNAL

"Official publication of the International Brotherhood of Electrical Workers." - JOURNAL

"Official publication of the National Association of Broadcast Employees and Technicians." - BROADCAST ENGINEERS' JOURNAL, THE

"Official publication of the National Association of Television Program Executives." - NATPE PROGRAMMER

"Official publication of the National Forensic League." - ROSTRUM

"Official publication of the National Press Photographers Association." - NEWS PHOTOGRAPHER

"Official publication of the New Theatre League, An." (Oct, 1936 - Sep/Oct, 1937). - THEATRE WORKSHOP

"Official publication of the Newspaper Guild (AFL-CIO, CLC)." - GUILD REPORTER, THE

"Official publication of the Photographers' Association of America." - PROFESSIONAL PHOTOGRAPHER, THE

"Official publication of the Photographic Society of America." - PSA JOURNAL

"Official publication of the Popular Literature Section of the Modern Language Association of America." - JOURNAL OF POPULAR CULTURE

"Official publication of the Professional Film and Video Equipment Association, The." - NEWSLETTER, THE

"Official publication of the Screen Actors' Guild." - SCREEN ACTOR HOLLYWOOD

"Official publication of Theta Sigma Phi." - MATRIX

"Official Publication: The Disney Afternoon." - DISNEY ADVENTURES

"Official publication, Washington Newspaper Publishers Association." - WASHINGTON NEWSPAPER, THE

"Official quarterly journal of the International Council for Educational Media, The." - EDUCATIONAL MEDIA INTERNATIONAL

"Official technical journal of ITT." - ELECTRICAL COMMUNICATION

"Official voice of the specialty advertising industry's one and only trade association." - SPECIALTY ADVERTISING BUSINESS

"Officially endorsed by the Photography Instructors Association." - CAMERA & DARKROOM PHOTOGRAPHY

"Oldest advertising journal in the world." - AMERICAN ADVERTISER

"Oldest continuously published media/marketing newsletter, The." - MEDIA INDUSTRY NEWSLETTER

"Oldest exclusively professional photographic publication in the Western hemisphere, The." - PROFESSIONAL PHOTOGRAPHER, THE

"Oldest magazine for literary workers, The." - WRITER, THE

"Oldest magazine for literary workers--founded in Boston 1887, The." - WRITER, THE

"Oldest photographic weekly in America." (? - Jun 24, 1931). - BULLETIN OF PHOTOGRAPHY

"On newsstands throughout the world." - DOWN BEAT

"On sale the 15th of each month in Woolworth stores." - NEW MOVIE MAGAZINE, THE

"On the fifth and twentieth." - NATIONAL EXHIBITOR, THE

"One Hundred Pictures for Ten Cents." - STAGE PICTORIAL

"One of the Tower Group of magazines." - NEW MOVIE MAGAZINE, THE

"Only authoritative weekly typographical paper published." (Jan 6, 1879? - Mar 24, 1879). - WOODCOCK'S PRINTERS' AND LITHOGRAPHERS' WEEKLY GAZETTE AND NEWSPAPER REPORTER

"Only film & videotape production magazine, The." - ON LOCATION

"Only film newspaper, The." - SCREEN INTERNATIONAL

"Only graphic arts newspaper serving the western United States, The." - PRINTEQUIP NEWS

"Only independent magazine in the field of visual instruction, The." (? - Apr, 1922). - MOVING PICTURE AGE

"Only independent magazine in the general field of visual instruction, The." (May, 1922). - MOVING PICTURE AGE

"Only independent weekly journal of newspapering, The." - EDITOR AND PUBLISHER

"Only indispensable movie monthly, The." - TELEVISION AND SCREEN GUIDE

"Only magazine for image-makers and their subjects, The." - PIC

"Only magazine for the serious dealer, The." - SATELLITE RETAILER

"Only magazine published exclusively for rural listeners, The." - RURAL RADIO

"Only national weekly serving the advertising, journalistic, printing and allied fields, including newspapers, magazines, trade press, outdoor publicity, commercial films, TV and radio, direct mail, advertising production and press and public relations, The." - CAMPAIGN

"Only publication devoted to talking pictures and television." (Oct, 1929). - TALKING PICTURE MAGAZINE

"Only publication exclusively for the radio manufacturer, The." (May, 1926 - ?). - RADIO INDUSTRIES

"Only serious quarterly devoted entirely to the art and history of the silent motion picture, The." - SILENT PICTURE, THE

"Only weekly journal of bookselling, The." - AB BOOKMAN'S WEEKLY

"Only weekly journal published treating on typography, lithography, bookbinding and stationery, The." (Mar 31, 1879 - ?). - WOODCOCK'S PRINTERS' AND LITHOGRAPHERS' WEEKLY GAZETTE AND NEWSPAPER REPORTER

"Only weekly publication of international television programming, The." - TELCO REPORT, THE

"Only weekly trade publication in the graphic arts industry, The." - PRINTINGNEWS

"Operations and marketing journal of the cable television industry, The." - MSO'S CABLE MARKETING

"Optical media review for information professionals, The." - CD-ROM LIBRARIAN

"Or 'Boz' in the boxes." - ODDFELLOW, THE

"Or critical and biographical illustration of the British stage for the year 1811, involving a correct register of every night's performances at our metropolitan theatres, and published with a view to sustaining the morality and dignity of the drama." (Jul, 1800 - Jun, 1801). - DRAMATIC CENSOR, THE

"Or monthly epitome of taste, fashion, and manners." (Jul, 1800 - Jun, 1801). - DRAMATIC CENSOR, THE

"Or weekly theatrical report." (Jan, 1800 - Jun 28, 1800). - DRAMATIC CENSOR, THE

"Organ of Association Western Union Employees." - TELEGRAPH WORLD

"Organ of British Advertising." - ADWEEK

"Organ of the Bulgarian Cinematography State Corporation." (1983+). - BULGARIAN FILMS

"Organ of the National Union of Journalists." - JOURNALIST

"Other movie magazine, The." - FILM THREAT

"Our motto: No refunds." - SIMPSONS ILLUSTRATED

"Over 100 cartoons from America's leading cartoonist." - NATIONAL FORUM, THE

"Over fifty years of service to the industry." - HOLLYWOOD REPORTER

"Overview of telecommunications news, An." - TELECOMMUNICATIONS ALERT

P

"Paper of the entertainment industry, The." - SCREEN INTERNATIONAL

"Paper quarterly for the graphic arts, The." - PRINTING PAPER

"Paving the way for the future." - STRANGE ADVENTURES

"People and careers in telecommunications." - PACTSHEET

"People in Camera." - PIC

"People magazine of the home electronics, appliance and personal electronics industry, The." - DEALERSCOPE

"Perfectionist's guide to fantastic video, The." - VIDEO WATCHDOG

"Performance art quarterly, The." - HIGH PERFORMANCE

"Performing arts news magazine." - INTERMISSION

"Performing arts weekly, The." - BACK STAGE

"Periodical of fact and opinion from NBC corporate and media relations, A." - OF SPECIAL INTEREST

"Periodical of the black theatre movement, A." - BLACK THEATRE

"Periodical of the International Federation of Journalists, A." - JOURNALIST'S WORLD

"Periodical review of films and videotapes made by artists and about the arts, A." - ART & CINEMA

"Perspectives on American underground film." (#1-1968 - ?). - CINEMA NOW

"Pertaining to agricultural newspaper advertising." - AGRICULTURAL ADVERTISING

"Petersen's Photographic shows you how..." - PETERSEN'S PHOTOGRAPHIC

"Philosophy of Communication Division Newsletter." - COMMUNIQUÉ

"Photographic journal of America, The." - CAMERA, THE

"Photographic monthly, A." - CAMERA CRAFT

"Photography, Cinematography, Sound & Image Recording." - PERSPECTIVE

"Photography / Independent Film / Video / Visual Books." - AFTERIMAGE

"Photography's how-to-do-it magazine." - CAMERA MAGAZINE

"Pictures and stories." - TV WORLD

"Pictures and stories of the top-flight band leaders." - BAND LEADERS

"Pioneer radio trade journal, The." (? - Oct, 1928). - RADIO DEALER, THE

"Plague on both your houses, A." - ODDFELLOW, THE

"Pleasure is all yours, The." - UNIVERSAL WEEKLY

"Pleasures of the past, The." (Nov, 1974 - ?). - NOSTALGIA ILLUSTRATED

"Political cartoon quarterly, The." - TARGET

"Popular culture scholar, The." - PCS, THE POPULAR CULTURE SCHOLAR

"Portrait and commercial weekly, The." (? - Jun 24, 1931). - BULLETIN OF PHOTOGRAPHY

"Poster magazine of teen stars, The." - TS

"Posters, prizes, interviews, gossip." - TV HITS

"Practical advertiser, A." (Jan, 1901 - Mar, 1902). - COMMON SENSE

"Practical, independent magazine, devoted to the photographic art, A." - PHOTOGRAPHER'S FRIEND, THE

"Practical manual for the busy advertising man in dry goods stores and newspaper offices, A." - ADVERTISING IDEAS

"Practical newsletter on agency management, The." - YELLOW SHEET, THE

"Practicle magazine for photographers, A." - CAMERA MAGAZINE

"Preeminent source of worldwide HDTV reporting, The." - HDTV NEWSLETTER

"Premium entertainment magazine, The." - CABLEVISION

"Prepress, sheetfed, web, postpress." - HIGH VOLUME PRINTING

"Presentation technology & applications." - AVC

"Presenting a condensed summary of the best material--written and spoken--on advertising and sales merchandising." - ADVERTISER'S DIGEST

"Presenting a condensed summary of the best material written and spoken, about the modern business scene." - ADVERTISER'S DIGEST

"Presenting the most important interviews, guides and reviews of daredevils in movies on television and print." - DAREDEVILS

"Pro audio applications magazine, The." - REP: RECORDING ENGINEERING PRODUCTION

"Proceedings of the Institution of Radio and Electronics Engineers, Australia. - PROCEEDINGS OF THE IREE AUSTRALIA

"Producing audio for tape, records, film, live performance, video & broadcast." - REP: RECORDING ENGINEERING PRODUCTION

"Product magazine for the consumer electronics market, The." (Jan, 1975 - ?). - CONSUMER ELECTRONICS PRODUCT NEWS

"Production and presentation technology." - AV VIDEO

"Production, engineering, distribution, radio, television, sound projection." (? - Oct/Nov, 1934). - RADIO INDUSTRIES

"Production magazine, The." - FILM & VIDEO

"Production management magazine of newspapers, The." - WEB

"Production Prospects." - SHOW BUSINESS

"Professional journal of business communications, The." - COMMUNICATIONS

"Professional journal of cable system operations, The." - CABLE TV BUSINESS MAGAZINE

"Professional journal of the cable television industry." - CABLE TV BUSINESS MAGAZINE

"Professional journal of the National Broadcast Editorial Association." - EDITORIALIST, THE

"Professional radio-TVman's magazine, The." - ELECTRONIC SERVICING & TECHNOLOGY

"Professional recording." - MIX

"Professional video from the inside out." - INVIEW

"Programming for profit." - MSO'S CABLE MARKETING

"Progressive magazine for up-to-date printers, A." (Nov, 1899). - PRACTICAL PRINTER, THE

"Promoting the Judeo-Christian ethic of decency in the American society with primary emphasis on television." - AFA JOURNAL

"Proudly published monthly in Humbold County, California. - COMIC RELIEF

"Public Telecommunications Review." - PUBLIC TELECOMMUNICATIONS REVIEW

"Publication, The." - ADVERTISING AGENCY

"Publication dedicated to the study and improvement of journalism in Washington, A." - WASHINGTON NEWSPAPER, THE

"Publication devoted to communication in human relations, A." - JOURNAL OF COMMUNICATION

"Publication for publishers and advertising managers, A." - AMERICAN ADVERTISER REPORTER

"Publication for the international recording community, A." - DASH WORLD

"Publication of Christians in the Arts Networking." - CANEWS

"Publication of FAIR (Fairness & Accuracy in Reporting), A." - EXTRA!

"Publication of film art fun, A." - MEDIA ARTS

"Publication of the American Association of Advertising Agencies, A." - AGENCY

"Publication of the American Business Communication Association, A." - BULLETIN OF THE ASSOCIATION FOR BUSINESS COMMUNICATION, THE

"Publication of the American Journalism Historians Association, The." - AMERICAN JOURNALISM

"Publication of the American Society of Composers, Authors and Publishers, A." - ASCAP IN ACTION

"Publication of the Broadcast Cable Financial Management Association, A." - BROADCAST CABLE FINANCIAL JOURNAL

"Publication of the Cinema Appreciation League." - CINEMA PROGRESS

"Publication of the Council on International Nontheatrical Events, A." - CINE NEWS

"Publication of the Eastern Communication Association, A." - COMMUNICATION QUARTERLY

"Publication of the entertainment law institute of the law center of the University of Southern California, A." - JOURNAL OF ARTS MANAGEMENT AND LAW, THE

"Publication of the Forum on Communications Law." - COMMUNICATIONS LAWYER

"Publication of the honorary professional society--American Cinema Editors, Inc, A." - AMERICAN CINEMEDITOR

"Publication of the IEEE Broadcast, Cable, and Consumer Electronics Society, A." - IEEE TRANSACTIONS ON CABLE TELEVISION

"Publication of the IEEE Communications Society, A." - IEEE TRANSACTIONS ON COMMUNICATIONS

"Publication of the Information Systems Division of the International Communication Association, A." - SYSTEMSLETTER

"Publication of The Institution of Radio and Electronics Engineers Australia, A." - MONITOR

"Publication of the International Documentary Association, A." - INTERNATIONAL DOCUMENTARY

"Publication of the National Association of College Broadcasters, A." - COLLEGE BROADCASTER

"Publication of the National Association of Educational Broadcasters, A." - PUBLIC TELECOMMUNICATIONS REVIEW

"Publication of the National Educational Closed-Circuit Television Association, A." - JOURNAL OF EDUCATIONAL TELEVISION

"Publication of the Photographic Resource Center at Boston University, A." - VIEWS

"Publication of the Society of Motion Picture and Television Engineers." - SMPTE JOURNAL

"Publication of the Speech Communication Association, A." - COMMUNICATION EDUCATION

"Publication of the Speech Communication Association, A." - CRITICAL STUDIES IN MASS COMMUNICATION

"Publication of the Speech Communication Association, A." - SPECTRA

"Publication of the Virginia Production Services Association, A." - REEL LIFE

"Published as the official organ of the Roxy Theatre." - ROXY THEATRE WEEKLY REVIEW

"Published bimonthly by the Asian Broadcasting Union." - ABU TECHNICAL REVIEW

"Published by and responsible to the National Newspaper Association." - PUBLISHER'S AUXILIARY

"Published by Pentax Family, Asahi Optical Company, Ltd." - PENTAX FAMILY

"Published by the Folger Shakespeare Library." - SHAKESPEARE QUARTERLY

"Published by the Freedom of Information Center, School of Journalism, University of Missouri." - FOI DIGEST

"Published by the International Federation of Journalists." - IFJ INFORMATION

"Published by the International Thespian Society." - DRAMATICS

"Published by the Printers' Ink Network of magazines." - BUSINESS ADVERTISING

"Published by the Reporters Committee for Freedom of the Press." - NEWS MEDIA & THE LAW, THE

"Published by the School of Journalism of the University of Iowa." - IOWA JOURNALIST

"Published by the Society of Motion Picture and Television Engineers, Inc." - SMPTE JOURNAL

"Published by the Society of Teachers of Speech and Drama." - SPEECH AND DRAMA

"Published every Wednesday." - AMATEUR PHOTOGRAPHER

"Published every week." - PICTURES MAGAZINE, THE

"Published for RAB Members." - SOUND MANAGEMENT

"Published for the dissemination of the best editorial thought of the day." - EDITORIAL

"Published for the old time wireless operator, historian, and collector." - OLD TIMER'S BULLETIN, THE

"Published for the Radio Industry." - RADIO BROADCAST

"Published for the Society of Cable Television Engineers." - COMMUNICATIONS ENGINEERING & DESIGN

"Published in the interests of employees of the Bell Telephone Company of Pennsylvania and the Diamond State Telephone Company." - TELEPHONE NEWS, THE

"Published monthly and devoted to promoting highest excellence in every-day typography." (Feb, 1902), (Jun, 1902). - PRACTICAL PRINTER, THE

"Published monthly for all newspaper boys." (Nov, 1936 - ?). - AMERICAN NEWSPAPER BOY, THE

"Published monthly in the interests of amateur motion pictures by the Eastman Kodak Company, Rochester, NY." - CINE-KODAK NEWS, THE

"Published quarterly by the National Broadcasting Company." (Oct, 1946 - Oct, 1947). - NBC DIGEST

"Published quarterly by the Nieman Foundation for Journalism at Harvard University." - NIEMAN REPORTS

"Published since 1883 to further the advancement of communications techniques." (Jan, 1965 - Feb, 1965). - WIRE & RADIO COMMUNICATIONS

"Published since 1935." - SCREEN ALBUM MAGAZINE

"Publishing, programming, broadcasting/cable TV, radio." - MEDIA BUSINESS

"Pulse of the motion picture industry, The." - BOX OFFICE

"Pulse of the motion picture industry, The." - BOXOFFICE

Q

"Quarterly digest of addresses of diversified interest broadcast over the Columbia network, A." (Jan, 1936 - ?). - TALKS

"Quarterly digest of addresses presented in the public interest by the Columbia network, A." - TALKS

"Quarterly for mass communications." - CLIO MAGAZINE

"Quarterly information service from the Centre for the Study of Communication and Culture, A." - COMMUNICATION RESEARCH TRENDS

"Quarterly journal, A." - COMBROAD

"Quarterly journal of film history, theory & criticism, A." - WIDE ANGLE

"Quarterly journal of film history, theory, criticism and practice, A." - WIDE ANGLE

"Quarterly journal of filmic art, A." - FILMING

"Quarterly journal of media research and resources, The." - MEDIA INFORMATION AUSTRALIA

"Quarterly journal of research, theory and application, A." - WRITTEN COMMUNICATION

"Quarterly journal of the graphic arts, A." - PRINT

"Quarterly journal of the IBA, The." - AIRWAVES

"Quarterly journal of the National Council for Children and Television." - TELEVISION & FAMILIES

"Quarterly journal of the theatre and film arts, A." (Oct, 1936 - Sep/Oct, 1937). - THEATRE WORKSHOP

"Quarterly journal of the World Media Study Group." - WORLD MEDIA REPORT

"Quarterly journal on microcomputer use in journalism and mass communication, A." - NEWS COMPUTING JOURNAL

"Quarterly look at modern communications and its impact on religious values, A." - MEDIA & VALUES

"Quarterly magazine, A." (Mar, 1924 - Nov, 1927). - JQ. JOURNALISM QUARTERLY.

"Quarterly magazine for the new arts audience, A." - HIGH PERFORMANCE

"Quarterly magazine of the Southeastern Theatre Conference." - SOUTHERN THEATRE

"Quarterly magazine published from 12-13 Little Newport St., London, WC2H 7JJ, A." - CINEMA

"Quarterly miscellany of the printing art, A." - ARS TYPOGRAPHICA

"Quarterly newsletter, A." - BROADCAST PIONEERS LIBRARY REPORTS

"Quarterly newsletter for media, advertising, and public relations professionals, The." - MEDIABRIEFS

"Quarterly newsletter published for the creators, writers, art directors, sponsors and broadcasters of programs, commercials, corporate films and special events, A." - VTA PLAYBACK

"Quarterly of discussion and analysis, A." - FILMS

"Quarterly of new drama, A." (winter-61/62 - ?) - DRAMA & THEATRE

"Quarterly of notes and research, A." (Oct, 1945 - ?). - THEATRE NOTEBOOK

"Quarterly of the Drama Teachers Association." - THEATRE AND SCHOOL

"Quarterly of typography and graphic arts, A." - ALPHABET AND IMAGE

"Quarterly presentation of your film favorites old and new, featuring exciting portraits and personal biographies, A." (Summer, 1948 - ?). - FILM ALBUM MAGAZINE

"Quarterly publication of the American Marketing Association, A." - JOURNAL OF MARKETING

"Quarterly publication of the National Conference of Editorial Writers, The." - MASTHEAD

"Quarterly resource for media literacy, A." - MEDIA & VALUES

"Quarterly review, A." (Feb, 1911 - ?). - DRAMA MAGAZINE, THE

"Quarterly review for newspapermen, A." - SEMINAR

"Quarterly review of dramatic literature, A." (Feb, 1911 - May, 1919). - DRAMA MAGAZINE, THE

"Quarterly review of marketing communications, The." - INTERNATIONAL JOURNAL OF ADVERTISING

"Quarterly review of media issues and trends, A." - MEDIA & VALUES

"Quarterly review of modern aids to learning, A." - SIGHT & SOUND

"Quarterly review of progress." - PERSPECTIVE

"Quarterly review of public relations, The." (Oct, 1955 - ?). - PUBLIC RELATIONS QUARTERLY

"Quarterly review of the communications business, A." - ADVERTISING AND GRAPHIC ARTS TECHNIQUES

"Quarterly review of the communications business, A." - ADVERTISING MAGAZINE

"Quarterly review of the serious, foreign-language cinema-TV-press, A." (winter, 1961/62 - ?). - CTVD

"Quarterly supplement of Monitor Magazine audio video broadcasting." - MONITOR INTERNATIONAL

"Quarterly theatre review, The." - DRAMA

"Quick reference picture chart, A." - FILM BUYER

R

"Radio amateur's journal, The." - CQ

"Radio and newspapers, film and theater." (1942). - AUDIO-VISUAL GUIDE

"Radio & Records." - R & R

"Radio broadcast, communications & Television Engineering and design practice." (Nov, 1941 - Mar, 1942). - COMMUNICATION ENGINEERING

"Radio-electronics in all its phases." - RADIO-ELECTRONICS

"Radio for every place and purpose." - RADIO BROADCAST

"Radio magazine, The." - PRACTICAL WIRELESS

"Radio magazine, The." - WIRELESS AGE, THE

"Radio manufacturers' monthly, The." (? - Oct/Nov, 1934). - RADIO INDUSTRIES

"Radio publication you're reading the most, The." - INSIDE RADIO

"Radio, Television, and Electronics." - ELECTRONICS WORLD + WIRELESS WORLD

"Radio television video broadcasting." - MONITOR INTERNATIONAL

"Radio trade journal for the radio business man, The." (? - Oct, 1928). - RADIO DEALER, THE

"Radio trade journal for the radio retailer, The." (May, 1922 - ?). - RADIO DEALER, THE

"Radio's best read newspaper." - RADIO WORLD

"Radio's greatest magazine." - ELECTRONICS WORLD

"Radio's management weekly." - PULSE OF RADIO

"Radio's technology magazine." - RADIO GUIDE

"Rain and shine and sleet and snow; it's all the same to us, you know." (Nov, 1936 - ?). - AMERICAN NEWSPAPER BOY, THE

"Rarities, retitlings, restorations." - VIDEO WATCHDOG

"Reaching all serious comic art fans and collectors." - COMICS BUYER'S GUIDE

"Reaching every radio TV service firm owner in the USA." - ELECTRONIC SERVICING & TECHNOLOGY

"Readers in 142 countries." - DOWN BEAT

"Recent release, classics, TV-nostalgia, special interest." - MOVIE MARKETPLACE

"Recent titles in telecommunications, information and media." - COMMUNICATION BOOKNOTES

"Record of BBC technical experience and developments in radio and television broadcasting, A." - BBC ENGINEERING

"Record of modern practice in architecture and technics, A." - IDEAL KINEMA, THE

"Recording industry magazine, The." - MIX

"Recording the electrical era." - JOURNAL

"Reflecting the magic of Hollywood." - SILVER SCREEN

"Relating recording science to recording art to recording equipment." - REP: RECORDING ENGINEERING PRODUCTION

"Report for editors provided in coordination with the newspaper readership council, A." - ANPA NEWS RESEARCH REPORT

"Report on broadcast rules and regulations presented by Broadcasting and the Law, Inc., a wholly owned company of the partners of Leibowitz & Spencer, a law firm practicing in the area of communications law, A." - BROADCASTING AND THE LAW

"Reporter of Direct Mail Advertising, The." - DIRECT MARKETING

"Reporting how the media work." - PRESS, THE

"Reporting on the marketing profession." - MARKETING NEWS

"Reporting on the marketing profession and its association." - MARKETING NEWS

"Reporting the technologies of broadband communications." - COMMUNICATIONS ENGINEERING & DESIGN

"Reports and interprets current court and FCC rulings affecting broadcasting practice and operations." - BROADCASTING AND THE LAW

"Research, analysis and comment on communication and mass media." - CANADIAN JOURNAL OF COMMUNICATION

"Research journal concerned with all that is involved with our being literate, The." - VISIBLE LANGUAGE

"Research, manufacturing, communications, broadcasting." - ELECTRONIC AGE

"Research, manufacturing, communications, broadcasting, television." - ELECTRONIC AGE

"Research publication of the Magazine Division, AEJMC, The." - MAGAZINES IN DEPTH

"Research Society for American Periodicals." - RSAP NEWSLETTER

"Resource for managers, A." - RADIOWEEK

"Resource newsletter of the National Sisters Communications Service, A." - MEDIA & VALUES

"Retailer and advertiser, The." - RETAIL EQUIPMENT AND MERCHANDISE

"Review journal of obscure, popular, independent, and foreign horror and fantasy cinema, The." - CINEFAN

"Review of books from independent and smaller presses, A." - SMALL PRESS BOOK REVIEW, THE

"Review of Cinema." - VELVET LIGHT TRAP

"Review of contemporary cinema, A." - JUMP CUT

"Review of contemporary media, A." - JUMP CUT

"Review of dramatic literature & the theatrical arts, A." (May, 1961 to date?). - DRAMA SURVEY

"Review of horror, fantasy, and science fiction films, The." - CINEFANTASTIQUE

"Review of independent cinema and video, A." - CANTRILLS FILMNOTES

"Review of Newspaper Journalism, A." - OVERSET

"Review of publications in religious communication, A." - HOMILETIC

"Review of puppets and related theatre, A." - ANIMATIONS

"Review of the advance-guard cinema." (Summer, 1933 - Winter, 1934). - FILM ART

"Review of the allied arts of the theatre, A." (Oct, 1925 - May, 1930). - DRAMA MAGAZINE, THE

"Review of the arts of animation in theatre, film and television, A." - ANIMATIONS

"Review of the International Radio and Television Organization." - RADIO AND TELEVISION

"Reviewing the graphic arts in the tri-state Philadelphia area." - MID-ATLANTIC GRAPHIC ARTS REVIEW

"Reviews, comment, criticism." - FILM GUIDE

"Revue canadienne de la telecommunication." - IN SEARCH

S

"Sales journal of periodical distribution, The." (? - Sep, 1960). - MAGAZINE & BOOKSELLER

"Satellite TV Week is America's most accurate and up-to-date listing of satellite TV programming." - SATELLITE TV WEEK

"Scenario writer's magazine, The." (Dec, 1921 - ?). - PHOTODRAMATIST, THE

"Scenic, travel, wildlife, sports." - OUTDOOR PHOTOGRAPHER

"School / people / public relations." - JOURNAL OF EDUCATIONAL PUBLIC RELATIONS

"School PR magazine, The." - JOURNAL OF EDUCATIONAL PUBLIC RELATIONS

"Science fiction, fantasy & horror in films." - CINEFAN

"Sciences, public address, education, communication, theatre, radio-TV- film, arts." - SPECTRA

"Scott Bruce's cereal box collecting magazine." - FLAKE

"Section of the Radio Dealer for radio manufacturers and engineers, A." (? - Oct, 1928). - RADIO MANUFACTURER, THE

"Semi-monthly journal devoted to land-line telegraphs, submarine cable interests, radio-telegraphy and allied industries, A." (1883 - 1909). - WIRE & RADIO COMMUNICATIONS

"Serious film journal, A." - CINEMONKEY

"Service newsletter about mass communication ethics, A." - MEDIA ETHICS UPDATE

"Service paper of the motion picture industry, The." - SHOWMEN'S TRADE REVIEW

"Serving amateur radio since 1945." - CQ

"Serving Canada's Communications Industry." - BROADCASTER

"Serving Canadian telephone and cable television systems." - CABLE COMMUNICATIONS MAGAZINE

"Serving public relations practitioners and educators and management." - PUBLIC RELATIONS JOURNAL, THE

"Serving: recording, broadcast and sound contracting fields." - DB

"Serving the Communications Industry Worldwide." - RADIO WORLD

"Serving the industry since 1903." - PULP & PAPER CANADA

"Serving the nations photo editors & photo illustrators." - PHOTOLETTER

"Serving the sun belt's advertising-marketing industry." - COMMUNIQUE

"Serving the world of comics every week." - COMICS BUYER'S GUIDE

"Serving theatre across America." - PLAYERS

"SF experts tell you what to rent & what to own!, The." - SCIENCE-FICTION VIDEO MAGAZINE

"Show news weekly, The." - DRAMATIC MIRROR, THE

"Show Place of the Nation." (Apr 3, 1933 - Nov 2, 1933). - RADIO CITY NEWS

"Showbiz magazine." - SOSYAL! MAGAZINE

"Sign post shows all the roads--the choice lies with the traveler, The." (Feb 5, 1949 - ?). - BROADWAY SIGN POST

"SMATV, MATV, MDS & DBS systems magazine, The." - PRIVATE CABLE

"Society of broadcast professionals contributing to the past, present and future of broadcasting, A." - SPARKS

"Something of interest for every member of the radio family." (Apr, 1926). - RADIO HOME, THE

"Sound and music production." - MIX

"Sound engineering magazine, The." - DB

"Sound Monthly, The." - HI-FI SOUND

"Southam business publication, A." - PULP & PAPER CANADA

"Southeast film & video news magazine, The." - MARKEE

"Southern States Communication Association Newsletter, The." - C-O-N-N-E-C-T-I-O-N-S

"Sparkling young journal, free and independent, was born to shine for all, The." - ST. LOUIS AND CANADIAN PHOTOGRAPHER

"Special interest group of the International Communication Association (ICA)." - COMMUNICATION LAW & POLICY NEWSLETTER

"Special medium of inter-communication for publishers, booksellers, and stationers, A." (Sep, 1869 - Aug 18, 1870). - PUBLISHER'S WEEKLY

"Specialist book trade weekly, The." - AB BOOKMAN'S WEEKLY

"Specialist weekly for the communicators, The." - CAMPAIGN

"Sport, Broadway, Hollywood." - PIC

"Spot news and features about newspapers, advertisers and agencies." - EDITOR AND PUBLISHER

"Stars, stories, gossip." - SOAP OPERA TIME

"Stereo, disc, tape." (Nov, 1967 - ?). - HI-FI SOUND

"Stills and stories of the films." - FILM ARTISTE

"Strategies, applications and solutions." (Sep, 1989+). - VIDEO MANAGEMENT

"Style and technology in harmony." - AUDIO/VIDEO INTERIORS

"Supplement to Industrial and Commercial Photographer." - GRAPHIC ARTS

"Surviving in the digital age." - DIGITAL RADIO NEWS

"Synergetic audio concepts." - SYN-AUD-CON NEWSLETTER

"Systems and Operation." - INTERNATIONAL BROADCASTING

"Systems, the market, the future, The." - VIDEOCASSETTE AND CATV NEWSLETTER

T

"Tabloid magazine of the screen, The." (Oct, 1931 - ?). - MOVIE CLASSIC

"Teaching with television." - CONNECT

"Technical magazine for the nineties, The." (Feb, 1990). - BME'S TELEVISION ENGINEERING

"Technical magazine that solves your hi-fi queries and problems, The." (? - Mar, 1984). - HI-FI ANSWERS

"Technical, professional, scientific." - BRITISH JOURNAL OF PHOTOGRAPHY

"Techniques magazine for professional video, The." - E-ITV

"Technological Horizons in Education." - THE JOURNAL

"Technology - video - stereo - computers - service." - RADIO-ELECTRONICS

"Telecom industry's favorite magazine, The." - TELECONNECT

"Television Business International." - TBI

"Television, communications, service, sound," - ELECTRONICS AND COMMUNICATIONS

"Television fanzine of science fiction, fantasy, and adventure, The." - EPI-LOG

"Television in the Eighties." - WATCH

"Television magazine, The." - PANORAMA

"Television magazine of science fiction, fantasy, and adventure, The." - EPI-LOG

"Television, parties, movies." - PREVIEW

"Television quarterly, The." - CONTRAST

"Television, radio, communication." - MILLECANALI INTERNATIONAL

"Television today & tomorrow." - PANORAMA

"There is already enough ignorance." - BLACK JOURNALISM REVIEW

"Three magazines in one covering the entire field of entertainment." - PIC

"Through high fidelity." - BETTER LISTENING

"Timely, critical review of communications resources, A." (Apr, 1976 - ?). - RELIGIOUS MEDIA TODAY

"To assess the performance of journalism, to help stimulate continuing improvement in the profession, and to speak out for what is right, fair, and decent." - COLUMBIA JOURNALISM REVIEW

"To generate more television sales." - SALES NEWS

"To help improve instruction through the more effective use of materials." (Feb, 1956 - ?). - TECHTRENDS

"To make the screen a greater power in education and business." (Jul, 1918 - ?). - MOVING PICTURE AGE

"To promote study, criticism, research, teaching, and applications of the principles of communications." - SPECTRA

"To see ourselves as others see us." (Dec, 1926 - ?). - MOVIE MAKERS

"Top selling video entertainment magazine, The." - VIDEO TODAY

"Top Tunes." - HIT PARADER

"Touring talent weekly, The." - PERFORMANCE

"Trade paper for exhibitors of motion pictures." - FILM JOURNAL, THE

"Trade weekly for all the entertainment industry, The." (Oct, 1969 - May 29, 1970). - ENTERTAINMENT WORLD

"Truth about uncut fantastic video, The." - VIDEO WATCHDOG

"Truth comes out, The." - FAST FORWARD

"Tune in to TV Radio Talk for the top stories first!" - TV RADIO TALK

"TV - AM - FM - sound." - ELECTRONIC SERVICING & TECHNOLOGY

"TV & film production, distribution & manufacturing marketplace of the Spanish-speaking world & Brazil, The." - PRODUCCIÓN Y DISTRIBUCIÓN

"Twenty years the authority." - DAYTIME TV

"Twice-monthly analysis of federal issues affecting the cable and broadcast industries, A." - TV & RADIO FAXLETTER

"Two great magazines for the price of one." - PHOTOPLAY COMBINED WITH MOVIE MIRROR

U

"Unabashed attempt to inspire advertising agency account executives, An." - AD • MENTOR, THE

"Underbelly of film history, The." - LOWBROW CINEMA

"Union of hearts and minds, The." - IBEW JOURNAL

"Unique reporting service on photography, art & communications books for libraries and book users, A." - ROTKIN REVIEW, THE

"Unique reporting service to libraries for photography, art, communications, and other visually-oriented books, A." - ROTKIN REVIEW, THE

"Universal has the pictures." - UNIVERSAL WEEKLY

"Up-to-the-minute weekly management news for radio executives." - INSIDE RADIO

"Users group newsletter." - ECHO BUSS

"Using direct response advertising to enhance marketing database." (? - Dec, 1989). - DIRECT MARKETING

"Using television to lead families to museums and libraries." - TEACHER'S GUIDE TO TELEVISION

V

"Variety paper for variety people, A." - VARIETY

"VCR guide, The." - HOME VIEWER

"Video, audio & computers." - ON!

"Video Camera user's magazine, The." - VIDEOMAKER

"Video-making magazine, The." - CAMCORDER USER

"Video, multimedia, audio-visual, interactive systems, industry, government." - COMMUNICATIONS INDUSTRIES REPORT, THE

"Visual communications magazine, The." - COMPUTER PICTURES

"Visual documentation & communication in science, technology & medicine." - FUNCTIONAL PHOTOGRAPHY

"Voice of letterpress printing and photoengraving, The." - MORE BUSINESS

"Voice of National Academy of Radio Arts & Sciences." - INTERNATIONAL RADIO REPORT, THE

"Voice of print advertising, The." - INSIDE MEDIA

"Voice of the box office, The." - PICTURE REPORTS

"Voice of the Canadian motion picture industry." - CANADIAN FILM DIGEST

"Voice of the direct market, The." - COMIC FANDOM'S FORUM

"Voice of the entertainment industry." - CANADIAN FILM DIGEST

"Voice of the imaging industry, The." - ADVANCED IMAGING

"Voice of the industry professional." - VIDEOPRO

"Voice of the industry since 1982, The." - TELEMARKETING

"Voice of the nation's capital." - NATIONAL EXHIBITOR, THE

"Voice of the radio broadcasting industry." - RADIO BUSINESS REPORT

"Voice of the telephone interconnect industry, The." - TELECONNECT

"Voted favourite hi-fi magazine by hi-fi shops nationwide." - HI-FI CHOICE

W

"Waldenbooks' news, reviews & exclusive interviews with today's hottest authors." - W • B

"We let the industry speak for itself." - COMICS INTERVIEW

"We show you how to do it." (Jun, 1891 - Oct 15, 1892 [and] Jan 15, 1893 - ?). - PROFITABLE ADVERTISING

"Weekly European satellite & space business newsletter." - INTERSPACE

"Weekly for leading users of communications products & services, The." - NETWORK WORLD

"Weekly magazine for the professional photographer, A." (Aug 14, 1907 - ?). - BULLETIN OF PHOTOGRAPHY

"Weekly magazine of advertising, marketing, and sales, The." - MARKETING / COMMUNICATIONS

"Weekly magazine of kinetic drama and literature, A." - REEL LIFE

"Weekly media employment newsletter, The." - JOB LEADS

"Weekly news service of TV and communications magazine, The." - VUE

"Weekly newsmagazine of radio, The." - BROADCASTING

"Weekly newspaper for advertisers and newspaper makers, A." (? - Nov 26, 1927). - FOURTH ESTATE

"Weekly newspaper for publishers, advertisers, advertising agents and allied interests, A." - FOURTH ESTATE

"Weekly newspaper for the makers of newspapers, A." (Mar 1, 1894 - ?). - FOURTH ESTATE

"Weekly publication devoted to newspaper men and publishers, A." (Mar 22, 1884 - ?). - JOURNALIST, THE

"Weekly publication of record for the magazine industry, The." - MAGAZINEWEEK

"Weekly record of offers and announcements, A." - KINETRADOGRAM, THE

"Weekly record of offers and announcements by the Kinematograph Trading Co., Ltd, A." - KINETRADOGRAM, THE

"Weekly record of the stage, A." (Mar 20, 1886 - Apr 27, 1893). - THEATRE, THE

"Weekly report to management." - MEDIA INDUSTRY NEWSLETTER

"Weekly resource for radio managers, A." - RADIOWEEK

"Weekly review and analysis of important regulatory and court decisions affecting broadcasters, A." - LINE MONITOR, THE

"Westward the star of empire takes its way." - ST. LOUIS AND CANADIAN PHOTOGRAPHER

"What to buy and what to watch." - WHAT SATELLITE

"What to buy; How to use it." - VIDEO ANSWERS

"What women are doing and thinking about the communications media." - MEDIA REPORT TO WOMEN

"What's happening in yearbooks." - TAYLOR-TALK

"What's new and how to magazine for the AV communicator, The." (Fall, 1978 - Sep/Oct, 1980). - AV VIDEO

"What's new in business publications, databases and research techniques." - BUSINESS INFORMATION ALERT

"Where art meets the real world." - DIRECTION

"Where marketing and media meet." - MEDIAWEEK

"Where show business begins." - CASTING CALL

"Where stars of tomorrow shine today!" - SHOWCASE WORLD

"Where the world gets the word on marketing." - ADVERTISING AGE

"Where to turn for design ideas & techniques... on a desktop or not." - IN HOUSE GRAPHICS

"Who's doing what, when, how, why, what for, in media?" - MEDIA INFORMATION AUSTRALIA

"Who's who in television." - TELEVISION PERSONALITIES

"Wisconsin's new photo monthly--a publication serving the photo-graphic enthusiast." - WISCONSIN PHOTOGRAPHER

"With which is incorporated Radio Manufacturers' Monthly." (Nov, 1929 - ?). - RADIO INDUSTRIES

"With which is incorporated 'The Lantern World.'" (Feb, 1897 - ?) - KINEMATOGRAPH WEEKLY

"Words and music." - RADIO HIT SONGS

"Working writer's newsletter, The." - SCRIPTWRITER NEWS

"Workshop publication for 16 mm film producers." - APERTURE, THE

"World Association for Christian Communication Newsletter." - ACTION

"World Association for Christian Communication. - MEDIA DEVELOPMENT

"World authority on consumer video, The." - VIDEO REVIEW

"World authority on home entertainment, The." - VIDEO REVIEW

"World authority on home video, The." - VIDEO REVIEW

"World Communication Association." - WCA NEWSLETTER

"World entertainment news daily." - HOLLYWOOD REPORTER

"World of after-dark entertainment, The." - STAGE

"World of animated films and comic art, The." - FUNNYWORLD

"World of location filming, The." - LOCATION UPDATE

"World of sound, The." - AUDIO

"World wide news of documentary and educational motion pictures." (Dec, 1940 - ?). - FILM & VIDEO NEWS

"World's biggest video publication." - VIDEO MAGAZINE

"World's first monster fan magazine, The." - FAMOUS MONSTERS OF FILMLAND

"World's first television journal, The." (Mar, 1928 - Jan, 1935). - ELECTRONIC ENGINEERING

"World's first television journal, The." - TELEVISION

"World's foremost amusement weekly, The." - BILLBOARD

"World's foremost source for television program information, The." - TELCO REPORT, THE

"World's headquarters for animated photography, The." - CINEMATOGRAPHY AND BIOSCOPE MAGAZINE

"World's largest circulation photography magazine, The." - POPULAR PHOTOGRAPHY

"World's largest electronic trade circulation." - ELECTRONIC TECHNICIAN/DEALER

"World's largest international audio-video trade association, The." - ITA NEWS DIGEST

"World's largest photo magazine." - POPULAR PHOTOGRAPHY

"World's largest-selling electronics magazine." (Jan, 1974 - Oct, 1982). - COMPUTERS & ELECTRONICS

"World's leading electronics magazine." (Aug, 1948 - Mar, 1957). - ELECTRONICS WORLD

"World's leading magazine for writers, The." - WRITER'S DIGEST

"World's leading newsweekly for commercial production, The." - BACK STAGE/SHOOT

"World's most complete home satellite TV listings." - SATELLITE ORBIT

"World's number one guide to buying hi-fi, The." - HI-FI CHOICE

"World's only real motion picture newspaper, The." - HOLLYWOOD FILMOGRAPH

"Worldwide coverage of television, film, video and cable." - MOVING PICTURES INTERNATIONAL

"Worldwide technology weekly, The." - ELECTRONICS

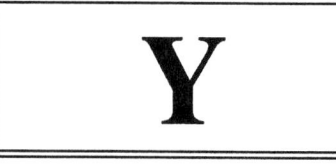

Y

"You stick to me, and I'll stick to you." - ADVERTISING OUTDOORS

"Your #1 NKOTB spot!" - SUPER TEEN

"Your complete guide to video." - VIDEO TIMES

"Your eye on the industry." - VIDEODISC MONITOR, THE

"Your guide to audio and video entertainment." - INTELLIGENT DECISIONS

"Your guide to creator-owned small press and independent comics." - COMICS FANDOM EXAMINER

"Your guide to the world of animation." - ANIMATOR

"Your journal of animation art and Disneyana collecting." - STORYBOARD / THE ART OF LAUGHTER

"Your monthly cable magazine." - ENTERTAINER, THE

"Your monthly guide to getting published." - WRITER'S DIGEST

"Your No. 1 guide to TV entertainment." - SATELLITE ORBIT

"Your shop-at-home source for 1000's of video subjects." - MOVIE MARKETPLACE

"Your watchdog of the news media." - AIM REPORT

Varies

This *VARIES* index provides a listing of all former titles, and their associated *ISSN* numbers as well as inclusive dates of publication when available. A title is listed here when direct lineage links together the *VARIES* title and the *MAIN TITLE*.

1

16 MM Film User - *Varied* Nov, 1946 - Oct, 1947 *under* AUDIO VISUAL

17th and 18th Century Theatre Research - *Varied* May, 1962 - Nov, 1962 *under* RESTORATION AND 18TH CENTURY THEATRE RESEARCH

3

35mm Photography (ISSN: 0265-7198) - *Varied* Aug, 1983 - Sep, 1986? *under* PHOTOGRAPHY

7

73 (ISSN: 0037-3036) - *Varied* Oct, 1960 - Jul, 1982 *under* 73 AMATEUR RADIO

73 Amateur Radio's Technical Journal (ISSN: 0745-080x) - *Varied* Aug, 1982 - Feb, 1985 *under* 73 AMATEUR RADIO

73 for Radio Amateurs (ISSN: 0883-234x) - *Varied* Mar, 1985 - Apr, 1986 *under* 73 AMATEUR RADIO

8

8 MM - *Varied* May, 1969 - Aug, 1970 *under* FILM MAKING

8 MM Movie-Maker - *Varied* Oct, 1957 - 1964? *under* EIGHT MM MOVIE MAKER AND CINE CAMERA

8mm Magazine - *Varied* 1962? - Apr?, 1969? *under* FILM MAKING

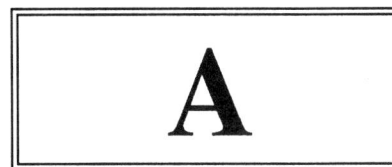

A

ABCA Bulletin, The (ISSN: 0001-0383) - *Varied* 1969 - Dec, 1984 *under* BULLETIN OF THE ASSOCIATION FOR BUSINESS COMMUNICATION, THE

ABCA Journal of Business Communication (ISSN: 0886-7216) - *Varied* Fall, 1969 - Summer, 1973 *under* JOURNAL OF BUSINESS COMMUNICATION, THE

Abels Photographic Weekly - *Varied* Dec 7, 1907 - Jan, 1934 *under* PROFESSIONAL PHOTOGRAPHER, THE

About Music & Writers - *Varied* ? - ? *under* BMI: MUSICWORLD

About Music and Writers (ISSN: 0740-8382) - *Varied* Oct, 1964 *under* BMI: MUSICWORLD

ABWA Bulletin - *Varied* May, 1937 - May, 1967 *under* BULLETIN OF THE ASSOCIATION FOR BUSINESS COMMUNICATION, THE

Academy of Motion Picture Arts and Sciences. Bulletin - *Varied* 1928 - 1946 *under* BULLETIN

Access Reports - *Varied* Jun 16, 1975 - 1981 *under* ACCESS REPORTS/FREEDOM OF INFORMATION

Actors by Gaslight - *Varied* Apr 21, 1838 - Dec 29, 1838 *under* ODDFELLOW, THE

Actor's Cues (ISSN: 7800-0081) - *Varied* Sep 30, 1941 - 1948 *under* SHOW BUSINESS

Ad Art Techniques - *Varied* Nov, 1968 - Aug, 1970 *under* ADVERTISING AND GRAPHIC ARTS TECHNIQUES

AD Assistant (ISSN: 0567-3607) - *Varied* Sep, 1965 - Oct, 1968 *under* ADVERTISING AND GRAPHIC ARTS TECHNIQUES

Ad Forum (ISSN: 0274-6328) - *Varied* Jun, 1980 - May?, 1985 *under* ADWEEK'S MARKETING WEEK

Ad-School, The - *Varied* Jan, 1901 - Mar, 1902 *under* COMMON SENSE

Ad Weekly - *Varied* Jun 6, 1969 - Oct 6, 1972 *under* ADWEEK

Advertiser, The - *Varied* Jul, 1933 *under* ADVERTISER MAGAZINE, THE

Advertiser's Gazette - *Varied* Dec, 1866 - Dec, 1870 *under* ADVERTISERS GAZETTE

Advertisers Magazine - *Varied* Oct, 1907 - Sep, 1910 *under* ADVERTISING ADVOCATE

Advertisers Weekly - *Varied* 1913 - May 30, 1969 *under* ADWEEK

Advertising (ISSN: 0141-8920) - *Varied* Summer, 1978 - Winter, 1979/1980 *under* ADVERTISING MAGAZINE

Advertising Abroad - *Varied* Dec, 1928 - Dec, 1929 *under* EXPORT ADVERTISER

Advertising Age [Electronic Media Edition] (ISSN: 0744-6675) - *Varied* May 3, 1982 - Jul ?, 1982 *under* ELECTRONIC MEDIA

Advertising Age and Mail Order Journal, The - *Varied* Apr, 1916 - Aug, 1921 *under* NATIONAL ADVERTISING

Advertising Age/Europe (ISSN: 0197-2359) - *Varied* Jan, 1979 - Dec, 1981 *under* FOCUS

Advertising Agency - *Varied* Oct 4, 1954 - Apr 4, 1955 *under* ADVERTISING AGENCY

Advertising Agency [Bristol, CT] - *Varied* Jan 3, 1958 - Aug 29, 1958 *under* ADVERTISING AGE

Advertising Agency and Advertising & Selling - *Varied* May, 1949 - Sep, 1954 *under* ADVERTISING AGENCY

Advertising Agency Magazine - *Varied* Apr 29, 1955 - Dec 20, 1957 *under* ADVERTISING AGENCY

Advertising Age's Focus (ISSN: 0264-1755) - *Varied* Jan, 1982 - Jan, 1985 *under* FOCUS

Advertising and Newspaper News (ISSN: 0001-8929) - *Varied* ? - ? *under* ADVERTISING NEWS

Advertising & Sales Promotion (ISSN: 0001-8937) - *Varied* May, 1961 - Dec, 24, 1973 *under* PROMOTION

Advertising & Selling - *Varied* May, 1926 - Aug, 1948 *under* ADVERTISING AGENCY

Advertising and Selling and the Advertising Agency - *Varied* Sep, 1948 - Apr, 1949 *under* ADVERTISING AGENCY

Advertising and Selling Fortnightly - *Varied* May 7, 1924 - Apr 21, 1926 *under* ADVERTISING AGENCY

Advertising & Selling Magazine - *Varied* Jan 15, 1921 - Aug 6, 1921 *under* ADVERTISING & SELLING

Advertising Management - *Varied* 1964 - Dec?, 1969 *under* ADVERTISING AND MARKETING MANAGEMENT

Advertising News and the Publishers' Guide, The - *Varied* Aug 18, 1916 - Aug 25, 1916 *under* ADVERTISING NEWS

Advertising Quarterly - *Varied* Autumn, 1964 - 1977 *under* ADVERTISING MAGAZINE

Advertising Requirements - *Varied* Feb, 1953 - Apr, 1961 *under* PROMOTION

Advertising Statistical Review (ISSN: 0065-3640) - *Varied* 1972 - 1975 *under* PRESS STATISTICAL REVIEW

Advertising Statistical Review of Press and Television Expenditures - *Varied* ? - 1972 *under* PRESS STATISTICAL REVIEW

Advertising Techniques (ISSN: 0001-0235) - *Varied* Sep, 1970 - Mar, 1983 *under* ADVERTISING AND GRAPHIC ARTS TECHNIQUES

Advertising World (ISSN: 0163-9412) - *Varied* 1974? - Jun, 1985 *under* INTERNATIONAL ADVERTISER

Adweek [National Marketing Edition] (ISSN: 0888-3718) - *Varied* Jul 1, 1985 - Sep 1, 1986 *under* ADWEEK'S MARKETING WEEK

Adweek/West - *Varied* Apr 12, 1982 *under* ADWEEK

AEG Progress - *Varied* ? - 1967 *under* AEG-TELEFUNKEN PROGRESS

AEJ Newsletter, The (ISSN: 0278-8179) - *Varied* 1968? - ? *under* AEJMC NEWS

AEJMC Newsletter, The - *Varied* 198u - Jul, 1983 *under* AEJMC NEWS

AERT Journal - *Varied* Oct, 1956 - May, 1957 *under* PUBLIC TELECOMMUNICATIONS REVIEW

AFFS Newsletter - *Varied* ? - ? *under* CRITIC

AFI Report - *Varied* Winter, 1973? - Summer, 1974 *under* AMERICAN FILM INSTITUTE. QUARTERLY.

AIGA Journal (ISSN: 0197-6907) - *Varied* 1947 - 1953 *under* AIGA JOURNAL OF GRAPHIC DESIGN

All About Television - *Varied* Summer, 1927 *under* TELEVISION

AM-FM Television - *Varied* Mar, 1954 - Apr, 1954 *under* RCA BROADCAST NEWS

Amateur Movie Maker - *Varied* ? - ? *under* EIGHT MM MOVIE MAKER AND CINE CAMERA

Amateur Movie Makers - *Varied* Dec, 1926 - May, 1928 *under* MOVIE MAKERS

Amateur Photographer & Cinematographer, The - *Varied* Aug 3, 1927 - Jun 13, 1945 *under* AMATEUR PHOTOGRAPHER

Amateur Photographer and Photography, The - *Varied* Jun 19, 1918 - Jul 27, 1927 *under* AMATEUR PHOTOGRAPHER

Amateur Radio - *Varied* Jan, 1977 - ? *under* CQ

Amateur Tape Recording - *Varied* 1959 - ? *under* HI-FI SOUND

Amateur Tape Recording & Hi-Fi - *Varied* Feb, 1961 - 1963 *under* HI-FI SOUND

Amateur Tape Recording, Video & Hi-Fi - *Varied* 1963? - Nov, 1967 *under* HI-FI SOUND

Amateur Wireless and Electrics - *Varied* No. 1 - 331 *under* AMATEUR WIRELESS AND RADIOVISION

American Federation of Film Societies. Newsletter - *Varied* Oct, 1956 - Jun, 1957 *under* CRITIC

American Film Institute Report (ISSN: 0044-7684) - *Varied* Jun, 1970? - Fall, 1973 *under* AMERICAN FILM INSTITUTE. QUARTERLY.

American Newspaper Reporter - *Varied* ? - ? *under* ADVERTISERS GAZETTE

American Newspaper Reporter and Advertiser's Gazette - *Varied* Jan, 1871 - ? *under* ADVERTISERS GAZETTE

American Newspapers and Printers Gazette - *Varied* ? - ? *under* WOODCOCK'S PRINTERS' AND LITHOGRAPHERS' WEEKLY GAZETTE AND NEWSPAPER REPORTER

American Photographer (ISSN: 0161-6854) - *Varied* Jun, 1978 - Dec, 1989 *under* AMERICAN PHOTO

American Printer and Lithographer (ISSN: 0192-9933) - *Varied* Jan, 1979 - Dec, 1981 *under* AMERICAN PRINTER

American Publishers' Circular and Literary Gazette - *Varied* Sep 1, 1855 - Oct 15, 1863 *under* AMERICAN LITERARY GAZETTE AND PUBLISHERS' CIRCULAR

American Society of Magazine Photographers Newsletter - *Varied* ? - ? *under* ASMP BULLETIN

American Society of Magazine Photographers. News (ISSN: 0361-9168) - *Varied* Aug, 1950 - Jan, 1952 *under* ASMP BULLETIN

Andy Warhol's Interview (ISSN: 0020-5109) - *Varied* 1972 - Feb, 1977 *under* INTERVIEW

Animation News - *Varied* Jan, 1987 - Jul, 1987 *under* ANIMATION MAGAZINE

Animation Newsletter - *Varied* Jan, 1978? - ?, 1983? *under* ANIMATOR

ANPA Newspaper Information Service Newsletter (ISSN: 0569-6712) - *Varied* ? - ? *under* ANPA PUBLIC AFFAIRS NEWSLETTER

Anti-Nazi News - *Varied* 1936 - Mar, 1937 *under* HOLLYWOOD NOW

Antiquarian Bookman - *Varied* Jan 3, 1948 - May 29, 1967 *under* AB BOOKMAN'S WEEKLY

Archiv der Elektrischen Ubertragung (ISSN: 0374-2393) - *Varied* Jul/Aug, 1947 - Dec, 1970 *under* AEU

Art Director & Studio News - *Varied* Jul, 1950 - Dec, 1955 *under* ART DIRECTION

Art Product News (ISSN: 0163-7460) - *Varied* Jan/Feb, 1979 - Nov/Dec, 1990 *under* ART & DESIGN NEWS

Artist & Advertiser, The - *Varied* Oct, 1930 - Jun, 1933 *under* ADVERTISER MAGAZINE, THE

ASCAP News (ISSN: 1043-3791) - *Varied* ? - 1967 *under* ASCAP IN ACTION

ASCAP Today (ISSN: 0001-2424) - *Varied* 1967 - Summer, 1979? *under* ASCAP IN ACTION

ASMP News - *Varied* ? - Jul, 1950 *under* ASMP BULLETIN

AT&T Bell Laboratories Technical Journal (ISSN: 0748-612x) - *Varied* Jan, 1984 - Dec, 1984 *under* AT&T TECHNICAL JOURNAL

Atlanta Art Workers Coalition Newspaper - *Varied* 1976? - Nov/Dec, 1980? *under* ART PAPERS

Atlas (ISSN: 0004-6930) - *Varied* Mar, 1961 - Apr, 1972 *under* WORLD PRESS REVIEW

Atlas World Press Review (ISSN: 0161-6528) - *Varied* May, 1974 - Feb, 1980 *under* WORLD PRESS REVIEW

Audio & Video News (ISSN: 0362-1162) - *Varied* Jan, 1973 - Dec, 1973 *under* AUDIO-VIDEO INTERNATIONAL

Audio Engineering (ISSN: 0275-3804) - *Varied* May, 1947 - Feb, 1954 *under* AUDIO

Audio-Visual Communication Review (ISSN: 0885-727x) - *Varied* Winter, 1953 - Nov/Dec, 1963 *under* EDUCATIONAL COMMUNICATION AND TECHNOLOGY

Audio Visual Communications (ISSN: 0004-7562) - *Varied* May, 1967 - Jun, 1989 *under* AVC

Audio Visual Directions (ISSN: 0746-8989) - *Varied* Nov/Dec, 1980 - Jan, 1984 *under* AV VIDEO

Audio-Visual Education - *Varied* Apr, 1957 - Jan/Mar, 1966 *under* NIE JOURNAL

Audio-Visual Media (ISSN: 0571-8716) - *Varied* Spring, 1967 - Mar, 1971 *under* EDUCATIONAL MEDIA INTERNATIONAL

Audio Visual Product News (ISSN: 0164-6834) - *Varied* Fall, 1978 - Sep/Oct, 1980 *under* AV VIDEO

Audiocraft - *Varied* Nov, 1955 - May, 1957 *under* AUDIOCRAFT FOR THE HI-FI HOBBYIST

AudioVideo (ISSN: 0093-6499) - *Varied* Jan, 1974 - Nov, 1974 *under* AUDIOVIDEO INTERNATIONAL

Audiovisual Instruction (ISSN: 0004-7635) - *Varied* Oct, 1956 - May, 1978 *under* TECHTRENDS

Audiovisual Instruction with/Instructional Resources (ISSN: 0191-3417) - *Varied* Sep, 1978 - Dec, 1979 *under* TECHTRENDS

Australian Film Guide - *Varied* Jun, 1966 - 1967 *under* FILM INDEX

Australian Media Notes - *Varied* Dec, 1975 *under* MEDIA INFORMATION AUSTRALIA

Author, The - *Varied* May 15, 1890 - Sep, 1926 *under* AUTHOR, THE

Author, Playwright and Composer - *Varied* Oct, 1926 - Winter, 1948 *under* AUTHOR, THE

AV Communication Review (ISSN: 0001-2890) - *Varied* Spring, 1964 - Winter, 1977 *under* EDUCATIONAL COMMUNICATION AND TECHNOLOGY

B

Back Stage Magazine Supplement/Business Screen - *Varied* Apr, 1979 - Jun, 1980 *under* COMPUTER PICTURES

Ballroom After Dark - *Varied* Apr, 1968 *under* AFTER DARK

Ballroom Dance Magazine - *Varied* Feb, 1960 - Mar, 1968 *under* AFTER DARK

BBC Empire Broadcasting - *Varied* ? - Sep 17, 1939 *under* BBC WORLD SERVICE LONDON CALLING

BBC Engineering Monographs (ISSN: 0005-2817) - *Varied* 1955? - 1969 *under* BBC ENGINEERING

BBC London Calling - *Varied* Apr, 1963 - Jun, 1981 *under* BBC WORLD SERVICE LONDON CALLING

Beacon - *Varied* 1889? - 1892? *under* PHOTO-BEACON, THE

Bell Laboratories Record (ISSN: 0005-8564) - *Varied* Sep, 1925 - May/Jun, 1983 *under* AT&T TECHNOLOGY

Bell System Technical Journal (ISSN: 0005-8580) - *Varied* Jul, 1922 - Dec, 1983 *under* AT&T TECHNICAL JOURNAL

Bell Telephone Company of Pennsylvania News, The - *Varied under* TELEPHONE NEWS, THE

Bell Telephone Magazine (ISSN: 0096-8692) - *Varied* Feb, 1941 - 1983? *under* AT&T MAGAZINE

Bell Telephone Quarterly (ISSN: 0270-5869) - *Varied* Apr, 1922 - Oct, 1940 *under* AT&T MAGAZINE

Bestseller Business - *Varied* Mar, 1972 - ? *under* MAGAZINE & BOOKSELLER

Bestsellers (ISSN: 0005-9730) - *Varied* Oct, 1960 - ? *under* MAGAZINE & BOOKSELLER

Better Broadcasts Newsletter (ISSN: 0409-283x) - *Varied* Oct, 1955 - ? *under* BETTER BROADCASTS NEWS

Better Listening Through High Fidelity - *Varied* ? - ? *under* BETTER LISTENING

Bill Poster, The - *Varied* Feb 22, 1896 - ? *under* ADVERTISING OUTDOORS

Bill Poster and Display Advertising, The - *Varied* ? - 1910 *under* ADVERTISING OUTDOORS

Billboard, The - *Varied* Apr, 1897 - Dec 26, 1960 *under* BILLBOARD

Billboard Advertising - *Varied* Nov, 1894 - Mar, 1897 *under* BILLBOARD

Billboard Music Week - *Varied* Jan 9, 1961 - Dec 22, 1962 *under* BILLBOARD

BKSTS Journal, The (ISSN: 0305-6996) - *Varied* Jan, 1974 - Jun, 1986 *under* IMAGE TECHNOLOGY

Black oracle (ISSN: 0045-2246) - *Varied* Mar, 1969 - Summer/Fall?, 1978 *under* CINEMACABRE

BM/E (ISSN: 0005-3201) - *Varied* Jan, 1965 - May, 1988 *under* BME'S TELEVISION ENGINEERING

BM/E's World Broadcast News - *Varied* Jan, 1978 - Jan, 1990 *under* WORLD BROADCAST NEWS

BME For Technical and Engineering Management (ISSN: 1043-7487) - *Varied* Jun, 1988 - Jan, 1990 *under* BME'S TELEVISION ENGINEERING

Book and Magazine Production (ISSN: 0273-8724) - *Varied* Nov/Dec, 1980 - May, 1982 *under* HIGH VOLUME PRINTING

Book Production Industry & Magazine Production (ISSN: 0192-2874) - *Varied* ? - Sep/Oct?, 1980 *under* HIGH VOLUME PRINTING

Book Research Quarterly (ISSN: 0741-6148) - *Varied* Spring, 1985 - Winter, 1990/1991 *under* PUBLISHING RESEARCH QUARTERLY

Boston Dramatic Review - *Varied* ? - Nov 25, 1899 *under* DRAMATIC REVIEW, THE

Brains - *Varied* Jan, 1905 - Aug 28, 1912 *under* RETAIL EQUIPMENT AND MERCHANDISE

British Institution of Radio Engineers. Journal - *Varied* 1939 - Dec, 1962 *under* ELECTRONICS & COMMUNICATIONS ENGINEERING JOURNAL

British Kinematography (ISSN: 0007-1358) - *Varied* 194u - Dec, 1965 *under* IMAGE TECHNOLOGY

British Kinematography, Sound and Television (ISSN: 0373-109x) - *Varied* Jan, 1966 - Dec, 1973 *under* IMAGE TECHNOLOGY

Broadcast Bibliophile Booknotes (ISSN: 0045-3188) - *Varied* Nov, 1969 - Aug, 1973 *under* COMMUNICATION BOOKNOTES

Broadcast Communications (ISSN: 0164-999x) - *Varied* ? - Sep, 1983 *under* TELEVISION BROADCAST

Broadcast Equipment Exchange (ISSN: 0194-2190) - *Varied* Jul, 1977 - Jun, 1980 *under* RADIO WORLD

Broadcast Equipment Today (ISSN: 0383-9338) - *Varied* Sep/Oct, 1975 - Dec, 1979 *under* BROADCAST + TECHNOLOGY

Broadcast Financial Journal (ISSN: 0161-9063) - *Varied* Mar, 1972 - ? *under* BROADCAST CABLE FINANCIAL JOURNAL

Broadcast News - *Varied* Oct, 1931 - Feb, 1954 *under* RCA BROADCAST NEWS

Broadcast News - *Varied* May, 1954 - Feb, 1968 *under* RCA BROADCAST NEWS

Broadcast Reporter - *Varied* Oct 17, 1932 - Jun, 1933 *under* BROADCAST REPORTER

Broadcast Sound (ISSN: 0263-5682) - *Varied* 198u - Feb, 1985 *under* BROADCAST SYSTEMS ENGINEERING

Broadcast Technology (ISSN: 0709-9797) - *Varied* Sep/Oct, 1979 - Sep, 1986 *under* BROADCAST + TECHNOLOGY

Broadcasters News Bulletin - *Varied* ? - Mar 4, 1933 *under* NARTB MEMBER SERVICE

Broadcasting - *Varied* Oct 15, 1931 - Feb 1, 1933 *under* BROADCASTING

Broadcasting, Broadcast Advertising - *Varied* Jul 1, 1936 - Nov 19, 1945 *under* BROADCASTING

Broadcasting, Combined With Broadcast Advertising - *Varied* Feb 15, 1933 - Jun 15, 1936 *under* BROADCASTING

Broadcasting Systems & Operations - *Varied* 1978 - Mar, 1980 *under* INTERNATIONAL BROADCASTING

Broadcasting, Telecasting - *Varied* Nov 26, 1945 - Oct 7, 1957 *under* BROADCASTING

Broadway Magazine - *Varied* Apr, 1898 - Nov, 1907 *under* HAMPTON MAGAZINE

Bulletin - *Varied* ? - Spring, 1979 *under* CSPAA BULLETIN

Bulletin - *Varied* 1945? - Dec?, 1957? *under* JOURNALISM EDUCATOR, THE

Bulletin. ASMP (ISSN: 0361-9168) - *Varied* ? - ? *under* ASMP BULLETIN

Bulletin d'Informations - *Varied* May, 1949 - Oct, 1965 *under* FIEJ-BULLETIN

Bulletin of ALPSP (ISSN: 0260-9428) - *Varied* 1977 - ? *under* LEARNED PUBLISHING

Bulletin of the Association of Departments & Administrators in Speech Communication - *Varied* Oct, 1972 - Apr, 1975 *under* ACA BULLETIN

Bulletin of the Columbia Scholastic Press Advisors Association - *Varied* Summer, 1979 - ? *under* CSPAA BULLETIN

Business and Home TV Screen - *Varied* Jan, 1978 - Feb, 1979 *under* COMPUTER PICTURES

Business Screen - *Varied* 1938 - Mar 1, 1946 *under* COMPUTER PICTURES

Business Screen - *Varied* October 1, 1968 - Nov, 1977 *under* COMPUTER PICTURES

Business Screen (ISSN: 0160-7294) - *Varied* Aug, 1980? - Dec?, 1982? *under* COMPUTER PICTURES

Business Screen Magazine - *Varied* Apr 23, 1946 - Aug 15, 1968 *under* COMPUTER PICTURES

Buyer's Guide for Comic Fandom, The - *Varied* 1971 - Feb 4, 1983 *under* COMICS BUYER'S GUIDE

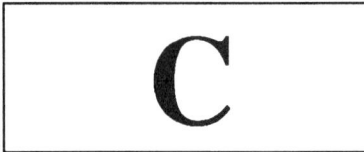

C

CA - *Varied* 1959 - 1966 *under* COMMUNICATION ARTS

CA Magazine (ISSN: 0884-0008) - *Varied* 1967 - 1969 *under* COMMUNICATION ARTS

Cable Communications (ISSN: 0824-8435) - *Varied* Jun/Jul, 1973 - Apr, 1979 *under* CABLE COMMUNICATIONS MAGAZINE

Cable Communications - *Varied* ? - ? *under* COMMUNICATIONS

Cable Strategies (ISSN: 1044-2820) - *Varied* Oct, 1987 - Aug?, 1989 *under* MSO'S CABLE MARKETING

Cable Television Business Magazine (ISSN: 0745-2808) - *Varied* Oct?, 1982 - Sep 15, 1989 *under* CABLE TV BUSINESS MAGAZINE

Cable Television Review - *Varied* Mar, 1965 - Aug, 1967 *under* VUE

Cablecasting and Educational Television (ISSN: 0574-9905) - *Varied* Sep, 1967 - Oct, 1968 *under* E-ITV

Camcorder Report (ISSN: 1047-8787) - *Varied* Apr, 1989 - Nov, 1989 *under* CAMCORDER

Camera - *Varied* Jul, 1897 - Feb, 1949 *under* CAMERA MAGAZINE

Camera 35 Photo World - *Varied* Aug, 1978 - Feb, 1979 *under* CAMERA 35 INCORPORATING PHOTO WORLD

Camera 35 With Photo World - *Varied* Jun, 1978 - Jul, 1978 *under* CAMERA 35 INCORPORATING PHOTO WORLD

Camera 35 With Photo World - *Varied* Mar, 1979 - Jun, 1979 *under* CAMERA 35 INCORPORATING PHOTO WORLD

Camera Owner - *Varied* 1963? - Jul, 1967 *under* CREATIVE CAMERA

Camera World - *Varied* Jun, 1955 - Apr, 1958 *under* 35MM PHOTOGRAPHY

Canadian Broadcaster, The (ISSN: 0319-1389) - *Varied* Jan, 1942 - Sep, 1969 *under* BROADCASTER

Canadian Cinematography (ISSN: 0576-4823) - *Varied* 1961 - May/Jun, 1967 *under* CINEMA/CANADA

Canadian Film and TV Bi-Weekly (ISSN: 0383-0233) - *Varied* May 26, 1965 - Dec 24, 1969 *under* CANADIAN FILM DIGEST

Canadian Film Weekly (ISSN: 0383-0225) - *Varied* 1936 - May 12, 1965 *under* CANADIAN FILM DIGEST

Canadian Film Weekly (ISSN: 0590-7918) - *Varied* Jan 14, 1970 - May 29, 1970 *under* CANADIAN FILM DIGEST

Canadian Printer & Publisher (ISSN: 0008-4816) - *Varied* ? - Aug, 1989 *under* CANADIAN PRINTER

Canadian Telephone and Cable Television Journal (ISSN: 0008-5162) - *Varied* Spring, 1966 - Apr/May, 1973 *under* CABLE COMMUNICATIONS MAGAZINE

Canadian Telephone Journal, The (ISSN: 0318-0050) - *Varied* May, 1934? - Dec, 1965 *under* CABLE COMMUNICATIONS MAGAZINE

Canyon Cinemanews (ISSN: 0008-5758) - *Varied* Jan, 1963 - Sep/Oct, 1976 *under* CINEMANEWS, THE

Captain George's Whizzbang - *Varied* Nov/Dec, 1968? - Vol 1, #6? *under* NEW CAPTAIN GEORGE'S WHIZZBANG, THE

Carleton Drama Review (ISSN: 0161-3936) - *Varied* 1955? - May?, 1957 *under* TDR

Catholic Film Newsletter (ISSN: 0008-8021) - *Varied* 1964 - Dec 30, 1975 *under* FILM & BROADCASTING REVIEW

Catholic Journalist Newsletter - *Varied* ? - ? *under* CATHOLIC JOURNALIST

CATV (ISSN: 0574-9204) - *Varied* Aug 14, 1967 - Oct 18, 1976 *under* VUE

CCJA Journalist - *Varied* Summer, 1983 *under* COMMUNITY COLLEGE JOURNALIST

Celebrity Focus (ISSN: 0896-8225) - *Varied* Jan, 1987 - Feb, 1988 *under* CELEBRITY PLUS

Central States Speech Journal (ISSN: 0008-9575) - *Varied* Nov, 1949 - 198u *under* COMMUNICATION STUDIES

CEPN - *Varied* Jan, 1975 - ? *under* CONSUMER ELECTRONICS PRODUCT NEWS

CETO News - *Varied* Oct?, 1963? - Jan, 1967? *under* MEDIA IN EDUCATION AND DEVELOPMENT

Channels of Communications (ISSN: 0276-1572) - *Varied* Apr/May, 1981 - Jul/Aug, 1986 *under* CHANNELS

Charles Austin Bates Criticisms - *Varied* Jan, 1897 - Mar, 1900 *under* CURRENT ADVERTISING

Christian Broadcaster (ISSN: 0577-9960) - *Varied* Oct, 1953 - Apr, 1968? *under* MEDIA DEVELOPMENT

Cinema - *Varied* Jul, 1921 - Nov, 1922 *under* SCREEN INTERNATIONAL

Cinema News and Property Gazette - *Varied* 1911 - Jul, 1921 *under* SCREEN INTERNATIONAL

Cinema News and Property Gazette, The - *Varied* May, 1923 - Feb, 1928 *under* SCREEN INTERNATIONAL

Cinema Quarterly - *Varied* Autumn, 1932 - Summer, 1935 *under* DOCUMENTARY FILM NEWS

Cinema TV Today - *Varied* Nov 13, 1971 - Aug, 1975 *under* SCREEN INTERNATIONAL

Cinemeditor (ISSN: 0069-4169) - *Varied* Winter, 1950 - Summer, 1971 *under* AMERICAN CINEMEDITOR

Class - *Varied* Jan, 1915 - Feb, 1927 *under* BUSINESS MARKETING

Class & Industrial Marketing - *Varied* Mar, 1927 - Jun, 1933 *under* BUSINESS MARKETING

Classic - *Varied* Sep, 1922 - Jan, 1924 *under* MOVIE CLASSIC

Classic Pictorial of Screen and Stage - *Varied* Feb, 1924 - Aug, 1924 *under* MOVIE CLASSIC

Clio Devoted to Commercials - *Varied* Oct, 1968 - ? *under* CLIO MAGAZINE

College Press Review (ISSN: 0010-1117) - *Varied* 1956 - Spring, 1983? *under* COLLEGE MEDIA REVIEW

College Public Relations - *Varied* Oct, 1947 - May/Jun, 1949 *under* COLLEGE & UNIVERSITY JOURNAL

College Public Relations Quarterly - *Varied* Oct, 1949 - Jul, 1956 *under* COLLEGE & UNIVERSITY JOURNAL

College Publicity Digest, The - *Varied* 1917 - Jul, 1942 *under* COLLEGE & UNIVERSITY JOURNAL

College Radio - *Varied* 1964 - 1969 *under* JOURNAL OF COLLEGE RADIO

Colorado Editor and the Intermountain Press - *Varied* ?, 1926 - Mar, 1942 *under* COLORADO EDITOR

Comic Relief Magazine (ISSN: 1042-1556) - *Varied* Jun, 1989 - ? *under* COMIC RELIEF

Comics Review - *Varied* 1983 - 1985 *under* COMICS REVUE

Comixscene - *Varied* Nov/Dec, 1972 - Sep/Oct, 1973 *under* PREVUE

Comm/Ent, A Journal of Communications and Entertainment Law - *Varied* Fall, 1977 - Summer, 1983 *under* HASTINGS COMMUNICATIONS AND ENTERTAINMENT LAW JOURNAL

Comm/Ent, Hastings Journal of Communications and Entertainment Law - *Varied* Fall, 1983 - Summer, 1988 *under* HASTINGS COMMUNICATIONS AND ENTERTAINMENT LAW JOURNAL

Commercial Camera Magazine - *Varied* Oct/Nov, 1947 - Aug, 1953? *under* COMMERCIAL CAMERA

Commercials Monthly (ISSN: 0194-5114) - *Varied* 1977 - 1982 *under* ENTERTAINMENT MONTHLY

Commonwealth Broadcasting Conference - *Varied* Jan, 1967 - Apr/Jun, 1974 *under* COMBROAD

Communication (ISSN: 0882-4088) - *Varied* Jul, 1972 - Sep, 1984 *under* WORLD COMMUNICATION

Communication: Journalism Education Today (ISSN: 0010-3535) - *Varied* 1967 - Summer?, 1977 *under* C: JET

Communication Reports - *Varied* Dec, 1984 *under* WORLD COMMUNICATION

Communications (ISSN: 0161-374x) - *Varied* Sep, 1937 - Dec, 1949 *under* TELEVISION ENGINEERING

Communications and Electronics - *Varied* Oct, 1954 - Apr, 1955 *under* BRITISH COMMUNICATIONS AND ELECTRONICS

Communications/Engineering Digest (ISSN: 1046-574x) - *Varied* Oct, 1975 - ? *under* COMMUNICATIONS ENGINEERING & DESIGN

Community College Journalist - *Varied* Fall, 1974 - Summer, 1981 *under* COMMUNITY COLLEGE JOURNALIST

Community Theatre Bulletin (ISSN: 0414-1520) - *Varied* Mar, 1955? - Sep, 1960 *under* THEATRE JOURNAL

Community Video Report - *Varied* Summer, 1973 - Autumn, 1974 *under* TELEVISIONS

Computers and Programming (ISSN: 0279-070x) - *Varied* Jul/Aug, 1981 - ? *under* COMMUNICATIONS WORLD

Consumer Electronics Monthly - *Varied* ? - ? *under* CONSUMER ELECTRONICS

COSMEP Newsletter (ISSN: 0007-8832) - *Varied* Aug, 1969 - May, 1980 *under* COSMEP NEWSLETTER

CPB Memo - *Varied* 1970? - Aug 23, 1974 *under* REPORT

CPB Report - *Varied* ? - May 10, 1982 *under* REPORT

Creative Camera Owner - *Varied* Aug, 1967 - Jan, 1968 *under* CREATIVE CAMERA

CSCC Newsletter - *Varied* ? - ? *under* COMMUNICATION RESEARCH TRENDS

Curtain - *Varied* Oct, 1969 - ? *under* DRAMATICS

D

DA (ISSN: 0011-4693) - *Varied* Jan, 1943? - #3, 1977 *under* PRINTING PAPER

Darkroom Photography (ISSN: 0163-9250) - *Varied* ? - Nov, 1990 *under* CAMERA & DARKROOM PHOTOGRAPHY

Darkroom Techniques (ISSN: 0195-3850) - *Varied* Fall, 1979 - Nov/Dec, 1983 *under* DARKROOM AND CREATIVE CAMERA TECHNIQUES

Daytimers (ISSN: 0744-3935) - *Varied* 198u - 198u *under* REAL LIFE/DAYTIMERS

Design & Art Direction - *Varied* ? - Jan 17, 1986 *under* DIRECTION

Digest of the University Film Association - *Varied* ? - Sep, 1981 *under* DIGEST OF THE UNIVERSITY FILM AND VIDEO ASSOCIATION

Digital Audio & Compact Disc Review (ISSN: 0743-619x) - *Varied* Sep, 1984 - ? *under* CD REVIEW

Digital Audio's CD Review (ISSN: 1041-8342) - *Varied* ? - ? *under* CD REVIEW

Direct Advertising (ISSN: 0740-9265) - *Varied* Spring, 1935 - Jan, 1943 *under* PRINTING PAPER

Direct Advertising and Sample Book of Mill Brand Papers (ISSN: 0740-9249) - *Varied* 1911 - Winter, 1934 *under* PRINTING PAPER

Documentary News Letter - *Varied* Jan, 1940 - Nov/Dec, 1947 *under* DOCUMENTARY FILM NEWS

Documentation and Information Bulletin of the International Broadcasting Organization - *Varied* Feb, 1960? - ? *under* RADIO AND TELEVISION

Documentation List - *Varied* Jan, 1972 - Jul/Oct, 1973 *under* MEDIA ASIA

Drama - *Varied* Jul, 1919 - Jul/Sep, 1939 *under* DRAMA

Drama Review, The (ISSN: 0012-5962) - *Varied* Spring, 1968 - Winter, 1987 *under* TDR

Drama, The [Chicago] - *Varied* Feb, 1911 - May, 1930 *under* DRAMA MAGAZINE, THE

Dramatic Mirror - *Varied* Feb 8, 1919 - Oct 9, 1920 *under* DRAMATIC MIRROR, THE

Dramatic Mirror and Theatre World - *Varied* Oct 16, 1920 - Dec 24, 1921 *under* DRAMATIC MIRROR, THE

Dramatic Mirror of the Stage and Motion Pictures - *Varied* Feb 17, 1917 - Feb 1, 1919 *under* DRAMATIC MIRROR, THE

Dramatics - *Varied* Oct, 1944 - May, 1948 *under* DRAMATICS

Dramatics' Curtain - *Varied* Feb, 1981 - Sep?, 1981 *under* DRAMATICS

E

Ear - *Varied* ? - ? *under* SOUND MANAGEMENT

EBU Bulletin - *Varied* 1954 - 1957 *under* EBU REVIEW. TECHNICAL.

EBU Documentation and Information Bulletin - *Varied* 1950 - 1953 *under* EBU REVIEW. TECHNICAL.

EBU Review. Part A: Technical (ISSN: 0423-9865) - *Varied* Jan, 1958 - Dec, 1971 *under* EBU REVIEW. TECHNICAL.

EBU Review. Part B: General and Legal (ISSN: 0012-7493) - *Varied* Feb, 1958 - Nov, 1971 *under* EBU REVIEW. PROGRAMMES, ADMINISTRATION, LAW.

EBU Review. Radio and Television Programmes, Administration, Law - *Varied* Jan, 1972 - 1982 *under* EBU REVIEW. PROGRAMMES, ADMINISTRATION, LAW.

Editor and Publisher - *Varied* Jun 29, 1901 - Jun 3, 1911 *under* EDITOR AND PUBLISHER

Editor and Publisher and Journalist - *Varied* Jun 10, 1911 - Apr 15, 1916 *under* EDITOR AND PUBLISHER

Editorial Research Reports (ISSN: 0013-0958) - *Varied* Jan, 1924 - Dec 26, 1986 *under* CONGRESSIONAL QUARTERLY'S EDITORIAL RESEARCH REPORTS

Educational & Industrial Television (ISSN: 0046-1466) - *Varied* 1972 - May, 1983 *under* E-ITV

Educational Broadcasting International (ISSN: 0013-1970) - *Varied* Mar, 1971 - Sep, 1981 *under* MEDIA IN EDUCATION AND DEVELOPMENT

Educational Broadcasting Review (ISSN: 0013-1660) - *Varied* Oct, 1967 - Jun, 1973 *under* PUBLIC TELECOMMUNICATIONS REVIEW

Educational-Instructional Broadcasting (ISSN: 0013-1776) - *Varied* 1968 - May, 1971 *under* EDUCATIONAL BROADCASTING

Educational Screen and Audio-Visual Guide - *Varied* Sep, 1956 - Nov, 1971 *under* AV GUIDE

Educational Television (ISSN: 0424-6101) - *Varied* Nov, 1968 - 1971 *under* E-ITV

Educational Television International - *Varied* Mar, 1967 - Dec, 1970 *under* MEDIA IN EDUCATION AND DEVELOPMENT

Educational Theatre Journal (ISSN: 0013-1989) - *Varied* Oct, 1949 - Dec, 1978 *under* THEATRE JOURNAL

Educators Guide to Media & Methods (ISSN: 0013-2063) - *Varied* Nov, 1967 - May, 1969 *under* MEDIA & METHODS

Electrical Engineering (ISSN: 0095-9197) - *Varied* Jan, 1931 - Dec, 1963 *under* IEEE SPECTRUM

Electrical Engineering and Telephone Magazine - *Varied* Aug, 1898 - Dec, 1899 *under* TELEPHONE MAGAZINE

Electrical Engingeering - *Varied* Jun, 1893 - Jul, 1898 *under* TELEPHONE MAGAZINE

Electrical Review International - *Varied* ? - ? *under* ELECTRICAL REVIEW

Electrical Worker, The - *Varied* 1902? - Jul, 1914 *under* IBEW JOURNAL

Electrical Worker, The - *Varied* May, 1901? - Jul, 1914 *under* JOURNAL

Electrical Workers' Journal, The - *Varied* Jan?, 1948 - Dec, 1971 *under* IBEW JOURNAL

Electrical Workers' Journal, The - *Varied* ?, 1893 - Apr, 1901 *under* JOURNAL

Electrical Workers' Journal, The - *Varied* 1948 - Dec, 1971 *under* JOURNAL

Electronic & Radio Engineer - *Varied* Jan, 1957 - Dec, 1959 *under* INDUSTRIAL ELECTRONICS

Electronic, Electro-Optic and Infrared Countermeasures (ISSN: 0148-6373) - *Varied* ? - Apr?, 1977 *under* MILITARY ELECTRONICS / COUNTERMEASURES

Electronic Products (ISSN: 0738-2553) - *Varied* Sep, 1962 - May, 1970 *under* ELECTRONIC PRODUCTS

Electronic Products Magazine - *Varied* Jun, 1970? - Feb?, 1981 *under* ELECTRONIC PRODUCTS

Electronic Products Magazine & Clip File - *Varied* 1958? - ?, 1962 *under* ELECTRONIC PRODUCTS

Electronic Publishing & Printing (ISSN: 1044-0852) - *Varied* Jan/Feb, 1986 - Aug/Sep, 1990 *under* COMPUTER PUBLISHING

Electronic Servicing (ISSN: 0013-497x) - *Varied* ? - ? *under* ELECTRONIC SERVICING & TECHNOLOGY

Electronic Technican (ISSN: 0013-4988) - *Varied* Nov, 1956 - Dec, 1967 *under* ELECTRONIC TECHNICAN/DEALER

Electronic Technology - *Varied* Jan, 1960 - Sep, 1962 *under* INDUSTRIAL ELECTRONICS

Electronics (ISSN: 0013-5070) - *Varied* Apr, 1930 - Jul 12, 1984 *under* ELECTRONICS

Electronics and Television & Short-Wave World - *Varied* Oct, 1939 - May, 1941 *under* ELECTRONIC ENGINEERING

Electronics & Wireless World (ISSN: 0266-3244) - *Varied* Oct, 1983 - Sep, 1989 *under* ELECTRONICS WORLD + WIRELESS WORLD

Electronics Week (ISSN: 0748-3252) - *Varied* Jul 23, 1984 - Jun 10, 1985 *under* ELECTRONICS

Elementary Electronics (ISSN: 0013-595x) - *Varied* 196u - Jan/Feb, 1981 *under* COMMUNICATIONS WORLD

Exhibitor's Herald and Moving Picture World - *Varied* Jan 7, 1928 - Dec 29, 1928 *under* EXHIBITORS HERALD WORLD

Experimental Wireless - *Varied* Oct, 1923 - Aug, 1924 *under* INDUSTRIAL ELECTRONICS

Experimental Wireless & the Wireless Engineer - *Varied* Sep, 1924 - Aug, 1931 *under* INDUSTRIAL ELECTRONICS

F

Falling for Stars News - *Varied* 1965 - May/Jun, 1974 *under* FALLING FOR STARS

Fantasy Illustrated - *Varied* ? - ? *under* FANFARE

Far East Film News - *Varied* Jun, 1953 - May, 1959 *under* MOVIE/TV MARKETING

Far East Film News - *Varied* Jul, 1959 - Dec, 1961 *under* MOVIE/TV MARKETING

Far East Film News and TViews - *Varied* May, 1953 *under* MOVIE/TV MARKETING

Federal Communications Bar Journal (ISSN: 0014-9055) - *Varied* Mar, 1937 - 1976 *under* FEDERAL COMMUNICATIONS LAW JOURNAL

Fifth Mode, The - *Varied* 198u - 1988? *under* SCSC XEROX PIPELINE

Film - *Varied* Spring, 1933 *under* FILM ART

Film - *Varied* Nov, 1961 - Feb, 1962 *under* FILM BULLETIN

Film and Audio-Visual Annual [NF] - *Varied* May, 1962 - ? *under* AVC

Film and Audio-Visual Communications - *Varied* Feb, 1967 *under* AVC

Film and Radio Discussion Guide - *Varied* Oct, 1942 - Jun, 1945 *under* AUDIO-VISUAL GUIDE

Film & Radio Guide - *Varied* Oct, 1945 - Jun, 1947 *under* AUDIO-VISUAL GUIDE

Film and Television Daily - *Varied* Mar 18, 1968 - Nov 14, 1969 *under* FILM TV DAILY

Film/AV News (ISSN: 0737-2582) - *Varied* Apr, 1958 - Sep 1, 1958 *under* FILM & VIDEO NEWS

Film Daily, The - *Varied* Jan 1, 1922 - Mar 17, 1968 *under* FILM TV DAILY

Film Library Quarterly (ISSN: 0015-1327) - *Varied* Winter, 1967/1968 - Fall, 1971 *under* FILM LIBRARY QUARTERLY

Film News (ISSN: 0015-1343) - *Varied* May, 1940 - Winter, 1957/1958 *under* FILM & VIDEO NEWS

Film News (ISSN: 0195-1017) - *Varied* Oct, 1960 - Fall, 1981 *under* FILM & VIDEO NEWS

Film News - *Varied* ? - ? *under* NATIONAL EXHIBITOR, THE

Film Review Now - *Varied* Jun, 1990 - Jul, 1990 *under* FILM REVIEW

Film Society Newsletter - *Varied* 1963 - Apr, 1965 *under* CRITIC

Film Society Review (ISSN: 0015-1408) - *Varied* Sep, 1965 - Mar/May, 1972 *under* CRITIC

Film Spectator, The - *Varied* Mar, 1926 - Jun 13, 1931 *under* HOLLYWOOD SPECTATOR

Film Study - *Varied* ? - Feb, 1955? *under* CINEMAGES

Film Teacher - *Varied* Summer, 1952 - ? *under* SCREEN

Film User (ISSN: 0015-1459) - *Varied* Nov, 1947 - Nov, 1971 *under* AUDIO VISUAL

Film World - *Varied* Feb, 1945 - Sep, 1951 *under* FILM WORLD AND A-V NEWS MAGAZINE

Film World (ISSN: 0015-1475) - *Varied* 1964 - Jul, 1975? *under* FILMWORLD

Film World and A-V World News Magazine - *Varied* Oct, 1951 - May, 1960 *under* FILM WORLD AND A-V NEWS MAGAZINE

Filmmakers (ISSN: 0194-4339) - *Varied* Oct, 1978 *under* FILMMAKERS FILM & VIDEO MONTHLY

Filmmakers (ISSN: 0194-4339) - *Varied* Feb, 1980 - ?, 1982 *under* FILMMAKERS FILM & VIDEO MONTHLY

Filmmakers Monthly - *Varied* Nov, 1978 - Jan, 1980 *under* FILMMAKERS FILM & VIDEO MONTHLY

Filmmakers Newsletter (ISSN: 0015-1610) - *Varied* Apr, 1968 - Sep, 1978 *under* FILMMAKERS FILM & VIDEO MONTHLY

Filmograph - *Varied* May?, 1923 - 1929 *under* HOLLYWOOD FILMOGRAPH

Films & Filming Incorporating Focus on Film - *Varied* ? - ? *under* FILMS AND FILMING

Films by Wid - *Varied* Apr 27, 1916 *under* FILM TV DAILY

Finland Filmland (ISSN: 0355-1539) - *Varied* 1978 - ? *under* FINNISH FILMS

First Stage (ISSN: 0885-047x) - *Varied* Winter, 1961/1962 - Winter, 1967/1968 *under* DRAMA & THEATRE

Florida Newspaper News - *Varied* 192u - Oct, 1947 *under* COMMUNIQUE

Florida Newspaper News and Radio Digest - *Varied* Nov, 1947 - Dec, 1969 *under* COMMUNIQUE

FLQ (ISSN: 0160-7316) - *Varied* Winter, 1971/1972 - ? *under* FILM LIBRARY QUARTERLY

FM - *Varied* Nov, 1940 - Feb, 1942 *under* COMMUNICATION ENGINEERING

FM and Television - *Varied* Apr, 1944 - Oct, 1948 *under* COMMUNICATION ENGINEERING

FM Electronic Equipment Engineering & Design Practise - *Varied* Mar, 1942 - Apr, 1942 *under* COMMUNICATION ENGINEERING

FM Radio-Electronic Engineering and Design - *Varied* May, 1942 - Feb, 1943 *under* COMMUNICATION ENGINEERING

FM Radio Electronics - *Varied* Mar, 1943 - Mar, 1944 *under* COMMUNICATION ENGINEERING

FM-TV - *Varied* Nov, 1948 - Jan, 1950 *under* COMMUNICATION ENGINEERING

FM-TV - *Varied* 1952 *under* COMMUNICATION ENGINEERING

FM-TV Radio Communication - *Varied* 1950 - 1951 *under* COMMUNICATION ENGINEERING

Focus: Chicago (ISSN: 0362-0905) - *Varied* Feb, 1967 - Spring/Summer, 1973 *under* FACETS FEATURES

For Film - *Varied* ? - Winter, 1962? *under* CRITIC

Frame By Frame - *Varied* Dec, 1982 - ? *under* PENCIL TEST

Freedom of Information News Digest - *Varied* May 25, 1954 - Apr, 1959 *under* FOI DIGEST

G

General Electric Company Review - *Varied* Mar 2, 1903 - Apr, 1907 *under* GENERAL ELECTRIC REVIEW

General Radio Experimenter, The (ISSN: 0095-9499) - *Varied* Jun, 1926 - Oct/Dec, 1970 *under* GR TODAY

Geo. P. Rowell & Co's Advertising Agency Circular - *Varied* Nov, 1866, *under* ADVERTISERS GAZETTE

Get Animated - *Varied* Feb, 1985 - ?, 1986 *under* GET ANIMATED! UPDATE.

Glenn Hauser's Independent Publication - *Varied* Mar, 1977? - ? *under* REVIEW OF INTERNATIONAL BROADCASTING

Global Movie Marketing - *Varied* Jan, 1962 *under* MOVIE/TV MARKETING

Gramophone (ISSN: 0017-310x) - *Varied* Apr, 1923 - ? *under* GRAMOPHONE

Gramophone Including Compact Disc News and Reviews - *Varied* ? - ? *under* GRAMOPHONE

Graphic Arts for Printers and Users of Printing - *Varied* Jan, 1911 - Apr, 1911 *under* GRAPHIC ARTS, THE

Graphic Arts Monthly and the Printing Industry (ISSN: 0017-3312) - *Varied* Jan, 1938 - Oct, 1987 *under* GRAPHIC ARTS MONTHLY

Graphic Arts Review - *Varied* Jan, 1938 - ? *under* MID-ATLANTIC GRAPHIC ARTS REVIEW

Graphic Arts Unionist (ISSN: 0017-3363) - *Varied* Nov, 1964 - Nov/Dec, 1977 *under* GRAPHIC COMMUNICATOR

Graphic Story Magazine - *Varied* 1964? - 1974 *under* FANFARE

Graphics Design, USA (ISSN: 0274-7499) - *Varied* May, 1980 - Jun, 1983 *under* GRAPHIC DESIGN: USA

Grassroots (ISSN: 0046-3541) - *Varied* ? - ? *under* GRASSROOTS EDITOR

Great TV Entertainment - *Varied* 1980 - 1982 *under* CABLE GUIDE, THE

Greater Amusements and International Projectionist - *Varied* Jul, 1965 - Dec, 1967 *under* GREATER AMUSEMENTS

Grossbild-Technik - *Varied* 1955 - 1959 *under* PHOTO TECHNIQUE INTERNATIONAL

Group Discussion Guide - *Varied* Feb, 1936 - Jun, 1942 *under* AUDIO-VISUAL GUIDE

H

Hampton-Columbian Magazine - *Varied* Oct, 1911 - Jan, 1912 *under* HAMPTON MAGAZINE

Hampton's Broadway Magazine - *Varied* Oct, 1908 - Jan, 1909 *under* HAMPTON MAGAZINE

Hampton's Magazine - *Varied* Feb, 1909 - Sep, 1911 *under* HAMPTON MAGAZINE

Hands-On Electronics (ISSN: 0743-2968) - *Varied* Summer, 1984 - Jan, 1989 *under* POPULAR ELECTRONICS

HDTV World Review (ISSN: 1044-9507) - *Varied* Winter, 1990 - ? *under* HD SYSTEMS WORLD REVIEW

Hi Fi & Music Review - *Varied* Feb, 1958 - Nov, 1958 *under* STEREO REVIEW

Hi-Fi News incorporating Record Review - *Varied* Oct, 1970 - Dec, 1970 *under* HI-FI NEWS AND RECORD REVIEW

Hi Fi Review - *Varied* Dec, 1958 - Jan, 1960 *under* STEREO REVIEW

Hi Fi/Stereo Review - *Varied* Feb, 1960 - Oct, 1968 *under* STEREO REVIEW

Hi-Fi Tape Recording - *Varied* Dec, 1956 - Mar, 1960 *under* TAPE RECORDING

High Fidelity & Audiocraft - *Varied* Dec, 1958 - Mar, 1959 *under* HIGH FIDELITY

High Fidelity Trade News (ISSN: 0046-7367) - *Varied* 1957 - Jun?, 1983 *under* PERSONAL ELECTRONICS

High School Thespian - *Varied* Oct, 1929 - May, 1944 *under* DRAMATICS

Highlights - *Varied* Jan, 1975 - ? *under* NAB HIGHLIGHTS

Holly Leaves - *Varied* 1913 - 1924 *under* HOLLYWOOD

Hollywood (ISSN: 0199-7866) - *Varied* Jul, 1980 - Jan, 1983 *under* SCREEN ACTOR HOLLYWOOD

Hollywood Close Up (ISSN: 0199-7866) - *Varied* Mar, 1980 - May/Jun?, 1980 *under* SCREEN ACTOR HOLLYWOOD

Hollywood Magazine - *Varied* 1925 - Jun, 1928 *under* HOLLYWOOD

Hollywood Movie Novels - *Varied* Jun, 1933 - Aug, 1933 *under* HOLLYWOOD

Hollywood Quarterly - *Varied* Oct, 1945 - Summer, 1951 *under* FILM QUARTERLY

Hollywood Screen Life - *Varied* Feb, 1939 - Feb, 1940 *under* HOLLYWOOD

Hollywood Spectator - *Varied* Jun, 1931 - Mar, 1932 *under* HOLLYWOOD SPECTATOR

Hollywood Star and the Hollywood Spectator - *Varied* Apr, 1932 *under* HOLLYWOOD SPECTATOR

Home Entertainment Quarterly (ISSN: 0746-2719) - *Varied* ? - ? *under* HOME ENTERTAINMENT

Home Movies Magazine - *Varied* 1934 - 1936 *under* HOME MOVIES

I

IABC Journal (ISSN: 0092-7384) - *Varied* Spring, 1973 - Winter, 1974 *under* JOURNAL OF COMMUNICATION MANAGEMENT

IABC News (ISSN: 0744-7612) - *Varied* Winter?, 1971/1972 - May?, 1982 *under* COMMUNICATION WORLD

IAM - *Varied* May, 1964 - Fall, 1975 *under* AM

IBI Newsletter - *Varied* ? - ? *under* INTERMEDIA

IBS Bulletin - *Varied* 1941 - 1955 *under* JOURNAL OF COLLEGE RADIO

IBS Newsletter - *Varied* 1955 - 1964 *under* JOURNAL OF COLLEGE RADIO

IEEE Transactions on Broadcast and Television Receivers (ISSN: 0018-9308) - *Varied* May, 1963 - Nov, 1974 *under* IEEE TRANSACTIONS ON CONSUMER ELECTRONICS

IEEE Transactions on Communication Technology (ISSN: 0018-9332) - *Varied* Sep, 1964 - Dec, 1971 *under* IEEE TRANSACTIONS ON COMMUNICATIONS

IEEE Transactions on Communications Systems (ISSN: 0096-1965) - *Varied* 1963 - Jun, 1964 *under* IEEE TRANSACTIONS ON COMMUNICATIONS

Implet - *Varied* Jan 20, 1912 - Jun 8, 1912 *under* UNIVERSAL WEEKLY

In-Plant Offset Printer - *Varied* Feb, 1961 - ? *under* IN-PLANT PRINTER & ELECTRONIC PUBLISHER

In-Plant Printer (ISSN: 0019-3232) - *Varied* ? - Aug, 1986 *under* IN-PLANT PRINTER & ELECTRONIC PUBLISHER

In-Plant Reproductions (ISSN: 0198-9065) - *Varied* Dec, 1979 - 198u *under* IN-PLANT REPRODUCTIONS

In-Plant Reproductions & Electronic Publishing (ISSN: 0886-3121) - *Varied* 198u - ? *under* IN-PLANT REPRODUCTIONS

Incorporation and Bylaws - *Varied* Jul, 1916 *under* SMPTE JOURNAL

Independent Broadcasting (ISSN: 0305-6104) - *Varied* Aug, 1974 - Nov, 1984 *under* AIRWAVES

Independent Film Journal (ISSN: 0019-3712) - *Varied* 1937 - Nov, 1979 *under* FILM JOURNAL, THE

Independent Publisher, The - *Varied* Jun, 1980 - Feb, 1981 *under* COSMEP NEWSLETTER

Index - *Varied* Spring, 1972 - ? *under* INDEX ON CENSORSHIP

Indian Listener - *Varied* ? - ? *under* AKASHVANI

Industrial and Commercial Photographer - *Varied* May, 1961 - Feb, 1980 *under* PROFESSIONAL PHOTOGRAPHER, THE

Industrial Film and Audio-Visual Annual [NF] - *Varied* May, 1961 *under* AVC

Industrial Marketing (ISSN: 0019-8498) - *Varied* Jun, 1935 - Mar, 1983 *under* BUSINESS MARKETING

Infinity (ISSN: 0019-9583) - *Varied* Feb, 1952 - Mar, 1973 *under* ASMP BULLETIN

Inkline Journal - *Varied* Jan/Feb, 1980? - Nov/Dec, 1986? *under* WRITERS' JOURNAL

Inland and American Printer and Lithographer, The (ISSN: 0096-2562) - *Varied* Nov, 1958 - Jul, 1961 *under* AMERICAN PRINTER

Inland Printer, American Lithographer (ISSN: 0020-1502) - *Varied* Aug, 1961 - Dec, 1978 *under* AMERICAN PRINTER

Inside Print (ISSN: 0886-9928) - *Varied* Jan, 1986 - Jul, 1989 *under* INSIDE MEDIA

Instructional Innovator (ISSN: 0196-6979) - *Varied* Jan, 1980 - Jan, 1985 *under* TECHTRENDS

Instructional Materials - *Varied* Feb, 1956 - Jun, 1956 *under* TECHTRENDS

Inter/View - *Varied* 1969 - Nov, 1972 *under* INTERVIEW

Interim Drama - *Varied* Nov, 1945 - Spring?, 1946 *under* DRAMA

International Journal of Communication Research (ISSN: 0340-0158) - *Varied* 1974 - ? *under* COMMUNICATIONS

International Journal of Instructional Media (ISSN: 0092-1815) - *Varied* Fall, 1973 - Summer, 1983/84// *under* INTERNATIONAL JOURNAL OF INSTRUCTIONAL MEDIA AND TECHNOLOGY

International Marketing Report (ISSN: 0193-9661) - *Varied* Jul, 1976 - Jun, 1980 *under* INTERNATIONAL ADVERTISER

International Marketing Report (ISSN: 0198-6228) - *Varied* ? - ? *under* INTERNATIONAL ADVERTISER, THE

International Photo Technik (ISSN: 0020-8280) - *Varied* 1960 - May, 1983 *under* PHOTO TECHNIQUE INTERNATIONAL

International Photo Technique - *Varied* Aug, 1983 - Nov, 1983 *under* PHOTO TECHNIQUE INTERNATIONAL

International Television (ISSN: 0737-3929) - *Varied* Jun, 1983 - Jul, 1986 *under* CORPORATE TELEVISION

Iowa Journalist, The - *Varied* Jan, 1925 - Dec, 1928 *under* IOWA JOURNALIST

Iowa Publisher, The - *Varied* Apr?, 1960 - Oct, 1967 *under* IOWA JOURNALIST

Iowa Publisher and the Bulletin of the Iowa Press Association, The - *Varied* Jan, 1929 - Mar, 1960 *under* IOWA JOURNALIST

IRE Transactions on Broadcast and Television Receivers (ISSN: 0096-1655) - *Varied* Jan, 1955 - Nov, 1962 *under* IEEE TRANSACTIONS ON CONSUMER ELECTRONICS

IRE Transactions on Broadcast Transmission Systems (ISSN: 0099-6866) - *Varied* Mar, 1955 - Dec, 1958 *under* IEEE TRANSACTIONS ON BROADCASTING

IRE Transactions on Broadcasting (ISSN: 0096-1663) - *Varied* Feb, 1959 - Mar, 1962 *under* IEEE TRANSACTIONS ON BROADCASTING

IRE Transactions on Communications Systems (ISSN: 0096-2244) - *Varied* ? - ? *under* IEEE TRANSACTIONS ON COMMUNICATIONS

IRE Transactions on Information Theory (ISSN: 0096-1000) - *Varied* 1955 - 1962 *under* IEEE TRANSACTIONS ON INFORMATION THEORY

IREE Monitor - *Varied* Oct, 1979 - Jun, 1980 *under* MONITOR

ITA Newsletter - *Varied* ? - ? *under* ITA NEWS DIGEST

ITC Desktop (ISSN: 1042-3923) - *Varied* Mar/Apr, 1989 - Mar/Apr, 1990? *under* DESKTOP COMMUNICATIONS

J

Jason Rogers' Advertisers' Weekly - *Varied* Jan 3, 1925 - Sep 26, 1925 *under* ADVERTISERS' WEEKLY

JEE (ISSN: 0021-3608) - *Varied* ?, 1964 - Aug, 1974 *under* JEE, JOURNAL OF ELECTRONIC ENGINEERING

Journal (ISSN: 0004-5438) - *Varied* Winter, 1967/1968 - 1985? *under* ARSC JOURNAL

Journal - *Varied* Jan, 1972 - Mar, 1987 *under* IBEW JOURNAL

Journal - *Varied* Jan, 1954 - Dec, 1954 *under* SMPTE JOURNAL

Journal des Telecommunications - *Varied* ? - ? *under* TELECOMMUNICATION JOURNAL

Journal of Advertising (ISSN: 0261-9903) - *Varied* Jan, 1982 - Mar, 1982 *under* INTERNATIONAL JOURNAL OF ADVERTISING

Journal of Applied Communications Research (ISSN: 0090-9882) - *Varied* Winter/Spring, 1973 - Summer/Fall?, 1972? *under* JOURNAL OF APPLIED COMMUNICATION RESEARCH

Journal of Broadcasting (ISSN: 0021-938x) - *Varied* Winter, 1956/1957 - Fall, 1984 *under* JOURNAL OF BROADCASTING & ELECTRONIC MEDIA

Journal of Business Communication (ISSN: 0885-2456) - *Varied* Oct, 1963 - Summer, 1969 *under* JOURNAL OF BUSINESS COMMUNICATION, THE

Journal of C4I Countermeasures [NC] - *Varied* *under* MILITARY ELECTRONICS / COUNTERMEASURES

Journal of Educational Communication (ISSN: 0745-4058) - *Varied* Jul/Aug, 1975 - Dec, 1983 *under* JOURNAL OF EDUCATIONAL PUBLIC RELATIONS

Journal of Educational Television - *Varied* Mar, 1975 - Nov, 1975 *under* JOURNAL OF EDUCATIONAL TELEVISION

Journal of Educational Television and Other Media - *Varied* Spring, 1976 - Winter, 1981 *under* JOURNAL OF EDUCATIONAL TELEVISION

Journal of Electrical Workers and Operators - *Varied* Aug, 1914 - Dec, 1947? *under* IBEW JOURNAL

Journal of Electrical Workers and Operators, The - *Varied* Aug, 1914 - 1948? *under* JOURNAL

Journal of Frankenstein, The - *Varied* ?, 1959 - Dec?, 1961 *under* CASTLE OF FRANKENSTEIN

Journal of Organizational Communications (ISSN: 0047-2646) - *Varied* Fall, 1971 - Winter, 1972/1973 *under* JOURNAL OF COMMUNICATION MANAGEMENT

Journal of Organizational Communication (ISSN: 0162-5659) - *Varied* Spring, 1975? - ?, 1981 *under* JOURNAL OF COMMUNICATION MANAGEMENT

Journal of Photographic Society of America (ISSN: 0096-5812) - *Varied* Mar, 1935 - Dec, 1946 *under* PSA JOURNAL

Journal of Popular Film (ISSN: 0047-2719) - *Varied* Winter, 1972 - 1978 *under* JOURNAL OF POPULAR FILM AND TELEVISION

Journal of Speech Disorders - *Varied* ? - Jan, 1948? *under* JOURNAL OF SPEECH AND HEARING DISORDERS

Journal of the AER - *Varied* Sep, 1941 - May, 1953 *under* PUBLIC TELECOMMUNICATIONS REVIEW

Journal of the AERT - *Varied* Oct, 1953 - May, 1956 *under* PUBLIC TELECOMMUNICATIONS REVIEW

Journal of the AIEE (ISSN: 0095-9804) - *Varied* ? - ? *under* IEEE SPECTRUM

Journal of the American Institute of Graphic Arts (ISSN: 0065-8820) - *Varied* 1965 - ? *under* AIGA JOURNAL OF GRAPHIC DESIGN

Journal of the Audio Engineering Society - *Varied* Jan, 1953 - Dec, 1985 *under* AES

Journal of the Institution of Electronic and Radio Engineers, The (ISSN: 0267-1689) - *Varied* Jan, 1985 - Dec?, 1988 *under* ELECTRONICS & COMMUNICATIONS ENGINEERING JOURNAL

Journal of the Screen Producers Guild - *Varied* Apr, 1952 - Dec, 1966 *under* JOURNAL OF THE PRODUCERS GUILD OF AMERICA, THE

Journal of the SMPTE (ISSN: 0361-4573) - *Varied* Jan, 1956 - Dec, 1975 *under* SMPTE JOURNAL

Journal of the Society of Motion Picture Engineers - *Varied* 1930 - 1949 *under* SMPTE JOURNAL

Journal of the Society of Motion Picture and Television Engineers - *Varied* 1950 - 1953 *under* SMPTE JOURNAL

Journal of the Television Society - *Varied* Jun, 1928 - Autumn, 1966 *under* TELEVISION

Journal of the University Film and Video Association (ISSN: 0734-919x) - *Varied* Winter, 1982 - Fall, 1983 *under* JOURNAL OF FILM AND VIDEO

Journal of the University Film Association (ISSN: 0041-9311) - *Varied* 1968 - ? *under* JOURNAL OF FILM AND VIDEO

Journal of the University Film Producers Association - *Varied* Mar, 1949 - ?, 1967 *under* JOURNAL OF FILM AND VIDEO

Journal of Typographic Research, The (ISSN: 0449-329x) - *Varied* Jan, 1967 - Autumn, 1970 *under* VISIBLE LANGUAGE

Journal Telegraphique [NE?] - *Varied* ? - ? *under* TELECOMMUNICATION JOURNAL

Journal UIT - *Varied* Jan, 1953 - Dec, 1961 *under* TELECOMMUNICATION JOURNAL

Journalism Bulletin, The (ISSN: 0197-2448) - *Varied* Mar, 1924 - Nov, 1927 *under* JQ. JOURNALISM QUARTERLY.

Journalism Quarterly (ISSN: 0022-5533) - *Varied* Jan, 1928 - Spring, 1971 *under* JQ. JOURNALISM QUARTERLY.

Journalist - *Varied* Fall, 1981 - Spring, 1983 under COMMUNITY COLLEGE JOURNALIST

JPF&T - *Varied* 1978 - Winter, 1984/1985 under JOURNAL OF POPULAR FILM AND TELEVISION

Junior College Journalist - *Varied* Summer, 1972 - Spring/Summer, 1974 under COMMUNITY COLLEGE JOURNALIST

K

Kine Weekly - *Varied* Sep 25, 1919 - ? under KINEMATOGRAPH WEEKLY

Kinematograph and Lantern Weekly, The - *Varied* May 16, 1907 - Sep 18, 1919 under KINEMATOGRAPH WEEKLY

Kodak Magazine, The - *Varied* Jun, 1920 - ? under KODAK

L

Law Enforcement Communications (ISSN: 0193-0540) - *Varied* 1974? - Jan/Feb, 1984 under LAW ENFORCEMENT TECHNOLOGY

Leica Fotografie (ISSN: 0024-0621) - *Varied* Jan?, 1951 - ?, 1989 under LEICA FOTOGRAFIE INTERNATIONAL

Leypoldt & Holt's Literary Bulletin - *Varied* Feb, 1869 - Jun, 1869 under PUBLISHER'S WEEKLY

Liberty (ISSN: 0024-208x) - *Varied* Summer, 1971 - Spring?, 1973 under LIBERTY, THEN AND NOW

Library Journal/School Library Journal Previews - *Varied* ? - Nov?, 1973 under PREVIEWS

Listener, The - *Varied* Jan 16, 1929 - Dec 31, 1959 under LISTENER

Listener and BBC Television Review, The - *Varied* Jan 7, 1960 - Jul 27, 1967 under LISTENER

Literary Bulletin, The - *Varied* Jul, 1869 - Aug, 1869 under PUBLISHER'S WEEKLY

Literature in Performance (ISSN: 0734-0796) - *Varied* ? - Oct, 1988? under TPQ

Liverpool and Manchester Photographic Journal - *Varied* Jan, 1857 - Dec?, 1858 under BRITISH JOURNAL OF PHOTOGRAPHY

Liverpool Photographic Journal - *Varied* Jan, 1854 - Dec?, 1856 under BRITISH JOURNAL OF PHOTOGRAPHY

LOC - *Varied* ? - ? under COMIC FANDOM'S FORUM

London Calling (ISSN: 0024-600x) - *Varied* Sep 24, 1939 - Mar 23, 1963 under BBC WORLD SERVICE LONDON CALLING

Look, Listen, Learn - *Varied* ? - 1966 under AUDIO VISUAL JOURNAL

Loyola of Los Angeles Entertainment Law Journal (ISSN: 0273-4249) - *Varied* Apr, 1981 - ? under LOYOLA ENTERTAINMENT JOURNAL

M

MAC - *Varied* Jul 17, 1967 - Dec 21, 1967 under ADWEEK

MAC/WA - *Varied* Jul 13, 1967 under ADWEEK

MAC/WA - *Varied* Dec 28, 1967? - Jan 4, 1970? under ADWEEK

MAC/Western Advertising - *Varied* Jan 12, 1970 - Mar 2, 1970 under ADWEEK

MAC/Western Advertising News (ISSN: 0194-4789) - *Varied* Mar 9, 1970 - Nov 17, 1980 under ADWEEK

Magazine Age (ISSN: 0194-2506) - *Varied* Jan, 1980 - Dec, 1985 under INSIDE MEDIA

Magazine Industry Newsletter - *Varied* Nov, 1947 - Sep 24, 1970 under MEDIA INDUSTRY NEWSLETTER

Magazine of the Oxford Film Society - *Varied* May, 1946 - ?, 1946 under SEQUENCE

Magnetic Film and Tape Recording - *Varied* Feb, 1954 - Oct, 1956 under TAPE RECORDING

Mail Order Connection - *Varied* ? - ? under DIRECT RESPONSE SPECIALIST, THE

Mail Order Journal - *Varied* 1897 - Mar, 1916 under NATIONAL ADVERTISING

Making Films in New York - *Varied* Mar, 1967 - Oct/Nov, 1975 under MAKING FILMS

Many Worlds of Music, The (ISSN: 0045-317x) - *Varied* Nov, 1964 - Fall, 1987 under BMI: MUSICWORLD

Marconigraph - *Varied* Oct, 1912 - Mar, 1913 under WIRELESS AGE, THE

Margaret Wentworth's Sign Post - *Varied* Oct 30, 1930 - May, 1948 under BROADWAY SIGN POST

Marketing & Media Decisions (ISSN: 0195-4296) - *Varied* May, 1979 - Dec, 1990 under MEDIAWEEK

Marketing Bestsellers (ISSN: 0164-9876) - *Varied* ? - Jan, 1982 under MAGAZINE & BOOKSELLER

Martial Arts Movies (ISSN: 0744-8430) - *Varied* Jan, 1981 - Oct, 1982 under ACTION FILMS

Maryland in Motion Film & Video Production Directory - *Varied* ? - ? under IN MOTION FILM & VIDEO PRODUCTION MAGAZINE

Mass Media Bi-Weekly Newsletter (ISSN: 0163-4968) - *Varied* Apr 3, 1972 - Apr 28, 1975 under MASS MEDIA NEWSLETTER

Mass Media Booknotes (ISSN: 0740-6479) - *Varied* Sep, 1973 - Jan, 1982 under COMMUNICATION BOOKNOTES

Mass Media Ministries Bi-Weekly Newsletter (ISSN: 0025-472x) - *Varied* 1964? - Mar 20, 1972 under MASS MEDIA NEWSLETTER

Master Printer - *Varied* May, 1903 - Apr, 1905 under NEWSPAPER WORLD AND ADVERTISING REVIEW

Media, Agencies, Clients - *Varied* Dec 19, 1951 - Jul 10, 1967 under ADWEEK

Media Business News (ISSN: 0898-283x) - *Varied* Jan, 1987 - ?, 1988? under MEDIA BUSINESS

Media Decisions (ISSN: 0025-6900) - *Varied* Sep, 1966 - Apr, 1979 under MEDIAWEEK

Media Management Monographs (ISSN: 0192-7663) - *Varied* ? - Dec, 1990? under PUBLISHING TRENDS & TRENDSETTERS

Media Probe (ISSN: 0384-1618) - *Varied* Mar, 1974 - Summer, 1977 under CANADIAN JOURNAL OF COMMUNICATION

Media Report - *Varied* ? - ? under MEDIA REPORTER, THE

Mediascene - *Varied* Nov/Dec, 1973 - May/Jun, 1980 under PREVUE

Mediascene Prevue (ISSN: 0199-9257) - *Varied* Jul/Aug, 1980 - ?, 1987 under PREVUE

Memo - Corporation for Public Broadcasting - *Varied* Aug 30, 1974? - ? under REPORT

MGM Short Story - *Varied* ? - Jan, 1939 under METRO-GOLDWYN-MAYER SHORT STORY

Miniature Camera World - *Varied* Dec?, 1936? - May, 1955 under 35MM PHOTOGRAPHY

Minicam - *Varied* Sep, 1937 - Jan, 1940 under MODERN PHOTOGRAPHY

Minicam Photography (ISSN: 0096-5863) - *Varied* Feb, 1940 - Aug, 1949 under MODERN PHOTOGRAPHY

Modern Recording (ISSN: 0361-0004) - *Varied* Oct/Nov, 1975 - Jun, 1980 under MODERN RECORDING & MUSIC

Modern Screen Magazine, The - *Varied* Nov, 1930 - ? *under* MODERN SCREEN

Monitor (ISSN: 0314-4321) - *Varied* Jan/Feb, 1976 - Dec, 1979 *under* PROCEEDINGS OF THE IREE AUSTRALIA

Monthly Bulletin - *Varied* Apr, 1916 *under* DRAMA LEAGUE MONTHLY

Monthly Filmstrip Review - *Varied* ? - Jan, 1950 *under* VISUAL EDUCATION

Monthly News Letter, American Association of Teachers of Journalism - *Varied* ? - ? *under* JQ. JOURNALISM QUARTERLY.

Morning Filmograph - *Varied* Apr, 1922 - May?, 1923 *under* HOLLYWOOD FILMOGRAPH

Motion Picture - *Varied* Dec, 1926 *under* MOTION PICTURE

Motion Picture, The - *Varied* Sep, 1925 - Jul, 1930 *under* SELECTED MOTION PICTURES

Motion Picture and Television Magazine - *Varied* Sep, 1951 - Sep, 1954 *under* MOTION PICTURE

Motion Picture Classic - *Varied* Dec, 1915 - Aug, 1922 *under* MOVIE CLASSIC

Motion Picture Classic - *Varied* Sep, 1924 - Aug, 1931 *under* MOVIE CLASSIC

Motion Picture Magazine - *Varied* Mar, 1914 - Nov, 1926 *under* MOTION PICTURE

Motion Picture Magazine - *Varied* Jan, 1927 - Aug, 1951 *under* MOTION PICTURE

Motion Picture Monthly, The - *Varied* Aug, 1930 - Dec, 1931 *under* SELECTED MOTION PICTURES

Motion Picture Projectionist - *Varied* Jan, 1928 - Jan, 1933 *under* MOTION PICTURE PROJECTION

Motion Picture Projectionist of the United States and Canada, The - *Varied* Oct, 1927 - Nov, 1927 *under* MOTION PICTURE PROJECTION

Motion Picture Story Magazine, The - *Varied* Mar?, 1911 - Feb, 1914 *under* MOTION PICTURE

Motion Picture Supplement - *Varied* Sep, 1915 - Nov, 1915 *under* MOVIE CLASSIC

Movie and Radio Guide - *Varied* Feb 23, 1940 - Sep 21, 1940 *under* MOVIE-RADIO GUIDE

Movie Life (ISSN: 0027-2698) - *Varied* Jan, 1938 - 197u *under* TONI HOLT'S MOVIE LIFE

Movie Marketing - *Varied* Feb, 1962 - Jan, 1966 *under* MOVIE/TV MARKETING

Movie Stars Parade - *Varied* Fall, 1940 - Dec, 1958 *under* MOVIE STARS

Movie Stars. TV Close-Ups - *Varied* ? - ? *under* MOVIE STARS

Movieland - *Varied* Feb, 1943 - Apr, 1958 *under* MOVIELAND AND TV TIME

Moving Picture Story Magazine - *Varied* Feb?, 1911 *under* MOTION PICTURE

Moving Picture Weekly - *Varied* 1915 - May, 1922 *under* UNIVERSAL WEEKLY

MSO (ISSN: 1046-3321) - *Varied* Sep?, 1989 - Aug, 1990 *under* MSO'S CABLE MARKETING

Multi-Images - *Varied* 1974? - Jan/Feb, 1986 *under* MULTI IMAGES JOURNAL

Music & Sound Output (ISSN: 0273-8902) - *Varied* Nov/Dec, 1980 - Dec, 1988 *under* STAGE & STUDIO

Mystery Newsletter, The - *Varied* ? - ? *under* SCARLET STREET

N

NAB Member Service - *Varied* Mar, 1949 - 195u *under* NARTB MEMBER SERVICE

NAB Reports - *Varied* Mar 11, 1933 - Feb 28, 1949 *under* NARTB MEMBER SERVICE

NAB Today [Television Edition] - *Varied* ? - ? *under* TV TODAY

NAEB Journal - *Varied* Oct, 1957 - Jul/Aug, 1967 *under* PUBLIC TELECOMMUNICATIONS REVIEW

NAEB Letter - *Varied* 1964 - Mar, 1979 *under* CURRENT

NAFBRAT Quarterly - *Varied* Summer, 1960 - Summer, 1963 *under* BETTER RADIO AND TELEVISION

NARND Bulletin - *Varied* Jan, 1947? - Nov, 1952 *under* COMMUNICATOR

National Association of Educational Broadcasters Newsletter (ISSN: 0027-8610) - *Varied* 19uu - 1964 *under* CURRENT

National Board of Review Magazine - *Varied* Feb, 1926 - Jan, 1942 *under* FILMS IN REVIEW

National Broadcast Reporter - *Varied* Nov, 1931 - Oct 8, 1932 *under* BROADCAST REPORTER

National Cinema Workshop and Appreciation League Bulletin - *Varied* Dec, 1935 - Jul, 1936 *under* CINEMA PROGRESS

National Federation for Decency Newsletter - *Varied* Aug, 1979 *under* AFA JOURNAL

National Press Photographer (ISSN: 0027-9935) - *Varied* Apr, 1946 - Aug, 1974 *under* NEWS PHOTOGRAPHER

National Professional Photographer, The (ISSN: 0734-7529) - *Varied* Sep, 1961 - Dec, 1963 *under* PROFESSIONAL PHOTOGRAPHER, THE

NAVA News - *Varied* 1946 - Aug, 1983 *under* COMMUNICATIONS INDUSTRIES REPORT, THE

NCCT Forum - *Varied* Winter, 1978 - Spring?, 1980 *under* TELEVISION & FAMILIES

Network News - *Varied* 1982 - ? *under* AP BROADCASTER

New Broadway Magazine - *Varied* Dec, 1907 - Sep, 1908 *under* HAMPTON MAGAZINE

New Developments for the Photographic Dealer and Photo Finisher - *Varied* ? - ? *under* PHOTO MARKETING

New Movies, The - *Varied* Feb, 1942 - Jan/Feb, 1949 *under* FILMS IN REVIEW

New Review of Books and Religion, The (ISSN: 0146-0609) - *Varied* Sep, 1976 - Jun, 1980 *under* BOOKS & RELIGION

New Show, The - *Varied* Mar/Apr, 1966 - ? *under* SHOW

New York Dramatic Mirror, The - *Varied* Jan 26, 1889 - Feb 10, 1917 *under* DRAMATIC MIRROR, THE

New York Mirror - *Varied* 1879? - ? *under* DRAMATIC MIRROR, THE

New York Printing News - *Varied* 1928 - Jan, 1931 *under* PRINTINGNEWS

New York State Community Theatre Journal (ISSN: 0548-8974) - *Varied* Dec, 1960 - Winter/Spring, 1970 *under* THEATRE JOURNAL

News - Action for Children's Television (ISSN: 0145-6822) - *Varied* ? - Summer, 1977 *under* RE:ACT

News & Views - *Varied* ? - ? *under* AWRT NEWS AND VIEWS

News From the American Film Center, Inc. - *Varied* Dec, 1939 - Apr, 1940 *under* FILM & VIDEO NEWS

News of the World - *Varied* Mar 20, 1937 - Nov, 1937 *under* HOLLYWOOD NOW

News Research Bulletin (ISSN: 0734-9238) - *Varied* ? - 1976 *under* ANPA NEWS RESEARCH REPORT

Newsdealer - *Varied* Mar, 1946 - Sep, 1960 *under* MAGAZINE & BOOKSELLER

Newsdealers' Bestsellers - *Varied* 1945? - ? *under* MAGAZINE & BOOKSELLER

Newsletter - *Varied* ? - ? *under* BETTER RADIO AND TELEVISION

Newsletter - *Varied* ? - ? *under* CMA NEWSLETTER

Newsletter - *Varied* ? - ? *under* FOLLOW FOCUS

Newsletter - *Varied* ? - Autumn, 1985 *under* IAMHIST NEWSLETTER

Newsletter - *Varied* ? - 1970? *under* REPORT

Newsletter / Broadcasters Promotion Association - *Varied* ? - ? *under* BPME IMAGE MAGAZINE

Newsletter - Historians Film Committee - *Varied* Mar, 1971 - Dec, 1971 *under* FILM & HISTORY

Newsletter - Media Institute (ISSN: 0270-3564) - *Varied* Fall, 1979 *under* BUSINESS AND THE MEDIA

Newsletter of the National Federation for Decency - *Varied* May?, 1979 *under* AFA JOURNAL

Newsletter: Rhetoric Society of America - *Varied* 1968 - 1975 *under* RHETORIC SOCIETY QUARTERLY

Newspaper Fund Newsletter - *Varied* Spring, 1960? - Nov, 1982 *under* DOW JONES NEWSPAPER FUND NEWSLETTER

Newspaper News and Advertising News? - *Varied* ? - ? *under* ADVERTISING NEWS

Newspaper Owner and Manager - *Varied* 1898 - May, 1903 *under* NEWSPAPER WORLD AND ADVERTISING REVIEW

Newspaper Owner and World - *Varied* Apr 8, 1905 - Jul 28, 1913 *under* NEWSPAPER WORLD AND ADVERTISING REVIEW

Newspaper Production (ISSN: 0148-9631) - *Varied* Nov, 1972 - Aug, 1976 *under* WEB

Newspaper Production for North and South America (ISSN: 0148-964x) - *Varied* Sep, 1976 - Sep, 1978 *under* WEB

Newspaper World - *Varied* Aug, 1913 - 1936? *under* NEWSPAPER WORLD AND ADVERTISING REVIEW

Newspaperdom - *Varied* Vol 1-40, No. 5 *under* ADVERTISING

NFD Informer - *Varied* ? - Sep, 1983 *under* AFA JOURNAL

NFD Journal - *Varied* ? - ? *under* AFA JOURNAL

NFD Newsletter - *Varied* Jun, 1979 - Jul, 1979 *under* AFA JOURNAL

NFD Newsletter - *Varied* Sep, 1979 - ? *under* AFA JOURNAL

NITA News - *Varied* ? - ? *under* INDUSTRIAL TELEVISION NEWS

Norton's Literary Advertiser - *Varied* May, 1851 - Jan, 1852 *under* AMERICAN LITERARY GAZETTE AND PUBLISHERS' CIRCULAR

Norton's Literary Gazette and Publishers' Circular - *Varied* Jan, 1852 - Sep 1, 1855 *under* AMERICAN LITERARY GAZETTE AND PUBLISHERS' CIRCULAR

Nostalgia Journal - *Varied* Jun?, 1974 - Dec, 1976 *under* COMICS JOURNAL, THE

Novum - *Varied* 1972? - 1974? *under* NOVUM GEBRAUCHSGRAPHIK

Novum - *Varied* 1980? - ? *under* NOVUM GEBRAUCHSGRAPHIK

Novum Gebrauchsgraphik (ISSN: 0302-9794) - *Varied* 1974 - 1979 *under* NOVUM GEBRAUCHSGRAPHIK

NSSC Newsletter - *Varied* ? - ? *under* ICA NEWSLETTER

NY Filmmakers Newsletter - *Varied* Nov, 1967 - Mar, 1968 *under* FILMMAKERS FILM & VIDEO MONTHLY

O

Official Doctor Who Magazine, The - *Varied* 1985? - ? *under* DOCTOR WHO MAGAZINE

OIR Information - *Varied* ? - ? *under* OIRT INFORMATION

On Communications (ISSN: 8750-7854) - *Varied* Nov, 1984 - Mar, 1986 *under* NETWORK WORLD

Optic Music (ISSN: 0889-5651) - *Varied* Feb, 1984 - May, 1987 *under* FILM & VIDEO

Optical Information Systems Update / Library & Information Center Applications (ISSN: 0886-019x) - *Varied* ? - Dec, 1986 *under* CD-ROM LIBRARIAN

Optical Lantern and Cinematograph Journal - *Varied* Nov, 1904 - May, 1906 *under* KINEMATOGRAPH WEEKLY

Optical Lantern and Kinematograph Journal - *Varied* Jun, 1906 - Apr, 1907 *under* KINEMATOGRAPH WEEKLY

Optical Magic Lantern Journal and Photographic Enlarger, The - *Varied* Jun 15, 1889 - Jun, 1903 *under* KINEMATOGRAPH WEEKLY

Optical memory Newsletter Including Interactive Videodisks (ISSN: 0731-9452) - *Varied* Jan, 1982 - Sep/Oct, 1983 *under* OPTICAL MEMORY NEWS

Opticmusic's Film & Video Production (ISSN: 0894-4423) - *Varied* Jun, 1987 - Oct, 1988 *under* FILM & VIDEO

Our Player's Gallery (ISSN: 0748-6634) - *Varied* Oct, 1900 - Jan, 1901 *under* THEATRE MAGAZINE

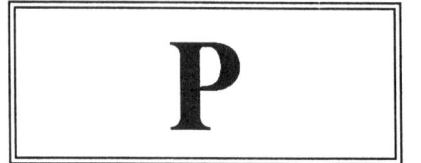

P

Pacific Radio News - *Varied* Jan, 1917 - Oct, 1921 *under* AUDIO

PC Publishing (ISSN: 0896-8209) - *Varied* Jan, 1986 - Mar, 1991 *under* PC PUBLISHING AND PRESENTATIONS

PD Cue (ISSN: 0193-0141) - *Varied* ? - ? *under* NATPE PROGRAMMER

Performance Newspaper (ISSN: 0746-9772) - *Varied* ? - ? *under* PERFORMANCE

Performing Arts Review (ISSN: 0031-5249) - *Varied* Winter, 1969 - 1981 *under* JOURNAL OF ARTS MANAGEMENT AND LAW, THE

Perry's Broadcasting and the Law (ISSN: 0161-5823) - *Varied* 1971 - Dec 1, 1984 *under* BROADCASTING AND THE LAW

Petersen's Photographic Magazine (ISSN: 0048-3583) - *Varied* May, 1972 - Oct, 1979 *under* PETERSEN'S PHOTOGRAPHIC

Photo Developments - *Varied* ? - Apr?, 1964? *under* PHOTO MARKETING

Photo-Era - *Varied* May, 1898 - Dec, 1920 *under* PHOTO-ERA MAGAZINE

Photo-Miniature, The - *Varied* Apr, 1899 - Jan, 1932 *under* NEW PHOTO-MINIATURE

Photo Playwright, The - *Varied* Apr, 1912 - Dec, 1912 *under* MOTION PICTURE ALBUM

Photographic Applications in Science and Technology (ISSN: 0031-871x) - *Varied* Winter, 1966/1967 - Spring, 1968 *under* FUNCTIONAL PHOTOGRAPHY

Photographic Applications in Science, Technology and Medicine (ISSN: 0098-8227) - *Varied* Summer, 1968 - Jul, 1975 *under* FUNCTIONAL PHOTOGRAPHY

Photographic Business and Product News - *Varied* Jan, 1968 - Jun?, 1975 *under* STUDIO PHOTOGRAPHY

Photographic Journal - *Varied* Jan, 1859 - Dec, 1859 *under* BRITISH JOURNAL OF PHOTOGRAPHY

Photographic Product News - *Varied* 196u - Dec?, 1967? *under* STUDIO PHOTOGRAPHY

Photographic Quarterly - *Varied* Fall, 1971 - Winter, 1971 *under* PETERSEN'S PHOTOGRAPHIC

Photographic Times, The - *Varied* 1871 - 1880 *under* PHOTOGRAPHIC TIMES, THE

Photographic Times, The - *Varied* 1895 - Apr, 1902 *under* PHOTOGRAPHIC TIMES, THE

Photographic Times and American Photographer, The - *Varied* 1881 - 1894 *under* PHOTOGRAPHIC TIMES, THE

Photographic Times-Bulletin, The - *Varied* May, 1902 - Dec, 1904 *under* PHOTOGRAPHIC TIMES, THE

Photography (ISSN: 0031-8809) - *Varied* Oct, 1965 - Jul?, 1983 *under* PHOTOGRAPHY

Photography - *Varied* Jan, 1952 - May, 1952 *under* POPULAR PHOTOGRAPHY

Photography - *Varied* Aug, 1952 - Jan, 1955 *under* POPULAR PHOTOGRAPHY

Photography Magazine - *Varied* Jun, 1952 - Jul, 1952 *under* POPULAR PHOTOGRAPHY

Photolith (ISSN: 0031-8825) - *Varied* 1950 - May, 1975 *under* PHOTOLITH, SCM

Photoplay - *Varied* Jan, 1986 - Mar, 1989 *under* FILM MONTHLY

Photoplay - *Varied* Jun, 1944 - ?, 1946 *under* PHOTOPLAY COMBINED WITH MOVIE MIRROR

Photoplay Movies & Video - *Varied* Jan, 1950? - Dec, 1985? *under* FILM MONTHLY

Picture-Play Weekly - *Varied* Apr, 1915 - Nov, 1915 *under* PICTURE PLAY MAGAZINE

Players Magazine (ISSN: 0162-394x) - *Varied* 1924 - Dec/Jan, 1967/1968 *under* PLAYERS

PM - *Varied* Sep, 1934 - May, 1940 *under* A-D

PMI, Photo Methods for Industry (ISSN: 0030-8110) - *Varied* Jan, 1958 - Aug, 1974 *under* PHOTOMETHODS

Polaroid Newsletter for Photographic Education, The - *Varied* Winter, 1983 - Spring/Summer, 1988 *under* PHOTOEDUCATION

Popular Electronics (ISSN: 0032-4485) - *Varied* Oct, 1954 - Dec, 1971 *under* COMPUTERS & ELECTRONICS

Popular Electronics (ISSN: 0032-4485) - *Varied* Jan, 1972 - Oct, 1982 *under* COMPUTERS & ELECTRONICS

Popular Electronics, Including Electronics World - *Varied* Jan, 1972 - Dec, 1973 *under* COMPUTERS & ELECTRONICS

Popular Photography - *Varied* May, 1937 - Dec, 1951 *under* POPULAR PHOTOGRAPHY

Popular Radio - *Varied* May, 1922 - Mar, 1928 *under* POPULAR RADIO AND TELEVISION

Postage and the Mailbag - *Varied* Sep, 1927 - Nov, 1937 *under* DIRECT MARKETING

Poster, The - *Varied* 1910 - Jan, 1930 *under* ADVERTISING OUTDOORS

PR - *Varied* Oct, 1955 - Summer, 1960 *under* PUBLIC RELATIONS QUARTERLY

Practical and Amateur Wireless - *Varied* ? - Aug 19, 1939 *under* PRACTICAL WIRELESS

Practical Newsletter on Agency Management - *Varied* ? - ? *under* YELLOW SHEET, THE

Practical Television - *Varied* Sep, 1934 - May, 1935 *under* PRACTICAL TELEVISION AND SHORT-WAVE REVIEW

Practical Wireless - *Varied* ? - ? *under* PRACTICAL WIRELESS

Practical Wireless and Practical Television - *Varied* ? - ? *under* PRACTICAL WIRELESS

Premium Channels (ISSN: 0273-561x) - *Varied* ? - ? *under* PREMIUM CHANNELS TV BLUEPRINT

Premi'ere (ISSN: 0274-7766) - *Varied* Sep, 1980 - Mar, 1981 *under* AMERICAN PREMIERE

Press Censorship Newsletter - *Varied* Mar/Apr, 1973 - Sep/Oct, 1976 *under* NEWS MEDIA & THE LAW, THE

Pride (ISSN: 0032-8197) - *Varied* Jan, 1957 - Jun, 1961 *under* COLLEGE & UNIVERSITY JOURNAL

Printer & Publisher (ISSN: 0317-1213) - *Varied* ? - ? *under* CANADIAN PRINTER

Printers' Ink (ISSN: 0196-1160) - *Varied* Jul 15, 1888 - Sep 8, 1967 *under* MARKETING / COMMUNICATIONS

Printing News (ISSN: 0032-8626) - *Varied* Jan, 1931 - Sep 30, 1989 *under* PRINTINGNEWS

Printing Paper Quarterly - *Varied* ? - ? *under* PRINTING PAPER

Proceedings, The - *Varied* Oct, 1926 - 1939 *under* ELECTRONICS & COMMUNICATIONS ENGINEERING JOURNAL

Proceedings - Institution of Radio and Electronics Engineers Australia (ISSN: 0020-3521) - *Varied* Jan, 1964 - Dec, 1971 *under* PROCEEDINGS OF THE IREE AUSTRALIA

Proceedings - Institution of Radio Engineers (ISSN: 0020-3521) - *Varied* 1937 - 1963 *under* PROCEEDINGS OF THE IREE AUSTRALIA

Proceedings of the Institute of Radio Engineers (ISSN: 0731-5996) - *Varied* ? - ? *under* PROCEEDINGS OF THE IEEE

Proceedings of the IRE (ISSN: 0096-8390) - *Varied* Jan, 1939 - Dec, 1962 *under* PROCEEDINGS OF THE IEEE

Proceedings of the IREE (ISSN: 0314-4313) - *Varied* Jan, 1972 - Dec, 1975 *under* PROCEEDINGS OF THE IREE AUSTRALIA

Producci on [NE] (ISSN: 1048-1869) - *Varied* Oct/Nov, 1989 - Volume 1, #2, 1990 *under* PRODUCCIÓN Y DISTRIBUCIÓN

Product Digest (ISSN: 0093-2132) - *Varied* Jun 6, 1973 - May 22, 1974 *under* MOTION PICTURE PRODUCT DIGEST

Production Committee Newsletter - *Varied* ? - ? *under* PD REPORT

Production Prospects - *Varied* ? - ? *under* SHOW BUSINESS

Professional Photographer, The - *Varied* Feb, 1934 - ? *under* PROFESSIONAL PHOTOGRAPHER, THE

Professional Publishing (ISSN: 0736-7457) - *Varied* ? - Sep?, 1985 *under* PERSONAL PUBLISHING

Professional Video (ISSN: 0264-1321) - *Varied* 1982? - 198u *under* BROADCAST SYSTEMS ENGINEERING

Progress in Photography - *Varied* 1949/1950? - ? *under* PERSPECTIVE

Public Telecommunications Letter - *Varied* Apr/May, 1979 - Jan/Feb, 1980 *under* CURRENT

Publicity Problems - *Varied* Sep, 1942 - May/Jun, 1946 *under* COLLEGE & UNIVERSITY JOURNAL

Publishers' and Stationers' Weekly Trade Circular - *Varied* Jan 18, 1872 - Dec 26, 1872 *under* PUBLISHER'S WEEKLY

Publishers' Guide, The - *Varied* 1893 - Jul 28, 1916 *under* ADVERTISING NEWS

Publishers' Guide and the Advertising News - *Varied* Aug 4, 1916 - Aug 11, 1916 *under* ADVERTISING NEWS

Publishing Technology (ISSN: 1040-9440) - *Varied* Jan, 1987? - Oct?, 1989 *under* PUBLISHING & PRODUCTION EXECUTIVE

Pulp & Paper Magazine of Canada (ISSN: 0033-4103) - *Varied* ? - ? *under* PULP & PAPER CANADA

Pulse of Broadcasting, The - *Varied* Jan 1, 1986? - Jan 20, 1989 *under* PULSE OF RADIO

Q

QP Herald (ISSN: 0090-2136) - *Varied* Jan 6, 1973 - May 5, 1973 *under* MOTION PICTURE PRODUCT DIGEST

Quarterly Journal of Public Speaking, The - *Varied* Apr, 1915 - Oct, 1917 *under* QUARTERLY JOURNAL OF SPEECH, THE

Quarterly Journal of Speech Education, The - *Varied* Jan, 1918 - Nov, 1927 *under* QUARTERLY JOURNAL OF SPEECH, THE

Quarterly of Film, Radio, and Television, The - *Varied* Fall, 1951 - Summer, 1957 *under* FILM QUARTERLY

Quarterly Review of Film Studies (ISSN: 0146-0013) - *Varied* Feb, 1976 - Feb, 1989 *under* QUARTERLY REVIEW OF FILM AND VIDEO

Varies INDEX 1024

Quarterly Review of Public Relations - *Varied* Fall, 1960 - Winter, 1963 *under* PUBLIC RELATIONS QUARTERLY

Quill of Sigma Delta Chi, The - *Varied* 1912 - Feb, 1930 *under* QUILL, THE

R

Radio - *Varied* Nov, 1921 - Feb/Mar, 1947 *under* AUDIO

Radio Age - *Varied* Oct, 1941 - ?, 1957 *under* ELECTRONIC AGE

Radio Album - *Varied* Summer, 1948 *under* RADIO ALBUM MAGAZINE

Radio Amateur News - *Varied* Jul, 1919 - Jun, 1920 *under* ELECTRONICS WORLD

Radio and Amusement Guide - *Varied* Jan 7, 1932 - ? *under* MOVIE-RADIO GUIDE

Radio & Electrical Appliance Dealer - *Varied* Feb, 1944 - Apr, 1944 *under* ELECTRONIC SERVICING & TECHNOLOGY

Radio and Electrical Review - *Varied* May 1, 1954 - Apr 1, 1964 *under* ELECTRONICS AND COMMUNICATIONS

Radio and Electronic Engineer, The (ISSN: 0033-7722) - *Varied* 1963 - Nov/Dec, 1984 *under* ELECTRONICS & COMMUNICATIONS ENGINEERING JOURNAL

Radio and Electronics - *Varied* Apr, 1946 - Apr, 1954 *under* ELECTRONICS AND COMMUNICATIONS

Radio & Television - *Varied* 1960 - May, 1966 *under* RADIO AND TELEVISION

Radio and Television Best - *Varied* Oct, 1949 - Aug, 1950 *under* TV SCREEN

Radio & Television Incorporating Foto-Craft - *Varied* Dec, 1939 - ? *under* RADIO & TELEVISION

Radio and Television Mirror - *Varied* Aug, 1939 - Oct, 1942 *under* TV RADIO MIRROR

Radio and Television Mirror - *Varied* Apr, 1948 - Feb, 1951 *under* TV RADIO MIRROR

Radio & Television News - *Varied* Aug, 1948 - Mar, 1957 *under* ELECTRONICS WORLD

Radio and Television Retailing - *Varied* Apr, 1939 - Dec, 1941 *under* TELEVISION RETAILING

Radio & Television Retailing - *Varied* Apr, 1944 - Jun, 1952 *under* TELEVISION RETAILING

Radio and TV News (ISSN: 0097-6660) - *Varied* Apr, 1957 - Apr, 1959 *under* ELECTRONICS WORLD

Radio Best - *Varied* Nov, 1947 - ? *under* TV SCREEN

Radio Best & Television Magazine - *Varied* Oct, 1950 - Dec, 1950 *under* TV SCREEN

Radio Constructor - *Varied* ? - ? *under* RADIO & ELECTRONICS CONSTRUCTOR

Radio-Craft - *Varied* Jul, 1929 - Oct, 1941 *under* RADIO-ELECTRONICS

Radio-Craft - *Varied* May, 1943 - Jun, 1948 *under* RADIO-ELECTRONICS

Radio-Craft Incorporating Radio and Television - *Varied* Nov, 1941 - Apr, 1943 *under* RADIO-ELECTRONICS

Radio-Craft, Radio-Electronics - *Varied* Jul, 1948 - Sep, 1948 *under* RADIO-ELECTRONICS

Radio Daily - *Varied* Feb 9, 1936 - Sep 6, 1950 *under* RTD

Radio Daily-Television Daily - *Varied* Sep 7, 1950 - Jan 5, 1962 *under* RTD

Radio Digest Illustrated - *Varied* Apr, 1922 - Feb, 1924 *under* RADIO FAN-FARE

Radio Digest Programs Illustrated - *Varied* ? - ?, 1933 *under* RADIO FAN-FARE

Radio, Electronics and Communications - *Varied* May 1, 1964 - Dec 1, 1971 *under* ELECTRONICS AND COMMUNICATIONS

Radio-Electronics Special Projects (ISSN: 0730-7616) - *Varied* ? - ? *under* POPULAR ELECTRONICS

Radio Guide - *Varied* Oct, 1931 - Dec, 1931 *under* MOVIE-RADIO GUIDE

Radio Guide - *Varied* ? - Feb 16, 1940 *under* MOVIE-RADIO GUIDE

Radio in the Home - *Varied* Jun, 1922 - Mar, 1926 *under* RADIO HOME, THE

Radio Manufacturers Monthly - *Varied* May, 1926 - Oct, 1929 *under* RADIO INDUSTRIES

Radio Mirror - *Varied* Nov, 1933 - Jul, 1939 *under* TV RADIO MIRROR

Radio Mirror - *Varied* Nov, 1942 - Mar, 1945 *under* TV RADIO MIRROR

Radio Mirror - *Varied* Dec, 1945 - Mar, 1948 *under* TV RADIO MIRROR

Radio News - *Varied* Jul, 1920 - Jul, 1948 *under* ELECTRONICS WORLD

Radio Retailing - *Varied* 1925 - Mar, 1939 *under* TELEVISION RETAILING

Radio Retailing Combined with Radio Today - *Varied* Jan, 1942 - Jul, 1942 *under* TELEVISION RETAILING

Radio Retailing Today - *Varied* Aug, 1942 - Mar, 1944 *under* TELEVISION RETAILING

Radio Romances - *Varied* Apr, 1945 - Nov, 1945 *under* TV RADIO MIRROR

Radio Service Dealer - *Varied* Apr, 1940 - Jan, 1944 *under* ELECTRONIC SERVICING & TECHNOLOGY

Radio Service Dealer - *Varied* May, 1944 - Jul, 1950 *under* ELECTRONIC SERVICING & TECHNOLOGY

Radio Television (ISSN: 0033-7676) - *Varied* Jul/Aug, 1966? - 1981 *under* RADIO AND TELEVISION

Radio-Television Daily - *Varied* Jan 12, 1962 - Aug 31, 1965 *under* RTD

Radio Television International Review (ISSN: 1015-8596) - *Varied* 1982 - 1984 *under* RADIO AND TELEVISION

Radio Television Mirror - *Varied* Mar, 1951 - Sep, 1951 *under* TV RADIO MIRROR

Radio-Television Service Dealer - *Varied* 195u - 195u *under* ELECTRONIC SERVICING & TECHNOLOGY

Radio-TV Mirror - *Varied* Oct, 1951 - Jul, 1954 *under* TV RADIO MIRROR

Radio World Newspaper - *Varied* Dec 15, 1985 - ? *under* RADIO WORLD

Record [Bell Laboratories] (ISSN: 0743-0205) - *Varied* Jul/Aug, 1983 *under* AT&T TECHNOLOGY

Record [AT&T Bell Laboratories] (ISSN: 0749-8152) - *Varied* Sep, 1983 - Mar, 1986 *under* AT&T TECHNOLOGY

Record Review (ISSN: 0198-8573) - *Varied* ? - ? *under* FRESH!

Recording Engineer/Producer (ISSN: 0034-1673) - *Varied* Apr/May, 1970 - May, 1990 *under* REP: RECORDING ENGINEERING PRODUCTION

Reel and Slide Magazine - *Varied* Mar, 1918 - Dec, 1919 *under* MOVING PICTURE AGE

Relay Engineer - *Varied* ? - ? *under* CABLE TELEVISION ENGINEERING

Religious Communication Today - *Varied* Sep, 1978 - 1986? *under* JOURNAL OF COMMUNICATION AND RELIGION, THE

Rengo Film News - *Varied* Jun, 1959 *under* MOVIE/TV MARKETING

Reporter of Direct Mail Advertising, The - *Varied* May, 1938 - Apr, 1968 *under* DIRECT MARKETING

Reports - *Varied* Spring, 1975 - ?, 1987? *under* BROADCAST PIONEERS LIBRARY REPORTS

Reproductions Review & Methods (ISSN: 0164-4327) - *Varied* 1951 - Nov, 1979 *under* IN-PLANT REPRODUCTIONS

Retail Equipment - *Varied* ? - ? *under* RETAIL EQUIPMENT AND MERCHANDISE

Retailer and Advertiser, The - *Varied* Oct 19, 1901 - Dec, 1904 *under* RETAIL EQUIPMENT AND MERCHANDISE

Review of Books and Religion, The (ISSN: 0732-5800) - *Varied* Sep, 1981 - Sep/Oct, 1984 *under* BOOKS & RELIGION

Rona Barrett's Daytimers (ISSN: 0199-1817) - *Varied* Apr, 1977? - ?, 198u *under* REAL LIFE/DAYTIMERS

Rona Barrett's Gossip (ISSN: 0199-1590) - *Varied* May, 1972? - Dec, 1980 *under* GOSSIP

Roundup, The (ISSN: 0035-855x) - *Varied* Apr, 1953 - Jun, 1988 *under* ROUNDUP QUARTERLY

Royal Television Society Journal, The (ISSN: 0035-9270) - *Varied* Winter 1966/1967 - Nov/Dec, 1975 *under* TELEVISION

RSGB Bulletin - *Varied* 194u - Dec, 1967 *under* RADIO COMMUNICATION

RTNDA Bulletin - *Varied* Dec, 1952? - Dec, 1970 *under* COMMUNICATOR

RTNDA Communicator (ISSN: 0033-7153) - *Varied* 1971 - Jul, 1988 *under* COMMUNICATOR

S

Sales Management (ISSN: 0885-9019) - *Varied* Apr 6, 1929 - Nov 3, 1975 *under* SALES & MARKETING MANAGEMENT

Sales Management and Advertisers' Weekly - *Varied* May 26, 1928 - Mar 16, 1929 *under* SALES & MARKETING MANAGEMENT

Satellite TV (ISSN: 0744-9739) - *Varied* Jul/Aug, 1982 - ? *under* PRIVATE CABLE

Scholastic Editor - *Varied* 1923 - Mar, 1968 *under* SCHOLASTIC EDITOR'S TRENDS IN PUBLICATIONS

Scholastic Editor (ISSN: 0279-8980) - *Varied* Sep, 1975 - May, 1982 *under* SCHOLASTIC EDITOR'S TRENDS IN PUBLICATIONS

Scholastic Editor Graphics/Communications (ISSN: 0036-6390) - *Varied* Apr, 1968 - May, 1975 *under* SCHOLASTIC EDITOR'S TRENDS IN PUBLICATIONS

School Paperback Journal - *Varied* Oct, 1964 - May, 1966 *under* MEDIA & METHODS

Science & Electronics (ISSN: 0279-585x) - *Varied* Mar/Apr, 1981 - May/Jun, 1981 *under* COMMUNICATIONS WORLD

Scintillation (ISSN: 0147-5789) - *Varied* Winter, 1975? - 1978? *under* CINEMONKEY

Screen, The - *Varied* ? - Jun 29, 1951 *under* SCREEN WEEKLY, THE

Screen Actor (ISSN: 0036-956x) - *Varied* Aug, 1959 - Nov/Dec, 1966? *under* SCREEN ACTOR HOLLYWOOD

Screen Actor News (ISSN: 0746-9225) - *Varied* Mar, 1983 - Jan, 1986 *under* SCREEN ACTOR HOLLYWOOD

Screen Actor News (ISSN: 0745-7243) - *Varied* ? - ? *under* SCREEN ACTOR HOLLYWOOD

Screen Actor Newsletter (ISSN: 0195-2684) - *Varied* ? - ? *under* SCREEN ACTOR HOLLYWOOD

Screen and Television Guide - *Varied* Jul, 1948 - Nov, 1949 *under* TELEVISION AND SCREEN GUIDE

Screen Education (ISSN: 0306-0691) - *Varied* Oct, 1959 - Sep/Oct, 1968 *under* SCREEN

Screen Education Notes - *Varied* Winter, 1971 - Winter, 1973/1974 *under* SCREEN

Screen Guide - *Varied* May, 1936 - Jun, 1948 *under* TELEVISION AND SCREEN GUIDE

Screen Guide - *Varied* Oct, 1949 *under* TELEVISION AND SCREEN GUIDE

Screen Guide - *Varied* Dec, 1949 - Apr, 1951 *under* TELEVISION AND SCREEN GUIDE

Screen International & Cinema TV Today - *Varied* Sep 6, 1975 - ? *under* SCREEN INTERNATIONAL

Screenland - *Varied* 1920 - Aug, 1952 *under* SCREENLAND PLUS TV-LAND

ScriptWriter (ISSN: 0197-9388) - *Varied* Jan, 1980 - May, 1980 *under* SCRIPTWRITER NEWS

SEE; World Film News - *Varied* Sep, 1938 - Nov, 1938 *under* DOCUMENTARY FILM NEWS

Selection of Recent Books Published in Great Britain - *Varied* Mar, 1940 - Apr, 1941 *under* BRITISH BOOK NEWS

Service for Company Publications - *Varied* Jul, 1955 - Feb, 1974 *under* SERVICE FOR COMPANY COMMUNNICATORS

Service for Employee Publications - *Varied* Sep, 1949 - Jun, 1955 *under* SERVICE FOR COMPANY COMMUNNICATORS

Shooting Commercials (ISSN: 0163-3236) - *Varied* 1978 - 1979 *under* SHOOTING COMMERCIALS

Shooting Commercials & Industrials (ISSN: 0199-0497) - *Varied* 1979 - 1980 *under* SHOOTING COMMERCIALS

Short Wave & Television - *Varied* Jan, 1937 - Sep, 1938 *under* RADIO & TELEVISION

Short Wave Craft - *Varied* Jun/Jul, 1930 - Dec, 1936 *under* RADIO & TELEVISION

Show; The Magazine of the Arts (ISSN: 0037-4296) - *Varied* Oct, 1961 - May, 1965 *under* SHOW

Showmen's Motion Picture Trade Review - *Varied* May 27, 1933 - Feb 10, 1940 *under* SHOWMEN'S TRADE REVIEW

Shutterbug Ads - *Varied* ? - Oct?, 1984 *under* SHUTTERBUG

Sidney Miller's Black Radio Exclusive (ISSN: 0161-1526) - *Varied* Jan 1, 1976? - ? *under* BLACK RADIO EXCLUSIVE

Sightlines (ISSN: 0037-4830) - *Varied* Sep/Oct, 1967 - Summer?, 1987? *under* AFVA BULLETIN

SMPTE Journal (ISSN: 0898-0438) - *Varied* Jan, 1955 - Dec, 1955 *under* SMPTE JOURNAL

Social Science Information Studies (ISSN: 0143-6236) - *Varied* ? - Feb?, 1986 *under* INTERNATIONAL JOURNAL OF INFORMATION MANAGEMENT

Society of Cinematologists. Journal. - *Varied* ? - ? *under* CINEMA JOURNAL

Society of Film Teachers. Bulletin - *Varied* ? - ? *under* SCREEN

Sound (ISSN: 0703-6930) - *Varied* Oct, 1970 - Oct, 1973 *under* SOUND & VISION

Sound & Picture Tape Recording Magazine - *Varied* Apr, 1971 - Sep/Oct, 1973 *under* TAPE

Sound Blast - *Varied* ? - Feb?, 1989 *under* PRODUCTION SOUND REPORT

Sound Canada (ISSN: 0383-6908) - *Varied* Nov, 1973 - Nov/Dec, 1984 *under* SOUND & VISION

Southern Speech Bulletin - *Varied* Oct, 1935 - Mar, 1942 *under* SOUTHERN COMMUNICATION JOURNAL, THE

Southern Speech Communication Journal, The (ISSN: 0361-8269) - *Varied* Fall, 1971 - Summer, 1988 *under* SOUTHERN COMMUNICATION JOURNAL, THE

Southern Speech Journal, The (ISSN: 0038-4585) - *Varied* Sep, 1942 - Summer, 1971 *under* SOUTHERN COMMUNICATION JOURNAL, THE

Southern Theatre News - *Varied* 1956 - Summer, 1962 *under* SOUTHERN THEATRE

Speech Monographs (ISSN: 0038-7169) - *Varied* 1934 - Winter?, 1975 *under* COMMUNICATION MONOGRAPHS

Speech Teacher, The (ISSN: 0038-7177) - *Varied* Jan, 1952 - Nov, 1975 *under* COMMUNICATION EDUCATION

SPLC Report - *Varied* Spring, 1986 - ? *under* STUDENT PRESS LAW CENTER REPORT

St. Louis Photographer (ISSN: 0735-5629) - *Varied* Jan, 1883 - Dec, 1887 *under* ST. LOUIS AND CANADIAN PHOTOGRAPHER

St. Louis Practical Photographer - *Varied* Jan, 1877 - Dec?, 1882 *under* ST. LOUIS AND CANADIAN PHOTOGRAPHER

Stage, The - *Varied* 1880 - Feb 12, 1959 *under* STAGE AND TELEVISION TODAY, THE

Stage Directory - *Varied* 1880 *under* STAGE AND TELEVISION TODAY, THE

Star Hits (ISSN: 8750-7234) - *Varied* ? - ? *under* SMASH HITS

Starlog Presents Comics Scene (ISSN: 0732-5622) - *Varied* Jan/Feb, 1981 - ?, 1982 *under* COMICS SCENE

Strandlight - *Varied* ? - ? *under* LIGHTS!

Student Forum (ISSN: 0148-589x) - *Varied* Nov, 1978 - ?, 1978 *under* PHOTOGRAPHER'S FORUM

Studies in the Anthropology of Visual Communication (ISSN: 0192-6918) - *Varied* Fall, 1974 - 1979 *under* STUDIES IN VISUAL COMMUNICATION

Studio News - *Varied* Winter, 1942 - Jun, 1950 *under* ART DIRECTION

Studio Sound - *Varied* May, 1973 - ? *under* STUDIO SOUND AND BROADCAST ENGINEERING

STV (ISSN: 0885-6745) - *Varied* Jan, 1983 - 198u *under* STV GUIDE

Successful Writing - *Varied* Dec, 1920 - Feb, 1921 *under* WRITER'S DIGEST

Super 8 Filmaker (ISSN: 0049-2574) - *Varied* Winter, 1972/1973 - Jul/Aug, 1981 *under* MOVING IMAGE

Super Television - *Varied* Jan, 1985? - Mar, 1989? *under* CAMCORDER

T

T & R Bulletin - *Varied* 1925? - ? *under* RADIO COMMUNICATION

Tan (ISSN: 0039-9345) - *Varied* Nov, 1952 - Oct, 1971 *under* BLACK STARS

Tan Confessions - *Varied* Nov, 1950 - Sep, 1952 *under* BLACK STARS

Tape and Film Recording - *Varied* Nov/Dec, 1953 *under* TAPE RECORDING

Tape Business - *Varied* May/Jun, 1987 - ? *under* TAPE/DISC BUSINESS

Tape Recorder, The - *Varied* Jan?, 1959 - ? *under* STUDIO SOUND AND BROADCAST ENGINEERING

Tape Recorder - *Varied* ? - Apr, 1973? *under* STUDIO SOUND AND BROADCAST ENGINEERING

Tape Recording - *Varied* May, 1960 - ? *under* TAPE RECORDING

Tape Recording and Hi-Fi Magazine - *Varied* Aug, 1958 - Aug 10, 1960 *under* TAPE

Tape Recording & High Fidelity Reproduction Magazine - *Varied* Dec, 1957 - Nov, 1958 *under* TAPE

Tape Recording and Reproduction Magazine - *Varied* Feb, 1957 - Nov, 1957 *under* TAPE

Tape Recording Fortnightly - *Varied* Aug 24, 1960 - 1961 *under* TAPE

Tape Recording Magazine (ISSN: 0039-9558) - *Varied* 1961 - Mar, 1971 *under* TAPE

TC, Theatre Crafts - *Varied* Mar/Apr, 1967 - ? *under* THEATRE CRAFTS

TDR (ISSN: 0273-4354) - *Varied* Fall, 1967 - Winter, 1968 *under* TDR

Teacher's Guide to Media and Methods - *Varied* Sep, 1966 - Oct, 1967 *under* MEDIA & METHODS

Tech Photo Pro Imaging Systems (ISSN: 1040-0141) - *Varied* Jun, 1988 - Sep?, 1988 *under* ADVANCED IMAGING

Technician - *Varied* Sep, 1953 - Dec, 1953 *under* ELECTRONIC TECHNICAN/DEALER

Technician - *Varied* Aug, 1956 - Oct, 1956 *under* ELECTRONIC TECHNICAN/DEALER

Technician & Circuit Digests - *Varied* Jan, 1954 - Jul, 1956 *under* ELECTRONIC TECHNICAN/DEALER

Tele-Screen Century Series - *Varied* 1942 - 1943 *under* TELESCREEN

Telecommunication Journal - *Varied* 1948 - 1952 *under* TELECOMMUNICATION JOURNAL

Telecommunications [Euro-global Edition] (ISSN: 0192-6209) - *Varied* Sep, 1981? - ? *under* TELECOMMUNICATIONS

Telecommunications [Global Edition] (ISSN: 0278-484x) - *Varied* ? - Mar, 1986 *under* TELECOMMUNICATIONS

Telefilm International - *Varied* ? - ? *under* TELEVISION INTERNATIONAL

Telefilm Magazine - *Varied* Nov, 1958 - Jun/Jul, 1963 *under* TELEVISION INTERNATIONAL

Telegraph Age - *Varied* 1883 - Dec 16, 1909 *under* WIRE & RADIO COMMUNICATIONS

Telegraph and Telephone Age - *Varied* Jan, 1910 - Jun, 1953 *under* WIRE & RADIO COMMUNICATIONS

Telegraph and Telephone Journal, The - *Varied* Oct, 1914 - Dec, 1933 *under* POST OFFICE MAGAZINE

Telegraph World, The - *Varied* Jan, 1919 - ? *under* TELEGRAPH WORLD

Telegraphic Journal and Electrical Review - *Varied* Jan, 1873 - Dec, 1891 *under* ELECTRICAL REVIEW

Telegraphic Journal and Monthly Illustrated Review of Electrical Science - *Varied* Nov 15, 1872 - Dec, 1872 *under* ELECTRICAL REVIEW

Telephone Worker - *Varied* May, 1941 - Jun, 1947 *under* CWA NEWS

Telescreen Century - *Varied* 1944 - Spring, 1945 *under* TELESCREEN

Telespan's BusinessTV (ISSN: 0896-3142) - *Varied* 1986 - Jul/Aug, 1990 *under* TELESPAN'S BUSINESSTV GUIDE

Television - *Varied* Mar, 1928 - Jan, 1935 *under* ELECTRONIC ENGINEERING

Television - *Varied* Spring, 1944 - Jan, 1949 *under* TELEVISION

Television Age - *Varied* Aug, 1953 - Dec, 1969 *under* TELEVISION/RADIO AGE

Television Age International - *Varied* Apr, 1984 - Jul?, 1985 *under* TELEVISION / RADIO AGE INTERNATIONAL

Television & Children (ISSN: 0276-7309) - *Varied* Summer, 1980 - Summer/Fall, 1984 *under* TELEVISION & FAMILIES

Television and Short-Wave World - *Varied* Feb, 1935 - Sep, 1939 *under* ELECTRONIC ENGINEERING

Television/Broadcast Communications (ISSN: 0746-5777) - *Varied* Oct, 1983 - Dec, 1983 *under* TELEVISION BROADCAST

Television Digest with Consumer Electronics (ISSN: 0897-4632) - *Varied* 1961 - ? *under* TELEVISION DIGEST WITH CONSUMER ELECTRONICS

Television Magazine - *Varied* Feb, 1949 - Apr, 1955 *under* TELEVISION

Television Mail - *Varied* ? - ? *under* BROADCAST

Television News - *Varied* Mar/Apr, 1931 - Sep/Oct, 1932 *under* RADIO REVIEW AND TELEVISION NEWS

Television/Radio Age International - *Varied* ? - Feb, 1984 *under* TELEVISION / RADIO AGE INTERNATIONAL

The Advisers Bulletin - *Varied* ? - ? *under* CSPAA BULLETIN

Theatre, The (ISSN: 0891-6861) - *Varied* May, 1901 - Jul, 1917 *under* THEATRE MAGAZINE

Theatre Arts Magazine - *Varied* Nov, 1916 - Oct, 1923 *under* THEATRE ARTS

Theatre Arts Monthly - *Varied* Jan, 1924 - Oct, 1939 *under* THEATRE ARTS

Theatre Communications (ISSN: 0275-5971) - *Varied* Apr, 1979 - Mar, 1984 *under* AMERICAN THEATRE

Theatre Communications Group Newsletter (ISSN: 0163-9137) - *Varied* Jan, 1973 - Mar, 1979 *under* AMERICAN THEATRE

Theatre Design & Technology (ISSN: 0040-5477) - *Varied* May, 1965 - Feb, 1968 *under* THEATRE DESIGN & TECHNOLOGY

Theatre Design and Technology (ISSN: 0040-5477) - *Varied* May, 1968 - Winter, 1977 *under* THEATRE DESIGN & TECHNOLOGY

Theatre Guild Bulletin - *Varied* Dec, 1923 - Nov, 1925 *under* STAGE

Theatre Guild Magazine - *Varied* Oct, 1928 - Apr, 1932 *under* STAGE

Theatre Guild Quarterly - *Varied* Dec, 1925 - Sep, 1928 *under* STAGE

Theatre Newsletter - *Varied* Jul 15, 1946 - Jan 19, 1952 *under* THEATRE

Theatre Quarterly (ISSN: 0049-3600) - *Varied* Jan/Mar, 1971 - Oct/Dec, 1981 *under* NEW THEATRE QUARTERLY

Theatre Today - *Varied* #1 - 7 *under* FILM AND THEATRE TODAY

TM (ISSN: 8755-3104) - *Varied* ? - ? *under* TS

Today's Cinema - *Varied* 1930? - Nov, 1971 *under* SCREEN INTERNATIONAL

Today's Cinema News and Property Gazette - *Varied* Feb, 1928 - 1930? *under* SCREEN INTERNATIONAL

Today's Speech (ISSN: 0040-8573) - *Varied* Apr, 1953 - Fall, 1975 *under* COMMUNICATION QUARTERLY

Tortfeasor - *Varied* ? - ? *under* MEDIA LAW NOTES

Trade Circular and Literary Bulletin, The - *Varied* Sep, 1869 - Aug 18, 1870 *under* PUBLISHER'S WEEKLY

Trade Circular and Publishers' Bulletin, The - *Varied* Sep 18, 1870 - Dec 26, 1871 *under* PUBLISHER'S WEEKLY

Transactions - *Varied* 1953 - 1954 *under* IEEE TRANSACTIONS ON INFORMATION THEORY

Transactions - *Varied* Oct, 1916 - May, 1929 *under* SMPTE JOURNAL

Transactions of the IRE Professional Group on Broadcast and Television Receivers - *Varied* Jul, 1952 - Oct, 1954 *under* IEEE TRANSACTIONS ON CONSUMER ELECTRONICS

Travel & Camera (ISSN: 0049-4542) - *Varied* Feb, 1969 - Dec/Jan, 1970/1971 *under* TRAVEL & LEISURE

Tulane Drama Review (ISSN: 0886-800x) - *Varied* Jun, 1957 - Summer, 1967 *under* TDR

TV & Communications - *Varied* Jan, 1964 - Dec, 1966 *under* CABLE TV BUSINESS MAGAZINE

TV Availabilities - *Varied* ? - ? *under* BILLBOARD TV PROGRAM AND TIME AVAILABILITIES, THE

TV Broadcast Communications - *Varied* Jan, 1984 - Dec, 1984 *under* TELEVISION BROADCAST

TV Communications (ISSN: 0039-8519) - *Varied* Jan, 1967 - Jun, 1976 *under* CABLE TV BUSINESS MAGAZINE

TV Entertainment Monthly (ISSN: 1044-0682) - *Varied* 198u - 198u *under* TV ENTERTAINMENT

TV People (ISSN: 0492-0538) - *Varied* ? - ? *under* TV PEOPLE AND PICTURES

TV Search - *Varied* Jan/Feb, 1983 - Nov/Dec, 1989 *under* TELEVISION HISTORY

TVC (ISSN: 0164-8489) - *Varied* Jul, 1976 - Oct?, 1982 *under* CABLE TV BUSINESS MAGAZINE

U

UFPA Journal - *Varied* Jan, 1951 *under* JOURNAL OF FILM AND VIDEO

Union Tabloid (ISSN: 0275-8342) - *Varied* Feb, 1978 - Jun 30, 1983 *under* GRAPHIC COMMUNICATOR

Universal Weekly - *Varied* Jun 22, 1912 - Jun, 1915 *under* UNIVERSAL WEEKLY

University Film Journal - *Varied* ? - ?, 1968 *under* UNIVERSITY VISION

U.S. Camera - *Varied* 1935 - ? *under* TRAVEL & LEISURE

U.S. Camera - *Varied* Aug, 1941 - 1949? *under* TRAVEL & LEISURE

U.S. Camera - *Varied* 1952? - Dec, 1963 *under* TRAVEL & LEISURE

U.S. Camera & Travel - *Varied* Jan?, 1964 - Jan, 1969? *under* TRAVEL & LEISURE

U.S. Camera Annual (ISSN: 0749-0275) - *Varied* 1950 - 1952 *under* TRAVEL & LEISURE

U.S. Camera Magazine - *Varied* ? - Jul, 1941 *under* TRAVEL & LEISURE

USC Spectator, The - *Varied* Spring, 1982 - Spring, 1987 *under* SPECTATOR, THE

V

VE-Time Drama - *Varied* May, 1945 - Jul, 1945 *under* DRAMA

Ventura Publishes - *Varied* ? - 1988 *under* VENTURA PROFESSIONAL!

Victorian Periodicals Newsletter (ISSN: 0049-6189) - *Varied* Jan, 1968 - Winter, 1978 *under* VICTORIAN PERIODICALS REVIEW

Video (ISSN: 0276-0835) - *Varied* 1980 - 1983? *under* VIDEO EIGHTIES MAGAZINE

Video (ISSN: 0147-8907) - *Varied* Winter, 1978 - Aug?, 1987 *under* VIDEO MAGAZINE

Video 80 - *Varied* ? - ? *under* VIDEO EIGHTIES MAGAZINE

Video and Audio-Visual Review - *Varied* Nov, 1974 - May, 1978 *under* VIDEO

Video Cassettes Newsletter - *Varied* Mar, 1971 - Feb, 1972 *under* VIDEOCASSETTE AND CATV NEWSLETTER

Video Cassettes; the Systems, the Market, the Future - *Varied* ? - ? *under* VIDEOCASSETTE AND CATV NEWSLETTER

Video Manager (ISSN: 0747-3745) - *Varied* Apr, 1984 - Aug, 1989 *under* VIDEO MANAGEMENT

Video Marketplace (ISSN: 0895-2892) - *Varied* Oct/Nov, 1987 - Jun/Jul, 1990 *under* MOVIE MARKETPLACE

Video Movies (ISSN: 0742-8111) - *Varied* Mar, 1984 - ?, 1984 *under* VIDEO TIMES

Video Software Dealer (ISSN: 0894-3001) - *Varied* Sep, 1985 - ?, 1989 *under* VIDEO SOFTWARE MAGAZINE

Video User (ISSN: 0273-7817) - *Varied* Aug, 1980 - Mar, 1984 *under* VIDEO MANAGEMENT

Video Users Marketplace - *Varied* 1978 - ? *under* VIDEO MANAGEMENT

Videodisc and Optical Disk (ISSN: 0742-5740) - *Varied* Mar/Apr, 1984 - Nov/Dec, 1985 *under* OPTICAL INFORMATION SYSTEMS

Videodisc/Teletext (ISSN: 0198-9456) - *Varied* Winter, 1981 - Spring, 1981 *under* OPTICAL INFORMATION SYSTEMS

Videodisc, Videotex (ISSN: 0278-9183) - *Varied* Summer, 1981 - Jan/Feb, 1984 *under* OPTICAL INFORMATION SYSTEMS

View - *Varied* Aug, 1965 - Jun/Jul, 1967 *under* E-ITV

Vision - *Varied* Spring, 1962 - Summer, 1962 *under* FILM COMMENT

VJ-Time Drama - *Varied* Oct, 1945 *under* DRAMA

VU Marketplace (ISSN: 0149-6832) - *Varied* May, 1979 - Jul, 1980 *under* VIDEO MANAGEMENT

W

WACC Journal (ISSN: 0092-7821) - *Varied* 1970 - 1979 *under* MEDIA DEVELOPMENT

War-Time Drama - *Varied* Winter?, 1939/1940? - Apr?, 1945 *under* DRAMA

Washington Journalism Review (ISSN: 0149-1172) - *Varied* Oct, 1977 - 1980 *under* WASHINGTON JOURNALISM REVIEW

Weekly Television Digest with Consumer Electronics (ISSN: 0897-5620) - *Varied* ? - May 21, 1984 *under* TELEVISION DIGEST WITH CONSUMER ELECTRONICS

Welford Beaton's Hollywood Spectator - *Varied* Jun, 1933 - Mar, 1934 *under* HOLLYWOOD SPECTATOR

Western Monthly [Kansas City] - *Varied* 1902 - Sep, 1907 *under* ADVERTISING ADVOCATE

Western Speech (ISSN: 0043-4205) - *Varied* 1937 - 1975 *under* WESTERN JOURNAL OF SPEECH COMMUNICATION

Western Speech Communication (ISSN: 0147-2216) - *Varied* Spring, 1975 - Fall, 1976 *under* WESTERN JOURNAL OF SPEECH COMMUNICATION

Wid's - *Varied* Jun 1, 1916 - May 2, 1918 *under* FILM TV DAILY

Wid's Daily - *Varied* May 8, 1918 - Dec, 31, 1921 *under* FILM TV DAILY

Wid's Films and Film Folk - *Varied* Oct 14, 1915 - May 25, 1916 *under* FILM TV DAILY

Wire and Radio Communications - *Varied* Jul, 1953 - Jan, 1959 *under* WIRE & RADIO COMMUNICATIONS

Wireless Engineer - *Varied* Jan, 1936 - Dec, 1956 *under* INDUSTRIAL ELECTRONICS

Wireless Engineer and Experimental Wireless - *Varied* Sep, 1931 - Dec, 1935 *under* INDUSTRIAL ELECTRONICS

Wireless World, The (ISSN: 0043-6062) - *Varied* Jul, 1932 - Sep, 1983 *under* ELECTRONICS WORLD + WIRELESS WORLD

Wireless World and Radio Review, The - *Varied* Apr, 1922 - Jun, 1932 *under* ELECTRONICS WORLD + WIRELESS WORLD

WJR (ISSN: 0743-9881) - *Varied* Jan/Feb, 1981 - Dec, 1982 *under* WASHINGTON JOURNALISM REVIEW

World Film News - *Varied* Apr, 1936 - ? *under* DOCUMENTARY FILM NEWS

World Film News - *Varied* Feb, 1937 - Aug, 1938 *under* DOCUMENTARY FILM NEWS

World Film News and Television Progress - *Varied* ?, 1936 - Jan, 1937 *under* DOCUMENTARY FILM NEWS

World's Fair Electrical Engineering - *Varied* Jan, 1893 - May, 1893 *under* TELEPHONE MAGAZINE

World's Press News - *Varied* 1929 - Oct, 1935 *under* CAMPAIGN

World's Press News and Advertiser's Review - *Varied* 1944 - Nov 13, 1964 *under* CAMPAIGN

World's Press News and Advertising - *Varied* Nov, 1935 - Aug, 19, 1937 *under* CAMPAIGN

WPN and Advertisers' Review - *Varied* Nov 20, 1964 - Sep 4, 1968? *under* CAMPAIGN

Writer's Digest, The - *Varied* Mar, 1921 - Aug, 1921 *under* WRITER'S DIGEST

Writer's Northwest Handbook Newsletter (ISSN: 0895-8971) - *Varied* ? - ? *under* WRITER'S NW

Writer's Northwest Newsletter (ISSN: 0895-898x) - *Varied* Winter, 1987 - Winter, 1988 *under* WRITER'S NW

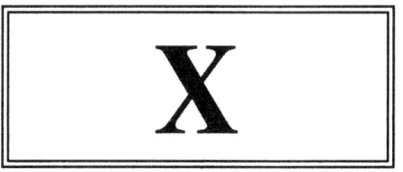

X

Xerox Ventura Pipeline - *Varied* 1988? - Vol 2, #1 *under* SCSC XEROX PIPELINE

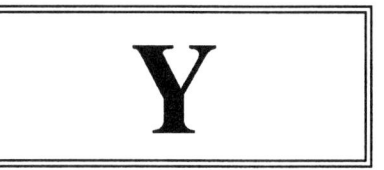

Y

Yale/Theatre (ISSN: 0044-0167) - *Varied* Spring, 1968 - Spring, 1977 *under* THEATER

Z

Zeiss Werkzeitschrift [English Edition] - *Varied* ? - ? *under* ZEISS INFORMATION

ZIP Target Marketing (ISSN: 0739-6953) - *Varied* Jan, 1978? - Jul, 1986? *under* TARGET MARKETING

VFOT

Varying Form of Title *(VFOT)* lists title variations as they might exist for a publication that utilizes initials, slang, non-standard punctuation, or non-English words in the *Main Title* or *Varies Title* listings. This list, therefore, provides titles which may appear under one or more alternate listings.

8

8mm Cine *See:* FILM MAKING

A

A/V Product News *See:* AV VIDEO
AA *See:* APPLIED ARTS QUARTERLY
AAAA Newsletter *See:* FOUR A NEWSLETTER
AAT *See:* ADVERTISING AND GRAPHIC ARTS TECHNIQUES
AB *See:* AMUSEMENT BUSINESS
ABA Communications Lawyer *See:* COMMUNICATIONS LAWYER
Academy Bulletin *See:* BULLETIN
Academy of Motion Picture Arts and Sciences. Bulletin *See:* BULLETIN
Access Reports/FOI Newsletter *See:* ACCESS REPORTS/FREEDOM OF INFORMATION
Access Reports/Freedom of Information Newsletter *See:* ACCESS REPORTS/FREEDOM OF INFORMATION
Accuracy in Media Report *See:* AIM REPORT
ACT News *See:* RE:ACT
Action for Children's Television News *See:* RE:ACT
AD *See:* ART DYNAMO
Ad Mentor, The *See:* AD • MENTOR, THE

Ad Week *See:* ADWEEK
Ad Week *See:* ADWEEK'S MARKETING WEEK
Ad Week/West *See:* ADWEEK
Ad Week's Marketing Week *See:* ADWEEK'S MARKETING WEEK
ADASC Bulletin *See:* ACA BULLETIN
Adventures *See:* DISNEY ADVENTURES
Advertising Ageurope *See:* FOCUS
Advertising and Marketing *See:* AM
Advertising & Marketing *See:* ASIAN ADVERTISING & MARKETING
Advertising Art Techniques *See:* ADVERTISING AND GRAPHIC ARTS TECHNIQUES
Advertising Assistant *See:* ADVERTISING AND GRAPHIC ARTS TECHNIQUES
Advertising Forum *See:* ADWEEK'S MARKETING WEEK
Advertising Mentor, The *See:* AD • MENTOR, THE
Advertising Sense *See:* AD SENSE
Advertising Techniques *See:* ADVERTISING AND GRAPHIC ARTS TECHNIQUES
Advertising Week *See:* ADWEEK
Advertising Week *See:* ADWEEK
Advertising Week/West *See:* ADWEEK
Advertising Weekly *See:* AD WEEKLY
Advertising Weekly *See:* ADWEEK
Advertising Week's Marketing Week *See:* ADWEEK'S MARKETING WEEK
AdvertisingWorld *See:* INTERNATIONAL ADVERTISER
AdWeekly *See:* AD WEEKLY
AFG *See:* FILM INDEX
AFI Close-Up *See:* CLOSE-UP
African-Asian Journalist *See:* AFRO-ASIAN JOURNALIST
After Image *See:* AFTERIMAGE

After Image *See:* AFTERIMAGE
Afternoon Television *See:* AFTERNOON TV
Air Brush Action *See:* AIRBRUSH ACTION
Alert *See:* BROADCAST ACCOUNTING ALERT
Allgemeine Elektricit ats-Gesselschaft Telefunken Progress *See:* AEG-TELEFUNKEN PROGRESS
Amalgated Wireless Australasia Technical Review *See:* AWA TECHNICAL REVIEW
Amateur Motion Picture Makers *See:* MOVIE MAKERS
Amateur Radio 73 *See:* 73 AMATEUR RADIO
Amateur Tape Recording and High-Fidelity *See:* HI-FI SOUND
Amateur Tape Recording, Video and High-Fidelity *See:* HI-FI SOUND
AMC Magazine *See:* AMERICAN MOVIE CLASSICS MAGAZINE
American Bar Association Communications Lawyer *See:* COMMUNICATIONS LAWYER
American Business Communication Association Bulletin *See:* BULLETIN OF THE ASSOCIATION FOR BUSINESS COMMUNICATION, THE
American Cinema Editor *See:* AMERICAN CINEMEDITOR
American College Theater Festival / Playwriting Awards Committee News *See:* ACTF / PAC NEWS
American Film and Video Association Bulletin *See:* AFVA BULLETIN
American Film Institute Education Newsletter *See:* AFI EDUCATION NEWSLETTER
American Film Institute Close-Up *See:* CLOSE-UP

American Institute of Graphic Arts Journal *See:* AIGA JOURNAL OF GRAPHIC DESIGN

American Institute of Graphic Arts Journal of Graphic Design *See:* AIGA JOURNAL OF GRAPHIC DESIGN

American Journalism Historians Association Intelligencer *See:* INTELLIGENCER

American Newspaper Publishers Association Research Report *See:* ANPA NEWS RESEARCH REPORT

American Newspaper Publishers Association Newspaper Information Service Newsletter *See:* ANPA PUBLIC AFFAIRS NEWSLETTER

American Newspaper Publishers Association Public Affairs Newsletter *See:* ANPA PUBLIC AFFAIRS NEWSLETTER

American Showcase *See:* LÜRZER'S INTERNATIONAL ARCHIVE

American Society of Composers, Authors and Publishers in Action *See:* ASCAP IN ACTION

American Society of composers, Authors and Publishers News *See:* ASCAP IN ACTION

American Society of composers, Authors and Publishers Today *See:* ASCAP IN ACTION

American Society of Magazine Photographers News *See:* ASMP BULLETIN

American Society of Journalism School Administrators. Bulletin *See:* JOURNALISM EDUCATOR, THE

American Telephone and Telegraph Magazine *See:* AT&T MAGAZINE

American Telephone and Telegraph Bell Laboratories Technical Journal *See:* AT&T TECHNICAL JOURNAL

American Telephone and Telegraph Technical Journal *See:* AT&T TECHNICAL JOURNAL

American Telephone and Telegraph Technology *See:* AT&T TECHNOLOGY

American Women in Radio and Television News and Views *See:* AWRT NEWS AND VIEWS

Amplitude Modulation-Frequency Modulation Television *See:* RCA BROADCAST NEWS

Animation *See:* ANIMATION MAGAZINE

Animation Film *See:* ANIMAFILM

Archiv fuer Elektronik und Uebertragungstechnik *See:* AEU

Archive *See:* LÜRZER'S INTERNATIONAL ARCHIVE

Art Director *See:* A-D

Art Director/Studio News *See:* ART DIRECTION

Art of Laughter, The *See:* STORYBOARD / THE ART OF LAUGHTER

Arts *See:* JOURNAL OF ARTS MANAGEMENT AND LAW, THE

Arts & Entertainment Program Guide *See:* A & E PROGRAM GUIDE

Arts & Entertainment Law Journal *See:* CARDOZO ARTS & ENTERTAINMENT LAW JOURNAL

Asia-Pacific Broadcasting Union Technical Review *See:* ABU TECHNICAL REVIEW

Asian Broadcasting Union Newsletter *See:* ABU NEWSLETTER

Asian Communication *See:* ASIAN JOURNAL OF COMMUNICATION

Asian Mass Communication Research and Information Centre. Documentation List *See:* MEDIA ASIA

ASIFA News *See:* ASIFA NOUVELLES

ASIFA Novosti *See:* ASIFA NOUVELLES

Associated Press Broadcaster *See:* AP BROADCASTER

Association for Business Communication. Journal of Business Communication *See:* JOURNAL OF BUSINESS COMMUNICATION, THE

Association for Communication Administration Bulletin *See:* ACA BULLETIN

Association for Education in Journalism and Mass Communication News *See:* AEJMC NEWS

Association for Education by Radio and Television Journal *See:* PUBLIC TELECOMMUNICATIONS REVIEW

Association for Recorded Sound Collections Journal *See:* ARSC JOURNAL

Association of American Publishers Monthly Report *See:* AAP MONTHLY REPORT

Association of Departments and Administrators in Speech Communication Bulletin *See:* ACA BULLETIN

Association of Learned and Professional Society Publishers Bulletin *See:* LEARNED PUBLISHING

Audio Engineering Society *See:* AES

Audio Phile *See:* AUDIOPHILE WITH HI-FI ANSWERS

Audio Video *See:* AUDIOVIDEO INTERNATIONAL

Audio Video Interiors *See:* AUDIO/VIDEO INTERIORS

Audio Video International *See:* AUDIO-VIDEO INTERNATIONAL

Audio-Visual Communications *See:* AVC

Audio Visual Communication Review *See:* EDUCATIONAL COMMUNICATION AND TECHNOLOGY

Audio-Visual Guide *See:* AV GUIDE

Audio Visual Instruction *See:* TECHTRENDS

Audio Visual Instruction with/Instructional Resources *See:* TECHTRENDS

Audio-Visual News Magazine *See:* FILM WORLD AND A-V NEWS MAGAZINE

Audio Visual Product News *See:* AV VIDEO

Audio Visual Video *See:* AV VIDEO

Audiocraft for the High-Fidelity Hobbyist *See:* AUDIOCRAFT FOR THE HI-FI HOBBYIST

Audiophile *See:* AUDIOPHILE WITH HI-FI ANSWERS

Audiovideo Video *See:* AV VIDEO

Audiovisual Directions *See:* AV VIDEO

Audit Bureau of Circulation News Bulletin *See:* ABC NEWS BULLETIN

Australasian Photo-Review *See:* APR

Australian Broadcasting Commission Weekly *See:* ABC WEEKLY

Australian Institution of Radio and Electronics Engineers *See:* PROCEEDINGS OF THE IREE AUSTRALIA

Australian Telecommunication Research *See:* ATR

AVideo *See:* AV VIDEO

AVPN *See:* AV VIDEO

B

B and R *See:* BOOKS & RELIGION

Back Stage Shoot *See:* BACK STAGE/SHOOT

Back Stage Supplement *See:* COMPUTER PICTURES

Ballet International *See:* BALLETT INTERNATIONAL

B&R *See:* BOOKS & RELIGION

BBB *See:* COMMUNICATION BOOKNOTES

BEA Educator News Notes *See:* BROADCAST EDUCATOR NEWS NOTES

BEA Management and Sales Committee Newsletter *See:* MANAGEMENT AND SALES DIVISION NEWSLETTER

BEA News Notes *See:* BROADCAST EDUCATOR NEWS NOTES

BEE *See:* RADIO WORLD

Bi-Weekly Newsletter - Mass Media Ministries *See:* MASS MEDIA NEWSLETTER

BIA *See:* BUSINESS INFORMATION ALERT

Billboard Television Program and Time Availabilities, The *See:* BILLBOARD TV PROGRAM AND TIME AVAILABILITIES, THE

Bioscope British Film Number *See:* BIOSCOPE, THE

Black Radio *See:* BLACK RADIO EXCLUSIVE

BM/E *See:* BME'S TELEVISION ENGINEERING

BMI Music World *See:* BMI: MUSICWORLD

BMI Musicworld *See:* BMI: MUSICWORLD

BMI, the Many Worlds of Music *See:* BMI: MUSICWORLD

BMU *See:* BOOK MARKETING UPDATE

Bookman's Weekly *See:* AB BOOKMAN'S WEEKLY

Booksellers Association of Great Britain and Ireland Book News *See:* BRITISH BOOK NEWS

Box Office *See:* BOXOFFICE

BP & P *See:* BROADCAST PROGRAMMING AND PRODUCTION

BPME Image *See:* BPME IMAGE MAGAZINE

BPME Newsletter *See:* BPME IMAGE MAGAZINE

British Broadcasting Corporation Engineering *See:* BBC ENGINEERING

British Broadcasting Corporation Quarterly, The *See:* BBC QUARTERLY, THE

British Broadcasting Corporation Empire Broadcasting *See:* BBC WORLD SERVICE LONDON CALLING

British Broadcasting Corporation London Calling *See:* BBC WORLD SERVICE LONDON CALLING

British Broadcasting Corporation World Service London Calling *See:* BBC WORLD SERVICE LONDON CALLING

British Kinematograph Sound and Television Society Journal *See:* IMAGE TECHNOLOGY

Broadcast Education Association Educator News Notes *See:* BROADCAST EDUCATOR NEWS NOTES

Broadcast Education Association Management and Sales Committee Newsletter *See:* MANAGEMENT AND SALES DIVISION NEWSLETTER

Broadcast Incorporating Television Weekly *See:* BROADCAST

Broadcast Management Engineering *See:* BME'S TELEVISION ENGINEERING

Broadcast Management Engineering's Television Engineering *See:* BME'S TELEVISION ENGINEERING

Broadcast Management/Engineering's World Broadcast News *See:* WORLD BROADCAST NEWS

Broadcast Plus Technology *See:* BROADCAST + TECHNOLOGY

Broadcast Promotion & Marketing Executives Image Magazine *See:* BPME IMAGE MAGAZINE

Broadcast Technology *See:* BROADCAST + TECHNOLOGY

BRQ *See:* PUBLISHING RESEARCH QUARTERLY

BSI *See:* BROADCAST SYSTEMS INTERNATIONAL

BTR *See:* BEYOND THE RATINGS/RADIO

BTR *See:* BEYOND THE RATINGS/TELEVISION

Bulletin *See:* BRITISH INSTITUTE OF RECORDED SOUND. BULLETIN.

Bulletin - American Society of Magazine Photographers *See:* ASMP BULLETIN

Business and Home Television Screen *See:* COMPUTER PICTURES

Business Bringer, The *See:* SCHEMER, THE

Business of Amusements, The *See:* AMUSEMENT BUSINESS

Business of Motion Pictures, The *See:* BUSINESS OF FILM, THE

Business Television *See:* TELESPAN'S BUSINESSTV GUIDE

Business Television Video Eight Guide *See:* BUSINESSTV VIDEO 8 GUIDE

Business Television Guide *See:* TELESPAN'S BUSINESSTV GUIDE

Business TV Video Eight Guide *See:* BUSINESSTV VIDEO 8 GUIDE

BusinessTV *See:* TELESPAN'S BUSINESSTV GUIDE

BusinessTV Guide *See:* TELESPAN'S BUSINESSTV GUIDE

C

C-ED *See:* COMMUNICATIONS ENGINEERING & DESIGN

C/Ed *See:* COMMUNICATIONS ENGINEERING & DESIGN

CA *See:* COMMUNICATION ARTS

Cable Age *See:* CABLEAGE

Cable Casting and Educational Television *See:* E-ITV

Cable, Cinema & Video Movie Digest *See:* CINEMA, VIDEO & CABLE MOVIE DIGEST

Cable International *See:* INTERNATIONAL CABLE

Cable Television *See:* VUE

Cable Television Advertising *See:* CABLE TV ADVERTISING

Cable Television and New Media: Law & Finance *See:* CABLE TV AND NEW MEDIA LAW & FINANCE

Cable Television Business *See:* CABLE TV BUSINESS MAGAZINE

Cable Television Programming *See:* CABLE TV PROGRAMMING

Cable TV Business *See:* CABLE TV BUSINESS MAGAZINE

Cable TV Business Magazine *See:* CABLE TV BUSINESS MAGAZINE

Cable Vision *See:* CABLEVISION

California Intercollegiate Press Association News *See:* CIPA NEWS

Camera *See:* TRAVEL & LEISURE

Camera & Darkroom *See:* CAMERA & DARKROOM PHOTOGRAPHY

Camera and Travel *See:* TRAVEL & LEISURE

Camera Annual *See:* TRAVEL & LEISURE

Camera Art *See:* CAMERART

Camera Magazine *See:* TRAVEL & LEISURE

Camera Thirty-five *See:* CAMERA 35

Camera Thirty-five *See:* CAMERA 35 INCORPORATING PHOTO WORLD

Camera Thirty-five Photo World *See:* CAMERA 35 INCORPORATING PHOTO WORLD

Camera Thirty-five with Photo World *See:* CAMERA 35 INCORPORATING PHOTO WORLD

Canadian Broadcasting Corporation Times *See:* CBC TIMES

Canadian Film and Television Bi-Weekly *See:* CANADIAN FILM DIGEST

Canadian Photographer *See:* ST. LOUIS AND CANADIAN PHOTOGRAPHER

Canadian Practical Photographer *See:* ST. LOUIS AND CANADIAN PHOTOGRAPHER

Canadian Pulp and Paper *See:* PULP & PAPER CANADA

Cartoon Quarterly *See:* KORKIS AND CAWLEY'S CARTOON QUARTERLY

Casting Magazine *See:* SPOTLIGHT CASTING MAGAZINE

CC Journalist *See:* COMMUNITY COLLEGE JOURNALIST

Center for Media and Public Affairs Media Monitor *See:* MEDIA MONITOR

Choice Video *See:* VIDEO CHOICE

Christians in Journalism *See:* GOOD NEWS: CHRISTIANS IN JOURNALISM

Christians in the Arts Networking News *See:* CANEWS

Cine Fan *See:* CINEFAN

Cine Fantastique *See:* CINEFANTASTIQUE

Cine Gram *See:* CINEGRAM

Cine Images *See:* CINEMAGES

Cine Magic *See:* CINEMAGIC

Cine Monkey *See:* CINEMONKEY

Cinema Canada *See:* CINEMA/CANADA

Cinema Editor *See:* AMERICAN CINEMEDITOR

Cinema Macabre *See:* CINEMACABRE

Cinema News, The *See:* CINEMANEWS, THE

Cinema Television Digest *See:* CTVD

Cinema Television Today *See:* SCREEN INTERNATIONAL

Cinema TV Digest *See:* CTVD

Cinematography Fan *See:* CINEFAN

Citizens Band Life *See:* CB LIFE

CLAP Newsletter *See:* COMMUNICATION LAW & POLICY NEWSLETTER

Claude Hall's International Radio Report *See:* INTERNATIONAL RADIO REPORT, THE

Clio Magazine for Mass Communications *See:* CLIO MAGAZINE

Collector of Postcards *See:* POSTCARD COLLECTOR

College Entertainment Guide *See:* AMPERSAND'S COLLEGE ENTERTAINMENT GUIDE
College Media Advisors Newsletter *See:* CMA NEWSLETTER
Color *See:* COLOUR
Columbia Scholastic Press Advisors Association Bulletin *See:* CSPAA BULLETIN
Comics F/X *See:* COMICS FANDOM EXAMINER
Comics Scene *See:* PREVUE
Comment *See:* HASTINGS COMMUNICATIONS AND ENTERTAINMENT LAW JOURNAL
Committee of Small Magazine Editors and Publishers Newsletter *See:* COSMEP NEWSLETTER
Commonwealth Broadcasting *See:* COMBROAD
Communication and Technology Newsletter *See:* CAT NEWS
Communication Arts Magazine *See:* COMMUNICATION ARTS
Communication: Journalism Education Today *See:* C: JET
Communications Research Center Newsletter *See:* CRC NEWSLETTER
Communications Satellite Corporation Technical Review *See:* COMSAT TECHNICAL REVIEW
Communications Week *See:* COMMUNICATIONSWEEK
Communications Workers of America News *See:* CWA NEWS
Community College Journalism Association Journalist *See:* COMMUNITY COLLEGE JOURNALIST
Compact Disc-Read Only Memory *See:* CD-ROM
Compact Disc-Read Only Memory Librarian *See:* CD-ROM LIBRARIAN
Compact Disc Review *See:* CD REVIEW
Congress-Span Update *See:* C-SPAN UPDATE
Connections *See:* C-O-N-N-E-C-T-I-O-N-S
Corporation for Public Broadcasting Memo *See:* REPORT
Corporation for Public Broadcasting Report *See:* REPORT
Council of Communication Libraries Newsletter *See:* FORUM
Council of Communication Libraries Forum *See:* FORUM
Council on International Nontheatrical Events News *See:* CINE NEWS
Countermeasures *See:* MILITARY ELECTRONICS / COUNTERMEASURES
CQ *See:* COMMUNICATION QUARTERLY
CQ *See:* KORKIS AND CAWLEY'S CARTOON QUARTERLY
CRR *See:* COMMUNICATION RESEARCH REPORTS

CSMC *See:* CRITICAL STUDIES IN MASS COMMUNICATION
CSSJ *See:* COMMUNICATION STUDIES

D

D/A *See:* PRINTING PAPER
Darkroom Techniques *See:* DARKROOM AND CREATIVE CAMERA TECHNIQUES
David Anthony Kraft's Comics Interview *See:* COMICS INTERVIEW
Daytime Television *See:* DAYTIME TV
Daytimers *See:* REAL LIFE/DAYTIMERS
Dealer Scope *See:* DEALERSCOPE
Decibel *See:* DB
Design *See:* RF DESIGN
Desk Top *See:* DESKTOP COMMUNICATIONS
Desk Top Communications *See:* DESKTOP COMMUNICATIONS
Desktop *See:* DESKTOP COMMUNICATIONS
Desktop Publishing *See:* PUBLISH!
Dialog Media Briefs *See:* MEDIABRIEFS
Direct Broadcast Satellite News *See:* DBS NEWS
Direct Marketing News *See:* DM NEWS
Disney Channel *See:* DISNEY CHANNEL MAGAZINE, THE
Distribution and Production *See:* PRODUCCIÓN Y DISTRIBUCIÓN
Division IV Newsletter *See:* ORGANIZATIONAL COMMUNICATION NEWSLETTER
Doctor Who Bulletin *See:* DWB
Dow Jones Newspaper Fund Adviser Update *See:* ADVISER UPDATE
Dow Jones Newspaper Fund Alumni Newsline *See:* ALUMNI NEWSLINE
Drama Review *See:* TDR
Drama Teachers' Bulletin *See:* THEATRE AND SCHOOL
Dramatic Censor *See:* MIRROR OF TASTE, AND DRAMATIC CENSOR, THE
Dynamic Art *See:* ART DYNAMO

E

E and ITV *See:* E-ITV
EC and TJ *See:* EDUCATIONAL COMMUNICATION AND TECHNOLOGY
EC & TJ *See:* EDUCATIONAL COMMUNICATION AND TECHNOLOGY

ECTJ *See:* EDUCATIONAL COMMUNICATION AND TECHNOLOGY
Educational and Industrial Television *See:* E-ITV
Educational Communication and Technology Journal *See:* EDUCATIONAL COMMUNICATION AND TECHNOLOGY
Educational Communication Technology Journal *See:* EDUCATIONAL COMMUNICATION AND TECHNOLOGY
Educational Film Library Association Bulletin *See:* AFVA BULLETIN
Educational-Industrial Television *See:* E-ITV
Educational Television Newsletter *See:* ETV NEWSLETTER
Educational Television Reporter *See:* ETV REPORTER
Eight Millimeter *See:* FILM MAKING
Eight Millimeter Cine *See:* FILM MAKING
Eight Millimeter Magazine *See:* FILM MAKING
Eight Millimeter Movie Maker and Cine Camera *See:* EIGHT MM MOVIE MAKER AND CINE CAMERA
EITV *See:* E-ITV
EJC *See:* EUROPEAN JOURNAL OF COMMUNICATION
Electronic and Radio Engineer *See:* INDUSTRIAL ELECTRONICS
Electronic Design *See:* STEP-BY-STEP ELECTRONIC DESIGN
Electronics and Communication *See:* AEU
Electronics and Communications *See:* ELECTRONICS & COMMUNICATIONS
Electronics Today International *See:* ETI
Electronics Week *See:* ELECTRONICS
EMI *See:* EDUCATIONAL MEDIA INTERNATIONAL
Enquirer, The *See:* NATIONAL ENQUIRER
Entertainment for the Home *See:* HOME ENTERTAINMENT
Entertainment Law Journal *See:* LOYOLA ENTERTAINMENT JOURNAL
Entertainment, Media & Intellectual Property Law Forum *See:* FORDHAM ENTERTAINMENT, MEDIA & INTELLECTUAL PROPERTY LAW FORUM
EP *See:* ELECTRONIC PRODUCTS
EP&P *See:* COMPUTER PUBLISHING
Epic Log *See:* EPI-LOG
Equalization *See:* EQ
ERR *See:* CONGRESSIONAL QUARTERLY'S EDITORIAL RESEARCH REPORTS
ETC *See:* EUROPEAN TRASH CINEMA
Ethics Update *See:* MEDIA ETHICS UPDATE
ETT *See:* EUROPEAN TRANSACTIONS ON TELECOMMUNICATIONS AND RELATED TECHNOLOGIES

European Broadcasting Union Review. Part B: General and Legal *See:* EBU REVIEW. PROGRAMMES, ADMINISTRATION, LAW.

European Broadcasting Union Review. Programmes, Administration, Law *See:* EBU REVIEW. PROGRAMMES, ADMINISTRATION, LAW.

European Broadcasting Union Review. Radio and Television Programmes, Administration, Law *See:* EBU REVIEW. PROGRAMMES, ADMINISTRATION, LAW.

European Broadcasting Union Bulletin *See:* EBU REVIEW. TECHNICAL.

European Broadcasting Union Documentation and Information Bulletin *See:* EBU REVIEW. TECHNICAL.

European Broadcasting Union Review. Part A: Technical *See:* EBU REVIEW. TECHNICAL.

European Broadcasting Union Review. Technical *See:* EBU REVIEW. TECHNICAL.

Experimental Wireless and the Wireless Engineer *See:* INDUSTRIAL ELECTRONICS

Export Polygraph International *See:* POLYGRAPH INTERNATIONAL

F

Falling for Stars Magazine *See:* FALLING FOR STARS
Fan Fare *See:* FANFARE
Fan Goria *See:* FANGORIA
Far East Film News and Television Views *See:* MOVIE/TV MARKETING
Federal Communications Commission Week *See:* FCC WEEK
Federation Internationale des Editeurs de Journaux-Bulletin *See:* FIEJ-BULLETIN
Federation News *See:* FILM
Feed Back *See:* FEEDBACK
Film and Film Folk *See:* FILM TV DAILY
Film and Video *See:* CHRISTIAN FILM & VIDEO
Film & Video: The Production Magazine *See:* FILM & VIDEO
Film/Audio Visual News *See:* FILM & VIDEO NEWS
Film Buff *See:* INTERNATIONAL FILM BUFF
Film Business *See:* BUSINESS OF FILM, THE
Film Fare *See:* FILMFARE
Film Fax *See:* FILMFAX
Film Land *See:* FILMLAND

Film Land's Famous Monsters *See:* FAMOUS MONSTERS OF FILMLAND
Film/Literature Quarterly *See:* LITERATURE/FILM QUARTERLY
Film Makers *See:* FILMMAKERS FILM & VIDEO MONTHLY
Film Makers Film and Video Monthly *See:* FILMMAKERS FILM & VIDEO MONTHLY
Film Makers Monthly *See:* FILMMAKERS FILM & VIDEO MONTHLY
Film Scientifique *See:* SCIENTIFIC FILM
Film Television Daily *See:* FILM TV DAILY
Film World *See:* FILMWORLD
Film World and Audio-Visual World News Magazine *See:* FILM WORLD AND A-V NEWS MAGAZINE
Filmis Index Cards {14938370} [NA] *See:* FILMIS
Filmis Mission *See:* FILMIS
Filmis Review *See:* FILMIS
Filmis Series *See:* FILMIS
Filmland Famous Monsters *See:* FAMOUS MONSTERS OF FILMLAND
Fine Line *See:* FINELINE
Flash *See:* MOVIE FLASH
Focus *See:* FOCUS
Folger Library Shakespeare Quarterly *See:* SHAKESPEARE QUARTERLY
Foresight Magazine *See:* 4SIGHT MAGAZINE
Fotografie International *See:* LEICA FOTOGRAFIE INTERNATIONAL
Four Color Magazine *See:* FOUR COLOR
Fourth Media Journal, The *See:* 4TH MEDIA JOURNAL, THE
Fourth Medium Journal, The *See:* 4TH MEDIA JOURNAL, THE
Freedom of Information Newsletter *See:* ACCESS REPORTS/FREEDOM OF INFORMATION
Freedom of Information Digest *See:* FOI DIGEST
Frequency Modulation *See:* COMMUNICATION ENGINEERING
Frequency Modulation and Television *See:* COMMUNICATION ENGINEERING
Frequency Modulation Electronic Equipment Engineering and Design Practise *See:* COMMUNICATION ENGINEERING
Frequency Modulation Radio-Electronic Engineering and Design *See:* COMMUNICATION ENGINEERING
Frequency Modulation Radio-Electronics *See:* COMMUNICATION ENGINEERING
Frequency Modulation-Television *See:* COMMUNICATION ENGINEERING
Frequency Modulation-Television Radio Communication *See:* COMMUNICATION ENGINEERING

FSIG Newsletter *See:* FEMINIST SCHOLARSHIP INTEREST GROUP NEWSLETTER OF THE INTERNATIONAL COMMUNICATION ASSOCIATION
Funny World *See:* FUNNYWORLD
Future Home Technology News *See:* FUTUREHOME TECHNOLOGY NEWS

G

Gannett Foundation Magazine *See:* GF MAGAZINE
General Radio Today *See:* GR TODAY
GF *See:* GF MAGAZINE
Gore Zone *See:* GOREZONE
Graphic Design, United States of America *See:* GRAPHIC DESIGN: USA
Graphics: United States of America *See:* GRAPHICS: U.S.A.
Grass Roots *See:* GRASSROOTS EDITOR
Grass Roots Editor *See:* GRASSROOTS EDITOR
Great Television Entertainment *See:* CABLE GUIDE, THE
GSM *See:* FANFARE

H

H&SR *See:* HOME & STUDIO RECORDING
HC Newsletter *See:* HEALTH COMMUNICATION NEWSLETTER
HCR *See:* HUMAN COMMUNICATION RESEARCH
HD TV Newsletter *See:* HDTV NEWSLETTER
HDTV Production *See:* HD PRODUCTION
HE *See:* HOME ENTERTAINMENT
HEQ *See:* HOME ENTERTAINMENT
Hi-Fi News & Record Review *See:* HI-FI NEWS AND RECORD REVIEW
High Definition Production *See:* HD PRODUCTION
High Definition Systems World Review *See:* HD SYSTEMS WORLD REVIEW
High Definition Television Production *See:* HD PRODUCTION
High Definition Television World Review *See:* HD SYSTEMS WORLD REVIEW
High Definition Television Newsletter *See:* HDTV NEWSLETTER
High Definition Television Report *See:* HDTV REPORT

High Definition TV Report *See:* HDTV REPORT

High Fidelity and Music Review *See:* STEREO REVIEW

High-Fidelity Answers *See:* HI-FI ANSWERS

High-Fidelity Choice *See:* HI-FI CHOICE

High-Fidelity Heretic *See:* HI-FI HERETIC

High Fidelity Magazine *See:* HIGH FIDELITY

High-Fidelity News and Record Review *See:* HI-FI NEWS AND RECORD REVIEW

High-Fidelity News Incorporating Record Review *See:* HI-FI NEWS AND RECORD REVIEW

High Fidelity Review *See:* STEREO REVIEW

High-Fidelity Sound *See:* HI-FI SOUND

High Fidelity/Stereo Review *See:* STEREO REVIEW

High-Fidelity Tape Recording *See:* TAPE RECORDING

High-Fidelity World *See:* HI-FI WORLD

High Technology Lifestyles *See:* HIGH TECH LIFESTYLES

Hit Songs of Radio *See:* RADIO HIT SONGS

HJC *See:* HOWARD JOURNAL OF COMMUNICATIONS, THE

Hollywood *See:* HOLLYWOOD STUDIO MAGAZINE

Hollywood Drama-Logue *See:* DRAMA-LOGUE

Hollywood Reporter Magazine *See:* HOLLYWOOD REPORTER

Hollywood Studio Magazine, Then and Now *See:* HOLLYWOOD STUDIO MAGAZINE

Hollywood Then and Now *See:* HOLLYWOOD STUDIO MAGAZINE

Home and Studio Recording *See:* HOME & STUDIO RECORDING

Home Motion Pictures *See:* HOME MOVIES

Home Motion Pictures Magazine *See:* HOME MOVIES

Horror Fan *See:* HORRORFAN

Hot Magazine *See:* SMASH HITS

HP *See:* HIGH PERFORMANCE

Hungarian Film Bulletin *See:* HUNGAROFILM BULLETIN

HVP *See:* HIGH VOLUME PRINTING

HVP *See:* HOME VIDEO PUBLISHER

I

I & I *See:* IMAGES & IDEAS BY PHOTOMETHODS

IBE International Broadcast Engineer *See:* IBE

ICA Communication and Technology Newsletter *See:* CAT NEWS

ICA Communication Law & Policy Newsletter *See:* COMMUNICATION LAW & POLICY NEWSLETTER

ICA Communique *See:* COMMUNIQUÉ

ICA Council of Communication Libraries Forum *See:* FORUM

ICA FSIG Newsletter *See:* FEMINIST SCHOLARSHIP INTEREST GROUP NEWSLETTER OF THE INTERNATIONAL COMMUNICATION ASSOCIATION

ICA Health Communication Newsletter *See:* HEALTH COMMUNICATION NEWSLETTER

ICA Intercultural & Development Communication Newsletter *See:* INTERCULTURAL & DEVELOPMENT COMMUNICATION NEWSLETTER

ICA Organizational Communication Newsletter *See:* ORGANIZATIONAL COMMUNICATION NEWSLETTER

ICA Political Communication Newsletter *See:* POLITICAL COMMUNICATION NEWSLETTER

ICA Public Relations Interest Group Newsletter *See:* PRIG

ICA Systems Letter *See:* SYSTEMSLETTER

IEE Electronics Letters *See:* ELECTRONICS LETTERS

IEEE Proceedings *See:* PROCEEDINGS OF THE IEEE

IFRA Newspaper Techniques *See:* NEWSPAPER TECHNIQUES

Illustrated Show Business *See:* SHOW BUSINESS ILLUSTRATED

Image Eleven *See:* IMAGE 11

Image Magazine *See:* BPME IMAGE MAGAZINE

Image Maker *See:* IMAGEMAKER

Images and Ideas *See:* IMAGES & IDEAS BY PHOTOMETHODS

In Motion *See:* IN MOTION FILM & VIDEO PRODUCTION MAGAZINE

In View *See:* INVIEW

In Vision *See:* INVISION

Industrial Advertising and Marketing *See:* AM

Information *See:* ZEISS INFORMATION

Information Systems Division Newsletter *See:* SYSTEMSLETTER

Information Theory *See:* IEEE TRANSACTIONS ON INFORMATION THEORY

Inland Printer/American Lithographer *See:* AMERICAN PRINTER

Institute of Electrical and Electronics Engineers Spectrum *See:* IEEE SPECTRUM

Institute of Electrical and Electronics Engineers Transactions on Broadcasting *See:* IEEE TRANSACTIONS ON BROADCASTING

Institute of Electrical and Electronics Engineers Transactions on Cable Television *See:* IEEE TRANSACTIONS ON CABLE TELEVISION

Institute of Electrical and Electronics Engineers Transactions on Communications *See:* IEEE TRANSACTIONS ON COMMUNICATIONS

Institute of Electrical and Electronics Engineers Transactions on Broadcast and Television Receivers *See:* IEEE TRANSACTIONS ON CONSUMER ELECTRONICS

Institute of Electrical and Electronics Engineers Transactions on Consumer Electronics *See:* IEEE TRANSACTIONS ON CONSUMER ELECTRONICS

Institute of Electrical and Electronic Engineers on Information Theory *See:* IEEE TRANSACTIONS ON INFORMATION THEORY

Institute of Electrical and Electronics Engineers - Proceedings *See:* PROCEEDINGS OF THE IEEE

Institute of Radio Engineers Transactions on Broadcasting *See:* IEEE TRANSACTIONS ON BROADCASTING

Institute of Radio Engineers Transactions on Broadcast and Television Receivers *See:* IEEE TRANSACTIONS ON CONSUMER ELECTRONICS

Institute of Radio Engineers Transactions on Information Theory *See:* IEEE TRANSACTIONS ON INFORMATION THEORY

Institution of Electrical Engineers Electronics Letters *See:* ELECTRONICS LETTERS

Institution of Radio and Electronics Engineers, Australia. Proceedings *See:* PROCEEDINGS OF THE IREE AUSTRALIA

Instructor Newsletter *See:* ILFORD PHOTO INSTRUCTOR NEWSLETTER

Inter Media *See:* INTERMEDIA

Inter-View *See:* INTERVIEW

Intercollegiate Broadcasting System Bulletin *See:* JOURNAL OF COLLEGE RADIO

Intercollegiate Broadcasting System Newsletter *See:* JOURNAL OF COLLEGE RADIO

Intercollegiate Religious Broadcasters Newsletter *See:* IRB

International Advertising Art *See:* NOVUM GEBRAUCHSGRAPHIK

International Animated Film Association News *See:* ASIFA NOUVELLES

International Archive *See:* LÜRZER'S INTERNATIONAL ARCHIVE

International Association of Business Communicators Journal *See:* JOURNAL OF COMMUNICATION MANAGEMENT
International Broadcast Engineer *See:* IBE
International Brotherhood of Electrical Workers Journal *See:* IBEW JOURNAL
International Cassette Association Newsletter *See:* ICA NEWSLETTER
International Communication Association Feminist Scholarship Interest Group Newsletter *See:* FEMINIST SCHOLARSHIP INTEREST GROUP NEWSLETTER OF THE INTERNATIONAL COMMUNICATION ASSOCIATION
International Communication Association Newsletter *See:* ICA NEWSLETTER
International Federation of Newspaper Publishers-Bulletin *See:* FIEJ-BULLETIN
International Federation of Journalists Information *See:* IFJ INFORMATION
International Literature *See:* INTERLIT
International Photographer *See:* INTERNATIONAL PHOTOGRAPHER MAGAZINE
International Press Institute Report *See:* IPI REPORT
International Press Institute Survey *See:* IPI SURVEY
International Radio and Television Organization Information *See:* OIRT INFORMATION
International Tape Association News Digest *See:* ITA NEWS DIGEST
International Theatre Institute World Theatre *See:* WORLD THEATRE
International Typeface Corporation Desktop *See:* DESKTOP COMMUNICATIONS
Internationale Zeitschrift fur Kommunikationsforschung *See:* COMMUNICATIONS
IPM *See:* INTERNATIONAL PHOTOGRAPHER MAGAZINE
IREE Australia, Proceedings *See:* PROCEEDINGS OF THE IREE AUSTRALIA
IREE Proceedings *See:* PROCEEDINGS OF THE IREE AUSTRALIA
IT *See:* INFORMATION TODAY
Italian Cinema *See:* SPAGHETTI CINEMA
ITI World Theatre *See:* WORLD THEATRE
IVTN *See:* INTERNATIONAL VIDEOTEXT TELETEXT NEWS

J

JACR *See:* JOURNAL OF APPLIED COMMUNICATION RESEARCH
James Bond 007 Fan Club *See:* BONDAGE
Japan Electronic Engineering *See:* JEE, JOURNAL OF ELECTRONIC ENGINEERING
JET *See:* C: JET
JIERE *See:* ELECTRONICS & COMMUNICATIONS ENGINEERING JOURNAL
JME *See:* JOURNAL OF MEDIA ECONOMICS
JMME *See:* JOURNAL OF MASS MEDIA ETHICS
Journal *See:* ELECTRONICS & COMMUNICATIONS ENGINEERING JOURNAL
Journal of Communication *See:* ASIAN JOURNAL OF COMMUNICATION
Journal of Communication European *See:* EUROPEAN JOURNAL OF COMMUNICATION
Journal of Electronic Engineering *See:* JEE, JOURNAL OF ELECTRONIC ENGINEERING
Journal of European Communication *See:* EUROPEAN JOURNAL OF COMMUNICATION
Journal of Information Management *See:* INTERNATIONAL JOURNAL OF INFORMATION MANAGEMENT
Journal of Marketing Research *See:* JMR, JOURNAL OF MARKETING RESEARCH
Journal of Photography in New England *See:* VIEWS
Journal of the Association for Education by Radio *See:* PUBLIC TELECOMMUNICATIONS REVIEW
Journal of the Association for Education by Radio and Television *See:* PUBLIC TELECOMMUNICATIONS REVIEW
Journal of the Federal Communications Bar Association *See:* FEDERAL COMMUNICATIONS LAW JOURNAL
Journal of the International Brotherhood of Electrical Workers *See:* JOURNAL
Journal - SMPTE *See:* SMPTE JOURNAL
Journal Union Internationale des Telecommunications *See:* TELECOMMUNICATION JOURNAL
Journalism Education Today *See:* C: JET
Journalism Education Association Newswire *See:* JEA NEWSWIRE
Journalism Quarterly *See:* JQ. JOURNALISM QUARTERLY.
JPF&T *See:* JOURNAL OF POPULAR FILM AND TELEVISION
JUFVA *See:* JOURNAL OF FILM AND VIDEO

K

Kappa Tau Alpha Newsletter *See:* KTA NEWSLETTER

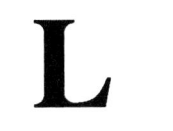

L

Law & Finance in Cable Television and New Media *See:* CABLE TV AND NEW MEDIA LAW & FINANCE
Leica Photografie *See:* LEICA PHOTOGRAPHY
Leica Photography International *See:* LEICA FOTOGRAFIE INTERNATIONAL
LFI *See:* LEICA FOTOGRAFIE INTERNATIONAL
Linkup *See:* LINK-UP
Listener and British Broadcasting Corporation Television Review *See:* LISTENER
Literary Bulletin *See:* PUBLISHER'S WEEKLY
LJ/SLJ Previews *See:* PREVIEWS
London Calling *See:* BBC WORLD SERVICE LONDON CALLING
LOOT *See:* LIES OF OUR TIMES
Low Power Television Report, The *See:* LPTV REPORT, THE
LSH *See:* LITTLE SHOPPE OF HORRORS
Lucas Film Fan Club *See:* LUCASFILM FAN CLUB, THE

M

M & MD *See:* MEDIAWEEK
Magazine Week *See:* MAGAZINEWEEK
Magnetic Tracks *See:* MAG TRACKS
Marketing Week *See:* ADWEEK'S MARKETING WEEK
Marquee *See:* MARKEE
Mass Communication and Society Newsletter *See:* MC&S NEWSLETTER
Mass Media Ethics *See:* JOURNAL OF MASS MEDIA ETHICS
McQ *See:* MANAGEMENT COMMUNICATION QUARTERLY
MCR *See:* MASS COMM REVIEW

MD&P *See:* MAGAZINE DESIGN & PRODUCTION
ME/C *See:* MILITARY ELECTRONICS / COUNTERMEASURES
MED *See:* MEDIA IN EDUCATION AND DEVELOPMENT
Media, Agencies, Clients/Western Advertising *See:* ADWEEK
Media and Methods *See:* MEDIA & METHODS
Media Anthropologist *See:* MEDIA ANTHROPOLOGIST NEWSLETTER
Media Briefs *See:* MEDIABRIEFS
Media Economics Journal *See:* JOURNAL OF MEDIA ECONOMICS
Media Mix Newsletter *See:* MEDIA MIX
Media Scene *See:* PREVUE
Media Scene Prevue *See:* PREVUE
Media Watch *See:* MEDIAWATCH
Media Week *See:* MEDIAWEEK
Media*Sight *See:* MEDIA SIGHT
Men's Guide to Fashion *See:* MGF
MF *See:* MOVIE FLASH
Mid Week Motion Picture News *See:* MIDWEEK MOTION PICTURE NEWS
Military Electronics *See:* MILITARY ELECTRONICS / COUNTERMEASURES
MIN *See:* MEDIA INDUSTRY NEWSLETTER
Miniature Camera Monthly *See:* MODERN PHOTOGRAPHY
Mirror of Taste *See:* MIRROR OF TASTE, AND DRAMATIC CENSOR, THE
MM *See:* MEDIA MONITOR
MME *See:* JOURNAL OF MASS MEDIA ETHICS
MMR *See:* MONDAY MORNING REPLAY
MMV *See:* MOVIE - THE VIDEO MAGAZINE
Monsters of Filmland *See:* FAMOUS MONSTERS OF FILMLAND
Monthly Report *See:* AAP MONTHLY REPORT
Motion Picture *See:* MOVIE
Motion Picture *See:* MOVIE
Motion Picture Action Magazine *See:* MOVIE ACTION MAGAZINE
Motion Picture Age *See:* MOVING PICTURE AGE
Motion Picture and Radio Guide *See:* MOVIE-RADIO GUIDE
Motion Picture Business *See:* BUSINESS OF FILM, THE
Motion Picture Classic *See:* MOVIE CLASSIC
Motion Picture Digest *See:* MOVIE DIGEST
Motion Picture Dream Guys *See:* MOVIE DREAM GUYS
Motion Picture Fan *See:* MOVIE FAN
Motion Picture Films and Filming *See:* FILMS AND FILMING
Motion Picture Fun *See:* FILM FUN
Motion Picture Geek *See:* MOVIE GEEK

Motion Picture Goer *See:* MOVIEGOER
Motion Picture Goer *See:* MOVIEGOER
Motion Picture Guide *See:* MOVIEGUIDE
Motion Picture Land *See:* FILMLAND
Motion Picture Land *See:* MOVIELAND AND TV TIME
Motion Picture Land and Television Time *See:* MOVIELAND AND TV TIME
Motion Picture Magazine, The *See:* MOVIE MAGAZINE, THE
Motion Picture Magazine, The *See:* NEW MOVIE MAGAZINE, THE
Motion Picture Makers *See:* MOVIE MAKERS
Motion Picture Mirror *See:* MOVIE MIRROR
Motion Picture News *See:* MIDWEEK MOTION PICTURE NEWS
Motion Picture-Play Magazine *See:* PICTURE PLAY MAGAZINE
Motion Picture-Radio Guide. *See:* MOVIE-RADIO GUIDE
Motion Picture Show *See:* MOVIE SHOW
Motion Picture Stars *See:* MOVIE STARS
Motion Picture Stars Parade *See:* MOVIE STARS
Motion Picture/Television Marketing *See:* MOVIE/TV MARKETING
Motion Picture World *See:* MOVIE WORLD
Motion Pictures and Ministry *See:* MOVIES AND MINISTRY
Motion Pictures and the People Who Make Them, The *See:* MOVIES AND THE PEOPLE WHO MAKE THEM, THE
Motion Pictures, The. *See:* MOVIES, THE
Motion Pictures United States of America *See:* MOVIES USA
Movie *See:* MOVIE - THE VIDEO MAGAZINE
Movie Fun *See:* FILM FUN
Movie Goer *See:* MOVIEGOER
Movie Goer *See:* MOVIEGOER
Movie Guide *See:* MOVIEGUIDE
Movie Land *See:* MOVIELAND AND TV TIME
Movie Land and Television Time *See:* MOVIELAND AND TV TIME
Movie/Television Marketing *See:* MOVIE/TV MARKETING
Movies International *See:* MOVING PICTURES INTERNATIONAL
Movies-Play Magazine *See:* PICTURE PLAY MAGAZINE
Movies United States of America *See:* MOVIES USA
Moyens Audio-Visuels *See:* EDUCATIONAL MEDIA INTERNATIONAL
MPCS Video Times *See:* VIDEO TIMES
MPI *See:* MOVING PICTURES INTERNATIONAL
MSN *See:* MOBILE SATELLITE NEWS
MT *See:* MONITORING TIMES
Multi Channel News *See:* MULTICHANNEL NEWS

Multiple System Operator *See:* MSO'S CABLE MARKETING
Multiple System Operator's Cable Marketing *See:* MSO'S CABLE MARKETING
Museum of Broadcasting News *See:* MB NEWS
Museum of Broadcasting Newsletter *See:* MB NEWS
Music/Sound Output *See:* STAGE & STUDIO
Music World *See:* BMI: MUSICWORLD
Musicline *See:* MUSIC LINE
MusicWorld *See:* BMI: MUSICWORLD
MVM *See:* MOVIE - THE VIDEO MAGAZINE

N

National Association for Better Broadcasting Quarterly *See:* BETTER RADIO AND TELEVISION
National Association for Better Radio and Television Quarterly *See:* BETTER RADIO AND TELEVISION
National Association of Radio News Directors Bulletin *See:* COMMUNICATOR
National Association of Broadcasters Highlights *See:* NAB HIGHLIGHTS
National Association of Broadcast Employees and Technicians News *See:* NABET NEWS
National Association of Broadcasters Reports *See:* NARTB MEMBER SERVICE
National Association of Broadcasters Member Service *See:* NARTB MEMBER SERVICE
National Association of Radio and Television Broadcasters Member Service *See:* NARTB MEMBER SERVICE
National Association of Television Program Executives Programmer *See:* NATPE PROGRAMMER
National Association of Educational Broadcasters Journal *See:* PUBLIC TELECOMMUNICATIONS REVIEW
National Association of Broadcasters Today *See:* TV TODAY
National Association of Broadcasters TV Today *See:* TV TODAY
National Broadcasting Company Digest *See:* NBC DIGEST
National Broadcasting Company Newsline *See:* NBC NEWSLINE
National Council for Children and Television Forum *See:* TELEVISION & FAMILIES
National Federation for Decency Informer *See:* AFA JOURNAL
National Federation for Decency Journal *See:* AFA JOURNAL

National Federation for Decency Newsletter *See:* AFA JOURNAL

National Forensic League Rostrum *See:* ROSTRUM

National Forum Editorial Cartoons, The *See:* NATIONAL FORUM, THE

National Industrial Television Association News *See:* INDUSTRIAL TELEVISION NEWS

National Institute of Audio-Visual Education Journal *See:* NIE JOURNAL

National Newspaper Association Publishers' Auxiliary *See:* PUBLISHER'S AUXILIARY

NCJ *See:* NEWS COMPUTING JOURNAL

New Motion Picture Magazine, The *See:* NEW MOVIE MAGAZINE, THE

New York Film Makers Newsletter *See:* FILMMAKERS FILM & VIDEO MONTHLY

News About BMI Music and Writers *See:* BMI: MUSICWORLD

News and Reviews of Non-Print Media *See:* PREVIEWS

News and the Law *See:* NEWS MEDIA & THE LAW, THE

News Digest - ITA *See:* ITA NEWS DIGEST

News From Associated Press Broadcasters *See:* NEWS FROM APB

News Inc *See:* NEWSINC.

News Incorporated *See:* NEWSINC.

News, The *See:* MIDWEEK MOTION PICTURE NEWS

Newsleads *See:* NEWS LEADS

Newsletter *See:* DOW JONES NEWSPAPER FUND NEWSLETTER

Newsletter of Kappa Tau Alpha *See:* KTA NEWSLETTER

Newsletter of the World Communication Association *See:* WCA NEWSLETTER

Newsletter. World Communication Association *See:* WCA NEWSLETTER

Nightime Television *See:* NIGHTTIME TV

NNA Pub Aux *See:* PUBLISHER'S AUXILIARY

NRJ *See:* NEWSPAPER RESEARCH JOURNAL

NTQ *See:* NEW THEATRE QUARTERLY

O

Official Fan Club Magazine of Star Trek *See:* STAR TREK: THE OFFICIAL FAN CLUB MAGAZINE

On Satellite *See:* ONSAT

Optical Memory Newsletter *See:* OPTICAL MEMORY NEWS

Opticmusic *See:* FILM & VIDEO

Our Times *See:* LIES OF OUR TIMES

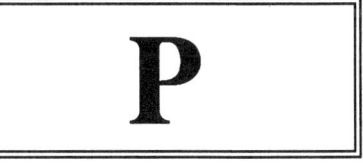

P

P/D *See:* PHOTO/DESIGN

PC *See:* PREMIUM CHANNELS TV BLUEPRINT

PCN *See:* PD REPORT

PCS *See:* PCS, THE POPULAR CULTURE SCHOLAR

PD *See:* PRODUCT DIGEST

People and Careers in Telecommunications *See:* PACTSHEET

Personal Computer Publishing and Presentations *See:* PC PUBLISHING AND PRESENTATIONS

PFVEA Newsletter *See:* FOLLOW FOCUS

Philcom Newsletter *See:* COMMUNIQUÉ

Phillips Mobile Satellite News *See:* MOBILE SATELLITE NEWS

Photo Design *See:* PHOTO/DESIGN

Photo Dramatist, The *See:* PHOTODRAMATIST, THE

Photo Education *See:* PHOTOEDUCATION

Photo Instructor Newsletter *See:* ILFORD PHOTO INSTRUCTOR NEWSLETTER

Photo Letter *See:* PHOTOLETTER

Photo Methods *See:* PHOTOMETHODS

Photo Methods for Industry *See:* PHOTOMETHODS

Photo Play *See:* PHOTOPLAY

Photo Play Combined with Motion Picture Mirror *See:* PHOTOPLAY COMBINED WITH MOVIE MIRROR

Photo Play Studies *See:* PHOTOPLAY STUDIES

Photo Pro *See:* PHOTOPRO

Photo Star *See:* PHOTOSTAR

PhotoDesign *See:* PHOTO/DESIGN

Photographic *See:* PETERSEN'S PHOTOGRAPHIC

Photographic Journal of America *See:* CAMERA, THE

Photographic Magazine *See:* PETERSEN'S PHOTOGRAPHIC

Photographic Society of America Journal *See:* PSA JOURNAL

Photography Laboratory Management *See:* PHOTO LAB MANAGEMENT

Photography Pro *See:* PHOTOPRO

Photography Professional *See:* PHOTOPRO

Photography Unique *See:* PHOTIQUE

Photomethods Images & Ideas *See:* IMAGES & IDEAS BY PHOTOMETHODS

Photonique *See:* PHOTIQUE

PI *See:* POLYGRAPH INTERNATIONAL

Pictorial *See:* STAGE PICTORIAL

Pictorial of the Stage *See:* STAGE PICTORIAL

Picture News *See:* MIDWEEK MOTION PICTURE NEWS

Pipeline *See:* SCSC XEROX PIPELINE

Play Back *See:* PLAYBACK

Play Bill *See:* PLAYBILL

Play Time *See:* PLAYTIME

Playshop *See:* PLAY SHOP, THE

Playwriting Awards Committee News *See:* ACTF / PAC NEWS

Political Cartoon Quarterly *See:* TARGET

Popular Culture Scholar *See:* PCS, THE POPULAR CULTURE SCHOLAR

Popular Electronics Including Hands-On Electronics *See:* POPULAR ELECTRONICS

Popular Film *See:* JOURNAL OF POPULAR FILM AND TELEVISION

Post Card Collector *See:* POSTCARD COLLECTOR

PQ *See:* PRODUCERS QUARTERLY

PR News *See:* PUBLIC RELATIONS NEWS

PR: The Quarterly Review of Public Relations *See:* PUBLIC RELATIONS QUARTERLY

Practical Photographer *See:* ST. LOUIS AND CANADIAN PHOTOGRAPHER

Premiere *See:* AMERICAN PREMIERE

Premium Channels *See:* PREMIUM CHANNELS TV BLUEPRINT

Premium Channels Television Blueprint *See:* PREMIUM CHANNELS TV BLUEPRINT

Press Time *See:* PRESSTIME

Print Equipment News *See:* PRINT-EQUIP NEWS

Printer and Lithographe *See:* AMERICAN PRINTER

Printing News. East *See:* PRINTINGNEWS

PrintingNews. East *See:* PRINTINGNEWS

Pro Imaging Systems *See:* ADVANCED IMAGING

Proceedings *See:* PROCEEDINGS OF THE IEEE

Proceedings *See:* PROCEEDINGS OF THE IREE AUSTRALIA

Proceedings - IRE *See:* PROCEEDINGS OF THE IREE AUSTRALIA

Proceedings of the Institute of Electrical and Electronics Engineers *See:* PROCEEDINGS OF THE IEEE

Proceedings of the Institute of Radio Engineers *See:* PROCEEDINGS OF THE IEEE

Production and Distribution *See:* PRODUCCIÓN Y DISTRIBUCIÓN

Professional Imaging Systems *See:* ADVANCED IMAGING

Professional Sound News *See:* PRO SOUND NEWS

Professional Videogram *See:* PRO VIDEOGRAM

Program Director Cue *See:* NATPE PROGRAMMER

Programmer *See:* NATPE PROGRAMMER

PRQ *See:* PUBLIC RELATIONS QUARTERLY

PSA *See:* PSA JOURNAL

PSN *See:* PRO SOUND NEWS

PTR *See:* PUBLIC TELECOMMUNICATIONS REVIEW

Pub Aux *See:* PUBLISHER'S AUXILIARY

Public Relations *See:* PUBLIC RELATIONS QUARTERLY

Public Relations Interest Group Newsletter *See:* PRIG

Public Relations Week *See:* PR WEEK

Public Service Advertising *See:* PSA

Publishers Mark ing Association Newsletter *See:* PMA NEWSLETTER

Pulse *See:* PULSE OF RADIO

PV *See:* PRO VIDEOGRAM

Q

QRFS *See:* QUARTERLY REVIEW OF FILM AND VIDEO

QRFV *See:* QUARTERLY REVIEW OF FILM AND VIDEO

Quarterly of Communication Management *See:* MANAGEMENT COMMUNICATION QUARTERLY

Quigley Publishing Herald *See:* MOTION PICTURE PRODUCT DIGEST

R

Radio Active *See:* RADIOACTIVE

Radio and Records *See:* R & R

Radio Corporation of America Broadcast News *See:* RCA BROADCAST NEWS

Radio Frequency Design *See:* RF DESIGN

Radio Land *See:* RADIOLAND

Radio Manufacturers Association Engineer *See:* RMA ENGINEER

Radio Report *See:* INTERNATIONAL RADIO REPORT, THE

Radio Rural *See:* RURAL RADIO

Radio Society of Great Britain Bulletin *See:* RADIO COMMUNICATION

Radio Songs *See:* RADIO HIT SONGS

Radio Television Daily *See:* RTD

Radio Television News Directors Association Bulletin *See:* COMMUNICATOR

Radio Television News Directors Association Communicator *See:* COMMUNICATOR

Radio Television Show *See:* TV RADIO SHOW

Radio TV Talk *See:* TV RADIO TALK

Radio Vision *See:* AMATEUR WIRELESS AND RADIOVISION

Radio Week *See:* RADIOWEEK

RadioWorld *See:* RADIO WORLD

Range Finder *See:* RANGEFINDER, THE

Range Finder, The *See:* RANGEFINDER, THE

RBR *See:* RADIO BUSINESS REPORT

Re: Action for Children's Television *See:* RE:ACT

RE/P *See:* REP: RECORDING ENGINEERING PRODUCTION

Real Life *See:* REAL LIFE/DAYTIMERS

Real Life *See:* REEL LIFE

Recherches Theatrales *See:* THEATRE RESEARCH

Recording, Engineering, Producing *See:* REP: RECORDING ENGINEERING PRODUCTION

Research Society for American Periodicals Newsletter *See:* RSAP NEWSLETTER

Retailer *See:* SATELLITE RETAILER

Retro Focus *See:* RETROFOCUS

Review *See:* ENTERTAINMENT REVUE

Review of Film and Video *See:* QUARTERLY REVIEW OF FILM AND VIDEO

Review of Film Studies *See:* QUARTERLY REVIEW OF FILM AND VIDEO

Review of Serials *See:* SERIALS REVIEW

Revue *See:* ENTERTAINMENT REVUE

RFDesign *See:* RF DESIGN

Rhetoric and Philosophy *See:* PHILOSOPHY AND RHETORIC

Rona Barretts Daytimers Television *See:* REAL LIFE/DAYTIMERS

Rona Barretts Daytimers TV *See:* REAL LIFE/DAYTIMERS

Ross Talent Report *See:* ROSS REPORTS TELEVISION

RSQ *See:* RHETORIC SOCIETY QUARTERLY

RW *See:* RADIO WORLD

RWN *See:* RADIO WORLD

S

S & MM *See:* SALES & MARKETING MANAGEMENT

SA *See:* STRANGE ADVENTURES

SAG Hollywood *See:* SCREEN ACTOR HOLLYWOOD

Saint Louis and Canadian Photographer *See:* ST. LOUIS AND CANADIAN PHOTOGRAPHER

Saint Louis Journalism Review *See:* ST. LOUIS JOURNALISM REVIEW

Saint Louis Practical Photographer *See:* ST. LOUIS AND CANADIAN PHOTOGRAPHER

Sample Book of Mill-Brand Papers *See:* PRINTING PAPER

Satellite News *See:* MOBILE SATELLITE NEWS

Satellite Television *See:* PRIVATE CABLE

Satellite Television Magazine *See:* PRIVATE CABLE

Satellite Television Week *See:* SATELLITE TV WEEK

Satellite Television *See:* STV GUIDE

Satellite Television Guide *See:* STV GUIDE

Satellite TV Magazine *See:* PRIVATE CABLE

SB/AL *See:* STORYBOARD / THE ART OF LAUGHTER

SBI *See:* SHOW BUSINESS ILLUSTRATED

Science Fiction Movieland *See:* SF MOVIELAND

Screen Actors Guild Hollywood *See:* SCREEN ACTOR HOLLYWOOD

Screen and Television Secrets *See:* TV AND SCREEN SECRETS

Screen International and Cinema Television Today *See:* SCREEN INTERNATIONAL

Screen Land *See:* SCREENLAND PLUS TV-LAND

Screen Land Plus Television-Land *See:* SCREENLAND PLUS TV-LAND

Screen Secrets *See:* TV AND SCREEN SECRETS

ScreenLand Plus Television-Land *See:* SCREENLAND PLUS TV-LAND

Screenwriting Coalition foR Industry Professionals and Teachers Newsletter *See:* SCRIPT NEWSLETTER

Script Writer News *See:* SCRIPTWRITER NEWS

SCSC Pipeline *See:* SCSC XEROX PIPELINE

SCTE Cable Television Engineering *See:* CABLE TELEVISION ENGINEERING

Secret Agent *See:* TOP SECRET

Security and Auto Sound *See:* AUTO SOUND & SECURITY

SEE; World Film News *See:* DOCUMENTARY FILM NEWS

Seen at the Movies *See:* SCENE AT THE MOVIES

Seventy-Three *See:* 73 AMATEUR RADIO

Seventy-Three Amateur Radio *See:* 73 AMATEUR RADIO

Seventy-Three Amateur Radio's Technical Journal *See:* 73 AMATEUR RADIO

Seventy-Three for Radio Amateurs *See:* 73 AMATEUR RADIO
Seybold Digital Media *See:* DIGITAL MEDIA
Shoot *See:* BACK STAGE/SHOOT
Show *See:* TV RADIO SHOW
Show *See:* TV SHOW
Show Business West *See:* SHOW BIZ WEST
Show Case World *See:* SHOWCASE WORLD
Show Magazine *See:* SHOW
Showbiz Magazine *See:* SOSYAL! MAGAZINE
Shutterbug Advertisements *See:* SHUTTERBUG
Shutterbug Advertisements Photographic News *See:* SHUTTERBUG
Sight Lines *See:* AFVA BULLETIN
Six Shooters *See:* SIXSHOOTERS
Sixty Seconds *See:* 60 SECONDS
SJR *See:* ST. LOUIS JOURNALISM REVIEW
Society and Discourse *See:* DISCOURSE & SOCIETY
Society for Scholarly Publishing Letter *See:* SSP LETTER
Society of Cable Television Engineers Cable Television Engineering *See:* CABLE TELEVISION ENGINEERING
Society of Motion Picture and Television Engineers Journal *See:* SMPTE JOURNAL
Society of Newspaper Design *See:* DESIGN
Sosyal! Showbiz Magazine *See:* SOSYAL! MAGAZINE
Sound News *See:* PRO SOUND NEWS
Southern States Communication Association Connections *See:* C-O-N-N-E-C-T-I-O-N-S
SP *See:* STAGE PICTORIAL
Spectrum *See:* IEEE SPECTRUM
Speech Communication Association Women's Caucus and Feminist & Women Studies Division Newsletter *See:* SCA WOMEN'S CAUCUS AND FEMINIST & WOMEN STUDIES DIVISION NEWSLETTER
Sports and Entertainment Lawyer, The *See:* ENTERTAINMENT AND SPORTS LAWYER, THE
SR *See:* SERIALS REVIEW
Standard Rate and Data Service Report, The *See:* SRDS REPORT, THE
Star Parade *See:* TV STAR PARADE
Starline Presents Teen Dream *See:* TEEN DREAM
Starlog Presents Fangoria *See:* FANGORIA
Stars *See:* STARZ
Stereo Choice *See:* HI-FI CHOICE
Story Board / The Art of Laughter *See:* STORYBOARD / THE ART OF LAUGHTER
Street & Smith's Picture-Play Magazine *See:* PICTURE PLAY MAGAZINE
STW *See:* SATELLITE TV WEEK

Super Eight Filmaker *See:* MOVING IMAGE
Synergetic Audio Concepts Newsletter *See:* SYN-AUD-CON NEWSLETTER
Systems Customer Support Center Xerox Pipeline *See:* SCSC XEROX PIPELINE
Systems Letter *See:* SYSTEMSLETTER

T

Talk *See:* TV RADIO TALK
Tape Recording and High-Fidelity Magazine *See:* TAPE
Taylor Talk *See:* TAYLORTALK
TC *See:* THEATRE CRAFTS
TCG Newsletter *See:* AMERICAN THEATRE
TD & T *See:* THEATRE DESIGN & TECHNOLOGY
TDRS *See:* DIRECT RESPONSE SPECIALIST, THE
Tech Trends *See:* TECHTRENDS
Technical Journal *See:* AT&T TECHNICAL JOURNAL
Technical Photo Professional Imaging Systems *See:* ADVANCED IMAGING
Technical Review of the Asian Broadcasting Union *See:* ABU TECHNICAL REVIEW
Technical Trends *See:* TECHTRENDS
Technological Horizons in Education Journal *See:* THE JOURNAL
Teen Stars *See:* TS
Tele Conference Magazine *See:* TELECONFERENCE MAGAZINE
Tele Screen *See:* TELESCREEN
Tele Screen Century *See:* TELESCREEN
Tele Span's Business Television *See:* TELESPAN'S BUSINESSTV GUIDE
Tele Span's Business Television Guide *See:* TELESPAN'S BUSINESSTV GUIDE
Tele-Vision Engineering *See:* TELEVISION ENGINEERING
Teleconferencing Magazine *See:* TELECONFERENCE MAGAZINE
TeleSpan's Business Television *See:* TELESPAN'S BUSINESSTV GUIDE
TeleSpan's Business Television Guide *See:* TELESPAN'S BUSINESSTV GUIDE
Television *See:* TV SHOW
Television and Appliance Mart *See:* TV & APPLIANCE MART
Television and Communications *See:* CABLE TV BUSINESS MAGAZINE
Television and Radio FAXletter *See:* TV & RADIO FAXLETTER
Television and Screen Secrets *See:* TV AND SCREEN SECRETS

Television Availabilities *See:* BILLBOARD TV PROGRAM AND TIME AVAILABILITIES, THE
Television Blueprint *See:* PREMIUM CHANNELS TV BLUEPRINT
Television Broadcast Communications *See:* TELEVISION BROADCAST
Television Bureau of Advertising Sales News *See:* SALES NEWS
Television Business International *See:* TBI
Television Communications *See:* CABLE TV BUSINESS MAGAZINE
Television Conference Magazine *See:* TELECONFERENCE MAGAZINE
Television Digest *See:* TELEVISION DIGEST WITH CONSUMER ELECTRONICS
Television-Electronic Technician *See:* TV-ELECTRONIC TECHNICIAN
Television Engineering *See:* BME'S TELEVISION ENGINEERING
Television, Etc *See:* TV, ETC.
Television, Etcetera *See:* TV, ETC.
Television Gold *See:* TV GOLD
Television Guide *See:* TV GUIDE
Television Guide *See:* TV GUIDE
Television Mirror *See:* TV MIRROR
Television People *See:* TV PEOPLE AND PICTURES
Television People and Pictures *See:* TV PEOPLE AND PICTURES
Television Program Investor *See:* TV PROGRAM INVESTOR
Television/Radio Age *See:* TELEVISION/RADIO AGE
Television Radio Mirror *See:* TV RADIO MIRROR
Television Radio Show *See:* TV RADIO SHOW
Television Radio Talk *See:* TV RADIO TALK
Television Screen *See:* TELESCREEN
Television Screen *See:* TV SCREEN
Television Screen Century *See:* TELESCREEN
Television-Screen Century Series *See:* TELESCREEN
Television Search *See:* TELEVISION HISTORY
Television Show *See:* TV SHOW
Television Star Parade *See:* TV STAR PARADE
Television Stars *See:* TV STARS
Television Technology *See:* TV TECHNOLOGY
Television Times *See:* TV TIMES
Television Today *See:* TV TODAY
Television World *See:* TV WORLD
Television World *See:* TV WORLD
Text and Performance Quarterly *See:* TPQ
TGIF Magazine *See:* TGIF
Thank Goodness It's Friday *See:* TGIF

Thank Goodness It's Friday Magazine *See:* TGIF
The Drama Review *See:* TDR
Theater News *See:* THEATRE NEWS
Theater Week *See:* THEATERWEEK
Thirty Five Millimeter Photography *See:* PHOTOGRAPHY
Thirty-Five Millimeter Photography *See:* 35MM PHOTOGRAPHY
TJ *See:* THEATRE JOURNAL
Today *See:* TV TODAY
Trade Circular *See:* PUBLISHER'S WEEKLY
Trans World Radio *See:* TWR
Transaction Periodicals Consortium Book Research Quarterly *See:* PUBLISHING RESEARCH QUARTERLY
Transactions on Broadcasting *See:* IEEE TRANSACTIONS ON BROADCASTING
Transactions on Telecommunications European *See:* EUROPEAN TRANSACTIONS ON TELECOMMUNICATIONS AND RELATED TECHNOLOGIES
Trash Cinema *See:* EUROPEAN TRASH CINEMA
Trends in Publications *See:* SCHOLASTIC EDITOR'S TRENDS IN PUBLICATIONS
TS *See:* TOP SECRET
Tulane Drama Review *See:* TDR
TV *See:* TV SHOW
TV Blueprint *See:* PREMIUM CHANNELS TV BLUEPRINT
TV, Etcetera *See:* TV, ETC.
TvB Sales News *See:* SALES NEWS
TVCommunications *See:* CABLE TV BUSINESS MAGAZINE
Twenty/Twenty *See:* 20/20

U

Unique Magazine *See:* UNIQUE
United Kingdom Press Gazette *See:* UK PRESS GAZETTE
United Press International Advance *See:* UPI ADVANCE
United States Camera *See:* TRAVEL & LEISURE
United States Camera and Travel *See:* TRAVEL & LEISURE
United States Camera Annual *See:* TRAVEL & LEISURE
United States Camera Magazine *See:* TRAVEL & LEISURE
University of Southern California Spectator, The *See:* SPECTATOR, THE
Upper and Lower Case *See:* U & LC

V

Ventura Publisher Users Group *See:* VENTURA PROFESSIONAL!
Victory in Europe-Time Drama *See:* DRAMA
Victory in Japan-Time Drama *See:* DRAMA
Video *See:* V
Video Cassette and Cable Television Newsletter *See:* VIDEOCASSETTE AND CATV NEWSLETTER
Video Cassette and CATV Newsletter *See:* VIDEOCASSETTE AND CATV NEWSLETTER
Video Cassettes *See:* V
Video, Cinema & Cable Movie Digest *See:* CINEMA, VIDEO & CABLE MOVIE DIGEST
Video Disc Design/Production Group. News *See:* VIDEODISC DESIGN / PRODUCTION GROUP. NEWS.
Video Disc Monitor, The *See:* VIDEODISC MONITOR, THE
Video Eighty *See:* VIDEO EIGHTIES MAGAZINE
Video Gram *See:* PRO VIDEOGRAM
Video Magazine, The *See:* MOVIE - THE VIDEO MAGAZINE
Video Maker *See:* VIDEOMAKER
Video Play Magazine *See:* VIDEOPLAY MAGAZINE
Video Pro *See:* VIDEOPRO
Video Store Magazine *See:* VIDEO STORE
Video Tools *See:* VIDEOTOOLS
Videocassettes *See:* V
Videogram *See:* PRO VIDEOGRAM
View Camera *See:* VIEWCAMERA
Visions *See:* VIZIONS
VPR *See:* VICTORIAN PERIODICALS REVIEW
VTN *See:* VIDEO TECHNOLOGY NEWS

W

WCA Communication Research Reports *See:* COMMUNICATION RESEARCH REPORTS
Weekly Review *See:* ROXY THEATRE WEEKLY REVIEW
Weekly Review of the Roxy Theatre *See:* ROXY THEATRE WEEKLY REVIEW
Weekly Theatrical Report *See:* DRAMATIC CENSOR, THE
Weekly Trade Circular *See:* PUBLISHER'S WEEKLY
Western Advertising News *See:* ADWEEK
Western States Communication Association News *See:* WSCA NEWS
Who's Who in Motion Pictures and Television *See:* WHO'S WHO IN MOVIES AND TV
Who's Who in Movies and Television *See:* WHO'S WHO IN MOVIES AND TV
Witty World *See:* WITTYWORLD
WJSC *See:* WESTERN JOURNAL OF SPEECH COMMUNICATION
WNW *See:* WRITER'S NW
World Association for Christian Communication Journal *See:* MEDIA DEVELOPMENT
World Communication Association Communication Research Reports *See:* COMMUNICATION RESEARCH REPORTS
World Communication Association Newsletter *See:* WCA NEWSLETTER
World of Fandom Magazine, The *See:* WORLD OF FANDOM, THE
World of High-Fidelity *See:* HI-FI WORLD
WOW *See:* WRITERS ON WRITING
Writer's Northwest *See:* WRITER'S NW

X

Xerox Pipeline *See:* SCSC XEROX PIPELINE

1992/1993 ed.

APR 0 8 1992